THIRTY-FIRST EDITION

KOVELS'

ANTIQUES & COLLECTIBLES

PRICE LIST

FOR THE 1999 MARKET

ILLUSTRATED

W9-AJS-451

Three Rivers Press New York

Published by Three Rivers Press, a division of Crown Publishers, Inc., 201 East 50th
Street, New York, New York 10022. Member of the Crown Publishing Group.

Random House, Inc. New York, Toronto, London, Sydney, Auckland

http://www.randomhouse.com/

THREE RIVERS PRESS and colophon are trademarks of Crown Publishers, Inc.

Printed in the United States of America
Library of Congress Catalog Card Number: 83-643618
ISBN 0-609-80344-1 (pbk.)
10 9 8 7 6 5 4 3 2 1

Books by Ralph and Terry Kovel

American Country Furniture 1780–1875

A Directory of American Silver, Pewter, and Silver Plate

Kovels' Advertising Collectibles Price List

Kovels' American Art Pottery: The Collector's Guide to Makers,
Marks, and Factory Histories

Kovels' American Silver Marks: 1650 to the Present

Kovels' Antiques & Collectibles Fix-It Source Book

Kovels' Book of Antique Labels

Kovels' Bottles Price List

Kovels' Collector's Guide to American Art Pottery

Kovels' Collectors' Source Book

Kovels' Depression Glass & Dinnerware Price List

Kovels' Dictionary of Marks—Pottery & Porcelain

Kovels' Guide to Selling, Buying, and Fixing
Your Antiques and Collectibles

Kovels' Guide to Selling Your Antiques & Collectibles

Kovels' Illustrated Price Guide to Royal Doulton

Kovels' Know Your Antiques

Kovels' Know Your Collectibles

Kovels' New Dictionary of Marks—Pottery & Porcelain

Kovels' Organizer for Collectors

Kovels' Price Guide for Collector Plates, Figurines,
Paperweights, and Other Limited Editions

Kovels' Quick Tips—799 Helpful Hints on
How to Care for Your Collectibles

The Label Made Me Buy It: From Aunt Jemima to Zonkers—
The Best-Dressed Boxes, Bottles & Cans from the Past

It is hard to believe that this is the 31st year we have compiled this price book. It has changed from a book with no illustrations and typewriter-style letters to this edition with hundreds of pictures and logos, about 50,000 prices, dozens of tips about care, and a special report on the emerging markets in the collecting world. And it is still being written by the original authors, Ralph and Terry Kovel.

READ THIS BEFORE YOU USE THIS BOOK—IT WILL HELP

This is a book for the average collector. All year we check prices, visit shops and shows, read our mail, check on-line computer services and the Internet, and decide what antiques and collectibles are of most interest. We concentrate on the average pieces in any category. We sometimes include one or two high-priced pieces in a category so you will realize that some of the rarities are quite valuable. For example, Chintz pottery listed this year includes a Marguerite teapot for $925 and a Queen Anne plate for $30.

Examples of furniture, silver, Tiffany, or art pottery may sell for more than $50,000; we list few of those examples. The highest price in this book is $96,000 for the Bank Teller mechanical bank. The lowest price is 50 cents for a paper baking cup. Most pieces we list cost less than $10,000. We even include the weird and wonderful, and this year you can find listings for a suppository machine made of iron and wood for $110; a Jayne Mansfield 1960s hot water bottle for $125; a Chapman's milk bottle marked "Dairy Cows milked in our parlor" for $65; a coin-operated toilet-seat-cover dispenser from the 1920s for $45; a chart picturing cow's teeth used to determine the age of a cow for $23; and an African bracelet made of elephant hair for $65. The smallest object is a 5/8-inch political button showing "King Lyndon I" for $15. The largest is a 110-foot-long Gothic-post iron fence with a gate for $2,700.

This year we have recorded a number of very high prices in the Bank, Mechanical section. These five- or six-digit prices are all from a single auction of a single bank collection. The banks were among the rarest known and most of them were in almost pristine condition, so the prices were higher than might have been expected. Other prices are up too. Some rare pieces of Bakelite jewelry sold for thousands of dollars. Art pottery continues to be popular, and pieces by the lesser-known factories like North Dakota School of Mines are up in price. Architectural tiles are also rising in price as they become a more popular collectible. Garden accessories, from statues and birdbaths to rakes, trowels, and pieces of old buildings to be used as sculpture, are selling well. And, of course, anything from the '50s to the '80s that is well designed sells. The many antiques malls that are springing up in all parts of the country and the many auctions and sales found on the Internet are also influencing prices. Small pieces that are inexpensive and easy to identify sell quickly.

The book is changed slightly each year. Categories are added or omitted to make it easier for you to find your antiques. New this year are Josef Originals (ceramic figurines), Office Technology (from calculators to stamp machines), Azalea (Japanese dinnerware), and prints by Icart. Several categories were renamed. American Dinnerware has been replaced by Dinnerware because we have listed some pieces popular in America but made elsewhere. Blue Willow has become Willow because there are more pink willow pieces selling. Blown Glass is now listed as Glass-Blown to help keep all of the glass items in one area. The book is kept at about 800 pages because it is written to go with you to sales. We try to have a balanced format—not too many glass, pottery, or collectible items, a variety of furniture from the 18th through the 20th centuries, not too many items that sell for more than $5,000. The prices are *from* the American market *for* the American market. Few European sales are reported. We take the editorial privilege of not including any prices that seem to result from "auction fever."

The computer-generated index is so complete it amazes us. Use it often. An internal alphabetical index is also included. For example, there is a category for "Celluloid." Most items made of celluloid will be found there, but if there is a toy made of celluloid, it will be listed under "Toy" and also indexed under "Celluloid." There are also cross-references in the listings and in the paragraphs. But some searching must be done. For example, Barbie dolls are found in the doll category; there is no Barbie category. And when you look at "doll, Barbie" you will see a note that tells you that Barbie is under "doll, Mattel, Barbie" because most dolls are listed by maker. All pictures and prices are new every year, except pictures that are pattern examples shown in "Depression Glass" and "Pressed Glass." The pictures have been computer-enhanced to make them as crisp as possible. Antiques pictured are not museum pieces but items offered for sale. We hate to waste space, so whenever computer-generated spaces appeared, we filled them with tips about care of collections, security, and other useful information. These tips are set in special type, a bit larger and easier to read. Leaf through the book and learn how to wash porcelains, store textiles, guard against theft, and much more. Don't discard this book when it is time to buy a new one next year. Old Kovels' price books should be saved for future reference, and for tax and appraisal information.

The prices in this book are reports of the general antiques market, not the record-setting examples. Each year, every price in the book is new. We do not estimate or "update" prices. Prices are actual asking prices, although a buyer may have negotiated a price to a lower figure. No price is an estimate. We do not ask dealers and writers to estimate prices. Experience has shown that a collector of one type of antique is prejudiced in favor of that item, and prices are usually high or low, but rarely a true report. If a price range is given, it is because at least two identical items were offered for sale at different times. The computer records prices and prints the high and low figures. Price ranges are found only in categories like "Pressed Glass," where identical items can be identified. If the price is from an auction, it includes the buyer's premium, but like all of the prices, it does not include sales tax. Some prices in *Kovels' Antiques & Collectibles Price List* may seem high and some may seem low because of regional variations. But each price is one you could have paid for the object.

If you are selling your collection, do not expect to get retail value unless you are a dealer. Wholesale prices for antiques are from 20 to 50 percent less than retail. Remember, the antiques dealer must make a profit or go out of business.

THE RECORD PRICES HYPE

The media loves to report record prices, amazing auctions, and other events that really have little to do with the antiques and collectibles market of the average collector. The death of Princess Diana, the movie *Titanic,* and the sales of an important collection of costume jewelry and another of mechanical banks impressed buyers, and prices went up.

The following section lists some record prices that might influence the everyday market for antiques.

BRONZES & OTHER SCULPTURES

- **Mahonri Mackintosh Young sculpture:** $106,950 for the bronze figural group, *Da Winna!,* depicting three French boxers arranged by the artist, Mahonri Mackintosh Young, *The Winner, The Referee,* and *The Loser,* modeled in Paris in 1927, 35 x 32 inches.
- **William Wetmore Story statue:** $250,510 for an over-life-size marble statue of Sardanapalus by William Wetmore Story.

CLOCKS & WATCHES

- **George Daniels watch:** $242,000 for an 18-karat yellow-gold Tourbillon pocket chronometer by George Daniels.
- **Patek Philippe "World Time" wristwatch with cloisonné enamel dial:** $946,830 for an 18-karat pink gold Patek Philippe "World Time" gentleman's wristwatch, with two crowns and a polychrome, cloisonné enamel dial representing the North American continent, made in 1953.
- **Patek Philippe "World Time" wristwatch with guilloché dial:** $662,500 for an 18-karat pink-gold Patek Philippe "World Time" gentleman's wristwatch with two crowns and a guilloché dial, made in 1965.
- **Patek Philippe wristwatch without complications:** $138,965 for a Patek Philippe *Calatrava* wristwatch without complications, 18-karat yellow-gold half-hunting case.
- **Patek Philippe yellow-gold wristwatch:** $1,100,000 for an 18-karat yellow-gold Patek Philippe wristwatch, with matt silver and applied gold indexes, perpetual calendar, and moon phases, c. 1961.

FOLK ART

- **Shore bird decoy:** $335,500 for a running, sickle-bill curlew shore-bird decoy by an unknown maker from Salem, Massachusetts, c. 1890, 21½ inches.

FURNITURE

- **Any piece of Japanned furniture:** $772,500 for a Queen Anne, flat-top, high chest of drawers, with original 18th-century, japanned decoration, Boston, c. 1740. This chest set several records at auction: for American japanning, a Massachusetts case piece, and a flat-top highboy.
- **Fornasetti work:** $140,000 for a tall bureau designed by Piero Fornasetti, called "Architettura," with a trompe l'oeil design hand-painted and lithographically printed on wood and metal and 15 lithographic zinc templates, 1952, 85½ x 31½ x 16 inches.
- **Gustav Stickley, Morris chair, no. 369:** $15,400 for a Gustav Stickley, drop-arm, Morris chair, no. 369, with original finish and a branded signature, and a black leather seat cushion and back, 39 x 32 x 37 inches.
- **Gustav Stickley sideboard, no. 816:** $4,400 for a Gustav Stickley sideboard, no. 816, with original finish, from the Stickley cottage.
- **L. & J.G. Stickley sideboard:** $13,200 for an L. & J.G. Stickley sideboard, with original finish, leaded glass doors on top, strap hinges, and lower paneled doors with brass handles.
- **Massachusetts bonnet-top highboy:** $690,000 for a Chippendale, carved and figured mahogany, bonnet-top highboy, with corkscrew finials, fan-carved center drawers, cabriole legs, carved ball-and-claw feet, and cast-brass hardware, Salem, Massachusetts, c. 1770, 7 feet 6 inches x 39¼ inches x 20½ inches.
- **New England easy chair:** $387,500 for a Queen Anne easy chair, with walnut legs and stretchers, Boston, c. 1740.
- **New York chair:** $387,500 for a New York armchair, with ruffled splat and eagle's head, upholstered seat, leaf-carved cabriole legs, and ball-and-claw feet, made between 1760 and 1780.
- **Nisbet piece of furniture:** $19,500 for a Thomas Nisbet, four-drawer, mahogany butler's chest, with a bird's-eye maple fitted interior, carved paw feet in front and turnip feet in back, and a top drawer that drops to form a desk, with a Thomas Nisbet label in the second drawer, made in New Brunswick, Canada, 45 x 49 x 22½ inches.
- **Ruhlmann/Art Deco furniture:** $662,500 for "Etat d'Angle," an ivory and ebony inlaid amboyna corner cabinet with a triangular case on three legs and bowed front, by Jacques-Emile Ruhlmann, 1916, 50⅛ x 32⅝ x 20½ inches.
- **Seymour desk:** $200,500 for a Federal, lady's tambour desk, mahogany veneer, attributed to John Seymour and Son, Boston, Massachusetts, 1794–1809.

- **Tall chest:** $87,000 for a Chester County tall chest with four arched drawers, a bold cornice, and paneled sides, 66⁹⁄₁₆ x 43⁷⁄₈ x 24⁵⁄₈ inches.

GLASS

- **Barber bottle:** $2,585 for a purple amethyst, Mary Gregory bottle depicting a woman in white at a fountain, with a pontil-scarred base and rolled lip, 8 inches high, 1885–1925.
- **Canning jar:** $11,000 for a deep cobalt blue petal jar, with a red iron pontil, 10 panels around the shoulder and neck, and an applied mouth, 8³⁄₈ inches high, blown at a midwestern glass house, 1850–1860.
- **Italian "Saturneo" vase:** $9,200 for a 1951, Italian "Saturneo" vase by Barovier & Toso Studios, freeblown bottle-form glass, five double rows of teal-green-aqua bull's-eye murrine, and lattimo (white) filigrana vertical rods, 11½ inches.
- **René Lalique piece of glass:** $409,500 for the *cire perdue* glass vase, "Roses," made by René Lalique, 12 inches high, c. 1913. (*Cire perdue* is an ancient form of casting, originating in Greece in the 6th century B.C., and most often used with bronze.)

JEWELRY

- **Bakelite charm pin:** $10,450 for a Bakelite, cigarette-shaped charm pin—an ivory cigarette in a black holder with nine red- , green- , and black-tipped match charms, 3 inches.
- **Bakelite clown pin:** $7,700 for a Bakelite googly eyed clown pin, with the ivory head, collar, and hat carved from one piece, painted highlights, 3 inches.
- **Bakelite "Philadelphia" bracelet:** $17,600 for a "Philadelphia" bracelet, with green, hinged body and laminated fins of black, orange, green, red, and yellow, 1½ inches wide.
- **Jadeite jewelry:** $9,400,000 for a single-strand jadeite-bead necklace from the stone "Doubly Fortunate." Twenty-seven matched jadeite beads, approximately ⁵⁄₈ inches each, in vivid emerald green color, with old, European-cut, diamond terminals, 18½ inches long, to the diamond, single-stone clasp.

LAMP

- **Tiffany/20th-century decorative arts:** $2,807,500 for a Pink Lotus lamp with a bronze and mosaic base, a two-part shade of waterlilies suspended from bronze tendrils, and an inner circle of tendrils holding eight Favrile-glass shades in the shape of lotus flowers, made by Tiffany Studios, c. 1905, 34³⁄₄ x 28 inches.
- **Tiffany "Laburnum" lamp:** $129,000 for a Tiffany "Laburnum" table lamp with a domed, favrile-glass shade of yellow cluster blossoms, brown branches, and green leaves against a sky-blue background, mounted on a reticulated bronze base, 27³⁄₄ inches high, shade diameter 22 inches.

METAL

- **Toleware coffeepot:** $33,000 (record hammer price) for a red-painted, tin, gooseneck, toleware coffeepot. (A red, decorated toleware coffeepot with a straight spout and flatter lid sold in June 1993 for $36,800 with a buyer's premium.)

MISCELLANEOUS

- **Telescope:** $14,950 for a 6-inch refractor telescope by Alvan Clark & Son of Cambridgeport, Massachusetts, with a counterweight equatorial mount, angle eyepiece tube, partial spotting scope, lens cover, and mahogany tripod, 1891, 92 x 87 inches.
- **Burt solar compass:** $17,250 for a Burt aluminum and brass, solar compass with detachable telescope, level vial, counterweight, compass in hourglass box, vernier scale, edge-engraved quadrant scale, and detachable sight vanes, W. & L.E. Gurley, Troy, N.Y., c. 1892, 18½ x 13½ x 7 inches.
- **Cheyenne lattice cradle:** $59,700 for a Central Plains, beaded, hide-and-tacked cradleboard, c. 1880.
- **Cigar-store soldier:** $46,750 for the wood-carved, cigar-store figure Corporal Joe, a soldier with black mustache, dark Havana cigar, and arms folded across his chest, wearing blue pants and a black jacket with two yellow stripes on the arm, c. 1865, approximately 6 feet tall.
- **Dresden ornament:** $8,250 for a Dresden cyclist ornament—two gentlemen wearing blue caps and shirts and gray riding trousers, seated on a two-seat bicycle made of hand-painted, stamped cardboard, Germany, c. 1900, 4¾ inches.
- **Scrimshaw tooth:** $50,600 for a sperm-whale tooth engraved by Frederick Myrick of the ship *Susan* of Nantucket, showing views of *Susan* on the coast of Japan and, on the reverse side, her homeward-bound passage. A colorful inscription reads "Death to the living, long life to the killers/Success to sailors wives & greasy luck to whalers."

MOVIE & CELEBRITY MEMORABILIA

- **One-sheet movie poster:** $21,850 for a one-sheet poster for the Humphrey Bogart classic *Casablanca* (Warner Bros., 1943), from the Royal Theater Collection.

MUSIC

- **Farotti Cello:** $68,500 for a violoncello by Celeste Farotti, with a two-piece poplar back, a medium curl maple scroll, and red-gold varnish, labeled and inscribed, Milan, 1912, 29¹⁵⁄₁₆ inches, with case.
- **Nicolas Maire violin bow:** $25,300 for a silver-mounted violin bow by Nicolas Maire of Paris, with the round stick stamped MAIRE at the butt, an ebony frog with pearl eye, and an ebony adjuster with two silver bands and pearl eye, weight 59 grams.

- **Piano:** $1,210,885 (£716,500) for a Steinway piano with an ebony and cedar case; other materials include ebony, sandalwood, ivory, boxwood, coral, and mother-of-pearl. The artist Edward Poynter was hired to paint a classical scene on the lid. The lid's parchment paneled interior is inscribed with signatures of musical celebrities, such as Sir Arthur Sullivan (of Gilbert and Sullivan), Richard Rodgers (of Rodgers and Hammerstein), and others who have played the piano created by Queen Victoria's furniture makers, Messrs. Johnstone, Norman & Co.

PAPER

- **American stock certificate:** $61,000 for an American stock certificate of the Standard Oil Company. This 1870 founder's certificate assigns 2,407 shares to John D. Rockefeller and is endorsed by him. It bears a revenue stamp and clearly indicates a capitalization of $1 million with 10,000 shares outstanding.
- **Bob Dalton–signed document:** $13,200 for an 1887 prisoner-certification document signed by lawman/outlaw Bob Dalton.
- **Medical book:** $1,652,500 for the first edition of a 16th-century medical book presented by its author, Antreas Vesalius, to Holy Roman Emperor Charles V in 1543.

PHOTOGRAPHY & CAMERAS

- **Fred Thompson photograph:** $577 for Fred Thompson's hand-colored photograph *Toiler of the Sea,* which pictures an old, heavily bearded fisherman in his rowboat, with fish at his feet, c. 1915, 14 x 17 inches.

POTTERY & PORCELAIN

- **American porcelain:** $291,500 for a pair of Tucker urns/vases. One has a view of Sedgley Park on one side and the Schuylkill River on the other. The other vase has a shipwreck scene with a man and woman fleeing on horseback and firing a gun at Indians. Each vase is gilt-decorated at the neck and ring, and has cast gilt-bronze griffin handles and a square-footed base, 21 inches high.
- **Anna Pottery "little brown jug":** $5,600 for an Anna Pottery jug, inscribed "Little Brown Jug," with an applied, detailed snake going up the back of the jug forming the handle and wrapping its head around the neck, dark brown glaze, dated 1884, 6 inches.
- **Regimental stein:** $17,469 for a porcelain, Regimental 6 Jäger stein, tree trunk body with two side scenes including Jägers on bicycles, a photograph of Jäger Elflein in the center, a St. Hubertus thumblift, and a horn and pewter helmet finial, 1912–1914, 8½ inches, ½ liter.
- **Shaving mug:** $6,600 for an occupational shaving mug made for Chas. J. Kiers showing a man operating an oil derrick–type machine inside a building, full pink wrap, 1885–1925, 3 5/8 inches high.

SPORTS

- **American handle reel:** $2,145 for a brass, American handle reel, P. A. Altimaire, Harrisburg, Pennsylvania, Patent November 9, 1869.
- **American wooden reel:** $1,210 for an Earnest H. Pflueger 1896-patented, wood, line-winder-type reel.
- **Babe Ruth rookie card:** $27,114 for Babe Ruth's 1914 rookie baseball card, minor-league Baltimore Orioles; reverse side has "at home" and "abroad" schedules.
- **Boxing gloves:** $32,200 for a pair of boxing gloves Muhammad Ali wore when he defeated Leon Spinks in New Orleans on September 15, 1978.
- **Boxing memorabilia:** $156,500 for the robe Muhammad Ali wore to face George Foreman in Kinshasa, Zaire, in 1974. The robe has a silk handkerchief stitched to the lining with an astrological prediction of the fight.
- **Boxing-related document:** $63,000 for Muhammad Ali's 1966 letter to the National Director of Selective Service as a petition to reclassify him for the draft.
- **Boxing shoes:** $59,700 for a pair of boxing shoes worn by Muhammad Ali during his 1974 fight against George Foreman in Kinshasa, Zaire.
- **Boxing trunks:** $57,500 for a pair of boxing trunks Muhammad Ali wore to face George Foreman in Kinshasa, Zaire, in 1974.
- **Heddon baits/wooden lure:** $9,900 for a Heddon #1400 Dowagiac Minnow lure, marked, 3 in.
- **Heddon Punkinseed lure:** $1,320 for a Heddon Punkinseed #730 lure in a rainbow finish.
- **Lure box:** $3,960 for an empty Redfin Floating Bait box with label, "A Casting and Trolling Bait For Bass and Pickerel."
- **Peerless Trout Reel no. 5 size:** $6,050 for an Edward Vom Hofe model 355 Peerless trout reel, handmade German silver and hard rubber, in the smallest size, no. 5, $1\frac{7}{8}$ inches.
- **Pflueger lure:** $4,840 for a Pflueger lure, no. 250, silver-and-green enamel, five-hook, wooden minnow, in the original "Hi Henry Special" box.
- **Reel oil bottle:** $935 for Milam's Reel Oil bottle and original cork stopper, labeled, unused bottle, full contents, B.C. Milam & Son, Frankfort, Kentucky.
- **Single-signed baseball:** $21,916 for a Christy Mathewson single-signed baseball, with a brown signature across the sweet spot.

TEXTILES

Navajo man's wearing blanket: $431,500 for a classic Navajo man's wearing blanket or sarape, in vivid lac-dyed crimson, indigo blue, and ivory handspun and raveled worsted wool, 82 x 59 in.

Any bank or toy: $426,000 for the Old Woman in the Shoe bank, in which the old woman stands in her shoe and swings a stick at a boy when a coin is deposited, cast iron, designed by W.S. Reed Co., Leominster, Massachusetts, patent 11/27/1883.

- **Barbie doll:** $8,800 for a 1959 Barbie doll wearing a zebra-striped, one-piece bathing suit, original box.
- **Cupola bank:** $1,125 for the 1869 cast-iron Cupola bank by J. & E. Stevens, large version.
- **Kachina doll:** $294,000 for a Hopi carved, polychrome, wood kachina doll, representing a dancing *Shalako Mana,* wearing an elaborately carved and painted tableta headdress, sculpted in an animated posture, 18 in.
- **Marionette:** $113,431 for an original 1950s Howdy Doody marionette referred to as "Photo Doody," which has no strings and was used for publicity stills, advertisements, and travel purposes. This is one of three originals.
- **"Miller Swirl" Golden Rebel marble:** $2,993 for a "Miller Swirl" Golden Rebel marble, c. 1927, with an opaque yellow base and aventurine, black, and opaque red swirls, 27/32 inches.
- **Moody & Sankey still bank:** $12,000 for the Moody & Sankey bank picturing Dwight Moody and Ira Sankey, made by Smith & Egge in 1870, 5 inches.

A NOTE TO COLLECTORS

You already know that this is a great overall price guide for all sorts of antiques and collectibles. Each entry is current, every picture is new, all prices are accurate.

But in the collecting world, things change quickly. Important sales produce new record prices. Rarities are discovered. Fakes appear. *Kovels on Antiques and Collectibles* is a monthly newsletter designed to keep up with these developments, with up-to-date information on the world of collecting. It is filled with color photographs, about forty to an issue. The newsletter reports prices, trends, auction results, and other pertinent news for collectors *as it happens.* For a free sample of *Kovels on Antiques and Collectibles,* fill out and mail the postage-paid postcard at the back of this book. We also have an informational Web site. Visit us at www.kovel.com to learn more.

KEEP READING— HOW TO USE THIS BOOK

There are a few rules for using this book. Each listing is arranged in the following manner: CATEGORY (such as Pressed Glass or Furniture), OBJECT (such as vase), DESCRIPTION (as much information as possible about size, age, color, and pattern). Some types of glass, pottery, and silver are exceptions to this rule. These are listed CATEGORY, PATTERN, OBJECT, DESCRIPTION. All items are presumed to be in good condition and undamaged, unless otherwise noted. If a maker's name is easily recognized, like Gustav Stickley, we try to include it near the beginning of the entry. If the maker is obscure, the name may be at the end. Because the descriptions are part of actual reports, we do not edit to make everything consistent in each entry. We try to edit enough to be sure that two items are not actually two descriptions of the same piece.

Several special categories were formed to make the most sensible listing possible. For instance, "Tool" includes special equipment because the casual collector might not know the proper name for an "adze." Many of the glass entries are in special categories: "Glass-Art," "Glass-Blown," "Glass-Contemporary," "Glass-Midcentury," and "Glass-Venetian." Major glass factories are still listed under the factory names, and well-known types of glass, such as cut, pressed, Carnival, and others, can be found in their own categories. The silver listings are also a bit different. You will find silver flatware in either Silver Flatware Plated or Silver Flatware Sterling. You will also find a section for Silver Plate, which includes coffeepots, trays, and other plated pieces. Solid or sterling silver is listed by country, so look for Silver-American, Silver-English, and others. Pottery and porcelain are usually listed by factory name or item, but some are found in Art Pottery, Art Nouveau, Art Deco, Arts & Crafts, Dinnerware, Kitchen, Pottery, or Porcelain.

Sometimes we make arbitrary decisions based on the number of entries or interest in a subject. Fishing has its own category, but hunting is part of the larger category called Sports. We have eliminated all guns except toy types. It is not legal to sell weapons without a special license, and so guns are not part of the general antiques market. Airguns, BB guns, rocket guns, and others are listed in the "Toy" section. Several idiosyncrasies of style appear because the book is printed by computer. Everything is listed according to the computer alphabetizing system. This means words such as "Mt." are alphabetized as "M-T," not as "M-O-U-N-T." All numerals are before all letters; thus 2 comes before "A." A quick glance will make this clear, as it is consistent throughout the book.

We made several editorial decisions. A bowl is a "bowl" and not a "dish," unless it is a special dish, such as a pickle dish. A butter dish is a "butter." A salt dish is called a "salt" to differentiate it from a saltshaker. It is always "sugar and creamer," never "creamer and sugar." Political collectors often refer to "pinbacks," the round celluloid or tin pins that are decorated with candidates' names and faces. The word "button" is sometimes used in this book instead of the word "pinback." Of course, the word "button" is also used when referring to the fasteners used on clothing. Where one dimension is given, it is the height; or if the object is round, the dimension is the diameter. The height of a picture is listed before width. Glass is clear unless a color is indicated.

Every entry is listed alphabetically, but the problem of language remains. Some antiques terms, such as "Sheffield" or "Pratt," have two meanings. Be sure to read the paragraph headings to know the meaning used. All category headings are based on the language of the average person at an average show, and we use terms like "mud figures" even if not technically correct.

This book does *not* include price listings of fine art paintings, antiquities, stamps, coins, or most types of books. *Big Little Books* and similar children's books *are* included. Comic books are *not* listed, but original comic art and cels *are* listed in their own categories.

All pictures in *Kovels' Antiques & Collectibles Price List* are listed with the prices asked by the seller. "Illus" (illustrated nearby) is part of the description if a picture is shown.

There have been misinformed comments about how this book is written. We *do* use the computer. It alphabetizes, ranges prices, sets type, and does other time-consuming jobs. Because of the computer, the book can be produced quickly. The last entries are added in June; the book is available in October. This is six months faster than would be possible any other way. But it is human help that finds prices and checks accuracy. We read everything at least three times, sometimes more. We edit from 80,000 entries to the 50,000 entries found here. We correct spelling, remove incorrect data, write category headings, and decide on new categories. We sometimes make errors. Information in the paragraphs is reviewed and updated each year. This year fifty-five corrections and additions were made in the category headings.

Prices are reports from all parts of the United States and Canada (translated to U.S. dollars at the rate of $1.46 U.S. to $1 Canadian) between June 1997 and June 1998. Prices are from auctions, shops, and shows. Every price is checked for accuracy, but we are not responsible for errors.

We cannot answer your letters asking for specific price information. But please write if you have any requests for categories to be included in future editions or any corrections to information in the paragraphs.

When you see us at the shows, stop and say hello. Don't be surprised if we ask for your suggestions for the next edition of *Kovels' Antiques & Collectibles Price List.* You can write to us at P.O. Box 22200-K, Beachwood, Ohio 44122 or visit us at our new Web site: www.kovel.com.

RALPH & TERRY KOVEL
Accredited Senior Appraisers
American Society of Appraisers
July 1998

ACKNOWLEDGMENTS

Special thanks should go to those who helped us with pictures and deeds: Alderfer Auction Co.; Allard Auctions Inc.; America West Archives; American Historical Auctions (Larry Richmond); American Social History & Social Movements; Andre Ammelounx; Antiquorum Auctioneers; Bill Bertoia Auctions; Block's Box; Butterfield & Butterfield; Christie's; Christie's East; Christie's South Kensington; Cincinnati Art Galleries; Collectors Auction Services; Craftsman Auctions; Dan Ripley Antiques; David Rago Auction Inc.; DeFina Auctions; DuMouchelle's Art Galleries; Dunbar Gallery; Dunning's Auction Service; Fink's Off the Wall Auction; Frank H. Boos Gallery; Garth's Auctions Inc.; Gene Harris Antique Auction Center Inc.; Glass-Works Auctions; Guyette and Schmidt Inc.; Henry/Peirce Auctioneers; Hewletts Antique Auctions; Horst Auctioneers; Jackson's Auctioneers & Appraisers; James D. Julia Inc.; Jay McCormick Auction Service; Ken Farmer Auctions; Kenneth S. Hays & Associates Inc.; Lang's Sporting Collectibles Inc.; Leland's; McMasters Doll Auction; Michael Ivankovich Antiques Inc.; Muddy River Trading Co.; Neal Auction Company; Norm's Auction Service; Norman C. Heckler & Co.; Northeast Auctions; O'Gallerie Inc.; Political Memorabilia Catalog; Rafael Osona; Richard Opfer Auctioneering Inc.; Robert C. Eldred Co. Inc.; Robert Edward Auctions; Skinner Inc.; Smith and Jones Inc.; Smith House; Sotheby's; Swann Galleries; Tim Isaac Antiques; Treadway/Toomey; Waddington's; Waverly Auctions Inc.; and Wolf's. An extra thank you for the special help given by Carmie Amata, Harriet Goldner, Lee Markley, James Measell, and Darryl Rehr.

To the others in the antiques trade who knowingly or unknowingly contributed to this book, we say "thank you!" We could not have done it without you. Some of you are: Adamstown Antique Gallery; Alice J. Schnabel; Allen's Collector Plates; American Potluck; Americana Resources Antiques & Collectibles; Antique Aquariums & Pet Related Items; Armbrook Antiques; Arnold Flynn; Arnold Moelk; Ashland Antique Jewelry; Auctions Unlimited; Audrey L. Yerger; Aunt Fay's Toys & Collectibles; Baker's International Antiques & Collectibles; Barry Abel; Betty Bennion; Bill & Linda Borchert; Bill Bassett; Bill Duncanson; Bittersweet Antiques & Collectibles; Black Sheep Antique Center; Blue Willow Antiques; Bob Christie; Bob Sanford; Bob Smith; Brad Baker; Briars Antiques; Brookside Antiques; Brown's; Buffalo Bay Auction Co.; Burmese Cruet; California Pottery Auction; California Pottery Trader; Cat's Paw Antiques; Cedars Antiques; Cerebro; Charles E. Kirtley; Cheryl Leaf Antiques & Gifts; Cindy Korth; Clinstman International Inc.; Coca-Cola Collector's News; Collage 20th Century Classics; Connie & Keith Dunn; Continental Hobby House; Crown Jewels of the Wire; Cup & Saucer; D. Richter; Dawson's Fine Jewelry; Depression Delights; Don Ptalis; Dorothy J. Hatfield; Dottie Milanoski; Eclectic; Edith Weber & Assoc. Antique Jewelry; Eric's Antiques; Fenner's Antiques; 52 Girls Collectibles; Freeman/Fine Arts of Philadelphia Inc.; Garry Beegle; Garthoeffner Gallery; George Kamm; Gibb & Bev Green; Ginny's Hutch Antiques; Glass Cupboard; Glenn Poch's Bottle Sales List; Grier & Sowden Antiques & Collectibles; Heather Irving; Heritage Harvest Antiques; Historic Originals; Irene Benesch; Jack & Nancy Kieffer; Jack & Norma Majewski; James Tabaska; Jeff Hooven; Jerry Fralick; Jerry's Antiques; Jimmy Blanton; Joe Maurath, Jr.; John Grogan; Joyce Taylor; Judy Dahl; Judy Geller; Judy Hesson; Judy Posner Collectibles; Keepers Antique Mall; Keith Haynes; Ken & Barbara Weaver; Kit Wittekind; L & J Antiques & Collectibles; L. A. Finders Keepers; Larry D. Wells; Lila deLellis; Lil-Bud Antiques; Lois Wood; Lu Dodemont/Jack Senander; Lucky Penny Collectibles; Luther Weaver; Lyndall's; Manion's International Auction House Inc.; Mark Wiskow; May's Antiques; Memories; Michael J. Urness; Michael's Memories; Modern; Morantiques; Mouse Man Ink; Nancy Revay; Norman's Olde Store; Norton Rustad; Old Paperphiles; Open Wire Supply; Paper Chaser; Paper Nut; Pat Warner; Perdue & Podner Antiques; Pete Niederberger; Philadelphia Print Shop, Ltd.; Plums & Lemon's; Postcards International; Posteritati; Pottery Collectors Express; Primarily Cookie Jars; Ray & Marilyn Sampson; Ray Vlach; Red Wing Collectors Society; Replacements, Ltd.; Rex Stark; Rita's Attic; Roanoke Antique Mall; Robert Simmons; Roger & Nancy Parsells; Ronald H. Anderson Antiques Art Pottery; Sanders' Antiques; Sandy Guide; Sari Blecker; Scot Douglas; Selma Sternheim; Sharon Bowman; Sierra Hills Antiques; Soda Pop & More; Southern Folk Pottery Collector's Society; Stephen Boyer; Susan Higgins; Susan Levine; Swan Tavern Antiques; Team Antiques; Ted Kromer; Temple's Antiques; Theriault's the Dollmasters; Tim Gaudet; Timeless Treasures Antique Mall; Tom & Jean Tierney; Tom Barker; Tom Waggoner; Tomlinson Antiques; Toy Bin; Toy Scouts Inc.; Toy Tokyo; Treasures & Trifles Inc.; 20th Century Arts; Unger Junction Antiques; Vernon Danison; Vickery Antiques & Collectibles; Vicki Luna; Virtual Bottle Shop; Warwick Henderson Gallery; Wayne Collins; Weschler's; Wesley's Inheritance; White Rose Antiques; William Fagan & Co.; William R. & Teresa F. Kurau; Winter Associates; Yankee Tools & Collectibles; Yesteryear Here; and York Town Auction Inc.

Thank you to everyone at Crown, especially Pam Stinson-Bell, who reads and rereads each entry, and to Chip Gibson, Steve Magnuson, PJ Dempsey, Karen Minster, Oona Schmid, Laura Duffy, John Sharp, and Laurie Stark. Further kudos to Merri Ann Morrell and Diane Dugal at Precision Graphics. More thanks to our photographers, Benjamin Margalit and Jay Brown, and to Kitty Busher, Grace DeFrancisco, Marcia Goldberg, Evelyn Hayes, Karen Kneisley, Eleanore Melzak, Gloria Pearlman, Nancy Saada, Cherrie Smrekar, Edie Smrekar, Virginia Warner, Jane Warner-Seik, and Ann Wochner. But most of all we thank Gay Hunter, who checked every word and so much more.

A. WALTER made pate-de-verre glass under contract at the Daum glass-works from 1908 to 1914. He started his own firm in Nancy, France, in 1919. Pieces made before 1914 are signed *Daum, Nancy* with a cross. After 1919 the signature is *A. Walter Nancy*.

Bowl, Boll Weevils & Pinecone Needles, Signed, 3 5/8 In.	5750.00
Bowl, Flying Fish Amid Seaweed, Emerald Green & Gray, Signed, c.1900, 9 1/4 In.	9200.00
Change Receiver, Blue, Mottled, Molded Moths, 11 x 4 In.	4600.00
Change Receiver, Orange & Black, Molded Lizard, 4 x 7 In.	5175.00
Dish, Beetle At Top, Yellow Shading To Amber, Signed, 4 1/2 In.	1150.00
Figurine, Faun Playing Flute, Signed A. Walter Nancy, 3 5/8 In.	1235.00
Figurine, Ice Blue, Yellow, Green Base, Marked, 1910, 8 5/8 In.	2100.00
Paperweight, Cicada Resting On Pine Branch, Signed, 4 3/4 In.	3000.00
Paperweight, Mouse Eating From Walnut, On Grassy Knoll, Signed, 3 1/2 In.	8495.00
Tray, Crab, Crustacean At Top, Heart Shape, Signed, 7 x 6 1/4 In.	5500.00
Tray, Nautical, Snail On Hermit Crab, Seaweed Branches, Freeform, Oval, 9 3/4 In.	8500.00
Tray, Partridge, Molded, Signed, c.1920, 7 3/4 In.	2300.00
Tray, Pen, Divided Oval Dish, Black Stag Horn Beetle At End, Signed, 9 1/2 In.	3700.00

ABC plates, or children's alphabet plates, were most popular from 1780 to 1860, but are still being made. The letters on the plate were meant as teaching aids for children learning to read. The plates were made of pottery, porcelain, metal, or glass. Mugs and other items were also made with alphabet decorations.

Bowl, Nursery Rhymes, Graphics, England	145.00
Cup, Boys Playing Soccer Transfer, 2 In.	110.00
Cup & Saucer, Pink Luster, Small	37.50
Dish, Little Bo Peep, Glass, Embossed	60.00
Dish, Mother Goose	85.00
Mug, Child At Desk	145.00
Mug, Green Transfer, Ship Scene, 3 In.	88.00
Planter, 3 Little Pigs, Gold Trim	50.00
Planter, Lamb	65.00
Planter, Puppy With Sock	10.00
Plate, A Happy New Year To You, Chicks Hatching, 8 In.	115.00
Plate, Aesop's Fables, Fox & Grapes	225.00
Plate, Baby Bunting & Dog Go Hunting	75.00
Plate, Birds On Branch, Enameled, Staffordshire, 1884	85.00
Plate, Boy & Girl In Touring Car, Transfer, 6 In.	75.00
Plate, Boy Selling Newspapers, Red Transfer, 1870s	75.00
Plate, Cat & Bird In Cage	185.00
Plate, Children With Hoop, Tin, 2 3/4 In.	225.00
Plate, Choo Choo Train, Pearlware Transfer, Edge & Malkin Co., 1900, 7 In.	275.00
Plate, Clock Center	250.00
Plate, Cock Robin, Embossed, Tin, c.1900	145.00
Plate, Court House, Minneapolis, Minn., Embossed Aqua Border	30.00
Plate, Crusoe At Work, c.1885	125.00
Plate, Crusoe Viewing Island, Staffordshire	185.00
Plate, Dog & Clown Doing Hat Tricks	125.00
Plate, Dr. Franklin's Maxims	325.00
Plate, Elephant, Fishing	195.00
Plate, Felix The Cat, England	100.00
Plate, Fisherman's Children, Embossed Floral Border, Staffordshire, 7 1/2 In.	82.00
Plate, Frolics Of Youth, Now I'm Grandmother, Black Transfer, Red Rim Strip, 7 3/8 In.	150.00
Plate, Garfield, Glass	85.00
Plate, General Gilmore	195.00
Plate, Girl With Dog, Holding Reins Of Saddled Horse, Staffordshire	140.00
Plate, Golden Crested Wren	210.00
Plate, John Gilpin	210.00
Plate, Mary, Mary Quite Contrary, Wood & Sons, England	20.00
Plate, Men Plowing, Embossed Alphabet, Staffordshire, 4 1/2 In.	93.00
Plate, Noah's Ark, Animals	35.00
Plate, Playing At Lovers	200.00

Plate, Pride Of The Barn Yard, Staffordshire, 7 In. 110.00
Plate, Punch & Judy, Dog, Embossed Alphabet, Brown & Green, C.A. Sons, England ... 165.00
Plate, Rabbits, 1940s, 9 In. 15.00
Plate, Rooster, Hen, Chicks, Germany 65.00
Plate, Sancho Panza, Frosted Glass, 6 In. 145.00
Plate, Soldier & Horse 115.00
Plate, Trap Bat & Ball, 3 Children, Staffordshire, 1890, 6 In. 170.00
Plate, Village Blacksmith 225.00
Plate, Virginia Troops, Staffordshire 375.00
Plate, Washington, Tin, 6 1/8 In. 145.00

ABINGDON POTTERY was established in 1908 by Raymond E. Bidwell
as the Abingdon Sanitary Manufacturing Company. The company
started making art pottery in 1934. The factory ceased production of
art pottery in 1950.

Bookend, Fish, 1 Piece 35.00
Bookends, Horse Head, Black ....55.00 to 58.00
Bookends, Horse Head, Pink 75.00
Bookends, Horse Head, White ....55.00 to 80.00
Bookends, Horse, Black ....55.00 to 75.00
Bookends, Sea Gull, No. 305 ....165.00 to 228.00
Bowl, Hibiscus, No. 528, Large 52.00
Bowl, Scroll, Dark Blue, No. 532, 11 In. 26.00
Bowl, Shell, Pink, Medium, No. 501, 11 In. 20.00
Bulb Bowl, Egg White, Oblong, Handle, No. 542, 11 In. 12.00
Candleholder, Double, Ring Divider, Ivory, 4 x 4 1/2 In. 39.00
Conch Shell, Pink, 9 In. 25.00
Console Set, Blue 35.00
Console Set, Pink, No. 564 & No. 575 .... 50.00
Cookie Jar, 3 Bears 300.00
Cookie Jar, ABC Lady Pig 60.00
Cookie Jar, Bo Peep ....395.00 to 410.00
Cookie Jar, Choo Choo Train, Turquoise ....150.00 to 200.00
Cookie Jar, Daisy, No. 677 .... 95.00
Cookie Jar, Fat Boy 425.00
Cookie Jar, Hippo, Blue 150.00
Cookie Jar, Hobby Horse, Original Label 250.00
Cookie Jar, Humpty Dumpty, Yellow ....195.00 to 300.00
Cookie Jar, Jack-In-The-Box ....295.00 to 390.00
Cookie Jar, Keebler Tree House 50.00
Cookie Jar, Little Girl, Wooden Top 65.00
Cookie Jar, Little Ol' Lady 175.00
Cookie Jar, Miss Muffet 425.00
Cookie Jar, Money Sack ....65.00 to 95.00
Cookie Jar, Mother Goose ....495.00 to 595.00
Cookie Jar, Pineapple ....115.00 to 150.00
Cookie Jar, Pumpkin 550.00
Cookie Jar, Train 225.00
Cookie Jar, Wigwam 395.00
Cornucopia, Single, Yellow, No. 474 .... 16.00
Cornucopia, White, Glossy Glaze 15.00
Flowerpot, Cattail, No. 150 .... 28.00
Planter, Jack O' Lantern, Striped, 1943, 6 x 7 In. 300.00
Planter, Mexican Siesta 35.00
Vase, Blue, Handles, 9 1/2 In. 75.00
Vase, Bluebird, 7 In. 40.00
Vase, Dolphin, 11 In. 80.00
Vase, Egret, 7 In. 175.00
Vase, Gazelle, Pink, 7 In. 50.00
Vase, Handle, Light Green, 9 In. 25.00
Vase, Horse Head, Blue, 10 In. 55.00
Vase, Seashell, Yellow, No. 507, 9 In. 30.00
Wall Pocket, Dutch Boy, Geese 110.00

ADAMS china was made by William Adams and Sons of Staffordshire, England. The firm was founded in 1769 and is still working. All types of tablewares and useful wares have been made through the years. Other pieces of Adams will be found listed under Flow Blue.

ADAMS
ENGLAND

Bough Pot, Pierced Cover, Jasperware, White, Acanthus Leaves, Marked, 7 In.	1725.00
Charger, Rose, Ironstone, Molded Deep Flange, Alberton, 14 In.	310.00
Creamer, English Scene, Dark Blue, 5 3/8 In.	165.00
Cup & Saucer, Peafowl, Red, Spatter	104.00
Muffineer, Dark Blue, White Hunt Scene, Silver Plated Lid	165.00
Plate, Bound To A Tree, Dr. Syntax, Pearlized Border, 9 1/2 In.	55.00
Plate, Headwaters Of Juniata, Pink, 10 1/2 In.	135.00
Plate, Kyber, Flow Blue, 10 In.	125.00 to 145.00
Plate, Old English Rural Scene, Blue Transfer, 10 1/8 In.	28.00
Plate, Peafowl, Blue Green, Red & Black, Red Spatter, 14 Sides, 9 1/2 In.	245.00 to 310.00
Plate, Shanghai, Flow Blue, 10 In.	90.00
Plate, Tonquin, Flow Blue, 9 In.	150.00
Platter, Black Beauty Cut, Central Floral, Spongeware, Late 19th Century, 12 1/4 In.	258.00
Platter, Cobalt Feather Edge, Incised On Reverse, 8 Sides, 15 1/2 x 12 In.	88.00
Platter, Minuet, Oval, 13 1/2 In.	48.00
Platter, Regents Quadrant, London, Dark Blue, 17 1/2 In.	950.00
Sugar, Cover, c.1820, 5 3/4 In.	350.00
Vase, Blue Jasperware, White Classical Relief, Leaf Handles, Marked, 1790, 9 7/8 In.	920.00
Vase, Cover, Jasperware, Dark Blue, Gladiators, Women's Head Handles, 1800, 10 In.	460.00

ADVERTISING containers and products sold in the old country store are now all collectibles. These stores, with the crackers in a barrel and a potbellied stove, are a symbol of an earlier, less hectic time. Listed here are many of the advertising items. Other similar pieces may be found under the product name, such as Planters Peanuts. We have tried to list items in the logical places, so large store fixtures will be found under the Architectural category, enameled tin dishes under Graniteware, paper items in the Paper category, etc. Store fixtures, cases, and other items that have no advertising as part of the decoration are listed in the Store category.

Apron, Reddy Kilowatt	25.00
Ashtray, Anheuser-Busch, Ceramic, 1950s, 5 In.	15.00
Ashtray, Budweiser Beer, Metal, 1960s, 4 x 6 In.	16.00
Ashtray, Congress Beer, Derby Cream Ale, Mottled Finish, 1930s, 5 1/2 In.	150.00
Ashtray, Goodyear, Life Raft, Figural	45.00
Ashtray, Island Lager Beer, Ceramic, 1980s, 7 In.	13.00
Ashtray, Lemp Beer, 5 1/2 In.	45.00
Ashtray, Pepsin Tutti-Frutti	37.00
Ashtray, Ruppert-Knickerson Brewery, Bottle Shape, Glass	80.00
Ashtray, Tennent's Lager Beer, Ceramic, Early 1900s	23.00
Ashtray, US Navigation Co.	25.00
Ashtray, Yuengling's Beer, Glass, 1940s, 4 In.	16.00
Bag, Hyde Park Beer, Paper, Unused, 1950s, 8 x 10 In.	3.50
Bag, Manru Beer-Ale, Paper, 1940s, 8 x 12 In.	18.00
Bag, Poppin' Fresh Doughboy, Canvas Handle	10.00
Baggage Sticker, Hotel Swastika, Raton, N.M., Gilt, Black, Red, Prewar, 3 In.	32.00
Banner, Bambi Bread, Mickey Mouse & Pluto, Tug Of War With Bread, 20 In.	295.00
Banner, Floral Festival, Woodland, California, May 12th & 13th, 1923, 14 x 31 In.	27.00
Banner, Mr. Peanut, Sale, Paper, 1950s, 15 x 36 In.	200.00
Banner, Rich Holiday Goods, Double Sided, Canvas, 42 x 78 In.	468.00
Banner, Van Heusen Wrinkle-Free Shirts, Hand, Iron, Trash Can, 16 x 36 In.	29.00
Banner, Whitman's Chocolates, Famous Since 1842, 36 1/2 x 57 1/2 In.	100.00
Banner, Wrangler Logo, Western Designs, Blue Denim, 1950s, 39 x 72 In.	1702.00
Bill Clip, Hoyt's Flintstone Belting, Globe, Celluloid Button, 1 3/4 In.	25.00
Bill Hook, Eagle Paint & Varnish, Celluloid, Eagle, Stars & Stripes, 1 3/4 In.	120.00
Bill Hook, Worcester Salt, Red & White Enamel On Tin, Hook On End, 7 In.	30.00
Bin, De Nobili Cigar, Counter, Red Lettering, Mustard Ground, Tin, 12 x 8 x 4 In.	53.00
Bin, Dilworth's Coffee, Tin Panel, Gilt Stenciling, 1920s, 32 x 21 x 19 In.	625.00

Bin, Sure Shot Chewing Tobacco, Counter 715.00
Blotter, Elsie, Borden's, 1940s 35.00
Blotter, Heidelberg Beer, Unused, 1948 .... 5.50
Blotter, Ink, Green River Whiskey, 1920, Set Of 2 .... 46.00
Blotter, Levi's 35.00
Blotter, Morton Salt, 1930s 35.00
Blotter, Snap, Crackle & Pop, Kellogg's, Vernon Grant 15.00
Blotter, Sunoco, Rounded Corners, Cardboard, Blue, 3 3/4 x 7 3/4 In. 5.00
Booklet, Duke's Cigarettes, General Winfield Scott, Knapp & Co., 1888 ...... 25.00
Booklet, Dutch Boy White Lead Paint, Painting The House That Jack Built, 1920 ...... 34.00
Booklet, Pictorial History Of The Vendo Company, 1952 .... 70.00
Bookmark, No. One Penny Chocolate Candies, Yellow, Red Tin, c.1890 .... 50.00
Books may be included in the Paper category.
Bottle Hanger, RC Cola, Santa Claus, 1950s 10.00
Bottle Openers are listed in their own category.
Bottle Topper, Dr Pepper, Edith Luce, With Empty Bottle 150.00
Bottle Topper, Dr Pepper, Sandy Carleson, With Full Bottle 195.00
Bottle Topper, Hires Root Beer, Healthful, Delicious 80.00
Bottle Topper, Smile, With Full Bottle, Paper Label 430.00
Bottle Topper, Virginia Dare Grape Punch, Cardboard, 4 3/4 x 7 1/2 In. 20.00
Bottle Topper, Whistle, Girl's Head, With Bottle 175.00
Bottles are listed in their own category.
Box, see also Box category.
Box, Big Yank Union Made Shirts, Orange, Black, 11 x 14 x 4 In. 35.00
Box, Blue Jay Rolled Oats, Blue Jay In Center, Red Lettering, Round, 42 Oz. 902.00
Box, Bull Durham, Black Lettering, Light Yellow Ground, Cardboard, 4 x 7 In. 25.00
Box, Butter, K & W Fancy Print Butter Carrier, Stenciled, Wooden, 4 Trays 175.00
Box, C.W.S. Congress Soap, Beautiful Woman, Black, Green & Red, 18 In. 22.00
Box, Caravan Condom, Cardboard, Holds 3 Doz. 42.00
Box, Cereal, Home Brand Rolled Oats, Cardboard 55.00
Box, Cereal, Kellogg's All Bran, Light Yellow Ground 43.00
Box, Cereal, Kellogg's Corn Flakes, Leave It To Beaver, 1984, 24 Oz. 50.00
Box, Cereal, Kellogg's Corn-Soya Shreds, New & Different, Light Yellow, 7 Oz. 27.50
Box, Cereal, Kellogg's Pepwheat Flakes, Baseball Player 100.00
Box, Cereal, Kellogg's Sugar Frosted Flakes, Tony The Tiger 125.00
Box, Cereal, Monadnock Rolled Oats 187.00
Box, Cereal, Morning Glory Oats 38.00
Box, Cigar, Benduro, Tax Stamp, 1917 .... 85.00
Box, Cigar, Black Hawk, Andy Dehner Cigar Co., 1894 .... 120.00
Box, Cigar, Christmas Victorian Scene, Celluloid, Small 50.00
Box, Cigar, Club Night, Enterprise Cigar Co., 1901 .... 85.00
Box, Cigar, Cody Special Extra Fresh, 8 3/4 x 5 1/2 x 2 1/2 In. 90.00
Box, Cigar, Coronas, Lancaster Country Club, Wooden, Brass Latch 75.00
Box, Cigar, Don Digo, Tax Stamps 85.00
Box, Cigar, Gay Boy, 10 Count, c.1901 .... 55.00
Box, Cigar, Hobson's Fearless, Naval, 1896 .... 75.00
Box, Cigar, Jose Morales, 1898, Box Of 25 .... 60.00
Box, Cigar, Mohawk Chief, Cardboard 80.00
Box, Cigar, Old Cabin, Jack Dunn's Special 65.00
Box, Cigar, Old Plantation, Black Works, Tobacco Fields, 3 x 11 1/4 x 5 1/2 In. 38.00
Box, Cigar, Pickwick Club, Tax Stamp, 1917 .... 85.00
Box, Cigar, Rail Splitter, 50 Count, c.1920 .... 55.00
Box, Cigar, Tempter, Devil & Lightning 120.00
Box, Cigar, Totem, Watt & Bond, Box Of 100 .... 55.00
Box, Cigar, X-Teddy, Cedar 60.00
Box, Cigarette, Egyptian Turkish, Stephano Bros., Hinged, 3 3/4 x 3 In. .... *Illus* 2.00
Box, Cigarette, London Life, Cardboard, 1910, 10s 20.00
Box, Cigarette, M. Melachrino & Co., Cardboard, 1909, 10s 25.00
Box, Cigarette, Schenasi Bros. Nat., Cardboard, 1909, 10s 15.00
Box, Clark's Honest Square Candy Bar, 1930s 45.00
Box, Cretor's Popcorn, Young Girl Eating Popcorn, Blue & Orange, 1929 ...... 10.00
Box, Early Peas, William P. Burt, Cardboard, 4 1/2 x 3 x 3/4 In. .... *Illus* 4.00
Box, Fairbanks Fairy Soap, 1898, 16 x 17 x 8 In. 175.00

Advertising, Box, Cigarette, Egyptian Turkish, Stephano Bros., Hinged, 3 3/4 x 3 In.

Advertising, Box, Early Peas, William P. Burt, Cardboard, 4 1/2 x 3 x 3/4 In.

Advertising, Box, Nasturtium Dwarf Seeds, Cardboard, 2 1/2 x 3 1/4 x 1 In.

Box, Fairbanks Fairy Soap, Christmas, Picture Inside Lid, Wooden, 17 In. 190.00
Box, Fairbanks Fairy Soap, Pure White Floating Soap, Wooden, 17 In. 230.00
Box, Fairbanks Gold Dust Washing Powder, Black Twins, Cardboard, Contents, 1930 . . . 95.00
Box, Fairbanks Gold Dust, Wooden, Stenciled Label, 27 In. 120.00
Box, Fun To Wash Washing Powder, Mammy, Cardboard, c.1910, 3 x 5 x 7 In. 34.00
Box, Gold Dust Washing Powder, Cardboard, Contents, 2 Lb. 4 Oz. 50.00
Box, Hill Country Butter, Brady & Fredericksburg, Texas, Waxed, 1/2 Lb. 4.50
Box, Ivory Snow, Procter & Gamble, Wooden Box, c.1930, 18 x 11 x 12 In. 95.00
Box, Kraft Cheese, Wooden, 11 3/4 In. . . . . .8.00 to 12.00
Box, Lenox Soap, Wooden, Stencil, 19 In. 45.00
Box, Magic White Soap, Wooden, Paper Label, 19 1/2 In. 45.00
Box, Mediar Co.'s Biscuits, Chromolithograph Labels, Wooden, 1 1/2 In. 247.00
Box, Mel-O-Bit Cheese, Great Atlantic & Pacific Tea Co., Wooden, 9 In. 8.00
Box, Milk, Koontz Dairy Products, Tin, Hinged Lid, 1950-1960, 12 x 10 x 13 In. 35.00
Box, Morning Glory Quick Oats, Teal Blue Ground, Round, 4 Oz. 45.00
Box, Nasturtium Dwarf Seeds, Cardboard, 2 1/2 x 3 1/4 x 1 In. . . . .*Illus* 3.00
Box, Old Dutch Cleanser, Wooden, Stenciled, Red, Black, 20 In. 35.00
Box, Old Style Lager Beer, Heileman Brewing, Cardboard, Dividers, 1950s 10.00
Box, Packing, Mason's Complete Fruit Jars, 1 Doz., 1858 Jar Picture On Crate 55.00
Box, Pickwick Rolled Oats, Gentlemen In Center, Black Lettering, Round, 4 Oz. 67.00
Box, Quaker Corn Meal, Cardboard, Price 9 Cents, Round, 6 1/2 In. . . . .*Illus* 8.00
Box, Saf-T Pops, 1 Cent Lollipops, Kids On Front, Unpunched, 1940s 98.00
Box, Seed, Printed Label, 13 x 27 In. 192.00
Box, Shelby's Bubble Gum 35.00
Box, Silica Soap, With 12 Individual Bars, 10 1/2 In. 28.00
Box, Smoky City Laundry Flakes, Contents, 8 1/4 In. 45.00
Box, Soap, Label, Seals Of 13 Colonies, Lafayette's Visit To America, 1824, 4 3/8 In. . . . 395.00
Box, Sterling Creamery Butter, Sterling, Kansas, Waxed, Dated 1935, 1 Lb. 6.00
Box, Sunny Monday Soap, White, Blue, Red, 13 1/2 In. 44.00
Box, Toothpaste, Carnation Creme, c.1910 . . . . 20.00
Box, Typewriter Ribbon, A & W, Black & Red, 1950s 9.50
Box, West Beach & Motor Hair Net, 3 Tiers, Tin Lithograph, 5 1/2 x 6 1/2 In. 175.00
Box, Wrigley's Juicy Fruit Gum, Cardboard, Holds 20 Packs 65.00
Brochure, N-A-T Flying Service, Inc., Tri-Motor Monoplane, 4 x 9 In. 64.00
Cabinet, American Railway Express, Wooden Countertop, 33 x 25 x 11 In. 58.00
Cabinet, Clark's Spool, Dime Store, Metal & Glass, 1950s, 10 x 23 In. 125.00
Cabinet, Diamond Dyes, Children With Balloons, Oak, 30 x 23 In. 1275.00
Cabinet, Diamond Dyes, Maypole 2000.00
Cabinet, Display, Carborundum, 2 Sides Glass, 2 Sides Wood, 41 1/2 x 22 In. 440.00
Cabinet, Display, Dr. Daniels', Tin Front, 15 Medicines 2205.00
Cabinet, Display, Humphreys' Veterinary Specifics, Farmyard Scene . . . . .3465.00 to 5000.00
Cabinet, Sauer's Extracts, Wood, Glass Front, 1910-15, 12 x 26 x 7 In. 1065.00

Cabinet, Spool, Clark's, Cherry, Black Letters On Gold, 21 x 16 x 17 In. 400.00
Cabinet, Spool, Clark's, Slant Front, Oak, Decal On Front, 24 x 32 x 9 In. 604.00
Cabinet, Spool, J. & P. Coats', Blue Tin, Glass Doors, Gold Lettering 135.00
Cabinet, Spool, J. & P. Coats', Top Slanted Front, Oak, 31 x 24 x 10 In. 1150.00
Cabinet, Spool, Richardson's, 4 Sides, 24 x 30 x 24 In. 1150.00
Cabinet, Spool, Walnut, 4 Drawers, Brass Pulls, 23 x 17 x 16 In. 275.00
Cabinet, Westinghouse Auto Bulbs, Countertop, 1930s 150.00
Cake Pan, Angel Food, Swans Down Cake Flour, 1923 . . . . 30.00
Calculator, Matchbook, Camel Joe 12.50
Calendars are listed in their own category.
Caliper, Steel, Leg, Compliments Of Snap-On Tools, Inc., 2 1/2 To 3 In., Set Of 4 . . . . . . 242.00
Can, Gunpowder, Snapshot, 1 Lb. 80.00
Can, Negro Head Shrimp, Image Of Black Man, Paper Label, 4 1/2 Oz. 440.00
Can, Niggerhead Oysters, Exaggerated Image, Paper Label 400.00
Can, Puffenjoy Tobacco, Lev-A-Lift Pry Lid, Paper Label, 1940s Tax Stamp 110.00
Can, Socony Kerosene, Embossed Lettering, 1 Gal., 15 In. 192.00
Can, Sunbrite Cleanser, 13 Oz. 22.00
Can, Thermo Antifreeze, 1 Gal., 8 In. 33.00
Can Opener, Blatz Beer, Slide Out, 1950s 20.00
Can Opener, Figural Bottle, Teachers Highland Cream 25.00
Can Opener, Pet Milk, Punch Type 22.00
Candy Dish, Pan American Airways, Metal, Winged Globe, Sweden, 4 In., 2 Piece 43.00
Canisters, see introductory paragraph to Tins in this category.
Cap, Driver's, Bunny Bread 40.00
Cards are listed in the Card category.
Carrier, Bottle, Dr. Pepper, Six Pack, Wire, Tin, 1930s-1940s 605.00
Carrier, Bottle, Olde Frothingslosh Ale, 6 Pack, 1950s 8.50
Carrier, Dr Pepper, Polished Aluminum, c.1930s-1940s 430.00
Carton, Bing Crosby Ice Cream, Bing's Picture, 1953 . . . . 7.00
Carton, Buttermilk, Sanders Dairy, Rogersville, Tenn., Wax, 1940s, 1 Qt. 10.00
Carton, Dad's Root Beer Flavored Milk, Cardboard, Unused, Flat, 1/2 Gal. 50.00
Carton, Milk, Hancock Co. Creamery, Ellsworth, Me., Wax, Cone Shape, 10 In. 25.00
Carton, Milk, Sanders Dairy, Rogersville, Tenn., Wax, 1940s, 1 Pt. 10.00
Carton, Oleomargarine, Tasti-Spred, Butterine Co., Baltimore, Wax, 1920s, 1 Lb. 16.00
Case, Ingersoll Pencil, Etched Front Glass, Opens From Back, Storage In Bottom 450.00
Case, Mansfield's Pepsin Gum, 1900-1910, 11 1/2 In. 1265.00
Case, Merrick's Six Cord Soft Finish Spool Cotton, Cylindrical, Oak, Glass 1100.00
Case, Shipping, Anheuser-Busch, Wood, 1920, 20 1/2 x 13 x 11 1/2 In. 35.00
Case, Zippo, Glass, 8 Sides, 5 Tiers, Lighted, Motorized, 23 In. 230.00
Chair, Folding, Piedmont Cigarettes, 2 Piece 230.00
Chalkboard, Knickerbocker Beer, Tin On Cardboard, Unused, 15 x 18 In. 16.00
Chalkboard, Orange Kist, Bottle, Tin, Embossed, c.1940s, 13 x 19 In. 265.00
Change Receiver, see also Tip Tray in this category.
Change Receiver, Wrigley's Gum, Arrow Shape, Glass, 1920s-1930s 265.00
Change Tray, Baby Ruth Gum, Glass 125.00
Charger, Malt Rainier, Pure Malt Tonic, 1904, 17 1/2 In. 275.00

Advertising, Dispenser,
Hires Root Beer, 1920,
14 x 8 In.

**Ultraviolet rays coming in a
window and fluorescent light
will fade tin signs and cans.
Plexiglass UF-1 or UF-3 will
cover the window and keep the
rays away from your collection.
There are also plastic sleeves
to cover fluorescent tubes.**

Advertising, Box, Quaker Corn
Meal, Cardboard, Price
9 Cents, Round, 6 1/2 In.

Cigar Band, Mark Twain, Pictorial, c.1930 .... 10.00
Cigar Cutter, Cast Iron, Colonial Soldier & Horse Design 245.00
Cigar Cutter, Desktop, Match Holder, Dickens Characters 425.00
Cigar Cutter, Donkey, Cast Iron, Pat. March 30, 1897, 8 x 7 In. 550.00
Cigar Cutter, Royal Seal, Countertop, Painted Light Gold, Iron, 1903, 18 x 9 In. 2200.00
Cigar Cutter, Star Tobacco, Countertop, Patent 1885, Iron 125.00
Clapper, Hand Held, Cherry's Ice Cream, Paper Cat, Cardboard, Die Cut, 6 In. 47.00
Clicker, Quaker State Motor Oil, Tin 35.00
Clocks are listed in their own category.
Coaster, Baltimore American Ale & Beer, Orange, Blue, Round, 4 In. 5.50
Coaster, Free State Beer, Yellow, Black & Orange, Round, 4 In. 6.50
Coaster, Knickerbocker Beer, Metal, 1950s, 4 In. 8.00
Coaster, Regal Supreme Beer, 1 Side, 1940s, 4 In. 13.00
Container, Lutted's S.P. Cough Drops, Log Cabin, Glass, 7 x 7 1/2 x 5 In. 350.00
Cookie Cutter, Elsie's Daughter, Buelah's Face, Borden's, Plastic, 2 1/4 In. 48.00
Cooler, Kist, Wooden, Metal Lined, Double-Hinged Top 350.00
Cooler, Nehi Soda, Floor Model, With 4 Nehi Signs 1350.00
Cooler, Orange Crush, Wooden, Zinc Lining, 1910s-1920s, 34 x 19 x 33 In. 431.00
Creamer, Sinclair Oil, Walker China, 1939 .... 100.00
Crock, Elkhorn Brand Cottage Cheese, 10 Lb. 185.00
Cup, Baker's Cocoa, Restaurant 60.00
Cup, Charlie Tuna, Plastic, 1977 .... 17.00
Cup, Measuring, Cream Dove Brand Peanut Butter Salad Dressing, Green, 1 Cup 40.00
Cup, Solitaire Peanut Butter, Tin 60.00
Cup & Saucer, Red Rose Tea, Fortune-Telling, Bone China 9.00
Decanter, Mennen, Construction Worker, Orange Hard Hat, 1960s, 9 1/2 In. 20.00
Dexterity Puzzle, Cherry Blossoms, Blooming Good Drink, Prewar, 1 1/4 In. 33.00
Dexterity Puzzle, Esskay Quality Meat Products, Metal, Plastic, 1950s, 2 In. 22.00
Dish, Howard Johnson's Ice Cream, Silhouette Logo, Gold Rim, 1950s, 4 In. 20.00
Dish, Mr. Peanut, 50th Anniversary, Diecasters, Ridgefield, N.J., 1956, 6 In. 105.00
Dispenser, Alka-Seltzer Powder, Cast Iron, 1920s 225.00
Dispenser, Buckeye Root Beer, Tree Trunk Shape 300.00
Dispenser, Cherry Smash, Bolt-On, Ruby Glass, c.1930s-1940s 575.00
Dispenser, Cherry Smash, Glass On Leaves, c.1920 .... 3450.00
Dispenser, Cherry Smash, Milk Glass Base, Gallon Jug, Label, 19 In. 546.00
Dispenser, Dalton's Orangeade & Lemonade, 2 Containers, Tub, Spigots, 1900 .... 110.00
Dispenser, Double Kay Salted Nuts, Porcelain, Kelling-Karel Co., 21 x 9 x 17 In. 242.00
Dispenser, Fan-Taz, Hand Pump, Ceramic Baseball, Bat & Slogans, 1910 .... 8625.00
Dispenser, Grape Smash, Ball Pump, 1918-1922 .... 10925.00
Dispenser, Green River, Trophy Style, 15 In. 230.00
Dispenser, Hires Root Beer, 1920, 14 x 8 In. ....*Illus* 1210.00
Dispenser, Hires, Bolt On Stainless & Porcelain, 1930s-1940s, 21 In. 230.00
Dispenser, Liberty Root Beer, Barrel, Oak, 1920s, 2 Ft. 402.00
Dispenser, Middleby Root Beer, Mug Shape, Amber, Bakelite Base, 16 In. 316.00
Dispenser, Mission Orange, Amber, Original Lid, Decals, 14 In. ....230.00 to 259.00
Dispenser, Mission, Green Glass, Chrome Base & Lid, 13 1/2 In. 75.00
Dispenser, Mission, Light Amber Glass, Chrome Base & Lid, 13 1/2 In. 172.00
Dispenser, Nesbitt's Soda, 1940s 250.00
Dispenser, Orange Crush, 1940s 1075.00
Dispenser, Oriental Tea Co., Boston, 26 1/2 In. 225.00
Dispenser, Paper Cone, For Soda Fountain, Brass, c.1920s, 11 In. 125.00
Dispenser, Ward's Lemon Crush, 8 3/4 In. 920.00
Dispenser, Ward's Lemon Crush, Pump, Marked Ball, 1915-1920, 13 1/2 In. 2645.00
Dispenser, Ward's Lime Crush, Green Base, Black Lettering, 13 1/2 In. 2185.00
Dispenser, Ward's Lime Crush, Porcelain, 12 1/2 In. 2760.00
Dispenser, Ward's Orange Crush, Syrup, 9 3/4 In. 690.00
Dispenser, Ward's, Orange Crush, 14 In. 1380.00
Dispenser, Wine-Dip, Glass, Silicone Sealed, 20 In. 230.00
Display, 7-Up, Bottle In Iceberg, 1940s-1950s 315.00
Display, 7-Up, Bottles, Mix Drinks, Stand-Up, Cardboard, 1950, 8 x 12 In. 70.00
Display, Aero-Lux Electric, Light-Up Figural Horsehead Interior 125.00
Display, Alka-Seltzer, Tin Lithograph, Advanced Display Co., 1950s, 12 x 12 x 6 In. 75.00
Display, Armour Soap, Glass, Embossed, Counter 250.00

Display, Arrow Collar, Vertical Collar, Glass, Brass Trim, 7 x 7 x 47 In. 632.50
Display, Box, Hoarhound & Wild Cherry Drops, Wooden, Stenciled, 4 1/2 In. 75.00
Display, Captain Morgan Spiced Rum, Wooden, Ceramic, 12 x 13 In. 73.00
Display, Clark's Teaberry Gum, Embossed, 7 x 5 x 3 In. 31.00
Display, Daisy Red Ryder, 50th Anniversary, Cardboard, 3 Ft. 50.00
Display, Dr. Morse's Indian Root Pills, Village, 3-Part Cardboard, 27 x 41 In. 690.00
Display, Eblings Goblet Extra, Etched, Colored, Frosted Top, 11 x 7 x 7 In. 67.00
Display, Gotham Watches, Hand Drops Tray Of Water, 1955 .... 300.00
Display, Gunther Beer, John L. Sullivan, 1950s 325.00
Display, Hamm's Beer, Polar Bear, Mechanical 1250.00
Display, Horseshoe Tobacco, Chalkware, Counter, 3-D, 1900 .... 200.00
Display, Jack Daniels, Figural, Basswood, Carved 45.00
Display, Keen Kutter Pocket Knife, Plywood, Metal Logo, Tag, 12 x 16 In. 70.00
Display, Lucky Lindy Perfume, 18 Bottles, Label With Name & Plane, Box 250.00
Display, Lucky Strike Cigarette, Walter Hagen, I Prefer Lucky Strikes, 6 x 10 In. ... 380.00
Display, Mobil Pegasus Fan Belt 100.00
Display, Monarch Soap, Cardboard 82.00
Display, Munsing Wear, Pretty Woman, Cardboard, 1928 .... 85.00
Display, Oily Bird Household Lubricant, Half Cage, Brass, Paper Back, Bottle 60.00
Display, Old Virginia Cheroots, Automated, Papier-Mache, Clockwork, 1900 ...... 4950.00
Display, Palmolive Soap, Keep That Schoolgirl Complexion, 19 3/4 In. 35.00
Display, Rosemarie Reid Swimsuits, Mannequin, White Wire, 1950s, 60 In. 125.00
Display, Sanford Inks, Pyramidal Oak, Glass Countertop, Ivory, 12 x 9 x 16 In. 498.00
Display, Slinky, Boy Holding A Slinky, 1956, 17 x 17 In. 750.00
Display, Squirt, Santa Claus As Jack-In-The Box, Stand In 6 Bottles, 1959, 15 In. ... 15.00
Display, Star Soap, Reverse Mirror, Countertop, 5 1/2 In. 440.00
Display, Sweetheart Soap, Baby, Bassinet, Composition, Figural, Animated, 32 In. 450.00
Display, Teacher's Highland Cream Scotch Liquor, Mortarboard, 15 In. 105.00
Display, Tinkertoy, Paddlewheel Model Of Tinkertoy Parts, 1940 .... 450.00
Display, Whistle, Elves, Cardboard, With Bottle, 1948, 13 x 11 In. 520.00
Dolls are listed in their own category.
Door Bar, Ken-L Ration Dog Biscuits, 1950s 489.00
Door Bar, Whistle, Wire, Tin, Adjustable, 30 In. 345.00
Door Bar & Handle Pull, Sunbeam Bread, Loaf, 1950s, 30 x 15 In. 316.00
Door Plate, Vicks, Porcelain, 8 x 4 In. 275.00
Door Pull, Cigar, Celluloid 200.00
Door Pull, Old Gold Cigarettes, Dancing 149.00
Door Push, 7-Up, Come In, 7-Up Likes You, Aluminum, c.1940s 98.00
Door Push, Budweiser, Bottle, 1940s-1950s 98.00
Door Push, Canada Dry Spur, Bottle, Tin, 1940s, 3 x 9 In. 30.00
Door Push, Dreikoorns Bread 75.00
Door Push, Ex-Lax, Colorful Tin, Dark Blue Plastic, 7 1/2 x 3 1/2 In. 40.00
Door Push, Frings Cigars, Tin Lithograph, 9 x 3 1/2 In. 88.00
Door Push, Grapette, Aluminum 220.00
Door Push, Hart Batteries, Porcelain, 3 1/4 x 32 In. 110.00
Door Push, Jena Glass Chimneys & Globes, Porcelain, 7 3/4 x 3 1/8 In. 275.00
Door Push, Ken-L-Ration Dog Biscuits, Navy Ground, Yellow Dog, 1950s 490.00
Door Push, Kist Beverages, 1940s-1950s 57.00
Door Push, Kool Cigarettes, Pack 69.00
Door Push, Korker Soda, Metal 55.00
Door Push, L & M Cigarettes, Pack, 1960s 69.00
Door Push, Lipton's Tea 60.00
Door Push, Mission Beverages, With Mirror, 3 1/2 x 12 In. 115.00
Door Push, Mission Orange, Bottle, Large Cap, Embossed 138.00
Door Push, Old Gold Cigarettes, Dancing 126.00
Door Push, Peter Pan Bread 80.00
Door Push, Robin Hood Flour, Porcelain 75.00
Door Push, Salada Tea Bags, Porcelain, 3 1/4 x 31 1/2 In. 110.00
Door Push, Salada Tea, 2 Sides, Porcelain, 3 1/8 x 32 In. ....45.00 to 50.00
Door Push, U.S. Royal Soles-Heels, Porcelain, 3 x 31 7/8 In. 130.00
Door Push, Vicks, Porcelain 75.00
Door Push, Voigts Crescent Flour 145.00
Dose Glass, Ginch Weiss Pharmacy, Philadelphia, Pa., Embossed Eagle 20.00

Dose Glass, Louis Klinzing Pharmacist, Rochester, N.Y. 22.00
Egg Separator, Hood's Dairy Products 45.00
Fans are listed in their own category.
Figure, Big Boy, Fat Model, Plastic, Vinyl, 1950s, 9 1/2 In. 80.00
Figure, Big Boy, Fat Model, Plastic, Vinyl, Niagara Plastics, 1980s, 8 1/2 In. 35.00
Figure, Big Boy, Plastic, Vinyl, Painted, Thin, 1973, 8 1/2 In. 36.00
Figure, Big Boy, Rubber, Cloth Shirt, Overalls, Dakin, Hong Kong, 1970, 8 In. 102.00
Figure, Big Boy, Rubber, Vinyl, First Edition, 1960s, 9 3/4 In. 79.00
Figure, Blatz Beer, Barrel Man Holding Mug, Metal, 8 In. 60.00
Figure, Dog, Nipper, RCA, 36 In. 2550.00
Figure, Hamm's Bear, Ceramic, Brazil, 1972 .... 125.00
Figure, Hohner Harmonicas, Boy On Large Ashtray Playing Music, Germany 350.00
Figure, Kentucky Fried Chicken, Colonel Sanders, Plastic, 1970s, 13 In. 40.00
Figure, Knap, Kellogg's, Plastic, White, Red, Yellow & Blue, 7 1/2 In. 55.00
Figure, McDonald's Grimace, Ceramic, 6 In. 45.00
Figure, Pabst Blue Ribbon Beer, Barber-Shop Quartet, Metal, 1960s, 11 In. 70.00
Figure, Reddy Kilowatt, Head Glows In Dark, Plastic Feet & Hands, 5 1/2 In. 265.00
Figure, Rolling Rock, Horse Rearing, Plaster, Raised Letters On Base, 1960s, 11 In. 65.00
Figure, Speedy, Alka-Seltzer, 8 In. 950.00
Figure, Tagamet, Stomach With Face, Vinyl, Pink, 5 In. 45.00
Figure, Texaco, Man, Wearing Uniform, Hat, Aluminum, 16 x 11 In. 19.00
Figure, Use Puritan Flour, Mannequin, Oilcloth Apron 475.00
Flashlight, Figural, Little Sprout, Green Giant 50.00
Flashlight, Schlitz Beer, Bottle Shape 15.00
Flyswatter, Straub's Beer, Plastic, 1950s 3.50
Foam Scraper, Knickerbocker Beer 9.00
Foam Scraper, Miller High Life Beer, 1 Side, 1930s 50.00
Foam Scraper, R & H Beer & Ale, Butterscotch Cantel, 1940s 55.00
Foam Scraper, Regal Amber Lager Beer, Wave, 1 Side, 1940s 18.00
Foam Scraper, Rheingold Beer 9.00
Foam Scraper, Schmidt's City Club Beer, 2 Sides, 1940s 28.00
Game, Dr. Pepper Puzzle Game, 2 Bent Nails, Celluloid Disks, 1905-1910 .... 1265.00
Game, Mail Pouch Tobacco, Mirrored Writing Game, Tin, 1920s-1930s, 4 x 5 In. 140.00
Glass, Blatz Pilsener Beer, Painted Label, 1950s, 4 In. 11.00
Glass, Broom Hilda, Reads The Sunday Funnies, Enameled 85.00
Glass, Dr Pepper, Cleveland Browns, Mike Pruitt 5.00
Glass, Elsie & Beulah Restaurant, Brown & Gold Stripes 80.00
Glass, Erin Brew, Cleveland, Post-Prohibition, Enameled, 1951 .... 370.00
Glass, Fink Brewing Company, Sandstone Finish, Pre-Prohibition, 3 1/2 In. 45.00
Glass, Louis Bergdoll Brewing, 60th Anniversary, 1909, 4 In. 55.00
Glass, Lucky Lager Beer, Brown & Red Painted Label, 1960s, 7 In. 4.00
Glass, McDonald's, Grimace, 1977, 16 Oz. 6.00
Glass, Orange Soda, Frosted, Bell Shaped 29.00
Glass, P.O.C. Beer, White Finish, Pre-Prohibition, 4 In. 96.00
Glass, Pillsbury Doughboy, 30th Birthday, Box, 6 Piece 30.00
Glass, Pizza Hut, Care Bear, Cheer Bear 3.00
Glass, Puritan Brewing, Stemmed, Etched, Pre-Prohibition, 6 1/2 In. 38.00
Glass, Regal, Tastes Better, Painted Label, 1960s, 3 1/2 In. 33.00
Glass, Schlitz, Painted Label, Stemmed, 6 1/2 In. 8.00
Glass, Welch's, Flintstone, Fred's Newest Invention, Wilma 4.00
Glass, Welch's, Road Runner, Yosemite Sam, Warner Bros. 5.00
Globe, Irvona Hardware Co., Quality & Service, 16 1/2 x 15 In. 330.00
Hat, Soda Jerk, Mountain Dew, Hillbillies On Mountain, Paper 20.00
Hat, Soda Jerk, Paper, Mountain Dew, Unused, 11 x 3 1/2 In. 29.00
Hat, Straw, International Harvester, White, Red Trim, 1950s-1960s, Size Small 20.00
Hat Box, Dobb's Felt, Salesman Sample, Cardboard 35.00
Humidor, Dill's Best Humidor & Yale Square, Green Ground 43.00
Humidor, Manuel Cigars, Glass Hinge Lid Counter Case, Tin, 9 1/2 x 16 x 12 In. 399.00
Ice Bucket, Alka-Seltzer, Vinyl, 1979, 11 In. 50.00
Ice Chest, Nehi Soda, 1930s 975.00
Ice Pick, Moosehorn Lake Ice, Worcester, Ma., Metal 25.00
Jacket, Jack Daniels, Black Nylon, Cotton Lining, Slash Pockets, Size 44 .... 24.00
Jacket, Joe Camel, Windbreaker, Large 50.00

Jar, Adams, Chewing Gum, Thumbnail Lid, 1915 .... 126.00

Jar, American Lady Coffee, 3 Lb. 45.00

Jar, Beater, With Beater, Wesson Oil, Stoneware 185.00

Jar, Carnation Malted Milk, Milk Glass, Aluminum Cover, 1940s-1950s 175.00

Jar, Easy Off Oven Cleaner, Attached Applicator Brush, Contents 6.00

Jar, Franklin Caro, Chewing Gum, Small Embossing 40.00

Jar, Franklin Manufacturing Company, Chewing Gum, Large Embossing 75.00

Jar, Horlick's Malted Milk, 11 In. 85.00

Jar, Old Judge Coffee, Embossed Glass, Paper Label 65.00

Jar, Squirrel Brand Salted Nuts, Embossed Name & Squirrel, 14 1/2 In. 475.00

Jar, Squirrel Salted Peanuts 92.00

Jar, Union Leader Tobacco, Cardboard Lid, Label, 1943 .... 45.00

Jug, Cherry Smash, Glass, Embossed, 1 Gal. 60.00

Jug, Schlitz Beer, Hand Blown, Metal Handle, Etched, 1880 .... 325.00

Jug, Shaker Ketchup, Stoneware 175.00

Jug, Syrup, Cherry Smash, Paper Label, Glass, 1930s 100.00

Kite, Jell-O, Unused 18.00

Kite, Mounds, Sometimes You Feel Like A Nut, Paper, Early 1970s, 22 x 28 In. 25.00

Label, Ale, Old Monterey Extra Dry, Monterey Brewing, Oval, Neckband, 11 Oz. 5.50

Label, Ale, U.S., Tivoli Union Co., 12 Oz. 28.00

Label, Apples, Wapato Fruit & Cold Storage Co., Wapato, Wash., 11 x 9 In. ...... *Illus* 12.00

Label, Beer, Blue & Gold Lager, Extra Strength, Neckband, 11 Oz., 2 Piece 33.00

Label, Beer, Fredericksburg Export, Pacific Brewing, Neckband, 11/16 Quart 17.00

Label, Beer, Log Cabin, Paper, Globe Brewing, Permit No. Calif. U-1116, 11 Oz. 28.00

Label, Beer, Marinoff, Red Bluff Brewing, 1 Full Quart, Middle Crease 5.50

Label, Cigar Box, Cherry Ripe, 2 Piece 130.00

Label, Cigar Box, Home Stock, 2 Piece 140.00

Label, Cigar Box, Sharpshooters, 2 Piece 190.00

Label, Cigar, Betsy Ross, Mild Pleasing Quality 8.00

Label, Cigar, Rosa Moro, 4 3/8 x 2 1/4 In. 6.00

Label, Cigar, Sonny Boy Quality, 6 1/2 x 2 1/4 In. 7.00

Label, Cigar, Uncle Jake's Nickel Seegar, 5 x 2 1/4 In. 7.00

Label, Cigars, Red Cloud, Picture Of Red Cloud On Horseback, 10 x 6 1/2 In. 25.00

Label, Cream Cheese, Armour's Veribest Full, 12 x 7 In. 6.00

Label, Hotel Taft, New York City, 1930s, 3 1/2 In. 12.00

Label, Root Beer, Yosemite, Yosemite Scenes, San Francisco, c.1930 .... 6.00

Label, Stringless Beans, Maryland Chief, 8 x 4 In. 2.50

Label, Tobacco, Navy Long Cut, Fashion Cut Plug, Monkeys, Cardboard, 8 x 11 In. 16.00

Lamps are listed in the Lamp category.

License, Boston Newsboy, Nickel, Black Lettering, No. 1909, 1973, 2 1/2 In. 30.00

License Plate, Big Smith Work Clothes, 1916-1956, 40 Years, Metal, 12 x 6 In. 81.00

License Plate, Eastern Airlines, Logo, Wings, Gold, Blue, White Ground, 12 x 6 In. 25.00

Lunch Boxes are listed in their own category.

Malted Milk Container, Borden's, Stainless Steel 138.00

Malted Milk Container, Carnation, Milk Glass 195.00

Malted Milk Container, Horlicks, Aluminum 161.00

Advertising, Label, Apples, Wapato Fruit &
Cold Storage Co., Wapato, Wash., 11 x 9 In.

Never wash a "flannel" (also called a
"blanket" or "felt"), the small piece
of fabric packed in cigar or cigarette
packs around 1914. Washing the small
fabric pieces will fade them. Put dry
flannels and a clean, dry towel in the
clothes drier set on the cool setting.
A few tumbles will remove dust.

Malted Milk Container, Horlicks, Glass ....138.00 to 149.00
Manual, Armour, The Business Of Being A Housewife, Color, Illustrated, 1921 .... 30.00
Manual, General Foods, Melvin Purvis Manual Of Instructions, 1936, 23 Pages 45.00
Matchbook, Wildroot Cream Oil, Fearless Fosdick, Lil' Abner, 1954 .... 45.00
Measure, Enna Jetticks, Foot Size, Width, Left & Right Foot, Metal, Brannock 65.00
Menu, Country Club Ice Cream, Cardboard, Frame, c.1950s, 10 x 20 In. 300.00
Menu Board, Dr Pepper, Bottle & Clock, 1940s 225.00
Menu Board, Frostie Root Beer, Tin Lithograph, 19 1/2 x 30 In. 120.00
Menu Board, Hambone Five Cent Cigar, Cardboard, 20 x 13 In. 132.00
Menu Board, Hires Root Beer, 1940s 275.00
Menu Mask, Child's, Howard Johnson's, Easter Bunny, 1950s, 10 x 14 In. 45.00

Advertising pocket mirrors range in size from 1 1/2 to 5 inches in diameter. Most of these mirrors were given away as advertising promotions and include the name of the company in the design.

Mirror, A. Wissel's Son, Cesspools & Toilets, Long Island, Pocket 38.00
Mirror, A.C. Boll Cafe, York's Best, Interior View, Pocket 77.00
Mirror, A.I. Root Company, Airline Bee Products, Pure Honey, Pocket 82.00
Mirror, ABC Power Washer, Altorfer Bros., Woman Washing Clothes, Pocket 187.00
Mirror, Adam Scheidt Brewing Company, Lotos Export, Pocket 175.00
Mirror, Ammon & Person, Creamery Butterine, Pocket 66.00
Mirror, Arnold's Brewery, Metal Rim, Pocket 77.00
Mirror, Arnold's Patent Flour, Pocket 49.00
Mirror, Ashland Brewing Company, Ashland, Wisconsin, Barrel Shape, Pocket 60.00
Mirror, Beaver Stoves & Furnaces, Coal & Gas, Danville, Pennsylvania, Pocket 38.00
Mirror, Beddeo, Clothing For Men, Women & Children, Open A Charge, Pocket 16.00
Mirror, Beeman's Pepsin Gum, Good For Digestion, Pocket 330.00
Mirror, Big Boy Soda, Bottle, Sunrise, Pocket 29.00
Mirror, Bjur Bros., & Gordon & Son, Pianos & Player Pianos, Pocket 65.00
Mirror, Bletzacker Furniture Company, Lancaster, Ohio, Pocket 165.00
Mirror, Bolton Shoe, Rochester, New York, Pocket 110.00
Mirror, Boston Herald, Paperboy With Papers, 1 3/4 In. 55.00
Mirror, Bromo-Seltzer, Cures All Headaches, Bottle Picture, Pocket 230.00
Mirror, Brotherhood Overalls, Girl, Dover, New Jersey, Pocket 242.00
Mirror, Buffalo Brand Overalls, Pants & Shirts, Pocket 55.00
Mirror, Butterine, Churned Fresh Daily, Boy & Cow, Pocket 180.00
Mirror, Carmen Complexion Powder, St. Louis, 1 3/4 In. 75.00
Mirror, Cascarets, Best For Bowels, 10 Cent, 25 Cent, 50 Cent, Pocket 88.00
Mirror, Cascarets, Cupid On Chamber Pot, Pocket, 2 In. 95.00
Mirror, Cedarburg Milk Company, Celluloid, Red, Black, Pocket 138.00
Mirror, Ceresota Flour, Prize Brand Flour Of The World, Child, Pocket 93.00
Mirror, Church & Company 's Soda, Arm & Hammer, Pocket 55.00
Mirror, Columbia Tool Steel Company, Clarite, U.S. Shield, Pocket 60.00
Mirror, Continental Cubes, Ready For Pipe, Nude Woman, Pocket 632.00
Mirror, Copper Clad, World's Greatest Range, Celluloid, Pocket, 2 3/4 In. 20.00
Mirror, Crowder Co., Best Coal, Germantown, Calendar Rim, Pocket 45.00
Mirror, Curtis Publishing Company, Saturday Evening Post, Oval, Pocket 93.00
Mirror, D.A. Fichter, Tonsorial Parlor, Wharton, New Jersey, Pocket 132.00
Mirror, DeBelle Grape Juice, Pocket 700.00
Mirror, Deluxe Ironer, Poland Laundry Machinery Co., Pocket, 3 1/2 In. 60.00
Mirror, Dixie Tailoring Co., Chicago, Statue Of Liberty, Oval, 2 3/4 In. 95.00
Mirror, Duffy Malt Whiskey, Pocket 50.00
Mirror, Duffy's Pure Malt Whiskey, 1915, Pocket, Set Of 6 ....69.00 to 80.00
Mirror, Duffy's Pure Malt Whiskey, Pure & Unadulterated, Oval, Pocket 95.00
Mirror, Duncan & Stenz, Silk Specialists, New York, Pocket 60.00
Mirror, Edward R. Harwood, Distributor Of High Grade Pianos, Pocket 110.00
Mirror, Enna Jettick, Shoes For Women, Pocket 35.00
Mirror, Ex-Lax, A Chocolate Laxative, Pocket 132.00
Mirror, Farmer's Band & Trust Company, Oval, Pocket 27.00
Mirror, First National Bank, Uniontown, Pennsylvania, Oval, Pocket 60.00
Mirror, Foot-Schulze Glove, Landscape Scene, Celluloid, Pocket, 2 3/4 In. 25.00
Mirror, Friedman-Shelby Leather Shoes, Monkey, See Other Side, Pocket 65.00
Mirror, Garland Stoves, Pocket 20.00

Mirror, Gerhard Lang Brewery, Buffalo, Pocket 105.00
Mirror, Graf's Soft Drinks, The Best What Gives, Pocket 6.00
Mirror, Greenings Big Nursery, Monroe, Michigan, Pocket 55.00
Mirror, Hackney's Seafood, Atlantic City, New Jersey, Pocket 165.00
Mirror, Hendrucks Club Rye, Chas. S. Gove Co., Boston, Pocket 82.00
Mirror, Hires Root Beer, Picture Of Girl Holding Mug With Ugly Kid, Pocket 300.00
Mirror, Hires Root Beer, Ugly Kid, Pocket ....150.00 to 200.00
Mirror, Hoff & Lynch, Operators Of Ferris Wheel, San Diego Exposition, Pocket 550.00
Mirror, Holeproof Hosiery, Pocket 30.00
Mirror, Hooker-Corser & Mitchell Company, Cantrihum, Overalls & Coats, Pocket 412.00
Mirror, Horlick's Malted Milk, Milk Maid, Cow, Celluloid, Pocket, 2 In. ....50.00 to 93.00
Mirror, Hotel Majestic, Philadelphia, Pocket 175.00
Mirror, J.H. Bell & Company, Mocha & Java Coffee, Chicago, Pocket 70.00
Mirror, Jacob Ruppert Beer, Colonial Man Leaning On Bottle, Pocket 155.00
Mirror, Jacob Ulmer Packing Company, Pottsville, Pennsylvania, Pocket 88.00
Mirror, James W. Wilcox, Artistic Tailoring, Albany, New York, Pocket 120.00
Mirror, Java Coffee Mills, Pocket 37.50
Mirror, Jewel Shop, Harrisburg, Pa., Glass, Celluloid, 1 3/4 x 3 3/4 In. 65.00
Mirror, John Morrell & Company, Meats, Pocket 45.00
Mirror, Keystone Overalls, Cleveland & Whitehill Company, Pocket 520.00
Mirror, King Arthur Flour, Minnesota, Knight On Horse, Pocket 198.00
Mirror, Kingan's, Hams, Bacon, Sausage, Lard, Pocket 143.00
Mirror, Kopkes Ports Wine, Barrel Shape, Celluloid, 2 3/4 In. 71.00
Mirror, Kratzer Vehicles, Pocket ....65.00 to 195.00
Mirror, Lava Chemical Resolvent Soap, Celluloid, Pocket, 2 In. 45.00
Mirror, Levi Brothers, The Berlin, Broadway's Big Store, Pocket 132.00
Mirror, Mahlon N. Haines, Shoe Wizard, Pocket 33.00
Mirror, Mascot, Crushed Cut Tobacco, Dog, Pocket 1100.00
Mirror, Mayflower Doughnuts, Optimist's Creed, Pocket 82.00
Mirror, McWatters-Dolan, Agents For Hart, Schaffner & Marx, Pocket 93.00
Mirror, Mennen's Toilet Powder, Violets, Man, Celluloid, 2 3/4 In. 53.00
Mirror, Monogram Stoves, Simonet Furn. & Carpet Co., Celluloid, 2 1/4 In. 64.00
Mirror, Morgan, Watch Repairs, We Know How, Pocket 45.00
Mirror, Morrell's Pride Meats, Heart, Delivery Man, Celluloid, 2 1/4 In. 53.00
Mirror, Murphy Ice & Fuel Company, Stockton, California, Pocket 70.00
Mirror, Ohio Blue Tip Matches, Factory Pictured, Pocket 185.00
Mirror, Old Dutch Cleanser, Pocket 12.00
Mirror, Old Green 10 Cent Cigar, Stoddard-Gilbert Company, Pocket 82.00
Mirror, Old Reliable Coffee, Always Good, Man, Smoking Pipe, Pocket 93.00
Mirror, Olympian Ice Cream, Westfield, New York, Pocket 143.00
Mirror, Omar Pearls, Woman, Draped In Pearl Necklaces, Pocket 220.00
Mirror, Paul F. Williams Garms, Salt, Rent, Exchange, New Jersey, Oval, Pocket 27.00
Mirror, Penn Mutual Life Insurance Company, Woman Reading To Child, Pocket 38.00
Mirror, Pennington County Bank, Rapid City, South Dakota, Pocket 33.00
Mirror, Perkasie Fire Department, Golden Jubilee, 1890-1940, Pocket 17.00
Mirror, Queen Quality Shoes, Pretty Woman, Pocket 160.00
Mirror, Razor, Gillette Safety Razor, Child Shaving, Calendar On Outer Rim, Pocket 175.00
Mirror, Royal Blend Coffee, Granger & Company, Pocket 120.00
Mirror, Ryan's Pure Beers, Syracuse, New York, Indian Head, Pocket 330.00
Mirror, S.E. Perlberg & Company, Wholesale Tailors, Chicago, Pocket 175.00
Mirror, Scharffer Pianos, 37 Years Experience, Michigan, Pocket 130.00
Mirror, Shane's Hats, Union Made, 2 Dollars, Pocket 82.00
Mirror, Shawmut Rubbers, A.H. Marshall, Rhode Island, Pocket 44.00
Mirror, Sidle Fletcher, Holmes Company, Granulated Sugar, Pocket 187.00
Mirror, Sill Stove Works, Sterling Range Has No Equal, Pocket 70.00
Mirror, Smith & Bussey, Clothiers, Skowhegan, Maine, Oval, Pocket 93.00
Mirror, Smith Premier Typewriters, Pictures Machine, Pocket 70.00
Mirror, Stacy's Chocolates, Sun Setting Over Water, 2 3/16 In. 95.00
Mirror, Stoddard, Gilbert & Company, Smoke The East Rock 10 Cent Cigar, Pocket 93.00
Mirror, Sunshine & Othello Enameled Ranges, Pocket 38.00
Mirror, Taxis Dumbo, Salesman's Sample, Flying Elephant, 2 1/4 In. 40.00
Mirror, Terre Haute Brewing Company, Girl & Bottle, Pocket 880.00
Mirror, Thatcher Furnace Company, Face Upside & Down, Frown & Smile, Pocket 143.00

Mirror, The Apple's, Quaint & Classic Furniture, Allentown, Pa., Pocket 105.00
Mirror, Tomson's Borax Soap, R.C. Tomson & Co., Philadelphia, Pocket 34.00
Mirror, Traveler's Insurance Co., Train, Celluloid, Pocket, 2 1/2 In. .... 55.00 to 85.00
Mirror, V. Linn & Son, Carriages Of Every Description, Brooklyn, New York, Pocket ... 187.00
Mirror, Valvoline Motor Oils, Barrel Form, San Francisco 330.00
Mirror, Victor, Pictures Dog Speaking Into Horn, Oval, Pocket 935.00
Mirror, Victrola, M. Steinert & Sons, Lowell, Massachusetts, Pocket 77.00
Mirror, Victrola, Millard's, Brooklyn, New York, Pocket 105.00
Mirror, Victrola, Sherman, Clay & Company, Sacramento, California, Pocket 105.00
Mirror, Walker's Cafe, Schenectady, New York, Nude Woman, Pocket 275.00
Mirror, Washburn-Crosby Co. Flour, Barrel, Celluloid, Pocket, 2 1/2 In. 55.00
Mirror, West End Brewing, Metal Trim, Pocket 122.00
Mirror, Weymann, Pianos, Victrolas, Everything Musical, Pocket 103.00
Mirror, White Cat Union Suits, Cooper Underwear Co., Celluloid, 2 3/4 In. 45.00
Mirror, William & Morgan, Quality Furniture, Utica, New York, Pocket 110.00
Mirror, William Stoffel Company, Made In Los Angeles, Pocket 132.00
Mirror, Woolf Bros., Kansas City, Brass, Round, 1 1/2 In. 41.00
Mirror, Workers Union, Wear Union Stamped Shoes, Pocket .... 25.00 to 38.00
Mirror & Comb, Lifesavers, Vinyl Case, 1970's, 5 In. 10.00
Money Clip, Hughes Tool, Sterling 95.00
Mug, A & W Root Beer, 6 In. 8.50
Mug, A & W Root Beer, Emblem, 4 1/4 In. 25.00
Mug, Anheuser-Busch, Commemorative, Gussie Busch, Cardinals, 1990, 5 In. 35.00
Mug, Budweiser, Clydesdales, Winter Scene, Ceramarte, 6 In. 19.00
Mug, Campbell's Soup, Plastic 25.00
Mug, Carnation Hot Cocoa Mix, Red 4.00
Mug, Cocoa Crush, Ceramic, 1920s, 4 1/2 In. 150.00
Mug, Dad's Root Beer, Barrel Shape, 5 1/4 In. 30.00
Mug, Elsie The Cow, Borden's Beulah 50.00
Mug, Hires Root Beer, Child Lithograph, Mettlach, Germany, c.1900 .... 185.00
Mug, Hires Root Beer, Stoneware, 1900s, 7 In. 60.00
Mug, Hires Root Beer, Ugly Boy, Mettlach 225.00
Mug, Leisy Brewing Co., Green, Name In Gold 50.00
Mug, Lincoln Malt & Hop, Blue 260.00
Mug, Moxie, Fluted, 1915-1920, 5 In. 50.00
Mug, Ovaltine, 50th Anniversary 15.00
Mug, Philadelphia Beer Brewers Union No. 5, Ceramic 15.00
Mug, Pillsbury Funny Face, Set Of 8 Different Faces, 1960s, 3 In. 75.00
Mug, Richardson's Root Beer Rich, Etched, 6 5/8 In. 40.00
Mug, Rochester Root Beer, Glass, Fluted, Double Bands, 1920s-1930s, 9 1/2 In. 195.00
Mug, Spuds Mackenzie, Blue & White, Beach-Party Animal Scene, Thermal, 16 Oz. 9.00
Notebook, White's Yucatan Gum, Celluloid, 1901 .... 175.00
Nut Dish, Mr. Peanut, Metal, 7 Piece 20.00
Opener, Cigar Box, Sether's Cigar, 5 1/2 In. 30.00
Pack, Cigarette, Camel, Unopened, 1940s 25.00
Pack, Cigarette, Head Play, Preakness Race Horses, 1933, Set Of 4 .... 200.00
Pack, Cigarette, Home Run, Liggett & Myers, 1960s 15.00
Pack, Cigarette, Johnnie Walker, American Tobacco Co. 12.50
Pack, Cigarette, Lucky Strike, Green, American Tobacco Co., 1939-1941 .... 45.00
Pack, Cigarette, Mecca, American Tobacco Co. 15.00
Pack, Cigarette, Spud Cigarette Tobacco, Unopened, 1950s 20.00
Pack, Cigarette, Top Score, Brown & Williamson, 1940s 12.50
Pack, Cigarette, Waldorf Astoria, American Tobacco Co. 15.00
Packet, Zinnia, W.D. Burt Co., 8 1/2 x 4 1/2 In. .... *Illus* 5.00
Pails are also listed in the Lunch Box category.
Pail, Candy, Merry Christmas From Santa, Tin 270.00
Pail, Candy, Peter Rabbit, Tin 340.00
Pail, Milk, Robinson Dairy Products, Chicago, Tin, Handle 35.00
Pail, Old Boy Peanut Butter, 1 Lb. 115.00
Pattern, Doll's, Crakle, Quaker Oats, 1930s .... 45.00 to 65.00
Pennant, Fatima Cigarettes, Felt, 31 x 11 In. 140.00
Pennant, John S. Beavon Coal Co., Albuquerque, Felt, 1912 .... 90.00
Pennant, Old Dutch Cleanser, Doesn'T Scratch, Cloth, 25 In. 22.00

Display your collections in a way that fits your lifestyle. Keep small breakables out of the reach of children or pets. Use wax, fishing line, or other barriers to keep small objects on shelves if you live in an area that has earthquakes or even if you live near a train track or highway. Continuous vibrations will make pieces "walk" toward the edge of the shelf and eventually fall off.

Advertising, Packet, Zinnia, W.D. Burt Co., 8 1/2 x 4 1/2 In.

Photograph, Quakerman, Quaker Oats, Radio Premium, 1930s	38.00
Pin, 7-Up, Zorro, Pinback	38.00
Pin, Bond Bread, Plastic, Famous Planes, Byrd's Floyd Bennett, 1930s, 1 1/2 In.	44.00
Pin, Eat Cherry-Ripe Ice Cream, Celluloid, White, Pinback, 3 In.	20.00
Pin, Elsie The Cow In Daisy, Borden Co., Plastic, Alwynn Products, 1 1/2 In.	55.00
Pin, Packard, Match Packard 120 Against The Field, Lapel	85.00
Pin, Quality Sausage, 3 Little Pigs, Lithograph, 2 1/2 In.	65.00
Pin, Red Goose Shoes, Wooden, Red & Yellow Enamel, Pinback, 2 In.	23.00
Pin, Reddy Kilowatt, Red, Lapel, 1 In.	30.00
Pin, Yellow Kid, High Admiral Cigarettes, I Am 1 Of De Princeton Tigers	65.00
Pitcher, Dewar's Scotch Whiskey, White, Wade, Regicor, London England, 7 In.	37.50
Pitcher, Hawaiian Punch, Blue	15.00
Plaque, Electric Cooperative, Bandera, Texas, Cast Aluminum, 12 In.	90.00
Plaque, Stroh's Beer, Chalkware, Hanging Cord, Round, 1950s, 12 In.	49.00
Plate, Bob's Big Boy, China, Big Boy Eating Burger, 1940s, 5 1/2 In.	55.00
Plate, Borden's Ice Cream Parlor, Paper, 1935	12.00 to 15.00
Plate, Delta Airlines, White, Red & Blue Logo, Porcelain, Abco Tableware, 8 In.	40.00
Plate, Fred Krug Brewing Co., 1859-1909, 9 3/4 In.	85.00
Plate, Pink Panther, Insulation Advertising, Christmas, 1985, Box	45.00
Plate, Reddy Kilowatt, Cafeteria, White, Red Figure, 1950, 9 In.	45.00 to 65.00
Plate, Ronald McDonald, McDonaldland Characters, Plastic, 10 In., 4 Piece	24.00
Pot Scraper, Forbes Baking Powder	40.00
Pouch, Union Workman, Free Sample, Cardboard, Contents, 3 Oz.	28.00
Print, Anheuser-Busch, Budweiser Girl, Marbolite, 1977, 21 In., Set Of 5	305.00
Print, Minnesota Chief Threshers, Custer's Last Fight, 1880s, 22 x 28 In.	1850.00
Pull Toy, Old Dutch Cleanser, Hubley, 1932	4100.00
Punch Board, Camel Cigarette, 1 Cent	55.00
Purse, Change, J.H. Cutter, Leather, Gold Letters, 1890-1910	65.00
Puzzle, Champion Spark Plug, Matted, Frame, 25 x 17 In.	85.00
Rack, Lenit & Lenit Cubanos, 100 Percent Imported Havana Cigars, Tin, 10 In.	99.00
Rattle, Heinz 57 Baby Food	40.00
Recipe Box, Bisquick, Slice Of Quiche, White	15.00 to 26.00
Recipe Box, Shredded Wheat, 1973	25.00
Reflector, Goodrich, Silvertown Safety League, Wing Motif, Steel, 1940s-1950s	37.00
Ruler, Hires, Blue On White, 12 1/4 In.	22.00
Sack, Flour, Bay State Milling Co., Early Boxer Pictured, 100 Lb.	38.00
Salt & Pepper Shakers are listed in their own category.	
Scales are listed in their own category.	
Screen Door Brace, Left Hand Side, 7-Up, Take Some Home Today, 1940s-1950s	195.00
Sharpening Stone, John C. Roberts Shoes For Men, Celluloid, 2 3/4 In.	42.00
Shoe, Hanover, Box, 2 In.	17.00
Shoe, Stetson, Box, 2 In.	25.00
Sign, 7-Up, Fresh Up With 7-Up, Porcelain, Canada, 1940s, 20 x 28 In.	402.00
Sign, 7-Up, Thermometer, Porcelain, 1948, 20 x 28 In.	115.00
Sign, All Jacks Cigarettes, Tin, 10 x 14 In.	55.00

Sign, Always Drink Foaler's Cherry Smash, Celluloid, Small 350.00
Sign, Arm & Hammer Brand Soda, Glazed, Hanging, 13 In. 22.00
Sign, Atlantic Ale & Beer, Pan American Clipper Plane, 1942, 27 x 22 In. 287.00
Sign, Baker Chocolate, Baker Maid, Self-Framed, 1910, 16 x 20 In. 661.00
Sign, Barber Shop, Haircut & Shave, 25 Cents, Cast Iron, 13 1/2 In. 165.00
Sign, Barber Shop, Red, White, Black, Porcelain, 14 1/2 x 24 In. 325.00
Sign, Barq's, Ice Cold, Gas & Oil, 1930s, 11 3/4 x 35 In. 632.00
Sign, Bell Helicopter Corporation, Service Station, 2 Sides, 18 In. 2645.00
Sign, Big Bear Ice Cream, Sundae, Tin, 20 In. 259.00
Sign, Bireley's Orange & Grape, Reverse Glass, Mirror, 1950s, 6 1/2 x 9 In. 138.00
Sign, Birthday Beverage, Hand, Bottle, Tin, 1930s-1940s, 9 x 11 In. 29.00
Sign, Black Horse Beer, Tin On Cardboard, 10 x 12 In. 5.00
Sign, Blatz Beer, Wooden, Metal Letters, 7 x 7 In. 18.00
Sign, Blatz, Light-Up, 8 x 8 In. 75.00
Sign, Bludwine, For Your Health's Sake, Flange, Tin, 1910-1915, 10 x 13 In. 575.00
Sign, Blue Ridge Velvet Ice Cream, Curb Service, Porcelain, 1940s, 20 x 28 In. 260.00
Sign, Bond Bread, Easter Greetings, Paper, Roll Down, 1930s-1940s, 13 x 38 In. 126.00
Sign, Breyers Ice Cream, Original Frame, Sidewalk, 2 Sides, 20 x 28 In. 315.00
Sign, Brownie Soda, Elf, With Bottle, Tin, 1950s, 20 x 28 In. 165.00
Sign, Buckeye Mowing Machines, Richardson Mfg., Lithographed, 13 x 19 In. 395.00
Sign, Budweiser Beer, Guitar Shape, 41 In. 150.00
Sign, Budweiser Beer, Lighted, Clydesdales, Pulling Wagon, 1964, 13 x 20 In. 200.00
Sign, Butter-Nut Bread, Cardboard, Little Girl With Loaf, 1920s, 17 x 12 In. 55.00
Sign, Buy Chesterfield Here, Enameled, 17 3/4 x 12 In. 40.00
Sign, Caledonian Insurance Company, Tin, 22 x 16 In. 135.00
Sign, Camay Toilet Soap, Tin Lithograph On Wood, 6 x 27 In. 542.00
Sign, Carnation Fresh Milk, Porcelain, 15 x 14 1/2 In. 235.00
Sign, Carnation Malted Milk, Red Lettering, Cream Ground, Milk Glass, 9 x 7 In. 202.00
Sign, Carnation Milk, Can, 1950s, 12 x 18 In. 224.00
Sign, Carnation Milk, Scalloped Design, 1950s, 22 In. 595.00
Sign, Carter's Union Made Overalls, Speeding Train, Porcelain, 6 x 15 In. 1350.00
Sign, Cetacolor Fabric, Woman, Black, Green, Red & White Fabric, 36 In. 38.00
Sign, Charles Gebhardt Undertaker, Horse Drawn Hearse, Printed, 12 3/8 x 10 In. 170.00
Sign, Cheer Up, Flange, Countertop, Vertical, Tin, 1940s-1950s, 10 x 12 In. 195.00
Sign, Chesterfield Cigarettes, Rhonda Fleming, Cardboard, 20 x 19 In. 85.00
Sign, Chevrolet Bow Tie, Porcelain, 6 7/8 x 20 1/4 In. 385.00
Sign, Child's Razor Blades, Man Lathered Up, With Son, 14 3/4 x 7 1/2 In. 50.00
Sign, Chiropractor, Gold On Black Ground, Molded Frame, 12 x 25 1/2 In. 375.00
Sign, Clairol, Woman's Head, Cardboard, Die Cut, Easel Back, 1941, 16 x 21 In. 11.00
Sign, Coble Milk, Reach For Me, Carton, Tin, Embossed, 1953, 15 x 24 In. 345.00
Sign, Colman's Starch, Porcelain, 62 In. 65.00
Sign, Combat Cigars, We Sell High Grade 5 Cent Cigars, Cardboard, 14 x 19 In. 375.00
Sign, Cooks Paint, Red & White, Porcelain, 36 x 24 In. 175.00
Sign, Coors Beer Wolf, Light Beer, Mirror, Wooden Frame, 1986, 17 x 17 In. 18.00
Sign, Copco Bath Soap, Children In Underwear Scene, 1894, 27 1/4 In. 200.00
Sign, Country Club Ice Cream, Sundae, Enamel Print On Masonite, 16 x 25 In. 40.00
Sign, Crockett, Bit & Spur Co., Oscar Crockett, 1916, 16 x 36 In. 695.00
Sign, Crystal White Soap, Porcelain, Curved, 20 1/2 In. 70.00
Sign, Cunard Line, Aquitania Steam Ship, Frame, A.F. Bishop, 33 x 43 In. 115.00
Sign, De Laval, Picture Of Separator, Flange, 2 Sides, 1905-1915, 18 x 26 In. 520.00
Sign, Decoret, Furniture Polish, Pull String, Can Goes Up & Down, 19 x 13 In. 2035.00
Sign, Delaware Punch, Bottle, Tin, 1940s, 12 x 38 In. 365.00
Sign, Delco Batteries, Made In U.S.A., Tin, Wooden Back, 70 1/2 x 18 1/2 In. 165.00
Sign, Dentist, Gold Lettering On Black, Reverse Painted, Frame, 12 1/2 x 26 In. 225.00
Sign, Display, Swatch, Plastic, Green, Pink, Neon, 1980s 53.00
Sign, Dixie Cola, Tin, 1940s, 10 x 26 In. 195.00
Sign, Dixie Spring Birch Beer, Cream Soda, Reverse Glass, 1930s-1940s, 6 x 12 In. 210.00
Sign, Domestic Sewing Machines, Light Green, Neon, 10 x 23 x 5 1/2 In. 220.00
Sign, Donald Duck Bread, Tin, 1940s-1950s, 20 x 39 In. 400.00
Sign, Donald Duck Cola, Die Cut, Easel Back, Canada, 1940s, 22 x 26 In. 175.00
Sign, Double Cola, Flange, Tin, 1947, 15 x 18 In. 660.00
Sign, Dr Pepper, With Chevron, Tin, Embossed, 1950s-1960s, 12 x 28 In. 105.00
Sign, Dr. A.C. Daniels' Medicines, For Home Treatment Of Cattle, 13 x 29 In. 550.00

Sign, Dr. Pepper, Drink A Bite To Eat, Tin, 1938, 18 x 54 In. 3795.0

Sign, Dr. Pepper, Woman, Cardboard, Shelf Display, 3-D, 1940s, 18 x 16 In. 1610.0

Sign, Dr. Pierce's Golden Medical Discovery, 38 x 25 In. 805.0

Sign, Dr. Swett's Root Beer, Tin, Embossed, Wood Graining, 1940s, 20 x 28 In. 315.0

Sign, Dress Making, Black On White, Scrollwork, Molded Frame, 12 1/2 x 50 In. 495.0

Sign, Drink Birchola, Bottles, Tin, Embossed, 10 x 28 In. 230.0

Sign, Drink Bireley's, Bottle Cap, Blue, White, Tin, Embossed, Round, 1950s, 30 In. .. 160.0

Sign, Drink Genie Cola, Tin, 10 x 26 In. 130.0

Sign, Drink Hires In Bottles, Tin, Horizontal, 1930s, 10 x 28 In. 345.0

Sign, Drink Moxie, Flange, No Holes, Tin, 1920s-1930s, 8 x 8 In. 375.0

Sign, Drink Moxie, White Lettering, Embossed, 1938, 27 x 19 In. 138.0

Sign, Drink Nehi Beverages, Bottle, Tin, Embossed, 1950s, 17 x 44 In. 230.0

Sign, Drink Nehi, Ice Cold, Bottle, Yellow, Tin, Embossed, 1940s-1950s, 15 x 42 In. 345.0

Sign, Drink Orange Crush, Bottle, Late 1930s-Early 1940s, 4 x 8 Ft. 315.0

Sign, Drink Orange Crush, Crushy Figure, Flange, 1930s-1940s, 18 x 18 In. 520.0

Sign, DuBois, Pa., Brewery, Colorful, Song Verse, Canvas, 1950, 21 x 32 In. 95.0

Sign, Electrician's, Gilt On Black, 1920s, 23 x 55 In. 650.0

Sign, Electro Freeze Ice Cream, Chrome Over Brass, Figural, Arched, 16 x 30 In. 290.0

Sign, Empress Ice Cream, Tin, 28 x 44 In. ....75.00 to 86.0

Sign, Enjoy Hires Root Beer, Bottle, Tin, Embossed, 1930s, 10 x 28 In. ....345.00 to 405.0

Sign, Enjoy Nesbitt's, Bottle, Center Circle, Tin, Square, 1940s-1950s, 33 In. 316.0

Sign, Esso Aviation Products, Stand Clear, Tin, 2 Sides, Round, 1940s-1950s 661.0

Sign, Estabrooks' Red Rose Coffee, Tin Lithograph, Square, 15 In. 220.0

Sign, Evinrude, Men Motoring Into Sunrise, Tin, 2 1/2 x 4 In. 675.0

Sign, Famosa Cigars, Just Think Famosa 5 Cent, Sheet Metal, 1920s, 36 x 11 In. 110.0

Sign, Florsheim Shoes, Brass, 9 1/2 x 9 1/2 In. 75.0

Sign, Freed Eisemann Radio, A.E. Meech, 2 Sides, 36 x 24 In. 750.0

Sign, Fresh Up With 7-Up, Bottle, Tin, Canada, 1950s-1960s, 18 x 54 In. 316.0

Sign, Fresh Up With 7-Up, Hand Holding Bottle, Tin, 1950, 16 x 54 In. 520.0

Sign, Get Kist Here, Orange & Other Flavors, 7 1/2 x 29 1/2 In. 120.0

Sign, Gettelman Beer, Duck Scene, Foil, Composite, Dated 1951, 10 x 16 In. 9.0

Sign, Gillette, Shape Of Box Of Blades, Plywood, 43 1/2 x 68 1/2 In. 950.0

Sign, Goebel Beer, Reverse On Glass, 5 x 9 In. 50.0

Sign, Gold Dust Powder, Frame, c.1930, 22 x 28 In. 275.0

Sign, Golden Quality Ice Cream, 28 x 44 In. ....75.00 to 98.0

Sign, Gooch's Egg Noodles, Tin, 1940s, 9 x 20 In. 100.0

Sign, Gordon's Gin, Yellow & Red Foil Style Logo, Glass, Countertop, 11 x 7 In. 23.0

Sign, Grape Smash, Tin, c.1915, 9 1/2 x 13 1/2 In. 605.0

Sign, Grapette, Thirsty Or Not, Woman, Cardboard, Frame, Round, 1940s, 17 In. 545.0

Sign, Great Atlantic & Pacific Tea Co., Cardboard, Young Girl, 10 x 12 In. 27.0

Sign, Green River Whiskey, Black Man, Frame, Tin, 30 x 40 In. 2300.0

Sign, Green River Whiskey, She Was Bred In Old Kentucky, Tin, 23 x 34 In. 330.0

Sign, Green River Whiskey, Whiskey Without Regrets, Cardboard, 1935, 25 In. 110.0

Sign, Green River, Tin Over Cardboard, String Hanger, 1920s, 3 x 9 1/2 In. 230.0

Sign, Green River, Whiskey Without A Headache, Frame, 30 x 40 In. 2850.0

Sign, Hambone 5 Cent Cigar, Cardboard, Chalkboard, 21 x 13 In. 70.0

Sign, Happy Headaches Tablets Cures All Kinds Of Pain, Paper, 14 x 5 In. 55.0

Sign, Hat, Copper & Tin, c.1930, 39 x 48 In. 2950.0

Sign, Heinz 57 Varieties, Marque, 17 x 14 x 7 In. 5940.0

Sign, Highball Ginger Ale, Bottle, Tin, String Hanger, 1915-1925, 6 1/2 x 6 1/2 In. 175.0

Sign, Hire's Root Beer, Bottle, Tin, Embossed, 1940s-1950s, 13 x 42 In. 430.0

Sign, Hires Root Beer, Die Cut, Embossed, 8 x 5 In. ....*Illus* 22000.0

Sign, Hires, Drink Hires, 2 Girls, Glasses, Tin, 20 x 24 In. ....*Illus* 4675.0

Sign, Hires, For Pleasure & Thirst, Tin, Embossed, Round, 1940s-1950s, 24 In. 430.0

Sign, Hoefler Ice Cream Co., Buffalo, N.Y., Tin, Round, 1915, 14 In. 1065.0

Sign, Honest Scrap, Dog & Cat, Cardboard, Frame, 1910s, 22 x 30 In. 1150.0

Sign, Honey Moon Tobacco, Tin Lithograph, Couple On Moon, 7 x 10 In. 290.0

Sign, Hood, Logo M-H Co., Embossed Tin, 34 7/9 x 28 1/2 In. 395.0

Sign, Horlacher's 9 Month Old Perfection Beer, Frame, 1910s, 12 x 18 In. 352.0

Sign, Horoscope, Man In Robes, Porcelain, 1940s-1950s, 12 x 15 In. 40.0

Sign, Hospital Razor Blades, Picture Of Box Of Blades, 12 x 10 1/8 In. 175.0

Sign, Howel's Root Beer, Brownie With Bottle On Tray, Metal, Embossed, 1930s 195.0

Sign, Howel's Root Beer, Tin, 18 x 36 In. 375.0

Sign, Hudson's Extract Soap, Standing Woman Picture, Porcelain, 22 x 12 In. 195.00
Sign, Hunt's Baking Powder, Lady, With Products, Cardboard, Bill Hook, 5 1/2 In. 75.00
Sign, Iron City Bock Beer, Pittsburgh Brewing Co., Cardboard, 1930s, 13 x 18 In. 130.00
Sign, Jacks Cookies, Pictures Happy Jack, Tin, 1950s, 7 x 22 In. 100.00
Sign, Jeweler, New Or Redeemed Watches, Milk Glass, 1920s, 46 x 20 In. 170.00
Sign, Joe's Tourist Court, Gainesville, Ga., Travel Trailer Form, 1935, 43 In. 2475.00
Sign, Johnson & Johnson Toilet & Baby Powder, 3 Babies On World, 3 Panels 950.00
Sign, Johnson & Johnson, Negroes Picking Cotton, Frame, 1894, 24 x 33 In. 550.00
Sign, Journeyman Barber's Union Shop, Eagle, Shield, Metal, 1920s, 7 x 9 In. 48.00
Sign, Kamm's Pilsener Light, Cardboard, Frame, Copyright 1940, 28 x 16 In. 95.00
Sign, Kickapoo Joy Juice, It's Out Of This World, Hillbilly & Indian, 22 x 28 In. 50.00
Sign, Kis-Me Chewing Gum, American Chicle Co., Cardboard, 15 1/2 x 9 1/2 In. 2805.00
Sign, Kis-Me Gum, Woman, Tin, Self-Framed, 1905-1915, 14 x 17 In. 633.00
Sign, Kist, Woman, Riding Outfit, Earl Moran Art, Paper, 1940s, 18 x 30 In. 320.00
Sign, Knox Gelatin, Mammy & Child, Harry Roseland, 1901, 26 x 20 In. 1375.00
Sign, Koch's Beer, Neon, 3 Colors, 1950s, 16 x 26 In. 177.00
Sign, Kuebler Beer-Ale Porter, Easton, Pa., Cardboard, 1930s, 14 x 19 In. 117.00
Sign, La Creosa Cigars, Painted Glass, Frame, 11 x 15 In. 60.00
Sign, Lemon Crush, Boy In Straw Hat, Norman Rockwell, 1930s, 9 x 12 In. 950.00
Sign, Levi Strauss & Co. Quality Socks, Pressed Wood, 2 Hooks, 15 x 12 In. 128.00
Sign, Life Savers, Porcelain, Metal Frame, 1920s, 27 x 60 In. 2415.00
Sign, Lime Crush, Tin, 1930s, 14 x 24 In. 150.00
Sign, LubriKups, Celluloid, Tin, Cardboard, Hanging, 1930s, 9 x 13 In. 460.00
Sign, Lucky Strike Cigarettes, Woman Boarding TWA Airliner, 13 x 21 In. 65.00
Sign, Lusitania, Tin Lithograph, Self-Framed, 27 x 38 In. 1600.00
Sign, Lux Fire Extinguishing Equipment, Flange, 2 Sides, 1940s-1950s, 18 x 13 In. 605.00
Sign, M.D. Morton, Fancy Goods, Confectionery, Toys, Wooden, Frame, 13 x 103 In. ... 770.00
Sign, Marathon Beer, Woman On Phone, Cardboard, Frame, Matted, 13 x 21 In. 290.00
Sign, Marlin Fire-Arms, Double & Single Edge, 19 1/4 x 9 1/2 In. 475.00
Sign, Mayo's Plug, Cock O' The Walk, 1910s-1920s, 6 1/2 x 13 In. 1207.00
Sign, Milliner's, Painted Iron, 19th Century, 12 In. 1150.00
Sign, Mission Orange, Bottle Picture, Tin Lithograph, 24 In. 35.00
Sign, Morrell's Boiled Hams, Sadistic Pig, Leaning On Cauldron, 10 x 11 In. 365.00
Sign, Morris Evans Remedies, Cardboard, Hanger, Britain, 1915-1920, 15 x 10 In. 92.00
Sign, Moxie, 2 Children Running, Bottle, Cardboard, Die Cut, Easel Back, 13 x 19 In. ... 40.00
Sign, Moxie, Man Pouring Glass For Lady On Bike, Tin, 28 x 20 In. 750.00
Sign, Moxie, Yes! We Sell Moxie, Frame, Tin, Oval, 27 x 19 1/2 In. 575.00
Sign, National Brewing Co., Ale & Porter, Red, White, Black, Porcelain, 17 x 15 In. 450.00
Sign, National Tobacco Works, Turkish Trophies Cigarettes, 33 x 23 1/2 In. 395.00
Sign, Nehi Beverages, Flange, Tin, 1940s, 14 x 18 In. 290.00
Sign, Nesbitt's Orange, Family At Cookout, Cardboard, 1940s, 2 x 3 Ft. 287.00
Sign, Nesbitt's Orange, Porcelain, Canada, 1950s, 12 x 25 In. 430.00
Sign, Nesbitt's, Boy Drinking, Cardstock, 1940s, 19 1/2 x 28 In. 65.00

Advertising, Sign, Hires, Drink Hires, 2 Girls, Glasses, Tin, 20 x 24 In.

Advertising, Sign, Hires Root Beer, Die Cut, Embossed, 8 x 5 In.

Sign, Nichol Kola, Sheet Metal, Lithographed, 1930s, 4 x 14 In. 26.00
Sign, Nichol Kola, Soda, Tin, Embossed, 1936, 8 x 24 In. 95.00
Sign, Nipper, His Masters Voice, Porcelain, RCA, 15 x 24 In. 825.00
Sign, Nu-Wood, House Amongst Tree, Porcelain, Veribrite Signs, 22 x 35 In. 115.00
Sign, Nugget Shoe Polish, Porcelain, 1920s, 41 x 17 In. 850.00
Sign, O Whiskies & Wines, Saloon Scene, R. Brand & Co., 1800, 17 x 23 In. 1450.00
Sign, Oh Boy Gum, 1 Cent, It's Pure, Tin, 1920s-1930s, 7 x 15 In. 375.00
Sign, Old Dutch Cleanser, Porcelain, c.1910, 3 1/2 x 26 In. 290.00
Sign, Old Joe's Beer, Porcelain, Round, Convex, 1905-1915, 18 In. 1955.00
Sign, Optometrist, Eye Center, Eyes Examined, Glasses Fitted, Light-Up, 18 In. 1250.00
Sign, Orange Crush, Ballerina, Walt Otto Artwork, Paper, Frame, 1936, 15 x 31 In. 325.00
Sign, Orange Crush, Eagle, Refreshment For Workers & Fighters, c.1930s-1940s 195.00
Sign, Orange Crush, Schoolgirl, 3-D Hand, Bottle, Die Cut, 1930s-1940s, 18 x 20 In. 430.00
Sign, Orange Crush, Woman & Puppy, Cardboard, 13 1/2 x 19 In. 205.00
Sign, Oscar Peterson's Fish Decoys Sold Here, Fish Shape, 52 In. 1760.00
Sign, Ox Head Beer, Beer Can Pouring Into Glass, Cardboard, 1930s, 15 x 8 In. 46.00
Sign, Pal Ade, Picture Of Bottle, Tin, 16 x 16 In. 75.00
Sign, Palmolive, Woman, Man, Soap Bar, Tin, 1940s, 14 x 28 In. 460.00
Sign, Pandora In Blue Jeans, Red, White, Black, Cardboard, 14 x 22 In. 75.00
Sign, Patterson's Paints, Woman Painting Kitchen, 1930s, 13 x 18 In. 50.00
Sign, Paul Jones' Havana Cigars, Wood Grain, Frame, 20 x 24 In. 800.00
Sign, Paul Jones' Whiskey, Game Hunting Scene, Gold Gilt Frame, 43 x 57 In. 865.00
Sign, Paul Jones, Temptation Of St. Anthony, Lithograph On Wood, 14 x 20 In. 2950.00
Sign, Pennfield Motor Oil, Oil-Derrick, Colorful, Tin, 19 1/2 x 14 In. 250.00
Sign, Penny Scale, A Penny A Day Shows You The Weigh, 1930s, 9 x 10 In. 23.00
Sign, Penslar Baby Bath Castile, Cardboard, Frame, 22 1/2 In. 35.00
Sign, Peters Shoes, Diamond Brand Shoes, Accordion Shape, 5 Tiers, 20 x 15 In. 160.00
Sign, Philip Morris Cigarettes, Cardboard, Easel Back, c.1940s, 21 x 29 In. 520.00
Sign, Pickwick Ale, Old Men, Toasting Beer At Table, Tin, Frame, 22 x 28 In. 345.00
Sign, Pipe, Gemutlicheit, White, Gold Trim, Painted Bell, Porcelain, 13 In. 750.00
Sign, Polar Bear Tobacco, Die Cut, 2 Sides, 12 x 8 1/2 In. 3135.00
Sign, Posey Cold Breakers, Reading, Pa., Cardboard, 1931, 21 x 11 In. 65.00
Sign, Purity Ice Cream, Woman With 3 Dishes Of Ice Cream, Die Cut, 8 x 12 In. 185.00
Sign, Purity Pretzels, Cardboard, Easel Back, c.1930s-1940s, 22 x 12 In. 105.00
Sign, Quaker Oats, Porcelain, 24 x 33 In. 1750.00
Sign, Quaker Oats, Porcelain, 42 x 23 7/8 In. 750.00
Sign, Quiz Scale, Porcelain, 12 x 15 In. 90.00
Sign, Rhinelander Butter, Tin Over Cardboard, Hanging String, Easel, 9 x 13 In. 160.00
Sign, Robin Hood Flour, Porcelain, 15 x 28 In. 175.00
Sign, Roe Buck, Fell, Northampton, 6 Point Buck, Oil On Panel, 38 x 27 In. 1210.00
Sign, Rolling Rock Beer, 3 Winning Horses Pictured, Composition, 14 x 16 In. 20.00
Sign, Royal Baking Powder, Gingerbread Man, 1930s, 20 x 29 In. 75.00
Sign, Royal Crown Cola, Bottle Shape, Tin, Embossed, 1951, 16 x 58 In. 355.00
Sign, Royal Crown Cola, Bottles, Tin, Embossed, 1951, 18 x 54 In. 400.00
Sign, Royal Crown Cola, RC Tastes Best!, Says Barbara Stanwyck, Blue, 28 x 11 In. 72.00
Sign, Royal Crown Cola, Take Home RC For Your Family!, Cardboard, 11 x 24 In. 44.00
Sign, Royal Crown, Bottle On Left, Tin, 11 1/2 x 29 1/2 In. 100.00
Sign, Silver Honey Blades, For A Sweet Shave, 5 For 10 Cents, 5 x 11 In. 40.00
Sign, Singer Sewing Machine, Koekelberg S.A., Porcelain, 36 x 24 In. 330.00
Sign, Singer Sewing Machine, T.P. Bruzelles, Porcelain, 35 1/4 x 23 1/2 In. 300.00
Sign, Singer Sewing Machines, Seamstress Logo, Porcelain, 1920s, 12 x 19 In. 950.00
Sign, Speer Ammo, Bicentennial, Applied Slugs, Frame, 11 1/2 x 21 1/2 In. 225.00
Sign, Spitz's Bread, Poster Board, 12 x 32 1/2 In. 125.00
Sign, Springfield Fire & Marine Ins. Co., Cardboard, Frame, 1926, 16 x 22 In. 225.00
Sign, Squeeze, Boys Playing Baseball, Die Cut, Easel Back, 1940s, 15 x 20 In. 460.00
Sign, Squeeze, Woman Archer, Cardboard, Frame, 1940s, 15 x 21 In. 430.00
Sign, Squirt, Bottle, Squirt Jumping Off, 1946, 18 x 53 In. 690.00
Sign, Squirt, It's In The Public Eye, Flange, Tin, 1942, 14 x 18 In. 345.00
Sign, Stag Beer, Flange, c.1954, 13 1/2 x 18 In. 125.00
Sign, Star Razor Blades, Yellow, 12 For 25 Cents, Box Of Blades, 21 x 14 In. 350.00
Sign, Star Soap, Extra Large, Porcelain, Curved, 26 In. 275.00
Sign, Stetson Hats, Porcelain, 1920s, 16 x 8 In. 475.00
Sign, Strip, Drink Double Cola, Tin, Embossed, 1930s-1940s, 4 1/2 x 20 In. 149.00

Sign, Strip, Railway Express, Porcelain, Board Backing, 1930s-1940s, 4 x 30 In. 400.00
Sign, Strip, Squirt, Bottle, Tin, Embossed, 1941, 4 x 18 In. 185.00
Sign, Stroehmann's Sunbeam Bread, Girl On Left, Tin, 1956, 6 x 30 In. 160.00
Sign, Stroh's, Life Preserver, Welcome Aboard Beer Lovers, Light-Up, 15 1/2 In. 65.00
Sign, Sun Crest, Woman & Grocer, Cardboard, Easel Back, 1940s, 20 x 21 In. 185.00
Sign, Sun Drop Lemonade, Girl, Cardboard, Die Cut, String Hanger, 16 x 16 In. 40.00
Sign, Sun Spot Orange Drink, Drink America's Favorite, Tin, 8 x 26 In. 160.00
Sign, Sunbeam Bread, Little Miss Sunbeam, Tin, 1953, 19 x 55 In. 776.00
Sign, Superior Stoves & Ranges, Porcelain, Round, 17 1/2 In. 120.00
Sign, Supplee Ice Cream, Porcelain, 1940s-1950s, 20 x 28 In. 150.00
Sign, Texas Punch, Tin, Embossed, 1940s, 7 x 27 In. 315.00
Sign, The Aviary Or Bird Fanciers Recreation, Blue, White, Frame, 28 x 30 In. 350.00
Sign, Thendora, The Bouquet Of Quality, Cardboard, 15 x 7 In. 65.00
Sign, Thirsty? Just Whistle, Orange Drink, Tin Lithograph, 30 x 26 In. 495.00
Sign, Triple Cola, Tin, 10 x 28 In. 110.00
Sign, True Ade, Bottle, Tin, 1940s-1950s, 18 x 54 In. 345.00
Sign, Valet Strop Safety Razor, Old Man, Sharpens Itself, 7 x 10 3/4 In. 250.00
Sign, Van Houten's Cocoa, Blue, Black Border, Porcelain, c.1905, 4 x 24 In. 315.00
Sign, Veep Soda, Bottle Picture, Tin, 12 x 28 In. 145.00
Sign, Velvet Ice Cream, Boy With 3 Cones, Frame, Matted, 16 x 27 In. 635.00
Sign, Victory Cigars, Frutiger Cigar Co., Self-Standing, 21 x 14 In. 60.00
Sign, Vienna Pudding, Dog, Running Between Butler's Legs, Paper, 12 x 19 In. 95.00
Sign, W. Shepherd, Serpentine Frame, Scroll Border, 1840s, 49 1/2 x 59 1/4 In. 3740.00
Sign, Warning, Amoco Pipeline Co., Oil Rigs In Background, 12 In. 225.00
Sign, Watch Repair, Metal Banded, Suspended From Brass Chain, 14 In. 1195.00
Sign, Watch Repair, Pocket Watch Form, Cast Zinc, 26 x 18 In. 725.00
Sign, Watchmaker, Painted, Metal, 37 x 23 1/2 In. 460.00
Sign, Welch's Grape Juice Juniors, Tin, Self-Framed, 1931, 18 x 40 In. 690.00
Sign, Welch's Grape Juice, Tin, Cardboard, Easel, String Hanger, 1930s, 6 x 9 In. 230.00
Sign, Welch's, Picnic Basket, Cardboard, c.1920s, 15 x 15 In. 100.00
Sign, Western Union, Telegraph Here, Flange, Porcelain, 1940s-1950s, 17 x 11 In. 290.00
Sign, Wheeler & Wilson Sewing Machine, Black, White, Porcelain, 20 x 20 In. 325.00
Sign, Whistle Soda, Cardboard, 1930s, 10 x 12 In. 24.00
Sign, White King Washing Machine Soap, Tin, 1930s, 10 x 14 In. 130.00
Sign, Willie Kool Cigarettes, 1941, 10 1/4 x 15 1/2 In. 25.00
Sign, Wilson Whiskey, Sample, Stand-Up, Tin, Die Cut, 1930s, 5 x 6 In. 40.00
Sign, Winchester Fishing Tackle, Oil On Tin, 20 x 14 In. 475.00
Sign, Winchester Shotgun Shells, String Hung Cardboard, 12 x 8 1/4 In. 2255.00
Sign, Winchester, Duck Hunters Eating Breakfast, Cardboard, 1954, 28 x 20 In. 135.00
Sign, Wonder Bread, Loaf Shape, Tin, Die Cut, 1950s, 20 x 42 In. 213.00
Soap, Peanuts Gang, Avon, Charlie Brown, Lucy, Snoopy, Figural, Box, 1970, 3 In. 31.00
Soup, Dish, American Airlines, Ceramic, White, Blue Stripe, 6 In. 18.00
Spoon, Duffy's Pure Malt Whiskey, Short Handle, Glass, 3 In. 8.50
Spoon, Measuring, Sunbeam Bread, 1950s 10.00
Spoon, Towle's Log Cabin, Cabin On Handle, 4 1/4 In. 25.00
Stickpin, Buffalo, North Dakota, 1906 . . . . 38.00
Stickpin, Case Tractors 32.00
Stickpin, Locket, National Of Hartford 45.00
Stickpin, Moline Plow 30.00
Stickpin, Swift's Silver Leaf Lard, Silver Finish, 1 In. 15.00
Straw Set, Soda Fountain, Mother Goose, Colored, Box 10.00
String Holder, Red Goose Shoes, Goose Form 8500.00
Sugar & Creamer, Elsie The Cow Creamer, Elmer With Hat Sugar . . . . 175.00 to 185.00
Sugar & Creamer, Lipton's Tea, Yellow 24.00
Syrup Jug, Mission, Light Amber, Aluminum Handle, Original Cork, 128 Oz. 200.00
T-Shirt, Joe Camel, Camel Cigarettes 20.00
Tap Knob, Coors, Lucite, 2 Sides 5.00
Tap Knob, E & B Ale, Plastic, Metal Inserts, 2 Sides, 1940s 60.00
Tap Knob, Krueger Beer, Plastic, Metal Insert & Stem, 1940s 20.00
Tap Knob, Old Shay Deluxe Beer, Plastic, Plastic Insert 66.00
Tap Knob, Ortlieb's Ale, Plastic 15.00
Tap Knob, Rheingold Beer, Chrome, Plastic Insert, 2 Sides 4.00
Tap Knob, Stegmaier's Beer, Ball, Plastic, Porcelain Insert 55.00

Thermometers are listed in their own category.
Tie Clasp, Reddy Kilowatt 25.00
Tie Clasp, Remington 8.00
Tie Tack, Bull Dog, Mack Trucks 20.00

Advertising tin cans or canisters were first used commercially in the
United States in 1819 and were called *tins*. The English language is
sometimes confusing. Today the word *tin* is used by most collectors to
describe many types of containers, including food tins, biscuit boxes,
roly poly tobacco containers, gunpowder cans, talcum powder sprin-
kle-top cans, cigarette flat-fifty tins, and more. Beer cans are listed in
their own category. Things made of undecorated tin are listed under
Tinware.

Tin, Abbots Bitters, Paper Label, Sample 25.00
Tin, Accent Flavor Enhancer, 10 Lb. 7.00
Tin, Alberty's Food For Children/Infants, Contents, 1 Lb. 20.00
Tin, Altex, Air Tested Prophylactic, 3 For 50 Cents, Yellow Lettering, Brown 322.00
Tin, American 3 Vees Turtle Food, 1930s 45.00
Tin, Archer Lubricants, Red, Black, Beige, Indian, Bow & Arrow, 2 Gal. 75.00
Tin, Aristocrat Reservoir End Condom, Contents, Black Ground, Midwest Drug Co. 550.00
Tin, Autocrat Coffee, Round, No. 3, 6 x 3 In. 80.00
Tin, Bachman Butter Pretzels, Red & Yellow, 7 1/4 x 7 1/2 In. 18.00
Tin, Bagdad Coffee, Red Ground, 12 x 5 In. 225.00
Tin, Bagdad Tobacco, Blue, 3 x 1 x 3 3/4 In. 165.00
Tin, Baker's Cocoa, Paper Label, Sample 185.00
Tin, Bee Brand Cloves 15.00
Tin, Ben Bey Superfine Cigar, Tin, Graphics On Inside Lid, 10 x 6 x 4 In. 55.00
Tin, Biscuit, Accordion, Jacobs, Harmonic Music When Closed, 5 In. 110.00
Tin, Biscuit, Bookcase Form, Brown, Huntley & Palmers, 4 x 4 1/2 In. 316.00
Tin, Biscuit, Books, Huntley & Palmers 195.00
Tin, Biscuit, Bus, Crawford's Biscuits, Tin 4200.00
Tin, Biscuit, Chest, 3 Drawers, Serpentine Front, Mahogany, Gold Trim, 4 x 7 In. 230.00
Tin, Biscuit, China Closet Shape, Brown, Red Trim, 3 x 5 1/4 In. 316.00
Tin, Biscuit, Elkes, Limited, Orange Flowers, England, Oval, 10 In. 1.00
Tin, Biscuit, Garden Sundial, William Crawford & Sons, 9 5/8 In. 165.00
Tin, Biscuit, Globe, Huntley & Palmers, 7 In. 105.00
Tin, Biscuit, Hamper, Huntley & Palmers 495.00
Tin, Biscuit, Huntley & Palmers, 6-Footed Stool Shape 250.00
Tin, Biscuit, Jacob Coronation Coach, W & R 415.00
Tin, Biscuit, Jacob's, Coach, 1937 .... 725.00
Tin, Biscuit, Loose-Wiles, Woman Feeding Deer On Lid, 10 In. 50.00
Tin, Biscuit, McVitie & Price, Sample, 3 x 1 In. 25.00
Tin, Biscuit, Suitcase, Huntley & Palmers, c.1904 .... 295.00
Tin, Biscuit, Tropical Bird, Beads For Eyes, McVitie & Price, 8 3/4 In. 242.00
Tin, Biscuit, Wagon, Gray, Dunn & Co., 5 1/2 In. 165.00
Tin, Breakfast Cheer Coffee, Campbell & Woods Co., Couple At Table, Red, 1 Lb. 2530.00
Tin, Cadbury's Chocolate, Flat, Rectangular 1.00
Tin, California Perfume, Jungle Jinks 75.00
Tin, Campfire Marshmallows Supreme, Heekin Can Co., Ohio, c.1915, 8 x 2 In. 40.00
Tin, Cascaret, For Use In Constipation, 1 1/2 x 2 1/2 In. 12.00
Tin, Caswell's National Crest, Red Lettering, Light Yellow Ground ....25.00 to 47.00
Tin, Charles Chips, Red, 1 Lb. 8.00
Tin, Charles Neubert & Company, Oyster Can, Mermaid, 1 Gal. 450.00
Tin, Chase & Sanborn Coffee, Pressure Packed, Drip Grind, Key, 1 Lb. 45.00
Tin, Chase & Sanborn Coffee, Standard Brands, N.Y., Embossed Lid, 1 Lb. 11.00
Tin, Chase & Sanborn Coffee, Twist Lid, NRA Code, Paper Label, 1 Lb. 34.00
Tin, Chicago Cubs Chewing Tobacco, Cylindrical, 1936 .... 68.00
Tin, Coats & Clark Thread, Round, Large 6.00
Tin, Colonial Coffee, Thomas Coffee Co., York, Pa., Blue, Soldier, 1 Lb., 6 x 4 In. 75.00
Tin, Compound Neatsfoot Harness Oil, Standard Oil Co., 1915, 1 Gal. 75.00
Tin, Condom, Ultex Platinum, Red & Silver, 2 x 1 1/2 In. 8.00
Tin, Coors Malted Milk, Round, 10 Lb. 150.00
Tin, Core-Ga, Dental Powder, Free Sample, 2 1/4 In. 20.00

Tin, De Telegraff, 100 Count Claro Cigar, Holland, 9 x 4 1/2 x 3 1/2 In. 44.00
Tin, Diamond Outboard Motor Oil, Woman In Skiff, 1 Qt. 35.00
Tin, Dixie Chop Cut, Allen & Ginter, Plug, Barrel, 4 1/2 x 3 In. 250.00
Tin, Doan's Ointment, Blue, White, Graphics, 1 Oz. 65.00
Tin, Dr. Hobbs Asparagus Kidney Pills, 1 1/2 x 1 5/8 In. 24.00
Tin, Dr. Scholl's Foot Powder, Contents, 1930s 38.00
Tin, Egg-O Baking Powder, Hamilton, Lid, Paper, 16 Oz. 10.00
Tin, Empress Coffee, Purple, Gold, Stone-Ordean-Wells Co., 9 In. 68.00
Tin, Epicure Oyster, 1 Gal. 125.00
Tin, Esskay Quality Lard, Red Ground, Blue Letter, Press On Top, 10 Lb. 85.00
Tin, Folger's, White Lettering, Red Ground, J.A. Folger & Co., 3 1/2 x 5 In. 77.00
Tin, Forest & Stream Tobacco, Ducks, 4 x 2 In. 500.00
Tin, French's Bird Biscuit, Yellow Canary, Red & Blue Ground, 1920-1930 .... 22.00
Tin, Gauztex Gauze For Sportsmen, Contents, 1939 .... 35.00
Tin, Gillies Coffee, Tin Lithograph, Press Top Lid, 7 x 4 x 4 In. 110.00
Tin, Glendora Spices, 4 x 2 In. 55.00
Tin, Gold Dust Scouring Cleaner ....48.00 to 65.00
Tin, Gold Dust Washing Powder, 2 Black Children In Tub, Pat. July 21, 1896 ......32.00 to 38.00
Tin, Gold Medal Coffee, Blue, Gold Letters, 6 In. 65.00
Tin, Golden Rule Coffee, Red, 10 Lb. 230.00
Tin, Grain Tobacco, Vertical Pocket, 3 x 3 In. 125.00
Tin, Grandmother's Tea, A & P, 1/2 Lb. 50.00
Tin, Hartz Mountain My-T-Mite Powder, Canary, Orange, 1930s 35.00
Tin, Hartz Mountain Wafer Fish Food, Orange, Box, 1930s 25.00
Tin, Hauswald's Lifetime Bread, Brooklandville, Md., Label, 12 Oz. 5.00
Tin, Heart's Delight Coffee, Blue, Red, 4 x 5 In. 245.00
Tin, Heine's Blend Smoking Tobacco, Dutchman, Windmill, 2 1/2 x 2 1/2 In. 25.00
Tin, Hi-Plane Tobacco, 2 Engines, Vertical Pocket, 4 x 2 In. 100.00
Tin, High Brown Face Powder, Black 48.00
Tin, Horlick's Malted Milk, Domed Cover, Square, 25 Lb. 43.00
Tin, Humpty Dumpty Potato Chips, Yellow, Red, White, Blue, 3 Lb. 22.00
Tin, Index Brand Breakfast Cocoa, Montgomery Ward & Co., Square 165.00
Tin, Jap Rose Talc, Woman's Face, 3 Oz. 75.00
Tin, Jergen's Talc, 4 x 2 x 1 In. 37.00
Tin, Jewel Tea Baking Powder, Red & Gold 95.00
Tin, Jewel Tea Spice, Gold, Tan 95.00
Tin, Kaffee Hag, Black, Red, 3 1/2 x 5 In. 17.00
Tin, Kellogg's Froot Loops, 1984 .... 15.00
Tin, Koskott Hair Cream, 1930 .... 45.00
Tin, Lady Hellen Coffee, Hellen Co., Lithographed Label, 1920s, 16 Oz. 65.00
Tin, Lincoln Highway Cigars, From Coast To Coast, Beige Ground, 4 x 4 In. 133.00
Tin, Lion Syrup, Bail Handle, Paper Label, Lion Center, 6 In. 12.00
Tin, Log Cabin Syrup, Woman & Child, Boy Cowboy On Reverse, 4 x 4 In. 60.00
Tin, Martinson's Coffee, Embossed, Cardboard, 9 1/2 In. 33.00
Tin, Maryland Club Tobacco, Orange, Flat Top, Pocket, 4 x 2 In. 265.00
Tin, Mayo's Plug Tobacco, Handle, 8 x 5 x 3 1/2 In. 30.00
Tin, Mentholatum Little Nurse, Green, Blue, White, Contents, 1 3/8 In. 40.00
Tin, Mexo-Rico Exports, Marcus Feder, Cleveland, 7 x 5 x 4 In. ....*Illus* 22.00
Tin, Milk Box, Koontz Dairy, Mother & Carriage, Hinged Lid, c.1950s, 12 x 13 In. 35.00
Tin, Monarch Marshmallows, 5 x 5 In. 125.00
Tin, Mrs. Dinsmore's Cough Drops, c.1879 .... 300.00
Tin, Nabisco Shredded Wheat 60.00
Tin, Nebraska Blossom Cigar, Pretty Girl, Wearing Cowboy Hat 2860.00
Tin, Nigger Hair Tobacco, Brown, 7 x 5 In. 300.00
Tin, Norian's Dear Brand Pistachio Nuts 325.00
Tin, Ontario Cracker Co., Buffalo 65.00
Tin, Oreo Cookies, Lady On Phone 60.00
Tin, Parodi Cigar Of New York, Inc., Red, Mustard Ground, 6 x 9 x 7 In. 132.00
Tin, Pat Hand Tobacco, 2 x 2 x 1 In. 200.00
Tin, Peacock Coffee, Slip Lid, Picture Of Peacock, Paper Label 92.00
Tin, Peanut Butter, Peter Rabbit, Peter Sitting, 4 x 2 In. 250.00
Tin, Peterman's Roach Poison, Marching Roaches 30.00
Tin, Pette Wormerveer Cacopoeder, Birds, Rectangular, 8 x 8 x 5 In. 28.00

Tin, Philip Morris Cigarette 25.00

Tin, Pickwick Coffee, Red Lettering, Off-White Ground, 4 x 5 In. 25.00

Tin, Pillsbury's Best XXX Flour, Eagle Front, 1982 . . . . 12.00

Tin, Pinkussohns Tobacco, Vertical Pocket, 3 x 2 In. 95.00

Tin, Prince Of Wales & Pilot Chewing Tobacco, Slip Lid, Green Ground, 6 x 4 In. 61.00

Tin, Princess Pat, Powder, With Puff, Package 18.00

Tin, Puck, Virginia Cigarette Tobacco, 2 Hockey Players, Lithographed, 3 3/4 In. 187.00

Tin, Queen Tex Condoms, Bullet Shape, Paper Label, Black 91.00

Tin, Radiance Devon Toffee, Hinged Top, 7 5/16 x 8 In. 65.00

Tin, Radway's Pills, Oval, Unopened, Contents, Small 25.00

Tin, Red Rooster Coffee, 2 Lb. 38.00

Tin, Reliance Fish Nutrition, Green, 1920s 35.00

Tin, Requa's Charcoal Tablets, No. 11 . . . . 20.00

Tin, Richard Hudnut 3 Flowers Dusting Powder, 2 3/4 x 4 In. 60.00

Tin, Richmond Gem Cigarettes 45.00

Tin, Roly Poly, Mammy, Mayo 795.00

Tin, Roly Poly, Satisfied Customer, Mayo 360.00

Tin, Rough Rider Baking Powder 110.00

Tin, Royal Purple Diarrhea Tablets, Poultry, Calves & Pigs 75.00

Tin, Sambo Axle Grease, 4 3/4 In. 75.00

Tin, Savabrush, 1918 . . . . 38.00

Tin, Sheik Condoms, 1 Dozen Sheik, No. 25, Orange Ground, 1931 . . . . 90.00

Tin, Shelter Island Oyster, 1/2 Gal. 50.00

Tin, Squirrel Salted Peanuts, Handle, Pail, 1905-1915, 10 Lb. 405.00

Tin, St. Laurent Peanut Butter, 2 Lbs. 125.00

Tin, Standard Chemical-Fumoil Inhalant For Poultry & Hogs, 1930 . . . . 30.00

Tin, Suds Flakes Soap, Tin, Handle, 8 1/2 In. 28.00

Tin, Superla, Cream Separator Oil, Dairy Cows, Children, 1930-1940, 1/2 Gal. 125.00

Tin, Sweet Cuba Tobacco, Cannister, 8 x 10 1/4 In. 525.00

Tin, Sweet Mist, Lid & Base, Round 165.00

Tin, Tarzan Tea, Red, Green, White & Gold Painted, 1920s 75.00

Tin, Tetley Tea, 150th Anniversary 22.00

Tin, Thornton's Coffee, 1 Lb. 245.00

Tin, Three Merry Widows, Condom 25.00

Tin, Three Sheik Condom Tin, Arab On Horseback, Julius Schmid, 1931 . . . . 35.00

Tin, Tiger Chewing Tobacco, Orange Red, 8 x 6 x 6 In. 250.00

Tin, Tip Top Tobacco, Man On Horse Drawn Fire Engine, Paper Label, 5 In. Diam. 250.00

Tin, Top Cigarette Tobacco, Press On Lid With Opener, Papers Inside, 7 Oz. 17.50

Tin, Towle's Log Cabin Syrup, Woman & Girl, No Cap, 12 Oz. 50.00

Tin, Tuxedo Tobacco, Pocket 25.00

Tin, Twenty Grand Aspirin 15.00

Tin, Union Leader Tobacco, Uncle Sam, Pocket, 1917 . . . . 95.00

Tin, Verona Needles, Image Of Nude 33.00

Tin, Wan-Eta Cocoa, Cover, Embossed 275.00

Tin, White House Coffee, Key Wind, 1 Lb. 55.00

Tin, White Rose Sprayer, Glass Bottle, Wooden Handle, 12 1/2 In. 33.00

Tin, White Trojans, White Center Ground, Red Outside Edges 60.50

Tin, Wilson Tennis Balls 33.00

Tin, Wish Bone, Yellow Lettering, Green Ground 75.00

Tin, Yale Coffee, Screw Top, Black Ground 55.00

Tin, Yellow Kid Ginger Wafers, Box 65.00

If you have a smelly tin, try filling it with fragrant peppermint tea for a few weeks. When you empty it, the tin will still smell, but like peppermint.

Advertising, Tin, Mexo-Rico Exports,
Marcus Feder, Cleveland, 7 x 5 x 4 In.

Tin, Zuane La Parot Talc, Picture Of Bird, Sun 30.00
Tin, ZuZu Ginger Snaps, 1982 .... 20.00

dvertising tip trays are decorated metal trays less than 5 inches in
ameter. They were placed on the table or counter to hold either the
ll or the coins that were left as a tip. Change receivers could be made
' glass, plastic, or metal. They were kept on the counter near the cash
gister and held the money passed back and forth by the cashier.
elated items may be listed in the Advertising category under Change
eceivers.

Tip Tray, 7-Up, Old Logo, Glass, 3 1/2 In. 40.00
Tip Tray, America's Pride, Stars & Stripes Border, C.D. Kenny, 4 1/4 In. 316.00
Tip Tray, American Brewing Company, 3 Monkeys 205.00
Tip Tray, American Steamship Line 350.00
Tip Tray, Apollinaris, Queen Of Table Waters 65.00
Tip Tray, Baby Ruth Gum 350.00
Tip Tray, Badger Sheboygan Ginger Ale, Indian, Headdress 305.00
Tip Tray, Bartels Lager, Ale & Porter, Syracuse, New York 110.00
Tip Tray, Bellrose Rye Whiskey, Showell & Fryer, Ltd., Philadelphia, 1930s, 4 In. 43.00
Tip Tray, Bettendorf, Steel Gear Wagon 305.00
Tip Tray, Bloomingdale's, Greatest Store, New York 182.00
Tip Tray, Borden's, Malted Milk In The Square Package 253.00
Tip Tray, Boston Herald, Sunday Herald, Newsboy 88.00
Tip Tray, Boston Tire & Rubber Company, Vulcanizing, Repairing 220.00
Tip Tray, Bricker's OK Bread 50.00
Tip Tray, Cardinal Beer, Real Hop Flavor, Girl, Roses Around Head 120.00
Tip Tray, Citizens Coal Company, Moose 33.00
Tip Tray, Clysmic Table Water, Woman, Stag, Waterfall, Oval, 4 1/2 x 6 1/2 In. 76.00
Tip Tray, Continental Life Insurance Co., St. Louis, Photo Of Building, 4 In. 25.00
Tip Tray, Cortez Cigars, Key West 275.00
Tip Tray, De Laval Cream Separator's, 1906, 4 1/4 In. .... 100.00 to 160.00
Tip Tray, Dorne's Carnation Gum, Floral 220.00
Tip Tray, Dubbleware, Overalls, Pants & Woolen Sportswear 38.00
Tip Tray, Eye Fix, Great Eye Remedy, Girl, Angel At Eye 275.00
Tip Tray, F.C. Wagner For Shoes, Monroe, Michigan, Child Center 93.00
Tip Tray, Fairy Soap, Little Girl, With Bouquet, On Soap Bar, 4 1/4 In. 55.00
Tip Tray, Ferro-Phos Company, 5 Cents, Pottstown, Pennsylvania 220.00
Tip Tray, Fome Las Exquisitas Cervezas High Life, Woman Tasting Beer, 4 1/4 In. 36.00
Tip Tray, Globe-Wernicke, Couple, Sorting Books, 4 1/4 In. 110.00
Tip Tray, Gottfried Krueger Brewing Co., High Grade Beer 110.00
Tip Tray, Grand Prize Beer, Aluminum, 1950s, 5 x 6 In. 31.00
Tip Tray, Hanlen Bros., Liquor Dealers, Harrisburg, Pennsylvania 145.00
Tip Tray, Hy-Roller Whiskey 75.00
Tip Tray, Incandescent Light & Stove Company, Cincinnati, Ohio 285.00
Tip Tray, Iroquois Brewery, Indian 295.00
Tip Tray, Iroquois Brewing, Buffalo, New York 132.00
Tip Tray, J.H. Beamer, President Suspenders 27.00
Tip Tray, Jenney Aero Gasoline, Cars & Airplane, 1930s, 4 1/4 In. .... 120.00 to 145.00
Tip Tray, John Weaver, 5 Cent Cigar, Philadelphia 285.00
Tip Tray, Junket, Have Some Junket, Hansens, N.Y., 4 1/4 In. 230.00
Tip Tray, King's Pure Malt, Barmaid & Awards, Oval, 6 In. 68.00
Tip Tray, King's Pure Malt, Nurse, In Vintage Garb Carrying Tray, 6 x 4 In. 86.00
Tip Tray, King's Pure Malt, Panama Pacific International Expo Emblem 310.00
Tip Tray, L.C. Smith & Brothers, Typewriter & Horses 305.00
Tip Tray, Lehnert Beer, Made In Catasauqua, Pennsylvania, Sad Dog 330.00
Tip Tray, Lehnert's Beer, Head Of Beautiful Woman, 4 1/4 In. 115.00
Tip Tray, Manure Spreader, Success, Horse Drawn Wagon 143.00
Tip Tray, March Brownback Stove Co., Bright Globe Range 175.00
Tip Tray, Mason's, Druggists, Philadelphia 187.00
Tip Tray, May Company, Ohio's Largest Department Store 100.00
Tip Tray, Modox, Made From Indian Herbs, Indian Head, Full Headdress Form 187.00
Tip Tray, Monroe Brewing Company, Knight, King Of Rochester Beers 35.00
Tip Tray, Moxie, Drink For Health 45.00

Tip Tray, Moxie, I Just Love Moxie Don't You?, Ivy Around Rim . . . . .160.00 to 247.00
Tip Tray, Moxie, I Like It, Girl With Tumbler Of Drink 187.00
Tip Tray, Mr. Thomas 5 Cent Cigar, Kitten Center 715.00
Tip Tray, Narragansett, Providence, R.I., Pre-Prohibition 57.00
Tip Tray, National Brewing Co., Pure Lager, Ales & Porter 165.00
Tip Tray, National Cigar Stands Company, Brands Around Rim 50.00
Tip Tray, North Western Bank, Portland Trust Company Of Oregon 105.00
Tip Tray, Old India Pale Ale, Green, Red, Race Horses On Rim, 4 1/4 In. 53.00
Tip Tray, Oscar Holmes, Rockford Watches 80.00
Tip Tray, Peter Doelger, Bottled Beer 175.00
Tip Tray, Plymouth, Dry Gin, Monk & Bottle 45.00
Tip Tray, Quick Meal Ranges, Ask Your Dealer, Chicks 110.00
Tip Tray, Red Raven, Child, Finger In Mouth 285.00
Tip Tray, Red Raven, Woman, Holding Large Bird 187.00
Tip Tray, Resinol Soap & Ointment, For All Your Diseases 198.00
Tip Tray, Rienzi Beer, Bottles Only, Cavalier On Horseback 143.00
Tip Tray, Rock Island Brewing Company, Lilly, Beverage, Bottle & Food 120.00
Tip Tray, Rockford High-Grade Watches, Oval, 4 1/2 In. . . . . .125.00 to 245.00
Tip Tray, Rockford Watches, Lady In Waiting, Sitting On Waters Edge, 5 x 3 In. 345.00
Tip Tray, S.W. Van Slyke & Norton, Peter Schuyler Perfecto Cigars 220.00
Tip Tray, Scranton Distributing Company, Chum's, Man, Dog 410.00
Tip Tray, Sen Sen Gum 25.00
Tip Tray, Shawut Furniture Company, R.Y. Tait 120.00
Tip Tray, Soulas Rathskeller, Betz Building, Bar Scene 33.00
Tip Tray, St. Louis-Texas Line, Along The Frisco 385.00
Tip Tray, Stegmaier Brewing Company, Wilkes Barre, Pennsylvania 155.00
Tip Tray, Taka-Kola, Every Hour, Clock Face, Girl Lifting Drink 357.00
Tip Tray, Tivoli, A Select Lager 77.00
Tip Tray, Universal Stoves & Ranges 130.00
Tip Tray, Walter Baker & Co., Ltd., Breakfast Cocoa, Established 1780 . . . . 210.00
Tip Tray, Welsbach, Assures Dependable Lighting Service 242.00
Tip Tray, White Rock Table Water, Topless Woman, 4 1/2 x 6 1/2 In. 69.00
Tip Tray, White Rock, World's Best Table Water, Girl Leaning Over Stream . . . . .143.00 to 330.00
Tip Tray, Young's Pier, Atlantic City 70.00
Tip Tray, Yuengling's Bottled Beer, Woman In Straw Hat . . . . .187.00 to 275.00
Tip Tray, Zipp's, Flavoring, Extracts 100.00
Tobacco Cutter, Bird Design On Cutter, Birds On Plaque, Stand, Wood, Brass, Copper . 555.00
Tobacco Cutter, Chew Flat Iron Plug, Figural Flat Iron, Scotten Dillon Co., 16 In. 1595.00
Token, Associated Tailors, Tailor Tools, Brass, 1907, 1 1/2 In. 29.00
Toothpick, Fink Pig, Boston Baked Beans 75.00
Towel, Cabin, Eastern Steamship, 1939 . . . . 20.00
Toy, All Dogs Go To Heaven, Action Figures, Wendy's, Bags, Box, 3 In., 6 Piece 44.00
Toy, Bear, Snuggles, Fabric Softener, Cloth 25.00
Toy, Big Boy, Bendable, On Card 8.00
Toy, California Raisin, Windup, Plastic, Nasta, On Card, 7 1/2 x 8 In. 24.00
Toy, Detective Disguises, Poll Parrot, Unpunched, 14 x 18 In. 75.00
Toy, Duck, Calvert Whiskey, Plush, 1985 . . . . 25.00
Toy, Felix The Cat, Post Toasties Corn Flakes, Tin Lithograph, c.1949 . . . . 50.00
Toy, Hawaiian Punch Guy, Hard Plastic, Yellow, 1976, 4 In. . . . . .65.00 to 98.00
Toy, Jet Plane, Squirt, Cardboard, Punch-Out, Free With 6-Pack, 1958 . . . . 22.00
Toy, Jetsons, Action Figures, In Saucers, Wendy's, Original Bags, Box, 2 In., 6 Piece .34.00 to 39.00
Toy, Michelin Man, Vinyl, Squeeze 65.00
Toy, Nestle Scotchie Chip, Plush, 1984 . . . . 11.00
Toy, Oscar Mayer Weinermobile, Hot Wheels, Plastic, 3 In. 3.00
Toy, Pedal Car, Sinclair, Dino Dinosaur, Woody Tow Truck, GMC Diesel Cab 1000.00
Toy, Raid Bug, Talking, Remote Control, 12 In. 150.00
Toy, Roger Raccoon, Roger's Dept. Store, 4 In. 98.00
Toy, Ronald McDonald, Plastic, Plush, Yarn Hair, Korea, 15 In. 40.00
Toy, Ship Spotter, Wonder Bread, World War II, Rotating Card, Printed Flags, 1943 . . . . . 28.00
Toy, Snow White, 7 Dwarfs, Complete Set, McDonald's Happy Meal, 8 Piece 38.00
Toy, Train, Coors Beer, Reefer, HO, Plastic Box, Unassembled 35.00
Toy, Train, Steam Beer, Reefer, HO, Wooden, Plastic, Unassembled, Box, 1960s 24.00
Toy, Treasure Chest, Captain Crunch, Coins, Shovel, Map, Plastic, 1975 . . . . 50.00

Toy, Wiener Mobile, Oscar Mayer, 4 x 9 In.	8.50
Toy, Wild Indian, Cal-Nev Machine Makers Mascot, Rubber, 6 1/2 x 7 In.	75.00
Trash Can, Wall's Ice Cream, Wire, 1930s, 30 In.	175.00
Tray, Tip, see Tip Trays in this category.	
Tray, Apollo Beer, Tam O'Shanter Ale, American Brewing Co., Rochester, N.Y., 12 In.	25.00
Tray, Atlas Beer, Porcelain, Eagle On Globe, Pre-Prohibition, 16 In.	400.00
Tray, Blatz Old Heidelberg Beer, 1930s, 11 x 13 In.	205.00
Tray, Boehmian Beer, Pre-Prohibition, 13 In.	28.00
Tray, Car Door, McDonald's, Art Combed Plastics, Kokomo, Ind., 1960, 4 x 8 In.	70.00
Tray, Cream City Brewing, Milwaukee, Wis., 1930s, 14 In.	213.00
Tray, Dobler Lager Beer, Lithograph, Oval, 13 1/2 x 16 1/2 In.	150.00
Tray, Dow Old Stock Ale, Porcelain On Steel, Red, White, 12 In.	32.00
Tray, Dr. Pepper, Woman In Center Holding 2 Bottles, 1940, 13 1/2 x 10 1/2 In.	320.00 to 350.00
Tray, E. Robinson's Sons, Pilsener Bottler Beer, Factory, Pre-Prohibition, 12 In.	103.00
Tray, Edelweiss Beer, Pre-Prohibition, Round, 13 In.	13.00
Tray, Elgin Ice Cream, Woman & Boy With Ice Cream, Round, 13 1/2 In.	980.00
Tray, Genesee Beer, Hemlock Lake, Round, 10 3/4 In.	15.00
Tray, Genesee Dickens Ale, Coach & Horses, 12 In.	25.00
Tray, Green River Whiskey, She Was Bred In Old Kentucky, Man, Horse, Tin, 24 In.	330.00
Tray, Gunthers Beer, Mid-1930s, Round, 13 In.	10.00
Tray, Hedrick Beer, Round, 12 In.	10.00
Tray, Hires Root Beer, 14 In., Pair	215.00
Tray, Hires, 5 Cents, Man Holding Glass, 1914, 13 In. ....*Illus*	1650.00
Tray, Hires, Girl In Oval, Tin, 13 x 10 In. ....*Illus*	660.00
Tray, Iroquois Indian Head Beer & Ale, Iroquois Chief, Since 1842, 12 In.	32.00
Tray, Iroquois Indian Head Beer, Round, 13 In.	28.00
Tray, Los Angeles Brewing Co., Oriental Woman With Umbrella, San Toy, 1912	40.00
Tray, Miller High Life Beer, 2 Sides, Round, 12 In.	5.00
Tray, Molson's Ale, Porcelain On Steel, 12 3/4 In.	43.00
Tray, Narragansett Lager-Ale, Hops & Grains Design On Rim, 12 In.	25.00
Tray, New Yorker Beer & Ale, Gentlemen In Tavern, Herbert Bohnert, 1936, 12 In.	31.00
Tray, Old Heidelberg Brew, 10 x 13 In.	17.00
Tray, Old London Ale & Beer, 1930s, 12 In.	90.00
Tray, Pabst-Milwaukee, Factory Scene, Horses, Trolleys, Beveled Rim, 17 x 12 In.	75.00
Tray, Palisades Beer, Wm. Peter Brewing, Pre-Prohibition, Oval, 17 x 14 In.	306.00
Tray, Pickwick Ale, Haffenreffer Brewing, 1940s, 12 In.	28.00
Tray, Pie Plate, Miller High Life Beer, 1910s, 13 In.	200.00
Tray, Revlon, Bamboo Handles, Black, Turquoise, Plastic, 15 x 5 3/4 In.	95.00
Tray, Rochester Based Brewery, Round, 13 In.	34.00
Tray, S. Babic Wholesale Liquor, Mildred Portrait, Metal, Round, 13 In.	390.00
Tray, Simon Pure Extra Pale Ale, Winged Hops Trademark, Buffalo, N.Y., 12 In.	26.00
Tray, Tally-Ho Beer, Coach, Koenig-Rauch-Paulsen Brewers, N.Y. City, 12 In.	25.00
Tray, Tam O'Shanter Lager Beer & Ales, Tartan Design, 13 In.	26.00
Tray, Velvet Ice Cream, Shake, Dish, Square, c.1915, 13 In.	195.00
Tray, Yuengling's Prize Beer, Round, 12 In.	240.00
Tray, Zippo Lighters, Cardboard, Indented Areas For Lighters, 10 x 12 In.	33.00

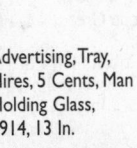

Advertising, Tray,
Hires, 5 Cents, Man
Holding Glass,
1914, 13 In.

Advertising, Tray,
Hires, Girl In Oval,
Tin, 13 x 10 In.

Tumbler, Dad's Root Beer, Black Cow, Box, 12 Piece 285.0
Umbrella, Golf, Timex, John Cameron Swayze's 60.0
Wallet, Child's, Froot Loops, Colored, 1984 .... 12.0
Whet Stone, Sloss Ladle-Mixed Pig Iron, Steel Mill, Pocket, 2 3/4 In. 45.0
Whiskey, Napier, Glass 75.0
Whiskey, W.R. Riley, Etched 18.0
Whistle, Oscar Meyer Wiener, Plastic, Red, Yellow, Cellophane Wrapper, 2 Piece 30.0
Whistle, Yellow Cab, Tin, Phone Cherry 1-4900 .... 40.0
Windmill, Wooden, Tin, Salesman, 32 In. 7250.0

AGATA glass was made by Joseph Locke of the New England Glass
Company of Cambridge, Massachusetts, after 1885. A metallic stain
was applied to New England Peachblow and the mottled design characteristic of agata appeared.

Bowl, Blue, Gold Highlights, Ruffled, 3 x 5 1/2 In. 600.0
Mug, Green, Gold Trim, New England, 2 1/2 x 3 In. 700.0
Spooner, New England, Peachblow, 4 1/2 In. 865.0
Tumbler, New England, 3 3/4 In. 620.0
Vase, Lily, Crimson, Random Black Splotches, Victorian, 8 In. 1085.0
Vase, Tan, Yellow, Brown, Green Striations, Marked, 5 1/2 In. 1380.0

AKRO AGATE glass was made in Clarksburg, West Virginia, from 1932
to 1951. Before that time, the firm made children's glass marbles,
which are listed in this book in the Marble category. Most of the glass
is marked with a crow flying through the letter *A*.

Ashtray, Car, Metal Fixtures, 3 3/4 In. 77.0
Bowl, Cereal, Interior Panel, Lemonade, Oxblood, 3 3/8 In. 48.0
Bowl, Cereal, Octagonal, Closed Handles, White, 3 3/8 In. 14.0
Bowl, Cereal, Stacked Disc & Interior Panel, Cobalt, 3 3/8 In. 40.0
Bowl, Cereal, Stacked Disc & Interior Panel, Marbleized Blue, 3 3/8 In. 48.0
Creamer, Chiquita, Cobalt, 1 1/2 In. 15.0
Creamer, Interior Panel, Marbleized Maroon, 1 3/8 In. 35.0
Creamer, Interior Panel, Marbleized Topaz, 1 3/8 In. 19.0
Creamer, Octagonal, Open Handle, Light Blue, 1 1/2 In. 25.0
Creamer, Stacked Disc & Interior Panel, Marbleized Blue, 1 1/4 In. 18.0
Creamer, Stacked Disc, Yellow, 1 1/4 In. 15.0
Creamer, Stippled Band, Green, 1 3/8 In. 26.0
Cup, Concentric Ring, Light Blue, 1 1/4 In. 12.0
Cup, Interior Panel, Marbleized Blue, 1 3/8 In. 32.0
Cup, Interior Panel, Marbleized Green, 1 3/8 In. 25.0
Cup, Octagonal, Closed Handle, Cobalt, 1 1/2 In. 10.0
Cup, Octagonal, Open Handle, Orange, 1 1/2 In. 20.0
Cup, Stacked Disc, Blue, 1 1/4 In. 20.0
Cup, Stacked Disc, Green, 1 1/4 In. 4.0
Cup & Saucer, Chiquita, Opaque Green, 1 1/2 In. 7.0
Cup & Saucer, Interior Panel, Marbleized Green, 1 1/4 In. 15.0
Cup & Saucer, Stacked Disc & Interior Panel, Cobalt, 1 1/4 In. 40.0
Cup & Saucer, Stippled Band, Green, 1 1/2 In. 28.0
Pitcher, Stacked Disc & Interior Panel, Green 18.0
Pitcher, Stacked Disc, Opaque Blue 27.0
Pitcher, Stippled Band & Interior Panel, Topaz 30.0
Planter, Lilly, Marbleized Green, 5 In. 6.0
Plate, Concentric Ring, Cobalt, 3 1/4 In. 8.0
Plate, Concentric Ring, Opaque Green, 4 1/4 In. 12.0
Plate, Interior Panel, Marbleized Blue, 4 1/4 In. 10.0
Plate, Interior Panel, Marbleized Green, 3 1/4 In. 9.0
Plate, Interior Panel, Marbleized Green, 4 1/4 In. 15.0
Plate, Octagonal, Closed Handle, Opaque Green, 4 1/4 In. 5.0
Plate, Octagonal, Cobalt, 4 1/4 In. 10.0
Plate, Stacked Disc & Interior Panel, Cobalt, 4 1/4 In. 21.0
Plate, Stacked Disc & Interior Panel, Opaque Yellow, 3 1/4 In. 13.0
Plate, Stacked Disc, Opaque Green, 3 1/4 In. 4.0
Plate, Stippled Band, Green, 3 1/4 In. 16.0

Plate, Stippled Band, Green, 4 1/4 In.	9.00
Powder Jar, Cover, Ivy, Marbleized Green	65.00
Saucer, Concentric Ring, Opaque Pink, 2 3/4 In.	6.00
Saucer, Interior Panel, Marbleized Green, 2 3/4 In.	12.00
Saucer, Interior Panel, Marbleized Red, 3 3/8 In.	12.00
Saucer, Octagonal, Closed Handle, Yellow & Orange, 2 3/4 In.	6.00
Saucer, Raised Daisy, Marbleized Yellow, 2 1/2 In.	16.00
Sugar, Cover, Interior Panel, Marbleized Green, 1 3/8 In.	41.00
Sugar, Cover, Octagonal, Opaque Yellow, 1 3/8 In.	21.00
Sugar, Cover, Stacked Disc & Interior Panel, Cobalt, 1 3/8 In.	60.00
Sugar, Interior Panel, Marbleized Green, 1 3/8 In.	30.00
Sugar, Octagonal, Open Handles, Opaque Blue, 1 1/4 In.	24.00
Sugar, Stacked Disc, Opaque Blue, 1 1/4 In.	15.00
Sugar & Creamer, Interior Panel, Marbleized Green, 1 1/4 In.	53.00
Sugar & Creamer, Stacked Disc & Interior Panel, Opaque Blue, 1 1/4 In.	38.00
Sugar & Creamer, Stacked Disc, Opaque Pink, 1 1/4 In.	45.00
Tea Set, Concentric Ring, Opaque, Box, 2 3/8 In., 21 Piece	450.00
Tea Set, Interior Panel, Marbleized Maroon, Box, 2 7/8 In., 21 Piece	500.00
Tea Set, Raised Daisy, Box, 19 Piece	700.00
Tea Set, Stacked Disc, Box, 21 Piece	275.00
Teapot, Cover, Chiquita, Opaque Green, 2 3/4 In.	16.00
Teapot, Cover, Interior Panel, Marbleized Blue, 2 5/8 In.	42.00
Teapot, Cover, Stacked Disc, Opaque Green, 2 3/8 In.	12.00
Teapot, Interior Panel, Marbleized Green, 2 3/8 In.	30.00
Teapot, Octagonal, Open Handle, Opaque Blue, 2 3/8 In.	25.00
Teapot, Raised Daisy, Opaque Blue, 2 3/8 In.	55.00
Teapot, Stacked Disc & Interior Panel, Cobalt, 2 3/8 In.	75.00
Teapot, Stacked Disc, Opaque Blue, 2 3/8 In.	21.00
Teapot, Stippled Band, Cobalt, 2 5/8 In.	90.00
Teapot, Stippled Band, Green, 2 3/8 In.	36.00
Teapot, Stippled Band, Topaz, 2 3/8 In.	25.00
Tumbler, Interior Panel, Marbleized Green, 2 In.	10.00 to 15.00
Tumbler, Octagonal, Opaque Green, 2 In.	16.00
Tumbler, Stacked Disc & Interior Panel, Green, 2 In.	10.00
Tumbler, Stacked Disc & Interior Panel, Opaque Blue, 2 In.	30.00
Tumbler, Stippled Band, Green Transparent, 2 In.	11.00
Tumbler, Stippled Band, Topaz, 2 In.	16.00
Urn, Marbleized Green, Beaded Top, Square Base, 3 1/4 In.	15.00
Water Set, Stacked Disc, Marbleized, Blue Pitcher, Pink Tumblers, 7 Piece	160.00
Water Set, Stippled Band, Topaz, 5 Piece	60.00

ALABASTER is a very soft form of gypsum, a stone that resembles marble. It was often carved into vases or statues in Victorian times. There are alabaster carvings being made even today. Because the alabaster is very porous, it will dissolve if kept in water, so do not use alabaster vases for flowers.

Bust, Woman, Spring, C. Scheggi, Italy, c.1880, 18 1/2 In.	1380.00
Bust, Young Girl, On Pedestal, A. Firlli, 1904, 23 In.	3450.00
Bust, Young Man, C. Augusto, Marked, Italy, 8 1/2 In.	72.00
Figurine, American Eagle, Rock-Like Pedestal Base, 17 In.	155.00
Figurine, Babushka Lady, Seated, With Billowing Headdress, Gray, 17 1/2 In.	630.00
Figurine, Dancer, Woman, With Braid, Revolving Mirror Base, Pink, 22 In.	465.00
Figurine, Nude Woman, Draped, Leaning Against Pedestal, Winged Griffin, 47 In.	9775.00
Figurine, Nude Woman, Seated, Hand To Cheek, Marble Base, 12 x 15 In.	2760.00
Figurine, Polar Bear, Black Formica Revolving Base, 13 1/2 In.	605.00
Figurine, Torso In Motion, Green, Brown, C. Schatzberg, 20 1/2 In.	350.00
Figurine, Woman, Bobbed Hair, Long Dress, 1920s, 20 1/2 In.	4140.00
Figurine, Woman, Cipriani, 19th Century, 32 In.	6325.00
Figurine, Young Boy, Dove, Mounted With Ivory Plaque, 23 1/2 In.	862.00
Figurine, Young Boy, Holding A Bird, 27 In.	1089.00
Figurine, Young Girl, Holding A Doll, Signed, Pugi Firenzi, 32 1/2 In.	3267.00
Lamp, Ribbon, Floral Design, Domed Shade, Hexagonal Base, Reeded Stem, Floor	2400.00
Lamp, Seated Woman On Top, Figural, 15 1/5 In.	995.00

Lamp, Urn Form, Stylized Intertwining Leaves, 1930s, 15 1/2 In. 6325.00
Tazza, Dish Form Top, Waisted Socle, Beaded Design, Ormolu, France, 10 x 15 In. 5462.00
Urn, Allegorical Figures At Base, Bronze Mounted, Louis Philippe, 11 In., Pair 2875.00
Urn, Fluted Campana Form, Classical Figures, c.1875, 17 1/2 In., Pair 6800.00
Urn, Woman Egyptian Torso, Louis XVI Style, Square Base, 14 3/4 In. 7475.00

ALEXANDRITE is a name with many meanings. It is a form of the mineral chrysoberyl that changes from green to red under artificial light. A man-made version of this mineral is sold in Mexico today. It changes from deep purple to aquamarine blue under artificial light. The Alexandrite listed here is glass made in the late nineteenth and twentieth centuries. Thomas Webb & Sons sold their transparent glass shaded from yellow to rose to blue under the name Alexandrite. Stevens and Williams had a cased Alexandrite of yellow, rose, and blue. A. Douglas Nash Corporation made an amethyst-colored Alexandrite. Several American glass companies of the 1920s made a glass that changed color under electric lights and this was also called Alexandrite.

Goblet, Honeycomb, Amber 725.00
Sherbet, Crystal Bowl, Incised Fuchsia Design 240.00
Vase, Honeycomb, Webb, 4 In. 2000.00

ALUMINUM was more expensive than gold or silver until the 1850s. Chemists learned how to refine bauxite to get aluminum. Jewelry and other small objects were made of the valuable metal until 1914, when an inexpensive smelting process was invented. The aluminum collected today dates from the 1930s through the 1950s. Hand-hammered pieces are the most popular.

Ashtray, Bamboo, On Stand, Everlast 90.00
Basket, Oval, Twisted 3-Wire Handles, J. Braun, 7 x 16 x 10 5/8 In. 130.00
Basket, Sunflower, Farber & Shlevin, 7 In. 1.00
Basket, Twisted Wire Handle, Oval, J. Braun 130.00
Bowl, Fruit, Grape Leaf, Shallow, West Bend, 14 In. 10.00
Bowl, Wheat, Gold Anodized, Arthur Armour, 11 In. 25.00
Box, Cover, Sailboat, Removable Partition, Wendell August Forge, 3 1/2 x 5 3/8 In. 45.00
Box, Dresser, Divided Interior, Kensington, 7 3/16 x 3 1/4 In. 65.00
Brooch, Ming Tree, Wendell August Forge, 1 1/2 x 2 1/4 In. 60.00
Cake Plate, Twisted Handle, Double, Buenilum 25.00
Candelabrum, 5-Light, Arched, Curly Y-Shaped Base, Wendell August Forge, 30 In. 1050.00
Candleholder, Farberware, 1940s, Pair 50.00
Candlestick, Y-Shaped Base, Wendell August Forge 100.00
Candy Dish, Chrysanthemum, Continental 38.00
Candy Dish, Green, Cut Grapes, Pedestal, Farberware 20.00
Canister Set, Flour, Cookies, Sugar, Coffee, Rice, Tea, Kromex, 6 Piece 60.00
Canister Set, Flour, Sugar, Coffee, Tea, Kromex, 1940s, 4 Piece 45.00
Casserole, Cover, Wild Rose, Continental, Box, 4 x 6 In. 27.50
Cocktail Shaker, West Bend 75.00
Dish, Coiled Handle, Square, Hand Wrought, Farber & Shlevin ....18.00 to 20.00

Never use the dishwasher to wash a disposable aluminum container that held food from the grocery store. If the container touches a piece of white china, it will leave a black mark. It will also harm pewter, brass, and bronze.

Aluminum,
Syrup Jug, Great
Northern Mfg.
Co., Chicago, 6 In.

Dish, Cover, Peapod, Everlast 3.00
Frame, Stylized Bird Corners, 6-Sided Rosettes, Otto Pisoni, 11 x 9 In. 2050.00
Ice Bucket, Bamboo, K-Shaped Waiter Finial, No Liner, Everlast 45.00
Ice Bucket, Chrome Lid & Base, Russel Wright 250.00
Ice Bucket, Chrysanthemum, No. 705, Continental 85.00
Lamp, Spherical Frosted Glass, Russel Wright, 12 x 27 In. 465.00
Pitcher, No. 453, Rodney Kent 23.00
Pitcher, Wild Rose, Continental 17.50
Platter Set, 12 Brass Zodiac Symbols In Center, Kensington, 18 In., 12 Piece 525.00
Server, Dogwood & Roses, Rectangular, 2 Tiers, Everlast, Bottom 11 x 7 1/2 In. 75.00
Silent Butler, Art Deco, 1930s 40.00
Snack Server, Bamboo, Ferris Wheel Shape, Glass Inserts, Everlast 65.00
Syrup Jug, Great Northern Mfg. Co., Chicago, 6 In. ....*Illus* 10.00
Tidbit, 2 Tiers, Everlast 24.00
Tidbit, Kromex, 1950s, 13 In. & 8 1/2 In., Pair 30.00
Tray, Chain Links, Everlast, 11 7/8 x 15 3/4 In. 90.00
Tray, Dagger Form Feet, Wendell August Forge, 14 3/4 In. 925.00
Tray, Daisy, Tab Handles, Bar Style, Everlast 35.00
Tray, Floral, Hammered Handles, Ball Footed, Everlast 65.00
Tray, Flowers & Fruit Around Sides, Cromwell, 17 In. 15.00
Tray, Geometric Border, Upturned Edge, 8 1/2 In. 25.00
Tray, Pine Cone, Wendell August Forge, 20 x 15 7/8 In. 345.00
Tray, Pussy Willow, Cut-Out Handles, Wendell August Forge, 13 1/2 x 24 In. 80.00
Tray, Rope, Loop & Bead Handles, Palmer Smith, 11 3/8 In. 55.00
Vase, Russel Wright, 9 In. 150.00
Wine Cooler, Grapes, With Stand, Everlast 140.00

AMBER, see Jewelry category.

AMBER GLASS is the name of any glassware with the proper yellow-brown shading. It was a popular color just after the Civil War and many pressed glass pieces were made of amber glass. Depression glass of the 1930s–1950s was also made in shades of amber glass. Other pieces may be found in the Depression Glass, Pressed Glass, and other glass categories. All types are being reproduced.

Compote, Thumbprint Bowl, Scalloped, Hexagonal Baluster Stem, 7 1/4 x 6 In. 120.00
Epergne, Sapphire Blue, Rigaree Trim, Enameled Flowers, 14 In. 395.00
Tumbler, 6 Panels, 2 7/8 In. 60.00
Tumbler, 8 Panels, 3 3/8 In. 120.00
Vase, Bud, Boy & Girl In Foliage, White Spatter, 7 x 2 1/2 In., Pair 550.00
Vase, Heart-Shaped Foot, 7 x 5 In. 295.00

AMBERETTE pieces are listed in the Pressed Glass category under the pattern name Amberette.

AMBERINA is a two-toned glassware made from 1883 to about 1900. It was patented by Joseph Locke of the New England Glass Company, but was also made by other companies. The glass shades from red to amber. Similar pieces of glass may be found in the Baccarat and Plated Amberina categories. Glass shaded from blue to amber is called *Blue Amberina* or *Bluerina*.

Basket, Ruffled Edge, Amber Foot & Handle, New England, 9 x 4 In. 475.00
Berry Bowl, Daisy & Button, Boat Shape, Hobbs, Brockunier & Co., 3 3/4 In. 395.00
Biscuit Jar, Thumbprint 135.00
Bowl, Alternating Panels Of Ribs & Diamond Points, 6 Pinched Corners, 9 In. 137.00
Bowl, Daisy & Button, Square, 9 x 3 In. 150.00
Bowl, Diamond-Quilted, Ruffled Edge, 3 1/2 x 8 1/4 In. 750.00
Bowl, Diamond-Quilted, Thorn Handle, 4 Applied Feet, 10 1/2 In. 435.00
Bowl, Diamond-Quilted, Thorn Handle, Ruffled Edge, New England Glass Co., 10 In. 495.00
Bowl, Hobstar Within Arches, 3 Feathered Buzz Saws, 8 In. 55.00
Celery Vase, 6 3/4 x 4 In. 100.00
Cracker Jar, Inverted Thumbprint, Amber Knob Finial, 1885, 8 x 5 3/4 In. 785.00
Dish, Ice Cream, Daisy & Button, 4-Cornered, Boat Shape, 10 x 8 In. 275.00
Finger Bowl, Fluted 385.00

Pitcher, Coinspot, Mt. Washington, 7 1/2 In. 250.0
Pitcher, Cream, Thumbprint, Amber Handle, 4 1/2 In. 143.0
Pitcher, Diamond-Quilted, Amber Ribbed Handle, 8 3/4 In. 330.0
Pitcher, Diamond-Quilted, Optic, Ruffled Edge, Crystal Handle, 7 1/4 In. 270.0
Pitcher, Inverted Thumbprint, Amber Handle, 3-Way Mouth, 8 1/2 In. 300.0
Pitcher, Inverted Thumbprint, Reeded Amber Handle 450.0
Pitcher, Thumbprint, Reeded Handle, 7 In. 145.0
Pitcher, Thumbprint, Ribbed Handle, 4 1/2 In. 110.0
Pitcher, Water, Swirl, Amber Handle, 6 x 6 In. 225.0
Sauce, Daisy & Button, Scalloped Edge, Hobbs Brockunier, Square, 5 In. 85.0
Toothpick, Daisy & Button, Footed 225.0
Toothpick, Diamond-Quilted 55.0
Toothpick, Inverted Thumbprint 245.0
Toothpick, Inverted Thumbprint, Flared Top 285.0
Toothpick, Swirl, Square Top 265.0
Toothpick, Thumbprint 125.0
Tumbler, Diamond-Quilted, 3 3/4 In. 66.0
Tumbler, Thumbprint, 4 In. .... 44.00 to 55.0
Vase, 9 Optic Panels, Flower Form Mouth, Marked, 11 In. 875.0
Vase, Blue Enameled, Berries, Gold, Bulbous Base, Late 19th Century, 10 1/4 In. ... 245.0
Vase, Calla Lilly Shape, Amber Foot & Spiral Trim, 12 1/4 In. 150.0
Vase, Diamond-Quilted, Satin, White Lining, Mt. Washington, 1880s, 8 In. 1250.0
Vase, Inverted Thumbprint, 6 3/4 x 3 1/2 In. 175.0
Vase, Lily, 8 1/4 In. 285.0
Vase, Swirl, Fluted Top, 8 In. 275.0
Vase, Wishbone Rigaree, 4 Berry Prunts, 5 x 5 1/2 In. 1500.0
Whiskey Taster, Diamond-Quilted, Fuchsia To Amber, 2 3/4 In. 60.0

AMERICAN DINNERWARE, see Dinnerware.

AMERICAN ENCAUSTIC TILING COMPANY was founded in Zanesville, Ohio, in 1875. The company planned to make a variety of tiles to compete with the English tiles that were selling in the United States for use in fireplaces and other architectural designs. The first glazed tiles were made in 1880, embossed tiles in 1881, faience tiles in the 1920s. The firm closed in 1935 and reopened in 1937 as the Shawnee Pottery.

Plaque, Cavalier, Frame, 6 x 18 In. 165.00
Plaque, Lion & Lioness, Dusty Rose, Pair 695.00
Tile, 2 Boys Carrying Deer On Pole, Green Glaze, 6 In. 235.00
Tile, Admiral Dewey, In Uniform, 6 x 6 In. 114.00
Tile, Boy Pulling Ram, H.C. Mueller, Frame, 1941, 6 x 16 In. 1700.00
Tile, Diana Reclining On Fox Rug, Green Glaze, 6 In. 245.00
Tile, Figure Of Woman, Detailed Dress, Signed, 18 x 6 In. 395.00
Tile, Lion & Lioness, 12 x 6 In., Pair 495.00
Tile, Maroon, Tan Glaze, Wide Oak Frame, Square, 6 In. 176.00
Tile, Peacock Under Green Glaze, 12 x 6 In. 265.00
Tile, Wintry Snow Scene, Arts & Crafts Style, 9 x 4 1/2 In. 880.00
Tray, Monk Scene, Brown, Marked, Paper Label, 6 x 5 In. 11.00

AMETHYST GLASS is any of the many glasswares made in the dark purple color of the gemstone called amethyst. Included in this category are many pieces made in the nineteenth and twentieth centuries. Very dark pieces are called *black amethyst* and are listed under that heading.

Bowl, Spreading Foot Foliate Border, Gothic Cast Rim, 12 x 13 1/4 In., Pair 9200.00
Box, Leaves On Hinged Cover, Enameled Leaves On Sides, 3 5/8 x 4 1/8 In. 195.00
Decanter, Whiskey, Tennis Scene, Silver Overlay, c.1920, 10 1/2 In. 375.00
Decanter, Wine, Satin, Enameled, Green, Tan Leaves, 13 In. 165.00
Goblet, Applied Twisted Stem, Allover Gold, 7 In. 130.00
Punch Bowl, Pinwheel Design, Clear Ladle, 12 Cups 90.00
Vase, 3-Printie Bowl, Hexagonal Base, 10 3/8 In. 3265.00
Vase, Enameled Lilies Of Valley, Leaves, Gold Trim, Scalloped Rim, 14 5/8 In. 225.00
Vase, Goldstone, Scalloped Top, Melon Shape, 4 3/4 In. 135.00
Vase, Hexagonal Paneled Bowl, Ruffled Edge, Square Base, 11 1/2 In. 1575.00
Vase, Hexagonal, 3-Printie Bowl, Scalloped Edge, 9 In. 1100.00

Vase, Lilies Of The Valley, White Enamel, Gold Leaves, 8 3/8 In. 110.00
Vase, Panel & Arch, Hexagonal Waterfall Base, Ruffled Edge, 11 1/2 In. 1695.00
Vase, Tulip, Paneled, Petal Rim, Octagonal Wafer Stem, 10 In. . . . . .1450.00 to 1870.00
Vase, White Swirls, Ribbed, Opalescent Foot, Stem, 10 1/2 In. 100.00

AMPHORA pieces are listed in the Teplitz category.

ANDIRONS and related fireplace items are included in the Fireplace category.

ANIMAL TROPHIES, such as stuffed animals, rugs made of animal skins, and other similar collectibles, are listed in this category. Collectors should be aware of the endangered species laws that make it illegal to buy and sell some of these items. Any eagle feathers, many types of pelts or rugs (such as leopard), ivory, and many forms of tortoiseshell can be confiscated by the government. Related trophies may be found in the Fishing category. Ivory items may be found in the Scrimshaw or Ivory categories.

Buffalo Head, Full Mount 550.00
Buffalo Horns, With Skull 275.00
Bull's Head, 19th Century 1898.00
Hawaiian Golden Owl, Plaque, 1963 . . . . 500.00
Moose Hide, Pyrography & Painted Scene, Wm. Betzeler, 1913, 7 x 5 Ft. 2600.00
Rhinoceros Foot, Humidor 1250.00
Rug, Bear Skin, 2 Missing Claws 685.00
Rug, Polar Bear, 1900s, 31 x 36 In. 150.00
Seal, 1870s 135.00
Steer, Longhorn, Bald Face, Shoulder Mount 1200.00
Steer, Texas Longhorn, Arizona, 1962, 5 Ft. 125.00
Steer Horns, Wood Base, 25 In. 50.00
Wolverine 715.00

ANIMATION ART collectibles include cels that are painted drawings on celluloid needed to make animated cartoons shown in movie theaters or on TV. Hundreds of cels were made, then photographed in sequence to make a cartoon showing moving figures. Early examples made by the Walt Disney Studios are popular with collectors today. Original sketches used by the artists are also listed here. Modern animated cartoons are made using computer-generated pictures. Some of these are being produced as cels to be sold to collectors. Other cartoon art is listed in Comic Art and Disneyana.

Cel, Bambi & Mother, Gouache, Hand-Painted Ground, 1942, 6 7/8 x 5 7/8 In. 1840.00
Cel, Bambi, Leaping Rabbits, Hand-Painted Ground, 1942, 7 3/8 x 9 1/8 In. 515.00
Cel, Beatles, Yellow Submarine, George With Arms Outstretched, 1968, 7 1/2 In. 450.00
Cel, Bugs Bunny, 2 Policemen With Belligerent Bugs, 10 1/2 x 11 In. 1380.00
Cel, Caveman, Hanna-Barbera 60.00
Cel, Chipmunk, 1960s, 9 1/4 x 11 3/4 In. 55.00
Cel, Donald Duck As Fireman, 11 1/2 x 15 In. 357.00
Cel, Donald Duck's Nephew, Disneyland, 11 x 13 In. 192.00
Cel, Donald Duck, Holds Key, Angry Expression, 8 x 12 In. 1150.00
Cel, Ferdinand The Bull, Peering Timidly Out From Wreath, 2 1/2 x 2 1/2 In. 460.00
Cel, Keebler, T.V. Commercial, 1970s 30.00
Cel, Lady & The Tramp, Peg Sings, 12 x 16 In. 1725.00
Cel, Ludwig Von Drake, Wonderful World Of Color, 1960s, 6 1/2 In. 285.00
Cel, Peter Pan, Mr. Smee Fumbles With Blunderbuss, 1953, 11 x 16 In. 805.00
Cel, Pink Panther, Signed By Friz Freleng & David DePatie, Frame 525.00
Cel, Pinocchio, Figaro Walks Happily Along, 4 1/2 x 5 In. 3450.00
Cel, Pinocchio, Gepetto & Pinocchio, Matted, 1940, 7 1/2 x 9 1/4 In. 2415.00
Cel, Pinocchio, Smiling As Walking Along, 12 1/2 x 16 In. 1380.00
Cel, Popeye & Olive Oyl, Halas & Bachelor Cartoon Studios 522.00
Cel, Rabbit From Winnie The Pooh, Day For Eeyore, 1980s, 1 1/4 In. 85.00
Cel, Rabbit, Winnie The Pooh, Unpainted, 1980s, 1 1/4 In. 45.00
Cel, Sleeping Beauty, Flora, Fauna & Merryweather, 7 x 4 1/2 In. 1380.00
Cel, Ugly Duckling, Breaks Out Of Shell, 6 1/2 x 6 1/2 In. 1380.00
Cel, Wendy & Peter Pan Telling Children A Story, 1953, 7 1/2 x 9 1/2 In. 870.00

Cel, Winged Scourge, Dopey Bends Over While Using Bug Spray, 7 x 11 In. 1495.00
Drawing, Mickey Mouse, In Tux & Hat, Flying Downwards, 1936, 3 1/2 In. 600.00
Drawing, Mickey Mouse, Riding Motorcycle, Black Pencil, 1934, 3 1/4 x 4 In. 600.00
Drawing, Pinocchio & Stromboli, Gustav Tengren, Signed, 1940 .... 675.00

ANNA POTTERY was started in Anna, Illinois, in 1859 by Cornwall and
Wallace Kirkpatrick. They made many types of utilitarian wares,
bricks, drain tiles, and giftware. The most collectible pieces made by
the pottery are the pig-shaped bottles and jugs with special inscriptions, applied animals, and figures. The pottery closed in 1894.

Anna Pottery

Flask, Pig, Kirkpatrick Brothers, Ill., World's Fair, 1893, 6 In. 1760.00
Flask, Pig, Railroad & River Guide, Stoneware, Cobalt Blue, 6 In. 5500.00
Pig, World's Fair, With A Little Good Rye, 1893, 7 1/4 In. 1760.00

APPLE PEELERS are listed in the Kitchen category under Peeler, Apple.

ARCHITECTURAL antiques include a variety of collectibles, usually
very large, that have been removed from buildings. Hardware, back-
bars, doors, paneling, and even old bathtubs are now wanted by collectors. Pieces of the Victorian, Art Nouveau, and Art Deco styles are
in greatest demand.

Altar Decoration, Scrolling & Entwining Acanthus Vines, Iron, Spanish, 34 In. 630.00
Backbar, Lion Head Over Each Arch, Oak, 144 x 98 In. 7500.00
Backbar, Oak, Saloon, 2 Arches With Lion Heads, Front, 144 x 96 In. 7500.00
Bracket, For 30-In. Sign, 1935 .... 345.00
Column, Regency, Mahogany, Brass, Circular Frieze, Block Feet, 43 In., Pair 1840.00
Cupola, Ship Weather Vane 475.00
Curtain Ring, Leaf Design, Gilt Metal, 6 Piece 495.00
Curtain Tieback, George III, Gilt Metal, Enameled, 6 Piece 775.00
Door, Carved, Divided Into Panels, Mythological Creatures, 92 1/2 In., Pair 1500.00
Door, Stained Glass, 94 x 55 In., Pair 8600.00
Door Handle, Figural, Hindu Head, France, 3 1/4 In. 165.00
Door Knocker, Brass, Hand Holding Ball, Victorian 115.00
Door Knocker, Dolphins Swallowing Bearded Mask, Iron, France, 5 1/2 In. 1840.00
Door Knocker, Form Of Sea Creatures, Pull Center, Iron, France, 6 3/4 In. 1725.00
Door Knocker, Ivy Post, No. 123, Cast Iron, Hubley 160.00
Door Knocker, Original Striker Plate, Iron Bolts, England, 18th Century 395.00
Door Lock, Original Key & Escutcheon, Hand Forged, 9 9/16 x 6 5/8 In. 145.00
Doorknob, Doggie, Pair 3600.00
Doorknob, Elk Heads, Backplate, Large 100.00
Doorknob, Floral, Bluebird & Owl, Aesthetic Style 475.00
Doorknob, Gothic, Heavy Bronze 70.00
Doorknob, Hummingbird, Rosettes, Gold Washed, Pair 550.00
Doorknob, Lion, Backplate, MCCC/R & E ....*Illus* 2300.00
Doorknob, New York City School, Oval 20.00

Architectural,
Doorknob, Lion,
Backplate, MCCC/R & E

Architectural, Doorknob,
Outline Of Man, Round, 2 In.

Architectural, Doorknob,
School Building, Oblong, 3 In.

Doorknob, Outline Of Man, Round, 2 In. .... *Illus*   15.00
Doorknob, Passage, Union County, N.J., Seal, Revolutionary Soldier 400.00
Doorknob, School Building, Oblong, 3 In. .... *Illus*   12.00
Doorknob, Starfish 325.00
Fan, Over-Door, White Paint 715.00
Fence, Gothic Posts, 1 Gate, Iron, 4 x 110 Ft. 2700.00
Fence, Weeping Willow, Iron, Cemetery, 8 Ft. 500.00
Finial, Molded Zinc, 24 In., Pair 258.00
Finial, Newel Post, Blue Cut To White, Brass Stem, 6 7/8 In. 160.00
Flag Pole, Eagle, Silver Paint, 19th Century, 7 1/2 Ft. 165.00
Gate, Iron, Ball & Spire Finials, Green-Black Paint, 50 x 35 In. 330.00
Gate, Iron, Central Man & Woman Musician, E. Brandt, 1925, 27 x 39 In., Pair   8625.00
Gate, Lattice Design, Mortise & Tenon Constructed Frame, Painted, 24 x 32 In. 172.00
Grate, Bank Teller's, Brass Bars, 8 Teller Openings, 2 1/2 Ft. x 40 In. 1350.00
Hinge, Aesthetic Style, Nashua, 3 x 6 In. 220.00
Hinge, Barn, Hand Forged, Green Paint, Early 1800s, 26 1/2 In., 2 Pair 160.00
Hitching Post, Horse Head, Black, Acanthus Leaves On Bottom, Cast Iron, 40 In. 2070.00
Hitching Post, Horse Head, Cast Iron, 20 In., Pair 660.00
Knob, Mirror, Brass, England, 2 1/4 In., Pair 285.00
Letter Slot, Neoclassical, Large 40.00
Lock, Fleur-De-Lis Border, Serpent-Form Hasp, Iron, France, 9 In. 2587.00
Lockplate, Rope Twist Borders, Iron, French Gothic, 1490s, 10 3/4 x 10 1/2 In. 1265.00
Mantel, Beveled Mirror, Slate Cover, Marbleized Painting, Oak, c.1900, 82 In. 2800.00
Mantel, Carved Marble, France, 1850s, 55 x 43 In. 9500.00
Mantel, Marble, Carved Shells, Shaped Top, Conforming Frieze, 42 1/2 x 47 In. 1265.00
Mantel, Striped Pine, Flight Of Athena Scene, 59 x 74 1/2 In. 2990.00
Newel Post, Millefiori 595.00
Ornament, Roof, Flame Finial, Tassels, Wooden, Carved, Red & Black Paint, 15 In. 172.00
Ornament, Roof, Gargoyle Head Form, Custom-Made Stand, Cast Iron, 7 5/8 In. 287.00
School Locker, Steel, 4 Over 4, Block Of 8, France, 8 Ft. 2800.00
Soda Fountain, Hamilton Beach, No. 32, Juice Extractor, Enamel, Chrome, 22 In. 100.00
Thumb Latch, Brass, 1780s, 7 1/2 In. 175.00

AREQUIPA POTTERY was produced from 1911 to 1918 by the patients
of the Arequipa Sanitarium in Marin County Hills, California. The
patients were trained by Frederick Hürten Rhead, who had worked at
the Roseville Pottery.

Bowl, Black High-Glaze Exterior, Mottled Blue Interior, Incised, 8 1/2 x 3 In. 209.00
Bowl, Blue High-Glaze Exterior, Yellow Interior, Incised, 9 x 2 1/2 In. 187.00
Bowl, Multitoned, Green Glaze, 9 In. 165.00
Vase, Bell-Shaped Flowers, Brown Glaze, Signed, 11 In. 770.00
Vase, Brown & Blue Semigloss Luster, Impressed Mark, 3 1/2 In. 355.00
Vase, Embossed Acanthus Leaves, Blue, Gray Matte Glaze, 3 1/2 x 2 In. 770.00
Vase, Mauve Over Blue, 6 In. 650.00

ARGY-ROUSSEAU, see G. Argy-Rousseau category.

ARITA is a port in Japan. Porcelain was made there from about 1616.
Many types of decorations were used, including the popular Imari
designs, which are listed under Imari in this book.

Figurine, Kannon With 2 Children, Lacquered Shrine, Gilt Interior, 12 In. 2075.00
Saucer, 2 Dragons, Central Snowflake, Late 17th Century, 8 3/4 In. 800.00
Vase, Ewer Shape, Landscape, 8 In. 700.00

ART DECO, or Art Moderne, a style started at the Paris Exposition of
1925, is characterized by linear, geometric designs. All types of furniture and decorative arts, jewelry, book bindings, and even games were
designed in this style. Additional items may be found in the Furniture
category or in various glass and pottery categories, etc.

Box, Cigarette, Wood Interior, Leather Base, Hinged Lid, Silver, 1935, 7 In. 1720.00
Cocktail Shaker, Chrome, Painted Black Ribs At Shoulder & Base, Chase, 11 1/2 In. 110.00
Coffee Service, Electroplated, Coffeepot, Sugar, Creamer, Stamped, England 2875.00
Figure, Nubian Nude Woman, Metal, 9 1/2 In. 115.00

Figure, Woman, Walking 2 Borzois, Simulated Ivory, Mexico, 12 x 10 1/2 In. 175.00
Tray, Bird's-Eye Maple, Inset Brass Plaque Of Man & Dog, 10 1/2 x 10 In. 121.00
Tray, Reverse Painted Design, Green, Black, White, Chrome Frame, 1930s, 18 x 12 In. ... 880.00
Tray, Reverse Painted Scene, Red, Black & White, Chrome Frame, 1930s, 18 x 12 In. 385.00
Vase, Cubist Form, Blue, Green, Yellow, Brown, White, A. Dubois, Belgium, 9 x 7 In. ... 154.00
Waste Basket, African Female Masks On Each Side, Copper, Brass 125.00

ART GLASS, see Glass-Art category.

ART NOUVEAU is a style of design that was at its most popular from
1895 to 1905. Famous designers, including Rene Lalique and Emile
Galle, produced furniture, glass, silver, metalwork, and buildings in
the new style. Ladies with long flowing hair and elongated bodies were
among the more easily recognized design elements. Copies of this
style are being made today. Many modern pieces of jewelry can be
found. Additional Art Nouveau pieces may be found in Furniture or in
various glass categories.

Centerpiece, Silver Plated, 2 Handles, Cut Glass Insert, Star & Fan, 6 x 13 In. 259.00
Comb, Sterling Silver, 5 x 4 1/2 In. 225.00
Decanter, Glass, Metal, WMF, Pair 775.00

ART POTTERY was first made in America in Cincinnati, Ohio, during
the 1870s. The pieces were hand thrown and hand decorated. The art
pottery tradition continued until the 1920s when studio potters began
making the more artistic wares. American, English, and Continental art
pottery by less well-known makers is listed here. Most makers listed
in *Kovels' American Art Pottery*, such as Arequipa, Ohr, Rookwood,
Roseville, and Weller, are listed in their own categories in this book.
More recent pottery is listed under the name of the maker or in the
Pottery category.

Bowl, Fruit, Floral Design, Green Matte Glaze, 8 x 3 In. 176.00
Bowl, Peacock Feather Design, Blue, Green, Cream Crackle Ground, 7 x 3 In. 165.00
Chamberstick, Collapsed Base, Mottled Glaze, W.J. Walley, 4 x 5 1/4 In. 110.00
Charger, Incised & Painted Roosters, J. Lurcat, 15 In. 495.00
Charger, Stylized Amber Rooster, White Ground, H. Diederich, c.1925, 15 1/4 In. 2200.00
Flask, Allover Dappled, Brown Glaze, Ribbon Handles, C. Dresser, 1880, 13 In. 750.00
Jar, Storage, Cover, Brown, Blue Floral Design, Lug Handles, Craven, 1983, 6 7/8 In. ... 110.00
Jardiniere, Molded Vertical Leaves, Green Matte Glaze, 12 x 9 In. 230.00
Mug, Devil's, Feathered Brown Glaze, Walley, Signed, 6 1/2 In. 920.00
Pitcher, Ribbed, Blue Matte Glaze, Light Tan, Brown, 6 1/2 In. 110.00
Plate, Stylized Female Figure, Marbleized Ground, J. Mayodon, 1926, 13 1/2 In. 715.00
Plate, Woman, Gray Curled Hair, White Robe, Alphonse Mucha, 1899, 16 1/2 In. 605.00
Tile, Profile Of Sitting Dog, White On Green Glaze Ground, Walley, 8 1/4 In. 315.00
Vase, 4-Lobed Twisted Form, Green Matte Glaze, Chicago Crucible, 8 In. 385.00
Vase, Black Glaze, Green, 2 Handles, 9 In. 121.00
Vase, Blue Matte, Impressed Cream Bands, Denver, 5 1/2 In. 110.00
Vase, Blue Matte, Zark, Impressed Mark, 9 In. 65.00
Vase, Blue Oxide Glaze Over White, Stoneware, Norweta, 7 3/4 In. 575.00
Vase, Branches Of Holly, Lustered Blue-Green Glaze, Dalpayrat, 8 In. 550.00
Vase, Brown Matte Glaze Over Raised Design, Markham, 3 1/2 x 2 1/2 In. 305.00

Art Pottery, Vase,
Indian, Turquoise
Ground, Khouri
& Cazaux,
France, 12 In.

Cleaning a lot of small figurines or
other collectibles? Line the sink
with a towel. Put the pieces in
the sink. Spray them with window
cleaner. Move them to another
towel on the counter to air dry.

Vase, Brown, Green, Blue, Tree Design, Pauline, 10 1/2 In. 1320.00
Vase, Brown, Turquoise & White, Flattened Globe, C. Dresser, Ault, 1890s, 7 In. 2610.00
Vase, Chrysanthemum, Lines At Edges, John Wareham, 1898 .... 2420.00
Vase, Crackled, Aubergine Glaze, Amber Base, C. Dresser, Linthorpe, 1880, 10 In. 335.00
Vase, Dark Green Matte Over Brown Clay Body, Frederick Rhead, 7 In. 2090.00
Vase, Dimpled, Brown, Turquoise, White Glaze, C. Dresser, Linthorpe, 1880, 11 In. 750.00
Vase, Dutch Scenes, Green, Austria, 10 1/8 In. 70.00
Vase, Frothy Green Matte Glaze, Chicago Crucible, 5 x 3 1/2 In. 330.00
Vase, Geometric Design, Green Matte Glaze, 4 1/2 In. 220.00
Vase, Green & Gun Metal Dripping Glaze, W.J. Walley, 10 In. 935.00
Vase, Green Luster Glaze Over Leathery Deep Brown, Walley, 9 x 6 In. 1980.00
Vase, Indian, Turquoise Ground, Khouri & Cazaux, France, 12 In. ....*Illus* 605.00
Vase, Light Blue Matte Glaze, Jervis, Incised Mark, 6 1/2 In. 110.00
Vase, Matte Mottled Mauve Glaze, Gourd Shape, Delaherche, 7 In. 440.00
Vase, Medium To Light Green Matte Glaze, Dark Brown, Frederick Rhead, 4 In. 1540.00
Vase, Molded Overlapping Leaves Design, Green, Yellow Matte Glaze, 9 In. 440.00
Vase, Mottled Green & Yellow Matte, Chicago Crucible, 8 In. 285.00
Vase, Red & Brown Matte Glaze Over Raised Design, Markham, Label, 4 1/2 In. 385.00
Vase, Red & Green Speckled Glaze, High Fired, Dalpayrat, 1900, 20 In. 6000.00
Vase, Robins, Butterflies & Dragonfly, Blossoms, T. Deck, c.1880, 22 In. 3450.00
Vase, Sculpted Vertical Leaves, Mustard Brown Matte, Chicago Crucible, 7 In. 286.00
Vase, Seed Pods Of Eucalyptus Tree, Rhead, 6 1/4 In. 1800.00
Vase, Striated Green-Brown Glaze, Handle Over Top, Oviform, Walley, 10 3/4 In. 862.00
Vase, Tapered, Mottled Green, Brown Glaze, Markham, 7 In. 825.00
Vase, Vertical Leaves, Green, Brown Matte Glaze, Chicago Crucible, 6 1/2 In. 385.00

ARTS & CRAFTS was a design style popular in American decorative arts
from 1894 to 1923. In the 1970s collectors began to rediscover
Mission furniture, art pottery, metalwork, linens, and light fixtures
from this period. The interest has continued. Today everything from
this era is collectible, including jewelry, graphics, and silverware.
Additional items may be found in the Furniture category, various glass
categories, etc.

Chafing Dish, Mixed Metal, 3 Bronze Rabbits Supports, 3 Burners, 13 1/2 In. 1850.00
Dinner Gong, Iron Frame, Bronze Strike, Floor Standing, 35 1/4 x 25 3/4 In. 435.00
Pitcher, Brass, Copper Trim, Hammered, 13 1/2 In. 195.00
Teapot, Geometric Design, Brass, Rattan Handle, 11 In. 253.00

AURENE glass was made by Frederick Carder of New York about 1904.
It is an iridescent gold, blue, green, or red glass, usually marked
Aurene or *Steuben*.

Bud Vase Holder, Blue-Green, Circular, 6 Bud Holes, No. 2775, 2 x 4 3/8 In. 489.00
Cologne, 8-Lobed Bottle, Tapered, Gold, Signed, Carder, 6 1/2 In. 805.00
Cup & Saucer, Gold Iridescent, Marked, Cafe Noir 300.00
Decanter, Gold 1480.00
Jar, Potpourri, Gold 875.00
Perfume Bottle, Atomizer, Cobalt Blue Finial, 9 1/2 In. 715.00
Shade, Intarsia Brown, 2 1/4 x 4 3/4 x 4 3/8 In. 443.00
Shade, Pulled Feather, 2 1/4 x 3 3/4 x 5 In. 413.00
Shade, White & Gold Pulled-Feather, Gold Aurene Interior, 5 3/4 In. Diam., Pair 375.00

AUSTRIA is a collecting term which covers pieces made by a wide variety of factories. They are listed in this book in categories such as Kauffmann, Royal Dux,
or Porcelain.

AUTO parts and accessories are collectors' items today. Gas pump
globes and license plates are part of this specialty. Prices are determined by age, rarity, and condition. Signs and packaging related to
automobiles may also be found in the Advertising category. Lalique
hood ornaments will be listed in the Lalique category.

Ashtray, Champion Spark Plug 100.00
Ashtray, Ford Dealer, Glass, Logo, 1950s 25.00
Ashtray, Mac Truck 50.00

Ashtray, Michelin Man, Art Deco Style, Bakelite, c.1930s, 5 x 2 In. ....95.00 to 115.00
Ashtray, Michelin Man, Figural, Art Deco Style, England, 6 x 5 x 5 In. 129.00
Banner, Esso Motor Oil, Cloth, 33 x 64 In. 125.00
Banner, New! Nifty! Thrifty! Edsel For 1960, Wall, 36 x 48 In. 150.00
Banner, Oilzum, Blue Ground, Triangle & Oilzum Man Logo, 1950s, 12 x 26 In. 550.00
Battery Tester, Auto-Lite Battery Service, Hard Rubber, 13 x 10 3/4 x 5 In. 11.00
Booklet, Texaco Town Talk, Paper, 7 x 5 In. 70.00
Bookmark, Texaco, Bastien Bros., Co., Rochester, N.Y., Celluloid, 1 3/4 x 3 3/4 In. 275.00
Can, Standard Oil, 5 Gal. 30.00
Catalog, DeSoto, Showroom, 1941, 9 x 11 1/2 In. 28.00
Catalog, Studebaker Auto, Light Six, 1922, 31 Pages, 8 x 11 In. 55.00
Clock, Elm City, Silver 50.00
Fender, Ornament, Whizzer, Box 110.00
First Aid Kit, Ford, Unused, 1962 .... 11.00
Flag Holder, Radiator Cap, 1920s 45.00
Gas Pump, Hand Operated, Glass Measure Tank, Model F, Hose 2500.00
Gas Pump, Metal, Glass, Plastic & Rubber, 7 1/2 Ft. 1000.00
Gas Pump, Phillips 66, National Model A-38, 87 x 21 x 16 In. 1870.00
Gas Pump, Shell, Light-Up, Electric, 86 x 23 x 14 In. 1320.00
Gas Pump, Sinclair H-C, Ethyl Signs, 74 In. 2420.00
Gas Pump, Sinclair, Bowser Rol-Way, Light-Up, 58 x 27 In. 990.00
Gas Pump, Sunoco, Blue, 6 Sides, 10 Gal. 975.00
Gas Pump, Texaco, Fire-Chief ....990.00 to 2000.00
Gas Pump Globe, American, Glass, 12 1/2 In. 230.00
Gas Pump Globe, Arco, Bird In Flight, 1935, 15 In. 1220.00
Gas Pump Globe, Dixie, Flags & Rebel Cap, Round 150.00
Gas Pump Globe, Esso Aviation, Wide Body, 13 1/2 In. 357.00
Gas Pump Globe, Gulf Dieselect Fuel, 12 In. 440.00
Gas Pump Globe, Imperial Ethyl Refineries, 13 1/2 In. 275.00
Gas Pump Globe, Imperial Premier, Metal, 16 1/2 In. 357.00
Gas Pump Globe, Imperial, 1950s 195.00
Gas Pump Globe, Kerosene Diesel Fuel, Blue & White Lens, Metal Base, 15 In. 320.00
Gas Pump Globe, Marathon, Copper Base, 13 1/2 In. 550.00
Gas Pump Globe, Mobil Kerosene, Metal, 16 1/2 In. 357.00
Gas Pump Globe, Mobilgas Special, Gill Body, Red Ripple, 1 Lens, 13 1/2 In. 990.00
Gas Pump Globe, Mobilgas, Metal, Repainted, 16 1/2 In. 357.00
Gas Pump Globe, Phillips 66 Flite Fuel, Plastic Body, Shield-Shaped Lens, 15 In. 467.00
Gas Pump Globe, Red Crown, Milk Glass, Metal Base, 16 1/2 In. 230.00
Gas Pump Globe, Red Crown, Milk Glass, Red, Gold, 16 x 16 In. 180.00
Gas Pump Globe, Shamrock, Plastic, 13 1/2 In. 330.00
Gas Pump Globe, Shell Oil, Glass, Decal Lettering, 20 x 19 1/2 In. ....375.00 to 700.00
Gas Pump Globe, Shell Super Oil, Shell Gas, Glass, 17 1/2 x 17 1/2 In. 600.00
Gas Pump Globe, Sinclair Dino Supreme, Plastic Body, 13 1/2 In. 170.00
Gas Pump Globe, Sinclair, Glass Hull Body, 13 1/2 In. 500.00
Gas Pump Globe, Sky Chief, Capolite No. 216 Body, 13 1/2 In. 220.00
Gas Pump Globe, Socony, Metal, 15 In. 495.00
Gas Pump Globe, X-Cel 98, Glass Insert, Plastic 300.00
Gas Pump Lens, D-X Lubricating, 13 1/2 In., Pair 120.00
Gas Pump Lens, Ryan's Jet Regular, 13 1/2 In. 132.00
Gas Pump Sign, Atlantic Kerosene, Porcelain, 17 x 13 1/2 In. 130.00
Gas Pump Sign, Atlantic Refining Company, Porcelain, 1930s, 9 x 9 In. 230.00
Gas Pump Sign, Mobilgas Special, Porcelain, 13 1/4 x 12 1/2 In. 170.00
Gas Pump Sign, Sunoco Dynafuel, Yellow Diamond Logo, 1930s, 8 x 12 In. 80.00
Gas Pump Sign, Texaco Sky Chief, Porcelain, 1947 .... 125.00
Gauge, Oil Pressure, Maxwell 45.00
Gauge, Tire, Schrader, Brass, 1909 .... 65.00
Grill Emblem, Chromed Metal, Knight Helmet, Shield, Motto, Je Suis Pret, 5 1/2 x 3 In. .. 40.00
Headlight, Dodge Bros., Glass, 8 In. 7.00
Headlight, Ford, Kerosene, 1914, Pair 55.00
Hood Ornament, Cadillac, Metal Mounted On Wood, 3 1/2 x 9 In. 65.00
Hood Ornament, Eagle, Metal, 3 1/2 x 6 1/4 In. 55.00
Hood Ornament, Indian, Light-Up 150.00
Hood Ornament, Jocko The Monkey, Gilt Bronze, Brunswick, c.1920 .... 1275.00

Hood Ornament, Mack Truck Bulldog, Chrome Plated, 4 1/2 x 5 1/2 In.	75.00
Hood Ornament, Mustang, Used On White Trucks, Metal, 7 1/2 In.	50.00
Hood Ornament, Nash, Flying Lady, 1948	90.00
Hood Ornament, Pelican, Silvered Spelter, France, c.1920	895.00
Hood Ornament, Pinup Girl	50.00
Horn, Brass, Bell Mouth, Insert Screen, Side Bolt, No Bulb	70.00
Jack, Model T Ford	15.00
Knob, Gear Shift, Akro Agate, Bakelite, Airedale Dog On Top, 1940s, 2 x 1 1/2 In.	35.00
Knob, Steering Wheel, Art Deco, Bakelite	55.00
License Plate, Arizona, 1970, Copper	30.00
License Plate, California, 1914	90.00
License Plate, California, 1915, Porcelain	40.00
License Plate, Illinois, 1912, Pair	425.00
License Plate, Illinois, 1913, Pair	300.00
License Plate, Maine, 1939, Tractor, Mailer	105.00
License Plate, Massachusetts, 1908, 5 1/2 x 12 In.	33.00
License Plate, Massachusetts, 1909, 5 1/2 x 12 In.	38.00
License Plate, Massachusetts, 1914, 5 1/2 x 16 In.	38.00
License Plate, North Dakota, 1934	12.00
License Plate, Oklahoma, 1936, 6 x 12 1/4 In.	38.00
License Plate, Pennsylvania, 1908	300.00
License Plate, Pennsylvania, 1913, Green & White	50.00
License Plate, Pennsylvania, 1915, Keystone Emblem Riveted	60.00
License Plate, Texas, 1968, Hemisfair	25.00
License Plate Attachment, Mobil Oil Co., Winged Horse, Red, White, Black, 6 x 5 In.	55.00
License Plate Attachment, Water Valley, Watermelon City	35.00
Manual, Chrysler 60, 1926	45.00
Manual, Mustang, 1965	25.00
Mileage Calculator, Sunoco Gas, 1958	8.00
Oil Can, Atlantic Extra Heavy Motor Oil, Cardboard Box, 5 Gal.	38.00
Oil Can, Atlantic Motor Oil Polarine, Handle, Square, 1 Gal.	50.00
Oil Can, Atlantic Polarine Motor Oil, Tin, 11 x 8 x 3 In.	45.00
Oil Can, En-Ar-Co Refinery Sealed Motor Oil, Toronto, Canada, 1 Imperial Qt.	50.00
Oil Can, Freedom Perfect Motor Oil, 5 Qt.	88.00
Oil Can, Gargoyle Mobiloil, Vacuum Oil Co., Paris, Square, 1 Imperial Gal.	44.00
Oil Can, Gibble Gas Motor Oil, Ribbed, Tin, 1 Qt.	40.00
Oil Can, Grand Champion, 2 Gal.	265.00
Oil Can, Gulf Electric Motor Oil, Tin, Lead Top, 1930s, 8 Oz.	35.00
Oil Can, Husky Motor Oil, Western Oil & Fuel Co., Minn., 5 1/2 x 4 In.	425.00
Oil Can, Kendall 2000 Mile, Tin, 5 Qt.	25.00
Oil Can, Lion Head, Unopened, 1 Qt.	115.00
Oil Can, Lubrite, Red Pegasus, 2 Gal.	45.00
Oil Can, Mercury Motor Oil, New Top, 1950s, 32 Oz.	16.00
Oil Can, Montgomery Ward's All Season Motor Oil, Tin, 1 Qt.	20.00
Oil Can, Mother Penn Motor Oil, Cardboard, Tin Lid, 1960s, 1 Qt.	10.00
Oil Can, Oilzum, 1 Gal.	50.00
Oil Can, Penntroleum, 5 Qt., 9 1/2 In.	198.00
Oil Can, Pennzoil Outboard Motor Oil, Tin, 5 1/2 x 4 In.	125.00
Oil Can, Pennzoil, Transcontinental Train On Back, 1 Qt., 5 1/2 In.	363.00
Oil Can, Pep Boys Western Motor Oil, 2 Gal.	300.00
Oil Can, Pure As Gold Motor Oil, Tin, 1 Qt.	225.00
Oil Can, Red & White Motor Oil, Single Engine Airplane, 2 Gal.	125.00
Oil Can, Richfield Lubricant, Grease Pail, 5 Lb., 6 1/2 In.	49.00
Oil Can, Sinclair Emerald, 2 Gal.	35.00
Oil Can, Standard Oil, Tank Wagon, 1920s, 5 Gal.	30.00
Oil Can, Supreme Heavy Auto Oil, Gulf Refining Co., Pittsburgh, Pa., Handle, Square	93.00
Oil Can, Texaco Turbine Oil, Display, 1 Qt., 5 1/2 In.	220.00
Oil Drum, Texaco, With Hand Pump, Galvanized Metal, 40 x 25 In.	990.00
Parking Meter, Double, 1, 5 & 10 Cents	125.00
Parking Meter, Each Penny-12 Minutes, Each Nickel-60 Minutes, 51 1/2 In.	94.00
Pennant, Buick, White, On Blue, Felt, 1915	150.00
Pennant, Gilmore Lion Head Motor Oil, Paper, 2 Sides, Gas Station Photo, 21 x 10 In.	567.00
Pin, Gulf Merit Award, Metal, Porcelain Enameled, 1 x 7/8 In.	65.00

Poster, Ford, Universal Car, Picture Of Model T, c.1915, 33 x 25 In. 375.0
Poster, Quaker State Motor Oil, Time To Change Summer Driving, Paper, 34 x 57 In. 200.0
Sign, A-C Spark Plug Cleaning Station, Metal, Flange, 15 1/4 x 10 1/2 In. 400.0
Sign, Atlantic Credit Cards Honored Here, 2 Sides, Metal, 10 x 15 In. 120.0
Sign, Atlantic Lubrication Service, Metal, 12 x 30 In. 80.0
Sign, BMW, Dealership, Porcelain, 1960s, 30 In. 750.0
Sign, Buick Sales & Service, 2 Sides, Porcelain, 14 x 30 In. 160.0
Sign, Champion Spark Plugs, Porcelain, 24 5/8 x 4 In. 425.0
Sign, Champion Spark Plugs, Tin, 14 1/2 x 30 In. 155.0
Sign, Chevrolet Super Service, Neon, Porcelain, 2 Sides, 57 x 73 In. 1210.0
Sign, Clean Restroom, Sinclair Gasoline, Porcelain, 2 Sides, 37 x 30 In. 93.0
Sign, Conoco In Motion, Porcelain, 8 x 15 In. 110.0
Sign, Conoco Minuteman, Gasoline, 15 In. 2200.0
Sign, Conoco, Danger Gas Line, Logo, Porcelain, 8 x 15 In. 125.0
Sign, Cooper Tires, Tin, Embossed, 14 1/2 x 23 1/2 In. 95.0
Sign, Essolube Motor Oil, Porcelain, 2 Sides, 30 In. 132.0
Sign, Firestone, Rack, 5 1/2 x 12 3/4 In. 35.0
Sign, Fisk Tires & Tubes, Wooden, 2 Sides, 14 x 29 1/2 In. 425.00
Sign, Ford Dealership, Neon, Oval, 6 x 3 In. 1600.00
Sign, Ford Sales Equipment Co., Detroit, Michigan, Neon, 2 Sides, 24 x 48 In. 2200.00
Sign, Gateway Motor Co., Ford Service, Hand Pointing, Tin, 1930s, 6 1/2 x 28 In. 290.00
Sign, Genuine Ford Parts, Porcelain, 2 Sides, 16 1/2 x 24 In. 385.00
Sign, Gill Piston Rings, Tin, Wood Frame, 8 x 20 1/2 In. 285.00
Sign, Golden State Automobile Club, Porcelain, 2 Sides, 27 x 14 x 2 In. 135.00
Sign, Goodwill, Pontiac Indian, Red On White, Porcelain, 36 x 36 In. 385.00
Sign, Goodyear Tires, Tin, Embossed, 1920s, 12 x 22 In. 260.00
Sign, Greyline Bus 24, Earth, See Everywhere, Porcelain 375.00
Sign, Greyline Bus, Porcelain, 20 In. 400.00
Sign, Hupmobile, Porcelain, 16 x 38 In. 390.00
Sign, Indian Gasoline, Pump 300.00
Sign, Jaguar Sales & Service, Porcelain, 1 Side, 40 1/2 x 38 In. 880.00
Sign, Jaguar Sales & Service, Porcelain, 19 3/4 x 18 1/2 In. 1300.00
Sign, Marine White Texaco, Embossed Tin, 10 x 15 1/4 In. 275.00
Sign, Mercedes Benz, Porcelain, 24 x 30 In. 475.00
Sign, Michelin Tyres, Tin, 1 1/2 x 18 1/2 In. 275.00
Sign, Minute Man Conoco Gasoline, Porcelain, 2 Sides, 25 1/4 In. 2950.00
Sign, Mobil, Glass Insert, Frame, 4 1/4 x 25 1/4 In. 27.00
Sign, Mobile, Horse, Flying With Mobile Oil Logo, Porcelain, 35 x 45 In. 460.00
Sign, Mobilgas Restroom, Porcelain, 1 Side, 7 1/2 x 8 In. 330.00
Sign, No Parking Here, Cast Iron, 5 In. 135.00
Sign, No Smoking, Texaco, Porcelain, c.1963, 4 x 23 In. 100.00
Sign, Oldsmobile Authorized Service, Porcelain, 2 Sides, 20 x 28 In. 2530.00
Sign, Packard, Walker & Co., Detroit, Neon, 30 x 22 1/2 In. 3300.00
Sign, Penn Seal Motor Oil, Tin, Embossed, 13 5/8 x 29 5/8 In. 180.00
Sign, Pennzoil Safe Lubrication, Tin, 2 Sides, 1950s, 11 3/4 x 16 1/2 In. 69.00
Sign, Pontiac Master Salesman, 3-Dimensional, 35 1/2 x 39 In. 375.00
Sign, Post Transportation Co., For Truck, Porcelain, 12 x 20 In. 140.00
Sign, Puroil Gasoline, Blue & White Indian Arrows, Porcelain, 2 Sides, 24 In. 400.00
Sign, Quaker State Cold Test Oil, Porcelain, 2 Sides, 9 x 26 1/2 In. 135.00
Sign, Red Indian Motor Oils, Porcelain, 1920s-1930s, 20 x 20 In. 2415.00
Sign, Route 66, Highway Department, Texas 295.00
Sign, Shell Motor Oil, Property Of Shell Company, Ltd., Porcelain, 11 x 17 3/4 In. . . .   500.00
Sign, Sinclair Opaline Motor Oil, Authorized Dealer, Porcelain, 20 x 48 In. 825.00
Sign, Sky Chief Gasoline, Red Lettering, Green Ground, Porcelain, 12 x 18 In. 79.00
Sign, Spears Station & Restroom, 2 Sides, Porcelain, 29 7/8 In. 160.00
Sign, Standard Esso Dealer, 1940s-1950s, 40 x 60 In. 400.00
Sign, Super Shell, Saves On Stop & Go Driving, Paper, Linen Backing, 32 x 57 In. 200.00
Sign, Texaco Restroom Sign, Key Chains, Metal, 12 x 9 In. 250.00
Sign, Texaco, Green-T Drum, 90 Wt. Oil, 27 In. 85.00
Sign, Tiolene Motor Oil Pure Oil Co., Porcelain, 2 Sides, 24 In. 400.00
Sign, Tydol-Veedol-Ize Your Car, Painted On Plywood, Frame, 1922, 39 3/4 x 17 1/2 In. . .   187.00
Sign, U.S. Route 6 Highway, Reflectors 200.00
Sign, United Service Motors, Neon, 28 x 48 x 6 In. 1100.00

Sign, Waverly Motor Oil, Porcelain, 2 Sides, 20 x 24 In. 250.00
Sign, Wolf's Head Heavy Oil Lube, Metal, 2 Sides, 8 1/4 x 7 In. 253.00
Sign, Wolf's Head Oil Medium Lube, Empire Refining Company, 8 1/4 x 7 In. 265.00
Sign, Wolf's Head Oil, Porcelain, 2 Sides, 20 x 30 In. 1650.00
Sign, Zerolene, Tin, 2 Sides, With Shipping Papers, Unused, 11 x 11 In. 195.00
Signal, Gas Station Drive, Run Over Hose & Bell Rings 150.00
Spark Plug, Beru, Pin Insulator, Spark Plug Logo 10.00
Spark Plug, Blue Crown X-Citer, 3 Times Indy 500 Winner, Box, 1950s, 2 1/2 In. 31.00
Spark Plug, Champion, 3X, Made In Canada, Model A Ford 40.00
Spark Plug, Champion, Franklin Script Logo 35.00
Spark Plug, Eveready, 18 mm 5.00
Spark Plug, Hastings, Aero Type, 2 Side Electrodes, Box 5.00
Spark Plug, Never Miss, No. 8, 1/2-In. Thread 35.00
Spark Plug, Red-Headed Big Boy, Red Lego 35.00
Spark Plug, Wizard, Twin Fire, Box 4.00
Tire Pump, ECO Tireflator Islander, Restored, 98 In. 2420.00
Tire Pump, ECO Tireflator, Cast Iron, Metal, Bennett Pump Division, 16 x 9 In. 300.00
Vase, Cone, Yellow, Pair 55.00
Vase, Hobstars, Curved 90.00

AUTUMN LEAF pattern china was made for the Jewel Tea Company
beginning in 1933. Hall China Company of East Liverpool, Ohio,
Crooksville China Company of Crooksville, Ohio, Harker Potteries of
Chester, West Virginia, and Paden City Pottery, Paden City, West
Virginia, made dishes with this design. Autumn Leaf has remained
popular and was made by Hall China Company until 1978. Some other
pieces in the Autumn Leaf pattern are still being made. For more information, see *Kovels' Depression Glass & Dinnerware Price List*.

Bean Pot, 1 Handle 650.00
Bowl, 6 1/2 In. ....15.00 to 29.00
Bowl, Radiance, 9 In. 25.00
Bowl, Vegetable, Divided, Oval ....100.00 to 125.00
Butter, Ruffled Top, 1 Lb. ....450.00 to 625.00
Butter, Square Top, 1/4 Lb. 1400.00
Cake Plate, Flat ....20.00 to 25.00
Cake Plate, Metal Base 140.00
Candleholder, 1988 .... 175.00
Candy Dish, Metal Base ....475.00 to 525.00
Canister Set, Square, 4 Piece 275.00
Clock, Electric ....475.00 to 525.00
Coffee Urn, Jewel Best, 30 Cup 575.00
Coffeepot, Drip, 8 Cup 95.00
Coffeepot, Drip, All China 250.00
Coffeepot, Electric Percalator ....350.00 to 475.00
Cookbook, 60th Anniversary ....20.00 to 25.00
Cookbook, Mary Dunbar ....20.00 to 35.00
Cookie Jar, Big Ear, Zeisel 250.00
Cookie Jar, Tootsie ....225.00 to 275.00
Cover, Mixer, Plastic 60.00
Cup, St. Denis 39.00
Cup, Tea, Ruffled 8.00
Cup & Saucer, Flat, 2 1/2 In. 49.00
Cup & Saucer, St. Denis 45.00
Custard Cup, Radiance 15.00
Drip Jar 24.00
Flour Sifter ....385.00 to 575.00
French Baker, 2 Pt. 15.00
French Baker, 3 Pt. ....25.00 to 28.00
Gravy Boat 30.00
Jug, Ball ....25.00 to 45.00
Mug, Irish Coffee ....125.00 to 165.00
Pie Plate 40.00
Pitcher, 6 3/4 In. 140.00

Plate, 6 1/4 In.	17.00
Plate, 7 3/4 In.	25.00
Plate, 9 In.	12.50
Plate, 10 In.	20.00
Platter, 13 1/2 In.	42.00
Platter, Oval, 11 1/2 In.	50.00
Reamer, Orange	80.00 to 125.00
Salt & Pepper, Casper, Large	48.00
Salt & Pepper, Casper, Small	25.00
Salt & Pepper, Range, Handle	25.00
Salt & Pepper, With Grease Bowl, Range, 3 Piece	75.00
Shelf Paper, 9 Ft. x 9 1/4 In.	215.00
Soup, Cream	45.00
Soup, Cream, 2 Handles	45.00
Soup, Dish	28.00
Stack Set, 4 Piece	100.00 to 125.00
Sugar & Creamer, Rayed, 1930s	95.00
Sugar & Creamer, Ruffled, 1940s	65.00
Tablecloth, 54 x 72 In.	125.00
Tea Kettle	325.00
Teapot, Aladdin	78.00
Teapot, Delivery Car	350.00
Teapot, Long Spout	50.00
Teapot, New York, 1984	725.00
Teapot, Newport, 1933	275.00
Thermos, Picnic	275.00
Tidbit, 3 Tiers, Box	175.00
Tray, Wooden, Glass	175.00
Tumbler, Frosted, 5 1/2 In.	65.00
Warmer, Oval	145.00 to 155.00
Warmer, Round	120.00 to 200.00

AVON bottles are listed in the Bottle category under Avon.

AZALEA dinnerware was made for Larkin Company customers from 1918 to 1914. Larkin, the soap company, was in Buffalo, New York. The dishes were made by Noritake China Company of Japan. Each piece of the white china was decorated with pink azaleas.

Bowl, Breakfast	17.00
Bowl, Salad, 9 3/4 In.	45.00
Bowl, Vegetable, Cover	540.00
Cake Plate, Open Handles, 9 3/4 In.	40.00
Casserole, Cover, Gold Finial	350.00
Celery Dish, 12 In.	50.00 to 65.00
Coffeepot, Demitasse	475.00
Condiment Set	50.00
Cup	14.00
Cup & Saucer	12.00 to 17.00
Eggcup	53.00 to 55.00
Gravy Boat	30.00 to 55.00
Grill Plate	160.00
Jam Jar, Cover	125.00
Lemon Tray, 2 Handles	24.00
Mayonnaise, 3 Piece	45.00
Plate, 5 1/4 In.	11.00
Plate, 7 1/2 In.	10.00 to 12.00
Plate, 8 1/2 In.	20.00
Plate, 10 In.	28.00
Plate, 13 In.	20.00
Platter, 12 In.	60.00
Relish, Divided	45.00
Relish, Oval	18.00
Salt & Pepper	30.00
Saucer, Fruit	10.00

Spoon Holder	85.00
Sugar & Creamer	40.00 to 50.00
Sugar & Creamer, Cover	40.00
Sugar & Creamer, Demitasse	105.00
Sugar & Creamer, Individual	450.00
Tea Tile	45.00 to 50.00
Teapot	110.00 to 120.00
Teapot, Child's	400.00
Toothpick	135.00
Vase, Fan, 5 1/2 In.	150.00

BACCARAT glass was made in France by La Compagnie des Cristalleries de Baccarat, located 150 miles from Paris. The factory was started in 1765. The firm went bankrupt and began operating again about 1822. Cane and millefiori paperweights were made during the 1860 to 1880 period. The firm is still working near Paris making paperweights and glasswares.

Ashtray, Rectangular, Flared, 7 In.	69.00
Biscuit Jar, Moss, Red Enameled Flowers, Leaves, 10 1/2 In.	1395.00
Candelabrum, 3-Light, Bobeche & Drip Pan Draped With Prisms, 20 In.	405.00
Candelabrum, 4-Light, Dolphin Base	3080.00
Candlestick, Satin Cherub Figural Stem, 11 In., Pair	250.00
Candlestick, Versailles, 2 Rings On Standard, Hexagonal Cup, 7 In., Pair	137.00
Champagne, Engraved Design, Gilt, 19th Century	158.00
Champagne, Provence	45.00
Chandelier, 6-Light, Trumpet Form, Hurricane Shades, 1850, 43 1/2 In.	6900.00
Clock, Gilt Bronze Dore, Marti Movement, c.1900, 14 1/2 In.	3950.00
Decanter, Harmonie, Faceted Base, Cube Stopper, 12 1/4 In.	206.00
Decanter, Moss Cut To Clear, c.1900, 17 In., Pair	2950.00
Decanter, Talleyrand, Flared Faceted Base, Stopper, 9 1/2 In.	105.00
Figurine, Baker, Box, 6 In.	110.00 to 125.00
Figurine, Duck, 5 1/2 In.	129.00
Figurine, Owl, Satin, 1982, 10 In.	3000.00
Figurine, Parrot, Signed, 6 In.	175.00
Figurine, Rabbit, Seated, 3 1/2 In.	115.00
Paperweight, Blue Primrose, Star Center, 2 1/4 In.	920.00
Paperweight, Butterfly, Alternating White Cane Garland, 3 1/8 In.	3737.00
Paperweight, Cauliflower, 3 In.	*Illus* 10000.00
Paperweight, Clematis, Garland, 2 3/8 In.	977.00
Paperweight, Clematis, Star Cut Base, 2 1/8 x 3 In.	2355.00
Paperweight, Close Concentric Millefiori, 7 Arrowheads, 5-Pointed Star, 2 3/8 In.	545.00
Paperweight, Millefiori, Canes Of Animals, Devil, Goose, Deer, Goat, 1884, 2 In.	860.00
Paperweight, Millefiori, Stardust Carpet Ground	9900.00
Paperweight, Pansy, 2 1/2 In.	775.00
Paperweight, Snake Coil, Muslin Ground, c.1845	7700.00

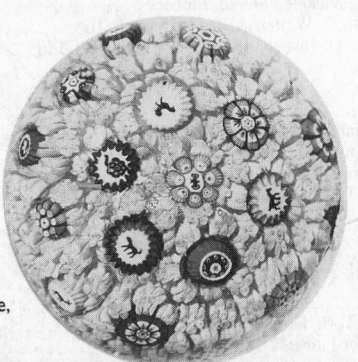

Baccarat,
Paperweight,
Cauliflower,
3 In.

Baccarat, Vase,
Bud, 9 In.

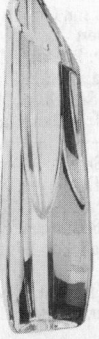

**Don't clean
coins. Collectors
want coins with
the patina
unchanged.**

Paperweight, Sulphide, Abraham Lincoln, 2 3/4 In. 325.00
Paperweight, Sulphide, Aquarius, Blue Ground, Signed, 2 3/4 In. 125.00
Paperweight, Sulphide, Aries, 1955 .... 165.00
Paperweight, Sulphide, Eleanor Roosevelt, 1950s 135.00
Paperweight, Sulphide, Lafayette, Blue Waffle Cut Base, 1950s 285.00
Paperweight, Sulphide, Lion, Royal Blue, 6 Facets 95.00
Paperweight, Sulphide, Pope John Paul II 135.00
Paperweight, Sulphide, Robert E. Lee, Clear Waffle Cut Base, 1950s 285.00
Paperweight, Sulphide, Virgo, 1955 .... 165.00
Paperweight, Sulphide, Washington, Green Waffle Cut Base, 1950s 285.00
Paperweight, Turtle, Clear, 3 3/4 In. 85.00
Perfume Bottle, Amethyst Cut To Clear Glass, Screw Stopper, 6 1/4 In. 110.00
Perfume Bottle, Blue, Flower Stopper, 7 In. 700.00
Perfume Bottle, Diamond Base, Stopper, Bulbous, 5 1/4 In. 402.00
Perfume Bottle, Diamond Base, Stopper, Bulbous, 6 In. 322.00
Perfume Bottle, Green, Stopper, 8 In. 400.00
Perfume Bottle, Primevera, Shell Style, 6 1/4 In. 180.00
Powder Jar, Diamond Handle, Base, Bulbous, 7 In. 253.00
Tumbler, Rose Swirl, 3 7/8 In. 38.00
Vase, Bud, 9 In. ....*Illus* 75.00
Vase, Gold Handles, 9 x 8 In. 675.00
Vase, Petal Form Rim, 7 1/4 In. 82.50

BADGES have been used since before the Civil War. Collectors search
for examples of all types, including law enforcement and company
identification badges. Well-known prison or law enforcement badges
are most desirable. Most are made of nickel or brass. Many recent
reproductions have been made.

Alaska Airlines, Wings, Gold Finish, Red & Blue Enamel Logo, Pinback, 3 1/4 In.113.00 to 141.00
American Airlines, Wings, AA & Eagle Logo At Center, Silver Finish, 3 In. 87.00
American Express, Brass Hat, Celluloid 475.00
Auxiliary Police, West Fairview, Pa., Shield, Pinback, Nickel Finish 25.00
Braniff Airline, Wings, Pilot, Star Above Center, Silver Finish, 3 1/4 In. 112.00
Braniff International Airlines, Wings, Pilot, Gold Finish, Clip Back, 3 In. 60.00
Buffalo Transit Company, Cap, Shield Shape, Buffalo Head, 2 1/2 In. 95.00
Central Cab Co., Shield Shape, Taxi In Circle, Silver Finish, 2 3/4 In. 85.00
Chauffeur, California, 1919 .... 50.00
Chauffeur, California, 1931 .... 55.00
Chauffeur, Illinois, 1936 .... 25.00
Chauffeur, Indiana, 1937, Metal, 1 x 1 1/4 In. 5.50
Chauffeur, Maine, 1933 .... 40.00
Chauffeur, New Hampshire, Diamond Shape, Gilt Brass, Pinback, 1921, 1 In. 20.00
Chauffeur, Virginia, 1937, Metal, 1 1/4 x 1 1/2 In. 33.00
D.C. Transit, Supervisor, Cap, Half Wing, Gold Finish, Green Enamel, 1930s, 2 3/4 In. .. 236.00
Delta Airlines, Wings, Captain, Gold Finish, Wreathed Star, Enamel Insignia, 3 3/8 In. .. 78.00
Deputy Game Protector, Penn., Silver Metal, Enameled State Crest, 2 1/2 In. 47.00
Fireman, Combination 1, Randolph, Mass., Nickeled Shield, Pinback 20.00
Fireman, Essex Veteran Firemen's Assn. No. 2, Whitehead & Hoag Eagle Top 60.00
Fireman, Volunteer, Shield, Lion On Scales Of Justice, Silver Finish, Pinback, 3 In. 20.00
Forest Fire Fighting Warden 45.00
Judge, American Pageant, ID, Ribbon, Medal 35.00
Junk License, Harrisburg, Pa., Nickel Finish, Pinback, 1935, 1 1/2 x 2 In. 31.00
Lee Riders, Deputy Sheriff, Star Shape, Pinback, Stamped Metal, 3 Piece 230.00
Massachusetts Motor Vehicle Examiner, Shield, Blue, Silver Finish, 2 1/2 In. 65.00
Montana Jaycees, Evel Knievel On Motorcycle, 1975, 2 1/2 In. 34.00
Ohio Bus Line Company, Shield, Yellow Ground, Green Map Of Ohio, 1950s 26.00
Pabst Brewing Company, Employee, No. 4916, Los Angeles, 1950s 3.50
Police, Cap, City Crest, Silver Finish, 2 1/2 In. 34.00
Police, Cap, New York City Patrolman, City Crest, Silver Finish 25.00
Police, Cap, Philadelphia, Scalloped Edge, No. In Center, 1920s, Oval, 3 In. 75.00
Police, Crestwood, Missouri 95.00
Police, Detective, County Of Nassau, New York, Gold Finish, Pinback, 1 1/2 In. 30.00
Police, New York City Transit, Shield, Silver Finish, 2 1/2 In. 45.00

Police, Patrolman, Michigan, 2 Stags Flanking State Shield, Nickel Finish 26.00
Police, PFC, Brass, Attached Copper Enameled Sections, Philippines, 3 1/2 In. 38.00
Police, Presentation, Longbranch, Shield, Dates Of Service 1904-1934, 2 3/4 In. 100.00
Police, Reserve, Buffalo, N.Y., Free-Standing Eagle, Pinback, 1930s 23.00
Police, San Bernardino, 7-Pointed Star, City Emblem, Silver Finish, Wallet 53.00
Police, Special Deputy Sheriff, St. Clair Co., Ill., Pinback, Silver Finish, 2 1/2 In. 33.00
Police, Special, Commonwealth Of Pennsylvania, Nickel Shield, 1940s 23.00
Police, Special, Nashville, Tennessee, 5-Pointed Star In Center, Pinback, 2 1/2 In. 35.00
Police, Wisconsin State Fair, Silver Metal, Incised 222, 1940s, 2 1/2 In. 115.00
Public Hack Driver, New York City, Nickel Shield, Black Paint, 1940 .... 38.00
Public Hack Driver, New York City, Nickel Shield, Double Loop Back, 1938 .... 46.00
Railway Express Agency, Brass, Black & White Letters, Red Enamel Ground, 1 7/8 In. .. 60.00
Recreational Commission, Ventnor City, N.J., Brass, Scrolled Border, 1 5/8 In. 23.00
Salvation Army, Woman, July 5, 1891 .... 40.00
Sheriff, Deputy, Queens County, Gold Plated, 1892 .... 75.00
Sheriff, Honorary Deputy, Hartford County, Conn., Shield, Eagle, Gold Finish 25.00
Sheriff, Honorary Deputy, Parish Of New Orleans, Louisiana, Crest In Relief, 2 1/2 In. .. 25.00
Sheriff, Lieutenant, Cap, Durham County, N.C., 5-Pointed Star, Eagle, 2 3/4 In. 53.00
Sheriff, Washburn County, Wisconsin, 7 Sided Star, State Seal, Silver, 2 In. 23.00
State Trooper, Louisiana, Gilt Metal, Shaped Like State, Enameled State Crest, 2 In. ... 52.00
Surface Transportation System, Operator 100.00
Texaco Oil Co., Employee 22.00
U.S. Army, Marksman, Sterling Silver 8.00
U.S. Army, Sharp Shooter, Rifle Bar 6.00
U.S. Army, Vehicle Driver & Mechanic 4.00
U.S. Post Office, Cap, Boise, Idaho, No. 6 .... 300.00
U.S. Post Office, Cap, Vehicle Service 75.00
Utah Oil Safety Committee, U Shape, Diagonal Pinback, 3/4 x 1 In. 36.00
Washington Electric Co., Guard, Bronze Shield, Chain, 2 Monogram Buttons, c.1917 . 23.00

BANKS of metal have been made since 1868. There are still banks,
mechanical banks, and registering banks (those that show the total
money deposited on the face of the bank). Many old iron or tin banks
have been reproduced since the 1950s in iron or plastic. Pottery, glass,
and plastic banks are also listed here. Mickey Mouse and other
Disneyana banks are listed in Disneyana. A group of selected high
prices from an acution of a major collection are included this year to
reflect the prices of the rarest banks in the best condition.

7-Up Delivery Truck, Cast Metal, Ertl, Box 50.00
Air Mail, Red, Cast Iron 675.00
Airplane, American Airlines, Lockheed Orion, 1933-1935 .... 33.00
Airplane, Spirit Of Savings, Brass Propeller, Cast Metal, 7 1/2 In. 500.00
Amish Boy, Black Overalls, Blue Shirt, John Wright, 1970s, 5 1/4 In. 65.00
Aunt Jemima, Hands On Hips, Cast Iron, Hubley, 1914-1946, 5 1/4 In. 135.00
Bab-O Cleanser, Cardboard & Tin 22.00
Baby In Cradle, Cast Iron & Tin, 4 In. 143.00
Barber Shop Pole, Ceramic, Painted, 1940s 65.00
Baseball, Detroit Tigers, Flying Horse, Original Closure 44.00
Baseball, Flying Horse, Cincinnati, Original Closure 71.50
Basset Hound, Cast Iron, Gold Paint, 3 In. 825.00
Battleship Maine, Cast Iron 375.00
Bear, Sitting Up, Glass, Tin Screw Cover, Snow Crest Beverages, Inc., 7 In. 22.00
Begging Bear, A.C. Williams, c.1920, 5 3/8 In. 55.00
Benjamin Franklin, Bust, Copper Tone, White Metal, 1950s, 5 13/16 In. 95.00
Big Boy, Hand Painted, Plastic, Package, 1960-1970 .... 75.00
Big Boy, Plastic, Movable Head, Marriott Corp., 1973, 8 3/4 In. .... .30.00 to 45.00
Big Boy, Rubber, California, 1977, 9 3/8 x 5 1/4 In. 15.00
Billiken, Cast Iron, A.C. Williams, Early 20th Century, 4 1/8 In. 55.00
Bionic Woman, Vinyl, 10 In. 45.00
Black Boy, 2 Faces, Cast Iron, Black & Gold, A.C. Williams, c.1910, 4 1/8 In. ....115.00 to 295.00
Bosco The Bear Chocolate Syrup, Glass, Plastic, 1950s, 8 In. 65.00
Boston Bull Terrier, Sitting, Cast Iron, Hubley, 4 1/2 In. 55.00
Boxer, Seated, Cast Iron, 4 In. 325.00

Boy, Dressed As Wizard, Insty Prints, Plastic, 1960s, 8 1/2 In. . . . . 65.0•
Brown Bear, Red Vest, Glass, 6 1/2 In. . . . . 20.0•
Building, Dollar Savings Bank, Metal, Pittsburgh . . . . .145.00 to 160.0•
Building, Double Door, Central Window, Bank Above, Cast Iron, A.C. Williams, 1905 . . 200.0•
Building, Independence Hall, Bronze Finish, Cast Iron, 7 1/2 x 9 1/4 In. . . . . 850.0•
Building, Mosque, Bronze . . . . 325.0•
Building, Nickel Plated, Coin Slot, Cast Iron, 3 3/4 x 3 3/4 In. . . . . 400.0•
Building, Villa, Cast Iron, Asphaltum Finish, Gold Striping, Kyser & Rex, 1882, 5 1/2 In. 375.0•
Building, Westminster Abbey, Cast Iron, Bronze Finish, England, c.1908, 6 1/4 In. . . . . . 247.0•
Bull, Aberdeen Angus, Aluminum, 1957, 4 1/2 x 7 3/8 In. . . . . 60.0•
Bullwinkle, Plastic, 1973 . . . . 35.0•
Cabbage Patch Girl, Vinyl, 8 In. . . . . 5.0•
Campbell's, 125th Anniversary . . . . 5.0•
Campbell's Airplane, 2nd . . . . 25.0•
Campbell's Vegetable Garden Soup Can, Metal, Seeds For Garden, Label, 1977, 5 In. 15.0•
Can, Metal, Li'l Abner & Daisy Mae, Large, 1953 . . . . 75.0•
Captain Crunch Pirates Chest, Plastic, Metal Handles . . . . 95.0•
Captain Kidd, Cast Iron, 5 5/8 In. . . . . 425.0•
Car, Nash Rambler, 1902 Model, Black Spoked Wheels, Cast Metal, Banthrico . . . . 65.0•
Car, Stanley Steamer, 1910 Model, Cast Metal, Banthrico . . . . 75.0•
Car, Yellow Cab, Coin Saver, Cast Iron, Arcade, 4 1/4 x 7 7/8 In. . . . . 3575.0•
Casper The Friendly Ghost, Ceramic 200.00
Cat With Bow, Cast Iron, 4 1/8 In. 55.00
Chewbacca, Star Wars, Ceramic, 10 In. 75.00
Chocolate Baker Man 22.00
Clown, With Crooked Hat, Yellow & Red, Cast Iron, 6 In. 300.00
Col. Sanders, Stand, Plastic, 10 In. . . . . .40.00 to 50.00
Colt 45 Beer Can, Steel 8.00
Columbian Safe Deposit, Black, Gold Trim, Cast Iron, 4 3/4 x 6 3/4 In. 225.00
Corky Pig, Glass 125.00
Cupola, Black, Red & Yellow Trim, Cast Iron, 5 1/2 In. 425.00
Del Monte, Clown 25.00
Devil, 2 Faces, Cast Iron, Arcade, 1911, 4 1/2 In. . . . . .700.00 to 1450.00
Dog, Fido, Hubley, Cast Iron, 5 In. 225.00
Dresser, Pewter, Hinged Lid, Lock, 3 5/8 In. 66.00
Drum Shape, Red, White, Blue, God Bless America On Top, Tin, Chein, 2 1/2 x 3 In. . . 50.00
Duck, Save For A Rainy Day, Hubley, 5 3/8 In. . . . . .265.00 to 310.00
Egyptian, Cast Iron, 4 1/2 x 3 1/2 In. 195.00
Eight-O'Clock Coffee, Tin, Red & Gold, 1940-1950 . . . . 45.00
Electrolux Vacuum Cleaner, Hard Plastic, Push Button Front Release, 1950s 95.00
Elephant, Sitting Up, Glass, Tin Screw Cover, Lucky Jumbo Bank, 7 In. 25.00
Elephant On Tub, Cast Iron, Hand Painted, John Wright, 1960s 125.00
Elmer Fudd At Tree Trunk, Coin Slot In Trunk, White Metal, Moss, 5 1/2 In. 80.00
Entenmann's Chef, With Donuts . . . . .50.00 to 75.00
Flat Iron Building, Cast Iron, Silver, Gold Trim, 5 1/4 In. 203.00
Foxy Grandpa, Cast Iron, John Wright, 1960s 95.00
Fruit Jar, Atlas Mason, Glass, 3 3/4 In. 30.00
Gas Pump, Esso, Red & White, Globe Lights When Coin Inserted, 6 1/2 In. 30.00
Gas Pump, Pennzoil, 1950s Style, Globe Lights When Coin Inserted, 6 1/2 In. 30.00
General Pershing, Cast Iron, Grey Iron Casting, 7 1/2 In. 130.00
George Washington, Bust, Preferred Bank Services Co., Cast Metal, 1920s, 5 7/8 In. . . 75.00
George Washington, Standing, Cast Iron, 7 1/2 In. 50.00
Give Me A Penny, Black Man, Cast Iron, 5 1/2 In. 300.00
Globe, Enterprise Manufacturing Co., 1880, Cast Iron, Eagle Finial, Painted, 5 1/2 In. . . 145.00
Globe Savings Fund, Cast Iron, Kyser & Rex, 1889, 7 1/8 In. 495.00
Graf Zeppelin, Cast Iron, A.C. Williams, 8 In. 650.00
Gumball Machine, Plastic, Coin Operated, Tarco Toys, 1960s 35.00
Happy Days, Tin Lithograph, Barrel Shape, Chein, 1930s, 3 3/4 x 3 In. 24.00
Hog, Harley-Davidson, Gray, 1982 . . . . 25.00
Huckleberry Hound, Box, 1960 . . . . 250.00
Humpty Dumpty, Chein, 6 In. 275.00
Ice Cream Freezer, Cast Iron, Hand Painted, 1960s 95.00
Inlaid Wood, Puzzle, 1929, 2 3/4 x 3 13/16 In. 235.00

Jeep, Play Pal Plastics, 11 In.	33.00
John F. Kennedy, Metal, Banthrico, 5 1/4 In.	30.00
Keebler Elf, Standing, Ceramic, 10 In.	75.00
Kitty, Cast Iron, Hubley, 1930s, 4 3/4 In.	135.00
Liberty Bell, Amber Carnival Glass, 1950s	48.00
Liberty Bell, With Yoke, Cast Iron, Arcade, 1925, 3 1/2 In.	125.00
Lindbergh, Bust, Aluminum, Gold Finished, Grannis & Tolton, 1928, 6 1/2 x 3 7/8 In.	295.00
Lion, Cast Iron, Gold Paint, Red Mouth, A.C. Williams, 1920s, 6 1/4 In.	46.00
Little Lulu, Figural, Plastic, Playpal, 1973, 10 1/2 In.	65.00
Log Cabin, Glass, Clear, Tin Screw Cover, 4 1/2 In.	40.00
Lucky Charms, Pot O' Gold, Musical, Plastic, Box, 5 In.	65.00
Lucky Savings, Tin, Pat. 1916	95.00
Magic Chef, Vinyl, 7 1/2 In.	15.00
Main Street Trolley, Cast Iron, A.C. Williams, 1920s, 3 x 6 3/4 In.	595.00
Main Street Trolley, Gold Paint, Cast Iron, Iron Wheels, 7 In.	220.00
Mammy, Chalkware, 7 In.	125.00
Mammy, Hands On Hips, Cast Iron, Hubley, 1914, 5 1/4 In.	295.00
Mammy, Turkey, Cast Iron, 3 1/2 In.	35.00
Mammy, With Spoon, Cast Iron, Original Paint, A.C. Williams, 5 7/8 In.	65.00

Mechanical banks were first made about 1870. Any bank with moving parts is considered mechanical. The metal banks made before World War I are the most desirable. Copies and new designs of mechanical banks have been made in metal or plastic since the 1920s. The condition of the paint on the old banks is important. Worn paint can lower a price by 90%.

Mechanical, Artillery, Union Officer, Firing At Fort, Cast Iron, Shepard Hardware	345.00
Mechanical, Bad Accident, Cast Iron, c.1888, J. & E. Stevens	2970.00 to 6600.00
Mechanical, Bank Of Education & Economy, Cast Iron, Proctor-Raymond	1150.00
Mechanical, Bank Teller, Patented September 1, 1876	96000.00
Mechanical, Birdie Putt, Richard Toys, 1950s	375.00
Mechanical, Boy Scout Camp, J. & E. Stevens, 1912-1917	4370.00
Mechanical, Boy Stealing Watermelons, Cast Iron, Kyser & Rex	3410.00
Mechanical, Bozo, Plastic, Banthrico Inc., Dated 1971, 6 3/4 In.	65.00
Mechanical, Bulldog, Cast Iron, Book Of Knowledge	225.00
Mechanical, Bulldog, J. & E. Stevens, 7 1/2 In.	8625.00
Mechanical, Butting Buffalo, Book Of Knowledge	175.00 to 325.00
Mechanical, Butting Buffalo, Kyser & Rex, 7 1/2 In.	5000.00
Mechanical, Cabin, Cast Iron, Green Building, J. & E. Stevens, 1885, 4 3/16 In.	460.00 to 495.00
Mechanical, Calamity Football, Cast Iron, 1960s	275.00
Mechanical, Calamity Football, Cast Iron, J. & E. Stevens, 1905	90500.00
Mechanical, Cast Iron, Cabin, Yellow Building, J. & E. Stevens, 1885, 4 3/16 In.	575.00
Mechanical, Cat & Mouse, Cast Iron, J. & E. Stevens	5445.00 to 6500.00
Mechanical, Chief Big Moon, Cast Iron, J. & E. Stevens	620.00
Mechanical, Circus Ticket Collector, Cast Iron, Judd	240.00
Mechanical, Clown On Globe, Cast Iron, Hand Painted, 1960s	275.00
Mechanical, Clown On Globe, Cast Iron, Red Clown, Yellow, J. & E. Stevens, 1890	1700.00
Mechanical, Clown On Globe, Cast Iron, Tan Base, J. & E. Stevens, 1890, 9 In.	2750.00
Mechanical, Coffin, Green Arm Deposits Coin, Skeleton Raises Head	50.00

Tell your heirs about your collection. Inventory items by category, and include what you paid. Then list names and addresses of people who might want to buy your collection or dealers you trust. Consider donating to a museum or charity.

Bank,
Mechanical,
Jolly Nigger,
Big Mouth,
1950s, 5 In.

Mechanical, Coffin, Skeleton's Hands Grabs Coin, Windup, Yone Toys, Japan, 1960s ...   195.00
Mechanical, Creedmoor, Cast Iron, Painted, J. & E. Stevens, 10 In. . . . . .345.00 to 430.00
Mechanical, Darktown Battery, Cast Iron, Book Of Knowledge 250.00
Mechanical, Darktown Battery, Pitcher, Cast Iron, J. & E. Stevens, 10 In. . . . . . .880.00 to 1750.00
Mechanical, Dentist, Cast Iron, Book Of Knowledge 375.00
Mechanical, Dentist, Cast Iron, Repaired Foot, 1880-1890 . . . . 20700.00
Mechanical, Dog On Turntable, Revolves, Deposits Coin Inside, Cast Iron, Judd .450.00 to 1210.00
Mechanical, Eagle & Eaglets, Cast Iron, J. & E. Stevens, 6 1/2 In. . . . . .650.00 to 1093.00
Mechanical, Eagle & Eaglets, Cast Iron, J. & E. Stevens, Green Grass, 6 1/2 In. 2185.00
Mechanical, Elephant & 3 Clowns, Cast Iron, J. & E. Stevens 1430.00
Mechanical, Elephant, Howdah, Cast Iron, White, Hubley 850.00
Mechanical, Ferris Wheel, Hubley 5060.00
Mechanical, Fisherman's Luck, Cast Iron, Hand Painted, Richard Toys, 1950s 1275.00
Mechanical, Football, John Harper & Co., Ltd., 1895, 10 x 4 In.   1250.00
Mechanical, Fortune Horserace Savings, Tin, Norton Brothers, Pat. 1897 . . . .   1100.00
Mechanical, Fortune Teller Savings Bank, Nickel Plate, Cast Iron, 4 1/2 x 5 x 4 In. 650.00
Mechanical, Frog Bank, 2 Frogs, Cast Iron, J. & E. Stevens, 1882 . . . .   1850.00
Mechanical, Frog On Rock, Cast Iron, Kilgore 1150.00
Mechanical, Girl Skipping Rope, Patented May 20, 1890 . . . . 28750.00
Mechanical, Golfing, Birdie Putt, Cast Iron, Utexiqual Products, 1970s, 8 3/4 In. 115.00
Mechanical, Hall's Excelsior, Building, Cast Iron & Wood, J. & E. Stevens, 1869 . . . . . .   475.00
Mechanical, Harold Lloyd, Tin Lithograph, Germany, 1920s 4500.00
Mechanical, Hen & Chick, Cast Iron, J. & E. Stevens 6500.00
Mechanical, Home Bank, Building With A Teller, Tin, Morrison's, 5 x 6 x 6 In. 172.00
Mechanical, Hoop-La, Clown, Holding Hoop, Cast Iron, John Harper, England 1092.00
Mechanical, Horse Race, Cast Iron, J. & E. Stevens, 1871 . . . .   3850.00
Mechanical, Humpty Dumpty The Clown, 1960s . . . . .145.00 to 175.00
Mechanical, Humpty Dumpty, Cast Iron, 7 3/4 In. 470.00
Mechanical, I Always Did 'Spise A Mule, Book Of Knowledge 295.00
Mechanical, I Always Did 'Spise A Mule, Boy On Bench, J. & E. Stevens . . . . .750.00 to 3450.00
Mechanical, I Always Did 'Spise A Mule, Rider On Donkey, Cast Iron, J. & E. Stevens .   1955.00
Mechanical, Indian & Bear, Book Of Knowledge, Cast Iron, 10 In. 450.00
Mechanical, Indian & Bear, Cast Iron, J. & E. Stevens, Pat. 1-7-1883, 10 In. . . .2000.00 to 2415.00
Mechanical, Initiating Bank, First Degree, Cast Iron, Mechanical Novelty Works, 1880 . .   9570.00
Mechanical, John Deere Blacksmith, Cast Iron, Painted, 1975 . . . .   650.00
Mechanical, Jolly Nigger, Big Mouth, 1950s, 5 In. . . . .*Illus*   55.00
Mechanical, Jolly Nigger, Cast Iron, Blue Shirt, Shepard, 1892, 4 3/4 In. . . . . . .285.00 to 475.00
Mechanical, Jolly Nigger, Cast Iron, Red Shirt, Shepard, 1892, 4 3/4 In. . . . . . . .315.00 to 640.00
Mechanical, Jolly Nigger, Plastic, 1950s 45.00
Mechanical, Jolly Nigger, Starkie, England, 1920s . . . . .325.00 to 650.00
Mechanical, Kool-Aid Character, Plastic, Red, 7 In. 30.00
Mechanical, Las Vegas Jackpot, Metal, Plastic Back, Pennies, Nickels & Dimes, 1950s . .   65.00
Mechanical, Leap Frog, Cast Iron, Shepard Hardware, 1891, 7 1/2 In. . . . . .2050.00 to 2150.00
Mechanical, Lion & Monkeys, Cast Iron, Kyser & Rex, 1883 . . . . .1035.00 to 2500.00
Mechanical, Magic Mouse, Tin, Yone, Japan 60.00
Mechanical, Magician, Cast Iron, J. & E. Stevens, 1901 . . . . .2640.00 to 3950.00
Mechanical, Magician, Grey Iron Manufacturing Co., Book Of Knowledge 375.00
Mechanical, Mama Katzenjammer, Cast Iron, Kenton Hardware, c.1912, 6 In. 5750.00
Mechanical, Mason, Cast Iron, Excelsior, Shepard Hardware, c.1890, 7 1/2 In. .5000.00 to 7475.00
Mechanical, Memorial Money Bank, Bell Rings, Liberty Enterprise, 1875 . . . .   675.00
Mechanical, Milking Cow, Book Of Knowledge, 1950s 495.00
Mechanical, Monkey & Coconut, Cast Iron, J. & E. Stevens, 1886 . . . .   3600.00
Mechanical, Monkey, Tips Had, Tin, Chein 35.00
Mechanical, Mouse Pushes Coin Into Shoe, Tin, Japan 70.00
Mechanical, Mule Entering Barn, Gray Barn, J. & E. Stevens, 1880, 8 1/2 In. 835.00
Mechanical, Multiplying Bank, J. & E. Stevens, c.1883, 7 In. 5175.00
Mechanical, One That Got Away, Cast Iron, Hand Painted, 1960s 175.00
Mechanical, Organ Bank, Cat & Dog, Cast Iron, Kyser & Rex, 1882 . . . . .805.00 to 1500.00
Mechanical, Organ Bank, Miniature, Cast Iron, Painted, Kyser & Rex, 1881, 4 In. 315.00
Mechanical, Organ Bank, Monkey, Boy & Girl, Cast Iron, Book Of Knowledge 450.00
Mechanical, Organ Grinder & Bear, Cast Iron, Kyser & Rex, 1882 . . . .   4255.00
Mechanical, Owl, Cast Iron, Kilgore, 1926 . . . .   950.00
Mechanical, Owl, Turns Head, Glass Eyes, Cast Iron, J. & E. Stevens, 1880, 4 In. 690.00

Mechanical, Paddy & Pig, Cast Iron, Grey Manufacturing Co., Book Of Knowledge 375.00
Mechanical, Paddy & Pig, Cast Iron, J. & E. Stevens, 1882 ....660.00 to 1540.00
Mechanical, Panorama, Cast Iron, Pictures In House Window, J. & E. Stevens, 1876 .... 8800.00
Mechanical, Penny Pineapple, Hawaii 50th State, 1960 .... 775.00
Mechanical, Picture Gallery, Cast Iron, Shepard Hardware, 1885 .... 4290.00
Mechanical, Pig In High Chair, Cast Iron, J. & E. Stevens, 1897 .... 660.00
Mechanical, Punch & Judy, 3 1/2 x 5 1/4 In. 360.00
Mechanical, Punch & Judy, Cast Iron, Grey Mfg. Co., Book Of Knowledge .....350.00 to 495.00
Mechanical, Punch & Judy, Cast Iron, Shepard Hardware, 6 1/8 In. ....800.00 to 1495.00
Mechanical, Punch & Judy, Tin, Box, England 550.00
Mechanical, Rabbit In Cabbage, Cast Iron, Kilgore, 1920s, 4 In. 412.00
Mechanical, Rabbit, Standing, Cast Iron, Small 770.00
Mechanical, Record Money Bank, Weight Scale, Tin, Red, Blue, Green, 6 1/2 In. 518.00
Mechanical, Rocket Ship, Cast Metal, 1950s 215.00
Mechanical, Rooster, Cast Iron, Kyser & Rex, 1890s, 6 In. 745.00
Mechanical, Safety Locomotive, Cast Iron, 1887, Semimechanical 495.00
Mechanical, Santa Claus At Chimney, Cast Iron, Hand Painted, 1950s ....350.00 to 375.00
Mechanical, Santa Claus, Cast Iron, Shepard Hardware, c.1890, 8 In. ....1610.00 to 4312.00
Mechanical, Santa Claus, On Roof, Tin, Felt, Plush, Electric, Japan, Box, 9 In. 115.00
Mechanical, Satellite, With Instructions & Maps, Box 260.00
Mechanical, Sav-O The Amazing Clown, Plastic, Box, 1950s 225.00
Mechanical, Southern Comfort, Civil War Soldier, Bottle, Hand Painted, 1950s ...95.00 to 215.00
Mechanical, Speaking Dog, Girl & Dog On Couch, Cast Iron, Shepard, 7 In. ..1610.00 to 3737.00
Mechanical, Squirrel & Tree Stump, Cast Iron, Mechanical Novelty Works, c.1881 ..... 3225.00
Mechanical, Stollwerk Chocolates Money Box, Tin, Glass Candy Dispenser, 1920s 400.00
Mechanical, Strike Bowling, Cast Iron, Hand Painted, Richard Toys, 1950s 750.00
Mechanical, Stump Speaker, Cast Iron, Shepard Hardware, c.1886, 10 In. 2300.00
Mechanical, Tammany, Brown Pants, J. & E. Stevens, 1873 ....550.00 to 1610.00
Mechanical, Tammany, Cast Iron, 5 1/2 x 3 1/4 In. ....1380.00 to 3220.00
Mechanical, Tammany, Cast Iron, Repro, 5 1/2 x 3 1/4 In. ....250.00 to 375.00
Mechanical, Tammany, Gray Pants, J. & E. Stevens, 1873 ....675.00 to 3220.00
Mechanical, Teddy & The Bear, Cast Iron, J. & E. Stevens ....880.00 to 1275.00
Mechanical, Tennis Players, Billy Jean King & Bobby Riggs, John Wright, 1975 .... 1300.00
Mechanical, Thing, Addams Family, Filmways TV Productions, Box, 1964 .... 195.00
Mechanical, Trick Dog, Cast Iron, 1960s ....75.00 to 175.00
Mechanical, Trick Dog, Cast Iron, Painted, Hubley, 1920s, 8 3/4 In. ....490.00 to 700.00
Mechanical, Trick Pony, Cast Iron, Shepard Hardware, 1885 .... 1400.00
Mechanical, Trick Pony, Grey Iron Manufacturing Co., Book Of Knowledge 325.00
Mechanical, Tricky Pig, Cast Iron, 7 1/2 In. 412.00
Mechanical, Try Your Weight, Scale Form, Tin, Red, Blue, Green, 6 1/2 x 3 1/4 In. 431.00
Mechanical, Uncle Bugs, Cast Iron, Warner Brothers, Box 150.00
Mechanical, Uncle Remus, Log Cabin, Policeman On Outside Waiting, Cast Iron 3450.00
Mechanical, Uncle Sam, Cast Iron, Book Of Knowledge 175.00
Mechanical, Uncle Sam, Cast Iron, Shepard Hardware, 1886 .... 9200.00
Mechanical, Uncle Tom, Cast Iron, Kyser & Rex, 1882 .... 585.00
Mechanical, Wild West, Cowboy At Saloon Door, Cast Metal, 1950s 215.00
Mechanical, William Tell, Cast Aluminum, Australia, 1930 .... 495.00
Mechanical, William Tell, Cast Iron, 1960s 275.00
Mechanical, William Tell, Cast Iron, J. & E. Stevens, 1896, 10 1/2 In. ....435.00 to 1650.00
Mechanical, Wireless Bank Building, Tin, Cast Iron, Wood, Battery Operated, John Hugo 50.00
Mechanical, Zoo Bank, Cast Iron, Hand Painted, 1960s 650.00
Merry-Go-Round, Cast Iron, 4 3/4 x 4 In. 59.00
Miner's Savings Bank, Lunch Pail Shape, Pittston, Pa. 55.00
Minstrel, Tin Lithograph, 1940s, 4 1/2 In. 88.00
Minuteman, White Metal, Bank Advertising, 8 1/8 In. 38.00
Mission Orange Drink Can, 1954, 12 Oz. Size 45.00
Mobile Midland, Blue, White, Clear Top, Rubber Tires, Dinky Toy 29.00
Nipper The Dog, RCA, Victor, Cast Iron, 1970s 95.00
Old Dutch Beer Can, Steel 8.00
Organ Grinder, Cast Iron, Hubley, Conversion From Toy 650.00
Oscar Mayer, Wienermobile, Plastic, 4 1/2 In. 25.00
Panda & Child, Metal, Glass 17.00
Peanuts, Charlie Brown, Composition, Wearing Baseball Hat, Glove & Ball, Japan, 1971 85.00

Peters Weatherbird, Cast Iron, Arcade, 4 1/4 In. 990.00
Pig, Ivory Soap, Plastic, 6 In. 20.00
Pig, Old Thompson Blended Whiskey, 2 Sides, Ceramic, 1950s, 7 x 8 In. 16.00
Pig With Drum, Tin Lithograph, Felt Clothes, Windup, 4 1/2 In. 320.00
Pistol Packing Pirate, Hand Painted, White Metal, Locking Coin Trap, 1930s 150.00
Pittsburgh Paints, Glass Block 45.00
Polar Bear, White, Cast Iron, 5 1/4 In. 325.00
Porky Pig, That's All Folks, Ceramic, Applause, Warner Bros., 1989, 8 In. 195.00
Prancing Horse, Cast Iron, 1930s 95.00
Puppo, Dog, Cast Iron, Hubley, 1920s 225.00
Radio, Hubley, c.1928 .... 165.00
Radio, Standing, Dark Japan Finish, Gold Trim, Pressed Steel, 4 x 2 1/2 In. 400.00
Red Goose Shoes, Goose, Cast Iron, 4 1/4 In. 75.00
Register, Easy Saver, Buddy L, Stamped Metal, Lithographed, 6 In. 24.00
Register, New York World's Fair, 1964, Dime 40.00
Register, Rooster, Cast Iron, 4 7/8 In. 133.00
Register, Uncle Sam, 3-Coin, Stamped Metal, Blue, 1940s 24.00
Rheingold Beer Can, Steel 12.00
Rival Dog Food, Tin Lithograph, 1930-1940 .... 65.00
Robot, Galaxy Spaceman, Glass, 1950s 30.00
Rocket, Metallic Plate, Vacumet, Inc. 95.00
Ronald McDonald, Plastic, 7 1/2 In. 15.00
Rooster, Cast Iron, Gold & Red Paint, 5 In. 170.00
Rooster, Cast Iron, Hubley, 4 3/4 In. 75.00
Saddle Horse, Cast Iron, Grey Iron Casting, c.1934, 4 3/8 In. 245.00
Safe, 2 Doors, Dark Bronze, Cast Iron, Kenton, 1896, 4 x 6 In. 400.00
Safe, 2 Doors, Nickel Plate, 1 Coin Slot, Cast Iron, 4 x 6 In. 200.00
Safe, Arabian, People & Camels Scene, Gold, Bronze, Cast Iron, 4 x 4 x 4 3/4 In. ... 115.00
Safe, Bakelite, Jack Benny's Picture On Dial 50.00
Safe, Colorful Flowers, Rectangular Base, Blue Trim, Cast Iron, 4 In. 175.00
Safe, Combination Lock, Bank Of Commerce, Cast Iron, 4 1/2 x 4 In. 200.00
Safe, Combination Lock, Black, Gold Trim, Cast Iron, 6 x 8 In. 225.00
Safe, Combination Lock, Royal Safe Deposit, Flowers, Black, Cast Iron 150.00
Safe, Diamond, Nickel Plate, Handle, Cast Iron, 5 1/4 x 7 1/2 In. 250.00
Safe, Fidelity Trust Vault, Cast Iron, J. Barton Smith Co., 1890, 6 x 6 x 5 In. 460.00
Safe, J.B. Barnaby Co.'s Boy's Savings Bank, Cast Iron, Nickel Plate, 3 1/2 x 3 In. 862.00
Safe, Young America, Cast Iron, Young Boys, Walking, Biking, Fishing, 3 x 3 x 4 In. ... 201.00
Santa Claus, Asleep In Chair, Metal, Painted, Banthrico, 1940-1950, 7 x 6 In. 60.00
Santa Claus, Overstuffed Chair, Chalkware, Painted, 8 1/2 x 7 1/2 In. 65.00
Santa Claus, Standing, Holding Christmas Toys, Cast Iron, 10 In. 95.00
Santa Claus, With Tree, Red, Cast Iron, Hubley, 1914, 5 7/8 In. 341.00
Save For A Rainy Day, Cast Iron, 5 1/4 In. 203.00
Seaman's Sailor Savings, Porcelain, Hand Painted, Metal Coin Trap, 1940s 65.00
Sharecropper, Cast Iron, A.C. Williams, 1901, 5 1/2 In. ....185.00 to 187.00
Shmoo, Li'l Abner, Figural, Plastic, On Card, 1948 .... 85.00
Singer Sewing Machines Book, Brass, Leather Bound Cover, 1930s 95.00
Snoopy, Doghouse, Glass 32.00
Snoopy, Figural, Porcelain, Italy, 1968, 6 1/2 In. 85.00
Snoopy, On Dog House, Molded Plastic, Red, White, 1966, 7 1/4 x 4 1/4 In. 35.00
St. Bernard, Black, Gold Trim, Cast Iron, 7 3/4 In. 126.00
State, Cast Iron, Locking Door, Japanned Finish, Gold Trim, Kenton, 1900, 5 7/8 In. 285.00
Statue Of Liberty, Copper Tone, White Metal, 1960s 95.00
Streetcar, H.J. Heinz 100.00
Sun-Maid Raisins, Vinyl 15.00
Sun-Proof Paints, Tin Lithograph, 1920s, 3 1/2 In. 55.00
Tabernacle Savings, Cast Iron, Keyless Lock Co., 2 1/2 x 5 In. 3410.00
Tarzan & Empire State Building, Warner Bros. 65.00
Thing, The Addams Family, Box, Dated 1964 .... 195.00
Three Little Pigs, Chein 175.00
Three Stooges, Bisque, 1960 .... 1375.00
Time Is Money, Clock, Embossed, Cast Iron, A.C. Williams, 1909-1931, 3 5/8 In. 105.00 to 115.00
Tractor, Campbell's Harvest Of Good Foods, Wooden, 1988, 6 1/4 x 3 3/4 x 5 In. 29.00
Truck, Texaco Diamond T Tanker Delivery, 1934 Model, Cast Metal, Ertl, Box 65.00

White City Puzzle Safe, Time Lock, Cast Iron, Bronze Finish, Nicol, 1/2 x 2 1/8 In. . . .   475.00
White City Savings, Cast Iron, Nichol, 1894 . . . .   895.00
Wimpy, Cast Iron 27.00
Wise Old Owl, Dark Amber Glass, 6 1/2 In. 30.00
Wonder Bread, Loaf Of Bread, Wrapped 225.00
Woodsy Owl, Glass 110.00
Woody Woodpecker, On Stump, Ceramic, Walter Lantz, Applause, 6 1/2 In. 45.00
World War II Pilot, Cast Iron, Tan Jacket, White Pants, Red Scarf, 8 3/4 In. 33.00
Yosemite Sam, Applause, 1988 . . . .   125.00
Ziggy & Dog, On Safe, Ceramic, 1982, 5 1/2 In. 40.00

ANKO, Korean ware, and Sumida are terms that are often confusing.
We use the names in the way most often used by antiques dealers and
collectors. Korean ware is now called *Sumida Gawa* or *Sumida* and is
listed in this book in the Sumida category. Banko is a group of rustic
Japanese wares made in the nineteenth and twentieth centuries. Some
pieces are made of mosaics of colored clay, some are fanciful teapots.
Redware and other materials were also used.

Coffeepot, Lighthouse Shape, Tapestry Design, Handle, Marked, 8 In. 145.00
Teapot, Form Of The Gods Of Good Fortune, 5 1/4 In. 210.00
Teapot, Head Shape, Dragonfly Handle, 6 In. 220.00
Teapot, Mandarin Duck Form, Early 20th Century, 8 In. 110.00
Teapot, Relief Flowers, Green Grass Design, Marked, 5 3/4 In. 100.00
Teapot, Relief Hawthorn Design, 19th Century, 6 1/4 In. 88.00
Vase, Double Gourd Form, Green, Blue Floral Design, Peeled Brown Ground, 18 In. 275.00
Vase, Insect Design, Gray Ground, Marked, 7 1/4 In., Pair 165.00
Wine Pot, Sparrow Form, Marked, Japan, 4 1/2 In. 88.00

BARBER collectibles range from the popular red and white striped pole
that used to be found in front of every shop to the small scissors and
tools of the trade. Barber chairs are wanted, especially the older models with elaborate iron trim.

Basin, Brass, Oval, Neck Cutout, Hanging Ring, England, c.1750, 11 1/2 In. 425.00
Bowl, Floral Pinwheel Center, Tom, 10 7/8 In. 220.00
Bowl, Oval, Elfin Figures, Overall Green Floral, Double Border, Faience, 13 In. 322.00
Bowl, Pewter, Oval Shape, Hanging Ring, England, 11 1/2 In. 395.00
Chair, Aluminum, Iron, 1930s, 48 In. 50.00
Chair, Kochs, Gold, Maroon Naugahyde Covered 995.00
Chair, Swan Head Armrests, 3 Ft. 10 In. x 2 Ft. 2 In. 330.00
Dispenser, Sanek Neck Strips, Metal, Cream Enameled, 4 1/2 x 3 x 2 1/8 In. 55.00
Dispenser, Shop Type, Porcelain, White, Crazed 65.00
Pole, Acorn Finials, Wooden, Red & White, 59 In. 467.00
Pole, Electric, Lighted 675.00
Pole, Pine, Half Round, Wall Mount, Red & White, 5 1/2 x 55 In.   420.00
Pole, Porcelain, Look Better-Feel Better, Wall Mount, 1/2 Round, 8 x 48 In. 265.00
Pole, Wooden, Turned, Red, White, Blue Paint, Over Varnish, Dowel Rods, 76 In. 825.00
Shaving Vase, Paper, Apple Green, Thumbprint Pattern, 7 1/4 In. 330.00
Strop, Razor, Kriss Kross, Box, c.1921 . . . .   55.00

BAROMETERS are used to forecast the weather. Antique barometers
with elaborate wooden cases and brass trim are the most desirable.
Mercury column barometers are also popular with collectors. It is difficult to find someone to repair a broken one, so be sure your barometer is in working condition.

Anaroid, P.F. Bollenbach Co., Ebonized Frame, Brass Face, Black Enamel, 22 In. 46.00
Angle, Mahogany, Ogee Borders, George III, 44 x 23 In. 2300.00
Banjo, Anthony Gatty, Shell & Flower Inlay, Mahogany, 38 1/2 In. 715.00
Banjo, Cort & Co., Figured Walnut Case, 38 In. 990.00
Banjo, T. & H. Doublet, Thermometer Dials, Mahogany, 1840s, 38 1/4 In. 747.00
Banjo, Walnut, Oil Painting Of Sail Ship, England, 43 In. 495.00
Banjo, Wheel, Oak, Foliage, C-Scrolls, Late 19th Century, 33 In.   230.00
Beaded Edge, Parquetry Trim, Mahogany, England, 1840s, 36 1/2 In. 660.00
Charles Wilder, Turned Wood Case, Metal Face, Peterboro, New Hampshire, 39 In. 1073.00

D.E. Lent, Walnut Case, Tramp Art, Metal Face, New York, 35 1/2 In. 825.C
G. Tagliabue, Mahogany Case, Circular Base, Metal Face, 37 In. 1210.C
Giltwood, Foliate Wreath Frame, Oval Painted Dial, Leaf Finial, Louis XVI, 35 In. 3162.C
Hygrometer, Thermometer & Level, Capella, Mahogany, c.1835, 45 1/2 In. 3450.C
L. Simon, Ivory, Brass, Arched Glazed Top, Brass Gimbal Bracket, 1800, 37 In. 1840.C
Meteorological, Henry J. Green, Brass, 1920s, 43 In. 310.0
Orbros, Wall, Fahrenheit Temperature, Barometric Pressure, 31 In. 86.0
Spencer Browning & Co., London, Mahogany, Gimbaled, 36 In. 5775.C
Stick, E. Kendall, Mahogany, Etched Steel Face, Signed, 34 In.   546.C
Stick, J. Ortelly, Brass Urn Finial, Inlaid Satin Wood Sides, Mahogany, 37 1/2 In. 275.C
Stick, Mahogany, Arch Pediment, England, Mid-19th Century, 38 In. 92.C
Thermometer, A. Peja, Inlaid Shell & Checkered Banding, c.1800, 48 In. 2875.C
Thermometer, Charles Wilder, Silver Wash, Wood Case, 1860, 37 1/2 x 4 3/8 In. 633.C
Thermometer, Currier & Simpson, Silver Wash, Front Mahogany Case, 16 In. 920.C
Thermometer, Red Marble, Brass Base, 8-Day, Enamel Dial, 1900, 9 In. 920.C
Thermometer, Wheel, Mahogany, Back Opening, Victorian, 12 In. 715.C
Thermometer, William IV, Mahogany, Swan's Neck, 1830, 37 1/2 In. 863.C
Thomas Shaw, Pierced Crest, Paper Dial, Rectangular Frame, 19th Century, 39 In. 690.C
Water Wheel, Gilt Metal Industrial, Stonework Arch, France, 1900, 14 In. 1380.C
Wheel, A. Ciapini, Inlaid Flowerheads & Shells, Victorian, 39 In. 430.C
Wheel, Bapt. Ronchet, Inlaid Mahogany Flower Heads, 38 In. 430.C
Wheel, Davis Optical, Rosewood, Mid-19th Century, 37 1/2 In.   287.C
Wheel, J. Testi, String Inlaid Mahogany, 38 In. 402.C
Wheel, Rosewood, Mother-Of-Pearl, Victorian, 39 In. 374.C
Wheel, Satinwood, 2 Prince Of Wales Plumes, George III, 1800, 35 In. 2587.C
Wheel, Victorian, Walteston & Co., Mid-19th Century, 44 In. 488.C
Windmill, Brass Industrial, Conical Top, 8-Day, France, 1900, 16 In. 2070.6

BASEBALL collectibles are in the Sports category, except for baseball cards, which
are listed under Baseball in the Card category.

BASKETS of all types are popular with collectors. American Indian,
Japanese, African, Shaker, and many other kinds of baskets can be
found. Of course, baskets are still being made, so the collector must
learn to tell the age and style of the basket to determine the value.

Apple, Bail Handle, Wooden Base, 15 In. 140.6
Apple, Swing Handle, 9 1/2 x 14 1/2 In. 357.C
Bamboo, Double Walled Rimloop Handle, 13 1/2 x 12 1/2 In.   165.C
Bamboo, Handle, Ikebana, Globular Form, 15 In. 357.C
Berry, Picket Fence, Wood, Wire & Tin, Bale Handles, 6 1/2 In. 275.C
Buttocks, Splint, 21 Ribs, Bentwood Handle, 3 1/2 x 8 x 8 In.   105.6
Buttocks, Splint, 22 Ribs, Bentwood Handle, Blue, 4 1/4 x 5 x 5 1/4 In. 578.C
Buttocks, Splint, 26 Ribs, Bentwood Handle, Red, Green, Natural Patina, 4 1/4 In. 220.C
Buttocks, Splint, 28 Ribs, Bentwood Handle, 10 x 12 x 6 1/4 In. 165.C
Buttocks, Splint, 30 Ribs, Bentwood Handle, Floral Design, Red, Orange, Green, 5 In. . .   440.C
Buttocks, Splint, 38 Ribs, Bentwood Handle, Natural Patina, 7 x 7 1/2 x 4 In. 138.6
Buttocks, Splint, 56 Ribs, Bentwood Handle, 7 x 8 In. 330.C
Buttocks, Splint, 58 Ribs, Twisted Handle, Old Orangish Tan, 12 1/2 x 12 1/2 x 6 In. . . .   550.6
Buttocks, Splint, Bentwood Handle, 5 3/4 x 7 7/8 x 3 1/2 In. 245.C
Buttocks, Splint, Bentwood Handle, 6 x 10 x 10 In. 94.C
Buttocks, Splint, Bentwood Handle, 11 x 11 1/2 x 6 1/2 In. 137.6
Buttocks, Splint, Bentwood Handle, 14 x 21 x 13 In. 149.C
Buttocks, Splint, Bentwood Handle, Gray Scrubbed Finish, 12 1/2 x 13 1/2 x 8 In. 99.6
Buttocks, Splint, Handle, Dark Brown, 3 1/2 x 4 In. 165.C
Buttocks, Splint, Natural Patina, 6 1/4 x 7 In. 165.C
Buttocks, Splint, Oak, Handle, 14 In. 154.C
Buttocks, Twig Handle, 18 x 16 1/2 In. 165.C
Cheese, Woven, Round, 9 1/4 In. 150.6
Coiled, Rye Straw, 2 Stripped Bentwood Handles, 10 1/2 x 22 1/4 In. 748.C
Egg, Splint, Bentwood Handle, Brown Patina, 3 1/2 x 3 In. 100.6
Eskimo, Chitamacha, Storage 400.6
Eskimo, Geometric Design, Brown, Cream, Black, Round, 3 1/4 x 7 In. 115.6
Field, Split Ash, Handle, Circular Collar, Tapering Sides, Bentwood Base, 12 x 18 In. . . .   230.C

Figural, Hen, Wire, 5 1/2 x 9 In. 40.00
Fruit, Finger Lapped, Slat Sides, Signed & Dated 1902, 9 1/2 In. 150.00
Fruit, Taghkanic, Brown Ash, 12 In. 265.00
Goose Feather, Double Lids, Wrapped Handle, Oblong, Red, Black Paint, 18 In. 248.00
Laundry, Splint, Bentwood Handles, 25 x 26 x 10 1/2 In. 357.00
Laundry, Splint, Rim Handles, Oblong, Scrubbed Finish, 18 x 21 x 11 In. 105.00
Market, Splint, Oak, Handle, 16 In. 82.00
Nantucket, 2 Turned Wooden Handles, Round, 7 1/2 In. 345.00
Nantucket, Cane & Splint, Bentwood Rim, 14 x 6 3/4 In. 2365.00
Nantucket, Cane & Splint, Swivel Bentwood Handle, Wooden Base, 8 1/2 x 3 3/4 In. 740.00
Nantucket, Cane & Splint, Swivel Bentwood Handle, Wooden Base, Boyer, 6 In. 2090.00
Nantucket, Cane, Bentwood Rim Handles, Wooden Base, 7 1/2 x 4 In. 990.00
Nantucket, Cane, Swivel Handle, Turned Wooden Base, Round, 5 1/2 In. 1320.00
Nantucket, Carved Swing Handle, Copper Pinned, Round, 8 1/2 In. 402.00
Nantucket, Dark Brown, Turned Wood Base, 7 1/2 In. 78.00
Nantucket, F. Sylvaro, Paper Label, 3 1/2 In. 550.00
Nantucket, Ivory Swing Handle, Turned Wood Base, Signed Corey, 1982, 2 1/4 x 2 In. . . 125.00
Nantucket, Mitchell Ray, Paper Label On Base, 20th Century, 5 1/4 x 8 1/4 In. 632.00
Nantucket, Nested, Handle, 6 Piece 12650.00
Nantucket, Stenciled Interior, R. Folger Maker, 4 x 6 In. 747.00
Nantucket, Swing Handle, 9 1/2 In. 880.00
Nantucket, Swing Handle, Harbor Scene, Medallion Over Wicker Basket, 6 3/4 In. 23.00
Pack, Adirondack, Blue Paint 160.00
Peach, Oak, Initials CMT, 11 1/2 x 14 In. 230.00
Picket Fence, Wood & Wire, Wire Bail Handles, Oblong, 16 3/4 x 33 In. 125.00
Rice Straw, Polychrome Floral Design, Oriental Export, 7 In. 38.00
Saddle, Split Ash, Bentwood Handle, Closed Horseshoe Shape Collar, 16 x 16 In. 345.00
Splint, 2 Carved Handles, Bowed Sides, Green Paint, 18 x 13 1/4 x 5 1/2 In. 949.00
Splint, 14 Melon Ribs, Bentwood Handle, Red, 6 x 6 3/4 x 3 1/4 In. 165.00
Splint, 20 Melon Ribs, Bentwood Handle, 8 x 8 1/2 x 4 1/4 In. 138.00
Splint, 20 Ribs, Bentwood Handle, 8 x 7 1/2 In. 93.00
Splint, 30 Ribs, Bentwood Handle, Applied Foot, Red, Black, Yellow, 6 1/4 In. 110.00
Splint, Applied Handles, Oak, Square, 9 3/4 x 8 1/2 x 10 In. 72.00
Splint, Bail Handle, Pin-Type Wood Connector, Indian Hills, 1929, 11 x 7 1/2 In. 230.00
Splint, Bentwood Handle, 10 1/2 x 16 1/2 x 6 1/4 In. 105.00
Splint, Bentwood Handle, Dark Worn Patina, 8 x 9 x 5 1/2 In. 149.00
Splint, Bentwood Handle, Old Green Paint, 13 1/4 x 7 In. 440.00
Splint, Bentwood Handle, Red, 6 1/4 x 6 3/4 x 4 In. 468.00
Splint, Bentwood Handle, Red, Blue, Natural, 10 1/2 x 17 x 10 1/2 In. 77.00
Splint, Bentwood Handle, Red, Yellow, Black Stripes, 6 1/2 x 7 3/4 x 3 1/4 In. 412.00
Splint, Bentwood Handles, White Paint, Brown Varnish, 20 1/2 x 35 x 10 In. 415.00
Splint, Bentwood Rim Handles, Oblong, 14 x 16 x 6 In. 220.00
Splint, Bentwood Rim Handles, Potato Print Design, Oval, 11 x 14 x 5 1/2 In. 495.00
Splint, Bentwood Swivel Handle, Round, 12 1/2 x 7 1/4 In. 520.00
Splint, Carved Handle, Square, 8 x 13 x 12 In. 115.00
Splint, Carved Wood Handle, Melon Shape, 3 x 5 1/2 In. 230.00
Splint, Carved Wood Handle, Oval, 8 x 13 x 8 In. 80.00
Splint, Colored Weave Sides, Round, 13 1/2 x 15 1/2 In. 144.00
Splint, Cover, Bentwood Handle, Potato Print Design, Round, 7 1/2 x 7 1/2 x 8 In. 355.00
Splint, Cover, Horizontal Dark Lines, Round, 1869, 15 x 18 In. 172.00
Splint, Curled, Upturned Handles, Blue, Round, 4 3/4 x 8 In. 173.00
Splint, Feather, Oak, Handles, 17 x 24 In. 412.00
Splint, Garden, Oak, Strap Handle, 7 x 13 x 7 In. 120.00
Splint, Handle, Oak, Melon Shape, 15 In. 82.00
Splint, Handle, Oak, Square, Painted Bands, 12 In. 345.00
Splint, Herb Drying, Openwork Sides, 11 x 11 3/4 x 5 1/4 In. 192.00
Splint, Hinged Handle, Blue, Green Accents, 8 x 9 3/4 In. 77.00
Splint, Hinged Handle, Oak, 7 x 12 In. 248.00
Splint, Pie Carry, Bentwood, Removable Wood Slat Lid, Signed, 14 x 8 x 13 In. 125.00
Splint, Red, Rectangular, 20 x 11 1/2 x 14 In. 144.00
Splint, Round Handle, Round, 5 x 10 1/2 In. 138.00
Splint, Strap Handle, Blue Accents, 6 1/4 x 8 1/2 In. 82.00

Splint, Strap Handle, Green, Orange, New England, 8 1/2 x 16 3/4 In. 248.00
Splint, Swing Handle, Bushwhacker Type, Brown Patina, c.1850, 14 1/2 x 11 In. 195.00
Splint, Swing Handle, Shaker Style, Round, 7 x 11 1/2 In. 460.00
Splint, Swivel Handle, Round, 7 1/2 x 4 3/4 In. 220.00
Splint, Vermont Woodstock, 6 1/4 x 5 In. 105.00
Splint & Cane, Compote Shape, Wooden Base, Varnish, 12 1/2 x 9 In. 385.00
Split Oak, 1 Handle, Miniature 220.00
Storage, Aleutian Islands, 21 x 13 In. 395.00
Straw, Rye, Oval, 8 1/2 x 10 3/4 x 4 1/2 In. 50.00
Sweet Grass, Cover, Woven Handle, Red Reverse Ends, Crimson Line Border, 2 x 4 In. . 40.00
Sweet Grass, Cover, Woven Handle, Zigzag Design, Brown, Green, Blue, 2 x 4 1/4 In. . 58.00

BATCHELDER products are made from California clay. Ernest
Batchelder established a tile studio in Pasadena, California, in 1909
and expanded until 1916. Then he built a larger factory with a new
partner. The Batchelder-Wilson Company made all types of architec-   **BATCHELDER**
tural tiles, garden pots, and bookends. The plant closed in 1932. In   **LOS ANGELES**
1936 Batchelder opened Batchelder Ceramics, also in Pasadena, and
made bowls, vases, and earthenware pots. He retired in 1951 and died
in 1957. Pieces are marked *Batchelder Pasadena* or *Batchelder Los
Angeles*.

Bowl, 1 1/2 x 15 In. 150.00
Bowl, Maroon Overglaze, Chartreuse, 13 In. 75.00
Tile, Artichoke, Gold & Blue Glazes, 3 In. 65.00
Tile, Floral, Multi-Diamond Shape 145.00
Tile, Geometric 125.00
Tile, Mythical Bird & Animals, Gray Underglaze, 6 In. 365.00

BATMAN and Robin are characters from a comic strip by Bob Kane that
started in 1939. In 1966, the characters became part of a popular tele-
vision series. There have been radio and movie serials that featured the
pair. The first full-length movie was made in 1989. The third movie
was made in 1995.

Adventure Set, Colorforms, Box, 1989 . . . . 15.00
Bank, Ralston Cereal, Plastic, Original Package, 1989 . . . . 25.00
Bank, Robin, Figural, Stopper & Sticker, 1960s 95.00
Bat Stickers, Package, 1966, 5 Piece 20.00
Batmobile, Boat & Trailer Set, Metal, Plastic, Corgi, 1960s, 3 1/2 x 4 1/2 In., 3 Piece . . . 360.00
Batmobile, Child's Barber Chair, Porcelain, 20 x 46 x 43 In. 1092.00
Batmobile, Exhaust Flame, Flip-Out Saw Blade, Corgi, 5 In. 126.00
Batmobile, Talking, Box, 1960s 175.00
Batplane, Irwin, Stickers, 1960s, 21-In. Wingspan 265.00
Boat, Black Plastic, Red Plastic Fin, Logo Decals, 1970s, 8 In. 83.00
Bottle, Soaky 65.00
Bracelet, Charm, On Card 75.00
Candy Container, PEZ, 9-In. Candy, Card, 1985 . . . . 20.00
Card Set, Come Along With Batman & Robin As They Battle Mr. Freeze, Box, 70 Cards . 45.00
Carton, Ice Cream, Empty, 1966, 1/2 Gal. 75.00
Clock, Alarm, Batman & Robin On Face, Charter Member, Westclox 295.00
Colorforms, Box, Booklet, 1966 . . . . 39.00
Coloring Book, Comedy Of Tears, Whitman, 1975, 11 x 14 In. 18.00
Command Console, Box, 1970s, 7 x 11 In. 100.00
Cookie Jar, Warner Bros. 85.00
Costume, Captain Action, Ideal, 1966 . . . . 45.00
Costume, Robin, Action Boy 675.00
Doll, Ace Novelty, 30 In. 40.00
Doll, Topps, 1964, 12 In. 295.00
Escape Gun, Red Plastic, Blister Pack, 1966 . . . . 45.00
Figure, Batman, Metal, Blister Pack, With Collector Card, Ertl, 1990, 2 In. 15.00
Figure, Batman, Robin & 3 Villains, Cardboard, Stand-Up, 1977, 6 In., 5 Piece 25.00
Figure, Penguin, In Corgi Car, Sealed, 1979 . . . . 60.00
Figure, Penguin, Metal, Blister Pack, Collector Card, Ertl, 1900, 2 In. 15.00

Game, Milton Bradley	35.00
Glass, Pepsi-Cola, 2 Logos, 1966, 6 In.	20.00
Jackknife, Batman Logo, Face In Red, Single Blade, 1972	200.00
Lunch Box, Batman & Robin, Metal, 1966	125.00
Lunch Box, Gray Plastic, 1982	30.00 to 50.00
Lunch Box Thermos, Batman & Robin, Aladdin, 1966	60.00 to 75.00
Marionette, Batman & Robin, Azelles, Box, Instructions, Pair	600.00
Mask, Bat Girl, 1970s	35.00
Model Kit, Batman & Robin, Keel Style, Plastic, Original Package, 1987	20.00
Model Kit, Batman, MPC, Box	50.00
Model Kit, Batman, Standing, Horizon, 1/8 Scale	45.00
Model Kit, Batmobile, AMT, Box, 1989	15.00
Model Kit, Batmobile, Aurora Kit, Box	250.00
Model Kit, Robin, Standing, Legs & Arms Out, Horizon, 1/8 Scale	45.00
Mug, Milk Glass, Batman's Head One Side, Body Other, 1966	24.00
Night-Light	140.00
Periscope, Cereal Premium	65.00
Radio, 1973	119.00
Radio, Alarm, AM-FM, Logo, 1988, Box	395.00
Radio, Clock, AM-FM, Neon	395.00
Radio, Micro-Bat	2210.00
Record, Batman & Superman, Golden, 45 RPM, 1966	18.00
Soaky, Batman, Catwoman & Penguin, Avon, 3 Piece Set	75.00
Soaky, Robin, Plastic, Black, Red, Flesh Tone, 1966, 9 1/2 In.	50.00
Squirt Gun	30.00
Telescope, 1966	150.00
Towel, With Robin	75.00
Toy, Ride-On Batmobile	150.00
Utility Belt, Batcuffs, Ideal, Box, 1966	55.00
Utility Belt, Rope & Grappling Hook, Other Tools, Ideal, Box, 1966	7300.00
Walkie-Talkies, 4 Transistor, Box, Set Of 2	25.00
Walkie-Talkies, Batman & Robin	225.00
Watch, Paper Face, Black Hands & Numbers, Die Cut Frame, Japan, c.1953	80.00
Wristwatch, Joker, On Card	15.00

BATTERSEA enamels, which are enamels painted on copper, were made in the Battersea district of London from about 1750 to 1756. Many similar enamels are mistakenly called *Battersea*.

Box, Floral, Egg Shape, Porcelain, 1 1/2 In.	285.00
Box, Hunt Scene On Cover, Porcelain, 1 3/4 In.	480.00
Box, Parable On Hinged Cover, Brass, 1 3/4 In.	90.00
Box, Scenic, Floral Design, Heart Shape, 2 1/2 In.	250.00
Box, Victory Of The Nile On Cover, 2 In.	140.00
Portrait, Medallion Of George II, Oval, 4 In.	1265.00
Snuffbox, English Warship On Cover, Blue, 1 1/2 In.	350.00
Snuffbox, Portrait Of Washington, Great Seal Inside Lid, 2 3/4 x 1 7/8 In.	4495.00
Snuffbox, Spaniel On Cover, 3 In.	1265.00
Tieback, Admiral Duncan, British Naval Commander, Sir Sidnay Smith, Pair	875.00
Tieback, Face In Brass Frame, Horseman Firing Pistol	295.00

BAUER pottery is a California-made ware. J.A. Bauer moved his Kentucky pottery to Los Angeles, California, in 1909. The company made art pottery after 1912 and dinnerwares marked *Bauer* after 1929. The factory went out of business in 1962.

Art Pottery, Vase, Matte Green, Louis Ipsen, 4 x 6 In.	75.00
Contempo, Casserole, Pumpkin, Tab Handle, Individual	125.00
Dutch, Pitcher, Red, 3 Qt.	195.00
Fish, Cookie Jar, Pink	225.00
Florist Ware, Console, Chartreuse, High Gloss, Rectangular, 11 1/2 In.	45.00
Florist Ware, Flowerpot, Tan Speckle Glaze, 8 x 13 In.	22.00
Florist Ware, Planter, Swan, White, 10 In.	55.00
Florist Ware, Vase, Brown Inside, Marbling Outside, Matt Carlton, 6 x 4 In.	77.00

Florist Ware, Vase, Green Glaze, Matt Carlton, 8 x 5 In. 100.00
Florist Ware, Vase, Ivory, Cylindrical, 10 In. 125.00
Florist Ware, Vase, Jade Green, Wavy Lip, Matt Carlton, 6 In. 375.00
Florist Ware, Vase, Olive Green Glaze, 8 x 10 In. 33.00
Florist Ware, Vase, Orange Red Glaze, Fred Johnson, 5 x 7 1/2 In. 55.00
Florist Ware, Vase, Wavy Lip, Yellow Glaze, Matt Carlton, 6 x 4 In. 90.00
Kitchen Ware, Oil Jar, Jade, Green, No. 100, 16 In. 650.00
Kitchen Ware, Spice Jar Set, Hand Painted, Marked, Largest 9 x 8 In., 6 Piece 225.00
La Linda, Bowl, Vegetable, Turquoise, 10 In. 35.00
La Linda, Teapot, Aladdin, Brown, 4 Cup 125.00
La Linda, Teapot, Aladdin, Orange, 4 Cup 65.00
La Linda, Tumbler, Assorted Colors, Set Of 6 .... 90.00
Monterey, Bowl, Fruit, Orange, Footed, 10 In. 125.00
Monterey, Cake Plate, Yellow, 10 1/2 In. ....250.00 to 325.00
Monterey, Gravy Boat, Orange 50.00
Monterey, Grill Plate, Chartreuse, 10 In. 35.00
Monterey, Teapot, Chartreuse, Individual 50.00
Moonsong, Casserole, Tan, Large 100.00
Pitcher, Black, 1 1/2 Pt. 85.00
Pitcher, Ice Lip, Light Green Glaze, Marked, 6 x 10 In. 165.00
Pitcher, Ice Lip, White Glaze, Marked, 6 x 10 In. 70.00
Plainware, Ashtray, Dark Blue, Sombrero, 4 In. 175.00
Plainware, Ashtray, Orange, 4 In. 60.00
Plainware, Bean Pot, Black, 1 Qt. 200.00
Plainware, Bean Pot, Yellow, 2 Qt. 120.00
Plainware, Beater Jar, Green, 4 3/4 In. 75.00
Plainware, Bowl, Pudding, Jade 80.00
Plainware, Carafe, Orange, 1935 .... 100.00
Plainware, Casserole, Yellow, 5 1/2 In. 45.00
Plainware, Mixing Bowl, No. 3, Yellow 95.00
Rebekah, Vase, Matt Carlton, 14 1/2 x 8 1/2 In. 905.00
Ring, Berry Bowl, Orange, 4 3/4 In. 40.00
Ring, Bowl, Salad, Low, 12 In. 200.00
Ring, Carafe, Orange, Copper Handle ....65.00 to 125.00
Ring, Carafe, Yellow, Copper Handle 95.00
Ring, Casserole, Black, 5 1/2 In. 60.00
Ring, Casserole, Red, 9 1/2 In. 235.00
Ring, Casserole, Red, With Rack, 5 1/2 In. 85.00
Ring, Chop Plate, Burnt Orange, 17 In. 250.00
Ring, Chop Plate, Orange, 12 In. ....65.00 to 90.00
Ring, Chop Plate, Orange, 14 In. ....100.00 to 125.00
Ring, Chop Plate, Yellow, 12 In. ....75.00 to 90.00
Ring, Coffee Server, Black Glaze, 9 x 9 In. 165.00
Ring, Coffee Server, Orange, Metal 110.00
Ring, Cookie Jar, Burnt Orange, Brown 375.00
Ring, Cup & Saucer, Green, After Dinner 300.00
Ring, Cup & Saucer, Yellow 30.00
Ring, Cup & Saucer, Yellow, After Dinner 300.00
Ring, Cup, Dark Blue, After Dinner 100.00
Ring, Dish, Pickle, Orange ....35.00 to 40.00
Ring, Goblet, Orange 125.00
Ring, Mixing Bowl, No. 9, Black 450.00
Ring, Mixing Bowl, No. 9, Red, 10 In. 65.00
Ring, Mixing Bowl, No. 12, Yellow, 9 In. 75.00
Ring, Mixing Bowl, No. 18, Chartreuse, 8 In. 75.00
Ring, Mixing Bowl, No. 30, Black, 6 In. 50.00
Ring, Pitcher, Turquoise, 1/2 Pt. 25.00
Ring, Place Setting, Orange, 5 Piece 100.00
Ring, Plate, Green, 10 1/2 In. 85.00
Ring, Plate, Serving, Yellow, 17 In. 175.00
Ring, Platter, Dark Blue, 17 1/4 x 17 1/4 In. 192.00
Ring, Punch Set, Jade Green, Pedestal, 14 Piece 2000.00
Ring, Refrigerator Set, Stacking, Olive Green, 4 Piece 165.00

Ring, Salt & Pepper, Barrel Shape, Yellow	70.00
Ring, Stacking Set, Yellow, Green & Red, Black Wooden Lids, Copper Stand	395.00
Ring, Sugar & Creamer, Cover, Miniature	65.00
Ring, Teapot, Orange, 6 Cup	95.00 to 100.00
Ring, Teapot, Yellow, 2 Cup	15.00
Ring, Tumbler, Dark Blue, 6 Oz.	40.00
Ring, Tumbler, Dark Blue, 12 Oz.	68.00
Ring, Tumbler, Green, 12 Oz.	68.00
Ring, Tumbler, Yellow, 3 Oz.	50.00
Ring, Vase, Black, Cylindrical, 8 In.	165.00
Ring, Vase, Burnt Orange, 8 In.	80.00
Ring, Vase, White, 10 In.	195.00
Swan, Figurine, White, Speckled Glaze	225.00
Swirl, Vase, Aqua, 12 1/2 In.	245.00
Wright, Bread Tray	500.00

EADED BAGS are included in the Purse category.

EATLES collectors search for any items picturing the four members of he famous music group or any of their recordings. Because these ems are so new, the condition is very important and top prices are aid only for items in mint condition. The Beatles first appeared on American network television in 1964. The group disbanded in 1971. Ringo Starr, George Harrison, and Paul McCartney are still performing. John Lennon died in 1980.

Autograph, John Lennon, Imagine Album	800.00
Bank, Make A Date	58.00
Book, I, Me, Mine, George Harrison's Life, Simon & Schuster, 1980	45.00
Book, Love You Make, 1984	7.00
Book, Monthly Magazine No. 3, October 1963, Signed By All Four	2875.00
Book, Shout, 1981, 415 Pages, 6 x 9 In.	7.00 to 10.00
Book, The Man Who Gave The Beatles Away, Macmillan, 1975	15.00
Book, Twilight Of The Gods, Meaning Of Their Music, Wilfrid Mellers, 1973	15.00
Cake Decoration, Swingers Music Set, Box	90.00
Card, Playing, Black & White Photo, Plastic Coated, Full Deck, Gemanco, Box	20.00
Decanter, John Lennon	170.00
Display, Counter, Stand-Up, For Complete Beatles Video Tape, 9 1/2 x 13 In.	28.00
Doll, Plastic, Large Vinyl Heads, Seltaeb Inc., 1964, 5 In., Set Of 4	280.00
Doll, Ringo Starr, Molded Plastic Body, Brush Bristle Hair, 4 1/2 In.	101.00
Doll, Ringo, With Drum	100.00
Figure, Ringo, Remco	125.00
Figure, Swinger Set, Unused, Early 1960s, 4 Piece	100.00
Flight Bag, TWA, Fab Four With Facsimile Autographs, Red, Vinyl, 1965, 10 x 14 In.	92.00
Game, Flip Your Wig, 1970s	145.00
Guitar, Paper Lithograph, Wooden, England	250.00
Hanger, Clothes, Yellow Submarine	150.00
Lunch Box, Thermos, Faces, Autographs, Stamped Steel, Aladdin, 1965	200.00 to 400.00
Magazine, Rolling Stone, Beatles On Cover, 1969	45.00
Magazine, The Beatles Forever, History As A Group, 1970s	24.00
Nodder, Box, 4 Piece	695.00
Pen & Holder Set, NEMS Ent., Ltd., Box, 1980s	22.00
Picture, Color, Folds, 19 x 29 In.	10.00
Pin, Guitar, Lennon Portrait, Fabulous Beatles Jewelry Brooch, Rego Design, 4 1/2 In.	54.00
Pin, Guitar, Tie-Tack, On Card, 1964	125.00
Pin, Yellow Submarine, 1968	98.00
Pin Set, Face Form, Pewter, 4 Piece	25.00
Puzzle, Unopened, 1967, 500 Piece	30.00
Record, Album, Introducing The Beatles, With Photograph, 33 RPM	100.00
Sheet Music, Ticket To Ride, Help, 1965	38.00
T-Shirt, Child's, John Lennon	35.00
Toy, Yellow Submarine, Corgi, Box, 5 1/4 In.	425.00
Video, Let It Be	150.00
Wallet, Vinyl, Day-Glo Pink, Autographed, Ramat & Co. Ltd., London, 1964	85.00

Beehive, Charger, Toilet Of Venus, Gold
Border, Gorner, 16 1/2 In.

**If you have a serious flood, be sure
to have the power to the house
turned off before you wade into the
water. If you must turn off the
power, wear rubber boots and dry
rubber gloves. Stand on a wooden
chair or ladder and use a broom
handle to flip the main switch.**

BEEHIVE, Austria, or Beehive, Vienna, are terms used in English-speaking countries to refer to the many types of decorated porcelain bearing a mark that looks like a beehive. The mark is actually a shield, viewed upside down. It was first used in 1744 by the Royal Porcelain Manufactory of Vienna. The firm made porcelains, called *Royal Vienna* by collectors, until it closed in 1864. Many other German, Austrian, and Japanese factories have reproduced Royal Vienna wares, complete with the original shield or *beehive* mark. This listing includes the expensive, original Royal Vienna porcelains and many other types of beehive porcelain. The Royal Vienna pieces include that name in the description.

Charger, Toilet Of Venus, Gold Border, Gorner, 16 1/2 In. ....*Illus* 2750.00
Cup & Saucer, Classical, Cloud Reserves, Gold Band, Midnight Blue, Marked 175.00
Cup & Saucer, Man & Woman Scene, Suhl, Signed, Saucer, 4 7/8 In. 125.00
Cup & Saucer, Square Handle, Scene Of Venus, Marked, 18th Century, 3 1/2 In. 690.00
Figurine, Dog, Greyhound, Reclining, Royal Vienna 650.00
Pitcher, Gilded, Pinched Spout, Cobalt Blue, Porcelain, 8 1/2 In. 65.00
Plate, Portrait, Woman With Rose In Hair, Gold Scrolling, Signed, 9 1/2 In. 1137.00
Tazza, Bearded Monk, Reading Bible, 3 Medallions Of Cherubs, Signed, 9 In. 715.00
Urn, Cover, 2 Handles, Red Ground, Beehive Mark, Signed, K. Wek, 11 In. 600.00
Vase, Blackberry, 5 In. 550.00
Vase, Garniture, Polychrome, Landscape, Figures, 10 1/2 In. 247.00
Vase, Portrait, Woman, Holding Roses, Lavender Ground, 1900, 33 In. 7475.00

BEER BOTTLES are listed in the Bottle category under Beer.

BEER CANS are a twentieth-century idea. Beer was sold in kegs or returnable bottles until 1934. The first patent for a can was issued to the American Can Company in September of that year; and Gotfried Kruger Brewing Company, Newark, New Jersey, was the first to use the can. The cone-top can was first made in 1935, the aluminum pop-top in 1962. Collectors should look for cans in good condition, with no dents or rust. Serious collectors prefer cans that have been opened from the bottom.

Alps Brau, Flat Top 90.00
Ballantine, Flat Top 15.00
Beverwyck Ale, Albany, N.Y., Cone Top 160.00
Blackhawk, Cone Top 175.00
Blatz, Old Heidleberg, Tin Litho 28.00
Brockert Pale Ale, Cone Top, 12 Oz. 295.00
Budweiser, 1936 .... 110.00
Budweiser, Flat Top 30.00
Burgermeister Beer, Flat Top, 15 Oz. 25.00
Busch, NASCAR, Atlanta, 12 Oz. 1.00
Busch Bavarian, Flat Top 15.00

Busch Light, NASCAR, Bristol, Black Car, 16 Oz. 1.50
Canadian Ace, Cone Top, 32 Oz. 65.00
Canadian Ace, Cone Top, Simulated Wood Lithograph, 12 Oz. 25.00
Clyde Cream Ale, Cone Top, 12 Oz. 225.00
Drewry's Ale, Flat Top 35.00
Dutch Lunch, Grace Bros. Brewing Co., Santa Rosa, California 120.00
Fox Deluxe Beer, Chicago 15.00
Genesee, Flat Top 15.00
Golden Crown, Tab Type 12.00
Grain Belt, Cone Top 25.00
Heileman's Old Style Lager Beer, Cone Top, 12 Oz. 505.00
Holburg Beer, Hofbrau Brewing 33.00
Iron City, Pittsburgh Pirates, 12 Oz. 1.00
Iroquois Indian Head Beer, Buffalo, N.Y., Cone Top 202.00
Lebanon Valley Beer, Rolled At Crown Company 106.00
Michelob, Golf 10th Hole, Pleasant Valley, 12 Oz. 1.50
Old Dutch Beer, Rolled At Crown Company, Eagle Brewery 67.00
Old Vienna, Tab Type 35.00
Pabst Big Cat Malt Liquor, Pull Tab, 16 In. 5.00
Pittsburgh Steelers, Championship Team, 1980 .... 4.50
Schlitz, Tab Type 10.00
Schlitz, Tall Boy, Flat Top, 1969, 24 Oz. ....9.00 to 28.00
Schmidt's, Cone Top 35.00
St. Ides Gold Premium Beer, 12 Oz. 1.25
Tam O Shanter Ale, Rochester N.Y., Flat Bottom 74.00
Western Gold, 16 Oz. 195.00

ELL collectors collect all types of bells. Favorites include glass bells,
figural bells, school bells, and cowbells. Bells have been made of
porcelain, china, or metal through the centuries.

Bicycle, Crown Jewel, 1950s 65.00
Bluejay, Towle, 5 In. ....*Illus* 20.00
Bronze, Gothic, Fleur-De-Lis, c.1530, 11 In. 2250.00
Bronze, Gothic, Medallions, Virgin Mary & Initials IHS, 1530-1560, 9 In. 2250.00
Elephant, Tap, Bronze 1200.00
Hand, Turned Walnut Handle, Brass, 7 3/4 In. 175.00
Nunnery, Attached Rope Arm, Cast Metal, 1850s, 8 In. 3600.00
School, Turned Curly Maple Handle, 10 1/4 In. 385.00
Sleigh, 19 Graduated Bells, No. 1 To No. 10, Key Type, Original Strap 300.00
Sleigh, 24 Graduated Bells, Double-Backed Leather Strap, 7 1/2 In. 425.00
Sleigh, 29 Bells, Leather Strap, 95 In. 300.00
Sleigh, 33 Graduated Bells, New Leather Strap, 1 1/8 To 3 5/8 In. 300.00
St. Peter's, Raised Figures Of Apostles, Cross Finial, Brass, 7 1/2 In. 125.00

BELLE WARE glass was made in 1903 by Carl V. Helmschmied. In
1904 he started a corporation known as the Helmschmied Manufacturing Company. His factory closed in 1908 and he worked on his own
until his death in 1934.

Box, Cover, Pink Roses & Buds, Signed, 3 x 4 1/4 In. 230.00
Jar, Sweetmeat, Roses & Buds, Textured Crystalline Finish, 7 In. 405.00

Most ceramics can be washed with soap or
detergent and water, but a few things should not
be. Any pieces that are repaired, damaged, or have
painted decorations should not be soaked in water.
Wipe them with a damp cloth after testing a small
area. Unglazed pieces should be dusted only.

Bell, Bluejay,
Towle, 5 In.

BELLEEK china was made in Ireland, other European countries, and the
United States. The glaze is creamy yellow and appears wet. The first
Belleek was made in 1857. All pieces listed here are Irish Belleek. The
mark changed through the years. The first mark, black, dates from
1863 to 1890. The second mark, black, dates from 1891 to 1926 and
includes the words *Co. Fermanagh, Ireland.* The third mark, black,
dates from 1926 to 1946 and has the words *Deanta in Eirinn.* The
fourth mark, same as the third mark but green, dates from 1946 to
1955. The fifth mark, green, dates from 1955 to 1965 and has an R in
a circle added in the upper right. The sixth mark, green, dates after
1965 and the words *Co. Fermanagh* have been omitted. The seventh
mark, gold, was used from 1980 to 1993 and omits the words *Deanta
in Eirinn.* The eighth mark, introduced in 1993, is similar to the second mark but is printed in blue. The word *Belleek* is now used only on
the pieces made in Ireland even though earlier pieces from other countries were sometimes marked *Belleek.* These early pieces are listed by
manufacturer, such as Ceramic Art Co., Haviland, Lenox, Ott &
Brewer, and Willets.

Ashtray, Thorn, 6th Mark, Green, 4 1/4 In.	17.00
Basket, Lily, Brown Veined Leaves, Pink Petals, 1st Mark, Black, 1885, 8 1/4 In.	2185.00
Basket, Shamrock Shape, 4 Strands, 6 1/2 In.	280.00 to 375.00
Biscuit Box, Ribbons & Bamboo, 6th Mark, Green	185.00
Biscuit Jar, Cover, Shamrock, 6th Mark, Green, 6 3/4 In.	165.00
Bowl, Cover, Shell, Coral Finial, 1st Mark, Black, 4 3/4 In.	805.00
Bowl, Limpet, 6th Mark, Green, 4 3/4 In.	228.00
Box, Trinket, Cover, Jack-On-Shore, 1st Mark, Black, 6 x 5 In.	2875.00
Bread Tray, Neptune, Handle, 4th Mark, Green, 11 1/4 In.	99.00
Cake Plate, Shamrock, 5th Mark, Green, 10 1/2 In.	75.00
Cake Plate, Shamrock, Basket Weave, 3rd Mark, Black, 10 1/4 In.	110.00
Cardium On Coral, 2nd Mark, Black, c.1910, 4 1/4 In.	632.00
Creamer, Shamrock, 6th Mark, Green	35.00
Cup & Saucer, Limpet, 3rd Mark, Black	65.00
Cup & Saucer, Shamrock, Harp Handle, 3rd Mark, Black	108.00
Cup & Saucer, Thistle, 2nd Mark, Black	225.00
Figurine, Cat, 7th Mark, Gold, 5 In.	40.00
Figurine, Pig, Sitting, 2nd Mark, Black, 2 3/4 x 4 1/2 In.	300.00
Figurine, Swan, Black Head, Yellow Bill, Gold Trim, 1st Mark, Black	195.00
Flower Holder, Sea Horse, Gilt & Bronze Design, 1st Mark, Black, 4 3/4 In., Pair	2530.00
Flowerpot, Applied Flowers, 3rd Mark, Black, 3 1/2 x 4 In.	260.00
Jam Jar, Cover, Shamrock, 7th Mark, Gold, 3 1/4 In.	60.00
Loving Cup, Floral, Pedestal, Handles, 1880-1910	385.00
Mug, Shamrock, Baby's, 3rd Mark, Black	100.00
Mug, Thorn, Twig Handle, 6th Mark, Green	16.00
Nut Dish, Neptune, 6th Mark, Green	16.00
Plate, Christmas, 1978, 1st Edition, 9 In.	75.00
Plate, Shell, Pink Trim, 4th Mark, Green	60.00
Plate, Tridacna, 1st Mark, Black, 6 In.	75.00
Sugar & Creamer, Ribbons, 4th Mark, Green	90.00
Teapot, Hexagonal, 2nd Mark, Black	635.00
Teapot, Neptune, Green Trim, 2nd Mark, Black	55.00
Vase, Aberdeen, Floral Design, 6th Mark, Green, 6 In.	145.00
Vase, Frog, 2nd Mark, Black, 5 In.	1000.00
Vase, Lily Pad Leaf, Cream, 3rd Mark, Black, 13 1/2 In.	385.00
Vase, Owl, 6th Mark, Green, 1965-1980, 8 1/4 In.	55.00
Vase, Prince Arthur, Applied Floral Design, 2nd Mark, Black, 10 1/2 In.	2415.00
Vase, Swan, 6th Mark, Green, 1965-1980, 5 3/4 x 4 1/4 In.	28.00
Vase, Swirl Pattern, Fluted Rim, Rose & Buds, 2nd Mark, Black, 4 1/2 x 5 In.	165.00

BENNINGTON ware was the product of two factories working in
Bennington, Vermont. Both the Norton Company and the Lyman
Fenton Company were out of business by 1896. The wares include
brown and yellow mottled pottery, Parian, scroddled ware, stoneware,
graniteware, yellowware, and Staffordshire-type vases. The name is

also a generic term for mottled brownware of the type made in Bennington.

Bed Pan, Brown Glaze, 1840-1860, 5 x 17 1/2 In.	22.00
Bottle, Coachman, Rockingham Glaze, Impressed 1849 Mark, 10 3/8 In.	250.00
Bowl & Pitcher Set, 12-Sided Bowl, Looped Edge Pitcher, 1849	3735.00
Candlestick, Column Form, Brown, Yellow, 9 1/2 In.	25.00
Coffeepot, Lid, 2-Hole Handle, Oatmeal, Golden Brown, Mottled	145.00
Crock, Dragonfly, No. 2	130.00
Crock, Spotted Dog, Ground Cover	3025.00
Figurine, Spaniel, Sitting On Raised Base, 10 In.	490.00
Flask, Book, Departed Spirits, Rockingham Glaze, Brown & Cream, 5 1/2 In.	200.00 to 425.00
Flask, Book, Life Of Kossuth, Brown, Green, Tan, Flint Enamel, 5 1/2 In.	748.00
Jug, E. Norton, Cobalt Blue Scroll, Applied Handle, 11 In.	385.00
Jug, Parrot, On Stump, Cobalt Blue, 2 Gal.	900.00
Pie Plate, Brown, Yellow, Cream Ground, 1849, 9 3/4 In.	225.00
Pitcher, Alternating Rib, Light Brown, Cream, 8 1/4 In.	50.00
Pitcher, Alternating Rib, Yellow, Brown, Black, Flint Enamel, 1849, 10 1/2 In.	460.00
Pitcher, Barrel Shape, Dark Brown, Cream, 6 In.	225.00
Pitcher, Tulip & Heart, Brown Highlights, Cream Ground, 1849, 7 In.	60.00
Pitcher & Bowl, 12-Sided Bowl, Scalloped Rim Pitcher	3737.00
Sugar, Cover, Alternate Rib, Brown, Yellow, Green, Flint Enamel, 1849, 6 1/2 In.	1610.00
Sugar, Flint Enamel, 19th Century	412.00
Teapot, Cover, Brown, Yellow, Cream, 9 In.	300.00
Tobacco Jar, Cover, Alternating Rib, Brown, Cream Glaze, 1849, 7 1/4 In.	350.00
Vase, Tulip, Protruding Ribs, Blue Green Highlights, Flint Enamel, 9 In.	195.00
Vase, White Grapes & Leaves, Blue Ground, 10 3/4 In.	400.00

BERLIN, a German porcelain factory, was started in 1751 by Wilhelm Kaspar Wegely. In 1763, the factory was taken over by Frederick the Great and became the Royal Berlin Porcelain Manufactory. It is still in operation today. Pieces have been marked in a variety of ways.

Plaque, Cavalier & Woman	3680.00
Plaque, Portrait, Profile Of Female, Oval, Giltwood Frame, 13 1/4 x 16 1/2 In.	1955.00
Plaque, Woodland Scene, 10 In.	3680.00
Plaque, Young Boy Holding Turnips, L. Kraus, Signed, 9 In.	2587.00
Plaque, Young Girl, Praying To Madonna, Signed, 10 x 16 In.	5175.00
Salt, Double, Shell, Gold & Blue Design, 6 1/2 In.	50.00

BESWICK started making earthenware in Staffordshire, England, in 1936. The company is now part of Royal Doulton Tableware, Ltd. Figurines of animals, especially dogs and horses, Beatrix Potter animals, and other wares are still being made.

Ashtray, Duck, No. 755, 4 In.	55.00
Bowl, Baby's, Humpty Dumpty	70.00
Cat, Ginger, Striped, No. 2559	85.00
Character Jug, Falstaff, No. 1126, 8 In.	175.00
Character Jug, Tony Weller, No. 281, 7 In.	175.00
Creamer, Pecksniff, No. 1117, 3 1/2 In.	25.00
Figurine, Amiable Guinea Pig, No. 2061, 3 1/2 In.	250.00 to 350.00
Figurine, Anna Maria, No. 1851, 3 In.	250.00 to 320.00
Figurine, Aunt Pettitoes, No. 2276, 3 3/4 In.	160.00
Figurine, Benjamin Bunny, No. 1105, 4 In.	55.00 to 120.00
Figurine, Bulldog, No. 1731, 2 1/2 In.	35.00
Figurine, Cat, White, No. 1876, 3 1/2 In.	75.00 to 80.00
Figurine, Cecily Parsley, No. 1941, 4 In.	55.00 to 150.00
Figurine, Cheshire Cat, No. 2480, 1 1/2 In.	625.00
Figurine, Chihuahua, No. 2454, 2 7/8 In.	55.00
Figurine, Chippy Hackee, No. 2927, 3 3/4 In.	70.00
Figurine, Cocker Spaniel, No. 967, 5 3/4 In.	45.00
Figurine, Cottontail, No. 2878, 3 1/2 In.	65.00
Figurine, Cousin Ribby, No. 2284, 3 1/4 In.	42.00
Figurine, Dachshund, No. 1460, 2 3/4 In.	85.00
Figurine, Dodo, No. 2545, 4 In.	265.00

Figurine, Fierce Bad Rabbit, No. 2586, 4 3/4 In. 120.00
Figurine, Flopsy, Mopsy Cottontail, No. 1274, 2 3/4 In. 290.00
Figurine, Foxy Whiskered Gentleman, No. 1277, 5 In. ....65.00 to 170.00
Figurine, Goody Tiptoes, No. 1675, 3 1/2 In. 170.00
Figurine, Gryphon, No. 2485, 3 1/4 In. 215.00
Figurine, Hunca Munca Sweeping, No. 2584, 3 1/8 In. 72.00
Figurine, Hunca Munca, No. 1198, 2 3/4 In. 42.00
Figurine, Indian, Elephant, Trunk Up, No. 1770, 12 In. 235.00
Figurine, Irish Setter, Sugar Of Wendover, No. 966, 5 3/4 In. 100.00
Figurine, Jemima Puddleduck, No. 1092, 4 1/4 In. ....30.00 to 85.00
Figurine, Johnny Townmouse, No. 1276, 3 1/2 In. ....50.00 to 95.00
Figurine, Lady Mouse, No. 1183, 4 In. 125.00
Figurine, Lady, Riding Donkey, No. 1244, 5 1/2 In. 225.00
Figurine, Lazybones, No. 2530, 1 5/8 In. 60.00
Figurine, Little Black Rabbit, No. 2586, 4 3/4 In. ....40.00 to 100.00
Figurine, Mad Hatter, No. 2479, 4 1/4 In. 295.00
Figurine, Mrs. Flopsy Bunny, No. 1942, 4 In. 125.00
Figurine, Mrs. Tiggy Winkle, No. 1107, 3 1/4 In. ....100.00 to 215.00
Figurine, Mrs. Tittlemouse, No. 1103, 3 3/4 In. ....80.00 to 125.00
Figurine, Old English Sheep Dog, No. 453, 8 1/2 In. 110.00
Figurine, Old Mr. Brown, No. 1796, 3 1/4 In. ....75.00 to 140.00
Figurine, Old Woman Who Lived In A Shoe, No. 2804, 3 In. ....50.00 to 125.00
Figurine, Owl, No. 2026, 4 1/2 In. 58.00
Figurine, Peter Rabbit, No. 1098, 4 1/2 In. ....60.00 to 90.00
Figurine, Pickles, No. 2334, 4 1/2 In. 350.00
Figurine, Pig-Wig, No. 2381, 4 In. 450.00
Figurine, Poorly Peter Rabbit, No. 2560, 3 1/2 In. 40.00
Figurine, Rebeccah Puddleduck, No. 2647, 3 1/4 In. ....30.00 to 45.00
Figurine, Sally Hennypenny, No. 2452, 4 In. 50.00
Figurine, Samuel Whiskers, No. 1106, 3 1/2 In. 50.00
Figurine, Shetland Pony, No. 1033, 5 3/4 In. 100.00
Figurine, Siamese Cat, Climbing, No. 2301, 4 1/2 In. 25.00
Figurine, Sir Isaac Newton, No. 2425, 3 7/8 In. ....200.00 to 395.00
Figurine, Squirrel Nutkin, No. 1102, 3 3/4 In. ....30.00 to 70.00
Figurine, Stallion, No. 1992, 5 1/2 In. 100.00
Figurine, Tabitha Twitchett, No. 1676, 3 1/2 In. ....165.00 to 220.00
Figurine, Tailor Of Gloucester, No. 1108, 3 3/4 In. ....95.00 to 140.00
Figurine, Thomasina Tittlemouse, No. 2668, 3 1/4 In. 90.00
Figurine, Timmy Tiptoes, No. 1101, 3 3/4 In. ....70.00 to 140.00
Figurine, Timmy Willie, No. 1109, 3 In. ....50.00 to 150.00
Figurine, Tom Kitten, No. 1100, 3 1/2 In. ....120.00 to 150.00
Figurine, Tom Thumb, No. 2989, 3 In. 200.00
Mug, Juliet, No. 1215, 4 In. 50.00
Pitcher, Robert Burns, Saying On Reverse, No. 1045, 8 In. 245.00
Salt & Pepper, Mr. Micawber, No. 690 & Sairey Gamp, No. 689 .... 75.00
Sugar & Creamer, Pecksniff 43.00
Teapot, Sairey Gamp, No. 691, 5 3/4 In. 80.00

BETTY BOOP, the cartoon figure, first appeared on the screen in 1931.
Her face was modeled after the famous singer Helen Kane and her
body after Mae West. In 1935, a comic strip was started. Her dog was
named Bimbo. Although the Betty Boop cartoons ended by 1938, there
was a revival of interest in the Betty Boop image in the 1980s and new
pieces are being made.

Big Little Book, Miss Gulliver's Travels, Betty, Max Fleischer, 1935, 286 Pages 92.00
Box, Cover, 60 Years 35.00
Clock, Alarm, Box, 5 In. 20.00
Clock, Betty & Bimbo 35.00
Cookie Jar, Betty's Kitchen 50.00
Cookie Jar, Holiday 50.00
Cookie Jar, Miranda, Vandor 995.00
Cookie Jar, Standing, Vandor 600.00

Dish, Class, Hand Painted, Nippon, 5 3/4 In. 45.00
Doll, Bobbin' Head 22.00
Figurine, Betty & Pudgy, In Red Convertible, Ceramic 32.00
Figurine, Candleholder, Betty In Flowing Gown, Vandor, 1981, 8 In. 65.00
Guitar, 1930s 325.00
Jewelry, Stickpin, Red Dress 76.00
Lunch Box 10.00
Mug, Head, 1981 . . . . 25.00
Napkin Holder 12.00
Night-Light, Betty, Wearing Pink Dress 80.00
Nodder, Cowgirl, Vandor, 7 In. 22.00
Ornament, Christmas, Betty, Sitting On Candy Cane 6.00
Salt & Pepper, Luster 35.00
Spoon Rest 10.00
String Holder, Vandor 65.00
Sugar & Creamer, Vandor 35.00
Tray, Betty As Santa Claus, Sack With Donald Duck Toy, Tin, 1950s, 6 1/4 x 3/4 In. 85.00
Vase, Betty Sitting On Piano, Vandor, 1981, 7 x 4 In. 115.00

BICYCLES were invented in 1839. The first manufactured bicycle was
made in 1861. Special ladies' bicycles were made after 1874. The
modern safety bicycle was not produced until 1885. Collectors search
for all types of bicycles and tricycles. Bicycle-related items are also
listed here.

Banner, Columbia Chainless Bicycles, Hanging, 40 x 84 In. 1380.00
Colson-Firestone, Bullnose, Girl's, Whitewall Tires, c.1939 . . . . .770.00 to 775.00
Columbia, 3-Star Deluxe, Boy's, c.1950, 26 In. 330.00
Columbia, Highwheel, 8 Ft. 4900.00
Columbia, Special Deluxe, Red, White, Original Labels, Rear Baskets, c.1940 . . . . 220.00
Firestone, Pilot, Boy's, Red & White, Basket, Carrier, 26 In. 165.00
Indian, Twin Bar, Waterbury Motor Clock On Handle Bars, 1937 . . . . 3450.00
J.C. Higgins, Deluxe, Boy's, With Spring, 1949 . . . . 550.00
J.C. Higgins, Girl's, Cream, Gray & Red, c.1948, 26 In. . . . . .90.00 to 110.00
Lamp, Carbide, Marked Lucas, Silver King, Birmingham, Brass, Nickel Plate, 5 In. 94.00
Lamp, Mathews & Williams, Oil, Bronze Burner, 1897 . . . . 180.00
Mead Cycle Co., Mead Price Ranger, 1953 . . . . 2185.00
Monark, Silver King, Gene Autry Westerner, 1950 . . . . 2990.00
Monark, Silver King, Girl's, Aluminum, 1938, 24 In. 1800.00
Poster, Cleveland Cycle, Indian, Riding Bicycle Looking Back, Paper, 58 x 43 In. 2015.00
Poster, Cleveland Cycle, Man, Riding Cleveland Bicycle, 49 x 36 In. 975.00
Roadmaster, Girl's, Blue 225.00
Schwinn, Black Phantom, Accessories 1650.00
Schwinn, Black Phantom, Model B-17 . . . . 9200.00
Schwinn, Cycle Truck, Large Front Basket, 1967 . . . . 2185.00
Schwinn, Green Phantom, 1954 . . . . 4370.00
Schwinn, Jaguar, Red, 3 Speeds 275.00
Schwinn, Man's, Cruiser, 5 Speeds, Blue, Whitewall Tires, Chrome Fenders 300.00
Schwinn, Orange Krate, 1968 . . . . 850.00
Schwinn, Panther, Blue & Green, 1958 . . . . 375.00
Schwinn, Stingray, Lemon Peeler, Gear Shift On Bars 3450.00
Schwinn, Whizzer, Maroon, Speedometer, Steering Lock, 1948 . . . . 6600.00
Schwinn, Woman's, Starlet, No. D-67, 1951, 73 1/2 x 23 x 42 In. 1100.00
Sears, Girl's, Wooden Rims, Fenders, Guards, All Original, 1906 . . . . 1000.00
Sherrell Classic, 1980 . . . . 3220.00
Sign, Raleigh Bicycle, Black Man, Riding Away On Bicycle, 24 x 36 In. 690.00
Tricycle, Child's, Black Metal Frame, Spoke Wheels, Wood Hand Grips, Leather Seat . . . 220.00
Tricycle, Firestone, Chrome, Black Paint, White Seat, 1950s, 25 In. 130.00
Tricycle, Garton, 1950s 50.00
Tricycle, Kilgore, Cast Iron 100.00
Velocipede, Horse, Cast Iron Head, Wooden Body, 28 In. 275.00

BING & GRONDAHL is a famous Danish factory making fine porcelains from 1853 to the present. Underglaze blue decoration was started in 1886. The annual Christmas plate series was introduced in 1895. Dinnerwares, stoneware, and figurines are still being made today. The firm has used the initials B & G and a stylized castle as part of the mark since 1898.

MADE IN
DENMARK

Bell, Christmas, 1st Edition	30.00
Bowl, Vegetable, Square	110.00
Bread Plate, Sea Gull	20.00
Cake Plate, Sea Gull, Dolphin Handles, Gold Design	60.00
Compote, Flying Seagulls, 3 Dolphins Base, Blue, White, 4 x 5 1/2 In.	50.00
Cup & Saucer, Sea Gull	48.00 to 50.00
Decanter, Cherry Heering	95.00
Figurine, Cat, Siamese, No. 2256, 7 1/2 In.	150.00
Figurine, Dog, Bulldog, No. 1676, 3 In.	95.00
Figurine, Dog, Cairn Terrier	200.00
Figurine, Dog, Terrier, No. 3170	225.00
Figurine, Dog, Wolfhound, Recumbent	120.00
Figurine, Else, No. 1574, 6 1/2 In.	275.00
Figurine, Goosegirl, No. 2254, 9 1/4 In.	350.00
Figurine, Gray Lamb, No. 2171, Signed KJ, 2 3/4 In.	55.00
Figurine, Love Refused, No. 1614	135.00
Figurine, Mary, No. 1721, 7 1/4 In.	300.00
Figurine, Penguin, No. 1822, 9 3/4 In.	400.00
Figurine, Reading Children, No. 1567, 3 3/4 In.	100.00
Plate, Arrival Of Christmas Guests, 1969	35.00
Plate, Christmas, 1900, Church Bells	950.00
Plate, Christmas, 1901, 3 Wise Men	500.00
Plate, Christmas, 1902, Interior Of Gothic Church	435.00
Plate, Christmas, 1907, Little Match Girl	165.00
Plate, Christmas, 1915, Dog Getting Double Meal	135.00
Plate, Christmas, 1922, Star Of Bethlehem	70.00
Plate, Christmas, 1934, Church Bell In Tower	250.00
Plate, Christmas, 1941, Horses Enjoying Christmas Meal	250.00
Plate, Christmas, 1942, Danish Farm On Christmas Night	250.00
Plate, Christmas, 1945, Old Water Mill	225.00
Plate, Christmas, 1950 To 1985, Collection	2000.00
Plate, Christmas, 1953, Royal Boat	125.00
Plate, Christmas, 1960, Danish Village Church	165.00
Plate, Christmas, 1961, Winter Harmony	115.00
Plate, Christmas, 1963, Christmas Elf	65.00 to 120.00
Plate, Christmas, 1968, Christmas In Church, 7 1/8 In.	11.00
Plate, Christmas, 1972, Christmas In Greenland	18.00
Plate, Christmas, 1980, Christmas In The Woods	30.00
Plate, Mother's Day, 1975	25.00

BINOCULARS of all types are wanted by collectors. Those made in the eighteenth and nineteenth centuries are favored by serious collectors. The small, attractive binoculars called *opera glasses* are listed in their own category.

Bausch & Lomb, FJA 7 x 50, Black, 1942, 7 x 5 In.	90.00
Bell & Howell, 8 x 40 In.	75.00
Crown, 10 x 50 In.	70.00
Leather Case, Tower Optics, 1938-1947	38.00
Lens Fold, L.A. Retni, c.1860	110.00
Naval, Marked U.S. Navy, B.O. Ships, World War II, Pair	16.00
Scope Pockette Folding Sports Glass, Model No. 2379, Box, Japan	20.00
Sears Roebuck, Case, 10 x 50 In.	65.00
Swift, Triton, 7 x 35 BCF, Black, Brown Case, Display Box, Japan, 5 x 6 In.	29.00
U.S. Army, Signal Corp, Bausch & Lomb	65.00
Zeiss, 6 x 30 In.	60.00

IRDCAGES are collected for use as homes for pet birds and as decorave objects of folk art. Elaborate wooden cages of the past centuries an still be found. The brass or wicker cages of the 1930s are popular /ith bird owners.

2 Tiers, Cleaning Tray, Wood & Wire, Painted Gray, 19th Century, 37 In.	210.00
Copper, Arts & Crafts, 1910	495.00
Dove, Green Paint	485.00
Hendryx, Brass, With Stand, Signed	250.00
Hendryx, Chinese Style, Brass Plated, Tubular Design, 2 Feeders, 1910-1920	125.00
Plastic, Metal Bottom Tray, 1950s, Small	85.00
Serpentine Crest, Giltwood Spread Winged Eagle, Mahogany, 23 x 30 3/4 In.	862.00
Tin, Cylindrical, Ring Handle, 20 In.	110.00
Tin, Painted, Victorian	175.00
Tin & Wire, Yellow, Blue & White, 16 In.	50.00
Wire, Wood, Domed Top, Hanging Spring Dangles, 23 In.	275.00
Wire, Yellow & Blue Paint, Revolving Treadmill	245.00
Wood, Birds, Pine, 1 Sliding Door, Victorian, 16 x 9 3/4 In.	1380.00

ISQUE is an unglazed baked porcelain. Finished bisque has a slightly andy texture with a dull finish. Some of it may be decorated with varous colors. Bisque gained favor during the late Victorian era when housands of bisque figurines were made. It is still being made. additional bisque items may be listed under the factory name.

Figurine, Boy & Ram, England, c.1840, 7 In.	2750.00
Figurine, Boy, Carrying Blue Hat, Blue Flower, Pastel Blue Clothes, 3 3/8 In.	145.00
Figurine, Cupid, Blue Wings, Hands On Green Shell, 4 1/2 x 3 1/2 In.	45.00
Figurine, Girl With Cat & Boy With Dog, Germany, 9 In., Pair	175.00
Figurine, Googly, Boy, Orange Suit, Holding Hat & Umbrella, Germany, 5 In.	28.00
Figurine, The Moon In Bad Spirits, Germany, 7 1/2 In.	94.00
Figurine, Woman, Naughty, Reclining, Long Blue Stockings, Germany, 3 3/4 In.	28.00
Match Holder, Colonial Man & Woman Leaning Out Window, Striker	45.00
Powder Box, Porcelain Angel, 4 1/2 In.	35.00

BLACK memorabilia has become an important area of collecting since he 1970s. The best material dates from past centuries, but many recent items are also of interest. F & F is the mark used on plastic made by Fiedler & Fiedler Mold & Die Works, Inc. in the 1930s and 1940s. Objects that picture a black person may also be listed in this book under Advertising; Tins; Banks; Bottle Openers; Cookie Jars; Salt & Pepper; Sheet Music; etc.

Album, Postcards, From 1920s, 1930s, 1940s, 75 Piece	3395.00
Album, Tip Top Entertainment & Minstrel Album, Songs, Wrapper, 1936, 66 Pages	57.00
Ashtray, Boy Sitting Over Bedpan, 1 1/2 x 3 In.	35.00
Ashtray, Boys On Clothesline, 2 x 2 In.	35.00
Ashtray, Coon Chicken Inn, Black Head, 1940-1951, 3 1/2 In.	20.00
Ashtray, Old Sambo, Cake, Logo, Man Smoking Pipe, Yellow Glass, 6 x 4 1/2 In.	82.00
Biscuit Jar, Mammy, Googly-Eye	975.00
Book, Little Black Sambo, c.1930	95.00
Booklet, Sex & Civil Rights, True Selma Story, 1965, 32 Pages, 8 1/2 x 11 In.	50.00
Box, Recipe, Mammy, Yellow Plastic	135.00
Card, Playing, St. Louis Southwestern Rwy., Cottonbelt Route, Box, 1903	500.00
Card, Thurgood Marshal, Autograph, 6 x 4 1/2 In.	110.00
Christmas Card, Mammy, With Poem, 1890, 3 x 4 In.	65.00
Clothespin Holder, Mammy, Doll Form	40.00
Coat Rack, Sambo's Restaurant	125.00
Container, Nigger Head Stove Polish, Tin, 3 In.	44.00
Cookie Jars are listed in the Cookie Jar category.	
Creamer, Mammy, Plastic, F & F Mold, 5 1/4 In.	85.00
Cup & Saucer, Child's, Golliwog, Children Playing, Radio Series, England	110.00
Cutout, Girl, 3-Dimensional Wheelbarrow, Painted, 11 1/2 In.	33.00
Diploma, Yazoo City, Miss. Colored School, Willis Laws, 1921, 12 x 16 In.	138.00

Dispenser, Cigarette 1250.00
Document, Slavery, Bill Of Sale, Hand Written, 1812, 7 3/4 x 12 1/4 In. 402.00
Doll, Baby, Cloth, Red Mouth, Red & White Striped Pants, Blue Coat, 1940s, 11 1/2 In. . 80.00
Doll, Bisque, Brown Sleep Eyes, Black Skin, Wig, Ball-Jointed Body, 17 In. 4500.00
Doll, Child, Wooden Head, Cloth Body, Fiber Hair, Apple On Shirt, 10 In. 30.00
Doll, Composition Head, Googly-Eye, Red Painted Mouth, Straw Stuffed, 19 In. 1250.00
Doll, Composition, Bent Limb, Jointed, Painted Eyes, 1930s, 10 In. 110.00
Doll, Golliwog, Red Velvet Jacket, Plays Music, Merry Thought, Tag On Foot, 18 In. 475.00
Doll, Mammy, Cloth Stuffed, Vinyl, Flowered Dress, White Scarf, Apron, 1930s, 17 In. .. 85.00
Doll, Mammy, Stitched Red Fabric Shoes, Flowered Dress, Apron, 1930s, 17 In. 85.00
Doll, Papier-Mache, Hinged Jaw, Muslin Body, Porter's Outfit, Germany, c.1885, 12 In. .. 500.00
Doll, Wax Head & Hands, Cloth Body, Googly-Eye, 17 In. 750.00
Fan, Darkie Toothpaste, Black Man In Top Hat, Wooden Handle, 13 In. 29.00
Figurine, Blackamoor With Tray, Cast Iron, Hoefinchoff & Lane Foundry Co., Cin., Oh. . 550.00
Figurine, Boy In Outhouse With Boy On Side, One Moment Please 35.00
Figurine, Boy, Eating Watermelon, 2 1/2 In. 35.00
Figurine, Boy, Hugging Toilet, Nest, Gloss Finish, 1 In. 35.00
Figurine, Boy, On Toilet, You're Next, 3 In. 35.00
Figurine, Man, Holding Guitar, Wooden, Metal, 7 In. 65.00
Flour Sack, Aunt Jemima, 1917-1932 .... 650.00
Game, Snake Eyes 60.00
Glass, Coon Chicken 70.00
Glass, Coon Chicken Inn, Black Head 30.00
Glass, Water, Coon Chicken Inn 10.00
Humidor, Minstrel Man, Bisque, c.1920 .... 750.00
Inkwell, Black Boy, Cast Iron 395.00
Jar, Dresser, Heart Shape, Butler On Top 350.00
Letter Opener, Darkie With Alligator, Head Pulls To Reveal Pencil, Celluloid, 5 3/4 In. . 82.00
Menu, Coon Chicken Inn 125.00
Menu, Coon Chicken Inn, Child's 45.00
Mug, Chocolate, Black Face, Large 25.00
Mug, Coffee, Sambo's Stars & Stripes 40.00
Nodder, Boy, Papier-Mache, Felt & Cotton Outfit, c.1900, 24 In. 1265.00
Note Pad, Mammy 35.00
Paperweight, Mammy, Lead, 2 1/2 In. 125.00
Pencil Holder, Boy & Girl, Chalkware, 10 In. 125.00
Photograph, Amos 'n' Andy, Sepia, 1930s, 7 x 5 In. 25.00
Pie Bird, Chef 75.00
Pin, Aunt Jemima Breakfast Club, Eat A Better Breakfast, 4 In. 35.00
Pin, Boy, With Pancakes, Employee, Sambo's Restaurant 45.00
Pip-Squeak, Composition Face On Wooden Chair, 4 1/4 In. 16.00
Pitcher, Syrup, Mammy, F & F, 6 In. 55.00
Place Mat, Coon Chicken Inn ....45.00 to 85.00
Planter, Plaid Mammy, Japan 60.00
Plaque, Little Black Sambo, Chalkware 30.00
Plate, Sambo's Restaurant, 8 1/2 In. 65.00
Postcard, Booker T. Washington, Biography, Titled Tuskegee Institute, Portrait 275.00
Postcard, Man, Striking Both Mother-In-Law & Turkey On Head, Color, 1930s 23.00
Postcard, Martin Luther King Memorial, I Have A Dream, King In Front Of Flag, 1968 . 4.00
Postcard, Sambo's Restaurant, Little Black Sambo, 8 Piece 65.00
Postcard, Thanksgiving, Black Chef Cooking Turkey, 1920 .... 20.00
Poster, Black Liberation, Sons Of Malcom, 1960s, 17 1/2 x 22 1/2 In. 80.00
Poster, Black Power, 1971, 21 x 23 In. 35.00
Poster, NAACP vs. A & P, Red & White Picket Line, 1969, 14 x 22 In. 25.00
Print, Edward W. Kemblekembeles Coons, Caricatures Of Black People, 1896 .... 100.00
Radio Script, Amos 'n' Andy, Amos' Wedding, Photo On Front, 1930s, 6 Pages 23.00
Radio Script, Amos 'n' Andy, Christmas 45.00
Shelf Sitter, Boy Eating Melon, Bisque, 1 In. 22.00
Shoeshine Box, Mason's Blacking, Labels 165.00
Shopping List, Pegboard, Wooden, Painted Mammy, We Needs, 1940s 60.00
Slave Badge, Copper, Marked 689 Servant, Charleston, South Carolina, 1815, 2 In. 2000.00
Snow Dome, Black Musician 45.00
Soup Spoon, Coon Chicken Inn, Silver Plate 75.00

Spice Set, Cat, Yellow Eyes, Wooden Rack, 6 Piece	110.00
Spoon, Boy, Silver Sterling	90.00
Spoon Rest, Mammy & Chef, Cast Iron, Pair	195.00
Spooner, Boy Eating Watermelon	125.00
Spooner, Winking Eye Mammy	95.00
Sprinkler Bottle, Mammy	325.00
String Holder, Plaid Apron, Polka Dot Shirt, Japan	185.00
Sugar & Creamer, Clown	50.00
Sugar Shaker, Mammy, Bulbous, Chalkware	45.00
Syrup, Dispenser, Aunt Jemima	75.00
Tag, Slave, Hand Engraved, Die Punched Registration Number, Copper, 1833	3975.00
Taxi, Amos 'n' Andy, Box, 3 1/2 x 5 1/2 x 8 In.	900.00
Teapot, Googly-Eyed	400.00
Thermos Only, Sambo's Restaurant, Brown, Beige Trim	38.00
Toaster Cover, Mammy	45.00
Toothpaste, Darkie, Box	26.00
Towel, Kitchen, 1940s	150.00
Tray, Mammy, Cast Iron, 8 3/4 In.	120.00
Tumbler, Coon Chicken Inn	50.00
Watch, Amos 'n' Andy, Pocket	145.00

BLACK AMETHYST glass appears black until it is held to the light, then a dark purple can be seen. It has been made in many factories from 1860 to the present.

Box, Rose On Hinged Cover, Enameled Leaf Sprays At Sides, 3 In., Pair	190.00
Loving Cup, Dancing Nudes, 2 Handles	110.00
Pomade Jar, Bear Shape, Eugene Bize & Fricke, 4 5/8 In.	465.00
Ring Tree, Lacy Gold Vines, Enameled Leaves & Flowers, 3 7/8 In.	88.00
Vase, Sterling Silver Overlay, c.1910, 10 1/2 In.	215.00

BLOWN GLASS, see Glass-Blown category.

BLUE GLASS, see Cobalt Blue category.

BLUE ONION, see Onion category.

BLUE WILLOW, see Willow category.

BOCH FRERES factory was founded in 1841 in La Louviere in eastern Belgium. The wares resemble the work of Villeroy & Boch. The factory is still in business.

Inkwell, Floral Design, White, Cobalt Blue, Stoneware, 1841-1889, 8 3/4 In.	110.00
Lamp, Art Deco, 21 In.	245.00

BOEHM is the collector's name for the porcelains of Edward Marshall Boehm. In 1953 the Osso China Company was reorganized as Edward Marshall Boehm, Inc. The company is still working in England and New Jersey. In the early days of the factory, dishes were made, but the elaborate and lifelike bird figurines are the best-known ware. Edward Marshall Boehm, the founder, died in 1969, but the firm has continued to design and produce porcelain. Today, the firm makes both limited and unlimited editions of figurines and plates.

Figurine, Baby Blue Bird, No. 442	70.00
Figurine, Baby Wood Thrush, No. 444	85.00
Figurine, Beverly Sills, 12 In.	1200.00
Figurine, Cocker Spaniel, 1961	120.00
Figurine, Cygnet On Lily Pad, 4 3/8 In.	137.00
Figurine, Fledgling Kingfisher, No. 449, 6 In.	115.00
Figurine, Fledgling Magpie, No. 476	60.00
Figurine, Fledgling Robin, No. 40231	88.00
Figurine, French Poodle, Lying, Bisque, 5 In.	75.00
Figurine, Giant Panda, Reclining, 8 x 6 In.	650.00
Figurine, Indigo Bunting, No. 429	60.00
Figurine, Koala, 9 x 8 1/2 In.	750.00

Figurine, Madonna La Pietz, 4 1/2 In. 112.00
Figurine, Nuthatch 270.00
Figurine, Rabbit At Rest, No. 400-87 . . . . 115.00
Figurine, Sleeping Baby Rabbit 175.00
Figurine, Sparrows, With Tulips, Pair 8625.00
Figurine, Tumbler Pigeon, 8 x 8 1/2 In. 750.00
Figurine, Woman, Kneeling, Arms Full Of Flowers, Dotted Head Scarf, 6 In. 105.00
Figurine, Young American Bald Eagle, Perched On Rock, 9 In. 230.00
Pitcher, White Rose Panel, 7 In. 150.00
Tureen, Cover, Duck Form, Water Lilies At Base, 9 x 13 In.. 630.00

BOHEMIAN GLASS is an ornate overlay or flashed glass made during
the Victorian era. It has been reproduced in Bohemia, which is now a
part of the Czech Republic. Glass made from 1875 to 1900 is preferred
by collectors.

Ashtray, Turtle, Crystal, Gold Labels, 4 Piece 35.00
Biscuit Jar, Arabic Oasis, Camel & Rider, Pyramid, Silver Plated Top, Signed 195.00
Bowl, Cover, Foliate Design, Gold, Red, Blue, Green, 5 1/2 x 6 1/2 In. 632.00
Bowl, Cranberry Cut To Clear, 9 x 3 1/2 In. 121.00
Brandy Set, Etched Vintage Grape, Decanter, 6 Footed Glasses, Ruby 195.00
Compote, Forest Scene With Deer, Scalloped Rim, Amber, 12 x 9 1/2 In. 525.00
Cordial Set, Hand Painted Blackheath Golfer, Stopper, 1920s, 5 Piece 350.00
Cracker Jar, Cover, Thumbprint, Deer, Foliate Motif, Amber, 8 3/4 In. 100.00
Creamer, Bird Scene 55.00
Decanter, Bird, Monkey, Flowers, Stopper, 15 1/2 In. 115.00
Decanter, Grape Design, Ruby, Frosted 75.00
Ewer, Ruby Engraved To Clear, 2 Deer In Landscape, 9 In. 100.00
Jar, Cover, Faceted Panels, Amber, 10 3/4 In. 345.00
Mug, Forest Scene With Deer, Applied Handle, Amber, 5 3/4 In. 250.00
Pitcher, Crystal, Gold Foliate Design, Applied Gold Blossoms, 6 1/4 In. 400.00
Sugar Shaker, Red To Clear, 6 In. 210.00
Urn, Domed Lid, Carved Forest Scene With Deer, Red Cut To Clear, 18 3/4 In. 850.00
Vase, Black Opaque, White Ibis, Blue Floral, 7 In., Pair 138.00
Vase, Blown Apple, Green, Red, Amber, Bulb Body, 12 In. 172.00
Vase, Conical Body, Gold Iridescent Interior, Applied Pedestal Foot, 6 In. 287.00
Vase, Griffins, Swags, Broad Medial Band, Gold Enamel, 10 In. 374.00
Vase, Iridescent Gold Tone Surface, 8 In. 260.00
Vase, Medallions, Enameled, Striated Blue, Green, Burgundy, Red, Oval, 8 3/4 In. 316.00
Vase, Pillow, Black Opaque, White Enamel Floral, Fauna, 8 1/4 In., Pair 110.00
Vase, Recessed Blossoms & Leaves, Lined In Frosted Ruby Red, 12 1/2 In. 400.00
Vase, Silver Leaf Design, Blue Birds, Flowers, 15 In. 412.00

BONE DISHES were considered a necessary part of a table setting for
the Victorian table. The crescent-shaped dish was kept at the edge of
the dinner plate so the bones removed from the fish could be stored
away from the uneaten food. Some bone dishes were made in more
fanciful shapes and many resemble fish.

Plate, Cobalt Blue Flowers, White Center, Gold Scalloped Trim, 1921, 8 In. 6.50
Flow Blue, Louise 25.00

BOOKENDS have probably been used since books became inexpensive.
Early libraries kept books in cupboards, not on open shelves. By the
1870s bookends appeared, especially homemade fret-carved wooden
examples. Most bookends listed in this book date from the twentieth
century. Bookends are also listed in other categories by manufacturer
or material.

Baby Shoes, Bronze Finish, Perma Plated Product, 6 1/2 x 3 3/4 In. . . . . *Illus* 15.00
Black Clown, Tambourine, Lute, Ceramic, 6 x 4 1/2 x 2 1/2 In. 30.00
Cat, Stretching, Copper Clad, Weighted 70.00
Chief Of Police, Bronze Finish, Cast Iron 60.00
Dartmouth College, Iron 43.00
Dog, Stylized, Art Deco, Bronze, Franklin 225.00
Elderly Gentleman, Reading, Seated, Bronze Finish, 7 x 6 In. 75.00

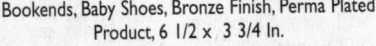

Bookends, Baby Shoes, Bronze Finish, Perma Plated Product, 6 1/2 x 3 3/4 In.

Bookends, Sailing Ship, Bronze Finish, G. Luntz Brass Foundry, Cleveland, 6 x 8 In.

End Of Trail, Cast Iron	65.00
Fish, Hand-Pounded Brass, E.T.C., 5 x 4 In.	125.00
Fisherman, With Rope, Old Salt, Painted, Iron	125.00
George Washington, Bradley & Hubbard, 5 3/8 x 4 1/2 In.	125.00
George Washington, Red, White & Blue Enamel, Brass, 1932	85.00
Golfers, Cast Iron	80.00
Grecian Woman Beside Urns, Embossed, Bradley & Hubbard	80.00
Horse, Rearing, Stylized, Cast Metal, Black Enamel Mane & Tail, Art Deco, 7 In.	575.00
Hunting Dog, Stamped Made In Austria, Bronze, c.1920, 6 In.	345.00
Hunting Dogs, Bronze, Rosewood Stand, Signed	795.00
Indian, Signed & Dated, West, Bronze Finish, 1913, 6 x 7 3/4 In.	185.00
Indian On Horse, Appeal To Great Spirit, Spelter	70.00
John F. Kennedy, White Metal, Brass Toned, Tan Onyx Base, New Diamond, 7 In.	55.00
Liberty Bell, Iron	125.00
Lincoln, Lincoln National Insurance, Bronze Finish, Metal	25.00
Lion's Head, Brass, Hollow, 4 1/2 x 5 In.	125.00
Monks Reading By Bookcase, Bronze Finish, 1922	40.00
Nudes, Full Figure, Cast Iron, 1930s	150.00
Owl, Sliding, Adjustable, Bronze Finish & Brass	125.00
Parrot, Cast Iron, 6 1/2 In.	350.00
Parrots On Fanned Books, White Metal, Painted, Pair	88.00
Penguin, Chromed Metal, 1940-1950, 4 1/4 In.	141.00
Pirate, Enamel Paint On Metal, 1940s	125.00
Rabbits, Lying Flat, Crystal, 5 3/4 In.	88.00
Ram's Head, Royal Copley	55.00
Rams At Gate, Patinated Copper Over Plaster, J.K. Krupka, 1914, 7 1/2 x 8 1/4 In.	575.00
Sailboats, Cast Iron	95.00
Sailing Ship, Bronze Finish, G. Luntz Brass Foundry, Cleveland, 6 x 8 In. ....*Illus*	55.00
Seated Antelope, Spray Of Leaves, Edgar Brandt, Bronze, 1920s, 6 5/8 In.	6560.00
Setters, Dexter Washer Advertising On Side, Hubley	175.00
Shakespeare, Bronzed Cast Iron, Bradley & Hubbard	140.00
Ship, Bradley & Hubbard	120.00
Snoopy & Woodstock, Heart Shaped Back, Ceramic, Base, Hong Kong, Pair	30.00
Stylized Pelican, Open Beak, Wrought Iron, Edgar Brandt, 1920s, 6 3/4 In.	4685.00
Sunbonnet Girl, Pink Dress, Cast Iron, 6 In.	350.00
Young Woman's Head With Butterfly, Wooden, Carved, Gold Paint, 7 3/4 In.	60.00

BOOKMARKS were originally made of parchment, cloth, or leather. Soon woven silk ribbon, thin cardboard, celluloid, wood, silver, tortoiseshell, and metals were used. Examples made before 1850 are scarce, but there are many to be found dating before 1920.

Butterfly Shape, Plastic & Paper, Treasure Island, Logo, Envelope	39.00
Calendar, 1901, Welsback Oil Lamps, Celluloid, Woman Reading	45.00
Cartier, Elephant Finial, 14K Yellow Gold, Engraved, Aug. 11, 1945, 3 5/8 In.	110.00
Columbus Commemorative, Silk, 1792-1892	70.00
John Wayne, Rio Lobo Style Clothes, Figural, Brass, 3 1/4 In., 5 Piece	26.00
Paris Exposition	32.00

BOSSONS character wall masks, plaques, figurines, and other decorative pieces are made by W.H. Bossons, Limited of Congleton, England. The company was founded in 1946 and is still working.

Wall Figure, Desert Hunters, 7 In.	50.00
Wall Figure, Lords Of Desert, 10 In.	60.00
Wall Figure, Pathan, 11 In.	60.00
Wall Mask, Kurd, 5 1/2 In.	40.00
Wall Mask, Mr. Bumble, Charles Dickens Series, 5 In.	30.00
Wall Mask, Pirate, Wearing Turban, Earring, 5 In.	100.00

BOSTON & SANDWICH CO. pieces may be found in the Sandwich Glass category.

BOTTLE collecting has become a major American hobby. There are several general categories of bottles, such as historic flasks, bitters, household, and figural. Pyro is the shortened form of the word pyroglaze, an enameled lettering used on bottles after the mid-1930s. For more bottle prices, see the book *Kovels' Bottles Price List* by Ralph and Terry Kovel.

Apothecary, Pillar Mold, 8 Ribs, Applied Finial Cover, Pittsburgh, 17 3/4 In.	1265.00
Apothecary, Stacking, Thick Glass, Turn Of The Century	230.00

Avon started in 1886 as the California Perfume Company. It was not until 1929 that the name *Avon* was used. In 1939, it became Avon Products, Inc. Avon has made many figural bottles filled with cosmetic products. Ceramic, plastic, and glass bottles were made in limited editions.

$\mathcal{A}$von

Avon, Bell, Dinner, 1980, Navarre	55.00
Avon, Bell, Dinner, Navarre, 1980	55.00
Avon, Charlie Brown, Bubble Bath, Plastic, 1970s, 6 In.	25.00
Avon, Dinosaur, Bubble Bath, Triceratops, Brontosaurus, Tyrannosaurus, Box, 3 Piece	20.00
Avon, Linus, Peanuts, Bubble Bath, Hard Plastic, Painted, Box, 1970s, 6 In.	20.00 to 35.00
Avon, Lucy, Peanuts, Bubble Bath, Hard Plastic, Painted, 1970s, 6 In.	25.00 to 30.00
Avon, Pistol, 1850 Pepper Box, Figural, Cologne, Box	35.00
Avon, Skunk, Plastic, Pinback, 1972	34.00
Avon, Sniffy, Linus, Shampoo, No-Tear, 1970, 4 Oz.	9.00
Avon, Stein, Blacksmith, 1985, 8 1/2 In.	6.00
Avon, Stein, Christopher Columbus, Box, 1992, 12 In.	12.00
Avon, Stein, Ducks Of American Wilderness, Box, 1988, 8 In.	26.00
Avon, Stein, Great American Football, Box, 1983, 9 In.	16.00
Avon, Stein, Shipbuilder, 1986, 8 1/2 In.	19.00
Avon, Stein, Tribute To Airplanes, 1981, 9 1/2 In.	10.00
Barber, Amethyst, White Victorian Woman, Mary Gregory Type, Bulbous, 7 1/2 In.	210.00
Barber, Bay Rum, Opaque Blue, Woman Label Under Glass, Gilt, 10 7/8 In.	990.00
Barber, Boy With Butterfly Net, Dark Green, Mary Gregory	275.00
Barber, Chas. L. Auger, Bay Rum, Milk Glass, Woman Label Under Glass, 11 In.	880.00
Barber, Clear Raised Ribs, Cobalt Blue Base, 1885-1925, 7 1/2 In.	330.00

Bottle, Barber, Witch Hazel, Amber, Label Under Glass, Pewter Stopper, 7 In.

To remove a bottle stopper that is stuck, mix 1/2 teaspoon salt, I teaspoon rubbing alcohol, and 1/2 teaspoon glycerin. Pour the mixture around the stopper and let it seep in for a day. Then remove the stopper. If it's still stuck, try to encourage it by gently tapping the neck of the bottle with a wooden spoon. Some stoppers may be impossible to remove.

Barber, Cranberry Opalescent, Daisy & Fern, Melon, 1870-1920, 7 In. 305.00
Barber, Cranberry Opalescent, Seaweed, Bulbous 345.00
Barber, Cranberry Opalescent, Stars & Stripes 285.00
Barber, Cranberry, Floral Design, Vertical Ribs, Globular, 1870-1920, 8 1/8 In. 275.00
Barber, Cranberry, Ribbed, Enameled, Pontil, 1885-1925, 7 3/8 In. 715.00
Barber, Cranberry, Stars & Stripes 350.00
Barber, Green, White & Orange Enameled, Pontil, 1885-1925, 8 1/4 In. 220.00
Barber, Hair Tonic, Milk Glass, Victorian Woman Label Under Glass, Cylindrical, 10 In. 990.00
Barber, Opalescent Lime Green, White Stripe, Smooth Base, Rolled Lip, 7 In. 440.00
Barber, Robin's-Egg Blue Opalescent, Daisy & Fern, Melon, 7 1/8 In. 230.00
Barber, Sapphire Blue, White Enamel Floral, Gilt, Pontil, 7 1/2 In. 260.00
Barber, Toilet Water, 3-Piece Mold, Tam-O'-Shanter Stopper, 6 3/4 In. 198.00
Barber, Topaz, Ribbed, Enameled Design, Waisted, Pontil, 7 7/8 In. 525.00
Barber, Turquoise, White, Mary Gregory Type, Bell Shape, 1885-1925, 7 1/2 In. 575.00
Barber, Vegederma, Amethyst, Woman Flowing Hair, Pontil 290.00
Barber, Witch Hazel, Amber, Label Under Glass, Pewter Stopper, 7 In. . . . .*Illus* 187.00
Barber, Witch Hazel, Milk Glass, 6 Sides 45.00

eam bottles were made to hold Kentucky Straight Bourbon, made by
e James B. Beam Distilling Company. The Beam series of ceramic
ottles began in 1953.

Beam, Australian Hobo, Swagman, 1979, 14 In. 38.00
Beam, Baseball's 100th Anniversary, 1969, 10 1/2 In. 35.00
Beam, Chevrolet, Camaro, 1969 Model, Reglued Steering Wheel, 1989 . . . . 33.00
Beam, Churchill Downs, Kentucky Derby, 98th, Horse & Rider, 1971 . . . . 25.00
Beam, Corvette Stingray, 1963 Model, Missing Back Bumper, 1987 . . . . 28.00
Beam, Executive, 1975, Reflections In Gold 25.00
Beam, Executive, 1976, Floro De Oro 25.00
Beam, Oldsmobile, 1904 Model, 1972 . . . . 28.00
Beam, Pearl Harbor Survivors, Blue, White, 1941-1972 . . . . 65.00
Beam, Republican Convention, Miami Beach, 1974 . . . . 15.00
Beam, Siamese Cat, 1967 . . . . 25.00
Beam, Stutz Bearcat, 1914 Model, 1977, Box 45.00
Beam, Train, Grant Locomotive, 1971-1986, 5 Piece 185.00
Beer, Anheuser-Busch Brewing Co., Pre-Prohibition, 12 Oz. 39.00
Beer, Anheuser-Busch Brewing Co., Watertown Branch, Amber, Eagle, Monogram 15.00
Beer, Canadian Ace, Cone Top, Simulated Wood Lithograph, 12 Oz. 25.00
Beer, Emmerling Brewing Co., Embossed, Pre-Prohibition, 12 Oz. 4.50
Beer, Falstaff Lemp, St. Louis, Embossed, Pre-Prohibition, 12 Oz. 11.00
Beer, Ferro-Phos Brewing, Embossed, Pre-Prohibition, 14 Oz. 4.50
Beer, Glennon's Beer, Pittston, Pa., Embossed 3.50
Beer, Indianapolis Brewing Co., Indianapolis, In., 1 Qt. 22.00
Beer, Iroquois Beverage, Indian Head, Pre-Prohibition, 12 Oz. 11.00
Beer, National, Jug, Plastic Handle, 1960s 13.00
Beer, Old Jug Bier, Stoneware, Logo, Label, Pre-Prohibition 5.50
Beer, People's Brewing Company, Embossed, Pre-Prohibition, 12 Oz. 8.00
Beer, Peter Hand's, Label, 1950s, 12 Oz. 3.50
Beer, Pfeiffer's Jumbo Beer, 1950s, 32 Oz. 11.00
Beer, Phil Scheuermann Brewery, Hancock, Mich., Amber, Round, 12 In. 10.00
Beer, Val Blatz, Milwaukee, Aqua, Embossed Star, Blob Top 15.00
Bitters, Amber, Bowling Pin, Applied Collar, 11 3/4 In. 45.00
Bitters, Bennet's Celebrated Stomach, San Francisco, Orange Amber 302.00
Bitters, Boneco Stomach, Paper Labels, Cork, Contents, 9 3/8 In. 255.00
Bitters, Bourbon Whiskey, Barrel, Deep Strawberry Puce, 9 1/4 In. 545.00
Bitters, Burdock Blood, T. Milburn & Co., Toronto, Ont., Aqua, Miniature 75.00
Bitters, Clarke's Compound, Mandrake, Aqua, 7 3/8 In. 75.00
Bitters, Curtis & Perkins Wild Cherry, Aqua, Round, Open Pontil 45.00
Bitters, Doyle's Hop, Semi-Cabin, Amber, Berries & Leaves, 9 1/2 In. 45.00
Bitters, Dr. Blake's Aromatic, New York, Light Aqua, Open Pontil, 7 1/4 In. 225.00
Bitters, Dr. H.C. Stewart's Tonic, Columbus, Ohio, Amber, Rectangular 80.00
Bitters, Dr. Harter's Wild Cherry, St. Louis, Amber, Embossed, 7 3/4 In. 45.00
Bitters, Dr. Henley's Wild Grape Root IXL, Olive Green, 12 1/2 In. 1760.00
Bitters, Drake's Plantation, 4 Log, Yellow Amber, 10 In. 375.00

Bitters, Drake's Plantation, 4 Log, Yellow Amber, Olive Tone, 10 In.	1495.0
Bitters, Drake's Plantation, 5 Log, Yellow Green, 1860-1880, 9 3/4 In.	550.0
Bitters, Drake's Plantation, 6 Log, Amber, 10 In.	110.0
Bitters, Drake's Plantation, 6 Log, Medium Yellow Amber, 1860-1880, 9 3/4 In.	80.0
Bitters, Excelsior Herb, Light Amber, 10 1/4 In.	1210.0
Bitters, Fish, W.H. Ware, Golden Amber, 1860-1880, 11 1/2 In.	170.0
Bitters, Greeley's Bourbon, Barrel, Moss Green, Square Mouth, 9 In.	1600.0
Bitters, Hall's, Barrel, Yellow Amber, 1860-1880, 9 1/8 In.	225.0
Bitters, Hartwig Kantorowicz Posen, Hamburg, Germany, Milk Glass, 10 3/4 In.	45.0
Bitters, Holtzerman's Patent Stomach, Cabin, Deep Orange Amber, 9 7/8 In.	140.0
Bitters, Kaiser Wilhem Bitters Co., Sandusky, Ohio, 10 1/4 In.	28.0
Bitters, Keystone, Cleveland, Ohio, Barrel, Amber, 3/4 Qt., 9 3/4 In.	575.0
Bitters, Lady's Leg, Red Amber, Embossed, 12 1/8 In.	48.0
Bitters, Lash's, Natural Tonic Laxative, Amber, Square, 9 1/2 In.	25.0
Bitters, Saint Jacob's, Honey Amber, 8 1/2 In.	220.0
Bitters, Sheetz's Celebrated Bitter Cordial, Phila., Aqua, 10 In.	45.0
Bitters, Simon's Centennial, Aqua, c.1876, 10 1/2 In.	850.0
Bitters, Smith's Druid, Barrel, Yellow Amber, Square Mouth, 1860-1880, 9 In.	660.0
Bitters, W.L. Richardson's, South Reading, Mass., Aqua, Flared Lip, Open Pontil, 7 In.	170.0
Bitters, William Allen's Congress, Aqua, Indented Panels, 1880, 10 In.	80.0
Black Glass, English Onion, Squatty, 1725-1730	550.0
Black Glass, Spirit, Flat Sides, England, 1680-1700	950.0
Blown Glass, 25 Melon Ribs, Honey Olive, Midwest, 8 In.	245.0
Coca-Cola bottles are listed in the Coca-Cola category.	
Cosmetic, C.S. Emerson American Hair Restorative, Cleveland, Oh., Oval, 6 1/2 In.	215.00
Cosmetic, Canadian Booster Hair Tonic & Dandruff Cure, Windsor, Ont., 6 1/2 In.	50.00
Cosmetic, E.S. Russell's Castanaine For The Hair, Nashua, N.H., Amber	50.00
Cosmetic, Owl Drug Co., Hair Tonic, Amethyst, 1 Wing, 8 3/4 In.	25.00
Cosmetic, Perry's Hungarian Balm For The Hair, Aqua, Pontil, 5 3/4 In.	75.00
Cosmetic, Rauchfuss Hair Invigorator, N.Y., Dark Aqua, Rectangular, Pontil, 7 In.	225.00
Cure, Holland Cough Consumption, Aqua, 6 In.	45.00
Cure, Kilmer's Swamp Root, Sample	10.00
Cure, Warner's Safe Rheumatic Cure, Amber, Late 1800s, 9 1/2 In.	50.00
Cure, Warner's Safe, London, Orange, Whittled, Bubbles, Slugplate Variant, Yellow, 7 In.	130.00
Cure, Wm. Radams No. 1 Cure, Jug, 1 Gal.	85.00
Cyrus Noble, Gambler's Lady, 1977, Miniature	40.00
Cyrus Noble, Miner's Daughter, 1975	40.00
Decanter, Cornflower Blue, 8 Panels, Applied Bulbous Lip, Stopper, 10 3/4 In.	825.00
Decanter, Etched Glass, Silver Mounted, Cherubs, Figural Finial Stopper, 8 1/2 In.	65.00
Decanter, Keene, Marlboro Street, Bright Forest Green, Pontil, 1 Pt.	630.00
Decanter, Old Tucker Whiskey, White Enamel, Fluted	95.00
Decanter, Pillar Mold, Clear, Cranberry Cased Interior, Panels & Notches, 11 1/4 In.	1045.00
Decanter, Pillar Mold, Cut Panels Neck & Ribs, Star Cut Base, Stopper, 11 In.	495.00
Decanter, Wine, 3-Piece Mold, Stopper, 8 1/2 In.	495.00
Demijohn, Blown, Offset Neck, Open Pontil, 10 1/2 In.	60.00
Demijohn, Green, Blown, 26 1/2 In.	80.00
Ezra Brooks, Badger, Football, 1974	35.00
Ezra Brooks, Max The Hat, Zimmerman, 1976	25.00
Ezra Brooks, Tennis Player, 1973	10.00
Ezra Brooks, Tiger, Bengal, 1979	30.00
Famous Firsts, Butterfly, 1971	12.00
Famous Firsts, Phonograph, 1969, Miniature	18.00
Famous Firsts, Telephone, French, White, 1973, Miniature	18.00
Figural, Bartender, Red Clay, Cork In Head, With 4 Whiskeys, 9 In., 5 Piece	85.00
Figural, Donald Duck's Head, Clear, No Lid, 4 1/4 In.	25.00
Figural, Fish, Sits On Tail & 2 Fins, Mouth Opening, 14 In.	20.00
Figural, Fish, W.H. Ware, Deep Red Amber, Pat. 1866, 11 1/2 In.	215.00
Figural, French Policeman, Cobalt Blue, 8 In.	175.00
Figural, General Boulanger, Painted, Depose, No Stopper, 1890-1915, 14 3/4 In.	75.00
Figural, Gun, Whiskey, Amber, 1895-1910	85.00
Figural, Hand Shape, Mennon Skin Bracer	12.00
Figural, Hand, Whiskey Nipper, Glad Hand Written In Palm, Cork	50.00
Figural, Heart, Paul Masson, Amber, Wood Covered Cork, 8 1/2 In.	10.00

Figural, Joan Of Arc, John Tavernier, Milk Glass, Stopper, France, 16 1/2 In. 305.00
Figural, John Tavernier, Saint Joseph Bonbon, France, Painted, 16 In. 110.00
Figural, Jules Grevy Bust, Jo Janvier, D & D Depose, France, 11 1/2 In. . . . . .75.00 to 135.00
Figural, Kummel Bear, Black Amethyst, Applied Top 90.00
Figural, Man In The Moon, Decanter, Topaz Carnival Glass, Painted, 11 1/8 In. 355.00
Figural, Monk, Ceramic, Cork In Head, West Germany, 8 In. 40.00
Figural, Moses, Poland Springs Water, Aqua, 1880-1890, 11 1/4 In. 85.00
Figural, Pig, Drink While It Lasts From The Hogs, 7 In. 150.00
Figural, Pig, Stoneware, 8 1/2 In. 2900.00
Figural, Policeman, Liqueur, Raspail, Paris, Cobalt Blue, Painted, 14 1/2 In. 85.00
Figural, President Harrison, Frosted Bust On Black Column 525.00
Figural, Scotch Lass With Scotty Dog 45.00
Figural, Statue Of Liberty 550.00
Figural, Woman, Partly Nude, Art Deco, Monterrey Cocktail, Mexico, 1940, 1/2 Gal. . . . 25.00
Flask, 16 Ribs, Yellow, Amber Tone, Club 3960.00
Flask, 36 Ribs, Swirled, Light Yellow Olive, Pontil, 5 1/2 In. 300.00
Flask, Byron & Scott, Portrait, Amber, Open Pontil, 1/2 Pt. 120.00
Flask, Chestnut, 10 Diamond, Yellow, Olive Tone 3190.00
Flask, Chestnut, 15 Vertical Ribs, Green, Sheared Lip, 4 3/4 In. 275.00
Flask, Chestnut, 16 Diamond, Aqua, Sheared Lip, 4 3/4 In. 385.00
Flask, Chestnut, 16 Vertical Ribs, Amber, Sheared Lip, 5 1/8 In. 220.00
Flask, Chestnut, 25 Swirled Ribs, Aqua, Ohio, 7 1/4 In. 190.00
Flask, Chestnut, New England, Yellow Olive, Pontil, 1783-1830, 8 3/4 In. 140.00
Flask, Chestnut, Yellow Olive, Applied Rim, Pontil, New England, 1783-1830, 5 1/2 In. . . 154.00
Flask, Chestnut, Zanesville, 24 Broken Swirl Ribs, Amber, Sheared Lip, 5 1/2 In. 1155.00
Flask, Chestnut, Zanesville, 24 Swirled Ribs, Amber, Sheared Lip, 4 1/2 In. 330.00
Flask, Chestnut, Zanesville, 24 Vertical Ribs, Green, Sheared Lip, Pot Stones, 5 In. 245.00
Flask, Cleveland & Stephenson, Barrel, Amber, Polished Pontil, 1/2 Pt. 305.00
Flask, Double Eagle, Applied Ring, Yellow Olive 220.00
Flask, Duffy's Crescent Saloon, Pig Shape, Aqua, 7 1/2 In. 1050.00
Flask, Eagle & Anchor, Ravenna Glass, Aqua, 1 Pt., 8 In. 140.00
Flask, Eagle & Cornucopia, Dark Olive, 1 Pt. 250.00
Flask, Eagle & Flag, Aqua, Sheared Mouth, Pontil, 1 Pt. 220.00
Flask, Eagle & Grapes, Aqua, Pontil, Coffin & Hay, 1/2 Pt. 285.00
Flask, Eagle & Indian, Shooting Bird, Aqua, Pittsburgh, Pa., 1860, 1 Qt. 110.00
Flask, Eagle & Tree, Olive Amber, 5 3/4 In. 1320.00
Flask, Eagle, Aqua, Applied Mouth, Pittsburgh, Pa., 1860-1880, 1 Pt. 250.00
Flask, Eagle, Medium Yellow, Olive, Willington Glass Works, 1860-1872, 1 Qt. 170.00
Flask, Eagle, Olive Amber, Open Pontil, Granite Glass Co., 1 Pt., 7 1/2 In. 345.00
Flask, Flora Temple, Horse, Greenish Amber, 1 Pt. 225.00
Flask, Franklin & Dyott, Aqua, Kensington Glass Works, Open Pontil, 1 Qt. 265.00
Flask, G.A.R., Label Under Glass, 19th National Encampment, 1895, 6 In. 635.00
Flask, Grandfather's, Zanesville, 24 Vertical Ribs, Amber, Sheared Lip, 8 1/8 In. 660.00
Flask, Holy Water, Picture, Bulged Neck, Pontil 225.00
Flask, Hunter & Fisherman, Calabash, Amber, Impressed Pontil, 1 Qt. 165.00
Flask, Lafayette-Dewitt Clinton, Aqua, Kensington Glass Works, 7 In. 195.00
Flask, Louis XVI, Pinch, Pewter Cap, 6 1/8 In. 125.00
Flask, Masonic & Eagle, Amber, Keene Glass Works, Semi-Open Pontil, 1 Pt. 110.00
Flask, Masonic & Seeing Eye, Yellow Olive, Stoddard, New Hampshire, 1 Pt. 210.00
Flask, Nutshell, Carved, Applied Handles, Chain For Stopper, 6 1/2 In. 220.00
Flask, Pitkin Type, 16 Broken Swirl Ribs, Green, Half Post Neck, Sheared Lip, 6 In. 550.00
Flask, Pitkin Type, 32 Broken Swirl Ribs, Peacock Green, Half Post Neck, 6 In. 495.00
Flask, Pitkin Type, 36 Broken Swirls, Olive Green, Half Post Neck, New England, 5 In. . . 355.00
Flask, Scroll, Golden Amber, Pontil, 1845-1860, 1 Pt. 325.00
Flask, Scroll, Sapphire Blue, Iron Pontil, 1845-1860, 1 Pt. 1950.00
Flask, Sheaf Of Wheat & Star, Bright Golden Amber, Applied Mouth, 1860, 1 Pt. 132.00
Flask, Sheaf Of Wheat & Westford, Olive Amber, 1/2 Pt., 6 In. 65.00
Flask, Soldier & Dancer, Aqua, 1860-1870, 1 Pt. 145.00
Flask, Stiegel Type, Floral, Engraved KRN, Teardrop, Pontil, 6 3/8 In. 330.00
Flask, Summer & Summer, Aqua, Open Pontil, 1 Pt. 100.00
Flask, Sunburst, Light Yellow, Green, Pontil, Keene, 1 Pt. 300.00
Flask, Taylor & Monument, Light Yellow, 1840, 1 Pt. 2310.00
Flask, Taylor & Monument, Pale Aqua, Pontil, Baltimore Glass Works, 1/2 Pt. 200.00

Flask, Taylor, Corn For The World, Baltimore Glass Works, Aqua, 1860-1870, 1 Qt. 240.00
Flask, Traveler's Companion & Star, Amber, Sheared Mouth, Iron Pontil, 1/2 Pt. 77.00
Flask, Union, Clasped Hands & Eagle, Light Yellow, 2 Qt., 8 3/4 In. 385.00
Flask, W.A. Reist, Colonial, York, Pa., Fluted, Hotel, Mold Blown, Pewter Cap, 1 Pt. 55.00
Flask, Washington & Eagle, Aqua, Open Pontil, Kensington Glass Works, 1 Pt. 165.00
Flask, Washington & Jackson, Olive Green, 1 Pt. 225.00
Flask, Washington & Jackson, Yellow Amber, Sheared Mouth, Pontil, 1848, 1/2 Pt. 210.00
Flask, Washington & Taylor, Aqua, Baltimore Glassworks, Reversed S, 1 Qt. 250.00
Flask, Wormser Bros., San Francisco, Orange Amber, 1867-1872, 8 1/2 In. 330.00
Flask, Zanesville, Chestnut, 24 Swirled Ribs, Aqua, 7 In. 148.00
Food, A.L. Murdock Liquid Food, Amber, Embossed 15.00
Food, California Fig Syrup Co., Sterling Products Inc., 1900, 6 7/8 In. 7.00
Food, Capital Queen Olives, Round 8.00
Food, Curtice Brothers Tomato Ketchup, Blue Label, Embossed, Small 15.00
Food, French's Mustard, Squeeze Bottle, Fred Flintstone, Barney & Dino, 1985 . . . . 7.00
Food, Jewel Tea Vanilla, 1917 . . . . 75.00
Food, Margaret O'Brien Candy Kitchen, Lemon Flavor, Label, 1 Oz. 40.00
Food, Parke Davis Orange Extract, For Soda Fountain Use, Label, Contents 40.00
Food, Watkins Extract Of Orange 6.00
Food, Watkins Lemon Extract, Large 9.00
Food, White Vanilla Lemon Extract 5.00
Fruit Jar, A. Stone & Co., Grooved Ring Wax Sealer, Tin Lid, Iron Pontil, 1845, 1 Pt. 1045.00
Fruit Jar, Atlas E-Z Seal, Aqua, Glass Lid, Clamp, 1 Qt. 5.00
Fruit Jar, Atlas E-Z Seal, Blue Green, Glass Lid, Wire, 1/2 Pt. 300.00
Fruit Jar, Atlas, Good Luck, Glass Lid, Clamp, Embossed, 4 Leaf-Clover, 1 Qt. 5.00
Fruit Jar, Ball Mason's, Patent Nov. 30th, 1858, Zinc Screw Lid, 1 Qt. 5.00
Fruit Jar, Ball Mason, Embossed Bicentennial Old North Bridge, Zinc Screw Lid, 1 Qt. . . 5.00
Fruit Jar, E.C. Flaccus Co., Deer & Flowers In Relief, 1 Pt. 115.00
Fruit Jar, Good Luck, Glass Lid, 1 Pt., 1 Qt., 1/2 Gal., 3 Piece 45.00
Fruit Jar, Jeannette Mason Home Packer, Zinc Screw Lid, J In Square, 1 Qt. 8.00
Fruit Jar, Mankley & Cartwright, East Liverpool, Ohio, Pottery, Wax Seal 250.00
Fruit Jar, Mason's, Patent Nov. 30, 1858, Green Aqua, Ground Lip, 1/2 Gal. 100.00
Fruit Jar, McDonald New Perfect Seal, Aqua, Glass Lid, Clamp, 1 Pt. 6.00
Fruit Jar, Peoria Pottery, Brown Bennington Type Glaze, 7 1/4 In. 35.00
Fruit Jar, Sterling Mason, Zinc Screw Lid, 1 Pt. 3.00
Garnier, Mocking Bird, 1970 . . . . 25.00
Garnier, Paris Monuments, 1966 . . . . 35.00
Garnier, Poodle, 1954 . . . . 15.00
Garnier, Roadrunner, 1969 . . . . 25.00
Garnier, Trout, 1967 . . . . 20.00
Gemel, Double Blown, Deep Green, Applied Rigaree Sides, Pontil 125.00
Gin, Case, Black, Square Face, 4 3/8 In. 79.00

Bottle, Ink, A.B. Laird, Blue
Green, Octagonal, Open
Pontil, 2 In.

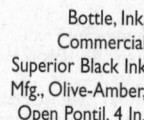

Bottle, Ink,
Commercial
Superior Black Ink
Mfg., Olive-Amber,
Open Pontil, 4 In.

Right: Bottle, Ink, Cabin,
Gold Amber, Label, 2 3/4

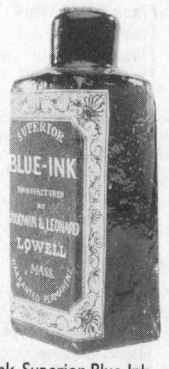

Bottle, Ink, Superior Blue Ink,
Goodwin & Leonard, Olive,
Open Pontil, 4 3/4 In.

Gin, Milshire Dry Gin, Heublein Bro., Hartford, Miniature 15.00
Ginger Beer, E.S. Shapley & Sons, Torquay Pure Home Made, Stoneware, 6 1/2 In. 35.00
Grenadier, Pancho Villa, Standing 10.00
Grenadier, Soldier, 1st Regiment, Virginia Volunteers, 1974, Miniature 14.00
Grenadier, Soldier, 6th Regiment, Wisconsin, 1975, Miniature 14.00
Hoffman, Blue Jay, 1979, Pair 40.00
Hoffman, Bobcat & Pheasant, 1978 .... 50.00
Hoffman, Buffalo Hunter, Russel, 1978 .... 44.00
Hoffman, Mr. Lucky, 1974, Miniature 10.00
Hoffman, Penguins, 1979 .... 50.00
Hoffman, Street Swingers, Bass Player, 1979, Miniature 12.00
Household, A. Richard's Glue & Cement, Cylinder, Aqua, 2 1/2 In. 35.00
Household, Eureka Mending Liquid, Cork, 1900s, 4 In. 15.00
Household, Plynine Ammonia, Stoneware Cap, 1 Qt. 235.00
Ink, 3-Piece Mold, Blown, Deep Olive Green, 2 3/4 In. 110.00
Ink, A.B. Laird, Blue Green, Octagonal, Open Pontil, 2 In. ....*Illus* 2530.00
Ink, Blown, Aqua, Applied Foot, Midwestern, 4 1/2 In. 220.00
Ink, Cabin, Gold Amber, Label, 2 3/4 In. ....*Illus* 1980.00
Ink, Carter's Ink Co., Jug, Stoneware, White & Brown, Blue Letters, 1 Gal. 100.00
Ink, Carter's, Cobalt Blue, 6 Sides, Cloverleaf Design, 6 1/4 In. 145.00
Ink, Carter's, Diamond, Cobalt Blue, Cork Top, 1920s 200.00
Ink, Commercial Superior Black Ink Mfg., Olive-Amber, Open Pontil, 4 In. ......*Illus* 246.00
Ink, Davids', Blue Green, Embossed, c.1870, 1 7/8 In. 2200.00
Ink, Favorite, Aqua, 2 1/4 In. 25.00
Ink, Harrison's Columbian Blue Black Writing Fluid, c.1840, 4 1/8 In. 1100.00
Ink, Harrison's Columbian, Aqua, 12 Sides, Pontil, 1845-1860, 7 1/4 In. 280.00
Ink, Horn, Copper Inlay, Horn Stopper, 18th Century 195.00
Ink, J. & I.E. Moore, Turtle, Aqua, Patent 1865 .... 65.00
Ink, Ma & Pa Carter, Ceramic, Germany, 1914, Pair 165.00
Ink, S. Fine Black Ink, Yellow Green, Inward Rolled Mouth, Pontil, 1840-1860, 3 In. ... 305.00
Ink, Sanford's, Boat, Aqua 20.00
Ink, Superior Blue Ink, Goodwin & Leonard, Olive, Open Pontil, 4 3/4 In. ....*Illus* 560.00
Ink, Umbrella, 8 Sides, Light Golden Amber, Pontil, 1840-1860, 2 1/8 In. 160.00
Ink, Worden Hyatts Fancy, Part Label, 2 5/8 In. 60.00
Jar, Apothecary, Diamond Dust, Label Under Glass, Stopper, Square, 1880-1900, 8 In. 165.00
Jar, Cover, Horlick's Malted Milk, 1 Gal. 150.00
Jar, Heinz Food, Figural Stopper, Logo, c.1900, 12 1/2 In. 295.00
Jar, Inhaler, Chemist's, Dark Green, Wide Mouth, Glass Stopper, 6 1/2 In. 50.00
Jar, Inhaler, S. Maw Son & Sons, London, England, White Stoneware, 6 1/2 In. 45.00
Jar, Squirrel Salted Nuts, 14 1/2 In. 450.00
Jug, Bauer Saloon, Peoria, Miniature, 1 Pt. 100.00
Jug, Bullivants Grocery, Miniature 75.00
Jug, Cambridge Springs Mineral Water, Miniature 110.00
Jug, Chas. D. Moul Wines & Liquors, York, Pa., Stoneware, 1/2 Gal. 165.00
Jug, H. Free & Co. Fine Wines & Liquors, York, Pa., Stoneware, White, Tan, 1/2 Gal. ... 195.00
Jug, Hirsch Bros. & Co., Vinegar & Cider, Pittsburg, Pa., Miniature 165.00
Jug, I.W. Harper Nelson Co. Kentucky Whiskey, White, Miniature 85.00
Jug, M.S. Herlihy & Co., Miniature 75.00
Lionstone, Professor, 1973, Miniature 9.00
McCormick, Pony Express, 1978 .... 50.00
McCormick, Spirit Of '76, 1977, Miniature 10.00
Medicine, Admirine Laxative, Label, Screw Cap, Nude Graphics, 1933 .... 45.00
Medicine, Ballard's Horehound Syrup, Label, 4 Oz. 6.00
Medicine, Brant's Indian Pulmonary Balsam, M.T. Wallace, Aqua, Open Pontil, 7 In. ... 70.00
Medicine, Bristol's Extract Of Sarsaparilla, Buffalo, Aqua, Pontil 50.00
Medicine, Clark Stanley's Snake Oil Liniment, Horse Liniment, 6 1/4 In. 100.00
Medicine, Dr. D. Jayne's Tonic Vermufuge, Embossed, Machine Made, Aqua, 6 1/2 In. .. 18.00
Medicine, Dr. Feely's Pine Shampoo For Dogs & Cats, Amber, 1940s 22.00
Medicine, Dr. M.M. Fenner's Peoples Remedies, Fredonia, N.Y., Amber, 10 1/4 In. 30.00
Medicine, E.T. Miller, York, Pa., Partial Label 35.00
Medicine, Fellows Laxative Tablets, Embossed, 2 3/4 In. 8.00
Medicine, Fink's Magic Oil, Springdale, Pa., Aqua, Indented Panels, 1890s, 5 1/2 In. ... 10.00
Medicine, Floraplexion, Cures Dyspepsia, Franklin Hart, Aqua, 1890s, 6 In. 10.00

Medicine, Golden State Liniment, B.F. Hewlett, Label, 5 In. 15.00
Medicine, H.C. Farrell's Arabian Liniment, Peoria, Aqua, Cylindrical, 4 In. 10.00
Medicine, Hick's Capudine Liquid For Headaches, Grip, Amber, Label, Stopper 260.00
Medicine, Hobsun's Mange Treatment For Dogs, Cattle, Pfeiffer Chemical Co., 8 In. 38.00
Medicine, Humphrey's Homeopathic No. 29 Fever Blisters, Large Logo, Wrapped 15.00
Medicine, J.W. Hawks, M.D., Manchester, N.H., Aqua, 12 Sided Emblem, 4 In. 75.00
Medicine, Kennel Comfort Sacuptic Mange Remedy For Dogs, Contents, 1960 .... 35.00
Medicine, Laughlins & Bushfield Druggists, Wheeling, Va., Dark Aqua, Pontil, 9 1/2 In. .. 400.00
Medicine, McLean's Volcanic Oil Liniment, Aqua, Applied Top, 1860s, 4 In. 15.00
Medicine, Mexican Mustang Liniment, Dark Aqua, Cylinder, Red Iron Pontil, 7 3/4 In. ... 250.00
Medicine, Owl Drug Co., Amber, Peroxide, 2 Wings, On Mortar & Pestle, 8 In. 60.00
Medicine, Owl Drug Co., Celluloid Cap, Duraglas, 6 Oz. 12.50
Medicine, Owl Drug Co., Milk Glass, 1 Wing, Square, Blown, 4 1/2 In. 65.00
Medicine, Phelp's Arcanum, Molded, Olive Amber, 1830, 8 3/4 In. 920.00
Medicine, Rouzer Funeral Home, Smelling Salts, Box 20.00
Medicine, Scott & Browne, Cherry Malt Phosphate, Lady's Leg, Amber, Round 55.00
Medicine, Sun Drug Co., Amber, Embossed, 4 1/2 In. 20.00
Medicine, USA Hospital Dept., Light Blue, 7 3/4 In. 130.00
Medicine, W. Day Pharmacist, Hopkinton, Mass., Amber, 5 In. 25.00
Medicine, Wonderfluff After Clip Lotion, For Dogs, 1960s 18.00
Medicine, Woodward Chemist, Nottingham, Light Cobalt Blue, 6 1/4 In. 20.00
Milk, Blue Boy Sparkle Vitamin-Mineral Fortified Milk, Fairy Picture, Amber, 1 Qt. 25.00
Milk, Borden Company, Southern Division, Gail Borden Picture, Amber, 1 Qt. 29.00
Milk, Borden's Milk & Cream, Red Pyro, Square, 1/2 Pt. 25.00
Milk, Boyes Dairy, Topeka Kansas, Amber, White Letters, Square, 1 Qt. 8.50
Milk, Burch Dairy Co., Health In Every Bottle, Florence, S.C., Orange Pyro, Round, 1 Qt. 40.00
Milk, Buzzelli Sons, Embossed Cow, 1/2 Pt. 20.00
Milk, Buzzelli Sons, Niagara Falls, Babyface, 1 Qt. 40.00
Milk, Chapman's Dairy, Cows Milked In Parlor, Greenville, S.C., Red Pyro, Round, 1 Qt. 65.00
Milk, Clover Dairy Products, 3-Leaf Clover, Embossed, Round, 1942, 1 Qt. 17.00
Milk, Creamer, Hillview Dairies Cream, Pouring Lip, Handle, 3 5/8 In. 15.00
Milk, Creamer, Jar, Lancashire Hygienic Dairies Ltd., Churn Shape, 2 7/8 In. 30.00
Milk, Crisp County Dairies, Cordele, Ga., Red Pyro, Round, 1 Qt. 45.00
Milk, Dairymen's Meadow Gold, Honolulu, Hawaii, Red & Orange, Square, 1 Qt. 45.00
Milk, Dellinger Dairy Farm, Gold Medal, Jeffersonville, Ind., Orange & Black, 1 Qt. 60.00
Milk, Diamond Dairy Farms, Salem, N.H., Orange Pyro, 1/2 Pt. 30.00
Milk, Dublin Co-Op Dairies, 5 Cent Deposit, Red Pyro, Round, Squatty, 1 Qt. 25.00
Milk, Dunville Dairy, Dunville, Ont., 1/2 Pt. 10.00
Milk, Fairview Dairy Quality Products, Antigo, Wis., Painted Label, 1/2 Pt. 14.00
Milk, Forest City Dairy, Rockford, Ill., 1 Qt. 15.00
Milk, Gold Spot Dairy, Enid, Okla., Enjoy Our Ice Cream, Orange, Square, 1 Qt. 26.00
Milk, Grady Farms, Waterloo, Iowa, Red Pyro, 1 Gal. 25.00
Milk, Gratzer Dairy, Syracuse, N.Y., Amber, Deposit, Square, 1 Qt. 25.00
Milk, Guernsey Dairy, Stockton, Ill., Embossed, 1/2 Pt. 8.00
Milk, H.G. Williams Co., Norfolk, Va., Embossed, 1/2 Pt. 15.00
Milk, Hampden Creamery Co., Cow's Head, Mass. Seal, Embossed, Tin Top, 1/2 Pt. 37.00
Milk, I.M. Smith's Dairy, Kinards, Red Pyro, Round, 1/3 Qt. 25.00
Milk, J.H. Belle, Long Ridge Dairy, Stamford, Conn., Embossed, 1/2 Pt. 22.00
Milk, King Farm Dairy, Rockford, Ill., Embossed, 1 Qt. 15.00
Milk, Kishwaukee Dairy, Rockford, Ill, Embossed, 1/2 Pt. 6.00
Milk, Lassig's Dairy, Rhinelander, Wis., 1/2 Pt. 8.00
Milk, Lions Club, Your Cows Will Keep Blind Family From Want, Red Pyro, 1/2 Pt. 25.00
Milk, Logstown Dairy, Aliquippa, Pa., Green Pyro, 1/2 Pt. 25.00
Milk, Luxerin Farms, Fond Du Lac, Wi., Blue Pyro, 1/2 Pt. 25.00
Milk, Metzcer's, Embossed Boy Child's Face, 1 Qt. 35.00
Milk, Modern Dairy Products Co., Rhinelander, Wis., Embossed, With Cap, 1 Qt. 10.00
Milk, Palm Milk & Cream, Red Circle, Green Border, Round, 1.5 Litre 24.00
Milk, Peckham's Dairy, North Adams, Mass., Embossed, Round, 1 Pt. 8.50
Milk, Pilleys Fine Dairy Products, Lion On Shield, Red Pyro, Round, 1 Qt. 22.00
Milk, Pinehurst Dairy Farm, Rockford, Ill., Embossed, 1 Qt. 8.00
Milk, Ruff's Dairy, St. Clair, Mich., Girl, Building Blocks, Round, 1 Qt. 8.50
Milk, S. End Dairies, Kline Bros., Cumberland, Md., Embossed, 1/2 Pt. 25.00
Milk, Serve Producers Ice Cream, Delicious, Crawfordsville, Ind., Black, Round, 1 Qt. .. 31.00

Milk, Seward Dairy, Seward, Alaska, Embossed, Round, 1 Pt. 125.00
Milk, St. Elizabeth's Hospital, Washington, D.C., 1/2 Qt. 75.00
Milk, Sunnycrest, Niagara Falls, Cop Top, 1 Qt. 150.00
Milk, W.J. Kennedy Dairy Co., Token, Baby Picture, Pat. Sept. 22, 1925, 1/4 Pt. 400.00
Milk, Wakefield, Cop The Cream, 1 Qt. 75.00
Mineral Water, Adirondack Spring, Westport, N.Y., Deep Emerald Green, 1875, 1 Qt. . . 265.00
Mineral Water, Artesian Spring Co., Olive Green, Sloping Double Collar, 1875, 1 Pt. . . 70.00
Mineral Water, Hopkins Chalybeate, Baltimore, Olive Green, Iron Pontil, 1855, 7 1/2 In. 360.00
Mineral Water, John H. Gardner & Son, Sharon Springs, Teal Blue, Double Collar, 1 Pt. 255.00
Mineral Water, Massena Spring, Amethystine Tint, Tooled Mouth, 1890, 1 Qt. 165.00
Mineral Water, Oak Orchard Acid Springs, Lockport, N.Y., Deep Green, 1765, 1 Qt. . . . 60.00
Mineral Water, Saratoga Spring Co., N.Y., Yellow Olive Green, Double Collar, 1 Pt. . . . 145.00
Mineral Water, Saratoga Spring, Emerald Green, Double Collar, 1875, 1 Qt. 145.00
Mineral Water, Saratoga Vichy Spouting Spring, Aqua, Double Collar, 1875, 1 Pt. 75.00
Mineral Water, Strumatic, P.S.M. Co., Deep Red Amber, Double Collar, 1880, 1 Pt. 550.00
Mineral Water, Tahoe Sparkling Water, Green, Painted Label, 1950s, 13 Oz. 9.00
Nursing, Allenbury's Feeder, Ploughshare Picture 40.00
Nursing, Aqua, 15 Diamond, 5 7/8 In. 50.00
Nursing, Blown, Vertical Ribs, Aqua, Midwest, 6 3/8 In. 80.00
Nursing, Crown Feeder, Turtle, Aqua, 1880, 5 1/2 In. 45.00
Nursing, Evenflo, 3 1/2 In. 30.00
Nursing, Figural, Milk Glass, Hard Rubber Nipple, France, 11 1/2 In. 120.00
Nursing, Hygeia, Embossed, Ball, Instructions, 4 Oz. 8.00
Nursing, Hygeia, Painted Label, Duraglas, Instructions, 8 Oz. 8.00
Nursing, Hygienic Feeder, Banana Shape, Standard Size 20.00
Nursing, Our Little Beauties, WH Monogram, Slipper Shape 35.00
Nursing, S. Maw & Thomson, London, England, Slipper Shape . . . . .30.00 to 40.00
Perfume bottles are listed in their own category.
Pickle, Cathedral, Applied Lip, Green, 13 1/2 In. 187.00
Pickle, Cathedral, Blue Aqua, Rolled Lip, Whittled, 1865, 13 3/4 In. 260.00
Pickle, Cathedral, Blue Green, Applied Mouth, Open Bubbles, 1865, 9 1/4 In. 210.00
Pickle, Cathedral, Molded Flower Baskets & Scrolls, 10 In. 11.00
Pickle, Cathedral, Teal Blue, 6-Sided, 1865-1875, 13 1/4 In. 240.00
Poison, Amber, 12 Vertical Grooves, Cylinder, 7 In. 15.00
Poison, Bottled By Jeyes, Green, Embossed, Oval, 6 In. 25.00
Poison, Burdall's LTD Manufacturing Chemist, Sheffield, Aqua, Ribbed 35.00
Poison, C.L.G. Co., Patent Applied For, Cobalt Blue, 7 1/2 In. 205.00
Poison, Carbolic Acid, Cobalt Blue, Embossed Warnings, Oval, 7 1/2 In. 10.00
Poison, Cobalt Blue, Quilted, Poison Stopper, Master, 5 1/2 In. 115.00
Poison, Embossed Not To Be Taken, Cobalt Blue, 2 Panels, 3 5/8 In. 12.00
Poison, Embossed Not To Be Taken, Cobalt Blue, Hexagonal, 4 Oz., 5 1/2 In. 15.00
Poison, Embossed Not To Be Taken, Cobalt Blue, Hexagonal, 6 3/4 In. 30.00
Poison, Figural, Skull, Cobalt Blue, Tooled Mouth, 1880-1900, 4 1/4 In. 935.00
Poison, Iodinol, Manor Remedies Co., Ltd., Newcastle, Aqua, Hexagonal, 6 1/4 In. 15.00
Poison, Manchester Royal Infirmary, Cobalt Blue, Hexagonal, Embossed, 4 In. 25.00
Poison, Medium Olive Green, Vertical Ribs Front, Oval, 7 In. 25.00
Poison, Owl Drug Co., 1 Wing, Cobalt Blue, Triangle, Mold, 3 5/8 In. 125.00
Poison, Sulpholine, Cobalt Blue, Embossed, Rectangular, 4 1/2 In. 12.00
Poison, Triloids-Poison, Cobalt Blue, Triangular, Hobnail Corners 30.00
Poison, Vasogen, Amber, Embossed, Hexagonal, 3 3/4 In. 12.00
Poison, Vorsicht, Skull & Crossbones, Light Turquoise, Hexagonal, Germany, 8 1/4 In. . . 165.00
Sarsaparilla, Dr. Townsend's, Albany, N.Y., Emerald Green, Iron Pontil, 9 3/8 In. 235.00
Sarsaparilla, Edwin W. Joy Co., San Francisco, Aqua, Square, 8 3/4 In. 35.00
Sarsaparilla, Old Dr. J. Townsend's, N.Y., Emerald Green, Iron Pontil, 9 1/2 In. 145.00
Seal, Black Coat Of Arms, England, 1720 . . . . 1350.00
Snuff, Agate, Leave, Vine Design, Red, Green Stone Stopper, 1900, 1 3/4 In. 154.00
Snuff, Agate, Mask, Mock Ring Handles, Coral Stopper, 2 In. 70.00
Snuff, Agate, Moss, Green, Red, Gray Ground, Green Stone Stopper, 2 1/8 In. 121.00
Snuff, Agate, Puddingstone, Carved Flower & Mask, Mock Ring Handle, 1 3/4 In. 785.00
Snuff, Agate, Puddingstone, Spade Shape, Carved Ducks, Green Stone Stopper, 2 In. 210.00
Snuff, Amber, Mask & Mock Ring Handles, Stopper, 3 1/4 In. 330.00
Snuff, Carnelian, Flat Sides, Plum Blossoms, Jade Stopper, 2 3/4 In. 103.00
Snuff, Chalcedony Agate, Brown, White Ground, Egg Shape, Pink Glass Stopper, 2 In. . . 275.00

Snuff, Coral, Branch Form, Flower, Leaf Design, Jadeite Stopper, 1 3/4 In. 176.0

Snuff, Crane Design, Sea-Root, Mother-Of-Pearl Stopper, 20th Century, 2 1/2 In. 176.0

Snuff, Crystal, Cameo Carved Bird, Prunus & Lotus, 19th Century, 2 1/4 In. 513.0

Snuff, Glass, Ruby, Pear Shape, Stopper, Early 19th Century, 2 1/4 In. 55.0

Snuff, Hornbill, Figural Carving On Natural Ground, 1920s, 1 3/4 In. 968.0

Snuff, Horsehide, 2 Side Handles, Scotland, c.1780, 2 1/2 x 1 In. 595.0

Snuff, Inkstone, Carved Dragon Design, Coral Stopper, 2 1/4 In.   484.0

Snuff, Ivory, Figure Seated Beneath Tree One Side, Bird On Other, Stopper, 2 3/4 In. 195.0

Snuff, Ivory, Flattened Urn Form, Etched Flowering Trees & Bushes, 1 3/4 In. 105.0

Snuff, Ivory, Leaping Carp Design, Stopper, 2 3/4 In. 121.0

Snuff, Ivory, Repeated Shou Design, Jade Stopper, 18th Century, 2 1/2 In. 5082.0

Snuff, Ivory, Swimming Carp Form, Conforming Stopper, c.1900 . . . .   1452.0

Snuff, Jade, Black, Flattened Egg Shape, Simulated Coral Stopper, 2 In. 605.0

Snuff, Jade, Celadon Green, Butterfly & Vine, Double Gourd Form, Stopper, 2 3/4 In. 220.0

Snuff, Jade, Crouching Mouse Eating Coral Kernel Of Rice, 2 1/2 In. 3630.0

Snuff, Jade, Man On Bull Near Rock, Amethyst Top, Brown Stone, 2 3/4 In. 575.0

Snuff, Jade, Man On Bull Near Rock, Orange Top, Blue, Handles, 2 3/4 In. 144.0

Snuff, Jade, Raised Calligraphic Design, 19th Century, 2 1/4 In.   121.0

Snuff, Jade, White, Rectangular, Raised Panel Sides, Green Jade Stopper, 2 1/4 In. 110.0

Snuff, Jadeite, Apple Green, Silver Mounts, Jadeite Stopper, 19th Century, 2 3/4 In. 1210.0

Snuff, Lapis Lazuli, Lion & Peonies, Pear Shape, Conforming Stopper, 3 3/8 In. 155.0

Snuff, Lapis Lazuli, Relief Peony Design, Spade Shape, Stopper, 1900, 2 1/4 In. 88.0

Snuff, Lapis Lazuli, Spade Shape, Blue Accents, Gray, Spade Shape, Agate Stopper, 2 In. . .   66.0

Snuff, Malachite, Leaping Carp Shape, Coral Stopper, 2 3/4 In. 220.0

Snuff, Mother-Of-Pearl, Woman With Lute, Spade Shade, Conforming Stopper, 3 In. 110.0

Snuff, Pilgrim Flask Form, Lapis Lazulil Stopper, 1 1/4 In. 66.0

Snuff, Pilgrim Flask Form, Pearl & Coral, Silver, Stopper, 19th Century, 2 5/8 In. 465.0

Snuff, Porcelain, 5-Claw Green Dragon Design, Tiger's Eye Stopper, Cylinder, 3 In. 522.0

Snuff, Porcelain, Blue, Gilt Bird, Floral Design, Agate Stopper, 20th Century, 2 1/4 In. . .   44.0

Snuff, Porcelain, Dark Green & Black Dragon, Jade Stopper, 3 In. 115.0

Snuff, Porcelain, Flower, Shou Lattice Design, Green, White, Spadeshape, Coral Stopper .   247.0

Snuff, Porcelain, Herdboy & Water Buffalo, Ivory Stopper, 18th Century, 2 7/8 In. 133.0

Snuff, Porcelain, Magpie Design, Cylinder, Coral Stopper, 1880, 2 1/2 In. 605.0

Snuff, Porcelain, Relief Gold Dragons, Turquoise Ground, Jadeite Stopper, 2 1/4 In. 121.0

Snuff, Porcelain, Salmon Red, Black Ground, Teardrop Shape, Coral Stopper, 2 3/4 In. . .   264.0

Snuff, Pressed Burl, Little Milkmaid On Lid, France, 1820, 3 x 1 In. 300.0

Snuff, Puddingstone, Egg Shape, Jadeite Stopper, Late 19th Century, 2 In. 465.0

Snuff, Rock Crystal, Women In Winter Landscape, Interior Painted, 1915, 2 1/2 In. 484.0

Snuff, Soapstone, Relief Hare Design, Jadeite Stopper, Early 20th Century, 2 In. 77.0

Snuff, Tortoiseshell, Crane & Pheasant Design, Stopper, Rectangular, 2 1/2 In. 265.0

Snuff, Tourmaline, Pink, Flower & Vine Design, Spade Shape, Stopper, 2 3/4 In. 2640.0

Snuff, Turquoise, Double Gourd Shape, Silver-Mounted, Coral Stopper, 2 1/4 In. 825.0

Snuff, Turquoise, Flattened Egg Shape, Glass Stopper, 2 1/4 In.   135.0

Snuff, Turquoise, Spade Shape, Butterfly, Floral Design, Stopper, 2 1/2 In. 440.0

Snuff, Turquoise, Spade Shape, Sage, Meijin Design, Stopper, 2 5/8 In. 220.0

Snuff, Turquoise, Temple Jar Shape, Bird, Flower Design, Stopper, 1 5/8 In. 165.0

Snuff, White, Mask, Mock Ring Handles, Coral Stopper, 19th Century, 2 In. 187.0

Snuff, Wooden, Seal Scene, Calligraphy, Spade Shape, Jadeite Stopper, 2 In. 1980.0

Soaky, Baloo, Colgate 75.0

Soaky, Bullwinkle Moose, Plastic, Red, Yellow Antlers, 1966, 10 In. 50.0

Soaky, Creature From The Black Lagoon, Plastic, Green, 10 In. 60.0

Soaky, Felix The Cat, Box 25.0

Soaky, King Louie, Colgate 75.0

Soaky, Mister Magoo, 1960s, 9 In. 35.0

Soaky, Tennessee Tuxedo 35.0

Soaky, Top Cat, Yellow, Hanna Barbera, Contents, 10 In. 45.0

Soaky, Tweety 68.0

Soda, 7-Up, Indianapolis 500, 1978 . . . .   35.0

Soda, Big Chief, Indian, Red & White Painted Logo, Price, Utah, 9 Oz. 85.0

Soda, Big Chief, Indian, White & Red Painted Logo, Raton, N.M., 6 1/2 Oz. 40.0

Soda, Big Shot Beverage, Cartoon, Man With Cigar, Red & White Painted Label, 12 Oz. .   35.0

Soda, Brownie Club Beverage, Little Brownie, White & Red Painted Logo, R.I., 12 Oz. .   85.0

Soda, Bryces Beverage, Butlers Holding Tray, Troy, N.Y., 7 Oz. 45.0

Soda, Canada Dry, Iridized, Paper Labels, 1920s 80.00
Soda, Carolina Moon Beverage, Green, Painted Red & Yellow Sun Rise Logo, 12 Oz. 75.00
Soda, Catawissa, Catawissa, Pa., Sexy Lady, White & Red Painted Logo, 12 Oz. 35.00
Soda, Celro-Kola Co., Portland, Ore, Light Amber, Square, 9 In. 35.00
Soda, Chicago Consolidated Bottling Co., Aqua, Dug, Large 12.00
Soda, Clicquot Club, Eskimo Boy, Red & White, 12 Oz. 6.00
Soda, Country Squire, Corieskill, N.Y., Man In Top Hat, Red Painted Logo, 8 Oz. 30.00
Soda, Daniel Boone Mix, Green, Daniel, Indian, Dog, White Painted On Logo, 7 Oz. ... 50.00
Soda, Dextrose-O-So-Grape-Oh So Good, Flat River, Mo., White Pyro, 8 In. 6.00
Soda, Double Cola, Oval Shield, Red & White, 1950s, 12 Oz. 7.00
Soda, Dr Pepper Seltzer, Etched 450.00
Soda, Eagle & Flags On Banner, Blue Green, Applied Mouth, Iron Pontil, Cylindrical ... 190.00
Soda, Elk Club, Elkton, Va., Black Elk, Red Painted Logo, 9 Oz. 100.00
Soda, Ewa Bottling Works, H.T., Hutchinson, Light Aqua 250.00
Soda, Frost King, Jackson, Miss., Snowman & Sports Figures, Blue Painted Logo, 7 Oz. . 45.00
Soda, Ginger Ale, Green, White Felix The Cat Picture, 1958 .... 198.00
Soda, Golden Valley, Gone With The Wind Scene, Red & White Painted Logo, 12 Oz. 30.00
Soda, Graba Gazzosa Beverage, Weird Hand, Pa., Green, White Painted Logo, 7 Oz. 35.00
Soda, H. Denhalter & Son, Salt Lake City, Aqua, Tombstone Slug Plate, Pony Blob, 6 In. 225.00
Soda, Harmony Club, Cleveland, Ohio, Pin Up Girl, Blue & White Painted Logo, 7 Oz. . 10.00
Soda, Hi Ho, Plymouth, Wis., Cartoon Of Kid, White & Red Painted Logo, 7 Oz. 50.00
Soda, Hill Billy Brew, Green, Hillbilly & Still, 10 Oz. 8.50
Soda, Hires, Salesman's Sample, Amber, 1910, 3 In. 230.00
Soda, Hosmer Mountain Beverage, House, Mountain, Red & White Painted Logo, 8 Oz. . 50.00
Soda, J. Hindle's Pop, Stoneware 75.00
Soda, Jet, Waco, Texas, Red Airplane, White Painted Logo, 8 Oz. 40.00
Soda, Jolly Beverage, Fitchburg, Ma., Boy & Glass, Green & White Painted Logo, 12 Oz. 35.00
Soda, K.C., Muskogee, Okla., Cowboy On Horse, White & Red Painted Logo, 10 Oz. ... 50.00
Soda, Kenoza Club Beverage, Methuen, Ma., Castle Scene, White Painted Logo, 7 Oz. .. 50.00
Soda, La Orange Cola, St. Louis, Mo., French Girl, White & Red Painted Logo, 9 1/2 Oz. 35.00
Soda, Lincoln Beverage, Chicago, Ill., Blue & Red Painted Logo, 7 Oz. 350.00
Soda, Mahaska, Oskaloosa, Iowa, Indian, Red & White Painted Logo, 10 Oz. 100.00
Soda, Martin Rancich, Union Glass Works, c.1858 .... 2750.00
Soda, Maui Soda Works, Hutchinson, Aqua, 7 3/4 In. 45.00
Soda, Mingo, Williamson, W.Va., Indian Princess, Red & Black Painted Logo, 9 Oz. 135.00
Soda, Mountain Dew, Green, Hillbilly With Gun, 10 Oz. 7.50
Soda, Mt. Lassen Beverages, Susanville, Calif., Red & White Pyro, 1920s, 8 1/2 In. 25.00
Soda, Nevada City Bottling, Nevada City, Cal., Embossed, 1920s, 9 1/2 In. 25.00
Soda, New Orleans Seltzer Co., Etched, Logo 50.00
Soda, Orange Crush-Dry, Black, Unopened, Paper Label, Gold Foil Seal, 1920-1930 .... 260.00
Soda, Owl Drug Co., Green, Crown Top, Machine Made, 9 3/4 In. 40.00
Soda, Park City Bottle Works, Utah, Crown Machine Made, 7 1/2 In. 18.00
Soda, Pep-Up, Green, Pixie Walking, Red & White Painted Logo, Sandusky, Ohio, 7 Oz. 65.00
Soda, Pittsburgher Beverage, Green, Street Scene, Red Painted Logo, 7 Oz. 85.00
Soda, Polar Cola, Salem, Mass., Owl, Red Painted Logo, 12 Oz. 40.00
Soda, Polar Pak Beverage, San Diego, Cartoon Bear, White & Green Painted Logo, 7 Oz. 45.00
Soda, Rancho, Glendale, Ca., Cowboy On Horse, Black & White Painted Logo, 10 Oz. .. 75.00
Soda, Ritz Beverage, St. Louis, Mo., Green, White Painted Logo, Man In Top Hat, 12 Oz. 45.00
Soda, Rob Roy, Canada, Green, Scottish Warrior, White & Red Painted Label, 12 Oz. ... 85.00
Soda, Scopel's, Benld, Ill., Couple Dancing, Blue & White Painted Logo, 12 Oz. 75.00
Soda, Seisler Beverage, St. Charles, Mo., Eskimo, Blue & White Painted Logo, 10 Oz. .. 100.00
Soda, Ski Beverage, Montreal, Skier, White & Green Logo, 12 Oz. 75.00
Soda, Skipper Beverages, Pittsburgh, Pa., Red & White Flag, 8 In. 5.00
Soda, Sour Schnapps, Oskaloosa, Ia., Green, Lady With Bottle, Red Painted Logo, 7 Oz. . 35.00
Soda, Spartan, Greenville, S.C., Roman Soldier, Red & White Painted Logo, 12 Oz. 85.00
Soda, Sun Dial Beverage, Aurora, Ontario, Red & Yellow Sun Dial Painted Logo 65.00
Soda, Whippers Beverage, Toronto, Green, Wrestler, Yellow & Red Painted Logo, 7 Oz. . 350.00
Soda, Wilson Mfg. Co., Sacramento, Cal., Aqua, Carbonated Drinks, 11 3/4 In. 18.00
Soda, Wood Wiltwyck Rondout, Aqua, Squatty 30.00
Soda, Yaky's Beverages, Aliquippa, Pa., Red & White Pyro, 8 In. 6.00
Soda, Yankee Beverage, R.I., Uncle Sam's Top Hat, Blue & White Painted Logo, 12 Oz. . 45.00
Soda, Zee Beverage, Flying Saucer, White & Blue Painted Label, 7 Oz. 30.00
Target Ball, Bogardus Glass Ball, Pat'd. Apr. 10, 1877, Yellow Amber, 2 3/4 In. 550.00

Target Ball, Grenade Unic Extinctrice, Medium Amber, Vertical Rib, France, 5 1/2 In. . .   305.00
Target Ball, Hayward's Hand Fire Grenade, Pat. Aug. 8, 1871, Turquoise, 6 3/8 In. 330.00
Target Ball, Hayward's Hand Grenade Fire Extinguisher, Yellow Olive, 6 In. 825.00
Target Ball, J.H. Johnston Great Western Gun Works, Pittsburgh, Tobacco Amber 4620.00
Target Ball, N.B. Glass Works Perth, Pale Green Aqua, England, 1880-1890, 2 3/4 In. . . .   105.00
Target Ball, Of The World, Green, Ground Pontil, 3 In. 550.00
Tonic, Schenck Seaweed, 9 In. 45.00
Tonic, Webb's Indian, Aqua, Tenpin 30.00
Vinegar, White House, Double Handle, Apple Jug, 1 Pt. 195.00
Whiskey, A.M. Bininger & Co., Cannon Barrel, Golden Amber, 1860-1880, 12 In. 525.00
Whiskey, Blood Wine, Worcester, Mass., 3 1/2 In. 20.00
Whiskey, Crown Distilleries, San Francisco, 5 3/4 In. 29.00
Whiskey, Deep Amethyst, Panels & Ovals, Applied Lip, Octagonal, 10 1/4 In. 1650.00
Whiskey, Free's Pure Rye Whiskey, York, Pa., Amber, 12 In. 45.00
Whiskey, German Peppermint Schnapps, 4 In. 50.00
Whiskey, Hirsch's Malt Whiskey, Reliable Stimulant In Circle, Amber, 10 3/4 In. 65.00
Whiskey, J.H. Cutter Old Bourbon, Orange Amber, Cylinder, Potstone In Top, 11 3/4 In. .   45.00
Whiskey, J.H. Cutter Old Bourbon, Orange Amber, Cylinder, Tooled Top, 11 5/8 In. 25.00
Whiskey, Kellogg's Nelson County Extra Kentucky Bourbon, Orange Amber, Stopper . . .   45.00
Whiskey, Old Cyprus, Dennis Donovan, Haverhill, Mass., Stoneware, 1 Pt. 22.00
Whiskey, Parker Rye, Decanter, Miniature 35.00
Whiskey, Udolpho Wolfe's Aromatic Schnapps, Light Amber, 9 5/8 In. 22.00
Whiskey, Udolpho Wolfe's Aromatic Schnapps, Yellow Green, Square, 9 3/4 In. 30.00
Whiskey, W.H. Co. Pride Of Kentucky, Cleveland, Ohio, Miniature 35.00
Whiskey, Wm. H. Spears & Co., Embossed Bear, c.1890 . . . .   6270.00
Wine, Dutch, c.1720, 7 1/2 In. 145.00
Wine, Porter Type, c.1780, 10 3/4 In. 145.00
Zanesville, 24 Broken Swirl Ribs, Aqua, Club Shape, Applied Lip, 8 1/2 In. 330.00
Zanesville, 24 Melon Ribs, Honey Olive, Applied Lip, 8 3/8 In.   550.00
Zanesville, 24 Swirled Ribs, Amber, Applied Lip, Globular, 7 In.   495.00
Zanesville, Chestnut, 24 Ribs, Aqua, Sheared Lip, 4 7/8 In. 247.00
Zanesville, Chestnut, 24 Ribs, Green Aqua, 4 In. 330.00

BOTTLE CAP collectors search for the printed cardboard caps used during the past 80 years. Unusual mottoes, graphics, and caps from dairies
that are out of business bring the highest prices.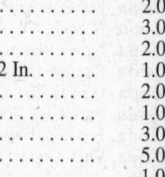

Canada Dry Black Cherry Beverage, Metal, Cork Lined 2.00
Cherry, Grape & Grapefruit, Cork Lined, 1950s, 4 Piece 3.00
Cherry Cola, Metal, Red & White 2.00
Fairview Dairy, Pasteurized Homogenized Milk, Zeeland, Mich., Green, 2 1/2 In. 1.00
Grapefruit Drink, Metal, Cork Lined 2.00
Highland Hill Dairy, Lowell, Mich., Purple & Yellow, 2 1/2 In. 1.00
Hires Root Beer, Metal, Cork Lined, Brown, White & Orange 3.00
Kist Punch, Metal, Red, Silver, Cork Lined 5.00
Lyle Johnson Farm Milk, Grandville, Mich., Yellow, Green, 1 3/8 In. 1.00
MalBert Cola, Please Daddy, Metal, Red, On Yellow 5.00
Mills Creamery Soft Curd Vitamin D Milk, Monday, Black, Orange, 1 3/8 In. 1.00
Old Red Eye, 1930-1950 50
Regal Lager Beer, Metal, 3 1/2 In. 15.00
Ritz Orange Pineapple Soda, Metal, Cork Lined 5.00
Sprite, Metal, Dark Green, On Silver & Light Green, Cork Lined 2.00
Sun Crest Strawberry Soda, Metal, Red & White, Cork Lined 3.00
True Fruit Flavored Pineapple Soda, Metal, Palm Tree Picture, Cork Lined 5.00

BOTTLE OPENERS are needed to open many bottles. As soon as the
commercial bottle was invented, the opener to be used with the new
types of closures became a necessity. Many types of bottle openers can
be found, most dating from the twentieth century. Collectors prize
advertising and comic openers.

4-Eyed Man, Cast Iron . . . . .85.00 to 90.00
4-Eyed Woman, Cast Iron 90.00
7-Up, Wall Mount, Metal Housing Catches Cap, White 70.00

If a bottle stopper is stuck, try using Liquid Wrench, an oil found at the hardware store, to loosen it.

If you find an old bottle with an unwanted old cork inside, pour ammonia into the bottle until it covers the cork. The cork will dissolve.

Bottle Opener, Ashtray,
Drunk Man, Lamppost, 5 In.

Amish Boy, Cast Iron	185.00
Ashtray, Drunk Man, Lamppost, 5 In. ....*Illus*	4.00
Ashtray, Football Player, Homecoming '56, L & L Favors	450.00
Bartle's Beer, Metal	28.00
Bear Head, Wall Mount	140.00
Beck's Beer, Wooden Handle, Metal, 1940s	4.50
Berghoff Beer	30.00
Bull's Head, Tail, Cast Iron, 6 1/4 In.	235.00
Canada Goose, Bronze	30.00
Canada Goose, Cast Iron	65.00
Chero-Cola, Boot Shape, 5 Cents	55.00
Clown's Head, Cast Iron	110.00
Cowboy, With Cactus, Cast Iron	300.00
Cowboy, With Guitar, Cast Iron	165.00
Dog, Brass	25.00
Dog, Pointer, Black & White, Cast Iron	110.00
Donkey, Brass	45.00
Donkey, Cast Iron	30.00
Drunk, Lamppost, Cast Iron ....45.00 to 65.00	
Drunk, Lamppost, White Metal ....20.00 to 60.00	
Drunk, Sign Post, Brass	50.00
Elephant, Brass, Canada	15.00
Eskimo, Cast Iron	495.00
False Teeth, Wall Mount	65.00
Fehr's Beer, Figural	30.00
Gosman's Ginger Ale, Wall Mount	15.00
Grand Prize, Star-X, Wall Mount	75.00
Grass Skirt Greek, Cast Iron	425.00
Graupner's Beer, 1930s	60.00
Horse's Rear, Cast Iron	40.00
Iron City Beer, Cast Iron	15.00
K-B Beer, Bottle Shape, 1940s	14.00
Mr. Dry, Man, Top Hat	65.00
Norwegian, Cast Iron	1200.00
Nude, Stamped On Base, Xmas T.C.A. '47	50.00
Old Snifter, Beer Drinker, Brass	45.00
Pabst Blue Ribbon Brew, Bottle Shape, 1930s	10.00
Parrot, Cast Iron ....25.00 to 45.00	
Pelican, Beak Up, Cast Iron	225.00
Pelican, Brass	45.00
Pickwick Ale, Tin ....22.00 to 35.00	
Ringler Brewers, Baseball Player, 1914	48.00
Sailor, Norfolk, Virginia Sign, Iron, 1940s	45.00
Seagull, Cast Iron ....50.00 to 60.00	
Walrus, Cast Metal, Germany	65.00

BOW is an English porcelain works started in 1744 in East London. Bow made decorated porcelains, often copies of Chinese blue and white patterns. The factory stopped working about 1776. Most items sold as Bow today were made after 1750.

Coffeepot, Cover, Blue, Chinaman, Bearing Satchel On Pole, 1760, 10 In.	7475.00
Dish, Pickle, Leaf, Shell Form, Aubergine, Brown, Red, Yellow, Blue, 4 1/4 x 4 In.	1850.00
Figurine, Air & Earth, Wearing White & Green Robe, Florets, 9 7/8 & 9 3/4 In., Pair	2875.00
Figurine, Allegorical Figures, Spring & Autumn, Holding Grapes, 7 1/2 & 7 In., Pair	2585.00
Figurine, Goldfinch, Pale Puce Plumage, Yellow Wings, Octagonal Base, 1765, 5 3/8 In.	865.00
Figurine, Harlequin, Columbine As Children, 1760-1765, 4 9/16 & 4 5/8 In., Pair	2760.00
Figurine, Mars & Venus, Sword, Green Sprigs, 1760, 9 11/16 & 9 5/16 In., Pair	1600.00
Figurine, Woman, Running, Puce Jacket, Puce Sprigged White Skirt, 1756, 4 3/8 In.	2760.00
Group, Allegorical Figure Of Autumn, Grape Wreath, Puce, Blue Edged Base, 8 In.	920.00
Plate, Powder Blue, Chinese Man, In A Punt On A River, Floral Roundels, 9 1/2 In.	575.00
Teapot, Blue Floral & Insect, Globular, 1760, 3 5/8 In.	375.00

BOXES of all kinds are collected. They were made of thin strips of inlaid wood, metal, tortoiseshell, embroidery, or other material. Additional boxes may be listed in other sections, such as Advertising, Battersea, Ivory, Shaker, Tinware, and various Porcelain categories. Tea Caddies are listed in their own category.

18K Gold, Flowers & Figures By Urn, Black Enamel, Continental, c.1900, 4 In.	1610.00
Allover Cherubs Holding Roses, Pierced Silver, Leather Hinged Lid, 1890, 6 1/4 In.	690.00
Apple, Walnut, Dovetailed, 19th Century	295.00
Baleen, 3-Finger, Pincushion Insert In Top With Wool Covering, Oval, 4 1/4 In.	275.00
Ballot, Pine, Dovetailed Drawer, With Marbles, Felt Lined, c.1864, 9 x 5 x 5 In.	155.00
Band, Decoupage Covered, Watercolor Design, Oval, 6 In.	193.00
Band, Poplar, Cover, Wallpaper Covered, Squirrels & Trees, 18 1/2 In.	1100.00
Band, Wallpaper Covered, American Flag Cover, Newspaper Interior, 17 1/2 In.	1070.00
Band, Wallpaper Covered, Blue, White, Gray, Orange, Brown, Amber, Oval, 9 1/4 In.	495.00
Band, Wallpaper Covered, Newspaper Lining, Bentwood, 16 1/2 x 13 1/2 In.	330.00
Band, Wallpaper Covered, Oval, Lined With Journals Of 1812, Hannah Davis, 11 In.	632.00
Band, Wallpaper Covered, Ribbon, Newspaper Lined, New Hampshire, 7 1/4 In.	175.00
Band, Wallpaper Covered, Tan, Green On White, Rectangular, 4 1/2 In.	38.00
Bentwood, Finger Construction, Green Paint, Round, 6 In.	302.00
Bentwood, Pine, Poplar, Yellow Paint, Red Graining, Round, 5 1/4 x 3 1/2 In.	193.00
Bentwood, Pinkish Gray Paint, Round, 19 1/2 In.	440.00
Berry, Triangle Of Air Holes Each Side, New England, 1 Qt.	190.00
Bible, Mahogany, Mortised Joints, Diamond Shape Inlays On Front, 19 3/4 In.	420.00
Bible, Walnut, Dovetailed, Walnut, Square, 19th Century, 18 x 7 In.	195.00
Bird's-Eye Burl Veneer, Line Inlay, Ivory Finial, Mirror Inside Lid, Octagonal, 9 In.	302.50
Bird's-Eye Maple, Walnut Veneer, Lift-Out Tray, 8 In.	38.00
Black Brushed Graining On Orange Ground, Sliding Lid, 4 3/4 x 6 7/8 In.	275.00
Blanket, Dark Blue Over Dark Red Paint Design, c.1860, Miniature	325.00
Bone & Wood, Figural, Native, Sitting, Tribal, Jointed Arms & Legs, Swivel Head, 6 In.	325.00
Book Form, Walnut, Carved Simulated Leather Front, Gilt-Edged Pages, 7 x 6 x 2 In.	195.00
Brass, Rampant Lions, Victorian, 11 In.	104.00
Brass, St. George Finial, Jewel Drawer, Russia, 6 x 5 In.	860.00
Brass Handle On Lid, Nailhead Trim, Leather Covered, 1850s, 3 1/2 x 6 3/8 In.	230.00
Candle, 2 Sections, Wood, Mustard, Red Striping, Dovetailed, Hanging, 20 In.	550.00
Candle, Blue-Green Paint, New England, c.1800, 9 x 13 1/2 In.	495.00
Candle, Chestnut, Dovetailed, Flame Graining, Raised Panel Sliding Cover, 8 x 12 In.	825.00
Candle, Double, Chestnut, Hand-Cut Backing Nails, c.1800, 14 1/2 x 17 5/8 In.	485.00
Candle, Fanback, Tin	325.00
Candle, Hanging, Oak, Dovetailed, Sliding Cover, Shaped Crest, 21 1/2 In.	165.00
Candle, Heavy Sheet Brass, Engraved Cover, England, 1760, 10 In.	1100.00
Candle, Hinged Lid, Shaped Backboard Pierced For Hanging, Walnut, 13 x 8 In.	184.00
Candle, Mahogany, Hinged Lid, Screw & Wire Nail Construction, 12 In.	330.00
Candle, Wall, Birch, Pine Secondary Wood, Drawer, 23 x 12 In.	935.00
Candle, Wall, Cylindrical, Punched Lid & Ends, Tin	265.00
Candle, Wall, Pine, Hinged Lid, Curved Crest, 12 1/4 In.	330.00
Candle, Wall, Pine, Old Brown Finish, Heart Crest, 11 3/4 x 7 x 21 In.	770.00
Candle, Wall, Pine, Shaped Crest, 2 Shelves, 24 x 13 1/2 In.	1061.00

Cartridge, Leather, Flap Punched With Date, 1702 .... 495.00
Carved Half Circles, Birds, Foliage, Oak, England, 17th Century, 8 7/8 x 18 1/2 In. 690.00
Cherry, Cover, Dovetailed, Landscape Scene, Applied Bone Heart, Zoar, Oh., 19 1/2 In. . 2805.00
Circular Rosette On Textured Lid, Louis XVI, Tricolor, 18K Gold Trim, 3 1/4 In. ... 2875.00
Comb, Walnut, Inlay, Incised Design, 19th Century, 11 1/2 In. 185.00
Cutlery, Pine, Dovetailed, Canted Sides, New England, 17 3/4 x 11 1/2 In. 172.00
Desk, Ebonized Hardwood, Molded, Section Top, Drawer Over Bracket Base 22.00
Document, Burled Elm, Figured Wood 165.00
Document, Chip Carved, Dark Varnish, Top Handle, 12 1/4 x 6 In. 440.00
Document, Embossed Leather, Wallpaper Interior, 18th Century, 9 3/4 In. 245.00
Document, Hide Covered, Early 19th Century, 9 3/4 In. 265.00
Document, Leather Covered, Brass Studs, 11 1/2 In. 110.00
Document, Leather, Brass Studs & Handle, Lock & Key, Paper Interior, 14 x 6 x 7 In. .. 110.00
Document, Mahogany, 3 Drawers, Paneled Front & Sides, Hinged Lid, 16 x 11 x 11 In. . 330.00
Document, Mahogany, Dovetailed, Diamond Shape Inlay, Bracket Feet, 12 x 6 In. 275.00
Document, Pine, Oak, Red, Carved Stars, Geometric Shapes, 1690-1730, 8 1/2 In. 2875.00
Document, Queen Anne, Sharkskin Covered, Brass Hardware, Red Silk Lining 650.00
Document, Revolutionary War, Brass Studs, Original Lock, 8 1/4 x 21 5/8 In. 165.00
Document, Walnut, Hinged Cover, 4 Paw Feet, Italy, 9 1/2 x 15 3/4 x 10 1/2 In. 1265.00
Dome Top, Black Grained Paint, Divided Interior, Till, Poplar & Butternut, 14 In. 330.00
Dome Top, Dark Green Design, Ocher Ground, Mid-19th Century, 6 x 3 1/4 In. 275.00
Dome Top, Pine, Dovetailed, Iron Bound, Painted Initials, 1869, 16 1/2 In. 60.00
Dome Top, Poplar, Worn Blue Paint, Iron End Handles, H.L.E.N. In Brass Tacks, 24 In. . 190.00
Ebony Frame Over Cedar, Ivory Pegs, Slide Top, Porcupine Quill, 7 1/4 x 3 7/8 In. 125.00
Egyptian Revival, 10 x 11 1/2 x 22 In. 795.00
Embroidered, Moosehair, c.1860, 2 1/2 x 3 1/2 In. 575.00
Game, Oak, Silver Plated Handle & Mounts, 2 Sections, 1880s, 16 x 17 In. 550.00
Gilt Metal, Hardstone, Footed, Rectangular, 4 In. 259.00
Glass, Sapphire Blue, Hinged Cover, Woman With Hat, 4 In. 375.00
Glove, Mahogany, Brass Handle, Lock & Hinges, 2 1/8 x 13 7/8 In. 110.00
Glove, Pyrography, Indian 60.00
Glove, Tufted Silk Interior, 5 x 13 In. 105.00
Hat, Leather, Travel Labels, Lining, Holds 3 Hats, 14 3/8 In. 165.00
Hearts, Doves & Cross On Each Side, Pennsylvania, 6 1/2 x 9 1/4 In. 675.00
Horn Stud, Silver Mounted Citrine Lid, 19th Century, 3 1/2 x 2 1/2 In. 265.00
Ivory & Tortoiseshell, Carving On Top & Sides, Inside Mirror, c.1865, 7 x 6 x 2 In. ... 325.00
Jewelry, Art Deco, Black & White Cover, Helena Rubinstein, 5 1/4 In. 90.00
Jewelry, Beveled Glass, Ormolu Mounting, Polychrome Picture, Lyon 1894 .... 95.00
Jewelry, Bone & Ivory Inlay, Tortoiseshell Veneer, Spain, 1680s, 6 x 11 In. 2875.00
Jewelry, Inlaid Olive Wood, 20th Century, 12 1/2 In. 93.00
Jewelry, Nacre Inlay, Black Lacquer, Fitted Interior, 11 1/4 In. 170.00
Jewelry, Plaques Of Roman Scenes, Micromosaic, Bird & Foliate Footed, 4 x 6 In. 4830.00
Jewelry, Sterling Silver & Elephant Hide 985.00
Jewelry, Tortoise & Ivory, Inlay, Handles, 2 Doors, 9 Drawer Interior, 12 x 13 In. 1725.00
Jewelry, Women & Child On Lid, Removable Tray, 4 Sections, Whalebone, 6 x 10 In. ... 5462.00
Jewelry Casket, Wood, Inlaid, Needlepoint Hinged Lid, George III Style, 4 x 5 In. 230.00
Knife, Ash, Bent Corner, Divided, Turned Handle, 8 1/4 x 13 In. 60.00
Knife, Checker Strung Mahogany, Serpentine Form, George III, 13 x 9 1/2 In. 431.00
Knife, Cherry, Dovetailed, Divider, 8 x 13 1/4 In. 275.00
Knife, Federal, Mahogany, Square Base 1430.00
Knife, Mahogany, Dovetailed, Scalloped, 10 x 14 1/4 x 6 3/4 In. 412.00
Knife, Mahogany, Ebony Herringbone Inlay, Serpentine, Hepplewhite, 1800, 14 In. 880.00
Knife, Poplar, Brown Paint, White, Yellow & Blue Design, 9 1/2 x 15 1/2 In. 330.00
Knife, Poplar, Salmon & White Paint, Curved & Scalloped Crest, Handle, 10 x 14 In. ... 220.00
Knife, Walnut, Inlaid, 1 Dovetailed Drawer, 9 3/4 x 14 x 8 In. 5565.00
Lehnware, Saffron, Strawberries & Flowers, 1840, 4 3/4 In. 795.00
Lid, Pine, Bird's-Eye Maple Geometric Overlay, 18 x 21 In. 1000.00
Lift Lid, Leather Strap Handles, 5 x 8 3/4 In. 165.00
Mahogany, Dovetailed, Flame Veneer Mahogany Lid, Rosewood Inlay, 17 In. 192.00
Mahogany, Maple, Inlaid Ovals & Shell, 10 1/2 In. 170.50
Money, Shopkeepers, Wooden, Till, Iron Hinges & Lock, Divided, 18th Century 650.00
Olive Wood, Bird & Floral Design, Russia, 4 1/2 x 7 In., Pair 287.00
Pantry, Carved F. Hardy Bros. On Cover, Late 18th Century, 6 1/2 In. 155.00

Papier-Mache, Marbleized, c.1880, 2 1/4 In. 98.00

Papier-Mache, Painted, Serpentine Outline, Mother-Of-Pearl Inlay, 6 x 14 In. 230.00

Patch, Glass, Black Amethyst, Butterfly On Lid, Gold Enamel Dots, 1 1/4 x 2 1/8 In. 170.00

Patch, Glass, Cobalt Blue, Multicolored Fan & Flowers On Lid, 1 x 2 In. 215.00

Patch, Glass, Cranberry, Encased In Gold Colored Metal Filigree, 1 3/8 x 2 1/2 In. 220.00

Patch, Glass, Cranberry, Gold Leaves Lid, 1 1/4 x 2 In. 225.00

Patch, Glass, Cranberry, Gold Scrolls On Lid & Bottom, 1 1/4 x 2 1/2 In. 205.00

Patch, Glass, Crystal, Light Blue Painted, Violets Lid, 1 1/4 x 2 In. 175.00

Patch, Glass, Crystal, Yellow Sand Effect, Violets & Flowers Lid, 1 1/4 x 2 1/8 In. 190.00

Patch, Glass, Medium Green, White & Orange Flowers Lid, 1 3/8 x 2 1/4 In. 110.00

Patch, Glass, Opalescent With Pink Stain, Multicolored Flowers Lid, 1 1/8 x 2 1/8 In. 120.00

Patch, Glass, Orange Amber, Floral Design Lid, 1 1/8 x 7 1/8 In. 150.00

Patch, Glass, Sapphire Blue, Enameled Trim, 7/8 x 2 1/8 In. 225.00

Pencil, Disappearing, Illustrated, Japan 90.00

Pencil, Kellogg's Tony Tiger School Bus, Pencils, 1978 .... 18.00

Pine, Acorn, Oak Leaves On Front, Oval Border, 4 1/2 In. 230.00

Pine, Double Wall, Brown Paint, F.A. Brimmer, Cot. 1860, 16 3/4 x 10 3/4 In. 1035.00

Pine, Dovetailed, Black & Red, Cream Striping, Baffles Groove Interior, 17 1/2 In. 175.00

Pine, Dovetailed, Cotter Pin Hinges, 2 Dividers, c.1840, 5 1/2 x 18 1/8 In. 190.00

Pine, Dovetailed, Red & Black Grained, Brass Ring Handle, Bone Escutcheon, 10 In. 170.00

Pine, Dovetailed, Red Brown Patina, 8 In. 440.00

Pine, Poplar, Dovetailed, Red Flame Graining, Wrought Iron Lock, 30 In. 220.00

Pine, Sliding Lid, Lollipop Crest, With Knitting Or Tatting Needles, 13 In. 605.00

Pine, Walnut, Cutout Designs, Soft Finish, 24 In. 132.00

Pipe, Carved Drawer, Bone Pull, Rose Head Nail On Bottom 150.00

Poplar, Dovetailed, Red & Black Graining, Wrought Iron Lock, 19 1/2 In. 110.00

Powder, Porcelain, Floral & Character Designs, 6 Sides, Marked Prussia, 1880s, 5 In. 221.00

Puzzle, Inlaid, China, 3 1/4 x 7 In. 33.00

Puzzle, Inlay Wood, Bird Scene, Japan, 1890 .... 195.00

Red & Green Tulip Design, Black Paint, Dovetailed, 9 1/2 In. 181.50

Rosewood, Mother-Of-Pearl, Oriental, Fitted Interior Tray, Round Top, 4 x 11 In. 690.00

Salt, Copper, Design, Late 18th Century, 9 1/2 In. 295.00

Salt, Lid, Birch, Cotter-Pin Hinges, Handmade Screws, 4 1/8 x 10 In. 120.00

Salt, Wall, Mahogany, Hinged Lid & Cutout Crest, Old Finish, 11 1/2 In. 605.00

Shell & Button Covered, House Shape, Alligatored Varnish, 8 1/2 In. 55.00

Shoeshine, Carved Shoe Form On Top, Blue Paint, c.1920, 13 x 16 In. 95.00

Silver & Shell, Mexico, 7 x 3 3/4 In. 44.00

Snuff, Engraved, Paktong, Original Silvering, England, c.1785, 3 In. 350.00

Soap, Treenware, Chestnut, America, Late 18th Century, Round, 4 In. 160.00

Spice, Bentwood, 8 Interior Canisters, Stenciled Labels, Round, 9 In. 385.00

Spice, Pine, Poplar, 4 Removable Containers, Inscribed Lid, Painted, Heart, 1869, 13 In. .. 825.00

Spice, Pine, Walnut, Design, 4-Part Interior, 10 1/4 In. 605.00

Spice, Wall, Ash, 8 Drawers, Old Varnish, Black Stenciled Labels, 11 x 19 In. 275.00

Spice, Wall, Beech, Oak, Poplar, 13 Drawers, Labels, Porcelain Knobs, 10 x 25 In. 220.00

Spice, Wall, Tin, 3 Sections, Embossed, 6 x 6 In. 175.00

Storage, Gilt Stencil, Iron Hardware, Chrome Yellow, Green Striping, 10 x 10 In. 675.00

Storage, Pine, Carved Bird Design, Dovetailed, 13 1/2 x 20 1/2 In. 975.00

Storage, Pine, Painted, Rectangular Hinged Top, Bracket Feet, 19th Century, 17 In. 400.00

Storage, Teakwood, Brass, 2 Doors, Lift Top, Early 20th Century, Japan, 50 x 24 x 27 In. 550.00

Strawwork, Dome Top, Compartmented, Drawer, Mirrored Lid, Dartmoor Prison, 1790 . 1450.00

Taper, Lighting Device, Brass, England, Late 18th Century 195.00

Ticket, Mahogany, Used At Ascot, Brass Finger Loop & Cover Latch, 9 5/8 x 4 1/4 In. .. 365.00

Ticket, Pine, Dovetailed, Hand-Cut Screws, Mid-1800s, 5 3/4 x 8 1/4 x 9 3/4 In. 110.00

Tinder, Dome Cover, Striker & Flint, Mid-18th Century 210.00

Tinder, Friesian Wood, Carved, Dated 1821, Flint & Striker, 9 1/2 In. 575.00

Tinder, Traveling, Brass, Iron Flint Striker, 1800 .... 695.00

Tobacco, Birchbark, Leather Pull Tabs 65.00

Tobacco, Brass, Engraved Boy Scene, Standing On Table, 4 3/8 In. 165.00

Tobacco, Brass, Engraved Scenes, Dutch Inscription, 6 3/8 In. 220.00

Tobacco, Brass, Engraved, Comical Man With Gun, 18th-19th Century, 5 x 3 x 1 In. 220.00

Tobacco, Brass, Parable From John, Good Shepherd, 1747, 2 3/4 x 4 5/8 In. 575.00

Toilet, Strawwork, Dome Top, Ivory Hardware, Dartmoor Prison, England, 1790 .... 875.00

Trinket, Exotic Wood, Heart Shape, Heart Shape Reserve On Lid, 3 In. 258.00

Trinket, Gold Filigree Work, Pink Carved Flowers, Glass Panels	85.00
Vanity, Man's, Mother-Of-Pearl Crest, Lift-Out Tray, Secret Drawer, 12 x 9 In.	800.00
Wall, 3 Sections, Mustard, Red Striping, Dovetailed Gray Blue Interior, 16 1/2 In.	440.00
Wall, Cherry, Lift Top, 1 Drawer, Dovetailed	575.00
Wall, Figured Tiger Maple, Dovetailed Construction, Late 18th Century, 12 In.	795.00
Wallpaper Covered, Boston Paper, 1833, 10 1/2 x 14 1/2 x 11 1/2 In.	275.00
Wallpaper Covered, Orange & White Design, Green Ground Paper Interior, 7 In.	1495.00
Walnut, Dovetailed, Wrought Iron Strap Hinges & Hasp, 10 3/8 In.	545.00
Walnut, Slant Top, Ed Wash, 7 1/2 x 16 In.	440.00
Walnut, Wire Nail Design, Square Footed, 11 In.	83.00
Whatnot, Bronze, Stars & Oval Cabochons, Velvet Lined, Agate Mounted, 5 In.	431.00
Wooden, Basket With Flowers On Top, Blue & Green Banding, 6 x 9 x 15 In.	90.00
Wooden, Brass, Embossed Tavern Scene, England	330.00
Wooden, Cricket, 3-Dimensional Vintage Design, China, 3 1/2 In.	140.00
Wooden, Figures In Landscape On Lid, Grain Painted Reserves, Decoupage, 13 7/8 In.	287.00
Wooden, Freeform, Hinged, Russel Wright, Signed, 2 3/4 x 9 1 /2 In.	1045.00
Wooden, Paint Decorated, Circular Design, Cobalt Blue Floral Cover, 8 1/2 In.	489.00
Wooden, Pine, Red, Conical Footed, 9 3/4 x 10 x 4 In.	303.00
Work, Embroidered Leather, Bombe Form, Scalloped Lid, 5 3/4 x 11 In.	230.00
Work, Quilter's, Burled Walnut & Wood Veneers, Stuffed Cushion, 1850s, 5 x 7 5/8 In.	288.00
Writing, Cherry, Slant Lid, 6 Compartment Interior, 2 Small Drawers, 10 1/2 x 24 In.	1495.00
Writing, Mahogany & Rosewood Lined, Inkwell, Leather Surface, Brass Mounts, 18 In.	440.00
Writing, Olive Wood Veneer, Mahogany Bands, Fitted Interior, Brass Lock & Key, 16 In.	220.00

BOY SCOUT collectibles include any material related to scouting, including patches, manuals, and uniforms. The Boy Scout movement in the United States started in 1910. The first Jamboree was held in 1937. Girl Scout items are listed under their own heading.

Ax, Steel Head, Wood Handle, Leather Carrier, Collins, 13 In.	20.00
Baby Spoon, Sterling Silver, Stork By Chimney, BSA Emblem On Chest, 4 In.	100.00
Badge, Explorer Post 590, Public Safety, White Metal Shield, Eagle, 2 1/2 In.	35.00
Badge, Junior Assistant Scoutmaster, Gold Metal Emblem, Green Bars, 1 In.	30.00
Badge, Layman, Blue Enamel Ground, Gold Toned Emblem, 3/4 In.	25.00
Bank, Boy Scout Camp, Mechanical, Cast Iron, J. & E. Stevens	1150.00 to 6600.00
Bank, Figural, Cast Iron, 1920s, 5 3/4 In.	100.00
Banner, National Jamboree, Cloth, 1954	45.00
Book, Boy Scouts Yearbook, Hard Cover, McGuire & Mathews, 1916, 269 Pages	40.00
Book, Matching Mountains With The Boy Scout Uniform, Edward Reimer, 1929	65.00
Book, Scout Circus, 1934, 192 Pages	35.00
Book, Scouting With Daniel Boone, 1914	5.00
Book, Woodcraft Lesson, 1913	25.00
Booklet, Scout Courtesy Customs & Drills, 1942, 95 Pages	30.00
Booklet, The Scoutmaster & His Troop, 1935	35.00
Booklet, Troop Spirit, 1930, 22 Pages	35.00
Box, Storage, Hinged, Tin, Green Enamel, BSA Eagle, Be Prepared, 9 x 6 x 3 1/2 In.	43.00
Brag Vest, Suede, Scouting Events Patches, Order Of The Arrow, 1950-1960	155.00
Brochure, Men Of Tomorrow, Large	10.00
Bugle, Rexcraft	35.00
Card, 3-Fold, Norman Rockwell, 1929	20.00
Card, Membership, Folder In Sleeve, 1940	27.00
Catalog, Boy Scouts Of American, Scouting Equipment, Uniforms, 1927, 32 Pages	75.00
Certificate, 3-Year Training Program, Monmouth, N.J. Council, 1956	23.00
Drum, Flag, Ship, Eagle, Tin, Celluloid, 1908, 6 1/2 In.	100.00
Drum, Tin, Scouts In Uniform, Boy Scout Band, Wood Bands, 2 Sticks, 12 In.	385.00
Figurine, Boy Scout, Pot Metal, Dated 1915	75.00
Handbook, Color Oilcloth Cover, 1923, 513 Pages	47.00
Handbook, For Boys, 1948	15.00
Handbook, For Boys, 2nd Edition, 1930	30.00
Handbook, For Boys, Hardcover, 1916, 656 Pages	25.00
Handbook, For Scoutmasters, Black & White Photos, 1927, 676 Pages	35.00
Handbook, For Scoutmasters, Official, 1920, 608 Pages	40.00
Handbook, Patrol Leader's, 1929	12.00
Handbook, Philmont Scout, 1958	5.00

Handbook, Wolf Cub, Paper Back, 1967	3.00
Hat, Sea Scout, Leader, Wool, Navy Blue, Black Visor, White Chin Strap, Size 7 1/4	57.00
Hatchet, Leather Case	50.00
Hatchet, Plumb, Leather Case	35.00
Jacket, Poplin, Green, National Jamboree, Valley Forge, 1964, Medium	34.00
Knife, Hunting, Ka-Bar, Tan Leather Sheath, BSA Logo, 5 1/4 In.	55.00
Knife, Ulster, 4 Blades, Pocket	45.00
Magazine, Koshare, 1955	5.00
Merit Badge Sash, Eagle Scout, Tan, 15 Badges, 1920-1930	398.00
Merit Badge Sash, Tan, 1937 National Jamboree Patch, Camporee Patches, 1930s	218.00
Merit Badge Sash, Tan, 9 Crimped-Edge Badges, 6 Patches, 1940s	26.00
Neckerchief, Order Of The Arrow, White Cotton, Embroidered, 7 1/2 x 5 1/2 In.	24.00
Patch, 50th Jubilee	15.00
Patch, Air Scout Squadron, Winged Emblem, World War II Era, 3 1/2 In., Set Of 5	345.00
Patch, Build Serve Achieve Roundup, 1961	5.00
Patch, National Jamboree, Washington D.C. 1937, 3 In.	85.00
Patch, Patrol, Flying Eagle, Red Felt, Black Embroidered Eagle, 2 In.	30.00
Photograph, Troop 65, 1964 National Jamboree, Valley Forge, 8 x 10 In.	25.00
Pin, Collar, Council Executive, Silver Outline, Eagle, Wreath, Red Ground, 1 In.	35.00
Pin, Webelos, Metal, Gold & Blue Bar, Ribbons	2.00
Plaque, Award, 1960, 6 x 9 In.	8.00
Poster, Boy Scout Jamboree, Canceled, Norman Rockwell, Unfolded, Frame, 1935	1000.00
Scarf, National Jamboree Valley Forge, 1957	25.00
Shirt, Explorer Scout, Dark Green Cotton Twill, Long Sleeves, 1950s	25.00
Shirt, Junior Assistant Scoutmaster, Tan Cotton Twill, Patches, 1940s	23.00
Shirt, Scoutmaster, Green, Long Sleeves, Pocket Flap Patch, Size Medium	25.00
Shirt, Sea Scout Explorer, Green, Long Sleeves, Patches, 1950s, Size 15	31.00
Statue, Scout, Cast Pewter, Hollow Base, Bronze Paint, 8 1/2 In.	22.00
Telegraph Set	75.00
Watch Fob, Bust Of Scout, Crossed Flags, Rifles, Bugle, Leather Strap, 1 1/4 In.	25.00

BRADLEY & HUBBARD is a name found on many metal objects. Walter Hubbard and his brother-in-law, Nathaniel Lyman Bradley, started making cast iron clocks, tables, frames, andirons, lamps, chandeliers, sconces, and sewing birds in 1854 in Meriden, Connecticut. The company became Bradley & Hubbard Manufacturing Company in 1875. Charles Parker Company bought the firm in 1940. Their lamps are especially prized by collectors.

Andirons, Block Tops, Geometric Figures, Brass Wash, 22 1/2 In.	275.00
Andirons, Cast Iron, Rounded Scrollwork, Twist Design, 16 3/4 In.	225.00
Andirons, Sunburst, Cast Iron, 16 1/2 In.	575.00
Andirons, Winged Griffin, No. 9537	2800.00
Ashtray, Gentleman Form, Polychrome, Signed, 6 In.	35.00
Cuspidor, Turtle Form, Step On Tail To Open, Signed, 11 In.	250.00 to 265.00
Inkwell, Silver Plated Stag Head Base, Square	467.50
Lamp, 6-Panel, White Slag Glass Shade, 14 In.	325.00
Lamp, Banquet, Pale Pink Globe, Reticulated, Base, 27 In.	650.00
Lamp, Gone With The Wind, Chrysanthemum Globe, Electrified, 22 In.	275.00
Lamp, Gone With The Wind, Flower, Brown, Yellow Ground, 22 In.	300.00
Lamp, Kerosene, Bronze, 8-Panel, Slag Glass Shade, 19 In.	475.00
Lamp, Kerosene, Student, Single	3300.00
Lamp, Lincoln Drape	375.00
Lamp, Oak Leaves, Acorn Design, Green Slag Glass, Bronze Shade, 11 In.	990.00
Lamp, Oil, Banquet, Hand Painted Holly Globe, Gilded Metal & Brass, 31 In.	412.00
Lamp, Oil, Banquet, White Onyx Base, Gilded Cast Metal, Electrified, 29 In.	330.00
Lamp, Oil, Brass, Rococo Openwork Handles, Electrified	175.00
Lamp, Table, Brass, Embossed Floral Design, Slag Glass Panes, 22 In.	610.00

BRASS has been used for decorative pieces and useful tablewares since ancient times. It is an alloy of copper, zinc, and other metals. Additional brass items may be found under Bell, Candlestick, Tool, or Trivet.

Beaker, Cast & Turned, Early 19th Century, 2 3/4 In.	105.00
Bed Warmer, Brass Pan, Punch Geometric Design, Wooden Handle, Child's, 33 In.	225.00

Brass can be polished with this homemade remedy: Make a paste of equal parts salt, flour, and vinegar. Rub the paste on the brass with a soft cloth. Rinse completely. Buff with a clean, dry, soft cloth.

Brass, Clock Pendulum, Glass Insert Center, White & Green Star, 2 1/4 x 6 1/2 In.

Brass, Clock Pendulum, Scrollwork, Building & Trees In Center, 2 1/2 x 6 1/4 In.

Bed Warmer, Extended Mahogany Handle, Floral Lid, Copper, 43 In.	45.00
Bed Warmer, Floral Engraved Cover, Turned Wooden Handle, Dark Finish, 43 In.	220.00
Box, Jewelry, Hinged Cover, Clear Glass, Plush Interior, Rectangular, 5 1/2 x 6 3/4 In.	195.00
Bucket, Ansonia Company, Large	55.00
Bucket, Ansonia Company, Small	35.00
Cannon, Laurel Wreath Motif, Wooden Caddy, Wheels, France, 12 In.	259.00
Card Holder, Figural Design, Early 20th Century, 9 1/4 x 4 1/2 In.	33.00
Chalice, Footed, 2 Handles, Ribbed, Hammered, Weiner Werkstatte, 1920-1925, 7 1/4 In.	5750.00
Chamberstick, Cast Stem, Push-Up Ejector, 1740-1780, 4 5/8 In.	165.00
Chamberstick, Flared Base, S-Shape Handle, Arts & Crafts, Benedict Studios, 6 In.	75.00 to 80.00
Chamberstick, Frying Pan, Design, Initials, Holland, 1718, 11 In.	395.00
Chamberstick, Original Patina, Carence Crafters, 4 1/2 In.	165.00
Clock Pendulum, Glass Insert Center, White & Green Star, 2 1/4 x 6 1/2 In. ......*Illus*	15.00
Clock Pendulum, Scrollwork, Building & Trees In Center, 2 1/2 x 6 1/4 In. ....*Illus*	10.00
Coffeepot, Classic Design, Acorn Finial, England, 18th Century, 9 In.	275.00
Coffeepot, WMF Secessionist Style, Woven Handle Cover, Brass Stand, 14 In.	300.00
Comb, Federal Style Eagle On Top, Late 18th Century, 4 1/2 In.	325.00
Crucifix, Priest's, Russia, 14 x 9 In.	750.00
Cup, Conical, Monogram, WHW, Hagenauer Wien, Signed, 10 1/4 In., Pair	2055.00
Cutter, Cigar, Ship's Wheel	225.00
Desk, Portable, Crystal Bottles, Rosewood Tray, Lock, Handmade Screws, c.1850	400.00
Door Knocker, Little Nell	110.00
Door Knocker, Sea Beast Form, Late 19th Century, 12 In.	863.00
Door Knocker, With Seated Lion, Polished, c.1770-1800, 10 In.	2250.00
Figurine, Dancing Woman, Patinated, WHW, Hagenauer Wien, Austria, 10 3/4 In.	1315.00
Figurine, Dragon, White, Long Twisted Tail, 5 1/4 In.	59.00
Figurine, Lion, White Marble Base, Parson Mark, 2 1/4 x 5 1/2 In.	28.00
Girandoles, Figural Stem, Faceted Prisms, White Marble Base, 14 1/2 In., Pair	175.00
Gong, Antler Mounted, Suede Covered Striker, Oak Base, c.1880, 21 In.	172.00
Kettle, Dome Cover, Bell Form, Beak Spout, Swing Handle, 1820, 21 In.	863.00
Kettle, Raised Stepped Cover, Pear Form, Lidded Spout, Swing Handle, 1800, 16 In.	690.00
Kettle, Spun, Iron Bale Handle, 14 In.	60.00
Kettle, Wrought Iron Bail, Seamless, 6 x 10 In.	195.00
Lighter, Pipe, Brass & Wood, Dutch, c.1740, 6 5/8 In.	425.00
Lock, Trunk, 1820s, 5 1/2 x 3 7/8 In.	95.00
Mantel Set, Gilt, Porcelain Insert, Key & Pendulum, France, 17 1/2 In., 3 Piece	990.00
Measure, Cast Brass, Marked Brampton Rd., 1/2 Pt., 4 In.	145.00
Mortar & Pestle, Brass Handles, Drugstore Size	125.00
Muffineer, Incised Bands, Domed Pierced Lid, Scroll Handle, Everted Rim, 1760, 4 In.	403.00
Ornament, Gilded, Heart In Hand, 4 7/8 In., Set Of 3	495.00
Pan, Jam, Spun Brass, Hand Wrought Iron Swing Handle, Scotland, 11 1/4 In.	55.00
Pan, Jam, Spun Brass, Wrought Iron Arch Handle, Scotland, Late 19th Century, 13 In.	120.00
Pan, Warming, Tulip Design, Basket Of Fruit & Flowers, Brass Lid, 1875, 42 In.	345.00
Pitcher, Incised Figural Design, Handwrought, Los Castillo, Taxco, Mexico, 11 3/4 In.	835.00
Planter, Flower Baskets On Sides, Double Lion Ring Handles, England, 10 x 9 1/2 In.	80.00

Porringer, 2 Fretted Ears, Tudor Rose In Base, c.1720, 7 1/4 In.	650.00
Samovar, 2 Handles, Undertray, Waste Bowl, Russia, Marked, 1870, 17 1/2 In.	310.00
Samovar, Urn, Bulbous, Dome Pedestal, 4 Ogee Bracket Feet, Russia, 16 In.	385.00
Samovar, Urn, Bulbous, Dome Pedestal, Bracket Feet, Russia, 15 In.	176.00
Samovar, Urn, Dome Base, Brass Handles, Raised On 4 Bracket Feet, Russia, 14 In.	440.00
Sconce, 1-Light, Wall, Mask, Foliate Design, Scrolled Arm, 19th Century, 15 In.	690.00
Sconce, 3-Light, Wall, Ornate, 1920s, 19 x 11 In.	250.00
Scuttle, Helmet Shape, England, c.1870	950.00
Spice Mill, Brass, Design, Folding Handle, Turkey, 1700	110.00
Spurs, Gal-Leg, Sterling Silver, M & W S.E., 1905, 4 x 6 In.	520.00
Still, Domed Top, Swing Handle, 18 In.	33.00
Still, Reeded Barrel Form, Spigots, Copper, 24 1/2 In.	55.00
Sundial, Globe Form, 11 In.	33.00
Teakettle, Gooseneck Spout, Turned Wooden Handle, H. Gordon & Co., 9 In.	85.00
Teakettle, Turned Wooden Handle, England, 19th Century, 4 In.	285.00
Tray, Bamboo Design, Original Patina, Carence Crafters, 9 x 5 In.	187.00
Tray, Engraved, Chased Handles, Removable Mahogany Base, c.1770, 16 3/4 In.	2200.00
Tray, Original Patina, Arts & Crafts, Carence Crafters, 9 In.	143.00
Wall Pocket, Copper Star Design, England, c.1840, 13 In.	495.00
Warmer, Butter Or Brandy, Wood Handle, Late 18th Century, 2 1/2 In.	165.00
Whistle, Leather Crop, Police, Equestrian, 18 In.	135.00
Whistle, Steam, 3 x 13 In.	225.00

BRASTOFF, see Sascha Brastoff category.

BREAD PLATE, see various silver categories, porcelain factories, and pressed glass patterns.

BRIDE'S BASKETS OR BRIDE'S BOWLS were usually one-of-a-kind novelties made in American and European glass factories. They were especially popular about 1880 when the decorated basket was often given as a wedding gift. Cut glass baskets were popular after 1890. All bride's baskets lost favor about 1905. Bride's baskets and bride's bowls may also be found in other glass sections. Check the index at the back of the book.

BRIDE'S BASKET, Blue, White, Amber, Blue, Gold Ruffles, 12 In.	412.00
Cased Glass, Plum To Custard, 11 1/2 In.	330.00
Cased Glass, White, Pink Interior, Floral Design In Bowl, 11 1/2 In.	225.00
Cranberry Opalescent Lattice, Frame, 9 In.	192.00
Delaware, Clear, Rose & Gold, Oval, Silver Frame	285.00
Diamond-Quilted, Pink & White Cased, Silver Plated Frame, 11 x 8 In.	605.00
Pink To White Glass, Ruffled Rim, Silver Plated Stand, 3 Cherubs, 11 In.	522.00
Portrait In Center, Ruffled Edge, Art Nouveau Style Stand, 13 x 12 In.	345.00
Salmon, White, Ruffled Edge, Quadruple Plate Frame	302.00
BRIDE'S BOWL, Cased Glass, Blue, White Flowers, Leaves, Ruffled Edge, 3 1/2 In.	195.00
Cased Glass, Dark To Light Pink Interior, Ruffled Edge, 8 1/2 x 2 3/8 In.	44.00
Cased Glass, Diamond-Quilted, Cranberry Opalescent, Square, 4 x 8 In.	165.00
Cased Glass, Pale Ivory, Red Border, Wavy Border, 10 x 2 3/4 In.	50.00
Cased Glass, Yellow, Fluted Edge, Tufts Silver Plated Holder	220.00
Cranberry, Applied Custard Ruffled Edge, Acid Finish, 10 In.	126.00
Flowers, Leaf Design, Off-White Ground, Ruffled Edge, Gold, Silver Sanded, 3 In.	165.00
Herringbone, Pink Fluted Border, 8 1/2 x 2 1/2 In.	33.00
Peachblow, 3 x 9 7/8 x 3 3/4 In.	245.00
Purple & White Flowers, Scalloped Edge, White Underside, 10 3/4 In.	210.00
Satin Glass, Enameled Gold Flower Design, 12 1/2 In.	298.00
White Satin, Yellow, Winged Cherubs Picking Fruit, 5 x 11 3/4 In.	330.00
Yellow & White Satin Glass, Cherubs, Meriden Silver Plated Holder, 5 In.	330.00

BRISTOL glass was made in Bristol, England, after the 1700s. The Bristol glass most often seen today is a Victorian, lightweight opaque glass that is often blue. Some of the glass was decorated with enamels.

Charger, Adam & Eve, Blue, c.1695, 13 1/2 In.	2050.00
Decanter, Butterfly, Enameled Flowers, Ruffled Stopper, 11 1/2 In.	75.00
Dresser Set, Lavender, 3 Piece	165.00

Finger Bowl, Clambroth, Applied Floral Design, 19th Century, 3 x 4 1/2 In.	33.00
Lamp, Kerosene, White, Electrified, 32 In.	86.00
Pitcher, Lacy Gold Sprays, Small Flowers, 5 1/4 In.	70.00
Pitcher, White Opalescent, Applied Handle, 8 In.	38.00
Sweetmeat Jar, Enameled Egrets, Silver Plated Top, Rim & Handle, 5 1/2 In.	135.00
Vase, Bud, 3 Cupids, Flowers, 7 3/4 In.	65.00
Vase, Clambroth, Floral Design, 8 In., Pair	27.00
Vase, Clambroth, Floral Design, Winged Cherubs At Play, 11 1/4 In.	66.00
Vase, Clambroth, Satin, Molded Silhouettes, Footed, 12 In., Pair	90.00
Vase, Coach & Horses, Scrolled, 14 In.	100.00
Vase, Cupid & Maiden Front, Rosette Back, 10 In.	130.00
Vase, Floral Design, Encrusted Gold, 10 3/8 In., Pair	55.00
Vase, Floral, Bee Design, 10 In.	8.50
Vase, Light Green, Floral Design, 14 In., Pair	137.00
Vase, Pink Cased, Ruffled Edge, 8 3/4 In.	55.00
Vase, Pink, Satin, Bands & Leaves, Applied Handle, Gold Trim, 6 3/8 In.	125.00
Vase, Polychrome Enameled Flowers, Gilt, 8 7/8 In.	66.00
Vase, Poppies, Red, Purple, 13 In.	100.00

BRITANNIA, see Pewter category.

BRONZE is an alloy of copper, tin, and other metals. It is used to make figurines, lamps, and other decorative objects. Pieces listed here date from the eighteenth, nineteenth, and twentieth centuries.

Ashtray, Figural, Male Tennis Player On Green Onyx	135.00
Ashtray, Meier, E., Figural, Boy Drinking From Shell, 6 In.	315.00
Bowl, Lotus, 2 Crabs, Resting On Lily Pad, Japan, 6 1/2 In.	1045.00
Box, Cover, Perenn, Classical Scene, Angel Musicians, Ball Footed, 6 1/2 x 7 3/4 In.	550.00
Box, Jewelry, Coach Shape, Enameled, 19th Century, Austria, 4 x 3 1/2 x 7 1/2 In.	2200.00
Brazier, Side Bacchic Masks, Hoof Feet, Paw Feet, 59 In., Pair	4315.00
Bust, Goder, H., Nymph In Flower, Variegated Red Marble Base, 9 In.	1035.00
Bust, Hannaux, E., Man, Helmet, Gilt, Marble Base, Jollet & Cie Bronzes, Paris, 5 In.	315.00
Bust, Houdon, George Washington, Arable Socle, 1778, 20 1/2 In.	4025.00
Bust, Kusher, Stuart, Cowboy, Marble Base, 7 In.	95.00
Bust, Man, Patinated, Marble Base, 8 In., Pair	747.00
Bust, Mars, Rouge Marble Plinth, Verde Antico Base, Signed, 9 1/4 In.	209.00
Bust, Pinedo, Napoleon, Gilt, Marble Stepped Base, Signed, France, 8 3/4 In.	575.00
Bust, Villanis, Delilah, Girl In Headscarf, Patinated, 16 3/4 In.	1315.00
Cannon, Mounted On Cast Iron Carriage, Wheels, 1-In. Bore, 1870s	1250.00
Cannon, Wooden Truck, Brass Wheels, 20 In.	275.00
Cauldron, St. George & Dragon, Saint Other Side, Germany, 1480s, 10 1/2 In.	1840.00
Champagne Bucket, Missile Form, Removable Liner, Silvered, April 6, 1879, 28 In.	4600.00
Compote, Neptune, Other Sea Gods & Serpents In Waves, 19th Century, 7 1/2 In.	175.00
Ewer, Man Watching Lovers Kiss, Base Dragons With Masks, 1880s, 36 In.	6325.00
Figurine, 3 Hunting Dogs, Attacking Stag, Vienna	1450.00
Figurine, Armbrister, David, Samurai, 20th Century, 20 In.	345.00
Figurine, Art Nouveau Woman, Flowing Toga, Places Branch On Pillar, 23 1/2 In.	2970.00
Figurine, Barbedienne, Classical Goddess, 26 1/4 In.	2185.00
Figurine, Barye, Antoine, Jaguar, Sleeping, Brown Patina, 12 In.	6325.00
Figurine, Barye, Antoine-Louis, Lion, Green Patina, Signed, France, 1850, 9 x 15 In.	605.00
Figurine, Barye, Lion, Attacking Serpent, 17 In.	2185.00
Figurine, Barye, Mother Pig & 5 Playful Piglets, 7 1/2 In.	2950.00
Figurine, Barye, Owl, Outstretched Wings, Signed, 19th Century, 4 x 6 In.	275.00
Figurine, Barye, Panther Of India, Antoine-Louis, Dark Green, Black Patina, 5 1/4 In.	495.00
Figurine, Barye, Theseus Slaying Centaur, 13 In.	4140.00
Figurine, Barye, Tiger Attacking Stag	6325.00
Figurine, Berge, Nymph, Standing, American Art Foundry, New York, 8 1/2 In.	975.00
Figurine, Bergman, Austrian Lizard, Mouth Opens When Leg Moves _Illus_	2530.00
Figurine, Bergman, Rooster, Glass Eyes, Painted, 8 1/2 In. _Illus_	1320.00
Figurine, Boar, 5 1/2 x 4 1/2 In.	140.00
Figurine, Bonheur, I., Pointer, Standing, Bronze, Brown, Patina, 1827, 32 In.	10350.00
Figurine, Bouraine, Marcel, Salome Presenting Head Of John The Baptist, c.1929	4500.00
Figurine, Bouval, Maurice, Seated Maiden, Nude, Gilt, Signed, 8 5/8 In.	1235.00

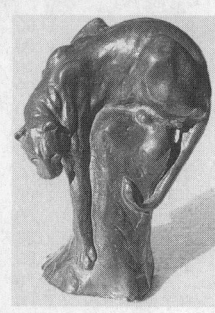

Bronze, Figurine,
Hyatt, Anna V.,
Mountain Lion On
Rock, 32 1/2 In.

Bronze, Figurine, Bergman, Austrian Lizard,
Mouth Opens When Leg Moves

Figurine, Brown, Joseph, Ballerina, Marble Base, 8 1/2 x 10 1/2 In.	330.00
Figurine, Brown, Linda, Bather, Marble Base, 17 In.	660.00
Figurine, Buffalo, Standing, Integral Bronze Base, Signed, 12 In.	175.00
Figurine, Carriere-Belleuse, Woman Reading, Ivory Face & Hands, 12 1/2 In.	1380.00
Figurine, Causse, J., Maiden Archer, No Bow, France, 19th Century, 31 1/2 In.	1210.00
Figurine, Chapu, H., La Jeunesse, Art Nouveau Woman, Reaching Up To Pillar	2970.00
Figurine, Cherub With Violin, 22 1/2 In.	300.00
Figurine, Colinet, Kneeling Egyptian Maiden, Marble Plinth, 14 In.	2310.00
Figurine, Corti, A., Seminude Maiden, Putting Toes In Water, Marble, 17 In.	750.00
Figurine, Dachshund, Marble Base, 6 In.	135.00
Figurine, Debut, Tunisian Boy, Carrying Water Jugs, 36 In. ....*Illus*	3850.00
Figurine, Deer, Inlaid Mixed Metals, China, 19th Century, 8 x 9 In.	525.00
Figurine, Dog, Oval Base, Gilt, Victorian, 3 1/2 x 4 In.	1250.00
Figurine, Dragon, Wooden Stand, 13 1/2 In.	90.00
Figurine, Dumaige, Man & Woman Warrior, 23 In., Pair	3220.00
Figurine, Eagle, Outstretched Wings, Pink Marble Base, 4 1/2 In.	287.00
Figurine, Elephant, Dark Brown Patinated, 10 x 13 In.	33.00
Figurine, Elephant, Raised Trunk, Japan, 45 x 45 In.	2750.00
Figurine, Falguiere, A., Woman Nude, Water Jug On Shoulder, 29 In.	2860.00
Figurine, Faure, Maurice, Crusader, Mail & Armor, Ivory Face & Hands, 13 1/4 In.	1495.00
Figurine, Foley, J.H., Gaelic Warrior, London, 31 In.	1320.00
Figurine, Fox, Lincoln, Indian, Quiver, Tomahawk, 1988, 14 In.	420.00
Figurine, Fratin, Dog, Setter With Bird In Mouth ....*Illus*	990.00
Figurine, Gatti, Young Boy Beside Cat & Mouse, 28 In.	1495.00
Figurine, Gerome, Jean-Leon, La Danse, Dancing Woman, Patinated, Paris, 20 1/2 In.	5750.00
Figurine, Girl, Examining Flower Blossom, Baton Under Arm, Signed, 16 1/2 In.	1265.00
Figurine, Girl, Playing Flute, Armor Bronze Co., Pair	120.00
Figurine, Goff, Male Nude, Seated On Rocky Base, 1891, 24 1/2 In.	3740.00
Figurine, Grisard, D., The Pose, 14 1/2 In.	980.00
Figurine, Hagenauer, African Dancer, 10 1/2 In., Pair	1600.00
Figurine, Heuvelmans, Lucienne, Madonna & Child, Signed, 11 1/2 In.	1840.00
Figurine, Hyatt, Anna V., Mountain Lion On Rock, 32 1/2 In. ....*Illus*	3190.00
Figurine, Jaeger, G., Blacksmith At Work, Marble Base, 13 1/2 In.	1250.00
Figurine, Johnson, C.H., Middle Eastern Dance, Seminude, 33 In.	3165.00
Figurine, Judd, Donald, Mythological Children, Walnut Mounted, 7 3/4 x 17 1/4 In.	50.00
Figurine, Kaespach, R., Shot-Putter, Gilt, Marble Base, Early 20th Century, 16 In.	1045.00
Figurine, Kaish, Luise Meyers, Horse, 1925, 8 In.	330.00
Figurine, Kuntze, Reinhold, Whimsical Jester & Pig, c.1925, 14 1/4 In.	1265.00
Figurine, Lambert, Jack Lincoln, Man, Brown Patina, 8 In.	475.00
Figurine, Laurent, E., Nymph, Winged, Black Marble Base, 10 1/2 In.	460.00
Figurine, Lavroff, Snarling Panther, Silvered, Marble, 1920s, 24 1/8 In.	5625.00
Figurine, Leyrer, C., Diana, On Deer, Patinated, Munich, 1900, 29 5/8 In.	5750.00
Figurine, Louis, 3 Mermen Holding Shell Aloft, 11 1/2 x 9 In.	3680.00
Figurine, Male Lion, Hollow Cast, 40 In., Pair	4180.00
Figurine, Martinus, Boy, Holding A Bird, Standing On Rocky Base, France, 38 1/2 In.	2125.00
Figurine, Mene, Pierre, Equestrian, After The Race, 20th Century, 17 1/2 x 21 In.	272.00
Figurine, Mene, Pierre, Horse, Standing, Bronze, Brown Patina, 1810, 17 In.	8050.00
Figurine, Mene, Pierre, Irish Wolfhound, Bronze, Brown Patina, 1807, 13 In.	6900.00

Figurine, Mene, Pierre, Reclining Stag, 19th Century, 5 In. 302.00
Figurine, Mercury, Marble Pedestal, 19 1/2 In. 165.00
Figurine, Moigniez, Jules, Boar Hunt, 12 3/4 In. 3300.00
Figurine, Moigniez, Jules, Horse, English Saddle, Marble Base, 12 1/4 In. 1100.00
Figurine, Moigniez, Jules, Horse, Side Saddle, Marble Base, 13 1/4 In. 850.00
Figurine, Monkey, Holding A Shell, Austria, 4 In. 230.00
Figurine, Moreau, Bacchanalian Group, 21 In. 4312.00
Figurine, Moreau, Mathurin, Female, Round Base, 43 In. 8825.00
Figurine, Muse, Dancing, Dark Brown Patina, Signed, Rome, 1946, 22 In. 605.00
Figurine, Nude Warrior, Ocher, Black Marble Plinth Base, 5 1/2 x 3 1/4 x 11 In. 880.00
Figurine, Nude Warrior, Swordsman Pose With Dagger, Black Marble Base, 6 In. 5500.00
Figurine, Nude, With Pole, Gilt, Black Marble Base, 9 1/4 In. 520.00
Figurine, Preiss, F., Con Brio, Ivory Woman, Painted Bikini, Marble, 1920s, 15 1/8 In. .. 9373.00
Figurine, Preiss, F., The Stile, Green Onyx Base, 10 In. 7475.00
Figurine, Preiss, Girl, Skipping Rope, Ivory, 6 3/4 In. 1610.00
Figurine, Preiss, Girl, With Casket, Ivory, 6 5/8 In. 2760.00
Figurine, Preiss, Parting, Ivory, Green Onyx Base, 7 In. 6325.00
Figurine, Preiss, Woman, Nude, Outstretched Arms, Green Onyx Base, 13 In. 2990.00
Figurine, Prost, Prowling Panther, Wedge Marble Base, 1930, 14 In. 2250.00
Figurine, Puppy, Recumbent, Brown, c.1920, Austria, 4 In. 290.00
Figurine, Rancoulet, Ernest, Renaissance Worker, 26 3/8 In. 2200.00
Figurine, Remington, Mountain Man, Marble Base, 27 In. 605.00
Figurine, Sadoux, A., Horse, 15 1/2 In. 2875.00
Figurine, Scholar, On A Mule, Reading From A Book, China, 12 1/2 In. 1840.00
Figurine, Sphinx, Recumbent, 26 1/2 In., Pair 1620.00
Figurine, Sphinx, Verde Antico Patina, 19th Century, 9 3/4 In. 660.00
Figurine, Stouffer, Edgar, J., Young Girl Nymph, Nude, Holding Rabbit, c.1915, 7 In. ... 575.00
Figurine, Tiger, 2-Tone, 10 x 17 In. 1500.00
Figurine, Weiss, Felix, Dancer, Woman On Tiptoe, Green, Patinated, 24 1/2 In. 2055.00
Figurine, Winged Victory, Black Marble, Europe, 40 x 24 In. 3575.00
Figurine, Woman, Nude, Kneeling, Patinated, Marble Base, Gorham Co., 4 In. 750.00
Figurine, Woman, Seated With Rose, Stepped Base, 12 1/4 In. 135.00
Figurine, Woman, With Dog, Pink Marble Base, 10 5/8 In. 190.00
Figurine, Zach, Bruno, Gladiators, 21 1/2 x 23 1/4 In. 5175.00
Garniture Set, Gilt, Figural Design, Cut Drop Prisms, 16 In., 3 Piece 345.00
Group, Couple, Courting, Austria, 4 1/4 In. 750.00
Group, Herd Boy Riding Water Buffalo, Japan, 7 x 9 In. 145.00
Group, Lavroff, Woman, Nude, Embracing Borzoi, Partly Silvered, Marble, 29 In. 9370.00
Group, Le Faguays, 3 Dancing Women, Grecian, Silvered, Marble, 1920s, 11 In. 1780.00
Group, Martinus, Young Girl, Feeding A Squirrel, France, 20 x 19 In. 2125.00
Group, Officer & Lady Astride Horse, Dark Brown Patina, 14 x 12 In. 865.00
Group, Poertzel, La Poupee, 15 In. 1495.00
Group, Schmidt-Felling, 2 Owls, Patinated, Inlaid Glass Eyes, 7 3/8 In. 655.00
Head, Elongated Face, Amadeo Modigliani Style, Black Patina, 16 1/2 In. 675.00
Humidor, Renaissance Style, Panels Of Figures & Foliage, 6 In. 430.00
Jar, Foo Dog Finial Lid, Oriental, 16 In. 165.00

Bronze, Figurine,
Debut, Tunisian
Boy, Carrying
Water Jugs, 36 In.

Bronze, Figurine, Fratin, Dog,
Setter With Bird In Mouth

Bronze, Figurine, Bergman,
Rooster, Glass Eyes, Painted,
8 1/2 In.

Jar, Incense, Reticulated Lid, 2 Birds Finial, Birds & Blossoms, Oriental, 19 1/2 In. 495.00
Jar, Man & Monkey Finial, Oriental, 17 In. 495.00
Jardiniere, Bamboo Design, Gilt Inlay, 4 x 11 x 17 In. 440.00
Letter Opener, Green Seahorse & Fish, Arts & Crafts, E.T. Hurley, 9 In. 265.00
Letter Opener, Williams & Peters Pittston Coal, Buffalo 38.00
Mask, Bougouin, E., Young Man, Marble Base, Paris, 15 In. 1645.00
Mirror, Buddha & Acolyte Seated Under Tree, Ming Dynasty, 6 In. 275.00
Mirror, Dragon Center, T'Ang Dynasty, 4 1/8 In. 495.00
Mirror, Dressing, Circular Plate On Classical Figure, 19th Century, 14 In. 3680.00
Mirror, Flower Form, 2 Figures Under A Tree, Ming Dynasty, 5 1/2 In. 220.00
Mirror, Lion, Bird Amongst Grapevine, Ming Dynasty, 4 1/4 In. 154.00
Mirror, Lion, Grapevine Design, Ming Dynasty, 3 1/2 In. 135.00
Mold, Spoon, For Pewter Spoons, 1824 & Initials J.S. In Handle, With Spoon, 9 In. 165.00
Mold, Spoon, With Flat Tablespoon, 7 3/4 In. 335.00
Mortar, Acanthus On Upper Rim, Scrollwork Band, Punched Ground, Italy, 2 7/8 In. . . .   1725.00
Mortar, English, Dated 1683, 3 1/2 x 4 3/8 In. 650.00
Obelisk, Cleopatra's Needle, Marble Base, 16 In. 660.00
Obelisk, Gilt, Mirrored Glass, Orb & Arrow Top, Footed, France, 1930, 54 In., Pair 9750.00
Oil Burner, Classical Design, 4 1/2 In. 115.00
Pedestal, Lion, Standing, Holding Marble Top, Round Base, 48 x 19 3/4 In. 1925.00
Pen Stand, Boy Playing Flute, Green Marble Base, Swan Pen, Austria, 1930s 395.00
Planter, 3 Atlantes Acanthus Base, Green Patina, 20th Century, 40 In. 320.00
Planter, Neoclassical, Reticulated Basket, Supported By 3 Sphinxes, Green, 34 1/2 In. . .   1045.00
Plaque, Eagle, Naval, 13 Stars, 7 x 7 1/4 In. 100.00
Plaque, Ivory Elephant's Head, Molded Skin, Ivory Tusks, Japan, 1910, 14 In. 1090.00
Sconce, Chabert, D., Dancer, With Flowing Dress For Backplate, 1900, 7 1/4 In., Pair . . .   2070.00
Tazza, 7 Cabochon Jewels, Cast Rope-Twist Borders, 19th Century, France, 10 In. 165.00
Tazza, Neoclassical, Rouge Marble Base, Square, France, 19th Century, 8 1/4 In. 490.00
Urn, Open Fretwork, Rectangular Base, c.1870, 35 In., Pair 2400.00
Vase, Blossom Design, Flared Lip, Japan, 14 In. 110.00
Vase, Handles, Japan, 1850s, 12 In. 300.00
Vase, Leaf Baluster Form, Mid-19th Century, 11 In., Pair 460.00
Vase, Leaping Carp Form, 16 1/2 In. 450.00
Vase, Offner, J., Day & Night, Sunflowers, Allegorical, Patinated, 12 1/2 In. 2055.00
Vase, Sorensen, Brown & Green Patina, Impressed Mark, 8 In. 330.00

BROWNIES were first drawn in 1883 by Palmer Cox. They are charac-
terized by large round eyes, downturned mouths, and skinny legs.
Toys, books, dinnerware, and other objects were made with the
Brownies as part of the design.

Bracelet, 1940s 35.00
Candlestick, Majolica 425.00
Lamp Base, Chalkware, Palmer Cox 35.00
Pencil Box, Rolling-Pin Shape, 15 Brownies In Boat 90.00
Pin Dish, Scalloped Gold Rim, Limoges, 3 1/2 x 3 In. 125.00
Platter, Palmer Cox, Oval 395.00
Sauce, 2 Brownies, Palmer Cox 45.00
Tray, Benham's Ice Cream, Tin Lithograph, H.D. Beach Co., 13 1/4 x 10 1/2 In. 172.00

BRUSH Pottery was started in 1925. George Brush first worked in 1901
in Zanesville, Ohio. He started his own pottery in 1907, but it burned
to the ground soon after. In 1909 he then became manager of the J.W.
McCoy Pottery. In 1911, Brush and J.W. McCoy formed the Brush-
McCoy Pottery Co. After a series of name changes, the company
became The Brush Pottery in 1925. It closed in 1982. Collectors favor
the figural cookie jars made by this company. Because there was a
company named Brush-McCoy, there is great confusion between
Brush and Nelson McCoy pieces. See McCoy category for more information.

MARK

Bank, Pig 325.00
Cookie Jar, Bear, Feet Together 75.00
Cookie Jar, Cinderella Pumpkin 250.00
Cookie Jar, Cow, Brown . . . . .75.00 to 175.00

Cookie Jar, Cow, With Cat On Back 125.00
Cookie Jar, Elephant, Ice Cream Cone In Trunk, Bonnet, Blond Curls .... 370.00 to 400.00
Cookie Jar, Formal Pig, Black Coat, Blue Vest 300.00
Cookie Jar, Granny 50.00
Cookie Jar, Humpty Dumpty, Beanie 295.00
Cookie Jar, Humpty Dumpty, Blue Belt 350.00
Cookie Jar, Humpty Dumpty, Cowboy Hat 275.00
Cookie Jar, Laughing Hippo 725.00
Cookie Jar, Little Red Riding Hood .... 150.00 to 275.00
Cookie Jar, Old Shoe 95.00
Cookie Jar, Peter Pan 700.00
Cookie Jar, Peter, Peter, Pumpkin Eater 230.00
Cookie Jar, Squirrel On Log 115.00
Jardiniere, Blended Basket Weave, Emerald Green Glaze, 7 3/4 In. 33.00
Mug, Peter Pan .... 85.00 to 100.00
Vase, 2 Handles, Blue, Art Vellum Glaze, 8 In. 33.00
Vase, Amaryllis, Cream, 7 1/2 In. 60.00
Vase, Floral Design, Mottled Turquoise, Green Glaze, 7 In. 27.00
Vase, Majolica Stylized Flowers, 4 1/2 In. 44.00
Vase, Mulberry Over Green, Art Vellum Glaze, 4 1/2 In. 27.00
Vase, Stylized Flowers, Faceted Body, Polychrome, 7 In. 770.00

BRUSH MCCOY, see Brush category and related pieces in McCoy category.

BUCK ROGERS was the first American science fiction comic strip. It
started in 1929 and continued until 1965. Buck has also appeared in
comic books, movies, and, in the 1980s, a television series. Any memorabilia connected with the character Buck Rogers is collectible.

Battle Cruiser, Tootsietoy 125.00
Big Little Book, Buck Rogers 25th Century A.D., 1933, 318 Pages 92.00
Book, Coloring, Some Pages Colored, 1979 .... 5.00
Card & Sticker Set, Color Photographs, 1979 .... 21.00
Communications Outfit, Box, 1950s 150.00
Costume, Pants, Jersey, Holster & Gun 895.00
Electric Casting Set, Buck Rogers Jr. 700.00
Gun, Liquid Helium 400.00
Kit, Space Ranger 155.00
Knife, Solar Scout 550.00
Lunch Box, Thermos .... 35.00 to 75.00
Pencil Box, Buck Rogers In The 25th Century, Cardboard, 1940-1950 .... 85.00
Pistol, 25th Century, Daisy Mfg. Co., 1930s, 9 1/2 In. ....*Illus* 138.00
Pistol, Atomic, Daisy Mfg. Co., Steel, 1930s, 9 1/2 In. ....*Illus* 273.00
Puzzle, Jigsaw, 1970s, Box, 10 x 14 In. 15.00
Record, Soundtrack, TV Pilot, Gil Gerard, Stereo, MCA, 1979 .... 18.00
Rocket, Police Patrol, Sparks, Rogers In Cockpit, Tin, 1930s, 12 In. 295.00
Rocketship, Tootsietoy 35.00
Strato-Kite, Graphics Of Buck, Envelope, 1940s 135.00
View-Master Set, Battle On The Moon, Cartoon, 1978 .... 21.00

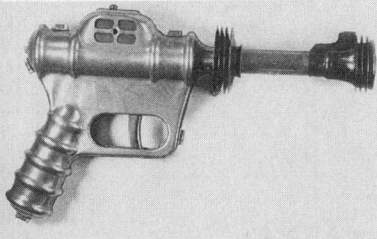

Buck Rogers, Pistol, Atomic, Daisy Mfg. Co.,
Steel, 1930s, 9 1/2 In.

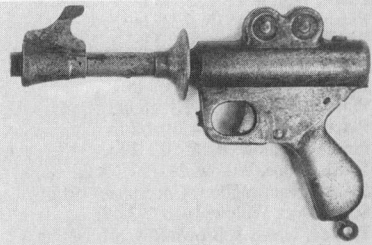

Buck Rogers, Pistol, 25th Century, Daisy Mfg. Co.,
1930s, 9 1/2 In.

BUFFALO POTTERY was made in Buffalo, New York, after 1902. The company was established by the Larkin Company, famous manufacturers of soap. The wares are marked with a picture of a buffalo and the date of manufacture. Deldare ware is the most famous pottery made at the factory. It has either a khaki-colored or green background with hand painted transfer designs.

BUFFALO POTTERY, Bowl, Dessert, Willow, 1916, 4 3/4 In.	30.00 to 40.00
Bowl, Sugar, Willow, 1911	140.00
Bowl, Vegetable, 9 1/4 In.	180.00
Bowl, Vegetable, Willow, 1911, 8 1/2 In.	160.00
Bowl, Vegetable, Willow, Cover, Rectangular, 1911	500.00
Bowl, Vegetable, Willow, Round, 1911	350.00
Bowl, Willow, 1911, 4 3/4 In.	40.00
Bowl, Willow, 1911, 6 1/2 In.	40.00 to 50.00
Bowl, Willow, 1914, 7 3/4 In.	50.00
Bowl, Willow, 1916, 4 3/4 In.	20.00
Bread Plate, Willow, 1911, 6 3/8 In.	30.00
Butter Chip, Blue Willow	30.00
Cup, Bouillon, Willow	40.00
Cup, Willow, 1911	40.00
Cup & Saucer, Willow, 1911	90.00
Cup & Saucer, Willow, 1916	90.00
George Washington, Cobalt Blue, Ink Mark, 1907, 7 1/2 x 7 1/4 In.	415.00 to 525.00
Gravy Boat, Willow	240.00
Pie Plate, Willow, 1916, 7 1/8 In.	40.00
Pitcher, Cinderella, 1907	650.00
Pitcher, John Paul Jones, Fredericksburg, Va., 1773, 9 3/8 In.	660.00
Pitcher, Roosevelt Bears, 1907, 8 x 8 In.	*Illus* 2550.00
Pitcher, Whaling City, New Bedford, Mass., 6 1/8 In.	880.00
Pitcher, With A Cane Superior Air, 1908	550.00
Plate, Christmas, Ebenezer Scrooge, 1953	25.00
Plate, Christmas, Good People Flocking Through The Streets, 1960	35.00
Plate, Christmas, Just In Time To Greet Father, 1955	50.00
Plate, Christmas, Mr. Fezziwig's Ball, 1954	25.00 to 50.00
Plate, Christmas, Noel, 3 Carolers, 1950	45.00
Plate, Christmas, Scrooge Buys A Christmas Turkey, 1957	50.00
Plate, Christmas, Season's Best Wishes, Horse Drawn Coach, 1952	25.00 to 50.00
Plate, Christmas, Season's Greetings, 3 Sledders, 1951	50.00
Plate, Christmas, Shoppers In Groceries, 1958	45.00
Plate, Christmas, The Best From The Dicken's Christmas Plates, 1962	125.00 to 150.00
Plate, Christmas, The Cratchits, 1959	50.00
Plate, Christmas, To The Spirit Of Christmas Past, 1956	35.00
Plate, Sail Boat Scene, Orange Peel, Abino, 1912, 9 1/4 In.	385.00
Plate, Statue Of Liberty, 7 3/4 In.	65.00
Plate, Willow, 1911, 6 1/2 In.	50.00
Plate, Willow, 1911, 10 In.	70.00
Plate, Willow, 1914, 9 1/4 In.	35.00 to 50.00
Plate, Willow, 1914, 10 In.	70.00
Plate, Willow, 1916, 2 3/8 In.	85.00
Plate, Willow, 1916, 6 3/8 In.	30.00
Plate, Willow, 1916, 9 1/8 In.	45.00
Plate, Willow, 1917, 8 3/8 In.	50.00
Platter, Oval, 1909, 14 1/8 In.	220.00
Platter, Willow, 1909, 9 5/8 In.	140.00
Platter, Willow, 1914, 10 1/2 In.	150.00
Platter, Willow, 1916, 10 1/2 In.	110.00
Soup, Coupe, Willow, 1911, 7 3/4 In.	50.00
Soup, Cream, Willow, Underplate, 1915	110.00
Soup, Dish, Willow, 1916, 7 3/4 In.	65.00
Teapot, Green & Brown Roycroft Design, Cream Ground, 1925, 4 In.	1320.00
Teapot, Tea Rose	195.00
Tray, Dresser, Boat, Seagulls, Peach Over Olive, Abino, 1912, 9 x 12 In.	990.00

Buffalo Pottery
Deldare, Pitcher,
Fallowfield Hunt,
Hunt Supper,
1908, 12 x 7 In.

Buffalo Pottery Deldare, Pitcher,
Fallowfield Hunt, Breaking Cover,
1908, 9 x 8 In.

Buffalo Pottery, Pitcher,
Roosevelt Bears, 1907, 8 x 8 In.

Vegetable, Cover, Willow, Rectangular, 1911	500.00
Vegetable, Willow, Round, 1911, 8 1/2 In.	160.00
Vegetable, Willow, Round, 1911, 9 1/4 In.	180.00
BUFFALO POTTERY DELDARE, Bowl, Ye Village Street, 9 In.	300.00
Chop Plate, An Evening At Ye Lion Inn, Signed, 1908, 13 1/2 In.	420.00 to 825.00
Chop Plate, Breakfast At Three Pigeons, Pink, 1920s, 11 3/8 In.	440.00
Chop Plate, Fallowfield Hunt, The Start, 14 In.	550.00 to 725.00
Cup & Saucer, Fallowfield Hunt, Ink Mark, 1909, 2 & 5 3/4 In.	305.00
Cup & Saucer, Ye Olden Days	175.00
Hair Receiver, Ye Village Street, Ink Mark, 1908, 2 3/4 x 4 3/4 In.	605.00
Humidor, Old Sailor	795.00
Mug, At The Three Pigeons, Olive Green Glaze, 1908, 4 1/3 x 5 In.	495.00
Mug, Fallowfield Hunt	250.00
Mug, I Give The Law, Emerald, 2 1/2 In.	875.00
Mug, Ye Lion Inn	320.00
Pitcher, Dr. Syntax Looking In Pond, Emerald, 7 x 6 In.	1430.00
Pitcher, Fallowfield Hunt, 7 3/4 In.	825.00
Pitcher, Fallowfield Hunt, Breaking Cover, 1908, 9 x 8 In. ....*Illus*	880.00
Pitcher, Fallowfield Hunt, Hunt Supper, 1908, 12 x 7 In. ....*Illus*	1760.00
Pitcher, Nautical Design, Cobalt Blue, 9 In.	412.00
Pitcher, To Becky's Hand He Gave, Emerald, 1911, 12 In. ....*Illus*	1430.00
Plaque, Fallowfield Hunt, Breakfast At Three Pigeons, 1908, 12 In.	330.00 to 525.00
Plaque, Friday Friars Dinner, M. Gerhardt, 1914, 12 In.	2000.00
Plaque, Ye Lion Inn, 1908, 12 1/2 In.	525.00
Plate, An Evening At Ye Lion Inn, Signed, 13 3/4 In.	625.00
Plate, Calendar, 1910	1900.00
Plate, Dr. Syntax Loses His Wig, Emerald, Signed, 10 In.	715.00 to 785.00
Plate, Dr. Syntax Misfortune At Tulip Hall, Emerald, 1911, 8 1/4 In.	485.00 to 660.00
Plate, Dr. Syntax Presenting Floral Offering, Emerald, Burgess, 6 In.	660.00
Plate, Fairview Country Club, 5 1/2 In.	35.00
Plate, Fallowfield Hunt, The Death, 1909, 8 1/4 In.	195.00
Plate, Fallowfield Hunt, The Start	150.00
Plate, Geometric Design, Emerald, Ink Mark, 8 1/4 In.	600.00
Plate, The Garden Trio, Emerald, Signed, 9 1/2 In.	770.00
Plate, The Garden Trio, L. Newman, 9 1/2 In.	847.00
Plate, Windmill & Boat, Abino, 6 1/8 In.	357.00
Plate, Ye Olden Times, Signed, 1909, 9 1/4 In.	82.00 to 175.00
Plate, Ye Town Crier	135.00
Plate, Ye Town Crier, Olive Green Glaze, 8 1/4 In.	165.00
Plate, Ye Village Gossips, 10 In.	165.00 to 225.00
Platter, Dancing Ye Minuet, 1909, 9 x 12 In.	750.00
Platter, Ye Lion Inn, 12 In.	480.00
Platter, Ye Lion Inn, 13 1/2 In.	500.00
Powder Jar, Ye Village Street, 4 1/8 In.	385.00
Salt & Pepper, Geometric Design, Red & Green, 3 In.	495.00
Shaving Mug, Ye Razor, Pole Sign, Crazed, 1910, 3 3/4 x 4 1/2 In.	1210.00
Soup, Dish, Fallowfield Hunt, Breaking Cover, Ink Mark, 2 x 9 In.	485.00
Sugar, Scenes Of Village Life, Ye Olden Days, Handles, 1909, 5 1/4 In.	135.00
Tankard, Fallowfield Hunt, Hunt Supper, W. Foster, 12 x 7 1/4 In.	1650.00
Tea Set, Fallowfield Hunt, 2 In., 6 Piece	250.00

Buffalo Pottery Deldare,
Pitcher, To Becky's Hand He
Gave, Emerald, 1911, 12 In.

Buffalo Pottery Deldare,
Vase, Kingfisher, Dragonflies,
Iris, Emerald, 1911, 7 x 6 In.

Teapot, Fallowfield Hunt, Breaking Cover, Signed, 4 1/2 In.	800.00
Teapot, Scenes Of Village Life In Ye Olden Days, 6 Sides, 8 1/4 In.	315.00
Teapot, Ye Olden Times, 5 3/4 In.	425.00
Tile, Dr. Syntax Taking Possession Of His Living, Emerald, 6 In.	660.00
Tile, Traveling In Ye Olden Days, 1908	320.00
Tray, Dresser, Dr. Syntax Rural Sports, B. Willon, Emerald, 12 In.	1540.00
Vase, 3 Women, Man & Woman Other Side, 1908, 8 x 7 1/2 In.	1320.00
Vase, Floral, Emerald, Ink Mark, 1911, 8 1/3 x 5 3/4 In.	1045.00
Vase, Kingfisher, Dragonflies, Iris, Emerald, 1911, 7 x 6 In. ....*Illus*	3190.00
Vase, Ye Village Schoolmaster, Ye Village Parson, 8 1/2 In.	990.00

BUNNYKINS, see Royal Doulton category.

BURMESE GLASS was developed by Frederick Shirley at the Mt.
Washington Glass Works in New Bedford, Massachusetts, in 1885. It
is a two-toned glass, shading from peach to yellow. Some pieces have
a pattern mold design. A few Burmese pieces were decorated with pictures or applied glass flowers of colored Burmese glass. Other factories made similar glass also called *Burmese*. Related items may be
listed in the Fenton category, the Gunderson category, and under Webb
Burmese.

Bowl, Mt. Washington, 2 x 5 1/4 In.	200.00
Condiment Set, Ribbed Pillar, Brown Top & Design, Mt. Washington	580.00
Creamer, Applied Handle, Mt. Washington, 3 3/4 x 2 1/2 In.	1400.00
Cruet, Enameled, Blue & White Flowers, Mt. Washington, 7 x 4 In.	1200.00
Cruet, Mushroom Stopper, 30 Ribs, Mt. Washington, 7 In.	1250.00
Cup, Diamond-Quilted, Shiny Finish, 3 1/4 In.	330.00
Cup & Saucer, Yellow Handle, Saucer, Mt. Washington, 5 1/2 In.	400.00
Fairy Lamp, Maple Leaf, 1 Piece	225.00
Fairy Lamp, Shade On Clear Clarke Base	220.00
Finger Bowl, 9 Crimped Top, Mt. Washington, 2 1/2 x 4 1/2 In.	210.00
Flower Frog, Mushroom Shape, Daisies On Top, Mt. Washington, 3 x 5 1/2 In.	287.00
Jar, Cover, Gold Wild Rose, Mt. Washington, 5 x 5 1/2 In.	1400.00
Lamp, Brass Frame, Base, Ruffled Top, Signed, 1973, 21 In.	325.00
Match Holder, Ribbon Candy Ruffled Rim, Ruffled Foot, 4 In.	450.00
Rose Bowl, Diamond-Quilted, Mother-Of-Pearl, 10 Panels, 2 3/4 x 4 1/2 In.	575.00
Saltshaker, Tomato Shape, Enameled Florals, Mt. Washington, 2 In.	39.00
Toothpick, Pine Cones, Needles & Branches, Mt. Washington, 1880s, 3 x 3 In.	675.00
Toothpick, Ruffled Hat Shape, 2 3/8 In.	550.00
Toothpick, Square Mouth, 2 5/8 In.	192.00
Toothpick, Square Top, Bulbous Bottom, Mt. Washington, 2 3/4 In.	325.00
Tumbler, Enamel English Ivy, Vines, Mt. Washington, 3 3/4 In.	395.00
Tumbler, Juice, Diamond-Quilted, 3 3/4 In.	150.00
Vase, 3 Roses Tulip, 11 x 6 In.	225.00
Vase, Gold Enamel Floral, Satin Finish, 3 1/2 x 5 In.	450.00
Vase, Grape, Enameled, 3 3/8 In.	412.00
Vase, Jack-In-The-Pulpit, Pleated Ruffled Top, 10 In.	518.00
Vase, Lily, Jack-In-The-Pulpit, Crimped Edge, 6 3/4 In.	230.00

Vase, Lily, Matte Finish, Mt. Washington, 15 In. 950.00
Vase, Painted Grape Design, Hexagonal Top, 3 3/8 In. 412.00

BUSTER BROWN, the comic strip, first appeared in color in 1902. Buster and his dog, Tige, remained a popular comic and soon became even more famous as the emblem for a shoe company, a textile firm, and others. The strip was discontinued in 1920, but some of the advertising is still in use.

Bandana, 1940 . . . . 50.00
Bank, Buster & Tige, Cast Iron, A.C. Williams, 1910-1932, 5 1/2 In. . . . . 115.00 to 375.00
Book, Dictionary 45.00
Button, Tige, Advertising Buster Brown Bread, Brown, Green, Yellow, 1 1/2 In. 30.00
Comic Book, Adventure Stories Of Andy Devine, 1950s 5.00
Cup, 2 1/8 In. 100.00
Doll, Advertising For Shoes, 1910, 14 In. 110.00
Doll Kit, Cloth 20.00
Flashlight 85.00
Locket, Buster Brown & Tige, Round, Opens For Photograph 125.00
Mirror, Vacation Days Carnival, Buster & Tige, Pocket . . . . 55.00 to 70.00
Periscope, Secret Agency, Lithograph, Cardboard, 1950, 20 In. 45.00
Playing Cards, Miniature, 51 Piece 35.00
Postcard, Buster Brown Shoes, Cartoon, 1950s 3.00
Postcard, His Bubble, A Good Bump, R.F. Outcault, 1903 . . . . 45.00
Ring, Flicker, Plastic, Red 8.00
Shoes, Boy's, 1950s, Box 35.00
Target Game, Buster Brown & Tige, Lithographed Paper, Wood, Bliss, 24 In. 575.00
Teapot, Tige 48.00
Yo-Yo, Metal 58.00

BUTTER CHIPS, or butter pats, were small individual dishes for butter. They were the height of fashion from 1880 to 1910. Earlier as well as later examples are known.

Glass, Crystalline, Amber Stained 12.00
Glass, Daisy & Button, Amber Stained Daisies 12.00
Glass, Shell & Tassel 14.00
Glass, Tree Of Life . . . . 12.00 to 30.00
Pottery, Blue Willow, Square, 3 In. 25.00

BUTTER MOLDS are listed in the Kitchen category under Mold, Butter.

BUTTON collecting has been popular since the nineteenth century. Buttons have been known throughout the centuries, and there are millions of styles. Gold, silver, or precious stones were used for the best buttons, but most were made of natural materials, like bone or shell, or from inexpensive metals. Only a few types are listed for comparison.

Bakelite, Green, 7 Piece 30.00
Bakelite, Yellow, 6 Piece 22.00
China, Toshikane, Tokyo, Card, 6 Piece 295.00
Pearl, Picture Of Man, Harvey, Chalmers & Sons, Set Of 2 . . . . 15.00
Plastic, 4-Leaf Flowers, Red, 3 Piece 3.50
Plastic, Blue, White Stripe, Self Shank, 6 Piece 4.00
Plastic, Floral Carved Type, 3 Piece 5.00
Plastic, Flower Shape, Navy, On Card, 6 Piece 10.00
Plastic, Rhinestone Around Rim, 4 Piece 2.00

BUTTONHOOKS have been a popular collectible in England for many years but only recently have gained the attention of American collectors. The buttonhooks were made to help fasten the many buttons of the old-fashioned high-button shoes and other items of apparel.

Metal, Marked Hanan & Son Pittsburgh 10.00
Silver Sterling, 9 In. 55.00
Victorian, Sterling Silver Handle 45.00

CALENDARS made to hang on the wall or to be displayed on a desk top have been popular since the last quarter of the nineteenth century. Many were printed with advertising as part of the artwork and were given away as premiums. Calendars with guns, gunpowder, or Coca-Cola advertising are most prized.

1878, Hires Root Beer, 12 Pages, 9 x 7 In.	*Illus*	2475.00
1889, Hood's Sarsaparilla, Young Girl, Bonnet		95.00
1890, Hood's Sarsaparilla, Beautiful Girl Profile		100.00
1894, Country Scene With Sheep, Clay Robinson & Company, Frame		15.00
1894, Puinniqiac Company Fertilizers, Boston, Indian, Fields, 9 x 13 In.		80.00
1895, Advertising, Die Cut Cardboard, 9 x 11 1/2 In.		36.00
1895, American Railway Supply Co., Metal Case, Cardboard, 2 3/4 x 2 In.		22.00
1898, Equitable Life Insurance, Victorian Couples		75.00
1898, Perry Mason, Fold-Out		25.00
1900, Armour & Co., August		7.00
1900, Babcock & Teague, Registered Druggists, Die Cut, 7 1/2 x 12 In.		134.00
1902, Davis Pianos, Organs & Sewing Machines, Boy, Watermelon, Frame		100.00
1903, Bel-Cap-Sie Plaster, Tri-Fold, Little Girl & Puppy In Water, 13 x 10 In.		52.00
1903, Hanson Drug Co., Chemist & Pharmacist, Granite Falls, Minn., 13 In.		82.00
1903, Hood's Sarsaparilla, Girl, Dogs, Donkey		120.00
1904, Anheuser-Busch, Pocket, Factory Scene, Pad, 3 x 5 In.		25.00
1904, Metropolitan Life Insurance Co., Pretty Girl, Cardboard, 7 x 20 In.		162.00
1905, Antikamnia		50.00
1905, Collins Baking Co., Little Girl, Bread Loaf, 11 x 14 In.		138.00
1905, German Fire Insurance Company, Pittsburgh, Pa., 10 1/2 x 13 1/2 In.		50.00
1905, Lady Golfer, Finishing Her Swing, Gray Lithograph Co., 10 x 13 In.		150.00
1906, Clark's Old Cumberland Rye Whiskey, Girl With Kitten, 6 x 3 In.		25.00
1906, Life's Calendar, June, Charles Dana Gibson		7.00
1907, Bennett & Hall, 18 x 11 3/4 In.		55.00
1907, Dupont, Original Hanger, E.H. Osthaus, 15 x 29 1/4 In.		696.00
1907, Indian Maiden, Lithograph		85.00
1907, Koehler & Hanson, Hardware, Frame, 13 x 22 In.		440.00
1907, Kreger's Baker & Ice Cream Parlor, Metal Strips, 13 x 20 In.		44.00
1908, Roycroft, Each Day Has A Motto, Iron Strap, 7 1/2 x 9 In.		2530.00
1909, Bennett & Hall, 18 1/4 x 12 In.		100.00
1910, Bennett & Hall, 19 1/4 x 11 3/4 In.		66.00
1910, May Pretty Girl		9.00
1912, Daily Record Newspaper, Race Car Driver & Lady, Cardboard, 16 In.		132.00
1912, Hood's Sarsaparilla, Victorian Lady		110.00
1912, Rising Sun Beer & Porter, 2 Women Scene, 15 x 22 In.		193.00
1914, Hood's, Madonnina, Little Mother, Unused		45.00
1918, Lowell Fertilizer Co., Beautiful Young Woman, Full Pad, 15 x 24 In.		100.00
1919, Swift's Premium, 4 Sheets, Woman Supporting, War Effort, 8 x 15 In.		85.00
1920, Prometheus, Edison Mazda, Maxfield Parrish		4325.00
1920, Van Dyke Fur Co., Harrison Fisher, 4 3/4 x 7 3/4 In.		25.00
1922, Coca-Cola		3800.00
1928, Edison Mazda, Parrish		2500.00
1929, Golden Hours, Edison Mazda, Maxfield Parrish For General Electric		3700.00
1929, Orange Crush, Woman In Rowboat, Frame, 11 x 24 In.		1897.00
1931, Life's Dog Calendar, Cardboard, 14 x 10 In.		50.00
1931, McCray Refrigerators, 12 Pages	28.00 to	30.00
1931, Morrell's Food, 12 Pages Of Products, 8 x 14 In.		50.00
1932, Eichler Brewing Co., Frame		35.00
1932, Goodyear Tires, Fisherman Pouring Water Out Of Black Boot		110.00
1936, American Store Co., Lithograph Of Girl, Calf, Pasture		45.00
1938, Lucky Strike, Pinup, 11 x 14 In.		8.00
1938, Richfield Motor Oil, Green & Tan, Truck, Cardboard, 14 x 10 In.		110.00
1939, Feed Store, Kissimmee, Florida		30.00
1941, Alka-Seltzer, Cartoons, 12 Pages		25.00
1941, Atlantic Petroleum Products, 28 3/4 x 16 In.		50.00
1941, Charles G. Copp Insurance, 3 In.	*Illus*	8.00
1941, Whistle, Rolf Armstrong Artwork, Matted, Frame, 15 x 32 In.		1210.00
1944, John Deere, 2 Children Looking Out Window, 16 x 10 3/4 In.		66.00

Calendar, 1878,
Hires Root Beer,
12 Pages, 9 x 7 In.

Calendar, 1962, Feather Parrot,
Kubik's Hotel & Lounge, Frame,
5 1/2 x 10 In.

Calendar, 1941, Charles G.
Copp Insurance, 3 In.

1945, Artist's Sketch Pad, K.O. Munson, 12 Pages, 9 x 14 In.	40.00
1945, For Men Of Letters, Pinup, 12 Pictures, Moran, 8 x 14 In.	75.00
1946, Atlantic Gasoline Motor Oil, Cardboard, Paper Pad, 17 x 10 In.	44.00
1946, Atlantic Refining Company, 28 1/2 x 16 In.	50.00
1946, Heavenly Bodies, Pinup, Blue Pennant Tire Co., Austin, Texas	65.00
1947, Esquire, Petty Girl	65.00
1947, Esquire, Petty Girl, Envelope	70.00 to 100.00
1947, Hercules Powder	75.00
1948, Dr Pepper, Cover Sheet	250.00
1948, Morrell Fairy Tales, Complete Pad	30.00
1948, Red & Black Envelope	150.00
1949, Kelly Tires, 34 x 16 In.	175.00
1949, Squirt	85.00
1950, Firestone, Dean Cornwell, 36 In.	75.00
1950, Koppers, Piston Ring Pin-Up, 16 x 33 In.	75.00
1951, Dr Pepper	175.00
1951, Goodyear, 28 x 20 1/2 In.	66.00
1952, Keen Kutter, Complete Pad	125.00
1953, Chevron, Pocket	10.00
1953, Day Herding, Frank Hoffman, Remembrance, 29 x 43 1/2 In.	65.00
1953, Nash	35.00
1953, Sinclair Oil	25.00
1954, Squirt, Girls, 6 Pages	25.00
1955, Earl Moran, Sounds Good, Salesman's Sample, 22 x 46 In.	45.00
1955, Marilyn Monroe, Nude Pinup, Color, Full Pad, 10 x 17 In.	25.00 to 30.00
1955, Mission Orange	85.00
1955, Playboy, Jayne Mansfield	20.00
1955, Zoe Mozert, Prom Date Picture, Salesman's Sample, 22 x 46 In.	35.00
1956, Fishing, Sales Sample	12.00
1959, Union Pacific Railroad, Logos & Trains, 12 x 22 In.	15.00
1961, United Airlines, Travel, Planes	20.00
1962, Feather Parrot, Kubik's Hotel & Lounge, Frame, 5 1/2 x 10 In. *Illus*	10.00
1964, Union Pacific Railroad, Logos & Trains, 12 x 22 In.	15.00
1966, Horlacher Beer, Full Pad, 16 x 33 In.	33.00
1968, Playboy	18.00

Calendar Plate, 1914, Rebbello & Fopiano, Boston, Mass., 8 1/2 In.

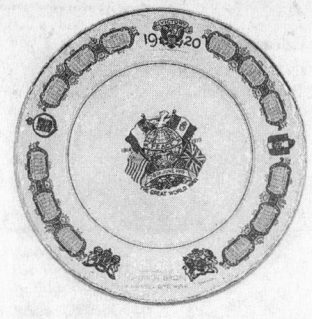

Calendar Plate, 1920, Great World War, 1914-1919, Church Bros., Minn. City, 9 In.

1969, Prior Beer, Packet Type, Unused, 4 x 6 1/2 In.	13.00
1970, Esso, Smith, Oil, Robbins, N.C., 13 Pages	8.00
1972, Esso, Still In Tube	22.00
1975, Artists In America	12.00
1977, Miss Piggy Cover Girl	25.00
1977, U.S. Taxpayers	10.00
1988, Norman Rockwell, Engagement, 9 x 6 1/2 In.	18.00
Perpetual, Walnut, c.1860	195.00

CALENDAR PLATES were very popular in the United States from 1906 to 1929. Since then, plates have been made every year. A calendar and the name of a store, a picture of flowers, a girl, or a scene were featured on the plate.

1908, Clarks, N.B.	50.00
1908, Deer, Full Color, Scalloped Rim, N.C. Company	25.00
1908, European Country Estate, M. Rachman, Groceries, Omaha, 9 1/8 In.	30.00
1909, Gibson Girl Center, Compliments Of W.A. Baughan, Wisconsin, 9 1/2 In.	22.00
1909, Grape Cluster, B.J. Blakely, Dealer In Fresh Meats, Darien, Wis., 7 5/8 In.	20.00
1909, Mountain Scene, Gold Band, First National Bank, S. Dakota, 8 1/8 In.	25.00
1909, Rose Design, Months Around Rim, 8 1/4 In.	10.00
1909, Rudolph Bros., Menomonee Falls, Wis., Imperial China, 8 In.	50.00
1910, Gibson Style Girl In Hat, 8 1/4 In.	46.00
1910, Kids Swimming, Verse, Syndicate Dept. Store, East End China, 9 1/4 In.	75.00
1911, Billiken, Advertising	80.00
1911, Months Hanging Above Car, Semiporcelain, 7 In.	93.00
1911, T. Roosevelt, Months At Rim, Merry Christmas, Princeton, Ill., 8 3/4 In.	80.00
1912, Indian Maiden Shucking Corn, Teepees, Dresden China, Ohio, 8 1/2 In.	50.00
1914, Rebbello & Fopiano, Boston, Mass., 8 1/2 In.	*Illus* 12.00
1920, Great World War, 1914-1919, Church Bros., Minn. City, 9 In.	*Illus* 45.00
1969, Currier & Ives, Green	18.00

CAMARK POTTERY started in 1924 in Camden, Arkansas. Jack Carnes founded the firm and made many types of glazes and wares. The company was bought by Mary Daniel. Production was halted in 1983.

Bowl, Fish, Bird On Logs, White	125.00
Bowl, Frog, Purple	30.00
Ewer, Orchid, 13 1/2 In.	135.00
Figurine, Bulldog, Gloss Black, Original Label, 12 1/2 x 11 In.	225.00
Figurine, Cat, White, 8 In.	50.00
Jug, Pure Corn, 9 In.	275.00
Pitcher, Yellow	20.00
Planter, Rooster, White Glaze, 2 Original Stickers, 8 3/4 In.	38.00
Vase, Aqua Matte, 14 In.	55.00
Vase, Blue Swirl, Miniature	8.00
Vase, Orange, Green, Triangular, 8 In.	25.00

Vase, Orange, Light Green Matte Glaze, Impressed Mark, 5 In. 60.00
Vase, White Morning Glories, 8 In. 165.00
Vase, Yellow & Green, 5 In. 65.00
Vase, Yellow, Ink Mark, 6 In. 60.00

CAMBRIDGE GLASS Company was founded in 1901 in Cambridge, Ohio. The company closed in 1954, reopened briefly, and closed again in 1958. The firm made all types of glass. Their early wares included heavy pressed glass with the mark *Near Cut*. Later wares included Crown Tuscan, etched stemware, and clear and colored glass. The firm used a C in a triangle mark after 1920. Some Cambridge patterns may be included in the Depression Glass category.

Apple Blossom, Bowl, 4-Footed, Green, 12 In. 129.00
Apple Blossom, Bowl, Green, 10 In. 125.00
Apple Blossom, Compote, Cheese, Amber 49.00
Apple Blossom, Jug, Ball, Amber 295.00
Apple Blossom, Pickle Tray, 7 In. 69.00
Apple Blossom, Plate, Crystal, 6 In. 8.50
Apple Blossom, Plate, Heatherbloom, 7 1/2 In. 125.00
Apple Blossom, Plate, Pink, 12 1/2 In. 50.00
Apple Blossom, Relish, 2 Sections, Blue 145.00
Apple Blossom, Relish, 5 Sections 89.00
Apple Blossom, Sandwich, Center Handle, Amber 30.00
Apple Blossom, Tumbler, Iced Tea, Heatherbloom 175.00
Bashful Charlotte, Flower Frog, Mandarin Gold 225.00
Bird & Butterfly Etch, Vase, Blue, 12 In. 395.00
Blue Bird, Plate, 8 1/2 In. 45.00
Caprice, Ashtray, Pink 13.00
Caprice, Bonbon, Footed, 6 In. 24.00
Caprice, Bowl, Belled, 4-Footed, Blue, 12 1/2 In. 125.00
Caprice, Bowl, Blue, 13 In. 145.00
Caprice, Bowl, Crimped, Blue, 5 In. 125.00
Caprice, Bowl, Crimped, Footed, 13 In. 47.00
Caprice, Bowl, Footed, Blue, 7 In. 65.00
Caprice, Candlestick, 2-Light, Pair 200.00
Caprice, Candlestick, 3-Light, Blue 250.00
Caprice, Candlestick, 3-Light, Mandarin Gold, 6 In., Pair 135.00
Caprice, Candlestick, Blue, Pair 135.00
Caprice, Candy Dish, Cover, 3-Footed, Blue .... 55.00 to 130.00
Caprice, Champagne 15.00
Caprice, Cocktail, 3 Oz. 20.00
Caprice, Cocktail, Blue, 3 1/2 In. 29.00
Caprice, Cruet, Oil, Stopper, 5 Oz. 70.00
Caprice, Cup & Saucer, Amber 36.00
Caprice, Dish, Mayonnaise, Spoon, Liner, Blue, 3 Piece 130.00
Caprice, Dish, Pickle, Blue, 9 In. 60.00
Caprice, Goblet, Water, 9 Oz. .... 18.00 to 27.00
Caprice, Goblet, Water, Blue, 10 Oz. 55.00
Caprice, Ice Bucket, Tongs, Blue 125.00
Caprice, Jelly, Crimped, Blue, 7 In. 65.00
Caprice, Lemon Plate, 3 Handles, 6 1/2 In. 11.00
Caprice, Parfait, Pink, 5 Oz. 169.00
Caprice, Pitcher, Ball Shape, Blue, 80 Oz. 395.00
Caprice, Plate, 4-Footed, 14 In. 30.00
Caprice, Plate, Amber, 8 1/2 In. 29.00
Caprice, Plate, Blue, 8 1/2 In. 35.00
Caprice, Plate, Blue, 14 In. 119.00
Caprice, Plate, Footed, Blue, 14 In. 95.00
Caprice, Relish, 3 Sections, Blue, 8 1/2 In. .... 45.00 to 69.00
Caprice, Salver, 4-Footed, Blue, 13 In. 65.00
Caprice, Saucer, Crimped, Blue, 5 In. 89.00
Caprice, Shaker, Flat, Blue, Individual, Pair 190.00
Caprice, Sherbet, Low, 5 Oz. 14.00

Caprice, Sherbet, Tall, 7 Oz.	12.00
Caprice, Sugar & Creamer, Blue	40.00 to 75.00
Caprice, Tumbler, Footed, 10 Oz.	20.00
Caprice, Tumbler, Footed, Blue, 10 Oz.	42.00
Caprice, Tumbler, Iced Tea, Footed, 12 Oz.	17.00
Caprice, Vase, Amber, 8 1/2 In.	189.00
Caprice, Vase, Blue, 8 1/2 In.	289.00
Caprice, Vase, Blue, 9 In.	255.00
Carmen, Mint Dish, 2 Handles, 6 1/2 In.	27.00
Carmen, Vase, Keyhole, Ivy, Ball	50.00
Cascade, Compote, 5 1/2 In.	20.00
Cascade, Sugar & Creamer, Emerald Green	35.00
Chantilly, Candlestick, Fleur-De-Lis, 6 In., Pair	450.00
Chantilly, Cocktail Shaker, Sterling Finial	155.00
Chantilly, Cocktail, 2 1/2 Oz.	28.00
Chantilly, Cordial, 1 Oz.	58.00
Chantilly, Lamp, Hurricane, Pair	295.00
Cleo, Candlestick, Pink, 4 In., Pair	95.00
Cleo, Cocktail, Green, Set Of 4	175.00
Cleo, Cup & Saucer, Round, Pink	25.00
Cleo, Goblet, Water, Green, Set Of 6	300.00
Cleo, Ice Bucket, Blue	275.00
Cleo, Tumbler, Footed, Green, 2 1/2 Oz.	65.00
Crown Tuscan, Bowl, Footed, Gold Encrusted Diane	350.00
Crown Tuscan, Box, Cigarette, Footed	56.00
Crown Tuscan, Dish, Shell, Cover, Marked	80.00
Crown Tuscan, Swan, Gold Trim, 3 In.	55.00
Crown Tuscan, Vase, Cornucopia, 3 3/4 In.	38.00
Decagon, Bouillon, Footed, Blue	20.00
Decagon, Bowl, Belled, Green, 5 1/2 In.	17.00
Decagon, Champagne, Blue	24.00
Decagon, Creamer, Green	25.00
Decagon, Cruet, Blue, 6 Oz.	195.00
Decagon, Cup & Saucer, Green	11.00
Decagon, Goblet, Water, Blue	32.00
Decagon, Jug, Green, 22 Oz.	32.00
Decagon, Plate, Green, 8 1/2 In.	10.00
Decagon, Plate, Pink, 6 1/4 In.	10.00
Decagon, Plate, Pink, 10 In.	45.00
Decagon, Server, Center Handle, Green	30.00
Decagon, Sugar Shaker, Pink	165.00
Decagon, Tray, Blue, Oval, 9 In.	35.00
Decagon, Tumbler, Footed, Blue, 12 Oz.	42.00
Diane, Bowl, 10 In.	225.00
Diane, Compote, Low, Green, 7 In.	495.00
Diane, Tumbler, Green, 12 Oz.	125.00
Diane, Tumbler, Heatherbloom, 12 Oz.	125.00
Draped Lady, Compote, 8 1/2 In.	375.00
Draped Lady, Flower Frog, 13 1/2 In.	180.00
Draped Lady, Flower Frog, Pink, 8 1/2 In.	95.00 to 145.00
Eagle, Flower Frog, Pink	365.00
Elaine, Ashtray, Individual, 3 1/4 In.	7.00
Elaine, Plate, 8 In.	14.00
Gloria, Candlestick, 3-Light, Keyhole, Pair	225.00
Gloria, Goblet, Water, Yellow, 10 Oz.	25.00
Helio, Candlestick, 6 1/2 In., Pair	75.00
Honeycomb, Compote, Moonlight, 8 1/4 In.	145.00
Marjorie, Pitcher	265.00
Martha Washington, Cake Plate	195.00
Martha Washington, Cup & Saucer, Amber	12.00
Martha Washington, Plate, Luncheon, Amber, 8 In.	12.00
Martha Washington, Sugar & Creamer	21.00
Moonlight, Flower Frog, Figural, 13 In.	750.00

Mt. Vernon, Bowl, 10 1/2 In.	26.00
Mt. Vernon, Candy Dish, Cover	46.00
Mt. Vernon, Decanter Set, Red, 7 Piece	365.00
Mt. Vernon, Ice Bucket	26.00
Mt. Vernon, Relish, 5 Sections, 12 In.	28.00
Mt. Vernon, Wine, 3 Oz.	14.00
Nude Stem, Flower Frog, Green	90.00
Portia, Cocktail, 3 Oz.	20.00
Portia, Cordial, 1 Oz.	90.00
Portia, Pitcher, 80 Oz.	140.00
Portia, Relish, 5 Sections, 10 In.	45.00
Portia, Sugar & Creamer	25.00
Portia, Vase, Keyhole, 12 In.	65.00
Pristine, Cocktail Shaker	89.00
Pristine, Torte Plate, 14 In.	24.00
Regency, Bowl, Oval, 10 In.	20.00
Regency, Champagne	13.00
Regency, Goblet, Water, 10 Oz.	15.00
Rose Point, Bowl, Footed, 12 In.	75.00 to 100.00
Rose Point, Candlestick, 2-Light, Pair	150.00
Rose Point, Cigarette Holder	295.00
Rose Point, Claret, 4 1/2 In.	40.00 to 125.00
Rose Point, Compote, 5 1/2 In.	50.00
Rose Point, Compote, 6 In.	44.00
Rose Point, Cruet, Oil, 6 Oz.	125.00
Rose Point, Decanter, Stopper, Gold Ball, 12 Oz.	325.00
Rose Point, Dish, Mayonnaise, Sterling Silver Base	350.00
Rose Point, Goblet, 10 Oz.	30.00 to 125.00
Rose Point, Nut Cup	56.00
Rose Point, Parfait, 5 Oz.	85.00
Rose Point, Pitcher, Martini, 32 Oz.	285.00
Rose Point, Plate, 8 1/2 In.	15.00 to 21.00
Rose Point, Plate, Footed, 12 In.	99.00
Rose Point, Plate, Handle, 6 In.	23.00
Rose Point, Relish, 2 Sections, 6 In.	29.00
Rose Point, Relish, 3 Sections	25.00
Rose Point, Relish, 5 Sections, 12 In.	100.00
Rose Point, Relish, Handle, 3 Sections, 8 In.	189.00
Rose Point, Relish, Handle, 6 1/2 In.	48.00
Rose Point, Salt & Pepper, Egg Shape, Pair	195.00
Rose Point, Sherbet, 6 Oz.	18.00 to 24.00
Rose Point, Sugar & Creamer	30.00 to 58.00
Rose Point, Sugar & Creamer, Individual	45.00 to 49.00
Rose Point, Tray, Center Handle, Yellow, 12 In.	35.00
Rose Point, Tray, Pickle, Gold Trim	50.00
Rose Point, Tumbler, 10 Oz.	30.00
Rose Point, Tumbler, Footed, 5 Oz.	27.00
Rose Point, Wine, 2 1/2 Oz.	55.00
Sign, Dealer's, Crystal & Frosted	235.00
Tally-Ho, Basket, Crystal Handle, Amber	75.00
Tally-Ho, Cocktail, Cobalt Blue	39.00
Tally-Ho, Cup & Saucer, Cobalt Blue	55.00
Tally-Ho, Sugar, Cobalt Blue	55.00
Tally-Ho, Tumbler, Carmen, 10 Oz.	20.00
Tally-Ho, Tumbler, Moonlight Blue, 9 Oz.	18.00
Two Kids, Flower Frog, Pink	225.00
Valencia, Bowl, Ram's Head	395.00
Wildflower, Candlestick, 2-Light	70.00
Wildflower, Candy Dish, Cover, 3 Sections, 8 In.	75.00
Wildflower, Claret, 4 1/2 In.	42.00 to 45.00
Wildflower, Cordial, 1 Oz.	60.00 to 75.00
Wildflower, Plate, Gold Trim, 8 In.	20.00
Wildflower, Tumbler, Iced Tea, 12 Oz.	28.00

Cameo Glass,
Vase, Rain Scene,
Brown, Burgundy,
Yellow, Michel,
France, 13 In.

There are many ecologically sound products made for care and repair of antiques. Look at the labels. Our ancestors cleaned pewter with wood ashes and oil. Be sure to dispose of paint thinners, harsh chemical cleaners, and other dangerous products in the approved manner. Don't just dump them in the sewer.

Wildflower, Vase, Footed, 11 In.	70.00
Wildflower, Wine, 3 1/2 In.	35.00

CAMBRIDGE POTTERY was made in Cambridge, Ohio, from about 1895 until World War I. The factory made brown glazed decorated art wares with a variety of marks, including an acorn, the name *Cambridge*, the name *Oakwood*, or the name *Terrhea*.

Ashtray, Donkey & Elephant, Under Our Flag, We Do Have A Choice, 6 In.	38.00
Mug, Green Matte, 5 In.	115.00
Vase, Pansies, Leaves, Terrhea, 6 In.	95.00

CAMEO GLASS was made in much the same manner as a cameo in jewelry. Parts of the top layer of glass were cut away to reveal a different colored glass beneath. The most famous cameo glass was made during the nineteenth century. Signed cameo glass pieces are listed under the glasswork's name, such as Daum or Galle.

Bowl, Green Favrile Stem On Base, Flaring, Yellow, Ovington, France, 11 In.	935.00
Plaque, Citron, White Flowers, England, 5 1/2 x 3 1/2 In.	1275.00
Vase, Blue Shades, Art Deco, Signed, 6 1/2 In.	687.00
Vase, Cranberry, White Sweet Peas, Corset, England, 7 x 5 In.	1750.00
Vase, Dandelion Blossoms & Leaves, Green & Frosted, F. Graveur, 9 1/2 In.	1890.00
Vase, Etched Blossoms, Opaque White Over Ruby, England, 6 In.	258.00
Vase, Etched Wild Roses, Squat Red Cased To Layered White, England, 2 1/2 In.	258.00
Vase, Rain Scene, Brown, Burgundy, Yellow, Michel, France, 13 In. ....*Illus*	1100.00
Vase, Red Floral, Orange Ground, 8 In.	385.00
Vase, Sailing Ship, Lighthouse, Flower Border, Michel, France, 10 1/4 In.	1220.00
Vase, Stick, Purple Flowers, Leaves, Signed, 1900, 11 1/2 x 4 1/2 In.	770.00

CAMPAIGN memorabilia is listed in the Political category.

CAMPBELL KIDS were first used as part of an advertisement for the Campbell Soup Company in 1906. The kids were created by Grace Drayton, a popular illustrator of the day. The kids were used in magazine and newspaper ads until about 1951. They were presented again in 1966; and in 1983, they were redesigned with a slimmer, more contemporary appearance.

Bank, Chef, Porcelain, White	8.00
Bank, Soup Can, 125th Anniversary	8.00
Clock, Boy Carrying Can, Red, Octagonal	19.00
Clock, Plastic, New Haven, Quartz	35.00
Cookie Jar	50.00
Dish, Feeding, Buffalo Pottery	75.00
Display, Advertising, Girl With Crayons, Cutout	5.00
Doll, Composition, Original Clothes, 1940s, 12 In.	325.00
Doll, Early American, 1976, Pair	150.00
Doll, Ideal, Rubber, 1950	65.00
Doll, Scottish Clothing, 10 In.	60.00
Mug, Bicentennial	7.00

Mug, M'm M'm Good, Thermal 2.50
Mug, Plastic, Insulated 4.00
Mug, Silver Plate 15.00
Mug, Tomato Soup 6.00
Plate, Olympics, 1984 .... 12.00
Poster, Advertising, 21 x 18 In. 55.00
Puzzle, 100 Piece 18.00
Salt & Pepper 95.00
Spoon, Pair 300.00
Thermometer, Figural, Plaster, 1940s, 7 1/2 In. 75.00
Thermos, 1984 Olympic Flag, Aladdin 12.00
Tin, Extra Large 7.00
Tool Caddy, Ceramic, Westwood, 11 1/2 In. 13.00

CANDELABRUM refers to a candleholder with more than one arm to
hold many candles; a candlestick is designed to hold one candle. The
eccentricity of the English language makes the plural of candelabrum
into candelabra.

2-Light, 2 Scrolled Arms, Sterling Silver, Georg Jensen, 1945, 5 In., Pair 3335.00
2-Light, Harlequin, Musical, Flowering Vines, Sitzendorff, 5 5/8 In., Pair 522.00
2-Light, Silver Plate, Fenestrated, Victorian, 13 1/2 x 10 1/2 In., Pair 198.00
2-Light, Sterling Silver, Hammered, Stylized Floral, Monogram, Friedell, 14 In. 1870.00
2-Light, Wrought Iron, Tripod Base, Penny Footed, Adjustable Arm, 22 In. 3750.00
3-Light, 3 Draped Maidens, Musical Instrument Supports, R. Rozet, 46 In. 9745.00
3-Light, Cobalt Blue Glass, Hexagonal Foot, 4 1/2 In. 29.00
3-Light, Cut Glass, Double Urn Shaft, Diamonds, Brass Arms, Prisms 165.00
3-Light, Gilt Bronze, Woman, Holding Cornucopia, France, 1820, 19 In., Pair 6050.00
3-Light, Glass Stem, Neoclassical, Cut Drop Prisms, 22 x 16 3/4 In., Pair 1380.00
3-Light, Hammered Silver, Square Base, Circle & Lines, WMF, 12 1/2 In., Pair 3700.00
3-Light, Roman Soldier, Clear Cut Prisms, White & Black Marble Base, 18 In. 253.00
3-Light, Silver Plate, Foliate, Floral Center Finial, Proceoe Roulz, Pair 855.00
3-Light, Sterling Silver, Duchin, 6 1/4 In., Pair 225.00
3-Light, Sterling Silver, John & Thomas Settle, England, 1814, 20 In., Pair 9775.00
3-Light, Sterling Silver, Weighted, Peru, 11 In., Pair 275.00
3-Light, White Metal, Gilt, Grape & Leaf Design, 16 3/4 In., Pair 198.00
4-Light, Wrought Iron, 3 Scrolled Arms, Center Pedestal, Tripod Base, 17 In. 110.00
5-Light, Brass, Urn Base, Black Marble, Gold Designs, 31 In., Pair 137.00
5-Light, Bronze, Gilt, With Figures, 26 In., Pair 920.00
5-Light, Classican, Sheffield, Silver Plate, 17 1/2 In., Pair 415.00
5-Light, Gilt Metal, Woman's Head, Orvit, Signed, 17 1/2 In. 5750.00
5-Light, Iron, Floral Fencing, Scrollwork, Italy, 17th Century, 33 1/4 In. 1610.00
5-Light, Rococo Style, Silver Plate, 15 3/4 In. 160.00
5-Light, Sterling Silver, Preisner, 15 1/2 In. 350.00
5-Light, Sterling Silver, Woman Holding Cornucopia, France, c.1875, 19 3/8 In. 4025.00
6-Light, Bronze, Cattails, Triton Figures, Foliate Branches, Beaded Foot, 32 In. 1840.00
6-Light, Flower Urn, Corinthian, Sheffield, Silver Plate, Electrified, 24 In., Pair 2860.00
Brass, Figural Female Stem, Marble Base, Prisms, 15 In., 3 Piece 190.00
Brass, Glass, Pendant Prisms, Electrified, 14 1/2 In., Pair 363.00
Brass, Marble, Figural Design, Prisms, 15 In., 3 Piece 154.00
Bronze, Figural Woman, Green Marble Base, Scalloped Bobeche, 22 In. 1980.00
Gilt, Brass Stems, 3 Birds, Clear Prisms, 15 In., Pair 220.00
Louis XV Style, Dore Bronze, c.1880, 27 In., Pair 6500.00
Wood & Metal, Carved & Painted, Flower Form, Pricket Arms, 38 In. 747.00

CANDLESTICKS were made of brass, pewter, glass, sterling silver,
plated silver, and all types of pottery and porcelain. The earliest candlesticks, dating from the sixteenth century, held the candle on a
pricket (sharp pointed spike). These lost favor because in times of
strife the large church candlesticks with prickets became formidable
weapons, so the socket was mandated. Candlesticks changed in style
through the centuries, and designs range from classic to rococo to Art
Nouveau to Art Deco.

Bell Metal, c.1750, 5 1/2 In., Pair 595.00

Bell Metal, c.1829, 19 In., Pair 275.00
Blown Glass, Pale Amber, Pair 165.00
Brass, Arts & Crafts, 14 In., Pair 210.00
Brass, Baluster Stem, Square Base, 7 1/2 In. 220.00
Brass, Beehive, Push-Up, Victorian, 7 1/2 In., Pair 65.00
Brass, Bobeche, Allover Engraving, E. Picard, c.1720, 6 In., Pair 1250.00
Brass, Capstan Base, 4 7/8 In. 660.00
Brass, Column Pedestal, Square Base, 4-Footed, 9 1/2 In. 44.00
Brass, Continental, 13 1/2 In., Pair 77.00
Brass, Continental, Neoclassical, c.1790-1810, 8 3/4 In., Pair 175.00
Brass, Cornelius & Company, c.1840, 10 In., Pair 72.00
Brass, Detachable Bobeche, Dutch, c.1680, 8 1/2 In., Pair 2250.00
Brass, Dome Base, 5 1/2 In., Pair 1760.00
Brass, Double Twist, England, c.1875, 20 In., Pair 5250.00
Brass, Drip Pan, Spain, c.1660, 10 1/2 In., Pair 2400.00
Brass, Drum Base, 5 In., Pair 2255.00
Brass, Etched Shades, Cut Prisms, 22 In., Pair 110.00
Brass, Federal, Slender Shaft, Square Base, 9 In., Pair 120.00
Brass, Fluted Shaft, Circular Spreading Foot, 14 3/4 In., Pair 1092.00
Brass, Gadrooned Fluted Column, England, c.1775, 11 5/8 In., Pair 2250.00
Brass, Geometric, Reimann, 5 x 9 In., Pair 440.00
Brass, Gothic Style, Ornate, France, 19th Century, 8 In., Pair 165.00
Brass, Marble Base, Clear Cut Prisms, 14 In., Pair 220.00
Brass, Medial Drip Pan, Dutch, 17th Century, 8 In. 170.00
Brass, Medial Drip Pan, Flemish, 7 In., Pair 121.00
Brass, Mid-Drip, Dutch, c.1700 .... 2750.00
Brass, Neoclassical, Side Push-Up, 8 1/2 In., Pair 120.00
Brass, Octagonal Base, 9 In. 275.00
Brass, Petal Base, England, c.1750, 7 1/4 In. 825.00
Brass, Petal Base, England, c.1750, 9 1/4 In., Pair 1500.00
Brass, Push-Up, Beehive, Diamond Design, Victorian, England, 9 5/8 In., Pair .. 140.00
Brass, Push-Up, Bulbous Turnings, 10 1/2 In., Pair 66.00
Brass, Push-Up, Saucer Base, 19th Century 120.00
Brass, Queen Anne, 8 3/4 & 8 7/8 In., Pair 440.00
Brass, Queen Anne, Petal Base & Bobeche, 9 In. 175.00
Brass, Queen Anne, Petal Base, Joseph Wood, 7 3/8 In., Pair 3740.00
Brass, Queen Anne, Petal Base, Scalloped Lip, 7 1/2 In. 247.00
Brass, Queen Anne, Scalloped Base, 7 3/4 In. 330.00
Brass, Queen Of Diamonds, Push-Up, Victorian, 11 1/2 In., Pair 330.00
Brass, Raised Acanthus Design, 12 In., Pair 130.00
Brass, Repousse Design, Scandinavian, c.1690, 8 1/2 In. 375.00
Brass, Seamed Construction, England, 1745, 7 1/4 In. 295.00
Brass, Semi-Shell Base, England, c.1740, 7 1/2 In., Pair 1500.00
Brass, Square Base, Octagonal Stem, 6 1/2 In. 660.00
Brass, Telescopic, Round Base, England, 18th Century, 7 In., Pair 201.00
Brass, Trumpet Form, Ribbed Stems, Raised Base, 1660, 6 1/2 In., Pair 5405.00
Brass, Victorian, 9 7/8 In., Pair 38.00
Brass, Vintage Design, Pendant Prisms, 14 1/2 In., Pair 275.00
Brass, Wavy Rim Base, England, c.1750, 9 3/4 In., Pair 1950.00
Bronze, Art Nouveau, 1 Bobeche Attached To Arm, 3 Pad Feet, 11 3/4 In. 600.00
Bronze, Charles X, Beaded Column, Gilt Metal Capital, 3-Legged, 21 In., Pair .. 2760.00
Bronze, Charles X, Gothic Arches, Drilled For Electricity, 26 1/2 In., Pair ... 8050.00
Bronze, Louis XVI, Gilt, Reed, Garland Design Standard, 10 1/4 In., Pair 690.00
Bronze, Mask Stem, Paw Feet, Mounted As Lamp, 12 1/2 In., Pair 2185.00
Bronze, Ormolu Masks On Pedestal, Electrified As Lamp, 19 3/4 In., Pair 8050.00
Bronze, William & Mary, Dutch, c.1695, 6 In., Pair 1700.00
Bronze, Winged Woman, Flowing Gown, Blossom Forms Spike, 26 In. 245.00
Coin Silver, Engraved Floral, 10 In., Pair 495.00
Copper, Hammered, Applied Crawfish & Rope Design, Arts & Crafts, 9 1/2 In. ... 190.00
Copper, Semicircular Flat Band, Chase, 6 x 6 1/2 In., Pair 550.00
Copper, Semispherical Bands, 4-Sided Shafts, Chase, 8 1/2 In., Pair 935.00

Copper, Silver Plated Overlay Design, 10 In., Pair	38.00
Copper Alloy, c.1765, 11 1 /4 In., Pair	1650.00
Copper Alloy, Heemskerk, Dutch, c.1640, 9 1/4 In.	2450.00
Copper Alloy, Petal Base, c.1740, 8 1/4 In., Pair	2500.00
Copper Alloy, Stepped Base, England, c.1755, 11 2/4 In., Pair	2600.00
Copper Alloy, Trumpet, England, c.1680, 7 1/2 In.	6900.00
Crystal, Flint, Hexagonal, Round Base, Pewter Insert, 9 1/2 In., Pair	190.00
Gilt, Medial Drip Pan, Dutch Indonesian, 17th Century, 8 1/2 In., Pair	1600.00
Glass, 2-Knop Stem, Hollow Socket, Pewter Insert, 8 3/4 In.	210.00
Glass, Canary, Petal Socket & Wafer, Hexagonal, Flint, 7 1/8 In.	110.00
Glass, Dolphin Base, Scalloped, Petal Socket, 6 5/8 In.	2060.00
Glass, Opalescent & Opaque Blue, Dolphin Base, Pittsburgh, 5 3/4 In., Pair	7810.00
Glass, Opaque Blue, Hexagonal, 9 In., Pair	1760.00
Glass, Opaque Blue, Loop Footed, Hexagonal Stem, Petal Socket, 6 7/8 In.	1550.00
Glass, Opaque Midnight Blue, Sanded Finish, Hexagonal, 7 In.	110.00
Glass, Purple, Hexagonal, Wafer, 7 1/2 In., Pair	1760.00
Glass, Rope Form, Scalloped Base & Bobeches, Seguso, 10 x 7 In., Pair	415.00
Glass, Smoky Amethyst, Wafer, 7 3/8 In., Pair	1870.00
Iron, Hog Scraper, 19th Century, 9 In.	140.00
Iron, Hog Scraper, Banded, A. Lear, 1800, 7 In.	450.00
Iron, Hog Scraper, Boothby & Hoole Co., c.1800, 7 1/4 In.	145.00
Iron, Twisted Shaft With Leaves, Samuel Yellin, 14 1/4 In.	1150.00
Marble, Louis XVI, Leaf Cast Nozzle, Drip Pan, 1780s, 13 1/4 In., Pair	9200.00
Ormolu, Doe & Stag, France, c.1800, 5 1/4 In., Pair	550.00
Paktong, Removable Bobeches, Fluted Shaft, England, c.1765, 10 In., Pair	3650.00
Pewter, Cast Paw Feet, Foliage Scrolls, Homan, Cincinnati, Ohio, 14 In., Pair	209.00
Pewter, Cornucopia Holder, Kneeling Nude Female Shaft, Denmark, 5 1/2 In., 4 Pc.	80.00
Pewter, Homan & Company, Cincinnati, 8 In., Pair	220.00
Porcelain, Figural, Man, Maiden With Bocage, Scroll Feet, 8 1/2 In., Pair	230.00
Pressed Glass, Canary, Hexagonal, Boston & Sandwich, 1840-1860, 7 3/4 In.	130.00
Pressed Glass, Hollow Blown Stem, 10 1/2 In.	465.00
Silver Plate, Crane Form, 8 3/4 In.	27.00
Sterling Silver, 1-Light, Inverted Shaft, Gorham, c.1950, 7 In., Pair	120.00
Sterling Silver, Bobeche, Sheffield, England, 7 In., Pair	110.00
Sterling Silver, Contemporary, Borgila, 7 In., Pair	870.00
Sterling Silver, Dolphin Body, Upturned Tails, Shells, Foliage, 9 1/2 In., Pair	2875.00
Sterling Silver, Engraved Floral Design, W. Breed, 10 In., Pair	605.00
Sterling Silver, Engraved Hurricane Shade, Pair	125.00
Sterling Silver, Flared Base, Edward VII, England, 1905, 6 In., Pair	2530.00
Sterling Silver, Gadrooned Pan, Paw Feet, JD, Germany, 1690, 3 1/2 In.	1955.00
Sterling Silver, Grapevine, Georg Jensen, 1945, 5 3/4 In., Pair	2760.00
Sterling Silver, Handle, Applied Borders, Peru, 2 1/2 In., Pair	176.00
Sterling Silver, Harvard University, Society Of Fellows, c.1930, Pair	2600.00
Sterling Silver, Pricket, Cluster Stem, R. Comyns, 1928, 12 3/4 In., Pair	3450.00
Sterling Silver, Profile Heads, Female Busts, France, c.1900, 9 1/4 In., Pair	2875.00
Sterling Silver, Queen Anne Profile Mark, 19th Century, 4 1/8 In., Pair	650.00
Sterling Silver, Repousse, S. Kirk & Son Co., 10 In., Pair	2200.00
Sterling Silver, Rococo, Foliate Design, Base, 10 1/2 In., Pair	172.00
Sterling Silver, S. Kirk & Son Co., 10 In., Pair	2310.00
Sterling Silver, Spiraling Design, Round Base, Spratling, 4 x 4 1/2 In., Pair	1870.00
Tin, Hog Scraper, Push-Up, 6 3/4 In.	110.00
Tin, Hog Scraper, Push-Up, 7 1/2 In.	110.00
Tin, Hog Scraper, Push-Up, Die Stamped Base, Dover Tin Company, 4 3/4 In., Pair	140.00
Tin, Hog Scraper, Push-Up, Lip Hanger, 7 1/4 In.	110.00
Tin, Hog Scraper, Push-Up, Lip Hanger, Brass Ring, 7 In.	495.00
Tin, Hog Scraper, Push-Up, Lip Hanger, Brass Trim, 8 1/2 In., Pair	495.00
Tin, Miner's, Sticking Tommy, Hand Forged, 12 1/2 In.	67.00
Victorian Sword Handle Shape, 3 Scroll Legs, Silver Plated, 12 1/2 In., Pair	1380.00
Whalebone, Carved, c.1870, Pair	1875.00

CANDLEWICK items may be listed in the Imperial and Pressed Glass categories.

When storing plastic toys and novelties like PEZ containers, keep them away from heat. They might melt. Don't store plastic items touching each other. The different types sometimes react, causing damage.

Candy Container, Cat, Witch's Head, Composition, c.1920, 5 1/2 In.

CANDY CONTAINERS have been popular since the late Victorian era. Collectors have long favored the glass containers, but now all types, including tin and papier-mache, are collected. Probably the earliest glass container sold commercially was the Liberty Bell made in 1876 for sale at the Centennial Exposition. Thousands of designs were made until the cost became too high in the 1960s. By the late 1970s, reproductions were being made and sold without the candy. Containers listed here are glass unless otherwise described. A Belsnickle is a nineteenth-century figure of Father Christmas.

Airplane, Liberty Motor, Clear Glass, Replaced Wheels 1100.00
Airplane, No. P-51, Glass, Yellow Paint, 1944-1945, 5 In. 165.00
Airplane, Original Wings & Propeller 50.00
Airplane, Plastic Wings, Closure 5.50
Airplane, Spirit Of Goodwill, Replaced Propeller 94.00
Amos & Andy Taxi, Victory Glass Co., c.1930, 4 1/2 In. ....620.00 to 770.00
Auto, 4 Door Sedan, Repainted 50.00
Baby In Shoe, Cloth Over Cardboard, 4 In. 60.00
Baby On Log Type, Poured Wax, 6 In. 450.00
Balancing Acrobats, Bisque Dolls On Chair, France, c.1890, 24 In. 4500.00
Barney Google, On Pedestal, Glass 385.00
Basket, Paper, Red Cloth, Germany, 1930s, 2 1/2 In. 33.00
Bear, Holding Windmill 750.00
Bear, On Circus Tub, Snap-On Tin Closure, Red Paint, 4 1/2 In. 825.00
Belsnickle, Holding Christmas Tree 143.00
Belsnickle, White, 13 1/2 In. 1550.00
Belsnickle, Yellow, 7 3/4 In. 595.00
Billiken, Painted, Original Closure 85.00
Binocular Case, Cardboard, Leather, Germany, 1930s, 3 1/2 In. 28.00
Bird, Real Feathers, 3 x 2 In. 100.00
Boat, Model Cruiser, Original Closure 33.00
Box, Christmas Tree, Candles, Cardboard, Triangular, USA, 1930s, 5 In. 45.00
Boy & Girl, Cardboard, Handle, Germany, 1930s, 4 1/2 In. 50.00
Candelabra, Amber 33.00
Car, Rear Trunk, Original Closure 55.00
Carpet Sweeper, Baby, Replaced Handle 286.00
Cat, Black & Gray, Composition, 3 1/4 In. 53.00
Cat, Glass Eyes 160.00
Cat, Witch's Head, Composition, c.1920, 5 1/2 In. ....*Illus* 803.00
Child, Sitting On Large Shoe, Closed Mouth, Blue Paperweight Eyes 1295.00
Child With Flowers, Cardboard, Handle, Germany, 1930s, 4 1/2 In. 60.00
Christmas Stocking, Die Cut, Red Hanging String, 1875, 4 3/4 x 11 In. 75.00
Coal Car, On Tender, New York Central, Original Closure 66.00
Deer, Germany, 19th Century 410.00
Dog, American Eskimo, Rabbit Fur, Head Lifts Off, Early 20th Century, 8 In. .. 200.00
Dog, Bulldog, Gold Collar, Metal Screw On Cap, 1930 .... 95.00
Dog, Bulldog, Oblong Base 11.00

Dog, Bulldog, Screw Closure 25.00
Dog, With Umbrella, Painted Glass 65.00
Dove On Nest 145.00
Egg, Boy, Girl, Chicks, Cardboard, Germany, c.1900, 4 1/2 In. 38.00
Egg, Boy, Girl, Rabbit, Cardboard, Germany, c.1900, 5 1/4 In. 33.00
Egg, Cardboard, Celluloid Rabbit, Baby 1907, Germany, 3 1/2 In. 112.00
Egg, Girl & Geese, Cardboard, Germany, c.1900, 3 1/4 In. 50.00
Egg, Rabbits, Cardboard, Germany, c.1900, 3 1/2 In. 50.00
Egg, Soldier Chicks, Cardboard, Celluloid Baby Inside, 1908, 4 In. 91.00
Elephant, Emerging From Egg, Composition, 5 In. 275.00
Elephant, GOP 363.00
Elephant, Standing, In Swallowtail Suit 393.00
English Telephone Booth, Tin Lithograph, Bank 48.00
Father Christmas, Glass, Painted, Tin Screw Closure, 5 1/4 In. 295.00
Feather Tree, Goose Feathers, Spring Candle Clips, Flower Pot, 6 In. 100.00
Felix, On Pedestal, Glass 4180.00
Fire Engine, Stough's 1914 .... 79.00
Firecracker, Germany, 4 1/2 In. 195.00
Fish, Papier-Mache, 14 In. 400.00
Flossie Fisher Furniture, Bed, Black Silhouettes On Yellow Tin .... 4355.00 to 5600.00
Flossie Fisher Furniture, Dresser, Black Silhouettes On Yellow Tin 2420.00
Flossie Fisher Furniture, Table 2540.00
Foxy Doctor, Candy Pills For All Ills, 4 Bottles, Holder 225.00
Gas Pump 650.00
George Washington, Cherry Tree, Ax, Germany, 5 In. 132.00
George Washington, Germany, 4 3/4 In. 69.00
George Washington, Holding Flag, 3 1/2 In. 58.00
George Washington, White Hair, Papier-Mache, 3 1/2 In. 230.00
Goblin, Luggage, Lithographed Cardboard, 2 1/4 In. 182.00
Greyhound Bus, Victory Glass Co. 330.00
Grocery Truck, Red & White 2300.00
Gun, Plastic, Millstein's 30.00
Hat Box, Travelling, Paper Lithograph On Cardboard, 1 1/4 In. 16.00
Hearse No. 1, Missing Radiator Cap 132.00
Hen Turkey, Papier-Mache, West Germany, 4 1/4 In. 22.00
Horn, 3 Valves 393.00
Horn, Striped Tube 30.00
House, William Penn's House, Cardboard, Acker's, 1908 .... 16.00
House Of Glass, Blue 303.00
House Of Glass, Clear 170.00
Independence Hall 393.00
Iron, Electric, Cord & Plug 85.00
Iron, Flat 755.00
Kiddie Kar 218.00
Kiddies Band, 3 Musical Horns, 6 7/8 x 7 1/2 In. 687.00
Knife, Glass 32.00
Ladder Truck 170.00
Lamp, Kerosene 61.00
Lantern, Barn Type No. 1 .... 36.00
Lantern, Barn Type No. 3, Souvenir, Brighton Fair 48.00
Lantern, Devil 950.00
Lawn Swing, Tin ....787.00 to 975.00
Liberty Bell, Original Closure 110.00
Library Lamp 756.00
Limousine, Green Taxi, Original Closure 660.00
Limousine, West Spec. Co., Replaced Closure 176.00
Locomotive, 999, Man In Window 91.00
Los Angeles Dirigible 100.00
Ma Rabbit, Holding Easter Basket, Cardboard, Germany, 10 1/2 In. 374.00
Mailbox 272.00
Man On Motorcycle, Side Car ....575.00 to 975.00
Man On Motorcycle, Side Car, See's Candies 42.00
Man's Head, Movable Eyes & Mouth, 5 1/2 In. 950.00

Mantel Clock, Ironwood, Mich. 120.00
Milk Bottle Carrier, 4 Bottles, Martha Washington 91.00
Milk Bottle Carrier, 6 Bottles, Younken Brothers, Des Moines 230.00
Motorcycle, Glass 125.00
Mule Pulling Barrel ....79.00 to 130.00
Musical Toy Airplane, Closure 28.00
Old Woman In Shoe, Santa Claus Giving Gifts, Tin, Handle, Rectangular 45.00
Opera Glasses, Paneled, Milk Glass 121.00
Oval Clock, Milk Glass, Little Falls, Minn. 230.00
Oval Clock, Milk Glass, Original Closure 110.00
Owl, Wings, Eyes, Blue Hobnail Body, 2 1/4 In. 66.00
Parlor Car, New York Central, Original Closure 575.00
Peanut, Dresden 60.00
Pencil, Baby-Jumbo 109.00
PEZ, Batgirl 225.00
PEZ, Batman, Cape 150.00
PEZ, Bozo, Die Cut 250.00
PEZ, Captain Hook 75.00
PEZ, Clown, With Collar ....85.00 to 100.00
PEZ, Cool Cat, Orange 25.00
PEZ, Doctor 165.00
PEZ, Duck With Flower, Green Face 100.00
PEZ, Dumbo 25.00
PEZ, Easter Bunny, Side Picture 300.00
PEZ, Elephant, Green Head 250.00
PEZ, Garfield, Cook 5.00
PEZ, Green Hornet 375.00
PEZ, Indian Brave, Brown Face 170.00
PEZ, Indian Chief ....100.00 to 135.00
PEZ, King Louie, Brown Face 75.00
PEZ, Lamb, White Head, Pink Stem, 4 1/2 In. 25.00
PEZ, Mr. Ugly 75.00
PEZ, Octopus 60.00
PEZ, Peter Pan 150.00
PEZ, Practical Pig 25.00
PEZ, Psychedelic Flower, Yellow 800.00
PEZ, Santa Claus, Full-Bodied ....65.00 to 150.00
PEZ, Sheik 35.00
PEZ, Smurfette 5.00
PEZ, Snowman 30.00
PEZ, Space Gun, Red, 1980s 65.00
PEZ, Space Trooper, Yellow 295.00
PEZ, Spaceman, Cocoa Marsh ....85.00 to 150.00
PEZ, Teenage Mutant Ninja Turtles, 4 Different Piece 15.00
PEZ, Tinkerbell 320.00
PEZ, Truck 23.00
PEZ, Uncle Sam 400.00
PEZ, Witch, Green Face 50.00
PEZ, Zorro ....100.00 to 110.00
Phonograph, Glass Horn, Ruby Flashed Record 303.00
Pierre Noel, Fur Covered, 21 In. 3200.00
Pumpkin, 4 Faces, 2 Sides, Composition & Cardboard, 3 In. 88.00
Rabbit, Basket On Arm, 1930, 5 1/2 In. 175.00
Rabbit, Begging ....65.00 to 70.00
Rabbit, Bisque 18.00
Rabbit, Crouching 212.00
Rabbit, Pushing Wheelbarrow, Germany 3900.00
Rabbit, With Basket, Hat, Composition, 7 1/2 In. 40.00
Rabbit In Tree Trunk ....1292.00 to 1513.00
Radio, Tune In, Glass, Tin Bottom, 4 1/2 In. 16.00
Rolling Pin 351.00
Rooster, Crowing, Germany, 1930s 95.00
Sailor, On Lemon, Composition ....*Illus* 688.00

Santa Claus, Bag On Chimney, Glass, Painted 70.00
Santa Claus, Composition, On Cardboard Box, Germany, 1930s, 2 5/8 In. 180.00
Santa Claus, Felt, Cardboard, Head On Spring, Germany, 13 In. 50.00
Santa Claus, Glass, Fur Beard, Wicker Basket, Feather Tree, 1920s, 12 In. 595.00
Santa Claus, Glass, Painted, Tin Screw Closure, 5 In. 275.00
Santa Claus, Holding Ball, Papier-Mache, Germany ....580.00 to 650.00
Santa Claus, Holding Feather Tree, Felt Over Cardboard, Germany, 13 In. 60.00
Santa Claus, In Boot, Silver Foil, Chenille Trim, Japan, 1920s, 6 In. 75.00
Santa Claus, In Chimney, Plastic 20.00
Santa Claus, Landing On Roof, In Airplane, Oval 30.00
Santa Claus, On Top Of Box, Revolves, Plays Music, 1940s 125.00
Santa Claus, Papier-Mache, 9 1/2 In. ....55.00 to 75.00
Santa Claus, Roly Poly, Cardboard, Mica, Composition Face, 10 x 6 In. 450.00
Santa Claus, Sack, Papier-Mache, White, Red & Green Trim, 8 In. 45.00
Santa Claus, Sitting On Papier-Mache Tree Stump, Felt Face, 4 1/2 In. 125.00
Santa's Boot, Red & Gold Chenille, Holly Sprig, Japan, 6 In. 80.00
Sewing Machine, Old Fashioned Treadle Type 587.00
Skookum, By Tree Stump 424.00
Snowball, Bisque Head Figure, Cotton 495.00
Snowman, Cardboard, Mica, Black Hat, Striped Cane, Germany, 9 In. 60.00
Snowman, Cardboard, Painted, Wire Arms, Germany, 1930s, 7 In. 82.00
Soldier, On Pickle, Composition ....*Illus* 550.00
Spark Plug ....120.00 to 330.00
Station Wagon, No Closure 16.00
Statue Of Liberty 2420.00
Stop & Go, Original Candy 484.00
Store, 5 & 10 Cent, Nothing Over 10 Cents, 2 Story, Tin, 2 7/8 In. 1650.00
Suitcase, Clear Glass 65.00
Suitcase, Milk Glass, Salem, Kansas, Embossed Stickers 109.00
Teddy Bear, Plush Fur, Glass Eyes, Unjointed, Head Lifts Off, 1920s, 21 In. 460.00
Telephone, Desk Type, Glass, Black Plastic Receiver, 1940s, 3 x 4 In. 30.00
Telephone, Desk Type, Tin 121.00
Telephone, Old Fashioned 450.00
Telephone, Old Fashioned, Wall Type 91.00
Telephone, West Bros. Co., 1907 .... 61.00
Tom Turkey, Papier-Mache, West Germany, 4 1/2 In. 38.00
Truck, Van, Cork On Front 242.00
Trunk, Rounded Top, Newark, N.Y., Glass 97.00
Uncle Sam, Fanny Farmer, 1944, 3 In. 120.00
Waltham Clock, Glass, Tin Back, 4 In. 38.00
Watermelon Face, Paper Lithographed Over Cardboard, 3 3/4 In. 143.00
Wax Half Doll, On Cardboard Box, Feather Plumes, France, c.1920, Box, 6 In. 550.00
Wheelbarrow, Large Wheel 133.00
World Globe On Stand, 3 1/2 In. 11.00

Candy Container, Sailor,
On Lemon, Composition

Candy Container, Soldier,
On Pickle, Composition

**Do not put water in a
pottery container with an
unglazed interior. The water
will be absorbed and
eventually stain the
container.**

CANES and walking sticks were used by every well-dressed man in the nineteenth century, but by World War I the style had changed. Today canes are used by few but the infirm. Collectors prize old canes made with special features, like hidden swords, whiskey flasks, or risqué pictures seen through peepholes. Examples with solid gold heads or made from exotic materials, such as walrus vertebrae, are among the higher priced canes.

Bone, Carved Dog's Head, Glass Eyes, Brass Ferule, 32 3/8 In. 247.00
Bronze, Octopus Head, Walnut, Signed T. Hochstetler 450.00
Cowhorn, Carved, Knobbie 150.00
Glass, Green, White, Scotland, 19th Century, 34 In. 44.00
Gold, Knot, Hand Chased, 36 In. 410.00
Gold, Presented To General George B. Hodge, Ebonized Shaft, 1864 .... 1900.00
Horn Handle, Gun, Pepperbox, Stiletto Points With Turn, Metal Ferrule, 33 In. 3960.00
Ivory, Cluster Of Monkeys, 4 1/2 In. 157.00
Ivory, Elephant Head 3640.00
Ivory, Greyhound, Mounted In Wood, Sterling Ferrule, 5 In. 350.00
Ivory, Knob, Monogrammed Silver Insert, Bamboo Shaft, J. Finley, 1797-1866, 34 In. ... 198.00
Ivory, Pistol Grip Handle, Silver Inlay & Ferule, Wooden Shaft, Ivory Tip, 33 1/4 In. 220.00
Ivory, Pug, Automaton, Turns Head & Opens Mouth 4400.00
Ivory, Smiling Woman, Flowing Hair, Ebony Shaft, 19th Century 2500.00
Pewter, Lady's Leg Handle, Presentation, Ebony, 36 1/2 In. 302.00
Rock Crystal & Tortoiseshell, Platinum Ring Set With 4 Sapphires, Coconut Shaft ... 3800.00
Silver & Ivory, Silver Bands, Carved Ivory Man's Head 275.00
Sterling Silver, Antler Shape, Ferule, Bark Shaft, 36 In. 198.00
Sword, Horn Tip 395.00
Sword, Leather Wrapped Shaft, Lead Fish Handle 90.00
Telescope 875.00
Topaz, Bulldog's Head Knob, Sapphire Eyes, Cherry Shaft 3000.00
Twisted Narwhal Tusk, Iron Ferrule 3400.00
Vertebrae Of Snake 150.00
Walking Stick, Alligator Handle, Hand Carved 225.00
Walking Stick, Bird Carved In The Round, Articulated Eyes, Metal Tip, 34 1/2 In. 1610.00
Walking Stick, Bird, Carved From A Root 632.00
Walking Stick, Black & Gold Painted Bird In Carved Hand, Painted, 37 1/2 In. 3220.00
Walking Stick, Blown Glass, Red & Blue Swirls, Applied Threading, 95 1/2 In. 1045.00
Walking Stick, Bone, Rope Twist, Sterling Silver Ferule, Bamboo Shaft, 34 In. 165.00
Walking Stick, Ebony, Gold Head, 33 1/2 In. 121.00
Walking Stick, Fully Carved Ram's Head Grip, Stripped Branch Shaft, 33 1/2 In. 748.00
Walking Stick, Incised & Twisted Dolphin's Body Grip, Stripped Shaft, 34 1/2 In. 316.00
Walking Stick, Ivory, Clenched Fist Handle 1650.00
Walking Stick, Ivory, Woman's Leg Handle, Baleen Shaft 715.00
Walking Stick, Mahogany, Leather Strap, Roycroft, 1903, 35 In. 550.00
Walking Stick, Man's Head Grip, Exotic Turban-Type Hat, Stripped Shaft, 37 1/4 In. ... 575.00
Walking Stick, Man's Head, Silhouette, Folds Into Seat, Wood, Polychrome Paint, 34 In. 110.00
Walking Stick, Octagonal Carved Knob, Rope Turned Shaft 1485.00
Walking Stick, Silver Plate, Inscribed Charles Bebber, Aug. 13, '98, 36 2/3 In. 38.00
Walking Stick, Steer's Head 575.00
Walking Stick, Twisting Grip Carved With Man's Face, Incised Hat, Eyes, 39 3/4 In. ... 345.00
Walking Stick, Walnut, Mustache & Turban On Man, 4 Serpent Forms Ascending Shaft . 5225.00
Walking Stick, Whalebone, Silver Handle, Presented To Dr. E. Hatton, Sr., 35 In. 950.00
Whalebone, 7 Sections Of Spiral Turnings, Inlaid Tortoiseshell Handle 1650.00
Wood, Carved Snake Spiraling Up To Man, Folk Art, 1913 Dime On Handle 90.00
Wood, Civil War Theme, U.S. Constitution, Snake, Attacking Man, Red Sealing Wax ... 975.00
Wood, Snake & 2 Lizards, 36 In. 33.00

CANTON CHINA is blue-and-white ware made near the city of Canton, in China, from about 1785 to 1895. It is hand decorated with Chinese scenes. Canton is part of the group of porcelains known today as Chinese Export Porcelain.

Basket, Birds Amid Flowers, Reticulated Sides, Woven Cane Handle 2100.00
Basket, Fruit, Underplate, Reticulated 880.00

Basket, Open Work Edges, Vertical Handles, 5 1/2 x 10 1/2 In. 1200.00
Bowl, Cut Corner, 9 1/2 In. 1100.00
Bowl, Fruit, Square Cut, 10 1/2 x 4 1/4 In. 1035.00
Bowl, Lobed, 8 1/2 In. 1250.00
Bowl, Reticulated, 9 In. 800.00
Bowl, Scalloped, 8 1/4 In. 460.00
Bowl, Scalloped, 10 In. 575.00
Bowl, Vegetable, 8 1/4 In. 245.00
Box, Cover, Square, 3 In. 1800.00
Cachepot, 7 x 5 In. 1450.00
Candlestick, 11 In., Pair 825.00
Dish, Hot Water, Octagonal 350.00
Dish, Leaf Form, 10 1/2 In. 431.00
Jug, Cider, Foo Lion Final Cover, Twisted Handle, Rain & Cloud Border 1870.00
Mug, Oriental Scene, 1860, 3 3/4 In. 425.00
Pitcher, Architectural Lake Scene, Foo Dog Finial, Ovoid, 8 1/2 In. 1870.00
Pitcher, Landscape Design, 1840, 6 In. 385.00
Pitcher, Milk, 7 1/2 In. 700.00
Plate, Hot Water, Octagonal, 9 In. 192.00
Platter, 16 1/4 In. 550.00
Platter, 18 3/4 In. 580.00
Platter, Cut Corners, 13 In. 165.00
Platter, Pagoda Design, Octagonal, 20 In. 65.00
Platter, Reticulated, 11 In. 335.00
Platter, Well & Tree, 17 In. 745.00
Sauceboat, Cover, Boar Head Handles, 7 1/4 In. 315.00
Teapot, 7 In. 330.00
Teapot, Globular, 6 In. 187.00
Tray, Quatrefoil, 8 x 10 3/4 In. 345.00
Trivet, Tile, 5 In. 420.00
Urn, Cover, Genre Scenes, Fruit Ground, Hand Painted, 15 1/2 In. 110.00
Urn, Cover, Lake Scene, 2 Handles, 11 In. 660.00
Vase, Flared, Cylindrical, 15 1/2 In. 1725.00
Vegetable, Cover, 9 1/4 In. 100.00
Vegetable, Cover, Deep, 9 x 8 In. 460.00

CAPO-DI-MONTE porcelain was first made in Naples, Italy, from 1743
to 1759. The factory moved near Madrid, Spain, reopened in 1771, and
worked to 1834. Since that time, the Doccia factory of Italy acquired
the molds and is using the crown and N mark. Societe Richard
Ceramica is a modern-day firm often referred to as Ginori or Capo-di-
Monte. This company uses the crown and N mark.

Bowl, Swans & Cranes, Late 19th Century, 5 3/4 In., Pair 200.00
Box, Classical Figure & Battle Relief, Brass Hinged Cover, Italy, 3 In. 431.00
Box, Cover, Typical Festive Scene 145.00
Box, Putti Design, 5 3/4 x 3 1/2 In. 402.00
Bust, Napoleon, Metal Base, 10 1/2 In. 201.00
Cachepot, Orange Glaze, Richard Ginori, 4 To 7 In., 4 Piece 144.00
Compote, Cover, Signed 145.00
Cup & Saucer, Cherub Design, Demitasse 165.00
Figurine, Bird Of Paradise, 21 In. 395.00
Figurine, Maiden, Carrying Basket Of Wash, Signed, 8 In. 270.00
Figurine, Victorian Couple, Early 1900s 285.00
Group, Diana & Nymph, Early 20th Century, 18 In. 630.00
Group, Europa & The Bull, Blanc-De-Chine, 20th Century, 8 3/4 In. 230.00
Helmet, Relief Scenes From Homer's Iliad, Crown & N Mark, c.1900 .... 632.00
Jar, Cherub, 5 In. 45.00
Lamp, Nude Infants, Brass Plinth, Matching Shade, 21 In., Pair 100.00
Lamp, Urn Form, Cherubs, White Metal Base, 30 In., Pair 66.00
Pitcher, 16 In. 125.00
Plaque, Shield Shape, Battle Scene, Rim Reserves Of Fruit & Armor, 23 In. 165.00
Plaque, Shield Shape, Tooled Leather Frame, Late 19th Century, 27 In. 862.00
Plate, Central Shield, Border Embossed With Figures, 10 In., 12 Piece 862.00

Stein, Painted Relief, People All Around Body, Boar Finial, Set-On Lid, 1 Liter 90.00
Urn, Cover, Playful Cherubs, Ram's Head Handles, Crown & N Mark, 15 In. 577.00
Urn, Diana & Endymion, Classical, Handles, Bronzed Plinth, 24 x 18 In. 3300.00
Urn, Standard Form, Raised Figural Design, Gilt, 7 In. 69.00
Vase, Cherub, 19th Century, 11 In. 385.00
Vase, Maid Milking Goat, Garland, Gilt Borders, Crown & N Mark, 13 1/2 In. 715.00

CAPTAIN MARVEL was introduced in February 1940 in Whiz comic
books. An orphan named Billy Batson met the wizard, Shazam, and
whenever he said the magic word he was transformed into a superhero.
A movie serial was released in 1940. The comic was discontinued in
1954. A second Captain Marvel appeared in 1966, a third in 1967.
Only the original was transformed by shouting *Shazam*.

Airplane, 1930s 90.00
Bank, Dime 250.00
Car, Racing, Partial Box 1095.00
Comic Book, Marvel Team Up, No. 128, 1983 . . . . 35.00
Comic Book, Whiz Comic, Fawcett, No. 68, 1945 . . . . 33.00
Game, Super Heroes Strategy, Marvel Comics, Milton Bradley, 1980 . . . . 15.00
Pennant 100.00
Race Car, White, Black Wheels, Windup 350.00
Race Car, Windup, 1947, 4 In. 195.00
Tippy Toy, Billy The Kid, Fawcett, 1940s 18.00
Whistle, Power Siren, 1940s 200.00
Wristwatch, Leather Band, Swiss, 1948 . . . . 100.00

CAPTAIN MIDNIGHT began as a radio show in September 1940. The
first comic book appeared in July 1941. Captain Midnight was really
the aviator Captain Albright, who was to defeat the Nazis. A movie serial was made in 1942 and a comic strip was published for a short time.
The comic book Captain Midnight ended his career in 1948. The radio
premiums are the prized collector memorabilia today.

Album, Stamp, Air Heroes, Captain Midnight & Skelly Logo 20.00
Album, Stamp, Complete 45.00
Badge, Mystery Dial, Code-O-Graphic 65.00
Badge, Secret Squadron Decoder 100.00
Book, Joyce Of The Secret Squadron, Whitman, 1942 . . . . 24.00
Cup, Ovaltine 45.00
Decoder, The Rifleman Gun, 1949 . . . . 82.50
Manual, Club, 1941 . . . . 125.00
Medal, Membership, Spinner, Brass, Skelly, 1940s, 1 1/4 In. 22.00
Mug, Shake-Up, Ovaltine 75.00
Pin, Decoder 85.00
Spy-Scope, Metal, Plastic Ends, Instructions & Mailing Tube, c.1947 . . . . 320.00

CARAMEL SLAG, see Chocolate Glass category.

CARDS listed here include advertising cards (often called trade cards),
baseball cards, playing cards, and others. Color pictures were rare in
the nineteenth century, so companies gave away colorful cards with
pictures of children, flowers, products, or related scenes that promoted
the company name. These were often collected and stored in albums.
Baseball cards also date from the nineteenth century when they were
used by tobacco companies as giveaways. Gum cards were started in
1933, but it was not until after World War II that the bubble gum cards
favored today were produced. Today over 1,000 cards are issued each
year by the gum companies. Related items may be found in the
Christmas, Halloween, Paper, Postcard, and Movie categories.

Advertising, Bank, Bear Hunt, J. & E. Stevens, Early 20th Century 55.00
Advertising, Bonanza Thresher Trade, 1895 . . . . 15.00
Advertising, Carriage Ad, Black Child Chef, 1880s 22.00
Advertising, Conack & Co., Buffalo, N.Y., Girl With Aquarium, 1890s 25.00
Advertising, D. Buchner, Butterflies & Bugs, 2 Piece 80.00

Don't buy baseball cards that have been trimmed, or cards with punch or staple holes— unless a card is so rare you may never find it again. Cards with holes, ink stains, tape stains, and trimmed edges don't have much value unless they are extremely rare.

Card, Advertising, Hires
Root Beer, 3 x 5 In.

Advertising, Dolly Madison Cigars, I.M. Carvalho, Mechanical, Peek A Boo, 6 x 4 In. ..	80.00
Advertising, Duke's Cigarettes, 2 Women Smoking Cigars, 3 x 5 In.	35.00
Advertising, Eureka Soap Company, Different Actor Or Actress, Playing	125.00
Advertising, Hires Root Beer, 3 x 5 In. ....*Illus*	275.00
Advertising, Hires Root Beer, Graphics Of Smiling Boy, Could I Have Another, 3 x 5 In.	14.00
Advertising, Kinney Bros., Butterflies Of The World, 1888, 17 Piece	140.00
Advertising, Larkin Soap, Buffalo, N.Y., Burro, Reverse Sweet Home, 8 x 9 In.	45.00
Advertising, Nolan Bro. Shoes, Mountain Scene, Palette Shape	10.00
Advertising, Old Judge Cigarettes, Goodwin & Co., Die Cut, 6 x 4 In.	50.00
Advertising, Pet Cigarettes, Allen & Ginter, Dogs, Children, Boy, 3 x 4 In., 12 Piece ...	130.00
Advertising, Quaker & Quaker, Jr. Rangers, Lt. Greeley Arrives At North Pole, 6 x 10 In.	38.00
Advertising, Saxe, The Hatter, Opera House Block, Omaha, Neb., Palette Shape	12.00
Advertising, Sub Rosa All Tobacco Cigarettes, Photograph Of Prostitute, 1888, 8 x 5 In..	120.00
Advertising, Sulphur Bitters, Portrait Of President Cleveland, 6 1/2 x 4 1/4 In.	16.00
Advertising, Welcome Cigarettes, Goodwin & Co., Die Cut Miss Liberty, 7 x 4 In.	50.00
Advertising, Yum Yum Cigarettes, Aug. Beck, Presidents Of U.S., 3 Piece	40.00
Baseball, Christy Mathewson, Turkey Red Cigarettes, Baseball-Actress Series, 1911	259.00
Baseball, J.T. Meyers, New York Giants, T206, Sweet Caporal Cigarettes, c.1911	22.00
Baseball, Jiggs Donohue, Chicago, T206, Piedmont Cigarettes, 2 3/4 x 1 1/2 In.	20.00
Baseball, Joe Birmingham, Cleveland, T206, Piedmont Cigarettes, 2 3/4 x 1 1/2 In.	23.00
Baseball, Mecca Double-Folder Series, Complete Set, 50 Cards, c.1911	3162.00
Baseball, Paul Davidson, Indianapolis, T206, Piedmont Cigarettes, 2 3/4 x 1 1/2 In.	20.00
Baseball, Philadelphia Caramel Co., E-95 Series, Complete Set, 25 Cards, c.1909	2070.00
Baseball, Ty Cobb, T206, Sweet Caporal Cigarettes, 3 Different Cards, c.1910	1495.00
Football, Jack Kemp, Fleer No. 79, 1962	220.00
Football, Robert Waterfield, L.A. Rams, No. 35, Bowman, 1948	30.00
Greeting, Valentine, 8-Pointed Rosette, 8 Romantic Verses, 1820s, 13 In.	2300.00
Greeting, Valentine, Heart Hunter, Ribboned Folder, Sender's Calling Card, 1908, 18 In.	100.00
Greeting, Valentine, Mechanical, 1920s	45.00
Greeting, Valentine, Watercolor, Ink & Cutout, Leafy Buds, Blossoms, 12 1/8 In.	1265.00
Hockey, Charlie Conacher, O-Pee-Chee, No. 34, 1933	525.00
Playing, American Red Cross, 1945	25.00
Playing, Beverly Hillbillies, Box, 1963	30.00
Playing, Boyertown Casket Co., We're Not Forgetting, World War II, 2 Decks	20.00
Playing, Fan Tan, Flying Girl	2.00
Playing, Horse Racing, Citation, 2 Decks	80.00
Playing, Horse Racing, Man O War, Leather Case	50.00
Playing, James J. Jeffries, Great White Hope, Boxing, 1909	675.00
Playing, Komponisten Quartett	40.00
Playing, Moosehead Beer, Embossed Tin Box, 2 Decks	15.00
Playing, Mork & Mindy	10.00
Playing, Munson Steamship Line	25.00
Playing, Petty Sailor Girl, Box	75.00
Playing, Pop Music, Elvis Presley To Beatles, 1960s	80.00
Playing, Rainier National Park	30.00
Playing, Ripley's Believe It Or Not, Each Different, 1950s	8.00
Playing, Stage Stars, 1897	90.00

Playing, Vargas, Esquire Double Deck, Sealed 40.0
Playing, Virginia Slims, Box 20.0
Playing, White Pass & Yukon Route, 1900, With Case 175.0
Playing, Yellowstone Park, 1920 .... 32.0
Playing, Yellowstone Park, 1926 .... 20.0
Trading, Star Wars Galaxy, 1983, 275 Piece 85.0
Trading, Star Wars, Topps, 1977, 385 Piece 395.0

CARDER, see Aurene and Steuben categories.

CARLSBAD is a mark found on china made by several factories in
Germany, Austria, and Bavaria. Many pieces were exported to the
United States. Most of the pieces available today were made after
1891.

Bowl, 3 Ladies & Children With Instruments, Cobalt Blue, Gold, 11 1/2 In. 195.0
Ewer, Purple & Yellow Floral Design, Ivory Ground, 11 3/4 In. 55.0
Plate, Portrait, French Dandy, Victorian 40.0
Platter, Fish, Pink Roses, 20 1/2 In. 125.0
Vase, Peacock On Balcony, Pedestal, Reticulated Handles, Aqua, Green, 10 1/2 In. 265.0

CARLTON WARE was made at the Carlton Works of Stoke-on-Trent,
England, beginning about 1890. The firm traded as Wiltshaw &
Robinson until 1957. It was renamed Carlton Ware Ltd. in 1958. The
company went bankrupt in 1995, but the name is still in use.

Biscuit Jar, Allover Colored Roses, Cobalt Blue Borders, 1909 .... 165.0
Bowl, Black, Ducks, Iris, Gold Trim, 13 1/4 x 6 1/2 x 6 1/2 In. 920.0
Bowl, Chinoiserie Design, Oriental Houses, Temples, Gold Border, 8 5/8 In. 350.0
Bowl, Exotic Scene, Birds & Flowers, Gold Trim, 2 1/8 In. 195.0
Bowl, Floral, Pedestal Foot, Soft Green Ground, Gold Trim, 3 1/4 x 12 3/8 In. 395.0
Bowl, Pagoda Scene, Enameled, Cobalt Blue, 7 1/2 In. 110.0
Bowl, Rouge Royale, Fancy Bird, Butterflies, Trees, 3 Gold Peg Feet, 10 x 3 In. 485.0
Bowl, Rouge Royale, Oriental Scene, 9 In. 95.0
Bowl, Shell Shape, Coralbells, Cobalt & Gold Trim, Pre-1921, 9 3/4 x 3 In. 270.0
Bowl, Tree On Pedestal, Orange Handles, Cream Ground, Scalloped, 7 x 12 In. 350.0
Bowl, Tropical Birds, Black Ground, 9 In. 190.0
Box, Birds, 2 1/2 In. 65.0
Candy Dish, Australian Pattern, Footed, 5 In. 30.0
Candy Dish, Australian Pattern, Single Tab Handle, Yellow, 4 1/4 In. 18.0
Demitasse Set, Art Deco, Gold Rims, Gold Interior, 15 Piece 495.0
Dish, Jelly, Anemone, Spoon, Box 45.0
Dish, Jelly, Foxglove, Spoon 35.0
Eggcup, Walking Feet 15.0
Ginger Jar, Raised Pagoda, People, Bridge, Boat & Birds, Gold Trim 195.0
Inkwell, Pen Tray, Egyptian Fan Pattern, Cobalt Blue, 2 1/4 x 8 In. 600.0
Jar, Cover, Birds In Flight, 10 In. 800.0
Jar, Cover, Oriental Man & Woman, Gold Trim & Bands, Signed, 9 In. 450.0
Jar, Potpourri, Oriental Buildings & People, Matching Reverse, 9 3/4 In. 425.0
Mug, Drinker's Verse 37.0
Mug, Man, Hanging Motto 25.0
Pitcher, Ivy & Figures, Dark Green Ground, 6 1/2 In. 95.0
Pitcher, Leaf Shape, Gold Edge 75.0
Pitcher, Rouge Royale Scene, 6 x 6 In. 195.0
Pitcher, Spider Web, Butterflies & Flowers 325.0
Plate, Water Lily, Handles, 7 In. 50.0
Relish, Anemone, Handles, 10 1/2 x 6 In. 115.0
Sugar & Creamer, Foxglove 45.0
Tazza, Flowers, Gold, Pink, Blue, Green Ground, 2 1/2 x 7 1/4 In. 225.0
Tea Set, Buttercup, Pink, 5 Piece 135.0
Tea Set, Foxglove, Green, 9 Piece ....400.00 to 425.0
Teapot, Bird In Tree, 7 In. 275.0
Teapot, Foxglove 100.0
Tray, Deviled Egg, 12 In. 35.0
Tray, Rouge Royale, 10 x 6 1/4 In. 35.0

Vase, Birds & Flowers, 11 In.	350.00
Vase, Cover, Oriental Scenes, White Lining, Egg Shape, 7 3/8 In.	265.00
Vase, Exotic Birds, 11 In.	250.00
Vase, Fantasia, Exotic Landscape, Long Tailed Birds, Blue, 7 In.	450.00
Vase, Flowers, Panels, Yellow, Green, Blue, Red Ground, 7 1/2 In.	920.00
Vase, Gold Oriental Temples, Homes, Gold Top Border, Aqua, Green Trim, 9 In.	395.00
Vase, Oriental Buildings, Orange Top Band, Gold Trim, 4 3/8 In.	110.00
Vase, Oriental Scene, Man & Woman, Orange Top, Black Satin Ground, 6 In.	150.00
Vase, Oriental Scenes, Dark Blue Ground, Mother-Of-Pearl Interior, 11 In.	395.00
Vase, Persian Scene, Multicolored Enamels, 10 1/2 In.	350.00
Vase, Persian Scene, Servants Serving Ruler, Trees, Birds, Animals, 10 1/2 In.	395.00
Vase, Pixies Blowing Bubbles, Pearl Ground, Orange, Matte Black, 6 In.	600.00
Vase, Rouge Royale, 5 In.	70.00
Vase, Rouge Royale, Cascades Of Leaves, Flowers & Butterflies, 8 In.	250.00

CARNIVAL GLASS was an inexpensive, iridescent, pressed glass made from about 1907 to about 1925. More than 1,000 different patterns are known. Carnival glass is currently being reproduced. Additional pieces may be found in the Northwood category.

Acanthus, Bowl, Green, 8 In.	75.00
Acanthus, Bowl, Ruffled Edge, Marigold, 8 In.	40.00
Acorn, Bowl, Marigold, 8 In.	100.00
Acorn, Bowl, Ruffled Edge, Marigold, 7 1/2 In.	55.00
Acorn Burrs, Punch Cup, Green	60.00
Acorn Burrs, Spooner, Amethyst	85.00
Acorn Burrs, Tumbler, Purple	60.00
Acorn Burrs & Bark pattern is listed here as Acorn Burrs.	
Amaryllis pattern is listed here as Tiger Lily.	
Banded Medallion & Teardrop pattern is listed here as Beaded Bull's Eye.	
Basketweave, Basket, Blue	95.00
Battenburg Lace No. 1 pattern is listed here as Hearts & Flowers.	
Battenburg Lace No. 2 pattern is listed here as Captive Rose.	
Battenburg Lace No. 3 pattern is listed here as Fanciful.	
Beaded Acanthus, Pitcher, Milk, Marigold	150.00
Beaded Bull's Eye, Vase, Amethyst	100.00
Beaded Cable, Rose Bowl, Amethyst	75.00
Beaded Cable, Rose Bowl, Ice Blue	800.00
Beaded Cable, Rose Bowl, White	465.00
Beaded Medallion & Teardrop pattern is listed here as Beaded Bull's Eye.	
Blossoms & Band, Bowl, Marigold, 7 1/2 In.	35.00
Boutonniere, Compote, Marigold	200.00
Brocaded Palms, Vase, 8 In.	400.00
Butterfly, Berry Set, Marigold, 5 Piece	200.00
Butterfly, Tumbler, Marigold	65.00
Butterfly & Berry, Berry Bowl, Amethyst	95.00
Butterfly & Berry, Bowl, Footed, Marigold, 8 1/2 In.	90.00
Butterfly & Berry, Tumbler, Cobalt Blue	95.00
Butterfly & Grape pattern is listed here as Butterfly & Berry.	
Butterfly & Stippled Rays pattern is listed here as Butterfly.	
Captive Rose, Plate, Marigold, 9 In.	570.00
Cattails & Water Lily pattern is listed here as Water Lily & Cattails.	
Cherry Chain, Bowl, Blue, 6 In.	50.00
Christmas Cactus pattern is listed here as Thistle.	
Christmas Plate pattern is listed here as Poinsettia.	
Chrysanthemum, Bowl, Footed, Blue, 10 1/2 In.	175.00
Chrysanthemum, Bowl, Footed, Marigold, 10 In.	200.00
Coin Dot, Pitcher, Clear & Opalescent, 11 In.	185.00
Colonial, Goblet, Marigold	85.00
Concave Diamonds, Tumbler, Celeste Blue	30.00
Corinth, Vase, Amethyst, 8 In.	45.00
Crackle, Water Set, Marigold, 14 Piece	275.00
Dahlia, Pitcher, Amethyst	750.00
Daisy & Drape, Vase, White	195.00

Daisy & Plume, Compote, Green 60.00
Daisy Band & Drape pattern is listed here as Daisy & Drape.
Dandelion, Tankard, White 4950.00
Dandelion Variant pattern is listed here as Panelled Dandelion.
Diamond & Rib, Vase, Green, 11 In. 80.00
Diamond Lace, Water Set, Amethyst, 7 Piece 595.00
Diamond Point Columns, Creamer, Marigold 28.00
Dogwood & Marsh Lily pattern is listed here as Two Flowers.
Double Loop, Sugar, Blue 165.00
Double-Stem Rose, Bowl, Dome Footed, White, 8 1/2 In. 105.00
Double-Stem Rose, Bowl, Footed, White, 9 In. . . . . .90.00 to 95.00
Dragon & Lotus, Bowl, Amber 169.00
Dragon & Lotus, Bowl, Black Amethyst 375.00
Dragon & Lotus, Bowl, Ruffled Edge, Peach 295.00
Dragon & Lotus, Bowl, White 1450.00
Embroidered Mums, Bowl, Blue, 9 In. 390.00
Embroidered Mums, Bowl, Marigold, 9 In. 525.00
English Hob & Button, Bowl, Blue, 10 In. 56.00
Fan & Arch pattern is listed here as Persian Garden.
Fanciful, Bowl, White, 8 In. 425.00
Fantasy pattern is listed here as Question Marks.
Feather & Hobstar pattern is listed here as Inverted Feather.
Fenton's Butterfly pattern is listed here as Butterfly.
Fisherman's Net pattern is listed here as Tree Bark.
Floral & Grape, Pitcher, Amethyst 130.00
Floral & Grape, Tumbler, Amethyst 70.00
Floral & Grapevine pattern is listed here as Floral & Grape.
Florentine, Candlestick, Amethyst, 8 In., Pair 125.00
Fluffy Bird pattern is listed here as Peacock.
Four Pillars, Vase, Squatty, Amethyst, 6 In. 250.00
Fruit & Flowers, Bonbon, Blue, 4 x 8 1/2 In., Pair 288.00
Fruit & Flowers, Dish, Ruffled Edge, Amethyst, 5 In. 40.00
Garden Path Variant, Bowl, Marigold, 7 1/2 In. 165.00
Good Luck, Bowl, Amethyst, 8 1/2 In. 350.00
Grape & Cable, Banana Boat, Amethyst, 12 In. . . . .*Illus* 225.00
Grape & Cable, Bowl, Amethyst, 8 In. . . . . .165.00 to 185.00
Grape & Cable, Bowl, Ice Blue, 7 1/2 In. 350.00
Grape & Cable, Bowl, Marigold, 9 In. 125.00
Grape & Cable, Bowl, Purple, 8 In. 400.00
Grape & Cable, Hatpin Holder, Amethyst 350.00
Grape & Cable, Hatpin Holder, Blue 375.00
Grape & Cable, Hatpin Holder, Purple 400.00
Grape & Cable, Punch Cup, Blue 80.00
Grape & Cable, Sweetmeat, Amethyst 165.00
Grape & Cable, Tray, Dresser, Marigold 135.00
Grape & Cable, Tumbler, Green 100.00
Grape & Cable, Tumbler, Marigold 35.00
Grape & Gothic Arches, Tumbler, Marigold 25.00
Grape Delight pattern is listed here as Vintage.
Grapevine Diamonds pattern is listed here as Grapevine Lattice.
Grapevine Lattice, Plate, White, 7 In. 145.00
Grapevine Lattice, Tumbler, Marigold 27.00
Hanging Cherry, Bowl, Ice Cream, Green, 10 In. 225.00
Hearts & Flowers, Bowl, Ice Blue, 8 In. 675.00
Hearts & Flowers, Plate, Marigold 1850.00
Heron & Rushes pattern is listed here as Stork & Rushes.
Hobnail pattern is listed in this book as its own category.
Holly, Bowl, Cobalt Blue 175.00
Holly & Whirl, Bowl, Rhodium Iridescent, 7 In. 143.00
Holly Spray pattern is listed here as Holly Sprig.
Holly Sprig, Bonbon, 2 Handles, Green 90.00
Horse Medallions pattern is listed here as Horses' Heads.
Horses' Heads, Bowl, Jack-In-The-Pulpit, Vaseline, 7 1/2 In. 175.00

Carnival Glass, Grape & Cable, Banana Boat, Amethyst, 12 In.

Carnival Glass, Soldiers & Sailors, Bowl, Berry & Leaf Circle, Marigold, 7 1/2 In.

Horses' Heads, Bowl, Marigold, 14 In.	120.00
Imperial Grape, Decanter, Wine, Stopper, Marigold	75.00
Imperial Grape, Tumbler, Marigold	45.00
Imperial Grape, Wine Set, Marigold, 7 Piece	250.00
Imperial Grape, Wine, Green	48.00
Inverted Feather, Cracker Jar, Green	250.00
Inverted Feather, Parfait, Marigold	65.00
Inverted Strawberry, Cuspidor, Woman's, 3 x 5 1/2 In.	862.00
Kimberly pattern is listed here as Concave Diamonds.	
Kittens, Bowl, Marigold, 5 1/2 In.	290.00
Kittens, Cup, Marigold	170.00
Kittens, Toothpick, Blue	550.00
Labelle Rose pattern is listed here as Rose Show.	
Lattice & Grape, Pitcher, Marigold	208.00
Lattice & Grape, Tumbler, Blue	25.00
Lattice & Grape, Tumbler, Marigold	25.00
Lattice & Grapevine pattern is listed here as Lattice & Grape.	
Leaf & Beads, Rose Bowl, Sapphire	800.00
Leaf Chain, Bowl, Ruffled Edge, White, 9 In.	125.00
Leaf Chain, Bowl, White, 9 In.	110.00
Leaf Medallion pattern is listed here as Leaf Chain.	
Lined Lattice, Vase, Purple, 9 1/2 In.	90.00
Lustre Rose, Bowl, Footed, Green, 12 In.	215.00
Lustre Rose, Bowl, Marigold 10 1/4 In.	32.00
Lustre Rose, Fernery, Blue	125.00
Lustre Rose, Table Set, Marigold, 4 Piece	137.00
Melinda pattern is listed here as Wishbone.	
Melon & Fan pattern is listed here as Diamond & Rib.	
Memphis, Punch Cup, Green	40.00
Memphis, Punch Cup, Marigold	12.00
Memphis, Punch Cup, Purple	20.00
Mums & Greek Key pattern is listed here as Embroidered Mums.	
Oak Leaf & Acorn pattern is listed here as Acorn.	
Orange Tree, Bowl, Marigold, Footed, 5 x 10 In.	125.00
Orange Tree, Bowl, White, 9 In.	110.00
Orange Tree, Hatpin Holder, Cobalt Blue, 7 In.	175.00
Orange Tree, Mug, Blue	95.00 to 120.00
Orange Tree, Mug, Marigold	45.00
Orange Tree, Plate, Bearded Berry Exterior, Marigold, 9 In.	135.00
Orange Tree, Rose Bowl, Marigold	42.00
Palm Beach, Sauce, Gooseberry Interior, White, 5 In.	80.00
Palm Beach, Sugar, White	105.00
Panelled Dandelion, Tumbler, Green	45.00
Pansy, Bowl, 9 In.	100.00
Pansy, Bowl, Marigold, 9 In.	40.00
Pansy, Nappy, Green	35.00

Pansy, Relish, Green 55.00
Panther, Bowl, Footed, Marigold, 5 In. 85.00
Peacock, Bowl, Green, 9 In. 350.00
Peacock, Bowl, Notched Rim, Pinched Sides, Aqua, 8 1/2 In. ... 2012.00
Peacock, Plate, Notched Rim, Electric Blue, 9 In. 1035.00
Peacock & Grape, Bowl, Green, 8 1/2 In. 175.00
Peacock & Urn, Sauce, Amethyst 100.00
Peacock At The Fountain, Bowl, Marigold, 9 In. 425.00
Peacock At The Fountain, Compote, White 650.00
Peacock At The Fountain, Punch Set, Amethyst, 10 Piece 1330.00
Peacock At The Fountain, Water Set, Blue, 5 Piece 950.00
Peacock On Fence pattern is listed here as Peacock.
Persian Garden, Plate, Marigold, 6 1/4 In. 85.00
Persian Medallion, Bowl, Amethyst, 9 In. 165.00
Petal & Fan, Berry Set, Peach, 7 Piece 650.00
Poinsettia, Pitcher, Milk, Marigold 170.00
Poinsettia & Lattice pattern is listed here as Poinsettia.
Question Marks, Bonbon, Blue 50.00
Rainbow, Compote, Ruffled Edge, Green Base, 5 1/2 In. 95.00
Raspberry, Pitcher, Milk, Amethyst 300.00
Raspberry, Pitcher, Milk, Green, 7 1/2 In. 177.00
Rays & Ribbons, Bowl, Marigold, 9 In. 135.00
Ripple, Vase, Amethyst, 11 In. 115.00
Rose Show, Bowl, Amethyst, 9 In. 700.00
Roses & Loops pattern is listed here as Double-Stem Rose.
Sailboat & Windmill pattern is listed here as Sailboats.
Sailboats, Bowl, Ruffled Edge, Marigold, 6 In. 75.00
Singing Birds, Mug, Amethyst, 3 1/2 In. 125.00
Singing Birds, Tumbler, Green 55.00
Singing Birds, Water Set, Marigold, 6 Piece 700.00
Single Flower, Bowl, Peach Opalescent, 7 1/2 In. 45.00
Ski Star, Bowl, Peach, 11 In. 95.00
Soda Gold, Pitcher, Smoky 270.00
Soldiers & Sailors, Bowl, Berry & Leaf Circle, Marigold, 7 1/2 In. .... *Illus* 1320.00
Spider Web pattern is listed here as Soda Gold.
Stag & Holly, Bowl, 3 Footed, Blue, 10 In. 425.00
Stag & Holly, Bowl, Blue, 9 In. 185.00
Stag & Holly, Bowl, Marigold, 10 In. 110.00
Star Medallion, Pitcher, Marigold 50.00
Star Of David & Bows, Bowl, Amethyst, 9 In. 185.00
Star Of David Medallion pattern is listed here as Star of David & Bows.
Stippled Flower, Bowl, Peach, 8 In. 145.00
Stippled Leaf & Beads pattern is listed here as Leaf & Beads.
Stippled Ribbons & Rays pattern is listed here as Rays & Ribbons.
Stork & Rushes, Basket, Marigold 140.00
Strawberry pattern is listed here as Wild Strawberry.
Sunflower pattern is listed here as Dandelion.
Thin Rib, Vase, Funeral, Marigold 150.00
Thistle, Banana Boat, Blue 495.00
Thistle, Banana Boat, Green 595.00
Thistle, Banana Bowl, Marigold 150.00
Three Fruits, Bowl, Aqua, 9 In. 150.00
Three Fruits, Bowl, Stippled, Marigold, 8 1/2 In. 125.00
Three Fruits, Plate, Amethyst, 7 1/2 In. 150.00
Three Fruits, Plate, Amethyst, 9 In. 245.00
Three Fruits Medallion, Bowl, Footed, Amethyst 175.00
Tiger Lily, Water Set, Marigold, 7 Piece 495.00
Tree Bark, Lemonade Set, Marigold, 7 Piece 100.00
Tree Bark, Mug, Amethyst 100.00
Tree Bark, Vase, Green, 8 1/2 In. 160.00
Tree Trunk, Vase, Blue, 8 In. 250.00
Two Flowers, Banana Boat, Fluted, Marigold 99.00
Two Flowers, Bowl, Ball Footed, Marigold, 10 1/2 In. 95.00

Two Flowers, Sauce, Amber	115.00
Two Fruits, Bonbon, Blue	75.00
Vintage, Bowl, Amethyst, 9 In.	155.00
Vintage, Fernery, Blue	65.00
Vintage, Rose Bowl, Amethyst	125.00
Vintage, Rose Bowl, Blue	115.00
Water Lily & Cattails, Butter, Cover, Marigold	325.00
Water Lily & Cattails, Tumbler, Marigold	40.00 to 95.00
Wild Strawberry, Plate, Purple, 9 In.	225.00
Windflower, Bowl, Marigold, 8 1/2 In.	75.00 to 80.00
Windflower, Bowl, Ruffled Edge, Marigold, 8 1/2 In.	22.00
Windmill, Ashtray, Marigold	25.00
Windmill, Water Set, Rubigold	335.00
Windmill Medallion pattern is listed here as Windmill.	
Wishbone, Bowl, Ruffled Edge, Marigold, 7 3/4 In.	85.00
Wishbone, Tumbler, Marigold, 9 In.	65.00
Wishbone & Spades, Plate, Purple, 6 In.	385.00

CAROUSEL or merry-go-round figures were first carved in the United States in 1867 by Gustav Dentzel. Collectors discovered the charm of the hand-carved figures in the 1970s, and they were soon classed as folk art. Most desirable are the figures other than horses, such as pigs, camels, lions, or dogs. A jumper is a figure that was made to move up and down on a pole; a stander was placed in a stationary position.

Cow, Old Park Paint, Bayol, 43 In.	5200.00
Goat, Running	*Illus* 17250.00
Goat, Tucked Head, Eagle's Head Saddle, Carved Wood, Outside Row, 1880s, 65 In.	4887.00
Horse, Allan Herschell Co., 1925, 60 In.	7800.00
Horse, Carved Rifle & Rabbit Pelt, Jewels, Parker	4500.00
Horse, Carved, Country Fair Style, Painted, North Tonawanda, New York, 57 x 48 In.	1540.00
Horse, Cast Iron, New Canopy, 110 Volt Motor, 1920s, 14 x 8 Ft., 15 Piece	17500.00
Horse, Indian, Park Paint, Herschell-Spillman, 68 In.	6700.00
Horse, Inner Row Jumper, Stein & Goldstein, c.1915, 38 x 43 1/2 In.	1955.00
Horse, Inside, 1930	4000.00
Horse, Jumper, Circus, Park Paint, Allan Herschell, 42 x 36 In.	3200.00
Horse, Jumper, Metal, Allan Herschell	1200.00
Horse, Outside Row, Dentzel, Restored	19500.00
Horse, Park Paint, Parker's, Metal, 54 x 24 In.	800.00
Horse, Prancer, Heyn, 38 x 43 In.	2500.00
Panel, Man Astride Horse, Painted On Tin, 41 1/2 x 53 In.	3375.00

CARRIAGE means several things, so this category lists baby carriages, buggies for adults, horse-drawn sleighs, and even strollers. Doll-sized carriages are listed in the Toy category.

Baby Buggy, Wicker, 1920s	185.00
Baby Buggy, Wicker, 32 x 30 In.	325.00
Baby Buggy, Wicker, 35 x 37 In.	450.00

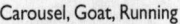

Carousel, Goat, Running

Carriage, Baby Stroller, Wicker, 2 Seats, Parasol

Baby Stroller, Wicker, 2 Seats, Parasol	*Illus*	850.00
Buggy, Doctor's, Restored		2500.00
Buggy, Pony, Parasol, Wicker		1900.00
Delivery, Milk & Ice, Horse Drawn, 1926		2500.00
Wagon, Peddler's, 6 Ft.		1850.00
Wagon, Popcorn, Horse Drawn, Cretors, Restored		850.00

CASH REGISTERS were invented in 1884 because an eye on the cash was a necessity in stores of the nineteenth century, too. John and James Ritty invented a large model that resembled a clock and kept a record of the dollars and cents exchanged in the store. John Patterson improved the cash register with a paper roll to record the money. By the early 1900s, elaborate brass registers were made. About World War I, the fancy case was exchanged for the more modern types.

Imperial, Nickel Finish, Osborn Cash Register Co., 18 1/2 x 19 In.	110.00
National, 15-Key, Metal Case, Mahogany Finish, Drawer, Milk Glass Slab, 17 In.	220.00
National, Embossed, Slanted Marquee, 11 x 21 x 15 In.	719.00
National, Model 5, Scroll Case, Metal Base, Glass Key Checks	2000.00
National, Model 79, Oak Base, Floor Model, 1904	3500.00
National, Model 130, Nickel Plate Bohemian Case, Name Lid Plate, 1904	1000.00
National, Model 138, Nickel Plate Art Nouveau Case	1750.00
National, Model 245, Copper Oxidized Fleur-De-Lis Case, 1908	1750.00
National, Model 313, Brass, Oak, Shave & Haircut 25 Cents, 21 x 10 x 15 In.	460.00
National, Model 313, Embossed Design, 1893-1908	1200.00
National, Model 332, Brass, Embossed, c.1913	575.00
National, Model 395, C.G. Hamm, Roodhouse, Ill, Nickel On Brass, 1888-1904	1500.00
National, Model 452, Nickel Over Brass, Oak Trim, 22 x 25 x 17 In.	385.00
National, Model 542-EL-4F, Recorder Clock, Floor Model, 1912	5000.00
National, Smith-Corona, Wooden Extended Base, Drawer, Wooden	39.00
St. Louis, Slide Type Opening Mechanism, c.1915	150.00

CASTOR JARS for pickles are glass jars about six inches in height, held in special metal holders. They became a popular dinner table accessory about 1890. Each jar had a top that was usually silver or silver plate. The frame, also of a silver metal, had a handle that arched above the jar and a hook that held a pair of tongs. By 1900, the pickle castor was out of fashion. Many examples found today have reproduced glass jars in old holders. Additional pickle castors may be found in the various Glass categories.

Pickle, Amber Glass, Silver Plated Frame	355.00

If the hinge that attaches the lid on a stein or other metal object is balky, try lubricating it with WD-40 (found in most hardware stores).

Castor, Pickle, Paneled Sprig, Cranberry, Enameled Floral, Colonial Silver Co.

Castor, Pickle, Cranberry, Enameled Flowers, Webster, No. 94

Pickle, Baby Inverted Thumbprint, Cranberry Base, Enameled Flowers 450.00
Pickle, Black Amethyst, Classical Designs, Etched, Silver Deposit Rim, 12 In. 105.00
Pickle, Blue Cut To Clear Insert, Grape Holder 175.00
Pickle, Button & Pineapple, Rockford Frame, Victorian, 12 In. 140.00
Pickle, Button & Star, Fish & Bird, Blue Glass Insert, Quadruple Plate, 12 In. 385.00
Pickle, Cathedral, 4 Arched Panels, Light Green, 1860-1880, 13 3/8 In. 200.00
Pickle, Cathedral, 4 Panels, Pale Teal, Blue, Green, 1860-1880, 11 3/4 In. 190.00
Pickle, Cranberry Glass, Tongs 550.00
Pickle, Cranberry, Enameled Flowers, Webster, No. 94 . . . .*Illus*   715.00
Pickle, Diamond, Amber, Lion Final Lid, Quad Plate Frame, Victorian, 10 1/2 In. 140.00
Pickle, Enamel Design, American Silver Holder, Tongs 1250.00
Pickle, Frosted Crystal Insert, Blue Flowers, Silver Frame, 9 3/4 In. 620.00
Pickle, Frosted Ivy Vine, Crystal Insert 175.00
Pickle, Green Glass, Silver Plated, 14 1/2 In. 580.00
Pickle, Inverted Thumbprint Insert, Mary Gregory Girl, Holding Flowers 495.00
Pickle, Inverted Thumbprint, Floral, Quad Plate Eastlake Frame, Victorian, 12 In. 440.00
Pickle, Optic, Corset Shape, Enameled Daisy, Green Leaves, Homan Frame, Tongs 295.00
Pickle, Paneled Sprig, Cranberry, Enameled Floral, Colonial Silver Co. . . . .*Illus*   850.00
Pickle, Quilted, Brooklyn Frame, Victorian, 11 1/2 In. 140.00
Pickle, Quilted, Roger's Bros. Frame, Victorian, 13 In. 140.00
Pickle, Rubina, Thumbprint, Coralene Butterflies, Bird Finial Cover, Silver, 7 In. 825.00
Pickle, Sapphire Blue Glass, Silver Plated Frame, 13 1/2 In. 380.00
Pickle, Silver Frame, Thomas Daniel, 1774, 5 1/2 In. 395.00

CASTOR SETS holding just salt and pepper castors were used in the seventeenth century. The sugar castor, mustard pot, spice dredger, bottles
for vinegar and oil, and other spice holders became popular by the
eighteenth century. These sets were usually made of sterling silver. The
American Victorian castor set, the type most collected today, was made
of silver plated Britannia metal. Colored glass bottles were introduced
after the Civil War. The sets were out of fashion by World War I. Be
careful when buying sets with colored bottles; many are reproductions.
Other castor sets may be listed in various porcelain and glass categories in this book.

2 Bottles, Sterling Silver Frame, Reeded Rims, Scroll Handle, P. Lamerie, George I 4600.00
3 Bottles, Elephant's Head, Salt, Pepper & Mustard 2310.00
4 Bottles, Gilt Papier-Mache Holder, Gilt Handle, England, 19th Century, 8 1/2 In. 121.00
4 Bottles, Silver, Electroplate, C. Dresser, Hukin & Heath, England, 1878, 7 In. 5995.00
6 Bottles, 3-Mold, Pewter Frame, With Tumble-Up Stopper, 8 In. 220.00

CATALOGS are listed in the Paper category.

CAUGHLEY porcelain was made in England from 1772 to 1814.
Caughley porcelains are very similar in appearance to those made at
the Worcester factory. See the Salopian category for related items.

Pitcher, Leaf Molded, Blue Floral, Mask Spout & Scrolled Handle, 1785, 7 1/2 In. 460.00
Plate, 4 Blue Floral Sprigs In Center, Blue Scalloped Rim, 8 In. 184.00

CAULDON Limited worked in Staffordshire, Great Britain, and went
through many name changes. John Ridgway made porcelain at
Cauldon Place, Hanley, until 1855. The firm of John Ridgway, Bates
and Co. of Cauldon Place worked from 1856 to 1859. It became Bates,
Brown-Westhead, Moore and Co. from 1859 to 1862. Brown-
Westhead, Moore and Co. worked from 1862 to 1904. About 1890, this
firm started using the words *Cauldon* or *Cauldon ware* as part of the
mark. Cauldon Ltd. worked from 1905 to 1920, Cauldon Potteries
from 1920 to 1962. Related items may be found in the Indian Tree
category.

Charger, 2 White Quail, Blue, White, Gilded Rim, Porcelain, 16 1/4 In. 75.00
Plate, Blue, Scalloped, Gilt Rim, Porcelain, 9 1/2 In., 11 Piece 161.00
Plate, Columbian Star, Dark Blue, 9 In. 175.00
Platter, Blue Floral Transfer, Tree & Well, J.R. Bentick, 21 1/2 In. 300.00

CELADON is the name of a velvet-textured green-gray glaze used by Chinese, Japanese, Korean, and other factories. The name refers both to the glaze and to pieces covered with the glaze. It is still being made.

Bowl, Bell Form, Incised Peony Design, Ming Dynasty, 7 1/2 In.	412.00
Bowl, Carved Carp, Lotus Design, Porcelain, 19th Century, 6 In.	55.00
Bowl, Carved Floral Design, Koryo Dynasty, 7 1/2 In.	330.00
Bowl, Concentric Ring Design, Koryo Dynasty, 7 1/4 In.	220.00
Bowl, Conical Form, Light Green, Song Dynasty, 7 Piece	690.00
Bowl, Everted Rim, Fluted Sides, Porcelain, Song Dynasty, 5 3/4 In.	165.00
Bowl, Form Of Six Leaves, Marked, 4 In.	44.00
Bowl, Peony, Cloud Design Exterior, Wave Design Interior, Ming Dynasty, 12 In.	165.00
Bowl, Porcelain, Early 19th Century, 6 1/2 In.	121.00
Cup, Libation, Allover Rice Pattern, 2 Handles, 19th Century, 5 In.	165.00
Dish, Central Shou Design, Porcelain, 18th Century, 10 In.	220.00
Dish, Leaf Design, Raised Double Fish Design Interior, 7 1/2 In.	192.00
Ewer, Floral Mogul Style, Metal Mounts, Jade, 19th Century, 3 5/8 In.	110.00
Figurine, Bird-Headed Creature, Brown, Jade, 3 In.	88.00
Figurine, Jui Fungus Relief, 3 3/4 In.	440.00
Figurine, Mandarin Duck, 8 In.	330.00
Ginger Jar, Wooden Cover & Base, Polychrome, 7 In.	275.00
Ginger Jar, Wooden Cover, Relief Dragon Design, Porcelain, Globular, 8 In.	522.00
Jar, Floral, 8 In., Pair	175.00
Lamp, Baluster, Drilled, 13 In.	230.00
Pitcher, Floral, Bird Design, Bamboo Handle, 5 In.	66.00
Snuff Bottle, Apple Green, Round Body, Flat Base, 2 1/8 In.	374.00
Vase, Baluster, Hexagonal, 11 1/2 In., Pair	92.00
Vase, Crackled, Blue Neck, Emile Decoeur, 1920-1925, 8 1/2 In.	1725.00
Vase, Hu Form, Dragon, Bat Design, Elephant Handles, 19th Century, 12 In., Pair	550.00
Vase, Kinuta Form, Bird Form Handles, Porcelain, Ming Dynasty, 9 1/2 In.	468.00
Vase, Stylized Dragon Banding, Trumpet Shape, 18th Century, 5 In.	385.00
Vase, Vertical Lines, Arched Border, Allover Olive Green Glaze, Song Dynasty	575.00

CELLULOID is a trademark for a plastic developed in 1868 by John W. Hyatt. Celluloid Manufacturing Company, the Celluloid Novelty Company, Celluloid Fancy Goods Company, and American Xylonite Company all used Celluloid to make jewelry, games, sewing equipment, false teeth, and piano keys. Eventually, the Hyatt Company became the American Celluloid and Chemical Manufacturing Company, the Celanese Corporation. The name *Celluloid* was often used to identify any similar plastic. Celluloid toys are listed under Toys.

Box, Collar, Child As Fairy Princess On Cover	125.00
Brush, Monroe Fox Co., Friendly Credit Clothiers, Chicago, Red, White, Black, 1924	32.00
Cake Topper, Bride & Groom, Box, 4 3/4 In., Pair	55.00
Cake Topper, Bride, Groom & Preacher, Box	125.00
Dresser Set, Child's, Green Marble, Cream, Box, 4 Piece	80.00
Dresser Set, Cream, 2 Sizes Hinged Boxes, Box, 8 Piece	95.00
Figurine, Couple, Dancing, Occupied Japan, 2 x 5 In.	50.00
Letter Opener, Full Bodied Warthog End	45.00
Letter Opener, Indian Chief, Winnipeg	25.00
Rattle, 3 Cats In Basket, Victorian	150.00
Rattle, Man In The Moon, Winking	160.00

CELS are listed in this book in the Animation Art category.

CERAMIC ART COMPANY of Trenton, New Jersey, was established in 1889 by J. Coxon and W. Lenox and was an early producer of American Belleek porcelain. It became Lenox, Inc. in 1906. Do not confuse this ware with the pottery made by the Ceramic Arts Studio of Madison, Wisconsin.

Coffeepot, Cobalt Blue, Silver Deposit, CAC In Wreath, 8 In.	325.00
Pitcher, Grapes, Leaves, 8 In.	150.00
Vase, Roses, Daisies, Gold Trim, 10 In.	300.00

ERAMIC ARTS STUDIO was founded about 1940 in Madison, Wisconsin, by Lawrence Rabbett and Ruben Sand. Their most popular products were expensive molded figurines. The pottery closed in 1955. Do not confuse these products with those of the Ceramic Art Co. of Trenton, New Jersey.

Bank, Tony The Barber, 4 3/4 In.	75.00 to 125.00
Bell, Lillibelle, 6 1/2 In.	42.00
Bell, Winter Bell, 5 1/4 In.	55.00
Figurine, Autumn Andy, Blue Pants, Black Hair, 5 In.	65.00
Figurine, Calico Cat, 3 In.	50.00
Figurine, Daisy Donkey, 4 3/4 In.	165.00
Figurine, Elsie, Elephant, 5 In.	95.00
Figurine, Fawn, Resting, 3 1/2 In.	40.00
Figurine, Fire Man & Fire Woman, Burgundy, 11 1/4 In., Pair	100.00
Figurine, Gay '90s Man, Blue Hat, 6 3/4 In.	30.00
Figurine, Gingham Dog, 2 3/4 In.	50.00
Figurine, Gypsy Man, With Gold Violin, 6 1/2 In.	75.00
Figurine, Gypsy Woman, Blue, Gold, 7 In.	125.00
Figurine, Inky & Dinky Skunks, 2 1/4 & 2 In., Pair	50.00
Figurine, Inky Skunk, 2 1/4 In.	30.00
Figurine, Isaac & Rebekah, 10 In., Pair	250.00
Figurine, Kangaroo Mother, Brown, 4 3/4 In.	90.00
Figurine, Little Boy Blue, 4 1/2 In.	30.00 to 45.00
Figurine, Mary & Lamb With Bow, 6 1/4 & 4 In., Pair	50.00
Figurine, Mouse & Snuggle, Cheese, 2 & 3 In., Pair	30.00
Figurine, Mr. Skunk, 3 In.	48.00 to 60.00
Figurine, Panda With Hat, 2 1/2 In.	45.00
Figurine, Pepita, Blue, 4 1/2 In.	45.00
Figurine, Pete Parrot & Polly Parrot, Green, 7 1/2 In., Pair	120.00
Figurine, Pioneer Sam, 5 1/2 In.	40.00
Figurine, Pioneer Susie, Green, 5 In.	48.00
Figurine, Pixie Girl On Toadstool, 4 In.	40.00
Figurine, Pixie Riding Snail, 4 3/4 In.	40.00
Figurine, Polish Boy, Yellow, 6 1/2 In.	50.00 to 55.00
Figurine, Rhumba Man & Woman, Blue, 7 1/4 & 7 In., Pair	125.00
Figurine, Sabu Elephant Boy, & Elephant, Snuggle, 2 3/4 & 5 In., Pair	325.00
Figurine, Sambo & Tiger, 3 1/2 & 5 In., Pair	500.00
Figurine, Square Dance Boy & Girl, 6 1/2 & 6 In., Pair	165.00
Figurine, Water Woman, 11 1/2 In.	95.00
Figurine, Wendy, Blond, 5 1/4 In.	70.00
Head Vase, Barbie & Bonnie, 7 In., Pair	150.00
Head Vase, Lotus, 7 3/4 In.	120.00
Head Vase, Mei-Ling, Green, Black Hair, 5 In.	150.00
Pitcher, George Washington, Green, 3 1/2 In.	50.00
Plaque, Attitude & Arabesque, Ballerinas, 9 1/2 & 9 1/4 In., Pair	125.00
Plaque, Harlequin, Black & White, 8 In.	65.00
Plaque, Harlequin, Black, Tan & Lime, 8 In.	55.00
Plaque, Harlequin, Red & Black, 8 In.	82.00
Salt & Pepper, Bear & Cub, Snuggle, White	38.00 to 48.00
Salt & Pepper, Blackamoors	125.00
Salt & Pepper, Calico Cat, Gingham Dog	85.00 to 90.00
Salt & Pepper, Chinese Boy & Girl	30.00 to 35.00
Salt & Pepper, Cocks Fighting	80.00
Salt & Pepper, Dutch Boy & Girl, Yellow, Brown Trim, 4 In.	95.00
Salt & Pepper, Elephant & Boy, Snuggle	130.00
Salt & Pepper, Elf & Toadstool	120.00
Salt & Pepper, Fish Up On Tails	85.00
Salt & Pepper, Frog & Toadstool	50.00 to 67.00
Salt & Pepper, Harry & Lillibeth, Browns	125.00
Salt & Pepper, Mama Cow, Baby Cow In Lap	120.00
Salt & Pepper, Monkey & Baby, Snuggle	60.00
Salt & Pepper, Mouse & Cheese, Snuggle	20.00 to 48.00
Salt & Pepper, Mr. & Mrs. Penguin	70.00 to 95.00

Salt & Pepper, Ram & Ewe 225.00
Salt & Pepper, Seahorse & Coral, Snuggle 65.00
Salt & Pepper, Siamese Cat & Kitten 45.00
Shelf Sitter, Banjo Girl 150.00
Shelf Sitter, Budgie Parakeet, Aqua & Teal 50.00
Shelf Sitter, Cat, Fluffy 85.00
Shelf Sitter, Cat, Tuffy 95.00
Shelf Sitter, Cowboy & Cowgirl, Brown, Green & Yellow, 4 3/4 In., Pair ... 135.00
Shelf Sitter, Dutch Boy & Girl, Blue 25.00
Shelf Sitter, Farm Boy Fishing & Farm Girl, 5 & 4 3/4 In., Pair ... 75.00
Shelf Sitter, Farm Girl, Green, 4 3/4 In. 50.00
Shelf Sitter, Pudgie Parakeet, Green 150.00
Shelf Sitter, Sun-Lin, White, Green & Red 25.00
Shelf Sitter, Young Love Girl, Green 50.00
Vase, Landscape Scene, Floral Bouquet, Enamel, Gilt, 1900, 18 In. ... 316.00

CHALKWARE is really plaster of Paris decorated with watercolors. One type was molded from Staffordshire and other porcelain models and painted and sold as inexpensive decorations in the nineteenth century. Figures of plaster, made from about 1910 to 1940 for use as prizes at carnivals, are also known as chalkware. Kewpie dolls made of chalkware will be found in their own category.

Ashtray, Rin Tin Tin 25.00
Bank, Bunny Pulling Egg In Cart 75.00
Bank, Cow, Articulated Horns, Ears & Tail, Yellow, Red Patches, Slot On Back ... 403.00
Bank, Dog, 19th Century 1450.00
Bank, Sailor, Black, Red & White, Allan-Madre, 1857, 14 In. 863.00
Bookends, Boy & Girl, Yellow, Green 72.00
Bookends, Santa Maria 35.00
Bust, George Washington, 5 1/4 In. 175.00
Figurine, 2 Doves, Conjoined At Beaks, Articulated Eyes, Feather & Wings, 6 In. ... 288.00
Figurine, Deer, Black & Brown Paint, 10 In. 210.00
Figurine, Dog, Brown & Black, c.1920, 8 x 7 In. 125.00
Figurine, Dog, Early 1840s, 5 In. 75.00
Figurine, Dog, Painted Facial Features, Ears, Tail & Collar, 8 In. ... 464.00
Figurine, Dog, Seated, Black, Green, Red, Yellow, 6 1/2 In. 110.00
Figurine, Dog, Standing, Open Legs, Red, Black, Yellow, Green, 7 7/8 In. ... 248.00
Figurine, Nude Girl, Sitting On Rock, Looking Into Bowl, Dolphins, 1930s, 15 In. ... 275.00
Figurine, Parrot, Green & Orange, 8 In. 412.00
Figurine, Ram, Standing, Open Legs, Red, Olive, Yellow, Black, 9 In. ... 935.00
Figurine, Squirrel, Painted Tail & Acorn, 6 In. 357.00
Figurine, Squirrel, With Nut, 6 3/4 In. 675.00
Figurine, Uncle Sam, Rolling Up Sleeve, 15 1/2 In. 100.00
String Holder, Bashful Girl & Debonair Boy, Pair 100.00
String Holder, Boy In Top Hat, Girl In Bonnet, Pair 175.00
String Holder, Chef 65.00
String Holder, Dutch Girl .... 45.00 to 70.00
String Holder, Sailor Boy 110.00
String Holder, Strawberry Face 75.00
Watch Case Holder, Napoleon, Columns, Painted, Gilt, American, 11 3/4 In. ... 230.00

CHARLIE CHAPLIN, the famous comic and actor, lived from 1889 to 1977. He made his first movie in 1913. He did the movie *The Tramp* in 1915. The character of the Tramp has remained famous, and in the 1980s appeared in a series of television commercials for computers. Dolls, candy containers, and all sorts of memorabilia picture Charlie Chaplin. Pieces are being made even today.

Candy Container, Borgfeldt 125.00
Candy Container, Glass, Paint Traces, Geo. Borgfeldt & Co. 100.00
Candy Container, Smith 187.00
Doll, Music Box, Porcelain Head, Hands & Feet, Play The Sting, 1970s, 18 In. ... 110.00
Doll, Vinyl, Present Co., Box, 11 In. 15.00
Game, Board, Chasing Charlie, Spears Games, England, 1920s, 7 1/4 x 10 In. ... 375.00

Magazine, Movie, England 50.00
Movie, The Love Friend, Unique Slide Co., 1918 .... 75.00
Pencil Box, Tin 65.00
Postcard, He Also Drinks Rossik, France 100.00
Toy, Walker, Tin Lithograph, Cast Iron Feet, Gunthermann, Germany, 8 In. 797.00
Toy, Windup, 1960-1970, Box, 6 In. 28.00

CHARLIE McCARTHY was the ventriloquist's dummy used by Edgar
Bergen from the 1930s. He was famous for his work in radio, movies,
and television. The act was retired in the 1970s.

Bank, Charlie With Suitcase, Cast Metal, 1930s 450.00
Decanter, Charlie McCarthy & Mortimer Snerd, Beam, 1976, Pair ....90.00 to 95.00
Doll, Advertising, Chase & Sandborn Coffee, Charlie's Doll, 1937 .... 12.00
Dummy, Ventriloquist's, Plastic, Wood, Fabric, Black Felt Top Hat, 34 In. 167.00
Figurine, Chalkware ....45.00 to 85.00
Game, Radio, 1930 .... 90.00
Pencil Sharpener, Bakelite 40.00
Pin, Plastic 37.00
Sheet Music, Speaking For Myself, 1939 .... 125.00
Toy, Car, Tin Lithograph, Windup, Waddles, Mouth Moves, 8 1/4 In. 305.00
Toy, Radio Characters, Directions, Complete, 1938 .... 75.00
Toy, Tin, Windup, Sways, Mouth Opens & Closes, Marx, 1930, 8 In. 650.00
Toy, Walker, Windup, Marx 350.00
Valentine, Mechanical, Cowboy 20.00

CHELSEA porcelain was made in the Chelsea area of London from
about 1745 to 1784. Some pieces made from 1770 to 1784 may include
the letter *D* for *Derby* in the mark. Ceramic designs were borrowed
from the Meissen models of the day. Pieces were made of soft paste.
The gold anchor was used as the mark but it has been copied by many
other factories. Recent copies of Chelsea have been made from the
original molds. Do not confuse Chelsea porcelain with Chelsea Grape,
the next category.

Bottle, Scent, Fruit Cluster, 2 Maroon Cherry Sprigs, Blue Plum, 1760, 3 3/8 In. 1150.00
Bowl, Finger, Pear Shape, Floral Bouquet, Yellow, Red, Blue, Green, 1755, 3 Piece 690.00
Bust, Portrait, Vine-Wreathed Satyr, Pedestal Base, 4 1/4 In. 230.00
Butter Tub, Lemon, 5 Floral Sprigs, 3 Insects, Notched Rim, 1755, 5 1/2 x 5 5/8 In. 2070.00
Dish, Basket, White, Honeycomb-Patterned Rim, 3 Vine Leaves, Oval, 1754, 12 In. 1092.00
Dish, Floral Sprigs, Butterfly, Crenellated Rim, Red, Blue, Purple, Yellow, 1753, 11 In. .. 747.00
Dish, Sunflower, 2 Rows Of Yellow Petals, Seed Center, Puce, Mauve, 1756, 8 In., Pair .. 1955.00
Dish, Sunflower, 2 Rows Of Yellow Petals, Turquoise, Green Handle, 1760, 8 In. 1840.00
Figurine, Dog In Front Of Gumdrop Tree, Signed, 4 In., Pair 357.00
Figurine, Musician, Green Leaf, 8 In. ....*Illus* 85.00
Figurine, Ram, 3 In. 88.00
Inkwell, Double, Angel Figure Center, White Porcelain, 6 x 5 In. 425.00

If you have an entry door with a large window,
put unbreakable glass in the window. The
easiest way for a burglar to enter your house
is by breaking the window in the door and
reaching in to unlock the door. Even a small
window in a door might be positioned so it is
possible to break it and reach the door knob.
Either put in unbreakable panes or install a
slide bolt that will be out of reach.

Chelsea, Figurine, Musician,
Green Leaf, 8 In.

Pitcher, Blue & White, 8 In. 65.00
Plate, Botanical, Melon, Yellow, Green, Brown Veins, Red Berries, 1759, 8 5/16 In. 517.00
Plate, Floral Bouquet, Scattered Sprigs, 4 Pair Of Birds On Rim, 1760, Pair 1610.00
Plate, Fruit, Peach, Pear, Sprigs Of Raspberries, Green Edge Rim, 1760, 8 7/16 In. 460.00
Plate, Scalloped, Gilt, Salmon, Purple, Gnarled Prunus Tree, 1753, 9 7/16 In. 575.00
Tureen, Birds Perched In Flight, Blue Sky, Sprigs Of Yellow Roses, Oval, 1755 .... 1150.00

CHELSEA GRAPE pattern was made before 1840. A small bunch of
grapes in a raised design, colored with purple or blue luster, is on the
border of the white plate. Most of the pieces are unmarked. The pattern is sometimes called *Aynsley* or *Grandmother*. Chelsea Sprig is
similar but has a sprig of flowers instead of the bunch of grapes.
Chelsea Thistle has a raised thistle pattern. Do not confuse these
Chelsea patterns with Chelsea Keramic Art Works, which can be
found in the Dedham category, or with Chelsea porcelain, the preceding category.

Coffeepot 200.00
Cup & Saucer 35.00
Plate, 8 In. 40.00

CHINESE EXPORT porcelain comprises all the many kinds of porcelain
made in China for export to America and Europe in the eighteenth,
nineteenth, and twentieth centuries. Other pieces may be listed in this
book under Canton, Celadon, Nanking, and Rose Medallion.

Bough Pot, Cover, Chamfered Square Body, 1785, 8 In., Pair 6900.00
Bowl, Bird, Bamboo Design, Blue, White, Bell Form, 5 1/2 In. 275.00
Bowl, Blue Geometric Floral Medallions, Birds, Famille Rose, 10 In. 253.00
Bowl, Butterflies, Famille Rose, 12 x 4 7/8 In. 935.00
Bowl, Dragon, Butterfly Design, Famille Verte, Octagonal, 4 3/4 In. 330.00
Bowl, Fish, Teakwood Stand, Famille Rose, c.1860 .... 2950.00
Bowl, Genre Panels, Famille Rose, Orange Peel Surface, 10 x 4 In. 1210.00
Bowl, Geometric Design Exterior, 1 Flower Interior, Famille Rose, 6 3/4 In. 105.00
Bowl, Herons, Flowers Exterior, Central Floral Design, Famille Verte, 6 In. 440.00
Bowl, Horses, Mandarin Palette, 1785, 5 5/8 In., Pair 1150.00
Bowl, Lotus Form, Insect, Floral Design, Famille Rose, 6 3/4 In., Pair 220.00
Bowl, Passion Flower Design, Blue, White, 10 1/2 In. 575.00
Bowl, Pine, Crane, Butterflies Around Lotus Pond, Famille Rose, 13 3/4 In. 403.00
Bowl, Sacred Birds, Butterflies, Characters, Iron Red, 19th Century, 11 In. 1955.00
Bowl, Scalloped Border, Famille Rose, Chien Lung Period, 7 In., Pair 402.00
Bowl, Underplate, Reserves Of Courtiers & Birds, Famille Rose, 10 1/2 In. 345.00
Bowl, Vegetable, Cover, Fruit Finial, Blue Armorial, Floral Swags, 14 In. 165.00
Box, Cover, Stylized Dragon, Floral Design, Famille Verte, Rectangular, 4 In. 155.00
Cache Pot, Allover Butterfly Design, Famille Rose, 9 1/2 In. 121.00
Candlestick, Insects, Plants, Blue, White, Silver Shape, 1720, 5 x 5 3/16 In. 6035.00
Candlestick, Trellis Border, Octagonal Base, 1765-1775, 7 1/2 In., Pair 5175.00
Charger, 2 Pairs Of Soldiers On Horseback, Famille Verte, 13 3/4 In. 1725.00
Charger, Bird, Floral Garden Center, Blue, White, Swatow, 16 In. 605.00
Charger, Peonies & Bamboo, Famille Rose, 1750, 15 1/2 In., Pair 4600.00
Charger, Peony Blossoms, Foliage, Black Ground, 21 1/2 In., Pair 8050.00
Coffeepot, Gilt Strawberry Finial, Fitzhugh, 10 In. 3190.00
Creamer, Helmet Shape, Fitzhugh Style Border, 5 1/4 In. 1430.00
Cup & Saucer, Peacock, Butterfly & Flower Design, Famille Rose, 4 Sets 22.00
Dish, Hot Water, Cover, Blue Fitzhugh, 19th Century, 13 1/2 In. 1035.00
Dish, Kakiemon-Style, Famille Verte, 1715-1925, 9 11/16 In. 3450.00
Dish, Mandarin Design, Spearhead Border, 18th Century, 5 1/4 In. 143.00
Dish, Rice, Blue, White, Yung Cheng, 10 1/2 In. 110.00
Dish, Winged Insects, Cricket, Famille Rose, 1740, 13 5/8 In. 575.00
Ewer, Figures Meeting In A Garden, Famille Rose, 5 1/4 In. 437.00
Figurine, Crane, Standing, 19th Century, 11 7/8 & 11 11/16 In., Pair 3160.00
Figurine, Spaniel, Seated, Grisaille Trim, 1760-1780, 6 9/16 In. 5290.00
Fishbowl, Floral Exterior, Green, Blue, Red, Scrollwork, Lappet Border, 8 In. 60.00
Garden Seat, Landscape Design, 18 In. 770.00
Garden Seat, Rose Medallion, 19th Century, 18 1/4 x 19 In. 3105.00

Chinese Export, Ginger Jar,
Mythological People,
Blue & White, 8 In.

Chinese Export, Jar, Cover,
Famille Verte, 9 In.

Chinese Export, Sauce,
Leaf Form, Blue & White,
Fitzhugh, 8 In.

Garniture Set, Mantel, White Peonies, Famille Rose, 8 To 9 In., 5 Piece	8050.00
Ginger Jar, Cover, Blue & White, 5 In., Pair	144.00
Ginger Jar, Mythological People, Blue & White, 8 In. ....*Illus*	330.00
Jar, Baluster, Blue, White, 6 3/4 In.	172.00
Jar, Chrysanthemums, Iron Red, Famille Verte, 1720, 13 13/16 In.	2585.00
Jar, Cover, Famille Verte, 9 In. ....*Illus*	1595.00
Jar, Cover, Figural Interior Reserves, 12 In., Pair	255.00
Jar, Cover, Scrolling Vine Design, Knob Finial, Blue, White, 24 In.	3450.00
Jar, Floral Design, Blue, White, 6 In.	385.00
Jar, Floral, Pearl Design, Blue, White, Globular, Ching Dynasty, 4 3/4 In.	121.00
Jar, Foo Lion, Peony Design, Blue, Inverted Pear Shape, 9 In.	440.00
Jar, Temple, 4 Phoenix Birds In Flight, Floral, 17 In., Pair	805.00
Jardiniere, Figural Design, Famille Rose, 7 x 9 1/4 In.	250.00
Jardiniere, Lion Handles, Famille Rose, Early 20th Century, 3 3/4 In., Pair	575.00
Jardiniere, Pink Honeycomb Pattern, Hexagonal, 6 1/4 x 11 1/4 In., Pair	9775.00
Jug, Cider, Cover, Walled Palace Compound Scene, Blue, White, 11 1/2 In.	1150.00
Jug, Cover, Chinese Woman, Famille Verte, 1735-1745, 8 7/8 In.	4025.00
Jug, Milk, Cover, Milkmaid, Pear Shape, 1740, 4 3/8 In.	2875.00
Lamp, Foliage & Symbols, Blue, White, 22 In., Pair	345.00
Lamp Base, Blue Medallions, Triple Gourd, Famille Jaune, 33 In.	316.00
Mug, Aquatic Plants, Famille Rose, 1745, 5 1/4 In.	1610.00
Mug, Family Scenes, Polychrome Enamel, Gilt, 6 1/4 In.	385.00
Mug, Satirical, Woman On Lap Of Man, S Scroll Handle, 1750, 6 1/4 In.	5175.00
Pitcher, Cream, Cover, Western Figural Design, Pear Form, 5 In.	440.00
Plaque, Oriental Groups, Mandarin Palette, 1780, 8 1/2 x 7 7/8 In.	860.00
Plate, Armorial, Shields In Well, Helmet, Cornucopia & Swag Rim, 9 In., Pair	1430.00
Plate, Birds Amid Foliage, Famille Rose, 19th Century, 9 In., Pair	316.00
Plate, Doctors' Visit, 1738, 8 15/16 In.	9775.00
Plate, Floral Design, Famille Verte, 1800, 10 In.	88.00
Plate, Floral, Flower Garden Scene Interior, Vine Design, Blue, White, 6 In.	110.00
Plate, Judgment Of Paris, Athena & Cupid, 1750-1755, 8 13/16 In.	860.00
Plate, La Dame Au Parasol, Blue & White, 1736-1738, 8 13/16 In.	5175.00
Plate, Lotus, Scalloped & Barbed Rim, 1745-1755, 8 7/8 In., Pair	975.00
Plate, Passion Flower, Famille Jaune, 8 1/2 In.	220.00
Plate, Prunus, Rockery Design, Pale Cafe-Au-Lait Ground, Famille Verte, 8 In.	330.00
Platter, Bird & Butterfly, Orange, Gold, Orange Peel Texture, 18 x 15 In.	1210.00
Platter, Brown Fitzhugh, Monogram, Oval, Pair	3335.00
Platter, Floral Design, White Ground, Gilt Rim, 20 In., Pair	690.00
Platter, Floral, Gilt Edge, Oval, 1785, 14 7/8 In.	1090.00
Platter, Flowering Plants, Chamfered, 1750-1760, 11 3/8 In.	1380.00
Platter, Polychrome Scene Of Woman In Garden, Blue & White, 13 x 10 In.	355.00
Platter, Pseudo Tobacco Leaf, Chamfered, Rectangular, 1785, 9 15/16 In.	1380.00
Platter, Tobacco Leaf, Oval, 1770-1780, 11 In.	7475.00
Platter, Tobacco Leaf, Oval, 1770-1780, 15 1/4 In.	7475.00
Punch Bowl, Famille Rose, 1780, 15 1/16 In.	2300.00

Punch Bowl, Floral Bouquets Interior & Exterior, Gilt, 10 1/4 In. 357.00
Punch Bowl, Fruit, Flower Design, Dolphin Feet, Famille Rose, 15 In. 2530.00
Sauce, Leaf Form, Blue & White, Fitzhugh, 8 In. ....*Illus* 385.00
Sauceboat, Fitzhugh, Braided Strap Handles, c.1800, 7 3/4 In. 77.00
Sauceboat, Underplate, Gilt & Copper Foliate Rim, c.1800, 7 1/2 In. 465.00
Saucer, Leaf & Ribbon Design, Blue Underglaze, Ming Dynasty, 6 In. 316.00
Saucer, Mythological, Gilt, 1745, 8 13/16 In. 1380.00
Saucer, Peony & Chrysanthemums, Famille Rose, 1730, 8 3/4 In. 5750.00
Saucer, Scholar In Boat, Blue Underglaze, Ming Dynasty, 5 In. 35.00
Ship, Blue & White, 19th Century, 9 x 11 In. ....*Illus* 2000.00
Soup, Dish, Mythological, Lion, Shepherd, Gilt Border, 1740, 8 5/8 In. 2300.00
Soup, Dish, Seamstress, Gold Dress, 1750, 8 13/16 In. 920.00
Sugar, Fruit Finial, Polychrome Floral, Twined Handles, 5 5/8 In. 330.00
Tea Set, Butterflies, Famille Rose, c.1910, 15 Piece 995.00
Tea Set, Grisaille Design, 21 Piece 1350.00
Teabowl & Saucer, Cockerels, Semi-Eggshell, Famille Rose, 1735 .... 1380.00
Teabowl & Saucer, Pink Peonies, Famille Rose, 1730-1735 .... 1955.00
Teapot, Calligraphy Design, Brown, Drum Form, 7 1/8 In. 66.00
Teapot, Cover, Cobalt Blue Fish, Fruit, Flowers, Famille Rose, 4 3/4 In. 748.00
Teapot, Cover, Raised Chrysanthemum Design At Foot, Famille Noire, 6 In. 605.00
Teapot, Gilt Strawberry Finial, Fitzhugh, 5 1/2 In. 1760.00
Teapot, Hawthorn Design, Red, Brown, Melon Form, Early 20th Century, 8 In. 66.00
Tureen, Cover, Figural, Dragon Headed Carp, 19th Century, 8 3/4 In. 8050.00
Tureen, Lotus Finial, Crossed Branch Handles, 11 x 14 In. 5225.00
Tureen, Soup, Armorial Design, 11 In. 357.00
Tureen, Stand, Gilt B In Shield, Chamfered, 1790, 14 1/8 In. 575.00
Vase, Allover Mottled Green Ground, Red Flecks, 8 In. 460.00
Vase, Bird, Flower Design, Famille Verte, Baluster, Blue Mark, 14 In. 550.00
Vase, Camellia Leaf Green Glaze, Bulbous, 9 1/2 In. 374.00
Vase, Cartouche, Figure & Bird, Famille Jaune, 19th Century, Square, 15 In. 143.00
Vase, Children In Mythical Landscape, Dragon Handles, Famille Rose, 17 In. 525.00
Vase, Chinese Scenes, Purple Ground, Baluster, 17 1/2 In., Pair 431.00
Vase, Dome Cover, Powder Blue, Fruited Finial, Strapwork Handles, 17 In. 6900.00
Vase, Dragon & Lotus, Blue & White, 15 3/4 In. ....*Illus* 715.00
Vase, Dragons, Cloud, Blue, Red, Leaf Rim, Footed, 8 In. 187.00
Vase, Famille Verte, Cartouche Panels, China, 19th Century, 14 In., Pair 460.00
Vase, Famille Verte, Double Blue Ring Mark, 14 In. ....*Illus* 550.00
Vase, Garniture, Mandarin Panels, Floral Border, Famille Rose, 12 1/2 In. 355.00
Vase, Green, Red, Beige Mottled, Seal Mark, 7 1/2 In. 460.00
Vase, Mille Fleurs Pattern, Electrified, Famille Rose, 26 3/4 In., Pair 3750.00
Vase, Oxblood, White Flecked Ground, 7 In. 201.00
Vase, Panels Of Birds, Flowers, Peking Opera, Famille Rose, 1820s, 24 In. 1380.00

Chinese Export, Ship, Blue & White,
19th Century, 9 x 11 In.

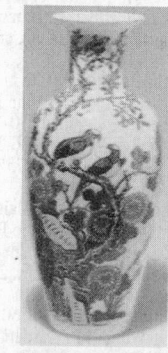

Chinese Export, Vase, Famille
Verte, Double Blue Ring
Mark, 14 In.

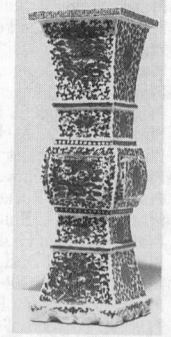

Chinese Export, Vase,
Dragon & Lotus, Blue
& White, 15 3/4 In.

Vase, Phoenix, Cloud Design, Garlic Mouth, Famille Verte, 17 3/4 In. 1100.00
Vase, Polychrome Floral, Famille Verte, Gilt Stand, K'Ang-Hsi, 11 In. 920.00
Vase, Potpourri, Trellis Pierced Cover, Blue, White, Ormolu Mounted, 7 In. 3450.00
Vase, Scrolled Vines, Rosettes, Rust Glaze, 11 In., Pair 2070.00
Vase, Stylized Dragon Design, Blue, White, Club Form, 1800, 6 In. 1705.00
Vase, Tulip, Boys, Panels Of Figure Scenes, Blue, White, Porcelain, 1753 .... 800.00
Vase, Warrior, Court Landscape, Cylinder, Famille Verte, 17 In. 1540.00
Vase, Warriors & Scholars, Chinese Figure At Ends, Famille Rose, 30 In., Pair 8050.00
Vase, White Women & Children Reserves, Blue Overglaze, Baluster, 18 In. 230.00
Washbowl, Famille Rose, Early 19th Century, 13 1/2 In. 55.00

CHINTZ is the name of a group of china patterns featuring an overall design of flowers and leaves. The design became popular with English makers about 1928. A few pieces are still being made. The best known are designs by Royal Winton, James Kent Ltd., Crown Ducal, and Shelley.

Apple Blossom, Relish, James Kent 175.00
Ascot, Plate, Crown Ducal, 8 In. ....110.00 to 225.00
Ascot, Soup, Cream, Crown Ducal 90.00
Ascot, Sugar & Creamer, Royal Ducal 225.00
Balmoral, Salt & Pepper, Tray 195.00
Balmoral, Tray, Breakfast, Royal Winton 150.00
Blue Chintz, Vase, Crown Ducal, 7 In. 300.00
Briar Rose, Plate, Diamond Shape, Lord Nelson, 12 x 7 In. 135.00
Clevedon, Sugar & Creamer, Royal Winton 185.00
Clyde, Relish, Royal Winton 75.00
Clyde, Tray, Grimwades, Royal Winton.................................... 185.00
Crocus, Toast Rack, 5 Bar, Royal Winton 450.00
Du Barry, Plate, James Kent, 6 1/2 In. 65.00
Du Barry, Sugar & Creamer 170.00
Du Barry, Teapot, James Kent, 6 Cup 775.00
Eleanor, Bowl, Royal Winton, 9 In. 225.00
Eleanor, Pin Dish, Royal Winton 45.00
English Rose, Plate, Square, Royal Winton, 5 In. ....95.00 to 125.00
Esther, Cup, For Stacking Teapot, Royal Winton 200.00
Evesham, Butter, Cover, Royal Winton.................................... 300.00
Evesham, Toast Rack, 2 Slice, Royal Winton 375.00
Florida, Cup & Saucer, Crown Ducal 145.00
Gold, Coffee Set, Royal Winton, 15 Piece 500.00
Green Tulip, Tray, Lord Nelson, 10 In. 245.00
Hazel, Cheese Dish, Royal Winton 300.00
Hazel, Cup & Saucer, Royal Winton ....100.00 to 125.00
Hazel, Jug, Royal Winton, 5 In. 575.00
Hazel, Plate, Royal Winton, 10 In. ....175.00 to 245.00
Hazel, Sugar & Creamer, Royal Winton, James Kent 175.00
Hazel, Tray, Royal Winton, 10 x 5 In. 250.00
Julia, Ashtray, Royal Winton, 4 In. 160.00
Julia, Butter, Cover, Royal Winton 475.00
Julia, Cup & Saucer, Royal Winton ....175.00 to 200.00
Julia, Tray, Breakfast, Royal Winton 400.00
June Festival, Salt & Pepper, Tray, Royal Winton 140.00
June Festival, Teapot, Royal Winton, 4 Cup 475.00
June Roses, Dish, Silver Trim, Royal Winton, 12 In. 325.00
Lord Nelson, Sugar & Creamer, Tray, Royal Brocade 95.00
Majestic, Bowl, Cereal, Royal Winton 125.00
Majestic, Cup & Saucer, Royal Winton 165.00
Majestic, Plate, Royal Winton, 6 In. 125.00
Marguerite, Cake Plate, Chrome Pedestal, Royal Winton, 8 In. 195.00
Marguerite, Cup & Saucer, Royal Winton 115.00
Marguerite, Jug, Bulbous, Royal Winton, 5 In. 325.00
Marguerite, Plate, 5 In. 65.00
Marguerite, Plate, Royal Winton, 7 In. 75.00
Marguerite, Teapot, Elite Shaped Trivet, Royal Winton 925.00

Marguerite, Teapot, Royal Winton, 4 Cup 650.00

Marigold, Sugar & Creamer, James Kent 95.00

Marina, Bowl, 2 Handles, Lord Nelson, 6 1/2 x 7 In. 175.00

Marina, Cup & Saucer, Lord Nelson, Demitasse 105.00

Marina, Sugar & Creamer 160.00

Marina, Sugar & Creamer, Lord Nelson 145.00

Marion, Plate, Royal Winton, 5 In. 95.00

Mayfair, Sugar & Creamer, Royal Winton 150.00

Melody, Plate, Dessert, Shelley, 7 In. ....70.00 to 95.00

Melody, Teapot, Shelley, 6 Cup 850.00

Mille Fleurs, Jam Jar, James Kent 245.00

Nantwich, Coffeepot, Royal Winton 795.00

Nantwich, Strainer, Royal Winton 225.00

Nantwich, Sugar & Creamer, Royal Winton 125.00

Old Cottage, Bowl, Royal Winton, 5 In. 135.00

Old Cottage, Cup & Saucer, Royal Winton 65.00

Old Cottage, Jam Pot, Cover, Undertray, Royal Winton 175.00

Old Cottage, Plate, Royal Winton, 8 In. 65.00

Old Cottage, Tile, Royal Winton 175.00

Old English Sampler, Creamer, Hollinshead & Kirkham, Ltd. 65.00

Paisley, Bowl, Royal Winton, 6 In. 125.00

Paisley, Cup & Saucer, Royal Winton 55.00

Paisley, Sugar & Creamer, Royal Winton ....150.00 to 155.00

Pekin, Jug, Black Ground, Royal Winton, 5 In. 150.00

Pekin, Tidbit, 2 Tiers, Royal Winton 135.00

Pelham, Plate, Royal Winton, 7 In. 35.00

Primula, Plate, Octagonal, Crown Ducal, 5 In. 65.00

Primula, Plate, Scalloped, James Kent, 5 In. 115.00

Queen Anne, Box, Cover, Royal Winton, Rectangular 165.00

Queen Anne, Cake Plate, Royal Winton, 10 In. 145.00

Queen Anne, Plate, Royal Winton, 6 In. 30.00

Queen Anne, Tray, Royal Winton, 11 In. 85.00

Rosalynde, Sugar & Creamer, 2 1/2 In. ....100.00 to 200.00

Rosetime, Cup & Saucer, Lord Nelson 150.00

Rosetime, Sugar & Creamer, Lord Nelson 160.00

Rosina, Cup & Saucer, China Co. Ltd. 125.00

Royal Brocade, Sugar & Creamer, Lord Nelson 75.00

Royal Brocade, Teapot, Stacking, Lord Nelson 695.00

Royal Brocade, Vase, Bud, Lord Nelson 85.00

Royalty, Plate, Royal Winton, 8 In. 150.00

Spring, Cup & Saucer, Royal Winton 135.00

Spring, Plate, Royal Winton, 10 In. 185.00

Summertime, Bowl, Royal Winton, 8 In. 135.00

Summertime, Coffeepot, Royal Winton, 7 In. 1100.00

Summertime, Creamer & Sugar, Royal Winton, 3 1/4 In. 175.00

Summertime, Cup & Saucer, Royal Winton ....85.00 to 110.00

Summertime, Jam Jar, Metal Lid, Royal Winton 135.00

Summertime, Plate, Royal Winton, 10 In. ....130.00 to 155.00

Summertime, Salt & Pepper, Royal Winton ....110.00 to 195.00

Summertime, Salt & Pepper, Tray, Royal Winton 180.00

Summertime, Sugar & Creamer, Royal Winton 195.00

Summertime, Sugar, Cover, Royal Winton 125.00

Summertime, Teapot, Royal Winton, 4 Cup 850.00

Sunshine, Plate, Royal Winton, 5 In. 70.00

Sunshine, Plate, Royal Winton, 9 In. 95.00

Sweet Pea, Plate, Royal Winton, 6 In. 95.00

Sweet Pea, Plate, Royal Winton, 9 In. 150.00

Tapestry, Plate, James Kent, 9 In. 75.00

Victorian Rose, Cup & Saucer, Royal Winton, Demitasse 145.00

Welbeck, Plate, Royal Winton, 5 In. 165.00

Welbeck, Sugar & Creamer, Royal Winton 275.00

White Hydrangea, Candy Dish, James Kent, 5 3/4 In. 325.00

White Hydrangea, Cup & Saucer, James Kent 125.00

Chocolate
Glass, Cactus,
Salt & Pepper,
3 1/4 In.

**Dust frequently if you live
near the seashore. Salt air
causes problems.**

HOCOLATE GLASS, sometimes mistakenly called caramel slag, was
made by the Indiana Tumbler and Goblet Company of Greentown,
ndiana, from 1900 to 1903. It was also made at other National Glass
ompany factories. Fenton Art Glass Co. also made chocolate glass
rom about 1907 to 1915. More recent pieces have been made by
mperial and others.

Animal Dish, Cat On Hamper, Greentown	595.00
Animal Dish, Hen, Greentown	1000.00
Cactus, Salt & Pepper, 3 1/4 In. ....*Illus*	275.00
Cactus, Sugar, Cover	125.00
Cactus, Tumbler	45.00
Chrysanthemum Leaf, Cruet	1275.00
Daisy, Butter, Cover, Greentown	225.00
Daisy, Creamer, Greentown	160.00
Geneva, Bowl, 10 1/2 In.	450.00
Leaf Bracket, Cruet, Greentown ....145.00 to 190.00
Leaf Bracket, Nappy, Triangular, 3-Footed, 5 3/4 In.	45.00
Pepper Box, Mug, Greentown	250.00
Shuttle, Butter, Cover	1100.00
Shuttle, Tumbler	70.00
Wild Rose With Bowknot, Cruet	325.00

CHRISTMAS collectibles include not only Christmas trees and ornaments listed below, but also Santa Claus figures, special dishes, and
ven games and wrapping paper. A Belsnickle is a nineteenth-century
igure of Father Christmas. A kugel is an early, heavy ornament made
f thick blown glass, lined with zinc or lead, and often covered with
olored wax. Christmas collectibles may also be listed in the Candy
Container category and in the Paper category under Greeting Card.
Christmas trees are listed in the section that follows.

Angel, Snow, Tinsel & Tree, Paper	35.00
Book, Fred & Jane With The Tiny Arcadians, Chromolithograph, Arcade, 1931	260.00
Candy Box, Feather Tree, Cardboard Candy Box, Germany, Prewar, 9 1/2 In.	133.00
Candy Box, Santa, Shaking Boy's Hand, Reg'Lar Fellers, Cardboard, 1935, 6 In.	60.00
Candy Container, Boot, With Candy	77.00

Christmas, Figure, Santa Claus,
Composition, Fur Beard,
Germany, Pre-1940, 6 In.

Christmas, Figure, Santa Claus, In
Sled, Composition, Papier-Mache,
Germany, 25 In.

Candy Container, Santa Claus & Chimney, Tin Lithograph, Handle, 1940s, 4 1/2 In. . . .   75.00
Candy Container, Santa Claus, Cardboard, Paper, 1940-1950, 8 In. 22.00
Candy Container, Santa Claus, On Sled, Germany 395.00
Candy Container, Santa Claus, Paneled Coat 182.00
Candy Container, Santa Claus, Plastic Head, Paper Label 61.00
Cracker, Paper & Foil, Germany, c.1900, 11 In. 28.00
Decoration, Angel, Chin On Hand, Die Cut Cardboard, Tinsel, Germany, 1920s, 2 In. . .   28.00
Decoration, Santa Claus In Auto, Die Cut Cardboard, Tinsel, Germany, 1920s, 4 In. 39.00
Decoration, Santa Claus, Die Cut Cardboard, Tinsel, Germany, 1920s, 4 1/4 In. 50.00
Decoration, Santa Claus, In Sleigh, Reindeer, Cardboard, Germany, Prewar, 15 x 9 In. . .   44.00
Decoration, Santa Claus, On Donkey, Die Cut Cardboard, Tinsel, Germany, 1920s, 6 In.   39.00
Doll, Mrs. Claus, Annalee, 1971 . . . .   400.00
Doll, Santa Claus, Annalee, 1971 . . . .   400.00
Figure, Candy Cane Humpty Dumpty, Japan, 1950s, 3 1/2 In.   24.00
Figure, Girl, On Mica Cardboard Sled, Spun Cotton, Japan, 5 In. 75.00
Figure, Santa Claus, Bisque, Germany, 1920-1930, 1 1/2 In. 50.00
Figure, Santa Claus, Blue Coat, Holding Feather Tree, Germany, 1920s, 5 In. 295.00
Figure, Santa Claus, Cardboard, Felt Clothes, Rabbit Fur Trim, Japan, 1950s, 10 In. . . .   66.00
Figure, Santa Claus, Celluloid Face, Bell, Chenille, 4 In. 55.00
Figure, Santa Claus, Celluloid, Germany, Prewar, 5 1/2 In. 28.00
Figure, Santa Claus, Cloth Suit, Plaster Face & Boots, 5 In. 40.00
Figure, Santa Claus, Composition, Cardboard, Foil, Japan, 1950s, 7 1/2 In. 60.00
Figure, Santa Claus, Composition, Fur Beard, Germany, Pre-1940, 6 In. . . . .*Illus*   110.00
Figure, Santa Claus, Fur Beard, Plaster, Cardboard Body, 5 In.   30.00
Figure, Santa Claus, In Sled, Composition, Papier-Mache, Germany, 25 In. . . . .*Illus*   330.00
Figure, Santa Claus, In Sleigh, Metal, Small 30.00
Figure, Santa Claus, Papier-Mache, Glass Eyes, Hat, Boots, Luffa Coat, 18 In. 3500.00
Figure, Santa Claus, Plaster, Painted, Japan, 1950s, 5 1/2 In.   55.00
Figure, Santa Claus, Plastic, Irwin USA, 1950s, 4 1/4 In. 22.00
Figure, Santa Claus, Snowman, House, Fur Tree, Mica Cardboard, Japan, 5 x 8 In. 55.00
Figure, Santa Claus, With Basket, Composition, Felt, Germany, 1920s, 8 In. . . . .*Illus*   532.00
Figure, Santa Claus, With Sack, Plastic, Irwin, 4 1/2 In. 20.00
Figure, Santa Claus, With Sleigh, Reindeer, Cardboard, 10 In.   25.00
Figurine, Santa Claus, On Motorcycle, Bisque, 2 In. . . . .*Illus*   182.00
Figurine, Santa Claus, Papier-Mache, Russia, c.1910, 18 In. 950.00
Kugel, Glass, Brass Cap, Brown, Germany, c.1900, 3 1/4 In. 152.00
Kugel, Glass, Brass Cap, Green, Germany, c.1900, 3 1/4 In. 152.00
Lantern, Santa's Head, Composition, Mica Trim On Hood, Paper Eyes & Teeth, 7 In. 935.00
Ornament, Wreath, Feather, With Bird, 7 In. 45.00
Plates that are limited editions are listed in the Collector Plate category or in the correct
factory listing.
Puppet, Santa Claus, Plush, Holding Bell, 1960s, 2 3/4 In. 18.00
Shelf Sitter, Elf, Japan, 1960s, 4 x 2 1/2 In. 15.00
Toy, Santa Claus & Sleigh, Reindeer, Windup, Tin, 1930s 57.00

Christmas, Figure, Santa Claus,
With Basket, Composition, Felt,
Germany, 1920s, 8 In.

Christmas, Figurine, Santa Claus, On
Motorcycle, Bisque, 2 In.

Christmas, Toy, Santa Claus, Tin
Lithograph, Windup, Arnold,
Germany, Pre-1940, 5 In.

Christmas, Toy, Santee Claus, Tin Lithograph,
Windup, F. Strauss, 1921, 11 In.

Christmas, Toy, Santa Claus, In Sled,
Occupied Japan, 1940s, 7 1/2 In.

Toy, Santa Claus, Battery Operated, 5 Actions, Light-Up Bulb In Hat, 12 In.	275.00
Toy, Santa Claus, Beats Drum, Rings Bell & Walks, Battery Operated, 1950s	275.00
Toy, Santa Claus, Drummer, Reindeer Graphics, Battery Operated, Alps, 10 In.	265.00
Toy, Santa Claus, In Sled, 2 Reindeer, Celluloid, Japan, 1950s, 10 1/2 In.	28.00
Toy, Santa Claus, In Sled, Deer, Composition, Germany, Early 20th Century, 25 In.	1059.00
Toy, Santa Claus, In Sled, Occupied Japan, 1940s, 7 1/2 In. ....*Illus*	121.00
Toy, Santa Claus, In Sled, Reindeer, Windup, Tin, Strauss, 1920s	850.00
Toy, Santa Claus, In Sleigh, Pull Toy, Tin Platform & Sleigh, Box, 6 x 2 1/2 In.	330.00
Toy, Santa Claus, In Sleigh, Pulled By Reindeer, Hubley	3800.00
Toy, Santa Claus, On Reindeer, 1950s	395.00
Toy, Santa Claus, On Sled With Sack, Deer, Wood, Painted, Germany, Prewar, 4 In.	55.00
Toy, Santa Claus, On Sled, Celluloid, Tin, Windup, 1950s	145.00
Toy, Santa Claus, On Sled, Reindeer, Windup, Celluloid, Metal, Japan, 1950s, 8 In.	85.00
Toy, Santa Claus, On Sled, Windup, Celluloid, Tin, 1930s	295.00
Toy, Santa Claus, On Tricycle, Windup, Celluloid, Tin Lithograph, Japan, c.1960, 3 In.	61.00
Toy, Santa Claus, Reading, Mechanical, Alps, Box	375.00
Toy, Santa Claus, Reading, Windup, Alps, 7 In.	175.00
Toy, Santa Claus, Reindeer Run Up & Down When Pulled, Tin & Pot Metal, Box	895.00
Toy, Santa Claus, Reindeer, Sleigh, Windup, Celluloid	170.00
Toy, Santa Claus, Roly Poly, Celluloid, 3 In.	30.00
Toy, Santa Claus, Roly Poly, Composition, 6 1/4 In.	485.00
Toy, Santa Claus, Roly Poly, Schoenhut, 11 In.	3800.00
Toy, Santa Claus, Tin Lithograph, Windup, Arnold, Germany, Pre-1940, 5 In. ......*Illus*	365.00
Toy, Santa Claus, Windup, Composition, Felt Clothes, Germany, Prewar, 6 In.	110.00
Toy, Santa Claus, With Sack, On Motorcycle, Bisque, 1920s, 2 In.	282.00
Toy, Santa Copter, Tin, Plastic, Battery Operated, Illco, Japan, 1960s, 9 1/2 In.	55.00
Toy, Santee Claus, Tin Lithograph, Windup, F. Strauss, 1921, 11 In. ....*Illus*	1349.00
Tray, Christmas Scene, Santa Claus, Brass, TS USA, Rectangular, c.1900, 5 1/4 In.	28.00
View-Master, Rudolph The Red-Nosed Reindeer, Booklet, No. 25, 1949	5.00
Wreath, Santa Claus, Celluloid, Cardboard, Box, 1950s, 12 1/2 In.	22.00
Wreath, Window, Red Cellophane	15.00

CHRISTMAS TREES made of feathers and Christmas tree decorations of
all types are popular with collectors. The first decorated Christmas tree
in America is claimed by many states, including Pennsylvania (1747),
Massachusetts (1832), Illinois (1833), Ohio (1838), and Iowa (1845).
The first glass ornaments were imported from Germany about 1860.
Dresden ornaments were made about 100 years ago of paper and tinsel. Manufacturers in the United States were making ornaments in the
early 1870s. Electric lights were first used on a Christmas tree in 1882.
Character light bulbs became popular in the 1920s, bubble lights in the
1940s, twinkle bulbs in the 1950s, plastic bulbs by 1955. In this book
a Christmas light is a holder for a candle used on the tree. Other forms
of lighting include light bulbs. Other Christmas memorabilia is listed
in the preceding section.

Aluminum, 48 1/2 In.	50.00

Candle Clip, Angel Playing Drum, Tin Lithograph, Germany, c.1900, 2 In. 22.00
Candle Clip, Castle, Tin Lithograph, Wire Holder, Germany, c.1900, 2 In. 28.00
Candle Clip, Cherub, Tin Lithograph, Wire Holder, Germany, c.1900, 1 1/2 In. 22.00
Candle Clip, Elf, Tin Lithograph, Wire Holder, Germany, c.1900, 1 3/4 In. 28.00
Candle Clip, Girl Eating Fruit, Tin Lithograph, Germany, c.1900, 1 3/4 In. 22.00
Candle Clip, Girl Holding Flowers, Tin Lithograph, Germany, c.1900, 1 3/4 In. 22.00
Candle Clip, Girl Throwing Snowballs, Tin, Wire, Germany, c.1900, 1 5/8 In. 28.00
Candle Clip, Girl With Bird In Hand, Tin Lithograph, Germany, c.1900, 1 3/4 In. 22.00
Candle Clip, Victorian House, Tin Lithograph, Germany, c.1900, 2 In. 22.00
Color Wheel 35.00
Feather, Eckardt Musical Stand, 2 Songs, Germany, 3 Ft. 625.00
Feather, With Ornaments, Blown Glass, Celluloid, Early 20th Century, 28 In. 345.00
Fence, Cast Iron, Green, Gold Trim, Victorian, 13 Sections, 4 Gate Sections 340.00
Fence, Flex, 19 Ft. 30.00
Fence, Wooden, Green & White, 3 x 12-In. Sections, 10 Piece 125.00
Fence, Wooden, Picket, Meany & Co., Phila., Pa., 35 x 36 In. 192.00
Garland, Glass Beads, 8 Ft. 15.00
Goose Feather, Victorian Ornaments, 24 In. 900.00
Holder, Santa Claus, Papier-Mache, Paint, Made To Hold Pole Or Tree, 41 In. 550.00
Light, Figural, King Edward Bust, Cobalt Blue, England, 1875-1895, 4 In. 330.00
Light, Figural, Queen Victoria Bust, Milk Glass, England, 1875-1895, 4 In. 220.00
Light, Floral, Blue Milk Glass, England, 1875-1895, 3 7/8 In. 330.00
Light, Tulip, Deep Cobalt Blue, England, 1875-1895, 3 5/8 In. 145.00
Light Bulb, Andy Gump . . . . .50.00 to 95.00
Light Bulb, Bakelite, 1930s, Set Of 8 . . . . 58.00
Light Bulb, Bell, With Santa Claus Face 12.00
Light Bulb, Clown, On Ball 15.00
Light Bulb, Humpty Dumpty . . . . .35.00 to 55.00
Light Bulb, Kewpie 40.00
Light Bulb, King Cole . . . . .30.00 to 45.00
Light Bulb, Little Girl 20.00
Light Bulb, Mickey Mouse, British Thomson-Houston Co., Box, 1930s, 16 In. 93.00
Light Bulb, Mickey Mouse, Noma, Decals On Light Covers, Box, 1930s . . . . . . .225.00 to 265.00
Light Bulb, Moon Mullins . . . . .50.00 to 100.00
Light Bulb, Multiple Lighting Set, Mazda Lamps, c.1940, Box, 12 1/2 x 7 In. 28.00
Light Bulb, Silly Symphony, Box, 1930s 225.00
Light Bulb, Smitty 75.00
Light Bulb, Twinkle, Transformer, Radiant Glass Fibers 50.00
Light Bulb, Yellow Songbird 12.00
Light Bulb Set, Snow White 50.00
Ornament, 3 Little Pigs, Glass, North American Glass, 1940s, 2 1/2 In. 15.00
Ornament, Alligator, Dresden 290.00
Ornament, Angel With Trumpet, 1988 . . . . 40.00
Ornament, Angel, Wax Over Composition, Cloth, Hair, Germany, c.1900, 6 In. 137.00
Ornament, Angel, Wax Over Composition, Hair, Cloth, Germany, c.1900, 3 3/4 In. 75.00
Ornament, Angel, Wax Over Composition, Hair, Silk Robe, Germany, c.1900, 5 In. 82.00
Ornament, Bambi, Glass, North American Glass, 1940s, 2 1/2 In. 15.00
Ornament, Bear In Cap, Blown Glass, 4 1/2 In. 8.00
Ornament, Bicycle, Glass 65.00

Christmas Tree, Ornament, Santa
Claus, Donkey, Cardboard, Tinsel,
Germany, 1920s, 6 In.

Christmas Tree, Ornament, Santas,
In Auto, Cardboard, Tinsel,
Germany, 1920s, 4 In.

Ornament, Bird In Cage, Stained White Metal, Red Gable, Germany, 2 1/2 In. 28.00
Ornament, Bird, Clip On, Bisque, 1930s 95.00
Ornament, Black Forest Doll, Wood, Man, Woman, Germany, Prewar, 2 In., Pair 28.00
Ornament, Butterfly, Glass 55.00
Ornament, Camel, Dresden, Pressed Cardboard, Germany, 2 In. 55.00
Ornament, Car, Blown Glass, Painted, Pink, Germany, 1940s, 5 In. 22.00
Ornament, Car, Blown Glass, Painted, Yellow, Germany, 1940s, 5 In. 28.00
Ornament, Card Shop, Hallmark, Box, 1988 .... 20.00
Ornament, Carousel, Hallmark, 1979, Box 75.00
Ornament, Casey Jones Locomotive, Hallmark, 1961 .... 55.00
Ornament, Charlie Brown, With Tree, 1966 .... 35.00
Ornament, Classical Angel, Hallmark, Box, 1984 .... 45.00
Ornament, Clown, Blown Glass, 3 1/2 In. 5.50
Ornament, Clown, On Ball, Blown Glass, 4 In. 16.50
Ornament, Cool Yule, Frosty Friends, Hallmark, 1980 .... 400.00
Ornament, Donkey, Cotton Batting, Painted Face, Germany, c.1900, 4 In. ... 91.00
Ornament, Fish, Dresden 110.00
Ornament, Garfield, Skier 35.00
Ornament, Grandchild's First Christmas, Hallmark, 1987 .... 10.00
Ornament, Grasshopper, Papier-Mache, Painted, Shellacked Wings, Germany, 4 In. 38.00
Ornament, Happy Hooligan, Composition, Painted, Germany, 1920s, 3 In. 22.00
Ornament, Heavenly Sounds, Hallmark, Box, 1980 .... 40.00
Ornament, Here Comes Santa, Hallmark, 1979 .... 295.00
Ornament, Holiday Scrimshaw Angel, Hallmark, 1979 .... 100.00
Ornament, Icicle, Blown Glass, Germany, Prewar, Box, 3 1/2 In., 30 Piece 55.00
Ornament, Icicle, Blown Glass, Germany, Prewar, Box, 4 In., 40 Piece 60.00
Ornament, Kugel, Grape Cluster, Amethyst 175.00
Ornament, Kugel, Grape Cluster, Cobalt Blue 175.00
Ornament, Kugel, Grape Cluster, Gold 145.00
Ornament, Kugel, Grape Cluster, Silver 145.00
Ornament, Lamb, Cotton Batting, Painted Face, Germany, c.1900, 4 In. 91.00
Ornament, Lighting The Tree, Light & Motion, Box, Hallmark, 1986 .... 20.00
Ornament, Locomotive, Tin, Hallmark, 1988 .... 200.00
Ornament, Man In The Moon, Crescent Form, c.1930, 4 In. 80.00
Ornament, Mosque, Cardboard, Painted, Czechoslovakia, Prewar, 4 1/4 In. 28.00
Ornament, Murray Atomic Missile, Hallmark, 1958 .... 55.00
Ornament, Murray Super Deluxe Fire Truck, Hallmark, 1962 .... 55.00
Ornament, Nativity Scene, Cardboard, Paper, Tinsel, Glass Tubing, Prewar, 3 1/2 In. ... 28.00
Ornament, Pear, Glass, 1930s 60.00
Ornament, Penguin, Blown Glass, Paper Label, Germany, Prewar, 4 In. 82.00
Ornament, Reindeer, Glass Eyes, Celluloid 20.00
Ornament, Rocking Horse, 1st Edition, Hallmark, 1981 .... 500.00
Ornament, Rooftop Deliveries, Hallmark, 1981 .... 90.00
Ornament, Sailboat, Dresden, Cardboard, Paper, Germany, c.1900, 4 In. 240.00
Ornament, Sailboat, Mast & Rider, Blown Glass, Blue 40.00
Ornament, Santa Claus & His Reindeer Set, Hallmark, 1992, 5 Piece 50.00
Ornament, Santa Claus Truck, Hallmark, 1981 .... 350.00
Ornament, Santa Claus, Cardboard, Tinsel Hanger, Germany, Prewar, 4 1/2 In. 22.00
Ornament, Santa Claus, Composition, Cloth, Felt, Japan, 1950s, 5 1/2 In. 22.00
Ornament, Santa Claus, Composition, Painted, Germany, Prewar, 3 1/2 In. 137.00
Ornament, Santa Claus, Donkey, Cardboard, Tinsel, Germany, 1920s, 6 In. ...... *Illus* 39.00
Ornament, Santa Claus, Riding Reindeer, Waving, Plastic, 7 1/2 In. 12.00
Ornament, Santa Claus, Standing, Sleigh, Plastic 8.00
Ornament, Santa Claus, Tin, Glow Light Corp, 8 1/2 In. 15.00
Ornament, Santa Claus, With Glossy Eyes, Blown Glass, 4 In. 6.60
Ornament, Santa On Rocket, Ceramic, Shafford, Foil Label, 1960s, 4 In. 35.00
Ornament, Santas, In Auto, Cardboard, Tinsel, Germany, 1920s, 4 In. .... *Illus* 39.00
Ornament, Sea Plane, Tin, 3 1/4 In. 6.75
Ornament, Shepherd With Lamb, 1987 .... 40.00
Ornament, Skiers, Cotton Batting, Crepe Paper, Germany, Prewar, 3 In., Pair 101.00
Ornament, Skyscraper, Cardboard, Painted, Czechoslovakia, Prewar, 4 1/4 In. 33.00
Ornament, Snoopy With Sock, 1966 .... 30.00
Ornament, Snow Fairy, Glass, Feet, Hands, Head & Body, 1930s 150.00

Ornament, Snowball, Face, Papier-Mache, Painted, Germany, Prewar, 2 In. .... 22.0●

Ornament, Snowman, Hallmark, 1976, Miniature .... 40.0●

Ornament, Spaniel, Begging, Blown Glass, 3 In. .... 6.5●

Ornament, Star, Dresden, Cardboard & Foil, Germany, c.1900, 3 3/4 In. .... 83.0●

Ornament, Stocking, Wax, 3 1/2 In. .... 25.0●

Ornament, Sun, Stained Tin, Red, Gold, Germany, Prewar, 2 In. .... 44.0●

Ornament, Virgin & Child, Blown Glass, 5 In. .... 16.5●

Ornament, Wine Bottle, Blown Glass, Paper Label, Germany, Prewar, 3 In. .... 22.0●

Ornament, Zeppelin, Glass .... 85.0●

Santa Claus Scene, Flat, Oval Shape .... 30.0●

Stand, Cast Iron, North Bros., Philadelphia, Black & Gold Paint, Victorian .... 35.0●

Stand, Plays 3 Tunes, Turns Tree, Key Wind .... 450.0●

CHROME items in the Art Deco style became popular in the 1930s. Collectors are most interested in high-style pieces made by the Connecticut firms of Chase Brass and Copper Company, and Manning Bowman.

Candleholder, Chrome Ball, Cobalt Base, Chase, Pair 95.00

Candlesnuffer, Chase, Bakelite & Brass, 15 1/2 In. 135.00

Candlestick, Chase, Sphere Shape, 2 1/2 x 2 1/2 In., Pair 125.00

Candy Dish, Chase, Insert 190.00

Canister Set, Kromex, Flour, Sugar, Coffee, Tea, 1940s, 4 Piece 45.00

Cigarette Case, Nude Figure, Reclining, Gold Wash Interior, Silver, 3 1/2 In. 990.00

Cocktail Cup Set, Chase, Doric, White Plastic Base, 3 x 2 3/8 In., 4 Piece 90.00

Cocktail Set, Chrome Shaker, Farber, Black Handle, Chrome Footed Cups, 7 Piece 80.00

Cocktail Shaker, Bell Shape, Wood & Chrome Handle, Pour Spout With Cap, 11 In. ... 75.00

Cocktail Shaker, Bowling Pin 250.00

Cocktail Shaker, Chase, Black Painted Ribs At Shoulder & Base, 12 In. 125.00

Cocktail Shaker, Chase, Black Painted Ribs At Shoulder & Base, Art Deco, 11 In. 75.00

Cocktail Shaker, Krome Kraft, Bakelite Handle, 12 1/2 In. 48.00

Cocktail Shaker, Penguin 400.00

Coffee Maker Set, Chase, Comet, Coffeepot, Covered Sugar, Creamer, 3 Piece 450.00

Cup, Chase, Liqueur, 2 3/8 In., 6 Piece 195.00

Cup, Fruit, Art Deco 110.00

Dish, Serving, Chase, 2 Sections, Glass Liner, Stationary Handle, 5 1/2 In. 45.00

Humidor, Robbins Co., Hammered, Black Plastic Handles, Bostonian, 7 3/4 x 5 3/4 In. ... 48.00

Ice Bucket, Penguins, West Band 24.00

Salt & Pepper, Chase, Russel Wright Design, 1930s, 1 3/4 & 1 1/8 In. 65.00

Stand, Smoker's, Chase, Lazy Boy, Polished Chromium, 22 In. 450.00

Sugar, Cover, Chase, Black Handle On Lid, 3 3/4 In. 22.00

Sugar & Creamer, Chase, Bakelite Banded Handles, Oval 95.00

Tray, Chase, 3 Tiers, Folding, Designs Of Fruit, Fish & Chicken, Ribbed Handle 70.00

CIGAR STORE FIGURES of carved wood or cast iron were used as advertisements in front of the Victorian cigar store. The carved figures are now collected as folk art. They range in size from counter type, about three feet, to over eight feet high.

Indian, Contrapasto, Feather Headdress, Red, Cream, Black, 59 In., Pair 19500.00

Indian, Princess, Carved Headdress & Beads, Kaspar, 72 1/2 In. 25850.00

Indian, Reclining, Plaster 350.00

Indian, Sioux, Capitol, Wooden, 1940s, 6 Ft. 1295.00

Soldier, Corporal Joe, Wooden, c.1865, 72 In. 46750.00

CINNABAR is a vermilion or red lacquer. Pieces are made with tens to hundreds of thicknesses of the lacquer that is later carved. Most cinnabar was made in the Orient.

Box, Cover, Oriental Couple, Bonsai Trees, Black Interior 100.00

Plate, Flower Form, Children Playing, China, 10 In. 58.00

CIVIL WAR mementos are important collector's items. Most of the pieces are military items used from 1861 to 1865. Be sure to avoid any explosive munitions.

Badge, 6th Corps, Silver, Brass, Blue Cloth Center, T-Bar Pin 550.00

Badge, Lincoln For President, Union & Liberty At Top, Paper, 1860, 3 1/4 x 1/4 In. 1982.00
Battle Rattle, Walnut, Brass 250.00
Book, Song, The Bugle Call, Root & Casy, 1863 .... 135.00
Book, The Civil War In Song & Story, 1865 .... 65.00
Boots, Drummer Boy's, Brass Tips, Pulls 365.00
Boots & Shako, Drummer Boy, 55th Illinois 1540.00
Box, Document, Eagle, Shield, Cannons, 1864 .... 1200.00
Box, Prisoner Made, Inlays 4 Sides, Stars, Shields On Top, Brass Lock, 12 x 17 In. 600.00
Box, Prisoner Made, Inlays Of Various Woods, Felt Lined, 5 1/4 x 12 1/8 In. 325.00
Canteen, Carved Pine, Oak Bands, 9 x 9 1/8 In. 520.00
Canteen, GAR Reunion 285.00
Canteen, Pewter Spout, I.D. Sgt. James A. Pettis, 1858, 8 3/4 In. 440.00
Canteen, Pottery, Blue Transfer Union Soldier, White Ground, 5 1/4 In. 255.00
Canteen, Union, Blue Birds, Nest With Eggs, Gray Ground, 1858, 8 1/2 In. 165.00
Canteen, Union, Decorated, Naval Scene, Homecoming Scene, 8 1/4 In. 385.00
Canteen, Walnut Staves, Iron Rope Band, Marked 64-65, Oval, 10 1/8 x 7 In. 420.00
Canteen, Wooden, Metal Banding, Hand Tooled Chain & Hardware, 4 1/4 x 9 In. 220.00
Card, In Memoriam, Abraham Lincoln In Center Circle, Phil Magee, 4 x 2 1/2 In. 81.00
Card, Lincoln Memorial, Tombstone, Embossed, 1865, 3 1/2 x 5 In. 110.00
Carpet Bag, Confederate, Multicolored, Large 175.00
Case, Dispatch, Strap, 11 1/2 x 8 In. 100.00
Case, Field, Surgeon's, Scalpels, Saw, Chisel & Knife, Mahogany Case, 8 1/4 In. 1600.00
Case, Map, Original Clasp, 6 3/4 x 13 In. 115.00
Checkers Kit, Rosewood Frame, Drawers, Wooden Checkers, Glass Cover 340.00
Coat, Frock, Trousers, 9 Buttons, I.W. Lt. 1250.00
Cup, Collapsible, Hard Rubber, Dated On Lid, 1860, 2 1/4 In. 125.00
Desk, Field, Contents, Quartermaster W.H.D. Blake 6160.00
Desk, Lap, Prisoner Made, Inlays All Sides, Interior Stars, Brass Hinges & Lock 485.00
Drum, Black Paint & Varnish, With Pine Sticks, J.C. Haynes & Co., 10 x 14 3/4 In. 600.00
Farrier's Set, Cavalry, W.C. Corsan & Co. 120.00
Fife 185.00
Kepi, Cord & Eagle Buttons, c.1870 .... 425.00
Kit, Field, Surgeon's, 11 Instruments, Tortoiseshell Handles, Folded, 2 x 6 1/2 In. 290.00
Kit, Shaving & Writing, Officer's, 10 Items, Pine Case, Mahogany Veneer, 9 1/8 In. 565.00
Knapsack, Tar Covered Canvas, Leather Straps 110.00
Knapsack, Treated Canvas, Leather Straps 295.00
Lantern, Conductor, Globe Marked P. Co., Brass, 1864 .... 900.00
Lantern, Conductor, Presentation, Globe Marked Casey, Seaboard, Keystone, 1904 ..... 1000.00
Letter, Signed By Robert E. Lee 4675.00
Letter, U.S. Army Captain, Pay Records, Requests Check, Fermamdoma Beach, Florida . 45.00
Pouch, Mail, Courier, Marked B & M RR , 5 In. 70.00
Powder Tin, Black Paint, Pewter Cap, 4 1/8 x 5 1/2 In. 85.00
Print, Bird's Eye View Of Andersonville, Lithograph, 1899 .... 300.00
Razor Kit, Sheath, Leather Strop, Tin Drawer, Marked Joseph Rogers & Sons 120.00
Ribbon, James Monroe, Memorial, Frame 977.00
Saddle Bag, U.S. Cavalry, Signal Corps 1500.00
Sash, Officer's, Confederate, Gold Bullion & Crimson Bands 50.00
Slide, Lee & His Generals After Appomattox 40.00
Sword, Col. S.C.K.D. & K.N.O., Scabbard, Metal, 41 1/2 In. 1045.00
Sword, Field Officer's, 1 Hook Scabbard, Emerson & Silver, 1863 .... 475.00
Sword, Foot Officer's, Folding Guard, Metal Scabbard, Jas. Hirsch & Son, 1860 .... 350.00
Sword, NCO, Horstman Philadelphia, 26 In. 450.00
Sword, Officer's, Engraved U.S., American Spread Eagle & Cannons ....465.00 to 485.00

CKAW, see Dedham category.

CLAMBROTH glass, popular in the Victorian era, is a grayish color and
is somewhat opaque, like clam broth. It was made by several factories
in the United States and England.

Candlestick, Acanthus, Blue Socket, Hexagonal, 9 1/2 In., Pair 1265.00
Candlestick, Dolphin, Opaque Blue Petal Socket, 9 1/2 In., Pair 2200.00
Candlestick, Hexagonal, 7 5/8 In., Pair ....110.00 to 220.00
Goblet, Button Arches, Souvenir 35.00

Hot Plate, Square, 5 In.	12.(
Jar, Pomade, Bear Shape, F.B. Strouse, N.Y., 3 3/4 In.	385.(
Lamp, Baluster Stem, Hexagonal Base, Sawtooth Font, Brass Collar, 10 5/8 In.	685.(
Lamp, Bristol, Brass Collar, 12 1/4 In.	110.0
Lamp, Ribbed, Gilt Brass Connector & Collar, 12 In.	2090.0
Mug, Colorado, Souvenir	22.(
Rolling Pin	125.(
Toothpick, Zipper, Opalescent	30.0

CLARICE CLIFF was a designer who worked in several English factories after the 1920s. She is best known for her brightly colored art deco designs. She died in 1972.

Biaritz, Plate, Sunburst, 8 x 11 In.	295.0
Bizarre, Bowl, Abstract Landscape Design, Newport Pottery, England, 8 x 4 In.	1100.0
Bizarre, Bowl, Crocus, Stylized Trees In Landscape, Signed, 5 1/4 In.	860.0
Bizarre, Bowl, Floral Design, Newport Pottery, England, 9 x 4 1/2 In.	1045.0
Bizarre, Bowl, Forest Glen, Landscape, Red Bleeding Glaze, Signed, 7 1/2 In.	690.0
Bizarre, Plate, 12 In.	120.0
Bizarre, Platter, 16 In.	395.0
Bizarre, Vase, Autumn, Trees In Landscape, Signed, 7 1/4 In.	1265.0
Bizarre, Vase, Cubist Form, Newport Pottery, England, 3 x 7 In.	1430.0
Bizarre, Vase, Delicia Citrus, Orange, Yellow, Blue, Green, White, Marked, 5 In.	500.0
Bizarre, Vase, Landscape, Trees, Flowers, 3-Footed, 7 In.	495.0
Bizarre, Vase, Stylized Black, Green Trees, Orange Sky, Yellow Ground, 6 x 3 In.	660.0
Bizarre, Wall Pocket, Geometric Design, Newport Pottery, England, 10 x 12 In.	319.0
Deco, Tureen, Orange, Black, Yellow, Marked, Newport Pottery, England, 9 x 8 In.	440.0
Fantasque, Jug, Lotus, Stylized Melons, Signed, 11 1/2 In.	1495.0
Fantasque, Pitcher, Orange, Yellow, Blue & Black, 7 In.	440.0
Garden City, Bowl, Ruffled, Orange, 8 In.	40.0
Indian Design, Teapot, Cone Shape, Greetings From Canada, 9 x 6 In.	605.0
Odeon, Bowl, Art Deco, Cover, 7 1/4 In.	450.0
Rhodante, Plate, Floral, Rectangular, 9 In.	295.0
Sunkissed Peaches, Plate, 8 1/2 In.	75.00 to 100.0
Toby, Sugar & Creamer	175.0
Vase, Cream, Conical, Green & Yellow Birds, 12 1/4 In.	410.0
Wall Pocket, White To Simulate Clouds, Bird In Flight	195.0
Winston Churchill, Toby Jug, And May God Defend The Right, 1941, 12 In.	1035.00 to 1380.0

CLEWELL ware was made in limited quantities by Charles Walter Clewell of Canton, Ohio, from 1902 to 1955. Pottery was covered with a thin coating of bronze, then treated to make the bronze turn different colors. Pieces covered with copper, brass, or silver were also made. Mr. Clewell's secret formula for blue patinated bronze was burned when he died in 1965.

Ashtray, Copper, Stylized Leaf & Blossom Design, Brown & Green Patina, 6 x 2 In.	230.0(
Bowl, Bronze, Marked, 3 1/2 x 10 1/2 In.	495.0(
Bowl, Copper, Brown & Green Patina, 9 x 3 1/2 In.	410.0(
Humidor, Copper Clad, Riveted Design, Finial Cover, 4 In.	385.0(
Mug, External Rivets, Copper Clad, Signed, 4 1/8 In.	140.00 to 180.0(
Mug Set, Copper, Panel & Rivet Design, Brown Patina, 4 1/2 In., 5 Piece	330.0(
Pitcher, Copper Clad, Organic, Marked, 6 In.	242.0(
Vase, Copper Clad, 4-Sided Swirled Form, Incised Flowers, Owens Art Blank, 5 1/2 In.	330.0(
Vase, Copper Clad, Bronze To Verdigris Patina, 5 x 3 In.	165.0(
Vase, Copper Clad, Brown To Green Patina, 15 1/2 In.	1870.0(
Vase, Copper Clad, Brown To Verdigris Patina, Classical Shape, 7 1/2 x 4 In.	330.0(
Vase, Copper Clad, Brown, Gold Patina, 6 In.	275.0(
Vase, Copper Clad, Brown, Green Patina, 5 1/2 In.	440.0(
Vase, Copper Clad, Ear Of Corn Design, Brown Patina, 10 In.	1100.0(
Vase, Copper Clad, Flared Petal Rim, 6 1/2 In.	467.0(
Vase, Copper Clad, Floral, Brown Patina, 7 In.	253.0(
Vase, Copper Clad, Green Patina, Orange To Blue, 5 In.	1320.0(
Vase, Copper Clad, Green To Brown Patina, 10 1/2 In.	450.00 to 715.0(
Vase, Copper Clad, Green To Orange Patina, Signed, 6 1/4 In.	770.0(

Vase, Copper Clad, Orange To Brown Patina, 7 1/2 x 4 In. 605.00
Vase, Copper Clad, Orange To Green Patina, 3 1/2 In. 209.00
Vase, Copper Clad, Orange To Green Patina, 6 In. 1430.00
Vase, Copper Clad, Stylized Leaves, Geometric Shape, 9 3/4 In. 660.00
Vase, Copper Clad, Waisted Shoulder, Flared, 9 In. 1210.00
Vase, Copper Clad, Water Lilies & Lily Pads, Water-Textured Ground, 8 x 8 In. 2640.00
Vase, Copper, Brown To Green Patina, Incised Mark, 6 1/2 In. 385.00
Vase, Copper, Brown To Green Patina, Incised Mark, 9 In. 935.00
Vase, Copper, Incised Geometric, Brown Patina, Incised Mark, 7 x 5 In. 990.00
Vase, Copper, Orange & Green Patina, Incised Mark, 11 In. 825.00
Vase, Copper, Raised Stylized Leaf & Column Design, Brown Patina, Footed, 4 1/2 In. ... 605.00
Vase, Deep Orange To Verdigris Patina, Organic Handles, 5 1/2 x 7 1/2 In. 880.00
Vase, Embossed Egyptian Design, Rich Brown Patina, 9 1/2 x 4 In. 495.00
Vase, Floor, Deep Green Patina, 17 x 9 1/2 In. 1540.00
Vase, Orange, Green Patina, Bulbous, 14 1/2 x 6 In. 1980.00
Vase, Rich Verdigris Patina, 2 Bronze Handles, 9 x 4 3/4 In. 1210.00

CLEWS pottery was made by George Clews & Co. of Brownhill
Pottery, Tunstall, England, from 1806 to 1861. Additional pieces may
be listed in the Flow Blue category.

Cup Plate, Landing Of Lafayette, Floral Border, 4 1/2 In. 220.00
Plate, Blue Transfer, Landing Of General LaFayette At Castle Garden, Pearlware, 10 In. . 330.00
Plate, Peace & Plenty, Basket Of Flowers, Scroll Border, 9 In. 220.00
Plate, Playing At Draughts, Dark Blue, 7 7/8 In. 250.00
Plate, Troy From Mt. Ida, Purple, 10 1/2 In. 225.00
Plate, Welcome Lafayette The Nation's Guest, Dark Blue, 8 3/4 In. 950.00
Platter, Hunt Scene, Dark Blue, 16 1/2 In. 550.00
Platter, Landing Of General Lafayette, Blue Transfer, 17 In. 1100.00
Platter, Landing Of General Lafayette, Dark Blue, 15 1/4 In. 1705.00
Platter, Landing Of General Lafayette, Dark Blue, 17 In. 1100.00
Platter, Peace & Plenty, Dark Blue, 15 In. 1100.00
Platter, Valentine, Dark Blue, 17 In. ....935.00 to 1210.00
Sauceboat, Foliage & Scroll, Fisherman By River, Dark Blue 295.00
Sauceboat, Undertray, Redgrave Hall & Euston Hall, 2 Piece 245.00
Soup, Dish, States Pattern, Blue, Staffordshire, 10 1/4 In. 225.00
Soup, Dish, States Pattern, Scalloped Edge, 8 3/4 In. 245.00
Soup, Dish, Winter View Of Pittsfield, Dark Blue, 10 3/8 In. 440.00
Teapot, American Eagle On Urn, Florals, Blue, 8 In. 550.00
Teapot, Floral, Medium Dark Blue 525.00
Wash Bowl, Vase Of Flowers, Dark Blue, 4 x 12 In. 467.00

CLIFTON POTTERY was founded by William Long in Clifton, New
Jersey, in 1905. He worked there until 1908 making a line called
Crystal Patina. Clifton Pottery made art pottery. Another firm,
Chesapeake Pottery, sold majolica marked *Clifton ware*.

Lamp Base, Geometric Homolobi Clay, Red Dark Umber, 8 x 11 In. 550.00
Lamp Base, Ocher Glaze, Celadon Matte Ground, 1906, 5 x 7 In. 275.00
Teapot, Indian Ware, 5 In. 275.00
Vase, Brown, Green Crystalline Glaze, Green, Carmel, Cream Drip, 1906, 5 x 6 1/2 In. ... 605.00
Vase, Bulbous, Tirrube, 5 In. 300.00
Vase, Celadon, Crystalline Glaze, Bottle Shape, 1905, 10 1/2 x 4 3/4 In. 303.00
Vase, Cream, Olive, Blue Crystalline Glaze, 1906, 4 1/2 In. 286.00
Vase, Crystal Patina, 7 In. ....350.00 to 400.00
Vase, Crystal Patina, Matte Green, 11 In. 385.00
Vase, Floral, Leaves, Brick Red, 12 In. 475.00
Vase, Geometric Design, Black, Brown, Cocoa, Red Ground, Incised, 9 x 7 In. 286.00
Vase, Indian Design, Black, Tan Swirls & Geometric, Red Ground, Arizona, 7 x 5 In. 220.00
Vase, Light & Dark Brown Matte Swirl Design, Marked, 4 x 1 1/2 In. 65.00
Vase, Light Green Crystalline Glaze, Bulbous Base, Artist, 1907, 7 In. 165.00
Vase, Matte Blue, Dark Blue, Green, 12 In. 295.00
Vase, Ocher Glaze, Golden Crystalline Ground, 1906, 8 1/2 x 6 In. 385.00
Vase, Ocher Matte Celadon Crystalline Glaze, Bottle Shape, 1905, 8 3/4 x 5 1/4 In. 303.00
Vase, Stylized Stem With Berries Design, Ivory Highlights, Light Green, 4 x 2 In. 176.00

Vase, Tan Crystalline Matte Glaze, Waisted, Elongated Neck, 1906, 8 In. 385.00
Vase, White Wild Rose, Green Leaves, Bisque Red Clay Ground, Flared, 5 3/4 x 3 In. 412.00

CLOCKS of all types have always been popular with collectors. The eighteenth-century tall case, or grandfather's clock, was designed to house a works with a long pendulum. In 1816, Eli Terry patented a new, smaller works for a clock, and the case became smaller. The clock could be kept on a shelf instead of on the floor. By 1840, coiled springs were used and even smaller clocks were made. Battery-powered electric clocks were made in the 1870s.

Advertising, 7-Up, Animated, Aluminum Case, 1950s, 20 In. 517.00
Advertising, 7-Up, Light-Up, 15 In. . . . . .350.00 to 395.00
Advertising, 7-Up, Rocker, Neon, Green 1250.00
Advertising, A & P Coffee, Round, Red, White & Black, 14 1/2 In. 250.00
Advertising, Allis-Chalmers, Neon, Red Lights, Electric, 21 1/2 x 21 In. 850.00
Advertising, Belfast Sparkling Water, Neon, Green, 14 In. 495.00
Advertising, Belfast Sparkling Water, Neon, Green, 21 In. 550.00
Advertising, Bireley's, Double Bubble, Light-Up 395.00
Advertising, Bisma Trex, Metal, Electric, 13 1/2 x 15 In. 348.00
Advertising, Borden, Elsie, Yellow, Square, 12 In. 100.00
Advertising, Boston Laundry Starch, Baird Tin & Wood, 32 In. 1650.00
Advertising, Budweiser, Label, Clydesdales, Plastic, Light-Up, 14 x 13 In. . . . . .55.00 to 110.00
Advertising, Burger Brau, Tin Face & Back, Wooden Frame, 1940s, 19 x 14 In. 40.00
Advertising, Campbell Soup 35.00
Advertising, Canada Dry, Light-Up, Square 175.00
Advertising, Canada Dry, Pam Clock Co., New Rochelle, N.Y., Light-Up, Metal, 15 In. . . 500.00
Advertising, Canadian Neon-Ray, 13 In. 650.00
Advertising, Charlie Tuna, Star Kist, Photo-Block, Box, 1972 . . . . 100.00
Advertising, Cheer Up, Light-Up 345.00
Advertising, Diet Rite, Light-Up, Rectangular 175.00
Advertising, Diet-Rite Cola, Double Back, Light-Up 250.00
Advertising, Dr Pepper, Light-Up, Square 175.00
Advertising, Dr Pepper, Regulator, Oak, Dealer, 1970s 600.00
Advertising, Dr. Pepper, Plastic, Light-Up, 1950s, 11 In. 115.00
Advertising, Dr. Pepper, Reverse Painted, Art Deco Style, 1930s, 17 x 22 In. . . . . . .*Illus* 4255.00
Advertising, Dr. Pepper, Telechron, Electric, Late 1930s-Early 1940s 402.00
Advertising, Duquesne Beer, Art Deco, Reverse Glass, Light-Up, 1930s, 24 x 18 In. 320.00
Advertising, Dutch Boy Lucas Paint, Bubble, Can Of Paint, Boy On Top, 15 In. 300.00
Advertising, Edwards & Bradford Lumber Co., Cast Iron, 5 x 3 1/2 In. 65.00
Advertising, Evervess Spring Water, Parrot, Late 1940s-Early 1950s 402.00
Advertising, Falstaff Beer, Bakelite, Gold Metal, Table 75.00
Advertising, Falstaff Beer, Plastic, Simulated Wood Grain, Light-Up, 13 x 11 In. 60.00
Advertising, Federal, Walnut, Gilt Eagle Crest, White Gilt Dial, Black Ground, 34 In. . . . 316.00
Advertising, Ferz Product, Ball, Swiveling, Bakelite, 2 1/4 In. 125.00

Clock, Advertising, Dr. Pepper, Reverse Painted, Art Deco Style, 1930s, 17 x 22 In.

Clock, Advertising, Red Goose Shoes, Telecron, Light-Up, 1930-1940

Advertising, Fresca, Wall, Logo & Snowflake, Plastic, 12 1/2 x 20 In.	70.00
Advertising, Frito-Lay, Digital, Small	15.00
Advertising, Gillette Tires, Polar Bear, Metal, White & Green Face, Round, 14 1/2 In.	95.00
Advertising, Gilt Edge Paint, 15 x 15 In.	125.00
Advertising, Glo-Dial, Neon	850.00
Advertising, Goodyear, Wall, Goodyear Blimp, Plastic, Battery Operated, 10 In.	48.00
Advertising, Grant Batteries, Glass, Metal, Round, 14 1/2 In.	465.00
Advertising, Grant Batteries, Light-Up, Square, 15 1/2 In.	198.00
Advertising, Gulf, Plastic, Light-Up, 22 x 22 In.	187.00
Advertising, Heinz Mr. Aristocrat, Figural, Talking Alarm	105.00
Advertising, International Harvester, Neon	300.00
Advertising, Jewelry Store, Bulova, Double Back Lighted, Curved Glass Front	80.00
Advertising, Joe Camel, Wearing Levis & Leather Jacket, Plastic, 1992	65.00
Advertising, John Deere Farm Equipment, Glass, Metal, Light-Up, 14 3/4 In.	600.00
Advertising, Keebler, Alarm, 2 Bells	20.00
Advertising, Kendall Racing Oil, Glass Face & Front, Metal Body, Light-Up, 15 In.	360.00
Advertising, Kit-Kat, Animated	55.00
Advertising, Kix, Alarm, Windup	65.00
Advertising, Leinen Kugells, Indian Maiden, Double Bubble	475.00
Advertising, Midwest Ice Cream, Cow Picture, Light-Up	325.00
Advertising, Milton, Auto Parts, Colorful, Art Deco, 1950s	100.00
Advertising, Monroe Shock Absorbers	40.00
Advertising, Mopar Parts Accessories, Neon, Metal & Glass, 18 1/2 x 18 1/2 In.	600.00
Advertising, Mountain Dew, 1972	125.00
Advertising, Nestle, Chocolate Chip Cookie, Alarm, Lafayette Watch Co., 5 1/2 In.	38.00
Advertising, Nu-Grape Soda, Telechron, Straight Up Bottle Face, Light-Up, 15 In.	300.00
Advertising, Old Mr. Boston	400.00
Advertising, Oldsmobile, Glass Front, Metal Body, Light-Up, 17 3/4 x 15 1/2 In.	275.00
Advertising, Olympia Light Beer, Plastic, Bottle Cap, Light-Up, 17 In.	85.00
Advertising, Orange Crush, Glass, Metal, New Rochelle, N.Y., Light-Up, 14 1/2 In.	170.00
Advertising, Pepsi-Cola, Tin Face, Light-Up	575.00
Advertising, Polly Stamps, Double Bubble, Light-Up, 1940s-1950s	1725.00
Advertising, Pontiac, Dealership, Indian, Light-Up	650.00
Advertising, Pontiac, Neon, Metal Hands, Case, Plastic, 18 3/8 In.	375.00
Advertising, Pontiac, Service, Electric, Metals Hands, Plastic, 15 In.	250.00
Advertising, Poppin Fresh, Plastic	20.00
Advertising, Postal Telegraph Synchronized Electric, Metal Face, 20 x 5 In., 1929	350.00
Advertising, Purina Chows Sanitation Products, Double Bubble, Light-Up, 1940s	374.00
Advertising, Quaker State, Neon, Chrome Ring, Glass Face, Metal, 16 x 19 In.	550.00
Advertising, Quaker State, Plastic, Light-Up, Box, Square, 15 3/4 In.	100.00
Advertising, Quaker State, Spinner, Neon	800.00
Advertising, RC Cola, Light-Up, Square	175.00
Advertising, Red Goose Shoes, Telecron, Light-Up, 1930-1940 ....*Illus*	460.00
Advertising, Royal Crown Cola, Glass Face & Front, Second Hand, Light-Up, 15 In.	230.00
Advertising, Schmidt's Beer Ale, Plastic Over Metal, Keystone Shape, 1950s, 14 In.	78.00
Advertising, Seagram's-7, Big Red 7, Chrome Ground	90.00
Advertising, Sealtest Ice Cream, Light-Up, Square	125.00
Advertising, Sinclair, Dino Dinosaur Gasoline, Metal, Light-Up, 1950s	500.00
Advertising, Speedy Alka-Seltzer, Holding Glass, Tin Face, 1950s	450.00
Advertising, Squirt, Light-Up, Square	200.00
Advertising, St. Joseph's Aspirin, Blue, White Glass Face	130.00
Advertising, Sun Crest, Light-Up, Square	175.00
Advertising, Sun Crest, Telechron, Bottle, 1940s	402.00
Advertising, Texaco, Second Hand, Wood Case, Round, 8 In.	60.00
Advertising, Travelers Express, Money Orders, Curved Glass, Light-Up, Square, 14 In.	230.00
Advertising, Trice Jewelers, Curved Glass, Bakelite	85.00
Advertising, U.S. Royal Tires, Glass Face & Front, Metal Body, Light-Up	357.00
Advertising, Vess, Double Bubble, Light-Up	575.00
Advertising, Western Auto, Electric, 12 In.	125.00
Advertising, Western Union, c.1898	200.00
Advertising, Wheaties, Dale Earnhardt	60.00
Alarm, Bugs Bunny, Talking, Windup & Battery, Plastic, 1974	28.00
Alarm, Cartier, Paris, Quartz, Travel, 4 In.	115.00

Alarm, Dunhill, 8-Day, Windup, Octagonal Shape, 1960s 150.00
Alarm, Hubert The Harris Lion 35.00
Alarm, Painted Dial, Marble Base, Signed Erte, Christople Jewelers, Paris 770.00
Alarm, Radio, G.E., Model 506, Ivory Plastic, Vacuum Tubes, 11 1/2 x 6 1/2 In. 65.00
Alarm, Snoopy & Charlie Brown, Talking, Windup, Battery, Equity, Hong Kong, 1974 .. 35.00
Alarm, Telechron, Clear Lucite Cube, Electric, 1930s 90.00
Alarm, Woody Woodpecker, Box 242.00
American Clock Co., Shelf, Brass Works, Key, Pendulum, 1856, 18 1/2 In. 770.00
Anglo-American, Carved & Inlaid, Pendulum, Hanging, 28 In. 260.00
Animated, Big Bad Wolf, 3 Little Pigs, Alarm, Ingersoll, 1930s, 4 In. 580.00
Animated, Black Poodle, Coly Clock Co. 85.00
Animated, Bugs Bunny, Alarm, Talking, White, Plastic, Gray Bunny, Janex Corp., 7 In. . 65.00
Animated, Children Swinging 225.00
Animated, Kit Kat, Jeweled Moving Eyes & Tail, Box, 1960s 325.00
Animated, Mighty Mouse, Alarm, 2 Bells, Bradley, 1985 .... 50.00
Animated, Rocking Granny, Cream & Red, Electric, Haddon 160.00
Animated, Swinging Girl, Marbleized Case, Electric, Mastercrafters, 1950s 225.00
Animated, Swinging Playmates, Electric, Mastercrafters 190.00
Animated, Three Little Pigs & Wolf, Paper Face, Ingersoll, 1930s 180.00
Animation, Ballerina, Wood & Metal 120.00
Ansonia, Chiming, 30-Day, 19th Century, 24 x 16 In. 375.00
Ansonia, Mantel, 8-Day, Time & Strike, Brass Movement, Paper Dial, 1880s 155.00
Ansonia, Mantel, Cast Iron, Metal Fittings, Enameled Face, 10 1/2 In. 137.00
Ansonia, Mantel, Embossed Filigree, Cavaliers, Enameled Base, 21 x 24 In. 1045.00
Ansonia, Mantel, Side Mirror, Walnut, 1883 .... 495.00
Ansonia, Mantel, Tambour, 8-Day Movement, Silveroid Dial, Beveled Bezel, 21 1/2 In. .. 50.00
Ansonia, Mantel, Veined Green Marble, Ormolu Mounts, 10 1/2 x 11 In. 121.00
Ansonia, Regulator, Visible Porcelain Escapement, Polish Brass, Gold Trim, c.1902 .... 1250.00
Ansonia, Tecumseh, Blue & White China, Gilt Brass Trim, 11 In. 300.00
Ansonia, Time & Strike, Flower Basket Finial, Muse On Side, 16 1/2 In. 522.00
Ansonia, Treason, Half-Hour Strike, Scene Of Cupids & Greek Women, 14 In. 635.00
Ansonia, Wall, Spring Wind, Brass Case, Porcelain Plaques 165.00
Ansonia, Wall, Time & Strike, Spring Driven, Oak Case 55.00
Atmos, Silvered Dial, Nickel Movement, Brass Case, J.L. Reutter, c.1930, 8 1/2 In. 3162.00
Austrian, French Movement, Brass, Beveled Glass Panels, Marble Base, 16 In. 990.00
Banjo, Chelsea, Panel Of Mt. Vernon 977.00
Banjo, Federal, Eglomise, Pierced Brass Fillets, Aaron Willard, 1815, 32 x 10 In. 6325.00
Banjo, Federal, Mahogany, Eglomise, White Painted Dial, 1810, 40 x 10 1/2 In. 2070.00
Banjo, Howard & Davis, Regulator No. 4, Boston, Mass., c.1842, 32 In. 1540.00
Banjo, Howard, E., Federal Revival, 20th Century 605.00
Banjo, Howard, No. 4, Red, Green & Black Glasses, Mahogany Case, 21 In. 660.00
Banjo, Ingraham, Treasure Island 695.00
Banjo, Mahogany Case, Brass Bezel, Painted Iron Dial, 8-Day, Edmund Currir, 41 In. ... 977.00
Banjo, Mahogany, Eagle Finial, Shield, Lake Erie-Perry's Victory, Sept., 10, 1813 ..... 920.00
Banjo, Mahogany, Eagle Panel, Pink, Blue, White, Black, Gold, 31 In. 720.50
Banjo, Mahogany, Frame Grain Veneer, Weight & Pendulum, 32 In. 800.00
Banjo, Mahogany, Gilded Facade, Gold Paint, 40 1/2 In. 853.00
Banjo, Mahogany, Prince Of Wales Carved, Woman With Lyre, Signed John Anderson .. 748.00
Banjo, Mahogany, Reverse Glass Panels, Brass Works, Weight & Pendulum, 33 In. 825.00
Banjo, Mahogany, Simon Willard & Son, No. 4700, 29 1/2 In. 690.00
Banjo, Mahogany, White Enamel Dial, Ball Finial, Boston, 1810, 33 1/2 x 10 In. 1150.00
Banjo, Reverse Painted, Mahogany, Harvard Clock Co., 29 In. 805.00
Banjo, Reverse Painting, Wallace Nutting, No. 61 .... 3190.00
Banjo, Rosewood, 8-Day Time Only, Brass Frets, Metal Dial, James Crofts, 29 In. 750.00
Banjo, Willard, Simon, Mahogany Case, Reverse Painted Sunburst, 29 3/4 In. 880.00
Banjo, Willard, Simon, Mahogany, 8-Day Time Only, Brass Frets, Metal Dial, 36 In. 900.00
Banjo, Willard, Simon, Painted Dial, 8-Day Brass Movement, c.1815, 32 1/4 In. 1955.00
Becker, Gustav, Wall, 8-Day Spring Wound, Walnut Case, Brass Pendulum, 52 3/4 In. ... 605.00
Becker, Gustav, Wall, Porthole Glass Door, Brass Pendulum & 2 Weights, 46 In. 522.00
Berthoud, Mantel, Tortoiseshell, 2 Keys & Winding Key, 25 x 14 In. 5175.00
Bigelow, Kennard & Co., Carriage, Beveled Glass, Gilt Metal, Alarm, Leather Case, 6 In. . 520.00
Black Forest, Cuckoo, 3-Weight Driven Movement, 7-Day, Walnut, Germany, 1840s ... 3800.00
Blinking Eye, Banjo Player, Cast Iron, 15 1/2 In. ....1500.00 to 2800.00

Blinking Eye, Sambo, Man With Banjo, 16 In.	3500.00
Blinking Eye, Sea Captain, 16 In.	1670.00
Blinking Eye, Topsy, Woman With Tambourine, c.1880, 16 In.	4500.00
Bracket, Regency, Double Fusee Movement, Hour Strike, Repeat Lever, 1800, 14 In.	1380.00
Brass, Stylized Flowers, Foliage, Corinthian Columns, Roman Numerals, 1850, 16 In.	1265.00
Bronze, Classical Revival, Gilt, Fruit Cornucopia Border, France, 1900, 15 In.	632.00
Bronze, Onyx & Ivory, Painted Dial, Desk, c.1920	1250.00
Bundy, W.H., Time, Oak, Time Card Rack, Patent 1902	402.00
Cahoon, R.E. Jr., Regulator, Painted Dial & Case, 49 In.	2860.00
Caldwell, Garniture, Onyx, Gilt Bronze, 2-Light Electrified Candelabras, 16 In., 3 Piece	3575.00
Carriage, Brass, Beveled Edge, Enamel Dial, Marked Medaille D'Argent 1889, 9 In.	385.00
Carriage, Brass, Dial Marked J.E. Caldwell & Co., France, 4 3/4 In.	522.00
Carriage, Brass, Quarter-Hour Repeater Movement, France, 6 1/4 In.	1430.00
Carriage, Brass, Quarter-Hour Strike, Made For Shreve, Crump & Low, France, 7 In.	770.00
Carriage, Columnar Supports, Alarm Dial & Bell, Brass & Glass, France, 5 In.	402.00
Carriage, Enamel Dial, Bell-Striking Movement, Corinthian Columns, 1885, 6 7/8 In.	2990.00
Carriage, Enamel Dial, Chinese Numerals, Bamboo Columns, 1895, 6 In.	2070.00
Carriage, Enamel Dial, Gilt Bronze, Gong-Striking Movement, 1895, 6 In.	2590.00
Carriage, Enamel Dial, Platform Lever Escapement, Roman Numerals, 7 In.	4315.00
Carriage, Enamel Dial, Roman Numerals, Enamel Panels, 1890, 6 7/8 In.	2990.00
Carriage, Enamel Panels, Painted Birds Amid Boughs, France, c.1900, 2 3/4 In.	3165.00
Carriage, Enameled Bronze, France, 5 1/2 In.	115.00
Carriage, Gilt Bronze, Alarm, Limoges Enamel Mounted	7475.00
Carriage, Greenleaf & Crosby, Brass, Key, Leather Case, 4 5/8 In.	110.00
Carriage, Mother-Of-Pearl Inlay, Lacquer, Animals For Hours, Japan, 19th Century	6325.00
Carriage, Repeating, Porcelain Mounted, Gilt Bronze, Arsene Margarine, c.1880, 5 In.	3165.00
Carriage, With Alarm, Portrait Profiles Of Women, Silver Dial, Purple, Green, 4 In.	7475.00
Cartel, Louis XVI, Enamel Dial, Drapery Swags, Ormolu, 1775, 34 In.	8625.00
Cartel, Walnut, Black, Starr & Frost, Female Terms, Center Putto Mask Base, 38 In.	2875.00
Cartel, Woman On Tree Trunk, Dog, Cherubs, Floral Garland Over Pendant, 39 In.	2530.00
Cathedral, Westminster Chime, 30-Day, Chimes Quarter Hour, Wertenberg, 15 x 12 In.	595.00
Character, Green Hornet, Wall	50.00
Character, Sesame Street, Big Bird	100.00
Character, Woody Woodpecker, Wall, Display Box	695.00
Cottage, Mahogany, Open Fretwork, Box Frame, Victorian, 1887, 35 In.	1840.00
Cuckoo, Quail, 1915	1895.00
Dasson, Henry, Dial Within Foliate Scroll Cast Case, c.1886, 23 1/2 In.	8625.00
Digital, Brushed Copper, Moon Crest, Decal, Desk, 4 x 8 1/2 In.	110.00
Dugardin Lille, Empire, Bronze & Black Marble, 1850, 25 x 20 In.	2300.00
Empire, Mahogany, 8-Day Hanging, Roman Numerals, Tin Clock Face, 32 x 16 x 5 In.	460.00
Ethan Allen, Stepped Pediment, Beveled Glass Door, Pendulum, Walnut Case, 47 In.	345.00
Figural, Garfield, Plastic, Box, 1978	55.00
Gilbert, Calendar, Black & Gilt Painted Door, Allusha Maranville, 1861, 31 In.	440.00
Gilded Beech, Metal & Alabaster Temple Form, Mirrored Back, Austria, 1840, 25 In.	2300.00
Gilles Martinot, Louis XIV, Tortoiseshell & Painted, Striking Movement, 23 In.	6900.00
Gravity, 1 Hour Hand, Minutes Estimated By Distance, 1920	3500.00
Guimard, Hector, Leaves & Berries On Round Face, Hanging, Chains, 1900, 11 1/2 In.	4685.00
Gybelin, Art Deco, Marble & Steel, Swiss Movement	6500.00
Hotchkiss, Shelf, Mahogany, 8-Day Time & Strike, Acanthus Leaf Columns, Wood Dial	500.00
Howard Miller, Brass Face, Mahogany, Brass Railing Sides, 13 1/2 x 3 x 5 1/2 In.	230.00
Howard Miller, Starburst, George Nelson	375.00
Howard Miller, Sunburst, Walnut Radiating Spokes, White Metal Center, 19 In.	385.00
Ingraham, Mantle, Time & Strike, Brass Movement, Metal Face, Oak, 1880s, 14 In.	77.00
Ithaca, 8-Day Time, Double Dial, 28 1/2 x 15 1/2 In.	1230.00
Ithaca, Calendar, Farmer's, Double Dial, No. 10	850.00
Jameshon, Engraved Silvered Face, Cast Brass Detail, 17 In.	550.00
Japy Freres, Mantel, 3 Acorn Plinths, 8-Day, Time & Strike, Chimes Hour & Half, 1880	2400.00
Japy Freres, Mantel, Marble & Brass, 8-Day Time & Strike, 19 x 19 In.	1000.00
Jerome, Mantel, 30-Hour, Ogee, Reverse Painted Door, Harbor Scene, 1800s, 15 x 25 In.	325.00
Johnson, William S., Ogee, Mantel, Alarm Dial, 26 x 16 In.	165.00
Junghans, Mantel, Mahogany, 8-Day Chime, Beehive Case, Silver Dial	175.00
Kienzle, Mantel, Westminster Chime, 5 Chimes, Beveled Glass Door, Rosewood Case	600.00
Kirner, R., Wag-On-Wall, Hand Painted Numerals, Belfast, 19th Century, 13 In.	230.00

Knox, Archibald, Mantel, Tudric, Pewter, Rectangle, Latin Inscription, 1913, 8 1/4 In. . . . 2055.00
Kroebler, Shelf, Walnut, 8-Day, Brass Angel Pendulum, Brass Dial 950.00
Launay, C., Inlaid Mother-Of-Pearl, Enameled Numerals, Ebonized Case, 19 In. 920.00
LeCoultre, Atmospheric, Gilt Brass, 9 1/4 In. 220.00
LeCoultre, Mantel, Book Form 450.00
Lefebvre & Fils, Marble, Wooden Base, Key, Pendulum, Brass Trim & Works, 20 In. . . . 1045.00
Lemasson, P., Marble, 2-Tubed Mercury Pendulum, 8-Day, Open Escapement, c.1870 . . 3200.00
Lenoir, Lyre, White Marble, Bronze Ormolu, Mock Gridiron Pendulum, 30 In. 6600.00
Lewis, B.B., Calendar, Perpetual, Reverse Painted Tablet, Rosewood Case 990.00
Louis XVI, Hanging, Walnut, Stepped Bombay Form, Gilt, 39 x 12 3/4 x 6 In. 1150.00
Louis XVI, Marble Lyre Form, Gilt Bronze, Acanthus, Roman Numerals, 14 In. 1955.00
Louis XVI, Marble Temple, Gilt Bronze, Corinthian Columns, Plinth Base, 13 1/2 In. . . . 805.00
Lux, 4-String Banjo, Gilt Iron, 7 1/2 In. 175.00
Lux, Golfer 125.00
Lux, Showboat 125.00
Mantel, Alabaster, Urn Top, Ribbons & Rosettes, Bun Feet, France, 16 1/2 In. 330.00
Mantel, Black Marble, Red Marble Inlays, Enamel Dial, Victorian, 10 x 12 In. 410.00
Mantel, Brass & Glass Champleve Enamel, Mercury Filled Pendulum, 12 In. 632.00
Mantel, Bronze Dancing Scene, Figural, Roman Numerals, Metal, Marble, 22 x 24 In. . . 690.00
Mantel, Bronze, Cathedral Style, Marble Base, Russia, 23 1/2 In. 2530.00
Mantel, Bronze, Siena Marble, Rectangular Case, France, 1840 . . . . 2420.00
Mantel, Charles X, Ormolu, Orpheus, Playing The Flute, Dolphins Mask Feet, 17 In. . . . 5175.00
Mantel, Cherubs, Allegorical Female Finial, Medallion Portraits, Bronze, 22 x 17 In. 2300.00
Mantel, Cherubs, Reclining, Brass, Marble, France . . . . *Illus* 1025.00
Mantel, Dore Bronze, Seated Boy With Flowers, Inscription, 15 1/2 x 16 In. 715.00
Mantel, Empire, Ormolu, Pegasus Rearing Amidst Clouds, Bronze, 19 In. 3737.00
Mantel, Figural, Baroque, Scrollwork, Lion Heads, France, 19th Century, 19 x 20 In. . . . 575.00
Mantel, Figural, Woman Reclining, Marble, Gilt Bronze, 17 3/4 x 25 In. 3450.00
Mantel, Foliate Enameled Borders, Mercury Pendulum, Green Onyx, 1900, 11 In. 489.00
Mantel, French Gothic Revival, Bronze, Enamel Numerals, 1900, 19 In. 431.00
Mantel, French Ormolu, Boy & Dove On Naturalistic Setting, 1840-1860, 13 In. 460.00
Mantel, Fruitwood, Beveled Glass Panel, Enamel Face, Late 19th Century 978.00
Mantel, Gilt Bronze, Leaf Molded Bezel, Bell-Striking Movement, 1840, 10 In. 2415.00
Mantel, Gilt Metal, Figural, Enamel Dial, 12 3/4 x 11 In. 115.00
Mantel, Gilt Metal, Mahogany, Brass Face, c.1900, 25 x 13 x 12 1/2 In. 2530.00
Mantel, Giltwood, White Enamel Dial, Shell Crest, Allegorical Figures, 29 1/8 In. 4600.00
Mantel, Gothic Revival, Bronze, Cathedral Facade, Beast Feet, France, 23 1/2 In. 6900.00
Mantel, Greek Civilization, Black Marble Dial, Roman Numerals, 1870, 18 3/4 In. 4025.00
Mantel, Ice Skater Top, Dore Bronze, Black Marble, France, 16 1/2 In. 2200.00
Mantel, Inset Panels, Metal Case, Gold Finish, Continental 220.00
Mantel, Japy Freres, Fleur-De-Lis & Scroll Top, Dore Bronze, 17 In. 2200.00
Mantel, Kneeling Women Either Side Clock, Cupid Top, Bronze, France, 1900, 13 In. . . 1210.00
Mantel, Louis XV, Boulle, Late 19th Century, 16 In. 805.00
Mantel, Louis XV, Silver Metal, Early 20th Century, 14 1/2 In. 345.00
Mantel, Louis XVI, Ormolu, White Enamel Dial, White Marble, Toupie Feet, 17 1/2 In. . 3450.00
Mantel, Marble, Art Deco, Brass Works, Round Chrome Face, 14 x 9 In. 120.00

Clock, Mantel, Cherubs, Reclining, Brass, Marble, France

An original stained clock dial
is more valuable than a
new repainted dial.

Fakers sometimes 'marry' a
clock works and a clock case.
Examine a clock carefully to be
sure the parts are all original.

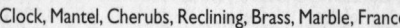

Mantel, Mosque, Domed Porcelain Top, Enamel Dial, 21 In. 4370.00
Mantel, Napoleon III, Gilt, Scrolled Foliate, Nozzle Feet, France, 1840, 14 In. 1380.00
Mantel, Neoclassical, Rosewood, Enameled Roman Numerals, Foliate Feet, 12 In. 431.00
Mantel, Onyx, Figures & Columns, 12 In. 374.00
Mantel, Papier-Mache, Polychrome & Gilt, Mother-Of-Pearl Inlay, c.1850, 17 In. 2070.00
Mantel, Pot Metal Figurine Holding Telescope, Black Marble Base, 23 x 18 In. 467.00
Mantel, Renaissance Revival, Black Marble, 1890, 14 1/2 In. 172.00
Mantel, Scroll Floral Relief Front, Hoof Feet, Dark Blue Ground, Germany, 15 1/2 In. .. 1035.00
Mantel, Scrolled Foliate Mounts, Birds, Cherubs On Sky Blue Ground, 20 In. 1380.00
Mantel, Temple Form, Mask Form Pendulum, Black Basalt & Bronze, 15 1/2 In. 575.00
Mantel, White Metal, Ormolu, Woman, Cupid, France, 19th Century, 11 x 13 In. 825.00
Morrison, W., Regulator, Wall, Mahogany Case, England, 66 1/2 In. 1955.00
Mourey, P.H., Mantel, Gilt Metal, Key & Pendulum, France, 18 1/4 In. 575.00
Muller, J., Enamel Dial, Cherubs, Mirrored, Alabaster Columns, c.1830, 24 In. 1380.00
Nast, Mantel, Charles X, Ormolu, White Enamel Dial, Rockwork Base, 1830, 9 In. 3450.00
Neoclassical, Fossilized Marble Case, Strike Movement, Russia, 1860s, 19 1/2 In. 6325.00
New Haven, Calendar, Time, Short Drop 495.00
New Haven, Calendar, Wall, Double Dial, Oak 1295.00
New Haven, Schoolhouse, Short Drop, c.1915 .... 175.00
New Haven, Shelf, Ogee, Brass Works, Reverse Design Glass With Beehive, 26 In. 100.00
Newark Clock Co., Kitchen, Ceramic, 8-Day 85.00
Oak, Castle Form, Gothic, Black Forest, Moving Carved Figure Of A Knight, 21 In. 2070.00
Pequegnat, Canadian Time, Schoolhouse, Pendulum, 1914 .... 750.00
Pratt Daniel, Jr., Shelf, Mirrored Door, Split Column, Label, 1839, 30 1/2 x 16 1/2 In. . 345.00
Purinton, William, Giltwood Mirror, 8-Day Brass Works 5800.00
Pyramid, Weights Suspended In Cabinet, Foliate Bars, Japan 4025.00
Radio, RCA Victor, AM, Levermatic, Beige, 1950s 75.00
Radio, Telechrom, Model 8H67 .... 20.00
Regulator, Brass, Glass, Mercury Pendulum, France, 10 1/2 In. 450.00
Regulator, Mahogany Veneer, Turned Columns, Composition Detail, Brass Works, 30 In. 120.00
Reliquary, Brass & Enamel, Woman Surrounded By Cherubs, 4 In. 302.00
Sessions, Bisque, Cherubs, Electric Works, Japan, 14 3/4 In. 66.00
Sessions, Kitchen, Shelf, Pressed Oak, Lion Head, Brass Works, Alarm, 22 3/4 In. 165.00
Sessions, Mantel, 8-Day, Black Iron, Brass Works, 1910 .... 150.00
Sessions, Mantel, Cathedral, Fretwork, Steeple Form, Bell Tower, 36 1/2 In. 467.00
Sessions, Regulator, Wall, Masonic Emblem On Bottom Glass 475.00
Sessions, Wall, Brass Works, Calendar, Eglomise Glass Door, Pendulum, 24 x 17 In. 110.00
Seth Thomas, Alarm, 8-Day, Reverse Painted Portrait Of Lady, 17 3/4 In. 192.00
Seth Thomas, Banjo, Images Of George Washington & Mount Vernon 425.00
Seth Thomas, Calendar, Oak Case, Ball Finial, Scrolls 1725.00
Seth Thomas, Enameled Movement, Reeded Columns, Mercury Pendulum, 11 1/2 In. .. 357.00
Seth Thomas, Hanging, Brass Works, Key & Pendulum, Paper Label, 21 1/2 In. 110.00
Seth Thomas, Mantel, Adamatine, Marbling Columns 235.00
Seth Thomas, Mantel, Beehive, Mahogany, Chime, 10 1/4 x 15 In. 154.00
Seth Thomas, Mantel, Mahogany, 8-Day, Pierced Overlay, Brass Dial 400.00
Seth Thomas, Mantel, Tambour, Mahogany Veneer Case, 8-Day, Chime, 9 1/4 x 20 In. ... 77.00
Seth Thomas, Pillar & Scroll, Wooden Works & Face, Reverse Painted, 31 In. 1265.00
Seth Thomas, Regulator, Glass, White Enamel Dial, Mercury Pendulum, 6 x 5 x 9 In. .. 220.00
Seth Thomas, Reverse Painted Design, Mahogany & Parcel Gilt Case, 28 1/2 In. 137.00
Seth Thomas, Rosewood Case, Turned Half Columns, Glass Door, 25 In. 110.00
Seth Thomas, Schoolhouse, Regulator, Wall 325.00
Seth Thomas, Shelf, Pillar & Scroll, Mahogany, Weights & Pendulum, 31 In. 825.00
Seth Thomas, Shelf, Walnut, With Key & Pendulum, 24 3/8 In. 165.00
Seth Thomas, Time & Strike, Napoleon Hat-Shaped Mahogany, 9 x 20 1/2 In. 110.00
Shelf, 8-Day Time & Strike, Mahogany Case, Bird's-Eye Maple, France, 19 x 9 In. 1435.00
Shelf, Draped Eagle Finial, Cupid, Striking, Austria, 19th Century, 17 In. 2800.00
Shelf, F.F. Bonnet, Beveled Glass Dial & Pendulum, Marble Case, 18 1/2 In. 605.00
Shelf, Federal, Metal Dial, Divided Door Case, 2 Faux Grain Columns, 25 x 15 In. 431.00
Shelf, Regency, Satinwood, Balloon, Stepped Plinth Base, 19th Century, 21 In. 2990.00
Shelf, Terry, Eli, Mahogany Veneer, Stenciled Florals, Wooden Works, 30 1/4 In. 275.00
Shelf, Terry, Samuel, Stenciled Crest, Reverse Painted Glass, 30-Hour, 28 In. 575.00
Shelf, Wm. K, Gilbert, Stepped Finials, Paned Door, Reverse Transfer, 19 1/4 In. 403.00
Shreve, Crump, Low, Mantel, Gilt Metal, Mirrored Borders, Columnar, 1920, 15 In. 1265.00

Clock, Tall Case, Bradley
Ilkiston, England, Late 18th
Century, 84 In.

Clock, Tall Case, Daniel Rose,
Walnut, 1749-1827, 8 Ft.

Clock, Tall Case, John Elliot,
Mahogany, 8-Day, 1890, 96 In.

Clock, Tall Case, Mahogany,
American, c.1800, 85 In.

Skeleton, Brass Works, Chain Driven, Marble Base, Glass Dome, 17 x 11 In. 990.00
Skeleton, Brass, 3-Train Chiming, 8 Bells, S-Scroll Plates, Block Feet, 15 1/2 In. 6900.00
Skeleton, Brass, Marble Base, England, 19th Century, 18 In. 550.00
Staton, J., Bracket, Arched Dial, Rosewood Case, Ring Handles, Ball Feet, 1845, 15 In. . . 920.00
Synchromatic, Broken Arch Pediment, Shaped Skirt, Electric, 20th Century 50.00
Tall Case, 8-Day, Date & Second Hand, Oak Case, Glasgow, Scotland, c.1812, 81 In. . . . 2200.00
Tall Case, Alex Frazer, Cross-Banded Mahogany, Mid-19th Century, 88 In. 1840.00
Tall Case, B. Johnson, Subsidiary Dial & Calendar, Striking Hour, 82 1/2 In. 7475.00
Tall Case, Benjamin Willard, Chippendale, Cherrywood, White Dial, 1800, 102 In. 7475.00
Tall Case, Bradley Ilkiston, England, Late 18th Century, 84 In. . . . .*Illus* 1870.00
Tall Case, Caleb Davis, Cherry, 8-Day Moon Phase, Applied Half Column, 97 In. 12000.00
Tall Case, Calendar, Floral Painted Scroll Board, Quarter Columns, 1790, 96 In. 6900.00
Tall Case, Charles Cooner, 8-Day Movement 7000.00
Tall Case, Cherry, Broken Arch Top, 8-Day, Painted Dial, Quarter Columns, 91 In. 1925.00
Tall Case, Cherry, Carved Apron, Arched Pediment, Splay Feet, 102 In. 2000.00
Tall Case, Chinoiserie Case, Brass Dial & Floral Spandrels, Calendar, 8-Day, 1780 . . . . 2145.00
Tall Case, Chippendale, Walnut, 30-Hour, Stylized Sunflower Rosettes, 1780, 106 In. . . . 9200.00
Tall Case, Chippendale, Walnut, Scrolled Rails, Stiles, Ogee Feet, 90 1/2 In. 2750.00
Tall Case, Colonial Clock Co., Walnut, 8-Day Movement, Westminster Chime, 82 3/4 In. 220.00
Tall Case, Country, Pine Case, Wood Works, Painted Face, Eagle, Fretwork Crest, 91 In. . 1540.00
Tall Case, Daniel Burnap, Glazed Tombstone Door, Silver Dial, 93 In. 7475.00
Tall Case, Daniel Oyster, Metal Dial, 8-Day Moon Phase, Beaded Waist Door, 95 In. . . . 6750.00
Tall Case, Daniel Rose, Walnut, 1749-1827, 8 Ft. . . . .*Illus* 8250.00
Tall Case, Edwardian, Mahogany, 8-Day, Spool Supports, Oval Panel On Base, 94 In. . . . 2250.00
Tall Case, Edwards-Ashby, 1-Day, Wooden Works, Strikes Hour & Half Hour, 1780 . . . . 6500.00
Tall Case, Ephraim Barber, Calendar, Freestanding Columns In Bonnet, Pine, 80 In. 3410.00
Tall Case, F. Herschede, Moon Dial, Brass Face, Westminster & Whittington Chimes . . . 8500.00
Tall Case, Federal, Acanthus Leaf Detail, 93 In. 75.00
Tall Case, Federal, Cherrywood, Brass Spread Eagle Finial, Roman Numerals, 91 In. 220.00
Tall Case, Federal, Mahogany, Brass Mounted Corinthian Supports, 99 In. 4600.00
Tall Case, Federal, Mahogany, Eagle Perched On Orb, 1810, 95 In. 10350.00
Tall Case, Federal, Maple Grain Paint, Flared Supports, Bracket Feet, 88 In. 10925.00
Tall Case, G. Parker, Cherry, Calendar, Tombstone Door, Iron Dial, 78 In. 9775.00
Tall Case, George III, Mahogany, Arch Door, Brass Dial, 18th Century, 88 In. 2760.00
Tall Case, George III, Mahogany, Enameled Dial, Late 18th Century, 85 In. 4313.00
Tall Case, George III, Mahogany, Enameled Dial, Roman Numerals, Bracket Feet 4600.00
Tall Case, George III, Mahogany, Oak Inlay, Painted Dial, c.1800, 94 In. 1495.00
Tall Case, George III, Mahogany, Subsidiary Dial, Plinth Base, 1800 . . . . 1610.00
Tall Case, George III, Mahogany, Swans Neck, 2 Columns, Central Door, 86 3/4 In. 2990.00
Tall Case, George III, Mahogany, Walnut Oyster, Arch Dial, 18th Century, 81 In. 2300.00
Tall Case, George III, Pine, Brass Mounted, Arched Brass Dial, Bracket Feet, 80 In. 1265.00
Tall Case, Gothic Revival, Walnut, Trefoil Crest, Walnut Clock Face, 99 In. 2300.00
Tall Case, Hepplewhite, Cherry, Alligator Finish, Ogee Feet, 91 In. 7150.00
Tall Case, Isaac Goddard, Rope Twist Columns, Brass Dial, Bracket Feet, 1690, 82 In. . . 7250.00

Tall Case, J. Stein, Broken Swan's Neck Pediment, Flowers, Pheasant, 1810s, 112 In. ... 9200.00
Tall Case, John Dalrymple, Dublin, 8-Day Movement, Brass Dial, c.1770, 92 In. 8500.00
Tall Case, John Elliot, Mahogany, 8-Day, 1890, 96 In. ....*Illus* 8800.00
Tall Case, John Fordham, Oak, Brass Mount, 8-Day, 2-Train Movement, 1790, 81 In. ... 5750.00
Tall Case, John Osgood, Cornice Over Glazed Door, Tombstone Opening, 1780s, 82 In. . 7475.00
Tall Case, Mahogany, American, c.1800, 85 In. ....*Illus* 3960.00
Tall Case, Mahogany, Beveled Glass Panel, Silvered Dial, Boston, 95 In. 4888.00
Tall Case, Mahogany, Inlay Chiming Automaton, Victorian, 19th Century, 95 In. 4600.00
Tall Case, Mahogany, Satinwood, Roman Numerals, England, 93 x 9 In. 3450.00
Tall Case, Martin Boswell, Calendar, Brass Works, Painted Metal Face, 81 1/2 In. 2145.00
Tall Case, Moon Phase Dial, Ornate Brass Hinges, Pennsylvania 5720.00
Tall Case, Musical Movement, Marquetry, 89 In. 8250.00
Tall Case, Oak, Rope Twist Columns, Silvered Face, Weights & Pendulum, 91 1/2 In. ... 385.00
Tall Case, Pennsylvania Hepplewhite, Turned Finials, Brass Works, Cherry, 91 1/2 In. ... 2310.00
Tall Case, Pine, Brass, Fluted Columns, Painted Face, Second Hand, Calendar, 87 In. .. 990.00
Tall Case, Pine, Scrolled Apron, Dovetailed Bonnet, Wooden Face, Cutout Feet, 87 In. .. 1540.00
Tall Case, Queen Anne, Walnut, 3-Lobed Volute Shells, Brass Dial, 1765, 83 In. 8050.00
Tall Case, Queen Anne, Walnut, 8-Day, Applied Molded Panel, Bulbous Feet, 87 In. ... 3250.00
Tall Case, Regency, Mahogany, 8-Day Moon Phase, Bracket Feet, 93 In. 2750.00
Tall Case, Regency, Mahogany, 8-Day Moon Phase, Brass Dial, 95 In. 2750.00
Tall Case, Regency, Mahogany, 8-Day, Conch Shell Inlay, Brass Dial, 88 In. 2250.00
Tall Case, Regency, Mahogany, 8-Day, Metal Dial, 3 Brass Finials, 1790s 4250.00
Tall Case, Riley Whiting, Painted, Brown Sponging, Wooden Works, 1830s, 85 In. 7200.00
Tall Case, Rolling Moon Dial, Mahogany, c.1780 .... 495.00
Tall Case, Scenic Arch, Tiger Maple, 8-Day, Sheraton Feet, 96 In. 7250.00
Tall Case, Shop Of The Crafters, Oak, Slag Glass Lamp Shade, Pink, Green, 24 x 77 In. . 1540.00
Tall Case, Silas Hoadley, 3 Finials, Painted Wood Dial, Faux Winding Holes 4200.00
Tall Case, Silas Hoadley, Pierced Fretwork Hood, Brass Urn Finials, c.1825, 91 In. 2530.00
Tall Case, Thomas Davies, George III, Mahogany, c.1780, 95 In. 4140.00
Tall Case, Tubular, Oak, Chime, Royal Crest, Anchor Motifs, 118 In. 18400.00
Tall Case, W.A. Williams, Mahogany, Glazed Door, Iron Moon Phase Dial, 1825, 100 In. 5175.00
Tall Case, Walnut, Fluted Quarter Columns, Brass Face, Ogee Feet, 86 3/4 In. 6875.00
Tall Case, Willard, Hepplewhite, Mahogany, Brass Fretwork Bonnet, Pendulum, 92 In. .. 16500.00
Tall Case, William Claggett, Thumbmolded Door, Brass Dial, 1740, 89 In. 19550.00
Terry, Eli, Pillar & Scroll, Painted Wooden Dial, Eglomise Tablet, 30 1/2 In. 977.00
Terry, Eli, Pillar & Scroll, Shelf, Brass Finials, Eglomise Panel, Mahogany 2200.00
Terry, Eli, Shelf, Pillar & Scroll, Mahogany Veneer, Reverse Painting, Pendulum, 31 In. . 1605.00
Terry, Shelf, Pillar & Scroll, Mahogany, 30-Hour Time & Strike, Brass Finials 1540.00
Tiffany clocks are listed in the Tiffany category.
Tortoise Shell & Brass Floral Inlay, Bronze Figures, France, 1890s, 41 1/4 In. 4400.00
Ulysse Nardin, Rose Quartz, Desk, c.1920 .... 1750.00
Uropa, Figural, World Map, Clock Inside, 7 Jewel, Hinged Lid For Winding 85.00
Vacheron & Constantin, 8-Day Wind, Sterling, Enamel & Bronze, Desk, c.1920 .... 3850.00
Vulliamy, Regulator, Mahogany, Seconds Ring, Deadbeat Escape Wheel 9200.00
Wag-On-Wall, Landscape Scene, Decoupage Village, 19th Century, 16 1/4 In. 287.00
Wag-On-Wall, Molded Brass Cherubs, Wheat Sheath, Roman Numerals, France, 57 In. ... 920.00
Wall, Blue Bird, Carved Wood Casing, Key Wound, American, Box, 3 1/2 x 4 x 2 In. 93.00
Wall, Mahogany Veneer, Composition Eagle Finial, Brass Works & Pendulum, 38 In. ... 302.00
Wall, Renaissance Revival, Oak, Round Dial, Roman Numerals, 36 x 16 x 6 In. 403.00
Wall, Renaissance Revival, Walnut, Scroll, Foliate, Roman Numerals, 41 x 20 In. 460.00
Walnut, Brass Works, Desk, 1950s, 5 1/2 In. 225.00
Wanamaker, John, Carriage, Brass, Clear Beveled Glass, Key, 5 In. 135.00
Waterbury, Calendar, Time, Short Drop 495.00
Waterbury, Figural, Dog, 1891, 5 In. 2115.00
Waterbury, Pinwheel Jeweler's Regulator, Oak 6000.00
Waterfall, Empire, Cut Crystal Basin For Fish, Gilt & Silvered Bronze, c.1840 .... 5950.00
Weinberg, Frederick, Bent Iron, Design Of Dancing Male & Female, c.1950, 27 In. 1100.00
Welch, Spring, Shelf, Double Dial Calendar, Month, Date, Day, Hour & Minute, 20 In. .. 550.00
Westclock, Bakelite, Large Stopwatch, Windup Top, 2 2/3 In. 125.00
Willard, Banjo, Eglomise Throat Glass, Mt. Vernon, 1840s, 39 In. 1380.00
Willard, Banjo, Reverse Painted Naval Scene On Door, Mahogany, c.1820, 40 1/2 In. 4312.00
Willard, Banjo, Reverse Painted Scenes, No. 1 .... 2750.00
Willard, Patent, Tablet With Naval Battle, Involving Constitution & Guerriere 2420.00

Willard, Simon, Painted Tablet, Wooden Inlay Case 2420.00
Winterholder & Hoffmeyer, Mantel, Oak, Quarter-Striking, Foliate Mounts, 16 In. ... 460.00

CLOISONNE enamel was developed during the tenth century. A glass enamel was applied between small ribbons of metal on a metal base. Most cloisonne is Chinese or Japanese. Pieces marked *China* are twentieth-century examples.

Box, Bird, Flowering Tree Design, Early 20th Century, 6 In. 275.00
Box, Cover, Round, 1920 .... 55.00
Box, Enameled Cover, Allover Florals, 4 x 1 In. 88.00
Box, Fan Form, Black Floral Ground, Round, Meiji Period, 2 1/2 In. 120.00
Box, Floral Design, Black, Aventurine Ground, Hexagonal, Enamel, 3 In. 145.00
Box, Thousand Flowers Pattern, Aventurine Ground, Rectangular, 5 In. 690.00
Candleholder, Panels Of Red & White Blossoms On Standard, 12 In., Pair 65.00
Charger, Red Crown Cranes, Brass, Base, Teakwood Stand, 26 In. 825.00
Charger, Types Of Chrysanthemums, Turquoise Ground, Brocade Rim, 14 1/2 In. ... 200.00
Charger, White Floral Design Center, Gilt Bronze, 16 In. 880.00
Clock, Mercury Pendulum, Cloisonne Design, Round, Gilt Metal, 15 In. 1100.00
Compote, Pink Floral Design, Birds, Butterflies, Apple Green, 4 In. 17.00
Ewer, Dragon Spout, Heads, Lappet Border, 19th Century, 10 1/2 In. 460.00
Figurine, Owl, Teakwood Stand, 6 In. 69.00
Incense Burner, Stork, 15 In., Pair 350.00
Jar, 1,000 Flowers, Black Ground, Globular, 6 In. 660.00
Jar, Cover, Floral Design, Spiral Stripes, 4 3/4 In. 115.00
Jar, Cover, Flowers & Butterflies, Blue Ground, 3 7/8 In. 50.00
Jardiniere, Foliage, Multicolored, Blue Ground, 10 x 11 1/2 In. 230.00
Lamp Base, Vase Form, Bronze, Multicolored Foliage, Mask Handles, 18 In., Pair 1840.00
Planter, Multicolored Foliage, Trelliswork, Bronze, France, 1880, 15 x 18 In. 4600.00
Plate, Bird, Flower & Fruit Design, 9 1/2 In. 120.00
Plate, Birds & Flowers, Gray Ground, Japan, 19th Century, 12 In. 115.00
Screen, 4-Panel, Bird & Flower Design, Red Foil Ground, 7 1/4 x 6 1/2 In. 605.00
Snuff Bottle, 2 Brown Dragons, Spade Shape, Yellow Ground, Enamel Stopper 120.00
Snuff Bottle, Saucer, Floral, Butterfly Design, White Ground, Coral Stopper, 2 In. ... 495.00
Teapot, Cherry Blossoms, White Ground, Brass, Japan, 3 In. 77.00
Tray, Center Medallion Of Morning Glories, Butterflies, Brocade Rim, 9 1/4 In. .. 690.00
Tray, Floral Design, Cloud Scroll Ground, Rectangular, China, 4 x 3 1/4 In. 70.00
Urn, Birds, Butterflies, Large Dragon Coiling Around Urn, Rust, Brown, 4 Scroll Feet ... 667.00
Urn, Dogwood Blossom & Branch, Red Ground, 19 1/2 In. 550.00
Vase, 3 Carp, Swimming, Gold, Gray, Silver Rim, Light Celadon Ground, 6 In. 2530.00
Vase, 3 Cranes, Black Ground, Meiji Period, 9 5/8 In. 1000.00
Vase, 4 Shields, Phoenix Birds, Dragon, Bands, Bulbous, Long Narrow Neck, 10 In. 385.00
Vase, Allover Design, Dark Ground, 24 1/2 In. 310.00
Vase, Allover Floral Design, Green, 16 In. 110.00
Vase, Alternate Dragons & Phoenix, Brocade Panels, Silver Wire, 6 1/2 In. 170.00
Vase, Asian Bird In Cherry Tree, Turquoise Ground, 6 In. 48.00
Vase, Blue To Pale Blue On Silver Foil, Geisha Girl, Fan & Flowers, Signed, 3 x 2 In. 330.00
Vase, Butterflies, Pink Flowers, Lacy Green Foliage, Dark Green Ground, 5 x 2 In. 125.00
Vase, Colorful Geisha Girl With Fan & Flowers, Sky Blue, Pale Blue, 3 1/2 x 2 In. 363.00
Vase, Dragon & Bird Design, 9 3/4 In., Pair 230.00
Vase, Dragon & Phoenix Bird In Panels, 19th Century, 10 1/2 In. 450.00
Vase, Dragons, Phoenix Art Deco, Blue Ground, Japan, 23 1/2 In. 925.00
Vase, Floral Design, Green Ground, Mid-19th Century, 9 In. 132.00
Vase, Floral, Gilt Bronze Rim & Base, Black Ground, 12 1/2 In. 90.00
Vase, Flowering Peonies Design, Yellow Ground, 20th Century, 9 1/2 In. 374.00
Vase, Guardian Lion Cartouches, Blue Ground, Rectangular, 10 1/2 In. 330.00
Vase, Intricate Floral Design, Birds & Butterflies, Blue Ground, 12 1/2 In. 159.00
Vase, Iris, Yellow Ground, Wireless, Silver Rim & Base Ring, Japan, 7 1/2 In. 90.00
Vase, Mount Fuji Scene, Pine Tree, 6 In. 385.00
Vase, Oriental Birds & Dragon Scene, Black, Rust, Late 19th Century, 8 In. 286.00
Vase, Pair Of Crows On Branch Of Persimmons, Brocade Borders, 10 In. 1495.00
Vase, Phoenix Birds, Dragons, 4 Shields, Apricot Band, Green, Gold, 10 In. 424.00
Vase, Phoenix, Dragon Lappets, Brown Ground, 9 1/2 In. 220.00
Vase, Pink Ground, Late 19th Century, 12 In. 303.00

Vase, Raised Bird Cages, Plum Tree, Pear Shape, 6 1/8 In., Pair 2090.00
Vase, Rust Band, Small Flowers, Bird In Flight, 8 1/2 In. 225.00
Vase, Stylized Lotus & Bat Design, Totai Shippo, Drilled For Lamp, 15 5/8 In. 410.00

LOTHING of all types is listed in this category. Dresses, hats, shoes,
nderwear, and more are found here. Other textiles are to be found in
he Coverlet, Movie, Quilt, Textile, and World War I and II categories.

Apron, Poodle, Uncut, 1950 .... 28.00
Bandana, Casey Tibbs, Blue, White, Rodeo Scenes, Lee Riders 138.00
Bathing Suit, Jantzen, Wool 36.00
Bathrobe, Beacon, Label 125.00
Belt, Carnelian, Leather, Brass, 56 x 2 3/4 In. 198.00
Belt, Hand Tooled, Studs, Rhinestones, Brass Buckle, Floral & Horseshoe Design 102.00
Belt, Red, White, Blue, Stretch Fabric, Pair Doves On Metal Buckle, Peter Max, 1970 ... 140.00
Belt, Sterling Silver, Open Mesh, Scalloped Floral & Leaf Design Buckle, c.1905 ...... 500.00
Belt, Tooled Leather, Cowhide, Rhinestones, Studs, Hickock, Size 30, Tag, Paper Box ... 137.00
Belt, Woman's, Leopard Fur, Size 26 .... 15.00
Belt Buckle, Silver, Longhorn Cattle Head, Mexico, 2 3/4 In. 40.00
Belt Buckle, Sterling Silver, Western Style, Hand Tooled Designs, Mexico, 1 3/4 In. 34.00
Blouse, Crocheted, Victorian, Ireland 165.00
Blouse, Gibson Girl, All Lace 55.00
Bonnet, Lace Rosettes, Beige Silk, White Lace, 19th Century 175.00
Bonnet, Quilted Silk, Green, Pale Pink Lining, American, 19th Century 145.00
Bonnet, Quilted Silk, Green, Pale Pink Lining, c.1790 .... 275.00
Bonnet, Woven Poplar, Green Gauze Trim 137.00
Boots, Cowboy, Black Leather, Applied Red & White Leather, Stitching, Code West 37.00
Boots, Cowboy, Black Leather, Scrollwork On Sides, Redwing Co., Size 10 1/2 D 52.00
Boots, Cowboy, Brown Leather, Stitched Design, Frye, 2-In. Heels, Size 8 1/2 D 23.00
Boots, Cowboy, Texas Ranger, Black Leather, White, Tex Tan Of Yoakam, Box, 1950s .. 95.00
Boots, Go-Go, Faux White Leather, Zipper Sides, Eskipets By Durham, Italy 80.00
Boots, Man's, High Top, Leather, Civil War 260.00
Boots, Ostrich Skin, Russet Brown, Pulls, Size 8 1/2 D 46.00
Breeches, Brown Velvet, Brass Buttons, Buckskin Pockets, 18th Century, Youth 1150.00
Cap, Bus Line, Interstate Motor Lines, Gray Twill, Black Patent Leather Visor 375.00
Cap, Night, Lace, Ribbons, Mercury Glass Pendants & Balls 75.00
Cape, Nurse's, Long, 1920s 50.00
Chaps, Cowboy's, Winter Black Woolies, 1920 .... 2150.00
Coat, Black Beaver, Long, Size 12-14 .... 45.00
Coat, Evening, Vinyl, White Knit Lining, White Mink Trim, Gres Label, 1960s 290.00
Coat, Factory Shop, Chevrolet-General Motors, White Herringbone Twill, Lee, 1950s ... 127.00
Coat, Mink, Natural Lunarine, With Russian Sable Collar, Robert Sidney, N.Y. 1559.00
Coat, Suede, Fringed, 1960s 50.00
Coat, Summer, Child's, Victorian 50.00
Coat, Trench, Man's, Wool, Large 35.00
Coat, Woman's, Leopard, Stroller Length, Koseff Johannesburg, 1955 .... 330.00
Coat, Woman's, Mouton, Lamb Fur, Black, Striped Satin Lining, Fair Labor Label, 1950 . 225.00
Collar, Different Raised Flower Designs, Crocheted, Irish 65.00
Costume, Vaudeville, Wool, Houndstooth Vest, Pants, 2 Black Frock Coats, 1903 ...... 25.00
Coveralls, Big Mac, Sanforized, Gray, Cotton, 6 Pockets, JC Penney, Size 38 .... 29.00
Coveralls, Dickies, Blue Denim, Embroidered, Stieben Service, Zipper Front, Size 42 ... 34.00
Coveralls, Sage Green, Cotton, Zipper Front, Snaps, Sanforized, Lee, Size 38 Long 92.00
Dress, Black Silk Taffeta, Beaded Strip Front, Back, Czechoslovakia, 1880, Size 12 ..... 140.00
Dress, Black Wool, Long Sleeves, Full Skirt, Anne Fogarty, 1950s 425.00
Dress, Christening, Built-In Petticoat, England, Early 20th Century, 38 In. 345.00
Dress, Cocktail, Black Lace Over Nude Silk Bodice, By Mainbocher, 1950s, Size 12 .... 385.00
Dress, Evening, Black Chiffon, Scalloped Tucks, Train, Jean Desses, 1954 .... 8625.00
Dress, Evening, Russet Changeante Taffeta, Givenchy, 1950s 4140.00
Dress, Evening, Wound Grosgrain Ribbon At Bodice, Chanel, 1930s 5750.00
Dress, Flapper, Beaded, Top, Turquoise, Pink, Gold Thread, Art Deco, Size 8-10 .... 403.00
Dress, Full-Length, Black Silk Taffeta, Crimped Waist, Beaded Strips, c.1890, Size 10 ... 250.00
Dress, Hawaiian, Deep Blue Cotton, Tiki Flower Pattern, Size Small, 1960s 65.00
Dress, Jeweled Suede, Fringe Hem, Native American Style, Yves Saint Laurent, 1960s .. 4025.00
Dress, Wedding, Chantilly Lace, 1948 .... 700.00

Dressing Gown, Copper Silk Trim, Black Net Ruffle, Worth, 1890s 3450.00
Dungarees, Tuff-Duck, Brown Denim, Zipper, Fly, Tool Loops, Paper Tags, Lee 58.00
Gloves, Beaded Rose, Kidskin, Opera Length, Paris 35.00
Gloves, White Kidskin, Opera Length 35.00
Gloves, White Leather, Mother-Of-Pearl Buttons, Victorian, 22 In. 23.00
Gloves, Woman's, Black Leather, Black Beads, Opera Length, 5th Ave., New York 35.00
Gloves, Woman's, White Soft Kid, Elbow Length, Small 12.00
Handkerchief, Fairmount Park Centennial, Brown Transfer, Red Border 125.00
Handkerchief, Scarlett, Gone With The Wind 100.00
Handkerchief, Upper & Lowercase Alphabet, Cotton, 11 1/4 x 10 7/8 In. 517.00
Hat, Beaver, Stetson, Light Gray, Box, 7 1/8 In. 165.00
Hat, Boater, Black Woven Band, Leather Sweatband, Dobbs 5th Ave., Italy, 1960s 57.00
Hat, Bowler, Stetson, Box, 7 1/8 Size 50.00
Hat, Child's, Motorcycle Style, I Pledge Safety, Green, Vinyl Visor, 1950s, Small 33.00
Hat, Cowboy, Felt, Texas Centennial, 1936 . . . . 550.00
Hat, Flowers At Band, Black Velvet, 1910 . . . . 198.00
Hat, Lace, Wide Brim, 1914 . . . . 175.00
Hat, Man's, Felt, Beaver 10.00
Hat, Toque, Satin, Colorful Feathers, 1915 . . . . 70.00
Jacket, Biker's, Black Leather, Zipper Front, Waist Belt, Quilted, Schott Brothers 330.00
Jacket, Bustle, Brown Plush, Large Ball Fringe, Victorian 65.00
Jacket, Campus, Dark Blue, Blue & Yellow Striped Collar, Bakelite Buttons, 1942 . . . . . 65.00
Jacket, Car Club, Majestics, So. Cal., Blue, Wool, Mother-Of-Pearl Buttons, Size 46 . . . . 90.00
Jacket, Child's, 7th Cavalry Insignia, Flags, Red Rayon, Korea, Souvenir, 1972-1973 . . . 52.00
Jacket, Delivery Driver, Falstaff Beer, Black Wool, Ike Style, 1940-1950, Small 34.00
Jacket, Denim, Copper Bull's Head Snaps, 2 Pockets, Wrangler Style 141.00
Jacket, Drizzler, Rain Repellent, Zipper Front, Tan, 2 Pockets, MacGregor, Size 44 . . . . . 41.00
Jacket, Farm Coat, Blue Denim, Red Quilted Lining, Big Mac, JC Penney, 1950s 29.00
Jacket, Flight, Brown, Child's, Vinyl, Plush Collar, Knit Trim, Patches, Zipper, Size 6 . . . 29.00
Jacket, Greyhound Bus Driver, Gray Wool, Blue Satin Lining, Zipper Front 41.00
Jacket, Jean, Big E Second Edition, Silver Buttons, Levi, 1950s, Size 34-36 . . . . 1092.00
Jacket, Jean, Blue Bell, Copper Buttons, 4 Pockets, Maverick, Size 40 . . . . 113.00
Jacket, Jean, Blue Denim, 4 Pockets, Copper Snap Buttons, Blanket Lining, Wrangler . . . 58.00
Jacket, Jean, Dungaree, Work Style, 2 Pockets, 1920s, Medium Size 126.00
Jacket, Jean, Indigo, Big E, Pocket, Pleated Button Front, Copper Riveted Belt, Levi 1590.00
Jacket, Jean, Light Tan, Snap Front, 2 Pockets, Levi, Size 40 . . . . 24.00
Jacket, Leather, A-2 Style, Brown, Zipper, 2 Pockets, Knit Cuffs, Red Quilted Lining . . . 47.00
Jacket, Leather, Horsehide, Brown, Green Lining, Zipper, 2 Slash Pockets, Size 40 . . . . . 109.00
Jacket, MGM Grand Hotel Grand Opening, Reversible, In Original Bag, Size M 79.00
Jacket, Police Uniform, Short, Ike Style, Brown Wool, Dacron, Polyester, Size 42 . . . . . . 24.00
Jacket, Runner's, Warm-Up, Nike Logo, White, Purple, Green, Black, Nylon, Large 83.00
Jacket, Service Station Attendant, Shell, Brown, Red Quilted Lining, Medium 62.00
Jacket, Snap Front, White, Blue Pinstripes, Blue Sleeves, Slash Pockets, Nike, Taiwan . . 113.00
Jacket, Suede, Tan, Button Front, Chest Pockets, Blue Lining, Tag, Californian, Size 40 . 37.00
Jacket, Woman's, Biker Style, Leather, Black Horsehide, Zipper Front, Quilted Lining . . 75.00
Jeans, 101-Z, Indigo, Zipper Fly, Selvedge, Lee Riders, 1960s, Size 33 x 30 In. 230.00
Jeans, 200-Z, Indigo, Zipper Fly, Unused, Paper Tags, Lee Riders, 1960s, 33 x 29 In. . . . 345.00
Jeans, 501, Akamimi, Red Levi Tab, Small E, Copper Rivets, Levi, 30 x 22 In. 130.00
Jeans, Denim, Bell Bottom, Blue, Zipper Fly, Paper Tags, Levi, Size 36 x 34 In. 24.00
Jeans, Denim, Blue, Button Fly, Unhemmed, 34-In. Waist 90.00
Jeans, Woman's, Flared Leg, 1960s, Size 12 . . . . 180.00
Jersey, Orange, Short Sleeve, Silkscreen, Harley-Davidson Logo, Champion, Large 25.00
Kimono, Checkerboard Design, Purple Ground, Silk 110.00
Lab Coat, Detroit Overall Co., Gray Herringbone, Blue Trim, 1950s, Size 36 . . . . 25.00
Mittens, Red Ryder, 6 Uncut Trading Cards, 1952 . . . . 95.00
Nightgown, Girl's, Brown Calico, c.1850 . . . . 75.00
Obi, Allover Flowers & Floral Medallions, Frame, Japan, 60 x 40 In. 85.00
Obi, Embroidered, Floral Design, Beige Ground, Silk 198.00
Overalls, Craftsman's, White, Cotton, Reinforced Double Knee, Paper Labels, Lee 72.00
Pajamas Set, Lounging, Satin, Aqua, Slippers In Satin Covered Box 35.00
Pants, Flare Leg, Corduroy, Big E, Tapestry Pattern, Brown, Gold, Blue, White, Levi . . . 25.00
Pants, Khaki, Army, Twill, Sanforized, Paper Tags, Size 33 x 30 In. 35.00
Peignoir, Ecru Lace, Satin Lining, 1920 . . . . 85.00

Petticoat, Girl's, Linsey-Woolsey, Dark Blue & Pumpkin, 18th Century, Small 350.00
Petticoat, Quilted, Yellow, Rose Lining, Early 19th Century 295.00
Pocket, Canvaswork, Blue, Pink, Red, Green, Linen Ground, Samson, 1773, 5 x 9 In. ... 4312.00
Pocket, Crewelwork, Green, Red, Blue, Yellow, Pink, Ocher, Linen Ground, 15 x 10 In. . 1495.00
Robe, Bishop's, Embroidered, Floral Design, Metallic Threads, France, 18th Century 385.00
Robe, Emperor In Waiting, Apricot Ground, Embroidered 8625.00
Robe, Hand Embroidered Repeating Butterflies, Red Ground, Silk, c.1880 .... 300.00
Robe, Satin, Embroidered Dragon Back, Black & Blue, 1920s, 56 x 38 In. 250.00
Romper Suit, Toddler, Blue, Cotton, Sanforized, Short Sleeves 23.00
Scarf, Abstract Design, Silk Twill, Emilio Pucci 200.00
Scarf, Bicycle Designs, Figures In Victorian Dress, Silk Twill, Hermes, Box 258.00
Scarf, Cowboy, Yellow, Blue, Purple, Bronco Riding, Bull Roping Designs, 1950s, 27 In. 25.00
Scarf, Paisley, Black, Pale Beige, Signed, Vera, 31 In. 35.00
Scarf, Rodeo, Bucking Bronco, Cowboy & Steer, White, Purple, 1920s, 28 x 28 In. 45.00
Scarf, Silk Twill, Abstract Design, Yellow, Pinks, Cream Ground, Emilio Pucci, 1960 ... 201.00
Scarf, Silk Twill, Figures, In Victorian Dress On Bicycles, Red Border, Hermes 259.00
Scarf, Silk, White, Black Border, Astrological Design, Earth Center, Peter Max, 1970s ... 95.00
Shawl, Paisley, Black Star Medallion, Scrolled Floral, Red, Gold, 134 x 60 In. 862.00
Shawl, Paisley, Black, Border, Fringe Damage, Centennial, Philadelphia, 30 x 120 In. ... 95.00
Shawl, Paisley, Red Field, Small Black Center, 19th Century, 61 x 120 In. 143.00
Shawl, Paisley, Victorian, 62 x 120 In. ....130.00 to 154.00
Shirt, Big E, Western Style, Blue & Tan Checks, Long Sleeves, Levi, 1970s 37.00
Shirt, Bowling, Black, White Collar, King Louie 52.00
Shirt, Bowling, Polyester, Blue, Ribbed, Short Sleeves, Zipper Top, King Louie, 1970s .. 20.00
Shirt, Bowling, Rayon, White, Green Collar, Trim, Broadway No. 2, Pins Logo, Dunhill . 52.00
Shirt, Bowling, Short Sleeves, Light Green, Dark Green Collar, Hilton, Large 29.00
Shirt, Bowling, Tan, Brown, Pocket, Radio Cab Co., Lord Penguin, Munsingwear, 1950s 34.00
Shirt, Bowling, Weber's, Yellow, Patch Pockets, UAW-CIO Local 887, 1950s 70.00
Shirt, Bowling, White, Short Sleeves, Omark Sales & Service Logo, Angeltown 34.00
Shirt, Child's, E.T., Yellow, Silkscreen, Screen Stars, In Sealed Original Bag, Size 14-16 . 29.00
Shirt, Hawaiian, Aloha, Blue, Coins, Stamps, Island Scenes, Coconut Shell Buttons 40.00
Shirt, Hawaiian, Aloha, Floral Designs, Sea Green, Olive, Coral, Cotton, Wood Buttons . 40.00
Shirt, Hawaiian, Aloha, Palm Tree, Beach Scene, Hand Screened, Size L 89.00
Shirt, Hawaiian, Orchid Design, White, Red, Pink, Cotton, King Kalakaua, Size M 45.00
Shirt, Hawaiian, Red, Tropical Flowers, Bamboo Buttons, 2 Pockets, Pali, 1940-1950 ... 157.00
Shirt, Man's, Homespun Linen, 3 Piece 690.00
Shirt, U.S.N., Blue, Cotton, Long Sleeves, 2 Pockets, World War II, Size 15 .... 126.00
Shirt, Uniform, Employee's, Jax Roller Rink, Jax, Fla., Black, Long Sleeves, 1940s 75.00
Shirt, Western, Black, Snap Buttons, Floral Pattern Yoke, Rockmount Ranch Wear 31.00
Shirt, Wool, Long Sleeves, Red, Blue & Green Plaid, 1 Pocket, Pendleton 24.00
Shirt, Wool, MacDuff Tartan, Red, Green, Blue, Black, Patch Pocket, Pendleton, Large .. 30.00
Shirt, Wool, Ruthven Tartan, Pendleton, Large 32.00
Shirt, Work Uniform, White, 2 Red & Blue Vertical Stripes On Front, 1970s 24.00
Shirt, Work, Khaki, Twill, Long Sleeves, 2 Pockets, Sanforized, Gold Star, Size 14 1/2 .. 41.00
Shoes, Athletic, O.J. Simpson Juicemobiles, White, Orange Cleats, New In Box, Size 5 .. 46.00
Shoes, Baby's, High Top, Pink, Ruching 100.00
Shoes, Baby's, Sport, Oxford Style, White Nylon, Gray Suede Trim, 1982, Size 3 .... 56.00
Shoes, High Heels, Ankle Straps, Rhinestones, Yves St. Laurent, 1970, Size 6 1/2 ...... 125.00
Shoes, Jogging, Men's, Blue, White, Nylon, Brushed Leather, Rubber Soles, Nike, 1985 . 46.00
Shoes, Low Top, Olive Green, Black, Leather, Rubber Sole, Nike, 1990, Size 11 .... 26.00
Shoes, Roadracer, Blue, Yellow, Unused, Nike, Size 6 .... 104.00
Shoes, Running, Dualist, Nylon, Leather, Nylon, Pink Swoosh, Nike, 1966, Size 9 ...... 63.00
Shoes, Tennis, Woman's, White, Gray, Blue, Leather, Rubber Soles, Adidas, 1970s 37.00
Shoes, White, Blue, Leather, Rubber Sole, Nike, 1982, Size 7 .... 98.00
Shoes, Woman's, High Top, Walkover Custom Made, Tan Leather, 9 1/2 In. High 110.00
Slip, Edwardian, Crocheted, Hand Made Eyelet Lace, Rows Of Tucks 45.00
Slippers, Baby's, Crocheted, 1930s 15.00
Spats, Brown Felt, With Buttonhook, Store Box 20.00
Stockings, Knitted By Wife Of Captain John Pitkin, Early 19th Century 135.00
Stole, Black Persian Lamb, Athens, Greece, 1960 .... 50.00
Stole, Mink, Evans, Paris, Chicago, New York 35.00
Suit, Woman's, Shantung, Navy Blue, Silk Flowers, Balenciaga Label, 1940, Size 8 ..... 3100.00
Sweater, Cardigan, Athletic Club, Black, Orange Trim, 2 Patch Pockets, 1940-1950 .... 59.00

Sweater, Letter, Football, Black, Orange Stripes, Button Front, Slash Pockets, 1950s	90.00
Sweater, Light Brown Wool, Wooden Buttons, Pendleton, Size XL	31.00
Sweater, Picture, Knit, Pheasant In Flight, Red Hunting Dogs, Cream Ground, 1950s ...	220.00
Sweater, Zipper Front, Wool, Geometric Pattern, Red, White, Gray, Black, 1950s	26.00
Sweatshirt, Cambridge Academy, Gray, Cotton, Ted Williams, Sears, Roebuck & Co. ...	56.00
Sweatshirt, Connecticut College, Logo, Champion Knitwear Co. Inc., 1950-1960	152.00
Sweatshirt, Hooded, U.S. Naval Academy, Gray, Pouch Pocket, Champion	34.00
Sweatshirt, Red, Gray & White Horizontal Stripes, Crocodile Logo, Izod Lacoste	30.00
Sweatshirt, Snoopy, Joe Cool, Leaning Against Lockers, Dark Maroon, Medium	55.00
Top Hat, Beaver Felt, Turned-Up Brim, Gold Bullion Star Cockade, Ostrich Feather	750.00
Top Hat, Silk, Collapsible	45.00
Top Hat, Stovepipe, Beaver, Name Inside, Civil War	245.00
Trousers, Khaki, Military, Cotton, Button Fly, 1951, Size 36 x 31 In.	46.00
Uniform, Grace Hill's Motor Maids From Indiana, Shirt, Tie, Pants, 1950s	160.00
Uniform, Police, Wool Gabardine, Navy Blue, Metal Buttons, Hamburg, Germany	20.00
Vest, Boy's, Wool, c.1890	75.00
Vest, Leather, Brown, Orange Lining, Button Front, 2 Pockets, Tony Lama, Size 42	24.00
Windbreaker, Pullover, Zipper Neck, Pouch Pocket, Gray, Blue, Red, Nike, Large	68.00

CLUTHRA glass is a two-layered glass with small air pockets that form white spots. The Steuben Glass Works of Corning, New York, made it in 1920. Kimball Glass Company of Vineland, New Jersey, made Cluthra from about 1925. Victor Durand signed some pieces with his name. Related items are listed in the Steuben category.

Dish, Heart Shape, Gilt, Copper, Victorian, 6 x 4 3/4 In.	45.00
Urn, Allover Bubbles, White, Signed, 8 1/2 x 7 1/2 In.	700.00
Vase, Allover Deep Green, Applied Clear Base, Signed, Steuben, 11 x 6 1/2 In.	1200.00
Vase, Black, White, 6 3/4 In.	175.00
Vase, Cone Pulled To Tall Neck, Green, C. Dresser, Couper, 1890s, 12 1/2 In.	6560.00
Vase, Deep Black, White, Flared Rim, Steuben, 6 1/2 x 7 In.	600.00
Vase, Deep Pink, White, Applied Crystal Foot, Signed, Steuben, 11 3/4 In.	1150.00
Vase, Globular Base, Tall Waisted Neck, C. Dresser, Couper, 1890s, 19 3/8 In.	9000.00
Vase, Green, White, Applied Handles, Steuben, 9 3/4 x 7 1/2 In.	1600.00
Vase, Horizontal Ribs From Waist To Top, Mottled Green, Durand & Kimble, 11 x 5 In. .	500.00
Vase, Light Amethyst, Signed, Steuben, 9 In.	1000.00
Vase, Mottled Amethyst, 9 5/8 In.	77.00
Vase, Mottled Apple Green, Bubble Design, Steuben, 1920, 10 1/8 In.	517.00

COALPORT ware has been made by the Coalport Porcelain Works of England from 1795 to the present time. Early pieces were unmarked. About 1810–1825 the pieces were marked with the name *Coalport* in various forms. Later pieces also had the name *John Rose* in the mark. The crown mark has been used with variations since 1881. The date 1750 is printed in some marks but it is not the date the factory started.

Ashtray, San Francisco Cable Car Scene, 5 In.	12.00
Box, Trinket, Christmas, Bright Holly, Mistletoe, White Gold Trim	20.00
Bread Tray, Rock, Acacia Tree, Peonies, Blue Underglaze, Red, Green, 1805, 15 In.	5175.00
Coffee Set, Japan, Gilt Berry-Vine Border, 1805-1810, 29 Piece	920.00
Creamer, Hunting Scene	85.00
Cup & Saucer, Enameled Mountain Scene, Turquoise Jewels, Miniature	132.00
Dessert Set, Stylized Flowers, Foliage, Blue, Red, Ocher, Yellow, 1810, 22 Piece	4887.00
Figurine, Clown, With Accordion	150.00
Figurine, Paddington Bear, Bath Time	45.00
Figurine, Peggy	65.00
Figurine, Prudence	85.00
Flowerpot, Ming Rose, 4 1/2 In.	60.00
Fruit Cooler, Cover, Gilt Foliate Scroll Handles, Brown, Gold Rim, 1800, 10 In., Pair ..	5175.00
Ginger Jar, Ming Rose, 7 In.	95.00
Pie Plate, Ming Rose, Gold Trim	75.00
Plate, Fruit Design, Hand Painted, Gold Scalloped Border, Signed, 9 In.	125.00
Plate, Twin Time Pattern, 5 3/4 In., 6 Piece	18.00
Plate Set, Ivory Reserves, Dark Blue Rim, Signed, 10 In., 12 Piece	3410.00
Platter, Rocktree, Blue Underglaze Branches On Rim, Red, Gilt Prunus, 1805, 18 In.	1610.00

Soup, Cream, Liner	35.00
Sugar, Cover, Hunting Scene	95.00
Vase, Campaniform Cupid, Bearing Torch, White Plants, 1805-1810, 9 1/2 In.	2070.00
Vase, Flower Encrusted, Cupid & Bird, Polychrome, England, c.1820, 12 In.	2850.00

COBALT BLUE glass was made using oxide of cobalt. The characteristic bright dark blue identifies it for the collector. Most cobalt glass found today was made after the Civil War. There was renewed interest in the dark blue glass in the late 1930s and dinnerwares were made.

Bowl, Centerpiece, 15 Golf Scenes, Sterling Rim, c.1925	825.00
Bowl, Cut To Clear, Polished Pontil, 12 1/2 In.	300.00
Bowl, Embroidered Mums, Fluted, 9 In.	400.00
Candlestick, 19th Century, 9 In.	66.00
Candlestick, Panel & Facet, Octagonal, 9 1/4 In., Pair	2175.00
Compote, Cut To Clear, 4 1/4 x 9 1/4 In.	125.00
Compote, Lacy, 5 1/8 x 3 In.	1850.00
Decanter, Cut To Clear, Stopper, 11 1/8 In.	225.00
Dish, Sweetmeat, Woven Silver Plated Trim, 8 1/2 x 5 3/8 In.	175.00
Glass Slipper, Cinderella, Impressed Picture, 1880	115.00
Goblet, Art Deco, Twisted Stem, Gold Trim, 7 In.	120.00
Goblet, Enameled, Pair	175.00
Lamp, Panel & Arch Font, Hexagonal Waterfall Base, Brass Collar, 10 1/8 In.	1575.00
Pitcher, Blown, Hollow Handle, Tooled Lip, Pittsburgh, 7 3/4 In.	4180.00
Pitcher, Clear Handle, 7 3/4 In.	125.00
Pitcher, Ice Lip, Crystal Handle, Weston	175.00
Salt, Hexagonal, 3 1/4 In., Pair	265.00
Sugar Basin, Honeycomb Pattern, 1760, 3 1/2 x 3 5/8 In.	950.00
Syrup, Tin Spout & Lid, 8 In.	66.00
Tankard, Golf Scene, Stoneware, Gerz, 1895	2950.00
Tumbler, Blown, Pillar Mold, 8 Ribs, 4 1/8 In.	365.00
Tumbler, Colonial Pattern, 6 Panels With Ovals, 3 3/4 In.	120.00
Tumbler, Figural, Fish, 3 3/4 In.	16.00
Tumbler, Juice, Weston, 6 Piece	70.00
Vase, Bigler Bowl, Ruffled, Square Octagonal Baluster Stem, 11 1/8 In.	1815.00
Vase, Fluted Top, Early 1900s, 6 1/2 In.	275.00
Vase, Mary Gregory Style, Man Standing In Foliage, Gold Trim, 2 1/2 x 1 1/2 In.	325.00
Vase, Silver Plated Mounts, Garland Design, England, 4 1/2 x 12 In., Pair	2200.00
Vase, Trumpet, Knop & Twisted Loop Bowl, Square Base, 10 1/2 In.	1650.00

COCA-COLA was first served in 1886 in Atlanta, Georgia. It was advertised through signs, newspaper ads, coupons, bottles, trays, calendars, and even lamps and clocks. Collectors want anything with the word *Coca-Cola*, including a few rare products, like gum wrappers and cigar bands. The famous trademark was patented in 1893, the *Coke* mark in 1945. Many modern items and reproductions are being made.

Airline Cooler, Stainless Steel Liner, 1950s	402.00
Apron, Cotton, White, Logo, Pocket, 32 x 31 In.	26.00
Bag, Cooler, White, With Red Lettering, Vinyl, 1960s	50.00
Bank, 1923 Model Chevy Delivery Truck, Cast Metal, Ertl, Box	75.00
Bank, Drink Machine, Tin, 1940-1950, 4 In.	65.00
Bank, Lockheed Air Express, Lockeed Airplane, Metal, Ertl, Box, 1929	65.00
Bank, Trolley, With Santa Claus, Cast Metal, Ertl, Box	50.00
Bank, Vending Machine, 1950s Style, Die Cast Metal, Box, 3 1/2 x 3 1/4 x 7 1/2 In.	41.00
Beach Umbrella, 1930s, Opens To 6 Ft.	220.00
Billboard Frame, Coke Insert, Be Really Refreshed, Plastic, 1950s-1960s, 4 x 6 In.	17.00
Binder, Sales, Sections On Profits, Stock, Coolers, Display	230.00 to 345.00
Blotter, Andrews Sisters, 1944	16.00 to 18.00
Blotter, Boy Scouts Pausing At Coca-Cola Ice Cooler Chest	12.00
Blotter, Girl, In Bobby Socks, 1942	18.00
Blotter, Sprite Boy, 4 x 8 In.	15.00
Blotter, Woman In Shorts, 1934	85.00
Booklet, Flower Arranging, 54 Pages, 1940	40.00
Booklet, Note Pad, 1940s, Unused, 8 x 10 In.	13.00

Coca-Cola, Clock, Light-Up, Wall, 15 In.

Coca-Cola, Calendar, 1909, Coca-Cola Helps The Tired Brain

Coca-Cola, Clock, Fishtail Logo, Not Working, 1960s, Box, 15 1/2 In.

Bookmark, Celluloid, Red, White, Black 625.00
Bookmark, Owl, Reading Book, Celluloid, 1906, 1 1/2 x 3 1/8 In. 750.00
Bottle, Applied Color Label, 64 Oz. 15.00
Bottle, Display, Christmas, 1930s, 20 In. 175.00
Bottle, Display, With Cap, Mexico, 1950s, 20 In. 172.00
Bottle, Porcelain, 1930s, 12 1/2 x 4 x 1/4 In. 138.00
Bottle, San Francisco, 75th Anniversary 15.00
Bottle, Syrup, Wreath Logo, Aluminum Cap, 1910 .... 431.00
Bottle, University Of Georgia, National Champs, 1980 .... 10.00
Bottle Cap, 1930s 12.00
Bottle Cap, 1950s 2.00
Bottle Opener, Chrome, Red Cap Catcher, 1950s 55.00
Bottle Opener, Spin To See Who Wins, Fish Shape, 1911-1930 .... 125.00
Bottle Opener, Starr X, Gray, Cast Iron, Box 30.00
Bottle Opener, Starr X, Wall Mounted, Cast Metal, Brown Mfg. Co., Box, 3 In. 23.00
Bottle Protector, Dated 1932 .... 10.00
Button, Always Coca-Cola, 1994, 18 In., Set Of 3 .... 287.00
Calendar, 1903, Hilda Clark 8000.00
Calendar, 1908, June, Woman In Red Dress, Frame, 7 x 14 In. 8280.00
Calendar, 1909, Coca-Cola Helps The Tired Brain ....*Illus* 12650.00
Calendar, 1914, June, Betty, With Bottle, Frame 3795.00
Calendar, 1918, Paper, Frame, 13 x 10 5/8 In. 160.00
Calendar, 1922, Woman In Pink Dress, Hat, Full Pad, Frame ....2070.00 to 3500.00
Calendar, 1923, Flapper Girl 1600.00
Calendar, 1925, Party Girl 1495.00
Calendar, 1930, Girl, In Bathing Suit, Pad, 1930, 24 1/4 x 12 In. 230.00
Calendar, 1932, Norman Rockwell, Full Pad, Cover Sheet, Frame 4255.00
Calendar, 1936, Girl & Sailor, Fiftieth Anniversary 920.00
Calendar, 1942, Boy & Girl With Snowman 138.00
Calendar, 1944, Hunting Dog, Harting Bros., Linton, In. Bottling Co., 11 x 14 In. 1035.00
Calendar, 1945, Thirst Knows No Season 633.00
Calendar Holder, Tin, With Unused 1988 Calendar Pad, 1950s, 8 x 20 In. 604.00
Calendar Top, 1914, Betty, Original Metal Strip, Frame, 12 3/4 x 27 1/4 In. 1150.00
Can, Classic Coke, Minnie Mouse, Disney World 15th Anniversary, 1986 .... 6.00
Can, Diet Coke, Figaro, Disney World 15th Anniversary, 1986 .... 6.00
Cap, Fountain Attendant, Card Stock, 2 Bottles With Figures, Small, Set Of 11 .... 24.00
Card, Playing, Airplane Spotter, Box, 1943, Full Deck 65.00
Card, Playing, Blue Deck, Box, 1939, Full Deck 65.00
Card, Playing, Couple In Swimsuits, Surfboard, Full Deck 55.00
Card, Playing, Unopened, 1950s 100.00
Card, Trade, Girl In Tub, Unfolds To Waitress Serving Coke, 1907 .... 1437.00
Card Set, Nature, 1930s, 96 Piece 40.00
Card Set, World War II Airplanes, Original Hanger, 1943, 13 x 15, 20 Piece 690.00
Carrier, 6-Pack, Aluminum, 1950s, 6 Oz. 65.00

Carrier, 6-Pack, Christmas, Cardboard, 1930s ....150.00 to 225.00
Carrier, 6-Pack, Wood, Yellow, Bottle On End Panel, 1930s 150.00
Carrier, 24-Bottle, Cardboard, Individual Tubes, 1940s 80.00
Case Insert, Sprite Boy, Cardboard, Die Cut, 1944, 10 x 13 In. 255.00
Chair, Folding, Metal, Embossed Logo 100.00
Change Receiver, Drink Coca-Cola, 5 Cents, Gold Leaf Reverse, Beige, 1904, 6 In. 352.00
Check, Payroll, Coca-Cola Bottling Works, Exmore, Va., Sept. 28, 1940 .... 75.00
Circus Cutout, How A Circus Comes To Town, Cardboard, 1932, 10 x 15 In. 40.00
Clock, Alarm, 2 Coke Bottles On Face, Ingraham, Copyright 1941 .... 295.00
Clock, Copper Finish, Burgundy Numbers, Dualite, 1940-1950, Round, 16 In. 345.00
Clock, Drink Coca-Cola, Light-Up, Gold Plate, Square, 9 x 19 1/2 In. 575.00
Clock, Fishtail Logo, Not Working, 1960s, Box, 15 1/2 In. ....*Illus* 460.00
Clock, Light-Up, Drink Coca-Cola, Glass, Metal, 1950s, 14 5/8 In. ....460.00 to 550.00
Clock, Light-Up, Please Pay When Served, Counter Type, 1950s ....*Illus* 865.00
Clock, Light-Up, Wall, 15 In. ....*Illus* 460.00
Clock, Reverse Glass, Metal Frame, Decal, Jump Start Motor, 1939-1942 .... 719.00
Clock, Stamped Label, Tin, 1954, 17 1/2 In. 130.00
Clock, Wall, Maroon, 1951, 17 1/2 In. 115.00
Coin-Operated Machine, Vendo, Model 27, Cavalier, 1940s 1500.00
Coin-Operated Machine, Vendo, Model 27, Have A Coke, 1948 .... 2500.00
Coin-Operated Machine, Vendo, Model GBV-50, Slider, Glasco, 1950-1960 .... 1750.00
Cookie Jar, Coke Can, McCoy 95.00
Cookie Jar, Coke Jug, Green Top 30.00
Cooler, Airline, Top Handle, Red Stainless Steel Inside, 1950s, 12 x 17 x 7 In. 395.00
Cooler, Executive, 10 3/4 x 17 3/4 x 9 In. 225.00
Cooler, Ice, Westinghouse Style, 1930s, 18 x 26 x 34 In. 891.00
Cooler, Picnic, Cardboard, 1930s 275.00
Cooler, Red Vinyl, 1940 .... 170.00
Cooler, Wood, Tin, 29 x 32 x 21 1/4 In. 1700.00
Cooler Bag, Vinyl, Insulated, 1950s 12.00
Crate, Wooden, Lake Geneva, Wi., 16 1/2 x 11 x 9 In. 38.00
Dispenser, 2 Sides, Porcelain, Metal Frame, 28 x 27 In. 850.00
Dispenser, Child's, Plastic, With 1 Glass, 10 In. 45.00
Dispenser, Cornelius, Countertop, Bolt-On, 2 Spigots, Coke & Sprite, 1950s 489.00
Dispenser, Drink Coca-Cola, Metal, 11 1/2 x 18 x 8 1/2 In. 210.00
Dispenser, Drink Coca-Cola, Metal, 22 x 8 1/2 x 19 In. 425.00
Dispenser, Fountain, 1930s 475.00
Dispenser, Fountain, Counter, Hardware, Booklets, Dole, Original Box 2415.00
Display, 6 Dummy Bottles, Cardboard Carton, King Size Coke 75.00
Display, Backbar, Girls' Heads, Cardboard, 1951, 5 Piece 4945.00
Display, Balancing, Double Carton, 2 Sides, Cardboard, 1954, 26 x 36 In. 805.00
Display, Santa In Rocket, Cardboard, Die Cut, Stand-Up, 1957, 8 In. 150.00
Display, Shadow Box, With Bottles, Centennial Celebration, Box 105.00
Display Element, Kay Displays, Battleship, Wooden, 1940s, 8 1/2 x 25 In. 719.00
Display Rack, Carton, 1930s, 55 In. 575.00
Doll, Buddy Lee, Plastic, Original Uniform, 1950s, 12 1/2 In. 720.00
Doll, Santa Claus, 1950s, 16 In. 95.00
Door Bar, Ice Cold, In Bottles, Porcelain, Red, Late-1950s, 34 In. 255.00
Door Bar, Iced Coca-Cola Here, Porcelain, Canada, 1950s, 32 In. 240.00
Door Bar Centerpiece, Porcelain, 1930s, 4 x 15 1/2 In. 430.00
Door Bar Centerpiece, Porcelain, Drink Coca-Cola, 1930s, 4 x 16 In. 460.00
Door Push, Bottle, Drink Coca-Cola, Tin, Embossed, 1931, 4 1/2 x 12 1/2 In. ...402.00 to 660.00
Door Push, Come In, Canada, 1940s, 4 x 11 1/2 In. 490.00
Door Push, Drink Coca-Cola, Iron Sides, Porcelain, 4 In. 700.00
Door Push, Thanks, Call Again, Canada, 1940s, 4 x 11 1/2 In. 490.00
Doorknob, Brass, From Baltimore, Md. Coke Plant, 1913-1915 .... 1150.00
Fan, Democratic Party Made Prosperity For Farmers, 1930 .... 121.00
Festoon, Lily Pads, 1935, 5 Piece 2990.00
Game Box, Marbles, Playing Cards, Dominos, Checkers, 1940s 175.00
Glass, Bell Shape, Pewter, 1930s 345.00
Glass, Flare, Etched, Syrup Line, 1904, 3 3/4 In. 661.00
Hat, Delivery, 100th Anniversary, Green, Black Brim, Coke Patch, 1986 .... 12.00
Ice Chest, Acton Manufacturing, Metal, Stainless Steel, 1950s, 6-Pack Size 316.00

Insert, For Lighted Menu Board, Foot Long Hot Dogs, Plastic, 1960s, 12 x 17 In. . . . .2.00 to 5.00
Insert, Sprite Boy, Quality In Cups, Cardboard, Frame, 1956, 12 x 15 In. 230.00
Jar, Chewing Gum, Embossed Lid, 1903-1905 . . . . 805.00
Jar, Pepsin Gum, Franklin Caro Lid, 1905-1911 .800.00 to 1300.00
Keg, Syrup, Original Paper Label Saying Cocaine Removed 205.00
Kickplate, Drink Coca-Cola, Sold Here Ice Cold, Canada, 1930s, 12 x 31 In. 747.00
Kickplate, Fountain Service, Porcelain, 1950s, 12 x 28 In. 1785.00
Kickplate, Tomese Coca-Cola, 2 Bottles, Spain, 1908, 12 x 36 In. 977.00
Knife, Pocket, Black Handle, Coca-Cola & Bottle Engraved On Sides 250.00
Knife, Salesman's Sample, No. 501, Pearlized Sides, Colonial, Prov., R.I., c.1935 . . . . . . 65.00
Lighter, Bottle Shape, Plastic, Steel, Brass, Unused, 1950-1960s, 2 1/2 In. 84.00
Lighter, Coke Bottle, Miniature 45.00
Lighter, Penguin, Red Celluloid Panel, Drink Coca-Cola, Box 55.00
Lighter, Shaving Cream Type Can 8.00
Machine, Bottle, Metal, 10 Cent, 65 In. 2195.00
Machine, Model WC44SK, Late 1950s 2200.00
Match Safe, Straight Bottle, Diamond Label, Whitehead & Hoag, 1908-1912 . . . . 8280.00
Match Striker, Canada, 1930s, Square, 4 1/4 In. 660.00
Menu Board, Green Chalk Board, Silhouette Girl, 1941, 20 x 28 In. 489.00
Mirror, Pocket, 1907 . . . . 750.00
Mirror, Pocket, 1909 . . . . 850.00
Mirror, Pocket, Woman At Beach, Oval, 1922, 1 3/4 x 2 3/4 In. 8280.00
Mobile, Person With Cup, Movies Are Better, Cardboard, 2 Sides, c.1957, 32 In. 490.00
Napkin, For Headache & Exhaustion, Rice Paper, Pre-1900, 14 In. 207.00
Necktie, Child's, Different Colored Bottle Caps, Red Ground 6.00
Notepad, Woman In Feathered Hat, Celluloid, 1902, 2 1/2 x 5 In. 949.00
Paperweight, People Inside, 1943 . . . . 1000.00
Pencil Case, 1937 . . . . 75.00
Pencil Sharpener, Bottle, Figural, Germany, c.1930 . . . . 45.00
Perfume Bottle, Coke Bottle Shape, Stopper, 1930s, Set Of 3 . . . . 150.00
Pin, 5 Year Service, Bottle Cap, Enameled, 1950s 30.00
Ping-Pong Set, Box, 1934 . . . . 185.00
Plate, Sandwich, Bottle & Glass In Center, Knowles China, 1931, 7 1/4 In. 460.00
Plate, Topless Girl, Vienna Art, 1908 . . . . 2800.00
Postcard, Original Design By Hamilton King, 1909 . . . . 2400.00
Postcard, Reminding Merchant To Order More Syrup, 1910 . . . . 220.00
Poster, 2 Teenagers On Picnic, Take Coke Along, Cardboard, Box, 1951, 16 x 27 In. 805.00
Poster, Cowgirl, Coke Time, Cardboard, Oak Frame, Matted, 1955, 16 x 27 In. 290.00
Poster, Santa Claus, Stock Up For The Holidays, Paper, 1950s, 19 x 34 In. 140.00
Poster, Stadium Vendor, Fans, Coke Time, Cardboard, Frame, 1954, 20 x 36 In. 1380.00
Pretzel Dish, 3 Bottles Around Edge, Aluminum, Metal, 1930s 290.00
Radio, AM, Cooler Shape, Red Bakelite 800.00
Radio, Bottle Shape, 1933, 24 In. 5750.00
Radio, Coca-Cola Cooler Shape, 1950s, 7 x 12 x 9 1/2 In. 633.00
Radio, Cooler, All Original, 1950s 1200.00
Sandwich Toaster, Electric, 1930s 1725.00
Scooter, Flyer, 3 Wheels 1500.00
Seat, Stadium, Cardboard 25.00
Service Pin, 25 Years, 5 Diamonds 126.00
Service Pin, 35 Years, 7 Diamonds 184.00
Shopping Cart, 2-Bottle Rack, Enjoy Coca-Cola While You Shop, 1950s 70.00
Sign, 1923 Bottle, Drink Coca-Cola, 1931, 11 1/2 x 34 1/2 In. 517.00
Sign, 3 Girls, Friendly Pause, Cardboard, 1948, 16 x 27 In. 1380.00
Sign, 6-Pack, Serve Coca-Cola At Home, Canada, Vertical, 1951, 17 x 53 In. 949.00
Sign, Arrow, Ice Cold, Sold Here, 2 Sides, Tin, Die Cut, 1927, 8 x 30 In. 2070.00
Sign, Bell Glass In Snow, Cardboard, Die Cut, Easel Back, 1930s, 17 x 27 In. 575.00
Sign, Betty, Tin, 1914, 31 x 41 In. 11155.00
Sign, Beverage Department, Sprite Boy, Masonite, Gold Frame, 1950s, 12 x 72 In. 891.00
Sign, Bottle & Diamond Can, Vertical, 1960s, 18 x 54 In. 1322.00
Sign, Bottle Of Coca-Cola With Coke Button Attached, 1950, 54 x 16 In. 690.00
Sign, Bottle Shape, Die Cut, October 1951, 9 In. 1207.00
Sign, Bottle, Drink Coca-Cola, Ice Cold, Aluminum Frame, 1934, 20 x 28 In. 747.00
Sign, Bottle, Hot Dog, Diminishing Logo, Cardboard, 3-D, 1932, 10 x 20 In. 1150.00

Sign, Bottle, Ice Cold Coca-Cola Sold Here, 1931, 20 x 28 In. 517.00
Sign, Bottle, Raised Gray Border, Tin, 1953, 18 x 33 In. 517.00
Sign, Button, Bottle, Tin, 1952, 24 In. 633.00
Sign, Button, Bottle, Tin, Alan Morrison Sign Co., Lynchburg, Va., 1950, 16 In. 1610.00
Sign, Button, Drink Coca-Cola, Tin, Original Paper Backing, 1951, 24 In. 520.00
Sign, Button, Protruding Soda Glass, Plastic, Hollis Press, 1950s, 12 x 14 In. 160.00
Sign, Button, Sign Of Good Taste, Porcelain, 1950s, 24 In. 375.00
Sign, Case, Take A Case Home Today, 1959, 20 x 28 In. 1150.00
Sign, Christmas Place Setting With Ham, Tastes So Good, 1954, 21 x 20 In. 38.00
Sign, Christmas, Santa Claus, Stand-Up, Cardboard, Die Cut, Easel, 1960s, 12 x 30 In. . . 98.00
Sign, Clown On Train With Cup, Vacu-Formed Plastic, c.1950s . . . . 150.00 to 265.00
Sign, Coca-Cola, Sign Of Good Taste, Bottle, Tin, Horizontal, 1960s, 18 x 54 In. 345.00
Sign, Counter, Please Pay Cashier, Glass, Plastic, 1950s, 18 1/2 x 8 In. 2990.00
Sign, Curb Service, Ice Cold Coca-Cola Sold Here, Tin, Embossed, 1938 . . . . 402.00
Sign, Dairy Queen, Menu Items, Coke Cup In Upper Right, 1950-1960, 22 x 28 In. 287.00
Sign, Delicious, Refreshing, Celluloid, Round, Late 1940s-Early 1950s, 9 In. 345.00
Sign, Dimensional, Bulletin, Porcelain, c.1950, 16 x 44 In. 400.00
Sign, Dispenser, Sidewalk, 2 Sides, Porcelain, 1950s, 27 x 28 In. 1265.00
Sign, Double 1915 Bottles, Cardboard, Tin Frame, 1910-1920, 21 x 60 In. 1035.00
Sign, Drink Coca-Cola In Bottles, 5 Cents, Tin, Embossed, 1920s, 6 x 23 In. 161.00
Sign, Drink Coca-Cola In Bottles, Bottle On Left, Tin, 1931, 10 x 28 In. 750.00
Sign, Drink Coca-Cola, 1923 Bottle, Tin, Embossed, 1931, 10 x 27 1/2 In. 977.00
Sign, Drink Coca-Cola, 2 Sides, Billiards, Outdoor, 1934, 63 x 49 In. 1495.00
Sign, Drink Coca-Cola, Bottle In Sun, Raised Framed Edge, 1946, 20 x 28 In. 660.00
Sign, Drink Coca-Cola, Bottle, Flange, 1941, 20 x 24 In. 660.00
Sign, Drink Coca-Cola, Bottle, Tin, Embossed, 1940, 20 x 28 In. 431.00
Sign, Drink Coca-Cola, Bottle, Tin, Horizontal, 1951, 18 x 54 In. 632.00
Sign, Drink Coca-Cola, Canada, Plexiglas, Wood, Desk, 1940-1950 . . . . 213.00
Sign, Drink Coca-Cola, Man, Woman, Tin, Outdoor, Wooden Frame, 1942, 32 x 68 In. . . 920.00
Sign, Drink Coca-Cola, Porcelain, Outdoor, Canada, 1938, 4 x 8 Ft. 1250.00
Sign, Drink Coca-Cola, Tin, Beveled Edges, String Hanger, 1930, 8 1/2 x 11 In. 2415.00
Sign, Drink Coca-Cola, Triangle, 2 Sides, Die Cut, Porcelain, 1935, 25 x 22 In. 9775.00
Sign, Drink Coke In Bottles, Porcelain, Round, 1950s, 24 In. 660.00
Sign, Drink Ice Cold Coca-Cola In Bottle, Tin, 1948, 11 x 24 In. 350.00
Sign, Drug Store, Sidewalk, 2 Sides, Porcelain, Frame, Fixtures, 1934, 3 x 5 Ft. . . 980.00 to 2185.00
Sign, Easel Back, Cardboard, Promotional, Kit Carson Kerchief, 1950s, 16 x 24 In. 200.00
Sign, Enjoy That Refreshing New Feeling, Flange, Tin, 1961, 18 x 15 In. 375.00
Sign, Fencing Girl, Join Me, Cardboard, Frame, 1947 . . . . 1208.00
Sign, Fishtail Logo Shape, Die Cut, Tin, 1962, 12 x 26 In. 460.00
Sign, Fishtail Logo, Bottle, Sign Of Good Taste, Tin, Horizontal, 1958, 18 x 54 In. 775.00
Sign, Fishtail Logo, Light-Up, Fluorescent, 2 Sides, 1960s, 38 x 20 x 9 In. 405.00
Sign, Fountain Service, Sidewalk, 2 Sides, Porcelain, 1950s, 55 x 60 x 5 In. 1495.00
Sign, Fountain Service, Sidewalk, Porcelain, Straps, Bracket, 1935, 34 x 44 In. 2185.00
Sign, Frozen Coca-Cola, Revolving, Light-Up, Plastic, 1960, 18 x 32 In. 546.00
Sign, Girl With Bottle, Raised Gold Border, Tin, Oval, 1926, 7 1/2 x 10 1/2 In. 5405.00
Sign, Have A Coke, Drink Coca-Cola, Light-Up, Metal Frame, 1950s, 8 x 19 In. 460.00
Sign, Ice Cold Coca-Cola Sold Here, Embossed, Round Sign, Tin, 1933, 19 1/4 In. 665.00
Sign, Ice Cold, Circle & Arrow, Tin, Flange, 1953, 18 x 22 In. 865.00
Sign, Kay Displays, 2 Glasses, Plywood, Metal, 1930s, 9 x 11 1/2 In. 950.00
Sign, Lillian Nordica, Celluloid, Metal Frame, Reverse Printed Back, Wall 10350.00

Clock, Light-Up, Please Pay When Served,
Counter Type, 1950s

Coca-Cola, Sign, Please Pay When Served,
9 1/2 x 19 In.

Sign, Logo, Raised Frame Edge, White, Red, Green, 1920s, 14 x 42 In. 862.00
Sign, Lunch-Soda, Plastic, Light-Up, Wall, 1956, 23 x 27 In. 1092.00
Sign, Motion, Glass, Plastic, Price Bros., Box, Circular, 1950s, 11 1/2 In. 1437.00
Sign, Navy Soldier, Woman On Roller Skates, Cardboard, 1943, 16 x 27 In. 1840.00
Sign, Painted Outdoor Scene, Tin, Round, 1950s, 16 In. 40.00
Sign, Patent Medicines, Drink Coca-Cola, Bottle, 1940, 3 x 6 Ft. 575.00
Sign, Pause, Light-Up, Motion, Counter, 1950s 1380.00
Sign, Pick Up 6 For Home Refreshment, Horizontal, 1964, 16 x 50 In. 517.00
Sign, Pick Up 6 For Home Refreshment, Vertical, 1954, 16 x 40 In. 920.00
Sign, Please Pay When Served, 9 1/2 x 19 In. ....*Illus* 862.00
Sign, Please Pay When Served, Light-Up, Counter, Clock, 1950s, 8 x 18 In. ......750.00 to 860.00
Sign, Please Place Empties Here, Metal, 16 x 7 In., Set Of 4 .... 45.00
Sign, Policeman Shape, Slow, School Zone 1495.00
Sign, Price Brothers, Glass Front, Light-Up, Wire Ground, Round, 1965, 14 In. 460.00
Sign, Race Card, Car No. 1, Indianapolis 500, 1960s 200.00
Sign, Refresh Yourself, Flange, 2 Sides, Porcelain, Canada, 1930s, 17 x 20 In. 1265.00
Sign, Santa Claus Sitting In Front Of Tree, 1970, 15 1/2 x 25 In. 27.00
Sign, School Slow, Girl's Silhouette, Tin, Round, 1958, 27 In., 2 Piece 405.00
Sign, School Zone, 2 Sides, Plywood, Metal Brackets, Base Ring, 1955 .... 805.00
Sign, Serve Coke At Home, Six-Pack, With Button, Tin, 1950s, 16 x 40 In. 640.00
Sign, Serve Coke At Home, Tin, 1948, 16 x 48 In. 632.00
Sign, Shop Refreshed, 2 Sides, Light-Up, Wall, 1950s 1555.00
Sign, Sign Of Good Taste, Flange, Tin, 1959, 18 x 15 In. 517.00
Sign, Sign Of Good Taste, Light-Up, Plastic, Metal Case, Circular, 1950s, 2 Piece 862.00
Sign, Six-Pack, Regular Size Circle, Tin, Die Cut, 1958, 11 x 12 In. 2070.00
Sign, Snowman, Holding Big Glass, Frame, 1953, 20 x 28 In. 920.00
Sign, Take A Case Home Today, Bottle Case, Tin, 1952, 20 x 28 In. 1035.00
Sign, Take Home A Carton, Six-Pack, Tin, Canada, 1942, 18 x 54 In. 835.00
Sign, Take Home A Coca-Cola, Canada, 1950, 53 x 35 In. 750.00
Sign, Things Go Better With Coke, Girl, On Roller Skates, 1960, 24 x 40 In. 185.00
Sign, Tin, Diminishing Logo, 1923 Bottle On Right, 1933, 20 x 28 In. 1150.00
Sign, Tire Rack, 2 Sides, Folding Legs, Adjustable Handle, Tin, 1952, 17 In. 3910.00
Sign, Wallace Beery, Cardboard, String Hanger, Frame, 1934, 14 x 29 1/2 In. 4370.00
Sign, Welcome Friend, Cardboard, Self-Framed, Beveled Edge, 1957, 11 x 14 In. 260.00
Sign, Woman Putting Coke In Icebox, Cardboard, Frame, 1948, 16 x 27 In. 920.00
Sign, Woman With Bottle, Drink Coca-Cola, 1940, 20 x 28 In. 460.00
Sign, Woman With Dance Card, Balloons, Cardboard, Frame, 1950s, 16 x 27 In. 1440.00
Sign, Work Refreshed, Frame, Cardboard, 29 x 50 In. 200.00
Syrup Can, Tin Lithograph, 1930s, 1 Gal. 865.00
Syrup Can, White Paper Label, 1950s, 1 Gal. 100.00
Telephone, Plastic, Electric, Model 5000, Arrow Trading Co., 9 3/4 In. 46.00
Thermometer, Bottle Shape, 1958, 17 In. 35.00
Thermometer, Bottle Shape, Gold, 1956, 7 1/2 In. 75.00
Thermometer, Bottle, Masonite, 1940s, 7 x 17 In. 978.00
Thermometer, Double Bottle, Gold Color, 1942, 7 x 16 In. 518.00
Thermometer, Pam, Red & Blue, Gold Bottle Logo, Round, 12 In. 719.00
Thermometer, Quality Refreshment, 1950s, 9 In. 460.00
Thermometer, Round, Fish Tail Logo, Glass Front, Box, 1959, 12 In. 690.00
Thermometer, Silhouette Girl, Porcelain, 1939, 5 1/2 x 18 In. 2530.00
Thermometer, Things Go Better, Round, 12 In. 225.00
Thermometer, Thirst Knows No Season, Porcelain, 18 x 6 In. 425.00
Thimble, Red Glass 35.00
Tip Tray, 1904, Lillian Nordica, With Glass, 4 In. 230.00
Tip Tray, 1907, Relieves Fatigue, 5 Cent, Girl Holding Glass 1155.00
Tip Tray, 1909, Exhibition Girl ....450.00 to 980.00
Tip Tray, 1912, Woman, In Vintage Clothing Drinking Coke, 6 x 4 1/4 In. 80.00
Tip Tray, 1914, Betty, Hat, Pink Dress, Shawl, Passaic Metalware Co., 4 1/4 x 6 In. 240.00
Tip Tray, 1916, Elaine, 6 x 4 1/4 In. 127.00
Tip Tray, 1920, Golfer Girl 490.00
Tip Tray, 1959, Woman, Black Hat & Gloves, Mexico, 13 1/4 In. 86.00
Towel, Coca-Cola Sign & Bottle, Linen 2.00
Toy, Airplane, Bi-Wing, Polar Bears In Cockpit, White Lettering 35.00
Toy, Car, Yesteryear, Die Cast, Matchbox, Box 45.00

Toy, Shopping Cart, Metal, Masonite, 1950s 290.00
Toy, Truck, Buddy L, 1950s 275.00
Toy, Truck, Metal Cab, Plastic Trailer, Coke Cases, Remco, 1987, 10 1/2 In. 40.00
Toy, Truck, Metal, Holds 6 Barrels, England, Box, 1967, 3 1/2 In. 30.00
Toy, Truck, Route, Tin, Battery Operated, Allen Haddock Works, Japan, 1960s, 12 In. 333.00
Toy, Truck, Tin Lithograph, Marx 385.00
Tray, 1905, Serving, Topless, 12 1/4 In. 4000.00
Tray, 1906, Relieves Fatigue, Oval, 4 In. .... 834.00 to 862.00
Tray, 1909, Exhibition Girl, 13 x 10 In. .... 2000.00 to 3450.00
Tray, 1910, Coca-Cola Girl, 13 1/4 x 10 1/2 In. .... 3100.00 to 3300.00
Tray, 1913, Hamilton King Girl, 13 1/4 x 10 1/2 In. 2400.00
Tray, 1913, Hamilton King Girl, Oval 719.00
Tray, 1914, Betty, 13 1/4 x 10 1/2 In. 550.00
Tray, 1914, Betty, Drink Coca-Cola, Delicious & Refreshing, Oval 316.00
Tray, 1916, Elaine, 8 1/2 x 19 In. .... 425.00 to 720.00
Tray, 1921, Golfer Girl 300.00
Tray, 1922, Summer Girl, 13 1/4 x 10 1/2 In. .... 950.00 to 1500.00
Tray, 1924, Smiling Girl, 13 1/4 x 10 1/2 In. 1600.00
Tray, 1925, Party Girl, 13 1/4 x 10 1/2 In. .... 395.00 to 520.00
Tray, 1926, Golfer, Wearing White Coat, Knickers, Pouring A Coke, F. Milen, 1926 ..... 825.00
Tray, 1928, Girl With Bobbed Hair, Black Ground 1150.00
Tray, 1929, Girl In Yellow Bathing Suit, Rectangular 374.00
Tray, 1930, Bather Girl, 13 1/4 x 10 1/2 In. .... 700.00 to 1100.00
Tray, 1932, Girl In Bathing Suit Sitting, England .... 800.00 to 1200.00
Tray, 1933, Francis Dee, England .... 800.00 to 1610.00
Tray, 1936, Hostess .... 300.00 to 350.00
Tray, 1937, Running Girl .... 200.00 to 300.00
Tray, 1938, Girl In Yellow Hat .... 144.00 to 246.00
Tray, 1939, Springboard Girl, 10 1/2 x 13 1/2 In. .... 195.00 to 250.00
Tray, 1941, Skating Girl .... 231.00 to 395.00
Tray, 1941-1942, 2 Girls At Car 325.00
Tray, 1950, Menu Girl, Holding Coke, Have A Coke, Thirst Knows No Season ..... 30.00 to 50.00
Tray, 1952, Girl With Bottle, Wind In Hair, Screened Ground 100.00
Tray, 1957, Bird House, Canada 45.00
Tray, 1957, Girl With Umbrella 375.00
Tray, 1957, Rooster 125.00
Tray, 1957, Sandwiches & Bottles 215.00
Tray, 1960, Girl With Bottle, Glass, Sandwich, Mexico 98.00
Tray, 1961, Pansies, Be Really Refreshed 140.00
Tray, 1964, Decorated Both Sides, Commemorative, 25 Anos, Plant, Mexico 345.00
Tray, 1985, Commemorative, Hoover Dam 50th Anniversary, 13 x 10 1/2 In. 20.00
Truck Grill Plate, Aluminum, Die Cut, Brown Manufacturing Mark, 7 x 17 In. 489.00
Umbrella, Cream Ground, Red Writing, Brown Bottles, 1930s, Opens To 5 Ft. 1035.00
Umbrella, The Pause That Refreshes, 1930s, Opens To 5 Ft. 1035.00
Uniform, Authentic, 2 Piece, White, Red Coke Emblem, Green Stripe, 1950s 75.00
Urn, 1972 Replica Of Early 1900s Urn, Box 750.00
Wall Sconce, Composition, Embossed, 1920-1930, 9 x 12 In. 980.00
Wallet, Pigskin, 1920s 28.00
Wristwatch, Woman's, Pink Coke, Light Blue Ground, Blue Band 14.00

COFFEE GRINDERS of home size were first made about 1894. They lost favor by the 1930s. Large floor-standing or counter-model coffee grinders were used in the nineteenth-century country store. The renewed interest in fresh-ground coffee has produced many modern electric and hand grinders, and reproductions of the old styles are being made.

Arcade, No. 4, Crystal, Original Glass Top 275.00
Arcade, No. 9035, Art Deco, Green Paint 280.00
Bates, D.L. & Bros., Brass, April 10, 1888, 35 In. 450.00
Bone & Ivory Knobs, Cast Brass Handle, 19th Century 475.00
Cast Iron, Enterprise Mfg. Co., Philadelphia, Pat'd. Dec. 9, 1873, 12 In. 585.00
Cherry Wood, Porcelain Drawer Pull, Lap Type 65.00
Elgin National, Eagle Finial, Red Paint, Gold Trim, Cast Iron, Tin Hopper, 30 In. 550.00

Elma, Cast Iron, 11 In. 245.00
Enterprise, 1 Heel, Complete, 12 In. 245.00
Enterprise, Cast Iron, Drawer, Red, Black, Gold, 13 In. 440.00
Enterprise, Double Wheel, Pedestal Base, Pinstripes, 1873 .... 1200.00
Enterprise, No. 00, Wall Mount, Cast Iron Cup 165.00
Enterprise, No. 1, Cast Iron, Black Paint, Wood Base, Philadelphia, 11 1/2 In. .. 165.00
Enterprise, No. 7, Eagle Finial On Lid, 16-In. Wheel 690.00
Enterprise, Red & Blue, Decals, Wooden Base, Drawer, Cast Iron, 22 1/2 In. ... 330.00
Ivory Knobs, Pierced Brass Handle, 10 In. 395.00
Landers, Frary & Clark, 2 Wheels, Cast Iron, 8 1/2 In. 1950.00
Landers, Frary & Clark, 2 Wheels, Decal, c.1870, Miniature 550.00
Landers, Frary & Clark, Cast Iron, Patent 1878 .... 425.00
Landers, Frary & Clark, No. 24, Crystal, Original Glass Top & Bracket 220.00
Lane Bros., Swift, No. 12, Repainted, 9-In. Wheel 450.00
Leinbrack Ideal, Lap, Germany 40.00
Mennonite, Dovetailed Walnut Case, Brass Hopper, Knob On Handle 175.00
National Specialty, Cast Iron, Red Paint, Wooden Base, Philadelphia, 13 In. .. 880.00
Parker, C., No. 314, Box Mill, Label 150.00
Poplar, Pewter Hopper, Cast Iron Fittings, 8 1/2 In. 115.00
Tillmann's Hawaiian, Wall Mount, Cast Iron 175.00
Wilson, Improved, Wall Mount, Hand Crank, On Wooden Plaque, 6 In. 35.00
Wooden, Czechoslovakia, c.1910 .... 85.00

COIN SPOT is a glass pattern that was named by the collectors for the spots resembling coins, which are part of the glass. Colored, clear, and opalescent glass was made with the spots. Many companies used the design in the 1870–1890 period. It is so popular that reproductions are still being made.

Bowl, Scalloped Top, Thorn Feet, Berry Prunt, Pink & Blue, 4 1/2 x 6 1/2 In. 750.00
Compote, Peach 85.00
Cruet, Cranberry 225.00
Dish, Jelly, Marigold Carnival 25.00
Jug, Cranberry Opalescent 110.00
Mustard, Floral, Red To Amber, Silver Plated Cover, Handle 60.00
Night-Light, Ball Shape, Candle Cup, Cranberry, Nickeled Brass Foot, 5 1/8 In. 175.00
Pitcher, Cranberry Opalescent 435.00
Pitcher, Cranberry, Ruffled Rim, Ribbed Crystal Handle, 9 1/2 In. 110.00
Salt & Pepper, Cranberry Opalescent .... 350.00 to 400.00
Sugar Shaker, Blue Opalescent, Ring Neck 160.00
Sugar Shaker, White 135.00
Tankard, 3 Tiers, Cranberry 1385.00
Toothpick, 9 Panels, Green 125.00
Tumbler, Blue Opalescent 21.00
Vase, Blue Opalescent, Flared, Egg Shape, 9 1/2 In. 35.00
Water Set, Green, 7 Piece 450.00

COIN-OPERATED MACHINES of all types are collected. The vending machine is an ancient invention dating back to 200 B.C. when holy water was dispensed in a coin-operated vase. Smokers in seventeenth-century England could buy tobacco from a coin-operated box. It was not until after the Civil War that the technology made modern coin-operated games and vending machines plentiful. Slot machines, arcade games, and dispensers are all collected.

Baseball, Heavy Hitter, Bally, Stand 875.00
Candy, Mutoscope, Old Mill 2200.00
Cille, Mascot Grip & Blow 6500.00
Dice, Bally, Reliance, 5 Cent 4500.00
Digger, Buckley, Jewel Box, Table Model 950.00
Digger, Electrohoist 1475.00
Digger, Esco, Crystal Palace 1800.00
Digger, Exhibit Supply, 25 Cent Player 2600.00
Digger, Skill Crane, Table Model 550.00
Digger, Treasure Chest, Floor Model 2200.00

Fortune Teller, Exhibit Supply, Card Vendor 2200.00
Fortune Teller, Granny, Oak Cabinet 3800.00
Fortune Teller, Napkin Dispenser, The Planet, Metal, 1950s, 10 x 7 In. 80.00
Gum, Adams Pepsin Tutti-Frutti, Porcelain Front Panel 325.00
Gum, Baker Boy, Manikin Vendor Company, c.1929 .... 5750.00
Gum, Kelley, Chicago, Glass Window, 1 Cent 2300.00
Gum, Kola Pepsin 3500.00
Gum, Simpson, 1 Cent 490.00
Gum, Wrigley's Spearmint, 5 Cent 150.00
Gum, Yellow Kid, Pulver's, Red, 1 Cent, 21 In. 775.00
Gumball, Baby Grand 55.00
Gumball, Masters, Red, Black Porcelain, 1923, 16 x 8 x 8 In. 259.00
Gumball, Victor, Topper ....90.00 to 95.00
Kiddie Ride, Motorcycle, 10 Cent 850.00
Kiddie Ride, Toonerville Trolley, 10 Cent 850.00
Match, Northwestern Vendor 475.00
Mutoscope, Mobile Amusement, 1950, 29 x 62 In. 287.00
Mutoscope, Wood, Iron Pedestal, Red, 74 In. 865.00
Mutoscope, Wood, Iron Pedestal, Sheet Metal, Yellow, 74 In. 870.00
Peanut, Northwestern 49er, 5 Cent 50.00
Peanut, Victor, Model B, 1 Cent 125.00
Peep Show, Cail-O-Scope 3000.00
Peep Show, Mills, Drop Card, Oak, Floor Model 1250.00
Pinball, Gottlieb, Liberty Bell, 1935 .... 2100.00
Popcorn, Holkum & Hoke, Peanut Roaster Below, Floor Model ....2200.00 to 2850.00
Punching Bag, Exhibit Supply 2200.00
Punching Bag, Mutoscope 3400.00
Scale, Peerless Weighing, 1 Cent, Porcelain, 1920, 69 In. 834.00
Shock Machine, 1920s 400.00
Shooting Gallery, Bally, Ranger, Cash Payout, c.1935 .... 3500.00
Shooting Gallery, Learn To Shoot, 5 Cent, Oak, Floor Model 2500.00
Shooting Gallery, Radio Rifle, Record Of Shooter & Shots, 5 Cent 5750.00
Slot, Bakers, Races 6500.00
Slot, Bally, Reliance, Automatic Dice, 5 Cent 4500.00
Slot, Buckley, Horse Race, 1930s, 19 x 44 x 40 In. 805.00
Slot, Caille, Baseball, 1 Cent 7900.00
Slot, Caille, Busy Bee 8400.00
Slot, Caille, Our Baby, Cherry, 5 Cent, 20 x 29 x 11 In. 4025.00
Slot, Dewery, 50 Cent, Miniature 4500.00
Slot, Electro, Three Slots, Nickel, Quarter, Dollar 2500.00
Slot, Golden Nugget, 25 Cent 1595.00
Slot, H.C. Evans, Wood, 36 x 45 x 22 In. 1035.00
Slot, Horse Race, 6 Horsemen, Eastlake Type Design, Table Model 2530.00
Slot, Jennings, Indian Chief, Silver Dollar, Stand 3300.00
Slot, Jennings, Little Duke, Cast Aluminum, 1 Cent, 1935 .... 1150.00
Slot, Jennings, Rockaway, Cash Box, Lock 1350.00
Slot, Jennings, Standard Chief, 5 Cent 1700.00
Slot, Mills, 20th Century, Upright, 1903, 25 x 65 In. 9775.00
Slot, Mills, 3 Reels, 5 Cent, 1931, 16 x 24 In. 805.00
Slot, Mills, 3 Reels, Spearmint, 5 Cent, 1930, 16 x 24 In. 1207.50
Slot, Mills, Admiral, Upright, 5 Cent 8500.00
Slot, Mills, Aluminum Casting, Oak Case, 5 Cent, 16 x 25 x 16 In. 575.00
Slot, Mills, Diamond Chrome, 50 Cent, 1950, 15 x 25 In. 1100.00
Slot, Mills, Judge, Upright, 1 Wheel, 5 Cents, 1899, 22 x 65 In. 8050.00
Slot, Mills, Liberty Bell, Cast Iron, 5 Cent ....7500.00 to 9000.00
Slot, Mills, Lion Front ....1380.00 to 2400.00
Slot, Mills, One-Armed Bandit, Figural 7700.00
Slot, Mills, Puritan Bell 650.00
Slot, Mills, Silent Mystery, Oak Cabinet, 5 Cent, 1930, 16 x 24 In. 1265.00
Slot, Money Honey, 25 Cent 1250.00
Slot, Mysterious Eye, 5 Cent 2900.00
Slot, Novoma, Metal Works & Attachments, British Pennies 192.00
Slot, Oak, Hinged Door, 11 1/4 x 9 1/2 x 15 1/2 In. 850.00

Slot, Rol-A-Top, Coin Front, 5 Cent 3995.00
Slot, Saratoga, Wood Cabinet, 5 Cent, 1930s, 32 x 43 x 23 In. 1205.00
Slot, Victor, Upright, 25 Cent, 1904 . . . . 7360.00
Slot, Watling, Blue Seal, 5 Cent 1595.00
Slot, Watling, Rol-A-Top, Bird Of Paradise 3700.00
Slot, Wurlitzer, Watling, Rol-A-Top, 10 Cent 2900.00
Stamp, Postage, Cast Iron Base, Sheet Metal Body 60.00
Strength Tester, Exhibit Supply, Grandfather's Clock 1700.00
Strength Tester, Exhibit Supply, Lighthouse 2200.00
Trade Stimulator, Bell & Bicycle Tires Rotate, Win Cigar, 5 Cent 4200.00
Trade Stimulator, Daval, Bell, Gum, 1938, 13 x 12 In. 345.00
Trade Stimulator, Daval, Heads & Tails, Gum, 1940, 8 x 10 In. 201.00
Trade Stimulator, Daval, Jiffy, Gum, 1 Cent, 8 x 10 In. 290.00
Trade Stimulator, Daval, Tally, Gum, 5 Cent, 1940, 9 x 14 In. 460.00
Trade Stimulator, Daval, Tit Tat Toe, Gum, Wood, 1937, 10 x 9 In. 489.00
Trade Stimulator, Exhibit Supply, Sweet Sally, Gum, 1935, 10 x 15 In. 290.00
Trade Stimulator, Garden City, Gum, 3 Reels, 1938, 9 x 12 In. 259.00
Trade Stimulator, Groetchen, Pok-O-Reel, Gum, 1933, 15 x 12 In. 400.00
Trade Stimulator, Groetchen, Royal Flush, Gum, 1939, 13 x 11 In. 345.00
Trade Stimulator, Groetchen, Twenty-One, Gum, 14 x 15 In. 489.00
Trade Stimulator, Groetchen, Zig Zag, Gum, 1935, 14 x 14 In. 661.00
Trade Stimulator, H.C. Evans, Saratoga Sweepstakes, Horse Race 750.00
Vending, Balba Mfg. Co., Perfume, 7 x 12 In. 144.00
Vending, Black Figure, Cigar, 21 x 32 x 17 In. 14375.00
Vending, Condom, Royal Knight, Knock Out V.D., 30 x 6 1/2 In. 275.00
Vending, Condom, Surete 895.00
Vending, Gillette Razor Blade, 15 Cent, 25 Cent, 7 x 13 In. 75.00
Vending, Griswold, Match Box, 1910, 6 x 16 In. 175.00
Vending, Hershey Bars, Beech-Nut Gum, 1 Cent, 1950 . . . . 115.00
Vending, Holly Engineering Co., Arcade, 1939, 7 x 13 In. 115.00
Vending, Jennings, Golf Ball, 25 Cent 6500.00
Vending, Northwestern, Ohio Book Matches, 1930, 13 In. 230.00
Vending, Toilet Seat Cover Dispenser, 1920s 45.00
Video, Star Wars, Stand-Up Version 500.00

COLLECTOR PLATES are modern plates produced in limited editions.
Some may be found listed under the factory name, such as Bing &
Grondahl, Royal Copenhagen, Royal Doulton, and Wedgwood.

Anri, Christmas, 1971, St. Jakob In Groden, Wood 30.00
Anri, Christmas, 1972, Pipers At Alberobello, Wood 34.00
Anri, Mother's Day, 1972, Children With Cradle, Wood 30.00
Avon, Betsy Ross With Congress, 1973 . . . . 9.00
Avon, Christmas, 1973, Christmas On The Farm 14.00
Avon, Christmas, 1974, Country Church 9.00
Avon, Christmas, 1977, Carolers In The Snow 7.00
Chambers, Annie & The Orphans, Annie, 1984 . . . . 40.00
Chambers, Daddy Warbucks, Annie, 1983 . . . . 50.00
Daniel, A Dream Is A Wish Your Heart Makes, Cinderella, 1988 . . . . 70.00
Daniel, Winter Travelers, Call Of The Wilderness, 1991 . . . . 75.00
Degrazia, Little Cocopah, 1980 . . . . 70.00
Degrazia, Morning Ride, 1986 . . . . 105.00
Degrazia, White Dove, 1981, Miniature 40.00
Gorham, Butter Girl, Norman Rockwell, 9 In. 23.00
Gorham, Christmas, 1974, God Bless Tiny Tim, Rockwell 30.00
Kaiser, Christmas, 1970, Waiting For Santa Claus 7.00
Kaiser, Christmas, 1972, Coming Home For Christmas 7.00
Kaiser, Mother's Day, 1971, Mare & Foal 7.00
Knowles, Christmas, 1976, Golden Christmas, Rockwell 24.00
Knowles, Goose That Laid The Golden Egg, 1988 . . . . 40.00
Knowles, Hare & The Tortoise, 1988 . . . . 40.00
Knowles, Heritage, Shipbuilder, Rockwell, 1980 . . . . 24.00
Knowles, Mother's Day, 1979, Reflections, Rockwell 24.00

Knowles, Valentine's Day, 1981, Rockwell	24.00
Porsgrund, Christmas, 1969, 3 Wise Men	17.00
Porsgrund, Christmas, 1970, Road To Bethlehem	9.00
Porsgrund, Christmas, 1972, Hark The Herald Angels	9.00
Porsgrund, Christmas, 1976, Jesus In The Temple	12.00
Porsgrund, Christmas, 1980, Preparing For Christmas	12.00
Porsgrund, Easter, Bird & Baby Chicks, 1973	12.00
Porsgrund, Father's Day, 1972, Father & Son Camping	5.00
Porsgrund, Father's Day, 1975, Dad Ice Skating With Daughter	7.00
Porsgrund, Mother's Day, 1971, Boy & Geese	5.00
Porsgrund, Mother's Day, 1974, Boy On Goat	7.00
Porsgrund, Mother's Day, 1977, Boy Feeding Chicks	7.00
Schmid, Christmas, 1975, Gift Exchange With Raggedy Andy	12.00
Schmid, Christmas, 1977, Peanuts & Snoopy, Box	25.00
Schmid, Christmas, 1977, Raggedy Ann By Christmas Tree	7.00
Schmid, Mother's Day, 1979, Raggedy Ann On Swing	7.00
Schmid, Valentine's Day, 1978, Raggedy Ann & Andy, With Hearts	7.00

COMIC ART, or cartoon art, is a relatively new field of collecting. Original comic strips, magazine covers, and even printed strips are collected. The first daily comic strip was printed in 1907. The paintings on celluloid used for movie cartoons are listed in this book under Animation Art.

Banner, Snoopy, Curse You Red Baron, Yellow Felt, 1987, 33 x 14 In.	65.00
Banner, Snoopy, I've Become Allergic To People, Orange Felt, 1967, 33 x 14 In.	80.00
Card, Envelope, Fontaine Fox, Congratulating Rollin Kirby, 1933, 3 3/8 x 5 In.	170.00
Drawing, Tarzan, Fighting, Leopard, Pen & Ink, 1970s, 14 x 10 In.	485.00
Drawing, VIP, Pen & Ink, Pencil Caption, Virgil Partch, Signed	29.00
Strip, Alley Oop, Oola, Under Arrest, V.T. Hamlin, April 18, 1949, 6 x 20 1/2 In.	240.00
Strip, Broom Hilda, Signed Best Wishes, Russel Myers, 1987, 4 x 13 In.	125.00
Strip, Gasoline Alley, Skeezix & Nina, Sunday, Nov. 25, 1945, 21 x 16 In.	1000.00
Strip, Nancy, With Sluggo, Ernie Bushmiller, March 18, 1944, 5 x 19 In.	190.00
Strip, Phantom, Jungle, Wilson McCoy, August, 7, 1960, 17 1/2 x 26 In.	725.00
Strip, Secret Agent Corrigan, Al Williamson, March 12, 1969, 5 1/2 x 19 In.	110.00
Strip, Secret Agent Corrigan, Al Williamson, Sept. 30, No Year, 5 x 16 In.	125.00
Strip, Terry & The Pirates, George Wunder, Sunday, May 7, 1950, 17 x 25 In.	535.00

COMMEMORATIVE items have been made to honor members of royalty and those of great national fame. World's fairs and important historical events are also remembered with commemorative pieces. Related collectibles are listed in the Coronation and World's Fair categories.

Beaker, Edward VII, Cranberry Glass	165.00
Book, Coloring, Princess Diana, 1982	50.00
Calendar, Princess Diana & Prince Charles, 1983	75.00
Cup & Saucer, Princess Charlotte, In Memoriam, 1819	225.00
Doll, Princess Diana & Prince Charles, Danbury, Box, Pair	1200.00
Figurine, Charles & Diana Wedding Study, Coalport, 1981	2395.00
Hot Plate Pad Set, Prince Of Wales Emblem, Wedding Date, 4 Piece	20.00
Loving Cup, Crowning Of Queen Elizabeth, Green, Minton, 4 In.	35.00
Mug, Diana, Royal Visit To Canada, Faces Of Charles & Diana, 1983	65.00
Mug, Princess Diana, Birth Of William, June 21, 1982, England	25.00 to 30.00
Mug, Royal Visit, Atlantic Canada, 1983	150.00
Mug, Royal Wedding, Prince Of Wales & Lady Diana Spencer	175.00
Paper Doll, Princess Diana, Book, 1985	35.00
Pin Dish, Princess Diana Wedding, With Photograph, 6 In.	30.00
Plate, John Glenn Portrait, First Moon Landing	10.00
Plate, Royal Birth, Charles, Diana, Heart, Cherubs, Wedgwood, 1982, 4 In.	34.00
Plate, University Of Notre Dame, Vernon Kilns, 10 1/2 In.	12.00
Sugar & Milk, Queen Victoria, Proclamation, 1837, Goodwin & Ellis	1595.00
Tray, Coronation Of Edward VII, Edward & Alexandra, 1902, 16 1/2 In.	40.00
Tumbler, Queen Elizabeth, Royal Visit, June 1959, Canada, Maple Leaf	25.00
Vase, Queen Victoria Jubilee, Doulton Lambeth, 1887	2395.00

COMPACTS hold face powder. A woman did not powder her face in public until after World War I. By 1920, the beauty parlor, permanent waves, and cosmetics had become acceptable. A few companies sold cake face powder in a box with a mirror and a pad or puff. Soon the compact was designed by jewelers and made of gold, silver, and precious materials. Cosmetic companies began to sell powder in attractive compacts of less valuable metal or plastic. Collectors today search for Art Deco designs, commemorative compacts from world's fairs or political events, and unusual examples. Many were made with companion lipsticks and other fittings.

Art Deco, Blue Mirror, Handle Holds Lipstick, Powder Shaker Top	100.00
Art Deco, Green, Black & Orange Ray Design, Mirror, Metal Perfume Bottle, Chain	90.00
Bakelite, Black, Screw-On Top, Inset Horse & Hansom Cab	45.00
Bakelite, Carved, Maroon, Metal Lid, Hand Painted, 18th Century Couple, Signed, 3 In.	135.00
Cameo Center, Lipstick Holder	40.00
Ciner, Glued-On Bears, Holding Pearl In Paws	90.00
Coty, Book Shape, Marked Puff	50.00
Djer Kiss, Set, Powder, Perfume & Small Compact In Gold Satin Pouch	75.00
Dorset, Dried Flowers Under Plastic Dome, Marked	33.00
Dorset, Gold Tone, Basket Of Flowers	40.00
Dorset, Red, Painted Flowers	28.00
Elgin, Green & Gold Design	25.00
Elgin, Mother-Of-Pearl, Pamphlet	50.00
Elgin, Musical, Brahms' Waltz	145.00
Elgin, Original Elgin Pouch, 1940s	40.00
Elgin, Red Top, Honeycomb Silver-Tone Mesh, Square	25.00
Evans, Enamel, Compartments For Loose Powder & Rouge, 2 1/4 In.	55.00
Evans, Lipstick On Chain, Red & Black	85.00
Evening In Paris, Blue Enamel, Chrome, 1930s	40.00
Evening In Paris, Vanity Case, Chain, 14 Piece	250.00
Flato, Birds, Pearl Bodies, Lipstick Case	95.00
Goldtone, Powder Section, Attached Money Clip, Coin Holder, 1914, 2 1/3 x 4 In.	110.00
Goldtone, Raised Venice Scene, Chain, 3 x 4 In.	35.00
Green Bakelite Top, Metal Bottom	40.00
Houbigant, Art Deco, Diagonal Lines, Octagonal, 3 1/2 In.	65.00
Hudnut, Powder & Rouge, 3 Flowers, Domed, Basket Weave Decor, Silvertone, 2 In.	45.00
Ice Carnival, Shrine	65.00
Lady Esther, Chrome, 1940s	14.00
Lipstick Case, Mirror, Gold & Black Beaded	15.00
Mercedes Logo On Top, Brushed Gold Tone, 3 1/2 In.	27.00
Metal, Opens To Powder, Rouge & Mirror, Scott On Front	75.00
Metalfield, Cover, Multicolored Florals, Loose Powder	35.00
Metalfield, Goldtone, Loose Powder, Pull-Out Drawer For Cigarettes, Currency	40.00
Montmartre, Hand Painted Scene, Lucite	60.00
Mother-Of-Pearl Top, Lipstick	20.00
Mt. Vernon, Blue, 3 1/2 In.	35.00
Navy Cap Shape, Sterling Silver	125.00
Painted Fishing Scene, Puff & Screen, Square Lucite	46.00
Pendant, Enamel Flower Basket Design, Silver Finish	75.00
Plastic, Brown Satin Fabric Top, Amber Color, Square	46.00
Plastic, Painted Flowers Surrounded By Clear Rhinestones, 1950s	45.00
Plastic, Tortoise Color, Etched Bee Design, Rhinestones, With Cigarette Case	38.00
Quinlan, Black Plastic, Rhinestone, Rectangular	20.00
Raised Goldfish, Sterling Silver	95.00
Silver, Chased, Molded Edge, Square	85.00
Silver, Reeded Compartmented Case, Gold Pieces, Channel Set Sapphires, Art Deco	288.00
Souvenir, Estes Park, Red, Plastic	30.00
Sterling Silver, Enamel Country Scene, People, Sheep, Powder Door	375.00
Sterling Silver, Mirror, Engraved Outlining, Flared Edge, Square, 3 3/4 In.	65.00
Sterling Silver & Enamel, Oval Reserve Of 3 Figures On Lid, Germany	110.00
Stratton, Black Enamel & Gold	20.00
Stratton, Three Graces	95.00
Vasher, 2 Compartments	55.00

Volupte, Box, Slip Cover	50.00
Volupte, Cigarette Case, Match Case, Lipstick Case, Faille Bag	25.00
Volupte, Mother-Of-Pearl Cover	20.00
Volupte, Rhinestones, Goldtone, Square	40.00
Wadsworth, Military Hat, Medium Blue, World War II	55.00
Watch Inset On Cover, Illinois	85.00

CONSOLIDATED LAMP AND GLASS COMPANY of Coraopolis, Pennsylvania, was founded in 1894. The company made lamps, tablewares, and art glass. Collectors are particularly interested in the wares made after 1925, including black satin glass, Cosmos (listed in its own category in this book), Martele (which resembled Lalique), Ruba Rombic (1928–1932 art deco line), and colored glasswares. Some Consolidated pieces are very similar to those made by the Phoenix Glass Company. The colors are sometimes different. Consolidated made Martele glass in blue, crystal, green, pink, white, or custard glass with added fired-on color or a satin finish. The company closed for the final time in 1967.

Bowl, Catalonian, Flared, Green, 8 In.	75.00
Bowl, Fruit, Lovebird, Brown	295.00
Bowl, Fruit, Nuthatch	125.00
Candleholder, Catalonian, Amber, Pair	135.00
Candleholder, Catalonian, Amethyst, Pair	100.00
Cookie Jar, Con Cora, Roses, 6 1/2 In.	125.00
Dish, Mayonnaise, Iris, Purple	22.00
Finger Bowl, Ruba Rombic, Smoky Topaz	175.00
Lamp, Cockatoo, Coral, Tan, Light Blue On Milk Glass	300.00
Lamp, Pine Cones, Brown	125.00
Plate, Catalonian, Green, 8 1/2 In.	65.00
Plate, Dancing Nymphs, Green, 8 1/2 In.	550.00
Plate, Five Fruits, Orange, 8 In.	30.00
Sundae, Catalonian, Amethyst	20.00
Sundae, Ruba Rombic, Smoky Topaz	195.00
Tumbler, Ruba Rombic, Smoky Topaz	175.00
Vase, Catalonian, Yellow, Flared Rim, 1931, 4 3/4 In.	172.00
Vase, Chickadee, Ruby, 6 1/2 In.	220.00
Vase, Dogwood, Gold On White, 11 In.	135.00
Vase, Dragonfly, 6 In.	115.00
Vase, Fan, Catalonian, Jade, 6 1/2 In.	70.00
Vase, Fan, Katydid, White Satin, 8 1/2 In.	175.00
Vase, Foxglove, Coral & Blue, Custard Glass, 10 1/2 In.	160.00
Vase, Katydid, White, 8 1/2 In.	44.00
Vase, Owls, Blue, 6 In.	125.00
Vase, Poppies, Tri-Color, White, 11 In.	275.00

CONTEMPORARY GLASS, see Glass-Contemporary.

COOKBOOKS are collected for various reasons. Some are wanted for the recipes, some for investment, and some as examples of advertising. Cookbooks and recipe pamphlets are included in this category.

15 Ways To A Man's Heart, Betty Crocker, 1932, Miniature	22.00
American Woman, Ruth Berolzheimer, Hard Cover, 1943	5.00
Betty Crocker Picture Cooky Book, 44 Pages, 1948, 6 x 9 In.	5.00
Borden's Book Of Magic Recipes, Elsie On Cover	20.00
Breakfast, Dinner & Tea, 351 Pages, 1860	30.00
California Magic With Cottage Cheese, California Dairy Industry, 24 Pages, 1956	6.00
Elsie's Magic Recipes, 1942	30.00 to 45.00
Every-Day Cookbook, 316 Pages, 1889	45.00
Excellent Recipes For Baking With Fleischmann's Yeast, 1910, 52 Pages, 6 In.	10.00
Fannie Farmer, Boston Cooking School, 1938	45.00
Favorite Recipes Of Famous Musicians, Photographs & Menus, 1941	20.00
General Mills Cake Recipe, 1950s, 6 x 8 In.	10.00
Good Things To Eat, Velvet Cake Flour, 1954	8.00
Granny, Beverly Hillbillies TV Series	125.00

Hotel St. Francis, 1919, 432 Pages .... .80.00 to 100.00
Illustrated Treasury Of Cooking, Loose-Leaf, 448 Pages 25.00
Jell-O Girl Entertains, Rose O'Neill Cover, 1914 .... 70.00
Karo Finer Fruits, 1946, 6 x 9 In. 10.00
Kate Smith's Breakfast Book, General Foods, 1941, 48 Pages, 8 x 10 In. 12.00
Kingan's Meat Recipe, 1950s, 6 x 8 In. 10.00
La Choy, 1925 .... 25.00
Ladies Home Journal, 1st Edition, Hard Cover, 728 Pages 40.00
Modern Family, Meta Given, Hard Cover, 1943 .... 5.00
Pillsbury, 100 Prize Winning Recipes, 1950 .... 40.00
Pot Luck, New York City Women's Council Of Navy League Of U.S., 80 Pages 18.00
Pyrex, Hard Cover, 1953 .... 6.00
Quaker, Art Of Cookery Made Plain & Easy, Hannah Glasse, 1786 .... 395.00
Ransom's, Buffalo, N.Y., 1885 .... 356.00
Rumford, Hardcover, 1928 .... 16.00
Savannah, Image Of Mammy On Cover, Harriet Ross Colquitt, 1933 .... 45.00
Swift's Little Cook, Swift & Co., Lift Hat To Reveal 36-Page Booklet, 1900 .... 20.00
The Gentleman's Companion Exotic Cookery, Leather Cover, 1946 .... 35.00
Uneeda Bakers 6th Cookbook Of Menu Magic, 1934 .... 10.00
Virginia Dare Wine, 1941 .... 30.00
Wurlitzer Centennial, 1956 .... 65.00

COOKIE JARS with brightly painted designs or amusing figural shapes
became popular in the mid-1930s. Many companies made them and
collectors search for cookie jars either by design or by maker's name.
Listed here are examples by the less common makers. Major factories
are listed under their own names in other categories of the book, such
as Abingdon, Brush, Hull, McCoy, Red Wing, and Shawnee. See also
the Black and Disneyana categories.

3 Bears, Gold Trim, Regal China 225.00
Airplane, Red Baron, California Originals 430.00
Alley Cat, Metlox 165.00
Apple, Metlox 90.00
Apple, Purinton, Oval, 9 1/2 In. .... .70.00 to 80.00
Aunt Jemima, Brown Face, Plastic, F & F .... .350.00 to 875.00
Baby Elephant, American Bisque .... .125.00 to 145.00
Balloon Lady, Pottery Guild 200.00
Barn, Regal China .... .150.00 to 285.00
Bart Simpson, With Cookie, Treasure Craft .... .50.00 to 55.00
Bear, On Blocks, Sierra Vista/Starnes 250.00
Bear, On Stump, California Originals 35.00
Bear, Sombrero, Metlox 75.00
Beaver, Metlox 185.00
Bert & Ernie Fine Cookies, California Originals 325.00
Betsy Ross, Enesco 75.00
Betty Crocker, Cylinder 75.00
Big Bird, Holding Cookie Jar, California Originals .... .95.00 to 125.00
Big Boy .... .400.00 to 800.00
Big Boy, Wolfe Studio, 1992 .... 395.00
Blackboard Boy, American Bisque 375.00
Blackboard Clown, American Bisque 225.00
Blue Bonnet Sue, Benjamin & Medwin .... .60.00 to 65.00
Brownie Scout, Metlox 175.00
Bubbles The Hippo, Yellow, Metlox 495.00
Buick, White, Appleman 895.00
Cadillac, Pink, Expressive Design, Box 120.00
Cat, Black & White, North American Ceramics 28.00
Cat, Standing, American Bisque 125.00
Cat-In-The-Hat 375.00
Century 21 House 675.00
Chalkboard Girl, Mustn'T Forget, American Bisque 325.00
Chef, Japan 400.00
Chef, Pearl China .... .450.00 to 850.00

Chef, White, Artistic Pottery 300.00
Children On Drum, Metlox 200.00
Churn Boy, American Bisque 225.00
Circus Tent, Brayton Laguna 295.00
Clock, Marshall Field 95.00
Coffee Grinder, California Originals 35.00
Cookie Book, California Cleminsons 175.00
Cookie House, California Cleminsons 150.00
Cool Cat 225.00
Corvette, Black & White, Appleman, 17 3/4 In. 605.00
Cottontailors, Fitz & Floyd 95.00
Cow, Purple, Metlox 425.00
Cow, Spots, Twin Winton 65.00
Cow, Yellow, Metlox 250.00
Cowboy Boots, American Bisque 225.00
Crowing Rooster, Metlox 395.00
Debutante, Blue Dress, Metlox 375.00
Diaper Pin Pig, Regal China 595.00
Dino, Flinstones, American Bisque ....800.00 to 895.00
Dolphin, With White Boy, A Little Company 175.00
Drummer Boy, Metlox 500.00
Dutch Girl, Regal China 695.00
Elsie The Cow, In Barrel, Pottery Guild ....375.00 to 475.00
Entenman's Chef ....140.00 to 150.00
Family Circus Billy, Starnes 450.00
Felix The Cat, Benjamin & Medwin 35.00
Fire Truck, Red, California Original 150.00
Fred Flintstone, Standing, Certified International 65.00
Fred Flintstone & Pebbles, Sitting In Chair, Vandor 325.00
Frog With Tie, Metlox 140.00
Frosty Penguin, Metlox 75.00
Fruit Basket, Metlox 80.00
Garfield, On Stack Of Cookies, Enesco 350.00
Goldilocks, Regal China ....195.00 to 350.00
Good Humors Truck 450.00
Graduate Owl, Doranne Of California 40.00
Grandma, Lime Collar, American Bisque 120.00
Grandma, Treasure Craft 45.00
Gumby & Pokey 50.00
Happy Bull, Twin Winton 65.00
Hearts & Flowers, Sigma 300.00
Hobby Horse, Sierra Vista 140.00
Homer Simpson 55.00
Homestead Provincial, Canister, Metlox 90.00
House, Smiley Face On Reverse Side, Sierra Vista 195.00
Human Bean, Enesco 165.00
Humpty Dumpty, Yellow Base, Regal China 265.00
I Love Lucy, Car 100.00
Jack-In-The-Box, American Bisque ....150.00 to 165.00
John Deere, Cylinder 50.00
Kangaroo, Twin Winton 200.00
Katy Cat, Metlox 85.00
Keebler Elf, Head, Plastic, F & F 100.00
Ken-L-Ration Dog, Plastic, F & F ....95.00 to 125.00
Kentucky Fried Chicken 95.00
Keystone Cop, Twin Winton 85.00
Kitten On Beehive, American Bisque ....80.00 to 130.00
Koala Bear, Metlox 80.00
Lighthouse, Metlox 600.00
Little Lamb, Twin Winton 30.00
Little Red Riding Hood, Metlox 1475.00
Little Red Riding Hood, Napco ....165.00 to 175.00
Little Red Riding Hood, Regal China 295.00

Maid, Black, Brayton Laguna 4000.00
Majorette, Regal China .... 325.00 to 475.00
Mammy, Mosaic Tile, Carol Gifford 950.00
Mammy, National Silver 300.00
Mammy, Pearl China .... 475.00 to 795.00
Mammy, Yellow, Gilner 1200.00
Mammy, Yellow, Mosaic Tile, Carol Gifford 545.00
Milk Wagon, American Bisque .... 80.00 to 225.00
Monk, Thou Shall Not Steal, Treasure Craft 45.00
Monkey In Barrel, Doranne Of California 150.00
Mother Hen, Metlox 175.00
Mr. Rabbit, American Bisque 175.00
Mrs. Fields Cookie Sack 70.00
Mrs. Rabbit, Metlox .... 75.00 to 175.00
Nestle's Toll House Cookie House 90.00
Ninja Turtle, Taiwan 60.00
Noah's Ark 150.00
Nun, DeForest 275.00
Old MacDonald Milk Pitcher 450.00
Old Red Truck, Treasure Craft 350.00
Oscar The Grouch, California Originals 60.00
Packard Convertible, White, Appleman 800.00
Paddington Bear, Yellow Hat, Eden Toys 450.00
Pancake Mammy, Carol Gifford 285.00
Panda Bear, Metlox 75.00
Parakeets In Cage 85.00
Pear, Green, Metlox 110.00
Peter Pumpkin Eater, Vallona Starr 510.00
Picadilly Circus, Marshall Field 495.00
Pig In A Poke, American Bisque .... 65.00 to 125.00
Pig With Overalls, Treasure Craft 33.00
Pillsbury All-Purpose Sack Of Flour 75.00
Pillsbury Doughboy, Benjamin & Medwin 60.00
Pink Panther, Treasure Craft .... 195.00 to 300.00
Pinnochio On Whale, Starnes 750.00
Poodle, At Cookie Counter, Twin Winton 95.00
Potbellied Stove, Black, California Cleminsons .... 160.00 to 165.00
Potbellied Stove, White, California Cleminsons 125.00
Professor Ludwig Von Drake, American Bisque 500.00
Prunella Pig, Fitz & Floyd 80.00
Puddles The Duck, Metlox .... 45.00 to 68.00
Puppy, California Originals 40.00
Quaker Oats, Regal China .... 85.00 to 145.00
Rabbit On Cabbage, Metlox 125.00
Raccoon Cookie Bandit, Metlox 215.00
Rag Doll, Metlox 135.00
Raggedy Andy, Metlox 180.00
Raggedy Ann, Metlox 175.00
Recipe Jar, American Bisque 95.00
Rose Petal Place, Teapot Shape, Treasure Craft 550.00
Rubbles House, American Bisque .... 475.00 to 750.00
Ruby, Black, Alfano Art Pottery 450.00
Sad Bear, Sierra Vista 25.00
Sailor Elephant, Twin Winton .... 65.00 to 135.00
Sandman Cookies, Flasher, American Bisque 100.00
Santa Claus, Black, Metlox 600.00
School Teacher, Kay Steindorf 325.00
Seal On Igloo, American Bisque 150.00
Shedd's Spread Crock 45.00
Skyway Taxi, Appleman, 1979 .... 825.00
Smokey The Bear, 50th Anniversary, Joyce Roerig .... 195.00 to 295.00
Snowman, California Originals 170.00
Sock Hoppers, Fitz & Floyd 265.00

Squirrel, On Barrel Of Nuts, Metlox	145.00
Sugar Plum Castle, Fitz & Floyd	165.00
Sylvester Head, Tweety, Applause, Warner Brothers	55.00
Tasmanian Devil, Football Player, Certified International, 1993	35.00
Tony The Tiger, Kellogg's, Plastic	45.00 to 100.00
Toucan, Treasure Craft	40.00
Transformers, Roman Ceramics	135.00
Treasure Chest, American Bisque	80.00
Tree Of Knowledge, Treasure Craft	950.00
Turtle, Doranne Of California	28.00
Walrus, Doranne Of California	125.00
Whale, White, Metlox	250.00
Woody Woodpecker, California Originals	700.00 to 995.00
Yellow Pear, Los Angeles Pottery	35.00
Yogi Bear, American Bisque	425.00 to 500.00
Yogi Bear, Head, Hanna-Barbera	975.00
Yorktowne, Cover, Pfaltzgraff	75.00
Ziggy On Stack Of Cookies, Sigma	225.00

COORS ware was made by a pottery in Golden, Colorado, owned by the Coors Beverage Company. Dishes and decorative wares were produced from the turn of the century until the pottery was destroyed by fire in the 1930s. The name *Coors* is marked on the back. For more information, see *Kovels' Depression Glass & Dinnerware Price List.*

COORS

U.S.A.

Ashtray, Anholt	20.00
Casserole, Cover, Orange, 7 In.	95.00
Casserole, Orange, Straight, Rack, 7 In.	80.00
Coffeepot, Thermos, Porcelain, Drip	250.00
Cookie Jar, Rosebud, Utility	85.00
Creamer, Poppy	30.00
Creamer, Rosebud, Red	60.00
Custard, Rosebud, 6 Piece	78.00
Jar, Utility, Cover, Orange, 2 1/2 Pt.	60.00
Jug, Water, Rosebud	100.00
Lamp, Pool Table, 3 Water Scenes, Plastic	48.00
Platter, Rosebud, Oval, 12 In.	45.00
Platter, Starburst, 15 In.	80.00
Ramekin, Rosebud	18.00
Salt & Pepper, Rosebud	40.00 to 45.00
Sugar Shaker, Rosebud	50.00
Teapot, Floree	90.00
Teapot, Rosebud, Green, 6 Cup	190.00
Tumbler, Rosebud, Footed, Blue	100.00
Vase, Cripple Creek, Green, White, 5 In.	50.00
Vase, Grecian Urn Style, 2 Handles, Mauve Glaze, 8 In.	44.00
Vase, Matte Yellow, 8 In.	95.00
Vase, Protruding Handles, Russet Glaze, Matte Green Interior, Signed, 8 In.	85.00
Vase, Rose Color, Marked, 6 3/4 In.	25.00
Vase, Salmon, 8 In.	90.00
Vase, Tan, Green Interior, Octagonal, 8 In.	25.00
Vase, Yellow, 6 In.	45.00

COPELAND pieces listed here are those that have a mark including the word Copeland used between 1847 and 1976. Marks include Copeland Spode and Copeland & Garrett. See also Copeland Spode and Royal Worcester.

Figurine, Summer, Young Man, Sacrificing Ram, Parian, 1875, 9 1/2 In.	90.00
Figurine, Winter, Old Man Carrying Firewood, Parian, 1875, 9 1/2 In.	110.00
Pitcher, Football, White Raised Figures, Blue Ground, 7 In.	325.00
Plate, Botanical, Mansard Border, 1910	35.00
Plate, Dinner, Gold & Cobalt Rim, 10 In., 8 Piece	115.00
Plate, Orchid, Plumed Bird In Center, England, 9 In.	11.00
Spoon Warmer, Majolica, Open Shell, By Coral, Impressed Mark, 1869, 4 5/8 In.	860.00

Sugar & Cream Jug, Red, Willow Pattern, Scalloped, Butterfly Border, 1851-1885 .... 255.00
Tea Set, White, Baskets & Green Floral Design, 19 Piece 121.00
Tumbler, Hunt Scene, White, Blue Ground, Impressed Mark 95.00

COPELAND SPODE appears on some pieces of nineteenth-century English porcelain. Josiah Spode established a pottery at Stoke-on-Trent, England, in 1770. In 1833, the firm was purchased by William Copeland and Thomas Garrett and the mark was changed. In 1847, Copeland became the sole owner and the mark changed again. W.T. Copeland & Sons continued until a 1976 merger when it became Royal Worcester Spode. Pieces are listed in this book under the name that appears in the mark. Copeland Spode, Copeland, and Royal Worcester have separate listings.

COPELAND
SPODE
ENGLAND

Bowl, Cobalt Blue, Iron Red Foliage, Imari Design, 11 In., Pair 173.00
Butter Chip, Gainsborough, Great Britain 80.00
Cup & Saucer, Maritime Rose, Green Mark 35.00
Cup & Saucer, Wicker Dell 12.00
Dish, Bird Pattern, 9 In. 560.00
Dish, Cobalt Blue, Mandarin Design, Gilt, 10 3/4 In., Pair 75.00
Gravy Boat, Camilla, Blue & White 40.00
Humidor, Grape Vine On Lid, White Figures On Base, Gray & Brown, 7 In. 137.00
Jam Jar, Allover Pink Gold, Floral, Silver Handled Top & Cover 200.00
Pitcher, Hunting Scene, Salt Glaze 165.00
Plate, Cream, Gold Rococo Rim, 9 In., 6 Piece 175.00
Plate, Floral Center, Basket Weave Border, 9 In., 12 Piece 100.00
Plate, Fruit, Flower Design, Signed, J. Price, 9 In. 325.00
Plate, Gilt Floral & Foliate Design, Blue Banded, 10 1/2 In., 12 Piece 375.00
Plate, Maritime Rose, Impressed Mark, 9 1/4 In. 30.00
Plate, Romantic Scene In Center, Black, White, 1844, 9 In. 52.00
Soup, Dish, Portland Vase Design, Early 20th Century, 6 Piece 495.00
Teapot, Cover, Earthenware, Cobalt Blue, Gray, White, 1894-1910, 5 In. 165.00
Tumbler, Hunt Scene, Blue, White, Early 20th Century, 4 In. ....65.00 to 90.00

COPPER has been used to make utilitarian items, such as teakettles and cooking pans, since the days of the early American colonists. Copper became a popular metal with the Arts & Crafts makers of the early 1900s, and decorative pieces, like bookends and desk sets, were made. Other pieces of copper may be found in the Arts & Crafts, Bradley & Hubbard, Kitchen, and Roycroft categories.

Ashtray, Hammered, Embossed With 4-Lobes, Round, G. Stickley, 5 1/4 In. 137.50
Ashtray, Hammered, Original Patina, Dirk Van Erp, 4 In. 88.00
Bed Warmer, Brass, Hot Water Bottle Style, Pat. 12/12/11 .... 95.00
Bed Warmer, Engraved Peacock Lid, Turned Wooden Handle, 31 In. 575.00
Bed Warmer, Engraved Star, Turned Figured Maple Handle 355.00
Bed Warmer, Floral Engraved Lid, Wooden Handle, 43 In. 220.00
Bed Warmer, Inner Cap To Ensure Watertight Seal, c.1820 .... 235.00
Bed Warmer, Punched Design, Maple Handle, 19th Century 275.00
Bowl, Hammered, Dark Brown Patina, Closed Form, Dirk Van Erp, 7 x 3 In. 885.00
Bowl, Hammered, Dark Brown Patina, Flared, Dirk Van Erp, 7 x 2 1/2 In. 825.00
Bowl, Hammered, G. Stickley, Impressed Mark, 7 x 2 1/2 In. 335.00
Bowl, Hammered, Kalo, Impressed Mark, 7 1/2 In. 385.00
Bowl, Hammered, Lobed Form, Silver Wash Interior, F. Novick, 6 1/2 x 2 In. 175.00
Bowl, Hammered, Tusk Handles, c.1915, 18 x 11 1/2 In. 2600.00
Bowl, Hammered, Waisted, H. Dixon, San Francisco, 1920, 5 x 2 1/2 In. 415.00
Box, 3 Coins Attached To Top, Original Patina, Dirk Van Erp, 11 x 3 1/2 x 1 1/2 In. 400.00
Box, Hammered, Wood Interior, Impressed Mark, Dirk Van Erp, 11 x 1/2 In. 190.00
Box, Hinged Rectangular Lid, Bending Trees In Front, Pa., 19th Century, 3 x 8 In. 2875.00
Box, Pill, Enameled Top, Opal Cabochon, Arts & Crafts, 1 1/4 x 3 1/4 In. 275.00
Box, Presentation, Floral Design, Georg Jensen, 1916, 3 1/4 x 7 1/2 x 5 3/4 In. 800.00
Bucket, Coal, Hammered, 2 Handles, Riveted, Benedict Studios, 11 x 12 In. 1500.00
Bucket, Cover, Dovetailed Flat Base, Iron Bale Handle 225.00
Cauldron, Apple Butter, Stirrer, Iron Stand, 19th Century, 25 x 25 In. 495.00
Chafing Dish, Metal Pan & Cover, Wooden Handles, Onondaga Shops, 14 x 13 In. 445.00

Chamberstick, Riveted Spade Shape Handle, Signed, G. Stickley, 9 x 7 In.	565.00
Chestnut Roaster, Wriggle-Work Design, 19th Century, 11 1/2 In.	190.00
Coal Hod & Shovel, Handle, Helmet Shape, 19th Century, 20 x 20 In.	230.00
Cocktail Shaker, Norman Bel Geddes, Revere	500.00
Cocktail Shaker, Zephyr, Revere	225.00
Coffeepot, Goose Neck Spout, Brass Finial, Incised Marking, 12 In.	65.00
Container, Dovetailed, Tab Handles, American, 1852, 6 1/2 x 7 1/2 In.	245.00
Desk Set, Trefoil Pattern, Sorensen, Signed, 4 Piece	165.00
Figurine, Mason Allen, Full Uniform, Etban, 18 1/2 x 6 1/2 In.	150.00
Figurine, Panda Bear, Signed, EMES No. 636, 12 3/4 In.	165.00
Frame, Picture, Hammered, Arts & Crafts, 6 1/2 x 10 In.	220.00
Humidor, Hammered Cover, Arts & Crafts, 7 In.	135.00
Jar, Cover, Hammered, Rivet Design, Onondaga, 6 In.	550.00
Jardiniere, Hammered, Tapered Base, Rolled Rim, Stickley Brothers, 7 3/4 x 11 In.	495.00
Jug, Ale, Dovetailed, England, c.1790, 4 1/8 In.	250.00
Kettle, Candy, Dovetailed, Steel Handles, 21 1/2 In.	247.00
Kettle, Dovetailed Seams, Hammered, Iron Bale Handle, 3-Legged Base, 20 x 21 In.	275.00
Kettle, Dovetailed, Brass Ears, Iron Bail Handle, Mid-18th Century, 11 1/2 In.	200.00
Kettle, Dovetailed, Iron Bale Handle, 13 x 9 In.	50.00
Kettle, Maple Sugar, Hand Hammered, c.1870, 7 1/2 x 16 1/4 In.	155.00
Letter Holder, Hammered, Sailing Ship, Medallion, Enamel, G. Twichell, 4 1/4 In.	800.00
Measure, Engraved Script 2 Gills, Dovetailed, Scotland, 19th Century, 4 1/4 In. . .145.00 to	175.00
Molds are listed in the Kitchen category.	
Mug, Dovetailed, Early 19th Century, 4 x 4 1/4 In.	185.00
Mug, Hammered, With Riveted Brass Strips, Lined In Tin, Stickley Brothers, 4 x 5 In.	275.00
Mug, Tavern, Dovetailed, Large Handle, 18th Century, 1 Pt., 4 1/4 In.	295.00
Pitcher, Protruding Lip, Angular Handle, Medium Patina, Chase, 9 3/4 x 8 In.	90.00
Plaque, Anointment Of Saul, Repousse, Gilded, Arched, Russia, 18th Century, 16 In.	275.00
Pot, Glue, Carpenter's, 6 1/2 x 5 3/4 In.	295.00
Pot, Glue, Joiner's, Inner Container, 1830s, 4 x 8 In.	275.00
Saucepan, Cover, Dovetailed, 19th Century, 8 x 5 1/2 In. . . . . .195.00 to	295.00
Scoop, Marked Master, Copper, 19th Century, 9 3/4 In.	145.00
Stein, Gasthaus Scene, Pewter Cover, 1 Liter	110.00
Still, Whiskey, Stilts	1100.00
Tankard, Hinged Lid, Brass Thumbpiece, c.1790, 8 1/2 In.	375.00
Tea & Coffee Set, Serving Pieces Lined In Sterling Silver, Joseph Heinrichs, 12 Piece	4950.00
Teakettle, Dovetailed, Brass Trim, 12 In.	138.00
Teakettle, Dovetailed, Swing Handle, Dutch, c.1750	750.00
Teakettle, Scandinavian, Marked PA Gundersen, 7 x 7 In.	175.00
Teakettle, Swivel Handle, 1840, 8 1/4 In.	192.00
Teapot, Brass Handle, W.A.S. Benson, c.1895	657.00
Teapot, Bulbous Shape, Hinged Handled, Gooseneck Spout, Finial, 7 In.	45.00
Tray, Hammered, Cleaned Patina, Rectangular, Gustav Stickley, 10 In.	225.00
Tray, Hammered, Raised Edge, Marked, Dirk Van Erp, 18 In.	1100.00
Tray, Hammered, Recessed Center, Green Highlights, Dirk Van Erp, 19 x 13 In.	470.00
Umbrella Holder, Hammered, 4 Ball Feet, Rectangular, Dirk Van Erp, 16 x 12 In.	1760.00
Vase, Continental, Rococo, Garniture, 8 1/2 In., Pair	950.00
Vase, Floral Design, Silver Overlay, Silver Crest, 6 In.	165.00
Vase, Hammered, Dirk Van Erp, 5 1/2 In.	1045.00
Vase, Hammered, Fluted, Ribbed Form, Pedestal Base, Marie Zimmerman, 19 In.	3850.00
Vase, Hammered, Original Patina, Dirk Van Erp, 7 In.	1430.00
Vase, Hammered, Original Patina, Dirk Van Erp, 11 x 17 In.	6600.00
Vase, Hammered, Rolled Rim, 7 1/2 In.	150.00
Vase, Hammered, Rolled Rim, Baluster Form, Dirk Van Erp, 10 In.	800.00
Vase, Hammered, Rolled Rim, Heinrichs, 15 1/2 In.	445.00

COPPER LUSTER items are listed in the Luster category.

CORALENE glass was made by firing many small colored beads on the outside of glassware. It was made in many patterns in the United States and Europe in the 1880s. Reproductions are made today.

Hatpin Holder, Woodland Pattern	395.00
Pin Tray, Beaded, 8 x 4 In.	200.00

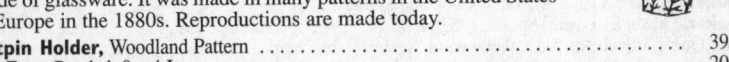

Pitcher, Peppermint Striped, Rose Interior, Tricorner Mouth, Amber Handle, 6 1/2 In. . . .	495.00
Sugar & Creamer, Quilted Blue, Seaweed	400.00
Vase, Deep Rose, Pale Pink, Yellow Crystal Beads, Gold Trim Top, Wheeling, 7 1/2 In. . .	600.00
Vase, Marked, 1909, 4 1/2 x 5 In.	168.00
Vase, Shaded Deep To Pale Pink, 7 1/2 In.	435.00
Vase, Yellow Seaweed, Applied Amber Feet, 6 In.	275.00
Water Set, White Satin, Flowers, Yellow, Brown Acorns, 7 Piece	395.00
Wine, Cranberry, Beaded Leaves	135.00

CORDEY China Company was founded by Boleslaw Cybis in 1942 in Trenton, New Jersey. The firm produced gift shop items. In 1969 it was acquired by the Lightron Corp. and operated as the Schiller Cordey Co., manufacturers of lamps. About 1950 Boleslaw Cybis began making Cybis porcelains, which are listed in their own category in this book.

Bust, Lady With Bonnet, Collar, Scroll Base, 14 In.	90.00
Bust, Woman, No. 5003, 14 In.	58.00
Figurine, Cat, Full-Bodied, Artist	160.00
Figurine, Colonial Man, No. 5042, 14 In.	125.00
Figurine, Man, Full Figure, 16 In.	125.00
Figurine, Oriental Woman, Serpent Entwined Around Her, Signed	450.00
Figurine, Poodle, 16 In.	250.00
Plate, Border Scene, Heavy Gold	45.00
Wall Pocket, Woman, Pair	325.00

CORKSCREWS have been needed since the first bottle was sealed with a cork, probably in the seventeenth century. Today collectors search for the early, unusual patented examples or the figural corkscrews of recent years.

Anheuser-Busch, Bottle Shape, Metal, Williamson Co., 2 3/4 In.	36.00
Anheuser-Busch, Chrome Bottle Shape, Brass Insignia, Pre-Prohibition	42.00
Anheuser-Busch, Wooden Handle, Williamson, c.1900	40.00
Antler, Stamped Germany	85.00
Bartender Head, Composition, Full Figure, 1930s, 7 1/2 In.	45.00
Drink Lemp Of St. Louis	150.00
Golf Club	23.00
Guchenheimer Rye Whiskey	15.00
Leering Bacchante Above 2 Herm Figures, Bronze, Victorian, 5 In.	400.00
Lemp Brewing, St. Louis, Bullet, Metal, Pre-Prohibition	33.00
Man, Composition, Syrocowood, 1930s, 8 1/2 In.	293.00
Mechanical, Brass, Whalebone Handle	352.00
Mermaid, Bent At Waist, Celluloid	375.00
Perpetual, Germany	250.00
Pig, Brass, Rhinestones, Box	45.00
Pixie, Pair Holding Hands Back To Back, Spelter Handle, 5 3/4 In.	88.00
Sailor Head, Celluloid, 1920s, 5 In.	50.00
Sea Serpent, Folding, Brass Handle, Steel Screw, 1920s, 3 In.	70.00
Silver & Ivory, Mathew Linwood, England, 19th Century	650.00
Steel, Wooden Handle, 7 1/2 In.	65.00
Viking Ship, Splayed Steel Shaft, 1930s, 3 1/2 In.	33.00
Vollstead, Wooden Handle	75.00
Zigzag, Plated Steel, France, 7 In.	38.00

CORONATION souvenirs have been made since the 1800s. Pottery, glass, tin, silver, and paper objects with a picture of the monarchs and date have been sold at many coronations. The pieces that mention King Edward VIII, the king who was never crowned, are not rare; collectors should be sure to check values before buying. Related pieces are found in the Commemorative category.

Beaker, Edward VIII, May, 1937, Copeland Spode	175.00
Beaker, Queen Elizabeth, Spode, 1953, 4 1/2 In.	32.00
Box, Queen Elizabeth, 1953, Wedgwood, Square, 4 In.	50.00
Box, Vesta, King Edward, Book Shape	77.00

Cup & Saucer, Queen Elizabeth, Perpetual, Hammersley, 1953	25.00
Figure Set, Johillco, Box, 1938, 54 Piece	195.00
Mug, King Edward VII, 1902, Moorcroft	825.00
Mug, Queen Elizabeth II, Royal Doulton	65.00
Pin Tray, Queen Elizabeth, 1953, 5 1/2 In.	38.00
Pitcher, Milk, George V & Mary, 1911, 5 In.	110.00
Pitcher, Pub, Queen Elizabeth, White Enameled Picture Around Crown, 1953	32.00
Plate, George V & Mary, 1911, 10 1/2 In.	138.00
Plate, Queen Elizabeth, Shelley China, 1953	23.00
Plate, Queen Elizabeth II, Silver Jubilee, 1952-1977	45.00
Toy, Coach, Horse Drawn, Cast Metal, In Case, Book, England	75.00

COSMOS is a pressed milk glass pattern with colored flowers made from 1894 to 1915 by the Consolidated Lamp and Glass Company. Tablewares and lamps were made in this pattern. A few pieces were also made of clear glass with painted decorations. Other glass patterns are listed under Consolidated Lamp and also in various glass categories.

Beverage Set, White Opaque Glass, Polychrome Florals, 7 Piece	360.00
Butter, Cover	185.00
Pitcher, Syrup, No Lid	165.00
Powder Jar, Colored Flowers	275.00

COVERLETS were made of linen or wool during the nineteenth century. Most of the coverlets date from 1800 to 1860. Four types were made: the double weave, jacquard, summer and winter, and overshot. Later coverlets were made of a variety of materials. Quilts are listed in this book in their own category.

Double Weave, Nine Star, Blue Green & Brick Red On Cream, 2 Piece, 103 x 75 In.	190.00
Double Weave, Summer-Winter, Snowflake, Pine Tree, 2 Piece, 71 x 87 In.	302.00
Jacquard, 4 Floral Medallions, Tree & Building Border, 74 x 84 In.	910.00
Jacquard, 4 Rose Medallions, Bird Borders & Corners, E. Spitler, 1848, 70 x 91 In.	665.00
Jacquard, 4 Rose Medallions, Bird, Rose Tree Border, Olive Green, 1843, 72 x 89 In.	165.00
Jacquard, 4 Rose Medallions, Flowers, Building Border, Eagle Corners, 72 x 82 In.	385.00
Jacquard, 4 Rose Medallions, Rose, Bird Borders, 1842, 70 x 85 In.	770.00
Jacquard, 4 Rose Medallions, Star & Bird House, Blue, 66 x 91 In.	220.00
Jacquard, 4 Rose Medallions, Stars, Compote Borders, 86 x 87 In.	1320.00
Jacquard, 4 Rose, Compass Star Medallions, Bird Border, 81 x 88 In.	825.00
Jacquard, 4 Rose, Star Medallion Center, Vintage Border, 65 x 81 In.	385.00
Jacquard, 4 Rose, Star Medallions, Bird Border, Blue, 71 x 89 In.	335.00
Jacquard, Center Floral Medallion, Eagles At Corners, 78 x 84 In.	165.00
Jacquard, Central Medallion, Cornucopias & Foliage Border, 78 x 86 In.	192.00
Jacquard, Double Lily Pattern, Blue, Red, Green, John Kaufman, 78 x 93 In.	525.00
Jacquard, Double Lily, Double Row Of 8 Pointed Stars, John Kaufman, 78 x 93 In.	575.00
Jacquard, Double Weave, Peacock Feeding, Blue & White, 73 x 82 In.	330.00
Jacquard, Eagle, Independence Hall Border, C.W. Jerman, 1835, 91 x 77 In.	630.00
Jacquard, Flag, Decorated, Capital Edge, 1869, 75 x 81 In.	1323.00
Jacquard, Floral & Acorn Medallions, Eagle Border, 1836, 74 x 94 In.	165.00
Jacquard, Floral & Starflower Medallions, Navy, Natural, Ohio, 1847, 72 x 90 In.	455.00
Jacquard, Floral Medallions, Bird Border, Red, Blue, 1835, 74 x 89 In.	445.00
Jacquard, Floral Medallions, Birds, J. Mellinger, 1839, 81 x 96 In.	525.00
Jacquard, Floral Medallions, Border, P. Warner, Carroll County, 80 x 90 In.	138.00
Jacquard, Floral Medallions, Building Border, 1845, 74 x 99 In.	1320.00
Jacquard, Floral Medallions, Christian & Heathen Border, 73 x 73 In.	165.00
Jacquard, Floral Medallions, Jacob & Michael Archer, 1860, 72 x 83 In.	385.00
Jacquard, Floral Medallions, Pinwheels, Roosters, Red, Blue, 76 x 82 In.	220.00
Jacquard, Floral Medallions, Scrolled Border, Natural, Blue, 1 Piece, 70 x 78 In.	165.00
Jacquard, Floral Medallions, Stripes, Rose Border, 1843, 70 x 88 In.	415.00
Jacquard, Floral Vines, Navy Blue, Red, White, 1 Piece, 75 x 90 In.	220.00
Jacquard, Floral, Star Medallions, Bird Border, 1847, 76 x 79 In.	605.00
Jacquard, Geometric Floral Medallions, Corner Dated 1854, 71 x 87 In.	275.00
Jacquard, Geometric Floral Medallions, Probst & Seip, 1847, 76 x 90 In.	495.00
Jacquard, Geometric Floral Medallions, Tree, Bird Borders, 1842, 73 x 84 In.	470.00

Jacquard, Geometric Floral, Navy, Tomato Red, White, 1850, 72 x 90 In. 300.00
Jacquard, Geometric Floral, Rose Border, 1848, 62 x 86 In. 470.00
Jacquard, Geometric Floral, Stars, Basket Of Flowers, Building Borders, 70 x 85 In. 1100.00
Jacquard, Mariner's Star Variation, Cream Ground, 19th Century, 85 x 84 In. 920.00
Jacquard, Medallion Design, For Emanuel Meily, M. Hosfater, 1837, 78 x 96 In. 230.00
Jacquard, Medallions, Tree Border, Navy, Hannah E. Knapp, 1844, 77 x 81 In. 300.00
Jacquard, Navy, White Florals, Octagons, 1825, 78 x 85 In. 330.00
Jacquard, Nesting Lovebirds, Floral, Red, Black & Mustard, 64 x 76 In. 200.00
Jacquard, Oak Leaf, Oak Tree Border, Blue On White, C. Fehr, 1838, 98 x 71 In. 220.00
Jacquard, Peacocks & Young, Floral Border, 1862, 70 x 88 In. 495.00
Jacquard, Rose Medallions, Geometric Floral, Ohio, 2 Piece, 1844, 76 x 93 In. 435.00
Jacquard, Rose Medallions, Rose Border, York County, Pa, 1846 . . . . 535.00
Jacquard, Roses, Flowers, Navy Blue, Natural, 1 Piece, 78 x 80 In. 165.00
Jacquard, Rough & Ready, Navy Blue, White, 1847, 75 x 82 In. 495.00
Jacquard, Rows Of Alternating Bands Of Floral Rosettes, 103 1/2 x 81 In. 1265.00
Jacquard, Rows Of Roses & Star Medallions, Rooster On Stump, 1842, 90 x 101 In. . . . 1380.00
Jacquard, Single Weave, Peacocks Feeding Young, Blue, White, 75 x 80 In. 550.00
Jacquard, Snowflake & Tile, Navy & White, 88 x 77 1/2 In. 175.00
Jacquard, Snowflake, Pine Tree, Navy Blue, White, 71 x 84 In. 195.00
Jacquard, Snowflakes, Roses, Pine Trees, Scene, Snowflake Border, 72 x 80 In. 250.00
Jacquard, Star Center, Floral Border, Red, Green, 1851, 79 x 99 In. 635.00
Jacquard, Star Medallions, Floral Border, Margret Snyder, 1867, 76 x 92 In. 250.00
Jacquard, Stars, Floral Medallion, Bird Borders, Blue, Red, 2 Piece, 71 x 88 In. 495.00
Jacquard, Various Winged Figures, Turkey Red, Late 19th Century, 80 x 63 In. 175.00
Jacquard, Vintage Center, Bird Border, Purple, Gold, Blue, 76 x 90 In. 950.00
Overshot, Burgundy & White, Faded, 2 Piece, 62 x 81 In. 165.00
Overshot, Geometric, Navy Blue, Natural, 84 x 100 In. 250.00
Overshot, Geometric, Navy Blue, Natural, Tied Fringe, 74 x 74 In. 138.00
Overshot, Geometric, Red & Natural, 62 x 84 In. 180.00
Overshot, Geometric, Salmon Red, Black Wool, Blue Cotton Warp, 82 x 90 In. 165.00
Overshot, Gold, Royal Blue & Natural, Faded, 2 Piece, 84 x 94 In. 165.00
Overshot, Scale Star Design, Pine Tree Border, Navy Blue, Olive, Gold, 70 x 92 In. 220.00
Summer, Winter, Homespun, Black, Purple & White, Squares, 90 x 98 In. 290.00

COWAN POTTERY made art pottery and wares for florists. Guy Cowan
made pottery in Rocky River, Ohio, a suburb of Cleveland, from 1913
to 1931. A stylized mark with the word *Cowan* was used on most
pieces. A commercial, mass-produced line was marked *Lakeware*.
Collectors today search for the Art Deco pieces by Guy Cowan, Viktor
Schreckengost, Waylande Gregory, or Thelma Frazier Winter.

Bookends, Little Boy & A Little Girl, Ivory Matte Glaze, 6 1/2 x 4 In., Pair 775.00
Bookends, Monks, Reading Books, Green Matte Glaze, 6 1/2 x 5 x 4 In. 550.00
Bookends, Sun Bonnet Little Girl, Ivory Matte Glaze, 7 1/4 x 4 In. 550.00
Bowl, Birds Head Exterior, Mottled Pink Interior, Yellow, Ivory, 15 x 4 In. 110.00
Bowl, Blue Luster, Fluted, No. 538 . . . . 60.00
Bowl, Pink, Cream, 9 In. 75.00
Bowl, Ribbed, Blue Interior, Yellow, Ivory, 11 x 3 1/2 In. 88.00
Bowl, Ribbed, Mottled Pink Interior, Yellow, Ivory, 9 1/2 x 4 In. 66.00
Bowl, Sea Horse, Yellow, Ivory, Blue Interior, 16 1/2 x 5 In. 66.00
Candlestick, Floral Base, Yellow, Ivory, 10 1/2 x 5 1/2 In. 66.00
Candlestick, Floral, Yellow, Ivory, 4 In. 66.00
Candlestick, Larkspur Glaze, Handle, Pair 65.00
Charger, Mermaid, Fish, Waves, Blue Green Crackled Glaze, W. Gregory, 1935, 14 In. . . 2970.00
Charger, Undersea Design, Fish & Plants, Signed, 11 1/4 In. 550.00
Compote, Ivory Glaze, Turquoise Glazed Interior, Footed, 3 x 9 3/4 In. 65.00
Compote, Sea Horse Base, Blue Interior Bowl, Yellow, Ivory, 6 x 3 1/2 In. 44.00
Decanter, Chinese Red Crystalline Red Glaze, Corked Stopper, 12 x 4 In. 550.00
Figurine, Girl, Dancing On Flower Frog Base, White Glaze, 12 x 6 x 3 3/4 In. 935.00
Figurine, Slender Nude Woman, Ivory Glaze, W. Gregory, 14 x 6 In. 3300.00
Figurine, Stylized Bird, Gunmetal Glaze, 8 1/2 x 3 1/2 x 4 In. 3575.00
Flower Frog, Nude, 8 In. 325.00
Flower Frog, Scarf Dancer, Woman, Nude, Swirling Scarf, Yellow, Ivory, 11 In. 1100.00

Flower Frog, Scarf Dancer, Woman, White, 7 In. 300.00
Flower Frog, Woman, Dancing With Scarf, White, 6 1/2 In. 220.00
Lamp, Russet, October Rocket 600.00
Match Holder, Sea Horse, Yellow, Ivory, 3 1/2 In. 55.00
Paperweight, Elephant, White 225.00
Plate, Southwest Scene, Ribbed, Tan, Ivory Ground, 8 In. .... .90.00 to 145.00
Trivet, Flowers & Leaves, Hexagonal, Ivory Mark, 7 In. 245.00
Urn, Grape Handles, Yellow, Ivory, Gold Trim, 10 In. 176.00
Vase, Blue Luster, 4 In. 38.00
Vase, Bud, Sea Horse Base, Yellow, Ivory Ground, 7 In. 55.00
Vase, Fan, Sea Horse Base, Pink, 6 In. 60.00
Vase, Fluted, Orange Luster, 6 1/2 In. 70.00
Vase, Green Mottled Glaze, Baluster, 12 x 5 1/2 In. 665.00
Vase, Mother-Of-Pearl Glaze, 9 In. 195.00
Vase, Orange, 7 1/4 In. 195.00
Vase, Pillow, Handles, Yellow, 5 In. 65.00
Vase, Raspberry Red Glaze, Marked, 11 3/4 x 6 In. 358.00
Vase, Sea Horse, Yellow, Ivory, 7 In. 55.00
Vase, Yellow, Gray Luster, Marked, 13 x 5 1/4 In. 825.00

CRACKER JACK, the molasses-flavored popcorn mixture, was first
made in 1896 in Chicago, Illinois. A prize was added to each box in
1912. Collectors search for the old boxes, toys, and advertising materials. Many of the toys are unmarked.

Belt & Buckle, Lee, 1974 .... 25.00
Car, Racing, Tin Lithograph, Meier, 3 1/2 In. 2900.00
Figure, Elephant, Plastic, 1950s, 1 1/2 In. 6.00
Mirror, Good To Eat, Can't Be Beat, Rueckheim Bros., & Eckstien, Pocket 175.00
Motorcycle, Side Car, Penny 1650.00
Postcard, Cracker Jack Bears, No. 6, 5 1/2 x 3 In. 30.00
Puzzle, Palm, Metal, Glass Top, Mirror Bottom, Germany, Box 65.00

CRACKLE GLASS was originally made by the Venetians, but most of the
ware found today dates from the 1800s. The glass was heated, cooled,
and refired so that many small lines appeared inside the glass. It was
made in many factories in the United States and Europe.

Vase, Blue, 1 In. 75.00
Water Set, Blue Handles 100.00

CRANBERRY GLASS is an almost transparent yellow-red glass. It resembles the color of cranberry juice. The glass has been made in Europe
and America since the Civil War. It is still being made, and reproductions can fool the unwary. Related glass items may be listed in other
categories, such as Northwood, Rubena Verde, etc.

Basket, Sweetmeat, Allover Enamel, Forget-Me-Nots, Fork Hook 295.00
Biscuit Jar, Puffy, Silver Mount & Cover, Beaded Melon Shape 195.00
Bottle, White Enameled Dot, Flowers Band, Teardrop Stopper, 10 In. 145.00
Bowl, Cover, Applied Crystal Feet, Flowers, Handles, Finial, 9 1/4 x 7 1/2 In. 660.00
Bowl, Floral Design, Ruffled, Blue, Yellow, 2 3/8 x 4 3/4 In. 125.00
Bowl, Mica Flecks, Scalloped Lip, White Cased, 4 3/4 x 4 In. 143.00
Bowl, Spatter Glass, Cranberry Interior, Goldstone, 4 1/4 x 8 1/2 In. 195.00
Box, Dresser, Landscape Scene, Boy & Girl, White, 4 In. 275.00
Celery Vase, Thumbprint, Enameled Flowers, Handles, Jas. Tufts Co., 10 In. 550.00
Creamer, Chrysanthemum Base, Speckled Satin 450.00
Creamer, Optic Pattern, Clear Applied Handle, Fluted, 5 x 2 3/4 In. 88.00
Cruet, Opalescent Swirl, Reverse Ribbed 300.00
Cruet, Thumbprint, Clear Reeded Handle 66.00
Cruet, Wine, Gold Roses, Crystal Handle, Cut Faceted Stopper, 13 In. 190.00
Decanter, Allover Dainty Leaf Design, Gold Bands, Cranberry Stopper, 8 In. 175.00
Decanter, Applied Flat-Ribbed Handle, Teardrop Steeple Stopper, 10 1/2 In. 165.00
Decanter, Blown, Matching Stopper, Early 1900's, 10 In. 135.00
Decanter, Claret, Figural, Duck, Silver Mounted, 9 In., Pair 198.00

We like this answering
machine message we just
heard: "Please leave a message
at the beep. The person now at
home does not speak English."
It is plausible and explains
why the house is occupied yet
the answering machine is on.

Cranberry Glass, Sugar
Shaker, 12 Panels, 5 1/2 In.

Cranberry Glass, Sugar
Shaker, Paneled, 6 In.

Decanter, Controlled Bubble Pattern, Stopper, 12 1/2 In. .... 16.0●
Decanter, Gold Enamel Flower Design, Clear Handle, Stopper, 10 3/4 In. .... 100.0●
Decanter, Gold Trim, Bubble Stopper, 8 1/2 In. .... 150.0●
Decanter, Horse Scene, Cut-Star On Reverse, Teardrop Stopper, 1869, 10 In. .... 978.0●
Epergne, Lily, 3 Twisted Canes, 1875, 15 In. .... 440.0●
Ewer, Bright Coralene Leaves & Flowers, Crystal Strap Handle, 16 1/4 In. .... 920.0●
Ewer, Floral & Leaf Pattern, Enameled, Clear Handle, 10 1/4 In. .... 121.0●
Ewer, Hawk Shape, Clear Ribbed Handle, Brass Fittings, 10 3/4 In. .... 275.0●
Finger Bowl, Heavy Clear Rigaree On Rim, 2 1/2 x 6 In. .... 77.0●
Jug, Cream, Paneled, Clear Handle, 4 1/2 In. .... 55.0●
Jug, Design, Crystal Handle, 2 In. .... 150.0●
Lamp, Kerosene, Herringbone, Nickeled Stem, Brass Burner, 10 1/2 In. .... 175.0●
Lamp, Stand, Snowflake, Opalescent, Large .... 750.0●
Lemonade Set, Raised Feather, 6 Piece .... 385.0●
Liquor Set, Decanter, 4 Piece .... 66.0●
Patch Box, Encased In Gold Filigree .... 200.0●
Pitcher, 6 Tumblers, Swirl, Ruffled Rim .... 250.0●
Pitcher, Applied Clear Handle, 7 1/2 In. .... 60.0●
Pitcher, Enameled Flowers, Blue, Yellow, Green, Applied Handle, 12 1/2 In. .... 165.0●
Pitcher, Ice Bladder, Bulbous, Clear Handle, 10 x 5 In. .... 210.0●
Pitcher, Leaf Umbrella .... 395.0●
Pitcher, Milk, Ribbed, Clear Reeded Handle, 5 1/4 In. .... 31.0●
Pitcher, Opalescent Spiral Swirls, Crystal Handle, 9 In. .... 192.0●
Pitcher, Overshot, White Drapery, Reeded Handle, 8 In. .... 170.5●
Pitcher, Ripple Pattern, Crystal Handle, Round Mouth, 6 1/4 In. .... 98.0●
Pitcher, Swirl Handles, 8 1/2 In. .... 198.0●
Pitcher, Water, Clear Loop Handle, Floral Enamel, 1895, 11 3/8 x 9 In. .... 275.0●
Pitcher, Windows, Ruffled Mouth, Opalescent .... 695.0●
Pitcher, Yellow Threading .... 55.00 to 66.0●
Salt & Pepper, Tapered Pillar, Enamel Floral, E.G. Wester Holder .... 385.0●
Sugar Shaker, 12 Panels, 5 1/2 In. .... *Illus* 165.0●
Sugar Shaker, Paneled, 6 In. .... *Illus* 176.0●
Syrup, Clear Opalescent .... 225.0●
Syrup, Windows, Swirl, Opalescent .... 1350.0●
Tumbler, Landscape Scene, Boy & Girl, White, Pair .... 80.0●
Vase, Applied Berry Design, 7 7/8 In. .... 28.0●
Vase, Applied Portrait Medallions, Gold, 6 5/8 In., Pair .... 962.0●
Vase, Elongated Twisted Neck, Bulbous Ribbed Base, Ground Pontil, 11 In. .... 85.0●
Vase, Embossed Swirl, Goldstone, 8 1/8 x 3 5/8 In. .... 135.0●
Vase, Gold Church, Flattened Bulbous Bottle Shape, 7 3/4 In. .... 125.0●
Vase, Rigori, Applied Vaseline Feet, 4 1/2 In. .... 100.0●
Vase, Thorny Tree Trunk, Victorian Novelty, 8 1/4 In. .... 110.0●
Vase, Thumbprint, Grotesque, 8 In. .... 22.0●
Vase, White Cased Bowl, Brass Stem, Marble Base, Scalloped, 11 3/8 In. .... 80.0●
Vase, White Enameled Leaf Design, 5 1/2 In. .... 16.0●

CREAMWARE, or queensware, was developed by Josiah Wedgwood about 1765. It is a cream-colored earthenware that has been copied by many factories. Similar wares may be listed under Pearlware and Wedgwood.

Bowl, Ormolu Mounts, Dragons & Garlands, Geschutzt, 8 3/4 In.	200.00
Bowl, With Stand, Latticework, Stamped Sewel, England, c.1820	1250.00
Butter Tub, Leaf Shape	650.00
Charger, Salem Harbor, Salem Marine Society, Certificate, 11 In.	1050.00
Coffeepot, Cauliflower, Floret Finial, Staffordshire, 18th Century, 8 In.	1495.00
Coffeepot, Cauliflower, Pear Shaped, S-Scroll Handle, Staffordshire	5175.00
Coffeepot, Crabstock Handle, Floral Spout, Staffordshire, 1770, 8 In.	3105.00
Coffeepot, Polychrome Enamel, 1870	395.00
Coffeepot, Vines, Cream Strap Handle, Spout, Staffordshire, 1755, 8 In.	9775.00
Compote, Reticulated Rim, Ormolu Garland Mounts, 9 1/2 x 8 In.	220.00 to 245.00
Cup & Saucer Set, Handleless, Washington, Lafayette, 6 Cups, 1 Saucer, 7 Piece	990.00
Dish, Botanical, Stylized Berry, Vine Border, Pink, Green, Gray, 1820, 7 11/16 In.	1265.00
Dish, Leaf Shape, Central Midrib, Gray Highlights, Bud Feet, Staffordshire, 8 In.	1380.00
Dish, Leaf Shape, Long Beaked Bird In Center, Manganese, Staffordshire, 12 In.	4312.00
Figurine, Cowl, Freeform Base, England, 1780, 5 In.	2300.00
Figurine, Cradle, Molded, Splashed Translucent Glaze, Late 18th Century, 4 In.	315.00
Figurine, Lion, Late 18th Century, 6 1/4 In.	745.00
Group, 2 Nude Children, Whieldon-Type, Staffordshire, 1765, 2 3/4 In., Pair	1035.00
Jug, Cover, Pineapple Form, Scroll Handle, 1765, 5 1/2 In.	4600.00
Matchbox, Striker, Dog On Cover, Signed	225.00
Mug, Red Brown Body, Blue Underglaze, Reeded Handle, Staffordshire, 4 In.	1725.00
Pepper Pot, Translucent Glaze, Staffordshire, 18th Century, 4 1/2 In.	315.00
Pitcher, House & Flowers, Purple & Pink Luster, 6 In.	220.00
Plaque, Blind Man, Another Man, St. John, Staffordshire, Oct. 1976, 5 x 7 In.	260.00
Plate, Cauliflower, Green Glazed Leaves, 1765, 9 1/2 In.	1380.00
Plate, Enameled Scene, Floral Rim, Dutch Inscription, 10 In., 4 Piece	2000.00
Plate, Ocher Basketwork Roundel Center, Basket Border, Staffordshire, 11 In.	1955.00
Plate, Ocher Basketwork Roundel, Teal Blue Center, Cream Panels, 1765, 8 In.	460.00
Plate, Scenic, Little Girl & Her Mother Buying Buns, Signed, Lessore, 1863, 9 In.	325.00
Platter, England, c.1820, 18 x 14 1/2 In.	635.00
Snuff Box, Cover, Chinese Man, Standing, Red, Black, Green, Yellow, 3 In.	1150.00
Tea Caddy, Cluster Of Shells On Sides, Dark Cream Ground, Greatbatch, 4 In.	1100.00
Tea Caddy, Green & Red Design, 18th Century	295.00
Teapot, Applied Vines, Flowers, Crabstock Handle, Staffordshire, 1775, 3 1/4 In.	920.00
Teapot, Central Floral Medallion, Crabstock Handle, Staffordshire, 6 In.	1495.00
Teapot, Cover, Beadwork Border, Foliate Handle, Green, Gray, Blue, Yellow, 5 In.	1840.00
Teapot, Cover, Black Transfer, Red, Green, Yellow, Purple, W. Greatbatch, 5 1/4 In.	1495.00
Teapot, Cover, Figures Under Parasol, Tortoiseshell Glaze, Staffordshire, 5 In.	1610.00
Teapot, Cover, Floral Spray Terminals, Fluted Spout, Strap Handle, Cream, 5 In.	1265.00
Teapot, Cover, Goddess In Her Chariot, Rose Red, Gray, Green, W. Greatbatch, 5 In.	635.00
Teapot, Cover, Green, Floral Terminals, Red Rose, Yellow, Blue, Green, 1775, 6 In.	635.00
Teapot, Cover, Prodigal Son, Black, Red, Green, Yellow, Greatbatch, 1770, 5 In.	1035.00
Teapot, Crabstock Handle & Spout, Globular, Staffordshire, 1780, 5 In.	2530.00
Teapot, Crabstock Handle, Spout, Staffordshire, 1760, 4 1/4 In.	483.00
Teapot, Floral Finial, Handle & Leaf Spout, England, 18th Century, 4 3/4 In.	630.00
Teapot, Floral, Leaf Molded Handle & Spout, Globular, Staffordshire, 5 1/4 In.	230.00
Teapot, Leaf Molded Spout, Crabstock Handle, Green, Staffordshire, 5 In.	4887.00
Teapot, Leaf Shape, Crabstock Handle & Finial, Staffordshire, 1760, 4 In.	1035.00
Teapot, Lobed Rim, Square, Staffordshire, 1765, 5 1/2 In.	860.00
Teapot, Oriental Figures Panel, Staffordshire, Late 18th Century, 5 1/2 In.	975.00
Teapot, Overlapping Green Leaves, Cream Florets, Staffordshire, 5 In.	1380.00
Teapot, Pineapple Shape, Yellow & Green Glaze, Staffordshire, 1760, 4 In.	3105.00
Teapot, Pineapple, Ocher Ground, Crabstock Handle, Staffordshire, 5 In.	5175.00
Teapot, Stylized Bark, Manganese Brown Roses, Green, Staffordshire, 4 In.	402.00
Toby Jug, Man Holding Foaming Beaker, Brown Jug, Loop Handle, 10 In.	690.00
Veilleuse, Spouted Bowl, 2 Handles, 18th Century, 2 Part, 7 3/4 In.	220.00
Wall Pocket, Bacchus, Brown & Green Glaze, Late 18th Century, 9 1/2 In.	460.00
Wall Pocket, Flora, Wearing Rose, Green Robe, Undulated Rim, 1765, 11 In.	690.00
Wall Pocket, Framed Mask Head, Staffordshire, 1760, 6 1/4 In.	460.00

CREDIT CARDS, credit tokens, metal charge plates, phone cards, and other similar collectibles that replace money are now part of the numismatic collecting hobby.

American Express, Green, 1970	25.00
Bloomingdales, 1980	6.00
Chevron, 1953	35.00
Mobil Gas, Station, 1950s	22.00
Standard Oil, 1971	15.00

CROWN DERBY is the name given to porcelain made in Derby, England, from the 1770s to 1935. Pieces are marked with a crown and the letter *D* or the word *Derby*. The earliest pieces were made by the original Derby factory, while later pieces were made by the King Street Partnerships (1848–1935) or the Derby Crown Porcelain Co. (1876– 1890). Derby Crown Porcelain Co. became Royal Crown Derby Co. Ltd. in 1890. It is now part of Royal Doulton Tableware Ltd.

Jug, Pakette, Pink Ground, Gold Trim, 1885, Pair	750.00
Sauceboat, Underplate, Cover, Imari Pattern, Lion, Paw Feet, 8 1/2 In., Pair	460.00
Soup, Dish, Gilt Foliate Design, Blue Ground Borders, 1810, 9 3/4 In., 8 Piece	400.00
Vase, Hand Designed, Tiffany & Co., N.Y., 1885, 9 1/2 In.	850.00
Vase, Ribbed Design, Gilt Chrysanthemums, 1875, 13 In.	230.00
Vase, Urn Form, Gilt Design, Blue Ground, 1875, 7 In., Pair	575.00

CROWN DUCAL is the name used on some pieces of porcelain made by A. G. Richardson and Co., Ltd., of Tunstall and Cobridge, England. The name has been used since 1916.

Charger, Pottery, Green, Blue, Yellow, C. Rhead, Mark, No. 3052, 13 In.	450.00
Charger, Purple, Blue Floral, Ivory Ground, Signed, C. Rhead, 12 1/2 In.	55.00
Cup & Saucer, Florida	145.00
Pitcher, Handle, Orange, Gray, Tan, 7 1/2 In.	39.00
Plate, Ivory Chintz, Octagonal, 8 1/2 In.	150.00
Plate, Peimula, Square, 5 In.	65.00
Plate, Pottery, Tan, Orange, Dark Brown, C. Rhead, Mark, No. 4926, 10 1/2 In.	430.00
Plate, Primula, Square, 5 In.	65.00
Soup, Cream, Underplate, Ascot	95.00
Teapot, Festival	500.00
Vase, Chintz, Cylinder, Early 1900s, 8 In.	215.00
Vase, Chintz, Trumpet, Blue, 7 In.	300.00
Vase, Fan, Orange Poppies, Orange Luster Interior, Black, 7 3/4 In.	150.00
Vase, Flared, Mottled, 6 In.	40.00

CROWN MILANO glass was made by Frederick Shirley at the Mt. Washington Glass Works about 1890. It had a plain biscuit color with a satin finish. It was decorated with flowers and often had large gold scrolls.

Biscuit Jar, Painted Acorns & Oak Leaves, Silver Plated Lid, Signed, 6 1/2 In.	495.00
Biscuit Jar, Silver Plated Lid, Signed	600.00
Bowl, Yellow, Purple Pansies, Gold Edge, Fluted Top, 11 1/2 In.	3650.00
Bride's Bowl, Yellow, Purple Pansies, Pairpoint Holder, 11 1/2 In. ....*Illus*	3630.00
Candlestick, Silver Plated Base, Woman, Maroon Ground, 8 x 4 In., Pair	1750.00
Cracker Jar, Bamboo Design, Green, Gold, Brown, Silver Hardware, 6 In. ......675.00 to 900.00
Ewer, Jeweled Shadow Flowers, Gold Scrolled Outline, Beige, Tan, 10 1/2 In.	1375.00
Ewer, Pillo, Scantly Clad Women, Reclining, Pale Beige Ground, 11 x 8 1/2 In.	500.00
Jar, Temple, Cover, St. George & Dragon Design, Brown, Beige, Green, 16 In.	10000.00
Vase, 5 Snow Geese In Flight, Blue, Green, Beige Ground, 14 x 5 1/2 In.	9000.00
Vase, Bulbous, Swirl, Yellow & Burgundy Dahlias, Gold Trim, 7 x 6 3/4 In.	2030.00
Vase, Cone Shape, Gilt Prunts, Gold, Fluted Top, Marked, 1893, 11 3/4 In.	770.00
Vase, Diamond-Quilted, Holly, Red Glass Berries, Marked CM, 3 3/4 In.	440.00
Vase, Guba Duck Design, Blue Enamel, 15 In. ....*Illus*	1650.00
Vase, Peony Blossom, 24 Swirling Ribs, Random Medallions, 6 In.	1240.00

Crown
Milano, Vase,
Guba Duck
Design, Blue
Enamel, 15 In.

Crown Milano, Bride's Bowl,
Yellow, Purple Pansies, Pairpoint
Holder, 11 1/2 In.

Cruet, Oil,
Pottery, Pixie,
Davar,
8 1/2 In.

ROWN TUSCAN pattern is included in the Cambridge glass category.

RUETS of glass or porcelain were made to hold vinegar, oil, and other
ondiments. They were especially popular during Victorian times and
ave been made in a variety of styles since the eighteenth century.
dditional cruets may be found in the Castor Set category and also in
arious glass categories.

Amber Glass, Applied Pewter, Cherubs Holding Hands, Pewter Stopper, 13 1/2 In.	231.00
Amber Glass, Blue, Apple Blossom	95.00
Amber Glass, Diamond & Cube	70.00
Blown Glass, Floral Design, Applied Handle, Stopper, Sterling Overlay, 11 In.	110.00
Blown Glass, Green, Milk Swirls, Pulled Glass Applied Handle, Pontil, 1850, 6 In.	85.00
Cranberry Glass, Inverted Thumbprint, Crystal Reeded Handle, Cut Stopper, 6 3/4 In. . .	375.00
Eureka, Ruby Stained	165.00
Fern, Cranberry Opalescent	895.00
Florette, Pink Satin Glass	225.00
Inverted Thumbprint, Bluerina To Deep Blue To Clear, Clear Faceted Stopper, Handle	175.00
Medallion Sprig, Amethyst	295.00
Oil, Pottery, Pixie, Davar, 8 1/2 In. . . . . *Illus*	45.00
Oil & Vinegar, Yellow, 2 Piece	125.00
Prism, Glass, Flint, Applied Handle	75.00
Stopper, Green, Slag	75.00
Victor, Glass, Green	150.00
X-Ray, Green, Gold Trim	175.00

UP PLATES are small glass or china plates that held the cup while a
iner of the mid-nineteenth century drank coffee or tea from the
aucer. The most famous cup plates were made of glass at the Boston
nd Sandwich factory located in Sandwich, Massachusetts. There have
een many new glass cup plates made in recent years for sale to gift
hops or limited edition collectors. These are similar to the old plates
ut can be recognized as new.

2 Children, Rust Transfer, Soft Paste	58.00
Animal Design, Tiger, Giraffe, Lion & 2 Monkeys, Staffordshire, 5 In., 5 Piece	330.00
Battery, New York, Trefoil Border, Staffordshire	345.00
Benjamin Franklin	7.00
Bird Perched On Branch, Green Spatter Foliage, Yellow Glaze, 4 1/4 In.	316.00
Blue Hill, Rowantrees	35.00
Blue Morning Glory Center, Spatterware, 5 1/8 In.	3245.00
Boreham House Essex, Dark Blue, Staffordshire, Stevenson	150.00
Boston State House, Dark Blue, Staffordshire, Wood	950.00
Butterfly, Enameled, Luster Trim	140.00

Cadmus, Trefoil Border, Dark Blue, Staffordshire, Wood 250.0
Customs House, Philadelphia, Blue, Ridgway 950.0
Eagle, Pearlware 660.0
Floral, Brown Band, Pearlware, 4 In. 1127.0
Flow Blue, Pagoda & Bridge In Center, Registry Mark On Base, 3 3/4 In., 6 Piece 115.0
Glass, Fine Diamond Point, Flint 9.0
Lady Of The Lake, Blue Transfer, Staffordshire, c.1830, 4 In. 140.0
Landing Of Pilgrims, Blue, Staffordshire, Wood 450.0
Polychrome Flowers, Scalloped Rim, Pearlware, 4 1/4 In. 1485.0
Remains Of Coventham, Essex, Dark Blue, Staffordshire, Stevenson 165.0
Three Weeks After Wedding 22.0
War Bonnet, 4 3/8 In. 525.0
Weehawk, Blue, Staffordshire 95.0
Woman Holding Wheat & Sickle, Building To Rear, Staffordshire 165.0

CURRIER & IVES made the famous American lithographs marked with
their name from 1857 to 1907. The mark used on the print included the
street address in New York City, and it is possible to date the year of
the original issue from this information. Earlier prints were made by N.
Currier and use that name from 1835 to 1847. Many reprints of the
Currier or Currier & Ives prints have been made. Some collectors buy
the insurance calendars that were based on the old prints. The words
large, *small*, or *medium folio* refer to size. The original print sizes were
very small (up to about 7 x 9 in.), small (8.8 x 12.8 in.), medium (9 x
14 in. to 14 x 20 in.), large (larger than 14 x 20 in.). Other sizes are
probably later copies. Other prints by Currier & Ives may be listed in
the Card category under Advertising and in the Sheet Music category.
Currier & Ives dinnerware patterns may be found in the Adams or
American Dinnerware categories.

American Country Life, May Morning, 1885, 20 5/16 x 28 5/16 In. 1380.0
American Country Life, Summer's Evening, Frame, 1855, Large Folio ......1540.00 to 2300.0
American Winter Scenes, Evening, Frame, 1854, 16 3/4 x 24 1/8 In. 2185.0
Autumn In New England, Cider Making, 14 7/8 x 25 1/4 In. 6210.0
Autumn On Lake George, Maple Veneer Frame, 13 1/4 x 17 1/4 In. 192.0
Battle Of Chancellorsville, Virginia, 12 x 16 In. 137.0
Battle Of Newburn, N.C., March 14, 1862, 9 1/2 x 14 In. 120.0
Battle Of Newburn, N.C., March 14, 1862, 12 x 16 In. 192.0
Beauty Of The Mississippi, 15 x 11 1/4 In. 55.0
Brush For The Lead, Frame, Large Folio 1870.0
Burning Of Chicago, Wooden Frame, 8 x 12 1/2 In. 265.0
California Scenery, Matted, 9 7/8 x 14 In. 60.0
Carrying Young Girl To Rescue, Fireman, 17 x 13 1/4 In. 805.0
Catching A Trout, Frame, 1854, Large Folio 3190.0
Celebrated Trotting Stallion George Wilkes, Frame, 17 1/8 x 26 3/4 In. 1150.0
Central Park, Winter, Skating Carnival, Frame, Small Folio 1650.0
City Of New York, Frame, 1876, 21 1/4 x 33 5/8 In. 5175.0
Clipper Ship, Sweepstakes, Frame, 16 x 23 1/2 In. 3450.0
Cross Matched Race, Matted, Frame, 22 1/2 x 28 In. 468.0
Declaration Of Independence July 4th, 1776, 1838-1856, 8 1/2 x 12 1/2 In. 425.0
Destruction Of Tea At Boston Harbor, Frame, Medium Folio 1760.0
Eventide, October, The Village Inn, Frame, 1867, 14 3/8 x 24 7/8 In. 2185.0
Farmyard, Winter, Frame, 1861, 16 1/4 x 23 1/2 In. 5175.0
Fashionable Turn-Outs In Central Park, Frame, 1869, 18 1/2 x 28 3/4 In. 2585.0
George Washington, Curly Maple & Mahogany Frame, 19 1/2 x 15 1/2 In. 440.0
Going To The Trot, Frame, 1869, 18 3/4 x 28 5/8 In. 1265.0
Great East River Suspension Bridge, Frame, 1877, 20 3/4 x 32 7/8 In. 1265.0
Hiawatha's Wedding, Walnut Frame, c.1858, 16 1/4 x 21 1/8 In. 245.0
Home In The Country, Frame, 10 x 12 In. 165.0
Home In The Wilderness, Frame, 10 x 14 In. 275.0
Home On The Mississippi, Matted, Frame, 16 3/4 x 20 3/4 In. 385.0
Home On The Mississippi, Shadowbox Frame, 14 x 17 In. 357.0
Hosing Down Flames, Fireman, 22 3/4 x 17 3/4 In. 690.0
Lady Suffolk & Lady Moscow, Frame, 1850, 17 3/4 x 26 3/8 In. 1495.0

Life Of A Fireman, Metropolitan System, Frame, 17 x 26 1/8 In. 2875.00
Life Of A Fireman, The Fire, Frame, 1854, 17 1/8 x 25 3/4 In. 980.00
Life Of A Fireman, The Race, Frame, 1854, 17 x 25 7/8 In. 1265.00
Life Of A Fireman, The Ruins, Frame, 1854, 17 x 26 In. 980.00
Life Of A Sportsman, Camping In Woods, Matted, Frame, 10 x 14 In. 385.00
Midnight Race On The Mississippi, Frame, 1860, 18 1/4 x 27 3/4 In. 8050.00
Narrows, New York Bay From Staten Island, 8 x 12 1/2 In. 650.00
New Brood, Frame, 12 3/4 x 16 1/2 In. ....192.00 to 225.00
Old Mill-Dam, Frame, 13 1/2 x 17 1/4 In. 192.00
Pasture, Noontide, Matted, Frame, 16 5/8 x 20 1/2 In. 275.00
Pointing At Fire With Horn, Fireman, 17 x 13 1/4 In. 805.00
Prairie Fires Of The Great West, Frame, 8 3/8 x 12 1/2 In. 1265.00
Pulling Fire Wagon, Fireman, White Matte Border, 17 x 13 In. 748.00
Race For Blood, 3 Sulkies With Riders Atop, Oak Frame, 21 x 29 In. 800.00
Rattling Heat, Matted, Frame, 22 1/2 x 28 In. 468.00
Ready For The Signal, 1872, 16 7/8 x 25 3/4 In. 1600.00
Road, Winter, Frame, 1853, 17 3/8 x 26 In. 6900.00
Road, Winter, On Stone, 1851, 17 5/16 x 26 1/16 In. 12650.00
Sacred Heart Of Jesus, 16 1/2 x 12 1/2 In. 100.00
Soldier's Home, The Vision, Frame, 12 1/4 x 16 In. 140.00
Staten Island & Narrows From Fort Hamilton, Frame, 21 1/2 x 26 1/2 In. 770.00
Staten Island & Narrows From Fort Hamilton, Maple Frame, 1861, 14 x 20 In. ... 3000.00
Summer In The Country, Frame, 15 3/4 x 19 1/2 In. 210.00
Sunnyside, On The Hudson, 11 x 15 In. 165.00
Sylvan Lake, 1868, 8 x 12 1/2 In. 225.00
Trotters On The Snow, Hand Colored, Frame, 13 1/2 x 17 1/2 In. 247.00
Trotting Cracks On The Snow, 18 15/16 x 27 1/2 In. 357.00
Trotting Cracks On The Snow, Frame, 1858, 16 5/8 x 28 In. 3162.00
Union Iron Clad Moniter vs. Nashville, Colored, 9 x 12 In. 185.00
View Of New York, 8 1/4 x 12 3/4 In. 750.00
View On Hudson River, Walnut Frame, 14 x 16 3/4 In. 110.00
Washington Columns, Yosemite Valley, 8 1/2 x 12 1/2 In. 650.00
Whale Fishery, The Sperm Whale, 1852, 16 1/4 x 23 7/8 In. 4885.00
William Penn's Treaty With Indians, Frame, Small Folio 80.00

CUSTARD GLASS is a slightly yellow opaque glass. It was first made in England in the 1880s and was first made in the United States in the 1890s. It has been reproduced. Additional pieces may be found in the Cambridge, Fenton, Heisey, and Northwood categories. Custard glass is called Ivorina Verde by Heisey and other companies.

Argonaut Shell, Compote ....80.00 to 120.00
Argonaut Shell, Creamer 150.00
Argonaut Shell, Sauce ....85.00 to 90.00
Argonaut Shell, Toothpick ....385.00 to 465.00
Argonaut Shell, Toothpick, Souvenir, 1898 .... 320.00
Chrysanthemum Sprig, Berry Bowl, Master 100.00
Chrysanthemum Sprig, Compote, Jelly, Gold Trim, 4 1/2 In. 60.00
Chrysanthemum Sprig, Compote, Sprig Jelly 45.00
Chrysanthemum Sprig, Cruet ....225.00 to 465.00
Chrysanthemum Sprig, Spooner ....135.00 to 150.00
Chrysanthemum Sprig, Sugar, Cover, Design 185.00
Chrysanthemum Sprig, Table Set, Green, Gold Trim, 4 Piece 575.00
Chrysanthemum Sprig, Toothpick 300.00
Delaware, Pin Tray, Blue Trim 65.00
Diamond With Peg, Pitcher, Tumbler, Roses, Gold Trim, Souvenir, Coney Island 300.00
Diamond With Peg, Salt & Pepper, Souvenir, Gettysburg, 1863 .... 138.00
Diamond With Peg, Toothpick, Souvenir, Gettysburg 65.00
Geneva, Berry Set, 5 Piece 225.00
Geneva, Butter, Cover 125.00
Geneva, Spooner 80.00
Georgia Gem, Table Set, 4 Piece 175.00
Georgia Gem, Toothpick, Footed, Turquoise 32.00
Grape & Cable, Creamer, Nutmeg Stained 125.00

Grape & Cable, Plate, 8 In. .... 40.0•

Grape & Cable, Sugar, Nutmeg Stained .... 58.0•

Grape Arbor, Dresser Tray, Nutmeg Stained 225.0

Grape Arbor, Vase, Hat Shape .... 40.0•

Heart & Thumbprint, Lamp, Enameled Floral, Burner, 6 In. 83.0

Intaglio, Butter Dish, Cover, Green, Gold Trim, 7 In. .... 95.0•

Intaglio, Spooner, Footed, Green, Gold Trim, 4 3/4 In. ....55.00 to 95.0•

Inverted Fan & Feather, Pitcher .... 545.0•

Inverted Fan & Feather, Sauce .... 45.0•

Inverted Fan & Feather, Spooner .... 65.0•

Inverted Fan & Feather, Toothpick, 2 1/2 In. .... 875.0•

Jackson, Tumbler, Water .... 45.0•

Little Gem, see Georgia Gem pattern in this category.

Louis XV, Butter, Cover, Gold Trim .... 150.0•

Louis XV, Creamer .... 45.0•

Louis XV, Cruet, Clear Faceted Stopper .... 85.0•

Louis XV, Salt & Pepper .... 350.0•

Louis XV, Spooner .... 65.0•

Maize is its own category in this book.

Maple Leaf, Butter, Cover, Green, Gold Trim .... 275.0•

Maple Leaf, Creamer ....100.00 to 125.0•

Maple Leaf, Pitcher, Water .... 300.0•

Maple Leaf, Spooner .... 100.0•

Maple Leaf, Sugar .... 225.0•

Ring Band, Water Set, 8 Piece .... 800.0•

Tiny Thumbprint, Butter, Cover .... 300.0•

Tiny Thumbprint, Spooner .... 58.0•

Wild Rose, Tumbler .... 35.0•

Winged Scroll, Butter, Cover ....83.00 to 150.0•

Winged Scroll, Table Set, 4 Piece ....275.00 to 385.0•

Winged Scroll, Toothpick ....100.00 to 115.0•

Winged Scroll, Water Set, 10 Piece .... 750.0•

CUT GLASS has been made since ancient times, but the large majority
of the pieces now for sale date from the brilliant period of glass design,
1880 to 1905. These pieces have elaborate geometric designs with a
deep miter cut. Modern cut glass with a similar appearance is being
made in England, Ireland, and the Czech and Slovak republics. Chips
and scratches are often difficult to notice but lower the value dramati-
cally. A signature on the glass adds significantly to the value. Other cut
glass pieces are listed under factory names.

Ashtray, Apple Form, Art V., France, 4 1/2 In. 115.00

Basket, 6 Large Cosmos, Daisy Flowers, Thistles, Leaves, Triple Notched Handle 1200.00

Basket, Flower, Hobstars, 3 1/2 x 3 1/2 In. 275.00

Basket, Fruit, Rope Handle, 7 x 7 In. 325.00

Basket, Hobstars, Diamond Point Fan, Double Notched Handle, 7 x 6 In. .... 100.0•

Basket, Hobstars, Pinwheels, Rope Handle, 5 1/2 x 7 In. .... 100.0•

Biscuit Jar, Daisy & Button, Blue, Cut To Clear Glass, Silver-Plate Hinged Cover 72.00

Biscuit Jar, Daisy & Button, Nickel Plate Cover, Handle, 7 1/2 In. .... 33.0•

Bottle, Ale, Brilliant, Florals, 10 1/2 In. 95.00

Bottle, Panel & Rib, 2 Rows, 3 Rings, Raised Bottom, 1 Qt. .... 100.0•

Bowl, Cane, Faceted Edge, Octagonal Scalloped Rim, Union Glass Co., 5 x 9 1/4 In. 3450.00

Bowl, Central Hobstar, Rows Of Alternating Stars, Snow Flakes, Notched Rim, 9 In. ..... 55.0•

Bowl, Cover, Russian, Diamond Point, Late 18th Century, 10 x 9 In. 484.00

Bowl, Eggnog, Hobstar, Fan, Crosshatch, Cane, Pedestal Base, c.1900, 10 In. 600.00

Bowl, Emu, Griffin Design, Animal Paw Feet, Sterling Silver Base, 11 1/2 In. 995.00

Bowl, Fleur-De-Lis, 8 In. 67.00

Bowl, Fruit, Allover Hobstars & Caning, Clapperton, 8 In. 137.00

Bowl, Fruit, Marquise, Hobstars, Cane, Notch Work, Maple City, 8 In. 110.00

Bowl, Fruit, Sunburst, Scalloped, Brilliant, Square, 8 1/2 In. 105.00

Bowl, Grape & Leaf Border, 4 Sections, Sterling Silver Mounted, 9 1/4 In. 374.00

Bowl, Hobstars, Alternating Bands Of Strawberry-Diamonds, 9 In. 345.00

Bowl, Napoleon Hat Shape, Imperial, 5 x 12 x 9 In. 785.00

Bowl, Nassau, Hoare, 10 In. 185.00
Bowl, Prima Donna, Dental Edge, 8 In. 185.00
Bowl, Russian, Brilliant, 9 x 4 1/4 In. 275.00
Bowl, Shallow, Vintage, 9 3/4 In. 575.00
Bowl, Waffle & Star, Paneled Foot, Scalloped Edge, 8 1/4 x 4 7/8 In. 125.00
Box, Allover Floral, Wheat, Geometric Design, Brilliant, Circular, 5 In. 103.50
Bucket, Crosshatch, Fans & Hobstars, 6 1/4 In. 172.00
Butter Chip, Hobstars, Elongated Thumb Hold, 4 Piece 200.00
Candlestick, Knob & Prism, Horizontal Step-Cut Petticoat Base, 10 In., Pair 175.00
Candy Dish, Birds, Flowers & Leaves, Curled Handles, 10 1/2 In. 225.00
Carafe, Russian, 7 1/2 x 6 In. 345.00
Celery Dish, 2 Hobstars, 11 1/2 x 5 1/2 In. 215.00
Celery Dish, Diamond, c.1900, 11 x 4 1/2 x 1 1/2 In. 165.00
Celery Dish, Florence, 11 In. 110.00
Celery Dish, Plaza, Empress, 13 x 5 In. 250.00
Celery Dish, Radiant Star, American Cut Glass Co., 11 1/2 x 6 In. 410.00
Centerpiece, Fans, Crosshatch, Footed, England, 20th Century, 10 3/4 In. .. 374.00
Champagne Cooler, Star, Chrome Liner, 8 1/2 In. 600.00
Cheese & Cracker Server, Serrated Edge, Allover Diamonds, Fans, 2 Tiers, 10 In. 235.00
Compote, 6 Alternating Hobstars, Crosshatch, Fans, Teardrop Stem, 6 In. 925.00
Compote, Diamond Band & Double Band, Stepped Foot, Baluster Stem, 8 x 7 In. 110.00
Compote, Floral, 7 3/4 x 6 3/4 In., Pair 489.00
Compote, Floral, 8 Panels, Reverse Baluster Stem, Pittsburgh, 4 3/4 x 5 In. 330.00
Compote, Hobstars, Crosshatch & Fans, Teardrop Stem, 10 In. 425.00
Compote, Hobstars, Fans, Buttons, Octagonal Notched Foot, 9 x 6 In. 150.00
Compote, Opaque White, Cut To Clear, Scalloped, Silver Plated Foot, 9 1/2 x 7 In. 55.00
Compote, Panels & Ovals, Engraved Blower Band, Applied Foot Panel, 9 3/8 In. 185.00
Compote, Straus Drape, 8 x 7 3/4 In. 375.00
Compote, Strawberry-Diamonds, Sawtooth, Rays & Fans, Applied Wafer Stem, 9 In. ... 545.00
Cruet, Hobstars, Trefoil Lip, Silver Stopper, Pair 250.00
Decanter, Acme, Sterling Stopper, Averbeck, 9 3/4 x 5 In. 685.00
Decanter, Allover Diamond Point, Matching Stopper, 11 In. 55.00
Decanter, Hobstar & Fan, Notched Handle, Hoare, 12 3/4 In. 85.00
Decanter, Hobstar Body, Zipper Neck, 10 In. 385.00
Decanter, Honeycomb, Paneled Base, 12 In. 1485.00
Decanter, Pinwheel & Star, Hexagonal Panel Stopper, Brilliant, 17 In. 350.00
Decanter, Prism Loops, Hobstar Thumb Rest, Sterling Silver Stopper, 8 3/4 In. 385.00
Decanter, Russian, St. Louis Diamond Neck, Tusks, 12 1/2 In. 375.00
Decanter, Split Vesica With Diamonds, Crosshatch, Tusks, 12 In. 320.00
Decanter, St. Louis Diamond Neck, Hobstar Stopper, 9 3/4 In. 400.00
Decanter, Star & Pineapple, Faceted Stopper, 11 In. 250.00
Decanter, Stars, Arches, Star & Mushroom Stopper, 11 1/2 In. 95.00
Dish, Comet, Scalloped Edge, Star Base, Oval, 8 3/4 In. 55.00
Dish, Hobstar, Bars Of Cane, 4 Sections, Sterling Silver Rim, 7 1/4 In. 225.00
Dish, Hobstar, Maple Leaf Mark, 11 In. 60.50
Dish, Olive, Sunburst, Geometric, Brilliant, 7 1/2 In. 69.00
Dish, Russian, Rayed Buttons, Hawkes, 6 In. 90.00
Dish, Whist, Spade Shape, Newark Glass Co., 5 1/4 x 5 In. 95.00
Ewer, Pinwheel & Ribs, Applied Handle, 10 1/4 In. 85.00
Goblet, Renaissance, Blue, Cut To Clear, Dorflinger 185.00
Ice Bucket, Allover Floral, Geometric, Brilliant, 6 1/2 In. 46.00
Ice Bucket, Hobstar & Fan, Liner, 5 1/2 x 5 In. 275.00
Jar, Apothecary, Floral, Crest & Crown, Stopper, 19th Century, 21 In., Pair 1000.00
Jug, Water, Pinwheels, Flat Stars, Fans, Crosshatch, Notched Spout, 10 In. 85.00
Lamp, Mushroom, 6 Jeweled Flowers, Star On Top, Ball Shape, 16 1/4 In. 1200.00
Lotus, Flower Center, Egginton, 5 1/2 x 6 1/2 In. 525.00
Nut Cup, Underplate, Sawtooth 82.00
Perfume Bottle, Floral Design, 5 In., Pair 201.00
Pitcher, 30 Point Hobstar Base, Zipper Cut Handle, 6 1/2 In. 300.00
Pitcher, Cider, Cane Hobstars & Fine Diamonds, Triple Notched Handle, 6 x 8 In. 425.00
Pitcher, Cider, Hobstar Base, 8 In. 350.00
Pitcher, Claret, Prisms, Hobstar Bottom, Honeycomb Handle, 13 In. 675.00
Pitcher, Crosshatch, Hobstars & Fans, Notched Spout, 7 1/4 In. 85.00

Cut Glass, Punch Set, Silver
Plated Ladle, 10 Piece

Pitcher, Hobstar Base, Cut Handle, Embossed Floral Sterling Silver Rim, 8 1/2 In. 550.00
Pitcher, Pineapple, Brilliant, Applied Handle, 10 In. 400.00
Pitcher, Pinwheel & Star, Applied Handle, 9 In. 100.00
Pitcher, Pinwheel, Scalloped Sawtooth Edge, Brilliant, Applied Handle, 13 In. 160.00
Pitcher, Royal, Hunt, 12 In. 675.00
Pitcher, Snowflakes, Cane & Diamonds, Hoare, 10 In. 220.00
Pitcher, Teutonic, Hawkes, 11 1/4 x 5 In. 750.00
Pitcher, Water, Pinwheel, 8 In. 95.00
Plate, Hobstars, Raised Fans & Stars, 12 In. 115.00
Punch Bowl, Brazilian, Hawkes, 6 3/4 x 12 1/2 In. 1575.00
Punch Bowl, Grape Clusters, Vines, Brilliant, Notched Ribs, 5 x 12 In. 1035.00
Punch Set, Silver-Plated Ladle, 10 Piece . . . .*Illus*   2310.00
Relish, Hobstar & Miter, 7 3/4 x 5 3/4 x 2 In. 75.00
Relish, Stars, Crosshatch & Fans, 7 1/2 In. 25.00
Rose Bowl, Classical Sphere, Russian Edge, Brilliant, 9 1/2 x 10 In. 575.00
Sugar, Roundels, Fans & Rays, Strawberry-Diamonds Cover, Footed, Pittsburgh 2530.00
Sugar & Creamer, Butterfly, Pedestal 235.00
Sugar & Creamer, Hobstar & Fine Cut, Eggington 77.00
Sugar & Creamer, Hobstars, Sunburst, Brilliant, Plantation Size 385.00
Sugar & Creamer, Sunburst, Geometric, Circular, Round, Libbey 81.00
Sugar Shaker, Strawberry-Diamond, Fan & Panels, Sterling Silver Top, 5 In. 250.00
Tray, Elongated Oval Petals, Fan, Scalloped Edge, 14 x 7 In. 575.00
Tray, Hobstar & Cane, Clark, 13 1/2 x 8 1/4 In. 675.00
Tray, Ice Cream, Allover Hobstars, Whirling Stars, Fans, Handles, Oval, 14 In. 275.00
Tumbler, Flutes & Diamond Band, Engraved Roses, Monogram, 3 3/4 In. 1815.00
Tumbler, Juice, Russian, Rayed Bottom, 6 Piece 275.00
Urn, Fluted, Diamond Scalloped Edge, Ireland, c.1850, 10 3/4 In., Pair 880.00
Vase, Allover Floral, Geometric, Round, Brilliant, 10 1/4 In. 69.00
Vase, Corset, Graduated Pinwheels, Crosshatch, Signed, 16 In. 1600.00
Vase, Corset, Hobstars, Cane, Notched Prisms, 10 x 4 3/4 In. 295.00
Vase, Daisies, Notched Edge, Globular Form, Clapperton, 7 1/2 x 8 In. 143.00
Vase, Daisy Button, Faceted Sides, Flared, 16 1/2 In. 155.00
Vase, Daisy Design, Hobstar & Notched Diamond Band, Roden, 19th Century, 10 In. . . .   60.00
Vase, Fan & Star, Sawtooth Edge, 15 1/2 In. 86.00
Vase, Feather, Hobstar, Tulip Shape, Flared, Footed, 10 In. 225.00
Vase, Flower, Large Hobstar Bottom, Step-Cut Neck, 8 In. 325.00
Vase, Flowers, Notched Edge, Hour Glass Shape, 1880s, 10 In.   70.00
Vase, Graduated Hobstars, Cylindrical, Flared, 16 In. 635.00
Vase, Harvard, Flower, 11 1/2 In. 295.00
Vase, Hobstars, Fans, Diamond-Point, Handles, 8 In. 525.00
Vase, Hobstars, Hobstar Bottom, Maple Leaf Mark, 15 In. 575.00
Vase, Hobstars, Thumbprints, Crosshatch, Notches, Flared, 20 In. 1150.00
Vase, Kalana, Lily Design, Dorflinger, 5 In. 160.00
Vase, Large Hobstars, Fans, Notched Neck, Goblet Form, 4 In. 60.00
Vase, Pineapple, 11 In. 88.00
Vase, Pinwheel & Star, Sawtooth Edge, 12 In. 100.00
Vase, Snowflake & Fan, Flared, Bulbous, 8 1/2 In. 577.00

UT VELVET is a special type of art glass, made with two layers of
lown glass, which shows a raised pattern. It usually had an acid fin-
sh or a texture like velvet. It was made by many glass factories during
he late Victorian years.

Basket, Diamond-Quilted Yellow, Pink Interior, Loop Handle, 11 In.	184.00
Bride's Bowl, Bird & Floral Holder, E. Webster, 12 1/2 x 12 3/4 In.	1380.00
Vase, Diamond-Quilted, Rose Spatter, Ruffled Edge, Mt. Washington, 11 x 4 In.	675.00
Vase, Mother-Of-Pearl, Turquoise, White Interior, 19th Century, 6 3/4 In.	110.00
Vase, Pink To White, Vertical Ribs, Mt. Washington, 9 1/2 In.	100.00
Vase, Purple & White Body, Diamond-Quilted, Ruffled & Crimped Edge, 10 In.	658.00
Vase, Stick, White Cased, Blue, 6 1/2 In.	75.00

YBIS porcelain is a twentieth-century product. Boleslaw Cybis came
o the United States from Poland in 1939. He started making porcelains
n Long Island, New York, in 1940. He moved to Trenton, New Jersey,
n 1942 as one of the founders of Cordey China Co. and started his
wn Cybis Porcelains about 1950. The firm is still working. See also
Cordey.

Figurine, Abigail Adams, 10 In.	675.00
Figurine, American Bullfrog, 6 1/2 In.	300.00
Figurine, Appaloosa Colt, Dappled Gray, 9 x 7 In.	325.00
Figurine, Beatrice, 12 In.	925.00
Figurine, Buffalo, 5 x 5 3/4 In.	65.00
Figurine, Burro, Fitzgerald, 7 In.	112.00
Figurine, Carousel Horse, 12 1/2 x 12 In.	900.00 to 1200.00
Figurine, Cinderella, 7 1/2 In.	315.00
Figurine, Circus Rider, On Base, 13 1/4 x 15 1/2 In.	350.00
Figurine, Eskimo, Child's Head, 10 1/2 In.	200.00
Figurine, Girl, Pandora, 5 In.	350.00
Figurine, Girl, Wendy, 6 1/2 In.	300.00
Figurine, Hansel, 9 In.	375.00
Figurine, Head Of Boy, Black Base, 10 In.	425.00
Figurine, Heidi, No. 432, 7 1/2 In.	175.00
Figurine, Kwan Yin, 1972	1000.00
Figurine, Lady Bug, Duchess Of Seven Rosettes, 2 x 5 x 4 In.	100.00
Figurine, Lady MacBeth, 13 In.	925.00
Figurine, Little Bo Peep, 10 1/2 In.	275.00
Figurine, Mandy, Baby Lamb, 4 1/2 x 4 In.	165.00
Figurine, Owl, 4 1/2 In.	35.00 to 95.00
Figurine, Pollyanna, 7 In.	225.00
Figurine, Priscilla, 14 In.	925.00
Figurine, Raccoon, Raffles, 7 1/2 In.	375.00
Figurine, Rapunzel, Lilac, No. 468L, 8 1/2 In.	450.00
Figurine, Sea King's Steed, Oceana, 14 x 14 1/2 In.	1750.00
Figurine, Squirrel, Mr. Fluffy Tail, Holding Nut, 8 In.	125.00
Figurine, Wood Wren With Dogwood, No. 336, 5 1/2 In.	250.00 to 425.00

DANIEL BOONE, a pre-Revolutionary War folk hero, was a surveyor,
trapper, and frontiersman. A television series, which ran from 1964 to
1970, was based on his life and starred Fess Parker. All types of Daniel
Boone memorabilia are collected.

Book, Comic No. 5, 1966	20.00
Book, Comic, Fess Parker, No.7, 1966	20.00
Game, Card, Fess Parker Wilderness Trail, Transogram, 1964	70.00
Puzzle, 1950	20.00
Transfer Set, Fess Parker, Rub-On Magic Picture, Hasbro, Box, 1964	25.00

DAUM, a glassworks in Nancy, France, was started by Jean Daum in
1875. The company, now called *Cristalleries de Nancy*, is still working. The *Daum Nancy* mark has been used in many variations. The
name of the city and the artist are usually both included.

Bottle, Apothecary, Violets, Mottled, Green, Yellow Enameled, Stopper, 4 In.	1495.00

Bottle, Stopper, Crocus Blossoms, Leafage, Rose, Lavender, Rust, Magenta, 1900, 4 In. . 5465.00
Bowl, Enameled, Flowering Primula, Pink, Amber, Overlaid In Yellow, 1905, 8 In. 1495.00
Bowl, Enameled, Wild Flowers, White, Yellow, Aubergine Base, Quatrefoil Rim, 8 In. . . . 2070.00
Bowl, Etched, Smoky Brown Glass, Frieze Semicircles, Dots, 1925, 9 1/8 In. 2760.00
Bowl, Fuchsia, Gray & White, Blue Base, Indented Quatrefoil, 1905, 5 3/4 In. 3000.00
Bowl, Hops Blossoms, Leafage, White, Purple Streaks, Amber, Oliver Green, Gray, 6 In. . 2185.00
Bowl, Orange Autumn Berries, Squatty Bulbous, 1905, 8 1/8 In. 7875.00
Bowl, Pink Flowers, White, Yellow Base, Indented Quatrefoil Rim, 1905, 5 1/8 In. 1690.00
Bowl, Wild Violets & Leaves, Indented Quatrefoil Rim, 1905, 5 3/4 In. 3560.00
Bowl, Yellow Wild Flowers, Indented Quatrefoil Rim, 1905, 4 5/8 In. 1500.00
Box, Cover, Enameled, Flowering Wild Orchids, Dappled Gold, Yellow, 1905, 4 In. 2990.00
Box, Cover, Wild Orchids, Dappled Ice Blue, Square, 1905, 6 In. 6000.00
Box, Cover, Wild Orchids, Spider Webs, Mottled Blue, 1905, 5 3/8 In. 9850.00
Cologne Bottle, Parfum De Vertus, Iris, Amethyst Ground, Marked, 1 1/2 In. . . . . . *Illus* 1430.00
Decanter, Bubbly Orange Color, Applied Aubergine Handle & Stopper, Signed, 9 In. . . . 795.00
Decanter, Croix De Lorraine, Turquoise Dots, Gilt, Signed, Stopper, c.1895, 7 7/8 In. . . . 6210.00
Decanter, Traveling, Exotic Plants, Yellow, Purple, Green Enamel, Signed, 6 1/2 In. 175.00
Dish, Blackberries, Mottled Gray Glass, Autumn Tones, Square, 1900, 7 5/8 In. 3750.00
Dish, Pink Sweet Peas, Brick-Orange Base, Raised Foot, Triangular, 1905, 5 7/8 In. 3190.00
Ewer, Convolvulus Blossoms, Rose, Red, Handle, 12 In. 4890.50
Figurine, Cat, Sitting, Gray-Green Glass, Signed, Pate-De-Verre, 10 3/4 In. 795.00
Goblets, Intaglio Etched, Thistle Blossoms, Gold Trim, 5 1/2 In., Set Of 6 . . . . 1020.00
Inkwell, Cover, Gray Acorns, Faceted Cabochons, Forest Green, Red, 1900, 5 In. 8625.00
Jar, Cover, Hinged, Raspberries, Leaves, Gilt, Etched, Signed, 1896, 4 x 2 3/4 In. 330.00
Jug, Cover, Chased With Irises, Buds, Overlaid In Purple, Etched, 1900, 12 5/8 In. 2875.00
Jug, Sprays Of Cornflowers, Yellow, Aubergine, 1900, 8 In. 5175.00
Lamp, 2-Light, 2 Gray Shades, Wrought Iron Square Base, 1925, 19 In. 7475.00
Lamp, Boudoir, Checkerboard, Bell-Shaped Shade, Pale Amber Base, 8 1/2 In. 6900.00
Lamp, Chandelier, Small & Large Shade, Etched Furrows, c.1925, 15 1/2 In. 6325.00
Lamp, Etched, Geometric Frieze, Cylindrical Base, 1925, 18 1/4 In. 7130.00
Lamp, Fruited Orange Branches, Wrought Iron Arms, 1910, 17 1/2 In. 11250.00
Lamp, Landscape, River, Leafy Trees, Lemon Yellow, Purple, Gray, 1900, 17 In. 8625.00
Lamp, Metal Base, 3 Arms, Art Glass Dome-Shaped Shade, Signed, 25 3/4 In. 660.00
Lamp, Purple Creeper Conical Shade, 3 Bronze Arms, 1905, 11 1/8 In. 6600.00
Lamp, Sailboats, Domed Shade, Tangerine, Yellow, Etched, Enameled, 19 1/2 In. 9775.00
Lamp, Waterlily, Gilt Bronze 3-Frog Base, Majorelle, 1900, 18 1/2 In. 6000.00
Lamp, Wooded River Shade, Iron Arms Above Baluster Base, 1900, 17 In. 7500.00
Lamp, Wrought Iron, Mushroom Glass Shade, Berge, 1920s, 20 1/4 In. 3185.00
Lemonade Set, Cut Branches Of Mistletoe, White Enamel, Signed, 9 Piece 6500.00
Paperweight, Cactus, Signed 125.00
Perfume Bottle, Amethyst Flower On Front 330.00
Perfume Bottle, Wild Violets & Leaves, Gilt, Flattened Stopper, 1905, 4 1/8 In. 5250.00
Powder Bowl, Cover, Fuchsia, Gilt, White Ground, 1905, 4 1/8 In. 4125.00
Tumbler, Dutch Scene On 1 Side, Windmill On Other, White, Signed, 3 1/4 In. 450.00
Vase, 2 Handles, Bulbous, Opalescent, Rose Branches, Etched, Signed, 6 1/2 In. 2055.00
Vase, Amber Streaked, Geometric Design, Signed, 13 In. 935.00
Vase, Amber, Black Speckles, Flared Foot, 9 x 6 1/2 In. 665.00
Vase, Aspen Leaves, Brown, Lavender & Gold, 10 1/2 In. 5900.00

Daum, Cologne Bottle,
Parfum De Vertus, Iris,
Amethyst Ground,
Marked, 1 1/2 In.

A ground-glass perfume bottle
stopper should be turned gently to
the right for a snug fit. To remove
the stopper, first turn it to the left
to 'unlock it' before pulling it out.

Vase, Asters, Orange & Brown Overlay, Frosted Ground, Etched, Signed, 6 1/4 In. 2300.00
Vase, Berry Branches, White, Cylindrical, 1900, 4 1/2 In. 1035.00
Vase, Blown Out Into Bronze Frame, Majorelle, 10 In. 1800.00
Vase, Blue Berries, Leaves, Globular To Tapering, Footed, Cameo, 1900, 9 1/2 In. 6748.00
Vase, Blue Wild Violets, Cylindrical, Flared Raised Foot, 1905, 8 5/8 In. 4875.00
Vase, Blue Wild Violets, Mottled White, 1905, 4 In. 4125.00
Vase, Blue, Circular Rim, Tapered Circular Foot, Octagonal, 10 In. 690.00
Vase, Bluebells, Gray & White Ground, 1905, 4 In. 1500.00
Vase, Bulbous, Dutch Scene, Windmills, Sailboats, Frosted, Black Enamel, Signed, 4 In. . 835.00
Vase, Butterfly Between Flowering Hydrangea, Green, Cherry Red, 1905, 7 In. 8050.00
Vase, Cabinet, Flowered Branches, Red, Green, Brown, Orange Matte Ground, 6 5/8 In. . 1955.00
Vase, Columbines, Sunset Ground, 5 In. 2500.00
Vase, Cornflower, Blue, Yellow, Deep Purple, Etched, 4 3/4 In. 2530.00
Vase, Crocus, Leaves, Purple Glass, Caramel, Yellow, Indigo Base, 1900, 12 In. 7820.00
Vase, Crowing Cock, Gray, Tomato-Red, Yellow, Overlaid Brown, c.1900, 5 In. 2300.00
Vase, Dahlia Blossoms, Leafage, Orange, Amethyst Streaks, Dusty Rose, 9 In. 3740.00
Vase, Dandelions & Leaves, Signed, c.1900, 4 5/8 In. 2760.00
Vase, Depictions Of Spring Trees, Hilly Landscape, Signed, 14 In. 4140.00
Vase, Diamond-Shaped Leaf, Gold, Ice-Green Glass, 1895, 4 3/4 In. 665.00
Vase, Dusky Pink Prunus, Amber Ground, Mold Blown, Cameo, 1900, 13 3/8 In. 13120.00
Vase, Enameled Bluebells, Mottled Blue & White, Footed, 1905, 18 In. 9000.00
Vase, Enameled, Pink Wild Flowers, Pink, Pale Yellow, Everted Rim, 1905, 13 In. 4600.00
Vase, Enameled, Sprays Of Red, Pink Blossoms, Milky White Glass, 1905, 9 1/8 In. 1725.00
Vase, Enameled, Wild Flowers, Tear Shape, Leaves, Caramel, Yellow, Mauve, 5 In. 1380.00
Vase, Etched & Enamel Flowers, Flattened Form, Gray & Tan Ground, 3 In. 1495.00
Vase, Etched & Enameled Wild Violets, Signed, 10 1/4 In. 5175.00
Vase, Etched & Enameled, Thistle Branch, Trumpet Form, Opalescent, 4 1/2 In. 805.00
Vase, Etched Floral, Leaf Design, Gold Accents, Green, Amethyst Body, 4 In. 1100.00
Vase, Etched, Bulbous Form, Wheel-Carved, Fluted Panels, Smoky Gray, 6 In. 575.00
Vase, Etched, Smoky Topaz, Skyscraper Design, Wheel Carved, Oviform, 14 1/2 In. 8050.00
Vase, Etched, Trees, Lake, Apricot Ground, Green Overlay, 10 1/4 In. 1840.00
Vase, Fall Landscape, Gray Walls, Baluster Form, Signed, 10 1/4 In. 5520.00
Vase, Figures In Boats, Venice Skyline, Sky Blue, Ochre, Brown, Signed, 7 1/4 In. 2055.00
Vase, Fleur-De-Lis, Gilt, Diamond Shape, Signed, 7 1/4 In. 595.00
Vase, Flock Of Butterflies, Light Blue, Rose Streaks, Purple, Orange, 10 In. 9775.00
Vase, Flowering Sprays Of Oleander, Yellow Buttercup, Pink, Aubergine Base, 18 In. ... 3450.00
Vase, Flowers, Red, Yellow, Green Stems, Leaves, Black Enamel Ground, 7 1/2 In. 2090.00
Vase, Foliate Design, Amethyst, Yellow, Signed, 7 1/2 In. 1000.00
Vase, Geometric Design, Amber, Etched, 1925, 7 In. 2070.00
Vase, Geometric Design, Symmetrical Progression, Topaz, 7 3/4 In. 375.00
Vase, Hops Blossoms, Leafage, White, Purple Streaks, Amber, Oliver Green, 1900, 11 In. 9200.00
Vase, Hydrangea Blossoms, Pale Gold, Foliate Cut Ground, Cylindrical, 6 In. 805.00
Vase, Infused With Gold Foil, Wrought Iron Mounts, Signed, c.1900, 10 In. 5465.00
Vase, Inverted Rim, Large Dot Design, Pale Green, Blue, Etched, 13 1/2 In. 8050.00
Vase, Landscape, Forest Scene, Lemon, Orange, Brown, White, Cylindrical, 1910, 6 In. .. 2040.00
Vase, Landscape, Leafy Trees In Foreground, Free-Form Rim, Signed, 6 1/4 In. 4630.00
Vase, Landscape, Leafy Trees, Orange, Crimson, Gray, Cameo, 1900, 16 3/8 In. 3740.00
Vase, Landscape, River, Lemon Yellow, Green, Brown, Cameo, 1900, 14 In. 3450.00
Vase, Landscape, River, Umbellifer Blossoms, Dragonflies, Signed, c.1900, 16 In. 2875.00
Vase, Landscape, Tranquil River, Crimson, Yellow, Green, Cameo, 1910, 11 7/8 In. 3450.00
Vase, Landscape, Tranquil River, Leafy Trees, Orange, Brown, Gray, Cameo, 1900, 11 In. 3450.00
Vase, Landscape, Trees By River, Red Enameled, Orange, Gray Streaks, 1900, 8 1/4 In. ... 1380.00
Vase, Landscape, Trees, Amber Sky Against Green Body Of Water, Cameo, 10 1/2 In. ... 2750.00
Vase, Leaf Branch, Berries, Russet, Black, Amber Base, Gray Mottled, 1900, 14 In. 1840.00
Vase, Leaves & Branches, Ruby Opalescent, Flared Foot, Signed, 6 x 6 In. 300.00
Vase, Lilacs, Leafage, Pale Purple, Pea Green, Gray, Cameo, 1900, 7 1/2 In. 4025.00
Vase, Maroon Tiger Lilies, White Shot With Amber, H. Berge, c.1915, 8 x 5 In. 1400.00
Vase, Mottled Amber & Green, Shoulder Handles, Enameled Berries, 1900, 12 In. 6375.00
Vase, Mottled Yellow, Green, Brown, Rose Hip Twigs, Frosted Ground, Signed, 8 In. ... 2465.00
Vase, Nicotiana Blossoms, Leafage, Lemon Yellow, Red, Gray, Cameo, 1900, 9 In. 4315.00
Vase, Nuts On Leafy Branch, Emerald Green, Marked, 6 3/4 In. 880.00
Vase, Orange, Brown Peonies, Yellow, Orange, White, Brown Ground, Cameo, 12 In. ... 2310.00
Vase, Orchids, Dark Violet Overlay, Frosted Ground, Footed, Signed, 11 In. 3290.00

Vase, Oriental Poppies, Mottled Yellow Ground, 6 1/4 In. 2365.00
Vase, Pendant, Leafy Branches, Mottled Gray Walls, Trumpet Form, Signed, 21 In. 5175.00
Vase, Pink & Amber Poppies, Gray Ground, Dark Footed, Cameo, 1914, 16 3/4 In. 9000.00
Vase, Pink & Orange Floral, Purple Base, Flared Bell Form, 1905, 11 1/8 In. 7335.00
Vase, Pink Sweetpeas, White Streaked Ground, Yellow Footed, Cameo, 4 In. 2500.00
Vase, Pink Wild Flowers, White Ground, Amber Base, Inverted Rim, 1905, 9 1/2 In. 5250.00
Vase, Poppies, Leafage, Salmon Pink, Green, Cameo, 1900, 5 In. 4600.00
Vase, Poppies, Leafage, Sea-Foam Green Streaks, Signed, c.1900, 25 3/4 In. 6325.00
Vase, Poppy Blossoms, Leafage, Pale Blue, Tangerine, Gray, Cameo, 1900, 12 In. 8625.00
Vase, Purple Crocus, Gray, White, Footed, Cameo, 1900, 7 In. 6000.00
Vase, Purple Wild Violets, Mottled White, Long Tapering Neck, 1905, 21 1/2 In. 15000.00
Vase, Rain Scene, Pink, Green Ground, Cameo, Signed, 2 1/4 x 1 In. 1800.00
Vase, Red & Maroon Blend, Flared Rim, Footed, 14 In. 1400.00
Vase, Red Flowers, Green Leaves, Purple Ground, 4 Sides, Cameo, Signed, 3 1/4 x 5 In. . 1650.00
Vase, Snowdrop, Blue, White Ground, Dark Base, Cameo, 1900, 11 3/8 In. 9375.00
Vase, Sprays Of Apple Blossoms, Buds, Leafage, Crimson, Green, Brown, Cameo, 12 In. 2875.00
Vase, Sprays Of Flowering Bluebells, Trumpet Form, Ice Blue, Purple, 1905, 21 In. 9200.00
Vase, Sprays Of Orange Flowers, Gray, White, Pink Base, Cameo, 1905, 4 7/8 In. 3000.00
Vase, Spring Flowers, White, Cobalt Blue, Purple, White, Cameo, 1910, 7 1/8 In. 6325.00
Vase, Spring Scene, Green & Black Trees, Green & Brown Leaves, Cameo, 4 1/2 In. 1650.00
Vase, Stylized Bellflowers, Berries, Overlaid Blue, Mottled White Ground, 12 In. 2300.00
Vase, Stylized Floral Motif, Upper Body With Dot Design, Blue, Etched, 14 1/2 In. 9200.00
Vase, Stylized Foliage, Amber Overlay, Black Metallic, Everted Rim, 1925, 11 In. 1380.00
Vase, Teardrop Form, Enameled Leaves, Trumpet Blooms, Flared Neck, 1905, 16 In. 4600.00
Vase, Thistle Blossoms, Leaf Design, Gilded Rim, Bulbous, Etched, 19 1/4 In. 5750.00
Vase, Thistle, Crosses Of Lorraine, Acid Cut, Enameled, Frosted, Signed, 11 3/4 In. 2630.00
Vase, Thistle, Spherical Form, Pedestal Foot, Arched Foliate Frames, Signed, 6 1/4 In. ... 1022.00
Vase, Tulip Blossoms, Leafage, Pale Pearl Gray, Green, Cameo, 1900, 9 In. 8625.00
Vase, Tulip, Green, Orange, Amber, Applied Gold Handles, 6 3/4 In. 2875.00
Vase, Vertical Ribbing, Turquoise, Spherical, 6 In. 8050.00
Vase, Vertical Stripes, Dots, Azure Blue Opalescent, Amber, Baluster, 16 In. 6325.00
Vase, Wheat, White, Deep Purple, Blue, Etched, Cameo, 10 3/4 In. 5750.00
Vase, Wheel-Carved, Etched, Clematis Blossom, Lavender Overlay, Cameo, 20 In. 6900.00
Vase, Wheel-Carved, Etched, Poppy Blossoms, Orange & Green Overlay, 9 1/4 In. 2300.00
Vase, Wild Orchids, Spider Webs, Mottled White, Conical, 1900, 9 1/8 In. 6748.00
Vase, Wild Violets & Leaves, Gilt, Square, 1905, 4 3/4 In. 2810.00
Vase, Wild Violets & Leaves, Mottled White, Blue Base, Cylindrical, 1905, 4 7/8 In. 2625.00
Vase, Wild Violets, White, Amber Base, 1905, 3 1/8 In. 3000.00
Vase, Wild Violets, White, Amber Base, Squatty Bulbous, 1905, 2 3/4 In. 1405.00
Vase, Winter Landscape, Etched, Enameled, Frosted, Signed, 9 3/4 In. 3290.00
Vase, Winter Scene, 4 Sides Form, Signed, 4 In. 1840.00
Vase, Winter Scene, Baluster Form, Signed, 1 3/4 In. 2000.00
Vase, Winter Scene, Baluster Form, Wide Mouth, Signed, 2 1/4 In. 1150.00
Vase, Winter Scene, Egg Shape, Signed, 4 In. 2300.00
Vase, Winter Scene, Flask Form, Cylindrical Mouth, Signed, 3 In. 1150.00
Vase, Winter Scene, Trees, Snow On Branches, Amber Body, Cameo, 5 In. 1430.00
Vase, Yellow & Purple Flowers & Leaves, Square, 1905, 4 7/8 In. 2625.00
Vase, Yellow Cowslips, Egg Shape, 1905, 10 1/4 In. 5810.00
Vase, Yellow Wisteria, Leaves, Pale Purple Highlights, Pale Green, Yellow, 15 x 4 In. ... 2600.00
Vase, Ziggurat Designs Above Zigzags, Signed, c.1925, 18 3/4 In. 3165.00
Wine Set, Wheel-Carved, Thistle Blossoms, Gilded, Pitcher, 6 Glasses, 7 Piece 2590.00

DAVENPORT pottery and porcelain were made at the Davenport factory
in Longport, Staffordshire, England, from 1793 to 1887. Earthenwares,
creamwares, porcelains, ironstone, and other ceramics were made.
Most of the pieces are marked with a form of the word *Davenport*.

DAVENPORT
LONGPORT
STAFFORDSHRE

Bowl, Cover, Amoy, Octagonal, 11 1/2 In. 500.00
Coffeepot, Amoy, Gooseneck Spout, 9 1/4 In. 247.00
Dish, Italian Verandah, Gilt Transfer, Powder Blue Ground, 1830, 12 1/2 In. 385.00
Gravy Boat, Ironstone 45.00
Idyllic Scene, Boat & Church, Purple Transfer, 19 1/8 In. 440.00
Jug, Fox Hunt, White-Smear Glaze, Basket-Weave Border, Impressed Mark, 6 In. 170.00
Platter, Blue & White Transfer, Mon Filla, Davenport, 15 x 19 In. 195.00

Platter, Blue Feather Edge, 12 x 15 1/2 In. 185.00
Platter, Friburg, 17 3/4 x 13 3/4 In. 287.00
Platter, Oriental Scene, Blue & White, 21 x 15 1/2 In. 660.00

AVY CROCKETT, the American frontiersman, was born in 1786 and
ied in 1836. The historical character gained new fame in 1954 when
he Walt Disney television show ran a series of episodes featuring Fess
arker as Davy Crockett. Coonskin caps and buckskins became popu-
ar and hundreds of different Davy Crockett items were made.

Bag, Shoulder, Picture, Fringe 50.00
Bandanna, Yellow, Red & Black Graphics, Square, 17 In. ....55.00 to 65.00
Bank, Shoot A-B'Ar, Mechanical, 1950s 495.00
Belt, Buckle 45.00
Bolo Tie 35.00
Book & Small Record, 1971 .... 6.00
Boots, Rain, Rubber, Fringe, Decal, Box 275.00
Bowl, Fire-King 15.00
Cap, Raccoon Skin 35.00
Coloring Book, White Lettering, Saalfield, 1950s 22.00
Cookie Jar, American Bisque 350.00
Cookie Jar, Brush 225.00
Cookie Jar, McCoy ....250.00 to 325.00
Doll, Cloth Body, Celluloid Face, 19 In. 95.00
Doll, Plastic Flintlock Rifle, Rawhide Pants, Jacket, Plastic Face, 8 In. 25.00
Doll, Squeeze, Rubber, 1950s 15.00
Drum Set, Sticks, 2-Tone Tom-Tom, A Right Time Toy, 11 1/2 x 5 In. 109.00
Figurine, Horse, Coonskin Cap, Saddle, Kaintuck Rifle, Knife, Hartland 375.00
Flashlight, Pictures Davy With Rifle, Yellow, Red & White, 3 1/4 In. 50.00
Game, Radar Action, Ewing, 1950s 145.00
Ge-Tar, Mattel, 1950s 65.00
Glass, Enameled, 16 Oz. ....15.00 to 18.00
Glass Set, In Canoe & On Horse, 6 Piece 60.00
Hat, Rabbit Fur Tail & Side, Plastic Top, 1950s 50.00
Jacket, Frontier Marshal, Denim, Tan, Walt Disney, Blue Bell, Frame, Size 8 .... 241.00
Knife, Pocket, Small 40.00
Lunch Box, Holtemp, 1955 ....100.00 to 125.00
Lunch Box, Metal, Canada, No Thermos, 1955 .... 400.00
Mobile, Swing Dings, Modern Toy Co., Instructions 48.00
Mug, Brown Decal 10.00
Mug, McCoy 75.00
Mug, Milk Glass, Red Decal ....10.00 to 35.00
Neckerchief 25.00
Nodder 295.00
Official Doll, Sleepy Eye, Plastic, WDP, Fortune Toy Corp., Box, 7 1/2 In. 230.00
Ornament, Christmas Tree, Blown Glass, 5 1/2 In. 22.00
Pistol, Marx, Box 125.00
Pistol & Knife Set 70.00
Planter, American Bisque 50.00
Planter, Little Boy 65.00
Plate, Oxford China 45.00
Puzzle, Siege Of The Fort, Jaymar, Box 35.00
Record, Ballad Of Davy Crockett, 78 RPM, Peter Pan, Wonderland, 1954 .... 9.00
Ring, Copper 20.00
Ring, Figural, Plastic, Silvertone 35.00
Scarf, 16 x 16 In. 25.00
Shirt, Fringe 45.00
Tie, Lariat, On Card 45.00
Toy, Pony, Wooden, Ride & Push 100.00
Vest, Plastic 50.00
Wallet, Davy At Fort, Light Brown 40.00
Wallet, Vinyl, Disney, 1950s 100.00
Wristwatch, Windup, U.S. Time, 1954 .... 125.00

DE MORGAN art pottery was made in England by William De Morgan from the 1860s to 1907. He is best known for his luster-glazed Moorish-inspired pieces. The pottery used a variety of marks.

Tile, Fanciful Birds, Blue & White, Square, 6 1/8 In.	202.00
Vase, Fish, Waves Ground, Waisted Neck, Luster, Pink, 8 7/8 In.	1593.00

DE VEZ was a signature used on cameo glass after 1910. E. S. Monot founded the glass company near Paris in 1851. The company changed names many times. Mt. Joye, another glass by this factory, is listed in its own category.

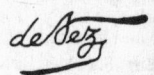

Bell, Floral, Leaf Design, Cranberry, Cast Brass Classical Hanger, Signed, 8 1/2 x 6 In.	2100.00
Vase, Green, Orange, Milky Green Ground, 8 1/4 In.	468.00
Vase, Harbor Scene, Houses On Land, Trees, Green, Red, Yellow Ground, 8 1/2 In.	358.00
Vase, Hyacinth, River Scene, 3 Cows Wading, Cloaked Figure, Signed, 6 In.	1190.00
Vase, Lake Scene, Blue, Yellow, Pink, 5 1/2 In.	275.00
Vase, Scenic, Young Maid Wearing A Cloak, Expansive Lake, Cobalt Blue, Blue, 7 In.	1450.00
Vase, Trees, Lake & Mountains, White & Yellow Overlaid In Red, Signed, 5 1/4 In.	1200.00

DECOYS are carved or turned wooden copies of birds, fish, or animals. The decoy was placed in the water or propped on the shore to lure flying birds to the pond for hunters. Some decoys are handmade, some are commercial products. Today there is a group of artists making modern decoys for display, not for use in a pond.

Black Duck, Lowhead, Hollow Carved, James Baker, 1910	2750.00
Black Duck, Resting Positions, Carved Bill, Inset Glass Eyes, 1900	230.00
Black Duck Drake, Painted Wood & Cork, 19 In.	375.00
Bluebill, Original Paint, Glass Eyes, Harold Dinham Waubaushene, Canada, 13 In., Pair	75.00
Bufflehead, Drake, Shot Scars, Inscription, Paul Gibson, c.1967, 12 1/4 In.	330.00
Canada Goose, Black Stain, Glass Eyes, John Castle, Birmingham, Michigan, 25 1/2 In.	200.00
Canada Goose, Blue Black Stain, Glass Eyes, John Castle, Michigan, 25 1/2 In.	120.00
Canada Goose, Carved Bill, Tack Eyes, Eugene Hendrickson, 1930	1380.00
Canada Goose, Carved Feathers, Glass Eyes, Signed Robert Sakota, Inscription, 18 In.	60.00
Canada Goose, Field, Standing, Roy Mill, P.E.I., c.1920	995.00
Canada Goose, Hollow Block, Glass Eyes, 20th Century, 22 In.	440.00
Canada Goose, Hollow Carved, Lloyd Sterling, 1930s	5225.00
Canada Goose, Original Paint, Alert Head, 24 In.	165.00
Canada Goose, Original Paint, Marked, Castle Haven, 22 In.	300.00
Canvasback Drake, Harry Fennimore, Bordentown, N.J., c.1928	2200.00
Canvasback Drake, Hollow Block, Glass Eyes, Alex Meldrum, Michigan, 16 3/4 In.	160.00
Drake & Duck, Baby On Base, Gort	500.00
Duck, Eider Drake, Inlet Head, Original Head, Maine, 1920	1265.00
Duck, Eider Drake, Upper Maine, Early 20th Century	345.00
Duck, Stamped Glen Burnie, Painted, c.1940, 6 1/2 x 13 In.	125.00
Duck, Willet, Raised Wing, Shoebutton Eyes, William Bowman, 1870	5460.00
Duck, Yellowlegs, Raised Wing, Shoebutton Eyes, Original Paint, W. Bowman, 1870	4890.00
Duckling, Lawrence Bethel, Black & White, 1940, 10 In.	285.00
Fish, Carved Wood, Metal Fins, Glass Eyes, Carl Christiansen, 9 3/4 In.	80.00
Goldeneye, Glass Eyes, Painted, Signed Good Hunting Josef Wooster '70, 14 1/2 In.	360.00
Goldeneye, Noah Sterling, c.1920	3300.00
Goldeneye Drake, Cork Body, Wood Tail, Bottom, S. Wheeler, 1900	1495.00
Goldeneye Hen, Sleeping, Ed Parsons	3850.00
Green-Winged Teal Hen, Joseph Paquette	1650.00
Mallard, Ben Schmidt, Pair	1375.00
Mallard, Factory, Polychrome Paint, Glass Eyes, 17 1/4 In., Pair	220.00
Mallard Drake, Glass Eyes, Leopold Koehler, 15 1/4 In.	225.00
Mallard Drake, Tack Eyes, Repaint, Duck Creek Hunt Club, Ontario, Canada, 17 1/2 In.	90.00
Mallard Hen, Herber	35.00
Mallard Hen, Preener, Hollow, Glass Eyes, Tobe Dawson, c.1920, 14 1/2 In.	350.00
Merganser Drake, Sheet Metal Comb, Early 20th Century	460.00
Muskie, Button Eyes, Wire Teeth, Miles Smith, 37 1/2 In.	247.00
Pigeon, Carved & Painted Wood, Early 20th Century, 12 1/4 In.	575.00
Pintail Drake, Delaware River, Blair School, c.1890	2000.00

Pintail Hen, Mason 4620.00
Red-Breasted Merganser, Roger Williams 4400.00
Red-Breasted Merganser, Willie Ross, Chebeague Island, Maine, 4 In. 260.00
Redhead Drake, Hollow Block, Glass Eyes, Alex Meldrum, Michigan, 16 3/4 In. 195.00
Shore Bird, Carved, Original Paint, Marked, T.L., 7 3/4 In. 165.00
Shore Bird, Plover, Black-Breasted, Original Paint, William Bowman, 1870 .... 4312.00
Shore Bird, Plover, Black-Breasted, Raised Wing, Captain Al Ketchum, 1870 .... 9200.00
Shore Bird, Plover, Black-Breasted, Raised Wing, Original Paint, W. Bowman, 1870 ... 5462.00
Shore Bird, Robin-Snipe, Paddle Tail, Original Paint, Captain Al Ketchum, 1870 ...... 1380.00
Swan, Red Eyes, Blue & Red, c.1920, 9 x 17 In. 175.00
Yellowlegs, Glass Eye, Painted, Mason 1800.00
Yellowlegs, Shore, Joseph W. Lincoln, c.1910 .... 1395.00
Yellowlegs, Wooden, Raised Wing Detail, New England, 20th Century 402.00

DEDHAM Pottery was started in 1895. Chelsea Keramic Art Works was
established in 1872 in Chelsea, Massachusetts, by members of the
Robertson family. The factory closed in 1889 and was reorganized as
the Chelsea Pottery U.S. in 1891. The firm used the marks *CKAW* and
CPUS. It became the Dedham Pottery of Dedham, Massachusetts. The
factory closed in 1943. It was famous for its crackleware dishes, which
picture blue outlines of animals, flowers, and other natural motifs.

5 Petals, Butter Chip, Raised Design, 3 1/4 In. 305.00
Azalea, Plate, 10 In. 465.00
Azalea, Punch Bowl, 12 In. 1800.00
Birds In Potted Orange Tree, Plate, Impressed, 10 In. 715.00
Bookends, Elephant, Raised Trunk, 3 1/3 x 5 1/2 In. 880.00
Butterfly, Plate, Alternating Flower, 10 In. 715.00
Butterfly, Plate, Stamped, 8 1/3 In. 385.00
Butterfly Border, Candlestick, Miniature Flowers, 1 1/2 In., Pair 1045.00
California Poppies Rim, Plate, Golden Gate, San Francisco 2600.00
Chick, Pitcher, Blue Border, 5 In. 3400.00
Crab, Plate, 10 In. 825.00
Crab, Plate, Claws Extending Over Rim, 8 1/3 In. 825.00
Dolphin, Plate, 8 1/2 In. 605.00
Dolphin, Plate, Blue Ink Stamp, 6 1/2 In. 430.00
Double Turtle, Plate, 6 In. ....715.00 to 1210.00
Duck, Plate, 10 In. 330.00
Duck, Plate, Stamped, 8 1/2 In. 305.00
Duck, Plate, White Glaze, 6 In. ....100.00 to 165.00
Elephant, Ashtray, Slots For Cigarettes, 3 3/4 In. 385.00
Elephant, Bowl, Rice, 2 x 3 1/4 In. 1045.00
Elephant, Plate, 9 3/4 In. 430.00
Elephant, Plate, Trunk Raised, 4 1/2 In. 605.00
Elephant, Sugar & Creamer, 2 x 5 1/2 In. 1150.00
French Mushroom, Pitcher, Spotted & Striped Mushrooms, 5 In. 1210.00
Grape, Bowl, 10 3/4 In. 385.00
Grape, Charger, 12 In. 355.00
Grape, Cup & Saucer, 2 3/4 & 6 In. ....355.00 to 385.00
Grape, Plate, 6 3/8 In. 70.00
Grape, Plate, 8 1/2 In. 195.00
Grape, Plate, Maude Davenport, 6 In. 220.00
Horsechestnut, Plate, 6 1/4 In. 165.00
Horsechestnut, Plate, Maude Davenport, 8 1/2 In. 305.00
Iris, Plate, Blue Rabbit Stamp, Maude Davenport, 10 In., 4 Piece 1150.00
Iris, Plate, Iris, 6 In. 247.00
Lobster, Plate, 6 In. ....660.00 to 825.00
Magnolia, Plate, 2 Double Buds, 9 3/4 In. 302.00
Magnolia, Plate, 8 1/2 In. 195.00
Mushroom, Plate, Blue Rabbit Stamp, Maude Davenport, 8 1/2 In. ....690.00 to 805.00
Mushroom & Wicket, Soup, Dish, 8 1/2 In. 990.00
Oak Leaves, Pitcher, Molded, Branches, Green Glaze, CKAW, 9 3/4 x 6 In. 935.00
Owl, Plate, Alternating Star & Half Moon, 8 1/3 In. 3960.00
Pinecone, Bowl, Teal, Footed, CKAW, 3 1/2 x 7 In. 525.00

Polar Bear On Icebergs, Plate, 8 1/2 In. 605.00
Poppy, Bowl, Chinese Cut, 3 3/4 x 8 1/2 In. 525.00
Poppy Pods, Plate, Large Poppy In Center, 8 1/2 In. 385.00
Rabbit, Bowl, 4 3/4 x 8 In. 355.00
Rabbit, Bowl, 5 1/2 In. 120.00
Rabbit, Bowl, 9 In. 170.00
Rabbit, Bowl, Maude Davenport, 2 1/2 x 6 In. 330.00
Rabbit, Bowl, Signed, 7 3/4 In. 75.00
Rabbit, Candlesnuffer, Bell Shape, 1 3/4 In. 880.00
Rabbit, Chamberstick 2300.00
Rabbit, Charger, Stamped, 12 In. 330.00
Rabbit, Coaster, Stamped, 4 In. 550.00
Rabbit, Creamer, Circular Handle, Partial Stamp, 3 x 3 1/3 In. 330.00
Rabbit, Cup & Saucer, After Dinner, 2 1/8 & 4 1/3 In. 275.00
Rabbit, Cup & Saucer, Blue Ink Stamp, 6 x 2 1/2 In. 100.00
Rabbit, Dish, 5 Sides, Stamped, 7 1/4 In. 495.00
Rabbit, Holder, Boot Shape, 5 In. 1870.00
Rabbit, Holder, Flower, Standing, Blue Trim, 6 x 4 1/4 In. 1320.00
Rabbit, Humidor, 6 1/3 x 5 1/2 In. 1210.00
Rabbit, Jar, Mustard, 2 3/4 x 2 1/2 In. 715.00
Rabbit, Pitcher, 4 1/2 In. 145.00
Rabbit, Pitcher, Band Of Rabbits At Base, 5 In. 550.00
Rabbit, Pitcher, Bulbous, White Glaze, Stamped, 8 1/2 x 7 In. 305.00
Rabbit, Plate, 8 1/3 In. 195.00
Rabbit, Plate, 9 3/4 In. 330.00
Rabbit, Plate, 10 In., Pair 275.00
Rabbit, Plate, Marked, 6 In. ....110.00 to 145.00
Rabbit, Plate, Yellow Glaze, Blue Rabbit Stamp, 6 In., Pair 2070.00
Rabbit, Platter, Roast, 17 1/4 x 10 1/4 In. 1980.00
Rabbit, Platter, Round, 11 1/2 In. 290.00
Rabbit, Salt & Pepper, Floral Band At Neck 440.00
Rabbit, Saucer, 7 In., Pair 285.00
Rabbit, Sugar, Cover, 2 Handles, Stamped, 4 1/4 x 4 1/2 In. 245.00
Rabbit, Teapot, 6 1/8 x 6 3/4 In. 1210.00
Rabbit, Tureen, Rabbit Handle, 5 x 9 1/4 In. 1650.00
Rabbit, Wash Basin, Inverted Center, Stamped, 3 x 12 In. 770.00
Rabbit, Water Tray, Signed MBD, 13 1/2 In. 2000.00
Rabbit Border, Tile, 4 1/2 x 4 1/2 In. 275.00
Rooster & Hens, Pitcher, Night & Morning, Blue Green Glaze, CKAW, 5 In. ...385.00 to 600.00
Scotty Dogs, Plate, Crouching, 8 1/2 In. 2640.00
Snowtree, Plate, 10 1/8 In. 135.00
Snowtree, Plate, Signed, 6 In. 225.00
Swan, Bowl, Rice, 2 x 3 1/4 In. 165.00
Swan, Dish, Oblong, Signed, 5 1/2 In. 560.00
Swan, Jam Jar, Cover, Cylindrical, 4 1/4 x 3 In. 880.00
Swan, Plate, Intertwined With Cattails, 8 3/4 In. 495.00
Swan, Plate, Stamped, 7 1/3 In. 385.00
Swan, Tile, Square, 4 3/4 In. 265.00
Turkey, Cup & Saucer, 3 1/4 In. 545.00
Turkey, Plate, 9 3/4 In. 385.00
Turkey, Plate, Centenary Mark, 6 In. 430.00
Turkey, Plate, Maude Davenport, 10 In. 525.00
Turtle, Paperweight, Decorated Blue Shell, Stamped, 3 1/3 In. 880.00
Vase, Applied Spider & Fly, Blue, Brown Glaze, CKAW, A. Robertson, 3 x 5 In. ... 1045.00
Vase, Blue & Plume Paint, Signed, 5 x 4 1/2 In. 1760.00
Vase, Burgundy Iridescent, Green Volcanic Glaze, Hugh Robertson, 8 In. 1495.00
Vase, Curdled Dripping Volcanic Glaze, Hugh Robertson, 8 1/2 In. 1210.00
Vase, Dripping Green Over Red Flambe Glaze, Hugh Robertson, 9 In. 880.00
Vase, Floral Panels, Crackle, 8 3/4 x 5 In. 550.00
Vase, Floral, Carved Bird On A Limb, Brown Body, Green Glaze, CKAW, 7 In. 825.00
Vase, Garnet To Green Lustered Flambe, Hugh Robertson, Signed, 6 1/2 x 5 In. ... 1320.00
Vase, Luster, Dripping Oxblood & Gunmetal Glaze, Signed, 9 In. 1430.00
Vase, Mauve Over Khaki, Volcanic Glaze, CKAW, 4 1/8 x 4 In. 525.00

Vase, Rabbit Wide Border, Hugh Cornwall Robertson, 2 1/4 x 4 1/4 In. 495.00
Vase, Red Oxblood To Gunmetal Glaze, Iridescent, CKAW, 4 In. 880.00
Vase, Sang-De-Boeuf, Hugh Robertson, 5 x 3 1/2 In. 825.00
Vase, Sang-De-Boeuf, Pigeon Feather Glaze, CKAW, 7 x 4 In. 1430.00
Vase, Volcanic, Blue, Black Glaze Over Ocher, H. Robertson, 8 In. 920.00
Vase, Volcanic, Oxblood Glaze, Signed, 4 x 2 1/4 In. 660.00
Walnut On Leaf, Salt, Bisque, CKAW, 1 1/4 x 3 1/4 In. 305.00

DEGENHART is the name used by collectors for the products of the Crystal Art Glass Company of Cambridge, Ohio. John and Elizabeth Degenhart started the glassworks in 1947. Quality paperweights and other glass objects were made. John died in 1964 and his wife took over management and production ideas. Over 145 colors of glass were made. In 1978, after the death of Mrs. Degenhart, the molds were sold. The D in a heart trademark was removed, so collectors can easily recognize the true Degenhart piece.

Bell, Bicentennial, Amethyst 8.00
Cup Plate, Heart & Lyre, Gold 18.00
Dish, Hen Cover, Green 22.00
Figurine, Owl, Dark Gray 50.00
Figurine, Priscilla, Amber 70.00
Pitcher, Vaseline, Miniature 25.00

DEGUE is a signature acid-etched on pieces of French glass made in the early 1900s. Cameo, mold blown, and smooth glass with contrasting colored rims are the types most often found.

Chandelier, Domed Shade, Blue, Yellow, Pink, Stylized Floral Design, 24 In. 825.00
Lamp, Wrought Iron, Stylized Clematis Blossoms, Trailing Leafage, Gray, 1930, 26 In. . . 7475.00
Night-Light, Arab & Camel, Metal Top, Switch On Cord, 6 1/2 In. 795.00
Vase, Arab & Camel Scene, Deep Maroon, Peach, Orange Satin, 6 1/2 In. 750.00
Vase, Brown House & Trees, Orange Ground, Signed, Cameo, 6 1/4 In. 644.00
Vase, Intaglio Cut Designs, Cobalt Blue, Signed, 11 1/2 In. 550.00
Vase, Row Of Trees, Light Blue Mottled, Blue Overlay, Cushion Foot, 1925, 21 In. 2750.00

DELATTE glass is a French cameo glass made by Andre Delatte. It was first made in Nancy, France, in 1921. Lighting fixtures and opaque glassware in imitation of Bohemian opaline were made. There were many French cameo glass makers, so be sure to look in other appropriate categories.

Vase, Azalea Design, Pink, Green Mottled, Signed, 13 x 5 In. 900.00
Vase, Cameo Etched Exotic Blossoms, Signed, 8 In. 690.00
Vase, Floral, Black, Blue, Green, Enamel, Blue Ground, 3 1/2 x 1 3/4 In. 100.00
Vase, Floral, Blue, Green Enamel, Orange Ground, 3 1/2 x 1 3/4 In. 100.00
Vase, Landscape, Lake, Trees, Red, Brown, Lime Green, Baluster, Signed, 8 In. 747.00
Vase, Nude Maiden Amid Forest Glen, Loop Handles, Signed, c.1920, 14 In. 1955.00
Vase, Oak Leaves, Acorns, Brown, Light Brown Over Burnt Orange, Signed, 9 1/2 In. 550.00

DELDARE, see Buffalo Pottery Deldare.

DELFT is a tin-glazed pottery that has been made since the seventeenth century. It is decorated with blue on white or with colored decorations. Most of the pieces sold today were made after 1891, and the name *Holland* appears with the Delft factory marks. The word *delft* also appears on pottery from other countries. Delft was made in England in the eighteenth century.

Basin, Flowering Tree Landscape, Cell Border, Blue, White, 1760, 13 3/4 In. 575.00
Bird Feeder, Exotic Birds Perched On Prunus Trees, Blue, White, Cylindrical, 8 In. 3162.00
Biscuit Jar, 2 Figures On Front, Amphora, Blue & White 110.00
Bowl, Bleeding, Cottage Painted Design, Heart-Pierced Handle, England, 1765, 6 1/2 In. . . 6325.00
Bowl, Blue & White, Oriental Design With Ducks, Lambeth, England, 9 x 3 3/4 In. 358.00
Bowl, Blue, Gold, Green, Brown, Purple, Bouquet Of Flowers, Leaf Border, 9 In. 58.00
Bowl, Blue, White, Yellow Rim, Landscape With House, Shallow, 14 In. 275.00
Bowl, Exotic Bird Perched On 2 Spreading Branches Of Prunus Tree, 1700, 12 In. 1380.00

Bowl, Insects Flitting Amidst Branches, Blue Manganese Interior, 1750, 10 5/8 In. 240.00
Bowl, Landscape, Figure Scene, Blue, White, Signed, Anno, 1671, England, 9 3/8 In. . . . 2990.00
Bowl, Man Seated, Holding Fishing Rod, Blue, White, 1740-1750, 11 3/4 In. 1610.00
Bowl, Pagodas Flanking Large Rock, Cluster Of Rocks, Blue, Red, Yellow, 10 1/4 In. . . . 460.00
Bowl, Peonies, Vine Branch, Grape Cluster Interior, Blue, White, 10 In. 575.00
Bowl, Polychrome, Yellow & Blue, 19th Century, 15 1/4 x 6 In. 165.00
Bowl, Squirrel Perched On Vine Branch, Grape Clusters, Blue, White, 1740, 12 In. 1725.00
Bowl, Yellow, Blue, Polychrome, 15 1/4 x 6 In. 72.00
Butter Tub, Blue & White, 2 Handles, 8 1/2 In. 231.00
Charger, Cell, Floral Border Panels, Yellow Enamel Trim, Blue, White, 1770, 14 In. 460.00
Charger, Coastal Landscape, Male & Female Figures With A Dog, Blue, White, 14 In. . . 259.00
Charger, Figure Of Flora, Amid Wooded Landscape, c.1730, 12 1/4 In. 1650.00
Charger, Floral Design, Polychrome, 13 3/4 In. 546.00
Charger, Floral Garden, Fence Landscape, Blue, White, 1770, 14 In. 345.00
Charger, Fruit, Flowers, Foliage, Blue, White, 1770, 13 3/4 In. 920.00
Charger, Pale Blue, Dutch, 17th Century, c.1660, 13 5/8 In. 2450.00
Charger, Stylized Oriental Dragon, Dot, Cell Border, Blue, White, 14 In. 345.00
Charger, Teaplant, Flower Before A Fence, Stylized Floral Lappets Border, 13 3/4 In. . . . 460.00
Charger, Warwick Castle, Blue & White, 19th Century, 14 In. 88.00
Charger, William & Mary Portrait, Bird, Landscape Border, Blue, White, 13 In. 690.00
Charger, William III, Polychrome, England, c.1688, 13 1/2 In. 2650.00
Coffeepot, Cover, Fluted Conical Form, L-Shape Spout, Blue, White, 10 1/2 In. 4830.00
Dish, Allover Scrolled Vine & Floral, Blue & White, Holland, 1780, 12 1/4 In. 230.00
Dish, Bird & Floral, Paneled Border, Blue & White, Holland, 1780, 13 1/2 In. 145.00
Dish, Blue & White, Oriental & Floral Design, Lobed, 18th Century, 13 3/4 In. 920.00
Dish, Center Foliate Medallion, Foliate Panels To Rim, c.17th Century, 12 In. 357.00
Dish, Cracked Ice, Blue & Manganese, England, 9 In. 1350.00
Dish, Man Astride Rearing Horse, Buff-Colored Body, Blue, White, 12 1/4 In. 1035.00
Dish, Spice, Columnar Center, 4 Compartments, Raised On 5 Bun Feet, 1780, 7 In. 748.00
Dish, Sponged Tree Among 4 Other Sponged Trees, Manganese White, 1730, 12 In. 345.00
Egg Timer, Germany, 1920 . . . . 75.00
Food Warmer, 4 Pierced Hearts, Alternating Leaves, Blue, White, 2 x 5 1/16 x 5 In. 345.00
Inkwell, 5 Quill Holders, Blue Dash Border, Cast Iron Masks, c.1640, 5 In. 695.00
Jar, Cover, Dog On Ball Finial, Panels Of Birds & Figures, Hexagonal, c.1720, 14 In. . . . 1475.00
Jar, Drug, Blue & White, Angels & Floral, U. Rub. Desi, England, 1770, 7 1/4 In. 860.00
Pitcher, Oval Medallions Of Houses, Mauve Field, Pear Shape, 1741, 9 1/2 In. 577.00
Plaque, Canal Scene, Lozenge Form, 14 x 13 In. 545.00
Plate, Brown, Red, Yellow, Blue, Green, Polychrome, Floral Center, 9 In. 250.00
Plate, Chinese Pavilion By Fence Beneath Willow Tree, Orange Rim, Blue, Green, 9 In. . . 345.00
Plate, Dutch, Floral Design, 18th Century, 8 1/2 In. 88.00
Plate, Farm Scene, c.1760, 8 3/4 In. 235.00
Plate, Fluted Edge, Turquoise Ground, 6 1/2 In. 1900.00
Plate, Foliate Medallion In Center, Manganese Blue, Striped Bands, 9 In. 460.00
Plate, Geometric & Floral Design, c.1750, 9 1/8 In. 185.00
Plate, Man Chasing Animal, Off-White Ground, Rust, Blue, Yellow, Green, 9 In. 633.00
Plate, Peacock, Under Tree, Sponged Landscape, England, Mid-18th Century, 8 1/2 In. . . 1840.00
Plate, Prince William Of Orange Portrait, Floral Border, Holland, 18th Century, 9 In. . . . 545.00
Plate, Resting Horse Center, Mid-18th Century, 8 3/4 In. 185.00
Plate, Youth Playing A Horn, c.1750, 9 In. 250.00
Platter, Floral Spray, Blue To Center, Blue, White Border, 15 In. 97.00
Platter, Oriental Coastal Landscape, Woman & Child On Boat, Blue, White, 1750 . . . . . 575.00
Platter, Oriental Vase Of Flowers, Floral Landscape, Blue, White, 1760, 14 In. 518.00
Pot, Posset Cover, Chinaman Beneath A Tree, Blue, White, England, 1700, 8 3/8 In. 4312.00
Punch Bowl, Blue & White, c.1730, 10 1/2 In. 2350.00
Punch Bowl, Continuous Scene, Blue & White, England, c.1750, 11 3/4 In. 4250.00
Punch Bowl, Polychrome, c.1740, 13 7/8 In. 250.00
Strainer, Cheese, Early 18th Century 265.00
Tea Bowl, Chinaman, Seated, Blue, White, 1680 . . . . 748.00
Teapot, Cover, Flowers, Gadrooned, Band Of Scrolls, Blue, White, England, 1720, 5 In. . 2990.00
Tile, Children Playing, 8 Different Scenes, Blue, 5 1/8 In., Set Of 8 . . . . 255.00
Tile, Manganese Water Fowl, Square, 1850s, 5 In., Pair 55.00
Tile, Picture, Canary Within Manganese Cage, Yellow Finials, Blue Feeder, 15 x 10 In. . . 1265.00
Tile, Picture, Clock, Manganese Border, Hour Glass & Crest, 1775, 15 1/2 x 10 In. 1265.00

Tile, Picture, Cow Within Landscape, 6 Tiles, 14 3/4 x 9 3/4 In.	1150.00
Tile, Rooster, Multicolored, 20th Century, 4 x 9 In.	44.00
Tile, Windmill Scene, Square, 20th Century, 4 In.	44.00
Vase, Blue & White, Tulip, De Twee Scheepjes, Allover Floral, 1770, 13 In.	375.00
Vase, Floral Design, Blue, White, 19th Century, 8 1/2 In.	165.00
Vase, Flowers, Diaper & Elongated Diamond Borders, England, c.1760, 11 In.	1100.00
Vase, Hexagonal Trumpet Form, Floral Design, Blue, White, 7 1/2 In.	72.00
Vase, Stylized, Oriental Blossoms, Foliage, Insects, Blue, White, 12 3/18 In., Pair	1095.00
Vase, Trumpet Form, 3 Bells Mark, Blue, White, 10 In., Pair	335.00
Wall Pocket, Chinese Man Standing Behind Garden Fence, Inverted Bell-Shaped Body	1400.00

DENTAL cabinets, chairs, equipment, and other related items are listed here. Other objects may be found in the Medical category.

Cabinet, Mahogany, 20 Drawers, 2 Doors, Bin, 53 x 41 In.	850.00
Cabinet, Mahogany, Glass Doors, Milk Glass Shelves, Marble Base	1100.00
Cabinet, Marble Work Surface, Upper Cupboard, Lower Cupboard, 1920s	1250.00
Catalog, Silverman's, Dental Tools & Supplies, 1969, 150 Pages	25.00
Chair, 1904	725.00
Chair, Traveling	425.00
Kit, Teeth, Dentist's Supply, N.Y., 400 Bioform Teeth, 9 Drawers, Sample, 6 3/8 In.	185.00
Mirror, Pocket, Hill's Dental Company, Paterson, New Jersey	155.00

DENVER is part of the mark on an American art pottery. William Long of Steubenville, Ohio, founded the Lonhuda Pottery Company in 1892. In 1900 he moved to Denver, Colorado, and organized the Denver China and Pottery Company. This pottery, which used the mark *Denver*, worked until 1905 when Long moved to New Jersey and founded the Clifton Pottery. Long also worked for Weller Pottery, Roseville Pottery, and American Encaustic Tiling Company.

DENVER
C &.
P Co

Vase, Alternating Chrysanthemums & Leaves, Green Matte Glaze, 1903, 6 x 6 In.	990.00
Vase, Alternating Dandelion Blossoms, Leaves, Green Glaze, 6 1/2 x 6 In.	3300.00
Vase, Carnations, Pink, White, Gray, Brown Ground, 6 x 8 In.	330.00
Vase, Daffodil, Embossed Stems, Olive, 9 In.	2860.00
Vase, Dogwood, Lonhuda, Eugene Roberts, 8 1/4 In.	440.00
Vase, Stylized Blossoms, Leaves, Petals Forming Scalloped Rim, Green Glaze, 6 In.	2860.00

DEPRESSION GLASS was an inexpensive glass manufactured in large quantities during the 1920s and early 1930s. It was made in many colors and patterns by dozens of factories in the United States. The name *Depression glass* is a modern one. For more descriptions, history, pictures, and prices of Depression glass, see the book *Kovels' Depression Glass & Dinnerware Price List*.

Adam, Ashtray, Green, 4 1/2 In.	24.00 to 27.00
Adam, Bowl, Cover, Pink, 9 In.	65.00 to 78.00
Adam, Bowl, Green, 4 3/4 In.	15.00 to 18.00
Adam, Bowl, Pink, 7 3/4 In.	26.00
Adam, Bowl, Vegetable, Oval, Pink, 10 In.	35.00
Adam, Butter, Cover, Green	285.00 to 315.00
Adam, Butter, Cover, Pink	80.00
Adam, Cake Plate, Footed, Green, 10 In.	23.00 to 30.00
Adam, Cake Plate, Pink, 10 In.	25.00 to 28.00
Adam, Candlestick, Green, 4 In., Pair	98.00
Adam, Candy Jar, Cover, Green	125.00
Adam, Creamer, Pink	20.00 to 25.00
Adam, Cup & Saucer, Pink	33.00 to 35.00
Adam, Grill Plate, Green, 9 In.	20.00 to 22.00
Adam, Pitcher, Green, 8 In.	50.00
Adam, Plate, Green, Square, 9 In.	20.00 to 35.00
Adam, Plate, Pink, 6 In.	9.00
Adam, Platter, Green, Oval, 11 3/4 In.	29.00
Adam, Salt & Pepper, Footed, Green, 4 In.	125.00
Adam, Sherbet, Footed, Pink, 3 In.	30.00
Adam, Sugar & Creamer, Cover, Pink	60.00 to 70.00

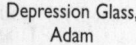

Depression Glass,
Adam

Depression Glass,
American Sweetheart

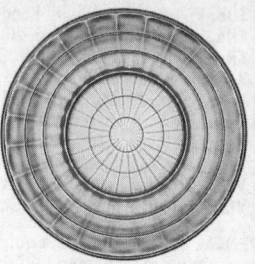

Depression Glass,
Block Optic

Adam, Tumbler, Green, 4 1/2 In. . . . . .28.00 to 32.00
Adam, Tumbler, Iced Tea, Pink, 5 1/2 In. 80.00
Adam, Vase, Green, 7 1/2 In. 85.00
Alice, Plate, Jadite, 10 In. . . . . .22.00 to 25.00
American Pioneer, Bowl, Handles, Green, 9 In. 27.00
American Sweetheart, Bowl, Monax, 6 In. 13.50
American Sweetheart, Bowl, Oval, Pink, 11 In. . . . . .72.00 to 79.00
American Sweetheart, Bowl, Pink, 9 In. . . . . .56.00 to 59.00
American Sweetheart, Bread Plate, Monax, 6 In. . . . . .4.00 to 10.00
American Sweetheart, Chop Plate, Monax, 11 In. 15.00
American Sweetheart, Console, Blue, 18 In. 2100.00
American Sweetheart, Console, Red, 18 In. 1900.00
American Sweetheart, Creamer, Monax 10.00
American Sweetheart, Cup & Saucer, Monax . . . . .11.00 to 13.00
American Sweetheart, Cup & Saucer, Pink . . . . .21.00 to 23.00
American Sweetheart, Pitcher, Pink, 60 Oz., 7 1/2 In. 950.00
American Sweetheart, Plate, Monax, 10 1/4 In. 25.00
American Sweetheart, Plate, Monax, 9 In. . . . . .11.00 to 18.00
American Sweetheart, Plate, Pink, 10 1/4 In. . . . . .34.00 to 40.00
American Sweetheart, Plate, Red, 8 In. 75.00
American Sweetheart, Platter, Oval, Monax, 13 In. 65.00
American Sweetheart, Platter, Oval, Pink, 13 In. . . . . .52.00 to 55.00
American Sweetheart, Salt & Pepper, Monax . . . . .375.00 to 399.00
American Sweetheart, Salt Shaker, Footed, Monax 205.00
American Sweetheart, Salver, Monax, 12 In. 16.00
American Sweetheart, Salver, Pink, 12 In. . . . . .20.00 to 28.00
American Sweetheart, Salver, Red, 12 In. 220.00
American Sweetheart, Sandwich Server, Blue, 15 1/2 In. . . . . .550.00 to 625.00
American Sweetheart, Sandwich Server, Monax, 15 1/2 In. 225.00
American Sweetheart, Sherbet, Footed, Pink, 4 1/4 In. . . . . .14.00 to 16.00
American Sweetheart, Soup, Cream, Monax 130.00
American Sweetheart, Soup, Cream, Pink, 4 1/2 In. . . . . .75.00 to 95.00
American Sweetheart, Soup, Dish, Pink, 9 1/2 In. . . . . .42.00 to 72.00
American Sweetheart, Sugar, Monax 9.00
American Sweetheart, Tidbit, 2 Tiers, Red 410.00
American Sweetheart, Tumbler, Pink, 5 Oz., 3 1/2 In. . . . . .85.00 to 110.00
American Sweetheart, Tumbler, Pink, 9 Oz., 4 1/4 In. . . . . .75.00 to 100.00
Anniversary, Bowl, 4 7/8 In. 5.00
Anniversary, Butter, Cover, Pink 52.00
Anniversary, Candlestick, 6 1/2 In., Pair 15.00
Anniversary, Candy Jar, Cover 22.00
Anniversary, Compote, 3-Footed 4.00
Anniversary, Creamer 6.00
Anniversary, Cup & Saucer 5.00
Anniversary, Plate, 6 1/4 In. 2.00
Anniversary, Sherbet 5.00
Anniversary, Soup, Dish, 7 3/8 In. 10.00

Anniversary, Sugar, Cover . . . . .9.00 to 12.00
Anniversary, Vase, 6 1/2 In. 10.00
Apple Blossom pattern is listed here as Dogwood.
Aunt Polly, Bowl, Blue, 4 3/4 In. 16.00
Aunt Polly, Butter, Cover, Blue 205.00
Aunt Polly, Pickle, Blue, Handle, 7 1/4 In. 38.00
Aunt Polly, Plate, Sherbet, Blue, 6 In. . . . . .9.00 to 14.00
Aunt Polly, Tumbler, Blue, 8 Oz., 3 5/8 In. 33.00
Aurora, Bowl, Cereal, Pink, 5 3/8 In. . . . . .15.00 to 18.00
Aurora, Bowl, Cobalt Blue, 4 1/2 In. 50.00
Aurora, Cup, Cobalt Blue 17.00
Aurora, Plate, Cobalt Blue, 6 1/2 In. 12.00
Aurora, Saucer, Cobalt Blue 6.00
Avocado, Plate, Pink, 8 1/4 In. 20.00
Avocado, Plate, Sherbet, Green, 6 3/8 In. 18.00
Avocado, Sherbet, Footed, Green 53.00
Avocado, Sugar & Creamer, Footed, Green 70.00
Ballerina pattern is listed here as Cameo.
Banded Rib pattern is listed here as Coronation.
Banded Rings pattern is listed here as Ring.
Basket pattern is listed here as No. 615.
Beaded Block, Pickle, 2 Handles, Green, 6 1/2 In. 12.00
Block pattern is listed here as Block Optic.
Block Optic, Butter, Cover, Green, 3 x 5 In. 45.00
Block Optic, Candy Jar, Cover, Low, Pink, 2 1/4 In. 65.00
Block Optic, Console, Rolled Edge, Pink, 11 3/4 In. 150.00
Block Optic, Creamer, Footed, Green, 4 1/4 In. 10.00
Block Optic, Cup, Green . . . . .6.00 to 7.00
Block Optic, Goblet, Green, 9 Oz., 5 3/4 In. 22.00
Block Optic, Goblet, Yellow, 9 Oz., 5 3/4 In. 30.00
Block Optic, Grill Plate, Green, 8 In. 4.00
Block Optic, Mug, Green 30.00
Block Optic, Pitcher, Bulbous, Green, 54 Oz., 7 5/8 In. 80.00
Block Optic, Pitcher, Green, 80 Oz., 8 In. 75.00
Block Optic, Plate, Green, 9 In. . . . . .10.00 to 22.00
Block Optic, Plate, Sherbet, Pink, 6 In. 4.00
Block Optic, Salt & Pepper, Yellow, Footed 85.00
Block Optic, Sandwich Server, Center Handle, Pink 68.00
Block Optic, Sherbet, Cone, Green . . . . .3.50 to 7.00
Block Optic, Sherbet, Pink, 4 3/4 In. 17.00
Block Optic, Sugar & Creamer, Footed, Green 24.00
Block Optic, Tumbler, Pink, 10 Oz., 5 In. 15.00
Bouquet & Lattice pattern is listed here as Normandie.
Bow Knot, Tumbler, 10 Oz., 5 In. 18.00
Bubble, Bowl, Blue, 4 1/2 In. 10.00
Bubble, Bowl, Blue, 5 1/4 In. . . . . .10.50 to 13.00
Bubble, Bowl, Blue, 8 3/8 In. . . . . .12.00 to 18.00
Bubble, Bread Plate, Blue, 6 3/4 In. 2.00
Bubble, Candlestick, Pair 15.00
Bubble, Creamer, Blue . . . . .38.00 to 40.00
Bubble, Cup & Saucer, Blue . . . . .4.00 to 7.00
Bubble, Cup & Saucer, Red 10.00
Bubble, Pitcher, Ice Lip, Red, 64 Oz. 60.00
Bubble, Pitcher, Red, 64 Oz. 52.00
Bubble, Plate, Blue, 9 3/8 In. . . . . .6.00 to 7.00
Bubble, Plate, Green, 9 3/8 In. 22.00
Bubble, Plate, Red, 9 3/8 In. 19.00
Bubble, Platter, Oval, Blue, 12 In. . . . . .15.00 to 17.00
Bubble, Sherbet, Green 9.00
Bubble, Soup, Dish, Blue, 7 3/4 In. . . . . .12.00 to 20.00
Bubble, Sugar, Blue 23.00
Bubble, Tumbler, Red, 12 Oz. 12.00
Bullseye pattern is listed here as Bubble.

Depression Glass,
Cameo

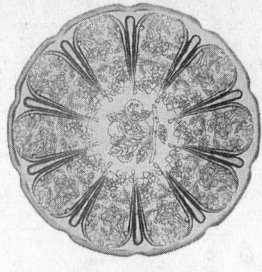

Depression Glass,
Cherry Blossom

Depression Glass,
Colonial

Butterflies & Roses pattern is listed here as Flower Garden with Butterflies.
Buttons & Bows pattern is listed here as Holiday.
Cabbage Rose pattern is listed here as Sharon.
Cameo, Bottle, Water, Green 25.00
Cameo, Bowl, Green, 5 1/2 In. 33.00
Cameo, Bowl, Vegetable, Oval, Green, 10 In. . . . . .33.00 to 35.00
Cameo, Butter, Cover, Green . . . . .220.00 to 235.00
Cameo, Cake Plate, 3-Footed, Green 22.00
Cameo, Candlestick, Green, 4 In., Pair 95.00
Cameo, Compote, Green, 5 In. 32.00
Cameo, Cookie Jar, Cover, Green 53.00
Cameo, Creamer, Green, 3 1/4 In. 20.00
Cameo, Decanter, Stopper, Green, 10 In. 210.00
Cameo, Grill Plate, Yellow, 10 1/2 In. . . . . .9.00 to 10.00
Cameo, Jam Jar, Cover, Green, 2 In. 195.00
Cameo, Pitcher, Green, 20 Oz., 5 3/4 In. 325.00
Cameo, Pitcher, Green, 56 Oz., 8 1/2 In. . . . . .60.00 to 85.00
Cameo, Plate, Green, 9 1/2 In. . . . . .20.00 to 21.00
Cameo, Plate, Yellow, 9 1/2 In. . . . . .9.00 to 11.00
Cameo, Platter, Green, 12 In. 20.00
Cameo, Salt & Pepper, Green 80.00
Cameo, Sherbet, Green, 4 7/8 In. . . . . .30.00 to 40.00
Cameo, Sugar, Green, 3 1/4 In. 20.00
Cameo, Tray, Domino, Green, 7 In. 145.00
Cameo, Tumbler, Footed, Green, 9 Oz., 5 In. . . . . .30.00 to 35.00
Cameo, Tumbler, Footed, Yellow, 9 Oz., 5 In. 19.00
Cameo, Vase, Green, 5 3/4 In. 185.00
Cameo, Vase, Green, 8 In. 34.00
Cameo, Wine, Green, 4 In. 65.00
Candlewick pattern is listed in the Imperial Glass category.
Cape Cod, Cake Plate, Candle 260.00
Cape Cod, Cruet, Stopper, 4 Oz. 24.00
Cape Cod, Salt & Pepper, Footed 22.00
Caprice pattern is included in the Cambridge Glass category.
Caribbean, Bowl, Blue, Handle, 7 In. 28.00
Caribbean, Bowl, Fruit, Blue, 5 In. 19.00
Charm, Bowl, Azurite, 4 3/4 In. 4.50
Charm, Cup & Saucer, Azurite 4.50
Charm, Plate, Azurite, 6 5/8 In. 5.00
Charm, Plate, Azurite, 10 In. 15.00
Cherry Blossom, Bowl, 2 Handles, Green, 9 In. 65.00
Cherry Blossom, Bowl, Green, 5 3/4 In. 45.00
Cherry Blossom, Bowl, Green, 8 1/2 In. . . . . .45.00 to 56.00
Cherry Blossom, Bowl, Pink, 8 1/2 In. . . . . .45.00 to 50.00
Cherry Blossom, Bowl, Vegetable, Oval, Pink, 9 In. 50.00
Cherry Blossom, Butter, Cover, Green 98.00
Cherry Blossom, Butter, Cover, Pink 70.00

Cherry Blossom, Cake Plate, Footed, Pink, 10 1/4 In. 31.00
Cherry Blossom, Child's Set, Delphite, 14 Piece .... 275.00 to 365.00
Cherry Blossom, Creamer, Child's, Pink .... 45.00 to 55.00
Cherry Blossom, Creamer, Green 18.00
Cherry Blossom, Cup & Saucer, Green 26.00
Cherry Blossom, Grill Plate, Pink, 9 In. 25.00
Cherry Blossom, Pitcher, Green 200.00
Cherry Blossom, Plate, Delphite, 9 In. 25.00
Cherry Blossom, Plate, Green, 7 In. .... 20.00 to 21.00
Cherry Blossom, Plate, Green, 9 In. 24.00
Cherry Blossom, Plate, Pink, 9 In. 25.00
Cherry Blossom, Plate, Sherbet, Green, 6 In. 7.00
Cherry Blossom, Platter, Oval, Green, 11 In. 50.00
Cherry Blossom, Sandwich Tray, 2 Handles, Delphite, 10 1/2 In. 19.00
Cherry Blossom, Sandwich Tray, 2 Handles, Green, 10 1/2 In. 25.00
Cherry Blossom, Sherbet, Footed, Green 18.00
Cherry Blossom, Sherbet, Footed, Pink .... 16.00 to 18.00
Cherry Blossom, Sugar & Creamer, Delphite 30.00
Cherry Blossom, Sugar, Cover, Green 34.00
Cherry Blossom, Tumbler, Footed, Delphite, 9 Oz., 4 1/2 In. 25.00
Cherry Blossom, Tumbler, Footed, Green, 4 Oz., 3 1/2 In. 18.00
Cherry Blossom, Tumbler, Footed, Pink, 4 Oz., 3 1/2 In. 15.00
Cherry Blossom, Tumbler, Footed, Pink, 9 Oz., 4 1/2 In. 35.00
Cherry-Berry, Plate, Sherbet, Pink, 6 In. 7.50
Cherry-Berry, Sherbet, Green 9.00
Chinex Classic, Plate, Ivory, Castle Decal, 9 3/4 In. 15.00
Circle, Water Set, Green, 80-Oz. Pitcher, 9 3/4 In., 7 Piece 150.00
Cloverleaf, Ashtray, Black, 4 In. 55.00
Cloverleaf, Cup & Saucer, Green .... 8.00 to 9.50
Cloverleaf, Cup & Saucer, Pink .... 10.00 to 15.00
Cloverleaf, Cup, Yellow 9.00
Cloverleaf, Plate, Green, 8 In. .... 6.50 to 8.00
Cloverleaf, Plate, Sherbet, Black, 6 In. 12.00
Cloverleaf, Sherbet, Footed, Yellow 10.00
Cloverleaf, Sugar & Creamer, Green 22.00
Colonial, Bowl, Green, 9 In. .... 25.00 to 28.00
Colonial, Butter, Cover 40.00
Colonial, Candy, Cover, Green 30.00
Colonial, Grill Plate, Green, 10 In. 25.00
Colonial, Plate, Green, 8 In. 9.00
Colonial, Sugar & Creamer, Pink 20.00
Colonial Fluted, Creamer, Green 8.00
Colonial Fluted, Sugar, Cover, Green 23.00
Columbia, Plate, 9 1/2 In. 9.00
Coronation, Berry Set, Red, 9 Piece 65.00
Coronation, Tumbler, Footed, Pink, 10 Oz., 5 In. 20.00
Cremax, Cup & Saucer, Cream Colored, After Dinner 15.00
Cube pattern is listed here as Cubist.
Cubist, Bowl, Green, 4 1/2 In. 7.00
Cubist, Butter, Cover, Green 50.00
Cubist, Candy Jar, Cover, Green 15.00
Cubist, Coaster, Green, 3 3/4 In. 5.00
Cubist, Pitcher, Pink, 45 Oz., 8 3/4 In. 245.00
Cubist, Plate, Sherbet, Pink, 6 In. 4.00
Cubist, Sherbet, Footed, Green 7.00
Cubist, Sugar, Cover, Green 22.00
Daisy pattern is listed here as No. 620.
Dancing Girl pattern is listed here as Cameo.
Decagon, Sandwich Server, Center Handle, Green 35.00
Della Robbia, Tumbler, Footed, 11 Oz. 21.00
Dewdrop, Butter, Cover 30.00
Dewdrop, Pitcher, 1/2 Gal. 20.00
Dewdrop, Punch Set, 15 Piece 75.00

Dewdrop, Tray, Lazy Susan, 13 In. 18.00
Diamond Pattern is listed here as Miss America.
Diamond Quilted, Compote, Pink, 6 x 7 1/4 In. 65.00
Diamond Quilted, Soup, Cream, Blue, 4 3/4 In. 20.00
Diana, Bread Plate, Pink, 6 In. 4.00
Diana, Cup & Saucer, Pink, After Dinner 45.00
Diana, Goblet, 9 Oz., 4 1/8 In. 35.00
Diana, Sugar & Creamer 25.00
Dogwood, Bowl, Pink, 5 1/2 In. ....24.00 to 30.00
Dogwood, Bowl, Pink, 8 1/2 In. 58.00
Dogwood, Cake Plate, Pink, 13 In. 125.00
Dogwood, Creamer, Thick, Pink 24.00
Dogwood, Creamer, Thin, Green 25.00
Dogwood, Cup & Saucer, Thick, Pink ....19.00 to 22.00
Dogwood, Cup & Saucer, Thin, Pink 18.50
Dogwood, Plate, Pink, 9 1/4 In. ....33.00 to 35.00
Dogwood, Sherbet, Pink ....31.00 to 34.00
Dogwood, Sugar & Creamer, Thin, Pink 30.00
Dogwood, Tumbler, Pink, 10 Oz., 4 In. 40.00
Doric, Bowl, Pink, 4 1/2 In. 8.00
Doric, Candy Dish, Cover, Pink 35.00
Doric, Creamer, Pink 10.00
Doric, Salt & Pepper, Pink 35.00
Doric & Pansy, Butter, Cover, Ultramarine 480.00
Doric & Pansy, Cup & Saucer, Ultramarine ....20.00 to 25.00
Doric & Pansy, Saucer, Pretty Polly, Ultramarine 8.00
Dutch Rose pattern is listed here as Rosemary.
Early American Rock Crystal pattern is listed here as Rock Crystal.
English Hobnail, Cheese & Cracker, Cover, 8 In. 8.00
English Hobnail, Cruet, Oil, 2 Oz. 20.00
English Hobnail, Cup & Saucer 18.00
English Hobnail, Lamp, Electric, 9 1/4 In. 75.00
English Hobnail, Toilet Bottle, Ice Blue, 5 Oz. 83.00
Fine Rib pattern is listed here as Homespun.
Fire-King, Bowl, Blue, 5 3/8 In. 13.00
Fire-King, Bowl, Teardrop, Jadite, 16 Oz. 27.00
Fire-King, Cake Pan, Square, Ivory, Pink Dogwood 11.50
Fire-King, Casserole, Cover, Blue, 1 Pt. ....8.50 to 12.00
Fire-King, Casserole, Cover, White, Hand Painted Fruit, 1 1/2 Qt. 11.00
Fire-King, Cup & Saucer, Blue 14.00
Fire-King, Custard Cup, Blue, 6 Oz. 3.00
Fire-King, Jar, Drippings, Tulip Cover, Jadite 50.00
Fire-King, Loaf Pan, White, Hand Painted Fruit 11.50
Fire-King, Measuring Cup, Blue, 8 Oz. 15.00
Fire-King, Mixing Bowl, Blue, 8 3/8 In. 17.00
Fire-King, Mixing Bowl, Ivory, Fruit, 6 7/8 In. ....9.00 to 14.00
Fire-King, Mug, White, Pink Dogwood 6.50

Depression Glass,
Cubist

Depression Glass,
English Hobnail

Depression Glass,
Holiday

Fire-King, Pie Plate, Blue, 9 In. 12.00
Fire-King, Pie Plate, Jadite, 5 3/4 In. 4.25
Fire-King, Pie Plate, Juice Saver, Blue, 10 3/8 In. . . . . .120.00 to 145.00
Fire-King, Refrigerator Jar, Cover, Thin, Jadite, 5 1/8 x 9 1 /8 In. . . . . .34.00 to 40.00
Flat Diamond pattern is listed here as Diamond Quilted.
Fleurette, Cup & Saucer 4.00
Fleurette, Sugar & Creamer 7.00
Floragold, Bowl, Ruffled, 12 In. 17.00
Floragold, Butter, Cover, Iridescent, Oval, 1/4 Lb. . . . . .25.00 to 34.00
Floragold, Creamer, Iridescent 9.00
Floragold, Pitcher, Iridescent, 64 Oz. 35.00
Floragold, Plate, 5 3/4 In. 12.00
Floragold, Sugar, Cover 14.00
Floragold, Tumbler, Footed, Iridescent, 10 Oz. 17.50
Floral, Bowl, Vegetable, Cover, Green, 8 In. 40.00
Floral, Butter, Cover, Green 105.00
Floral, Coaster, Green . . . . .7.00 to 10.00
Floral, Coaster, Pink . . . . .13.00 to 14.00
Floral, Cup & Saucer, Green . . . . .20.00 to 27.00
Floral, Pitcher, Pink, 48 Oz., 10 1/4 In. 275.00
Floral, Plate, Pink, 9 In. . . . . .16.00 to 25.00
Floral, Platter, Green, 10 3/4 In. 17.00
Floral, Platter, Pink, 10 3/4 In. 25.00
Floral, Refrigerator Dish, Cover, Green, Square, 5 In. 48.00
Floral, Relish, 2 Sections, Oval, Green . . . . .15.00 to 19.00
Floral, Salt & Pepper, Footed, Green, 4 In. 52.00
Floral, Salt & Pepper, Footed, Pink, 4 In. 43.00
Floral, Sugar, Cover, Green 29.00
Floral, Tray, Square, Green, 6 In. 35.00
Floral, Tumbler, Footed, Pink, 7 Oz., 4 3/4 In. . . . . .17.00 to 18.00
Floral, Tumbler, Lemonade, Pink, 9 Oz., 5 1/4 In. . . . . .45.00 to 52.00
Floral & Diamond Band, Creamer, Green, 4 3/4 In. 20.00
Florentine No. 1, Bowl, Vegetable, Cover, Yellow, 9 1/2 In. 50.00
Florentine No. 1, Coaster, Green, 3 3/4 In. 10.00
Florentine No. 1, Creamer, Cobalt Blue, Ruffled 65.00
Florentine No. 1, Creamer, Pink 15.00
Florentine No. 1, Plate, Yellow, 10 In. 15.00
Florentine No. 2, Bowl, Yellow, 4 1/2 In. 20.00
Florentine No. 2, Butter, Cover, Green 100.00
Florentine No. 2, Butter, Cover, Yellow . . . . .129.00 to 140.00
Florentine No. 2, Candlestick, Yellow, 2 3/4 In., Pair 60.00
Florentine No. 2, Creamer, Yellow 7.00
Florentine No. 2, Cup & Saucer, Yellow 13.50
Florentine No. 2, Gravy Boat, Yellow 100.00
Florentine No. 2, Pitcher, Cone, Footed, Yellow, 24 Oz., 6 1/4 In. 145.00
Florentine No. 2, Pitcher, Cone, Footed, Yellow, 28 Oz., 7 1/2 In. . . . . .25.00 to 30.00
Florentine No. 2, Plate, Sherbet, Yellow, 6 In. 6.00
Florentine No. 2, Plate, Yellow, 8 1/2 In. 10.00
Florentine No. 2, Plate, Yellow, 10 In. 14.00
Florentine No. 2, Platter, Oval, Green, 11 In. 19.00
Florentine No. 2, Relish, 3 Sections, Yellow, 10 In. . . . . .30.00 to 32.00
Florentine No. 2, Salt & Pepper, Green 40.00
Florentine No. 2, Salt & Pepper, Yellow . . . . .45.00 to 50.00
Florentine No. 2, Sherbet, Footed, Green 10.00
Florentine No. 2, Sherbet, Footed, Yellow 10.00
Florentine No. 2, Soup, Cream, Yellow, 4 3/4 In. 21.00
Florentine No. 2, Tumbler, Footed, Green, 12 Oz., 5 In. 32.00
Florentine No. 2, Tumbler, Footed, Yellow, 5 Oz., 3 3/8 In. 21.00
Florentine No. 2, Tumbler, Water, Yellow, 9 Oz., 4 In. 21.00
Florentine No. 2, Vase, Yellow, 6 In. . . . . .51.00 to 60.00
Flower & Leaf Band pattern is listed here as Indiana Custard.
Flower Garden With Butterflies, Candy, Cover, Pink 140.00

Depression Glass,
Iris

Depression Glass,
Mayfair Open Rose

Forest Green, Batter Bowl, With Spout	25.00
Forest Green, Bowl, 4 3/4 In.	5.50
Forest Green, Bowl, Square, 6 In.	10.00
Forest Green, Bowl, Vegetable, Oval, 8 1/2 In.	24.00
Forest Green, Cup	5.00
Forest Green, Pitcher, Juice, 36 Oz.	27.00
Forest Green, Punch Set, 12 Cups, 14 Piece	85.00
Fruits, Cup & Saucer, Green	13.00
Georgian, Bowl, Deep, Green, 6 1/2 In.	45.00
Georgian, Butter, Cover, Green	80.00
Georgian, Creamer, Footed, Green, 3 In.	11.00
Georgian, Plate, Green, 9 1/4 In.	28.00
Georgian, Platter, Green, 11 1/2 In.	70.00
Georgian, Sugar & Creamer, Cover, Green, 3 In.	63.00
Georgian, Sugar & Creamer, Green, 4 In.	25.00
Georgian, Tumbler, Green, 9 Oz., 4 In.	56.00 to 57.00
Georgian, Tumbler, Green, 12 Oz., 5 1/4 In.	165.00
Hairpin pattern is listed here as Newport.	
Harp, Cake Stand, 9 In.	22.50
Harp, Cup & Saucer	25.00
Harp, Vase, 6 In.	22.50
Heritage, Bowl, 5 In.	3.00
Heritage, Bowl, 10 1/2 In.	6.00 to 15.00
Heritage, Creamer	10.00
Heritage, Cup	3.00 to 7.00
Heritage, Plate, 9 1/4 In.	4.00 to 12.00
Heritage, Sandwich Plate, 12 In.	6.00
Heritage, Saucer	1.00
Heritage, Sugar	6.00
Hex Optic pattern is listed here as Hexagon Optic.	
Hexagon Optic, Tumbler, Green, 12 Oz., 5 In.	7.00
Hobnail pattern is listed in the Hobnail category.	
Holiday, Bowl, Pink, 5 1/8 In.	14.00
Holiday, Candlestick, Pink, 3 In., Pair	115.00
Holiday, Creamer, Pink	10.00
Holiday, Pitcher, Milk, Pink, 4 3/4 In.	59.00
Holiday, Plate, Pink, 9 In.	16.00 to 18.00
Holiday, Saucer, Pink	2.50
Holiday, Tumbler, Footed, Pink, 4 In.	45.00
Holiday, Tumbler, Footed, Pink, 6 In.	165.00
Homespun, Bowl, Pink, 8 1/4 In.	20.00
Homespun, Cup & Saucer, Pink	12.00
Homespun, Plate, Pink, 9 1/4 In.	14.00
Homespun, Saucer, Pink	2.50
Homespun, Tumbler, Footed, Pink, 5 Oz., 4 In.	15.00
Homespun, Tumbler, Pink, 12 1/2 Oz., 5 3/8 In.	12.00
Honeycomb pattern is listed here as Hexagon Optic.	
Horizontal Ribbed pattern is listed here as Manhattan.	
Horseshoe pattern is listed here as No. 612.	
Indiana Custard, Bowl, Ivory, 6 1/2 In.	20.00

Indiana Custard, Butter, Cover, Ivory 60.00
Indiana Custard, Creamer, Ivory 16.00
Indiana Custard, Plate, Ivory, 9 3/4 In. 25.00
Indiana Custard, Platter, Oval, Ivory, 11 1/2 In. 30.00
Indiana Custard, Sugar, Cover, Ivory ....20.00 to 35.00
Iris, Berry Bowl, Beaded Edge, 8 In. 80.00
Iris, Bowl, Beaded Edge, 4 1/2 In. ....40.00 to 45.00
Iris, Bowl, Beaded Edge, Iridescent, 5 In. 12.00
Iris, Bowl, Sauce, Ruffled, 5 In. 10.00
Iris, Bowl, Straight Edge, 11 In. 16.00
Iris, Butter, Cover, Iridescent 42.00
Iris, Candlestick, Iridescent, Pair 43.00
Iris, Cup & Saucer, Iridescent 26.00
Iris, Cup, After Dinner 40.00
Iris, Goblet, 8 Oz., 5 3/4 In. 25.00
Iris, Lamp Shade, Frosted, 11 1/2 In. 125.00
Iris, Pitcher, Footed, 9 1/2 In. ....24.00 to 37.50
Iris, Plate, Iridescent, 9 In. 45.00
Iris, Sherbet, Footed, 2 1/2 In. 32.00
Iris, Sugar & Creamer, Cover, Iridescent ....32.00 to 40.00
Iris, Tumbler, Footed, 6 In. ....12.00 to 22.00
Iris, Tumbler, Footed, Iridescent, 6 In. 18.00
Iris, Vase, Iridescent, 9 In. 29.00
Iris, Wine, Iridescent, 3 Oz., 4 1/2 In. ....26.00 to 29.00
Iris & Herringbone pattern is listed here as Iris.
Jadite, Batter Bowl, Colonial 35.00
Jadite, Bowl, 5 7/8 In. 14.00
Jadite, Bowl, Restaurant Ware, 4 3/4 In. 5.00
Jadite, Pitcher, Milk, 20 Oz. 50.00
Jadite, Skillet, 1 Spout 77.00
Jamestown pattern is listed here as Tradition.
Jane-Ray, Bowl, Jadite, 5 1/8 In. 8.50
Jane-Ray, Bowl, Vegetable, Jadite, 8 1/4 In. 13.00
Jane-Ray, Cup & Saucer, Jadite ....2.75 to 3.75
Jane-Ray, Cup & Saucer, Jadite, After Dinner ....75.00 to 85.00
Jane-Ray, Plate, Jadite, 8 In. ....5.50 to 7.00
Jane-Ray, Platter, Oval, Jadite, 9 x 12 In. ....14.00 to 35.00
Jane-Ray, Sugar & Creamer, Cover, Jadite 21.00
Jubilee, Bowl, Footed, Yellow, 11 1/2 In. 150.00
Jubilee, Creamer, Footed, Yellow 20.00
Jubilee, Plate, 3-Footed, Yellow, 14 In. 200.00
Jubilee, Plate, Yellow, 7 In. ....5.00 to 14.00
Jubilee, Sugar & Creamer, Yellow 38.00
Jubilee, Tumbler, Footed, Yellow, 10 Oz., 6 In. 35.00
Knife & Fork pattern is listed here as Colonial.
Lace Edge, Bowl, Pink, 6 3/8 In. 22.00
Lace Edge, Butter, Cover 72.00
Lace Edge, Compote, Footed, 7 In. 300.00
Lace Edge, Creamer, Pink 25.00
Lace Edge, Cup & Saucer, Pink 37.00
Lace Edge, Plate, Pink, 10 1/2 In. 24.00
Lace Edge, Sugar & Creamer, Pink 45.00
Laurel, Bowl, Green, 5 In. 7.00
Laurel, Plate, Green, 9 1/8 In. 15.00
Lorain pattern is listed here as No. 615.
Lorna pattern is included in the Cambridge Glass category.
Louisa pattern is listed here as Floragold.
Lovebirds pattern is listed here as Georgian.
Madrid, Bowl, Amber, 9 1/2 In. 30.00
Madrid, Bowl, Vegetable, Oval, Green, 10 In. 20.00
Madrid, Cookie Jar, Amber 75.00
Madrid, Creamer, Amber 9.00
Madrid, Cup & Saucer, Green 16.00

Madrid, Plate, Amber, 7 1/2 In. 11.00
Madrid, Plate, Amber, 8 7/8 In. 8.00
Madrid, Plate, Blue, 8 7/8 In. 18.00
Madrid, Salt & Pepper, Amber, Flat, 3 1/2 In. 40.00
Madrid, Salt & Pepper, Green, 3 1/2 In. 70.00
Madrid, Sherbet, Blue 15.00
Madrid, Sherbet, Green 13.00
Madrid, Sugar, Cover, Green 58.00
Madrid, Tumbler, Amber, 9 Oz., 4 1/4 In. ....15.00 to 30.00
Madrid, Water Set, Square Pitcher, Pink, 7 Piece 225.00
Manhattan, Ashtray 24.00
Manhattan, Bowl, Handles, 4 1/2 In. 9.00
Manhattan, Candlestick, 4 1/2 In., Pair 15.00
Manhattan, Candy Dish, Pink 12.00
Manhattan, Compote, Pink, 5 3/4 In. 38.00
Manhattan, Cup 18.00
Manhattan, Pitcher, 24 Oz. 25.00
Manhattan, Relish, Tray, Ruby Inserts, 14 In. 60.00
Manhattan, Salt & Pepper, Square, 2 In. 25.00
Manhattan, Sugar & Creamer, Pink 22.00
Many Windows pattern is listed here as Roulette.
Martha Washington pattern is included in the Cambridge Glass category.
Mayfair Open Rose, Bowl, Deep, Green, 12 In. 45.00
Mayfair Open Rose, Bowl, Pink, 5 1/2 In. ....20.00 to 28.00
Mayfair Open Rose, Bowl, Vegetable, 2 Handles, Pink, 10 In. 50.00
Mayfair Open Rose, Bowl, Vegetable, Oval, Blue, 9 1/2 In. 70.00
Mayfair Open Rose, Cake Plate, Footed, Blue, 10 In. 70.00
Mayfair Open Rose, Cake Plate, Footed, Pink, 10 In. 32.00
Mayfair Open Rose, Candy Dish, Cover, Pink 56.00
Mayfair Open Rose, Celery Dish, Divided, Blue 65.00
Mayfair Open Rose, Cookie Jar, Cover, Pink 50.00
Mayfair Open Rose, Cup & Saucer, Blue 74.00
Mayfair Open Rose, Cup & Saucer, Ringed, Pink 60.00
Mayfair Open Rose, Decanter, Stopper, Pink, 32 Oz. 165.00
Mayfair Open Rose, Goblet, Pink, 9 Oz., 5 3/4 In. 68.00
Mayfair Open Rose, Grill Plate, Pink, 9 1/2 In. 35.00
Mayfair Open Rose, Pitcher, Pink, 37 Oz., 6 In. ....50.00 to 57.00
Mayfair Open Rose, Pitcher, Pink, 80 Oz., 8 1/2 In. ....100.00 to 130.00
Mayfair Open Rose, Plate, Pink, 9 1/2 In. ....52.00 to 60.00
Mayfair Open Rose, Plate, Sherbet, Blue, 6 1/2 In. 25.00
Mayfair Open Rose, Platter, Oval, Open Handles, Pink 30.00
Mayfair Open Rose, Relish, 4 Sections, Pink, 8 3/8 In. 37.00
Mayfair Open Rose, Sandwich Server, Center Handle, Pink ....42.00 to 53.00
Mayfair Open Rose, Sherbet, Footed, 3 In. 14.00
Mayfair Open Rose, Sherbet, Footed, Pink, 3 In. 18.00
Mayfair Open Rose, Soup, Cream, Pink, 5 In. ....43.00 to 53.00
Mayfair Open Rose, Sugar & Creamer, Blue 185.00
Mayfair Open Rose, Tumbler, Footed, Pink, 6 1/2 In. 36.00
Mayfair Open Rose, Tumbler, Pink, 9 Oz., 4 1/4 In. 30.00
Mayfair Open Rose, Vase, Sweet Pea, Blue ....85.00 to 102.00
Mayfair Open Rose, Vase, Sweet Pea, Pink 220.00
Miss America, Bowl, Pink, 6 1/4 In. 24.00
Miss America, Candy Jar, Cover, Pink, 11 1/2 In. ....144.00 to 155.00
Miss America, Celery Dish, Pink, 10 1/2 In. 30.00
Miss America, Creamer, Pink 22.00
Miss America, Cup, Pink 26.00
Miss America, Goblet, Pink, 10 Oz., 5 1/2 In. 47.00
Miss America, Grill Plate, Pink, 10 1/4 In. ....24.00 to 25.00
Miss America, Plate, Pink, 10 1/4 In. ....30.00 to 34.00
Miss America, Platter, Oval, Pink, 12 1/4 In. 26.00
Miss America, Relish, 4 Sections, Pink, 8 3/4 In. 28.00
Miss America, Salt & Pepper, Pink 62.00
Moderntone, Butter, Cover, Cobalt Blue 95.00

 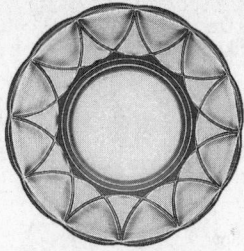 

Depression Glass,
Miss America

Depression Glass,
Newport

Depression Glass,
No. 615

Moderntone, Creamer, Cobalt Blue	....	11.00
Moderntone, Cup, Cobalt Blue	....	11.00
Moderntone, Little Hostess Party Set, Creamer, Pink, White Interior	....	12.00
Moderntone, Little Hostess Party Set, Sugar, Green	....	12.00
Moderntone, Little Hostess Party Set, Tea Set, Burgundy, Box, 16 Piece	....	220.00
Moderntone, Little Hostess Party Set, Tea Set, Pastels, Box, 14 Piece	....	143.00
Moderntone, Plate, Cobalt Blue, 6 3/4 In.	....	11.00
Moderntone, Plate, Cobalt Blue, 8 7/8 In.	...............................18.00 to	20.00
Moderntone, Plate, Pink, 8 7/8 In.	....	9.00
Moderntone, Platter, Oval, Cobalt Blue, 11 In.	....	47.00
Moderntone, Salt & Pepper, Cobalt Blue, Metal Lid	....	37.50
Moderntone, Sandwich Server, Cobalt Blue, 10 In.	....	68.00
Moderntone, Sherbet, Cobalt Blue	...............................13.00 to	14.00
Moderntone, Soup, Cream, Cobalt Blue	.............................20.00 to	22.00
Moderntone, Sugar & Creamer, Cobalt Blue	....	20.00
Moderntone, Tumbler, Cobalt Blue, 5 Oz.	....	50.00
Moderntone, Tumbler, Cobalt Blue, 9 Oz.	....	37.50
Moderntone Platonite, Cup & Saucer, Lemon	....	10.00
Moderntone Platonite, Plate, Lemon, 8 7/8 In.	....	11.00
Moondrops, Console, Winged, Red, 13 In.	....	125.00
Moondrops, Cordial, Cobalt Blue, 3/4 Oz., 2 7/8 In.	....	39.00
Moondrops, Tumbler, Red, 9 Oz., 4 7/8 In.	....	19.00
Moondrops, Whiskey, Amethyst	....	20.00
Moonstone, Bon Bon, Heart, Handle	....	12.00
Moonstone, Bowl, Crimped, 9 1/2 In.	....	20.00
Moonstone, Candlestick, Opalescent, Pair	....	18.00
Moonstone, Cigarette Bowl, Cover	....	25.00
Moonstone, Goblet, 10 Oz., 5 1/2 In.	....	8.00
Moonstone, Plate, 8 In.	....	15.00
Moonstone, Relish, Divided, 7 In.	....	12.00
Moonstone, Sandwich Server, 10 In.	....	27.00
Moonstone, Sugar & Creamer	....	18.00
Moonstone, Vase, Bud, 5 In.	....	10.00
Mt. Vernon pattern is included in the Cambridge Glass category.		
New Century, Sugar, Cover, Green	....	23.00
New Century, Tumbler, Amethyst, 5 Oz., 3 1/2 In.	....	12.00
New Century, Tumbler, Amethyst, 9 Oz., 4 1/4 In.	....	15.00
New Century, Tumbler, Amethyst, 12 Oz., 5 1/4 In.	....	25.00
Newport, Bowl, Amethyst, 5 1/4 In.	....	35.00
Newport, Cup & Saucer, Amethyst	....	15.00
Newport, Plate, Sherbet, Amethyst, 5 7/8 In.	....	6.00
Newport, Sherbet, Cobalt Blue	....	15.00
Newport, Soup, Cream, Amethyst, 4 3/4 In.	....	18.00
Newport, Sugar & Creamer, Amethyst	....	28.00
Newport, Tumbler, Cobalt Blue, 9 Oz., 4 1/2 In.	....	40.00
No. 601 pattern is listed here as Avocado.		
No. 610, Ice Tub, Pink	....	70.00

No. 610, Pitcher, Yellow 835.00
No. 610, Tumbler, Footed, Green, 8 Oz. 48.00
No. 612, Bowl, Vegetable, Oval, Yellow, 10 1/2 In. 27.00
No. 612, Bowl, Yellow, 7 1/2 In. 32.00
No. 612, Bowl, Yellow, 9 1/2 In. 35.00
No. 612, Cup & Saucer, Green 11.00
No. 612, Plate, Green, 8 3/8 In. 10.00
No. 612, Platter, Oval, Yellow, 10 3/4 In. 25.00
No. 612, Relish, 3 Sections, Yellow .... 31.00 to 35.00
No. 612, Sherbet, Green 13.00
No. 612, Sugar, Green 12.00
No. 615, Bowl, Vegetable, Oval, Yellow, 9 3/4 In. 60.00
No. 615, Bowl, Yellow, 7 1/4 In. 65.00
No. 615, Creamer, Green 18.00
No. 615, Cup & Saucer, Yellow .... 20.00 to 34.00
No. 615, Plate, Green, 8 3/8 In. 18.00
No. 615, Plate, Yellow, 8 3/4 In. 30.00
No. 615, Sugar & Creamer, Yellow 45.00
No. 615, Tumbler, Footed, Yellow, 9 Oz., 4 3/4 In. 28.00
No. 616, Creamer, Footed, Yellow 25.00
No. 618, Bowl, 6 In. 23.00
No. 618, Bowl, Vegetable, Oval, 10 In. 15.00
No. 618, Compote, Diamond 12.00
No. 618, Plate, 9 3/8 In. 15.00
No. 618, Saucer 6.00
No. 618, Sherbet, Footed 20.00
No. 618, Sugar & Creamer, Diamond 13.00
No. 618, Tumbler, 8 Oz., 4 1/4 In. 40.00
No. 620, Bowl, Vegetable, Amber, 9 3/8 In. 16.00
No. 620, Creamer, Amber 8.00
No. 620, Cup & Saucer, Amber 5.00
No. 620, Plate, Amber, 9 3/8 In. 9.00
No. 620, Sherbet, Footed, Amber 9.00
No. 622 pattern is listed here as Pretzel.
Normandie, Cup & Saucer, Pink 10.00
Normandie, Tumbler, Amber, 5 Oz., 4 In. 24.00
Normandie, Tumbler, Pink, 9 Oz., 4 1/4 In. .... 45.00 to 50.00
Old Cafe, Candy, Red, 8 In. 10.00
Old Cafe, Plate, Pink, 10 In. 40.00
Old Colony pattern is listed here as Lace Edge.
Old English, Eggcup 10.00
Old Florentine pattern is listed here as Florentine No. 1.
Open Lace pattern is listed here as Lace Edge.
Open Rose pattern is listed here as Mayfair Open Rose.
Ovide, Sugar & Creamer, White, Red Trim 36.00
Parrot pattern is listed here as Sylvan.
Patrician, Bowl, Amber, 5 In. .... 11.00 to 12.00
Patrician, Bowl, Amber, 8 1/2 In. 45.00
Patrician, Bowl, Vegetable, Oval, Amber, 12 In. 22.00
Patrician, Bowl, Vegetable, Oval, Green, 12 In. 35.00
Patrician, Butter, Cover, Amber 90.00
Patrician, Cup & Saucer, Amber 17.00
Patrician, Grill Plate, Amber, 10 1/2 In. .... 12.00 to 13.00
Patrician, Jam Dish, Amber, 6 1/2 In. 35.00
Patrician, Pitcher, Amber, 75 Oz., 8 In. 120.00
Patrician, Plate, Amber, 9 In. 11.00
Patrician, Platter, Oval, Amber, 9 1/2 In. 22.00
Patrician, Salt & Pepper, Amber 55.00
Patrician, Sherbet, Footed, Green 8.00
Patrician, Soup, Cream, Amber, 4 3/4 In. 16.00
Patrician, Sugar, Cover, Amber 65.00
Patrician, Tumbler, Amber, 14 Oz., 5 1/2 In. 32.00
Patrician, Tumbler, Footed, Amber, 14 Oz., 5 1/2 In. ..... 43.00 to 45.00

Depression Glass, Patrician

Depression Glass, Royal Lace

Patrician, Tumbler, Footed, Green, 8 Oz., 5 1/4 In. . . . . .48.00 to 55.00
Patrician, Water Set, Footed, Box, 8 In., 7 Piece 360.00
Petal Swirl pattern is listed here as Swirl.
Petalware, Salver, Monax, 11 In. 8.00
Petalware, Salver, Pink, 11 In. 30.00
Pineapple & Floral pattern is listed here as No. 618.
Pinwheel pattern is listed here as Sierra.
Poinsettia pattern is listed here as Floral.
Popeye & Olive, Candlestick, Light Blue, Low 30.00
Poppy No. I pattern is listed here as Florentine No. 1.
Poppy No. 2 pattern is listed here as Florentine No. 2.
Pretty Polly Party Dishes, see also the related pattern Doric & Pansy.
Pretzel, Olive Dish, Leaf, 7 In. 2.00
Pretzel, Plate, 8 3/8 In. 2.00
Pretzel, Relish, 2 Handles, 8 1/2 In. 2.00
Pretzel, Sandwich Server, 11 1/2 In. 6.00
Pretzel, Soup, Coupe, 7 1/2 In. 6.00
Primrose, Cake Pan, Round 7.00
Primrose, Creamer 3.00
Primrose, Sugar, Cover 5.00
Princess, Bowl, Oval, Green, 10 In. 30.00
Princess, Bowl, Topaz, 10 In. 45.00
Princess, Candy Dish, Footed, Green 25.00
Princess, Cookie Jar, Green 55.00
Princess, Cup, Pink 15.00
Princess, Cup, Topaz 8.00
Princess, Pitcher, Green, 37 Oz., 6 In. 55.00
Princess, Plate, Green, 8 In. 14.00
Princess, Platter, Closed Handles, Green, 12 In. 25.00
Princess, Relish, Divided, Green, 7 1/2 In. 25.00
Princess, Saucer, Topaz 4.00
Princess, Tumbler, Footed, Green, 10 Oz., 5 1/4 In. 32.00
Prismatic Line pattern is listed here as Queen Mary.
Provincial pattern is listed here as Bubble.
Pyramid pattern is listed here as No. 610.
Queen Mary, Butter, Cover 25.00
Queen Mary, Candlestick, Double, 4 1/2 In., Pair 14.00
Queen Mary, Creamer 5.00
Queen Mary, Plate, Pink, 6 In. 8.00
Queen Mary, Plate, Pink, 9 3/4 In. 50.00
Queen Mary, Sugar, Pink 30.00
Queen Mary, Tumbler, Pink, 5 Oz., 3 1/2 In. . . . . .9.00 to 10.00
Radiance, Butter, Cover, Cornflower Etched 85.00
Radiance, Punch Cup, Ice Blue, 12 Piece 125.00
Radiance, Punch Ladle, Amber 65.00
Radiance, Vase, Cobalt Blue, 10 In. 75.00
Ring, Bowl, Green, 5 In. 6.00
Ring, Sandwich Server, Center Handle, Green 35.00
Ring, Tumbler, Footed, Platinum Bands, 10 Oz., 4 3/4 In. 10.00

Ring, Water Set, Pink, 7 Piece 100.0
Rock Crystal, Cup & Saucer 22.0
Rock Crystal, Goblet, Low Footed, 8 Oz. 15.0
Rock Crystal, Pitcher, 1/2 Gal., 7 1/2 In. 95.0
Rock Crystal, Tumbler, Concave, Red, 9 Oz. 40.0
Rope pattern is listed here as Colonial Fluted.
Rose Cameo, Tumbler, Footed, 5 In. 18.0
Rosemary, Bowl, Vegetable, Oval, Pink, 10 In. 34.0
Rosemary, Creamer, Pink 12.0
Rosemary, Sugar, Footed, Green 8.0
Roulette, Cup & Saucer, Green 11.0
Roulette, Plate, Green, 8 1/2 In. 6.0
Roulette, Plate, Sherbet, Green, 6 In. 4.5
Roulette, Sherbet, Green ....5.00 to 6.0
Roulette, Tumbler, Green, 5 Oz., 3 1/4 In. 22.5
Round Robin, Sugar & Creamer, Green 15.0
Roxana, Tumbler, Yellow, 9 Oz., 4 1/4 In. 18.0
Royal Lace, Bowl, 3-Footed, Straight Edge, Cobalt Blue, 10 In. 105.0
Royal Lace, Bowl, Cobalt Blue, 10 In. 100.0
Royal Lace, Bowl, Pink, 5 In. 65.0
Royal Lace, Butter, Cover, Green 325.0
Royal Lace, Cookie Jar, Cobalt Blue ....350.00 to 495.0
Royal Lace, Creamer, Footed, Cobalt Blue 62.0
Royal Lace, Creamer, Footed, Pink ....18.00 to 25.0
Royal Lace, Cup & Saucer, Green 35.0
Royal Lace, Pitcher, Ice Lip, Cobalt Blue, 48 Oz. 175.0
Royal Lace, Plate, Cobalt Blue, 9 7/8 In. 45.0
Royal Lace, Plate, Sherbet, Green, 6 In. 15.0
Royal Lace, Platter, Oval, Pink, 13 In. 38.0
Royal Lace, Salt & Pepper, Green 128.0
Royal Lace, Soup, Cream, Cobalt Blue, 4 3/4 In. ....35.00 to 47.0
Royal Lace, Sugar & Creamer, Cover, Green 132.0
Royal Lace, Sugar, Footed, Green 22.0
Royal Lace, Sugar, Footed, Pink ....14.00 to 18.0
Royal Lace, Tumbler, 9 Oz., 4 1/8 In. 11.0
Royal Lace, Tumbler, Cobalt Blue, 9 Oz., 4 1/8 In. 54.0
Royal Lace, Tumbler, Pink, 9 Oz., 4 1/8 In. 39.0
Royal Ruby, Bowl, Handle, Round, 4 1/2 In. 5.0
Royal Ruby, Cup & Saucer 7.0
Royal Ruby, Pitcher, Upright, 3 Qt. 45.0
Royal Ruby, Punch Cup 3.0
Royal Ruby, Sugar 5.0
Royal Ruby, Tumbler, 9 Oz., 4 In. 65.0
Royal Ruby, Tumbler, Footed, 3 In. 6.0
Royal Ruby, Vase, Etched, Scotty, 9 In. 16.0
Royal Ruby, Vase, Rachael, 10 In. 55.0
Sandwich Anchor Hocking, Bowl, Scalloped, Royal Ruby, 6 1/2 In. 20.0
Sandwich Anchor Hocking, Butter, Cover 45.0
Sandwich Anchor Hocking, Cookie Jar, Amber 35.0
Sandwich Anchor Hocking, Creamer 6.0
Sandwich Anchor Hocking, Cup & Saucer, Amber 6.0
Sandwich Anchor Hocking, Custard Cup, Liner, Forest Green 3.0
Sandwich Anchor Hocking, Plate, Amber, 9 In. 9.0
Sandwich Anchor Hocking, Punch Set, 14 Piece 70.0
Sandwich Anchor Hocking, Sugar 36.5
Sandwich Anchor Hocking, Tumbler, Footed, Forest Green, 9 Oz. 5.0
Sandwich Indiana, Bowl, 8 1/2 In. 12.0
Sandwich Indiana, Butter, Domed, Cover 25.0
Sandwich Indiana, Cup & Saucer 5.0
Sandwich Indiana, Plate, 8 3/8 In. 6.0
Sandwich Indiana, Plate, 10 1/2 In. 9.0
Saxon pattern is listed here as Coronation.
Sharon, Bowl, Pink, 5 In. 13.0

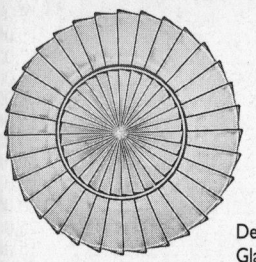

Depression
Glass, Sierra

Depression Glass, Sharon

Sharon, Bowl, Vegetable, Oval, Pink, 9 1/2 In.	25.00 to 35.00
Sharon, Butter, Cover, Amber	46.00
Sharon, Cake Plate, Footed, Pink, 11 1/2 In.	25.00
Sharon, Cake Plate, Pink, 11 1/2 In.	40.00
Sharon, Candy Jar, Cover, Pink	50.00
Sharon, Cup & Saucer, Pink	21.00
Sharon, Plate, Bread Plate, Pink, 6 In.	6.00
Sharon, Plate, Pink, 9 1/2 In.	17.00 to 18.00
Sharon, Platter, Oval, Pink, 12 1/2 In.	28.00 to 30.00
Sharon, Soup, Cream, Pink, 5 In.	45.00
Sharon, Tumbler, Footed, Pink, 15 Oz., 6 1/2 In.	42.50
Sierra, Bowl, Green, 8 1/2 In.	34.00
Sierra, Cup & Saucer, Green	25.00
Sierra, Plate, Pink, 9 In.	20.00
Sierra, Sugar & Creamer, Cover, Pink	55.00
Spiral, Butter Tub, Green	26.00
Spiral, Pitcher, Green, 58 Oz., 7 5/8 In.	30.00
Spoke pattern is listed here as Patrician.	
Spun, Pitcher, Blue Green, 8 In.	110.00
Spun, Tumbler, Blue Green, 15 Oz., 5 In.	25.00
Strawberry, Bowl, Pink, 4 In.	14.00
Strawberry, Compote, Pink, 5 3/4 In.	24.00
Sunflower, Cake Plate, 3 Footed, Green, 10 In.	15.00
Sunflower, Cake Plate, 3 Footed, Pink, 10 In.	14.00
Sunflower, Cup & Saucer, Green	26.00
Sunflower, Plate, Green, 9 In.	19.00 to 22.50
Sunflower, Plate, Pink, 9 In.	15.00
Sunflower, Tumbler, Footed, Pink, 8 Oz., 4 3/4 In.	25.00
Sunflower, Tumbler, Green, 8 Oz., 4 3/4 In.	40.00
Swirl, Bowl, Ultramarine, 5 1/4 In.	14.00 to 15.00
Swirl, Butter, Cover, Ultramarine	275.00
Swirl, Candy, Cover, Ultramarine	135.00
Swirl, Creamer, Ultramarine	15.00
Swirl, Cup, Ultramarine	15.00
Swirl, Plate, Ultramarine, 9 1/4 In.	18.00
Swirl, Sandwich Server, Ultramarine, 12 1/4 In.	27.50
Swirl, Soup, Lug Handles, Ultramarine	45.00
Swirl, Sugar, Delphite	7.00
Swirl, Sugar, Ultramarine	15.00
Swirl, Tumbler, Footed, Ultramarine, 9 Oz., 4 5/8 In.	45.00
Swirl, Vase, Footed, Ultramarine, 8 1/2 In.	27.50
Swirl Fire-King, Bowl, Jadite, 4 7/8 In.	13.00
Swirl Fire-King, Creamer, Jadite	9.50
Swirl Fire-King, Cup & Saucer, Ivory	6.00
Swirl Fire-King, Cup, Ivory, Gold Trim	12.00
Swirl Fire-King, Mixing Bowl, Ivory, 9 In.	13.00
Swirl Fire-King, Plate, Azurite, 7 3/8 In.	5.00
Swirl Fire-King, Plate, Ivory, Gold Trim, 9 1/8 In.	5.00 to 12.00
Swirl Fire-King, Plate, Jadite, 7 1/4 In.	8.50
Swirl Fire-King, Platter, Jadite, 12 x 9 In.	17.00

Swirl Fire-King, Soup, Dish, Jadite, 7 5/8 In. 19.00
Swirl Fire-King, Sugar & Creamer, Cover, Ivory 18.00
Sylvan, Bowl, Vegetable, Oval, Green, 10 In. 57.00
Sylvan, Cup & Saucer, Green 61.00
Sylvan, Plate, Green, 9 In. 48.00
Sylvan, Sugar & Creamer, Cover, Green 285.00
Sylvan, Tumbler, Green, 12 Oz., 5 1/2 In. 160.00
Tea Room, Ice Bucket, Pink 65.00
Tea Room, Saltshaker, Green . . . . .25.00 to 40.00
Tea Room, Sherbet, Low-Footed, Green 20.00
Tea Room, Sherbet, Low-Footed, Pink 25.00
Tea Room, Sugar, Cover, Footed, Green 15.00
Tea Room, Tray, Center Handle, Pink 190.00
Tea Room, Vase, Green, Ruffled, 9 1/2 In. 125.00
Thistle, Cup & Saucer, Green 33.00
Thistle, Plate, Green, 8 In. 18.00
Threading pattern is listed here as Old English.
Tradition, Goblet, Water, Pink 20.00
Tulip, Plate, Blue, 9 In. 35.00
Turquoise Blue, Bowl, Vegetable, 8 In. 14.00
Turquoise Blue, Creamer 5.00
Turquoise Blue, Cup & Saucer 5.00
Turquoise Blue, Mixing Bowl, Round, 1 Qt. 12.75
Turquoise Blue, Mixing Bowl, Round, 2 Qt. 12.50
Turquoise Blue, Mixing Bowl, Round, 3 Qt 16.50
Turquoise Blue, Mug, 8 Oz. 10.00
Turquoise Blue, Plate, 7 In. 9.50
Turquoise Blue, Relish, 3 Sections, Gold Trim, 11 1/8 In. 11.00
Twisted Optic, Candlestick, Green, 3 In., Pair 21.00
Vernon pattern is listed here as No. 616.
Vertical Ribbed pattern is listed here as Queen Mary.
Victory, Creamer, Green 12.00
Victory, Sugar & Creamer, Black 75.00
Waffle pattern is listed here as Waterford.
Waterford, Bowl, Pink, 5 1/2 In. 33.00
Waterford, Butter, Cover, Pink 220.00
Waterford, Pitcher, Tilted, 80 Oz. 32.00
Waterford, Plate, 7 1/8 In. 7.00
Waterford, Plate, Pink, 9 5/8 In. 20.00
Waterford, Sherbet, Footed 5.00
Waterford, Sherbet, Footed, Pink 11.00
Waterford, Sugar, Cover 12.00
Waterford, Tumbler, Footed, 10 Oz., 4 7/8 In. 12.00
Wheat, Bowl, 4 5/8 In. 2.50
Wheat, Cake Pan, Round, 8 In. 9.00
Wheat, Casserole, Cover, 2 Qt. 13.00
Wheat, Plate, 10 In. 8.00
Wheat, Platter, 9 x 12 In. 10.00
Wild Rose pattern is listed here as Dogwood.

Depression Glass, Windsor

If the metal top on your saltshaker won't unscrew, try this: Turn the saltshaker upside down in a small bowl of white vinegar. Let it soak for about 12 hours. The cap should then be loose. Rub soap on the inside of the cap to keep it from sticking again.

Windsor, Bowl, Vegetable, Oval, Pink, 9 1/2 In.	22.00
Windsor, Chop Plate, Green, 13 5/8 In.	45.00
Windsor, Coaster, Green, 3 1/4 In.	15.00
Windsor, Pitcher, Green, 52 Oz., 6 3/4 In.	70.00
Windsor, Plate, Pink, 7 In.	20.00
Windsor, Plate, Pink, 9 In.	20.00
Windsor, Sugar & Creamer, Cover, Pink	45.00
Windsor, Tumbler, 11 Oz., 4 5/8 In.	30.00
Windsor, Tumbler, Green, 12 Oz., 5 In.	30.00 to 65.00
Windsor Diamond pattern is listed here as Windsor.	
Woolworth, Sugar, Pink	10.00
X Design, Butter, Cover, Green, 1/4 Lb.	55.00
X Design, Reamer, Green	35.00

DERBY has been marked on porcelain made in the city of Derby, England, since about 1748. The original Derby factory closed in 1848, but others opened there and continued to produce quality porcelain. The Crown Derby mark began appearing on Derby wares in the 1770s.

Basket, Landscape, Man, Wearing Red Coat, Lady, Wearing Rose Dress, 1756, 6 In.	1380.00
Bowl, Chestnut, Cream, 8 Flowering Plants, Red, Puce, Purple, 5 In.	2645.00
Bowl, Cover, Rose, Purple, Blue, Brown, Gray, Fruit, D Mark In Gold, 1775, 8 In.	2530.00
Candlestick, Birds In Branches, 2 Yellow, Purple, Perched Finches, 1765, 9 In.	865.00
Coffee, Tea Set, Gilt Floral Sprigs, Vine Border, Salmon Border, 1825, 22 Piece	920.00
Coffee Can, Saucer, Young Mother, Wearing Yellow Hat, Red Shawl, 1794, 3 In.	2530.00
Dessert Set, Stylized Floral, Tureen, Cover, 6-Sided Dish, 1810, 8 Piece	275.00
Dinner Set, Fruit Cooler, Cover, D Mark In Iron Red, 1815, 26 Piece	9775.00
Dish, Center Flowers, Foliate Scrolls, Dots, Garland Border, Rectangular, 1820, 11 In.	1610.00
Dish, Scalloped, Yellow Apple, Purple, Green, Purple Twig, Russet Rim, 1760, Pair	3740.00
Figurine, Songbirds, Goldfinch, Brown Mottled Back, Yellow Wings, 7 In.	1092.00
Plate, Botanical, Pink, Yellow, Purple, Poppy, William Pegg, 1858, 8 3/4 In.	3740.00
Plate, Dessert, Japan, Underglaze Blue, Iron Red, Gold In Center, 1825, 26 Piece	2100.00
Tea Set, Topographical, Waste Bowl, Gilt Oval, Scrollwork, 1815, 17 Piece	5465.00
Vase, Imari Pattern, 3 1/2 In.	44.00

DICK TRACY, the comic strip, started in 1931. Tracy was also the hero of movies from 1937 to 1947 and again in 1990, and starred in a radio series in the 1940s and a television series in the 1950s. Memorabilia from all these activities are collected.

Badge, Detective Club, Brass, Embossed, Leather Pouch, 1937, 3 x 3 In.	110.00
Badge, Inspector General, Brass, 1939, 2 1/2 In.	700.00
Book, Big Little Book, Chains Of Crime, Chester Gould, 1936	31.00
Book, Big Little Book, Dick Tracy Solves The Penfield Mystery, Whitman, 1934	45.00
Book, Comic, Dick Tracy Meets The Blank, 1939	155.00
Book, Comic, No. C-40, 1975	15.00
Book, Pop-Up, 1935	125.00
Book, Secret Code, Envelope, 3 x 6 In.	27.00
Bottle, Soaky	40.00
Car, Squad, Friction, Green Tin, Box, Marx, 1950s	550.00
Car, Squad, Windup, Tin, Marx, 11 In.	175.00
Card, Playing, Walter H. Johnson Candy Co., Framed, 1930s	150.00
Cards, Decoder, Green, Post Cereal, 1957	15.00
Doll, Bonny Braids, Toothbrush, Box, Ideal, 1951, 14 In.	450.00
Filmviewer, Acme, 3 Rolls Of Film, Box	90.00
Flashlight, Secret Service, Pocket, Metal & Plastic, 1939	55.00
Game, Crimestopper, Ideal	75.00
Game, Dick Tracy Electronic Target, Box	250.00
Handcuffs, For Jr., John Henry Products, On Card, 1940-1960, 5 x 10 In.	65.00
Kit, Crimestopper Club, Mailer, 1961	75.00
Kit, Secret Detecto, Mailer, Quaker Cereals, 1938	150.00
Lunch Box, Metal, Aladdin, 1967	90.00
Lunch Box, Thermos, 1967	195.00
Pistol, Click-Type, Black Aluminum, 3 Fake Rubies, Dick Tracy Jr., Marx	120.00
Pistol, Siren	95.00

Play Set, Dick Tracy, Ideal, 1973	85.00
Ring, Silvered Brass, Quaker, 1938	125.00
Sheet Music, What Did Dick Tracy Do Today?, Chester Gould Characters, 1947	108.00
Suspender Set, Dick Tracy Braces, Box, 1940s	125.00
Valentine, 1940	25.00
Watch, In Police Car, Omni, 1981	195.00
Wrist, Radio, 2-Way Electronic, Plastic, 2 Radios, Wire Cord, Remco, Box	75.00

DICKENS WARE pieces are listed in the Royal Doulton and Weller categories.

DINNERWARE used in the United States from the 1930s through the 1950s is listed here. Most was made in potteries in southern Ohio, West Virginia, and California. A few patterns were made in Japan, England, and other countries. Dishes were sold in gift shops and department stores, or were given away as premiums. Many of these patterns are listed in this book in their own categories, such as Autumn Leaf, Azalea, Coors, Fiesta, Franciscan, Hall, Harker, Harlequin, Red Wing, Riviera, Russel Wright, Vernon Kilns, Watt, and WIllow. For more information, see *Kovels' Depression Glass & Dinnerware Price List.*

Antique Grape, Canister, Flour, Metlox	95.00
Antique Grape, Canister, Sugar, Metlox	85.00
Apple, Creamer, Purinton	62.00
Apple, Jug, Purinton, 2 Pt., 5 3/4 In.	55.00
Apple, Pitcher Set, Purinton, 4 Large Tumblers	145.00
Apple, Teapot, Purinton, 6 Cup, 6 1/2 In.	60.00
Apple, Water Set, Purinton, 5-Pt. Jug, 5 Piece	130.00
Apple Blossom, Platter, Homer Laughlin, 14 In.	40.00
Aztec, Celery Dish, Metlox	50.00
Aztec, Pitcher, Water, Metlox	200.00
Aztec, Sugar & Creamer, Cover, Metlox	70.00
Blossom Top, Salt & Pepper, Red Flower, Blue Ridge	35.00
Blue Fish, Ashtray, Catalina	135.00
Blue Heaven, Casserole, Cover, Royal	35.00
Blue Heaven, Coffeepot, Royal	40.00
Blue Heaven, Gravy Boat, Liner, Royal	18.00
Blue Heaven, Pie Plate, Royal	15.00
Blue Heaven, Salt & Pepper, Royal	12.00
Blue Heaven, Teapot, Royal	50.00
Blue Heaven, Tumbler, Water, Royal	7.00
Brown Intaglio, Chop Plate, Purinton, 12 In.	40.00
California Ivy, Dinner Set, Metlox, 8 Place Setting, 44 Piece	450.00
California Ivy, Platter, Metlox, 13 1/4 In.	40.00
California Ivy, Salt & Pepper, Metlox	24.00
California Ivy, Water Set, Metlox, 9 Piece	225.00
California Provincial, Bowl, Metlox, 6 In.	11.00
California Provincial, Bowl, Vegetable, Divided, Metlox	50.00
California Provincial, Canister, Flour, Metlox	105.00
California Provincial, Casserole, Hen On Nest Cover	70.00 to 135.00
California Provincial, Coffeepot, Metlox	60.00
California Provincial, Gravy Boat, Metlox	40.00
California Provincial, Mug, Large	20.00
California Strawberry, Bowl, Metlox, 5 1/2 In.	10.00
California Strawberry, Cup & Saucer, Metlox	20.00
California Strawberry, Plate, Metlox, 6 In.	5.00
California Strawberry, Soup, Dish, Metlox	12.50
California Strawberry, Sugar, Cover, Metlox	20.00
California Strawberry, Teapot, Metlox	35.00
Cashmere, Bowl, Vegetable, Cover, Homer Laughlin	75.00
Cashmere, Bowl, Vegetable, Oval, Homer Laughlin	25.00
Cashmere, Cup & Saucer, Homer Laughlin	5.00
Cashmere, Plate, Homer Laughlin, 10 In.	11.00
Cashmere, Platter, Homer Laughlin, 8 1/2 In.	12.00

Cashmere, Platter, Homer Laughlin, 15 In. 40.00
Cashmere, Sugar, Cover, Homer Laughlin 18.00
Cat-Tail, Cup & Saucer, Universal 18.00
Cat-Tail, Plate, Luncheon, Universal, 8 In. 8.00
Catalina, Bowl, Fluted, White, 14 In. 120.00
Cavalier, Teapot, Pink Rose, Homer Laughlin 35.00
Chrysanthemum, Sugar & Creamer, Blue Ridge 40.00
Coaching Scenes, Cup & Saucer, Blue, Johnson Brothers 8.00
Coaching Scenes, Platter, Blue, Johnson Brothers, 14 In. 45.00
Colonial Homestead, Bowl, 9 In. 7.00
Colonial Homestead, Bowl, Royal, 5 In. 2.00
Colonial Homestead, Casserole, Cover, Royal 12.00
Colonial Homestead, Cocktail, Royal 15.00
Colonial Homestead, Gravy Boat, Liner, Metlox 16.50
Colonial Homestead, Salt & Pepper, Royal 8.00
Colonial Homestead, Sherbet, Royal, 6 1/2 In. 1.00
Colonial Homestead, Teapot, Royal . . . . .65.00 to 97.00
Currier & Ives, Bowl, Royal, 5 1/2 In. . . . . .2.00 to 9.00
Currier & Ives, Bowl, Royal, 9 In. 9.00
Currier & Ives, Bowl, Vegetable, Red, Round, 9 In. 17.00
Currier & Ives, Bowl, Vegetable, Red, Round, 10 In. 20.00
Currier & Ives, Casserole, Cover, Blue 88.00
Currier & Ives, Chop Plate, Red, 11 In. 18.00
Currier & Ives, Cup & Saucer, Royal 3.00
Currier & Ives, Cup, Red 7.00
Currier & Ives, Cup, Royal 2.00
Currier & Ives, Lamp, Oil 145.00
Currier & Ives, Pie Plate, Christmas, Royal 15.00
Currier & Ives, Pie Plate, The Road Winter, Blue 12.00
Currier & Ives, Pie Plate, Winter, Royal 15.00
Currier & Ives, Plate, Red, 10 In. 12.00
Currier & Ives, Plate, Royal, 10 In. . . . . .3.50 to 4.00
Currier & Ives, Platter, Bucks County, Round, 13 In. 20.00
Currier & Ives, Platter, Royal, Oval, 13 In. 25.00
Currier & Ives, Salt & Pepper, Royal 12.00
Currier & Ives, Soup, Dish, Royal 14.00
Currier & Ives, Teapot, Cover, Blue 125.00
Daisy, Mug, Metlox 15.00
Della Robbia, Coffeepot, Metlox 35.00
Dogwood, Soup, Dish, Homer Laughlin 9.00
El Rancho, Chop Plate, Catalina, 12 In. 25.00
Epicure, Plate, Dawn Pink, Homer Laughlin, 10 In. 20.00
Epicure, Saucer, Charcoal, Homer Laughlin 4.00
Epicure, Saucer, Dawn Pink, Homer Laughlin 4.00
Flowering Berry, Berry Bowl, Blue Ridge, 5 1/4 In. 6.00
Flowering Berry, Plate, Blue Ridge, 7 In. 8.00
Flowering Berry, Soup Dish, Blue Ridge, 8 In. 18.00
Friendly Village, Bowl, Johnson Brothers, 6 1/8 In. 10.00
Friendly Village, Cup & Saucer, Johnson Brothers 15.00
Friendly Village, Plate, Johnson Brothers, 10 In. 14.00
Friendly Village, Platter, Johnson Brothers, Oval, 12 In. 34.00
Friendly Village, Sugar, Cover, Johnson Brothers 22.00
Friendly Village, Teapot, Johnson Brothers 45.00
Fruit, Pitcher, Purinton 35.00
Fruit, Teapot, Purinton, 4 Cup 35.00
Happily Ever After, Teapot, Blue Ridge 135.00
Happy Time, Chop Plate, Metlox, 12 In. 22.00
Hawaiian Flowers, Plate, Blue Ridge, 9 In. 25.00
Homestead Provincial, Bowl, Metlox, 6 In. . . . . .8.00 to 10.00
Homestead Provincial, Bowl, Vegetable, Tab Handles, Metlox, 8 1/2 In. 50.00
Homestead Provincial, Butter, Cover, Metlox 20.00
Homestead Provincial, Creamer 20.00

Homestead Provincial, Cruet Set, Metlox, 5 Piece 145.00
Homestead Provincial, Cup & Saucer, Metlox 12.00
Homestead Provincial, Cup, Metlox 10.00
Homestead Provincial, Gravy Boat, Metlox 30.00
Homestead Provincial, Mug, Large 300.00
Homestead Provincial, Plate, Metlox, 10 In. . . . . .10.00 to 13.00
Homestead Provincial, Platter, Metlox, 13 1/2 In. . . . . .37.00 to 45.00
Homestead Provincial, Salt Box, Poppy Trail, Metlox 85.00
Jade, Cup, Platinum Trim, Homer Laughlin 12.00
Jade, Plate, Platinum Trim, Homer Laughlin, 7 In. 9.00
Jubilee, Teapot, Green, Homer Laughlin 18.00
Liberty Blue, Gravy Boat, Liner, Johnson Brothers 50.00
Liberty Blue, Tureen, Soup, Cover 330.00
Lu-Ray, Breakfast Set, Pink, Service For 4, Taylor, Smith & Taylor, 20 Piece 150.00
Lu-Ray, Chop Plate, Yellow, Taylor, Smith & Taylor 35.00
Lu-Ray, Cup & Saucer, Pink, Taylor, Smith & Taylor, After Dinner 35.00
Lu-Ray, Cup, Blue, Taylor, Smith & Taylor, After Dinner 35.00
Lu-Ray, Eggcup, Double, Pink, Taylor, Smith & Taylor 22.00
Lu-Ray, Grill Plate, Yellow, Taylor, Smith & Taylor 45.00
Lu-Ray, Platter, Persian Cream, Taylor, Smith & Taylor, 12 In. . . . . .12.00 to 15.00
Lu-Ray, Teapot, Yellow, Taylor, Smith & Taylor 125.00
Mandarin Yellow, Plate, Catalina, 10 In. 55.00
Medallion, Bowl, Vegetable, Red, Divided, Metlox 30.00
Medallion Red, Plate, Metlox, 10 In. 10.00
Old Curiosity Shop, Bowl, 5 1/2 In. 2.00
Old Curiosity Shop, Creamer, Royal 6.00
Old Curiosity Shop, Cup & Saucer, Royal . . . . .3.00 to 10.00
Old Curiosity Shop, Cup, Royal 2.00
Old Curiosity Shop, Pie Plate, Royal 35.00
Old Curiosity Shop, Plate, Royal, 10 In. 7.50
Orange, Pitcher, Pfaltzgraff 65.00
Orange Tree, Bowl Set, Graduated, Turquoise, Homer Laughlin, 4 Piece 175.00
Plaid, Bowl, Pacific, 15 In. 75.00
Poppy Trail, Coffeepot, Metlox 100.00
Poppy Trail, Ladle, Soup, Red 65.00
Poppy Trail, Teapot, Red 75.00
Provincial Blue, Bowl, Metlox, 11 3/8 In. 75.00
Provincial Blue, Bowl, Metlox, 6 In. 13.00
Provincial Blue, Creamer, Cover, Metlox 30.00
Provincial Blue, Gravy Boat, Handle, Metlox 30.00
Provincial Blue, Plate, Metlox, 10 In. 15.00
Provincial Blue, Sugar, Cover, Metlox 30.00
Provincial Rose, Bowl, 2 Sections, Rectangular, Metlox, 12 In. 55.00
Provincial Rose, Platter, Rectangular, Metlox, Large 45.00
Red Rooster, Bowl, Poppy Trail, Metlox, 11 1/2 In. 50.00
Red Rooster, Bread Plate, Metlox 60.00
Red Rooster, Canister, Sugar, Metlox 75.00
Red Rooster, Creamer, Metlox 15.00
Red Rooster, Mug, Metlox, 8 Oz. 19.00
Red Rooster, Pitcher, Figural, Metlox, 14 In. . . . . .500.00 to 1000.00
Red Rooster, Plate, Metlox, 7 1/2 In. 8.00
Red Rooster, Plate, Metlox, 10 In. 8.00
Red Rooster, Platter, Metlox, 13 1/2 In. 13.00
Red Rooster, Salt & Pepper, Metlox 45.00
Red Rooster, Soup, Dish, Metlox 12.00
Rhythm Rose, Teapot, Homer Laughlin 45.00
Ridge Daisy, Bowl, Blue Ridge, 5 1/4 In. 5.00
Ridge Daisy, Bread Plate, Blue Ridge 4.00
Ridge Daisy, Plate, Blue Ridge, 9 1/4 In. 12.00
Ridge Daisy, Platter, Blue Ridge, 15 In. 30.00
Rodeo, Bowl, Wallace, 5 1/2 In. 42.00
Rodeo, Cup & Saucer, Wallace 6.00

Dinnerware, Streamline, Sugar, Cover,
Orange, Salem China

Dinnerware,
Serenade, Bowl,
Cronin China, 5 In.

Sculptured Daisy, Bowl, Metlox, 12 1/4 In.	95.00
Sculptured Daisy, Coffeepot, Metlox	85.00
Sculptured Daisy, Compote, Cover, Poppy Trail, Metlox	42.00
Sculptured Daisy, Jar, Apothecary Cover, Metlox	125.00
Sculptured Daisy, Mug, Metlox, Small	33.00
Sculptured Daisy, Pitcher, Metlox, 1 Pt.	85.00
Sculptured Daisy, Teapot, Metlox	75.00
Sculptured Daisy, Tumbler, Metlox	32.00
Sculptured Grape, Bowl, Metlox, 10 1/8 In.	90.00
Sculptured Grape, Compote, Metlox	80.00
Serenade, Bowl, Cronin China, 5 In. ....*Illus*	10.00
Serenade, Pitcher, Blue Ridge, 6 In.	65.00
Silhouette, Bowl, Salad, Crooksville, 9 In.	25.00
Silhouette, Coffeepot, Five Band, Crooksville	125.00
Silhouette, Coffeepot, Medallion, Crooksville	150.00
Silhouette, Leftover, Square, Crooksville	75.00
Silhouette, Saucer, Crooksville	10.00
Streamline, Sugar, Cover, Orange, Salem China ....*Illus*	20.00
Sunbright, Platter, Blue Ridge, 11 In.	18.00
Suntone, Cup & Saucer, Child's, Brown, Homer Laughlin	15.00
Town & Country, Cup & Saucer, Chartreuse, Eva Zeisel	36.00
Town & Country, Cup & Saucer, Rust, Eva Zeisel	42.00
Town & Country, Gravy Boat, Liner, Chartreuse, Eva Zeisel	45.00
Town & Country, Plate, Chartreuse, Eva Zeisel, 10 3/4 In.	34.00
Town & Country, Plate, Rust, Eva Zeisel, 6 1/4 In.	12.00
Town & Country, Plate, Rust, Eva Zeisel, 10 3/4 In.	38.00
Town & Country, Relish, Chartreuse, Eva Zeisel, 5 x 6 In.	16.00
Town & Country, Relish, Rust, Eva Zeisel, 5 x 6 In.	18.00
Town & Country, Soup, Dish, Chartreuse, Eva Zeisel, 6 In.	22.00
Town & Country, Soup, Dish, Rust, Eva Zeisel, 6 In.	24.00
Tropicana Fish, Bowl, Metlox, 12 In.	80.00
Tropicana Fish, Tray, Metlox, 25 In.	125.00
Virginia Rose, Place Setting, Homer Laughlin, 8 Sets	135.00
Westward Ho, Bread Plate, Boots & Saddles, Wallace, 7 In.	6.00
Westward Ho, Plate, Boots & Saddles, Wallace, 10 In.	12.00
Wild Strawberry, Berry Bowl, Blue Ridge, 5 1/4 In.	6.00
Wild Strawberry, Plate, Blue Ridge, 8 1/2 In.	14.00
Witch, Teapot, Polka Dot, Fitz & Floyd	150.00
Yorktowne, Bowl, Pfaltzgraff, 8 1/2 In.	16.00
Yorktowne, Creamer, Pfaltzgraff	17.00
Yorktowne, Cup & Saucer, Pfaltzgraff	10.00
Yorktowne, Plate, Pfaltzgraff, 6 In.	4.00
Yorktowne, Sherbet, Footed, Pfaltzgraff	8.00
Yorktowne, Tray, Pfaltzgraff, 3 1/2 x 7 1/2 In.	15.00

DIONNE QUINTUPLETS were born in Canada on May 28, 1934. The publicity about their birth and their special status as wards of the Canadian government made them famous throughout the world. Visitors could watch the girls play; reporters interviewed the girls and the staff. Thousands of special dolls and souvenirs were made picturing the quints at different ages. Emilie died in 1954, Marie in 1970. Yvonne, Annette, and Cecile still live in Canada.

Book, Paper Doll, All Aboard For Shuteye Town	95.00
Book, We're 2 Years Old, Soft Cover, 1936	50.00
Calendar, Print, 1939	35.00
Doll, Composition, Madame Alexander, With Bed, 6 Piece, c.1935, 7 In.	495.00
Doll, Emilie, Madame Alexander, c.1935, 17 In.	450.00
Doll Set, All In Swing, Madame Alexander, 5 Piece	2800.00
Doll Set, In Chair, Bent Limb, Composition, Arranbee, 1936, 6 1/2 In.	1035.00
Lawn Swing, Awning, Names	675.00
Magazine, Look, October 11, 1938	15.00
Mirror, Palmolive Soap, Pocket	98.00
Paper Doll, Uncut	85.00
Sign, Palmolive Soap, Quintuplets Picture, Cardboard, 21 In.	45.00
Spoon Set, c.1935, 5 Piece	100.00

DISNEYANA is a collector's term. Walt Disney and his company introduced many comic characters to the world. Collectors search for examples of the work of the Disney Studios and the many commercial products modeled after his characters, including Mickey Mouse, Donald Duck, and recent films, like *Beauty and the Beast* and *The Little Mermaid*.

Apron, Snow White, Plastic, 1950s	22.00
Badge, Host, Disney World, Gilt Metal, Pinback, Walt Disney Productions, 1 3/4 In.	45.00
Bag, Flour, Snow White, 1950s, 5 Lb.	20.00
Bank, 2nd National Duck Bank, Tin Lithograph, Chein, 1950s, 6 1/2 In.	100.00
Bank, Cinderella, American Bisque	195.00
Bank, Dopey, Ceramic, Rubber Stopper, Painted, 1960s, 6 In.	45.00
Bank, Elmer Elephant, Drum, Bisque, 1930s, 5 In.	300.00
Bank, Mickey & Minnie Mouse, Sitting On Stools, Pair	85.00
Bank, Mickey Mouse, Drum Major, Movable Arms	45.00
Bank, Mickey Mouse, On Drum, Tin, Lead, Germany, c.1940, 5 In.	302.00
Bank, Mickey Mouse, On Haunted Island, 1950, 5 1/2 x 3 1/4 In.	45.00
Bank, Mickey Mouse, Small Book Form, Mickey On Cover, 4 1/4 x 3 In.	1035.00
Bank, Minnie Mouse, At Christmas Tree	25.00
Bank, Winnie The Pooh, Tree House	95.00
Birthday Card, Brown Paper, Inked Name, 1936, 19 x 23, Folds To 5 1/2 In.	75.00
Birthday Card, Mickey Mouse, As Sailor, Hallmark, 1930s	40.00
Birthday Card, Mickey Mouse, Brown Paper, Hallmark, 1936, 4 1/2 x 5 1/2 In.	75.00
Biscuit Tin, Mickey & Minnie Mouse, 1931, 10 x 7 x 8 In.	1450.00
Blotter, Donald Duck & Goofy Fishing, Paper Company Bottom, 1940s, 9 x 4 In.	45.00
Blotter, Donald Duck, Sunoco, 1940s	35.00
Book, 3 Little Wolves, Whitman, 1937, 13 x 9 1/2 In.	65.00
Book, Better Little Book, Mickey Mouse & The 'Lectro Box, 1946	50.00
Book, Better Little Book, Mickey Mouse Bell Boy Detective, No. 1483, 1945, Small	40.00
Book, Big Little Book, Mickey Mouse The Mail Pilot, Whitman Publishing, 1933	38.00
Book, Big Little Book, The Boys, Donald Duck, Whitman, 1948, 96 Pages	22.00
Book, Clock Clowns Mickey & Donald, Whitman, 1938, 12 1/4 x 9 1/4 In.	90.00
Book, Coloring, Snow White, 1938	30.00
Book, Donald's Lucky Day, Color Illustrations, Whitman, 1939	45.00
Book, Famous Seven Dwarfs, Whitman, 1938	45.00
Book, Guide, Disneyland, 1957	75.00
Book, Guide, Disneyland, 1960	60.00
Book, Hiawatha, 1938	40.00
Book, Lady & The Tramp, 1954	8.00
Book, Little Golden Book, 101 Dalmatians, 1985	12.00
Book, Little Golden Book, Babes In Toyland, Green Background Cover, 1961	14.00
Book, Little Golden Book, Detective Mickey Mouse, 1985	8.00

Book, Little Golden Book, Mickey & The Beanstalk, 1988 .... 10.00
Book, Little Golden Book, Mickey Mouse's Picnic, 1st Printing, 1950 .... 18.00
Book, Little Golden Book, Winnie The Pooh & The Honey Tree, 1965 .... 16.00
Book, Little Golden Book, Winnie The Pooh Meets Gopher, 1964 .... 18.00
Book, Little Pigs Picnic, Heath Books, 1939 .... 25.00
Book, Mickey & The Beanstalk, Story Hour, 1948 .... 16.00
Book, Mickey Mouse & Pluto The Pup, Whitman, 1936 .... 270.00
Book, Mickey Mouse Alphabet, A To Z, Whitman, 1936 .... 175.00
Book, Mickey Mouse Fire Brigade, Cartoon, Whitman, 1936 .... 258.00
Book, Mickey Mouse On Haunted Island, 1950 .... 45.00
Book, Mickey Never Fails, Heath, 1939 .... 30.00
Book, Paint, Bambi, Whitman, No. 664, Some Coloring, 1942 .... 29.00
Book, Paint, Mickey Mouse, Color Cover, W.D. Prod., 1946 .... 26.00
Book, Paint, Pinocchio, Whitman, Some Painted Pages, 1939 .... 40.00
Book, Photograph, Dopey, Doc, Vinyl, Paper, Snapshots, 1930s, 8 x 10 1/2 In. 40.00
Book, Pinocchio Paint Book, Whitman, 1938 ....40.00 to 50.00
Book, Pop-Up, Mickey Mouse Presents His Silly Symphonies, Blue Ribbon, 1933 ...... 685.00
Book, Pop-Up, Minnie Mouse, Blue Ribbon, 1933 .... 500.00
Book, Snow White & Seven Dwarfs, Whitman, No. 925, 1938 ....17.00 to 30.00
Book, Snow White Song, Illustrated, France, 1938 .... 58.00
Book, Sword In The Stone, By Top Tap Tales, Whitman, 1963 .... 15.00
Book, Uncle Scrooge McDuck, His Life & Times, Carl Barks, 375 Pages, 1981 ...615.00 to 650.00
Book, Walt Disney's Bambi Paint Book #664, Whitman, 1942 .... 35.00
Book, Walt Disney's Famous Seven Dwarfs, Whitman, 1938 .... 50.00
Book, Walt Disney's Sleeping Beauty Castle, Color Illustrations, 1957 .... 30.00
Book, Walt Disney's The Sword In The Stone, Top Tap Tales, Whitman, 1963 ...... 15.00
Book, Walt Disney's Version Of Pinocchio, Collins Of England, 1940s 25.00
Book, Wise Little Hen, Donald Duck, Linen, 1937 .... 60.00
Book Plate, Mickey Mouse, Minnie, Santa, England, 1930s, 13 1/2 x 14 1/2 In. 250.00
Booklet, Sleeping Beauty Castle, Illustrations, 4 Pages, 1957 .... 30.00
Bottle Cap, Horace Horsecollar, Enamel, Lemon Benzoate Soda, 1930s, 1 In. 60.00
Bottle Cap, Horace Horsecollar, Tin, Lemon Benzoate Soda, 1920s-1930s, 1 In. 46.00
Bowl, Fish, Gold, No. 121, Vernon Kiln, 1940s 400.00
Bowl, Mushroom, No. 120, Rectangular, Dancing Mushrooms, Vernon Kilns, 1940 ..... 300.00
Box, Music, Snow White Dancing, Ceramic, Some Day My Prince Will Come, 9 In. 35.00
Box, Paint, Donald Duck, Mickey, Tin Lithograph, Transogram, 1948 .... 50.00
Box, Paint, Mickey Mouse, Tin Lithograph Case, 80 Watercolors, England, 12 In. 34.00
Box, Walt Disney Characters Embroidery Set, 1930s, 6 x 9 x 1 In. 85.00
Bracelet, Charm, Zorro, Gold Color, Black Paint, Box, 1950s 75.00
Bread Wrapper, Donald Duck, Debus, 1950s, 16 x 17 In. 10.00
Bust, Donald Duck, Long Ski Nose, Chalkware 40.00
Calendar, 1942, Morrell Hams 150.00
Calendar, Mickey Mouse, Glow In Dark 20.00
Calendar, Wall, Chromolithograph, Shrink-Wrapped, Morrell, 1942, 18 x 8 In. 1150.00
Camera, Donald Duck, Box 100.00
Camera, Donald Duck, Plastic, 127, Herbert-George Co., WDP, 1946, 4 1/2 x 3 In. 25.00
Camera, Mick-A-Matic Camera, With Flash, Box, Unused 225.00
Can, Donald Duck, Cone Top 150.00
Candy Container, Mickey Mouse, Papier-Mache, String Tail, 1930s 110.00
Candy Container, Minnie Mouse 385.00
Candy Container, PEZ, Mickey Mouse, On Card 10.00
Candy Container, PEZ, Scrooge McDuck 48.00
Car, Dipsy, Mickey Mouse, Metal Ears, Windup, Linemar 550.00
Card, Christmas, 101 Dalmatians Panorama, 1961 Calendar, 1960 .... 85.00
Card, Christmas, Corporate, Mickey, Donald, Goofy, Pluto, Tree, Epcot Opening, 1982 .. 18.00
Card Box, Bubble Gum, Davy Crockett, Topps, Walt Disney, 1950s 400.00
Carpet Bag, Mary Poppins, Red & Blue Floral, Red & Blue 135.00
Cel, see Animation Art category.
Certificate, Mickey Mouse Club Membership, No Name, WDP, 11 x 8 1/2 In. 26.00
Charm Bracelet, Zorro, Gold Color, Zorro, Horse, Lariat, Carriage, Z For Zorror, 1950s 75.00
Clock, Alarm, Mickey Mouse & Goofy, Bradley 45.00
Clock, Alarm, Mickey Mouse, Enesco 325.00
Clock, Alarm, Mickey Mouse, Ingersoll, WDP, Box, 1949, 4 x 4 1/2 x 2 In. 287.00

Clock, Alarm, Mickey Mouse, Pie-Eyed, All Metal, Bradley 70.00
Clock, Alarm, Mickey Mouse, Talking, Bradley Time, Box 15.00
Clock, Donald Duck, Wall, Wristwatch Shape, Black Band, Box, Bradley, 26 In. 65.00
Clock, Mickey Mouse & Friends, Talking Alarm, Bradley, 1970s 245.00
Clock, Mickey Mouse, Lorus, Battery Operated, Japan, Sealed 22.00
Clock Radio, Mickey Mouse, AM-FM, Youth Electronics, G.E. 135.00
Comic Strip, Mickey Mouse, Pluto, Walt Disney Studio, May 14, 1942, 5 x 23 In. 1275.00
Comic Strip, Mickey Mouse, Walt Disney Studio, May 7, 1942, 5 x 23 In. 1090.00
Cookie Jar, Aladdin, With Lamp 35.00
Cookie Jar, Cinderella's Coach, 1930s 170.00
Cookie Jar, Cinderella, Napco, 9 3/4 In. ....165.00 to 200.00
Cookie Jar, Donald Duck, Sitting, American Bisque 2650.00
Cookie Jar, Donald Duck, Standing, Pastel, American Bisque 350.00
Cookie Jar, Dumbo's Greatest Cookies, California Originals 800.00
Cookie Jar, Eeyore 850.00
Cookie Jar, Goofy Cookie Co., California Originals 2200.00
Cookie Jar, Mickey & Minnie Mouse, Turnabout, Leeds 175.00
Cookie Jar, Mickey Mouse Alarm Clock, Enesco 355.00
Cookie Jar, Mickey Mouse, Joan, Box 30.00
Cookie Jar, Minnie Mouse, Sitting, Treasure Craft 48.00
Cookie Jar, Pinocchio Head, Metlox 50.00
Cookie Jar, Pinocchio, Sitting, Arms Crossed, California Originals 1400.00
Cookie Jar, Winnie The Pooh, California Originals ....100.00 to 150.00
Cookie Jar, Winnie The Pooh, Classic, Beehive Hunny, Treasure Craft 48.00
Costume, Mask, Pluto, Ben Cooper, Vinyl, Plastic, Box, 1982, Tiny Tot Size 2-3 ...... 37.00
Costume, Mickey Mouse, Wornova Play Clothes, Box, 1930s, 7 x 11 1/2 x 12 In. 431.00
Creamer, Pluto & Figaro, Gold Rim, Beswick, 1940s, 2 In. 85.00
Creamer, Rabbit, Regal China 425.00
Doll, Bashful, Knickerbocker, 1930s, 11 In. 165.00
Doll, Donald Duck, Felt, Sawdust Stuffed, Japan, 1950-1960, 7 In. 26.00
Doll, Grumpy, Knickerbocker, 1930s, 8 In. 245.00
Doll, Grumpy, Original Clothing, Belt, Hat, Coat, Pants, Knickerbocker, 1930s, 8 In. .. 245.00
Doll, Happy, Snow White, Composite Face, Stuffed Body, Head Pivots, 1930s, 15 In. ... 122.00
Doll, Jiminy Cricket, Composition, Knickerbocker, 1939, 10 In. ....*Illus* 1100.00
Doll, Mickey Mouse, Gund, 26 In. 65.00
Doll, Mickey Mouse, Hollow Rubber, Pie-Eyed, France, 1930s, 9 In. 350.00
Doll, Minnie Mouse, Felt, Sawdust Stuffed, Japan, 1960-1970, 7 In. 24.00
Doll, Pinocchio, Composition, Knickerbocker, 16 In. 450.00
Doll, Pinocchio, Composition, Knickerbocker, 1939, 10 In. ....*Illus* 900.00
Doll, Pinocchio, Ideal, 20 In. 850.00
Doll, Pinocchio, Painted Eyes, Red Romper, Yellow Gloves, Knickerbocker, 10 In. 900.00
Doll, Pinocchio, Wooden, Ideal, 10 In. ....*Illus* 200.00
Doll, Puppet, Hand, Dopey, Composition Head, Cloth Body & Hat, 1930s 125.00
Doll, Sleepy, Snow White, Composition, Green, Yellow, Orange, Black, 8 In. 126.00

Disneyana, Doll,
Pinocchio,
Composition,
Knickerbocker,
1939, 10 In.

Disneyana, Doll,
Jiminy Cricket,
Composition,
Knickerbocker,
1939, 10 In.

Disneyana, Doll, Pinocchio,
Wooden, Ideal, 10 In.

Doll, Snow White, Composition, Knickerbocker, No Clothes, 1930s, 12 1/4 In. 100.00
Doll, Toyland Soldier, Rubber Head, Plush Body, Gundikins, With Tag, 1961, 9 1/2 In. .. 40.00
Egg Timer, Doc, Figural, England, c.1937 .... 295.00
Eggcup, Mickey Mouse, Figural, Black & White 185.00
Figurine, Bambi, Bug On Tail, Goebel, 1980s, 3 3/8 In. 75.00
Figurine, Bambi, Butterfly On Tail, Japan, 1970s, 5 1/2 In. 75.00
Figurine, Bashful, Ceramic, Enesco, 1960s, 4 1/2 In. 30.00
Figurine, Dachsie The Dachshund, Lady & The Tramp, Hagen-Renaker, 1950s, 1 In. 200.00
Figurine, Doc, Ceramic, Enesco, 1960s, 4 1/2 In. 35.00
Figurine, Doc, Pewter, Hudson, 1980s, 2 In. 18.00
Figurine, Donald Duck, Bisque, 1930s, 2 In. 45.00
Figurine, Donald Duck, On Trapeze, Windup, Celluloid, Box 550.00
Figurine, Dopey, Bisque, 1930s, 3 In. 45.00
Figurine, Dopey, Bisque, 1930s, 5 In. 75.00
Figurine, Dopey, Ceramic, Enesco, 1960s, 4 1/2 In. 35.00
Figurine, Dopey, Goebel, 1980s, 3 In. 125.00
Figurine, Dumbo, Sitting, Yellow Bonnet, American Pottery, 1940s, 5 In. 100.00
Figurine, Dumbo, Vernon Kilns, 1941 .... 225.00
Figurine, Fauna, Sleeping Beauty, Hagen-Renaker, 1950s, 2 In. 250.00
Figurine, Ferdinand, Bisque, Black & White Face, 1930s, 3 In. 45.00
Figurine, Figaro, Hagen-Renaker Designer's Work, 1950s, 2 1/2 In. 375.00
Figurine, Figaro, Sitting Up, Paws Over Ball, Goebel, Bee In V Mark, 1950s, 4 In. 375.00
Figurine, Flora, Sleeping Beauty, Hagen-Renaker, 1950s, 2 In. 250.00
Figurine, Geppetto, Hand On Chin, Multi-Products, Sirocco, 1940s, 5 1/2 In. 95.00
Figurine, Grumpy, Bisque, 1930s, 3 In. 50.00
Figurine, Grumpy, Pewter, Hudson, 1980s, 2 In. 18.00
Figurine, Happy, Ceramic, Enesco, 1960s, 4 1/2 In. 30.00
Figurine, Honest John The Fox, Pinocchio, Multi-Products, 1940s, 7 In. 175.00
Figurine, Jaq The Mouse, Hagen-Renaker, 1950s, 1 3/8 In. 300.00
Figurine, Jock, Lady & The Tramp, Hagen-Renaker, 1950s, 1 3/8 In. 100.00
Figurine, Mad Hatter, Evan K. Shaw, 4 1/2 In. 325.00
Figurine, Merryweather, Fairy, Sleeping Beauty, Hagen-Renaker, 1950s, 2 In. 200.00
Figurine, Merryweather, Sleeping Beauty, Hagen-Renaker, 1950s, 1 3/4 In. 200.00
Figurine, Mickey Mouse Sitting In Canoe, Donald Duck On Right, Bisque, 1930 ...... 1000.00
Figurine, Mickey Mouse, Bendable, Hong Kong, On Card 15.00
Figurine, Mickey Mouse, Camphor Glass, 4 1/2 In. 60.00
Figurine, Mickey Mouse, Donald Duck, Sitting In Canoe, Facing Left, 1930s 1000.00
Figurine, Mickey Mouse, Sled, Bisque, Walt Disney Productions, 1970s, 4 In. 18.00
Figurine, Mickey Mouse, Vinyl, Dakin, 1970s 18.00
Figurine, Mickey Mouse, Windsor Canada On Canoe, Bisque, 1930s 1350.00
Figurine, Minnie Mouse, Broom, American Pottery, Worn Label, 1940s, 7 In. 225.00
Figurine, Minnie Mouse, Golf Clubs, Bisque, Walt Disney Productions, 1970s, 4 In. .18.00 to 20.00
Figurine, Peg, Lady & The Tramp, Hagen-Renaker, 1950s, 1 In. 275.00
Figurine, Peter Pan, Paper Hat, Weather Bird Shoes, 1950s, 8 In. 35.00
Figurine, Pinocchio, Honest John, Bisque, 1930s, 3 In. 40.00
Figurine, Pinocchio, Honest John, Multi-Products, Sirocco, 1940s, 7 In. 125.00
Figurine, Pluto, On Tricycle, Windup, Celluloid, Linemar 350.00
Figurine, Puppy, Standing, Lady & The Tramp, 1950s, 1 In. 55.00
Figurine, Shaggy Dog, Pajamas, Enesco, Label, 1960s, 5 In. 45.00
Figurine, Si The Cat, Lady & The Tramp, Hagen-Renaker, 1950s, 1 3/4 In. 200.00
Figurine, Sleepy, American Pottery, Label, 1930s, 5 1/2 In. 275.00
Figurine, Sleepy, Ceramic, Enesco, 1960s, 4 1/2 In. 30.00
Figurine, Sneezy, Enesco, 1960s, 4 1/2 In. 30.00
Figurine, Snow White & Seven Dwarfs, Bisque, 1930s, Box, 3 & 4 In., 8 Piece 300.00
Figurine, Snow White, Deer, Brayton Laguna, 1930s, 6 3/8 In. 275.00
Figurine, Snow White, Goebel, 1980s, 5 1/2 In. 175.00
Figurine, Sprite, Fantasia, No. 12, Vernon Kilns, 4 1/2 In. 240.00
Figurine, Stork From Dumbo 3850.00
Figurine, Trusty, Lady & The Tramp, Hagen-Renaker, 1950s, 2 In. 100.00
Figurine Set, 101 Dalmatians, Plastic, Unpainted, 1960s, 8 Piece 35.00
Fishbowl, Fantasia, Dark Pastel Pink, Vernon Kilns, 1940 .... 325.00
Flashlight, Mickey Mouse, 1930s 85.00
Flashlight, Zorro, Wrist, Vinyl Band 50.00

Flippers, Swimming, Mickey Mouse, Vinyl, 1960s 20.00
Game, Bowling, Mickey Mouse Soldier Set, Marbles, Marks Bro., 1930 .... 750.00
Game, Card, Donald Duck, Walt Disney's Disneyland, Box, 1955 .... 30.00
Game, Disneyland Monorail, Board, 1960 .... 50.00
Game, Donald Duck Bean Bag, Parker Brothers, Box, 1939 .... 200.00
Game, Magic Kingdom Pinball, Wolverine 30.00
Game, Mickey Mouse Club Bagatelle, Wolverine, 10 x 15 In. 200.00
Game, Mickey Mouse Hoop-La, Box, 1930s 258.00
Game, Mickey Mouse Pop-Up, Steeple Chase With Horses, 1982 .... 36.00
Game, Mickey Mouse Soldier Set, Box, Marks Brothers Toys, 1930s 725.00
Game, Peter Pan, Board 75.00
Game, Pinocchio, Card, Box, 1939 .... 45.00
Game, Pinocchio, Walt Disney, General Mills, 1971 .... 30.00
Game, Snow White & The Seven Dwarfs, Board, Milton Bradley, 1937 .... 295.00
Game, Tomorrowland, Rocket To The Moon, Parker Brothers, 1956 .... 65.00
Game, Zorro, Board, Unused, 1965 .... 61.00
Glass, Bianca, The Rescuers, Pepsi Series, 1977, 6 1/4 In. 6.00
Glass, Doc, Snow White & Seven Dwarfs 30.00
Glass, Donald Duck, Full Going Going Gone, Blue & Yellow Image, 1950s, 4 3/4 In. ... 20.00
Glass, Dopey, Snow White & Seven Dwarfs 30.00
Glass, Evinrude, The Rescuers Pepsi Series, 1977, 6 1/4 In. 6.00
Glass, Magic Kingdom Castle, Walt Disney World, 4 x 3 In. 2.00
Glass, Mickey Mouse Club, Mickey, Pluto, 1970s, 7 In. 10.00
Glass, Mickey's Christmas Carol, Goofy, Mickey, Scrooge, 1982, 6 In., 3 Piece 25.00
Glass, Monorail, Walt Disney World, 4 x 6 In. 2.00
Glass, Sleepy, Musical Note, Green Image, 1930s, 4 3/4 In. 55.00
Glass, Sneezy, Orange, 1930s, 4 1/4 In. 20.00
Glass, Snow White & Seven Dwarfs, 1930s, 8 Piece Set 195.00
Glass, Snow White, Red, 1930s, 4 1/4 In. 20.00
Goldfish Bowl, # 121, Pink, Vernon Kilns, 1940 .... 400.00
Guide, Disneyland, 1957 .... 60.00
Handkerchief, Sleepy & Happy Figures, Names, White, 1930s, Pair 10.00
Hat, Paper, Mickey, Minnie, Pluto, 3 Pigs, Wolf, Walt Disney Enterprises, 1930s ... 145.00
Head Visor, Disneyland, Elastic Strap, Pink, Pictures Tinkerbell, 1950s 75.00
Jar, Lollipop, Mickey Mouse, 1961 .... 375.00
Juice Set, Donald Duck, 4 Piece 95.00
Kid's Tattoos, Cockamamies Skin Pictures, Dynamic Toys, Unopened Box, 1969 ...... 23.00
Kitchen Set, Snow White, Wolverine, 3 Piece 110.00
Label, Bread, Donald Duck, Yellow, 1950s 6.00
Label, Bread, Hiawatha, Yellow, 1950s 6.00
Label, Bread, Pluto, Yellow, 1950s 6.00
Label, Bread, Sneezy, Yellow, 1950s 6.00
Lamp, Dumbo, Leeds 175.00
Lighter, Disneyland, Enameled Magic Kingdom Logo, WDP, Zippo, 1971 .... 191.00
Lighter, Mickey Mouse, Impressed, Polished Stainless Steel, Zippo, 1971 .... 382.00
Lunch Box, Disneyland Castle, 1957 .... 175.00
Lunch Box, Jungle Book, Metal, Aladdin, 1968 .... 85.00
Lunch Box, Ludwig Von Drake, Metal, Aladdin, 1962 .... 80.00
Lunch Box, Mickey Mouse Swinging Bridge 25.00
Lunch Box, Mickey Mouse, Original Tag 990.00
Lunch Box, Mickey's Head, With Thermos 35.00
Lunch Box, School Bus, Dome, Metal, 1969 .... 70.00 to 95.00
Magazine, Fortune Magazine, 8-Page Article On Disney & Silly Symphonies, 1934 .... 25.00
Map, Santa Fe & Disneyland Railroads, Paper, Black & White, 1950s, 10 x 12 In. 50.00
Mask, Donald Duck, Starched Linen 25.00
Mask, Dwarf Happy, Fishback, 1930s 75.00
Mask, Grumpy, Cloth, 1940s 45.00
Mask, Mickey Mouse, Cardboard, Frame, 8 1/2 x 7 In. 60.00
Mask, Snow White, Paper, 1937 .... 25.00
Menu, Carnation Ice Cream Parlor, Color Illustrations, Disneyland, 1955 .... 60.00
Mirror, Pocket, Mickey Mouse 10.00
Model Kit, Robin Hood, Royal Coach, Elephant, Prince John, Revell, Box, 1970s 65.00
Movie, Cinderella, Super 8 Silent, Box, 1960s 50.00

Movie Program, Fantasia, 1940s 38.00
Mug, Coffee, Donald Duck, Circus Vendor Selling Ice Cream, Patriot China, 1930 ...... 110.00
Mug, Disney Epcot Center, Plastic, 1982 .... 9.00
Mug, Doc, Ceramic, Raised Image, Handleless, Enesco, 1960s, 3 3/4 In. .... 35.00 to 45.00
Mug, Minnie Mouse, Face, Ceramic, Raised Image, Enesco, 1960s 30.00
Music Box, Snow White, Dopey, Sneezy, Ceramic, Schmid, 1970s, 9 In. 35.00
Night-Light, Sleepy Dwarf, Figural, Plaster, Painted, 1930s, 5 In. 20.00
Nodder, Pluto, Composition, Japan, 6 In. 115.00
Paperweight, Mickey Mouse, c.1935 .... 500.00
Pencil, Donald Duck Bread 20.00
Pencil, Mechanical, Mickey Mouse, Bakelite & Metal, Inkrograph Co., 1930s 120.00
Pencil, Mickey Mouse, Decal 80.00
Pencil Case, Mickey Mouse, Dixon 60.00
Pencil Case, Mickey Mouse, Donald, Pluto, Off To School, Hasbro, 1950s 30.00
Pencil Sharpener, Donald Duck 75.00
Pencil Sharpener, Mickey Mouse, Celluloid, Black, Red, 1930s, 3 In. 155.00
Pencil Sharpener, Snow White, Bakelite 65.00
Photo, Press, Tommy Kirk Being Kissed By Annette Funicello, Shaggy Dog, 1960 ..... 20.00
Picture, Luminous, Wynken, Blynken & Nod, Silly Symphony, Citroen, 1940s 45.00
Pin, Dopey, Wood Composition, Hand Painted, Brier Manufacturing, 1930s, 1 1/2 In. ... 45.00
Pin, Epcot Center Space Ship Earth, 1988, 2 1/4 In. 2.00
Pin, Jiminy Cricket Official Conscience Medal, Brass, Pinback, 1 1/4 In. 46.00
Pin, Little Mermaid, White Lettering, 1980s, 3 In. 3.00
Pin, Mickey Mouse Globe Trotter, Eat Freihofer's Perfect Loaf, 1930s 55.00
Pin, Mickey Mouse, Figural, Brier Manufacturing Co., Cloisonne, 1930s 85.00
Pin, Minnie Mouse, Evening Ledger Comics, Celluloid, 1 1/4 In. 714.00
Pin, Star Tours, Disneyland, C3PO & R2-D2, 1980s, 3 In. 15.00
Pin, Star Tours, Tokyo Disneyland, C3PO & R2-D2, 1980s, 3 1/2 In. 30.00
Pin, Star Tours, Walt Disney World, C3PO & R2-D2, 1980s, 3 In. 15.00
Pin, Tinkerbell, Figural, Colorful, 1960s 69.00
Pitcher, King Of Hearts, Regal 875.00
Planter, Bambi, Double Log 74.00
Planter, Bambi, Standing, Enesco 50.00
Planter, Dancing Mushroom, Fantasia, Vernon Kilns, 1940 .... 120.00
Planter, Donald Duck 95.00
Planter, Mickey Mouse, Ceramic, 1930s, 7 In. 70.00
Planter, Mickey Mouse, Cowboy, Leeds, Pre-1954, 6 1/2 In. .... 115.00 to 195.00
Planter, Mickey Mouse, Flowers & Figure 36.00
Planter, Mickey Playing Sax, Figural, Lusterware, 1930s, 4 In. 75.00
Planter, Thumper, Gold Trim 70.00
Plaque, Thermometer, Walt Disney Sportsman, Donald Duck Bowling, No. 1841 ...... 60.00
Plate, Christmas, 1977, Down The Chimney, Schmid, Box, 7 1/2 In. 75.00
Plate, Christmas, 1979, Santa Surprise, Schmid, Box, 7 1/2 In. 65.00
Plate, Christmas, 1981, Happy Holidays, Schmid, Box, 7 1/2 In. 50.00
Plate, Christmas, 1982, Winter Games, Schmid, Box, 7 1/2 In. 50.00
Plate, Christmas, 1983, Sneak Preview, Schmid, Box, 7 1/2 In. 50.00
Plate, Christmas, 1984, Command Performance, Schmid, Box, 7 1/2 In. 50.00
Plate, Christmas, 1985, Snow Biz, Schmid, Box, 7 1/2 In. 35.00
Plate, Christmas, 1987, Merry Mouse Medley, Schmid, Box, 7 1/2 In. 35.00
Plate, Christmas, 1988, Warm Winter Ride, Schmid, Box, 7 1/2 In. 35.00
Plate, Christmas, 1990, Holly Jolly Christmas, Schmid, Box, 7 1/2 In. 30.00
Plate, Disneyland, Castle, Open Slots In Rim, Gold Trim & Lettering, 1950s, 7 In. 20.00
Plate, Donald Duck, Ceramic, Made To Look Like Clock, 8 1/4 In. 44.00
Plate, Donald Duck, Circus Act, Patriot China, 3 Sections, 1930s, 8 In. 150.00
Plate, Fantasia, Nutcracker Suite, Blues & Yellows, Vernon Kilns, 7 1/2 In. 225.00
Plate, Hanging, Disneyland, Castle In Center, Round, 1960s, 7 In. 45.00
Plate, Minnie Mouse, Pluto, Patriot China, 3 Sections, 1930s, 8 In. 175.00
Play Set, Mickey Mouse, Pirate Ship, Ideal, Box 295.00
Postcard, Mickey Mouse, Planning Christmas Shopping, Sweden, 1940s 25.00
Postcard, Seven Dwarfs, At Mine, French, 1930s 28.00
Postcard, Snow White, Prince, Valentine & Sons, Ltd., England, 1930s 25.00
Postcard, Snow White, Seven Dwarfs, Singing, Valentine & Sons, Ltd., England, 1930s . 23.00
Poster, Goofy In A Boat, 17 x 23 In. 334.00

Poster, Pinocchio, Coco-Malt, 1939, 10 x 16 In. 90.00
Potty, Mickey & Minnie At Piano, Enamelware, Germany, 1932 .... 475.00
Projector, Donald Duck, Film 45.00
Projector, Mickey Mouse, Keystone, With 2 16mm Films, Box, c.1935, 10 In. 220.00
Puppet, Donald Duck, Die Cut Cardboard, Bread Promo 41.00
Puppet, Hand, Dopey, Composition Head, Cloth Body & Hat, 1930s 125.00
Puppet, Hand, Minnie Mouse, Gund 20.00
Puppet, Hand, Pinocchio, Composition Head, Cloth Body, 1930s 125.00
Puppet, Push-Up, Mickey Mouse, Original Package, 1978 .... 20.00
Purse, Donald Duck, Squeak, Vinyl, 1970s, 5 In. 15.00
Purse, Mickey Mouse, Mesh, Pie-Eye Mickey, 3 In. 137.00
Purse, Minnie Mouse & Pluto, 1950s 12.00
Puzzle, Interlocking, Sleeping Beauty, Jaymar, 1960s 20.00
Puzzle, Jigsaw, Mickey & Minnie Mouse In House Trailer, Jaymar, 1940s 40.00
Puzzle, Mickey Mouse Diving, Frame, 1950, 11 x 15 In. 35.00
Puzzle, Peter Pan, Flying To Neverland, Tray, Jaymar, 1950s 18.00
Puzzle, Sleeping Beauty, Interlocking Picture, Jaymar, Box, 1960s 20.00
Radio, Mickey Mouse Playing Cello, Emerson, Walt Disney, 1940, 5 x 7 In. 715.00
Raincoat, Child's, Mickey Mouse Club, Vinyl, Yellow, Fabil, Hong Kong, Size T2 .... 33.00
Record, Lady & The Tramp, Bella Notte, 78 RPM, Little Golden, 1955 .... 18.00
Record, Little Engine That Could, Booklet, Disneyland, 1969 .... 8.00
Record, Mickey Mouse Picture House Song, 78 RPM, Little Golden, 1950s 15.00
Record, Mouseketeer, 78 RPM, 1950s 38.00
Record Player, Mickey Mouse Club, Lionel Toy Corp., 13 x 11 1/4 x 6 In. 65.00
Ring, Sword In The Stone, Cereal Premium, Blue Plastic, 1970s 12.00
Rug, Minnie Mouse & Mickey Mouse, Fringed, 41 x 21 In. 105.00
Salt & Pepper, Figaro, Yellow, National Porcelain, 1940s, 2 1/2 In. 75.00
Salt & Pepper, Hop Low Mushroom, Vernon Kilns, 1940s ....110.00 to 300.00
Salt & Pepper, Napkin Holder, Snow White, Enesco, 3 Piece 535.00
Salt & Pepper, Sneezy, Bashful, Ceramic, Rubber Stopper, 1980s, 5 In. 50.00
Sheet Music, Bibbidi-Bobbidi-Boo, Cinderella 23.00
Sheet Music, Der Fuehrer's Face, Donald Duck, Disney 10.00
Sheet Music, Heigh-Ho, Snow White & Seven Dwarfs 15.00
Sheet Music, Make Mine Music, Johnny Fedora & Alice Blue Bonnet, 1946 .... 20.00
Sheet Music, Reluctant Dragon, Movie, 1941 .... 38.00
Sheet Music, Snow White & Seven Dwarfs, Australia, 1937 .... 16.00
Sheet Music, Sooner Or Later, Song Of The South, 1946 .... 15.00
Sheet Music, Story Of Robin Hood, Whistle My Love, 1950 .... 25.00
Sheet Music, That Darn Cat, Cat On Cover, 1964 .... 20.00
Sheet Music, The World Owes Me A Living, Silly Symphony, 1934 .... 90.00
Sheet Music, Two Silhouettes, Make Mine Music, Red Cover, 1945 .... 15.00
Sheet Music, Whistle My Love, Story Of Robin Hood, Live Action, 1950 .... 25.00
Sheet Music, Wringle Wrangle, Westward Ho The Wagons, Fess Parker, 1956 ....16.00 to 25.00
Shoe Dye, Scuffy, Brushless, Glass Bottle, WDP, Unused, Box, 4 In. 29.00
Shoes, Shower, Child's, Donald Duck, Mickey Mouse & Goofy, 8 In. 10.00
Soaky, Pinocchio, Figural, Red Plastic, WDP, 10 In. 25.00
Soap, Elmer Elephant, Figural, Lightfoot Schultz Co., 1930s, 3 3/4 In. ......20.00 to 25.00
Soap, Geppetto, Figural, Castille Soap, Lightfoot Schultz, Box, 1940, 3 1/2 In. 85.00
Soap, Geppetto, Modeled In Castile Soap, By Lightfoot Schultz Co., 4 In. 85.00
Soap, Mickey Mouse, Figural, Lightfoot Schultz, Box, 1930s, 4 1/2 In. 145.00
Soap, Pluto, Figural, Cussons Of England, Box, 1940s, 4 In. 95.00
Soap, Snow White, Figural, Decal Premium, Ben Rickert Inc., Box, 1980, 5 In. 32.00
Soap, Snow White, Set In Storybook Box, 1938 .... 200.00
Spoon, Mickey Mouse, Silver Plate, Branford, 1930s 25.00
Spoon & Fork, Mickey & Minnie, Silver Plate, Wm. Rogers & Son, Box, 1930s, 5 In. .. 325.00
Stamp Pad, & 2 Stamps, Minnie Mouse, Fulton Specialty Co., 1930s, 3 Piece 50.00
Store Display, Clarabelle Cow, Old King Cole, 15 1/2 In. 2200.00
Store Display, Goofy, Old King Cole, 13 x 12 In. 2350.00
Store Display, Pluto, Papier-Mache, Old King Cole, 15 x 11 In. 950.00
Sweatshirt, Mickey Mouse, Gray, Black, Red, Knit Trim, Size Child's Large 61.00
Switch Plate, Electric, Pinocchio, Hallmark, 4 3/4 x 7 3/4 In. 18.00
Tablet, School, Snow White & Seven Dwarfs, Hilroy Similar, 1938 .... 50.00
Tea Set, Mickey Mouse, Luster, Japan, 7 Piece 295.00

Tea Set, Snow White & Seven Dwarfs, Chein, Box, 10 Piece 110.00
Teacup, Donald Duck, Dancing, Wadeheath Of England, 1930s, 2 In. 100.00
T-shirt, Mickey Mouse, Black, Yellow, Red, Disney Character Fashion, Size Small 53.00
Thermometer, Donald Duck, Ceramic Tile, Walt Disney, 6 x 6 In. 50.00
Ticket, Epcot Opening Day, Oct. 1, 1982, Commemorative, In Silver Envelope 10.00
Toothbrush, Mickey Mouse 65.00
Toothbrush Holder, 3 Little Pigs, Porcelain, You'll Be Sorry, Brush Teeth, 1950 . . . . . .   350.00
Toothbrush Holder, Donald Duck, Profile, Bisque, Green Base, 1930s 255.00
Toothbrush Holder, Three Little Pigs 270.00
Toothbrush Holder, Three Little Pigs, Porcelain, Plaque, Evan K. Shaw, 1950s 350.00
Toy, Candy Factory, Mickey Mouse, Remco, 24 Molds, Box, 1973 . . . .   95.00
Toy, Cinderella & Prince Charming Dance, Windup, Box, 1960s 140.00
Toy, Doc & Dopey Dwarfs, Banging Drum, On Cart, #770, Fisher Price, 1937 . . . .   450.00
Toy, Donald Duck & Pluto Cart, Celluloid, Windup, Japan, Box 4070.00
Toy, Donald Duck, Car, Dipsy, Windup, Tin Lithograph, Japan, Box 1400.00
Toy, Donald Duck, Car, Friction, Tinplate, Linemar 200.00
Toy, Donald Duck, Cup & Saucer, Ohio Art 25.00
Toy, Donald Duck, Dapper, Fisher-Price, No. 460, 1936 . . . .   575.00
Toy, Donald Duck, Dapper, Pull Toy, Lithograph, #460, Fisher Price, 1936 . . . .   575.00
Toy, Donald Duck, Delivery Truck, Celluloid, Tin, Friction Drive, Linemar, 6 In. 585.00
Toy, Donald Duck, Doughboy, Between 2 Cannons, Fisher-Price, No. 744, 1942 . . . .   1200.00
Toy, Donald Duck, Drummer, Linemar 650.00
Toy, Donald Duck, Handcar, Pluto, Metal Doghouse, Lionel, 1930s, 10 1/2 In. 402.00
Toy, Donald Duck, On Scooter, Disney Delivery, Windup, Plastic, WDP, 1950s, 5 In. 172.00
Toy, Donald Duck, On Tricycle, Windup, Tin Lithograph, Celluloid Figure, Linemar 575.00
Toy, Donald Duck, Plush, Germany, 1950s 62.00
Toy, Donald Duck, Squeeze, Molded, Enamel Paint, Dell, 1950, 6 1/2 In. 32.00
Toy, Donald Duck, Truck, Delivery, Celluloid, Tin, Friction Drive, Linemar, 6 In. 585.00
Toy, Donald Duck, Walker, Metal, Painted, Creation Toys Of France, Box 1075.00
Toy, Donald Duck, Walking, Plastic 30.00
Toy, Ferdinand The Bull, Tin Lithograph, Windup, Marx, 1938 . . . .   185.00
Toy, Hand Car, Track, Mickey & Minnie, Windup, Tin, Composition, Lionel, 1930s, 9 In.   575.00
Toy, March Hare, Bendable, Clothing, Marx, 1960s, 6 In. 75.00
Toy, Mickey Mouse & Minnie Mouse, Acrobats, Windup, Celluloid, Japan, Box, 11 In. . .   1035.00
Toy, Mickey Mouse Trapeze, Windup, Plastic, Wire, c.1930s, 5 1/2 In. 525.00
Toy, Mickey Mouse, Airplane, Mickey's Airmail, Sun Rubber, 1940s, 6 In. 100.00
Toy, Mickey Mouse, Banjo Player, Windup, Celluloid, Disney, 1930s 1575.00
Toy, Mickey Mouse, Drummer, Battery Operated, Linemar, Box, 1950s, 10 In. 1400.00
Toy, Mickey Mouse, Drummer, Windup, Tin Lithograph, 1930s, 6 5/8 In. 546.00
Toy, Mickey Mouse, Fun-E-Flex, Pie-Eyed, Walt E. Disney, Standing, 5 In. 395.00
Toy, Mickey Mouse, Magic Show, Box 75.00
Toy, Mickey Mouse, Moving Van, Mousekemovers, Friction, Linemar, Box 1250.00
Toy, Mickey Mouse, On Trapeze Between Wooden Trees, Windup, 1930s 1950.00
Toy, Mickey Mouse, Plush, c.1940, 25 In. 55.00
Toy, Mickey Mouse, Pull Toy, Wooden Wagon, Toy Kraft Co., 1930s, 5 x 9 In. 250.00
Toy, Mickey Mouse, Riding Bucking Horse, Windup 5400.00
Toy, Mickey Mouse, Rolling Action, Key Wind, Gabriel, 1978 . . . .   75.00
Toy, Mickey Mouse, Rolykin, Ball Bearing, 1960s 12.00
Toy, Mickey Mouse, Train Set, Meteor, No. 932, Marx 650.00
Toy, Mickey Mouse, Typewriter, Mouseketeers, A.T. Cohn, Box 58.00
Toy, Mickey Mouse, Walking Phone 50.00
Toy, Mickey Mouse, Whirligig, Windup, Celluloid, Long Snout, Pie Eyes, 7 In. 1995.00
Toy, Mickey Mouse, Windup, Plastic, WDP, Marx, Japan, 4 1/2 In. 57.00
Toy, Mickey Mouse, Windup, Tumbles, Velvet, Metal-Frame, Metal Eyes, 4 In. 525.00
Toy, Minnie Mouse, In Rocking Chair, Tin, Windup, Linemar, c.1950, 6 In. 319.00
Toy, Minnie Mouse, On Trapeze Between Wooden Trees, Windup, 1930s 1950.00
Toy, Minnie Mouse, Rocking, Knitting, Tin Lithograph, Windup, Mar Line Toys 450.00
Toy, Minnie Mouse, Umbrella, Bisque, 1930s, 4 In. 100.00
Toy, Pinocchio The Acrobat, Walt Disney Prod., 1939 . . . .   875.00
Toy, Pinocchio, Plays Cymbals, Windup, Tin, Japan, 11 1/2 In. 150.00
Toy, Pinocchio, Waddles, Eyes Move, Windup, Tin, Marx, 1939 . . . .   475.00
Toy, Pinocchio, Walker, Marx, Box 1150.00
Toy, Pinocchio, Walker, Windup, Linemar, Box 925.00

Toy, Pinocchio, Walker, Windup, Metal, Creation Toys Of France, Box 975.00
Toy, Pinocchio, Xylophone 295.00
Toy, Pluto, Battery Operated, Plastic, Illco, 9 In. 85.00
Toy, Pluto, Drum Major, Tin 530.00
Toy, Pluto, Squeaker, Plush, Molded, Walt Disney Prod., 1960s, 11 x 4 x 12 In. 185.00
Toy, Pluto, Twirling Tail, Molded Plastic, Yellow, W.D. Prod., Marx, Box, 5 1/2 In. 133.00
Toy, Pluto, Windup, Blows Party Horn, Tin, Rubber, Linemar, Japan, 6 1/2 In. 395.00
Toy, Pluto, Windup, Tin Lithograph, Tin Ears, Rubber Tail, 1950s, 5 In. 340.00
Toy, Pongo, Anita, Roger, Cruella, Horace, Jasper, Plastic, White, Marx, 1960s, Set Of 8 . 35.00
Toy, Ramp Walker, Donald Duck, With Wheelbarrow 30.00
Toy, Snow White & Seven Dwarfs, Top, Chein 100.00
Toy, Telephone & Lamp, Mickey Mouse, Rotary Dial, 1973, 26 In. 160.00
Toy, Telephone, Mickey Mouse, 14 In. ....55.00 to 62.00
Toy, Telephone, Mickey Mouse, Brass Dial Ring, 1976, 15 In. 125.00
Toy, Train, Casey Jr., Plastic Engine, 3 Tin Lithograph Cars, Disney Characters, Marx ... 155.00
Transfer, Donald Duck, McCall Kaumagraph, 2 Large Patterns, Envelope, 1940 ...... 35.00
Umbrella, Mickey Mouse & Minnie Mouse 120.00
Viewer, Mickey Mouse, 13 Filmstrips 145.00
Wall Hanging, Bambi & Thumper In Woods, Tapestry, Belgium, 44 x 60 In. 55.00
Waste Can, Mickey Mouse, Minnie In Car, Out Of Gas Sign, Tin Lithograph 90.00
Watch, Pocket, Mickey Mouse, Fob, Ingersoll, Box, 2 In. 330.00
Watch Fob, Mickey Mouse 125.00
Wrapper, Bubble Gum, Mickey Mouse, 1930s 145.00
Wrapper, Mickey Mouse Toasted Nut Chocolate, 1930s 115.00
Wristwatch, Cinderella, White Plastic Strap, In White Plastic Slipper, Bradley, 1970s ... 35.00
Wristwatch, Goofy, Arms Revolve In Reverse, Helbros, 1972 .... 570.00
Wristwatch, Mickey Mouse, Birthday Cake Box, 1947 .... 600.00
Wristwatch, Mickey Mouse, Bradley 85.00
Wristwatch, Mickey Mouse, Chrome Body, Yellow Leather Band, Ingersoll 65.00
Wristwatch, Mickey Mouse, Expansion Band, Ingersoll, WDP, 1950s 255.00
Wristwatch, Mickey Mouse, Ingersoll, Metal, Plastic Crystal, Vinyl Band, c.1950 ..... 302.00
Wristwatch, Mickey Mouse, Mickey On Metal Band, Ingersoll, 1930s 375.00
Wristwatch, Mickey Mouse, Red Trousers, Mickey Forms Each Side, Ingersoll 500.00
Wristwatch, Mickey Mouse, U.S. Time, Blue Plastic Band, No Crystal 45.00
Wristwatch, Tron, LCD Quartz, Clear Plastic Box, 1970s 50.00
Writing Paper, Envelopes, Box, Donald Duck, Whitman Publishing, 1949, 5 x 4 In. ... 30.00
Xylophone, Box 235.00

DOCTOR, see Dental; Medical

DOLL entries are listed by marks printed or incised on the doll, if possible. If there are no marks, the doll is listed by the name of the subject or country or maker. Notice that Barbie is listed under Mattel. G.I.
Joe figures are listed in the Toy section.

A.M., 5, Mabel, Bisque, Kid Body, Sleep Eyes, Open Mouth, 4 Teeth, c.1910, 21 In. 55.00
A.M., 6/0, Baby Betty, Bisque, Papier-Mache, Sleep Eyes, 4 Teeth, Box, c.1912, 12 In. ... 650.00
A.M., 12, Mabel, Bisque, Kid Body, Open Mouth, 5 Teeth, Black Dress, c.1910, 13 In. ... 77.00
A.M., 15, Lilly, Bisque, Kid Body, Open Mouth, 4 Teeth, Lace Dress, c.1910, 13 In. 77.00
A.M., 200, Googly, Fat-Cheeked Face, Sleep Eyes To Side, Tip Of Tongue, 10 In. 3100.00
A.M., 211, Floradora, Bisque, Cork-Stuffed Body, Sleep Eyes, 3 Teeth, 1895, 22 In. 121.00
A.M., 233, Bisque, Composition Body, Sleep Eyes, Open Mouth, 2 Teeth, 8 In. 247.00
A.M., 241, Googly, Boy, Bisque Head, Side-Glancing Eyes, Jointed, c.1920, 12 In. 2400.00
A.M., 310, Just Me, Bisque Head, Sleep Eyes, 5 Piece Composition Body, 9 In. .....*Illus* 1050.00
A.M., 323, Bisque Head, Googly, Girl, Side-Glancing Sleep Eyes, Dress, 1920, 8 In. 800.00
A.M., 323, Googly, Side-Glancing Sleep Eyes, Toddler Body, 9 1/2 In. 1500.00
A.M., 326, Boy, Toddler, Original Cotton Romper, 15 In. 450.00
A.M., 341, Bisque, Cotton Body, Sleep Eyes, White Gown, c.1910, 12 In. 110.00
A.M., 351, Black, Glass Eyes, 2 Teeth, 5 In. 425.00
A.M., 353, Bisque, Little Emperor, Sleep Eyes, Amber Tinted Solid Dome, 12 In. 1250.00
A.M., 370 M-2 Ox, Bisque, Kid Body, Sleep Eyes, Open Mouth, 4 Teeth, 1900, 17 In. ... 121.00
A.M., 370, Bisque, Cloth, Composition Limbs, Sleep Eyes, 4 Teeth, c.1910, 13 In. 88.00
A.M., 370, Bisque, Kid Body, Blond, Sleep Eyes, Open Mouth, 4 Teeth, 1910, 19 In. 181.00
A.M., 370, Bisque, Kid Body, Blue Sleep Eyes, Open Mouth, 4 Teeth, c.1910, 18 In. 99.00

A.M., 370, Bisque, Kid Body, Open Mouth, 5 Teeth, Red Lace Dress, c.1910, 15 In. 110.00
A.M., 370, Bisque, Kid Body, Sleep Eyes, Open Mouth, 4 Teeth, Gray Skirt, 1910, 19 In. .   73.00
A.M., 370, Child, Bisque, Fixed Eyes, Open Mouth, Teeth, Kid Body, Not Dressed, 22 In.   145.00
A.M., 390, Bisque, Black, Composition Body, 26 In. 1950.00
A.M., 390, Bisque, Composition Body, Sleep Eyes, Open Mouth, 4 Teeth, 1910, 16 In. 151.00
A.M., 390, Bisque, Composition, Sleep Eyes, Open Mouth, 4 Teeth, c.1900, 14 In. 66.00
A.M., 390, Bisque, Composition, Sleep Eyes, Open Mouth, 4 Teeth, c.1910, 28 In. 220.00
A.M., 390, German Dancer, Bisque, Composition, Sleep Eyes, 4 Teeth, c.1900, 24 In. 275.00
A.M., 390, Nun, Bisque Head, Sleep Eyes, 4 Teeth, Jointed Body, 20 In. 295.00
A.M., 590, Boy, Character, Bisque, Composition, Wood, Jointed, Sleep Eyes, 1912, 16 In.   1350.00
A.M., 590, Child, Character, Open-Close Mouth, Jointed Body, 18 In. 1900.00
A.M., 640, Bisque, Kid Body, Painted Eyes, Black Pants, Jacket, c.1910, 13 In. 192.00
A.M., 990, Baby, Character, Composition Body, 26 In. 1250.00
A.M., 1894, Bisque, Composition, 4 Teeth, Mushroom-Gathering Outfit, 1895, 10 In. 302.00
A.M., 3200, Bisque, Kid Body, 4 Teeth, Open Mouth, White, Green Outfit, c.1910, 14 In. .   77.00
A.M., A-7-M, Floradora, Child, Bisque, Open Mouth, Teeth, Kid Body, 23 In. 155.00
A.M., Alma, Bisque, Kid Body, Brown Eyes, Open Mouth, 4 Teeth, 1910, 12 In. 73.00
A.M., Baby Kiddiejoy, Bisque, Cotton Body, Brown Sleep Eyes, c.1910, 14 In. 165.00
A.M., Baby, 5 Piece Composition Body, Open Mouth, 2 Teeth, 17 In. 695.00
A.M., Child, Bisque Head, Kid Body, Bisque Arms, Old Clothes, 12 In. 192.00
A.M., Dream Baby, Bisque Head, Cloth Body, Composition Hands, 21 In. 345.00
A.M., Floradora, Bisque, Kid Body, Sleep Eyes, Open Mouth, 4 Teeth, 1910, 20 In. 121.00
A.M., Floradora, Bisque, Kid Body, Sleep Eyes, Open Mouth, 4 Teeth, c.1900, 17 In. 121.00
A.M., Floradora, Bisque, Kid Body, Sleep Eyes, Open Mouth, 4 Teeth, c.1910, 16 In. 99.00
A.M., Floradora, Bisque, Kid Body, Sleep Eyes, Open Mouth, 4 Teeth, c.1910, 25 In. 99.00
A.M., Googly, Blue Eyes, Blond Mohair Wig, Cotton Frock, 12 In. 1495.00
A.M., Googly, Nobbie Kid, Blue Eyes, Nurse's Outfit, 7 In. 995.00
A.M., Lilly, Bisque, Kid Body, Blond, Sleep Eyes, Open Mouth, 5 Teeth, 1910, 11 1/2 In.   109.00
A.M., M-370, Child, Bisque, Kid Jointed Body, Open Mouth, Teeth, Dressed, 29 In. 220.00
A.M., Mabel, Kid Body, Brown Sleep Eyes, Open Mouth, 4 Teeth, 1905, 13 In. 73.00
Adolf Hulss, 156/6, Toddler, Bisque Head, Sleep Eyes, Open Mouth, Blond, 14 In. ..*Illus*   700.00
Advertising, Bart Simpson, Burger King, Paper Surfboard, Poly Bag 10.00
Advertising, Big Boy, Cloth, Vinyl Head, EBR Inc., 9 In. 10.00
Advertising, Blue Bonnet Sue, Cloth, 1986, 13 In. ....15.00 to 20.00
Advertising, Bud Man, Rubber, Flesh Color, Red Outfit, Budweiser Back, 1960s, 18 In. .   155.00
Advertising, Bunny, Nestle's Quik, Plush 45.00
Advertising, Campbell's Soup, Cloth, Military Uniforms, World War II, 11 In., Set Of 2 .   240.00
Advertising, Cap'n Crunch, Quaker, Stuffed, 1992, 18 In. 28.00
Advertising, Captain Scarlet, Sugar Smacks Box, 1967 ....   250.00
Advertising, Dairy Queen, 1974, 12 1/2 In. 25.00
Advertising, Elsie The Cow, Borden's, Pink Plush, Rubber Head, Moos 90.00
Advertising, Eskimo Pie, Pillow, 1970s, 15 In. 15.00
Advertising, Holland America Cruises, Sailor, Rag Doll, 1950s, 11 In. ....46.00 to 65.00
Advertising, Hotpoint, Wooden, Painted, Movable Joints, 14 In. 320.00

Doll, A.M., 310, Just Me, Bisque Head, Sleep Eyes, 5 Piece Composition Body, 9 In.

Doll, Adolf Hulss, 156/6, Toddler, Bisque Head, Sleep Eyes, Open Mouth, Blond, 14 In.

Advertising, Huggins, By Hallmark, Dressed, 1985 .... 5.00
Advertising, Jolly Green Giant, Stuffed, 1960s, 16 In. 24.00
Advertising, Jolly Green Giant, Vinyl, Box, 1970s 195.00
Advertising, Li'l Sprout, Talking, Plush, 1980s 45.00
Advertising, Milky, Nestle, Stuffed, 1984, 4 In. 18.00
Advertising, Mr. Crisp, Mount Olive Pickle, Pillow, 1970s, 14 In. 20.00
Advertising, Nabob Coffee, Canadian 95.00
Advertising, Northern Tissue, White, Package, 17 In. 25.00
Advertising, Ronald McDonald, Cloth 15.00
Advertising, Squirt, Vinyl, 1961 .... 210.00
Advertising, Tony The Tiger, Frosted Flakes, Vinyl 95.00
Alexander dolls are listed in this category under Madame Alexander.
Alf, Talking, Box, 1980s 250.00
Alt, Beck & Gottschalck, 83/125/16 1/2, Bisque, Sleep Eyes, Open Mouth, 1911, 7 In. 109.00
Alt, Beck & Gottschalck, 1362, Bisque, Child, 4 Upper Teeth, Silk Dress, 22 In. 250.00
Amberg, Newborn Babe, Bisque, Muslin, Sleep Eyes, Mama Squeaker, Label, 1914, 6 In. 400.00
American, Baby, Rubber, c.1940, 15 In. 27.00
American, Bisque, Crying Face, Tag, By Claire Mueller, Bozeman, Montana, 9 In. 55.00
American, Hard Plastic, Molded Hair, Sleep Eyes, 4 Teeth, Squawk Box, c.1945, 25 In. .. 66.00
American, Papier-Mache, Molded Hair, Leather Cotton-Stuffed Body, c.1860, 21 In. 110.00
American Character, Sweet Sue, Vinyl Head, Sleep Eyes, Adult Body, Box, 19 In. *Illus* 305.00
Armand Marseille dolls are listed in this category under A.M.
Art Fabric Mills, Topsy, Printed Cotton, Uncut, Shrinkwrapped, 1900, 19 In. 345.00
Automaton, Boy, Playing Violin, Head Turns, Sleep Eyes, Papier-Mache, France 2995.00
Automaton, Dancing Gypsy Girl, Body Turns Side To Side, Hand Shakes Tambourine .. 4795.00
Automaton, Rabbit, Cabbage, Fur Cover, Papier-Mache, France, 19 In. ....*Illus* 9000.00
Automaton, Woman, Papier-Mache, Metal Base, Circles Around, Vichy, c.1850, 10 In. . 1500.00
Averill, Bonnie Babe, Bisque Head, Blue Sleep Eyes, Brown Curly Hair, 1920, 11 In. ... 950.00
Averill, Bonnie Babe, Bisque Head, Blue Sleep Eyes, Open Mouth, Composition, 16 In. . 1200.00
Averill, Bonnie Babe, Bisque Head, Cloth Body, Celluloid Hands, Old Clothes, 12 In. . 440.00
Averill, Bonnie Babe, Celluloid Head, Muslin Body, 2 Teeth, Tongue, c.1925, 18 In. 1300.00
Averill, Character, Child, Sonny, Bisque, Label On Chest, 5 5/8 In. 195.00
Averill, Little Lulu, Cloth, Painted, Yarn Hair, 1930s, 36 In. 200.00
Baby, All Bisque, Jointed Hips & Shoulders, Attached Bottles, Germany, 5 1/2 In. 55.00
Baby, Black, Composition, Molded Hair, 3 Yarn Tufts, Painted Eyes, Jointed, 10 In. 22.00
Baby, Celluloid, Flesh Toned, Painted Face Features, 1940s, 1 3/4 In., Set Of 3 .... 34.00
Baby Peggy, Kid Body, Bisque Hands, Child Movie Star, Autographed, 20 1/2 In. 2350.00
Baby Sandy, Composition, 11 In. 250.00
Bahr & Proschild, 204, Bisque, Blue Sleep Eyes, Open Mouth, 10 1/2 In. 1150.00
Bahr & Proschild, 261, Blue Spiral Threaded Eyes, Open Mouth, Blond Wig, 15 In. ... 1800.00
Bahr & Proschild, 275, Bisque Socket Head, Brown Eyes, Open Mouth, 1888, 11 In. .. 1050.00
Bahr & Proschild, 513, Bisque Head, Mohair, Old Clothes & Hat, 36 In. 1150.00
Bahr & Proschild, 520, Girl, Bisque, Composition, Wood, Jointed, c.1912, 13 In. 2500.00
Bahr & Proschild, 620, Boy, Toddler, Character, Bisque, Sleep Eyes, Jointed, 12 1/2 In. 546.00
Barbie dolls are listed in this category under Mattel.
Barrois, Bisque Swivel Head, Kid Fashion Body, Jointed, c.1865, 14 In. 2600.00
Belton, Bisque, Brown Paperweight Eyes, Closed Mouth, Cabinet Size 1950.00
Belton, Bisque, Wig, Paperweight Eyes, Nurse's Uniform, Extra Clothes, 15 In. 2995.00
Belton, Closed Mouth, Paperweight Eyes, Dressed, 11 In. 1100.00
Bergmann dolls are also in this category under Simon & Halbig.
Bisque, 2-Face Baby, Crying 1 Side, Smiling Other, Nursing Gown & Cap, 12 In. 1295.00
Bisque, Baby, Seated, Naked, Scowling, Blue Side-Glancing Eyes, Germany, 5 In. 500.00
Bisque, Baby, Young Boy, Seated, Blue Side-Glancing Eyes, Orange Cap, 1910, 5 In. ... 425.00
Bisque, Blue Glass Eyes, Blond Hair, Closed Mouth, 1880, 21 In. 2100.00
Bisque, Head & Torso, Blue Painted Eyes, Closed Mouth, Germany, 1915, 6 In. 250.00
Bisque, Hinged Shoulders & Hips, Closed Mouth, Mohair Wig, Germany, 3 3/4 In. 60.00
Bisque, J.M. 4/0 Mark, Composition & Wood Body, Jointed, France, c.1880, 13 In. 8500.00
Bisque, Mignonette, Bride, Groom, Jointed Limbs, France, c.1900, 2 In., Pair 400.00
Bisque, Mignonette, Jointed, Communion Costume, Original Box, France, c.1880, 3 In. . 325.00
Bisque, Plump Cheeks, Paperweight Eyes, Period Clothes, Shoes, 14 In. 2600.00
Bisque, Polichinelle, Head, Straw Arms & Legs, Carved Feet, France, 1890, 13 In. 1500.00
Bisque, Polichinelle, Padded Limbs, Wooden Feet, Silk Costume, France, c.1885, 22 In. . 2600.00
Bisque, Polichinelle, Socket Head, Original Costume, Wood Feet, France, c.1880, 18 In. . 2800.00

Doll, American
Character, Sweet
Sue, Vinyl Head, Sleep
Eyes, Adult Body,
Box, 19 In.

Doll, Automaton,
Rabbit, Cabbage, Fur
Cover, Papier-Mache,
France, 19 In.

Bisque, Shoulder Head, Paperweight Eyes, Cloth Body, Late 19th Century, 15 In.	375.00
Bisque, Sleep Eyes, Brown Wig, Composition Body, 21 In.	690.00
Bisque, Sleep Eyes, Open Mouth, Auburn Wig, Jointed Composition Body, 12 In.	165.00
Bisque, Swivel Shoulder Head, Sleep Eyes, Mohair Wig, Cloth Body, Kid Arms, 24 In.	750.00
Black dolls are included in the Black category.	
Borgfeldt, Chanticleer, Rooster, Child's Face, Mohair Plush, Celluloid, c.1905, 10 In.	450.00
Boudoir, Carmen Miranda, Original Outfit, 28 In.	650.00
Bru Jne, Bisque Head, Walking, Crying, Upper Teeth, Composition Body, 21 In.	1495.00
Bru Jne, Bisque Swivel Head, Patented Wood Body, Jointed, c.1869, 17 In.	9000.00
Bru Jne, Fashion, Bisque Swivel Head, Kid Body, Bisque Hands, c.1867, 15 In.	4000.00
Bruno Schmidt, Tommy Tucker, Sleep Eyes, Closed Mouth, Ball-Jointed Body, 24 In.	2450.00
Bucherer, Mutt & Jeff, Composition, Metal, Jointed, c.1925, 6 1/2 & 8 In.	550.00
Bucherer, Peter Rabbit, Metal, Composition Ball-Jointed, 8 In.	660.00
Buddy Lee, Plastic, Lee On Hat, Painted Eyes, 12 In. ....*Illus*	350.00
Bugs Bunny, Masked Face, Felt Body, Partial Tag, 1930s, 26 In.	100.00
Butler Brothers, Bertha, China Head, Kid Body, Blue Dress, Germany, c.1905, 24 In.	99.00
Butler Brothers, Marion, China Head, Kid Body, Blond Hair, Germany, c.1905, 24 In.	110.00
Bye-Lo, Baby, 1-Piece Head, Light Brown Baby Hair, Closed Mouth, 1925, 4 In., Pair	800.00
Bye-Lo, Baby, Bisque Head, Brown Sleep Eyes, Brown Hair, Germany, 1923, 12 In.	575.00
Bye-Lo, Baby, Bisque Head, Celluloid Hands, Cloth Body, Undressed, 9 3/4 In.	357.00
Bye-Lo, Baby, Bisque Head, Sleep Eyes, Cloth Body & Legs, Putnam, 1920s, 13 In.	375.00
Bye-Lo, Baby, Bisque, Cotton Body, Blue Sleep Eyes, Putnam, c.1923, 10 In.	275.00
Bye-Lo, Baby, Bisque, Sleep Eyes, Cloth Body, Christening Dress, Putnam, 1920s, 10 In.	400.00
Bye-Lo, Baby, Blue Sleep Eyes, Cloth Body & Legs, Celluloid Hands, Putnam, 13 In.	375.00
Bye-Lo, Baby, Closed Mouth, Painted Hair, Cloth Body, Celluloid Hands, Dressed, 13 In.	350.00
Bye-Lo, Baby, Sleep Eyes, Cloth Body, Celluloid Hands, Putnam, 16 In.	460.00
Bye-Lo, Bisque, Cloth Body, Celluloid Hands, Grace S. Putnam, 10 In. ....185.00 to	275.00
Bye-Lo, Factory Clothes, Signed Body, 13 In.	650.00
Bye-Lo, Toddler, Layette, Box, 12 In.	2500.00
Cabbage Patch, Preemie, Pacifier, Signed, 1983	120.00
Carrie, Little House On Prairie, Box, 1978, 14 In.	85.00
Casimir, Bisque Swivel Head, Kid-Lined Shoulder Plate, Feathered Brows, 12 In.	7000.00
Celluloid, Baby, Jointed Arms & Legs, Painted Eyes, Molded Hair, Dressed, 10 In.	70.00
Celluloid, Fat Jointed Cloth Body, Original Outfit, 12 In., Pair	1250.00
Celluloid, Sleep Eyes, Antique Embroidered Dress, 13 In.	50.00
Celluloid, Woman, Painted Features, Shoes, Socks, Original Clothes, 1920s, 12 In.	75.00
Chad Valley, Pirate, Felt, Glass Eyes, Painted Features, Original Clothing, 20 In.	1380.00
Chad Valley, Princess Elizabeth, Portrait, Glass Eyes, 14 In.	950.00
Character, Baby, Bisque, Intaglio Eyes, Painted Hair, Germany, 9 In.	105.00
Character, Jockey, Bisque Head, Mustache, Cloth Body, Germany, 8 In.	195.00
Character, Sweet Sue, 9-Piece Walker Body, Sunday Best Outfit, c.1955, 24 In.	1100.00
Character, Vinyl Head, Toni Bride, 6-Piece Body, Bridal Gown, c.1958, 19 In.	225.00
Chase, Baby, Ball-Jointed, Weighted Body, 22 In.	895.00

Chein, Krazy Kat, Jointed, Wood, Stenciled Face, Decal On Foot, 7 In. 632.00

China, Civil War, Cloth Body, Germany, 13 1/2 In. 165.00

China, Glass Eyes, Gusseted Kid Body, China Lower Limbs, Wool Dress, 14 In. 1840.00

China, Shoulder Head, Cloth Body, Original Dress, Germany, 11 In. 145.00

Cloth, Alabama Baby Type, Oil Painted Stockinet Head, Coarse Hair, 21 In. ....*Illus* 925.00

Cloth, Boy, Harry, Round Arms & Legs, Printed Union Suit, Socks & Shorts, 15 1/2 In. . 172.00

Cloth, Felt Hat, Dress, Shoes, Auburn Mohair Wig, Germany, 17 In. 268.00

Coleco, Thidwick The Big Hearted Moose, Dr. Seuss, 1983, 16 In. 90.00

DEP, 15, Bisque Socket Head, Sleep Eyes, 4 Teeth, Human Hair, Jointed, c.1900, 35 In. .. 2900.00

DEP, Bebe Tete, Child, Bisque, Paperweight Eyes, Composition, Jointed, 18 In. 550.00

DEP, Bisque, Blue Eyes, Old Clothes, 23 In. 2095.00

Dollhouse, Bisque, Molded Hair, Cloth Body, Germany, 4 1/2 In. 85.00

Dollhouse, China Head, Shoulder Head, Wavy Molded Hair, Germany, 6 In. 75.00

Dollhouse, Man, Bisque, Molded Top Hat, Black Felt Suit With Tails, 3 1/2 In. 22.00

Dressel, Bisque, Composition, Jointed, Sleep Eyes, Open Mouth, 2 Teeth, c.1910, 14 In. . 363.00

Dresser, Black Bodice, White Lace Sleeves, Roses On Skirt, Japan, 6 x 4 In. 175.00

Effanbee, Anne Shirley, Composition Head, Composition Body, 27 In. 500.00

Effanbee, Bubbles, Composition Shoulder Head, Molded Hair, Muslin Torso, 16 In. 300.00

Effanbee, Bubbles, Composition, Molded Hair, Tin Sleep Eyes, 2 Teeth, c.1924, 18 In. 176.00

Effanbee, Charlie McCarthy, Working Mouth, Black Tuxedo, Bow Tie, Top Hat, 17 In. .. 500.00

Effanbee, George & Martha Washington, Tiltable Heads, Period Clothing, 9 In., Pair 390.00

Effanbee, Honey, Hard Plastic, c.1950, 16 In. 27.00

Effanbee, Honey, Walker, Bride, Blue Sleep Eyes, Blond Saran Wig, 1954, 14 1/2 In. .. 225.00

Effanbee, Jackie Gleason, Honeymooners, Plastic, Bus Driver Uniform, 1966, 16 In. 40.00

Effanbee, Patricia, Composition, c.1930, 14 In. 110.00

Effanbee, Patsy Ann, Tin Sleep Eyes, Lashes, Original Outfit, c.1928, 19 In. 575.00

Effanbee, Patsy Ann, With Pooh Bear, Original Dress, Shoes & Socks, 1930, 15 In. 300.00

Effanbee, Patsy Lou, Composition Head, Sleep Eyes, Molded Hair, 22 In. ....*Illus* 500.00

Effanbee, Patsy Mae, Composition, Sleep Eyes, Mohair Lashes, Closed Mouth, 30 In. ... 1200.00

Effanbee, Patsyette, 9 In. 275.00

Effanbee, Popeye, Corn Cob Pipe, Cloth, 16 In. 1850.00

Effanbee, Sweetie Pie, All Composition, White Organdy Dress, Pink Trim, 20 In. 350.00

Effanbee, Walker, Honey, Plastic, Rabbit Fur Coat, Muff, Trunk, 14 In. 435.00

Effanbee, Wee Patsy, Composition, 1930s, 6 In. 200.00

Endelman, 12, Bisque, Composition, Sleep Eyes, Open Mouth, 2 Teeth, 1921, 24 In. ... 220.00

Fashion, Cobalt Blue Glass Eyes, Pierced Ears, Striped Dress, France, 17 In. 4650.00

Felix, Glass Eyes, Metal Nose, Squeaker, 1920s, 15 In. 485.00

Flintstones, Fred, Hanna-Barbara Productions, 1960, 12 In. 31.00

Folk, Black, Cloth, Painted Face, Early 19th Century, 25 In. 66.00

Franz Schmidt, Bisque Head, Sleep Eyes, Jointed, With Trunk, Clothes, 1920s, 11 In. .. 1495.00

Fred Flintstone, Cloth, 1972, 7 1/2 In. 15.00

Fred Flintstone, Vinyl, 1960, 13 In. 85.00

Doll, Buddy Lee, Plastic,
Lee On Hat, Painted Eyes,
12 In.

Doll, Cloth, Alabama Baby Type, Oil
Painted Stockinet Head, Coarse
Hair, 21 In.

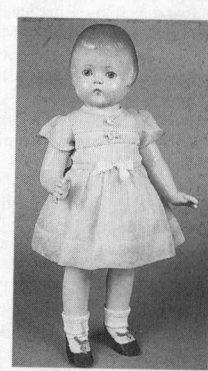

Doll, Effanbee, Patsy Lou,
Composition Head, Sleep
Eyes, Molded Hair, 22 In.

French, Bisque, Blond Wig, Paperweight Eyes, Ball-Jointed Body, 17 In. 3737.00
French, Bisque, Blue Paperweight Eyes, Wheat Blond Hair, Striped Aqua Frock, 16 In. . . 1800.00
French, Bisque, Cobalt Blue Enamel Eyes, Almond Shape, Blond Mohair Wig, 12 In. . . . 2000.00
French, Bisque, Composition & Wood Body, Jointed, Paris 4 Mark, c.1885, 10 1/2 In. . . . 3300.00
French, Bisque, Portrait, Napoleonic Style Man's Clothes, c.1910, 19 In. 1800.00
French, Bisque, Socket Head, Amber Brown Spiral Threaded Eyes, Closed Mouth, 14 In. 4600.00
French, Bisque, Socket Head, Brown Paperweight Eyes, Open Mouth, 1912, 16 In. 1800.00
French, Bisque, Socket Head, Dark Blue Sleep Eyes, Open Mouth, 1895, 31 In. 2100.00
French, Bisque, Swivel Head, Blue Glass Enamel Inset Eyes, Closed Mouth, 1870, 19 In. 5000.00
French, Bisque, Swivel Head, Blue Glass Inset Eyes, Closed Mouth, Taffeta Gown, 17 In. 3200.00
French, Bisque, Swivel Head, Kid & Wood Body, Jointed, Swivel Waist, c.1860, 17 In. . . 7000.00
French, Bisque, Swivel Head, Kid Body, Jointed, Couturier Outfit, c.1870, 19 In. 4600.00
French, Bisque, Swivel Head, Kid Body, Pierced Ears, Silk Gown, c.1865, 19 In. 3200.00
French, Bisque, Swivel Head, Patented Clement Leather Body, c.1866, 17 In. 6000.00
French, Bisque, Swivel Head, Wood Articulated Body, Wedding Gown, c.1867, 18 In. . . . 5400.00
French, Fashion, Porcelain Shoulder Head, Kid Body, J 111 Mark, c.1850, 16 In. 750.00
French, Fashion, Wax Shoulder Head, Fuchsia Wool Jacket, Silk Skirt, 1914, 11 In. 650.00
French, Fashion, Wax Shoulder Head, Silk Crepe Skirt, Black Straw Hat, 1914, 11 In. . . . 900.00
French, Fortune Teller, Bisque Swivel Head, Kid & Wood Body, c.1870, 15 In. 4300.00
French, Hard Plastic, Blue Sleep Eyes, Pink Dress, c.1960, 19 In. 38.00
French, Mignonette, Bisque Swivel Head, Jointed Limbs, Elbows, c.1880, 5 In. 2700.00
French, Mignonette, Bisque, Jointed, 18th-Century Clothes, Wood Box, c.1880, 6 x 6 In. 2100.00
French, Porcelain, Black Hair, Blue Painted Eyes, Closed Mouth, 1860, 11 In. 650.00
Freundlich, Character, Wolf, Grandma's Clothes, Composition, Jointed, 11 In. 165.00
Freundlich, Red Riding Hood Set, Girl, Grandmother, Wolf, Box, 1934, 3 x 11 x 10 In. . 805.00
Frozen Charley, China Head & Body, Stiff Neck, Molded Hair, Hands In Fists, 8 1/2 In. 175.00
Frozen Charley, Closed Mouth, Arms Extended, Green Knit Suit, 14 1/2 In. 300.00
Frozen Charley, Porcelain, Blond, Blue Eyes, Germany, Mid 19th Century, 15 In. 315.00
Frozen Charlotte, China, Black Molded Hair, Teal Blue Dress, Germany, c.1890, 7 In. . 110.00
Fulper, 5-10, Bisque, Kid Body, Open Mouth, 2 Teeth, Blond Wig, 1918, 21 In. 145.00
G.I. Joe figures are listed in the Toy category.
Galoob, Mr. T, Talking, With Tool Box, 1983, 12 In. 48.00
Gans & Seyforth, Bisque, Sleep Eyes, Human Hair Wig, Silk Dress & Undies, 24 1/2 In. 775.00
Gaultier, 2, Pierrot, Bisque Swivel Head, Kid Body, On Candy Box, c.1885, 19 In. 2500.00
Gaultier, 5, Bisque, Composition & Wood Body, Jointed, Pierced Ears, c.1884, 12 In. . . . 3600.00
Gaultier, Bisque Head, Blue Paperweight Eyes, Blond Mohair Wig, 1886, 9 In. 2800.00
Gaultier, Bisque Head, Blue Paperweight Eyes, Closed Mouth, 1890, 12 In. 4900.00
Gaultier, Bisque, Blue Paperweight Eyes, 5-Piece French Body, 16 In. 2795.00
Gaultier, Bisque, Blue Paperweight Eyes, Closed Mouth, 16 In. 2495.00
Gaultier, Closed Mouth, Paperweight Eyes 995.00
Gaultier, Nun & Schoolchildren, Bisque, Kid & Muslin, c.1875, 14 & 11 In., 5 Piece . . . 7250.00
Gebruder Heubach dolls are also in this category under Heubach.
Gebruder Heubach, 6970, Girl, Bisque, Socket Head, Glass Sleep Eyes, 1910, 19 In. . . 4100.00
Gebruder Heubach, 6970, Pouty Child, Glass Eyes, Jointed Body, 12 In. 2150.00
Gebruder Heubach, 8894, Bisque, Pouty Toddler, Jointed Legs, Bent Arms, 10 In. 220.00
Gebruder Heubach, Baby Stuart, Intaglio Eyes, Closed Mouth, Bisque, 1910, 7 In. 955.00
Gebruder Heubach, Bisque Head, Indian Male, Painted Features, Leather Outfit, 14 In. 1150.00
Gebruder Heubach, Bisque, Girl, Brown Curly Bobbed Hair, Brown Eyes, 1915, 9 In. . 2400.00
Gebruder Heubach, Bisque, Intaglio Dark Blue Eyes, Closed Mouth, 1915, 20 In. 1650.00
Gebruder Heubach, Bisque, Pouty Character, Velvet Suit, Snap Shoes, 17 In. 1000.00
Gebruder Heubach, Character Child, Glass Eyes, Jointed Body, 18 1/2 In. 1900.00
Gebruder Heubach, Shipmates, 13 In. 1495.00
Gebruder Heubach, Whistler, Bisque, Composition Body, c.1900, 11 In. 440.00
Gebruder Kuhnlenz, 47-22, Bisque, Kid Body, Blue Eyes, Blond Wig, 1895, 13 In. . . . 272.00
Gebruder Kuhnlenz, Bisque, Gray Spiral Eyes, Composition Body, 15 In. 1495.00
Gebruder Kuhnlenz, Bisque, Swivel Head, Blue Sleep Eyes, Open Mouth, 1895, 9 In. . 2800.00
German, 63, Bisque, Composition Body, Sleep Eyes, Open Mouth, 4 Teeth, 1915, 22 In. . 109.00
German, 134, Flirty Eyes, Ethnic, Composition, Chunky Toddler, 17 In. 995.00
German, 1039, Child, Bisque Head, Brown Sleep Eyes, Open Mouth, 1900, 14 In. 850.00
German, Bisque, Baby, Brown Glass Sleep Eyes, Brunette Mohair Bobbed Wig, 11 In. . . 850.00
German, Bisque, Blond Sculpted Hair, Blue Eyes, Spiral Threaded, 1885, 14 In. 575.00
German, Bisque, Brown Sleep Eyes, Blond Mohair Wig, 14 In. 325.00
German, Bisque, Cobalt Blue Inset Eyes, Brunette Mohair Wig, 1870, 18 In. 1400.00

German, Bisque, Composition Body, Baby, Sleep Eyes, Open Mouth, c.1915, 14 In. 110.00
German, Bisque, Composition Body, Brown Eyes, White Dress, 1909, 10 In. 467.00
German, Bisque, Composition Body, Molded Wig, Blue Outfit, c.1920, 12 In. 2145.00
German, Bisque, Composition, Open Mouth, 5 Teeth, Green Dress, c.1915, 15 In. 121.00
German, Bisque, Composition, Painted Face, 206 D.R.G.M. Mark, c.1910, 8 In. 286.00
German, Bisque, Composition, Sleep Eyes, Open Mouth, Green Outfit, c.1900, 8 In. 275.00
German, Bisque, Cotton Body, Brown Eyes, Open-Close Mouth, c.1910, 18 In. 467.00
German, Bisque, Kid Body, Brown Eyes, Brown Wig, Pink Dress, c.1910, 16 In. 36.00
German, Bisque, Kid Body, Brown Eyes, Floral Dress, c.1920, 15 In. 154.00
German, Bisque, Kid Body, Brown Sleep Eyes, Open Mouth, 4 Teeth, c.1915, 19 In. ... 66.00
German, Bisque, Kid Body, Open Mouth, 4 Teeth, Pierced Ears, Blue Dress, 1910, 19 In. 143.00
German, Bisque, Kid Body, Sleep Eyes, Open Mouth, 4 Teeth, Lace Dress, c.1920, 18 In. 93.00
German, Bisque, Kid Body, Sleep Eyes, Open Mouth, Lavender Dress, c.1900, 19 In. ... 231.00
German, Bisque, Kid Body, Sleep Eyes, Open Mouth, Pierced Ears, c.1895, 18 In. 231.00
German, Bisque, Mohair Body, Stitch Jointing, Folk Wedding Costume, c.1890, 13 In. .. 625.00
German, Bisque, Muslin, Baby In Gown, Original Bed, Pillow, c.1865, 4 In. 750.00
German, Bisque, Woman, Sculpted Hair, Muslin Body, Leather Arms, c.1875, 23 In. 2500.00
German, Blue Eyes, Closed Mouth, Muslin Gown With Gigot Sleeves, 1860, 24 In. 13500.00
German, Celluloid Head, Seated In Sleigh, White Winter Coat, c.1920, 4 In. 88.00
German, Celluloid Shoulder Head, Kid Body, Open Mouth, 4 Teeth, c.1920, 20 In. 38.00
German, Child, Bisque, Blond Hair, Closed Mouth, Bridegroom Costume, 4 In. 220.00
German, Child, Bisque, Brown Sleep Eyes, Bridegroom Costume, 1920, 17 In. 500.00
German, Child, Bisque, Composition, Sleep Eyes, Open Mouth, 2 Teeth, c.1920, 17 In. . 247.00
German, Child, Blue Sleep Eyes, Black Mohair Wig, Joint, 26 In. 800.00
German, China Head, Black Hair, Blue Eyes, Brown Dress, c.1870, 7 In. 286.00
German, China Head, Black Molded Hair, Kid Body, Pink Striped Dress, c.1870, 14 In. . 275.00
German, China Head, Black Spiral-Shaped Hair, Lavender Dress, c.1870, 9 In. 340.00
German, China Head, Kid Body, Black Hair, Brown Checkered Dress, c.1880, 26 In. 145.00
German, China Head, Kid Body, Black Molded Curly Hair, Blue Dress, c.1800, 14 In. ... 121.00
German, China Head, Kid Body, Black Molded Hair, Blue Eyes, c.1870, 17 In. 154.00
German, China Head, Kid Body, Black Molded Hair, Green Dress, c.1880, 17 In. 55.00
German, China Head, Kid Body, Black Molded Hair, Green Dress, c.1880, 19 In. 165.00
German, China Head, Kid Body, Black Molded Hair, Molded Boots, c.1880, 17 In. 88.00
German, China Head, Kid Body, Black Molded Hair, Red Dress, c.1900, 17 In. 77.00
German, China Head, Kid Body, Blond Molded Hair, c.1905, 20 In. 99.00
German, China Head, Kid Body, Blond Molded Hair, Green Outfit, c.1880, 17 In. 132.00
German, China Head, Kid Body, Blond Molded Hair, Tan Dress, c.1920, 22 In. 165.00
German, China Head, Kid Body, Bun Molded Hair, Black & Floral Dress, c.1870, 12 In. 198.00
German, China Head, Kid Body, Leather Hands, Feet, Orange Dress, c.1870, 20 In. 165.00
German, Composition, Blond Wig, Brown Glass Eyes, Green Dress, c.1930, 22 In. 27.00
German, Marked Alice No. 191, Bisque, Cork-Stuffed Body, 4 Teeth, 1925, 19 In. 77.00
German, Our Pet, Wears Banner, Chicago Miss Century Of Progress 1933, Box, 14 In. .. 302.00
German, Papier-Mache Head, Cotton-Stuffed Body, Brown Floral Dress, c.1870, 20 In. . 80.00
German, Papier-Mache Head, Kid Body, Wood Limbs, Blue Net Dress, 1835, 14 In. 605.00
German, Parian Head, Molded Hair, Cotton Body, Red Floral Dress, c.1880, 21 In. 192.00
German, Parian, Kid Body, Molded French-Twist Hair, Blue Dress, c.1870, 25 In. 165.00
German, Porcelain, Adult Woman, Blue Downcast Eyes, Closed Mouth, 16 In. 1500.00
German, Porcelain, Blue Eyes, Closed Mouth, Accented Nostrils, 1860, 4 In. 3900.00
German, Porcelain, Blue Painted Eyes, Brown Modeled Hair, Closed Mouth, 20 In. 750.00
German, Porcelain, Intaglio Blue Eyes, Gray, Brown Hair, Black Brimmed Bonnet, 8 In. 1200.00
German, Porcelain, Jointed Arms, Head Inclined Into Torso, Silk Dress, c.1860, 9 In. ... 2200.00
German, Stone Bisque, Bonnet Head, c.1870, 7 1/2 In. 80.00
German, Stone Bisque, Bonnet Head, c.1900, 8 In. 45.00
German, Tauflinge Baby, Painted Hair, Face, Muslin Tauflinge, Early 19th Century, 8 In. 200.00
German, Windup, Dances, Plastic, Navy Style Uniform, 6 1/2 In. 175.00
Germany, Bisque Head, Dark Blue Eyes, Closed Mouth, Jointed, 1912, 12 In. 1200.00
Giebeler-Falk, 18, Metal Head, Composition, Open Mouth, Painted Teeth, 1920, 19 In. .. 145.00
Golliwog, Celluloid Eyes, Furry Type Hair, Printed Cloth Clothes, 16 In. 275.00
Golliwog, Cloth, Celluloid Disc Googly Eyes, Merrythought, England, c.1940, 14 In. ... 225.00
Golliwog, Original Pants & Jacket, Tag, 1920s, 22 In. 350.00
Googly, Composition Mask Face, Smiling Mouth, Pink Dress, Pinafore, Bonnet, 12 In. .. 1008.00
Greiner, Papier-Mache Head, Black Curly Hair, Pale Blue Eyes, Jointed, 1865, 40 In. ... 900.00
Grodner Tal, Wood, Cameo Face, Jointed, c.1840, 5 1/2 In. 625.00

Grodner Tal, Wood, Painted Hair, Jointed, Original Gown, c.1830, 13 In. 1300.00
Half Dolls are listed in the Pinchushion category.
Handwerck, 6/0, Bisque, Kid Body, Blue Sleep Eyes, Open Mouth, 6 Teeth, 1910, 16 In.   133.00
Handwerck, 7, Bisque, Composition, Sleep Eyes, Open Mouth, 4 Teeth, c.1890, 31 In. . . .   330.00
Handwerck, 10, Bisque, Kid Body, Open Mouth, 5 Teeth, Lace Dress, c.1915, 14 In. 99.00
Handwerck, 69, Bisque, Composition, Sleep Eyes, Pierced Ears, 4 Teeth, c.1900, 24 In. .   550.00
Handwerck, 69, Child, Light Blue Sleep Eyes, Blond Human Hair Wig, 24 In. 1175.00
Handwerck, 79, Bisque, Composition, Sleep Eyes, 4 Teeth, Pierced Ears, c.1900, 18 In. .   357.00
Handwerck, 79, Brown Sleep Eyes, All Original, 16 1/2 In. 675.00
Handwerck, 79, Child, Bisque Head, Blue Sleep Flirty Eyes, Open Mouth, 17 In. 900.00
Handwerck, 99, Child, Bisque, Light Blue Sleep Eyes, Dress, Hat, 33 In. 2250.00
Handwerck, 99, Sleep Eyes, Human Hair Wig, Ball-Jointed Body, Old Clothes, 22 In. . . .   795.00
Handwerck, 109, Bisque, Blue Eyes, Jointed Composition Body, Dressed, 31 In. 1675.00
Handwerck, 109, Bisque, Brown Sleep Eyes, White Dress, 30 In. 1650.00
Handwerck, 109, Bisque, Old Clothes Of Tucking & Lace On Ecru Net, 23 In. 1050.00
Handwerck, 109, Bisque, Sleep Eyes, 4 Teeth, Composition & Wood, c.1900, 16 In. 1000.00
Handwerck, 109, Child, Bisque, Blue Sleep Eyes, Auburn Wig, 25 In. 1175.00
Handwerck, 119, Bisque Head, Child, Ball-Jointed Body, Old Clothes, 28 In. 660.00
Handwerck, 283, Bisque, Composition, Sleep Eyes, 4 Teeth, Striped Dress, 1920, 20 In. .   165.00
Handwerck, 283, Bisque, Composition, Sleep Eyes, Open Mouth, 3 Teeth, c.1900, 19 In.   110.00
Handwerck, Bisque Head, Ball-Jointed, Fixed Eyes, Open Mouth, Dressed, 6 1/2 In. . . .   605.00
Handwerck, Bisque Head, Composition, Jointed, Blue Sleep Eyes, Open Mouth, 30 In. .   518.00
Handwerck, Bisque, Blue Sleep Eyes, White Antique Dress, 30 In. 1050.00
Handwerck, Bisque, Composition, Sleep Eyes, 4 Teeth, Pierced Ears, c.1900, 24 In. 550.00
Handwerck, Bisque, Kid Body, Open Mouth, 5 Teeth, Brown Dress, c.1885, 21 In. 55.00
Handwerck, Bisque, Sleep Eyes, 4 Teeth, Composition & Wood, c.1900, 18 In. 700.00
Handwerck, Googly, Molded Helmet, Glass Eyes, Open Watermelon Mouth, 11 In. 1850.00
Handwerck, Walker, Bisque Socket Head, 4 Upper Teeth, 27 In. 575.00
Happifats, All Bisque, Jointed Arms, Kate Jordan, Box, Germany, c.1915, 4 In., Pair . . .   850.00
Happy Hooligan, Wood & Composition, Jointed, Label On Foot, 1924, 9 In. 1250.00
Hartmann, Bisque, Sleeping, Glass Eyes, Open Mouth, Kid Body & Legs, 1920s, 26 In.   287.00
Hasbro, Charlie's Angels, Jill, Sabrina, Kelly, Poseable, Mint On Cards, 1978, 8 1/2 In. . .   155.00
Head, Redware, Sculpted Face & Hair, 11 Mark, Pennsylvania, Mid-19th Century, 3 In. .   175.00
Hertel Schwab, 172, Boy, Bisque, Socket Head, Closed, Smiling Mouth, 15 In. 4000.00
Hertel Schwab, 198, Baby, Dimples, 12 1/2 In. 1850.00
Hertel Schwab, Bisque, Baby, Bent Leg, 13 1/2 In. 550.00
Hertel Schwab, No. 142, Baby, Open Close Mouth, Painted Eyes, Dome Head, 12 In. . .   350.00
Heubach dolls are also in this category under Gebruder Heubach.
Heubach, 275, Bisque, Kid Body, Brown Sleep Eyes, 4 Teeth, Blue Dress, c.1890, 15 In.   99.00
Heubach, 275, Bisque, Kid Body, Brown Sleep Eyes, Open Mouth, 4 Teeth, c.1890 . . . .   88.00
Heubach, 275, Bisque, Kid Body, Sleep Eyes, Open Mouth, 4 Teeth, c.1890, 15 In. 88.00
Heubach, 275, Bisque, Kid Body, Sleep Eyes, Open Mouth, 4 Teeth, c.1905, 12 In. 99.00
Heubach, 275, Bisque, Shoulder Head, Brown Sleep Eyes, Mohair Wig, Kid Body, 18 In.   170.00
Heubach, 321, Bisque, Composition, Sleep Eyes, Open Mouth, 2 Teeth, c.1910, 9 In. . . .   143.00
Heubach, 1900 3/0, Bisque, Kid Body, Brown Eyes, Open Mouth, 5 Teeth, 1910, 20 In. .   73.00
Heubach, 1900, Bisque, Composition, Open Mouth, 4 Teeth, Lace Dress, 1895, 9 In. . . .   121.00
Heubach, 7631, Bisque Head, Baby, 5 Piece Body, Painted Eyes & Hair, 8 In. 120.00
Heubach, Bisque, Pouty, Sleep Eyes, Braided Wig, With Trousseau Trunk, 6 1/2 In. . . .   3250.00
Heubach, Character, Baby, Molded Hair, Intaglio Eyes, Lower Teeth, Sunburst, 8 5/8 In. .   345.00
Heubach, Character, Boy, Bisque Head, Molded Hair, Intaglio Eyes, Jointed, 13 1/2 In. . .   400.00
Heubach, Napoleon & Josephine, 17 In., Pair 2495.00
Heubach, Toddler, Tubby Body, Leather Shoes, Dressed, 8 In. 750.00
Heubach Kopplesdorf, 250, Bisque, Composition, Sleep Eyes, 4 Teeth, c.1900, 21 In. . . .   247.00
Heubach Kopplesdorf, 250, Porcelain Head, Composition Body, 2 Teeth, 9 In. 82.00
Hilda Ege, Carved Wood, Stockinet-Over-Wire Body, Folklore Dress, c.1920, 12 In. . . .   250.00
Hippy Turtle, Animal Crackers, Mighty Star, Attached Tag, 1978, 9 In. 18.00
Horsman, Baby Dimples, Composition, Cloth Body, Crazed Head, 21 In. 85.00
Horsman, Babyland Rag, Muslin, Hand Painted, Leather Slippers, c.1893, 14 In. 1300.00
Horsman, Babyland Rag, Topsy-Turvy, Printed Face, Original Clothes One Side, 12 In. .   357.00
Horsman, Cynthia, Composition, 1938, 18 In. 185.00
Horsman, Ella Cinders, Composition Head, Arms & Legs, Original Outfit, 1925, 18 In. .   237.00
Horsman, Poor Pitiful Pearl, 17 In. 65.00
Horsman, Snowbell, Composition Head & Hands, Original Costume, 1916, 13 In. 200.00

Doll, Ideal, Mary
Hartline, Plastic
Head, 5-Piece
Body, Rayve,
Baton, Box, 16 In.

Doll, Jumeau,
Bisque Socket
Head,
Paperweight Eyes,
Open Mouth,
1907, 29 In.

Ideal, Archie Bunker's Grandson, Joey Stivic, Baby, Box, 14 In. 25.00
Ideal, Bam-Bam, Flintstones, Hanna-Barbera Productions, 16 In. 40.00
Ideal, Betsy McCall, Blue Sleep Eyes, Brunette Wig, Chemise, Box, 1958, 8 In. .. 325.00
Ideal, Betsy McCall, Blue Sleep Eyes, Red Wig, Pink Dress, Fashion Case, 1958, 14 In. . 650.00
Ideal, Betsy McCall, Brown Sleep Eyes, Pink Dress, Tag, Curlers, 1952-1953, 14 In. 450.00
Ideal, Betsy McCall, Brown Sleep Eyes, Yellow Dress, Tag, Box, 1952-1953, 14 In. 600.00
Ideal, Deanna Durbin, Box, 20 In. 1700.00
Ideal, Deanna Durbin, Brown Eyes, Human Hair Wig, Original Dress, 21 In. 675.00
Ideal, Fanny Brice, As Baby Snooks, Original Clothes, 12 In. 350.00
Ideal, Judy Garland, As Dorothy, Wizard Of Oz, Composition, 15 In. 1450.00
Ideal, Mary Hartline, 8 In. 58.00
Ideal, Mary Hartline, Plastic Head, 5-Piece Body, Rayve, Baton, Box, 16 In. ....*Illus* 700.00
Ideal, Miss Curity, Hat, Dress, 14 In. 195.00
Ideal, Patti Playpal, Blond Hair, 35 In. 350.00
Ideal, Patti Playpal, Box, 1981, 34 In. 250.00
Ideal, Patti Playpal, Vinyl, Checked Dress, 36 In. 130.00
Ideal, Patty Playpal, Honey Blond Wig, Original Dress, 1960, 35 In. 275.00
Ideal, Toni, Blue Sleep Eyes, Blond Nylon Wig, Tagged Dress, Curlers, Box, 1949, 14 In. 525.00
Indian dolls are listed in the Indian category.
J.D.K. dolls are also listed in this category under Kestner.
J.D.K., 260, Bisque, Chubby Long Cheeks, Jointed Composition Body, 36 In. 2750.00
Jane Mansfield, Articulated, 20 In. 750.00
Japanese, Wooden, Carved, Jointed, Silk Costume, Early 20th Century, 15 In. 1300.00
Jeanson, Bisque, Glass Eyes, Blond Curls, Jointed Body, Dressed, Leather Boots, 27 In. . 3500.00
Jester, Clapping, Windup, Bisque Head 395.00
Joanny, J 4, Bisque Head, Steiner Sleep Eyes, Composition, Jointed, c.1880s, 15 In. 5000.00
Joanny, J 7, Bisque Socket Head, Composition & Wood, Jointed, c.1880s, 17 In. 6750.00
John Wright, Gretel Brinker, Felt Swivel Head, Felt Body, 20 In. 950.00
John Wright, Hans Brinker, Felt Swivel Head, Felt Body, 20 In. 950.00
Jumeau, 4, Bisque Swivel Head, Kid Body, Jointed, Fashion Gown, c.1875, 18 In. 3900.00
Jumeau, 7, Bisque, Almond-Shaped Paperweight Eyes, Long Wig, 8 Ball Body, 16 In. .. 9500.00
Jumeau, 301, Dressed, Paperweight Eyes, Blond Human Hair Wig, Jewelry, 28 In. 2250.00
Jumeau, 1907, Walking Body, Paperweight Eyes, Human Hair Wig, Dress, 17 In. 1900.00
Jumeau, Bisque Head, Baby, Blue Paperweight Eyes, Closed Mouth, 1888, 17 In. 4500.00
Jumeau, Bisque Head, Baby, Blue Paperweight Eyes, Closed Mouth, Jointed, 11 In. 3100.00
Jumeau, Bisque Head, Baby, Blue Paperweight Eyes, Mohair Wig, 1888, 22 In. 6000.00
Jumeau, Bisque Head, Baby, Blue Sleep Eyes, Open Mouth, Jointed, 1895, 10 1/2 In. ... 1400.00
Jumeau, Bisque Head, Baby, Dark Blue Paperweight Eyes, Closed Mouth, 1886, 19 In. .. 4900.00
Jumeau, Bisque Socket Head, Paperweight Eyes, Open Mouth, 1907, 29 In. ....*Illus* 2300.00
Jumeau, Bisque Socket Head, Sleep Eyes, Composition, Human Hair, 24 In. ......*Illus* 3200.00
Jumeau, Bisque Socket Head, Sleep Eyes, Wood & Composition Body, 31 In. .....*Illus* 2900.00
Jumeau, Bisque, Long Curls, Stationary Eyes, Open Mouth, Dress, 1907, 30 In. 2900.00
Jumeau, Bisque, Sleep Eyes, 6 Upper Teeth, Jointed Body, Dressed, 31 In. 2900.00
Jumeau, Child, Brown Paperweight Eyes, Pale Pink Silk, Shoes, 12 1/2 In. 4750.00
Jumeau, Opaque Bisque, Fashion Lady, Firm Body, Paperweight Eyes, 17 In. 3795.00

Jumeau, Paperweight Eyes, Mohair Wig, 23 In. 4500.00
Jumeau, Paperweight Eyes, Open Mouth, 6 Upper Teeth, 1907, 14 In. 2300.00
Jumeau, Set Glass Eyes, Long Curls, Composition Body, Dress, Lace Cap, Purse, 30 In. . 2795.00
Jutta, Bisque, Child, Big Blue Eyes, 25 In. 1795.00
K * R, 30, Walker, Bisque, Sleep Eyes, 4 Teeth, Painted Socks & Shoes, 11 1/2 In. 575.00
K * R, 58, Bisque, Composition, Ball-Jointed, Flirty Sleep Eyes, 4 Teeth, c.1910, 22 In. . 632.00
K * R, 100, Baby, Brown Eyes, 15 In. 495.00
K * R, 100, Character, Baby, Celluloid, Composition Bent-Limb Body, c.1915, 16 In. ... 700.00
K * R, 101, Elise, Blue Intaglio Eyes, Blond Mohair Wig, Jointed, 9 In. 4500.00
K * R, 101, Marie, Blue Inset Eyes, Blond Mohair Wig, Jointed, 14 1/2 In. 4500.00
K * R, 101, Peter, Bisque Head, Gray Gazing Eyes, Closed Mouth, Jointed, 15 In. 4000.00
K * R, 114, Gretchen, Bisque Head, Composition Body, Painted Eyes, Costume, 8 1/4 In. 1760.00
K * R, 115, Phillip, Sculpted Hair, Sleep Eyes, Jointed, Linen Romper Suit, c.1910, 16 In. 4800.00
K * R, 115, Pouty Character Boy, Bisque, Painted & Molded Hair, 15 1/2 In. 6300.00
K * R, 115A, Poochie Cheeks, Auburn Mohair Wig, Toddler Body, Original Outfit, 14 In. 6850.00
K * R, 116, Bisque, Open-Closes Mouth, Holding Steiff Teddy Bear, 21 In. 1950.00
K * R, 116/A, Baby, Bisque, Sleep Eyes, Painted Lashes, Bent Limb, 1912, 15 In. 1500.00
K * R, 116A, Bisque Head, Blue Sleep Flirty Eyes, Blond Mohair Wig, 1910, 15 In. 1200.00
K * R, 117, Mein Liebling, Bisque Head, Human Hair, Composition Body, c.1912, 28 In. 6800.00
K * R, 117N, Bisque, Blue Glass Sleep Eyes, Closed Mouth, Brunette Human Hair, 30 In. 5750.00
K * R, 117N, Bisque, Blue Glass Sleep Flirty Eyes, Open Mouth, Jointed, 26 In. 2400.00
K * R, 119, Baby, Bisque Head, Ball-Jointed Composition Body, Sleep Eyes, 25 In. 9350.00
K * R, 121, Bisque Head, Brown Sleep Eyes, Mohair Wig, Jointed, 1912, 15 In. 950.00
K * R, 121, Bisque Head, Sleep Eyes, Open Mouth, Fleeced Wig, 14 In., Pair 1700.00
K * R, 121, Bisque, Composition, Sleep Eyes, Open Mouth, 2 Teeth, c.1910, 11 In. 577.00
K * R, 121/50, Character, Baby, Bisque, Blond Mohair, Sleep Eyes, Composition Body .. 660.00
K * R, 122, Baby Toddler, Bisque Head, Sleep Eyes, Movable Tongue, 1912, 24 In. 1550.00
K * R, 122, Toddler, Blue Sleep Eyes, Open Mouth, Antique Dress, 13 In. 1850.00
K * R, 126, Bisque Head, Toddler, Flirty-Eyed, Toddler Clothes, 20 In. 880.00
K * R, 190, Child, Bisque, Composition & Wood Body, Jointed, c.1890, 7 In. 750.00
K * R, Baby, Molded Hair, Painted Hair, 2 Upper Teeth, Bent-Limb Body, 16 In. 2587.00
K * R, Bisque Head, Intaglio Gray Eyes, Closed Mouth, Composition, 1910, 20 In. 875.00
K * R, Bisque Head, My Darling Baby, Open Mouth, Upper Teeth, Bent Limb, 20 In. ... 1150.00
K * R, Bisque Head, Shaded Blue Eyes, Closed, Pouty Mouth, 1910, 18 In. 5100.00
K * R, Bisque, Brown Inset Eyes, Brown Mohair Wig, White Hat, 29 In. 1495.00
K * R, Bisque, Molded Eyebrows, 33 In. 1695.00
K * R, Bisque, Sleep Eyes, Open Mouth, Mohair Wig, Composition Body, Jointed, 8 In. . 230.00
K * R, Bisque, Socket Head, Blue Glass Sleep Eyes, Open Mouth, Jointed, 1915, 31 In. . 1800.00
K * R, Bisque, Socket Head, Brown Glass Sleep Eyes, Auburn Mohair Wig, 19 In. 1000.00
K * R, Child, Bisque Head, Ball-Jointed Body, Sleep Eyes, Wigged & Dressed, 19 In. ... 522.00
K * R, Child, Bisque Head, Blue Sleep Eyes, Blond Mohair Wig, Jointed, 1915, 16 In. .. 650.00
K * R, Child, Bisque Head, Blue Sleep Eyes, Open Mouth, Composition, 1915, 21 In. ... 800.00
K * R, Child, Bisque Head, Blue Sleep Flirty Eyes, Brunette Mohair Wig, 1912, 25 In. .. 850.00
K * R, Child, Bisque, Marine Blue Sleep Eyes, Blond Braided Wig, 28 In. 1650.00
K * R, Child, Bisque, Socket Head, Brown Glass Sleep Eyes, Open Mouth, 1915, 26 In. . 900.00
Kallus, Baby Bo-Kaye, Bisque, Muslin, Composition, Sleep Eyes, 2 Teeth, c.1920, 14 In. 1500.00
Kathe Kruse, 3134, Series 1, Girl, All Cloth, Painted Hair, Jointed Legs, c.1915, 17 In. . 5700.00

Doll, Jumeau,
Bisque Socket
Head, Sleep Eyes,
Composition,
Human Hair,
24 In.

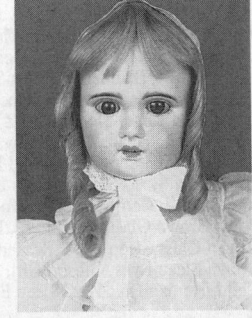

Doll, Jumeau,
Bisque Socket
Head, Sleep Eyes,
Wood &
Composition
Body, 31 In.

Kathe Kruse, Boy, Kleines Du Mein, 28415, All Cloth, 1927-30, 15 In. 4200.00
Kathe Kruse, Brown, Green Eyes, Closed, Pouty Mouth, Jointed, 1935, 18 In. 2100.00
Kathe Kruse, Character, Boy, Oil Painted Face, All Cloth, Series I, c.1915, 17 In. 2600.00
Kathe Kruse, Child, Blue Inset Eyes, Pouty Mouth, 1910-1929, 16 In. 3500.00
Kathe Kruse, Cloth, Gray Eyes, Closed Mouth, Pouty, 17 In. 2200.00
Kathe Kruse, Cloth, Painted Face & Hair, Dress, Underwear, 1950s, 16 In. 700.00
Kathe Kruse, Cloth, Painted Face & Hair, Underwear & Jacket, 1930s, 16 In. 655.00
Kathe Kruse, Girl, Kleines Du Mein, 29906, All Cloth, 1927-30, 15 In. 4300.00
Kestner dolls are also in this category under J.D.K.
Kestner, 7, Bisque, Composition Body, Painted Hair, Open Mouth, c.1900, 11 In. 412.00
Kestner, 9, Child, Bisque, Composition & Wood Body, Sleep Eyes, c.1890, 16 In. 1900.00
Kestner, 10, Bisque, Closed Mouth, Paperweight Eyes, Feathered Brows, 22 In. 1295.00
Kestner, 143, Bisque Head, Blue Sleep Eyes, Open Mouth, Blond Mohair Wig, 16 In. . . . 1000.00
Kestner, 143, Bisque Head, Brown Sleep Eyes, Brunette Mohair Wig, 1910, 20 In. 850.00
Kestner, 143, Bisque, Composition, Jointed, Sleep Eyes, 4 Teeth, c.1910, 7 In. 632.00
Kestner, 143, Bisque, Sleep Eyes, Human Hair Wig, Signed Body, Original Shoes, 25 In. 2450.00
Kestner, 146, Bisque, Excelsior Body, 24 In. 925.00
Kestner, 147, Bisque, Riveted Kid Body, Crepe De Chine Dress, c.1892, 21 In. 695.00
Kestner, 148, Bisque, Plaster Pate, Blue Eyes, Layers Of Clothes, 20 In. 695.00
Kestner, 152, Bisque, Composition, Sleep Eyes, Open Mouth, 2 Teeth, c.1890, 12 In. . . . 357.00
Kestner, 154 DEP 8, Bisque, Kid Body, Sleep Eyes, Open Mouth, 4 Teeth, 1905, 21 In. . . 230.00
Kestner, 154 DEP, Bisque, Composition, Sleep Eyes, Open Mouth, 4 Teeth, 1910, 28 In. 484.00
Kestner, 154 DEP, Bisque, Kid Body, Sleep Eyes, Open Mouth, 4 Teeth, 1895, 18 In. . . . 212.00
Kestner, 154, Bisque Shoulder Head, Hands, Sleep Eyes, Jointed Kid Body, 16 1/2 In. . . 260.00
Kestner, 154, Bisque, Kid Body, Brown Sleep Eyes, 4 Teeth, Green Dress, 1895, 28 In. . 231.00
Kestner, 154, Bisque, Kid Body, Sleep Eyes, Open Mouth, 4 Teeth, 1885, 18 In. 133.00
Kestner, 154, Bisque, Kid Body, Sleep Eyes, Open Mouth, 4 Teeth, c.1900, 21 In. 302.00
Kestner, 154, Bisque, Kid Body, Sleep Eyes, Open Mouth, 4 Teeth, c.1910, 19 In. 231.00
Kestner, 154, Blue Sleep Eyes, Brown Hair, Open Mouth, Composition, 28 In. 950.00
Kestner, 154.14, Child, Bisque Head, Sleep Eyes, Open Mouth, Teeth, Kid Body, 26 In. . 330.00
Kestner, 155, Bisque, Socket Head, Brown Glass Sleep Eyes, Open Mouth, 10 In. 950.00
Kestner, 155, Child, Bisque, Socket Head, Brown Glass Sleep Eyes, Open Mouth, 19 In. 900.00
Kestner, 160, Bisque, Sleep Eyes, 4 Teeth, Composition & Wood, Jointed, c.1900, 16 In. 950.00
Kestner, 164, Child, Bisque, Sleep Eyes, Open Mouth, Teeth, Composition Body, 27 In. . 410.00
Kestner, 164, Oriental, Ball-Jointed Olive-Toned Body, Kimono, 15 In. 1950.00
Kestner, 167, Bisque, Brown Eyes, Open Mouth, Hair Wig, Composition Body, 16 In. . . 460.00
Kestner, 168, Ball-Jointed Composition Body, Old Clothes, Human Hair Wig, 22 In. 750.00
Kestner, 168, Bisque, Brown Eyes, Blond Mohair Wig, Composition Body, 19 In. 630.00
Kestner, 169, Bisque Head, Brown Sleep Eyes, Blond Mohair Wig, Jointed, 13 1/2 In. . . 2185.00
Kestner, 171, Bisque, Ball-Jointed Body, Dressed, 21 In. 650.00
Kestner, 171, Bisque, Composition, Jointed, Open Mouth, 4 Teeth, c.1900, 26 In. 363.00
Kestner, 171, Child, Bisque, Blue Sleep Eyes, Pale Pink Mouth, 30 In. 1150.00
Kestner, 179, Character Child, Thick Mohair Wig, Braided Buns, Shoes, 15 In. 5500.00
Kestner, 183, Bisque, Socket Head, Painted Blue Eyes, Blond Mohair Wig, 1912, 15 In. . 3300.00
Kestner, 211, Child, Bisque Head, Blue Eyes, Open Mouth, Brunette Wig, 12 In. 550.00
Kestner, 214, Child, Bisque, Sleep Eyes, Open Mouth, Teeth, Ball-Jointed Body, 30 In. . 412.00
Kestner, 221, Googly, Bisque Socket Head, Jointed Wood, Composition, 12 In. . . . .*Illus* 7200.00
Kestner, 243, Baby, Bisque, Socket Head, Brown Glass Sleep Eyes, Open Mouth, 16 In. . 6000.00
Kestner, 245, Bisque, Hilda, Sleep Eyes, 2 Upper Teeth, Tongue, Mohair Wig, 16 In. . . . 2900.00
Kestner, 247, Baby, Bisque Head, Blue Sleep Eyes, Mohair Wig, Germany, 19 In. 2600.00
Kestner, 247, Child, Blue Sleep Eyes, Blond Mohair Wig, 19 In. 2995.00
Kestner, 249, Character, Bisque, Composition, Jointed, Sleep Eyes, 4 Teeth, 1909, 14 In. 522.00
Kestner, 257, Character, Baby, Bent Limb Body, Sleep Eyes, Open Mouth, 1920s, 9 In. . 431.00
Kestner, 260, Bisque Head, Blue Sleep Eyes, Open Mouth, Composition, 1915, 21 In. . . 950.00
Kestner, 260, Bisque Socket Head, Sleep Eyes, 2 Teeth, Tongue, Jointed, c.1910, 34 In. . 1650.00
Kestner, Baby, Domed Bisque Head, Blond Baby Hair, Brown Sleep Eyes, 10 In. 950.00
Kestner, Bisque Head, Brown Sleep Eyes, Blond Baby Hair, Open Mouth, 1914, 22 In. . 3100.00
Kestner, Bisque Head, Gray Sleep Eyes, Mohair Bobbed Wig, Composition, 28 In. 950.00
Kestner, Bisque Socket Head, Composition & Wood Body, Jointed, c.1885, 12 In. 2200.00
Kestner, Bisque, Baby, Brown Glass Sleep Eyes, Blond Painted Baby Hair, 1912, 16 In. . 2050.00
Kestner, Bisque, Brown Glass Sleep Eyes, Brunette Mohair Wig, 1915, 13 In. 700.00
Kestner, Bisque, Brown Sleep Eyes, Gibson Girl, Blond Mohair Wig, 19 In. 2800.00
Kestner, Bisque, Child, Human Hair Wig, Sleep Eyes, Old Shoes, 26 In. 1350.00

Clean the dust from a doll's wig by blowing it with a hair dryer set on low or cool.

Don't get water into the eyes of a doll with glass eyes.

Doll, Kestner, 221, Googly,
Bisque Socket Head, Jointed
Wood, Composition, 12 In.

Kestner, Bisque, Child, Jointed Arms & Legs, Glass Eyes, Painted Socks & Shoes, 5 In. .	135.00
Kestner, Bisque, Gibson Girl, Smiling Mouth, Mohair Wig, Organdy Dress, 10 In.	650.00
Kestner, Bisque, Painted Face, Open Mouth, c.1900, 7 In.	109.00
Kestner, Bisque, Painted Square Teeth, Sleep Eyes, White Dress, Blue Belt, 16 1/2 In. . .	1400.00
Kestner, Bisque, Shoulder Head, Blue Glass Sleep Eyes, Composition, 1915, 14 In.	750.00
Kestner, Bisque, Socket Head, Brown Glass Inset Eyes, Brunette Mohair Wig, 23 In. . . .	750.00
Kestner, Bisque, Swivel Head, Blue Glass Sleep Eyes, Jointed, Antique Costume, 16 In. . .	1600.00
Kestner, Black, Jointed Body, Brown Sleep Eyes, 11 1/2 In.	1950.00
Kestner, Brown Glass Sleep Eyes, Brown Mohair Wig, Antique Dress, 15 In.	15000.00
Kestner, Child, Bisque, Blond Sculpted Hair, Blue Eyes, Antique Muslin Gown, 22 In. . .	1800.00
Kestner, Child, Bisque, Sleep Eyes, Open Mouth, Blond Wig, Kid Body, 17 In.	305.00
Kestner, Gibson Girl, Silk Ensemble, Heeled Leather Shoes, 21 In.	4000.00
Kestner, Hilda, Brown Bisque Socket Head, Sleep Eyes, Baby Gown, c.1914, 15 In.	2900.00
Kestner, No. 226, Bisque Head, Baby, Sleep Eyes, White Dress & Bonnet, 11 1/2 In. . . .	575.00
Kewpie dolls are listed in the Kewpie category.	
Kley & Hahn, 62 Special, Bisque, Composition, Blue Sleep Eyes, 4 Teeth, 1905, 26 In. .	393.00
Kley & Hahn, 250, Walkure, Bisque, Composition, Sleep Eyes, 4 Teeth, 1905, 24 In. . . .	393.00
Kley & Hahn, Bisque, Sleep Eyes, Jointed Composition Body, 34 1/2 In.	1625.00
Kling, 123-6, Bisque Shoulder Head, Kid Body, Bisque Forearms, c.1885, 14 In.	1600.00
Knickerbocker, Raggedy Andy, 15 In.	25.00
Knickerbocker, Raggedy Andy, 30 In.	100.00
Knickerbocker, Raggedy Ann, 45 In.	95.00
Knight, Composition, Tin, c.1910, 12 In.	88.00
Knoch, Bisque Head, Glass Sleep Eyes, Open Mouth, Henna Mohair Wig, 1920s, 24 In. .	143.00
Konig & Wernicke, Toddler, Flirty Eyes, 5-Piece Composition Body, 20 In.	450.00
Koppelsdorf, Character Baby, Open Nostrils, 12 In.	275.00
Kuhnlenz, Black, Pupiless Set Eyes, Painted Shoes & Socks, 8 1/2 In.	750.00
Lafitte-Desirat, Fashion, Au Theatre, Wax Shoulder Head, Ivory Dress, 1912, 13 In. . . .	1000.00
Lafitte-Desirat, Fashion, Silk & Lace Dress, Cap With Plume, France, 1911, 11 In.	1300.00
Lafitte-Desirat, Fashion, Wax Shoulder Head, Crepe Blouse, Silk Skirt, 1912, 13 In. . . .	950.00
Lafitte-Desirat, Fashion, Wax, Velvet Dress, Muff, Wide Hat, France, 1912, 11 In.	850.00
Lanternier, Bisque, Paperweight Eyes, Mohair Wig, 20 In.	1295.00
Lanternier, Cherie, Paperweight Blue Eyes, Human Hair Wig, Dressed, 18 In.	1400.00
Lanternier, Lady, Paperweight Eyes, Slender, 15 In.	895.00
Laurel & Hardy, Seated On Metal Bench, 26 In.	300.00
Lavallee-Peronne, Bisque Swivel Head, Lily, Articulated Wood Body, France, 17 In. . . .	4700.00
Lenci, Bride, Pressed & Painted Face, Blond Wig, Felt Outfit, 36 In.	747.00
Lenci, Child, Swivel Head, Red Flowered Dress, Felt Coat & Hat, 17 In.	625.00
Lenci, Chubby Cheeks, Rosebud Mouth, 11 1/2 In.	750.00
Lenci, Cloth, Felt Swivel Head, Blue Side-Glancing Eyes, Black Mohair, 1930, 17 In. . . .	1900.00
Lenci, Girl, Felt Swivel Head, Blue Side-Glancing Eyes, Closed Mouth, 1930, 18 In.	1500.00
Lenci, Girl, Side-Glancing Eyes, Original Clothes, Blue Felt Dress, 13 In.	375.00
Lenci, Girl, Southern Belle, Organdy & Lace, Felt Flowers, Hat, 18 In.	1900.00
Lenci, Harlequin, Pressed & Painted Head, Colored Costume, 1930s, 28 In.	862.00
Lenci, Impish Character, Dressed, Tag, 12 In.	1200.00
Lenci, Mascotte, Stamp & Label Inside Dress, 9 In.	350.00

Lenci, Plaid Dress, Hat, Original Clothes, c.1930, 12 In. 525.00
Lenci, Swivel Head, Closed Mouth, 1-Piece Underwear, Oilcloth Coat, 16 In. 450.00
Little Lulu, Cloth, Mask Face, Original Clothing, 13 In. 200.00
Lola Hanson, Bisque, Cotton Body, Red Wig, Blue Eyes, Pierced Ears, 1978, 16 In. 60.00
Madame Alexander, Alice In Wonderland, Alexanderkin, Walker, 1954, 8 In. 220.00
Madame Alexander, Alice In Wonderland, Human Hair Wig, Organdy Pinafore, 13 In. . 525.00
Madame Alexander, Cisette, Hard Plastic, Formal Gown, c.1957, 10 In. 132.00
Madame Alexander, Cynthia, 14 In. 750.00
Madame Alexander, Cynthia, 18 In. 950.00
Madame Alexander, Dutch Boy, 9 In. 200.00
Madame Alexander, Dutch Girl, 9 In. 230.00
Madame Alexander, Elise, Pink Formal, 17 In. 200.00
Madame Alexander, Eskimo, Sleep Eyes, Tagged Outfit, Wrist Tag, 1966, 8 In. 175.00
Madame Alexander, Fairy Princess, Composition, Original Dress, c.1942, 14 In. 44.00
Madame Alexander, Hawaiian, Sleep Eyes, Tagged Outfit, Box, 1966, 8 In. 150.00
Madame Alexander, Lissy, White Organdy Blouse, Checked Skirt, 11 1/2 In. 195.00
Madame Alexander, Lissy, Yellow Organdy Party Dress, Hat, 11 1/2 In. 225.00
Madame Alexander, Little Shaver, 15 In. 220.00
Madame Alexander, Little Women, Tagged Outfits, Boxes, 1948-49, 8 In., 4 Piece 2600.00
Madame Alexander, Margot Ballerina, Blue Sleep Eyes, Pink Tagged Tutu, 1954, 18 In. 650.00
Madame Alexander, Marie, Toddler, Straight Leg, 8 In. 275.00
Madame Alexander, Mary Hoyer, Hard Plastic, c.1940, 14 In. 66.00
Madame Alexander, Mary Martin, South Pacific Sailor Costume, c.1950, 18 In. 725.00
Madame Alexander, Mother & Me, Blue Sleep Eyes, Tagged Dress, 1940s, 14 In. 275.00
Madame Alexander, Plastic Head, Mary Louise, Walker Body, Booklet, c.1954, 8 In. .. 1500.00
Madame Alexander, Prince Charles, Hard Plastic Head, Blue Sleep Eyes, 8 In. 575.00
Madame Alexander, Scarlett O'Hara, Composition, Tag, c.1937, 11 In. 88.00
Madame Alexander, Sonja Henie, Composition, Tag, c.1939, 21 In. 302.00
Madame Alexander, Sonja Henie, Hard Plastic, Original Dress, c.1939, 14 In. 209.00
Madame Alexander, Susie Q, Cloth, Blue Glancing Eyes, Closed Pouty Mouth, 16 In. ... 750.00
Madame Alexander, Susie Q, Cloth, Tag, c.1935, 13 In. 385.00
Madame Alexander, Treena Ballerina, Original Outfit, 1952, 14 In. 650.00
Madame Alexander, Wendy Ann, Composition, Missing Label, c.1936, 11 In. 88.00
Mae Starr, Composition Shoulder Head, Cloth, Sleep Eyes, Open Mouth, 1928, 29 In. ... 125.00
Mannequin, Wax Bust, 12 In. 99.00
Marion Kaulitz, Character Girl, Composition, Jointed, Folklore Costume, 1900s, 17 In. . 5750.00
Marseille, 323, Bisque, Googly, Impish Smile, Papier-Mache Body, Muslin Frock, 8 In. . 750.00
Marseille, 323, Bisque, Socket Head, Blue Glass Googly Eyes, Closed Mouth, 7 1/2 In. . 1150.00
Marseille, 323, Googly, Bisque, Socket Head, Blue Glass Googly Sleep Eyes, 11 In. 1350.00
Marseille, 590, Bisque Head, Brown Sleep Eyes, Brunette Mohair, 12 In. 1200.00
Marseille, Bisque Head, Blue Sleep Eyes, Blond Mohair Wig, 1915, 13 In. 1600.00
Marseille, Bisque Head, Blue Sleep Googly Eyes, Brunette Mohair Wig, 10 In. 1400.00
Marseille, Just Me, 310, Sleep Eyes, Ginny By Vogue Costume, Germany, c.1930, 8 In. . 1550.00
Martha Chase, Blond Hair, Brown Eyes, 24 In. 375.00
Martha Chase, Painted Stockinet Body, Painted Blond Hair, 21 In. 345.00
Martha Thompson, Portrait, Empress Carlotta, Bisque, Muslin, 1954, 20 In. 1900.00
Mary Francis Woods, Portrait, American Indian, Muslin, Early 20th Century, 14 In. ... 600.00
Mary Hoyer, Gigi, Sleep Eyes, Red Saran Wig, Pink Gown, Box, Mid 1950s, 18 In. 2600.00
Mary Hoyer, Green Sleep Eyes, Brunette Wig, Carol Outfit, Box, c.1950, 14 In. 450.00
Mary Hoyer, Plastic Head, 5-Piece Body, Formal Gown, 1950s, 14 In. 550.00
Mary Hoyer, Plastic Head, Gigi, c.1953, 18 In. 500.00
Mary Poppins, Cloth, Composition, 10 1/2 In. 16.00
Mattel, Baby First Step, Battery Operated, Skates, Box, 1960s 35.00
Mattel, Barbie, 1st Valentine 45.00
Mattel, Barbie, 35th Anniversary, Blond ....20.00 to 35.00
Mattel, Barbie, 5th Anniversary 525.00
Mattel, Barbie, American Girl, Box 1250.00
Mattel, Barbie, Anniversary, 35th, Brunette 135.00
Mattel, Barbie, Black Patent Ballet Case, 1960s 50.00
Mattel, Barbie, Black Patent Wallet Carryall, 1965 .... 85.00
Mattel, Barbie, Blue Rhapsody Barbie, Porcelain, c.1986 .... 265.00
Mattel, Barbie, Brunette, Vinyl Head, Blue Eyes, Box, 1960 .... 650.00
Mattel, Barbie, Bubble Cut, American Airlines Outfit 200.00

Mattel, Barbie, Bubble Cut, Blond, Pink Lips, Let's Dance Dress, c.1961 . . . . 105.00
Mattel, Barbie, Busy Gal, Box 50.00
Mattel, Barbie, Coca-Cola 175.00
Mattel, Barbie, Enchanted Evening, Gown & Stole, Red Hair, Bubble Cut 300.00
Mattel, Barbie, Flight Time Gift Set, Flight Attendant Uniform, Party Skirt, Box, 1989 . . 40.00
Mattel, Barbie, Greek, International Series, c.1985 . . . . 55.00
Mattel, Barbie, Happy Holidays Barbie, White Dress, Fur Trim, 1989 . . . . .195.00 to 200.00
Mattel, Barbie, Happy Holidays, 1990 . . . . 200.00
Mattel, Barbie, Harley-Davidson 150.00
Mattel, Barbie, Holiday, 1st Edition, 1988 . . . . 695.00
Mattel, Barbie, Little Debbie 98.00
Mattel, Barbie, Live Action, Blond, Rooted Eyelashes, Original Outfit, 1973 . . . . 155.00
Mattel, Barbie, Living Barbie, Brunette, Original Silver & Gold Swimsuit, 1970 . . . . 70.00
Mattel, Barbie, Loves Elvis 64.00
Mattel, Barbie, Mardi Gras 75.00
Mattel, Barbie, Maria 40.00
Mattel, Barbie, Navy, Stars & Stripes Special Edition, Box, 1990 . . . . 30.00
Mattel, Barbie, No. 1, Brunette, Ponytail, Hoop Earrings, Black & White Swimsuit 4100.00
Mattel, Barbie, No. 3, Brunette, Ponytail, Pearl Earrings, Black & White Swimsuit 1700.00
Mattel, Barbie, No. 4, Brunette, Ponytail, Finger & Toe Paint, Blue & White Swimsuit . . 235.00
Mattel, Barbie, No. 5, Blond Hair, Ponytail, Black & White 1-Piece Swimsuit 180.00
Mattel, Barbie, Peppermint Princess . . . . .58.00 to 80.00
Mattel, Barbie, Ponytail, Red Jersey Swimsuit, High Heels, Pearl Earrings, 1962 . . . . 375.00
Mattel, Barbie, Purple Passion, Box 35.00
Mattel, Barbie, Queen Of Hearts 200.00
Mattel, Barbie, Radio Shack 45.00
Mattel, Barbie, Rapunzel 43.00
Mattel, Barbie, Rhapsody, Porcelain 650.00
Mattel, Barbie, Ribbons & Roses, Box 40.00
Mattel, Barbie, Royal Elegance, Box 38.00
Mattel, Barbie, Scarlett, Flowered 65.00
Mattel, Barbie, Scarlett, Green 65.00
Mattel, Barbie, Scarlett, Red 65.00
Mattel, Barbie, Snow Princess . . . . .125.00 to 150.00
Mattel, Barbie, Soda Fountain 150.00
Mattel, Barbie, Starlight Waltz 85.00
Mattel, Barbie, Summer Splendor 90.00
Mattel, Barbie, Swan Lake, Box 250.00
Mattel, Barbie, Swirl Ponytail, Box 425.00
Mattel, Barbie, Terri Lee, Brunette 295.00
Mattel, Barbie, Titian Ponytail, Ponytail, Pearl Earrings, Black & White Swimsuit 450.00
Mattel, Barbie, Vinyl Head, Blue Eyes, Rooted Blond Hair, Box, 1960 . . . . 750.00
Mattel, Barbie, Vinyl Head, Blue Eyes, Rooted Blond Hair, Box, 1961, 11 In. 400.00
Mattel, Barbie, Vinyl Head, Blue Eyes, Rooted Blond Hair, Box, 1962, 11 In. 550.00
Mattel, Barbie, Wedding Day, Pink Bridesmaid Dress, Box, 1990 . . . . 40.00
Mattel, Beany, Large Vinyl Head, 1960s, 15 In. 65.00
Mattel, Growing Up Skipper, Move Arm, Bust Grows, 1975, 9 1/2 In. 45.00
Mattel, Ken, Box, 1961, 12 In. 195.00
Mattel, Ken, Braniff Airlines Pilot Uniform, 12 In. 35.00
Mattel, Ken, Sport & Shave 25.00
Mattel, Larry The Lion, Talking, Cloth, Molded Vinyl, 1962, 12 In. 45.00
Mattel, Lucy, Skeddidle Kiddle, Peanuts, Plastic, Blue Fabric Dress, 5 In. 40.00
Max Oscar Arnold, 200, Bisque, Composition, 6 Teeth, Scottish Dancer, c.1920, 11 In. . . 60.00
Mego, Captain Kirk, Spock, Lt. Uhura, Mr. Scott, Klingon, On Card, 1974, 8 In., 5 Piece . 325.00
Mego, Cher, Poseable, Plastic, Vinyl, Box, 1976, 12 In. 85.00
Mego, Fonzie, Happy Days, Thumbs-Up Lever Action, Box, 1976, 8 In. 30.00
Mego, Wonder Woman, Linda Carter, Box, 12 In. 250.00
Mignonette, Bisque, Boy, Girl, Original Glass-Front Box, France, c.1890, 2 In., Pair . . . 250.00
Mignonette, Bisque, Swivel Head, 6 Wood Lambs, Box, France, 1890, 3 x 4 In. 700.00
Minerva, Metal Head, Cloth Body, Painted Eyes, Molded Hair, Germany, 16 In. 35.00
Molly-'es, Raggedy Andy, Mark On Front Torso, 1935-38, 20 In. 522.00
Morimura, 2, Bisque, Composition, Sleep Eyes, Open Mouth, 2 Teeth, c.1915, 10 In. . . . 66.00
Morimura, Baby, Character, Bisque Head, Sleep Eyes, Mohair Wig, 1920, 11 In. 115.00

Morimura, Janon, Bisque, Kid Body, Sleep Eyes, Open Mouth, 4 Teeth, c.1920, 17 In. . . . 71.00
Mulatto, Bisque, Shoulder Head, Closed Mouth, Painted Eyes, Cloth Body, 7 In. 90.00
Nancy Ann Storybook, Black, 1950s, 6 In. 138.00
Nancy Ann Storybook, Muffie, Groom, Plastic Head, Walker Body, Box, c.1953, 8 In. . . 250.00
Nancy Ann Storybook, Muffie, Plastic Head, Toddler Body, Box, c.1953, 8 In. . . .195.00 to 325.00
Nancy Lee, Ice Skater, Hard Plastic, Wrist Tag, 4 Outfits, 18 In. 255.00
Neapolitan, Black Man, Molded Face, Composition Body, Silk Shirt, c.1880, 16 In. 275.00
Neapolitan, Peasant Woman, Wax, 17 In. 66.00
Nippon, Boy, Bisque, Cloth Sawdust-Stuffed Body, 5 In. 90.00
Nippon Novelty, Japanese, Bisque, Composition, Sleep Eyes, 2 Teeth, 1925, 11 In. 97.00
Norah Wellings, Black, Islander, Grass Skirt, Glass Eyes, Tag, 38 In. 775.00
Norah Wellings, Lady, Cloth, Painted Face, Felt & Velvet Cloths, Tag, 14 In. 220.00
Norah Wellings, Sailor, Fabric, Cap Marked S.S. Stratheden, England, c.1930, 8 In. 33.00
Oriental, Composition, Dark Brown Sleep Eyes, Brown Hair, 12 In. 595.00
Oriental, Composition, Swivel Head, Glass Eyes, Mohair Wig, 24 In. 185.00
Paper dolls are listed in their own category.
Papier-Mache, Baby, Painted Swaddling, France, c.1830, 14 In. 1250.00
Papier-Mache, Cameo Face, Sculpted Hair, Kid Body, Germany, c.1840, 7 1/2 In. 400.00
Papier-Mache, Ethnic Features, Glass Eyes, 11 1/2 In. 375.00
Papier-Mache, Girl, Holz-Masse, 40 In. 1295.00
Papier-Mache, Kid Body, Separated Fingers, Provincial Costume, France, c.1840, 11 In. 650.00
Papier-Mache, Marotte, On Wooden Stick, Silk Ribbons, French Market, c.1890, 14 In. . 325.00
Papier-Mache, Molded & Painted Head, Blond Hair, Kid Hands, Calico Dress, 17 1/2 In. 201.00
Papier-Mache, Nun, Muslin Body, Brown Wool Habit, Rope Belt, France, 1845, 16 In. . 850.00
Papier-Mache, Paperweight Eyes, Blond Mohair Wig, Jointed Arms, 4 1/2 In. 325.00
Papier-Mache, Polichinelle, Plays Cymbals, Wood Body, France, c.1890, 15 In. 1000.00
Papier-Mache, Polichinelle, Straw-Filled Limbs, Silk Costume, France, c.1885, 17 In. . . 850.00
Parian, Blond Molded Hair, Blue Eyes, Pink Dress, Germany, c.1870, 17 In. 66.00
Parian, Glass Eyes, Leather Hands, Molded Hair With Bow, Pierced Ears, 16 In. 1650.00
Parian, Princess Eugenie, Snood Hair Net, c.1860, 15 In. 1250.00
Parian, Snood Over Hair, Painted Intaglio Eyes, Cloth Body, Kid Lower Limbs, 19 In. . . 460.00
Parian, Woman, Shoulder Head, Cloth Body, Molded Features, Blond Flat Top, 7 1/2 In. . 75.00
Parian, Woman, Upswept Hair, Pulled Back In Braids, Cloth Body, Spoon Hands, 17 In. . 950.00
Paris, Heart-Shaped Face, Oversized Paperweight Eyes, 16 In. 4200.00
Pincushion dolls are listed in their own category.
Pintel & Godchaux, Large Paperweight Eyes, Dressed, 24 In. 3850.00
Princess Diana, Wedding Dress, Box, 18 In. 1000.00
Princess Leia, Star Wars, Vinyl, White Dress, 1978, 12 In. 50.00
Puppet, Bisque Head, Punichello, Pull String At Head, Arms & Legs Move 2200.00
Puppet, Black Man, Glass Eyes, c.1900 . . . . 1285.00
Puppet, Finger, 3 Stooges, Larry, Moe, Curly, Molded Plastic, 3 To 3 1/2 In., 3 Piece . . . 40.00
Puppet, Finger, Adventure Boy, With Skymobile, Remco, Box, 1970 . . . . 65.00
Puppet, Finger, Davy, Monkees . . . . .25.00 to 30.00
Puppet, Gizmo, Gremlins, Plush, Original Care Tag, 11 In. 86.00
Puppet, Grandpa Munster, Vinyl, Fabric, Karyo-Vue Productions, Ideal, 1964, 10 1/2 In. 110.00
Puppet, Hand, Alvin, Knickerbocker, 1963, 12 In. 48.00
Puppet, Hand, Bert & Ernie, Pair 80.00
Puppet, Hand, Bob Hope 65.00
Puppet, Hand, Cap'n Crunch, Vinyl, 1960s, 8 In. 28.00
Puppet, Hand, Cecil, Talks, 1962 . . . . 75.00
Puppet, Hand, Dutch Boy Paints 40.00
Puppet, Hand, Gumby, Cloth 40.00
Puppet, Hand, H.R. Pufnstuf 275.00
Puppet, Hand, Jell-O, Mr. Wiggles, 1966 . . . . 185.00
Puppet, Hand, Lamb Chop, Original Package, Ideal Toy Co., 1960 . . . . 25.00
Puppet, Hand, Laurel & Hardy, Knickerbocker, Pair 65.00
Puppet, Hand, Loopy Wolf, Identification, Steiff 165.00
Puppet, Hand, Monkees, 4 Plastic Heads, Cloth Sleeve, Mattel, 1966 . . . . 100.00
Puppet, Hand, Mr. Ed, Pull-String Talker 95.00
Puppet, Hand, Mr. Ed, Talking Horse, Mattel, 1962 . . . . 85.00
Puppet, Hand, Peter Pan 15.00
Puppet, Hand, Planet Of The Apes 65.00
Puppet, Hand, Robin, Vinyl, Ideal, 1966, 11 In. 50.00

Puppet, Hand, Talking Mister Ed, Molded Vinyl, Cloth, Pull String, Mattel, 1962, 11 In.	40.00
Puppet, Hand, Wendy The Good Little Witch	15.00
Puppet, Lamb Chop, Ideal Toy Co., 1960, Original Package	25.00
Puppet, Movable Jaw, Wooden, c.1900	985.00
Puppet, Pokey, Orange Head, Vinyl, 1960s	95.00
Puppet, Push Up, Robot, Wooden, Tilts & Dances, Spring & String Control	8.00
Puppet, Star Wars, Yoda, Soft Plastic, White Hair, 1981, 8 1/2 In.	40.00
Quan Quan Co., Chinese, Composition, Black Hair, Oriental Outfit, c.1930, 12 In.	71.00
Queen Mother Mary Of England, Stone Bisque, Kid Body, England, c.1890, 20 In.	275.00
Recknagel, Googly, Glass Eyes, 10 In.	1295.00
Resi Brandl, 22/118, Bisque, Kid Body, Sleep Eyes, Open Mouth, 4 Teeth, c.1923, 14 In.	77.00
Rheinesche Gummi, Celluloid, Interchangeable Heads, 3 Girls, 1 Cat, 1913, 10 In.	2000.00
Rockwell, Little Sister, Original Clothes, 1927	495.00
Roger Rabbit, Plush, Red Corduroy Jumper, 16 In.	25.00
Rohmer, Bisque, Kid & Wood Body, Jointed, Bisque Limbs, Bare Feet, c.1860, 17 In.	4700.00
Rohmer, Bisque, Zinc Body, Wood, Jointed, Cotton Gown, Stamped Mark, c.1860, 18 In.	6000.00
Ronald McDonald, Plastic, Cloth Clothes, Remco, Hong Kong, 1976, 8 In.	40.00
Roullet Et Decamps, L'Intrepide Bebe, Clockwork Mechanism, Box, 1895, 13 In.	1900.00
S & H dolls are listed here as Bergmann and Simon & Halbig.	
S.F.B.J., 236, Bisque Head, Baby, Jointed Body, 2 Upper Teeth, Nursing Gown, 12 In.	895.00
S.F.B.J., 236, Toddler, Sleep Eyes, Open-Close Mouth, 2 Upper Teeth, 23 In.	1895.00
S.F.B.J., 251, Character Baby, Flirty Blue Eyes, 24 In.	2500.00
S.F.B.J., 301, Ball-Jointed Body, Composition Head, Dressed, 24 In.	450.00
S.F.B.J., 301, Walker, Bluette, Sleep Eyes, Pierced Ears, Mohair Wig, 1920s, 19 1/2 In.	920.00
S.F.B.J., Bisque Head, Child, Jointed Body, Wigged & Dressed, 21 In.	550.00
S.F.B.J., Bisque, Blue Eyes, Chunky Body, 28 In.	2600.00
S.F.B.J., Bisque, Socket Head, Amber, Brown Inset Eyes, Open Mouth, 1907, 25 In.	2200.00
S.F.B.J., Bisque, Socket Head, Blue Paperweight Eyes, Auburn Human Hair, 1907, 24 In.	2500.00
S.F.B.J., Bisque, Socket Head, Blue Paperweight Eyes, Blond Mohair Wig, 18 In.	1300.00
Sandy McCall, Original Clothes, 35 In.	530.00
Scarecrow, Cloth, Rubber Face, 1950, 18 In.	125.00
Schmidt, 1255, Character Baby, Painted Fuzzy Hair, Solid Dome, Dimples, 13 In.	1700.00
Schmidt, Bisque, Brown Sleep Eyes, Brown Human Hair Wig, 30 In.	1150.00
Schmidt & Fils, Bisque, Almond Paperweight Eyes, 1879, 19 In.	13500.00
Schmitt & Fils, Bisque, Human Hair, Composition & Wood Body, Jointed, 1884, 15 In.	7750.00
Schoenau & Hoffmeister, 1909, Bisque Head, Sleep Eyes, Open Mouth, 24 In.	259.00
Schoenau & Hoffmeister, 4000, Sleep Eyes, 4 Teeth, Folklore Costume, c.1900, 15 In.	900.00
Schoenau & Hoffmeister, Bisque Head, Brown, Toddler, Lei, Grass Skirt, 1920s, 8 In.	230.00
Schoenau & Hoffmeister, Bisque Head, Fixed Glass Eyes, Teeth, Kid Body, Hat, 22 In.	55.00
Schoenau & Hoffmeister, Bisque Head, Infant, White Dress, Lace Trim, 12 In.	200.00
Schoenau & Hoffmeister, Bisque, Brown Sleep Eyes, Antique Dress, 24 In.	800.00
Schoenau & Hoffmeister, Child, Brown Sleep Eyes, Mohair Wig, 11 In.	225.00
Schoenau & Hoffmeister, Princess Elizabeth, 19 In.	1400.00
Schoenhut, Dolly Face, 15 In.	275.00
Schoenhut, Dressed As Scottish Lad, 2 Extra Outfits, 17 In.	1250.00
Schoenhut, Girl, Carved Hair, Rear Bow, Original Dress & Shoes, 16 In.	595.00
Schoenhut, Girl, Sober Face, Blond Mohair, Philadelphia, 1911, 13 1/2 In.	375.00
Schoenhut, Girl, Sober Face, Brown Eyes, Blond Mohair, 18 1/2 In.	375.00
Schoenhut, Girl, Wooden, Socket Head, Carved Braids, Blue Bow, Jointed, 1912, 18 In.	1500.00
Schoenhut, Ko-Ko Clown, Wood, Jointed, 10 1/2 In.	1045.00
Schoenhut, Wooden, Painted Eyes, Spring-Jointed Wooden Body, Pink Dress, 21 In.	977.00
Schuetzmeister & Quendt, 251, Character, Black, Sleep Eyes, 2 Teeth, c.1920, 12 In.	1200.00
Selchow & Righter, Merrie Marie, Printed Cotton, Uncut, Shrinkwrapped, 1900, 25 In.	230.00
Shindana Toys, Flip Wilson, Geraldine Honey, Stuffed Cloth, Talking, 1970s, 16 In.	175.00
Shirley Temple dolls are included in the Shirley Temple category.	
Simon & Halbig dolls are also listed here under Bergmann.	
Simon & Halbig, 719, Bisque Head, Sleep Eyes, Pierced Ears, Mohair Wig, 23 3/4 In.	1495.00
Simon & Halbig, 719, Bisque Socket Head, 6 Teeth, Composition & Wood, 1895, 21 In.	2800.00
Simon & Halbig, 719, Bisque, Blue Paperweight Eyes, Long Tail Mohair Wig, 24 In.	2875.00
Simon & Halbig, 740, Bisque, Brown Eyes, Closed Mouth, Brunette Mohair Wig, 11 In.	1700.00
Simon & Halbig, 886, Mignonette, Bisque, Jointed, 4 Teeth, Red Silk Suit, c.1890, 5 In.	950.00
Simon & Halbig, 908, Bisque, Open Mouth, 12 In.	1500.00
Simon & Halbig, 939, Bisque Head, Blond Human Hair, Jointed Body, 30 In.	1035.00

Simon & Halbig, 939, Bisque Swivel Head, Blue Eyes, 1890, 16 In. 1700.00
Simon & Halbig, 939, Brown Bisque Head, 4 Teeth, Jointed, c.1900, 13 In. 1800.00
Simon & Halbig, 939, Child, Bisque Head, Blue Sleep Eyes, Composition, 14 In. 1050.00
Simon & Halbig, 939, Child, Bisque, Kid Body, Jointed, Human Hair, c.1890, 12 In. . . . 2000.00
Simon & Halbig, 949, Bisque Socket Head, 4 Teeth, Composition & Wood, 1895, 38 In. . 3400.00
Simon & Halbig, 949, Bisque, Auburn Human Hair Wig, Victorian Dress, 42 In. 6400.00
Simon & Halbig, 949, Bisque, Composition & Wood Body, Jointed, c.1890, 12 In. 1800.00
Simon & Halbig, 949, Bisque, Composition & Wood Body, Straw Hat, c.1890, 11 In. . . . 3100.00
Simon & Halbig, 1078, Bisque Head, Walking Undressed, 9 In. 247.00
Simon & Halbig, 1078, Bisque, Antique Clothes, 17 In. 825.00
Simon & Halbig, 1078, Bisque, Composition, Sleep Eyes, 4 Teeth, c.1910, 28 In. 385.00
Simon & Halbig, 1078, Black, Brown Set Eyes, Painted Socks, 8 1/2 In. 950.00
Simon & Halbig, 1079, Bisque, Blond Mohair Wig, Open Mouth, 32 In. 1795.00
Simon & Halbig, 1079, Bisque, Child, Antique Clothing, 31 In. 450.00
Simon & Halbig, 1079, Bisque, Composition, Open Mouth, 5 Teeth, c.1910, 10 In. 165.00
Simon & Halbig, 1079, Bisque, Kid Body, Pierced Ears, 4 Teeth, 1915, 23 In. 1633.00
Simon & Halbig, 1079, Original Hair & Body, Dressed, 28 In. 1450.00
Simon & Halbig, 1249, Bisque, Composition, Jointed, Sleep Eyes, Open Mouth, 18 In. . 748.00
Simon & Halbig, 1249, Bisque, Sleep Eyes, Open Mouth, Human Hair, c.1900, 26 In. . . 2200.00
Simon & Halbig, 1249, Original Hairnet, 31 In. 1995.00
Simon & Halbig, 1249, Santa Claus, 24 In. 1495.00
Simon & Halbig, 1299, Bisque Socket Head, Sleep Eyes, 2 Teeth, c.1910, 18 In. 1500.00
Simon & Halbig, 1329, Bisque, Woman, Oriental, Dimono, 16 In. 2375.00
Simon & Halbig, Bisque Head, Black, Brown Wig, Sleep Eyes, Upper Teeth, 16 1/2 In. . 1265.00
Simon & Halbig, Bisque, Composition, Open Mouth, Jointed, c.1900, 31 In. 575.00
Simon & Halbig, Bisque, Swivel Head, Cobalt Blue Inset Eyes, Closed Mouth, 8 In. . . . 850.00
Simon & Halbig, Child, Bisque Head, Blue Sleep Eyes, Open Mouth, 1900, 23 In. 650.00
Simon & Halbig, Child, Fully Jointed Body, Sleep Eyes, Dimples, 15 In. 950.00
Simon & Halbig, Evelyn, Sleep Eyes, Open Mouth, Jointed, S & H 17 Mark, 42 In. 2070.00
Simon & Halbig, Mignonette, Bisque, Sleep Eyes, Painted Black Stockings, 1890, 5 In. . 650.00
Simon & Halbig, Woman, Asian, Bisque, Socket Head, Brown Glass Sleep Eyes, 16 In. . 1300.00
Skippy Doll Corp., Little Debbie Eve, Pink Lace Outfit, Baby Bottle, 1950s, 20 In. 100.00
Skookum, With Baby, With Blanket Over Shoulder, 1926, 11 & 7 In., 2 Piece 235.00
Sonja Henie, 19 In. 695.00
Steiff, All Felt, Swivel Head, Jointed, Wool Skirt, Dutch Cap, Shoes, c.1920, 13 In. 1500.00
Steiff, Micki & Mecki, 6 1/2 In., Pair 125.00
Steiner, Bisque Head, Baby, Blue Eyes, Closed Mouth, Blond Mohair Wig, 1890, 10 In. . 455.00
Steiner, Bisque Head, Blue Glass Side-Glancing Googly Eyes, Composition, 1920, 8 In. . 500.00
Steiner, Bisque Head, Clockwork, Paperweight Eyes, Lambskin Wig, 1880s, 20 In. 1035.00
Steiner, Bisque Head, Dark Blue Enamel Eyes, Closed Mouth, Composition, 9 In. 4200.00
Steiner, Bisque Head, Kid Body, Brown Sleep Eyes, Open Mouth, 5 Teeth, c.1922, 14 In. 66.00
Steiner, Bisque Head, Set Eyes, Mohair Wig, Jointed Body, Dress, Shoes, 11 1/2 In. 1850.00
Steiner, Majestic, Bisque, Composition, Open Mouth, 4 Teeth, c.1900, 18 In. 154.00
Steiner, Round Face, Paperweight Eyes, Mohair Wig, Composition Body, 23 In. 5900.00
Steiner, Series C, Bisque, Composition & Wood Body, Jointed, c.1885, 10 In. 6500.00
Strawberry Shortcake, Outfit With Hat & Stockings, 1979, 4 In. 4.00
Sun Rubber, Baby, Squeeze Toy, Squeaking Sound, Yellow, Tan, 10 In. 29.00

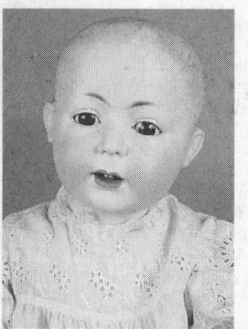

**If you buy an old cloth doll, put
it in a closed box with an insect
strip for 48 hours to be sure
there are no insects. Be sure the
strip does not touch the doll.**

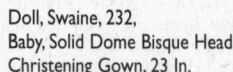

Doll, Swaine, 232,
Baby, Solid Dome Bisque Head,
Christening Gown, 23 In.

Sun Rubber, Gerber Baby, Glass Eyes, Bottle, Cries 125.00
Swaine, 232, Baby, Solid Dome Bisque Head, Christening Gown, 23 In. ....*Illus* 1500.00
Swaine, Bisque, Composition Body, Blue Sleep Eyes, Stamped, c.1910, 9 In. 440.00
Swaine, Bisque, Socket Head, Intaglio Blue Eyes, Closed Mouth, Brunette Wig, 15 In. .. 5200.00
Terrene, Bisque, Swivel Head, Kid Over Wood Body, Jointed, France, c.1875, 18 In. ... 5300.00
Terri Lee, Plastic Head, Ballerina, Curled Wig, Ballerina Outfit, c.1952, 16 In. 550.00
Terri Lee, Plastic Head, Saran Wig, Red Bow Box, Tagged Outfit, c.1952, 16 In. 600.00
Terri Lee, Red Play Suit, Long Beach Coat, 16 In. 250.00
Tete Jumeau, Bisque Socket Head, Jointed Body, Wig Over Cork Pate, 21 In. 3700.00
Tete Jumeau, Bisque, Almond-Shaped Eyes, Teeth, Lace-Trimmed Dress, 24 In. 3125.00
Tete Jumeau, Bisque, Blue Saucer-Like Eyes, Blond Mohair Wig, 10 1/2 In. 4200.00
Tete Jumeau, Bisque, Child, Blue Paperweight Eyes, Closed Mouth, 20 In. 5900.00
Tete Jumeau, Bisque, Large Eyes, Old Clothes, 20 In. 5500.00
Tete Jumeau, Bisque, Paperweight Eyes, Closed Mouth, Shoes, 16 In. 4495.00
Tete Jumeau, Bisque, Paperweight Eyes, Original Shoes, 16 In. 4495.00
Tete Jumeau, Blond Human Hair Wig, Paperweight Eyes, Box, 29 In. 9500.00
Tete Jumeau, Child, Bisque, Paperweight Eyes, Open Mouth, Composition Body, 27 In. 940.00
Tete Jumeau, Closed Mouth, Almond Paperweight Eyes, Antique Dress, 17 In. 4850.00
Tete Jumeau, Original Clothes, Shoes & Wig, Box, 17 In. 7500.00
Tinkerbell, Pivoted Arms & Legs, Glass Eyes, Hanging Bracket, Soft Vinyl, 12 In. 225.00
Troll, Wishnik, Felt Clothes, Brown Hair, 1964, 5 1/4 In. 12.00
Uneeda, Baby, Black, Cloth Body, Rubber Head & Hands, Sleep Eyes, Undressed, 15 In. 12.00
Unique, Elly Mae Clampett, Fashion, 1960s, 8 In. 80.00
Ventriloquist, Jerry Mahoney, Composition Head & Hands, Dressed, Juro, Box, 1950s . 350.00
Ventriloquist Dummy, Danny O'Day, Jimmy Nelson, With Record 95.00
Vogue, Ginny, Composition, Original Clothes, 8 In. 395.00
Vogue, Ginny, Coronation Queen, Walker, Sleep Eyes, Red Wig, 1953, 8 In. 2200.00
Vogue, Ginny, Green Gingham Pinafore, Walker, Hard Plastic, 8 In. 100.00
Vogue, Ginny, Kindergarten, Blue Sleep Eyes, Blond Poodle Wig, 1952, 8 In. 400.00
Vogue, Ginny, Plastic Head, Black, Organdy Party Dress, c.1953, 8 In. 1900.00
Vogue, Ginny, Plastic Head, Cheryl, Auburn Wig, Toddler Body, Tagged Dress, 1953, 8 In. 1000.00
Vogue, Ginny, Walker, Alaska, Sleep Eyes, Eskimo Outfit, Box, 1959, 8 In. 475.00
Vogue, Ginny, Walker, Black, Brown Sleep Eyes, Tagged Yellow Dress, 1954, 8 In. 2100.00
Vogue, Ginny, Walker, Sleep Eyes, Blond Wig, Tagged Dutch Outfit, 1954-56, 8 In. 325.00
Vogue, Toddies, Composition, 1930s, 7 1/2 In. 225.00
Volland, Raggedy Ann, Muslin, Hand Painted, Cardboard Heart, 1920, 16 In. 850.00
Walker, Charlie Chaplin, Iron Feet, Windup, 1920s 950.00
Walker, Cloth Head, Stiff Neck, Closed Mouth, Striped Dress, White Apron, 18 In. 700.00
Walkure, Closed Mouth, Jumeau Mold, 14 In. 3400.00
Wax, Child, Blue-Gray Spiral Eyes, All Original, 20 In. 1995.00
Wax, Child, Brown Inset Eyes, Closed Mouth, Brunette Mohair Wig, 1865, 22 In. 850.00
Wax, Child, Cobalt Blue Glass Eyes, 20 In. 1995.00
Wax Over Composition Head, Cloth Body, Mid-19th Century, 21 In. 230.00
Woman, Bisque, Shoulder Head, Molded Hair, Painted Face, Cloth Body, Germany, 9 In. 275.00
Wooden, Carved Socket Head, Jointed, Continental, Late 18th Century, 24 In. 5250.00
Wooden, Jointed, Painted Face, Mason Taylor Type, Black & Gray Dress, c.1880, 12 In. . 143.00
Wooden, Peg Joints, Painted Head, Shoulders, Forearms & Lower Legs, 11 In. 100.00
Yolanda Rello, Bisque, Sleeping Form, 12 1/2 In. 33.00
Zinner & Sohne, Clown, Bisque, Wire, Wood, Cymbals, Eyes Blink, c.1890, 16 In. 1500.00

DONALD DUCK items are included in the Disneyana category.

DOORSTOPS have been made in all types of designs. The vast majority
of the doorstops sold today are cast iron and were made from about
1890 to 1930. Most of them are shaped like people, animals, flowers,
or ships. Reproductions and newly designed examples are sold in gift
shops.

Amish Woman, With Basket 150.00
Amos 'n' Andy, Check & Doublecheck, Cast Iron, 1930s, 8 1/2 In. 175.00
Aunt Jemima, Hubley, 1920s 175.00
Basket, Iron, Painted 275.00
Bathing Beauties, Fish Shape 3000.00
Bell Shape, Coalbrookdale, Cast Iron 195.00

Bird, Polychrome, Cast Iron, 7 1/2 In. 190.00
Black Bellhop 1500.00
Camel, Cast Iron 95.00
Cat, 3 Kittens, Bradley & Hubbard 675.00
Cat, Black, Red Bow, Green Eyes, Hubley 265.00
Cat, Hollow Back, Gray & Pink Paint, Iron, 7 3/4 In. 220.00
Cat, Marked Mickey On Back, Painted, 20th Century, 13 In. 345.00
Cat, Reclining, Cast Iron 130.00
Cat, Seated, Cast Iron 345.00
Cat, Sleeping, Hubley 600.00
Cat, Waverly, 1920 .... 100.00
Cat, With Ribbon & Cushion, Black, Red Paint, Cast Iron, 7 3/4 In. 190.00
Dog, 3 Puppies, 19th Century, Cast Iron, 6 1/2 x 8 1/4 In. 196.00
Dog, Boston Terrier, Cast Iron, 9 1/2 In. 132.00
Dog, Boston Terrier, Full Bodied, White, Brown & Black Paint, Cast Iron, 10 1/2 In. 80.00
Dog, Bulldog, Glass, Cobalt Blue, Solid 175.00
Dog, Dachshund, Hubley 575.00
Dog, Dalmatian, Cast Iron 23.00
Dog, Doberman, Hubley, Cast Iron, 8 In. 150.00
Dog, Ohio Red Clay, Solid Cast, Impressed Label, Superior, Uhrichsville, O., 10 1/4 In. ... 385.00
Dog, Pekinese, Hubley, Large 1975.00
Dog, Pointer, Cast Iron, 15 In. 88.00
Dog, Scotty, Cast Iron, 11 In. 138.00
Dog, Twin Scotties, Painted, Cast Iron, 6 x 9 In. ....150.00 to 220.00
Doll, Standing, Yellow Dress, Hubley 395.00
Duck, Full Figure, Worn Black Paint, Cast Iron, 11 1/2 In. 635.00
Duck, Mallard, Black, 13 In. 250.00
Duck, Sheet Iron, 7 1/2 In. 95.00
Duck, Wedge, Marked EMG 806 On Back, 10 In. 175.00
Dutch Girl, With Pails, Cast Iron 295.00
Dutch Windmill, Cast Iron 245.00
Eagle, Black Paint, Cast Iron, 7 In. 275.00
Eagle, Stars On Base, Reddish Brown Paint Traces, Cast Iron, 1866, 6 3/4 In. 275.00
Elephant, Cast Iron, 10 1/4 x 11 In. 220.00
Elephant, Palm Tree, 1920s, 14 In. 200.00
Elephant, Palm Tree, Cast Iron, 7 3/4 x 7 5/8 In. 185.00
English Coach, Horses, Cast Iron 100.00
Flower Basket, Petunias & Daisies, Hubley 90.00
Flower Basket, Tulips, Cast Iron, 8 1/2 In. 300.00
Flower Basket, Zinnias, Hubley 165.00
Flowerpot, Zinnias, Hubley 245.00
Flowers, Oval, Bradley & Hubbard 100.00
Footmen, In Livery, Worn Repaint, Hubley, Iron, 12 In. 275.00
Galleon Ship, Iron, 10 x 10 In. 145.00
Galleon Ship, Polychrome, Painted, Golden Eagle Masthead, 1930, 12 x 11 In. 245.00
General Lafayette, On Rearing Horse, Cast Iron, 9 x 11 5/8 In. 345.00
Golfer, Red Hat & Vest, Cast Iron, 9 3/4 In. 465.00
Heron 225.00
Horse, Hoof, Silver Plate, Blue Rock, Early 20th Century, 1905-1923 .... 1035.00
Horse, Hubley, Cast Iron 95.00
Horse, King's Genius, Racehorse, Iron, 1938 .... 95.00
Horse, Prancing, Scrolled & Molded Base, Glasgow, 19th Century, 11 In. 172.00
Horse, Standing, With Saddle, Cast Iron, 8 3/4 x 7 3/4 In. 140.00
Indian Chief, A.A. Richardson, Marked, Cast Iron, Copyright 1927 .... 1235.00
Indian Head, Full Headdress, Original Paint, Cast Iron 850.00
Jiggs, Bringing Up Father, Folk Art 100.00
Lamb, Reclining, Cast Iron 2400.00
Lion, Full Figure, Cast Iron, 9 In. 55.00
Lion, Recumbent, Bronzed Metal, 9 In. 35.00
Mail Coach, England, Iron 90.00
Mammy, Colorful Clothes, Cast Iron, 12 1/2 In. 135.00
Mammy, Painted, Hubley, 1920s, 9 In. 345.00
Naughty Lady, Cast Iron 65.00

Nude, Standing, Bronze 245.00
Old Salt, Cast Iron, 7 In. 82.00
Ostrich, Cast Iron, 8 1/2 x 9 In. 143.00
Parrot, Bradley & Hubbard, Cast Iron 375.00
Parrot, Polychrome Repaint, Cast Iron, 7 5/8 In. 275.00
Peacock, Painted, Cast Iron 50.00
Pelican, Cast Iron 675.00
Pheasant, Fred Everett 550.00
Punch, All Black 500.00
Rabbit, Full Figure, White Paint, Cast Iron, 9 In. 605.00
Rabbit, Full Figure, White Repaint, Pink, Cast Iron, 10 3/4 In. 135.00
Rabbit, In Cabbage Patch, Cast Iron 475.00
Ram, Cast Iron, 10 1/2 x 8 In. 220.00
Sailing Ship, Chalkware 45.00
Scottish Highlander, Hubley 250.00
Skunk, Cast Iron 975.00
Squirrel, Cast Iron 150.00
Stagecoach, Green Coach, Salmon Wheels, Dated 1930, 7 1/4 x 8 3/4 In. 250.00
Three Kitties, Bradley & Hubbard 675.00
Tropical Woman, Holding Basket, Cast Iron 575.00
Vase Of Tulips, Hubley 350.00
Woman, With 2 Floral Pompons, Cast Iron, 9 In. 195.00

DORCHESTER POTTERY was founded by George Henderson in 1895 in Dorchester, Massachusetts. At first, the firm made utilitarian stoneware, but collectors are most interested in the line of decorated blue and white pottery that Dorchester made from 1940 until it went out of business in 1979.

DORCHESTER POTTERY WORKS BOSTON, MASS.

Candlestick, Half Scroll Pattern, High Luster, Round, 5 1/3 In. 135.00
Casserole, Cover, 7 In. 235.00
Charger, Stylized Pussy Willow Branch, Blue Swirl Ground, 12 1/4 In. 825.00
Charger, Teardrop Repeated Design, Starburst Center, 12 1/4 In. 550.00
Cup & Saucer, Smiling Whale, Blue Swirl Glaze Saucer, 2 3/4 & 6 1/8 In. 75.00
Jug, Egg Shape, Speckled Cerulean Blue Glaze, Handle, 15 In. 330.00
Mug, Donkey, Blue, Ivory Glaze Ground, 3 In. 135.00
Plate, Blue Whale Design, Waves, High Luster, 10 1/3 In. 165.00
Sugar, Cover, Full Scroll Design, Bulbous, Handles, 4 3/4 x 5 1/2 In. 135.00
Sugar & Creamer, Cover, Half Scroll Design, Bulbous, 3 & 3 1/2 In. 110.00
Wall Pocket, Sailing Ship, On Waves, Knesseth Denisons, 5 x 5 1/4 In. 110.00

DOULTON pottery and porcelain were made by Doulton and Co. of Burslem, England, after 1882. The name *Royal Doulton* appeared on their wares after 1902. Other pottery by Doulton is listed under Royal Doulton.

Bank, Soldier Bunny 75.00
Biscuit Jar, Geometric, Stoneware, Metal Lid, Lambeth, E. Adams, 1879, 7 x 4 3/4 In. ... 400.00
Biscuit Jar, Silver Mounts, Brown & Tan 170.00
Bouillon, With Saucer, Blue & Gilt Floral Design, 24 Piece 220.00
Charger, Head Of Woman In Center Surrounded By Flowers, 1881, 20 In. 715.00
Figurine, Man, Burslem, Noke, 1895, 17 1/2 In. 630.00
Flask, Moon, Faience, Girl Frieze Borders, Artist, 1885, 9 1/2 In. 630.00
Jug, Lion, Grooming, Landscape, Hannah Barlow, Lambeth, 1878, 10 1/2 In. 745.00
Jug, Washington & Columbus, Cobalt Blue & Buff Ground, Lambeth, 7 3/8 In. 400.00
Lamp, Yellow, Turquoise, Blue, Milk Glass Shade & Frame, Lambeth, 12 1/2 In. 585.00
Loving Cup, Raised Figural Scene, 3 Handles, Tan, Brown, 1894, 6 In. 190.00
Pitcher, Christopher Columbus, Columbian Fair Souvenir, White Lettering On Sides 375.00
Pitcher, Good Measure Heavens Treasure, Blue Transfer, Lambeth 121.00
Pitcher, Overall Floral, Foliate Design, Lambeth, 11 In. 385.00
Pitcher, Pastoral Scene, Deer, Grasslands, Beaded & Floral Border, Salt Glaze, 9 In. 855.00
Pitcher & Bowl, Flow Blue, Burslem ....*Illus* 990.00
Plate, Madras, Flow Blue, 6 1/2 In. 60.00
Plate, Madras, Flow Blue, 10 In. 100.00
Plate, Madras, Polychrome, 10 In. 70.00

Plastic bubble wrap can ruin the glaze on old ceramics. If the wrap touches the piece for a long time in a hot storage area, it may discolor the glaze or adhere to the surface in an almost permanent glob.

Doulton, Pitcher & Bowl, Flow Blue, Burslem

Plate, Persian Garden, Flow Blue, 10 1/2 In.	60.00
Plate, Rose & The Thistle, 10 1/2 In.	70.00
Plate, Willow, 1891-1902, 10 1/2 In.	55.00
Platter, Meat, Willow, 1882-1903, 13 x 11 In.	165.00
Platter, Well & Tree, Watteau, 1900, 20 x 16 In.	632.50
Soup, Dish, Gold Trim, Flow Blue, 1903, 10 1/2 In.	20.00
Tureen, Watteau, Flow Blue, Inside & Outside Scene	275.00
Vase, Flambe, Veining, Noke, 6 In.	475.00
Vase, Horse Profile, Mottled Brown Ground, Hannah Barlow, Lambeth, 8 1/2 In.	575.00
Vase, Lions, Lambeth, 14 In.	800.00
Vase, Relief Patterns, Lambeth, 1882, 6 1/2 In.	200.00
Vase, Scenic, Flambe, 2 In.	195.00
Vase, Scenic, Sheep, W. Odkinson, 7 1/2 In.	575.00
Vase, Stylized Leaves, Stippled Dandelions, Glossy Blue Ground, 1889, 10 In.	385.00

DRAGONWARE is a form of moriage pottery. Moriage is a type of decoration on Japanese pottery. Raised white designs are applied to the ware. White dragons are the major raised decorations on the moriage called *dragonware*. The background color is gray and white, orange and lavender, or orange and brown. It is a twentieth-century ware.

Cup & Saucer, Lithophane	25.00
Humidor	50.00
Plate, 7 In., 4 Piece	42.00
Plate, Cup & Saucer, Lithophane	12.50
Tea Set, 13 Piece	150.00
Tea Set, 17 Piece	325.00
Tea Set, Occupied Japan, 11 Piece	225.00
Teapot, Cup & Saucer, Doll's, 3 Piece	35.00

DRESDEN china is any china made in the town of Dresden, Germany. The most famous factory in Dresden is the Meissen factory. Figurines of eighteenth-century ladies and gentlemen, animal groups, or cherubs and other mythological subjects were popular. One special type of figurine was made with skirts of porcelain-dipped lace. Do not make the mistake of thinking that all pieces marked *Dresden* are from the Meissen factory. The Meissen pieces usually have crossed swords marks, and are listed under Meissen. Some recent porcelain from Ireland, called *Irish Dresden*, is not included in this book.

Bowl, Floral, Lattice, Handles, 9 In.	105.00
Bowl, Flowers, Polychrome & Gilt, Marked, 9 1/2 x 3 1/2 In.	165.00
Box, Salt, Hanging, Wooden Lid, Stenciled Salz & Mehl, 8 In. & 12 1/4 In., Pair	220.00
Cake Plate, Floral, Gilt Design, 6 Piece	325.00
Cake Stand, Polychrome Flowers, Reticulated Rim, Marked, 9 x 6 In.	176.00
Candlestick, Gilt, Floral Design, 6 1/2 In., Pair	190.00
Candy Container, Alligator	290.00
Compote, Applied Florets On Bowl, 2 Figures Of Children On Stems, 14 1/4 In.	345.00

Compote, Multicolored Floral Swag Design, Pink, Gilt Highlights, Off-White Ground .. 170.00
Cup & Saucer, Cover, Blue, Gilt Floral Motif, Flower Finial, 5 1/2 x 4 In. 144.00
Cup & Saucer, Neoclassical, 19th Century 357.50
Dish, Basket Form, Floral Design, Porcelain, 8 x 3 1/2 In. 80.00
Dish, Lobster Motif, Serpent Handle, 12 x 5 1/2 In. 60.00
Dish, Shell Form, Floral & Gold Design, White Ground, 4 x 12 In. 165.00
Dish, Sweetmeat, Cover, 4 Open Wells, Handle, 14 1/2 x 6 1/2 In. 495.00
Figurine, Flamenco Dancer, 5 In. 210.00
Figurine, Group, Diana The Huntress, c.1900, 29 In. 2760.00
Figurine, Spanish Dancer, 6 In. 180.00
Jar, Ginger, Birds, Gold, 5 In. 235.00
Lamp, Table, Faces, Cherubs, Flower Motif, Fancy Openwork, 3 Scroll Feet, 38 In. 747.00
Plaque, Virgin Mary & Christ, Crossed Swords Mark, Porcelain, Frame, 13 x 10 In. 1452.00
Plate, Dinner, Courting Scene, No. 7559, 10 In., Set Of 12 .... 230.00
Wall Pocket, Whisk Broom, Pale Lavender Floral & Gold 95.00

DUNCAN & MILLER is a term used by collectors when referring to glass
made by the George A. Duncan and Sons Company or the Duncan and
Miller Glass Company. These companies worked from 1893 to 1955,
when the use of the name *Duncan* was discontinued and the firm
became part of the United States Glass Company. Early patterns may
be listed under Pressed Glass.

Adoration, Wine, 3 Oz. 23.00
American Way, Basket, Pink, 12 1/2 x 7 1/2 In. 165.00
American Way, Candy, Cover, Satin 75.00
Canterbury, Ashtray, Rectangular 10.00
Canterbury, Bowl, Black, 6 1/4 In. 30.00
Canterbury, Bowl, Oval, 12 In. 45.00
Canterbury, Candy Dish, Cover, Flat 33.00
Canterbury, Cocktail 10.00
Canterbury, Compote 20.00
Canterbury, Finger Bowl 9.00
Canterbury, Sugar & Creamer, 7 Oz. 15.00
Caribbean, Bowl, Blue, 5 In. 30.00
Caribbean, Console Set, Bowl, 2-Light Candlestick, Blue, 3 Piece 225.00
Caribbean, Goblet, Water, Blue 40.00
Caribbean, Relish, 2 Sections, Blue, 6 In. 25.00
Cookie Jar, Nautical, Pink 150.00
Cornucopia, Ruby 125.00
Duck, Ashtray, Cranberry Stained 60.00
Figurine, Donkey 120.00
Figurine, Dove 120.00
Figurine, Fat Goose 245.00
Figurine, Swan, Chartreuse, 7 In. 27.00
Figurine, Swan, Green Neck, Milk Glass Body, 8 In. 400.00
Figurine, Swan, Solid Back Body, 6 1/2 In. 25.00
First Love, Bonbon, Handle 24.00
First Love, Bottle, Salad Dressing 195.00
First Love, Bowl, Flared, 11 In. 60.00
First Love, Candy Dish, Cover 60.00
First Love, Champagne, 5 Oz. 22.00
First Love, Cocktail 19.00
First Love, Compote, 6 In. 30.00
First Love, Goblet, 10 Oz. 25.00
First Love, Pitcher, Ice Lip 150.00
First Love, Plate, Square, 7 1/2 In. 30.00
First Love, Relish, 4 Sections, 9 In. 45.00
First Love, Vase, Cornucopia, 8 In. 60.00
First Love, Vase, Urn, 7 In. 50.00
Hobnail, Bowl, Crimped, Pink Opalescent, 12 In. 40.00
Hobnail, Goblet, Pink Opalescent 25.00
Hobnail, Powder Jar, Cover, Green, 3 In. 35.00
Hobnail, Punch Set, Bowl, Underplate, 12 Cups, Ladle, Box 200.00

Hobnail, Sherbet, Pink Opalescent	15.00
Hobnail, Tumbler, Pink Opalescent, 5 In.	25.00
Indian Tree, Candlestick, 2-Light	45.00
Passion Flower, Sugar & Creamer	45.00
Sandwich, Ashtray, Square, Individual	8.00
Sandwich, Bowl, Crimped, Milk Glass, 11 1/2 In.	110.00
Sandwich, Coaster, 5 In.	12.00
Sandwich, Compote, 7 In.	25.00
Sandwich, Cup & Saucer	14.00
Sandwich, Plate, 8 In.	10.00
Sanibel, Plate, Hors D'Oeuvre, Blue, 14 In.	125.00
Sanibel, Plate, Salad, Pink, 8 1/2 In.	18.00
Sanibel, Relish, 3 Sections, Yellow Opalescent, 12 In.	55.00
Spiral Flutes, Bowl, Pink, 9 In.	26.00
Spiral Flutes, Cup & Saucer, Pink	14.00
Spiral Flutes, Plate, Pink, 10 1/2 In.	25.00
Spiral Flutes, Platter, Pink, 13 In.	42.00
Teardrop, Ashtray, Individual	4.00
Teardrop, Bowl, 12 In.	40.00
Teardrop, Butter, Cover, Morning Glory Silver Overlay	90.00
Teardrop, Candlestick, 2-Light, 4 1/2 In., Pair	62.00
Teardrop, Compote, Footed, 4 1/2 In.	12.00
Teardrop, Cruet, 3 Oz.	26.00
Teardrop, Mayonnaise, Footed, Spoon	24.00
Teardrop, Plate, 8 In.	7.00
Teardrop, Relish, 2 Sections, Heart Shape	17.00
Teardrop, Sugar & Creamer, With Tray	22.00
Teardrop, Tumbler, Juice, Footed, 4 1/2 Oz.	7.00
Teardrop, Wine, 4 3/4 In.	14.00
Terrace, Ashtray, Red, 3 In.	30.00
Terrace, Relish, 3 Sections	35.00
Tropical Fish, Candlestick, Pair	600.00
Venetian, Vase, Green, 6 In.	48.00

DURAND art glass was made from 1924 to 1931. The Vineland Flint Glass Works was established by Victor Durand and Victor Durand, Jr. in 1897. In 1924 Martin Bach, Jr., and other artisans from the Quezal glassworks joined them at the Vineland, New Jersey, plant to make Durand art glass.

Bowl, White Head, Vine Design, Blue Iridescent, 2 x 4 1/4 In.	575.00
Candlestick, Transparent Ambergris, Baluster Form, 10 In., Pair	595.00
Lamp, King Tut, Orange, Pink, Silver Stem, 1900, 15 In., Pair	1430.00
Lamp, Pulled Hearts & Feathers, Silk Shade, 14 In.	1000.00
Rose Bowl, Wreath Of Ferns, Fringed Flowers, Yellow, Amber Iridescent, 1900, 5 In.	1100.00
Vase, Blue Iridescent, 7 1/4 In.	675.00
Vase, Crackled & Iridized Surface, Gold Luster, Signed, 8 1/2 In.	1850.00
Vase, Heart & Vine, Trumpet Form, Deep Blue, White Hearts, 7 In.	605.00
Vase, King Tut, Gold & Green, Signed, 4 In.	750.00
Vase, Peacock Feather, Intaglio-Cut Flower, Cranberry, 8 1/4 In.	1045.00
Vase, Peacock, Blue Iridescent, Ambergris Handles, 12 In.	2310.00
Vase, Pulled Feather, Blue-Tipped Feathers, Iridescent Gold, Gold Threads, 10 In.	1390.00
Vase, Webbed Vines, Horizontal Stripes, Pale Red, 6 1/2 In.	1045.00

ELFINWARE is a mark found on Dresden-like porcelain that was sold in dime stores and gift shops. Many pieces were decorated with raised flowers. The mark was registered by Breslauer-Underberg, Inc. of New York City in 1947. Pieces marked *Elfinware Made in Germany* had been sold since 1945 by this importer.

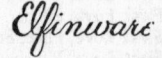

Basket, Forget-Me-Nots On Base, 6 1/2 x 5 1/2 In.	225.00
Box, Cover, Germany	25.00
Holder, Place Card, 8 Piece	225.00
Powder Box, Flowers On Cover, Green, 3 x 5 In.	125.00
Slipper, Flowers	145.00

ELVIS PRESLEY, the well-known singer, lived from 1935 to 1977. He became famous by 1956. Elvis appeared on television, starred in twenty-seven movies, and performed in Las Vegas. Memorabilia from any of the Presley shows, his records, and even memorials made after his death are collected.

Book, Poster, Giant, 1977	18.00
Calendar, 1968, Pocket	10.00
Card Set, Colored, Donruss, 1978, 66 Piece	40.00
Key Holder, Hold To Light, 1960s	22.00
Photograph, With Sold Out Concert Map On Back, 1974, 8 x 10 In.	20.00
Poster, Elvis In Las Vegas, 1976, 24 x 36 In.	16.00
Poster, Jailhouse Rock, Full Color, 28 x 37 In.	45.00
Radio, Figural, AM, Battery Powered, Box, Hong Kong, After 1977, 8 In.	50.00
Record, Album, Fun In Acapulco, 1963, 33 RPM	20.00
Record, Album, Pot Luck, 1965, 33 RPM	15.00
Record, Love Me Tender, 45 RPM	10.00
Sheet Music, Life, 1969	25.00
Toy, Hound Dog, Musical, Box, 1986	50.00
Wristwatch, Commemorative, Replica Of Postal Stamp, Box, 1992	40.00
Wristwatch, Donruss, Unopened Wax Box, 1978	40.00

ENAMELS listed here are made of glass particles and other materials heated and fused to metal. In the eighteenth and nineteenth centuries, workmen from Russia, France, England, and other countries made small boxes and table pieces of enamel on metal. One form of English enamel is called *Battersea* and is listed under that name. There was a revival of interest in enameling in the 1930s and a new style evolved. There is now renewed interest in the artistic enameled plaques, vases, ashtrays, and jewelry. Enamels made since the 1930s are usually on copper or steel, although silver was often used for jewelry. Graniteware is a separate category, and enameled metal kitchen pieces may be included in the Kitchen category.

Ashtray, Flowers, Birds, 1960s, 4-In. Diam.	20.00
Beaker, Imperial Eagle, Black On 1 Side, Cylindrical, Russia, 1896, 4 1/8 In.	1150.00
Bowl, Dutch Girl Feeds Black Cat, Germany, 5 In.	45.00
Box, Cover, Floral, Aviary, Brass, Green, 1 1/2 In.	35.00
Box, Dresser, Conical Cover, Floral, Diaper Enamel, White, Chased Brass Frame, 5 In.	200.00
Box, Dresser, Forget-Me-Knot Design, Bulbous, 3 3/4 In.	150.00
Box, Egg, Marked, 88, Russia, 3 In.	165.00
Box, Floral & Figural Design In Cartouches, China, 19th Century, 5 x 3 1/2 x 3 In.	50.00
Candlestick, Floral Spray, Lobed Domed Base, White Ground, 1770, 9 1/2 In., Pair	1840.00
Cigarette Box, Gold, Lacquered Black, Agate Base, Rectangular, 1930, 4 In.	1840.00
Cigarette Case, Black Enameled Stripes, Wiener Werkstatte, Square, 1920s, 3 1/8 In.	3560.00
Cigarette Case, Pastel Rural Scene, Figure, In Colonial Dress, Brass, 3 1/4 In.	60.00
Cigarette Case, Silver, Half Portrait, Woman, Seminude, 3 1/2 x 3 3/4 In.	2090.00
Cigarette Case, Silver, Red, Small Green & Gold Frog, 3 3/4 x 3 In.	357.00

Enamel, Plate, Car, Orange,
Blue & Gray, 6 3/4 In.

Enamel, Plate, Owl, On Branch,
Thelma Winter, 10 In.

Cigarette Case, With Lighter, Engraved Map Mount Fuji, Japan, Korea, Blue 125.00
Lipstick Case, Silver, Courting Couple, 2 1/4 In. 44.00
Plate, Car, Orange, Blue & Gray, 6 3/4 In. . . . . *Illus* 10.00
Plate, Owl, On Branch, Thelma Winter, 10 In. . . . . *Illus* 100.00
Plate, Wild West Chuck Wagon, Brands, Monterrey Western Ware, 10 In., 4 Piece 65.00
Vase, Hexagonal, Stylized Bird Design, Champleve, Japan, Late 19th Century, 18 In. 110.00
Vase, Hu Form, Passion Flower, Calligraphy, Champleve, 19th Century, 16 In. 165.00

ERPHILA is a mark found on Czechoslovakian and other pottery and
porcelain made after the 1930s. The mark was used on items imported
by Eberling & Reuss, Philadelphia, a giftware firm that is still operating in Pennsylvania. The mark is a combination of the letters *E* and *R*
(Eberling & Reuss) and the first letters of the city, Phila(delphia).
Many whimsical figural pitchers and creamers, figurines, platters, and
other giftwares carry this mark.

Box, Ski, Art Deco 75.00
Figurine, Bear, 4 1/2 In. 35.00
Figurine, Colts, Pair 45.00
Figurine, Dogs, Sitting, 5 1/2 In., Pair 75.00
Figurine, Donkey, 4 1/2 In. 45.00
Figurine, Elephant, 4 In. 50.00
Figurine, Girl's Head, Red Hair 195.00
Figurine, Lion 35.00
Pitcher, Cat, Orange, Black 1000.00
Pitcher, Orange Flowers, Czechoslovakia 70.00
Pitcher, Ram, Orange, Black, 9 In. 250.00
Planter, 3 Graduated Spheres On Each End, 10 In. 50.00
Platter, Chintz, Hand Painted, 11 1/4 In. 75.00
Powder Box, Madame Pompadour, Green Dress 100.00
Teapot, Brown Dog 140.00
Teapot, Cat, 7 In. 75.00
Teapot, Rabbit 150.00

ES GERMANY porcelain was made at the factory of Erdmann
Schlegelmilch from 1861 to 1937 in Suhl, Germany. The porcelain,
marked *ES Germany* or *ES Suhl*, was sold decorated or undecorated.
Other pieces were made at a factory in Saxony, Prussia, and are
marked *ES Prussia*. Reinhold Schlegelmilch made the famous wares
marked *RS Germany*.

Cup & Saucer, Madame Recamier, Portrait 150.00
Cup & Saucer, Mother-Of-Pearl Luster, Woman, With Roses, Yellow, Footed 175.00
Cup & Saucer, Napoleon, Matching 95.00
Plate, Scenic, Ships, Lighthouse, Dark Sky, 9 In. 85.00
Sugar, Napoleon Cover 250.00
Vase, Lady & Peacock, Marked, Art Nouveau, 7 1/2 In. 325.00

ESKIMO artifacts of all types are collected. Carvings of whale or walrus teeth are listed under Scrimshaw. Baskets are in the Basket category. All other types of Eskimo art are listed here.

Busk, Whalebone, Inked Designs, 9 13/16 In. 175.00
Cribbage Board, Arctic Mammals Design, Scrimshaw, Ivory, 1920, 19 In. 4313.00
Cribbage Board, Scrimshaw Design, Polar Bear, Eating A Seal, 20th Century, 7 In. 1380.00
Cribbage Board, Whale's Tooth 1380.00
Doll, Elder Duck Feather Jacket, Reindeer Hide, 1930s, 11 In. 275.00
Doll, Greenland, Wooden, Sealskin Mukluks, c.1900, 18 In. 550.00
Doll, Mother, Sealskins, Colored Leather, Leather Boots, Child In Hood, 1920s 1800.00
Doll, Reindeer Fur Parka, Wolverine Fur Hood, 1930s, 12 In. 247.50
Effigy, Seal, Ivory Handle, Large 150.00
Figurine, Human, Arms Crossed On Torso, Feet Joined, Ivory, 9 3/4 In. 1840.00
Figurine, Hunter Stalking Seal, Stone, 2 3/4 In. 40.00
Figurine, Polar Bear, Carved, 1930s, 2 1/4 & 1 1/2 In., Pair 110.00
Figurine, Walrus, 1 Mounted On Ivory Plinth, 4 1/4 & 3 1/2 In., Pair 93.50
Fire-Starting Device, Driftwood Base, Wooden Shaft, Leather Thong, 6 In. 690.00

Goggles, Snow, Carved Wood	100.00
Knife, Skinning, Bone, Curved To Hand, 18th Century, 1 Piece, 2 1/2 In.	175.00
Mask, Ceremonial, Whalebone	100.00
Model, Bone Carving, Oosik Wand, Bear Head At One End, Walrus At Other, 23 In.	345.00
Model, Kayak, 1882, 43 In.	1925.00
Model, Kayak, Sealskin, Wood Frame, Bow Split, Late 19th Century, 49 In.	161.00
Model, Kayak, Sealskin, Wooden, Carved Bone Trim, 19th Century, 23 In., Pair	230.00
Mukluks, Hand Sewn Sealskin & Caribou Hide, 19th Century, 5 7/8 In.	215.00
Sash, Winnebago, Beaded	500.00
Soapstone, Eskimo & Sled Being Pulled By Dog, 7 1/2 x 3 In.	144.00
Soapstone, Fisherman	100.00
Soapstone, Fox, Green, 1950s, 3 In.	115.00
Soapstone, Sea Otter, 1970, 6 In.	200.00

FABERGE was a firm of jewelers and goldsmiths founded in St. Petersburg, Russia, in 1842, by Gustav Faberge. Peter Carl Faberge, his son, was jeweler to the Russian Imperial Court from about 1870 to 1914. The rare Imperial Easter eggs, jewelry, and decorative items are very expensive today.

ФАБЕРЖЕ

КФ

Bell Push, Rose Pink Over Guilloche Ground, Moonstone Push Border, 1910, 2 In.	5175.00
Bell Push, Rose Pink Over Guilloche Ground, Pale Blue Borders, 3 Bun Feet, 3 In.	18400.00
Bowl, Anthemion Design, Ribbon Tied Laurel Wreaths, Silver Rim, Green, 1900, 3 In.	7475.00
Cake Basket, Gilded Interior, Molded Rim, Swing Handle, Moscow, 1910, 10 1/4 In.	1840.00
Card Case, Pictorial, King Of Clubs, Double-Headed Eagle, Silver, Signed, c.1908	5750.00
Cigarette Case, 2-Tone Gold, Red Body, Hinged Cover, Wigstrom, 1900, 3 5/8 In.	4600.00
Cigarette Case, Gilded Silver, Tubular, Apple Green, Gold Borders, 1910, 3 1/2 In.	12650.00
Cigarette Case, Gold Thumbpiece, Cabochon Sapphire, Julius Rappoport, 1910, 4 In.	4600.00
Cigarette Case, Gold, Cabochon Sapphire Thumbpiece, St. Petersburg, 1910, 4 In.	3165.00
Cigarette Case, Gold, Imperial Eagle Set, Diamonds, Cabochon Ruby, 1910, 4 In.	6325.00
Cigarette Case, Gold, Sunburst, Cabochon Sapphire Thumbpiece, 1890, 3 1/4 In.	6050.00
Cigarette Case, Hound, Pursuing A Wild Boar, Gold Tip, St. Petersburg, 1910, 3 In.	3165.00
Cigarette Case, Royal Blue Over Guilloche Ground, August Hollming, 1910, 4 In.	4900.00
Cigarette Case, Yellow Gold, Red Panels, Diamond Set Thumbpiece, 1910, 3 1/4 In.	8050.00
Figurine, Deerhound, Standing In Attentive Posture, Ruby Eyes, 1900, 2 5/8 In.	5750.00
Inkwell, Traveling, Sterling Silver, 1908	4025.00
Kovsh, Pale Blue Over Guilloche Ground, Hook Handle, Anders Nevalainen, 1900	5750.00
Letter Opener, Dagger Form, Silver, Red Stone Cabochon Mounted, Fluted Handle	5465.00
Letter Opener, Gold Handle, Flower Head, Leaf-Tip Design, 1900, 10 5/8 In.	8625.00
Lighter, Cigar, Silver, Samovar Shape, Square Base, St. Petersburg, 1890, 4 In.	4315.00
Pendant, Icon, Kazan Mother Of God, Silver Frame Set, Sapphires, Ruby, 1910, 2 In.	5175.00
Pill Box, Silver, Chased With Flowers, Foliage On Sides, Hinged Cover, Moscow, 2 In.	6325.00
Pin, 14K Gold, Enameled Blue, Sunburst Ground, Moscow, 1900, 1 1/4 In.	18400.00
Pin, 14K Gold, Flower Head Form, Diamonds, A. Hollming, 1900, 1 In. Diam.	4315.00
Pin, 14K Gold, Nephrite Leaf, Gold Flowers, Pearl, Moscow, 1900, 1 3/8 In.	8050.00
Vase, Oriental Fish, Foliate, 3 1/4 In.	50.00
Vase, Pale Blue Over Guilloche Ground, Leaf Tip Gold Border, 1900, 6 1/2 In.	4600.00

FAIENCE refers to tin-glazed earthenware, especially the wares made in France, Germany, and Scandinavia. It is also correct to say that faience is the same as majolica or Delft, although usually the term refers only to the tin-glazed pottery of the three regions mentioned.

Charger, Duke Of Schleswig-Holstein, Jeweled Crown, Blue, White, 18 & 19 In., Pair	6900.00
Charger, Floral, Leaf In Center, Blue, Purple, Blue Border, Cream Ground, 14 In.	115.00
Desk Set, Enameled, Artist, Portugal, 9 1/2 In.	165.00
Dish, Chinaman, Seated Amidst Rocks, Grasses, Pale Blue Glaze, 11 & 12 In., Pair	747.00
Dish, Lobed, Chinaman Seated Beside Garden Fence, Nonagonal Center, Blue, White	747.00
Dish, Oriental Couple & Child Playing In Rocky Garden, Rose, Blue, Yellow, Green	1610.00
Dish, Satyr Figure Pushing 2 Bacchic Putti In Wheelbarrow, Blue Border, 16 In.	8050.00
Figurine, Bagpiper, Wearing Plumed Blue Manganese Hat, Blue Pipe, 1730, 7 In.	2300.00
Inkwell, Lobed Form, Polychrome Design, Europe, 19th Century, 2 x 4 1/2 In.	33.00
Jar, Apothecary, Baluster Form, Landscape Scene, Urbino, 19th Century, 8 1/4 In.	93.00
Jug, Cover, Figural, Owl, Crest On Torso, Europe, Late 18th Century, 10 In.	400.00
Jug, Cover, Green Floral, Men, Blowing Horn, France, 18th Century, 9 1/2 In.	515.00

Jug, Peacocks, Floral, Blue & White, Silver Cover, Germany, 18th Century, 8 3/4 In.	1380.00
Plaque, Bird Design, Persia, Oval, 19th Century, 13 1/2 x 9 1/2 In.	66.00
Plaque, Calligraphic Design, Persia, Oval, 19th Century, 10 x 7 In.	27.00
Plate, 3 Sprigs, 2 Small Insects, Rose, Yellow, Turquoise, Green, Blue Center, 9 In.	1956.00
Plate, Death Of Louis XVI, Late 19th Century, 9 1/2 In.	72.00
Plate, Ten Walnuts In Center, Octagonal Rim, 3 Green Leaf Sprigs, 10 In.	1092.00
Pot, Bough, Polychrome Enamel, Floral Panels On Sides, Figures In Landscape, 7 In.	175.00
Salt, Double, Woman, Mark Of Geo. Martel, 7 1/4 In.	121.00
Stein, Blue Floral Design, Sponge Work On Both Sides, Pewter Cover, 1/5 Liter	550.00
Stein, Horse, Leaping, Pewter Cover, 19th Century, 1 Liter	660.00
Stein, Large Floral Design, Blue Sponge On Both Sides, Pewter Cover, 1 Liter	1801.00
Stein, Stag, Leaping, Trees On Both Sides, Pewter Base, Cream, 1783, 1/4 Liter	982.00
Sugar, Polychrome Design, Europe, 19th Century, 3 1/2 In.	44.00
Tankard, 2 Chinese Men Holding Vessels Amidst Trees, Blue, Green, Yellow, Red, 9 In.	1150.00
Tankard, Floral Sprig, Stylized Flower Heads, Blue, Red, Blue Scrollwork Band, 10 In.	1380.00
Tankard, Landscape Floral Cartouche, Stylized Blue White Flower, 7 1/2 In.	345.00
Tankard, Stylized Flowers, Red, Green, Blue Manganese Vines, Ocher Rim, 9 1/2 In.	805.00
Tile, Pinecone, Square, 6 In.	295.00
Tureen, Cover, Floral Spray, Rose, Blue, Mustard Yellow, Green Loop Handle, 15 In.	920.00
Tureen, Cover, Large Floral Spray, Rose, Purple, Blue, Yellow, Green, 1765, 8 1/2 In.	690.00
Tureen, Cover, Yellow, Green Fruit Handle, Yellow, Blue Band Border, France, 9 In.	483.00
Vase, Blue, Aqua & Reddish Brown, Figural Dragon On Side, Burmantofts, 14 In., Pair	950.00
Vase, Blue, Red Clay Body, Marked, 11 In.	467.50
Vase, Chinoiserie Figure Standing Amidst Trees, Blue Scrollwork Handle, Blue, White	805.00
Vase, Chinoiserie Figures Amidst Rocks, Dentil Border, Blue, White, 1700, 7 3/4 In.	690.00
Vase, Deer, Flower Design, 23 In.	157.00
Vase, Urn, Serpent Handles, Champleve Neck, Base, France, 19th Century, 7 In., Pair	880.00
Wall Pocket, Climbing Cat, France, c.1890, 16 In.	285.00

FAIRINGS are small souvenir china boxes and figurines that were sold at country fairs during the nineteenth century. Most were made in Germany. Reproductions of fairings are being made, especially of the famous *twelve months of marriage* series.

Box, Pin, Chest Of Drawers, Mirror, Watch	200.00
Box, Trinket, 19th Century Couple	125.00
Box, Trinket, Figural Bust, U.S. Grant On Cover, Eagle At Base, Staffordshire	100.00
Box, Who Is Coming	110.00
Figurine, Baby's First Step, 3 Children Holding Hands	195.00
Figurine, Returning At 1 O'Clock	250.00
Figurine, Shall We Sleep Or What	150.00

FAIRYLAND LUSTER pieces are included in the Wedgwood category.

FAMILLE ROSE, see Chinese Export category.

FANS have been used for cooling since the days of the ancients. By the eighteenth century, the fan was an accessory for the lady of fashion, and very elaborate and expensive fans were made. Sticks were made of ivory or wood, set with jewels or carved. The fans were made of painted silk or paper. Inexpensive paper fans printed with advertising were giveaways in the late nineteenth and early twentieth centuries. Electric fans were introduced in 1882.

Advertising, Birchola, Couple At Soda Fountain, Cardboard	86.00
Advertising, Cuba Advertising, Child's, 1920s	43.00
Advertising, Drink Moxie, Celluloid, 1910s	52.00
Advertising, Goodyear Tire	25.00
Advertising, Infallible Coffee, Roasted By Leflore Coffee Co., Cardboard & Wood	35.00
Advertising, Kool Cigarettes	38.00
Advertising, Moxie, Bottle On Handles, Boy & Dog	15.00
Advertising, Moxie, Celluloid, Ribbons Connect Blades, White, Black Letters, 1920s	55.00
Advertising, Moxie, Eileen Percy, Music On Back, Cardboard	69.00
Advertising, Moxie, Eileen Percy, TNT Cowboy On Back, Cardboard	103.00
Advertising, Moxie, Francis Pritchard, Pink Hat, Music On Back, Cardboard, 1910s	63.00
Advertising, Moxie, Frank Archer, Boy On Rocking Horse On Back, Cardboard	86.00

Advertising, Moxie, Laura Walker, Blue Dress, Music On Back, Cardboard 75.00
Advertising, Moxie, Lillian MacKensie, 1919 .... 60.00
Advertising, Moxie, Pretty Woman, Glass Of Moxie & Moxie Clerk 40.00
Advertising, Moxie, Sketch Of Couple In Canoe, Club House In Background, 1916 .... 33.00
Advertising, Pur-Ox Syrups, 2 Toasting Couples At Dinner Table, Cardboard 126.00
Advertising, Reid's Ice Cream, Little Girl With Ice Cream Cone, Cardboard ...... 86.00 to 90.00
Advertising, Sinclair Opaline, Cardboard, 10 1/2 x 7 1/2 In. 93.00
Black Lace, Abalone, Inlaid Brass Birds On Ribs, Frame, 1890, 18 1/2 x 30 1/2 In. 247.00
Bone & Chiffon, Black, Silver Sequins, Stylized Laurel Wreath, Floral, Mourning 50.00
Bone Handle, Hand Painted Birds On Silk, Feather Edge 180.00
Brass Tipped Handles, Linen, Folding, Mourning 55.00
Electric, ArticAire, Desk, Gooseneck, Art Deco Base, 10 In. 65.00
Electric, Cool Spot, Pedestal, Floor, Bullet Back, 10 In. 165.00
Electric, Dayton, Ceiling, Ornate Brass Base Plate & Switch Housing, 48 In. 645.00
Electric, Dayton, Ceiling, Ornate Brass Base Plate & Switch Housing, 56 In. 700.00
Electric, Diehl, Ceiling, Plain, No Brass Parts, 52 In. 200.00
Electric, Emerson, Ceiling, 6 Blades, Brass Fern Leaf Plate, Switch Housing, Oil Cup .. 1200.00
Electric, Emerson, Desk, Oscillating, Brass Blades, 12 In. 150.00
Electric, Emerson, Desk, Step Base, New Windings & Bearings, 8 In. 345.00
Electric, Emerson, Jr., Desk, Oscillating, Ivory, 8 In. 160.00
Electric, Emerson, Trojan, Ceiling, Ribbed Base Plate, Switch Housing, Oil Cup, 56 In. . 285.00
Electric, Eskimo, Desk, Oscillating, Bullet Back, 10 In. 35.00
Electric, Galvin, Brass Blades, 10 In. 55.00
Electric, General Electric, Ceiling 195.00
Electric, General Electric, Desk, Brass Blades, Restored, 6 In. 175.00
Electric, General Electric, Metal, Cast Iron, 16 1/2 x 13 In. 325.00
Electric, Hunter R-52, Ceiling 150.00
Electric, Hunter, Ceiling, All Chrome, Adaptair Feature, 52 In. 500.00
Electric, Hunter, Ceiling, Brass Cover Plate, Canopy, Spiral Pipe, 52 In. 350.00
Electric, KM, Jack Frost, Desk, 8 In. 35.00
Electric, Polar Cub, Desk, Brass Blades, 6 In. 135.00
Electric, Power Pakt, Microphone, 8 In. 60.00
Electric, Singer, Ribbonaire, 2-Speed, 10 x 7 In. 225.00
Electric, Turek, Ceiling, Concave Brass Base Plate, 52 In. 450.00
Electric, Verity, Orbit, Desk, England, 220 Volts, 16 In. 1500.00
Electric, Western Electric, Model No. 6304, Brass Blades 295.00
Electric, Western Electric, Oscillating, Brass Blades, 12 In. 125.00
Electric, Westinghouse, Ceiling, Ornate, 56 In. 695.00
Electric, Westinghouse, Ceiling, Sidewinder, Ornate, 52 In. 400.00
Electric, Westinghouse, No. 149575, Brass Cage, Blades, Original Paint, Tag .... 195.00 to 210.00
Electric, Wizard Deluxe, Western Auto Supply Co., 4 Blades, Blue Metal Base, 11 In. ... 83.00
Feather, 17 Large Feathers, Gold Handle 85.00
Feather, Butterfly & Flower, Silk Leaf Design, Bone Sticks, Late 19th Century, 13 In. .. 143.00
Feather, Daisies & Blossom Design, Chiffon Leaf, Applied Sequins, 9 In. 220.00
Feather, Gauze Leaf Design, Green Mother-Of-Pearl Sticks, Early 20th Century, 9 In. ... 154.00
Feather, Lady & Gentleman Garden Scene, Crimson Leaf, Bone Sticks, 1870, 11 In. 198.00
Feather, Ostrich, Blond Tortoiseshell Sticks, 1890, 17 1/2 In. 248.00
Feather, Ostrich, Ivory Spokes, Cawston Farm, South Pasadena, Box, 16 x 12 In. 125.00
Feather, Stylized Flower, Leaves, Blossom Design, Bone Stick, 1890, 13 1/2 In. 198.00
Fontange, Sequins, Silk Leaf, Flame Stitch, Duvelleroy, Frame, c.1910, 10 1/4 In. 1120.00
Hot Air, Motor On Sterling Engine, Pierced Tin Housing, Nickel Flywheel, Jost 4500.00
Ivory, 19 Blades, Filigree Cutwork, Painted, Floral Design, France, c.1870, 5 In. 275.00
Ivory, Brise, 1870, 8 1/2 In. 358.00
Ivory, Brise, Carved, Pierced, Figures, Tassel, Mid-19th Century, Lacquer Box, 9 In. 825.00
Ivory, Carved, European, c.1880 .... 1875.00
Ivory, Lace On Satin, Mother-Of-Pearl Button, Fan-Shaped Frame, 1825, 9 In. 330.00
Ivory, Musical Courtship Scene, Carved Guards, England-Flanders, c.1740, 11 In. 467.00
Ivory, Paper, Continental, Classical Musical Scene, Instruments, Flowers, c.1820, 10 In. . 165.00
Ivory, Silk Gauze, Courting Couple, Gold Sequins, Signed Innis, c.1850 .... 143.00
Ivory, Silk, Brussels Lace Leaf, 1890, 14 1/2 In. 132.00
Ivory, Silvered Paper, Embossed Floral, Inset Mirror On Front Guard, c.1800 .... 33.00
Ivory & Paper, Youth Giving Lamb To Shepherdess, Painted Flowers, 19 x 24 In. 231.00
Ivory & Silk, Pastel Floral Spray, Hand Painted, Pierced Sticks 55.00

Ivory Sticks, Classical Scene, Polychrome & Gilt, Frame, 25 In. 345.00
Lace, Black Chantilly, Tortoiseshell Sticks, 1870, 13 In. 165.00
Lace, Hand Painted Flowers, Bone Handle 230.00
Lace, Leaf With Spangles, Tulip, Leaf Design, Blond Tortoiseshell Sticks, 1890, 9 1/2 In. 412.00
Lace, Mother-Of-Pearl Sticks, Guards, Button, Monogram, c.1825, 16 x 23 In. 220.00
Lace & Mother-Of-Pearl, c.1750, 19 x 24 In. 225.00
Lace & Mother-Of-Pearl, Cream, Gold, Flowers, Brass Loop, 1860, 11 In. 165.00
Lacquer, Brise, Black, Gold, Court Scene, Tassels, Box, China, c.1820 .... 165.00
Linen, Young Couple, Sheet Music, Hanging Fan Shape Frame, 22 1/4 x 15 1/4 In. 380.00
Mother-Of-Pearl, Beige Silk, Black Lace, Rhinestone Jewel, c.1920 .... 143.00
Mother-Of-Pearl, Inlaid, Women, Children, Animals Scene, Gilt, 1880, 10 1/2 In. 201.00
Mother-Of-Pearl, Lace On Silk, Rhinestone Jewels, Velvet Box, c.1890 .... 121.00
Mother-Of-Pearl, Satin, Lace, Bride & Groom Vignette, c.1820, 9 1/2 In. 176.00
Mother-Of-Pearl, Silk Gauze, Courting Scene, Gold Sequins, Flowers, c.1850, 8 1/2 In. . 176.00
Mother-Of-Pearl, Silk, Hand Painted, Carved, Men & Women, Riverbank, c.1850, 10 In. 385.00
Mother-Of-Pearl Sticks, Continental, Voile Leaf, Guards, Silver Sequins 33.00
Mother-Of-Pearl Sticks, Silk Leaf Painted Putti & Girls In Chariot, 11 3/4 In. 630.00
Olive Wood, Telescope, Mirror, Bird, Waxed Paper With Lace Transfer Design, Italy .. 88.00
Painted Sticks With Cranes, Blossom, Grasses, Clouds, Reverse Butterflies, c.1850 .. 1955.00
Paper, Abalone Shell Ribs, Classical Scene, E.P. Joyce, Frame, 14 x 22 1/2 In. 220.00
Paper, Flag, 48 Stars, 28 In. 115.00
Paper, Hand Painted, French Colonial Courtyard Scenes, Lacquered Sticks, Initialed L.M. 33.00
Paper, Pierced Carved Bone Ribs, Metallic Inlay, Frame, 13 3/4 x 23 In. 165.00
Parchment, Bone Handle, 10 Blades, Carved Floral, Painted, France, c.1850, 4 In. 200.00
Raffia, Rattan Hoops, Carved Wooden Grip, India 20.00
Sandalwood, Carved, Satin Stitched Birds, Butterflies, Silk, 12 x 20 In. 110.00
Sandalwood, Fan Of 1000 Faces, Silk, Ivory & Peacock Feathers, Box, 16 1/2 In. 950.00
Sandalwood, Paper, Painted, Port Scenes, Hong Kong, Canton, Shanghai, 1750, 11 In. .. 4400.00
Sandalwood, Peacock Feather, Painted Paper, Court Scenes, Lacquer Box, c.1840, 14 In. 275.00
Silk, Sequin Design, Black Gauze Leaf, Horn Sticks, 1910, 7 1/2 In. 143.00
Silver Filigree, Central Shield Of Bird & Flower, Oval Medallions, c.1820, 7 1/2 In. 2185.00
Tortoiseshell, Black Lace, Scrolled Leaf & Feather, Floral Designs, 8 In. 132.00
Tortoiseshell, Brise, Pierced, Hand Painted, Gilt Highlights, c.1740, 8 1/2 In. 220.00
Tortoiseshell, Brise, Silver Inlay Of Medallion, Signed, 1870, 9 1/2 In. 95.00
Tortoiseshell, Ivory, Sandalwood, Figures In Pavilions, Painted, Canton, c.1860, 11 In. . 660.00
Tortoiseshell & Black Ostrich Feather, Vine, Flowers, Henrik Wigstrom, 19 1/2 In. .. 4400.00
Wood, Chiffon, Hand Painted, Flowers, Butterfly, Sequins, France, c.1890, 14 In. 105.00
Wood & Silk, Hunt Scene, Cherries, Cherry Trees, Hand Painted, Tassel, Japan, c.1890 . 110.00

FAST FOOD COLLECTIBLES may be included in several categories, such as Advertising, Coca-Cola, Toy, etc.

FEDERZEICHNUNG is the very strange German name for a pattern of mother-of-pearl satin glass. The pattern had irregularly shaped sections of brown glass covered with a pattern of gold squiggle lines. It was first made in the late nineteenth century.

Vase, Ruffled Top, Pat. 9159, 7 3/4 In. 2500.00

FENTON Art Glass Company, founded in Martins Ferry, Ohio, by Frank L. Fenton, is now located in Williamstown, West Virginia. It is noted for early carnival glass produced between 1907 and 1920. Some of these pieces are listed in the Carnival Glass category. Many other types of glass were also made. Spanish Lace in this section refers to the pattern made by Fenton.

Apple Tree, Water Set, 5 Piece 130.00
Apple Tree, Water Set, Marigold, 6 Piece 425.00
Aqua Crest, Basket, Handle, 5 In. 119.00
Aqua Crest, Bowl, 13 In. ....77.00 to 129.00
Aqua Crest, Bowl, 9 1/2 In. 30.00
Aqua Crest, Cake Stand, Low 70.00
Aqua Crest, Jug, Rose Design, Handle, 9 In. 69.00
Aqua Crest, Saucer, White, Blue, 6 In. 9.00
Aqua Crest, Vase, Square, 8 In. ....49.00 to 59.00
Blue Opalescent, Basket, Handle, 4 In. 37.00

Burmese, Basket, Medium	65.00
Burmese, Bowl, 8 In.	70.00
Burmese, Lamp, Courting, Daisy & Fern, 10 1/2 In.	375.00
Burmese, Lamp, Student, Hand Painted, Gloria Finn, 1973	695.00
Burmese, Pitcher, Dragonfly	165.00
Burmese, Vase, Bud, 8 In.	100.00
Burmese, Vase, Bud, 11 In.	75.00
Burmese, Vase, Queen's Bird	250.00
Burmese, Vase, Rose, 5 In.	65.00
Cactus, Basket, Yellow Opalescent, 7 In.	100.00
Cactus, Water Set, Aqua Opalescent, 7 Piece	375.00
Coin Dot, Basket, Opalescent, 7 In.	55.00
Coin Dot, Goblet, 5 1/2 In.	13.00
Coin Dot, Lamp, Boudoir, Pair	100.00
Coin Dot, Lamp, Red & White, Shade	250.00
Coin Dot, Pitcher, Water, Cranberry Opalescent	275.00
Coin Dot, Vase, 1925, 6 In.	40.00
Coin Dot, Vase, Blue Opalescent, 2 Handles, 11 In.	159.00
Coin Dot, Vase, Cranberry Opalescent, 8 1/2 In.	65.00
Coin Dot, Vase, Double Crimped, Blue Opalescent, 11 In.	159.00
Cosmos, Variant, Syrup, Milk Glass, Design	245.00
Cranberry Opalescent, Vase, Crimped, 5 In.	50.00
Cranberry Opalescent Swirl, Rose Bowl, c.1939	95.00
Daisy & Button, Pitcher, Water, Yellow Opalescent	275.00
Daisy & Fern, Tumbler, Barrel, Cranberry Opalescent, 4 In.	35.00
Daisy & Fern, Tumbler, Cranberry Opalescent, 4 In.	35.00
Danielle, Vase, Teal Sand Etched 1920s Era Woman & Birds	240.00
Diamond Lace, Epergne, Champagne Satin, Teal Rim, Art Glass, 11 In.	75.00
Diamond Optic, Cup	20.00
Diamond Optic, Tumbler, Ruby Overlay, 10 Oz.	30.00
Diamond Optic, Water Set, Cut Flowers, Green, 6 Piece	170.00
Dot Optic, Sugar Shaker, Cranberry Opalescent	90.00
Emerald Crest, Basket, Dot French Opalescent, 7 In.	50.00
Emerald Crest, Bowl, 10 In.	55.00
Emerald Crest, Compote, 6 In.	72.00
Emerald Crest, Compote, 7 x 3 5/8 In.	30.00
Emerald Crest, Compote, Blue Opalescent, 7 In.	35.00
Emerald Crest, Cup & Saucer, Set Of 8	55.00
Emerald Crest, Mustard, Metal Frame	145.00
Emerald Crest, Tray, Sandwich, Handle, 10 In.	159.00
Fan, Vase, Black, 1920s, 6 In.	35.00
Forget-Me-Not, Cruet Set, Blue Opaque, 4 Piece	250.00
Forget-Me-Not, Sugar Shaker, Blue Opaque	165.00
French Opalescent, Ginger Jar	70.00
Georgian, Cocktail, Ruby, 4 In.	9.00
Georgian, Cup & Saucer, Footed, Ruby	20.00
Georgian, Goblet, Cocktail, Ruby	17.00
Georgian, Goblet, Pink, 10 Oz.	9.00
Georgian, Sherbet, Ruby, 4 In.	17.00
Georgian, Sugar & Creamer, Green	35.00
Georgian, Sugar, Ruby	13.00
Georgian, Tumbler, Juice, Ruby, 3 1/4 In.	14.00
Gold Crest, Rose Bowl	15.00
Gold Crest, Vase, 6 1/2 In.	30.00
Hanging Heart, Vase, Iridized Pearl Hearts & Vines, Signed, 1981	225.00
Hanging Heart & Vine, Vase, Applied Handles, Antique Green, 9 In.	1750.00
Hobnail, Basket, 4 1/2 In.	59.00
Hobnail, Basket, Blue Opalescent, 7 In.	25.00
Hobnail, Basket, Cranberry Opalescent, 7 In.	95.00
Hobnail, Basket, Cranberry, 10 In.	125.00
Hobnail, Basket, Handle, Blue Opalescent, 10 1/2 In.	48.00
Hobnail, Blue Opalescent, 10 In.	70.00
Hobnail, Bonbon, Green Opalescent, 5 In.	22.00

Hobnail, Bowl, Blue Opalescent, 10 In. 60.00
Hobnail, Bowl, Blue Opalescent, 11 In. ....46.00 to 70.00
Hobnail, Cake Plate, White, Pedestal, Piecrust Edge 50.00
Hobnail, Cologne Bottle, No Stopper 25.00
Hobnail, Compote, Blue Opalescent 50.00
Hobnail, Epergne, 3-Lily, 10 In. 175.00
Hobnail, Jar, Apothecary, Milk Glass, 11 In. 175.00
Hobnail, Jug, Blue Opalescent, 4 1/2 In. 69.00
Hobnail, Jug, Blue Opalescent, Squat, 5 1/2 In. 45.00
Hobnail, Jug, Cranberry Opalescent, 5 1/2 In. 75.00
Hobnail, Pitcher, Cranberry Opalescent 65.00
Hobnail, Pitcher, Plum Opalescent, 5 1/2 In. 85.00
Hobnail, Pitcher, Yellow Opalescent, 5 In. 75.00
Hobnail, Plate, French Opalescent, 8 In. 15.00
Hobnail, Punch Set, Vaseline, 9 Piece 675.00
Hobnail, Salt & Pepper, Blue Opalescent, Pair 45.00
Hobnail, Salt & Pepper, Footed, Blue Opalescent 65.00
Hobnail, Salt & Pepper, Footed, Cranberry Opalescent 70.00
Hobnail, Shade, Cranberry Opalescent, Fluted, 2 1/4 x 4 1/4 x 5 1/2 In. 110.00
Hobnail, Shaker, Cranberry Opalescent 70.00
Hobnail, Sugar & Creamer, Blue Opalescent 40.00
Hobnail, Sugar & Creamer, Blue Opalescent, Individual 21.00
Hobnail, Tumbler, Blue Opalescent, 3 1/2 In. 9.00
Hobnail, Tumbler, Cranberry Opalescent, 9 Oz. 35.00
Hobnail, Tumbler, Juice, Blue Opalescent 8.00
Hobnail, Vase, 8 In. 90.00
Hobnail, Vase, 11 In. 115.00
Hobnail, Vase, Blue Opalescent, Footed, 4 In. 28.00
Hobnail, Vase, Cranberry Opalescent, 4 In. 30.00
Hobnail, Vase, Cranberry Opalescent, 4 1/2 In. 50.00
Hobnail, Vase, Cranberry Opalescent, 8 In. 125.00
Hobnail, Vase, Crimped, Cranberry Opalescent, 5 In. 50.00
Hobnail, Vase, Fan, Blue Opalescent, 6 In. 35.00
Hobnail, Vase, Fan, Blue Opalescent, 6 1/4 In. 42.00
Hobnail, Vase, Fan, Cranberry Opalescent, 4 1/2 In. 50.00
Hobnail, Vase, Flared, Blue Opalescent, 4 1/2 In. 9.00
Hobnail, Vase, Footed, Blue Opalescent, 8 In. 59.00
Lamp, Gone With The Wind, Poppy, Ruby 175.00
Lincoln Inn, Cup & Saucer, Red 26.00
Lincoln Inn, Goblet, Water, Red 30.00
Moonstone, Urn, Cover, Dancing Ladies, 7 In. 300.00
Orange Tree, Bowl, Large, 3-Footed, Marigold 100.00
Orange Tree, Plate, Stylized Center, Blue Opalescent 450.00
Paperweight, Lovebirds 36.00
Peach Blow, Bowl, Ruffled, 13 1/2 In. 100.00
Peach Blow, Epergne, 1 Lily 100.00
Peach Crest, Bowl, 8 In. 50.00
Peach Crest, Bowl, 10 1/2 x 4 In. 35.00
Peach Crest, Bowl, 14 In. 90.00
Peach Crest, Bowl, Double Crimped, 10 In. 89.00
Peach Crest, Bowl, Double Crimped, 13 In. ....149.00 to 259.00
Peach Crest, Bowl, Ruffled, 10 In. 75.00
Peach Crest, Vase, 13 1/2 In. ....129.00 to 149.00
Peach Crest, Vase, Crimped Edge, 5 In. 69.00
Peach Crest, Vase, Hand, 10 1/2 In. 359.00
Peach Crest, Vase, Jack-In-The-Pulpit, 8 1/2 In. 75.00
Peacock, Bookends, Green 300.00
Peacock, Bowl, With Urn, Blue Opalescent 275.00
Peacock & Urn, Plate, White, 9 In. 425.00
Rosalene, Epergne, 4 Trumpets 500.00
Rosalene, Lamp, Fairy, c.1977 .... 95.00
Rose Crest, Vase, Fan, 8 1/2 In. 69.00
Rose Crest, Vase-Candle Cornucopia, 6 In. 45.00

Ruby Overlay, Basket, Handle, 7 In.	75.00
Ruby Overlay, Bowl, Ruffled, 8 In.	75.00
Ruby Overlay, Vase, Optic, Ruffled, 6 1/2 In.	60.00
Silver Crest, Banana Bowl, Footed, High	70.00
Silver Crest, Banana Bowl, Footed, Low	50.00 to 60.00
Silver Crest, Basket, 7 In.	35.00 to 39.00
Silver Crest, Basket, Handle, 6 In.	35.00
Silver Crest, Bonbon, 5 In.	10.00
Silver Crest, Bowl, 10 In.	49.00
Silver Crest, Bowl, Red, Flower Form, 9 In.	35.00
Silver Crest, Bowl, Ruffled, 13 In.	46.00
Silver Crest, Cake Salver, 12 In.	35.00 to 40.00
Silver Crest, Cake Stand, Footed	45.00
Silver Crest, Candlestick, Red, Flower Form	20.00
Silver Crest, Compote, Ruffled, Pair	75.00
Silver Crest, Compote, White, Small	5.50
Silver Crest, Cornucopia Candle, Pair	69.00
Silver Crest, Nappy, White	8.50
Silver Crest, Nut Dish, Footed	17.00
Silver Crest, Relish, 2 Sections	55.00 to 60.00
Silver Crest, Relish, Heart Shaped, Handle	30.00
Silver Crest, Rose Bowl, Footed, 6 In.	55.00
Silver Crest, Rose Bowl, White	5.50
Silver Crest, Ruffled, 13 In.	90.00
Silver Crest, Salt & Pepper, Ruffled Bottom	125.00 to 130.00
Silver Crest, Salver, Footed, Low	35.00
Silver Crest, Shaker, Footed, Pair	110.00
Silver Crest, Tidbit, 2 Tiers	47.00
Silver Crest, Vase, 6 1/4 In.	20.00
Silver Crest, Vase, 8 In.	45.00 to 49.00
Silver Crest, Vase, Fan, 8 1/2 In.	35.00
Silver Crest, Vase, Fan, 12 In.	90.00 to 95.00
Silver Crest, Vase, Ruffled, 13 In.	90.00
Snow Crest, Hurricane Shade, Emerald Green	95.00
Snow Crest, Pot & Saucer, Emerald Green	95.00
Spiral Optic, Vase, Cranberry, 4 1/2 In.	85.00
Stretch, Console Set, Blue, 3 Piece	75.00
Stretch, Vase, Fan, Footed, Green, 5 1/4 In.	35.00
Swirl, Cruet, Cranberry, Clear Swirl Stopper	125.00
Swirled Ribs, Cruet	65.00
Thumbprint, Candlestick, Amber, 8 1/2 In., Pair	40.00
Thumbprint, Candy Dish, Cover, Oval, Pink	29.00
Thumbprint, Goblet, Water, Ruby	15.00
Thumbprint, Iced Tea, Blue, 13 Oz.	19.00 to 22.00
Thumbprint, Pitcher, Water, Cranberry, Reeded Handle, Ruffled Top	110.00
Thumbprint, Plate, Ruby, 8 In.	20.00
Thumbprint, Sherbet, Ruby	14.00
Thumbprint, Wine, Blue	20.00
Thumbprint, Wine, Ruby	19.00 to 20.00
Violets In The Snow, Bowl, Double Ruffle, Paper Label, Signed, 11 In.	130.00
Water Lily, Bowl, Ruffled, Footed, Green, 5 In.	225.00
Wild Rose, Epergne, 4 Trumpets, Pink Iridized Stretch, 75th Anniversary	325.00
Winking Cat, Teapot	125.00

FIESTA, the colorful dinnerware, was introduced in 1936 by the Homer Laughlin China Co., redesigned in 1969, and withdrawn in 1973. It was reissued again in 1986 in different colors and is still being made. The simple design was characterized by a band of concentric circles, beginning at the rim. Cups had full-circle handles until 1969, when partial-circle handles were made. Harlequin and Riviera were related wares. For more information and prices of American dinnerware, see the book *Kovels' Depression Glass & Dinnerware Price List.*

Chartreuse, Ashtray, 5 1/2 In.	65.00 to 85.00

Chartreuse, Bowl, Cereal, 5 1/2 In. 30.00
Chartreuse, Bowl, Dessert, 6 In. 40.00
Chartreuse, Bowl, Fruit, 4 3/4 In. 30.00
Chartreuse, Chop Plate, 13 In. 95.00
Chartreuse, Chop Plate, 15 In. 135.00
Chartreuse, Coffeepot 585.00
Chartreuse, Cup & Saucer 18.50
Chartreuse, Eggcup . . . . .125.00 to 135.00
Chartreuse, Jug, Water, 2 Pt. 150.00
Chartreuse, Mug 90.00
Chartreuse, Pitcher, Disk 280.00
Chartreuse, Pitcher, Juice . . . . .185.00 to 395.00
Chartreuse, Plate, 6 In. 7.00
Chartreuse, Plate, 9 In. 22.00
Chartreuse, Plate, 10 In. 50.00
Chartreuse, Platter, 12 In. 50.00
Chartreuse, Saucer 6.00
Chartreuse, Soup, Cream 85.00
Chartreuse, Sugar 8.00
Chartreuse, Sugar & Creamer, Cover, Tray, 3 Piece 275.00
Chartreuse, Sugar, Cover 65.00
Cobalt Blue, Bowl, Cereal, 5 1/2 In. 25.00
Cobalt Blue, Bowl, Dessert, 6 In. 35.00
Cobalt Blue, Bowl, Fruit, 4 3/4 In. 25.00
Cobalt Blue, Bowl, Fruit, 11 3/4 In. 485.00
Cobalt Blue, Cake Server, Kitchen Kraft, 10 7/8 In. 185.00
Cobalt Blue, Candleholder, Bulb 110.00
Cobalt Blue, Candleholder, Tripod, Pair 950.00
Cobalt Blue, Carafe . . . . .226.00 to 375.00
Cobalt Blue, Casserole, Cover, Kitchen Kraft, Individual . . . . .75.00 to 110.00
Cobalt Blue, Chop Plate, 13 In. 35.00
Cobalt Blue, Coffeepot 200.00
Cobalt Blue, Coffeepot, After Dinner 550.00
Cobalt Blue, Compote, 12 In. 115.00
Cobalt Blue, Compote, Sweets, 5 1/8 In. 80.00
Cobalt Blue, Cup & Saucer . . . . .25.00 to 27.00
Cobalt Blue, Cup & Saucer, After Dinner 75.00
Cobalt Blue, Eggcup . . . . .56.00 to 70.00
Cobalt Blue, Jar, Cover, Kitchen Kraft 495.00
Cobalt Blue, Jar, Marmalade . . . . .265.00 to 330.00
Cobalt Blue, Jug, Water, 2 Pt. 120.00
Cobalt Blue, Mixing Bowl, No. 2 . . . . 190.00
Cobalt Blue, Mixing Bowl, No. 3 . . . . 170.00
Cobalt Blue, Mixing Bowl, No. 4 . . . . 225.00
Cobalt Blue, Mixing Bowl, No. 5 . . . . 195.00
Cobalt Blue, Mixing Bowl, No. 7 . . . . 650.00
Cobalt Blue, Mug, Tom & Jerry . . . . .35.00 to 55.00
Cobalt Blue, Mustard 325.00
Cobalt Blue, Nappy, 8 1/2 In. 50.00
Cobalt Blue, Pie Plate, Kitchen Kraft, 9 In. 65.00
Cobalt Blue, Pitcher, Disk 95.00
Cobalt Blue, Plate, 6 In. 7.00
Cobalt Blue, Plate, 10 In. 38.00
Cobalt Blue, Saucer 4.00
Cobalt Blue, Soup, Onion, Cover 550.00
Cobalt Blue, Spoon, Kitchen Kraft 170.00
Cobalt Blue, Sugar & Creamer 75.00
Cobalt Blue, Sugar & Creamer, Cover, Tray, 3 Piece 350.00
Cobalt Blue, Teapot, 8 Cup 335.00
Cobalt Blue, Tumbler, Juice 45.00
Cobalt Blue, Tumbler, Water . . . . .60.00 to 65.00
Cobalt Blue, Vase, 8 In. 800.00
Cobalt Blue, Vase, 10 In. 1150.00

Cobalt Blue, Vase, Bud, 6 1/4 In. 125.00
Forest Green, Ashtray, 5 1/2 In. 72.00
Forest Green, Bowl, Cereal, 5 1/2 In. 30.00
Forest Green, Bowl, Dessert, 6 In. 40.00
Forest Green, Bowl, Fruit, 4 3/4 In. ....25.00 to 30.00
Forest Green, Casserole, Cover 435.00
Forest Green, Coffeepot 228.00
Forest Green, Cup, Tea, Inside Rings 20.00
Forest Green, Eggcup ....130.00 to 150.00
Forest Green, Gravy Boat 75.00
Forest Green, Mixing Bowl, No. 3 .... 120.00
Forest Green, Mixing Bowl, No. 4 .... 100.00
Forest Green, Pitcher, Disk 275.00
Forest Green, Plate, 9 In. 11.00
Forest Green, Platter, 12 In. 45.00
Forest Green, Saltshaker 10.00
Forest Green, Sauceboat ....35.00 to 90.00
Forest Green, Saucer 3.00
Forest Green, Soup, Cream ....53.00 to 95.00
Forest Green, Teapot, 8 Cup 325.00
Forest Green, Tumbler, Water 50.00
Gray, Ashtray, 5 1/2 In. 90.00
Gray, Bowl, Dessert, 6 In. ....28.00 to 40.00
Gray, Bowl, Fruit, 4 3/4 In. ....26.00 to 30.00
Gray, Chop Plate, 13 In. 95.00
Gray, Coffeepot ....550.00 to 750.00
Gray, Compartment Plate, 10 1/2 In. 95.00
Gray, Creamer 38.00
Gray, Cup 38.00
Gray, Eggcup 135.00
Gray, Nappy, 8 1/2 In. 50.00
Gray, Pitcher, Disk 370.00
Gray, Plate, Deep 48.00
Gray, Saltshaker ....17.50 to 20.00
Gray, Sauceboat 75.00
Gray, Soup, Cream ....65.00 to 95.00
Gray, Sugar, Cover 75.00
Green, Fork, Kitchen Kraft ....75.00 to 115.00
Green, Nappy, 9 1/2 In. 55.00
Ivory, Bowl, Cereal, 5 1/2 In. ....25.00 to 28.00
Ivory, Bowl, Dessert, 6 In. ....35.00 to 45.00
Ivory, Bowl, Fruit, 4 3/4 In. 21.00
Ivory, Bowl, Fruit, 11 3/4 In. 300.00
Ivory, Candleholder, Tripod, Pair ....600.00 to 950.00
Ivory, Chop Plate, 15 In. 60.00
Ivory, Coffeepot ....135.00 to 450.00
Ivory, Coffeepot, After Dinner 432.00
Ivory, Compote, 12 In. 225.00
Ivory, Creamer 20.00
Ivory, Creamer, Stick Handle 60.00
Ivory, Eggcup ....48.00 to 75.00
Ivory, Jar, Marmalade 175.00
Ivory, Jug, Water, 2 Pt. 120.00
Ivory, Mixing Bowl, No. 2 .... 230.00
Ivory, Mixing Bowl, No. 3 .... 70.00
Ivory, Mixing Bowl, No. 4 ....130.00 to 225.00
Ivory, Mixing Bowl, No. 5 .... 275.00
Ivory, Mixing Bowl, No. 6 .... 360.00
Ivory, Mug, Tom & Jerry, Gold Trim 65.00
Ivory, Pitcher, Ice Lip 155.00
Ivory, Plate, 6 In. 5.00
Ivory, Plate, 7 In. 8.00
Ivory, Plate, 9 In. 15.00

Ivory, Plate, 10 In. ....30.00 to 40.00

Ivory, Plate, Calendar, 1954, 10 In. 45.00

Ivory, Plate, Calendar, 1955, 9 In. 50.00

Ivory, Plate, Deep 40.00

Ivory, Saucer 4.00

Ivory, Soup, Cream 60.00

Ivory, Soup, Onion, Cover 1200.00

Ivory, Stack Unit, Kitchen Kraft 175.00

Ivory, Sugar & Creamer, Cover 75.00

Ivory, Syrup 600.00

Ivory, Tumbler, Water 75.00

Ivory, Vase, 8 In. 895.00

Ivory, Vase, 10 In. ....729.00 to 1185.00

Ivory, Vase, Bud, 6 1/4 In. 95.00

Light Green, Bowl, Cereal, 5 1/2 In. 20.00

Light Green, Bowl, Fruit, 4 3/4 In. ....18.00 to 20.00

Light Green, Bowl, Fruit, 11 3/4 In. 345.00

Light Green, Cake Plate, Kitchen Kraft, 10 7/8 In. 50.00

Light Green, Cake Server, Kitchen Kraft 150.00

Light Green, Candleholder, Bulb 40.00

Light Green, Carafe 325.00

Light Green, Casserole, Cover 165.00

Light Green, Casserole, Cover, Kitchen Kraft, Individual ....145.00 to 150.00

Light Green, Chop Plate, 15 In. 40.00

Light Green, Coffeepot 275.00

Light Green, Coffeepot, After Dinner ....215.00 to 495.00

Light Green, Creamer, Individual 12.00

Light Green, Creamer, Stick Handle 45.00

Light Green, Cup & Saucer 25.00

Light Green, Cup & Saucer, After Dinner ....59.00 to 85.00

Light Green, Eggcup ....45.00 to 50.00

Light Green, Jar, Marmalade ....295.00 to 395.00

Light Green, Mixing Bowl, No. 1, Cover 895.00

Light Green, Mixing Bowl, No. 3 ....130.00 to 160.00

Light Green, Mixing Bowl, No. 5 .... 165.00

Light Green, Mixing Bowl, No. 6 ....200.00 to 375.00

Light Green, Nappy, 8 1/2 In. ....33.00 to 40.00

Light Green, Pitcher, Disk ....85.00 to 115.00

Light Green, Plate, 9 In. ....8.50 to 12.00

Light Green, Plate, 10 In. ....22.00 to 32.00

Light Green, Platter, 12 In. 18.00

Light Green, Sauceboat 35.00

Light Green, Soup, Cream 35.00

Light Green, Soup, Onion, Cover 795.00

Light Green, Sugar, Cover 40.00

Light Green, Teapot, 6 Cup 195.00

Light Green, Tumbler, Water ....65.00 to 75.00

Light Green, Vase, 8 In. 525.00

Light Green, Vase, 10 In. ....750.00 to 975.00

Light Green, Vase, 12 In. 1095.00

Light Green, Vase, Bud, 6 1/4 In. 85.00

Medium Gray, Teapot, 6 Cup ....125.00 to 325.00

Medium Green, Bowl, Cereal, 5 1/2 In. ....60.00 to 65.00

Medium Green, Chop Plate, 13 In. 625.00

Medium Green, Creamer 110.00

Medium Green, Cup 45.00

Medium Green, Cup & Saucer 65.00

Medium Green, Cup & Saucer, Inside Rings 95.00

Medium Green, Mug 95.00

Medium Green, Mustard 185.00

Medium Green, Pitcher, Disk ....650.00 to 1600.00

Medium Green, Plate, 6 In. ....30.00 to 35.00

Medium Green, Plate, 7 In. ....20.00 to 45.00

Medium Green, Plate, 9 In. ....40.00 to 65.00
Medium Green, Plate, 10 In. ....135.00 to 150.00
Medium Green, Salt & Pepper 270.00
Medium Green, Sauceboat 250.00
Medium Green, Saucer 9.00
Medium Green, Soup, Cream 8500.00
Medium Green, Sugar, Cover 265.00
Medium Green, Syrup 325.00
Pink, Mug, Bugs Bunny, Looney Tunes 15.00
Red, Ashtray, 5 1/2 In. ....45.00 to 90.00
Red, Bowl, Cereal, 5 1/2 In. ....26.00 to 34.00
Red, Bowl, Dessert, 6 In. 45.00
Red, Bowl, Fruit, 4 3/4 In. ....28.00 to 35.00
Red, Cake Server, Kitchen Kraft 190.00
Red, Candleholder, Bulb 65.00
Red, Candleholder, Bulb, Pair ....90.00 to 110.00
Red, Candleholder, Tripod, Pair 795.00
Red, Carafe ....190.00 to 395.00
Red, Casserole 150.00
Red, Chop Plate, 15 In. 40.00
Red, Coffeepot ....225.00 to 295.00
Red, Coffeepot, After Dinner ....340.00 to 650.00
Red, Compote, 12 In. 90.00
Red, Creamer ....22.00 to 35.00
Red, Creamer, Individual ....265.00 to 350.00
Red, Creamer, Stick Handle 48.00
Red, Cup & Saucer 25.00
Red, Eggcup ....70.00 to 75.00
Red, Gravy Boat ....50.00 to 60.00
Red, Jar, Marmalade 235.00
Red, Mixing Bowl, No. 1 .... 275.00
Red, Mixing Bowl, No. 1, Cover 1400.00
Red, Mixing Bowl, No. 2 ....165.00 to 190.00
Red, Mixing Bowl, No. 3 .... 200.00
Red, Mixing Bowl, No. 4 .... 220.00
Red, Mixing Bowl, No. 5 .... 100.00
Red, Mixing Bowl, No. 6 .... 90.00
Red, Mug 75.00
Red, Mug, Tom & Jerry 70.00
Red, Mustard 395.00
Red, Nappy, 8 1/2 In. 65.00
Red, Pie Plate, Kitchen Kraft, 9 In. 55.00
Red, Pitcher, Disk 90.00
Red, Pitcher, Ice Lip 185.00
Red, Pitcher, Juice 500.00
Red, Plate, 10 In. 32.00
Red, Plate, Deep, 8 In. 42.00
Red, Platter, 12 In. 40.00
Red, Relish 55.00
Red, Salt & Pepper 24.00
Red, Sauceboat 85.00
Red, Saucer, After Dinner 25.00
Red, Soup, Cream 75.00
Red, Soup, Onion, Cover 460.00
Red, Spoon, Kitchen Kraft ....175.00 to 180.00
Red, Syrup 425.00
Red, Teapot, 8 Cup 285.00
Red, Tumbler, Juice ....50.00 to 75.00
Red, Tumbler, Water ....60.00 to 65.00
Red, Vase, 8 In. 985.00
Red, Vase, Bud, 6 1/4 In. ....100.00 to 125.00
Rose, Bowl, Cereal, 5 1/2 In. 26.00
Rose, Bowl, Fruit, 4 3/4 In. 25.00

Rose, Casserole, Cover 325.00
Rose, Chop Plate, 15 In. ....95.00 to 150.00
Rose, Coffeepot 100.00
Rose, Creamer 38.00
Rose, Creamer, Individual 23.00
Rose, Cup 8.00
Rose, Cup & Saucer, After Dinner 695.00
Rose, Eggcup 135.00
Rose, Jug, Water, 2 Pt. 150.00
Rose, Mug 95.00
Rose, Pitcher, Disk 295.00
Rose, Plate, 7 In. 6.50
Rose, Plate, 9 In. ....8.50 to 19.00
Rose, Sauceboat 70.00
Rose, Soup, Cream ....60.00 to 95.00
Rose, Sugar, Cover 75.00
Rose, Teapot, 6 Cup 270.00
Rose, Tumbler, Juice 95.00
Turquoise, Ashtray 34.00
Turquoise, Bowl, Cereal, 5 1/2 In. 25.00
Turquoise, Bowl, Dessert, 6 In. 125.00
Turquoise, Bowl, Fruit, 5 1/2 In. 22.00
Turquoise, Cake Plate, 10 In. 600.00
Turquoise, Candleholder, Bulb, Pair 110.00
Turquoise, Candleholder, Tripod, Pair 560.00
Turquoise, Carafe 380.00
Turquoise, Casserole, Cover 135.00
Turquoise, Chop Plate, 15 In. 55.00
Turquoise, Coffeepot 35.00
Turquoise, Compartment Plate, 10 1/2 In. 40.00
Turquoise, Cup 22.00
Turquoise, Cup & Saucer ....25.00 to 29.00
Turquoise, Cup & Saucer, After Dinner 65.00
Turquoise, Jar, Marmalade ....175.00 to 325.00
Turquoise, Mixing Bowl, No. 1 .... 275.00
Turquoise, Mixing Bowl, No. 4 .... 120.00
Turquoise, Mixing Bowl, No. 5 ....120.00 to 195.00
Turquoise, Mug, Tom & Jerry 45.00
Turquoise, Mustard 275.00
Turquoise, Pitcher, Disk ....95.00 to 100.00
Turquoise, Pitcher, Ice Lip 195.00
Turquoise, Salt & Pepper 135.00
Turquoise, Sauceboat 38.00
Turquoise, Soup, Cream 35.00
Turquoise, Sugar & Creamer 25.00
Turquoise, Sugar, Cover 36.00
Turquoise, Syrup 265.00
Turquoise, Teapot, 6 Cup 65.00
Turquoise, Teapot, 8 Cup 280.00
Turquoise, Tray, Utility 30.00
Turquoise, Tumbler, Water 75.00
Turquoise, Vase, 8 In. 600.00
Yellow, Ashtray, 5 1/2 In. 36.00
Yellow, Bowl, Cereal, 5 1/2 In. ....18.50 to 20.00
Yellow, Bowl, Fruit, 4 3/4 In. ....18.00 to 20.00
Yellow, Cake Plate, 10 In. 490.00
Yellow, Cake Plate, Kitchen Kraft, 10 7/8 In. 50.00
Yellow, Cake Server, Kitchen Kraft ....180.00 to 190.00
Yellow, Candleholder, Bulb, Pair ....90.00 to 100.00
Yellow, Carafe 250.00
Yellow, Casserole 275.00
Yellow, Casserole, Cover, Kitchen Craft, Individual 150.00
Yellow, Casserole, French, Cover, Stick Handle ....215.00 to 300.00

Yellow, Chop Plate, 13 In. 35.00
Yellow, Chop Plate, 15 In. 75.00
Yellow, Coffeepot 135.00
Yellow, Coffeepot, After Dinner 275.00
Yellow, Compote, 12 In. 50.00
Yellow, Creamer, Stick Handle 50.00
Yellow, Cup 5.00
Yellow, Cup & Saucer 26.00
Yellow, Cup & Saucer, After Dinner 55.00
Yellow, Eggcup ....43.00 to 50.00
Yellow, Fork, Kitchen Kraft 210.00
Yellow, Jar, Cover, Kitchen Kraft 360.00
Yellow, Jar, Marmalade 250.00
Yellow, Mixing Bowl, No. 1 .... 325.00
Yellow, Mixing Bowl, No. 2 ....35.00 to 80.00
Yellow, Mixing Bowl, No. 2, Cover 1150.00
Yellow, Mixing Bowl, No. 4 .... 145.00
Yellow, Mixing Bowl, No. 4, Cover 850.00
Yellow, Mixing Bowl, No. 7 .... 175.00
Yellow, Mug, Tom & Jerry 50.00
Yellow, Pitcher, Disk ....60.00 to 90.00
Yellow, Pitcher, Ice Lip 130.00
Yellow, Pitcher, Juice ....38.00 to 55.00
Yellow, Plate, 9 In. 8.50
Yellow, Plate, Deep ....26.00 to 42.00
Yellow, Platter, 12 In. 30.00
Yellow, Relish 55.00
Yellow, Salt & Pepper 18.00
Yellow, Sauceboat ....35.00 to 39.00
Yellow, Soup, Cream 35.00
Yellow, Syrup ....325.00 to 425.00
Yellow, Tumbler, Juice 30.00
Yellow, Tumbler, Water 50.00
Yellow, Vase, 10 In. ....860.00 to 900.00
Yellow, Vase, Bud, 6 1/4 In. 50.00

FINCH, see Kay Finch category.

FINDLAY ONYX AND FLORADINE are two similar types of glass made by Dalzell, Gilmore and Leighton Co. of Findlay, Ohio, about 1889. Onyx is a patented yellowish white opaque glass with raised silver daisy decorations. A few rare pieces were made of rose, amber, orange, or purple glass. Floradine is made of cranberry-colored glass with an opalescent white raised floral pattern and a satin finish. The same molds were used for both types of glass.

Spooner, Silver Design 375.00
Sugar Shaker 450.00
Toothpick, Raised Leaf Designs, Green, 2 1/2 In. 475.00

FIREFIGHTING equipment of all types is wanted, from fire marks to uniforms to toy fire trucks. It is said that every little boy wanted to be a fireman or a train engineer 75 years ago and the collectors today reflect this interest.

Alarm Box, Star Electric Co., Milwaukee, Iron, Ornamental, 1916, 7 Ft. 1400.00
Ax, Bent Spiked Poll, Colt's Footed Handle, Round Blade, 13 1/2 In. 325.00
Bag, Linsey-Woolsey, Original Tie, 19x 39 In. 140.00
Booklet, Babcock Portable Fire Extinguisher, N.Y., Chicago, 1870s, 16 Pages 45.00
Box, Alarm, Cast Iron, Attached Hammer & Chain, Ostrander, 5 x 3 In. 65.00
Bucket, Black & White Letters, No. 1, T. Mumford, 1792 .... 950.00
Bucket, Black Leather, Handle, 11 1/2 In. 70.00
Bucket, Copper Riveted, Black Leather, Tanner's Mark, 16 In. 225.00
Bucket, Gold Bands, Handle, 10 1/8 In. 110.00
Bucket, Leather, Painted Green, Yellow Lettering, M.T. Richards No. 2, 13 In. 385.00

Bucket, Leather, Swinging Bail Handle, Marked, W.F.C., 1847, 13 In. 2300.00
Bucket, Painted Green, Red & Gold, Aaron D. Williams, No. 2, 1828, 13 In. 385.00
Bucket, Painted Red, Franklin Hook & Ladder Co., 1823, 12 In., Pair 1200.00
Bucket, Publico No. 3 Thomas Briggs, 1802, 13 1/2 In. 2760.00
Bucket, United Fire Society, Yellow Letters Outlined In Brown, 1837 .... 885.00
Buckle, Silver Toned, Red Painted Fire Truck, Fireman's Emblem, 3 x 2 In. 20.00
Cap, Fire Brigade, Essex County, Cloth, Plastic Brim, 7 1/4 x 11 In. 50.00
Extinguisher, Babcock Hand Grenade, Cobalt Blue, 1875-1895, 7 1/2 In. 1430.00
Extinguisher, General Quick Aid, Model T515, Brass 95.00
Extinguisher, Magic Fire Extinguisher Co., Yellow Amber, Bubbles, 6 1/4 In. 465.00
Extinguisher, Phoenix Compound, Metal Canister, April 25, 1899, 21 7/8 In. 100.00
Extinguisher, Portable, Heavy Vehicle, Pump Style, Brass, Pyrene Brand, 14 In. 25.00
Extinguisher, Rockford Kalamazoo Automatic & Hand Fire, Cobalt Blue, 11 In. 470.00
Extinguisher, Systeme Labbe Grenade Extincteur, Topaz, France, 5 1/2 In. 305.00
Fire Mark, Hand Pumper, F.L. Co., Cast Iron 195.00
Fire Mark, Hydrant & Hose, F.A., Iron, Oval, 11 3/4 x 7 1/4 In. 45.00
Grenade, Harden, Turquoise Blue, Contents, 1884, 7 In. 320.00
Hat, Fireman's, Dress, Lake Carmel 45.00
Hat, Leather, Painted Red, Label Hooked Onto Brass Plate, 25 3/4 In. 425.00
Hat, Uniform, Blue Wool Shell, Leather Visor, Metal Chin Strap, 1940s-1950s, Small ... 23.00
Helmet, Aluminum, Eagle Head At Front Top, 1926, 10 3/4 x 14 1/2 In. 195.00
Helmet, Hand Sewn, Brass Eagle, Velvet Liner, Black Leather, c.1860 .... 425.00
Helmet, USA-FD, Black, 1940s 175.00
Horn, Lifeline, Bellows, Brass, 12 7/8 x 20 1/2 In. 665.00
Key Ring, Boyer Fire Apparatus, Leather 6.00
Light, Helmet, U.S. Govt. Forester, Red Battery Box, 1950s, 2 1/2-In. Light 35.00
Nozzle, Brass Handle & Tip Of Nozzle, 25 3/4 In. 60.00
Nozzle, Brass, 15 In. 22.00
Paper, Catalog, Dayton Fire Equipment Co., No. 33, 1940s, 28 Pages 50.00
Pin, I'm Helping Smokey Prevent Forest Fires, Tin Lithograph, Fold 30.00
Pin, Join Smokey's Campaign Prevent Forest Fires, Smokey 40.00
Plaque, Hose & Hydrant, Cast Iron, Oval, 11 1/2 x 7 1/4 In. 325.00
Trumpet, Britannia Silver, c.1890, 14 1/2 In. 535.00

FIREGLOW glass is attributed to the Boston and Sandwich Glass Company. The light-tan-colored glass appears reddish brown when held to the light. Most fireglow has an acid finish and enamel decoration, although it was also made with a satin finish.

Pitcher, Apple Blossoms, 8 In. 225.00
Tumbler, Ribs 100.00
Vase, Ruffled Top, Red Glow, 3 In. 130.00
Vase, White Mary Gregory Type Enameled Figure, 9 1/4 In. 90.00

FIREPLACES were used to cook food and to heat the American home in past centuries. Many types of tools and equipment were used. Andirons held the logs in place, firebacks reflected the heat into the room, and tongs were used to move either fuel or food. Many types of spits and roasting jacks were made and may be listed in the Kitchen category.

Andirons, Brass, Ball & Dog Finials, 15 1/2 In. 365.00
Andirons, Brass, Ball Finial, 14 3/4 In., Pair 220.00
Andirons, Brass, Ball Top, 13 1/4 In., Pair 275.00
Andirons, Brass, Ball Top, Spurred Cabriole Legs, Slipper Feet, 13 1/2 In. 415.00
Andirons, Brass, Belted Ball Top, 19th Century, 18 In. 402.00
Andirons, Brass, Belted Ball Top, Skidmore, New York, 13 1/4 In. 920.00
Andirons, Brass, Dogs, Double Urn Form, Attached To Metal Log Holder, 17 In., Pair .. 115.00
Andirons, Brass, Double Lemon Top, 19 1/4 In. 495.00
Andirons, Brass, Double Urn Top, Swag & Acorn Finials, Federal, 18 1/2 In. 440.00
Andirons, Brass, Empire, Multiturned With Drop Skirt, Cabriole Legs, 14 1/2 In. 165.00
Andirons, Brass, Engraved, Ball Top, Engraved Plinths, R. Wittingham, 22 In. 4887.00
Andirons, Brass, Faceted & Turned Top & Shaft, Cabriole Legs, Empire, 20 In. 330.00
Andirons, Brass, Fire Dog, Penny Feet, Urn Finial With Spire, 12 3/4 In. 385.00
Andirons, Brass, Flame Finial, Pad Feet, Georgian, 19th Century, 21 In., Pair 184.00

Andirons, Brass, Greyhounds, Art Deco, 14 In. 168.00
Andirons, Brass, In Shape Of Birds & Flowers, 18 x 19 In., Pair 132.00
Andirons, Brass, Lacquer Traces, Rostand, 20th Century, 28 1/2 In. 110.00
Andirons, Brass, Lemon Top, Paneled Shaft, Spurred Cabriole Legs, 15 1/2 In. 495.00
Andirons, Brass, Music Note, Splayed Feet, 20th Century, 17 In., Pair 1150.00
Andirons, Brass, Ring Turned Shaft, 19th Century, 18 In. 55.00
Andirons, Brass, Ring Turned Supports, Bracket Feet, 19th Century, 11 x 23 In., Pair ... 770.00
Andirons, Brass, Scroll Panels, Reed, Floral Apron, 2 Legs, Continental, 24 In., Pair 920.00
Andirons, Brass, Signed Hunneman, Boston, Massachusetts, c.1835, 11 1/2 In. 1050.00
Andirons, Brass, Sphere Steeple Finial, Shovel & Tongs, 22 1/2 In. 2585.00
Andirons, Brass, Spiral Flame Finials, Baluster, Arched Legs, Ball Feet, 23 In., Pair 6900.00
Andirons, Brass, Steeple Top, c.1800, 20 1/2 In. 690.00
Andirons, Brass, Urn Form, Openwork Base, Pair 176.00
Andirons, Brass, Urn Top, 20th Century, 32 In. 137.00
Andirons, Brass, Urn Top, Scrolled Legs, Ball Feet, Federal, 23 In. 275.00
Andirons, Brass, Wrapped With Dolphin 715.00
Andirons, Bronze & Cast Iron, Dolphin, 14 In. 650.00
Andirons, Bronze, Dolphin Form, Pair 1650.00
Andirons, Bronze, Dragon Form, Winged & Breasted Beast, Paw Feet, 31 In. 4600.00
Andirons, Bronze, Female Allegorical Figure, Seated On Pierced Sphere, 25 In. 2300.00
Andirons, Bronze, Figural, Female Term, Leaf-Tip & Mask Cast Base, 15 3/4 In. 2587.00
Andirons, Bronze, Flower-Filled Horn, Ram's Head Base, Robsjohn-Gibbings, 1937 .... 4600.00
Andirons, Bronze, Washington, 20th Century, 20 In., Pair 28.00
Andirons, Cast Iron, Baseball Player, 1 Holding Bat, Other Holding Ball, 9 3/4 In. 1430.00
Andirons, Cast Iron, Boxer, Yellow, Black Glass Eyes, Seated On Pedestal, 17 In. 920.00
Andirons, Cast Iron, Comic Black Men, 16 1/2 In. 192.00
Andirons, Cast Iron, Dachshund, On Its Haunches, Head Down, 13 1/4 In., Pair .800.00 to 920.00
Andirons, Cast Iron, Flower Bouquet Finial, Haven Iron Works, Cincinnati, O., 12 In. 110.00
Andirons, Cast Iron, Hessian Soldier Form, Plumed Hats, Swords, 20 1/4 In. 403.00
Andirons, Cast Iron, Hessians, Flesh Face & Handle, Black, White Swords, 19 7/8 In. 530.00
Andirons, Cast Iron, Indian Warrior, With Bow & Arrows, 13 In., Pair 225.00
Andirons, Cast Iron, Monk Faces, Arts & Crafts, 24 1/2 x 13 1/4 x 23 1/2 In. 315.00
Andirons, Cast Iron, Owl, Stand On Tree Branches, Amber Glass Eyes, 1920s 1850.00
Andirons, Cast Iron, Washington Commemorative, 21 1/2 In. 345.00
Andirons, Forged Iron, Square Columns, Scrollwork Design, Large Iron Rings, 21 In. 300.00
Andirons, Gilt Bronze, Floral Finial, Rosette Base, Empire, France, 13 In., Pair 1035.00
Andirons, Gilt Bronze, Louis XV Style, Foliate Scrolls, 15 1/4 In. 2587.00
Andirons, Iron, Ball Finial, Large Penny Feet, Penna., 1750-1780, 4 1/2 In. 850.00
Andirons, Steel, Scrolled Feet, Brass Ball Finials, 24 In. 165.00
Andirons, Wrought Iron & Bell Metal, Cabriole Legs, 1800, 18 1/2 In., Pair 2300.00
Andirons, Wrought Iron & Brass, Ball Finial, R. Whittingham, 1821, 22 In., Pair 1495.00
Andirons, Wrought Iron & Brass, Urn Form Finial, 1800, 18 x 17 In., Pair 1495.00
Andirons, Wrought Iron, Double Snake, 1880s, 17 In. 2400.00
Andirons, Wrought Iron, Gooseneck, Octagonal Heads, 18 1/2 In. 165.00
Andirons, Wrought Iron, Gooseneck, Penny Feet, 37 x 27 1/2 In., Pair 1150.00
Andirons, Wrought Iron, Holland, Miniature, 17th Century, 4 In. 3200.00
Andirons, Wrought Iron, Knife Blade, Penny Footed, Brass Urn Finial, 20 In. 330.00
Andirons, Wrought Iron, Knife Blade, Penny Footed, Brass Urn Finial, 23 In. 440.00
Andirons, Wrought Iron, Urn Finial, Knife Blade, Brass Trim, Penny Feet, 19 1/2 In. ... 785.00
Bellows, Fruit, Foliage Design, Yellow, Gold, Green, Black, Red, Brass Nozzle, 18 In. .. 880.00
Bellows, Leather, Turtle Back, Stencil & Floral Design, Brass Nozzle, 17 1/2 In. 355.00
Bellows, Mechanical, Brass & Mahogany, 19th Century, 22 1/4 In. 2012.00
Bellows, Red Paint, 2-Tone Gold With Black, Sheet Brass Nozzle, 17 3/4 In. 220.00
Bellows, Turtleback, Original Stenciling, Leather, 19th Century, 17 3/4 In. 145.00
Box, Log, Hinged Slant Front, Embossed Genre Panels, 22 x 28 In. 385.00
Box, Tinder, Hanging, Raised Design, Hinged Lid, Rolled Wire Rim, Sheet Metal, 13 In. .. 460.00
Brazier, Hammered Brass Bowl, Wrought Iron Frame, Wood Handle, 1750, 6 1/4 In. 495.00
Broiler, Rotary, Wrought Iron, Late 18th Century, 23 1/2 In. 245.00
Carrier, Embers, Tinned Iron, Slanted Style, Perforated Hinged Cover, 1820 .... 150.00
Coal, Hod, Floral Transfer Design, Gold Stenciling, Tole, Iron Fittings, 24 1/2 In. 192.00
Coal, Hod, Hammered Finish, Brass, 15 In. 165.00
Coal Hod, Blue Enameled Lid, Cast Iron, 22 1/2 In. 247.00
Coal Hod, Urn Shape, Hawk Head Handles, Brass, 15 1/2 In. 286.00

Coal Scuttle, Brass Shovels, Stylized Flowers, Copper, 18 x 22 x 13 In. 275.00

Coal Scuttle, Brass, Tapered Form, 2 Hinged Lids, Scrolled Foliage, 20 In. 289.00

Coal Scuttle, Iron Handle, Brass, 7 x 12 In. 155.00

Coal Scuttle, Mahogany, Floral, Foliate Design, Foliate Handle, Bracket Feet, 17 In. . . . 218.50

Coal Scuttle, Nautilus Shell Form, Painted & Stenciled, 21 In. 517.00

Coal Scuttle, Tapered Form, Scrolled Base, Removable Liner, Painted Tin, 25 In. 230.00

Coal Scuttle, Upright Handle, Pierced Scoop, Brass, England, 19 x 19 In. 288.00

Damper, Weight Balance, Grouse On Tree Branch Form, Wrought Iron, 8 1/2 In. 805.00

Fender, Brass & Wire, Brass Finials, 1840s, 45 In. 1495.00

Fender, Brass, 2-Tier Cross Rails, 9 1/2 x 58 x 13 In. 715.00

Fender, Brass, Circular Metal Frame, Arched Base, 25 1/2 In., Pair 402.50

Fender, Brass, England, 19th Century, 40 In. 172.50

Fender, Brass, Tubular, 42 x 13 x 9 In. 143.00

Fender, Brass, With Kettle Shelf, Home Sweet Home, Reticulated Top, 18 In. 50.00

Fender, Pierced Brass, Footed, 8 x 41 1/2 In. 165.00

Fender, Pierced Upright Sides, 8 Lyres Within Laurel Wreaths, Brass, 6 x 42 In. 258.00

Fender, Rail Cresting, Gadrooned Body, Paw Feet, Brass, 49 In. 460.00

Fender, Sheet Metal, Cast Iron Legs, Gilded Swags & Cherubs, Tole, 18 1/2 x 31 In. 522.00

Fender, Spindle Gallery Over Pierced & Foliage Body, Paw Feet, Brass, 19 x 41 In. 385.00

Fender, Wire Grill, Brass Top, Finial, 55 In. 660.00

Fire Curb, Napoleon III, Fruiting Scrolls, Putti On Base, Bronze, c.1870, 51 In. 2875.00

Firedog, Iron, Formalized Whiplash Design, Hector Guimard, 11 In., Pair 7125.00

Fork, Finial With Shepherd's Crook Hook On Back, 18th Century, 16 In. 365.00

Fork, Inset Heart, 18th Century, 27 1/4 In. 3400.00

Fork, Notch File Work Above Tines, Late 18th Century, 19 1/2 In. 350.00

Fork, Punchwork Design On Handle, Marked POK On Back, 18th Century, 18 In. 1200.00

Fork, Punchwork, 18th Century 550.00

Fork, Roasting, Brass Top Band, 2 Pointed Tins, Iron, Engraved 1819, 11 1/2 In. 805.00

Fork, Roasting, Wrought Iron, With Rest 203.00

Fork, Scroll Back Finial, Late18th Century, 23 1/2 In. 285.00

Fork, Toasting, Blacksmith Made, Late 18th Century, 29 In. 95.00

Fork, Toasting, Mahogany, Brass & Steel, c.1780, 25 1/2 In. 425.00

Fork & Strainer, Brass Inlay On Handles, 1828 . . . . 2750.00

Grate, Cast Iron Fireback, Cut Brass Fender, Eagles On Urn, Brass, 33 x 29 1/2 In. 4312.00

Grate, Cast Iron, Patinated Orbs, Applied Brass, Late 19th Century, 44 x 28 In. 1380.00

Griddle, Cast Iron, c.1800, 9 3/4 In. Diam., 17 3/4 In. 95.00

Griddle, Cast Iron, c.1800, 23 In. 195.00

Griddle, Hanging, Cast & Wrought Iron, c.1800, 12 1/2 x 16 In. 245.00

Griddle, Hanging, Cast Iron, c.1800, 13 1/2 In. 245.00

Griddle, Watch Fob, Hand Forged Iron, 12 1/4 In. 245.00

Grill, Crosshatch Handle, 3 Legs, 1860s 150.00

Grill, Hanging, Cast Iron, 8 7/8 In. 165.00

Holder, Skewer, 6 Hand Wrought Skewers, Diamond-Shaped Back, Curled Ends 295.00

Kettle, 3 Legs, Initials SK Over Sunburst, Cast Iron, 9 3/4 In. 225.00

Kettle, Rendering, Firebox, Cattle Heads, Ears Of Corn, Cast Iron, 45 Gal., 36 In. 1100.00

Kindling Container, Brass, Copper, Arts & Crafts, Spade Feet, Embossed, 13 x 15 In. . . 385.00

Ladle, Brass Bowl Attached With Copper Nails, Stamped J. Schneaar, 17 1/2 In. 863.00

Ladle, Hammered Round Bowl, 3 Copper Nails, Wrought Iron & Brass, 9 1/4 In. 345.00

Mantel is listed in the Architectural category.

Oven, Fireside Reflector, Wrought Iron Spit, Tin, 19 In. 110.00

Peel, Lollipop Handle, Iron, 1920s, 37 1/2 In. 150.00

Pie Lifter, Wrought Iron, c.1840, 14 In. 265.00

Pole Screen, Mahogany, Petit Point Floral Panel, Barley Twist, Tripod, 1860, 60 In. 850.00

Pot, Forged Triple Copper Tip-Proof Rivets, Cast Iron, c.1845 . . . . 275.00

Roaster, Bird, Adjustable, Rat Tail Ends, Spade Feet, Turned Finial, Wrought Iron, 34 In. 975.00

Roaster, Chestnut, Brass, Shaped Handle, Late 18th Century, 20 In. 295.00

Roaster, Chestnut, Hand-Hammered Copper Pan & Cover, Iron Shaft, 13 1/4 In. 280.00

Roaster, Coffee, Wooden Handle, c.1800, 40 In. 245.00

Screen, 3 Leaded Glass Panels, Tulip Design, 30 3/8 x 29 1/2 In. 522.00

Screen, 3 Panels, Expandable, Damask, Dolphins & Ducks, c.1880, 42 x 25 In. 859.00

Screen, 4 Panels, Overgrown Ivy, Berries Opening To Leafy Branches, Red, 7 In. 5750.00

Screen, 6 Panels, Silver Leaf, Figural Design, Art Deco, 84 1/2 In. 316.00

Screen, Ball Feet, Jamb Hooks, Signed, W.T., Federal, 30 x 47 In. 1800.00

Screen, Bamboo, Painted On Canvas Little Girl & Dog	125.00
Screen, Brass, Iron, Folding, Victorian	165.00
Screen, Brass, Wire, Federal, 24 x 41 1/2 In.	415.00
Screen, Bronze, Rococo, S-Scroll Frame, C-Scroll Feet, 20th Century, 30 In.	172.00
Screen, Candle, Gilt Frame, Needlepoint, 20 In., Pair	330.00
Screen, Enameled, Stained Glass & Brass, Victorian, c.1870	3450.00
Screen, Gilt Carved Wood, Tapestry, Crest, Musical Trophy, Louis XVI, 45 x 25 In.	2800.00
Screen, Hinged Door, Grill Work, Classical Figures, Cast Iron, 33 1/2 In.	605.00
Screen, L, Scene Of 2 Bucking Stags, Flanked With Lunging Hound, Iron, 67 1/2 In.	2760.00
Screen, Mahogany Veneer, Floral Stitchwork, 3 Feet, Barley Twist, Empire, 65 In.	632.00
Screen, Mahogany, Gilded Form Frame, Gold Floral, Ball Feet, 4 Ft. 11 In.	2875.00
Screen, Mahogany, Needlework, Wallpaper Backing, 1760s, 33 x 26 1/2 In.	4200.00
Screen, Needlework Panel, Pair Of Exotic Figures Within Landscape, 24 x 29 In.	920.00
Screen, Needlework, On Walnut Pole, Victorian, 57 1/2 In.	88.00
Screen, Ormolu, Empire, France, c.1820	385.00
Screen, Pole, George III, Mahogany, Petit-Point Panel, Foliage, 1785, 5 Ft.	3162.00
Screen, Pole, Rosewood, Needlepoint Shield, Floral Spray, Tripartite Base, 5 Ft.	575.00
Screen, Rounded Crest Rail, Upholstered Panel, Reeded Legs, Louis XVI, 36 x 34 In.	207.00
Screen, Stylized Flower & Calligraphic Devices, Wrought Iron, France, 34 x 28 In.	3450.00
Screen, Tapestry Front, Oak, 33 x 31 In.	375.00
Screen, Walnut, Gros Point & Petit Point Panel, 37 1/2 In.	632.00
Screen, Walnut, Needlework, Victorian, 44 In.	220.00
Screen, Wrought Iron, Gilt Bird, Branch In Beak, Edgar Brandt, 1925, 26 x 36 In.	4875.00
Shelf, Pot, Sheet Iron, Iron Hanger, c.1860	165.00
Shelf, Warming, Forged Iron, Crane Hook, 12 3/8 In.	185.00
Shovel, Ash, Heart Finial, 21 1/2 In.	135.00
Shovel, Ash, Penny Foot, 24 1/2 In.	115.00
Shovel, Brass Steeple Top Handle, Hand Forged, 27 In.	130.00
Shovel, Ember, Placing Hot Coals In Pipe Lighters, 18th Century, 8 3/4 In.	195.00
Shovel & Tongs, Wrought Iron, Brass Handles, 31 1/2 In., Pair	100.00 to 265.00
Skimmer, Wrought Iron Handle, J. Schmidt, 1842, 20 In.	247.00
Spatula, Hooked Terminus, Attached With 3 Copper Nails, 11 3/4 In.	518.00
Spatula, Pierced Copper Blade, Wrought Iron Handle, 24 In.	49.00
Spit, Roasting, Clockwork, Brass & Iron	3300.00
Stand, Kettle, Brass, Tall Iron Feet, Pair	100.00
Stand, Kettle, Cresset Burner, Scrolled & Twisted, Wrought Iron, 1780s, 18 3/4 In.	450.00
Strainer, Brass, Handle, 18th Century, 6 3/4 In.	295.00
Strainer, Pierced Bowl, Wrought Iron, Stamped Schmidt 1843, 19 1/2 In.	460.00
Surround, Carved Giltwood, Venetian Rococo	4400.00
Surround, Scroll Design, Dixon & Sons, Cast Iron, 32 2/4 x 34 In.	1597.00
Teapot, Hand Wrought Copper, Tinned Inside	85.00
Toaster, Iron, 32 x 15 1/4 In.	875.00
Toaster, Twisted Handle, Wrought Iron, 26 In.	110.00
Tongs, Ember, Brass, 18th Century, 12 In.	175.00
Tongs, Ember, Used To Light Pipe, Spring In Handle, 18th Century, 8 In.	285.00
Tongs, Shovel, Brass, Steel, Acorn Finial, Faceted Handle, N.Y., 1800, 32 In.	287.00
Tongs, Shovel, Brass, Steelpipe, Acorn Finial, Penny Footed, Pa., 17 1/2 In., Pair	2300.00
Tool Set, Peacock Andirons, Wrought Iron, Edgar Brandt, 1925	6375.00
Tools, Baroque Style, Steel, Shovel, Tongs & Poker	575.00
Trammel, Sawtooth Adjustable Hanging Hook, Wrought Iron, 1780s, 11 In.	403.00
Waffle Iron, Early 19th Century	175.00
Warming Shelf, Hand Form Crane, Spoon Holder, 10 7/8 x 17 In.	220.00

FISCHER porcelain was made in Herend, Hungary, by Moritz Fischer. The factory was founded in 1839 and continued working into the twentieth century. The wares are sometimes referred to as *Herend* porcelain.

MF

Bowl, Bird, Butterflies & Insects, Branch, 11 1/2 In.	140.00
Box, Cover, Open Floral, Gilt Highlights, 3 In.	77.00
Coffeepot, Rothschild Bird, 10 Cup	325.00
Cup & Saucer, Fruit & Flower Pattern, 10 Piece	220.00
Figurine, 2 Duck Molds, Porcelain, 15 x 8 In.	402.00
Figurine, Boy, Hunting Outfit, Signed, 8 In.	125.00

Jug, Enameled Florals & Butterflies, Oriental Style, Multicolored, 10 3/4 In. 200.00
Pitcher, Floral, 2 In. 50.00
Tray, Polychrome, Butterfly & Flower Design, 16 In. 242.00
Tureen, Queen Victoria, Bird Handle, 4 Qt. 950.00
Vase, Hand Painted Flowers & Butterflies, 7 1/4 In. 70.00
Vase, Oriental Scenes, Footed Pedestal, 1946, 3 In. 175.00

FISHING reels of brass or nickel were made in the United States by 1810. Bamboo fly rods were sold by 1860, often marked with the maker's name. Lures made of metal, or metal and wood, were made in the nineteenth century. Plastic lures were made by the 1930s. All fishing material is collected today and even equipment of the past thirty years is of interest if in good condition with original box. Other fishing equipment may be listed in the Sports category.

A.L. & W., Fishrite Duel, Spinning 1 Brass Blade, 1 Copper Blade, 2 1/2 In. 10.00
A.L. & W., Popeye, Spinning Brass, Red Glass Bead, 4 In. 15.00
American, Spinning Half Nickel & Half Brass Blade, 2 In. 55.00
Bottle, Reel Oil, Horton Mfg., For Meek Reels, Box ....*Illus* 550.00
Bottle, Reel Oil, Milam's ....*Illus* 935.00
Box, Tackle, Green Paint, Tin 115.00
Box, Tackle, Illustration Of Fish Inside, Outing Mfg., 1933 .... 298.00
Catalog, B.F. Gladding & Co., Fishing Line, 1939, 14 Pages 75.00
Catalog, Creek Chub Bait Co., 1947 .... 250.00
Catalog, Edward Vom Hofe, 1928 .... 275.00
Catalog, Heddon, 1911 .... 1650.00
Catalog, Pflueger, Fishing Tackle, No. 196, Reels, Rods, Lures, 1960, 50 Pages 35.00
Catalog, Shakespeare, 1928 .... 315.00
Catalog, South Bend Tackle Co., Fishing Tackle, 1963, 40 Pages 35.00
Creel, Adirondack, 19th Century 175.00
Creel, Algonquin, 1880 .... 625.00
Creel, Hinged Lid, Birch Bark, Leather Case, 6 Hooks Inside 495.00
Creel, Split Willow 88.00
Creel, Turtle, Leather Bound 935.00
Creel, Wicker, Leather & Canvas Strap, 1930s 85.00
Creel, Willow, Leather Bound ....65.00 to 145.00
Creel, Wooden Pegged Latch, Rawhide Belt 85.00
Gaff, Blubber, Hand-Forged Iron, Wood Handle, 33 5/8 In. 225.00
Gaff, Blubber, Oak Shaft, 7 3/4 In. 185.00
Harpoon, Hand Held, Hand Forged, Early 1800s, 44 1/8 In. 395.00
Harpoon, Toggle, For Walrus & Seals, c.1900, 15 In. 115.00
Ke-Ad, Dual Teardrop, Spinning Brass Blade, 1 Copper Blade, Box Swivel 18.00
License, Combination Hunting & Fishing, Connecticut, 1927 .... 100.00
Lure, Al Foss, Oriental Wiggler, 18 Blades, Red & White Finish 18.00
Lure, Arbogast, Fly Rod Hula-Popper, Perch Finish, Rubber Tail, Plastic, 1 1/4 In. 15.00
Lure, Arbogast, Wood Jitterbug, White Finish, 2 3/4 In. 10.00
Lure, Best-O-Luck, Tango Type, Red & White, Cardboard Box, 2 5/8 In. 30.00
Lure, Black Sambo, Box ....100.00 to 135.00
Lure, Bud Stewart, Pollywog Pad Hopper, Black Back, Gold Sides, Plastic, 3 1/4 In. 25.00

Fishing, Bottle, Reel Oil, Milam's

Fishing, Bottle, Reel Oil, Horton Mfg., For Meek Reels, Box

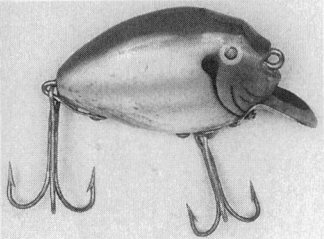

Fishing, Lure, Heddon, Punkinseed, No. 730,
Rainbow Finish

Fishing, Print, John Walsh, American
Sporting Scene, Trout Fishing, 1870

Lure, Comstock, Flying Helgramite	7500.00
Lure, Comstock, Flying Helgramite, Type II, Unmarked Wings	6000.00
Lure, Frog, Lou Rhead, Handmade, 1920s	1430.00
Lure, Grasshopper, 1 1/4 In.	990.00
Lure, Hargrett's, Cat's Paw, Depress Belly Plate, 2 Single Hooks Spring Out	35.00
Lure, Heddon, Meadow Mouse	40.00
Lure, Heddon, Punkinseed, No. 730, Rainbow Finish ....*Illus*	1320.00
Lure, Hunt, Charmer, Decal Eyes, Green Scale Finish, Box	20.00
Lure, Jenson, Kicker, Frog, Rubber Legs Kick, Plastic, 3 1/2 In.	18.00
Lure, L & S, Pike-Master, Gold Scales, White Ribs, Plastic, 3 3/4 In.	15.00
Lure, Makinen Makilure Jr., Red & White Finish, Cardboard Box, Catalog	20.00
Lure, Makinen, Holi-Comet, Silver Scales, 3 3/4 In.	10.00
Lure, Michigan Life-Like, Minnow, c.1908	880.00
Lure, Minnow, Weighted	660.00
Lure, P & K, Fly Rod Mouse, Gray, White Belly, Rubber, 1 1/2 In.	12.00
Lure, Paw Paw, Crippled Killer, Silver Flash Finish, 3 In.	20.00
Lure, Paw Paw, Torpedo, Pike Scale Finish, 3 3/4 In.	15.00
Lure, Pflueger, Minnow, Green Back, Red Glass Bead, 1 1/4 In.	15.00
Lure, Pfluger, Monarch Minnow, 3 Treble Hooks, Rainbow Finish	235.00
Lure, Pod Pad Hopper, Red Plastic Weed Guards, Frog Finish, 2 In.	45.00
Lure, Redeye, Legion	22.00
Lure, Sea Witch, Shakespeare	95.00
Lure, Shakespeare, Minnow, Wooden, Submerged, Box, 3 In.	1650.00
Lure, South Bend, Bass-Oreno, Red & White, Box	35.00
Lure, South Bend, Better Bass-Oreno, Red & White Arrow, 3 3/4 In.	15.00
Lure, South Bend, Panatella Minnow, 3 Side Hooks, Yellow Perch Finish, 4 1/2 In.	75.00
Lure, Virgin Mermaid, Box	100.00
Motor, Outboard, Trolling, Sea King, Montgomery Ward, 31 In.	71.00
Paul Bunyan, Centipede, Spinning Copper, Red Dots, 4 1/2 In.	85.00
Pflueger, Multilite, Spinning Brass Blade, 12 Red Glass Beads, 5 1/4 In.	30.00
Poster, Pflueger Fishing Tackle, 1926	550.00
Poster, Winchester Tackle, 1920s	385.00
Print, John Walsh, American Sporting Scene, Trout Fishing, 1870 ....*Illus*	1045.00
Reel, Alcedo, Micron, Spinning	100.00
Reel, Ambassadeur, Sweden	65.00
Reel, Billy Hatch, Salmon, Mounted, 1928	495.00
Reel, Chubb, Henshall-Van Antwerp, Black Bass, c.1887	4070.00
Reel, Cozzone Squidder	88.00
Reel, Edward Vom Hofe, Perfection, No. 3, Trout	6050.00
Reel, Edward Vom Hofe, Salmon, 2/0	1375.00
Reel, Empire City, No Handle	16.00
Reel, Heddon, Pal P-41	85.00
Reel, Heddon, Pal, Box	95.00
Reel, Hendryx Safety, Fly	990.00

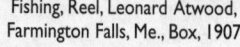

Fishing, Reel, Leonard Atwood,
Farmington Falls, Me., Box, 1907

Fishing, Reel, Meek & Milam, Bait
Casting, No. 6, German Silver

Reel, Holiday, Model 40, Spinning 100.00
Reel, Julius Vom Hofe, Fly, Narrow Spool 990.00
Reel, Leonard Atwood, Farmington Falls, Me., Box, 1907 ....*Illus* 1400.00
Reel, Meek & Milam, Bait Casting, No. 6, German Silver ....*Illus* 3520.00
Reel, Meek, No. 3 .... 300.00
Reel, Ocean City, Ike Walton Club, 300 Yard 120.00
Reel, Ocean City, No. 1600, Open Reel, Green Finish 29.00
Reel, Pflueger, Medalist, No. 1495, Box 50.00
Reel, Pflueger, Summit, No. 1993L 30.00
Reel, Pflueger, Supreme, No. 1573, Level Wind, Anti-Backlash, Original Box .. 29.00
Reel, Robert Haskell, Fly, Naples, Me., Titanium 1320.00
Reel, Shakespeare, Marhoff, Level, Winding, Casting Drag, Box, Papers 59.00
Reel, Shakespeare, Superior, Model DK, Open Body, Copper Finish, 1906 ..... 40.00
Reel, South Bend, No. 300, Model E, Open Body, Stainless Steel 33.00
Reel, T.H. Bates, Trout, German Silver, N.Y., c.1860 .... 1265.00
Reel, Winchester, No. 4350 .... 95.00
Reel, Winchester, No. 4850 .... 110.00
Rod, Fly, Orvis, Model 772, Split Bamboo, Cork Handle, Case, 9 1/2 In. 1200.00
Rod, Fly, Winchester, Bamboo, Cloth Bag, 9 Ft. 350.00
Rod, Garrison, Model 204, Trout, 7 Ft. 9350.00
Rod, Gillum, Trout, Custom Built, 7 Ft. 8660.00
Rod, H.L. Leonard, No. 37, Fly, 6 Ft. 2200.00
Rod, Hardy, Alnwich, England, For Yannin & Son, Caledonia, N.Y., With Net, 9 Ft. 357.00
Rod, Jim Payne, No. 102-L, Fly, 8 Ft. 2200.00
Rod, Leonard, Tournament, With Extra Tip, 8 Ft. 6 In., 3 Piece 220.00
Rod, Leonard, Tournament, With Extra Tip, 8 Ft., 3 Piece 275.00
Rod, Ogden Smith, Warrior, London, England, With Extra Tip, 8 Ft. 6 In., 2 Piece 55.00
Rod, Paul H. Young, Perfection, Fly, 7 1/2 Ft. 3300.00
Rod, Rodcraft, With Extra Tip, 9 Ft., 5 1/2 Oz., 3 Piece 55.00
Rod, Sam Carlson, Housatonic Model, Fly, 7 1/2 Ft. 4400.00
Trap, Minnow, C.F. Orvis 150.00
Trap, Minnow, Woven Splint, 7 In. 90.00
Trophy, Bass, On Oval Wooden Plaque 155.00

FLAGS are included in the Textile category.

FLASH GORDON appeared in the Sunday comics in 1934. The daily
strip started in 1940. The hero was also in comic books from 1930 to
1970, in books from 1936, in movies from 1938, on the radio in the
1930s and 1940s, and on television from 1953 to 1954. All sorts of
memorabilia are collected, but the ray guns and rocket ships are the
most popular.

Air Gun, Box 1095.00
Book, Better Little Book, Flash Gordon & Red Sword Invaders, 1945, 350 Pages 92.00
Book, Big Little Book, Power Men Of Mongo, Whitman, 1943 .... 29.00
Book, Big Little Book, Water World Of Mongo, 1937, 425 Pages 32.00
Button, Sword Fight With Ming, Celluloid, Raymond, 1974 .... 20.00

Coloring Book, 1952	100.00
Comic Book, Adventure With Flash, The Lost Continent, King, 1967	17.00
Comic Strip, Pluto's Icy Surface, Mac Raboy, Sunday, Sept. 3, 1967, 14 x 21 In.	550.00
Comic Strip, Venus Flight Ship, Mac Raboy, Sunday, Jan. 16, 1966, 14 x 21 In.	405.00
Lunch Box, Dome, Plastic	40.00
Puzzle, Defenders Of The Earth Slide, Ja-Ru, On Car, 1985	18.00
Ray Gun, Arresting	475.00
Shade, Christmas Bulb, Colored Plastic, Noma, 1930s, 1 1/2 x 1 1/2 In., Set Of 6	60.00
Tray, TV	20.00
Viewmaster, Reels	18.00

FLORENCE CERAMICS were made in Pasadena, California, from World War II to 1977. Florence Ward created many colorful figurines, boxes, candleholders, and other items for the gift shop trade. Each piece was marked with an ink stamp that included the name *Florence Ceramics Co.* The company was sold in 1964, and although the name remained the same the products were very different. Mugs, cups, and trays were made.

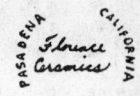

Ashtray, Breast-O-Chicken Tuna, Fish Shape	25.00
Bust, Pamela & David, 9 1/2 & 9 3/4 In., Pair	550.00
Figurine, Abigail, 8 In.	145.00 to 160.00
Figurine, Amber, 9 1/4 In.	850.00
Figurine, Ann, 6 In.	90.00
Figurine, Ava, 10 1/2 In.	200.00
Figurine, Bea, Gold Trim, 7 1/4 In.	85.00
Figurine, Betsy, White, Gold Trim, 7 1/4 In.	80.00
Figurine, Blue Boy & Pinkie, 12 In., Pair	500.00 to 650.00
Figurine, Blue Boy, 12 In.	275.00
Figurine, Charmaine, Blue, 8 1/2 In.	175.00
Figurine, Child Ballerina, 6 3/4 In.	175.00
Figurine, Cindy, 8 In.	375.00
Figurine, Claudia, Gray Over Pink, 8 1/4 In.	250.00
Figurine, David, White, Gold Trim, 7 1/2 In.	150.00
Figurine, Delia, Gray, 7 1/4 In.	150.00
Figurine, Delia, White, 7 1/4 In.	165.00
Figurine, Edith, Blue, 7 1/4 In.	128.00
Figurine, Elaine, Sage Green, 6 In.	122.00
Figurine, Elizabeth, Seated, 8 1/4 x 7 In. ....*Illus*	425.00
Figurine, Ellen, 7 In.	120.00
Figurine, Gibson Girl, White, Gold Trim, 10 In.	275.00
Figurine, Grace, Light Green, 7 3/4 In.	220.00
Figurine, Her Majesty, 7 In.	150.00
Figurine, Irene, 6 In.	65.00 to 75.00
Figurine, Jenette, Olive, 7 3/4 In.	140.00
Figurine, Jim, 6 1/4 In.	75.00
Figurine, Joy, Child, 6 In.	65.00
Figurine, Joyce, 9 In.	800.00
Figurine, Laura, 7 1/2 In.	175.00
Figurine, Leading Man, 10 1/4 In.	275.00
Figurine, Lillian, Rose, 7 1/4 In.	185.00
Figurine, Madame Pompadour & Louis XV, Red, Pair	1250.00
Figurine, Madonna, With Child Bust, 4 3/4 In.	225.00
Figurine, Masquerade, 8 1/4 In.	800.00
Figurine, Melanie, Beige, Green, 7 1/2 In.	110.00
Figurine, Pamela, 7 1/4 In.	400.00
Figurine, Priscilla, Gray, 7 1/4 In.	170.00
Figurine, Rebecca, Sitting, Brown, Green, 7 In.	175.00
Figurine, Rebecca, Sitting, Turquoise, 7 In.	165.00 to 325.00
Figurine, Sarah, 7 1/2 In.	115.00
Figurine, Scarlet, 8 3/4 In.	175.00
Figurine, Sue Ellen, Gray, Maroon, 8 1/4 In.	160.00
Figurine, Sue, 6 In.	65.00 to 75.00
Figurine, Susanna, White, 8 3/4 In.	325.00

Rearrange lamps, figurines, vases, and other knickknacks on tabletops. If you don't, the exposed wood will be lighter than the covered sections under the ornaments.

Florence Ceramics, Figurine,
Elizabeth, Seated, 8 1/4 x 7 In.

Figurine, Victoria, On Sofa, Burgundy Dress, 8 1/4 x 7 In. 250.00
Figurine, Vivian, Pink, 10 In. ....250.00 to 375.00
Figurine, Vivian, Purple, 10 In. 195.00
Figurine, Wynkin, Blynkin, 5 1/2 In. 105.00
Flower Holder, Jerry, Base 85.00
Flower Holder, Joy, Harp 145.00
Flower Holder, Kay, 7 In. 33.00
Flower Holder, Polly, 6 In. 50.00
Flower Holder, Twin Girl & Boy, 6 1/2 In., Pair 85.00
Frame, Picture, Cream, Rosebud, Pair 95.00
Lamp, TV, Dear Ruth, 9 In. 1500.00
Plaque, Cameo, Lady & Gentlemen 85.00
Vase, Angel Fish, Green & Brown, 8 1/4 In. 75.00
Vase, Cornucopia, Gray, Pink & Rose, 7 In. 95.00

FLOW BLUE, or flo blue, was made in England about 1830 to 1900. The
plates were printed with designs using a cobalt blue coloring. The
color flowed from the design to the white plate so that the finished
plate has a smeared blue design. The plates were usually made of ironstone china.

Bell, Kaiser, Nativity Scene, Gold Trim Border, 7 In. 35.00
Bone Dish, Marguerite, W.H. Grindley 55.00
Bone Dish, Rose, W.H. Grindley 60.00
Bone Dish, Touraine ....75.00 to 90.00
Bowl, Colonial, J. & G. Meakin, 5 In. 30.00
Bowl, Conway, New Wharf Pottery, 9 In. 55.00
Bowl, Cover, Eclipse, 11 In. 200.00
Bowl, Cover, Somerset, Round, W.H. Grindley 225.00
Bowl, Cyrene, Scalloped, Vegetable, Adams 95.00
Bowl, Delph, Wood & Son, 9 In. 70.00
Bowl, Fairy Villas, 7 In. 70.00
Bowl, La Belle, Ruffled, Wheeling Potteries, 9 In. 125.00
Bowl, Louise, 6 1/4 In. 30.00
Bowl, Manilla, Ed. Challinor, c.1842, 13 3/4 In. 1100.00
Bowl, Muriel, Oval, Upper Hanley Potteries, 9 In. 90.00
Bowl, Serving, Conway, New Wharf Pottery 125.00
Bowl, Touraine, Stanley Pottery Co., 8 1/2 In. 125.00
Bowl, Vegetable, Oregon, Johnson Bros. 190.00
Bowl, Vegetable, Pelew, Ed. Challinor, 7 5/8 In. 165.00
Bowl, Vegetable, Touraine, Oval, Stanley Pottery Co., 9 In. 115.00
Bowl, Victoria, Fluted, 10 In. 200.00
Box, Marinated Herring, Dresden Pattern, 1900s 695.00
Butter, Cover, Argyle 495.00
Butter, Cover, La Francais, French China Co. 95.00
Butter, Cover, Oregon, 12 Sides 515.00
Butter Chip, Alaska, W.H. Grindley 48.00
Butter Chip, Grace, W.H. Grindley ....10.00 to 40.00

Butter Chip, La Francais, French China Co. 15.00
Butter Chip, Lorne, W.H. Grindley 55.00
Butter Chip, Melbourne, W.H. Grindley 48.00
Cake Stand, Chusan, c.1850 .... 225.00
Casserole, Cover, Colonial, J. & G. Meakin 215.00
Celery Dish, Kyber 125.00
Charger, La Belle, Wheeling Potteries, 12 In. 350.00
Charger, La Belle, Wheeling Potteries, 14 In. 450.00
Chocolate Pot, Abbey 275.00
Coffeepot, Manilla, Podmore, Walker, 9 In. 330.00
Creamer, Chusan, J. Clements, 5 3/4 In. 121.00
Creamer, Florida, Johnson Bros. 195.00
Creamer, Florida, W.H. Grindley 165.00
Creamer, India, Villeroy & Boch 225.00
Creamer, Lorne, W.H. Grindley ....150.00 to 165.00
Creamer, Nonpareil ....200.00 to 225.00
Creamer, Pandy, Embossed Design, Warwick 225.00
Creamer, Scinde, J. & G. Alcock 695.00
Creamer, Sobroan, 1850, 5 1/4 In. 431.00
Creamer, Touraine, 4 In. ....125.00 to 275.00
Creamer, Waldorf, New Wharf Pottery 250.00
Cup & Saucer, Arcadia 85.00
Cup & Saucer, Cashmere 250.00
Cup & Saucer, Duchess 70.00
Cup & Saucer, Gironde, W.H. Grindley 70.00
Cup & Saucer, Harwood, New Wharf Pottery 75.00
Cup & Saucer, Idris, W.H. Grindley 65.00
Cup & Saucer, Touraine ....105.00 to 110.00
Cup Plate, Nino Po, R. Hall & Co. 100.00
Cup Plate, Scinde 150.00
Dessert Set, Alton, Service For 12, W.H. Grindley, 45 Piece 2750.00
Dessert Set, La Francais, French China Co., 7 Piece 150.00
Dinner Set, Florida, Service For 12, Johnson Bros., 98 Piece 9250.00
Dinner Set, Janette, With Serving Pieces, W.H. Grindley, 83 Piece 3500.00
Dish, Pelew, Oblong, Ed. Chalinor, 7 5/8 In. 110.00
Dish, Warwick 175.00
Eggcup, Athol, Burgess & Leigh 110.00
Eggcup, Corey Hill, E. Walky 150.00
Eggcup, Touraine 195.00
Gravy Boat, Amoy 395.00
Gravy Boat, Chapoo, Interior & Exterior Pattern, Wedgwood 260.00
Gravy Boat, Colonial 65.00
Gravy Boat, Lorne, W.H. Grindley ....150.00 to 155.00
Gravy Boat, Royal, F. Winkle 145.00
Gravy Boat, Scinde 295.00
Jardiniere, Cashmere, 14 In. 475.00
Jug, Brush Stroke Painted, 12 In. 795.00
Ladle, Sauce, Nonpareil, Burgess & Leigh, 1891 .... 230.00
Muffin, Dish, Royal Blue, Burgess & Campbell 325.00
Nut Dish, La Belle, Wheeling Potteries 395.00
Pitcher, Abbey, 7 In. 60.00
Pitcher, Idris, W.H. Grindley 285.00
Pitcher, La Belle, Wheeling Potteries, 4 In. 85.00
Pitcher, La Belle, Wheeling Potteries, 6 In. 425.00
Pitcher, Manilla, Podmore, Walker, 5 In. 550.00
Pitcher, Manilla, Podmore, Walker, c.1834, 12 3/4 In. 1200.00
Pitcher, Milk, Grenada, Henry Alcock & Co. 575.00
Pitcher, Milk, Hamilton, John Maddock & Son, 6 1/2 In. ....395.00 to 575.00
Pitcher, Portrait, Belle China .... *Illus* 770.00
Pitcher, Sobraon, Alcock, 8 In. 700.00
Pitcher, Sphinx, Face On Spout, Charles Meigh, 8 In. 400.00
Pitcher, Wild Rose, 3 3/4 In. 125.00
Pitcher & Bowl, Iris, S. Hancock & Sons, 1906-1912, 11 1/2 In. 2000.00

ℰℛ

**Ironstone and porous pottery
can be cleaned with wig
bleach purchased from a
beauty salon.**

ℰℛ

Flow Blue,
Pitcher, Portrait,
Belle China

Plate, Abbey, George Jones & Son, 7 1/2 In.	65.00
Plate, Arcadia, 10 In.	70.00
Plate, Beaufort, Scalloped, W.H. Grindley, 6 3/4 In.	30.00
Plate, Beauties Of China, Meller, Venables & Co., 7 1/2 In.	75.00
Plate, Colonial, J. & G. Meakin, 9 In.	65.00
Plate, Conway, Oval, New Wharf Pottery, 10 1/2 In.	95.00
Plate, Cookie, Melbourne, W.H. Grindley	395.00
Plate, Duchess, 9 In.	50.00
Plate, Fairy Villas, W. Adams Co., 10 1/2 In.	90.00
Plate, Formosa, Thos., John & Joseph Mayer, 8 In.	98.00
Plate, Formosa, Thos., John & Joseph Mayer, 10 1/4 In.	185.00
Plate, Holland, 8 1/2 In.	65.00
Plate, Kremlin, Red Band, Reticulated Rim, Samuel Alcock & Co., 9 1/8 In.	110.00
Plate, Lancaster, 6 1/2 In.	90.00
Plate, Lois, New Wharf Pottery, 9 In.	80.00
Plate, Lorne, W.H. Grindley, 10 In.	70.00
Plate, Normandy, Johnson Bros., 9 In.	80.00
Plate, Normandy, Johnson Bros., 10 In.	110.00
Plate, Pelew, Ed. Challinor, 10 3/4 In.	132.00
Plate, Rhoda Gardens, Hackwood, 9 1/4 In.	77.00
Plate, Scinde, 7 1/4 In.	110.00
Plate, Scinde, J. & G. Alcock, 9 1/2 In.	82.00
Plate, Shanghai, 9 In.	50.00
Plate, Tonquin, 8 In.	110.00
Plate, Tonquin, Hancock, 8 In.	100.00
Plate, Touraine, J. & G. Alcock	58.00
Plate, Touraine, Stanley Potteries, 8 3/4 In.	60.00
Plate, Virginia, 9 3/4 In.	85.00
Plate Set, Manilla, Podmore, Walker, 8 In., 12 Piece	605.00
Plate Set, Washington Vase, Podmore, Walker, 9 3/4 In., 12 Piece	1350.00
Platter, Amoy, 20 In.	1135.00
Platter, Carlton, 19 x 15 1/2 In.	200.00
Platter, Celtic, W.H. Grindley, 21 In.	450.00
Platter, Chapoo, John Wedgwood, 15 3/4 In.	3402.00
Platter, Chapoo, John Wedgwood, c.1850, 20 1/4 x 15 3/4 In.	2760.00
Platter, Eddo, Oriental Fan In Center, Gold, Oval, 21 1/2 x 17 In.	220.00
Platter, Florence, New Wharf Pottery, 16 In.	245.00
Platter, Formosa, 11 1/2 x 15 1/2 In.	385.00
Platter, Gothic, Boote, 14 x 18 In.	895.00
Platter, Grace, W.H. Grindley, 15 1/2 In.	275.00
Platter, Kenworth, Johnson Bros., 12 1/4 In.	125.00
Platter, Kyber, 10 1/4 In.	140.00
Platter, Kyber, 7 1/2 x 10 In.	185.00
Platter, Lorne, Boote, 14 In.	250.00
Platter, Lorne, W.H. Grindley, 12 In.	150.00 to 165.00
Platter, Lorne, W.H. Grindley, 14 In.	250.00
Platter, Lorne, W.H. Grindley, 16 In.	265.00
Platter, Manilla, Podmore, Walker, 18 In.	750.00 to 795.00
Platter, Manilla, Podmore, Walker, 20 In.	1095.00
Platter, Melbourne, W.H. Grindley, 16 In.	285.00 to 295.00

Platter, Nonpareil, Burgess & Leigh, 13 x 15 1/2 In. . . . . .395.00 to 467.00
Platter, Nonpareil, Burgess & Leigh, 1891, 12 1/4 x 10 In. 201.00
Platter, Normandy, Johnson Bros., 16 In. 365.00
Platter, Oregon, Johnson Bros., 14 1/2 x 11 In. 350.00
Platter, Oregon, Johnson Bros., 18 x 14 In. 575.00
Platter, Oriental Design, Marked With Urn Of Flowers, 18 x 14 In. 260.00
Platter, Oriental, Transfer, John Alcock, 10 In. 150.00
Platter, Paisley, Mercer, 11 3/4 In. 135.00
Platter, Rhone, T.E. & Company, 18 x 14 In. 178.00
Platter, Saxon, Clementson Bros., 15 x 11 In. 75.00
Platter, Scinde, 16 1/2 x 12 1/2 In. 850.00
Platter, Scinde, 20 In. 1540.00
Platter, Scinde, Podmore, Walker, 16 1/2 x 12 In. 550.00
Platter, Touraine, 15 In. 295.00
Platter, Touraine, 1898, 8 3/4 x 6 In. 290.00
Platter, Watteau, 15 1/2 In. 165.00
Platter, Well & Tree, Dagger Border, Minton & Boyle, c.1840 . . . . 525.00
Sauce, Amoy 65.00
Saucer, Touraine 12.50
Soup, Dish, Touraine, Stanley Pottery Co., 7 1/2 In. 80.00
Sugar, Cover, Manila, 8 1/2 In. 247.00
Sugar, Cover, Manilla, Podmore, Walker 550.00
Sugar, Cover, Scinde . . . . .302.00 to 695.00
Sugar, Cover, Scinde, Hall 695.00
Sugar, La Belle, Wheeling Potteries 395.00
Sugar & Creamer, Amoy 145.00
Sugar & Creamer, Amoy, Handle 195.00
Sugar & Creamer, Chen-Si, John Meier 180.00
Sugar & Creamer, Melbourne, W.H. Grindley 475.00
Syrup, La Belle, Silver Lid, Wheeling Potteries 375.00
Syrup, Undertray, La Belle, Wheeling Potteries 695.00
Tea Set, Chinese, Child's, 14 Piece 4500.00
Teapot, Amoy, 10 1/4 In. 825.00
Teapot, Chapoo, John Wedgwood, 9 In. . . . . .460.00 to 695.00
Teapot, Coburg, John Edwards 1025.00
Teapot, Hamilton, John Maddock & Son, 8 In. . . . . .695.00 to 895.00
Teapot, Hong Kong, 8 In. 850.00
Teapot, Kaolin, Podmore, Walker 895.00
Teapot, Nonpareil, Burgess & Leigh 750.00
Teapot, Oriental 995.00
Teapot, Vinranka 450.00
Toothbrush Holder, Glenwood, Johnson Bros. 175.00
Tray, Scinde, J. & G. Alcock, 8 1/4 In. 165.00
Tureen, Cover, Normandy, Oval, Johnson Bros. 400.00
Tureen, Cover, Sevres, Wood & Son, 10 In. 295.00
Tureen, Fairy Villas 1500.00
Tureen, Sauce, Bochara, John Edwards, 3 Piece 525.00
Tureen, Sauce, Cashmere, Underplate 395.00
Tureen, Sauce, Melbourne, W.H. Grindley 395.00
Tureen, Sauce, Vincennes, John Alcock, 3 Piece 525.00
Tureen, Soup, Anemone, Branches, Cones On Lid, Handles, 11 1/2 x 11 1/2 In. 385.00
Tureen, Soup, Blue Danube, Johnson Bros. 595.00
Tureen, Soup, Burleigh, Burgess & Leigh 495.00
Tureen, Soup, Cover, Oriental, Handles, 6 1/2 x 12 In. 460.00
Tureen, Soup, Floral, Thom. Hughes & Son 495.00
Tureen, Soup, Hampton Spray, W.H. Grindley 795.00
Tureen, Soup, Tivoli, Thom. Furnival . . . . .1395.00 to 1795.00
Tureen, Vegetable, Touraine, 1898, 9 1/2 x 6 3/4 In. 57.50
Underliner For Tureen, Scinde, 15 In. 2310.00
Vase, Minister, Floral, 6 In. 75.00
Waste Bowl, Chapoo, Boote 195.00
Waste Bowl, Conway, New Wharf Pottery 125.00
Waste Bowl, Touraine, Large 150.00

FLYING PHOENIX, see Phoenix Bird category.

FOLK ART is also listed in many categories of this book under the actual name of the object. See categories such as Box, Cigar Store Figure, Paper, Weather Vane, Wooden, etc.

Alligator, Lady Litigator, Bottle Cap Eyes, Rusty Nails For Teeth, 18 In.	125.0
Apple, Beaded	5.0
Ark, 8 Lithographed Animals, 6 1/2 x 14 x 4 1/2 In.	82.0
Ashtray, Bear, Carved, Wooden	120.0
Banana, Beaded	5.0
Banner, Carnival, The Hammer Of Death, Signed J. Sigler, 1950s, 10 x 10 Ft.	2500.0
Basket, Beaded, Gold & Amber, 12 In. ....*Illus*	5.0
Basket, Bottle Cap, Silver Paint, Oversized	135.0
Benjamin Franklin, Carved & Painted, M.D. Rumbaugh, 27 In.	250.0
Bird, Bobbing, Wood Carving, c.1900, 6 x 3 1/2 In.	245.0
Bird, Carved, 5 Birds, Multicolored, Wooden, Signed, D & BS, 17 In.	190.0
Bird, Carved, 6 Painted Birds, Wooden, Signed, D & BS, 19 In.	190.0
Bird, Carved, On Swing, Wire Perch, Wooden, Signed, 6 1/4 In.	82.0
Birdhouse, Face Form, Mixed Metals, Parts, Painted, 20th Century, 37 3/4 In.	440.0
Birdhouse, Mounted On White Metal Stand, Gray Boot, Pitched Roof, 25 1/2 In.	2875.0
Birdhouse, Seacoast House Design, Red, Gray, Blue, White, Green, Kittery, Me., 24 In.	1815.0
Birdhouse, Wooden, Signed Whorf, 11 x 10 1/2 In.	495.0
Bust, Aged Black Man, Smoking Pipe, Polychromed, Ed. Mudiwa, 4 In.	195.0
Cup Hook & Towel Hanger, Love Birds, Wall Bracket, Wooden, Painted, 11 1/2 In.	33.0
Doll, Witch, Abbottstown, 1880-1890	5000.0
Dollhouse, Furniture, Car, Cat, Dog, 48-Star Flag, 38 x 22 x 27 In.	750.0
Drummer Boy, Carved Wood, 1920s, 4 1/2 Ft.	950.0
Eagle, Stylized Eagle, Tail Down, Wings Out, Green Glass Eyes, S. Polaha, 15 1/2 In.	632.0
Figure, Bird, Standing, Silvio Zoratti ....*Illus*	187.0
Figure, Carved, Man & Woman, Kissing, Wooden	40.0
Figure, Carved, Man With Black Top Hat, Smoking Cigar, Wooden	55.0
Figure, Cow, Standing, L. Barker, Poplar, 1990, 18 1/2 In.	385.0
Figure, Doll & Chair, Walnut, Carved Wood, American, 19th Century, 8 In.	300.0
Figure, Eagle, Wooden, Carved, Silvio Zoratti ....*Illus*	143.0
Figure, George Washington, Holding Cane Coiled By Snake, E. Patton, 17 1/2 In.	495.0
Figure, Man & Dog, Polychrome, Carved, Signed, Charles Crookes, Ohio, 9 In.	140.0
Figure, Mouse, Wooden, Carved, Silvio Zoratti ....*Illus*	275.0
Figure, Shorebird, Old Paint, Replaced Beak, 11 In.	220.0
Figure, Woman, Busty, Carved From Bedpost, 10 In.	80.0
Fort, Prisoner Of War, Built By French Soldier, 11 2/3 In.	9020.0
Frame, Animal Horns	50.0
Fruit, Apple, Orange, Strawberry, Walnut, Pear, Peach, Stone, 6 Piece	77.0
Fruit, Orange, Peach, Lemon, Tomato, Strawberry, Lemon, Stone, 6 Piece	165.0
Fruit, Peach, Beaded	5.0

Folk Art, Basket, Beaded, Gold & Amber, 12 In.

Folk Art, Scene, Coal, Carving, Painted Background, Frame, c.1900, 9 3/4 x 7 3/4 In.

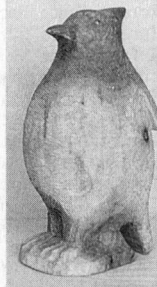

Folk Art, Figure, Bird, Standing, Silvio Zoratti

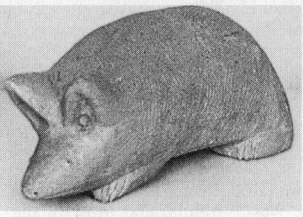

Folk Art, Figure, Mouse, Wooden,
Carved, Silvio Zoratti

Folk Art, Figure, Eagle,   Folk Art, Retablo, Priest
Wooden, Carved,   Overlooking Bullfight Scene,
Silvio Zoratti   Tin, 1927, 8 x 6 3/4 In.

Fruit, Strawberries, Lemon, Apples, Stone, 5 Piece	70.00
Hand, Sign, Holding Open Cup, Carved Wood	550.00
Jug, Devil Face, Flaring Neck, Strap Handle, Green Glaze, B. Craig, 20th Century	850.00
Jug, Memoryware, Various Buttons, Watch Parts, Jewelry, Stoneware, 11 In.	345.00
Lamp, Constructed Of Wooden Sucker Sticks, 26 In.	82.00
Locomotive, Scrap Iron & Brass, Made By Prisoner, 1920s, 22 In.	485.00
Mirror, Carved Bone, Shields, Crests, Prisoner Of War, France, 19th Century, 21 In.	7500.00
Mirror, Welsh Farm, Oak, 27 x 14 In.	245.00
Pen Holder, Bear, Carved, 5 In.	135.00
Pig Dog, Carving, Gray Paint Over Pink, Black Trim, 20th Century, 13 In.	165.00
Retablo, Priest Overlooking Bullfight Scene, Tin, 1927, 8 x 6 3/4 In. *Illus*	75.00
Root Snake, Brown, Yellow, Lead Band Rattles, Nail Head Eyes, Copper Wire Tongue	138.00
Root Snake, Red Design, Nail Head Eyes, Wire Tongue, 38 In.	28.00
Scene, Coal, Carving, Painted Background, Frame, c.1900, 9 3/4 x 7 3/4 In. *Illus*	195.00
Shelf, Comb, Cigar Box Construction, Chip Carved, Hanging, 16 1/4 In.	185.00
Tin Man, Weathered Tin & Wood, 8 1/2 Ft.	2500.00
Turkey, Thin Copper Skin, Plaster Interior, Worn White Paint, Red Trim, 9 1/2 In.	635.00
Watch Safe, Tall Case Clock Form, Overpaint, Shenandoah Valley Origin	72.00
Whirligig, 2 Men, Sawing Tin As Pin Wheel Spinning, 33 In.	440.00
Whirligig, 5-Prop Airplane, Red, White & Blue, 2- Ft. Wingspan	205.00
Whirligig, Airplane	1250.00
Whirligig, Black Woman Churning Butter, Wood, Wire & Sheet Metal, 24 In.	115.00
Whirligig, Boy On Bicycle, Pedals Revolve, Painted, Cut From Tin Cans	890.00
Whirligig, Covered Wagon, Pulled By 2 Horses, Riders, Wooden Blades	325.00
Whirligig, High-Wheel Cyclist, Wood & Rubber, 18 In.	6600.00
Whirligig, Indian Brave, Pine, Wearing Single Feather In Headband, 24 In.	1035.00
Whirligig, Indian In Canoe, Weathered Wood, 19th Century	650.00
Whirligig, Italian Soldier, Red, Green, Gold & Black Uniform, 19th Century, 45 In.	2970.00
Whirligig, Italian Soldier, Wooden, Weathered Paint, 15 In.	1970.00
Whirligig, Man In Leather Suit & Cap, 10 Blades, Late 19th Century, 18 1/2 In.	1100.00
Whirligig, Man Sawing Wood	22.00
Whirligig, Man With Pick & Another With Saw, Wooden, Some Paint	250.00
Whirligig, Mountie, Blades For Arms, 1940s, 18 In.	713.00
Whirligig, Policeman, New York City, Wearing Black Uniform, Black Cap, 20 1/4 In.	805.00
Whirligig, Stationary Tin Horse, Red, White & Blue Revolving Blade	260.00
Wind Indicator, Biplane, Sheet Metal, Wooden Struts	605.00

FOOT WARMERS solved the problem of cold feet in past generations.
Some warmers held charcoal, others held hot water. Pottery, tin, and
soapstone were the favored materials to conduct the heat. The warmer
was kept under the feet, then the legs and feet were tucked into a blanket, providing welcome warmth in a cold carriage or church.

Blue & White, Stoneware, Logan Pottery Company	105.00
Cherry, Pierced Designs	345.00
Crockery, Screw-In Stopper	40.00

Pine, Tin Lined, Cut Holes, Slat Top, Bail Handle 195.00
Punched Circle & Diamond Design, Pinched Tin, Hardwood Frame, 8 1/2 In. 154.00
Punched Hearts & Circles, Tin, Walnut Frame, Wire Bale, Inside Pan, 5 3/4 In. 192.00
Punched Tin, Pinwheel Circle Designs, Wooden Frame, Corner Posts, 7 3/4 In. 115.00
Punched Tin, Wooden Frame, Hinged End Door, Interior Pan, 7 x 16 1/4 In. 275.00
Walnut, c.1830 . . . . 350.00

FOOTBALL collectibles may be found in the Card and the Sports categories.

FOSTORIA glass was made in Fostoria, Ohio, from 1887 to 1891. The
factory was moved to Moundsville, West Virginia, and most of the
glass seen in shops today is a twentieth-century product. The company
was sold in 1983; new items will be easily identifiable, according to
the new owner, Lancaster Colony Corporation. Additional Fostoria
items may be listed in the Milk Glass category.

American, Ashtray, With Match Stand, Oval 25.00
American, Bell 650.00
American, Biscuit Jar 600.00
American, Bottle, Water 600.00
American, Bowl, Floral, Oval, 11 In. 55.00
American, Butter, Cover, Rectangular, 1/4 Lb. 27.00
American, Cake Plate, 2 Handles, 10 In. 32.00
American, Cake Stand, Square . . . . .45.00 to 75.00
American, Candlestick, 2-Light 39.00
American, Candlestick, Bell Shape 125.00
American, Centerpiece, Tri-Corner, 11 In. . . . . .38.00 to 55.00
American, Cocktail, Oyster, Footed 17.50
American, Compote, Cover, 9 In. . . . . .25.00 to 35.00
American, Creamer, 9 1/2 Oz. 13.00
American, Cruet, Oil 45.00
American, Cup & Saucer 12.00
American, Decanter, Wine 85.00
American, Dish, Mayonnaise, Underplate, Spoon, 3 Piece 38.00
American, Goblet, Water . . . . .12.00 to 18.00
American, Hair Receiver 850.00
American, Hurricane Lamp, Chimney 325.00
American, Ice Bucket, Tongs 70.00
American, Ice Tub, Large 90.00
American, Mug, Beer 75.00
American, Oyster Cocktail 16.00
American, Plate, 6 In. 12.00
American, Plate, 10 1/2 In. 24.00
American, Plate, Center Ring, 11 1/2 In. 34.00
American, Platter, Oval, 12 In. 55.00
American, Pomade Set, 3 Piece 875.00
American, Punch Bowl, Tom & Jerry 250.00
American, Punch Cup, Flared 10.00
American, Relish, 3 Sections, 6 x 9 In. 35.00
American, Ring Tree 750.00
American, Sherbet 8.00
American, Soup, Cream, 5 In. 55.00
American, Sugar & Creamer, Small 20.00
American, Syrup 75.00
American, Tray, 5 Sections, Cobalt, 14 1/8 In. 195.00
American, Tumbler, Footed, 9 Oz. 12.00
American, Vase, Bud, Flared, Milk Glass, 8 1/4 In. 65.00
American, Vase, Cupped, 10 In. 235.00
American, Vase, Footed, Square, Milk Glass, 9 In. 125.00
American Lady, Champagne 23.00
American Lady, Goblet 15.00
American Lady, Sherbet 12.00
Argus, Tumbler, Juice, Blue 9.00
Atlanta, Berry Bowl 25.00

Baroque, Bonbon, 3-Footed, Topaz 30.00
Baroque, Bowl, Nut, Blue, 3-Footed 65.00
Baroque, Candlestick, Topaz, 5 1/2 In. ....28.00 to 32.00
Baroque, Celery Dish, Azure Blue, 11 In. 45.00
Baroque, Cocktail Shaker, Cover, Topaz 32.00
Baroque, Compote, Topaz, 6 1/2 In. ....40.00 to 45.00
Baroque, Cruet, Oil, Blue 600.00
Baroque, Dish, Mayonnaise, Underplate, Ruffled Edge, Topaz 70.00
Baroque, Ice Bucket, Topaz 125.00
Baroque, Jam Jar, Cover, Blue 85.00
Baroque, Mustard, Cover, Topaz 110.00
Baroque, Plate, Topaz, 8 1/2 In. 13.00
Baroque, Platter, Blue, Oval, Large 100.00
Baroque, Punch Bowl, Blue 1200.00
Baroque, Relish, 3 Sections, Topaz 20.00
Baroque, Rose Bowl, Topaz 95.00
Baroque, Sugar & Creamer, Topaz 40.00
Baroque, Sweetmeat, Footed, Blue, 6 In. 48.00
Baroque, Torte Plate, Topaz 20.00
Baroque, Tumbler, 9 Oz. 13.00
Buttercup, Candle, 4 In. 30.00
Buttercup, Goblet 24.00
Buttercup, Plate, 7 1/2 In. 17.00
Buttercup, Plate, 10 In. 50.00
Buttercup, Relish, 3 Sections 36.00
Buttercup, Tumbler, Juice 18.00
Camellia, Cocktail 24.00
Camellia, Plate, 7 1/2 In. 10.00
Camellia, Sherbet 10.00
Camellia, Tumbler, Juice 18.00
Century, Basket, Reed Handle 80.00
Century, Bowl, 2 Handles, Oval, 8 In. 55.00
Century, Bowl, Fruit, Flared, 12 In. 50.00
Century, Dish, Olive, 8 In. 24.00
Century, Goblet ....12.00 to 20.00
Century, Mustard, Cover 30.00
Century, Pitcher, Pint 50.00
Century, Relish, Oval 14.00
Century, Tumbler, Water 28.00
Chintz, Candlestick, 3-Light, Pair 90.00
Chintz, Candy Dish, Cover, 3 Sections 150.00
Chintz, Champagne 25.00
Chintz, Cheese Dish 50.00
Chintz, Cup & Saucer 28.00
Chintz, Goblet, 7 3/4 In. 30.00
Chintz, Pitcher, Footed, 48 Oz. 375.00
Chintz, Plate, 7 In. 17.00
Chintz, Sugar & Creamer, Footed 35.00
Chintz, Tray, Center Handle, 11 1/2 In. 35.00
Chintz, Tumbler, 10 Oz. 25.00
Chintz, Wine 45.00
Coin, Bowl, Blue, 7 1/4 In. 60.00
Coin, Candy Jar, Cover, Amber 28.00
Coin, Cruet, Amber 75.00
Coin, Jelly, Footed 16.00
Coin, Sauce, Green, Handle 38.00
Coin, Sugar, Cover 29.00
Colonial Dame, Goblet, Green Bowl, 11 Oz. 16.00
Colonial Dame, Sherbet, Green Bowl, 6 1/2 Oz. 12.00
Colony, Butter, Cover, 1/4 Lb. 32.00
Colony, Candlestick, Trumpet Shape, 9 In. 50.00
Colony, Cruet ....45.00 to 55.00
Colony, Dish, Mayonnaise, Ladle 30.00

Colony, Goblet, 9 Oz.	13.50
Colony, Ice Bowl, Footed	200.00
Colony, Jam Jar, Cover, Footed	50.00
Colony, Oyster Cocktail, 4 Oz.	12.00
Colony, Pitcher, Ice, Lip, Footed, 3 Pt.	200.00
Colony, Platter, Oval	50.00
Colony, Salt & Pepper, Tray, Individual	30.00
Colony, Sandwich Server, Center Handle	40.00
Colony, Sherbet	9.00
Colony, Sugar & Creamer, Tray	25.00
Colony, Tumbler, Juice	18.00
Colony, Urn, Cover	85.00
Corsage, Iced Tea, Footed, 6 In.	28.00
Corsage, Torte Plate, 2 Handles, 13 In.	45.00
Cynthia, Cordial	20.00
Cynthia, Tumbler, Water	22.00
Cynthia, Wine	20.00
Daisy, Vase, 9 1/2 In.	98.00
Drape, Punch Cup	10.00
Fairfax, Ashtray, Pink, 4 In.	17.00
Fairfax, Bouillon, Underplate, Green	18.00
Fairfax, Bowl, Fruit, Underplate, Blue	40.00
Fairfax, Butter, Cover, Rose	125.00
Fairfax, Candlestick, Blue, 2 In.	36.00
Fairfax, Cheese Plate, Footed, Green	15.00
Fairfax, Cup & Saucer, Green	12.00
Fairfax, Dish, Mayonnaise, Footed, Pink	20.00
Fairfax, Finger Bowl, Blue	9.00
Fairfax, Finger Bowl, Underplate, Topaz	20.00
Fairfax, Ice Bucket, Blue	45.00
Fairfax, Plate, Green, 9 1/2 In.	20.00
Fairfax, Relish, 2 Sections, Oval, Pink	16.00
Fairfax, Salt & Pepper, Footed, Glass Top, Topaz	55.00
Fairfax, Sandwich Server, Center Handle, Amber	25.00
Fairfax, Sugar & Creamer, Green, Individual	23.00
Fairfax, Tumbler, Footed, Blue, 9 Oz.	20.00
Florentine, Vase, 6 In.	45.00
Foster Block, Rose Bowl	50.00
Heather, Bonbon, 3-Footed	30.00
Heather, Cake Stand, 12 In.	68.00
Heather, Plate, 8 In.	17.00
Heather, Sherbet	13.00
Heirloom, Console, Blue, 13 1/2 In.	45.00
Hermitage, Berry Bowl, 5 In.	6.00
Hermitage, Cup & Saucer	8.00
Hermitage, Pitcher, Amber, 3 Pt.	60.00
Hermitage, Plate, 10 In.	10.00
Hermitage, Tumbler, Footed, Amber, 9 Oz.	10.00
Holly, Cocktail	20.00
Holly, Goblet	13.00
Jamestown, Goblet, Amber, 10 Oz.	10.00
Jamestown, Ice Tea, Footed, Amber, 12 Oz.	10.00
Jamestown, Pitcher, Amber	60.00
Jamestown, Tumbler, Green	8.00
June, Berry Bowl, Yellow	38.00
June, Candlestick, 3-Footed, Topaz, Pair	75.00
June, Champagne, Topaz	24.00
June, Compote, Blue, 6 1/2 In.	110.00
June, Console, Pink	140.00
June, Cup & Saucer, Pink, After Dinner	195.00
June, Goblet, Blue	60.00
June, Ice Bucket, Rose	120.00
June, Pitcher, Topaz	425.00

June, Plate, Topaz, 8 1/2 In. 19.00
June, Sherbet, Azure, High, 6 In. 35.00
June, Sherbet, Topaz, High, 6 In. 20.00
June, Sugar & Creamer, Topaz, After Dinner 150.00
June, Tumbler, Water 22.00
Kashmir, Berry Bowl, Blue 37.50
Kashmir, Celery Dish, Blue 85.00
Lafayette, Cup & Saucer, Wisteria ....32.00 to 40.00
Lafayette, Sugar & Creamer, Wisteria 80.00
Manor, Ashtray 10.00
Mayflower, Bonbon 20.00
Mayflower, Candlestick, Pair 65.00
Mayflower, Pitcher, 60 Oz. 250.00
Meadow Rose, Cruet 275.00
Meadow Rose, Salt & Pepper, 2 1/4 In. 54.00
Milkweed, Relish, 3 Sections, 10 In. 35.00
Morning Glory, Bowl, Fruit, Amber, 13 In. 38.00
Navarre, Cake Plate, 2 Handles 45.00
Navarre, Candlestick, 2-Light 45.00
Navarre, Champagne 23.00
Navarre, Compote, 4 1/2 In. 45.00
Navarre, Cup & Saucer ....20.00 to 29.00
Navarre, Goblet, Wine 32.00
Navarre, Iced Tea, Footed, Azure Blue 55.00
Navarre, Plate, 7 1/2 In. 18.00
Navarre, Relish, 3 Sections 28.00
Navarre, Sugar & Creamer 39.00
Navarre, Wine 20.00
Needlepoint, Tumbler, Old Fashion 18.00
Oak Leaf, Bonbon, Green 40.00
Oak Leaf, Tray, Luncheon, Octagonal, Green 65.00
Orchid, Sugar, Cover 90.00
Pine, Iced Tea, Footed 10.00
Pioneer, Cup & Saucer, Topaz 8.00
Pioneer, Plate, Topaz, 9 1/2 In. 7.00
Priscilla, Creamer, Green 45.00
Regency, Cordial, 1 Oz. 30.00
Robin Hood, Pitcher, c.1898 .... 80.00
Romance, Bowl, 12 In. 40.00
Romance, Cocktail 18.00
Romance, Cup & Saucer 27.50
Romance, Sherbet 13.00
Romance, Sugar & Creamer 30.00
Romance, Tumbler, Water 24.00
Royal, Candlestick, Green, 3 In., Pair 50.00
Royal, Cup & Saucer, Amber 14.00
Royal, Plate, Amber, 9 1/2 In. 16.00
Royal, Sherbet, Amber 12.00
Royal, Tumbler, Juice, Amber 14.00
Seville, Centerpiece, 2 Sections, Oval, 13 In. 135.00
Seville, Plate, Amber, 10 In. 12.00
Seville, Platter, Amber 30.00
Spartan, Cocktail, Amber 15.00
Spartan, Sherbet, Amber 16.00
Sunray, Bowl, Handle, 12 In. 45.00
Sunray, Compote, Topaz 16.00
Sunray, Decanter, Bourbon 50.00
Sunray, Relish, Handle, 2 Sections 20.00
Trojan, Cup & Saucer, Topaz, After Dinner 45.00
Trojan, Parfait, Topaz, 6 Oz. 35.00
Trojan, Plate, 7 1/2 In. 8.00
Vernon, Sherbet, 6 Oz. 10.00
Vernon, Tumbler, Water 15.00

Versailles, Ashtray, Blue 40.00
Versailles, Bouillon, Topaz 20.00
Versailles, Candlestick, Scroll, Topaz, 5 In. 60.00
Versailles, Centerpiece, Footed, Blue, 12 In. 70.00
Versailles, Champagne, Pink 40.00
Versailles, Cruet, Topaz 3500.00
Versailles, Cup & Saucer, Pink, After Dinner 42.00
Versailles, Dish, Mayonnaise, Underplate, Topaz 40.00
Versailles, Goblet, Topaz 30.00
Versailles, Ice Bucket, Blue 125.00
Versailles, Lemon Dish, Blue 35.00
Versailles, Oyster, Cocktail, Topaz 25.00
Versailles, Pitcher, Green 350.00
Versailles, Plate, Topaz, 8 1/2 In. ....12.00 to 18.00
Versailles, Relish, 2 Sections, Topaz, 8 1/2 In. ....28.00 to 39.00
Versailles, Salt & Pepper, Blue 225.00
Versailles, Soup, Cream, Underplate, Blue 55.00
Versailles, Sugar & Creamer, Blue, Individual 55.00
Versailles, Tumbler, Pink, 12 Oz. 45.00
Vesper, Bowl, Footed, Amber, 10 In. 85.00
Vesper, Candy Dish, Cover, Green, 1/2 Lb. 119.00
Vesper, Cup & Saucer, Amber 25.00
Vesper, Ice Bucket, Amber ....65.00 to 100.00
Vesper, Plate, Amber, 9 1/2 In. 25.00
Vesper, Wine, Green 45.00
Victoria, Relish, Boat Shape 45.00
Virginia, Tumbler, 6 Oz. 15.00
Westchester, Cordial, Ruby 50.00
Westchester, Sherbet, Ruby Bowl, 5 In. 32.00
Willow, Cordial 39.00
Willow, Pitcher, Footed 359.00
Willow, Plate, 9 1/2 In. 55.00
Willow, Sugar & Creamer 35.00
Willowmere, Bowl, Salad, Underplate, 10 In. 75.00
Willowmere, Champagne 25.00
Willowmere, Console, 12 1/2 In. 35.00
Willowmere, Cup & Saucer 14.00
Willowmere, Dish, Mayonnaise, Liner, 7 1/2 In. 42.00
Willowmere, Goblet, 10 Oz. 19.00
Willowmere, Relish, 3 Sections 60.00
Willowmere, Sugar & Creamer, Individual ....40.00 to 49.00
Willowmere, Torte Plate, 14 In. ....40.00 to 70.00
Wilma, Goblet, Claret, Blue 38.00

FOVAL, see Fry category.

FRAMES are included in the Furniture category under Frame.

FRANCISCAN is a trademark that appears on pottery. Gladding, McBean
and Company started in 1875. The company grew and acquired other
potteries. They made sewer pipes, floor tiles, dinnerwares, and art pottery with a variety of trademarks. In 1934, dinnerware and art pottery
were sold under the name Franciscan Ware. They made china and
cream-colored, decorated earthenware. Desert Rose, Apple, El Patio,
and Coronado were best-sellers. The company became Interpace
Corporation and in 1979 was purchased by Josiah Wedgwood & Sons.
The plant was closed in 1984 but a few of the patterns are still being
made. For more information, see *Kovels' Depression Glass &
Dinnerware Price List.*

Apple, Ashtray, Individual 13.00
Apple, Ashtray, Oval 55.00
Apple, Ashtray, Square 125.00
Apple, Baking Dish, 1 1/2 Qt. 95.00
Apple, Bowl, 5 1/4 In. 10.00

Apple, Bowl, 6 In. . . . . .12.00 to 16.00
Apple, Bowl, 10 In. . . . . .68.00 to 95.00
Apple, Bowl, 11 In. 45.00
Apple, Bowl, Batter, 10 1/4 In. 225.00
Apple, Bowl, Vegetable, 7 3/4 In. 50.00
Apple, Bowl, Vegetable, 8 1/4 In. 38.00
Apple, Bowl, Vegetable, Divided, 10 3/4 In. 45.00
Apple, Butter, Cover . . . . .25.00 to 40.00
Apple, Candleholder, Pair, 3 In. 65.00
Apple, Casserole, Cover, 2 Qt. . . . . .50.00 to 90.00
Apple, Chop Plate, 12 In. . . . . .45.00 to 60.00
Apple, Chop Plate, 14 In. . . . . .55.00 to 75.00
Apple, Compote, 8 In. . . . . .50.00 to 85.00
Apple, Cookie Jar . . . . .225.00 to 290.00
Apple, Creamer . . . . .20.00 to 28.00
Apple, Cup 10.00
Apple, Cup & Saucer 66.00
Apple, Cup & Saucer, After Dinner 55.00
Apple, Eggcup . . . . .20.00 to 39.00
Apple, Ginger Jar, Cover 150.00
Apple, Gravy Boat . . . . .23.00 to 50.00
Apple, Grill Plate, 11 In. 100.00
Apple, Jam Jar 450.00
Apple, Mixing Bowl Set, 3 Piece . . . . .275.00 to 350.00
Apple, Mug, 7 Oz. 25.00
Apple, Pitcher, Cream 19.00
Apple, Pitcher, Milk, 1 Qt. . . . . .70.00 to 80.00
Apple, Pitcher, Water, 2 Qt. 175.00
Apple, Plate, 6 1/2 In. 6.00
Apple, Plate, 8 1/2 In. 12.00
Apple, Plate, 10 1/2 In. . . . . .16.00 to 27.00
Apple, Plate, 12 In. 39.00
Apple, Platter, 4 In. 40.00
Apple, Platter, 12 1/2 In. 50.00
Apple, Platter, 14 In. 70.00
Apple, Platter, 19 In. 295.00
Apple, Relish, 3 Sections . . . . .45.00 to 75.00
Apple, Salt & Pepper 24.00
Apple, Salt & Pepper Mill, 6 In. . . . . .225.00 to 250.00
Apple, Sherbet . . . . .17.00 to 20.00
Apple, Sherbet, Footed, 8 Piece 240.00
Apple, Sugar 18.00
Apple, Sugar & Creamer, Cover . . . . .25.00 to 35.00
Apple, Teapot 100.00
Apple, Teapot, Flask Spout 50.00
Apple, Tidbit, 3 Tiers 150.00
Apple, Tumbler, Juice 35.00
Cafe Royale, Cookie Jar 250.00
Cafe Royale, Tea Canister 80.00
Cafe Royale, Thimble Box 60.00
Catalina, Plate, Orange, 9 1/2 In. 80.00
Coronado, Candy Dish, Cover, Coral 150.00
Coronado, Creamer, Yellow Gloss 10.00
Coronado, Plate, Burgundy Gloss, 9 1/4 In. 13.00
Coronado, Plate, Yellow Gloss, 6 1/4 In. 5.00
Coronado, Sugar, Cover, Yellow 15.00
Daisy, Bowl, 7 1/4 In. 12.00
Daisy, Bowl, Salad, 11 In. 75.00
Daisy, Bowl, Vegetable, Divided . . . . .35.00 to 45.00
Daisy, Butter, Cover . . . . .35.00 to 65.00
Daisy, Creamer 15.00
Daisy, Dish, Child's, 8 3/4 In. 30.00
Daisy, Pitcher, Milk, 8 1/2 In. . . . . .65.00 to 78.00

Daisy, Pitcher, Water, 10 In. 35.00
Daisy, Plate, 8 1/2 In. 10.00
Daisy, Plate, 10 In. 14.00
Daisy, Platter, 14 In. 30.00
Daisy, Platter, 19 In. 65.00
Daisy, Salt & Pepper 150.00
Daisy, Salt & Pepper, Small 20.00
Daisy, Sugar & Creamer 58.00
Daisy, Teapot ....50.00 to 75.00
Daisy, Tumbler, Juice, 8 Oz. 18.00
Desert Rose, Ashtray 20.00
Desert Rose, Ashtray, Individual ....11.00 to 20.00
Desert Rose, Ashtray, Oval 50.00
Desert Rose, Ashtray, Square ....80.00 to 125.00
Desert Rose, Baking Dish, 1 1/2 Qt. 75.00
Desert Rose, Bell, Danbury 48.00
Desert Rose, Bell, Dinner, 6 In. 85.00
Desert Rose, Bowl, 5 1/4 In. 7.00
Desert Rose, Bowl, 6 In. ....8.00 to 13.00
Desert Rose, Bowl, 8 1/2 In. 35.00
Desert Rose, Bowl, Microwave, Square, 1 1/2 Qt. 245.00
Desert Rose, Bowl, Salad, 10 In. 115.00
Desert Rose, Bowl, Sugar 11.00
Desert Rose, Bowl, Vegetable, 8 In. ....17.00 to 25.00
Desert Rose, Bowl, Vegetable, 9 In. 19.00
Desert Rose, Bowl, Vegetable, Divided, 10 3/4 In. ....37.00 to 55.00
Desert Rose, Box, Cigarette, Original Label 135.00
Desert Rose, Box, Heart, 4 1/2 In. ....135.00 to 165.00
Desert Rose, Candleholder, 3 In., Pair 75.00
Desert Rose, Candy Dish, Oval, 7 In. 315.00
Desert Rose, Canister, Tea ....250.00 to 295.00
Desert Rose, Casserole, Cover, 1 1/2 Qt. 27.00
Desert Rose, Chop Plate, 12 In. ....45.00 to 75.00
Desert Rose, Coffeepot ....70.00 to 85.00
Desert Rose, Coffeepot, After Dinner 195.00
Desert Rose, Compote, 8 In. 60.00
Desert Rose, Cookie Jar ....265.00 to 300.00
Desert Rose, Creamer 50.00
Desert Rose, Cup & Saucer ....5.00 to 12.00
Desert Rose, Cup & Saucer, After Dinner 55.00
Desert Rose, Cup & Saucer, Jumbo ....35.00 to 55.00
Desert Rose, Cup, 4 1/2 In. 50.00
Desert Rose, Dish, Heart, 5 3/4 In. 85.00
Desert Rose, Eggcup 36.00
Desert Rose, Ginger Jar 275.00
Desert Rose, Goblet 225.00
Desert Rose, Gravy Boat 32.00
Desert Rose, Grill Plate, 11 In. ....75.00 to 125.00
Desert Rose, Ladle, 10 1/2 In. 275.00
Desert Rose, Mug, 7 Oz. ....17.00 to 25.00
Desert Rose, Mug, 10 Oz. ....30.00 to 55.00
Desert Rose, Mug, 12 Oz. ....25.00 to 50.00
Desert Rose, Napkin Ring 36.00
Desert Rose, Pastry Tray, 8 In. 30.00
Desert Rose, Piggy Bank 300.00
Desert Rose, Pitcher, Milk 95.00
Desert Rose, Pitcher, Syrup, 1 Qt. ....65.00 to 75.00
Desert Rose, Pitcher, Water, 2 Qt. ....95.00 to 100.00
Desert Rose, Plate, 6 1/2 In. ....4.00 to 8.00
Desert Rose, Plate, 8 1/2 In. 12.00
Desert Rose, Plate, 9 1/2 In. ....12.00 to 20.00
Desert Rose, Plate, 10 1/2 In. 16.00
Desert Rose, Platter, 12 3/4 In. ....30.00 to 55.00

Desert Rose, Platter, 14 In. 22.00
Desert Rose, Platter, 19 In. .... 245.00 to 295.00
Desert Rose, Porringer, 6 In. 195.00
Desert Rose, Relish, 3 Sections .... 40.00 to 65.00
Desert Rose, Salt & Pepper 18.00
Desert Rose, Salt & Pepper, Tall .... 40.00 to 65.00
Desert Rose, Soup, Dish, Rimmed 28.00
Desert Rose, Sugar & Creamer .... 17.00 to 30.00
Desert Rose, Sugar, After Dinner 65.00
Desert Rose, Sugar, Cover .... 18.00 to 45.00
Desert Rose, Teapot 100.00
Desert Rose, Thimble 33.00
Desert Rose, Thimble, Original Box 95.00
Desert Rose, Tidbit, 2 Tiers 185.00
Desert Rose, Tidbit, 3 Tiers 195.00
Desert Rose, Toast Cover 195.00
Desert Rose, Tray, TV 150.00
Desert Rose, Trivet 180.00
Desert Rose, Tumbler, 10 Oz. .... 20.00 to 50.00
Desert Rose, Tureen, 8 1/4 In. 595.00
Desert Rose, Vase, Bud, 2 In. .... 70.00 to 85.00
El Patio, Eggcup 35.00
El Patio, Gravy Boat, Gray 35.00
El Patio, Sugar & Creamer, Orange, After Dinner 45.00
Forget-Me-Not, Bowl, Fruit 22.00
Forget-Me-Not, Bowl, Vegetable, 8 3/4 In. 45.00
Forget-Me-Not, Creamer .... 17.00 to 25.00
Forget-Me-Not, Cup 9.00
Forget-Me-Not, Cup & Saucer 14.00
Forget-Me-Not, Platter, 14 In. .... 69.00 to 95.00
Fruit, Plate, Salad, 8 1/2 In. 35.00
Huntington, Cup & Saucer 25.00
Ivy, Bowl, Salad, 11 1/4 In. .... 120.00 to 140.00
Ivy, Bowl, Vegetable, 7 1/4 In. 50.00
Ivy, Bowl, Vegetable, 8 1/4 In. 58.00
Ivy, Bowl, Vegetable, Divided, 12 1/4 In. .... 55.00 to 60.00
Ivy, Casserole, 1 1/2 Qt. 150.00
Ivy, Coffeepot 195.00
Ivy, Cup & Saucer .... 21.00 to 25.00
Ivy, Gravy Boat, Underplate 75.00
Ivy, Ivy 39.00
Ivy, Jam Jar 35.00
Ivy, Plate, 6 In. 10.00
Ivy, Plate, 10 In. 20.00
Ivy, Platter, 18 In. 275.00
Ivy, Platter, 19 In. 265.00
Ivy, Relish, Pickle, 11 In. 55.00
Ivy, Tile 95.00
Meadow Rose, Bowl, Vegetable, 9 In. 38.00
Meadow Rose, Butter, Cover 43.00
Meadow Rose, Cup 10.00
Meadow Rose, Platter, 14 In. 49.00
Meadow Rose, Sugar & Creamer, Cover 37.00
October, Bowl, 7 In. 18.00
October, Creamer 15.00
October, Cup & Saucer .... 14.00 to 25.00
October, Napkin Ring 20.00
October, Platter, 14 In. 40.00
October, Saucer 3.00
October, Sugar, Cover 25.00
Poppy, Ashtray 35.00
Poppy, Chop Plate, 12 In. 125.00
Poppy, Cup & Saucer .... 25.00 to 40.00

**When stacking dinner plates, put a
piece of felt or paper between each
plate. Never put more than
24 in one stack.**

Franciscan,
White Stone,
Plate, 10 1/4 In.

Poppy, Plate, 6 1/4 In.	12.00
Poppy, Plate, 10 In.	34.00 to 40.00
Poppy, Salt & Pepper	95.00
Shasta, Cup & Saucer, After Dinner	12.00
Starburst, Bonbon	65.00
Starburst, Bowl, Salad, 12 In.	145.00
Starburst, Bowl, Vegetable, Cover, 8 In.	250.00
Starburst, Canister Set, 4 Piece	665.00
Starburst, Casserole, Cover	55.00
Starburst, Casserole, Large	85.00
Starburst, Chop Plate, 13 In.	50.00 to 85.00
Starburst, Coffeepot	225.00 to 325.00
Starburst, Gravy Boat	45.00
Starburst, Ladle, Gravy Boat	28.00 to 35.00
Starburst, Pitcher, 7 1/2 In.	55.00 to 95.00
Starburst, Plate, TV	75.00
Starburst, Platter, 13 In.	125.00
Starburst, Platter, 15 In.	140.00
Starburst, Salt & Pepper, Bullet Shape	50.00
Starburst, Soup, Dish	30.00
Starburst, Spoon Holder	44.00
Starburst, Sugar & Creamer	9.00
Starburst, Tray, Condiment	50.00
Sunburst, Butter, Cover	75.00
Sunburst, Teapot	125.00
Swirl, Toothpick, Frosted	195.00
White Stone, Plate, 10 1/4 In.	*Illus*
Wildflower, Ashtray, Mariposa Lily	90.00 to 95.00
Wildflower, Bowl, 6 In.	70.00
Wildflower, Chop Plate, 12 In.	225.00 to 350.00
Wildflower, Chop Plate, 14 In.	320.00
Wildflower, Gravy Boat	250.00
Wildflower, Plate, 6 1/2 In.	35.00
Wildflower, Plate, 8 1/2 In.	85.00
Wildflower, Plate, 9 1/2 In.	75.00 to 85.00
Wildflower, Plate, 10 1/2 In.	95.00
Wildflower, Platter, 14 In.	325.00 to 375.00
Wildflower, Sugar, Cover	125.00
Wildflower, Tumbler, 10 Oz.	100.00

FRANCISWARE is the name of a glassware made by Hobbs, Brockunier
and Company of Wheeling, West Virginia, in the 1880s. It is a clear or
frosted hobnail or swirl pattern glass with amber-stained rim. Some
pieces were made by a pressed glass method, others were mold blown.

Finger Bowl, Frosted, Amber	27.50
Toothpick, Frosted, Amber	65.00

FRANKART, Inc., New York, New York, mass-produced nude *dancing lady* lamps, ashtrays, and other decorative Art Deco items in the 1920s and 1930s. They were made of white lead composition and spray-painted. *Frankart Inc.* and the patent number and year were stamped on the base.

Ashtray, Bear Holding Honey Pot, 5 1/2 In.	125.00
Bookends, Female Heads, Shoulder-Length Hair, Floral Headband	235.00
Bookends, Ponies	175.00
Lamp, 2 Nudes, Kneeling, Holding Globe, 9 In.	450.00

FRANKOMA POTTERY was originally known as The Frank Potteries when John F. Frank opened shop in 1933. The factory is now working in Sapulpa, Oklahoma. Early wares were made from a light cream-colored clay from Ada, Oklahoma, but in 1956 the company switched to a red burning clay from Sapulpa. The firm makes dinnerwares, utilitarian and decorative kitchenwares, figurines, flowerpots, and limited edition and commemorative pieces.

Ashtray, Advertising, Broadmoor, Ada Clay	40.00
Ashtray, Dogwood, Red Clay	6.00
Ashtray, Dutch Shoe, Desert Gold, Sapulpa Clay, 6 In.	20.00
Ashtray, Fish, Red Clay	15.00
Baker, Wagon Wheel, 1 1/2 Qt.	12.00
Bank, Lamb	37.00
Bean Pot, Wagon Wheel, Desert Gold, Sapulpa Clay, Individual	40.00
Bookends, Bronco, Green, Ada Clay	150.00
Bookends, Chargers	50.00
Bookends, Dreamer Girl	550.00
Bookends, Indian Maiden, Black	125.00
Bookends, Irish Setter	85.00
Bookends, Irish Setter, Desert Gold	145.00
Bookends, Mountain Girl, Orange Glaze	150.00
Bookends, Standing Horse, Jade Green, Ada Clay	225.00
Boots, Desert Gold, 4 In.	7.50
Bowl, Cactus, Desert Gold, Ada Clay, Round, 5 In.	20.00
Bowl, Cactus, Prairie Green, Ada Clay, Oblong, 6 In.	35.00
Bowl, Cereal, Lazybones, Brown, Sapulpa Clay	5.00
Bowl, Desert Gold, Footed, 6 In.	15.00
Bowl, Mayan-Aztec, 5 1/2 In.	10.00
Bowl, Plainsman, 5 1/2 In.	7.00
Bowl, Prairie Green, 10 In.	395.00
Bowl, Swirl, Prairie Green, Ada Clay, 12 In.	20.00
Butter, Cover, Lazybones	20.00
Casserole, Wagon Wheel, Desert Gold, Sapulpa Clay	35.00
Cornucopia, Desert Gold, Ada Clay, 12 In.	20.00
Cornucopia, Prairie Green, Tall	25.00
Creamer, Plainsman, Flame	5.00
Creamer, Wagon Wheel	8.00
Creamer, Wagon Wheel, Ada Clay, Miniature	15.00
Cup, Gracetone	2.50
Cup, Plainsman, Prairie Green, Ada Clay, Demitasse	10.00
Dish, Leaf, Prairie Green, Red Clay, 7 In.	5.00
Ewer, Prairie Green, 8 In.	45.00
Figurine, Black Panther, On Haunches, 7 In.	125.00
Figurine, Indian Bowl Maker, Sitting, Black, 6 In.	60.00
Figurine, Indian Madonna, Willard Stone	20.00
Figurine, Kid Flower Girl, Prairie Green, Ada Clay	95.00
Figurine, Madonna	18.50
Figurine, Mare & Colt	15.00
Figurine, Ponytail Girl, Desert Gold	30.00
Figurine, Ponytail Girl, Red Clay	95.00
Figurine, Puma, Reclining, Red Clay	52.00
Figurine, Puma, Seated, Prairie Green	15.00

Figurine, Squirrel 10.00
Gravy Boat, Plainsman 4.50
Juice Set, Guernsey, Pitcher, 6 Cups, Prairie Green, Ada Clay 40.00
Lazy Susan, Desert Gold, Sapulpa Clay 40.00
Match Holder, Lazybones, Royal Blue, 1942 .... 40.00
Mug, Barrel, Sorghum Brown, Ada Clay, 1942 .... 15.00
Mug, Donkey, 1975, Autumn Yellow ....18.00 to 35.00
Mug, Donkey, 1976, Centennial Red 20.00
Mug, Donkey, 1979, Brown Satin 40.00
Mug, Elephant, 1968, White ....20.00 to 50.00
Mug, Elephant, 1969, Flame ....45.00 to 60.00
Mug, Elephant, 1971, Black 60.00
Mug, Elephant, 1973, Desert Gold 40.00
Mug, Elephant, 1978, Woodland Moss 18.00
Mug, Elephant, 1980, Terra Cotta 40.00
Mug, Elephant, 1984 .... 35.00
Mug, Lazybones, 16 Oz. 5.00
Mug, U.S. Postal Service 15.00
Mug, Wagon Wheel, Desert Gold, Ada Clay, 16 Oz. 12.00
Pitcher, Aztec, Onyx Black, Miniature 25.00
Pitcher, Bank, Mayan Aztec, Prairie Green 25.00
Pitcher, Batter, Desert Gold, Ada Clay 30.00
Pitcher, Cover, Guernsey, Onyx Black, Ada Clay, 6 1/2 In. 60.00
Pitcher, Cover, Guernsey, Prairie Green, 1940s, 6 1/2 In. 55.00
Pitcher, Eagle, Desert Gold, Ada Clay 25.00
Pitcher, Guernsey, Prairie Green, Ada Clay 25.00
Pitcher, Juice, Guernsey, Desert Gold 40.00
Pitcher, Lazybones, Prairie Green, Sapulpa Clay, 24 Oz. 15.00
Pitcher, Round, 1 Qt. 25.00
Planter, Mallard, Lazybones, Yellow 10.00
Plaque, Wall, Indian Head, Yellow, Pair 85.00
Plate, 50th Anniversary, Desert Gold 20.00
Plate, Anniversary, 1898-1973 .... 25.00
Plate, Bicentennial, 1975 .... 8.00
Plate, Buffalo, 1979 .... 75.00
Plate, Christmas, 1965, Good Will Towards Men ....240.00 to 300.00
Plate, Christmas, 1968, Flight Into Egypt ....18.00 to 29.00
Plate, Christmas, 1969, Laid In A Manger ....10.00 to 14.00
Plate, Christmas, 1970, King Of Kings 20.00
Plate, Christmas, 1971, No Room In The Inn 10.00
Plate, Christmas, 1974, She Loved & Cared 10.00
Plate, Christmas, 1983, Wise Men Bring Gifts 20.00
Plate, Conestoga Wagon 150.00
Plate, Grace Madonna 20.00
Plate, Jubilee, 1975 .... 20.00

Frankoma, Salt & Pepper, Oil Derrick, Ivory &
Sage, 1950-1960, 3 In.

**The water for your dishwasher
should be set at over 120 degrees
to help prevent the spread of
disease, but it should be under
140 degrees to avoid unnecessary
stress and damage on old dishes.**

Plate, Phoenix, 1985	17.00 to 25.00
Plate, Plainsman, Desert Gold, 8 In.	5.00
Plate, Plainsman, Desert Gold, 10 1/2 In.	12.00
Plate, Rural Letter Carrier, Desert Gold, Ada Clay, 1951	75.00
Plate, Squirrel, 1977	80.00
Plate, Statue Of Liberty, 1986	20.00 to 25.00
Plate, Wagon Wheel, Desert Gold, Ada Clay, 9 In.	13.00
Plate, Wagon Wheel, Desert Gold, Ada Clay, 10 In.	10.00
Plate, We The People, 1987	20.00
Platter, Plainsman, Prairie Green, 13 In.	8.00
Salt & Pepper, Barrel, White Sand, Ada Clay	30.00
Salt & Pepper, Dutch Shoes, Red Clay	60.00
Salt & Pepper, Lazybones, Prairie Green	10.00
Salt & Pepper, Mayan Aztec, Desert Gold, Ada Clay	15.00
Salt & Pepper, Oil Derrick, Ivory & Sage, 1950-1960, 3 In.	*Illus* 15.00
Salt & Pepper, Pink Elephant	65.00
Salt & Pepper, Plainsman, Brown	6.00
Salt & Pepper, Wagon Wheel, Prairie Green	12.00 to 16.00
Salt & Pepper, Wheat Shock	30.00
Saucer, Plainsman	3.50
Stein, Lazybones	8.00
Stein, Plainsman, Prairie Green, Sticker	8.00
Sugar, Wagon Wheel, Desert Gold, Ada Clay	15.00
Sugar & Creamer, Cover, Mayan Aztec, Prairie Green, Ada Clay	30.00
Sugar & Creamer, Wagon Wheel, Desert Gold, Ada Clay, Miniature	20.00
Sugar & Creamer, Wagon Wheel, Desert Gold, Sapulpa Clay	25.00
Tea Set, Desert Gold, 3 Piece	40.00 to 55.00
Teacup, Plainsman, Desert Gold, 5 Oz.	8.00
Teapot, Green Aztec	22.00
Teapot, Mayan Aztec, 2 Cup	40.00
Teapot, Wagon Wheel, Desert Gold, Ada Clay	20.00 to 35.00
Teepees, Prairie Green, Ada Clay	40.00
Toby Jug, Cowboy, Prairie Green, 1977	15.00
Toby Jug, Uncle Sam, 1976	12.00
Toothbrush Holder, Owl, Tan	58.00
Tray, 50th Anniversary, Prairie Gold, Oval, 1983	35.00
Trivet, Republican, Grand Old Party, Prairie Green, 1975	10.00
Trivet, Wagon Wheel, Prairie Green, 1957	65.00
Vase, Attached Pottery Black Stand, Bottle Shape, J.F. Roman, 16 In.	165.00
Vase, Blue, Bulbous, 4 1/4 In.	6.00
Vase, Bud, Crocus, Prairie Green, Sapulpa Clay	15.00
Vase, Cactus, Prairie Green, Ada Clay	30.00
Vase, Crocus, Prairie Green	15.00
Vase, Pillow, Prairie Green, 7 In.	27.00
Vase, Swan, Prairie Green, Sapulpa Clay	15.00
Wall Pocket, Acornada	45.00
Wall Pocket, Circus Horse	90.00
Wall Pocket, Gardener Girl	90.00
Wall Pocket, Phoebe, Black	128.00

FRATERNAL objects that are related to the many different fraternal organizations in the United States are listed in this category. The Elks, Masons, Odd Fellows, and others are included. Furniture is listed in the Furniture category. Shaving mugs decorated with fraternal crests are included in the Shaving Mug category.

Eastern Star, Bookmark, World's Fair Day, San Francisco, Metal, 2 1/2 In.	26.00
Eastern Star, Cup & Saucer	25.00
Elks, 21st Annual Reunion, John Wanamaker	110.00
Elks, July 1909, 45th Reunion, Grand Lodge, Los Angeles	27.00
Elks, Mirror, Elk Held, Barrel Shape, Oval, Pocket	70.00
Elks, Mug, Burnt Artware, Blue, Gold Trim, Early 1900s	45.00
Elks, Mug, Golden Anniversary, 1954	35.00
Elks, Pin, Elk Head & Symbol	7.00

Elks, Plate, 1910, 7 In.	35.00
Elks, Stein, Logo, Cream Colored, Gray Domed Lid, Germany, Early 1900s, 8 1/2 In.	30.00
Elks, Watch Fob, Cigarette Paper Case, Sterling Silver	125.00
Elks, Watch Fob, Gold Mount, BPOE Clock, Hands On 11	75.00
Knights Of Columbus, Postcard	22.00
Masonic, Apron	125.00
Masonic, Ashtray, Gold Trim, 1923	45.00
Masonic, Book, Masonic Encyclopedia Of Free Masonry, Mackey, 2 Volumes	110.00
Masonic, Chair Set, Masonic Emblem On Crest, Curved Arms, 33 In., 4	374.00
Masonic, Chair Set, Stenciled Emblem On Crest, 33 1/2 In., 1 Armchair, 6	1452.00
Masonic, Lighter, Gold-Toned Wreathed Emblem, Brushed Finish, Zippo, 1958	29.00
Masonic, Plate, Shenango, Desert Scene, Gold Border, Signed, DeLan, 10 1/2 In.	175.00
Masonic, Razor, Straight, Wade & Butcher, Box, 1860	170.00
Masonic, Sword, Kenning, London, 30 1/8-In. Blade	185.00
Masonic, Sword, Wrapped Handle, Engraved Blade With Masonic Designs	33.00
Masonic, Watch, Triangle, Swiss, 15 Jewel, 3 Adjustments, Silver	1475.00
Odd Fellows, Ax, Painted Design, c.1870	895.00
Odd Fellows, Badge, Lewis & Clark Exposition, Portland, 1905	85.00
Odd Fellows, Badge, San Francisco World's Fair, Silver Plate, Bronze, 1915, 3 In.	18.00
Odd Fellows, Lectern, Poplar, Red Flame Grained, Crescent Moon, 40 x 15 In.	1045.00
Odd Fellows, Magazine, 1846	15.00
Odd Fellows, Motto, Oil On Canvas, Frame, 23 1/4 x 20 In.	2645.00
Odd Fellows, Shoulder Boards, Gold Braid, Red Wool, Brass Clip, Mc Lilley & Co.	22.00
Odd Fellows, Watch Fob	22.00
Odd Fellows & Knights Of Pythias, Shaving Mug, Double Emblems, Gold Names	225.00
Shriner, Carte-De-Visite, Black Martin's Ferry Buckeye Band, Frame, 10 x 35 In.	75.00
Shriner, Wine, Pittsburgh Syrian Temple, Gold Buffalo & Date, 1899	195.00

FRY GLASS was made by the H. C. Fry Glass Company of Rochester, Pennsylvania. The company, founded in 1901, first made cut glass and other types of fine glasswares. In 1922, they patented a heat-resistant glass called *Pearl Oven glass*. For two years, 1926–1927, the company made Fry Foval, an opal ware decorated with colored trim. Reproductions of this glass have been made. Depression glass patterns made by Fry may be listed in the Depression Glass category. Some pieces of cut glass may also be included in the Cut Glass category.

FRY, Aquarium, Golden Glow	100.00 to 150.00
Basket, Angelica, Loop Crystal Rope Handle, Signed, 8 x 8 1/2 In.	630.00
Basket, Candy, Beaver, Whirling Stars, Crosshatch, Notched Rim, 6 x 4 In.	225.00
Bowl, Ivy, Amber	48.00
Bread Baker, 6 x 10 In.	30.00
Candlestick, Azure Blue Threading At Stems, Blue, Signed, 11 In., Pair	385.00
Candlestick, Spiral Looping, Blue Collar & Ring, Signed, 10 7/8 In., Pair	275.00
Clock, Clear Cut Case, Aristocrat Works, 5 1/2 In.	55.00
Compote, Opalescent Blue Lip & Stem, 4 1/4 x 9 1/2 In.	220.00
Compote, Threading Bubbles	165.00
Decanter, Petal Foot, Royal Blue Stopper, 14 In.	225.00
Goblet, Diamond Optic, Green Threading, Twist Stem	95.00
Grill Plate, Royal Blue, 10 In.	35.00
Iced Tea, Underplate, Floral Spray	58.00
Reamer, Opalescent	75.00
Reamer, Ruffled	175.00
Sugar, Underplate, Stippled, Blue Handles	195.00
Vase, Fan, Golden Glow, 5 1/2 In.	195.00 to 235.00
Vase, Threaded Diamond Optic, Black, 10 In.	165.00
FRY FOVAL, Bowl, Blue Rim, 9 In.	125.00
Champagne, Blue Stem	75.00
Cup & Saucer, Blue Handle	61.00
Grill Plate, 10 1/2 In.	40.00
Lamp, Ceiling, 9 In.	80.00
Pitcher, Tankard, Delft Blue Loop Handle, Footed, 10 1/2 In.	675.00
Plate, Pink Shading, 7 3/4 In.	35.00
Plate, Pink Shading, Turned Sides, 8 In.	65.00

Sugar & Creamer, Silver Overlay, Green Trim 240.00
Vase, Bud, Delft Blue Knop Stem, 6 1/4 In. 195.00
Vase, Silver Overlay, Green Foot, Marked, Rockford 225.00
Vase, Sweet Pea, Jade Foot 295.00
Vase, Trumpet, Green Foot, 12 In. 400.00

FULPER Pottery Company was incorporated in 1899 in Flemington,
New Jersey. They made art pottery from 1910 to 1929. The firm had
been making bottles, jugs, and housewares from 1805. Doll heads were
made about 1928. The firm became Stangl Pottery in 1929. Stangl
Pottery is listed in its own category in this book.

Basket, Applied Rose, Off-White, Twisted Rope Handle, 7 1/4 x 15 In. 325.00
Bookends, Ship, Pair 275.00
Bowl, Blue Flambe, Matte Green Glaze, Vertical Ink Mark, 11 x 3 In. 110.00
Bowl, Blue, Green High Glaze Over Pink, Vertical Ink Mark, 11 x 2 1/2 In. 355.00
Bowl, Cat's Eye Flambe, Brown, Deep Yellow, Vertical Ink Mark, 9 x 2 In. 143.00
Bowl, Chinese Blue Flambe Glaze, Blue, Black, Pink, Vertical Ink Mark, 9 x 2 In. .. 355.00
Bowl, Chinese Blue, Exhibited At Panama-Pacific Intl. Exposition, 1915 .... 550.00
Bowl, Chinese Blue, White Flambe Glaze, Square Vertical Mark, 4 1/2 x 8 In. 374.00
Bowl, Cobalt Blue Over Famille Rose Glaze, Green Flambe Interior, 3 1/8 x 7 1/2 In. ... 90.00
Bowl, Cucumber Crystalline Glaze, Scalloped Rim, Vertical Ink Mark, 15 x 3 In. 385.00
Bowl, Effigy, 3 Crouching Figures Hold Bowl, Cafe-Au-Lait Exterior, Signed, 10 1/2 In. .. 825.00
Bowl, Effigy, 3 Squaty Figures, Famille Rose, Gray Matte Glaze, Blue Green, 7 x 10 In. .. 330.00
Bowl, Effigy, Blue, Gray, Signed, 7 1/2 In. 522.00
Bowl, Effigy, Brown Flambe Over Brown, Blue, Cream, Vertical Ink Mark, 7 In. 465.00
Bowl, Flared, Blue, 3 x 8 In. 225.00
Bowl, Flemington Green Glaze, Green, Gray, Black, Vertical Ink Mark, 8 x 2 In. 187.00
Bowl, Green Flambe, Cream, Blue Matte Glaze, 1920-1930, 9 1/2 In. 330.00
Bowl, Mission Matte Flambe Over Alice Blue, Purple Wisteria Interior, 8 3/4 In. ... 135.00
Bowl, Moss Green Crystalline Glaze, Closed-In Rim, 5 x 12 In. 355.00
Bowl, Olive Flambe Over Green Glaze, Cat's Eye Interior, 3 1/2 x 6 3/4 In. 110.00
Bowl, Pale Yellow Flambe Glaze, Inverted Flat Lip, 8 7/8 In. 220.00
Bowl, Scarab Flower Frog Design, Chinese Blue Crystalline Glaze, 5 x 11 1/4 In. ... 350.00
Candlestick, 3-Light, Famille Rose, Alice Blue Over Antique Green, 6 In., Pair 275.00
Candlestick, Chinese Blue Flambe Glaze, Ivory, Brown, 10 3/4 x 4 1/4 In., Pair 605.00
Candlestick, Mint Green Crystalline Glaze, Olive, Vertical Ink Mark, 3 1/2 In., Pair 209.00
Centerpiece, Effigy, Light & Dark Black Glaze, Blue & Olive Flambe, 7 1/2 x 10 3/4 In. .. 525.00
Chamberstick, Chinese Red Matte Glaze, Incised Vertical Mark, 7 In. 305.00
Chamberstick, Purple Matte Glaze, 6 x 2 1/4 In. 176.00
Coaster Set, Coat Of Arms, Cafe Au Lait Matte Glaze, 4 In., 4 Piece 165.00
Flagon, Flower, Pear Shape, Braided Handle, Flambe, 10 3/8 In. 375.00
Flower Frog, Duck, Blue Crystalline 200.00
Humidor, Gun Metal Glaze, Signed, 6 1/4 x 7 In. 330.00
Jug, Colonial Revival Ware, Handle, 6 In. 125.00
Jug, Musical, Elephants' Breath Glaze 95.00
Jug, Sterling Silver Overlay, Sports Figures, Pinched Spout 425.00
Lamp, Green Crystalline, Wicker Shade, 1909, 17 In. 2600.00
Lamp, Green Crystalline, Wicker Shade, 27 In. 2600.00
Lamp, Perfume, Ballerina 275.00
Lamp, Striated Butterscotch Glaze, Cylindrical Neck, Flared Base, 15 1/2 In. 593.00
Lamp Base, Flemington Green Flambe Glaze, 2 Angular Handles, 7 1/2 x 9 1/2 In. 355.00
Mug, Blue Matte, Scroll Handle, 4 x 5 In. 90.00
Pitcher, Blue Flambe, Green, Gunmetal, 11 In. 253.00
Pitcher, Blue Snowflake Crystalline Glaze, Signed, 6 3/8 In. 220.00
Powder Jar, Egyptian 475.00
Powder Jar, Figural, Woman 250.00
Urn, Blue Flambe Glaze, Green, Blue Matte Ground, 4 Footed, 16 1/2 x 5 1/2 In. 935.00
Urn, Chinese Blue Microcrystalline Glaze, 2 Buttressed Handles, 10 x 6 1/4 In. 250.00
Urn, Chinese Blue, Olive Green Flambe Glaze, 2 Embossed Handles, 10 x 8 1/2 In. ... 1430.00
Vase, 3 Buttress Handle Shape, Green, Speckled Ivory, Rose Ground, 6 1/2 x 4 In. ... 330.00
Vase, 4 Buttresses Under Flambe Glaze, Signed, 8 1/4 In. 255.00
Vase, 4 Open Handles, Purple, Blue Matte Glaze, 9 x 8 In. 2530.00
Vase, 6 Sides, Turquoise Crystalline & Moss Flambe Glaze, Signed, 11 In. 330.00

Vase, 7 Sides, Frothy Mirror & Ivory Flambe Glaze, 10 In. 440.00
Vase, 8 Sides, Green Matte Glaze Over Ivory Matte Ground, 8 x 6 3/4 In. 660.00
Vase, Applied Rose Design, Blue, Green Highlights, Vertical Ink Mark, 6 In. 175.00
Vase, Applied Roses & Leaves, Green Matte Glaze, Vertical Ink Mark, 7 In. 143.00
Vase, Baluster, Blue Wisteria Glaze, Blue Speckled, 8 3/4 x 5 3/4 In. 245.00
Vase, Barrel, Flemington Green Flambe Glaze, 7 1/4 x 5 In. 440.00
Vase, Bee Hive, Caramel Flambe Over Black Copper Dust Glaze, 6 1/2 In. 220.00
Vase, Blossoms, Leaves, Cutout Design, Matte Green Glaze, Incised Mark, 5 x 3 In. 110.00
Vase, Blue & Green Flambe Glaze, Handles, Vertical Ink Mark, 6 In. 440.00
Vase, Blue & Lavender Crystalline High Glaze, Vertical Ink Mark, 9 In. 770.00
Vase, Blue Crystalline Glaze, 12 x 7 In. 990.00
Vase, Blue Snowflake Crystalline Glaze, 2 Handles, Signed, 4 3/4 In. 275.00
Vase, Blue, Bullet, Ivory Flambe Glaze, Vertical Ink Mark, 10 x 6 In. 660.00
Vase, Blue, Rose Striated Matte Glaze, 2 Handles, Tapered Base, 5 1/2 x 7 1/2 In. 230.00
Vase, Bottle, Brown & Tan Drip Crystalline Glaze, Incised Mark, 7 3/4 x 5 3/4 In. 245.00
Vase, Brown & Green Crystalline High Glaze, Handles, Vertical Ink Mark, 9 In. 770.00
Vase, Brown Flambe Over Blue, Gunmetal Flambe, Cream, Tan, 7 In. 355.00
Vase, Brown Flambe, Swirled Fern Design, Cream, Blue, 8 In. 88.00
Vase, Brown Matte Glaze, 2 Handles, Vertical Prang Mark, 4 1/2 In. 410.00
Vase, Bud, Frothy Ivory Crystalline Glaze, Mustard Matte Ground, 5 1/4 x 3 3/4 In. 330.00
Vase, Bud, Glossy Green Glaze, Blue Matte Ground, 8 x 3 In. 330.00
Vase, Bud, Mission Matte Flambe Over Antique Verte Green, Vertical Ink Mark, 5 In. . . . 135.00
Vase, Bulbous, Mirrored Black Crystalline Glaze, Signed, 7 3/4 In. 660.00
Vase, Bullet, Elephant's Breath Flambe Glaze, 3 Buttressed Handles, 6 1/2 x 4 In. 440.00
Vase, Bullet, Thick Glossy Green Over Green Glaze, Signed, 6 3/4 In. 357.00
Vase, Buttress, Chinese Blue Flambe, Signed, 8 In. 467.00
Vase, Cat's-Eye Flambe Glaze, Signed, 12 x 9 1/2 In. 1100.00
Vase, Cat's-Eye Flambe Glaze, Signed, 13 1/4 In. 660.00
Vase, Cat's-Eye Flambe Over Mustard Glaze, Signed, 4 5/8 In. 302.00
Vase, Chinese Blue Crystalline Glaze, 2 Angular Handles, 11 x 4 1/2 In. 415.00
Vase, Chinese Blue Flambe Over Famille Rose Glaze, Signed, 9 In. 522.00
Vase, Chocolate Brown, Blue Glaze Over Mustard, 4 Fin Handles, 1920, 10 In. 1725.00
Vase, Classical, Periwinkle Blue Crystalline Glaze, 12 x 5 In. 440.00
Vase, Copper Dust Crystalline & Gunmetal Flambe Glaze, 7 In. 440.00
Vase, Copper Dust Crystalline Glaze To Mirror Black Glaze, 12 x 7 3/4 In. 2090.00
Vase, Copper Dust Crystalline Glaze, 2 Angular Handles, 5 x 6 In. 465.00
Vase, Copper Dust Crystalline To Green Flambe Glaze, 2 Buttressed Handles, 9 x 6 In. . . 465.00
Vase, Copper Dust Crystalline, Green Flambe Glaze, Angular Handles, 9 1/2 x 7 In. 525.00
Vase, Corset, Black, Mustard Drip Glaze, Cobalt Blue Flambe Interior, 7 1/2 x 4 In. 305.00
Vase, Corset, Bronze Drip Glaze Over Green Glaze, Vertical Ink Mark, 7 1/2 x 4 In. 355.00
Vase, Corset, Striated Black Glaze, Green Ground, 10 x 5 In. 198.00
Vase, Cream & Blue Flambe, Handles, Incised Mark, 6 x 4 In. 175.00
Vase, Cream & Gray Flambe, Brown, Caramel, Incised Mark, 7 1/2 In. 410.00
Vase, Famille Rose, Verte Green Glaze, Handles, 7 1/2 x 5 3/4 In. 330.00
Vase, Flemington Green Flambe Glaze, Collared Rim, 4 1/2 x 6 1/2 In. 495.00
Vase, Flemington Green Flambe Glaze, Reticulated Triangles, 13 x 7 1/2 In. 4400.00
Vase, Flemington, Olive High Glaze, 8 In. 605.00
Vase, Frothy Elephants Breath, Textured Caramel Glaze, 7 1/3 x 4 1/4 In. 415.00
Vase, Frothy Gunmetal & Hare's Fur Glaze, Protruding Shoulder, 13 x 11 In. 4125.00
Vase, Futura Type, Bronze Flambe Over Blue & Lavender Wisteria, 4 3/4 x 6 1/4 In. 185.00
Vase, Gray Crystalline Glaze, Caramel, Green, 5 1/2 In. 605.00
Vase, Gray Gunmetal Flambe Glaze, Closed-In Rim, 8 x 5 1/2 In. 220.00
Vase, Green Crystalline Flambe Glaze, Elephant's Breath, 8 1/2 x 5 3/4 In. 605.00
Vase, Green Flambe Glaze, Gunmetal Rectangles Around Rim, Vertical Ink Mark, 8 In. . . 525.00
Vase, Green Flambe Over Cream, Incised Mark, 17 In. 1210.00
Vase, Green Flambe, 2 Squared Handles, Vertical Ink Mark, 4 1/2 In. 465.00
Vase, Green Flambe, Brown, Blue Matte Glaze, 2 Handles, 8 In. 605.00
Vase, Green Glaze, White Highlights At Rolled Rim, Signed, 7 In. 345.00
Vase, Green Matte Glaze, Cream, Brown Ground, Vertical Ink Mark, 5 x 6 In. 316.00
Vase, Gunmetal Crystalline Glaze Over Green, 2 Handles, Vertical Ink Mark, 6 x 4 In. . . . 385.00
Vase, Lavender & Caramel Flambe, Tan, Gray, Prank Mark, 6 1/2 x 4 1/2 In. 385.00
Vase, Leopard-Skin Crystalline Glaze, Signed, 12 In. 440.00
Vase, Melon, Famille Rose, Elephant's Breath Mouth, 5 1/4 x 5 In. 165.00

Vase, Mirrored Brown, Purple Flambe Glaze, Closed-In Rim, 8 x 5 In. 495.00
Vase, Moss Green Crystalline Glaze, Ink Mark, 12 1/2 x 6 In. 550.00
Vase, Mushroom Frieze, Ivory, Brown, Purple Flambe Glaze, 9 1/2 x 4 1/2 In. 935.00
Vase, Olive & Caramel Crystalline Flambe Over Streaked Alice Blue, 9 1/2 x 6 1/2 In. . . 550.00
Vase, Oxblood Glaze, Mottled Green, 6 In. 157.00
Vase, Pear, Blue Blush Flambe Glaze, 2 Buttressed Handles, Signed, 9 1/2 In. 467.00
Vase, Periwinkle Blue Crystalline Glaze, Flat Shoulder, 7 x 8 In. 440.00
Vase, Pink Flambe Glaze, Frothy Gray, 12 x 7 In. 275.00
Vase, Pink To Green Flambe, Gunmetal Glaze, 8 In. 935.00
Vase, Pumpkin Shape, White & Elephant's Breath Flecks, Spatter, 5 1/2 x 7 1/2 In. 245.00
Vase, Purple Flambe, Rust, Tan, 3 Handles, 6 1/2 In. 357.50
Vase, Ribbed, Light Green Crystalline Glaze, 13 In. 522.50
Vase, Rose Green Flambe Glaze, 4 Handles, 13 x 10 In. 990.00
Vase, Rose Matte Glaze, Blue Drip, Green, 3 Handles, 6 1/2 In. 440.00
Vase, Rose, Bulbous, Green Matte Glaze, Vertical Ink Mark, 8 1/2 x 6 In. 285.00
Vase, Silvery Flemington Green Glaze, Signed, Vasecraft, 5 In. 412.00
Vase, Spherical, Cucumber Green Matte Glaze, 3 Handles, 6 1/2 x 7 1/2 In. 465.00
Vase, Spherical, Flemington Green Flambe Glaze, Rolled Rim, 6 x 6 1/2 In. 385.00
Vase, Spherical, Frothy Green, Black Glaze, 3 Handles, 6 1/2 x 8 In. 525.00
Vase, Spherical, Gunmetal Glaze, Vertical Ink Mark, 5 3/4 x 7 In. 410.00
Vase, Spherical, Leopard-Skin Crystalline Glaze, 3 Handles, 6 1/2 x 9 In. 770.00
Vase, Striated Green Glaze, Intertwining Handles, Signed, 4 3/4 x 8 1/2 In. 396.00
Vase, Tan Crystalline Glaze, Gunmetal Glaze, Brown, Cream, 2 Open Handles, 12 In. . . . 1540.00
Vase, Taupe Crystalline Glaze, Mocha Brown Matte Glaze, Cream, Purple, 12 In. 715.00
Vase, Trumpet Neck, Cobalt Blue Crystalline Clusters, Purple Wisteria, 9 1/2 x 6 In. . . . 305.00
Vase, Trumpet, Elephant's Breath Flambe, Caramel, 2 Handles, 7 x 6 3/4 In. 195.00
Vase, Turquoise Green Crystalline Glaze, Ring Handles, Vertical Ink Mark, 12 x 8 In. . . . 550.00
Vase, Urn Shape, Mission Flambe, Mirror Finish, Square Handles, 4 3/4 x 6 In. 220.00
Vase, White Glossy Glaze, Thick Cobalt Blue, Oyster Matte Ground, 9 x 5 1/2 In. 350.00
Vessel, Bell Pepper Shape, Blue Flambe Over Mustard Speckled Glaze, Signed, 4 In. . . . 990.00
Wall Pocket, Leaves Covered In Green Flambe, 7 In. 275.00

FURNITURE of all types is listed in this category. Examples dating from the seventeenth century to the 1950s are included. Prices for furniture vary in different parts of the country. Oak furniture is most expensive in the West; large pieces over eight feet high are sold for the most money in the South, where high ceilings are found in the old homes. Condition is very important when determining prices. These are NOT average prices but rather reports of unique sales. If the description includes the word *style*, the piece resembles the old furniture style but was made at a later time. It is not a period piece. Garden furniture is listed in the Garden Furnishings category. Related items may be found in the Architectural, Brass, and Store categories.

Armchairs are listed under Chair in this category.
Armoire, Bird's-Eye Maple, Double Door, 2 Full-Length Locking Doors, 72 In. 330.00
Armoire, Eastlake, Walnut, Mirrored Door, Carved Crest, Drawer Base, 101 In. 1760.00
Armoire, Fruitwood Veneer, Glass Paneled Doors, Bookcase Shelving, 86 x 58 In. 1760.00
Armoire, Fruitwood, Foliate Crest, Scrolled Feet, 101 x 50 In. 920.00
Armoire, Fruitwood, Walnut, Foliate Crest, 2 Arched Doors, 78 1/2 x 47 In., Pair 747.00
Armoire, Louis XV, Oak, Central Frieze With Lovebirds, Cabriole Legs, 90 In. 3220.00
Armoire, Louis XV, Oak, Laurel Wreath Flanked By Swags, 90 x 55 In. 5175.00
Armoire, Louis XVI Style, Lion's Pelt Over Mirrored Door, Scrolled Legs, Paw Feet . . . 4600.00
Armoire, Louis XVI, Mahogany, Beveled Mirror, 2 Doors, 3 Drawers, 95 x 76 In. 2750.00
Armoire, Natural Wood, Zodiac-Shaped Ornaments, 1 Door, Quebec 920.00
Armoire, Oak, Drapery-Carved Frieze, Carved Fruit-Filled Baskets 6900.00
Armoire, Oak, Foliate, Floral Frieze, Bellflower Corners, 90 x 59 x 26 In. 5060.00
Armoire, Oak, Louis XV, Foliate-Carved Top Crest, 3 Shelves, 1830s, 89 1/2 In. 4600.00
Armoire, Pine, Light Blue, 19th Century, 62 x 41 In. 1980.00
Armoire, Walnut, 2 Mirrored Doors, Victorian, 89 x 66 In. 1936.00
Armoire, Walnut, Figured Veneer, Beveled-Mirror Door, 99 In. 3300.00
Armoire, Walnut, Round Cornice, 2 Paneled Doors, Fitted Interior, 90 1/2 In. 2300.00
Backbar, Oak, Saloon, Arches, Lions' Heads Over Each Arch, 66 x 72 In. 7500.00
Bed, Arbus, Bateau-Shaped, Mahogany Veneered, 1935-1940, Double, 58 In. 7500.00

Bed, Arts & Crafts, Peaked Top Rail, 5 Slats, 46 x 81 x 44 In. 187.00

Bed, Brass, Original Rails, 42 x 72 In. 245.00

Bed, Cannonball, Cherry, Rope, Scrolled Headboard, Turned Posts, 74 x 46 In. 385.00

Bed, Cannonball, Scroll Cutout Head & Footboard, Youth, 39 1/2 x 69 1/2 In. 825.00

Bed, Canopy, Birch, Pencil Post, Lamb's-Tongue Detail, 35 1/2 x 76 1/2 In. 550.00

Bed, Canopy, Mahogany, Spiral Acanthus Leaf & Pineapple Posts, 62 1/2 x 78 In. 1725.00

Bed, Cherry, Turned & Reeded Posts, Carved Swags & Tassels, Full Size 550.00

Bed, Cherry, Turned, Carved & Reeded Posts, 88 1/2 x 48 1/4 In. 1210.00

Bed, Day, Rococo, Giltwood, Blue Silk, Sweden, 35 1/2 x 81 1/4 In. 3740.00

Bed, Empire, Mahogany, Paneled Head & Footboards, Boat-Shaped Rail, 81 In. 7475.00

Bed, Field, Sheraton, Birch, Turned Legs, Hinged Canopy, 56 x 69 x 66 In. 5445.00

Bed, Four-Poster, Federal, Maple, Pine, Red, Tapered Legs, 1850, 5 Ft. 7 In. x 4 Ft. . 805.00

Bed, Four-Poster, George III, Mahogany, Spiral Reeded Finials, Bracket Feet 546.00

Bed, Four-Poster, Mahogany, Carved, Canopy 8250.00

Bed, Four-Poster, Mahogany, Pineapple Finial, Mid-1800s 455.00

Bed, Four-Poster, Mahogany, Poplar Headboard, Splayed Feet, 1810, 66 In. 1495.00

Bed, Four-Poster, Maple, Mid-19th-Century, Full Size 1750.00

Bed, Fruitwood, Carved Cupids & Scrollwork, Italy, 74 In. 550.00

Bed, G. Stickley, Leather Mattress On Rope Foundation, Child's, 56 3/4 In. 9255.00

Bed, G. Stickley, Oak, Crested Head, Footboard, 1910, Double, 51 In. 4600.00

Bed, G. Stickley, Oak, Vertical Slats, Red Decal, 1910, 44 In., Pair 4600.00

Bed, Herter Brothers, Aesthetic Movement, Inlaid & Gilt Rosewood, c.1881 .... 10925.00

Bed, Jenny Lind Style, Walnut, 40 x 68 1/2 x 42 1/2 In. 165.00

Bed, Maple, Pine, Low Post, Carved Pineapples, Punched Stars, 44 1/4 In. 258.00

Bed, Oak, Panel Headboard, Scroll Carved, c.1885, 72 In. 280.00

Bed, Oak, Rectangular-Panel Headboard, Scroll Carving, Victorian, c.1885, 72 In. 280.00

Bed, Opium, Rosewood, c.1850 .... 8500.00

Bed, Rope, Cherry, Maple, Ball Finials, Turned Feet, 71 In. 415.00

Bed, Rope, Deer & Dog In Crest, Yellow Foliage, Seymour Lindsey, 51 x 54 In. 6050.00

Bed, Rope, Hardwood, Red Stain, Turned Posts, High Feet, 51 x 69 x 32 In. 385.00

Bed, Rope, Mahogany, Empire, Turned Posts, Acorn Finials, 47 3/4 x 47 1/2 In. 247.00

Bed, Rope, Maple, Cutout-Eagle Headboard, Ohio, 1788-1888, 52 1/2 In. 3025.00

Bed, Rope, Maple, Square Posts, Turned Finials, 49 x 70 In. 110.00

Bed, Rope, Poplar, Turned Posts, Ball Finials, Shaped Headboard, 41 x 69 In. 302.00

Bed, Rope, Poplar, Turned Posts, Crosshatch Carving On Acorn Finials, 75 In. 495.00

Bed, Rope, Red Wash Finish, 48 x 80 In. 595.00

Bed, Rosewood, Marquetry, Snake Shape, Acanthus Scroll Crest, 1895, Full Size 2300.00

Bed, Sheraton, Curly Maple, Turned Posts & Finials, Removable Side, Baby's 660.00

Bed, Sheraton, Tall Post, Curly Maple, Reeded, Rope End Rails, 52 x 70 x 82 In. 4400.00

Bed, Sheraton, Tall Post, Mahogany, Swags & Tassels, Canopy, 67 x 82 x 99 In. 2090.00

Bed, Steel, Directoire Style, Brass, Rosettes, 37 x 80 In. 1840.00

Bed, Tall Post, Curly Maple, Cherry, Scrolled Headboard, 55 x 68 1/4 In. 302.00

Bed, Tester, Cherry, Acanthus Carving, Reeded Legs, 1830, 95 In. 4950.00

Bed, Tester, Federal, Birch, Red, Arched Headboard, 1810, 84 x 78 In. 1955.00

Bed, Tester, Federal, Maple, Poplar, Red Stain, Tapered Legs, 1810, 84 x 72 In. 1150.00

Bed, Tester, George III, Satinwood, Late 19th Century, 93 x 83 x 71 In. 8625.00

Bed, Tester, Printed Cotton Fabric Headboard, 95 1/2 x 57 In. 4600.00

Bed, Tester, Regency, Mahogany, Reeded, 4 Turned-Head Posts, 1830, 97 In. 1210.00

Bed, Trundle, Cherry, Low Head & Footboards, Side Rails, 16 x 64 1/2 In. 110.00

Bed, Vase-Form Posts, Ball Finials, Thimble Feet, Grain Painted, 1850s, 3/4 Size 555.00

Bed, Walnut, Burl Veneer, Moldings, Carved, Victorian, 58 x 72 x 80 1/2 In. 440.00

Bed, Walnut, Curved Head & Footboards, Victorian, 55 1/2 x 51 x 72 In. 250.00

Bed, Walnut, Inlay, Ormolu Mounts, France, 20th Century, 63 In., Pair 990.00

Bed, Walnut, Spool Turned, 67 1/2 x 56 1/2 In. 385.00

Bed, Walnut, Varnish Over Alligatored Finish, Victorian, 53 1/2 x 73 1/2 x 61 In. 385.00

Bed Steps, Second Step Slides Out With Chamber Pot, 19th Century 1795.00

Bedroom Set, Cottage, Pine, Black Walnut Trim, 4 Piece 1395.00

Bedroom Set, Oak, Curved Fronts, Beveled Mirrors, 3 Piece 4000.00

Bedroom Set, Oak, Robert Thompson, 1940-1950, 3 Piece 12185.00

Bedroom Set, Upholstered, Art Deco, 1935, 80 1/2 In. 115.00

Bedroom Set, Walnut, Marble Top Dresser, Tall-Post Bed, Victorian, 2 Piece 2200.00

Bench, Art Deco, Mahogany, Upholstered, Slab Legs, France, 1928, 48 In. 3450.00

Bench, Baroque, Walnut, Needlepoint, 81 1/2 x 45 x 17 1/4 In. 865.00

Bench, Baroque, Walnut, Upholstered, Scrolled Legs, 55 1/2 In. 1983.00
Bench, Bucket, Dovetailed Case, 4 Graduated Shelves, Cutout Feet, 46 x 48 In. 495.00
Bench, Bucket, Poplar, Green Wash Over Gray, Wire-Nails, 37 3/4 In. 522.00
Bench, Bucket, Wooden, Gray & Green Paint, Cutout Hearts On Legs, 60 In. 230.00
Bench, Bugatti, Oak, Applied Strips Of Patinated Metal, 1900, 52 x 40 1/4 In. 3450.00
Bench, Cricket, Bootjack Feet, Tiny Cut Square Nails, Red Paint 175.00
Bench, Cricket, Scroll Top, Mortised & Pegged, 4 3/4 x 18 In. 185.00
Bench, Deacon's, Brown Paint, Stenciled Design, 75 In. 1430.00
Bench, Dressing, Cast Iron, Pierced Scroll Skirt, Acanthus Knees, Claw Feet, 21 In. 165.00
Bench, Empire, 2 Stylized Urchins On Arch, Spherical Feet, 31 1/4 In. 374.00
Bench, G. Nakashima, Black Walnut, Plant Top, 4 Doweled Legs, 95 1/2 In. 1540.00
Bench, Giltwood, Flower Heads, Foliate Scrolls, Upholstered Arms & Seat, 31 In. 1610.00
Bench, Hall, Blue & White Striped Seat, 51 1/2 In. 400.00
Bench, Hardwood, Pine, Fireside High Back, 72 x 44 In. 550.00
Bench, Hitchcock, Gold Design, Black, Turned Spindles, Legs, 77 In. 770.00
Bench, Kneeling, Beaded Cushion, Black, Gray & White, 5 Melon Feet, 47 x 10 In. 440.00
Bench, Kneeling, Pine, Cutout Feet, Apron, Red Paint, Black Graining, 6 x 43 In. 300.00
Bench, Leather, Steel, Flat Steel, F. Knoll, 71 1/2 In. 718.00
Bench, Library, Hinged Seat, Metamorphic, Opens To 4 Treads, 21 x 30 In. 5750.00
Bench, Louis XIV, Hardwood, Cabriole Legs, Silk Top, 18 1/2 x 41 In. 522.00
Bench, Louis XIV, Hardwood, Caned Back & Seat, Velvet Cushion, 78 In. 3100.00
Bench, Louis XV Style, Beechwood, Needlepoint Seat, c.1910, 42 In. 1400.00
Bench, Mammy's Arrow Back, Baby Guard, Black Paint, Yellow Striping, 73 In. 550.00
Bench, Mammy's, Mustard Paint, Black Stencil, Arms, 72 In. 1100.00
Bench, Maple, Carved Ribbons On Arm Supports, Upholstered Back, 78 In. 3450.00
Bench, Maple, Hitchcock-Type, Backless, Cane Seat, Turned Feet, 1830s, 72 In. 1610.00
Bench, Meetinghouse, Plank Seat, Red Paint, 84 x 33 x 11 3/4 In. 115.00
Bench, Oak, Carved Geometric Backrest, Plank Seat, Scrolled Arms, 1680s, 80 In. 920.00
Bench, Oak, Gothic Revival, Continental, 62 x 43 3/4 In. 6325.00
Bench, Piano, Oak, Lift Seat, Square Tapering Legs, 35 In. 385.00
Bench, Pine, 2 Splats, Plank Seat, 19th Century, 32 1/2 x 74 x 17 In. 635.00
Bench, Pine, 24 Splats, Plank Seat, Turned Legs, Painted, 34 1/2 In. 1610.00
Bench, Pine, Cutout Ends, Curved Braces, Red, 9 x 46 x 19 In. 660.00
Bench, Pine, Cutout Hearts, 45 In. 15.00
Bench, Pine, Green, 10 x 56 x 19 In. 220.00
Bench, Pine, Lift Seat, 19th Century 132.00
Bench, Poplar, Mustard Yellow Paint, Wire Nails, 60 In. 300.00
Bench, Regency, Mahogany, 19th Century, 19 x 12 x 10 In. 400.00
Bench, Regency, Pine, Polychromed 6875.00
Bench, Shaker, Poplar, Natural Patina, 6 3/4 x 36 In. 300.00
Bench, Walnut, Bird's-Eye Veneer On Apron, Upholstered, 20 1/2 x 23 In. 275.00
Bench, Water, Pine, Mustard Yellow Paint, Bootjack Feet, 12 x 30 x 30 In. 385.00
Bench, Water, Poplar, Gray Paint, 37 x 10 x 31 In. 465.00
Bench, Water, Poplar, Red Paint, 32 3/4 x 38 In. 357.00
Bench, William & Mary, Walnut, H-Form Stretcher, 16 x 26 1/2 In. 632.00
Bench, Windsor, T. Ash, Bowed Seat, Turned Spindles, Posts, N.Y., 73 In. 770.00
Bench & Chair, Crisscrossed Back & Seat, Cross-Shaped Arms, 40 In. 575.00
Bench & Chair Set, Bugatti, Painted Vellum Drum Back, Arms, 1900, 3 Piece 18745.00
Bookcase, Art Nouveau, Walnut, Carved Thistle & Pinecone, 1900s, 74 x 86 In. 2300.00
Bookcase, Arts & Crafts, Oak, 4 Shelves, Vertical Slat Sides, 39 In. 77.00
Bookcase, Biedermeier, Birch, Peaked Pediment, Dentil Molding, Glazed Doors 8625.00
Bookcase, Cahoon, Brown & Yellow, 2 Hinged Doors, 1944, 67 x 42 In. 11500.00
Bookcase, Camden Cabinet Co., Oak, Stacked, 3 Sections, 44 1/2 In. 302.00
Bookcase, Curly Maple, Walnut, Full Turned Pilasters, Beveled Glass Doors, 59 In. 715.00
Bookcase, Cushman, 4 Shelves Over 2 Doors, Pine Color, 79 1/2 In., Pair 110.00
Bookcase, Duncan Phyfe Style, Eglomise Panes 9200.00
Bookcase, Ebonized, Silk, Brass Trellis, Victorian, 37 1/2 In., Pair 12650.00
Bookcase, G. Stickley, 2 Doors, Original Hardware, Decal, 56 1/4 In. 7935.00
Bookcase, G. Stickley, No. 715, 16-Pane Door, Keyed Tenon Sides, Decal, 56 In. 6050.00
Bookcase, George III, Mahogany, Glazed Mullioned Doors, Shelves, 82 In. 9775.00
Bookcase, Globe-Wernicke, Barrister, Step Back, Sliding Glass Doors 632.00
Bookcase, Globe-Wernicke, Mahogany, 3 Sections, Label, 35 x 11 x 50 In. . . . . . .330.00 to 412.00
Bookcase, Globe-Wernicke, Mahogany, Stacked, 4 Sections, 61 x 34 1/2 In. 440.00

Bookcase, Golden Oak, 5 Levels Of Open Shelves, Plank Sides, c.1890, 61 In. 357.00
Bookcase, Golden Oak, Acanthus Leaves On Columns, Glass Door, 4 Shelves, 53 In. 495.00
Bookcase, Golden Oak, Paw Feet, Scrolled Apron, 1-Pane Door, 58 1/2 In., Pair 825.00
Bookcase, Jean Prouve, Aluminum, Lacquered, Ash, 1952, 72 x 60 In. .... *Illus* 17600.00
Bookcase, L. & J.G. Stickley, No. 641, 8-Pane Door, Keyed Tenon Sides, 55 In. 7150.00
Bookcase, L. & J.G. Stickley, Oak, 3 Doors, Red Decal, 1908, 55 1/4 In. 1495.00
Bookcase, Lawyer's, Walnut, Step Back, 2 Glass Doors On Top, Ohio, 59 In. 2640.00
Bookcase, Lifetime, Mahogany, 3 Shelves, Paine Furniture Co., 45 x 13 x 55 In. 1540.00
Bookcase, Limbert, 2 Doors, 3 Adjusting Shelves, Dark Brown Finish, 58 In. 2645.00
Bookcase, Limbert, No. 358, 2 Doors, 2 Vertical Panes, Casters, Label, 59 x 48 In. 3500.00
Bookcase, Mahogany, 2 Parts, 2 Doors, Leather-Bound Books, Shelves, 1820s 4600.00
Bookcase, Mahogany, 3 Shelves, 2 Glazed Doors, Dividers, Ball & Claw Feet 412.00
Bookcase, Mahogany, Figural Carving, 3 Open Shelves, 2 With Doors, 65 In. 247.00
Bookcase, Mahogany, Open Shelf, Ogee Frieze Drawer, 60 x 35 x 14 In. 248.00
Bookcase, Mahogany, Panels In Double Doors, 2 Lower Drawers, Korea, 44 1/4 In. 187.00
Bookcase, Mahogany, Tambour, Hinged Door, c.1790, 80 In. 8500.00
Bookcase, Mahogany, Wire-Grill Front, Bronze Mounted, 48 x 58 3/4 In. 3105.00
Bookcase, Mission, 3 Sections, Leaded Glass Top, 19 Drawers ....*Illus* 715.00
Bookcase, Mission, Oak, 2 Doors, 58 x 43 x 15 In. 465.00
Bookcase, Mission, Oak, 2 Doors, Glass Sides ....*Illus* 770.00
Bookcase, Mission, Oak, Revolving, Open Storage, 4-Prong Base, 69 x 26 In. 920.00
Bookcase, Oak, 2 Drawers, Openwork Leaf Carving, 65 x 42 x 13 In. 825.00
Bookcase, Oak, 3 Adjustable Shelves, 2 Long Doors With Glass, 55 In. 175.00
Bookcase, Oak, Crenellated Top, 2 Shallow Shelves, 1855, 48 x 58 1/2 In. 7130.00
Bookcase, Oak, Open Front, Adjustable Shelves, 2 End-To-End Drawers, 60 x 60 In. ... 770.00
Bookcase, Oak, Single Astragal Glazed Door, Side Brass Handles, 25 In. 40.00
Bookcase, Oak, Stacked, 3 Horizontal Sections, Glass Panel Door, 47 3/8 In. 550.00
Bookcase, Oak, Stylized Floral Inlay, 1910, 65 1/2 x 67 In. 483.00
Bookcase, Oak, Swivel, Square, X-Shaped Base, Casters, 60 1/2 In. 488.00
Bookcase, Ormolu Mounted, Ebonized, Glazed Doors, 4 Shelves, 83 1/4 In. 4887.00
Bookcase, Queen Anne, Mahogany, 2 Glazed Doors, Mirrored Back, 44 x 80 In. 350.00
Bookcase, Queen Anne, Walnut, Beveled-Mirror Door, Bracket Feet, 68 In. 17250.00
Bookcase, Regency, Mahogany, Walnut, 2 Doors, 87 x 85 In. 2300.00
Bookcase, Roycroft, Mahogany, 12-Pane Door, Original Finish, 56 In. 6050.00
Bookcase, Sheraton, Mahogany, Astragal Doors, Bracket Feet, 89 x 46 x 20 In. 1840.00
Bookcase, Urn Finial, 2 Glazed Doors, Shelves, Mirrored Back Over Drawer, 80 In. 385.00
Bookcase, Urn Finial, 2 Glazed Doors, Shelves, Mirrored Back, 80 In. 385.00
Bookcase, Walnut, 2 Drawers, Adjustable Shelves, Crest, 60 1/2 In. 2035.00
Bookcase, Walnut, Carved Frieze Over 2 Glazed Doors, Blind Doors, 53 x 84 In. 1035.00
Bookrack, Arts & Crafts, Arched Sides, Cutouts, Tenon Construction, 22 x 7 In. 165.00
Bookrack, G. Stickley, 4 Compartments, Cutout Handle, Square, 13 x 9 1/2 In. 1320.00
Bookrack, G. Stickley, No. 74, Light Brown Finish, 30 3/4 x 32 x 10 In. 1150.00
Bookshelf, L. & J.G. Stickley, Oak, 3 Shelves, Yellow Decal, 55 x 34 In. 4600.00
Bookstand, Georgian, Mahogany, Revolving, Early 20th Century, 53 In. 1840.00
Bookstand, Palisander, Ebony, Bone Inlay, Ratchet Mechanism, A. Giroux 6325.00
Bookstand, Roycroft, Mahogany, Dovetailed, 18 x 4 1/2 x 5 1/2 In. 1320.00

Furniture, Bookcase,
Mission, Oak, 2 Doors,
Glass Sides

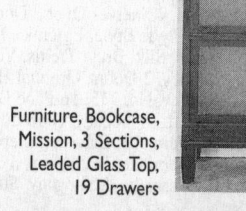

Furniture, Bookcase,
Mission, 3 Sections,
Leaded Glass Top,
19 Drawers

To get rid of mildew on wooden furniture, wipe the wood with a cloth dipped in this mixture: 1 cup water mixed with 1 tablespoon bleach and 1 tablespoon liquid dishwashing detergent. Then dry the wood with a clean cloth.

Furniture, Bookcase, Jean Prouve, Aluminum, Lacquered, Ash, 1952, 72 x 60 In.

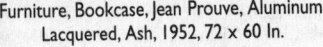

Bookstand, Roycroft, Mahogany, Little Journeys, 2 Shelves, 26 In.	660.00
Breakfront, Empire, Mahogany, 2 Sections, 2 Drawers, 81 x 64 x 16 In.	1840.00
Breakfront, George III, Mahogany, Dentiled, Gadrooned Plinth Base	1265.00
Breakfront, Mahogany, 5 Doors, 3 Drawers, 54 x 15 x 80 In.	1045.00
Breakfront, Pine, Central Astragal Doors, Plinth Base	920.00
Breakfront-Bookcase, George III, Mahogany, Late 18th Century, 83 1/2 In.	3740.00
Breakfront-Bookcase, Glazed Mullioned Doors, Shelves, Pigeonholes, 89 1/2 In.	8625.00
Breakfront-Bookcase, Ribbons & Swags, Diamond Mullioned Doors, 108 In.	8625.00
Breakfront-Bookcase, Rosewood, 4 Doors, 1825, 90 1/2 In.	6900.00
Buffet, Burl Walnut, Hand-Carved Figures On Front Legs, Claw Feet, 1800s	1500.00
Buffet, Empire Revival, Mahogany, 2 Secret Doors	1450.00
Buffet, Heywood-Wakefield Co., 3 Drawers, Tambour Door, 49 In.	660.00
Buffet, L. & J.G. Stickley, No. 740, Oak, Rack, 2 Drawers, 2 Shelves, 1910, 48 In.	3750.00
Buffet, Louis XV, Fruitwood, Plate Rack, Lower Cupboard, c.1780, 77 In.	4500.00
Buffet, Mennonite, Pine, Butternut, c.1840, 64 x 49 In.	4250.00
Bureau, Boulle Style, Brass Scroll Surface, Gilt Metal Edge, 30 x 56 x 30 In.	3450.00
Bureau, Empire, Bird's-Eye Maple, Serpentine Front, 5 Drawers, 47 x 24 x 35 In.	1870.00
Bureau, French Style, Mahogany, 1 False Over 2 Long Drawers, Marble Top	3520.00
Bureau, Leather Top, 1 Long & 2 Short Drawers, Bronze Mounted, 68 In.	5775.00
Bureau, Louis XVI, Oak, Cylindrical	4890.00
Bureau, Mahogany, Bowfront, 4 Veneered Drawers, Brass Pulls, 40 x 43 In.	1210.00
Bureau, Mahogany, Mirror, Carved Feet, 2 Large & 2 Small Drawers, 73 x 60 In.	198.00
Bureau, Mahogany, Slant Front, String Inlay, Fitted Interior, 42 1/4 In.	2300.00
Bureau, Maple, Shagreen, 2 Small Drawers, Block-Shaped Legs, 1930s, 29 1/2 In.	1150.00
Bureau, Neoclassical, Walnut, Marquetry	5290.00
Bureau, Oak, 2 Short Drawers Over 4 Graduated Drawers, Scrolled Feet	55.00
Bureau, Rosewood Veneer, Dutch Kettle Base, Barrel Front, 42 x 45 In.	1760.00
Butler's Desk, Walnut, 15 Drawers, Hidden Drawer, 55 x 39 x 20 In.	660.00
Cabinet, 2 Glazed Doors Flanked By Columns, Plinth Base, 74 x 69 x 20 In.	1150.00
Cabinet, Beveled Glass, Pagoda-Style Top, Glazed Doors, Black Paint, 88 x 47 In.	575.00
Cabinet, Biedermeier, Walnut, Stepped Cornice, 2 Doors, Block Feet, 69 x 47 In.	2300.00
Cabinet, Black Lacquer, Curving Shelf, 2 Doors, Silvered Handles, 1941, 35 1/2 In.	2530.00
Cabinet, Black Lacquer, Double Doors With Allegorical Figures, 30 1/4 In., Pair	175.00
Cabinet, Brass, Shagreen, Birch-Lined Interior, Stand, 48 In.	5520.00
Cabinet, Butternut, 4 Upper Doors, 10 Base Drawers, 84 x 60 In.	3500.00
Cabinet, Charles X, Fruitwood, Hinged Top, Octagonal, 1825, 35 x 18 In.	99.00
Cabinet, Cherry, Beveled Mirrors, Shelves, Towel Rack, c.1880, 75 In.	3500.00
Cabinet, Cherry, Slant Front, Kettle Body, Upper Doors, Small Drawers, 89 In.	1375.00
Cabinet, China, Arts & Crafts, 3 Shelves, 2 Glass Doors, Brass Pulls, 60 In.	660.00
Cabinet, China, Arts & Crafts, 3 Shelves, Top Glass Pane, Original Finish, 61 In.	990.00
Cabinet, China, Burl Walnut, Bowed Beveled-Glass Doors	1250.00
Cabinet, China, Dome Top, Shell-Shaped Crest, Glazed Doors, 76 In.	770.00
Cabinet, China, Drexel, Mahogany, Upper Bowfront Glass Door, Center Drawers	605.00
Cabinet, China, Frankl, Mahogany, Cork Trim, X Handles, 1949	2500.00
Cabinet, China, Fruitwood, Grilled & Paneled Doors, Shelves, 2 Piece, 79 In.	247.00

Cabinet, China, G. Stickley, 12-Pane Glass Door, 4 Glass Side Panels, 63 x 38 In. 6050.00
Cabinet, China, G. Stickley, No. 815, 16 Panes, 2 Doors, Red Decal, 39 x 64 In. 10450.00
Cabinet, China, Heywood-Wakefield Co., Bombe Glass Doors, 4 Drawers 1210.00
Cabinet, China, Heywood-Wakefield Co., Open Top, 2 Piece, 53 x 18 x 72 In. 660.00
Cabinet, China, Limbert, 1 Door, 3 Small Panes, 44 x 16 x 58 In. 7150.00
Cabinet, China, Mahogany, 2 Glass Top Doors, 1 Long Drawer Over 2 Base Doors 325.00
Cabinet, China, Mahogany, Curved Glass Door & Sides, Ball & Claw Feet, 55 1/2 In. . . 660.00
Cabinet, China, Oak, Beveled Curved Glass Sides & Front, Large Claw Feet 3650.00
Cabinet, China, Oak, Quartersawn, Curved Glass, 64 1/2 In. 525.00
Cabinet, China, Renaissance Revival, Oak, Carved Classical Men, 58 x 63 In. 1430.00
Cabinet, China, Shell-Shaped Carved Crest, 2 Glazed Doors, Cabriole Legs, 76 In. 770.00
Cabinet, Chinese Chippendale, Mahogany, Glass, Pagoda Top, Side Door, 91 1/2 In. 4600.00
Cabinet, Corner, Burl Walnut, 2 Mirrored Shelves, Marble Top, 77 In. 1300.00
Cabinet, Corner, Edwardian, Painted, c.1910, 73 In. 3800.00
Cabinet, Corner, George III, Black Lacquer, Late 18th Century, 36 In. 1150.00
Cabinet, Corner, Mahogany, Hanging, 1 Lattice Door, 4 Shelves, 44 x 27 1/2 In. 687.00
Cabinet, Corner, Pine, Relief-Cut Diamond, 1 Shelf, Molded Base, 55 In. 1095.00
Cabinet, Curio, Bronze, 2 Doors, France, 18 x 12 In. 775.00
Cabinet, Curio, Golden Oak, Quartersawn Veneer, Bowed Glass Sides & Door, 62 In. . . . 825.00
Cabinet, Curio, Inlaid Veneer, Ormolu Trim, Lighted, 2 Glass Shelves, 59 In. 550.00
Cabinet, Curio, Mahogany, Scenic Panels, Curved Glass, 2 Glass Shelves, 57 1/2 In. 1870.00
Cabinet, Curio, Rosewood, 12 Shelves, Mirrored Backdrop, Glass Door, 31 3/4 In. 275.00
Cabinet, Empire, Walnut, Molded Cornice, 20th Century, 68 x 42 1/2 x 14 In. 1150.00
Cabinet, File, Oak, 6 Drawers, 4 Tall Legs, 36 x 18 1/2 In. 220.00
Cabinet, Franco-Flemish, Tortoiseshell & Ivory Inlay, Plinth Base, 19th Century 2070.00
Cabinet, Frank Lloyd Wright, 2 Doors, Original Finish, 21 x 20 x 28 In. 1200.00
Cabinet, Fruitwood, 3 Painted Ivory Panels, Tortoiseshell Drawer Fronts 5225.00
Cabinet, G. Nelson, Birch Veneer, 4 Drawers, Label, 34 x 29 x 24 In. 605.00
Cabinet, G. Nelson, Birch, 2 Doors With Hook Pulls, Open Storage, 29 x 34 In. 430.00
Cabinet, G. Nelson, Rosewood, 3 Drawers, Aluminum Pulls & Legs, 31 In. 1760.00
Cabinet, G. Nelson, Walnut Veneer, 4 Drawers, Aluminum Pulls, 24 x 30 In. 660.00
Cabinet, G. Nelson, Walnut Veneer, 8 Drawers, Aluminum Pulls, 57 x 30 In. 935.00
Cabinet, G. Nelson, Walnut, 2 Doors, 4 Drawers, Herman Miller, 29 x 56 In. 450.00
Cabinet, George III, Mahogany, Swan's-Neck Crest, 2 Drawers, 90 1/2 In. 1610.00
Cabinet, George III, Satinwood, 4 Drawers, Foliate Panels, 53 In. 4600.00
Cabinet, Hanging, Biedermeier, Bird's-Eye Maple, Moire Silk Lining, 32 In., Pair 2090.00
Cabinet, Herman Miller, Birch Veneer, 4 Drawers, 1 Door, 56 x 19 x 30 In. 1210.00
Cabinet, Herman Miller, Paldao Veneer, 2 Doors, Sculpted Pulls, 40 x 17 x 42 In. 525.00
Cabinet, Herman Miller, Walnut Veneer, 3 Drawers, Wooden Knob, Label, 29 In. 385.00
Cabinet, I.F. Dubut, Tulipwood, Purplewood, Marble Top, 2 Doors, 32 In. 2875.00
Cabinet, Knoll, Walnut Veneer, Chrome Base, 5 Drawers, 1958, 108 x 20 x 29 In. 1430.00
Cabinet, Mahogany, 25 Dovetailed Drawers, 25 x 30 In. 795.00
Cabinet, Mahogany, 3 Sections, Cabriole Legs, Paw Feet, 68 x 65 In. 2070.00
Cabinet, Mahogany, Bowfront, Curved Glass, 40 1/2 x 16 1/2 x 62 In. 495.00
Cabinet, Mahogany, D-Shape, Marquetry, 1880-1900, 58 x 16 In. 4290.00
Cabinet, Mahogany, Fluted Pedestal, Black Marble Top, 15 x 29 In., Pair 990.00
Cabinet, Maple, 4 Drawers, 6 Pigeonholes, Penna., 19th Century, 30 1/2 In. 4600.00
Cabinet, Maple, Radiating Fluted-Medallion Doors, Canada 3575.00
Cabinet, Marquetry, Lovers Scene On Door, 6 Small Drawers, 1920, 11 In. 632.00
Cabinet, Mounted Ivory & Brass Inlay, Gadrooned Border, Paneled Door, 40 In. 2587.00
Cabinet, Music, Aesthetic Movement, Carved 1100.00
Cabinet, Music, Bird's-Eye Maple Front, 2 Doors 275.00
Cabinet, Music, Flip Door, Diamond Disc, Edison 525.00
Cabinet, Music, French Style, Mahogany, Brass Gallery, Serpentine Inlay 495.00
Cabinet, Music, Oak, Cylinder, Half Round 1150.00
Cabinet, Music, Oak, Phonograph, Grand Piano Shape 3800.00
Cabinet, Music, Renaissance Revival, Walnut, Carved, Drawers, Door, 43 x 23 In. 2750.00
Cabinet, Music, Rosewood, Mahogany, Marquetry, c.1870 . . . . 2200.00
Cabinet, Napoleon III, Ebonized, Rosette Frieze, Plinth Base, 41 x 60 In. 2990.00
Cabinet, Oak, 2 Paneled Parquetry Doors, Iron Hinges, 62 x 45 In. 1320.00
Cabinet, Oak, Louis XVI, Paneled Door, 73 x 41 x 18 1/2 In. 1380.00
Cabinet, Oak, Music, Quartersawn Oak, Door Concealing 2 Shelves, 31 1/2 In. 120.00
Cabinet, Oak, Paneled Ends, Carved Facade, Foliage Rails, Lion's Heads, 38 1/2 In. 3575.00

Cabinet, Open Shelf With Mirror Back, 2 Doors, Inlay, Austria, 1905, 32 x 69 In. 7125.00
Cabinet, Painted Reliquary, 1 Door Over 1 Drawer, Baby In Casket, 1804, 20 In. 975.00
Cabinet, Phonograph, Peter Hunt, 47 1/2 x 22 1/2 In. 880.00
Cabinet, Pierre-Paul Montagnac, Rosewood, Marble, 4 Drawers, 20 x 57 In. 7475.00
Cabinet, Pine, 1-Board & Batten Door, 5 Shelves, 57 3/4 In. 55.00
Cabinet, Pine, Rectangular Cornice, Red, Early 19th Century, 85 1/2 x 48 In. 5175.00
Cabinet, Prairie School, 3 Side Drawers Both Sides, Spindled Sides, 30 3/4 In. 1430.00
Cabinet, Regency Revival, Mahogany, 38 x 48 19 1/4 In. 995.00
Cabinet, Regency Revival, Mahogany, Gilt-Metal Frieze, 1 Cupboard Door, 38 In. 995.00
Cabinet, Regency Style, Marble Top, Black Paint, Leaf-Carved Feet, 37 1/2 In., Pair 5750.00
Cabinet, Renaissance Revival, Oak, Gothic Tracery, Columnar Legs, 61 In. 1035.00
Cabinet, Rosewood, Burl Panels, 3 Cabinet Doors, N.Y., 1865, 57 x 77 x 19 In. 470.00
Cabinet, Rosewood, On Stand, 5 Drawers, Carrying Handles, Portuguese, 57 3/4 In. 9775.00
Cabinet, Rosewood, Stepped Top, Door, 2 Lower Cabinets, France, c.1930, 52 In. 5750.00
Cabinet, Satinwood, Burl Walnut, Reeded Columns, Turned Feet, 43 x 66 x 17 In. 4600.00
Cabinet, Sheet Music, Eastlake, Black Lacquer, Concealed Safe, 49 1/4 x 20 In. 1875.00
Cabinet, Side, Empire, Mahogany, Pullout Shelves, 52 x 20 x 16 1/4 In. 750.00
Cabinet, Side, Mahogany, Mother-Of-Pearl, 2 Side Doors, Leleu, 1940s, 56 x 51 In. 7475.00
Cabinet, Side, Napoleon III, Marble Top, Late 19th Century, 43 x 33 In. 575.00
Cabinet, Smoker's, Stickley Brothers, 1 Drawer, Mackmurdo Feet, Round, 26 In. 990.00
Cabinet, Softwood, Blind Door, Panel Doors, 6 Divided Compartments, Red Wash 550.00
Cabinet, Spice, 2 Center Doors, Black Paint, 16 1/2 x 14 1/2 In. 518.00
Cabinet, Swans On Mullioned Doors, Bracket Feet, 1880 .... 2415.00
Cabinet, Tiger Maple, 2 Glazed Doors, 3 Shelves, 3 Long Drawers, c.1825, 88 In. 5175.00
Cabinet, V. Kagan, Burl Maple Veneer, 6 Doors, 2 Shelves, 96 x 108 In. 935.00
Cabinet, Wall, Curio, Golden Oak, Glass Door, Configured Shelving, 17 x 24 In. 290.00
Cabinet, Wall, Oak, Scrolled Crest, Paneled Door, Bun Feet, 24 1/2 x 14 x 8 In. 300.00
Cabinet, Walnut, 2 Paneled Doors, Block Feet, 45 x 43 1/2 In. 437.00
Cabinet, Walnut, 3 Glass Doors, Floral & Scroll Carving 1210.00
Cabinet, Walnut, 8 Drawers, 2 Cupboards, Projecting Panels, 17th Century, 80 In. 6325.00
Cabinet, Walnut, Mirrored Back, Adjustable Shelves, Lower Drawers, 96 In. 3000.00
Cabinet, William & Mary, Walnut, Rectangular, 24 x 26 x 14 In. 805.00
Candlestand, Birch, Hepplewhite, Tripod Base, Snake Feet, 28 x 17 In. 990.00
Candlestand, Birch, Square Top, Ovolo Corners, Splayed Feet, c.1820, 29 In. 690.00
Candlestand, Cherry Top, Birch, 3 Curved Legs, 27 1/2 x 15 1/4 x 15 1/2 In. 920.00
Candlestand, Cherry, Double Arm, Wood Screw, Cast Brass Candle Sockets, 15 1/2 In. .. 875.00
Candlestand, Cherry, Snake Feet, Turned Column, Round 1-Board Top, 17 x 24 In. 495.00
Candlestand, Cherry, Spider Legs, 28 1/2 x 16 3/4 In. 1210.00
Candlestand, Cherry, Vase & Ring-Turned Legs, 1840s, 28 1/2 In. 1840.00
Candlestand, Chippendale, Brown Finish, Tripod, Square 1-Board Top, 14 x 26 In. 880.00
Candlestand, Chippendale, Cherry, 4 Drawers, Down-Swept Legs, 1770, 26 In. 1610.00
Candlestand, Chippendale, Cherry, Snake Feet, Round, Dish Top, 15 x 28 In. 715.00
Candlestand, Chippendale, Cherry, Tripod Base, Slipper Feet, 28 x 17 In. 6325.00
Candlestand, Chippendale, Cherry, Tripod Base, Snake Feet, Square Top, 16 x 17 In. ... 550.00
Candlestand, Chippendale, Cherry, Tripod, Chip-Carved Knees, Gallery, 15 x 26 In. ... 1540.00
Candlestand, Chippendale, Curly Maple, 1-Board Top, Tripod, 15 x 24 In. 1045.00
Candlestand, Chippendale, Mahogany, Circular Top, Claw Feet, 29 In. 4025.00
Candlestand, Chippendale, Mahogany, Dish Top, Snake Feet, 27 1/4 In. 4600.00
Candlestand, Chippendale, Maple, 1-Board Dish Top, Tripod, 15 x 27 In. 990.00
Candlestand, Chippendale, Red, 1-Board Top, Tripod, Snake Feet, 13 In. 880.00
Candlestand, Classical, Mahogany, Hinged Top, Acanthus Legs, N.Y., 1825, 19 In. 1495.00
Candlestand, Curly Maple, Mahogany Inlay, Urn On Post, Carved Swags 3450.00
Candlestand, Dish Top, Walnut, Birdcage, Slipper Feet, Pennsylvania, 1770, 30 In. 4250.00
Candlestand, Federal, Cherry, 3 Down-Swept Feet, 1800, 28 In. 575.00
Candlestand, Federal, Mahogany, Shaped Top, Spiral Shaft, Saber-Reeded Legs 440.00
Candlestand, Federal, Maple, Octagonal Top, Spider Legs, 1800, 28 x 16 In. 1265.00
Candlestand, Federal, Maple, Square Top, Vase & Ring Post, Pad Feet, 25 In. 805.00
Candlestand, Federal, Tilt Top, Mahogany, Oval, Snake Feet, 1790, 28 In. 1265.00
Candlestand, Federal, Tilt Top, Mahogany, Reeded Legs, N.Y., 1810, 28 x 17 In. 1035.00
Candlestand, Hepplewhite Style, Tilt Top, Birch, c.1810, 41 1/2 In. 1400.00
Candlestand, Hepplewhite, Cherry Base, Pine Top, Tripod Base, 28 In. 385.00
Candlestand, Hepplewhite, Cherry, 1-Board Top, Ovolo Corner, 17 x 17 In. 2300.00
Candlestand, Hepplewhite, Cherry, Tripod, 1-Board Top, Refinished, 28 In. 385.00

Most furniture should be moved by two people. Ask for help. Dragging a table or chair is hard on the legs and arms. Arms are made to withstand downward force, not the upward force of lifting. Carry the chair by the bottom frame. Large cabinets should not be pushed across a floor. Remove drawers and loose shelves and lock any doors or tie them shut. I possible, lift the piece off the floor to move it.

Furniture, Chair, Belter, Laminated
Rosewood, Cornucopia, 1840s

Candlestand, Hepplewhite, Curly Maple, Tripod, Spider Legs, 16 x 17 x 27 In. 6325.0
Candlestand, Hepplewhite, Tilt Top, Curly Maple, 1-Board Top, Refinished, 15 In. 2915.0
Candlestand, Hepplewhite, Tilt Top, Mahogany, Checkerboard Insert, 18 1/2 In. 550.0
Candlestand, Hepplewhite, Tilt Top, Mahogany, Spider Legs, 16 x 28 In. 385.0
Candlestand, Mahogany, Circular Top, 3 Splayed Legs, 20 x 28 In. 489.0
Candlestand, Maple, Shaped Top, Cabriole Legs, Pad Feet, 26 3/4 In. 632.0
Candlestand, Maple, Square Top, Tripod Base, Slipper Feet 412.0
Candlestand, Queen Anne, Mahogany, Round, Dish Top, Tripod Legs, 28 In. 6900.0
Candlestand, Queen Anne, Maple, Cherry, Round Top, 18th Century, 27 In. 747.0
Candlestand, Queen Anne, Round Top, 15 x 15 1/2 In. 6820.0
Candlestand, Rohlfs, Oak, Hammered-Copper Fitting, 38 x 7 x 6 1/2 In. 1650.0
Candlestand, Scratch-Beaded Edge, Cabriole Base, Late 18th Century, 28 1/2 In. 862.0
Candlestand, Shaker, 3 Spider Legs, 18 x 17 1/2 In. 1150.0
Candlestand, Sheraton, Mahogany, 3 Legs, Oval Top, 19th Century, 27 In. 85.0
Candlestand, Tiger Maple, Square Top, Pedestal, Pad Feet, 19th Century, 25 1/2 In. 1150.0
Candlestand, Tilt Top, Cherry, Diamond-Shaped Inlay, Cock-Beaded Edge 300.0
Candlestand, Tilt Top, Cherry, Figured-Wood Veneer, 29 x 18 1/2 In. 247.0
Candlestand, Tilt Top, Chippendale, Birch, Tripod Base, 15 x 15 1/2 x 27 1/2 In. 470.0
Candlestand, Tilt Top, Mahogany, Serpentine, Ring-Turned Post, c.1810, 28 In. 430.0
Candlestand, Tilt Top, Queen Anne, Mahogany, Philadelphia, 1760 . . . . 9200.0
Candlestand, Tilt Top, Walnut, Spider Legs, Cut Corners, 17 1/2 x 23 In. 275.0
Candlestand, Windsor, Butternut, Poplar, Red Stain, Tripod Base, Dish Top, 29 In. 220.0
Canterbury, Burl Walnut, Victorian, c.1880, 40 1/2 x 30 In. 2400.0
Canterbury, Divided Top, Out-Scrolled Sides, Drawer, Ball Feet, 1860s, 25 In. 3450.0
Canterbury, Divided Top, Spindle Insets, Drawer, Casters, 1820s, 39 x 18 1/4 In. 5175.0
Canterbury, Regency Style, Rosewood, 1 Drawer, 20 x 21 x 13 1/3 In. 1380.0
Canterbury, Rosewood, Divided Top, Carrying Handle, Drawer, Casters, 18 3/4 In. 4312.0
Canterbury, Rosewood, Divided Top, Handhold, Fitted Drawer, 19 1/2 x 13 3/4 In. 4885.0
Canterbury, Walnut, 5 Sleeves, 4 Turned Ends, Drawer, Casters, 20 1/2 In. 770.0
Case, Map, Lid, Carved Ship's Wheel, 25 1/2 x 39 In. 605.0
Cellarette, Federal, Cherry, Hinged Rectangular Top, 1795, 37 3/4 In. 4600.0
Cellarette, Federal, Mahogany, Crossbanded Cuffs, Brass Caps, 1800, 27 In. 11500.0
Cellarette, George III, Mahogany, Boxwood, Ebony Stringing, Hinged Top, 3 Trays 1725.0
Cellarette, George III, Mahogany, Brassbound, Lead Lined, Sectioned, 28 x 18 In. 2875.0
Cellarette, George III, Mahogany, Brassbound, Octagonal, 15 1/4 x 13 x 13 In. 316.0
Cellarette, Georgian, Mahogany, Coffin Top, Centennial 1100.0
Cellarette, Hinged Arched Top, Plaque, Fitted Interior, Casters, 21 x 30 In. 1495.0
Cellarette, Mahogany, Panels With Lion's Masks, Ring Handles, 20 3/4 In. 8625.0
Cellarette, Mahogany, Stepped & Canted Lift Top, Tin Interior, 22 x 30 In. 2145.0
Cellarette, Majorelle, Marquetry, 3 Tiers, 1910, 49 In. 3375.0
Cellarette, Regency, Mahogany, Sarcophagus Shape, Paw Feet, 1820 . . . . 1265.0
Chair, Aalto, Birch, Web Seat & Back, 24 x 28 x 30 In. 90.0
Chair, Adams, Hepplewhite, Oval Backrest, 3 Vertical Straps, Carved Arms, 1800 . . . . . 1200.0
Chair, Adnet, Mahogany, High Square Back, Upholstered, Arms, 1930s, Pair 7475.0
Chair, Antler, Carved Animal Legs, Silk Seat, 36 In. 825.0

Chair, Arched Back, Down-Swept Padded Arms, Painted, Upholstered 4025.00
Chair, Arched Backrest, Aubusson, Down-Swept Padded Arms, Pair 4600.00
Chair, Arched Caned Back Continuing To Sides, Caned Seat, Green & Gray Paint 9200.00
Chair, Arched Top Rail, Reeded Supports, Painted, Upholstered Back, Padded Arms 5750.00
Chair, Arne Jacobsen, Swan, Fiberglass Shell, Wool, 30 x 20 x 30 In. 385.00
Chair, Arrow Back, Painted Freehand Floral & Fruit, Arms, 1820s, 33 1/2 In. 1380.00
Chair, Arrow Back, Yellow Striping, Floral On Crest, Arms, 44 1/2 In. 275.00
Chair, Art Deco, Bentwood, Upholstered Seat, Back, Arms, France, 1930s, 23 In. 230.00
Chair, Art Deco, Oak, Red Leatherette, 1930s, 30 x 36 In. 770.00
Chair, Art Deco, Square Backs, Tapered Legs, Rolled Arms, Pair 3737.00
Chair, Arts & Crafts, 3-Slat Back, Saddle Seat, Arms, Pair 185.00
Chair, Arts & Crafts, Cube, 4 Vertical Back Slats, 3 Slats Each Side, 33 x 33 In. 550.00
Chair, Arts & Crafts, Cube, 6 Slats, Screw Supports, 28 x 33 In. 220.00
Chair, Arts & Crafts, Cutout Top, 5 Spindle Back, Tacked-Down Leather, 36 In. 550.00
Chair, Arts & Crafts, Cutout Wide-Board Back, Plank Seat, 43 In. 220.00
Chair, Arts & Crafts, Quartersawn Oak, 9 Vertical Spindles, 36 In. 730.00
Chair, Balloon Back, Walnut, Carved, Cabriole Legs, Peg Feet, Pair 575.00
Chair, Banister Back, Black Paint, Gold Striping, 19th Century, 39 In. 210.00
Chair, Banister Back, Red Paint, Splint Seat, c.1800, Child's 165.00
Chair, Barcelona, Chrome Base, Leather, 29 x 30 x 32 In. 300.00
Chair, Baroque Revival, Walnut, Floral Brocade, 38 3/4 In., Pair 605.00
Chair, Baroque Style, Leather, Brass Tacks, Arms, c.1900 .... 5175.00
Chair, Baroque, Walnut, Continental, 18th Century, 47 In. 1725.00
Chair, Baroque, Walnut, Upholstered, Spain, 18th Century, 39 1/4 In., Pair 115.00
Chair, Beaded Edge On Crest & Stiles, Set Rail, 18th Century, 37 1/2 In., Pair 1610.00
Chair, Beechwood, Leather Back, Padded Arms, Voluted Supports, 1760s 9200.00
Chair, Beechwood, Louis XV, Upholstered Back, Carved Toes, 1750s 3740.00
Chair, Beechwood, Louis XV, Upholstered Back, Down-Swept Arms 2875.00
Chair, Beechwood, Rectangular Back, Upholstered, Padded Arms, 1730s, Pair 9200.00
Chair, Beechwood, Upholstered Foliate Back, Padded Arms, Pair 4890.00
Chair, Belter, Laminated Rosewood, Applied Crest, Arms 4500.00
Chair, Belter, Laminated Rosewood, Cornucopia, Arms ....*Illus* 10100.00
Chair, Bertoia, White Wire, Aluminum Cat's-Cradle Base, Pads, Pair 300.00
Chair, Bertoia, Wire Mesh, Chrome Base, Gold Fabric, 29 1/2 In. 82.00
Chair, Biedermeier, Fruitwood, Curved Open Back, Leather Seat, 1840 .... 1750.00
Chair, Biedermeier, Shaped Open Back, Upholstered Seat 115.00
Chair, Bow Back, Fretwork, Carved, Floral Design, Center Medallion 110.00
Chair, Brass Rococo Style, Scroll & Trellis Over Padded Back & Seat, Arms, Pair 2415.00
Chair, Brass, Vertical Splat, Butterflies On Grid, Needlepoint Cushion, c.1900 ...... 522.00
Chair, Bruno Mathesson, Bentwood, Woven Rope Support, 36 In. 660.00
Chair, Bugatti, Allover Inlay, Pewter, Bone, Vellum Seat, 1900, Pair 6560.00
Chair, Bugatti, Applied Strips Of Beaten Copper, Vellum Seat, 1900 .... 2070.00
Chair, Bugatti, Drum Back, Painted Vellum Sling, 1900, 2 Piece 5625.00
Chair, Bugatti, Ebonized Wood, Parchment, Copper, Pewter Inlay, 1900 .... 3160.00
Chair, Cabinetmaker's Sample, Plank Seat, Brown, Yellow, 1830-1850, 14 In. 2587.00
Chair, Campechy, Oak, Carved Crest, Casters, Late 19th Century 2310.00
Chair, Carved Figures Of Pharaoh & Priestess Back, Arms, Pair 8625.00
Chair, Carved Scrolled Border Surrounding Caned Slat Back, Caned Seat 82.00
Chair, Carved Shell, Leaf Design, Shield Back, Upholstered Seat 110.00
Chair, Cherry, Arched Curved Back, Pierced Splat, Open Arms, Rush Seat 550.00
Chair, Chestnut, Carved, Damask, Open Arms, 37 1/4 In. 990.00
Chair, Chippendale Style, Mahogany, Carved, Leather, Arms, 38 In. 410.00
Chair, Chippendale Style, Mahogany, Slip Seats, Pair 550.00
Chair, Chippendale, Birch, Cherry Finish, Slip Seat, Square Legs, 37 1/2 In., Pair 4620.00
Chair, Chippendale, Cedar, Serpentine Crest, Square Legs, 1760-1800, 18 x 38 In. 2530.00
Chair, Chippendale, Mahogany, 4 Pierced Ladders, Curved Arms 775.00
Chair, Chippendale, Mahogany, Ball & Claw Feet, 1760, Pair 1380.00
Chair, Chippendale, Mahogany, Cabriole Legs, Ball & Claw Feet, New York, 39 In. 1650.00
Chair, Chippendale, Mahogany, Carved Scroll, Pierced Splat, Upholstered, 39 In. 415.00
Chair, Chippendale, Mahogany, Compass Slip Seat, Ball Feet, 1750, 38 In. 17250.00
Chair, Chippendale, Mahogany, Crest, Pierced Shaped Splat, Molded Seat 495.00
Chair, Chippendale, Mahogany, Crest, Pierced Splat, Slip Seat, Ball & Claw Feet 1100.00
Chair, Chippendale, Mahogany, Flared Pierced Splat, Molded Seat, Stretcher 550.00

Chair, Chippendale, Mahogany, H-Stretcher, Pierced Splat, Upholstered Seat, 38 In. 138.00
Chair, Chippendale, Mahogany, Open Back, Serpentine Arms, Upholstered, Pair 1650.00
Chair, Chippendale, Mahogany, Pierced Corner Brackets, Pair 1760.00
Chair, Chippendale, Mahogany, Pierced Strapwork Splat, Pad Feet, Pair 690.00
Chair, Chippendale, Mahogany, Ribbon Slats & Crest, Rush Seat, 39 1/4 In. 93.00
Chair, Chippendale, Mahogany, Ribbonback, Upholstered Seat, 38 In. 315.00
Chair, Chippendale, Mahogany, Serpentine Crest, Boston, 1770, 17 x 37 In., Pair 8050.00
Chair, Chippendale, Mahogany, Serpentine Shell Crest, Bowfront Seat, 1770 .... 1840.00
Chair, Chippendale, Mahogany, Slip Seat, Claw & Ball Feet, Pair 2750.00
Chair, Chippendale, Walnut, Acanthus, Shell Seat, Cabriole Legs, 1755 .... 3740.00
Chair, Chippendale, Walnut, Ball Feet, Penna., 1760, 17 x 40 1/2 In. 3450.00
Chair, Chippendale, Walnut, Cartouche Crest, Rocaille Seat, 47 In. 400.00
Chair, Chippendale, Walnut, Carved Crest, Vase Splat, Ball & Claw Feet, c.1755 .... 2750.00
Chair, Chippendale, Walnut, Poplar, 3-Ribbed Pierced Splat, Slip Seat 245.00
Chair, Chippendale, Walnut, Serpentine Crest, Slip Seat, 1740-1760, 40 In. 9200.00
Chair, Chippendale, Walnut, Slip Seat, Cabriole Legs, 1770, 17 In. 5175.00
Chair, Choir, Oak, Curved Top Rail, Shaped Hinged Seat, France 920.00
Chair, Circular Wicker Seat, Canvas Back, Black Enamel, Tubular, Pair 1045.00
Chair, Classical, Mahogany, Tub-Shaped, Curved Back, 4 Turned Legs 605.00
Chair, Corner, Bugatti, Parchment, Copper Inlay, c.1900 .... 7475.00
Chair, Corner, Chippendale Style, Mahogany, Pierced Slats, Slip Seat, 30 3/4 In. 632.00
Chair, Corner, Chippendale, Rush Seat, Original Red Paint, 33 In. 1350.00
Chair, Corner, Chippendale, Walnut, Cabriole Legs, Vase Splats, Slip Seat, 32 In. 3630.00
Chair, Corner, Eastlake, Upholstered, c.1880 .... 385.00
Chair, Corner, George III, Elm, Drop-In Seat, 4 Chamfered Legs, 18th Century 1095.00
Chair, Corner, George III, Oak, Elm, 4 Turned Legs, Early 19th Century 3220.00
Chair, Corner, Rohlfs, Cutout Vine Scroll Legs, Original Finish, 28 x 19 In. 3850.00
Chair, Curved Crest Rail, Bamboo Slat Seat 110.00
Chair, Curved Hoop Back, Spindles, Plank Seat, Child's, 27 1/2 In. 65.00
Chair, D. Deskey, Upholstered Back, Seat, Cream, Light Brown Curved Arms, 1931 .... 5175.00
Chair, E. Wormley, Mahogany, Upholstered, 22 x 20 x 34 In. 770.00
Chair, E. Wormley, Mahogany, Velvet Tufted, 32 In. 65.00
Chair, E. Wormley, Sculpted Walnut, Upholstered, Arms, 29 In., Pair 1320.00
Chair, Eames, Fiberglass, Watermelon-Colored Shell, Rope Outline, X-Shaped Base 138.00
Chair, Eames, Soft Pad, Tan Leather, Aluminum, Arms, 32 In. 665.00
Chair, Eames, Time Life, Leather Cushions, Cast Aluminum, 4-Prong Base, 33 In. 546.00
Chair, Eames, Wire, Black Fiberglass Shell, Zinc Struts, 25 x 18 x 24 In. 385.00
Chair, Eames, Womb, Upholstered 1600.00
Chair, Eastlake, Carved Crest, Medallion Backrest, Upholstered 38.00
Chair, Eastlake, Sawtooth Inlay, Carved Crest, Arms, Skirt 187.00
Chair, Easy, Mahogany, Carved, Loose Cushion Seat, Padded Arms, 1930s 445.00
Chair, Ebony, Mermaids Over Spindle Back, Caned Seat, Indo-Portuguese, 1690s 2875.00
Chair, Edwardian, Black Paint, c.1900, 36 In., Pair 430.00
Chair, Empire, Crest Over Straight Stiles, Caned Seat, 19th Century, Pair 259.00
Chair, Empire, Mahogany, Saber Leg, Slip Seats, Arms, 34 In., Pair 715.00
Chair, Eykes, Morris, Open Arms, Drop-In Seat, Saddle Leather, Label, 37 x 29 In. 660.00
Chair, F. Albini, Maple, Open Square Arms, Upholstered, 29 1/2 In., Pair 880.00
Chair, Fanback, Serpentine Crest Rail, 7 Spindles, Saddle Seat, Arms, Painted, 1780 ... 546.00
Chair, Faux Rosewood, Out-Scrolled Top Rail, Down-Swept Arms, Tufted 1430.00
Chair, Faux Rosewood, Reclining, Padded Adjustable Backrest & Seat, 1860s 6900.00
Chair, Federal, Mahogany, Bowed Seat, Upholstered, 17 In. 4600.00
Chair, Federal, Mahogany, Serpentine Crest, Slip Seat, Side, N.Y., 1795, 18 In., Pair 1035.00
Chair, Flint Co., Mahogany, 10 Vertical Back Slats, 8 Vertical Side Slats, 36 In. 460.00
Chair, Floral Crest, Pierced Cartouche-Shaped Splat, Shaped Seat, Painted, Pair 575.00
Chair, Floral Crest, Pierced Handhold, Plank Seat, Mustard Paint, 34 1/2 In. Pair 920.00
Chair, Folding, George III, Mahogany, Caned Metamorphic, 1800, 33 1/4 In. 316.00
Chair, Folding, Yoke Arms, Paneled Splat, Red & Gold Lacquer 715.00
Chair, Frank Lloyd Wright, Hexagonal Back, Upholstered, 1930s, 38 In. 5225.00
Chair, Frank Lloyd Wright, Naugahyde, Arms, 20 x 22 x 41 In. 2200.00
Chair, Fruitwood, Fluted Supports, Padded Arms, Upholstered, Pair 6325.00
Chair, G. Gaw, Bamboo Turnings, Birdcage Arms, 1798-1824 .... 440.00
Chair, G. Stickley, 4 Horizontal Slats, Arched Stretcher, Rope Seat, 37 In. 350.00
Chair, G. Stickley, H-Back, Drop-In Seat, 40 In. 440.00

Chair, G. Stickley, Ladder Back, 3 Slat Back, Rush Seat, 38 In. 200.00
Chair, G. Stickley, Ladder Back, Rush Seat, Red Decal, Arms, 35 1/2 In., Pair 715.00
Chair, G. Stickley, Leather Seat & Back, 27 x 23 x 37 In. 665.00
Chair, G. Stickley, Leather Tacks, Yellow, 35 x 26 x 21 3/4 In. 750.00
Chair, G. Stickley, No. 306, Ladder Back, Leather Seat, 1904, 36 In. 495.00
Chair, G. Stickley, No. 308, H-Back, Drop-In Seat, 17 x 15 x 40 In. 360.00
Chair, G. Stickley, No. 324, 5 Slats, Leather, 29 x 39 In. 1760.00
Chair, G. Stickley, No. 328, Cube, Wide-Slat Side & Back, 28 In. 3300.00
Chair, G. Stickley, No. 360, Quartersawn Oak, Arms, Red Decal, 37 x 27 In., Pair 3965.00
Chair, G. Stickley, No. 366, 3 Vertical Slats, Red Decal, Arms, 26 x 22 In., Pair 1540.00
Chair, G. Stickley, No. 369, Vertical Slats Under Arms, Drop-In Seat, 38 x 32 In. 6600.00
Chair, G. Stickley, No. 376, Mahogany, Cushion, 11-Slat Back, 9-Slat Arms, 49 In. 2860.00
Chair, G. Stickley, No. 1295, Leather, Tacks, 19 x 17 x 34 In. 3300.00
Chair, G. Stickley, No. 1303, Leather, Tacks 550.00
Chair, G. Stickley, Oak, Arms, 1906-1908, Pair 1800.00
Chair, G. Stickley, Oak, Roped Seat, Red Decal, 1903, 36 1/2 In. 7475.00
Chair, G. Stickley, Rabbit-Ear Design, Red Decal, Arms, 23 x 18 In., Pair 935.00
Chair, George I, Walnut, Shepherd's Crook Arms, Drop-In Seat, Pair 2990.00
Chair, George II, Mahogany, Balloon Seat, Volute Cabriole Legs, Pad Feet 2587.00
Chair, George II, Walnut, Shell-Carved Crest, Open Arms, Needlepoint 8050.00
Chair, George II, Walnut, Slip Seat, Cabriole Legs, 1750 .... 660.00
Chair, George II, Walnut, Upholstered Seat, Cabriole Legs, 1730, 50 1/4 In. 3450.00
Chair, George III, Giltwood, Serpentine Seat, Padded Backrest & Arms, 1775 .... 2300.00
Chair, George III, Giltwood, Shield Back, Upholstered Seat, Carved Arms, 1780 .... 5750.00
Chair, George III, Mahogany, Arched Back, Down-Swept Arms, 37 In. 1100.00
Chair, George III, Mahogany, Arms, Upholstered, 1730s, 36 In. 1495.00
Chair, George III, Mahogany, Caned, Loose Leather Cushions, 40 In. 3105.00
Chair, George III, Mahogany, Padded Arms & Back, c.1770 .... 3450.00
Chair, George III, Mahogany, Ribbonback, Celadon Silk Seat, Pair 750.00
Chair, George III, Mahogany, Scrolled Arms, Needlepoint Seat, Square Legs 5520.00
Chair, George III, Mahogany, Serpentine Backrest, Square Legs, 19th Century 10350.00
Chair, George III, Mahogany, Upholstered, Arms, 1800, 3 1/2 In. 2100.00
Chair, George III, Molded Flower Head, Padded Arms & Back, c.1770 .... 3450.00
Chair, George III, Walnut, Ladder Back, Serpentine Splat, Chamfered Square Legs 290.00
Chair, Gillow & Co., Aesthetic Movement, Ebony, Spindled Crest, Pair 2860.00
Chair, Giltwood, Curved Back, Sides & Seat, Upholstered, Padded Arms 8050.00
Chair, Giltwood, Paneled Back Continuing To Padded Arms, c.1900, Pair 5175.00
Chair, Giltwood, Slipper, Cut Velvet, 1880-1890, 34 In. 375.00
Chair, Giltwood, Upholstered Back, Arched Top Rail, Padded Arms, 1780s 6325.00
Chair, Gio Ponti, Walnut, Sculptural, Upholstered Seat, Arms, 21 x 21 x 31 In. 90.00
Chair, Gothic Revival, Oak, Quatrefoil-Cutout Back Slat, Arms, 36 1/2 In. 275.00
Chair, Greene & Greene, Mahogany, 10-Slat Back, Flint Co., 36 In. 485.00
Chair, Guitar, Piero Fornasetti, Hand Painted, Pair 5900.00
Chair, Half Spindle, Plank Seat, Tan Paint, Flowers, Penna., 32 In., Pair 495.00
Chair, Harden, Vertical Slats To Back & Sides, Leather Seat, Arms, 40 x 30 In. 220.00
Chair, Hardwood, Banister Back, Turned Legs, Rush Seat, 17 3/4 x 43 1/2 In. 525.00
Chair, Hepplewhite Style, Arrow Back, Crewel Embroidery 385.00
Chair, Hepplewhite, Mahogany, Upholstered Seat, Tapered Legs, 19 x 40 In. 40.00
Chair, Herman Miller, Tubular Metal Legs, Black Wool, 25 x 30 x 29 In. 550.00
Chair, Hickory, Ash, Chestnut, Comb Back, Carved Terminals, Handholds 5465.00
Chair, Hitchcock, Black Paint, Gold Stenciling, Bamboo Turnings, Plank Seat, Pair 185.00
Chair, Hitchcock, Stencil, Vase-Form Splat, Turned Legs, 19th Century, Pair 805.00
Chair, Horn, Victorian, 19th Century, 39 1/2 In. 920.00
Chair, Huret, Metal, Velvet, Spiral Legs, Rounded Back, c.1865, Child's, 20 In. 2800.00
Chair, Italian Rococo Style, Giltwood, Upholstered Backrest, & Seat, Miniature 2300.00
Chair, Jabes Delano, Molded Crest Rail, 7 Spindles, Arms, Plank Seat 1950.00
Chair, Jacaranda, Rococo, Pierced Foliate, Cabriole Legs, Pad Feet, Pair 9200.00
Chair, Jacobean Style, Walnut, Carved Back, Turned Columns, Arms, 19th Century 250.00
Chair, Jacobsen, Egg, Fritz Hansen, Sculptured, Wool, Aluminum Tilt Base, 42 In. 1760.00
Chair, Joe Columbo, Elda, Swiveling, Fiberglass Shell, Leather, Arms, 1970s, 40 In. 1100.00
Chair, L. & J.G. Stickley, Corbel Supports, Drop-In Seat, 27 x 22 x 37 In. 360.00
Chair, L. & J.G. Stickley, No. 420, 4-Slat Back, Cushions, Arms, 31 x 30 x 42 In. 1210.00
Chair, Ladder Back, Black Paint, 4 Slats, Rush Seat, 16 1/2 x 44 In. 220.00

Chair, Ladder Back, Green Paint, 4 Slat Back, Rush Seat, Philadelphia, c.1840 . . . . 1980.00

Chair, Ladder Back, Maple, 5 Arched Slats, Turned Legs, Rush Seat, 41 In. 715.00

Chair, Ladder Back, Maple, Red Stained, Rush Seat, Turned Legs, 18 x 40 In. 1150.00

Chair, Ladder Back, Oak, Mushroom Finials, Brown, Black, Yellow, 15 x 43 In. 920.00

Chair, Ladder Back, Red Paint, White Striping, 3 Slats, Paper Rush Seat, 34 In. 100.00

Chair, Ladder Back, White Paint, Splint Seat, 13 In. 195.00

Chair, Le Corbusier, Chrome, Tubular, Vinyl, Arms, c.1968, 25 In. 460.00

Chair, Limbert, Cutout Handle, Plank Back, Leather Seat, 34 In. 3300.00

Chair, Limbert, Drop-In Seat, Arms, Branded, 38 In. 255.00

Chair, Limbert, Horizontal Slat Back, Upholstered, Label, 35 In. 455.00

Chair, Limbert, No. 693, 4-Slat Back, Corbel Under Arms, Leather Cushion, 37 In. 1430.00

Chair, Limbert, No. 827, 5-Slat Back, Drop-In Seat, Branded, 38 In. 255.00

Chair, Limbert, No. 1833, Leather Seat, 23 x 16 3/4 In. 627.00

Chair, Limbert, Notched Top Rail, Arched Support, 15 x 40 In. 880.00

Chair, Limbert, Slant Arms, Plaid Fabric Cushion, 36 x 31 In. 2910.00

Chair, Lolling, Chippendale, Mahogany, Acanthus Knees, Hairy Ball & Claw Feet 1210.00

Chair, Lolling, Chippendale, Mahogany, Square Legs, 39 In. 1760.00

Chair, Lolling, Federal, Mahogany, Serpentine Crest, Tapered Legs, 1795 . . . . 4025.00

Chair, Lolling, Federal, Mahogany, Upholstered Seat, Tapered Legs, 1790, 43 In. 980.00

Chair, Lolling, Mahogany, H-Stretcher, Wool, 45 In. 2750.00

Chair, Louis XIII, Floral, Square Seat, Block Turned Legs, Acanthus Arms 1725.00

Chair, Louis XV Style, Walnut, Upholstered, Late 19th Century, Child's 632.00

Chair, Louis XV, Cartouche Backrest, Foliate Rail, Cabriole Legs, Pale Blue, Arms 8050.00

Chair, Louis XV, Floral Crest Rail, Cabriole Legs, Padded Arms, Pair 3680.00

Chair, Louis XV, Floral Crest, Floral Skirt, Cabriole Legs, Arm 575.00

Chair, Louis XV, Fruitwood, Foliate Scroll Crest, Cabriole Legs, Arms, Pair 385.00

Chair, Louis XV, Giltwood, Padded Arms, Cabriole Legs, 1754 . . . . 4600.00

Chair, Louis XV, Mahogany, Foliate-Carved Crest Rail, Cabriole Legs, Arms 207.00

Chair, Louis XV, Pierced Floral Crest, Rosette Skirt, Fluted Legs, Side 605.00

Chair, Louis XV, Upholstered Backrest, Padded Arms, Upholstered Seat, Pair 4600.00

Chair, Louis XV, Walnut, Arched Ladder Backrest, Cabriole Legs, 1750s, Pair 3165.00

Chair, Louis XV, Walnut, Parcel Gilt, Arms, Late 19th Century, 34 /12 In. 290.00

Chair, Louis XV, Walnut, Scrolled Crest, Damask, Arms, 38 In. 1150.00

Chair, Louis XVI Style, Carved, Upholstered, Arms, 34 3/4 In. 330.00

Chair, Louis XVI Style, Giltwood, Arched Crest Rail, Curved, Padded Arms, Pair 7475.00

Chair, Louis XVI Style, Mahogany, Chinoiserie, Needlepoint, Black, Arms 1840.00

Chair, Louis XVI Style, Mahogany, Ribbon Carved, Chinoiserie, Black Ground, Arms . . . 1380.00

Chair, Louis XVI Style, Oval Back, Upholstered 630.00

Chair, Louis XVI, Beechwood, Creme Silk, Arms, 36 1/2 In. 800.00

Chair, Louis XVI, Carved, Cane Back & Seat, Arms, 1920s, 31 In. 220.00

Chair, Louis XVI, Floral Seat, Tapered Legs, Padded Arms 575.00

Chair, Louis XVI, Giltwood, Oval Back, Carved Leaf Tips, Upholstered, Pair 4025.00

Chair, Louis XVI, Mahogany, Cream, Cotton Seat, Padded Arms 431.00

Furniture, Chair, Mission, Oak,
Pool Hall, Pair, 1 shown

Furniture, Chair, Queen Anne,
Walnut, Vase Splat, Rush Seat, Arms

**Inept restorers should
remember that fresh
bloodstains can be
removed from wood
with a rag soaked in
hydrogen peroxide.**

Chair, Louis XVI, Mahogany, Vertical Splats, Arms, Upholstered Seat 9200.00
Chair, Louis XVI, Oval Back, Leaf-Carved Rail, Upholstered, Pair 2300.00
Chair, Louis XVI, Silk Damask Seat, Padded Arms, Pair 865.00
Chair, Louis XVI, Tapered Backrest, Padded Arms, Painted, Pair 2875.00
Chair, Louis XVI, Walnut, Serpentine Seat, Upholstered Oval Backrest, Miniature 4312.00
Chair, Mahogany, Adjustable Bookrest, Gothic Backrest, Upholstered Seat 9200.00
Chair, Mahogany, Arched Back, Bowfront Seat, Stop-Fluted Legs, Upholstered, Pair 9775.00
Chair, Mahogany, Balloon Back, Padded Arms, Pair 357.00
Chair, Mahogany, Carved Splat, Floral Needlepoint, 1930s 65.00
Chair, Mahogany, Carved, Shaped Back, Shield-Shaped Seat, Curved Arms 132.00
Chair, Mahogany, Cherub Profiles, Medallion, Hand Carved, Griffin Arms 1745.00
Chair, Mahogany, Cock Fighting, Collapsible & Adjustable Back Shelf, Leather 2200.00
Chair, Mahogany, Colored Wooden Flowers & Birds Inlay, 19th Century, 46 In. 1485.00
Chair, Mahogany, Foliate & Scroll Crest, Tufted Backrest, Padded Arms, 1835, Pair 8050.00
Chair, Mahogany, Foliate-Carved Crest, Saber Legs, 1840, Pair 1430.00
Chair, Mahogany, Hooded, Carved, Horsehair, Arms 6037.00
Chair, Mahogany, Loose Cushioned Seat, Padded Arms, 1880s, Pair 9775.00
Chair, Mahogany, Metamorphic, Flips To Become Steps, c.1820 .... 5900.00
Chair, Mahogany, Shaped Crest Rail, Acanthus Legs, Open Arms 1485.00
Chair, Mahogany, Wheel Back, Caned Front, Open Arms, Cushion, 1770s 2300.00
Chair, Maple, Ash, Poplar, Low Back, Vase & Ring Turnings, Saddle Seat, Arms 1265.00
Chair, Maple, Ash, Turned Stiles, 3 Arched Slats, Mushroom Handholds, 38 1/2 In. 2415.00
Chair, Maple, Birch, Shouldered Splat Over Vase-Form Splat, Rush Seat, 1730 .... 805.00
Chair, Marcel Breuer, Tubular Chrome, Hard Black Leather Arms, Pair 935.00
Chair, Mingazzi, Figural, Iron, Wicker Seat, 1950, Child's, 38 In., Pair 600.00
Chair, Mission, Oak, Pool Hall, Pair ....*Illus* 715.00
Chair, Morris, 18-Spindle Arms 1150.00
Chair, Morris, Arts & Crafts, 4-Slat Back, 4 Slats Under Arms, 30 x 40 In. 1210.00
Chair, Morris, C. Stickley, Adjustable Back, 4 Slats Under Arms, 39 In. 770.00
Chair, Morris, J.M. Young, 5 Vertical Disc Slats, Paper Label, 35 x 29 x 37 In. 2245.00
Chair, Morris, L. & J.G. Stickley, No 410, Leather Cushion, Bent Arms, 39 In. 6000.00
Chair, Morris, L. & J.G. Stickley, No. 470, Adjustable Back, Cushions, 40 In. 2530.00
Chair, Morris, L. & J.G. Stickley, Paddle Arms, Drop-In Spring Seat 6600.00
Chair, Morris, Lifetime, Quartersawn Oak, Leather Cushions, Arms, 41 1/2 In. 3305.00
Chair, Morris, McHugh, Adjustable Back, x Design Under Arms & Back, 42 In. 240.00
Chair, Morris, Quartersawn Oak, Out-Turned Arms, Spindle Supports, Paw Feet 110.00
Chair, Morris, Walnut, 4 Slats, Spring Cushion, Paper Label, 32 x 36 x 42 In. 2970.00
Chair, Morris, Walnut, Adjustable Back, 38 x 46 x 44 In. 360.00
Chair, Musical, Plays When Seated, Cane Bottom, Victorian 475.00
Chair, Musical, Walnut, Goat & Reindeer Design, Child's, 28 In. 172.00
Chair, N. Cherner, Bentwood, Continuous Seat & Back, Pair 865.00
Chair, Neoclassical, Walnut, Caned, Arms, Italy, c.1775, 39 1/2 In. 1840.00
Chair, Neoclassical, Walnut, Urn, Wheat-Carved Splat, Tapered Legs, Italy, 34 In. 1100.00
Chair, Oak, Leather Back, Carved & Tooled Leather Seat, 1880s, 57 In. 605.00
Chair, Oak, Ogee Arches, Carved Floral Motif, England, 1870s 1380.00
Chair, Old Hickory, Arms, 35 x 24 1/2 In. 725.00
Chair, Openwork Splat, Rush Seat, Saber Legs, Italy, Pair 375.00
Chair, Oriental, Emperor & Empress, Rosewood, Carved, Arms, Victorian, Pair 2475.00
Chair, Otto Wagner, Bentwood, Bowed Back, Paneled Seat, 1906 .... 1150.00
Chair, Out-Scrolled Back, Down-Swept Arms, Fluted Supports, Upholstered, Pair 4600.00
Chair, Out-Scrolled Back, Down-Swept Padded Arms, Painted, Upholstered, Pair 6325.00
Chair, Padded Oval Backrest, Padded Open Arms, Leather, 1780 .... 4600.00
Chair, Painted, Freehand Flower, Foliage, Plank Seat, c.1820, Pair 400.00
Chair, Painted, Parcel Gilt, Scrolled Rail, Pierced Back Splat, Dolphins, Pair 2875.00
Chair, Papier-Mache, Overall Mother-Of-Pearl Inlay, Peg Feet 260.00
Chair, Papier-Mache, Painted Landscape Vignette 7425.00
Chair, Pennsylvania Dutch, Oak, Floral Square Medallion, Square Legs 635.00
Chair, Pine, Hinged Seat, Raised On Trestle Supports, 28 In. 2530.00
Chair, Plattner, Wire Base, Brown Wool, 30 1/2 x 36 In. 360.00
Chair, Porter's, Mahogany, Paneled Back, Sides, Upholstered Arms, 1880s, 72 In. 9200.00
Chair, Pottier & Stymus, Renaissance Revival, Walnut, Arms, New York, 1870, 38 In. 1100.00
Chair, Prairie, Phoenix, 13-Spindle Back, 11-Spindle Arms, Leather, 36 In. 3575.00
Chair, Queen Anne, Cherry, Maple, Yoke Crest, Pad Feet, 1730, 18 1/2 In. 3162.00

Chair, Queen Anne, Mahogany, Balloon Seat, Pierced Splat, Crest, Ball & Claw Feet 1210.00
Chair, Queen Anne, Mahogany, Balloon Slip Seat, Pad Feet, Boston, 1755, 39 In. 5175.00
Chair, Queen Anne, Mahogany, Horseshoe Slip Seat, Cabriole Legs, 41 In. 13800.00
Chair, Queen Anne, Mahogany, Red Velvet Slip Seat, Miniature, 24 1/2 In. 165.00
Chair, Queen Anne, Mahogany, Upholstered Compass Seat, 1740, 45 In. 2185.00
Chair, Queen Anne, Maple, Carved Yoke Crest, Rush Seat, 1740-1760, 40 In. 10925.00
Chair, Queen Anne, Maple, Red Stain, Rush Seat, 1740, 17 3/4 In. 575.00
Chair, Queen Anne, Maple, Spoon Back, Spanish Feet, Rush Seat, 18th Century 880.00
Chair, Queen Anne, Shell-Carved Crest, Balloon Seat, c.1740 .... 2750.00
Chair, Queen Anne, Walnut, Back-Scrolled Crest, Vase-Form Splat, Drop-In Seat 7495.00
Chair, Queen Anne, Walnut, Block & Turned Stretcher, Pair 3850.00
Chair, Queen Anne, Walnut, Carved Base Splat, Cabriole Legs, 18th Century 770.00
Chair, Queen Anne, Walnut, Pierced Splat & Crest, Cabriole Legs, Slip Seat, Boston 3870.00
Chair, Queen Anne, Walnut, Upholstered Arms, 18th Century, 43 In. 1725.00
Chair, Queen Anne, Walnut, Upholstered Seat, Pad Feet, 39 In. 1035.00
Chair, Queen Anne, Walnut, Vase Splat, Rush Seat, Arms ....*Illus* 2420.00
Chair, Queen Anne, Walnut, Vase-Form Splat, Cabriole Legs, 18 In. 3740.00
Chair, Rectangular Padded Back, Upholstered Seat & Arms, Pad Feet 690.00
Chair, Regency Style, Painted, Gilt Design, Open Arms, Pair 1955.00
Chair, Regency, Japanned, Painted Crest Rail, Caned Seat 460.00
Chair, Regency, Mahogany, Brass Inlay, Scroll, Foliate Design, Saber Legs, Pair 920.00
Chair, Regency, Mahogany, Curved Paneled Crests, Slip Seat, 1820, Pair 1760.00
Chair, Regency, Walnut, Padded Arms, Serpentine Seat, Leaf Feet 2300.00
Chair, Renaissance Revival, Oak, Throne, Carved 4000.00
Chair, Ribbon-Carved Splats, Scrolled Arms, Upholstered Seat, Pair 920.00
Chair, Rocker, is listed under Rocker in this category.
Chair, Rococo Revival, Floral, Nut-Carved Crest, Cabriole Legs, 1870 .... 1725.00
Chair, Rococo, Rosewood, Scroll, Rocaille Design, Cabriole Legs, N.Y., 1850-1860 ..... 3300.00
Chair, Rohde, Bentwood, Upholstered Seat & Back, 16 x 19 x 32 In. 45.00
Chair, Rosewood, Peach-Shaped Splat, Carved Peonies & Butterflies, Pair 198.00
Chair, Roycroft, No. 030 1/2, Wide-Slat Back, Leather Seat, 40 In. 550.00
Chair, Roycroft, No. 030, Hourglass Back Panel, Mackmurdo Feet, 43 In., Pair 2750.00
Chair, Roycroft, Oak, 3 Vertical Slats, 4 Legs, 1906, 47 In. 2070.00
Chair, S. Courtois, Painted, Padded Arms, Fluted Supports, 1780s, Pair 3162.00
Chair, Satinwood, Continuous Arms, 18th Century 3450.00
Chair, Savonarola, Lion's-Head Hand Rests, 19th Century 247.00
Chair, Scroll Crest, Needlepoint Seat, Victorian 60.00
Chair, Serpentine Front, Painted, Upholstered Backrest, Out-Scrolled Arms, Pair 5750.00
Chair, Shaker Style, Wooden Peg Construction, Rush Seat, 38 1/2 In. 55.00
Chair, Shaker, Harvard, Child's, 24 In. 495.00
Chair, Shaker, Ladder Back, 3 Horizontal Slats, Cloth Seat, 40 x 16 In. 144.00
Chair, Shaker, Maple, Turned Acorn Finials, Rush Seat, 19th Century 115.00
Chair, Shaker, No. 4, Maple, Taped Seat, Label, 35 1/2 In. 632.00
Chair, Sheraton, Curly Maple, Cane Seat, 34 In., Pair 945.00
Chair, Sheraton, Floral, Red & Black Graining, 33 3/4 In., Pair 495.00
Chair, Sheraton, Maple, Balloon Seats, 33 1/2 In., Pair 220.00
Chair, Shop Of The Crafters, Stylized Flower, Splayed Legs, 18 x 19 x 43 In. 4180.00
Chair, Sleepy Hollow, Turned Feet, Beaded Molding, Brocade, Arms 55.00
Chair, Slipper, Rococo Revival, Rosewood, Upholstered Seat, 1860 .... 1395.00
Chair, Spindle Arms & Apron, Plank Footrest, Chinese, 35 1/2 In. 220.00
Chair, Spindle Back, Brace Back, Saddle Seat, Continuous Arms, 34 1/2 In. 770.00
Chair, Steamer, Teakwood, Brass Fittings, Oil Finish 375.00
Chair, Stickley Brothers, No. 2422, Round Top, Flared Base, 4 Leaves, 54 In. 2310.00
Chair, Stickley Brothers, Oak, Horizontal Crest Rail, 3 Vertical Splats, Pair 137.00
Chair, Studio 65, Foam, Ionic Capital, Capitello, 1971, 44 x 52 x 30 In. 1100.00
Chair, Teakwood, Carved Dragon Figures On Back Slat, Upholstered Seat, Oriental 220.00
Chair, Teakwood, Carved Elephants, Birds, Fish & Man, Pierced Back, 47 3/4 In. 220.00
Chair, Teakwood, Red-Brown Lacquer Traces, Arms, China, 46 1/2 In., Pair 1430.00
Chair, Thomas Brooks, Gothic Revival, Rosewood, Pair 1650.00
Chair, Thonet, Bentwood, 3 Holes Above 3 Dowel Spindles, 20 1/2 In., Pair 3680.00
Chair, Thonet, Bentwood, Stacking, Cutout Handle On Back, Child's, Pair 440.00
Chair, Throne, Upholstered Backrest, Carved Top Rail, Down-Swept Arms 2875.00
Chair, Tiger Maple, Maple, Serpentine Crest Rail, Rush Seat, 1790s, 39 In. 430.00

Chair, Tiger Maple, Maple, Shaped Crest Rail, Trapezoidal Rush Seat, 1780s, 42 In. 632.00
Chair, Vase-Form Splat, Rush Seat, Paintbrush Feet, Pair 9200.00
Chair, Wainscot, Chip-Carved Back Panel, Floral Design, Arms, Pair 440.00
Chair, Wallace Nutting, No. 456, Arms 1265.00
Chair, Wallace Nutting, Windsor, No. 408, Knuckle Arms 715.00
Chair, Walnut, Bronze Finials, Upholstered, Pair 1375.00
Chair, Walnut, Cartouche-Shaped Back, Scrolled Toes, Upholstered Seat, 38 In. 258.00
Chair, Walnut, Carved & Incised Back, 2 Vertical Splats, Needlepoint Spring Seat 55.00
Chair, Walnut, Carved Front Legs, Tapestry, 19th Century 660.00
Chair, Walnut, Finger Carved, Fruit & Foliage Crest, Needlepoint, 41 In. 470.00
Chair, Walnut, Finger Carved, Upholstered, Arms, Victorian, 44 In. 305.00
Chair, Walnut, Floral Roundel, Drop-In Rush Seat, 1905, Pair 1125.00
Chair, Walnut, Leather Seat, Brass Studs, Rope Turnings 80.00
Chair, Walnut, Open Back, Suspended Leather Seat, Scrolled Arms, Spain, Pair 1265.00
Chair, Walnut, Padded Back, Acanthus Finials, Wooden Arms, Upholstered Seat 7475.00
Chair, Walnut, Pierced Splat, Cabriole Legs, England, c.1800, Child's, 26 In. 2250.00
Chair, Walnut, Rosewood Graining, Fruit & Foliage Crest, Tufted Seat & Back, Arms ... 210.00
Chair, Walnut, Serpentine Spooned Crest Rail, Vase-Form Splat, Slip Seat, c.1740 ...... 4600.00
Chair, Walnut, Shaped Crest, Vase-Form Splat, Down-Scrolled Arms, 37 In. 115.00
Chair, Walnut, Shaped Shell & Foliate Crest, Caned Center & Seat 200.00
Chair, Walnut, Sleepy Hollow, Finger Carved, Brocade, Arms, 40 1/2 In. 100.00
Chair, Walnut, Sleepy Hollow, Floral Brocade, 35 3/4 In. 330.00
Chair, Walnut, Vase-Form Splat, Out-Swept Scrolled Arms, Rush Seat 2420.00
Chair, Walnut, Yorkshire, 19th Century, Child's, Pair 690.00
Chair, Westport Type, Light Green Over Dark Green 485.00
Chair, William & Mary, Birch, Square-Board Seat, Stump Feet, 37 x 18 1/4 In. 1840.00
Chair, William & Mary, Black Paint, Banister Back, Rush Seat, 44 In. 1725.00
Chair, William & Mary, Ebonized, Scroll Back, Damask Seat, 53 1/2 In. 2415.00
Chair, William & Mary, Oak, Caned, Arms, Late 19th Century, 49 In., Pair 865.00
Chair, William & Mary, Pierced Crest Over Caned Backrest, Arms, c.1695 .... 4600.00
Chair, William & Mary, Slat Back, Woven Seat, Turned Arms, New Jersey 1210.00
Chair, William & Mary, Walnut, Scrolled Crest, Foliate, 47 In. 1380.00
Chair, Windsor, 6 Spindles, Statehouse, Arms, Hartford, Conn. 9775.00
Chair, Windsor, 7 Spindles, Black Paint, Splayed Base, Saddle Seat 3265.00
Chair, Windsor, 7 Spindles, Upturned Pad Ears, Plank Seat, Black, 34 3/4 In. 2100.00
Chair, Windsor, 8 Spindles, Elm, Central Cutout Panel, England 275.00
Chair, Windsor, 8 Spindles, Pierced Splat With Star, England 415.00
Chair, Windsor, Bamboo Turnings, 7 Spindles, Dark Finish, Shaped Seat, 33 In., Pair ... 440.00
Chair, Windsor, Bamboo Turnings, Arrow Back, Black Finish, 17 In. Seat, 34 In. 165.00
Chair, Windsor, Bamboo Turnings, Birdcage Arms, Stamped G. Gaw, 1810 .... 440.00
Chair, Windsor, Bamboo Turnings, Black Paint, Yellow Striping, Decal, 35 In. 195.00
Chair, Windsor, Bamboo Turnings, Brown Finish, Child's 165.00
Chair, Windsor, Bamboo Turnings, Brown Paint, Splayed Legs, H-Stretcher, 34 In. 385.00
Chair, Windsor, Bamboo Turnings, Rabbit-Ear Finials, Plank Seat, 34 In., Pair 220.00
Chair, Windsor, Birdcage, Bamboo Turnings, Splayed Legs, Black, Gold, 35 In. 144.00
Chair, Windsor, Bow Back, 7 Spindles, Bamboo Turned Legs, Saddle Seat 137.00
Chair, Windsor, Bow Back, 7 Spindles, Bamboo Turnings, Black Paint, 37 In. 300.00
Chair, Windsor, Bow Back, 7 Spindles, Black Paint, Saddle Seat, 38 In. 330.00
Chair, Windsor, Bow Back, 7 Spindles, Brown Finish, Saddle Seat, 38 In. 330.00
Chair, Windsor, Bow Back, 7 Spindles, Red Paint, Yellow Striping, 37 In., Pair 1100.00
Chair, Windsor, Bow Back, 7 Spindles, Saddle Seat, 37 1/2 In. 192.00
Chair, Windsor, Bow Back, 7 Spindles, Splayed Base, H-Stretcher, 37 In. 110.00
Chair, Windsor, Bow Back, 9 Bamboo-Turned Spindles, Scrolled Arms, Red Paint 978.00
Chair, Windsor, Bow Back, 9 Spindles, Saddle Seat, Black Paint, 37 1/4 In. 385.00
Chair, Windsor, Bow Back, Bamboo Turnings, Label, Arms, Philips Mill, Penna. 1650.00
Chair, Windsor, Bow Back, Black Over Green Paint, Branded 750.00
Chair, Windsor, Bow Back, Dark Finish, Saddle Seat, Splayed Base, R.I., 38 In. 605.00
Chair, Windsor, Bow Back, Oval Seat, Knuckle Arms, 34 In. 195.00
Chair, Windsor, Bow Back, Red Paint, Arms, Late 18th Century, 36 1/2 In. 1150.00
Chair, Windsor, Bow Back, Splayed Base, Brown Paint, Turned Legs, 33 1/2 In. 440.00
Chair, Windsor, Bow Back, Splayed Base, Knuckle Arms, 38 3/4 In. 2530.00
Chair, Windsor, Bow Back, Splayed Base, Saddle Seat, 15 1/2 x 36 In. 330.00
Chair, Windsor, Bow Back, Splayed Base, Saddle Seat, 17 x 34 1/2 In. 495.00

Sometimes when there has been damage, an armchair is reworked into a side chair. The new chair can be detected because an armchair would be wider than a side chair and the incorrect proportions indicates it is a fake.

Furniture, Chair, Windsor,
Fanback, 7 Spindles,
Red-Brown Finish

Chair, Windsor, Bow Back, Splayed, H-Stretcher, Shaped Arms, 38 In. 385.00
Chair, Windsor, Brace Back, 9 Spindles, Black & Green Paint, Continuous Arms 4400.00
Chair, Windsor, Brace Back, Brown Finish, Saddle Seat, Continuous Arms 1695.00
Chair, Windsor, Brace Back, Mahogany Finish, Rush Seat, 37 In., Pair 110.00
Chair, Windsor, Brace Back, Mahogany, Saddle Seat, Continuous Arms, 18 x 36 In. 1540.00
Chair, Windsor, Brace Back, Saddle Seat, Spindle Back, 38 1/4 In. 3850.00
Chair, Windsor, Brace Back, Spindle Back, Shaped Seat, Continuous Arms, 37 In. 745.00
Chair, Windsor, Brace Back, Splayed Base, Turned Legs, H-Stretcher, 16 x 36 In. 1210.00
Chair, Windsor, Chicken Coop, Pine 187.00
Chair, Windsor, Comb Back, 7 Spindles, Flowers, Philadelphia, c.1760 . . . . 7475.00
Chair, Windsor, Comb Back, 9 Spindles, Plank Seat, Pine, Arms, 41 In. 1800.00
Chair, Windsor, Comb Back, Bamboo Turnings, Oval Seat, Spindle Back & Arms 275.00
Chair, Windsor, Comb Back, Bamboo Turnings, Shaped Arms, 36 3/4 In. 440.00
Chair, Windsor, Continuous Arms, Brick Red Paint, Plank Seat, Pair 9050.00
Chair, Windsor, E. Tracy, Fanback, Yoke Crest, Splayed Base, Saddle Seat, 36 In. 990.00
Chair, Windsor, Elm, Ash, Mid-19th Century, England, 45 1/2 In. 285.00
Chair, Windsor, Fanback, 5 Spindles, Oval Plank Seat, Black, 35 In. 5750.00
Chair, Windsor, Fanback, 6 Spindles, Saddle Seat, New England, c.1780, 39 In. 2070.00
Chair, Windsor, Fanback, 7 Spindles, Red-Brown Finish . . . . *Illus* 880.00
Chair, Windsor, Fanback, 7 Spindles, Saddle Seat, Painted, 37 1/4 In. 3000.00
Chair, Windsor, Fanback, Black Paint, Leatherized Cloth Seat, 39 In. 3465.00
Chair, Windsor, Fanback, Bulbous Legs, H-Stretcher, Saddle Seat, 36 In., Pair 1320.00
Chair, Windsor, Fanback, Bulbous Turned Legs, Saddle Seat, Arms, 41 In. 3850.00
Chair, Windsor, Fanback, Hickory, Maple, Arms, 1790-1800 . . . . 4025.00
Chair, Windsor, Fanback, Painted, Serpentine Crest Rail, Saddle Seat, c.1780, 39 In. 2070.00
Chair, Windsor, Fanback, Splayed Base, Curved Crest With Ears, 35 3/4 In. 110.00
Chair, Windsor, Fanback, Splayed Base, Oval Seat, 17 1/2 x 43 1/2 In. 3960.00
Chair, Windsor, Gilbert Gaw, Bamboo Turnings, Spindle Back, Butterfly, Stamped 220.00
Chair, Windsor, Gilbert Gaw, Bamboo Turnings, Spindle Back, Stamped, Arms, Pair 800.00
Chair, Windsor, Maple, Hickory, Poplar, Arms, 34 1/4 In. 495.00
Chair, Windsor, Sack Back, 5 Spindles, U-Shaped Armrest, 26 1/2 In. 1495.00
Chair, Windsor, Sack Back, 7 Spindles, Plank Seat, Black, 19th Century 575.00
Chair, Windsor, Sack Back, Arched Crest, Saddle Seat, Salmon, Green, 17 In. 1840.00
Chair, Windsor, Sack Back, Black Paint, Turned Legs, Saddle Seat, Arms, 38 In. 2420.00
Chair, Windsor, Sack Back, Black, Splayed Base, Bulbous Turned Legs, Saddle Seat 1300.00
Chair, Windsor, Sack Back, Dark Green, Arms 5225.00
Chair, Windsor, Sack Back, Saddle Seat, Late 1700s 1155.00
Chair, Windsor, Sack Back, Splayed Base, H-Stretcher, Arms, Conn., 28 1/2 In. 2750.00
Chair, Windsor, Sack Back, Thick Seat, Turned Spindles & Legs, Arms 715.00
Chair, Windsor, Saddle Seat, Green Paint, Continuous Arms, 36 In. 2090.00
Chair, Windsor, Spindle Back, Saddle Seat, Dark Green Paint, Continuous Arms, R.I. . . . 1090.00
Chair, Windsor, Step-Down, Mahogany-Color Paint, 1830s, 35 1/2 In., Pair 517.00
Chair, Windsor, Stephen Kilbourn, Bamboo Turnings, Red & Black Graining, 35 In. 1320.00
Chair, Wing, Chippendale, Barrel, Mahogany, Upholstered, Arms, 44 In. 1595.00
Chair, Wing, Chippendale, Cabriole Legs, Upholstered, England, 48 In. 465.00
Chair, Wing, Chippendale, Mahogany, Loose-Fitted Cushion, 1780, 20 x 50 In. 3165.00

Chair, Wing, Chippendale, Mahogany, Upholstered, Arms, R.I., 46 In. 5775.00
Chair, Wing, Chippendale, Mahogany, Yellow Brocade, 45 In. 4675.00
Chair, Wing, Federal, Mahogany, Serpentine Seat, Penna., 1790, 18 x 43 In. 2590.00
Chair, Wing, George I, Walnut, Out-Scrolled Arms, Needlepoint 8625.00
Chair, Wing, George I, Walnut, Padded Backrest, Out-Scrolled Arms, c.1725 . . . . 3740.00
Chair, Wing, Hepplewhite, Mahogany, Upholstered, Arms, Phila., 44 In. 7150.00
Chair, Wing, Mahogany, Shell-Carved Knees, Claw & Ball Feet 495.00
Chair, Wing, Queen Anne, Mahogany, Upholstered 1760.00
Chair, Wing, Queen Anne, Mahogany, Upholstered, 42 1/2 In. 1650.00
Chair, Wing, Walnut, Out-Scrolled Arms, Padded Backrest, 1720s 5175.00
Chair, Writing Arm, Ladder Back, 3 Slats, Woven Splint Seat 270.00
Chair, Yoke Back, Out-Curved Arms, Paneled Seat, Chinese, 41 1/2 In. 495.00
Chair, Yoke Crest, Vase-Form Splat, Rush Slip Seat, Spanish Feet 440.00
Chair, Zebra Wood, Slab Sides, Leather, c.1930, Pair 7475.00
Chair & Ottoman, Barcelona, Leather Cushions, Chrome Bases, 29 1/2 x 29 In. 1870.00
Chair & Ottoman, H. Bertoia, Wire Mesh, Chrome Bases, Upholstered, 38 In. 522.00
Chair & Ottoman, Saarinen, Womb 1006.00
Chair & Stool, Van Der Rohe, Barcelona, Chrome, c.1960, 29 1/2 In. 375.00
Chair Set, Arrow Back, Brown Paint, Yellow Striping, Crest Design, 1830s, 6 . . . . 805.00
Chair Set, Biedermeier, Walnut, Fanback, Shaped Stiles, Upholstered, 1810, 4 . . . . 1500.00
Chair Set, Birdcage, Curved Crests, Incised Spindles & Seat, Black Paint, 1800s, 6 . . . . . 6325.00
Chair Set, Bow Back, 9 Spindles, Saddle Seat, Archer Brown, Virginia, 37 In., 6 . . . . . . 2145.00
Chair Set, Chippendale Style, Mahogany, Pierced Carved Back Splat, 6 . . . . 1870.00
Chair Set, Dan Johnson, Sculptural Cast Aluminum, 1960s, 4 . . . . 3300.00
Chair Set, Dupre-Lafon, Palissandre, Leather Back & Seat, 1930, 12 . . . . 9775.00
Chair Set, Eames, Ash, Streamline Style, Black Feet, 4 . . . . 1450.00
Chair Set, Eames, Fiberglass Shell, Eiffel Tower Base, 3 Armchairs, 6 . . . . 4300.00
Chair Set, Eames, Molded Ash Plywood Seat, Back, Metal, 4 . . . . 1210.00
Chair Set, Elon Wycome, Stick Back, c.1830, 6 . . . . 3600.00
Chair Set, Empire, Cherry, Mahogany Veneer, Slip Seat, Carved Crest, 6 . . . . 530.00
Chair Set, Faux Rosewood, Stenciled Crest, Plank Seat, 10 . . . . 1380.00
Chair Set, G. Stickley, 3 Horizontal Back Slats, Leather Seat, Paper Label, 6 . . . . 4297.00
Chair Set, G. Stickley, No. 306, Ladder Back, Leather Seat, 1 Armchair, 6 . . . . 6600.00
Chair Set, George III, Mahogany, Damask, 2 Armchairs, 7 . . . . 2300.00
Chair Set, George III, Mahogany, Pierced Splat, Drop-In Seats 5750.00
Chair Set, Georgian Style, Mahogany, 2 Armchairs, 12 . . . . 8625.00
Chair Set, Georgian Style, Mahogany, Walnut, Wheel Back, 8 . . . . 4600.00
Chair Set, Giltwood, Tapestry Back & Seat, Padded Arms, 6 . . . . 7475.00
Chair Set, Gunlock Chair Co., Chippendale, Walnut, 36 1/2 In., 6 . . . . 192.00
Chair Set, H. Bertoia, Molded Fiberglass Shells, Metal, 4 . . . . 172.00
Chair Set, H. Bertoia, Plastic-Coated Wire, Black Metal Base, Child's, 20 In., 4 . . . . 440.00
Chair Set, Half-Spindle Back, Angel-Wing Crest Rail, Bluebirds, Fruit, Yellow, 9 . . . . . . 4800.00
Chair Set, Hepplewhite Style, Mahogany, Satin Brocade, 1 Armchair, 5 . . . . 962.00
Chair Set, Hepplewhite, Mahogany, 18th Century, 6 . . . . 8500.00
Chair Set, Heywood-Wakefield Co., Wheat Finish, 2 Armchairs, 6 . . . . 605.00
Chair Set, Ilmari Tapiovaara, Stacking, Blond Wood, Laminated Seat & Back, 1950, 4 . . 770.00
Chair Set, Jaems Shoolbred, Mahogany, Shaped Back Slats, 1900, 6 . . . . 2250.00
Chair Set, Javier Cavajal-Ferrer, Swivel, Black Leather, 8 . . . . 990.00
Chair Set, Laminated Birch, Tripod Legs, Square Seat, 42 In., 4 . . . . 605.00
Chair Set, Light Green Paint, Red & Black Striping, Plank Seat, Penna., 33 In., 6 . . . . . . 2310.00
Chair Set, Louis XV Style, Walnut, Pink Velvet, 3 . . . . 575.00
Chair Set, Louis XV, Carved Flower Head Backrest, Caned Seat & Back, 1750s, 5 . . . . . 5750.00
Chair Set, Louis XV, Walnut, Cartouche-Shaped Backrest, Padded Arms, 4 . . . . 4600.00
Chair Set, Low Back, Slightly Curved Crest, 6-Spindle Back, 1850s, 3 . . . . 3680.00
Chair Set, Mahogany, Carved & Figural, Serpentine Crest Rail, 2 Armchairs, 6 . . . . 2185.00
Chair Set, Mahogany, Carved Square Crest, Lyre Splat, Square Seat, Upholstered, 4 . . . . 1035.00
Chair Set, Mahogany, Gondola, Concave Scroll Over Vase-Form Splat, Slip Seat, 4 . . . . 1150.00
Chair Set, Mahogany, Ladder Back, Looped & Acanthus Carved Splat, 6 . . . . 1725.00
Chair Set, Mahogany, Pierced Back Over Trapezoidal Slip Seat, c.1765, 3 . . . . 4887.00
Chair Set, Mahogany, Pierced Back, Prince Of Wales Plumes, Upholstered, 3 . . . . 3450.00
Chair Set, Mahogany, Regency, Oval Crest On Backrest, Plank Seat, 6 . . . . 8050.00
Chair Set, Mahogany, Saber, Upholstered, Slip Seat, 2 Armchairs, 7 . . . . 962.00
Chair Set, Mahogany, Serpentine Crest, Pierced Splat, 2 Armchairs, 12 . . . . 7187.00

Chair Set, Mahogany, Shaped Back, Foliate-Carved Crest, 1860s, 4 . . . . 6325.00
Chair Set, Mahogany, Shaped Crest Rail, Vase-Form Splat, 2 Armchairs, 8 . . . . 4950.00
Chair Set, Mahogany, Shaped Splat, Inset Cushion, 4 . . . . 155.00
Chair Set, Mahogany, Tablet Crests, Pierced Horizontal Splats, Saber Legs, 6 . . . . 4070.00
Chair Set, Mahogany, Upholstered Slip Seat, 33 1/4 In., 4 . . . . 528.00
Chair Set, Majorelle, Mahogany, Chicory, Upholstered Back & Seat, c.1900, 8 . . . . 6900.00
Chair Set, Norman Cherner, Walnut, Sculpted, 2 Armchairs, 6 . . . . 2100.00
Chair Set, Paul McCobb, Wrought Iron, Walnut Back & Arms, 4 . . . . 465.00
Chair Set, Pierced Vertical Splats, Upholstered, 19th Century 540.00
Chair Set, Pierre Paulin, Sculptural, Upholstered, Chrome Disk Base, 4 . . . . 2640.00
Chair Set, Pressed Back, Solid Seat, 4 . . . . 660.00
Chair Set, Queen Anne Style, Mahogany, 10 . . . . 1650.00
Chair Set, Queen Anne, Mahogany, Spoon Back, Cabriole Legs, 10 . . . . 1760.00
Chair Set, Regency Style, Black Japanned, Caned Back & Seat, Arms, 6 . . . . 7475.00
Chair Set, Regency, Mahogany, Pierced Backrest, Leather Seat, 6 . . . . 5520.00
Chair Set, Regency, Mahogany, Upholstered Seat, England, 1810, 34 In., 6 . . . . 2800.00
Chair Set, Robsjohn-Gibbings, Walnut, Upholstered Cushion & Back, 3 . . . . 1045.00
Chair Set, Rosewood, Grained, Patriotic & Floral Stencil, 4 . . . . 300.00
Chair Set, Shaker, Watervliet Finials, Chamfered Slats, 1850s, 4 . . . . 750.00
Chair Set, Shaped Crest, Baluster Splat, Turned Posts, Plank Seat, Painted, 6 . . . . 4600.00
Chair Set, Sheraton, Cream Paint, Rush Seats, Bentwood Edging, 17 x 34 In., 8 . . . . 1716.00
Chair Set, Sheraton, Red & Yellow Scroll Crests, Woven Seat, New England, 5 . . . . 600.00
Chair Set, Slat Back, Yellow Paint, 6 . . . . 3600.00
Chair Set, Spindle Back, Cane Seat, Saber Legs, Rosewood Graining, 33 1/2 In., 4 . . . . . 330.00
Chair Set, Stickley Brothers, 2 Vertical Slats, Arched Crest Rail, 1 Armchair, 6 . . . . 2300.00
Chair Set, Swivel, Tufted Leather, White Enamel, Wheels, 4 . . . . 440.00
Chair Set, Thonet, Bentwood, Bistro, Embossed Seat, Label, 1886, 4 . . . . 375.00
Chair Set, Tiger Maple, Maple, Horizontal Splat, c.1830, 33 1/2 In., 8 . . . . 2645.00
Chair Set, Walnut, Hickory, Spindle Back, Cantilevered Seat, Shoe Feet, 6 . . . . 7475.00
Chair Set, Walnut, Padded, Carved Lion Masks, Upholstered Seat, 2 Armchairs, 8 . . . . . 2875.00
Chair Set, William IV, Mahogany, c.1835, 1 Armchair, 6 . . . . 1600.00
Chair Set, William Turner, Mahogany, Padded Backrest, Serpentine Seat, c.1835, 6 . . . . . 2587.00
Chair Set, Windsor, Bow Back, 9 Spindles, c.1810, 36 1/2 In., 4 . . . . 4887.00
Chair Set, Windsor, Brace Back, Saddle Seat, 37 In., 4 . . . . 2420.00
Chair Set, Windsor, Fanback, 6 Spindles, Shaped Saddle Seat, 1793, 4 . . . . 4312.00
Chair Set, Windsor, Spindle Back, Bamboo Turnings, Step-Down Crest, 4 . . . . 1210.00
Chair Set, Windsor, Spindle Back, Plank Seat, 32 1/2 In., 9 . . . . 2227.00
Chair Set, Windsor, Step-Down, Maple, Pine, Early 19th Century, 34 1/2 In., 6 . . . . 2875.00
Chair Set, Windsor, Step-Down, Rod Back, Bamboo Turnings, 6 . . . . 950.00
Chair Set, Wrought Iron, Art Metal Grapevines, Clusters Of Grapes, Rush Seat, 6 . . . . . . 660.00
Chair-Table, Pine, Demilune Cutout Ends, Hinged Top, Painted Base, 1830s, 29 In. 1495.00
Chair-Table, Pine, Maple, 26 1/2 x 46 1/2 In. 3000.00
Chaise Longue, Beechwood, Upholstered Back, Padded Arms, Flower Heads 5175.00
Chaise Longue, Biedermeier, Fruitwood, Gooseneck, Upholstered 4600.00
Chaise Longue, Eames, 6 Black Leather Pillows, Enameled Metal Base, 64 In. 2200.00
Chaise Longue, Eames, Model LCW, Plywood, Rubber, Herman Miller, 1946, 25 In. . . . 400.00
Chaise Longue, Eames, No. 670, Molded Rosewood, Upholstered, Arms, 31 In. 465.00
Chaise Longue, Eames, Rosewood, Aluminum, Upholstered, 32 In. 935.00
Chaise Longue, Eastlake, Walnut, Incised Floral Design, 69 In. 220.00
Chaise Longue, G. Nelson, Steel, Chrome, Channeled Black Wool, 31 In. 1430.00
Chaise Longue, Giltwood, Scrolled Head & Footboards, 73 In. 8625.00
Chaise Longue, Herman W. Ladd, Swinging, Adjustable 1250.00
Chaise Longue, Le Corbusier, Atelier International, 1968, 67 In. 500.00
Chaise Longue, Louis XVI Style, Giltwood, Aubusson Back, 1880s, 36 1/2 In. 632.00
Chaise Longue, R. Thompson, Oak, Leather Thongs, Cushion, Shaped Arms, c.1950 . . . 4500.00
Chaise Longue, Rattan, Upholstered Cushions, White Paint 82.00
Chaise Longue, Saarinen, Grasshopper, Walnut, Upholstered, Knoll & Assoc., 34 In. . . . 920.00
Chaise Longue, Shell & Scroll Crest, Down-Swept Arms, Carved Apron, 72 In. 345.00
Chaise Longue, Van Der Rohe, Cantilevered, Leather Strap Supports 4370.00
Chaise Longue, Van Der Rohe, Wood Supports, Leather Back & Sides, 26 In. 1850.00
Chaise Longue, Wegner, Chrome, Enameled Steel, Rope, Attached Headrest, 1949 . . . . . 4730.00
Chaise Longue, Wicker, Carved Arms & Back, 62 In. 110.00
Chaise Longue, Widdicomb, Walnut, Upholstered Seat & Back, 31 In., Pair 1045.00

Chaise Longue & Footstool, Vladimir Kagan, Walnut, Teal Leather, 1955	3800.00
Chaise Longue & Ottoman, Eames, No. 670, Rosewood Shell, Leather, 33 In.	1540.00
Chaise Longue & Ottoman, Eames, Rosewood, Black Leather, Signed, 1970, 32 In. . .	1150.00
Chaise Longue & Ottoman, Herman Miller, Rosewood Veneer, Leather	1320.00
Chaise Longue & Ottoman, Eames, Rosewood Shell, Black Leather, 32 1/2 In.	1150.00
Chest, 4 Recessed Drawers, Peach Mirror, Glass Base, England, 1930s, 43 x 46 In.	2435.00
Chest, Bachelor's, George III, Mahogany, 2 Drawers, 3 Cabriole Legs, 30 1/2 In.	3450.00
Chest, Bachelor's, George III, Mahogany, 4 Graduated Drawers, 31 x 34 In.	4370.00
Chest, Bachelor's, Mahogany, 2 Small & 3 Long Shallow Drawers, 26 3/4 In.	120.00
Chest, Bachelor's, Mahogany, 3 Shallow Drawers, Brass Bail Handles, 27 3/4 In.	155.00
Chest, Bachelor's, Mahogany, 4 Graduated Drawers, Brass Handles, 30 1/2 In.	355.00
Chest, Bachelor's, Mahogany, 6 Graduated Drawers, Victorian, 50 1/2 x 36 In.	460.00
Chest, Bachelor's, Oak, Faux Bamboo, c.1880, 31 x 18 In.	795.00
Chest, Baroque, Rosewood, 3 Graduated Drawers, Marble Top, 33 x 45 x 20 In.	750.00
Chest, Biedermeier Style, Walnut, 2 Short Over 3 Long Drawers, 17 x 11 1/2 In.	172.00
Chest, Biedermeier, Fruitwood Veneer, 4 Drawers, Marble Top, 48 x 25 x 43 In.	1540.00
Chest, Biedermeier, Walnut, 2 Long Drawers, Block Feet, 19th Century, 15 x 9 In.	1955.00
Chest, Blanket, Applied Molded Side Cleats, Robin's-Egg Blue, 19 1/2 x 45 In.	1380.00
Chest, Blanket, Bird & Floral Design, Trap Hinges, 1793, 24 1/2 x 50 In.	2970.00
Chest, Blanket, Blue Paint, Strap Hinges, 6-Board, 27 x 46 In.	1250.00
Chest, Blanket, Brown Over Yellow Putty Grained, Cutout Feet	375.00
Chest, Blanket, C. Selzer, Stars On Lid, Till, Painted Front Panels, 1750s, 52 In.	9200.00
Chest, Blanket, Cherry, Dovetailed, Iron Strap Hinges, Miniature	715.00
Chest, Blanket, Chestnut, Dovetailed, Bracket Feet, 2-Panel Top	300.00
Chest, Blanket, Chippendale, Maple, 2 Drawers, Hinged Lid, 1780, 42 x 36 In.	2100.00
Chest, Blanket, Chippendale, Oak, Bracket Feet, 3 Raised Panels, Till, 45 In.	825.00
Chest, Blanket, Chippendale, Pine, Red Paint, 1-Board Top, Penna., 42 x 16 x 22 In.	825.00
Chest, Blanket, Chippendale, Poplar, Red Paint, 50 x 23 x 26 In.	385.00
Chest, Blanket, Chippendale, Walnut, Red Traces, Till, Initials C.H., 50 x 24 In.	935.00
Chest, Blanket, Hinged Top, 1 Long, 2 Short & 2 Simulated Drawers, 29 x 38 In.	1725.00
Chest, Blanket, Lift Top, 2 Lower Drawers, Painted, New England, 38 x 42 In.	1495.00
Chest, Blanket, Oak, Pine, Handles At Each End, 1909, 17 x 67 In.	5175.00
Chest, Blanket, Pine, 1 Drawer, Brown, Black, Bracket Feet, 34 x 42 x 18 In.	1380.00
Chest, Blanket, Pine, 2 Green Drawers, Sponged Brown Over Mustard, 55 1/2 In.	1345.00
Chest, Blanket, Pine, 3 Drawers, Ocher, Brown, Red, 33 1/2 In.	9775.00
Chest, Blanket, Pine, Angels & Doves On Basket Of Fruit, 1825, 24 In.	4315.00
Chest, Blanket, Pine, Brown & Yellow Striping, Original Staple Hinges, 48 1/2 In.	797.00
Chest, Blanket, Pine, Brown Grain, Cedar Interior, Metal Floral Pulls, 31 In.	1100.00
Chest, Blanket, Pine, Brown Paint, Rectangular Hinged Top, 27 x 44 x 19 In.	805.00
Chest, Blanket, Pine, Circular Brown, Black Pattern, 19th Century, 24 1/2 In.	1610.00
Chest, Blanket, Pine, Dark Brown Over White Paint, Floral, 12 1/2 In.	5810.00
Chest, Blanket, Pine, Grain Design, Bracket Feet, Iron Hinges, 41 x 19 x 22 In.	330.00
Chest, Blanket, Pine, Grain Painted, Brown, Black, Bracket Feet, 21 1/2 In.	920.00
Chest, Blanket, Pine, Grain Painted, Turned Feet, Dovetailed Case, 50 x 24 In.	275.00
Chest, Blanket, Pine, Open Till, Dovetailed, Lock, Mid-19th Century, 8 x 14 In.	425.00
Chest, Blanket, Pine, Painted, Red, Navy Blue, Flower Baskets, 1841, 50 x 27 x 25 In. . .	55.00
Chest, Blanket, Pine, Poplar, 3 Drawers, Hinged Lid, Penna., 1810, 31 In.	7475.00
Chest, Blanket, Pine, Poplar, Brown & Yellow Paint, Penna., 44 x 21 x 24 In.	525.00
Chest, Blanket, Pine, Poplar, Dovetailed, 2 Drawers, 28 x 40 In.	1155.00
Chest, Blanket, Pine, Poplar, Flame Grained, Paneled, Penna., 43 x 21 x 26 In.	715.00
Chest, Blanket, Pine, Poplar, Red Paint, Smoke Decorated White Panels, 38 x 21 In.	300.00
Chest, Blanket, Pine, Rope-Twist Border, Yellow Sides, 16 x 35 x 17 In.	489.00
Chest, Blanket, Pine, Till With Smaller Till Inside, Lids, Iron Nails, 37 1/2 In.	180.00
Chest, Blanket, Pine, Till, Inside Secret Drawer, 2 Drawers, Initials A.R., 1763	7500.00
Chest, Blanket, Pine, Turned Feet, Till, Dovetailed, 38 1/4 In.	467.00
Chest, Blanket, Pine, Wrought-Iron Rose-Head Nails, 52 x 17 x 58 In.	605.00
Chest, Blanket, Poplar, 2 Dovetailed Drawers, Red, Brown Graining, 50 x 22 In.	5610.00
Chest, Blanket, Poplar, 2 Lower Drawers, Fitted Till, Iron Hinges, Painted, 50 In.	8050.00
Chest, Blanket, Poplar, Blue Paint, Bracket Feet, 12 3/4 In.	1430.00
Chest, Blanket, Poplar, Brown Varnish, 2 Drawers Attached To Base, 42 In.	600.00
Chest, Blanket, Poplar, Floral Designs, Turned Feet, Brown Finish, 24 In.	770.00
Chest, Blanket, Poplar, Grain Painted, Till, Lebanon County, 1816, 25 1/2 x 46 In.	550.00
Chest, Blanket, Poplar, Mustard Grained, Black Trim, Till, 40 x 19 x 21 In.	935.00

Furniture, Chest, Empire, Cherry, Banding,
Painted Columns

Furniture, Chest, Empire, Curly Maple,
2 Over 4 Drawers, Turned Columns

Chest, Blanket, Poplar, Red Paint, Turned Feet, 25 1/2 x 14 1/4 x 21 In. 770.00
Chest, Blanket, Poplar, Red Stain, Turned Feet, Edge Molding, 42 x 20 x 28 In. 360.00
Chest, Blanket, Poplar, Red Wash, Dovetailed, Bracket Feet, 24 x 16 x 12 In. 1700.00
Chest, Blanket, Poplar, Turned Feet, Dovetailed, Penna., 38 x 19 x 23 In. 250.00
Chest, Blanket, Poplar, Walnut, Red Paint, Blue, Green Trim, 43 x 19 x 23 In. 4400.00
Chest, Blanket, Red Grained Over Mustard, Early 19th Century 1650.00
Chest, Blanket, Shaker, Maple, Butternut, Bottle-Shaped Legs, 26 x 40 In. 4600.00
Chest, Blanket, Softwood, Red & Yellow Feathered Design, Bracket Feet, Penna. 275.00
Chest, Blanket, Sponge Painted, Panel & Post, Secret Drawer Under Till, Penna. 2895.00
Chest, Blanket, Tiger Maple, 2 Drawers, 18th Century 1500.00
Chest, Blanket, W. Shinn, Pine, 6-Board, White, Bracket Feet, 1865, 6 x 13 x 5 In. 605.00
Chest, Blanket, Walnut, Inlay, 2 Drawers, Till With Lid, Penna., 44 x 20 x 27 In. 4960.00
Chest, Blanket, Walnut, Punch & Chip-Carved Floral Design, Ohio, 41 x 20 x 26 In. 3135.00
Chest, Block Front, Mahogany, 4 Drawers, Dust Shields, Original Brasses, 1780 . . . . 8900.00
Chest, Bowfront, Federal, Cherry, 4 Graduated Drawers, 1800, 31 In. 2185.00
Chest, Bowfront, George III, Mahogany, 3 Graduated Drawers, French Feet 1380.00
Chest, Bowfront, Mahogany, Bird's-Eye Veneer, 4 Drawers, Inlaid Edge, 34 x 38 In. 4890.00
Chest, Bowfront, Mahogany, Bow Front, 4 Graduated Drawers, 1785, 33 1/2 In. 9775.00
Chest, Butler's, Mahogany, Fitted Interior, 3 Drawers, Wood Pulls, 44 x 44 1/2 In. 990.00
Chest, Campaign, Drop Front, Fitted Top, 46 x 22 In. 5460.00
Chest, Campaign, Mahogany, 2-Part, Brass, Mid-19th Century, 42 x 40 x 18 In. 1265.00
Chest, Campaign, Walnut, Brass Corners, Cedar Interior, Swing Handles, 38 1/2 In. 522.00
Chest, Camphor, Blanket, Carved On All Sides, Chinese, 40 In. 160.00
Chest, Captain's, Lift Top, Painted Maritime View, Rope Handles, 17 x 40 In. 550.00
Chest, Cedar, Lane, Mahogany Veneer, Compartments, 47 3/8 In. 110.00
Chest, Cedar, Lane, Queen Anne Style, Lift Top, 32 x 45 In. 148.00
Chest, Cedar, Lane, Turned Gallery, Hand-Painted Floral Crest, Late 1920s 80.00
Chest, Cedar, Strap Hinges, Stippled Paint, c.1850 . . . . 1850.00
Chest, Cherry Top, 4 Tiger-Maple Veneer Drawer Fronts, 29 x 34 In. 1610.00
Chest, Cherry, 4 Dovetailed Drawers, Beaded Edge, 39 x 20 x 41 In. 825.00
Chest, Cherry, 4 Graduated Drawers, Red Paint, 1790s, 42 1/2 x 40 1/4 In. 1265.00
Chest, Cherry, 4 Overlapping Drawers, Dovetailed Case, Original Brasses, 44 In. 715.00
Chest, Cherry, 7 Graduated Drawers, Bail Brasses, c.1800, 56 In. 3100.00
Chest, Cherry, Bowfront, Mahogany Veneer, 4 Drawers, Original Brasses, 37 In. 2185.00
Chest, Cherry, Chippendale, Fluted Quarter Columns, 3 Drawers, 34 1/8 In. 4312.00
Chest, Cherry, Empire, Bone Inlay, c.1830, 26 x 20 1/4 In. 1750.00
Chest, Cherry, Federal, Mahogany Veneer, 4 Drawers, Turned Front Feet, 38 1/2 In. 942.00
Chest, Cherry, Mahogany Veneer, Serpentine Top, 4 Graduated Drawers, 33 1/4 In. 2300.00
Chest, Cherry, Tiger-Maple Drawer Fronts, 40 1/4 x 43 In. 1380.00
Chest, Cherry, Willett, 4 Drawers, Dovetailed Case, 30 3/4 In. 236.00
Chest, Cherry, Yellow Pine, 2 Over 3 Drawers, 46 x 45 In. 500.00
Chest, Chippendale, 4 Overlapping Drawers, Replaced Brass Bale, 40 x 37 In. 2060.00
Chest, Chippendale, Birch, 4 Graduated Drawers, Ogee Feet, 1780, 37 In. 1380.00

Chest, Chippendale, Cherry, 10 Dovetailed Drawers, Ogee Feet, 65 1/2 In. 3960.00
Chest, Chippendale, Cherry, 5 Graduated Drawers, 1775, 37 x 55 In. 6325.00
Chest, Chippendale, Cherry, 6 Lipped Drawers, Dovetailed, 37 x 55 x 19 In. 1210.00
Chest, Chippendale, Cherry, Pine, 4 Dovetailed Drawers, Bracket Feet, 39 In. 2200.00
Chest, Chippendale, Mahogany, 2 Small Over 3 Dovetailed Drawers, 37 x 35 In. 1870.00
Chest, Chippendale, Mahogany, 4 Dovetailed Beaded Drawers, 39 x 40 x 33 In. 4125.00
Chest, Chippendale, Maple, 4 Graduated Drawers, Ogee Bracket Feet, 1790, 36 In. 8050.00
Chest, Chippendale, Walnut Veneer, 3 Drawers, England, 36 x 20 x 32 In. 690.00
Chest, Chippendale, Walnut, 3 Drawers, Ogee Feet, 1780, 63 1/2 In. 4600.00
Chest, Chippendale, Walnut, 3 Over 3 Drawers, Dovetailed, Reeded, 38 x 40 In. 3575.00
Chest, Chippendale, Walnut, 4 Graduated Drawers, Ogee Feet, 38 x 20 x 33 In. 1650.00
Chest, Chippendale, Walnut, 6 Dovetailed Drawers, Ogee Feet, 46 1/2 In. 1100.00
Chest, Chippendale, Walnut, Graduated Drawers, Philadelphia, c.1770, 38 x 60 In. 9500.00
Chest, Curly Maple, Poplar, 4 Drawers, Divided Top Drawer, 21 x 33 x 37 In. 770.00
Chest, Dower, Pine, Ornate Iron Lock, Continental, 18th Century, 52 x 21 x 20 In. 80.00
Chest, Empire, 2-Gallery Top Over 4 Drawers, Column Front 595.00
Chest, Empire, Cherry, 4 Dovetailed & 2 Glove Top Drawers, Douglas, Mich., 41 In. . . . 715.00
Chest, Empire, Cherry, 4 Dovetailed Drawers, 41 x 42 x 47 In. 600.00
Chest, Empire, Cherry, 4 Dovetailed Drawers, Red Paint, Turned Feet, 48 In. 440.00
Chest, Empire, Cherry, Banding, Painted Columns . . . . *Illus* 770.00
Chest, Empire, Cherry, Mahogany Veneer, 2 Short Over 4 Long Drawers, 48 x 63 In. . . . 330.00
Chest, Empire, Cherry, Pine, 4 Drawers, Scrolled Feet, 46 In. 220.00
Chest, Empire, Cherry, Turned Feet, 4 Dovetailed Drawers, 42 x 44 In. 220.00
Chest, Empire, Curly Maple, 2 Over 4 Drawers, Turned Columns . . . . *Illus* 715.00
Chest, Empire, Curly Maple, 4 Dovetailed Drawers, 20 x 44 x 44 In. 935.00
Chest, Empire, Curly Maple, Cherry, 4 Drawers, 45 x 45 1/2 In. 605.00
Chest, Empire, Curly, Bird's-Eye Maple, 1 Large Over 3 Small Drawers, 44 x 50 In. 715.00
Chest, Empire, Mahogany, 4 Drawers, Acanthus Columns, Paw Feet, 44 1/2 In. 2070.00
Chest, Empire, Mahogany, Baluster Pendants, 2 Drawers, 38 x 42 In. 460.00
Chest, Empire, Pine, Figural Mahogany Veneer, 1820, Miniature, 10 x 7 x 9 In. 550.00
Chest, Empire, Poplar, 4 Dovetailed & 2 Step Back Drawers, 41 x 45 In. 305.00
Chest, Empire, Poplar, Cherry, 4 Drawers, Full Round Columns, 46 In. 330.00
Chest, Empire, Poplar, Red Graining, Turned Feet, 24 In. 715.00
Chest, Federal, 3 Shallow Drawers, Fluted, Turned Legs, 32 x 36 x 18 1/2 In. 1150.00
Chest, Federal, 5 Drawers, Walnut, Pine, Bundled Column Pilasters, 21 x 42 In. 440.00
Chest, Federal, Birch, 4 Graduated Drawers, Tapered Feet, 37 1/4 In. 5175.00
Chest, Federal, Bowfront, Mahogany, 2 Doors, Bracket Feet, 33 1/4 In. 550.00
Chest, Federal, Bowfront, Mahogany, 4 Drawers, Peg Feet, 1810, 40 1/2 In. 2185.00
Chest, Federal, Cherry, 1810-1830 . . . . *Illus* 1100.00
Chest, Federal, Cherry, 6 Dovetailed Drawers, 42 x 49 In. 495.00
Chest, Federal, Cherry, Serpentine Top, 4 Drawers, Conn., 1795, 39 x 41 In. 3160.00
Chest, Federal, Mahogany, 6 Drawers, Wood Knobs, Turned Feet, 50 In. 460.00
Chest, Federal, Mahogany, Bowfront, Tapered Legs, 41 1/2 In. 6325.00
Chest, Federal, Walnut, 4 Drawers, Sawtooth Apron, 1790, 41 1/2 x 22 In. 6325.00
Chest, Federal, Walnut, 4 Graduated Cock-Beaded Drawers, 38 x 37 1/4 x 20 In. 2070.00

Furniture,
Chest,
Federal,
Cherry,
1810-1830

Furniture,
Chest, Tiger
Maple, R.I.

Chest, Federal, Walnut, 4 Graduated Cock-Beaded Drawers, Ringed Legs, 42 In. 1725.00

Chest, Federal, Walnut, Cherry, 4 Dovetailed Drawers, Glass Knobs, 43 x 52 In. 600.00

Chest, Fruitwood, Marble Top, Bowfront, 4 Drawers, Side Marquetry, 36 1/4 In. 3680.00

Chest, G. Nelson, Birch Veneer, 5 Drawers, Ebonized Legs, Herman Miller, 40 In. 990.00

Chest, G. Nelson, Rosewood, Drop Front Desk, 5 Drawers, Porcelain Pulls, 41 In. 2990.00

Chest, G. Stickley, Oak, 3 Long Drawers, 1904, 43 1/4 In. 1265.00

Chest, G. Stickley, Oak, 3 Long Drawers, Wooden Knobs, 1907, 50 In. 575.00

Chest, Gallery Wood Top, 6 Drawers, Old Red Paint, 15 1/2 x 48 3/4 In. 1610.00

Chest, George I, Olive Wood, Oyster Veneered, Boxwood Stringing, 1740s, 36 In. 9200.00

Chest, George I, Walnut, Crossbanded, 2 Drawers, Bun Feet, 24 In. 4025.00

Chest, George I, Walnut, Mahogany, 3 Graduated Drawers, 34 x 35 x 18 In. 1095.00

Chest, George II, Walnut, 2 Short Over 3 Long Drawers, Lining, 63 1/2 In. 8050.00

Chest, George II, Walnut, 3 Feather-Banded Drawers, Bracket Feet, 60 In. 8050.00

Chest, George II, Walnut, 3 Graduated Drawers, Bracket Feet, 37 In. 1610.00

Chest, George III, Bowfront, Mahogany, 3 Graduated Drawers, 35 x 37 In. 1495.00

Chest, George III, Mahogany, 3 Graduated Drawers, Bracket Feet, 37 In. 2550.00

Chest, George III, Mahogany, 4 Graduated Drawers, Brass Inlay, Ogee Feet 1150.00

Chest, George III, Mahogany, Bowfront, 32 x 36 1/2 x 20 1/2 In. 4025.00

Chest, George III, Mahogany, Brass Inlay, Camphorwood Interior 575.00

Chest, George III, Walnut, 4 Graduated Drawers, Reeded Columns, 38 x 40 In. 2530.00

Chest, Georgian, Walnut, 2 Short, 3 Long Drawers, Bracket Feet, 35 1/2 In. 1840.00

Chest, Hepplewhite Style, Mahogany Veneer, 4 Drawers, 31 x 18 x 30 In. 275.00

Chest, Hepplewhite, Bowfront, Cherry, 4 Graduated Drawers, Molded Edge, 42 In. 4180.00

Chest, Hepplewhite, Bowfront, Mahogany Veneer, Dovetailed Drawers, 41 x 37 In. 1210.00

Chest, Hepplewhite, Bowfront, Pine, Poplar, Mahogany Veneer, 4 Drawers, 37 In. 2090.00

Chest, Hepplewhite, Cherry, 4 Dovetailed Drawers, Inlay, French Feet, 20 x 41 In. 2475.00

Chest, Hepplewhite, Cherry, 4 Graduated Drawers, Eagle Brasses, 37 x 40 x 37 In. 4400.00

Chest, Hepplewhite, Cherry, 5 Dovetailed Drawers, French Feet, 39 x 41 In. 715.00

Chest, Hepplewhite, Mahogany, 4 Dovetailed Drawers, Carved Edge, 25 x 30 In. 990.00

Chest, Hepplewhite, Walnut, 4 Drawers, Dovetailed, 39 x 34 x 22 In. 3025.00

Chest, Herman Miller, 5 Drawers, Metal Legs, 40 x 19 x 38 In. 1650.00

Chest, Herman Miller, Macassar Ebony, Figured Maple Veneer, 4 Drawers, 46 In. 2650.00

Chest, Heywood-Wakefield Co., Mirror, 5 Drawers, Champagne Finish, 1952, 46 In. 425.00

Chest, Immigrant's, Amanda Lindgren, Pine, Dovetailed Domed Top, 29 1/4 In. 192.00

Chest, Immigrant's, Oak, Dome Top, Dovetailed, Weathered Finish, 45 In. 70.00

Chest, Immigrant's, Pine, Black & Red Paint, Bear-Trap Lock, Strap Hinges, 49 In. 165.00

Chest, Immigrant's, Pine, Painted, Red, Green, Compass Stars, 1815, 49 In. 275.00

Chest, Ivory Inlay, Stylized Foliage, Geometric Design, France, 1925, 39 x 18 In. 5175.00

Chest, J. Ross, Walnut, 9 Drawers, Lamb's Tongue Corners, 1805, 69 In. 220.00

Chest, Louis XV, Tulipwood, Kingwood, Drawer At Side, 28 1/4 In. 8625.00

Chest, Louis XVI, Fruitwood, 2 Drawers, Cabriole Legs, D-Shaped Marble Top, 30 In. . . 520.00

Chest, Mahogany Veneer, Scrolled Mirror Supports, 1810, 58 3/4 In. 862.00

Chest, Mahogany, 6 Drawers, Cigar Box Construction, Porcelain Pulls, 18 x 12 In. 140.00

Chest, Mahogany, Lace Maker's, Compartmented Drawer, 1830s, 11 5/8 In. 977.00

Chest, Mahogany, Lace Maker's, Drawer Filled With Lace Bobbins, 12 x 21 In. 1400.00

Chest, Marble Top, 3 Drawers, Victorian, 78 x 60 x 24 In. 1495.00

Chest, Marble Top, 4 Drawers, Mother-Of-Pearl Inlay, Syria, 50 x 45 In. 4600.00

Chest, Mule, Chestnut, Hepplewhite, 2 Dovetailed Drawers, 38 1/2 In. 1375.00

Chest, Mule, Jacobean, Oak, 2 Short Drawers, Paneled Front, 30 x 51 In. 2300.00

Chest, Mule, Pine, Brown Graining, Scrolled Apron, 2 Drawers, 39 1/2 In. 1280.00

Chest, Mule, Pine, Green, Yellow Stripes, 2 Dovetailed Drawers, 34 In. 880.00

Chest, Mule, Poplar, Cherry Finish, Drawer, Lift Top, Scrolled Apron, 37 In. 385.00

Chest, Oak, Burl Veneer, Double Doors, 4 Drawers, Korea, 34 In. 165.00

Chest, Oak, Hinged Paneled Top, 4 Recessed Panels, Gothic Tracery, 22 x 46 In. 8625.00

Chest, Oak, Hinged Top Over 2 Square Panels, Vase & Tulips Inlay, England, 33 In. 1380.00

Chest, Pawlonia, Wedding, Characters, Wrought-Iron Latch, Korea, 30 1/4 In. 470.00

Chest, Pine, 4 Graduated Drawers, Wood Knobs, 13 x 11 1/2 x 8 1/4 In. 230.00

Chest, Pine, 6-Board, Blue, Bracket Feet, Vermont, 23 x 47 x 15 1/2 In. 1035.00

Chest, Pine, 6-Board, Cleat Lifts Over Lidded Till, Blue Paint, 23 1/2 In. 1150.00

Chest, Pine, Blanket, Fish-Shaped Lock, South Korea, Child's, 28 In. 192.00

Chest, Pine, Blanket, Lift Top, Bracket Base, 32 x 43 In. 495.00

Chest, Pine, Wave & Spot Pattern, Rectangular Hinged Top, 13 x 33 x 12 In. 489.00

Chest, Pine, Wedding, Wrought-Iron Lock, Hasp & Handles, Korea, 24 1/2 In. 300.00

Chest, Pine, Woman's, Sliding Doors, Brass Fittings, Korea, 21 1/2 In., Pair 330.00
Chest, Poplar, 3 Drawers, 2 Step Back Drawers, Floral Design, 23 x 13 x 25 In. 770.00
Chest, Poplar, 3 Drawers, Red Grained, Yellow Ground, 43 x 21 x 41 In. 1340.00
Chest, Poplar, Dovetailed, Red-Umber & Brown, Grain Painted, 17 1/2 In. 430.00
Chest, Queen Anne Style, Walnut Veneer, 4 Drawers, Serpentine Facade, 33 x 30 In. 1595.00
Chest, Queen Anne, 2 Over 4 Graduated Drawers, Dark Patina, 50 In. 5175.00
Chest, Queen Anne, Cherry, Chestnut, 7 Dovetailed Drawers, 51 3/8 In. 4125.00
Chest, Queen Anne, Maple, 3 Thumb-Molded Drawers, Pad Feet, 74 x 39 In. 11500.00
Chest, Queen Anne, Maple, 4 Graduated Drawers, 1740, 79 x 39 In. 12650.00
Chest, Queen Anne, Maple, 6 Graduated Drawers, Molded Cornice, 36 x 53 In. 9075.00
Chest, Queen Anne, Walnut, 4 Graduated Drawers, Bracket Feet, 1750-1770, 32 In. 6900.00
Chest, Regency, Bowfront, Mahogany, Brass Pulls, Carved Bracket Feet, 40 1/2 In. 750.00
Chest, Regency, Mahogany, Ormolu Mounts, 4 Drawers, 33 x 51 x 24 In. 785.00
Chest, Rosewood, Cast-Brass Drawer Pulls, Portugal, 1820s, 35 x 40 In. 2645.00
Chest, Saarinen, Bird, 5 Drawers, Aluminum Pulls, Label, 32 x 20 x 46 In. 770.00
Chest, Shaker, 4 Graduated Drawers, Center Knobs, 36 1/2 x 30 In. 1150.00
Chest, Sheraton, 4 Drawers, Reeded Legs, Cookie Corners, c.1820 . . . . 1800.00
Chest, Sheraton, Bowfront, Birch, Mahogany, 4 Dovetailed Drawers, 38 In. 1320.00
Chest, Sheraton, Cherry, 3 Bird's-Eye Maple Drawer Fronts, 39 In. 7700.00
Chest, Sheraton, Cherry, 6 Dovetailed Drawers, Beaded Edge, 39 x 19 x 40 In. 990.00
Chest, Sheraton, Walnut, 2 Over 3 Drawers, Star Inlay On Drawers 1350.00
Chest, Sugar, Cherry, 2 Shallow Drawers At Bottom 1250.00
Chest, Sugar, Walnut, c.1820 . . . . 6800.00
Chest, Sugar, Walnut, Dovetailed Drawer, Hinged Lid, 24 x 15 x 34 In. 3245.00
Chest, Tiger Maple, 2 Thumb-Molded Drawers, 4 Long Drawers, 46 x 36 In. 3450.00
Chest, Tiger Maple, 5 Graduated Drawers, Molded Top, 42 x 37 x 19 In. 2015.00
Chest, Tiger Maple, R.I. . . . . *Illus* 4400.00
Chest, Traveler's, Walnut, Hinged Lid, Brass Fitted, Side Straps, 29 In. 220.00
Chest, Tulipwood, Fruitwood, 2 Drawers, Hipped Legs, 19th Century, Miniature 3680.00
Chest, Walnut, 2 Dovetailed Drawers, Scrolled Crest, 16 1/2 In.   660.00
Chest, Walnut, 2 Drawers, Mid-19th Century, 11 3/4 x 12 In. 395.00
Chest, Walnut, 4 Drawers, Graduated Spheres Trailing Floral Vines, 49 x 20 In. 110.00
Chest, Walnut, 4 Graduated Drawers, Reeded Stiles, 36 In. 3740.00
Chest, Walnut, 5 Dovetailed Drawers, Turned Feet, 14 3/4 In. 495.00
Chest, Walnut, Burl Walnut, 2 Small Drawers Over 3 Drawers, 35 In. 2185.00
Chest, Walnut, England, 19th Century, 8 1/2 x 14 x 11 1/2 In. 698.00
Chest, Walnut, Hinged Side Lock, 6 Large & 2 Small Drawers, Brass Knobs, 62 In. 1100.00
Chest, Wedding, Lift Top, Ditty Box, Painted Florals, Scandinavia, 16 1/2 x 33 In. 1760.00
Chest, Wedding, Pennsylvania Dutch, 6-Board, 24 x 23 x 50 In. 1450.00
Chest, William & Mary, Maple, Pine, 5 Dovetailed Drawers, 42 1/2 In. 5225.00
Chest, William & Mary, Walnut, Feather Banded, 2 Short & 3 Long Drawers, 36 In. 9775.00
Chest-On-Chest, Empire, Dovetailed Drawers, Child's, 34 x 19 1/2 In. 3250.00
Chest-On-Chest, Empire, Walnut, 2 Over 3 Drawers, Turned Feet, 34 In. 2310.00
Chest-On-Chest, George III, Mahogany, Chamfered Fluted Corners, 1760, 71 In. 6600.00
Chest-On-Chest, George III, Mahogany, Late 18th Century, 39 x 37 1/4 In. 4025.00
Chest-On-Chest, Mahogany, 2 Half & 3 Long Drawers, 71 1/2 In. 3850.00
Chest-On-Chest, Mahogany, 8 Drawers, Bracket Feet, 45 x 22 x 73 1/2 In. 4000.00
Chest-On-Chest, Mahogany, 8 Drawers, Dentil Molding, England, 40 x 19 x 68 In. 1650.00
Chest-On-Stand, 3 Short & 3 Long Drawers, Bun Feet, 64 In. 2590.00
Chest-On-Stand, George III, Mahogany, c.1800 . . . .   975.00
Chest-On-Stand, William & Mary, Walnut, Floral Marquetry, 1880s, 63 1/2 In. 2760.00
Chiffonier, Bowfront, Mahogany, Ebony Medallions, 6 Drawers, 59 In. 6325.00
Chiffonier, Fruitwood, Veined Marble Top, 7 Drawers, 44 3/4 In. 5750.00
Chiffonier, Louis XVI, Tulipwood, 3 Drawers, Tapered Legs, 27 x 19 In. 2530.00
Chippendale, Chair, Carved Crest, Serpentine Slip Seat, Ball & Claw Feet, Arms, Pair . 3630.00
Chippendale, Chair, Mahogany, 4-Ribbed Pierced Splat, Molded Crest Rail, Slip Seat . .   440.00
Coat Rack, Buffalo Horn 195.00
Coat Rack, Horn, Mirror 1625.00
Commode, Burl Birch, Elm Border, 3 Long Drawers, 1740s, 33 x 45 . . . . 9775.00
Commode, Durand, Tulipwood, Purplewood, Serpentine, Marble Top, Door, Pair 8625.00
Commode, Dutch Rococo, Walnut, Seaweed Marquetry, 4 Drawers, 32 x 34 In. 8050.00
Commode, Empire, Mahogany, 3 Long Drawers, Ormolu Mounted, 36 3/4 In. 5750.00
Commode, Empire, Mahogany, Fruitwood, Ebonized, 1840s, 37 x 53 In. 3335.00

Commode, Faux Marble Top, 2 Short Over 2 Long Drawers, Painted, 33 x 45 In. 8625.00
Commode, George III, Mahogany, 2 Doors, Apron Front, 30 x 21 x 19 In. 980.00
Commode, George III, Mahogany, 2 Faux Drawers, Square Feet, 31 In. 805.00
Commode, Georgian, Mahogany, Apron, Cabriole Legs, Claw Feet, 21 x 20 In. 345.00
Commode, Holland, Mahogany, Hinged Top, Well, Tambour Doors, 33 1/2 In. 8050.00
Commode, I.B. Hedouin, Tulipwood, Kingwood, Marble Top, Drawers, 33 1/4 In. 5175.00
Commode, Kingwood, Mottled Marble Top, 2 Short & 2 Long Drawers, 52 In. 6900.00
Commode, Lift Top, Grain Painted, 1 Drawer, 31 x 24 In. 275.00
Commode, Louis XV, 3 Aligned Drawers, Scrolled Vines, 29 In., Pair 400.00
Commode, Louis XV, Bronze Mounted, Marble Top, 37 x 39 x 18 1/4 In. 865.00
Commode, Louis XV, Walnut, Serpentine, Carved, 51 In. 8625.00
Commode, Louis XVI, Rectangular Marble Top, 1 Door, 31 In., Pair 552.00
Commode, Louis XVI, Walnut, Rectangular Top, 3 Drawers, 32 x 47 1/2 In. 5175.00
Commode, Mahogany, Tray Top, Pierced Handles, Doors, 1 Drawer, 30 1/2 In. 880.00
Commode, Mottled Marble Top, 2 Short Over 2 Long Drawers, Parquetry 7475.00
Commode, Neoclassical, Mahogany, 3 Drawers, Square Tapered Legs, 32 In. 231.00
Commode, Neoclassical, Walnut, 2 Drawers, Tapered Legs, 35 x 46 x 22 In. 3450.00
Commode, Oak, Mirror, Candleholders, 2 Drawers & Doors 160.00
Commode, Oak, Serpentine, Towel Bar, 3 Drawers, 1 Door, 48 x 32 x 19 In. 230.00
Commode, Pine Top, Spoon Feet, Square, 20th Century 38.00
Commode, Poplar, 1 Door, 3 Drawers, Backsplash, 38 1/2 x 30 In. 253.00
Commode, Regency, Rosewood, Oblong Thumbnail Marble Top, 32 x 48 In. 8050.00
Commode, Rococo Style, Serpentine Top, 2 Drawers, 30 x 23 x 14 1/2 In. 345.00
Commode, Rococo, Ormolu, Serpentine, Burnt Orange Marble Top, 35 In. 11500.00
Commode, Rococo, Tulipwood, Walnut, Mid-18th Century, 31 x 21 In. 10350.00
Commode, Rococo, Walnut, Black Walnut, Fruitwood Border, 32 In. 8050.00
Commode, Rococo, Walnut, Fruitwood, 3 Drawers, Splayed Legs, 10 x 17 In. 2875.00
Commode, Rococo, Walnut, Fruitwood, Mid-18th Century, Italy, 35 In. 2185.00
Commode, Rococo, Walnut, Mid-18th Century, Italy, 33 x 43 x 18 In. 2415.00
Commode, Serpentine, 3 Long Drawers, Parcel Gilt, Painted, 34 x 51 In. 4315.00
Commode, Walnut, 3 Dovetailed Drawers, Cutout Feet, 17 x 31 In. 385.00
Commode, Walnut, 3 Dovetailed Drawers, Fruit Pulls, Victorian, 31 x 15 x 31 In. ... 355.00
Commode, Walnut, Marble Top & High Backsplash, Shelves, Victorian 935.00
Commode, Walnut, Marble Top, Parquetry & Marquetry, 60 In. 8625.00
Commode, Walnut, Poplar, 3 Dovetailed Drawers, Victorian, 28 x 16 x 30 In. 220.00
Commode, White Marble Top, 1 Shelf, 19th Century, 43 x 31 x 21 In. 425.00
Console, Adam Style, D-Shape, Painted, Pair 5175.00
Console, Art Deco, Wrought Iron, Hammered Columns, Glass Top, 1935, 29 In. 3450.00
Console, Art Deco, Wrought Iron, Scrolled Supports, Charles Piquet, 1925, 36 In. 5462.00
Console, Baroque Revival, Walnut, Crest, 60 x 20 x 48 In. 1375.00
Console, Demilune, Pier Mirror, Ebonized, 1 Door, 1 Drawer, Painted, 2 Piece 1540.00
Console, Ebonized, Parcel Gilt, Greek Key Border, Ball Feet, 30 In., Pair 6900.00
Console, Empire, Eglomise, Mythological Creatures, 32 1/4 In. 865.00
Console, Mahogany, Fruitwood Doors, Marble Inset, African Scenes, 40 In. 8050.00
Console, Oak, Gray & White Marble Top, Serpentine Frieze, 1750s, 35 3/4 In. 9200.00
Console, Rococo Revival, Walnut, Baluster Stem, 3 Scrolled Feet, 35 x 37 In. 1035.00
Console, Walnut, Marble Top, Foliate Frieze, Flowering Vines, 33 1/2 In. 9200.00
Console, Walnut, Marble Top, Parchment Back Panel, France, 1928, 48 In. 4890.00
Console, Wrought Iron, Marble, Scrolled Tendrils, 1930, 36 x 29 In. 1725.00
Costumer, G. Stickley, Original Finish & Hardware, 65 1/2 In. 3305.00
Couch, Tufted Back, Scrolling Top, Carved Giltwood Sphinx Supports, 92 In. 8625.00
Couch, Wicker, White, Seat Cushion, 70 In. 350.00
Cradle, Bentwood, Wheels, Silver Stripes, Gold Stenciling, Ford Johnson, 54 In. 605.00
Cradle, Cherry, Dovetailed, 42 1/2 In. 220.00
Cradle, Hooded, Painted Interior, 19th Century 300.00
Cradle, Mahogany, Hooded, Rockers, 40 In. 550.00
Cradle, Mattress Made From Sugar Sack, Mid-19th Century 470.00
Cradle, Oak, Hooded, 36 In. 190.00
Cradle, Walnut, Curly Maple Brackets, Scrolled, Square Posts, Penna., 40 1/2 In. 970.00
Cradle, Walnut, Rocking, Turned Finials, 40 In. 110.00
Credenza, Baroque, Walnut, Italy, 33 1/2 x 25 1/2 x 12 1/2 In. 1725.00
Credenza, Birch, 10 Drawers, 2 Doors, Metal Pulls, Paul McCobb, 72 x 18 x 26 In. 1540.00
Credenza, Empire, Mahogany, 2 Columns, 1 Drawer, New York, 34 x 33 x 14 In. 330.00

Credenza, G. Nelson, Walnut, Sliding Black Masonite Doors, Chrome Legs, 24 In. 495.00
Credenza, Walnut, 2 Doors Flanking 4 Drawers, Formica Top, c.1960, 74 In. 935.00
Credenza, Walnut, 2 Short & 1 Long Drawer, Paneled Doors, Fitted Interior, 61 In. 6325.00
Credenza, Walnut, 3 Short Drawers, 3 Doors, Masks & Scrolls, 47 3/4 x 79 In. 4025.00
Credenza, Walnut, Hinged Top, Well, Cupboard Doors, 33 1/4 x 56 In. 8050.00
Credenza, Walnut, Leaded Beveled Glass Doors, Marble Top, Brass, Hardware 4250.00
Credenza, Walnut, Lift Top, Frieze, 2 Panel Doors, Italy, 35 x 31 1/2 In. 1980.00
Credenza, Walnut, Marble Top, Convoluted Scroll Stretcher, Shelf, 58 1/2 In. 4510.00
Crib, Brass, Victorian 1500.00
Crib, Walnut, Victorian, Casters, 41 1/2 x 41 1/2 In. 190.00
Cupboard, 2 Doors, Molded Panels, 4 Shelves, Painted, Canada, 70 x 63 In. 690.00
Cupboard, Baroque, Oak, Walnut, 2 Doors, 17th Century, Germany 1300.00
Cupboard, Cherry, Scalloped Apron, 4 Doors, 47 x 52 x 85 In. 1045.00
Cupboard, Chimney, Painted White, Black Feet, Pegged Construction, 75 7/8 In. 4300.00
Cupboard, Chimney, Pine, 1 Paneled Door, Mustard Grained, Cornice 1045.00
Cupboard, Chimney, Pine, Blue Paint, Wire Nails, 17 x 38 In. 335.00
Cupboard, Chimney, Pine, Blue, Board Door, Cutout Feet, 18 x 24 x 67 In. 396.00
Cupboard, Cloak, 2 Paneled Doors, Red Over Dark Blue, 64 In. 4600.00
Cupboard, Corner, 1 Chamfered Panel Door, Painted 1250.00
Cupboard, Corner, 4 Paneled Doors, Olive Green Paint, Molded Cornice 2750.00
Cupboard, Corner, 9 Panes, 1 Paneled Door, Red Paint, Child's, 1 Piece 1000.00
Cupboard, Corner, Blue Paint, 108 In., 1 Piece 7750.00
Cupboard, Corner, Cherry, 16 Panes, Crown Molding, 1 Piece 2860.00
Cupboard, Corner, Cherry, 2 8-Light Doors Over 2 Paneled Doors, 82 In. 3740.00
Cupboard, Corner, Cherry, 2 Cathedral Doors, Cornice, Fluted Side Columns 2090.00
Cupboard, Corner, Cherry, 2 Doors & 2 Drawers Over 2 Doors, Turned Legs, 52 In. 3740.00
Cupboard, Corner, Cherry, 3 Drawers, Lower Doors, Upper Shelves, 1780s, 87 In. 7750.00
Cupboard, Corner, Cherry, Alligatored Varnish, 2 Glass Doors, Cornice, 88 In. 2750.00
Cupboard, Corner, Cherry, Curly Maple Drawer Fronts, 2 Piece, 80 3/4 In. 2640.00
Cupboard, Corner, Cherry, Glazed Doors, Raised Panel Doors, 1 Piece 3740.00
Cupboard, Corner, Cherry, Molded Cornice, 2 Drawers, 1830, 88 In., 2 Piece 2640.00
Cupboard, Corner, Cherry, Panel, Glass Top Doors, 2 Drawers, 1 Piece 3410.00
Cupboard, Corner, Cherry, Paneled Doors, 2 Dovetailed Drawers, 12 Panes, 87 In. 4070.00
Cupboard, Corner, Cherry, Paneled Doors, 6 Panes, 47 x 50 x 82 In. 2035.00
Cupboard, Corner, Cherry, Paneled Doors, Beaded, 46 x 79 In., 1 Piece 1000.00
Cupboard, Corner, Cherry, Poplar, Glass & Paneled Doors, 48 x 92 In. 4950.00
Cupboard, Corner, Cherry, Rounded, 12 Panes, 2 Base Doors, Cornice, 80 In. 1650.00
Cupboard, Corner, Cherry, Tiger Maple Inlay, 3 Shelves, Panel Door, 89 In. 1610.00
Cupboard, Corner, Hanging, R. Cahoon, Jr., Prince Albert On Horseback On Door 1100.00
Cupboard, Corner, Hepplewhite, Poplar, Paneled Doors, 2 Drawers, 41 x 86 In. 3520.00
Cupboard, Corner, Mahogany Veneer, Inlay, 2 Glass Doors, 47 x 91 In., 2 Piece 2540.00
Cupboard, Corner, Pine, 12 Panes, 2 Paneled Doors, 89 In. 1100.00
Cupboard, Corner, Pine, 2 Door, 2 Drawers, 3 Panes, 86 In. 1485.00
Cupboard, Corner, Pine, 2 Raised Paneled Doors, Cornice, 50 x 88 In. 2915.00
Cupboard, Corner, Pine, Double-Panel Doors, 2 Short Drawers, French Feet, 91 In. 6325.00
Cupboard, Corner, Pine, Green Paint, Quebec, 1860 . . . . 2015.00
Cupboard, Corner, Pine, Red Paint, Yellow Trim, Blue Interior, 77 3/4 In. 3575.00
Cupboard, Corner, Poplar, 12 Panes, Plate Rail, 1 Paneled Base Door 1320.00
Cupboard, Corner, Poplar, Cutout Feet, Board & Batten Doors, 80 1/2 In. 330.00
Cupboard, Corner, Softwood, 12 Panes, 1 Drawer, Hanover, Penna., 82 In. 1760.00
Cupboard, Corner, Walnut, 16 Panes, 2-Door Base, 89 1/2 In., 2 Piece 1540.00
Cupboard, Corner, Walnut, Molded Cornice, 1 Paneled Door, 34 x 35 x 22 In. 1035.00
Cupboard, Corner, Walnut, Pine, Paneled Doors, Applied Moldings, 83 In. 1320.00
Cupboard, Corner, Walnut, Wood Pinned Construction, Porringer Shelves 2300.00
Cupboard, Corner, William & Mary, Walnut, 2 Doors, Ball Feet, 74 1/2 In. 8050.00
Cupboard, Grain Painted, 3 Open Shelves, Lower Doors, 1840s, 80 In. 5462.00
Cupboard, Hanging, Pine, 2 Doors, Painted Birds, Penna., 29 x 25 x 8 In. 745.00
Cupboard, Hanging, Pine, Red Finish, Beaded Edges, 24 x 8 x 15 In. 330.00
Cupboard, Hanging, Pine, Wrought-Iron Hinges, Shelves, Pigeonholes, 17 x 24 In. 1155.00
Cupboard, Hanging, Poplar, Butternut, Dark Brown, Alligatored, 18 x 10 x 30 In. 520.00
Cupboard, Hanging, Poplar, Paneled Door, Gallery & Crest, 16 3/8 x 30 In. 165.00
Cupboard, Hanging, Poplar, Paneled Door, Yellow, Green, Brown, Red, 18 In. 4025.00
Cupboard, Hanging, Poplar, Pine, Dark Cherry Finish, 24 x 11 x 26 In. 440.00

Cupboard, Hanging, Walnut, 1 Drawer & Door, 1 Pane, 31 3/8 In. 308.00
Cupboard, Hanging, Walnut, Scrolled Detail, Paneled Door, 14 x 5 x 22 In. 220.00
Cupboard, Jelly, Cherry, Walnut, Poplar Door Panels, 18 1/2 x 44 1/2 x 55 In. 880.00
Cupboard, Jelly, Pine, 4 Interior Shelves, 47 1/2 In. 1600.00
Cupboard, Jelly, Pine, Bluish Gray Paint, 2-Board Door, 41 1/2 x 13 3/4 x 47 In. 412.00
Cupboard, Jelly, Pine, Board & Batten Door, Painted Interior, 35 x 12 x 33 In. 385.00
Cupboard, Jelly, Pine, Flame Painted, 63 In. 4620.00
Cupboard, Jelly, Pine, Hand Dovetailed, c.1830 . . . . 1095.00
Cupboard, Jelly, Pine, Painted, Wire Nails, Board & Batten Doors, 39 1/2 x 51 In. 385.00
Cupboard, Jelly, Pine, Raised Panel Doors, Applied Moldings, 18 x 43 x 42 In. 605.00
Cupboard, Jelly, Pine, Red Flame Graining, Scalloped Base, Brass Latch, 63 In. 4620.00
Cupboard, Jelly, Pine, Yellow Paint, 2 Doors, Hinged Top Drawer, 18 x 37 x 72 In. 1155.00
Cupboard, Jelly, Poplar, Alligatored, Scene Painted On Doors, 40 x 42 x 63 In. 1045.00
Cupboard, Jelly, Poplar, Black Paint, Cutout Feet, Raised Panel Doors, 71 1/2 In. 1210.00
Cupboard, Jelly, Poplar, Board & Batten Doors, Drawers, Crest, 39 x 50 In. 577.00
Cupboard, Jelly, Poplar, Paneled Door, Cast-Iron Latch, Porcelain Knob, 39 In. 535.00
Cupboard, Jelly, Poplar, Red & Blue Paint, Yellow Interior, 73 In. 415.00
Cupboard, Jelly, Poplar, Red Paint, 1 Paneled Door, Gallery, 50 In. 770.00
Cupboard, Jelly, Sheraton, 2 Drawers Over 2 Doors, 44 1/2 In. 990.00
Cupboard, Kitchen, Golden Oak Era, Paneled Doors, 2 Drawers, Crest, 37 x 75 In. 440.00
Cupboard, Kitchen, Pine, Rounded Front, 2 Doors, 2 Bins, 64 x 44 x 26 In., 2 Piece 195.00
Cupboard, Kitchen, Pink, Pumpkin, 2 Base & 2 Top Glass Doors, Gallery, 84 x 48 In. . . . 330.00
Cupboard, Oak, Blind Fretwork, Globular Finials, 2 Doors, 17th Century, 61 1/2 In. 3450.00
Cupboard, Oak, Broken Pediment Over Floral-Carved Case, 1 Door, 1890s, 48 In. 490.00
Cupboard, Oak, Turned Legs, Open Shelf, 2 Glass Sides & Doors, 30 x 19 x 35 In. 385.00
Cupboard, Open Shelf, Blind Door, Scalloped Trim, Blue Paint, Child's, 1 Piece 495.00
Cupboard, Pewter, 3 Drawers, Reeded Pilasters, Molded Cornice 4345.00
Cupboard, Pewter, Pine, Open Top, Dovetailed Case, 78 1/2 x 40 In. 1792.00
Cupboard, Pewter, Pine, Poplar, Open Shelves, 2 Paneled Doors, 69 In. 1100.00
Cupboard, Pewter, Red Tulips On Blue & Green Ground, 72 x 50 In. 1100.00
Cupboard, Pine, 2 Doors, 16 Inside Drawers, Blue Paint, 19th Century 247.00
Cupboard, Pine, 2 Doors, Bracket Feet, 82 x 63 x 20 1/2 In. 1495.00
Cupboard, Pine, Corner, 2 Doors Over 2 Doors, Raised Panels 3400.00
Cupboard, Pine, Corner, Glazed Doors, 3 Interior Shelves, 19th Century, 87 In. 2415.00
Cupboard, Pine, Corner, Pickled Finish, Double Doors Top & Bottom, 87 In. 1320.00
Cupboard, Pine, Corner, Stepped Cornice, Twin Panels, Doors, c.1790, 87 In. 2750.00
Cupboard, Pine, Jelly, Board & Batten Door, 1 Drawer, 45 x 35 1/4 In. 550.00
Cupboard, Pine, Paneled Doors, Single Shelf, Blue, 33 x 48 1/4 x 20 1/4 In. 4600.00
Cupboard, Pine, Poplar, 2 Paneled Doors, Shelved Interior, 60 7/8 In. 9200.00
Cupboard, Pine, Red Stain, Bow Front, Step-Back Base, Hanging, 40 In. 190.00
Cupboard, Pine, Step Back, Upper Doors, 2 Drawers, Yellow, Brass Pulls, 79 In. 2090.00
Cupboard, Poplar, 2 Glass Doors, Brown Graining, Mustard Ground, 86 In., 2 Piece 1870.00
Cupboard, Poplar, 6 Raised Panel Doors, 3 Drawers, Pie Shelf, 85 1/4 In. 2530.00
Cupboard, Poplar, Chimney, Grayish Beige Paint, 1927, 62 In. 360.00
Cupboard, Poplar, Cock-Beaded Paneled Doors, 2 Drawers, 88 3/4 In. 2970.00
Cupboard, Poplar, Paneled Doors, Pie Shelf, 2 Drawers, 83 In., 2 Piece 1000.00
Cupboard, Raised Paneled Doors, Red Wash, Early 19th Century, 83 x 52 In. 5950.00
Cupboard, Satinwood, c.1900-1910, 33 1/4 x 14 x 13 1/2 In. 2300.00
Cupboard, Shaker, Interior Pegs, Grained Red Over Blue 4600.00
Cupboard, Shaker, Mustard Paint, 1 Door, Wood Knob, 54 x 26 1/2 In. 2070.00
Cupboard, Step Back, c.1870, Miniature, 22 1/2 In. 1450.00
Cupboard, Step Back, Cherry, Poplar, 2 Dovetailed Drawers, 89 In. 4070.00
Cupboard, Step Back, Chippendale, Mahogany, 3 Base Drawers, 36 x 73 In. 605.00
Cupboard, Step Back, Chippendale, Walnut, Pennsylvania 6900.00
Cupboard, Step Back, Glazed Doors On Top, 2 Drawers Over 2 Doors, 86 In. 376.00
Cupboard, Step Back, Oak, 2 Glass Doors, Drawers Below, 1800s 1500.00
Cupboard, Step Back, Pine, 2 Panel Doors, 2 Doors In Lower Section, 78 In. 1210.00
Cupboard, Step Back, Pine, Poplar, Blue Paint, 3 Base Drawers, 36 x 71 In., 1 Piece 605.00
Cupboard, Step Back, Poplar, 4 Paneled Doors, 4 Spice Drawers, 85 In. 1430.00
Cupboard, Step Back, Poplar, Curly Maple Front, 2 Glass Doors, 81 In. 1755.00
Cupboard, Step Back, Poplar, Pewter, Open Shelves, 2 Lower Doors, 75 1/4 In. 770.00
Cupboard, Step Back, Red, 2 Doors, Vermont 950.00
Cupboard, Step Back, Walnut, Curly Maple, Poplar Door Panels, 1850s, 80 In. 450.00

Cupboard, Step Back, Walnut, Double Doors, Drawers In Base, Pie Shelf, 82 In. 2970.00
Cupboard, Step Back, Walnut, Paneled Doors, 2 Drawers, Brass Latches, 81 1/4 In. 1980.00
Cupboard, Teakwood, Serpentine, Carved Animal Feet, Pierced Doors, India, 37 In. 605.00
Cupboard, Walnut Veneer, Carved Ornaments, Adjustable Shelves, 1910s, 50 1/2 In. 165.00
Cupboard, Walnut, 2 Plank Doors, Feet, Blue Paint 1300.00
Cupboard, Walnut, Pinned Construction, 45 In. 2350.00
Daybed, Arts & Crafts, Oak, Shaped Panels, Fitted Mattress, c.1910, 82 In. 1300.00
Daybed, Birch, Iron, Upholstered Seat & Back, Paul McCobb, 73 In. 1100.00
Daybed, Birch, Loose Velvet Cushion, Velvet, Denmark, 76 In. 525.00
Daybed, Dominique, Nickled Bronze, Upholstered, 1930s, 90 In. 9775.00
Daybed, Empire, Cherry, Out-Scrolled Arms, Bracket Feet 1495.00
Daybed, G. Nelson, Walnut, Metal, Upholstered Slab Seat & Back, 42 In. 990.00
Daybed, G. Stickley, Original Pegs, Brown Leather, 34 x 83 1/2 In. 4627.00
Daybed, Knoll, Walnut, Chrome, Tufted Leather Cushion, Round Pillow, 80 x 40 In. 4950.00
Daybed, L. & J.G. Stickley, No. 291, Slanted Headrest, Cushion, Decal, 76 x 30 In. 1000.00
Daybed, Lift Top, Sliding Lower Drawer, Grain Painted 1000.00
Daybed, Mahogany, Shaped Head & Footboards, Triple-Pierced Splats 275.00
Daybed, Maple, Blue Velvet Cushion 95.00
Daybed, Neoclassical Style, Scrolled Arms, Reeded Legs, Italy, 74 1/4 In. 1265.00
Daybed, Red Scroll, Ivory Linen, 53 x 33 In. 2990.00
Daybed, Robsjohn-Gibbings, Walnut, Strap-Woven Seat, 4 Post Legs, 84 In. 575.00
Daybed, Rococo, Walnut, Late 18th Century, Italy, 34 x 84 In. 2760.00
Daybed, Stickley Brothers, No. 3752, 3-Slat Headboard, Cushion, 72 x 28 In. 330.00
Daybed, Walnut, Spool Turned, Open Arms, 1 Loose Cushion, Trundle, 72 In. 250.00
Daybed, William & Mary, Walnut, Leather, Straw Stuffing 7475.00
Daybed, Yamasaki, Orange, Purple Plaid Cushions, 1960, 72 x 26 In. 770.00
Desk, 2 Tambour Drawers, Document Door, 2 Long Drawers, 20th Century, 43 1/2 In. 860.00
Desk, 3 Drawers, Cabriole Legs, Carved, Cane Seat, Woman's 495.00
Desk, Architect's, Walnut, Back Rail & Bookrack, 4 Drawers, 57 x 84 In. 1725.00
Desk, Biedermeier, Drop Front, Veneers, Secret Drawer, 1825 .... 8950.00
Desk, Birch, Slant Front, Red Stain, Oxbow Front, Canted Ogee Bracket Feet, 36 In. 8050.00
Desk, Bugatti, Wood, Parchment, Copper Inlay, 6 Drawers, c.1900, 38 1/2 x 21 In. 6325.00
Desk, Burl Walnut, Painted Scroll & Foliate Medallion, Pullout Slide, 38 In. 2760.00
Desk, Butler's, Cherry, Walnut Veneer, Drawer Dated 1825, 54 In. 4620.00
Desk, Butler's, Curly Maple Veneer, Fitted Interior, 28 x 19 3/4 In. 1540.00
Desk, Butler's, Curly Maple, Mahogany, 2 Drawers, Pigeonholes, Mirror, 43 x 50 In. ... 1540.00
Desk, Butler's, Empire, Maple, Mahogany, Mirror, Pigeonhole, 43 x 22 x 50 In. 1540.00
Desk, Butler's, Federal, Fall-Front, Cherry, Pigeonholes, c.1820, 20 x 48 x 46 In. 1100.00
Desk, Butler's, Mahogany, 4 Drawers, Fitted, 8 Small Drawers, Bracket Feet 825.00
Desk, Butler's, Rosewood Veneer, 3 Drawers, Pullout Desk Drawer, 40 x 38 In. 715.00
Desk, Butternut, Stand-Up, Hinged Lid, 1 Drawer, 19th Century, 39 x 40 In. 517.00
Desk, Campaign, British Colonial, Camphorwood, Brassbound, Fitted Interior, 8 In. 750.00
Desk, Campaign, Gothic Style, Naval Officer, Lieutenant Commander Feitz 2200.00
Desk, Centennial, Drop Front, Mahogany, Fitted Interior Over 1 Drawer, 44 In. 2145.00
Desk, Cherry, 3 Side-By-Side Inlaid Drawers, 48 x 38 1/2 In. 4840.00
Desk, Cherry, Drop Front, Fitted Interior, 4 Drawers, Brass Handles, 45 1/2 In. 1980.00
Desk, Cherry, Slant Front, 4 Interior Drawers, c.1790, 43 1/2 In. 8050.00
Desk, Chestnut, Escutcheons On All 4 Panels, 28 1/2 x 35 1/2 In. 375.00
Desk, Chippendale, Cherry, 2 Short Drawers, Green Writing Surface, 48 In. 4312.00
Desk, Chippendale, Poplar, 3 Drawers, Ogee Feet, 14 In. 715.00
Desk, Chippendale, Slant Front, 1790, 40 x 39 x 18 In. ....*Illus* 880.00
Desk, Chippendale, Slant Front, Cherry, 4 Dovetailed Drawers, Ogee Feet, 31 In. 3025.00
Desk, Chippendale, Slant Front, Cherry, 4 Drawers, Fitted, Chamfered Corners, N.Y. 2200.00
Desk, Chippendale, Slant Front, Cherry, 4 Graduated Drawers, R.I., 1770, 42 In. 4315.00
Desk, Chippendale, Slant Front, Mahogany, 4 Dovetailed Drawers, 33 1/4 In. 6050.00
Desk, Chippendale, Slant Front, Mahogany, 4 Dovetailed Drawers, R.I., 43 In. 9350.00
Desk, Chippendale, Slant Front, Maple, 3 Graduated Drawers, 1770, 40 In. 10925.00
Desk, Chippendale, Slant Front, Maple, 4 Overlapping Dovetailed Drawers, 41 In. 1650.00
Desk, Chippendale, Slant Front, Maple, Ball & Claw Feet, Mass., 37 x 18 x 43 In. 7700.00
Desk, Chippendale, Slant Front, Walnut, Pigeonholes, Drawers, 40 x 20 x 41 In. 2530.00
Desk, Cylinder, Bookcase Base, 2 Doors, Victorian ....*Illus* 1980.00
Desk, Cylinder, Drop Front, Mahogany Veneer, Label, Germany, Early 19th Century 9950.00
Desk, Cylinder, Walnut, Victorian, 40 x 44 In. 885.00

Furniture, Desk, Mahogany, Slant Front, Serpentine, 18th Century Style

Furniture, Desk, Chippendale, Slant Front, 1790, 40 x 39 x 18 In.

Furniture, Desk, Cylinder, Bookcase Base, 2 Doors, Victorian

Desk, Davenport, Bird's-Eye Maple, Oak 1325.00
Desk, Davenport, Lift Top, Walnut, Drawers In Gallery, 40 1/2 In. 550.00
Desk, Davenport, Walnut, Burl Walnut, c.1860 .... 1850.00
Desk, Double Pedestal, Pencil Slot, Built-In Seat, Italy, Child's, 31 x 43 In. 1725.00
Desk, Drop Front, Birch, Interior Drawers, 4 Graduated Drawers, Child's, 21 In. 4315.00
Desk, Drop Front, Tiger Maple, Fitted Interior, 4 Drawers, 41 x 38 In. 3410.00
Desk, Dutch Neoclassical, Walnut, Floral Marquetry, Kidney Shape, 30 3/4 In. 2760.00
Desk, Eames, Birch Top, L-Shaped, Chrome Supports, 2 File Drawers, 60 In. 6875.00
Desk, Eastlake, Lift Top, Walnut, Molded, Relief Carved, Leather Inset, 27 x 35 In. 275.00
Desk, Eastlake, Mahogany, Oak, Floral Door, 19th Century, 53 x 39 x 22 1/2 In. 865.00
Desk, Edwardian, Mahogany, Two Drawers, Pigeonholes, Inlay, 1905 .... 715.00
Desk, Empire, Step Back, Figured Cherry, Fold-Down Desk Box, 36 x 24 x 41 3/4 In. 880.00
Desk, Frankl, Mahogany, Cork Trim, 1949, 26 x 60 In. 6500.00
Desk, French Style, Walnut Veneer, Kidney Shape, 20th Century, 50 x 23 x 31 In. 385.00
Desk, G. Nelson, Walnut, Cantilevered Section, Drawer & File Unit, 30 x 60 In. 2310.00
Desk, G. Nelson, Walnut, Leather Top, Sliding Doors, Steel, 1948, 54 In. 4675.00
Desk, G. Stickley, 1 Drawer, Copper Hardware, 28 x 18 x 35 In. 2530.00
Desk, G. Stickley, Chalet, Keyed Tenon Sides, Shoe Feet, 1902, 11 x 16 x 46 In. 2200.00
Desk, G. Stickley, Desk, Leather Top, 9 Drawer, Keys & Tenons, 30 12 In. 6236.00
Desk, G. Stickley, Drop Front, Hammered Copper Hinges, Red Brown, 49 x 26 In. 8625.00
Desk, G. Stickley, No. 505, Chalet, Mahogany, Shoe Feet, 24 x 16 x 46 In. 1320.00
Desk, G. Stickley, No. 518, 2 Shelves, Hammered Copper Hinges, 52 x 26 In. 3300.00
Desk, G. Stickley, No. 550, 2 Half Drawers, 1 Drawer, Red Decal, 33 In. 4400.00
Desk, G. Stickley, No. 721, Drop Front, Chestnut, Slab Sides, 29 x 14 x 37 In. 990.00
Desk, G. Stickley, Oak, 2 Drawers, Tapered Legs, 1910, 30 x 40 In. 2415.00
Desk, G. Stickley, Oak, Rectangular Top, 8 Legs, 1912, 36 1/4 In. 1150.00
Desk, George I, Slant Front, Walnut, Burl Walnut, c.1720, 41 In. 8000.00
Desk, George II, Slant Front, Walnut, Hinged Writing Surface, 2 Drawers, 40 In. 715.00
Desk, George III, Satinwood, Reeded Legs, Woman's, 55 x 34 x 21 In. 5060.00
Desk, George III, Slant Front, Mahogany, 4 Graduated Drawers, 39 x 43 In. 1265.00
Desk, George III, Slant Front, Mahogany, 42 x 36 1/4 x 19 1/2 In. 865.00
Desk, Governor Winthrop Style, Oxbow Slant Front, Mahogany, Fitted Interior 302.00
Desk, Hepplewhite, Slant Front, Cherry, 4 Graduated Drawers, 41 1/2 In. 1725.00
Desk, Hepplewhite, Slant Front, Cherry, Inlay, Barber Pole Drawer Dividers, 41 In. 2200.00
Desk, Hepplewhite, Slant Front, Walnut, 4 Drawers, Inlaid Interior, c.1790, 45 In. 1200.00
Desk, Herman Miller, Walnut Veneer, 3 Side Drawers, Steel, 40 x 24 x 29 In. 880.00
Desk, Kidney Shape, Painted, Flowers, Birds, Yellow Ground, 30 In. 1840.00
Desk, Kneehole, George III, Mahogany, 7 Drawers, Bracket Feet, 30 1/2 In. 2875.00
Desk, Kneehole, Louis XV, 3 Drawers, Scroll Skirt, Cabriole Legs, 48 x 20 In. 230.00
Desk, Kneehole, Oak, 4 Drawers, 1906, 38 1/4 In. 1035.00
Desk, L. & J.G. Stickley, Drop Front, 2 Drawers, Arched Apron, 43 x 40 1/2 In. 460.00
Desk, L. & J.G. Stickley, Drop Front, Gallery, 2 Small Drawers, Base Shelf 1950.00
Desk, L. & J.G. Stickley, No. 400, Copper Pulls, Through Tenon, 42 x 30 In. 1100.00

Desk, L. & J.G. Stickley, No. 512, Walnut, 2 Shelves On Each Side, 40 x 26 In. 1100.00
Desk, Lap, Camphor, Folding Section, Secret Drawer, Brassbound, 9 x 21 In. 1375.00
Desk, Lap, Lacquer, Hinged Cover, Bottles, Wells, Drawer, Chinese Export, 28 1/2 In. 316.00
Desk, Lap, Mahogany, 1 Side Drawer, Banded Line Inlay, 7 x 20 In. 300.00
Desk, Lap, Mahogany, Brass Hardware Banding, 19th Century, 6 x 14 x 9 In. 86.00
Desk, Lap, Pine, Painted Tin Inset, 2 Inkwells, Pen Holder, Velvet Lined, 15 In. 515.00
Desk, Lap, Satinwood, Marquetry, Landscape Scene, 14 1/2 x 12 In. 635.00
Desk, Lap, Walnut, Banded Top, Name Plate, Tooled Leather Surface, 7 1/4 x 18 In. 175.00
Desk, Limbert, No. 701, Chalet Shape, Woodburned Portrait In Center, 44 In. 1100.00
Desk, Louis XV, Mahogany, Tulipwood, 2 Drawers, 38 x 30 In. 1610.00
Desk, Louis XV, Marquetry, Floral, Colored Woods Gallery, Woman's 3290.00
Desk, Louis XVI, Mahogany, Satinwood Borders, Russia, 31 x 53 x 28 In. 6900.00
Desk, Louis XVI, Slant Front, Tulipwood, Serpentine, Cabriole Legs, 37 x 28 In. 1150.00
Desk, Louis XVI, Walnut, 1 Drawer, Tapered Legs, 39 x 27 x 17 In. 865.00
Desk, Mahogany, 3 Drawers In Frieze, Tapered Legs, Woman's 385.00
Desk, Mahogany, Carlton House, Inlay, England 2640.00
Desk, Mahogany, Leather Surface, 1 Long & 3 Short Drawers, Writing Slides, 52 In. 4887.00
Desk, Mahogany, Leather Top, Double Pedestal, c.1920, 30 x 60 In. 2500.00
Desk, Mahogany, Slant Front, 2 Drawers, Pale Blue Interior, Brown, 1810, 10 In. 2415.00
Desk, Mahogany, Slant Front, Serpentine, 18th Century Style ....*Illus* 495.00
Desk, Maple, Slant Front, Scrolled Compartments, 2 Small Drawers, 44 x 37 In. 6325.00
Desk, Metal, George Nelson, 1955 .... 950.00
Desk, Mother-Of-Pearl Inlay, Ormolu Mounts, 19th Century, Woman's 935.00
Desk, Neoclassical, Central Star Design, 6 Aligned Drawers, 32 x 47 x 23 In. 3000.00
Desk, Neoclassical, Roll Top, Walnut, 1790-1810, Italy, 43 x 43 1/2 x 24 In. 4600.00
Desk, Oak, Double Pedestals, 8 Square Tapering Legs, 60 In. 120.00
Desk, Parquetry, Brown Leather Writing Surface, 2 Drawers, France, 30 x 77 In. 7475.00
Desk, Partner's, 8 Drawers, Ball & Claw Feet, Late 19th Century 2200.00
Desk, Partner's, Applied Scroll & Leaves, Carved Women On Corners, 19th Century 2420.00
Desk, Partner's, Carved Gadrooned Border, Push-Pull Drawers, Felt Top 3300.00
Desk, Partner's, Chippendale Style, Bowfront, Mahogany, 54 x 30 x 29 In. 1100.00
Desk, Partner's, L. & J.G. Stickley, Walnut, 1 Drawer, 48 x 30 x 30 In. 2200.00
Desk, Partner's, Limbert, No. 739, Slant Top, Trestle, 36 x 40 In. 3300.00
Desk, Partner's, Mahogany, Carved Border, Rounded Corners, 54 x 34 x 28 In. 1100.00
Desk, Partner's, Mahogany, Chippendale, Red Leather Top, c.1870 .... 3950.00
Desk, Partner's, Mahogany, Inset Leather Top, 3 Drawers, Lyre Legs, 30 1/4 In. 3910.00
Desk, Partner's, Oak, 2 Graduated Drawers, Green Leather Inset, 1870, 60 x 44 In. 6900.00
Desk, Partner's, Oak, Glass Over Leather Top, 14 Drawers, 48 x 60 In. 495.00
Desk, Partner's, Oak, Lion's Head & Claw Feet, 36 x 54 In. 9750.00
Desk, Partner's, Saarinen, Walnut Sides, White Rectangular Top, 42 x 30 x 31 In. 330.00
Desk, Pedestal, Charles X, Mahogany, Inset Leather Top, Gilt Metal Feet, 31 In. 2300.00
Desk, Pedestal, George III, Mahogany, 9 Drawers, Molded Plinth, 29 1/2 In. 9775.00
Desk, Pedestal, George III, Mahogany, Leather-Lined Top, 6 Drawers, 47 In. 6325.00
Desk, Pedestal, Mahogany, Gilt Tooled Leather Inset, 6 Drawers, Victorian 3450.00

Have you ever pulled a drawer
handle and had it fall off the
drawer? This problem is not
uncommon for very old furniture
with bail handles. The best way to
get the handleless drawer open is
to use a plunger, the plumber's
friend. Stick it to the front of the
drawer, then pull.

Furniture, Desk, Roll
Top, Cylinder Lock,
Bookcase
Top, Pressed
Wood Design

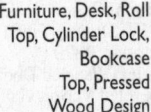

Furniture, Desk, Slant Front,
Fruitwood, Mahogany, Woman's
Head In Crest

Furniture, Desk, Secretary,
Chippendale Style, Mahogany,
Bookcase Top

Furniture, Desk, William & Mary
Style, Walnut, Adolf Kilsch, 1870,
58 x 42 x 25 In.

Desk, Plantation, Walnut, 1 Drawer, Fruit Pulls, Double-Door Top, 83 x 43 In. 935.00
Desk, Portable, Rosewood, Blown Glass Ink Bottles, Brasses, Felt Lined, c.1850 . . . . 300.00
Desk, Presentation, Renaissance Revival, Walnut, Gilt, 1865 . . . . 286.00
Desk, Queen Anne, Walnut, Knee Hole, 7 Drawers, Crossbanded, England, 34 In. 330.00
Desk, Regency, Mahogany, 3 Drawers, Trestle Supports, 30 x 48 x 32 In. 1095.00
Desk, Renaissance Revival, Shoe Feet, Cutout Ends, 3 Drawers, Woman's, 36 x 30 In. . . . 248.00
Desk, Renaissance Revival, Walnut, 3 Drawers, 2 Doors, 27 1/4 x 57 x 30 In. 360.00
Desk, Rococo Revival, Slant Front, Walnut, 38 1/2 x 36 3/4 In. 2300.00
Desk, Roll Top, 2 Roll, Oak, 2 Pedestals, 4 Drawers, 1 Door, 50 x 44 In. 440.00
Desk, Roll Top, Cylinder Lock, Bookcase Top, Pressed Wood Design . . . .*Illus* 1045.00
Desk, Roll Top, Derby Desk Co., S Roll, Oak, Fitted Interior, 4 Drawers, 43 1/2 In. 715.00
Desk, Roll Top, Eastlake, Shelf, Crest Rail 770.00
Desk, Roll Top, Oak, Divided Interior, Tapered Legs, c.1900, 39 x 32 x 23 In. 210.00
Desk, Roll Top, S Roll, Oak, 8 Drawers, Fitted Interior, 49 x 59 1/2 In. 1375.00
Desk, Roll Top, S Roll, Quartersawn Oak, 3 Side Drawers, Oak Chair, 42 x 51 In. 935.00
Desk, Roll Top, Walnut, Oak, Fitted Interior, 19th Century 9800.00
Desk, Satinwood, Carlton House, 1 Drawer, Leather Writing Slide, 1880s, 51 In. 8625.00
Desk, Schoolmaster's, Cherry, Dovetailed, Drawer, Fitted Interior, 25 x 41 In. 275.00
Desk, Schoolmaster's, Slant Front, Cherry, Lift Top, Turned Legs, 30 x 24 x 37 In. 330.00
Desk, Schoolmaster's, Slant Front, Pine, Drawer, 41 x 20 x 39 In. 220.00
Desk, Schoolmaster's, Slant Front, Walnut, Fitted Interior, 39 x 38 In. 825.00
Desk, Secretary, Chippendale Style, Mahogany, Bookcase Top . . . .*Illus* 550.00
Desk, Secretary, Mahogany, 2 Serpentine Doors, 4 Base Drawers, 1890, 1 Piece 2640.00
Desk, Sheraton, Mahogany, 2 Gothic Glass Doors, 3 Base Drawers, Woman's, 79 In. 3575.00
Desk, Slant Front, Bookcase Top, 2 Paneled Doors, Grain Painted 800.00
Desk, Slant Front, Figured Maple, Stepped Interior, Valanced Pigeonholes 6050.00
Desk, Slant Front, Fruitwood, Mahogany, Woman's Head In Crest . . . .*Illus* 2420.00
Desk, Slant Front, Mahogany, 4 Overlapping Drawers, New England, 9 x 43 In. 3740.00
Desk, Slant Front, Maple, 7 Drawers, Pigeonholes, Graduated Drawers, 39 x 41 In. 2015.00
Desk, Slant Front, Pegged Construction, Painted, 1 Inner Compartment, 1840 . . . . 395.00
Desk, Slant Front, Pine, Red Design Against Black Ground, 9 x 15 x 14 1/2 In. 520.00
Desk, Slant Front, Rosehead Nails, Backboard Signed, F.B. 1805, 14 In. 1275.00
Desk, Slant Front, Rupp Type, 12 Interior Drawers, 1861 . . . . 2900.00
Desk, Slant Front, Tiger Maple, Cherry, Document Drawers, 4 Drawers, c.1750 . . . . 5175.00
Desk, Slant Front, Walnut, Light Top, Drawers Behind Drawers, 41 x 29 In. 1500.00
Desk, Slant Front, Wavy Birch, Oxbow, Inside Drawers, Graduated Drawers, 44 In. 5175.00
Desk, Typewriter Drawer, Fill Drawer, Fitted Interior, Leather, Wood, Metal, 1946 . . . . . . 6500.00
Desk, Walnut, Boston, Victorian, 1870 . . . . 6050.00
Desk, Walnut, Carved Pilasters, Paneled Doors, Fold-Down Lid, Fitted, 55 In. 440.00
Desk, Walnut, Cylinder, Beveled Mirror, Gallery Top, 65 x 31 1/4 In. 1850.00
Desk, Walnut, Drop Front, c.1870 . . . . 850.00

Desk, Walnut, Drop Front, Pigeonholes, Carved Drawers, Belgium, 1930s 270.00
Desk, Wicker, White Paint, Glass Top, Chair 400.00
Desk, William & Mary Style, Walnut, Adolf Kilsch, 1870, 58 x 42 x 25 In. .... *Illus* 3575.00
Desk, Wooton, Oak, Spindle Gallery 8000.00
Desk, Work, Walnut, Compartment Interior, 1 Drawer, Victorian, 31 In. 425.00
Desk Bookcase, Mahogany Veneer, Shelves Over Drawers, Fold-Out Surface, 1885 .... 1495.00
Dinette Set, Chrome, Green, 4 Chairs, 1950s 400.00
Dining Set, Duncan Phyfe Style, Mahogany, 1 Armchair, 8 Piece 605.00
Dining Set, Herman Miller, Aluminum, Laminated, Naugahyde Chairs, 5 Piece 2090.00
Dining Set, Johnson Furniture, Birch Veneer, 4 Upholstered Curved Chairs 3575.00
Dining Set, Oak, Round Table, 6 Leather Chairs, 5 Leaves 1200.00
Dining Set, Peter Hunt, Ladder Back, Rush Seat, 9 Piece 3080.00
Dining Set, Quartersawn Oak, 6 Matching Chairs, Buffet, Table 5500.00
Dining Set, Renaissance Revival, Burl Mahogany, 7 Piece 660.00
Dresser, 14 Divided Drawers, Oak, Quartersawn, 30 1/2 x 22 x 78 In. 1125.00
Dresser, Arts & Crafts, Mahogany, 3 Short Drawers, 2 Full Drawers, Mirror, 71 In. 990.00
Dresser, Bird's-Eye Maple, Serpentine Front, Framed Oval Beveled Mirror 300.00
Dresser, Burl Walnut, Veneer, Marble Top, Mirror, Victorian, 88 3/4 In. 302.00
Dresser, Burl Walnut, Wishbone Mirror, c.1880 .... 400.00
Dresser, Cherry, Convertible Marble Sink, Water Reservoir, Towel Racks, 1876 .... 3495.00
Dresser, Chippendale, Mahogany, 3 Graduated Cock-Beaded Drawers, 36 In. 1610.00
Dresser, E. Wormley, Walnut, 3 Drawers, 30 x 36 In. 660.00
Dresser, G. Nelson, Rosewood, 10 Drawers, Hourglass Steel Pulls & Legs, 33 In. 5060.00
Dresser, G. Nelson, Rosewood, 4 Drawers, Stainless Steel Pulls, Pad Feet, 33 In. 1380.00
Dresser, G. Stickley, No. 911, Iron Pulls, 48 x 22 x 67 In. .... *Illus* 12100.00
Dresser, Limbert, 2 Half Drawers 2 Full Drawers, 40 x 22 x 67 In. 1870.00
Dresser, Mahogany, 2 Small & 2 Large Drawers, Swing Mirror, 1920s, 50 In. 360.00
Dresser, Oak, 4 Shallow Shelves, Rectangular Top, 84 x 99 x 20 In. 7360.00
Dresser, Oak, Beveled Mirror, 2 Dovetailed Drawers, 30 x 17 1/2 In. 550.00
Dresser, Oak, Beveled Side Mirror, Side Storage .... *Illus* 440.00
Dresser, Oak, Cornice Over Open Shelves & Doors, 2 Banks Of Drawers, 85 In. 2300.00
Dresser, Pine, Molded Cornice, Plinth Base, 19th Century, 66 x 40 In. 1380.00
Dresser, Renaissance Revival, Burl Walnut, Incised Designs, Marble Top, 93 In. 635.00
Dresser, Walnut, 2 Short & 2 Long Drawers, Bracket Feet, 33 1/2 x 39 1/2 In. 198.00
Dresser, Walnut, 3 Dovetailed Drawers, 3 Hankie Drawers, Victorian, 40 x 75 In. 305.00
Dresser, Walnut, 3 Drawers, 2 Step-Back Drawers, Victorian, 38 x 17 x 68 In. 245.00
Dresser, Walnut, 3 Drawers, Marble Top, 2 Step-Back Boxes, Victorian, 62 In. 375.00
Dresser, Walnut, 3 Drawers, Marble Top, Brass Pulls, Casters, 33 x 35 In. 330.00
Dresser, Walnut, 4 Drawers, Fruit Pulls, Masonite Back, 43 1/2 In. 187.00
Dresser, Walnut, Figured Veneer, Matching Mirror, Fruit Pulls, Marble Top, 40 In. 605.00
Dresser, Welsh, Oak, 2 Drawers, 2 Paneled Doors, 18th Century, 61 x 79 In. 3500.00
Dresser, Welsh, Oak, 2 Upper Shelves, Central Drawer, Pad Feet, 74 1/2 In. 1090.00

Furniture, Dresser, Oak, Beveled
Side Mirror, Side Storage

Furniture, Highboy, Queen
Anne Style, Mahogany

Furniture, Dresser, G. Stickley, No.
911, Iron Pulls, 48 x 22 x 67 In.

Dresser, Welsh, Oak, Cabriole Legs, 3 Drawers, Open Shelves, 63 x 72 In., 2 Piece 1430.00
Dresser, Welsh, Oak, Lower Pot Board, 83 In. 8500.00
Dresser, Welsh, Queen Anne Style, Oak, 2 Shelves, Drawer, Stepped Cornice, 75 In. 950.00
Dry Sink, Cherry, Oak, 19 x 59 x 17 1/2 In. 335.00
Dry Sink, Dark Gray, Red Panels, c.1900, Child's, 19 x 24 In. 950.00
Dry Sink, Oak, Drop-Down Work Surface, Door & 3 Drawers On Side 1250.00
Dry Sink, Pine, 1 Long Drawer Over 2 Doors, Knobs, Shelved Backsplash 50.00
Dry Sink, Pine, 2 Drawers, 2 Paneled Doors, 47 x 20 x 33 In. 715.00
Dry Sink, Pine, Amish, 1870s, 31-In. Front, 49-In. Back 1400.00
Dry Sink, Pine, Blue Paint, Cutout Feet, Shelf, 39 x 30 1/2 In. 770.00
Dry Sink, Poplar, Brown Grained, 1-Board Ends, 2 Doors, 41 x 17 In. 1150.00
Dry Sink, Poplar, Cutout Feet, 2 Paneled Doors, 1 Lower Drawer, 36 1/2 In. 412.00
Dry Sink, Poplar, Drawer, Paneled Doors, Raised Back, Shelf, 54 x 43 In. 525.00
Dry Sink, Tin-Lined Sink, Mustard Yellow Paint 890.00
Dry Sink, Walnut, Red, Cutout Feet, 1-Board Ends, 1 Paneled Door, Ohio, 15 x 24 In. ... 4235.00
Dry Sink, Yellow Paint, Scalloped Sides, Zinc Top & Backsplash, Ohio, 1800s 695.00
Dumbwaiter, George III Style, Mahogany, Brass Feet On Casters, 46 1/2 In. 375.00
Dumbwaiter, Mahogany, 3 Tiers, Urn-Tuned Shaft, Cabriole Legs, 1870s, 44 In. 2875.00
Easel, Rococo Revival Style, Mahogany, Carved, Painted Gold Scrollwork, 84 In. 198.00
Easel, Rococo Revival, Brass, Tripod, Sliding Adjustable Support Bracket 247.00
Etagere, Biedermeier, Walnut, Columnar Supports, Leaf-Tip Terminals, 56 1/4 In. 2300.00
Etagere, Burl Walnut, c.1880, 48 In. 1900.00
Etagere, Cherry, Beveled Mirror, Ball-Turned Supports, 1880-1900, 55 1/2 In. 1150.00
Etagere, Corner, Mahogany, 5 Rounded Shelves 137.00
Etagere, Eastlake, Mirror, Lower Shelf, 1900 .... 780.00
Etagere, George III, Mahogany, 3 Tiers, Turned Legs, Brass Casters, 1800, 48 In. 415.00
Etagere, Louis XV, Walnut, Scalloped Edge, Cabriole Legs, 26 1/2 In. 184.00
Etagere, Mahogany, 4 Tiers, Drawer In Lowest Section, 53 1/2 x 18 In. 4312.00
Etagere, Mahogany, 5 Tiers, Ring-Turned Supports, Victorian, 62 In. 3737.00
Etagere, Mahogany, 5 Tiers, Ring-Turned Supports, Victorian, 77 In. 4312.00
Etagere, Regency, Mahogany, Ribbed Legs, Paw Feet, 42 x 18 In. 4025.00
Etagere, Rosewood, 3 Tiers, Down-Swept Legs, Casters, 37 3/4 In. 4312.00
Etagere, Rosewood, Foliate Crest, Scroll Supports, Legs, 1860, 92 x 62 x 20 In. 4830.00
Etagere, Tiger Maple, 3 Drawers, 3 Shelves, Turned Posts, c.1830, 53 x 39 In. 3220.00
Etagere, William IV, Mahogany, Reeded Legs, 48 x 20 x 15 3/4 In. 2760.00
Footstool, American Empire, Mahogany, Upholstered Cushion, 17 1/2 In. 632.00
Footstool, Bird's-Eye Maple, 19th Century 875.00
Footstool, Chippendale, Mahogany, Slip Seat, Cabriole Legs, 27 x 21 In. 328.00
Footstool, Curly Maple Legs, Oval Upholstered Top, 9 1/2 x 14 1/2 In. 300.00
Footstool, Curly Maple, Old Finish, Curly Maple Graining, Pine Legs, 6 x 11 In. 770.00
Footstool, Eastlake, Walnut, Burl Inlay, 4 Carved Legs, Round, Upholstered, 18 In. 165.00
Footstool, G. Stickley, 17 1/4 x 19 3/4 x 16 In. 374.00
Footstool, G. Stickley, Leather, 12 1/2 x 12 1/2 In. 373.00
Footstool, G. Stickley, No. 300, Arched Apron, 20 x 15 In. 1320.00
Footstool, George III, Walnut, Cabriole Legs, Ball Feet, 18 1/2 x 22 3/4 In. 297.00
Footstool, J.M. Young, Arched Apron, Leather Top, Paper Label, 17 x 18 In. 330.00
Footstool, Louis XV Style, Walnut, Elongated, Floral Apron, 6 1/4 x 25 1/2 In. 575.00
Footstool, Louis XV Style, Walnut, Needlepoint, 12 x 14 In. 92.00
Footstool, Mahogany, Concave Over-Upholstered Top, 1810, 15 x 21 In. 977.00
Footstool, Mahogany, Salem Type, Octagonal, Upholstered, 1810, 12 x 8 1/2 In. 695.00
Footstool, Pierced Cast Iron, Floral Needlepoint, 8 x 14 1/2 In. 385.00
Footstool, Pine, Legs Mortised Through Top, 7 x 12 x 6 1/2 In. 150.00
Footstool, Pine, Red Paint, Cutout Feet, Fluted Apron, 8 1/2 x 20 x 11 In. 220.00
Footstool, Ribbon, Printed Velvet, P. Paulin, 15 x 27 1/2 In., Pair 357.00
Footstool, Robsjohn-Gibbings, Walnut, Square Seat, Rounded, Flaring Dowel Legs 747.00
Footstool, Shaker, Mt. Lebanon, Dark Finish 350.00
Footstool, Smoker's, Limbert, No. 225, 1 Drawer, Leather Top, 12 x 18 x 12 In. 600.00
Footstool, Walnut, Drop-In Seat, Paper Label, 20 x 14 x 15 In. 495.00
Footstool, Walnut, Figured, Shaped Aprons, Splayed Feet, 7 In. 255.00
Footstool, Walnut, Foliate-Carved Edge, Cabriole Legs, Victorian, 42 In. 345.00
Footstool, Windsor, Black, 14 In. 72.00
Frame, Birch Bark, Deer Horns, 48 In. 1800.00
Frame, Giltwood, Carved Foliate, Wavy Inner Border, Spain, 4 1/2 x 7 In. 2587.00

Frame, Giltwood, Easel-Shaped, Micromosaic, 16 In. 670.00
Frame, Giltwood, Pierced Foliage Around Beaded Border, Spain, 16 x 11 In. 4887.00
Frame, Giltwood, Strapwork, Scrolls, Ribbon-Bound Husks, Italy, 42 x 36 In. 2875.00
Frame, Parquetry, Stepped, 19th Century, 36 x 32 In. 980.00
Hall Stand, Golden Oak, Lift Seat, Paneled Back, Beveled Mirror, 78 In. 580.00
Hall Stand, Mahogany, Mirrored Sides & Center, Brass Trim, 6 Hooks, 85 In. 1650.00
Hall Tree, Arts & Crafts, Tapered Cruciform Stem, 4 Hooks, 4 Feet, 70 In. 220.00
Hall Tree, Golden Oak, Side Umbrella Stand, Arms, Tin Drip Pans, Lift Seat, 69 In. 467.00
Hall Tree, Oak, Hooks, Umbrella Hold, Drip Pan 2850.00
Hall Tree, Thonet, Bentwood, 69 1/4 In. 330.00
Hat Rack, 3 Sets Of Buffalo Horns 375.00
Hat Rack, Walnut, Ships Wheel, Mirror, Porcelain Capped Peg Hooks, 37 In. 270.00
High Chair, Arrowhead, Bamboo-Turned Legs, Gold Striping, 37 In. 247.00
High Chair, Captain's Chair Back, 30 1/4 In. 137.00
High Chair, Converts To Play Table, Decals & Beads 600.00
High Chair, Early 1800s, 18-In. Seat 525.00
High Chair, Eastlake, Walnut, Burl Veneer, Cane Seat, 36 In. 110.00
High Chair, Figural Elephant Design, 40 1/2 In. 250.00
High Chair, Ladder Back, Woven Splint Seat, 33 In. 148.00
High Chair, Mahogany, French-Style Painted Design, Cane Back, 1910 . . . .   550.00
High Chair, Maple, Hickory, Rush Seat, 31 In. 3625.00
High Chair, Oak, On Wheels, Folds To Become Walker, 40 In. 148.00
High Chair, Oak, Pressed Back, Cane Seat, 40 1/4 In. 135.00
High Chair, Windsor, Thumb Back, Green Paint, Black Bandings 236.00
Highboy, Mahogany, Walnut, Fan Carved, Beaded Drawers, Shaped Skirt 9350.00
Highboy, Marvel Furniture Co., Tag On Back, 1903 . . . .   1500.00
Highboy, Queen Anne Style, Mahogany . . . . .Illus   385.00
Highboy, Queen Anne Style, Tiger Maple, Charles Arena, Summit, N.J., 30 In., 2 Pc. 2587.00
Highboy, Queen Anne, 11 Drawers, Reconstructed Base, American 5500.00
Highboy, Queen Anne, Cherry, 4 Graduated Drawers, Cabriole Legs, 70 In. 9775.00
Highboy, Queen Anne, Cherry, 5 Overlapping Drawers, Fan-Carved Base, 78 In. 5775.00
Highboy, Queen Anne, Cherry, Maple, Birch, Cabriole Legs, 80 3/4 In. 8250.00
Highboy, Queen Anne, Cherry, Pennsylvania House, 42 x 82 In., 2 Piece 990.00
Highboy, Queen Anne, Maple, 1 Top Drawer, Mock Twin Drawers, 63 1/2 In. 8250.00
Highboy, Queen Anne, Maple, Flat Top, 4 Drawers, 1750, 70 In.   6000.00
Highboy, Walnut, Fan-Carved Drawer, 3 Full Drawers, 72 In. 5500.00
Highboy, William & Mary, Maple, Frame, c.1710, 64 x 39 In. 7200.00
Highboy, William & Mary, Walnut, 4 Upper & 3 Lower Drawers, 70 In. 2750.00
Humidor, On Stand, Columns Each Corner, Drawer, A. Dunhill, c.1900, 34 In. 2645.00
Huntboard, Pine, Brown Paint, Square Legs, 3 Drawers, 25 x 41 x 37 In. 880.00
Hutch, Harvest, Pine, 4 Upper & Lower Doors, 85 x 66 x 19 In., 2 Piece 635.00
Hutch, Maple, Upper Shelves, Vertical Cabinets, Brass Fillet Doors, 68 5/8 In. 143.00
Hutch, Pine, 2 Open Shelves, 2 Drawers Over 2 Cabinet Doors, 84 In. 1610.00
Hutch, Pine, 3 Open Shelves, Lower Short Drawers, Stretcher Shelf, 79 1/2 In. 330.00
Hutch, Pine, 3 Shelves Over 2 Paneled Doors, 79 1/2 x 52 In. 1100.00
Hutch, Step Back, Maple, Bird's-Eye Maple, c.1920, 66 x 18 In. 625.00
Hutch, Watch, Carved & Painted Wood, 1830s, 8 1/4 In. 1610.00
Ice Cream Set, Cast Iron, Marble Top, Scrollwork, 1950s, 3 Piece 285.00
Ice Cream Set, Oak, Quartersawn Veneer Top, 2 Chairs, 29 x 30 In. 330.00
Ice Cream Set, Table, 2 Chairs, Round Table, 20 x 29 In., 1915-1925 . . . .   920.00
Kas, Poplar, Varnish Over Red, Raised Panel Doors, Applied Moldings, Ohio, 73 In. 3025.00
Kas, Walnut, Crossbanded Doors, Corinthian Columns, Germany, 90 x 76 In. 8050.00
Lazy Susan, Mahogany, Piecrust Top, Circular Feet, Late 19th Century, 22 In. 345.00
Library Steps, Mahogany, 2 Drawers 395.00
Library Steps, Stretcher-Shaped Steps, 1780s, 19 x 37 In. 4600.00
Linen Press, Flame Mahogany, 2 Top Doors, 3 Graduated Drawers, 1800, 38 In. 3800.00
Linen Press, George III, Mahogany, Panel Inset Doors, 52 x 24 In. 8050.00
Linen Press, Mahogany, Marquetry, 3 Shelves, Late 18th Century, 87 In. 9200.00
Linen Press, Mahogany, Oval Paneled Doors, 2 Short Over 2 Long Drawers, 82 In. 9775.00
Linen Press, Walnut, 2 Top Drawers, 2 Paneled Doors, 1845 . . . .   2400.00
Love Seat, Le Corbusier, Vinyl, 25 1/2 x 46 In. 490.00
Love Seat, Mahogany Veneer, Armless, Velvet, 1845, 45 1/8 In. 187.00
Love Seat, Rococo, Walnut, Carved Grape Design, Victorian, c.1860 . . . .   1550.00

Love Seat, Walnut, Carved, Victorian Style, 53 In. 440.00
Love Seat, Walnut, Thumb-Molded Crest, Upholstered, Victorian 847.00
Love Seat, Wicker, Basket-Weave Back & Arms, Upholstered Cushion, 56 In. 145.00
Love Seat, Windsor, Maple, Thumb Back, Rush Seat, c.1820 . . . . 1500.00
Lowboy, Cherry, Drawer Over Center Drawer, Carved Shell, 30 x 36 In. 715.00
Lowboy, Chippendale, 2 Drawers, Cabriole Legs, Ball & Claw Feet 275.00
Lowboy, Chippendale, Walnut, 4 Drawers, Shell Design On Front, 36 x 31 x 20 In. 250.00
Lowboy, Jacobean, Oak, Floral Geometric Frieze, Baluster Legs, 51 x 44 x 17 In. 978.00
Lowboy, Oak, Pine, Scrolled Front Edge, 1 Drawer, 30 x 31 In. 440.00
Lowboy, Queen Anne Style, Mahogany, Cedar-Lined Interior, Lane Furniture Co. 155.00
Lowboy, Queen Anne, Hardwood, Mahogany Finish, 3 Drawers, Child's 275.00
Lowboy, Walnut, Figured Veneer, 3 Drawers, 1920s, 28 1/2 x 26 1/4 In. 550.00
Mirror, 2 Small Center Arrows, Helmets On Corners, Turquoise, 1940, 30 x 21 In. 63.00
Mirror, 3 Tiers Of Carved Framing, Beveled Mirror, 53 x 43 In. 330.00
Mirror, Arched Crest, Floral Border, Beveled Glass, 48 In. 415.00
Mirror, Architectural, Reverse Painted, Gold Paint, 24 x 13 In., 2 Piece 440.00
Mirror, Architectural, Reverse Painted, Gold Paint, 33 x 20 In., 2 Piece 1320.00
Mirror, Art Deco, Chrome, Black Lacquered Base, Round, 16 x 9 x 18 In. 65.00
Mirror, Baroque, Basket-Weave Border, Rectangular, 97 x 88 1/2 In. 5175.00
Mirror, Baroque, Foliate-Carved Crest, Serpentine, Italy, 30 x 18 In. 546.00
Mirror, Baroque, Fruitwood, Pierced Foliate, 41 x 36 In. 1100.00
Mirror, Chinese Chippendale Style, Giltwood, Pair 4370.00
Mirror, Chippendale, Mahogany, Base Crown, Scrollwork, 20 x 11 In. 440.00
Mirror, Chippendale, Mahogany, Giltwood Reserve, 1760, 28 In. 1495.00
Mirror, Chippendale, Mahogany, Giltwood, C-Scroll, Foliate Crest, 49 x 27 In. 1840.00
Mirror, Chippendale, Mahogany, Giltwood, Phoenix, Inlay, Gilt Liner, 38 In. 660.00
Mirror, Chippendale, Mahogany, Giltwood, Pierced Crest, 30 x 18 In. 374.00
Mirror, Chippendale, Mahogany, Giltwood, Scroll, Phoenix, 28 x 7 1/2 In. 1595.00
Mirror, Chippendale, Mahogany, Giltwood, Scroll, Phoenix, 45 x 25 In. 1090.00
Mirror, Chippendale, Mahogany, Scroll, Prince Of Wales Feather Ornament, 29 In. 330.00
Mirror, Chippendale, Tiger Maple, Scrolled Crest, 36 1/2 x 19 In., Pair 1150.00
Mirror, Chippendale, Walnut, Scrolled, 22 1/2 x 13 1/4 In. 715.00
Mirror, Classical, Giltwood, Beveled Glass, 24 1/2 x 36 In. 82.00
Mirror, Classical, Giltwood, Ebonized Half Columns, Boston, 62 x 33 In. 330.00
Mirror, Classical, Giltwood, Free-Standing Pilaster, Cornice, 26 x 43 In. 1650.00
Mirror, Classical, Giltwood, Girandole, Early 19th Century 5750.00
Mirror, Courting, Pine, Black, Gold, Floral Arabesque, 14 1/2 x 11 1/4 In. 440.00
Mirror, Curly Maple, Corner Blocks, Worn Silvering, 15 1/4 x 12 3/8 In. 740.00
Mirror, Decorated, Yellow & Black Paint, Half Columns, 12 3/4 x 10 3/4 In. 165.00
Mirror, Double-Arched Crest, Mother-Of-Pearl And Ivory Inlay, Syria, 63 In. 2875.00
Mirror, Dressing, Queen Anne, Recessed Center, 3 Drawers, 27 In. 1725.00
Mirror, Dutch Baroque, Ebonized, Beveled Glass, 49 x 39 In. 690.00
Mirror, Eagle At Top, Floral-Carved Sprays, Rosette Corner Blocks, 40 x 24 In. 440.00
Mirror, Empire, Brass Rosettes, Reverse Painted Church & Lake, 27 1/2 In. 330.00
Mirror, Empire, Giltwood, Beveled Glass, 24 x 40 In. 605.00
Mirror, Empire, Mahogany Veneer, Reverse Painted Fruit, 28 x 15 1/2 In. 302.00
Mirror, Federal, Eglomise, Floral, Black, Gold, Green Border, 1815, 43 In. 6325.00
Mirror, Federal, Eglomise, Shells, Coral, Floral, Beaded Base, 1815, 41 In. 805.00
Mirror, Federal, Giltwood, Convex, Leaf, Cornucopia, Floral & Eagle Finial, 40 In. 4400.00
Mirror, Federal, Giltwood, Half Columns, 4 Rosettes, Painted Bridge Scene, 34 In. 247.00
Mirror, Federal, Mahogany, Floral Sprays, Rectangular, 19th Century, 60 In. 2875.00
Mirror, Federal, Mahogany, Reeded & Ring-Trimmed Columns, 46 1/4 x 24 1/2 In. 302.00
Mirror, Federal, Mahogany, Twist Columns, Painted Tablet, Buildings, 19 x 39 In. 467.00
Mirror, Federal, Pine, Red & Yellow Grained, Reeded Pilasters, 21 x 13 In. 305.00
Mirror, Federal, Reverse Lithograph, Engraved Top, England, 20 x 36 In. 300.00
Mirror, Federal, Reverse Painted, Napoleon On Top, 15 x 29 In. 247.00
Mirror, Federal, Stenciled, Reverse Painted Table, 32 1/2 x 14 In. 275.00
Mirror, Foliate Crest, Panel Of Lovers In Country, Scrolled, 40 x 38 In. 345.00
Mirror, French Directoire, Garland & Flower Crest, c.1800, 58 x 25 In. 3400.00
Mirror, Fruitwood, Divided Plate, Flanked By 2 Mahogany Columns, 55 In. 1610.00
Mirror, G. Stickley, 6 Triple Hooks, Crested Top Rail, 28 x 36 1/2 In. 2310.00
Mirror, G. Stickley, Mahogany, Full-Length Swivel, Red Decal, 1904, 68 In. 7700.00
Mirror, George II, Giltwood, Cabochon-Shaped Crest, Flower Heads, 49 x 27 In. 9200.00

Mirror, George II, Mahogany, Parcel Gilt, 58 x 29 1/2 In. 4025.00
Mirror, George III, Giltwood, C-Scrolls & Leafy Branches Surround, Oval, 34 In. 3737.00
Mirror, George III, Giltwood, Pierced Foliate & C-Scroll, c.1760, 52 x 29 In. 9200.00
Mirror, George III, Giltwood, Scroll, Rocaille Design, 19th Century, 46 In. 2990.00
Mirror, George III, Mahogany, Giltwood Rococo Ornament, 52 In. 4200.00
Mirror, Georgian, Walnut, Swan Neck, Scrolled Borders, 57 x 25 1/2 In. 3220.00
Mirror, Giltwood, Divided Plate, Serpentine Cresting, Sweden, 1750s, 77 x 35 In. 8050.00
Mirror, Giltwood, Divided Plate, Serpentine Top Rail, 74 1/4 x 45 3/4 In. 2875.00
Mirror, Giltwood, Foliate & Acanthus Scrolls, 18th Century, 40 x 27 In. 1760.00
Mirror, Giltwood, Leaf Carved, Brass Candle Arms At Base, 25 3/4 x 23 In. 6325.00
Mirror, Giltwood, Oval, Palm Fronds & Flower Heads, 19th Century, 48 In. 3450.00
Mirror, Giltwood, Reverse Painted, Shipping Scene, Rectangular 330.00
Mirror, Giltwood, Ribbon Surmount, Oval, 19th Century, 36 x 25 In. 231.00
Mirror, Giltwood, Ribbon-Tied Branches, Long Leaves, 42 x 25 In. 6325.00
Mirror, Giltwood, Scrollwork Crest, Painted Flowers, 40 x 28 In. 380.00
Mirror, Giltwood, Split Baluster, Tablet Of Woman, c.1830, 32 x 16 In. 750.00
Mirror, Girandole, Eagle Pediment, 2 Candle Arms, Convex Glass, 32 x 24 In. 5940.00
Mirror, Girandole, Walnut, Carved Eagle On Pedestal, 19th Century, 48 In. 4830.00
Mirror, Gothic Arches, Glass Top, Polished Brass, 1940s, 44 x 25 1/2 In. 4312.00
Mirror, Green, Yellow, Black, Red Ground, Penna., 19th Century, 9 1/2 x 6 In. 2587.00
Mirror, Hector Guimard, Gilt Plaster, 1900, 41 x 50 In. 8435.00
Mirror, Italian Rococo Style, Carved, Foliage & Flowers, 76 x 60 In. 4312.00
Mirror, Italian Rococo, Giltwood, Scrolls, Flower Heads, 2 Candle Branches, 48 In. 3450.00
Mirror, L. & J.G. Stickley, Hanging Chains, 39 In. 1980.00
Mirror, L. & J.G. Stickley, Mahogany, Arched Top, Frame, 45 x 26 In. 2200.00
Mirror, Louis XVI, Giltwood, Berried Laurel Wreath, Foliate Swags, 71 In. 6900.00
Mirror, Louis XVI, Giltwood, Gesso, Garland, Leaf Crest, Beveled, 44 x 31 In. 1840.00
Mirror, Louis XVI, Giltwood, Love Trophy Under Floral Wreath, 31 x 18 In. 2875.00
Mirror, Mahogany Veneer, Giltwood Garlands, Eagle Finial, 29 3/4 x 18 In. 440.00
Mirror, Mahogany, Giltwood, Gesso, Fret Scroll, Eagle, 19th Century, 50 x 24 In. 1760.00
Mirror, Mahogany, Scroll Top, Eglomise Panel, 43 1/2 In. 430.00
Mirror, Mahogany, Seated Eagle On Crest, 51 1/2 x 20 1/2 In. 50.00
Mirror, Maple, Broken Arch Pediment, Turned Crest, 26 x 48 In. 77.00
Mirror, Molded, Paneled Backboards, Victorian, 1850s, 87 x 29 1/2 In. 1125.00
Mirror, Napoleon III, Mahogany, Marquetry, Gilt-Metal Foliate, 71 1/2 In. 920.00
Mirror, Napoleon III, Strapwork Cartouche Crest, Swag Flowers, 1850, 84 In. 121.00
Mirror, Nautical Picture Top, Beveled Glass, 19th Century, 29 x 14 In. 495.00
Mirror, Neoclassical Style, Mahogany, Brass Mounted, Russia, 60 x 25 1/4 In. 2300.00
Mirror, Neoclassical, Bead Molded, Berried Laurel Branches, 55 In. 8050.00
Mirror, Neoclassical, Giltwood, Molded Border, Foliate Swags, 34 1/4 In. 1150.00
Mirror, Neoclassical, Giltwood, Portrait Medallion, Foliate Scrolls, 45 In. 12650.00
Mirror, Neoclassical, Giltwood, Rosettes, Stepped Beading, Ogee, 62 In. 220.00
Mirror, Neoclassical, Mahogany, Molded Urn, Scrolled Apron, 18th Century, 39 In. 1380.00
Mirror, Neoclassical, Mahogany, Swan Design, Leaf-Tip Border, 65 In. 8625.00
Mirror, Neoclassical, Stylized Corinthian Capitals, Baltic, 50 In., Pair 3450.00
Mirror, Oak Back Panel, Brass Screws, Jean-Michel Frank, 1930, 68 1/4 In. 4600.00
Mirror, Pier, Baroque Revival, Giltwood, 74 3/4 x 33 In. 390.00
Mirror, Pier, Baroque Revival, Giltwood, Marble Top, 101 In. 220.00
Mirror, Pier, Beveled Glass, Diamond Frieze, 20th Century, 24 x 89 In. 522.00
Mirror, Pier, Eastlake, Walnut, Burl Veneer, Shelf, Drawer, Stone Top, 27 x 82 In. 440.00
Mirror, Pier, Eastlake, Walnut, Rosewood, White Marble Shelf, 28 1/2 In. 1045.00
Mirror, Pier, Mahogany, Brass Inlay, Stand, 60 x 30 In. 550.00
Mirror, Pier, Rococo Revival, Giltwood, Victorian, 87 1/2 x 36 In. 715.00
Mirror, Pier, Walnut, Burl Veneer Stiles, 68 3/4 In. 305.00
Mirror, Queen Anne, Arched Top, Double Plate Mirror, 48 x 22 In. 489.00
Mirror, Queen Anne, Ebonized, Arched Beveled Plate, Frame, 1710, 40 1/2 In. 1035.00
Mirror, Queen Anne, Mahogany, Scroll, 16 1/4 x 9 5/8 In. 385.00
Mirror, Queen Anne, Maple, Scroll Crest, Engraved Swan, Flowers, 15 x 10 In. 485.00
Mirror, Queen Anne, Shell-Carved Crest, 23 x 12 In. 1265.00
Mirror, Queen Anne, Walnut Veneer, Giltwood Ornaments & Liner, 25 x 11 3/8 In. 935.00
Mirror, Queen Anne, Walnut Veneer, Scroll, Ornaments, Gold Paint, 31 x 13 In. 1210.00
Mirror, Queen Anne, Walnut Veneer, Scroll, Prince Of Wales Feather, 36 x 14 In. 550.00
Mirror, Queen Anne, Walnut, Arched Beveled Plate, Foliate, 1710, 47 1/2 In. 1725.00

Mirror, Queen Anne, Walnut, Scrolled Crest, Beveled, 1760, 30 1/2 In. 1610.00
Mirror, Queen Anne, Walnut, Scrolled Crest, Oblong, Beveled, 1750, 30 In. 1265.00
Mirror, Regency, Convex, Carved Eagle Crest, 2 Candleholders, 40 In. 1320.00
Mirror, Regency, Giltwood, Convex, Spherule Mounted, Eagle At Top, 41 In. 3450.00
Mirror, Regency, Giltwood, Convex, Spread-Winged Eagle Design, 55 In. 770.00
Mirror, Regency, Giltwood, Garland Frieze, 4 Fluted Columns, 28 x 61 1/2 In. 2760.00
Mirror, Renaissance Revival, Giltwood, Gesso, Oval, 52 x 35 In., Pair 5300.00
Mirror, Reverse Painted, Fruit Basket, Stenciled, Folk Art, 20 x 11 In. 300.00
Mirror, Reverse Painted, Man & Woman Seated At Table Having Tea, 23 x 33 In. 1265.00
Mirror, Rococo Style, Giltwood, Leaf-Carved Surround, 33 1/2 x 33 In. 500.00
Mirror, Rococo, Cut Glass, Serpentine Side Border, 63 In. 5175.00
Mirror, Rococo, Giltwood, Floral, Scroll Design, 31 x 19 In. 575.00
Mirror, Rococo, Openwork Crest, Pendant Foliage, 18th Century, 35 In. 1100.00
Mirror, Rosewood, Baroque, Vine Inlay, Open Leaf Spandrels, 106 x 73 In. 1760.00
Mirror, Scrolled Crest, Gilt Incised Liner, 2-Part Beveled Glass, 40 x 16 In. 8525.00
Mirror, Shaving, Empire, Mahogany, Marble Top, 25 x 29 1/2 In. 248.00
Mirror, Shaving, Federal, Mahogany Veneer, 5 Dovetailed Drawers, Bowed Center 415.00
Mirror, Shaving, Mahogany Veneer, Bowfront, 3 Drawers, Oval, 22 In. 192.00
Mirror, Shaving, Maple, 2 Turned Standards, Rectangular Base, 25 3/4 In. 100.00
Mirror, Shaving, Maple, Mahogany Veneer, Bowfront, 3 Drawers, 24 In. 192.00
Mirror, Shaving, Polychrome Paint, Cast Iron, 18 In. 302.00
Mirror, Shaving, Sheraton, Table Top, Pedestal Base, 26 1/2 In. 297.00
Mirror, Shaving, Walnut, Molded Side Posts, Curved Top, Victorian, 25 x 30 In. 220.00
Mirror, Sheraton, Giltwood, Ball Drop Cornice, Corner Rosettes, 43 In. 330.00
Mirror, Sheraton, Giltwood, Ball Drop Cornice, Reverse Painted, 41 x 23 In. 1320.00
Mirror, Sheraton, Mahogany, Carved Crest, Reeded Columns, 44 x 22 In., 2 Piece 357.00
Mirror, Silver Mounted, Chased Bird & Flower Design, Beveled, 19 x 15 In. 825.00
Mirror, Tabernacle, Reverse Painted, Still Life With Fruit, 32 x 17 1/2 In. 715.00
Mirror, Traveling, Folding, Mahogany, Rectangular, 17 x 13 In. 259.00
Mirror, Tulipwood, Floral Marquetry, Gilt-Bronze Mounted, 31 In. 2587.00
Mirror, Venetian Baroque Style, Oval Plate, Floral Designs, 64 1/2 x 39 1/2 In. 5750.00
Mirror, Venetian Glass, Etched Floral Design, Geometric, 47 x 28 In. 1150.00
Mirror, Walnut Veneer, Ogee Molded, Cut Corners, 18 x 26 In. 82.00
Mirror, Walnut, Carved Cherubs, Flower Heads, Mid-19th Century, 64 In. 9200.00
Mirror, Walnut, Ebony, Chevron Inlay, Barnsley, 31 x 25 In. 2070.00
Mirror, Walnut, Molded Surround, Giltwood Foliage, Pierced Crest, 42 x 20 In. 4025.00
Mirror, Walnut, Monkeys Centering Shield, Bamboo Carved, France, 39 In. 3740.00
Mirror, Walnut, Reeded, Curly Maple Corner Blocks, 21 x 17 5/8 In. 190.00
Mirror, Walnut, Scrolled Ears, Pediment & Apron, Giltwood Bezel, 44 x 26 In. 1320.00
Mirror, William & Mary, Oyster Veneer, Flower-Shaped Crest, Rectangular, 1690 ...... 2530.00
Mirror, Wreath, Overlapping Ivy Leaves, Bow-Tied Swag, Cast Iron, 29 x 23 In. 3165.00
Ottoman, Art Deco, Walnut, Green Velvet, 18 x 16 x 14 In. 245.00
Ottoman, Walnut, Tapestry Cushion, In-Turned Base, Victorian, 17 1/4 In. 130.00
Ottoman, William & Mary, Triangular Sections, Circular Seat, Tapestry 4900.00
Parlor Set, Colonna, Extended Back, Upholstered, 1900, 5 Piece 10870.00
Parlor Set, Colonna, Extended Back, Upholstered, Arms, 1900, 3 Piece 14750.00
Parlor Set, Eastlake Style, Walnut, Upholstered, Victorian, 2 Piece 2400.00
Parlor Set, Louis XVI, Walnut, Padded Arms, Floral Chenille, Settee, 4 Chairs 3220.00
Parlor Set, Mahogany, Scrolled Arms, Settee, Rocking Chair, c.1900, 3 Piece 550.00
Parlor Set, Oval Back, Padded Arms, Aubusson Tapestry, 3 Piece 9775.00
Parlor Set, Triple Chair Back, Fruit Clusters, Rush Seat, c.1790, 2 Piece 5700.00
Parlor Set, Walnut, Finger Carved, Velvet, Victorian, 4 Piece 935.00
Parlor Set, Wicker, Chintz Cushions, c.1910, 2 Piece 950.00
Parlor Set, Wicker, Loose Cushions, Love Seat, 2 Armchairs, Coffee Table 187.00
Pedestal, Empire, Mahogany, Marble Top, Conforming Frieze, Paw Feet, 36 1/2 In. 2012.00
Pedestal, Mahogany, 3 Fixed Shelves, 49 1/4 In. 3450.00
Pedestal, Oak, Reeded Stand, Circular Base, Victorian, 34 x 13 In. 115.00
Pedestal, S. Roche, Plaster, Twisted Foliage, Square Top, 1935, 47 In., Pair 7500.00
Pedestal, Tulipwood, Marble Top, Parquetry, Male & Female Busts, 59 In., Pair 2300.00
Pie Safe, Cherry, 2 Drawers Over 2 Doors, Empire Turnings, 46 x 40 In. 815.00
Pie Safe, Cherry, Walnut, 2 Drawers Over 2 Doors, Punched Tin Panels, 51 In. 6160.00
Pie Safe, Hanging, Poplar, Punched Tin Panels, 34 In. 577.00
Pie Safe, Pine, 12 Punched Tin Panels, 70 x 38 In. 350.00

Pie Safe, Pine, 2 Drawers, Punched Tin Panels, Red Paint, 41 In. 875.00
Pie Safe, Pine, Bootjack Ends, 68 x 34 In. 495.00
Pie Safe, Pine, Diamonds On Door, Star Design, Blue, Green Paint, 46 In. 2420.00
Pie Safe, Poplar, 12 Punched Tin Panels, 57 In. 825.00
Pie Safe, Punched Tin Panels, Interior Shelves 1300.00
Pie Safe, Walnut, 12 Punched Tin Panels, Blue Paint 3400.00
Pie Safe, Walnut, 3 Heart & Star Panels, 1 Dovetailed Drawer, 58 In. 1000.00
Pie Safe, Walnut, Pegged, Lift-Off Doors 2800.00
Planter, Wicker, Natural, Victorian, 28 x 12 x 71 In. 225.00
Rack, Baker's, Charles X, Wrought Iron, Brass, Stamped Echalie Paris 862.00
Rack, Magazine, E. Wormley, Walnut, Triangular Top, Leather Straps, 23 x 24 In. 440.00
Rack, Magazine, Eastlake, Victorian 605.00
Rack, Plate, Arts & Crafts, Maple, Hanging, Arched Top, 1905, 22 x 40 In. 550.00
Rack, Plate, Shoe Feet, Gray Wash 1175.00
Rack, Quilt, Pine, 4 Parts, 66 In. 230.00
Recamier, Charles X, Rosewood, Scrolled Side, Floral Urn, Vine Inlay, 36 x 80 In. 660.00
Recamier, Classical, Mahogany, Gadroon Border, Leaf Legs, 1825, 74 In. 8625.00
Recamier, Classical, Mahogany, Stylized Dolphin Terminal, Reeded Legs, 32 In. 470.00
Recamier, Undulating Backrest, Out-Scrolled Sides, Upholstered Seat 3737.00
Rocker, Adirondack, Bent-Oak Slats, Natural Timber, 41 x 21 x 33 In. 835.00
Rocker, Adirondack, Bent-Oak Slats, Timber Supports, 37 x 24 In. 2115.00
Rocker, Arrow Back, Red Over Green Paint, Cheese-Cutter Rockers, Child's 595.00
Rocker, Arts & Crafts, 3 Vertical Back Slats, 3 Vertical Side Slats, 39 3/4 In. 460.00
Rocker, Arts & Crafts, Walnut, 5 Vertical Slats, Naugahyde Cushion, 28 In. 330.00
Rocker, Black Paint, White & Gold Striping, Polychrome Stencil, Arms, 24 In. 110.00
Rocker, Boston, Pine, 19th Century, 40 In. 154.00
Rocker, Captain's, Child's, 15 1/2 In. 60.00
Rocker, Eames, Fiberglass Shell, Bent-Metal Support, Birch Runners, 26 1/2 In. 575.00
Rocker, Eames, Fiberglass Shell, Birch Runners, Herman Miller, 27 In. . . . . . . .1045.00 to 1430.00
Rocker, Eames, Fiberglass Shell, Wire Base, Arms, 28 In. 825.00
Rocker, Eastlake, Walnut, Allover Carving, Crushed Velvet, 43 In. 110.00
Rocker, Eastlake, Walnut, Platform, Incised Design 70.00
Rocker, Edwardian, Mahogany, Satinwood, Crest Rail, 2 Circular Legs 400.00
Rocker, Faux Bamboo, Ladder Back, Rush Seat, Woman's 316.00
Rocker, Flower Design, Lyre Back, Bellevue, Ohio, 35 1/2 In. 195.00
Rocker, G. Stickley, 3-Slat Back, Leather Seat, Red Decal, 32 In. 275.00
Rocker, G. Stickley, 5 Vertical Back Slats, Dark Finish, 34 x 25 3/4 x 28 In. 605.00
Rocker, G. Stickley, H-Back, Rush Seat, Decal, 34 1/2 In. 412.00
Rocker, G. Stickley, Loose Back Pillow, Drop-In Seat, 38 x 29 1/4 In. 990.00
Rocker, G. Stickley, No. 323, 5 Wide Slats Under Arms, Cushions, 37 In. 1980.00
Rocker, G. Stickley, No. 343, 3-Slat Back, Leather Seat, Branded, Child's, 25 In. 410.00
Rocker, G. Stickley, No. 365, 3 Vertical Back Slats, Leather Seat, 38 x 26 In. 775.00
Rocker, G. Stickley, No. 1627, 2-Board Back, Thornden Arms, Rush Seat, 32 In. 440.00
Rocker, G. Stickley, No. 2603, 3-Slat Back, Open Under Arms, 36 In. 495.00
Rocker, Hunzinger, Walnut, Gold-Filled Line Carving, Silk, 1869 . . . . .1250.00 to 1500.00
Rocker, L. & J.G. Stickley, Inverted-V Back, 5 Vertical Slats, 34 x 26 In. 1122.00
Rocker, L. & J.G. Stickley, Walnut, 5-Slat Back, Spring Cushion, 30 x 36 In. 1540.00
Rocker, Ladder Back, 4-Slat Back, Carved, Woven Splint Seat, Arms, Ohio, 44 In. 2200.00
Rocker, Ladder Back, Arms, Child's 220.00
Rocker, Ladder Back, Rush Seat, Arms, Child's 300.00
Rocker, Ladder Back, Splint Seat, Arms, Child's, 26 1/2 In. 190.00
Rocker, Ladder Back, Traces Of Old Red Paint, Woven Splint Seat, Arms, 38 In. 170.00
Rocker, Limbert, 4 Horizontal Back Slats, Dark Finish, 27 x 32 x 32 In. 286.00
Rocker, Limbert, No. 828, 5-Slat Back, Drop-In Seat, Arms, Label, 33 In. 275.00
Rocker, Low Back, Mustard-Color Paint, Black Paint Accents, 1850s, 26 1/2 In. 635.00
Rocker, Nursing, Ladder Back, Maple, 5-Slat Back, Rush Seat, Turned Legs 80.00
Rocker, Oak, Mission, Lift-Out Seat, Webster Chair Mfg., c.1915 . . . . 187.00
Rocker, Oak, Pressed Back, Round Spokes, 1890s 250.00
Rocker, Oak, Spindle Back, Pressed Splat, North Wind Image, Open Arms, Cushion 175.00
Rocker, Plank Seat, Star & Circle Base, Green Paint, 32 In. 200.00
Rocker, Platform, Mahogany, Velvet Arms, 19th Century 165.00
Rocker, Platform, Oak, Upholstered Cushion Seat & Back Panel, c.1900 . . . . 65.00
Rocker, Red & Yellow Striping, Gold Stenciled Flowers & Fruit, Arms, 38 1/2 In. 104.00

Rocker, Roycroft, Corseted Back Slat, Leather Seat, Arms, 35 1/2 In. 825.00

Rocker, Shaker, 6 Mushroom-Type Arms, 42 x 17 In. 975.00

Rocker, Shaker, No. 1, Cherry, Mt. Lebanon, c.1875, Child's 1095.00

Rocker, Shaker, No. 1, Red Paint, Rush Seat, Child's, 30 x 15 In. 392.00

Rocker, Shaker, No. 3, Cherry, Web Back, Taped Seat, Label, Mt. Lebanon, 36 In. 460.00

Rocker, Shaker, No. 4, Armless, Label, Mt. Lebanon 415.00

Rocker, Shaker, Red & Black Tape Seat & Back, Arms, Mt. Lebanon, 37 3/4 In. 495.00

Rocker, Shaker, Taped Seat & Back, Arms, 38 In. 275.00

Rocker, Stickley Brothers, 3 Horizontal Slats, Rush Seat, Arms, 31 1/2 In. 230.00

Rocker, Stickley Brothers, Oak, Contoured Seat, Child's 100.00

Rocker, Walnut, Grape-Carved Crest, Molded Arms 27.00

Rocker, Walnut, Raised Panels, Upholstered, Victorian, 19th Century 66.00

Rocker, Walnut, Tufted Back, Finger Carved, Silk Brocade, 36 In. 220.00

Rocker, Wicker, Caned Back & Seat, 32 In. 165.00

Rocker, Windsor, Comb Back, Bamboo Turnings, Bentwood Arms, 45 In. 220.00

Rocker, Windsor, Comb Back, Bamboo, Black Paint, Striping, Arms, 43 In. 880.00

Rocker, Windsor, Comb Back, Bamboo-Turned Legs, Arm Posts, 43 In. 385.00

Rocker, Windsor, Comb Back, Brown Paint, Bamboo Turnings, 41 In. 1320.00

Rocker, Windsor, Comb Back, Reddish Brown Paint, Yellow Striping, Arms, 43 In. 605.00

Rocker, Windsor, Fanback, 7 Tapering Spindles, Plank Seat, 1780, 39 In. 585.00

Rocker, Windsor, Grain Painted, Stenciled 82.00

Rocker, Wire, Woven Vinyl Seat & Back, Child's 55.00

Rocker-Stroller, Oak, Collapsible 275.00

Screen, 2-Panel, Bone & Mother-Of-Pearl Inlay, Lacquered, 33 1/2 In. 80.00

Screen, 2-Panel, Mahogany, Leather, Chinoiserie Figures, Foliage, 50 1/2 In. 1725.00

Screen, 3-Panel, Arts & Crafts, Polychrome Stylized Flowers, Leaves, 68 x 31 In. 1760.00

Screen, 3-Panel, Arts & Crafts, Scenic River Valley, 72 1/4 x 96 In. 665.00

Screen, 3-Panel, Central Mirror Flanked By Glazed Landscapes, 24 x 21 In. 460.00

Screen, 3-Panel, Chinoiserie, Walnut, Chinese Figures, Flowers On Reverse, 49 In. 4600.00

Screen, 3-Panel, Colored French Print Over Fabric, Carved 412.00

Screen, 3-Panel, Giltwood, Aubusson, Floral-Filled Basket, 72 x 81 In. 9200.00

Screen, 3-Panel, Leather, Painted Scenes & Designs, France, 1900, 68 1/2 In. 2000.00

Screen, 3-Panel, Pseudo-Frosted Texture, Panels Of Leaded Glass, 61 1/2 x 66 In. 825.00

Screen, 3-Panel, Walnut, Carved Foliage, Silk Brocade, Arts & Crafts, 54 x 20 1/4 In. . . . 495.00

Screen, 3-Panel, Walnut, Floral & Figural Tapestry, 73 x 66 1/2 In. 1610.00

Screen, 4-Panel, Bamboo & Stream Design, Gold Ground 685.00

Screen, 4-Panel, Black & Red Lacquer, Birds & Flora In Shell, 47 1/2 In. 80.00

Screen, 4-Panel, Canvas, Wood, Leather Edging, 69 1/2 In. 1430.00

Screen, 4-Panel, Edgar & Dale, Perched Cats & Birds, Stylized Floral, 48 In. 2990.00

Screen, 4-Panel, Landscape With Birds & Flowering Trees, 90 In. 575.00

Screen, 4-Panel, Mahogany, Tooled Leather Upper Section, 115 x 78 In. 2625.00

Screen, 4-Panel, Oriental, Carved Lacquer, 70 1/2 In. 360.00

Screen, 4-Panel, Painted Leather, Continuous Street Scene, 72 x 21 In. 3450.00

Screen, 4-Panel, Tapestry, Fruit, Vases, Vine Border, Flemish, c.1600, 73 x 22 In. 5750.00

Screen, 4-Panel, Village Scene, Lacquered Black Ground, Gold Trim, 36 x 12 In. 80.00

Screen, 4-Panel, Wood, Figures & Cloud-Strewn Landscape, 30 5/8 In. 265.00

Screen, 6-Panel, Black Lacquer, Relief-Carved Oriental Figures, 18 x 84 In. 305.00

Screen, 6-Panel, Herman Miller, Grained Veneer, Canvas Hinges, 60 x 68 In. 4400.00

Screen, 6-Panel, Lacquered, Hardstone, Jade Animals, Mother-Of Pearl, China, 72 In. . . . 1150.00

Screen, 8-Panel, Coromandel, China 3450.00

Screen, 8-Panel, Coromandel, Warriors, Pavilions, Reverse Of Flowers, 76 x 124 In. 865.00

Screen, 9-Panel, Scarlet Japanned, Parcel Gilt, Chinese Figures, 84 x 23 In. 8050.00

Screen, Arts & Crafts, Folding, Oak, Square Posts, Upholstered, 68 3/4 In. 258.00

Screen, French Style, Carved, Gilt, Tapestry Insert, Boy Fishing, 43 In. 715.00

Screen, Jade, Carnelian & Amethyst Branches, Teakwood Base, 6 1/4 x 4 In. 405.00

Screen, Walnut, Triptych, 3 Damask Panels, 55 x 66 In. 470.00

Secretary, Baroque, Walnut, Italy, 94 x 39 x 23 In. 14950.00

Secretary, Biedermeier, Carved Fruit, Multiple Center Drawers 6325.00

Secretary, Biedermeier, Cherry, 3 Graduated Drawers, Plain Feet 1150.00

Secretary, Biedermeier, Rosewood, Ebonized, Satinwood Interior, 4 Legs, 1830 . . . . 330.00

Secretary, Cherry, 3 Drawers, Mid-19th Century, 40 x 82 In. 4200.00

Secretary, Chippendale, Cherry, Pine, 4 Dovetailed Drawers, 83 In. 8800.00

Secretary, Classical, Mahogany, Pilasters, Fitted, 2 Glass Doors, 38 x 23 x 77 In. 2530.00

Secretary, Drop Front, Belgian Granite Top, Laurel Sprays, 54 1/2 In. 9200.00
Secretary, Drop Front, Robsjohn-Gibbings, Walnut Veneer, 2 Glass Doors, 62 In. 1320.00
Secretary, Drop Front, Tulipwood, Kingwood, Marble Top, 58 In. 3740.00
Secretary, Drop Front, Walnut, 2 Arched Doors, Plinth Base, Victorian, 93 x 45 In. 1610.00
Secretary, Empire, Figured Mahogany Veneer, Fold Down, 3 Drawers, 37 x 79 In. 1100.00
Secretary, Empire, Gilt Bronze, 2 Cupboard Doors, Columns, 49 1/4 x 44 In. 1955.00
Secretary, Federal, Figured Mahogany, Serpentine Base, Glass Doors On Top, N.Y. 14300.00
Secretary, Federal, Mahogany, 2 Panel Doors, Scroll Legs, 40 x 20 x 87 In. 1050.00
Secretary, Federal, Mahogany, 3 Drawers, New England, 1815, 2 Piece 1955.00
Secretary, Gothic Revival, Mahogany, Paneled Doors, Pullout Desk, 40 x 88 In. 2860.00
Secretary, Louis XV, Fruitwood, Fitted Interior, Delorme, 54 3/4 In. 4600.00
Secretary, Mahogany, Blind Front, Shelves, Pigeonholes, Drawers, 1810, 52 In. 1650.00
Secretary, Mahogany, Gilt-Bronze Mounted, Granite Top, 49 x 41 In. 3450.00
Secretary, Marquetry, Holland, 18th Century 4125.00
Secretary, Pine, Mahogany Veneer, 2 Dovetailed Drawers, Bracket Feet, 14 In. 660.00
Secretary, Poplar, 4 Dovetailed Drawers, Fold-Down Lid, Fitted Interior, 86 In. 2420.00
Secretary, Rococo, Mahogany Veneer, 71 1/4 In. 2420.00
Secretary, Side By Side, Carved Oak, Center Mirror, Sears Roebuck, 1900 . . . . 4250.00
Secretary, Tulipwood, Marble Top, Leather Surface, Parquetry, 31 In. 9200.00
Secretary, Walnut, 3 Dovetailed Drawers, Cutout Feet, 80 In. 1325.00
Secretary-Bookcase, Biedermeier, Walnut, Fitted Interior, 3 Drawers, 86 In. 2970.00
Secretary-Bookcase, Chinoiserie, Gold & Polychrome, 20th Century, 95 In. 880.00
Secretary-Bookcase, Chippendale Style, Drop Front, Fretwork, Glazed Doors 525.00
Secretary-Bookcase, Chippendale, Cherry, 2 Doors, Bracket, 1760, 90 In. 8625.00
Secretary-Bookcase, Chippendale, Cherry, Bonnet Top, Connecticut 9200.00
Secretary-Bookcase, Chippendale, Fall Front, Cherry, 4 Drawers, c.1770, 84 In. 8800.00
Secretary-Bookcase, Federal, Mahogany, 4 Short Drawers, 1810, 90 In. 13800.00
Secretary-Bookcase, Federal, Mahogany, Bracket Feet, 70 In. 4600.00
Secretary-Bookcase, Federal, Mahogany, Tambour Doors, 1805, 86 x 42 In. 3450.00
Secretary-Bookcase, George II, Walnut, 18th Century, 78 1/2 x 39 x 22 In. 5750.00
Secretary-Bookcase, George II, Walnut, 4 Graduated Drawers, 78 1/2 In. 4600.00
Secretary-Bookcase, George III, Drop Front, Mahogany, Inlaid Drawer, 89 In. 6900.00
Secretary-Bookcase, Governor Winthrop Style, Mahogany Veneer, 76 x 31 1/2 In. 575.00
Secretary-Bookcase, Governor Winthrop, Mahogany, Monitor Furniture Co., 80 In. . . . 715.00
Secretary-Bookcase, Hepplewhite, French Feet, 90 x 24 In. 5225.00
Secretary-Bookcase, Mahogany, 3 Inlaid Doors, Bracket Feet, 88 In. 9200.00
Secretary-Bookcase, Mahogany, Glazed Doors, Fitted Interior, Drawers, 75 1/2 In. 8050.00
Secretary-Bookcase, Neoclassical, 3 Graduated Drawers, 43 1/4 x 37 1/2 In. 920.00
Secretary-Bookcase, Oak, Curved Glass, Carved Man, Mirror, 74 x 40 In. 1430.00
Secretary-Bookcase, Queen Anne, Walnut, 2 Graduated Drawers, 83 In. 12650.00
Secretary-Bookcase, Red Paint, Nail Construction, 86 In. 2420.00
Secretary-Bookcase, Slant Front, Queen Anne Style, Oak 9200.00
Secretary-Bookcase, Slant Front, Walnut, Fretwork Over Glass Doors, 76 In. 330.00
Server, Figured Walnut, 3 Drawers, England, 19th Century, 47 x 21 x 35 In. 990.00
Server, G. Stickley, No. 802, 2 Drawers, Dark Chocolate Finish, 39 In. 7475.00
Server, G. Stickley, No. 819, 3 Over 1 Long Drawer, Iron Pulls, 48 x 20 In. 3190.00
Server, Heywood-Wakefield Co., Wheat Finish, 2 Doors, 34 x 17 x 33 In. 660.00
Server, L. & J.G. Stickley, 3 Drawers Above Shelf, Signed, 39 1/2 In. 2380.00
Server, Limbert, Oak, Metal Fittings, Key, Ebony Inlay, 41 1/4 In. 2960.00
Server, Mahogany Veneer, Removable Butler's Tray, 2 Bottom Doors 275.00
Server, Mahogany, 3 Drawers, Inlay, Early 20th Century, 42 x 37 In. 140.00
Server, Mahogany, Inlay, 1920s, 31 x 41 1/2 In. 215.00
Server, Mirrored Backsplash, 2 Drawers Over Paneled Doors, Lower Drawer 192.00
Server, Scrolled Top, 2 Drawers, 2 Doors, Black, Red Paint, Figural Scenes, 33 In. 172.00
Server, Stickley Brothers, No. 8406, 2 Drawers Over 1, Mirrored Back, 49 1/2 In. 1840.00
Settee, Arched Top Rail, Incurved Arms Headed By Eagle Masks, 63 In. 5465.00
Settee, Biedermeier, Walnut, Double Chair Back, Fan Crest, Gilt-Metal, 47 In. 5980.00
Settee, Bird's-Eye Maple, Cane Seat & Back, 19th Century, 76 1/2 In. 990.00
Settee, Bugatti, Wood, Parchment, Copper & Pewter Inlay, c.1900, 48 In. 8625.00
Settee, Carved, Scrolled Backrest & Arms, Cabriole Legs, Victorian 312.00
Settee, Chesterfield, Tufted Leather, Loose Cushions, 73 In. 5750.00
Settee, Chippendale, Wallace Nutting, No. 525, Upholstered 1650.00
Settee, Empire, Mahogany, Curved Backs, 2-Seat, Hoof-Form Feet 2070.00

Settee, Federal, Mahogany, Bow Knot, Cane Seat, Reed Legs, 1815, 72 In. 9775.00
Settee, Federal, Prince Of Wales Motif Splat, Upholstered Spring Seat 330.00
Settee, Federal, Scrolled Arms, Blue & White Floral Seat, Saber Legs, 54 In. 1035.00
Settee, Fruit & Floral Stencil, Painted, Early 19th Century, 32 In. 1725.00
Settee, Fruitwood, Birch, Vase-Form Splats, Angels On Supports, 80 1/2 In. 5175.00
Settee, George II Style, Walnut, Camelback, Needlepoint, 78 In. 6325.00
Settee, George II, Mahogany, Rectangular Back, Damask, 60 In. 1150.00
Settee, George III Style, Mahogany, Serpentine Crest, Scrolling Arms, 30 x 53 In. 1400.00
Settee, George III, Camelback, Cushion Seat, White, Blue Floral, 84 In. 2300.00
Settee, George III, Mahogany, Late 18th Century, 38 x 48 1/4 In. 7475.00
Settee, George III, Satinwood, Striped Silk, 35 x 54 In. 3740.00
Settee, Herman Miller, Wool, Square Foam Cushion, Metal Legs, 29 In. 715.00
Settee, Hitchcock Style, Stenciled Fruit At Crest, Black, 20th Century 135.00
Settee, Jacobean, Oak, Foliate Crest Rail, Cane Seat, Rope-Twist Legs, 48 x 68 In. 1610.00
Settee, Limbert, 2 Vertical Back Slats, Leather Seat, 39 x 40 1/2 x 19 In. 1320.00
Settee, Louis XV, Blonde Wood, Muslin, 51 In. 1430.00
Settee, Louis XVI Style, Mahogany, Striped Velvet, 56 In. 275.00
Settee, Louis XVI Style, Wool, Early 20th Century, 31 x 65 In. 1035.00
Settee, Louis XVI, Mahogany, Ribbon Carved, Needlepoint, Black 2300.00
Settee, Mahogany, Barley-Twist Uprights, Upholstered, 1875, 78 x 35 x 32 In. 4500.00
Settee, Mahogany, Dolphin & Floral Carving, Paw Feet, Silk 110.00
Settee, Mahogany, Double Chair Back, Pierced Vase Splat, Out-Scrolled Arms 575.00
Settee, Mahogany, Serpentine Back, Upholstered Out-Turned Sides, c.1775, 84 In. 4600.00
Settee, Mahogany, Straight Crest Rail, Flaring Arms & Seat, Damask 1650.00
Settee, Neo-Classical, Gothic Arch, Caned Seat, Tapered Legs, Italy, 33 1/2 In. 1150.00
Settee, Padded Arched Back, Out-Scrolled Arms, White Splayed Legs, 33 1/2 In. 4025.00
Settee, Painted & Parcel Gilt, Padded Backrest, Upholstered, 62 In. 4600.00
Settee, Parcel Gilt, Painted, Stepped Back, Sweden, 72 1/2 In. 920.00
Settee, Pierced Back Splats, Wooden Arms, Painted Wheat Sheaves, 37 1/2 In. 2875.00
Settee, Pine, Arrow Back, 16 Spindles 550.00
Settee, Pine, Empire, Loose Cushion, Bolsters, Casters, c.1830, 68 In. 1100.00
Settee, Polychrome Fruit Stencil, Painted, 72 In. 1955.00
Settee, Regency, Ebonized, Gilt, 3 Panels, Foliate Scrolls, Cane Seat, 27 In. 5750.00
Settee, Regency, Walnut, Padded Arms, Serpentine Back, Aubusson, 81 In. 4945.00
Settee, Rococo, Walnut, Stylized Shell, Serpentine Top Rail, Cabriole Legs, 84 In. 2875.00
Settee, Serpentine Crest Rail, Down-Swept Arms, Italy, 59 In., Pair 1840.00
Settee, Walnut, C-Scroll Floral Arms, Cabriole Legs, Victorian, 69 x 38 In. 460.00
Settee, Walnut, Finger Carved, Open Arms, Oval Back, Velvet, 56 In. 715.00
Settle, Arrow Back, Black Paint, Scrolled Arms, Turned Legs & Posts, 78 In. 495.00
Settle, Arts & Crafts, 11 Vertical Back Slats, 3 Slats Under Arms, 80 In. 865.00
Settle, Arts & Crafts, Walnut, 11 Slats, 91 x 36 x 36 In. 660.00
Settle, Free-Hand Flowers, Yellow, Brown & Black Striping, 78 1/2 In. 4950.00
Settle, G. Nakashima, Black Walnut, Doweled Legs, Loose Seat & Back, 71 1/2 In. 2750.00
Settle, G. Stickley, No. 208, 8-Slat Back, Through Tenon, Cushion, Arms, 77 In. 6600.00
Settle, G. Stickley, Oak, 3 Slats Under Each Arm, 1906, 60 In. 4025.00
Settle, G. Stickley, Oak, 22 Vertical Back Slats, Canted Sides, 1910, 79 In. 4830.00
Settle, G. Stickley, Oak, 22 Vertical Back Slats, Post Legs, 1910, 34 1/2 In. 750.00
Settle, George III, Pine, Limed, Down-Swept Arms, Lift Seat, 60 x 72 x 21 In. 635.00
Settle, Half-Spindle Back, Stenciled Flowers & Fruit, Scrolled Arms, 69 In. 1375.00
Settle, Harden, Even Arms, Slat Back, Spring Seat, Label, 34 3/4 x 79 1/2 In. 2970.00
Settle, Hardwood, Pine, Steel Rods In Arms, 83 1/2 In. 220.00
Settle, L. & J.G. Stickley, 5-Slat Back, 1 Slat Each Side, Drop-In Seat, 72 In. 2420.00
Settle, L. & J.G. Stickley, No. 215, 7-Slat Back, Cushion, Arms, Decal, 72 In. 2310.00
Settle, L. & J.G. Stickley, No. 229, Horizontal-Board Back, Cushion, 71 x 26 In. 3300.00
Settle, Limbert, Drop-In Seat, 68 x 28 x 36 In. 1320.00
Settle, Limbert, No. 578, 3 Back Panels, Drop Arms, Brown Leather, 68 In. 2750.00
Settle, Oak, 3 Narrow Back Slats, Tapered Posts, 1905, 39 1/2 In. 1265.00
Settle, Plank Seat, Painted Designs 2090.00
Shelf, 3 Tiers, Square Nails, Stenciling, Green Paint 200.00
Shelf, Carved Eagle Bracket, Black Paint, Gilt, 9 1/4 x 7 5/8 x 14 In. 4055.00
Shelf, Corner, Black Lacquer, Folding, Gilt Lions, 11 1/2 In., Pair 75.00
Shelf, Corner, Carved Deer Head, c.1940 . . . . 675.00
Shelf, Corner, Hanging, Pine, 2 Shelves, Brown Stain, Hinged Door, 24 x 37 In. 4400.00

Shelf, Corner, Hanging, Walnut, Truncated Sides, Graduated Shelves, 23 x 50 In. 3190.00
Shelf, Hanging, Acorn Finials, Scalloped Skirt, 2 Drawers 385.00
Shelf, Hanging, George III, Mahogany, 4 Graduated Shelves, Bracket, 45 1/2 In. 805.00
Shelf, Hanging, Mahogany, 3 Dovetailed Drawers, 1 Shelf, 24 x 36 1/2 In. 3740.00
Shelf, Hanging, Oak, 1 Door, Beveled Glass, Shaped Shelves 250.00
Shelf, Hanging, Pine, 2 Dovetailed Drawers, England, 28 x 5 x 35 In. 190.00
Shelf, Hanging, Pine, 3 Shelves Over 2 Side-By-Side Drawers, 29 x 28 In. 45.00
Shelf, Hanging, Pine, Dovetailed, Blue, 31 1/2 x 7 x 25 In. 2090.00
Shelf, Mahogany, Whale End, 4 Shelves, Early 19th Century, 1830s, 36 x 31 In. 920.00
Shelf, Walnut, 2 Tiers, Stepped Form, 18th Century, 9 In. 805.00
Sideboard, Art Deco, Rosewood, Marble Top, 3 Doors, 1928, 43 In. 805.00
Sideboard, Arts & Crafts, 2 Drawers Over 2 Doors, Mirrored Gallery, 48 x 58 In. 990.00
Sideboard, Arts & Crafts, 5 Drawers, 2 Doors, Copper Pulls, Mirror, 48 x 54 In. 1045.00
Sideboard, Bird's-Eye Maple, Carved Crest, Paw Feet, 52 x 81 In. 5800.00
Sideboard, Chestnut, Burl Walnut, Nuts & Fruit Clusters, Marble Top, 54 x 84 In. 3500.00
Sideboard, Classical, Mahogany, 3 Drawers, Acanthus Columns, 1830, 51 In. 3450.00
Sideboard, Classical, Mahogany, Brass Mounted, 2 Drawers, 1830, 62 In. 2300.00
Sideboard, Classical, Mahogany, Ormolu Mounted, Marble Top, 1825, 50 In. 9775.00
Sideboard, Empire, Mahogany, 3 Silver Drawers Over 1 Long Drawer, 46 In. 880.00
Sideboard, Empire, Mahogany, Double Pedestal, 2 Doors, 3 Drawers, 74 x 68 In. 855.00
Sideboard, Empire, Mahogany, Poplar, Paneled Doors, 3 Drawers, 48 x 22 x 41 In. 330.00
Sideboard, Federal, Cherry, Bowfront, 4 Drawers, Beaded, Crossbanded, 38 In. 4315.00
Sideboard, Federal, Mahogany, 2 Concave Doors, Tapered Legs, 36 x 78 In. 3740.00
Sideboard, Federal, Mahogany, 2 Drawers, Brass Hardware, 1810, 40 x 60 In. 8050.00
Sideboard, Federal, Mahogany, 2 Frieze Drawers, 2 Doors, Tapered Legs, 41 In. 6325.00
Sideboard, Federal, Mahogany, 3 Drawers, Splayed Feet, 51 x 78 In. 2990.00
Sideboard, Federal, Mahogany, Cherry, Serpentine Top, 1790, 40 In. 9200.00
Sideboard, G. Nakashima, 2 Sliding Doors, 2 Slab Feet, 1958, 21 x 83 In. 5750.00
Sideboard, G. Stickley, Long Drawer Over 3 Center Drawers, Doors, 45 1/4 In. 2875.00
Sideboard, G. Stickley, No. 814 1/2, 4 Drawers, Side Doors, Plate Rail, 56 In. 6600.00
Sideboard, G. Stickley, No. 814, 3 Drawers, Side Strap-Hinged Cabinets 6600.00
Sideboard, George III, Mahogany, Angled Drawers, Tapered Legs, 37 x 66 In. 2530.00
Sideboard, George III, Mahogany, Breakfront Top, Lead-Lined Cellarette, 84 In. 5175.00
Sideboard, George III, Mahogany, Center Drawer, Leaf Legs, Splayed Feet, 38 In. 3680.00
Sideboard, George III, Mahogany, Frieze Drawer, Tapered Legs, 37 1/2 In. 5520.00
Sideboard, George III, Mahogany, Satinwood, Bowed Top, N.Y., 35 1/2 x 66 In. 7590.00
Sideboard, George III, Mahogany, Serpentine Front, 3 Drawers, Cupboard, 41 In. 690.00
Sideboard, Grand Rapids Chair Co., Hepplewhite, Mahogany, Band Inlay, 70 In. 605.00
Sideboard, Harden, Quartersawn Oak, Felt-Lined Drawer, Backsplash, 52 1/8 In. 925.00
Sideboard, Hepplewhite, Mahogany, Curved Doors & Drawers, Tambour, 40 In. 13200.00
Sideboard, Hepplewhite, Mahogany, Flame Veneer, New York, 81 x 30 x 41 In. 1320.00
Sideboard, Herman Miller, Mahogany, 3 Drawers, 2 Doors, 75 x 18 x 33 In. 1760.00
Sideboard, Kimbel & Cabus, Gothic Revival, Walnut, New York, 1875, 73 x 39 In. 9775.00
Sideboard, L. & J.G. Stickley, Plate Rail Backsplash, 48 In. 5620.00
Sideboard, Leleu, Satinwood, Parchment, Shelved Interior, 1930, 84 In. 6900.00
Sideboard, Limbert, Mirrored Back, 6 Drawers, 2 Doors, 57 x 60 In. 4890.00
Sideboard, Limbert, No. 1320, Paneled Sides, Arched Apron, Signed, 51 3/4 In. 2910.00
Sideboard, Limbert, Oak, Plate Rail, 2 Drawers Over 2 Doors, 44 3/4 In. 2515.00
Sideboard, Mahogany, 2 Paneled Doors, 2 Drawers, Rounded Fronts, 42 In. 550.00
Sideboard, Mahogany, Curved Front & Legs, 2 Middle Drawers, Cupboard Sides 2000.00
Sideboard, Mahogany, Regency, Brass Rail, Drawer Over Door, Ebony Inlay, 93 In. 8625.00
Sideboard, Mahogany, Side Cabinets, 1 Large, 2 Small Drawers, Ivory Keyhole 9200.00
Sideboard, Majorelle, Mahogany, Foliate Mounts, Glazed Doors, 1900, 76 In. 6325.00
Sideboard, Oak, 4 Cupboard Doors, 2 Small Drawers, Scroll Moldings, 87 5/8 In. 275.00
Sideboard, Oak, Carved Lions' Heads, Columns, Marble Top . . . . *Illus* 1980.00
Sideboard, Oak, Griffin Mirror, 2 Short & 1 Long Drawer, Doors, 65 x 44 In. 335.00
Sideboard, Oak, Marble, Mirror Backsplash, Pillars, Carved, 82 x 59 x 20 In. 715.00
Sideboard, P. Evans, Patchwork Enameled Squares, Slate Top, 4 Doors, 96 In. 1100.00
Sideboard, Peaked Backboard, Gallery, 2 Drawers, 2 Doors, c.1820, 44 x 58 In. 3105.00
Sideboard, Pine, Poplar, Red, Plank Table, 2-Board Doors, 18 x 83 x 54 In. 55.00
Sideboard, Regency, Mahogany, Ebony Inlay, Arched Backsplash, 54 x 90 x 25 In. 165.00
Sideboard, Renaissance Revival, 3 Paneled Doors, Black Marble Top, 38 In. 1725.00
Sideboard, Renaissance Revival, Oak, Geometric Doors, 38 x 65 In. 980.00

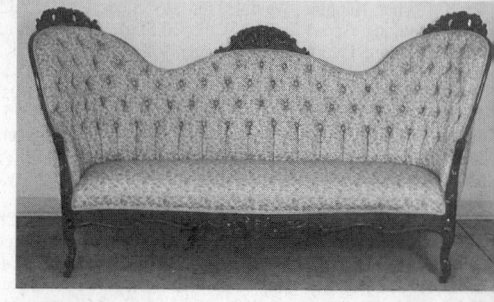

Furniture, Sideboard, Oak,
Carved Lions' Heads,
Columns, Marble Top

Furniture, Sofa, Louis XV,
Pierce-Carved Crest, Tufted,
American, 1860

Sideboard, Rohde, Burl, 4 Drawers, 1 Cabinet Door, Chrome Pulls, 45 In. 1210.00
Sideboard, Rohde, Mahogany Case, 4 Doors, 1937, 72 x 21 x 33 In. 3190.00
Sideboard, Serpentine Front, Frieze Drawer, Patera & Fan Inlay, 35 x 49 In. 9775.00
Sideboard, Sheraton, Mahogany, Pine, Poplar, Turned Feet, 48 1/2 In. 1320.00
Sideboard, Sheraton, Mahogany, Satinwood Veneer, Boston, 80 In. 4125.00
Sideboard, Sheraton, Mahogany, Serpentine Front, 39 x 74 x 29 In. 5175.00
Sideboard, Tiger Oak, Beveled Mirrors, Claw Feet, Carved, 1800s 3500.00
Sideboard, Widdicomb, Walnut Veneer, 3 Doors, Dowel Legs, Inside Drawers, 72 In. . . . 715.00
Sofa, 3 Sections, Loose Cushioned Backs & Seats, Bolster Arms, 164 In. 6325.00
Sofa, Biedermeier, Walnut, Ebonized, Arch Backrest, Pilaster Legs, 59 1/4 In. 1725.00
Sofa, Chippendale Style, Camelback, Ball & Claw Feet, Crewel, 77 In. 275.00
Sofa, Chippendale, Camelback, 6 Molded Legs, Upholstered 5170.00
Sofa, Chippendale, Carved Wood Trim, Camelback, Wooden Legs, Ball Feet 275.00
Sofa, Classical, Mahogany, Reeded Columnar Arms, Reeded Seat, 1820, 80 In. 920.00
Sofa, Classical, Mahogany, Reeded Crest, Scrolled Terminal & Feet, 36 In. 330.00
Sofa, Classical, Mahogany, Scrolled Crest, Tapered Legs, 1825, 84 In. 1610.00
Sofa, Contemporary, Oak, 3 Splats, Leather Seat, 82 x 36 x 33 In. 55.00
Sofa, Curved Backrest, Bun Feet, Upholstered, Wooden Arms, 70 In. 6325.00
Sofa, Curved Crest Rail, Carved Paw Feet, Upholstered Back, Seat & Arms 1840.00
Sofa, Cylinder Crest Foliate Ends, Urn-Carved Arm Support Panels, Melon Feet 5060.00
Sofa, Dunbar, Wooden Legs, Tufted Wool Seat, 1950, 84 x 33 x 29 In. 2530.00
Sofa, E. Wormley, Tufted Seat & Back, Upholstered, 89 x 28 In. 1210.00
Sofa, E. Wormley, Walnut, Upholstered, Dunbar, 84 x 29 x 29 In. 1650.00
Sofa, Eames, Aluminum, Slat Seat & Back, 73 x 26 x 33 In. 2310.00
Sofa, Eames, Black Metal, Chrome, Off-White Naugahyde, 36 In. 1100.00
Sofa, Empire, Mahogany Veneer, Serpentine, Velvet, 95 In. 357.00
Sofa, Empire, Mahogany, Claw Feet, Upholstered, 1820s 2350.00
Sofa, Empire, Mahogany, Turned Feet, Rope-Carved Arm Posts, Scrolled Arms, 73 In. . . . 1540.00
Sofa, Federal Style, Mahogany, Loose Seat Cushions, c.1940, 90 In. 1150.00
Sofa, Federal, Duncan Phyfe, Reeded Mahogany, Serpentine Arms, 77 In. 11550.00
Sofa, Federal, Mahogany, Bird's-Eye Maple, Brass Caps, Casters, 1815, 87 In. 2300.00
Sofa, Federal, Mahogany, Bowfront Seat, Splayed Feet, 1795, 84 In. 2875.00
Sofa, Federal, Mahogany, Leaf-Carved Reeded Legs, Peg Feet, 1810, 86 In. 4600.00
Sofa, Federal, Mahogany, Upholstered Seat, Reed Legs, 78 In. 1840.00
Sofa, Federal, Mahogany, Upholstered, 76 3/4 In. 1045.00
Sofa, Federal, Mahogany, Vase-Form Supports, 19th Century, 75 In. 385.00
Sofa, Florence Knoll, Stainless Steel, Tufted Seat & Back, 84 x 30 x 30 In. 525.00
Sofa, George Nelson, Marshmallow, c.1956 . . . . 7000.00
Sofa, George Nelson, Sling, 2 Seats, Leather, Chrome, Herman Miller, 58 x 33 In. 1760.00
Sofa, Hepplewhite, Mahogany, Camelback, Serpentine, Upholstered, Phila., 67 In. 5445.00
Sofa, Hunzinger, Signed & Dated, 1880s, 66 In. 1500.00
Sofa, Louis XV, Beechwood, Serpentine Top Rail, Down-Swept Arms, 1750s, 75 In. 9200.00
Sofa, Louis XV, Pierce-Carved Crest, Tufted, American, 1860 . . . . *Illus* 1320.00
Sofa, Louis XVI, Carved Crest Rail, Down-Swept Arms, Circular Legs, 53 In. 368.00

Sofa, Louis XVI, Foliate Arch, Scrolled Reeded Arms, Legs, 36 In. 805.00
Sofa, Louis XVI, Giltwood, Fortuny Fabric, Late 19th Century, 36 x 55 In. 1610.00
Sofa, Louis XVI, Giltwood, Ribbon-Tied Husks, Cabriole Legs, 36 x 48 In. 690.00
Sofa, Mahogany Veneer, Carved Foliage On Crest, Velvet, 76 In. 220.00
Sofa, Mahogany, Acanthus & Fruit, Flame Veneer Crest, Bolster Pillows, 67 In. 550.00
Sofa, Mahogany, Allover Carved Design, Bowed Crest Rail, Scrolled Arms, 88 In. 1045.00
Sofa, Mahogany, Camelback, Scrolled Arms, Seat Cushion, 84 In. 5170.00
Sofa, Mahogany, Carved Shell, Floral Fabric, Scroll Arms, Victorian 1870.00
Sofa, Mahogany, Empire, Rolled Arms, Back, Seat & Bolsters, Crewel 440.00
Sofa, Mahogany, Gadroon Crest Rail, Scrolled Arms, Hairy Paw Feet, Upholstered 605.00
Sofa, Mahogany, Medallion & Arches On Back, Enclosed Arms, 65 3/4 In. 305.00
Sofa, Mahogany, Shaped Back Rail, In-Turned Arms, 1830s, 76 3/4 In. 330.00
Sofa, Mahogany, Shaped Reeded Crest Rail, Scrolled Arms, c.1815, 78 In. 1495.00
Sofa, Mirror Back, Walnut, Carved Crest Rail, Oxbow Front, Victorian 660.00
Sofa, Mission Style, Oak, 3-Cushion Seat & Back, c.1905, 84 In. 4730.00
Sofa, Neoclassical, Walnut, Fortuny Fabric, Reeded Arms, Legs, Italy, 36 In. 2530.00
Sofa, Olive Wood, Mahogany, Folds Into Bed, Drawer Under Seat, 84 In. 330.00
Sofa, Porcelain Plaques, Mark Twain, Scalamandre Silk 1870.00
Sofa, Regency, Burl Walnut, 2 Drawers, Splayed Legs, 29 x 58 In. 2990.00
Sofa, Ritts Co., Rattan, 4-Piece Sectional, 1950, 98 In. 825.00
Sofa, Robsjohn-Gibbings, Walnut, Strap, Upholstered Back, Round, 89 In. 1955.00
Sofa, Rosewood, Fruit-Carved Crest, Applied Grape Clusters, Velvet 550.00
Sofa, Rounded Back & Arms, Cushioned Seat, Upholstered, 64 In. 4600.00
Sofa, Sheraton, Mahogany, Satinwood Panels, Peg Feet, c.1810, 76 In. 3850.00
Sofa, V. Kagan, Sculptured, Triform Legs, Upholstered, 96 x 32 In. 1650.00
Sofa, Walnut, Carved & Molded, Scroll Arms, Quilted, 81 In. 412.00
Sofa, Walnut, Carved Rose Crest, Tufted Back, Velvet, 54 In. 467.00
Sofa, Walnut, Oval Back, Padded Open Arms, Velvet, 2 Pillows 155.00
Sofa, Walnut, Tufted Back, Casters, Velvet, 67 In. 190.00
Sofa, Wicker, Painted, 3 Cushions, 4 Pillows, c.1900, 77 x 23 In. 650.00
Sofa, William & Mary, Velvet, 3 Feather Cushions, 31 3/4 In. 1849.00
Sofa, William IV, Rosewood, Carved, c.1835, 84 In. 1800.00
Stand, 1 Drawer, Single Turned Stretcher, Grain Painted 50.00
Stand, 4 Tiers, Spiral & Spindle Turnings, Late 19th Century 275.00
Stand, Artek, Birch Veneer, 1 Door, Wooden Pull, Stamped, 20 x 15 x 22 In. 175.00
Stand, Baroque, Mahogany, 1 Drawer, Panel Door, 30 x 17 x 15 In. 489.00
Stand, Biedermeier, Mahogany, Circular Top, 4 Square Legs, Feet, 36 x 12 In. 345.00
Stand, Biedermeier, Walnut, 1 Drawer, 4 Saber Legs, Rectangular Top, 31 1/3 In. 575.00
Stand, Biedermeier, Walnut, Circular Top, 4 Tapered Legs, 31 x 13 1/2 In. 345.00
Stand, Carved Spread-Winged Eagle, Mounted Shelf, 20 In. 1045.00
Stand, Cherry, 1 Dovetailed Drawer, 2-Board Top, 19 x 19 x 28 In. 355.00
Stand, Cherry, 1 Drawer, Serpentine Rim, Cut Corners, 1830s 1375.00
Stand, Cherry, 1 Drawer, Turned Legs, 1-Board Top, 17 x 20 x 28 In. 440.00
Stand, Cherry, Bird's-Eye Maple, c.1815 . . . . 745.00
Stand, Cherry, Maple, Tilt Top, Round, Tripod Base, Spider Legs, 30 In. 193.00
Stand, Cherry, Paneled Doors, Marble Top, 30 x 14 x 14 In. 259.00
Stand, Cherry, Spool-Turned Legs, Dovetailed Drawer, 16 x 18 x 29 In. 192.00
Stand, Cherry, Tiger Maple, Burl Drawer, Brass Ring Pull, 29 x 17 In. 460.00
Stand, Chippendale, Cherry, Tripod, 1-Board Top, Chapin, 16 1/2 x 16 7/8 x 25 In. 1090.00
Stand, Colonial Revival, Maple, Walnut, 4 Graduated Drawers, 18th Century, 68 In. 385.00
Stand, Curly Maple, 1 Drawer, Baluster Turned, South, 1830, 14 x 13 In. 1800.00
Stand, Curly Maple, Drop Leaf, 2 Drawers . . . .*Illus* 715.00
Stand, Drop Leaf, Walnut, Pencil-Post Legs, Drawer, 17 x 22 1/2 x 8 1/2 In. 495.00
Stand, Empire, Cherry, 1 Dovetailed Drawer, Dark Finish, 28 3/4 In. 805.00
Stand, Empire, Cherry, 2 Drawers, Turned Legs, 22 x 23 x 29 In. 550.00
Stand, Empire, Tiger Maple, Bird's-Eye Maple, Adjustable Mirror, 1835 . . . .*Illus* 1100.00
Stand, Federal, Cherry, Turned & Carved Legs, 2 Dovetailed Drawers, 19 x 26 In. 300.00
Stand, Federal, Mahogany, 2 Dovetailed Drawers, Biscuit Corners, 18 x 20 x 28 In. 770.00
Stand, Federal, Mahogany, Thumb-Molded Edge, Singe Drawer, 1780, 29 In. 1380.00
Stand, Federal, Maple, 1 Drawer, Reeded Legs, Bottle-Form Feet, 1820, 27 1/2 In. 2875.00
Stand, Federal, Walnut, 1 String Drawer, Squared Feet, 29 x 17 x 16 1/2 In. 1100.00
Stand, Federal, Wavy Birch, Overhanging Top, 2 Drawers, Glass Pulls, 28 1/2 In. 460.00
Stand, Fern, Mahogany, Carved Leaf & Rope Standard, Ball & Claw Feet 165.00

Furniture, Stand, Tiger
Maple, 1 Drawer

Furniture, Stand, Curly Maple,
Drop Leaf, 2 Drawers

Furniture, Stand, Empire, Tiger
Maple, Bird's-Eye Maple, Adjustable

Stand, Fishbowl, 2 Mermaids, Blown, 1920s, Marked Verona Pat., Iron	750.00
Stand, Folio, Mahogany, Hinged Sides, 2 Legs Ending In Paw Feet, 43 x 39 In.	8625.00
Stand, G. Nelson, Rosewood Veneer, 1 Drawer, Shelf, Aluminum Legs, 24 In.	465.00
Stand, G. Stickley, 2 Drawers, Red Decal, 1910, 29 x 20 In.	2645.00
Stand, George III, Mahogany, Baluster Support, Tapered Legs, 19 x 12 In.	690.00
Stand, Hat, Child's, Wooden, Art Deco, 3 Piece	85.00
Stand, Hepplewhite Style, Curly Maple, Dovetailed Drawer, Ohio, 13 x 28 In.	275.00
Stand, Hepplewhite, 1 Drawer, Line Inlay, 1810, 21 x 16 x 29 In.	2950.00
Stand, Hepplewhite, Cherry, 1 Dovetailed Drawer, 18 x 18 x 27 1/4 In.	330.00
Stand, Hepplewhite, Cherry, Dark Varnish, 1-Board Top, 19 x 20 In.	605.00
Stand, Hepplewhite, Pine, 2-Board Top, Tapered Legs, 19 x 24 x 29 In.	90.00
Stand, Hepplewhite, Tilt Top, Cherry, Tripod Base, Spider Legs, 28 1/2 x 21 In.	412.00
Stand, Hepplewhite, Walnut, Poplar, 1 Dovetailed Drawer, 29 In.	305.00
Stand, Hepplewhite, Walnut, Square Tapered Legs, 2-Board Top, 27 In.	247.00
Stand, Heywood-Wakefield Co., 1 Drawer, Whalebone Flaring Legs, Koh-I-Noor	192.00
Stand, Jacobean, Walnut, 1 Drawer, Carved Supports, Stretcher, Bun Feet, Victorian	220.00
Stand, L. & J.G. Stickley, Overhanging Top, 1 Drawer, Label, 29 x 20 x 18 In.	1100.00
Stand, Lakeside Craft Shops, Plant, 3 Side Slats, Cutout Handles, Label, 20 In.	632.00
Stand, Lifetime, No. 1203, Copper Pull, Arched Apron, 29 3/4 In.	660.00
Stand, Lift Top, Walnut, Diamond Pattern Marquetry, 26 In.	385.00
Stand, Limbert, No. 138, Cutout Design, Slab Legs, 17 x 17 x 29 In.	825.00
Stand, Limbert, No. 238, Round Hanging Top, Shelf, Cruciform Base, 16 x 26 In.	1760.00
Stand, Louis XVI, Marquetry, 3 Drawers, Circular, 28 x 20 In., Pair	690.00
Stand, Magazine, Arts & Crafts, 4 Shelves, Through Tenon Construction, 40 In.	230.00
Stand, Magazine, Brooks, Pointed Back, Slanted Sides, Cutouts, 5 Shelves, 46 In.	715.00
Stand, Magazine, G. Stickley, No. 547, Mahogany, Paneled Sides, 15 x 35 In.	4950.00
Stand, Magazine, G. Stickley, No. 548, 4 Shelves, Paneled Sides, 15 x 44 In.	2860.00
Stand, Magazine, Knaus Mfg. Co., 4 Shelves, Arched Cross Supports, 22 x 42 In.	660.00
Stand, Magazine, L. & J.G. Stickley, 3 Shelves, Side Slats, Signed, 24 x 44 In.	2100.00
Stand, Magazine, Lakeside Craft Shops, 3 Shelves, Book-Trough Top, 18 x 33 In.	440.00
Stand, Magazine, Limbert, 3 Open Shelves, 29 x 10 x 30 In.	3575.00
Stand, Magazine, Limbert, No. 300, Cutout Slab Sides, 20 x 14 x 37 In.	825.00
Stand, Magazine, Limbert, No. 304, 3 Shelves, 16 x 12 x 42 In.	1540.00
Stand, Magazine, Michigan Chair Co., 2 Vertical Slats, Keys, Tenons, Label, 33 In.	1122.00
Stand, Magazine, Michigan Chair Co., Birch, 4 Shelves, Chamfered Top, 33 In.	440.00
Stand, Magazine, Widdicomb, Walnut Shelf, X-Shaped Base, Label, 30 x 24 x 22 In.	130.00
Stand, Mahogany, 1 Drawer, Open Front, Splayed Feet, 28 1/4 In., Pair	225.00
Stand, Mahogany, Acanthus-Carved Legs, 3 Drawers, Banded Veneer, 29 In.	775.00
Stand, Mahogany, Fruitwood Line Inlay, 2 Tiers, Lower Drawer, c.1810, 32 In.	1095.00
Stand, Maple, Bird's-Eye Maple, 1 Drawer, Glass Pulls, c.1830, 27 1/2 In.	1265.00
Stand, Maple, Poplar, 1 Dovetailed Drawer, 1-Board Top, 19 x 19 1/2 In.	385.00
Stand, Marble Top, Mahogany Veneer, Wooden Pulls, 1830s, 32 x 24 In.	460.00

Stand, Music, Rosewood, Leaf-Carved Octagonal Post, Double Sided, c.1830, 48 In. 1955.00
Stand, Music, Rosewood, Walnut, Swivels, Adjustable, Candlestands, 43 In. 3850.00
Stand, Music, Thonet, Bentwood, Triangular Top, Adjustable Tray, 51 1/2 In. 2300.00
Stand, Oak, Slant Front, Wheels, 1860s 650.00
Stand, Pine, Drop Leaf, Allover Decoupage Design, 2 Drawers, 27 1/2 In. 1760.00
Stand, Pine, Poplar, 3 Tiers, Green Paint, Semicircular, 48 In. 330.00
Stand, Pine, T-Shaped Base, Red Wash 345.00
Stand, Plant, 4 Tiers, 4 Swing Arms, Shell & Vine Base, 44 In. 143.00
Stand, Plant, Brass, Beveled Glass Shelf, White Onyx Top, 32 x 14 In. 247.00
Stand, Plant, Inset Ceramic Tile, Center Flowers, Tile Standard, c.1880, 34 In. 4025.00
Stand, Plant, Iron, 9 Movable Arms, 42 In. 275.00
Stand, Plant, Iron, Free Form, 3 Supports, Signed, A.S. Aiman, 41 3/4 In. 300.00
Stand, Plant, Limbert, Round Top, Arched Aprons, Square Tiers, Signed, 33 In. 990.00
Stand, Plant, Walnut, Marble Top, Columnar Base, Marble Shelf, 40 In. 45.00
Stand, Plant, White Marble Top, Carved, 3 Turned Columns, Victorian, 40 In. 550.00
Stand, Poplar, Maple, 1 Dovetailed Drawer, Turned Legs, 19 x 21 x 29 In. 330.00
Stand, Poplar, Red Wash, Embossed Brass Pull, 1-Board Top 300.00
Stand, Queen Anne, Hardwood, Pine, Duck Feet, Cutout Apron, 27 1/4 x 21 In. 715.00
Stand, Robsjohn-Gibbings, Walnut Veneer, 1 Drawer, Brass Legs, 20 x 23 In. 230.00
Stand, Rosewood, Faceted Bulbous Standard, 27 In. 100.00
Stand, Rosewood, Marble Top, Carved Frieze, Carved Legs, China, 24 In. 257.00
Stand, Rosewood, Walnut, Marble Top, 6 Drawers, 16 x 14 x 35 In. 290.00
Stand, Shaker, Cherry, 1 Drawer, Carved Handle, Tapered Leg, 26 1/4 In. 4025.00
Stand, Shaving, Mahogany, Swivel Mirror, Bowfront Base, 2 Drawers, Ball Feet 330.00
Stand, Shaving, Nickeled Silver, Mirror, Milk Glass Cup, Embossed Base, 16 In. 100.00
Stand, Shaving, Swivel Mirror, Bowfront Base, 2 Drawers, 1850s 247.00
Stand, Shaving, Swivel Mirror, Carved, Drawer, Turned Pedestal, Victorian, 69 In. 960.00
Stand, Sheraton, Birch, Pine, Poplar, Dovetailed Drawer, 17 x 17 1/2 In. 165.00
Stand, Sheraton, Bird's-Eye Maple, 2 Dovetailed Drawers, 16 x 18 x 28 In. 1650.00
Stand, Sheraton, Checkerboard Top, Red Paint, Turned Legs, 28 x 18 In. 3565.00
Stand, Sheraton, Cherry, 1 Walnut Veneer Drawer, Curly Maple Top, 19 In. 495.00
Stand, Sheraton, Cherry, Bird's-Eye Maple, 2 Dovetailed Drawers, 29 In. 715.00
Stand, Sheraton, Cherry, Drawer, Turned Legs With Rope Spiral, 21 x 24 x 28 In. 935.00
Stand, Sheraton, Cherry, Mahogany, Rope Carving, 2 Drawers, 1-Board Top, 28 In. 605.00
Stand, Sheraton, Dragoon Edge, 2 Dovetailed Drawers, Glass Knobs, 21 x 18 x 29 In. .. 440.00
Stand, Sheraton, Drawer, Black & Red Grain Painted, 29 x 16 x 17 In. 1265.00
Stand, Sheraton, Mahogany, 2 Figured Veneer Drawers, Turned Posts, 17 x 19 In. 2540.00
Stand, Sheraton, Mahogany, Drop Leaf, 2 Drawer, 33 1/2 x 18 In. 690.00
Stand, Sheraton, Maple, 2 Dovetailed Drawers, 16 1/2 x 20 1/2 x 28 3/4 In. 825.00
Stand, Sheraton, Maple, Birch, Drop Leaf, 2 Drawers, Turned Legs, New England 275.00
Stand, Sheraton, Maple, Cherry, 2 Dovetailed Drawers, Lion's-Head Handles, 30 In. 2100.00
Stand, Sheraton, Maple, Medium Brown Finish, Turned Legs, 19 1/2 x 22 x 29 In. 990.00
Stand, Sheraton, Pine, Poplar, Grain Painted, 1 Drawer, 17 x 19 x 28 In. 1045.00
Stand, Smoking, Dog Shape, Crackled Paint, Brass Ashtray, 1920s, 11 x 9 In. 125.00
Stand, Smoking, Warren McArthur, Aluminum, Bakelite Top, 10 x 25 In. 715.00
Stand, Smoking, William & Mary, Walnut, Baluster-Turned Legs, 18 x 14 In. 400.00
Stand, Square Top, 4 Square Legs, Square Stem, Plinth Base, Vienna, 44 x 12 In. 230.00
Stand, Teakwood, Carved, Soapstone Insert, Round Top, China, 36 In. 385.00
Stand, Teakwood, Soapstone Insert, Square Top, China, 19 x 19 x 31 In. 355.00
Stand, Tiger Maple, 1 Drawer ...._Illus_ 1980.00
Stand, Tiger Maple, Curved Drawer Front, Turned Legs 1200.00
Stand, Umbrella, Black Forest, Bear-Shaped, c.1890 .... 7950.00
Stand, Umbrella, Brass, Iron, Black Paint, Victorian, 24 In. 145.00
Stand, Umbrella, Cast Iron, Black Paint, 19th Century, 51 3/4 In. 400.00
Stand, Umbrella, G. Stickley, Hammered Copper, Repousse, 2 Handles, Signed, 24 In. .. 4400.00
Stand, Umbrella, Metal Cylinder, Black Map Of Florence, Red Ground, 20 x 23 In. 285.00
Stand, Umbrella, Stickley Brothers, No. 168, Hexagonal, 26 In. 725.00
Stand, Umbrella, Thonet, Paper Label, 28 1/2 x 15 1/2 In. 290.00
Stand, Walnut Base, Cherry Top, Square Tapered Legs, 27 x 20 In. 165.00
Stand, Walnut, 1 Drawer, String Inlay & Cuffs, Kentucky, 28 x 18 1/2 In. 1456.00
Stand, Walnut, Figured Veneer, Drop Leaf, 2 Drawers, Wooden Pulls, 29 1/2 In. 275.00
Stand, Walnut, Natural Patina, Square Segmented Legs, 18 x 21 x 29 In. 72.00
Stand, Walnut, Tapered Pencil-Post Legs, Dovetailed Drawer, 14 x 14 x 25 In. 165.00

Stand, Walnut, Tilt Top, Suppressed Ball On Cabriole Leg Base, 29 x 17 3/4 In. 6325.00
Stand, Walnut, Turned Legs, 2 Dovetailed Drawers, 2-Board Top, 18 x 20 In. 165.00
Stand, Wash, Sheraton, Cherry, Poplar, Spool Legs, Shelf, Drawer, 27 x 33 In. 165.00
Stand, Wavy Birch, Tilt Top, 1820s, 29 1/2 In. 287.00
Stand, Wig, Mahogany, England, 18th Century 1295.00
Stool, Arts & Crafts, Walnut, Through Tenon, 24 x 12 x 12 In. 360.00
Stool, Barcelona, Knoll, Stainless Steel, Leather Sling Seat, 23 x 22 In., Pair 1870.00
Stool, Black Lacquer Top, Clustered Bamboo Legs, China, Pair 6900.00
Stool, Black Lacquer, Parcel Gilt, Openwork Body, 1890s, 20 x 14 1/2 In. 4025.00
Stool, Butterfly, Sori Yanagi, Molded Rosewood Veneer, 1956, 16 x 16 In. 1540.00
Stool, Chippendale, Mahogany, Cabriole Legs, Upholstered Top 805.00
Stool, Chippendale, Mahogany, Slip Seat, Beaded Legs, 1780, 18 1/2 In. 1495.00
Stool, Eames, Lifetime, Walnut, 14 1/2 In. 805.00
Stool, Empire, Ball Feet, Floral Needlepoint 285.00
Stool, Empire, Desmalter, White Paint, Gilt, X-Shape, Padded Seat, 1804, 24 In. 2990.00
Stool, Federal, Cherry, Square Tapered Legs, Upholstered Slip Seat, c.1790 . . . . 580.00
Stool, Federal, Mahogany, Curule Shape, Rectangular Seat, 1815, 18 In., Pair 4887.00
Stool, Figural, Mother-Of-Pearl & Ivory Inlay, Upholstered Oval Seat 6900.00
Stool, George II, Mahogany, Rectangular, Cabriole Legs, Pad Feet, 15 In., Pair 9200.00
Stool, Giltwood, Serpentine Seat, Scrolled Toes, Upholstered, 19 In., Pair 6325.00
Stool, Giltwood, Upholstered Seat, Shell-Carved Rails, Hoof Feet, 16 x 21 1/2 In. 2590.00
Stool, Jacobean, Oak, 18th Century, 22 x 17 1/2 x 10 1/2 In. 635.00
Stool, Jacobean, Oak, 19 x 17 x 7 1/2 In. 489.00
Stool, Kneeling, Turned Mahogany Legs, Upholstered, 28 x 12 x 10 In. 275.00
Stool, Louis XV, Giltwood, Carved Flower-Head Knees, Velvet, 20 1/4 In., Pair 9200.00
Stool, Louis XVI, Square Seat, Carved Corners, Gray Paint, Upholstered 2300.00
Stool, Louis XVI, Square Top, Stop-Fluted Legs, Mauve Paint, Upholstered, 13 In. 3165.00
Stool, Mahogany Veneer, Upholstered, 1950s 175.00
Stool, Mahogany, Upholstered Top, Blind Fret-Carved Legs, 1780s, 16 1/2 In., Pair 8050.00
Stool, Piano, Bugatti, Parchment, Mother-Of-Pearl & Bronze, c.1900, 27 1/2 In. 9775.00
Stool, Piano, Center Post, Iron & Glass Claw & Ball Feet 110.00
Stool, Piano, Central Octagonal Stem, Scroll Feet, Upholstered Top, Vienna 690.00
Stool, Piano, Eureka, Sherman & Hyde, 1873 . . . . 145.00
Stool, Piano, Mahogany, Backrest, Dolphin Supports, Adjustable Height 3850.00
Stool, Piano, Mahogany, Paneled Back, Dolphin Sides, Penna., 1825, 24 In. 198.00
Stool, Piano, Mahogany, Reeded Seat Rail, Spiral-Carved Legs, 1820s, 19 In. 402.00
Stool, Piano, Mahogany, Serpentine, Carved Bracket Feet, 17 In. 330.00
Stool, Poplar, Ebony, Upholstered Seat, Out-Scrolled Sides, 25 1/2 In., Pair 5175.00
Stool, Rohde, Z-Shaped, 1920s, Pair 700.00
Stool, Roycroft, Maple, Marked, 10 1/4 x 15 x 9 In. 230.00
Stool, Square Stop-Fluted Legs, Painted & Parcel Gilt, Upholstered, 17 1/2 In. 1840.00
Stool, Steer Horn, Horsehair Stuffing, Velvet, 12 x 8 x 8 In. 225.00
Stool, Tapered Fluted Legs, Blue & White Paint, Upholstered Top, 15 1/2 In. 2875.00
Stool, Walnut, 4 Turned Legs, Pad Feet, Padded Seat, Pair 2875.00
Stool, Walnut, Joined By Chrome Wire Strut Work, Rockers, 1954, 16 1/4 x 14 In. 3680.00
Stool, William & Mary Style, Upholstered, Bulbous Legs, Bun Feet, 14 x 14 In. 405.00
Stool, William & Mary, Walnut, Rectangular, Floral Needlepoint Seat, 18 In. 6900.00
Stool, William & Mary, Walnut, Semicircular Seat, 15 x 17 x 9 In. 230.00
Stool, William & Mary, Walnut, Semicircular Seat, 3 Chamfered Legs, 17 In. 250.00
Stool, Windsor, Bamboo, Stamped J.C. Hubbard On Seat Bottom, 32 In. 412.00
Stool, Windsor, Red & Black Graining, Yellow Striping, 13 1/2 x 13 1/2 In. 250.00
Storage Cube, G. Nelson, Oak Veneer, 3 Lift Sections, Ebonized Legs, 34 x 23 In. 715.00
Table, 1 Drawer, Red Base, Child's 280.00
Table, Aalto, Laminated Plywood, Bowed, 2 Shelves, 1936, 33 x 21 x 12 In. 5250.00
Table, Aesthetic Movement, Walnut, Greek Key & Floral Band Inlay, 48 In. 4890.00
Table, Architect's, Mahogany, Ratchet Support, Sectioned Interior, 36 In. 3450.00
Table, Art Deco, Bird's-Eye Maple, Fruitwood, Marquetry, 29 1/2 In. 1840.00
Table, Art Deco, Black Circular Top, Gold Star Design, 1930, 18 In. 2300.00
Table, Art Deco, Burl Walnut, Circular Top, Stepped Standard, 1930, 22 In. 2070.00
Table, Art Deco, Green Marble Top, 3 Wrought Iron Legs, R. Subes, 1925, 24 x 36 In. . . 3200.00
Table, Art Deco, Walnut, Black Trim, 2 Tiers, 24 x 12 x 50 In. 132.00
Table, Art Deco, Wrought Iron, Marble, Rectangular Marble Top, 1925, 18 In. 1840.00
Table, Biedermeier, Mahogany, Ebonized Banded Border, Hexagonal Standard 5175.00

Furniture, Table, Card, Federal, Mahogany,
Satinwood Inlay, D-Shape, 1800, 36 x 18 In.

Furniture, Table,
Dressing, G.
Stickley, No. 914,
Iron Pulls, 1904,
36 x 18 x 54 In.

Table, Black Slate Top, Colored Stone Inlay, Floral Spray, c.1860, 24-In. Diam.		3450.00
Table, Brohdt, Mahogany, Demilune, Hinged Top, 29 3/4 x 32 In.		470.00
Table, Card, Cherry, Bird's-Eye Maple, Early 19th Century, 30 5/8 In.		1380.00
Table, Card, Cherry, Swing Top, Spool Turned, 29 1/2 x 32 In.		210.00
Table, Card, Chippendale, Folding Top, Accordion-Fold Apron, 38 In. Open		2035.00
Table, Card, Chippendale, Mahogany, 6 Brackets, Molded Edge, 28 In.		2750.00
Table, Card, Chippendale, Mahogany, Beaded Edge, Marlboro Legs, 28 1/2 In.		5175.00
Table, Card, Classical, Mahogany, Acanthus Carving, Serpentine Apron, 18 x 36 In.		2530.00
Table, Card, Empire, Walnut, Veneer, Serpentine Base, Swing Top, 17 x 34 x 29 In.		220.00
Table, Card, Federal, Mahogany Veneer, Beaded Edges, 28 3/8 x 36 In.		980.00
Table, Card, Federal, Mahogany, Hinged Oblong Top, Peg Feet, 30 x 35 x 18 In.		980.00
Table, Card, Federal, Mahogany, Inlaid Edge, Mass., 1800, 29 1/2 In.		1610.00
Table, Card, Federal, Mahogany, Satinwood Inlay, D-Shape, 1800, 36 x 18 In.	*Illus*	4620.00
Table, Card, Federal, Mahogany, Skirt Divided Into 3 Panels, c.1800, 29 1/2 In.		1380.00
Table, Card, Federal, Mahogany, Trick Leg, Hinged Elliptical Top, 1815, 30 In.		2875.00
Table, Card, Galle, Marquetry, Folding Top, Twist Legs, 1900, 31 x 30 x 18 In.		9375.00
Table, Card, George III, Satinwood, Baize-Lined Top, Square Legs, 36 In.		6325.00
Table, Card, Hepplewhite, Mahogany, Inlay, 30 x 39 x 36 In.		580.00
Table, Card, Hepplewhite, Mahogany, Inlay, Philadelphia, c.1790, 34 x 17 x 29 In.		2950.00
Table, Card, Hepplewhite, Mahogany, Tapered Legs, Newport, R.I., 28 1/4 In.		2475.00
Table, Card, Hepplewhite, Walnut, Stringing, Dovetailed Drawer, 18 x 36 In.		385.00
Table, Card, Mahogany Top, Crossbanded, Inlay, Felt		1400.00
Table, Card, Mahogany, Bowfront, D-Shape, Boston, 36 In., Pair		5225.00
Table, Card, Mahogany, Claw & Egg Feet, Center Post, 19th Century		2300.00
Table, Card, Mahogany, Crotch Mahogany Apron, Double-Line Inlay, c.1790		4700.00
Table, Card, Mahogany, Flame Birch Veneer, Inlaid Skirt Panel, c.1800, 29 1/2 In.		8050.00
Table, Card, Mahogany, Flame Birch Veneer, Ovolo Corners, c.1800, 30 In.		1955.00
Table, Card, Mahogany, Line Inlay, Massachusetts, 1800		4620.00
Table, Card, Mahogany, Satinwood, Serpentine Top, Inlay, Ring-Turned Legs		8625.00
Table, Card, Rosewood, Hungarian Ash, Mahogany, Dynamique, 1928, 36 1/2 In.		1650.00
Table, Card, Sheraton, Mahogany Veneer, Convoluted Apron, 17 x 35 x 28 In.		1430.00
Table, Card, Sheraton, Mahogany, D-Shaped Ends, 41 x 30 1/2 In. Open		220.00
Table, Card, Sheraton, Mahogany, Inlay, Hinged Leaf, Mass., 36 x 17 x 28 In.		7425.00
Table, Card, Walnut, Lyre Base, Swivel Top, Victorian, 35 x 28 1/2 In.		220.00
Table, Card, Walnut, Swing Top, Square Tapered Legs, Folds, 16 x 33 x 28 In.		190.00
Table, Center, Baroque, Pine, Linenfold Apron, S-Curved Legs, 33 x 51 x 35 In.		1725.00
Table, Center, Carved Walnut, White Marble Top, Victorian, 42 x 30 x 30 In.		2310.00
Table, Center, Chippendale Style, Mahogany, Ireland, c.1870, 28 x 42 x 22 In.		2100.00
Table, Center, Classical, Mahogany, Tilt Top, 4 Scrolled Feet, 1830-1840, 29 In.		275.00
Table, Center, Eastlake, Carved Walnut, Marble Top, 35 x 23 x 29 1/2 In.		495.00
Table, Center, Eastlake, Walnut, Burl Veneer, Marble Top, 30 1/4 In.		302.00
Table, Center, Eastlake, Walnut, Burl Walnut, Marble Top, 28 1/2 x 30 1/2 In.		60.00
Table, Center, Eastlake, Walnut, White Marble Top, Victorian, 20 x 28 x 30 In.		330.00
Table, Center, Empire, Mahogany, Marble Top, Plinth Base, 20 x 40 In.		575.00
Table, Center, George II, Mahogany, Rectangular Gray Marble Top, 32 In.		6900.00
Table, Center, George III, Mahogany, 31 1/2 x 36 x 21 1/2 In.		2875.00

Table, Center, Herter Brothers, Gilt, Rosewood Inlay, c.1872 . . . . 17250.00
Table, Center, Mahogany, Marble Checkerboard Turtle Top, Victorian, 20 x 31 In. 660.00
Table, Center, Mahogany, White Marble Top, 24 Triangles On Border, 30 1/2 In. 4025.00
Table, Center, Neoclassical, Walnut, Fruitwood, Foliate Reserve, Italy, 29 In. 575.00
Table, Center, Regency, Giltwood, Dolphin-Shaped Supports, 29 x 38 In. 2645.00
Table, Center, Renaissance Revival, Walnut, Italy, 29 x 34 x 33 In. 1610.00
Table, Center, Renaissance Revival, Walnut, Scrolled Supports, 30 x 32 In. 460.00
Table, Center, Rococo, Elm, Leaf-Carved Support, Scrolled Legs, 28 In. 1440.00
Table, Center, Rococo, Marble Top, Carved Garland, Acanthus Legs, 31 x 25 In. 920.00
Table, Center, Rosewood, Barley-Twist Legs, 1850s 1960.00
Table, Center, Rosewood, Marble Top, Solid Pedestal Base, c.1850 . . . . 7000.00
Table, Center, Scene Of Ruins, Marble Border, Splayed Legs, 28 3/4 In. 8050.00
Table, Center, Thomas Brooks, Marble Top, Brooklyn, N.Y. 2200.00
Table, Center, Walnut, Oak Leaves, Carved Stylized Fox, Paw Feet, 43 x 31 In. 3740.00
Table, Center, Walnut, Turned Base, Shelby, Ohio, 24 1/4 x 36 x 27 1/2 In. 300.00
Table, Center, Walnut, Victorian, 30 x 32 3/4 In. 220.00
Table, Charles X, Mahogany, Bird's-Eye Maple Inlay, Bun Feet, 53 In. 5750.00
Table, Cherry, Demilune, String Outlining Top Edge, Drawer, 29 1/2 x 33 /2 In. 1840.00
Table, Cherry, Empire, Scroll Legs, 36 In. 425.00
Table, Cherry, Rope-Carved Legs, 1 Drawer, 2-Board Top, 31 x 36 In. 300.00
Table, Cherry, Tiger Maple, Cookie Cutter Corners, 30 x 19 In. 400.00
Table, Chippendale, Mahogany, Piecrust, Cabriole Legs, 31 x 32 In. 1495.00
Table, Chippendale, Mahogany, Tilt Top, Claw Feet, 19th Century, 26 In. 121.00
Table, Chippendale, Wallace Nutting, No. 693B, Piecrust 2860.00
Table, Classical, Mahogany, Marble Top, Brass Paw Feet, Casters, 29 In. 330.00
Table, Coffee, Adnet, Salmon Pink, Blue, Gray, Marble Slab Stop, 1930, 37 x 14 In. 1610.00
Table, Coffee, Art Deco, Veneered Cube, Black Plinth Base, Square, 36 x 19 In. 550.00
Table, Coffee, Black Wire Corseted Base, Glass Top, W. Plattner, 15 1/2 x 42 In. 440.00
Table, Coffee, Florence Knoll, Walnut, Chrome Base, Round Top, 42 x 16 In. 440.00
Table, Coffee, Frankl, Mahogany, Round Cork Top, Square Legs, 48 x 14 In. 1540.00
Table, Coffee, Frankl, Rectangular Cork Top, Triangular Base, 48 x 24 x 14 In. 275.00
Table, Coffee, G. Nelson, White Laminate, Black Steel, 30 x 16 In. 165.00
Table, Coffee, Glass Top, Walnut Legs, Dunbar, 1950, 57 x 31 x 16 In. 2530.00
Table, Coffee, Herman Miller, White Laminate, Folding Steel Legs, 50 x 14 In. 165.00
Table, Coffee, I. Noguchi, Adjustable Lacquer Base, Elliptical Glass Top, 40 In. 16550.00
Table, Coffee, I. Noguchi, Plywood, Paddle Fin, 2 Metal & 2 Wood Legs, 50 In. 5225.00
Table, Coffee, Jens Rison, Walnut, Cutout Top For Magazine Holder, 17 x 52 In. 165.00
Table, Coffee, Laminated Birch, Lead, Circular Glass Top, 1930, 16 x 43 1/4 In. 8625.00
Table, Coffee, Louis XVI, Fruitwood, Brassbound Marble Top, 19 x 31 In. 220.00
Table, Coffee, Louis XVI, Marble Top, Oval, 50 x 25 In. 173.00
Table, Coffee, Mahogany, Glass Tray Top, 25 1/4 x 26 In. 412.00
Table, Coffee, Nickel Plate, Tubular Steel, 1930, 24 1/2 x 23 5/8 In. 9775.00
Table, Coffee, Painted White Metal Base, Marble Top, Knoll International, 15 In. 430.00
Table, Coffee, Poillerat, Wrought-Iron, Rectangular Marble Top, 1940, 22 In. 11500.00
Table, Coffee, Richard Fahnkow, Rosewood, 4 Square Legs, Germany, 1930, 19 In. 2875.00
Table, Coffee, Robsjohn-Gibbings, Walnut Veneer, Square, 1954, 30 x 16 In. 65.00
Table, Coffee, Rohde, Circular Glass Top, Leatherette Legs, 27 x 16 In. 605.00
Table, Coffee, W. Plattner, Chrome Wire, Round Glass Top, Knoll, 35 x 16 In. 605.00
Table, Coffee, Walnut Veneer, Framed Base, c.1960, 48 In. 385.00
Table, Coffee, Widdicomb, Walnut Veneer, Lazy Susan, Towel Base, 39 In. 220.00
Table, Coffee, Yamasaki, Rectangular Stone Top, Wrought Iron, 50 x 18 x 10 In. 440.00
Table, Colonna, Mahogany, Round, Carved Linear Design, 1900, 28 In., Pair 6560.00
Table, Console, Art Deco, Black Lacquer, Chrome, Lower Shelf, 60 x 22 In. 825.00
Table, Console, Bugatti, Hammered-Copper Strips, Rectangular Top, 35 In. 4370.00
Table, Console, Chippendale, Mahogany, Plum Pudding, 34 In. 2300.00
Table, Console, George Fry, Steel Top, Frosted Glass Inserts, 1937, 60 In. 7050.00
Table, Console, Gothic Revival, Mahogany, Stenciled, c.1910, 32 x 16 In. 345.00
Table, Console, Green, Gold Paint, Swag, France, 18th Century, 40 x 18 x 31 In. 2310.00
Table, Console, Ico Parisi, Burl Veneer, Walnut, 1948, 71 x 20 x 30 In. 4125.00
Table, Console, Louis XVI, Fruitwood, Giltwood, Acanthus Leaves, 31 x 41 In. 1265.00
Table, Console, Louis XVI, Marble Top, Carved Acanthus Leaves, Gray, 34 x 45 In. 9200.00
Table, Console, Mahogany, Louis XVI, Marble Top & Stretcher, 1780s, 52 1/4 In. 6325.00
Table, Console, Marble Top, Drawer, Stop-Fluted Legs, 19th Century, 37 1/4 In. 3740.00

Table, Console, Neoclassical, Faux Marble Top, Foliate Swag, Italy, 33 1/4 In. 5750.00
Table, Console, Regency, Rosewood, Parcel Gilt, Marble Top, Mirrored Back 2300.00
Table, Console, Wrought Iron, Floral Panels, Marble Top, 1925, 38 x 58 x 25 In. 11245.00
Table, Copper, Painted & Parcel Gilt, Demilune, Foliage & Vase Center, 35 In. 4600.00
Table, Corner, Heywood Wakefield, Blond Finish, 2 Tiers 150.00
Table, Dinette, I. Noguchi, Laminated Plywood, Chrome Wire, Knoll, 36 In. 1100.00
Table, Dining, Arts & Crafts, Quartersawn Oak, 4 Leaves, 48 In. 1325.00
Table, Dining, Biedermeier, Maple, Circular Top, Stepped Plinth, 28 x 43 In. 3000.00
Table, Dining, Birch, Triangular Top, Steel Hairpin Legs, Rudder Supports, 51 In. 8510.00
Table, Dining, Cherry, Federal, Walnut-Veneered Skirt, Spiral Legs, 84 1/4 In. 1380.00
Table, Dining, Chippendale, Mahogany, 6 Molded Legs, Dovetailed 440.00
Table, Dining, Classical, Mahogany, Circular Top, Volute Feet, 1830, 32 In. 5750.00
Table, Dining, Drop Leaf, Cherry, Swing Leg, Ring & Spool-Turned Legs, c.1810 . . . . . . 220.00
Table, Dining, Drop Leaf, Mahogany, Square Vase-Form Pedestal Base, 42 In. 275.00
Table, Dining, Drop Leaf, Queen Anne, Mahogany, Pad Feet, 1750, 27 In. 2300.00
Table, Dining, Duncan Phyfe Style, Mahogany, 66 x 44 x 30 In., 2 11-In. Leaves 300.00
Table, Dining, Duncan Phyfe, Mahogany, Brass Paw Feet, 3 Part, 41 x 79 In. 1540.00
Table, Dining, E. Wormley, Walnut, Mahogany Base, 4 Leaves, 48 x 29 In. 2200.00
Table, Dining, Eames, Painted Undercarriage, 4 Tapering Dowel Legs, 53 1/4 In. 460.00
Table, Dining, Eames, Walnut, Plywood Legs, 1945, 54 x 34 x 29 In. 2310.00
Table, Dining, Federal, Cherry, Alligatored, 1-Leaf End Table, 3 Part, 113 In. 2640.00
Table, Dining, Federal, Cherry, Crossbanded Frieze, 1810, 2 Part, 30 In. 7475.00
Table, Dining, G. Stickley, No. 647, Rectangular Top, Keyed Tenon, 40 x 28 In. 1760.00
Table, Dining, G. Stickley, Octagonal Apron, Circular Top, 30 x 54 In. 4950.00
Table, Dining, G. Stickley, Overhanging Top, 5 Legs, 4 Leaves, 54 In. 3190.00
Table, Dining, G. Stickley, Round Top, Pedestal, Corbel Supports, 48-In. Diam. 2200.00
Table, Dining, George II, Mahogany, Brass Inlay, Lobed Dish Top, 27 In. 11500.00
Table, Dining, George III, Drop Leaf, Mahogany, Tapered Legs, Pad Feet, 28 In. 3450.00
Table, Dining, George III, Mahogany, 4 Pedestals, Reeded Edge, 28 x 17 x 2 In. 4830.00
Table, Dining, Heywood-Wakefield Co., Drop Leaf, Wheat Finish, 27 x 40 x 29 In. 465.00
Table, Dining, Jacobean, Oak, Geometric Apron, 65 x 35 x 21 In. 1840.00
Table, Dining, Knoll, Bird's-Eye Maple Top, Original Green Finish, 78 x 28 In. 1760.00
Table, Dining, Knoll, Smoked-Glass Top, Geometric Chrome Base, 1970, 54 x 29 In. . . . 250.00
Table, Dining, Knoll, Walnut Veneer, Bronze Finish, Wire Base, 36 x 28 In. 550.00
Table, Dining, Lifetime, Extension, Gateleg, Circular Top, Casters, 29 3/4 x 54 In. 2090.00
Table, Dining, Mahogany, 2 Pedestal, 2 Leaves, Down-Swept Reeded Legs, 106 In. 8050.00
Table, Dining, Mahogany, 3 Pedestals, Ring-Turned Standards, 2 Leaves, 54 In. 9200.00
Table, Dining, Mahogany, Beechwood, 2 Pedestal, 2 Leaves, Late 19th Century, 72 In. . . 5175.00
Table, Dining, Mahogany, D-Shaped Ends, England, 17-In. Leaf, 38 x 19 x 28 In. 690.00
Table, Dining, Mahogany, Double Pedestal, 3-Board, 105 In. 1375.00
Table, Dining, Mahogany, Double Pedestal, Rounded Corners, 3 Leaves, 64 In. 1020.00
Table, Dining, Mahogany, Extension, Hinged Top, 1 Leaf Over Frieze, 1820s, 66 In. 2875.00
Table, Dining, Mahogany, Regency, 2 Pedestals, Brass Feet, Casters, 2 Leaves, 92 In. . . . 4600.00
Table, Dining, Oak, Oblong Panel Top, Self-Storing Leaf Each End, 41 1/2 In. 275.00
Table, Dining, Queen Anne Style, Mahogany, 2 20-In. Leaves, 44 x 29 In. 715.00
Table, Dining, Queen Anne, Maple, Overhanging Top, 4 Block-Turned Legs, 39 In. 2760.00
Table, Dining, Queen Anne, Maple, Shaped Skirt, Pad Feet, 1750s, 29 x 47 1/2 In. 2530.00
Table, Dining, Ralph Rapson, Thick Walnut, Steel, 1950s, 88 x 46 x 30 In. 1870.00
Table, Dining, Regency, Mahogany, 2 Pedestals, Brass Caps, Casters, 28 In. 3190.00
Table, Dining, Regency, Mahogany, 4 Turned Columnar Supports, 29 x 95 1/2 In. 3680.00
Table, Dining, Regency, Mahogany, Reeded Edge, Legs, Paw Feet, 28 1/4 In. 3450.00
Table, Dining, Renaissance Revival, Walnut, 4 Panels, Scrolled Legs, 1875, 46 In. 1840.00
Table, Dining, Rohde, Tilt Top, Veneer, Chrome Tubes, Hinged Leaves, 48 In. 1650.00
Table, Dining, Sheraton, Mahogany, Reeded Edge, Ring-Banded Legs, 29 In. 2300.00
Table, Dining, Walnut, Drop-Leaf Extension, Out-Curved Legs, 29 1/2 x 100 In. 3450.00
Table, Dining, Walnut, Molded Top Edge, Pedestal Base, 28 x 23 1/4 In. 2665.00
Table, Dining, Widdicomb, Fruitwood, Columnar Legs, Upholstered Seat, 29 In. 3165.00
Table, Dining, Widdicomb, Walnut Veneer, X-Shaped Base, 1951, 58 x 38 x 29 In. 605.00
Table, Dinning, George III, Mahogany, Hinged Flaps, Molded Legs, 25 1/4 In. 550.00
Table, Dressing, Beau Brummel, Mahogany, Fitted Interior, Mirror, 2 Drawers, 35 In. . . . 920.00
Table, Dressing, Cherry, Maple, 2 Dovetailed Drawers, 36 1/4 In. 1815.00
Table, Dressing, G. Stickley, No. 914, Iron Pulls, 1904, 36 x 18 x 54 In. . . . .*Illus* 6600.00
Table, Dressing, George I, Oak, Walnut, 28 1/2 x 30 x 18 3/4 In. 690.00

Table, Dressing, George II, Oak, 3 Drawers, Apron, Cabriole Legs, 26 x 30 In. 1495.00
Table, Dressing, Hepplewhite, Pine, Dovetailed Drawer, Crest, 33 x 28 In. 660.00
Table, Dressing, Kingwood, Tulipwood Veneer, Floral Sprays, 29 x 17 3/4 In. 4600.00
Table, Dressing, Mahogany, Hinged Lid, Brass Inlay, Fitted Interior, 34 In. 1095.00
Table, Dressing, Mahogany, Lift Top, 2 Rectangular Drawers, Lyre-Shaped Pedestal 275.00
Table, Dressing, Mahogany, Lift Top, Geometric Inlay, 2 Drawers, Mirror, 29 In. 605.00
Table, Dressing, Mother-Of-Pearl Inlay, Mirror, Cane-Seat Chair, Victorian 440.00
Table, Dressing, Queen Anne, Maple, Thumb-Molded Drawer, Pad Feet, 31 In. 5175.00
Table, Dressing, Sheraton, Butternut, Poplar, 2 Drawers, 37 x 20 x 57 In. 4850.00
Table, Dressing, Sheraton, Pine, Poplar, 3 Drawers, Step Back, Crest, Stencil, 40 In. 2970.00
Table, Dressing, Tiger Maple Veneer, Center Drawer, 2 Side Square Doors 110.00
Table, Dressing, Tiger Maple, Simulated Walnut Veneers, Bandy Legs, 28 In. 360.00
Table, Dressing, Walnut, 2 Long Drawers, Pointed Slipper Feet, 27 x 31 1/2 In. 2875.00
Table, Dressing, Wicker, Reed, Oval Mirror, 2 Drawers, Spiral Legs, 58 1/2 In. 330.00
Table, Dressing, William & Mary, Pine, 3 Drawers, Ball Feet, 32 x 40 In. 575.00
Table, Dressing, William & Mary, Walnut, 31 x 35 3/4 x 18 In. 750.00
Table, Drink, George III, Mahogany, 3 Splayed Legs, Pad Feet, 27 1/2 In. 2530.00
Table, Drink, Stickley Brothers, No. 2615, Round Copper Top, Splayed Legs, 18 In. 1045.00
Table, Drop Leaf, Birch, Turned Posts, Castor Feet, Maine, 30 In. 345.00
Table, Drop Leaf, Cherry, Ring-Turned Legs, c.1815 . . . . 300.00
Table, Drop Leaf, Cherry, Spool Turned Swing Legs, 27 In. 275.00
Table, Drop Leaf, Cherry, Swing Leg, Leaves, 28 1/2 In. 385.00
Table, Drop Leaf, Cherry, Turned Legs, 19 x 39 x 12 /12 In. 166.00
Table, Drop Leaf, Chippendale, Mahogany, Cutout Apron, Ball & Claw Feet, 47 In. 1155.00
Table, Drop Leaf, Chippendale, Maple, Red Paint, Square Swing Legs, 45 1/4 In. 990.00
Table, Drop Leaf, Curly Maple, 6 Legs, 21 1/2 x 49 1/2 In. 1870.00
Table, Drop Leaf, Curly Maple, Turned Legs, Leaves, 17 x 37 x 29 In. 1320.00
Table, Drop Leaf, Empire, Flame Mahogany, Pedestal, 1840, American, 28 In. 1100.00
Table, Drop Leaf, Empire, Mahogany, Acanthus Pedestal, 1 Drawer, 24 x 42 In. 1870.00
Table, Drop Leaf, G. Stickley, No. 443, Through Tenons & Pegs, 30 x 40 x 42 In. 5460.00
Table, Drop Leaf, Gateleg, Walnut, Late 19th Century 330.00
Table, Drop Leaf, George II, Mahogany, 28 x 31 x 9 3/4 In. 920.00
Table, Drop Leaf, George II, Oak, Swivel Top, Pad Feet, 28 x 41 In. 1955.00
Table, Drop Leaf, George III, Mahogany, Spider Legs, Mid-19th Century 865.00
Table, Drop Leaf, George III, Mahogany, Tapered Legs, 29 In. 3450.00
Table, Drop Leaf, Hepplewhite, Cherry, Square Swing Legs, 13 x 14 In. 440.00
Table, Drop Leaf, Hepplewhite, Cherry, Square Tapered Legs, 23 x 48 In. 300.00
Table, Drop Leaf, Hepplewhite, Mahogany, 6 Tapered Legs, 18 x 44 x 22 In. 250.00
Table, Drop Leaf, Mahogany, 1 Drawer, Claw Feet, 27 3/4 x 24 In. 402.00
Table, Drop Leaf, Mahogany, 1 Drawer, Paw Legs, 26 x 40 In. 316.00
Table, Drop Leaf, Mahogany, 6 Swing Legs, Leaves, 20 x 46 1/2 In. 935.00
Table, Drop Leaf, Mahogany, Breakfast, Drawer, c.1810 . . . . 2070.00
Table, Drop Leaf, Mahogany, Carved Horse's-Hoof Feet 1650.00
Table, Drop Leaf, Mahogany, In-Cut Corners, Cut Corner Plinth, Hairy Paw Feet 880.00
Table, Drop Leaf, Mahogany, Spiral Acanthus Carving, 29 x 39 In. 440.00
Table, Drop Leaf, Maple, Breakfast, 4 Legs, 32 x 49 1/8 In. 75.00
Table, Drop Leaf, Maple, Turned Pad Feet, Painted, 28 x 40 In. 8625.00
Table, Drop Leaf, Pembroke, Hepplewhite, Cherry, Serpentine, New England, 33 In. 7810.00
Table, Drop Leaf, Pembroke, Hepplewhite, Mahogany, Banded Apron, 18 x 31 In. 3300.00
Table, Drop Leaf, Pembroke, Mahogany, Inlay, Drawer, 20th Century, 28 1/4 In. 275.00
Table, Drop Leaf, Queen Anne, Mahogany, 1 Drawer, Cabriole Legs, 12 x 35 In. 3080.00
Table, Drop Leaf, Queen Anne, Mahogany, Dovetailed, Pad Feet, 42 x 53 x 28 In. 1210.00
Table, Drop Leaf, Queen Anne, Maple, Scalloped Apron, Duck Feet, 27 In. 2475.00
Table, Drop Leaf, Queen Anne, Walnut, Hinged Oval Top, Pad Feet, 1750, 25 In. 2300.00
Table, Drop Leaf, Regency, Mahogany, Acanthus Baluster, Paw Feet, 27 In. 1840.00
Table, Drop Leaf, Sheraton, Mahogany, 1 Dovetailed Drawer, Reeded Legs, 29 In. 275.00
Table, Drop Leaf, Walnut, 6 Swing Legs, 1 Drawer, 1-Board Top, 19 x 47 In. 465.00
Table, Drop Leaf, Walnut, Marquetry, Triangular, 19th Century, 29 3/4 In. 865.00
Table, Drop Leaf, Walnut, Oval Top, 2 Opposing Drawers, 31 x 42 In. 3450.00
Table, Drop Leaf, Walnut, Swing Legs, 20 x 44 In. 245.00
Table, Drop Leaf, William & Mary, Maple, 8 Baluster Legs, Red, Black, 28 In. 10925.00
Table, Drop Leaf, William & Mary, Walnut, Rectangular Top, Turned Legs, 25 In. 980.00
Table, Drum, George III, Mahogany, 4 Drawers, 3 Reeded Legs, 29 x 24 In. 920.00

Table, Drum, George III, Mahogany, Faux Drawers, Tooled Leather Top, 31 In. 8625.00
Table, Dunbar, Bleach Mahogany, Trapezoidal, 26 x 25 x 22 In. 165.00
Table, E.S. Rehour, Mahogany, Kidney-Shaped Top, Brass Border, 29 x 38 In. 9200.00
Table, Eames, Lafonda, Slate Top, 4-Prong Aluminum Base, 30 In. 400.00
Table, Eames, Molded Plywood, Mahogany Veneer, Dish Top, Round, 34 In. 1045.00
Table, Eames, Surfboard, Laminated Plywood, Zinc Wire Struts, 89 In. 2420.00
Table, Eames, Walnut Veneer Top, Metal Post, Conference 470.00
Table, Elm, Brown Lacquer, Fretwork, China, 37 x 38 x 33 1/2 In. 245.00
Table, Federal Style, Mahogany, 2 Drawers, Casters, Splayed Legs 750.00
Table, Federal, Tiger Maple, 4 Drawers, 28 x 47 1/2 In. 6325.00
Table, Frank Lloyd Wright, Hexagonal, Tri-Slab Base, Taliesin, 20 x 17 In. 1045.00
Table, Frankl, Chrome Banding, Drawer, Shelves, 1930s, Pair 4500.00
Table, Frieze Drawer, Lion Masks, Scenes, Chinese Export, 41 1/2 In. 8970.00
Table, Fruitwood, Frieze Drawer, Rectangular Top, Mid-19th Century, 30 x 23 In. 345.00
Table, G. Nakashima, Black Walnut, Tripod Legs, 15 x 36 In. 522.00
Table, G. Nakashima, Free-Form, 3 Legs, 12 x 20 x 13 In. 522.00
Table, G. Nelson, Walnut Veneer, 1 Drawer, Lower Shelf, Steel Base, 24 In. 100.00
Table, G. Stickley, Drawer, Copper V-Shaped Pull, Lower Shelf, Decal, 20 x 30 In. 880.00
Table, G. Stickley, Ebonized, Middle Shelf, Trestle Sides, 28 In. 3630.00
Table, G. Stickley, Maple, 8 Legs, 3 Leaves, 48 In. 1200.00
Table, G. Stickley, No. 2508, Recessed Circular Shelf, Apron, 29 1/2 x 30 In. 990.00
Table, G. Stickley, Oak, 6 Chamfered Post Legs, 1912, 29 In. 5980.00
Table, Galle, 2 Tiers, Floral Inlay, 2 Tiers, 1900, 37 x 33 x 26 In. 9000.00
Table, Game, Art Deco, Aluminum, Cork Checkerboard Top, Square, 20 x 24 In. 715.00
Table, Game, Checkerboard Top, Spiral Turned Legs, 1 Drawer 675.00
Table, Game, Chestnut, Oak, Radiating Starburst On Top, Foliate Legs, 28 In. 2760.00
Table, Game, Classical, Mahogany, Lyre-Shaped Support, Scrolled Legs, 29 In. 1760.00
Table, Game, Classical, Rosewood, Swing Top, Pedestal, Felt Top, 18 x 36 x 29 In. 1375.00
Table, Game, Empire, Mahogany, Swivel Top, Pedestal, Spiral Columns, Saber Legs 660.00
Table, Game, Empire, Mahogany, Tilt Top, Carved Egg & Dart On Base, 34 x 30 In. 195.00
Table, Game, Federal, Birch, Maple, Inlay, 1800, 29 1/2 x 36 1/2 In. 1725.00
Table, Game, Federal, Curly Maple, Mahogany Inlay, Hinged Top, c.1805, 36 In. 625.00
Table, Game, Federal, Mahogany, C Shape, Conch Shell Inlay, Tapered Legs, 30 In. 1100.00
Table, Game, Federal, Mahogany, Hinged Rectangular Top, 1800, 29 x 36 In. 3740.00
Table, Game, Federal, Mahogany, Inlaid Panel, Mass., 1800, 30 x 36 In. 1610.00
Table, Game, George I, Mahogany, Cabriole Legs, Pad Feet, 28 x 32 x 28 In. 1300.00
Table, Game, George II, Mahogany, Rectangular Foldover Top, 29 In. 2990.00
Table, Game, George II, Walnut, Triangular Top, Mid-18th Century, 29 1/2 In. 1100.00
Table, Game, George III, Mahogany, Felt-Lined Surface, Fretwork Arches, 28 3/4 In. . . . 287.00
Table, Game, George III, Mahogany, Foldover Serpentine Top, 29 x 35 x 35 In. 1150.00
Table, Game, George III, Mahogany, Foldover Top, Beaded Drawer, 28 x 36 In. 1035.00
Table, Game, George III, Satinwood Inlay, Swing Leg, 29 x 36 x 17 In. 4370.00
Table, Game, George III, Walnut, Crossbanded, Scroll, Acanthus Legs, 28 x 29 In. 1150.00
Table, Game, Georgian, Mahogany, 1 Drawer, Circular Legs, 33 x 16 In. 1840.00
Table, Game, Hepplewhite, Mahogany, Medallion Inlay, Tapered Legs, New England . . . 885.00
Table, Game, Ivory, Mother-Of-Pearl, Swiveled Base, 4 Feet, 23 x 33 In. 490.00
Table, Game, Lacquered, Bi-Fold, China, 19th Century, 29 In. 2700.00
Table, Game, Mahogany, 1 Drawer, Bail Brasses, Tapered Legs, Philadelphia 990.00
Table, Game, Mahogany, Foldover Top, Gilt Leather & Green Baize, 1820s, 29 In. 8625.00
Table, Game, Mahogany, Storage Space Between 4 Turned Legs, 29 In. 440.00
Table, Game, Mahogany, Triple-Action, Foldover Top, 32 1/4 In. 2587.00
Table, Game, Oak, Octagonal, Carved Rosettes & Borders, Pedestal, 48 In. Diam. 210.00
Table, Game, Regency, Rosewood, Flared Columns, Paw Feet, 27 3/4 x 36 In. 2530.00
Table, Game, Regency, Walnut, Splayed Legs, Brass Feet, 36 x 17 In. 1495.00
Table, Game, Rococo Revival, Walnut, 4 Cabriole Legs, 31 x 35 x 17 In. 805.00
Table, Game, Rosewood, Foldover Top, Baize Lined, Paw Feet, 28 x 36 In. 1725.00
Table, Game, Rosewood, Regency, Brass Inlay, Baize Lined, 29 In. 2875.00
Table, Game, Sheraton, Mahogany, Satinwood Inlay, Fluted Legs, 35 x 32 x 17 In. 220.00
Table, Game, Sheraton, Maple, Mahogany, Shaped Top, Reeded Legs, 30 1/2 In. 2310.00
Table, Game, Walnut, Baroque Marquetry, Spiral-Turned Legs 4140.00
Table, Game, Walnut, Damask Lining, c.1740, 29 x 29 1/4 In. 5800.00
Table, Game, Walnut, Queen Anne, Baize Interior, 1830s, 28 1/2 x 34 In. 1380.00
Table, Game, William IV, Rosewood, Swivel Top, Acanthus Support, 28 x 36 In. 3000.00

Table, Gateleg, Cherry, Folded Leaf, Rope Legs, 44 x 87 In. 1150.00
Table, Gateleg, Oak, Mortised & Pinned Stretchers, Oval Top, England, 15 x 45 In. 415.00
Table, Gateleg, Oak, Oval Hinged Top, Leaves, England, 17th Century, 29 In. 920.00
Table, Gateleg, Oval Drop Leaf, Mahogany, Drawer, Pointed Pad Feet 3740.00
Table, Gateleg, Sheraton, Cherry, Drawer, Leaves, 29 1/2 x 19 1/2 x 41 In. 247.00
Table, Gateleg, Walnut, Beaded Skirt, 29 3/4 x 60 1/2 In. 440.00
Table, Gateleg, William & Mary Style, Oak, Barley-Twist Legs, 30 x 55 x 17 In. 955.00
Table, Gateleg, William & Mary, D-Shaped Leaves, Drawers, Turned Legs, 29 In. 1610.00
Table, George II, Mahogany, Marble Top, Gadrooned Frieze, 27 1/2 x 44 1/4 In. 7475.00
Table, George III Style, Mahogany, Silver, Columnar Legs, 30 x 35 In. 9775.00
Table, George III, Mahogany, 2 Drawers, Trestle Supports, 28 x 33 In. 1725.00
Table, George III, Mahogany, Cabriole Legs, Pad Feet, 27 1/2 In. 980.00
Table, George III, Mahogany, Down-Swept Reeded Legs, Brass Feet, 43 In. 460.00
Table, George III, Tilt Top, Mahogany, Cabriole Legs, Pad Feet, 28 x 33 In. 770.00
Table, George III, Tilt Top, Mahogany, Tripod, Late 19th Century, 29 x 32 In. 1265.00
Table, George III, Walnut, Elm, 25 1/4 x 27 In. 520.00
Table, Gilt Metal, Marble Top & Center Shelf, Pair 4600.00
Table, Giltwood, Japanned, Chinoiserie Landscape, 42 1/4 In. 9200.00
Table, Hall, Federal, Mahogany, D-Shape, Acanthus, Carved Floral Urn Aprons, Pair 4950.00
Table, Handkerchief, 4-Part Hinged Top, Satinwood Inlay, 20th Century, 28 In. 4890.00
Table, Handkerchief, Hinged Brass Top, 1 Drawer, Parquetry, 1880s, 29 3/4 In. 3740.00
Table, Handkerchief, P. Sormani, Kingwood, Rotating Top, Hinged Panels, 29 In. 8050.00
Table, Hardwood, Brown Finish, China, 35 x 35 1/2 x 21 1/4 In. 275.00
Table, Hepplewhite, Cherry, Mortised & Pinned Apron, 1 Drawer, 26 3/4 In. 605.00
Table, Hepplewhite, Cherry, Square Tapered Legs, 24 x 36 x 28 In. 440.00
Table, Hepplewhite, Mahogany, Copper Jardiniere Insert, Inlay, Oval, 18 x 23 In. 190.00
Table, Hepplewhite, Tilt Top, Mahogany, Gilt Checkerboard Top, Tripod, 16 x 23 In. 1430.00
Table, Herman Miller, Girard Striped Top, Steel Base, Square, 32 x 28 In. 415.00
Table, Herman Miller, Oak, Brushed Chrome Base, 1938, 18 1/2 x 24 In. 3000.00
Table, Hoffman, Coffee, Chromed Steel, Glass, c.1934 . . . . 2900.00
Table, Hunt, Gateleg, Mahogany, Oval Top, D-Shape Drop Leaves, 28 x 60 In. 2530.00
Table, Hutch, Pine, Dark Green Paint, 3-Board Top, 35 x 70 x 25 In. 1375.00
Table, I. Noguchi, Laminate, Chrome Wire, Black Metal Pedestal, 30 x 47 In. 1650.00
Table, Ice Cream Set, Wire Chairs, Braided Seat, c.1935, 3 Piece 155.00
Table, J. De Moulin, Tortoiseshell, Brass Mounted, Marquetry, 28 1/2 In. 5750.00
Table, L. & J.G. Stickley, No. 543, Round, Low Shelf, Through Tenons, 36 In. 1320.00
Table, L. & J.G. Stickley, No. 544, Oak, 4 Exposed-Tenon Legs, 29 1/2 In. 1380.00
Table, Lacquer, Dragons & Scrolling Top, Cabriole Legs, 15 x 46 1/2 In. 5175.00
Table, Library Golden Oak, Quartersawn, 2 Drawers, Carved Top Edge, 48 In. 910.00
Table, Library, Arts & Crafts, Walnut, 2 Wide Side Slats, 48 x 28 x 28 In. 165.00
Table, Library, Birch, Ormolu, Applied Moldings, 3 Drawers, Door, 30 x 42 In. 412.00
Table, Library, C. Rohlfs, 2 Drawers, Paneled Sides, Dark Finish, 30 x 60 In. 3300.00
Table, Library, Classical, Mahogany, Oblong Top, Acanthus Paw Feet, 1825, 29 In. 3450.00
Table, Library, Drop Leaf, Oak, Mahogany Veneer, 2 Dovetailed Drawers, 25 x 34 In. . . . 825.00
Table, Library, G. Stickley, No. 407, Arched Cross Stretchers, 29 1/4 In. 7500.00
Table, Library, G. Stickley, No. 616, 2 Drawers, 30 In. 6050.00
Table, Library, G. Stickley, No. 616, Drawers, Iron Pulls, Corbel Legs, 54 x 32 In. 5230.00
Table, Library, George III, Mahogany, Leather, 2 Real, 2 False Drawers, 28 In. 4887.00
Table, Library, L. & J.G. Stickley, No. 521, 1 Drawer, 4 Legs, 42 x 28 x 29 In. 1870.00
Table, Library, L. & J.G. Stickley, No. 522, 48 x 30 x 29 In. 1540.00
Table, Library, L. & J.G. Stickley, No. 659, 3 Drawers, Spindle Sides, 54 x 29 In. 8800.00
Table, Library, Lifetime, Slat Sides, Lower Shelf, 1 Drawer, Tag, 29 x 42 In. 825.00
Table, Library, Limbert, No. 133, Faux Drawer, Flared Side Slats, Decal, 42 In. 550.00
Table, Library, Limbert, No. 164, 2 Drawers, Long Corbels, 48 x 34 x 29 In. 1430.00
Table, Library, Limbert, No. 1129, Copper Pull, Signed, 48 x 28 x 29 In. 1045.00
Table, Library, Mahogany, Base Shelf, Cabriole Legs & Apron, 2 Drawers, 5 In. 880.00
Table, Library, Mahogany, Base Shelf, Lion's-Head Legs, Paw Feet, 46 In. 1210.00
Table, Library, Mahogany, Cabriole Legs, Secret Drawer 300.00
Table, Library, Mahogany, Mother-Of-Pearl & Brass Inlay, 2 Drawers, 72 In. 6900.00
Table, Library, Mahogany, Sienna Marble Top, 2 Drawers, Gothic Finial, 50 1/4 In. 5175.00
Table, Library, Oak, 1 Drawer, Stretcher, Curled Legs, 29 x 42 x 26 In. 55.00
Table, Library, Oak, Scalloped Skirt, Ball Feet, c.1750 . . . . 9900.00
Table, Library, Roycroft, 2 Drawers, Rectangular Top, Mackmurdo Feet, 30 In. 3300.00

Table, Library, Walnut, 1 Dovetailed Drawer, Turned Legs, 22 3/8 x 38 In. 440.00
Table, Library, Walnut, Ebony, Mahogany, 4 Columnar Legs, England, 1870, 27 In. 1265.00
Table, Lifetime, No. 930, Circular Top Over Lower Shelf, Paper Label, 18 x 29 In. 715.00
Table, Limbert, Hammered-Copper Cutout Tulips, Green Slag Glass Panels 3080.00
Table, Limbert, No. 111, Splayed Legs, 24 x 24 x 29 In. 990.00
Table, Limbert, No. 146, Oval Top, Splayed Slab Sides, 45 x 22 x 29 In. 2200.00
Table, Limbert, Rectangular Top, 2 Half Drawers Over 1 Long Drawer, 29 In. 3080.00
Table, Louis XIV, Serpentine Faux Marble Top, Leaf Legs, 31 x 55 In. 805.00
Table, Louis XV Style, Marquetry & Parquetry Veneered Panels, 29 1/4 In. 3165.00
Table, Louis XVI Style, Gilt, Onyx Top, Late 19th Century, 28 x 33 1/2 In. 660.00
Table, Louis XVI Style, Tulipwood, 1 Drawer, Geometric Inlay, 29 1/2 x 32 1/2 In. 4900.00
Table, Louis XVI, Cherry, Rectangular Top, Cabriole Legs, 30 In. 920.00
Table, Louis XVI, Marquetry, 2 Tiers, Ormolu Mounts, 36 x 31 1/2 In. 750.00
Table, Louis XVI, Marquetry, Ormolu Mounts, Oval, 24 x 26 In. 546.00
Table, Louis XVI, Walnut, Rosettes Frieze, Tapered Legs, 23 x 29 x 15 In. 719.00
Table, Mahogany, 2 Tiers, Scalloped Edge Top, Stylized Orchids, 34 In. 4600.00
Table, Mahogany, Bird's-Eye Maple, Trefoil Top, 3 Legs, Floral Mounts, 30 1/2 In. 9775.00
Table, Mahogany, Birdcage Support, Dish Top, c.1780, 21 In. 4800.00
Table, Mahogany, Brass Mounted, Inlay, Metamorphic, 1870s, 30 1/2 In. 980.00
Table, Mahogany, Copper Inlay, Oval, 20th Century, 26 1/4 x 23 1/2 In. 360.00
Table, Mahogany, Drop Leaf, 2 Drawers, Salesman's Sample, 1820, 28 x 42 In. 1150.00
Table, Mahogany, Ebony Inlay, Top Flaps, 2 Drawers, Brass Casters, 39 1/4 In. 4025.00
Table, Mahogany, Green & Gilt Leather Surface, 3 Drawers, 30 1/2 x 58 In. 6050.00
Table, Mahogany, Marble Top, Fluted Center Column, Square 2750.00
Table, Mahogany, Mottled Marble Top, 2 Drawers, 2 Candle Slides, 27 In. 3450.00
Table, Mahogany, Oval, Concave Stem, Quatrefoil Base, Rosettes, 53 1/2 In. 3740.00
Table, Mahogany, Pedestal With Claw & Ball Feet, 60 In. 800.00
Table, Majorelle, Mahogany, Trefoil, Molded Edge, 3 Legs, 30 1/2 In. 8050.00
Table, Maple, Turned Legs, Reeded Edge Apron, 2-Board Top, Oval, 25 x 31 In. 1760.00
Table, Marble Top, Black Marble Border, Monopodial Supports, 29 1/8 In., Pair 4890.00
Table, Marble Top, Marquetry Apron, Bronze Mounts, 28 x 26 In. 2415.00
Table, Marble Top, Octagonal Stem, Tripartite Base, 8 1/2 In. 3165.00
Table, Marquetry, Mythological Scene, Carved Incised Stretcher, 30 3/4 In. 8625.00
Table, Metal, Wire Mesh, Propeller Group, 28 x 33 In. 550.00
Table, Michigan Chair Co., Splayed Legs, Keyed Tenon, Shelf, 72 x 36 In. 3850.00
Table, Micro Mosaic Top, Butterfly & Lilac Spray Inlay, 22 1/2 x 30 In. 6900.00
Table, Mission Oak, 3 Splayed Legs, Pinned Stretchers 550.00
Table, Napoleon III, Burl, Brass-Trimmed Edge, 41 x 40 x 22 In. 1320.00
Table, Nesting, Black Lacquer, Carved, Oriental, 16 1/2 In. To 26 In., 4 Piece 400.00
Table, Nesting, Drop Leaf, Gateleg, Walnut, 30 1/2 In. 205.00
Table, Nesting, E. Wormley, Walnut Veneer, Brass Stretchers, 28 In., 3 Piece 770.00
Table, Nesting, Edwardian, Mahogany, Crossbanding, Checkered Banding, 3 Piece 1495.00
Table, Nesting, Galle, Marquetry, Wisteria, Tulips, Rectangular, 1900, 4 Piece 9375.00
Table, Nesting, Hepplewhite Style, Mahogany, Inlay, 18 x 28 x 29 In., 4 Piece 275.00
Table, Nesting, Mahogany, Carrying Holes, Splayed Legs, England, 2 Piece 300.00
Table, Nesting, Russel Wright, Conant-Ball, 1930s 475.00
Table, Nesting, Zebra Wood, Slab Legs, Fan-Shaped, 24 x 32 In., 5 Piece 4890.00
Table, Oak Top, Twig, 26 x 47 In. 78.00
Table, Oak, Demilune, Top Opens To Full Circle, Swing Leg, 48 1/2 In., Open 2310.00
Table, Oak, Sausage-Turned Legs, Cast-Iron Brackets Supporting Stretcher Shelf 110.00
Table, Onyx Top, 3 Civil War Rifles Legs, Cannonball & Bayonet Stretchers, 1885 . . . . . 1870.00
Table, Onyx Top, Wrought Iron & Brass Base, 24 x 24 In. 460.00
Table, Painted, Cusped Corners, Splayed Legs, Red & Blue, 30 In. 1150.00
Table, Pembroke, Cherry, 2 Drawers, Leaves, 30 x 36 In. 440.00
Table, Pembroke, Cherry, Inlay, Shaped Leaf, Drawer, 29 x 35 x 16 1/2 In. 520.00
Table, Pembroke, Federal, Mahogany, Bowed Ends, Inlaid Carrot Legs, 1795, 28 In. 9200.00
Table, Pembroke, Federal, Mahogany, Chamfered Legs, Early 19th Century, 28 In. 1045.00
Table, Pembroke, Federal, Mahogany, New York, 1795, 28 In. 2590.00
Table, Pembroke, Federal, Mahogany, Tapered Legs, Marlborough Feet, 20 x 34 In. 1500.00
Table, Pembroke, George III, Cherry, 2 Drop Leaves, Tapered Legs, 28 x 32 In. 1610.00
Table, Pembroke, George III, Hardwood, Satinwood, & Kingwood, c.1775, 29 In. 8050.00
Table, Pembroke, George III, Mahogany, Acanthus Brackets, 1760, 29 In. 3450.00
Table, Pembroke, George III, Mahogany, Bird's-Eye Maple, 29 x 37 In. 2530.00

Table, Pembroke, George III, Mahogany, Frieze Drawer, Tapered Legs, 27 In. 1035.00
Table, Pembroke, George III, Mahogany, Rectangular Top, Block Feet, 29 3/4 In. 2990.00
Table, Pembroke, George III, Mahogany, Satinwood, 1780, 28 1/2 In. 3165.00
Table, Pembroke, Hepplewhite, Cherry, Square Legs, 28 1/2 In. 990.00
Table, Pembroke, Hepplewhite, Mahogany, 1 Drawer, X-Stretcher, Brass Cuffs 715.00
Table, Pembroke, Hepplewhite, Mahogany, Oval Medallions On Posts, 29 In. 5500.00
Table, Pembroke, Hepplewhite, Mahogany, Tapered Legs, Drawer, 21 x 33 In. 770.00
Table, Pembroke, L. Tarr, Federal, Mahogany, Brass Caps, Casters, 1795, 28 x 19 In. 5750.00
Table, Pembroke, Mahogany, 1 Drawer, Rope-Turned Legs, Casters, 28 1/2 In. 550.00
Table, Pembroke, Mahogany, Trifid Feet, Drawer, 2 Leaves, 18 1/2 x 30 1/2 In. 1595.00
Table, Pembroke, Tiger Maple, Rectangular Top, 28 x 36 x 15 1/4 In. 2300.00
Table, Pembroke, Wallace Nutting, No. 628-B 1430.00
Table, Pembroke, Walnut, Reeded Tapered Legs, 2 Leaves, 21 1/2 x 30 In. 1540.00
Table, Pier, Mahogany, Serpentine, Cabriole Legs, Carved Knees, Whorl Feet, 30 In. 305.00
Table, Pine, 2 Drawers, Square Tapered Legs, 30 1/2 x 60 In. 660.00
Table, Pine, 3-Board Top, 2 Short Drawers, Red Paint, 28 1/2 x 51 3/4 In. 1955.00
Table, Pine, Breadboard Ends, Drawer In Base, Walnut Stretcher, 27 1/2 x 38 In. 1380.00
Table, Pine, Figural, Standard Shaped Like Draped Youth, 40 In., Pair 4315.00
Table, Pine, Lazy Susan Center, c.1890 . . . . 6500.00
Table, Pine, Walnut, Ring & Column Turned Legs, Red, 1840s, 79 In. 4600.00
Table, Pub, Tilt Top, Oak, Shoe Feet, Mortised, Round, 26 1/2 x 38 1/2 In. 885.00
Table, Pub, Yew Wood, Oak, Faux Leather Inset, Square Legs, Pad Feet 460.00
Table, Queen Anne Style, 4 Panels, Sports Scenes, South American, 48 x 30 In. 995.00
Table, Queen Anne, Hard & Softwood, Red Paint, Square Top, 12 x 24 In. 180.00
Table, Queen Anne, Mahogany, Cutout Apron, Dark Finish, Duck Feet, 28 In. 470.00
Table, Queen Anne, Walnut, Pine Top, 2 Drawers, Beaded Skirt, 51 x 32 In. 1430.00
Table, R. Fahnkow, Coffee, Walnut, Inset Glass Top, Square Legs, Germany, 23 In. 3740.00
Table, Refectory, Baroque, Walnut, Shaped Stretchers, Bun Feet, 31 x 119 In. 7475.00
Table, Refectory, Jacobean, Oak, Turned Legs, 19th Century, 28 x 62 3/4 In. 2300.00
Table, Refectory, Oak, 2 Drawers, Turned Legs, Continental, c.1700, 91 x 27 In. 1100.00
Table, Refectory, Oak, Drawer, Heart-Shaped Wrought-Iron Handle, 85 3/4 In. 1340.00
Table, Refectory, Oak, Planked Top, Block Feet, England, 157 1/2 In. 9200.00
Table, Refectory, Oak, Planked Top, Frieze On 6 Baluster Legs, 31 x 132 In. 7475.00
Table, Refectory, Oak, Trestle, Early 20th Century, 71 1/2 In. 275.00
Table, Refectory, Walnut, 6 Faceted Columnar Legs, 17th Century, 109 In. 9775.00
Table, Refectory, Walnut, Turned Columnar Supports, Continental, 30 x 90 In. 230.00
Table, Regency, Brass, Mahogany, 3 Tiers, Oval, Top Cut For Bowl, 34 In. 600.00
Table, Regency, Mahogany, 2 Tiers, 2 Shelves, Tapered Legs, Casters, 29 x 15 In. 690.00
Table, Regency, Rectangular Top, Reeded Legs, 44 1/2 x 30 In. 460.00
Table, Regency, Rosewood, Walnut, 19th Century, 19 x 36 In. 1725.00
Table, Renaissance Revival, Walnut, Ebonized, 1865-1875, 30 1/2 In. 750.00
Table, Renaissance Revival, Walnut, Marble Top, Shield & Medallion, 22 x 39 In. 770.00
Table, Roger Fry, Walnut, Square Border, 4 Square Legs, 1915, 34 x 30 In. 2875.00
Table, Rohde, Round Front, 1 Drawer, Tapered Octagonal Legs, 15 x 24 In. 230.00
Table, Rosewood Top, Starburst Tortoiseshell Panels, 19 1/2 x 19 In. 5750.00
Table, Rosewood, Carved Busts Of Man & Woman, 2 Drawers, Urn Center Finial 3300.00
Table, Rosewood, Inlaid Marble Top, China, 19th Century, 15 x 15 x 22 1/2 In. 575.00
Table, Rosewood, Tripod, Paneled Top, 1 Drawer, 23 1/2 In. 135.00
Table, S. Marx, Square Top, Block Legs, Acid-Spot Finish, Lacquered, 21 In. 690.00
Table, Sawbuck, 1-Board Top, Breadboard Ends, c.1800, 29 x 39 In. 1295.00
Table, Sawbuck, Painted, Scrubbed Top, Vermont, 1900, 60 In. 775.00
Table, Sawbuck, Pine, 1 Drawer, Lime Green Paint, 15 x 30 1/4 In. 862.00
Table, Sawbuck, Pine, 2-Board Top, 26 x 31 1/4 In. 660.00
Table, Sawbuck, Pine, Breadboard Ends, 24 In. 3740.00
Table, Sawbuck, Pine, Red Stain On Base, Varnish On 3-Board Top, 30 x 49 x 29 In. . . . 880.00
Table, Serving, George III, Mahogany, Bowed Top, Tapered Legs, 1800 . . . . 1725.00
Table, Sewing, Birch, Pine, Square Tapered Legs, Mortised & Pinned Apron, 26 In. 440.00
Table, Sewing, Black Lacquer, Fitted Compartment, Rectangular Hinged Top, 28 In. 980.00
Table, Sewing, Chippendale, Walnut, Square Molded Legs, 39 x 87 x 28 In. 605.00
Table, Sewing, Classical, Mahogany Veneer, 2 Drawers, 16 x 19 x 30 In. 550.00
Table, Sewing, Classical, Mahogany, Rectangular Top, 2 Drawers, Brass Paw Feet 220.00
Table, Sewing, Classical, Tilt Top, Mahogany, Tray, 1 Faux & 2 Drawers, 16 x 20 In. 660.00
Table, Sewing, Classical, Tilt Top, Rosewood Veneer, Bowfront Drawer, 19 x 31 In. 2750.00

Table, Sewing, Federal, Mahogany, 2 Drawers, 4 Reeded Legs, Boston, 1815, 30 In. 2875.00
Table, Sewing, Federal, Mahogany, 2 Drawers, Rope Carving, Wool Bag, 19 x 23 In. . . .   300.00
Table, Sewing, Federal, Mahogany, Brass Hardware, Reeded Legs, 1810, 30 1/4 In. 1380.00
Table, Sewing, Hepplewhite, Cherry, Square Legs, 21 x 38 1/4 x 30 In. 635.00
Table, Sewing, Hepplewhite, Pine Top, Red Paint, Square Legs, 26 x 43 In. 715.00
Table, Sewing, Heywood Bros. & Co., Basket, Stretcher Shelf, Rattan 275.00
Table, Sewing, Lift Top, Walnut, Bird's-Eye Maple Fitted Interior, 29 x 24 In. 224.00
Table, Sewing, Mahogany, 2 Bird's-Eye Maple Veneer Drawers, 1815, 29 In. 2875.00
Table, Sewing, Mahogany, Inlaid Crossbanded Top, Basket, Casters, c.1810, 29 In. 4600.00
Table, Sewing, Mahogany, Overhanging Top, 1 Drawer, c.1800, 27 1/4 In. 1495.00
Table, Sewing, Mahogany, Satinwood Inlay, Fitted Interior, Brass Casters, 1840 . . . .   1750.00
Table, Sewing, Mahogany, Turret Corners, 1 Drawer 5465.00
Table, Sewing, Martha Washington Style, Maple, Drawers, 20th Century . . . . .50.00 to 100.00
Table, Sewing, Parquetry Panel Over Drawer, Sliding Door, Center Mirror, 28 In. 2300.00
Table, Sewing, Satinwood, Crossbanding, Fitted, Octagonal, England, 1790, 16 In. 4950.00
Table, Sewing, Shaker, 1 Drawer, Splayed Tapered Legs 4025.00
Table, Sewing, Shaker, Pine, Maple, 2-Board Top, Turned Legs, c.1840, 28 x 20 In. 550.00
Table, Sewing, Sheraton, 3 Dovetailed Beaded Drawers, 40 x 23 x 30 In. 550.00
Table, Sewing, Sheraton, Cherry, Pine, 1 Drawer, Bag, X-Stretcher, New England 715.00
Table, Sewing, Sheraton, Mahogany, Turret Corners, 2 Drawers 8050.00
Table, Sewing, Tiger Maple, 2 Drawers, Ring-Turned Legs, c.1830, 28 3/4 x 20 In. 1150.00
Table, Sewing, Tiger Maple, 2 Graduated Drawers, Vase & Ring Post, c.1825, 29 In. 1095.00
Table, Sewing, Vose Cabinet Shop, Classical, Mahogany, 2 Drawers, 1825, 30 In. 6325.00
Table, Sewing, Vose Cabinet Shop, Classical, Mahogany, 3 Drawers, 1825, 29 In. 1840.00
Table, Sewing, Walnut, 1 Drawer, Turned Legs, 22 x 28 x 18 In. 165.00
Table, Sewing, Walnut, Inlay, Lyre-Shaped Base, Octagonal Top, Hinged Lid, 29 In. 110.00
Table, Sewing, Walnut, Pin Top, Molding At Bottom Of Apron & Corners Of Legs 1500.00
Table, Shaker, 1 Drawer, Turned Wooden Knob, Red, 29 x 42 In. 1725.00
Table, Sheraton, Pine, Poplar, Brown Paint, Drawer, 22 x 29 x 28 In. 275.00
Table, Sheraton, Tiger Maple, 2 Dovetailed Drawers, 48 x 28 In. 2100.00
Table, Side, Burl Mahogany, Trestle Supports, Cabriole Legs, 27 x 38 x 20 In. 800.00
Table, Side, C. Stickley, 1 Drawer, Dark Finish, 30 x 19 1/2 x 30 In. 600.00
Table, Side, Empire, Fruitwood, Brass Corners, 4 D-Shaped Leaves, Peg Feet, 28 In. 1840.00
Table, Side, Empire, Fruitwood, Marquetry, Scroll Corners, Peg Feet, 28 x 18 In. 1840.00
Table, Side, George II, Mahogany, 1 Drawer, Cabriole Legs, Pad Feet, 1750-1770 . . . . . .   1540.00
Table, Side, George III, Oak, 3 Drawers, Chamfered Legs, 1790, 30 x 36 x 20 In. 110.00
Table, Side, Louis XVI, Marble Top, Early 20th Century, 29 x 23 x 15 In. 230.00
Table, Side, Mahogany, Frieze Drawer, Trestle Support, Victorian, 34 In. 4315.00
Table, Side, Neoclassical, Walnut, Fruitwood, Tapered Legs, Italy, 27 1/4 In. 1035.00
Table, Side, Pine, 1 Drawer, Splayed Tapered Legs, 1800, 29 x 20 x 29 In. 90.00
Table, Side, Queen Anne, Mahogany, 2 Drawers, Cabriole Legs, 30 x 26 In. 375.00
Table, Side, Renaissance Revival, Drawer, Carved Cat's-Head Pulls, 25 x 32 In. 550.00
Table, Side, Renaissance Revival, Octagonal, 3 Fluted Legs, Fringed Velvet, 24 In. 385.00
Table, Side, Renaissance Revival, Walnut, Italy, 26 x 25 x 17 In. 400.00
Table, Side, William & Mary, Walnut, Piecrust Edge, Hoof Feet, 24 x 26 In. 375.00
Table, Side, Wood Grained, Plain Frieze, 1 Drawer, 28 x 19 x 18 In. 635.00
Table, Steel, Foliage Apron, Brass Fittings, Marble Top, 34 x 79 1/4 In. 3080.00
Table, Stickley Brothers, Mahogany, Leather Top, Vase-Form Column, 1930s, 26 In. 330.00
Table, Stickley Brothers, No. 2828, Square Overhanging Top, Lower Shelf, 18 In. 440.00
Table, Stickley Brothers, No. 402, Circular Top & Shelf, Through Tenons, 30 In. 865.00
Table, Tavern, Birch, Rectangular Top, Chamfered Legs, 19th Century, 27 In. 920.00
Table, Tavern, Block, Vase & Ring-Turned Legs, Gray Paint, 25 1/2 x 43 In. 6325.00
Table, Tavern, Cherry, Pine, Oval Top, Baluster Legs, 24 1/4 x 33 In. 4600.00
Table, Tavern, Cherry, Plank Top, Ball Feet, 28 x 35 1/2 In. 605.00
Table, Tavern, Cherry, Rectangular Top, 2 Short Drawers, 30 In.   2875.00
Table, Tavern, Chestnut, Poplar, 1 Overlapping Drawer, 26 x 41 In. 1595.00
Table, Tavern, Chippendale, Birch, Pine Top, Drawer, 26 x 41 x 28 In. 935.00
Table, Tavern, Cricket, Pine, Round 2-Board Top, England, 29 x 28 1/2 In. 645.00
Table, Tavern, Curly Maple, Pad Feet, Original Drawer Knob, Red Paint 5635.00
Table, Tavern, Hepplewhite Style, Red Base, Pine Breadboard Top, 23 x 33 x 29 In. 80.00
Table, Tavern, Hepplewhite, Birch, Pine, Red, Green, 25 x 44 x 29 In. 880.00
Table, Tavern, Oak, Pine, Drawer On Ring & Baluster Turned Legs, Painted, 1740s 4025.00
Table, Tavern, Pine, Cherry, Breadboard Ends, 1 Drawer, 27 1/2 x 43 In. 460.00

Table, Tavern, Pine, Drawer, Square Moldings, Padded Dutch Feet, 27 x 41 In. 1540.00
Table, Tavern, Pine, Maple, 4 Baluster Legs, Reel & Turned Feet, 25 x 29 In. 3680.00
Table, Tavern, Pine, Maple, Green, Red Paint, 1740-1770, 24 1/2 In. 7475.00
Table, Tavern, Pine, Oval Top, Splayed Legs, Ball Feet, Gray, 27 In. 3165.00
Table, Tavern, Pine, Red & Black, 1860s, 25 1/2 x 36 1/2 In. 475.00
Table, Tavern, Pine, Scrubbed Top, Red Finish, 28 1/2 x 26 1/2 In. 1150.00
Table, Tavern, Queen Anne, Cherry, Oval Top, Pad Feet, 1740-1760, 27 x 28 In. 3450.00
Table, Tavern, Queen Anne, Hardwood, Pine, 1 Drawer, 1-Board Top, 26 1/2 In. 1100.00
Table, Tavern, Queen Anne, Hardwood, Pine, 1 Drawer, Button Feet, 25 x 36 In. 880.00
Table, Tavern, Queen Anne, Hardwood, Pine, Turned Legs, Apron, 21 x 30 In. 3025.00
Table, Tavern, Walnut, 2 Drawers, Bottle-Shaped Legs, 1750, 30 x 34 1/2 In. 3450.00
Table, Tavern, Walnut, Cherry, 2-Board Top, Corner Wings, 28 3/4 x 31 3/4 In. 990.00
Table, Tavern, Walnut, Molded Skirt With Drawer, Early 18th Century, 28 1/4 In. 2530.00
Table, Tavern, Walnut, Oval Top, Thumb-Molded Drawer, Reel & Bun Feet, 30 In. 6325.00
Table, Tavern, Walnut, Thumb-Molded Drawer, Ring & Baluster Turned Legs, 29 In. 2760.00
Table, Tavern, Walnut, Turned Legs, 2-Board Top, Drawer Face, 26 x 22 In. 300.00
Table, Tavern, William & Mary, Double Baluster Turned Legs, Painted, 23 In. 2070.00
Table, Tavern, William & Mary, Molded Frieze, Disc Feet, 1740, 26 3/4 In. 2300.00
Table, Tavern, William & Mary, Oak, Frieze Drawer, Turned Legs, 28 x 31 In. 980.00
Table, Tea, Cherry, Maple, Oval Top, Cutout Skirt, 18th Century, 25 3/4 In. 4900.00
Table, Tea, Chippendale, Mahogany, Piecrust, Ball & Claw Feet, 28 3/4 In. 2750.00
Table, Tea, Chippendale, Mahogany, Tripod, Slipper Feet, Penna., 32 x 28 In. 4125.00
Table, Tea, Chippendale, Maple, Dish Top, Down-Swept Legs, 9 1/4 In. 345.00
Table, Tea, Chippendale, Tilt Top, Mahogany, Round, Dish Top, 27 1/4 In. 1265.00
Table, Tea, Chippendale, Tilt Top, Mahogany, Snake Feet, 25 1/2 x 27 1/2 In. 550.00
Table, Tea, Chippendale, Walnut, 2-Board Top, Tripod, Snake Feet, Penna., 30 In. 1210.00
Table, Tea, G. Stickley, No. 604, Round Top, 4 Square Legs, 1910, 26 In. 1380.00
Table, Tea, George III, Mahogany, Octagonal Top, Leaf-Carved Legs, 26 In. 1100.00
Table, Tea, Mahogany, Ball & Claw Feet, Shaft, Cabriole Legs, Molded Rim, 33 In. 1210.00
Table, Tea, Mahogany, Knee Brackets & Stretchers Pierced Fretwork, Baker Co. 300.00
Table, Tea, Mahogany, Serpentine Top, Tripod Base, 27 3/4 In. 862.00
Table, Tea, Mahogany, Shell-Carved Dish Top, Feathered Ball & Claw Feet 660.00
Table, Tea, Queen Anne, Hardwood, Pine, Red, 24 x 32 x 28 In. 3300.00
Table, Tea, Queen Anne, Mahogany Veneer, 4 Side Aprons, 1 Drawer, England, 19 In. . . . 770.00
Table, Tea, Queen Anne, Mahogany, 1 Dovetailed Drawer, Duck Feet, 25 In. 3025.00
Table, Tea, Queen Anne, Walnut, Cabriole Legs, Pad Feet, 26 x 28 In. 11500.00
Table, Tea, Regency, Needlework Under Glass Top, White & Black, Gilt, 29 x 35 In. 9350.00
Table, Tea, Tilt Top, Birdcage, 3-Board Dish Top, Mahogany, 32 x 29 In. 3025.00
Table, Tea, Tilt Top, Cherry, Dish Top, Birdcage, Fan Carvings, 29 In. 775.00
Table, Tea, Tilt Top, Chippendale, 20th Century, England, 29 1/2 x 29 1/2 In. 605.00
Table, Tea, Tilt Top, Chippendale, Walnut, Dish Top, Birdcage, 29 x 33 1/2 In. 862.00
Table, Tea, Tilt Top, Empire, Walnut, Cutout Legs, Turned Column, 33 x 35 x 31 In. 220.00
Table, Tea, Tilt Top, Medallion Inlay, 4 Outside Columns, Carved, 29 x 40 In. 300.00
Table, Teakwood, Cube, Pickled Finish, Glass Top, 16 3/4 x 16 3/4 x 16 1/4 In. 38.00
Table, Teakwood, Elm Insert, Red Lacquer, Square Legs, China, 25 x 85 x 20 1/2 In. 715.00
Table, Tilt Top, Cedar Wood, Tripod, Bermuda, 1760-1790, 28 x 32 3/4 In. 1725.00
Table, Tilt Top, Chippendale, Mahogany, Acanthus Carvings, Square Top, 28 In. 275.00
Table, Tilt Top, Chippendale, Mahogany, Piecrust Edge, Cabriole Legs, 30 1/4 In. 770.00
Table, Tilt Top, Chippendale, Mahogany, Snake Feet, 27 x 26 1/4 In. 550.00
Table, Tilt Top, Chippendale, Maple, Red Curl, Snake Feet, 26 1/2 x 26 In. 2090.00
Table, Tilt Top, Federal, Mahogany, Scimitar Legs, Cut Corners, 18 3/4 x 5 In. 250.00
Table, Tilt Top, Hepplewhite, Birch, Natural Finish, Tripod Base, 29 In. 110.00
Table, Tilt Top, Heywood-Wakefield Co., Maple, Turned Pedestal, Tripod Snake Feet . . . 195.00
Table, Tilt Top, Mahogany, Circular Support, Splayed Cabriole Legs, 26 3/4 In. 2185.00
Table, Tilt Top, Mahogany, Down-Swept Legs, 20 x 19 3/4 x 15 3/4 In. 430.00
Table, Tilt Top, Mahogany, Satinwood, Tripod, Leather Top, 1890s, 30 1/4 In. 7475.00
Table, Tilt Top, Mahogany, Tripod, Reeded Scimitar Legs, 1-Board Top, 20 x 29 In. 1045.00
Table, Tilt Top, Wallace Nutting, No. 644, Mahogany, 3 Legs 825.00
Table, Tilt Top, Walnut, Baluster-Turned Standard, 3 Legs, Victorian, 29 1/2 In. 185.00
Table, Tilt Top, Yew Wood, Tripod, Fowl In Landscape Painted On Top, 1780s, 29 In. 2300.00
Table, Tray, Black Japanned & Parcel Gilt Stand, Chinoiserie, Pontypool, 29 In. 9200.00
Table, Tray, Butler's, Burl, Inlay, Sand-Burned Oval Medallion, Scalloped Gallery 465.00
Table, Tray, George III, Mahogany, Brassbound, Scrolled Cabriole Legs, 21 In. 1035.00

Table, Tray, Herman Miller, Molded Ash Plywood, Chrome, 15 x 19 In.	605.00
Table, Tray, Mahogany, Butler's, X-Frame Floor Stand, Pierced Handles	110.00
Table, Tray, Mahogany, Table Top, 4 Cutout Heart Handles, 18 1/2 x 15 In.	440.00
Table, Tray, On Stand, Painted Ships At Sea, 1850s, 21 x 27 1/2 In.	3165.00
Table, Tray, On Stand, Papier-Mache, Fruit & Foliage, Black, 21 x 30 1/2 In.	4315.00
Table, Tray, Papier-Mache, Mother-Of-Pearl Inlay, Ebonized Stand, 18 1/2 x 26 In.	230.00
Table, Trestle, G. Nelson, Walnut, Solid Plank Top, Enameled Supports, 72 In.	885.00
Table, Trestle, G. Stickley, Keyed Tenon, Dark Finish, 60 x 36 x 30 In.	2310.00
Table, Trestle, G. Stickley, No. 639, Paper Label, Child's, 22 1/2 x 36 In.	2515.00
Table, Trestle, Wallace Nutting, No. 614, Maple	605.00
Table, Trestle, Walnut, Scrolling Trestles, Carved Stretcher, 17th Century, 31 In.	7475.00
Table, Tripod, George II, Mahogany, Lobed Circular Top, Paw Feet, 27 In.	4830.00
Table, Tulipwood, Floral Painted Inset Top, Marquetry Shelf, 28 1/2 In.	3450.00
Table, Tulipwood, Kidney-Shaped Top, Leather Writing Surface, 1740s, 29 In.	4600.00
Table, Tulipwood, Marble Top, Pierced Gallery, 2 Drawers, 2 Candle Slides, 30 In.	4900.00
Table, Tulipwood, Purplewood, Marble Top, Pierced Sides, Veneered Panels, 31 In.	7475.00
Table, Tulipwood, Purplewood, Serpentine Side, Floral Spray Veneer, Drawer, 28 In.	7475.00
Table, Vitrine, Mahogany, Gilt Bronze Mounted, 1880s, 32 x 24 In.	230.00
Table, W. Plattner, Birch, Laminated Top, Corseted Wire, 18 1/2 x 20 In., Pair	935.00
Table, Walnut, Dentil Molding, Box Stretcher, 1920s, 18 1/2 x 19 3/4 In.	315.00
Table, Walnut, Micro Mosaic Top, Central Medallion, Roman Scenes, 19 3/4 In.	5750.00
Table, Walnut, Oval Top, Foliage Inlay, 1860s, 54 In.	4600.00
Table, Walnut, Turned Medallions, Marble Top, Round, 30 x 49 In.	4455.00
Table, Wicker, Upholstered, Glass Top, 29 1/2 x 48 In.	435.00
Table, Widdicomb, Overhanging Doweled Top, Spindled Shelf, 19 1/2 x 24 In.	385.00
Table, William IV, Rosewood, Octagonal Standard, Animal-Shaped Feet, 29 In.	8050.00
Table, Wine Tasting, Drop Leaf, Mahogany, Brass Rail & Brass Panels, 1780s, 72 In.	4025.00
Table, Wine Tasting, Oval Well, 2 Short Drawers, Painted Mounts, Paw Feet, 30 In.	8050.00
Table, Writing, Baroque, Walnut, 18th Century, 30 x 41 3/4 x 26 In.	2875.00
Table, Writing, Baroque, Walnut, Continental, 18th Century, 29 1/2 x 38 In.	2530.00
Table, Writing, Drop Leaf, Jacobean, Graduated Lobed Legs, 48 x 36 In.	400.00
Table, Writing, George III, Mahogany, Leather Rectangular Top, 28 1/2 In.	5465.00
Table, Writing, Mahogany, Parquetry Top, 1 Drawer, c.1900, 29 1/2 x 44 In.	8625.00
Table, Writing, Mahogany, Tooled Leather Top, 2 Drawers, c.1790, 30 In.	3500.00
Table, Writing, Serpentine Apron, Central Drawer, 29 x 36 In.	1955.00
Table, Writing, Tilt Top, Tooled Leather Top, Side Drawers, Toupie Feet, 43 In.	1725.00
Table, Writing, William IV, Mahogany, 3 Frieze Drawers Each Side, 1840s, 72 In.	8050.00
Table, Wrought Iron, Amber Iridescent, Black Steuben Glass Tiles, 1915, 20 In.	5750.00
Table, Wrought Iron, Marble Top, Pierced Frieze, Foliate Medallion, 32 1/2 In.	2100.00
Table, Yew Wood, Oak, Tripod, Pad Feet, 26 1/2 In.	3165.00
Table Set, Oak, Square Pedestal, 6 Leather Chairs, 5 Leaves, 1890s	1200.00
Table-Chair, Baluster & Ring Supports, Drawer, Red & Black Graining, 28 1/2 In.	4900.00
Table-Chair, Hutch, Pine, 3-Board Round Top	350.00
Table-Chair, Tilting, Storage Compartment Under Seat, Red Paint	1295.00
Tabouret, Baroque, Fruitwood, Rectangular, Upholstered Top, Turned Legs	635.00
Tabouret, G. Stickley, Arched Cross Stretcher, Red Mark, 16 x 14 In.	725.00
Tabouret, L. & J.G. Stickley, Arched Stretcher, Clipped Corners, 20 x 17 In.	795.00
Tabouret, L. & J.G. Stickley, Arched Stretcher, Handicraft Label, 17 x 15 In.	920.00
Tabouret, L. & J.G. Stickley, Mahogany, Octagonal, 20 x 18 In.	1210.00
Tabouret, L. & J.G. Stickley, Square Top, 4 Splayed Legs, 12 x 19 In.	396.00
Tabouret, Limbert, No. 234, Mahogany, 2 Square Cutouts, Cube Base, 24 x 29 In.	2470.00
Tabouret, Roycroft, Mahogany, 4 Splayed Legs, Square Top, 12 x 12 x 19 In.	605.00
Tabouret, Thick Round Top, Reversed Tapered Legs, Tobey, 15 x 19 In.	300.00
Tea Cart, Aalto, Bentwood, Enameled Wooden Wheels, 29 1/2 x 33 In.	525.00
Tea Cart, Iron, Lyre Form, Wooden Top & Lower Shelf, Early 20th Century	385.00
Tea Cart, Walnut, Turned Detail, Glass Tray Top, 19 x 34 x 29 In.	210.00
Teapoy, George IV, Walnut, Mahogany, 2 Caddies, 2 Bowls, 28 1/2 In.	2875.00
Teapoy, Regency, Mahogany, Hinged Lid, 4 Tin Compartments, 1820, 29 In.	286.00
Teapoy, Rosewood, Hinged Top, Silk-Lined Interior, Bramah Lock, 31 1/2 In.	1840.00
Teapoy, Walnut, 2 Storage Containers, Mid-19th Century, Victorian, 29 In.	1265.00
Vanity, Art Deco, 6 Semicircular Drawers, Mirror, Upholstered Stool, 55 x 67 In.	880.00
Vanity, Art Deco, Chrome, Glass Shelves, Lighted Mirror, 1920s, 45 x 56 In.	605.00
Vanity, Art Deco, Metal, Black Lacquer, Round Mirror, Swivel Stool, 48 In., 2 Piece	55.00

To remove an unpleasant smell from an old chest of drawers, try this: Put the piece outside in the shade. Plug in a fan and blow air through the drawers and frame. If that does not work after several days, fill the drawers with baking soda, cat litter, or charcoal chips that may absorb the odor.

Furniture, Whatnot
Shelf, Mission,
Oak, 5 Shelves

Vanity, Edwardian, Mahogany, Swag Inlay, c.1910, 62 x 43 1/2 In. 3400.00
Vanity, Louis XV Style, Kneehole, 7 Drawers, 8 Short Cabriole Legs, 30 x 48 In. 300.00
Vanity, Mahogany, Sheraton, Backsplash, 2 Stepped Over 2 Drawers, 29 x 34 In. 220.00
Vanity, Majorelle, Mahogany, Lilac, 57 1/4 In. 5750.00
Vanity, Majorelle, Mahogany, Mirror, Candleholders, 36 x 61 In. 1760.00
Vanity, Mirror, Floor-Length, Blond Drum Sides, Leatherette Stool, 1934 .... 3900.00
Vanity, Painted Metal, Glass Top, Rope & Tassel, 1940s, Chair, 30 x 37 In. 605.00
Vanity, Rohde, 2 Circular Cabinets, Center Mirror, Chrome, 52 x 64 In. 1540.00
Vanity, Sikes, 4 Drawers, Round Mirror, Label, 53 x 52 1/2 In. 357.00
Vitrine, Bow Front, Marquetry, S-Shaped Sides, 2 Glass Shelves, Gallery 2960.00
Vitrine, Colonna, Mahogany, Mirror Back, Velvet Shelves, 1900, 40 x 65 x 13 In. 8435.00
Vitrine, G. Stickley, Oak, 3 Shelves, Wrought-Iron Handles, 1905, 24 x 56 In. 3450.00
Vitrine, Louis XV, Giltwood, Bowed Glass On Each Side, Cabriole Legs, 38 In. 800.00
Vitrine, Louis XV, Mahogany Inlay, Glazed Front, Cabriole Legs 2530.00
Vitrine, Louis XV, Mahogany, 2 Shelves, Cabriole Legs, 31 x 15 In. 230.00
Vitrine, Louis XV, Tulipwood, Gilt Bronze, Glazed Hinged Top, 26 3/4 x 26 In. 1380.00
Vitrine, Louis XVI, Gilt Metal, Early 20th Century, 30 x 26 x 37 1/4 In. 1150.00
Vitrine, Louis XVI, Ormolu Mounted, Parquetry, 3 Shelves, 53 x 22 In. 490.00
Vitrine, Louis XVI, Satinwood, Bacchanal Scene Flanked By Garlands 9085.00
Vitrine, Louis XVI, Walnut, 1 Door, Floral Ormolu Design, Fluted Legs, 28 x 21 In. .. 2760.00
Vitrine, Mahogany, Brass Gallery, Mirrored Back, 1 Door, 21 x 16 x 39 In. 275.00
Vitrine, Napoleon III, Acanthus, Reeded Border, Paw Feet, 44 x 34 In. 2530.00
Vitrine, Rene Prou, Wrought-Iron Legs, Glass, Arched Top, 1940s, 67 x 27 x 15 In. 5465.00
Vitrine, Tulipwood, Serpentine, Marble Top, 3 Drawers, Bronze Mounts, 51 x 20 In. 2070.00
Vitrine, Walnut, Foliate Crest, 2 Glazed Doors, Cartouche Feet, 99 x 52 x 18 In. 1725.00
Wardrobe, Chestnut, Mirrored Door, 75 x 38 In. 395.00
Wardrobe, Eastlake, Walnut, Drawer In Base, Paneled Door, 19 x 38 x 82 In. 605.00
Wardrobe, Eastlake, Walnut, Figured Veneer, Double Doors, Mirrors, 87 3/4 In. 880.00
Wardrobe, Georgian, Mahogany, Gothic Arch, Double Paneled Doors, 76 In. 1100.00
Wardrobe, Golden Oak, Quartersawn Veneer Door Panels, 2 Drawers, 90 1/2 In. 1265.00
Wardrobe, Mahogany, Oak Veneer, Paneled, Cornice, 1870s, 48 x 72 x 19 In. 2810.00
Wardrobe, Pine, 2 Panel Doors, Drawer, Painted, Interior Shelf, 50 x 85 In. 165.00
Wardrobe, Pine, Drawer, 2 Paneled Doors, 20 x 24 x 82 In. 415.00
Wardrobe, Pine, Poplar, Blind-Door, 2 Drawers, Pennsylvania, c.1850, 70 In. 2750.00
Wardrobe, Poplar, Red Finish, 2-Panel Door, Scrolled Apron 1450.00
Wardrobe, Walnut, 1 Drawer, Paneled Doors, Arched Rails, 20 x 56 x 83 In. 960.00
Wardrobe, Walnut, Full-Length Convex Door, Dressing Mirror Inside, 75 1/2 In. 145.00
Wardrobe, Walnut, Scrolled Base, 2 Drawers, Victorian, 20 x 57 x 83 In. 935.00
Washstand, Cherry, Base Shelf, 1 Drawer, Dovetailed Gallery, 28 3/4 In. 195.00
Washstand, Classical, Mahogany, Recessed Shelf, N.Y., 1830, 37 x 21 x 21 1/4 In. 176.00
Washstand, Corner, Hepplewhite, Out-Curved Feet, Gallery, 41 x 24 In. 605.00
Washstand, Corner, Mahogany, 1 Drawer, 2 Simulated Drawers, c.1790, 43 1/4 In. 895.00
Washstand, Corner, Pine, Triangular Top, Medial Shelf With Drawer, 38 In. 485.00
Washstand, Cottage Design, Lift Top, Brown, Yellow, Red, Drawer, Door, 18 x 29 In. .. 360.00
Washstand, Curly Maple, Mahogany Veneer On Drawers, Brass Pulls, 29 In. 825.00

Washstand, Edwardian, Oak, Marble Top, c.1910, 40 x 32 x 16 In. 275.00
Washstand, Federal, Mahogany, Backsplash, Basin Well, Paw Feet, 42 In. 495.00
Washstand, George III, Mahogany, Corner, Bow Front, Saber Legs, 40 1/2 In. 345.00
Washstand, Mahogany, 2 Candlestick Columns, Tilt Mirror, Victorian Style, 48 In. .. 100.00
Washstand, Mahogany, Lift Top, Mirror, Tin Bowl, Candlesticks, Brass Inlay, 37 In. ... 4025.00
Washstand, Mahogany-Stained, Turned Legs, Base Shelf, Drawer, 28 1/4 In. 88.00
Washstand, Sheraton, Cherry, Base Shelf, 1 Drawer, 20th Century, 28 1/2 In. 250.00
Washstand, Sheraton, Cherry, Scalloped Bottom Shelf, 33 1/4 In. 220.00
Washstand, Sheraton, Hardwood, Mahogany Veneer, 1 Drawer, 33 1/4 In. 385.00
Washstand, Sheraton, Pine, Poplar, Yellow Paint, Stencil, 18 1/2 x 17 x 30 1/2 In. 690.00
Washstand, Sheraton, Pine, Yellow Paint, Stencil, Drawer, Scrolled Crest, 37 In. 275.00
Washstand, Sheraton, Poplar, Dovetailed Drawer, Turned Legs, 37 In. 250.00
Washstand, Sheraton, Walnut, 1 Dovetailed Drawer, 33 3/4 In. 385.00
Washstand, Walnut, Marble Top, 3 Drawers, Candlestand, Victorian 685.00
Washstand, Walnut, White Marble Top, Backsplash Crest, Double Doors, 38 1/4 In. 525.00
Wastebasket, G. Stickley, Slats Riveted To Interior Bands, 14 x 12 In. 1870.00
Wastebasket, J. Hoffmann, White Paint, Hexagonal, Pierced, 1905, 19 In. 2250.00
Wastebasket, Maple, 4 Slats Over Caned Panel, Arts & Crafts, 12 x 12 x 18 In. 185.00
Whatnot, Corner, Walnut, Turned & Fret-Cut Detail, 56 1/2 In. 165.00
Whatnot Shelf, Brass, Wrought Iron, 4 Tiers, Pie Wedge Shape, 72 In. 220.00
Whatnot Shelf, Hanging, Georgian, Pine, Mid-19th Century, 36 x 7 3/4 In. 1035.00
Whatnot Shelf, Mahogany, 3 Tiers, Ring-Turned Supports, 39 1/2 In. 632.00
Whatnot Shelf, Mission, Oak, 5 Shelves ....*Illus* 770.00
Whatnot Shelf, Walnut, 4 Shelves, Victorian, 39 x 49 In. 90.00
Window Seat, Chamfered Square Legs, Tapestry, 1770s, 46 1/2 In. 5750.00
Window Seat, Louis XVI, Cane Seat, Fluted Tapered Legs, 21 x 39 x 14 In. 55.00
Window Seat, Mahogany, Upholstered Side & Seat, Cabriole Legs, c.1780, 37 In. 5750.00
Window Seat, Neoclassical Style, Gilt Design, Swag Drapery Below Seat 2070.00
Window Seat, Neoclassical, Mahogany, Scrolled Arms, Fluted Legs, 29 In. 1760.00
Window Seat, Paneled Legs, Needlepoint Seat, 20 1/2 x 47 In. 1035.00
Window Seat, Regency, Mahogany, Ebony, Padded Seat, 25 1/2 In. 1840.00
Window Seat, Tiger Maple, Carved Skirt, c.1840, 46 In. 1700.00
Window Seat, Walnut, Cabriole Legs, Needlepoint, 29 3/4 In. 155.00
Window Seat, William IV, Mahogany, Rectangular Molded Top, 4 Turned Legs 420.00
Wine Cooler, Oak, Parcel Gilt, Inset Paneled Side, Coat Of Arms, 17 x 25 1/2 In. 8625.00

G. ARGY-ROUSSEAU is the impressed mark used on a variety of objects
in the Art Deco style. Gabriel Argy-Rousseau, born in 1885, was a
French glass artist.

G-ARGY-ROUSSEAU

Ashtray, Lotus Flowers, Teal Blue, Purple, Gray, Pate-De-Verre, 1924, 3 In. 2760.00
Bowl, Violet, Hunting Scene, Boar, Deer, Fowl, Pate-De-Cristal, 4 x 6 In. 9487.00
Box, Cover, Ibis, Lappets & Bouquet Borders, Signed, c.1923, 4 1/2 In. 5175.00
Lamp, Stylized Flower Heads, Triangular Borders, Iron Mounts, 7 3/8 In. 2587.00
Plaque, Display, Les Pates-De-Verre, Brown Lettering, 4 4/5 x 2 5/8 In. 2910.00
Vase, Conical Bud, Stylized Birds Of Prey, Golden Amber & Brown, 5 In. 4625.00
Vase, Doves, Bubbled Clear Glass, Pate-De-Verre, 1932, 7 3/8 In. 10310.00
Vase, Enameled Nude Figures, Partly Silvered Ground, 1920s, 6 3/4 In. 3750.00
Vase, Molded Berry Branches, White & Violet, Pate-De-Verre, 4 In. 8337.00
Vase, Rondels Enclosing Thistles, Signed, c.1922, 3 3/8 In. 4312.00

GALLE was a designer who made glass, pottery, furniture, and other Art
Nouveau items. Émile Galle founded his factory in France in 1874.
After Galle's death in 1904, the firm continued to make glass and furniture until 1931. The name *Galle* was used as a mark, but it was often
hidden in the design of the object. Galle glass is listed here. Pottery is
in the next section. His furniture is listed in the Furniture category.

Galle

Bowl, Amber & Amethyst Cabochons, Mica Flakes, Stages Of Life Of Sunflower, 6 In. ... 6600.00
Bowl, Water Lilies, Blue & Violet, Frosted Ground Overlay, Etched, Cameo, 11 In. 1495.00
Bowl, Wild Rose Blossoms, Lemon Yellow, Crimson Overlay, Frosted Ground, 4 In. 4025.00
Box, 2 Dragonflies On Cover, Etched Waterlily Pond Scene, Signed, 10 In. 4600.00
Box, Etched Allover Blossoming Plants Cover, Frosted Amber-Yellow Base, 3 1/2 In. ... 1455.00
Centerpiece, Landscape, Lakeside, Trees, Brown Overlaid, Pale Yellow, White, 11 In. .. 2415.00
Chalice, Poppies, Leafage, Red, Blue, Green, Plum, Enameled, Cameo, 10 1/2 In. 5465.00

Jug, Bell Shape Body, Milk White Glass, Pink, Green, White Sprays, Cameo, 1900, 10 In.   3450.00
Lamp, Flowering Chrysanthemums Shade, Milky Yellow, Cameo, 1900, 20 In. 6670.00
Lamp, Hanging, Flowering Poppies, Orange Rim, Spherical Gray Shade, Cameo, 10 In. .   2760.00
Lamp, Inverted Trumpet Form Base, Yellow, Blue, Brown, Dragonfly Shade, 26 In. . . .   17250.00
Lamp, Wrought Iron Base, 3 Hanging Shades, Yellow Overlay, Flowers, Cameo, 14 In. . .   7475.00
Lamp Base, Baluster Form, Amber To White, Reeds, Flowers, Cameo, Signed, 11 1/2 In. .   1070.00
Pilgrim Flask, Hydrangea Blossoms, Leafage, Pink, White, Purple, Green, 1904, 5 In. . .   1380.00
Plate, Insect, Fruit, Vegetation Scene, Enameled, 19th Century, 9 In., 11 Piece 1495.00
Salt Tub, Green Frosted, Enameled Flower, Cameo, Silver Base, 1 1/2 x 1 3/4 In. 600.00
Shade, Hanging, Amber, Poppies, Iron Mount, Chains, Cameo, 1900, 19 1/2 In. 6000.00
Shade, Magnolia Blossoms, Leafage, Lemon Yellow, Pink, Deep Amber, Cameo, 11 In. . . .   9775.00
Tazza, Lotus Flowers, Shallow Conical Form, Yellow Body, Green, Blue, Cameo, 5 In. . .   5520.00
Toothpick, Green Fern & Vine, White Ground, 2 In. 396.00
Vase, 2 Open-Mouth Interlocked Fish, 11 7/8 In. 3450.00
Vase, 2-Tone Green Branch, Pink Ground, 4 1/4 In. 275.00
Vase, 5 Large Clematis, Deep Purple Vines, Buds, White Layer Over Purple Layer, 5 In. .   7750.00
Vase, Acorns, Oak Leaf Design, Peach To White Ground, Cameo, 8 In. 935.00
Vase, Alpine Landscape, Frosted, Blue, Yellow, Amethyst, Cameo, Signed, 10 In. 3290.00
Vase, Amber To Yellow, Narrow Neck, Flared Rim, Cameo, Signed, 11 1/4 In. 1265.00
Vase, Berry Branches, Pale Blue, Rose Overlay, 1900, 3 3/8 In. 635.00
Vase, Berry, Purple, Leafy Branches, With Berries, Cameo, 6 In.   750.00
Vase, Blossoming Lilies, Foliage, Pumpkin Orange, Frosted Yellow, Etched, 4 1/2 In. . . .   4025.00
Vase, Blue & Violet Daisies, Yellow Ground, Overlay, Etched, Cameo, Signed, 10 In. . . .   4600.00
Vase, Branches, Laden With Pinecones & Needles, Etched, Signed, 16 In. 2300.00
Vase, Bud, Enameled Vine, Pale Green, Pink Shade, Cameo, Early 20th Century, 7 In. . .   285.00
Vase, Bud, Mahogany, Amber, Bulbous Base, 8 In. 600.00
Vase, Butterflies Above Stylized Landscape, Etched, Aqua Blue Ground, 9 3/4 In. 10350.00
Vase, Cabinet, Leaf Branches, Ocher, Milk White, Squat, 1900, 7 7/8 In. 1265.00
Vase, Carved Scenic Mountain Landscape, Gray Walls, Signed, 14 In. 6900.00
Vase, Chrysanthemums, Cabochons, Fire Polished, Cameo, Signed, 12 1/4 In. 8220.00
Vase, Chrysanthemums, Transparent Emerald Green, Etched, Bulbous, 5 In. 1495.00
Vase, Clematis Sprays, Etched, Yellow, Purple, Blue, Cameo, 1900, 20 In. 3370.00
Vase, Cut Irises, Purple, Gray Overlay, Cushion Foot, 1900, 5 3/4 In. 1035.00
Vase, Cut Morning Glory Blossoms & Leaves, Pink & Purple Overlay, Signed, 4 5/8 In. .   2587.00
Vase, Cut With Spider Chrysanthemums & Leaves, Signed, 13 3/4 In. 2875.00
Vase, Delphinium Blossoms, Leafage, Amber, Gray, Cameo, 1900, 9 1/2 In. 2185.00
Vase, Double Overlay, Frosted, Wisteria, Violet, Brown, Yellow, Signed, 10 5/8 In. 1068.00
Vase, Dragonfly Above Lily Pond, Russet Overlay, Yellow, Gray, 1900, 6 5/8 In. 1725.00
Vase, Enameled Fleur-De-Lis, Gold Accents, 12 In. 1120.00
Vase, Enameled Tiger Lilies, Etched Ferns, Green, Cylindrical, 1900, 14 1/8 In. 3000.00
Vase, Enameled Wild Flowers, Green Tinted Clear Glass, Rectangular, 1895, 6 3/4 In. . . .   6000.00
Vase, Fig Tree, Raised Rim, Oval Body, Leafed Branches, 5 3/4 In. 1335.00
Vase, Fire Polished, Oak Leaf, Acorn, Wide Cylindrical Neck, Cameo, Signed, 10 In. . . .   1235.00
Vase, Floral Cartouches, Etched, Multicolored, Amber Ground, 1885, 8 3/4 In. 9775.00
Vase, Floral Motif, Lavender, Signed, 10 In. 1000.00
Vase, Floral Motif, Maroon, Brick-Red, Etched, Oval, Cameo, 3 3/4 In. 635.00
Vase, Floral, Leafy Stems, Red, Gray, Spherical, 1900, 4 In. 920.00
Vase, Flowering Clematis, Cherry Red, Blue Sky, Yellow, Bulbous, Cameo, 1900, 17 In. .   1955.00
Vase, Flowering Clematis, Overlaid In Yellow, Green, Brown, Yellow, Cameo, 9 1/2 In. . . .   2875.00
Vase, Flowering Irises, Purple, Ocher, Slender-Shouldered Body, Cameo, 18 In. 3220.00
Vase, Fruiting Sprays, Overlaid Cherry Pink, Slender Neck, 1900, 7 5/8 In. 1850.00
Vase, Geranium Blossoms, Leafage, Orange, Olive Green, Gray, Cameo, 1900, 9 1/2 In. .   2875.00
Vase, Gourd Shape, Pendent, Blossoms, Leafage, Deep Amber, Pale Crimson, 1920, 8 In.   6325.00
Vase, Hydrangea Blooms, Pink, White, Green, Mauve, Everted Rim, Cameo, 18 In. 2300.00
Vase, Hydrangea, Leaves, Purple, Gray Overlay, 1904-1910, 5 3/4 In. 750.00
Vase, Iris Blossoms, Buds, Spiked Leaves, 12 1/2 In. 2300.00
Vase, Irises, Lily Pond, Etched, Yellow, Purple, Cameo, Slender, 1900, 9 5/8 In. 2815.00
Vase, Japonesque Floral Design, Pastel, 3-Footed, 6 1/4 In. 315.00
Vase, Lady's Slipper Flowers, Caramel, Peach, Yellow, Frosted, Cameo, Signed, 5 In. . . .   660.00
Vase, Lake Landscape, Mountains, Tree In Foreground, Signed, 8 In. 2695.00
Vase, Lake, Mountains, Blue & Violet Overlay, Yellow Ground, Etched, Cameo, 8 In. . . .   2300.00
Vase, Landscape, 2 Boats, Trees, Lake, Green, Pale Yellow Opalescent, 14 In. 3100.00
Vase, Landscape, Blue Mountains, Yellow Ground, Footed, Signed, 19 1/4 In. 575.00

Vase, Landscape, Forest, River, Lime Green, Brown, Gray, Cameo, 1900, 20 In. 7475.00
Vase, Landscape, Lakes & Mountains, Yellow Body, Blue, Purple, Everted, 1900, 12 In. . 5520.00
Vase, Landscape, Leafy Verdant, Apricot, Pale Pink, Oliver Green, Cameo, 1900, 14 In. . . 2990.00
Vase, Landscape, Mountainous, Lofty Conifers, Lavender, Deep Amber, 1900, 5 1/2 In. . . . 3740.00
Vase, Landscape, River, Salmon, Lime Green, Brown, Gray, Cameo, 1900, 20 In. 6900.00
Vase, Landscape, Wooded River Scene, Gray Glass, Green, Brown, Cameo, 1900, 14 In. . 2300.00
Vase, Landscape, Yellow Body, Blue, Purple Mountains, Raised Foot, Cameo, 1900, 9 In. 3220.00
Vase, Lantana Blossoms, Leafage, Deep Amber, Gray, Cameo, 1900, 13 3/8 In. 2875.00
Vase, Leaf Design, Amber, Greens, Orange & Frost, 8 In. 1430.00
Vase, Leafy Blossoming Plants, Turquoise, Blue, Magenta, Red, Etched, Cameo, 2 x 4 In. 750.00
Vase, Leaves, Bud Design, Deep Brown, Yellow Ground, Cameo, 5 1/2 In. 825.00
Vase, Leaves, Floral Buds, Green, Light Green, Amber Ground, Signed, 5 In. 385.00
Vase, Lilac Sprays, Etched, Gray, Red, Slender Swollen Body, Cameo, 1900, 21 In. 3560.00
Vase, Lily Pads, Blooming Flowers, Signed, 11 3/4 In. 1955.00
Vase, Magnolia Blossoms, Etched, Foliage, Yellow Overlaid In Crimson, 13 In. 8050.00
Vase, Mountain Scene, Peach, Blue, Green, Brown, Cameo, 1900, 5 3/4 In. 920.00
Vase, Orchids, Mushrooms, Pink, Brown, Turquoise, Green, White, Red, 1900, 10 1/2 In. 1955.00
Vase, Overall Blossoming Plants, Etched, Signed, 23 1/4 In. 3220.00
Vase, Overlaid In Purple, Blue, Fuchsia Sprays, Cameo, 1900, 12 In. 5750.00
Vase, Painted Shells & Fronds, Milky Aqua Glass, Baluster, 1900, 8 7/8 In., Pair 8435.00
Vase, Pendant Vines, Laden With Squash, Blossoms & Foliage, Signed, 13 5/8 In. 830.00
Vase, Pine Branches, Dark Brown To Blue, Cone Shape, Cameo, Signed, 6 1/2 x 5 1/2 In. 4775.00
Vase, Plant, Red, Blue, Green Stems, 4 Applied Yellow Loop Handles, 1900, 4 In. 980.00
Vase, Poppies, Bulbous, Turquoise Ground, Tangerine, Etched, Cameo, 5 1/4 In. 1495.00
Vase, Poppies, Green, Ferns, Green, Yellow, White Ground, Cameo, 13 In. 1650.00
Vase, Prunus Blossoms, Leafage, Orange Rust, Lemon Yellow, Cameo, 1900, 13 5/8 In. . . 8050.00
Vase, Purple Clematis, White Ground, Cameo, 7 1/2 In. 1045.00
Vase, Purple Flowering Irises, Inverted Trumpet Form, Milky Ground, Cameo, 22 In. . . . 4600.00
Vase, Pussy Willow & A Bee, Yellow, Brown, Bulbous, Flared, 1900, 4 1/4 In. 2590.00
Vase, Raised Star Above Gold Centered Pink Blossoms, Angular Rim, Etched, 3 x 5 In. . . 1840.00
Vase, Red Thistles, Red, Gold Cream, Amber Ground, Cameo, 11 x 5 1/2 In. 1430.00
Vase, River Landscape, Trees In Foreground, Signed, c.1900, 13 1/2 In. 3160.00
Vase, River Landscape, Trees, Crouching Fisherman, Signed, 1904, 9 1/4 In. 4025.00
Vase, Riverside Landscape, Mountains, Tall Fir Trees, Cameo, 11 1/2 In. 2645.00
Vase, Rose, 5 Petal Flowers, Rose Overlay, Yellow, Gray, 1900, 9 1/4 In. 2185.00
Vase, Seedpods On Leaf Vines, Deep Brown, Amber, Signed, 1900, 7 1/8 In. 4025.00
Vase, Spiked Blossoms, Etched, Arising From Leafy Mound, Signed, 16 In. 2185.00
Vase, Spirals Of Daisies, Spider Web, Signed, c.1900, 18 In. 3737.00
Vase, Sprays Of Apple Blossom, White, Pink, Pale Yellow Body, Cameo, 14 In. 5750.00
Vase, Sprays Of Delicate Wild Flowers, Beige Interior, 1900, 13 In. 3220.00
Vase, Sprays Of Flowering Angels' Trumpets, Amber, White, Scarlet, Cameo, 13 In. 4370.00
Vase, Sprays Of Magnolia, Deep Red, Deep Yellow Body, Blue Interior, Cameo, 18 In. . . 5175.00
Vase, Stick, Yellow, Brown Floral Design, Cylindrical, Signed, 13 In. . . . . .1210.00 to 1320.00
Vase, Stylized Thistle Pods, Spiked Leaves, Signed, 17 3/4 In. 2415.00
Vase, Stylized Wildflowers, Leafage, Blue, Brown, Yellow, Green, White, 1900, 5 In. . . . 2760.00
Vase, Sunflower Blossoms, Leafage, Yellow, Ocher, Lime Green, Cameo, 1900, 23 In. 5175.00
Vase, Sunflowers In Differing Stages Of Bloom, Etched, Pale Amber, 6 1/4 In. 6900.00
Vase, Swiss Landscape, Matterhorn, Acid Cut, Frosted, Cameo, Signed, 6 1/4 In. 2465.00
Vase, Trailing Blossoms, Buds, Red, Orange, Cameo, 6 In. 575.00
Vase, Trees, Mountains, Blue & Green, Yellow Ground, Overlay, Etched, Cameo, 12 In. . 3450.00
Vase, Trumpet Form, Ferns, Shaded Peach, Green & Brown Overlay, Cameo, 10 In. 1725.00
Vase, Tulips, Orange, Amethyst, Overlaid Milky White, Pink Glass, Cameo, 1900, 9 In. . . 1955.00
Vase, Water Lily & Flower, Orange Over Blue Frost, 3 3/4 In. 885.00
Vase, Wooded River Scene, Pink, Brown, Cameo, 1900, 11 3/4 In. 3560.00
Vase, Woodland Landscape, Flattened Teardrop, Cameo, 1900, 20 1/8 In. 8250.00
Vase, Yellow & Red, Cameo, Signed, 13 1/2 In. 6325.00

GALLE POTTERY was made by Emile Galle, the famous French
designer, after 1874. The pieces were marked with the initials *E. G.*
impressed, *Em. Galle Faiencerie de Nancy,* or a version of his signature. Galle is best known for his glass, listed above.

Bowl, Cattle, Landscape, Partly Folded Edge, Signed E. Galle, 7 In. 660.00
Bowl, Duck, Figural Bird, Stylized Painted Florals, Signed, 6 3/4 x 8 1/4 In. 1335.00

Candelabrum, 4-Light, Lion, Holding Castle With Light, Faience, 25 In., Pair 4125.00
Figurine, Cat, Black & Yellow, c.1890, 8 1/2 In. 520.00
Figurine, Cat, Sitting, Faience, Blue Hearts, Yellow Ground, 1880s, 13 In. 7875.00
Pitcher, Costumed Dancers In Pastoral Setting, Hand Painted, Signed, 8 In. 1058.00
Plaque, Bucolic Landscape, 4 Cows, Black Underglaze, 12 1/2 In. 748.00
Plaque, Peacock, Stylized Gray, Amber, Blue Birds, Shield Form, 12 1/2 x 14 In. 575.00

GAME collectors like all types of games. Of special interest are any
board games or card games. Transogram and other company names are
included in the description when known. Other games may be found
listed under Card, Toy, or the name of the character or celebrity featured in the game.

12 O'Clock High, Box, Ideal, 1965 .... 20.00
77 Sunset Strip, 1959 .... 35.00
Addams Family, Board, 1964 .... 100.00
Addams Family, Card, 1965 .... 75.00
Air Defense, Illustrated Planes, Ships, Artillery Units, Wolverine, 1940s 100.00
Air Mail, Milton Bradley, Board, 1929 .... 90.00
Air Raid Defense, Dart Game, Wyandotte 75.00
Air-Attack Fighting Planes In Action, Box, Corey Game Division, 1943 .... 90.00
Alexander The Great, Avalon Hill, Board, 1974 .... 25.00
Alfred Hitchcock Presents, Mystery, Milton Bradley, 1958 .... 28.00
All American Action Football Game, Lowell, 1955 .... 65.00
America's Yacht Race, McLoughlin Bros., Early 20th Century, 19 3/4 x 10 1/2 In. ... 630.00
And Awa-a-y We Go, Jackie Gleason, Box 45.00
Andy Gump, His Game, Graphics On All Sides, Milton Bradley 65.00
Archie Bunker, Card, Milton Bradley, 1972 .... 20.00
Auf Der Eisenbahn, German Railroad, Die Cast Metal Pieces, Locomotive, Board, 1900 110.00
Barbie Queen Of The Prom, Mattel, 1960 .... 75.00
Baseball, Babe Ruth's, Milton Bradley, 1930s 460.00
Baseball, The Great American Game, Tin Lithograph, Frantz, 1920 .... 150.00
Baseball, Whitey Herzog, Autographed, Box, 1977 .... 100.00
Beat 'Em Out, Pinball Type, Bagatelle, Box 200.00
Beat The Clock, Milton Bradley, 1969 .... 25.00
Bello Or Lucky Quoits, 5 Figures, Children Playing On Box Top, J.W.S. & S. 255.00
Bermuda Triangle, Board, 1976 .... 25.00
Black Beauty, Retracing Beauty's Life, Transogram, Board, 1958 .... 24.00
Blow Football, Box, Spear Works, Box, 5 1/4 x 10 1/4 In. 93.00
Board, Drawn On Polychrome Clock Face, Graphite, 1860s, 12 x 12 In. 115.00
Board, Fox & Geese, Lollipop Form, 15 Pegs, 19th Century 120.00
Board, Green, 2 Children & Cat, White & Yellow 3400.00
Board, Hold 5 To 12 Marbles 15.00
Board, Mahogany, Birch & Pine Inlays, Walnut, Round, 22 1/8 In. 220.00
Board, Masonic Elements, Yellow Paint On Maroon Ground, 17 5/8 x 10 1/4 In. 977.00
Board, Numbers, Walnut, Square, Original Finish, 11 In. 175.00
Board, Pine, 3-Board, Red & Red, Square Nail Construction 1150.00
Board, Pine, Cut Nails, Corner Holes, Red & Black Over Mustard, 23 x 29 3/4 In. 255.00
Board, Plywood, Pine Frame, Polychrome Surface, 31 x 31 In. 412.00
Board, Polychrome Clock Face, Graphite & Paint, 12 x 12 In. 115.00
Board, Red & Black Paint, D. Clark On Reverse, Late 19th Century, 14 1/2 x 14 1/2 In. . 1380.00
Board, Red & Green Paint, Early 20th Century, 10 x 10 In. 287.00
Board, Red, Black & Green Paint, Yellow Field, Late 19th Century, 14 1/2 x 14 1/2 In. ... 862.00
Board, Red, White, Blue & Black On Frame, Pine, Square, 16 In. 190.00
Board, Yellow & Black Paint, Green Field, Late 19th Century, 16 x 20 3/4 In. 1150.00
Bocci Ball Set, Black Lacquered & Gilt Box, 1880s, 13 Balls 205.00
Bull Run, Avalon Hill, Board, 1983 .... 20.00
Bunk Bar, Dice, 1900 .... 50.00
Cabby!, Die Cast Taxi Markers, Box, Selchow & Righter, 1938 .... 35.00
Captain America, Milton Bradley, Board, 1977 .... 15.00
Captain Video, Space, Milton Bradley, Board, Box 175.00
Casper, Board, 1959 .... 12.00
Cattlemen, Woman & 2 Cowmen, Selchow & Righter, Box, 1977 ....20.00 to 38.00
Charlie McCarthy, Whitman, Card, Box, 1937 .... 50.00

Checkerboard, 2 Sides, Tin, Red & Black 175.00
Checkerboard, Black, Yellow & Red Alligatored Paint, Canada Decal, 19 x 30 In. 645.00
Checkerboard, Board, 2 Sides, Painted Game On Reverse, 16 1/2 x 16 In. 690.00
Checkerboard, Brown & Mustard, 26 3/4 x 19 In. 475.00
Checkerboard, Cameo Paintings Of Steamships 2475.00
Checkerboard, Chestnut, Brass Corners, Property Of Ens. Wm. Ashley, 16 x 20 5/8 In. . 240.00
Checkerboard, Pine, Painted Red & Yellow, 15 1/2 x 16 In. 302.00
Checkerboard, Pine, Red & Black Paint, 17 3/4 x 30 1/2 In. 357.00
Checkerboard, Poplar, Black Cream Paint, Green Border, 14 1/4 x 17 3/4 In. 300.00
Checkerboard, Red & White, Separate Blocks, Blue Frame, 1927, 16 x 16 1/4 In. 55.00
Checkerboard, Walnut, Cherry, Maple, Painted Backgammon On Reverse, 16 x 16 In. ... 440.00
Checkerboard, Wooden, Painted, Black, White, Red Gallery Edge, 14 1/2 x 15 In. 220.00
Chess Set, Anodized Aluminum, Modern, Man Ray, Manufactured Board, 2 In. 3450.00
Chess Set, Black & Blond Men, Carved Wood, 1860 .... 165.00
Chess Set, Carved Wood, Natural & Red, Lacquered Checkerboard Case, Oriental, 16 In. 385.00
Chess Set, Fitted Case, Chess Board, c.1940 .... 8500.00
Chess Set, Ivory, Fitted , Ivory Wooden Box, 24 x 24 In. 1150.00
Chess Set, Ivory, White & Opposing Brown Sides, Warriors & Animals, Parquetry Box . 920.00
Chess Set, Portable, Plastic Box, Russia, 1967, 3 3/4 x 3 3/4 In. 30.00
Chess Set, Staffordshire, 1850s 300.00
Cheyenne, Milton Bradley, Board, 1958 .... 75.00
Chinese Checkers, Glass Marble, Wooden, 7 1/4 In. 44.00
Chutes & Ladders, Milton Bradley, Board, 1956 .... 20.00
Cleveland Browns, Board, 1978 .... 10.00
Clue, Board, 1949 .... 40.00
Combat Board, Vic Morrow, Rick Jason On Cover Of Box, Ideal, 1963 .... 45.00
Cootie, 1949 .... 18.00
Cribbage Board, Brass, England, c.1750, 9 1/2 In. 195.00
Cribbage Board, Brass, Heart & Crescent Design, England, Late 18th Century, 9 In. ... 285.00
Cribbage Board, Horseshoe Shape, 5 x 6 In. 135.00
Cribbage Board, Ivory, Carved Buddha Top, 6 1/4 In. 95.00
Cribbage Board, Traveling, Folds, Leather 25.00
Cribbage Board, Traveling, Leather 35.00
Croquet Set, Wooden, Original Varnish, E-Z Stow-Away 135.00
Croquet Set, Wooden, Polychrome Paint 66.00
Croquet Wickets, Cast Iron, Figural, Jockeys, Painted, 17 1/2 In., 9 Piece 2475.00
Cross-Up, Milton Bradley, Board, 1974 .... 25.00
Croupier Stick, For Gambling Table, Hickory, Leather Sleeve, 1900s 135.00
Cut-Up Shopping Spree, Milton Bradley, 1969 .... 65.00
Dark Shadows, Board, Trying To Resurrect Barnabas' Remains, Milton Bradley, 1969 .. 29.00
Dart, Air Raid Defense, Box 75.00
Dart Board, Get Those Japs, Lithographed Plywood, Wartime Art, 16 x 16 In. 126.00
Dave Dawson Pacific Battle Game, Box, American Toy Works, 1942 .... 85.00
Deputy, Henry Fonda TV Series, Milton Bradley, Board, 1960 .... 89.00
Dexterity Puzzle, Boy On Moon, Metal Frame, Glass Front, Germany, Prewar, 1 1/8 In. 67.00
Dexterity Puzzle, Boy On Sled, Metal Frame, Glass Front, Germany, Prewar, 1 1/8 In. . 137.00
Dexterity Puzzle, Boy Riding Duck, Metal Frame, Germany, Prewar, 1 1/8 In. 44.00
Dexterity Puzzle, Butterfly, Metal Frame, Glass Front, Germany, Prewar, 1 1/4 In. 44.00
Dexterity Puzzle, Chickens Eating, Metal, Glass, Germany, Prewar, 2 1/4 In. 33.00
Dexterity Puzzle, Chimney Sweep, Metal Frame, Glass Front, Germany, Prewar, 1 In. . 112.00
Dexterity Puzzle, Couple Drinking, Metal Frame, Glass Front, Germany, Prewar, 2 In. . 67.00
Dexterity Puzzle, Couple In Old Auto, Metal, Glass Front, W. Germany, 1950s, 3 In. .. 82.00
Dexterity Puzzle, Football Players, Metal & Wood Frame, Glass Front, 1950s, 3 In. ... 22.00
Dexterity Puzzle, Girl With Deer, Metal Frame, Glass Front, Germany, Prewar, 1 1/8 In. 67.00
Dexterity Puzzle, Girl With Dice, Metal, Glass Front, Plastic Dice, Germany, 2 1/4 In. . 28.00
Dexterity Puzzle, Man Smoking, Glass Front, Mirror Back, Germany, Prewar, 2 In. ... 44.00
Dexterity Puzzle, Men In Old Auto, Metal, Glass, W. Germany, 1950s, 2 1/4 In. 113.00
Dexterity Puzzle, Metal Frame, Glass Front, Mirror Back 27.00
Dexterity Puzzle, Movie Star, Metal Frame, Mirror Front, Prewar, 2 1/4 In. 67.00
Dexterity Puzzle, Rabbits Hunting Fox, Metal Frame, Glass Front, Germany, 1 3/4 In. . 93.00
Dexterity Puzzle, Seal With Fish, Metal Frame, Glass Front, Japan, 1950s, 2 In. 82.00
Dexterity Puzzle, Squirrel In Tree, Metal Frame, Glass Front, Prewar, 1 1/8 In. 67.00
Dexterity Puzzle, Wedding Ring, Monkey On Reverse, Cardboard, Japan, 1950s, 3 In. . 33.00

Dexterity Puzzle, Woman With Hat, Metal Frame, Glass Front, Prewar, 1 1/8 In. 38.00
Dice, Shake-Em, 5 Cent Poker Hand Game, Box, 1950, 16 x 16 x 8 In. 11.00
District Messenger Boy, Folding Game Board, Spinner, McLoughlin, 1890s, 17 In. ... 86.00
Dominoes, 28 Bone-Backed Dominos, Wooden, Book-Shaped Box, 4 1/4 In. 220.00
Dominoes, Box, Cribbage Game On Border, c.1810 .... 1800.00
Dominoes, Brownies On Box Top, Germany 40.00
Dominoes, Carved Slide Top, Bakelite 75.00
Dominoes, Civil War, Wooden, 33-Star Flag, Red White & Blue, 28 Piece 175.00
Dominoes, Ivory & Ebony, Box, 8 1/4 In., 28 Piece 60.00
Dominoes, Ivory & Ebony, Box, 9 In., 28 Piece 70.00
Dominoes, Marbleized Wood Egg Form Case, Painted Bone, 19th Century, 2 1/2 In. 345.00
Dr. Seuss, Game Of Yertle The Turtle, Revell, 1960 .... 170.00
Dracula Mystery, Hasbro, Board, 1963 .... 300.00
Dragnet Target, Knickerbocker, No. 643, 1955 .... 35.00
Dukes Of Hazzard, Milton Bradley, Board, 1976 .... 15.00
Ed Wynn Fire Chief 95.00
Electronic Radar Search Game, Box, Ideal, 1969, 12 x 11 x 3 1/2 In. ....23.00 to 25.00
Ellsworth Elephant, Selchow & Righter, Board, 1960, 10 x 20 In. 295.00
Famous 500 Mile Race, Board 20.00
Fast Mail Railroad, Milton Bradley 165.00
Felix The Cat, 1968 .... 12.00
Fibber McGee, 1936 .... 25.00
Fibber McGee, 1940 .... 30.00
Finance, Parker Brothers, Board, 1962 .... 15.00
Flinch, Parker Brothers, Card, 1950s 6.00
Flintstones Big Game Hunt, Footprints, Cards, Animal Target, Whitman, Board, 1962 . 90.00
Flintstones Stone Age Game, Transogram, Cardboard Box, Board, 1962 .... 20.00
Flip Lid, Hasbro, Board, 1950s 25.00
Flipper Flips, Mattel, Board, 1965 .... 56.00
Flying Nun, Milton Bradley, Box, 1968 .... 50.00
Flying The Beam, Parker Brothers, Box, 1940s, 18 1/4 x 9 1/2 In. 33.00
Football, Electric, Metal, Plastic, Plug-In, Tudor, 1950s Or 1960s, Box, 26 x 16 In. 25.00
Football, Electric, Tudor Tru-Action, Box, 1940s 100.00
Football, Rose Bowl, 24 Plastic Players, 1949, Unused 29.00
Foresight, Milton Bradley, Board, 1967 .... 15.00
Fortune Teller, Fortune Teller On Cover, Card Wheel, Milton Bradley, c.1905 .... 125.00
Fox And Hounds, Parker Brothers, Board, 1948 .... 30.00
G.I. Joe, Card, 1960s 5.00
G.I. Joe, Combat Infantry 25.00
G.I. Joe, Navy Frogman 25.00
Game Counter, Ivory, 2 Tiers 295.00
Game Of Besieging, Germany, Box, 1800-1820, 13 1/4 x 12 5/8 In. 260.00
Game Of Boy Scouts, Milton Bradley Co., Box, 1910, 22 x 10 1/2 In. 285.00
Game Of Jack & The Beanstalk, McLoughlin Bros., Box, 1898, 19 3/4 x 10 1/2 In. ... 860.00
Game Of Merry Christmas, J. H. Singer, Box, 1 1/2 x 13 1/2 x 7 In. 920.00
Game Of Politics, Parker Brothers, Box, 1952 .... 40.00
Game Of Robbing The Miller, McLoughlin Bros., 1888, 15 1/2 x 8 In. 375.00
Gee-Wiz, Racing, Wolverine 210.00
Get Smart, Exploding Time Bomb, Ideal, 1965 .... 145.00
Gettysburg, Avalon Hill, Board, 1977 .... 15.00
Gidget, Fortune Teller, Sally Field Picture On Box, Board, 1965 .... 48.00
Gilligan's Island, New Adventures Of Gilligan, Milton Bradley, 3-D, 1974 .... 48.00
Global Air Race, World Globe, Magnetic, Box, 1952 .... 175.00
Go For Broke, Selchow & Righter, Board, 1965 .... 15.00
Godzilla, King Of The Monsters, Lurking In Outer Space, Board, 1978 .... 69.00
Goldilocks, Board, 1973 .... 20.00
Great American Game, Baseball Game, Tin, Frantz, 1920s, 13 1/2 x 9 x 3 In. 150.00
Great American Game, Baseball, Tin, Hustler Toy Corp. ....132.00 to 175.00
Gumps At Seashore 75.00
Gun, Skill Target, World War II Theme, Daval 1050.00
Hank Aaron Baseball, Ideal, 1973 .... 100.00
Heckle & Jeckle Ski Trail, Board, 1971 .... 35.00
Hendrik Van Loon's Wide World Game, Box, Parker Brothers, 1933, 26 1/2 x 17 In. .. 30.00

Hokum, Parker Brothers, 1927 .... 50.00
Hollywood Squares, Ideal, 1974 .... 28.00
Honors, Camp Fire Girls 25.00
House That Jack Built, Paper Lithograph On Wood Pieces, Box, Shepherd, 11 x 12 In. . 172.00
Huckleberry Hound Western, Milton Bradley, Board, 1959 .... 25.00
Hunting In Jungle, Hunting Scene On Box Top, A. Gropper 125.00
I Dream Of Jeannie, Art Of Jeannie On The Box, Milton Bradley, Board, 1965 .... 69.00
I Love Lucy, Board, 1990 .... 25.00
I Spy, Ideal, Board, Card, 1966 .... 55.00
I Spy, Picture Of Culp & Cosby On The Box, Ideal, Board, 1965 .... 77.00
I've Got A Secret, Lowell, 1958 .... 24.00
Intercollegiate Football, Hustler Toy Corp. & Franz Hardware, Early 1920s ..... *Illus* 200.00
James Bond 007, 1964 .... 40.00
Joe Namath Football, Electric, GPS, Pressed Steel Corp., 1960s 85.00
Johnny Apollo Moon Landing, Bagatelle 25.00
Jolly Marble, Paper Lithograph On Wood, Tilting Figures, 1892, 19 3/4 In. 110.00
Kreskin ESP Game, Milton Bradley, Board, 1966 ....25.00 to 30.00
Land Of Cotton, Board, 1978 .... 25.00
Land Of The Giants, Cast On The Cover, Ideal, Board, 1968 .... 250.00
Laverne & Shirley 30.00
Les Joyeux Acrobates, Wood Acrobats Fit Together, France, c.1871, Box, 9 x 11 In. ... 800.00
Life Magazine Remembers, Selchow & Righter, 1985 .... 30.00
Little House On The Prairie, Board, 1978 .... 40.00
Little Marksman, Gun & Target 80.00
Little Noddy's Taxi Game, Ceramic Pieces, Parker Brothers, 1956 .... 75.00
Lotto Game, Lock, Paper Label, Contents, Wood Box, Germany, 1893 .... 35.00
M*A*S*H, Milton Bradley, Board, 1981 ....15.00 to 31.00
Mad Magazine, Parker Brothers, Board, 1979 ....10.00 to 40.00
Magilla Gorilla, Magilla, On The Box, 8 Drawings On Board, Ideal, Board, 1964 .... 135.00
Magnetic Pie Toss, Laurel & Hardy 170.00
Man From U.N.C.L.E., Thrush Ray Gun Affair, 3-D, Ideal, 1965 .... 195.00
Man From U.N.C.L.E. Illya Kuryakin, Milton Bradley, Board, 1966 .... 25.00
Mandrake The Magician Magic Kit, Box, Gilbert Toys, 1955 .... 60.00
Marathon, Dice, Sports Game Co., Box, 1978, 11 x 5 In. 20.00
Marble, Jumpright, Bakelite, Box 65.00
Margie, Game Of Whoopee!, Milton Bradley, 1961 .... 40.00
Marx Brothers, Groucho, You Bet Your Life Quiz, Lowell, 1955 .... 195.00
Melvin Moon Man, Remco, 1960s 120.00
Mother Hen Target, Tin Lithograph, Box 55.00
Mouse Trap, Ideal, 1963 .... 40.00
Mr. Magoo Visits Zoo, Lowell, Board, 1961 .... 25.00
Mr. Ree The Fireside Detective Thriller Game, Selchow & Righter Co., 1937 ...... 65.00
My Favorite Martian, Transogram, Board, Box, 1963 .... 65.00
Mysterio, Brownies Playing On Box Top, Charles Graham Co., 1929 .... 38.00
Mystic Finger, 1923 .... 35.00
Name That Tune, Milton Bradley, Board, 1959 ....25.00 to 36.00

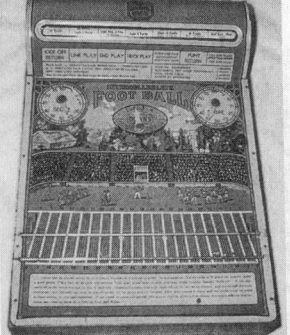

We hung a 1950s L'il Abner game board on the wall near a window. The sun removed all of the yellow color in a year. The grass in the print is now blue.

Game, Intercollegiate
Football, Hustler Toy
Corp. & Franz Hardware,
Early 1920s

NBC Peacock, Selchow & Righter, 1966 .... 76.00
NBC-TV News, With Chet Huntley, On Cover Of Box, Dadan, Board, 1962 .... 95.00
New Howard H. Jones Collegiate Football Game, Box, 2 x 26 x 13 In. 85.00
Newlywed, ABC TV Show, Hasbro, Board, 1968 .... 30.00
Park & Shop, Milton Bradley, Board, Box, 1960 .... 60.00
Partridge Family, Milton Bradley, Board, 1974 .... 10.00
Pennant Winner, Baseball Game, Tin, Box, Sandy Andy, Wolverine, 25 x 18 In. 75.00
Perry Mason, Case Of The Missing Suspect, Transogram, 1959 .... 48.00
Peter Coddles Trip, Instructions & Playing Strips, Milton Bradley 35.00
Peter Gunn, Board, 1960 .... 15.00
Peter Pan, Transogram, Board, 1953 .... 75.00
Peter Potamus, Ideal, Board, 1964 .... 485.00
Peter Rabbit, Gabriel Soons & Co., Box, c.1920 .... 92.00
Phalanx, War Game, Greek Military Strategies, Whitman, Board, 1964 .... 26.00
Pin Tail Donkey, Whitman, 1940s 10.00
Pinball, Boom Boom, Pocket Edition, Wood, Glass, Harvey Mfg. Co., 4 1/2 x 6 1/2 In. ... 20.00
Pinball, Gumball Game, Wood, Glass, 9 x 12 1/2 In. 25.00
Pinball, Poosh-M-Up Jr., Table Top, Northwestern Products Co., Box, 1930s 50.00
Play Ball-Batter Up, Made & Printed In U.S.A., 1960s, 8 x 4 In. 24.00
Play Football, Cast Iron Figures, Yellow Novelty Co., Schenectady, New York 2990.00
Playful Trails, Gumby & Pokey 100.00
Poker Chips, Bakelite, Red, Yellow & Navy, Black Cardboard Box, 200 Piece 175.00
Poker Chips, Caddy, 300 Bakelite Chips, Yellow, Green, Red, Tartan Tweed Box 195.00
Poker Chips, Catlin, Box 275.00
Poker Chips, Clay, Engraved, Woman, Flowing Hair, Wooden Rack, 100 Piece 145.00
Poker Chips, Engraved, Spread Eagle & Stars, Wooden Chest With Rack, 200 Pieces ... 395.00
Poker Chips, Standard Oil 75th Anniversary, Plastic, Box, 1954 .... 20.00
Politics, Parker Brothers, 1952 .... 45.00
Punchboard, Garcia Grande Cigars, Baseball, 5 Cent 20.00
Puzzle, Adventures Of Gulliver, Whitman, 1969, 11 x 14 In. 35.00
Puzzle, Battle Ship, Block, Paper Lithograph, 1900, 10 x 13 In. 495.00
Puzzle, Bee Gees, 1979, 11 x 17 In. 30.00
Puzzle, Block, Germany, Box, Late 19th Century, 1 1/2 x 4 x 4 In. 60.00
Puzzle, Boodle Alderman, Tin Lithograph, 3 3/4 In. 231.00
Puzzle, Bringing Up Father, Maggie & Jiggs, Saalfield, Lithograph Box, 1930s 85.00
Puzzle, C3PO & R2D2, Star Wars, Box, 1977 .... 20.00
Puzzle, Chase & Sanborn Coffee, New England Country Grocery Store, Box 68.00
Puzzle, Combat, Beach Landing, Jaymar, 1960s, 14 x 19 In. 18.00
Puzzle, Combat, Tank Corps, Tanks In Action On The Desert, Jaymar, 1960s, 14 x 19 In. ... 18.00
Puzzle, Eddie Cantor, We Want Cantor, Radio Stars, Einson, 1933 .... 28.00
Puzzle, Farrah Fawcett, Swimsuit Pose, 1977, 12 x 20 In. 25.00
Puzzle, Flintstones, Wilma & Dino With Pebbles, Bamm-Bamm In Yard, 14 x 18 In. 24.00
Puzzle, Incredible Hulk 8.00
Puzzle, James Bond 007, Goldfinger, 1965 .... 100.00
Puzzle, Jonny Quest, Blazing Harbor, 1964 .... 100.00
Puzzle, Kenobi-Vader Duel, Star Wars, Box, 1977 .... 20.00
Puzzle, Les Animaux Savants, Cardboard, France, Box, Prewar, 12 x 9 In., 4 Puzzles ... 218.00
Puzzle, Little Lulu & Tubby, Box, 1960 .... 48.00
Puzzle, Maggie & Jiggs, Bringing Up Father, Saalfield, Box, 1930s 95.00

Game, Witch-ee, Fortune
Teller, Selchow & Righter
Co., 1920s

Puzzle, Moon Landing 20th Anniversary Stamp, With Houston Cancellation Stamps 29.00
Puzzle, Multi-Piece 3-D Wooden Rocket, Stackman, New York, Japan, Box, 6 x 1 3/4 In. 36.00
Puzzle, Old Mother Hubbard, Lithographed Paper On Wood Cubes, McLoughlin, 1900 .. 225.00
Puzzle, Panama Canal, Pass Ball Through Locks, Box, 4 1/2 In. 11.00
Puzzle, Rainy Day & Balloon Puzzle, Hood's, 2 Sides, Framed, Box, 1891 .... 110.00
Puzzle, Spiro Agnew 35.00
Puzzle, The Impossibles, Beating Up Villains Along The Beach, 1967, 11 x 14 In. 24.00
Puzzle, Train, McLoughlin Bros., 1887, 22 x 13 In. 475.00
Puzzle, Twinkles, Frame, Whitman, 1962, 11 x 14 In. 65.00
Puzzle, Underdog, Frame Tray 35.00
Puzzle, Victory Soldier, Wooden 47.00
Puzzle, World War I Army Scenes, Oak Frame, Double Sided, Milton Bradley 145.00
Puzzle, Wyatt Earp, Box 25.00
Quick Draw McGraw, Private Eye 50.00
Raggedy Ann's Magic Pebble 50.00
Raider, Marx, Target, Box 175.00
Raiders Of The Lost Ark, Parker Brothers, Unplayed 45.00
Rex Morgan M.D., Ideal, 1972 .... 28.00
Ricochet-Rabbit & Droop-A-Long Coyote, 1964 .... 150.00
Ring Toss, Numbers On Red & Black Target, Metal Hooks, Square, 13 In. 195.00
Ring Toss, Soldier, Wooden 95.00
Ripley's Believe It Or Not, Milton Bradley, Board, 1984 .... 20.00
Road Runner, Coyote, Road Runner, Tweety & Sylvester, Milton Bradley, Box, 1968 ... 35.00
Roly Poly Popeye Target, Cork Gun, 6 Different Characters On Roly Polys, 1940s 275.00
Rook, Card, Box, 1936 .... 25.00
Rough Riders, Lithographed Box, Clark & Sowdon, Box, 19 1/2 x 10 1/2 In. 385.00
Rudolph The Red Nosed Reindeer 330.00
Scrabble For Juniors, Board, Selchow & Righter, 1958 .... 5.00
Sherlock Holmes, Holmes & Crime Scene, Cadaco, Box, 1982 .... 38.00
Simpson's, Wrist LCD, Original Display Card, Unopened, Tiger Electronics 25.00
Six Million Dollar Man, Parker Brothers, Board, 1975 .... 20.00
Sleeping Beauty, Bradley 20.00
Slugger Poosh-M-Up Baseball, 1940s 85.00
Smack-A-Roo, Play Baseball, Bowling & Smack It, Mattel, 1964, 24 x 16 In. 40.00
Snagglepuss, Yogi, Boo-Boo & Snagglepuss, Transogram, Box, 1961 .... 60.00
Snoopy Come Home, Board, 1966 .... 20.00
Snow White & The Seven Dwarfs, Cadaco, Board, 1977 .... 10.00
Snowballing, Cardboard & Wood, Celluloid Balls, Chad Valley, England, 1940s 331.00
Spot-A-Plane, Bomber, Board Game, 48 Cards, 2nd Series, Toy Creations, 1942 .... 125.00
Star Trek, Original TV Series, Limited Edition, Box 29.00
Steeple Chase, E.P. Malaret & Co., Paris, Felt Cloth, Box, Late 1800s, 50 x 34 In. 450.00
Stock Market, Whitman, Board, 1968 .... 25.00
Ten Pins, Military, Soldiers, Painted Wood & Lithographed Paper, Box, 1885, 8 In. 975.00
Texas Ranger, All-Fair, 1936 .... 55.00
The New Zoo Revue, Show's Characters On The Box, Ungame, Board, 1981 .... 18.00
Thunderbirds, Waddington, Board, 1965 .... 85.00
Tortoise & Hair, Russel Mfg., Co., Multicolored Lithograph On Cover, 1922 .... 120.00
Trick-Track, Mahogany & Walnut, Board, Box 1380.00
Twenty-One, From TV Game Show, Jack Barry On Lid 34.00
Uncle Wiggily, Board, Wrapped, 16 x 16 In. 50.00
Varsity, Scientific Football, Board, Cadaco, 1953 .... 20.00
Waltons, Faces Of All The Families, Milton Bradley, 1974, 17 x 19 In. 20.00
We Girls Can Do Anything, Barbie Career Game, Sealed Box, Golden, 1986 .... 12.00
Wheel, Bicycle Tire Style With Spokes, Painted, c.1900, 36 In. 425.00
Wheel Of Fortune, Parker Brothers, Board, 1985 .... 5.00
Which Witch, Milton Bradley, Board, 1970 .... 50.00
Whodunit, Selchow & Righter, Board, 1972 .... 18.00
Winnie-The-Pooh, Parker Brothers, Board, 1933 .... 40.00
Witch-ee, Fortune Teller, Selchow & Righter Co., 1920s ....*Illus* 303.00
Wizard Of Oz, Cadaco, Board, 1974 ....20.00 to 55.00
Woody Woodpecker's Moon Dash, Whitman, Board, 1976 .... 20.00
Yogi Bear, Milton Bradley, Board, 1971 .... 30.00
Yogi Bear, Target, 1960s 15.00

Yogi Bear, Yogi & Boo-Boo, Milton Bradley, Box, 1980 .... 20.00

GAME PLATES are plates of any make decorated with pictures of birds, animals, or fish. The game plates usually came in sets consisting of twelve dishes and a serving platter. These sets were most popular during the 1880s.

Birds In Marsh, France, 10 In. 65.00
Duck, Flying From Water, Gold Irregular Edge, Limoges, 9 1/2 In. 110.00
Fish Set, Platter, 6 Plates, Different Fish Underwater Each Plate, Bavaria 1200.00
Stag In Woods, 12 In. 175.00
Trout Jumping, Blue & Gold Border, 10 In. 85.00

GARDEN FURNISHINGS have been popular for centuries. The stone or metal statues, wire, iron, or rustic furniture, urns and fountains, sundials, and small figurines are included in this category. Many of the metal pieces have been made continuously for years.

Aviary, Arched Roof, Scalloped Edge, Painted, Wire, 93 x 72 1/2 In. 2300.00
Bench, 3 Seat, Double-Sided, Foliate Scrolls, c.1900, 75 In. 2415.00
Bench, Backrest & Seat On Winged Lion Supports, Italian Marble, c.1900, 52 In. 13800.00
Bench, Biomorphic Design, Cast Iron 2310.00
Bench, Cast Iron, Scotland, 1850 .... 8700.00
Bench, Demilune Seat, Winged & Breasted Lion Supports, Marble, 41 1/4 In. 1610.00
Bench, Fern Design, Pierced Shaped Back, Lime Green Paint, Cast Iron, 36 In. 2310.00
Bench, Grain Painted, France 2050.00
Bench, Iron, Rococo, Rusted White Repaint, 45 In. 550.00
Bench, Laurel Leaf Pattern, Cast Iron 1900.00
Bench, Lion's Paw Supports, Stylized Dolphins & Acanthus, Marble, 60 In., Pair 10925.00
Bench, Shell, Foliate Design, C & S Scroll Form Base, Stone, 15 1/2 x 47 x 18 In. 288.00
Bench, Slatted Wood, Painted White 4200.00
Bench, Twisted Wire, Rusted White Paint, Victorian, 54 In. 245.00
Bench, Vintage Design, White, Cast Iron, Painted, 42 In. 440.00
Bird Bath, Alice In Wonderland, Concrete 225.00
Bird Bath, Figural, Female Figure, Topped By Dish, Stone, 33 1/2 In. 10300.00
Chair, Cast Iron, 27 1/4 In., 4 Piece 198.00
Chair, Fern Design, Cast Iron, Arms, James W. Carr, 29 3/4 In. 330.00
Chair, Fern Pattern, Arms, Iron 302.00
Chair, Fern, James W. Carr, Richmond, Va., Iron, 30 In. 412.00
Chair, Pierced Allover With Interlacing Scrolls, Cast Iron, Painted, Pair 575.00
Chair, Wire Work, Victorian, 48 In., Pair 1035.00
Chair Set, Pierced Back With Fruited Festoons, Center Medallion, Cast Iron, 4 .... 4025.00
Figure, Boy, Riding Snail, Bronze, 20th Century, 36 In. 1265.00
Figure, Child, Draped, Stone, 28 In. 460.00
Figure, Dancing Gardener, Lead, 60 In. 2875.00
Figure, Eagle's Head, Stone, 15 1/2 In. 977.00
Figure, Eagle, Wings Outstretched, Lead, 19 1/4 In. 690.00
Figure, Elf, Green Apron, Green Booties, Cast Iron, 1910, 27 In. 1100.00
Figure, Girl, Small Bird On Shoulder, Marble, 48 In. 2300.00
Figure, Grecian Female, With Flowers, Stone, 39 1/2 In. 489.00
Figure, Lion, Recumbent, Full Mane, Cast Iron, Painted, 41 In., Pair 3162.00
Figure, Lion, Seated On Hind Legs, Right Or Left, Marble, 19th Century, 16 In., Pair ... 3220.00
Figure, Maiden, Flowing Garment, Holding Bunch Of Flowers, Metal, 40 In. 2645.00
Figure, Modeled After Neptune, Stone, 41 In. 259.00
Figure, Putto, Reclining Beside Stylized Dolphin, Cast Iron, 15 1/2 In. 4887.00
Figure, Retriever, Reclining On Rectangular Base, Cast Iron, 42 In., Pair 9785.00
Figure, Sea Turtle, Cast Cement, 28 x 20 x 11 In. 467.00
Figure, St. Francis, Bird Resting In Hand, Lead, 20th Century, 19 In. 373.00
Figure, Swan, Swimming, Hinged Between Wings For Plant, Copper, 35 In. 8912.00
Figure, Venus, Cast Cement, 38 In. 90.00
Figure, Youth & Maiden, Sowing Seed, Semeose & Semeur, Cast Zinc, Paint, 40 In. 990.00
Fountain, Child Seated On Urn, Shell Form Bowl, Pump, Cement 192.00
Fountain, Dolphin Form, Mouth Plumbed For Water, Gilt Metal, 18 In. 2587.00
Fountain, Leaping Frog, Bronze, Mouth Plumbed For Water, 26 In. 3450.00
Fountain, Open Lotus Flower Form, Indian Marble, Drilled For Water, 41 In. 14950.00

Fountain, Seminude Female, Basin, Lower Smaller Basin, Cast Iron, c.1880, 58 In. 4600.00
Fountain, Wall, Shell Form Backplate, Dolphin, Plumbed For Water, Marble, 35 In. 8625.00
Gate, Border Of Flowering Scrolls, Squirrels & Birds, Wrought Iron, 72 x 56 In. 9200.00
Jardiniere, Formalized Whiplash Design, Hector Guimard, Iron, 1900, 39 3/4 In. 11655.00
Jardiniere, Loop Handles, Waisted Footed, Squaty, Iron, Hector Guimard, 1900, 23 In. .. 12745.00
Jardiniere, Lotus Form, Indian Marble, 12 In., Pair 4025.00
Jardiniere, Oval, Foliate Scrolled Handles, Bronze, 14 1/2 In., Pair 920.00
Mask, Lion, Open Mouth Plumbed For Water, Marble, 16 In. 3737.00
Ornament, Foo Dog, 31 In., Pair 1265.00
Pedestal, Lion Shape, Iron, White Paint, 23 x 42 In., Pair 825.00
Pedestal, Sundial, Acanthus Leaf Above Fluted Baluster, Italian Marble, 46 In. 6325.00
Pedestal, Tree Trunk Form, Allover Berry Vines, 1 Nesting Bird, Marble, 44 In. 5750.00
Plant Stand, Scroll Design, Wrought Iron, 51 1/4 In. 137.00
Planter, Cast Iron, Footed, Painted Black, Rectangular, 28 x 14 x 15 In., Pair 220.00
Planter, Circular Basket, Flower Heads, Scrolled Base, Wrought Iron, 25 1/2 In., Pair ... 1380.00
Planter, Folky Sphinx, Concrete, White Paint, 24 In., Pair 110.00
Planter, Roman Style, Cast Cement, 14 In., Pair 187.00
Planter, Rustic Wood, Adirondack 1850.00
Plinth, Fruit Designed Panels, Terra-Cotta, 28 In., Pair 1380.00
Seat, Blue, White Paint, Scrolled Foliage, Chinese Porcelain, 19 In. 345.00
Seat, Tree Surround, Demilune, Pierced Triple Arch Back, Slatted Seat, Wrought Iron ... 1150.00
Set, Bench, 2 Chairs, Central Star Medallion, Dolphin Support Arms, Teakwood Seat ... 2760.00
Settee, Fern, James W. Carr, Richmond Va., Cast Iron, 39 In. 660.00
Settee, Leaves, Grapes, Vines, Cast Iron, 38 In. 250.00
Settee, Pierced With Scrolls Within Floral Border, Cast Iron, Painted, 43 In., Pair 5462.00
Settee, Rustic Twig Pattern, Cast Iron 2695.00
Settee, Vintage, White, Cast Iron, 57 In. 165.00
Sprinkler, Claw Footed, Cast Iron 225.00
Sprinkler, Cowboy Twists Lariat When Water Turned On, Cast Iron, 32 In. 2950.00
Sprinkler, Duck Form, Cast Iron, Painted, 13 In. 805.00
Sprinkler, Frog On Ball Form, Cast Iron 1550.00
Sundial, Cast Bronze, Mounted On Clay Chimney Pot, 33 In. 220.00
Sundial, Lyre Form Back Plate, Tooled Brass Dial, 40 In. 545.00
Sundial, Thomas Wright Fecit, Square, 1748, 7 In. 550.00
Table, 6 Chairs, Plate-Glass Top, Acorn & Oak Leaf, Wrought Iron, 29 1/4 x 60 In. 412.00
Table, Dolphin Form, Glazed Terra-Cotta, Green & White, 25 In. 2070.00
Table, Reticulated Top, 4 Legs, White Paint, Cast Iron, 40 x 26 In. 110.00
Urn, Band Of Leaf Tips, Scrolled Handles, Swags On Base, Cast Iron, 56 1/2 In., Pair ... 3335.00
Urn, Campana Form, Satyr Mask, Loop Handles, Terra-Cotta, 31 In. 5175.00
Urn, Foliate Relief Design, Stone, 23 1/2 In. 145.00
Urn, Lion's Head Handles, Cast Iron, Black Paint, 24 x 19 In., Pair 665.00
Urn, Relief Swags, Lion's Heads, Cast Iron, Black Paint, 24 x 17 1/2 In., Pair 660.00
Urn, Rococo Floral, Iron, Graff Hugus & Co., Pittsburgh, Green Paint, 24 In., Pair 605.00

GAUDY DUTCH pottery was made in England for America from about
1810 to 1820. It is a white earthenware with Imari-style decorations of
red, blue, green, yellow, and black. Only sixteen patterns of Gaudy
Dutch were made: Butterfly, Carnation, Dahlia, Double Rose, Dove,
Grape, Leaf, Oyster, Primrose, Single Rose, Strawflower, Sunflower,
Urn, War Bonnet, Zinnia, and No Name. Other similar wares are called
Gaudy Ironstone and *Gaudy Welsh*.

Coffeepot, Dome Cover, Single Rose 3025.00
Creamer, Dove 1150.00
Cup & Saucer, Grape 247.00
Cup & Saucer, Handleless, Butterfly ....495.00 to 660.00
Cup & Saucer, Handleless, Single Rose ....330.00 to 533.00
Cup & Saucer, Saucer Is Carnation, Cup Is Grape 192.00
Cup & Saucer, Single Rose, Pair 852.00
Cup & Saucer, Sunflower 357.00
Cup & Saucer, War Bonnet ....247.00 to 395.00
Pitcher, Cream, Double Rose, 4 x 5 1/2 In. 1073.00
Plate, Butterfly, 8 3/8 In. 385.00
Plate, Double Rose, 8 1/4 In. 577.00

❦

**If you are remodeling or
redecorating, think about
antiques and collectibles
displayed in the work area.
A workman will hammer on a
wall without worrying about
the shelves on the other side.**

❦

Gaudy
Ironstone,
Plate,
Rabbits &
Trees
Border, Rim

Plate, Double Rose, 10 In.	935.00
Plate, Dove, 7 1/2 In.	770.00
Plate, Grape, 6 1/4 In.	577.00
Plate, Grape, 9 3/4 In.	1045.00
Plate, Oyster, 7 1/2 In.	523.00
Plate, Sunflower, 10 In.	1100.00
Plate, Urn, 8 1/4 In.	1100.00
Plate, War Bonnet, 5 1/4 In.	660.00
Plate, War Bonnet, 8 1/2 In.	650.00 to 880.00
Soup, Dish, Double Rose, 9 3/4 In.	1595.00
Soup, Dish, War Bonnet	1600.00
Teapot, Dove, C Handle	8000.00
Teapot, Oyster	3000.00
Teapot, War Bonnet	3300.00

GAUDY IRONSTONE is the collector's name for the ironstone wares
with the bright patterns similar to Gaudy Dutch. It was made in
England for the American market. There may be other examples found
in the listing for Ironstone or under the name of the ceramic factory.

Bowl, Floral, Villeroy & Boch, 8 In.	44.00
Bowl, Red Roses, Green Leaves, Gold, Cobalt Rim, 10 1/2 In.	185.00
Chop Plate, 9 Rabbits, 4 Frogs, Black Transfer Flowers, 12 3/4 In.	990.00
Pitcher, Lion Head Snake Handle, Mason, 7 1/2 In.	330.00
Plate, 6 Rabbits, 3 Frogs, Black Transfer Flowers, 9 3/8 In.	467.00
Plate, 8 Rabbits, Black Transfer, Circular Design In Center, 9 3/8 In.	350.00
Plate, 9 Rabbits, 3 Cabbages, 3 Frogs & 3 Trees, 9 3/8 In.	385.00
Plate, Floral, Staffordshire, 1825, 8 In.	22.00
Plate, Floral, Stick Spatter, Yellow Zig-Zag Border, Red, Blue, 10 In.	165.00 to 182.00
Plate, Morning Glory, Blue & Green, 8 1/2 In., Pair	440.00
Plate, Rabbit Transfer, Brown, Stick Spatter, Yellow Floral Border, 9 1/4 In.	385.00
Plate, Rabbits & Trees Border, Rim ....*Illus*	253.00
Plate, Urn Pattern, 8 5/8 In., Set Of 6	869.00
Platter, Blue Floral Transfer, Polychrome Enamel, 12 3/4 In.	313.00
Platter, Dark Blue Oriental Floral Transfer, 11 7/8 In.	154.00
Platter, Floral Border, Medallion With Insect, 21 3/4 x 17 1/4 In.	160.00
Platter, Floral Design, Yellow Transfer, Black Enameling, 13 In.	385.00
Platter, Medallion With Insect, Floral Border, 21 3/4 x 17 1/4 In.	176.00

GAUDY WELSH is an Imari-decorated earthenware with red, blue,
green, and gold decorations. Most Gaudy Welsh was made in England
for the American market. It was made after 1820.

Biscuit Jar, Sponged Floral Design, Silver Plated Fittings, 5 3/4 In.	93.00
Cup & Saucer, Columbine	75.00
Pitcher, Oyster, 3 3/4 In.	65.00
Plate, Polychrome & Luster, 9 1/4 x 10 In., Pair	330.00
Plate, Tulip, 5 x 6 In., 4 Piece	40.00
Platter, Tree & Well, Urn, Flower Pattern, Blue, 21 1/2 In.	550.00

Tea Set, 18 Piece	525.00
Tea Set, Child's, Oyster, 1870, 6 Piece	2800.00
Tea Set, Oyster, c.1900, 3 Piece	150.00

GEISHA GIRL porcelain was made for export in the late nineteenth century in Japan. It was an inexpensive porcelain often sold in dime stores or used as free premiums. Pieces are sometimes marked with the name of a store. Japanese ladies in kimonos are pictured on the dishes. There are over 125 recorded patterns. Borders of red, blue, green, gold, brown, or several of these colors were used. Modern reproductions are being made.

Chocolate Set, Beaded Design, 7 Piece	235.00
Creamer	20.00
Cup, Chocolate, 5 Piece	165.00
Mustard	22.00
Sugar	22.00

GENE AUTRY was born in 1907. He began his career as the *Singing Cowboy* in 1928. His first movie appearance was in 1934, his last in 1958. His likeness and that of the Wonder Horse, Champion, were used on toys, books, lunch boxes, and advertisements.

Book, 30 Cowboy Songs, 1932	35.00
Book, Better Little Book, Gene Serenading Champion, Whitman, 1943	52.00
Book, Coloring, Whitman, 1951, 12 x 15 In.	43.00
Book, Comic, Champion, No. 14, 1954, 10 Cents	10.00
Book, Comic, Dell, No. 44	27.00
Book, Comic, Dell, No. 65	25.00
Book, Comic, No. 86, 1954	15.00
Book, Gene Autry Cowboy Songs, 1932	25.00
Book, Ghost Riders, Whitman, 1955	20.00
Book, Sgt. Gene Songbook	35.00
Cap Gun, Cast Iron, Pistol Grip Handle	35.00
Cap Gun, Goldtone, Box, Leslie Henry, 9 1/2 In.	165.00 to 375.00
Clock, With Horse, Electric	200.00
Cookie Jar	300.00
Doll, Portrait, Plastic, Open Mouth, Rodeo Outfit, Terri Lee, 1950-51, 16 In.	3100.00
Guitar, Melody Ranch, 1950s	225.00
Neckerchief, Square, 1995, 21 1/2 In.	10.00
Pencil Sharpener	5.00
Photograph, Gene Autry With Horse, Autographed, 8 x 10 In.	175.00
Puzzle, Jigsaw	25.00
Record, Album, Western Classics, Columbia, 78 RPM, 1947	45.00
Record, Peter Cottontail, 45 RPM, Columbia, 1950	8.00
Sheet Music, I'm Oscar-I'm Pete, Phantom Empire, 5 Movie Scenes, 1935	15.00
Sheet Music, Poison Ivy, 1950	15.00
Sheet Music, Songs & Scenes, Republic Pictures, Western Music, 1940, 15 Pages	30.00
Song Book, 95 Pages, 1938	35.00
Thermos, For Lunch Box	160.00 to 185.00
Watch, Six-Shooter	225.00
You're The Only Star, Picture Of Autry On Cover, 1938	7.00

GIBSON GIRL black-and-blue decorated plates were made in the early 1900s. Twenty-four different 10 1/2-inch plates were made by the Royal Doulton pottery at Lambeth, England. These pictured scenes from the book *A Widow and Her Friends* by Charles Dana Gibson. Another set of twelve 9-inch plates featuring pictures of the heads of Gibson Girls had all-blue decoration. Many other items also pictured the famous Gibson Girl.

Creamer	75.00 to 85.00
Plate, Calendar, 1909, 10 1/2 In.	35.00
Plate, Failing To Find Rest In The Country	125.00
Plate, Miss Babbles Brings A Copy	125.00 to 140.00
Plate, She Goes To The Fancy Dress Ball	115.00

GILLINDER pressed glass was first made by William T. Gillinder of Philadelphia in 1863. The company had a working factory on the grounds at the Centennial and made small, marked pieces of glass for sale as souvenirs. They made a variety of decorative glass pieces and tablewares.

GILLINDER

Mug, Historical, Bell Shape, Camel Handle 150.00

GIRL SCOUT collectors search for anything pertaining to the Girl Scouts, including uniforms, publications, and old cookie boxes. The Girl Scout movement started in 1912, two years after the Boy Scouts. It began under Juliette Gordon Low of Savannah, Georgia. The first Girl Scout cookies were sold in 1928.

Blouse, Khaki, Dark Bronze Finish Buttons, GS Collar Insignia, 2 Pockets 45.00
Book, Little Woodcrafter's Book, Doran Co., 1917 .... 14.00
Book, Song, Pocket, 1956 .... 20.00
Book, Woodcraft Girls At Camp, 1916 .... 16.00
Calendar, 1934, Hintermeister, 11 x 23 In. 225.00
Calendar, 1948 .... 22.00
Catalog, 1940 .... 35.00
Catalog, Girl Scout Equipment, Uniforms, Supplies, 1960, 40 Pages 25.00
Compact, Brass, Green & White Trefoil, Unused, Pilcher, 1950s, 3 1/4 In. 115.00
Compass, Taylor, Box, 1930s 35.00
Doll, Brownie Scout, Plastic, Vinyl Head, Brownie Outfit, 1950s, 8 In. 65.00
Doll, Extra Brownie Clothes, Effanbee, 1950s, 8 In. 60.00
Guide, Leader's, Brownie Scout Program, Hard Cover, 1950 .... 3.00
Handbook, Girl Scout, Inc., National Headquarters, Reprinted 1932 .... 18.00
Handbook, Hard Cover, 1959 .... 3.00
Hat, Senior Scout, Patch, Pin, 1943 .... 20.00
Jacket, Pantaloons, Scout Leader, Twill, Tan, Metal Buttons, Size Medium 60.00
Kit, First Aid, Metal Box, Johnson & Johnson 20.00
Knife, Celluloid Grips, Brownie Logo, Safety Verse, Kutmaster, 5 1/2 In. 25.00
Knife, Green 2.50
Knife, Pocket, Utica, Featherweight, Black Plastic Grips, Double Bladed, 3 1/4 In. 26.00
Pin, Brownie Girl On It 18.00
Pin, Wing, Wing Scout Pilot Rating, Silver Colored, Pinback, 1 1/4 In. 152.00
Record, 12,000 Girls Sing 8 National Favorites, 45 Size, 33 RPM., 1965 .... 12.00
Spoon, Sterling Silver 22.00
Thermos, Plastic, 1970 .... 25.00
Trophy, Copper, Plastic Base, 1965 .... 10.00
Uniform, 3 Merit Badges On Sleeve, 1920s 225.00
Uniform, Blue & White, Zipper Neck, Green Emblem On Collar, Medallion, 1940s 45.00
Uniform, Dress, Belt, Buckle, Beret, 2 Scarves, 3 Patches On Sleeve, Late 1950s 23.00
Uniform, Pins, Stars, Badges, Tie, 1953 .... 45.00

GLASS-ART. Art glass means any of the many forms of glassware made during the late nineteenth or early twentieth century. These wares were expensive and production was limited. Art glass is not the typical commercial glass that was made in large quantities, and most of the art glass was produced by hand methods. Later twentieth-century glass is listed under Glass-Contemporary, Glass-Midcentury, or Glass-Venetian. Even more art glass may be found in categories such as Burmese, Cameo Glass, Tiffany, Venini, and other factory names.

Basket, Amber, Cream & Brown Spatter, Gold, Cranberry, 4 1/2 x 6 1/2 In. 355.00
Basket, Cackle Exterior, Blue Interior, V-Shaped Thorn Handle, 7 1/2 In. 143.00
Basket, Clear, Loop Pink & White Latticinio Stripes Handle, Footed, 8 3/4 In. 850.00
Basket, Diamond Quilted, Blue Satin, Applied Frosted Foot & Thorn Handle, 10 In. 400.00
Basket, Pink, Yellow Spatter, White Interior, Clear Thorn Handle, 6 x 6 1/2 In. 250.00
Basket, Spatter, White Interior, Clear Thorn Handle, Rectangular, 6 1/2 x 6 In. 250.00
Biscuit Jar, Black, Purple & White Slag, Wood Finial, 4 1/2 x 8 3/4 In. 310.00
Bowl, Barber's, White Enameled Stylized Leaves, Green Base, 7 1/2 x 5 1/2 In. 750.00
Bowl, Gold, Blue Oil Drop Pattern, Ruffled Rim, 1900, 2 1/2 x 7 In. 120.00
Bowl, Green Opaque, Agata Stained, Victorian, 8 x 4 In. 1150.00
Bowl, Hand Painted Beetle In Base, Cobalt Blue Rim, 9 3/4 In. 190.00

Bowl, Sapphire Blue, Icicle, Victorian, 4 x 8 In. 875.00
Candlestick, Green Iridescent, Molded Stretch Glass, c.1920s, 9 1/2 In., Pair 90.00
Candy Dish, Cover, Yellow Vertical Stripes, Fachschule Haida, 7 1/2 x 6 5/8 In. 820.00
Carafe, Pinch, Purple, R. Tahm, 1971, 9 In. 55.00
Decanter, Amber, Cobalt Blue, Paperweight, 10 1/4 In. 150.00
Decanter, Liquor, Diving Helmet, Copper Colored Glass 34.00
Ewer, Latticinio, Blue, White & Clear, 8 In. 150.00
Flask, Latticinio, Pink, Green, White & Yellow Canes, c.1850, 3 1/2 In. 495.00
Jug, Claret, Periwinkle Blue, Optic Pattern, Hinged Pewter Cover & Handle, 13 In. 225.00
Pitcher, Gilt Floral Motif, Ruby Handle, Base, 8 In. 210.00
Pitcher, Molded Ribbed Design, Light Brown To Yellow, Green Handle, 7 1/2 In. 250.00
Pitcher Set, Green To Purple, Enameled Floral, Applied Green Handle, 3 Piece 850.00
Place Cards, Hostess, Mirrored, Raised Floral Design, 8 Piece 20.00
Punch Set, Enameled Blossoms, Rib-Molded Bowl, Cupped Pedestal, Ladle, 6 Piece ... 260.00
Rose Bowl, Opal, Crystal Feet, Crimped Pink Rim, 4 1/2 x 5 1/4 In. 285.00
Urn, Iridescent Ultramarine, Round Foot, Flared, American, 10 1/4 In. 600.00
Vase, 3 Applied Cherries, Gold Favrile, Pinched & Threaded Sides, 7 1/4 In. 635.00
Vase, Amber Opalescent, Slender Standard, American, 11 3/4 x 5 1/2 In. 825.00
Vase, Amber, Blue Applied Pattern, Cylindrical, 6 1/4 In. 360.00
Vase, Amber, Green, Red Iridescent, Signed, 1 3/4 In. 525.00
Vase, Amethyst Shaded To Green, Allover Enameled Floral, Applied Handles, 4 In. 375.00
Vase, Applied Blue Button, Black Gridlines, Signed, 5 1/2 x 4 In. 145.00
Vase, Applied Blue Snake, Button Design, Orange, Yellow, Cylindrical, 4 1/2 x 4 In. 935.00
Vase, Baluster Shape, Leaf Green Feathers, Pinched Rim, Harrach, c.1900, 15 In. 2300.00
Vase, Blue & Cranberry, Applied Feet, White Enamel, Gold Trim, 9 In. 110.00
Vase, Blue Opalescent, Pillar Mold, Presentation, Gilt, Scalloped, Pontil, 9 1/2 In. 10230.00
Vase, Bud, Green, Purple Iridescent, 5 1/2 In. 84.00
Vase, Clear, Black Enameled Neck, White Dot Border, Handles, Vienna, 1920s, 11 In. ... 1780.00
Vase, Clear, Frosted Lion Frieze, Otto Hoffner, J. & L. Lobmeyr, c.1905, 7 In. 985.00
Vase, Clear, Gold Leaf Handles, Flower Band Murrhina, 1930s, 8 In. 605.00
Vase, Cylindrical, Iridescent, Wilhelm Kralik Sohn, c.1905, 10 3/8 In. 1150.00
Vase, Enameled Birds & Water Lilies, Bohemia, c.1880, 6 1/4 In. 750.00
Vase, Floral Cut To Clear, Crenelated Rim, St. Louis, c.1860, 8 In. 550.00
Vase, Free-Form Rim, Blue, Red, Beige, Aqua, Deep Purple Stripes, Italy, 7 x 5 In. 1265.00
Vase, Gold, Brown Pulled String Motif, Ruffled Rim, Flared Base, 6 1/2 In. 220.00
Vase, Green Foliate Border, Red Iridescent, 3 1/2 In. 3050.00
Vase, Green, Internal Blue, Yellow & Amber Swirls, Flat Sides, Medina, 1948, 8 In. 145.00
Vase, Green, Oil Drop Pattern, Bulbous, 5 1/2 In. 72.00
Vase, Heavy Crystal, Yellow Butterflies, Blue Leaves, Enamel Dots, 8 In. 310.00
Vase, Iridescent Trailings, Gilt Metal Mount, Open Work, Austria, 25 In. 4370.00
Vase, Olympia, Green Stained, 3 Applied Handles, Josef Hoffman, 1900, 7 3/8 In. 2465.00
Vase, Peacock On Branch, Hand Painted, Gilt Rim, Victorian, 12 In., Pair 86.00
Vase, Pulled Feather Design, Amber, Green, Marked, 5 In. 1550.00
Vase, Ruby Iridescent, Silver Heart, Thread Design, 6 In. 135.00
Vase, Serpentine Design, Gunnel Nyman, 1947 .... 1800.00
Vase, Trumpet, Orange, Brown, Yellow Design, Inscribed Foot, Schneider, 15 1/2 In. 1380.00
Vase, Trumpet, Red, White, Opalescent Green, Stem Base, Fluted, 11 In. 60.00

GLASS-BLOWN was formed by forcing air through a rod into molten
glass. Early glass and some forms of art glass were hand blown. Other
types of glass were molded or pressed.

Bottle, 24 Swirled Ribs, Honey Amber, Kent, 5 In. 1210.00
Bottle, Blue, Rope Of Blue Glass Coiled At Neck, 16 x 6 In. 35.00
Bottle, Engraved Floral & Brandy, 3 Applied Rings, 9 1/2 In. 60.00
Bottle, Ludlow, Green, Applied Lip, 8 1/2 In. 200.00
Bottle, Swirled To Left, Globular, Outward Rolled Mouth, 1820-1840, 8 1/2 In. 715.00
Bowl, 3-Piece Mold, Diamond Pattern, Rayed Base, 7 1/4 x 2 1/4 In. 25.00
Bowl, Amber, 3 3/8 x 2 3/8 In. 355.00
Bowl, Green, Applied Foot, Hollow Stem, 12 7/8 In. 95.00
Bowl, Green, Folded Lip, 3 1/2 x 2 3/4 In. 715.00
Bowl, Light Green, Applied Foot, Folded Rim, 7 1/4 x 4 7/8 In. 1650.00
Bowl, Milk, Pale Yellow, Folded Rim, 9 1/2 x 3 In. 2090.00
Canister, Cover, Clear, 2 Applied Blue Rings, Blue Finial, 10 In. 605.00

Celery Vase, Etched Vines, Acorn & Foliate, Ball Knop Stem, 1820, 8 3/8 In. 517.00
Celery Vase, Etched Vines, Swag & Florals, Paneled Base, 7 1/2 In. 977.00
Compote, Applied Foot, Baluster Stem, Roundels, Pittsburgh, 9 x 7 In. 82.50
Compote, Dark Green, Applied Foot & Baluster Stem, 5 1/2 x 2 3/4 In. 715.00
Compote, Emerald Green, 9 3/4 x 5 1/4 In., Pair 250.00
Compote, Green, Applied Foot, Hollow Stem, 11 1/4 x 6 3/4 In. 440.00
Compote, Olive Green, Applied Foot, Baluster Stem, 5 x 4 5/8 In. 220.00
Compote, Swirled Violet & Amethyst, Applied Foot & Stem, 7 1/2 x 6 1/2 In. 7700.00
Condiment Jar, Notched Lid, Sterling Rim, 4 3/4 In. 140.00
Creamer, 8 Swirled Ribs, Applied Foot & Handle, 3 5/8 In. 245.00
Creamer, Applied Foot & Handle, Hollow Stem, 5 In. 465.00
Creamer, Aqua, Applied Hollow Handle, Tooled Lip, 4 3/4 In. 2475.00
Cuspidor, Amber, With Witch's Ball Cover, 5 1/2 In. 220.00
Decanter, Applied Rings & White Looping, Applied Foot, Stopper, 8 1/8 In. 495.00
Decanter, Applied Triple Neck Rings, Wafer Stopper, Flint, Polished Pontil 110.00
Decanter, Cut Panels & Diamonds, Star Cut Base, Stopper, 9 5/8 In. 110.00
Decanter, Cut Panels & Star Base, 3 Applied Rings, Flared Lip, Stopper, 7 In. 65.00
Decanter, Cut Panels, Circles & Fans, 3 Applied Rings, Stopper, 8 3/8 In. 40.00
Decanter, Molded, Stopper, Porcelain Liquor Label, 19th Century, 14 In., Pair 100.00
Decanter, Pillar Mold, Cobalt Blue, Applied Handle, Pewter Jigger Cap, 10 In. 7920.00
Decanter, Swag & Tassel, 8 In. 195.00
Egg, Darning 70.00
Fish Bowl, Victorian, c.1860, 8 In. 425.00
Fly Trap, 3 Feet, Deep Green, 8 1/8 In. 185.00
Goblet, Emerald Green, 1760, 4 5/8 In., Pair 450.00
Goblet, Red & Cotton Twist, Latticinio, 5 5/8 In. 220.00
Horn, Opalescent Looping, 11 1/2 In. 275.00
Hourglass, Pine & Oak Frame, Whittled Baluster Posts, 7 In. 275.00
Jar, Cover, Amber, Applied Foot, Egg Shape Bowl, 7 7/8 In. 1210.00
Jar, Storage, Tin Lid, Late 1800s, 9 1/4 In. 225.00
Lamp Shade, Bell Shape, Aqua, Gold Spattering, Hanging 55.00
Mug, Aqua, Applied Handle, 5 1/2 In. 1155.00
Pitcher, Applied Foot & Hollow Handle, Pittsburgh, 7 1/2 In. 220.00
Pitcher, Applied Handle, Ruffled Edge, Amber, 9 1/4 In. 60.00
Pitcher, Applied Handle, Silver Overlay, Foliate Motif, 8 1/4 In. 115.00
Pitcher, Applied Ring & Hollow Handle, Pittsburgh, 8 3/8 In. 385.00
Pitcher, Cobalt Blue, Applied Hollow Handle, Tooled Lip, 8 In. 3080.00
Pitcher, Lily Pad Design, Bulbous, Golden Amber, 1840, 5 1/2 In. 7700.00
Pitcher, Lily Pad, Light Green, Applied Foot & Handle, Ellenville, N.Y., 7 3/4 In. 4400.00
Pitcher, Pink, White Overlay, Applied Handle, 8 In. 160.00
Pokal, Cover, Engraved, Cranberry Twist In Stem, 10 1/2 In. 143.00
Rolling Pin, A Token Of Love, 1866, 30 1/2 In. 650.00
Smoke Bell, Cranberry, Clear Applied Ring, Pontil, 1850-1870, 7 1/8 In. 440.00
Smoke Bell, Pink, Milk Glass & Clear, Ruffled Rim, 1860-1890, 3 3/8 In. 330.00
Sugar, Cover, Aqua, Gallery, Applied Finial, Folded Lip, 5 3/4 In. 5500.00
Sugar, Flange Lid, Plain Finial, Cobalt Blue, 1780s, 5 3/4 In. 517.00
Sugar, Light Green, Swan Finial On Lid, Square Base, Double Handles, 7 3/8 In. 6050.00
Sugar, Yellow Green, Applied Foot, Bulbous, Folded Lip, 3 1/4 In. 115.00
Sweetmeat Jar, Cover, Applied Cobalt Rings, 10 In., Pair 460.00
Vase, Amethyst, 12 Molded Panels, Flared Lip, Open Blister, 8 In. 5500.00
Vase, Aqua, Lily Pad, Applied Handles, Threaded Neck, 8 In. 330.00
Vase, Clear, Cranberry Looping Cased In White, Applied Foot, 11 1/8 In. 1705.00
Vase, Enameled, Woman & Cherub, Fireglow, Mid-19th Century, 15 In., Pair 154.00
Vase, Floral Design, Mandarin, Signed, 3 1/2 In. 425.00
Vase, Looped Design, Ruby Red Band On Rim, Footed, 8 In. 3680.00
Vase, Pinch, Amber, Signed, 1 1/2 In. 125.00
Vase, Pink & White Spatter Base, Green Acid-Etched Neck, Gilt, 10 In. 192.00
Vase, Ribbed Features, Ruffled Edge, Amber, Signed, 2 1/4 In. 175.00
Vase, Trumpet, Amethyst, 3 Knop Stem With Wafers, Pontil, 12 1/2 In. 2750.00
Vase, Trumpet, Amethyst, Baluster Stem With Wafers, Folded Lip, 9 In. 1980.00
Vase, Trumpet, Cobalt Blue, Applied Foot & Stem, Ruffled Edge, 12 1/4 In. 4730.00
Vase, Trumpet, Opaque White, Red Looping Bowl, Footed, Ruffled Edge, 9 In. 1375.00
Vase, Trumpet, Peacock Green, 3 Knop Stem With Wafers, Folded Lip, 13 In. 3410.00

Vial, Sapphire Blue, White Combed Swirls, Pewter Cap, 2 1/2 In. 2365.00
Witch's Ball, Clear, White Coin Spots, 1870-1890 . . . . 80.00
Witch's Ball, Cobalt Blue, Pulled Feather, 10 In. 75.00
Witch's Ball, Cobalt Blue, White Spattered, Open Pontil, 4 7/8 In. 195.00
Witch's Ball, Light Green, 1870-1890 . . . . 45.00
Witch's Ball, Stand, Opalescent White Looping, Sheared Mouth, Rim, Pontil, 14 In. 825.00
Witch's Ball, Wig Stand, Cobalt Blue, 5 1/4 x 11 1/8 In. 300.00
Witch's Ball & Stand, Amber, 7 x 5 x 12 In. 1155.00

GLASS-CONTEMPORARY includes pieces by glass artists working after 1975. Many of these pieces are free-form, one-of-a-kind sculptures. Paperweights by contemporary artists are listed in the Paperweight category. Earlier studio glass may be found listed under Glass-Midcentury or Glass-Venetian.

Aquarium Block, 3 Fish, Cenedese, 5 x 8 1/4 In. 605.00
Bowl, Clear, Red & Opalescent Loops, Signed Gary C. Rhiel, 4 In. 55.00
Chalice, Twisted Air Stem, Light Green, c.1968 . . . . 1900.00
Figurine, Indian Squaw, Crystal, 10 In. 230.00
Sculpture, Blue Band Fused, Tom Patti, 1987, 2 3/8 In. 1955.00
Vase, Amber, Yellow Fronds, Labino, 1983 . . . . 900.00
Vase, Blue, Silver, Pulled Feather Design, Signed, Warren, 1979, 5 In. 2310.00
Vase, Cased, Yellow Putty & Clear, Signed Marty Christy '80, 4 7/8 In. 85.00
Vase, Conical Body, Applied Black Rim, Yellow, Tagliapietra, 1985, 10 In. 825.00
Vase, Green Waves, 5 1/2 x 5 In. 143.00
Vase, Loop Design, Iridescent Gold, 7 1/2 In. 60.00
Vase, Opaque, Red & Blue Looping, Cased, Halem, Kent, Ohio, 1974, 4 7/8 In. 40.00
Vase, Orange-Red, Yellow & Opalescent Swirls, Signed Baker, 1982, 7 In. 195.00
Vase, Pinch Design, Smeltz, 1979 . . . . 600.00
Vase, Yellow Festoons, Labino, 1980, 5 1/4 In. 700.00

GLASS-MIDCENTURY refers to art glass made from the 1950s to the 1980s. Some glass factories, such as Baccarat or Orrefors, are listed under their own categories. Earlier glass may be listed in the Glass-Art and Glass-Contemporary categories. Italian glass may be found under Venini and Glass-Venetian.

Ashtray, Birds, Higgins, 14 1/2 x 12 In. 145.00
Bowl, Blue Edge, Battuto, De Santillana, c.1960, 5 x 3 In. 275.00
Bowl, Cobalt Blue, Aventurine Swirl Interior, Signed, Vizner, 3 x 18 In. 385.00
Bowl, Gold & Pink Petals, Peacock Feather Ground, Higgins, 5 In. 715.00
Bowl, White Luster, Ocher, Smokey Gray Ground, Higgins, 3 1/2 x 12 In. 140.00
Compote, Amethyst Twist, Blenko, Large 40.00
Pitcher, Deep Blue Body, Label, Kaj Franck, 1960s, 9 In. 300.00
Tumbler, Cranberry Flashed, Gold, Georges Briard, 6 3/4 In., Set Of 7 . . . . 30.00
Tumbler, Heavy Gold Scroll, Georges Briard, 5 5/8 In., Set Of 6 . . . . 50.00
Urn, Everted Lip, Circular Body, Square Base, Sweden, 7 1/4 x 10 1/2 In. 3162.00
Vase, Crimson Lines, Orange Ground, Higgins, 4 x 6 In. 275.00
Vase, Kantarelli, Flared, Vertical Lines, 1956, Tapio Wirkkala Iittala, 9 In. 1100.00
Vase, Opaque Orange Bottle Form, Kaj Franck, 1960s, 7 In. 330.00
Wall Pocket, Fin-Shaped Dangle, Brass Hanger, Orange, Higgins, 35 x 7 In. 360.00
Wall Pocket, Leaf-Shaped Dangles, Brass Hanger, Cobalt Blue, Higgins 360.00

GLASS-VENETIAN. Venetian glass has been made near Venice, Italy, since the thirteenth century. Thin, colored glass with applied decoration is favored, although many other types have been made. Collectors have recently become interested in the Art Deco and 1950s designs. Glass was made on the Venetian island of Murano from 1291. The output dwindled in the late seventeenth century but began to flourish again in the 1850s. Some of the old techniques of glassmaking were revived, and firms today make traditional designs and original modern glass. Since 1981, the name *Murano* may only be used on glass made on Murano Island. Other pieces of Italian glass may be found in the Glass-Contemporary, Glass-Midcentury, and Venini categories of this book.

Ashtray, Purple, Bubbles, Paper Label, 5 In. 20.00

Ashtray, Red, Gold Flecks, Paper Label, Individual 25.00
Ashtray, Scattered Cane Pieces, 4 1/2 In. 25.0C
Block, 3 Internal Fish & Seaweed, Clear, Cenedese, 1950s, 4 x 9 In. 330.00
Bottle, Blue, Green, Clear Stripes, Flat Stopper, Canne, 13 1/2 x 3 1/2 In. 935.00
Bottle, Conical Body, Yellow, Black, Yellow Conical Stopper, 1950, 14 In. 825.0C
Bottle, Latticinio Glass, Spherical Stopper, Fratelli Toso, 13 In., Pair 770.00
Bottle, White & Gray Vertical Canes, Ball Stopper, Fratelli Toso, 1950s, 18 In. 220.0C
Bottle, Yellow, Black, Yellow Conical Stopper, 1950s, 19 In. 1210.00
Bowl, 3 Layers, Red, Pearl, Crystal, Shallow, 1925, 7 In. 230.00
Bowl, Center, Flowered Stem, Yellow Body, Blue Borders, 4 1/4 x 12 1/4 In. 60.00
Bowl, Owl Form, Light Green Body, Red Stars, Cenedese, 1960, 13 x 4 In. 220.00
Bowl, Pink, White, Gold Dust Latticinio, Ribbon Canes, Zanfirico, Fratelli Toso 150.00
Bowl, Wavy Rim, Flaring Eggplant Sommerso, Flavio Poli, 5 x 15 In. 1100.00
Bowl, White, Internal Patches, Dino Martens, AVEM, 1950s, 10 x 3 In. 230.00
Carafe, Pink & Orange, Fratelli Toso, 8 In. 192.00
Card Holder, Swan, Gold Flecked, 8 3/4 In. 172.00
Cigarette Holder, Gold Flecked, Aqua Interior, Scalloped Edge 35.00
Compote, Dolphins, Amber, Gold Trim, 8 In. 175.00
Decanter, Cobalt Blue, Paper Label, Pair 95.00
Dish, Green Zanfirico Caning, 7 In. 195.00
Dish, Pink & White Latticinio, Salviati, c.1920, 11 14/ In. 137.00
Figure, Musketeer, Opaque White, Black, Green, Gold Leaf, Murano, 11 In. 275.00
Figurine, Dancer, Pink & Blue Gold Foil Skirt, Seguso, 13 In. 880.00
Figurine, Dog, Red Controlled Bubbles, Amber Ears & Tail, Gold Trim, 8 In. 295.00
Figurine, Duck, Emerald To Apple Green, Gold Flecks, 10 In. 115.00
Figurine, Fish, Clear, White, Black, Murano, 9 7/8 x 2 1/8 In. 150.00
Figurine, Pheasant, Raised Tail, Multicolored, Gold Speckles, Murano, 16 In. 125.00
Figurine, Road Runner, White & Gold, Yellow, 13 1/2 In. 77.00
Figurine, Woman, Period Costume, Latticinio Caning, Gold Foil Overall, 9 In. 220.00
Goblet, Blue, White, Swan-Shape Stem, Gilt, Enameled Design, 3 In., 6 Piece 605.00
Paperweight, Orange, Yellow, Cialde, 1960s, 5 In. 220.00
Paperweight, White, Cobalt Murrine Band, Light Blue Sommerso, 6 x 3 In. 470.00
Plate, Red Opaque, Ludovico Diaz De Santillana, c.1960, 8 In. 8250.00
Salt, Master, Swan Form, Green, Gold, 19th Century, 3 In., Pair 120.00
Sculpture, Bull, Iridescent, Deep Amethyst, Label, Ermanno Nason, 1972, 7 In. 240.00
Swizzle Sticks, Parrot 50.00
Vase, Abstract Bivalve Form, Amethyst, Seguso, 1954, 6 5/8 In. 1265.00
Vase, Anse Volante, Green, 3 Pulled Holes, Iridescent, Ferro, Avem, 1952, 11 In. 935.00
Vase, Applied Handles, Blue Money Pouch, Fratelli Toso, 5 1/2 x 5 In. 165.00
Vase, Applied Handles, Bulbous, Vetri Scavo, 7 x 6 In. 357.50
Vase, Applied Spheres On Each Shoulder, Red Trails, Barbini, 1960, 10 In. 575.00
Vase, Black Body, Applied Red Scalloped Handles, Martinuzzi, 1932, 8 In. 1760.00
Vase, Black Body, Mica Flecks, Applied Curled Handles, Martinuzzi, 13 In. 770.00
Vase, Black Body, Red Circle Murrine, Scalloped, Ribbon Handles, Toso, 10 In. 1210.00
Vase, Black Body, Vertical Ribs, Appied Red Handles, Martinuzzi, 11 In. 4675.00
Vase, Black, Red, Fratelli Toso, 1950s, 7 In. 220.00
Vase, Black, White Pioggia Stripes, 1950, 8 3/4 In. 1380.00
Vase, Blue Body, Gold Leaf, Ribbon Handles, Barovier & Toso, 11 In. 440.00
Vase, Blue, Gold Accents, 4-Sided, Cenedese, 7 1/2 In. 80.00
Vase, Blue, White, Orange, Murrine, Rotellato, Barovier & Toso, 1969, 11 In. 5500.00
Vase, Bulbous Form, Cobalt Blue, Handles, Acid Etched, Seguso Soffiato, 11 In. 1150.00
Vase, Classic Shape, Green & White Spiraling Canes, F. Toso, 13 In. 330.00
Vase, Clear To Deep Amber, Frosted, Square, Murano, 1950s, 10 In. 275.00
Vase, Clear, Blue Internal Layer, Canes, Cenedese, Bianconi, Square, 1958, 5 In. 2310.00
Vase, Cobalt Blue, Applied Gold Design, Fratelli Toso, 1920, 9 x 5 In. 330.00
Vase, Controlled Bubbles, Gold Leaf, Handles, Barovier & Toso, 1930s, 8 In. 275.00
Vase, Corseted, Pink & White Zanfirico, D. Martens, 8 1/2 In. 165.00
Vase, Cranberry & Blue, Alternating Red, Murano, Fratelli Toso, 5 In. 165.00
Vase, Deep Green Conical Body, Red Vertical Canes, Martinuzzi, 1920, 11 In. 990.00
Vase, Fasce, Lemon Yellow, 2 Applied Opaque White Bands, Vistosi, 1960s, 11 In. 990.00
Vase, Fine Vertical Inciso, Carlo Scarpa, 1960, 5 In. 2990.00
Vase, Fish Shape, White & Black, 4 x 5 In. 75.00
Vase, Intarsia, Blue, Red Triangles, Barovier & Toso, 1960s, 14 1/2 In. 1045.00

Vase, Light Blue Body, Horizontal Ribs, N. Martinuzzi, c.1925, 12 In. 1100.00
Vase, Mica Flecked Body, Applied Orange Loop Handles, Martinuzzi, 8 In. 1100.00
Vase, Mosaic, Stylized Flowers, Golden Amber, Sapphire, Blue Tessera, 9 In. 2530.00
Vase, Multicolored Cane Segments, Black Body, Ferro, Figlio, 1880, 5 In. 495.00
Vase, Opaque Blue, White Interior, Handles, Zecchin-Martinuzzi, 1930s, 12 In. 465.00
Vase, Opaque Light Blue Body, Applied Black Handles, Zecchin, 15 In. 715.00
Vase, Pillow Form, Pink, Gold Leaf, Tomaso Buzzi, 1930s, 12 In. 1870.00
Vase, Pink & White Roses, Cobalt Blue, Murrine, Barovier, 1920s, 9 In. 7187.00
Vase, Pulegoso Glass, Floating Patched, D. Martens, c.1950, 12 In. 2200.00
Vase, Purple Body, Applied Foot, Vittorio Zecchin, 1925, 12 In. 1760.00
Vase, Red, Clear Applied Prunts & Collar, Gold Leaf, Murano, 1920s, 10 In. 155.00
Vase, Red, Yellow, Aventurine, Francesco Ferro & Figlio, 1870, 4 x 7 In. 440.00
Vase, Ribbed Vessel, Applied Blue Foot, Amber Curled Handles, 1920s, 8 In. 358.00
Vase, Ribbed, White, Gold, Barovier & Toso, 5 1/2 x 6 1/2 In. 110.00
Vase, Ruby Red, Applied Handles, Fratelli Toso, 8 1/2 x 4 1/2 In. 275.00
Vase, Salmon, Pink Body, Applied Handles, N. Martinuzzi, 1930, 11 In. 1760.00
Vase, Sommerso Free Form, Clear, Amber & Blue, Salviati, 7 In. 110.00
Vase, Sommerso Layers, Blue & Green, Seguso Vetri D-Arte, Flavio Poli, 6 x 4 In. 175.00
Vase, Sommerso, Amber Body, Green Internal Layer, Flavio Poli, 1950, 15 In. 715.00
Vase, Sommerso, Clear, Internal Yellow & Amber Layers, Murano, 1960s, 10 In. 155.00
Vase, Sommerso, Cube, Yellow, Deep Blue Internal Layer, Murano, 4 1/2 In. 120.00
Vase, Sommerso, Red, Purple Internal Layer, Flavio Poli, 1950, 12 In. 1650.00
Vase, Swirling Copper Specks & Orange Band, 1950s, Fratelli Toso, 9 In. 285.00
Vase, Swirling White & Plum Canes, Corset, Fratelli Toso, 1950s, 10 In. 100.00
Vase, Tear Shape, Yellow & Red Sommerso Glass, Salviati, 13 1/2 In. 440.00
Vase, Transparent Blue Body, Vertical Segmented Ribs, V. Zecchin, 8 In. 825.00
Vase, White & Purple Interior, Sommerso Flame Shape, Salviati, 11 In. 880.00
Vase, White Laguna, Gold Foil, Seguso, c.1935, 7 1/2 In. 110.00
Vase, White, Acid-Etched, 11 1/2 x 4 1/2 In. 440.00
Vase, White, Pink, Blue Pansies, Violets, Snapdragons, Everted Rim, 5 1/8 In. 345.00
Vase, Yellow & White Latticinio, Fratelli Toso, 15 1/2 In. 330.00
Vase, Zanfirico & Latticinio Canes, Gold Leaf Handles, Murano, 1950s, 9 In. 220.00

GLASSES for the eyes, or spectacles, were mentioned in a manuscript in 1289 and have been used ever since. The first eyeglasses with rigid side pieces were made in London in 1727. Bifocals were invented by Benjamin Franklin in 1785. Lorgnettes were popular in late Victorian times. Opera glasses are listed in their own category.

Goggles, Yellow Lenses, Tortoise Color Celluloid Frame, Steel Case, 1930s-1940s 30.00
Lorgnette, 14K Yellow Gold 345.00
Plastic, Tortoise Color, Fold Down & Out To Open 105.00
Spectacles, 3 1/2-In. Folded 150.00
Spectacles, Brass Frames, Benz, Case, 5 1/8 In. 245.00
Spectacles, Brass Frames, Mahogany Case, 1830s 195.00
Spectacles, Iron Frame, Original Lenses, Large Ribbon Loops, Mid-18th Century 295.00

GOEBEL is the mark used by W. Goebel Porzellanfabrik of Oeslau, Germany, now Rodental, Germany. Many types of figurines and dishes have been made. The firm is still working. The pieces marked *Goebel Hummel* are listed under Hummel in this book.

Ashtray, Friar Tuck 40.00
Ashtray, Swiss Boy, Red Crown Mark 35.00
Bookends, Colonial Couple 75.00
Breakfast Set, Meridian, Service For 4 .... 100.00
Creamer, Cardinal Tuck, 5 1/2 In. 168.00
Creamer, Double Crown Mark 55.00
Creamer, Elephant, Orange 90.00
Decanter, Greyhound, Crown Mark 85.00
Decanter, Scottish Man On Barrel, Crown Mark 48.00
Figurine, Angel, Kneeling, No. HE 20, 2 1/2 In. 20.00
Figurine, Atta Boy, Charlot Byj, No. 7, 4 In. 85.00
Figurine, Cat, Tabby, 4 In. 45.00
Figurine, Disney Dwarfs, 1940s 150.00

Goldscheider, Figurine, Easter Parade, Woman, Pink Dress, 6 1/2 In.

If a white powder forms on a piece of glass or pottery decorated with a lead glaze, immediately remove the piece from your house. The powder is poisonous. Consult an expert conservator if the piece is valuable and should be saved. Do the ecologically correct thing if you must dispose of the piece.

Figurine, E-E-Eek, Charlot Byj, No. 9, 4 1/4 In.	135.00
Figurine, Figaro, Ball, Sitting On Hind Legs, 1950s, 4 In.	375.00
Figurine, Figaro, Sitting, Holding Ball In Front Paws, 1950s, 4 In.	325.00
Figurine, Figaro, Sitting, Label, 1950s, 2 1/2 In.	125.00
Figurine, Guardian Angel, Standing Over Baby In Carriage, Tag, 3 1/2 In.	20.00
Figurine, Off Key, Charlot Byj, No. 22, 3 3/4 In.	150.00
Figurine, Palomino Horse	125.00
Figurine, Putting On The Dog, Charlot Byj, No. 25, 4 3/4 In.	135.00
Figurine, Rooster, 17 In.	350.00
Figurine, Sea Breezes, No. 75	250.00
Figurine, Sparrow, Signed	225.00
Figurine, The Kibitzer, Charlot Byj, No. 23	150.00
Figurine, Tyrolean Boy, Full Bee	100.00
Honey Pot	55.00
Lamp, Perfume, Bambi	375.00
Lamp, Perfume, Owl	120.00 to 150.00
Mug, Beer, Nude Handle, Signed	50.00
Mustard, Friar Tuck	65.00
Napkin Ring, Friar Tuck	35.00
Plaque, Gnome, Full Bee	40.00
Salt & Pepper, Black Musicians	150.00
Salt & Pepper, Chipmunks, Full Bee	45.00
Salt & Pepper, Clowns, Marked, 3 In.	40.00
Salt & Pepper, Flower, Disney, Full Bee & Crown	95.00
Salt & Pepper, Friar Tuck	30.00
Salt & Pepper, Hugging Cat	50.00
Salt & Pepper, Poodle, Full Bee	45.00
Salt & Pepper, Santa Claus	100.00
Salt & Pepper, Turkey On Nest, Full Bee	45.00
Sign, Dealer, Figural Bird On Plaque, Marked	120.00
Sugar & Creamer, Friar Tuck	90.00 to 95.00
Tea Set, Child's, Porcelain, White, Green Stripes, c.1950, 3 3/4 In. Tray, 8 Piece	125.00
Timer, Egg, Double, Rooster	65.00

GOLDSCHEIDER has made porcelains in three places. The family left Vienna in 1938 and started factories in England and in Trenton, New Jersey. The New Jersey factory started in 1940 as Goldscheider-U.S.A. In 1941 it became Goldscheider-Everlast Corporation. From 1947 to 1953 it was Goldcrest Ceramics Corporation. In 1950 the Vienna plant was returned to Mr. Goldscheider, and the company continues in business. The Trenton, New Jersey, business, now called *Goldscheider of Vienna*, imports all of the pieces.

Bust, Madonna, 9 In.	115.00
Bust, Young Ladies, Curly Orange Hair, Green Dress, 8 In., Pair	247.00
Clock, Table, Theodora, Sarah Bernhardt, On Throne, Stamped, 22 3/4 In.	11500.00
Figurine, Austrian Dancer, 6 1/4 In.	250.00

Figurine, Birds, On Pinecones, 8 In., Pair	195.00
Figurine, Blackamoor, Couple, Dancers, 15 1/2 In. Pair	395.00
Figurine, Captured Bird, Dancer Niddy Impekoven, Lorenzl, c.1923, 18 In.	1645.00
Figurine, Doe's Head, Fawn, White, Yellow Craquelle Glaze, Green, 15 1/4 In.	28.00
Figurine, Duchess Of Devonshire, 6 In.	75.00
Figurine, Easter Parade, Woman, Pink Dress, 6 1/2 In. ....*Illus*	75.00
Figurine, Horse & Colt, Base, 9 x 7 In.	260.00
Figurine, Lady Caller, P. Porcher, 6 1/2 In.	75.00
Figurine, Lady, In Red Dress, 14 1/2 In.	259.00
Figurine, Madonna & Child, 14 In.	200.00
Figurine, Prince Of Wales, 6 1/2 In.	75.00
Figurine, Southern Lady, Blue, 7 In.	100.00
Figurine, Woman, Blue Gown, 15 In.	300.00
Figurine, Woman, Oriental, 11 1/2 In.	89.00

GOLF, see Sports category.

GONDER Ceramic Arts, Inc., was opened by Lawton Gonder in 1941 in Zanesville, Ohio. Gonder made high-grade pottery decorated with flambe, drip, gold crackle, and Chinese crackle glazes. The factory closed in 1957. From 1946 to 1954, Gonder also operated the Elgee Pottery, which made ceramic lamp bases.

Basket, Leaves, Coral, Turquoise, 7 In.	45.00
Figurine, Panther, Reclining, Green, 19 In., Pair ....165.00 to 225.00
Planter, Swan, Pink	25.00
Vase, Turquoise, Pink, 10 In.	25.00

GOSS china has been made since 1858. English potter William Henry Goss first made it at the Falcon Pottery in Stoke-on-Trent. The factory name was changed to Goss China Company in 1934 when it was taken over by Cauldon Potteries. Production ceased in 1940. Goss china resembles Irish Belleek in both body and glaze. The company also made popular souvenir china, usually marked with local crests and names.

W. H. GOSS

Figurine, Ann Hathaway's Cottage	100.00
Figurine, Lorna, Bonnet	295.00
Mug, Little Jack Horner	68.00
Pitcher, Corfe Castle, 3 In.	15.00
Vase, St. Nicholas Chapel	35.00

GOUDA, Holland, has been a pottery center since the seventeenth century. Two firms, the Zenith pottery, established in the eighteenth century, and the Zuid-Hollandsche pottery made the brightly colored wares marked *Gouda* from 1880 to about 1940. Many pieces featured Art Nouveau or Art Deco designs.

PLAZUID
GOUDA
HOLLAND

Bowl, Black, Brown, Tan, Cream, Handle, Marked, 1895-1910, 8 1/2 In.	82.00
Bowl, Floral Center, Multicolored, Cream Ground, Shallow, 13 In.	66.00
Bowl, Glossy Florals, Deco Style, Signed, 3 x 10 In.	225.00
Bowl, Peacock Feather Design, 1920s, 10 In.	650.00
Candy Dish, Stylized Flowers, Multicolored, Dark Green Finish, Applied Handle	60.00
Chamberstick, 10 1/2 In.	185.00
Chamberstick, Matte, 5 In.	175.00
Inkwell, With Insert, 7 x 4 In.	140.00
Jug, Orchid Cover, Spout, Handle, White, Gold, Green, 10 1/2 In.	385.00
Match Holder, Matte Florals, Side Striker, Center Medallion Silhouette Airplane	95.00
Pitcher, Black, Brown, Tan, Cream, Marked, 1895-1910, 4 1/2 In.	70.00
Pitcher, Matte Black, Art Nouveau Hibiscus, Wide Base, 7 In.	195.00
Plate, Deco Flowers & Foliage, Cream Ground, Brown Trim, 9 7/8 In.	165.00
Plate, Floral Center, Orange Rim, Wall Hanger, 7 1/4 In.	50.00
Smoke Set, Ashtray, Match Striker, Round Tray, Aurora	145.00
Vase, Art Deco Florals, Matte Black, 4 In.	75.00
Vase, Art Deco Flower Designs, Signed, 6 1/8 In.	110.00
Vase, Floral, Green Interior, Signed, 4 In.	120.00

GRANITEWARE is an enameled tinware that has been used in the kitchen from the late nineteenth century to the present. Earlier graniteware was green or turquoise blue, with white spatters. The later ware was gray with white spatters. Reproductions are being made in all colors.

Bowl, Refrigerator, Red Swirl, 1960s, Set Of 4	585.0
Can, Cream, Wood Bail Handle, 7 1/2 In.	195.0
Can, Milk, Gray, 2 Qt.	50.0
Casserole, Cover, Swirled Lid, Black & White	85.0
Chamber Pot, Cover, Cobalt Trim, Wire Bail, Wooden Handle, Austria	240.0
Chowder Set, Child's, Covered Pot, Platter, Sauceboat On Underplate, Relish	195.0
Coffeepot, Crane In Pond, Pewter Top, Lid, Handle & Spout, 11 In.	345.0
Coffeepot, Green & White Swirl	105.00 to 160.0
Coffeepot, Painted Castle , Pewter Trim, 12 In.	225.0
Coffeepot, Red Swirl, 1960s	235.0
Colander, Gray	28.0
Colander, Red & White	12.5
Creamer, Cobalt Blue, White Swirl, Strap Handle	345.0
Cup, Measuring, White, 2 In.	18.0
Cuspidor, Gray Swirl, 4 x 7 1/4 In.	95.0
Egg Poacher Set, Navy, White Specks, Single, 3 Pieces	75.0
Jug, Gooseneck Petroleum, 2 Liter	225.0
Kettle, Granite On Cast Iron, Wrought Iron Range Co., Blue & White	450.0
Ladle, Blue & White	100.0
Ladle, Blue & White Outside, White Interior, Black Handle	35.0
Match Holder, Mottled Gray, Double	395.0
Mixing Bowl, Red Swirl, c.1960	175.0
Mixing Bowl Set, Nesting, Red, 1930s, Set Of 4	155.00 to 165.0
Mold, Melon, Footed, Gray, 6 1/2 x 7 1/2 In, Pair	185.0
Muffin Pan, White Interior, Blue, 6 Cups	165.0
Pan, Pudding, Blue Swirl	40.0
Pie Plate, Blue, White	40.0
Poacher, Fish	125.0
Refrigerator Bowl, Red Swirl, 1960s, Set Of 4	585.0
Soap Dish, Blue, White	75.0
Strainer, Wire Handle, Brown & White	45.0
Syrup, Gray	175.0
Teakettle, On Cast Iron, Wrought Iron Range Co., Blue & White	450.0
Teapot, Blue, 1890, 2 Cup	350.0
Teapot, Red, Cobalt, Orange, Black, c.1900	325.0
Water Pail, Lime Green, Brown, White, Early 1900s	225.0

GREENTOWN glass was made by the Indiana Tumbler and Goblet Company of Greentown, Indiana, from 1894 to 1903. In 1899, the factory became part of National Glass Company. A variety of pressed glass was made. Additional pieces may be found in other categories, such as Chocolate Glass, Holly Amber, Milk Glass, and Pressed Glass.

Brazen Shield, Tumbler, Blue	48.0
Cord Drapery, Cruet, Vinegar, Original Stopper	200.0
Daisy, Mustard, Frosted Crystal	50.0
Holly, Toothpick, Frosted Crystal	65.0
Leaf Bracket, Berry Bowl, 5 In.	50.0
Teardrop & Tassel, Tumbler, Nile Green	225.0
Wheelbarrow, Salt, Nile Green	350.0

GRUEBY Faience Company of Boston, Massachusetts, was incorporated in 1897 by William H. Grueby. Garden statuary, art pottery, and architectural tiles were made until 1920. The company developed a matte green glaze that was so popular it was copied by many other factories making a less expensive type of pottery. This eventually led to the financial problems of the pottery.

Bowl, Matte Green Glaze, Finger Ridges, 6 1/2 In.	360.0
Bowl, Matte Green Glaze, Impressed Mark, 7 1/2 In.	330.0

Bowl, Pale Green Matte Glaze, 3 1/2 x 2 In. 330.00
Jardiniere, Tooled & Applied Full-Length Leaves, Curdled Green Glaze, 5 x 8 1/4 In. 1980.00
Paperweight, Scarab, Matte Green Enamel, 3 x 2 In. 2090.00
Tile, Brown & Cream Marine Bird, Green Water, Matte Glaze, Square, 7 In. 660.00
Tile, Butterscotch, Cream Glaze, Square, Signed, 6 In. 1840.00
Tile, Cherub With Cornucopia, Square, 6 In. 175.00
Tile, Eros, Square, 6 In. 315.00
Tile, Knight On Horseback, Blue, Green, Cream, Yellow, Brown, Square, 8 x 15 In. 4025.00
Tile, Landscape In Blues, Greens & Yellow, Signed, Square, 4 In. 935.00
Tile, Monk, Playing Cello, Unglazed Terra-Cotta, Square, 6 In. 175.00
Tile, Oak Tree, Blue Sky, Dark Green Against Light Green Ground, Oak Frame, 6 In. ... 2310.00
Tile, Sailing Ship, Pink, Purple, White Sails, Brown Hull On Teal, Light Blue Sky, 6 In. . 990.00
Tile, Scenic, Pine Trees, Hills In Background, 6 x 6 In. 1980.00
Tile, Ship, Matte Blue, Green, Butterscotch, Cream, Brown, Square, 8 1/2 In. 460.00
Tile, Ship, White Sails, Blue Sky, Matte Glaze, Square, 6 In. 1540.00
Tile, Stylized Monk At A Lectern, Bisque Red Clay, Ocher Matte Ground, Frame, 6 In. .. 440.00
Tile, Tulip, Yellow Bud, Light, Dark Green Ground, Square, 6 In. 1035.00
Vase, Applied & Carved Leaves, Yellow Matte Glaze, Impressed ER, 4 In. 1650.00
Vase, Applied Full-Length Leaves Alternating With Light Green Buds, 9 x 4 In. 3850.00
Vase, Applied Full-Length Leaves, Matte Light Green Glaze, 5 1/2 x 4 In. 3932.00
Vase, Applied Leaves & Flowers, Matte White Crocus, Matte Green Glaze, 5 In. 2750.00
Vase, Applied Leaves Alternating With Buds On Stems, Matte Green Glaze, 11 In. 4950.00
Vase, Applied Leaves At Bottom, Matte Green Glaze, 7 In. 2640.00
Vase, Applied Leaves At Bottom, Sculpted Stems, Matte Green Glaze, 8 1/2 In. 1760.00
Vase, Applied Leaves, Carved Stems, Buds, Matte Green Glaze, 7 1/2 In. 2420.00
Vase, Applied Leaves, Ivory Buds, Flared Top, Matte Green Ground, 12 In. 7700.00
Vase, Applied Leaves, Matte Medium Green Glaze, 6 In. 2970.00
Vase, Applied Leaves, Reticulated Design Near Top, Green Matte Glaze, 7 1/2 In. 3190.00
Vase, Applied Leaves, Ribbed Cylindrical Neck, Matte Blue Glaze, Paper Label, 12 In. .. 2860.00
Vase, Applied Leaves, Yellow Buds, Matte Green Glaze, 6 1/2 In. 715.00
Vase, Applied Vertical Leaves, Green Matte Glaze, Impressed Mark, 8 In. 2640.00
Vase, Broad Leaves, Matte Green Glaze, Signed, 8 In. 2540.00
Vase, Carved & Applied Leaves Alternating With Buds, Green Matte Glaze, 7 x 5 In. ... 1210.00
Vase, Carved & Applied Rounded Leaves, Leathery Matte Glaze Post, 7 1/2 x 4 In. 1650.00
Vase, Carved Iris, Rolling Rim, 1901, 11 1/2 In. 6500.00
Vase, Carved Leaves, Matte Green Glaze, 8 x 6 In. 2750.00
Vase, Carved Vertical Leaves, Blue Matte Glaze, Impressed Mark, 6 1/2 In. 2860.00
Vase, Embossed 5-Petal Flowers, Alternating Flat Leaves, Signed, 6 x 9 In. 4510.00
Vase, Incised Leaf Design, Green Matte Glaze, Impressed Mark, 6 In. 1540.00
Vase, Leaf Design, 5 Vertical Lines, Light Green Glaze, Signed, 7 1/2 x 4 3/4 In. 980.00
Vase, Overlapping Vertical Leaves, Oatmeal Glaze, Impressed Mark, 7 1/2 In. 1760.00
Vase, Rings At Shoulder, Matte Oatmeal Glaze, 5 1/2 x 3 In. 825.00
Vase, Sculpted & Applied Leaves, Green Matte Glaze, Impressed Mark, 6 1/2 In. 1100.00
Vase, Thick Dark Mustard Matte Glaze, Impressed Mark, 9 1/2 In. 1100.00
Vase, Tooled Daffodils, 6 Sides Rim, Organic Matte Green Enamel, 11 1/4 In. 8500.00
Vase, Vertical Leaves In Groups Of Three, Ruth Erickson, 9 In. 2070.00
Vase, Vertical Leaves, Matte Green Glaze, Impressed Mark, Signed, 4 In. 825.00
Vase, Vertical Panels, Matte Green Glaze, 7 In. 2200.00
Wall Pocket, Sculpted Leaves, Matte Dark Green Glaze, 7 x 5 In. 1100.00

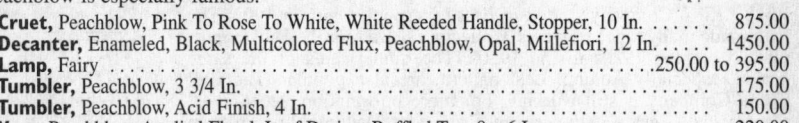

GUNDERSON glass was made at the Gunderson-Pairpoint Glass Works
of New Bedford, Massachusetts, from 1952 to 1957. Gunderson
Peachblow is especially famous.

Cruet, Peachblow, Pink To Rose To White, White Reeded Handle, Stopper, 10 In. 875.00
Decanter, Enameled, Black, Multicolored Flux, Peachblow, Opal, Millefiori, 12 In. 1450.00
Lamp, Fairy ....250.00 to 395.00
Tumbler, Peachblow, 3 3/4 In. 175.00
Tumbler, Peachblow, Acid Finish, 4 In. 150.00
Vase, Peachblow, Applied Floral, Leaf Design, Ruffled Top, 8 x 6 In. 220.00

GUNS that may be classed as toys, such as BB guns, air rifles, and cap guns, are
listed in the Toy category.

GUSTAVSBERG ceramics factory was founded in 1827 near Stockholm, Sweden. It is best known to collectors for its twentieth-century art wares, especially a green stoneware with silver inlay called *Argenta*.

Gustafsberg

Bowl, Fish Blowing Bubbles, Silver Overlay, Green Ground, Argenta, 6 1/4 In. . . .145.00 to 250.00
Bowl, Fish Design, Trailing Bubbles, Silver Scalloped Border, Argenta, 7 x 2 In. 345.00
Bowl, Mottled Green Glaze, Art Deco, 6 In. 137.00
Bowl, Stoneware, Berndt Friberg, 10 In. 1200.00
Charger, Silver Overlay Mermaid, Argenta 2250.00
Figurine, Farsta, Stoneware, Wilhelm Kage 1800.00
Figurine, Maiden, Kneeling On Stand, Circular Base, Sweden, 16 1/2 In. 575.00
Figurine, Woman, Seated, Lisa Larsen 125.00
Jug, Lion, 6 1/2 In. 450.00
Vase, Bud, Bellflower, 8 1/2 In. 150.00
Vase, Carved, Blue & Turquoise Leaves, Signed JE, 6 In. 185.00
Vase, Child, With Garland, 6 In. 500.00
Vase, Floral Design, Argenta, 5 3/4 x 5 In. 185.00
Vase, Landscape, Green Trees, Lime Green Ground, 1902, 5 In. 350.00
Vase, Nude, With Veil, Handles, 10 In. 1250.00
Vase, Robin's-Egg Blue, Stylized Scene, Mother & Child, Signed, 7 In. 165.00
Vase, Stylized Florals, Blue On Green Ground, Signed, 1921, 10 1/2 In. 575.00

GUTTA-PERCHA was one of the first plastic materials. It was made from a mixture of resins from Malaysian trees. It was molded and used for daguerreotype cases, toilet articles, and picture frames in the nineteenth century.

Case, Daguerreotype, 2 Men, 1/9 Plate 100.00
Case, Daguerreotype, Man Picture, 1/6 Plate 110.00
Case, Tintype, Man, 1/6 Plate 85.00

HAEGER Potteries, Inc., Dundee, Illinois, started making commercial art wares in 1914. Early pieces were marked with the name *Haeger* written over an *H*. About 1938, the mark *Royal Haeger* was used. The firm is still making florist wares and lamp bases.

Ashtray, Century Of Progress 50.00
Bowl, Light Chocolate Agate Glaze, Handle, Signed, 15 x 6 In. 48.00
Candlestick, Swan, Mauve Agate Glaze, Pair 175.00
Cookie Jar, Fireplug, Rust Color, Glen Richardson, 1970s 200.00
Cookie Jar, Gleep 200.00
Ewer, Floral, 15 In. 85.00
Figurine, Bull, Red 275.00
Figurine, Cocker Spaniel, Seated, 8 1/2 In. 55.00
Figurine, Cowboy On Bronco, Cactus 295.00
Figurine, Golfer, Pink 26.00
Lavabo & Basin, Gold Tweed 135.00
Planter, Green, 9 x 3 1/2 In. 25.00
Planter, Moss Agate, 2 Tigers 225.00
Planter, Red Rooster, 10 In. 50.00
Sign, Dealer, Bronze, 8 In. 40.00
Vase, Bud, Brown Wrap, Bulbous, 11 In. 60.00
Vase, Green High Glaze, 2 Square Handles, Martin Stangl, 1917, 5 1/2 In. 110.00

HALF-DOLL, see Pincushion Doll category.

HALL CHINA Company started in East Liverpool, Ohio, in 1903. The firm made many types of wares. Collectors search for the Hall teapots made from the 1920s to the 1950s. The dinnerwares of the same period, especially Autumn Leaf pattern, are also popular. The Hall China Company is still working. For more information, see *Kovels' Depression Glass & Dinnerware Price List*. Autumn Leaf pattern dishes are listed in their own category in this book.

Blue Blossom, Casserole, Thick Rim, 8 In. 30.00
Blue Blossom, Cookie Jar, Sundial 458.00
Blue Garden, Cookie Jar, Sundial 275.00

Brown, Mug, Tapered 5.00
Cactus, Batter Bowl, 5 Band, 6 In. 40.00
Crocus, Bowl, Radiance, 9 In. 45.00
Crocus, Bowl, Salad, 9 In. 35.00
Crocus, Coffeepot, Terrance 100.00
Crocus, Flour Shaker, Handle 130.00
Crocus, Platter, 11 In. 30.00
Crocus, Sugar, Cover, Art Deco 40.00
Crocus, Tidbit, 3 Tiers 65.00
Fantasy, Gravy Boat 60.00
Five Band, Pitcher, Red, 5 In. 35.00
Game Bird, Mug 32.00
Golden Glo, Cup, Irish Coffee, 6 Piece 115.00
Green, Creamer, Individual 6.00
Jonquil, Coffeepot, Drip, Waverly 25.00
Morning Glory, Bowl, Oval, 10 In. 45.00
Morning Glory, Cake Plate, 9 3/8 In. 95.00
Morning Glory, Coffeepot, Step Down 95.00
Morning Glory, Plate, 7 In. 22.00
Morning Glory, Plate, 8 In. 25.00
Morning Glory, Plate, 9 In. 25.00
Morning Glory, Platter, 11 In. 35.00
Morning Glory, Platter, 13 In. 45.00
Mt. Vernon, Bowl, Fruit 8.00
Mt. Vernon, Creamer 10.00
Mt. Vernon, Gravy Boat 20.00
Mt. Vernon, Plate, 10 In. 14.00
Mt. Vernon, Platter 20.00
Ning Po, Creamer, 1845, 5 In. 230.00
Peach Blossom, Jug, Small 75.00
Phoenix Blue, Butter, Cover, Westinghouse 45.00
Poppy, Bean Pot 95.00
Poppy, Bean Pot, Hand 110.00
Poppy, Bowl, Vegetable, 9 In. 27.00
Poppy, Coffeepot, S-Lid 65.00
Poppy, Custard Cup 10.00
Poppy, Jar, Pretzel ....125.00 to 150.00
Poppy, Plate, 7 In. 7.00
Poppy, Platter, 13 In. 25.00
Poppy, Salt & Pepper, Range, Handle 45.00
Poppy, Soup, Dish 27.00
Poppy, Spoon 130.00
Poppy & Wheat, Jug, Cover 100.00
Primrose, Pie Plate 20.00
Radiance, Casserole, Cover 45.00
Radiance, Mixing Bowl, 8 1/4 In. 39.00
Red, Batter Bowl 20.00
Red, Canister, Coffee, Radiance 168.00
Red, Cookie Jar 125.00
Red, Jug, Ball 40.00
Red Poppy, Coffeepot 45.00
Red Poppy, Gravy Boat 75.00
Red Poppy, Jug, Radiance, No. 5 .... 22.00
Red Poppy, Salt & Pepper 55.00
Rose Parade, Bean Pot ....75.00 to 95.00
Rose Parade, Jug, Pert, 5 In. 25.00
Rose Parade, Mixing Bowl, Straight Sides, 9 In. 26.00
Rose Parade, Pepper Shaker ....15.00 to 20.00
Rose Parade, Salt & Pepper, 4 1/2 In. 69.00
Rose Parade, Sugar & Creamer 50.00
Rose White, Jug, Pert, 7 1/2 In. 32.00
Royal Rose, Casserole, Cover 40.00
Royal Rose, Casserole, Thick 35.00

Royal Rose, Pepper Shaker, Handle 12.0

Springtime, Bowl, 5 1/2 In. 7.0

Springtime, Gravy Boat 22.0

Springtime, Plate, 7 1/4 In. 10.0

Springtime, Plate, 9 In. 18.0

Springtime, Soup, Dish 9.0

Star Design, Cookie Jar, Cadet 55.0

Sundial, Syrup, Cover, Red 125.0

Sunlight Yellow, Creamer, Hotel New Yorker, Individual 18.0

Taverne, Coffeepot, Banded 55.0

Teapot, Airflow, Cobalt, Gold Trim, 6 Cup 75.0

Teapot, Airflow, Cobalt, Gold Trim, 8 Cup 90.0

Teapot, Airflow, Red 120.0

Teapot, Airflow, Turquoise, Gold Trim 75.0

Teapot, Aladdin, Blue Bouquet 110.0

Teapot, Aladdin, Cadet Blue, White Floral Cover, Infuser, 11 In. 60.0

Teapot, Aladdin, Canary, 6 Cup 30.0

Teapot, Aladdin, Cobalt Blue 65.0

Teapot, Aladdin, Cobalt Blue, Gold Trim, 6 Cup ....50.00 to 110.0

Teapot, Aladdin, Yellow, Infuser 65.0

Teapot, Albany, Black 35.0

Teapot, Albany, Cobalt Blue 95.0

Teapot, Apple, Sky Blue 100.0

Teapot, Birdcage, Maroon 375.0

Teapot, Birdcage, Maroon, Gold 315.0

Teapot, Boston, Black 45.0

Teapot, Boston, Poppy 300.0

Teapot, Boston, Red 95.0

Teapot, Crocus ....200.00 to 225.0

Teapot, Donut, Ivory 450.0

Teapot, Donut, Poppy ....400.00 to 500.0

Teapot, Globe, Hook Cover, Cadet Blue, Gold Trim 65.0

Teapot, Hook, Cover, Red 135.0

Teapot, Kansas, Emerald Green, Gold Trim 250.0

Teapot, Lipton, Maroon 45.0

Teapot, Los Angeles, Green, Gold Trim 45.0

Teapot, McCormick, Maroon, Infuser 40.0

Teapot, Melody, Cobalt Blue 150.0

Teapot, Melody, Poppy ....298.00 to 400.0

Teapot, Melody, Red 250.0

Teapot, New York, Black, Gold Trim, 2 Cup 35.0

Teapot, New York, Red 225.0

Teapot, New York, Red Poppy 95.0

Teapot, Parade, Yellow, Gold Trim 39.0

Teapot, Philadelphia, Cadet Blue, 4 Cup 40.0

Teapot, Philadelphia, Marine, Gold Trim, 6 Cup 40.0

Teapot, Streamline, Blue 70.0

Teapot, Streamline, Poppy 350.0

Teapot, Streamline, Red 100.0

Teapot, Twinspout, Red 160.0

Teapot, Washington, Stock Green 18.0

Teapot, Wildfire, Pert 395.0

Teapot, Windshield, Golden Clover 163.0

Teapot, Windshield, Poppy 400.0

Teapot, World's Fair 275.0

Tom & Jerry Set, Cobalt Blue, 13 Piece 90.0

Tomorrow's Classic Bouquet, Bowl, Vegetable, Square, 8 3/4 In. 45.0

Tomorrow's Classic Bouquet, Creamer, After Dinner 30.0

Tomorrow's Classic Bouquet, Jug, 1 1/4 Qt. 85.0

Tomorrow's Classic Bouquet, Soup, Coupe 35.0

Tulip, Cup 13.0

Washington, Coffeepot, Brown, 6 Cup 35.0

Wildfire, Berry Bowl 11.0

Wildfire,	Bowl, Vegetable, 9 1/4 In.	38.00
Wildfire,	Coffeepot, S-Lid	60.00
Wildfire,	Gravy Boat, D-Line	38.00
Wildfire,	Plate, 7 In.	18.00
Wildfire,	Plate, 9 In.	18.00
Wildfire,	Platter, 11 In.	32.00
Wildfire,	Platter, 13 In.	38.00
Wildfire,	Sugar & Creamer, Cover	49.00
Zeisel,	Ashtray, Mulberry	25.00
Zeisel,	Bowl, Mulberry, 5 3/4 In.	8.00
Zeisel,	Cookie Jar, Star Design, Gold Label	60.00
Zeisel,	Cup & Saucer, Mulberry	15.00
Zeisel,	Plate, Mulberry, 6 In.	7.00
Zeisel,	Plate, Mulberry, 8 In.	10.00
Zeisel,	Plate, Mulberry, 11 In.	15.00
Zeisel,	Platter, Mulberry, 15 In.	25.00
Zeisel,	Platter, Mulberry, 17 In.	30.00

HALLOWEEN is an ancient holiday that has changed in the last 200 years. The jack-o'-lantern, witches on broomsticks, and orange decorations seem to be twentieth-century creations. Collectors started to become serious about collecting Halloween-related items in the late 1970s. The papier-mache decorations, now replaced by plastic, and old costumes are in demand.

Banner,	Halco Halloween Costumes, Jack-O'-Lantern, Cloth, 1930s	450.00
Box,	Costume, Captain Action Phantom Costume	110.00
Candleholder,	Pumpkin, Papier-Mache, Paper Liner, 1940-1950, 2 1/2 In., Pair	75.00
Candlestick,	Devil's Head On Hawk Foot, Pair	125.00
Candy Container,	Devil's Head, Composition, Painted, Germany, 1930s, 5 In.	203.00
Candy Container,	Devil's Head, Germany, 1910, 6 In.	418.00
Candy Container,	Jack-O'-Lantern, Black Cat	45.00
Candy Container,	Jack-O'-Lantern, Champagne Ice Bucket, Germany, 3 1/4 In.	1540.00
Candy Container,	Jack-O'-Lantern, Man Riding Squash, Germany, 4 x 4 In.	715.00
Candy Container,	Jack-O'-Lantern, Pop-Eyed, Bail	575.00
Candy Container,	Jack-O'-Lantern, Squinting, Germany, 4 In.	550.00
Candy Container,	Jack-O'-Lantern, Tin Screw On Lid	436.00
Candy Container,	Witch, Pumpkin Head	787.00
Candy Container,	Witch, Red Costume, Germany, 1930s, 10 In.	825.00
Cookie Cutter Set,	Trick Or Treat, Metal, Box, 1950s	28.00
Costume,	Aquaman, Ben Cooper, Small	225.00
Costume,	Archie, Comic Strip, Ben Cooper, 1969	69.00
Costume,	Army Uniform, With G.I. Joe Canteen	50.00
Costume,	Barbie, Jewel Secrets, Vinyl, Plastic Mask, Ben Cooper, 1986	40.00
Costume,	Beatnik, Box, 1960s	65.00

Halloween, Game, Pick A Pumpkin, 12 In. Diam

Halloween, Lantern, Pumpkin Man, Orange, Papier-Mache, 7 1/2 In.

Halloween, Lantern, Witch, Papier-Mache, 1920s, 18 In.

Halloween, Light Bulb Set, Pumpkin, Noma

Halloween, Toy, Devil,
Mechanical, Germany, 9 In.

Costume, C3PO, Star Wars, With Mask, Box, 1977	65.00
Costume, California Raisin, On Hanger	15.00
Costume, Captain America	50.00
Costume, Captain Kirk, Star Trek, Box	32.00
Costume, Captain Nemo, 20,000 Leagues Under The Sea, Ben Cooper, Box, 1950s	66.00
Costume, Catanooga, Ben Cooper, Box, 1969	65.00
Costume, Darth Vader, Star Wars, Mask, Ben Cooper, Box, 1977, Large ....35.00 to 65.00	
Costume, Frankenstein, Ben Cooper, Box, 1960s	88.00
Costume, Fred Flintstone, Box	22.00
Costume, Future Man, Halco, September, 1949, 45 In.	55.00
Costume, Great Grape Ape, Ben Cooper, 1976	65.00
Costume, Gumby Cowboy Adventure, Lakeside, 1965	50.00
Costume, Hagar The Horrible, Box	35.00
Costume, Lost In Space, Ben Cooper, 1966	300.00
Costume, Maverick, Cowboy, Rifle & Pistols, Box	650.00
Costume, Monsters Mutant	145.00
Costume, Pink Panther, Mask, Ben Cooper, Box, 1977, Medium	30.00
Costume, Rusty The Boy, Rin Tin Tin, Box	35.00
Costume, Warrior, Planet Of The Apes, Plastic, Ben Cooper, Box, Size 12-14	20.00
Costume, Wicket, Star Wars, 1983	25.00
Costume, Witch Doctor, Box	50.00
Figure, Dracula, Long Fangs, 1939, 4 In.	2.00
Figure, Owl, Orange, Black, Glass Eyes, Papier-Mache, 10 In.	110.00
Figure, Scarecrow, Plastic, 4 1/2 In.	20.00
Figure, Skeleton, Stand Up, Die Cut, 1930s, 9 1/2 In.	125.00
Figure, Witch On Pumpkin, Stand, Black, Orange, Pink, Papier-Mache, 5 5/8 In.	250.00
Game, Black Cat Ring Toss	255.00
Game, Cat & Witch, Board, Whitman, 1940s	60.00
Game, Pick A Pumpkin, 12 In. Diam ....*Illus*	941.00
Garland, Bats, Witches, Ghosts, Scarecrow, Cardboard, Die Cut, 1950s, 80 In.	44.00
Garland, Black Cats, Cardboard, Die Cut, American, 1950s, 50 In.	50.00
Horn, Devil, Composition, Painted, Germany, 1930s, 11 In.	181.00
Horn, Witch & Bats & Black Cats, Dark Green Ground, Tin, Japan, 5 1/2 In.	220.00
Jack-O'-Lantern, Clown, Die Cut, Germany, Box, 15 In., Pair	605.00
Jack-O'-Lantern, Composition, Black Doll Inside, 20th Century, 10 In.	66.00
Jack-O'-Lantern, Halloween Greetings, Light Orange Ground, 1920s, 3 x 3 In.	110.00
Jack-O'-Lantern, Painted, Paper Face, Papier-Mache, 1940-1950, 7 1/2 In.	154.00
Jack-O'-Lantern, Paper Face, Bail Handle, Papier-Mache, 1940-1950, 4 1/2 In.	100.00
Jack-O'-Lantern, Paper Face, Papier-Mache, Orange, Green, 4 3/4 In., Set Of 3	250.00
Jack-O'-Lantern, Plastic, Handle, Union Products Inc., 1950s, 4 x 3 In.	45.00
Jack-O'-Lantern, Pug Face, 5 In.	360.00
Jack-O'-Lantern, Scarecrow, Devil, Black Cat, Cardboard, 9 1/2 In.	165.00
Jack-O'-Lantern, Skull Head, Papier-Mache, Germany, 1920s	825.00
Jack-O'-Lantern, Stand Up, Die Cut, 1920s, 16 In.	176.00
Jack-O'-Lantern, U.S. Metal Toy Mfg. Co., 1958, 6 In.	70.00
Jack-O'-Lite, 2-Way, Papier-Mache	300.00
Lantern, Cat On Fence	95.00
Lantern, Chinaman, Germany, 1910, 4 In.	715.00

Lantern, Pumpkin Man, Orange, Papier-Mache, 7 1/2 In. .... *Illus* 145.00
Lantern, Pumpkin, Glass, Metal Base & Frame, Hong Kong, Box, 1960s, 5 1/2 In. 67.00
Lantern, Pumpkin, Paper Eyes, Hevy 240.00
Lantern, Witch, Owl, Orange Cardboard, Crepe Paper, Folding, 1950s, 10 1/2 In. 91.00
Lantern, Witch, Papier-Mache, 1920s, 18 In. .... *Illus* 990.00
Light Bulb Set, Pumpkin, Noma .... *Illus* 660.00
Mask, Chewbacca, Star Wars, Rubber, Plush, Don Post, 12 In. 25.00
Mask, Green Hornet, Sticker To Apply On Mask, Elastic Band, 1967 .... 100.00
Mask, Kiss, Gene Simmons, 1970s 50.00
Mask, Laurel & Hardy, Rubberized, Color, Pair 34.00
Mask, Old Virginia Catsup, Mammy With Products Displayed, 9 x 10 1/4 In. 250.00
Mask, Skull, Rubber, Covers Complete Head, Don Post, 1965 .... 75.00
Mask, Tip-Top Bread 25.00
Mask, Witch, Cardboard, Crepe Paper, 1930s 85.00
Nodder, Witch, West Germany, 1970s, 10 In. 30.00
Noisemaker, On Stick, Cardboard 30.00
Noisemaker, Whistle Handle, Rotating Wood, Brass Trim 165.00
Picture, Tinsel, Boy In Costume, Pumpkins, Owl, Frame, 7 1/2 x 9 In. 55.00
Plaque, Devil, Germany 125.00
Poster, Black Cat, Die Cut, 1930s, 23 x 10 In. 100.00
Poster, Cupcakes In Pumpkin Patch, Hostess Cupcakes, 42 x 30 In. 660.00
Poster, Pumpkin Festival During Thanksgiving, Frame, 1896, 13 x 19 In. 121.00
Pumpkin Lights, Bulb Set, Witches On 1 Side, Plastic, 1930s, 8 Piece 660.00
Skull, Papier-Mache 575.00
Tambourine, Black Cats On Wall, Tin, Chein, 1920, 7 In. 225.00
Tambourine, Children In Pumpkin Patch, 1920, 7 In. 360.00
Tambourine, Devil's Head, Tin, Lithographed, American, 1940-1950, 6 In. 112.00
Tambourine, Mother Goose Flying, Orange Ground, Tin, 1920s, 7 In. 305.00
Tambourine, Witch & Cat 95.00
Toy, Devil, Mechanical, Germany, 9 In. .... *Illus* 3080.00
Toy, Sam The Strolling Skeleton, Windup, Tin, Mikuni, Japan, 1950s, 5 1/2 In. 240.00
Toy, Witch On Rocket, Orange, Black Cat, Wheels, Plastic, American, 1950s, 4 1/8 In. 112.00
Whirligig, Witch, Wooden, Polychrome, 13 1/2 In. 55.00
Whistle, Trick Or Treat, Jack-O'-Lantern, Plastic, Black, Orange, 2 1/2 In. 30.00

HAMPSHIRE pottery was made in Keene, New Hampshire, between 1871 and 1923. Hampshire developed a line of colored glazed wares as early as 1883, including a Royal Worcester-type pink, olive green, blue, and mahogany. Pieces are marked with the printed mark or the impressed name *Hampshire Pottery* or *J.S.T. & Co., Keene, N.H.* Many pieces were marked with city names and sold as souvenirs.

Bowl, Deep Matte Green Glaze, Flat Rim, Incised Mark, 2 1/4 x 8 3/4 In. 220.00
Bowl, Deep Matte Green Glaze, Repeated Leafy Bushes, Incised Mark, 3 x 9 In. 305.00
Bowl, Embossed Buds, Leaves, Green Matte Glaze, 3 x 10 In. 495.00
Bowl, Leaves, Stems & Buds, Green Matte Glaze, Incised Mark, 10 x 2 1/2 In. 825.00
Bowl, Matte Green Glaze Over Indian Design, 7 x 2 1/2 In. 245.00
Bowl, Matte Green Glaze, Marked, 6 1/4 x 3 1/2 In. 460.00
Bowl, Matte Green Glaze, Oblong Repeated Design, Incised Mark, 6 1/4 In. 495.00
Bowl, Matte Green, Embossed Indian Peace, Gray Flecks, Incised Mark, 5 1/2 In. 220.00
Bowl, Swastika, Matte Green, 2 x 4 In. 250.00
Chamberstick, Matte Green Glaze, Applied Handle, Incised Mark, 5 1/2 In. 275.00
Chocolate Set, Olive Green Glaze, Bamboo Handle & Finial, 9 1/4 In., 4 Piece 245.00
Compote, Leaves Design, Green Matte Glaze, 2 Handles, Impressed Mark, 6 In. 355.00
Creamer, Brown, Crown, Volcanic Glaze 155.00
Inkwell, Cover, Liner, 3 1/2 In. 345.00
Lamp Base, Matte Green Glaze, Molded Flower Heads, Electrified, 10 1/4 In. 1320.00
Mug, Cathedral Drive Scene, Raised Leaf Design, Green, Brown, Gold, 5 1/2 In. 28.00
Pitcher, Milk, Cream Ground, Raised Light Green Leaf Design, Gilt Handle, 8 In. 55.00
Stein, Matte Green, Holly Berry Neck, Beaded Handle, Incised Mark, 5 1/2 In. 185.00
Toothpick, Matte Green Glaze, Corseted, Incised Mark, 3 x 1 3/4 In. 275.00
Vase, Alligator Matte Glaze, Ivory Over Mocha & Brown, Incised, 4 1/2 x 3 In. 665.00
Vase, Aqua To Green, Black Veining, Squatty, 4 1/4 x 4 1/2 In. 330.00
Vase, Bag, Matte Green Glaze, Ripples In Foil Bag, 11 x 5 In. 495.00

Vase, Blue Feathered Matte Glaze, Incised Mark, Artist, 10 1/2 In. 605.00
Vase, Bud, Lavender Over Dove Gray, Gray Speckled, Brown Interior, 5 x 2 3/4 In. 245.00
Vase, Butterscotch Matte Glaze, Raised Leaves & Stems, Incised Mark, 8 1/2 In. 410.00
Vase, Cerulean To Navy Matte Glaze, Trumpet Neck, Incised Mark, 5 1/2 x 4 In. 275.00
Vase, Cobalt Blue Glaze, Aqua & Gray, Buds & Blade Leaves, Incised Mark, 7 In. 550.00
Vase, Deep Matte Green Glaze, Gourd Shape, Incised Mark, 2 1/2 In. 245.00
Vase, Deep Matte Green, Embossed Water Lily, Egg Shaped, Incised Mark, 7 1/8 In. 660.00
Vase, Embossed Leaves & Buds, Bronze-Like Glaze, Signed, 6 1/2 In. 467.00
Vase, Embossed Leaves Alternating With Buds, Teal Blue Matte Glaze, 6 x 4 In. 660.00
Vase, Foliate Design, Matte Green Glaze, White Highlights, Marked, 6 x 3 1/2 In. 633.00
Vase, Geometric Design, Matte Green Glaze, 2 1/2 x 5 1/2 In. 374.00
Vase, Green Glaze, Trumpet Neck, Gray Flecks, Incised Mark, 9 1/2 x 6 1/4 In. 1100.00
Vase, Green Matte Glaze, Drip Design Around Base, 7 x 4 In. 305.00
Vase, Incised Scroll Design, Mottled Blue & Gray, Scroll Design, Signed, 7 1/2 In. 560.00
Vase, Incised Wave Design, Thick Green Matte Glaze, Artist, 5 1/2 x 2 In. 230.00
Vase, Leaf & Flower Form, Smooth Green Glaze, Signed, 6 3/4 In. 625.00
Vase, Matte Blue Glaze, Cream, Pink, 9 In. 935.00
Vase, Matte Green Glaze, Cloth Form, Flared Rim, 11 In. 520.00
Vase, Matte Green Glaze, Corn In Husks, Incised Mark, 5 1/3 x 5 In. 880.00
Vase, Matte Green Glaze, Tulips, Leaves, Incised Mark, 8 1/2 x 6 3/4 In. 1210.00
Vase, Molded Floral, Brown Glaze, Bulbous Base, Incised Mark, 6 1/2 In. 550.00
Vase, Molded Leaves, Stems & Buds, Brown Matte Glaze, Flared, Marked, 6 1/2 In. 660.00
Vase, Molded Stems, Leaves, Matte Yellow Glaze, 8 1/2 In. 495.00
Vase, Molded Vertical Leaves, Brown, Tan Matte Glaze, 7 In. 520.00
Vase, Mottled Azure Glaze, White Neck, White, Gray & Black Flecks, 7 1/4 In. 465.00
Vase, Mottled Matte Green Glaze, Hints Of Brown & Yellow, 7 In. 386.00
Vase, Mottled Sea Green To Aqua Glaze, Double Leaf Design, Base Hole, 8 1/4 In. 440.00
Vase, Stylized Tulips & Leaves, Light Brown Matte Glaze, Bulbous, 8 1/2 In. 550.00
Vase, Swastikas, Green Matte Glaze, Incised Mark, 5 1/2 x 2 In. 275.00
Vase, Thick Blue Feathered Matte Glaze, Round, Impressed Mark, 5 In. 385.00
Vase, Trumpet, Blue & Aqua Glaze, Horizontal Design, Incised Mark, 5 1/4 In. 220.00

HANDEL glass was made by Philip Handel working in Meriden, Connecticut, from 1885 and in New York City from 1893 to 1933. The firm made art glass and other types of lamps. Handel shades were made not only of leaded glass in a style reminiscent of Tiffany but also of reverse painted glass. Handel also made vases and other glass objects.

Humidor, 2 Owls On Branch, Glass Cover, Signed 1450.00
Humidor, Cover, Pipe Form, Dog & Horse Hand Painted On Exterior 1050.00
Lamp, 2 Center Bands Of Apple Blossoms, Geometric Amber Ground, 18 In. 3450.00
Lamp, 4 6-Sided Glass Shades, Mahogany, Prairie School Design, 14 x 19 In. 2310.00
Lamp, Black, Roses, Parrots, 16 In. . . . .*Illus* 15525.00
Lamp, Bronzed Metal Overlay Over Caramel Slag, Conical Shade, 16 x 8 In. 2420.00
Lamp, Brown, White Zigzag Design, Butterscotch Shade, Bronze Base, 7 In. 2310.00
Lamp, Cattails, Green, Brown, Bronze Overlay, Bronze Base, Slag Glass Ground, 24 In. . 3190.00
Lamp, Ceiling, 3 Gilt Metal Chains, Affixed To Center Mount, Signed, 16 In. 430.00
Lamp, Chipped Ice Shade, Autumn Leaves, Green, Brown, Purple, Beige Ground, 22 In. . 2400.00
Lamp, Chipped Ice Shade, Green Floral Design, Bronze Metal Base, 10 1/2 x 14 In. 1760.00
Lamp, Conical Shade, Grapes & Leaves, Bronzed Metal Base, Signed, 21 1/2 In. 3680.00
Lamp, Demilune, Blue Border, Metal Leaf Rim, 22 In. 1200.00
Lamp, Diamond Pattern On Exterior, Domed Shade, Cream Glass, Bronze Base, 20 In. . . 1650.00
Lamp, Dogwood, Red, Amber Centers, Bronze Patina Base, 25 In. 2700.00
Lamp, Domed Green Chipped Ice Shade, Bronze Harp Base, 14 x 57 In. 3570.00
Lamp, Globe, Hanging, Obverse Painted Birds, Trees, Tassel, 9 1/2 In. 2910.00
Lamp, Heraldic, Acid Etched, Coat Of Arms, Metal Base, 67 In. 400.00
Lamp, Leaded Glass Shade, Cream, Yellow, Green, Bronze Base, 23 x 19 In. 2530.00
Lamp, Leaded Glass Shade, Dogwood, Silk Label, Signed, 24 In. 1980.00
Lamp, Parrot, 4 Tapered Panels, Orange Parrots, Brown, Amber Jungle Leafage, 28 In. . . 4025.00
Lamp, Parrot, Large Butterfly Amidst Blossoming Peonies, Blue Ground, 23 1/2 In. 11000.00
Lamp, Pink Wild Roses, Green, Blue Leaves, Signed, 13 1/2 x 7 In. 2400.00
Lamp, Reverse Painted Chrysanthemums, Frosted Shade, Signed, 19 In. 2150.00
Lamp, Reverse Painted Shade, Basket Weave, Wild Rose, Domed, 22 x 15 In. 2185.00

Handel, Lamp, Black, Roses,
Parrots, 16 In.

Handel, Lamp, Reverse Painted
Shade, Wooded Landscape, 18 In.

**Never unplug an
electrical cord by
pulling the cord.
Always hold the
plastic part of
the plug. A loose
plug may spark,
causing a fire.**

Lamp, Reverse Painted Shade, Bird Of Paradise, Yellow, Green Foliage, Black, 24 In.	11500.00
Lamp, Reverse Painted Shade, Broad Landscape, Adjustable, Bronzed Base, 56 In.	3450.00
Lamp, Reverse Painted Shade, Daffodil, 3 Socket, Metal Base, Signed, 23 1/2 In.	6612.00
Lamp, Reverse Painted Shade, Domed, Harbor Scene, 14 1/2 x 7 In.	2415.00
Lamp, Reverse Painted Shade, Domed, Landscape, 8 Ribs, Signed, 24 1/2 x 18 In.	9255.00
Lamp, Reverse Painted Shade, Domed, Naturalistic, Footbridge, Stream, Signed, 23 In.	4887.00
Lamp, Reverse Painted Shade, Domed, Riverscape, Signed, 22 In.	4627.00
Lamp, Reverse Painted Shade, Floral Border, Bronzed Metal Base, Cloth Label, 22 In.	4125.00
Lamp, Reverse Painted Shade, Landscape, Signed, No. 6236A, c.1910, 12 x 8 In.	862.00
Lamp, Reverse Painted Shade, Meadow Scene, 14 x 7 In.	2645.00
Lamp, Reverse Painted Shade, Orange Flowers, Green Leaves, Bronze Base, 14 In.	2090.00
Lamp, Reverse Painted Shade, Pond Lilies, 13 1/2 x 7 In.	1840.00
Lamp, Reverse Painted Shade, Purple Asters, Pale Yellow, Pale Orange Ground, 21 In.	1700.00
Lamp, Reverse Painted Shade, Tree Landscape, Brown, Green, Bronze Base, 22 In.	7150.00
Lamp, Reverse Painted Shade, Wild Roses, Brown, Red, Green Ground, 9 x 14 In.	990.00
Lamp, Reverse Painted Shade, Wooded Landscape, 18 In. ....*Illus*	5200.00
Lamp, Reverse Painted Shade, Yellow Daffodils, Black, Green, Bronze Base, 24 In.	7700.00
Lamp, Scenic, Wooded Landscape, Birch, Oak Trees, Russet, Green, Brown, 24 In.	5400.00
Lamp, Stylized Green Leaf Shade, Tam-O'-Shanter, Cast Metal Base, 19 x 12 In.	546.00
Lamp, Yellow Glass Shade, Green Enamel Design, Stylized Metal Base, 13 In.	287.00
Lamp, Yellow Roses, Green Leaves On Trellises, Metal Overlay, 26 In.	2250.00
Shade, Bluebird, Ball Shape, Landscape, 2 Birds In Flight, Orange Interior, 6 x 3 In.	1495.00
Shade, Egg, Floral Design, Pale Amethyst Ground, 7 x 5 In.	300.00
Shade, Frosted Panels, Enameled, Black, Green, Red, Signed, 4 1/2 x 5 3/4 In.	350.00
Shade, Obverse, Chipped Ice Shade, Stylized Leaves, Scrolls, Signed, 25 1/2 In.	2300.00
Vase, Stylized Floral Motif, Gold, Amber Etch, 11 In.	1150.00
Vase, Teroma, Landscape Design, Brown, Trees, White Mountains, Signed, 8 x 4 In.	100.00
Vase, Wooded Landscape Scene, Enameled, 8 In.	690.00

HARDWARE, see Architectural category.

HARKER Pottery Company of East Liverpool, Ohio, was founded by
Benjamin Harker in 1840. The company made many types of pottery
but by the Civil War was making quantities of yellowware from native
clays. They also made Rockingham-type brown-glazed pottery and
whiteware. The plant was moved to Chester, West Virginia, in 1931.
Dinnerwares were made and sold nationally. In 1971 the company was
sold to Jeannette Glass Company and all operations ceased in 1972.
For more information, see *Kovels' Depression Glass & Dinnerware
Price List.*

Amethyst, Rolling Pin	95.00
Amy, Pie Plate	15.00
Amy, Rolling Pin	95.00
Autumn Brown, Cup & Saucer	30.00
Calico Tulip, Spoon	22.00
Cameoware, Rolling Pin, Blue	75.00

Cameoware, Salt & Pepper, Range 90.00
Country Cousins, Tidbit, Ring Handle, 10 In. 15.00
Daisy, Tidbit, Ring Handle, Yellow, 10 In. 25.00
Ivy, Pitcher 20.00
Mallow, Pie Plate 28.00
Meadow Green, Platter, 14 In. 45.00
Oriental Poppy, Teapot 40.00
Petit Point, Rolling Pin 75.00
Petit Point I, Casserole, Cover 20.00
Puritan, Jug, Honey 50.00
Red Apple, No. 2, Bowl, 4 In. ....7.00 to 8.00
Red Apple, No. 2, Custard 6.00
Red Apple, No. 2, Deep, Handle, 7 In. 7.00
Red Apple, No. 2, Pie Lifter 30.00
Red Apple, No. 2, Saucer 3.00
Red Apple, No. 2, Sugar & Creamer, Cover 24.00
Spring Time, Plate, 10 In. 10.00
Terra-Cotta, Cup & Saucer 30.00

HARLEQUIN dinnerware was produced by the Homer Laughlin Company from 1938 to 1964, and sold without trademark by the F. W. Woolworth Co. It has a concentric ring design like Fiesta, but the rings are separated from the rim by a plain margin. Cup handles are triangular in shape. For more information, see *Kovels' Depression Glass & Dinnerware Price List*.

Blue, Eggcup 12.00
Chartreuse, Casserole, Cover 240.00
Chartreuse, Pitcher, 22 Oz. 50.00
Chartreuse, Pitcher, 32 Oz. 75.00
Dark Green, Teapot 290.00
Gold, Figurine, Cat, Maverick 40.00
Gold, Figurine, Lamb, Maverick 55.00
Gray, Ashtray, Basketweave 90.00
Gray, Cup 10.00
Gray, Pitcher, 22 Oz. 95.00
Gray, Sugar, Cover 45.00
Gray, Teapot 185.00
Green, Creamer, Individual 125.00
Green, Plate, 7 In. 45.00
Maroon, Bowl, 5 1/2 In. 12.00
Maroon, Casserole, Cover 215.00
Maroon, Figurine, Cat 275.00
Maroon, Figurine, Donkey 275.00
Maroon, Figurine, Duck ....130.00 to 275.00
Maroon, Figurine, Penguin 285.00
Maroon, Gray, Yellow, Tidbit, 3-Tier, Metal 80.00
Maroon, Sugar & Creamer, After Dinner 195.00
Maroon, Sugar, Cover 45.00
Maroon, Teapot 195.00
Mauve, Ashtray 36.00
Mauve, Eggcup, Double 19.00
Mauve, Figurine, Donkey ....70.00 to 275.00
Mauve, Figurine, Lamb 160.00
Mauve, Figurine, Penguin 195.00
Mauve, Platter, 13 In. 25.00
Mauve, Teapot, Cover 95.00
Medium Green, Nappy 195.00
Medium Green, Plate, 7 In. 45.00
Medium Green, Plate, 10 In. ....135.00 to 195.00
Red, Ashtray 90.00
Red, Creamer, Individual 25.00
Red, Cup 14.00
Red, Jug, Ball 95.00

Red, Tumbler 42.00
Rose, Ashtray, Basketweave 65.00
Rose, Blue, Eggcup 12.00
Rose, Creamer, Novelty 25.00
Rose, Cup 4.50
Rose, Eggcup ....12.00 to 25.00
Rose, Eggcup, Double, 4 Piece 75.00
Rose, Nut Dish 95.00
Rose, Pitcher, 22 Oz. 50.00
Rose, Platter 18.00
Rose, Shaker 9.50
Rose, Tea Cup ....9.00 to 10.00
Rose, Tumbler 40.00
Spruce Green, Cup ....12.00 to 13.00
Spruce Green, Eggcup 23.00
Spruce Green, Figurine, Duck 275.00
Spruce Green, Figurine, Fish 275.00
Spruce Green, Figurine, Penguin 275.00
Spruce Green, Pitcher, Syrup 470.00
Spruce Green, Pitcher, Water 70.00
Spruce Green, Shaker 7.50
Spruce Green, Teapot, Cover 95.00
Tangerine, Eggcup 30.00
Tangerine, Pitcher, Water 70.00
Turquoise, Ashtray, Basketweave 30.00
Turquoise, Bowl, Nut, Basketweave 14.50
Turquoise, Creamer 10.00
Turquoise, Cup & Saucer, After Dinner 40.00
Turquoise, Gravy Boat 20.00
White, Figurine, Fish, Maverick, Gold Trim 55.00
Yellow, Casserole, Cover 75.00
Yellow, Cup & Saucer 9.50
Yellow, Figurine, Cat 195.00
Yellow, Figurine, Cat, Gold Trim 135.00
Yellow, Figurine, Donkey 175.00
Yellow, Figurine, Duck ....175.00 to 195.00
Yellow, Figurine, Duck, Gold Trim 99.00
Yellow, Figurine, Lamb 175.00
Yellow, Mauve, Bowl 18.50
Yellow, Pitcher, Ball 55.00

HATPIN collectors search for pins popular from 1860 to 1920. The long pin, often over four inches, was used to hold the hat in place on the hair. The tops of the pins were made of all materials, from solid gold and real gemstones to ceramics and glass. Be careful to buy original hatpins and not recent pieces made by altering old buttons.

Abalone Inlay, Sterling Silver Top, 7 In. 30.00
Faceted Clear Crystal Top, 3 In. 20.00
Faux Pearl 7.00
Red Bakelite, Uncarved, Screw-On Tip, 6 In., Pair 75.00
Square Top, Engraved, 14K Gold, 6 1/2 In. 40.00
Triple Floral Top, Rhinestone Set In Center, 8 In. 55.00

HATPIN HOLDERS were needed when hatpins were fashionable from 1860 to 1920. The large, heavy hat required special long-shanked pins to hold it in place. The hatpin holder resembles a large saltshaker, but it often has no opening at the bottom as a shaker does. Hatpin holders were made of all types of ceramics and metal. Look for other pieces under the names of specific manufacturers.

Art Nouveau, Woman's Face, Pink Bisque 275.00
Greenaway Girl, Tray 95.00
Pink Bisque, Schafer & Vater 325.00
White Poppy, Figural, Royal Bayreuth 500.00

HAVILAND china has been made in Limoges, France, since 1842. The factory was started by the Haviland Brothers of New York City. Pieces are marked *H & Co.*, *Haviland & Co.*, or *Theodore Haviland*. It is possible to match existing sets of dishes through dealers who specialize in Haviland china. Other factories worked in the town of Limoges making a similar chinaware. These porcelains are listed in this book under Limoges.

HAVILAND & CO.

Bowl, Floral Design, Scalloped Edge, Gold Rim, 9 In.	95.00
Bowl, Hand Painted Holly, L.C. McGarry, 1904, 9 7/8 In.	247.00
Box, Cover, White Forget-Me-Nots, Green Foliage, 13 x 4 1/2 x 3 3/4 In.	350.00
Bread Plate, My Garden, 8 x 6 1/2 In.	65.00
Chamber Pot, Child's	225.00
Chocolate Pot, Hand Painted Holly, 8 7/8 In.	220.00
Cup & Saucer, Green, Red Scrolled Floral Design, Gilt Edge, Demitasse	88.00
Feeder, Invalid, Red Berries, Green Holly, Hand Painted, 1877, 5 1/4 x 3 In.	200.00
Fish Set, 28-In. Platter, 10 1/2-In. Plate, 9 Piece	1175.00
Head, Aphrodite Emergeant Des Flots, Model Antoine Bourdelle, 1900, 8 1/4 In.	5250.00
Jardiniere, Sculptured Flowers, Terra-Cotta, Signed, H. & Co., 14 In.	1600.00
Ornament, Christmas, Angel, 1971, Box	6.50
Ornament, Christmas, Angel, 1978, Box	6.50
Plate, Christmas, 1971	20.00
Plate, Dinner, Wedding Ring, 1870	240.00
Plate, Luncheon, Floral, Painted, Scalloped Border, Gilt & Cobalt Rim, 12 Piece	316.00
Plate, Pink Floral Design, Gold Center, Scrolled Gold Band, 10 In.	5.50
Plate, Roses, Scalloped Border, Gold, Green, Gold Trim, 9 3/4 In., 12 Piece	1500.00
Plate, Soup, Scalloped Edge, White, France, 9 1/2 In.	120.00
Plate, The Burning Of The Gaspee, 10 In.	25.00
Platter, Yale, 8 1/2 x 11 3/4 In.	36.00
Punch Cup, Large Pink Roses, 4 Piece	300.00
Vase, 2 Oval Scenes Of Woman, Baskets & Garlands Of Flowers, 5 1/2 In.	245.00
Vase, Pillow, Roses, Buds & Leaves, Mottled Brown To Tan, 5 1/2 x 16 In.	1350.00

HAWKES cut glass was made by T. G. Hawkes & Company of Corning, New York, founded in 1880. The firm cut glass blanks made at other glassworks until 1962. Many pieces are marked with the trademark, a trefoil ring enclosing a fleur-de-lis and two hawks. Cut glass by other manufacturers is listed under either the factory name or in the general Cut Glass category.

Basket, Allover Scrolls & Leaves, Quadruple Notched Handle, Signed, 12 1/2 In.	1035.00
Basket, Engraved Floral & Panels, Signed, 11 In.	290.00
Basket, Floral & Bow Engraving, Sterling Silver Base, 12 x 6 In.	150.00
Bowl, 5-Pointed Star, Rays, Signed, 6 In.	65.00
Bowl, Devonshire, 9 In.	225.00
Bowl, Greek Key Rim, Crystal, 9 3/8 In.	137.00
Box, Hinged Cover, 6 1/2 In.	395.00
Candleholder, Intaglio Floral On Base, 4 In., Pair	130.00
Champagne, Raised Diamonds, Leaf Design Around Perimeter, 5 In., 6 Piece	275.00
Cocktail Shaker, Mallard Duck Over Marsh, Sterling Silver Rim & Cover, 12 1/2 In.	240.00
Compote, Candy, Green Teardrop Stem, Foot, 6 1/2 x 7 In.	95.00
Compote, Opalescent, Sterling Silver Base, 6 x 7 1/2 In.	363.00
Compote, Strawberries & Foliage, Hexagonal Cut Stem, Hobstar In Base, 6 1/2 In.	225.00
Creamer, Hobstar Chain, Vertical Pinstripes	85.00
Cruet, Oil & Vinegar, Floral, Leaf Design, Signed, 8 In.	100.00
Decanter, Etched Grape Fine & Leaf, Stopper, Signed, 12 In., Pair	495.00
Decanter, Etched, Face, Smiling, Winking Radiant Sunburst, 11 1/4 In.	315.00
Decanter, Whiskey, Golf Scene, The 19th Hole, Golf Holes, Flags, Greens, 1900, 12 In.	300.00
Decanter, Whiskey, Middlesex, Signed, 12 In.	395.00
Nappy, Hobstar & Strawberry, Loop Handle, 6 1/4 In.	55.00
Plate, Centauri, 9 3/4 In.	475.00
Salt & Pepper, Strawberry Cut Diamonds, Plastic Covers	33.00
Vase, Blue Exterior, White Tree Branch, Dot-Blossoms, Gold Rim, Signed, 9 3/4 In.	316.00
Vase, Engraved Dragon, Sterling Silver Rim, Signed, 10 1/4 In.	285.00
Vase, Etched, Square Foot, Sterling Silver Base, 10 1/2 In.	165.00

Vase, Floral Deign, 6 1/4 In.	242.00
Vase, Thumbprint Band, 8 In.	75.00
Vase, Trumpet, Floral, Leaf Pattern, Deep Ribbed Amethyst, Signed, 11 x 4 In.	350.00
Vase, Venetian, Trumpet Shape, 14 In.	750.00
Wine, Grapes & Vintage Cut Flint, Signed, 4 1/2 In., Set Of 6	395.00

HEAD VASES, generally showing a woman from the shoulders up, were used by florists primarily in the 1950s and 1960s. Made in a variety of sizes and often decorated with imitation jewelry and other lifelike accessories, the vases were manufactured in Japan and the U.S.A. Less elaborate examples were made as early as the 1930s. Religious themes, babies, and animals are also common subjects. Other head vases are listed under manufacturers' names and can be located through the index at the back of this book.

Baby, Bonnet, Holding Dog, 5 In.	95.00
Baby, Bonnet, Hull	50.00
Bam Bam, Flintstones	12.00
Blond, Napco, Small	65.00
Blue Blouse, Earrings, Necklace, Napcoware, 6 In.	40.00
Blue Flower On Shoulder, Earrings, Paper Label, Ucagco., 5 3/4 In.	50.00
Child, Germany, Wall	70.00
Christmas, Napco, 7 In.	110.00
Christmas Girl, Inarco, 4 1/2 In.	30.00
Cinderella	125.00
Collie Dog, 5 1/2 In.	35.00
Delsey Girl, Blonde, Enesco	85.00
Girl, Holding Umbrella, Blue & White Dress	95.00
Girl, Pale Yellow, 7 In.	55.00
Glamour Girl, Napco, 6 In.	60.00
Glamour Girl USA, Turned Head, Gold Highlights, Impressed Mark, 6 1/4 In.	20.00
Gloria Swanson, 7 1/2 In.	185.00 to 395.00
Gold Bow On Blouse, Relpo, 4 5/8 In.	35.00
Green Hat, Fingers, Ring, 7 In.	195.00
Green Top & Hat, Pink Flowers On Hat, 4 1/4 In.	15.00
Hand In Front Of Face, Big Lashes, Paper Label, Enesco, 5 1/2 In.	80.00
Hedda Hopper, 2 Hands, Relpo, 5 In.	115.00
High Collar Blouse, Earrings, Real Lashes, Paper Label, Napco, 5 1/2 In.	55.00
Howdy Doody	25.00
Jackie Kennedy, Hand To Cheek, Black Glove, Inarco, 6 In.	250.00 to 385.00
Jean, Pigtails, Plaid Dress, 7 In.	40.00
Kaye, California	65.00
Lady Aileen, Gold & Green Tiara, Painted Necklace, Inarco, 5 1/2. In.	175.00
Lavender Hat, Napco, 7 In.	175.00
Majorette	250.00
Nichols, 6 3/4 In.	330.00
Pearl Brooch, Earrings, Napcoware, Marked, 6 In.	45.00
Pebbles, Flintstones	12.00
Posegay, No. 142	140.00
Posegay, No. 216	95.00
Rubens, 7 In.	125.00

Don't use rubber gloves when washing figurines with protruding arms and legs. The gloves may snag and cause damage.

Head Vase, Woman, Black Hat, Long Eye Lashes, Pearl Earrings, Inarco, 7 In.

Shoulderless Blouse, Gold & White Bow On Black Hat, Napco, 5 1/8 In. 55.00
Teen, Blue, 8 1/2 In. 1500.00
White & Gold Ruffled Top, Paper Label, Napcoware, 6 1/8 In. 35.00
Woman, Black Hat, Long Eye Lashes, Pearl Earrings, Inarco, 7 In. . . . . *Illus* 25.00
Woman, Bonnet, Inarco, 4 1/2 In. 75.00
Woman, Earrings, Necklace, Gloved Hand, Bow, Pierced Hat, Inarco, 7 7/8 In. 165.00
Woman, Earrings, Necklace, Relpo, Paper Label, 7 In. 210.00
Woman, Hat, Hair, Pearls, Napco, 5 1/2 In. 95.00
Woman, Holding Fan, Jewelry 75.00
Woman, Madge, Blue Hat, Faux Pearl Choker, Napco, 5 3/4 In. 45.00
Woman, Pearl Brooch, Earrings, Napcoware, Marked, Paper Label, 6 In. 45.00
Woman, Tilted Hat, Fingers, Jewelry, Napco, 4 1/2 In. 125.00
Young Girl With Braids, 5 1/2 In. 45.00

HEDI SCHOOP Art Creations, North Hollywood, California, started
about 1945 and was working until 1954. Schoop made ceramic figurines, lamps, planters, and tablewares.

Hedi Schoop S

Ashtray, Duck, Green, Gold, 5 x 6 1/2 In. 30.00
Bowl, Gray, Pink Flower Design, Pink Interior, 14 In. 55.00
Cookie Jar, Darner Doll, Striped Skirt 265.00
Cookie Jar, Queen & King 2000.00
Figurine, Chinese Couple, With Buckets, 11 1/2 In. 98.00
Figurine, Chinese Girl, With Lantern, 11 1/2 In. 75.00
Figurine, Dutch Boy & Girl, With Buckets, 11 1/2 In. 95.00
Figurine, French Peasant Couple, 13 In. 195.00
Figurine, Girl, Ponytail, Short Blue Skirt, Gray Poodle Dog, 9 1/2 In. 145.00
Figurine, Oriental Woman, With Umbrella, Green On White, 11 1/2 In. 65.00
Figurine, Peasant Woman, Ruffled Dress, White Bonnet, Drawstring Purse, 10 In. 85.00
Figurine, Poodle, Black & White, Base, 12 1/4 In., Pair 325.00
Figurine, Rooster, 13 In. 165.00
Planter, Hobby Horse 50.00
Planter, Peasant, With Beret, 13 In. 70.00
Planter, Woman With Book, 9 1/8 In. 45.00
Tray, Figural Woman, Skirt Forms Tray 145.00
Vase, Speckled Pink & Green, Ruffled, 7 In., Pair 75.00
Vase, Yellow Flowers, Gray, 8 1/2 In. 55.00

HEINTZ ART Metal Shop made jewelry, copper, silver, and brass in
Buffalo, New York, from 1906 to 1935, when a new company name
was taken and the mark became *Silvercrest.* The most popular items
with collectors today are the copper desk sets and vases made with
applied silver designs.

Ashtray, Attached Match Safe, Sterling Silver On Bronze, 8 In. 125.00
Bowl, Floral Design, Silver On Copper, Original Patina, 9 x 3 In. 253.00
Bowl, Roses, Silver On Copper, 7 1/2 x 3 1/2 In. 110.00
Box, Cigarette, Flying Geese, Silver On Bronze, Brown Patina, 7 1/2 x 4 1/2 x 3 In. 175.00
Box, Cigarette, Stylized Silver On Bronze, Original Patina, 4 x 4 x 2 In. 286.00
Candlestick, Floral Design, Sterling On Bronze, Green, Brown Patina, 5 In., Pair 275.00
Candlestick, Foliate Silver On Bronze, Flared Base, Signed, 14 1/2 In. 1022.00
Candlestick, Sterling On Bronze, Greek Letters & Stylized Design, 8 In., Pair 385.00
Charger, Presentation To Ohio Ladies Of The GAR, Original Patina, 1911, 13 In. 121.00
Cup, Presentation, Stylized Floral Design, Silver On Bronze, 1919, 17 x 10 1/2 In. 220.00
Desk Set, Blotter Corners, Silver Sea Gulls Recessed Into Copper, 6 Piece 192.00
Desk Set, Plant Design, Silver On Bronze, Pat. Aug. 27, '12, 3 Piece 240.00
Desk Set, Silver On Bronze, Tree Design 350.00
Humidor, Overlaid Fox Hunting Scene, Sterling On Bronze, Signed, 6 3/4 In. 715.00
Lamp, Bronze Helmet, 3 Silver Flowers, Coral Center, 9 3/4 In. . . . . 775.00 to 885.00
Lamp, Landscape Design, Deer, Being Chased By Dogs, Sterling On Bronze, 13 In. 1045.00
Lamp, Stylized Flower, Repeated In Silk Shade, Sterling On Bronze, 14 1/2 In. 2420.00
Lamp, Table, Silhouetted Dancing Figures, Silk Lined Shade, Foil Label, 12 1/2 In. 770.00
Plate, Advertising, Heintz Bros., Makers Of Rings, Acid Etched Copper, 7 In. 165.00
Vase, Copper, Sterling Cattails & Bamboo Design, Pat. Aug. 27, '12, 6 In., Pair 200.00
Vase, Iris Design, Sterling On Bronze, Impressed Mark, 15 x 5 In. 230.00

Vase, Landscape, Trees, House, Clouds, Windmill, Silver On Bronze, 11 In. 605.00
Vase, Overlaid Flowers, Commemorative Message, Sterling On Bronze, 10 3/4 In. 330.00
Vase, Pinecone, Needle Design, Silver On Bronze, Original Patina, 6 In. 230.00
Vase, Silver Bamboo Design, Cylindrical, 9 In. 286.00

HEISEY glass was made from 1896 to 1957 in Newark, Ohio, by A. H.
Heisey and Co., Inc. The Imperial Glass Company of Bellaire, Ohio,
bought some of the molds and the rights to the trademark. Some Heisey
patterns have been made by Imperial since 1960. After 1968, they
stopped using the *H* trademark. Heisey used romantic names for colors,
such as *Sahara*. Do not confuse color and pattern names. The Custard
Glass and Ruby Glass categories may also include some Heisey pieces.

Animal, Asiatic Pheasant 125.00
Animal, Colt, Standing 75.00
Animal, Fighting Rooster 90.00
Animal, Giraffe ....150.00 to 170.00
Animal, Ring Neck Pheasant 125.00
Animal, Sparrow 95.00
Athena, Dish, Mayonnaise, Underplate 39.00
Banded Flute, Chamberstick 45.00
Banded Flute, Eggcup 32.00
Banded Flute, Saltshaker 50.00
Banded Flute, Wine, 4 In. 50.00
Carcassone, Tumbler, Alexandrite, 8 Oz. 120.00
Coarse Rib, Mustard, Cover, Amber, Stained 65.00
Colonial, Cocktail, Stem 10.00
Colonial, Punch Cup, 1 3/4 x 2 1/4 In. 15.00
Colonial, Sherbet 12.50
Colonial, Straw Holder 125.00
Colonial, Tumbler, Footed, 6 Oz. 50.00
Creole, Goblet, Alexandrite 195.00
Crystolite, Bowl, Salad 69.00
Crystolite, Candlestick, 3-Light, Pair 75.00
Crystolite, Celery Dish, 2 Sections 30.00
Crystolite, Cheese Dish, Footed, 5 1/2 In. ....20.00 to 29.00
Crystolite, Cigarette Box, Cover 30.00
Crystolite, Cigarette Holder 25.00
Crystolite, Coaster 7.00
Crystolite, Cruet, Oil, 3 Oz. 35.00
Crystolite, Mustard, Paddle 35.00
Crystolite, Plate, 8 1/2 In. 15.00
Crystolite, Plate, Cheese, 2 Handles, 8 In. 45.00
Crystolite, Plate, Salad, 7 In. 9.00
Crystolite, Puff Box, Cover, 4 3/4 In. 55.00
Crystolite, Punch Cup ....10.00 to 12.00
Crystolite, Punch Set, 14 Piece 200.00
Crystolite, Sugar & Creamer ....25.00 to 50.00
Crystolite, Vase, Footed, 5 1/4 In. 30.00
Cut Block, Toothpick, Custard 200.00
Daisy & Leaves, No. 480, Basket, Handle, Round, 9 1/2 x 8 In. 200.00
Double Rib & Panel, No. 417, Basket, Handle, Flamingo, 8 1/2 x 6 In. .. 143.00
Empress, Bowl, Flamingo, 4 1/2 In. 19.00
Empress, Celery Dish, Moongleam, Marked, 13 In. 30.00
Empress, Creamer, Dolphin Footed, Flamingo 40.00
Empress, Cruet, Sahara 200.00
Empress, Cup & Saucer, Sahara ....36.00 to 40.00
Empress, Dish, Mayonnaise, Empress Etch, Flamingo 50.00
Empress, Goblet, Flamingo 70.00
Empress, Ice Bucket, Arctic Etch 169.00
Empress, Iced Tea, Footed, Flamingo 50.00
Empress, Lemon Server, Oval 50.00
Empress, Nasturtium Bowl, Sahara, 7 1/2 In. 100.00
Empress, Nut Cup, Sahara ....20.00 to 26.00

Empress, Plate, Alexandrite, Square, 8 In. 95.00
Empress, Plate, Moongleam, 6 In. 17.00
Empress, Plate, Sahara, Square, 7 In. 15.00
Empress, Punch Cup, Moongleam 40.00
Empress, Relish, 3 Sections, Moongleam, 7 In. 35.00
Empress, Soup, Cream, Sahara 37.00
Empress, Sugar & Creamer 60.00
Fancy Loop, Cracker Jar, Cover 275.00
Fancy Loop, Punch Bowl, Base 325.00
Fancy Loop, Saltshaker, Metal Top 23.00
Fancy Loop, Sauce, 5 1/2 In. 11.00
Fancy Loop, Tumbler, Souvenir, Mt. Clemens, 1898 .... 50.00
Fandango, Bowl, 9 3/4 In. 65.00
Fandango, Cruet, Faceted Stopper, 8 Oz. 65.00
Fandango, Wine, 3 Oz. 95.00
Fish, Bookends 125.00
Flat Panel, Toothpick 45.00
Gascony, Decanter, Cobalt & Crystal, 1 Pt. 595.00
Georgian, Candlestick, 9 In., Pair 175.00
Greek Key, Compote, 5 1/2 x 6 1/2 In. 65.00
Greek Key, Cruet, No. 8 Stopper 65.00
Greek Key, Goblet 75.00
Greek Key, Plate, 5 In. ....13.00 to 18.00
Greek Key, Punch Bowl, Base, 14 1/2 x 15 In. 260.00
Greek Key, Punch Cup 15.00
Greek Key, Salt & Pepper 95.00
Greek Key, Sherbet, 3 In. 15.00
Greek Key, Sugar & Creamer, Oval 100.00
Helmet, No. 467, Basket, Leaf & Floral, Gold & Blue Enamel, 10 1/2 x 10 1/2 In. ... 115.00
Horsehead, Bookends 325.00
Ipswich, Candy Jar, Cover, 1 Lb. 150.00
Ipswich, Cruet 225.00
Ipswich, Finger Bowl, Underplate 18.00
Ipswich, Goblet, Flamingo 275.00
Ipswich, Plate, 8 In. ....18.00 to 25.00
Ipswich, Sherbet 25.00
Ipswich, Tumbler, 5 Oz. 23.00
Ipswich, Tumbler, Footed, 8 Oz. 59.00
Jamestown, Cordial, 1 Oz. 60.00
Lariat, Ashtray, Coaster 9.00
Lariat, Bowl, Floral, Scalloped Edge, 11 In. 75.00
Lariat, Candlestick, 2-Light, Pair 50.00
Lariat, Coaster ....8.00 to 10.00
Lariat, Cocktail, 4 1/2 Oz. 17.00
Lariat, Iced Tea, Footed 28.00
Lariat, Plate, 8 In. ....12.00 to 25.00
Lariat, Punch Set, Bowl, Underplate, 48 Cups 375.00
Lariat, Relish, 2 Handles, 2 Sections, 11 In. 40.00
Lariat, Sugar & Creamer 45.00
Lariat, Tray, Moonglo Cutting, Oval, 15 In. 48.00
Lariat, Vase, Bud, Swung, 15 In. 185.00
Lariat, Wine, 5 1/2 Oz. 22.00
Locket On Chain, Cake Stand, 9 1/2 In. ....110.00 to 145.00
Locket On Chain, Gaslight Shade 135.00
Locket On Chain, Toothpick, Green 3190.00
Mercury, Candlestick 35.00
Minuet, Goblet 40.00
Narrow Flute, Mustard, Cover 55.00
Narrow Flute, Nut Dish, Marked, Patent Date 15.00
Narrow Flute, Sugar, Cover 28.00
Narrow Flute, Wine, 5 1/2 In. 15.00
New Era, Candlestick, 2-Light, Pair 170.00
New Era, Champagne, 4 1/2 In. 12.00

New Era, Cordial . . . . .40.00 to 48.00
New Era, Cup & Saucer . . . . .50.00 to 60.00
New Era, Goblet, 6 1/2 In. 18.00
New Era, Plate, 6 In. 25.00
New Era, Sherbet 20.00
Oak Leaf, Coaster, Hawthorne 120.00
Octagon, Frozen Dessert, Flamingo 20.00
Octagon, Frozen Dessert, Moongleam 30.00
Old Colony, Bowl, Flamingo, 7 3/4 In. 62.00
Old Colony, Compote, Sahara, Oval, 7 In. 135.00
Old Colony, Cup & Saucer, Flamingo 33.00
Old Colony, Plate, Flamingo, 10 In. 30.00
Old Colony, Relish, 3 Sections, Flamingo 28.00
Old Colony, Tumbler, Flamingo, 9 Oz. 18.00
Old Dominion, Champagne, Alexandrite 110.00
Old Dominion, Wine, Alexandrite 160.00
Old Glory, Wine, 2 Oz. 37.50
Old Sandwich, Ashtray, Individual 10.00
Old Sandwich, Bowl, Flamingo, 11 In. 98.00
Old Sandwich, Candlestick, Sahara, Pair 130.00
Old Sandwich, Goblet, Sahara 37.00
Old Sandwich, Mug, Sahara, 18 Oz. 250.00
Old Sandwich, Plate, 7 In. 9.00
Old Sandwich, Tumbler, Footed, Sahara, 16 Oz. 35.00
Old Sandwich, Whiskey, Sahara 100.00
Old Williamsburg, Candelabrum, 2-Light, Pair 275.00
Old Williamsburg, Cherry Jar, 9 Oz. 95.00
Old Williamsburg, Cocktail, Stem 10.00
Old Williamsburg, Creamer, 4 1/2 In. . . . . .22.00 to 28.00
Old Williamsburg, Horseradish Jar, Lid, 6 Oz. 95.00
Old Williamsburg, Iced Tea, Footed 20.00
Old Williamsburg, Wine 14.00
Orchid, Cocktail Shaker, 1 Pt. 295.00
Orchid, Sugar & Creamer, Individual 45.00
Orchid, Syrup 150.00
Orchid, Tumbler, 10 Oz. 30.00
Orchid Etch, Ashtray, 3 In. 30.00
Orchid Etch, Bottle, French Dressing 170.00
Orchid Etch, Candlestick, Cascade, 3-Light, Pair 195.00
Orchid Etch, Cascade, Candlestick, 3-Light 60.00
Orchid Etch, Champagne, 6 Oz. 32.00
Orchid Etch, Cocktail Shaker, Sterling Silver Base, Silver Clad Stopper 350.00
Orchid Etch, Cup & Saucer, Footed 40.00
Orchid Etch, Goblet 34.00
Orchid Etch, Jam Jar, Silver Sterling Cover 95.00
Orchid Etch, Sandwich Server, Center Handle, 13 In. 150.00
Orchid Etch, Sherbet, Flared, 6 Oz. 20.00
Orchid Etch, Tumbler, Footed, 7 3/4 In. 60.00
Orchid Etch, Vase, Fan, Lariat, 7 In. 135.00
Orchid Etch, Wine 58.00
Patrician, Candlestick, 7 1/2 In., Pair 160.00
Peerless, Pitcher, 2 Qt. 165.00
Peerless, Plate, 5 1/2 In. 12.00
Peerless, Sherbet, Flamingo 55.00
Peerless, Toothpick 50.00
Picket, No. 458, Basket, Jeweled Rose Cut & Engraving, 11 1/2 x 8 1/2 In. 218.00
Pied Piper, Goblet, Wine 45.00
Pied Piper, Pitcher, 9 In. 350.00
Pineapple & Fan, Mug 35.00
Pineapple & Fan, Toothpick, Gold Trim 45.00
Pineapple & Fan, Tumbler 35.00
Pineapple & Fan, Vase, 6 1/2 In. 30.00
Pinwheel & Fan, Basket, 7 In. . . . . .225.00 to 395.00

Pinwheel & Fan, Bowl, Flamingo, Marked, 8 1/2 In. 215.00
Plantation, Candelabra, 2-Light, Pair 275.00
Plantation, Candle Block, Pair 225.00
Plantation, Cruet 50.00
Plantation, Goblet, 9 Oz. 38.00
Plantation, Parfait, 5 Oz. 35.00
Plantation, Pitcher 575.00
Plantation, Plate, 8 In. 35.00
Plantation, Punch Bowl 950.00
Plantation, Punch Cup . . . . .18.00 to 27.00
Plantation, Punch Set, Dr. Johnson, Bowl, 6 Cups, Ladle, 8 Piece . . . . .1000.00 to 1200.00
Plantation, Salt & Pepper 80.00
Plantation, Sherbet, 6 Oz. 25.00
Plantation, Sugar & Creamer 70.00
Plantation, Syrup 80.00
Plantation, Wine, 4 7/8 In. 55.00
Pleat & Panel, Candy Dish, Cover, Footed Flamingo, Low 65.00
Pleat & Panel, Cup & Saucer, Flamingo 27.50
Priscilla, Mustard, Cover 30.00
Priscilla, Toothpick 45.00
Prism Band, Decanter, Moongleam 265.00
Prison Stripe, Butter, Cover 125.00
Prison Stripe, Spooner, Crystal 85.00
Provincial, Bowl, Zircon, Marked, 5 1/2 In. 40.00
Provincial, Cigarette Set, Box & 2 Ashtrays 75.00
Provincial, Cruet, No. 6 Stopper, Marked, 4 Oz. 45.00
Provincial, Goblet, 10 Oz. 15.00
Provincial, Juice, Zircon, 6 Oz. 60.00
Puritan, Box, Cigarette, Horsehead Cover, 6 In. 80.00
Puritan, Claret, 4 Oz. 20.00
Puritan, Iced Tea, Footed 35.00
Puritan, Punch Cup, Footed 7.00
Puritan, Tankard, Silver Overlay, 9 In. 300.00
Queen Ann, Candlestick, 8 In. 75.00
Queen Ann, Cruet, No. 6 Stopper 75.00
Queen Ann, Cup & Saucer 45.00
Queen Ann, Ice Bucket, Bail & Tongs 265.00
Queen Ann, Jug, Dolphin, Footed, 3 Pt. 65.00
Queen Ann, Nut Dish, Dolphin Footed 22.00
Queen Anne, Ashtray, 7 In. 20.00
Recessed Panel, Jam Jar, Cover 65.00
Regency, Candlestick, 2-Light, Pair 98.00
Renaissance, Claret, 4 Oz. 52.00
Renaissance, Goblet, 9 Oz. 40.00
Ridgeleigh, Candlestick, Square, 2 In., Pair 78.00
Ridgeleigh, Champagne 25.00
Ridgeleigh, Cigarette Box, Cover, 4 x 2 3/4 x 1 3/4 In. 145.00
Ridgeleigh, Coaster, Zircon 45.00
Ridgeleigh, Cruet 48.00
Ridgeleigh, Mustard, Cover 35.00
Ridgeleigh, Plate, Sandwich, 14 1/2 In. 55.00
Ridgeleigh, Sherbet 19.00
Ridgeleigh, Sugar & Creamer 35.00
Ring Band, Butter, Cover, Gold Trim 245.00
Ring Band, Toothpick, Custard 60.00
Rococo, Candlestick, 2-Light, Marked 225.00
Rose Etch, Cordial 165.00
Rose Etch, Goblet 45.00
Rose Etch, Relish, 3 Sections, Oval 75.00
Rose Etch, Salt & Pepper . . . . .50.00 to 75.00
Rose Etch, Sandwich Server, Center Handle, 14 In. . . . . .215.00 to 245.00
Rose Etch, Sherbet 35.00
Rose Etch, Torte Plate, 14 In. 97.00

Rose Etch, Wine, 3 Oz.	95.00
Round Colonial, No. 459, Basket, Butterfly & Floral Engraving, 13 1/2 x 7 In.	200.00
Saturn, Cruet	45.00
Saturn, Goblet, Zircon	85.00
Saturn, Mustard, Cover, Silver Finial	27.50
Saturn, Plate, Zircon, 7 In.	35.00
Saturn, Sugar & Creamer, Zircon	295.00
Sweet Ad-O-Line, Goblet, 14 Oz.	300.00
Tangerine, Goblet, Water	200.00
Trident, Candlestick, 2-Light, Tea Rose Etch, 5 In., Pair	75.00
Tudor, Bonbon, 2 Handles, Moongleam	27.00
Tudor, Dish, Mayonnaise	30.00
Tudor, Mustard, Cover, Moongleam	145.00
Tudor, Pitcher, 5 7/8 In.	50.00
Tudor, Tumbler, Straight, 8 Oz.	15.00
Twist, Bowl, Marigold, 8 In.	45.00
Twist, Celery Dish, Flamingo, 13 In.	40.00
Twist, Cheese Plate, 2 Handles, Moongleam, 6 In.	17.50
Twist, Cruet, Flamingo	75.00
Twist, Cup & Saucer, Lightning Handle, Marigold	40.00
Twist, Mustard, Cover, Underplate, Moongleam	90.00
Twist, Plate, Moongleam, 7 In.	14.00
Twist, Relish, 3 Sections, Moongleam	28.00
Twist, Sauce, Flamingo, 4 1/2 In.	60.00
Twist, Soup, Cream, Flamingo	23.00
Victorian, Champagne	15.00
Wampum, Plate, Torte, 14 In.	49.00
Warwick, Match Holder, Cornucopia, Sahara, 2 1/2 In.	40.00
Warwick, Vase, Cornucopia, 7 In.	25.00
Waverly, Relish, 3 Sections, 11 x 8 In.	50.00
Waverly, Sugar & Creamer, Footed	70.00
Whirlpool, Candy Dish, Cover, Footed	75.00
Yeoman, Bowl, Tan Enameled Band, 10 In.	30.00
Yeoman, Cup & Saucer, Hawthorne	42.00

HEREND, see Fischer category.

HEUBACH is the collector's name for Gebruder Heubach, a firm working in Lichten, Germany, from 1840 to 1925. It is best known for bisque dolls and doll heads, their principal products. They also manufactured bisque figurines, including piano babies, beginning in the 1880s, and glazed figurines in the 1900s. Piano babies are listed in their own category. Dolls are included in the Doll category under *Gebruder Heubach* and *Heubach*. Another factory, Ernst Heubach, working in Koppelsdorf, Germany, also made porcelain and dolls. These will also be found in the Doll category under Heubach Koppelsdorf.

Bowl, Man & Woman, Mermaids, Iridescent Purple, 4 x 7 In.	495.00
Figurine, Boy & Girl, In Nightgowns, Dog & Cat, 4 1/2 In., Pair	500.00
Figurine, Cat, Lying On Side, White, 9 1/2 In.	300.00
Figurine, Dachshund, Seated, Shaded Gray, 7 1/2 In.	325.00
Figurine, Dancing Girl, Green Dress, Signed, 8 1/2 In.	195.00
Figurine, Farmer Boy, Farmer Girl, 12 1/2 In., Pair	750.00
Figurine, Girl, With Bonnet, 8 In.	350.00
Tray, Indian, On Horseback, Chased By Buffalo, 6 x 5 In.	145.00
Vase, Jonquil, Reticulated, 10 1/2 In.	500.00
Vase, Young Boy, Blue Bathing Suit, Exiting Cabana At High Tide, Signed, 6 In.	27.00

HIGBEE glass was made by the J. B. Higbee Company of Bridgeville, Pennsylvania, about 1900. Tablewares were made, and it is possible to assemble a full set of dishes and goblets in some Higbee patterns. Most of the glass was clear, not colored. Additional pieces may be found in the Pressed Glass category by pattern name.

Ladle, Tree	45.00
Plate, Child's, ABC, Dog Center, Bee Mark, 6 In.	55.00

HISTORIC BLUE, see factory names, such as Adams, Clews, Ridgway, and Staffordshire.

HOBNAIL glass is a style of glass with bumps all over. Dozens of hobnail patterns and variants have been made. Clear, colored, and opalescent hobnail have been made and are being reproduced. Other pieces of hobnail may also be listed in the Duncan & Miller, Fenton, and Francisware categories.

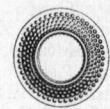

Basket, Amberina, Thorn Handle, Gold Enameled Floral, New England Glass, 11 In.	500.00
Basket, Cranberry, Silver Mica, Applied Thorn Handle, Rigaree, 11 x 8 x 10 In.	350.00
Bowl, Ruffled Edge, Opalescent, 6 x 2 3/4 In.	35.00
Cake Stand, Square	85.00
Cruet, Blue, Stopper, Small	75.00
Decanter, Wind, Plum Opalescent, Handle	300.00
Epergne, Plum Opalescent, 3 Trumpets	400.00
Pitcher, Milk, Anchor Hocking, 18 In.	20.00
Pitcher, Oval Star, Creamer	5000.00
Saltshaker, Blue	11.00
Smoke Bell, Cranberry, Applied Ring, Ruffled, Boston & Sandwich, 1880, 4 1/2 In.	525.00
Spooner, Ruffled Edge, Opalescent	27.00
Syrup, Cranberry Opalescent	895.00
Tray, Water, Blue, 11 1/2 In.	40.00
Tumbler, Pale Green, 7 1/2 In.	55.00
Tumbler, Water, Blue	25.00
Water Set, Blue, 6 Piece	125.00

HOCHST, or Hoechst, porcelain was made in Germany from 1746 to 1796. It was marked with a six-spoke wheel. Be careful when buying Hochst; many other firms have used a very similar wheel-shaped mark.

Bowl, Cover, Sprays, Sprigs, Puce Scrollwork, Fan-Shaped Handles, 8 3/4 In.	3162.00
Cup & Saucer, 2 Boys Tussling Before Distant Cottage, Puce, Gilt Rim, 2 x 5 In.	345.00
Cup & Saucer, Ogee Bird Perched On Branch, Red, Yellow, Rose, Green, 1770, 2 In.	1955.00
Figurine, Boy, Running To Embrace Girl, Signed, 19th Century, 5 1/4 In.	172.00
Figurine, Farmer Wearing Black Hat, With Eggs, Carrying Wicker Basket, 6 1/16 In.	5462.00
Figurine, Girl In Bonnet, Carrying Basket Of Fruit, 6 In.	143.00
Figurine, Girl In Hat, Goose & 2 Goslings, Signed, 19th Century, 4 3/4 In.	115.00
Figurine, Girl With Fruit, Wearing Turquoise Hair Bow, Blue Bodice, 1755, 4 3/4 In.	1495.00
Figurine, Lady With Cat, Wearing Pink Dress, Holding Brown & White Cat, 4 In.	1955.00
Figurine, Pilgrim & White Biscuit Bust Of Venus, Scalloped Shells, 4 7/16 & 7 In.	460.00
Figurine, Woman Carrying Goose In Basket, Man With Parcel, Signed, 6 1/2 In.	115.00
Vase, Cover, Potpourri, Pear-Shaped Body, 4 Rose Flower Heads On Cover, 1765, 6 In.	575.00

HOLLY AMBER, or golden agate, glass was made by the Indiana Tumbler and Goblet Company of Greentown, Indiana, from January 1, 1903, to June 13, 1903. It is a pressed glass pattern featuring holly leaves in the amber-shaded glass. The glass was made with shadings that range from creamy opalescent to brown-amber.

Butter, Cover	1875.00
Compote	1250.00
Cruet	1850.00 to 2100.00
Plate, 7 3/8 In.	385.00
Syrup	2500.00
Toothpick	795.00

HOLT HOWARD was an importer who started working in 1949 in Stamford, Connecticut. He sold many types of table accessories, such as condiment jars, decanters, spoon holders, and saltshakers. The figures shown on some of his pieces had a cartoon-like quality. The company was bought out by General Housewares Corporation in 1969. Holt Howard pieces are often marked with the name and the year or HH and the year stamped in black. There was also a black and silver label.

Ashtray, Butler	40.00
Ashtray, Cozy Kitten, Metal Stand For Matches	100.00 to 110.00

Ashtray, Mouse 25.00
Bottle, Italian Dressing, Pixie .... 295.00 to 300.00
Bottle, Russian Dressing, Pixie .... 175.00 to 295.00
Bowl, Rooster, 6 In. 18.00
Box, Stinky Cheese Mouse .... 55.00 to 65.00
Breakfast Set, Rooster, Service For 4, 16 Piece 95.00
Cake Topper, Bride, Box 65.00
Candle Hugger, Santa Claus 45.00
Candleholder, Angel 35.00
Candleholder, Angel, Pair 70.00
Candleholder, Bride & Groom, Box 40.00
Candleholder, Christmas, Pair .... 45.00 to 70.00
Candleholder, Praying Children 32.00
Candleholder, Santa Claus, 4 In., Pair 35.00
Candlestick, Figural, Horses, Christmas, Pair 30.00
Candlestick, White, Pink, Blue, With Blue Bird Ring 28.00
Candlestick Holder, Rooster 40.00
Cheese Keeper, Cats Cottage 45.00
Cocktail Shaker, The Bartender, Stirrer, Tumblers, 6 Piece 160.00
Coffee Set, Rooster, 6 Matching Mugs, Pitcher, 9 1/2 In. 75.00
Coffeepot, Chicken, Electric 100.00
Container, Ketchup, White, Orange & Green, Square, 4 x 4 In. ...... *Illus* 75.00
Cookie Jar, Rooster .... 75.00 to 85.00
Dish, Butter, Cover, Cats, White, Plaid Base 95.00
Dish, Butter, Cover, Rooster 42.00
Dish, Butter, Cozy Kitten .... 155.00 to 225.00
Dish, Christmas Tree, 9 3/4 In. 10.00
Dish, Christmas Tree, Divided, 13 3/4 In. 20.00
Dish, Cottage Cheese, Cat, White 45.00
Dish, Cottage Cheese, Cover, Kissing Cats, Standing 95.00
Dish, Feeding, Child's, Horsehead 200.00
Dispenser, Tape, Pelican 130.00
Eggcup, Rooster .... 15.00 to 18.00
Figurine, Angel Musician, Feather Body, Reads Music, Paper Label, 8 In. ... 29.00
Figurine, Camel 45.00
Head Vase, Christmas Lady, 4 In. 65.00
Head Vase, Holiday 125.00
Holder, Letter, Kozy Kitten 145.00
Inkwell, Bird, Tail Feathers Pen 75.00
Jar, Cherries, Pixie 195.00
Jar, Cocktail Olives, Pixie .... 225.00 to 295.00
Jar, Coffee, Instant, Pixie 375.00
Jar, Coffee, Pixie, No Spoon 135.00
Jar, Jam 'n Jelly, Pixie .... 40.00 to 100.00
Jar, Jam 'n Jelly, Rooster 22.00
Jar, Ketchup, Cat 450.00
Jar, Ketchup, Pixie, 4 1/2 x 6 In. .... 78.00 to 110.00
Jar, Mayonnaise, Pixie .... 145.00 to 150.00
Jar, Mustard, Cat 450.00
Jar, Mustard, Pixie, 1958 .... 110.00 to 125.00
Jar, Olive, Pixie .... 95.00 to 185.00
Jar, Onion, Pixie 100.00
Letter Holder, Cat .... 65.00 to 100.00
Match Holder, Cat 110.00
Mug, Christmas 10.00
Mug, Tan & Brown Glaze, Signed, 5 x 5 In. 11.00
Napkin Holder, Cat, White 70.00
Napkin Holder, Rooster 40.00
Pepper Shaker, Rooster, Large 18.00
Pin Box, Cozy Kitten, Measuring Tape In Cat's Mouth 200.00
Pitcher, 4 Matching Cups, Santa Claus 90.00
Planter, Duck, Hole In Head For Plant, Label, Box 75.00
Plate, Rooster, 8 1/2 In. 10.00

Holt Howard, Container, Ketchup, White,
Orange & Green, Square, 4 x 4 In.

Holt Howard, String Holder, Cozy Kitten With
Scissors, 4 1/2 In.

Relish, Tree Shape, Divided 25.00
Salt & Pepper, Cats, 1958, 4 1/4 In. .... .30.00 to 45.00
Salt & Pepper, Cozy Kitten 40.00
Salt & Pepper, In Napkin Holder 135.00
Salt & Pepper, Morton 32.00
Salt & Pepper, Pixie .... .350.00 to 625.00
Salt & Pepper, Rock 'n' Roll Kids, On Spring 95.00
Salt & Pepper, Rooster .... .25.00 to 40.00
Salt & Pepper, Santa Claus .... .30.00 to 35.00
Salt & Pepper, White Cat, Mink Coat 250.00
Salt & Pepper, Woman Head, On Spring 100.00
Shaker, Paprika, Cat's Head 28.00
Shaker, Sugar, Cat, White 95.00
Spice Set, Wire Rack 325.00
Spoon Rest, Rooster, 5 1/2 In., Pair 55.00
String Holder, Cat, Marked, 1958, 4 1/2 In. .... .45.00 to 75.00
String Holder, Cozy Kitten With Scissors, 4 1/2 In. ....*Illus* 45.00
String Holder, White Cat, Box 110.00
Sugar & Creamer, Cat, White, Stacking .... .95.00 to 175.00
Sugar & Creamer, Christmas 25.00
Sugar & Creamer, Pixie .... .225.00 to 235.00
Tray, Hors D'Oeuvre Boy, Pixie, Green 595.00
Trivet, Rooster, Metal & Tile .... .16.00 to 35.00
Vase, Bud, Cat, White 165.00
Vase, Bud, Rooster 28.00
Wall Pocket, Cat 175.00
Wall Pocket, Cat, Climbing, Box 95.00

HOPALONG CASSIDY was a character in a series of twenty-eight books
written by Clarence E. Milford, first published in 1907. Movies and
television shows were made based on the character. The best-known
actor playing Hopalong Cassidy was William Lawrence Boyd. His
first movie appearance was in 1919, but the first Hopalong Cassidy
film was not until 1934. Sixty-six films were made. In 1948, William
Boyd purchased the television rights to the movies, then later made
fifty-two new programs. In the 1950s, Hopalong Cassidy and his
horse, named *Topper*, were seen in comics, records, toys, and other
products. Boyd died in 1972.

Album, Bread Label, Hoppy, Unused, 1950s 110.00
Binoculars, Black, 2 Decals, Strap .... .90.00 to 175.00
Book, Little Golden Book, Hopalong Cassidy & The Bar 20 Cowboys, 1952 .... 25.00
Button, Pinback, Green 20.00
Button & Postcard, Bank Savings Program, 1950s, 2 Piece 35.00
Camera, Galter, Box, 1941 .... 40.00
Cap Gun, Wyandotte, Gold Wash, Black Grips .... .325.00 to 400.00

Coloring Book, 120 Pages, 1951 .... 35.00
Compass, Wrist, Original Band 100.00
Container, Cottage Cheese ....30.00 to 42.00
Cookie Jar ....450.00 to 825.00
Costume, Girl's, Blouse & Skirt 250.00
Costume, Girl's, Vest, Skirt, Gloves, Belt, Silk Tie With Slide 325.00
Dental Kit, Dr. West, Toothpaste Tube, Toothbrush 250.00
Figure, Windup, Rocker Base, Marx 395.00
Film, False Colors, 2 Reel, 1954 .... 350.00
Film Strip Gun 45.00
Game, Shooting Gallery, Box 275.00
Gun & Holster Set, 2 Guns, Schmidt 650.00
Hair Trainer 75.00
Hat, Deputy 175.00
Holster & Belt 225.00
Horseshoe, Good Luck, Boyd, 1950 .... 48.00
Ice Cream Carton, 1950 .... 17.00
Knife, 3 Blades, With Key Ring, 1950s, 4 In. 125.00
Knife, Pocket, Black, 3 Blades, Hopalong On Topper, Hammer Brand 35.00
Lamp, Figural, Holster With Gun, Picture 750.00
Lamp, Motion 467.00
Light, Wall, Aladdin 375.00
Linoleum, Full Roll, Original Tube With Label, 9 x 12 Ft. 3500.00
Lobby Card Set, Dangerous Venture, Movie, Mailer, 8 Piece 225.00
Lunch Box, Blue, Cisco Kid & Dale Evans Decal 145.00
Mug, Milk Glass, Green Illustration Of Hoppy, 1950s 36.00
Napkin, Original Wrapper & Label, Reeds, Package Of 32 .... 90.00
Neckerchief Slide, Longhorn Steer Shape, Silvered Finish, 1950s, 1 3/4 In. 25.00
Night-Light, Gun & Holster, Aladdin ....325.00 to 340.00
Paper Plate, Original Wrapper & Label, Reeds, Package Of 8, 6 In. 75.00
Pen, Figural 125.00
Pencil Case, Red, Zipper, Cardboard 40.00
Pennant, Felt 25.00
Plate, Blue Decal, WS George, 10 In. 75.00
Postcard, Chrysler Plymouth, Hoppy With Station Wagon, 1942 .... 31.00
Potato Chip Bag 65.00
Puzzle, Hopalong Cassidy On Horse, Frame, 1950, 9 x 12 In. 25.00
Radio, Arvin, Black 625.00
Rocker, Chrome, Vinyl Covered, Hoppy & Topper Decal, Child's, 1950s ....925.00 to 970.00
Scarf, Red & Black, 1950 .... 35.00
Scrapbook, Pictured On Cover 175.00
Shirt, Black, Hoppy Label 135.00
Shooting Gallery, Tin, Steel Shot, Box 495.00
Slate, School 125.00
Stationery Set, Folder, Unused 90.00
Store Display, Butternut Bread Loaf 75.00
Sweater, Brown Knit, Short Sleeve, Hoppy Front, Topper Back, Child's 95.00
Tumbler, 5 In. 40.00
Tumbler, Miss Dairylea 150.00
Wristwatch, Good Luck From Hoppy On Back, U.S. Time, 1950s ....600.00 to 1750.00
Wristwatch, Hoppy, Steel Frame, Leather Band, Saddle Box Bottom, 1950s 160.00

HOWARD PIERCE has been working in Southern California since 1936.
In 1945, he opened a pottery in Claremont. His contemporary-looking
figurines are popular with collectors. Pieces are marked with his name.
He stopped making pottery in 1991.

Howard
Pierce

Bowl, Free-Form, Tan & Brown, 13 In. 30.00
Figurine, Bird, Sparrow 35.00
Figurine, Cat, Brown, White, 8 1/2 In. 125.00
Figurine, Deer 80.00
Figurine, Doves, Wood Base, Pair 150.00
Figurine, Giraffe, Stylized, Black, 8 In. 75.00
Figurine, Girl, Kneeling, Feeding Swan, Brown Glaze, 7 In. 120.00

Figurine, Mother Quail, White, Brown, With 2 Chicks .... 65.0•
Figurine, Mouse .... 25.0•
Figurine, Native Couple, Dark Brown On White, Man, 7 1/2 In., Woman, 7 In. .... 275.0•
Figurine, Owl, 5 In. .... 65.0•
Figurine, Owl, Brown, White, 3 In. .... 60.0•
Figurine, Peasant Girl, Brown, Gray, 9 In. .... 110.0•
Figurine, Quail Family, Speckled Bellies, 1950s, 5 1/2 & 3 1/2 In., 3 Pieces ...... 48.00 to 50.0•
Figurine, Raccoons, Brown, White, Pair .... 225.0•
Figurine, Roadrunner, Gray, 12 1/2 In. .... 130.0•
Flower Frog, Bird On Rock, Gray, 5 In. .... 75.0•

HOWDY DOODY and Buffalo Bob were the main characters in a children's series televised from 1947 to 1960. Howdy was a redheaded puppet. The series became popular with college students in the late 1970s when Buffalo Bob began to lecture on campuses.

Album, Bread Label, Wonder Balloon Parade, 1950s .... 145.0•
Bandage Box .... 40.0•
Bank, Figural, Howdy Standing On Base, Plastic .... 65.0•
Bank, Howdy On T.V. .... 75.0•
Bank, Sitting On Pig, Porcelain .... 395.0•
Birthday Cake Decoration Set, Figural, Tee-Vee Toys, Inc. & Kagran, 6 Piece ...... 65.0•
Book, Coloring, Whitman, No. 2018, 1954 .... 15.0•
Book, Funbook, 1950s, Unused .... 45.0•
Book, Little Golden Book, Howdy Doody & Princess, 1952 .... 35.0•
Bookends, Box .... 85.0•
Bowl, 5 1/2 In. .... 45.0•
Cookie Jar, Purinton .... 495.0•
Display, Stand, Easel, Die Cut, 40 In. .... 845.0•
Doll, Goldberger, Box .... 150.0•
Doll, Ventriloquist, Box, 24 In. ....65.00 to 175.0•
Figure, Clarabel, Plastic, 4 In. .... 15.0•
Figure, Jointed Arms & Legs, Tin, Signed, 8 In. .... 150.0•
Figure, Phono-Go-Round .... 75.0•
Figurine, Driving Go-Cart, Windup, Nylint .... 350.0•
Fixture, Ceiling, Color Lithographs .... 375.0•
Game, Time Teacher, Pictorial, Package, 1960s, 10 x 20 In. .... 35.0•
Lamp, Figural, Howdy, Sitting, Missing Bulb, 6 1/4 x 3 3/4 In. .... 60.0•
Lamp, Wall, Howdy Sitting On Santa's Lap, Box, 10 x 14 In. .... 175.0•
Lunch Box, Metal, 1954 ....125.00 to 295.0•
Make It Yourself Bee-Nee Kit, Conn. Leather Co., Kagran, Box, 1950s .... 90.0•
Marionette, Princess Summerfall-Winterspring, Box ....95.00 to 135.0•
Mug, Shake-Up, Ovaltine .... 40.0•
Night-Light, Figural, Head, Leco, Box, 1950s .... 145.0•
Night-Light, Sitting Figure, Wood Base, Plastic, 6 In. ....60.00 to 65.0•
Paint Set, Kagran, Unused .... 250.0•
Pipe, Plastic, 4 1/2 In. .... 24.0•

Howdy Doody, Puppet,
Howdy, Wood, Jointed,
Holds NBC Mike,
Kohner, 1960s, 5 In.

When cleaning dolls or furniture or other wooden pieces, use the foam from a mixture of I tablespoon soap and I quart water. Whip the mixture with a beater and clean with the foam.

Poster, Blue Bonnet Margarine, Howdy, Clarabel, Princess, 1953, 12 x 40 In. . . . .100.00 to 150.00
Puppet, Howdy, Wood, Jointed, Holds NBC Mike, Kohner, 1960s, 5 In. . . . . *Illus* 335.00
Puzzle, Frame, 1952, Large 16.00
Puzzle, Poll-Parrot, Howdy & Friends, Copyright 1952 . . . . 58.00
Ring, Flasher, Howdy Doody & Poll Parrot 125.00
Ring, Flicker, Poll Parrot, Blue Plastic, 1950s 550.00
Salt & Pepper, Plastic 225.00
Spoon, Ice Cream 40.00
Table, Play, Lift Top, Wooden, Metal, With Attached Seat, 1950s 245.00
Top, Tin, Germany, 1970s 55.00
Toy, Acrobat, Windup, Arnold, Box 750.00
Toy, Head, Figural, Box, 1950s 68.00
Toy, Stands, Then Falls To Knees, Jointed, Wooden, 5 1/2 In. 95.00

HULL pottery was made in Crooksville, Ohio, from 1905. Addis E. Hull bought the Acme Pottery Company and started making ceramic wares. In 1917, A. E. Hull Pottery began making art pottery as well as the commercial wares. For a short time, 1921 to 1929, the firm also sold pottery imported from Europe. The dinnerwares of the 1940s, including the Little Red Riding Hood line, the high gloss artwares of the 1950s, and the matte wares of the 1940s, are all popular with collectors. The firm officially closed in March 1986.

Apple, Cookie Jar 55.00
Apple, Teapot, 6 Cup 45.00
Athena, Cornucopia 35.00
Barefoot Boy, Cookie Jar 150.00
Basket, Cookie Jar, Closed, Decals 300.00
Blossom Flite, Basket, Black Trim, 10 1/4 In. 85.00
Blossom Flite, Candleholder 35.00
Blossom Flite, Console, 16 1/2 In. 75.00
Blossom Flite, Pitcher 40.00
Blossom Flite, Vase, 9 1/2 In. 55.00
Bluebird, Clock, Sessions Movement 195.00
Bluebird, Wall Pocket, Clock 400.00
Bow Knot, Basket, 6 1/2 In. 225.00
Bow Knot, Basket, Pink, Blue, 10 1/2 In. 595.00
Bow Knot, Candlesticks, Pair 180.00
Bow Knot, Console, 13 1/2 In., Pair 675.00
Bow Knot, Cornucopia, 7 1/2 In. . . . . .125.00 to 175.00
Bow Knot, Cup & Saucer . . . . .195.00 to 245.00
Bow Knot, Flowerpot, Saucer 150.00
Bow Knot, Plate, Original Label 1275.00
Bow Knot, Tea Set, Pink 800.00
Bow Knot, Tea Set, Turquoise & Pink, 3 Piece 800.00
Bow Knot, Teapot 235.00
Bow Knot, Vase, 8 1/2 In. 168.00
Bow Knot, Vase, 10 1/2 In. 335.00
Bow Knot, Vase, Double Cornucopia, 13 In. 225.00
Bow Knot, Wall Pocket, Cup & Saucer . . . . .195.00 to 250.00
Bow Knot, Wall Pocket, Green Groom, 8 In. 295.00
Bow Knot, Wall Pocket, Iron . . . . .245.00 to 295.00
Bow Knot, Wall Pocket, Whisk Broom 295.00
Calla Lily Leaf, Candleholder 68.50
Cat, Planter 30.00
Chickadee, Planter, Green 10.00
Continental, Basket, 14 1/2 In. 85.00
Continental, Ewer 125.00
Continental, Vase, Bud, Persimmon 35.00
Corky Pig, Bank, Brown . . . . .40.00 to 50.00
Corky Pig, Bank, Miniature 225.00
Corky Pig, Bank, Raised Slot . . . . .135.00 to 225.00
Corky Pig, Figurine, Brown, Sitting 55.00
Corky Pig, Figurine, Yellow, Blue 80.00

Cornucopia, Vase, Pink To Blue, 1946, Paper Label, 8 1/2 In. 90.00
Dancing Lady, Planter 65.00
Diamond Quilt, Casserole, Cover, Turquoise, Nuline Bak-Serve, 7 1/2 In. 30.00
Dogwood, Basket, 7 1/2 In. 250.00
Dogwood, Ewer, 8 1/2 In. 285.00
Dogwood, Teapot ....255.00 to 325.00
Ducks, Planter, No. 94, 10 In. 45.00
Early Art, Jardiniere, 1920s, 6 1/2 In. 65.00
Ebb Tide, Basket, 6 In. 180.00
Ebb Tide, Basket, Pink & Green, 16 1/2 In. 160.00
Ebb Tide, Console, Snail, Shrimp 135.00
Ebb Tide, Ewer, Olive, Plum, 8 In. 75.00
Ebb Tide, Jar, Pretzel 200.00
Ebb Tide, Teapot, Wine 200.00
Flutist, Figurine, Swing Band, Gold Trim 175.00
Forget-Me-Not, Pitcher, Stippled 55.00
Gingerbread Boy, Cookie Jar, Brown ....125.00 to 375.00
Gingerbread Boy, Cookie Jar, Gray 450.00
Gingerbread Man, Bowl, Child's 125.00
Gingerbread Man, Cup, Child's 125.00
House 'n Garden, Casserole, Duck 65.00
House 'n Garden, Casserole, Hen, No. 592 .... 60.00
House 'n Garden, Coffeepot 35.00
Iris, Basket, No. 408, 7 In. 250.00
Iris, Candlestick, 5 In. 115.00
Iris, Pitcher, 9 In. 200.00
Iris, Rose Bowl, Pink, 6 In. 235.00
Little Red Riding Hood, Bank, Hanging 2400.00
Little Red Riding Hood, Bank, Standing ....595.00 to 725.00
Little Red Riding Hood, Butter ....250.00 to 395.00
Little Red Riding Hood, Canister Set, Flour, Sugar, Coffee & Tea 3195.00
Little Red Riding Hood, Canister, Cereal 1480.00
Little Red Riding Hood, Canister, Coffee ....750.00 to 850.00
Little Red Riding Hood, Canister, Flour 850.00
Little Red Riding Hood, Canister, Pretzel 7100.00
Little Red Riding Hood, Canister, Sugar 700.00
Little Red Riding Hood, Canister, Tea 850.00
Little Red Riding Hood, Clock, Sessions Movement ....225.00 to 300.00
Little Red Riding Hood, Cookie Jar, Gold Basket 425.00
Little Red Riding Hood, Cookie Jar, Gold Stars On Apron ....350.00 to 450.00
Little Red Riding Hood, Cookie Jar, Pink Roses, Gray Leaves 385.00
Little Red Riding Hood, Cookie Jar, Poinsettia ....450.00 to 950.00
Little Red Riding Hood, Creamer, Head Pour ....400.00 to 450.00
Little Red Riding Hood, Creamer, Pantaloons 275.00
Little Red Riding Hood, Creamer, Side Pour ....125.00 to 135.00
Little Red Riding Hood, Creamer, Tab Handle ....350.00 to 395.00
Little Red Riding Hood, Jar, 9 1/2 In. 375.00
Little Red Riding Hood, Jar, Dresser ....510.00 to 700.00
Little Red Riding Hood, Jar, Grease, Yellow Wolf ....695.00 to 895.00
Little Red Riding Hood, Jar, Spice, Cinnamon 695.00
Little Red Riding Hood, Jar, Spice, Cloves 695.00
Little Red Riding Hood, Lamp, With Shade 1900.00
Little Red Riding Hood, Match Safe, Wall, Hanging 895.00
Little Red Riding Hood, Mustard ....250.00 to 385.00
Little Red Riding Hood, Pitcher, Batter ....400.00 to 550.00
Little Red Riding Hood, Pitcher, Milk ....300.00 to 335.00
Little Red Riding Hood, Salt & Pepper, 3 1/2 In. ....55.00 to 140.00
Little Red Riding Hood, Salt & Pepper, 5 1/2 In. ....115.00 to 225.00
Little Red Riding Hood, Shaker, 4 1/2 In. 750.00
Little Red Riding Hood, Stringholder 2200.00
Little Red Riding Hood, Sugar & Creamer, Side Pour ....175.00 to 300.00
Little Red Riding Hood, Sugar, Cover 295.00
Little Red Riding Hood, Sugar, Crawling ....225.00 to 475.00

Little Red Riding Hood, Teapot	.265.00 to 375.00
Little Red Riding Hood, Wall Pocket	.450.00 to 700.00
Lusterware, Vase, Orange, 8 In.	75.00
Lusterware, Vase, Orange, 10 In.	200.00
Magnolia, Cornucopia, Gloss, 8 1/2 In.	80.00
Magnolia, Cornucopia, Matte, 8 1/2 In.	70.00
Magnolia, Ewer, 4 1/4 In.	30.00
Magnolia, Ewer, 13 1/2 In.	275.00
Magnolia, Ewer, Blue & Pink, 13 1/2 In.	225.00
Magnolia, Mug, Happy Days	35.00
Magnolia, Planter, Flower Cart, Green	20.00
Magnolia, Tea Set, 3 Piece	225.00
Magnolia, Teapot	95.00
Magnolia, Vase, Blue, Pink, 15 In.	450.00
Magnolia, Vase, Matte, 6 1/2 In.	45.00
Magnolia, Vase, No. 13, 4 3/4 In.	40.00
Magnolia, Vase, Pink To Blue, 8 1/2 In.	100.00
Magnolia, Vase, Winged Handles, Yellow, 12 1/2 In.	185.00
Magnolia Matte, Basket, Paper Label, 10 1/2 In.	345.00
Mermaid, Figurine, Sitting On Sea Shell, Green, Maroon	68.00
Nuline, Pitcher, Batter, Peach	42.00
Open Rose, Console Set	450.00
Open Rose, Cornucopia, 8 1/2 In.	150.00
Open Rose, Ewer, No. 105, 7 In.	200.00
Open Rose, Sugar & Creamer, Pink To Blue	150.00
Open Rose, Vase, 8 1/2 In.	110.00
Orchid, Basket, 7 In.	600.00
Orchid, Vase, 8 In.	135.00
Orchid, Vase, 10 In.	200.00
Parchment & Pine, Pitcher	135.00
Parchment & Pine, Vase, 10 In.	50.00
Pine & Parchment, Basket, Large	150.00
Pink, Vase, Handles, Matte, 16 In.	350.00
Poppy, Cornucopia, 8 In.	250.00
Poppy, Vase, 6 1/2 In.	.175.00 to 220.00
Poppy, Wall Pocket, 9 In.	300.00
Rosella, Ewer, 7 In.	50.00
Rosella, Planter, Hanging	85.00
Royal Woodland, Ewer, Glossy Rose, 13 1/2 In.	.75.00 to 95.00
Royal Woodland, Ewer, Mottled Pink, 13 1/2 In.	125.00
Royal Woodland, Wall Pocket, Gray	75.00
Seashell, Planter, No. 201, Pink, 8 x 4 In.	40.00
Serenade, Ashtray, Yellow, Large	85.00
Serenade, Basket, Pink, 12 In.	300.00
Serenade, Cookie Jar, Basket	300.00
Serenade, Planter, Pink	40.00
Serenade, Teapot	155.00
Serenade, Vase, Gold Traced, 8 In.	75.00
Serenade, Vase, Pink, 12 In.	275.00
Serenade, Window Box	75.00
Siamese Cat, Figurine, Mother & Babies, Large	55.00
Stars & Sprig, Cookie Jar, Border	369.00
Sunglow, Bell, Pink Loop Handle	125.00
Sunglow, Cornucopia, Pink, Yellow, 8 1/2 In.	58.00
Sunglow, Grease Jar	25.00
Sunglow, Vase, Pink, Yellow, Green Flowers, Handles, 8 1/2 In.	65.00
Sunglow, Wall Pocket, Cup & Saucer	55.00
Swan, Figurine, Yellow, Green, 8 1/2 In.	65.00
Swans, Planter	25.00
Thistle, Vase, Blue, 6 1/2 In.	105.00
Tokay, Basket, 8 In.	85.00
Tokay, Cornucopia, Footed	55.00
Tokay, Pitcher, 12 In.	225.00

Tuba Player, Figurine, Swing Band, Gold Trim 175.0

Tulip, Ewer, Cream & Blue, Colorful Tulips 275.0

Tulip, Jardiniere, Blue, 5 In. 85.0

Tulip, Vase, 8 In. 150.0

Water Lily, Basket, Pink, 10 1/2 In. 300.0

Water Lily, Candlestick, 4 1/2 In., Pair 60.0

Water Lily, Flowerpot, Saucer, Sticker, 6 3/4 In. 160.0

Water Lily, Pot & Saucer, Sticker, 6 3/4 In. 160.0

Water Lily, Tea Set, Apricot & Cream, 3 Piece 225.0

Water Lily, Vase, 9 1/2 In. 100.0

Water Lily, Vase, 10 1/2 In. 135.0

White, Jardiniere, 7 In. 60.0

Wildflower, Basket, 10 1/2 In. ....230.00 to 375.0

Wildflower, Cornucopia, Pink & Blue, 8 1/2 In. 155.0

Wildflower, Ewer, 13 1/2 In. 875.0

Wildflower, Vase, 6 1/2 In. 58.0

Woodland, Basket, Glossy Pink To Chartreuse, 10 1/2 In. ....175.00 to 265.0

Woodland, Candleholder, Pair 150.0

Woodland, Cornucopia, Blue 40.0

Woodland, Cornucopia, Double, White Gloss 200.0

Woodland, Jardiniere, 5 1/2 In. 150.0

Woodland, Teapot 150.0

Woodland, Vase, 8 1/2 In. 135.0

Woodland, Vase, Gold Trim, 5 1/2 In. 35.0

Woodland, Vase, High Glaze, 7 1/2 In. 40.0

Woodland, Wall Pocket 100.0

Woodland, Window Box, Glossy 50.0

Yellow, Vase, Tan Ground, Open Handles, 12 1/2 In. 175.0

HUMMEL figurines, based on the drawings of the nun M.I. Hummel (Berta Hummel), are made by the W. Goebel Porzellanfabrik of Oeslau, Germany, now Rodenthal, Germany. They were first made in 1934. The mark has changed through the years. The following are the approximate dates for each of the marks: *Crown* mark, 1935 to 1949; *U.S. Zone, Germany*, 1946 to 1948; *West Germany*, after 1949. The company added the *bee* marks in 1950. The *full bee* with variations, was used from 1950 to 1959; *stylized bee*, 1960 to 1972; *three line mark*, 1968 to 1972; *last bee*, sometimes called *vee over gee*, 1972 to 1979. In 1979 the V bee symbol was removed from the mark. The *Goebel, W. Germany* mark, called the *missing bee* mark, was used from 1979 to 1991; *Goebel, Germany* was used from 1991 to the present. Porcelain figures inspired by Berta Hummel's drawings were introduced in 1997. These are marked BH followed by a number. They are made in the Far East, not Germany. Other decorative items and plates that feature Hummel drawings have been made by Schmid Brothers, Inc., since 1971.

Ashtray, Let's Sing, Reverse Mold 455.0

Bookends, No. 61A & No. 61B, Playmates, Full Bee, Pair 350.0

Bookends, No. 252/A & B, Apple Tree Girl & Boy, Stylized Bee Mark 150.0

Figurine, No. 2/0, Little Fiddler, Three Line Mark ....69.00 to 180.0

Figurine, No. 3, Accordion Boy, Three Line Mark 82.5

Figurine, No. 3, Goose Girl, Three Line Mark 71.5

Figurine, No. 3, Little Helper, Three Line Mark 49.5

Figurine, No. 6/0, Sensitive Hunter, Three Line Mark 135.0

Figurine, No. 6/1, Sensitive Hunter, Three Line Mark 168.0

Figurine, No. 7/II, Merry Wanderer, Stylized Bee 850.0

Figurine, No. 8, Book Worm, Full Bee 225.0

Figurine, No. 8, Book Worm, Stylized Bee 225.0

Figurine, No. 10/I, Flower Madonna, Open Halo, Full Bee 330.0

Figurine, No. 11/2/0, Merry Wanderer, Stylized Bee 60.0

Figurine, No. 12/2/0, Chimney Sweep, Three Line Mark ....78.00 to 105.0

Figurine, No. 12/I, Chimney Sweep, Three Line Mark 147.0

Figurine, No. 15/0, Hear Ye, Hear Ye, Stylized Bee 325.0

Figurine, No. 15/I, Hear Ye, Hear Ye, Last Bee 140.0

Figurine, No. 17/0, Congratulations, Three Line Mark . . . . .135.00 to 165.00
Figurine, No. 18, Christ Child, Three Line Mark . . . . .96.00 to 120.00
Figurine, No. 21/0, Heavenly Angel, Full Bee 50.00
Figurine, No. 23/I, Adoration, Three Line Mark 120.00
Figurine, No. 28/II, Wayside Devotion, Three Line Mark 175.00
Figurine, No. 47/II, Goose Girl, Crown Mark 600.00
Figurine, No. 49/3/0, To Market, Full Bee 275.00
Figurine, No. 53, Joyful, Stylized Bee 135.00
Figurine, No. 53, Joyful, Three Line Mark 50.00
Figurine, No. 56/A, Culprits, Full Bee 325.00
Figurine, No. 56/A, Culprits, Three Line Mark 240.00
Figurine, No. 57, Chick Girl, Crown Mark 151.00
Figurine, No. 57/0, Chick Girl, Three Line Mark 162.00
Figurine, No. 63, Singing Lesson, Three Line Mark . . . . .81.00 to 99.00
Figurine, No. 65, Farewell, Full Bee 300.00
Figurine, No. 65, Farewell, Three Line Mark . . . . .144.00 to 159.00
Figurine, No. 66, Farm Boy, Three Line Mark 156.00
Figurine, No. 67, Doll Mother, Full Bee 255.00
Figurine, No. 67, Doll Mother, Three Line Mark . . . . .138.00 to 180.00
Figurine, No. 71, Stormy Weather, Stylized Bee 225.00
Figurine, No. 73, Little Helper, Three Line Mark . . . . .99.00 to 120.00
Figurine, No. 74, Little Gardener, Three Line Mark . . . . .78.00 to 99.00
Figurine, No. 80, Little Scholar, Three Line Mark . . . . .144.00 to 180.00
Figurine, No. 82/0/I, School Boy, Full Bee 350.00
Figurine, No. 82/II, School Boy, Stylized Bee 130.00
Figurine, No. 84/0, Worship, Stylized Bee 79.00
Figurine, No. 85/II, Serenade, Last Bee 250.00
Figurine, No. 88/II, Heavenly Protection, Last Bee 425.00
Figurine, No. 89/I, Little Cellist, Full Bee 40.00
Figurine, No. 89/I, Little Cellist, Stylized Bee 60.00
Figurine, No. 94/3/0, Surprise, Three Line Mark 126.00
Figurine, No. 94/I, Surprise, Three Line Mark 225.00
Figurine, No. 96, Little Shopper, Three Line Mark 96.00
Figurine, No. 99, Eventide, Three Line Mark 216.00
Figurine, No. 127, Doctor, Three Line Mark 102.00
Figurine, No. 128, Baker, Three Line Mark 165.00
Figurine, No. 129, Band Leader, Full Bee 179.00
Figurine, No. 129, Band Leader, Three Line Mark 165.00
Figurine, No. 133, Mother's Helper, Three Line Mark .165.00 to 210.00
Figurine, No. 141, Apple Tree Girl, Full Bee . . . . .425.00 to 495.00
Figurine, No. 141/V, Apple Tree Girl, Missing Bee 675.00
Figurine, No. 142/3/0, Apple Tree Boy, Three Line Mark 120.00
Figurine, No. 142/I, Apple Tree Boy, Three Line Mark 96.00
Figurine, No. 142/V, Apple Tree Boy, Three Line Mark 810.00
Figurine, No. 158/0, Auf Wiedersehen, Missing Bee 210.00
Figurine, No. 170, School Boys, Full Bee 1500.00
Figurine, No. 170/I, School Boys, Missing Bee 660.00
Figurine, No. 171, Little Sweeper, Three Line Mark 96.00
Figurine, No. 184, Bermuda News, Three Line Mark 695.00
Figurine, No. 185, Accordion Boy, Three Line Mark 126.00
Figurine, No. 186, Sweet Music, Three Line Mark . . . . .135.00 to 210.00
Figurine, No. 195/2/0, Barnyard Hero, Full Bee . . . . .70.00 to 121.00
Figurine, No. 195/2/0, Barnyard Hero, Three Line Mark 150.00
Figurine, No. 195/I, Barnyard Hero, Three Line Mark 210.00
Figurine, No. 197/I, Be Patient, Stylized Bee 88.00
Figurine, No. 198/2/0, Home From Market, Three Line Mark . . . . .102.00 to 120.00
Figurine, No. 198/I, Home From Market, Three Line Mark . . . . .150.00 to 180.00
Figurine, No. 199, Feeding Time, Full Bee 115.00
Figurine, No. 200/0, Little Goat Herder, Full Bee 80.00
Figurine, No. 201/I, Retreat To Safety, Full Bee 300.00
Figurine, No. 203/1, Signs Of Spring, Three Line Mark . . . . .150.00 to 195.00
Figurine, No. 226, Mail Is Here, Last Bee 298.00
Figurine, No. 226, Mail Is Here, Three Line Mark 475.00

Figurine, No. 238/A, Angel With Lute, Three Line Mark 36.00
Figurine, No. 238/B, Angel With Accordion, Three Line Mark 36.00
Figurine, No. 238/C, Angel With Trumpet, Three Line Mark 36.00
Figurine, No. 240, Little Drummer, Three Line Mark 99.00
Figurine, No. 255, A Stitch In Time, Three Line Mark ....78.00 to 195.00
Figurine, No. 261, Angel Duet, Three Line Mark 147.00
Figurine, No. 308, Little Tailor, Three Line Mark 165.00
Figurine, No. 311, Kiss Me, Three Line Mark 355.00
Figurine, No. 312/1, Honey Lover, Three Line Mark 230.00
Figurine, No. 315, Mountaineer, Three Line Mark ....144.00 to 150.00
Figurine, No. 319, Doll Bath, Three Line Mark 210.00
Figurine, No. 322, Little Pharmacist, Missing Bee 135.00
Figurine, No. 322, Little Pharmacist, Stylized Bee 650.00
Figurine, No. 322, Little Pharmacist, Three Line Mark 162.00
Figurine, No. 330, Baking Day, Three Line Mark 186.00
Figurine, No. 331, Crossroads, Three Line Mark 270.00
Figurine, No. 334, Homeward Bound, Three Line Mark 270.00
Figurine, No. 345, A Fair Measure, Three Line Mark 195.00
Figurine, No. 346, The Smart Little Sister, Stylized Bee 850.00
Figurine, No. 355, Autumn Harvest, Last Bee 140.00
Figurine, No. 355, Autumn Harvest, Three Line Mark 135.00
Figurine, No. 376, Little Nurse, Three Line Mark 162.00
Figurine, No. 378, Easter Greetings, Three Line Mark 135.00
Figurine, No. 384, Easter Time, Three Line Mark 165.00
Figurine, No. 385, Chicken Licken, Three Line Mark 186.00
Figurine, No. 399, Valentine Joy, Missing Bee 150.00
Figurine, No. 420, Is It Raining?, Missing Bee 88.00
Plaque, No. 92, Merry Wanderer, Three Line Mark 100.00
Plaque, No. 125, Vacation Time, Three Line Mark 125.00
Plaque, No. 126, Retreat To Safety, Three Line Mark 125.00
Plaque, No. 134, Quartet, Three Line Mark 170.00
Plaque, No. 140, The Mail Is Here, Three Line Mark 170.00
Plate, Anniversary, 1975, Stormy Weather 800.00
Plate, Annual, 1971, Heavenly Angel, Box ....325.00 to 350.00
Plate, Annual, 1972, Hear Ye, Hear Ye ....21.00 to 44.00
Plate, Annual, 1973, Globe Trotter, Box ....60.00 to 80.00
Plate, Annual, 1974, Goose Girl 40.00
Plate, Annual, 1975, Ride Into Christmas 40.00
Plate, Annual, 1976, Apple Tree Girl 40.00
Plate, Annual, 1978, Happy Pastime 40.00
Plate, Annual, 1979, Singing Lesson 30.00
Plate, Annual, 1980, School Girl 40.00
Plate, Annual, 1981, Umbrella Boy 44.00
Plate, Annual, 1982, Umbrella Girl 100.00
Plate, Annual, 1983, Postman With Love Letter 150.00
Plate, Annual, 1985, Chick Girl 70.00
Plate, Annual, 1986, Rabbit Boy 130.00
Plate, Annual, 1988, Little Goat Herder, Box 60.00
Plate, Annual, 1991, Just Resting 140.00
Plate, Christmas, 1972, Angel With Flute, Schmid 8.00
Plate, Christmas, 1976, Sacred Journey, Schmid 8.00
Plate, Christmas, 1978, Golden Tranquility, Schmid 40.00
Plate, Christmas, 1980, Parade Into Toyland, Schmid 12.00
Plate, Christmas, 1992, Sweet Blessings, Schmid 30.00
Plate, Mother's Day, 1972, Playing Hooky, Schmid 5.00
Plate, Mother's Day, 1973, Little Fisherman, Schmid 14.00
Plate, Mother's Day, 1978, Afternoon Stroll, Schmid 8.00

HUTSCHENREUTHER Porcelain Company of Selb, Germany, was established in 1814 and is still working. The company makes fine quality
porcelain dinnerwares and figurines. The mark has changed through
the years, but the name and the lion insignia appear in most versions.

Figurine, 2 Dancers, Signed Werner, 11 1/2 In. 265.00

Figurine, Cupid, On Gold Ball, 6 1/2 In. 240.00
Figurine, Dachshund, Standing 190.00
Figurine, Deer, Small 125.00
Figurine, Doe, Reclining 174.00
Figurine, Donkey, Dog, Cat, Chicken, 7 In. 66.00
Figurine, Eagle, Signed, Tutter, 11 x 11 In. 30.00
Figurine, German Shepherd, Lying Down 190.00
Figurine, Man Playing Violin, Woman On Knee, Signed, 8 1/2 x 8 1/2 In. 350.00
Figurine, Owl, On Tree Limb, 3 1/2 In. ....65.00 to 125.00
Figurine, Poodle, Sitting, White 245.00
Figurine, Schnauzer, Gray, 6 1/4 x 7 In. 175.00
Figurine, Two Mallard Ducks, 3 In. 78.00
Group, Children's Round Dance, White, Gold Flowers, K. Tutter, 7 1/4 In. 495.00
Plate, Roses Of Redoute, Box 8.00
Vase, Bud, White, Gold Rim, 9 In. 35.00
Vase, Center Victorian Scene Medallion, 15 In. 85.00
Vase, Morning Glories, Bulbous, Silver Overlay, 5 In. 50.00
Vase, Nude Women Each Side, Large Flowers, R. Lunghard, 1947, 10 1/2 In. 430.00

ICONS, special, revered pictures of Jesus, Mary, or a saint, are usually Russian or Byzantine. The small icons collected today are made of wood and tin or precious metals. Many modern copies have been made in the old style and are being sold to tourists in Russia and Europe.

Anastasis, Descent In Hell & Resurrection, Russia, 19th Century, 14 x 11 2/3 In. 430.00
Apostle Matthew, Round Wood Panel, 9 1/4 In. 220.00
Archangel Gabriel, Gilded Silver, Russia, 1890, 15 x 12 In. ....*Illus* 4620.00
Burning Bush, Applied Metal Border, Russia, 18th Century, 12 1/4 x 10 1/2 In. 920.00
Christ & Mary, Diptych, Gilt Frame, Flemish, Each Image 4 3/4 x 3 1/4 In. 980.00
Christ Enthroned, Saviour, Flanked By Holy Virgin, Russia, 19th Century, 13 x 10 In. .. 2070.00
Christ Pantocrator, Beaded, Jeweled Cover, Russia, 19th Century, 10 5/8 x 9 In. 1150.00
Cross, Walnut, Ironwood Corpus, INRI In Gold Leaf, Carrying Type, 17 x 28 1/2 In. 350.00
Crucifixion, Panel Inset, Brass Cross, 19th Century, 20 1/2 x 16 1/4 In. 1035.00
Dormition Mother Of God, Beaded, Leather On Wood, Russia, 19th Century, 14 In. .. 775.00
Dormition Of Holy Virgin, 19th Century, Russia, 11 1/2 x 13 1/4 In. 2185.00
Fierce Eye Of Christ, Old Style Paint, 20 x 16 In. 2000.00
Fiery Ascension Of Elijah The Prophet, 19th Century, 12 1/4 x 10 1/2 In. 1210.00
Holy Trinity, 19th Century, 24 x 21 In. 2590.00
Holy Trinity, Russia, Early 19th Century, 10 1/2 x 9 1/8 In. 1150.00
Jesus & Mary, Silver Riza, Bros. Zaharov, Frame, 1900 .... 3300.00
Jesus & Saint, Greek, Painted Wood, 19th Century, 11 1/2 x 8 3/4 In. 295.00
John The Baptist, Holding Platter, Gilded Silver, 1813, 12 3/4 x 10 1/2 In. 4625.00
Joy Of All Who Sorrow, Russia, c.1840, 12 x 10 1/2 In. 1000.00

Icon, Archangel Gabriel, Gilded Silver,
Russia, 1890, 15 x 12 In.

Icon, Lord Almighty, Gilded Silver,
Moscow, Late 19th Century, 12 x 10 In.

Kazan Mother Of God, Gilded Silver, Jeweled Veil, Sata, 1851, 12 In. 7700.00
Kazan Mother Of God, Russia, 19th Century, 15 3/4 x 13 1/4 In. 1610.00
Kazan Mother Of God, Tin, Russia, 18th Century, 12 x 10 1/4 In. 2200.00
Lord Almighty, Gilded Silver, Moscow, Late 19th Century, 12 x 10 In. . . . .*Illus* 4950.00
Madonna & Child, Gilt Frame, Wood Panel, 19th Century, 27 3/4 x 16 In. 550.00
Madonna & Child, Metal Over Wood, Gilt, Russia, 1895, 8 3/4 x 7 In. 440.00
Madonna Surrounded By Host Of Saints & Angels, Russia, 1888, 14 x 12 In. 260.00
Mother Of God, Softener Of Evil Hearts, Russia, 19th Century, 13 x 11 In. 2185.00
Mother Of God Iverskaya, Chased Brass Oklad, Russia, 19th Century, 5 1/2 In. 260.00
Pokrov, Russia, 19th Century, 12 1/4 x 10 1/2 In. 1955.00
Portrait, Christ, Engraved Silver Oklad, Painted, Russia, 19th Century, 10 1/2 x 9 In. . . . 605.00
Presentation Of The Holy Virgin In The Temple, 19th Century, 13 1/2 x 11 1/2 In. . . 2185.00
Russian Saint, Oil On Board, 19th Century, 12 x 10 1/2 In. 195.00
St. George, Slaying Dragon, Rearing His Horse, Red Cape, Greece, 1765, 16 x 15 In. . . . 2587.00
St. John The Baptist, Silvered Metal Overlay, 19th Century, 12 1/4 x 10 1/4 In. 550.00
St. Mark, Evangelist, Holding His Gospel, Russia, 18th Century, 12 x 10 1/4 In. 1725.00
St. Nicholas, Delivers A Blessing, Silver, 19th Century, 12 1/4 x 10 1/2 In. 1650.00
St. Nicholas, Gilded Silver Oklad, Russia, 19th Century, 12 1/4 x 10 3/8 In. 920.00
St. Nicholas, Silver Oklad, Halo With Foliage, Blue, Green, Russia, 1910, 11 x 8 In. 1725.00
St. Vladimir & Mother Of God, Gilded Silver Oklad, Foliage, 1874, 12 x 10 In. 1150.00
Tichvin Mother Of God, Russia, 18th Century, 21 x 17 1/2 In. 2590.00
Transfer Of St. Nicholas Relics, c.1800, 18 1/4 x 21 1/2 In. 3575.00
Triptych, Saints, Late 18th-Early 19th Century, 3 Panels, 3 x 1 1/2 In., 2 1/2 x 5 In. 470.00
Virgin & Child, Russia, 1800, 12 1/4 x 10 1/8 In. 1265.00
Virgin & Child, Russia, 19th Century, 17 1/2 x 14 1/2 In. 1495.00
Virgin & Child, Veneered Frame, Silver Plate, Spain, 20 x 14 3/4 In. 860.00

IMARI patterns are named for the Japanese ware characteristically decorated with orange, red, green, and blue stylized designs. The bamboo,
floral, and geometric patterns on the Japanese ware became so familiar that the name *Imari* has come to mean any patterns of this type. It
has been copied by Asian, European, and American factories since the
eighteenth century. It is still being made.

Beaker, Armorial, Trellis Diaper Border, Early 18th Century, 2 3/4 In. 400.00
Biscuit Jar, Cover, Florals, Hand Painted, Red, Blue, Silver Plated Handle, 7 In. 38.00
Biscuit Jar, Nickel Plated Cover, Ironstone China Handle, Porcelain, 7 In. 70.00
Bowl, Black Ship Design, Everted Rim, 9 In. 1000.00
Bowl, Butterfly & Chrysanthemum Design, Lobed Form, 6 In. 88.00
Bowl, Fluted, Porcelain, 9 In. 110.00
Bowl, Fruit, Scalloped, 10 In. 155.00
Bowl, Honeycomb, 19th Century, 7 In. 765.00
Bowl, Landscape Scene, Passion Flower Border, Octagonal, 19th Century, 5 1/2 In. 38.00
Bowl, Nesting, Chidori Design, Kitani, 7 In., 8 1/2 In., 9 1/2 In., 3 Piece 330.00
Bowl, Plant-Stand Center, Floral Spray Reserves, 19th Century, 5 x 13 In. 935.00
Charger, 3 Panels Of Foliate Design, Blue Exterior, Blue Design, White Ground, 18 In. . 520.00
Charger, 3 Panels, Bird On Branch With Flowers, Butterfly, Blue, Rust Floral Spray 345.00
Charger, Blue Bird, Floral, Foliate Design, Off-White Ground, 18 In. 170.00
Cup & Saucer, Floral Design, Porcelain, 19th Century 60.50
Dish, Blue, Red, Green Floral Design, Tree, Floral Exterior, 19th Century, 3 1/2 In., Pair . 77.00
Dish, Chrysanthemum, Scalloped, 8 In., Pair 65.00
Dish, Crane, Floral Design, 18th Century, 4 1/2 In., Pair 143.00
Dish, Passion Flower, Rectangular, 8 1/2 In. 192.00
Dish, Serving, Flower Basket Center Surrounded By Phoenix & Flowers, 18 1/2 In. 825.00
Ginger Jar, Floral Panels, Ribbed Ground, Early 19th Century, 14 1/2 In. 605.00
Jar, Temple, Foo Lion Finial, 20 In., Pair 2990.00
Plate, Flower Shape, Brocade Design, Raised Chrysanthemum Center, 19th Century, 9 In. 66.00
Plate, Flower Shape, Floral Center Surrounded By Brocade Design, 8 1/4 In. 66.00
Plate, Flower Shape, Floral Transfer Design, Flower Border, 19th Century, 8 1/2 In. 33.00
Plate, Flower Shape, Garden Design, 11 In., 9 Piece 770.00
Plate, Foo Dog & Bird Reserves, Fluted, 8 1/2 In. 55.00
Plate, Gadroon Border, Ironstone, Geo. Ashworth, 1920s, 8 Piece 900.00
Plate, Kirin Center, Surrounded By Fans, 7 1/2 In., 5 Piece 137.00

Plate, La Dame Au Parasol, China, 1770-1775, 9 1/8 & 9 3/8 In., Pair 3735.00
Plate, Prunus, Bamboo, Chrysanthemums, Polychrome, Late 19th Century, 8 1/4 In. 33.00
Platter, Ironstone, 19th Century, 20 1/4 In. 316.00
Teapot, Floral Design, Globular, 19th Century, 5 In. 66.00
Tray, Polychrome, Montplaisir, Brussels, 1786-1790, 14 1/2 In. 137.00
Tureen, Oval, Scenic Medallion, Handles, 12 3/4 In. 575.00
Urn, Allover Floral Design, 12 In., Pair 900.00
Vase, 4 Diapered Panels, Alternating Groups, Floral & Dragon Reserves, 7 1/2 In. 220.00
Vase, Baluster Form, 6 1/2 In., Pair 220.00
Vase, Bird, Floral Designs, Dragon In Relief, Late 19th Century, 26 3/4 In. 1034.00
Vase, Bud, Flared Rim, Vasiform Top, Base Fitted With 4 Holes, 5 3/4 In., 2 Part 144.00
Vase, Dragon, Bird, Signed, 19 In. 295.00
Vase, Fowl, Lacquered Panels, 13 1/2 In., Pair 110.00

IMPERIAL GLASS Corporation was founded in Bellaire, Ohio, in 1901. It became a subsidiary of Lenox, Inc., in 1973 and was sold to Arthur R. Lorch in 1981. It was sold again in 1982, went bankrupt that same year, and some of the molds and assets were sold. The Imperial glass referred to by the collector is freehand art glass, carnival glass, slag glass, stretch glass, and other top-quality tablewares. Tablewares and animals are listed here. The others may be found in the appropriate sections.

Animal, Dish, Lion, Amber 35.00
Animal, Duck, Cover, Purple Slag, Matte, 4 1/2 In. 75.00
Art Glass, Vase, Amethyst, 5 In. 140.00
Candlewick, Ashtray, Cranberry, 6 In. 5.00
Candlewick, Ashtray, Mason Insignia, 6 In. 25.00
Candlewick, Ashtray, Round 6.00
Candlewick, Ashtray, Satin & Clear 45.00
Candlewick, Bowl, 10 1/2 In. 48.00
Candlewick, Bowl, Fruit, Footed, 10 In. 200.00
Candlewick, Bowl, Heart Shape, 5 1/2 In. 20.00
Candlewick, Bowl, Heart Shape, 9 In. ....135.00 to 165.00
Candlewick, Bowl, Heart Shape, Caramel Slag, 5 1/2 In. 185.00
Candlewick, Bowl, Ruby, 9 In. 300.00
Candlewick, Cake Plate, 10 In. 39.00
Candlewick, Cake Plate, Birthday, 72 Candle Holders, 13 In. ....325.00 to 675.00
Candlewick, Candlestick 16.00
Candlewick, Candy Dish, Cover, 3 Sections, 7 In. 180.00
Candlewick, Candy Dish, Cover, 5 1/2 In. ....80.00 to 110.00
Candlewick, Champagne 12.00
Candlewick, Cigarette Set, Ruby Stained, Box, Cover, 4 Ashtrays 75.00
Candlewick, Cologne Bottle, Gold Trim 425.00
Candlewick, Compote, 8 1/2 In. 210.00
Candlewick, Creamer, Individual 7.00
Candlewick, Cruet, 4 Oz. 45.00
Candlewick, Cup & Saucer 10.00
Candlewick, Dish, Mayonnaise, 2 Sections, 2 Ladles 50.00
Candlewick, Dish, Mayonnaise, Underplate 18.00
Candlewick, Egg Plate 185.00
Candlewick, Eggcup 55.00
Candlewick, Goblet, 9 Oz. 16.00
Candlewick, Gravy Boat, Underplate ....160.00 to 200.00
Candlewick, Ladle 11.00
Candlewick, Lamp, Hurricane, 3 Piece 315.00
Candlewick, Paperweight, Logo 125.00
Candlewick, Pitcher, 1 Pt. 135.00
Candlewick, Plate, 6 In. ....7.00 to 8.00
Candlewick, Plate, 8 In. ....49.50 to 55.00
Candlewick, Plate, 9 In. 90.00
Candlewick, Plate, 10 In. 34.00
Candlewick, Platter, 16 In. 225.00

Candlewick, Relish, 4 Sections, 8 1/2 In. 22.00
Candlewick, Relish, 4 Sections, 10 1/2 In. 35.00
Candlewick, Relish, 5 Sections, 13 1/2 In. 77.50
Candlewick, Rose Bowl 250.00
Candlewick, Salt & Pepper, Footed .... .80.00 to 110.00
Candlewick, Salt, 1 /34 In. 7.00
Candlewick, Sandwich Server, Center Handle, 11 In. .... .35.00 to 37.00
Candlewick, Sherbet, Tall 28.00
Candlewick, Snack Set, Oval, Cup, Plate 25.00
Candlewick, Sugar & Creamer, Blue Iridescent 375.00
Candlewick, Sugar & Creamer, Tray 25.00
Candlewick, Tray, Kidney Shape, 6 1/2 In. 15.00
Candlewick, Tray, Lemon, Center Handle 45.00
Candlewick, Tray, Pastry, 11 In. .... .30.00 to 35.00
Candlewick, Tray, Pastry, Lily Of The Valley, Silver Overlay 125.00
Candlewick, Tumbler, 9 Oz. 16.00
Candlewick, Tumbler, Ruby, 9 Oz. 125.00
Candlewick, Vase, Bud, Footed, 7 In. 375.00
Cape Cod, Basket, Crimped Edge, Green, 9 In. 175.00
Cape Cod, Bowl, Flared, 5 1/2 In. 12.00
Cape Cod, Cake Stand 40.00
Cape Cod, Coaster 8.00
Cape Cod, Cocktail 6.00
Cape Cod, Compote, 4 1/4 In. 28.00
Cape Cod, Cruet, 4 Oz. 21.00
Cape Cod, Decanter, 30 Oz. 62.00
Cape Cod, Decanter, Square, 24 Oz. 50.00
Cape Cod, Dish, Spider, Handle, 6 1/2 In. 25.00
Cape Cod, Goblet, 6 Oz. .... .7.00 to 65.00
Cape Cod, Goblet, 10 Oz. 25.00
Cape Cod, Gravy, Underplate 55.00
Cape Cod, Jam Jar, Cover 22.00
Cape Cod, Plate, 6 In. 5.00
Cape Cod, Plate, 8 In. 8.00
Cape Cod, Punch Set, 14 Piece 125.00
Cape Cod, Relish, 4 Sections, Handle 30.00
Cape Cod, Salt & Pepper, Cranberry, Pair 10.00
Cape Cod, Sugar & Creamer, Footed 35.00
Cape Cod, Tray, Pastry, Yellow 145.00
Cape Cod, Tumbler, Juice, Footed, Amber, 6 Oz. 20.00
Cape Cod, Vase, 11 1/2 In. 60.00
Cathay, Bookends, Jade Green 225.00
Cathay, Bowl, Chinese Junk Shape, Marked 175.00
Crucifix, Candlestick 95.00
Diamond Quilted, Bowl, Rolled Edge, Green, 10 1/2 In. 28.00
Diamond Quilted, Candlestick, Pink 10.00
Diamond Quilted, Creamer, Black 15.00
Diamond Quilted, Cup, Pink 8.00
Diamond Quilted, Sugar, Amber 15.00
Grape, Tumbler, Milk Glass, 4 3/4 In. 8.00
Iris, Flowerpot, 5 In. 120.00
Katy, Bowl, Blue Opalescent, 9 In. 87.00
Katy, Creamer, Blue Opalescent 37.00
Katy, Cup & Saucer, Blue Opalescent 47.00
Katy, Plate, Blue Opalescent, 8 1/2 In. 27.00
Mug, Elephant Handle, Blue Carnival 25.00
Pillar Flute, Compote, Footed, Blue 30.00
Pillar Flute, Plate, Blue, 8 In. 20.00
Pillar Flute, Saucer, Blue 8.00
Vase, Freehand, Orange Luster, Cobalt Blue Loops, 10 1/2 In. 600.00
Windmill, Bowl, Milk Glass 30.00
Windmill, Water Set, 6 Piece 175.00

NDIAN art from North America has attracted the collector for many ears. Each tribe has its own distinctive designs and techniques. askets, jewelry, pottery, and leatherwork are of greatest collector nterest. Eskimo art is listed in another category in this book.

Armband, Beaded, Buffalo Hide, Geometric Design, Fringe, c.1890, 2 x 12 In., Pair	605.00
Awl Case, Sioux, Beaded, Chrome, Yellow Leather, Tin Cone Drops, c.1890, 15 In.	375.00
Ax, Southeastern, Grooved, Large	75.00
Baby Carrier, Hupa, Basketry, Miniature	110.00
Bag, Arapaho, Fully Beaded	375.00
Bag, Athabascan, Beaded, Wool, Colored Beads, c.1890, 9 1/2 x 6 In.	675.00
Bag, Beaded, Woodlands, Deerskin, 10 1/2 x 10 In.	440.00
Bag, Micmac, Beaded Floral, Red Beaded Border, Looped Beaded Fringe	1350.00
Bag, Nez Perce, Twined Corn Husk, Geometric Design, c.1900, 21 x 15 1/2 In.	1375.00
Bag, Pipe, Lakota, Beaded, Quilled, c.1870	5175.00
Bag, Pipe, Plains, Beaded, Quilled & Fringed Hide, 1860s	5290.00
Bag, Plateau, Floral Beaded, Corn Husk Back, Large	400.00
Bag, Plateau, Full-Beaded, Stylized Floral, Rectangular, 1940, 22 x 14 In.	187.00
Bag, Saddle, Woodlands, Beaded, Deerskin, Square, 17 In.	330.00
Basket, Algonquin, Birchbark, Flared Rim, 10 1/2 x 13 In.	225.00
Basket, Apache, Burden, 9 In.	145.00
Basket, Apache, Coiled, Black Parallel V Design, c.1940, 6 1/2 x 9 In.	550.00
Basket, Apache, Coiled, Meandering Design, c.1920, 2 1/2 x 9 In.	385.00
Basket, Apache, Polychrome Whirlwind Pattern, c.1920, 14 3/4 In.	400.00
Basket, Cherokee, Multicolored Oak Splints, Boat Shape, 11 x 15 In.	90.00
Basket, Haida, Plaited, Chest Cover, Zoomorphic Design, 13 x 17 x 22 In.	495.00
Basket, Hopi, 3 Large Mother Heads, 2 Small Mudheads, 1 Mad Face, 8 1/2 x 9 1/2 In. .	660.00
Basket, Hopi, Bundle Coil, Brown, Red, Black, Round, 5 3/4 x 9 1/2 In.	86.00
Basket, Horsehair, Triple Snake, 4 In.	415.00
Basket, Hupa, Stepped Cross Columns In Black Fern Stems, 7 1/2 x 10 In.	2035.00
Basket, Maidu, Coiled, Redbud Geometric Designs, c.1900, 4 1/2 x 9 In.	467.00
Basket, Makah, Birds, Blue, Red, Green, Blue Stripe Border, 3 x 4 1/4 In.	230.00
Basket, Makah, Cover, 4 Birds Design, Colored Finial, 3 1/2 x 4 In.	175.00
Basket, Makah, Cover, Black Zigzag Stripe, Black Sawtooth Circles On Top, 2 x 3 In. . .	55.00
Basket, Nootka-Makah, Ducks & Boats, 1920s, 11 x 5 In.	425.00
Basket, Papago, Brown Dogs Circling Baskets, Brown Border, Tan Ground, 2 3/4 In. . . .	144.00
Basket, Papago, Cylindrical, Terraced Zigzag, 4-Coil Split Handle, 8 1/2 x 10 1/2 In. . . .	175.00
Basket, Papago, Geometric Design, Dark Martynia, Yucca, 5 7/8 x 11 1/4 In.	85.00
Basket, Papago, Geometric, Dark Brown, Wheel Design To Bottom, 4 x 7 In.	86.00
Basket, Penobscot, Ash Splint, Braided Sweet Grass, c.1930, 3 x 5 In.	27.00
Basket, Penobscot, Birch Splints, Projecting Twist, 2 Bentwood Handles, 9 1/2 In.	44.00
Basket, Pima Alternating Dark Rectangular Bands, 10 In.	50.00
Basket, Pima, Coiled, Fret Design, Rectangular Shape, c.1930, 3 x 7 In.	137.00
Basket, Pima, Geometric Maze Design, Round, Early 20th Century, 2 x 8 1/4 In.	259.00
Basket, Pima, Linear Stacked Cross Design, Martynia, Willow, 1930, 7 x 11 In.	195.00
Basket, Pomo, Geometric Designs, Horizontal Diamonds, Black, Round, 7 1/2 In.	115.00
Basket, Salish, Fraser River, Salish Carrying Basket, c.1920, 8 x 9 In.	330.00
Basket, Salish, Star & Cross Motif, Cover, Handles, Rectangular, 13 x 12 x 21 In.	550.00
Basket, Seed, Washo, 5 3/4 x 2 1/2 In.	225.00
Basket, Storage, Papago, Coiled, 22 x 17 In.	1375.00
Basket, Storage, Salish, Fraser River, Cover, 12 x 10 In.	440.00
Basket, Tlingit, Twined, Brown, Orange Line Design, Straight Sided, 5 x 5 1/2 In.	825.00
Basket, Trinket, Northwest Coast Makah, 4 1/2 x 2 1/2 In.	275.00
Basket, Wall, Woodlands, 3 Sections, 18 x 15 1/2 In.	1500.00
Basket, Washo, Coiled, Black Geometric Designs, c.1910, 4 x 10 1/2 In.	550.00
Basket, Woodlands, Conical Shape, Spiral Design, Woven, 12 In.	86.00
Basket, Yokut, Coiled, 2 Bands Of Rattlesnake Design, Quail Feathers, c.1910, 4 x 9 In. .	825.00
Basket, Yokut, Polychrome, 8 1/2 In.	2970.00
Battle Ax, Cylindrical Turned Stone Head, Wood Shaft, Rawhide Wrap, 18 In.	200.00
Belt, Beaded, 1900, 44 1/2 In.	85.00
Belt, Choctaw, Beaded, 1920s	225.00
Belt, Navajo, Concha, Buckle, Bear Claw Pattern, Sterling & Turquoise	112.00
Blanket, Camp, Indian Design With Fringe, 1920, 64 x 66 In.	140.00

Blanket, Cree, Wool, Floral Beadwork, Brown, Gray, Fringe, c.1880s, 32 x 55 In. 1430.00
Blanket, Navajo, Double Saddle, Greek Key & Geometric, 20th Century, 34 x 50 In. 440.00
Blanket, Navajo, First Phase Design, Child's, c.1870, 31 x 36 In. 450.00
Blanket, Saddle, Navajo, Red, Black, Gray, Natural, c.1930, 52 x 25 In. 165.00
Blanket, Saddle, Woodlands, Painted Deerskin, 70 In. 275.00
Blanket, Woven, Striped, Yellow, Tan, Brown, Black, Red, Green, Fringed, 57 x 90 In. .. 59.00
Book, Gill's Chinook Dictionary, Chinook Language, J.K. Gill Co., Small Format, 1909 . 20.00
Bottle, Modoc, Overall Geometric Beadwork, c.1894, 16 In. 962.00
Bottle Basketry, Tlingit, c.1900, 7 In. 285.00
Bow, Yurok, Klamath River, Carved, 1850, 52 x 3 In. 440.00
Bowl, Apache, Coil Star, 5-Pointed Star, Geometric, 2 x 8 In. 460.00
Bowl, Apache, Coiled, 4-Petal Rosette Design, 20th Century, 2 1/2 x 10 1/2 In. 805.00
Bowl, Apache, Coiled, Rosette Motif, Geometric, 1900, 7 1/2 In. 750.00
Bowl, Cherokee, Hickory, Vegetable Dye, 1820-1860 .... 3700.00
Bowl, Dough, Acoma, c.1920, 7 In. 325.00
Bowl, Hopi, Diagonal Bands, Segmented, Rondina Huma, 4 1/2 x 6 1/2 In. 1725.00
Bowl, Hopi, Hand Painted, Roberta Silas, 1950s, 4 x 14 In. 196.00
Bowl, Hopi, Woven Fiber, 30 Concentric Rings, Brown, 13 1/2 In. 80.00
Bowl, Maidu, Natural, Peeled Redbud, Coiled, 4 3/4 x 8 3/4 In. 1100.00
Bowl, Pima, Coiled, Dark Brown Devil's Claw & Willow, Flared, 4 x 16 1/2 In. 1380.00
Bowl, Pima, Maze Motif, Braided Rim, 20th Century, 13 In. 400.00
Bowl, Southwestern, Blackware, Carved Relief Of Water Serpent, Marked, 8 In. 1035.00
Bowl, Southwestern, Blackware, Pottery, Marked Anna, 3 x 5 In. 750.00
Bowl, Zuni, Dough, Geometric & Curvilinear Designs, Bird, c.1870, 5 x 11 In. 1100.00
Box, Cover, Birchbark, Applied Flowers, 11 1/2 x 5 1/2 In. 75.00
Box, Micmac, Porcupine Quill Side Design, Fish On Lid, 2 1/2 x 5 In. 275.00
Box, Woodlands, Cover, White Over Red Paint, Handle, Oval, 27 1/2 x 18 x 11 In. 405.00
Bracelet, Navajo, Turquoise, Silver, 1950, 6 In. 85.00
Bridle, Navajo, Horsehair, 4 Hand Wrought Silver Conchas, Woven Reins, c.1920 ...... 550.00
Brooch, Zuni, Needlepoint, Turquoise, 4 In. 203.00
Canoe, Birchbark, 28 x 5 3/4 In. 100.00
Canoe, Ojibway, Birchbark, Quill Design, Incised, 1900, 7 x 2 In. 33.00
Canteen, Navajo, Tobacco, Brass 110.00
Canteen, Tobacco, Navajo, Incised Silver 250.00
Cape, Santee Sioux, Beadwork On Hide, Contrasting Color Beads, 19th Century 5500.00
Cradle, Doll's, Northeast, Birchbark, Twig & Splint, c.1900, 7 1/2 x 10 In. 145.00
Cradle, Nez Perce, Beaded Floral & Eagle Design, c.1910, 8 x 23 In. 660.00
Cradle, Paiute, Twined Willow, Bead Design On Sunshade 522.00
Cradle, Penobscot, Ash Splint, Rocker & Sun Shade, c.1910, 8 x 17 In. 1045.00
Cradle, Penobscot, Splint, Woven, 23 x 11 x 11 In. 425.00
Cradle, Salish, Baby, c.1890, 9 x 27 In. 550.00
Cradle Board, Ute, Hooded, White Hide & Brown Reeds 2500.00
Doll, Bust, Apache, Painted Clay, Human Hair, 4 In. 285.00
Doll, Hopi, Kachina, Badger, c.1940, 12 In. 825.00
Doll, Hopi, Kachina, Black Mask, Red & White Body, 11 1/2 In. 357.00
Doll, Hopi, Kachina, Carved Cottonwood, Straw Wreath, Bulbous Eyes, 12 In. 1380.00
Doll, Hopi, Kachina, Dance Costume, Snake In Mouth, Walter Howato, 23 In. 495.00
Doll, Hopi, Kachina, Germ God, Ah-Hula, c.1983, 18 In. 550.00
Doll, Hopi, Kachina, Leather Cape & Cuffs, Holds Flute & Gourd Rattle, 16 In. 330.00
Doll, Hopi, Mudhead, Rattle & Fan, Metal Base, c.1940, 28 In. 412.00
Doll, Hopi, Pot Carrier, Kachina, Polychromed Wood, Inscribed, 12 3/4 In. 1265.00
Doll, Iroquois, Corn Husk, 1940, 9 In. 75.00
Doll, Navajo, Female, Beaded Jewelry, Red Velvet Shirt, Cotton Skirts, 1930, 9 In. 86.00
Doll, Navajo, Traditional Dress, 1940, 16 In. 94.00
Doll, Painted Face, Leather Fringed Jacket, Beaded Trim, 15 1/2 In. 230.00
Doll, Plains, Buckskin, Beaded Dress & Belt, Painted Face, 12 In. 1540.00
Doll, Sioux, Fully Costumed, Quilled & Beaded, 20th Century, 17 In. 1705.00
Doll, Sioux, Muslin, Buffalo Hair, Original Dress, Mid-19th Century, 10 In. 1400.00
Doll, Southwestern, Kachina, Carved Cottonwood, Rainbow Headdress, 1920, 15 In. 2070.00
Doll, Southwestern, Kachina, Yellow Case Mask, White, Black Garb, 1920, 10 In. 750.00
Dress, Sioux, Beaded & Fringed Rawhide, Stepped Triangles, Hawk Bells, Child's 5500.00
Drum, Plains, Deer Hide, Birchbark 66.00
Fetish, Bear, Zuni, Turquoise 55.00

Fez, Nez Perce, Geometric Design, Corn Husk, Pre-1900 .... 800.00
Gauntlets, Beaded, 1920s 150.00
Gauntlets, Sioux, Floral Design, Fringed With Beaver Trim, 1920s 425.00
Goblet, Pima, Basketry, 3 x 2 1/2 In. 165.00
Hat, Hupa, 3-Color Twine, Concentric & Geometric Design, 6 1/2 In. 316.00
Hat, Iroquois, Floral Pattern, c.1860 .... 2100.00
Hatchet, Fraternal, Blade Stamped Eagle & T.O.T.E., Order Of The Eagle, c.1870 ..... 195.00
Head Covering, Woven Grass, Brown & Natural Facial Features, Long Grass Beard 45.00
Jacket, Children's, Chimayo Blanket, White, Red Corduroy Collar, Sleeves 201.00
Jar, Acoma, Geometric & Curvilinear Designs, c.1920, 11 In. 550.00
Jar, Acoma, Squared Shoulder, Black On White Slip Ground, 9 1/2 In. 2970.00
Jar, Blackware, Marked, 4 3/4 x 6 In. 1265.00
Jar, Hopi, Pottery, Seed, Adele Nampeyo, 1965, 4 x 5 In. 85.00
Jar, Hopi, Umber & Red Ocher Design, Verna Nahee, 6 1/2 x 8 1/2 In. 412.00
Jar, Pueblo, Tesuque Type, Plant Forms & Seed Pods On Body, White Slip 5610.00
Jar, Water, Santa Domingo, Black, Signed, 16 x 15 In. 650.00
Jar, Wedding, Pueblo, Blackware, Inverted Rainbow On Shoulder, 9 1/2 In. 110.00
Jar, Wedding, Santa Clara, Polished Blackware, 12 1/4 x 9 1/8 In. 247.00
Knife, Micmac, Skinner, 4 1/2 In. 70.00
Knife, Plains, Elk Horn Haft, Buffalo-Hide Sheath, Sun Type Design, 7 1/4 In. 185.00
Knife Case, Cheyenne, Beaded, Parfleche Liner, Tin Cone Suspensions 500.00
Knife Case, Plains, Beaded, Red, White, Blue, Leather Fringe, Copper Handle, 11 In. ... 115.00
Knife Sheath, Sioux, Beaded 295.00
Ladle, Iroquois, Otter Head Effigy, Ash, c.1900 .... 575.00
Leggings, Nez Perce, Red Trade Cloth, Beaded Floral Designs, Woman's, c.1900, 12 In. . 550.00
Leggings, Northern Plains, Men's, 1890s, Large 4200.00
Mask, Inuit, Hand Carved & Painted Cedar, 19th Century, 6 1/2 x 9 1/2 In. 330.00
Mask, Iroquois, False Face Society, Carved, Metal Eyes & Horns, c.1950, 18 x 14 In. .. 137.00
Mask, Iroquois, False Face Society, Ceremonial, Hair, c.1940, 13 x 9 In. 375.00
Mirror Bag, Nez Perce, Fully Beaded, Beaded Strap, Elk Hide, 19th Century 825.00
Moccasins, Beaded, Yellow, Orange, Blue, Suede, Brown, 1930s 42.00
Moccasins, Blackfoot, Fully Beaded, Geometric Designs, c.1890, 4 x 10 In. 935.00
Moccasins, Cheyenne, Blue & Red Tassel Design, White Background, Child's, Size 7 ... 575.00
Moccasins, Crow, Beaded, Sinew Sewn 275.00
Moccasins, Kiowa, Child's, Beaded, Yellow Ocher, 1900, 6 x 3 In. 140.00
Moccasins, Plains, Beaded Buckskin, Circular Design, Lazy Stitch Border, 10 In. 143.00
Moccasins, Plains, Geometric, Green, Red, Blue, Turquoise, Yellow, 9 1/2 In. 259.00
Moccasins, Plains, Green Beads, Butterflies, Yellow Ground, 1880, 8 1/2 In. 805.00
Moccasins, Plains, Green Beads, Thunderbirds, White Ground, 1900, 11 1/2 In. 805.00
Moccasins, Plains, Navy Blue, White Beads, Deep Blue Field, 1890 .... 980.00
Moccasins, Shoshone, Beaded, High Top, Soft Soles 81.00
Moccasins, Sioux, Beaded & Quilled, c.1890 .... 650.00
Moccasins, Sioux, Fully Beaded, Sinew Sewn On Buffalo Hide, c.1890, 4 x 11 In. 1265.00
Moccasins, Southern Plains, Buckskin, Seed Beads, German Silver Buttons, 15 In. 5500.00
Moccasins, Woodlands, Beaded, Tan Leather, Black Velvet Trim, Dated 1877 .... 235.00
Model, Canoe, Cree, Birch Bark, 3 Fish One Side, 4 Birds Other Side, 22 In. 175.00
Necklace, Black Foot, Painted Buffalo Tooth, Glass Trade Beads, c.1870, 26 In. 247.00
Necklace, Buffalo Bone, 2 Strand Trade Beads, 19th Century, 25 In. 330.00
Necklace, Hopi, Silver Squash Blossoms, Inlaid Turquoise, Coral & Jet 210.00
Necklace, Navajo, Silver Squash Blossom, 17 Pieces Of Turquoise 357.00
Necklace, Navajo, Silver, Naja, Turquoise Stone, 1940, 30 In. 220.00
Necklace, Navajo, Silver, Pendant Cross, Single Turquoise Stone, 1940, 34 In. 415.00
Necklace, Osage, Bead, White Blue, Salmon, Fringe, 1916 .... 190.00
Necklace, Southwestern, Shell Fetish, Turquoise, 13 In. 115.00
Necklace, Southwestern, Strung Turquoise Stones, Shells, 20th Century, 18 In. 575.00
Necklace-Tie, Sioux, Bolo Style, Beaded, Rosette, Orange, Yellow, Blue, White, Black .. 34.00
Olla, Apache, Allover Pattern, 19th Century, 15 1/2 x 17 In. 4200.00
Olla, Casas Grandes, Polychrome Red Ocher & Umber, Nicola Silvei, 9 1/2 x 9 In. 137.00
Olla, Hopi, 5 Different Kachina Faces, c.1950, 10 x 9 1/2 In. 605.00
Olla, Zuni, 2 Rows Of Heart-Line Deer, 1880s, 8 x 10 In. 2200.00
Olla, Zuni, Squash Blossom & Deer Design, Pine Base, 9 x 11 1/2 In. 3500.00
Panel, Leggings, Sioux, Lakota Style, Pair 770.00
Pipe, Arapaho, Carved, Quilled Stem 5000.00

Pipe, Iroquois, Effigy, Pottery, c.1650, 6 1/2 In. 675.00
Pipe, Plains, Pewter Inlay, Black Stone T Bowl, Beaded, 20th Century, 21 x 4 In. 165.00
Pipe, Puzzle, Potawatomi, Pierced Stem With 3 Balls 2000.00
Pipe, Sioux, Carving Of Elk, Turtle & Buffalo, c.1890 .... 1200.00
Pipe, Sioux, Catlinite, Eagle Foot Design, Carved Wooden Stem, c.1920, 30 In. 275.00
Pipe, Sioux, Snakes Carved On Wooden Stem 6000.00
Pipe Bag, Cheyenne, Buffalo Hide, Geometric Design, Fringe, c.1870, 7 x 20 In. 687.00
Pipe Bag, Lakota, Green, Yellow, White Beads, 1890, 24 In. 980.00
Pipe Bag, Sioux, 1890s 3200.00
Plate, Black Matte Pueblo, Leaves Design, Marie & Santana, Incised Mark, 6 In. 440.00
Plate, Plains, Beaded, Buffalo Bone Breast, Blue Beads, Leather Fringe, 38 In. 575.00
Pot, San Ildefonso, Blackware, Marie & Julian, 6 1/4 In. 22.00
Pottery, Quapaw, Pot In A Pot, Gray, Prehistoric, 7 x 10 In. 330.00
Pouch, Apache, Strike A Light, 5 Bead Colors, c.1890 .... 575.00
Pouch, Northeast Lake Region, Floral Beadwork, Velvet Trim, 2 Pockets, 14 In. 330.00
Pouch, Northern Plains, Beaded & Fringed Hide 1725.00
Pouch, Sioux, Quilled Hide 3450.00
Powder Horn, Algonquin, Double S Curve Scrolls, Mermaid & Elk, 18th Century 7000.00
Purse, Iroquois, Beaded Both Sides, c.1870 .... 290.00
Purse, Iroquois, Niagaraware, Beaded, Crossed American Flag, Star, c.1890 .... 175.00
Purse, Yakima, End Of The Trail, Fully Beaded 31.00
Ring, Zuni Arrow, Inlaid, Old Pawn 165.00
Rug, Blue, Red, Black & White Design, Tassels, 80 x 50 In. 120.00
Rug, Navajo, 2 Geometric Forms In Middle, Red, White, Gray, 46 x 24 In. 258.00
Rug, Navajo, 4 Different Storm Patterns, c.1975, 80 x 49 In. 1100.00
Rug, Navajo, Black, White & Gray, Greek Key Border, 1950, 150 x 68 In. 2200.00
Rug, Navajo, Black, White, Brown Arrow Shafts, Serrated Border, 86 x 63 In. 3265.00
Rug, Navajo, Central Serrated Double Diamond Design, Tan, Black, 25 1/2 x 36 In. 110.00
Rug, Navajo, Diamond Stripe Pattern, Serrated Edge, Black, Gray, 26 x 44 In. 55.00
Rug, Navajo, Double Diamond Center, Red, Brown, Tan, Gray Ground, 72 x 52 In. 575.00
Rug, Navajo, Ganado, Diamond Designs, Red, Natural, Black, Brown, 1910, 35 x 57 In. .. 330.00
Rug, Navajo, Ganado, Diamond, Stepped Terrace, Early 20th Century, 39 x 52 In. 385.00
Rug, Navajo, Geometric Designs, Bows & Arrows, Red, Gray, White, 71 x 45 In. 1495.00
Rug, Navajo, Geometric, Black, White, Red, Gray, Fret Design Border, 73 x 54 In. 2415.00
Rug, Navajo, Ivory, Beige, Red & Black, 41 x 65 In. 330.00
Rug, Navajo, Klagetoh, Sunrise Pattern, Star, Tan, Gray, Black, Red Outline, 28 x 49 In. .. 209.00
Rug, Navajo, Klagetoh, Triple Diamond, Stripes, Red, Gray, Black, White, 38 x 68 In. ... 440.00
Rug, Navajo, Natural Wool, Brown, White, Gray, 1920, 58 x 88 In. 605.00
Rug, Navajo, Pine Springs, Interwoven Central Design, Vegetable Dye, 1960, 82 x 49 In. .. 495.00
Rug, Navajo, Red Cross, Surrounding Central Stepped Cross, Gray Field, 41 x 56 In. 65.00
Rug, Navajo, Serrated Diamond Body, 1920s, 38 x 64 In. 440.00
Rug, Navajo, Serrated Diamonds At Corners, Gray, White, Brown, Red, 59 x 36 In. 172.00
Rug, Navajo, Serrated Lines Forming Diamond In Center, Brown, White, 76 x 44 In. 330.00
Rug, Navajo, Storm Pattern, White, Black, Russet Brown, 44 x 72 In. 495.00
Rug, Navajo, Sunrise Center, Mesa Design, Gray, Black, Red Ground, 25 x 36 In. 82.00
Rug, Navajo, Triangle Bands, Red, Natural, Brown, Black, Gray Ground, 29 x 58 In. 115.00

Indian, Totem Pole,
Carved, Painted,
Signed L.M.

**Clean Indian arrowheads with soap
and water and a toothbrush only
if they are very dirty. Handle
arrowheads carefully—they are
made of surprisingly fragile material
and will break if dropped.**

Rug, Navajo, Two Gray Hills, Diamond & Stepped Terrace Borders, 32 x 70 In.	220.00
Rug, Navajo, Vallejo Stars In Center Panel, Red, Gold, Black, Green, 51 x 84 In.	1760.00
Rug, Rhomboid Bands, Stripes, Gray, Black, Red, White, 19 x 36 In.	110.00
Saddle Cover, Plains, Buffalo Hide, 1850s	100.00
Sampler, Navajo, Germantown, Eye Dazzler, Diamond, Red, Green, Black, 1890s, 22 In.	550.00
Sash, Floral Beaded Design, White Beaded Ground, Colorful Tassels, 53 In.	360.00
Scabbard, Rifle, Trade Cloth, Beaded, 1700s, 47 In.	145.00
Shield, Arapaho, Ghost Dance, Fully Beaded, Buffalo Hide, c.1890, 9 In.	880.00
Skirt, Hopi, Ceremonial, Fringed	175.00
Skull Cracker, Blackfoot, Ceremonial, Beaded	495.00
Snowshoes, Algonquin Cree, Spider Web, Red & Blue Striping, Tassels	295.00
Souvenir, Iroquois, Beaded, Niagara Falls, Boot Shape, Early 20th Century, 8 In.	28.00
Spear, Chippewa, Muskrat, Double Barbed	350.00
Spear, Chippewa, Sturgeon, 5 Tine	175.00
Spear, Chippewa, Sturgeon, 6 Tine	275.00
Spoon, East Coast Canada, Moose On Top, 1850	3200.00
Spoon, Plains, Buffalo Horn, Mid-1800s, 10 In.	110.00
Teepee Bag, Sioux, Sinew Sewn On Buffalo Hide, Geometric Designs, c.1890, 22 In.	4900.00
Tomahawk, Trade, Wood Shaft, Steel Blade With Pipe Bowl, Hollow Tube, 16 1/2 In.	546.00
Totem Pole, Carved, Painted, Signed L.M. ....*Illus*	440.00
Tray, Apache, Black Geometric Patterns, Round, 12 In.	575.00
Tray, Apache, Checkered With Flower Petals, Woven & Coiled, 14 3/4 In.	2250.00
Tray, Hopi, Coil, Kachina Figure, Rainbow & Corn, c.1950, 14 In.	357.00
Tray, Navajo, Wedding, Brown, Black Woven Design, 12 1/2 In.	69.00
Tray, Pima, Geometric Hooked Spiral Motif, Early 20th Century, 6 3/4 In.	546.00
Vase, Hopi, Pottery, Birds & Flowers, Cream Slip, Red Band, Sofia Medina, 8 x 9 In.	605.00
Vase, Hopi, Pottery, Red & Black Scroll, Feathered Rim, Priscilla Nampeyo, 5 x 9 In.	770.00
Vase, Hopi, Pottery, Thunderbird, Burnished Orange Ground, Corn Signed, 10 In.	825.00
Vase, Hopi, Stylized Parrot, 20th Century, 12 In.	3385.00
Vase, Pueblo, Geometric & Curved Design, Black Matte, Marie & Santana, 7 In.	660.00
Vase, Santa Clara, Wedding, Blackware, Pottery, 1900, 12 In.	460.00
Vest, Nez Perce, Fully Beaded Panel, Cut Bead Stylized Floral, c.1900, 17 x 13 In.	1015.00
Vest, Sioux, Pictorial Quilled Hide, American Flags, Buffaloes & Blossoms	6900.00
Wall Pocket, Cree, Floral Beaded Design, c.1910, 6 x 7 In.	165.00
War Club, Penobscot, Ceremonial, Boot Ball Head, 18 In.	95.00
War Club, Plains, Root	550.00
War Shirt, Arapaho, Beaded Strips	4200.00
Water Pot, Zuni, Overall Insects, Butterflies, Dragonflies, Frogs, 1920	3250.00
Weaving, Navajo, Browns, Red, Black, Natural, Geometric Designs, c.1930, 35 x 29 In.	185.00
Whistle, Northern Plains, Bone, Beaded	105.00

INDIAN TREE is a china pattern that was popular during the last half of the nineteenth century. It was copied from earlier Indian textile patterns that were very similar. The pattern includes the crooked branch of a tree and a partial landscape with exotic flowers and leaves. Green, blue, pink, and orange were the favored colors used in the design.

Cup & Saucer, Johnson Brothers	12.00
Cup & Saucer, Rust, Copeland	25.00
Gravy Boat, Maddox	32.00
Plate, Johnson Brothers, 10 In.	12.00
Plate, Rust, Copeland, 6 In.	17.00
Plate, Rust, Copeland, 8 In.	25.00
Sugar & Creamer, Cover, Rust, Copeland	95.00
Sugar & Creamer, Wood	180.00

INKSTANDS were made to be placed on a desk. They held some type of container for ink, and possibly a sander, a pen tray, a pen, a holder for pounce, and even a candle to melt the sealing wax. Inkstands date to the eighteenth century and have been made of silver, copper, ceramics, and glass. Additional inkstands may be found in these and other related categories.

Brass, Hinged Lid, Floral Panel, 6 Porcelain Panels, 10 In.	300.00
Brass, Pierced Figural Masks, Griffin Wells, Crown-Form Finials, 6 x 22 In.	143.00

Bronze, Center Mythological Seated Figure, 2 Wells, Paw Feet, 17 3/4 In. 2300.00
Bronze, Gilt & Patinated, Ram's Mask Handles, Malachite Base, 28 In. 5750.00
Bronze, Gilt, Serpent, Pierced Scroll Foliate Border, 2 Wells, Glass Liners, 16 In. 201.00
Bronze, Marble, Retriever, Flanked By Foliates, Oval Base, 16 In. 431.00
Bronze, Reserve Of Courting Couple, Floral Edge, Porcelain Base, 8 1/2 In. 165.00
Bronze Gilt, Floral Scrolls, Snail Turtle & Salamander, 14 In. 315.00
Flower Encrusted, 2 Wells, Jacob Petit, c.1845, 10 3/8 In. 2300.00
Ivory, Carved, Flowers, 2 Glass Inkwells, Pen, Dieppe, France, c.1875, 1 3/4 In. 425.00
Painted Metal, Dog Across Top, Hinged Stump, Pen Rest, 4 x 5 In. 235.00
Pewter, Ink & Pounce Pots, Cornucopia Quill Holder, Continental, c.1750, 8 In. 275.00
Silver, Shell & Scroll Border, 4 Shell Feet, Robinson, Edkins & Astor, 13 1/4 In. 977.00
Silver Plate, 2 Cut Glass Inkwells, Candleholder, Sheffield, 13 x 7 x 5 In. 345.00
Silver Plate, Horse, Double Inkwells, Artist Signed, 1871, 11 x 7 x 8 In. 290.00
Stoneware, Holds 5 Quills, 18th Century, 2 5/16 x 3 1/16 In. 125.00

INKWELLS, of course, held ink. Ready-made ink was first made about
1836 and was sold in bottles. The desk inkwell had a narrow hole so
the pen would not slip inside. Inkwells were made of many materials,
such as pottery, glass, pewter, and silver. Look in these categories for
more listings of inkwells.

Brass, Glass Bottle, Brass Cover, Hand-Painted Floral Design Base, 2 x 3 7/8 In. 45.00
Brass, Glass Receptacle, England, c.1870, 3 1/2 x 3 x 3 In. 145.00
Brass, Imp On Stump, Toadstools Around Base 225.00
Brass, Ornate Handles & Covers, Winged Creatures, Master, 5 x 13 5/8 In. 160.00
Bronze, Agate & Gilt, E.F. Caldwell, 12 1/4 In. 1495.00
Bronze, Bear, Reclining With Bear Cub Climbing, A. Sokolov, Russia, 1876, 20 In. 4312.00
Bronze, Gilt & Patinated, Basket Of Fish, Japan, c.1900, 2 3/4 In. 460.00
Bronze, Gilt Patina, 2 Setter Dogs Hunting, Gornik, 18 In. 515.00
Bronze, Napoleonic Hat, Hinged, Marble Base, Marengo, 5 1/2 In. 690.00
Bronze, Reclining Putto Form Lid, Birds & Bouquet, Laurel Leaf Trim, 3 1/2 x 2 1/2 In. .. 630.00
Copper & Brass, Stag Head, Painted Pot Metal, 5 x 6 1/2 In. 325.00
Enamel, Gilt Cover, Poppy Pod Form, Peacock Feathers, Feuillatre, 1898, 3 3/4 In. 10310.00
Enamel, Green, Red & Blue, Arts & Crafts, 3 1/4 x 7 In. 315.00
Gilt Metal, Louis XV, Inkpot, Hinged Lid, Leafy Melon Feet, 9 In. 2300.00
Glass, 3 Applied Chickens, 24 Ribs, Swirled To Right, Aqua, 3 5/8 In. ....*Illus* 165.00
Glass, 3-Mold, Dark Olive-Amber, 19th Century, 2 5/8 In. 150.00
Glass, Amber, Hinged Amber Top, Square, 3 1/2 In. 210.00
Glass, Amber, Square Hinged Top, Dimples Sides, Brass Mounts, 4 1/8 In. 235.00
Glass, Black Bell Form, Green Neck, Black Rope Canes, Ettore Sottsass, 9 In. 1870.00
Glass, Cobalt Blue, Diamond, Metal Collar & Cap, 1860-1900, 2 3/4 In. 120.00
Glass, Copper & Enamel Lid Of Sailing Ship, Arts & Crafts, 2 1/2 In. 396.00
Glass, Hinged Top, Brass Connections, Dimpled Sides, Square, Coral Pink, 4 3/8 In. 235.00
Glass, Mold Blown, Aqua, Barrel Shape, Handle, 1840-1860, 2 1/4 In. 440.00
Glass, Silver Mounted, Bun Feet, Hallmarked, 4 1/4 x 5 In. 402.00
Glass, Teakettle, Forest Green, 1830-1860, 2 In. 385.00
Glass, Teakettle, Sapphire Blue, Octagonal, Panels, Fluted Corners, 1830-1860, 2 In. 305.00
Lapis & Onyx, Sterling Silver Mounts, 6 1/2 x 4 3/4 In. 220.00
Pewter, Ink & Pounce Pots, Cornucopia Form Quill Holder, c.1760, 8 1/2 In. 475.00

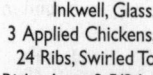

**Switch dishwasher detergent
brands periodically. This helps
to keep the inside of the
dishwasher and the dishes free
of any chemical buildup.**

Inkwell, Glass,
3 Applied Chickens,
24 Ribs, Swirled To
Right, Aqua, 3 5/8 In.

Pewter, Marble, Benjamin Franklin, Colonial Hat, 1900, 3 1/2 In. 125.00
Porcelain, Eagle, Polychrome & Gilt, Marked D.B., 5 1/8 In. 135.00
Porcelain, Lavender & Yellow Flowers, Gold Accents, White, 3 x 3 x 2 1/2 In. 125.00
Pot Metal, Lion, Head Lifts To Reveal Inkwell, Original Paint, 6 x 5 1/2 x 4 1/2 In. 170.00
Pottery, Carved Floral Design, Blue, Green, White Matte Glaze, A.F. Simpson, 3 x 3 In. . 715.00
Pottery, Dog, Whippet, Staffordshire 250.00
Silver, Leaf & Shell, Inscribed S, Victorian, Square, 1 1/2 x 2 1/4 In. 440.00
Silver Plate, Boy, Riding Dog, With Cart, Reed & Barton 350.00

INSULATORS of glass or pottery have been made for use on telegraph
or telephone poles since 1844. Thousands of different styles of insula-
ors have been made. Most common are those of clear or aqua glass;
most desirable are the threadless types made from 1850 to 1870.

American Telegraph & Telephone Co., No. 121, Purple 15.00
Armstrong, No. 122, Clear 2.00
Brookfield, No. 9, Aqua, Light Snow Flurry 20.00
Brookfield, No. 36, Aqua 15.00
Brookfield, No. 102, Aqua 2.00
Brookfield, No. 145, Teal, Amber Streaks 15.00
Cable, No. 4, Aqua 100.00
H.G. Co., Light Lavender, Pat'd May 2, 1893 . . . . 60.00
Hemingray, No. 106, Aqua . . . . 2.50 to 15.00
Hemingray, No. 106, Dark Yellow Olive Green 28.00
Hemingray, No. 115, Ice Blue 3.00
Hemingray, No. 214, 7-Up Green 24.00
Kerr T.S., No. 129, Steel, Ice 5.50
Light Green, Patented December 19, 1871 . . . . 15.00
Lynchburg, No. 106, Aqua 5.00
Maydwell, No. 115, Clear 6.00
Maydwell, No. 115, Light Green 3.00
Maydwell, No. 122, Light Green 5.00
N.E.G.M. Co., Medium Bright Blue, 1890 . . . . 140.00
Santa Ana, No. 178, Yellow Green 50.00
W.F.G. Co., No. 121, Medium Lavender, Seed Bubbles 280.00
Whitall Tatum, No. 5, Peach 6.00
Whitall Tatum, No. 154, Peach 10.00
Whitall Tatum, No. 154, Purple 20.00

IRISH BELLEEK, see Belleek category.

IRON is a metal that has been used by man since prehistoric times. It is
a popular metal for tools and decorative items like doorstops that need
as much weight as possible. Items are listed here or under other appropriate headings, such as Bookends, Doorstop, Kitchen, Match Holder,
or Tool. The tool that is used for ironing clothes, an iron, is listed in the
Kitchen category under Iron and Sadiron.

Boot Scraper, Eagle, Woman, Wearing Classical Attire, 10 1/2 x 16 In. 302.00
Boot Scraper, Lyre Form, American, c.1850, 13 x 11 1/2 x 9 1/2 In. 550.00
Boot Scraper, Scotty, 1920s, 7 x 7 1/2 In. 145.00
Box, Inlaid, Deer, Crane & Lotus Design, Korea, Square, 3 3/4 In. . . . . *Illus* 1045.00
Candle Bracket, Adjustable, Wall Bracket, 18th Century 975.00
Candleholder, Hanging, Twisted Shaft, 15 In. 355.00
Candleholder, Spring Clamp, Twisted & Shaped Saucer, Socket, Handle, 9 1/2 In. 247.00
Candleholder, Spring Clip, 3 Footed, Hanger, 7 3/4 In. 192.00
Candleholder, Tommy, Sticking, 12 1/2 In. 275.00
Candleholder, Wall Mounted, Griffin, c.1910, 16 1/2 In. 945.00
Candlestand, Table Top, Weight-Held Rushlight, Wooden Base, 18th Century, 27 In. . . . 1395.00
Chamberstick, Heart-Shaped Pan, Crimped Edge, Ring Handle, 19th Century, 2 1/2 In. . 110.00
Cigar Cutter, Reclining Nude, Brass Plated Kerosene Lamp, Etched Glass Globe 975.00
Cigar Cutter, Ship's Wheel 225.00
Cigar Cutter, Somebody Always Loses, Black Boy In Barrel After Losing Craps 125.00
Cigar Cutter, Woman, In Outhouse 175.00
Cigar Cutter, Woman, On Chamber Pot 335.00

Cross, Crucified Christ, Winged Angels, 62 x 34 1/2 In. 950.00

Dog, Greyhound, Life-Size, 61 1/2 x 21 x 14 In. 4500.00

Dog, Greyhound, Lying Down, 49 In., Pair 8250.00

Door Knocker, Charles Dickens, His Works On Scrolls Around Bust 65.00

Door Knocker, Hand Holding Ball, Strike Plate, 6 1/2 In. 235.00

Door Knocker, Mission Inn, Tiny Bell Hangs In Center, Cast Iron, 3 3/4 In. 45.00

Doormat, 186 Hearts, 19th Century, 15 x 23 1/2 In. 395.00

Duck, Shooting Gallery, Spring Base, Silver Paint, 4 1/2 In. 105.00

Figure, Eagle, Snowbird, Original Bracket, 1800s, 5 1/8 In. 125.00

Figure, Eagle, Spread Wings, 30 1/2 In. 515.00

Figure, Frog, Worn Polychrome, 11 In. 785.00

Figure, Hawk On Stump, Copper Flashing, 14-In. Wing Span, 15 1/2 In., 4 Piece 375.00

Figure, Unicorn Head, 19th Century, 8 In. 402.00

Figure, Weightlifter, Plaster Of Paris, 1930s, 15 x 20 In. 260.00

Finial, Stove, Reticulated Lid, Eagle, 10 1/2 In. 99.00

Flint Striker, Goose, 18th Century, 5 1/2 In. 350.00

Frame, Mirror, Interlocking Scrolls, Twisted Rope, Paul Kiss, c.1925, 42 In. 3600.00

Handcuffs, Forged, Chain Link, Key 35.00

Handcuffs, Yuma Prison, Hand Wrought, Pair 156.00

Hitching Post, Horse Head, 44 In., Pair 495.00

Hitching Post, Jockey, Square Base, Painted, 44 1/2 In. 3450.00

Hitching Post, Jockey, White Figure, Cream Jacket & Cap, J.L. Mott, 1850s 3500.00

Hutch, Watch, Leafy Scroll Work, Eagle, Cast Iron, Black Paint, 10 1/4 In. 85.00

Leg Cuffs, Hampton Jail 29.00

Notary Seal, Lion Head, Black, Gold Trim, 9 1/2 In. 40.00

Paperweight, Dog, Fido, Hubley 190.00

Paperweight, Doughboy Hat, 3 In. ....60.00 to 150.00

Paperweight, Elephant, Hubley 195.00

Paperweight, Figural, Man's Head, Gold Paint, 3 1/4 In. 66.00

Paperweight, Frog, Green & Black Spots, 4 In. 60.00

Paperweight, Kitty, Hubley 95.00

Paperweight, Pig, A. Pluemer & Co. Cin'Ti, O., Gold Paint, 2 1/4 In. 72.00

Plaque, 1792, Relief Image Of Eagle, Red Oxidized Finish, 11 x 8 1/4 In. 126.00

Plaque, Classical Scene, 9 1/4 x 12 1/2 In., Pair 120.00

Rod, Butcher's, Wrought, Scrolled Ends, 16 Hooks, 96 3/4 In. 410.00

Seat, Tractor, Buckeye 85.00

Seat, Tractor, Deering ....45.00 to 100.00

Seat, Tractor, Fuller Johnson 100.00

Seat, Tractor, Massey, Toronto 80.00

Seat, Tractor, McCormick 55.00

Seat, Tractor, Parlin & Orendorff, Canton, Il. ....90.00 to 100.00

Seat, Tractor, Rock Island Plow Co., 2 Stars 100.00

Seat, Tractor, Solid Comfort 98.00

Shears, Forged, 19th Century, 9 In. 85.00

Shovel, Oven, Hand Forged, c.1800, 28 1/4 In. ....110.00 to 115.00

Spring Latch, With Keeper, Mounted On Wood Block, Penna., 8 1/2 In. 165.00

Iron, Box, Inlaid, Deer, Crane & Lotus Design,
Korea, Square, 3 3/4 In.

Clean a very dirty cast-iron pot the old-fashioned way. Put it in a hot wood fire in a fireplace or barbecue pit for several hours. After it is cool, wash with hot water, soap, and a stiff scrubbing brush. Then season with oil.

Spurs, Forged Iron, Nickel Finish, Line & Leaf Design, Star Rowel, Crocket 90.00
Stand, Pocket Watch, Hand Forged, Flower & Leaf, 1890s 395.00
Step, Wagon, Blacksmith Made, Heart Design, Late 18th Century, 7 1/4 In. 295.00
Striker Flint, Curled Top Handle, 18th Century, 5 In. 250.00
Sundial, Griswold 500.00
Target, Shooting Gallery, Elephant Form, 1900s, 6 1/2 x 8 3/4 In. 185.00
Windmill Weight, Bobtail Horse, 15 x 16 In. 500.00
Windmill Weight, Crescent With Eclipse, Fairbanks, Morse & Co., 10 1/2 In. ...235.00 to 275.00
Windmill Weight, Horse, Painted, Dempster Mill Mfg. Co., 1970s, 6 1/2 In. 645.00
Windmill Weight, Rooster, Hummer, Elgin Wind, Power & Pump Co., 13 1/2 In. 605.00

IRONSTONE china was first made in 1813. It gained its greatest popularity during the mid-nineteenth century. The heavy, durable, off-white pottery was made in white or was decorated with any of hundreds of patterns. Much flow blue pottery was made of ironstone. Some of the decorations were raised. Many pieces of ironstone are unmarked, but some English and American factories included the word *Ironstone* in their marks. Additional pieces may be listed in other categories, such as Chelsea Grape, Chelsea Sprig, Flow Blue, Gaudy Ironstone, Moss Rose, Staffordshire, and Tea Leaf Ironstone.

Bank, Piggy, Black Spatter Spots, 5 In. 110.00
Bowl, Cover, Laurel Wreath, Elsmore & Forster, 7 3/4 x 10 3/4 In. 175.00
Bowl, Cover, Sydenham, 10 1/2 x 9 In., Pair 550.00
Bowl, Fruit, Blue & White, Pedestal Base, Twin Handles, 11 x 6 1/2 In. 165.00
Chamber Set, Imari Design, Pitcher & Basin, Figural Handle, 14 In. 210.00
Chamberstick, Arcadian Chariots, Blue, 1860s, Pair 950.00
Commode, Paneled Shape, Embossed Berries & Leaves, Anthony 110.00
Cup & Saucer, Snowflake 95.00
Dinner Set, Floral, Tureen, J. Meigh & Sons, 1830, 11 Piece 935.00
Gravy Boat, Wheat, Turner, Goddard & Co., 1867 .... 75.00
Pitcher, Black Musicians, Sally Is Girl For Me, Black Transfer, 8 1/8 In. 275.00
Pitcher, Gilt Flowers, White Baskets 100.00
Pitcher, Peony Sprays, Pagoda, England, Pair 242.00
Plate, Eagle & Shield, Blue Transfer, 9 1/4 In. 60.00
Plate, Holly, 8 5/8 In. 22.00
Plate, Polychrome Eagle, Shield, National Emblems, Frank Beardmore & Co. 140.00
Plate, Youth Balancing Bundle Of Flowers On Head, Black Transfer 8 5/8 In. 137.00
Platter, Archipelago, Light Blue Transfer, F & M, Label, 19 In. 100.00
Platter, Boy Near River, 15 In. 105.00
Platter, Columbine, Red Border, 12 3/8 In. 550.00
Platter, Floral, Blue Transfer, Praying Mantis, Polychrome Enamel, 21 In. 440.00
Platter, Floral, Transfer, Luster Accents, Purple Spatter Border, 15 In. 425.00
Platter, Lily Of The Valley, 1860s 95.00
Punch Bowl, Ming Pattern, 19th Century, 20 x 8 In. 484.00
Soup, Dish, Lady In The Window, 9 In., 12 Piece 175.00
Syrup, Grape Molding At Top, Gold Line Design, 9 In. 88.00
Tea Set, Grape Cluster Finial, White, Raised Leaf Borders, 15 Piece 450.00
Tea Set, Pansy Pattern, C.M. & S., 15 Piece 330.00
Tea Set, Sprig, 1840, 9 Piece 525.00
Tea Set, Stag, Blue, Allerton, 1880, 15 Piece 595.00
Tea Set, White, Gold Banding, 1880, 9 Piece 420.00
Teapot, Colbridge, Alcock & Co. 175.00
Tureen, Cover, Undertray, Lady In The Window, Polychrome, 14 In. 110.00
Tureen, Gravy, T. & R. Boote 275.00
Tureen, President, 13 1/4 x 13 3/4 In. 650.00
Tureen, Sauce, Ceres Wheat 200.00
Tureen, Sauce, Wheat, Turner, Goddard & Co., 1867 .... 65.00
Tureen, Soup, Cover, Floral Design, Black Transfer, England, 1847, 13 1/2 In. 1265.00
Tureen, Soup, Cover, Rambling Rose, Lily Pad Knop, 1850, 14 In. 1450.00
Tureen, Soup, Underplate, Wheat, Thomas Hughes & Son, 1920s 165.00
Tureen, Soup, Wheat & Blackberry, Meakin 300.00
Turkey Set, Dark Blue Transfer Platter, 6 Plates, Florence Bistro, England, 7 Piece 385.00
Vase, Chinoiserie Floral Design, Dragon Handles, Blue Ground, Electrified, 19 In. 2900.00

Vase, Cover, Gold Insects Between Gilt Borders, Blue Ground, 1820, 21 In., Pair 6900.00
Water Purifier, Meerschaum Filters, 22 x 9 1/2 In., 3 Piece 385.00

ISPANKY figurines were designed by Laszlo Ispanky, who began his
American career as a designer for Cybis Porcelains. In 1966, he established his own studio in Pennington, New Jersey; since 1976, he has
worked for Goebel of North America. He works in stone, wood, or
metal, as well as porcelain. The first limited edition figurines were
issued in 1966.

Figurine, Romeo & Juliet, Pink & Green, Pair, 1967 . . . . 250.00
Figurine, Spirit Of The Sea, 1972 . . . . 135.00
Figurine, Swan Lake, Pedestal Base, 16 3/4 In. 2500.00

IVORY from the tusk of an elephant is thought by many to be the only
true ivory. To most collectors, the term *ivory* also includes such natural materials as walrus, hippopotamus, or whale teeth or tusks, and
some of the vegetable materials that are of similar texture and density.
Other ivory items may be found in the Scrimshaw and Netsuke categories. Collectors should be aware of the recent laws limiting the buying and selling of elephant ivory and scrimshaw.

Amulet, For Robe, Monkey In Palm Of Hand, Japan, 1 5/8 x 1 3/8 In. 100.00
Crucifix, Christ In Agony, 19th Century, Original Box, 13 1/4 In. 880.00
Cutter & Turner, Page, Silver Mounted, Fox On Handle, England, 1891, 19 1/2 In. 1725.00
Dice Cup, Engraved, Large Ship On Reverse, 4 Aces, Amelia With Banner 675.00
Figurine, 2 Dragons, Mother-Of-Pearl Eyes, Meiji Period, 4 5/8 In. 385.00
Figurine, Bison, Taisho Period, 4 1/2 In. 402.00
Figurine, Buddha & 6 Children, Red & Green, 10 1/2 In. 635.00
Figurine, Chinese Fisherman, Holding Fish & Pole, 9 In. 220.00
Figurine, Deer, Recumbent On Reeded Base, Ivory Borders, Metal Case, 7 In. 1725.00
Figurine, Doctor's Doll, Lying On Palm Leaf, Wooden Stand, 9 1/2 In. 770.00
Figurine, Ecstasy, Green Onyx Base, Ferdinand Preiss, 8 3/4 In. 6325.00
Figurine, Elephant, Being Attacked By 3 Lions, 8 1/4 In. 187.00
Figurine, Equestrian Figure, Full Armor, 18 In., Pair 2070.00
Figurine, Fish Seller, Carrying Fish & Baskets, Kichikawa, 4 In. 415.00
Figurine, Fisherman & Child, Signed, 6 3/4 In. 385.00
Figurine, Fisherman Casting Net, Masayuki, 5 1/2 In. 165.00
Figurine, Fisherman Holding Cormorant, Orchid Plant, Signed, 10 1/2 In. 520.00
Figurine, Fisherman, Casting Net From Rocky Shore, Signed, 6 In. 1815.00
Figurine, Fisherman, Child & Fishing Birds, Signed, 10 1/4 In. 1100.00
Figurine, Goddess, On Lotus Flower Base, 20 In. 1035.00
Figurine, Hotoi, Seated, Wooden Base, 6 In. 65.00
Figurine, Madonna & Child, Gothic Style, 12 1/2 In. . . . . *Illus* 5170.00
Figurine, Madonna With Infant Jesus, 19th Century, 7 1/2 In. 430.00
Figurine, Man, Lying On Treasure Sack Holding 2 Scrolls, 4 1/4 In. 275.00

Ivory, Figurine,
Madonna &
Child, Gothic
Style, 12 1/2 In.

Ivory, Group, Minstrel Band, Continental, 18th Century, 13 x 8 In.

Figurine, Man, With Rake, Puppy At Feet, Signed, 7 3/4 In. 825.00
Figurine, Monkey, Stirring Rice In Bowl, Ivory, Meiji Period, 3 1/2 In. 1265.00
Figurine, Nun, Holding Dove In Each Hand, Signed, 10 3/8 In. 385.00
Figurine, Oriental Woman With Flowers, Wooden Base, 10 In. 467.00
Figurine, Peasant Girl, Carrying Wooden Spoon, Wooden Base, 19th Century, 6 1/4 In. . . 690.00
Figurine, Poet, Li Po Holding Fan In Left Hand, Scroll In Other, Rosewood Stand, 8 In. . 430.00
Figurine, Quan Yin, Standing, Lotus Blossoms, Teakwood Base, China, 1900, 14 1/2 In. . 880.00
Figurine, Sage With Deer, Red Seal Signature, 19th Century, 14 1/2 In. 1380.00
Figurine, Woman, Holding Parrot & Basin, Continental, 9 1/2 In. 862.00
Figurine, Woman, Nude, Seated On Rockery, Arranging Hair, Masanobu, 4 1/2 In. 715.00
Figurine, Young Man, Basket Of Melons & Ax, 5 1/4 In. 220.00
Group, 3 Graces, Carved, Oval Concave Base, Continental, 8 1/2 In. 1840.00
Group, Minstrel Band, Continental, 18th Century, 13 x 8 In. . . . . *Illus* 3300.00
Group, Woman, Seated Against Tree, Cupid On Her Knee, Late 19th Century, 6 1/2 In. . . 1725.00
Handle, Parasol, Frogs, Gyokusai, 5 1/2 In. 192.00
Letter Opener, Alligator 36.00
Needle Case, Carved, Full Figure Of Lady Wearing Bonnet & Apron, 1790, 3 In. 1095.00
Night-Light, Indian, 12 In., Pair 360.00
Pacifier, Large Ring, Victorian, 2 Piece 50.00
Page Turner, Stag Carved In Handle, 13 3/4 In. 195.00
Panel, Carved, Indian Deities, 19th Century, 9 3/4 In., Pair 110.00
Pepper Mill, Turned, 3 3/4 In. 70.00
Puzzle Ball, 6 Rings, Pedestal, China, 11 1/2 In. 625.00
Puzzle Ball, Intertwining Dragons, Stand, 12 In. 920.00
Sewing Accouterment, Carved, Screw For Table Mounting, China, 5 1/2 In. 176.00
Tusk, Procession Of Animals & Figures, Pierced End, 26 In. 375.00

JACK ARMSTRONG, the all-American boy, was the hero of a radio serial from 1933 to 1951. Premiums were offered to the listeners until the
mid-1940s. Jack Armstrong's best-known endorsement is for
Wheaties.

   Hike-O-Meter . . . . .22.00 to 35.00
   Magic Answer Box 40.00

JACK-IN-THE-PULPIT vases, oddly shaped like trumpets, resemble the
wild plant called jack-in-the-pulpit. The design originated in the late
Victorian years. Vases in the jack-in-the-pulpit shape were made of
ceramic or glass, and the complete list of page references can be found
in the index.

   Vase, Blue, Purple Stem, Blue Iridescent Circular Foot, Peaked Rim, 17 In. 8050.00
   Vase, Cranberry Glass, White Opalescent Rim, Wheeling Hobbs, 9 In. 425.00
   Vase, Incised Lines, Italy, 9 x 7 1/2 In. 468.00
   Vase, Italy, 5 1/2 x 4 1/2 In. 220.00
   Vase, Raindrop, Mother-Of-Pearl, Gold, Footed, White Lining, 7 3/8 In. 200.00

JADE is the name for two different minerals, nephrite and jadeite.
Nephrite is the mineral used for most early Oriental carvings. Jade is a
very tough stone that is found in many colors from dark green to pale
lavender. Jade carvings are still being made in the old styles, so collectors must be careful not to be fooled by recent pieces. Jade jewelry
is found in this book under Jewelry.

   Basket, Berry Design, Applied Alabaster Handle, Green, 8 1/2 x 7 5/8 In. 330.00
   Bowl, Bell Form, Green, 4 1/2 In. 330.00
   Box, Carved Relief Of 3 Rams On The Body, 1 Ram Figure As A Finial On Cover, 6 In. . 880.00
   Box, Kylin, Crouching, Exotic Animals & Birds Carved On Back, Sung Dynasty, 6 In. . . . 7700.00
   Box, Silver Metal, Rectangular, Early 20th Century, 3 3/8 In. 316.00
   Figurine, Buffalo, With Head Facing Left, Carved Back, Ming Style, 23 In. 8050.00
   Figurine, Carved Mountain, 2 Sages, Pine Trees Beneath Mountains, Gray, 3 3/4 In. 825.00
   Figurine, Dog, Lying With Head Resting On His Tail, Spotted Brown Coat, 12 3/4 In. . . . 154.00
   Figurine, Meiren, Standing With Head Tilted, Brown Flecks, Light Green, 9 In. 253.00
   Figurine, Mountain Of Tigers, 5 Cats Biting, Climbing Each Other, Light Green, 5 In. . . . 1725.00
   Figurine, Seal, Dragon Finial, 9 Characters Engraved On Base, White, Square, 2 In. 1430.00
   Figurine, Seal, Foo Lion Finial, Amber, Rectangular, 19th Century, 2 In. 825.00

Figurine, Young Buddha, Mutton Fat, Reclining On Lotus Leaf, 19th Century, 2 x 1 In. . . . 350.00
Jar, Urn Form, Horned Dragon, Loose Ring Handles, Green, 18 In. 1610.00
Pendant, 3 Chih Lung Dragon Design, White, 2 1/4 In. 220.00
Pendant, Shou Design, White, Early 19th Century, 2 1/2 In. 143.00
Snuff Bottle, Crane Amid Lotus, Apple Green, Conforming Stopper, 1 7/8 In. 374.00
Snuff Bottle, Spade Shape, White, 19th Century, 2 In. 605.00
Vase, 2 Stalks Of Bamboo With Bird, Foliage, Brown, White, 19th Century, 5 In. 660.00
Vase, 4 Buddhistic Lions, Raised On Carved Base, Handles, Gray, Green, 5 1/2 In. 368.00
Vase, Dragons, Classical Lotus Scrollwork, Handles, Round, Lavender, 9 In. 1495.00
Vase, Foliage, Falcons & Dragons, Flattened Oval, Light Green, 13 1/2 In. 805.00
Vase, Horned Dragon, Loose Ring Handles, Deep Green Stone, 14 1/4 In. 437.00
Vase, Horned Dragon, Loose Ring Handles, Green Stone, 18 In. 1150.00
Vase, Landscape Design, Dragon Handles, Gray, White, 19th Century, 5 1/4 In. 110.00
Vase, Phoenix Form, Celadon, Apple Green, 19th Century, 6 1/2 In., Pair 690.00
Vase, Smiling Mask, Loose Ring Handles, Wood Stand, White, 18th Century, 7 7/8 In. . . 5500.00

JAPANESE WOODBLOCK PRINTS are listed in this book in the Print category under Japanese.

JASPERWARE can be made in different ways. Some pieces are made from a solid colored clay with applied raised designs of a contrasting colored clay. Other pieces are made entirely of one color clay with raised decorations that are glazed with a contrasting color. Additional pieces of jasperware may also be listed in the Wedgwood category or under various art potteries.

Biscuit Jar, White Classical Scenes, Dark Blue 220.00
Bough Pot, Blue, White Classical, Neale & Co., 18th Century, 5 1/2 In. 975.00
Bough Pot, Cover, Woman's Heads, Classical, Blue, Turner, 1785, 8 In. 2530.00
Candlestick, Blue, White Classical Figures, Lear, 6 7/8 In., Pair 155.00
Flower Frog, Mermaid 165.00
Jug, Solid Blue, Classical Relief, Turner, 1785, 7 In. 1150.00
Pitcher, Dancing Figures, Dark Blue 75.00
Pitcher, Golf, Green 195.00
Plaque, Chief Painted Horse, Full Headdress, Border Of Owls, Green, White Trim 125.00
Plaque, Man & Woman In White Relief, Blue Ground, Germany, 11 1/2 x 9 1/4 In. 165.00
Teapot, Black & White Design, 5 In. 250.00
Teapot, Blue, Classical Relief, Leaf Border, Turner, 1785, 5 In. 1840.00
Vase, Cover, White Classical, Blue, Black Basalt Base, Neale & Co., 1785, 10 In. 460.00
Vase, Cover, White Classical, Pale Blue, England, 8 3/4 In., Pair 2070.00
Vase, Potpourri, Pierced Cover, White Classical, Turner, 7 1/2 In. 920.00
Wall Pocket, Cuckoo Clock 55.00

JEWELRY, whether made from gold and precious gems or plastic and colored glass, is popular with collectors. Values are determined by the intrinsic value of the stones and metal and by the skill of the craftsmen and designers. Victorian and older jewelry have been collected since the 1950s. More recent interests are Art Deco and Edwardian styles, Mexican and Danish silver jewelry, and beads of all kinds. Copies of almost all styles are being made. American Indian jewelry is listed in the Indian category.

Bracelet, 5 Emeralds, 18K Gold Mesh, 7 1/2 x 1/2 In. 632.00
Bracelet, 8 Strands With Oval Cylinders, Floral Clasp, 18K Gold, 1950s, 7 1/4 In. 700.00
Bracelet, Amethyst, Seed Pearls, 14K Yellow Gold, Early 20th Century, 7 In. 605.00
Bracelet, Angelskin Coral, 4 Strands, Coral Clasp, 14K Yellow Old Mount 345.00
Bracelet, Aquamarine, Red Garnet, Amethyst & Peridot, 4 Each, 14K Gold, 7 In. 154.00
Bracelet, Articulated Snake, Sterling Silver, Elsa Peretti, 1970s 245.00
Bracelet, Aztec Symbol Design, 9 Oval Silver Discs, Turquoise Inlay, Mexico, 6 In. 36.00
Bracelet, Bangle, Bakelite, 8 Sides, Cutout Circles, Pink, Purple, 1940s, 3 In. 70.00
Bracelet, Bangle, Bakelite, Fall Colored Leaves, On Metal Links, 7 In. 135.00
Bracelet, Bangle, Bakelite, Polka Dot 150.00
Bracelet, Bangle, Bakelite, Polka Dot, Red With Black Dots 400.00
Bracelet, Bangle, Bakelite, Round Inside, Squared Outside, 7/16 In. 30.00
Bracelet, Bangle, Carved Bakelite, Green, 1/2 In. Wide 96.00
Bracelet, Bangle, Engraved Large Shell Cameo, Coro 70.00

Bracelet, Bangle, Flexible Wrap, Platinum, Oriental Pearls, Diamond, c.1915 .... 5800.00
Bracelet, Bangle, Flowers & Leaves, 18K Yellow, Green & Rose Gold, 1920s 200.00
Bracelet, Bangle, Herring Bone Engraving, 18K Gold, 1940s 350.00
Bracelet, Bangle, Hinged, 18K Yellow Gold, Lalaounis, Greece 747.00
Bracelet, Bangle, Lucite, Carved, Red, 2 Clear Rhinestones, 1/2 In. Wide 48.00
Bracelet, Bangle, Ruby, Applied Gold Beads, 18K Yellow Gold 1495.00
Bracelet, C Design, Safety Chain, Open Back, Tapered, 18K Gold, France, 1940s 600.00
Bracelet, Chain Link, Reeded Links, 18K Yellow Gold, Italy, 20th Century, 8 In. 990.00
Bracelet, Chain, 12 Rectangular Florentine Links, 18K Yellow Gold 978.00
Bracelet, Charm, 13 Airplanes, 14K Gold, c.1960 .... 1975.00
Bracelet, Charm, 14 Traveler's Links, Enamel Accents, 14K Gold 230.00
Bracelet, Charm, 14K Yellow Gold, 6 Charms, Multicolored Stones 230.00
Bracelet, Charm, Art Deco, Diamonds & Colored Stones, Platinum 6900.00
Bracelet, Charm, Baseball Charms, Enamel, 14K Gold, 1950s 2250.00
Bracelet, Charm, Dogs, Horseshoe, 4 Leaf Clover, Heart, Bell, 14K Gold, Tiffany, 1940s 1800.00
Bracelet, Charm, Double Circle Links, 7 Charms, 14K Yellow Gold 345.00
Bracelet, Charm, Double Circle, 8 Charms, 14K Yellow Gold 316.00
Bracelet, Charm, Ocean Liner, Sailing Ships, 14K Gold, 1960s 1975.00
Bracelet, Charm, Poodle, 4-Leaf Clover, Horseshoe, Tiffany, 14K Gold, 1940s 1800.00
Bracelet, Charm, Scotty, Poodle, Horseshoe, Heart, Bell, Tiffany, 14K Gold, 1950s 1800.00
Bracelet, Charm, Silver Metal, 6 Charms, Fireman Motif, Hydrant, Truck, Axe, 2 1/2 In. 20.00
Bracelet, Charm, Small Plated Charms, 14K Yellow Gold 431.00
Bracelet, Charm, Textured, Link, Scroll Motif Frame, 14K Yellow Gold, 1880 .... 345.00
Bracelet, Charm, Trefoil Form, Chased Trace Link, Victorian, 14K Yellow Gold 402.00
Bracelet, Christmas Tree, Garland, Eisenberg 75.00
Bracelet, Circle & Figure Eight Link Design, 18K Rose Gold, Amethyst Enhancer, 1935 1600.00
Bracelet, Coin Silver, Eagle, Signed LH 25.00
Bracelet, Copper Wide Mesh, Renoir 25.00
Bracelet, Copper, Link, Figural Medallion, Rebajes, 7 In. 415.00
Bracelet, Cuff, Clear Lucite, Reverse Carved Floral, Lavender & White 85.00
Bracelet, Cuff, Inlaid Abalone, Mosaic Aztec Bird-Like Figure, Mexico 225.00
Bracelet, Cuff, Lucite, Frosted Swirled Front Piece, 2 In. Wide 42.00
Bracelet, Cuff, Silver, Spratling 950.00
Bracelet, Cultured Pearls Linked By 18K Yellow Gold Safety Chain, 1950s, 7 In. 150.00
Bracelet, Cultured Pearls, 4 Strands, 14K Gold Clasp, 6 1/2 In. 110.00
Bracelet, Diamond, Ruby & Emerald, White Gold, 1950s 3800.00
Bracelet, Diamond, Ruby, 18K Gold, Scalloped Fan, Rope Designs, Victorian, 1850s ... 900.00
Bracelet, Diamonds & Seed Pearls, White Gold, Crisscross Design, Art Deco, 1920s ... 1800.00
Bracelet, Double Figure Eight Links, 18K Green Gold & Rose Gold, 1930s 1000.00
Bracelet, Double Strand, Black Glass Beads, On Wire To Maintain Shape 25.00
Bracelet, Double-Headed Snake, Twisted Rope Body, 18K Gold, 1940s 550.00
Bracelet, Dual Links, Alternating With Triple Links, Rose Gold, France, 7 3/8 In. 935.00
Bracelet, Egyptian Revival, Plique-A-Jour, Sterling Silver, c.1900 .... 4950.00
Bracelet, Elephant Hair, Adjustable, Africa 60.00
Bracelet, Expandable, Garnet Set Into Center Medallion, Marked Solid Gold 200.00
Bracelet, Expansion, Bakelite, Flower Petals, Rectangular Links, Brown, 1930s-1940s .. 20.00
Bracelet, Figure Eight Flexible Link, 18K Pink Gold & Green Gold, 1950s 2000.00
Bracelet, Figure Eight Links, 18K Rose Gold & Green Gold, 1940s, 7 In. 450.00
Bracelet, Flexible Figure Eight Links, Side Clasp, 18K Gold, 1930s, 7 In. 350.00
Bracelet, Floral Engraved Center Links, Crescent Outer Links, 18K Gold, c.1915 ...... 500.00
Bracelet, Floral Motif, Diamonds, Rubies, Emeralds, Yellow & White Gold, 1950s 4000.00
Bracelet, Floral Pattern, Silver & Lapis Link, Georg Jensen, 7 1/2 In. 770.00
Bracelet, Floral Spray Motif, 10 Strands, 18K 3-Color Gold, Art Nouveau, c.1910 ..... 700.00
Bracelet, Garnet, Seed Pearls, 18K Gold, Victorian 247.00
Bracelet, Gold Hollow Work, Hair, Hand Engravings, Gold 375.00
Bracelet, Hair, Gold, Memorial, Bangle, Floral & Swirl, Leaf Cutout, Victorian, 1890s .. 550.00
Bracelet, Interconnecting Figure 8 Link, 18K Rose Gold & Green Gold, 1950s 1000.00
Bracelet, Ivory, With 15 Tiny Elephants 55.00
Bracelet, Jade Beads, 3 Strands, 14K Gold, Diamond & Enamel Clasp, 1930s 575.00
Bracelet, Jade, 6 Dark Green Ovals, 5 Diamonds Links, 14K White Gold 1092.00
Bracelet, Lacquered, Geometric Form, Black & Red, Jean Dunand, 1924, 2 3/4 In. 14060.00
Bracelet, Leaf & Floral Motif, 7 Strands, Pearl, 3-Color Gold, Art Nouveau, c.1910 .... 900.00
Bracelet, Lucite, Embedded Lavender & Purple Flowers, Hinged 38.00

Bracelet, Mesh, Heart-Shaped Padlock Closure, Victorian, 9K Yellow Gold 230.00
Bracelet, Orchid & Flower Motif, 8 Links, Pearls, 18K Gold, Art Nouveau, 1905 . . . . . . 600.00
Bracelet, Oriental Faces On Each Panel, Damascene 85.00
Bracelet, Oval Floral Design, Pearl, Wide Band, Hinged, 14K Gold, c.1910 . . . . 300.00
Bracelet, Pearls, 5 Strands, Diamonds, Stacked Star Shapes, 18K Gold, 1950s 1500.00
Bracelet, Plastic, Red Ball-Shaped Beads, Elastic 8.00
Bracelet, Plastic, Yellow, Carved Design, 1/2 In. Wide 10.00
Bracelet, Rhinestones & Pearls, Rhodium Plated, Bogoff, 7 In. 19.00
Bracelet, Rows Of Diamonds, Centered By French-Cut Sapphires, Art Deco 10925.00
Bracelet, Scrolled Links, Openwork, Plaques, Sterling Silver, Georg Jensen No. 62 . . . . . 350.00
Bracelet, Sterling Silver Links, Lily Pad Design, Danecraft, Marked 70.00
Bracelet, Sterling Silver, Cabochon Green Stones, Fish, Los Castillo, Taxco, Mexico . . . 373.00
Bracelet, Sterling Silver, Filigree Panels, Carved Black Onyx, H. Santana, 7 In. 165.00
Bracelet, Sterling Silver, Jade Cuff, Green Jade Flat Stone, 2 1/4 In. Wide 250.00
Bracelet, Sterling Silver, Turquoise Stone, Heavy, Mexico 65.00
Bracelet, Stylized Birds, Sterling Craft, Coro 65.00
Bracelet, Sweetheart, U.S. Naval Aviator Wing, LGB, World War II Era, 7 In. 125.00
Bracelet, Swirl Link, 18K Gold, Hanging Balls, Amethyst, Carnelian, Jade, 1945 . . . . . . 400.00
Bracelet, Wide Band, Raised Mesh, Silver Floral Pattern, Marked, Whiting Davis, Box . . 25.00
Bracelet, Wide Double Rope Twist Chain, 14K Yellow Gold 920.00
Buckle, Boot, Brass, c.1800, 3 5/8 x 2 1/8 In., Pair 65.00
Buckle, Dragon's Mark, Serpent Having Foliate Body, Jade, 3 1/2 In. 58.00
Buckle, Garter, Jasper & Agate, Sterling Silver, Scotland, 2 In. 875.00
Buckle, Silver & Agate, Central Star Set With Cairngorm, Scotland, c.1860, 1 1/2 In. 425.00
Casket, Woman In Arbor On Lid, Embroidered, Baroque Silk, Metallic Thread, 9 In. 3450.00
Charm, Merry-Go-Round, Horses, Movable, 1960s 125.00
Charm, Musical, Church Scene, Engraved, Music Hath Charm, 14K Gold, 1950s 350.00
Chatelaine, Clip & Large Purse, Star-Shaped Mesh, Dangles, Silver Plate, Early 1900s . . 100.00
Chatelaine, Dutch Sterling Silver, c.1880 . . . . 1400.00
Chatelaine, Floral Engraves, Chain, Slap, English Hallmark, 1898 . . . . 375.00
Chatelaine, Hook Suspending Oval Mirror, Floral Repousse Frame, Tiffany 258.00
Chatelaine, Ivory Crochet Hook, Sterling Silver, England, Victorian, 11 1/2 In. 995.00
Chatelaine, Red & Turquoise Enamel Powder Box, Perfume Holder, Lipstick, Chain 255.00
Chatelaine, Silver Hook, Inverted Heart Shape, Bright-Cut Border, Adam, 1800, 2 In. . . . 805.00
Chatelaine, Tape Measure, Pincushion, Thimble Holder, England, c.1870, 12 In. 698.00
Chatelaine, Umbrella Form Clasp, Scalloped Bottom, Foliage, F. West, 18 In. 1725.00
Cigar Case, Brass, Tortoise, Mother-Of-Pearl Inlaid, Accordion Sides, 19th Century 110.00
Cigar Cutter, Elongated Oval Shape, 18K Yellow Gold 250.00
Cigar Cutter, Horse's Head Opposite Cutter, Branch, White Metal, 20th Century, 6 In. . . . 172.00
Cigarette Case, Dragonfly In Center Design, Diamond Wings, 14K Yellow Gold 862.00
Cigarette Case, Souvenir, Enamel Design, Japanese Scenery & Map, 3 x 4 In. 18.00
Cigarette Case, Sterling, Nautical Code Flags, Enameled, Charles Thomas & Son, Inc. . 460.00
Cigarette Case & Lighter, Ronson, Pal, Black, Floral Design, Monogram, 4 In. 55.00
Cigarette Case & Lighter, Stratton Of London, Mottled Brown Enamel, 4 1/4 In. 45.00
Cigarette Holder, Dragon, Garnets, Sterling Silver 15.00
Cigarette Holder, Telescopic, Red Rhinestone 75.00
Clip, 7 Stones Each Clip, Kramer, 1 In., Pair 17.00
Clip, 20 Flower Heads, Suspended On Wire Frame, Sterling Button Co., 1930s 29.00
Clip, Cherub, Napier 22.00
Clip, Confetti Lucite, 1 In. 15.00
Clip, Dress, Blue Stones, Leaf Design, Trifari 25.00
Clip, Dress, Carved Leaves, Bakelite, 2 1/4 In., Pair 65.00
Clip, Dress, Flower, Red Bakelite, 2 1/4 x 1 1/4 In. 85.00
Clip, Dress, Leaf Shape, Bakelite, Butterscotch, Pair 35.00
Clip, Fur, Cuckoo Clock, Coro 45.00
Clip, Fur, Ice Blue Stones, Eisenberg 250.00
Clip, Sterling Silver, Red & Clear Rhinestones, Trifari, 1930s, 4 In. 95.00
Collar Studs, 18K Gold, Flat Disc Shape, Velvet Lined Box, Tiffany 275.00
Cuff Links, 22K Gold, English 1/2 Sovereigns, Marquis-Shaped Back, 1920s 225.00
Cuff Links, Applied Textured Fish Design, 14K Yellow Gold 345.00
Cuff Links, Black Plastic, Studded, Kenneth Lane, 1970 . . . . 50.00
Cuff Links, Earth Mover, Bulldozer With Front-End Scraper 30.00
Cuff Links, Enamel, Fox Head, 18K Gold, Hallmarked 1925 . . . . 1750.00

Cuff Links, Enamel, National Parks Centennial, Old Faithful, 1972 .... 45.00
Cuff Links, Honeywell, Step Up Award, c.1950 .... 45.00
Cuff Links, Lapis, 18K Gold, Round Stones, Engraved Border, S-Link, c.1910 .... 275.00
Cuff Links, Pharaoh Heads, Obelisks, Hieroglyphs, Gold & Polychrome, 1920s 450.00
Cuff Links, Playboy Club, Bunny Logo, Double Sided 75.00
Cuff Links, Rectangular Herringbone Design, Gold 110.00
Cuff Links, Red Motor On Black Background, A.O. Smith Logo 30.00
Cuff Links, Salamanders Sunning On Emerald Green Stones 35.00
Cuff Links, Square, Platinum, Sapphire, Diamond, 18K Gold, Art Deco, 1920s 300.00
Cuff Links, Stock Market, Red Stone Eye Accents, 14K Yellow Gold 374.00
Cuff Links, Triangular, Stepped Levels, Sterling Silver, B. Pepper 287.00
Cuff Links, World Book Encyclopedia, Award, 10K Gold, Enameled 60.00
Cuff Links & Shirt Stud Set, Mother-Of-Pearl, Diamond, 18K Rose Gold, Box, 1910 . 500.00
Earrings, Amethyst, Teardrop, Suspended By 7 Diamonds, 18K White Gold, 1920s 1000.00
Earrings, Angelskin Coral, 14K Yellow Gold, Circular 88.00
Earrings, Black On Front, Clear Back, Lucite, 1 In. 20.00
Earrings, Black Pearl, 14K Gold, Starburst Motif Enhancers, 1940s 250.00
Earrings, Black Pearl, 20 Diamonds In A Half Circle, 14K Gold, 1950s 1150.00
Earrings, Brushed Goldtone, Center Green Cabochons, Napier, 1 1/4 In. 25.00
Earrings, Circular Design, Turquoise, 14K Yellow Gold 110.00
Earrings, Clear Stones Emulate Flower, Kramer, 7/8 In. 25.00
Earrings, Clear Stones, Rhodium Plated, Hollycraft, Square, 1 In. 35.00
Earrings, Clip, Sapphire & Diamond, Platinum, c.1930 .... 6800.00
Earrings, Clip, Starburst, Rhinestones, Sterling Silver Frame, Eisenberg, 1940 ... 525.00
Earrings, Cluster Of Seed Beads & Rhinestones, Dangles Each Piece, Robert, 1 1/2 In. ... 35.00
Earrings, Dangle, Button Motif, 18K Gold, Diamonds, Marquis-Shape Link, 1920s 325.00
Earrings, Drop, Carnelian, Carved, c.1920, 2 1/2 In. 125.00
Earrings, Drop, Diamonds Around Oval Sapphire, 18K Gold, c.1910 .... 3900.00
Earrings, Drop, Emerald, Pear Shape, 18 Diamonds, Platinum, 1920s 6500.00
Earrings, Emerald, Pearl, 14K White Gold, Pair 632.00
Earrings, Floral Design, White Enamel, Aurora Borealis Rhinestones, Lisner, 1 In. 8.00
Earrings, Flower Form, Silver Screw Backs, Box, Georg Jensen 115.00
Earrings, Iridescent, White Swirled Glass, Hattie Carnegie 16.00
Earrings, Leaf, Marquise-Shaped Crystals, Gold Filled, Miriam Haskell, Marked, Pair .. 45.00
Earrings, Lucite, Diamond Shape, Bowling Ball & Pin, Clip, 1950s, 3/4 In. 38.00
Earrings, Pansy Shape, Enamel, Goldtone & Topaz Colored Stones, Nattie Rosenstein .. 27.00
Earrings, Pave Diamonds Hoops, Lapis Lazuli, 18K Yellow Gold, Cartier 1265.00
Earrings, Pearl, Diamonds, Platinum, Drop Setting, 1920s 3000.00
Earrings, Pearl, Drop, 8 Diamonds, Screw Back Design, 1930s, 1/2-In. Pearl 3000.00
Earrings, Plastic, Moon & Star Design, Green, Pink, Blue Rhinestones, Round, 1 1/4 In. .. 8.00
Earrings, Ring & Pendant Set, Silver Metal, Enamel Center, Teardrop, Flowers, Russia .. 89.00
Earrings, Rubies & Sapphires In Grape Bunch Motif, Diamonds, 18K Gold, 1920s 600.00
Earrings, Silver Horse, Abalone Ground, Shield Shape, Screw Post Type, Mexico 45.00
Earrings, Silver, Shell Design, Screw Back, Spratling, 1 1/2 In. 120.00
Earrings, Snake Head Design, Cross Figure Eight, 18K Gold, Diamond, Ruby, 1940s ... 600.00
Earrings, White, Pink Rhinestones, Hand Painted Flower Design, Bakelite, 1950s, 2 In. . 20.00
Earrings & Pin, Ivory, Carved, Flowers & Leaves, 19th Century, 3 Piece 247.00
Fish Clip, Sterling Silver, Incised Animal, William Spratling, Mexico, c.1931, 2 In. 345.00
Hairpin, Edwardian, Blue Enamel, 18K Gold, Seed Pearl, 1905, Pair 300.00
Hairpin, Flying Insect, Red Rhinestone Eyes, Turquoise Beads, 2 1/8-In. Wingspan 65.00
Hatpins are listed in this book in the Hatpin category.
Lavaliere, Diamond & Fresh Water Pearls, Center Shamrock, Chain, c.1910 .... 435.00
Locket, 14K Gold, Emerald, Onyx, Pearl, Flower Motif, 1880s 800.00
Locket, Black Onyx, Turquoise, Diamond, Pearl, 18K Gold, 1870s 700.00
Locket, Egyptian Goddess, Shield Shape, Cairo, 1900s 400.00
Locket, Engraved Covers, Prince Of Wales Hairwork Inside, Gold 275.00
Locket, Gold Dust Washing Powder, 2 Black Children In Tub 55.00
Locket, Gutta-Percha, Molded Design, 2 In. 165.00
Money Clip, Cartier, Bread, Cutout, 14K Yellow Gold, Original Case 345.00
Necklace, 14K Gold, Pearls, Teardrop-Shaped Links, Cutout Circles, 1930s, 15 In. 400.00
Necklace, 18K Yellow Gold, Chianpesan, Italy, 15 In. 862.00
Necklace, 2 Large Purple Stones, Art Deco, Chromium 45.00
Necklace, 6 Floral Plaques, Enamel Clasp, 18K Gold, c.1850 .... 2500.00

Necklace, Alternating Coral Beads, Large Oval Gold Beads, 18K Yellow Gold 1495.00
Necklace, Amber Beads, Alternating Ivory Beads, 1900, 22 In. 135.00
Necklace, Amber, Hand-Cut Graduated Oval Beads, 1900, 23 In. 155.00
Necklace, Angel Skin Coral, Triple Strand, Coral Floral Clasp, 14K Yellow Gold, 26 In. . 373.00
Necklace, Aurora Borealis Stones, Weiss, 16 1/2 In. 75.00
Necklace, Bakelite, Carved Brown Rose Pendant, Fake Pearls, Silver Links, 1940s 41.00
Necklace, Bracelet & Earrings, Pink & White, Hobe 225.00
Necklace, Celluloid, Cameo Pendant, Brown & Black, 30 In. 110.00
Necklace, Chain & Fob, Oval Link Chain, Swivel Hook, T-Bar & Coin Fob, 13 1/2 In. . . 316.00
Necklace, Chain & Slide, Swivel Hook, Applied Seed Pearls, 14K Yellow Gold 1380.00
Necklace, Chain, Link, Platinum, Diamond, Graduating Round Diamonds, Open Frame . 8625.00
Necklace, Chain, Links Of Floral & Scroll Design, 14K Yellow Gold, 30 In. 1150.00
Necklace, Chain, Lorgnette, 17K Gold, 50 In. 440.00
Necklace, Choker, Baroque Pearls, Almandine Garnet, Pearl Clasp, 14 In. 431.00
Necklace, Choker, Coral & Pearl, Miriam Haskell 125.00
Necklace, Citrine, Emerald Cut, 8 Diamonds, 14K Gold, 1960s 500.00
Necklace, Convex Links, Conform To Neck, Onyx Cubes, Sterling Silver, Taxco 517.00
Necklace, Coral Beads, 3 Strands, Red Coral Pendant, Dragon, Pheasant, 1930s 1000.00
Necklace, Coral Holy Man In 18K Gold Pagoda, 1950s, 20-In. Chain 400.00
Necklace, Disks & Cylinders, Bakelite, 32 In. 150.00
Necklace, Double Strand, Jet Beads & Gray Pearls, Haskell, 40 In. 225.00
Necklace, Faceted Amethyst Beads, 29 14K Gold Beads, 21 In. 66.00
Necklace, Faux Carved Lapis, Lucite, Brilliants, Hattie Carnegie 150.00
Necklace, Faux Pearl, Hobe, Box 125.00
Necklace, Fish Bowl, Lucite, Goldtone Chain, 24 In. 120.00
Necklace, Floral Design Links, Amethyst Clasp, 14K Gold, Germany, c.1840, 34 In. 7500.00
Necklace, Gold, Mother-Of-Pearl, Jade Beads, Case, C.R. Ashbee, 1905 . . . . 2245.00
Necklace, Heavy Links, Crackled, Silvertone, 16 In. 95.00
Necklace, Leaf, Sterling Silver, Danecraft, 18 In. 55.00
Necklace, Marcasites, Chrysophase, Sterling Silver, Germany, 1930s 112.00
Necklace, Mourning, Cameo, Black Faceted Glass, Shell, Victorian 480.00
Necklace, Opal, Cabochon Cut, 13 Diamonds, 18K Gold, Chain, 1940s, 18 In. 625.00
Necklace, Pearls, Double Strand, Bouquet Clasp, Gold, Ruby, Sapphire, 1930s, 34 In. . . 900.00
Necklace, Pearls, With Teardrop Amethyst, Pearl & Gold Enhancer, 1950s, 25 In. 600.00
Necklace, Pendant, Filigree, 18K Gold, Seed Pearls & Rubies, Victorian, 18 In. 715.00
Necklace, Pink Glass Stones, Serpentine Brass Chain, 1930s, 6 In. Wide 31.00
Necklace, Plastic, 1 Strand, Amber, Coro, 14 In. 45.00
Necklace, Plastic, Red, Trifari 8.00
Necklace, Silver Sterling, Ceramic Beads, Arrowheads, Los Castillo, 12 In. 605.00
Necklace, Snakes, Ruby Eyes, Fine Mesh Double Strand Design, 18K Gold, 1940s 2500.00
Necklace, Square Black Plastic Beads, Silvertone Chain, Trifari, 8 In. 8.00
Necklace, Star Ruby, 30 Diamonds, Platinum, Millegrain Edge, Art Deco, 1920s 900.00
Necklace, Sterling Silver & Moonstone, Kalo 976.00
Necklace, Sterling Silver, Link, Geometric, Ballesteros, 1940s, 8 In. 330.00
Necklace, Water Lily Pendant, Haskell 135.00
Necklace, White Beads, Layered Look, 1930s, 18 In. 35.00
Necklace & Bracelet, Black Plastic, White Stones, Kramer Of New York, 14 1/2 In. . . . 150.00
Necklace & Bracelet, Buddha & Carved Floral Charms, Gold Link Chain, 18 & 9 In. . . 245.00
Necklace & Bracelet, Ice Blue Rhinestones, Hollycraft 125.00
Necklace & Bracelet, Red Coral, 3 Strands, Cameo Style Clasp, 1920s, 15 & 8 In. 600.00
Necklace & Bracelet, Sterling Silver, Blue Stones, Signed, Mexico 750.00
Necklace & Cameo, Rectangular Links, Diamond Design, Floral, 10K Gold, 1880s 550.00
Necklace & Earrings, 14K Gold, Scrimshaw, 7 Teeth, Sailing Ship, 1940s, 15 In. 1200.00
Necklace & Earrings, Clear Stones, Pendant, Snake Chain, Trifari, 19 In. 55.00
Necklace & Earrings, Pendant, Green/Purple Stone, Pearls, Miriam Haskell, 1950s 350.00
Necklace & Earrings, Sterling Silver, Green Onyx & Pearls, Velvet Rope, Antonio 550.00
Necklace & Earrings, Sterling Silver, Link, Floral Medallions, McClelland & Barclay . . 120.00
Necklace & Earrings, White & Green Beads, Screw Back Earrings, Miriam Haskell . . . 60.00
Pendant, Amber, Bug & Leaf Specks, Silver Chain, 10 In. 101.00
Pendant, Art Nouveau Floral & Fruit, Enamel & Sterling Silver, DM & Co., 1 1/2 In. . . 55.00
Pendant, Black & White Onyx Cameo, Young Man In Profile, Gold Filled, c.1880 . . . . . 315.00
Pendant, Black Pearl & Diamonds, 18K Gold, Teardrop, 1950s, 3/4 x 1 1/4 In. 3500.00
Pendant, Book Locket Form, Vinaigrette, 18K Gold, c.1820 . . . . 2500.00

Pendant, Cameo, 18K Gold, Lava, Tan, Cherub With Horn On Deer, Chain, 1880s 750.00
Pendant, Cameo, Carved Amethyst, Diamonds, 14K Gold, Chain, 1880s, 1 x 3/4 In. 800.00
Pendant, Crescent Moon, With Nude Woman, Sterling Silver, Art Nouveau, 1 1/2 In. ... 50.00
Pendant, Dangles & Filigree, Colored Cabochon, Hollycraft, Chain 16.00
Pendant, Diamond, Ruby, Dragonfly Design, Rose-Cut Diamonds, Victorian 2300.00
Pendant, Enamel, Young Woman Giving Virgin Mary A Rosary, 18K Gold, 1910 ...... 400.00
Pendant, Heart, 13 Rubies, Braided Hair Under Glass, Georgian, c.1810, 15 In. 1500.00
Pendant, Holds Perfume, India Design, Florenza 15.00
Pendant, Horseshoe, Coral Buddha, 5 Rubies, 18K Gold, 1950s, 18-In. Chain 350.00
Pendant, Jasperware, 4 Colors, Blue, White Ground, Beadwork, Metal Frame, 7/8 In. ... 230.00
Pendant, Lapis Cabochon On Paperclip Link Chain, Kalo, 1 1/4 x 3/4 In. 665.00
Pendant, Leaf Form, Paperclip Link Chain, Sterling Silver, AMS, 1 3/4 x 1 1/4 In. 85.00
Pendant, Pagoda, 18K Gold, Jade Adornments, 14K Gold Chain, 1950s, 24 In. 350.00
Pendant, Painting On Ivory, Holds World's Smallest Dictionary, 15K Gold, c.1870 ..... 1800.00
Pendant, Peacock, 14K Gold, Opal, Ruby, Sapphire, Emerald, 1950s, 26-In. Chain 400.00
Pendant, Serpents, Entwined Snake Form, Blue, Lalique, Signed, 1920, 1 3/4 In. 495.00
Pendant, Strawberry, 18K Gold, Box, Steuben, 14K Gold Chain 700.00
Pendant, Tortoiseshell Fish, Bakelite 125.00
Pendant & Bracelet, Sterling Silver, Black Labradrite, William Spratling, Mexico 345.00
Pin, 18K Gold, Enamel, Raised Gold & Black Belt Design, Seed Pearls, 1890s 400.00
Pin, 18K Gold, Moss Agate, Rectangular, Heart & Swirl Border Design, 1900s 225.00
Pin, 18K Yellow Gold, Pearl, Turquoise Filigree, Mid-Victorian 185.00
Pin, 3 Horseshoes, Rhinestones, Weiss, 1 7/8 x 2 In. 95.00
Pin, 3-Line Design, Center Circle Motif, Diamonds, Seed Pearls, 14K Gold, 1920s 250.00
Pin, 4 Flower Heads, Collet Set Lapis Accents, Silver, Georg Jensen, c.1933 .... 977.00
Pin, 61 Diamonds, Flame Tip Design, 18K White Gold, Art Deco, 1920s 1500.00
Pin, Abstract Design, Silver Movable Bead, Rebajes, 3 In. 195.00
Pin, Abstract Flower, Red Plastic Circles, Rhinestones, Wired, 1930s 55.00
Pin, Alternating Pearls & Graduating Sapphires, 14K Yellow Gold, Fisher 230.00
Pin, Art Deco Bow, Green Plastic, 2 1/2 In. 45.00
Pin, Art Nouveau, Floral, Purple Poppy, Green Leaf, Pearl, Enamel & 18K Gold, 1910 .. 300.00
Pin, Bakelite, Orange Triangles, Brass Studs, Butterscotch Circles, 2 In. 40.00
Pin, Bar, 18K Yellow Gold, Enameled Maiden & Putto, Amethysts, France, 1850 .... 1800.00
Pin, Bar, Carved Brown Bangle, Bakelite, Pair 50.00
Pin, Bar, Center Circle Design, Diamonds, 24 Rubies, 18K Gold, Art Deco, 1930s 450.00
Pin, Bar, Cluster Mounting, 9 Mine-Cut Diamonds, 18K Gold, 1900s 325.00
Pin, Bar, Diamond Circle, 18K Gold, Platinum-Finished Front, 1920s 750.00
Pin, Bar, Flower & Leaf Shape, 18K Gold, Center Diamond, 1920s, 5/8 x 1 7/8 In. 225.00
Pin, Bar, Foliage & Berries, Sterling Silver, Georg Jensen 185.00
Pin, Bar, Sapphire, 2 Diamonds, Swirl Design, 14K Rose Gold, c.1925 .... 450.00
Pin, Bar, White Celluloid Bell-Shaped Dangling Flowers, Lucite, 3 x 3 1/2 In. 55.00
Pin, Bird In Flight, No. 334, Sterling Silver, Arc-Shaped Top, Georg Jensen, c.1950s ... 260.00
Pin, Bird In Wreath Of Foliage, Georg Jensen, 1 3/4 In. 192.00
Pin, Bird On Wing, Red Celluloid, 2 x 5 1/4 In. 75.00
Pin, Black Opal & Diamond, 18K Gold, Carved Flower, Floral Spray, 1930s 2200.00
Pin, Blue Center Stone, Surrounded By Blue & Clear Stones, Hobe, 2 1/2 In. 350.00
Pin, Boeing, 20 Years, Diamond 85.00
Pin, Brown Hair Under Glass, Black Enamel Frame, c.1860, 1 In. 95.00
Pin, Butterfly, Japanned Setting, Weiss, 1 1/2 In. ....30.00 to 50.00
Pin, Cameo, Attached To Square Ground, Black Bakelite 125.00
Pin, Cameo, Bezel Stone, 18K Gold, Rectangular, Swirl Design, Victorian, 1890s 375.00
Pin, Cameo, Classical Figures, Flower, Leaf Surround, Wedgwood, Sterling Silver, 2 In. . 165.00
Pin, Cameo, Diana, Sardonyx, Set In Yellow Gold With Seed Pearls, 1 3/4 x 1 3/8 In. ... 1385.00
Pin, Cameo, Georgian, Stone, 18K Gold, Raised Relief Swirl Design Bezel, 1820s, 1 In. . 450.00
Pin, Cameo, Helen Of Troy, Gold Filled 75.00
Pin, Cameo, Ivory, Female Profile, 18K Yellow Gold Frame 747.00
Pin, Cameo, Lady In Profile, 14K Rose Gold, Marta Igeregia 185.00
Pin, Cameo, Magnetic Stone, 14K Yellow Gold, Detailed Carving, c.1890, 1 1/2 In. 400.00
Pin, Cameo, Muse Calliope, 14K White Gold Mounting, Italy, 1900 .... 650.00
Pin, Cameo, Profile Of Woman, Crescent Moon In Hair, 10K Rose Gold, 1 1/4 In. 175.00
Pin, Cameo, Shell, 14K White Gold, Figure Eight & Floral Motifs, Art Deco, 1930s 325.00
Pin, Cameo, Shell, Nativity Scene, Fitted Box, P. Russo 430.00
Pin, Cameo, Shell, Rope Twist Frame, Late 19th Century 310.00

422

Pin, Cameo, Stone, 10K Rose Gold, Polished Finish, c.1885, 1 x 1 1/2 In. 425.00
Pin, Cameo, Stone, 18K Gold, Twisted Ribbon Motif Border, 1880s, 1 1/2 In. 600.00
Pin, Cameo, Tortoiseshell, Young Woman, Hair Ornament, Silver Frame 402.00
Pin, Cameo, White Woman's Profile, Black Plastic, 1 In. 14.00
Pin, Cameo, Woman Facing Left, Sterling Silver Frame, Brass Pin & Catch, Italy, 1 In. . . . 41.00
Pin, Cameo, Woman, Side View, Ivory, Yellow Gold 2000.00
Pin, Carved, Black, Raised Flowers, Coiled Gold Metal Frame, Bakelite 150.00
Pin, Carved, Floral, Black, Bakelite 135.00
Pin, Celluloid, Woman Lounging In Hammock, Blue Rhinestones, 1 1/2 x 2 In. 48.00
Pin, Child's Head, Leaves, Red Coral, Carved, Drop Pendant, 19th Century, 3 x 2 In. 1375.00
Pin, Christmas Tree, Emerald Marquis Stones, Eisenberg 75.00
Pin, Christmas Tree, Mylu 15.00
Pin, Christmas Tree, Wise 65.00
Pin, Cigarette, 5 Matches, Bakelite 975.00
Pin, Cocker Spaniel, Sterling, Embossed Details, Cini, 2 x 3 In. 85.00
Pin, Crab, Dark Pink Coral, 2 Small Full-Cut Diamonds, 18K Yellow Gold 145.00
Pin, Crown, Sterling, Red & Green Cabochons, Corocraft, 2 In. 90.00
Pin, Diamond, Platinum, Formal Swirl Design, 2 Piece, Clip, 1920s, 1 x 2 1/2 In. 5500.00
Pin, Diamonds, Rubies, Emerald, Peridots & Opal, 14K Gold, c.1885 . . . . 2250.00
Pin, Dog Running, Panetta 35.00
Pin, Donkey, Hattie Carnegie 195.00
Pin, Double Clip, Rhinestones, Coro 35.00
Pin, Double, Rhinestone, Silver Gray Tone Celluloid, 3 1/2 x 2 1/4 In. 46.00
Pin, Dove Within Foliate Wreath, Georg Jensen, 1933 . . . . 431.00
Pin, Dragonfly, Wirework Wings, Clear Pave Body, Monet, 1 7/8 x 1 3/4 In. 17.00
Pin, Duck, Top Hat, Green Stone, Hattie Carnegie, Italy 25.00
Pin, Elephant, Trunk Around Emerald Stone, Sterling Silver Mount, Corocraft, 3 In. 975.00
Pin, Eye Of Time, Round & Baguette Diamonds, Platinum Mount, Dali 5290.00
Pin, Face, Modern, Plastic, Lea Stein, 2 1/2 x 1 1/2 In. 95.00
Pin, Fan, Gilt Overlay, Copper Background, Shakudo, c.1880 . . . . 320.00
Pin, Feather, Miriam Haskell 40.00
Pin, Figural Eye, Sterling Silver, Yellow Glass Pupil, Sam Kramer, 3 In. 3300.00
Pin, Filigree Bow, Shell Cameo, Diamonds, 14K White Gold, 1870s 300.00
Pin, Fish, Cultured Pearl, 1 Small Diamond, Yellow & White Gold 85.00
Pin, Fish, Sterling Silver, Los Castillo, Mexico 150.00
Pin, Floral & Ribbon Motif, Diamonds, Platinum, 1940s, 1 7/8 x 2 5/8 In. 4500.00
Pin, Floral Spray, Sterling, Rose Gold, Clear Stones, Trifari, 1940, 3 In. 95.00
Pin, Floral, Green, Carved, Bakelite, 3 In. 120.00
Pin, Flower Shape, Green Petals, Goldtone Setting, Coro, 2 In. 35.00
Pin, Flower, Red Rhinestones, Enameled Bowl, Chanel, 3 1/2 x 2 1/2 In. 585.00
Pin, Flowers, Orange, Oval, Hand Painted, Bakelite, 2 1/5 x 3 1/2 In. 70.00
Pin, Foliate Design, Around Moonstones, Sterling Silver, Mary Gage, 2 3/4 In. 330.00
Pin, Foliate Design, Coral Centerpiece, 14K Yellow Gold 125.00
Pin, Frog, Marcasite, Sterling Silver 20.00
Pin, Fruit Basket, Bakelite, 2 3/4 x 2 1/2 In. 375.00
Pin, Gaping Fish, Eisenberg 1200.00
Pin, Gold Shield, Lions, Miriam Haskell 55.00
Pin, Goony Bird, Carved Tail & Head Feathers, Wooden, 2 3/4 In. 30.00
Pin, Grape, Silver, Georg Jensen, 1 1/2 x 2 3/4 In. 495.00
Pin, Hand Holding Coral Ball, 14K Gold, 1900s, 1 x 3/8 In. 250.00
Pin, Hat, Marbleized, Red Cord, Bakelite, 3 x 3 In. 350.00
Pin, Heart & Bird Design, Georg Jensen 230.00
Pin, Heart Shape, Red Sparkle, Brushed Gold & Clear Baguettes, Trifari, 2 In. 22.00
Pin, Horsehead, Wooden, Painted Face, Lucite Mane, 3 x 2 1/8 In. 65.00
Pin, Horseshoe, Sterling Silver & Agate, c.1850 . . . . 235.00
Pin, Indy 500, 1947 . . . . 350.00
Pin, Invisible Set Ruby, Sapphire & Diamond, Mickey Mouse Golfer, 18K Gold 4950.00
Pin, Jasper Dip, Classical Relief, Blue, Wedgwood, Late 18th Century, 3 7/8 In. 345.00
Pin, JMR Initials, Black Bakelite, Oval 95.00
Pin, Kilt, Scotch Agate, Citrine, Jasper & Agate, 1 5/8 In. 695.00
Pin, King Of Diamonds, Sterling Silver, McClelland Barclay 125.00
Pin, Lapel, Delta Airlines, 10 Years Service, Winged Red Ball, Red Stone, 1 In. 78.00
Pin, Lion's Head Shape, Diamond Eyes, 14K Yellow Gold 1092.00

Pin, Lion's Head, Trifari 95.00
Pin, Lizard Crawling In Clam Shell, Shell & Rose Diamond, 19th Century 440.00
Pin, Lizard, Gilt, Green & Black Enamel, Gold Tone Chain, 1920s-1930s, 2 1/4 In., Pair . 30.00
Pin, Locket, Reversible, Bevel Glass, Seed Pearls, Garnets, 14K Gold, Floral, 1890s 550.00
Pin, Lucite & Celluloid, Carved, Egyptian Design, 1 3/4 x 2 In. 85.00
Pin, Magnolia Blossom, Moonstone Accent, Georg Jensen 373.00
Pin, Memorial, Mourning Scene, Woman In Wilderness On Ivory, Gold Mount 460.00
Pin, Mermaid, Sterling Silver, William Spratling 825.00
Pin, Micromosaic, 14K Yellow Gold, Cherub, Blue Ground, Daisy Border 1775.00
Pin, Moon, Celluloid, Cream, Black Rhinestones, 1/2 x 2 1/2 In. 72.00
Pin, Mosaic, Lily-Of-The-Valley Design, 14K Gold, Oval, Late 19th Century, 2 1/4 In. .. 412.00
Pin, Mushrooms, 18K Yellow Gold & Diamond, Signed Laykin & Co. 3162.00
Pin, Opal, Diamonds, Platinum Frame, Art Deco Period 8000.00
Pin, Open Heart, Ribbon & Flower Design, Sterling Silver, 2 1/8 x 2 1/4 In. 30.00
Pin, Openwork Foliate Design, Sterling Silver, Panis, 2 In. 165.00
Pin, Over The Rainbow, Laminated Plastic, Square, Lea Stein, 1 1/2 In. 95.00
Pin, Parrot, Rose-Cut Diamonds, Rubies, Pearl, Victorian, c.1870 .... 2500.00
Pin, Pearl Swirl Design, 14K Yellow Gold 374.00
Pin, Pegasus, Coro, 1 1/2 x 2 In., Pair 41.00
Pin, Perfume, Carved Bakelite 325.00
Pin, Petal Shape, Cultured Pearls On Stem, Diamonds, Ruby, 14K Gold, 1950s 225.00
Pin, Pink & Purple Stones, Trifari 25.00
Pin, Pique Inlaid, Gold, Silver Starburst Design, 1865 .... 144.00
Pin, Poodle, Red Enamel Eyes & Nose, Blue Enameled Collar 120.00
Pin, Quarter Moon, Scales, Enameled, DeNicola 145.00
Pin, Red, Heart, Bakelite 1550.00
Pin, Revival Style, Egyptian, Blue Stone, Arts & Crafts, 1910 .... 75.00
Pin, Ribbon Form, Seed Pearls, Yellow Gold, c.1900 .... 187.00
Pin, Rooster, Diamonds, Pearl, Synthetic Rubies, 18K White & Yellow Gold, 1900s 2500.00
Pin, Sapphire Wings, Ruby Accents, Freshwater Pearls, 3 Pearl Drops, 18K Gold 747.00
Pin, Sapphire, Oval Cut, 15 Diamonds, 18K Rose Gold, c.1910 .... 950.00
Pin, Scotch Agate, Silver Mount, Curled Ribbon Design, 3 In. 302.00
Pin, Scottie, Plastic, Cream & Pin, Occupied Japan, 2 x 2 In. 55.00
Pin, Screw Post, Sterling & Conch Shell Inlay, Mexico, 3/4 x 1 1/2 In. 30.00
Pin, Scroll Motif Frame, Freshwater Pearls, Art Nouveau, 14K Yellow Gold 460.00
Pin, Seed Pearls, Violet Stones, Coro 50.00
Pin, Serpent, Double, Schrager 85.00
Pin, Snow White, Rhinestone, Wendy Gell 150.00
Pin, Spray Of Leaves, Rhinestone, Adele Simpson, 1950s, 3 In. 360.00
Pin, St. Peter, With Gate Keys, Sterling Silver, Los Castillo, 3 In. 165.00
Pin, Star, Aquamarines & Sapphires, Trifari 45.00
Pin, Sterling Silver & Moonstone, Tulip Design, Kalo 575.00
Pin, Stylized Tulips, Cabochon Blue Stone, Sterling Silver, Beaded Rim, Georg Jensen .. 460.00
Pin, Swallow Form, 18K Yellow Gold, Turquoise & Seed Pearls, Persia, 1880 .... 1800.00
Pin, Sweater, Silver Metal Frame, Rhinestones, Pinback, Oval, 3 1/2 In., Pair 31.00
Pin, Swirls, Sterling Silver, Monet, 3 In. 40.00
Pin, Three Parrots, Green Cabochons, Sterling Silver, 1 3/4 x 2 In. 55.00
Pin, Thumper With One Foot Up, Painted, Bakelite 245.00
Pin, Tree Of Life, Silvertone, 16 Pink Stones, Sarah Coventry 25.00
Pin, Tulip, Sterling Silver, Hobe 345.00
Pin, Turtle, Alice Caviness 30.00
Pin, Twin Dolphin, Blue & Red Enamel, 18K Yellow Gold 85.00
Pin, Victorian Mansion, Platinum, Diamond, Signed, Cartier, c.1930, 1 1/2 In. 6050.00
Pin, Violin, Lucite, 3 In. 65.00
Pin, Wheat Stalk Bundle, 18K Gold, 14 Diamonds, 1930s 750.00
Pin, Winged Dragon, Silver, Taxco 373.00
Pin, Wings, Flight Attendant's, Hawaiian Airlines, 2 1/2 In. 15.00
Pin, Wire Scrolls, Stylized Leaves Surrounding Moonstones, Arts & Crafts, 2 In. 3950.00
Pin, Woman On Horseback In Forest, Sterling Silver, 3 x 2 In. 115.00
Pin, Woman With Basket, Figural, Silver, Frederick Davis, Mexico, 2 In. 460.00
Pin, Wooden Carved Conestoga Wagon, Apple Juice Insert, Bakelite Wheels, 2 1/2 In. 350.00
Pin & Earrings, Abstract Design, Sterling Silver, Screw Back, Miraglia, 2 1/2 In. 165.00
Pin & Earrings, American Beauty Rose, Lucite, Black Ground, Screw Back Earrings ... 85.00

Pin & Earrings, Faceted, Laguna 125.00

Pin & Earrings, Satin Glass Blue Leaves, Schiaparelli 175.00

Pin & Earrings, Sterling Silver, Heart, Georg Jensen, Box 225.00

Pin & Earrings, Turquoise, Sterling Silver, Mary Gage 325.00

Pin-Pendant, Bow Top, Heart Locket, Butterfly, Flower, Enamel, 18K Gold, 3 In. 800.00

Pin-Pendant, Butterfly, Enamel, Diamond, 3.36 Carat, 18K Gold, c.1880 .... 19500.00

Pin-Pendant, Cupids, Enamel, Oriental Pears, Tiffany & Co., 18K Gold, c.1880 ...... 3800.00

Ring, 1 Large & 2 Small Diamonds, Platinum, Filigree Design, Art Deco, 1920s 2500.00

Ring, 1 Large & 6 Small Diamonds, Stair Step Design, 18K White Gold, c.1910 ...... 2500.00

Ring, 12.5 Ct. Emerald, Cushion Cut, 28 Channel-Set Diamonds, 14K Gold, 1960s 9500.00

Ring, 14 Diamonds, 18K White Gold, Swirl Motif, Victorian, 1900s 600.00

Ring, 2 Diamonds, 18K White Gold, Swirl Design, c.1910 .... 450.00

Ring, 2 Diamonds, Synthetic Ruby, 18K Gold, Linear Design, 1940s 450.00

Ring, 2 Pear-Shape Emeralds, Diamonds, Leaf Design, 14K White Gold, 1960s 500.00

Ring, 2 Rubies, 3 Diamonds, Linear Setting, 18K Rose Gold, 1930s 225.00

Ring, 2 Triangular Sapphires, 2 Diamonds, Sunburst Designs, 18K Gold, 1930s 500.00

Ring, 3 Diamonds, Collet Set, 4 Sapphires, 12 Small Diamonds, 18K Gold, c.1910 .... 400.00

Ring, 3 Diamonds, Flush Setting, Linear, 18K Gold, 1940s 625.00

Ring, 3 Flowers, Pearls, 18K White & Yellow Gold, Diamonds, 1940s 225.00

Ring, 3 Freshwater Pearls, Rose-Cut Diamonds, Austria, c.1880 .... 1900.00

Ring, 3 Sapphires, Linear Motif, 14K Gold, Swirl & Circle Designs, 1920s 350.00

Ring, 4 Fish & Seaweed Motif, 18K Gold, Ruby Eyes, Diamonds, 1960s 400.00

Ring, 8 Opals, 10 Diamonds, Floral Design, 18K Gold, 5-Wire Band, 1950s 750.00

Ring, 9 Rubies, Raised Design, 6 Diamonds, Flush Set, 14K Gold, Retro, 1940s 350.00

Ring, Anniversary, 5 Diamonds, 18K White Gold, Line Motif At Each End, 1950s 550.00

Ring, Anniversary, 5 Diamonds, Floral Prong Setting, Linear, 18K White Gold, 1940s ... 800.00

Ring, Anniversary, 5 Diamonds, Raised Prong Setting, Linear, 18K White Gold, 1940s .. 400.00

Ring, Aquamarine & Diamond, Deco, 18K Rose Gold, 1920s, Size 6 1/4 .... 500.00

Ring, Aquamarine, 10 Full-Cut Diamonds, 14K Gold, Openwork, 1950s 1500.00

Ring, Aquamarine, 18K Gold, Bezel Set, Burle Max, 1950s 500.00

Ring, Aquamarine, 3 Diamonds On One Side, One On The Other, 18K Gold, 1940s 525.00

Ring, Aquamarine, 35 Carat, Square Cut, Diamonds, 18K Gold, 1930s 2500.00

Ring, Aquamarine, 4 Rubies At Corners, Diamonds, 18K Rose Gold, Art Deco, 1920s ... 800.00

Ring, Aquamarine, 4 Rubies, 2 Diamonds, 18K Rose Gold, Art Deco, 1920s 550.00

Ring, Aquamarine, Cushion Cut, Diamonds, 18K Rose Gold, Openwork Floral, 1940s ... 750.00

Ring, Black Onyx, Cameo, Soldier & Woman, Intaglio, 18K Gold, Tiffany, 1920s 550.00

Ring, Black Opal, 6 Diamonds In Triangle Motif, 14K White Gold, 1940s 4000.00

Ring, Black Opal, 6 Diamonds, 18K White & Yellow Gold, Leaf & Floral Motif, 1930s .. 625.00

Ring, Black Pearl, 18 Channel-Set Diamonds, 18K Gold, 1930s 800.00

Ring, Black Pearl, Diamonds, Teardrop Design, 18K Gold, 1950s 3500.00

Ring, Blue Enamel, Diamonds, Stylized Floral Design, 14K Gold, c.1910 .... 1500.00

Ring, Buckle, Floral Engraved, 18K Gold, Hallmarked 1898 .... 895.00

Ring, Cameo, Classical Male, 18K Gold Mounting, c.1830 .... 3800.00

Ring, Cartier, Cigar Band, Corona Corona, Red Enamel, 18K Gold, 1920s 1400.00

Ring, Carved To Resemble Floral, Bakelite, Size 6 1/2 .... 85.00

Ring, Center Cluster Of Seed Pearls, 1 Diamond, Mourning, Size 4 3/4 .... 430.00

Ring, Cigar Band, 18K Gold, Corona Corona, Cartier No. 38544, 1920s 1400.00

Ring, Class, Roseville, Mich. High School, 10K Gold, Blue Stone, 1976 .... 23.00

Ring, Cluster Of Seed Pearls, Rose-Cut Diamond, Black, Enamel, Mourning, 4 3/4 In. ... 430.00

Ring, Cluster, Half-Pearls Flanked By Quartz Set, 1840, 14K Yellow Gold 230.00

Ring, Cocktail, Emerald, Yellow Gold, 22 Diamonds ....*Illus* 4400.00

Ring, Cocktail, Sapphire, Oval Cut, 76 Diamonds, Marquis Shape, Platinum, 1960s 6000.00

Ring, Coral Saddle, Coral Center, Signed, Cartier, Paris, 18K Yellow Gold 575.00

Ring, Cross-Over Design, Cabochon Emerald, Diamonds, 18K White Gold, 1940s 2000.00

Ring, Diamond Cluster, 18K Gold, Floral Burst Design, 1890s 650.00

Ring, Diamond, Pearl, Signed, J.E. Caldwell 2875.00

Ring, Diamonds & Sapphires, Platinum, Openwork, Swirl & Leaf Designs, 1890s 1000.00

Ring, Diamonds, 14K White Gold, Swirl & Bloom Design, 1930s 1800.00

Ring, Diamonds, Filigree, 18K White, Yellow Gold, Floral Band, Art Nouveau, 1910 .. 1300.00

Ring, Diamonds, Rubies, Gold, T Design With Crescent Motif, Art Nouveau, 1920s 300.00

Ring, Dragon & Serpent, 5 Diamonds, Ruby Eyes, 14K Gold, c.1880 .... 2900.00

Ring, Emerald, 13 Diamonds, 18K Gold, Leaf & Swirl Designs, Art Deco, 1920s 4000.00

Ring, Emerald, 16 Diamonds, Navette Motif, Teardrop Shanks, 1910 .... 1000.00

Jewelry, Ring,
Cocktail, Emerald,
Yellow Gold,
22 Diamonds

Jewelry, Ring,
Man's, Brilliant
Cut Diamond,
14K Gold,
Size 14

Ring, Emerald, 2 Diamonds, 14K White Gold, 1940s 900.00
Ring, Emerald, 28 Diamonds, Navette Motif, Rose Gold, 1900s 1300.00
Ring, Emerald, 5.4 Ct., Bezel Set, 18K Rose Gold, Polished Band, 1930s 1200.00
Ring, Emerald, Cabochon Cut, 14K Gold, Floral & Swirl Designs, Art Deco, 1920s 1500.00
Ring, Emerald, Cabochon Cut, 28 Diamonds, 18K White Gold, Expandable, 1930s 2500.00
Ring, Emerald, Cabochon Cut, Diamonds, 18K Gold, Leaf & Swirl Pattern, 1930s 1250.00
Ring, Emerald, Cabochon Cut, Diamonds, 18K Gold, Twisted Rope Design, 1930s 1800.00
Ring, Emerald, Pear Shape, 4 Diamonds, Platinum, 1930s 700.00
Ring, Emerald, Rubies, 3 Flowers On Sides, 18K Rose & Green Gold, 1940s 2900.00
Ring, Floral Bloom Pattern, 20 Diamonds, 18K Gold, Twisted Rope Design, 1940s 1300.00
Ring, Flower, 18K Gold, Diamonds On Petal Edges & Pistils, Hinged Petals, 1940s 900.00
Ring, Ford Motor Car Co. Marketing Award, Gold Toned, Logo, Early Auto, With Case .. 50.00
Ring, Garnet, Assay Mark, 1950s 15.00
Ring, Garnet, Otsby & Barton, 10K White Gold, 1920 .... 225.00
Ring, Georgian, Yellow Crown Rose-Cut Diamond, 2.35 Ct., c.1770 .... 10800.00
Ring, Gold, 3 Diamonds, Old Mine Cut, Bowtie Form Setting, France 357.00
Ring, Gold, Diamond, Anchor K Mark, Late Victorian 198.00
Ring, Green Foiled Beryl, Georgian, England, 15K Gold, c.1770 .... 4500.00
Ring, Green Sapphire, Emerald Cut, 2 Diamonds, White & Yellow Gold, 1920s 500.00
Ring, Green Sapphire, Oval Cut, 14K Gold, 5 Raised Crescent Shapes, 1950s 350.00
Ring, Hidden Mistress, Folding Key, 15K Gold, England, c.1830 .... 2500.00
Ring, High School, Mitchell, South Dakota, 1915 .... 50.00
Ring, Man's, 3 Diamonds, Linear Setting, 18K Gold, Swirl & Sunburst Design, 1930s ... 500.00
Ring, Man's, Black Onyx, Rectangular, Rounded, Center Diamond, 18K Gold, 1960s ... 425.00
Ring, Man's, Black Opal, 10 Diamonds, 18K Gold, Engraved Floral Design, 1930s 800.00
Ring, Man's, Black Opal, Oval Cut, 6 Diamonds, 18K Gold, Floral Designs, 1940s 800.00
Ring, Man's, Brilliant Cut Diamond, 14K Gold, Size 14 ....*Illus* 22000.00
Ring, Man's, Buckle Motif, Sapphire, Diamond, 18K White & Yellow Gold, 1930s 800.00
Ring, Man's, Elongated Oval, 19 Diamonds, 18K Gold, Hammered Finish, 1960s 600.00
Ring, Man's, Emerald, Rectangular, 2 Diamonds, 18K Gold, Sunburst Motif, 1940s 2000.00
Ring, Man's, Ruby, Cabochon Cut, 10 Diamonds, 18K White & Yellow Gold, 1930s 800.00
Ring, Man's, Ruby, Cabochon Cut, 4 Diamonds, 18K Gold, Twisted Rope Design, 1910 . 750.00
Ring, Man's, Ruby, Cabochon Cut, 6 Diamonds, 18K White & Yellow Gold, 1930s 700.00
Ring, Man's, Sapphire, 6 Diamonds, 18K White & Yellow Gold, 1930s 900.00
Ring, Man's, Square Top, 16 Diamonds, 18K Gold, Carved Leaf Design, 1940s 600.00
Ring, Marquis Shape, 2 Pearls, 6 Diamonds, 18K Gold, Floral Engraved Band, 1910 .... 250.00
Ring, Marquis Shape, Diamonds, 5 Demantoid Garnets, 14K Gold, 1920s 550.00
Ring, Marquis Shape, Emerald, Marquis Cut, 48 Diamonds, 14K White Gold, 1960s 3500.00
Ring, Memorial, Hair, Glass Center, Oval, Gold, White & Black Enamel, 1830s 550.00
Ring, Natural Blue Zircon, 10K Gold, J.R. Wood & Sons, 1920 .... 155.00
Ring, Portrait, Painting Of Grace Strangeways On Ivory, Diamonds, 1765 .... 4800.00
Ring, Rectangular 20 Ct. Emerald, 27 Diamonds, 18K White Gold, 1940s 8000.00
Ring, Rhinestone Center, Carved Flower Design, Bakelite, 1 1/4 In. 165.00
Ring, Round Carving Of Flower, End Of Day Swirl, Bakelite, 6 1/2 To 7 Size 70.00
Ring, Ruby & Diamond, Cabochon Ruby, 12 Diamonds, Platinum, c.1930 .... 9800.00
Ring, Sapphire, 2 Diamonds, 18K White & Yellow Gold, Vertical Bands, 1930s 800.00
Ring, Sapphire, Bezel-Set Round Diamonds, 18K Yellow Gold, 1950s 150.00
Ring, Sapphire, Cabochon Cut, 14 Diamonds, 18K Gold, Openwork, 1920s 1500.00
Ring, Sapphire, Cabochon Cut, 14K Gold, Embossed Tiger Design, 1930s 400.00
Ring, Sapphire, Cabochon Cut, 15 Diamonds, 18K White & Yellow Gold, 1870s 900.00
Ring, Sapphire, Cabochon Cut, 16 Diamonds, 18K Rose Gold, Floral Band, 1940s 900.00
Ring, Sapphire, Oval Cut, 9 Diamonds, 18K Gold, Fleur-De-Lis Band, Victorian, 1890s .. 1800.00
Ring, Sapphire, Oval, 24 Prong-Set Diamonds, 18K White Gold, 1950s 1800.00

Ring, Sapphire, Oval, Engraved Platinum & Diamond Mounting, c.1910 .... 6800.00
Ring, Scarab, Red Glass, Gold Swivel Type Mount, 14K Yellow Gold 175.00
Ring, Seal, Compartment For Wax, England, 18th Century 795.00
Ring, Snake, With Diamond & Sapphire, 9K Rose Gold, Hallmarked 1902 .... 1250.00
Ring, Topaz, 45 Carat, Emerald Cut, 18K Gold, Geometric Circular Design, 1945 ...... 425.00
Ring, Twist, Mixed-Cut Diamonds, Platinum & 18K Gold, c.1900 .... 3500.00
Ring, Victorian, 22 Carat Emerald, Cabochon Cut, 22 Diamonds, 18K Gold, 1900s 9500.00
Ring, Wreath & Fan Design, Pearls, Diamonds, 18K White & Yellow Gold, 1940s 300.00
Ring, Yellow Sapphire, Rose-Cut Diamonds, Platinum & Gold, c.1905 .... 4200.00
Ring & Earrings, Flower Motif, Diamonds, 18K Gold, 1890s 4500.00
Rosary, 18K Gold, Mother-Of Pearl Beads, Gold Openwork Design, Cross, 30 In. 500.00
Rosary, Black Onyx Beads, 14K Gold, Crucifix, Disc With Mary & Child, 1940s, 22 In. . . 250.00
Rosary, Coral Beads, Silver Floral, Silver Filigree Beads, Crucifix, 1915, 44 In. 350.00
Service Pin, Douglas Aircraft, 20 Years, 4 Diamonds 110.00
Shoe Buckle, Pewter & Steel, Punch-Decorated Design, 18th Century, 2 In., Pair 150.00
Slide Chain, 14K Yellow Gold, Victorian, 40 In. 920.00
Stickpin, 1 Oval Baroque Cultured Pearl, 18K White Gold 67.00
Stickpin, Black Opal, 14K Gold, Art Nouveau, c.1915, 2 3/4 In. 500.00
Stickpin, Black Opal, 18K Gold Mount, Marcus & Co. 2645.00
Stickpin, Cameo, Woman's Head, 10K Gold 82.00
Stickpin, Corkscrew Design, 7 Diamonds, Pearl, Emerald, 18K Rose Gold, 1900s 300.00
Stickpin, Crescent Moon, 7 Diamonds, 14K Gold, 1900s 250.00
Stickpin, Fountainhead Design, Diamonds, 3 Seed Pearls, 18K Gold, 1920s 300.00
Stickpin, Gold, Diamond, Pearl 71.00
Stickpin, Head Of Viking, Polychrome Enamel Winged Helmet, 14K Yellow Gold 805.00
Stickpin, Horseshoe Set With Mine-Cut Diamonds, Center Row Of Rubies, 18K Gold .. 345.00
Stickpin, Lava Cameo, 14K Gold 150.00
Stickpin, Malachite Cabochon, Carved As Scarab, Kalo 247.00
Stickpin, Pear-Shaped Sapphire In Diamond-Set Keyhole, Platinum Frame 402.00
Stickpin, Platinum, Diamond & Multicolored Enamel, 18K Yellow Gold 690.00
Stickpin, Profile Of Female, Diamond, Seed-Pearl Set Headdress, 14K Yellow Gold 632.00
Stickpin, Question Mark Shape, 12 Diamonds, 18K Rose Gold, 1920s, 2 In. 250.00
Stickpin, Woman's, 21 Single Cut Diamonds, 14K Yellow Gold 503.00
Stickpin, Woman's, Horseshoe, 14K Yellow Gold, 21 Diamonds 500.00
Stud Set, Double-Sided Onyx Cuff Links, 3 Studs, Platinum Frames, Larter & Sons 201.00
Tie Bar, Cowboy Boot Form, Sterling Silver & 10K Gold 25.00
Tie Bar, Cowboy Boot, Inset Turquoise Stone, Sterling Silver 18.00
Tie Bar, Pacific Electric Safety Award, 10K Gold, With Diamond 395.00
Tie Bar, Snap-On Tools, Ratchet, Socket Design, c.1950 .... 10.00
Tie Bar, Teardrop Shape, Sapphire & Mine-Cut Diamond, 18K Gold, 1930s 200.00
Tie Bar, TWA, Transcontinental, Sterling Silver, Dangle Chain Logo 150.00
Tie Set, Cuff Links, Tie Bar, Tie Tac, Sunbeam Bread, Logo, Enameled, c.1950 .... 80.00
Tsuba, Copper, Storm Over Mountains Scene, Fish Roe Ground, Oval, 3 In. 475.00
Tsuba, Iron, 2 Riobitsu, Bridge, With Rocks, Silver Trim, Oval, 2 3/4 In. 275.00
Tsuba, Iron, Celestial Design, Fish Roe Ground, Gold Lines, Aoi Shape, 3 3/4 In. 450.00
Tsuba, Iron, Riobitsu Shaping To Jar, 2 7/8 In. 325.00
Tsuba, Iron, Riobitsu, Large Flowers, Oval, 2 3/4 In. 250.00
Tsuba, Iron, Riobitsu, Large Foliage, Birds In Flight, Round, 2 7/8 In. 145.00
Watches are listed in their own category.
Watch, Chain, Floral Design Links, Swivel Hook & T-Bar, Shakudo, 15 1/2 In. 747.00
Watch, Chain, Gold Nugget, Diamond, 1880s 2500.00
Watch Chain, Blacksmith's Anvil & Hammer Fob, Gold Filled 195.00
Watch Chain, Braided Mesh, 14K Gold, 19 1/2 In. 125.00
Watch Chain, Hair 70.00
Wristwatches are listed in their own category.

JOHN ROGERS statues were made from 1859 to 1892. The originals
were bronze, but the thousands of copies made by the Rogers factory
were of painted plaster. Eighty different figures were created. Similar
painted plaster figures were produced by some other factories. Rights
to the figures were sold in 1893 and they were manufactured for several more years by the Rogers Statuette Co. Never repaint a Rogers figure because this lowers the value to collectors.

Group, Coming To The Parson 1000.00

Josef Originals,
Figurine, Girl, With
Kitten, Pottery, 5 In.

**August is the peak month
for residential burglaries.
April has the fewest home
break-ins. Most home
burglaries occur in the
daytime. The average
break-in lasts 17 minutes.**

Group, Politics	....	1100.00
Group, Private Theatricals	....	650.00
Group, Uncle Ned's School	....	800.00
Group, Village Schoolmaster	....	950.00

JOSEF ORIGINALS ceramics were designed by Muriel Joseph George. The first pieces were made in California from 1945 to 1962. They were then manufactured in Japan. The company was sold to George Good in 1982 and he continued to make Josef Originals until 1985. The company was then sold to Southland Corporation. The name is now owned by Applause.

Cookie Jar, Birthday Girl	....	25.00
Figurine, Angel, 16 Years	....	25.00
Figurine, Angel, 9 Years	....	25.00
Figurine, August Girl, Peridot	....	20.00
Figurine, Elephant Family, 3 Piece	....	95.00
Figurine, Fuzzy Rabbit	....	20.00
Figurine, Girl, With Kitten, Pottery, 5 In.	.......Illus	22.00
Figurine, Girl, With Poodle	....	25.00
Figurine, Kangaroo, 6 In.	....	55.00
Figurine, Mouse	....	8.00
Figurine, Wu Chu, Oriental, Large	....	75.00

JUDAICA is any memorabilia that refers to the Jews or the Jewish religion. Interests range from newspaper clippings that mention eighteenth- and nineteenth-century Jewish Americans to religious objects, such as menorahs or spice boxes. Age, condition, and the intrinsic value of the material, as well as the historic and artistic importance, determine the value.

Beaker, Kiddish, Hebrew Dedication Inscription, German Silver, 1766, 4 1/8 In.	....	6900.00
Beaker, Wine, Chased Overall, Hebrew Dedicatory Inscription, Polish Silver, 3 1/4 In.	..	2070.00
Binder, Torah, Hebrew Inscriptions, Birds, Painted Linen, 112 In.	....	750.00
Box, Charity, Engraved Silver Panels, German & Hebrew, Handle, 6 1/8 In.	....	8050.00
Box, Charity, Synagogue Form, Hinged Top, Hebrew Inscription, Silver Lock, 11 In.	..	6900.00
Box, Charity, Synagogue Form, Hinged Door, Coin Slot In Roof, 1868, 5 5/8 In.	..	3310.00
Candlestick, Foliate & Griffin's Heads, Paw Feet, German Silver Plate, 14 In., Pair	....	345.00
Candlestick, Foliate Skirt, Rose Design On Square Base, Polish Silver, 9 3/8 In., Pair	...	2070.00
Candlestick, Overall Floral & Foliate, Floral Form, German Silver, 1880s, 13 In., Pair	.	1360.00
Candlestick, Sabbath, Brass, Warzawa, Plewkiewicz, 10 3/4 In., Pair	....	50.00
Candlestick, Traveling, Bright Cut Design, Hebrew Text, Sterling Silver, 4 1/2 In., Pair	.	1092.00
Circumcision Set, Hebrew Letters, Child, Silver & Amethyst, German, c.1900	....	6900.00
Container, Etrog, Embossed & Chased Rose Clusters, Hinged Lid, Marked, 4 1/2 In.	...	630.00
Container, Spice, Rooster Finials, Dolphin Form Legs, English Silver, 1808, 4 1/4 In.	....	747.00
Cookbook, How To Cook In Palestine, Dr. Erna Meyer, c.1925	....	143.00
Crown, Torah, 6 Rows Of Flowers, Pendant Bells, Polish Silver, 1880s, 13 1/2 In.	....	1035.00
Crown, Torah, Bells, Bird Finial, Fitted Interior, Russian Silver, 1882, 16 In.	....	2990.00
Cup, Marriage, Grapevines, Coats Of Arms On Base, Gilt Interior, Silver, 5 1/8 In., Pair	.	920.00

Cup, Passover, Scene Of Seder, Temple In Jerusalem, German Silver, 2 3/4 In. 575.00
Curtain, Ark, Gold Threads On Velvet, Calcutta, India, 1918, 89 x 55 1/2 In. 670.00
Finials, Torah, Filigree, 2 Rows Of Bells, Egyptian Silver, 19th Century, 14 7/8 In. 4025.00
Goblet, Wine, Ceremonial, Silver, Flared, Star Of David, Hebrew Lettering, 5 In. 101.00
Goblet, Wine, Remember The Sabbath, Floral Band, German Silver, c.1900, 4 7/8 In. 745.00
Haggadah, Memory Of Holocaust, 12 Prints, 31 Illuminated Pages, 20 x 15 In. 2415.00
Kiddish Cup, Foliate Designs, Hebrew Text, German Silver, 20th Century, 5 1/2 In. 9200.00
Kiddish Cup, Inscribed Blessing, Sterling Silver, 6 In. 272.00
Kiddish Cup, Sterling Silver, 5 1/2 In. 195.00
Knife, Circumcision, Inlaid Handle, Horn Handle, Mother-Of-Pearl Inlay, 7 1/8 In. 975.00
Manuscript, Pentateuch, 160 Leaves, Italian Cursive Hebrew, Italy, 16th Century 1360.00
Map, Copperplate, Palestine, 12 Tribes, Moses Receiving Law, 19 1/2 x 22 1/2 In., Pr. 1150.00
Menorah, 7 Candlesticks, Brass, 16 1/2 In. 55.00
Menorah, Hanukkah, Arched Backplate, Row Of 8 Oil Fonts, Italian, Bronze, 5 In. 1725.00
Menorah, Hanukkah, Bird Finial, Grasses & Fruits, Servant Light, German Silver, 10 In. 2825.00
Menorah, Hanukkah, Hebrew Ten Commandments, Oil Pitcher, German Silver, 12 In. .. 1380.00
Menorah, Hanukkah, Lion & Crowns Stamped Backplate, 8 Holders, Brass, 9 In. 1265.00
Menorah, Hanukkah, Silver, Crowned Lions, Star Of David, Horowitz, Germany, 7 In. ... 2200.00
Menorah, Moses, Candlestick & Stag, Silver Plate, 19th Century, 11 3/4 In. 1380.00
Mezuzah, Hand & Scroll Case Set With Gemstones, Ottoman Silver & Stone 4.00
Mezuzah, Painted Star, Gilt Metal Mounts, Limoges, 20th Century, 5 3/4 In. 805.00
Plaque, Copper, Rabbi Medal Medallion, Stand, Hebrew Signed, 14 In. 125.00
Plate, Central Floral, Hebrew On Rim, Pewter, 18th Century, 8 1/2 In. 85.00
Plate, Seder, Man Carrying Kid, Symbols Painted In Hebrew, Ceramic, 1880s 460.00
Pointer, Torah, Open Filigree Design, Bands Of Flowers, Russian Silver, 1885, 10 In. 1035.00
Pointer, Torah, Openwork & Etched Design, Austro-Hungarian Silver, 12 In. 745.00
Scroll, Esther, Crown Finial, North African Silver & Copper, 15 1/4 In. 860.00
Scroll, Esther, Parchment, Silhouettes Of Men, Silver Filigree Case, 42 In. 2300.00
Shield, Crown Over Griffins, Lions & Tablets, Chain, Hungarian Silver, 1880s, 14 In. ... 747.00
Snuffbox, Painted Biblical Scenes, French Silver, 19th Century, 2 1/4 In. 2185.00
Snuffbox, Painted Biblical Scenes, German Silver, Enamel, 18th Century, 3 In. 1380.00
Spice Tower, Chased Flowers & C Scrolls, Spire & Pennant, German Silver, 8 1/4 In. 1090.00
Spice Tower, Filigree Spice Section, 5 Eagles With Bells, Russian Silver, 1889, 12 In. 1380.00
Spice Tower, Filigree, Pennant With Hebrew Word Zion, Jerusalem Silver, 7 In. 2165.00
Spice Tower, Pierced & Fitted Hinged Door, 4 Paw Supports, Spanish, 8 7/8 In. 1035.00
Spice Tower, Silver & Vermeil, 10 1/2 In. 605.00
Spice Tower, Spire With Pendant Over Compartment, Floral Panels, 1890s, 7 1/4 In. 632.00
Tray, Challah, Chased Braided Bread, Hebrew Verses, Austro-Hungarian Silver, c.1900 .. 6840.00
Yarmulke, Black Velvet, Silver Threading, 1890s 125.00

JUGTOWN Pottery refers to pottery made in North Carolina as far back
as the 1750s. In 1915, Juliana and Jacques Busbee set up a training and
sales organization for what they named *Jugtown Pottery*. In 1921, they
built a shop at Jugtown, North Carolina, and hired Ben Owen as a potter in 1923. The Busbees moved the village store where the pottery
was sold to New York City. Juliana Busbee sold the New York store in
1926 and moved into a log cabin near the Jugtown Pottery. The pottery
closed in 1959. It reopened in 1960 and is still working near Seagrove,
North Carolina.

Bean Pot, Orange 20.00
Bowl, Angular, Frogskin Black Variation, Interior Yellow, Green Exterior, 3 x 7 In. 192.50
Bowl, Chinese Blue Glaze, Oxblood, Blue, 1940s, 3 1/8 x 9 In. 1265.00
Bowl, Chinese Blue Glaze, Signed, 4 1/4 In., Pair 467.00
Bowl, Chinese Blue Glaze, Yellow, Cream Crystalline Interior, Flared, Angular, 9 In. 550.00
Bowl, Oriental Shape, Chinese Blue Glaze, 1 7/8 In. 247.00
Bowl, Rice, Overall Crimson Red, Turquoise Glaze, Signed, 1940s, 1 7/8 x 4 3/4 In. 132.00
Candlestick, Brown, Marked, 12 In. 55.00
Candlestick, Gray Speckled Glaze, 11 1/2 x 4 3/4 In., Pair 825.00
Doorstop, Figural, Chicken, Incised Neck, Wings, Tail, Orange Peel Glaze, 7 In. 305.00
Inkwell, Chinese Blue Glaze, Albany Slip Glaze, Chocolate Interior, 1940s, 3 In. 412.50
Jar, Chinese Blue Glaze, Albany Slip Glaze, Chocolate Interior, Crimson, 7 In. 1375.00
Pitcher, Cobalt Blue Floral Blossoms, 3 Lines On Shoulder, 1930-1940, 3 1/4 In. 110.00
Urn, Olive-Green Luster, Ocher Glaze, Brown Clay Body, 2 Handles, 9 x 7 In. 880.00

Vase, Chinese Blue Flambe Glaze, Signed, 3 3/4 x 2 1/2 In. 357.00
Vase, Chinese Blue Glaze, Angular Shape, Overall Red, Aqua, Busbee, 1940, 3 x 6 In. 495.00
Vase, Chinese Blue Glaze, Applied Dogwood Blossoms, White, 1940s, 7 5/8 In. 1045.00
Vase, Chinese Blue Glaze, Dark Brown Body, 5 1/4 x 5 1/2 In. 935.00
Vase, Chinese Blue Glaze, Egg Shape, Crimson, Turquoise Highlights, 1940s, 4 In. 220.00
Vase, Chinese Blue Glaze, Flared, 6 1/2 x 7 In. 2200.00
Vase, Chinese Blue Glaze, Multi-Tone Red, Speckled Blue, 4 In. 319.00
Vase, Chinese Blue Glaze, Ovoid, Signed, 7 1/2 x 4 1/2 In. 935.00
Vase, Chinese Blue Glaze, Pastel, Crimson Highlights, Incised Lines On Top, 8 In. 990.00
Vase, Chinese Blue Glaze, Pear Shape, Turquoise, 5 3/4 x 4 1/2 In. ....275.00 to 385.00
Vase, Chinese Blue Glaze, Red, Turquoise, 5 1/2 x 4 1/2 In. 660.00
Vase, Chinese Blue Glaze, Speckled Red, 5 In. 1045.00
Vase, Chinese Blue Glaze, Turquoise Matte Glaze, 7 1/2 x 6 In. 1045.00
Vase, Chinese Blue Glaze, Turquoise, Red, 5 1/2 x 6 1/2 In. 935.00
Vase, Chinese Blue Glaze, Turquoise, Red, Purple, Squat, 5 1/4 x 6 1/4 In. 825.00
Vase, Chinese Red Glaze, Speckled Blue, Turquoise, 6 In. 1045.00
Vase, Chinese Red Glaze, Turquoise, Impressed Mark, 7 1/2 In. 1100.00
Vase, Green, Brown Glaze, 4 Handles, Impressed Mark, 8 1/2 In. 275.00
Vase, Matte Mustard Glaze At Top, Clear Coating Bottom, Handles, 8 3/4 In. 935.00
Vase, Salt Glaze Celadon Blue, Red Glaze Low, 1930s, 3 1/4 x 4 3/8 In. 385.00
Vase, White, Marked, 7 1/2 In. 220.00

JUKEBOXES play records. The first coin-operated phonograph was demonstrated in 1889. In 1906 the *Automatic Entertainer* appeared, the first coin-operated phonograph to offer several different selections of music. The first electrically powered jukebox was introduced in 1927. Collectors search for jukeboxes of all ages, especially those with flashing lights and unusual design and graphics.

Electra, Holcomb & Hoke 2500.00
Mills, Throne Of Music 1250.00
Rock-Ola, Model 1426F, 3 Coin Boxes, 1 Wall Speaker, 1947 .... 7200.00
Rock-Ola, Model 1504, Wall Box 400.00
Seeburg, Model DS 160, 1961 .... 3000.00
Seeburg, Model J 4800.00
Seeburg, Vogue 950.00
Wurlitzer, Chrome Metal Housing, Curved Glass Window, Wall Box, 1958 .... 250.00
Wurlitzer, Hi-Fidelity, 48 Songs, 55 x 32 x 28 In. 1870.00
Wurlitzer, Model 61, Table Model, 22 x 24 x 21 In. 2875.00
Wurlitzer, Model 165, c.1953 .... 3250.00
Wurlitzer, Model 500, Coin Operated, 36 x 61 In. 6612.50
Wurlitzer, Model 750, 24 Selection, Bubble Tubes, Walnut Veneered Case, 55 3/4 In. 5175.00
Wurlitzer, Model 1015, 24 Song Selection, Walnut Veneered Case, 59 1/2 In. 6900.00
Wurlitzer, Model 1050, Plays 45 RPM Records, 1974 .... 5500.00
Wurlitzer, Model 1250, Plays 78 RPM Records, Restored, 1952 .... 47500.00
Wurlitzer, Model 2510 .... 1500.00
Wurlitzer, Victory, 16 Selections 6500.00

KATE GREENAWAY, who was a famous illustrator of children's books, drew pictures of children in high-waisted Empire dresses. She lived from 1846 to 1901. Her designs appear on china, glass, and other pieces. Figural napkin rings depicting the Greenaway children may also be found in the Napkin Ring category under Figural.

Book, Little Ann-A Book 225.00
Bookends, Children, Bronzart 85.00
Bowl, Boy & Girl With Flowers On Bowl, Applied Handle, Orange, 6 x 8 In. 195.00
Doll, Big Sister 40.00
Doll, Small Sister 40.00

KAY FINCH Ceramics were made in Corona Del Mar, California, from 1935 to 1963. The hand-decorated pieces often depicted whimsical animals and people. Pastel colors were used.

Kay Finch
CALIFORNIA

Ashtray, Leaf 100.00
Bank, Pig, Smiley, With Strawberries, No. 164, 6 3/4 x 8 In. 140.00

To find a small crack in porcelain or glass, try this: Put the piece on a table. Tap it with your fingernail. A cracked piece gives off a dull thud, a perfect piece will "ring." Learn to recognize the sound by practicing on some pieces you know are broken.

Kay Finch, Figurine, Penguin, Pete, No. 466, 7 1/2 In.

Cookie Jar, Yorky Pup, No. 4615	275.00
Creamer, Cow	45.00
Figurine, Angel, No. 114A, 4 1/4 In.	95.00
Figurine, Caress, 11 In.	450.00
Figurine, Cat With Cradle	125.00
Figurine, Cat, Ambrosia, No. 155, 10 3/4 In.	600.00
Figurine, Cat, Jezebel & Mehitabel, No. 179 & No. 181, Pair	675.00
Figurine, Cat, Jezebel, Pink, Green & Teal, No. 179, 6 x 9 In.	275.00 to 425.00
Figurine, Cat, Mehitable, No. 181, 8 In.	375.00
Figurine, Choir Boy, Standing, Blonde, No. 210, 7 1/2 In.	128.00
Figurine, Court Prince, Mandarin, No. 451, 11 In.	225.00
Figurine, Dog, Cocker Spaniel, Vicki, No. 455, 11 In.	975.00
Figurine, Dog, Poodle, Sitting, Pearl White, Gold Bow, Incised Mark, No. 5262, 8 In.	195.00
Figurine, Dog, Yorky Pup, No.171, 5 1/2 In.	295.00 to 375.00
Figurine, Dog, Yorky, Reclining, No. 831, Rare	495.00
Figurine, Duck, Jeep & Peep, No. 178B & No. 178A, 4 In., Pair	115.00
Figurine, Godey Man & Lady, No. 122, 1 1/2 In., Pair	275.00
Figurine, Godey Man & Lady, No. 160, 7 1/2 In., Pair	160.00 to 185.00
Figurine, Godey Man, Pink Jacket, Hat, No. 122, 9 1/2 In.	75.00 to 85.00
Figurine, Kitten, Muff, Sleeping, No. 182, 3 1/4 In.	75.00
Figurine, Kitten, Puff, Playful, No. 183, 3 1/4 In.	85.00
Figurine, Lamb, Prancing, No. 168, 10 1/2 In.	550.00
Figurine, Mr. Dickey Bird, No. 4905A, 4 In.	65.00
Figurine, Oriental Sage & Maiden, On Base, No. 4854 & No. 4855, 5 In., Pair	275.00
Figurine, Oriental Woman, Brown Glaze, Gold Trim, 10 In.	150.00
Figurine, Owl, Toot, No. 188, 5 3/4 In.	45.00 to 75.00
Figurine, Owl, Tootsie, No. 189, 3 3/4 In.	155.00
Figurine, Peasant Boy & Girl, No. 117 & No. 113, 6 3/4 In., Pair	125.00
Figurine, Peasant Boy, Blue & White, No. 113, 6 3/4 In.	85.00
Figurine, Peasant Boy, Lavender Vest, No. 117, 8 1/2 In.	85.00
Figurine, Peasant Girl, No. 11, 6 3/4 In.	90.00
Figurine, Penguin, Pete, No. 466, 7 1/2 In. ....*Illus*	300.00
Figurine, Pig, Grumpy, No. 165, 6 x 7 1/2 In.	250.00
Figurine, Pig, Sassy, No. 166, 3 1/2 x 4 1/2 In.	30.00 to 135.00
Figurine, Pig, Smiley, Pink & Floral, 8 x 6 3/4 In.	350.00
Figurine, Pig, Smiley, With Strawberries, No. 164, 6 3/4 x 8 In.	475.00
Figurine, Rooster, Chanticleer, No. 129, 11 In.	650.00 to 750.00
Figurine, Scandie Boy, No. 127, 5 1/4 In.	45.00
Figurine, Scandie Girl, No. 126, 5 1/4 In.	85.00 to 125.00
Mug, Kitten, Blue, No. B5415, 3 1/2 In.	165.00
Mug, Missouri Mule	200.00
Planter, Baby's First Teddy Bear	95.00
Planter, Lamb On Block, No. 5118, 4 In.	85.00
Sugar & Creamer, Briar Rose	95.00
Tray, 2-Tone, 13 1/2 x 10 1/2 In.	35.00
Tureen, Soup, Turkey, Ladle	495.00
Wall Planter, Ancestor Man, Turquoise, No. 5775, 26 In.	275.00

KAYSERZINN, see Pewter category.

KELVA glassware was made by the C. F. Monroe Company of Meriden, Connecticut, about 1904. It is a pale, pastel-painted glass decorated with flowers, designs, or scenes. Kelva resembles Nakara and Wave Crest, two other glasswares made by the same company.

KELVA

Box, Bishop's Hat, Pink Flowers, Green Ground, Square, 4 In.	425.00
Box, Bright Blue, Pink Daisies, Round, 6 In.	815.00
Box, Hinged, White Lily Design, Pink Ground, 4 x 6 In.	450.00
Box, Hinged, White Lily Design, Red Ground, 3 x 4 In.	500.00
Box, Mottled Enamel Flowers On Cover, Signed, 3 x 4 In.	630.00
Tray, Violets, Mottled Orange Ground, Gold Finish Metal Trim, 5 x 6 In.	287.00
Vase, Pink Blossoms, Gold Scrolls, Baluster, C.F. Monroe, 8 1/2 In.	489.00
Vase, Pink Roses, Batis Ground, Green, C.F. Monroe, 1904, 11 In.	1650.00

KENTON HILLS Pottery in Erlanger, Kentucky, made art wares, including vases and figurines that resembled Rookwood, probably because so many of the original artists and workmen had worked at the Rookwood plant. Kenton Hills opened in 1939 and closed during World War II.

Vessel, Coupe Shape, Blue-Green Aventurine Glaze, 5 3/4 x 5 In.	360.00

KEW BLAS is the name used by the Union Glass Company of Somerville, Massachusetts. The name refers to an iridescent golden glass made from the 1890s to 1924. The iridescent glass was reminiscent of the Tiffany glass of the period.

Vase, Gold Iridescent Feathers, Iridized Rim, 7 In.	978.00
Vase, Green Hook & Pull Feathers, Oyster Ground, Gold Iridescent Trim, 6 1/2 In.	1450.00
Vase, Symmetrically Looped Design, Signed, 8 In.	488.00
Vase, Trumpet, Amber Ribs, Pulled Emerald Green Design, 4 1/4 x 5 1/4 In.	805.00
Vase, Vertical Stripes, Gold & Green, Tapered Cylinder, 9 1/2 In.	460.00

KEWPIES, designed by Rose O'Neill, were first pictured in the *Ladies' Home Journal*. The figures, which are similar to pixies, were a success, and Kewpie dolls started appearing in 1911. Kewpie pictures and other items soon followed. Collectors search for all items that picture the little winged people.

Arms Folded On Chest, Rose O'Neill, 2 In.	190.00
Bell, Brass	65.00
Bisque, Arms Raised, Black Helmet With Gold Spike, Eagle, Germany, c.1910, 2 In.	625.00
Bisque, Baby, Red Heart	18.00
Bisque, Blunderboo, Lying On Back, Arms Out, Leg Kicking, Germany, 1912, 3 In.	900.00
Bisque, Doodle Dog, Pink Nose, Head To Side, Germany, 1912, 1 In.	1200.00
Bisque, Doodle Dog, Rose O'Neill, 1910s	1750.00
Bisque, Farmer, Rake, Hat, 2 Labels, O'Neill, Germany, Original Box, c.1910, 5 In.	1550.00
Bisque, Farmer, Sun Hat, Wooden Rake, O'Neill, Germany, c.1912, 4 In.	700.00
Bisque, Holding Bouquet Of Flowers, 2 1/2 In.	195.00
Bisque, Hottentot, Thin Smile, Jointed Arms, O'Neill, Germany, c.1910, 5 In.	1000.00
Bisque, Huggers, Glancing To Side, Germany, 1912, 3 In.	340.00
Bisque, Huggers, Reading Books, Germany, 1912, 3 In.	800.00
Bisque, Jointed Arms, Edwardian Human Hair Wig, O'Neill, c.1912, 5 In.	425.00
Bisque, Jointed Arms, O'Neill, 5 In.	110.00
Bisque, Jointed Hips, Shoulders, 5 In.	350.00
Bisque, Jointed Shoulders, Arms Loose, 7 1/2 In.	250.00
Bisque, Jointed, Label, Germany, c.1915, 5 In.	725.00
Bisque, Kewpie & Doodledog On Log, Holding Mandolin, c.1912, 3 In.	3100.00
Bisque, Muslin Body, Starfish Hands, 9268 Mark, Germany, c.1915, 5 In.	1200.00
Bisque, Painted Shoes With Bows & Garters, Rose O'Neill	495.00
Bisque, Playing Mandolin, 2 1/2 In.	195.00
Bisque, Reclining, Head Tilted, O'Neill 1861 B Mark, Paper Label, c.1912, 4 In.	850.00
Bisque, Scootles, Head Tucked In, Jointed Arms, Rose O'Neill, Germany, 1912, 5 In.	1650.00
Bisque, Seated In Yellow Chair, Arms Folded, Label, Germany, c.1912, 2 In.	425.00
Bisque, Seated, Arm Outstretched, Plush Bumblebee, Germany, c.1912, 4 In.	2800.00
Bisque, Seated, Bent Knees, Cloverleaf, Paper Label, Germany, c.1912, 1 1/2 In.	400.00

Bisque, Seated, Head Tilted, Fly On Foot, Side-Glancing Eyes, Germany, c.1912, 3 In. .. 900.00
Bisque, Seated, Holding Pen, Stamped Mark, Germany, 1912, 2 In. 700.00
Bisque, Seated, Holding Pencil, Signed, Germany, c.1912, 2 In. 700.00
Bisque, Seated, Holding Rose, Tulips In Pot, Signed, Germany, c.1912, 1 1/2 In. 500.00
Bisque, Seated, Knees Drawn Up, Bunny In Basket, c.1912, 1 1/2 In. 600.00
Bisque, Seated, Reading Book, Arm Outstretched, Germany, 1912, 3 In. 650.00
Bisque, Seated, With Book, Blue Vase, Paper Label, Germany, 1912, 1 1/2 In. 600.00
Bisque, Seated, With Book, Side-Glancing Eyes, Germany, c.1912, 1 3/4 In. 400.00
Bisque, Seated, With Mandolin, Side-Glancing Eyes, Germany, c.1912, 1 3/4 In. 300.00
Bisque, Seated, With Turkey, Arms Outstretched, c.1912, 1 1/2 In. 450.00
Bisque, Seated, With Yellow Chick, Germany, 1912, 1 1/2 In. 600.00
Bisque, Side-Glancing Googly Eyes, Starfish Hands, O'Neill, c.1910, 10 In. .. 1250.00
Bisque, Socket Head, Glass Eyes, Lace Costume, Signed, Kestner, c.1910, 12 In. 6200.00
Bisque, Standing, Arms Over Head, 2 1/2 In. 195.00
Bisque, Standing, Jointed Arms, 2 Paper Labels, O'Neill, Germany, 1912, 8 In. 575.00
Bisque, Standing, Jointed Arms, Side-Glancing Eyes, O'Neill, Germany, c.1912, 10 In. .. 700.00
Bisque, Standing, Jointed Arms, Side-Glancing Eyes, O'Neill, Germany, c.1912, 8 In. ... 450.00
Bisque, Thinker, 4 In. 300.00
Bisque, Thinker, Eyes Glancing Right, O'Neill, Germany, 1910, 5 In. 550.00
Bisque, Thinker, Googly Eyes Glancing Left, Label, O'Neill, Germany, c.1910, 6 In. ... 800.00
Bisque, Thinker, Rose O'Neill Sticker, Signed, 4 In. 325.00
Bisque, Traveler, Umbrella, Valise, Germany, c.1915, 3 In. 450.00
Bisque, Traveler, Umbrella, Valise, Side-Glancing Eyes, Germany, c.1912, 3 In. 425.00
Bisque, Traveler, Umbrella, Valise, Side-Glancing Eyes, Germany, c.1912, 4 1/2 In. 900.00
Bisque Head, Kestner, 221, Googly-Eye, Boy, Wood, Jointed, c.1912, 13 In. 6800.00
Bisque Shoulder Head, No Body, 9208, Germany, c.1915, 2 In. 425.00
Candy Container, By Barrel 133.00
Candy Container, On Radio 787.00
Celluloid, Bride & Groom, Celluloid, With Ice Cream 10-In. Book, O'Neill, 5 In. 50.00
Celluloid, Bride, Groom & Priest, Paper Clothes, 3 Piece 100.00
Celluloid, Movable Arms, Knit Outfit, Pointed Cloth Cap, 1920s, 3 In. 20.00
Composition, Blue Wings, Jointed, 11 In. 275.00
Creamer, Signed 155.00
Frame, Marked, 1923 .... 95.00
Glass, Painted Features, 4 In. 195.00
Inkwell, Seated, Holding Pen, Germany, 1912, 4 In. 850.00
Lithograph, Kewpie Easter, Painting Egg, O'Neill, Parker-Brawner, 30 x 20 In. 1800.00
Lithograph, On Your Way—Take Some Home, Chocolate Sundae, Signed, No. 683 .... 600.00
Mold, Chocolate, 12 x 6 1/2 In. 485.00
Napkin Ring, Kewpie Standing In Front Of Ring, Silver Plate 115.00
Paper Doll, Folder, 1963 .... 90.00
Paper Doll, Kewpiekin, 1962 .... 90.00
Pin Box, Blue Wicker Basket Shape, 2 1/2 In. 600.00
Plate, Part Of Child's Set, Blue Sky Ground, 4 In. 135.00
Plate, Signed Rose O'Neill, 8 In. 45.00
Postcard, Kewpie Writing Christmas Letter, Gibson Art Co. 30.00
Powder Box, Heart Shaped, Kewpie On Lid, c.1912, 4 In. 1900.00
Rattle, Celluloid 48.00
Salt & Pepper, Ceramic, Japan 98.00
Scootles, Composition, Original Shoes & Socks, Rose O'Neill, 13 In. 600.00
Scootles, Green Sleep Eyes, 22 In. 1995.00
Sticker, 2 Sheets 5.00
Stickpin Holder, With Umbrella 125.00
Sugar, Cover, Bavaria 125.00
Tea Set, White Ground, Rose O'Neill, Wilson, Germany, c.1915, 4 In., 15 Piece 1100.00
Tea Set, White Porcelain, Rose Shading, Rose O'Neill, Wilson, 1912, 6 In., 17 Piece ... 2300.00
Toy, Ostrich, Carved Body & Tail Feathers, Jointed Legs, Schoenhut, c.1910, 10 In. 350.00
Tray, DeCoursey's Ice Cream, Kansas City, Standing Kewpie Eating Ice Cream 950.00
Tray, Purity Ice Cream, Kewpie With Racket 950.00
Vinyl, Black, Cameo, Tag 5.50

KIMBALL, see Cluthra category.

KING'S ROSE, see Soft Paste category.

Emerging Markets

Today's collectors don't treasure the same things people collected fifty years ago. In those days, Victorian was bad taste, majolica was garish, and Mission furniture was best used as kindling wood. Collectors thought that only university-trained museum experts and antiques dealers knew what was suitable for a home furnished in good taste. By the mid-1950s, collecting stopped being elitist. People didn't have to inherit antique furniture to admire the look of Williamsburg, and "amateurs" started to use their own judgment to buy pieces at house sales. They became experts on their own. Newspaper columns, magazines, and books about antiques, written for the average person, became popular. Collectors discovered they often knew more than the "experts" about specialized fields of collecting, such as toys, advertising, mechanical banks, art pottery, or bottles—fields that are still often ignored by museums. A bottle auction in 1975 set at least ten records for prices. The top price was $26,500 for a Jared Spencer flask. Collectors spent tens of thousands of dollars, with few dealers to help distinguish good from great. The rules regarding values of commercially produced bottles were developed by collectors who knew a good find when they saw one.

Why are some previously ignored collectibles and antiques becoming popular with collectors? Sales are influenced by fashion designers and by media exposure in radio, movies, TV, magazines, and books. Buyer selections are based on nostalgia, historic interest, low price, usefulness, and amusement. The strongest influences are decorator magazines and their pictures of country kitchens and Victorian bedrooms. Visual images of collectibles create a demand. *The Thin Man* movies of the 1930s and 1940s are the basis for "movie deco." Current movies and TV shows, as well as reruns, add to the return of '50s chic. Rooms filled with blond furniture have the *Leave It to Beaver* look. Major designers like Ralph Lauren have caught the essence of every antique style from the 19th-century English gentleman, with yachting and hunting accessories, to the prep-school students of the early twentieth century. Disney World in Orlando, Florida, is a place of make-believe antiques. The hotels are too large in scale; buildings on Main Street are too small to house many real antiques. But tourists are training their eyes to see the size, shape, and color of Disney "antiques" as correct. Disney decorating is one of the reasons oversized, unusual pieces have high-dollar value in the collectibles market.

Lifestyles have changed. Antiques and collectibles used to be objects of respectful admiration from afar. Now collectors live with and enjoy them. Collectors are younger and prefer less-formal pieces, often because they have families that include rambunctious children. Mix and match is in. An informal mixture makes it easier to find replacements when a set is broken up.

Educated amateurs are determining emerging markets. The average collector wants to buy such items as modern glass, art glass, Depression-era glass, old advertising, perfume bottles, robot space toys, California pottery of the '60s, '50s high-style furniture, American studio silver jewelry, and Shelley and other English dinnerwares. Even works by '70s and '80s designers are selling at antiques and collectibles shows. These items tend to be mass-produced and are replacing earlier rare or one-of-a-kind interests like 18th-century Meissen porcelain or period furniture made before 1880.

Why is this happening? How can collectors spot a trend? A comparison of *Kovels' Complete Antiques Price List* (the first one done in 1968) and the newest *Kovels' Antiques & Collectibles Price List* (the 31st edition) shows how tastes seem to have changed. Even with the changes, however, some basic patterns remain. Pieces from celebrities' collections, household furnishings, colorful or humorous accessories, and historic items at low prices still attract buyers. To understand the interests of today's collectors—and to help you spot current bargains—study market trends, fashion influence, and popular tastes.

Spotting New Trends

We read the collector newsletters, more than 1,000 different titles, to see what the knowledgeable buyers and specialized collectors are paying for things these days. A 1970s Prayer Lady soap dish goes for $38 (the matching cookie jar is $300). In the daily paper, a dark blue Peanut the Elephant Beanie Baby was advertised for $1,700.

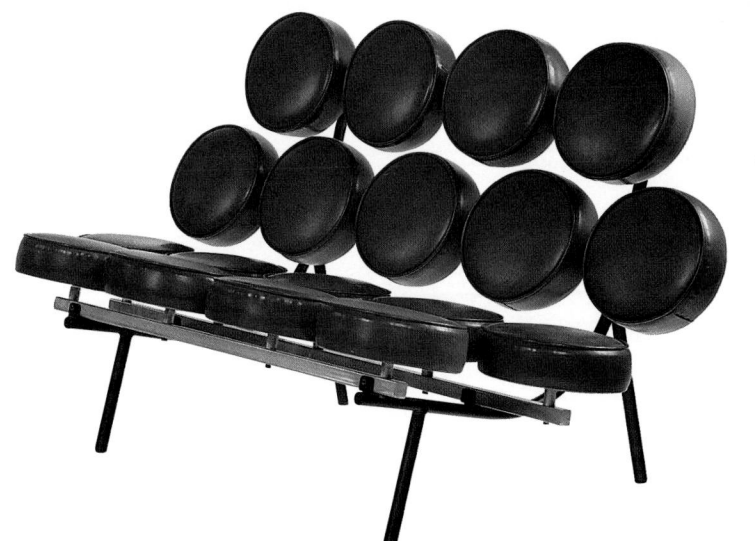

Treadway Gallery, Inc. and Toomey Gallery

Upscale '50s design is becoming the high-end "antique" of the '90s. George Nelson Associates' Marshmallow Sofa was produced by Herman Miller from 1956 to 1965, and only a few hundred were made. This one with original Naugahyde cushions sold for $5,000 in 1997.

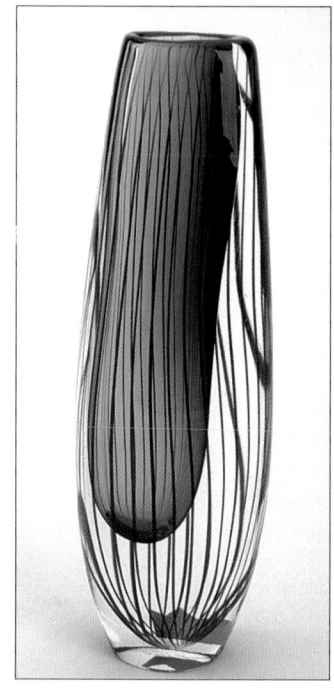

Mid-century glassware is popular now. A handcrafted vase by Kosta is worth $100 to $500. Items signed by designers, like Vicke Lindstrand, are higher priced.

The 1960s buyer liked 18th-century figurines, such as the Chelsea man, which is marked with a gold anchor, worth $250 in 1968. Today it is worth $800. But 1990s buyers will spend nearly as much for a Kay Finch pig, made in California from 1935 to 1963. It sells for $625.

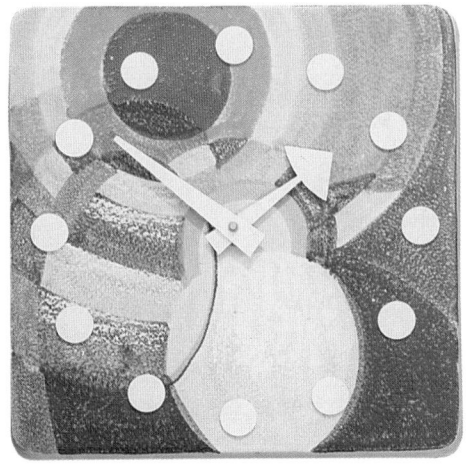

Christie's New York

A clock is a perfect example of a Kovelism: "If it moves and makes noise, it is worth more money." Old grandfather clocks, mantel clocks, and carriage clocks have long been expensive, but today '50s clocks are drawing the amazing prices. The George Nelson designs sell for $500 to $1,500. This Nelson-designed Raymor clock, made in Italy for Howard Miller, sold for $633 in 1995.

Colorful majolica is considered decorative now, not garish. Prices were beginning to rise in 1983 when the Minton mermaid compote sold for $350. It is now worth thousands. That same year, the square cup with saucer was $110 and the French peacock vase was $165—bargain prices today.

Gene Harris Antique Auction Center

At the time of
our first book,
the best known
of the English
wares was
Wedgwood.
The Wedgwood
Jasperware pitcher
(above), $30 in 1968, sells today for $140.
It does not entice buyers the way it used to.
The English ware that attracts the most attention today is art pottery like this Ruskin vase
(right), worth $950, or the Martinware two-
faced pitcher (below), at $1,500 or more.

Blown flasks and bitters bottles were important thirty years ago. Old-time collectors looked for bottles like the Chapin & Gore 1876 sour mash bottle (above left), now selling for $130, and the Tippecanoe bitters bottle (above center), now worth $400 to $500. The emerging bottles for new collectors include the telephone-shaped candy container, listed at $400.

Coin silver hollow ware is out of favor with many young buyers. A mid-19th-century pitcher by Mulford & Wendell of Albany, New York, is worth $375. But new collectors would rather have a 1930s Marshall Field sterling bowl, a good find for $350.

Christie's New York

Colonial pewter was big in the 1960s. The teapot from Philadelphia (above) that could be purchased for $200 in 1968 would sell for thousands of dollars today. New collectors priced out of that market want inexpensive hammered aluminum, like the Buenilum leaf-shape dish (below right), which sold for $17, and even unmarked items, like the square dish, which sold for $10. Kensington aluminum, with more modern designs, is gaining in popularity too.

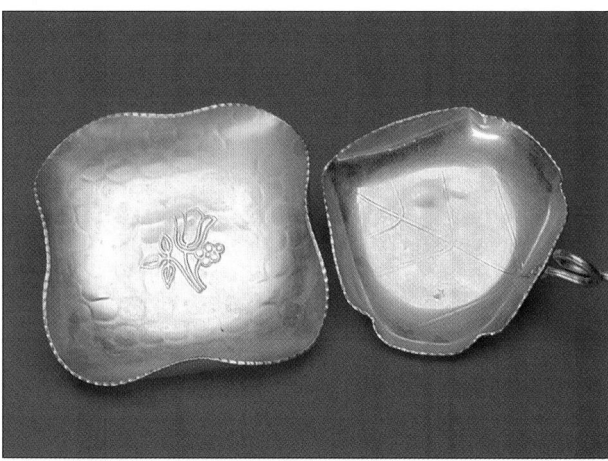

Expensive Victorian jewelry has traditionally been a good buy when compared to new fine jewelry. But today's young collector spends big money on costume jewelry. In 1998, a Trifari "fruit salad" pin (below left) sold for $1,210 at auction. Even Bakelite jewelry can be worth thousands. This "Philadelphia" bracelet (right) in the same 1998 auction sold for $9,250.

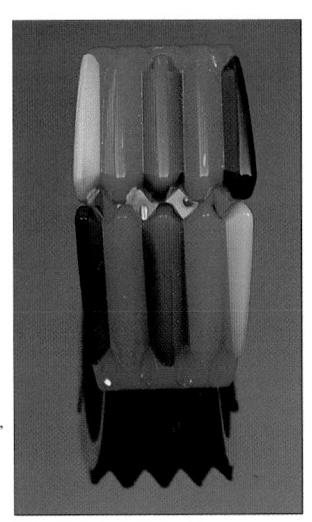

Treadway Gallery, Inc., Toomey Gallery, and Dan Ripley Antiques.

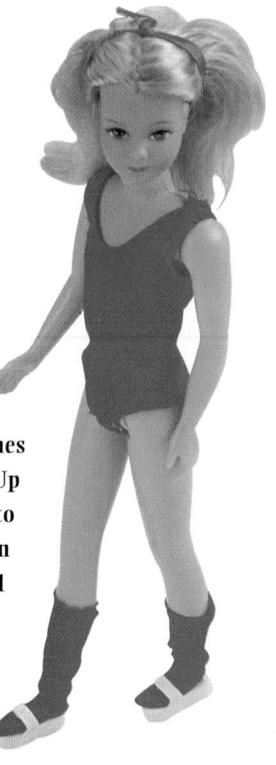

Fashion dolls from the 19th-century still attract older collectors, but the dolls collectors remember from their childhood are the ones rising in price. Barbie's friend, Growing Up Skipper, from 1975, is now selling at $60 to $70. The doll had breasts that grew bigger when you turned her arm. These dolls did not sell well originally, so they are scarce today. Watch as other less-than-forty-year-old dolls, such as Betsy Wetsy, Chatty Cathy, and Terri Lee, go up in price.

Toys like this mid-19th-century drum, which sold for $415 in 1996, used to be popular but are now hard to find. Today's collectors have moved on to battery-operated toys and space toys. A collector paid $10,650 for the Giant Sonic Train Robot in 1996. It was worth less than $50 in 1968. The mechanical Mama bear sells for $250.

Beaded purses were barely mentioned in our early books and were difficult to sell. Now purses of all sorts—leather, plastic, needlepoint, big-name designers, and novelty—merit their own separate category in Kovels' price lists. The beaded handbag (right), made around 1910, sold for $935 last year. The plastic tortoiseshell purse (below), labeled Bergdorf Goodman, is worth $100. The novelty bag made in the 1930s or 1940s from folded cigarette packs (below right) sells for $100.

Copake Auctions, Inc.

Most Victorian furniture was unfashionable in the 1960s. The only popular styles were the early Belter types. Few collectors wanted eccentric examples like a Hunzinger chair priced today at $1,500 or this Egyptian Revival sofa by Pottier & Stymus that would sell for $45,000.

Thirty years ago Mission furniture had almost no resale value—it was a thrift-shop bargain. Today exceptional pieces are selling for record prices, like $34,650 for a two-door Gustav Stickley bookcase and $29,900 for a woman's desk. An L. & J.G. Stickley Morris-style rocking chair is a more common find. This one sold for $1,610 at a 1997 auction.

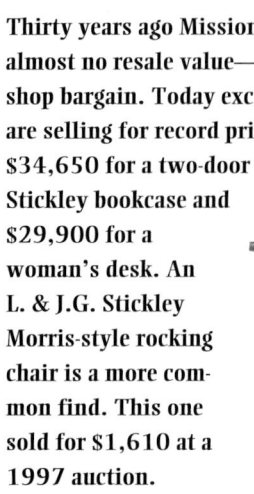

Skinner, Inc.

One of the most amazing "growth" categories listed in our first book was advertising memorabilia. Back then, most pieces were throwaways, but now they are high priced. This coffee sign sold recently for $5,000. And one of the biggest collectibles available on the Internet is commemorative tins—the new ones found at grocery stores. Prices for older ones—those from the 1980s—are now rising. The 1987 Nabisco animal crackers tin is worth $10 to $15.

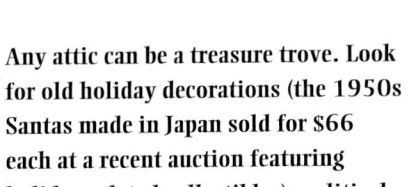

Any attic can be a treasure trove. Look for old holiday decorations (the 1950s Santas made in Japan sold for $66 each at a recent auction featuring holiday-related collectibles); political buttons (the one shown left was $10, and rare ones are worth much more); and

old cigarette lighters worth $25 to $100 (a 1933 Zippo might fetch as much as $10,000).

Christie's New York

Today's collectibles are appreciated from the viewpoint of the collector, not the museum curator. A long-lost Van Gogh painting is obviously valuable. However, auctioneers are selling other non–fine art items for unexpectedly high prices, such as $23,000 for a pair of cast iron baseball player andirons (left) and $363,000 for Lou Gehrig's 1927 New York Yankees uniform.

Using the Trends to Your Advantage

Wolfs

Collect to furnish the house. There is what is called "use" value. Price everything against new; add value for age and quality. Every recognized period from William and Mary to Mid-Century Modern is collected. A collector bought this 18th-century New England cherry secretary in 1946 at a Parke Bernet auction for $750. It sold in Cleveland in 1997 for $112,500. Don't forget furniture from "made-up" categories like country, rustic, folk art, and fantasy. All have value among the right buyers. And the rules are different for each—worn paint is good on country, bad on Sheraton.

Collect a set. Assembling a set provides a challenge for the collector and adds value to the final grouping. Even dining room chairs are bought and sold as a mix-and-match grouping. Shelley and other English dinner sets, even works from the '70s and '80s, are appearing at shows. Liberty Blue dishes, such as the one at right, were a 1976 grocery-store premium, and sell today for $8 to $12 a plate; a soup tureen is $500.

Follow the "philosophy of the series." Start with the new, then collect back to older years. Buy stamps, coins, Royal Doulton, Department 56 cottages, and Christmas plates. This Bing & Grondahl 1895 plate, the first in the series, is worth $5,000 (later plates are worth $25 to $100). The rare and scarce items in a series command very high prices. The complete set is worth more than the sum of its parts.

Collect technology—learn as you go. These items may be some of the toughest collectibles to acquire because sources of information are hard to find. Keep slide rules, typewriters, computers, toasters, blenders, and irons. This 1930s waffle iron was part of a coffee set by Royal Rochester that was a $200 "steal" at a recent show.

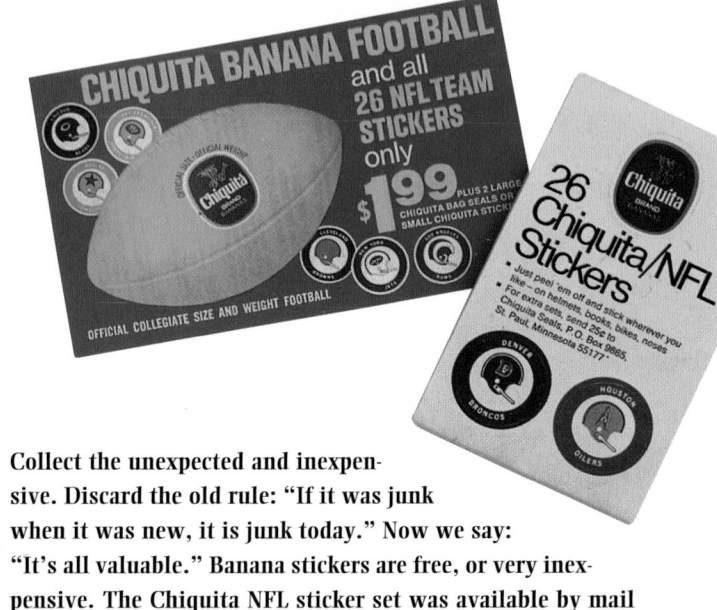

Collect the unexpected and inexpensive. Discard the old rule: "If it was junk when it was new, it is junk today." Now we say: "It's all valuable." Banana stickers are free, or very inexpensive. The Chiquita NFL sticker set was available by mail order in 1984 for $1.99 and is highly regarded among banana-sticker collectors today. Collect fast-food toys or memorabilia. This McDino Changeables Tri-Shake-Atops from McDonald's is worth $1.50 alone, $2.50 in the original plastic bag. Traditional collecting rules apply here: complete sets, rarity, and design increase the value. Sometimes ugly or bizarre is best.

TCHEN utensils of all types, from eggbeaters to bowls, are collected day. Handmade wooden and metal items, like ladles and apple peel-s, were made in the early nineteenth century. Mass-produced pieces, ke iron apple peelers and graniteware, were made in the nineteenth ntury. Other kitchen wares are listed under manufacturers' names or der Advertising, Iron, Tool, or Wooden.

Basket, Pastry, Cream Enamel, Blue Trim, Tin, 3 1/4 x 2 In.	175.00
Beater, Table Clamp, Pump Handle, Iron, Brooklyn, No. 5, 16 x 10 In.	1200.00
Beater Jar, Wesson Oil	55.00
Blender, Blend King, Brown Metallic Base, Yellow Plastic, Treman Elec., 1950s, 12 In.	50.00
Blender, Osterizer Deluxe, Chrome & Glass, 1950s	95.00
Board, Cutting Pine, Arch For Handing, 36 x 20 In.	178.00
Board, Cutting, Cherrywood, Winged Crest, Show & Work Side, Penna., 21 x 15 In.	195.00
Bowl, Chopping, Maple, Indian Red Paint, Vermont, 19th Century, 15 In.	550.00
Bowl, Mixing, Yellow, Girl Watering Flowers, Large	75.00
Bowl, Pyrex, Delphite, 9 In.	17.00
Box, Salt, Hanging, Stave Wood Construction, Strips Of Ash & Laburnum, c.1890	575.00
Box, Salt, Hinged Lid, Exposed Dovetails, Molded Drawer, Walnut, 11 1/2 In.	920.00
Box, Salt, White, Dark Blue Trim, Wooden Lid, France, 10 In.	165.00
Box Mangle, 4 Wooden Rollers, 16 In.	275.00
Bread Box, White Enamel, Brass Handle & Latch, Round, 14 In.	85.00
Bread Maker, Table Clamp, Universal, Gold Medal Winner, St. Louis Exposition, 1904	125.00
Broiler, Rotary, Wrought Iron, Tooled Handle, P.B., 12 1/2 x 21 3/4 In.	145.00
Broiler, Wrought Iron, Attached Drip Pan, Heart Handle, 10 1/2 x 16 In.	575.00
Broom, Corn, 19th Century	185.00
Butter Mold, look under Mold, Butter in this category.	
Butter Stamp, Beaver, Screw Handle, 2 3/8 In.	160.00
Butter Stamp, Cow On Stamp Face, 5 On Shell, 4 3/4 In.	165.00
Butter Stamp, Cow, Screw Handle, 2 3/16 In.	140.00
Butter Stamp, Crown Design, Wooden, 1 Piece Turned Handle, Scrubbed, 4 1/4 In.	110.00
Butter Stamp, Dasher Type, Pine, Turned Handle, Natural Finish, 22 In.	201.00
Butter Stamp, Eagle, Branch & Star, Self Handle, Round, 4 1/4 In.	190.00
Butter Stamp, Flower & Fern	65.00
Butter Stamp, Flower & Leaves	30.00
Butter Stamp, Geometric Star Flowers Both Sides, 3 In.	110.00
Butter Stamp, Heart, Geometric Design, Scrubbed Finish, 5 1/2 In.	220.00
Butter Stamp, Lollipop, Carved Flowers & Initals, 6 5/8 In.	247.00
Butter Stamp, Starflower Both Sides, Lollipop, 8 1/2 In.	190.00
Butter Stamp, Starflower, Zigzag & Swags, Lollipop, 7 In.	135.00
Butter Stamp, Stylized Tulip, 1 Piece Turned Handle, Round, 3 7/8 In.	165.00
Butter Stamp, Stylized Tulip, Scrubbed Star, Small Knob Handle, 4 In.	110.00
Butter Stamp, Tulip & Stars, Dark Finish, 1 Piece Turned Handle, 4 7/8 In.	220.00
Butter Stamp, Tulip, Leaves & Heart, Dark Varnish, Missing Handle, 4 In.	110.00
Butter Stamp, Tulip, Walnut, Lollipop, 6 3/4 In.	330.00
Butter Stamp, Wheat Sheath, Round Ball Top, Wooden	30.00
Cake Pan, Primrose, Fire-King	8.00
Cake Pan, Snoopy, 1965	40.00
Can Opener, Bull, Cast Iron	95.00
Can Opener, Wearever, Hand Cranked, 1950s	15.00
Canister Set, Glass, Tin Lids, 6 3/4, 7 3/4, 8 1/4, 10 In., 4 Piece	495.00
Canister Set, Gold Lettering, Cafe, Riz, Chicoree, Farine, White, 4 Piece	395.00
Canister Set, Old MacDonald, Regal China, 6 Piece	1800.00
Canister Set, Yellow Enamel, 8 3/4 In., 8 In., 7 In., 6 1/4 In., 4 Piece	85.00
Carafe, Turquoise, Insulated, Thermos, 10 In.	5.00
Cheese Strainer, Heart Shaped, Punched Tin, 3 Feet	165.00
Cherry Pitter, Enterprise, No. 12	85.00
Cherry Pitter, Mt. Joy, Automatic, Cast Iron	285.00
Chest, Flour, Cream & Green Paint, c.1880	895.00
Chopper, Food, Copper, Steel, Wooden, Horse-Shaped Body, 12 1/2 In.	270.00
Churn, A Square Deal Churn, Cast Iron, Hand Crank, Pat. 1911	165.00
Churn, Butter, Dazey, No. 4, 4 Qt.	125.00
Churn, Butter, Dazey, No. 10, 1 Qt.	1250.00
Churn, Butter, Dry Buttermilk Color, Green Trim	265.00

Churn, Butter, Lightning, 1917, 2 Qt. .... 125.
Churn, Dazey, 2 Qt. .... 325.
Churn, Dazey, 3 Qt. 150.0
Churn, Dazey, 4 Qt. 90.0
Churn, Dazey, Beveled Edge, 1 Qt. 3250.0
Churn, Dazey, Bull's-Eye, 1 Qt. .... 2500.
Churn, Dazey, No. 30, 1922 Pat. Date 650.0
Clothesline, Zippo, Box .... 20.
Clothespins, Hand Carved, Late 18th Century, 7 In., Pair .... 135.
Coffee Grinders are listed in their own category.
Coffee Set, Art Deco, Manning Bowman, 1930s .... 195.
Coffee Set, Golden Pheasant, Royal Rochester, 4 Piece .... *Illus* 85.0
Coffeepot, Kilbane, 12 In. 450.0
Coffeepot, Porcelier, Blown-Out Woman, Flowers .... 65.
Coffeepot, Tin, Parrot Beak Spout, Pewter Finial, 10 1/2 In. 192.0
Coffeepot, Tin, Tapered Cylindrical Form, Domed Lid, Applied Strap Handle, 11 In. ..... 2875.
Coffeepot, Tin, Wrigglework Eagle & Floral, 10 1/2 In. 6710.0
Colander, Chicken Wire, Germany .... 58.
Colander, Redware, 2 Handles With Daubs Of Manganese Glaze, 11 1/2 In. 2760.0
Colander, Straw Flower Design, Enamelware, 5 x 10 In. 85.0
Condiment Set, Fish, With Spoon, Lusterware, Germany, 3 1/4 x 6 1/2 In. 95.0
Condiment Set, Steamship, Covered Condiments, Open Salt & Pepper, 3 1/2 x 8 In. ... 95.0
Container, Canned Milk, Yellow Plastic, Piercing Red Flip Lid, E-Z-Canned Milk, 5 In. . 18.0
Cookie Board, 12 Blocks, Animals, C.G. Weiss, 1843, 7 1/4 x 5 1/2 In. 6325.0
Cookie Board, Cornucopia, Cast Iron, 3 7/8 x 5 1/4 In. 77.0
Cookie Board, Dancing Couple, Mahogany, Conger, 10 5/8 x 10 3/4 In. 1875.0
Cookie Board, Man On Horse, Mahogany, J. Conger 2540.0
Cookie Board, Maple, 9 Carved Sections, Animal, Bird, Fish, Insect, 4 3/4 x 7 In. 275.0
Cookie Board, New York State Arms, Excelsior, Mahogany, J. Conger, 11 In. 3510.0
Cookie Board, Wheat, Windmill, Rooster, Farmer & Owl, Wooden, 24 In. 275.0
Cookie Cutter, Dog, Tin, 10 In. 95.0
Cookie Cutter, Eagle, Sheet Iron, 19th Century, 4 1/2 x 4 1/4 In. 125.0
Cookie Cutter, Eagle, Tin, Wingspan 4 In. 44.0
Cookie Cutter, Heart Within Oval, Tin, Handmade 40.0
Cookie Cutter, Heart, Sheet Iron, Pennsylvania, 19th Century, Small 180.0
Cookie Cutter, Leaf, Tin 20.0
Cookie Cutter, Profile Of Man, Top Hat, 1 Raised Arm, Tinned Sheet Metal, 11 1/4 In. . 1265.0
Cookie Cutter, Santa Claus, Tin, Cake Art, Germany, 11 3/8 In. 143.0
Cookie Cutter, Star, Tin, Handmade 35.0
Cookie Plaque, Cast Iron, Pineapple & Dotwork Geometric Design, 1930s, 4 x 6 In. ... 150.0
Cookie Press, Pineapple, Cast Iron 130.0
Corer, Apple, Bone, England, 16th Century 95.0
Corer, Apple, Sheepbone 40.0
Cranberry Scoop, Wood & Canvas, Wire Teeth, 8 3/4 x 10 In. 126.0
Crumb Brush Set, Prayer Lady 40.0
Cup, Measuring, Clear Green, c.1920-1930, 2 Cups 29.0
Cup, Measuring, Copper, Marked 1/2 Gill GR, 19th Century, 2 In. 125.0

Kitchen, Coffee Set, Golden
Pheasant, Royal Rochester, 4 Piece

Curd Cutter, Cheesemaker's, 4 Spring Steel Blades, Wood Handle, Marked, 21 3/8 In. . .	110.00
Cutter, Cabbage, Heart Handle, Walnut, Pennsylvania, 22 In.	110.00
Cutter, Cabbage, Sliding Hopper, Walnut, Signed Blade, 9 3/4 In.	60.00
Cutter, Cabbage, Walnut, Heart Cutout, Pennsylvania, 19th Century, 23 In.	295.00
Dipper, Wrought Iron, C.W.K. On Handle, 24 In.	110.00
Dough Box, Dark Red Surface, Dovetailed, c.1820, 36 x 29 x 18 In.	1065.00
Dough Box, Pine, Square Legs, 28 x 35 In.	357.00
Dough Box, Poplar, 1-Board Lid, Dovetailed, 24 x 38 3/4 In.	242.00
Dough Box, Stand, Cover, Exposed Dovetails, Painted Red, 1820s, 28 3/4 In.	1380.00
Dough Box, Walnut, Turned Legs, 31 x 41 In.	418.00
Dough Tray, Community, Yellowish Brown Paint, 29 3/4 x 54 1/2 In.	5100.00
Doughnut Cutter, Maple, 2 Part, Pat. 3/26/01, 2 1/2 x 4 1/4 In.	120.00
Dryer, Herb, c.1820, 21 x 17 1/2 In.	650.00
Dutch Oven, Griswold, No. 7	90.00
Dutch Oven, Griswold, No. 9, Tite-Top	125.00
Dutch Oven, Griswold, No. 11, Tite-Top, Raised Letters	275.00
Dutch Oven, Griswold, No. 13	195.00
Dutch Oven, Wagner, No. 10, Flat Top	90.00
Egg Cooker, No. 815, Electric, Hankscraft, 5 Egg Cups	48.00
Egg Cutter, Rooster, Nickel & Sterling Silver, c.1890, 5 3/4 In.	95.00
Egg Timer, Figural, Boy, Ceramic, See-Through Plastic Head, 3 1/4 In.	25.00
Egg Timer, Prayer Lady	150.00
Egg Timer, Windmill With Bird On Top, Pale Yellow, Germany	40.00
Eggbeater, Big Bingo No.71, Aunt Jamena, White Wood Handle	12.00
Flat Iron, With Heat Block, Gooseneck Handle, Slide Trap Door	55.00
Flatiron, Interchangeable Handle, Pair	35.00
Flatiron, Teardrop Shape, Flower Box, 7 In.	60.00
Flue Cover, Porcelain, Ebony Frame	85.00
Flue Cover, Victorian Couple	75.00
Fluter, Brass, Nickel Plate On Cast Iron, Theodore Tucker, Pat. Feb. 7, 1871, 9 In.	330.00
Food Grinder, Winchester	65.00
Fork, Iron, 2 Prongs, Shaped Handle, Initialed E.G., Elizabeth Gottshalk, 1823	495.00
Fork, Roasting, Rattail Hook, Heart-Shape Handle, Wrought Iron, c.1800, 14 In.	180.00
Fruit Press, Tin Cones & Braces, Wood Frame, 24 x 16 In.	235.00
Fryer, Tom Thumb, Aluminum Cover, Guardian	125.00
Frying Pan, Cast Iron, 3 Legs, Rattail Handle	165.00
Frying Pan, Griswold, No. 12	80.00
Frying Pan, Rolled Rivet Construction, Dutch, c.1650, 14 1/2 In.	310.00
Funnel, Light Blue-Gray, 7 1/2 x 5 1/2 In.	40.00
Game Rack, Iron, Dutch Crown, American, 18th Century	395.00
Grater, Acme Safety Grater & Vegetable Juicer, Wrapper, 13 In. . . . . *Illus*	8.00
Grater, Coleslaw, Hardwood, Signed, Tucker & Dorsey Mfg. Co.	65.00
Grater, Coleslaw, Wooden, Tucker & Dorsey Mfg. Co.	45.00
Grater, Enameled Stanchion, Tin Revolving Grater, Wood Pusher	120.00
Grater, Erika, Blue Windmill On Front, Iron Bottom, Enameled, 14 In.	135.00
Grater, Horseradish, Walnut, Hand-Forged Iron Fittings, c.1860	335.00
Grater, Nutmeg, Cover, Compartment, Monogram, Jacobi & Jenkins, 1900, 5 In.	860.00
Grater, Nutmeg, Hinged Cover, Matthew Linwood, 1809, 1 Troy Oz.	750.00
Grater, Nutmeg, Long Tin Handle, Patented February 27, 1877	834.00
Grater, Nutmeg, Nut Shape Handle, Tin, Wood, 5 1/4 x 3 In.	69.00
Grater, Nutmeg, Tin Handle, Wood, Round, 1877, 6 In.	835.00
Grater, Soap, Fels-Naptha	15.00
Griddle, Griswold, No. 7, Pattern Number 907	60.00
Griddle, Griswold, No. 10, Handle, Erie	45.00
Griddle, Iron, Hanging, 19th Century, 8 3/4 x 9 1/2 In.	175.00
Griddle, Wagner, No. 4, Flop . . . . .225.00 to	300.00
Grinder, Spice, Folding Handle, c.1800, 12 1/2 In.	190.00
Grinder, Winchester No. 12	65.00
Hair Dryer, Handy Hannah, Enamel, Light Blue, Wood Handle, Metal Base, Box	33.00
Hair Dryer, Stand, Metal, Enamel Painted, Yellow, No. 559.8710, Kenmore, 8 x 10 In. . .	29.00
Hair Dryer, Star-Rite, Chrome, 1930s	40.00
Heater, Iron, Pressed Steel, Tall Legs, 19 In.	65.00
Heater, Liquid Fuel, Wick, Edy Georg Haller, Cast Iron, Enameled, 10 1/4 In.	70.00

Heater, Prometheus, Rocking Natural Gas, With 2 Ox Tongue Irons, 10 1/4 In. 230.00
Heater, Sadiron, Cast Iron, Holds 5 Irons, 14 1/2 In. 175.00
Holder, Napkin, Prayer Lady, Blue & White, 6 In. . . . . *Illus* 32.00
Holder, Scouring Pad, Prayer Lady, Pink 40.00
Holder, Soap Dish, Prayer Lady, Pink & White, 6 In. 38.00
Holder, Straw, Pink Glass 850.00
Ice Chest, Oak, 3 Large Doors, 2 Lower Doors 1800.00
Ice Cream Sandwich Maker, Metal Scoop, Wood Handle, 12 1/4 In. 125.00
Ice Crusher, Ice-O-Matic, White, Chrome Stripe, Rival, 10 1/2 In. 40.00
Ice Crusher, Iceramic, Black Plastic, Yellow Metal Top, Chrome Lid, Dazey, 10 x 4 In. . . 38.00
Ice Tongs, Double Points, Hand Forged, 12 1/2 In. 45.00
Ice Tongs, Sherwood Ice Co., Rubber Handles, 11 3/4 In. 35.00
Icebox, Oak, Lion-Head Corners, Paw Feet, 54 In. 1785.00
Iron, Alcohol, Feldmeyer Brilliant, 7 In. 60.00
Iron, Alcohol, Jubilee, Revolving Catch, Detachable Handle, 10 In. 200.00
Iron, American Elec'L Heater Co., Detroit, Electric, 5 1/2 In. 22.00
Iron, Brass, With Brass Insert, 18th Century 495.00
Iron, Charcoal, Bird Latch, 6 1/2 In. 145.00
Iron, Charcoal, Stand, Cast Iron, Wood Handle, 9 In. 260.00
Iron, Charcoal, T & C Clark & Co., Heat Shield, 8 1/4 In. 50.00
Iron, Fluting, Geneva, 1868 . . . . 95.00
Iron, Gasoline, Royal Iron, Self-Heating Iron Co., Key, 10 In. 35.00
Iron, Goffering, Brass, Brass Heater, 3-Footed Base, 5 In. 660.00
Iron, Goffering, Cast Metal, Ornate Base, 4 1/4 In. 175.00
Iron, Goffering, Triple, 3 Heater Slugs, Tripod, 17 1/4 In. 935.00
Iron, Kerosene, Coleman, Model 615, Black Enamel, Green Tank, 9 1/2 In. 175.00
Iron, Natural Gas, American Gas Machine Co., 7 1/4 In. 245.00
Iron, Polishing, Keystone, Name On Handle, 5 In. 175.00
Iron, Silver Streak, No.1038, Electric, Red, 9 In. 935.00
Iron, Slug, J.J. Siddons, Westbromwich, 5 1/2 In. 60.00
Iron, Smoothing, Cast Brass, Turned Wooden Handle, 4 1/2 x 5 In. 145.00
Iron, Smoothing, Turned Wood Handle, Dutch, 1840s, 4 1/2 x 5 In. 175.00
Iron, Steam, Leko Turex, Mixed Metal & Wood, 8 In. 38.00
Iron, Tailor's, 18th Century, 10 1/2 In. 135.00
Iron, Tailor's, Gas, New York Pressing Iron Co., 8 1/2 In. 38.00
Iron, Travel, Alcohol, Chrome Plated, Trivet, Leather Case, 9 In. 175.00
Iron Fluter, J. & A.M. Albert, Long Base, 2 Piece, 14 1/2 In. 525.00
Iron Fluter, Manville's Patent Machine, Yellow Stenciling, 10 In. 825.00
Iron Fluter, Mrs. Susan B. Knox, Saverbier & Son, 1866, 7 1/2 In. 145.00
Iron Fluter, Pennsylvania, Pat. 1880, Gold & Red Pinstriping, 14 In. 130.00
Iron Fluter, Rocker, Erie Fluter, 6 In. 230.00
Iron Fluter, Welcome, Pat. 1880, American Machine Co., 14 In. 130.00
Iron Fluter-Roller, With Slug, Stirrup Handle, Patent Applied For, 6 In. 220.00
Jack, Clockwork, Brass & Steel, Ornate Design, England, 18th Century 550.00

Kitchen, Holder, Napkin, Prayer
Lady, Blue & White, 6 In.

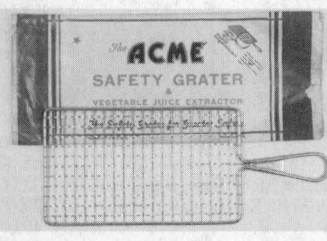

Kitchen, Grater, Acme Safety Grater &
Vegetable Juicer, Wrapper, 13 In.

Kitchen, Jar, Ketchup, Pixie, With
Bowtie, 5 1/4 In.

Jar, Instant Coffee, Prayer Lady, Pink 65.00
Jar, Ketchup, Pixie, With Bowtie, 5 1/4 In. ....*Illus* 42.00
Juicer, Measuring Cup, Cobalt Blue, 4 1/4 x 5 In. 42.00
Kettle, Black Iron, Mears, O.L. Haber & Co., Patent 1887 .... 250.00
Kettle, Footed, Cleveland Superior, 3 1/2 In. 55.00
Kettle, Interior Lined With Porcelain, Cast Iron, T & C Clark, 6 Pt., 8 3/4 In. 225.00
Kettle, Iron, Elongated Gate, Wrought Iron Handle, Footed, 18th Century, 10 x 6 In. 195.00
Kettle, Iron, Sampson & Tisdale, 19th Century, 8 In. 143.00
Kettle, Jelly, Cast Brass, 11 x 10 In. 67.00
Kettle, Preserve, Wheel-Turned Brass, Iron Handle, 14 In. 145.00
Kettle Stand, Wrought Iron, Tripod Base, Brass Top, Scalloped Edge, 8 x 10 1/2 In. ... 275.00
Kit, Wine Tasting, Floats With Mercury, Brass Beaker, Felt-Lined Case, 16 1/2 x 9 In. ... 155.00
Knife Sharpener, Batwing Design, 1870 .... 95.00
Ladle, Blue, White Speckled Enamel, 14 In. 10.00
Ladle, Pudding, Ash Burl, c.1790, 5 1/2 x 6 In. 675.00
Ladle, Turquoise, White Specks, Enamelware 39.00
Ladle & Skimmer, Iron, Blacksmith Made, 19th Century, Penna., 8 1/2 In., Pair 450.00
Linen Press, All Wood Construction, Primitive, 12 In. 85.00
Mangle Board, Horse Handle, Geometric Flower Design, Leather Strap, 29 1/2 In. 415.00
Match Holders can be found in their own category.
Match Safes can be found in their own category.
Measuring Set, 1 Cup, 1/2 Cup, 1/3 Cup, 1/4 Cup, Blue, Jeannette Glass, 1930s 200.00
Meat Grinder, Countertop, Tin-Plated Metal, Salesman's Sample, Rollman, 7 In. 70.00
Meat Tenderizer, Wildflower, Stoneware 240.00
Meat Tenderizer, Wooden Handle, Dated 12-25-1877, 8 In. 50.00
Mixer, Mayonnaise, Glass, Borden's, 1957 .... 25.00
Mixer, Milkshake, Green Porcelain, Hamilton Beach, 1940s 126.00
Mixer, Milkshake, Hamilton Beach, 2-Speed, Cream Porcelain 165.00
Mixer, Milkshake, Hamilton Beach, Green, Porcelain, Chrome Top, Container, 1940s 125.00
Mixer, Milkshake, Hamilton Beach, Polished Brass, Marble Base, c.1915-25 .... 315.00
Molds may also be found in the Pewter and Tinware categories.
Mold, Aspic, Gothic Form, Tinned Iron, 19th Century 100.00
Mold, Butter, Cow, Wooden, Worm Holes, 13 In. 148.00
Mold, Butter, Crescent Shape, Wheat Sheaf & Star, 7 In. 143.00
Mold, Butter, Pineapple, April 17, 1866 .... 215.00
Mold, Cake, Fluted, Copper, 11 In. 90.00
Mold, Cake, Rabbit, Griswold 250.00
Mold, Cake, Rudolph The Red Nose Reindeer, 1939, 8 Piece 40.00
Mold, Cake, Santa Claus, Griswold 575.00
Mold, Candle, see Tinware category.
Mold, Candy, Carved Fish, 2 Parts, Pine, Hinged, 11 3/4 In. 305.00
Mold, Cheese, Heart Shaped, Tin Cover 632.00
Mold, Chocolate, Baby In Bunting, Herman Walter, Berlin, 9 x 4 1/2 In. 395.00
Mold, Chocolate, Bride & Groom, Pair 125.00
Mold, Chocolate, Double Rabbit 70.00
Mold, Chocolate, Duck, Long Bill, 1930s, 7 x 5 3/8 In. 55.00
Mold, Chocolate, Elephant, Double Hinged, 6 x 7 1/2 In. 275.00
Mold, Chocolate, Elephant, Germany, 2 1/2 x 3 7/8 In. 145.00
Mold, Chocolate, Hen On Nest, Tin, 4 1/2 x 4 1/2 In. 95.00
Mold, Chocolate, Horse, Anton Reiche, Dresden, 5 1/2 x 7 In. 285.00
Mold, Chocolate, Lambs With Party Hats, 13 x 7 1/2 In. 165.00
Mold, Chocolate, Lion, 2 Piece 65.00
Mold, Chocolate, Rabbit With Basket, Tin, 3 1/2 x 3 In. 145.00
Mold, Chocolate, Rabbit, Medium 60.00
Mold, Chocolate, Rabbit, Small 45.00
Mold, Chocolate, Rabbit, Tin, Eppelsheimer & Co., 11 1/4 In. 148.00
Mold, Chocolate, Rocking Horse, Tin, 4 1/2 x 5 1/2 In. 165.00
Mold, Chocolate, Rooster 75.00
Mold, Chocolate, Santa Claus On Motorcycle, Bag Of Toys, Holland, 5 x 5 In. 245.00
Mold, Chocolate, Santa Claus, Marked H. LeCerf, Germany, 8 In. 350.00
Mold, Chocolate, Scotty Dog, 1930s, 4 x 4 1/8 In. 145.00
Mold, Chocolate, Scotty Dog, Large 125.00
Mold, Chocolate, Stork, Serpent Mark, France, 5 3/4 x 4 In. 225.00

Mold, Chocolate, Train 65.00
Mold, Chocolate, Walking Bear, Walters, Tin, Berlin, 3 3/4 x 6 1/4 In. 245.00
Mold, Copper, Food, Eagle With Arrows & Laurel, Round, 7 3/4 In. 385.00
Mold, Crispy Corn Stick, Griswold, No. 273 .... 50.00
Mold, Food, Copper Lion Top, Oval, 8 In. 220.00
Mold, Food, Grape Cluster, Mid-19th Century, 5 1/2 In. 110.00
Mold, Food, Heart Shaped, Yellow-Crowned Griffins, Germany, c.1740, 11 x 9 In. 295.00
Mold, Food, Lion, Tin & Copper, 7 1/2 x 6 1/2 In. 275.00
Mold, Food, Rose, Tin & Copper, 4 3/4 x 7 In. 250.00
Mold, Gelatin, Christmas Tree, Barfield 95.00
Mold, Ice Cream, see Pewter category.
Mold, Ice Cream, Eskimo 110.00
Mold, Ice Cream, George Washington 75.00
Mold, Ice Cream, Turkey 75.00
Mold, Maple Sugar, 2 Piece 185.00
Mold, Maple Sugar, Carved To Form Heart, 2 Piece, Late 19th Century 158.00
Mold, Maple Sugar, Double Heart 400.00
Mold, Patty, Bonley Wat-L-Ette, Box, Recipe Sheet 20.00
Mold, Patty, Griswold, Box 30.00
Mold, Pudding, Man In The Moon Face, Crescent Shape, Tin 65.00
Mold, Pudding, Steam, Kreamer, 5 1/2 x 4 In. 40.00
Mold, Pudding, Sunflower Design, Pineapple Form, Rectangular Handles, Tin, Pair 179.00
Mold, Pumpkin & Gourds, Mid-19th Century, 5 1/4 In. 130.00
Mold, Rabbit, Griswold 525.00
Mold, Redware, Brown Glaze, Black Design, 6 In. 82.00
Mold, Redware, Candle, 24 Tubes, Pine Frame, A. Wilcox, 8 x 23 1/2 x 13 1/2 In. 990.00
Mold, Redware, Ear Of Corn, Crimped Edge, Arched Sides, Sponging On Rim, 7 7/8 In. . 440.00
Mold, Redware, Jelly, Fish Shape, Articulated Features, Bootjack Feet, 11 1/2 In. 575.00
Mold, Redware, Jelly, Fish Shape, Inner Glaze, Footed, 12 1/4 In. 330.00
Mold, Redware, Turk's Head, Butterscotch Glaze, 9 In. 135.00
Mold, Redware, Turk's Head, Swirled Design, Brown Sponging, John Bell, 8 1/4 In. 1210.00
Mold, Redware, Turk's Head, Tobacco Spit Design 105.00
Napkin Holder, Prayer Lady ....35.00 to 42.00
Nipper, Sugar, Iron, 9 1/2 In. 121.00
Nipper, Sugar, Mounted On Base 166.00
Nipper, Sugar, Serrated Cutters, Brass Picor, 5 7/8 In. 210.00
Nipper, Sugar, Wrought Steel, 7 1/4 In., Set Of 2 .... 220.00
Pan, Breadstick, Griswold 40.00
Pan, Breadstick, Whole Wheat, Griswold, No. 8028 .... 250.00
Pan, Bundt, Griswold 900.00
Pan, Bundt, Wagner, Style B, Marked 250.00
Pan, Cake, Heart Shaped, Tin, 3 Graduated Sizes, 12, 15, & 18 In. 295.00
Pan, Corn Stick, Griswold 35.00
Pan, Corn Stick, Nickel Plated, Wagner, T-Size 45.00
Pan, Crispy Corn Stick, Griswold 95.00
Pan, French Roll, Griswold, No. 11 .... 45.00
Pan, Muffin, Griswold, No. 8, Pattern Number, Erie, Aluminum 50.00
Pan, Muffin, Griswold, No. 14, Turk's Head 1100.00
Pan, Muffin, Griswold, No. 947 .... 100.00
Pan, Muffin, Turk's Head, Wagner, 6 Cups 275.00
Pan, Muffin, Waterman 48.00
Pan, Popover, Erie, No. 10 .... 50.00
Pan, Popover, Griswold, No. 18, Erie, 6 Cup ....70.00 to 75.00
Pan, Roasting, Black, Pour Spout, Enamelware, 12 1/2 In. 55.00
Pan, Roasting, Gray Speckled Enamel, Oval, 9 1/2 x 7 In. 85.00
Pan, Spider, Bronze, Handle, 7 1/4 x 7 1/2 In. 55.00
Pan, Vienna Roll, Wagner, Aluminum 125.00
Pastry Wheel, Pierced Handle, 17th Century 285.00
Patty Mold Set, Griswold, Box 25.00
Peeler, Apple, Belt-Driven, Wood, Forged Iron, Mortised & Pegged, 8-In. Wheel 175.00
Peeler, Apple, Cast Iron Gears, Wood Base, c.1850 .... 145.00
Peeler, Apple, Hudson 65.00
Peeler, Apple, Lackey & Howland, Pat. Date 1856 .... 110.00

Peeler, Apple, Sargen & Foster, Iron, Wood Base, 1850s 225.00
Peeler, Apple, White Mountain, Box 35.00
Peeler, Fruit, Cast Iron 50.00
Peeler, Potato, Nu-Way 50.00
Pie Bird, 2-Headed Black Crow 87.00
Pie Bird, Benny The Baker, Tester & Cutter, Box 150.00
Pie Bird, Bird, Yellow, Pink Trim 30.00
Pie Bird, Black Chef, Holding Rabbit By Ears 75.00
Pie Bird, Dragon, Green 75.00
Pie Bird, Duck, Long Neck, Yellow, 5 In. 95.00
Pie Bird, Frog 35.00
Pie Bird, Morton Pottery, 5 In. 75.00
Pie Bird, Rabbit 35.00
Pie Bird, Rooster, Cleminson 30.00
Pie Bird, Rooster, Long Neck, White 128.00
Pie Bird, Turtle 80.00
Pie Cover, Screen 28.00
Pie Crimper, Brass, England, Tag On Bottom, 9 1/2 In. 305.00
Pie Crimper, Cast Iron, Brass, Green Paint Traces, 8 3/4 In. 240.00
Pie Crimper, Iron, Birch Handle, 7 3/8 In. 110.00
Pie Crimper, Ivory & Maple, 4 7/8 In. 65.00
Pie Crimper, Ivory, Short-Horned Unicorn, 7 1/8 In. 4600.00
Pie Crimper, Union Machine, Red & Green, Black Ground, Pat. 1880, 13 1/4 In. 110.00
Platter, Tree, Griswold 40.00
Pleating Board, Wooden, Metal Pusher, Instruction On Reverse, 11 3/4 In. 45.00
Pleating Board, Wooden, With Wires, 1876-1879, 20 1/4 In. 11.00
Pleating Machine, Singer Mfg., Hand Or Belt Driven, Catalog Sheet, 21 1/2 In. 185.00
Porringer, Iron, A. Kenrick & Son, 7 1/2 In. 245.00
Porringer, Iron, Bellevue, Signed T Clark On Bottom, 1840s, 4 1/2 In. 195.00
Pot, Copper, Long Iron Handle, Wood End, American, Late 18th Century, 23 In. 195.00
Pot, Forged Copper Tip-Proof Rivets, c.1845 .... 275.00
Pot, Iron, Elongated Wrought Bail, 18th Century, 6 1/4 x 7 In. 185.00
Pot Lifter, Iron, Hand Forged, 12 7/8 In. 70.00
Potato Baker, Stove Top, Tin, 1940s 40.00
Potato Slicer, Mechanical, Cast Iron, Clamp-On, Eagle Engineering Co., 1918 .... 60.00
Press, Fruit, Griswold, 4 Qt. 85.00
Pricker, Biscuit, Twisted Wire 145.00
Rack, Drying, Horseshoe, American Wringer Co., New York, Painted 110.00
Rack, Food, Hand Carved, Cotter Pin Ends, Hung From Pantry Ceiling, 10 1/8 In. 110.00
Rack, Utensil, 5 Hooks, Iron, Hand Forged, 21 In. 325.00
Rack, Utensil, Wrought Iron, Scrolled Crest, 5 Hooks, 22 x 17 In. 121.00
Rack, Utensil, Yellow, Rose & Green Pinstripe, Enamel, 20 1/2 In. 185.00
Raisin Seeder, Cast Iron, Enterprise, Dated 1895 .... 100.00
Raisin Seeder, The Everett 50.00
Reamers are listed in their own category.
Refrigerator Box, Pearl, Cover, Fry, 12 In. 65.00
Roaster, Green Enamel, Black Trim, 15 1/2 x 11 In. 25.00
Roaster, Griswold, No. 5, Smooth Top, Aluminum, Oval 55.00
Roaster, Griswold, No. 7, Oval 395.00
Roaster, Peanut, Kerosene Burner, Wrought Iron Crank, E. Tauney Mfg. Co. 686.00
Roaster, Wagner, No. 7, Oval 225.00
Rolling Pin, Blown Glass, Aqua, Wooden Handles 225.00
Rolling Pin, Brass Handles, Wooden 66.00
Rolling Pin, Candy, Tin 295.00
Rolling Pin, Colonial Pattern, Stoneware 1400.00
Rolling Pin, Glass, Art & Sentiment Design, Cobalt Blue, 1850s, 36 In. 1200.00
Rolling Pin, Hollow Brass, Dovetailed Construction, Weights Inside 295.00
Rolling Pin, Kelvinator, Porcelain 90.00
Rolling Pin, Louisville Pottery 75.00
Rolling Pin, Stoneware, Blue & White 225.00
Rolling Pin, Tiger Maple, Late 18th Century 100.00
Rolling Pin, Wild Flower, Stoneware, Advertising Undertaking Supplies 750.00
Sadiron, Child's, 5 In. 65.00

Sadiron, Child's, Trivet, 3 1/2 In. 75.0

Sadiron, For Ruffles, Blacksmith Made, 18th Century, 5 1/4 In. 285.0

Sadiron, Howell, Trivet 55.0

Sadiron, Serpent Head Handle, Patent 1873 .... 55.0

Sadiron, Winchester, Electric 285.0

Salt & Pepper Shakers are listed in their own category.

Scissors, Aluminum, 22 In. 130.0

Scoop, Butter, Curly Maple, 19th Century, 9 1/4 In. 145.0

Scoop, Carved Heart On End Of Handle, Maple, 18th Century, 11 1/2 In. 750.0

Scoop, Cranberry, Maple, Steel Tines & Springs, Brass Screws, T.P. On Side 220.0

Scoop, Ice Cream, Beaver Tail, Geer 135.0

Scoop, Ice Cream, Benedict Indestructo, No. 6, Red Handle 95.0

Scoop, Ice Cream, Block, Mayor 325.0

Scoop, Ice Cream, Brass, Model 31, Nickel Plated, Gilcrest 32.0

Scoop, Ice Cream, Brass, Wooden, 19th Century 195.0

Scoop, Ice Cream, Dover, Springless, Size 24 .... 125.0

Scoop, Ice Cream, Gilchrist, No. 30, Squeeze Type ....25.00 to 65.0

Scoop, Ice Cream, Gilchrist, No. 31, Wooden Handle ....35.00 to 75.0

Scoop, Ice Cream, Gilchrist, No. 33 .... 175.0

Scoop, Ice Cream, Icy, Wood Handle, Automatic Cone Co., Cambridge, Mass. 310.0

Scoop, Ice Cream, Newgen, Wood Handle, Made In U.S.A., Trenton, N.J. 50.0

Scoop, Ice Cream, Sandwich, Mayer, 12 In. 360.0

Scoop, Ice Cream, White Metal, Brass Grip, Dairy Fresh Mark, 1920s, 10 In. 25.0

Scoop, Ice Cream, White Metal, Wood Handle, Gilcest, 11 In. 30.0

Scraper, Dough, Steel & Brass, Marked P.D. 25, 1850, 4 In. 545.0

Scrubbing Stick, Red Oak, 18th Century, 15 1/2 In. 245.0

Seed Measures, Wooden, Painted Handles, 7 Colors, Milford, Conn., 7 Piece 1375.00

Shaker, Allspice, Jadite 130.00

Shaker, Ginger, White, Black, Paper Label 35.00

Shaker, Ovaltine, Aluminum 1750.00

Shaker, Paprika, White, Black, Square 30.00

Sieve, Cheese, Heart Shaped, Tin, 4 1/2 In. 203.00

Sieve, Cheese, Woven Splint, 26 In. 357.00

Sieve, Fabric Mesh, Rosehead Nails, 18th Century 95.00

Sifter, Flour, Wooden, Blood's 275.00

Skillet, Erie, No. 3 .... 30.00

Skillet, Erie, No. 12 .... 115.00

Skillet, Griswold, No. 2 .... 800.00

Skillet, Griswold, No. 8, Cover 100.00

Skillet, Griswold, No. 11 .... 125.00

Skillet, Griswold, No. 12 .... 65.00

Skillet, Griswold, No. 14, Bailed 800.00

Skillet, Griswold, No. 14, Heat Ring 150.00

Skillet, Griswold, No. 15, Oval Fish, Prototype Lid 1200.00

Skillet, Griswold, No. 20, Hotel, Large Block Erie, Pa. U.S.A. 550.00

Skillet, Wagner, No. 2 .... 125.00

Skillet, Wagner, No. 8, Heat Ring, Center Logo 55.00

Skimmer, 8 Small Hearts Punched On Handle, Penna., Early 19th Century 295.00

Skimmer, Brass Bowl, Iron Handle, Jessie Cornelius Of Union Co., 18 1/4 In. 165.00

Skimmer, Rattail Handle, Wrought Iron, Signed, J. Schmidt 1843, 19 In. 66.00

Skimmer & Ladle, Rattail Handle, Wrought Iron, 17 In. 33.00

Slicer, Bean, 4 Beans Each Time, Cast Iron & Wood 250.00

Slicer, Bean, Vaughn's, Box 35.00

Slicer, Cheese, Forged Iron, Turned Wooden Handle, 19th Century 125.00

Slicer, Cucumber, 4 Blades, Clamps To Table, Cast Iron 60.00

Slicer, Meat, Iron, Hand Crank, Sterling Slicer No. 20, Rochester, N.Y. 110.00

Spice Box, 6 Interior Sections, Mahogany, 10 1/2 In. 60.00

Spice Box, 8 Labeled Spice Boxes, Bentwood, Tin Banded, 1858 .... 325.00

Spice Box, 8 Matching Interior Canisters, Labels, Bentwood, 9 1/2 In. 192.00

Spice Box, Cherry & Mahogany, Ivory Inlay, Hearts, Diamonds, Lid, 9 x 6 1/2 In. 532.00

Spice Box, Dovetailed, Sliding Top, Zoar 295.00

Spice Box, Pegged & Nailed, Finger Lapped, Oval, 4 In. 150.00

Spice Box, Pine, Hanging, Dovetailed Drawer, 6 Compartments, Lift Lid, 11 1/2 In. 550.00
Spice Cabinet, 5 Drawers, Mahogany 375.00
Spice Cabinet, 8 Drawers, Ball Feet, Brass Pulls, 19th Century, Poplar, 10 3/4 In. 495.00
Spice Cabinet, 8 Drawers, Original Pulls, Mahogany 350.00
Spice Cabinet, Chippendale, Mahogany, Door, Drawers, England, c.1760, 7 x 7 x 9 In. . 2750.00
Spice Cabinet, Oak, Mahogany, Inlay, 8 Interior Drawers, 14 x 9 x 11 In. 715.00
Spice Chest, Pine, 6 Dovetailed Drawers, Painted Design, 14 1/2 x 6 3/4 x 9 In. 1100.00
Spice Chest, Pine, 9 Drawers, Bracket Feet, 12 1/2 x 10 1/2 In. 495.00
Spice Chest, Walnut, 16 Drawers, Porcelain Pulls, 12 x 12 3/4 x 17 1/4 In. 1475.00
Spice Set, 6 Hens Hang By Neck, Wooden Rack, 3 3/4-In. Shaker 75.00
Spice Set, Cutie Pie, Blue, With Rack, NAPCO 155.00
Spoon, Serving, Iron, Rattail Hanger, Hand Forged, 18 In. 85.00
Spoon, Tasting, Carved Design On Handle, Wooden, 18th Century, 6 1/4 In. 265.00
Spoon Holder, Prayer Lady 45.00
Spoon Rack, Scroll Cut Sides, Valanced Shelves, Red Paint, 36 Spoons, 16 x 16 1/2 In. . 137.00
Spoon Rest, Handy Flame, Ceramic, 6 1/4 In. 28.00
Spoon Rest, Prayer Lady 45.00
Spoon Rest, Woman's Face, Cleminson 14.00
Sprinkler Bottle, Black Mammy, 6 3/4 In. 130.00
Sprinkler Bottle, Chinese Man, Cleminson Art Studios 65.00
Sprinkler Bottle, Chinese Man, Holding Iron, Sprinkle Plenty . . . . 95.00 to 158.00
Sprinkler Bottle, Clothespin 250.00
Sprinkler Bottle, Clothespin, Painted Face, 8 In. 155.00
Sprinkler Bottle, Clothespin, Red 40.00
Sprinkler Bottle, Crystal, Hocking, 2 Qt. 22.00
Sprinkler Bottle, Dutch Girl 145.00
Sprinkler Bottle, Elephant, Pink & Gray 55.00
Sprinkler Bottle, Elephant, Trunk Straight Up 85.00
Sprinkler Bottle, Hand-Painted Floral, Red 45.00
Sprinkler Bottle, Mammy, 7 In. 495.00
Sprinkler Bottle, Pig, Crazing, 7 1/2 In. 90.00
Sprinkler Bottle, Poodle, Gray, Cardinal 120.00
Sprinkler Bottle, Sadiron, Woman Ironing 75.00
Sprinkler Bottle, Siamese Cat, Tan 150.00
Squeezer, Lard, Wrought Hinges 60.00
Squeezer, Lemon, Metal Box Type, Pat. May 3, '81 . . . . 19.00
String Holder, 6 Black Women 145.00
String Holder, Apple, Chalkware 60.00
String Holder, Apple, Red Berries 65.00
String Holder, Apple, Worm 85.00
String Holder, Baby Face, Chalkware 95.00
String Holder, Beehive, Ceramic 30.00
String Holder, Boxer 150.00
String Holder, Cat . . . . 40.00 to 95.00
String Holder, Cat's Head . . . . 45.00 to 75.00
String Holder, Cat, Chalkware . . . . 75.00 to 85.00
String Holder, Cat, England 65.00
String Holder, Cat, String Out Of Paw 148.00
String Holder, Chef, Chalkware . . . . 60.00 to 75.00
String Holder, Dutch Girl, Blue Dots 85.00
String Holder, Fox, Pottery 90.00
String Holder, Frog On Shell, Ceramic, Countertop, Japan 65.00
String Holder, Girl & Boy, Pair 160.00
String Holder, Granny, Fitz & Floyd, 1978 . . . . 80.00
String Holder, Housewife 40.00
String Holder, I Hate Housework 160.00
String Holder, Kitten, Holding Ball Of String, 6 In. 55.00
String Holder, Little Girl, Finger To Mouth, Chalkware 85.00
String Holder, Mammy, Blue & White Dress 185.00
String Holder, Mammy, Full-Bodied, Composition 120.00
String Holder, Mammy, Ty-Me 395.00
String Holder, Man With Top Hat & Pipe, 9 In. 65.00

String Holder, Mexican Man, Chalkware . . . . .60.00 to 65.00

String Holder, Mouse 30.00

String Holder, Mouse & Owl 65.00

String Holder, Prayer Lady, Enesco 195.00

String Holder, Pumpkin Face 158.00

String Holder, Sailor, Chalkware 70.00

String Holder, Soldier Boy, Chalkware 75.00

String Holder, Spaniel Dog's Head 65.00

String Holder, Victorian Lady 95.00

String Holder, Wishing Well 55.00

String Holder, Witch In Pumpkin 200.00

String Holder, Woman In Chair 158.00

String Holder, Woman, Flowered Dress . . . . .150.00 to 160.00

String Holder, Woman, Mexican, Comb, Flower 150.00

Sugar Block Cutter, Imbed Spike, Chip With Hatchet, Marked, 18th Century, 13 In. 190.00

Sugar Devil, Hand Forged, Wood Handle, 16 1/2 In. 230.00

Tamale Warmer, Copper, 17 x 14 In. 298.00

Teakettle, Griswold, Cast Aluminum, 6 Qt. 85.00

Teakettle, Iron, Bail Handle, Late 18th Century, 7 x 6 1/2 In. 295.00

Teakettle, Iron, Willow Tree & Rain Design, Relief Frog, Japan 225.00

Teapot, Aladdin, Jewel T 45.00

Teapot, Iron, Relief Scene, Boatmen Over Rolling Waves, Bronze Cover & Handle, 8 In. 165.00

Teapot, Prayer Lady, Blue . . . . .80.00 to 90.00

Tester, Cheese, Late 18th Century, 7 1/2 In. 80.00

Tie Press, Handle, Leckie, Graham & Co., Glasgow, 17 1/4 In. 11.00

Timer, Egg, Black Chef, Germany 65.00

Timer, Egg, Pennsylvania Dutch Girl On Bench 35.00

Timer, Prayer Lady 60.00

Toaster, Electric, Side Loader, Series 687, c.1930 . . . . 35.00

Toaster, Electric, Single Slice, MOD1A4, McGraw Toastmaster, c.1930 . . . . 60.00

Toaster, Electric, Style No. 1101, Dominion Electric Mfg., c.1930 . . . . 45.00

Toaster, Estate, Model 77, Swing Toast Holders 150.00

Toaster, Flip, Iron, With Maple Handle, c.1800, 26 1/2 x 12 1/2 In. 245.00

Toaster, Hand, Iron, American, Mid-18th Century, 9 1/4 In. 285.00

Toaster, Radiant Control, 2-Slice, Chrome, Electric, Sunbeam, 11 x 6 x 7 In. 20.00

Toaster, Samson 50.00

Toaster, Toastmaster, Chrome 35.00

Toaster, Toastmaster, Model LB14, Chrome, Black Bakelite Handles 70.00

Toaster, Wire, Folds Over, Double Handles, 9 x 10 In. 68.00

Toaster, With Toaster Oven, Dual Controls, Chromed Metal, General Electric, 12 x 6 In. . 37.00

Trivet, Iron, Child's, Cast Iron, Wooden Handle 85.00

Utensil Rack, Wrought Iron, 19th Century, 53 x 29 In. 330.00

Wafer Iron, Seal Of United States, Germany, c.1800, 5 1/4 In. 546.00

Waffle Iron, Electric, Manning-Bowman, 1920s 15.00

Waffle Iron, Forged, c.1840, 28 5/8 In.-Handles, 5 x 8 In.-Batter Bed 160.00

Waffle Iron, Griswold, No. 7, Button Hinge, Patent Date 1880 . . . . .89.00 to 115.00

Waffle Iron, Griswold, No. 8 . . . . 80.00

Waffle Iron, Griswold, No. 9 . . . . 45.00

Waffle Iron, Manning-Bowman, Double 100.00

Waffle Iron, Winchester 325.00

Waffle Iron Set, Griddle, Fry Pan, Cast Iron, Wagner-Ware, Child's, 4 Piece 115.00

Washboard, Bristol Glaze, Bull's-Eye Cobalt Design 575.00

Washboard, Enamel, Soap Saver, NRS Member, We Do Our Part 120.00

Washboard, Graniteware, Cobalt Blue 70.00

Washboard, Mother Hubbard 225.00

Washboard, National 30.00

Washboard, Pitsawn Birch, Soap Tray, 12 1/8 x 18 7/8 In. 120.00

Washboard, Redware Insert, Albany Slip 575.00

Washboard, Soapsaver, Cobalt Blue 110.00

Washboard, Wooden, 25 In. 230.00

Washing Machine, Hand Operated, Red Paint, 1880s 184.00

Washing Machine, Stove Top, Drum Type, 1886 . . . . 250.00

Wick Trimmers, Steel, England, c.1690-1720, 6 In. 165.00

KNIFE collectors usually specialize in a single type. In the 1960s, the United States government passed a law that required knife manufacturers to mark their knives with the country of origin. This seemed to encourage the collectors, and knife collecting became an interest of a large group of people. All types of knives are collected, from top quality twentieth-century examples to old bone- or pearl-handled knives in excellent condition.

Belt, Trapper, Carved Bone Haft, 7 7/8-In. Blade	180.00
Blubber, Steel Blade, c.1880, 28 In.	185.00
Bowie, Antler Handle	195.00
Bowie, Collins Blade No. 18, Wood Handle, Eagle Shaped Pommel, 9-In. Blade	39.00
Bowie, Edward Barnes, 8 1/2-In. Blade	3000.00
Bowie, Etched, Woodhead Howard St. Sheffield, Gold Rush Era	1600.00
Bowie, Handmade, Brass Guard, Thick Hide-Wrapped Haft, 10 In.	285.00
Bowie, Horn & German Silver Mounts, 9-In. Blade	2750.00
Bowie, Iron Ferrule, Wooden Grip, Confederate, 10 3/4-In. Blade	875.00
Bowie, IXL, S-Guard, 8 1/2-In. Blade	2750.00
Bowie, Stag Haft, Pistol & Heart, Sheffield, 6 In.	210.00
Bowie, Wooden Plaque, Long Blade	175.00
Bowie Style, Fighting, Handmade, W. Marples & Sons, Brass Guard, Horn Haft	240.00
Buck, Budweiser, Box, 1992, 9 In.	68.00
Butcher's, J. Russell Green River, 15 In.	185.00
Butcher's, Winchester, 7 In.	47.50
Colonial Skinner, Curved Blade, Carved Wood Hat, Pewter Ferrule, 5 3/8 In.	165.00
Curved, Made From Horseshoe, One End Sharpened Into Blade, Hand Forged, 6 In.	54.00
Dagger, Continental, North Country, Steel, 16th Century, 13 3/4 In.	373.00
Dagger, Luftwaffe, Medallion Pommel, Leather & Wire Wrapped Handle, 12 In.	192.00
Dagger, Sheath, Steel, No. 6, Brass Guards, Buffalo Horn Grips, Sheffield, 19th Century	40.00
Dirk, Brass Guard, Bone Handle, Brass & Pewter Spacers, 9 5/8 In.	230.00
Esso Standard Oil, Gas Pump Shape, Metal, 2 7/8 In.	60.00
Fish, Blue Marbleized Plastic Handle, 9 In.	12.00
Folding, Buck, No. 110, Wood Grips, Brass Fittings, Leather Pouch, Belt Loop, 5 In.	60.00
Folding, Case, Hammerhead, Shark On Blade, Wood Grip, Leather Sheath, Box, 1978	59.00
Folding, Case, Pattern 6227, 2 Blades, Simulated Stag Grips, 1976	23.00
Folding, Sod Buster Jr., Black Composition Grips, Plow On Blade, 1977	24.00
Folding, Ulster, Stag Grips, 1930s, 4 In.	30.00
GAR, Button End Cap, Bone Handle, Brass Fittings, 5 1/2-In. Blade	170.00
Hart Batteries, Leather Pouch, 3 5/8 In.	22.00
Hide Scraper, C.S. Osborne & Co., Half Moon Shaped, Steel, Leather Sheath, 3 x 5 In.	25.00
Hunting, Stag Handle, Metal Knobbed Pummel Cap, Black Leather Sheath, 10 In.	70.00
Hunting, Utility, Double Edge Blade, Wood Grip, Brown Leather Scabbard, 17 In.	30.00
Hunting, XX Rio Grande Camp Knife, Bowie Style Blade, Leather Sheath, 15 In.	87.00
Jack, Max Rosinstock, Sioux City, Iowa	16.00
Jack, Remington, Pearl Handle, No. 6484	60.00
Kelly, Civil War, 10-In. Blade	450.00
Machete, Horn Grip, Form Of Horse Head, Tooled Leather Sheath, 28 In.	80.00
National Hunting Association, Germany, 1933	1100.00
Novelty, Pen Shape, Aluminum, Sides Open To Reveal 4-In. Blade	43.00
Paper, Dog-Headed Sea Monster On Handle, Wooden, 8 1/4 In.	425.00
Pen, Case, Pattern 3201, Yellow Celluloid Grips, 1973	26.00
Pig Sticker, Handmade, Brass Guard & Band, Mahogany Haft, 5 7/8 In.	140.00
Pocket, Bathing Beauty, Bronze, Art Nouveau	70.00
Pocket, Budweiser, Clydesdales, Box, 1970s, 3 1/2 In.	40.00
Pocket, CKO, Orange & Black Rippled Plastic Grip, 2 Blades	5.00
Pocket, Coors Beer	14.00
Pocket, J. Nowil & Sons, Black Grips, 2 Blades, Sheffield, England, 3 1/2 In.	24.00
Pocket, John Deere Implements, Salesman's Sample, Pearlized Sides, 3 1/4 In.	30.00
Pocket, Kent N.Y. City, 2 Blades, Clear Plastic Handle	10.00
Pocket, L.L. Bean, Push Button, Striated Celluloid Grips, Leather Case, After 1916	172.00
Pocket, Mother-Of-Pearl, Gold, Signed George Dobson	75.00
Pocket, Old King Beer, With Bottle Opener & Corkscrew, 1930s	30.00
Pocket, Planter's Peanuts, White Celluloid Grips, Colonial, Prov., R.I.	20.00
Pocket, Shell Oil, Celluloid Grips, 2 Blades, File, Scissors, Germany, 1930s, 2 3/4 In.	20.00

Pocket, Space Shuttle, Enamel 65.00
Saber, Memelluke, Officer's, Horn Grips, Pigskin Over Wood Scabbard, 1801, 28 In. ... 985.00
Schrade, French Ivory, 5 In. 48.00
Shell, Mileage Is Our Business, With Scissors, 3 3/8 In. 55.00
Skinning, Bone Handle, Buffalo & Elk Scrimshaw Handle 185.00
Star Brand Shoe 55.00
Steak, White Celluloid, Set Of 6 .... 33.00
Sterling Silver, Allover Deep Engraved, Pocket 75.00
Swiss Army, 4 Blades, Black Handle, 3 3/4 In. 55.00
Trench, Knuckle Guard, Scabbard, U.S. 1918, 12 1/4 In. 110.00
Utility, Chip Carved Handle, R.W., Brass Wire, 10 In. 495.00
Wooden Handle, Form Of Fleur-De-Lis, Man With Human Head, 12 In. 1505.00
Woodsman's, Patch Cutter, Bone Handle 125.00

KNOWLES, TAYLOR & KNOWLES items may be found in the KTK and Lotus Ware categories.

KOREAN WARE, see Sumida.

KOSTA, the oldest Swedish glass factory, was founded in 1742. During the 1920s through the 1950s, many pieces of original design were made at the factory. The firm is still working.

KOSTA

Bowl, Opalescent, Signed, 4 3/4 x 9 1/2 In. 175.00
Candlestick, Lindstrand, Large, Pair 295.00
Decanter, Pheasant, Carved Feathers, Head Stopper, Vicke Lindstrand, 8 1/4 x 8 In. 402.00
Figurine, Cat, Frosted, 3 1/2 In. 65.00
Figurine, Dinosaur, P. Huff 150.00
Figurine, Whale, Etched Eye, Baleen At Mouth, Signed, 20th Century, 18 In. 80.00
Plate, Raised Madonna & Child, Gold, Cobalt Blue, Signed 85.00
Prism, Clowns, Vicke Lindstrand, 1960s 2000.00
Vase, After The Bath, Vicke Lindstrand, 1955 .... 650.00
Vase, Applied Disk Foot, Wing Type Handles 11.00
Vase, Blue & Red, 10 In. 800.00
Vase, Boda, Blue Trees, Blue Birds, Cameo, 8 3/4 x 4 5/8 In. 150.00
Vase, Clear, Blue Internal Layer, Cut Optic Windows, Paper Label, 6 1/2 In. 440.00
Vase, Clear, Internal Bubble, Surround Amethyst Swirl, Vicke Lindstrand, 1950s, 8 In. .. 110.00
Vase, Flattened Teardrop Shape, Blue Interior, Vicke Lindstrand, 1962-1963, 5 3/4 In. ... 265.00
Vase, Gray, Blue, Purple, Vicke Lindstrand, 1959, 6 1/2 In. 358.00
Vase, Internal Mauve Stripes To Depict Fish Net, Signed, 5 1/4 In. 287.00
Vase, Multicolored Shards, Bertil Vallien, 6 3/4 In. 316.00
Vase, Purple Internal Spirals, Vicke Lindstrand, 10 In. 330.00
Vase, Rose Bowl Sphere, Raised Stylized Floral Panels, 4 x 7 In. 489.00
Vase, Striations, Balluen, 5 1/2 x 5 1/2 In. 55.00
Vase, Stylized Base, Square, Vicke Lindstrand, 11 x 4 In. 990.00
Vase, Teal Blue, Circular Facets, Vicke Lindstrand, 4 1/4 x 6 1/2 In. 575.00
Vase, Teardrop Form, Girl, Skipping Rope, Vicke Lindstrand, 6 In. 33.00
Vase, Trees In The Fog, Black Tree Forms, White Design, Vicke Lindstrand, 1950s, 9 In. . 1430.00
Vase, Vallien, Pink, 2 In. 40.00
Vase, Wheel-Cut, Bright Emerald Green, Circle Interior, 6 1/4 In. 288.00

KPM refers to Berlin porcelain, but the same initials were used alone and in combination with other symbols by several German porcelain makers. They include the Konigliche Porzellan Manufaktur of Berlin, initials used in mark, 1823–1847; Meissen, 1723–1724 only; Krister Porzellan Manufaktur in Waldenburg, after 1831; Kranichfelder Porzellan Manufaktur in Kranichfeld, after 1903; and the Kister Porzellan Manufaktur in Scheibe, after 1838.

K.P.M

Candlestick, 2 Putti, Fluted Columnar Shafts, Gold Trim, Scepter Mark, 12 In., Pair 1210.00
Chocolate Pot, Art Deco, Peacock Eyes, Signed, 9 In. 135.00
Creamer, Porcelain, White Paste, Gold Overlay, 1825-1850, 6 1/2 In. 11.00
Cup, Lid, Scene From Opera On Side, 3 3/4 In. 100.00
Cup, Picture From Bartered Bride On Side, Gold Rim, 3 3/4 In., Pair 150.00
Cup & Saucer, Cover, Overall Gilt Design, Cobalt Ground, Porcelain, 5 1/2 In. 345.00
Dish, Lobster, Pink Luster 150.00

Figurine, 4 Elements, Putto, Fire, Water, Earth & Air, Scepter Mark, 8 In., 4 Piece 1760.00
Figurine, Poodle, 7 1/2 In. 45.00
Figurine, Woman, Flower In Hair, Signed, 3 3/4 In. 525.00
Figurine, Young Lady, Empire Style Dress, Hat & Fan, Signed, 8 1/2 In. 175.00
Figurine, Young Man, Cocked Hat, Long Coat, Signed, 8 1/2 In. 175.00
Jar, Potpourri, Pierced Cover, Fluted, Cobalt Blue, Gold Trim, Scepter Mark, 4 1/2 In. ... 605.00
Lithophane, see also Lithophane category.
Plaque, 20 People Enjoying Outing, Wooded Mountain, Signed, 7 1/2 x 9 7/8 In. 5950.00
Plaque, Konigin Louise, Carved & Gilded Frame, 9 1/2 x 6 1/4 In. 2035.00
Plaque, Maiden, Reading, Signed, Late 19th Century, 9 1/2 x 6 1/4 In. 1610.00
Plaque, Marguerite, After Berraud, Porcelain, c.1890, 12 7/8 x 7 3/4 In. 3105.00
Plaque, Portrait, Girl In White, Oval, 8 1/2 x 6 1/4 In. 1430.00
Plaque, Sorrowful Magdalene, Facing Heaven, Signed, 10 1/2 In. 3750.00
Plaque, Virgin Mary, Eyes Averted Upward, Signed, 20.12.99, 8 1/2 In. 980.00
Plate, Cake, Floral Design, Signed, 12 In. 65.00
Teakettle, Polychrome Floral Design, Stand, Germany, 14 In. 374.00
Vase, Cobalt Blue, 18 In. 75.00

KTK are the initials of the Knowles, Taylor & Knowles Company of East Liverpool, Ohio, founded by Isaac W. Knowles in 1853. The company made many types of utilitarian wares, hotel china, and dinnerwares. They made the fine bone china known as Lotus Ware from 1891 to 1896. The company merged with American Ceramic Corporation in 1928. It closed in 1934. Lotus Ware is listed in its own category in this book.

K.T.&K.
CHINA

Jug, Diamond Club Whiskey 115.00

KU KLUX KLAN items are now collected because of their historic importance. Literature, robes, and memorabilia are available. The Klan is still in existence, so new material is found.

Book, Exposed, Klansmen On Cover, 1922 .... 40.00
Booklet, Women's Membership, Rally At Roswell Public Park, 1920, 6 x 9 In. 49.00
Broadside, For Klan Field Day, Red On White, Auburn, N.Y., 9 x 12 In. 65.00
Candy Container, Hooded Robe, 1920s 825.00
Document, Charter Honor, Imperial Palace Invisible Empire Knights 875.00
Dues Notice, Exalted Cyclops, Red, Black, 1928, 7 1/2 x 11 In. 83.00
Medal, Hero Cross, Head Of KKK Founder, 1866, 1 1/4 x 1/4 In. 165.00
Paperweight, Ball, One Flag, One School, Red Schoolhouse, 3 1/2 In. 475.00
Penny, Elongated, 1944 Penny, Slogan, KKK For God Race & Country 41.00
Photograph, Klan Preacher, Child In Robe, Press Photo, 1920s, 8 x 10 In. 85.00
Pin, With Bell, Ladies Of Klan 575.00
Record, Dear Mr. President-Veteran's Plea, Happy Fats, 45 RPM, 1960s 57.00
Record, Flight NAACP 105-The Voice Of Alabama, Son Of Mississippi, 1960s 57.00
Robe, Hood, Cape, Belt, Patch 450.00
Robe, Yellow Cross, Child's 410.00
Uniform, c.1930 .... 50.00

KUTANI ware is a Japanese porcelain made after the mid-seventeenth century. Most of the pieces found today are nineteenth-century. Collectors often use the term *kutani* to refer to just the later, colorful pieces decorated with red, gold, and black pictures of warriors, animals, and birds.

Bowl, Bronze, Green Patina, Yi Dynasty, 5 x 7 In. 578.00
Bowl, Conical, Foliate, Green, Black Exterior, Mustard-Yellow, Green Interior, 6 In. 2300.00
Bowl, Cover, Floral & Fowl Design, Bamboo Top Handle, 8 1/4 In. 110.00
Bowl, Cover, Ring About The Cover, Raised Foot, Silver, Bronze, Koryo Dynasty, 6 In. ... 176.00
Bowl, Deep Coin Relief Design Exterior, Bronze, 19th Century, 3 3/4 In. 46.00
Bowl, Gilt Figures, 9 1/4 x 3 1/4 In. 165.00
Bowl, Raised Leaf Design On Exterior, Celadon, 7 In. 660.00
Bowl, Roses, Hand Painted, Gold Design, Marked, Japanese Chop Mark, 8 3/4 In. 11.00
Bowl, Scattered Floral Design, White, Celadon, Koryo Dynasty, 7 1/2 In. 605.00
Bowl, Tea, Temmoku Glaze, Sung Dynasty, 4 5/8 In. 440.00
Box, Cover, Wood Storage, Brass Fish Form Lock, Cylindrical, 12 In. 65.00

Charger, Robed Warrior Carrying A Sword, Beneath Pine Tree, Pink, Brown, 15 In. 127.00
Charger, Samurai, Mounted, On The Shore, Floral Panels, Red Ground, 17 3/4 In. 201.00
Cup & Saucer, Butterfly, Floral Design, Marked, 19th Century 44.00
Dish, Flat, Raised Bird, Floral Design, Gilt Landscape, Lacquered, 11 1/2 In. 58.00
Dish, Green, Aubergine Enamel Leaf Design, Brown Crackle, Ivory Ground, 9 In. 3220.00
Dish, Peach Shape, Porcelain, 5 1/4 In. 77.00
Dish, Saucer, Pheasant, Perched On Bamboo, Blue Underglaze, 8 1/4 In. 1265.00
Jar, Bamboo Design, Red Glaze, Globular, Yi Dynasty, 4 In. 330.00
Jar, Black, Brown Glaze, Honan, Globular, Sung Dynasty, 5 1/4 In. 165.00
Jar, Peony Design, Blue, White, Globular, 19th Century, 6 In. 3190.00
Jar, Tea, Karako & Flowers, Red, 6 In. 88.00
Rose Jar, Floral Pattern, Marked, Late 19th Century, 5 1/4 In. 120.00
Teapot, Lohan Design, Skirted Form, 6 1/2 In. 110.00
Vase, Applied Foo Dogs, 12 Round Figural Reserves, Converted To Lamp, Baluster 185.00
Vase, Applied Foo Dogs, Rings & Rope, Courtyard Figures, Tapering Cylindrical, 12 In. . 110.00
Vase, Bottle Shape, Ashes-Of-Roses, Teakwood Stand, Lavender Crystal Finial, 7 In. 104.00
Vase, Bottle Shape, Sunspot, Pickled Gold Patina Exterior, 11 In. 345.00
Vase, Bottle, Black Underglaze, Koryo Dynasty, 11 In. 935.00
Vase, Dragon, Turquoise Glaze, 19th Century, 24 In. 99.00
Vase, Gray, White Glaze, Choson Period, 19th Century, 10 1/2 In. 172.50
Vase, Incised Crane Design, Meiping Form, 1900, 10 1/2 In. 137.50
Vase, Moss Green, Teakwood Stand, Lavender Rock Crystal Finial, 8 In. 149.50
Vase, Raised Polychrome Design, 19th Century, 17 In. 121.00
Vase, Seated Elders, Gold & Enamel, c.1900, 12 1/4 In. 70.00
Vase, White Glaze, Carved Wooden Stand, 20th Century, 11 In. 110.00
Vase, Woodland Pond, Swans, Raised Gold Floral Enamel, 18 In. 154.00

LACQUER is a type of varnish. Collectors are most interested in the Chinese and Japanese lacquer wares made from the Japanese varnish tree. Lacquer wares are made from wood with many coats of lacquer. Sometimes the piece is carved or decorated with ivory or metal inlay.

Box, Dome Top, Mother-Of-Pearl, Korea, 20th Century, Round, 13 x 6 1/2 In. 121.00
Box, Painted Armored Knight On Horseback, Russia, 1973, 3 x 4 In. 165.00
Box, Peony & Butterfly, Black & Gold, 12 1/4 x 10 1/2 In. 935.00
Box, Wedding, Gilt Design, Red, China, Late 19th Century 155.00
Box, Writing, Fish & Fruit Design, 10 3/4 In. 187.00
Card Case, Black, Storming Palace At Monterey, Decoupage, 5 3/8 In. 575.00
Case, Lily Exterior, Butterfly Interior, Black, Gold, Early 20th Century, 9 1/2 In. 135.00
Tray, Chinese Scenes, Black, Gilt, China, 23 In. 170.00
Tray, Gold Peacocks & Peonies, Gold Mashiji Ground, 15 1/2 x 23 1/2 In. 220.00

LADY HEAD VASE, see Head Vase.

LALIQUE glass was made by Rene Lalique in Paris, France, between the 1890s and his death in 1945. The glass was molded, pressed, and engraved in Art Nouveau and Art Deco styles. Pieces were marked with the signature *R. Lalique*. Lalique glass is still being made. Pieces made after 1945 bear the mark *Lalique*. Jewelry made by Rene Lalique is listed in the Jewelry category.

LaLiQue

Ashtray, Koi Fish Motif, France, 4 In. 115.00
Atomizer, Cariatides, Females, Standing Hand In Hand, Gilt Metal 675.00
Bookends, Tete D'aigle, Frosted Eagle, Head Mounted On Stepped Base, 4 3/4 In. 862.00
Bowl, Champs-Elysees, Leaf Form, 1960, 18 In. 460.00
Bowl, Gui No. 2, Mistletoe Berries, Branches, Opalescent, After 1921, 8 In. 410.00
Bowl, Margeurites, Daisy Pattern, Raised Rim, Low, 13 1/4 In. 489.00
Bowl, Martigues, Fish, 1930s, 14 1/2 In. 2530.00
Bowl, Nemours, 10 In. 460.00
Bowl, Nemours, Flower Heads, Intaglio, Blue, Enameled, Stained, Frosted, 10 In. 986.00
Bowl, Perruches, Frieze Of Parakeets Amid Branches, Signed, 1931, 9 1/8 In. 2300.00
Bowl, Pinsons, Finches, Foliate Motif, Acid-Stamped, 1947-1951, 9 1/4 In. 272.00
Bowl, Poissons No. 1, Spiral Fish, Frosted, Opalescent, After 1931, 11 1/2 In. 410.00
Box, Cover, Primeveres, Wild Roses, Frosted, Opalescent, After 1927, Round, 6 1/4 In. . . 986.00
Carafe, Masques, Male Mask, Pink, Brown Patina, Silver Metal Stopper, 12 In. 2587.00

Centerpiece, 2 Love Birds, With Spread Wings, Plant Frog In Center, 8 1/4 In. 373.00
Centerpiece, Bammako 1045.00
Centerpiece, Fish, Frosted Glass, Signed, 1950s 2350.00
Chandelier, Charmes, Domed Shade, Leaf Design, Frosted, Molded, R. Lalique, 13 In. . . . 4600.00
Clock, Cinq Hirondelles, 5 Swallows Amidst Leafy Branches, Navy Blue, 1920, 6 In. . . . 4025.00
Dish, Swan Form, 4 In. 82.00
Figurine, Bamara, Seated Lion, Signed, 8 1/4 In. 550.00
Figurine, Caroline, Turtle Form, 5 3/4 In. 143.00
Figurine, Gregoire, Frog, Green . . . . .250.00 to 275.00
Figurine, Kneeling Nude, Stretching Backward, 5 In. 258.00
Figurine, Salamandre, Salamander, Green 250.00
Hood Ornament, Eagle Head, Clear & Frosted, Signed, 4 In. 395.00
Hood Ornament, Grande Libellule, Dragonfly, Signed, After 1928, 8 1/8 In. 2875.00
Hood Ornament, Hirondelle, Swallow, Signed, 6 In. 650.00
Hood Ornament, Tete D'aigle, Eagle Head, 4 1/2 In. 630.00
Hood Ornament, Tete D'aigle, Stylized Feathered Eagle Head, Signed, 1928, 4 1/2 In. . . 1380.00
Hood Ornament, Victoire, Maiden's Head, Windswept Hair, After 1928, 10 1/8 In. 6575.00
Lamp, 6-Light, Leaf Motif, Applied 6 Leaves, Chrome Frame, Rods, 17 1/2 In. 4025.00
Lamp, Fabric Shade, Gold Hardware, Frosted Doves On Base, Signed, 15 In. 1995.00
Lamp, Perfume, Band Of Doves, Frosted & Clear, Signed, 5 1/2 In. 395.00
Lighter, Lion, Lion's Head Motif Design, Crystal, Etched, 4 1/2 x 4 In. 1100.00
Paperweight, Chouette, Owl, Clear Frost, Incised Lalique France, 3 1/2 In. 192.00
Paperweight, Coq Nain, Rooster Form, Clear, 8 In. 145.00
Paperweight, Sanglier, Wild Boar, Clear Frost, Incised Lalique France, 2 3/4 In. 120.00
Paperweight, Tete D'aigle, Eagle Head 500.00
Perfume Bottle, Amphitrite, Colorless, Nautilus Seashell Shape, Signed, 3 3/4 In. 1092.00
Perfume Bottle, Band Of Nude Figures, Amid Foliage, 24K Gold Plated, 4 1/2 In. 5750.00
Perfume Bottle, Coeur Joie, Nina Ricci, Open Heart Shape, 5 In. . . . . .275.00 to 285.00
Perfume Bottle, Coty, Bee Above A Vessel, Pale Blue Glass, Stopper, 2 3/4 In. 2070.00
Perfume Bottle, L'Air Du Temps, Dove Swirl, Factice, Signed, Unopened, 13 In. 895.00
Perfume Bottle, L'Air Du Temps, Swirl, Signed, Sealed Box 675.00
Perfume Bottle, Pomme, Leaf Stopper, 5 In. 339.00
Plate, Annual, 1965, Paper Label, France, 8 1/4 In. 440.00
Plate, Annual, 1966, Paper Label, France, 8 1/4 In. 55.00
Plate, Annual, 1969, Box 67.00
Plate, Annual, 1975, 2 Goldfish, In Presentation Box, 1975, 8 1/2 In. 86.00
Plate, Volutes, Spiral Design, Signed, 10 1/2 In. 1188.00
Platter, Martigues, Scalloped, 10 In. 515.00
Vase, Archers, Birds, Baluster Form, Clear & Frosted, Signed, 10 1/2 In. 3735.00
Vase, Bacchantes, Band Of Nude Female Figures Dancing About, Brown, 1927, 10 In. . . 5750.00
Vase, Bammako, Cabochons, Frosted, Opalescent, Signed, After 1934, 7 1/8 In. 2300.00
Vase, Biches, Deer Herd, Foliage, Cobalt Blue, Stamped, 1932, 6 1/2 In. 1840.00
Vase, Biches, Deer In Various Poses Amidst Wild Flowers, Acid-Stamped, 1951, 6 In. . . . 220.00
Vase, Borromee, Overlapping Peacock Heads, Ovoid, Signed, 9 1/4 In. 4025.00
Vase, Ceylan, 4 Pairs Of Lovebirds, Perched On Branches, Signed, 9 In. . . . . . .4370.00 to 4627.00
Vase, Ceylan, 8 Parakeets, Frosted, Opalescent, Signed, After 1924, 16 1/2 In. 2630.00
Vase, Chamois, Antelope In Relief, Amber Stained, 1931, Signed, 4 7/8 In. 2300.00
Vase, Claude, Flared Lobed Base, Etched, 13 3/4 In. 357.50
Vase, Coqs Et Plumes, Frosted Oval, 12 Strutting Cock Roosters, Signed, 6 1/4 In. 920.00
Vase, Coqs Et Raisins, Cockerels, Vines, Frosted, Blue Stained, After 1928, 6 1/8 In. . . . 904.00
Vase, Cover, Tourterelles, Pair Of Lovebirds Amidst Foliage, 1925, 11 1/4 In. 6900.00
Vase, Dahlias, Overlapping Flower Heads, Black Wash Center, Signed, 5 In. 1610.00
Vase, Danaides, Female Nudes Pouring Water, Blue, Opalescent, R. Lalique, 7 1/4 In. . . . 2875.00
Vase, Danaides, Female Nudes Pouring Water, Green Patina, 7 In. 977.00
Vase, Danaides, Female Nudes Pouring Water, Opalescent, 1926, 7 In. 2300.00
Vase, Escargot, Snail Design, Blue, Signed, 8 1/4 In. 4900.00
Vase, Ferrieres, 5 Rings Of Flowers, Blue Patina, 1929, 6 5/8 In. 977.00
Vase, Formose, Fish, Red, Frosted, Spherical, Intaglio Signed, After 1924, 6 5/8 In. 6165.00
Vase, Gui, Pattern Of Mistletoe Leaves, Berries, Deep Green, 1920, 6 5/8 In. 4600.00
Vase, Ivoines, Peonies, Recessed Areas With Sepia Patina, Signed, 10 1/2 In. 5520.00
Vase, Lievres, Band Of Leaping Rabbits, Scrolled Ferns, Spherical, 1923, 6 1/4 In. 1265.00
Vase, Montlhery, Rows Of Inverted Arches, Signed, 1926, 5 1/2 In. 3680.00
Vase, Ormeaux, Frosted Sphere, Overlapping Leaves, Signed, 6 5/8 In. 488.00

Vase, Ornis, Chalice Form, 2 Birds, Smoky Topaz, Wheel-Carved R. Lalique, 7 1/2 In. . . 1150.00

Vase, Oursin, Horizontal Bands Of Various Prunts, Spherical, 1935, 7 In. 546.00

Vase, Penthievre, Deep Amber, Stylized Fish, 1928, 10 1/8 In. 6325.00

Vase, Pierrefonds, Scrolling Thorny Handles, Gray, 1926, 6 1/8 In. 4600.00

Vase, Raisins, Grapes On Scrolled Vines, Tapered, Cylindrical, 1928, 6 1/4 In. 1610.00

Vase, Rampillon, Frosted, Opalescent, Sienna Stained, After 1927, 5 1/8 In. 822.00

Vase, Ronces, Branches, Butterscotch, Opalescent, Signed, After 1921, 9 1/2 In. 1645.00

LAMPS of every type, from the early oil-burning Betty and Phoebe lamps to the recent electric lamps with glass or beaded shades, interest collectors. Fuels used in lamps changed through the years; whale oil (1800–1840), camphene (1828), Argand (1830), lard (1833–1863), turpentine and alcohol (1840s), gas (1850–1879), kerosene (1860), and electricity (1879) are the most common. Other lamps are listed by manufacturer or type of material.

Advertising, Charlie Tuna, 1970 . . . . 125.00

Aladdin, B-70, Solitaire, White Moonstone, 1938 . . . . 3500.00

Aladdin, B-76S, Tall Lincoln Drape, Alacite, 1940-1949 . . . . 2250.00

Aladdin, B-77F, Tall, Lincoln Drape, Alacite, Ruby Crystal 575.00

Aladdin, B-83, Beehive, Ruby Crystal, 1937 . . . . 600.00

Aladdin, B-91, Quilt, White Moonstone Font, Rose Moonstone Foot, 1937 . . . . 375.00

Aladdin, B-111, Cathedral, Green Moonstone, 1934-1935 . . . . 180.00

Aladdin, B-115AG, Corinthian, Green Moonstone, Jade, 1935-1936 . . . . 180.00

Aladdin, B-121, Majestic, Rose Moonstone, 1935-1936 . . . . 450.00

Aladdin, B-122, Majestic, Green Moonstone, 1935-1936 . . . . 425.00

Aladdin, B-133, Oriental, Silver Plate, 1935-1936 . . . . 250.00

Aladdin, E-302, Peach 250.00

Aladdin, G-16, Alacite 600.00

Aladdin, G-24, Cupid, Alacite . . . . 400.00 to 450.00

Aladdin, Oil, Leaded Glass Shade, Cast Iron Base, 24 In. 415.00

Argand, Brass, 1-Light, 2 Tiers Of Crystal Prisms, J. & I. Cox, Electrified, 23 In., Pair . . 2800.00

Argand, Patinated Bronze, Labeled Alfred Welles & Co., 1850s, 16 In. 805.00

Astral, 2 Arms, Brass, Clear Shades, Prisms, Marble, Electrified, 20 3/4 In., Pair 990.00

Astral, Blue Cut To White To Red, Brass Base & Font, Stepped Marble, Prisms, 28 In. . . . 2860.00

Astral, Brass, Marble Base, Glass Shade, Etched, Faceted Prisms, 26 In. 500.00

Astral, Brass, Marble Base, Glass Shade, Etched, Faceted Prisms, 33 1/2 In. 2500.00

Astral, Burner Removed, Electric Socket Added, Frosted Globe, 18 1/4 In. 121.00

Astral, Cornelius & Baker, Brass, Stepped Marble Base, Prisms, Electrified, 19 1/2 In. . . 605.00

Astral, Gilded Brass & Marble, Clear Cut Prisms, Frosted Shade, 20th Century, 24 1/2 In. 2275.00

Astral, Gilt, Fluted Columnar Support, Baluster Shade, 19th Century, 32 In. 605.00

Astral, Gilt, Original Oil Burner, Sans Shade, Baluster, 1840, 18 In. 1540.00

Astral, Kerosene, Cut Prisms, Clear Globe, Cornelius Label, 25 1/2 In. 440.00

Betty, Copper, Hanger, 4 1/4 In. 135.00

Betty, Hinged Lid, Hanging Spike, Wick Pick On Chain, Sheet Metal, 10 1/4 In. 345.00

Betty, Puritan Period, Hand Forged, On Gimbal, Adjustable, Twisted Iron Stand, 1740s . . 650.00

Betty, Wrought Iron, Hanger & Pick, 4 1/4 In. 302.00

Betty, Wrought Iron, On Sawtooth Trammel, 20 1/2 In. 330.00

Betty, Wrought Iron, Semicircular Crest, Hinged Lid, Hanger, 3 3/4 In. 220.00

Betty, Wrought Iron, Stand, Handle, Hinged Lid, Hanging Hook, Scrolling Feet, 9 1/2 In. 690.00

Bouillotte, 2 Candle Branches, Raised On Dish Form Base, Paw Feet, 22 1/2 In., Pair . . 3162.00

Bouillotte, 2-Light, Brass, Metal Shades, Candle Snuffers, 14 In., Pair 489.00

Bouillotte, 3 Foliate Arms, Gilt Bronze, Electrified, 23 1/4 In. 517.00

Bouillotte, 3 Swan Candle Branches, Stepped Circular Base, Ball Feet, Empire, 26 In. . . 2185.00

Bouillotte, 3-Light, Fluted Standard, Bronze, 24 In. 1840.00

Bradley & Hubbard lamps are included in the Bradley & Hubbard category.

Camphene Burner, Weighted Tin 145.00

Candelabrum, 2-Light, Bronze Male Or Female Satyr, Electrified, 20 1/2 In. 3162.00

Candelabrum, 3-Light, Bronze, Eagles' Heads Branches, Marble Base, 25 1/2 In., Pair . . 6325.00

Candelabrum, 3-Light, Female, Holding Leaf Cast Rim, Charles X, Square Base, 25 In. . . 8625.00

Candelabrum, 3-Light, Flame Finial Fitted With Candle Arms, Ormolu, 1830s, 13 In. . . . 5750.00

Candelabrum, 3-Light, Louis XV Style, Gilt Bronze & Rock Crystal, 18 1/2 In. 8050.00

Candelabrum, 3-Light, Louis XVI Style, Foliate Scrolled Branches, Electrified, 24 In. . . . 4600.00

Candelabrum, 4-Light, Bronze, Cupids, Holding Candlecups, Wreath Base, 22 In., Pair . 1540.00

Candelabrum, 4-Light, Louis XVI Style, Satyr, Bronze & Marble, Pair 3450.00
Candelabrum, 5-Light, Empire, Gilt Bronze, 1880 . . . .   405.00
Candelabrum, 5-Light, Held By Winged Victory, Bronze Pedestal, 40 1/2 In., Pair 9200.00
Candelabrum, 5-Light, Scrolled Arms, Multicolored Marble Base, France, 23 In., Pair . .   515.00
Candelabrum, 5-Light, Silver On Copper Candlestick 303.00
Candelabrum, 5-Light, Silver Plated, Christofle, c.1900, 19 1/4 In. 2012.00
Candelabrum, 8-Light, Bronze, Cage Form, Scrolled Supports, Amber, 44 In. 2300.00
Candelabrum, Cherub Figural Stem, 4 Acanthus Scrolled Arms, Gilt Metal, 22 In., Pair .   885.00
Candelabrum, Circular Base Rising To Fluted Stems, 2 Branches, 1940s, 14 In. 2875.00
Candelabrum, Louis XV, Gilt Metal, Marble, Acorn Finial, Foliate Grape, 12 In., Pair .   489.00
Candlescreen, Brass, Two Branch, Brocade Floral Crest Screen, Marble Base, Electrified   745.00
Chandelier, 3-Light, Brass, Double Hoops, Openwork, Austria, c.1905, 41 3/4 In. 2300.00
Chandelier, 3-Light, Bronze, Cast Leaf Arms, Raised Acanthus Design, 27 In. 3850.00
Chandelier, 3-Light, Regency, Cut Glass 4830.00
Chandelier, 4-Light, Arts & Crafts, Wrought Iron, Copper Disc, Hanging, 31 In. Diam. . .   1690.00
Chandelier, 4-Light, Copper, Brass, Central Stem, Opalescent Glass Shades, 1900, 45 In.   4600.00
Chandelier, 4-Light, Crystal, Amethyst Drops, 21 In. 745.00
Chandelier, 4-Light, Leafy Branches, Porcelain Flowers, Tulip Form Nozzle, Tole, 27 In.   2875.00
Chandelier, 5-Light, Beaded & Strung, Turquoise Drops, 25 In.   345.00
Chandelier, 5-Light, Intertwined Cherries, Red & Green Paint, Wrought Iron, 24 In. 138.00
Chandelier, 6-Light, Acanthus Corona Over Foliate Standard, Musical Trophies, 31 In. . . .   1610.00
Chandelier, 6-Light, Berried Foliate Body, Tassel Form Finial, Gilt Metal, 34 In. 2875.00
Chandelier, 6-Light, Brass Rods, Glass Beads, T. Parzinger, c.1958, 18 1/2 In. 3162.00
Chandelier, 6-Light, Brass, Dutch, 1940s, 33 In. 3800.00
Chandelier, 6-Light, Brass, Gilt, Acanthus Leaf & Tassel, Frosted Glass Shades 110.00
Chandelier, 6-Light, George II, Scrolling Candle Arms, 14 x 21 In. 6325.00
Chandelier, 6-Light, Gilt Brass Frame, Clear & Amethyst Prisms, 29 In. 660.00
Chandelier, 6-Light, Ormolu, Acanthus Leaves, Circular Border, Berried Finial, 38 In. . . .   5175.00
Chandelier, 6-Light, Painted Arms, Sheet Metal Bobeches, Iron & Wood, 12 1/2 In. 2300.00
Chandelier, 6-Light, Steel, Acorn & Leaf Center Core, Small Bulbs In Core, 32 In. 1155.00
Chandelier, 6-Light, Tin, Conical Punched Center, Charles Weir, 13 1/2 In. 125.00
Chandelier, 8-Light, Brass, Figural Shaft & Ball Drop, Electrified 385.00
Chandelier, 8-Light, Bronze, Renaissance Revival, Pine Cone Finial, 24 x 28 In. 4140.00
Chandelier, 8-Light, Cut Glass Flower Heads, Cut Glass Ropes, Gilt Metal, 36 In. 5175.00
Chandelier, 8-Light, Napoleon III, Gilt Metal, Roped Prisms, Circular Base, 31 In. 2530.00
Chandelier, 8-Light, Neoclassical, Circular Corona, Foliate Stem, 3 Link Chains, 24 In. . .   3737.00
Chandelier, 10-Light, 2 Tiers Of S-Scrolled Arms, Drops & Chains, 28 In. 460.00
Chandelier, 10-Light, Baluster Turned Standard, Within Scrolled Birdcage Frame, 40 In.   2415.00
Chandelier, 10-Light, Louis XV Style, Gilt Bronze & Crystal 2415.00
Chandelier, 12-Light, Neoclassical, Cut Crystal, Gilt Metal, Leaf Design, 35 x 25 In. . . .   920.00
Chandelier, 16-Light, 2 Tiers Of Arms, Bird Finial, Brass, Dutch, Electrified, 50 In. 3960.00
Chandelier, 16-Light, Stag Horns, Electrified, 44 x 58 1/2 In. 4400.00
Chandelier, 16-Light, Wrought Steel, Electric Candles, Chain, 42 x 32 1/2 In. 1155.00
Chandelier, 18-Light, Cage Form, 2 Tiers Of Candle Arms, Beaded Chains, 54 In. 5750.00
Chandelier, 30-Light, Bronze, Scrolling Arms, Flowers & Foliage, 36 In. 4600.00
Chandelier, Crystal & Bronze, 2 Tiers, 48 In. 2300.00
Chandelier, Ormolu, 4 Scrolled Arms, Frosted Shades, 19 In. 410.00
Chandelier, Rock Crystal & Bronze, 20 x 15 In. 460.00
Chandelier, Satin Glass Shade, Floral Design, Brass Mount, Frame 303.00
Chandelier, Scrolled Corona, Glass Chains, Prisms, Gilt Metal, 13 1/2 In., Pair 2345.00
Chandelier, Tole, With Lemons, 32 x 15 In. 402.00
Chocolate Glass, 8 Panels, Ornate Bronze Base, 21 In. 286.00
Desk, 7-Up, Metal Bottle, Swing Out 65.00
Electric, 8-Panel, Slag Glass & Floral Filigree, 20-In. Shade 305.00
Electric, Adnet, Chromed Metal Base & Shade, Glass Strips, 1930s, 66 3/4 In. 3750.00
Electric, Amber Corroso, Fittings & Shade, Seguso, 20 In. 275.00
Electric, Amoco, Plastic, Metal, 18 1/4 x 8 1/2 In. 148.00
Electric, Arched Chrome, Spherical Shade, Black Rectangular Base, 60 In. 247.00
Electric, Art Deco, Bucking Bronco, Rider, Chalkware, Glass, 1930s, 15 1/2 In. 175.00
Electric, Art Deco, Chrome, Black Lacquered Base, Nude Glass Panels, 20 In., Pair 330.00
Electric, Art Deco, Copper Colored Base, Green Enamel Hood 1125.00
Electric, Art Deco, Figural, Airplane, Glass, Metal, 14 1/2 x 10 In. 300.00
Electric, Art Deco, Stacked Disks, White & Black Plastic, Aluminum Base, 10 In., Pair .   55.00

Electric, Art Deco, White Enameled Shade, Chrome Arm, 1950s, 24 x 10 x 16 In. 55.00
Electric, Art Nouveau, Bronze, Exotic Bird Holding Shade In Beak & Claw, 19 In. 2760.00
Electric, Art Nouveau, Green & Pearl Shade, Vintage Fabric, Tin, 25 1/2 In. 1695.00
Electric, Art Nouveau, Woman, Holding Globe 175.00
Electric, Art Nouveau, Woman, Light Bulbs In Hair & On Gown, White Metal, 36 1/2 In. 660.00
Electric, Arts & Crafts, Leaded Shade, 14 In. 695.00
Electric, Bach, Bronze, Arrowhead Finial, 4 Arched Legs, Parchment Shade, 1925, 71 In. 7475.00
Electric, Banquet, Cobalt Blue, Stem, Marble Foot, Oregon Frosted Shade, 22 1/2 In. ... 600.00
Electric, Banquet, White, Cranberry Font, Stem, Frosted Oregon Style Shade, 25 In. 5000.00
Electric, Banquet, White, Floral Embossed Brass Foot, White Milk Glass Shade, 23 In. .. 600.00
Electric, Barovier & Toso, Orange & Black Spheres, Internal Bubbles, 6 x 20 In. 495.00
Electric, Bisque Ceramic, Figures In Village Landscape, 15 In. 4140.00
Electric, Black Panther, 1950s 30.00
Electric, Boudoir, Slag Glass Shade, c.1920 .... 110.00
Electric, Brandt, Wrought Iron, Leaves & Berries, Daum Shade, 1920s, 66 In. 15935.00
Electric, Brass, Adjustable Arm, Repainted Turquoise Shade, Metal Base, 1950s, 17 In. . 155.00
Electric, Brass, Samovar, Impressed Lion Mark, 20 In. 110.00
Electric, Brass, Student, Double, Yellow Satin Shade, 24 In. 520.00
Electric, Bronze, Alabaster Shade, Fluted Base, 1930, 66 3/4 In. 5250.00
Electric, Bronze, Allegorical Female, Urn On Shoulder, Marble Pedestal, 27 1/2 In., Pair 6325.00
Electric, Bronze, Bouval, Maurice, Nymph, Standing Amidst Bulrushes, Gilt, 17 In. 1265.00
Electric, Bronze, Figural, Winged Dragon, Lantern, Leaded Shade, Austria, 20 x 27 In. .. 2310.00
Electric, Bronze, Figural, Woman, Holding Alabaster Bowl, Partly Silvered, 1920, 27 In. 8250.00
Electric, Bronze, Frosted Glass Shades, Triple Flange Stem, Perzel, 1930, 74 3/4 In. .. 8625.00
Electric, Bronze, Variety Of Geometric Shapes On Stem, Birds & Dragons, 72 In. 747.00
Electric, Bronze, Woman, Holding Textile Over Head, Larche, 12 3/4 In. 10350.00
Electric, Brushed Chrome, Swing Arm, Adjustable, Milk Glass Shade, Nessen, 52 In. 110.00
Electric, Bubble, George Nelson, Fiberglass, Metal Frame, Tripod Base, 17 In. 330.00
Electric, Cactus, Cholla, Double Cacti, Brace Bar, Shade, 1950s 43.00
Electric, Candlestick, Sterling, Shade, Shreve & Co., 1920, 14 In., 4 Piece 6900.00
Electric, Ceiling, 5-Light, Amber Colored Glass Shades, 21 x 16 In. 495.00
Electric, Ceiling, Slag Glass, Octagonal Form, Green Prism Drops, 30 x 20 In. 58.00
Electric, Charlie The Tuna 85.00
Electric, Chrome Swinging Arch, Tube Light, Plexiglas Tip, Square Base, 48 1/2 In. 357.00
Electric, Chrome, L-Shape, Circular Base, Soneman, 46 In. 385.00
Electric, Column Pedestal, Slag Glass Panel Shade, 22 In. 1265.00
Electric, Copper, Cone Shape, Cluthra-Type Glass Lining, 1905, 13 3/4 In. 3185.00
Electric, Copper, Hammered, Tortoise-Back Shade, Arts & Crafts, 10 In. 1320.00
Electric, Copper, Wood Scene, Moose In Woods, Wicker Shade, Arts & Crafts, 61 In. ... 1540.00
Electric, Dancing Figures At Base, Shade, Porcelain, Germany, 25 In. 1495.00
Electric, Dennis The Menace, Composition, Dennis Playing With Ruff On Base, 1961 .. 145.00
Electric, Ebony Ball, Oak Base, Beaten Copper Shade, 1925, 38 In. 2070.00
Electric, Figural, Green Marble Base, Art Deco, 59 In. 109.00
Electric, Figural, Woman, Nude, Pottery, Metal, Blue Glass Shade, Art Deco, 12 In., Pair 160.00
Electric, French Poodle, White, Sitting, Pink Pillows, Shades, Pair 295.00
Electric, Gordon's Gin, Figural, Original Shade 25.00
Electric, Grand Tour, Napoleon's, Column Stepped Base, Continental, 8 In. 805.00
Electric, Green Gazelle Design, Art Deco, c.1930 .... 110.00
Electric, Hammered Copper, 4 Sockets, Arms, Copper Shade, Dirk Van Erp, 23 x 19 In. . 17600.00
Electric, Hammered Copper, Broad Conical Shade, 4 Mica Panels, Dirk Van Erp, 20 In. . 1495.00
Electric, Hammered Copper, Rolled Rim, Original Patina, Dirk Van Erp, 20 1/2 x 19 In. . 4315.00
Electric, Hanging, Artichoke, Enameled Metal Leaves, Paul Henningsen, 21 x 24 In. 2400.00
Electric, Hanging, Brass Frame, Milk Glass Shade & Font, Hunt Scenes, Prisms, 30 In. . 302.00
Electric, Hanging, Leaded Slag Glass, Ceiling Plate, Prairie School, 20-In. Shade 935.00
Electric, Hanging, Onion, Tin & Glass, 18 1/2 In. 132.00
Electric, Jean Harlow, Bronze, 1930s 225.00
Electric, Jefferson, Reverse Painted, Brown House, Trees, Bronzed Metal, 24 In. 935.00
Electric, Leering Baccante, Bronze, Black Marble Base, 29 In. 1725.00
Electric, Lithophane Shade, 5 Sides, Butterflies & Leaves, Scenes, Cast Iron, 18 In. 520.00
Electric, Lotton, Cranberry Glass, Glass Shade, 30 In. 2800.00
Electric, Metal Base, Lions' Heads, Etched Frosted Green Shade, Mappin & Webb, 9 In. 500.00
Electric, Modernistic, Kopp, Red Glass Base, Silk Covered Shade, c.1929, 14 1/2 In. ... 425.00
Electric, Moe Bridges, Birds Of Paradise, No. 184 .... 5500.00

Electric, Moe Bridges, Reverse Painted Primitive Landscape, 13 In. 373.00
Electric, Mosque, Mouth Blown, Gold Design, 1920s 200.00
Electric, Motion, Blacksmith & Forge 165.00
Electric, Motion, Campfire Scene 450.00
Electric, Motion, Christmas Tree, Econolite 50.00
Electric, Motion, Dancing Devils 425.00
Electric, Motion, Fire Scene 600.00
Electric, Motion, Fountain Of Youth, Roto-Vue 140.00
Electric, Motion, Horses On Drum 600.00
Electric, Motion, Locomotive, Econolite, 1956 .... 65.00
Electric, Motion, Niagara Falls, Econolite, 1930s 85.00
Electric, Motion, Niagara Falls, L.A. Goodman, 1956 .... 110.00
Electric, Motion, Niagara Falls, Oval 190.00
Electric, Motion, Santa Claus, Christmas Tree, Box 100.00
Electric, Motion, Watch Tower 75.00
Electric, Oak, Paneled Slag Shade, Arts & Crafts ....*Illus* 355.00
Electric, Open Scroll Mounts, Cylindrical Alabaster Shade, Edgar Brandt, 1925, 12 In. ... 1610.00
Electric, Parzinger, Wrought Iron, Star Finial, Black Marble Table, 1945, 7 Ft. 2 In. 4025.00
Electric, Parzinger, Wrought Iron, Stylized Star-Form Finial, 1945, 6 Ft. 7 In. 3450.00
Electric, Patinated Bronze, Nautilus, Shell Form Shade, Wood Base, Austria, 13 3/4 In. ... 2630.00
Electric, Patinated Bronze, Sirene & Nautilus, Gustav Gurschner, 1899, 17 3/8 In. 14790.00
Electric, Paul McCobb, Yellow Enamel, Perforated Metal Top, Rod Standard, 17 In., Pair 440.00
Electric, Piano, Cast Iron, White Metal, Milk Glass Globe, Transfer Flowers, 56 In. 440.00
Electric, Piano, Gold Designs, Pink 1430.00
Electric, Poulson, Visor, Gray Metal Frame, Adjustable Shade, Arne Jacobsen, 50 In. ... 605.00
Electric, Reverse Painted, Landscape, Chipped Ice Shade, Jefferson 1320.00
Electric, Rose Quartz, Figural, Griffin, Finial, 17 In. 259.00
Electric, Samuel Yellin, Riveted Triangular Base, Twisted Stem, Wrought Iron, 10 In. ... 1650.00
Electric, Silvered Bronze, Flowerhead Shape, Stem & Leaf Design, Crepin, 17 3/4 In. .. 2300.00
Electric, Skeleton, Lavender & Blue Trim, Green Glass Eyes, Foreign Burner, 5 1/2 In. ... 4250.00
Electric, Slag Glass Shade, 6 Panel, Pittsburgh, Cast Metal Base, c.1910, 17 In. 625.00
Electric, Snoopy, Ceramic Base, Plastic Shade, United Features, 1966 .... 110.00
Electric, Standard, Walnut, Ebony, Raised Octagonal Base, Edward Barnsley, 74 In. 4370.00
Electric, Swirling White & Aventurine Acanne Glass, A. Toso, 17 In. 192.00
Electric, Telephone Form, Clock Dial, Louvered Shade, Metal, 1950, 18 In. 125.00
Electric, Television, Siamese Cats, Blue Eyes, 12 x 12 In. 75.00
Electric, Texaco, Plastic, Metal, 18 1/4 x 8 1/2 In. 308.00
Electric, Turned Wooden Base, Green & Ruby Leaded Shade, 16 x 23 In. 385.00
Electric, Urn Form, Malachite Base, Gilt Bronze Mounted Rock Crystal, 21 1/2 In., Pair . 6900.00
Electric, Wicker, White Paint, Dome Shade ....*Illus* 355.00
Electric, Wrought Iron, 4 Upswept Arms, Raised On 4 Arched Legs, 6 Ft. 5 In. 3450.00
Fairy, Blue Satin Glass 40.00
Fairy, Figural, Dog's Head, Blue Eyes, 4 1/4 In. 520.00
Fairy, Pink Dome, Cleveland Swirl, Clarke Signed Cup, Fluted Rim, 5 3/8 In. 190.00
Fat, Carved From Soapstone Block, American, 1706 .... 1400.00
Fat, Pedestal Style, Single Handle, Wick Pick, Tin, 7 3/4 In. 176.00

Lamp, Electric, Oak,
Paneled Slag Shade,
Arts & Crafts

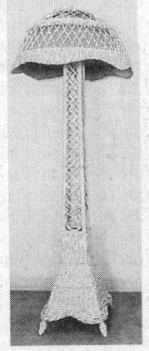

Lamp, Electric
Wicker, White Paint,
Dome Shade

Fat, Tin, 1850s 225.00

Fat, Tin, Separate Burner & Reservoir 285.00

Fluid, Blue, 8 In. 1100.00

Fluid, Brass, Marble Base, Without Burner, 9 In. 55.00

Fluid, Cobalt Cut To Clear Font, Frosted Shade, Brass, Early 19th Century, 16 3/4 In. ... 170.00

Fluid, Crystal, Hexagonal Foot, 9 1/2 In. 82.00

Fluid, Floral Engraved Font, 8 Panel, Brass Stem, Marble Foot, 10 In. 143.00

Fluid, Horn Of Plenty, Amber Font, Milk Glass Pedestal Base 110.00

Fluid, Juno, Brass, Electrified 55.00

Fluid, Pewter, Flower Goddess Figurine, China, Leo Gould, 18th Century, 18 In., Pair ... 977.00

Girandole, 6-Light, Scrolled Arms, Pendants, Bronze & Rock Crystal, 25 In., Pair . 3162.00

Girandole, George & Martha Washington, Prisms, Marble Base, 1880s, 16 1/4 In., Pair .. 110.00

Girandole, Gilt Brass, Marble Base, Cut Pans & Prisms, 27 In., Pair 770.00

Grease, Ohio Pottery, Saucer Base, Dark Glaze, 3 1/4 In. 330.00

Grease, Wrought Iron, Sawtooth Trammel, Twisted Rod, 26 In. 330.00

Handel lamps are included in the Handel category.

Hanging, Kerosene, Floral Design Shade, Bass Font, Electrified 143.00

Hanging, Kerosene, Prism, Painted Shades, Fonts, 14 In. 227.00

Hanging, Majolica Font, Brass Kerosene Burner, Milk Glass Shade, Cast Iron Frame 330.00

Kerosene, 3 Medallions, Gibson Type Girls On Base, 9 1/2 In. 28.00

Kerosene, Baluster Form, Green, Red Damask Cover Seats, Saber Legs, 37 1/2 In., Pair . 978.00

Kerosene, Banquet, Bronze Base, Hoof Footed, Ram's Heads, Electrified, 1887, 32 In. .. 895.00

Kerosene, Banquet, Floral Etched Ruby Ball Shade, Brass, Electrified, 28 1/2 In. . 575.00

Kerosene, Beaded Bull's-Eye, Green 115.00

Kerosene, Blue Opaline Font, Brass Stem, Marble Base, 9 In. 60.00

Kerosene, Brass, Classical, Milk Glass Shade, Messinger's Patent, 26 1/4 In., Pair 495.00

Kerosene, Brass, Frosted Chimney, Wall Bracket, 14 1/2 In. 220.00

Kerosene, Caramel Slag Glass, Geometric Design, Wooden Base, Arts & Crafts, 27 In. ... 165.00

Kerosene, Cobalt Overlay, White, Blue, Gold Tucker Top Shade, 18 1/4 In. 500.00

Kerosene, Dark Pink, White, Brass Stem, Marble Base, 20 1/4 In. 1450.00

Kerosene, Dolphin Overlay, White, Yellow, Green, Oregon Style Shade, 18 1/2 In. . 14000.00

Kerosene, Eaton, Blue Clam Broth Font, Blue Base, 13 1/4 In. 500.00

Kerosene, Eaton, Green Clam Broth Font, Stem, Footed, 13 In. 1200.00

Kerosene, Eaton, White, Blue Clam Broth Font, Light Blue Base, 14 3/8 In. 400.00

Kerosene, Engraved Writing On Top, Wooden Handle At Side, Brass, 6 x 10 In. 23.00

Kerosene, Finger, Cranberry Markham Swirl Band Opalescent, Silver Interior, 4 In. 2000.00

Kerosene, Finger, Hobbs Coin Dot, Blue Opalescent, 3 In. 600.00

Kerosene, Finger, Hobbs Coin Dot, Cranberry Opalescent, 4 3/4 In. 200.00

Kerosene, Finger, Opalescent Swirl, Crystal 325.00

Kerosene, Finger, Princess Feather, Cobalt Blue 485.00

Kerosene, Finger, Ripley, White Clam Broth Font, Blue Handles, Base, Footed, 5 In. . 700.00

Kerosene, Finger, Snowflake, Cranberry Opalescent, 3 In. ....200.00 to 500.00

Kerosene, Finger, Snowflake, Cranberry Opalescent, Footed, 5 In. 1150.00

Kerosene, Finger, Snowflake, Opalescent, 3 In. ....200.00 to 400.00

Kerosene, Finger, Snowflake, Sapphire Blue Opalescent, 3 In. 600.00

Kerosene, Firefly, Box, 6 In. 50.00

Kerosene, Frosted Font, Bristol Glass Stem, 1920s 68.00

Kerosene, Frosted Glass, Figural, Man & Woman Stem, Open Burner, 11 3/4 In., Pair ... 220.00

Kerosene, Gone With The Wind, Blown-Out Iris, Shade, Burner, 26 In. 385.00

Kerosene, Gone With The Wind, Blue Satin Opalescent, Scalloped, Electrified, 24 In. ... 385.00

Kerosene, Gone With The Wind, Gilt Floral, Green 60.50

Kerosene, Gone With The Wind, Green Rose Shade, 18 In. 110.00

Kerosene, Gone With The Wind, Green, Pink, Yellow Chrysanthemums, 26 In. 245.00

Kerosene, Gone With The Wind, Leaves, Yellow, Brass Font, Iron Base, 15 In. 22.00

Kerosene, Gone With The Wind, Pink & Blue Flowers Shade, 26 In. 137.50

Kerosene, Gone With The Wind, Pink Wild Roses, Green Leaves, Yellow, White, 22 In. . 300.00

Kerosene, Gone With The Wind, Pink, Blue Flowers, Pink Globe 28.00

Kerosene, Gone With The Wind, Pink, Flowers In Panels, Ball Shade, Victorian, 24 In. . 2200.00

Kerosene, Gone With The Wind, Red Satin, Complete 700.00

Kerosene, Gone With The Wind, White Leaf, Floral Design, Tan Shade, Green Base 165.00

Kerosene, Hanging, Angle, Double Milk, Glass Rib Shades, 18 1/2 In. 200.00

Kerosene, Hanging, Blue Cut Velvet Shade, Jeweled Frame, 14-In. Shade 1760.00

Kerosene, Hanging, Brass, Ruby Swirl Shade, Cast Iron 55.00

Kerosene, Honeycomb Font, Brass Connector, Opaque White Base, 10 1/8 In. 110.00
Kerosene, Hurricane, Silver Plate, Glass Shade, Copper Base, Sheffield, 16 In., Pair 330.00
Kerosene, Miller, Nickel Plate On Brass, Embossed Scrolls, Art Glass Shade, Victorian .   250.00
Kerosene, Moorish Windows, White, Cranberry Font, White Base, 12 1/2 In. 500.00
Kerosene, Neoclassical, Black Paint, Gilt Metal, Bristol Glass Globe, 31 In. 374.00
Kerosene, Newel Post, 3-Light, Peasant Youth, Cast Metal, Amber Flame Pulls, 25 In. . .   412.00
Kerosene, Nickel Finish, With Diffuser, Gimball Mount, England 95.00
Kerosene, Opaque White, Lime Green Font, Lime Green Base, 11 In. 385.00
Kerosene, Porcelain, Hand Painted, White, Gold, Rust, Ornate Brass Base, 1920s 165.00
Kerosene, Rayo, Nickel Plate, Milk Glass Shade . . . . .60.00 to 70.00
Kerosene, Ripley, Marriage, Opaque White & Blue, Brass Connector, 1868, 11 1/2 In. . . .   880.00
Kerosene, Skater's, The Jewel, Brass, Cobalt Blue Lens, 6 1/2 In. 365.00
Kerosene, Student, Double, Opaque White Shades, Brass, 17 1/2 In. 247.00
Kerosene, Student, Rochester, Cased Green Shade, 1880, 22 In. 595.00
Kerosene, Tomato Overlay, White, Checkerboard, Gold, White Base, 13 1/2 In. 1050.00
Kerosene, Tomato Overlay, White, Ruby Stem, Marble Base, 21 3/4 In. 1100.00
Lace Maker's, Green Tole & Brass, F.A. Walker, 19th Century, Pair 650.00
Loom, 1 Candle Socket, Wrought Iron, Spring Trammel, 24 In. 845.00
Loom, 1 Candle, Push Up, Wrought Iron, Sawtooth Trammel, 27 In. 120.00
Loom, 2 Candle Sockets, Wrought Iron, Sawtooth Trammel, Oval Shelf, 27 In. 210.00
Loom, Forged, Cone Socket, c.1800 . . . .   225.00
Miner's, Autolite 20.00
Miner's, Carbide, 1920s 125.00
Miner's, Carbide, Brass, Polished Reflector, Universal Lamp Co., Springfield, Ill. 25.00
Miner's, Chicken Finial, Cast & Wrought Iron, 7 3/8 In. 110.00
Miner's, Dewar Mfg. Co., Carbide, 9 1/4 In. 30.00
Miner's, Guys Dropper, Carbide, Brass, 4 1/4 In. 40.00
Miner's, Justrite, Carbide, Brass, 4 In. 22.00
Miner's, Nickel 325.00
Motion, Fountain Of Youth 175.00
Night-Light, Diamond-Quilted Ball Shape, Beaded Brass Rim, 6 1/2 In. 125.00
Night-Light, Globe, Brass Stand, Candle Placed Inside, Austria, 9 1/2 x 3 3/4 In. 395.00
Oil, Aladdin, Gold Decal, With Burner, 1947 . . . .   575.00
Oil, Amethyst Glass, Octagonal Baluster Stem, Knop & Bigler Font, Square Base, 10 In. .   2860.00
Oil, Apollo, Amber, 7 1/2 In. 350.00
Oil, Banquet, Moss Green Glass Ball Shade, Embossed, 1895, 21 In. 595.00
Oil, Beaded Loop, Milk Glass, Pedestal Base, 10 In. 50.00
Oil, Bellflower, Inside Ribs, Flint, Marble Base 450.00
Oil, Blown Glass, Hollow Stem, Puce Font, Drapery Swags, Brass Collar, 10 3/8 In. 840.00
Oil, Blown In Mold Font, Hexagonal Base, Incurving Sides, Electrified 55.00
Oil, Blue Cut To White To Clear Font, Gilt, Brass Stem, Marble Base, 9 3/4 In. 605.00
Oil, Blue Cut To White To Clear, Stepped Marble, Brass Base, 11 3/8 In. 905.00
Oil, Brass, Clear Font, Opaque White Looping, Stepped Marble Base 300.00
Oil, Brass, Ormolu Mounted, Floral Finial, Baluster Shade, 1825, 16 In., Pair 3162.00
Oil, Bronze, Convex Column, French, c.1580 . . . .   3000.00
Oil, Bull's-Eye & Fleur-De-Lis, Flint, Tin Can Font, 11 In. 450.00
Oil, Cathedral, Blue, Amber, Clear Shade 425.00
Oil, Clear Pressed Font, Rockingham Base, Brass Collar, 9 7/8 In. 410.00
Oil, Coach, Repousse Floral Design, Beveled Glass Windows, Brass, 27 In., Pair 2995.00
Oil, Cobalt Blue Glass, Hexagonal Base, Loop Font, Brass Collar, 9 3/4 In. 1265.00
Oil, Cobalt Blue Glass, Hexagonal Waterfall Base, Arch & Panel Fans, 10 In., Pair 3300.00
Oil, Columbian Coin, Milk Glass 595.00
Oil, Cranberry Font, White Looping, Marble Base, Brass Stem & Collar, 8 1/4 In. 485.00
Oil, Cranberry Overlay, Sandwich Glass, Burner & Shade, c.1860, 19 In. 2265.00
Oil, Crystal Wedding, Square Collar, 3 1/2 In. 245.00
Oil, Daisy & Button With V Ornament, Blue Stained Stem 75.00
Oil, Daisy & Button, 10 In. 210.00
Oil, Dewdrop With Star, 1876, 8 1/2 In. 145.00
Oil, Double Peg, 2 Webb Shades 1600.00
Oil, Double, Hanging, Brass, Quilted Cranberry Shades, Victorian, 36 In. 550.00
Oil, Finger, Hobbs, Blue, c.1880, 3 In. 475.00
Oil, Finger, Windows, Coin Dot 695.00
Oil, Glass, Square Lacy Base, Blown Pear Shaped Font, Brass Collar, 8 1/8 In. 970.00

Oil, Grapes, Leaves & Vines, Hester Pillsbury, Signed, Weller . . . . 1100.0•
Oil, Greek Key, Ruby Red, Cast Iron Pedestal Base, 10 In. . . . . 66.0•
Oil, Hand, Emerald Green, Loop Pattern, Brass Collar, 3 3/8 In. . . . . 880.0•
Oil, Hanging, Amber Base, Brass Tone Hanging Globe . . . . 55.0•
Oil, Hanging, Spout, Iron, c.1790 . . . . 195.0•
Oil, Heart With Thumbprint, 10 1/4 In. . . . . 225.0•
Oil, Lamp, Parcel Gilt, Black Opaline Glass, Baluster Base, 1850s, 21 In., Pair . . . . 4025.0•
Oil, Log Cabin . . . . 625.0•
Oil, Loop, Flint, Scalloped Base, 7 1/2 In. . . . . 155.0•
Oil, Malachite, Green Cut To Clear Chimney, 1928 . . . . 1400.0•
Oil, Mary Gregory Figures On Sides, Removable Inner Font . . . . 950.0•
Oil, Moon & Star, Finger, Flint, 4 3/4 In. . . . . 325.0•
Oil, Moon & Star, Ruby Stained . . . . 265.0•
Oil, Nickel Plate, On Brass, Hand Painted Shade, Dated 1899 . . . . 195.0•
Oil, One-Hundred-One, Finger . . . . 85.0•
Oil, Opalescent Snowflake, Blue . . . . 850.0•
Oil, Opaque Blue Base, White Cut To Clear Font, Brass Connector & Collar, 10 In. . . . . . 300.0•
Oil, Palmette . . . . 75.0•
Oil, Paneled Fern . . . . 210.0•
Oil, Pedestal, Saw Tooth Pattern, Flint Glass, 9 1/2 In., Pair . . . . 135.0•
Oil, Periwinkle, 6 3/4 In. . . . . 175.0•
Oil, Periwinkle, Brass Pedestal, Marble Base, 9 In. 44.00
Oil, Pink Cut To White To Clear Font, Brass Base, Stepped Marble Base, 11 7/8 In. 550.00
Oil, Pink Cut To White To Clear Font, Opalescent Base, 13 1/2 In. 880.00
Oil, Pink Marble, Gilt Metal, Foliate & Cornucopia Motif, Socle Base, 16 1/2 In., Pair . . . 862.00
Oil, Portrait, Female, Floral, Globe, Shell, White Overlay, Blue, 19 1/4 In. 635.00
Oil, Ruby Cut To Clear, Frosted Leaves, Ornate Gilt Brass, Pat. Sep. 20, 1870, 19 3/8 In. . . 715.00
Oil, Sabbath, Sawtooth Trammel, Brass, 33 In. 357.00
Oil, Terra-Cotta, Hand Painted Detail, 21 1/2 In. 998.00
Oil, Trefoil, Ruby Red Flashed Font, Cast Iron Pedestal Base, 11 In. 99.00
Pairpoint lamps are in the Pairpoint category.
Peg, Clear Cut Front, Brass Collar & Candlestick . . . . 200.00•
Peg, Interior Ribbed Font, Floral Design, Ice Chipped Shade 165.00
Peg, Whale Oil, Blown Glass, Spherical, Tin Drop, 4 1/4 In., Pair 495.00
Pocket, Koopman's Magic, Pat. Oct. '89 & Dec. '90 . . . . 300.00
Rush & Candle, Wrought Iron, Heart Shaped Base, 3 Feet, Loop Handle, 9 1/2 In. 465.00
Rush & Candle, Wrought Iron, Tripod Base, 16 In. 355.00
Rushlight, Candle, Double, Adjustable, Iron, Penny Feet, 1730s, 31 In. 1375.00
Rushlight, Heart Form Pincers, Penny Feet, Steel, c.1750, 7 3/4 In. 650.00
Sconce, 2-Light, Foliate Scrolled Backplate, Dragon Branches, Bronze, 16 1/4 In. 3450.00
Sconce, 2-Light, Gilt Metal, Beveled Glass, 17 In. 115.00
Sconce, 2-Light, Silvered Bronze, Lotus, Ruhlmann, 1925, 10 1/4 In., Pair 9375.00
Sconce, 2-Light, Voluted Backplate, Pierced Candle Arms, Brass, 21 In., Pair 4025.00
Sconce, 3-Light, Cast Metal, Winged Mermaid, Worn Gilt, 20th Century, 14 3/4 In., Pair . 385.00
Sconce, 3-Light, Ribbon & Foliate Backplate, Tulip Form Arms, Bronze, 15 In., Pair 2070.00
Sconce, 3-Light, Shield Backplate, Berried Branches, Bronze, 21 In. 4600.00
Sconce, 4-Light, Gilt & Patinated Bronze, Electrified, 34 In. 5175.00
Sconce, 5-Light, Wrought Iron, c.1910, 17 1/2 x 13 In. 1250.00
Sconce, 6-Arm, Bronze, Center Handle, Wooden Back, France, 1810, 22 x 20 In., Pair . . 2475.00
Sconce, Arts & Crafts, Dolphin, England, 14 1/2 x 9 In. 295.00
Sconce, Basket Form, Scrolled Supports, Wrought Iron, 16 In., Pair 172.00
Sconce, Brass, Dutch, c.1760, 11 3/8 In., Pair 3300.00
Sconce, Candle, Beveled Mirror Back, Crystal Cut Prisms, Cast Iron, 22 3/4 In. 550.00
Sconce, Continental, Gilt Metal, 3 Scrolled Arms, Crystal Prisms, Bobeche, 15 In., Pair . . 489.00
Sconce, Cut Crystal, Gilt Metal, Mirror Back, 3 Prong Mount, 2 Arms, 13 1/2 In., Pair . . 747.00
Sconce, Gilt, Wood, Carved, Shell Form, 6 1/2 x 11 In., Pair 230.00
Sconce, Gothic Dragon Form, Cast Iron, 46 x 24 In. 3575.00
Sconce, Heart Shape Finial, 4 Scrolled Arms, Prisms, Flowerhead Chain, 31 1/2 In., Pair . 3162.00
Sconce, Louis XV, Bronze, Gilt, Bow & Garland, 3 Acanthus Arms, 26 In., Pair 1265.00
Sconce, Louis XV, Bronze, Gilt, Late 19th Century, Pair 1150.00
Sconce, Reflector, American, Mid-19th Century, 8 In., Pair 1950.00
Sconce, Theater, Aluminum, Brass, Glass & Red Bakelite, 1930s, 34 In., Pair 4500.00
Searchlight, Rushmore Dynamo Works, Polished Brass, 22 In. 302.00

Shade, Daisy & Button, 9 In. 19.50
Shade, Daisy & Button, Yellow, Scalloped Edge 75.00
Shade, Leaded Glass, Garlands, Striated Amber Ground, Jeweled Flowers, 23 In. 1035.00
Shade, Mother-Of-Pearl, Satin Glass, Ruffled Edge, White Lining, 3 1/2 x 5 1/4 In. 250.00
Skater's, Amethyst Globe, Tin, 7 In. 474.00
Skater's, Aqua Globe, Tin, 6 1/4 In. 330.00
Skater's, Electric Blue Globe, Black Paint, Gold Design, Tin, 7 In. 365.00
Skater's, Emerald Green Globe, Tin, 6 1/2 In. 485.00
Tiffany lamps are listed in the Tiffany category.
Tin, Built-In Reflector, Green Paint, Paper Label, Mason's Factory, 11 1/2 In. 93.50
Torchere, Brass Bowl, Fluted Column, Disk Base, 1940s, 61 In. 22.00
Torchere, Carved Wood, Beaded Dish, 2 Panels Of Floral Bouquets, 64 In., Pair 3450.00
Torchere, Scrolled Standard, Splayed & Pierced Top, Wrought Iron, 4 Piece, 49 1/4 In. ... 1092.00
Whale Oil, Aqua, Sunbright Embossed Around Top, 3 1/8 In. 20.00
Whale Oil, Bigler, Flint, 9 1/2 In. 195.00
Whale Oil, Blown Glass, Single Brass Burner, Cranberry, Union Ratchet, 6 In. 132.00
Whale Oil, Cable, Flint, 8 1/2 In. 225.00
Whale Oil, Chamber, Pewter, American, 5 1/4 In. 115.50
Whale Oil, Copper, Handle, 1825, 5 3/8 x 3 In. 195.00
Whale Oil, Engraved Glass Bowl, Stepped Pedestal, 10 In. 60.00
Whale Oil, Etched Drapery, Free-Blown Font, Pewter Collar, Sandwich Glass, 9 In. 225.00
Whale Oil, Excelsior With Maltese Cross, Flint ....180.00 to 325.00
Whale Oil, Glass, Diamond Quilted, Columnar Stem, Replaced Brass Collar, 8 3/4 In. .. 145.00
Whale Oil, Glass, Star & Punty Font, Hexagonal Base, Brass Collar, 9 1/2 In. 180.00
Whale Oil, Hand, Loop Pattern, Pewter Collar, Pewter & Tin Burner, 3 1/2 In. 250.00
Whale Oil, Harp, Flint, 9 In. 225.00
Whale Oil, Horn Of Plenty, Flint, 9 1/2 In. 275.00
Whale Oil, Lee, Flint, 18 In. 295.00
Whale Oil, Pewter, Burner, Yale & Curtis, N.Y., 8 1/4 In. 220.00
Whale Oil, Pewter, Mark Of Eben Smith, 6 1/2 In. 247.00
Whale Oil, Pressed Glass, Free-Blown Conical Font, Brass Collar, Pontil, 8 3/8 In. 120.00
Whale Oil, Pressed Glass, Light Bulb Font, Pontil, Boston & Sandwich Glass, 6 1/2 In. . 55.00
Whale Oil, Pressed Stepped Base, Blown Font With Wafers, 7 3/4 In. 175.00
Whale Oil, Pressed Waterfall Design Base, Blown Stem, Pewter, 9 3/8 In., Pair 495.00
Whale Oil, Star & Punty, 10 In. 330.00
Whale Oil, Tin, Early 19th Century 435.00

LANTERNS are a special type of lighting device. They have a light
source, usually a candle, totally hidden inside the walls of the lantern.
Light is seen through holes or glass sections.

2-Candle Pan, Old Glass, Brass, Dutch, c.1670 .... 6500.00
All American, Green 525.00
Art Glass Panels, Bronze, Square, Crowned Top, L.M. Co., 1920s 195.00
Barn, Hardwood & Pine, Tin Candle Holder, Wooden, Wire Bale, 10 1/2 In. 473.00
Barn, Pine, Green & Brownish Red Paint, Wooden Door, Glass Panes, 14 1/2 In. 300.00
Barn, Pine, Tin & Wire Fittings, 12 In. 275.00
Barn, Pine, Wooden, 12 In. 192.50
Barn, Tin Candle Socket & Heat Shield, Pink & Oak, 16 1/2 In. 385.00
Barn, Tin Candle Socket, Hinged Door, Bail Handle, Wooden, 12 In. 440.00
Barn, Tin, Hooded Canopy, Green Paint, 19th Century 80.00
Barn, Wire Bail, Tin Heat Shield, Pine, 7 1/4 In. 385.00
Barn, Wooden, Tin Door & Candle Holder, Threaded Finial, Wire Bail Handle, 9 In. 300.00
Brass, 2-Light, Hinged Bail Handle, Vented Lid, Ball Feet, 18th Century, 16 x 9 In. 2587.00
Brass, Glazed Sides, Movable Arm, 16 In. 1955.00
Brass, Ship's Oil, 1900, 19 x 10 In. 350.00
Candle, Folding, Brass, Folds Into Book Form, 19th Century, 7 x 4 x 4 In. 935.00
Candle, Pierced Tin, 15 In. 275.00
Candle, Pierced Tin, 1830s, 16 In. 275.00
Candle, Pierced, Hanging Ring, 19th Century, 10 In. 275.00
Carbide, 4 1/2 In. 65.00
Carriage, Red Globe, Diaz 60.00
Copper, Verdigris Surface, France, 26 In. 363.00
Covered Bridge, Tin, Glass & Oil Tank, Back Hangers, Carrying Handle, 24 1/4 In. 500.00

Dietz, WPA Ohio, 12 In. 200.00
Electric, Glass, Knop Finial, Hammered Metal Collar, Smoke Shade, 18 In. 2587.00
Folding, Traveler's, Copper Alloy, c.1780, 5 1/2 In. 1200.00
Foliate Corona, 4 Supports, Pierced Frame, Glass Panels, Bronze, 33 In., Pair 1265.00
Hall, 4 Panes Of Curved Glass, Gilded Brass, 36 x 16 In. 770.00
Hall, Bell Form, Domed Smoke Shade, Etched Flowers, 3-Light, Electrified, 23 In. 4315.00
Hall, Pewter & Brass, England, c.1790, 12 x 20 1/2 In. 2950.00
Hand Blown Globe, Double Burner, Glass Reservoir, Pierced Tin 425.00
Hanging, 3-Sided Bronze, 3-Sided Ceiling Plate, Arts & Crafts, 13 x 7 1/2 In. 385.00
Hanging, Blown Glass, Painted, Germany, Victorian, 3 In. 28.00
Hanging, Octagonal Black Frame, Clear Frosted Glass, 20th Century, 36 In. 300.00
Mast Head, Cranberry Glass Shade, Removable Fuel Container, 1851, 23 In. 4600.00
Parade, Tin, Etched Glass, Red, Blue, Clear, Wrought Iron Lyre, Wood Handle 140.00
Parade Torch Hat, Shiny Heavy Tin Plate, Filler Holes, 11 3/4 In. 220.00
Pine, Glass In 4 Sides, Candle Access From Top, Wooden, Wire Bail Handle, 9 1/2 In. .. 685.00
Prairie School, Cutout Design, Ivory Glass, 6 x 9 In. 880.00
Red Base, Green Base, Tin Reflector, c.1870, 9 1/2 In. 150.00
Scrolled Frame, Beveled Glass Panels, Pair 920.00
Skater's, Brass Front, Tin Top & Bail 120.00
Skater's, Kerosene, Brass, Handle, 2 3/4 x 4 1/2 In. 125.00
Skater's, Kerosene, c.1870, 7 1/2 In. 140.00
Spherical Shape, Smoke Shades, Victorian, Brass Mounted, 15 In., Pair 2300.00
Spire-Form Finial, 4 Glass Panels, Wall Plate, Outdoor, c.1950, 40 In., Pair 745.00
Strap-Hanging Loop, Pierced Pyramidal Dome, Sliding Door, Sheet Metal, 15 In. 1035.00
Tin, Clear Glass Globe, Dietz Sport, 7 3/4 In. 192.00
Tin, Cranberry Globe, Engraved C.R.R., Ring Handle, 12 1/2 In. 1100.00
Tin, Dome Top, Single Candle, Loop Handle, 9 In. 55.00
Tin, Glass Enclosed, Dome Top, Loop Handle, Candle, 9 In. 50.00
Tin, Hanging Tab, Crimped Top, Hinged Door, Rectangular Sides, 19th Century, 19 In. .. 1150.00
Tin, Hanging Tab, Molded Conical Top, Hinged Door, 19th Century, 19 In. 1380.00
Tin, Pressed Globe, Pewter Collar, Whale Oil Burner, Ring Handle, 9 1/2 In. 220.00
Tin, Punched Circle Design, Semicircular, Candle, Handle, 12 1/4 In. 415.00
Tin, Punched, Black Paint, 5 1/2 In. 209.00
Tin, Serpentine Top, Chimney In Center, Triangular, 11 1/2 In. 110.00
Tin, Spring Handle, Glass Globe, 13 x 4 1/2 In., Pair 95.00
Tin, Spurred Conical Top, Door Opening To Candle Socket, 19th Century, 19 In. 517.00
Tin, Triangular, Conical Crest, 2 Glass Sides, Wire Guards, Ring Handle, Candle, 12 In. . 395.00
Underground Tunnel Connecting Buildings, Fort In Laprairie, Quebec, 19th Century 217.00

LE VERRE FRANCAIS is one of the many types of cameo glass made in
France. The glass was made by the C. Schneider factory in Epinay-sur-
Seine from 1920 to 1933. It is a mottled glass, usually decorated with
floral designs, and bears the incised signature *Le Verre Francais*.

Perfume Bottle, Cameo, 6 1/2 In. 625.00
Vase, 3 Scarab Beetles, Tortoise Shell, Acid-Cut Back, Cameo, 1900, 6 In. 880.00
Vase, Cobalt, Red-Orange, Cameo, Signed, 1900s, 18 In., Pair ....*Illus* 4180.00
Vase, Stylized Flower Heads, Thorny Stems, Signed, c.1925, 31 In. 5750.00

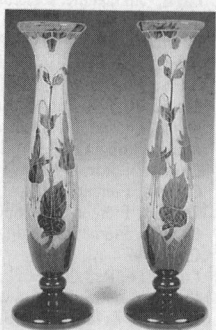

Le Verre Francais,
Vase, Cobalt,
Red-Orange, Cameo,
Signed, 1900s,
18 In., Pair

Vase, Stylized Flowers, Turquoise, Red, Orange, 1900, 17 3/4 In.	2200.00
Vase, Stylized Fruit Trees, Red, Orange Overlay, Blue Mottled, 7 In.	805.00

.EATHER is tanned animal hide and it has been used to make decora-
ive and useful objects for centuries. Leather objects must be carefully
preserved with proper humidity and oiling or the leather will deterio-
ate and crack. This damage cannot be repaired.

Bag, Shotgun Shell, Shoulder Strap	150.00
Bull Whip	30.00
Calf Cover, For Riding, Pigskin, Late Victorian, Pair	35.00
Card Carrier, C. Stegmaier & Son, Celluloid, 1892	18.50
Cowboy Cuffs, Studded, Engraved, 1920-1940, 7 x 4 In., Pair	255.00
Donkey, Store Display, 26 x 19 In.	400.00
Gauntlets, Bear Hide, Tan	125.00
Helmet, McKinley High School, Canton, Ohio, White, Name Cut In	595.00
Holster, 11 Mercury & Roosevelt Dimes, Dating From 1940 To 1948	125.00
Holster, Double, Saddle, Revolutionary War, Dyed Black, 12 1/8 In., Pair	400.00
Holster, To Hold 7 1/2-In. Barrel Peacemaker, Bauer Bros. Mfg. Co., Early 1900s	75.00
Jacket, Harley-Davidson, Local Gang Member, 1980, Size 40	198.00
Saddle, Breast Collar & Bridle, Silver Mounted, Olsen Noltie, Pair	6700.00
Saddle, High Back, Wood Stirrups, Metal Rosette Trim, Late 1800s	300.00
Saddlebag, Brass Letters, T.H. Burtturf	44.00
Valise, Traveling, Fitted Interior, Louis Vuitton, 191 4 x 19 1/2 In.	230.00
Wallet, Folding, c.1860, 4 x 7 In.	95.00

LEEDS pottery was made at Leeds, Yorkshire, England, from 1774 to
1878. Most Leeds ware was not marked. Early Leeds pieces had distinctive twisted handles with a greenish glaze on part of the creamy
ware. Later ware often had blue borders on the creamy pottery. A   **LEEDS POTTERY.**
Chicago company named Leeds made many Disney-inspired figurines.
They are listed in the Disneyana category.

Bottle, Pig	45.00
Candy, Cover, Creamware Portrait Of Lady, Threaded Interior, Teal Blue, 2 In.	2875.00
Coffeepot, Grapes, Leaves, Brown Tendrils, High Dome Cover, c.1800, 10 In.	450.00
Coffeepot, Pearlware, Batavian Ware, Double Intertwined Handles, 1800, 11 In.	745.00
Creamer, 3-Color Floral, Shell-Molded Spout, Barrel Form, 4 1/2 In.	295.00
Creamer, Blue, Gray Design, Handle, 4 In.	66.00
Creamer, Brush-Stroke Florals, Pedestal Foot, Blue & White	350.00
Creamer, Swirl, Ribbed & Waisted Shape, Blue Carnation	295.00
Cup & Saucer, Fluted Body, Brown & Ocher	145.00
Figurine, Andromache, Pearl Glaze	1210.00
Plate, 4-Color Florals In Center, Green Edge, 7 3/4 In.	525.00
Plate, Creamware, Grape Cluster, Green Glaze, Feather Border, 1800, 4 3/8 In.	430.00
Plate, Floral, Foliage Green Feather Edge, Scalloped, Blue, Green, Yellow, Tan, 9 In.	1705.00
Plate, Peafowl, Green Feather Edge, Blue, Yellow, Tan, Brown, Octagonal, 7 1/2 In.	1210.00
Plate, Peafowl, Green Foliage, Black Branches, Spatterware, c.1820, 7 1/2 In.	230.00
Plate, Strawberry, Blue Feather Edge, Polychrome, c.1770, 6 5/8 In.	395.00
Platter, Floral, Feather Edge, Blue, White, 18 1/2 x 15 In.	52.00
Pot, Cover, Horizontal Wavy Lines, Reeded Handle, 1765-1775, 10 In.	2070.00
Saucer, Tulip, 6 In.	275.00
Sugar & Saucer, Domed Lid, Peafowl, Green Spatter Foliage, 1830s, 5 1/4 In.	575.00
Tankard, Green, Yellow & Brown, Small	650.00
Teapot, Cover, Creamware, Tortoiseshell Glaze, Strap Handle, Beadwork Border	1092.00
Teapot, Green, Brown Spring Design, Ocher, Brown, Yellow Border	250.00
Urn, Pineapple, Green Feather Edge, Scalloped, Green Foliage, Brown Highlights, 7 In.	1070.00

LEFTON is a mark found on many pieces. The Geo. Zoltan Lefton
Company has imported pottery, porcelain, glass, and other wares to be
sold in America since 1940. The firm is still in business. The company
mark has changed through the years; but because marks have been
used for long periods of time, they are of little help in dating an object.

Ashtray, Swan, Pink	40.00
Bank, Hubert The Lion	25.00 to 45.00

Bank, Humpty Dumpty 45.00
Bank, Kewpie 50.00
Butter, Cover, Miss Priss, Cat .... 200.00 to 225.00
Candy Dish, Cover, White & Green Holly, Berries, Red Bow Handle 30.00
Compote, Floral 20.00
Cookie Jar, Bee 95.00
Cookie Jar, Blue Bird 195.00
Cookie Jar, Christmas Elf 110.00
Cookie Jar, Dainty Miss 150.00
Cookie Jar, Girl In Bunny Suit 395.00
Cookie Jar, Miss Cutie Pie, Pink 85.00
Cookie Jar, Old Lady 110.00
Cookie Jar, Pixie Baby 125.00
Cookie Jar, Santa Claus 180.00
Cookie Jar, Young Lady 95.00
Creamer, Bluebird 35.00
Creamer, Puppy 20.00
Cup & Bowl, Christmas, Box, Child's 35.00
Cup & Saucer, Fruit Design 35.00
Decanter & Mug Set, Santa, 7 Piece 70.00
Eggcup, Americana 45.00
Eggcup, Blue Paisley, 3 Piece 50.00
Eggcup, Bluebird 35.00
Eggcup, Miss Priss, Cat 40.00
Figurine, Angel, February 20.00
Figurine, Balinese Dancer, Man, 8 1/2 In. 55.00
Figurine, Bee, Sitting On Rose Petal, Pale Yellow Center Rose 30.00
Figurine, Bluebird 20.00
Figurine, Bridesmaid, 3 3/4 In. 25.00
Figurine, Cardinal 20.00
Figurine, Colonial Woman, No. 341 .... 50.00
Figurine, Continental, Man, Artillery 65.00
Figurine, Couple, On Park Bench, No. 5240, 7 1/2 x 7 In. 75.00
Figurine, French Woman, 6 1/4 In. 40.00
Figurine, Hummingbird 20.00
Figurine, Mallard, 4 3/4 In. 20.00
Figurine, Napoleon 80.00
Figurine, Nurse, Hot Water Bottle, Stamped, KW895C, 1955 .... 25.00
Figurine, Oriole 20.00
Figurine, Pekinese, Tan To Reddish Brown, H7328, 4 3/4 x 5 In. 25.00
Figurine, Pelican, 6 x 5 In. 25.00
Figurine, Pinkie & Blue Boy, 8 In., Pair 40.00
Figurine, Pixie, White Luster, 4 In. 15.00
Figurine, Poodle Puppy 50.00
Figurine, Praying Boy 20.00
Figurine, Senior Golfing Couple, Seated On Bench, No. 7269, 1970s, 7 x 6 In. 75.00
Figurine, Sun Girl, 1957 .... 55.00
Head Vase, Pink Top, Sash On Head, 6 In. 60.00
Head Vase, Woman, No. 2251, 6 In. 90.00
Jam Jar, Cat 45.00
Lantern, Holly Christmas, Green 60.00
Mug, Bluebird .... 75.00 to 85.00
Nut Dish, Miss Priss, Cat 175.00
Pitcher, Milk, Cow's Head, Large 35.00
Pitcher, Milk, Miss Priss, Cat 95.00
Pitcher & Bowl, Fruit Pattern 20.00
Planter, Bluebird 165.00
Plaque, Horse Head, Gray, 8 In., Pair 110.00
Plaque, Mermaid, Pair 80.00
Plaque, Mermaid, Rides Sea Horse, 2 Fish Swim Nearby, Box, 3 Piece 45.00
Plaque, Wall, Puppy, Flowers 25.00
Plaque, Wall, Rooster 35.00
Plate, Salad, Rose Chintz 25.00

Salt & Pepper, Birthday Boys 30.00
Salt & Pepper, Dog 30.00
Salt & Pepper, Heritage Fruit 30.00
Salt & Pepper, Holly Berry, Pair 20.00
Salt & Pepper, Miss Priss, Cat ....20.00 to 45.00
Salt & Pepper, Rose 25.00
Salt & Pepper, Rustic Daisy 20.00
Salt & Pepper, Thumbelina 20.00
Snack Set, Holly Berry 20.00
Sugar, Cover, Bluebird 25.00
Sugar, Cover, Golden Wheat 10.00
Sugar & Creamer 65.00
Sugar & Creamer, Americana 55.00
Sugar & Creamer, Holly Berry 55.00
Sugar & Creamer, Lady Head 80.00
Sugar & Creamer, Miss Priss, Cat 50.00
Sugar & Creamer, Rose Chintz 50.00
Sugar & Creamer, Violet 30.00
Tea Set, Roses, Hand Painted, Gold Trim, 21 Pieces 475.00
Teabag Holder, Miss Priss, Cat 25.00
Teapot, Bee 85.00
Teapot, Blue 40.00
Teapot, Dutch Girl 150.00
Teapot, Eastern Star 65.00
Teapot, Honey Bee 110.00
Teapot, Miss Priss, Cat ....85.00 to 155.00
Teapot, Rose Chintz ....75.00 to 100.00
Tray, Honey Bee 20.00
Tray, Tidbit, Miss Priss, Cat, 2 Sections 110.00
Vase, Cat's Head 45.00
Wall Pocket, Girl, Blond Hair 55.00
Wall Pocket, Green Hat, Blue Flowers, Brown Ribbon 120.00
Wall Pocket, Parrots On Limb 120.00

EGRAS was founded in 1864 by Auguste Legras at St. Denis, France. It is best known for cameo glass and enamel-decorated glass with Art Nouveau designs. Legras merged with Pantin in 1920 and became the Verreries et Cristalleries de St. Denis et de Pantin Reunies.

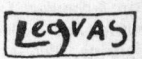

Bowl, Autumn Leaves, Cameo, 6 In. 600.00
Bowl, Holly, Signed, 4 3/4 In. 170.00
Rose Bowl, Enameled Grapes & Vine Over Acid Finish, Signed, 9 In. 165.00
Tray, Winter Scene, Framed In Conforming Wood Holder, Signed, 5 x 9 In. .. 345.00
Vase, Acid Cut Leaves & Berries, Mottled Peach, Gray Walls, Signed, 8 In. 460.00
Vase, Acid Cut Pendant Blossoming Branches, Signed, 13 3/4 In. 805.00
Vase, Berry Branch, Turquoise, Fuchsia, Brown Overlay, Caramel, 1900, 6 In. 575.00
Vase, Bird, White, Green, Floral Design, Mottled White, Blue Ground, Signed, 6 In. 176.00
Vase, Branch Design, Acid Finish, Enameled, Variegated Butterscotch Ground, 8 In. 385.00

If you display your collection at a library, museum, or commercial store, do not let the display include your street address or city name. It's best if you don't even include your name. A display is an open invitation to a thief. Be sure the collection will be guarded and fully insured.

Legras, Vase, Enameled, Trees & Lake, 4 Sides, 8 1/2 In.

Vase, Branches, Fruit, Aubergine Overlay, Pale Orange Acid Ground, White, 24 In. 1495.C
Vase, Brown Leaves, Stems, Green Leaves, Mottled Yellow Ground, 7 1/2 In. 412.C
Vase, Cameo, Etched Floral Design, Signed, 8 3/8 In. 575.C
Vase, Enameled Landscape, Fall Foliage, Sail Boats, Signed, 15 1/2 In. 440.C
Vase, Enameled Purple Grapes, Leaves, Signed, 1910-1920, 10 In. 360.C
Vase, Enameled, Trees & Lake, 4 Sides, 8 1/2 In. ....*Illus* 1488.C
Vase, Fernery Form, Scenic Design, Naturalistic Enamel Colors, Signed, 4 1/4 In. 1265.C
Vase, Hydrangea Bouquet, Purple, Acid Etched Pink Ground, 1900, 15 1/2 In. 1035.C
Vase, Landscape, Trees By A Lake, Green, Ecru, Terra-Cotta, Brown, 1910, 13 3/4 In. ... 747.C
Vase, Overall Maroon & Pink Flowering Blossoms, Signed, 12 In. 546.C
Vase, Pink & Red, Cameo, Signed, Base Stamped Made In France, 8 In. 287.C
Vase, Pink, Maroon Flowering Branches, Etched, Oval, 8 1/2 In. 575.C
Vase, Purple & Green Violets, Slender Neck, Signed, 5 1/2 In., Pair 345.C
Vase, Scenic, Orange, Yellow, Green Ground, Trees, Boats, Enameled, 15 3/4 x 4 In. 350.0
Vase, Scenic, Waterfront, With Sailboats, Squared Rim, Etched, 3 1/2 In. 316.0
Vase, Tiger, Tan Mottling, Goldstone Throughout, Amber Ruffled Top, 4 x 8 7/8 In. 295.0

LENOX is the name of a porcelain maker. Walter Scott Lenox and
Jonathan Cox founded the Ceramic Art Company in Trenton, New
Jersey, in 1889. In 1906, Lenox left and started his own company
called *Lenox*. The company makes a porcelain that is similar to Irish
Belleek. The marks used by the firm have changed through the years
and collectors prefer the earlier examples. Related pieces may also be
listed in the Ceramic Art Co. category.

Bookends, Trojan Horse Head 350.0
Bowl, Fruit, Ming .... 38.0(
Bowl, Patriot, Commemorative, 1776-1976, 24K Gold Trim, 9 1/2 In. 150.0
Cake Stand, Gold Trim, Footed, 8 1/2 In. 90.0
Candleholder, Lyre Shape, Blue Wreath, 8 1/2 In. 40.0
Coffeepot, Silver Overlay, Nouveau Design 275.0
Creamer, Figural, George Washington, 1890s .... 695.0(
Cup & Saucer, Demitasse, Princess .... 48.0(
Cup & Saucer, Rhodora .... 20.0(
Cup & Saucer, Springdale .... 12.5(
Cup & Saucer, Tuscany .... 100.0(
Dinner Set, Bellevue, Plates, Soups, Undertrays, Cups, Saucers, Teapot, 47 Piece ...... 357.0(
Figurine, Blue Jay .... 35.0(
Figurine, Breasted Grosbeck .... 35.0(
Figurine, Bulldog, Standing, Green Mark, 6 x 8 1/2 In. .... 1195.0(
Figurine, Chickadee .... 35.0(
Figurine, Chipping Sparrow .... 35.0(
Figurine, Cleopatra, Box .... 110.0(
Figurine, Golden Crowned Kinglet .... 35.0(
Figurine, Leda And The Swan, Bisque Finish, Signed, 1929, 10 1/2 In. .... .250.00 to 295.0(
Figurine, Rapunzel, 9 In. .... 105.0(
Figurine, Swan, Gold Mark, 6 x 8 In. .... 145.0(
Figurine, Tea At The Ritz, American Fashion Series, Box, 1984 .... 135.0(
Night-Light, Leda & Swan, Cream Bisque, Full Figure .... 895.0(
Ornament, Christmas, Ivory, Gold, 1983 .... 35.0(
Pitcher, Lemonade, 6 Red Apples, Leaves, Repeat Branches, Gold Handle, 5 1/2 In. .... 220.0(
Pitcher, Molded Patriot, Ivory Matte, Blue Enamel, 8 7/8 In. .... 75.0(
Pitcher, Romeo & Juliet, Ivory Matte, Gilt Trim, Ispanky, 9 1/2 In. ...... 95.0(
Plate, Amish Autumn .... 12.0(
Plate, Golf Tournament, U.S. Seniors Golf Assn., Lyford Gay Club Invitational, 1976 ... 20.0(
Plate, Little Quilters .... 12.0(
Plate, Red Feather, D. Crowley .... 10.0(
Plate, Spirit Rider, M. Fields .... 10.0(
Platter, Dessert, Fleur-De-Lis, Gold Trim, 1 1/2 In. .... 125.0(
Platter, Serving, Overall Embossed Grape Leaves, Cold Trim, 12 3/4 In. ...... 95.0(
Salt & Pepper, Nipper .... 50.0(
Salt & Pepper Mill, Urn, Floral Design, Brass Tops, Signed, 7 3/4 In. ..... 22.0(
Sugar, Cover, Mount Vernon, Roses In Basket, Aqua Jewels, Green Mark .... 65.0(
Tea & Coffee Set, Cobalt Blue, Sterling Silver Overlay, After Dinner Cups, 14 Piece ... 2200.0(

Toby Mug, William Penn, Indian Handle, Green Mark 250.00
Vase, Comical, Black, 8 In. 85.00
Vase, Corseted Shape, Pink Orchids, Green Lenox Stamp, 11 3/4 In. 850.00
Vase, Embossed Vertical Lines, Gold Trim, 8 3/4 In. 60.00
Vase, Intaglio Rose, Gold Pierced-Heart Border, Wreath Mark, 1/2 In. 38.50
Vase, Leaf Base, Circular, 10 5/8 In. 57.50
Vase, Rose, 13 In. 275.00

ETTER OPENERS have been used since the eighteenth century. Ivory
nd silver were favored by the well-to-do. In the late nineteenth cen-
ury, the letter opener was popular as an advertising giveaway and
any were made of metal or celluloid. Brass openers with figural han-
les were also popular.

Basket Of Flowers, Serpent On Reverse Side, Carved, Ivory, 10 1/4 In. 70.00
Brass, Hammered, Original Patina, Carence Crafters, 8 In. 110.00
Buffalo, Williams & Peters Pittston Coal, Bronze 38.00
Buick, Bronze & Ceramic 135.00
Carolina Marble & Tile Co., Winston-Salem, N.C., Brass 15.00
Carved & Pierced Handle, Screw Cap At Tip, 8 1/2 In. 35.00
Copper, Hammered, Cutout Work, Original Patina, Arts & Crafts, 9 In. 121.00
Desk Set, Ivory & Brass, 10 1/4 In., China, 4 Piece 590.00
Engraved Design On Handle, Copper, 4 1/2 In. 5.50
Fish, Compliment Of Ettlinger Commission Co., U.S. Yards, Chicago 78.00
Handle Embossed As Ticket To Fiddler On The Roof, Bronze Color, 1972, 7 1/2 In. 25.00
Hennis Freight Lines, White Handle, Chrome, 7 1/2 In. 4.50
Ivory, 2 Points, Floral Strapwork, Leather Case, Froment-Meurice, 1895, 23 In. 3750.00
Josephine, Lalique, 12 3/4 In. 120.00
Lawrence Welk 18.00
Lee Co., Food Brokers, Brass 9.00
Owl, Brass 15.00
Rococo Handle, Brass 40.00
Schlorer Delicatessen, Philadelphia, Steel, Engraved Handle, 9 In. 9.00
Sheffield Steel, Sterling Silver Handle 85.00
Spiral Design, Sterling Handle, Ivory, England 95.00
Sword, Knight Hilt, Brass 85.00
Turkey Foot Feather Blade, Cast Iron 95.00

IBBEY Glass Company has made many types of glass since 1888,
ncluding the cut glass and tablewares that are collected today. The
temwares of the 1930s and 1940s are once again in style. The Toledo,
Ohio, firm was purchased by Owens-Illinois in 1935 and is still work-
ng under the name *Libbey* as a division of that company. Additional
ieces may be listed under Amberina, Cut Glass, and Maize.

Basket, Carnation Flower, Cut Handle, Signed, 14 1/2 x 9 3/4 In. 1150.00
Basket, Roses, Band Of Diamond Point & Leaves, Signed, 19 1/2 In. 920.00
Basket, Star & Feather, Signed, 1896-1900, 14 In. 300.00
Bowl, Floral, Branch Pattern, Signed, 3 1/4 x 8 In. 193.00
Bowl, Hobstar, Fan & Fine Cut, Signed, 4 x 8 In. 330.00
Bowl, Hobstars & Diamond, Intaglio Border Of Fruit, 10 1/4 In. 750.00
Bowl, Stylized Flowers, 4 Cut Petals, 8 In. 450.00
Celery Dish, Laurent, Signed, 11 3/4 x 4 1/2 In. 250.00
Cocktail, Kangaroo, 6 Piece 495.00
Compote, Clear, Ruby Loops, Flared Flower Shape, 10 1/2 x 4 In. 595.00
Dish, Hobstar & Notch, Central Knob Handle, 3 3/4 x 5 In. 120.00
Finger Bowl, Jewel, Crossed Ellipse, Signed, 4 1/4 In. 75.00
Jug, Rum, Flute, Blue Cut To Clear, 6 x 5 1/4 In. 925.00
Pitcher, Diamond Optic, Blue Threading, Ice Lip, c.1933 .... 250.00
Plate, Love Birds, Signed, 7 In. 1200.00
Plate, Luncheon, Galway, 8 In. 18.00
Rose Bowl, Beige Cut, Pansies & Leaves, White Beaded, Signed, 2 1/2 x 3 1/2 In. 550.00
Tumbler, Galway 18.00
Tumbler, Iced Tea, Galway 18.00
Vase, Bud, Thorn Stems, Florals, Leaves, Signed, 12 In. 150.00
Vase, Fuchsia, Signed, 1917, 11 1/4 In. 1200.00

Vase, Opalescent Green, 8 3/4 In. 400.0
Vase, Zipper, Amber Ribbed, Internal Green Dotted Lines, 6 In. 255.0

LIGHTERS for cigarettes and cigars are collectible. Cigarettes became
popular in the late nineteenth century, and with the cigarette came
matches and cigarette lighters. All types of lighters are collected, from
solid gold to the first of the recent disposable lighters. Most examples
found were made after 1940. Some lighters may be found in the
Jewelry category in this book.

Afelo, Sterling Silver, Scroll Engraved Case 23.0
Airplane, Chrome 90.0
Aladdin, Table, Lamp Shape, Blue Enamel Painted Shade, Japan, 3 1/2 In. 24.0
Aladdin's Lamp Shape, Table, Occupied Japan 45.0
Art Deco, Bowman-Manning, Chrome, 1928 .... 85.0
Beer Can, 6-Pack, Pearl 24.0
Beer Can, Ballantine Beer, 12 Oz. 3.0
Beer Can, Falls City Beer, 12 Oz. 7.0
Beer Can, Falstaff Beer, 12 Oz. 5.0
Big Boy, Catalin, France 65.0
Bowling Pin, Cream Color, Red Band, Kem, Detroit, Mi., 3 In. 22.0
Brass, Pipe, Turned Wooden Handle, Curved Rod Legs, 18th Century 143.0
Calibri, Polished Chrome & Gold, Table Type, Box, England 65.0
Calibri, Table Size, Display Model 55.0
Camera Form, On Tripod, Occupied Japan 175.0
Charm, Rhinestone, Ring For Attachment, 1 x 1 In. 55.0
Chesterfield, Royalite 28.0
Cigar, Countertop, Gas Nozzle On Back, Hooks To Gas Line, Metal, 17 1/2 In. 2200.00
Cigar, Gas, Victorian Wall Mount, Brass, Woman's Hand Holding Glass Globe, 1880 .... 3175.00
Cigar, Midland Jump Start, Model L, Country Store, Davenport Mfg. 195.00
Cigar, Mixed Metal, Hammered Finish, 1880 .... 950.00
Cigar, Reclining Nude On Dolphin, Brass Lamp, Red Globe 975.00
Cigar, Risque Dancing Woman, Countertop, 1880s 2750.00
Cigar, Stachelbert, Cuspidor Shape 375.00
Cigar, Stag Horn & Sterling Silver, Swivels, c.1900, 13 In. 595.00
Cigar, Striker, Man On Horse, Countertop 450.00
Cigar, Swirl Glass, Electric 165.00
Cities Service, Gas Station, Box 32.00
Clark, Firefly, Lift Arm, Brass, Lizard-Skin Style Wrap 54.00
Comet, Wristwatch Shaped, Lighter Under Watch Cover, Japan 174.00
Danny Thomas, 1966 .... 85.00
Demley, Surelite, Trench Style, Brass, Austria, c.1912, 3 In. 52.00
Dunhill, Diamond Pattern, Sterling Silver, Pocket 75.00
Dunhill, Gold Plated, Box, Switzerland, 1960 .... 175.00
Dunhill, Pipe, Silver Plate 250.00
Dunhill, Rollalite, Chrome 100.00
Dunhill, Sterling Silver, Box 65.00
Dunhill, Sterling Silver, Navy Style, Tube Form 90.00
Dunhill, Tankard 245.00
Elgin, Matching Cigarette Case, Sterling Silver, Gift Box 100.00
Elgin, Studebaker Logo 32.00
Escort, Black Enamel, Chrome, Box 75.00
Evans, Gold Plated, Box, c.1940 .... 125.00
Evans, Hammered Panels, With Cigarette Case 60.00
Fire Pumper, Cast Metal, Red, Wheels Turn, 4 x 4 1/2 In. 125.00
Foxhole & Blackout, Fluid & Flameless, Instructions, Box, 4 In. 45.00
Girl With Bird, Girl With Flower, Memory Of Okinawa, Brushed Finish, Japan 29.00
Godzilla, Flame Shoots Out Of Mouth, Box, c.1984 .... 35.00
Horse, Art Deco, With Tag 65.00
Indian Wars, Military Markings, Brass, Round 495.00
Marathon, Combination With Compact 125.00
Master Case, Combination 50.00
Mickey Mouse, Silver Colored, Mouseketeers Club Emblem 210.00
Mirth Is King, Box 40.00

Park, Alcoa Thomas Brokerage Co., Zippo Style, Goldtoned Brushed Finish 23.00
Parker, Black Crackle Finish, Windproof, Zippo Style, Cardboard Box, World War II Era   75.00
Penguin, U.S. Air Force, Officers' Open Mess Yokota Air Base Japan, Plane, 1950s 64.00
Pipe, Brass, Dutch, c.1730, 6 1/2 x 8 1/4 In. 575.00
Pipe, Tongs To Light Clay Pipes, Beading, France, 2 7/8-In. Bowl 325.00
Pistol, Silver Finish, Mother-Of-Pearl Grips, 1 1/4 In. 26.00
Playboy 45.00
Pocket Watch Case, Lighter Inside, Horse Jumping Fence, Engraved, Australia, 2 In. . .   127.00
Regal, Lift Arm, Brushed Textured Finish, England 34.00
Ronson, Bartender 2200.00
Ronson, Blue Wedgwood Case With Angels, Polished Finish Top, Table, 3 1/4 In. 49.00
Ronson, Crown, Table 6.00
Ronson, Decanter, Silver Finish, Scrollwork Base, 4 1/2 In. 46.00
Ronson, Essex, Chrome, Flip Base To Fuel 20.00
Ronson, Fish Scene, Minton, Signed 200.00
Ronson, Front Covered With Rhinestones 85.00
Ronson, Frosted, Spherical Design, Table 195.00
Ronson, Georgian, Silver Plated, Green Felt Pad, Table, 3 1/4 In.   59.00
Ronson, Leona, Green Glass, Brass 45.00
Ronson, Mastercase, Cigarette Case, Silver Metal, Brown Celluloid Panels, Box 69.00
Ronson, Pal, Cigarette Case, Floral & Monogram, 4 In. 55.00
Ronson, Pencilighter, Lighter On Mechanical Pencil, Polished Finish, 5 1/4 In. 65.00
Ronson, Princess, Polished Finish, Engine-Turned Body, Purple Felt Bag, Box 59.00
Ronson, Queen Anne, Engraved 58.00
Ronson, Regal, Polished Finish, Green Felt Pad, Table, 3 1/4 In. 64.00
Ronson, Silver Plated Ashtray & Stepped Base 750.00
Ronson, Spartan, Table 40.00
Ronson, Sport, Black Textured Case, Maroon Felt Bag, Plastic Box 46.00
Ronson, Streamline, Black & Chrome, Box, Instructions 500.00
Ronson, Triumph, Polished Engine-Turned Body, Cream & Black Plastic Box 44.00
Ronson, U.S. Army, Silver Metal, Applied Bronze Great Seal Design, World War II Era .   52.00
Ronson, Varaflame Comet, Automatic, Windproof, Unused, Plastic Box, 2 1/2 In. 39.00
Ronson, Viking, Pocket 35.00
Ronson, Wedgwood Style, Pottery, Blue, Classical Woman Design, Table, 5 In. 49.00
Ronson, Whirlwind Imperial, Brushed Finish, Crest Logos, Wind Screen, Plastic Box . . .   46.00
Ronson, Zeus, Box, Wedgwood 125.00
Scotty Dog, Pulling On Leash, Green 25.00
Scripto, Ballantine, Plastic, Metal, Clear Base 37.00
Scripto, Black Label, Plastic 18.00
Scripto, Vu-Lighter, Martin's Rat Hole Drilling, Inc., Enid, Okla., Blue Band 41.00
Scripto, Vu-Lighter, Raytheon, Clear Plastic Case, Silver Lid, Red Band 46.00
Scripto, Vu-Lighter, Ship, USS San Pablo AGS-30, Clear Plastic Case, Blue Band 46.00
Scripto, Vu-Lighter, Tulsa Pipe Coating Inc., Clear Plastic Body, Red Band 36.00
Ship's Wheel, Nickeled Metal Base, Wheel Turns, 5 x 2 3/4 In. 52.00
St. Dupont, Paris, Gold Filled 100.00
Thorens, Cigarette Case, Brass, Hinged, Engraved Tartan Design, 1930s, 3 x 4 1/2 In. . . .   70.00
Tornado G, Trench Style, Bright Nickel Finish, Austria 46.00
Tube Style, Brass, Wick R, Kem Inc., Detroit, Mich., Early 1900s, 2 In. 28.00
Zippo, 10K Gold Plated, Slim, Globe With Red T, Engine Turned Case, 1960 . . . .   76.00
Zippo, 18-Wheeler Semitruck, Engraved, Professional Truck Driver, 1977 . . . .   34.00
Zippo, 40th Anniversary, Thank You Statement From George Blaisdell, 1971 . . . .   68.00
Zippo, 50-Year Commemorative, 50 Years & Glowing Strong, 1932-1982, Brass 100.00
Zippo, A.M. Collins Mfg. Co., Division Of International Paper Co., 1959 . . . .   41.00
Zippo, Ace Dodge Plymouth, Brooklyn, N.Y., Brushed Finish, 1950s 68.00
Zippo, Air Force, 25th Anniversary 95.00
Zippo, Anheuser-Busch, Chrome Display Stand, Each Different, 8 Piece 150.00
Zippo, Apollo Moon Landing, Astronauts, Lander, Commemorative, July 1969 . . . .   190.00
Zippo, Army Air Corps Pilot Wings, Steel, Black Crackle Finish, 1942 . . . .   250.00
Zippo, Atwater Mfg. Co., Plantsville, Conn., Red & Blue Enamel, Brushed Finish, 1958 .   63.00
Zippo, B.F. Goodrich Logo, Engraved, Painted, Brushed Finish, 1959 . . . .   69.00
Zippo, B.F. Goodrich, Smileage, Smiling Tire, Brushed Finish, 1959 . . . .   145.00
Zippo, Barcroft, 3rd Model, Chromed Finish, Plain Case, Table, 3 1/4 In. 182.00
Zippo, Barcroft, 4th Model, Safety Warning, Brushed Finish, Felt Pad, Table, 3 1/4 In. . .   185.00

Zippo, Barcroft, 4th Model, USS Albany Logo, Painted, Black Felt Pad, Table, 3 1/4 In. . . 205.00
Zippo, Bennet-Rogers Pipe Coating Inc., Engraved, Brushed Finish, 1963 . . . . 30.00
Zippo, Big West Oil Co. Of Montana, Brushed Finish, Enamel, Box, 1965 . . . . 39.00
Zippo, Black Crinkle Finish, 3-Barrel Hinge, Paper Box, 1943-45 . . . . 345.00
Zippo, Blue Cross & Blue Shield Logo, Brushed Finish, 1959 . . . . 45.00
Zippo, Brass Drawn Case, U-Shaped Cam Stop, Polished Finish, 1938-39 . . . . 291.00
Zippo, Camel, Embossed 30.00
Zippo, Car, C.B. Operator, Got Your Ears On Good Buddy, Brushed Finish, 1976 . . . . . . 47.00
Zippo, Chase Manhattan Bank N.A., Brushed Finish, White & Gold Box, 1974 . . . . 70.00
Zippo, Chrome Finish, Vertical Lines, Blank Panel, 5-Barrel Hinge, World War II Era . . . 92.00
Zippo, Dr Pepper Logo, Red Enamel, Polished Finish, Slim, Box, 1975 . . . . 201.00
Zippo, Engraved Facsimile Signature, Jane Rittenhouse, Brushed Finish, Late 1940s 40.00
Zippo, Engraved Picture Of Golfer, Brushed Finish, 1972 . . . . 59.00
Zippo, Equitable Of Iowa, Box, 1956 . . . . 45.00
Zippo, Fisherman Catching Fish, 5-Barrel Hinge, Loop, 1958 . . . . 50.00
Zippo, FM Fairbanks Morse, Engraved, Blue Enamel, Brushed Finish, 1951 . . . . 103.00
Zippo, G.E. Logo, Engraved, Brushed Finish, 1959 . . . . 70.00
Zippo, General Paper, Old Truck 35.00
Zippo, Golden Light Webster Cigars, Engraved, Brushed Finish, Slim, 1962 . . . . 28.00
Zippo, Goldtone U.S. Army Eagle, Nickel Case, Brushed Finish, Late 1940s 70.00
Zippo, International Harvester, Engraved, Red & Black Enamel, Striped Box, 1950s 109.00
Zippo, J.C. Nichols Construction, Etched, 3-Barrel Hinge, 1947 . . . . 76.00
Zippo, Johnstown Express, Pittsburgh, Brushed Finish, 1968 . . . . 64.00
Zippo, Kent Cigarettes 28.00
Zippo, Knickerbocker Hospital, Box, 1960s 35.00
Zippo, Krispy Kreme, 1943 . . . . 95.00
Zippo, Lifetime Guarantee, Polished Chrome 13.00
Zippo, Marines Raising Flag On Iwo Jima, Engraved, Brushed Finish, 1961 . . . . 59.00
Zippo, Marlboro Cigarettes 21.00
Zippo, Masonic, German Silver Case 100.00
Zippo, Moderne, Chrome, Black Felt Pad, Table, 4 1/4 In. 127.00
Zippo, Monkey Mountain, Vietnam 45.00
Zippo, NBC News, Printed, White Enamel Side, Polished Finish, Table, 1979, 3 1/4 In. . . 195.00
Zippo, Oakdale Yarn & Twine 1865-1965, Polished Finish, Slim, White & Gold Box 59.00
Zippo, Olympic, Silver Plate, 100th Anniversary, 1996 . . . . 25.00
Zippo, Painted, Black Crinkle Finish, World War II 231.00
Zippo, Phillips 66 Shield Logo, Polished Finish, Slim, 1967 . . . . 40.00
Zippo, Pioneer Club, Polished Finish, Pearl Opalescent Body, Table, 1960-66, 4 In. 175.00
Zippo, Plain Case, 3-Barrel Hinge, Brushed Finish, Late 1940s 98.00
Zippo, Plane, Boeing 727, Cruziero Logo, Polished Finish, Slim, 1973 . . . . 68.00
Zippo, Polished Finish, 3-Barrel Hinge, 1936-40 . . . . 383.00
Zippo, Rectangle, Stepped Base, Table, 3 1/4 In. 50.00
Zippo, Reddy Kilowatt Character, Engraved, Brushed Finish, 1958 . . . . .72.00 to 95.00
Zippo, Rose Art, Brass, Dark Marble, Table, 1958, 4 1/2 In. 317.00
Zippo, Rose Art, Brass, Wood, Table, 1967, 4 1/2 In. 179.00
Zippo, Sealtest Dairies Logo, Brushed Finish, 3-Barrel Hinge, Late 1940s 93.00
Zippo, Shell Oil Co., Shell Logo, Brushed Finish, 1958 . . . . 82.00
Zippo, Shell Oil Co., Shell Logo, Brushed Finish, Slim, 1963 . . . . 33.00
Zippo, St. Regis Envelope Division, Polished Finish, Slim, 1964 . . . . 25.00
Zippo, Steel Case, Brushed Finish, Early 1950s 37.00
Zippo, United States Military Academy West Point, Enamel Painted Emblem, 1962 . . . . . 47.00
Zippo, USS Hector AR 7, Engraved, Brushed Finish, 1960 . . . . 36.00
Zippo, Venetian, Holder 18.00
Zippo, W.G. Rankin Eight Air Force Outstanding Crew, December 1955, January 1956 . . 46.00
Zippo, Westinghouse Electric Logo On Lid Above Hinge, Slim, Box, 1966 . . . . 43.00
Zippo, Winchester-Western, Flying Duck, Brushed Finish, Partial Box, 1958 . . . . 230.00
Zippo, World War II Battleship USS Robinson Emblem 30.00
Zippo, Your Next Move Call Selinsky, Brushed Finish, 1962 . . . . 41.00

LIGHTNING ROD BALLS are collected for their variety of shapes and
colors. These glass balls were at the center of the rod that was attached
to the roof of a house or barn to avoid lightning damage.

 Cone, Red, Sheared Collar, 1920, 4 5/8 In. 250.00

Electra, Cobalt Blue, Embossed Letters, 1870-1920, 4 1/2 In. 175.00
Electra, Red, Embossed Letters, 4 1/2 In. 200.00
Gray Green, Quilted Flattened Diamond, 1870-1920, 5 In. 100.00
Kretzer, Gold Mercury, 1870-1920, 4 1/2 In. 120.00
Kretzer, Quilted Diamond, Gold Mercury, Metal Collar, 5 In. 300.00
Kretzer, Quilted Diamond, Silver Mercury, 5 In. 300.00
Moon & Star, Red, 1870-1920, 4 3/8 In. 230.00
Orange Milk Glass, Sheared Collar, 1870-1920, 4 1/2 In. 360.00
Quilted Diamond, Red, 1870-1920, 5 In. 250.00
Quilted Diamond, Silver Mercury, Sheared Metal Collar, 5 In. 330.00
Red, Chestnut, Sheared Mouth, 1920, 4 In. 210.00

LIMOGES porcelain has been made in Limoges, France, since the mid-
nineteenth century. Fine porcelains were made by many factories,
including Haviland, Ahrenfeldt, Guerin, Pouyat, Elite, and others.
Modern porcelains are being made at Limoges and the word *Limoges*
as part of the mark is not an indication of age. Haviland, one of the
Limoges factories, is listed as a separate category in this book.

Asparagus Plate, Gold Border, 3 Sections, Hand Painted, Signed Durand, 9 In. 165.00
Biscuit Jar, Cover, Hand-Painted Gold Enameling, Beige Body, c.1885, 6 1/2 In. 275.00
Bowl, Enamel, Interior & Exterior Design, Art Deco, Signed, 4 1/2 x 2 1/4 In. 330.00
Bowl, Grape Design, Hand Painted, 9 1/2 In. 205.00
Box, Cover, Violets & Leaf Sprays, Free-Form Art Nouveau, 9 x 5 1/2 In. 145.00
Box, Egg Form, Opens To 2 Scent Bottles, Gold, White, 5 In. 109.00
Box, Floral Inside & Out, Gilt Trim, Signed Pate De Limoges, 12 x 8 x 4 In. 895.00
Box, Patch, Father Christmas Figure On Cover, 3 1/2 In. 100.00
Box, White, 7 Pink Roses, Green Wreath, Gold Trim, Signed 85.00
Centerpiece, Hand Painted Grapes & Leaves, Gold, White Art Co. 275.00
Chamberstick, Floral, Gold Trim, Signed, M. Redon 160.00
Charger, Hanging, Loving Couple Scene, Gold Rococo Border, Signed DuBois, 13 In. .. 450.00
Charger, Pink Roses, Signed, 15 In. 750.00
Cup & Saucer, Pansies, After Dinner 20.00
Dinner Set, Gilt, White, Porcelain, 90 Piece 3680.00
Dinner Set, The St. Quentin, Floral Scroll, Blue Edge, Gold Trim, 1930, 81 Piece 750.00
Dish, Dutch Scene, Blue & White, Artist Initials, Aug.19, '96, 16 In. 110.00
Dresser Set, Cabbage Rose Design, 5 Piece 285.00
Dresser Tray, Purple Violets, 10 1/2 x 8 5/8 In. 33.00
Ewer, Gold Design, Beige Ground, 5 In. 110.00
Fish Set, Enameled Fish, Gilt Rims, 12 Plates, Sauceboat & Underplate, Oblong Tray ... 1870.00
Fish Set, Fish & Seaweed Transfer, Gold Rim, Sauceboat & Underplate, 16 Piece 1100.00
Fish Set, Pastel Blue & Green, R. Rico, Serving Platter, 10 Plates 1050.00
Fish Set, Platter, 8 Plates, Sauceboat & Underplate, 19th Century 2200.00
Fish Set, Platter, 8 Small Plates 950.00
Game Set, Different Birds, Sponged Gold Rim, 18-In. Platter, 12 Plates 1250.00
Glove Box, Cover, Enameled Forget-Me-Nots, Pink Ground, 13 x 4 3/4 In. 325.00
Gravy Boat, Turquoise Border, 10 In. 29.00
Ice Cream Set, Forget-Me-Nots, Rosebuds, Scroll & Scallop Border, Tray, 10 Dishes ... 450.00
Jardiniere, Children, Birds & Flowers, Hand Painted, 9 x 9 1/4 In. 330.00
Jardiniere, Hand Painted Poppies, Gilded Elephant Handles, 12 In. 880.00
Oyster Plate, Floral Design, 6 Piece 330.00
Oyster Plate, Hand Painted, 8 3/4 In. 93.00
Oyster Plate, Molded Shells Circle Center Sauce Well, 9 In. 75.00
Pin Tray, Green 75.00
Pitcher, Figure Of Woman, Gilt, Cream, White, Cylindrical, Signed Baumy, 11 1/2 In. .. 316.00
Pitcher, Platinum Mistletoe Berries & Leaves, Gray, Pink Ground, 6 x 5 1/8 In. 145.00
Pitcher, Seagull & Ocean, Signed, 5 1/2 x 9 In. 205.00
Pitcher, Water, Grape Design, Hand Painted, 14 1/2 In. 36.00
Plaque, Couple, Courting, Enameled, 11 In. 125.00
Plaque, Crucifixion, Arch Shape, Penicaud, Frame, 1530s, 3 3/4 In. 2875.00
Plaque, Landscape, Enamel, Signed, Frame, 3 1/2 x 4 1/2 In. 201.00
Plaque, Peacocks, Floral, Fruit, Gold Banded, M. Miller, 1911, 14 In. 137.50
Plaque, Sea Gulls, Ocean Surf, Ships Ground, Gold Rim, Signed, 11 1/2 In. 200.00
Plaque, Seascape, Mother & Child, Gold Trim, Signed, Puisoyer 395.00

Plaque, Stags & Does, Heavy Gold Rococo Border, Dubois, 13 1/4 In., Pair	845.0
Plaque, Winter Scene With Steeple, Blue, White, Gold, G. Tave, 11 1/2 In., Pair	640.0
Plate, 2 Pheasants Center, Irregular Gold Rim, 10 3/8 In.	110.0
Plate, Cavalier Smoking, Pierced, Coudert, 10 In.	160.0
Plate, Deer, Dog, Gold Trim, Marked, 10 In.	135.0
Plate, Flower Circle Wreath, Pink Flowers, White, Gold Edge, Blue Ribbon Trim, 9 In.	5.5
Plate, Game Bird, 2 Quail With 3 Young, Natural Colors, Blue Sky, 14 1/4 In.	195.0
Plate, Game Bird, Quail On 1, 2 Pheasants On Other, Hand Painted, 9 1/2 In., Pair	210.0
Plate, Game Bird, Signed, Dubois Coronet, 10 In.	120.0
Plate, Gold Floral, 8 1/2 In., 4 Piece	280.0
Plate, La Cloche, Gilt With Floral Design, 11 Piece	247.0
Plate, Monk, Coronet, Pair	285.0
Plate, Old Testament Scenes, Portrait Medallion, Signed, 8 1/4 In., 10 Piece	5462.0
Plate, Orchids, Dark Green Ground, 9 1/2 In.	30.0
Plate, Quail, Peony Motif, Scalloped, Porcelain, 12 In.	120.0
Plate, Shanghai Chicken, 2 Chicks, Pres. R.B. Hayes, 1879, 10 In.	1955.0
Platter, Aquatic Motif, 21 1/2 In.	150.0
Portrait, Woman In Red Kerchief, Gilt Metal Oval Frame	295.0
Powder Jar, Blue Boy & Girl	200.0
Sugar & Creamer, Cover, Romantic Scene, Gold Finial Handle, Green Glaze	22.0
Sugar & Creamer, Roses, Gold Trim	75.0
Tea Set, Hand Painted, Tray, Coffeepot, Sugar, Creamer, Cups, Saucers, 12 Piece	209.0
Teapot, Gilt, Floral Design, 9 1/8 In.	36.0
Tray, Hand Painted Scene, Bow Shape, Openwork Handle, 12 In.	210.0
Tray, Snow Scene, Old House	110.0
Urn, Art Deco Design, Cobalt Blue, Gold Trim, 19 1/2 In., Pair	650.0
Vase, Birds, Flowers, Enameled, Signed, C. Faure, 3 x 3 In.	910.0
Vase, Enamel, Birds & Flowers, Iridescent Ground, Signed, C. Faure, 3 x 3 In.	825.0
Vase, Enameled Geometric Chevron Design, Lavender Shading To Brown, 7 1/2 In.	1725.0
Vase, Enameled Geometric Chevron, Yellow Ground, Signed, 11 In.	2300.0
Vase, Floral Design, Gold, Black, Peach, Signed, Bess M. Sanders, 1906, 8 1/4 In.	80.5
Vase, Floral Design, Hand Painted, 12 In.	72.0
Vase, Pillow, Violets, Orange Blossoms On Back, 9 x 6 x 3 In.	270.0
Vase, Pink & Yellow Roses, Signed, 9 1/2 In.	325.0
Vase, Raised Daisies, Buds, Cream, Buff, Brown, Rust, Green, Maroon Ground, 7 In.	396.0
Vase, Red Roses, Signed, 17 In.	600.0
Vase, Stick, Enamel, Signed, Marty Faure, 7 In.	360.0

LINDBERGH was a national hero. In 1927, Charles Lindbergh, the aviator, became the first man to make a nonstop solo flight across the Atlantic Ocean. In 1932, his son was kidnapped and murdered, and Lindbergh was again the center of public interest. He died in 1974. All types of Lindbergh memorabilia are collected.

Bank, Lindy Bank, Bust Of Lindbergh, Aluminum, Grannis & Tolton, 1928, 4 x 6 In.	295.0
Candy Container, Airplane, Spirit Of St. Louis	412.0
Etching, Col. Charles A. Lindbergh, West, 1927, 8 7/8 x 7 In.	75.0
Game, Lindy Flying, Parker Bros., Complete	40.0
Mirror, Pictures Head, Eiffel Tower & Statue Of Liberty, Pocket	330.0
Plate, Spirit Of St. Louis, 1927, Limoges	65.0
Plate, Yellow, Square, 1927	48.0
Sheet Music, Lucky Lindy, 1927	15.00 to 25.0
Spoon, Souvenir	15.0
Tapestry, New York To Paris, France, 18 1/2 x 55 In.	120.0

LITHOPHANES are porcelain pictures made by casting clay in layers of various thicknesses. When a piece is held to the light, a picture of light and shadow is seen through it. Most lithophanes date from the 1825–1875 period. A few are still being made. Many lithophanes sold today were originally panels for lampshades.

Panel, Boy & Girl Kneeling Before A Shrine, Colored, 6 1/4 x 4 1/2 In.	305.0
Panel, Figures Viewing Sculpture, Colored, 4 1/2 x 3 3/4 In.	85.0
Panel, Interior Scene, Family, Metal Frame, 6 1/2 x 4 3/4 In.	288.0
Panel, Lake Itasca, Metal Frame, 4 1/2 x 4 1/2 In.	345.0

Panel, Mother & Child, Knitting Lesson, Metal Frame, With Candleholder	295.00
Panel, Woman Reading Book, Metal Frame, 3 1/2 x 2 1/4 In.	58.00
Puzzle Mug, Relief Leaves, Ribbed, Branch Handle, Germany	95.00
Stein, Bicycle Design, Pewter Fittings, Musterschutz, 6 5/8 In.	385.00
Stein, Regimental, Germany, 1909	500.00
Tea Warmer, Scenes Of West Point, 4 1/2 In.	1143.00

IVERPOOL, England, was the site of several pottery and porcelain fac-
·ries from 1716 to 1785. Some earthenware was made with trans-
·r decorations. Sadler and Green made print-decorated wares from
·756. Many of the pieces were made for the American market and
·ature patriotic emblems, such as eagles, flags, and other special-
·terest motifs. Liverpool pitchers are always called Liverpool jugs by
·ollectors.

Bowl, 3-Masted Ship, Reserves Of Armaments, Portrait Of Washington, 8 7/8 In.	403.00
Bowl, Exotic Birds Perched On Fence Amidst Peonies, Blue Band Rim, 12 In.	1035.00
Bowl, Peony Sprigs Alternating With Flowers, Cell Diaper Border Rim, 12 In.	460.00
Bowl, Washington, Lafayette & Franklin, 8 In.	176.00
Castor Set, 5 Bottles, Eagle Handled Holder, Late 18th Century, 11 In.	1430.00
Castor Set, Black Transfer Design, Round Stand	1430.00
Charger, Flowering Plant, Bamboo Beside Garden Wall, Blue, White, 1760, 17 In.	575.00
Cup & Saucer, Peacock Within Landscape, Plain White Body, 1765, 2 In.	195.50
Flower Brick, Flowering Peony, Rocks, Tree By Fence, Blue, White, 1750, 6 1/8 In.	575.00
Flower Brick, Flowers, Bamboo, Fenced Garden, Blue, White, 1750, 6 In.	690.00
Flower Brick, Tower Between 3 Small Houses, Blue, White, 1750, 6 In.	575.00
Jug, 11 Masonic Transfers, Large	1250.00
Jug, American Militia, Reverse U.S. Ship, Sailor's Adieu At Spout, 9 1/2 In.	3500.00
Jug, Faith, Hope & Charity, Figure Of Religion On Reverse, 10 In.	530.00
Jug, Gretna Green, The Red Hot Marriage, Shooting On Reverse, 7 3/4 In.	895.00
Jug, Masonic Transfers, Seal Of United States Under Spout, 10 1/2 In.	1100.00
Jug, Profile George Washington, He In Glory, America In Tears, 9 1/2 In.	3950.00
Jug, Reserve Of Ships, L'Insurgent & Constellation, Creamware, 7 3/4 In.	1265.00
Jug, Success To Trade, Clipper Ship Flying American Flag, Waterman Verse, 8 In.	750.00
Jug, Transfer Of Ship On One Side, Washington In Glory On Reverse, 9 In.	770.00
Jug, Wine Cannot Cure Pain I Endure, Women & Men Toasting, 8 In.	1495.00
Mug, Iron Bridge, Over River, 5 In.	395.00
Mug, Jemmy's Farewell	350.00
Mug, Transfer Of 3-Masted Ship, Under Sail, Figure Of Hope, Creamware, 6 In.	747.00
Plaque, Black Transfer, George Washington, Herculaneum, c.1800, 5 In.	2500.00
Plate, Black Transfer, U.S. Ship, 10 In.	375.00
Plate, Pike-Be Always Ready To Die For Your Country, 10 In.	1200.00

LADRO is a Spanish porcelain. Juan, Jose, and Vicente Lladro opened
· ceramics workshop in Almacera in 1951. They soon began making
·gurines in a distinctive, elongated style. In 1958 the factory moved to
·abernes Blanques, Spain. The company makes stoneware and porce-
·in figurines and vases in limited and unlimited editions. Dates given
·e first and last years of production.

Figurine, A Mother's Way, Box, No. 5946, 1993-1996	675.00
Figurine, Aerobics, Scissor Figure, No. 5336, 1985-1988	210.00
Figurine, Boy Meets Girl, No. 1188, 1972-1989	550.00
Figurine, Boy With Drum, No. 4616, 1969-1979	375.00
Figurine, Boy, On Carousel Horse, No. 1470, 1985	600.00
Figurine, Boys, Playing With Goat, No. 1129.30, 1971-1975	875.00
Figurine, Bull, Head Down, No. 1062, 1969-1975	460.00
Figurine, Camelot, No. 1458, 1985	895.00
Figurine, Cinderella & Fairy Godmother, No. 7553, Retired	798.00
Figurine, Cinderella, No. 4828, 1972	295.00
Figurine, Couple From Arctic, No. 2038, 1971-1982	475.00
Figurine, Demureness, No. 3020, 1989	625.00
Figurine, Dentist, No. 4762, 1971-1985	245.00
Figurine, Devotion, No. 1278, 1974-1990	600.00
Figurine, Don Quixote, No. 1030, 1969	800.00

Figurine, Donkey In Love, No. 524, 1969-1985 . . . . 450.0

Figurine, Duck, Running, No. 1263, 1974 . . . . 60.0

Figurine, Dutch Boy With Pails, No. 4811, 1972-1988 . . . . 275.0

Figurine, Eve, No. 1482, 1985-1988 . . . . 490.0

Figurine, Garden Classic, No. 7617, 1991 . . . . 249.0

Figurine, Gentleman Equestrian, No. 5329, 1985-1988 . . . . 265.0

Figurine, Girl Ironing, No. 4981, 1977-1985 . . . . 295.0

Figurine, Girl Sitting With Roses, No. 5127, 1982-1985 . . . . 350.0

Figurine, Girl With Flowers, No. 1088, 1969-1989 . . . . 550.0

Figurine, Girl With Goose & Dog, No. 4866, 1974-1995 . . . . .225.00 to 250.0

Figurine, Girl With Lamb, No. 1010, 1969-1993 . . . . 200.0

Figurine, Girl With Lamb, No. 4505, 1969-1985 . . . . 125.0

Figurine, Girl With Lamb, No. 4835, 1972-1991 . . . . 200.0•

Figurine, Girl With Milk Pail, No. 4682, 1970-1991 . . . . 400.0

Figurine, Girl With Slippers, No. 4523, 1969-1995 . . . . 100.0

Figurine, Jesters Serenade, Box, No. 5932, 1993-1995 . . . . 1000.0

Figurine, Land Of Giants, No. 5716, 1990-1995 . . . . .325.00 to 330.0

Figurine, Little Boy Bullfighter, No. 5115, 1982-1985 . . . . 390.0

Figurine, Little Eagle Owl, No. 2020, 1971-1985 . . . . 425.0

Figurine, Little Girl With Turkeys, No. 1180, 1971-1981 . . . . 375.0

Figurine, Little Leaguer, No. 5289, 1985-1990 . . . . 350.0

Figurine, Little Traveler, No. 7602, 1986 . . . . 895.0

Figurine, Mimi, No. 4985, 1978-1980 . . . . 475.0

Figurine, Obstetrician, No. 4763, 1971-1975 . . . . 325.0

Figurine, Old Dog, No. 1067, 1969-1978 . . . . 350.0

Figurine, Peter Pan, Box, No. 7529, 1993-1995 . . . . 850.0•

Figurine, Phyllis, No. 1356, 1978-1995 . . . . 125.0

Figurine, Promenade, No. 5685, 1990 . . . . 239.0

Figurine, Puppy Love, No. 1127, 1971-1996 . . . . 300.0

Figurine, Sancho With Bottle, No. 5165, 1982-1990 . . . . 325.0

Figurine, Sea Captain, No. 4621, 1969-1995 . . . . 260.0

Figurine, Seesaw, No. 1255, 1974-1995 . . . . 575.0

Figurine, Shepherdess With Goats, No. 1001, 1969-1987 . . . . 450.0

Figurine, Sisters With Flowers, No. 5013, 1978-1991 . . . . 845.0

Figurine, Sunning, No. 1481, 1985-1988 . . . . 345.0

Figurine, Valencian Boy, No. 1400, 1982-1988 . . . . 350.0•

Figurine, Voyage Of Columbus, No. 5847, Retired . . . . .875.00 to 995.0

Figurine, Waltz Time, No. 4856, 1974-1985 . . . . 450.0•

Figurine, Woman Carrying Water, No. 1212, 1971-1983 . . . . 575.0

Figurine, Woman, No. 4761, 1971-1995 . . . . 200.0•

Plate, Christmas, 1972 . . . . 50.0•

LOCKE ART is a trademark found on glass of the early twentieth century. Joseph Locke worked at many English and American firms. He designed and etched his own glass in Pittsburgh, Pennsylvania, starting in the 1880s. Some pieces were marked *Joe Locke*, but most were marked with the words *Locke Art*. The mark is hidden in the pattern on the glass.

Compote, Grape Vintage, 4 1/4 x 5 1/4 In. 175.0

LOETZ glass was made in many varieties. Johann Loetz bought a glassworks in Austria in 1840. He died in 1848 and his widow ran the company; then in 1879, his grandson took over. Most collectors recognize the iridescent gold glass similar to Tiffany, but many other types were made. The firm closed during World War II.

Loetz
Austria

Biscuit Jar, Green Iridescent, Random Threading, Nickel Plated Lid & Rim 260.0

Biscuit Jar, Lava Glass, Brass Collar, Cover, Handle, c.1900, 6 In. 935.0

Bowl, Deep Ruby To Green, 4-Lobed, Swirled, 9 1/2 x 4 In. 550.0

Bowl, Dimpled, Square, 4 x 3 In. 393.0

Bowl, Iridescent, Cylindrical, Ruffled Rim, Orange, Inside, Green To Silver Exterior, 6 In.   690.0

Bowl, Iridescent, Green & Blue, Shell Form, 7 1/2 In. 1955.0

Bowl, Oil Spot Design, Scalloped Rim, Spherical Body, 4 1/4 In., Pair 632.0

Bowl, Trailed Iridescence, Ribbed, Dimpled, Square, 4 x 3 In. 357.0

Bride's Basket, Ornate Frame, Victorian 490.00
Candlestick, Green, 12 In. 175.00
Cup, Opaque White, Aubergine Stripes, Applied Aubergine Rim, c.1914, 2 3/4 In. 655.00
Dispenser, Rose Water, Snake Design, Green, Cerise Oil Spots, Papillon Ground, 10 In. .. 665.00
Inkwell, Triangular Shape 495.00
Lamp, Lobster, Oil Spot, Crimson Feathers, Amber Opalescent, 1900, 16 1/4 In. 8395.00
Lamp, Phanomen Gre, Iridescent, Blue Garland, Silver Plated Brass, c.1902, 16 In. 8215.00
Pitcher, Branch Design, Rainbow Essence Handle, Iridescent, Polished Pontil, 6 In. 275.00
Shade, Peacock Feather Design, Green, Blue, Gold Iridescent, 4 1/2 x 2 1/4 In. 300.00
Shade, Yellow, Green, White Hooked Design, Gold, 4 1/2 x 2 1/4 In. 195.00
Vase, 3 Applied Feet, Gold, Blue Iridescent, 5 1/2 In. 715.00
Vase, 3 Stalks Of Star Flowers Connected With 3 Puffed Silver Raindrops, 5 1/4 In. 1870.00
Vase, 6 Applied Gold Prunts With Tails, Pale Green, Gold Iridescent, 10 x 4 1/2 In. 250.00
Vase, Amber Pulled Vertical Fingers, Horizontal Striping, Yellow, Silver Accents, 5 In. .. 7187.50
Vase, Amber, Light Green, Oil Spots, Corseted Beaker Form, Bronze, 6 3/4 In. 13800.00
Vase, Amber, Purple, Web, Blue Iridescent, Amber Crimped Circular Foot, 6 In. 460.00
Vase, Amber, Silvery Blue Waves, Silver Drips, Dimpled Sides, 1900, 7 In. 2875.00
Vase, Ambergris Interior, Pulled Rose, Ribbon Exterior, Flared, Oval, Iridescent, 10 In. .. 5175.00
Vase, Amberina, Tricorned, Rolled Rim, Iridescent Oil Spotting, 6 In. 475.00
Vase, Apple Green Design, Trefoil Mouth, Yellow Iridescent, 1900, 8 1/4 In. 402.00
Vase, Apricot, Silver-Blue Wave Design, 9 1/2 In. 770.00
Vase, Blue Oil-Spot Design, Ewer Form, Pinched, Art Nouveau Metal Stand, 11 In. 1725.00
Vase, Blue Stain, Silver-Yellow Iridescent, c.1898-1900, 9 1/2 In. 1810.00
Vase, Blue, Dimpled Shoulder, Rolled Rim, Iridescent, 6 In. 10925.00
Vase, Blue, Green, Dimpled, Ruffled Edge, 6 In. 395.00
Vase, Blue, Pink, Green, Silver-Blue Oil Spots, Applied 2 Gilded Handles, 1900, 4 1/4 In. 2300.00
Vase, Bud, Orange, Blue Base, Indented Lip, Double Gourd Shape, 9 In. 96.00
Vase, Bud, Papillon, Double Gourd Shape, Mirror Oil Spot, 5 In. 110.00
Vase, Citron, Blue Oil Spots On Shoulder, Neck, Aubergine Base, 8 1/4 In. 1452.00
Vase, Cobalt Blue, Silver-Blue Oil Spot, Peaked Rim, Iridescent, 10 1/4 In. 1725.00
Vase, Creta Pampas, Green Stained, Clear Glass Threads, Iridescent, c.1898, 12 In. 1070.00
Vase, Creta Papillon, Green Stained, Applied Iridescent Oil Spots, c.1900, 6 1/2 In. 575.00
Vase, Creta Papillon, Green Stained, Iridescent Oil Spots, c.1899, 8 1/4 In. 985.00
Vase, Creta Rusticana Silberiris, Tree Bark, Satin, Blue, 1900, 8 1/2 In. 182.00
Vase, Daffodils, Oil Spots, Whiplash Leafage, Pulled Trailings, Purple, Blue, Silver, 8 In. 5465.00
Vase, Damascene, Gold Ribbon, Cobalt Blue, Polished Pontil, 4 1/2 x 6 In. 385.00
Vase, Deep Cranberry Iridescent, 4 1/4 x 3 In. 250.00
Vase, Gold, Pinched Cylinder, Orange Spots, Iridescent, 9 3/4 In. 805.00
Vase, Green Coiled Serpent, Tree Trunk Form, Gold Iridescent, 11 3/4 In. 16100.00
Vase, Green To Amethyst, Silver Overlay, 11 1/2 In. ....*Illus* 1870.00
Vase, Green, Applied Buds & Stems, Iridescent, 7 3/8 In. 155.00
Vase, Green, Bulbous, Pierced, Tapered Stem, Clear Bowl, 3 Rope Supports, 11 In. 1480.00
Vase, Green, Drip Design, Iridescent, Engraved Loetz Austria, 6 In. 1840.00
Vase, Green, Gold Iridescent, Lavender Highlights, Flared, 5 In. 180.00

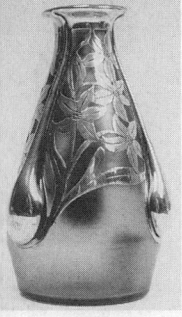
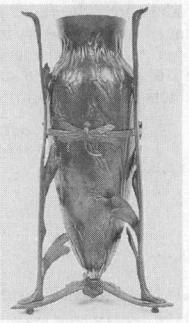

Loetz, Vase, Green To
Amethyst, Silver Overlay,
11 1/2 In.

Loetz, Vase, Red Thistle,
Bronze Dragonfly Holder,
13 1/2 In.

**Antique glass should be
handled as if it has been
repaired and might fall apart.
Hold a pitcher by the body,
not the handle. Pick up
stemware by holding both the
stem and the bowl. Hold plates
in two hands, not by the rim.**

Vase, Green, Narrow Twisted Panels, Iridescent, 6 1/2 In., Pair 165.00
Vase, Internal Tulip & Leaves, Signed, 7 1/4 In. 8625.00
Vase, Jack-In-The-Pulpit, Gold Iridescent, 10 In. 632.50
Vase, Jack-In-The-Pulpit, Ruffled Edge, Gold Iridescent, 14 In. 402.50
Vase, Lavender Rose, Oil Spots, Pinched Dimples, Iridescent, 11 3/4 In. 715.00
Vase, Lavender, Purple Cased, 4 In. 350.00
Vase, Luna, Green & Blue Stained, Optical Vertical Ribs, Iridescent, 11 3/4 In. 2300.00
Vase, Nautilus, Gold, Bronze Iridescent, 5 1/2 x 8 In. 450.00
Vase, Olive Green, Basket Shaped, 2 Handles, Iridescent, 1900, 10 In. 275.00
Vase, Opaque Blue, Applied Bright Red Trails, M. Powolny, 1915, 3 3/4 In. 1685.00
Vase, Orange Snakeskin, Collapsed Form, Iridescent, 12 1/2 In. 255.00
Vase, Pale Amber, Oil Spots, Silver Blue Iridescent, 1900, 7 In. 2645.00
Vase, Pampas, Blue-Green, Bronze, Tapered, Thin Neck, Trefoil Crimped Rim, 9 1/2 In. . 820.00
Vase, Paperweight, Iridescent Rose Railings, Clear Cased, 8 In. 1380.00
Vase, Papillon, Cobalt Stained, 2 Handles, Iridescent Oil Spots, 1900, 8 In. 1645.00
Vase, Papillon, Cobalt Stained, Footed, Silver-Yellow Iridescent, c.1918, 4 3/4 In. 985.00
Vase, Papillon, Cobalt, Footed, Flared Rim, Iridescent, 1916-1917, 7 1/2 In. 1070.00
Vase, Papillon, Round Ball, Mirror Oil Spots, 4 In. 110.00
Vase, Papillon, Ruby Red Stained, Silver-Yellow Iridescent, c.1898, 8 5/8 In. 2465.00
Vase, Papillon, Silver Swirl, Iridescent, 3 1/4 In. 1092.00
Vase, Pulled Feathers, Swirled, Burgundy, Iridescent, 7 3/4 x 4 1/2 In. 250.00
Vase, Purple Threaded, 8 In. 410.00
Vase, Purple, Blue Waves, Silver-Blue Oil Spots, 1900, 10 1/2 In. 3450.00
Vase, Purple, Blue, Gold, Banded Feather Design, Swirl, Iridescent, 9 x 8 In. 400.00
Vase, Purple, Blue, Green Surface, Iridescent, 7 1/4 x 4 1/2 In., Pair 325.00
Vase, Raindrop, Blue Highlights, Iridescent, 10 x 6 In. 100.00
Vase, Raindrop, Gold Highlights, Signed, 5 x 4 1/2 In. 100.00
Vase, Red Overlay, Mottled White Ground, Gold Highlights, 9 In., Pair 1070.00
Vase, Red Thistle, Bronze Dragonfly Holder, 13 1/2 In. .... *Illus* 1760.00
Vase, Roses On Leaf Branches, Green, Purple Overlay, Baluster, Flared Lip, 1925, 13 In. .. 1380.00
Vase, Salmon Pink, Silver Waves, Pinched Sides, Quatrefoil Rim, 14 1/2 In. 1725.00
Vase, Serpentine, Green, Iridescent, 9 1/4 In. 275.00
Vase, Silver-Blue Oil Spots, Iridescent, c.1900, 7 In. 1840.00
Vase, Silver-Blue Oil Spots, Thick Amber Handles, c.1936, 9 3/4 In. 2587.00
Vase, Silver-Blue Swirls, Cobalt Blue Interior, Tricornered, Polished Pontil, 1900, 7 In. ... 1540.00
Vase, Silver-Blue Trailings, Cobalt Blue, Iridescent, Beaker Form, Flared Rim, 9 In. 6900.00
Vase, Silver-Blue Trailings, Green, Iridescent, 1900, 7 1/4 In. 3105.00
Vase, Silver-Blue Waves, Apricot, 9 1/2 In. 847.00
Vase, Silver-Blue, Amber, Silver Overlay Whiplash Design, 1900, 6 In. 3737.00
Vase, Silver-Blue, Cobalt Blue, Iridescent, 1900, 7 In. 2875.00
Vase, Swirl Design, Amethyst, Cameo, 1900, 8 In. 495.00
Vase, Tadpoles, Crackled Surface, 5 1/2 In. 220.00
Vase, Trumpet, Apple Green, Applied Serpentine Design, 1900, 17 1/2 In. 862.00
Vase, Yellow, Bright Blue Iridescent, 7 x 6 In. 1200.00

LONE RANGER, a fictional character, was introduced on the radio in 1932. Over three thousand shows were produced before the series ended in 1954. In 1938, the first Lone Ranger movie was made. Television shows were started in 1949 and are still seen on some stations. The Lone Ranger appears on many products and was even the name of a restaurant chain for several years.

Badge, Premium, 1939 .... 75.00
Bank, Leather Cover, Metal, T.L.R., Inc., 1938, 3 3/8 x 3 1/8 In. 110.00
Book, Big Little Book, 1968 .... 15.00
Book, Whitman, 1940 .... 175.00
Boots, Endicott Johnson, Box 1200.00
Box, Official School Kit, 1940s 55.00
Brush Set, Box 150.00
Card Set, Hi-Yo Silver!, Lone Ranger & Tonto On Cover, Box, 72 Cards 40.00
Coloring Book, Whitman, 1959 .... 36.00
Comic Book, The Lone Ranger, No. 57, 1953, 10 Cents 25.00
Doll, Original Tag, 1938 .... 650.00
Figure, Chalkware, 1940s, 16 In. 98.00

Figure, Horse Silver, Plastic, Gabriel, 1977, Box, 15 In. 15.00
Figure, Tonto, Gabriel, On Card 75.00
Flashlight Pistol, Instructions & Mailer 120.00
Flashlight Pistol, Signal Siren, Silver Bullet Secret Codes, Box ....175.00 to 275.00
Frontier Town, 4 Punch-Out Buildings, 4 Mailing Envelopes, Cheerios Premium 1300.00
Frontier Town, Northwest Section, Cheerios Premium, Uncut, c.1948 .... 217.00
Game, Hi-Yo Silver Lone Ranger Target, Box, 1939 .... 175.00
Game, The New Lone Ranger, Board, 1956 .... 100.00
Guitar, Pressed Wood, Supertone, c.1940 .... 150.00
Gun, Clicker 100.00
Holster, Fiber & Cardboard, Red Jewel On Pocket, 1945 .... 40.00
Holster Set, 2 Pistols, Plastic Grips, Rubber Holster, Mattel, 1960s 180.00
Lantern, Chuck Wagon, Box 225.00
Lunch Box, Red Trim, 1954 ....230.00 to 280.00
Lunch Box, Thermos, Legend Of Lone Ranger & Tonto, Aladdin, 1980 .... 15.00
Mask, Wheaties Box 295.00
Neckerchief, Red, With Mask 115.00
Outfit, Tonto, Headdress, Buckle, Die Cast Hubley Tex Gun, Knife, TLR, Inc., 1950s ... 630.00
Pen, Figural, 1940s 75.00
Pin, Bond Bread Safety Club, 1953 .... 50.00
Play Set, Blizzard Adventure, Gabriel, Box, 1973 .... 21.00
Puppet, Push 85.00
Puzzle, Story, 4 Puzzles, Box 115.00
Ring, Cereal Premium 71.50
Ring, Filmstrip Saddle, Gold Metal, View In The Dark, 1951-1956 .... 290.00
Ring, Flashlight ....75.00 to 85.00
Sneakers, Unused, 1970s 45.00
Snow Dome ....65.00 to 105.00
Soap, Figural, Lone Ranger, Castile, Box, 4 In. 66.00
Soap, Figural, Silver, Hi-Yo Silver, Castile, Box, 4 In. 60.00
Stamp Set, 1985, On 6 x 7 In. Card 12.00
Thermos, Red, Metal 100.00
Toothbrush Holder 55.00
Toy, Lone Ranger On Horse, Windup, Tin, Cloth, Japan, 4 5/8 x 4 1/4 In. 33.00
Watch, Pocket, 1939 .... 550.00
Wristwatch 200.00

LONGWY Workshop of Longwy, France, first made ceramic wares in 1798. The workshop is still in business. Most of the ceramic pieces found today are glazed with many colors to resemble cloisonne or other enameled metal. Many pieces were made with stylized figures and art deco designs. The factory used a variety of marks.

Ashtray, Liberation, 1945 .... 150.00
Charger, Enameled Bird, Signed, 14 In. 695.00
Salt & Pepper, Barrel Shape, 2-Piece Top, 4 1/2 In. 110.00
Tile, Art Deco Lady, Shield & Crown, Square, 8 In. 395.00
Vase, Crackle Type Enamel On Ceramic, 1920s, 11 3/4 In. 1250.00
Vase, Pillow, Incised Medallion Of Medusa, Dark Blue Over Gray, 12 In. 440.00

LONHUDA Pottery Company of Steubenville, Ohio, was organized in 1892 by William Long, W. H. Hunter, and Alfred Day. Brown underglaze slip-decorated pottery was made. The firm closed in 1896. The company used many marks; the earliest included the letters *LPCO*.

Ewer, Flowers, Handle, 10 1/2 In. 82.00
Sugar & Creamer, Clover Blossoms 290.00

LOTUS WARE was made by the Knowles, Taylor & Knowles Company of East Liverpool, Ohio, from 1890 to 1900. Lotus Ware, a thin porcelain which resembles Belleek, was sometimes decorated outside the factory. Other types of ceramics that were made by the Knowles, Taylor & Knowles Company are listed under KTK.

Bowl, Nasturtiums, Leaves, Gold Trim, 5 In. 300.00
Cracker Barrel, Cover, Fishnet, Gold Trim, 6 1/2 In. 600.00

Ewer, Raised Flowers, Gold, 6 In. 350.00
Pitcher, Daisies, Green, Gold, Twig Handle, 5 In. 475.00
Teapot, Applied Net, Flowers 300.00
Vase, Fishscale, Applied Flowers, 8 In. 925.00
Vase, White, Ball Footed, Netted, KTK, 7 7/8 In. 385.00

LOW art tiles were made by the J. and J. G. Low Art Tile Works of
Chelsea, Massachusetts, from 1877 to 1902. A variety of art and other
tiles were made. Some of the tiles were made by a process called *natural*, some were hand modeled, and some were made mechanically.

J.&J.G.LOW

Tile, Bird Landing On Branch, Square, 7 7/8 In. 325.00
Tile, Ceres Figure, Frame, 1886, 4 1/2 x 9 In. 225.00
Tile, Greek Man & Woman, 2 Florets, 4 Piece 425.00

LOY-NEL-ART, see McCoy category.

LUNCH BOXES and lunch pails have been used to carry lunches to
school or work since the nineteenth century. Today, most collectors
want either early tobacco advertising boxes or children's lunch boxes
made since the 1930s. These boxes are made of metal or plastic. Boxes
listed here include the original Thermos bottle inside the box unless
otherwise indicated. Movie, television, and cartoon characters may be
found in their own categories.

LUNCH BOX, Alvin, King Seeley Thermos, 1963 .... 140.00
Adam 12, Embossed, Aladdin, 1972 .... 64.00
Addams Family, 1964 .... 260.00
Addams Family, Metal, King Seeley Thermos, 1974 .... 90.00
America On Parade, Metal, Aladdin, 1976 .... 50.00
Annie Oakley & Tagg, Metal, Aladdin, 1955 .... 300.00
Astronauts, Metal, Aladdin, 1969 .... 100.00
Atom Ant, Metal, King Seeley Thermos, 1966 .... 200.00
Banana Splits, Vinyl, King Seeley Thermos, 1969 .... 475.00
Barbie, Vinyl, King Seeley Thermos, 1962 .... 250.00
Barbie & Francie, Black, Vinyl, King Seeley Thermos, 1965 .... 65.00 to 105.00
Barn, With Open Door, Aladdin, Thermos 35.00
Battle Star Galactica, Metal, Aladdin, 1978 .... 50.00
Bee Gees, Barry Gibb, Metal, King Seeley Thermos, 1978 .... 45.00
Betty Boop, Tin 10.00
Beverly Hillbillies, Metal, 1963 .... 150.00
Bionic Woman, Aladdin, 1978 .... 45.00
Bless Our Happy Home, Vinyl, Hallmark, 1973 .... 65.00
Bonanza, Green Rim, Metal, Aladdin, 1963 .... 185.00
Bond XX Secret Agent, Metal, Ohio Art, 1966 .... 150.00
Bozo The Clown, Dome Top, Metal, Aladdin, 1963 .... 65.00
Buccaneer, Pirate Scenes, Dome Top, Metal, Aladdin, 1957 .... 160.00
Buck Rogers, Metal, Aladdin, 1979 .... 75.00
Bugaloos, Metal, Aladdin, 1971 .... 75.00
Bullwinkle, Vinyl, King Seeley Thermos, 1962 .... 150.00
Cable Car, Dome Top, Aladdin, 1962 .... 165.00
Captain Astro, Metal, Ohio, 1966 .... 195.00
Captain Kangaroo, Vinyl, King Seeley Thermos, 1964 .... 100.00
Casey Jones, Dome Top, Universal, 1960 .... 165.00
Charlie's Angels, Metal, Aladdin, 1978 .... 60.00 to 150.00
Chitty Chitty Bang Bang, Metal, King Seeley Thermos, 1969 .... 75.00
Chuck Wagon, Dome Top, Metal, Aladdin, 1958 .... 175.00
Daniel Boone, Fighting Bear, Metal, Aladdin, 1965 .... 150.00
Deputy Dawg, Vinyl, Thermos, 1964 .... 200.00
Dr. Seuss, Metal, Aladdin, 1970 .... 250.00
Drummer Boys Patriotic, Metal, Ohio Art, 1974 .... 125.00
Dukes Of Hazzard, Metal, Aladdin, 1980 .... 35.00
E.T., Metal, Aladdin, 1982 .... 25.00
Early West, Oregon Trail, Metal, Ohio Art, 1982 .... 60.00
Emergency, Metal, Aladdin, 1973 .... 60.00
Evel Knievel, Metal, Aladdin, 1974 .... 75.00

Fall Guy, Metal, Aladdin, 1981 .... 18.00
Fat Albert, Metal, King Seeley Thermos, 1973 .... 50.00
Flipper, Metal, King Seeley Thermos, 1966 ....50.00 to 125.00
George Washington, Box Style, Metal 95.00
Get Smart, Metal, King Seeley Thermos, 1966 ....75.00 to 175.00
Gomer Pyle, Metal, Aladdin, 1966 ....60.00 to 225.00
Great Wild West, Metal, Universal, 1959 .... 165.00
Green Hornet, Metal, King Seeley Thermos, 1967 .... 200.00
Gremlins, Metal, Aladdin, 1984 ....30.00 to 50.00
Grizzly Adams, Dome Top, Metal, Aladdin, 1977 .... 140.00
Gunsmoke, Matt Dillon U.S. Marshal, Metal, Aladdin, 1959 .... 160.00
Gunsmoke, Matt Dillon U.S. Marshall, With Double LLs, Metal, Aladdin, 1959 .... 60.00
Gunsmoke, Metal, 1973 .... 125.00
Happy Days, Metal, American Thermos, 1977 .... 35.00
Heathcliff, Metal, Aladdin, 1982 .... 25.00
Hometown Airport, Dome Top, Metal, King Seeley Thermos, 1960 .... 165.00
Hot Wheels, Plastic, Thermos, 1984 .... 35.00
Indiana Jones Temple Of Doom, Metal, King Seeley Thermos, 1984 .... 33.00
Jetsons, Dome, Metal, Aladdin, 1963 .... 475.00
Junior Miss, Metal, Aladdin, 1966 .... 45.00
King Kong, Metal, American Thermos, 1977 .... 39.00
Knight Rider, Metal, King Seeley Thermos, 1984 ....85.00 to 135.00
Krofft Supershow, Aladdin, 1976 ....42.00 to 60.00
Lawman, Metal, King Seeley Thermos, 1961 .... 140.00
Lion In Van, Vinyl, King Seeley Thermos, 1978 .... 125.00
Little Dutch Miss, Metal, Universal, 1959 .... 250.00
Little House On The Prairie, Metal, King Seeley Thermos, 1978 .....95.00 to 100.00
Monkees, Vinyl, King Seeley Thermos, 1967 ....95.00 to 450.00
Monsters, Universal Movie, Metal, Aladdin, 1979 .... 85.00
Munsters, Metal, King Seeley Thermos, 1965 ....65.00 to 95.00
Muppet Movie, Metal, King Seeley Thermos, 1979 .... 100.00
Osmonds, Metal, Aladdin, 1973 .... 60.00
Paladin, Metal, Aladdin, 1960 .... 190.00
Partridge Family, Metal, King Seeley Thermos, 1971 .... 43.00
Peanuts, Charlie Brown, Snoopy, Woodstock, Metal, King Seeley Thermos, 1966 ...30.00 to 35.00
Peanuts, Red, Vinyl, King Seeley Thermos, 1967 .... 54.00
Peanuts, Snoopy, Charlie Brown, Metal, No Thermos, King Seeley Thermos, 1970s 40.00
Peanuts, Snoopy, Woodstock, Sunglasses, Plastic, Thermos, 1971 .... 25.00
Penney Post Tobacco, Metal 220.00
Planet Of The Apes, Metal, No Thermos, Aladdin, 1974 .... 75.00
Pussycats, Red, Vinyl, Aladdin, 1968 .... 260.00
Rambo, Metal, King Seeley Thermos, 1985 .... 15.00
Return Of Jedi, Metal, King Seeley Thermos, 1983 ....30.00 to 110.00
Rifleman, Metal, Aladdin, 1961 .... 350.00
Robin Hood, Metal, Aladdin, 1956 .... 35.00
Ronald McDonald, Metal, Aladdin, 1982 .... 25.00
S.W.A.T., Dome Top, Plastic, Thermos, 1975 .... 45.00
Satellite, Metal, King Seeley Thermos, 1960 .... 125.00
Sensible Tobacco, Navy Cut For Pipe Or Cigarettes, Tin, 2 Metal Handles 50.00
Shari Lewis, Vinyl, Aladdin, 1963 .... 425.00
Snoopy, Dome Top, Metal, King Seeley Thermos, 1968 .... 65.00
Space Shuttle, King Seeley Thermos, 1977 .... 155.00
Speedy Turtle, Vinyl, Drawstring Bag, 1978 .... 65.00
Star Trek, Dome Top, Aladdin, 1968 .... 495.00
Star Trek The Next Generation, Blue, Plastic, Thermos, 1989 ....35.00 to 45.00
Star Wars, Metal, Characters On Band, King Seeley Thermos, 1978 .....45.00 to 65.00
Star Wars, Metal, Stars On Band, King Seeley Thermos, 1977 .... 130.00
Strawberry Shortcake, Metal, Aladdin, 1980 .... 15.00
Super Heroes, Metal, Aladdin, 1976 .... 45.00
Tammy & Pepper, Vinyl, Aladdin, 1965 .... 125.00
Tarzan, Metal, Aladdin, 1966 .... 75.00
Three Little Pigs, Metal, Ohio Art, 1982 .... 85.00
Tom Corbett, Blue, Metal, Lithograph, Aladdin, 1954 .... 525.00

Tom Corbett Space Cadet, Metal, Aladdin, 1950	85.0
Tom Corbett Space Cadet, Red, Metal, No Thermos, Aladdin, 1952	85.0
Transformers, Plastic, Aladdin, 1986	20.0
Union Commander Cut Plug	330.0
Union Leader Cut Plug, Black Eagle In Center, Red Ground	60.5
Wayne Gretzky, Aladdin, 1980	15.00
Wild, Wild West, Metal, Aladdin, 1969	250.00
Winner Cut Plug, Smoke & Chew, Graphics Of 20th Century Auto Race	200.00
Wonder Woman, Blue, Vinyl, Aladdin, 1977	225.00
Wonder Woman, Yellow, Vinyl, No Thermos, Aladdin, 1977	165.00
Woody Woodpecker, Metal, Aladdin, 1972	80.00
Yellow Submarine, King Seeley Thermos, 1968	500.00
Ziggy, Vinyl, Aladdin, 1979	95.00
LUNCH BOX THERMOS, Barbie, Thermos, 1990	45.00
Barbie & Midge, King Seeley Thermos, 1965	24.00
Beany & Cecil, King Seeley Thermos, 1962	50.00
Captain Kangaroo, King Seeley Thermos, 1964	90.00
Dukes Of Hazzard, Aladdin, 1980	15.00
G.I. Joe, King Seeley Thermos, 1967	60.00
Get Smart, King Seeley Thermos, 1966	85.00
Gunsmoke, Plastic, Aladdin, 1972 ....15.00 to 35.00	
Happy Days, American Thermos, 1977	45.00
Hee Haw, King Seeley Thermos, 1971	35.00
Keny Cars, Plastic, Mexico	25.00
Kiddles	45.00
King Kong, Plastic, American Thermos, 1977	20.00
Lance Link, King Seeley Thermos, 1971	45.00
Monkees, King Seeley Thermos, 1967 ....60.00 to 90.00	
Partridge Family, Metal, King Seeley Thermos, 1971	55.00
Patchwork Quilt, Plastic, 1970	20.00
Rat Patrol, Aladdin, 1967	45.00
Star Wars, King Seeley Thermos, 1978 ....15.00 to 20.00	
Transformer, Aladdin, 1984	3.00
Vanguard IV, Universal	75.00
Welcome Back Kotter, Aladdin, 1977	25.00
Wild Wild West, Aladdin, 1969	55.00
LUNCH PAIL, Cino Cigar, Tin, Revenue Stamp, 1917	28.00
Climax Peanut Butter, Tin, 1923	125.00

LUSTER glaze was meant to resemble copper, silver, or gold. It has been used since the sixteenth century. Most of the luster found today was made during the nineteenth century. The metallic glazes are applied on pottery. The finished color depends on the combination of the clay color and the glaze. Blue and orange luster decorations were used in the early 1900s. Tea Leaf pieces have their own category.

Copper, Ashtray, Man's Head, Bee On Nose	55.00
Copper, Bowl & Pitcher, Amber Band, Flowers, 1850s, 10-In. Pitcher, 14-In. Bowl	1035.00
Copper, Bowl, 6 In.	45.00
Copper, Creamer, Under Spout, Welcome Lafayette, Nation's Guest	695.00
Copper, Cup & Saucer, 5 1/2-In. Saucer	16.50
Copper, Mug, People, Animals In Relief, 4 In.	95.00
Copper, Pitcher, 2 Reserves Of Genre Scenes, Yellow Ground, 7 1/2 In.	172.00
Copper, Pitcher, Blue Bells, 6 1/4 In.	65.00
Copper, Pitcher, Blue Design, Molded Rim, Pear Shaped, Woods, 8 1/2 In.	22.00
Copper, Pitcher, Girl In Landscape, On Blue Band, 5 1/2 In.	75.00
Copper, Pitcher, Little Jockey, Royal Child Riding Dog	250.00
Copper, Pitcher, Pink Bubble Band, Beaded Rim, Pedestal, 6 In.	125.00
Copper, Pitcher, Primrose & Feather, White Band, 5 1/4 In.	110.00
Copper, Pitcher, Relief Molded, 14 1/2 In.	2587.00
Copper, Salt, Tan Band, Blue Design, Footed, 3 1/4 In.	95.00
Copper, Tumbler, Floral & Blue Band, 4 x 4 In.	70.00
Copper, Waste Bowl, Ochre Band, Luster Rose Design	45.00
Fairyland luster is included in the Wedgwood category.	

Orange, Tea Set, Blue Anemones, Cover, 7 1/4 In. 55.00
Pink, Cup, Saucer & Plate, Boy Feeding Swans 58.00
Pink, Jug, Hunt, Deer Both Sides, c.1815 .... 325.00
Pink, Pitcher, Hunters, Raised Dogs, 6 1/4 In. 450.00
Pink, Plate, Canary Yellow Rim, Be Always Ready To Die For Your Country, Pike, 10 In.   1350.00
Pink, Tea Set, House Pattern, 9 Cups & Saucers, Plate, Creamer, Waste Bowl, 12 Piece .. 165.00
Silver, Candlestick, Neptune 495.00
Silver, Mustard, Reeded Embossed Body 165.00
Soap Dish, 3 Mermaids, Shell Shaped Dish, 1950s, 5 1/2 x 3 1/2 In. 39.00
Sunderland luster pieces are listed in the Sunderland category.
Tea Leaf luster pieces are listed in the Tea Leaf Ironstone category.

LUSTRE ART GLASS Company was founded in Long Island, New York,
n 1920 by Conrad Vahlsing and Paul Frank. The company made lampshades and globes that are almost indistinguishable from those made
by Quezal. Most of the shades made by the company were unmarked.

Peacock Feather, Gold, Ceramic, Austria, 7 3/4 In. 440.00
Scenic Enameled Panels, Cut-Spear Prisms, Green, 12 In., Pair 1000.00
Shade, Gold Iridescent, 5 In. 100.00

LUSTRES are mantel decorations or pedestal vases with many hanging
glass prisms. The name really refers to the prisms, and it is proper to
refer to a single glass prism as a lustre. Either spelling, luster or lustre,
s correct.

Cranberry, Gold & Floral Design, Prisms, 14 1/2 In., Pair 550.00
Cut Glass, Beaded, Faceted Pendants, Stepped Round Base, Late Regency, 9 In., Pair ... 977.00
Deer & Castle, Red Cut To Clear, Pair 975.00
Enameled Design, Green Glass, Prism, 14 In., Pair 440.00
Enameled Flowers, Gilt Scalloped Rim, Crystal Prism, c.1870, 13 1/2 In., Pair 895.00
Lime Green, Gold Leaves & Trim, Prisms, 10 x 6 1/2 In., Pair 420.00
Milk Glass, Gilt Design, Pendant Prisms, 19th Century, 13 1/2 In., Pair 385.00
Red-Turquoise, Urn, Wrought Metal Mount, Emile Muller, 1905, 26 5/8 In., Pair 13120.00
Ruby Red, Bohemian, Enameled, Brass Standard, Electrified, 23 In. 192.00
Stepped Base, Gilt Foliage & Geometric Designs, Prisms, 14 In., Pair 345.00

MAASTRICHT, Holland, was the city where Petrus Regout established
the De Sphinx pottery in 1836. The firm was noted for its transfer-
printed earthenware. Many factories in Maastricht are still making
ceramics.

Bowl, Green Transfer, 4 1/2 x 9 In. 27.00
Bowl, Green, Gold, Red Transfer, P. Regout, 5 1/8 In. 11.00
Bowl, Serving, Abbey Pattern, Petrus Regout & Co., 1914 .... 16.00
Ladle, Soup, Ironstone, 13 In. 16.00
Plate, Scroll Border, Gold Edge, Blue, Black, Rose, Green Ground, 8 1/2 In. 50.00

MAIZE glass was made by W.L. Libbey & Son Company of Toledo,
Ohio, after 1889. The glass resembled an ear of corn. The leaves were
usually green, but some pieces were made with blue or red leaves. The
kernels of corn were light yellow, white, or light green.

Celery Vase, 6 1/2 In. 99.00
Condiment Set, 4 Piece 770.00
Condiment Set, Green Leaves, Holder, 5 3/4 x 6 In. 425.00
Cruet, Yellow Leaves, Stopper, Tall 875.00
Syrup, Green Leaves, Pewter Lid, Applied Handle, 7 In. 795.00
Toothpick, Blue Husks 750.00
Tumbler 120.00

MAJOLICA is a general term for any pottery glazed with an opaque tin
enamel that conceals the color of the clay body. It has been made since
the fourteenth century. Today's collector is most likely to find Victorian
majolica. The heavy, colorful ware is rarely marked. Some famous
makers include Wedgwood; Minton; Griffen, Smith and Hill (marked
Etruscan); and Chesapeake Pottery (marked *Avalon* or *Clifton*).

Ashtray, Match Holder, Russian Cossack Holding Rifle, Green, Beige, 8 x 5 1/2 In. 325.00

Bank, Penny, Lady's Head 55.00
Barrel, Biscuit, Cottage Scene, England 75.00
Basket, Bread, Wire Mounted, 10 1/2 x 8 1/2 In. 220.00
Basket, Green & Gold, Handle, 12 In. 350.00
Basket, Strawberry, Basket Weave, Flowers, Insects, George Jones & Sons, 11 1/4 In. 2415.00
Bottle, Figural, Woman With Violin 55.00
Bowl, Basket Weave, Scalloped, Brown With Flowers, Turquoise Interior, 8 In. 225.00
Bowl, Blackberries, Aqua Ground, Lion's Head Handles, Anchor Mark, 13 1/2 x 7 In. 275.00
Bowl, Cover, Allover Leaf, Geometric Design, Green, Blue, Ball Handle, 16 x 13 In. 3738.00
Bowl, Pale Blue, Brown Center, Brown Edges, Marked, Germany, 11 1/4 In. 66.00
Bowl, Shell & Seaweed, 8 3/4 In. 995.00
Bowl, Wave Edge, Man Seated On Rocks, Water Sprite, Oval, 12 1/2 In. 55.00
Box, Lucifer, Branch Of Green Oak Leaves, Chartreuse, Ocher, Acorns, Jones, 4 In. 517.00
Box, Sardine, Overlapping Fish On Cover, Boat Form Plank Dish, G. Jones, 9 1/8 In. 546.00
Box, Sardine, Stand, Green Stiff Leaves Border, Turquoise Glaze, George Jones 402.00
Cake Plate, Daisy & Leaf, Footed, 9 1/2 In. 275.00
Candleholder, Figural, Black Man & Woman, Candle Holds Basket, 6 In., Pair 625.00
Charger, Angels, Dolphins & Plant Life, Continental, 14 1/2 In. 242.00
Charger, Cobalt Blue, Pink, Green Flowers, Signed, 16 In. 33.00
Charger, Neptune & Sea Nymphs, Allegorical Animal Forms Border, Italy, 24 In. 805.00
Charger, Salamanders, Looking At Gray Speckled Snake, Palissy, 8 1/2 x 9 In. 1000.00
Cheese Dish, Cover, Bird, Berry, Leaf Design, Green, Purple Lining Inside Cover 33.00
Compote, Footed, Lily Pattern Top, Pedestal With Bird, 6 x 10 In. 172.00
Compote, Waterlily, 9 In. 150.00
Cream Jug, Corn Pattern, Green & Yellow, American, c.1900, 4 In. 80.00
Creamer, Sunflower, Etruscan, Griffen, Smith & Co., 4 1/4 In. 385.00
Cup, With Fan, Aqua Interior 150.00
Dessert Set, Fruit, Berry Design, Yellow, Green Ground, Germany, 7 Piece 16.00
Dish, Asparagus, Pastel Green Glaze, Gilt Accents, Late 19th Century 1430.00
Dish, Crab, Shells & Seaweed, Palissy Style, 13 In. 345.00
Dish, Dogwood Blossoms & Leaves, Bird Perched On Edge, Oval, 7 1/2 x 4 1/2 In. 575.00
Dish, Game, Minton, c.1877, 14 In. 1610.00
Dish, Leaf Mold, Squirrel Eating Nut, 9 3/4 In. 275.00
Dish, Leaf, Embossed, Floral, Pink, 1870, 8 In. 110.00
Dish, Strawberry, Strawberries, Bird Shaped Handle, George Jones, c.1879, 10 In. 302.00
Ewer, Tulip Relief, Art Nouveau, 14 1/4 x 5 1/4 In., Pair 550.00
Ewer, Young Boy, Helping Young Girl Over Fence, Multicolored, 7 3/4 In. 121.00
Figurine, Cat & Dog, Seated On Blue Love Seat, 2 1/4 In. 145.00
Figurine, Neptune Riding On Top Of Dolphin, 19th Century, 33 In. 3950.00
Figurine, Victorian Woman, France, 10 In. 50.00
Figurine, Young Woman, Seated On Bench With A Cat, 7 x 5 In. 215.00
Humidor, Brown Bear, Blue Coat, Holding Large Pipe, 5 1/2 In. 350.00
Humidor, Bust Of Victorian Boy, Green Jacket, Ear Flaps, Incised 1959 Over 12, 5 In. ... 165.00
Humidor, Castle Shape, England ....155.00 to 225.00
Humidor, Dog's Head, With Hat & Cigar, Green 350.00
Humidor, Head Of Englishman, Cigar In Mouth, Night Hat, 7 In. 250.00
Humidor, Monk's Head, Incised 1585 Over 27, 6 3/4 In. 225.00
Humidor, Monkey's Head Shape, Germany, 5 In. 148.00
Humidor, Owl, Full Figure, 7 In. 350.00
Humidor, Tobacco, Turk's Head 425.00

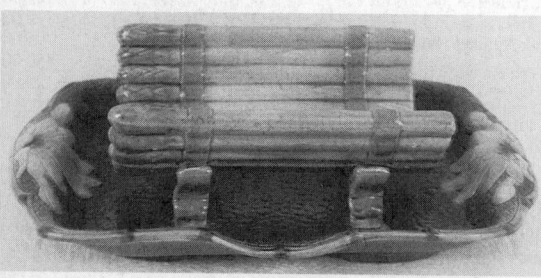

Majolica, Server, Asparagus,
Mustard, Green, Water Lily
Handles, Holdcroft

Inkwell, White Poodle, On Blue Pillow, Opens To Tortoiseshell Well & Tray 525.00
Jar, Flowers, Portrait Of Woman, Italy, 7 1/2 In. 50.00
Jardiniere, 3 Pegasus Figures, Molded Acanthus, Oriental Masks, 30 x 18 In. 358.00
Jardiniere, Cherubs, 10 In. 950.00
Jardiniere, Grape Leaf Design, Embossed, Green, Brown, Red Variegated Glaze, 7 In. ... 40.00
Jardiniere, Horses, Scrolled Acanthus Design, Burnt Orange, Blue, Yellow, 14 In. 550.00
Jardiniere, Paneled Design, Pinwheel Rosettes, Green, Amber, Brown, 10 In. 35.00
Jardiniere, Pedestal, Acorn Design, Embossed, Yellow, Green Over Blue Glaze, 12 In. .. 75.00
Jardiniere, Stand, Polychrome Glazed Foliate, 1880s, 13 1/8 In. 1265.00
Jug, Green Leaves, Yellow Flowers, 11 In. 250.00
Jug, Relief Of Classical Females, Columned Panels, Late 19th Century, 14 1/2 In. 500.00
Lamp, Castle Shape, Brass Collar & Burner, Milk Glass Globe, Kosmos, 8 3/8 In. 220.00
Lamp, Parrot, 12 In. 123.00
Match Safe, Black Child Sitting On Fancy Pillow 300.00
Mug, Bacchus Revelry, Satyr Figural Handle, 6 1/2 In. 85.00
Nut Dish, Heart Shape, Leaves, Acorn On Branches, George Jones, c.1875, 10 In. 805.00
Nut Dish, Squirrel, 10 In. 325.00
Oyster Plate, George Jones, 1864-1907, 9 In. 1795.00
Pie Dish, Game, Molded Game Designs, Rabbit Finial, Wedgwood, 10 In. 1127.00
Pitcher, Bee, Butterfly & Bamboo Design, 1800s, 7 In. 225.00
Pitcher, Bird On Branch 175.00
Pitcher, Corn, Cream, 4 1/4 In. 75.00
Pitcher, Drinking Scene Relief, Gargoyle Spout, 10 In. 175.00
Pitcher, Fish, Green, England, 9 1/2 In. 45.00
Pitcher, Fish, Pink Interior, Turned-Up Tail Handle, 9 In. 200.00
Pitcher, Floral & Basket Weave, 6 In. 95.00
Pitcher, Oriental Fan & Bird With Apple Blossoms, 8 In. 345.00
Pitcher, Oriental Fan, 6 In. 265.00
Pitcher, Owl, 11 In. 250.00
Pitcher, Palm Tree, Yellow, 7 In. 85.00
Pitcher, Pink Interior, Blue, Green, Yellow, Brown, Applied Brown Handle, 7 In. 105.00
Pitcher, Raspberry, Avalon Faience, 10 In. 70.00
Pitcher, Rooster, Marked, St. Clement, France, c.1890, 11 In. 250.00
Pitcher, Shell, Fielding, 8 In. 265.00
Pitcher, Village Blacksmith, Burgess & Leigh, 9 In. 145.00
Plate, Asparagus, France, 16 1/2 In. 1898.00
Plate, Bacchus Wine Scene, Beaded Scrolls, Gold Trim, 6 1/4 In. 55.00
Plate, Begonia, 8 In. 95.00
Plate, Bird & Dragonfly, 8 In. 145.00
Plate, Dog In Doghouse, 8 In. 145.00
Plate, Dog, Girl & Rabbit, 8 In. 120.00
Plate, Green Leaf, 8 In. 26.00
Plate, Green Leaves, Red Tips, Gold Ground, Germany, 7 1/2 In. 100.00
Plate, Green Leaves, Red Tips, Gold Ground, Germany, 11 1/2 In. 150.00
Plate, House, Trees, Fence, Signed, 6 3/8 In. 115.00
Plate, Leaf Shape, Green, 8 In. 35.00
Plate, Leaf Shape, Green, 9 1/4 In. 60.00
Plate, Leaf Shape, Wedgwood, 1960s, 8 In. 40.00
Plate, Palissy Style, Snake, Beetle, Moth, Portugal, 10 In. 1025.00
Plate Set, Green Glaze, Raised Water Lily Design, Stamped 12, 1850, 9 In., 5 Piece 154.00
Plate Set, Molded Butterfly, Leaf Design, Scalloped, 19th Century, 7 In., 10 Piece 489.00
Platter, 4 Lobsters On Leaf Base, 2 Branch Handles, 12 1/2 x 9 3/4 In. 388.00
Platter, Alternating Bands Of Geometric Designs, Green, Black, White, 20 x 12 In. 165.00
Platter, Cake Plate, Shell, Etruscan, 13 1/2 In. 900.00
Platter, Shell & Seaweed, 13 1/2 In. 995.00
Server, Asparagus, Mustard, Green, Water Lily Handles, Holdcroft ....*Illus* 715.00
Server, With Underplate, Asparagus 795.00
Smoke Set, Peasant Woman, Arms On Hips, Austria, 8 In. 137.00
Tazza, Trumpet Floral, Napkin Design, Brown, Green Border, 8 1/2 x 3 In. 110.00
Teapot, Chicken On Nest, Chick Finial, Twig Handle, Holdcroft 125.00
Teapot, Isle Of Man, Sailor Figure, Brownfield, 1880, 8 1/2 In. 517.00
Teapot, Raspberry, White Flowers, Pink Berries, Finial, 6 1/2 In. 375.00
Tobacco Jar, Arab, Brown, Beige Glaze, 6 x 8 In. 250.00

Tobacco Jar, Figural, Man In Top Hat, 5 3/4 In. 155.00

Tobacco Jar, Green Cigar, Pink, Blue 179.00

Toby Jug, Falstaff, Edward Steele, 1885, 10 1/2 In. 515.00

Tray, Barrel Staves & Flowers, Diamond Shape, 11 1/4 x 9 1/4 In. 85.00

Tray, Dessert, Brown Squirrel Crouching With Nut, Georg Jones, 1870, 14 In. 2070.00

Tureen, Undertray, Snail Finial, Cabbage Shape, Portugal 325.00

Umbrella Stand, Berries, Vines, Terra-Cotta Body, Cobalt Blue, Ocher, 22 In. ... 425.00

Umbrella Stand, Molded Floral, Art Nouveau, 10 1/2 In. 275.00

Umbrella Stand, Molded Floral, Glazed, 22 In. 275.00

Umbrella Stand, Raised Berry & Leaf Design, 1870s, 25 In. 460.00

Umbrella Stand, Tree Stump Form, Signed, 27 In. 2500.00

Urn, Blue, Yellow, Renaissance Design, Scroll Handle, 1920, 14 1/2 x 7 In. ... 264.00

Urn, Continuous Design Of Peasants In Landscape, 13 1/2 In. 345.00

Urn, Cover, Laurel Swags, Foliate Scrolls, Robin's-Egg Blue, 23 In. 3680.00

Urn, Peasants In Landscape, 14 1/2 In., Pair 920.00

Urn, Village Landscape, Foliated Border, 19th Century, 14 In., Pair 920.00

Vase, 6-Panels, Flowers, Scrolls, Green Ground, 14 In. 110.00

Vase, Applied Orchids, No. 6206, 12 1/4 In. 49.00

Vase, Applied Plums, Leaves, Twig Handles, 1890, 12 1/2 x 6 In. 85.00

Vase, Bennington Brown Glaze, Green, Blue, 19th Century, 8 1/2 In. 110.00

Vase, Classical Mask Heads, Cherubs, Animal Forms, Scrolled Vines, Berries, 30 In. 748.00

Vase, Cobalt, Ivy, Gold Handle, 12 In. 675.00

Vase, Floral, Green Shades, 10 In. 400.00

Vase, Overall, Mask, Foliate Raised Design, Beige, Green, Handle, Round, 13 In. .. 115.00

Vase, Portrait, Dragon Handles, Burgundy, 12 In. 250.00

Vase, Roses & Leaves, Blue-Green Flambe Glaze, 10 In. 82.00

MAPS of all types have been collected for centuries. The earliest known printed maps were made in 1478. The first printed street map showed London in 1559. The first road maps for use by drivers of automobiles were made in 1901. Collectors buy maps that were pages of old books, as well as the multifolded road maps popular in this century.

Alabama, Home & Landseekers Brochure, Dept. Of Agriculture, 1894, 20 x 26 In. 85.00

Alaska, State Issued, 1973 .... 2.00

American Airlines System, 1950s, Folds Out To 24 x 34 In. 20.00

Americas, Colonies, Red, Yellow, Black Chenille, Ann E. Colson, 1809, 25 x 27 3/8 In. .. 8050.00

City Of New Bedford, In 19th Century, Oil On Canvas, J.E. Aldred, 1928, 37 x 51 In. .. 1155.00

Connecticut, Hand Colored, 1855, 13 x 16 In. 95.00

Counties Of Barnstable, Duke & Nantucket Mass., 1858, 64 1/4 x 59 1/2 In. 220.00

Dakota Territory, Register Of Deeds, Wahpeton, N. Dakota, 1890s, 8 1/2 x 11 In. 25.00

Florida & Cuba, Metropolitan Areas, Gulf Gas, 1950s 12.00

Germany, Michelin, Tin, 31 x 23 In. 60.00

Globe, Celestial & Terrestrial, W. & S. Jones, Calculated To 1828, 10-In. Horizon Ring .. 6325.00

Globe, Celestial, Mahogany Stand, Downswept Legs, Casters, c.1800, 31 In. 4600.00

Globe, Celestial, Mahogany Tripod Stand, Bardin, 16 In. 4600.00

Globe, Celestial, Table, On Cherrywood Stand, Gilman Joslin, 1840, 6 In. 4025.00

Globe, Nautical, Newton & Son, London, 1831, 12 In. 2860.00

Globe, Stand, E. Wormley, 1953 Rand McNally Globe, Dunbar, 35 x 19 In. 495.00

Globe, Terrestrial & Celestial, Embroidered, Painted & Inked Silk, 5 1/2 In., Pair 8625.00

Globe, Terrestrial, Brass Clawed Stand, John Wanamaker, 30 x 18 In. 990.00

Globe, Terrestrial, Carved Giltwood Eagle, Ebonized Base, Signed, J. Felkl, 33 1/4 In. .. 2070.00

Globe, Terrestrial, Cast Metal Stand, Paw Feet, J.L. Hammett & Co., 1920s, 12 In. 165.00

Globe, Terrestrial, Dark Walnut, Ebonized Stand, England, c.1920, 11 In. 630.00

Globe, Terrestrial, Geographic Educator, Puzzle-Form Layers, c.1927, 6 In. 172.00

Globe, Terrestrial, Metal Stand, Art Nouveau, 1900, 18 In. 2990.00

Globe, Terrestrial, Napoleon III, Ormolu & Onyx, Stepped Ormolu Base, Bertaux, 16 In.. 4025.00

Globe, Terrestrial, Regency, Stand, Bardin Of London, 1817, 16 In. 1380.00

Globe, Terrestrial, Treen Base, Nims & Co., Troy, N.Y. 1700.00

Gloucestershire, England, 1712, 18 x 22 In. 95.00

Greater Cleveland, Official Arrow City Map, City Directory, 1947 .... 15.00

Hagstrom's Map Of Brooklyn, New York, 1929 .... 11.00

Hagstrom's Map Of New York City, 1928 .... 9.00

Hawaiian, Island, 1950 .... 60.00

Ireland, Michelin Tires, 1972, 34 1/2 x 25 In.	45.00
Louisiana, Hand Colored, 1855, 15 x 19 In.	95.00
Maine, State Highway Commission, 1963	3.00
McNally World Atlas, 1882	200.00
Michigan, City Services, 1940s	25.00
Missouri, Hand Colored, Cowperthwait, 1850, 13 x 16 In.	95.00
Mother Load Of California, Mining Areas, Mining Camps, 1949, 20 x 24 In.	47.00
New England, Pennsylvania & Ohio Valley, Hand Colored, 1757, 12 x 8 1/2 In.	225.00
New England, Socony, 1925	12.00
New England & Wales, Needlework, Linen, Jane Jones, 1798, 20 1/4 x 16 In.	253.00
New Mexico, Pocket Map & Shippers' Guide, 1890 Census Data, Folded, 1898, 4 x 6 In.	25.00
New York, Calco Gas, 1960s	1.00
North & South Carolina, Esso Gas, 1960s	1.00
Ohio, Engraved & Hand Colored, John Kilbourn, Jan. 1821, Frame, 21 3/4 x 20 1/8 In.	755.00
Oklahoma, Population, Counties, Major Cities, Rand McNally, 9 x 11 In.	12.00
Pan-American, World Airways, c.1956, 16 x 23 In.	7.50
Pictographic, Comic Images, Woodsman, Euto Industry, Michigan, 1935, 9 x 12 In.	25.00
Pictographic, Hicks, Farmers, Workers, Blacks Picking Cotton, 1937, 9 x 12 In.	25.00
Pike's Peak, Men & Women, Colorado, 9 x 12 In.	25.00
San Francisco Street Map, Oakland, Thomas Brothers, 1945	8.00
South Dakota, Self-Mailer, P.I. Neister & Co., Sioux Falls, Folded, 1909, 17 x 22 In.	39.00
South Dakota, Showing Railroad Lines, Butte County, Folded, 1900, 3 x 5 In.	62.00
Tellurian, Domed, Raised Cast Iron Base, Signed, J. Felkl, 26 1/4 In.	2587.00
Texas, Oklahoma & Indian Territory, Rand McNally, 9 x 11 In.	25.00
U.S.A. & Texas Republic, Historic, 1838	475.00
Utah, Comic Images Of Indians, Miners, Mormons, 1937, 9 x 12 In.	25.00
World, Culver Twin Hemisphere, Typus Orbis Terrarum, c.1680	1788.00
World, Roll, S. Augustus Mitchell, Publisher, 1838, 51 x 76 In.	154.00

MARBLE collectors pay highest prices for glass and sulphide marbles. The game of marbles has been popular since the days of the ancient Romans. American children were able to buy marbles by the mid-eighteenth century. Dutch glazed clay marbles were least expensive. Glazed pottery marbles, attributed to the Bennington potteries in Vermont, were of a better quality. Marbles made of pink marble were also available by the 1830s. Glass marbles seem to have been made later. By 1880, Samuel C. Dyke of South Akron, Ohio, was making clay marbles and The National Onyx Marble Company was making marbles of onyx. The Navarre Glass Marble Company of Navarre, Ohio, and M. B. Mishler of Ravenna, Ohio, made the glass marbles. Ohio remained the center of the marble industry, and the Akron-made Akro Agate brand became nationally known. Other pieces made by Akro Agate are listed in this book in the Akro Agate category. Sulphides are glass marbles with frosted white figures in the center.

Bumble Bee, Big Boy, Black & Yellow, 1 In., 500 Piece	45.00
Handmade, Dark Blue, Red & White Stripes, 5/8 In.	85.00
Latticinio Swirl, Yellow Core, 2 5/16 In.	200.00
Lutz, End Of Day, 2 1/4 In.	1882.00
Onionskin, 9 Colors	3000.00
Onionskin, Confetti, 2 3/8 In.	1575.00
Onionskin, Mica	1075.00
Onionskin, Segmented, 2 1/8 In.	185.00
Peppermint, Red, White, Blue, 1 1/2 In.	48.00
Slag, Akro Agate, Red, Box	1350.00
Sulphide, Angel	220.00
Sulphide, Boy On Hobbyhorse	400.00
Sulphide, Deer	145.00
Sulphide, Girl Petting Dog	450.00
Sulphide, Kissing Love Birds	750.00
Sulphide, Lamb	145.00
Sulphide, Perched Eagle, 1 7/8 In.	230.00
Sulphide, Spread-Winged Eagle, 2 1/8 In.	270.00
Sulphide, Wild Boar, 2 3/8 In.	670.00

**Where to put a marble bust? Not near a window—
the outdoor pollutants will discolor it.
Not near a fireplace—the smoke will be absorbed.
Not near a hot radiator or vent—it may scorch or
crack. And not in too damp an environment.**

Marble Carving, Statue,
Woman, Carrara Marble,
E. Gazzeri, Roma, 1901, 60 In.

Sulphide, Wild Boar, Amber 950.00
Swirl, Indian, Blue Bands, 1 1/16 In. 3550.00
Uranium Oxide, Bag, 21 Piece 9.00

MARBLE CARVINGS, such as large or small figurines, groups of people
or animals, and architectural decorations, have been a special art form
since the time of the ancient Greeks. Reproductions, especially of large
Victorian groups, are being made of a mixture using marble dust.
These are very difficult to detect and collectors should be careful.
Other carvings are listed under Alabaster.

Basin, Neoclassical, Everted Rim, Oval Top, Ring Handles, Italy, 12 3/4 In. 5750.00
Bust, Babrielle Claude Martine De Polastron, Boero, 36 In. 4887.00
Bust, Beatrice, 19th Century, 16 1/2 In. 770.00
Bust, Classical Woman, Round Base, 29 1/2 In. 5750.00
Bust, Cleopatra, Round Base, 22 In. 4025.00
Bust, Lions, Recumbent, Each Head Turned Slightly To Side, 21 In., Pair 9775.00
Bust, Renaissance Maiden, Laurel Wreath In Hair, Necklace, 16 1/2 In. 1035.00
Bust, Susan B. Anthony, Chauncey B. Ives, 1847, 23 In. 2875.00
Bust, Winged Maiden, Butterfly On Shoulder, Waisted Socle, 22 In. 5462.00
Bust, Woman, Tricolor, Neoclassical, Marble Socle Base, 19 1/2 In. 805.00
Bust, Young Man, Napoleon, Raised On White Marble Socle, Canova, 22 In. 2875.00
Classical Maiden, Holding Basket Of Flowers, 32 In. 3450.00
Girandole Set, Woman, Child, Ormolu, Prisms, 19th Century, 9 In., 3 Piece 154.00
Group, Infants Warming Themselves At Fire, A. Viviani, 25 1/4 In. 3737.00
Jardiniere, White, Berried Foliage, 19th Century, 20 In., Pair 17250.00
Jardiniere, White, Floral Swags, Arched Center, 29 1/2 In. 4370.00
Lamp, 3 Graces Holding Hands At Base, Scenes Of Children Shade, 70 In. 8250.00
Pedestal, Carrara Marble, 60 In., Pair 15400.00
Pedestal, Gilt Metal, Corinthian Support, Brown Mottled Column, 40 In. 1265.00
Pedestal, Gray & White Streaks, Square Base, Octagonal Top, 36 In. 330.00
Pedestal, Spiral Column, Black, 42 In. 715.00
Pedestal, Tri-Column, Marble Top, Painted Wooden Column, 35 In., Pair 575.00
Pedestal, Tri-Column, White Round Top, Plinth Base, 38 1/2 In. 630.00
Pedestal, Venus, Crouching, 20th Century, Italy, 20 x 15 x 77 In. 7475.00
Plaque, 3 Putti Standing By Urn, 18th Century, Italy, 16 x 16 1/2 In. 825.00
Plaque, Bust, Man, Neoclassical, 24 x 18 In. 1840.00
Statue, Aphrodite, Draped Cloth At Waist, Rocky Pedestal, 38 In. 4887.00
Statue, Boy, Tom Sawyer Look-Alike, Signed, F. Vichi, 36 In. 2860.00
Statue, Classic Woman, Standing, E. Gazzeri, Roma, 1901, 60 In. 15400.00
Statue, Neoclassical Nude, 20th Century, 25 1/2 In. 69.00
Statue, Neoclassical Nude, Standing, 20th Century, 26 In. 201.00
Statue, The Dance, Nude Woman & 2 Children, Charles Hafner, 78 In. 17600.00
Statue, Woman, Carrara Marble, E. Gazzeri, Roma, 1901, 60 In. ....*Illus* 15400.00
Statue, Young Woman Drying After Bath, White, 31 1/2 In. 2970.00
Tazza, Art Nouveau, Yellow, 2 White Doves On Base, 10 x 13 1/2 In. 875.00
Tazza, Neoclassical, Everted Rim, Raised Tapering Socle, Square Base, 12 In. 4600.00

Urn, Leaf Design Throughout, Figures In Relief, Wooden Base, 38 In. 4400.00
Woman, Seminude, Floral Garland Caressed By Winged Putto, 33 In. 6900.00
Woman, Seminude, Stepping Into Water, Carmello Fontona, 39 In. 2587.00
Women, Seminude, Floral Garland, Barcaglia, 42 In. 6900.00

MARBLEHEAD Pottery was founded in 1905 by Dr. J. Hall as a rehabil-
tative program for the patients of a Marblehead, Massachusetts, sanitarium. Two years later it was separated from the sanitarium and it continued operations until 1936. Many of the pieces were decorated with
marine motifs.

Basket, Hanging, Blue Matte, 5 In. 395.00
Basket, Hanging, Ruffled Top, With Chains, Green Matte Glaze, 4 x 5 In. 220.00
Bookends, Stylized Owl Form, Brown Matte Glaze, 5 x 6 In. 770.00
Bowl, Blue, 1 3/4 x 3 1/2 In. 145.00
Bowl, Brown, Yellow Glaze, Impressed Mark, 6 In. 770.00
Bowl, Flower Frog, Blue, 3 In. 100.00
Bowl, Flower Frog, Matte Blue Glaze, Spherical, Ship Mark, 2 x 8 1/2 In. 250.00
Bowl, Flower Frog, Matte Medium Blue Glaze, Ship Mark, 3 1/2 x 7 1/2 In. 440.00
Bowl, Flower Frog, Mottled Ocher Glaze, Low, 2 x 5 3/4 In. 330.00
Bowl, Matte Blue Glaze, 4 1/2 In. 495.00
Bowl, Matte Blue Glaze, Closed Mouth, Turquoise Interior, Ship Mark, 5 1/2 In. 330.00
Bowl, Matte Mustard Glaze, Caramel Drip Design Base, Ship Mark, 7 3/4 In. 330.00
Bowl, Matte Rose Glaze, Speckled Baby's Breath Pink Interior, 2 1/2 x 6 1/2 In. 185.00
Bowl, Matte Yellow Exterior, Green To Blue Interior, Signed, 7 3/4 In. 302.00
Bowl, Stylized Design, Dark Brown, Oatmeal Ground, 7 x 3 1/2 In. 4675.00
Chamberstick, Hooded . . . . .350.00 to 400.00
Chamberstick, Yellow Matte Glaze, Impressed Ship Mark, 4 x 4 1/2 In. 275.00
Lamp, Caramel, Cerulean Blue, Ivory Interior, Ship Mark, 4 3/4 x 3 In. 305.00
Pitcher, Chartreuse Mottled Veined, Ivory Ground, Melon, 7 1/4 x 5 1/3 In. 220.00
Pitcher, Cobalt Blue Matte, Speckled, Robin's Egg Interior, Bulbous, 3 3/4 In. 185.00
Pitcher, Ribbed, Lavender, 4 3/4 In. 195.00
Planter, Hanging, Blue, Lavender Glaze, Purple Interior, 3 Handles, 3 x 5 1/2 In. 173.00
Planter, Speckled Rose Matte, White Speckled Interior, 3 Handles, 3 1/2 x 5 In. 165.00
Tile, Dark Brown Ocher Rooster, Speckled Gray Ground, Ship Mark, 5 In. 1100.00
Tile, Dark Green Cluster Of Trees, Blue Overcast Sky, 4 1/4 In. 880.00
Tile, Full Masted Ship, Blue Matte Ground, Ship Mark, 4 3/4 In. 415.00
Tile, Incised Image Of Egyptian Figure, Blue, Green, Glaze, Marked, 7 x 4 In. 460.00
Tile, Landscape Scene, Dark Green Trees Reflected In A Lake, 4 1/4 In. 770.00
Tile, Large Tree In Forest, Matte Brown Umber Glaze, Moss Green Ground, 6 In. 1430.00
Tile, Red, Green Flowers In Purple Basket, Matte Black Ground, 6 In. 660.00
Tile, Sailing Ship, Brown, White Sails, Blue, Green Sea, Square, 6 In. 415.00
Tile, Ship, Blue, Green, Brown, White, Marked, Square, 4 1/2 In. 460.00
Tile, Stylized Flowers, Still Life, 7 Colors, Arthur Baggs & Hannah Tutt, 5 7/8 In. 935.00
Vase, 5 Incised Moths, Charcoal Gray, Matte Green Ground, Cylindrical, 7 In. 4400.00
Vase, Blue Matte Glaze, Cylindrical, 7 In. 660.00
Vase, Bud, Matte Dove Gray, Sky Blue Glaze Interior, Ship Mark, 6 x 3 In. 220.00
Vase, Bulbous, Matte Speckled Ocher Glaze, Ship Mark, 4 3/4 x 3 3/4 In. 495.00
Vase, Cabot, Caramel Glaze, Mustard, Caramel Interior, Ship Mark, 3 1/3 In. 220.00
Vase, Cone Shape, Mauve, 5 1/2 In. 125.00
Vase, Floral Design, Tan, Brown Against Tobacco Ground, 5 1/2 x 3 1/2 In. 990.00
Vase, Geometric Design At Top, Matte Blue Glaze, Gray Ground, 6 In. 1430.00
Vase, Grape & Leaf Design, Speckled Tobacco Brown & Mustard Glaze, 8 In. 5620.00
Vase, Green Vertical Stylized Leaves, Blue Matte, Impressed Mark, 4 1/2 x 7 In. 4125.00
Vase, Incised Foliate, Blue, Brown & Green Glaze, Logo, Signed, 5 1/4 x 6 1/2 In. 3305.00
Vase, Incised Stem Design, Leaves, Flowers, Matte Blue Glaze, Gray, 6 In. 4125.00
Vase, Incised Tree, Pine Cone, Green Ground, 11 1/2 In. 3175.00
Vase, Incised, Painted Geometric Design, Dark Brown, Green Ground, 4 1/2 In. 3300.00
Vase, Matte Blue Glaze, Flattened Ribbed Form, 7 x 6 In. 330.00
Vase, Matte Brown Glaze, 6 x 4 1/2 In. 385.00
Vase, Matte Brown Glaze, 9 In. 1980.00
Vase, Matte Dark Green Glaze, Cylindrical, 7 In. 550.00
Vase, Matte Dark Green Glaze, Light Green Ground, Hannah Tutt, 8 3/4 x 4 In. 935.00
Vase, Matte Gray Glaze, Blue Highlights, Impressed Mark, 3 1/2 In. 440.00

Vase, Matte Gray Glaze, Light Blue Interior, Ship Mark, 9 x 6 1/2 In. 770.00
Vase, Matte Green Glaze, 7 In. 467.50
Vase, Matte Green, Brown Glaze, 7 In. 1045.00
Vase, Matte Green, Flared, Label, 3 In. 250.00
Vase, Matte Light Purple Glaze, Impressed Mark, 5 1/2 In. 210.00
Vase, Matte Moss Green Glaze, 2 Handles, Ship Mark, 2 3/4 x 3 3/4 In. 495.00
Vase, Matte Mustard Glaze, Sea Green Interior, Ship Mark, 5 1/4 x 3 In. 165.00
Vase, Matte Purple Glaze, 3 1/2 In. 440.00
Vase, Matte Purple Glaze, Impressed Mark, 9 In. 1320.00
Vase, Matte Purple Glaze, Paper Label, 4 1/2 x 2 1/4 In. 355.00
Vase, Matte Purple, Green Glaze, Bulbous Shoulder, 2 1/2 In. 77.00
Vase, Matte Yellow Glaze, Cylindrical, Impressed Mark, 4 1/2 In. 770.00
Vase, Matte Yellow Glaze, Tapered, 6 In. 231.00
Vase, Matte Yellow Glaze, Tapered, 7 In. 880.00
Vase, Mauve, 5 1/2 In. 175.00
Vase, Midnight Blue Matte, Sky Blue Interior, Speckled, Corset, 4 1/3 In. 185.00
Vase, Mocha Glaze, Salmon Matte, Maroon & White Speckled Interior, 5 1/2 In. 465.00
Vase, Mocha Matte Brown, Speckled, Red Mahogany Drip Glaze, 3 1/2 In. 275.00
Vase, Mottled Ocher Glaze, Paper Label, 11 3/4 x 7 In. 1210.00
Vase, Mustard Brown Glaze, Tapering Cylindrical Shape, 8 In. 920.00
Vase, Red Clay Body, Matte Green Glaze, 10 1/2 In. 835.00
Vase, Smooth Blue Glaze, Egg Shape, Signed, 6 3/4 In. 412.00
Vase, Smooth Speckled Green & Brown Glaze, Signed, 7 In. 440.00
Vase, Stylized Gray Leaves, Yellow Matte Ground, Impressed Mark, 7 In. 7150.00
Vase, Stylized Landscape, Brown, Green Ground, 6 1/4 x 3 3/4 In. 2860.00
Vase, Stylized Large Flower, Green Field, Ship Mark, 8 3/4 In. 2850.00
Vase, Stylized Leaves & Stems, Forest Green Matte, Gray Matte, 3 1/2 x 4 In. 770.00
Vase, Stylized Trees & Yellow Flowers, Speckled Ground, Signed, 5 1/4 In. 1650.00
Vase, Stylized Trees, Brown On Green Ground, Signed, 6 1/4 In. 1760.00
Vase, Thistles, Light Purple Ground, Impressed Mark, 5 In. 2090.00
Vase, Tobacco Brown Glaze, Cylindrical, 4 1/2 In. 525.00
Vase, Trees, Green Vertical Trunks, Orange Berries, Navy Blue Ground, 7 In. 1100.00
Wall Pocket, Matte Blue Glaze, Semicircular Rim, Ship Mark, 5 3/4 x 6 3/4 In. 440.00
Wall Pocket, Matte Lavender Glaze, Speckled Lavender White Interior, 5 In. 305.00

MARTIN BROTHERS of Middlesex, England, made Martinware, a salt-
glazed stoneware, between 1873 and 1915. Many figural jugs and
vases were made by the three brothers. Of special interest are the fanciful birds, usually made with removable heads.

Martin Bro.
London

Ewer, 3 Sides, Incised Birds On 2 Sides, With Flowers, Gray, Tan, 1895, 9 In. 2760.00
Ewer, 3 Spiky Fish, Brown, Blue, Cream, 1896, 9 3/4 In. 2070.00
Ewer, Incised Smiling, Pursed-Lipped Face, Green, Brown, 1890, 4 3/4 In. 1725.00
Ewer, Stylized Broad Leafage, Wildflower Branches, Brown, Blue, 1900, 8 In. 800.00
Figurine, Bird, Looking Straight Ahead, Blue, Pale Brown, 1913, 3 1/2 In. 3100.00
Figurine, Fish, Flounder, Brown, Black Slip, 11 In. 2875.00
Humidor, Grotesque Bird Shape, 1903, 7 3/4 x 3 1/4 In. 2530.00
Inkstand, Amusing Fish Shape, Curling Tail To Support Pen, 1883, 3 In. 1725.00
Jar, Bird, Cover, Dour Little Bird, Blue, Tan, Black, Green Slip, 1906, 9 In. 9200.00
Jar, Bird, Cover, Owl-Like Bird, Brown, Blue, Black Wooden Base, 1901, 11 In. 9775.00
Jar, Bird, Cover, Solemn-Eyed Bird, Brown, Blue, Green, Black Slip, 1904, 9 In. 7475.00
Jar, Bird, Cover, Standing Bird, Cobalt Blue, Tan, Ocher, Mauve, 1913, 8 In. 8050.00
Jar, Bird, Cover, Standing Bird, Feather, Cobalt Blue, 1913, 9 In. 7475.00
Jar, Bird, Cover, Standing Bird, Tan, Blue, Gray, Brown, 1905, 9 In. 9775.00
Jar, Bird, Cover, With Oversized Beak, Brown, Green, Pale Blue Slip, 7 In. 6900.00
Jar, Chimpanzee, Cover, Crouching, Brown, Black, White, 1890, 10 In. 8050.00
Jar, Fantastic Creature, Cover, Brown, Cream, 1900, 5 1/4 In. 5175.00
Jar, Toby Dog, Cover, Seated, Wearing White Frilled Collar, 1890, 4 7/8 In. 6990.00
Jug, 2 Grinning, Craggy Faces, Tan, Brown, White, 1900, 9 1/2 In. 5179.00
Jug, 2 Smiling Faces, Tan, Brown, 1903, 6 3/4 In. 3162.00
Jug, Cream, Brown Leaf Design, Incised Mark, 1894, 2 1/2 In. 200.00
Jug, Marine, Grotesque Spiky Fish, Plants, Brown, Gray, Black, 10 In. 2590.00
Jug, Smiling Face, Black Slip, Globular, 1890, 6 1/2 In. 3162.00
Jug, Smiling Sun Visage & Verso, Light Brown, Tan, Cream, 1896, 6 1/2 In. 3910.00

Jug, Smiling, Laughing Face, Brown, Tan, 1910, 7 3/4 In.	9775.00
Mug, 2 Faces, Smiling, Gray Glaze, 1900, 4 1/2 In.	2590.00
Mug, Smiling, Pursed Lipped Face, Cream, Gray, Brown, 1900, 4 3/4 In.	2415.00
Pitcher, 2 Faces, Old Man, Brown, R.W. Martin & Sons, 8 In.	3000.00
Vase, Brown, Black Striations, 3 Lizard Handles, 1900, 11 In.	4025.00
Vase, Bud, 4 Sides, Storks, Foliage, Brown, Blue, Yellow, Gray, Cream, 5 1/2 In.	1840.00
Vase, Eel, School Of Ferocious Eels, 2 Handles, Brown, Black, Tan, 1887, 8 In.	4025.00
Vase, Incised Aquatic Figures, Flying Fish, Brown, Cobalt Blue, 1897, 11 In.	8625.00
Vase, Incised Winged Dragons, Tan, Blue, Gray, 1896, 8 1/2 In.	2587.00
Vase, Marine, Incised Crabs, Oysters, Shrimps, Green, Brown, Blue, 9 In.	3162.00
Vase, Renaissance, Stylized Foliage, Sparrows, Phoenix, Gray, Brown, 9 In.	1495.00
Vase, Sgraffito Veined Pattern, 2 Handles, Amber Ground, 1903, 9 x 4 In.	1100.00
Vase, Swirl Design, Brown, Black Glaze, 1903, 9 1/4 x 6 1/4 In.	1870.00
Vase, Swirl Design, Incised Mark, 1913, 4 1/8 In.	375.00

MARY GREGORY is the name used for a type of glass that is easily identified. White figures were painted on clear or colored glass as the decoration. The figures chosen were usually children at play. The first glass known as Mary Gregory was made about 1870. Similar glass is made even today. The traditional story has been that the glass was made at the Sandwich Glass works in Boston by a woman named Mary Gregory. Recent research suggests that it is possible that none was made at Sandwich. In general, all-white figures were used in the United States, tinted faces were probably used in Bohemia, France, Italy, Germany, Switzerland, and England. Children standing, not playing, were pictured after the 1950s.

Bell, Cranberry	85.00
Bottle, Barber, Girl Hitting Tennis Ball, 8 1/8 In.	302.00
Bottle, Barber, Purple, Woman At Fountain, 8 In.	2585.00
Bottle, Barber, Tennis Player, Cobalt Blue, 8 In. ....*Illus*	355.00
Box, Glove, Sapphire Blue, Oriental Figures, 11 1/2 x 3 3/4 x 3 1/4 In.	1470.00
Box, Hinged Cover, Boy Holding Bird, Amber, 3 1/2 x 3 3/4 In.	245.00
Box, Powder, Cobalt Blue	275.00
Box, Trinket, Landscape Scene, Girl, Holding Basket Of Cherries, Blue, 4 x 2 In.	525.00
Carafe, Water, Cranberry, 10 In.	325.00
Creamer, Tree, With Cupid, Green	175.00
Cup, Girl, Holding Basket, Amber, Child's, 2 1/2 In.	66.00
Decanter, Presentation Of Girl With Flower, Stopper, 12 In.	86.00
Flask, Woman's, Emerald Green, 3 1/2 In.	295.00
Goblet, Engraved White Elk, Emerald Green Ground, 8 In.	85.00
Jar, Powder, Hinged Cover, Green	245.00
Jug, Glass, Girl Design, 2 In.	230.00
Lamp, Girl Holding Flower, Black Amethyst & Milk Glass, 17 1/2 In.	1420.00
Liquor Set, Decanter & 4 Cordials, 5 Piece	137.00
Mug, Girl, Applied Handle, White Enamel, Cranberry, 3 5/8 In.	115.00
Mug, Iridescent Topaz, Child's, 3 In.	155.00

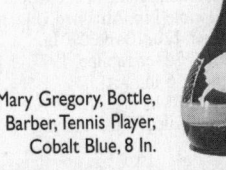

To make a quick 'photo' of your old bottle, try using a photocopying machine. Put the bottle on the machine, then cover it with white paper or cloth to block out any extra light. Lower the cover gently and take the picture.

Mary Gregory, Bottle, Barber, Tennis Player, Cobalt Blue, 8 In.

Pitcher, Boy With Basket, Trees, Cranberry 440.00
Pitcher, Inverted Thumbprint, Amber, Square Mouth, Blue Handle 245.00
Pitcher, Landscape Scene, Victorian Lady With Staff, Ruffled Rim, White, 7 In. 300.00
Plate, Cupids, Cobalt, 9 In. 195.00
Plate, Girl On Swing With Dog, Black, Opaque, 9 In. 45.00
Stein, Girl, Tinted Face In White Dress, Flip Lid, Amber 175.00
Tray, Dresser, Boy, With Hat, Girl, With Hat, 10 1/2 In. 245.00
Tumbler, Amethyst 95.00
Tumbler, Boy & Girl, Enamel, Amber, 19th Century, 5 3/4 In., Pair 38.00
Tumbler, Boy & Girl, White Enamel, Cranberry, 6 1/2 In., Pair 245.00
Tumbler, Juice, Cranberry 95.00
Tumbler, Sailor Boy, Holding Oar 55.00
Urn, Girl, White, Landscape With Gold Highlights, Purple, 11 1/2 In. 110.00
Vase, Amber, Girl In Forest, Other Side Floral, 6 3/4 x 3 In. 225.00
Vase, Blue Agate, Cylinder, 6 1/4 In. 275.00
Vase, Boy & Girl Holding Flower Chains, White & Brick Red, 10 3/4 In., Pair 970.00
Vase, Boy Blowing Bubbles, Deep Cranberry, 10 In. 325.00
Vase, Boy With Cane, Cranberry, White Enamel, 9 1/8 In. 245.00
Vase, Boy, All White, Green, Crystal Shell Trim, 6 1/2 In. 145.00
Vase, Boy, All White, Scalloped Top, Sapphire Blue, 9 In. 295.00
Vase, Boy, All White, Shell Trim Down Sides, Emerald Green, 6 1/2 In. 145.00
Vase, Boy, Girl, Facing Each Other, Amber, 7 3/4 In., Pair 350.00
Vase, Boy, White, Sapphire Blue, 8 5/8 x 3 5/8 In. 195.00
Vase, Boy, With Pink Face, Cranberry, 5 In. 80.00
Vase, Cupid, Emerald Green, 8 In. 85.00
Vase, Girl & Flowers, Amber Paneled, 5 3/4 In. 55.00
Vase, Girl Carrying Butterfly Net, Lime Green, 10 5/8 In. 180.00
Vase, Girl, Ruffled Top, Amber, 8 1/4 In. ....160.00 to 175.00
Vase, Lady Strolling, Red, 9 In., Pair 200.00
Vase, Scalloped Top, Gold Trim, Blue Handles, Sapphire Blue, 9 In. 295.00
Water Set, Sapphire Blue & Amber, Pitcher, 3 Girl & 3 Boy Goblets, 7 Piece 1345.00
Water Set, Sapphire Blue, 5 Piece 375.00
Wine Bottle, Girl Standing By Fence, Bubble Stopper, 9 3/4 In. 350.00
Wine Bottle, Girl With Scarf Around Her Neck, White, Stopper, 9 In. 195.00

MASON'S IRONSTONE was made by the English pottery of Charles J.
Mason after 1813. Mason, of Lane Delph, was given a patent for this
improved earthenware. He usually called it "Mason's Patent Ironstone
China." It resisted chipping and breaking so it became popular for dinnerwares and other table service dishes. Vases and other decorative
pieces were also made. The ironstone was decorated with orange, blue,
gold, and other colors, often in Japanese inspired designs. The firm had
financial difficulties but the molds and the name Mason were used by
many owners through the years, including Francis Morley, Taylor
Ashworth, George L. Ashworth, and John Shaw. Mason's joined the
Wedgwood group in 1973 and the name is still found on dinnerwares.

Bowl, Oriental Design, c.1870, 10 1/2 In. 495.00
Bowl, Oval, 8 3/4 In. 95.00
Centerpiece, Mandalay Star 500.00
Compote, Maroon Oriental Design, Hand Painted, 7 x 13 In. 450.00
Creamer, Vista 125.00
Dinner Service, Ashworth, 1890-1910, 150 Piece 3680.00
Dish, Cover, Imari Design, 11 In. 440.00
Eggcup, Vista, Large 65.00
Eggcup, Vista, Small 55.00
Garniture Set, Countryside Scene, Blue, 2 10-In. Vases, 16-In. Urn, 3 Piece 330.00
Gravy Boat, Double Lip, Attached Underplate 150.00
Jar, Ginger, Cover, Fruit Basket, 7 In. 95.00
Jar, Ginger, Royal Silver Jubilee, 1977, 5 1/2 In. 80.00
Jug, Manchu Mark, 6 In. 170.00
Ladle, Vista, Red, 10 In. 150.00
Pitcher, Golden Azalea, 6 In. 70.00
Plate, Oval, 11 In. 255.00

Plate, Square, 10 1/2 In.	255.00
Plate, Vista, 10 3/4 In.	50.00
Plate Set, Imari, Printed Marks, c.1830, 10 1/4 In., 12 Piece	805.00
Platter, Blue Vista, 1900, 17 1/2 In.	295.00
Platter, Blue Willow, 15 In.	110.00
Platter, Chinoiserie, Black Transfer Rose, Yellow, Staffordshire, 21 In.	920.00
Platter, Game Birds, 17 x 13 1/2 In.	150.00
Platter, Vista, 11 In.	90.00
Platter, Vista, 14 In.	115.00
Platter, Vista, 17 1/2 In.	250.00
Platter, Vista, Pink, Oval, 15 In.	70.00
Soup, Dish, Blue Pheasants, 9 1/2 In.	250.00
Sugar, Cover, Vista	125.00
Tureen, Cover, Multicolored, Ironstone, 12 x 14 In.	800.00
Tureen, Sauce, Ladle	450.00
Tureen, Soup, Blue Vista, 1900, 17 1/2 In.	295.00
Urn, Landscape, Pagoda, Leafy Branches, Green Foot, 1820, 18 In.	3450.00

MASONIC, see Fraternal category.

MASSIER, a French art pottery, was made by brothers Jerome, Delphin, and Clement Massier in Vallauris and Golfe-Juan, France, in the late nineteenth and early twentieth centuries. It has an iridescent metallic luster glaze that resembles the Weller Sicardo pottery glaze. Most pieces are marked *J. Massier.*

J.MASSiER fils

Charger, Mediterranean Bay Scene, Pine Trees, 13 In.	1430.00
Jardiniere, Siren, Waves Ground, Coppery Luster Glaze, 1900, 15 In.	3185.00
Vase, 4 Mushroom Stalks, Turquoise & Ruby Luster Glaze, 1900, 14 In.	9375.00
Vase, Leaf & Flower Design, Signed, 5 3/8 In.	660.00
Vase, Painted Swirls On Surface, Metallic Glaze, Signed, 7 3/4 In.	247.00

MATCH HOLDERS were made to hold the large wooden matches that were used in the nineteenth and twentieth centuries for a variety of purposes. The kitchen stove and the fireplace or furnace had to be lit regularly. One type of match holder was made to hang on the wall, another was designed to be kept on a tabletop. Of special interest today are match holders that have advertisements as part of the design.

Bearded Man With Turban & Sword, Striker, Porcelain	325.00
Black Boy, Holding Watermelon, Wooden, Wall	450.00
Black Boy, Majolica, Striker	275.00
Blue, Gold & White, Side Striker, 3 1/4 In.	55.00
Box, Hoglund Brothers	40.00
Boy, With Basket, Bisque, Chalkware Type, 7 1/2 x 6 3/4 x 6 1/4 In.	160.00
Colonial Man, Holding Musket, Deer Behind Of Wood Pile, Brass, 4 1/2 In.	145.00
De Laval, Tin, 4 In.	325.00
Double, Acorn Leaves, Cast Iron, 8 In.	75.00
Dutch Boy Paint, Figural	450.00
Elephant, Bisque, Germany, 8 x 9 In., Pair	550.00
Elwood Steel Fences	195.00
Fireplace, Cast Metal, Holds Whole Box Of Large Matches	110.00
Griswold, Ashtray, Skillet Shape	75.00
Grotesque Man With Comic Nose, Hat, Cast Iron, Black Paint, 5 1/4 In.	165.00
Horse, Looking Through Collar, Yellow Ground	675.00
Lacey Cast Iron, Weighted Self Closing, Wall, 4 1/2 x 5 3/4 In.	220.00
Mammy, Wooden, 1930s	85.00
Milwaukee Harvester, Tin	425.00
Owl Form, Hand Carved Wood, Glass Eyes, 6 5/8 In.	325.00
Purol Tiolene, Metal	93.00
Rooster & Basket, Lid Up On Baskets, Bisque, 4 In.	110.00
Shoe, White, Rectangle Base, Cast Iron, Victorian, 5 1/4 x 4 1/4 In.	87.00
Tooled Leather, Oak Leaf & Acorn Pattern, 2-Piece Form, Marked, c.1912	880.00
Umbrella, Nickel Plated Brass, For Hanging Lamp, 1 5/8 x 3 1/2 In.	95.00
Wooden Strike, Texaco Logo, Green Metal	40.00

MATCH SAFES were designed to be carried in the pocket. Early matches were made with phosphorus and could ignite unexpectedly. The matches were safely stored in the tightly closed container. Match safes were made in sterling silver, plated silver, or other metals. The English call these *vesta boxes.*

Alligator, Brass	165.00
Anheuser-Busch, Metal, Embossed	95.00
Bartholomay Brewing Co., Brass, Silver Metal Finish, 2 1/2 x 1 1/2 In.	60.00
BPOE, Pocket	57.00
Calendar, When In Trouble Use Pabst's Okay Specific, Celluloid, 2 1/4 In.	18.00
Compliments Of Empire Worsted Mills, December 25, 1901, 1 1/2 x 2 1/2 In.	55.00
Counter, Bird Picks Up Match In Beak	185.00
Cow's Foot, Brass	175.00
Dentist Pulling A Tooth, Porcelain	33.00
Fitzsimmons Bros. Restaurant, Nude Woman, Steel, Celluloid, c.1900	83.00
Flit Top, Striker, Burled Sycamore, 19th Century	85.00
Frog Form, Advertising, Michigan Stove Co.	132.00
Jack Daniel's	125.00
Mermaid, Sterling Silver	195.00
Pan-American Exposition, Electric Tower & Dancing Woman	85.00
Pocket Knife, Nickel Plate, White Celluloid Sides	350.00
Prince Albert, Brass, Ornate	65.00
Rainier Beer, Aluminum, Embossed	83.00
Red Ribbon Beer, Spring Loaded Door Flips In Front, Matches	132.00
Rochester Brewery, Seldom Equaled Never Excelled Logo	75.00
San Felice	75.00
Schlitz Beer, Cigar Cutter On Bottom	75.00
Seminude, In Garden With Babes & Tiger, Silver Plate	90.00
Socony, Embossed Metal, Hinged, 1920s	65.00
Suspended From Box Link Chain, 14K Yellow Gold, 30 In.	201.00
Venus & Attendants, Bas Relief Design, Art Nouveau, Rectangular, 2 7/8 In.	230.00
Woodrow Wilson, 2 x 3 In.	100.00

MATSU-NO-KE was a type of applied decoration for glass patented by Frederick Carder in 1922. There is clear evidence that pieces were made before that date at the Steuben glassworks. Stevens & Williams of England also made an applied decoration by the same name.

Candlestick, Pair	475.00
Glass, Green Handle, Cat	290.00
Tumbler, Green Handle	290.00
Vase, Rosa Design, Cat, 6 In.	290.00 to 340.00

MATT MORGAN, an English artist, was making pottery in Cincinnati, Ohio, by 1883. His pieces were decorated to resemble Moorish wares. Incised designs and colors were applied to raised panels on the pottery. Shiny or matte glazes were used. The company lasted less than two years.

Umbrella Stand, Blue Gloss Glaze, Gold Highlights, Signed, 20 3/8 In.	605.00
Vase, Cobalt Blue, Gold Accents, 5 In.	475.00

MCCOY pottery was made in Roseville, Ohio. Nelson McCoy and J.W. McCoy established the Nelson McCoy Sanitary and Stoneware Company in Roseville, Ohio, in 1910. The firm made art pottery after 1926. In 1933 it became the Nelson McCoy Pottery Company. Pieces marked *McCoy* were made by the Nelson McCoy Pottery Company. Cookie jars were made from about 1940 until December 1990, when the McCoy factory closed. In 1990 the McCoy mark was put back on pottery by a firm unrelated to the original company. Because there was a company named Brush-McCoy, there is great confusion between Brush and Nelson McCoy pieces. See Brush category for more information.

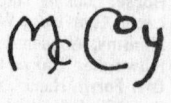

Bank, Eagle, Immigrant Industrial Savings	45.00 to 50.00
Bean Pot, Cover, Brown	8.00
Bookends, Lily	135.00

Bowl, El Rancho, Box .... 335.00 to 400.00
Bowl, Heinz, Brown, Tab Handle 35.00
Bowl, Treat, Cover, Unipet, Orange, White, Bell In Cover To Call Pet, 5 In. 35.00
Candy Dish, Gold Cascade 40.00
Canister, Cover, Stonecraft, Pink & Blue Banded, Small 25.00
Coffee Server, El Rancho 150.00
Coffee Server Set, El Rancho, 4 Mugs, Candle Warmer 375.00
Cookie Jar, Apollo 950.00
Cookie Jar, Apple, Yellow, Red 55.00
Cookie Jar, Astronauts, 1963 .... 550.00 to 750.00
Cookie Jar, Banana Bunch 125.00
Cookie Jar, Barnum's Animal Crackers 295.00
Cookie Jar, Bean Pot .... 50.00 to 75.00
Cookie Jar, Bobby The Baker 215.00
Cookie Jar, Boy On Football 195.00
Cookie Jar, Bugs Bunny Decal 700.00
Cookie Jar, Chairman Of The Board, 1985 .... 500.00 to 895.00
Cookie Jar, Christmas Tree 395.00
Cookie Jar, Clown, Bust .... 250.00 to 255.00
Cookie Jar, Clyde Dog .... 275.00 to 300.00
Cookie Jar, Coalby Cat 100.00
Cookie Jar, Covered Wagon 95.00
Cookie Jar, Crayola Kids .... 195.00 to 375.00
Cookie Jar, Dalmatians, Rocking Chair .... 35.00 to 45.00
Cookie Jar, Early American Frontier Family .... 155.00 to 165.00
Cookie Jar, Friendship 7, 1962-1968 .... 40.00
Cookie Jar, Fruit In Basket 300.00
Cookie Jar, Globe 135.00
Cookie Jar, Hamm's Bear 385.00
Cookie Jar, Harley-Davidson Hog .... 35.00 to 100.00
Cookie Jar, Have A Happy Day, Happy Face 140.00
Cookie Jar, Hobby Horse 180.00
Cookie Jar, Humpty Dumpty, Peeked Hat .... 285.00 to 400.00
Cookie Jar, Indian 400.00
Cookie Jar, Jack-O'-Lantern .... 50.00 to 75.00
Cookie Jar, Keebler Tree House .... 50.00 to 60.00
Cookie Jar, Kissing Penguins .... 80.00 to 95.00
Cookie Jar, Kitten On Basket Weave .... 595.00 to 600.00
Cookie Jar, Kittens In Basket 95.00
Cookie Jar, Koala Bear 185.00
Cookie Jar, Lamb On Cylinder 40.00
Cookie Jar, Lantern, Coleman Style, Hand Painted, 10 In. 40.00
Cookie Jar, Lazy Pig, Quigley 1250.00
Cookie Jar, Leprechaun, Red 80.00
Cookie Jar, Little Boy Blue, Carousel 75.00
Cookie Jar, Little Clown 265.00
Cookie Jar, Mammy 950.00
Cookie Jar, Mammy With Cauliflower 190.00
Cookie Jar, Mammy, Cookies 595.00
Cookie Jar, Mammy, Yellow, Cookies .... 36.00 to 75.00
Cookie Jar, Nabisco 75.00
Cookie Jar, Owl, Brown, Black, Tan 200.00
Cookie Jar, Panda Bear 40.00
Cookie Jar, Pepper, Green 40.00
Cookie Jar, Picnic Basket 100.00
Cookie Jar, Rabbit On Cabbage 125.00
Cookie Jar, Sad Clown .... 600.00 to 850.00
Cookie Jar, Stage Coach, White & Brown .... 25.00 to 35.00
Cookie Jar, Strawberry 35.00
Cookie Jar, Tea Kettle .... 225.00 to 435.00
Cookie Jar, Teepee, Slant Cover .... 20.00 to 35.00
Cookie Jar, Thinking Puppy 850.00
Cookie Jar, Touring Car ....

Cookie Jar, Tulip Flower Pot 275.00
Cookie Jar, Upside Down Bear 300.0
Cookie Jar, W.C. Fields ....150.00 to 400.0
Cookie Jar, Winking Pig ....175.00 to 195.0
Cookie Jar, Wishing Well ....40.00 to 55.0
Cookie Jar, Woodsy Owl ....195.00 to 345.0
Creamer, Daisy 22.0
Dispenser, Iced Tea, El Rancho 195.0
Flower Frog, Kingfisher 75.0
Flower Holder, Gnome, Yellow, 3 In. 150.0
Flowerpot, Saucer, Green, 1961, 4 x 4 1/4 In. 15.0
Flowerpot, Saucer, Lotus Leaf, Cream, Painted Leaves 95.0
Jar, Oil, Maroon, 12 In. 100.0
Jardiniere, Aqua, Hanson 65.0
Jardiniere, Basketweave, Green 10.0
Jardiniere, Basketweave, Pink ....15.00 to 30.0
Jardiniere, Black, Gloss, Marked 65.0
Jardiniere, Diamond, Brown, 9 In. 80.0
Jardiniere, Foliage, Quilted, Green, Large 125.0
Jardiniere, Leaf & Berry, Matte White, 7 In. 50.0
Jardiniere, Loy-Nel-Art, With Bird, 8 In. 45.0
Jardiniere, Pedestal, Orange Poppy, Brown, 29 1/2 In. 550.00
Jardiniere, Spring Wood, Mint Green, 10 In. 68.00
Jardiniere, Swirl, Aqua, 5 In. 25.0
Lamp, Cowboy Boot 45.0
Mug, Buccaneer, Green 30.0
Mug, Corn, Signed Cusick 45.00
Mug, El Rancho ....45.00 to 100.00
Pitcher, Fish, Blue 55.00
Pitcher, Matte Green, Shield Mark, Hanson, 13 1/2 In. 40.00
Pitcher, Seashell, Green 40.00
Pitcher, Spirit Of '76 .... 18.00
Pitcher, Vat, No. 69, White, Gold, 5 1/2 In. 50.00
Planter, Apple 50.00
Planter, Attached Liner, Brown, 6 In. 50.00
Planter, Bird Dog, 1954 .... 195.00
Planter, Bird, Green, 1940s, 4 1/2 x 4 1/2 In. 20.00
Planter, Black Spotted Hunting Dog 50.00
Planter, Brown Boot 30.00
Planter, Car, Brown 20.00
Planter, Clown, With Pig, Hanson 55.00
Planter, Duck Pulling Cart, Yellow 45.00
Planter, Duck With Umbrella 130.00
Planter, Elephant, Ivory 25.00
Planter, Fawn, 12 x 8 In. 275.00
Planter, Flower Shape, Purple, Blue, 13 x 5 In. 55.00
Planter, Frog & Lotus, Green, Yellow, 1940s 25.00
Planter, Frog, Green 30.00
Planter, Fruit, Orange, Green Base, 1954 .... 65.00
Planter, Hobnail, Turquoise 25.00
Planter, Humpty Dumpty, Aqua 35.00
Planter, Kitten Basket 90.00
Planter, Kitten On Side 50.00
Planter, Liberty Bell ....225.00 to 250.00
Planter, Loy-Nel-Art, Ivory 50.00
Planter, Pheasant 48.00
Planter, Plow Boy 80.00
Planter, Pony, Blue 65.00
Planter, Quail 43.00
Planter, Rocking Chair 40.00
Planter, Rodeo Cowboy 135.00
Planter, Seashell, Round 50.00
Planter, Sheep, Grass Growing 65.00

Planter, Squirrel, Gray	25.00
Planter, Swallows, Hanson	25.00
Planter, Swan, Tricolor Trim	55.00
Planter, Tangerine, 5 In.	15.00 to 18.00
Planter, Tour Car, 1945, 9 x 4 1/2 In.	45.00
Planter, Tree Stump, Green, With Initials	13.00
Planter, Trolley Car	45.00
Planter, Turtle, Green	40.00
Planter, Turtle, Green, 1950, 8 x 5 In.	45.00
Planter, Wagon Wheel	35.00
Planter, Well With Bucket	15.00
Planter, Western Log, With Rifle	55.00
Planter, Wild Rose, Yellow, Hanson, 8 x 3 1/2 In.	50.00
Planter, Wishing Well	22.00 to 37.00
Planter, Yellow	12.00
Server, Iced Tea, El Rancho, Box	195.00 to 200.00
Soup Pot, Cover, Metallic Brown, Copper Handle, 1971, 7 x 7 In.	40.00
Spooner, Butterfly	125.00
Stein, Buccaneer, Green, 5 In.	12.00
Tankard Set, Buccaneer, Brown High Glaze, 9 Piece	165.00
Tea Set, Pine Cone, 3 Piece	40.00
Teapot, Sugar & Creamer, Pine Cone	125.00
Teapot, Sunburst, Sugar & Creamer, Gold	140.00
Tureen, Soup, Pink & Blue, Bands, Ladle, Cover	55.00
Umbrella Stand, Lady With Dove	375.00
Vase, Bird Bath, El Rancho, 6 In.	38.00
Vase, Blossom Time, 8 In.	45.00
Vase, Butterfly, Aqua, Hanson, 6 1/4 In.	30.00
Vase, Butterfly, Green, White, 1940s, 9 In.	25.00
Vase, Butterfly, Ivy, Hanson, 4 1/2 In.	40.00
Vase, Daisies, Pink & Green, 10 1/2 In.	20.00
Vase, Fan, Burgundy, Hanson, 6 1/2 In.	55.00
Vase, Fan, Green, 14 1/2 In.	100.00
Vase, Gray, 10 In.	303.00
Vase, Lizard Handle, Brown & Green, 9 In.	250.00
Vase, Loy-Nel-Art, Iris, Orange, Green, Yellow Leaves, Brown Ground, 14 1/2 In.	350.00 to 385.00
Vase, Obelisk, Matte Green, 10 1/4 In.	400.00
Vase, Olympia Acorn, J.W., 5 In.	275.00
Vase, Peach, Hanson, 8 In.	50.00
Vase, Peacock, Green, 8 In.	90.00
Vase, Rustic, 9 In.	60.00
Vase, Sand Dollar, Matte White, 14 In.	125.00
Vase, Tulip, Double, 8 In.	75.00
Vase, White, Hanson, 8 In.	45.00
Wall Pocket, Apple	65.00
Wall Pocket, Birdbath	85.00
Wall Pocket, Blossom Time, Yellow	110.00
Wall Pocket, Fan, Blue	85.00
Wall Pocket, Grapes	195.00
Wall Pocket, Lady With Bonnet, Hanson	60.00
Wall Pocket, Owls	85.00

MCKEE is a name associated with various glass enterprises in the
United States since 1836, including J. & F. McKee (1850), Bryce,
McKee & Co. (1850 to 1854), McKee and Brothers (1865), and
National Glass Co. (1899). In 1903, the McKee Glass Company was
formed in Jeannette, Pennsylvania. It became McKee Division of the
Thatcher Glass Co. in 1951 and was bought out by the Jeannette
Corporation in 1961. Pressed glass, kitchenwares, and tablewares were
produced. Jeannette Corporation closed in the early 1980s. Additional
pieces may be included in the Custard Glass category.

Bowl, Jade Green, 9 In.	30.00
Bowl, Refrigerator, Cover, Opal, Red Ships, 5 x 8 In.	22.00

Bowl, Seville Yellow, 4 1/4 In.		12.0
Bowl, Skokie Green, Scalloped Edge, 8 1/2 In.		26.0
Butter, Child's, Tappan, Clear		75.0
Clock, Tambour Art Glass, Amber		175.0
Cup & Saucer, Rock Crystal		18.0
Dish, Sunbeam, Jade Green, Upturned Corners, Square		25.0
Jug, Tankard, Toltec, 8 1/2 In.		130.0
Lamp, Rose Pink, Frosted, Flared Base, Art Deco, 11 In.		333.0
Measuring Cup Set, Seville Yellow, 4 Piece		125.0
Pitcher, Rock Crystal, Green		95.0
Pitcher, Sunburst		65.0
Plate, Rock Crystal, 10 In.		10.0
Saltshaker, Poudre Blue, Square		100.0
Shaker, Flour, Poudre Blue, Square		125.0
Toothpick, Britannic, Ruby Stained		85.0
Tumbler, Whiskey, Bottoms-Up		90.0

MECHANICAL BANKS are listed in the Bank category.

MEDICAL office furniture, operating tools, microscopes, thermometers, and other paraphernalia used by doctors are included in this category. Medicine bottles are listed in the Bottle category. There are related collectibles listed under Dental.

Amblyoscope, Optician, Train's Eye Muscle Balance, Worth's, 1935, 6 x 5 3/4 In.		58.00
Aspirator, Infant, Favol		12.00
Bag, 2 Sections, Leather, Double Brass Locks, Civil War		160.00
Bag, Doctor's, Alligator		350.00
Bleeder, 6-Glass Suction Cups, Brass Suction Pump, 1860s		633.00
Bottle, Hot Water, Cat Shape, Child's		20.00
Bottle, Hot Water, Cello, Brass, 1912		100.00
Bottle, Hot Water, Jayne Mansfield, 1960, 22 x 8 In.		125.00
Bottle, Hot Water, Red Riding Hood, Light Blue, Rubber, Metal Screw Top, 1908		150.00
Bottle, Hot Water, This Little Piggy, Pink, Rubber, Child's		15.00
Box, Comedic Pills, Vicar & Moses, Hobby Horse, Metal, 2 x 1 5/8 In.		805.00
Box, Motto Pills, Inspirational Phrase Design, Metal, England, 1 3/4 In.		575.00
Box, Nephrite, Pills, Stylized Floral Design, Gold Mount, 1 5/8 In.		575.00
Box, Pill, Classical Domestic Scene, Silver, Round, France, 1 3/4 In.		288.00
Brace, Turned Rosewood Handle, Steel, France, 8 1/4 In.		700.00
Cabinet, Apothecary, 12 Drawers, 24 x 67 In.		995.00
Cabinet, Apothecary, Mahogany, 15 Drawers, Pine Base, Brass Fittings, 25 In.		165.00
Cabinet, Apothecary, Mahogany, Fitted Interior, Bottles Victorian, 19 1/2 In.		1150.00
Cabinet, Apothecary, Pine, Oak Grained, 7 Drawers, Labels, 16 x 8 x 18 In.		715.00
Cabinet, Apothecary, Poplar, 9 Drawers, Wooden Pulls, 11 x 7 1/2 In.		407.00
Cabinet, Apothecary, Shaker, 6 Dovetailed Drawers, Case, 34 1/4 x 8 x 7 In.		1035.00
Cabinet, Apothecary, Teakwood, 8 Dovetailed Drawers, Oriental, 35 x 23 x 44 In.		1320.00
Case, Leather, Vet, 11 Glass Vials, Parke Davis, 1900		25.00
Catalog, Budge Uniforms, For Doctors, Nurses, 50 Pages, 1961		25.00
Chest, Apothecary, Interior Fitted For Bottles, Victorian, 19th Century, 11 x 9 In.		345.00
Counter, Pill, For 144 Pills, Iron, Wooden Handle, 19th Century		145.00
Crutches, Mortise & Tenon Construction, 18th Century, Child's, 33 In.		200.00
Dilator, Uterine, Steel, Codman & Shurtleff, Late 1800s, 10 1/2 In.		35.00
Drill, Bone, Trepanning Brace, 4 Numbered Bits, Sklar, 12 In.		175.00
Eye Cup, John Bull, 1917		38.00
Fleam, Bone Handle, C. Croory On Blade, 3 Different Sizes		265.00
Fleam, Brass, Marked Morris, Mid-1800s		125.00
Fleam, Horn On Brass, Mid-1800s		110.00
Forceps, Placenta, Steel, Codman & Shurtleff, Late 1800s, 12 In.		35.00
Head, Phrenology, Paper Labels Identify Sections, Fowler & Wells		250.00
Head, Phrenology, Pharmaceutical Advertising, Miniature		170.00
Hearing Aid, Ear Trumpet, Ivory Earpiece, Copper, Instructions, Rein & Son, London		1500.00
Hearing Aid, Ear Trumpet, Tin, Painted, Turn-Of-The-Century, 4 1/2 In.		167.00
Hearing Aid, Flexible Woven Cloth Cord, Plastic Pipe Stem, Horn Funnel, 43 1/2 In.		385.00
Hearing Aid, Wrapped Black Cord Ear Piece, Brass Funnel		85.00
Heart, Anatomical		225.00

Kit, Nursing, Anti-Colic, Includes Old Glass Bottle With Nipple, Original Box	24.00
Kit, Surgeon's, Pocket, U.S. Army, 6 Steel Instruments, Canvas Case	120.00
Kit, Surgeon's, Pocket, U.S. Army, 12 Steel Instruments, Leather Case	245.00
Lancet, Gum, With Pick, Tortoiseshell Handle, Tiemann, c.1860	165.00
Lancet, Spring, Brass, Engraved Both Sides, 2 1/16 In.	340.00
Mirror, Pocket, N.C. Rublee, Optometrist	22.00
Model, Heart, Anatomical, 2 Sections, Hand Painted, 3 Dimensional, Stand	590.00
Mortar, Bell Metal, Heraldic Symbols, Royal Cipher, 1690, 4 1/8 In.	285.00
Mortar & Pestle, Burl Ash, Early 18th Century, 7 In.	850.00
Mortar & Pestle, Iron Banded, Birch, Early 19th Century	100.00
Mortar & Pestle, Wooden, Hand Turned, 6 In.	75.00
Otoscope, Bakelite Box, 1924	85.00
Pill Crusher, Amber, Hand Made, 5 In.	35.00
Pill Roller, Walnut, Brass, With Tray, 19th Century	365.00
Probe, Bullet, Wooden Handle, Late 1700s	265.00
Probe, Nickel Silver, Leach & Greene, No. 23, Early 1900s	23.00
Quack Device, Violet Ray, Mahogany Power Box, Instructions	125.00
Quack Machine, Eye Surgeon's Tools, 5-Drawer Mahogany Case, 1900, 8 x 4 In.	201.00
Quack Machine, Nickel Silver Violet Ray, Static Accessories, Fitted Case, 12 In.	173.00
Saddle Bag, Doctor's, Homeopathic, 19th Century	425.00
Saddle Bag, St. Louis, January 18, 1870, 7 x 5 1/2 In., Pair	850.00
Saw, Amputation, Finger, 18th Century, 7 1/4 In.	390.00
Saw, Amputation, Hilcer & Sons, 19 3/4 In.	265.00
Saw, Bow, Amputation, 13 1/8 In.	165.00
Scalpel, Fleam, Ebony Handle	40.00
Scalpel, Surgeon's, Folding, Steel Blade, Bone Handle, Marked Netwood, 3 13/16 In.	165.00
Scalpel, With Cover, Sheffield, 6 1/4 In.	39.00
Skull, Human, Papier-Mache	450.00
Suppository Machine, Iron, Wooden Base, W.T. & Co., No. 3	110.00
Syringe, Flushing, Brass, Tips, Felt Plunger, Brass Handle, 1860, 6 3/4 x 1 1/4 In.	230.00
Table, Examination, Black Leather, Wood, Salesman's Sample, c.1920	425.00
Tenaculum, Artery Hook, Wooden Handle, Late 1700s	255.00
Thermometer, Asepto Certified Fever Thermometer, Box	20.00
Trepan, Skull Borer, Horn Handle, Retractable Point, Blued Steel, Brass	195.00
Trephine, Surgeon's	170.00
Tweezers & Nail Clippers, Pearl Handle, From Doctor's Bag	75.00
Vaccinator, Folding Place, Ivory	150.00
Vaginal Depressor, Double Ended, Codman & Shurtleff, Early 1900s	18.00
Vaporizer, Vapo Cresolene, Box, Late 1800s	130.00
Vibrator, Electric, Blue, Steel, Wooden Handle, Rubber Heads, Box, Gilbert, c.1952	40.00
Vibrator, Electric, Gray Enamel, Wooden Handle, Box, Polar Cub, 1920s, 5 x 7 In.	45.00
Wheel Chair, Oak Frame, Single Rear Steel Wheel, Caned Seat & Back	500.00

MEERSCHAUM is a soft white, gray, or cream-colored mineral named magnesium silicate. The name comes from the German word for seafoam, because it was sometimes found floating in the Black Sea and people thought it was petrified seafoam. Pipes and other pieces of carved meerschaum listed here date from the nineteenth century to the present.

Cigarette Holder, 2 Children With A Dog, Unused, 7 In.	288.00
Cigarette Holder, Hunter, With Game & Dogs	374.00
Cigarette Holder, Stag & Tree Design	230.00
Pipe, 2 Indians	475.00
Pipe, Amber Stem & Case	60.00
Pipe, Bust, Victorian Lady With Hat, No Stem	115.00
Pipe, Diana The Huntress, With Dog, Case, 9 1/2 In.	230.00
Pipe, Doghouse Shape, Case, 8 x 3 In.	430.00
Pipe, Eagle	225.00
Pipe, Figure Of Bearded Gentleman, Wearing A Fez, Case, 5 1/2 x 2 1/2 In.	115.00
Pipe, Figure Of Hand Holding The Bowl, Case, 7 x 2 1/2 In.	115.00
Pipe, Gypsy Lady With Large Earrings, Scarf, 6 1/2 x 3 In.	316.00
Pipe, Horse & Tree Stump	115.00
Pipe, Horse, Chased By 3 Wolves, In Case	345.00

Pipe, Horse, Standing, Amber Stem, Repaired Stem, Fitted Case, 4 In. 325.0

Pipe, Lady, With A Fan, Case, 6 x 2 1/2 In. 288.0

Pipe, Lion's Head Shape, Baring Teeth & Tongue, 7 In. 259.0

Pipe, Nude, Large 500.0

Pipe, Nude, Mermaid 250.0

Pipe, Sailor, Leaning Against A Stump, Holding An Oar, 7 1/2 In. 287.0

Pipe, Snarling Animal Head, Hand Carved 65.0

Pipe, Victorian Lady Shape, Wearing Feathered Hat, No Stem, Red, Case, 4 In. 287.0

Pipe, Victorian Lady With Elegant Carved Coiffure, Wearing A Hat, 5 x 2 In. 175.0

MEISSEN is a town in Germany where porcelain has been made since 1710. Any china made in the town can be called Meissen, although the famous Meissen factory made the finest porcelains of the area. The crossed swords mark of the great Meissen factory has been copied by many other firms in Germany and other parts of the world. Pieces of Meissen dinnerware in the Onion pattern are listed in their own category in this book.

Basket, Blue Floral, Reticulated, Branch Handles, Blue Crossed Swords, 13 In. 605.0

Basket, Chestnut, Gilt Trim, Floral Center, 11 1/2 In. 450.0

Bowl, Straw Flowers, Blue, White, Footed, 1880s, 6 1/2 In. 295.0

Box, Lemon, Cover, 1 Green Leaf, Looped-Stem Handle, 1755, 4 3/16 In. 2012.0

Box, Lemon, Cover, Naturalistic Scene, 3 Green Leaves, Yellow, Oval, 4 In., Pair 3162.0

Box, Sugar, Cover, 2 Exotic Birds Amidst Fences, Puce Herringbone Border, 5 In. 7475.0

Box, Sugar, Cover, Exotic Bird In Flight, Stylized Rockwork, Red, Turquoise, 4 1/8 In. . . . 1725.0

Candelabrum, 4-Light, Woman Figural Supports, Putti & Shields Base, 22 In. 2300.0

Candlestick, Figural, Harvest Of Wheat, Pair . . . . *Illus* 3000.0

Candlestick, Man & Woman, Cherubs, Pair 3000.0

Centerpiece, 3 Reticulated Tiers, Finial Of Girl With Basket, Red Roses, 21 In. 2070.0

Centerpiece, Underglaze, Crossed Swords, 12 In. 850.0

Chocolate Pot, Cover, 3 Clusters Of Fruit, Flowers, Handle, 1765, 7 5/8 In. 1035.0

Clock, Flowers, Multicolored, Scrolled Base, c.1880, 11 In. 1955.0

Coffeepot, Cover, Winged Dragon In Flight, Brown, Yellow, Green Ground, 7 7/8 In. . . . 9200.0

Compote, Floral Medallions, Pedestal Base, Signed, Crossed Swords, 9 In. 400.0

Compote, Painted Coat Of Arms, Reticulated Rim, Gold Trim, 9 x 11 In. 275.0

Cup & Saucer, 4 Panels, Demitasse 75.0

Cup & Saucer, Coffee, 2 Peasants Conversing Near Cottage, 1740, 2 15/16 In. 1724.0

Cup & Saucer, Courting Couple Scene, Cobalt Blue, Factory Marks 288.0

Cup & Saucer, Ribbed Body, Enamel Floral & Insect, Signed, 5-In. Saucer 230.0

Cup & Saucer, Tea, 3 Figures Conversing Before Distant Ruin, 1740, 2 x 5 3/16 In. 920.0

Dessert Set, Fired Gold Leaves Below White Leaves, Sawtooth Rim, 6 Piece 860.0

Dinner Service, Floral Sprays & Moths, Osier Borders, Blue Crossed Swords 4025.0

Dish, Center, Reticulated Rim, Gold Trim, White Ground, Signed, 14 1/2 x 9 In. 400.0

Dish, Gilt Floral Design, Cobalt Blue, Low, 6 In. 58.0

Dish, Serving, Fruit Cartouches, Enameled, Gilt Trim, 20th Century, 12 In., Pair 431.0

Meissen, Candlestick, Figural, Harvest Of Wheat, Pair

When using antiques on a holiday table, be careful. Wax from candles can stain a cloth. Dishes may stain from cranberry or other fruits. Flower containers are easily water stained. Vases and plants often stain wood; be sure to use a coaster or dish. Greens draped on pictures or marble can stain. Cellophane tape will leave a mark.

Ewer, Allover Mermaids, Seahorse & Neptune, Dragonflies At Neck, 30 In. 4312.00
Figurine, 18th Century Woman, Plumed Hat, Blue Crossed Swords, 6 1/4 In. 715.00
Figurine, Allegory Figure Of A Woman, Holding A Script, Germany, 16 1/2 In. 2990.00
Figurine, Allegory Figure Of A Woman, Holding A Staff, Germany, 16 1/2 In. 3220.00
Figurine, Alpheus, Nude Torso, Signed, 20th Century, 10 In. 1155.00
Figurine, Animal, 2 Clashing Antelopes, Tan, White, Green, Signed, 11 1/4 In. 920.00
Figurine, Boy, Holding A Basket Of Grapes, Crossed Swords, 5 1/2 In. 201.00
Figurine, Boy, With Recorder & Dog, 5 1/2 In. 600.00
Figurine, Columbine Dancing, Red Bow, White Skirt, Yellow Slippers, Signed, 5 In. 5462.00
Figurine, Columbine, Playing Hurdy-Gurdy, Signed, c.1745, 4 15/16 In. 1840.00
Figurine, Court Dancer, Signed, 7 1/2 In. 990.00
Figurine, Courtesan, With Hurdy-Gurdy, 7 1/4 In. 1000.00
Figurine, Cupid With A Birdbath, Late 19th Century, 7 In. 1495.00
Figurine, Cupid, Fanning Flame Of Lovers Hearts, Signed, c.1877, 7 1/4 In. 1350.00
Figurine, Dove Perched On Green Mound Base, Orange Beak, Feet, 1 3/8 In. 690.00
Figurine, Flower Sellers, Woman With Garland, With Man, Flowers In Hat, 6 In., Pair . . 488.00
Figurine, Gentleman Wearing Cape, 19th Century, 4 1/4 In. 175.00
Figurine, Girl With Doll Carriage, Polychrome, Crossed Swords, c.1910, 5 1/8 In. 1070.00
Figurine, Girl, Basket Of Flowers, 5 1/4 In. 650.00
Figurine, Girl, On Tumbling Basket Of Flowers, Dirndl, 4 1/2 In. 800.00
Figurine, Girl, Playing Bowls, Green Draped Costume, c.1924, 12 In. 3400.00
Figurine, Goddess, Dancing Pose, Signed, 4 3/4 In. 460.00
Figurine, Goose, Applied Tiny Blossoms, Leaves, 3-Color Gold Border, 1 1/2 In. 520.00
Figurine, Group, Bacchus, Late 19th Century, 12 1/2 In. 1150.00
Figurine, Harlequin & Columbine, Seated, Signed, 5 1/2 In., Pair 4035.00
Figurine, Harlequin Dancing, Bows On Breeches, Red Shoes, 1745, 5 11/16 In. 4312.00
Figurine, Harlequin, Playing Bagpipes, Tricorn, Puce Jacket, 1737, 4 5/8 In. 1380.00
Figurine, Hound, Standing, Blue Collar, Rocky Plinth, 7 3/4 In. 245.00
Figurine, Hunter, Dog With Game Bird In Mouth, c.1900, 16 1/4 In. 1265.00
Figurine, Hunter, Gun & Dog, 5 1/2 In. 600.00
Figurine, Indian On Horseback, Charging Buffalo, Signed, 1903, 14 x 14 In. 3910.00
Figurine, Je Les Unis, Cupid, Uniting 2 Hearts, Column, Blue Crossed Swords, 5 In. . . . 605.00
Figurine, Man, Adorned With Bow, Arrow, Woman, Carrying A Basket, 13 In., Pair 4600.00
Figurine, Musicians & Putti In Landscape, Signed, 15 In. 4025.00
Figurine, Nobleman, Leaning On Tree, Floral Jacket, Pants, Signed, 1720s, 8 3/4 In. 2070.00
Figurine, Nude Woman, With Cupid, 17 In. 3800.00
Figurine, Partially Nude, Seated, Waist-Length Hair, 17 In. 3100.00
Figurine, Peasant Man & Woman, Gold Base, Blue Crossed Swords, 5 3/4 In., Pair 660.00
Figurine, Tailor, Seated On Gray Goat, 9 1/4 In. 1650.00
Figurine, Woman With Flowers & Courtier, Blue Mark, 19th Century, 19 In., Pair 770.00
Figurine, Woman, Holding A Stringed Instrument, Germany, 16 1/2 In. 2990.00
Figurine, Woman, Wearing A Colorful Lace Dress, Wide-Brimmed Hat, 8 1/2 In. 290.00
Group, 4 Classical Figures & A Mule, 19th Century, 8 x 8 In. 2300.00
Group, Birth Of Venus, Surrounded By Cherubs & Mermaids, Signed, 10 1/2 In. 1035.00
Group, Couple, With A Cage & Doves, Germany, 19th Century, 8 1/2 In. 85.00
Group, Spring, Woman & Bird, Woman & Birdcage, Man & Urn, Signed, 9 In. 1380.00
Incense Burner, Raised Columns To Corners, Scrolled Gallery, Woman Bust Finial 795.00
Plate, 200 Years Of The Meissen Co., Porcelain, Blue On White, 1710-1910, 9 In. 176.00
Plate, 25th Anniversary Of The Kaiser, Eagle In Center With Flags, Brass, 14 In. 180.00
Plate, Central Peony Sprig, 5 Lotus Sprigs, Blue Band, 1730, 8 5/16 In. 2070.00
Plate, Fox Flying Above Squirrel, Nibbling Grapes, Red, Blue, Turquoise, Yellow 1150.00
Plate, Leaf Pattern, 8 1/2 In. 105.00
Plate, Military, Yellow, Red Apple, Blue On White, 9 1/4 In. 230.00
Plate, Scalloped, Floral & Gold Panels On Edge, Floral Center, Signed, 11 1/2 In. 395.00
Salt Dish, Figural, Boy & Girl, Atop Baskets, Foliate Sides, Signed, 4 3/4 x 5 In., Pair . . 1035.00
Stein, Courting Scene, Trellis, Pink & White Ground, 19th Century, 6 1/2 In. 1650.00
Tea Caddy, Cover, Bird On Puce Plateau, Red, Blue, Turquoise Blossoms, 1735, 4 In. . . . 3152.00
Tea Caddy, Cover, Floral Sprig, Puce, Red, Yellow, Green, Ocher Feather Edges, 5 In. . . 460.00
Tea Service, Exotic Bird Perched On Flowering Branch, Brown Rim, 1740, 14 Piece 5175.00
Tea Set, Vine Wreath, Green 375.00
Teabowl, Saucer, Figures Moving Cargo, Puce Landscape, Roundel, 1740, 3 x 5 In. 1840.00
Teapot, Branch Handle, Drum Shape, Blanc De Chine 245.00
Teapot, Cover, Couple Conversing In Landscape, Octagonal, Loop Handle, 5 In. 3450.00

Tureen, Cover, Clusters Of Flowers, Fruit, Vegetables, Vine Border Rim, Oval, 6 1/2 In. . . 635.0
Tureen, Cover, Swirled Form, Molded Asparagus Sprigs, Gilt Edge, 1755, 9 1/4 In. 2070.0
Tureen, Soup, Phoenix In Flight, Perched On Prunus Branches, Red, Blue, 14 In. 7475.0
Tureen, Soup, Sprays Of Flowers, Putti Finial, 20th Century, 14 In. 1380.0
Urn, Decorative Bands, 2 Snake Handles, Blue Crossed Swords, 15 1/2 In. 770.0
Vase, 3 Quatrefoil Panels, Blue, White, 18 1/4 In., Pair 172.0
Vase, Applied Garland Of Flowers, Polychrome, 6 In., Pair 287.0
Vase, Baluster Form, Spray Of Blooms, Insects, Mounted As Lamp, 8 1/8 In., Pair 5175.0
Vase, Courting Scenes, Panels Of Floral Sprays, Augustus Rex, 13 1/2 In., Pair 2530.0
Vase, Floral Spray, Snake Handles, Blue Crossed Swords, 11 In., Pair 1265.0
Vase, Foliage Design, Cobalt Blue Ground, 20th Century, 10 In. 259.0
Vase, Gilt, White, Snake Handle, 20th Century, 11 In., Pair 345.0
Vase, Polychrome Enamel Floral Bouquets, Snake Handles, 15 3/8 In. 690.0
Waste Bowl, Fels & Vogel, 2 Floral Sprigs, Gentleman Seated On Tuffet, 6 3/4 In. 3162.0

MERCURY GLASS, or silvered glass, was first made in the 1850s. It lost favor for a while but became popular again about 1910. It looks like a piece of silver.

Bowl, Butler's Ball, Round Sphere, Baluster Round Foot, 6 1/2 In. 150.0
Chalice, Gold, Etched, Signed, 1869, 12 1/2 In. 231.0
Perfume Bottle, Floral Design, Enamel, 3 1/2 x 1 1/2 In. 450.0
Scent Bottle, Shaped Oval Panels, Cobalt Blue, Silver Mounted 316.0
Stand, Wig, 19th Century, 11 3/4 In. 225.0
Vase, Blue Painted Banding, Gold Relief Painted Design, 12 In. 1500.0
Vase, Painted Floral, 9 In., Pair 220.0

MERRIMAC POTTERY Company was founded by Thomas Nickerson in Newburyport, Massachusetts, in 1902. The company made art pottery, garden pottery, and reproductions of Roman pottery. The pottery burned to the ground in 1908.

Bowl, Applied Lily Pads, Water Lilies, Green Matte Glaze, Gray, 9 x 5 In. 1760.00
Pitcher, Matte Green Glaze, 6 3/4 x 6 1/2 In. 330.00
Vase, Apple Leaves, Brown, Green, Dead Matte Glaze, 6 x 5 In. 1430.00
Vase, Applied Leaves, Leathery Green Black Matte Glaze, Leaf Edge, 10 x 5 1/2 In. 2420.00
Vase, Applied Leaves, Stems, Flowers, Green, Gunmetal Glaze, 12 In. 4675.00
Vase, Brown, Green Glaze Over Mustard Body, Paper Label, 7 1/4 x 4 1/2 In. 1650.00
Vase, Feathered Matte Green & Gunmetal Glaze, 4 x 3 1/2 In. 495.00
Vase, Flaring Rim, Matte Green Glaze, Signed, 5 x 3 In. 172.00
Vase, Leathery Dark Green Celadon Crystalline Glaze, 12 1/4 x 9 3/4 In. 2090.00
Vase, Matte Green Glaze, Dripping Over Yellow Body, 10 x 9 In. 2640.00
Vase, Mottled Green Gunmetal Glaze, Beaker Shape, 7 3/4 x 7 In. 825.00
Vase, Stylized Flowers, Leathery Green Matte Glaze, Bulbous, 9 x 9 In. 4510.00

METTLACH, Germany, is a city where the Villeroy and Boch factories worked. Steins from the firm are known as Mettlach steins. They date from about 1842. *PUG* means painted under glaze. The steins can be dated from the marks on the bottom, which include a date-number code. Other pieces may be listed in the Villeroy & Boch category.

Beaker, No. 2327, 1/4 Liter, Hannover 91.00
Beaker, No. 2327, 1/4 Liter, Man & Woman, Tyrolean Village Printed On Rear 175.00
Beaker, No. 2327, 1/4 Liter, Milwaukee City Hall 120.00
Beaker, No. 2327, 1/4 Liter, Stuttgart 96.00
Charger, No. 2549, Profile Of Woman, Flowing Hair With Orchids, Chevroton, 18 In. 935.00
Plaque, No. 1044, Dog, Hunting, Gold, 17 In. 462.00
Plaque, No. 1044, Portrait Of Shakespeare, Blue, White, 17 In. 345.00
Plaque, No. 1044-1067, Water Wheel On Side Of Building, PUG, 17 1/2 In. 545.00
Plaque, No. 1044-5171, Dutch Scene, Delft Blue, 12 In. 95.00
Plaque, No. 1365, Castle On Rhine, Gold Edge, 1909, 17 In. 795.00
Plaque, No. 1384, Knight Carrying Flag, Signed, 14 1/2 In. . . . . .695.00 to 700.00
Plaque, No. 1770, William Tell, After Shooting Apple, Signed, 15 In. 1400.00
Plaque, No. 2022, Young Man, Playing Lute, Floral Border, Brown, 20 In. 745.00
Plaque, No. 2322, Knight, Trying To Kiss Maiden, 1900, 14 1/2 In. 795.00
Plaque, No. 2361A, Wartburg Castle, Etched, 17 In. 814.00

Plaque, No. 2362, Heidelberg Castle, Etched, 17 In. 770.00
Plaque, No. 2445, Children Playing Flute & Mandolin, Singing, Oval, 10 x 7 In. 640.00
Plaque, No. 2518, Town Scene Of Meissen, 17 1/2 In. 1675.00
Plaque, No. 2542, Art Nouveau, Girl's Portrait, Signed, Etched, 16 In. 750.00
Plaque, No. 2622, Cavalier Holding Glass, 1910, 7 3/4 In. 235.00
Plaque, No. 3225, Great Britain, Blue Ground, 11 x 13 In. 578.00
Plaque, No. 3225, Italy, Light Brown, Blue, 11 x 13 In. 778.00
Plaque, No. 7032, Cameo, Woman's Profile, Oval, 1900, 7 1/2 x 8 3/4 In. 295.00
Punch Bowl, No. 2843, Man With Flute, Lady, Seated, Couple Dancing, 8 3/4 In. 1955.00
Punch Bowl, No. 3364, Etched Blue & Gold Motif, 4 x 8 1/2 In. 260.00
Stein, 3 Figure Panels, Allover Birds, Berries, 14 In. 485.00
Stein, 3.3 Liter, 3 Scenes, Noah's Ark, Gray, Cream, Tan, Inlaid Lid 138.00
Stein, No. 32, 1 1/2 Liter, Castle Turret, Inlaid Lid 127.00
Stein, No. 285, 1/2 Liter, Student Society, Pewter Lid, Dated 1908-1909 .... 445.00
Stein, No. 485, 1/2 Liter, Musicians, Dancers, 8 3/8 In. 330.00
Stein, No. 675, 1/2 Liter, Barrel Form, Multicolored Marble, Inlaid Lid 116.00
Stein, No. 812, 1/2 Liter, 3 Hunting Scenes, Blue, Tan, Brown, Pewter Lid ......160.00 to 165.00
Stein, No. 1027, 1/2 Liter, Floral Design Face, Beige, Rust, Green, Inlaid Lid ....215.00 to 225.00
Stein, No. 1028, Brown & White, Pewter Fittings, Villeroy & Boch, 6 5/8 In. 110.00
Stein, No. 1100, 1/4 Liter, People, Walking, Pedestal Base, Inlaid Lid 162.00
Stein, No. 1265, 1/4 Liter, 3 Scenes, Tan, Brown, Gray, Inlaid Lid 73.00
Stein, No. 1370, 1/2 Liter, People & Verse Scene, Tan, Gray, Inlaid Lid 139.00
Stein, No. 1395, 1/2 Liter, French Card Design, Inlaid Lid 305.00
Stein, No. 1453, 1/2 Liter, Dwarf, Sitting In Nest, Inlaid Lid 205.00
Stein, No. 1453, 1/2 Liter, Hunters, Boars, Dogs, Inlaid Lid 809.00
Stein, No. 1476, 1/2 Liter, Gnomes Planting Grape Vines, Inlaid Lid 762.00
Stein, No. 1478, 1/5 Liter, Gnomes Constructing Barrels, Inlaid Lid 808.50
Stein, No. 1526, 1/2 Liter, Man, Serenading Woman, Pewter Lid 89.00
Stein, No. 1526, 1/2 Liter, Man, Smoking, Pewter Lid 132.00
Stein, No. 1526, 1/2 Liter, Military Figure, PUG, Pewter Lid 380.00
Stein, No. 1526, 1/2 Liter, Student Society, Pewter Lid, 1929 ....139.00 to 187.00
Stein, No. 1526, 1/2 Liter, Tosetti Brewing Co., Chicago, PUG, Pewter Lid 315.00
Stein, No. 1526, 1/5 Liter, Chicago, Pewter Lid, 1909 .... 140.00
Stein, No. 1527, 1 Liter, Cavaliers Drinking At Table, Woman & Shield, Pewter Lid 550.00
Stein, No. 1641, 1/2 Liter, Cavalier With Jug Of Wine, Inlaid Lid 296.00
Stein, No. 1655, 1/2 Liter, Young People Dancing, Inlaid Lid 578.00
Stein, No. 1662, 1 Liter, Blacksmith, Inlaid Lid 380.00
Stein, No. 1861, 1/2 Liter, Frederick III, Inlaid Lid 462.00
Stein, No. 1909, 1/2 Liter, 2 Men Confiscating Beer Barrel, PUG, Pewter Lid 380.00
Stein, No. 1909, 1/2 Liter, Old Man Bowling, Pewter Lid 127.00
Stein, No. 1909, 1/2 Liter, Old Soldier, PUG, Pewter Lid 380.00
Stein, No. 1972, 1/4 Liter, 4 Ladies, 4 Panels, Representing Seasons, Inlaid Lid 215.00
Stein, No. 2001B, 1/2 Liter, Book, Medicine, Inlaid Lid 670.00
Stein, No. 2002, 1 Liter, Town Of Munich, Verse, Inlaid Lid 450.00
Stein, No. 2025, Cherubs At Play, Inlaid Lid 317.00
Stein, No. 2028, 1 Liter, Tavern Scene, 10 Men Drinking, Inlaid Lid 751.00
Stein, No. 2044, Pub Scene, Inlaid Lid, 8 In. 275.00
Stein, No. 2057, 1/2 Liter, Dancing Figures With Steins, Inlaid Lid ....325.00 to 425.00
Stein, No. 2076, 2 Liter, 4 Panels, With Eagles, Owls, Shield, Terra-Cotta, Inlaid Lid 162.00
Stein, No. 2083, 1/2 Liter, Boar Hunt Scene, Inlaid Lid 730.00
Stein, No. 2090, 1/3 Liter, Man, At Table, In Club, With Verse, Inlaid Lid 186.00
Stein, No. 2100, 1/2 Liter, Knight With Stein, Man In Furs, Inlaid Lid 924.00
Stein, No. 2101, 1/2 Liter, Man Carrying Stein, Boar's Head On Tray, Inlaid Lid 347.00
Stein, No. 2134, 1/3 Liter, Gnome, Sitting In Nest, Inlaid Lid 205.00
Stein, No. 2140, Regimental Unit, 1894 .... 250.00
Stein, No. 2176, 2 Liter, Festive Drinking Scene, Pewter Lid 265.00
Stein, No. 2204, 1 Liter, Prussian Eagle, Inlaid Lid ....495.00 to 1395.00
Stein, No. 2231, 1/2 Liter, Tavern, Men Drinking At Table, Inlaid Lid 287.00
Stein, No. 2277, 1/2 Liter, Nurnberg, Inlaid Lid 525.00
Stein, No. 2373, 1/2 Liter, St. Augustine, Florida, Alligator Handle, Inlaid Lid ....440.00 to 675.00
Stein, No. 2382, 1 Liter, Knight Drinking In Cellar, Riding Away 1100.00
Stein, No. 2382, 1/2 Liter, Thirsty Rider, Body Forms Tower, Inlaid Lid 885.00
Stein, No. 2391, 1/2 Liter, Lohengrin, Wedding, March Of Swan Knight, Inlaid Lid 1085.00

Stein, No. 2481, 1 4/10 Liter, Hildegund Aiding Wounded, Inlaid Lid .... 303.0●
Stein, No. 2580, 1/2 Liter, Knight In Castle, Conical Inlaid Lid ....695.00 to 888.0●
Stein, No. 2581, 1/2 Liter, Ladies In Music Room .... 550.0●
Stein, No. 2585, 1 Liter, Munich Child, Standing On World, Etched, Relief, Inlaid Lid .. 950.0●
Stein, No. 2599, 1 Liter, Man Shooting At Target, Pewter Lid .... 365.0●
Stein, No. 2715, 1/2 Liter, 3 Musical & Dancing Scenes, Floral Design, Pewter Lid ..... 390.0●
Stein, No. 2778, 1/2 Liter, Festive Carnival Scene, Player & Drinkers, Pewter Lid ...... 695.0●
Stein, No. 2782, 4 1/2 Liter, Cavalier Drinking, Pewter Lid, 17 3/4 In. .... 490.0●
Stein, No. 2828, 1/2 Liter, Town Of Wartburg, Etched, Castle Form Inlaid Lid .... 913.0●
Stein, No. 2922, 1 Liter, Hunter Drinking Around Camp Fire, Etched .... 693.0●
Stein, No. 2938, 1/2 Liter, Hunter With Dog, Inlaid Lid .... 1015.0●
Stein, No. 2939, 1/2 Liter, Bavarian Waitress, Brown, Inlaid Lid .... 800.0●
Stein, No. 3085, 1/2 Liter, Tapestry, Postman, Sitting At Table, Pewter Lid .... 595.0●
Stein, No. 3135, 1/2 Liter, American Flag & Eagle .... 995.0●
Stein, No. 3170, 1/2 Liter, Men Walking, On Winter Night, Verse, Inlaid Lid .... 1216.0●
Stein, No. 3236, 1/2 Liter, Art Nouveau, Blue & White .... 575.0●
Stein, No. 5001, 4 1/2 Liter, Faience Type, Coat Of Arms, Pewter Lid .... 850.0●
Stein, No. 5013, 1 Liter, Munchen, Pewter Lid .... 1395.0●
Stein, No. 5013, 1/2 Liter, Man, Toasting, Pewter Lid .... 166.0●
Vase, Foliate Design, Stoneware, Germany, Early 20th Century, 10 In., Pair .... 230.0●
Vase, No. 1416, Women, 2 Scenes, Handles, c.1899, 18 In., Pair .... 1495.0●
Vase, No. 3040, Girls, 4 Panels, 12 In. .... 405.0●
Vase, No. 7000, Jardiniere, Grecian Men & Women In Carriage, 5 1/2 In. .... 395.0●

MILK GLASS was named for its milky white color. It was first made in
England during the 1700s. The height of its popularity in the United
States was from 1870 to 1880. It is now correct to refer to some colored glass as blue milk glass, black milk glass, etc. Reproductions of
milk glass are being made and sold in many stores. Related pieces may
be listed in the Cosmos, Vallerysthal, and Westmoreland categories.

Bowl, Acanthus 45.00
Bowl, Open Lattice, Design, 9 In. 25.00
Bust, Admiral Dewey, Spanish American War, 5 1/2 In. 225.00
Butter, Cover, Cosmos, Enameled Flowers 230.00
Candy Dish, Domed Cover, Della Robbia, Hand Painted, Signed 48.00
Compote, Atlas, Cover, 6 x 9 3/4 In. 65.00
Compote, Jenny Lind 130.00
Compote, Sawtooth, Flint, 11 1/4 x 8 3/4 In. 85.00
Compote, Scroll, Hexagonal Bowl, 8 x 8 1/4 In. 50.00
Compote, Shell & Dolphin, Enameled Foliage & Berries, Gold Trim, 7 x 7 1/2 In. 330.00
Creamer, Gooseberry 25.00
Creamer, Grape With Overlapping Foliage 40.00
Creamer, Paneled Wheat 25.00
Creamer, Swan, 5 1/2 In. 35.00
Cruet, Tree Of Life 45.00
Cup, Grape & Cable 10.00
Dish, Admiral Dewey Cover, 1895-1915, 4 1/4 In. 60.00
Dish, Battleship Oregon Cover 50.00
Dish, British Lion Cover 150.00
Dish, Cat On Drum Cover, Blue, 4 3/4 In. 75.00
Dish, Choy Dog Cover 400.00
Dish, Crawfish Cover, Octagonal Base, Tab Handles 200.00
Dish, Dewey Cover 90.00
Dish, Elephant Cover, Black, 7 1/2 In. 70.00
Dish, Fish On Skiff, 7 In. 25.00
Dish, Monkey On Grass Mound Cover, Leaf & Scroll Base, 6 1/4 In. 1800.00
Dish, Moses In Bullrushes Cover, 6 In. 200.00
Dish, Rabbit Cover, Marked, Pat'd. March 9, 1886, 6 1/4 In. 260.00
Dish, Swan Cover, Pair 425.00
Dish, Turtle With Snail On Back Cover, Blue, 7 1/2 In. 600.00
Dish, Uncle Sam On A Battleship Cover 65.00
Eggcup, Birch Leaf 18.00
Eggcup, Double, American Hobnail 12.00

Goblet, Blackberry 35.00
Jar, Cover, Owl, Glass Eyes .... .85.00 to 98.00
Muffineer, Netted Oak, Northwood 55.00
Plate, Cupid & Psyche, 7 In. 40.00
Plate, Dewey, Atterbury, 7 In. 40.00
Plate, Frank Brothers, Club & Shell, 7 1/8 In. 57.00
Plate, Little Red Hen, 7 1/4 In. 100.00
Plate, McKinley' Campaign, Eagle, Stars & Crossed Flags Border, 7 3/8 In. 192.00
Plate, Open Lattice, Enameled, 10 1/2 In. 23.00
Punch Bowl, Grape & Cable, Ladle 275.00
Punch Cup, Nursery Rhyme 25.00
Salt, Blackberry, Master 25.00
Salt, Flying Fish, Master 110.00
Salt, Sawtooth, Flint, Master 20.00
Salt & Pepper, Leaf, Footed 25.00
Saltshaker, Vine With Flower 15.00
Sauce, Basket Weave, 4 In. 9.00
Sauce, Blackberry, 4 In. 8.00
Sauce, Grape, 4 In. 6.00
Sauce, Paneled Wheat, 4 In. 5.00
Sauce, Strawberry, 4 In. 11.00
Spooner, Grape With Overlapping Foliage 30.00
Spooner, Paneled Hobnail, Blue 28.00
Spooner, Princess Feather 75.00
Sugar, Birch Leaf, Flint 29.50
Sugar, Cover, Gooseberry 50.00
Sugar, Cover, Netted Oak, Northwood 16.50
Sugar Shaker, Acorn 85.00
Table Set, Child's, Wild Rose, 4 Piece 275.00
Tankard, Beaded Circle 85.00
Tom & Jerry Set, Enameled Red Lettering, 12 Piece 40.00
Toothpick, Beaded Belt 25.00
Toothpick, Palm Leaf, Footed, Green Trim 45.00
Toothpick, Shell & Seaweed, Enameled 85.00

MILLEFIORI means, literally, a thousand flowers. Many small pieces of glass resembling flowers are grouped together to form a design. It is a type of glasswork popular in paperweights and some are listed in that category.

Figurine, Unicorn 200.00
Teapot, Italy 350.00
Vase, Multicolored, Handles, 8 In. 145.00
Vase, Ruffled Edge, 10 In. 195.00

MINTON china has been made in the Staffordshire region of England from 1793 to the present. The firm became part of the Royal Doulton Tableware Group in 1968, but the wares continued to be marked *Minton*. Many marks have been used. The one shown dates from about 1873 to 1891, when the word *England* was added.

Cache Pot, 9 x 11 1/2 In. 895.00
Charger, Mermaids, Cobalt Band, Majolica, 1861, 10 3/4 In. 475.00
Compote, Geometric Design, Green Glaze, Registry Mark, 7 x 11 In. 192.00
Cooler, Wine, Mermen With Entwined Tails, Nautilus Shells, c.1865, Pair 7762.00
Cup & Saucer, Ancestral, 12 Piece 1200.00
Dish, Game, Hare & Duck On Lid, Tin Liner, Majolica, Signed 3800.00
Figurine, Beauty, Seated On A Stump, Parian, 1850, 15 In. 230.00
Figurine, Dorothea, 1868, 14 In. 488.00
Figurine, Young Boy, Grape Harvester, Resting On Basket, 1870, 9 3/4 In. 630.00
Garden Seat, Body Modeled As Ribbon Wrapped Caned Seat, 1880s, 17 1/2 In. 460.00
Garden Seat, Hexagonal Baluster Form, Panels Of Foliate Scroll Work, 20 In. 4600.00
Jardiniere, Black & White Japanese Crane, C. Dresser, 1880, 7 5/8 In. 1215.00
Jardiniere, Flowers, Leaves, Brown, 7 1/2 x 10 In. 135.00
Jug, Malachite, Allover Green Glaze, Agate Ground, Globular, 1862, 9 1/2 In. 230.00

Mug, Cat, Playing With Broken Ball & Cup Toy, 3 In. 302.0

Mug, Quaker Man & Woman 4600.0

Pedestal, Majolica, Marble Top, Winged Satyr, Roman Clothes, Square Plinth, 45 In. ... 1322.0

Perfume Bottle, Enameled, Cobalt Blue, Flask Inside, 18th Century 715.0

Pie Dish, Majolica, Game On Basketweave Body, 1877, 14 In. 1610.0

Plate, Service, Floral Design, Light Blue Ground Banded Border, 11 In., 24 Piece 3450.0

Platter, Well & Tree, Oriental Design, Rust, Orange, 19th Century, 21 x 17 In. 545.0

Stirrup Cup, Boxer Head, Glazed Interior 675.0

Teapot, Majolica, Lemon, Mushroom Cover & Finial, 1868, 4 5/8 In. 1495.0

Tile, Shakespeare, 9 x 9 In., 2 Piece 150.0

Tile, Storks, Frame, 8 x 8 In. 65.0

Tureen, Soup, Cover, Landscape, Oriental Garden, Black Transfer, 1882, 14 1/4 In. 402.0

Vase, Majolica, 3 Figures On Pedestal, Lions On Urn Holding Wheat Garlands, 20 In. ... 9650.0

Vase, Majolica, Duck Hunter, In Boat, Blue High Glaze, 8 In. 170.0

Vase, Majolica, Peacock, Turquoise, Glaze, Impressed Mark, 1871, 9 5/8 In. 170.0

Vase, Majolica, Stylized Iris, Whiplash Stems, Closed-In Rim, Blue, Flambe, 7 x 5 In. ... 355.0

Vase, Majolica, Yellow Glaze, Blue Transfer, Geometric Banding, Handles, 23 3/4 In. ... 460.0

MIRRORS are listed in the Furniture category under Mirror.

MOCHA pottery is an English-made product that was sold in America during the early 1800s. It is a heavy pottery with pale coffee-and-cream coloring. Designs of blue, brown, green, orange, black, or white were added to the pottery and given fanciful names, such as *Tree*, *Snail Trail*, or *Moss*.

Bedpan, White Band, Blue Seaweed, Brown Stripes, 8 1/4 In. 200.0

Bowl, Blue Seaweed Design, White Band, Brown Stripes, 8 1/2 x 4 In. 245.0

Bowl, Earthworm, Green Band, Canary Yellow Ground, Ear Handle, 4 3/4 x 3 1/2 In. ... 110.0

Bowl, Green Seaweed Design, 12 In. 485.0

Cream Pot, Seaweed 495.0

Creamer, Blue Seaweed Design, Brown Stripes, White Band, 4 3/4 In. 440.0

Creamer, Green Seaweed Design, Black Stripes, White Band, 3 7/8 In. 165.0

Cup, Earthworm, Brown & White, Blue Ground, 19th Century, 2 7/8 In. 373.0

Jar, Cover, Earthworm, Cat's White Eyes, Pale Blue Band, Black Stripes, 4 In. 495.0

Measure, Pint, Tankard, Black Seaweed, Black & Blue Stripes, Gray Band, 4 7/8 In. 135.0

Measure, Quart, Tankard, Black Seaweed, Black & Blue Stripes, Gray Band, 6 1/2 In. .. 94.0

Mug, Earthworm, Blue, White, Tan, Dark Brown Band, Leaf Handle, 3 3/4 In. 550.0

Mug, Seaweed, Blue Bands, c.1850, 6 1/2 In. 350.0

Pepper Pot, Earthworm 1750.0

Pitcher, Barrel, Applied Handle, White Glaze, Green & Black Bands, England, 5 In. 525.0

Pitcher, Black Seaweed, Green, Dark Brown Band, Leaf Handle, 4 5/8 In. 440.0

Pitcher, Blue Seaweed, Ribbed Strap Handle, White Band, Brown Stripes, 8 3/4 In. 770.0

Pitcher, Brown & White Mocha Banding, 8 In. 595.0

Pitcher, Milk, Earthworm, Blue Band, Black, Blue Stripes, 4 7/8 In. 190.0

Pitcher, Polkadots, Yellow & Green, c.1820, 5 1/2 In. 195.0

Salt, White Wavy Lines, Gray Band, Black Stripes, 3 x 2 1/8 In. 330.0

Shaker, Black Seaweed, Orange Band, Brown Stripes, 4 1/8 In. 462.0

Shaker, Black Seaweed, Tan Bands, Brown Stripes, 4 1/8 In. 220.0

Shaker, Blue & Brown Stripes, White Ground, 4 3/4 In. 357.0

Shaker, Earthworm, Blue Band, Black Stripe, Blue Top, 4 7/8 In. 330.0

Tankard, Green Tree On Brown Ground, 6 x 4 1/2 In. 195.0

Waste Bowl, Black Earthworm, White, Blue, Stripes, Orange Band, 5 3/8 x 2 7/8 In. ... 245.0

Waste Bowl, Black Seaweed, Amber Band, Green Lip Band, 5 In. 275.0

Waste Bowl, Earthworm & Stripes, Blue, White, Dark Brown, Orange, Tan Band, 3 In. . 550.0

Waste Bowl, Seaweed, Tan Band With Black Stripes, 6 1/4 x 3 1/4 In. 55.0

MONMOUTH Pottery Company started working in Monmouth, Illinois, in 1892. The pottery made a variety of utilitarian wares. It became part of Western Stoneware Company in 1906. The maple leaf mark was used until 1930. If *Co.* appears as part of the mark, the piece was made before 1906.

Urn, Orange Crystal Glaze, Ring Handles, 6 In. 110.0

Vase, Blue, No. 270, 8 In. 100.0

Vase, Incised Band At Shoulder, Matte Blue, 16 x 10 In. 495.0

ONT JOYE, see Mt. Joye category.

OORCROFT pottery was first made in Burslem, England, in 1913.
'illiam Moorcroft had managed the art pottery department for James
acIntyre & Company of England from 1898 to 1913. The Moorcroft
ottery continues today, although William Moorcroft died in 1945. The
arlier wares are similar to the modern ones, but color and marking
ill help indicate the age.

Ashtray, Clematis, Cobalt Ground, Signed, 4 1/2 In.	60.00
Bowl, Grape, Blue, Green, Signed	195.00
Bowl, Hibiscus, Footed, 4 In.	110.00
Bowl, Hibiscus, Green, 2 x 5 1/2 In.	195.00
Bowl, Pansy, 12 In.	895.00
Box, Cover, Anemone, Pale Green To Blue Ground, Cylindrical, 1945, 3 1/2 In.	255.00
Box, Cover, Floral, Blue Ground, 1928, 5 x 3 1/2 In.	.185.00 to 195.00
Box, Cover, Hibiscus Design, Red, Yellow, Green, Blue Ground, Round, 6 In.	325.00
Candlestick, Anemone, Dark Blue Ground, Impressed Mark, 1925, 4 1/4 In., Pair	690.00
Candlestick, Pomegranate, Silver Plated Trim, 1925, 6 1/2 In., Pair	690.00
Compote, Florian Ware, Formalized Flowers, Foliage, Yellow, Blue, Green, 8 In.	1030.00
Compote, Hibiscus, White Ground, 6 In.	150.00
Cup & Saucer, Pomegranate, Impressed Mark, 1930, 5 1/2 In.	430.00
Dish, Grape & Leaf, 4 1/2 In.	200.00
Jar, Cover, Landscape, Trees, Hills, Moonlit Blue, Powder Blue Ground, 10 In.	5544.00
Jardiniere, Toadstool Design, 14 In.	4025.00
Lamp, Orchid Flambe, 8 1/2 In.	1300.00
Lamp, Orchid Flambe, 13 1/2 In.	1300.00
Plate, Black Tulip, 4 In.	95.00
Plate, Flowers, Cobalt Blue, Paper Label, Signed, 1950, 12 In.	550.00
Plate, Hibiscus, Blue & Maroon, Paper Label, Signed, 10 1/4 In.	310.00
Plate, Orchids, Red, Blue, Green Leaves, Yellow, Blue, Green Ground, 1955, 9 In.	317.00
Sugar & Creamer, Pomegranate, 1913-1925, 4 1/2 x 4 1/2 In.	1210.00
Tobacco Jar, Blue Poppies, Green & Blue Ground, Screw-On Lid, Signed, 3 3/4 In.	1650.00
Vase, Anemone, Multicolored Flowers, Cobalt Blue, c.1935	230.00
Vase, Blue Cornflowers, Marked, 6 1/4 x 4 1/2 In.	1320.00
Vase, Carp, Under Water Scene, Globular Body, Red & Gold, Bernard Moore, 10 In.	600.00
Vase, Claremont, Blue Toadstools, Red, Green, Ocher, Purple, 1925, 10 In.	3326.00
Vase, Clematis, 12 1/2 In.	600.00
Vase, Cornflower, Powder Blue, 2 Handles, Artist, 1927, 12 3/4 In.	4885.00
Vase, Eventide, Landscape, Hills, Tufts Of Grass, Red, Brown, Green, Blue, 14 In.	11088.00
Vase, Flambe Glaze, Signed, William Moorcroft, 12 1/8 In.	770.00
Vase, Flambe, Landscape, Waving Corn, Wheat, Brown, Cream, Red, 1934, 13 In.	4435.00
Vase, Flambe, Spring Flowers, Red Ground, 1960, 7 In.	713.00
Vase, Floral, Gold, Blue, Green, Olive Green Ground, Macintyre, 6 In.	990.00
Vase, Floral, Red, Blue, Yellow, Fluted Top, 10 1/4 In.	550.00
Vase, Floral, White Ground, Gilt Trim, Handles, Macintyre, 7 1/2 In.	1150.00
Vase, Florian Ware, Formalized Flowers, Leaves, Blue, Macintyre, 1898, 10 In.	1306.00
Vase, Florian Ware, Stylized Peacock Feathers, Yellow, Blue, Green, 1900, 10 In.	3088.00
Vase, Fruit, Floral Design, Yellow, Blue, Red, Green, 8 1/2 In.	330.00
Vase, Fruit, Leaves, Blue Green Ground, 1928-1934, 8 x 6 In.	520.00
Vase, Hibiscus, 6 3/4 In.	250.00
Vase, Iris Glaze, 10 In.	2530.00
Vase, Landscape, Blue Trees, Blue, Yellow Ground, Bulbous, 6 x 5 1/4 In.	2200.00
Vase, Landscape, Signed, Alison Neale & Jennifer James, 7 1/2 In.	522.00
Vase, Landscape, Trees, Moonlit Blue, Green Ground, Baluster, 12 In.	4118.00
Vase, Mottled Green & Brown Glaze, 2 Handles, 20th Century, 6 3/4 In.	230.00
Vase, Orange Luster, c.1920, 6 In.	137.00
Vase, Orchid, 6 1/2 x 5 1/2 In.	650.00
Vase, Orchid, 8 1/2 x 6 1/2 In.	950.00
Vase, Orchid, Blue, Red, Green, Cream Ground, Globular, 1940, 18 1/2 In.	950.00
Vase, Orchid, Cobalt Blue, 3 5/8 In.	110.00
Vase, Orchid, White, 9 In., Pair	1100.00
Vase, Pansy, 4 1/4 In.	250.00
Vase, Pansy, 7 1/2 In.	.750.00 to 800.00

Vase, Pansy, Blue Ground, Purple, Blue Flowers, Red, Yellow, 1928, 14 1/2 In. 871.0
Vase, Pansy, Blue Ground, Red, Purple, Blue Flowers, Yellow Centers, 6 In. 475.0
Vase, Pansy, Buds, 5 1/2 x 6 In. 650.0
Vase, Pansy, Bulbous Upper Portion, Signed, William Moorcroft, 9 1/8 In. 467.0
Vase, Pansy, Flowers, Leaves, Red, Blue, Green, Pale Green Ground, 1972, 11 In. 713.0
Vase, Pomegranate, 2 Handles, Signed, William Moorcroft, 8 1/4 In. 660.0
Vase, Pomegranate, Baluster, 8 In. ....775.00 to 850.0
Vase, Pomegranate, Burslem, 6 x 5 In. 1200.0
Vase, Pomegranate, Grapes, Leaves, Red, Green, Blue, Ocher, Gray, Squaty, 7 1/4 In. ... 747.0
Vase, Pomegranate, Signed, 12 14 In. 633.0
Vase, Pomegranate, Trumpet, 8 1/2 In. 900.0
Vase, Poppy, Blue, Macintyre, 3 1/2 In. 450.0
Vase, Poppy, Cobalt Blue, Signed, c.1935 .... 550.0
Vase, Poppy, Flowers, Leaves, Red, Ocher, Blue, Purple, Brown, 1920, 12 1/3 In. 3010.0
Vase, Poppy, Red, Marked, 10 x 7 In. 4400.0
Vase, Spanish, Red, Ocher, Blue Flowers, Scrolled Stems, Macintyre, 1910, 11 In. 2693.0
Vase, Spring Flowers, Pale Flambe Glaze, Signed, Walter Moorcroft, 7 In. 550.0
Vase, Trumpet, Pomegranate, 8 1/2 In. 900.0
Vase, Wisteria, 5 In. 303.0
Vase, Wisteria, Flambe, 6 In. 1200.0
Vase, Wisteria, Flambe, Drilled, Signed, c.1930, 16 In. 977.0

MORIAGE is a special type of raised decoration used on some Japanese
pottery. Sometimes pieces of clay were shaped by hand and applied to
the item; sometimes the clay was squeezed from a tube in the way we
apply cake frosting. One type of moriage is called *Dragonware* and is
listed under that name.

Basket, Lorals, Nippon, 8 1/2 In. 248.0
Candy Dish, Hawaii, Hula Maids, Heart Shaped, 5 In. 35.0
Cup & Plate Set, Desert, Geisha, Lithograph, Japan, 12 Piece 150.0
Dish, Purple Iris, Open Handles, Fluted, 8 In. 75.0
Humidor, Gold & Multicolored Jewels, Sage Green & White, Nippon 395.0
Humidor, Squirrel Finial, Nippon 550.0
Mug, Dragon, Mottled Gray, 6 In. 195.0
Plate, Hanging, Birds On Tree Branch, Leaves, 10 1/4 In. 62.0
Rose Bowl, White Slip Work, Turquoise Ground, Signed 225.0
Tea Set, Dragon, 11 Piece 120.0
Teapot, c.1880 .... 185.0
Vase, Violets, 2 Handles, Royal Moriye Nippon, 9 In. 190.0

MOSAIC TILE COMPANY of Zanesville, Ohio, was started by Karl
Langerbeck and Herman Mueller in 1894. Many types of plain and
ornamental tiles were made until 1959. The company closed in 1967.
The company also made some ashtrays, bookends, and related giftwares. Most pieces are marked with the entwined *MTC* monogram.

Tile, Ship On The Water, Taupe, Orange, Green, Dark Blue Sky, Frame, 6 In. 440.0
Tile, Windmill, 6 In. 250.0

MOSER glass is made by Ludwig Moser und Sohne, a Bohemian
(Czech) glasshouse founded in 1857. Art Nouveau-type glassware and
iridescent glassware were made. The most famous Moser glass is dec-
orated with heavy enameling in gold and bright colors. The firm,
Moser Glassworks, is still working in Karlsbad, West Czech Republic.
Few pieces of Moser glass are marked.

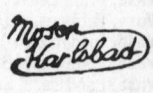

Bell, Cranberry Cut To Clear, Gold Scrolling, 5 1/2 In. 110.0
Bottle, Enameled Floral, Cobalt Blue, Stopper, 9 1/2 In. 165.0
Bottle, Platinum Design, Amethyst Gold, 9 In. 385.0
Bowl, Band Of Amazon Warriors, Gold Overlaid, Signed, 4 1/2 x 9 In. 373.0
Bowl, Intaglio Cut Floral, Lavender Shaded To Clear, Signed, 7 1/2 x 2 1/2 In. 475.0
Bowl, Raised Fish & Dragonfly, Blue, 3 In. 395.0
Bowl, Sunflower Cover, Leaves On Sides, Green, 4 x 6 In. 275.0
Bowl, Wine, Reversible Wedding, Raised Gold Morning Glory Vines, Gold, 6 3/4 In. 195.0

Box, Applied Pink Berries, Fern Leaves, Lime Green, 4 In.	585.00
Box, Cover, Yellow Custard, Applied Gold Design, 2 1/2 x 1 1/2 In.	165.00
Box, Dresser, Enameled, Hinged Lid, 3 In.	350.00
Box, Fern Leaves, 19 Berries, Lime Green, 4 In.	585.00
Box, Jewel, Dragon, Floral Design, Brass Hinge, Amethyst, 1900, 6 x 4 1/4 In.	275.00
Candlestick, Warriors, Faceted Sides, Purple, Signed, Pair	550.00
Centerpiece, 4 Pendants, 2 Cartouches, Floral Ribbons, Sprays, Oval, H. Jean, 10 In.	690.00
Cup & Saucer, Cranberry, Opaque White Cabochons, Hand Painted Floral, 2 1/2 In.	485.00
Cup & Saucer, Flowers, Gilt, Amber, White, Demitasse	100.00
Ewer, Gold, Rose, White Baroque Enameling, Rubena, 7 1/2 In.	210.00
Mug, Crackle Glass, Topaz, Gold Handle, Base, 4 Applied Insects, Polychrome, 5 In.	345.00
Pitcher, Cranberry Glass, Enameled Scrolling Flower, Gold, Clear Handle, 10 1/4 In.	660.00
Pitcher, Gold Enameled Branches, Gold Outlined Flowers, Blue, 10 In.	325.00
Pitcher, Storks & Cattails, Crackle Glass, 5 1/2 In.	475.00
Rose Bowl, Blue, Enameled Fish & Sea Foliage, 3 1/2 In.	345.00
Salt, 4 Applied Acorns, Cranberry	485.00
Salt & Pepper, Applied Fish, Enamel, 4 1/2 In.	465.00
Sugar & Creamer, Branch Handles, Green, Gold	650.00
Tankard, 4 Ales, Green, 12 In.	700.00
Tankard, Shaded Apple Green To Crystal, Intaglio-Cut Floral Design, 12 1/4 In.	765.00
Toothpick, Cased Crystal Panels, Gold Etched Band, Signed	295.00
Toothpick, Cranberry To Clear, Signed	145.00
Tumbler, Juice, Chardon No. 95, Green, Set Of 6	600.00
Tumbler, Juice, Gold Overlay, Gold Rim, Signed, 4 In.	110.00
Tumbler, Juice, Green, Gold Trim	135.00 to 145.00
Vase, 6 Women, Bathing, 4 In Water, 2 Seated, Surrounded By Trees, 9 3/4 In.	6325.00
Vase, Applied Flowers, Turquoise, Signed, 12 In.	335.00
Vase, Butterflies On Crystal, Florals, 8 1/2 In.	290.00
Vase, Cameo, Sea Scene, Ship, Sailing, Bahama Brown, Pale Yellow, Green, 8 In.	1540.00
Vase, Enameled Pansies, Green Shaded To Clear, 14 In.	650.00
Vase, Floral Bands, Amethyst Ribbed, 6 In., Pair	1100.00
Vase, Floral Design, Trees, Bees, Bird, Amber, Enameled, Signed, 11 In.	385.00
Vase, Floral, Cranberry, Marked, 10 1/2 In.	250.00
Vase, Goblet Form, Amazon Women Scene, Gold Medial Band, Flared, 6 In.	405.00
Vase, Gold Leaves, Elegant Lady Scene, 9 3/4 In.	200.00
Vase, Green Tassels Design, Green Bands, Enameled, Square, 6 x 2 5/8 In.	195.00
Vase, Green To Red-Brown, Canted Out, Heinrich Mussman, 1929-1930, 9 1/2 In.	495.00
Vase, Hand Painted Flowers & Gold Heart, Emerald Green, 14 In.	117.00
Vase, Karlsbad, Yellow, Deep Intaglio Floral, 1 Large Orange Flower, 5 7/8 In.	550.00
Vase, Marquetry, Intaglio Floral, Large Orange Flower, Opalescent Yellow Body, 6 In.	550.00
Vase, Nature Scene, 8 Sides, Kelly Green, Light Blue, Green, Marked, 6 In.	990.00
Vase, Pansy, 14 In.	1000.00
Vase, Rose Branches, Intaglio, Purple Rim, Acid Stamp, Early 20th Century, 12 In.	316.00
Vase, Stylized Flowers, Leaf Design, Acid Cutback, Emerald Green, 8 3/4 In.	1100.00
Vase, Thumbprint Type Texture, Amethyst Flowers, Gold Banding, c.1900, 12 1/4 In.	230.00
Vase, Warriors With Bows, Arrows, Purple, Gold Iridescent, 9 In.	198.00
Wine, Fluted, Tapering Conical Bowl, Josef Hoffman, Weiner Werkstatte, 12 3/4 In.	3120.00

MOSS ROSE china was made by many firms from 1808 to 1900. It has typical moss rose pictured as the design. The plant is not as popular now as it was in Victorian gardens, so the fuzz-covered bud is unfamiliar to most collectors. The dishes were usually decorated with pink and green flowers.

Butter, Cover	50.00
Coffeepot	110.00
Pitcher & Bowl, Ironstone, Lion & Unicorn Mark, 13 x 14 1/4 In.	165.00
Platter, 12 In.	38.00
Platter, 14 In.	45.00
Reamer, 2 Piece	50.00
Soup, Dish, Gold Trim, Green Mark	18.00
Sugar & Creamer	38.00

MOTHER-OF-PEARL GLASS, or pearl satin glass, was first made in the 1850s in England and in Massachusetts. It was a special type of mold-blown satin glass with air bubbles in the glass, giving it a pearlized color. It has been reproduced. Mother-of-pearl shell objects are listed under Pearl.

Beverage Set, Satin Coin Spot, Cranberry, 6 Piece	385.0
Biscuit Jar, Light Blue, Wide Ribbon Pattern, 6 x 7 1/2 In.	730.0
Jardiniere, Waisted Form, Frieze Design, Bun Feet, 5 x 12 1/4 In., Pair	5175.0
Nappy, Diamond-Quilted, White, Allover Gold Design, Crimped, 6 x 2 1/2 In.	425.0
Pitcher, Raspberry To Pink, 8 In.	30.0
Plate, Shaded Blue To White, 7 In.	145.0
Rose Bowl, White Lining, 7-Crimp, Blue Swirl, 2 3/4 x 3 1/4 In.	265.0
Rose Bowl, White Lining, Frosted Wafer Foot, 3 1/8 x 2 3/4 In.	165.0
Salt, Diamond-Quilted, Rainbow, Pink, Yellow, Blue, Apricot, White, 1 1/4 In.	795.0
Shade, Lamp, Ruffled, White Lining, 4 1/2 x 7 In., Pair	495.0
Sugar, Stationary Handle, Diamond-Quilted, Pink, 7 1/2 x 4 1/2 In.	455.0
Tumbler, Diamond-Quilted, Pink, Gunderson, 3 5/8 In.	55.0
Tumbler, Raindrop, Pink, 3 5/8 In.	33.0
Vase, Blue Swirl, Melon Sectioned, Ormolu Feet, White Lining, 7 In.	195.0
Vase, Diamond-Quilted, Dragonflies, Blue Satin, Enameled, 8 1/2 In.	415.0
Vase, Diamond-Quilted, Pink Satin, 5 3/4 In.	55.0
Vase, Diamond-Quilted, Pink Satin, Ground Pontil, 7 1/2 In.	195.0
Vase, Elongated Polkadot, Blue Satin, Flared Rim, 4 In.	80.0
Vase, Leaf Pattern, Fern Leaf Coralene Design, Yellow, White, 7 1/2 In.	1055.0

MOTORCYCLES and motorcycle accessories of all types are being collected today. Examples can be found that date back to the early years of the twentieth century. Toy motorcycles are listed in the Toy category.

Banner, Harley-Davidson, Dealer's, Paper, White, Orange, Black, 86 x 33 In.	75.0
Banner, Harley-Davidson, Dealer's, Vinyl, Fat Boy Style Logo, 12 x 2 Ft.	115.0
Belt, Kidney, Studded & Jeweled, Accordion Pockets Each Side, Black Leather	236.0
Belt Buckle, Harley-Davidson, Live To Ride, Ride To Live, Eagle, 1978	25.0
Belt Buckle, Harley-Davidson, Police Badge, Shield & Eagle, Dark Gold Finish	40.0
Booklet, Indian, Riders' Instruction Book, 1952, 42 Pages, 5 x 7 In.	70.0
Helmet, Fiber Shell, Leather Lined, Fiber Brim, Decal, AGY A-4, 1950s	40.0
Helmet, Fiberglass Shell, Black Leather Earflaps, Nylon Chinstrap, 1968	41.0
Jacket, Horsehide, Indian Motorcycle Patch, Size 42	950.0
Jacket, Leather, Mid-Thigh Length, Waist Belt, Taubers Of California	115.0
Jacket, Racing, Harley-Davidson, Nylon, Red, Black Stripes, Quilted Lining, 1980s	50.0
Jacket, Windbreaker, Harley-Davidson, Eagle, Over Bar & Shield, 14 x 16 In.	65.0
Kidney Belt, Leather, White Metal Studs, Plastic Stones, 38 In.	145.0
Lamp, Carbide, Jeweled Reflectors, Mounting Clamp, Nickel Plated, 4 x 4 1/2 In.	230.0
Lamp, Fender, For Indian, Indian Face, Original	275.0
License Plate, Pennsylvania, 1915, 4 1/2 x 8 1/4 In.	55.0
Motorcycle, Indian, 1917	16500.0
Patch, Harley-Davidson Motorcycle, Embroidered, Silver Wings, 1950s, 2 x 4 In.	85.0
Patch, Wings, Harley-Davidson Motorcycles, Black Felt, 1950s	85.0
Pin, Wings, Indian, Indian Head, Pinback, Sterling Silver, 1930s, 2 1/2 In.	180.0
Postcard, One Cylinder Motorcycle, 2 Women Riding Tandem, 3 1/2 x 5 1/2 In.	65.0
Sign, Harley-Davidson, Sales, Service & Parts, Glass, 6 3/4 x 19 In.	1320.0
Visor, Harley-Davidson Logo, Leather	33.0
Wallet, Harley-Davidson, Cowhide, Harley Eagle, Chain, Belt Loop, Tags, 6 x 3 In.	43.0
Wallet, Harley-Davidson, Logo	7.0
Whistle, Policeman's, Plastic, 3 3/4 In.	105.00 to 165.0

MOUNT WASHINGTON, see Mt. Washington category.

MOVIE memorabilia of all types is collected. Animation cels, games, sheet music, toys, and some celebrity items are listed in their own section. Listed here are costumes and paper collectibles. A lobby card is 11 by 14 inches. A set of lobby cards includes seven scene cards and one title card. A one sheet, the standard movie poster, is 27 by 41 inches. A

ree sheet is 81 by 40 inches. A half sheet is 22 by 28 inches. A win-
ow card, made of cardboard, is 14 by 22 inches. An insert is 14 by 36
iches. A herald is a promotional item handed out to patrons. A press
ook was sent to newspapers and magazines to promote a picture.

Air Freshener, Marilyn Monroe, In Plastic, Unused	25.00
Banner, Morocco, Marlene Dietrich, Paramount, 1930	9200.00
Book, Coloring, Doris Day, Whitman, No. 1867, Colored, 1953, 12 Pages	13.00
Book, Flip, Dance Lessons, 1940s	30.00
Box, Tin, Pola Negri, Round, 1920s, 7 1/2 In.	95.00
Chair, Cecil B. DeMille, Arms, White Fabric, Used At Paramount Commissary	230.00
Costume, Mutiny On The Bounty, Charles Laughton As Captain Bligh, 1935	310.00
Cuff Links, 14K Gold, Property Of Marlene Dietrich	5462.00
Doll, Marilyn Monroe, Lorelei, Gentlemen Prefer Blondes, Dress, Franklin Mint, 20 In.	125.00
Dress, Cocktail, White Linen, Rhinestones, Sophia Loren, 1951	925.00
Dress, Pucci, Jersey, Self Belt, Beaded Tassel, Marlene Dietrich	747.00
Fan, Harold Lloyd, 1920s	55.00
Figure, Laurel & Hardy, Plastic, Poseable Arms, Dakin, 1960s, 8 In., Pair	48.00
Figure, Marx Brothers, Groucho, Chico & Harpo, Standing On Film Can, Vinyl, 3 Piece	45.00
Film, Home, Chilly Willy, Rockabye Legend, 8mm, 1960s, 200 Ft.	15.00
Hat, Indiana Jones, Stetson, Brown	25.00
Jacket, Smoking, Lawrence Olivier, 1930	250.00
Jersey, Baseball, Major League, Charlie Sheen, Autographed, 1989 ....*Illus*	2185.00
Lighter, Dunhill, Bette Davis, All About Eve, Inscribed Bette On Lid, Leather Case	2070.00
Liquor Cork, W.C. Fields, Head Shape, Mechanical, Box, 1930s	90.00
Lobby Card, An American In Paris, Gene Kelly, 1951	45.00
Lobby Card, Bad Sister, Humphrey Bogart, 1931	1200.00
Lobby Card, Ben Hur, Ramon Novarro, Crowd Scene, 1926	250.00
Lobby Card, Black Pirate, Fairbanks Sr., Swashbuckling Scene, 1926	250.00
Lobby Card, Call Of The Canyon, Richard Dix, 1923	150.00
Lobby Card, City Lights, Chaplin, 1931	450.00
Lobby Card, Colossus Of New York, 1958	295.00
Lobby Card, Elephant Walk, Elizabeth Taylor, 1954, 3 Piece	150.00
Lobby Card, Gone With The Wind, Portraiture Art, 1939	425.00
Lobby Card, Haunted House, Vincent Price, Autographed	21.00
Lobby Card, It's A Wonderful Life, James Stewart & Donna Reed, 1946	250.00
Lobby Card, Jet Pilot, Janet Leigh Autograph, John Wayne, 1957	95.00
Lobby Card, Queen Of Outer Space, 1958	250.00
Lobby Card, Return Of Doctor X, Humphrey Bogart, 1939	875.00
Lobby Card, Return Of The Fly, Vincent Price, 1959	50.00
Lobby Card, The Terror From Beyond Space, 1958	295.00
Lobby Card, Time Machine, 1960	295.00
Lobby Card, Track Of The Cat, Robert Mitchum, No. 2, 1954	15.00
Lobby Card, Two Mrs. Carroll's, Humphrey Bogart, 1947	95.00
Lobby Card Set, Jackie Robinson Story, 1950, 8 Piece	300.00
Mirror, Mary Pickford, Pocket	90.00

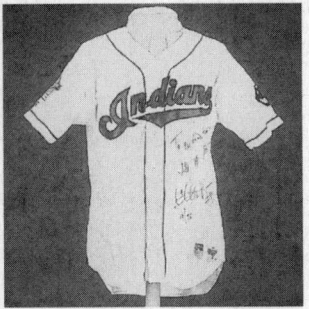

Movie, Jersey, Baseball, Major League,
Charlie Sheen, Autographed, 1989

**If you are buying a game-worn jersey,
look for signs of wear at the belt-line.
Check the buttonholes to make sure
they're not too tight. Sleeve patches
that are perfectly flat are on a jersey
that has never been washed. Even
minimal play leaves traces of wear.
Stains, rips, and pulls show that the
jersey was worn a lot.**

Money Clip, No. 21 Horseshoe, Joan Crawford, I. Magnin 1035.00
Note Pad, Hermes, Red Leather, Property Of Marlene Dietrich 2875.00
Photograph, Ann Blyth, Autographed, 11 x 13 In. 30.00
Photograph, Annette Funicello, With Pizza, Black & White, Autographed, 8 x 10 In. 34.00
Photograph, Camelot, Richard Burton, Autographed 90.00
Photograph, Hayley Mills, In Pigtails, Black & White, Autographed, 8 x 10 In. 25.00
Photograph, John Wayne, Black & White, Autographed, 8 x 10 In. 400.00
Photograph, Old Yeller, Tommy Kirk, Black & White, Autographed, 1957, 8 1/2 x 10 In. 10.00
Photograph, Otto Preminger, Autographed, 8 x 10 In. 45.00
Photograph, Robert Redford, Navy Uniform, Black & White, 8 x 10 In. 86.00
Photograph, Singing In The Rain, Gene Kelly Autograph 90.00
Picture, Pastel, Frank Sinatra, Cardboard Frame, Autographed, 8 x 10 In. 50.00
Portfolio, Empire Strikes Back, 24 Prints, Ralph McQuarrie, Ballantine Books, 1980 ... 25.00
Postcard, Hoot Gibson, Color Photo, Autographed 95.00
Poster, Cannes Film Festival, Marlene Dietrich, Autographed, 20 x 15 In. 6325.00
Poster, Cinderfella, Rockwell Art, 1960, One Sheet 200.00
Poster, Citizen Kane, Reissue, 1956, One Sheet 250.00
Poster, Cleopatra, Elizabeth Taylor, 1963, Three Sheet 100.00
Poster, Doctor & The Girl, Glenn Ford & Gloria DeHaven, 1949, One Sheet 275.00
Poster, Fighting Seabees, John Wayne, Susan Hayward, Swedish Release, 33 x 24 In. ... 25.00
Poster, Guns Of Navarone, Gregory Peck, Anthony Quinn, David Niven, Insert 45.00
Poster, High Noon, Gary Cooper, 1952, Half Sheet 449.00
Poster, I Passed For White, 1960, One Sheet 75.00
Poster, Jackie Robinson Story, 1950, One Sheet 575.00
Poster, Joan Crawford, 1930s, Half Sheet 1200.00
Poster, Little Rascals, 1959, 23 x 29 In. 25.00
Poster, M*A*S*H, Elliot Gould, 1969, One Sheet 15.00
Poster, National Velvet, Elizabeth Taylor, 1944, One Sheet 450.00
Poster, Queen Of Outer Space, Zsa Zsa Gabor, 1958, One Sheet 450.00
Poster, Raintree County, Elizabeth Taylor, 1957, Half Sheet 85.00
Poster, Sundown In Santa Fe, Allan Lane & Stallion Black Jack, Frame, 30 x 18 In. 575.00
Poster, The Further Perils Of Laurel & Hardy, Both Riding A Lion, 27 x 41 In. 45.00
Poster, Then Came Bronson, 1969, One Sheet 242.00
Poster, Three Stooges, Palace Theater In England, June 1939, 24 x 12 1/2 In. 575.00
Poster, Wild Angels, Peter Fonda, Nancy Sinatra, 15 Hell's Angels, 1966, One Sheet ... 253.00
Poster, Yakuza, Robert Mitchum, 1975, One Sheet 20.00
Poster, Yellow Cab Man, Red Skelton, 1949, One Sheet 250.00
Press Book, Gone With The Wind, Reissue, 1967 .... 10.00
Press Book, Jackie Robinson Story, 1950 .... 45.00
Press Book, Mary Poppins, 1964 .... 30.00
Press Book, Reflections In A Golden Eye, Elizabeth Taylor, 1967 .... 25.00
Program, Birth Of A Nation, England, 1916, 4 Pages 150.00
Program, Covered Wagon, 1923 .... 85.00
Program, It's A Mad, Mad, Mad, Mad World, Jack Davis Art On Cover, 1963, 40 Pages . 28.00
Program, Lawrence Of Arabia, 1962, 40 Pages 35.00
Program, Movie, Hell's Angel, Jean Harlow, 1930 .... 75.00
Program, Song Of Bernadette, Premier, Rockwell Art, With Original Ticket 145.00
Radio, Philco, Leather & Bakelite, Property Of Marlene Dietrich, 10 3/8 In. 402.00
Souvenir, Hollywood & Movie Star Homes, Box, 1940s, 20 Piece 38.00
Speaker, Drive-In Theater, Hanger Bracket, Pair 40.00
Thimble, Marilyn Monroe, Pink 25.00
Window Card, City Lights, Charlie Chaplin, 1931 .... 3500.00
Window Card, Crucifer Of Blood, Sherlock Holmes, Artcraft Litho 700.00
Window Card, Devil's Playground, Richard Dix, Dolores Del Rio, 1936 .... 150.00
Window Card, Glass Key, Hammett, George Raft, 1935 .... 750.00
Window Card, Louis vs. Schmelling, Fame, 1930s 750.00

MT. JOYE is an enameled cameo glass made in the late nineteenth and
twentieth centuries by Saint-Hilaire Touvier de Varraux and Co. of
Pantin, France. This same company made De Vez glass. Pieces were
usually decorated with enameling. Most pieces are not marked.

Vase, Cameo, Acorn Leaves, Silver, Golden Leaves On Base, Emerald Green, 13 In. 2200.00
Vase, Cameo, Gilt Floral, Green, 10 In. 375.00

Vase, Cameo, Purple & White Iris, Gilt, Pale Green, 10 In.	190.00
Vase, Enameled Flowers, Green, Gilt, Plum Body, 1920-1930, 11 1/2 In.	1045.00
Vase, Etched Floral Design, Enameled Pink, White & Black, 10 3/4 In.	517.00
Vase, Floral Design, Leaves, Stems, Chartreuse, Diamond Form, 12 x 5 In., Pair	650.00
Vase, Gold Enamel, Bead Design, Dark Green, 5 5/8 In.	360.00
Vase, Gold, Bead Design, Dark Green Ground, 5 5/8 In.	250.00
Vase, Gold, Silver Rose Hips, Transparent Green Ground, 10 In.	475.00
Vase, Pink, Yellow & Gilt Chrysanthemums, Sea Green, 12 1/2 In., Pair	575.00
Vase, Yellow, Pink & Gilt Floral, Bulbous Cylindrical Form, 9 1/4 In., Pair	575.00

MT. WASHINGTON Glass Works started in 1837 in South Boston,
Massachusetts. In 1870 the company moved to New Bedford,
Massachusetts. Many types of art glass were made there until 1894,
when the company merged with Pairpoint Manufacturing Co.
Amberina, Burmese, Crown Milano, Cut Glass, Peachblow, and Royal
Flemish are each listed in their own category.

Basket, Daffodil, Herringbone, Satin Loop Handle With Thorns, 9 1/2 In.	288.00
Basket, Deep Pink Cut To Clear, Allover Hobnails, Silver Mica, 6 3/4 In.	375.00
Basket, Diamond-Quilted, Blue To White, Ruffled Edge, 6 3/4 x 6 In.	395.00
Basket, Hobnail, Satin, Peach, Blue & Yellow, Flattened, 5 3/4 In.	1975.00
Biscuit Jar, Enameled Sea Creature, Sea Plants, Signed, 6 1/2 x 7 1/2 In.	1400.00
Biscuit Jar, Enameled, Pale Blue Blossoms, Yellow Outlining, 7 1/2 In.	525.00
Biscuit Jar, Yellow To Peach Painted Background, Shadow Flowers, Leaves	815.00
Bottle, Dresser, Lusterless White, Mushroom Body, Blown Stopper, 10 In.	200.00
Bowl, Diamond-Quilted, Applied Berry Prunt, Gold, 6 x 7 In.	5000.00
Bowl, Winged Griffin Design, Ruffled Edge, Blue On White, 3 3/4 x 8 In.	500.00
Bowl, Woman Portrait, White, Pink, 4 1/2 x 10 In.	651.00
Bride's Bowl, Lusterless White, Pink Roses, Gold Interior, Scrolls, 12 In.	2750.00
Celery Vase, Herringbone, Blue To Pale Blue, White Lining, Melon Shape, 5 In.	325.00
Cologne Bottle, Allover Floral Design, Opal, 9 In.	115.00
Cookie Jar, Shell Mold, Gold Enameled	475.00
Cracker Jar, Melon Ribbed	350.00
Cracker Jar, Raised Swirl, Enameled Beading, Silver Plate Fittings, 7 x 5 In.	200.00
Cracker Jar, Yellow To Purple Pansies, Pale Yellow, Orange Ground	250.00
Cruet, Pink, Blue, White, Applied Loop Handle, 7 1/4 In.	1450.00
Cruet, Stopper, Double Gourd Shape, Sticker, 5 1/2 In.	750.00
Epergne, Amber, Vertical Ribbed Pattern, Rose, 9 x 6 In.	2000.00
Ewer, Gold Chrysanthemum, Pale Blue, Lavender, Handle, 12 x 5 In.	3000.00
Ewer, Pillow, Landscape, Shepherd, Sheep Scene, Beige, Green Ground, 10 In.	3750.00
Flower Frog, Pale Blue, Mushroom Shape, White Floral Design, 3 x 5 In.	220.00
Jug, Mother-Of-Pearl, Polka Dot, Pink, White Air Traps, Loop Handle, 6 In.	475.00
Lamp, Banquet, Rampant Lion On A Coat Of Arms Design, 38 In.	900.00
Lamp, Parlor, Gold, Pansy Design, Basket Weave Ground, 21 x 10 In.	1800.00
Mug, Jewel Band Of Leaves & Berries, Blue Band, Gold Rope Handle, 7 In.	3050.00
Mustard, Enameled Apple Blossom, Silver Plated Cover, Brass Handle, 3 In.	200.00
Pickle Castor, Hobnail, White Enameled Flowers, 9 In.	1500.00
Pin Tray, Enameled Blue Forget-Me-Nots, Footed Frame, 3 In.	75.00
Pitcher, Cream, Hobnail, Rose, Blue, White, Peachblow Handle, 6 x 4 In.	2500.00
Pitcher, Daisy, Cranberry, Lily Of The Valley, Blue Floral Design, 9 x 7 In.	475.00
Pitcher, Diamond-Quilted, Satin, Loop Camphor Handle, 6 x 3 In.	325.00
Pitcher, Floral Design, Applied Reeded Crystal Handle, 8 x 5 In.	325.00
Pitcher, Mother-Of-Pearl, Coinspot, Pastel Pink, Blue, Peach, 8 In.	400.00
Pitcher, Mother-Of-Pearl, Cranberry, Diamond-Quilted, 8 In.	175.00
Pitcher, Syrup, Enameled, Blue, Yellow Spider Mums, 6 x 3 In.	3500.00
Pitcher, Syrup, Melon Ribbed, Pale Pink, Gold Floral Design, Signed, 6 In.	2500.00
Pitcher, Water, Alice, Blue Cut Velvet, Sapphire Reeded Handle, 9 x 6 In.	895.00
Rose Bowl, Blue, Pink, Inner White Casing	2000.00
Rose Bowl, Burmese Rigaree, 3 1/2 x 3 1/2 In.	400.00
Rose Bowl, Pink, Blue, White, 2 1/4 x 5 3/4 In.	900.00
Rose Bowl, Yellow, Enameled Red Berries, Ribbed Swirls, 4 x 5 In.	145.00
Salt & Pepper, Egg Shape, 1893 Columbian Exhibition, 3 In.	90.00
Salt & Pepper, Egg Shape, Floral Enameled	325.00
Salt & Pepper, Fig Shape, Floral Enameled, Metal Top, 2 5/8 In.	302.00

Salt & Pepper, Inverted Ribs, Dark Amber, Floral Enameled, Floral Top, 4 In. 72.00
Saltshaker, Beet Shape, Cranberry, Floral Enameled 475.00
Saltshaker, Tomato Shape, Light Blue, Enameled Florals, 2 In. 39.00
Tumbler, Mother-Of-Pearl, Diamond-Quilted, Yellow To White, 1880s, 4 In. 145.00
Tumbler, Mother-Of-Pearl, Herringbone, Blue, 1880s, 4 In. 145.00
Vase, Coat Of Arms Design, Heraldic Handle, Rust, Green Panels, 12 1/2 In. 2000.00
Vase, Colonial Ware, Lilies, Water Jug Shape, Loop Handle, Signed, 13 In. 1750.00
Vase, Daisy Design, Beige, Brown, Green Panels, 2 Handles, 10 x 6 1/2 In. 900.00
Vase, Diamond-Quilted Pattern, Cut Velvet, Purple, 14 x 8 In. 895.00
Vase, Enameled Flowers, Opal, Numbered, 13 1/2 In. 495.00
Vase, Enameled Seaweed Design, Brown To Gold, Satin, 11 1/4 In. 550.00
Vase, Fish, Green Sea Plants, Blue, Rust, Tan, Brown, 14 x 4 1/2 In. 13000.00
Vase, Glossy Opal, Persian Water Jug Shape, Loop Handle At Top, 12 3/4 In. 1750.00
Vase, Gold, Red, Raspberry Design, 10 x 4 In. 1850.00
Vase, Herringbone, Deep Rose, Yellow & Blue, 5 Colors, 7 3/4 x 5 In. 1750.00
Vase, Herringbone, Pink, Yellow, Blue, Beige, White, 5 x 5 1/2 In. 600.00
Vase, Hobnail, Blue, White Lining, Rolled Edge, 5 3/4 x 4 1/4 In. 675.00
Vase, Jack-In-The-Pulpit, Pink, Rose, Blue, White, 7 1/4 In. 3100.00
Vase, Large Griffin, Lavender, Blue, Green, Gold, 14 x 7 In. 5500.00
Vase, Lava, Irregular Patches Of Color, Allover Speckles, 5 3/4 In. 1915.00
Vase, Mother-Of-Pearl, Applied Satin Opal Edge, 6 1/2 x 3 In., Pair 550.00
Vase, Mother-Of-Pearl, Cut Velvet, Ruffled Edge, 6 x 9 In. 675.00
Vase, Mother-Of-Pearl, Herringbone, Pink, Yellow, Blue, 7 In. 850.00
Vase, Muslin, Alice Blue, Satin, Bulbous, 8 x 7 In. 675.00
Vase, Napoli, Frog Sitting In Bulrushes, Blue, Green, Rust, 8 1/2 In. 975.00
Vase, Pale Blue, Berries, Leaves, Thorns, Red Maroon Vines, 9 In. 4500.00
Vase, Pink Interior, Satin, Bulbous, Gourd Shape, 6 1/4 In. 4500.00
Vase, Posy, Pleated, Ruffled Edge, 2 1/4 In. 137.50
Vase, Prunis, Burmese Egyptian Handle, 7 x 4 In. 75.00
Vase, Satin Spatter, White Lining, Ruffled Edge, Bulbous, 7 3/4 x 5 In. 675.00
Vase, Stick, Floral, Serpent Head Design, Pale Green, Tan, Gold, 11 x 8 In. 900.00
Vase, Stick, Opal, Gold Design, Allover Vine & Berry, Signed, 11 7/8 In. 550.00
Vase, White, Pink Flowers, Brown, Green Leaves, Bulbous, 7 x 6 1/2 In. 550.00
Vase, Winged Serpent & Dragon, Maroon, Green Ground, 10 1/2 x 8 In. 3500.00
Vase, Yellow Hood Rose, Gold Leaves, Gourd Shape, 8 1/2 x 4 In. 4250.00
Water Set, Diamond-Quilted, Coralene Seaweed Design, 4 Piece 750.00
Water Set, Herringbone, Rose To Pink To White, 1880s, 5 Piece 1750.00

MUD FIGURES are small Chinese pottery figures made in the twentieth
century. The figures usually represent workers, scholars, farmers, or
merchants. Other pieces are trees, houses, and similar parts of the landscape. The figures have unglazed faces and hands but glazed clothing.
They were originally made for fish tanks or planters. Mud figures were
of little interest and brought low prices until the 1980s. When the
prices rose, reproductions appeared.

Man, Beard, Fishing Pole, 4 1/4 In. 25.00
Man, Seated, 4 In. 20.00
Woman, Holding Fruit, 4 In. 35.00

MULBERRY ware was made in the Staffordshire district of England
from about 1850 to 1860. The dishes were decorated with a reddish
brown transfer design, now called *mulberry*. Many of the patterns are
similar to those used for flow blue and other Staffordshire transfer
wares.

Bowl, Potato, Rhone Scenery, 11 In. 195.00
Creamer, Flowers 95.00
Cup & Saucer, Eagle On Shell, Hall 250.00
Ewer, Sir Walter Scott, 1 Side, Abbotsford Other, J. & M.P. Bell, 1860, 8 In. 425.00
Gravy Boat, Washington Vase 185.00
Plaque, Little Star 85.00
Plate, Corean, 10 In. 55.00
Plate, Medina, England, 9 5/8 In. 45.00
Plate, Pelew, Castle Scenery, 10 In. 115.00

Plate, Rhone Pattern, 9 In.	75.00
Plate, Vincennes, 9 1/4 In.	55.00
Platter, Floral, T. Walker, 15 1/4 x 12 In.	75.00
Sugar, Cover, Flowers	95.00
Teapot, Neva, Challinor	225.00
Teapot, Pagoda Design, Tree & Boat, 8 Sides, Ironstone, 9 1/2 In.	170.00
Teapot, Pelew	385.00 to 425.00
Tureen, Soup, Peru	3400.00
Urn, Cover, Vegetable	135.00

MULLER FRERES, French for Muller Brothers, made cameo and other glass from about 1895 to 1933. Their factory was first located in Luneville, then in nearby Croismare, France. Pieces were usually marked with the company name.

Muller Fres
Luneville

Lamp, Base, Landscape, Pine Trees, Mountains, Dark Purple, Gray, 1910, 14 In.	747.00
Lamp, Overlapping Leaves, Lavender, Pink, Green, Mottled Blue, 14 In.	990.00
Vase, Etched Cyclamen Blossoms, Buds & Leaves, Signed, 42 x 23 In.	1715.00
Vase, Etched Trumpet Shaped Blossoms & Spiked Leaves, Signed, 5 1/4 In.	660.00
Vase, Landscape, River, With A Village, Pale Lemon Yellow, Red, 1900, 12 1/2 In.	4887.00
Vase, Poppies, Blue Overlay, Cream Ground, Etched, Cameo, 21 In.	6440.00
Vase, Red, Orange, Royal Blue, Footed, 12 3/4 In.	750.00
Vase, Scenic Lake Front, Purple Landscape, Cameo, Signed, Luneville, 6 In.	2145.00
Vase, Trumpet Form, White Body, Wheel Cut As Poppy Pods, Signed, 10 In.	2645.00

MUNCIE Clay Products Company was established by Charles Benham in Muncie, Indiana, in 1922. The company made pottery for the florist and giftshop trade. The company closed by 1939. Pieces are marked with the name *Muncie* or just with a system of numbers and letters, like *1A*.

MUNCIE

Bowl, Closed Tab Handle, Blue Drip Over Blue, 5 In.	75.00
Bowl, Orange, Green Matte Glaze, 6 x 4 In.	475.00 to 495.00
Lamp, 6 Panels, Different Views Of Nude, Nude Finial, Signed, 9 3/4 In.	605.00
Lamp, Figural, Nude Panel, Orange & Green Glaze	495.00
Lamp, Nude Figure, Mauve & Green, Original Finial	675.00
Lamp, Nude Figure, Rust, Brown Glaze	475.00
Pitcher, Uranium Orange Glaze, Signed, 6 1/8 In.	110.00
Vase, Green Dripping Over Violet, 6 In.	95.00
Vase, Katydid, Burnt Orange, Mottled Green, 6 In.	145.00
Vase, Orange Peel, 9 In.	225.00
Vase, Rotary International Sticker, 8 1/2 In.	55.00
Vase, Turquoise Dripping Over Wine, 5 1/2 In.	95.00
Vase, Vessel, Cubist, Orange Glaze, 1930s, 2 1/2 x 9 In.	770.00
Vase, White, 7 1/2 In.	50.00

MURANO, see Glass-Venetian category.

MUSIC boxes and musical instruments are listed here. Phonograph records, jukeboxes, phonographs, and sheet music are listed in other categories in this book.

Accordion, Guillette, Plays Accordion & Piano Music	6000.00
Accordion, Scandalli, Marble-Finish Plastic, 1955	130.00
Accordion, Wurlitzer, Rhinestone & Mother-Of-Pearl Trim, Case, c.1930	140.00
Album, Photograph, Music Box In Back, Record Of Victoria's Reign, 5 Discs, c.1901	895.00
Autoharp, Favorite, Zimmerman	55.00
Banjo, Gibson Mastertone, 5 Strings, Inlaid Pearl Neck	175.00
Banjo, No. 961, 5 Strings, Mother-Of-Pearl Inlay On Neck, 1888	137.00
Banjo, Tenor, Ambassador Deluxe, Gold Plated Tone Ring & Pot, Pearl Inlay Peghead	747.00
Banjo, Vega Co., 30-Bracket Rim, Ivoroid Ebony Finger Board, Case, 1912	1035.00
Banjo Uke, Stella, Skin Head	100.00
Bassoon, Guillaume Triebert & Sons, Maple, Nickel-Plated Keys, Paris, 52 3/16 In.	1035.00
Bassoon, Maple Body, Brass Mounts, 6 Brass Keys, England, 1830, 50 In.	546.00
Bassoon, Milhouse, 8 Keys, Pearwood, Bronze Mounts, Brass Keys, 1835, 49 In.	460.00
Bow, Violin, A. Vigneron, Silver Mounted, Ebony Frog With Parisian Eye, France	920.00

Bow, Violin, F.N. Voirin, Gold Mounted, Ebony Frog With Parisian Eye, Gold Adjuster .. 1380.0
Bow, Violin, Wm. Koucky, Silver Mounted, Ebony Frog With Pearl Eye 630.0
Bow, Violoncello, John Norwood Lee, Gold Mounted, Ebony Frog With Pearl Eye 1265.0
Bow, Violoncello, Nickel Mounted, Ebony Frog With Pearl Eye 490.0
Box, 6 Tunes, Double Barrel, Change-Repeat Levers, Maple, Switzerland, 31 In. 3162.0
Box, 10 Tunes, 4 Tunes For 5 Cents, Gold Oak, Switzerland, 14 x 39 In. 6900.0
Box, Burled Veneer, Mother-Of-Pearl, 6 Tunes, 11-In. Cylinder, Switzerland, 21 In. ... 1430.0
Box, Crank, Nickel-Plated Drum Case, 2 Tunes, Switzerland 130.0
Box, Criterion, Mahogany, Shell & Poppy Design, Single Comb, 15 1/2-In. Disc 2530.0
Box, Cylinder, 3-Bell, Mahogany, Inlaid Floral Design On Lid 374.0
Box, Cylinder, Bells, Drum, 12 Tunes, Switzerland 3500.0
Box, Cylinder, Mahogany, 10 Tunes, Repeat, Crank Wind, Tune Sheet, 18 In. 1100.0
Box, Face Powder, Woman's Face, Brass, Lift Lid 125.0
Box, Floral Inlay, 6 Tunes, Switzerland, 14 1/2 x 8 x 5 1/2 In. 440.0
Box, Grain Decorated Case, 6 Tunes, Switzerland, 6 3/4 x 4 3/4 In. 522.0
Box, Hurdy-Gurdy, Mechanical, Primitive 440.0
Box, Instrumental Stencil & Line Inlay, 8 Tunes, Switzerland, 19 x 10 x 7 1/2 In. 880.0
Box, Kalliope, Single Comb, 13 & 15 3/4-In. Discs, 13 In. 920.0
Box, Lecoultre, 4 Tunes, Key Wind, 5-In. Cylinder 1500.0
Box, Lever Wind Cylinder, Stop, Play & Repeat, 4 Tunes, Wooden Case, 6 x 11 1/2 In. .. 750.0
Box, Lucia, Crank Operated, Painted Green, Discs, 7 1/2 x 10 In. 137.0
Box, Mira, Cabinet, 8 Discs, 18 1/2 In. 5000.0
Box, Mira, Coffin-Form Case, 20 Discs, 15 1/2-In. Disc 1650.0
Box, Nicole Freres, Cartel, 12 Tunes, 13-In. Cylinder 1800.0
Box, Nonpareil Mandolin Zither, 10 Songs, Switzerland, 1880s, 9 1/2 x 22 In. 2200.0
Box, Paillard, Orchestral, Drum, Belts, Wooden Block, 17-In. Cylinder 7500.0
Box, Paillard, Zither Attachment, Walnut Inlaid Case, 20 In. 1035.0
Box, Piano, Metal, With 5-In. Celluloid Doll 110.0
Box, Polichinelle Doll On Base, Bisque Head, Germany, French Market, c.1900, 8 In. 950.0
Box, Raggedy Andy, On Top, Close To You 20.0
Box, Raggedy Ann, On Top, Let Me Call You Sweetheart, 1973 .... 20.0
Box, Regina, Cherry, 24 Discs, 19th-20th Century, 22 x 20 1/2 x 12 In. 2860.0
Box, Regina, Disc Changer, 27-In. Discs 21500.0
Box, Regina, Double Comb, Oak, 24 Discs 2875.0
Box, Regina, Figured Mahogany, Double Comb, Table Top, 20 3/4-In. Disc 5950.0
Box, Regina, Mahogany Case, Original Storage Stand, 1880-1895, 15 1/2 In. 7800.0
Box, Reginaphone, Griffins, 15 1/2-In. Disc 7000.0
Box, Reuge, Waltzes Of Old Vienna, 5 Interchangeable Cylinders, 15 1/2 In. 630.0
Box, Singing Bird, Bird Cage, Yellow Birds, No. 321, Windup Key, France 1650.0
Box, Singing Bird, Birdcage, Windup, 20 x 11 In. 2070.0
Box, Singing Bird, In Metal Cage, Giltwood Base, Octagonal, 1870, 21 In. 1725.0
Box, Singing Bird, Spritzer & Fuhermann, Lake Scene, Flaps Wings, Sings, 4 In. 3680.0
Box, Singing Bird, Sterling Silver, Signed 3800.0
Box, Singing Birds, Birdcage, Gilt, Windup, 19th Century, 11 x 21 In. 1430.00
Box, Sports Car Shape, Schuco, Radio 4012 Made In U.S. Zone Germany, Schuco 500.00
Box, Stella, Rosewood, Stop-Start, Slow-Fast Levers, Drawer, Crank, 28 In. 4312.00
Box, Symphonion, Rococo Case, 11 3/4-In. Disc 6500.00
Box, Symphonion, Rosewood, Sublime Harmonie Combs, 9-In. Disc 1800.00
Box, Thorens, Lacquered Wood Case, 4 Tunes 200.00
Box, Toby Jug, Blue Danube Waltz, 7 In. 120.00
Box, Tremolo Zither, Inlaid Marquetry Case, Cylinder, 24 1/2 In. 880.00
Box, Triangular Table Style, Inlaid, Swiss Movement, Italy, 17 x 15 1/2 x 15 1/2 In. 60.00
Box, Veneer, Line Inlay, 8 Tunes, Mandolin-Harp, 10 Bell Strikes, Switzerland, 14 In. ... 3300.00
Bugle, Salesman's Sample, Brass Bell, Copper Tubing, Case, Pair 235.00
Calliope, Parade Outfit, Brass Parade Carriage, 30 A Rolls, Weather Cover 8000.00
Case, Double, Violin, Interior Mahogany, Silk Trim, Brass Fittings 488.00
Celestina, Crank, 3 Rolls 1000.00
Cello, Giovanni Beggianina, Interior Lavabel, Anno, 1895 .... 385.00
Clarinet, J. Ashton, Ivory Mounts, 5 Brass Keys, Boxwood Body, 23 1/4 In. 632.00
Cornet, Dupont, Paris, Silver 325.00
Drum, Child's, Tin, Embossed, 13 Stars, Flags, Wooden Bands, Late 19th Century, 13 In. 385.00
Drum, H.W. Maynard, Painted Reserve Of Musical Instruments, 13 5/8 x 17 In. 460.00
Drum, Marching, American Eagle, Shield, E Pluribus Unum 2300.00

Drum, Military, Frank Mehman, Wooden, 1892, 13 1/2 x 18 In. 215.00
Drum, Snare, Military, Shell Of 1 Piece Of Wood, c.1740, 11 In. 1800.00
Drum, Snare, Russell & Patee, Mid-19th Century, 12 x 15 In. 1955.00
Dulcimer, Pete Stanley, No. 16, Blond & Red Mahogany, Inside Label, 37 1/2 In. 225.00
Flute, Henry Hill, Rosewood, 8 Silver Keys, Mounts, 1829-1845, 23 1/8 In. 299.00
Flute, Ivory Mount, Boxwood, 4 Ivory Keys, Box, 22 1/8 In. 230.00
Flute, J.F. Boie, Blackwood, 8 Silver Keys, Ivory Mounts, 1809, 22 13/16 In. 805.00
Flute, Nickel Mount, Grenadella Body, 12 Nickel Keys, Adjustable Stopper, 27 In. 230.00
Flute, Richard Potter, Boxwood, 1-Key, Ivory Mounts, 1806, 21 1/16 In. 1380.00
Flute, Rudall & Rose, Boxwood, 8 Silver Keys, Pewter Plugs, 1821-1852, 23 In. 1840.00
Flute, Telescopic, 4 Finger Holes, Embossed Silver Knob, 15 3/4 In. 920.00
Flute, Wm. S. Haynes, Silver Mounts, C-Foot Joint, 1914, 26 15/16 In. 2185.00
Flute, Wm. S. Haynes, Silver Mounts, C-Foot Joint, Boston, 1914, 26 7/8 In. 1495.00
Flute, Wm. S. Haynes, Sterling Silver, C-Foot Joint, 1925, 26 1/2 In. 1265.00
Fork, Tuning, B. Hood, Steel, 3 1/8 In. 65.00
Guitar, Acoustic, Eagles, Signed By Band, 1995 .... 2300.00
Guitar, Acoustic, Hondo, Signed By 4 Members Of Country Group Alabama 172.00
Guitar, Bird's-Eye Maple Ribs, Ebony, Ivory Bands, Ivory Pegs, France, 1840, 17 In. ... 414.00
Guitar, C.F. Martin, Figured Koawood, Inlaid Strip, 1927, 19 1/16 In. 2090.00
Guitar, Darche Sucr, Rosewood Veneer Back & Sides, France, c.1835, 17 5/8 In. 1035.00
Guitar, Electric, Gibson, Rosewood Finger Board, 18 1/2 In. 862.00
Guitar, Fender, Coronado II, Electric, Blue, Yellow Trim, 1960s 1500.00
Guitar, Gibson, Les Paul Gold Top, Case, 1952 .... 4500.00
Guitar, Gibson, Sunburst Flamer Maple, 1948 .... 6500.00
Guitar, John D'Angelico, Maple Back, Sides & Neck, Pearl Inlay, 1954, 21 1/4 In. 1380.00
Guitar, Lacote School, Bird's-Eye Maple Body, Ivory Pegs, France, 1830, 17 13/16 In. .. 241.00
Guitar, Maple, Ebony, Black, Gold, Pin Bridge, Reverse Pegs, France, 1820, 17 1/8 In. .. 1955.00
Guitar, Metzler & Co., Maple Ribs, Mother-Of-Pearl Chevrons, 17 5/16 In. 805.00
Guitar, Panormo, Rosewood Ribs, Pin Bridge, England, 1838, 17 11/16 In. 1955.00
Guitar, Panormo, Rosewood Ribs, Pin Bridge, Ivory Pegs, England, 1843, 18 In. 1610.00
Guitar, Preston, Maple Ribs, Square Finial, England, 1775, 26 7/8 In. 391.00
Harmonica, Amorette, Spranger 45.00
Harmonica, Figural, Banana, I Went Bananas In San Francisco 10.00
Harmonica, Hohner, Ironclad, Box 50.00
Harmonica, Hohner, No. P4-A440, Wooden, Metal, Hohner's Trutone Pitch Pipe, Box .. 35.00
Harmonica, M. Hohner, Super Chromonia, Metal, Wooden, Box, Germany, 1900, 6 In. .. 45.00
Harp, Deires, 7 Bird's-Eye Maple Ribs, 4 Brass Lion's Paw Feet, 1850, 6 Ft. 1/4 In. 5175.00
Harp, Erard, Satinwood Body, Gilt Line Design, Spiraled Column, 1899, 5 Ft. 10 In. 5520.00
Hurdy-Gurdy, Pierced & Painted Front, Mahogany Case, 16 x 19 In. 440.00
Hurdy-Gurdy, Victor, Chlappa, 2 Barrel Cylinders 9000.00
Lute, Maple, 9 Maple Ribs, Ebony Fingerboard, Italy, 21 x 27 7/16 In. 2760.00
Lute, Rosewood, 3 Maple Ribs, 12 Ivory Frets, England, 1815, 31 1/4 In. 575.00
Mando-Cello, Gibson, Birch Back, Faux Tortoiseshell Sides, 18 1/2 In. 1880.00
Mandolin, 61 Narrow Sycamore Ribs, Mahogany, Scrollwork, Sicily, 1910, 25 In. 2760.00
Mandolin, Rosewood Ribs, Tortoiseshell Scratch Plate, Bone Pegs, 1900, 24 In. 1495.00
Melodia, Orguinette Co., New York Roller, Walnut, 12 Paper Rolls 275.00
Melody Player, Painted Tin, Crank Handle, 15 Rolls Of Tunes, 7 1/4 x 6 1/2 In. 425.00
Nickelodeon, Cremona, Style G, Keyboard Style, Player Piano, 29 Flute Pipes 13800.00
Nickelodeon, Regina Sublimo, With 5 Rolls 6000.00
Nickelodeon, Seeburg E, With Xylophone, Oak 9000.00
Nickelodeon, Seeburg, Quartersawn Oak, Leaded Glass Front, 8 Ten-Tune Rolls 9900.00
Nickelodeon, Stained Glass, Burled Walnut 4900.00
Nickelodeon, Western Electric, Mascot Cabinet, 2 Rolls 8000.00
Oboe, Delusse, 3 Keys, Ivory Finial, Round Touchpiece, 1785, 22 In. 2300.00
Oboe, Grundmann & Flot, Boxwood, 10 Keys, Silver, Ivory Mounts, 1800, 22 1/16 In. .. 506.00
Oboe, Heinz Roessler, Boxwood, 2 Keys, Brass, Ivory Mounts, 22 5/8 In. 264.00
Oboe, Sattler, Boxwood, Brass Keys, Fishtailed Touchpiece, 22 3/4 In. 4600.00
Organ, Band, 150 Spec., 129 Pipes With Drums, Cymbal 29500.00
Organ, Bijon Orchestrone, G.L. Wild & Bros., Oak, Pressed Leaf Borders, 7 Rolls 330.00
Organ, Celestina, Mechanical Orguinette Co., New York, Walnut, 6-In. Spool 385.00
Organ, Estey, Style J.J., Portable, Folding, Solid Oak, 1920s 300.00
Organ, Gem Roller, Gilt Letters, 6 1/2-In. Cobb 385.00
Organ, Grand, Oak, Black Letters, 13 1/4-In. Cobb, 9 Cobbs 3410.00

Organ, Monkey, 23 Keys 5500.00
Organ, Monkey, 31 Keys 7500.00
Organ, Monkey, Molinari, 1912, 16 x 17 x 10 In. 4800.00
Organ, Monkey, Molinari, American Songs 5500.00
Organ, Page Organ Co., Lima, Ohio 950.00
Organ, Pla Rola, Tin Lithograph Roller, Box 185.00
Organ, Portable, Circuit Preacher's, Pump, Carrying Case, 29 x 12 x 10 In. 235.00
Organ, Pump, Hamilton, High-Back Mirror, Swivel Stool, c.1891 .... 1100.00
Organ, Pump, Hillier, Baby, c.1910, 36 1/2 x 52 In. 700.00
Organ, Roller, Chautauqua, 9 Rolls, Early 1900s 1700.00
Organ, Roller, Chautauqua, Staff For Grinder's Use, Case, 18 x 15 In. 302.00
Organ, Roller, Walnut, Pressed Bands, Gold Stenciled, 8 Paper Rolls, 13 x 14 x 10 In. 385.00
Organ, Vincent Llinares, Faventia Hurdy-Gurdy, Spain, 1940-1950 .... 495.00
Organ Grinder's Box, Diorama, Animated, Germany, Late 19th Century, 8 x 14 x 7 In. .. 860.00
Organette, Ariston, Vertical, 4 Discs, 21 x 11 1/2 In. 805.00
Piano, Baldwin, Walnut, Grand, 60 x 76 In. 5750.00
Piano, Bernhardt, Mahogany, Boxwood Molding, 24 Keys, Paris, 1820, 25 1/2 In. 4140.00
Piano, Broadwood & Son, Mahogany, Satinwood Nameboard, 1802, 5 Ft. 5 In. 1437.00
Piano, Bush & Gerts, Baby Grand, 300 Rolls, 1925 .... 13000.00
Piano, Chickering, No. 163906, Mahogany, Baby Grand, 1938, 59 In. ....3750.00 to 4125.00
Piano, Chickering, Rosewood, Square, 1859 .... 3500.00
Piano, Coin-Operated, Peerless, Pneumatic 4750.00
Piano, Edwards, Mahogany, Satinwood Nameboard, 6 Reeded Legs, 1815, 4 Ft. 8 In. 1840.00
Piano, Ganer, Mahogany, Maple Nameboard, 2 Brass Handstops, 1785, 5 Ft. 2 In. 115.00
Piano, Grand, Grovesteen & Fuller, Square, Music Stand & Lyre 2500.00
Piano, Grand, Howard Piano Co., Quartersawn Oak Cabinet, c.1903, 54 3/4 In. 550.00
Piano, Grand, Marshall & Wendall, Model 7746, 1885 .... 5500.00
Piano, Kimball, Welte, Louis XVI, Matching Bench, 72 In. 2800.00
Piano, Mahogany, Player, Original Ivory Keys, Ampico, Grand, Bench, 6 1/2 In. 14500.00
Piano, Marshall & Wendall, Square Back, Grand, Albany, N.Y., 1885 .... 5500.00
Piano, Marshall & Wendell, Mahogany Case, Baby Grand, Bench, 60 In. 460.00
Piano, Mason & Hamlin, Player, Mahogany, Walnut, Grand, 69 x 62 In. 2185.00
Piano, Mehlin, Upright, Embossed Copper Floral Front, Bench, Walnut, 1891, 53 In. .. 2000.00
Piano, Orchestrelle Style V, 50 Rolls 6800.00
Piano, Player, Cable-Nelson, Burl Walnut 1750.00
Piano, Player, Chute & Butler, Dark Wood 1500.00
Piano, Player, Euphona, Bench, Roll Cabinet, 50 Rolls 2450.00
Piano, Player, Grand, Marshall & Wendell, 66 In. 2000.00
Piano, Player, Steinway, Duo-Art, Grand, 6 Ft. 1 In. 16000.00
Piano, Player, Weber, Upright, 1910 .... 1500.00
Piano, Pohlman, Mahogany, Nameboard, 2 Brass Covers, 1770, 4 Ft. 11 1/4 In. 1035.00
Piano, Reproducing, Ampico, Grand, 5 Ft. 8 In. 9000.00
Piano, Reproducing, Ampico, Knabe, Grand, 5 Ft. 4 In. 11000.00
Piano, Reproducing, Ampico, Mahogany, Grand, New Rolls, Bench, 6 1/2 Ft. 14500.00
Piano, Reproducing, Haines Ampico, Upright, Roll Cabinet, Matching Bench 9500.00
Piano, Reproducing, Steinway, Duo-Art, Upright 4995.00
Piano, Samuel Neilson, Mahogany, Rosewood, Recessed Keyboard, 69 x 27 x 36 In. 475.00
Piano, Seeburg, Pipe Organ, Wide Rolls 4575.00
Piano, Spinet, Cable-Nelson, Mahogany Veneer Case 357.00
Piano, Steinway, Black Lacquered, Reeded Baluster Turned Legs, Grand, 39 x 57 In. .. 13225.00
Piano, Steinway, No. 54804, Eastlake Carving, Baby Grand, 85 Keys, 54 x 71 In. 1100.00
Piano, Street, Cart, 1925, 22 x 11 x 24 In. 1600.00
Piano, Weber, Duo-Art Player, Grand, 6 Ft. 2 In. 12000.00
Pianoforte, Crisi, Mahogany, 4 Pedals, 3 Square Tapered Legs, 6 Ft. 11 In. 5980.00
Pianoforte, Loud & Brothers Label 4250.00
Piccolo, Wm. S. Haynes, Silver, With Case, 1920 .... 748.00
Pitch Pipe, Wooden, Late 18th Century 195.00
Pochette, Staved Back Veneered In Ivory & Tortoiseshell, Wood & Ivory Pegs, 9 In. ... 4887.00
Rolmonica, Roll Operated, Germany, 4 Rolls 225.00
Saxophone, Baritone, Adolphe Sax & Cie, Brass Tube, Keys, Paris, 40 1/2 In. 1380.00
Saxophone, Tenor, Buescher, Nickel Plated, 27 1/4 In. 100.00
Symphanola, Seeburg, Model 146M 1500.00
Tambourine, Canvas Cover, Hand Painted Landscape With Tree, 10 In. 50.00

Viola, Broad Curl, Medium Ribs, Dark Brown Finish, Mid-18th Century, 15 3/16 In. 1092.00
Viola, Enzo Arassi, Fine Grain, Brown Varnish, Case, 1921, 15 3/4 In. 2990.00
Viola, Scott L. Tribby, Fine Grain, Orange Varnish, Case, 1988, 16 1/2 In. 2415.00
Violin, Albert Deblaye, Medium Curl Scroll, Yellow, Brown, 1918, 13 15/16 In. 2070.00
Violin, Alfredo Gianotti, Medium Narrow Curl, Orange Varnish, Italy, 1976, 14 In. 3680.00
Violin, Carved African Head, Geometric Design On Back, 2-Tone Brown Finish, 24 In. ... 110.00
Violin, Edward Maday, Plain Scroll, Gold, Brown Varnish, 13 15/16 In. 862.00
Violin, Ernst Heinrich Roth, Medium Curl Scroll, Red, 1924, 14 In. 2760.00
Violin, Franz Angerer, Narrow Curl Scroll, Orange, Brown Varnish, 1906, 14 3/16 In. ... 1955.00
Violin, John L. Fawick, Bird's-Eye Maple, 1951, 14 1/8 In. 690.00
Violin, John Terry, Medium Narrow Curl, Red Varnish, 1980, 13 15/16 In. 2645.00
Violin, Joseph Delaglio, Fine Grain, Brown Varnish, Case, France, 1790, 14 In. 1380.00
Violin, Medium Curl Back, Bakelite Volume Knob, National Dobro, 14 1/8 In. 1150.00
Violin, Medium Ribs, Gold, Brown Finish, Early 19th Century, 13 15/16 In. 575.00
Violin, Mittenwald, Fine Grain, Brown Varnish, Case, 1880, 13 7/8 In. 750.00
Violin, Mittenwald, Narrow Ribs, Carved Lion's Head, Geometric Design, 14 3/16 In. .. 690.00
Violin, Vuillaume, Curl Scroll, Orange, Brown Varnish, France, 1889, 14 3/16 In. 805.00
Whistle, Pitch, Birch, American, 1 5/16 x 3 1/2 In. 45.00
Zither, Case, Pine, Rosewood Graining, White Stripes, Yellow Stars, Red Designs, 45 In. 275.00
Zonophone, Grand Opera, Glass Side 3200.00

MUSTACHE CUPS were popular from 1850 to 1900 when the large, flowing mustache was in style. A ledge of china or silver held the hair out of the liquid in the cup. This kept the mustache tidy and also kept the mustache wax from melting. Left-handed mustache cups are rare but are being reproduced.

Flowers, Gold Trim, Remember Me 50.00
Red Roses, Green, RS Prussia 200.00
Rolls-Royce 20.00
Roses, Green Leaves, Germany 55.00

NAILSEA glass was made in the Bristol district in England from 1788 to 1873. It was made by many different factories, not just the Nailsea Glass House. Many pieces were made with loopings of either white or colored glass as decoration.

Bottle, Wine, Matching Cranberry Bubble Stopper, 12 1/2 In. 245.00
Bowl, Red, Ruffled Clover Rim, 19th Century, 8 In. 468.00
Flask, Blue & White, 9 In. 275.00
Flask, Elongated Teardrop Form, Milk Glass, Blue, Rose Loopings, Pontil, 8 In. 300.00
Flask, Pink & White, 8 1/2 In. 250.00
Flask, Red & Blue Looping, Opaque White, 7 1/4 In. 165.00
Flask, Ruby Red, White Herringbone Loopings, Pontil, Oval, 1880, 7 1/8 In. 400.00
Flask, Teardrop Form, Teal Green, White Loopings, Pontil, 8 3/4 In. 240.00
Flask, White & Colorless, Double, 7 In. 275.00
Lamp, Fairy, White Loops On Medium Blue, 3 Sections, 6 1/2 x 7 In. 900.00
Nappy, Blue & White, 6 1/4 In., Pair 44.00
Pitcher, White, Pale Blue Opaque Loopings, Clear Applied Handle, 8 x 4 1/4 In. 150.00
Powder Horn, Milk Glass, Yellow Green Looped, 1850-1880, 13 In. 155.00
Rolling Pin, Aqua, Robin's-Egg Blue To Sapphire Looped, Pontil, 1850-1890, 13 In. ... 305.00
Rolling Pin, Patriotic, Red, White & Blue, 15 1/2 In. 575.00
Vase, Applied Handles, Skirted Bases, Green Satin, Flared, 10 In., Pair 440.00

NAKARA is a trade name for a white glassware made about 1900 by the C. F. Monroe Company of Meriden, Connecticut. It was decorated in pastel colors. The glass was very similar to another glass made by the company called *Wave Crest*. The company closed in 1916. Boxes for use on a dressing table are the most commonly found Nakara pieces. The mark is not found on every piece.

NAKARA

Box, Bishop's Hat, Enamel Bead Work & Apple Blossoms, 4 x 4 1/4 In. 460.00
Box, Bishop's Hat, White Flowers, Pink Centers, Yellow, Orange Ground, 5 x 5 1/2 In. .. 550.00
Box, Burmese Coloring, 18th Century Courting Couple, 6 In. 1370.00
Box, Cover, Cupid Design, Green, 3 x 6 In. 575.00
Box, Crown Mold, Green, Pink Roses, Scroll Trim, Cupid Feet, 6 1/4 x 8 In. 2100.00

Box, Dresser, Painted Pink Floral, Scroll, Blue Ground, Marked, 3 1/4 x 6 In. . . . . 725.0•
Box, Hinged Cover, Purple Iris Design, Yellow, Orange Ground, 4 x 6 In. . . . . 550.0•
Box, Hinged Cover, Purple Iris On Tan Ground, 6 In. . . . . 1035.0•
Box, Hinged, Ring, Pink, White, Signed, C.S.M. Co., 2 1/2 x 2 1/2 In. . . . . 500.0•
Box, Jewelry, Hinged Cover, Purple Violets, Yellow Ground, 4 1/2 In. . . . . 675.0•
Box, Orchid On Lid, Green, 3 1/8 x 2 3/4 In. . . . . 315.0•
Box, Pink, Hexagon, Footed, 3 In. . . . . 350.0•
Box, Portrait Of Princess Louise, Pink, Yellow Ground, Signed, 4 x 4 1/2 In. . . . . 750.0•
Box, Portrait, Gibson Girl, Blue, Yellow Ground, 4 1/2 x 2 3/4 In. . . . . 500.0•
Box, Portrait, Woman In Blue Dress With Orange Poppies, Green, Marked, 4 x 3 In. . . . . 650.0•
Box, Ring, Couple Ice Skating, Blue, Amber, 2 1/2 In. . . . . 880.0•
Box, Ring, Man & Woman In Foul Weather, Yellow, Pink Ground, Marked, 3 x 2 In. . . . . 1300.0•
Humidor, 7 Mum-Type Flowers, Enamel Centers, Shelf For Sponge, 5 3/4 In. 1495.00
Humidor, Old Sport, Transfer Of Bulldog & Mug, Silver Plated Lid, 5 In. . . . . 460.0•
Humidor, Portrait, Indian Chief, Headdress, Bead Work, Brass Lid, 7 1/2 In. 1725.00
Humidor, Whimsical Owl Perched On Tree Branch, Inverted Pear Shape, 5 1/2 In. 1495.00
Jar, Tobacco, B.P.O.E., With Elk, Lift-Off Glass Lid 1495.00

NANKING is a type of blue-and-white porcelain made in Canton, China, since the late eighteenth century. It is very similar to Canton, which is listed under its own name in this book. Both Nanking and Canton are part of a larger group now called *Chinese Export* porcelain. Nanking has a spear-and-post border and may have gold decoration.

Bowl, Scalloped Rim, Orange Peel Glaze, 10 1/4 In. 825.00
Gravy Boat, 7 In. 220.00
Platter, Coastal Village Landscape, Floral Border, Blue, White, 8 1/4 x 11 1/4 In. 200.00
Relish, Leaf Form, 8 In. 165.00
Tureen, Cover, Oval, 7 3/4 In. 82.00
Tureen, Underliner, 19th Century, 15 In. 3400.00

NAPKIN RINGS were in fashion from 1869 to about 1900. They were made of silver, porcelain, wood, and other materials. They are still being made today. The most popular rings with collectors are the silver plated figural examples. Small, realistic figures were made to hold the ring. Good and poor reproductions of the more expensive rings are now being made and collectors must be very careful.

Figural, 2 Birds, Nest, Eggs, Resting On Tree Limbs, Silver Plate, Victorian, 3 1/2 In. . . . 220.00
Figural, 2 Cockatoos, Between Rings, Silver Plate 415.00
Figural, 2 Dog Supports Ring, Silver Plate 415.00
Figural, 2 Serpents, Supporting Ring Between Tails, Quadruple Plate, Victorian 303.00
Figural, 2 Swans Supporting Ring, Silver Plate 65.00
Figural, Bird, Ring On Back, Silver Plate 33.00
Figural, Boy Feeds Dog, Silver Plate 55.00
Figural, Boy Pushes Ring With Barrel, Silver Plate 415.00
Figural, Boy Pushing Ring, Kate Greenaway, Silver Plate 750.00
Figural, Boy Rolling A Hoop, Quadruple Plate, Victorian, 2 1/2 In. 192.00
Figural, Cat Beside Ring, Silver Plate 33.00
Figural, Cherub Pulling Cart, Ring On Top, Silver Plate 100.00
Figural, Cherubs Dancing, Floral Garlands, Shreve & Co., Silver Plate, c.1900, 2 In. 345.00
Figural, Deer, Ring On Back, Silver Plate 800.00
Figural, Dog At Base Of Ring, Cat Above, Silver Plate 302.00
Figural, Engraved Canadian Rifle League, Barrel Shape, Silver Plate 54.00
Figural, Girl Supporting Toothpick Holder, Floral Base, Quadruple Plate, 5 In. 385.00
Figural, Horse Drawn Cart, Floral Chased, Quadruple Plate, Meriden, Victorian 303.00
Figural, Hunting Dog, Supporting Ring, Silver Plate 253.00
Figural, Kate Greenaway Style Girl, Next To Ring, Middletown, Silver Plate 65.00
Figural, Kate Greenaway Style Sailor Boy, Next To Ring, Silver Plate 55.00
Figural, Large Chick Beside Ring, Silver Plate 415.00
Figural, Little Bopeep, Silver Plate 195.00
Figural, Nude Child Pushing Ring, Rogers, Silver Plate 45.00
Figural, Open Rose, Leaves & Stem, Silver Plate 165.00
Figural, Owl, Glass Eyes, Wilcox, Silver Plate 250.00
Figural, Parrot Beside Engraved Ring, Silver Plate 231.00

Figural, Pear, Leaf Pedestal, Quadruple Plate, Victorian, 3 In.	165.00
Figural, Squirrel Holding Nut, Reed & Barton	150.00
Figural, Squirrels With Nuts, Each Side Of Ring, Oval Base, Hartford Silver Plate Co.	145.00
Figural, Winged Cherub Next To Ring, Southington, Silver Plate	77.00
Figural, Winged Cherub On Each Side Of Ring, Webster, Silver Plate	55.00
Figural, Winged Cherub Pulling Ring On Sled, Silver Plate	33.00
Figural, Woman On Rock, Next To Ring, Meriden, Silver Plate	120.00
Plastic, Chicken, Yellow, Bright Orange Beak, 2 1/2 x 3 In.	30.00
Plastic, Rocking Horse, Inlaid Eye	72.00
Plastic, Round, Carved	15.00
Plastic, Scotty Dog, Yellow	35.00

NASH glass was made in Corona, New York, from about 1928 to 1931.
A. Douglas Nash bought the Corona glassworks from Louis C. Tiffany
in 1928 and founded the A. Douglas Nash Corporation with support
from his father, Arthur J. Nash. Arthur had worked at the Webb factory
in England and for the Tiffany Glassworks in Corona.

NASH

Bowl, Scalloped Rim, Gold Iridescent, Signed, 8 3/4 In.	303.00
Candlestick, Uneven Golden Luster, Walled Ribbed Holder, Signed, 3 3/4 In., Pair	575.00
Cordial, Red, Silver Chintz, 4 In.	650.00
Dish, Molded Leaf Design, Lustrous Gold Iridescence Overall, Amber, 5 In.	295.00
Vase, Alternating, Wide & Narrow Vertical Silver Stripes, Red, 5 1/2 In.	978.00
Vase, Black, Brown, Gray Striped Herringbone Design, 5 1/2 In.	172.00
Vase, Purple, Blue, Green, Oil Spot Design, Everted Rim, 1920s, 8 1/4 In.	517.00
Vase, Swags, Blue, Green Stripes, Signed, 9 1/2 x 4 1/2 In.	425.00

NAUTICAL antiques are listed in this category. Any of the many objects
that were made or used by the seafaring trade, including ship parts,
models, and tools, are included. Other pieces may be found listed
under Scrimshaw.

Anchor, Iron, Early 19th Century, 60 x 36 In.	695.00
Anchor, Spade Ends, 33 1/2 In.	125.00
Anchor, W.C. & Co., Navy, Salesman's Sample, Cast Iron, Pat. 1912, 12 x 6 1/2 In.	60.00
Ashtray Set, Holland America Line, 6 Piece	135.00
Ax, Boarding, Belt, Revolutionary War Era, 6 1/8-In. Blade	285.00
Ax, Boarding, Naval, Revolutionary War, 15 3/4 In.	795.00
Baggage Tag, Cunard White Star Line, Depicts Queen Mary, c.1951, 6 1/2 x 4 In.	34.00
Bell, Brass, Iron Clapper & Terminal, 19th Century, 11 1/2 x 12 In.	800.00
Bell, Schatz, Mahogany & Brass Ship's Wheel Form, 13 In.	325.00
Bell, Solid Bronze, 19th Century, 16 x 14 In.	2200.00
Bellows Foghorn, Military, Japan, 1943	230.00
Cannon, Hutchinson, Mahogany Carriage, Leather Bound Wheels, 26-In. Barrel	6600.00
Canoe, Birch Bark, 14 Ft.	2400.00
Canoe, Maker Old Hickory, Metal, 4 Sections, Patent 1894	1800.00
Cask, Water, Lifeboat, Handle, Wooden	65.00
Chain, Anchor, Hand Forged, Early 1800s	75.00
Chest, Lift Top, Interior Ditty Box, Painted Green, 18 x 41 1/2 In.	247.00
Chest, Painting Of Full-Rigged Sailing Ship On Lid	1980.00
Chest, Pine, Sailor's, Domed Lid, Seal Skin Cover, Handmade Nails & Hardware, 24 In.	275.00
Chronometer, Hamilton, Marine Deck, Quartz, Mahogany Box, 4 1/2 In.	1150.00
Clock, Chelsea, 24-Hour Dial, Dated 1965	275.00
Clock, Chelsea, Bronze Case, Silvered & Sealed Dial	2585.00
Clock, Chelsea, Bronze Case, Silvered Dial, 5 1/2 In.	295.00
Clock, Knoblich, Brass Mounts, Fitted In Mahogany Box, Glass Window, 10 x 12 In.	1215.00
Clock, Seth Thomas, 31-Day Wind, Solid Brass & Wood, 1950s, 9 x 10 1/2 In.	265.00
Clock, Seth Thomas, U.S. Navy, Mark 1, Plastic, 3 7/8 x 5 In.	55.00
Clock, Trophy, Ship's Wheel Frame, New Haven Yacht Club, June 1886	1850.00
Compass, Brass, Colored Ball Handles, 13 x 20 1/2 In.	385.00
Compass, Stanley, Interior Mirrored Cover, Hinged Guide, Brass, 3 1/4 In.	198.00
Compass, Wooden Box, A. Lietz Co., San Francisco, 4 3/4 x 9 1/4 In.	185.00
Deck Chair, R.M.S. Queen Mary, Teakwood, Vertical Slats, 33 1/2 In., Pair	3220.00
Diorama, Sailboat, Lighthouse, Dinghy, Shadow Box, 1900, 18 x 12 In.	325.00
Document, Maritime, Boston Area, 1770s, 8 Piece	95.00

Figurehead, Angel Of Waves, Brass 660.00

Flare Gun, Trumpet Barrel, Operable 75.00

Flenser, Cast Steel, H.N. Dean, c.1850, 33 In. 290.00

Flenser, Hand Forged, 8 7/8 x 11 In. 130.00

Foghorn, Brass Horn & Crank, Wooden Case 250.00

Gun, Flare, To Assist In Emergencies 330.00

Harpoon, 3 Toggle, 19th Century, 23 1/4 To 36 1/4 In. 1495.00

Harpoon, Toggle, Mounted On Pole, 19th Century, 99 1/2 In. 1265.00

Harpoon, Whaler's, Wooden, Steel & Brass Shaft, Rope Tie, 93 In. 805.00

Helmet, Diving, TSK Diving Co., Japan, Pre-1944 .... 2695.00

Helmet, Diving, Window At Top & Sides, Galvanized Iron 825.00

Horn, Steamship, Brass, 20 In. 275.00

Horn, Swedish Label, Tyfon Patent, Brass, 22 1/4 In. 302.00

Kettle, Box Shape, English, c.1875 .... 1200.00

Knife, Sailor's, Horn Handle, Folding, Blade, 2 7/16 In. 95.00

Knife, Sailor's, Horn Handle, Folding, Blade, 3 7/8 In. 130.00

Lamp, Boat Bow, Kerosene, Patent 1913 .... 145.00

Lamp, Port & Starboard, Brass, Pair 1250.00

Lantern, Masthead, Cranberry Lens, Reverse Coin Dot Design, 1850s 4600.00

Lodestone, Oval Sterling Silver Container, Inside Magnetic Rock, 1 In. 7700.00

Medical Chest, Burled Mahogany, Felt Liner, 16 Bottles, Glass Mortar & Pestle, 8 In. .. 1800.00

Megaphone, Sailing Ship, Tin, 17 7/8 In. 135.00

Menu, SS Manhattan, United States Lines, Arch Of Triumph, 4 Pages, 6 x 10 In, 4 Piece . 28.00

Model, 2-Masted Schooner Yacht, Painted, Case, c.1900, 38 x 39 1/2 In. 2760.00

Model, 2-Masted Schooner, Shades Of Purple & Black, 76 x 84 In. 977.00

Model, 2-Masted Schooner, Under Sail, Shadowbox, 15 3/8 x 24 In. 546.00

Model, 3-Decked Steamboat, Livonia, Boiler, Furniture, Tin Lifeboat, Anchors, 43 In. 5959.00

Model, 3-Masted Schooner, Painted, 20th Century, 2 3/4 x 5 1/8 In. 287.00

Model, 3-Masted, Rigging & Sails, Dories 55.00

Model, America's Cup Yacht, Cased, 23 In. 1870.00

Model, Australian Clipper, Champion Of The Seas, Glass Case, 19 In. 305.00

Model, Boat Hull, Emily, With Rudder, Dark Finish, 26 In. 1430.00

Model, Cabin Cruiser, Sea Commander, Radio Controlled, Unused, 36 In. 595.00

Model, Canal Dredging Barge, Wood & Tin, c.1930, 15 1/2 In. 125.00

Model, Canoe, 1 Piece Pine, Mortised Seats & Deck, 1930, 12 5/8 In. 85.00

Model, Chris Craft Cabin Cruiser, Wooden, 1955 .... 750.00

Model, Clipper Ship, Ivory, Anchors, Boats, Glass Mahogany Box, 6 1/4 x 5 1/2 In. 920.00

Model, Half-Hull, Dark Hull, Cream Sails On Blue, Red Frame, 15 x 19 In. 750.00

Model, Half-Hull, Stained Wood, 19th Century, 37 1/2 In. 690.00

Model, Paris River Yacht, Clockwork Mechanism, Carette Hull, Enameled Tinplate 2200.00

Model, Prisoner Of War, 3-Masted, 82 Guns, Bone & Baleen, Mirrored Case, 11 In. ... 9775.00

Model, Sailing Ship, America, Sterling Silver, Wooden Base, 13 1/4 In. 357.00

Model, Sailing Ship, Bone, c.1870 .... 9750.00

Model, Sailing Ship, Intrepid, Sterling Silver, Wooden Base, 13 In. 265.00

Model, Sailing Ship, Wooden Sails, P. Rey, 1860s, 45 x 32 In. 435.00

Model, Ship In Bottle, 13 In. 65.00

Model, Ship, 3-Masted, Pine Hull, Cabins, 2 Lifeboats, 38 In. 70.00

Model, USS Constitution, 50 Mounted Cannons, Copper At Waterline, Case 2970.00

Model, USS Maine, Rigged Masts, Searchlight, Anchors, Display Case, 17 x 40 In. ... 2070.00

Model, Whaling Longboat, Whalebone, Held All Equipment, 1870s 1430.00

Model, Yacht, Steam, Sail, Brass Mounts, Original Engine ....*Illus* 2860.00

Model, Yacht, W.W. Massie, Case, Early 20th Century, 38 In. ....*Illus* 2860.00

Motor, Outboard, Johnson, 1929, 1/2 Hp. 300.00

Motor, Outboard, Johnson, 1934, 3 Hp. 200.00

Navy Transit, Surveyor's, Keuffel & Esser Co., Wooden Box, 1869, 14 1/4 In. 385.00

Nut Dish, Cunard Line, Foley Bone China, Small, 5 Piece 60.00

Paddle, North Star Canoe, Painted Design 75.00

Plate, Eastern Steamship Lines, Black Glass, Gold Letters, Caribbean Map, 5 x 8 In. 3.00

Propeller, Brass, 16 1/2 In. 55.00

Propeller, Mercury-Kiehaeffer, Brass, Box 50.00

Quadrant, Edmund Gunter, Brass, Stamped Latitude & Months, 1600s 6325.00

Quadrant, Gunner's, Wooden Box, 6 x 7 In. 85.00

Rule, Dolland, London, Brass, Engraved Tables, Scales & Angles, 1800s, 6 1/4 In. 145.00

Nautical, Model, Yacht, Steam, Sail, Brass
Mounts, Original Engine

Nautical, Model, Yacht, W.W. Massie, Case,
Early 20th Century, 38 In.

Sailor's Valentine, Forget-Me-Not, Shells & Colors, 18 In.	2310.00
Sailor's Valentine, Nude In A Nautilus, Shellwork, B.A. Woodman, 20 In.	5500.00
Scissors, Cutting Sail Canvas, Brass Handles, 13 In.	154.00
Sea Chest, Painted House & Farm Scenes, 1880s, 18 x 30 x 20 In.	1125.00
Sextant, Simex Mariner, Brass, Felt-Lined Mahogany Box, Japan, 9 1/2 In.	460.00
Sextant, Whitehead, London, Brass, Eye Pieces, Mahogany Case, 19th Century, 10 In.	440.00
Ship Model, see Nautical, Model.	
Shoes, Diver's, Canvas, Back & Heel Reinforced Leather, Toe Plate, Corrugated Sole	330.00
Sight, Brass Compass Plate, Bubble Level, Gimbal Mounted, Wooden Base	190.00
Sugar & Creamer, Cunard Steamship, Foley Bone China	35.00
Sundial, Diptych, Joanne Murero Tigurino, 1611, 2 5/8 x 3 5/8 In.	4125.00
Sundial, Silver Plate Base, Pierced Shadow Triangle, Brass & Tortoiseshell Case	3850.00
Telegraph, Engine Room, Bell Rang To Signal Bridge	450.00
Telegraph, Jos. Harper & Son Co., New York, NY, Brass, 16 1/2 x 21 In.	460.00
Telegraph Wheel, Teleflex Products Ltd., London Ships, Iron, Metal, 12 x 3 1/2 In.	220.00
Telescope, 4-Draw, Brass, Sliding Eyepiece Protector	125.00
Telescope, Alidade MKIII Model, Brass, 5 1/2 x 15 1/2 In.	45.00
Telescope, Dolland, London, Brass	2750.00
Telescope, H.C.M., Saegmuller's Pat. Mar. 17, 1908, 16 1/2 x 2 In.	90.00
Telescope, Hayward Lumber & Inv. Co., U.S. Navy, Wooden Box, 30 1/2 x 2 1/2 In.	320.00
Telescope, Navy, Brass, 7 x 12 1/8 x 8 In.	55.00
Theodolite, Meteorology Or Navigation, Improved Compass, Eames, c.1835	6105.00
Timetable, Grand Trunk Pacific Steamships To Alaska, 1916	65.00
Timetable, Pacific Steamship Co., 1923	45.00
Tip Tray, American Line, Philadelphia, Queenstown, Liverpool	210.00
Tip Tray, Cleveland & Buffalo, Daily, 8 P.M.	210.00
Watch, Deck, Waltham, 8-Day Movement, Gimbal Mounted In Mahogany Case	550.00
Wheel, Ship's, Carving Of Captain With Pipe Center	95.00
Wheel, Ship's, John Hastie & Company, Wood & Brass	695.00
Wheel, Ship's, Mahogany & Brass, 30 In.	265.00
Wheel, Ship's, Mahogany & Oak, Brass Screws, c.1900, 48 In.	550.00
Wheel, Ship's, Mahogany, Brass Inlaid, 27 In.	230.00
Wheel, Ship's, Pegged Joinery, Spokes Set In Hub, Extended Through Hub, Mahogany	4400.00
Whistle, Brass, 4 x 15 In.	350.00
Yacht, Pond, Gaff Rigged, 36 x 26 In.	1175.00

NETSUKES are small ivory, wood, metal, or porcelain pieces used as toggles on the end of the cord that held a Japanese money pouch. The earliest date from the sixteenth century. Many are miniature, carved works of art.

Amber, Dozing Figure With Fan, Signed, 2 In.	460.00
Bamboo, Herd Boy Resting On Back Of Water Buffalo, 19th Century	358.00
Bone, Ball Form, Endless Knot Design, 19th Century	165.00
Bone, Man, Wearing A Cape	165.00
Bone, Nio, Standing, Early 19th Century	220.00
Bone, Sennin, Holding Lotus Blossom, Standing	165.00
Boxwood, 2 Mushroom Heads, Single Stem, 19th Century, 1 3/4 In.	316.00
Boxwood, Cobra, Coiled Position, Inlaid Eyes, 19th Century, 1 3/4 In.	374.00

Boxwood, Gourd, Lobed Form, Single Curling Stalk, 19th Century, 1 1/2 In. 201.00
Coral, Fish, Swimming, Horn Inlaid Eyes 220.00
Ebony, Deer Form, Horn Inlaid Eyes, Signed 220.00
Horn, Kappa With A Gourd Bottle, Riding On Thunder Fish, Signed, Koetsu 220.00
Ivory, 2 Men Neck Wrestling, Signed, 1 3/4 In. 143.00
Ivory, 2 Shishi, 1 Emerging From A Brocade Ball, Signed, Anraku 880.00
Ivory, 2 Stirrups, 19th Century 550.00
Ivory, 7 Shells Piled Together, Signed, Korai, 19th Century 440.00
Ivory, Badger Priest, Signed 275.00
Ivory, Clam's Dream With Crab Detail, 1900 .... 275.00
Ivory, Deity, Man's Body, Boar's Head, Signed 180.00
Ivory, Demon, Stomping Through Flower Garden, Signed, Ryugyoku, 1800 .... 2200.00
Ivory, Dog With Bell, 19th Century, 1 1/4 In. 1380.00
Ivory, Dutchman, With A Hailing Trumpet, 19th Century 3080.00
Ivory, Evil Spirits, Humanoid Bodies, Horned Heads, Seiji, 2 In. 3450.00
Ivory, Figure, Standing, Hiding A Double Gourd Behind His Back, 19th Century 770.00
Ivory, Group Of Gourds & Vines, Early 19th Century 688.00
Ivory, Guardian Lion, Loose Ball In His Mouth, 19th Century 330.00
Ivory, Horse, Feeding, Kyoto School Figure, 18th Century 1595.00
Ivory, Jutsusai, Apsara In Flight, Lotus Blossom In Her Hands, Signed, 19th Century ... 1870.00
Ivory, Karako, Climbing A Bamboo Shoot, 18th Century 2145.00
Ivory, Karako, Wearing A Fox Mask, Meiji Period, Shomin 990.00
Ivory, Kenzan, Standing, Leaning Against Her Broom, Original Patina, 18th Century 1540.00
Ivory, Kintaro, Back Of Large Boar, Signed, Tama, 20th Century 385.00
Ivory, Kirin, Stands Upon An Oval Base, Early 19th Century 468.00
Ivory, Kneeling Woman, Holding Pipe, 1 5/8 In. 92.00
Ivory, Longevity Figure, Small Child Alongside, 2 In. 115.00
Ivory, Man Brewing Pot Of Tea, 1 5/8 In. 110.00
Ivory, Man Drinking From Double Gourd Bottle 63.00
Ivory, Man Holding Badger Down, 1 3/4 In. 546.00
Ivory, Man, Employing A Back-Scratcher, Signed, Early 19th Century 412.00
Ivory, Man, Leaves, Signed 225.00
Ivory, Mo/So, The Dutiful Son, Japan, 2 1/4 In. 633.00
Ivory, Monkey, Wearing A Brocade Jacket, Holding Onto A Tree Branch, Kachoku 358.00
Ivory, Pile Of Decaying Coins, 1800 .... 688.00
Ivory, Pumpkin, Movable Worm Appearing From Hole, 18th Century 143.00
Ivory, Rabbit, Japan, 2 1/4 In. 748.00
Ivory, Rat Form, Horn Inlaid Eyes, Using Abacus, 19th Century 468.00
Ivory, Rat, Seated, Holding His Own Tail, Signed, Tomokazu, Late 19th Century, 2 In. .. 660.00
Ivory, Seated Boy, Arms Folded, Large Hat, Signed, 2 In. 230.00
Ivory, Seated Man, Making Sake, 2 In. 172.00
Ivory, Seated Man, With Drum & Monkey Perched On Shoulder, 1 5/8 In. 115.00
Ivory, Sennin, Riding On Back Of Thunderfish, Signed, Tomotada, 20th Century 248.00
Ivory, Shishi, Seated On Flower Form Pedestal, 19th Century 412.00
Ivory, Sparrow, Tongue-Cut, Inlaid Eyes, Signed, Gyokuyosai, Early 19th Century 715.00
Ivory, Tea Whisk Form, Bamboo Handle, 19th Century 440.00
Ivory, Tortoise Emerging From Pile Of Shells, 18th Century 880.00
Ivory, Two Men Locked In Combat, 19th Century 862.00
Ivory, Warrior, Holding A Shield, 2 1/2 In. 1650.00
Wood, 2 Clam Shells, Resting On Awabi Shell, Signed, Tomonobu 990.00
Wood, 3 Puppies, Ball Shape, Signed, Tomokazu 1100.00
Wood, 9 Shiitake Mushrooms, Flower Form, 18th Century 192.00
Wood, Blind Man Threshing Wheat Using Tree Stump, 19th Century 220.00
Wood, Bone, Bird's Skull Form 220.00
Wood, Man, Wearing Geta, Holding A Lantern, 18th Century 770.00
Wood, Oni Leaning On Stump, Horn Inlaid Eyes, Signed, 1 1/16 In. 297.00
Wood, Peach Boy Emerging From A Peach, Signed, Jugyoku, Early 19th Century 550.00
Wood, Sage, Riding On A Mule, Seal Type, 18th Century 605.00
Wood, Shishi, Seated On Rectangular Platform, Signed, Koen, 19th Century 385.00
Wood, Shojo Figure, Sleeping, Signed, 19th Century 825.00
Wood, Shojo, Seated, Holding A Dipper, Signed, Shuzan, 19th Century 165.00
Wood, Stylized Bat In Flight, Signed, 19th Century 495.00

NEW HALL Porcelain Manufactory was started at Newhall, Shelton, Staffordshire, England, in 1782. Simple decorated wares were made. Between 1810 and 1825, the factory made a glassy bone porcelain sometimes marked with the factory name. Do not confuse New Hall porcelain with the pieces made by the New Hall Pottery Company, Ltd., a twentieth-century firm.

New Hall

Coffee, Tea Service, Blue, White, Floral Border, Gilt Edge Rim, 1782, 8 Piece	1035.00
Coffee, Tea Service, Blue, White, Fluted, Underglaze Blue, Twisted Tree, 11 Piece	345.00
Coffee, Tea Service, Wedge Shape, Underglaze Blue, 1785, 9 Piece	2645.00
Cream Jug, Floral Spray, Sprigs, Rose Trelliswork Border	1100.00
Tea Set, Polychrome Floral, Border Design, 18 Piece	1430.00
Teapot, Pink & Green Florals & Sprigs, Pearlware, 1790, 6 1/2 In.	375.00

NEW MARTINSVILLE Glass Manufacturing Company was established in 1901 in New Martinsville, West Virginia. It was bought and renamed the Viking Glass Company in 1944. In 1987 Kenneth Dalzell, former president of Fostoria Glass Company, purchased the factory and renamed it Dalzell-Viking.

Bookend, Clipper Ship, Crystal, Pair	125.00
Bowl, Janice, Blue, 9 In.	65.00
Bowl, Prelude, Crimped Edge, 14 1/2 In.	45.00
Butter, Metal Cover, Moondrops, Red	75.00
Cake Salver, Prelude	57.00
Candlestick, 2-Light, Janice, Blue, Pair	125.00
Cologne, Pink, Stopper, Octagonal	95.00
Decanter Set, Moondrops, 8 In., 6 Piece	80.00
Dish, Mayonnaise, Moondrops, Light Green	50.00
Dresser Set, Tray, Pink, 4 3/4 x 9 1/4 In.	27.00
Figurine, 2 Seals With Ball	100.00
Figurine, Baby Bear	50.00
Figurine, Baby Bear, Sun Colored	35.00
Figurine, Horse, Head Up	90.00
Figurine, Mama Bear	225.00
Figurine, Papa Bear	200.00
Figurine, Papa Bear, Satinized	225.00
Figurine, Piglet, Standing	145.00
Figurine, Squirrel, On Base	45.00
Figurine, Swan, Janice, 12 In.	55.00
Figurine, Tiger, Head Up	175.00
Goblet, Cordial, Moondrops, Cobalt	45.00
Plate, Prelude, 16 In.	85.00
Punch Bowl, Radiance, Flared, 14 1/2 In.	100.00
Server, Center Handle, Prelude	55.00 to 60.00
Torte Plate, Prelude, 15 In.	60.00

NEWCOMB Pottery was founded by Ellsworth and William Woodward at Sophie Newcomb College, New Orleans, Louisiana, in 1895. The work continued through the 1940s. Pieces of this art pottery are marked with the printed letters *NC* and often have the incised initials of the artist as well. Most pieces have a matte glaze and incised decoration.

Bowl, 6 Pink Flowers, Green Leaf Design, Light Green Band, Pink Ground, 5 x 4 In.	605.00
Bowl, Blue Flower Frog, Yellow Flowers, Blue Ground, Sadie Irvine, 8 x 3 In.	1210.00
Bowl, Buffalo, Blue, Cream Ground, 4 1/2 x 3 In.	665.00
Bowl, Flowers, White, Yellow, Blue, Green Leaves, Anna F. Simpson, 7 x 2 1/2 In.	1000.00
Bowl, Green, Blue Flowers, Cream, Blue Ground, Mary Butler, 3 x 6 In.	4400.00
Bowl, Painted Leaves, Blue High Glaze, May Louise Dunn, 8 1/2 x 3 In.	1320.00
Bowl, Pink Flowers, Green Leaves, Blue Ground, Joseph Meyer, 1924, 9 1/2 In.	9200.00
Bowl, White, Yellow Flowers, Green Leaves Top Edge, 6 1/2 x 4 1/2 In.	1210.00
Coaster, Lily Design, 3 1/2 In.	500.00
Flower Frog, Shell, Cream, Light Blue Matte Glaze, Marked, C.L., 3 x 2 In.	285.00
Inkwell, Bell Shape, Green, White Flowers, Blue, Yellow Ground, M. Butler, 3 x 3 In.	1430.00

Jar, Temple, Lily-Of-The-Valley Design, Light Blue Ground, A. Simpson, 1930, 6 In. 1650.00

Mug, 5 Rabbits Running, Seated In The Woods, Blue Ground, J. Meyer, 4 x 5 In. 4315.00

Pitcher, Green Glaze, Speckled Blue, Handle, 4 In. 190.00

Pitcher, Milk, Orange Stylized Blossoms, Dark Blue, Blue Green, Payne, 5 x 4 In. 3850.00

Plaque, Scenic Design, Hanging Spanish Moss, Oak Tree, H. Bailey, Frame, 14 In. 1650.00

Tile, Roses, Deep Pink, Yellow Centers, Green Leaves, Blue Ground, S. Irvine, 3 In. 825.00

Tile, Unglazed Squares Design, Henrietta Bailey, Square, 4 1/2 In. 410.00

Toothpick Holder, Floral, White, Blue, Yellow Matte Glaze, Sadie Irvine, 3 x 2 In. 775.00

Trivet, Incised Border Of Leaves, Dark Blue, Light Blue Matte Ground, 4 In. 825.00

Tyg, Painted Stylized Blossoms, Blue, H. Joor & J. Meyer, 7 x 6 In. 7150.00

Vase, 2 Mountain Goats On Brown Hillside, Brown, Blue Ground, 6 1/4 In. 880.00

Vase, 3 Spanish Moss Trees, Large Moon, Henrietta Bailey, 6 x 8 In. 920.00

Vase, 5 Live Oak Trees With Spanish Moss, Deep, Light Blue, A. Simpson, 5 x 6 In. 4600.00

Vase, Abstract Linear, Cobalt Blue, Blue Green, White Ground, Wells, 1904, 6 In. 3850.00

Vase, Band Of Stylized Flowers, White Ground, Sabrina Wells, 1904, 9 1/2 In. 8250.00

Vase, Berry Design, Wine, Cylindrical, Joseph Meyer, 1909, 6 1/4 In. 3850.00

Vase, Blue Cypress Trees, Full Moon, Anna Frances Simpson, 1916, 4 In. .... *Illus* 1760.00

Vase, Blue Matte Glaze, Hand Thrown, Joseph Meyer, 4 1/2 In. 385.00

Vase, Blue, Rose Matte Glaze, Blue, Red, Green Drip, Joseph Meyer, 8 1/2 In. 885.00

Vase, Canopy Of Spanish Moss, Transparent Glaze, Joseph Meyer, 6 1/2 In. 3680.00

Vase, Carved & Painted Blossoms, Pink & Blue, Simpson & Holt, 5 1/2 In. 1650.00

Vase, Carved & Painted Blue Trees, Matte Glaze, Irvine & Holt, 4 In. 1650.00

Vase, Carved & Painted Jonquil Band, Dark Blue Ground, Bailey & Meyer, 7 x 4 In. 1320.00

Vase, Carved & Painted Light & Blue Columns & Blossoms, LeBlanc, 6 x 4 In. 2310.00

Vase, Carved Floral Sprays, Light Green, Blue, Bulbous, 8 1/4 x 5 In. 2300.00

Vase, Carved Panel Design, Pink, Blue Matte Glaze, Sadie Irvine, 3 1/2 In. 935.00

Vase, Carved Pink, Yellow, Green Butterflies, Grass, 4 1/4 In. 1760.00

Vase, Carved, Painted Landscape Design, Pine Trees, Marked, M. LeBlanc, 12 In. 6600.00

Vase, Carved, Painted Spanish Design, Green, White, Blue, Sadie Irvine, 4 x 3 In 1540.00

Vase, Carved, Painted White Lily Of Valley, Light Blue Ground, May Dunn, 2 In. 2310.00

Vase, Carved, Painted, Landscape Design, Moss Oaks, Blue, Sadie Irvine, 3 x 2 In. 2310.00

Vase, Cotton Plants, Light Blue Ground, Mazie T. Ryan, 1904, 6 In. 6325.00

Vase, Cream, Blue, Pale Green, Blue Ground, Mary Sheerer, 1909, 10 In. 4125.00

Vase, Daffodil Design, Cream, Blue, Green Stems, Leaves, Green, Blue Glaze, 6 In. 1650.00

Vase, Floral, Blue, Light Green Stems, Leaves, 9 In. 1210.00

Vase, Flowers, Orange To Dark Green, 6 x 3 1/2 In. 495.00

Vase, Geometric Design, Blue, Rose, Green, Signed, Anna Simpson, 7 In. 2530.00

Vase, Green High Glaze Drip Over Orange Matte, Hand Thrown, J. Meyer, 4 1/2 In. 600.00

Vase, Green Sheaves Of Wheat, Blue Ground, Henrietta Bailey, 1909, 9 1/2 In. 4125.00

Vase, Green, Gunmetal Drip Glaze Over Blue Matte Glaze, Joseph Meyer, 3 In. 230.00

Vase, Green, Gunmetal Drip Glaze Over Cream, 2 1/2 In. 275.00

Vase, Green, Gunmetal Drip Glaze Over Red Clay Body, Joseph Meyer, 3 1/2 In. 465.00

Vase, Green, Gunmetal To Brown Glaze, Impressed Mark, 3 In. 385.00

Vase, Incised Cypress Design, Blue, Green, Joseph Meyer, 1910, 12 1/2 In. 2300.00

Vase, Incised Design, Sky Blue, White Clay Body, 1932, 2 1/2 In. 600.00

Vase, Incised Drooping Daffodils, Green Leaves, Blue Matte Glaze, 6 In. 2970.00

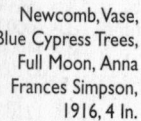
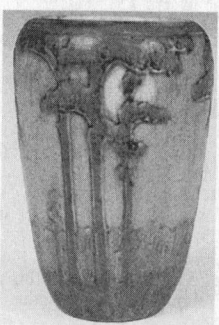
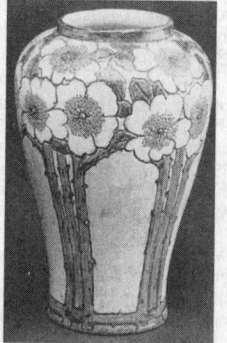

Newcomb, Vase,
Blue Cypress Trees,
Full Moon, Anna
Frances Simpson,
1916, 4 In.

Newcomb, Vase,
White & Amber
Roses, Hattie Joor,
1903, 9 x 5 1/2 In.

Vase, Ivory, Brown, Green Glaze, Marked, Joseph Meyer, 8 In. 330.00
Vase, Landscape, Southern Pine Trees, Blue, Green Matte Glaze, A. Simpson, 9 In. 3850.00
Vase, Landscape, Tall Pines, Blue Trunks, Pink, Blue Sky, Sadie Irvine, 10 1/2 In. 8250.00
Vase, Landscape, Trees, Green Leaves, Blue Trunks, Yellow Moon, S. Irvine, 5 1/2 In. ... 2860.00
Vase, Light Blue Irises, Dark Blue, Green Leaves, Sadie Irvine, 9 x 3 1/4 In. 3300.00
Vase, Moon & Spanish Moss, White Clay Body, Sadie Irvine, 10 5/8 In. 8250.00
Vase, Moon Peaking Through Live Oaks, Spanish Moss, H. Bailey, 1933, 3 x 5 In. 2860.00
Vase, Moon Shining Through Tree, Draped In Moss, 7 In. 3500.00
Vase, Oak Trees, Spanish Moss, Celadon & Blue, Sadie Irvine, 1928, 6 1/4 In. 1800.00
Vase, Painted Blossoms, Blue & Green Ground, H. Bailey & J. Meyer, 5 1/2 In. 2860.00
Vase, Painted Landscape, Blue & Green Matte Glaze, Sadie Irvine, 8 In. 2750.00
Vase, Pale Blue Blossoms, Blue & Green Ground, 4 Handles, C. Labouisse, 4 1/2 In. 2200.00
Vase, Palm Trees, Blue, Green Matte Glaze, 1913, 14 x 8 In. 2750.00
Vase, Pear Shape, Pink Pussy Willows, Purple Ground, Sadie Irvine, 5 x 4 In. 2310.00
Vase, Purple Berries, Green Leaves, Blue Ground, A. Mason, 3 x 3 1/2 In. 1650.00
Vase, Rose Colored Flowers, Cream Centers, Navy Blue Ground, S. Irvine, 8 In. 4400.00
Vase, Rose Colored Pinecones, Green Needles, Blue Ground, H. Bailey, 10 1/2 In. 4950.00
Vase, Southern Pines, Outlined On Blue Ground, Sadie Irvine, 1918, 13 1/2 In. 7700.00
Vase, Spanish Moss Over Live Oak Scene, Squat, 1920, 6 1/2 x 8 In. 5225.00
Vase, Stylized Blue Flowers, White Columns, Marie LeBlanc, 4 1/2 In. 3300.00
Vase, Stylized Floral Design, Cream, Blue, Green Matte Glaze, 5 1/2 In. 1650.00
Vase, Stylized Leaves, Tapered Top, Blue Ground, 1926, 8 1/2 x 3 1/2 In. 1980.00
Vase, Stylized Tulip Design, Blue, Green Glaze, White Clay Body, 7 7/8 In. 4675.00
Vase, Stylized Wild Roses, White, Green Stems, White Ground, H. Joor, 1903, 9 In. 14300.00
Vase, Trees, Blue Hills & Sky, Yellow Moon, Anna Simpson, 5 In. 1430.00
Vase, Urn Shape, Yellow, Green Yucca Plants, Light Blue, Green Ground, 7 x 3 In. 7150.00
Vase, White & Amber Roses, Hattie Joor, 1903, 9 x 5 1/2 In. ....*Illus* 14300.00
Vase, White, Yellow Roses, Blue, Green Ground, Henrietta Bailey, 1914, 3 x 6 In. 1870.00
Vase, Yellow Daisies, Ivory, Light Blue Ground, Desiree Roman, 1903, 5 x 5 In. 7150.00

NILOAK Pottery (Kaolin spelled backward) was made at the Hyten Brothers Pottery in Benton, Arkansas, between 1909 and 1946. Although the factory did make cast and molded wares, collectors are most interested in the marbleized art pottery line made of colored swirls of clay. It was called *Mission Ware*. By 1931 the company made cast-ware, and many of these pieces were marked with the name Hywood.

NILOAK

Ashtray, Match Holder 300.00
Candlestick, Mission Ware, 8 1/4 In., Pair 395.00
Candlestick, Swirl, 8 In., Pair 550.00
Chamberstick, Handle 300.00
Ewer, Hywood, Light Green, 7 In. 20.00
Ewer, Marbleized, Handle, Blue, Rose, Gray, Tan, 7 In. 2335.00
Humidor, Cover, Swirl 550.00
Pitcher, Mission Ware, Corset Shape, 10 1/2 In. 495.00
Planter, Hywood, Cannon, Tan, Green 50.00
Planter, Hywood, Kangaroo, Tan ....40.00 to 45.00
Planter, Hywood, Parrot, Tan ....40.00 to 45.00
Planter, Hywood, Pelican 75.00
Planter, Hywood, Wishing Well 50.00
Salt & Pepper, Blue, Label, 3 In. 35.00
Vase, Hywood, Blue, Handles, 7 In. 30.00
Vase, Hywood, Everted Rim, Signed, 4 1/2 In. 80.00
Vase, Hywood, Fan, Pink, Marked, 5 In. 20.00
Vase, Hywood, Fan, Tan, Sticker, 6 In. 25.00
Vase, Hywood, Fuchsia & Green, Glazed, 9 In. 60.00
Vase, Hywood, Yellow, 7 In. 45.00
Vase, Marbelized, Blue, Gray, Cream, Terra-Cotta, Die Stamp, 8 1/2 x 5 In. 230.00
Vase, Marbleized, Blue, Brown, Cream, Red Swirl Design, 6 1/2 In. 165.00
Vase, Marbleized, Blue, Brown, Ivory Clay, 8 x 8 1/2 In. 660.00
Vase, Marbleized, Blue, Brown, Red, Cream Swirl Design, 8 1/2 In. 165.00
Vase, Marbleized, Blue, Cream, Brown, Red Swirls, Hourglass Form, 11 In. 412.50
Vase, Marbleized, Blue, Green, Tan, Swirled Clay, Impressed Mark, 5 1/2 In. 88.00
Vase, Marbleized, Blue, Red, Brown, Cream Swirl Design, Flared Foot, 8 In. 198.00

Vase, Marbleized, Blue, Red, Brown, Cream, Flared Foot, 8 In. 165.0
Vase, Marbleized, Brown, Blue, Red, Cream Clay, 6 1/2 In. 220.00
Vase, Marbleized, Cream, Blue, Brown, Red Swirls, Flared Neck, Bulbous, 10 In. 385.00
Vase, Marbleized, Cream, Blue, Brown, Red Swirls, Flared Shoulder, 14 In. 550.00
Vase, Marbleized, Red, Brown, Blue, Cream Swirl Design, 8 In. 220.00
Vase, Marbleized, Red, Brown, Blue, Tan Swirl Design, Cylindrical, 9 In. 330.00
Vase, Marbleized, Red, Brown, Ivory, Blue Clay, 10 1/2 x 12 In. 1760.00
Vase, Marbleized, Red, Cream, Blue, Brown Clay, 4 In. 66.00
Vase, Marbleized, Red, Cream, Brown, Blue, Paper Label, 12 In. 440.00
Vase, Marbleized, Swirled Blue, Brown, Cream, Rust, Paper Label, 2 In. 120.00
Vase, Marbleized, Swirled Brown, Cream, Red, Blue Clay, 8 In. 120.00
Vase, Marbleized, Swirled Cream, Brown, Red, Blue, Green Clay, 10 In. 176.00
Vase, Marbleized, Swirled Red, Cream, Blue, Brown Clay, 4 1/2 In. 66.00
Vase, Mission Ware, Brown & Tan Swirl, Impressed Mark, 10 In. 255.00
Vase, Mission Ware, Brown, Gray, Tan & Blue Swirl, Impressed Mark, 7 1/2 In. 440.00
Vase, Mission Ware, Brown, Tan, Gray, Blue & Cream Swirl, 8 In. 330.00
Vase, Mission Ware, Egg Shape, Signed, 5 3/4 In. 70.00
Vase, Mission Ware, Swirl, 11 7/8 In. 330.00
Vase, Mission Ware, Swirl, 4 x 5 In. 110.00
Vase, Mission Ware, Swirl, 8 1/2 In. 145.00
Vase, Mission Ware, Swirled Blue, Brown, Cream & Tan, Marked, 4 1/2 In. 90.00
Vase, Mission Ware, Swirled Tan, Gray & Brown Clay, Marked, 6 1/2 In. 165.00
Vase, Mission Ware, Tan, Brown, Blue & Cream Swirl, Impressed Mark, 6 1/2 In. 145.00
Wall Pocket, Mission Ware 400.00

NIPPON porcelain was made in Japan from 1891 to 1921. *Nippon* is the
Japanese word for *Japan*. A few firms continued to use the word
Nippon on ceramics after 1921 as a part of the company name more
than as an identification of the country of origin. More pieces marked
Nippon will be found in the Dragonware, Moriage, and Noritake categories.

Ashtray, Blown-Out Dog 350.00
Ashtray, Junk Boats, Islands, 4 Cigarette Rests, 4 x 4 x 2 In. 57.00
Basket, Tapestry, Landscape, 9 In. 1870.00
Biscuit Jar, Cover, Indian In Canoe Shooting Elk, Green Wreath Mark, 8 In. 495.00
Biscuit Jar, Iris 295.00
Biscuit Jar, Pinecones & Flowers, 2 Handles, 5 1/2 In. 165.00
Biscuit Jar, Rose Design, Melon Shape, Mark, 6 In. 66.00
Biscuit Jar, Roses, 3-Footed, Gold Trim 525.00
Bowl, Acorn Motif, 2 Handles, Green M In Wreath, 7 In. 82.00
Bowl, Allover Molded Leaves & Acorn Design, Oval, 7 1/2 In. 75.00
Bowl, Bowtie Shape, Stream In Meadow Scene, Green M In Wreath, 9 In. 22.00
Bowl, Brown Peacock, Cobalt Blue Flowers, Orange, Pink, Scalloped, Gold Trim, 8 In. ... 38.00
Bowl, Center Medallion, Gold, Green, Fringe, Fluted Molded Body, Jeweled, 7 1/2 In. 425.00
Bowl, Cobalt, Gold, Red Roses, Blue Maple Leaf Mark, 7 In. 77.00
Bowl, Daffodils, Hand Painted, Footed, 6 1/4 In. 35.00
Bowl, Floral Center, Gold Scroll, Winged Bird Border, Blue, Green M In Wreath, 8 In. .. 137.50
Bowl, Gaudy Orchid Design, Gold, 11 In. 220.00
Bowl, Gold, Black On White, M In Wreath, 6 1/2 In. 60.00
Bowl, Gold, Lychee Nuts, Scalloped, Open Handles, 7 x 5 1/2 In. 75.00
Bowl, Turquoise Tapestry Design, Purple Violets, Green Beaded Leaves, 9 1/2 In. 148.00
Bowl, Violets, Gold Lace, Fluted, Maple Leaf Mark, 8 In. 95.00
Box, Heart Shaped, Gold, Green, Pink Floral, 4 In. 44.00
Box, Powder, Rose Medallions, Green, Gold Ground, 5 1/2 In. 66.00
Cake Plate, Floral Medallion Border, Maple Leaf Mark, 10 In. 38.00
Cake Plate, Gold On Wheat, Pierced Handles, 10 In. 75.00
Cake Plate, Hand Painted, Windmill & Yellow Poppies, Cobalt Blue Border, 11 3/4 In. .. 88.00
Celery Set, Celery Stalk Motif, Green, M In Wreath, 12 In. 110.00
Chocolate Pot, Roses, 9 3/4 In. 145.00
Chocolate Set, Green Mark, 9 1/2 In., 13 Piece 225.00
Coffee Set, Cobalt Blue, Roses, 11 Piece 125.00
Coffeepot, Purple Violets, 9 3/4 In. 50.00
Cup & Saucer, White, Gold Rim, Demitasse, Set Of 5 .... 130.00

Dish, Boat Scene, Clover, 3 Handles, Green M In Wreath 85.00
Dish, Winter Cabin Scene, 6 1/2 x 4 1/2 In. 28.00
Dish, Yellow Rose Interior, 2 1/4 x 4 3/4 In. 11.00
Ewer, 3 Oval Cartouches, Floral & Madame Recamier 125.00
Ewer, Floral Design, Raised Enamel, Handle, OkE Circle Mark, 10 1/2 In. 192.00
Hair Receiver, Floral Design, Blue Maple Leaf Mark, 5 In. 38.00
Hair Receiver, Floral Design, Raised Enamel, Footed, Blue Rising Sun Mark, 3 3/4 In. ... 50.00
Hair Receiver, Floral Design, Raised Enamel, Unmarked, 3 1/2 In. 33.00
Hair Receiver, Overall Applied Gold Floral Design, Apple Green, Beige, 4 1/2 In. 44.00
Hair Receiver, Roses, Gold Scroll, Beaded Edge, 3-Footed 225.00
Hair Receiver, Woodland Scene, Green M In Wreath, 5 In., 2 Piece 192.00
Hatpin Holder, Closed, Floral, Beaded Bands, Enameled, Porcelain, 4 3/4 In. 38.00
Hatpin Holder, Gold Floral Design, Green M In Wreath, 5 In. ....40.00 to 55.00
Hatpin Holder, Open, Floral Design, Blue Maple Leaf Mark, 5 In. 60.00
Hatpin Holder, Open, Mountain Scene, Floral Medallion, Enameled, Porcelain, 5 In. ... 40.00
Hatpin Holder, Open, Twisted Mold, Green M In Wreath, 5 In. 50.00
Humidor, 4 Golf, Tennis Scenes, Hand Painted, 5 In. 600.00
Humidor, Bizarre, Stylized Flowers 235.00
Humidor, Cherries, Gold & Brown Ground, Cobalt Blue 495.00
Humidor, Cover, House In Meadow, Green M In Wreath, 4 1/2 In. 138.00
Humidor, Hunt Scene ....*Illus* 1760.00
Humidor, Man, In Sailboat Scene, Hand Painted 300.00
Humidor, Outdoor Scene, Old Model Convertible With Occupants 169.00
Jug, Whiskey, Egyptian Design, Advertises E.M. Higgins Old Velvet, Signed, 6 1/2 In. ... 825.00
Jug, Whiskey, Gold Beading, Jeweled 400.00
Jug, Whiskey, Valley Scene, Square, Green M In Wreath, 7 1/2 In. 770.00
Jug, Wine, Elk Design, 8 In. ....*Illus* 1100.00
Jug, Wine, Scenic, Woman & Child By Lake 700.00
Muffineer, Floral Design, Unmarked, 5 In. 55.00
Mug, Gold Oriental Design, Blue Maple Leaf Mark, 5 In. 50.00
Mustard Jar, Geese, Flying, Gold Design, Green M In Wreath, 4 1/2 In. 82.00
Nut Dish, Floral, Gold Trim, Beaded 12.00
Pitcher, Milk, Cobalt Blue With Roses, Pagoda Mark, 6 In. 110.00
Pitcher, Rose, Gold Leaf Grape, Signed, Nishiki Nippon, 14 In. 475.00
Plaque, 5 Horse Heads, Horseshoe Trim Border, 10 1/2 In. 990.00
Plaque, Lake Scene, Autumnal Colors, 10 In. 165.00
Plaque, Man On Camel, Enameled Border, Green M In Wreath, 10 3/4 In. 1100.00
Plaque, Sailboats, Windmill Scene, Orange Sunset, 10 In. 100.00
Plaque, Wall, Fall Scene, 10 In. 140.00
Plate, Hanging, Sheepherder, 10 1/4 In. 125.00
Platter, Flying Phoenix, Dark Blue, 15 In. 110.00
Powder Box, Rose Medallion Design, Green, Gold Ground, 5 1/2 In. 66.00
Punch Bowl, Floral Design, Maple Leaf Mark, 2 Piece ....*Illus* 550.00
Rolling Pin, Geisha Girl 200.00
Salt & Pepper, Floral, Beaded, Jewels, Green Mark 45.00
Sauce Boat, Gold On Wheat, Footed, Small 40.00
Snuff Jar, Cover, Moriage Design, 6 1/2 In. 385.00
Spoon Holder, House In Meadow, Green M In Wreath, 8 In. 95.00
Sugar, Creamer & Teapot, Cobalt Blue, Gold Trim, Signed 475.00
Tankard, Maroon & Purple, Heavy Gold, 15 1/2 In. 420.00
Tea Set, Gold Pattern, White Ground, Green M In Wreath, 13 Piece 100.00
Toothpick, Scene, Pedestal, 1 Handle 75.00
Tray, Black, Gold On White, Handle, 17 1/2 x 6 1/2 In. 75.00
Tray, Dresser, Geese & Pond, Painted, Jewel Border, 6 3/4 x 10 1/4 In. 44.00
Tray, Fish Shape, Floral Design, Gold Scrolled, 15 1/2 In. 60.00
Tray, Meadow Scene, Gold Florals, Rolled Edge, 2 Handles, Green M In Wreath, 8 In. .. 50.00
Trivet, Scenic, House, Bridge, Trees 45.00
Tumbler, Satin Finish, Desert Camel, Palm Trees, Green M In Wreath 95.00
Urn, Medallion Depicting Peace Bringing Abundance, 11 In. 2200.00
Urn, Mill Scene, 2 Handles, Green M In Wreath, 10 In. 412.00
Vase, Bird, Cottage, Winter Scene, 2 Handles, Royal Nippon Mark, 10 In. 82.00
Vase, Coralene, 2 Handles, Kinran Mark, 8 1/2 In. 715.00
Vase, Egyptian Design, Handles, 11 In. 935.00

Nippon, Jug, Wine, Elk Design, 8 In.; Nippon,
Punch Bowl, Floral Design, Maple Leaf Mark, 2
Piece; Nippon, Humidor, Hunt Scene

Nippon, Vase, Mountain
Scene, Blue Maple Leaf
Mark, 17 1/2 In.

Vase, Egyptian Warship, Scrolled Gold Moriage Design, Green M In Wreath, 11 In.	935.00
Vase, Enameled, Floral Design, 2 Handles, Green M In Wreath, 8 1/2 In.	110.00
Vase, Floral Design, 2 Handles, Green M In Wreath, 7 In.	50.00
Vase, Floral, Diamond Shape, 10 1/2 In., Pair	775.00
Vase, Floral, Gold Design, 12 1/2 In.	90.00 to 195.00
Vase, Gold Dragon, Green Eyes, Tail Over Head, Green M In Wreath, 12 x 6 In., Pair	325.00
Vase, Grapes In Basket, Blown-Out, Blue M In Wreath, 6 In.	660.00
Vase, Greek Key Bands, Middle & Top, Roses On Medallions, Gold Handles, 9 1/2 In.	290.00
Vase, Hand Painted Sunflowers, 15 In.	200.00
Vase, Hand Painted Vines, Gilt, Beaded, 3 Handles, 8 In.	165.00
Vase, House In Meadow, 2 Handles, Green M In Wreath, 6 1/2 In.	55.00
Vase, House In Meadow, Grape Clusters, 2 Handles, Green M In Wreath, 12 In.	165.00
Vase, Lake Scene, Blue Maple Leaf Mark, 2 Handles, 14 In.	550.00
Vase, Lake Scene, Open Roses, 2 Handles, Blue Maple Leaf Mark, 11 In.	132.00
Vase, Large Poppies, 2 Handles, Gold	395.00
Vase, Melon Poppies, Blue Flowers Design, Maple Leaf Gold Top, 16 In.	1650.00
Vase, Morieye, Fern Leaf Design, Cobalt Blue & Gold Top, 10 In.	575.00
Vase, Mountain Scene, Blue Maple Leaf Mark, 17 1/2 In. ....*Illus*	7480.00
Vase, Mountain Scene, Red Tulips, 2 Handles, Green M Wreath, 8 In.	88.00
Vase, Mountain Scene, Red Tulips, 2 Handles, Green M Wreath, 10 In.	93.50
Vase, Open Roses, 2 Handles, Green M Wreath, 9 3/4 In.	82.00
Vase, Orchid Design, Double Gold Handles, Fluted Gold Top, 12 In.	770.00
Vase, Ostriches, Blue, Gold Trim, 13 In.	1195.00
Vase, Pictorial Lake Scene, 10 In.	880.00
Vase, Pink Roses On White, Gold Handles, 8 In.	95.00
Vase, Poppies, Handle, Baluster, 7 1/2 In.	150.00
Vase, Portrait Of Madame Recamier, Pedestal, Handle, Cobalt Blue, 7 1/2 x 7 In.	415.00
Vase, Red Floral Design, 2 Handles, Royal Kinran Mark, 6 In.	105.00
Vase, Rose Medallion, Turquoise Beads, Feet Handles, 5 x 6 In.	225.00
Vase, Scene, Coralene, 7 1/2 In.	550.00
Vase, Stylized Design, Raised Enamel, Blue Maple Leaf Mark, 2 Handles, 6 In.	70.00
Vase, Stylized Roses, Mauve Ground, Gold Neck, 5 1/2 In.	225.00
Vase, Tulips, Gold, Green Ground, 4 Handles, 7 1/2 In.	275.00
Vase, Yellow Roses, Burnt Orange, Green M Wreath, 10 1/2 In.	135.00

NODDERS, also called nodding figures or pagods, are porcelain figures with heads and hands that are attached to wires. Any slight movement causes the parts to move up and down. They were made in many countries during the eighteenth, nineteenth, and twentieth centuries. A few Art Deco designs are also known. Copies are being made. A more recent type of nodder is made of papier-mache or plastic. These often represent sports figures or comic characters.

Ashtray, Black Boy, Smoking Cigar 195.00

Bank, Holding Fruit, Earrings, Black, 7 In. 100.00
Baseball, Los Angeles Angels, White Uniform 285.00
Baseball Player, With Bank, Plastic, 1976 .... 45.00
Bisque, 2 Couples, 4 Nodding Heads, Playing Cards, Gold Trim, 7 1/2 x 8 1/4 In. 1200.00
Bisque, Turk With Sword, Germany 95.00
Black Cat 235.00
Bouncing Bum 95.00
Bowler, Seated, Best Bowler Award, Japan 25.00
Bugs Bunny, Composition, 1960s 225.00
Bull & Matador 140.00
Canadian Mountie 75.00
Charlie Brown, Composition, Lego 195.00
Chicago Bulls, Little Black Dribblers, Plastic, Box 65.00
Chickens, With Condiment 70.00
Chinese Boy & Girl, Plaster, Hand Decorated, Japan, 6 In., Pair 24.00
Chinese Man 15.00
Cleveland Indians, Baseball, Green Base, Plastic 225.00
Clown, Bisque 45.00
Colonel Sanders, 1960s 75.00
Comical Man In Top Hat, Wood & Papier-Mache, 6 3/8 In. 137.00
Creature From Black Lagoon 80.00
Denny Dimwit, Box, 1948 .... 495.00
Detroit Tigers, Plastic 150.00
Donkey & Elephant, Pair 120.00
Donkeys 60.00
Dr. Ben Casey, Box 210.00
Elephant, Celluloid, Occupied Japan 65.00
Elephant, Head & Tail Nod, Papier-Mache, German 165.00
Farmer 75.00
Flamingos 60.00
Foxy Grandpa, Cast Iron, Kenton, 1910, 6 1/4 In. 345.00
Girl, Head Turns, Smile 1 Side, Frown Other, 2 In. 85.00
Happy Hooligan, Seated, Bisque 125.00
Happy Hooligan, With Donkey Cart, Iron 795.00
Hillbilly, Composition 120.00
Hippie 75.00
Houston Oilers, Football, Ear Pads, Plastic 325.00
Indian, Scenes 80.00
Indian Maiden, Kiss Me 45.00
Indians, In Drum 70.00
Joe Cool, 1970s 50.00
Kangaroo 80.00
Kansas City Chiefs, Mascot, Sports Specialty Corp., Box, 1975, 7 In. 31.00
Man, Turban & Sword, Stars On Robe, Germany 245.00
Marilyn Monroe 60.00
Mickey Mouse, Tin & Celluloid, Windup, 1930s 1975.00
Monk, Bisque 135.00
Monk, With Umbrella, Basket Of Flowers, Bisque 35.00
Monkey On Spike 125.00
Monkeys 225.00
Mr. Bibb 245.00
Mummy 80.00
New York Knicks, Little Black Dribblers, Box 65.00
Nun, Enesco 75.00
Oriental, Kissing, Japan 75.00
Oriental Man, Planter 180.00
Pig, Walking 250.00
Player, Pittsburgh Pirates, Roberto Clemente, Box 2200.00
Pluto, Celluloid 40.00
Policeman 75.00
Priest & Choir Boy, Full Figure, 1903, Pair 1200.00
Rabbit, Seated, Composition, Dappled Gray & White, Painted Face 95.00
Rachel, Bisque, Comic Strip Gasoline Alley, Germany, 1930s, 3 1/2 In. 285.00

Roger Maris	625.00
Salt And Pepper Shakers are listed in the Salt & Pepper category.	
Santa, Papier-Mache, Sheepskin Hair & Beard, Germany, 1930s, 25 1/2 In.	630.00
Santa Claus, Kissing	125.00
Skull	95.00
Snake Charmer	290.00
Snoopy, 1970s	50.00
Turtle, Tin	55.00
Tweety Bird	22.00
Uncle Walt, Gasoline Alley, Bisque, Germany	75.00
Victorian Woman, Planter	85.00
Willie Mays, Celluloid	625.00

NORITAKE porcelain was made in Japan after 1904 by Nippon Toki Kaisha. The best-known Noritake pieces are marked with the M in a wreath for the Morimura Brothers, a New York City distributing company. This mark was used until 1941. There may be some helpful price information in the Nippon category, since prices are comparable. Noritake Azalea is listed in its own category in this book.

Bowl, Blue Floral, Handles, 9 In.	22.00
Bowl, Dresden, Scalloped, Floral, Gold Trim, 10 1/2 In.	50.00
Bowl, Luster, Cottage Scene, 6 In.	55.00
Bowl, Table, Rolled Scalloped Edge, Rose Interior, Gold Scrolled, Green M In Wreath	33.00
Bowl, Vegetable, 2 Pierced Handles, Oblong, 10 x 7 1/2 In.	95.00
Breakfast Set, Light Blue, Pale Yellow, Set For 2	115.00
Butter, Cover, Westward Ho	135.00
Coffeepot, Tree In Meadow, Demitasse	225.00
Compote, Cover, Westward Ho, 6 In.	115.00
Creamer, Westward Ho	95.00
Cruet, Greek Key	100.00
Decanter Set, Cobalt Blue, Gold Trim, 8 Piece	350.00
Dish, Lemon, Bird Design	48.00
Fernery, Scenic, Blown Out, Signed	275.00
Flower Frog, Bird, Blue & Yellow	24.00
Jam Jar, Cherries On Notched Cover, Basket Style, Overhead Handle	55.00
Plaque, Morning Glories, Gold Rim, Pieced For Hanging, Signed, 10 1/2 In.	65.00
Plate, Birds, Gold, 9 1/2 In.	40.00
Plate, Lemon	20.00
Plate, Yellow Roses, Cobalt Blue, Gray, Gold Beaded Edge, Gold Border, 7 In., Pair	190.00
Spooner, Hand Painted Flowers, 8 In.	55.00
Sugar & Creamer, Scenic, Brown Beaded Rim	120.00
Vase, Bird Of Paradise, Hand Painted, Green M In Wreath, 8 In.	33.00
Vase, Bird On Branch, Multicolor Roses, Blue Ground, 10 In.	120.00
Vase, Mums, Stylized Neck In Floral Design, 8 1/2 In.	325.00
Wall Pocket, Bird Of Paradise, Blue, Marigold Ground, Marked, H. Paulownia, 8 In.	38.50
Whiskey Set, Cobalt Blue, Gold, 9 Piece	150.00

NORSE Pottery Company started in Edgerton, Wisconsin, in 1903. In 1904 the company moved to Rockford, Illinois. The company made a black pottery, which resembled early bronze relics of the Scandinavian countries. The firm went out of business in 1913.

Bowl, Butterfly Design, Hammered, Dark Brown To Black Matte Glaze, 2 x 7 In.	77.00
Jardiniere, Incised Geometric, 3-Footed Base, 2 Applied Handles, 11 1/2 x 7 1/2 In.	1100.00
Vase, Green, Gunmetal Glaze, Orange Clay Body, 2 Handles, 5 In.	66.00
Vase, Stylized Scalloped Design, Gold, Black & Green Matte Glaze, Footed, 4 1/2 In.	130.00

NORTH DAKOTA SCHOOL OF MINES was established in 1892 at the University of North Dakota. A ceramic course was included and pieces were made from the clays found in the region. Students at the university made pieces from 1909 to 1949. Although very early pieces were marked *U.N.D.*, most pieces were stamped with the full name of the university.

Ashtray, 6 Sides, Brown Over Geometric Design, 4 In.	66.00

Bookends, Planter, Ivy Leaves, Dora Whitman, 3 3/4 x 5 1/2 In.	825.00
Bowl, Dark Green Drip Design, Light Green, 3 1/2 x 1 In.	66.00
Charger, Stylized Flower, Polychrome Cuerda Seca, 10 In.	770.00
Curtain Pull, Indian & Papoose, Yellow	95.00
Figurine, Cowboy, Brown, Black, 4 3/4 x 3 In.	305.00
Figurine, Hawk, Yellow, Black Stripes, 5 x 3 3/4 In.	880.00
Humidor, Profiles Of 6 Native Americans, 7 3/4 In.	2090.00
Jar, Cover, Oak Leaves & Acorns, Shaded Green, Signed, 6 In.	495.00
Mug, Dear Katie, Blue, 1945, 3 In.	192.50
Mug, Poor Dave, 1945, 3 In.	192.50
Paperweight, Rebekah Assemblies	95.00
Pitcher, Children, Playing, Incised, Franc Freeman, 5 x 5 In.	605.00
Tile, Incised Geometric Border, 1930, 6 1/4 In.	325.00
Trivet, Bird, Polychrome, Circular, 6 In.	440.00
Trivet, Incised Flowers, Dark Blue, Light Blue Ground, 5 In.	192.50
Vase, American Indian Heads, Devil's Lake, Blue, 5 x 3 In.	275.00
Vase, Blue Irises, Green Ground, Margaret Cable, 7 x 3 In.	2970.00
Vase, Carved, Bulbous, 6 In.	300.00 to 425.00
Vase, Carved, Bulbous, 8 In.	425.00
Vase, Green Glaze On A Light Green Ground, 6 In.	330.00
Vase, Green Trees, Blue, Gray Ground, 1923, 8 1/2 x 5 In.	4125.00
Vase, Konishe, 4 1/2 In.	200.00
Vase, Light Blue Dots On Bands, Indigo Ground, 4 x 5 In.	385.00
Vase, Prairie Dogs, Wheat Stalks, Signed, 5 1/4 In.	512.00
Vase, Red, White Daisies, Caramel Ground, 1924, 6 x 4 In.	3300.00
Vase, Rose To Brown, 9 x 6 In.	430.00
Vase, Trees Against Orange Sky, 1917, 14 x 7 1/2 In.	9350.00

NORTHWOOD Glass Company was founded by Harry Northwood, a glassmaker who worked for Hobbs, Brockunier and Company, La Belle Glass Company, and Buckeye Glass Company before founding his own firm. He opened one factory in Indiana, Pennsylvania, in 1896, and another in Wheeling, West Virginia, in 1902. Northwood closed when Mr. Northwood died in 1923. Many types of glass were made, including carnival, custard, goofus, and pressed. The underlined N mark was used on some pieces.

Alaska, Tumbler, Forget-Me-Nots	54.00
Argonaut Shell, Sugar & Creamer, Cover, Custard	290.00
Argonaut Shell, Toothpick, Custard, 1898	320.00
Banquet Grape, Punch Set, Marigold, 10 Piece	1500.00
Beaded Shell, Butter, Cover, White	95.00
Cherries & Little Flowers, Tumbler, Cobalt, Set Of 6	360.00
Cherry & Cable, Dish, Butter	125.00
Chrysanthemum Sprig, Bowl, Cover, Green, Gold Design, 6 1/2 In.	66.00
Cornflower, Decanter Set, Green & Gold, 5 Piece	125.00
Cornflower, Wine Set, Green, Gold Trim, 5 Piece	65.00
Dancing Nudes, Shade, Custard, Nutmeg Stain, 1918, 12 1/2 x 11 1/2 In.	950.00
Diamond Point, Vase, Amethyst, 10 In.	55.00
Epergne, Blue Opalescent, 4 Trumpets, Fluted, Stippled, 17 x 11 In.	1200.00
Fine Cut & Roses, Rose Bowl, Amethyst	225.00
Fine Cut & Roses, Rose Bowl, White	195.00
Grape & Cable, Berry Set, Amethyst, 7 Piece	395.00
Grape & Cable, Plate, Custard, Nutmeg Stain, 10 In.	60.00
Grape Frieze, Bowl, Amethyst, Gold Trim, 3 1/4 x 10 1/2 In.	100.00
Intaglio, Pitcher, Custard, Blue & Gold Trim	275.00
Inverted Bull's-Eye, Pitcher, Applied Reed Handle Amber, 8 1/4 In.	60.00
Inverted Fan & Feather, Creamer, Green	35.00
Inverted Rib, Cracker Jar, Aurora	325.00
Lily Of The Valley, Pitcher, Blue, Ruffled, Gold Trim, 12 3/4 In.	110.00
Maple Leaf, Compote, Green Opalescent	30.00
Memphis, Table Set, 4 Piece	350.00
Mikado, Berry Set, Master, 4 Piece	110.00
Paneled Cherry, Butter, Dome Cover	65.00

Peach, Water Set, Green & Gold, 5 Piece 300.00
Peacocks, Plate, Light Green, 10 In. 900.00
Peacocks On Fence, Plate, Amethyst, 9 In. 750.00
Poinsettia, Bowl, Ice Blue, 10 In. 650.00
Singing Birds, Tumbler, Green 150.00
Spatter, Bowl, Ribbed, Pink, White, 3 x 8 1/2 In. 44.00
Stretch, Bowl, Raised, Square Pedestal Base, c.1926, 10 In. 99.00
Swirl, Pitcher, Opalescent 275.00
Tumbler, Oriental Poppy 55.00
Utopia Optic, Sugar, Cranberry 120.00

NU-ART see Imperial category.

NUTCRACKERS of many types have been used through the centuries. At first the nutcracker was probably strong teeth or a hammer. But by the nineteenth century, many elaborate and ingenious types were made. Levers, screws, and hammer adaptations were the most popular. Because nutcrackers are still useful, they are still being made, some in the old styles.

Alligator, Cast Aluminum, 1920s, 8 In. 75.00
American Eagle Head, Carved, c.1870 .... 895.00
Bearded Man With Cap, Walnut, 19th Century 325.00
Dog, Full-Bodied, Iron, 12 1/2 In. 165.00
Elephant, Cast Iron, Red & Black, 9 3/4 In. 220.00
Face, Carved, Wooden, c.1940, 9 In. 125.00
Figural, Dog With Tray, Cast Iron, 12 1/2 In. 350.00
Horse & Jockey On Stand, Brass 85.00
Lion, Walking, Tail Controls Crushing Mouth, Brass, 6 3/4 In. 100.00
Man, Long Nose, Cast Iron, Green Paint, 7 In. 248.00
Parrot, Green Paint, Cast Iron, 5 3/4 In. 247.00
Rooster 45.00
Squirrel 35.00
St. Bernard, 5 1/2 x 11 In. 165.00
White Smith Steel, England, 18th Century 115.00
Woman's Legs, Brass 65.00

NYMPHENBURG, see Royal Nymphenburg

OCCUPIED JAPAN was printed on pottery, porcelain, toys, and other goods made during the American occupation of Japan after World War II, from 1945 to 1952. Collectors now search for these pieces. The items were made for export.

Bowl, Iris Pattern, Earth Tones, Marked, 10 In. 20.00
Chalice, Cover, White, Cobalt Blue Insert, Metal 35.00
Creamer, Cow, Brown, White 17.00
Creamer, Indian Chief Head 45.00
Cup & Saucer, Hand Painted Flowers 12.00
Figurine, Colonial Man & Woman, Single Base, 4 1/2 In. 35.00
Figurine, Couple, Bisque, Victorian, 2 1/2 In. 14.00
Figurine, Fish Bowl, Black Boy Fishing, Blue Suit, 3 In. 30.00
Figurine, Fish Bowl, Hanging Cat, White, Brown Stripes, 1930-1940 ...... 85.00
Lighter, Camera Shape, Black Plastic, Metal, Removable Tripod, 2 1/2 In. .. 35.00
Lighter, Photo-Lite, Camera Shape, 2 1/2 x 1 1/2 x 1/2 In. 46.00
Lighter, Table, Camera Shape, With Tripod, Orion, Cardboard Box, 3 1/2 In. .. 70.00
Lighter, Toby Jug, Ben Franklin, Brass-Toned Lighter Insert, 3 In. 32.00
Plate, San Francisco, Cable Car Scene, Golden Gate Bridge, Stand, 4 In. .. 59.00
Tea Set, Floral, Gold Design, 6 Piece 600.00
Teapot, Mammy Head 350.00
Teapot, Pagoda Scenes, Blue 75.00
Toy, Bear, Windup, Celluloid, 7 In. 30.00
Toy, Dalmatian, Rubber, White, 3 In., 3 Piece 30.00
Toy, Ostrich, Walking, Windup, Plush, Tin, Box, TN Trademark, 5 1/2 In. .. 130.00
Toy, Santa Claus In Sled, Reindeer, Windup, Celluloid, Metal Sled, Box, 7 1/2 In. 121.00

FFICE TECHNOLOGY includes office equipment and related products, **** ch as adding machines, calculators, and check-writing machines. ypewriters are in their own category in this book.

Adding Machine, Gem Pocket, Fitted Morocco Case, 4 1/2 x 3 In.	316.00
Adding Machine, Lighting Co., Los Angeles, Flat Metal, 1920s	35.00
Arithma Addiator, Metal, Vinyl Pouch, Germany, 6 1/4 In.	23.00
Calculator, Commodore 796M, 19 Red, White & Blue Keys	30.00
Calculator, Commodore 899A	35.00
Calculator, Nystrom's, W. Young, Brass, Silver Plate, 1855, 9 x 5 In.	10350.00
Calculator, Pocket, Spiral Logarithmic Scales, Cardboard Case, 1907	259.00
Calculator, TI-30, Case, Instruction Manual	18.00
Calculator, Wire, Frank A. Short, Diamond Electrical, Copyright 1931	85.00

HR pottery was made in Biloxi, Mississippi, from 1883 to 1918 by **** eorge E. Ohr, a true eccentric. The pottery was made of very thin clay **** at was twisted, folded, and dented into odd, graceful shapes. Some **** eces were lifelike models of hats, animal heads, or even a potato. **** thers were decorated with folded clay *snakes*. Reproductions and **** eworked pieces are appearing on the market. These have been **** glazed, or snakes and other embellishments have been added.

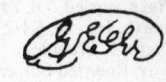

Bowl, Crimped Edge, Gunmetal Volcanic Glaze, 2 1/4 x 4 1/2 In.	995.00
Candleholder, Green, Raspberry, Ribbed Base, Pinched Ribbon Handle, Signed, 6 1/2 In.	1400.00
Candleholder, Pinched Ribbon Handle, Body Twist, Ribbed Base, Script Mark, 6 1/2 In.	3300.00
Chamberstick, Twist Body, Folded Handle, Signed, 5 1/2 In.	415.00
Cup, Green, Cobalt & Raspberry Glaze, Demitasse, Stamped, 2 1/2 In.	1500.00
Mug, Gunmetal Green, Brown, Peacock Blue, Protruding Handle, 5 1/4 x 6 1/2 In.	935.00
Mustache Cup, Occupational, Built As Shirt Cuff, Ribbon Handle, Blue, 3 In.	2000.00
Pitcher, Gunmetal Glaze, Pinched, Cutout Handle, Signed, 3 3/4 x 4 3/4 In.	1870.00
Pitcher, Gunmetal Volcanic Glaze, Bulbous, 3 1/2 x 4 3/4 In.	1430.00
Pitcher, Light Clay, Cupped Top, Bisque, 4 3/4 x 4 3/4 In.	550.00
Pitcher, Pinched & Folded, Green & Red Speckled Glaze, Signed, 4 x 5 1/4 In.	4950.00
Vase, Black Drip & Specks On Green Glaze, c.1890, 3 5/8 In.	475.00
Vase, Black Gunmetal Glaze, Folded Rim, Impressed Mark, 3 1/2 In.	445.00
Vase, Black-Brown Glaze Dimpled Rim, 3 x 5 1/4 In.	935.00
Vase, Bottle Shape, Mottled Raspberry, Purple, Cobalt, Green, Shallow Ring, 10 x 4 In.	2500.00
Vase, Brown Swirl Design, Cream Ground, Signed, 3 In.	600.00
Vase, Buff Clay Long Vertical Flutes Bisque, 5 3/4 x 4 1/2 In.	715.00
Vase, Gunmetal Glaze, Folded & Pinched, Asymmetrical, 3 x 4 1/2 In.	2750.00
Vase, Gunmetal Glaze, Signed, 4 1/2 In.	2200.00
Vase, Gunmetal Khaki Speckled Glaze, Bulbous, 6 1/4 x 5 1/2 In.	2650.00
Vase, Gunmetal Speckled Khaki Glaze, Dimpled 4-Sided Rim, 4 x 4 1/2 In.	1000.00
Vase, Indigo Green Sponge Pattern, White Glaze, Raspberry Ground, 3 x 4 In.	2640.00
Vase, Khaki Green Speckled Glaze, Deep-In-Body Twist, Cylindrical, 6 3/4 x 3 3/4 In.	1760.00
Vase, Loosely Folded Body, Tightly Folded Rim, Red Clay, Bisque, 2 1/2 x 5 1/2 In.	1540.00
Vase, Mottled Glaze, Closed-In Rim, Gourd Shape, Signed, 4 3/4 In.	1430.00
Vase, Red Clay Bisque, 2 3/4 x 3 3/4 In.	225.00
Vase, Ribbed, Gunmetal Glaze, Signed, 3 1/2 In.	495.00
Vase, Scroddled Clay, In-Body Twist, Exaggerated Bisque, 3 1/4 x 4 In.	400.00
Vase, Swirlware, Thin Walled, Signed, 1890s, 2 x 3 1/2 In.	880.00
Vessel, Gunmetal Glaze, Folded Rim, Dimpled Body, Signed, 3 1/4 x 3 3/4 In.	935.00

LD IVORY china was made by the Ohme Porcelain Works in Silesia, **** ermany, a factory working from 1882 to 1928. The china had an vory matte background and was usually decorated with flowers or **** ruit. Dinner sets, fish sets, mustache cups, and souvenir pieces were **** lso made. Pieces were marked with a crown, the cipher OH, and the vord *Silesia.* Some pieces are also marked with the words *Old Ivory.* **** he pattern numbers appear on the base of many pieces.

OLD IVORY
84

Berry Bowl, No. 29, Individual	65.00
Berry Bowl, No. 40, Individual	75.00
Bowl, White & Green Poppy Center, Buds At Edge, 6 In.	143.00
Chocolate Pot, No. 11, Double Handle, Pedestal, 9 1/2 In.	445.00

Chocolate Set, 6 Piece	800.0
Cracker Jar, Barrel Shape, Silesia, No. 16, 8 x 6 1/2 In.	488.0
Cup, Signed, No. 16	38.0
Cup & Saucer, No. 84	48.0
Dish, Berry, 5 In.	75.0
Plate, 3 Sections, Scalloped Rim, Gold Trim, Roses, Leaves, 7 1/2 In.	95.0
Plate, 6 1/4 In.	80.0
Plate, 7 1/2 In.	45.0
Plate, Alice Blank, 8 1/2 In.	22.0
Plate, Cookie, No. 113, 10 1/4 In.	160.0
Plate, Holly, 6 1/4 In.	50.0
Plate, No. 113, 8 1/4 In.	45.0
Plate, Pink & White Daisies, Gold Trim, 6 1/4 In.	90.0
Plate, Signed, No. 16, 7 3/4 In.	37.0
Plate, Signed, No. 16, 8 1/4 In.	44.0
Plate, Signed, No. 84, 8 3/4 In.	48.0
Relish, Handle, 6 1/2 In.	53.0
Sugar & Creamer	145.0
Tray, Rounded Corners, No. 84, 12 x 7 In.	150.0

OLD PARIS, see Paris category.

OLD SLEEPY EYE, see Sleepy Eye category.

ONION PATTERN, originally named *bulb pattern*, is a white ware decorated with cobalt blue or pink. Although it is commonly associated with Meissen, other companies made the pattern in the late nineteenth and the twentieth centuries. A rare type is called *red bud* because there are added red accents on the blue-and-white dishes.

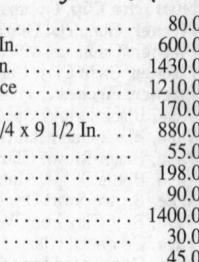

Ashtray, Crossed Swords, Round, Meissen, 5 In.	80.0
Bowl, Bamboo Pattern, Reticulated, Pedestal, Meissen, c.1888, 6 x 7 1/4 In.	600.0
Bowl, Nut, Reclining Woman & Man, Signed, Meissen, 19th Century, 7 In.	1430.0
Coffee Set, Rose Finial, Cartouche Shape Tray, Marked, Meissen, 17 Piece	1210.0
Colander, Applied Handle, Blue, White, Porcelain, 5 3/4 In.	170.0
Compote, Floral, Reticulated Sides, Twisted Base, Marked, Meissen, 7 3/4 x 9 1/2 In.	880.0
Cookie Jar, Cover	55.0
Cup & Saucer, Deep Saucer, Czechoslovakia	198.0
Cup & Saucer, Demitasse, c.1890	90.0
Desk Set, 2 Lidded Inkwells, Scalloped Tray, Meissen, 8 1/2 x 12 In.	1400.0
Dish, One Handle, Meissen, 8 1/2 In.	30.0
Feeder, Invalid	45.0
Lamp, Kerosene, Urn Form, Double Rope Handles, Marked, Meissen, 24 In., Pair	1430.0
Plate, Czechoslovakia, 6 In.	42.0
Plate, Floral Center, Scalloped, Meissen, Blue Crossed Swords, 9 1/2 In., 21 Piece	1000.0
Plate, Meissen, Mid-1800s	185.0
Plate, Red Bulbs, Gold Trim, Meissen, 7 1/4 In. ....*Illus*	100.0
Plate Set, Salad, Floral Center, Scalloped, Meissen, 8 1/2 In., 13 Piece	665.0
Platter, Crossed Swords, Meissen, 13 x 10 In.	295.0

Onion, Plate, Red Bulbs, Gold Trim,
Meissen, 7 1/4 In.

If your home has just been robbed, don't immediately give the police a list of the stolen items and damage. Sit down later and make a detailed list. This police copy is the one your insurance company will use to settle any claims. Take photographs of the damage as soon as possible.

Platter, Fish, Blue Crossed Swords Mark, 11 3/4 x 24 In. 520.00
Platter, Fish, Meissen, c.1880, 24 In. 895.00
Platter, Meissen, 13 1/2 In. 120.00
Platter, Meissen, Blue & White, Crossed Swords Mark, 8 x 11 In. 175.00
Platter, Scalloped Edge, Blue Shield With Crown, 2 Handles, Meissen, 15 In. 247.00
Soup, Dish, Scalloped, Meissen, Crossed Swords, 9 1/4 In., 16 Piece 1100.00
Teapot, Blue Flowers On Body & Cover, Rose On Top, Meissen, 4 1/4 In. 115.00

PALESCENT GLASS is translucent glass that has the tones of the opal
emstone. It originated in England in the 1870s and is often found in
essed glassware made in Victorian times. Opalescent glass was first
ade in America in 1897 at the Northwood glassworks in Indiana,
ennsylvania. Some dealers use the terms *opaline* and *opalescent* for
y of these translucent wares. More opalescent pieces may be listed
Hobnail, Northwood, Pressed Glass, Spanish Lace, and other glass
tegories.

Alaska, Creamer, Vaseline 298.00
Alaska, Sauce, White 20.00
Alaska, Sugar Shaker, Blue 75.00
Alaska, Sugar, Open, Vaseline 190.00
Beaded Acanthus, Creamer, Blue 65.00
Beaded Shell, Butter, Green 145.00
Beatty Rib, Creamer, Blue 40.00
Beatty Rib, Toothpick, Blue 35.00
Bubble Lattice, Celery Vase, Cranberry ....235.00 to 255.00
Bubble Lattice, Water Set, Cranberry, 5 Piece 1350.00
Buckeye Lattice, Creamer, Cranberry 450.00
Bull's-Eye, Spill, Hexagonal, 5 In. 785.00
Buttons & Braids, Pitcher, Blue ....220.00 to 245.00
Buttons & Braids, Tumbler, Green 40.00
Christmas Snowflake, Pitcher, Water, Cranberry 2100.00
Christmas Snowflake, Water Set, Cobalt Blue, 6 Piece 395.00
Chrysanthemum Base Swirl, Cruet, White 115.00
Circled Scroll, Sugar, Creamer & Spooner, Blue, 3 Piece 200.00
Coinspot, Creamer, Blue 65.00
Coinspot, Pitcher, Cranberry, Ruffled Edge 300.00
Coinspot, Pitcher, Ruffled Edge, Blue 225.00
Coinspot, Pitcher, Yellow 150.00
Coinspot, Syrup, Blue 145.00
Criss-Cross, Toothpick, Cranberry 225.00
Daisy & Fern, Cruet, Apple Blossom Stopper, Blue 150.00
Daisy & Fern, Pitcher, Cranberry 110.00
Daisy & Fern, Pitcher, White, Reeded Handle, Ruffled Edge 77.00
Daisy & Fern, Sugar Shaker, Blue 330.00
Daisy & Fern, Sugar Shaker, Cranberry ....220.00 to 480.00
Daisy In Criss-Cross, Syrup, White 550.00
Diamond Spearhead, Goblet, Yellow 125.00
Diamond Spearhead, Jam Jar, Cobalt Blue 225.00
Diamond Spearhead, Sugar, Cover 225.00
Diamond Spearhead, Toothpick, Vaseline 75.00
Diamond Spearhead, Tumbler, Blue 110.00
Everglades, Creamer, Vaseline 150.00
Everglades, Saltshaker, Vaseline 50.00
Everglades, Tumbler 25.00
Everglades, Water Set, Gold Trim, Blue, 7 Piece 630.00
Fern, Cruet, Cranberry 350.00
Fern, Sugar Shaker, Cranberry 795.00
Fluted Scrolls, Creamer, Blue 45.00
Fluted Scrolls, Cruet, Blue 250.00
Fluted Scrolls, Cruet, Vaseline 150.00
Fluted Scrolls, Powder Jar, Blue 45.00
Fluted Scrolls, Tumbler, Blue 75.00
Gonterman Swirl, Toothpick, Yellow 250.00

Hobbs Hobnail, Pitcher, Cranberry 315.0
Hobnail & Paneled Thumbprint, Spooner, Vaseline 55.0
Honeycomb & Clover, Butter, Cover, Blue 95.0
Intaglio, Cruet, Blue 145.0
Inverted Fan & Feather, Candy Dish, Green 175.0
Inverted Fan & Feather, Cuspidor, Woman's, White 150.0
Inverted Fan & Feather, Rose Bowl, Blue 150.0
Iris With Meander, Toothpick, Yellow 125.0
Jewel & Fan, Relish, Green 25.0
Jewel & Flower, Cruet, Blue 450.0
Lattice, Pitcher, Cranberry 950.0
Leaf Umbrella, Celery Vase, Cranberry 350.0
Palm Beach, Plate, Blue 490.0
Persian Medallion, Cuspidor, Vaseline 35.0
Piasa Bird, Bowl, Blue, Footed 85.0
Poinsettia, Tankard, Blue 425.0
Poinsettia, Tankard, Cranberry 2500.0
Raised Swirl, Bottle, Barber, Raised Swirl, Cranberry 395.0
Raised Swirl, Cruet, Cranberry 375.0
Raised Swirl, Pitcher, Cranberry 695.0
Reverse Swirl, Mustard, Cranberry 395.0
Reverse Swirl, Pitcher, Blue 450.0
Reverse Swirl, Sugar Shaker, White 125.0
Reverse Swirl, Syrup, Blue 335.0
Reverse Swirl, Syrup, Cranberry .... 1105.
Reverse Swirl, Toothpick, Cranberry .... 350.
Reverse Swirl, Water Set, Cranberry, 7 Piece 1550.0
Ribbed Lattice, Cruet, White ....100.00 to 135.
Ribbed Lattice, Salt & Pepper, Cranberry 245.0
Ribbed Lattice, Sugar Shaker .... 285.
Ribbed Lattice, Sugar Shaker, Cranberry .... 325.
Ribbed Lattice, Syrup, Blue 350.0
Ribbed Opal Lattice, Spooner, Cranberry 229.0
Ribbed Spiral, Toothpick 75.0
Riverside Reward, Butter, Cover, Green 250.0
Seaweed, Bottle, Barber, Tapered, Cranberry 475.0
Seaweed, Cruet, Blue 325.0
Seaweed, Cruet, Cranberry .... 685.
Seaweed, Pitcher, Water, White .... 195.
Smoke Bell, Clambroth, Lime Green Threading, Ruffled, 1870-1900, 5 In. .... 240.
Spanish Lace, Sugar Shaker .... 285.
Spanish Lace, Sugar Shaker, Blue, Bulbous .... 285.
Stars & Stripes, Cruet, Cranberry .... 685.
Strawberry, Bonbon, White .... 100.
Sunburst Medallion, Cuspidor, Vaseline .... 35.
Sunburst-On-Shield, Breakfast Set, Blue .... 140.
Sunburst-On-Shield, Sugar, Breakfast, Blue .... 70.
Swirl, Bottle, Barber, Blue .... 225.
Swirl, Vase, Green, Flower & Leaves, 15 x 4 3/4 In. .... 425.
Toothpicks are listed in the Toothpick category.
Tree Stump, Mug, Blue .... 70.
Waterlily With Cattails, Creamer, Green .... 45.
Windows, Pitcher, Cranberry .... 495.
Windows, Sugar Shaker, Blue .... 330.
Wreath & Shell, Tumbler .... 75.

OPALINE, or opal glass, was made in white, green, and other colors.
The glass had a matte surface and a lack of transparency. It was often
gilded or painted. It was a popular mid-nineteenth-century European
glassware.

Centerpiece Set, Urn Shape, Silver, Handles, France, 19th Century, 9 In., 3 Piece 1320.0
Urn, Campana, Scrolled & Mark Handles, Bronze Border Plinth, 18 1/4 In., Pair .... 7475.
Vase, Allover Gold, White Fern Design, Turquoise, Gold Rim, 8 1/2 In. .... 80.

OPERA GLASSES are needed because the stage is a long way from some of the seats at a play or an opera. Mother-of-pearl was a popular decoration on many French glasses.

Bardow & Son, Brass & Mother-Of-Pearl		75.00
LaTour, Mother-Of-Pearl, Leather Case		75.00
Mother-Of-Pearl, Gilt Brass, Lorgnette Handle, Signed Le Fils, Paris		225.00
Mother-Of-Pearl, Original Fitted Case, Signed, Le Fils, Paris, 4 1/4 In.		259.00
Telescoping Handle, France, 1890s		195.00

ORPHAN ANNIE first appeared in the comics in 1924. The redheaded girl and her friends have been on the radio and are still on the comic pages. A Broadway musical show and a movie in the 1980s made Annie popular again and many toys, dishes, and other memorabilia are being made.

Ashtray, Sandy, Figural, Ceramic, Famous Artists Syndicate, Japan, 1930s, 4 In.		120.00
Badge, Mysto-Matic Decoder, Brass		55.00
Badge, Radio, Decoder, 1939		100.00
Book, Big Little Book, Little Orphan Annie & The Secret Of The Well, 1947		26.00
Book, Big Little Book, Little Orphan Annie-Punjab The Wizard, 1935		26.00
Book, Pop-Up, 1935		85.00
Decoder Pin, Shield, Secret Compartment, Brass, 1936, 1 3/4 In.		30.00
Doll, Cloth, Georgene, Tin Eyes, Yarn Hair, Black Boots, 1950, 44 In.		1200.00
Doll, Composition, Original Clothes, 1930s, 10 1/2 In.		450.00
Doll, Oilcloth, 13 In.		150.00
Figurine, Annie With Sandy, Enesco, 1972, 15 x 9 In.		100.00
Foto Reel, Film Inside, c.1938		115.00
Game, Little Orphan Annie, Cardboard, Metal & Wood, Milton Bradley		60.00
Game, Little Orphan Annie-Pursuit, Elchow & Righter, 1978		12.00
Kit, Secret Society, 1939		135.00
Light Bulb, Christmas, Sandy, The Dog		75.00
Light Bulb, Orphan Annie & Sandy		50.00
Lunch Box, Annie, Metal, Thermos, With Tags, 1981		45.00
Mug, Ceramic		35.00
Mug, Ovaltine, Plastic		75.00
Mug, Shake-Up, Ovaltine, Blue Plastic, Fitted Lid, Annie & Arf Dancing, 5 In.		71.00
Pin, Decoder, Radio, Secret Compartment, 1936		28.00
Pin, Little Orphan Annie Pep, Premium, 1945		35.00
Plate, Bowl & Tumbler, Plastic, Brookpark, 1974		35.00
Purse, Leather, Mirror, 1930		22.00
Ring, Signet, Brass Base, Initials, Ovaltine Premium, 1937		60.00
Sheet Music, Chicago Tribune, c.1930		5.00
Stove, Red		70.00
Tea Set, Lusterware, Japan, 1930, 7 Piece		295.00
Teapot, Lusterware, Licensed By Famous Artists Syndicate, 1930s, 3 1/2 In.		69.00 to 95.00
Toothbrush Holder, Sandy On Couch		250.00
Toy, Sandy, With Briefcase, Windup		595.00
Whistle-Badge, Tin Lithograph, Red, White & Blue		35.00

ORREFORS Glassworks, located in the Swedish province of Smaaland, was established in 1898. The company is still making glass for use on the table or as decorations. There is renewed interest in the glass made in the modern styles of the 1940s and 1950s. Most vases and decorative pieces are signed with the etched name.

Orrefors

Bowl, Center, Raised On Solid Glass Pedestal, Teardrop Aperture, 6 3/4 x 12 In.		345.00
Bowl, Corona, 7 3/8 In.		111.00
Bowl, Fluted, Pink Ruffled Edge, Signed, 10 In.		460.00
Bowl, Moonstone, Sven Palmquist, 1950s, 8 In.		286.00
Bowl, One Thousand Windows, 9 1/2 In.		800.00
Bowl, Simon Gate 3 Graces, 1920, 5 In.		875.00
Bowl, Slip, Graal, Edward Hald, 1955		1200.00
Bowl, Tomato Red, 3 x 1 3/4 In.		85.00
Cocktail Shaker, Nude		400.00

Decanter, Romeo & Juliet, 1 Lover On Reverse Panel, Square, 1880, 11 3/4 In. 170.00
Decanter, Stopper, Square Cut, Paper Label, 9 3/4 In., Pair 220.00
Dish, Boat Shape, Blown & Cut, Naked Sprites In Woods, Engraved Mark, 11 1/4 In. . . . 355.00
Jardiniere, Trolleholm Castle, Signed, 1970s, 6 1/2 In. 645.00
Perfume Bottle, Heart Stopper 95.00
Plate, Westminster Abbey, Gold, Signed, 1971 . . . . 95.00
Vase, 2 Graceful Skaters, Signed, 1937, 9 1/4 In. 750.00
Vase, Alexandrite, Etched, Blue-Lilac, 6 In. 65.00
Vase, Angle Fish & Bubbles, Etched, 9 1/2 In., Pair 950.00
Vase, Bulbous, Signed, Smalland, 1942, 6 1/2 x 8 1/2 x 3 1/4 In. 275.00
Vase, Crystal, Paneled Cut, Signed, 9 1/2 In. 165.00
Vase, Crystal, Woman, Nude, Releasing A Dove, Signed, Lindstrand, 11 In. 330.00
Vase, Engraved 3 Seagulls In Flight, 9 1/2 In. 209.00
Vase, Engraved Pair Of Skaters, Angular Body, Arthur Diessner, 1937, 10 In. 750.00
Vase, Faceted Sommerso, Green & Clear, Signed, Paper Label, 11 In. 247.00
Vase, Festival In Forest, Blue Cut Back To Frosted Clear, Signed, 7 In. 690.00
Vase, Fish, Aquatic Plants, Pale Green, Edward Hald, Oval, 5 In. . . . . .900.00 to 975.00
Vase, Geometric Design, Deep Amber Layers, Ariel, 1965, 6 In. 1650.00
Vase, Internal Geometric Pattern, Clear Crystal, Signed, 8 3/4 In. 1610.00
Vase, Pearl Diver, Wavy Interior, Square, 7 In. 231.00
Vase, Profile Portrait Of Dove, Floral Surround, Signed, 7 In. 2760.00
Vase, Romeo & Juliet, American Senior Golf Assoc., 1935, 8 In. 595.00
Vase, Slip, Graal, Royal Blue Vertical Lines, Pale Peach Horizontal Lines, 7 3/4 In. 2070.00
Vase, Smoke, Signed, Nils Landberg, 7 1/2 In. 303.00
Vase, Smoke, Somerso Design, Signed, Nils Lindsberg, Square, 8 In. 150.00
Vase, Squares Of Triangles In Blue & Clear, Signed, 5 1/4 In. 690.00
Vase, Top Half Blue, Lower Half Blue Festoons & Controlled Bubbles, 11 1/2 In. 1610.00
Vase, Vertical Panels, Signed, Edvin Ohrstrom, Mid-20th Century, 5 1/4 In. 633.00
Vase, Vertical Strips, Aubergine, Blue, Applied Foot, 2 3/4 x 4 1/2 In. 400.00
Vase, Woman, With Basket Of Flowers, 1953, 5 x 7 In. 440.00

OTT & BREWER Company operated the Etruria Pottery at Trenton,
New Jersey, from 1863 to 1893. They started making belleek in 1882.
The firm used a variety of marks that incorporated the initials *O & B*.

Cup & Saucer, Demitasse 145.00
Cup & Saucer, Shell Ribbed Exterior, Gold Acorns On Handles, Gold Trim 195.00
Cup & Saucer, Yellow, Red Mark, After Dinner 30.00
Tazza, Gilt Paste Ferns, Red Mark, c.1876, 8 In. 875.00
Vase, Tree Trunk Shape, Floral Transfer, Polychrome, 5 In. 450.00

OVERBECK pottery was made by four sisters named Overbeck at a pottery in Cambridge City, Indiana. They started in 1911. They made all
types of vases, each one-of-a-kind. Small, hand-modeled figurines are
the most popular pieces with today's collectors. The factory continued
until 1955, when the last of the four sisters died.

Bowl, Incised Geometric Design, Pink Matte, Green Ground, Marked, 3 1/2 In. 825.00
Box, Cover, Carved Geometric Design, Olive, Blue Matte Glaze, 3 1/2 In. 1430.00
Figurine, Colonial Gentleman, Gloss & Matte Glazes, Signed, 5 3/4 In. 192.00
Figurine, Elephant, White, Pink, 4 x 7 In. 1430.00
Figurine, Goose, White, Pink, 3 x 5 In. 880.00
Figurine, Portly Gentleman, Blue Striped Trousers, 5 3/4 x 4 1/2 In. 660.00
Figurine, Postman, Brown Uniform, 5 1/2 x 2 1/2 In. 1925.00
Figurine, School Teacher, Brown Jacket, Blue Pants, 6 x 2 1/2 In. 165.00
Vase, Carved Floral, Olive Green, Aqua, Blue Matte Ground, 7 In. 5500.00
Vase, Floral, Mustard Ground, Matte Glaze, Initials E.H., 4 In. 5500.00
Vase, Geometric Floral Design, Tobacco Brown, Light Green Matte, 4 1/2 In. 1760.00
Vase, Hosta Flowers, 14 1/4 In. 22000.00
Vase, Incised Stylized Flowers, Green, Brown Matte, Blue, Yellow, 6 In. 1540.00
Vase, Stylized Florals, Tan & Pale Orange, Signed, 11 3/8 In. 8800.00
Vase, Stylized Trees, Purple, Brown Matte, Charcoal Gray Panels, 7 1/2 In. 2860.00
Vase, Stylized White Crows, Blue Gray Matte Ground, 6 x 6 In. 3960.00

WENS Pottery was made in Zanesville, Ohio, from 1891 to 1928. The
rst art pottery was made after 1896. Utopian Ware, Cyrano, Navarre,
roza, and Henri Deux were made. Pieces were usually marked with
form of the name *Owens*. About 1907, the firm began to make tile
d discontinued the art pottery wares.

Basket, Salt Glaze, White Interior, 1 Handle, 1973-1974, 6 1/2 x 9 In.	100.00
Bowl, Incised Lines, Crimson Haze, Chinese Blue Glaze, 7 1/4 In.	825.00
Figurine, Bear, Incised Claws, Slit-Type Nose, Orange Glaze, 1976, 3 1/4 x 5 3/4 In.	415.00
Jar, Cover, Ocher Matte Dark Green Speckled Glaze, 2 Handles, 6 1/2 x 5 In.	220.00
Mug, Utopian, Berry, Leaf Design, Caramel, Cream, Green, Brown, 5 In.	66.00
Pitcher, Alpine, Clover Blossoms, Spout, 5 1/2 In.	55.00
Pitcher, Blue Glaze, 3 Incised Lines On Shoulder, Late 1970s, 6 1/2 In.	66.00
Pitcher, Grape Design, Yellow, Brown, Green, Brown To Green Ground, 17 In.	1045.00
Pitcher, Lotus Blossom, Wading Bird, 8 5/8 In.	357.00
Pitcher, Lotus Blossom, Wading Bird, Signed, 6 In.	412.00
Pitcher, Rebekkah, Yellow & Green Glaze, Coggle Wheel Design Shoulder, 14 1/4 In.	165.00
Pitcher, Salt Glaze, Cobalt Blue Grapes, Green Leaf, Thumb Grooved Handle, 8 1/4 In.	250.00
Pitcher, Yellow, Brown Blossoms, Green Stems, Dark Brown Ground, 6 1/2 In.	143.00
Sugar & Creamer, Incised Lines, Sugar Handles, 1940-1950, 2 1/2 In.	190.00
Teapot, Cover, Allover Gray, Blue Highlights, Signed, 7 1/2 In.	121.00
Tile, Ship On The Water, Ocher, Brown, Cuenca, Arts & Crafts Frame, Square, 11 3/4 In.	1540.00
Vase, Alpine, Roses, Bottle Shape, Tot Steele, 9 3/4 In.	715.00
Vase, Berries & Leaves Design, Pottery, Signed, 5 In.	165.00
Vase, Corona, Leaves, Butterfly Design, Copper Clad, 15 In.	5000.00
Vase, Floral, Black, Blue, Cream, 3 Handles, 7 1/2 In.	143.00
Vase, Florals, Light Matte Glaze, Signed, 9 3/4 In.	266.00
Vase, Flowers, Pink, Black Ground, Squatty, 4 In.	357.00
Vase, Frogskin Olive Green Matte Glaze, 6 1/2 x 4 1/4 In.	220.00
Vase, Green Spattered Colors, Red Clay Ground, Signed, 6 1/2 x 7 1/2 In.	345.00
Vase, Lotus Flower, 15 In.	975.00
Vase, Pine Cones, 15 In.	1500.00
Vase, Purple Blossoms, Green Leaves, Squatty, 4 In.	358.00
Vase, Rust Pansies, Yellow, Brown, Signed, 8 In.	245.00
Vase, Utopian, Clover Blossoms, Bulbous, 14 In.	248.00
Vase, Utopian, Floral, Orange To Brown Ground, Signed, 6 x 4 In.	80.00 to 110.00
Vase, Utopian, Floral, Signed, Tot Steele, 11 In.	275.00
Vase, Utopian, Floral, Yellow, Blue, Green Leaves, Brown, Green Ground, 8 In.	143.00
Vase, Utopian, Grape Design, Brown Glaze, Signed, A. Haubrich, 11 In.	275.00
Vase, Utopian, Horse's Head Design, Pillow, Mae Timberlake, 12 In.	990.00
Vase, Utopian, Pine Cone, 15 In.	950.00
Vase, Utopian, Signed, Tot Steele, 10 1/2 In.	450.00
Vase, Utopian, Yellow Poppies, Brown Ground, 17 1/2 In.	715.00
Vase, Utopian, Yellow Roses, Delores Harvey, 4 1/4 In.	82.00
Vase, White Matte Glaze, Circular Stamp, 4 x 5 In.	165.00

YSTER PLATES were popular from the 1880s. Each course at dinner
as served in a special dish. The oyster plate had indentations shaped
ke oysters. Usually six oysters were held on a plate. There is no
eater value to a plate with more oysters, although that myth contin-
es to haunt antiques dealers. There are other plates for shellfish,
cluding cockle plates and whelk plates. The appropriately shaped
dentations are part of the design of these dishes.

4 Wells, France, 8 3/4 In.	100.00
5 Wells, Floral & Gold, Painted Trim, Haviland, 7 3/4 In.	143.00
5 Wells, Gold Design, Gutherz, Carlsbad, 7 1/2 In.	50.00
6 Wells, Blue & Gold Design, Haviland, 8 1/2 In.	165.00
6 Wells, Embossed Blue Design, 8 In.	80.00
6 Wells, Sea Creature, Shell Design, Limoges, 1880, 9 In., 8 Piece	1540.00
6 Wells, Sea Creatures, 9 In.	85.00
Blanc De Chine, Limoges	125.00
Crescent Shape, Polychrome Design, 9 In., Pair	215.00
Glass, 6 Piece	75.00
Half Moon, Haviland	175.00

Hand Painted, Naturalistic, Limoges, 1876, 9 In., 12 Piece 1650.0
Pink, Cream, Gilt Design, Porcelain, 1885, 8 1/2 In., 12 Piece 935.C
Sea Creature Design, Pale Blue, 8 x 9 In., Pair 180.C
Turkey, Lavender Tinge, Limoges, 8 1/2 In., 8 Piece 1380.C

PADEN CITY Glass Manufacturing Company was established in 1916 at Paden City, West Virginia. The company made more than seventy different colors of glass. The firm closed in 1951.

Bowl, Black Forest, Green, Rolled Edge, 13 1/4 In. 300.0
Bowl, Black Forest, Pink, Rolled Edge, 11 3/4 In. 250.0
Bowl, Crow's Foot, Black, 12 In. 305.0
Bowl, Cupid, 2 Handles, Amber 150.0
Bowl, Gazebo, Flat, 13 In. 75.0
Candlestick, Crow's Foot, Black 175.0
Champagne, Penny, Red 12.0
Compote, Cupid, Pink 220.0
Compote, Lela Bird, Green, Tall 65.0
Compote, Red, 11 In. 75.0
Cup, Black Forest, Red 120.0
Cup, Party, Cheriglo 12.5
Cup, Penny, Red .... .15.00 to 20.0
Cup & Saucer, Crow's Foot, Red 12.0
Dish, Mayonnaise, Ardith, Footed, Black 58.0
Figurine, Bunny, Cotton Dispenser, Ears Down, Pink, 5 In. ....95.00 to 150.0
Figurine, Pheasant, Blue, 13 3/4 In. 150.0
Figurine, Pony, Blue, 12 In. .... .125.00 to 185.0
Figurine, Rooster, Barn Yard, Blue, 8 3/4 In. 200.0
Ice Bucket, Black Forest, Pink 200.0
Ice Tub, Black 60.0
Pitcher, Black Forest, Pink 650.0
Pitcher, Cupid, Pink, 10 In. 1195.0
Pitcher, Peacock & Wild Rose, 10 1/2 In. 75.0
Plate, Crow's Foot, Amber, 8 3/4 In. 26.0
Plate, Gazebo, Fan-Shaped Handle, Gold Trim, 13 In. 50.0
Plate, Gazebo, Footed 125.0
Salt & Pepper, Caliente, Tangerine 12.0
Saucer, Party, Cheriglo 6.0
Saucer, Penny, Red 5.0
Server, Largo, Center Handle, Red 95.0
Soup, Cream, Crow's Foot, Amber 7.0
Tray, Crowsfoot, Milk Glass, Handles, Square, Tiny Applied Roses 45.0
Tumbler, Black Forest, Footed, 9 Oz. 35.0
Tumbler, Crow's Foot, Black 100.0
Vase, California Poppy, Pink, 12 In. 260.0
Vase, Peacock & Wild Rose, Black, 8 1/2 In. 135.0
Vase, Peacock & Wild Rose, Pink, 10 In. 148.0

PAINTINGS listed in this book are not works by major artists but rather decorative paintings on ivory, board, or glass that would be of interest to the average collector. Watercolors on paper are listed under Picture. To learn the value of an oil painting by a listed artist you must contact an expert in that area.

Oil On Board, Boy In Blue Dress With Drum, Frame, 43 x 27 In. 550.0
Oil On Board, Canadian Fishing Cove, Harry Leith-Ross, 7 1/4 x 15 1/2 In. 2640.0
Oil On Board, Dory Rowing To Ship, Gilt Frame, Chas. Mozin, 1847, 7 x 10 1/2 In. ... 862.0
Oil On Board, Farm House, Pastoral Setting, Mason, Frame, 16 x 20 In. 158.0
Oil On Board, Fruit Basket, Lobster, Fish, Scallops, Marcus Stone, 19 x 36 In. 2550.0
Oil On Board, Indian Chief With Spear, Winsor & Newton, Frame, 14 x 10 In. 605.0
Oil On Board, Landscape, Cabin, Frame, 13 1/2 x 19 1/2 In. 55.0
Oil On Board, Landscape, Chickens, W. Hammerson, 6 x 8 In. 230.0
Oil On Board, Landscape, Country Cottage, c.1900, 11 x 15 1/2 In. 150.0
Oil On Board, Landscape, Farm House, Frame, 10 x 14 In. 230.0
Oil On Board, Landscape, Fisherman, J.G. Beitl, Frame, 1893, 8 1/2 x 12 In. 517.0

Oil On Board, Landscape, Northern California Mountains, J. Cromwell, 9 x 12 In. 130.00
Oil On Board, Landscape, Old Man & Dog Beside Cabin, Gilt Frame, 12 x 16 In. 770.00
Oil On Board, Landscape, Winter, Temple Hills, Wm. J. Kaula, Frame, 29 x 33 In. 2750.00
Oil On Board, Passengers On Subway, Frame, 20th Century, 15 3/4 x 28 1/4 In. 400.00
Oil On Board, Portrait, Ebenezer Harvey, Beveled Frame, 17 x 13 In. 715.00
Oil On Board, Rural Scene, Mill & Millrace, 22 x 13 In. 55.00
Oil On Board, Seascape, Gulf Stream, Hermann Dudley Murphy, 11 x 16 In. 495.00
Oil On Board, Still Life, Floral, Earle B. Winslow, 22 x 16 In. 110.00
Oil On Board, Still Life, Floral, Schmidt, 1920, 8 3/4 x 8 1/4 In. 80.00
Oil On Board, Still Life, Tin Lunch Pail With Strawberries, Gilt Frame, 13 x 16 In. 275.00
Oil On Board, Woman, Playing Musical Instrument, Thulin Frame, 8 x 4 1/2 In. 550.00
Oil On Canvas, 2 Children, Woman Washing, Europe, 19th Century, 28 x 36 In. 1760.00
Oil On Canvas, 2 Men In Turbans, 1 Feather Trimmed Hat, 7 x 9 In. 110.00
Oil On Canvas, A Walk On The Road, Sunset, Vincenzo, 1927, 18 x 24 In. 230.00
Oil On Canvas, Black Man In Formal Attire, Thos. Fox, 1902, 19 1/4 x 10 In. 690.00
Oil On Canvas, British Country Home, W. Macleod, 19th Century, 19 x 30 In. 4400.00
Oil On Canvas, Canal & City Scene, Gustave Mascart, 1834-1914, 18 x 24 In. 1980.00
Oil On Canvas, Classical Scene, Figures, Early 19th Century, 144 x 60 In. 350.00
Oil On Canvas, Clipper Ship, J. Rule, 1917, 9 1/2 x 16 1/4 In. 920.00
Oil On Canvas, Courting Couple On Terrace, 18 x 23 In. 475.00
Oil On Canvas, Double Portrait, Men, Europe, 19th Century, Frame, 27 x 22 In. 450.00
Oil On Canvas, Figures On Path By Mountain Stream, Frame, 25 x 30 In. 865.00
Oil On Canvas, Fishing Boats Returning To Shore, Frame, 16 x 26 3/4 In. 690.00
Oil On Canvas, Forest Scene, Birch Tree, C.A. Pierce, 1889, Frame, 33 x 22 3/4 In. ... 215.00
Oil On Canvas, Fox With Prey, 12 1/2 x 15 1/4 In. 172.00
Oil On Canvas, Gentlemen, In Black Suit, Conant, Shadowbox Frame, 36 x 41 In. 800.00
Oil On Canvas, Girl At Well, Italy, 19th Century, 17 1/2 x 9 1/2 In. 110.00
Oil On Canvas, Interior Courting Scene, B. Sachs, Frame, 16 1/2 x 20 1/2 In. 770.00
Oil On Canvas, Island Trees, Charles Murray Foster, 1959, 18 x 25 In. 325.00
Oil On Canvas, Landscape, 18th Century Type, Fisherman, Gilt Frame, 36 x 45 In. 715.00
Oil On Canvas, Landscape, 2 Figures, 18th-19th Century, 19 x 26 In. 1375.00
Oil On Canvas, Landscape, Autumn, Christopher H. Shearer, 1924, 15 x 22 In. 1650.00
Oil On Canvas, Landscape, Cattle, American, G. Milone, 16 x 24 In. 175.00
Oil On Canvas, Landscape, Cottages Beside Stream, Frame, 20 x 30 In. 635.00
Oil On Canvas, Landscape, Desert, Stream, Cacti, David Swing, 1918, 22 x 14 In. 150.00
Oil On Canvas, Landscape, English Winter, Cottage, Gilt Frame, 19 3/4 x 26 3/4 In. 225.00
Oil On Canvas, Landscape, Farm, Mary Cable Butler, Unsigned, 24 x 32 In. 550.00
Oil On Canvas, Landscape, Fisherman, A.T. Oakes, 1852, 18 1/2 x 24 1/2 In. 770.00
Oil On Canvas, Landscape, Herdsman, Hunter, Peasants, Frame, 36 x 54 In. 1150.00
Oil On Canvas, Landscape, House, Albert Insley, 12 x 18 In. 115.00
Oil On Canvas, Landscape, Hudson River Valley, E. Alsdorf, 1891, 24 x 40 In. 195.00
Oil On Canvas, Landscape, Lake, Indians, M. King, 1882, Frame, 30 x 37 In. 495.00
Oil On Canvas, Landscape, Looking Through The Orchard, Gilt Frame, 12 x 19 In. 1870.00
Oil On Canvas, Landscape, Panorama De Rouen, A. Malet, 18 x 22 In. 935.00
Oil On Canvas, Landscape, Pastoral, Gilt Wood Frame, L.A. Reed, 12 x 20 In. 55.00
Oil On Canvas, Landscape, Shepherd With Sheep & Cottage, 23 x 35 In. 110.00
Oil On Canvas, Landscape, Sunset Scene, R.A. Blakelock, 11 x 9 1/2 In. 150.00
Oil On Canvas, Landscape, Village With Lake, Mountains, 1889, 29 1/2 x 39 1/2 In. ... 305.00
Oil On Canvas, Landscape, White Mountains, Gilt Frame, C.W. Knapp, 22 x 30 In. 4125.00
Oil On Canvas, Landscape, Winter, Pine Trees, Mountains, Gilt Frame, 12 x 17 In. 250.00
Oil On Canvas, Lane To The Village, C. Kuwassait, Frame, 17 x 28 In. 330.00
Oil On Canvas, Mallard Ducks In Flight At Sunset, Mayberg, 15 x 45 In. 165.00
Oil On Canvas, Man On Horse, Tea Leaking From Barrel, England, 1854, 12 x 15 In. ... 575.00
Oil On Canvas, Middle Eastern Scene, Gilt Gesso Frame, 10 x 14 In. 175.00
Oil On Canvas, Mountain River Valley, Sailboat, Repainted Gold Frame, 22 x 36 In. 445.00
Oil On Canvas, Mountain, Cascades, Signed J.B. Smith, Frame, 30 x 25 3/4 In. 575.00
Oil On Canvas, Mythological Scene, 19th Century, Frame, 26 1/2 x 19 1/2 In. 1375.00
Oil On Canvas, New York Harbor, Early 19th Century, Frame, 25 x 30 In. 2600.00
Oil On Canvas, Old Homestead Of Henry Wombaugh, Frame, 10 x 12 In. 245.00
Oil On Canvas, Paris Evening Scene, A. Branchard, Frame, 20 x 24 In. 4400.00
Oil On Canvas, Peasant & Horse Cart, Through The Woods, Carl Dietze, Frame, 30 In. . 865.00
Oil On Canvas, Pepper Pot Bridge, Arthur Clifton Goodwin, Frame, 17 x 21 In. 4150.00
Oil On Canvas, Portrait, Baby In White Dress, 18 x 18 In. 145.00

Oil On Canvas, Portrait, Boy, Blond, Landscape Ground, Gilt Frame, 34 x 29 In. 1375.00
Oil On Canvas, Portrait, Chinese Nobleman, Early 19th Cent., 16 1/2 x 13 In. 3740.00
Oil On Canvas, Portrait, Gentleman In Frock Coat, Gilt Frame, 14 3/4 x 11 1/4 In. 330.00
Oil On Canvas, Portrait, Gentleman, Distinguished Member Of Bar, Frame, 38 In. 660.00
Oil On Canvas, Portrait, George Washington, Gilt Frame, 31 x 25 3/4 In. 550.00
Oil On Canvas, Portrait, Girl, Blue Dress, E. Bowens, Frame, 36 x 29 In. 880.00
Oil On Canvas, Portrait, Jacob Joshua Freeman, Harold Dunbar, Frame, 22 x 18 In. 155.00
Oil On Canvas, Portrait, Man, Top Coat, Beard, Frame, 19th Century, Oval, 16 x 13 In. . 110.00
Oil On Canvas, Portrait, Mrs. Elizabeth Elliston, Age 53, W.R. Cooper, 27 1/2 In. 525.00
Oil On Canvas, Portrait, Woman, Blue Dress, Gilt Frame, 26 3/4 x 22 1/2 In. 190.00
Oil On Canvas, Portrait, Woman, Frame, I.S. Compton, 10 x 8 In. 55.00
Oil On Canvas, Portrait, Woman, Gilt Wood Frame, Leon Lippert, 16 x 20 In. 90.00
Oil On Canvas, Portrait, Young Man, High White Collar, Gilt Frame, 29 3/4 x 26 In. ... 425.00
Oil On Canvas, Scene Of Lake, Row Boat, Gilt Frame, 10 1/2 x 15 In. 209.00
Oil On Canvas, Seascape, California, Signed, 11 3/4 x 15 1/2 In. 165.00
Oil On Canvas, Seascape, Sail Boats, Samuel P. Dyke, 22 x 36 In. 165.00
Oil On Canvas, Self-Portrait, Woman, Ironing, S. Veronica Burleigh, Frame, 23 In. 135.00
Oil On Canvas, Ship With 3 Masts, Flying Cloud, P.D. Miller, Frame, 22 x 31 In. 1815.00
Oil On Canvas, Still Life, Apples In Basket, Shadowbox Frame, 25 1/4 x 31 In. 600.00
Oil On Canvas, Still Life, Berries In Basket, Signed, J. Bower, 1864, 9 3/4 x 7 1/2 In. .. 300.00
Oil On Canvas, Still Life, Floral, C.A. Ricciardi, 24 x 30 In. 187.00
Oil On Canvas, Still Life, Fruit, Flowers, Loving Cup, Gilt Frame, 13 3/4 x 17 In. 385.00
Oil On Canvas, Venetian Canal Scene At Dusk, D. De Ribcowsky, Frame, 16 x 24 In. ... 600.00
Oil On Canvas, Victorian House, Southern Scene, Gold Painted Frame, 9 x 14 In. 600.00
Oil On Canvas, View Of Nahant, Marine Scene, Rainbow, Darius Cobb, 18 x 30 In. 315.00
Oil On Canvas, View Of The Village By The Lake, Frame, 1866, 19 x 27 3/4 In. 1380.00
Oil On Canvas, Village Street Scene, Melville F. Stark, 20 x 30 In. 2300.00
Oil On Canvas, Waterfall Scene, C. Brenner, 1883, Shadowbox Frame, 16 x 22 In. 2100.00
Oil On Canvas, Woman, Blue Robe, Reading Book, 19th Century, 10 1/2 x 15 In. 577.00
Oil On Canvas, Woman, Green Dress, Red Shawl, Frame, 32 x 30 In. 1980.00
Oil On Canvas, Woman, Nude Before A Drape, Wolcott, Oval Frame, 29 x 24 1/2 In. ... 385.00
Oil On Canvas, Woman, Seated, Playing Guitar, Signed, 14 x 17 In. 4180.00
Oil On Canvas, Young Woman, Lace Collar, Brooch, Frame, 26 3/8 x 21 1/2 In. 220.00
Oil On Copper, Portrait, Spanish Nobleman, Frame, 19th Century, 5 x 4 In. 122.00
Oil On Linen, Landscape, Hudson River Highlands, Chadler, 1840, 17 3/4 x 23 5/8 In. .. 285.00
Oil On Panel, German Man Smoking Pipe, Gilt Foliate Frame, 10 1/2 x 8 1/2 In. 430.00
Oil On Panel, Saint George, Slain Dragon, 15th Century Style, Italy, 10 1/2 x 20 In. 275.00
Oil On Panel, Woman At Her Mirror, 19th Century, Frame, 12 1/2 x 10 In. 275.00
Oil On Plywood, Landscape, Cottage & Cart, England, Gilt Frame, 22 x 30 In. 110.00
Oil On Porcelain, Seminude Woman, Ornate Gilt Frame, Germany ....*Illus* 2000.00
Oil On Tin, Landscape, Winter, Horse Drawn Sleigh, Frame, 20 1/2 x 26 1/4 In. 210.00
Oil On Tin, Man, Red Hair, Fancy Vest, Jewelry, Frock Coat, Frame, 10 x 8 1/2 In. 330.00
On Board, Horse Head, W. Wampler, Shadowbox Frame, 1955, 24 x 20 In. 195.00
On Board, Portrait, Man, Black Frock Coat, Watercolor, Prior, Frame, 16 x 12 In. 995.00

Painting, Oil On Porcelain, Seminude
Woman, Ornate Gilt Frame, Germany

If you must move a painting in a car trunk, be careful. Put cardboard on each side of the canvas to keep it from being punctured by a tool or holder in the trunk. Close the trunk lid slowly. A quick slam may build up the air pressure and rip the canvas. If you are going on a long trip through several temperature zones, remember that a very hot, then very cold temperature will damage the painting.

On Board, Portrait, Man, Prior-Hamblin School, Mahogany Frame, 20 x 16 In. 1650.00
On Canvas, Portrait, Woman, Bell, Ink & Marker, B. Godie, Frame, 1908, 19 x 19 In. ... 775.00
On Canvas Sugar Sack, Girl With Goats, Signed, 19 x 27 In. 275.00
On Ivory, Child, Light Brown Hair, Engraved Pin, Died Jan. 23, 1844, 2 3/16 In. 1270.00
On Ivory, Dutch Village Scene, Inlaid Ivory Frame, 19th Century, 5 x 6 In. 335.00
On Ivory, George Washington, Parchment Backing, Matte, Frame, Hall, 3 1/4 In. 1100.00
On Ivory, Landscape, Farm, Animals, Georgian Style Homes, Frame, 1 1/2 x 2 7/8 In. .. 230.00
On Ivory, Madonna & Child, Velvet Lined Frame, M. Halk, 19th Century, 7 1/2 In. 550.00
On Ivory, Portrait, 2 Children, 1 Red & 1 Green, Together In Frame, 10 x 14 In. 2750.00
On Ivory, Portrait, Madame Pompadour, On Chaise, Brass Frame, 5 1/4 x 6 7/8 In. 275.00
On Ivory, Portrait, Man & Woman, Gold Case, Hair In Back, Case, 8 3/8 In., Pair 3400.00
On Ivory, Portrait, Man, Black Frock, Waistcoat, Gold Case, Hair Back, 2 3/8 x 2 In. ... 445.00
On Ivory, Portrait, Man, Frock Coat, Gray Hair, Rose Gold Case, 2 1/2 x 1 3/16 In. 545.00
On Ivory, Portrait, Marie Antoinette, Plumed Hat, Bezel Set Twisted Wire, 2 1/8 In. 150.00
On Ivory, Portrait, Officer, Ebonized Frame, Signed Caban, 6 1/4 x 4 3/4 In. 220.00
On Ivory, Portrait, Woman In Red Chapeau, Oval, G. Cerart, Metal Frame 155.00
On Ivory, Portrait, Woman, 18th Century Costume, Brass Frame, 2 1/4 x 3 1/4 In. 120.00
On Ivory, Portrait, Woman, Black Dress, Gutta Percha Case, 3 x 2 1/2 In. 995.00
On Ivory, Portrait, Woman, Gold Case, Chain, L. Thewentetti, 19th Century, 2 3/8 In. ... 550.00
On Ivory, Portrait, Woman, Polka Dot Dress, Gold Colored Case, 2 5/8 x 2 1/8 In. 995.00
On Ivory, Portrait, Young Man, Frock Coat, Gilt Frame, 3 1/2 x 2 3/4 In. 335.00
On Ivory, Portrait, Young Man, Gold Pendant Frame, Hair Locket Back, 1820s, 2 In. ... 800.00
On Ivory, Portrait, Young Woman, Purple Dress, N. Stiele, Ivory Frame, 3 3/8 In. 335.00
On Ivory, Portrait, Young Woman, White Dress, P. Legfreid, Brass Frame, 6 In. 275.00
On Panel, Saint Joseph & Christ Child, 15th Century, 11 x 9 In. 715.00
On Panel, Tiger, Folk Art, Black Flame Grained Ground, 9 1/2 x 29 1/2 In. 665.00
On Porcelain, Madame Elizabeth, Dietrich, Florentine Frame, 8 x 6 1/4 In. 140.00
On Porcelain, Young Woman, Blond Hair, M. Meline, Brass Frame, 5 5/8 x 3 3/4 In. ... 55.00
On Silk, Kyoto Woman, Black Kimono, Kiriwood Box, 14 1/4 x 2 3/4 In. 140.00
On Silk, Sage Standing Under Pine Tree, Tea Jar Seal, 39 1/2 x 14 1/4 In. 335.00
On Silk, Sailboats On River, Snow Scene, Kiriwood Box, 41 x 13 1/2 In. 225.00
On Velvet, Girl With Flute, Bird, Song Book, Gilded Frame, 14 1/2 x 18 In. 1100.00
Pastel On Canvas, Landscape, Ruins & Lake, May E. Chapin, Frame, 24 x 30 In. 600.00
Reverse On Glass, Castle Ruins On Lake, 18 x 22 In. 55.00
Reverse On Glass, Landscape, Dutch, Windmill, Frame, 19 1/2 x 27 1/2 In. 110.00
Reverse On Glass, Landscape, Outdoor Tavern, River, Frame, 1859, 17 1/4 x 20 In. 275.00
Reverse On Glass, Portrait, Daniel Webster, Frock Coat, Frame, 12 x 9 1/2 In. 1100.00
Reverse On Glass, Portrait, George Washington, Shadowbox, 27 1/2 x 23 1/4 In. 275.00
Reverse On Glass, Portrait, H. Clay, Blue Frock Coat, Frame, 12 x 9 1/4 In. 775.00
Reverse On Glass, Portrait, Jackson, Uniform, Frame, 13 3/4 x 10 1/2 In. 1100.00
Reverse On Glass, Portrait, Louise, Colorful Clothes, Frame, 15 x 11 3/4 In. 495.00
Reverse On Glass, Portrait, Man, Blue Coat, H.V. Enghiem, 8 1/8 x 5 5/8 In. 195.00
Reverse On Glass, Portrait, Martin Van Buren, Green Ground, Frame, 12 x 9 3/4 In. ... 600.00
Reverse On Glass, Portrait, Nicolaus On Horse, Uniform, Frame, 14 3/4 x 11 3/4 In. ... 600.00
Reverse On Glass, Vase Of Flowers, Gilt Frame, 10 x 7 In. 110.00
Watercolor, At Angmering Sussex, Cottage, Flowers, James Matthews, 14 x 10 In. 250.00

PAIRPOINT Manufacturing Company started in 1880 in New Bedford, Massachusetts. It soon joined with the glassworks nearby and made glass, silver-plated pieces, and lamps. Reverse-painted glass shades and molded shades known as *puffies* were part of the production until the 1930s. The company reorganized and changed its name several times but is still working today. Items listed here are glass or glass and metal. Silver-plated pieces are listed under Silver Plate.

Basket, Gadroon Edge, Twisted Open Work Handle, 9 1/4 x 8 In. 83.00
Bowl, Opal Swirl, Rosaria Rim, Stripes, Silver Plate Holder, 7 3/4 In. 197.00
Bowl, Ruby, 15 In. 235.00
Box, Dresser, Hinged Cover, Red, Yellow Rose Design, Bracket Floral Feet, 7 3/4 In. 523.00
Box, Dresser, Roses, Silver Mounted, Oval, 19th Century, 7 In. .... *Illus* 525.00
Box, Hinged Cover, Aqua, White, Scrolls & Roses, Metal Base, Oval, 7 x 4 x 4 In. 675.00
Candle Lamp, Puffy, Pansy Design, Mahogany Pedestal, 8 In. 1060.00
Candy Jar, Cover, Flame & Urn, 1907, 12 In. 695.00
Centerpiece, Silsbee, Flared Design, 4 Large Flowers, Leaves, Stems, 3 x 14 In. 210.00

Pairpoint, Box, Dresser, Roses, Silver Mounted,
Oval, 19th Century, 7 In.

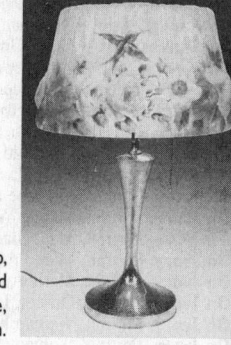

Pairpoint, Lamp,
Puffy, Hummingbird
& Rose, Silver Base,
Signed, 1907, 25 In.

Compote, Chelsea, 6 1/4 x 6 1/4 In.	85.00
Compote, Cobalt, 6 In.	65.00
Compote, Green Bowl & Stem, Controlled Bubble Ball Connector	65.00
Compote, Rosaria, Diamond Optic, Clear Controlled Bubble Ball Connector, 7 In.	325.00
Console Set, Flambeau, Mushroom Candlesticks, 1915, 12-In. Bowl, 3 Piece	1950.00
Cracker Jar, Allover Hand Painted Roses, Green & Gold Trim	385.00
Decanter, Wheat, Diamond Point, Notched Handle, Stopper, 10 x 4 In.	520.00
Dish, Cover, Controlled Bubble Ball Connector, Finial, Black Amethyst, 9 x 6 In.	55.00
Lamp, Bird, Blue Plumage, Flying Among Garden, Pink, Yellow Blossoms, 23 In.	5500.00
Lamp, Carlisle Shade, New Bedford Scene, 14 In.	2400.00
Lamp, Ceiling, Courting Cupids, Pastel Pink, White Cupids, Signed, 13 x 21 In.	6800.00
Lamp, Copley Shade, Flowers, Pink, Green, Yellow, Purple, Yellow, 13 In.	1500.00
Lamp, Copley Shade, Painted Exterior, Stylized Tree Border, 14 1/2 In.	690.00
Lamp, Daffodil, Leaded Panels Of Reds, Signed, 16 In.	9500.00
Lamp, English Forest Countryside, 15 In.	2750.00
Lamp, Exeter Shade, Garden Scene, Statues & Archways, Soft Green, 21 In.	700.00
Lamp, Exeter Shade, Team Of Horses Pulling Haywagon, Signed, 21 In.	2875.00
Lamp, Floral Design, Purple, Orange, Green, Blue, Red Flowers, Signed, 16 In.	750.00
Lamp, Landscape, Trees, Leaves, Brown, Green, Blue, 18 3/4 In.	1300.00
Lamp, Oriental Poppies, Pink, Orange, Yellow Borders, 26 In.	1600.00
Lamp, Puffy, Hummingbird & Rose, Silver Base, Signed, 1907, 25 In. *Illus*	10450.00
Lamp, Puffy, Multicolored Roses, Silver Plate Base, 7 In.	1350.00
Lamp, Puffy, Rose Bonnet, Trunk Base, 10 1/2 In.	4500.00
Lamp, Reverse Painted, 14 Ducks In Flight, Pale Blue Ground, 20 1/2 In.	4450.00
Lamp, Reverse Painted, Butterflies, Clusters Of Roses, Blue, White, 16 In.	4025.00
Lamp, Reverse Painted, Chrysanthemum Embossed Base, 22 1/2 In.	1200.00
Lamp, Reverse Painted, Exeter Shape, Autumn Harvest Scene, D. Hass, 23 In.	2000.00
Lamp, Reverse Painted, Floral, Pink, Blue, Green Ground, Signed, 14 1/2 In.	700.00
Lamp, Reverse Painted, Landscape Scene, Bronze Base, 22 1/2 In.	3025.00
Lamp, Reverse Painted, Landscape, Satin Shade, Bronze Base, Signed, 17 3/4 In.	2750.00
Lamp, Reverse Painted, Landscape, Trees, Pond With Deer, 23 In.	1210.00
Lamp, Reverse Painted, Parrot, Yellow, Soft Green, Blue Ground, 17 1/2 In.	4650.00
Lamp, Reverse Painted, Stylized Drapery, Yellow, White, 1920, 14 In.	5460.00
Lamp, Reversed Painted, Palm Shade, Closed Top, Gristmill Riverscape, 15 In.	5175.00
Lamp, Seville Shade	3800.00
Lamp, Spatterwork Shade, Clear Controlled Bubble Ball Connector, Onyx, 26 In.	2415.00
Lamp, Viscaria, Prisms, Shade, Silver Plated Fittings, 10 x 20 In.	1250.00
Lamp, Whale Oil, Cobalt, Melon Shape, 9 In.	1195.00
Pickle Castor, Chased & Engraved Silver Plated Holder, Green Jar Insert, Tongs	600.00
Plate, Coleus, 10 In.	115.00
Shade, Butterflies In Landscape, 19 In.	115.00
Shade, Roses, Pink, Yellow, Purple Butterflies, Pink, Purple, White Ground, 16 In.	300.00
Vase, Cornucopia, Peachblow	250.00
Vase, Daisy & Butterfly, 20th Century, 8 In.	104.00

Vase, Jack-In-The-Pulpit, Peachblow, White Opalescent, Enameled, 9 In.	165.00
Vase, Silsbee, Deeply Cut Leaves, Floral Design, Flared, 12 1/2 x 5 1/2 In.	300.00
Vase, Tavern, Ship Design	165.00
Vase, Trumpet, Ruby, 13 In.	335.00
Wine, Flambeau, 5 1/4 In.	50.00

ALMER COX, BROWNIES, see Brownies category.

PAPER collectibles, including almanacs, catalogs, children's books,
some greeting cards, stock certificates, and other paper ephemera, are
listed here. Paper calendars are listed separately in the Calendar category. Paper items may be found in many other sections, such as
Christmas and Movie.

Almanac, Mobil Flying Red Horse, 1940	25.00
Almanac, Standard Oil, 1922	15.00
Almanac, Swampott, Advertising For Dr. Kilmers, 1939	12.00
Almanack, Nathaniel Lower, Printed At Boston, 32 Pages, 1806, 7 x 4 1/2 In.	140.00
Blotter, Pinup, Scottie, Elvgren, Nov. 1949, 4 x 9 In.	15.00
Bond, Old Colony Railroad Company, Sheet, Cancelled Jan. 19, 1903, 16 1/2 x 11 In.	33.00
Book, Activity, Battlestar Galactica Adventure, Coloring, Puzzles, Games, 8 1/4 x 10 In.	8.00
Book, Activity, Push Out & Paste Without Paste, Saalfield Publishing Co., Ohio, 1946	8.00
Book, Big Little Book, Flipper	20.00
Book, Big Little Book, G-Man, 1936	25.00
Book, Big Little Book, Red Ryder & Little Beaver, Hoofs Of Thunder, 1939	35.00
Book, Blue Book Of Bulldogs, Pacific Bulldog Club, 119 Pages, 1938	125.00
Book, Coloring, 50 States	10.00
Book, Coloring, Bobbsey Twins, Unused, 1954	20.00
Book, Coloring, Cap'n Crunch	25.00
Book, Coloring, Chatty Baby, Whitman, 1962, 8 x 11 In.	16.00
Book, Coloring, Doris Day, Whitman, Partially Colored, 1956	16.00
Book, Coloring, Empire Strikes Back, Darth Vader, 2 Storm Troopers, 1982	9.00
Book, Coloring, G.I. Joe, 1965, 128 Pages	30.00
Book, Coloring, Green Hornet, Bruce Lee	80.00
Book, Coloring, Jonny Quest, 1960s	173.00
Book, Coloring, Lucille Ball, Whitman, 1953	40.00
Book, Coloring, My Mother The Car, Saalfield	45.00
Book, Coloring, Nancy & Sluggo, Saalfield, 1955	22.00
Book, Coloring, Wild Bill Hickok & Jingles, Saalfield, 1953	45.00
Book, Dick Daring's New Bag Of Tricks, Quaker Oats, 1934	18.00
Book, Little Golden Book, How To Tell Time, Gruen Watch Co.	65.00
Book, Paint, Ferdinand The Bull, 32 Pictures, Silly Symphony, Dell Publishing, 1938	50.00
Book, Pittsburgh Plate Glass Co., Glass-Paints, Large Format, 1923, 180 Pages	40.00
Book, Pop-Up, Jolly Jump-Ups Vacation Trip	22.00
Book, Pop-Up, Journey Through Space, 1952	60.00
Book, Pop-Up, Little Showman's Summer, Diorama	248.00
Book, Pop-Up, Night Before Christmas	20.00
Book, Pop-Up, Roosevelt In The Jungle	330.00
Book, Pop-Up, Terry & Pirates	475.00
Book, Pop-Up, Tim Tyler, Jungle, 1940s	90.00
Book, Sticker, Rocky & Bullwinkle, Whitman, 1961, Large Format, 5 Pages	20.00
Book, Tri City Dairy, Durand, Wis., $1.00 Value, Unused, 1950	12.00
Book, Trip Through Postumville, Postum Cereal Co., Hard Cover, 1920	45.00
Book, Webster's Dictionary, Given By Red Goose Shoes, Arenz Shoe Co., 1924	28.00
Booklet, Dickinson's Witchal, Beautiful Red Witch	15.00
Booklet, Handford Mfg. Co., Veterinary First Aid Hints, 1935, 24 Pages, 3 x 6 In.	15.00
Booklet, Hartz Mountain Pet Care, 1930s, 31 Pages, 4 3/4 x 6 3/4 In.	18.00
Booklet, Humphrey's Veterinary Guide, Medicines, Cures, 1911, 64 Pages	15.00
Booklet, Pratts, New Poultry, Pratt Food Co., 1907, 68 Pages	18.00
Booklet, Spratt's Hints On The Care & Feeding Of Dogs, 1930s, 50 Pages, 5 x 7 1/2 In.	45.00
Booklet, Star Wars, La Guerre Des Etoiles, General Mills, Canada, 1983, Set Of 8	57.00
Bookplate, Flower & Stem, Watercolor, Pin-Pricked Outline, 7 3/4 x 4 1/2 In.	11.00
Box, Betty Brithe Bakecups, Cardboard	.50
Brochure, Greyhound Bus Lines, The Amazing America, 1938, 24 Pages	30.00

Catalog, A.S. Aloe Co., Surgical & Medical Instruments, 1930s, 400 Pages, 7 x 10 In. .. 75.0
Catalog, Abercrombie & Fitch, 1940s 24.0
Catalog, Abercrombie & Fitch, Camping & Boating Equipment, 1938, 116 Pages 60.0
Catalog, Advance Stores Toys & Gifts, 1965, 63 Pages 30.0
Catalog, Advertising Book Matches, Salesman's Sample Book, 76 Pages 29.0
Catalog, Aldens, Spring & Summer, 1936 . . . . 70.0
Catalog, Allied Radio Corp, Chicago, 1929 . . . . 35.0
Catalog, Ansco Amateur Cameras, Supplies, 1920, 48 Pages 50.0
Catalog, Bausch & Lomb Optical Co., Rochester, N.Y., Binoculars, 1922, 20 Pages 50.0
Catalog, Bedell Co. Spring Ladies Fashions, 1913, New York, N.Y., 96 Pages 90.0
Catalog, Ben Franklin Store, 1960, Toytown, Christmas, 16 Pages 25.0
Catalog, Butterick, Spring, Pattern, 1960, 64 Pages 15.0
Catalog, California Perfume Co., Color Illustrations, 1920s, 33 Pages 180.0
Catalog, Carson Pirie Scott, Sewing Notions, Jewelry, Clothing, 1914, 538 Pages 125.0
Catalog, Colt Firearms, 1929, Illustrations, Prices 30.0
Catalog, Daisy Red Ryder, 1940 . . . . 125.0
Catalog, Detroit Carriage Mfg., 1902, 35 Pages 85.0
Catalog, E.I. DuPont Chemical Co., Explosives, Gun Powders, 1918, 236 Pages, 5 x 8 In. 50.0
Catalog, Eastman Kodak Co., Rochester, N.Y., Cameras & Supplies, 1917, 64 Pages 70.0
Catalog, Eaton's, Fall & Winter, Fashions, 1970, Canada, 820 Pages 40.0
Catalog, Eddie Bauer, 1976, Gift Book, Men's & Ladies Outdoor Clothing, 60 Pages . . . 20.0
Catalog, Emerson Electric Co., 1940, Electric Fans, 24 Pages 75.0
Catalog, F.A.O. Schwartz, Christmas, 1967 . . . . 65.0
Catalog, Firestone, Toys For 1958, Christmas, 1958, 60 Pages 100.0
Catalog, Frederick's Of Hollywood, Spring, 1962 . . . . 12.0
Catalog, General Electric, Duplex Lighting, No. DP-12, 1919, 24 Pages 60.0
Catalog, Great Meadow Farm, Trotting Stock, 1890, Washington County, N.Y., 49 Pages . 25.0
Catalog, H. Channon Co., Chicago, Tents, Camp Supplies, 1911, 112 Pages 45.0
Catalog, H. May, New York City, Safety & Straight Razors, 1890s, 18 Pages 40.0
Catalog, Imperial Wheel Co., Tires, Jackson, Michigan, 1901 . . . . 20.0
Catalog, International Harvester, 1921, Hay Machines & Stackers, 264 Pages 70.0
Catalog, J.C. Penney, Christmas Sale, 1929, Clothing, Gifts, Toys, 32 Pages 50.0
Catalog, J.C. Penney, Spring & Summer, 1964 . . . . 40.0
Catalog, Jewel Tea Co., Spring & Summer, 1955, Fashions, 100 Pages 25.0
Catalog, Joseph Harris Co., Seeds, 1932, 100 Pages 35.0
Catalog, Kalamazoo Stove Co., 1938, 36 Pages 18.0
Catalog, Kohler Co., The Victory, Newly Built Bathtub, 1915, 16 Pages 35.0
Catalog, Krantz & Sell Co., Inc., Honesdale, Pa., Rich Cut Glass, 1880s, 16 Pages 200.0
Catalog, L & C Mayers Jewelry, 1930, New York 50.0
Catalog, L.L. Bean, Fall, Outdoor Clothing, Camping, 1952, 108 Pages 50.0
Catalog, Lane Bryant Fashions For Stout Ladies, Spring & Summer, 1926, 104 Pages . . . 50.0
Catalog, Larkin, 1935 . . . . 35.0
Catalog, Larkin, Plan No. 102, Fashions, Furniture, 1929, 224 Pages 75.0
Catalog, Larkin, Spring & Summer, 1936, 184 Pages 23.0
Catalog, Lee Wards Mills Crafts & Supplies, Fall & Winter, 1954, 44 Pages 25.0
Catalog, Magee Carpet Company, Soft Cover, 40 Pages, 1932, 9 1/4 x 12 1/4 In. 14.0
Catalog, McCall Style News, May, 1938, Snow White & Seven Dwarf, Dolls, 24 Pages . 10.0
Catalog, McCormick Harvesting Machine Co., 1883, 32 Pages, 7 x 9 In. 100.0
Catalog, McCormick Harvesting Machine Co., 1901, 30 Pages 75.0
Catalog, Mendel, Berman & Co., Cincinnati, Oh., Spring & Summer, 1909, 64 Pages . . . 40.0
Catalog, Montgomery Ward, Fall & Winter, 1955-1956 . . . . 40.0
Catalog, Montgomery Ward, Fall & Winter, No. 58, 1895, 674 Pages 200.0
Catalog, Montgomery Ward, Groceries, Sep. & Oct., 1910, 74 Pages 40.0
Catalog, Montgomery Ward, No. 69, General Merchandise, 1901, 1124 Pages 175.0
Catalog, Montgomery Ward, Spring & Summer, 1941 . . . . 60.0
Catalog, Montgomery Ward, Spring & Summer, 1959 . . . . 40.0
Catalog, Moore's Auto Supply, Toys, Appliances, 1955, 67 Pages 27.50
Catalog, Moto-Mowers, Lawn Mowers, 1931, 20 Pages 35.00
Catalog, Neiman Marcus, Christmas, 1967 . . . . 30.00
Catalog, Norge Electric Ranges, 1937, 16 Pages 25.00
Catalog, Nursery & Seed, Folio, 1941 . . . . 12.00
Catalog, Oldsmobile, 1936 . . . . 45.00
Catalog, Paasch & Larson Company, Dairy Machinery, 1931, Denmark, 3 Languages . . . 40.00

Catalog, Peck, Stow & Wilcox Co., Fireplace Items, 1906, Stonington, Ct., 40 Pages	60.00
Catalog, Plymouth, 1935	45.00
Catalog, RCA Victor, Bluebird Phonograph Records, 1943, 500 Pages	50.00
Catalog, RCA, Radio, 1922	45.00
Catalog, S.S. Kresge Co., Radio Sets, Supplies, 1925, 32 Pages	75.00
Catalog, Schoenhut Toy Company, Humpty Dumpty Circus, Illustrated, 1918	185.00
Catalog, Scholl Mfg. Co., Dr. Scholl's Foot Comfort Remedies, 1935, 48 Pages	80.00
Catalog, Sears Roebuck, 1901, Drugs, Invalid Chairs, Veterinary, 53 Pages	125.00
Catalog, Sears Roebuck, 1902, No. 112, Hard Bound, 1200 Pages	250.00
Catalog, Sears Roebuck, 1909, Nov. & Dec., Our Grocery List, 50 Pages	40.00
Catalog, Sears Roebuck, 1918, Fall & Winter, General Merchandise	175.00
Catalog, Sears Roebuck, 1947, Spring & Summer	15.00
Catalog, Sears Roebuck, 1948, Spring & Summer	15.00
Catalog, Sears Roebuck, 1949, Christmas, 267 Pages, 8 x 11 In.	40.00
Catalog, Sears Roebuck, 1951, Spring & Summer	55.00
Catalog, Sears Roebuck, 1953, 450 Pages	11.00
Catalog, Sears Roebuck, 1961, Toy	60.00
Catalog, Sears Roebuck, 1966, Christmas Wish	25.00
Catalog, Sears Roebuck, 1978, Christmas Wish	25.00
Catalog, Sears Roebuck, 1981, Christmas Wish	25.00
Catalog, Spiegel, 1942, Christmas	100.00
Catalog, Spiegel, May & Stern, Fall, Furniture, Rugs, Stoves, 1925, No. 120, 120 Pages .	70.00
Catalog, SS White Porcelain Teeth, 1909	65.00
Catalog, Stanley Tools, c.1911, No. 110, Hard Cover, 52 Pages ....375.00 to 420.00	
Catalog, Stevens Shotguns, 1929	40.00
Catalog, Studebaker Wagons, South Bend, Indiana, 16 In.	85.00
Catalog, Wards, 1941, Mid-Summer Sale	40.00
Catalog, Western Auto, 1929, Order Blank, Envelope, 127 Pages	42.00
Catalog, Western Auto, Spring & Summer, 1932, Auto Supplies, Radios, 132 Pages	40.00
Catalog, Whole Earth, 1971	35.00
Catalog, Yield House, Friendly Pine, Furniture, Wall Racks, 1973, 48 Pages	15.00
Chart, 14 Drawings Of Cows' Teeth, Used To Determine Age Of Cow, 13 x 16 In.	23.00
Deed, Rowley, County Of Essex & Province Of Mass. Bay, June 1763, 8 x 15 In.	110.00
Fraktur, Baptismal, Polka Dots & Pinpricks, Margareth, 2 October 1820, 8 x 12 In.	3225.00
Fraktur, Birth & Baptismal Certificate, Susan Rebecca Wolf, Michael Wolf, A.D. 1857 ..	5060.00
Fraktur, Birth & Baptismal, Christian Vogely, Born 23 October 1770, 13 x 15 3/4 In.	2530.00
Fraktur, Birth & Baptismal, Ink & Tin Foil, Lydia Vogle, Born 18 April 1803, 13 In.	575.00
Fraktur, Birth & Baptismal, Marcobus Hartman, 11 September, 1809, 12 1/4 In.	3450.00
Fraktur, Birth & Baptismal, Phillip Schaeffer, 13 August 1823, 12 1/2 x 15 1/2 In.	5750.00
Fraktur, Birth & Baptismal, Scrolling Flowers, John Moll, 13 November 1796, 12 In.	750.00
Fraktur, Birth Record, Berks Country, Pen & Ink, Watercolor, Woven Paper, 12 x 10 In. .	715.00
Fraktur, Birth Record, Ephraim Herman, Born 1808, Frame, 13 1/2 x 12 1/2 In.	385.00
Fraktur, Birth Record, Esther Guthard, Berks County, November 22, 1803, 12 3/4 In. ...	1050.00
Fraktur, Birth Record, Heart, Floral, Birds, Dauphin County, Frame, 1801, 17 x 21 In. ..	495.00
Fraktur, Birth Record, J. Bauman, Ephrata, Watercolor Tulips, Frame, 1816, 17 x 20 In. .	600.00
Fraktur, Birth Record, Montgomery County, Pennsylvania, 1835, 18 1/4 x 16 In.	220.00
Fraktur, Birth Record, Pen & Ink, Watercolor, Frame, 1777, 15 x 15 1/2 In.	785.00
Fraktur, Birth Record, Verse, Johann Elchbach, Born 20 September, 1815, 7 x 12 In. ...	1840.00
Fraktur, Birth Record, Watercolor & Ink, Red, Black, Yellow, Frame, 1795, 7 In.	1760.00
Fraktur, Bookplate, Catarina Hersche, Lancaster County, Sepia & Blue, c.1800	1375.00
Fraktur, Interlace Calligraphic Figure Eight, Angel Heads In Corners, 9 1/2 x 7 In.	3740.00
Fraktur, Stylized Tulips, M.S.M.K., Pencil, Watercolor, Frame, 1847, 8 1/2 x 6 7/8 In. ...	880.00
Fraktur, Tulip & Compass Stars, Pen & Ink, Watercolor, Frame, 6 5/8 x 3 7/8 In.	365.00
Fraktur, Watercolor Tulip, Pinprick Horse Head, Frame, 9 1/2 x 11 1/2 In.	415.00
Guide, Greyhound, 1939	15.00
Harley Baking Cup	.50
House Blessing, Illuminated, Printed 1785, 16 1/2 x 13 In.	4100.00
Invoice & Envelope, Levi Strauss & Co., November 29, 1884	175.00
Label, Trunk, Grand Union Hotel, Opposite Grand Central Depot, N.Y.C., 1880s	20.00
Land Grant, Carroll Country, Indiana, Andrew Jackson, Frame, 1830, 11 x 17 In.	165.00
Land Grant, Carroll Country, Indiana, Martin Van Buren, Frame, 1837, 11 x 17 In.	72.00
Land Grant, For Eastern Shawnee Indian Woman, Ottawa County, Okla., 1919, 14 In. ..	150.00
Land Grant, Preble Country, Ohio, Martin Van Buren, Frame, 1838, 11 x 17 In.	100.00

Magazine, National Geographic, December, 1904 . . . . 275.0●
Manual, Buick Marquette Specifications & Adjustments, 1930, 8 1/2 x 11 In., 64 Pages . . 35.0●
Marriage Contract, Quaker, Massachusetts, Frame, 1798, 16 x 13 In. . . . . 150.0●
Membership Card, Temperance Union Membership, Carrie Nation's Picture . . . . 50.0●
Page, Harper's Weekly, A Shell In The Rebel Trenches, Winslow Homer, 1863 . . . . 40.0●
Press Pass, Pan American Airlines, 1940 . . . . 15.0●
Program, Barnum & Bailey Circus, Wizard Prince Of Arabia, 1914 . . . . 165.0●
Program, Buffalo Bill's Wild West, Frederick Remington, 1900, 7 1/2 x 9 1/2 In. . . . . . . 330.0●
Program, Cleopatra, Taylor, Burton, Harrison . . . . 10.0●
Program, Cole Bros. Circus, Cisco Kid & Pancho Cover, 1953 . . . . 23.0●
Program, Miss America Pageant, Atlantic City Steel Pier, 1954 . . . . 85.0●
Program, Pawnee Bill's Show, 1904 . . . . 350.0●
Program, Ringling Bros. Circus, 1923 . . . . 8.0●
Program, Tenth Olympiad, Los Angeles, 1932, 32 Pages . . . . 25.0●
Program, Woman Suffrage Procession In Washington, D.C., 1913 . . . . 363.0●
Songbook, 3 Registers, Belongs To Abraham Meyer, 1835, 3 2/3 x 6 In. 4025.00
Songbook, Jeanette McDonald, 1940 . . . . 5.00
Stock Certificate, Boston, Clinton Fitchburg, New Bedford R.R., 1877 . . . . 10.00
Stock Certificate, Felix Grundy Mining Co., N.Y., Factory Picture, 1882 . . . . 20.00
Stock Certificate, Frank Fehr Brewing Company, 1942 . . . . 19.00
Stock Certificate, Kansas City, Mexico Orient Railway Co., Aug. 5, 1904, 9 x 11 In. . . . 27.00
Stock Certificate, King Productions Inc., Workers, 1940s, 10 x 16 In., Book Of 26 . . . . 110.00
Stock Certificate, Los Angeles Real Estate Co., 1886 . . . . 25.00
Stock Certificate, North Butte Mining Co., Minnesota, Miners Picture, Green, 1909 . . . 6.00
Ticket, Circus, Ringling Brothers Barnum & Bailey, 1956 . . . . 3.00
Ticket, Woodstock Music & Art Fair, 3 Days, Green, Red, Black Letters, 1969, 2 x 6 In. . 50.00

PAPER DOLLS were probably inspired by the pantins, or jumping jacks, made in eighteenth-century Europe. By the 1880s, sheets of printed paper dolls and clothes were being made. The first paper doll books were made in the 1920s. Collectors prefer uncut sheets or books or boxed sets of paper dolls. Prices are about half as much if the pages have been cut.

2 Teens, Lowe, 1974, Uncut 15.00
Alice Faye 48.00
Around The World, Saalfield, 1940, Uncut 45.00
Baby Betty, Queen Holden, Whitman, 1937, Uncut 75.00
Bewitched, Samantha, Magic Wand, Box, 1965, Cut 89.00
Charmin' Chatty, Uncut 25.00
First Family, Ronald Reagan, 1981, Uncut 15.00
Gilda Radnor, Cut 22.00
Glamour Girl, Whitman, 1941, Uncut 75.00
Hair-Do, Queen Holden, Whitman, Uncut 60.00
Harry S. Truman, Cut 5.00
Heidi, Whitman, Box 35.00
Heidi & Peter, Saalfield, Uncut 40.00
Irish Girl & Boy, Cut 3.00
Jimmy Carter, Cut 5.00
June Allyson, Book, 1950s 30.00
Little Maids, Raphael Tuck, Cut 4.00
Lucille Ball, Desi Arnaz & Little Ricky, Whitman, 1953, Cut 70.00
Lucille Ball & Desi Arnaz, Whitman, 1953, Cut 55.00
Majorette, Carnation Ice Cream, 3 Costumes, 1950, 8 x 10 In. 2.00
Malibu Barbie, 1974 . . . . 20.00
Marilyn Monroe, 1978, Uncut 30.00
Metropolitan Fashions, Butterick, 1892, Cut 12.00
Mother Goose 35.00
Patsy Ann, Cardboard Trunk, 16 In. 125.00
Peggy Pryde's, Little Brother Peter, Magazine Sheet 15.00
President Clinton & Family, Cut 5.00
Princess Diana, Golden Book, 1985, Uncut 10.00
Ronald Reagan, Uncut 25.00
Singer World's Fair Dress Up Book, New York, 1964-1965, 10 x 14 In. 23.00

Sleeping, Queen Holden, 1944, Uncut 55.00
Sleeping, Queen Holden, Whitman, 1945 . . . . 50.00
Sonja Henie 48.00
Storybook Dolls, Merrill, Uncut 45.00
Storyland, Saalfield, Uncut 35.00
Sunbonnet Babies, Uncut 23.00
Susan Dey, Partridge Family, Saalfield, 1972, Uncut 55.00
Tonette, Punch-Out, Toni Company, Copyright 1952, 5 x 3 In. 35.00
Tricia Nixon, Uncut 35.00
Turn-About Twins, Lowe, 1943 . . . . 45.00
Two-Gun Pete, Magnetic, Milton Bradley, Box, 1950s 45.00
Waltons, 1975, Cut 45.00
White House Party Dresses, Merrill, 1961, Uncut 40.00
Winnie Winkle, Coloring Book, 1953 . . . . 10.00

PAPERWEIGHTS must have first appeared along with paper in ancient
Egypt. Today's collectors search for every type, from the very expensive French weights of the nineteenth century to the modern artist
weights or advertising pieces. The glass tops of the paperweights
sometimes have been nicked or scratched, and this type of damage can
be removed by polishing. Some serious collectors think this type of
repair is an alteration and will not buy a repolished weight; others
think it is an acceptable technique of restoration that does not change
the value. Baccarat paperweights are listed separately under Baccarat.

Advertising, 1000 Mile Club, Wooden, 2 Side Slats For Calling Cards 22.00
Advertising, Ames Sword Co., William Skinner & Son, Metal, 19th Century, 2 3/4 In. . . 55.00
Advertising, Amherst Stove, 1890s 75.00
Advertising, Chardonnay Vineyard, Randall Grubb, 3 In. 250.00
Advertising, Charles Cockshutt & Co., Iron Shape, Gold & Black Paint, 4 In. 275.00
Advertising, Coors Beer, Glass, Round, 1970s, 2 In. 14.00
Advertising, Duparquet, Huot & Moneuse French Ranges, 1890s 75.00
Advertising, Duplex Bicycle, Glass & Paper 250.00
Advertising, Electric Wire Clamp, Brass, Copper, 1937-1938, 3 x 3 1/2 In. 35.00
Advertising, Elephant, Cast Iron, Crane Co., 1905 . . . . 48.00
Advertising, Franklin Fire Insurance Company, Bronze, 1919, 3 In. 94.00
Advertising, Groton Bridge & Mfg. Co., Iron & Steel Bridges, 1890s 75.00
Advertising, Hartford Insurance, Bronze 50.00
Advertising, Horn's Trucking Co., Truck Shape, Gray, Red, Cast Metal, 5 In. 36.00
Advertising, Kearns Bottling Works, Dome Shape, Round 95.00
Advertising, London & Lancashire Fire Department 75.00
Advertising, Mirror, Lorenze Bros. Macaroni, Celluloid, 4 In. 70.00
Advertising, National Lead Co., Phoenix Metal, Dutch Boy, Lead, Round, 3 1/2 In. 41.00
Advertising, Neiman-Marcus, Venetian Tortoiseshell Glass, Bronze Stand 50.00
Advertising, No Flies On Green, Joyce & Co.'s Hosiery, Cast Iron, 4 1/2 In. 385.00
Advertising, Reid Brothers, At The Sign Of Red Goose, Tailor's, Iron Shape, 3 In. 305.00
Advertising, Zenith, Wallace E. James, 3 1/2 In. 60.00
Ayotte, Ballerina, 2 1/4 In. 350.00
Ayotte, Butterfly & Blossoms, 3 1/2 In. 862.00
Ayotte, Floral Bouquet, Lady Slipper Leaves, Signed, 3 1/2 In. 690.00
Banford, Floral Bouquet, Stylized Pansy, Green Leaves, Signed, 2 7/8 In. 402.00
Banford, Snake, Spotted Black On Yellow Ground, 2 3/4 In. 460.00
Buzzini, Bindweed & Wild Flax, Morning Glories, Signed, 3 In. 805.00
Buzzini, Floral Bouquet, Asters, Bud, Green Leaves, Brown Stems, Signed, 3 In. 575.00
Buzzini, Floral Bouquet, Wild Roses, Buds With Green Leaves, Signed, 3 In. 518.00
Buzzini, Potpourri Bouquet 1430.00
Casiun, Silhouettes Of Blue Ground, Pedestal 660.00
Cenedese, Lime, Internal Red Bubble, Ball Shape, On Pedestal, 1960s, 5 In. 240.00
Clichy, 8 Roses, Open Concentric, Turquoise Ground, 1 5/8 In. 920.00
Clichy, Bouquet, Pink Rose, Clematis Blossoms, 1845 . . . . *Illus* 17600.00
Clichy, Nosegay, Floral Canes, 5 Green Leaves & Stems, 2 In. 690.00
Clichy, Pink & Green Rose, Millefiori Ground, 2 1/8 In. 560.00
Clichy, Ring Of Roses, Roses, Purple Canes, Millefiori Ground, 1 3/4 In. 920.00
Clichy, Scattered Millefiori, Blue Ground, 3 In. 2045.00

Clichy, Star Cane Center, 2 In. 230.0

Cristal D'Albert, General Douglas MacArthur, 3 In. 90.0

Decorchemont, Stylized Insect, Signed, 2 1/2 In. 1725.0

End Of Day, Mr. & Mrs. Thos. Rowland, To Mr. & Mrs. John Rowland, 4 In. 40.0

Figural, Bat Head, Carved, Rosewood 225.0

Figural, Cannon Barrel, Dewey, Plaster, 5 1/2 In. 65.0

Gillinder, Lion, Satin Glass 125.0

Gillinder, White House, Impressed Picture 350.0

Kaziun, Rose, 16 Petal Blossom, Pedestal, 2 3/8 In. 805.0

Kaziun, Shamrock Center, Heart Canes, Cobalt, Green Twist, Pedestal, 2 In. 525.0

Labino, Internal White Flower Form, Signed 230.0

Labino, Smoky Mauve, Controlled Bubbles, Signed, 1972 .... 288.0

Lilies, Red & White, Green Ground, 4 1/2 In. 72.0

Lundberg, Orange Flowers, Black Vines, Iridescent Blue, Signed, 3 1/4 In. 110.0

Lundberg, Pink Lotus, Pond With Bud, Lily Pads, Blue Water, 3 5/8 In. 320.0

Lundberg, Wild Rose & Bud, Internal & External, 3 3/8 In. 450.0

Major General Zachary Taylor, Buena Vista, Feb. 22 & 23, 1847, 3 1/2 In. 150.0

Milk Glass, Alamo, Enclosed In Clear Rectangle, 1880 .... 165.0

Millifiori, 3 Stemmed Flowers, Signed 85.0

Millifiori, Flowers, Double View, 3 1/2 In. 65.0

New England Glass, Leaf Spray, Latticinio Ground, 2 1/2 In. 230.0

Olma, Purple & White Flowers, Green Leaves, 1983, 3 3/4 In. 40.0

Orient & Flume, Millefiori, Blue & White, Cane Center, May 1978, 3 In. 30.0

Perthshire, Butterfly Center, Blue Ground, 1997, 3 In. 295.0

Perthshire, Ice Skater On White Lace, Rings Of Millefiori Canes, 3 1/16 In. 413.0

Perthshire, Millefiori Butterfly, 3 In. 125.00

Perthshire, Millefiori Piedouche, 1990 .... 770.00

Raos, Spring, Monet Series, 3 In. 150.00

Rosenfeld, 3 Daffodils, 2 Buds, 2 Ladybugs, Green Ground, 3 1/4 In. 550.00

Rosenfeld, Spring Bouquet, Blue, Pink, White Flowers, Claret Ground, 3 1/4 In. 345.00

Rosenfeld, Vegetable Garden, 3 1/4 In. 300.00

Salazar, Moon & Stars, 2 1/8 In. 90.00

Sandwich, Poinsettia, Pink Blossom, Jasper Ground, 2 1/2 In. 200.00

Selkirk, Spellbound, 2 3/4 In. 130.00

Sherburne Glass Studio, Starry Night, 3 1/2 In. 260.00

Sinclair, Figural, Bluebird 48.00

Snow Dome, Advertising Tractors 55.00

Snow Dome, Atlantic City Steel Pier, Convention Hall 18.00

Snow Dome, Atlantic City, Convention Hall 20.00

Snow Dome, Cleveland, Ohio, Old Stadium 50.00

Snow Dome, Concorde Jet, With Angel 25.00

Snow Dome, Easter Rabbit, Eggs 10.00

Snow Dome, Faneuil Hall, Cradle Of Liberty 25.00

Snow Dome, Frog Prince, Germany 30.00

Snow Dome, Garfield Graduate 18.00

Snow Dome, Garfield Party, Big Fat Hairy Deal 18.00

Snow Dome, Gingerbread Castle 24.00

Snow Dome, Man Throwing Money 65.00

Snow Dome, Niagara Falls, Maid Of The Mist 17.00

Snow Dome, Royal Canadian Mounted Police 15.00

Snow Dome, San Francisco, 2 1/2 In. ....*Illus* 25.00

Snow Dome, Santa Claus, Figural, Carolers, 1950s 55.00

Snow Dome, Vancouver, Canada, Exposition, 1986 .... 22.00

Snow Dome, Washington D.C., Globe, Bakelite Base 49.00

Snow Globe, Paper Boy, Salesman Award 50.00

St. Clair, Multicolored Floral 35.00

St. Clair, Pear Shape, Green, Signed 65.00

St. Louis, Clematis, 12 Petals On Leafy Stem, 3 In. 296.00

St. Louis, Fruit Bouquet, Apple, 2 Pears, 3 Cherries, 2 1/2 In. 920.00

St. Louis, Fruit Cluster, White Latticinio Base, Mushroom Shape, Signed, 3 1/2 In. 745.00

St. Louis, Pear, Square Cookie Base, 2 3/4 In. 345.00

St. Louis, Rose Spray, Thorny Branch, 1976, 3 In. 197.00

Staffordshire, Tulip, Purple, Striated Yellow Blossom, Green Stem, 1835, 3 In. 977.00

Paperweight, Snow Dome,
San Francisco, 2 1/2 In.

Paperweight, Clichy,
Bouquet, Pink Rose,
Clematis Blossoms, 1845

Stankard, Blueberries & Butterfly, 3 1/4 In.	2185.00
Stankard, Blueberry & Spirit, Pink Blossoms, Yellow Flowers, 3 1/4 In.	2415.00
Stankard, Botanical	6050.00
Stankard, Dogwood, 4-Petal Blossoms, 2 1/4 In.	1118.00
Stankard, Floral Bouquet, Pink Roses, 3 Pink Buds, Signed, 3 In.	1725.00
Stankard, Lady's Slipper	1495.00
Stankard, Lady's Slipper, 2 Blossoms, Green Leaves On Stem, 1981, 3 1/4 In.	1719.00
Stankard, Stylized Flower, 14 Striped Blossoms, 2 1/8 In.	1120.00
Steuben, Crystal Spiral, Marked, Tompson, 3 1/2 In.	345.00
Sulphide, Acorn, Chris Buzzini, 3 3/8 In.	1200.00
Sulphide, Ben Franklin, Bust, Blue Diamond Base, 1954	85.00
Sulphide, Classic Greek Bust, Twisted Peppermint Candy Canes	120.00
Sulphide, Coronation Elizabeth II, St. Louis	375.00
Sulphide, Floral Garland, Blue & Yellow Flowers, Bandford, 3 In.	550.00
Sulphide, Grover Cleveland, Cobalt Blue, St. Clair, 1971, 3 In.	16.00
Sulphide, John & Jackie Kennedy, Blue, D'Albret	150.00
Sulphide, Man Reciting Soliloquy To Woman, St. Louis	10450.00
Sulphide, William Shakespeare, Clear Ground, 2 In.	143.00
Tarsitano, 12 Red American Beauty Roses, Green Leaves, 2 1/4 In.	575.00
Tarsitano, Crocus, Full Plant, 3 Blossoms, Leaves, 2 3/4 In.	575.00
Tarsitano, Dahlia, Yellow Stamens, Green Leaves, Star Cut Base, Signed, 3 In.	750.00
Tarsitano, Yellow, Pink Blossom, Blue Center, Blue Flowers, 3 In.	400.00
Trabucco, Red Trumpet Flower, Yellow Centers, 1 Bud On Branch, Signed, 3 In.	460.00
Trabucco, Spring Floral Bouquet, Signed, 1986, 3 3/4 In.	745.00

PAPIER-MACHE is made from paper mixed with glue, chalk, and other
ingredients, then molded and baked. It becomes very hard and can be
painted. Boxes, trays, and furniture were made of papier-mache. Some
of the nineteenth-century pieces were decorated with mother-of-pearl.
Furniture made of papier-mache is listed in the Furniture category.

Angel, Gilt Over Gesso, Wire Hanger, 9 3/8 In., Pair	265.00
Bank, Piggy, Sitting, 8 In.	110.00
Bowl, Mother-Of-Pearl Inlay, Black Ground, Europe, 19th Century, 11 In.	88.00
Box, Cover, 2 Gentlemen In Pub, Round, 5 In.	230.00
Candy Container, English Bulldog, Tan, Glass Eyes, Germany, 1900, 4 1/2 In.	875.00
Figurine, Bird, Pipsqueak In Felt, 7 1/2 In., Pair	165.00
Figurine, Pig, Pink, Curly Tail, Brown, Painted Hooves, Germany, c.1910, 9 In.	500.00
Figurine, Rabbit, Brown, Black & White Spots, Glass Eyes, F.N. Burt Co., 9 1/4 In.	48.00
Mask, Goliath, Horse Hair Beard, Mustache, Odd Fellows Lodge, 1900	195.00
Plate, Gold Siamese Design, 1920-1930, 9 x 9 1/4 In., Pair	5.50
Stand, Hat, Figural, Woman's Head, Polychrome Paint, Sylvia, 15 In.	465.00
Tray, Scroll, Black Lacquer & Gilt, Center Medallion, Landscape, 30 1/4 In.	247.00
Urn, Bamboo, Flowers, Chinese Characters In A Landscape, 27 1/2 In.	6325.00

PARASOL, see Umbrella category.

PARIAN is a fine-grained, hard-paste porcelain named for the marble it resembles. It was first made in England in 1846 and gained in favor in the United States about 1860. Figures, tea sets, vases, and other items were made of Parian at many English and American factories.

Bracket, Eagle Shape, 1850s, 7 x 7 1/2 In., Pair	1250.00
Bust, Charles Dickens, c.1900, 8 1/2 In.	125.00 to 140.00
Bust, Liszt, 7 1/4 In.	40.00
Bust, Napoleon, After Boudent, Cobalt Blue Pedestal, M. Imp. Le De Sevres, 24 In.	2750.00
Figurine, Boy, Doing A Handstand, 7 1/2 In.	69.00
Figurine, Fast Asleep, 11 1/2 In.	69.00
Figurine, Girl, Basket Of Flowers, Gold Trim, Victorian, 16 In.	225.00
Figurine, Girl, Mending A Net, 19th Century, Stamped, J. & T.B., 11 1/2 In.	97.00
Figurine, Sleeping Cupid, Lying On Side, Bow & Quiver, 12 1/4 In.	330.00
Figurine, Woman, Classic Clothes, 13 1/2 In., Pair	135.00
Group, 2 Owls On Tree Log, Matchmaking Title, 1871, 7 3/4 x 5 3/8 In.	195.00
Group, Young Man & Woman, With Dog & Lamb, White, Colonial Dress, 9 In.	125.00
Pitcher, Green, White, 1850, 9 In.	220.00
Pitcher, Pewter Lid, England, c.1850	250.00
Vase, Grape & Berry, Handle, 4 1/4 In.	55.00

PARIS, Vieux Paris, or Old Paris, is porcelain ware that is known to have been made in Paris in the eighteenth or early nineteenth century. These porcelains have no identifying mark but can be recognized by the whiteness of the porcelain and the lines and decorations. Gold decoration is often used.

Basket, Fruit, Openwork, Scrolled Foliate Designs, Blue Enamel Medallions, 14 x 6 In.	230.00
Bottle, Figural, Women, Pair	1350.00
Cachepot, Hand Painted Bird, Florals, 6 x 6 In.	60.00
Centerpiece, Lozenge Shape, Pierced, Gold & White Stripes, c.1820, 11 7/8 In.	2990.00
Cup, Putti Riding Snail, Swan, Painted In Multicolors, 6 In., Pair	632.00
Dish, Sweetmeat, Dolphins Supporting Shells, 4 3/4 In., Pair	1840.00
Dish, Vegetable, Cover, Polychrome Flowers, Gilt, Octagonal, 9 In.	66.00
Gravy Boat, Underplate	80.00
Ice Bucket, Raised Gilt Flowers, Beadwork, Festoon Border, Blue Ground, 7 x 7 3/8 In.	575.00
Jardiniere, Stand, Trumpet Shape, Painted Griffins, Urn Of Flowers, 1800, 8 3/16 In.	8050.00
Lamp, Angel Form Support, Green Ground, 2 Handles, Electric, 12 In., Pair	920.00
Pitcher, Floral Sprigs, Gold Trim, 9 3/8 In.	143.00
Pitcher & Bowl, Painted, Gilt, c.1840, 11 x 13 In.	230.00
Plate, Ornithological, Center Bird, Perched On Small Tree, 1810, 8 3/8 In., Pair	8050.00
Plate Set, Center Uniformed Soldier, Rural Landscape, c.1835, 9 3/8 In., 6 Piece	13800.00
Scent Bottle, Cavalier Figure, 1840, 10 1/2 In.	1760.00
Tea Set, Floral Bouquets, Bands, Gilt Ground, Enamel, France, 3 Piece	460.00
Teapot, Bunny Center On Rooster	325.00
Urn, Gilt, Caryatid Handles, Cobalt, 1815, 5 In., Pair	935.00
Urn, Scenic Design, Swing Shaped Handles, 1820, 20 x 7 In.	990.00
Vase, Floral Cartouches, Grapevine Handles, Blue Ground, France, 14 1/2 In., Pair	575.00
Vase, Floral Design, Peach, Gold Scalloped Top, White, Gold Ornate Handles, 14 1/2 In.	385.00

If you leave the house for a vacation or even a day, try to make it look occupied. Put a dog dish on the front porch even if you don't have a dog. Use two or more timers to light lamps in different rooms in the house. Set them at times to suggest you have turned the lights off, walked to another room, then turned lights on.

Paris, Vase, Flowers, 14 In., Pair, 1 Shown

Vase, Floral, Blue & Gold Design, 11 3/4 In., Pair 143.00
Vase, Flowers, 14 In., Pair ....*Illus* 3000.00
Vase, Foliate Sprays, Gilt, Chimera Handles, Blue Ground, 1880, 11 1/2 In., Pair 805.00
Vase, Landscape Scene, Topographical, White, 19th Century, France, 12 In. 345.00
Vase, Mercury In Oval, Trumpet Neck, Burgundy Ground, 1820, 16 13/16 In., Pair 4890.00
Vase, Pink Roses, Butterfly On Back, Blue Ground, France, 8 In. 80.00
Vase, Turquoise Faces At The Base Of Each Handle, Pink, Black, 2 Handles, 11 1/2 In. ... 195.00

PATE-DE-VERRE is an ancient technique in which glass is made by
blending and refining powdered glass of different colors into molds.
The process was revived by French glassmakers, especially Galle,
around the end of the nineteenth century.

Bowl, Green Horse Chestnut Leaves, Pink-Winged Insect, Despret, 1900, 6 In. 1610.00
Clock, Nude Maiden Amidst Foliage, Lemon Yellow, Blue, Green, 1925, 5 In. 4312.00
Dish, With Conch Shell, Pale Yellow, Turquoise, Blue, H. Berge, 1920, 4 In. 6325.00
Lamp, Wrought Iron, Blossoms, Tendrils, Amber, Orange, Brown, 1920, 8 In. 3105.00
Lamp, Wrought Iron, Stylized Aquatic Plants, Red, Purple, Gray, 1924, 12 In. 10350.00
Night-Light, 3 Purple Blossoms, Red Centers, Gray, Lavender, 8 1/4 In. 5290.00
Paperweight, Frog, Seated Upon Lily Pad, Emerald Green, Yellow, 1925, 5 In. 3450.00
Vase, Lizard, Green, Black Around Stem, Yellow, Amber, Green Base, 9 In. 6325.00
Vase, Spiders & Brambles, 2 Black Spiders Spinning Webs, 4 3/4 In. 2990.00

PATE-SUR-PATE means paste on paste. The design was made by painting layers of slip on the ceramic piece until a relief decoration was
formed. The method was developed at the Sevres factory in France
about 1850. It became even more famous at the English Minton factory about 1870. It has since been used by many potters to make both
pottery and porcelain wares.

Box, Cover, Enamel Nude With Dove, Green Ground, c.1950, 2 x 4 3/4 In. 115.00
Box, Cover, Figure On Chariot, White Relief, Cobalt Blue Rim, 7 3/4 In. 172.00
Compote, Cover, Chained Putti, Buff & Green Slip Trim, c.1865, 9 1/2 In. 6325.00
Flask, Angel Releasing Cherubs From Sack, Louis Solon, c.1870, 10 1/4 In. 8050.00
Medallion, Self-Portrait, Profile, Louis Solon, c.1892, 3 7/8 In. 1265.00
Plaque, Neptune Holding Vessel With Fish, France, 19th Century, 6 3/4 In. 980.00
Plaque, Seminude Woman, With Lantern, Putto Lights Torch, c.1870, 11 x 16 In. 2760.00
Plate, Child, Nude, Behind A Net, Supported By 2 Small Trees, 1885, 9 In. 748.00
Tile, Figural, Cherub, Green, White, Gilded Frame, 14 1/4 x 5 3/4 In. 3300.00
Tray, Woman Dancing, Blue Ground, 3 1/2 x 5 In. 165.00
Vase, Leaf Design, Celadon Ground, Minton, 1885, 7 3/4 In., Pair 546.00
Vase, Maiden In Rain Storm, Gilded Ring Handles, A. Birks, 9 1/2 In. 17525.00
Vase, White Women Figures, Mauve Ground Cartouches, 2 Handles, 7 In., Pair 748.00

PAUL REVERE POTTERY was made at several locations in and around
Boston, Massachusetts, between 1906 and 1942. The pottery was operated as a settlement house program for teenage girls. Many pieces were
signed *S.E.G.* for Saturday Evening Girls. The artists concentrated on
children's dishes and tiles. Decorations were outlined in black and
filled with color.

Bowl, Band Of Trees, Light Blue Ground, Label, 6 3/4 In. 522.00
Bowl, Breakfast, Repeated Goose, Pale Green, F. Levine, 1910, 2 1/4 In. 2200.00
Bowl, Duck, Black Lining, Skyline, Semiclosed, Manchini, 1910, 2 3/4 In. 990.00
Bowl, Green, Blue Mottled Glaze, Original Paper Label, Marked, 13 x 5 In. 412.00
Bowl, Landscape, Green, Blue, Black Outline, Ivory Ground, S.E.G., 4 x 2 1/2 In. 605.00
Bowl, Landscape, Green, Blue, Yellow, 6 In. 220.00
Bowl, Landscape, Green, Brown, Blue, Medium Blue Ground, S.E.G., 5 x 4 In. 1210.00
Bowl, Rose Glaze, Signed, S.E.G., 5 x 2 1/2 In. 110.00
Bowl, Water Lilies, Dark Green, Light Green Ground, S.E.G., 5 1/2 x 2 1/2 In. 770.00
Bowl, White Lilies, Green Leaves, Blue Sky, Yellow Ground, 9 In. 495.00
Bowl, White Water Lilies, Black Against Blue Ground, S.E.G., 8 1/2 x 2 1/2 In. 885.00
Bowl, White Water Lilies, Yellow Ground, S.E.G., 5 1/2 In. 550.00
Bowl, Yellow Flowers, Black Outline, S.E.G., 2 1/4 x 6 3/4 In. 430.00
Candlestick, Blue, Green Mottled Glaze, Ink Mark, 2 In., Pair 176.00
Chocolate Pot, Cover, 7 In. 185.00

Creamer, Mottled Blue, Brown Glaze, S.E.G., 3 In. 45.00
Cup & Saucer, Ivory Lotus, Buttercup Glaze, Eva Geneco, 1920, 2 In. 245.00
Cup & Saucer, Pinecone, Green, Black, Brown, White Ground, S.E.G., 5 x 3 In. .200.00 to 220.00
Cup & Saucer, Stylized Flowers & Leaves, Tan Ground, S.E.G., 7 1/2 In. 750.00
Cup & Saucer, Stylized Flowers, Leaves, Dark Blue, Green, Tan, S.E.G., 6 In. 750.00
Dish, Floral, Yellow, Green & Black, Blue Ground, S.E.G., Signed, 10 In. 205.00
Holder, Calendar, Landscape, Steel Blue Ground, JMD, 1919, 3 1/4 In. 465.00
Honey Pot, Stylized Bees, S.E.G., 5 1/2 x 5 1/2 In. 2070.00
Humidor, Blue Matte, S.E.G., 7 1/2 In. 645.00
Humidor, Matte Blue Glaze, Pink Interior, 6 1/4 x 5 3/4 In. 440.00
Jar, Cover, Lotus Flowers, Ivory Glaze, Eva Geneco, 1912, 5 x 3 3/4 In. 220.00
Mug, 2 Roosters Crowing In Front Of Rising Suns, 1911, S.E.G., 4 x 4 1/4 In. 4125.00
Pitcher, 6 Squirrels, Black Outline, Blue Ground, S.E.G., 1911, 4 1/2 x 4 3/4 In. 865.00
Pitcher, Band Of Trees Against Blue Sky, Green Matte Ground, Bulbous, 5 x 3 In. 550.00
Pitcher, Blue Drip Glaze, 7 In. 385.00
Pitcher, Blue Exterior, Yellow, Brown Over Blue Interior, 7 In. 498.00
Pitcher, Cream, Landscape Trees, Mountains, Green, Brown, S.E.G., 1909, 3 In. 715.00
Pitcher, Goose, Jade Green Panel Around Mouth, ELW, 1920, 4 1/4 In. 715.00
Pitcher, Milk, Band Of White Lotus Blossoms, Green Leaves, 1935, 4 3/4 x 6 In. 825.00
Pitcher, Rabbits & Tortoises, Pear Shape, Ocher, Blue, Green, S.E.G., 5 x 4 In. 3300.00
Plate, 8 Ducks, White Outline, Black Against Blue & White Ground, S.E.G., 6 In. 605.00
Plate, Band Of Trees, Green Center, S.E.G. 1913, 7 3/4 In. 1210.00
Plate, Band Of White Houses, Green Center, Green Trees, S.E.G., 1919, 7 1/2 In. 1100.00
Plate, Band Of White Rabbits, Flowers, Blue, Brown Ground, S.E.G., 1917, 7 In. 990.00
Plate, Billy His-Plate, Buttercup Yellow Band, JMD, 1919, 7 1/3 In. 330.00
Plate, Cottage Design, Black Lining, EW, 1927, 7 1/2 In. 605.00
Plate, Dessert, Incised Landscape Of Trees, Blue Sky, 1912, 7 In. 650.00
Plate, Dessert, Incised Windmills, Blue On Green, 1911, 8 In. 950.00
Plate, Dessert, Windmills, Blue On Green, White Center, S.E.G., 1911, 7 In. 950.00
Plate, Landscape, Green, Blue, Yellow, 1926, 10 In. 1045.00
Plate, Pinecone, Brown, Green, Black, White Ground, S.E.G., 8 In. 235.00
Plate, Pinecones, Brown, Green Leaves, Cream Ground, S.E.G., 7 1/2 In. 355.00
Plate, Rabbits & Tortoises, Cuerda Seca, 1917, S.E.G., 7 1/2 In. 1430.00
Plate, Repeated Singing Chicks, Canary Ground, ECT, 1921, 6 1/4 In. 880.00
Plate, Stylized Pinecones, Ivory Ground, E. Geneco, 1917, 6 1/4 In. 250.00
Plate, White Duck, Mottled Skyline Ground, Black Lining, 7 1/2 In. 935.00
Plate, White Goose, Dark Blue, Gray, Green, Yellow, S.E.G., 1914, 7 1/2 In. 880.00
Saucer, Band Of Bright Green Trees Against Blue Sky, 1928, 5 In. 385.00
Saucer, Pinecones, Brown, Green Leaves, Cream Ground, S.E.G., 5 1/2 In. 121.00
Sugar Tongs, Shell Terminals, Floral Pendants, Monogram, 1790, 6 In., Pair 8050.00
Teapot, Band Of Sailboats, Yellow Sky, S.E.G., 4 1/2 x 9 In. 770.00
Teapot, Cover, Medium Blue, Light Blue, White Drippings On Top, 7 In. 225.00
Teapot, Repeat Landscape, Black Lining, JMD, 1918, 4 3/4 x 5 1/4 In. 465.00
Teapot, Stylized White Bands, Black Lining, Chicory Blue, 1923, 4 1/2 In. 275.00
Tray, Jade Green Tree & Brown Trunks, Frame, Geneco, 1921, 15 x 8 In. 1210.00
Tray, Ring, Band Of Trees, Blue-Gray Ground, S.E.G., 4 In. 302.00
Trivet, White House In Landscape, S.E.G., 5 1/2 In. 1510.00
Vase, Birds Soaring Against Water, Green, Aqua, Light Blue, Yellow, S.E.G., 9 In. 2750.00
Vase, Blue, August 1923, 6 1/2 In. 195.00
Vase, Floral, 4 Sides, Paneled, Steel Blue Glaze, Manchini, 1918, 3 3/4 In. 1870.00
Vase, Geometric Design, Green, Black On Light Green Ground, S.E.G., 4 In. 825.00
Vase, Landscape, 6 Trees, Black Outline, Speckled Ground, S.E.G., 6 3/4 In. 717.00
Vase, Landscape, Chicory Blue, Ivory To Sage Green, JM, 1922, 4 3/4 In. 770.00
Vase, Landscape, Green, Brown, Blue, Green Ground, S.E.G., 8 In. 1430.00
Vase, Mottled Light, Dark Green, 5 1/2 In. 44.00
Vase, Stylized Landscape, Black Outline, Glossy Green Ground, S.E.G., 2 x 5 In. 770.00

PEACHBLOW glass originated about 1883 at Hobbs, Brockunier and
Company of Wheeling, West Virginia. It shades from yellow to peach
and is lined with white glass. New England peachblow is a one-layer
glass shading from red to white. Mt. Washington peachblow shades
from pink to blue. Reproductions of all types of peachblow have been
made. Some are poor and easy to identify as copies, others are very

accurate reproductions and could fool the unwary. Related pieces may be listed under Gunderson and Webb Peachblow.

Biscuit Jar, Cover, Enameled, Roses	468.00
Bowl, Floral Design, Portrait Medallions, Mt. Washington, 8 1/8 x 9 3/4 In.	550.00
Bowl, Tricornered, Mt. Washington, 2 1/2 x 5 In.	2250.00
Celery Vase, Wild Rose, Raspberry, Square Top, New England, 7 x 4 In.	785.00
Creamer, Wishbone, Footed, Raspberry Prunt, Mt. Washington, 3 3/4 x 5 In.	575.00
Jar, Diamond Quilted, Repousse Floral Design, Sterling Silver Lid, 3 1/2 In.	110.00
Pear, Whimsy, Blown, Red & Yellow, Wheeling, 5 x 3 In.	900.00
Pitcher, Hobnail, Applied Camphor Reeded Handle, Satin, 6 1/2 In.	275.00
Pitcher, Matte Finish, Rib Handle, New England, 4 1/2 In.	865.00
Punch Cup, Deep Rose To White, White Reeded Handle, New England	395.00
Punch Cup, Wild Rose	385.00
Shade, Gold, 13 1/2 In.	460.00
Sugar Shaker, Wheeling, Pewter Lid, 5 1/4 In.	2805.00
Toothpick, New England, Silver Plated Kate Greenway Holder, 5 In.	1075.00
Toothpick, Wheeling, Glossy, 2 3/4 In.	80.00
Tumbler, Wheeling	300.00
Tumbler, Wheeling, 4 In.	300.00
Tumbler, Yellow Seaweed Coraline Design, 3 5/8 In.	33.00
Vase, Amber Griffin Holder, Morgan, 10 In.	900.00
Vase, Applied Floral, Leaf Design, Ruffled Edge, 8 x 6 In.	220.00
Vase, Bud, Wheeling, 8 1/8 In.	415.00
Vase, Coralene, Seaweed, Applied Amber Feet, 6 In.	275.00
Vase, Deep Rose Shade To Pink, Cream Lining, Gold, 7 x 3 1/2 In.	375.00
Vase, Landscape, Bird Design, Oriental, Enamel, 4 1/2 In.	460.00
Vase, Lily, Deep Rose, Tricornered, New England, 9 1/2 In.	374.00
Vase, Lily, Satin, New England, 7 In.	945.00
Vase, Teardrop, Gourd Shape, Wheeling, 8 3/4 x 3 1/2 In.	875.00
Vase, Wheeling, 10 3/4 x 6 In.	1750.00
Vase, Wild Rose, Bulbous, New England, 10 1/2 x 5 In.	1250.00
Vase, Wild Rose, Flared, New England, 3 1/4 x 2 1/2 In.	550.00
Vase, Wild Rose, Raspberry To White, 4 Dimples, Gourd Shape, New England, 10 In.	1450.00

PEARL items listed here are made of the natural mother-of-pearl from shells. Such natural pearl has been used to decorate furniture and small utilitarian objects for centuries. The glassware known as mother-of-pearl is listed by that name. Opera glasses made with natural pearl shell are listed under Opera Glasses.

Case, Calling Card, Floral Inlay Tortoiseshell, 18th Century	135.00
Knife Set, Butter, Sterling Silver Ferrule, 5 1/2 In., 6 Piece	175.00
Lap Desk, Inlaid, Gold Tracery, Fitted, Victorian	265.00

PEARLWARE is an earthenware made by Josiah Wedgwood in 1779. It was copied by other potters in England. Pearlware is only slightly different in color from creamware and for many years collectors have confused the terms. Wedgwood pieces are listed in the Wedgwood category in this book.

Pearl

Bowl, Luster, Fan Shaped Blossoms, 8 Orange Squiggly Vertical Lines, 11 5/8 In.	460.00
Bowl, Peafowl, Inner Green Spatter Branch, Outer Leafy Branches, 1820, 7 1/2 In.	690.00
Bowl, Pheasant Type Design, 9 3/8 In.	2750.00
Coffeepot, Blue Oriental Landscape, England, 1800, 3 5/8 In.	805.00
Coffeepot, Dome Cover, Black Oriental Transfer, 11 1/2 In.	132.00
Coffeepot, Dome Cover, Cream, Blue, Light Mocha, Grooved Strap Handle, 9 In.	3737.00
Cream Pot, Peafowl, On Branch, Green Foliage, Leeds, 19th Century, 4 1/4 In.	862.00
Creamer, Peafowl, Sponged Tree, 3 1/2 In.	137.00
Creamer, Ribbed Handle, Blue & White Leeds Oriental Design, 3 1/4 In.	220.00
Cup, Bacchus Head Shape, Staffordshire, 3 1/2 In.	220.00
Cup & Saucer, Gaudy Floral, Pink Luster	148.00
Cup & Saucer, Handleless, Blue & White Floral, Impressed Wood	290.00
Cup & Saucer, Handleless, Salopian Black Transfer, Flowers & Birds	82.00
Cup & Saucer, Songbird, 5 Colors, Polychrome	2000.00
Dish, Serving, Cover, Flowers On Ends & Handle, Blue Feather Edge, 12 In.	385.00

Figurine, Woman With Bow & Arrow, Quiver, Staffordshire, 7 1/4 In.	489.00
Inkwell, Blue, Yellow, Gold, Double, 11 1/2 In.	330.00
Mug, Bleeding Heart Flower Design	2000.00
Mug, Vertical Banding, Blue & Brown Spatterware, c.1820, 4 3/4 In.	1840.00
Pitcher, 3 Colors, 8 1/4 In.	990.00
Pitcher, Gaudy Floral, Red, Blue, Green & Black, 6 5/8 In.	110.00
Pitcher, Name John Hodgkinsen, 1797	4025.00
Pitcher, Sprigged Design, Wood & Caldwell, 8 In.	2185.00
Plate, 5-Color Florals, Scalloped Rim, Brown Vine Border, 8 1/4 In.	935.00
Plate, Expedition D'Orient, Black Transfer, Reticulated, 2 Scenes, 7 5/8 In., Pair	120.00
Plate, Finding Of Moses, England, 8 1/4 In.	133.00
Plate, Hot Water, Blue Feather Edge, 10 In.	248.00
Plate, Peafowl, Blue Feather Edge, 7 1/2 In.	605.00
Plate, Toddy, Chicken Transfer, 4 1/2 In.	550.00
Platter, Molded Blue Feather Edge, Leed's Type, 17 In.	45.00
Pot, Blue & White Floral Design, 11 In.	358.00
Soup, Dish, S. Tams	1100.00
Sugar, Seal Of The U.S., Brown, c.1820	325.00
Tea Set, Floral Sprig Pattern, White With Green, Orange & Brown, 11 Piece	800.00
Teapot, Flowers & Insects, Flower Finial, Crossed Swords, 6 In.	355.00
Toby Jug, Man Seated In Manganese Chair, Holding Brown Jug, 9 13/16 In.	1035.00
Toby Jug, Man, Green Waistcoat, Holding Pear-Shaped Tankard, 10 In.	1495.00
Toby Jug, Man, Rose, Spotted Face, Black Tricornered Hat, 1820, 10 In.	1725.00
Toby Jug, Yorkshire Man, Maroon Waistcoat, Buttons, 9 1/4 In.	805.00
Tureen, Sauce, Scrolled Ferns, Foliage, Blue Transfer, England, 8 In.	144.00

PEKING GLASS is a Chinese cameo glass first made popular in the eighteenth century. The Chinese have continued to make this layered glass in the old manner, and many new pieces are now available that could confuse the average buyer.

Bottle, Lobed, Pale Turquoise, Quianlong Period, 5 3/4 In.	2990.00
Bottle, Red, Green & Amber, Jeweled Filigreed Metal Cap, 3 Piece	260.00
Bottle, Royal Blue, Late 19th Century, 4 In.	115.00
Bottle, Snuff, Red Vining Design, Jade Stopper, Oval, 3 In.	125.00
Bottle, Snuff, Various Animals, Flowering Tree, Mask & Ring Handles, 3 1/4 In.	1495.00
Bowl, 4-Lobed Shape, Pale Pink, 7 In.	143.00
Bowl, 4-Lobed Shape, Yellow, 3 x 9 In.	300.00
Bowl, Bell Shape, Cobalt Blue, 19th Century, 3 1/8 In., Pair	176.00
Bowl, Bell Shape, Prunus, Peony Design, Yellow, 19th Century, 6 1/8 In., Pair	990.00
Bowl, Lotus Shape, Green, 1900, 2 1/2 In., Pair	176.00
Bowl, Pale Blue, Gray, Early 20th Century, 4 1/4 In.	518.00
Bowl & Server, Rice, White, Apple Green Tint, 3 Piece	75.00
Box, Cover, Buddhist Design, Milk White, Round, 3 1/2 In.	1100.00
Candlestick, Floriform Socle, Wrought Iron Claw Base, 6 In.	90.00
Jar, Cover, Double Gourd Form, Allover Gourds & Vines, 11 In.	345.00
Jar, Rose, Carved Bird On Hawthorn Tree, Cameo Cover, 7 1/2 In.	373.00
Snuff Bottle, 2 Dragons, Red Overlay, Flattened, 19th Century, 2 1/2 In.	172.00
Snuff Bottle, Carved Dragon & Phoenix, Green Jade Stopper, 3 In.	345.00
Snuff Bottle, Chih Lung Dragons, Blue Overlay On White, 1920s, 3 In.	865.00
Snuff Bottle, Man On Bridge Fishing From Boat, Red, Jade Stopper, 2 3/4 In.	345.00
Snuff Bottle, Pear Shape, Red Fish, Yellow Ground, Agate Stopper, 2 In.	685.00
Snuff Bottle, Snowflake, Red Overlay, Green Stem Form Stopper, 3 In., Pair	345.00
Snuff Bottle, Stylized Archaic Dragons, Lappet Border, Pink, 2 3/16 In.	400.00
Vase, Birds & Fish Design, Yellow, Cameo, 10 In.	165.00
Vase, Blue & White, Applied Flowers, Butterflies, 12 In.	490.00
Vase, Blue Fish, Fauna, White, 13 1/2 In.	500.00
Vase, Bottle, Squirrel, Maple Tree Design, Club Form, Yellow, 8 In.	220.00
Vase, Double Gourd Shape, Amethyst, 18th Century, 4 1/2 In.	660.00
Vase, Duck, Amidst Scrolled Foliage, Red, White, China, 11 In., Pair	230.00
Vase, Green Crane, Lotus Design, White Ground, 19th Century, 7 In., Pair	880.00
Vase, Hand Carved Florals & Butterflies, 11 1/2 In.	1100.00
Vase, Peony, Passion Flower Design, White Ground, 1800, 7 In., Pair	3080.00
Vase, Vine Winding About Body, Deep Amethyst, 18th Century, 5 1/2 In.	2750.00

PELOTON glass is a European glass with small threads of colored glass rolled onto the surface of clear or colored glass. It is sometimes called spaghetti, or shredded coconut, glass. Most pieces found today were made in the nineteenth century.

Basket, Crystal Rigaree Rim, Wishbone Feet, Rope Thorn Handle, 8 In.	575.00
Bowl, Allover Brown & Yellow Coconut Shreds, White Ground, Footed, 6 x 6 1/2 In.	325.00
Dish, Sweetmeat, Cover, Ribbed Body, Coconut Threading, Pairpoint Lid, 5 1/2 In.	230.00
Vase, Embossed Ribbing, Coconut Strings Over Body, 4 1/2 In.	225.00
Vase, Embossed Ribbing, Coconut Strings, Pinched Middle, 3 1/2 In.	189.00
Vase, Tricornered Top, Coconut String Over Ribbed Body, 4 In.	275.00

PENS replaced hand-cut quills as writing instruments in 1780 when the first steel pen point was made in England. But it was 100 years before the commercial pen was a common item. The fountain pen was invented in the 1830s but was not made in quantity until the 1880s. All types of old pens are collected.

PEN, Conklin, Crescent Filler, Brown Hard Rubber, Gold Pocket Clip, 1918, 6 In.	90.00
Conklin, Fountain, Black Composite Body, Incised Wavy Design, Gold Band, c.1903	57.00
Conklin, Fountain, Black, Gold Filled Trim, 14K Gold Nib, 1930	90.00
Dip, Oyster Bay, Mother-Of-Pearl, Souvenir, Victorian, Box	68.00
Esterbrook, Marked Bell System Property	22.00
Eversharp, Fountain, Lever Fill, Black Bakelite, Gold Tone Trim, Pocket Clip	20.00
Eversharp, Wahl, Marbleized Green, 1930	50.00
Moore, Fountain, Lever Self-Filling, Brown, 14K Gold Tip	47.00
Mother-Of-Pearl, Victorian	80.00
Parker, Cartridge, Brown & Gold Toned Ring Design, 5 In.	35.00
Parker, Fountain, Duofold, Long Black Stripes Over Shelllike Design, 5 In.	59.00
Parker, Model 15	3700.00
Parker Duofold Jr., Lucky Curve, Orange	85.00
Sheaffer, Bakelite Holder	68.00
Sheaffer, Black Body, 14K Gold Tipped, 5 In.	25.00
Sheaffer, Junior, No. 275, Fountain, Black Plastic, Pearlescent Inlay	29.00
Sheaffer, Lifetime, Fountain, Celluloid Body, Jade Color, Gold Tone Clip, 1930s	25.00
Sheaffer, White Dot, Clipper, Box	50.00
Waterman, Fountain, Hundred Year Pen, Dark Burgundy Celluloid	59.00
PEN & PENCIL, Combination, Remington, Pen One End, Pencil Other, Celluloid, Gold Nib	25.00
Cross, Allied Signal, 14K, Box	35.00
Cross, Coca-Cola Logo Gift Box	65.00
Eversharp, 14K Gold Nib Fountain Pen, Black Barrels, Gilt Fittings, Case	22.00
Eversharp, Original Case, Marked, Skyline, 14K Yellow Gold	172.50
Morrison's, Gold Filled, 14K Gold Nib, Blue Fitted Case	92.00
Parker, Black Plastic, Gilt Banding	75.00
Parker, Brushed White Metal, Case, Cardboard Box	30.00
Sheaffer, ZD Boeing, Green Plastic, Ball-Point, Case	12.00
Tiffany, 14K Gold, 1960s Design	495.00
Waterman's, Sterling Filigree, Mechanical Pencil, 1920s	425.00
Wearever, 14K Gold Nib, Gray & Gold Tone Design, Black Stripes, Box, 5 1/4 In.	25.00

PENCILS were invented, so it is said, in 1565. The eraser was not added to the pencil until 1858. The automatic pencil was invented in 1863. Collectors today want advertising pencils or automatic pencils of unusual design. Boxes and sharpeners for pencils are also collected.

PENCIL, Atlas, Green & Black Plastic, 5 3/4 In.	12.00
Bullet, A. Dalton Box Co., Celluloid, 1910-1920, 3 3/8 In.	26.00
Bullet, Winchester	20.00
Kendall, Mechanical, Oil Can Top, 1940	40.00
Mechanical, Century, Gold Filled, c.1930	75.00
Mechanical, Cunard Liner Mautetanis, Metal Clip, Illustration Of Ship, 1930s	24.00
Mechanical, Gold, Blue, Turquoise, Victorian	45.00
Mechanical, Le Tourmeau	6.00
Mechanical, Mo-Pal Eagle	45.00
Mechanical, Parker, Blue & Black Ring Design, Arrowhead Pocket Clip, 4 1/2 In.	25.00

Pencil Sharpener, Brass, Simplex, Pat.1906, 2 In.

Fishing line is strong and almost invisible and can be used to tie fragile items to a base or wall. This will prevent damage from earthquakes, two-year-olds, and dogs with wagging tails.

Mechanical, Revolver, Metal, Moving Parts, 1 In.	31.00
Mechanical, Rifle, Moving Parts, 4 In.	30.00
Mechanical, Rio Grande	45.00
Mechanical, Salz, Pocket Clip, Purple Alligator Skin Plastic	10.00
Mechanical, Sheaffer, Model 300, O.G. Pyless, Dark Maroon, Gilt Fittings	25.00
Mechanical, Sylvania, Rotating Camera Settings, Black & White Celluloid	34.00
Parker Duofold, Red	95.00
Pencil Box, Our Gang	68.00
Royal Air Force Wing Shape, 14K Yellow Gold	345.00
Wahl, Gold Filled, For Chain	14.00
PENCIL SHARPENER, Alarm Clock	35.00
Baker's Chocolate Girl	100.00
Brass, Simplex, Pat. 1906, 2 In. ....*Illus*	8.00
Car	18.00
Clock, Germany ....20.00 to 40.00	
Cowboy, 1950s	40.00
Dexter, 1921	65.00
Dirigible, Metal, 5 In.	35.00
Dog's Head	35.00
Flip The Frog, Green Bakelite	65.00
Golfer	18.00
Gun, Die Cast Metal, Opens To Eraser In Handle, Japan, 1930s ....18.00 to 25.00	
Life Savers Candy Shape	12.00
Man, Metal, Germany	88.00
Monkees	16.00
Oriental Boy	8.50
Pocket Watch	35.00
Radio, Metal, Japan	45.00
Rubber Dog Face, Hasbro, Handle	35.00
Scotty, Bakelite	22.00
Snoopy, Ceramic	35.00
Spanky, Bakelite, 1930s, 1 1/8 In.	63.00
Spanky, Our Gang, Bakelite, 1930s	35.00
Timothy Mouse	40.00
Typewriter, Remington, 2 3/4 In.	15.00
W. Baker	40.00
Wizard Automatic Pencil Sharpener Co., Mounted, 1918	195.00

PENNSBURY Pottery worked in Morrisville, Pennsylvania, from 1950 to 1971. Full sets of dinnerware as well as many decorative items were made. Pieces are marked with the name of the factory.

Pennsbury Pottery

Amish, Ashtray, Couple, 5 In.	18.00
Amish, Cruet, Man & Woman, Pair	125.00
Amish, Cruet, Oil & Vinegar, 2 Piece ....65.00 to 125.00	
Amish, Cruet, Stopper, Pair	150.00
Amish, Cruet, Women	50.00
Amish, Pitcher, Couple, Medium	20.00
Amish, Pitcher, Woman & Heart, 4 In.	25.00

Amish, Plate, Couple	35.00
Ashtray, Don't Be So Doppish, 5 In.	24.00
Ashtray, Outen The Light	22.00
Black Rooster, Tureen, Cover, Ladle	125.00
Figurine, Bird, Nuthatch, No. 110, Black	110.00
Figurine, Rooster	139.00
Figurine, Rooster & Hen, White, 11 1/2 In., Pair	425.00
Gay Nineties, Mug, Beer, 4 1/2 In.	35.00
Plaque, Central R.R. Of New Jersey, Star, First Issue, 1870	150.00
Quartet, Bowl, Pretzel	40.00
Red Barn, Cookie Jar	100.00
Red Barn, Mug	65.00
Red Rooster, Ashtray, 5 In.	25.00
Red Rooster, Candleholder	35.00
Red Rooster, Creamer, 4 In.	22.00
Red Rooster, Mug, Cider, 4 1/2 In., Pair	75.00
Red Rooster, Pitcher	42.00
Red Rooster, Snack Set	30.00 to 35.00
Red Rooster, Sugar, Cover	22.00
Sign, Dealer's, Bird, Brown & White, 4 1/2 x 4 In.	375.00
Sweet Adeline, Bowl	65.00
Tray, 3 Sections, Christmas Tree Shape, Hexagonal Design	75.00
Tray, National Education Assoc., 1857-1957	50.00
Tulip, Pitcher, 3 Qt., 9 3/4 In.	100.00 to 145.00
Tulip, Relish	95.00

PEPSI-COLA, the drink and the name, was invented in 1898 but was not trademarked until 1903. The logo was changed from an elaborate script to the modern block letters on the 1970 Pepsi label. Several different logos have been used. Until 1951, the words *Pepsi* and *Cola* were separated by 2 dashes. These bottles are called *double dash*. In 1951 the modern logo with a single hyphen was introduced. All types of advertising memorabilia are collected, and reproductions are being made.

6-Pack, Indiana Jones	90.00
Bank, Biplane, Red, White & Blue, Pete Logos, Stearman	37.00
Bank, Truck, Cast Metal, Plastic, Box	48.00
Bank, Vending Machine, Plastic, Marx, Box, 1945	315.00
Bottle, Clemson University, Contents, 1974	10.00
Bottle, Commemorative, Amber, 1970s	85.00
Bottle, Nebraska Cornhuskers Commemorative, 1974	20.00
Bottle, Syrup, Contents, 1942	90.00
Bottle Cap, 7-Up, Coca-Cola, Cork Lined, 1950s, 3 Piece	5.00
Bottle Cap, Have A Pepsi, Yellow	155.00
Bottle Cap, Woodward Bros., Early 1900s	100.00
Bottle Display, Red, White, Blue, Gold Foil, 1940s, 8 x 14 In.	950.00
Bottle Display, With Bottle, Double Size, 5 Cents, 1930s, 6 1/2 x 13 1/2 In.	545.00
Bottle Opener, Bottle Shape, 1940	40.00
Button, Bottle Cap Shape, Made For World's Fair Uniforms, 1964, 1 In.	5.00
Calendar, 1941, Woman With Bottle, Full Pad, 15 x 23 In.	490.00
Calendar, 1947, Unused, Metal Strip, Introduction Letter	98.00
Calendar, 1956, 9 x 12 In.	575.00
Can, Cone Top, 1951	290.00
Carrier, 6-Pack, With Bottles, Bigger, Better, Cardboard, 1930s	65.00
Carrier, 6-Pack, Wood, 1930-1940	80.00
Carton, Family Case, Cardboard, 1940s	150.00
Cash Register Topper, Cardboard, Original Box, 1930-1940	632.00
Clock, Bottle Cap, Yellow Face, Light-Up, 1950s	374.00
Clock, Cloverdale Beverages, Electric, Wood Case, Square, 1930-1940, 15 1/2 In.	575.00
Clock, Double, Light-Up, 15 In.	350.00
Clock, Double-Bubble, Round, Black Numbers, Bottle Cap Shape, 1950s, 10 In.	1000.00
Clock, Electric, Sessions, Time For Pepsi-Cola, Square, 1930-1940, 14 In.	287.00
Clock, Glass, Metal, Light-Up, 14 1/2 In.	225.00

Pepsi-Cola, Clock, Light-Up, Wall

Pepsi-Cola, Clock, Telechron, Double Dot, Light-Up, 1940s

Clock, Light-Up, Wall .... *Illus* 375.00
Clock, Neon 190.00
Clock, Telechron, Double Dot, Light-Up, 1940s .... *Illus* 345.00
Clock, The Light Refreshment, Plastic, 1950s 690.00
Cooler, Aluminum, Blue Label Design, Carrying Handles, 1959, 22 x 16 In. 175.00
Cup, Paper, Full Box, 1960s 50.00
Dispenser, Countertop, Service Men's Center, 1940s, 16 x 16 x 12 In. 2185.00
Door Handle, Enjoy Pepsi-Cola, Bigger, Better, 1940s 167.00
Door Pull, Bakelite Handle, 1930-1940, 3 x 12 In. 405.00
Door Push, Bottle Caps, Pick A Pepsi, Tin, Canada, 1940s, 3 1/2 x 13 1/2 In. 430.00
Door Push, Buvez Pepsi-Cola Glace 55.00
Door Push, Drink Pepsi-Cola, 5 Cents, Worth Twice Its Price, Yellow, 1930s 1100.00
Door Push, Straight Bottle, 5 Cents, Tin, Raised Edge, 1930s, 3 1/2 x 13 1/2 In. 1092.00
Drum, Syrup, Tin, White, Red, Drum Cord Design, 10 Gal., 16 1/2 In. 120.00
Fan, Ceiling, Corrugated, 1960s, 11 In. 65.00
Glass, Anchor Hocking, Hits The Spot, Syrup Line, Box, 1930, 7 Oz., Set Of 12 .... 315.00
Glass, Flash, 1976, 16 Oz. 25.00
Glass, Green Lantern, 1976, 16 Oz. 35.00
Glass, Red & White Logo, Syrup Line, Box, c.1940, 10 Oz., Set Of 12 .... 290.00
Glass, Riddler, 1976, 16 Oz. 35.00
Glass, Road Runner, 1973, 16 Oz. 7.00
Glass, Slow Poke Rodriguez, 1973, 16 Oz. 50.00
Glass, Underdog, 1970s, 12 Oz. 25.00
Glass, Wile E. Coyote, 1973, 16 Oz. 7.00
Glass, Wonder Woman, 1976, 16 Oz. 15.00
Hat, Fountain, Paper, Pepsi-Cola, Say Pepsi, Please, Unused, 11 1/2 x 5 1/2 In. 25.00
Ice Pick & Bottle Opener, Box 28.00
Kick Plate, Refreshing & Healthful, Tin, Embossed, 1930s, 11 1/2 x 23 In. 430.00
Lighter, Musical, 1950s 175.00
Menu Board, Enjoy Teem Lemon-Lime Drink, Chalkboard, Metal, 26 x 22 In. 40.00
Menu Board, Red, White, Blue, Enamel Painted, Chalk Board, 1960s, 30 x 19 1/2 In. .. 54.00
Menu Board, Say Pepsi Please, Chalk Board, Yellow Enamel, Metal, 30 x 19 In. 124.00
Mug, Coffee, 1973 .... 8.00
Plaque, Woman, Mirror, 1940s, 13 1/2 x 6 In. 78.00
Poster, Santa With Bottle, Your Good Old Friend, Frame, 1940s, 20 x 26 In. 345.00
Radio, Cooler, Electric, 1967, 12 x 5 x 5 In. 460.00
Radio, Dispenser, Leather Carrying Straps, 1950s, 7 In. 230.00
Radio, Pepsi Dispenser, Box 495.00
Radio, Transistor, Soda Fountain Cooler Shape, Plastic, Leather Strap, 1930s 375.00
Record, With Mailing Folder, 1943 .... 60.00
Salt & Pepper, Bottle Shaped, Glass, Plastic Lid, 4 1/4 In. 36.00
Sign, 6-Pack Picture, Take Home A Carton Of Pepsi-Cola, 1930s, 23 x 11 In. 2100.00
Sign, Bag Rack Cover, Cops, Drink Pepsi-Cola, 13 x 24 In. 1495.00
Sign, Bottle Cap Shape, Celluloid, c.1945, 9 In. 160.00
Sign, Bottle Cap Shape, Porcelain, Slanted, Beveled, Canada, 1950s, 19 In. 545.00
Sign, Bottle Cap, Bottle, Tin, 1950s, 18 x 48 In. 431.00
Sign, Delicious, Delightful, Tin, Embossed, c.1910, 3 1/2 x 10 In. 255.00

Sign, Enjoy A Pepsi, Porcelain, 29 x 12 In.	525.00
Sign, Flange, Bottle Cap, Tin, Canada, 1940s, 16 x 18 In.	517.00
Sign, French, Glass Front, Light-Up, Canada, Round, 1950s	690.00
Sign, Glass, Wooden Base, Bottle Cap, Yellow Ground, 1950-1960, 17 x 12 In.	241.00
Sign, Hanging, Celluloid, Ice Cold, Round, Late 1930s-Early 1940s, 9 In.	489.00
Sign, Ice Cold Drinks, Polar Bear, Tin, 1950s, 23 In.	253.00
Sign, Ice Cold, Flange, Tin, Round, 1940s, 16 In.	2070.00
Sign, Pepsi-Cola Cap Trail, Tin, 14 x 37 In.	230.00
Sign, School Crossing Guard, Original Base & Pole, 1950s, 30 x 60 In.	2185.00
Sign, Straight Bottle, 5 Cents, Celluloid Over Tin, 1930s, 5 1/4 x 12 1/2 In.	1265.00
Sign, Tin On Cardboard, Stand-Up, 8 x 12 In.	83.00
Sign, Wall Flange, Hanging Bottle, Cardboard, 16 x 9 In.	520.00
Sign, Wall, Bottle Cap Shape, Metal, 20 In.	280.00
Sign, Woman, Winter Outfit, Bottle, Cardboard, Self-Framed, 1950s, 21 x 26 In.	345.00
Straws, Unopened Box, Picture Of Straight-Sided Bottle, 500 Piece	747.00
Syrup Drum, Concentrate, 1930s, 10 Gal.	120.00
Tap Knob, Musical, 1940s	240.00
Thermometer, Bigger, Better, 1930s, 6 x 16 In.	575.00
Thermometer, Bottle Logo, Late 1930s-Early 1940s, 6 1/2 x 16 In.	460.00
Thermometer, Round, Glass Front, Box, 1960-1970, 18 In.	161.00
Thermometer, Wall, Say Pepsi Please, Stamped Metal, 7 x 28 In.	50.00
Tip Tray, Woman, Green Dress, Feathered Hat, Holding Glass, 1909	1265.00
Toy, Carton Of Pepsi, 6-Pack, Glass Bottles, Child's Play Set, 1958	100.00
Toy, Picnic Bear, Drinks Pepsi, Battery Operated, Japan, Box, 1950s	345.00
Toy, Pull, Dog Riding Hot Dog Cart, Wood, Metal Umbrella, Cass Toys, 1945	230.00
Toy, Truck, 1951, 4 In.	125.00
Toy, Truck, Plastic, Metal Insert, Bottles, 1945, 7 1/2 In.	92.00
Tray, Enjoy, Hits The Spot, 1940s, 14 x 11 In.	195.00
Tray, Map, Bottle, Bigger & Better, Coast To Coast, Rectangular, 1930s	402.00
Tray, Scene, Round, 13 In.	22.00
Truck, Buddy L, Steel, Plastic, 15 x 6 1/4 x 7 In.	20.00
Vending Machine, Double Dot, Ideal 55	1400.00
Watch Fob, 1908	265.00

PERFUME BOTTLES are made of cut glass, pressed glass, art glass, silver, metal, enamel, and even plastic or porcelain. Although the small bottle to hold perfume was first made before the time of ancient Egypt, t is the nineteenth- and twentieth-century examples that interest oday's collector. DeVilbiss Company has made atomizers of all types since 1888 but no longer makes the perfume bottle tops so popular with collectors. These were made from 1920 to 1968. The glass bottle may be by any of many manufacturers even if the atomizer is marked *DeVilbiss*. The word *factice*, which often appears in ads, refers to store display bottles. Glass or porcelain examples may be found under the appropriate name such as Lalique, Czechoslovakia, etc.

Atomizer, Cobalt Blue, Enamel Design, Czechoslovakia, 7 3/4 In.	82.00
Balenciaga, LeDix, Contents	23.00
Berard, Butterfly, Leaves, Apple Design, Gilded Wax, 1 7/8 In.	270.00
Black Opaque Glass, Frosted Nude & Swan, Green Porcelain Stopper, 3 In.	185.00
Blue Iridescent, Peach, Blossom, Mirror Stopper, Carder, Steuben, 7 In.	1840.00
Blue Iridescent, Peach, Mirror Black Stopper, Carder, Steuben, 7 In.	1610.00
Bourday, Double Nudes On Stopper, Green, 1920s	295.00
Bourjois, Evening In Paris, Cobalt Blue Flacon, Blue Floral, 2 In.	254.00
Bourjois, Evening In Paris, Cobalt Blue Flacon, Teardrop Stopper, 2 7/8 In.	286.00 to 516.00
Bourjois, Evening In Paris, Cobalt Blue, Art Deco, Talc, 3 1/2 Oz.	50.00
Bourjois, Evening In Paris, Cobalt Blue, Talc, 3 1/2 Oz.	35.00
Bourjois, Evening In Paris, Cobalt Blue, White, Red Box, 2 1/3 In.	254.00
Bourjois, Evening In Paris, Spray Cologne, Cobalt Blue, 1 Oz.	45.00
Caron, Bellodgia, Faceted Glass Topper, 2 1/2 In.	40.00
Ciro, New Horizons, Box, 3 1/2 In.	20.00
Cologne, Crystal-Faceted Stopper, 7 1/2 In.	170.00
Coty, A Suma, Flacon, Floral Design, Matching Stopper, Spherical, 2 In.	436.00 to 635.00
Coty, Imprevu, Box, 2 1/4 In.	15.00

Coty, L'Amaint, Box 35.00
Coty, Styx, Frosted Stopper, Gilded Paper Box, Lalique Flacon 713.00
Cranberry Glass, Crystal Faceted Stopper, Band Of Gold, Frosted, 4 1/2 In. 145.00
Cranberry Glass, Holder, Marble Base, Signed Riker, 8 1/4 In. 72.00
Crystal Bird, Imbedded Heart, Zellique Studio, 1991 . . . . 125.00
Cupid & Woman, Malachite, Czechoslovakia 400.00
Cut Glass, Art Deco, Stopper, 8 In. 125.00
Cut Glass, Vanity Jar, Floral Repousse Cover, Sterling Silver 355.00
Cut Panels, Gilt, Ruby Flash, Stopper, 5 1/4 In. 220.00
D'Orsay, Toujours Fidele 275.00
DeVilbiss, Atomizer, Gold Plate, Original Base Label, 4 1/2 In. 16.50
DeVilbiss, Atomizer, Marigold, Stopper 400.00
DeVilbiss, Atomizer, Original Bulb, 4 1/2 In. 60.00
DeVilbiss, Black Oval Body, Gilt Vertical Stripes, Pedestal, c.1920, 9 In. 255.00
DeVilbiss, Blue, Black Atomizer, Original Bulb, 5 1/2 In. 65.00
DeVilbiss, Clear Atomizer, Paper Label 35.00
DeVilbiss, Floral, Foliate Design, Blue Aurene, Black Finial, 9 1/2 In. 920.00
DeVilbiss, Gilt Metal Anthemion Band, Gilt Vertical Stripes, Black, 9 In. 253.00
DeVilbiss, Marigold, Atomizer, Stopper 400.00
DeVilbiss, White Rabbit, Atomizer, Lenox 350.00
Elizabeth Arden, It's You, Hand Holding Bud Vase Shape, Baccarat Flacon 2380.00
Elysian Chemists & Perfumers, Detroit, Cobalt Blue, 6 1/2 In. 30.00
Enamel Coat Of Arms, Enamel Green Trim Stopper, Germany, 2 In. 55.00
Estee Lauder, Panda, Enameled 85.00
Faberge, Act IV, Goldtone, Bell-Shaped Top, 2 3/8 In. 30.00
Figural, Elephant, Turban Rider Cover, 3 x 2 In. 30.00
Figural, Guitar, Emerald Green, 6 In. 25.00
Flask, Black Glass, Brass Filigree 40.00
Flask, Crystal, Chased Silver Mounts, Europe, 19th Century, 10 In. 412.00
Floral, Pedestal, Limoges 170.00
Flowering Poppies, Enameled, Signed, Galle, 5 In. 4150.00
Forever Amber, Katheryn 45.00
Francois Villon, Tryst, Red Flacon, Skyscraper Shape, Black Stopper, 3 In. 357.00
Fuller Brush, Bird In Swing Cage, With Chain 75.00
Gala De Paris, 5 Assorted Bottles, Gold Presentation Box, 1 1/2 In. 35.00
Gardenia, Palmer, Box, 3 1/4 In. 15.00
Gold, Grape, Cameo, Vandermark 260.00
Gold, Playful Putti, Greek Key Borders, Brick Red, Black, 1930, 2 1/2 In. 2185.00
Gold Cranberry Bubble Stopper, Lacy Gold Leaves & Foliage, 6 In. 145.00
Guerlain, Gardenia, Cobalt Blue, Lantern Shape, Trapezoid Shape 793.00
Guerlain, Muguet, Vase Shape, Hollow Stopper, Ribbon At Neck 1110.00
Harriet Hubbard Ayer, Muguet, Flacon, Heart Shape, Brass Cap, 2 In. 381.00
Hattie Carnegie, Beige, Contents 30.00
Hattie Carnegie, Carte Verte, Box, 4 1/2 In. 25.00
Hattie Carnegie, Pink, Silk Box, 4 1/2 In. 85.00
Helena Rubinstein, Emotion, Box, 2 In. 15.00
Helena Rubinstein, Heaven Sent, Box, 2 5/8 In. 15.00
Hires Cologne, Philadelphia, Aqua, Triangular 55.00
Houbigant, Chantilly, Box, 2 3/4 In. 15.00
Ingrid, Flacon, 2-Tone Opaque Green, Bakelite Screw Cap, 2 1/2 In. 515.00
Jergens, Atom Bomb, Bomb Shape 35.00
Joe St. Clair, Paperweight, Signed 70.00
Kwan Yin, Lotus, Blue 24.00
Lancombe, Magie, Purse, Polished Glass Teardrop, 3 1/2 In. 65.00
Lanvin, My Sin, Cylindrical, Gold, Cartier On Box, 2 1/2 In. 25.00
Leaf Branches, Purple, Brown, White, Atomizer, Cameo, Galle, 5 In. 800.00
Lentheric, Miracle, Contents 28.00
Lightners Jockey Club, Label Under Glass, Stopper 315.00
Lubin, Kismet, Elephant Shape, Mahout Rider, Baccarat Flacon 6741.00
Lucien LeLong, Jabot, 5-In. Base 300.00
Lucien LeLong, Jabot, Ruffle Shaped, Stopper With Dauber 635.00
Lucien LeLong, Opening Night, Pyramid Shape, 1920s, 6 In. 160.00
Mary Dunhill, Flacon, White Serigraphy, Gold, Green Box, Ball Stopper, 2 In. 357.00

Max Factor, Flower Bouquet	100.00
Milk Glass, Chinaman, Seated, Metal Atomizer Head, 1860-1890, 5 3/4 In.	275.00
Millefiori, Paperweight, Dipper, Bulbous, 5 In.	70.00
Myon, 3 Passions, Black, Gold Myon Label, Black Bakelite Screw Cap, 1 In.	190.00
Nailsea, Cobalt Body, Opaque White Swirls, Brass Hinged Lid	390.00
Nina Ricci, Coeur-Joie, Purse Flacon, Suede Leather Pouch, Brass Cap, 4 In.	634.00
Nina Ricci, Douce, Scalloped Frieze, Glass Ball Stopper, 2 1/4 In.	182.00
Nina Ricci, Farouche, Heart Shape, Red Silk Box, Lalique Flacon	355.00
Nina Ricci, Sunburst, Scalloped Front, Green Apple, White Paper Label, 1 In.	175.00
Paperweight, Blown Glass, Red & White Floral Design, Stopper, 9 1/4 In.	105.00
Prince Matchabelli, Green Enamel, 1 Oz.	200.00
Prince Matchabelli, Maria, Box, 3 In.	95.00
Prince Matchabelli, Purse Flacon, Elongated Crown, Brass Cap, 2 7/8 In.	205.00
Prince Matchabelli, Stradivari, Box, 1 1/2 In.	65.00
Purse, Pop-Up, Door On Top, Plastic Case, 1 7/8 In.	45.00
Ralph Lauren, Chaps, Factice	65.00
Revillon Freres, Carnet De Bal, Twisted Bulb Shape, Bakelite Screw Cap, 1 In.	183.00
Richard Hudnut, Gemey, Flacon, Tester, 4 Vertical Panels, Disc Stopper, 2 In.	278.00
Rochas, Femme, Box	28.00
Roger & Gallet, Bridalis, Crystal, Frosted Stopper, Baccarat Flacon	278.00
Scent, Pinwheel, Aqua, Open Pontil	450.00
Schiaparelli, Pipe, 5 1/2 In.	875.00
Schiaparelli, Shocking, Glass Flowers In Dome, 6 In.	245.00
Shandra, Stopper, Plastic Box, 1920s, 3 In.	40.00
Star & Punty, Canary, Stopper, 5 5/8 In.	135.00
Star & Punty, Yellow Green, Stopper, 5 1/8 In.	330.00
Steuben, Alabaster, Gilt Foot	300.00
Steuben, Lime Green Iridescent, Oriental Village Design, Etched, 5 In.	187.00
Stone, Carved, Bird Shape, 3 3/4 In.	431.00
Thousand Eye Honeycomb Cutting, Hinged Silver Rim & Cap, Amethyst	700.00
Tic-Tox, Box, 4 In.	38.00
Toilet Water, Matching Undertray, Pomegranate Form, 1860, 8 In.	770.00
Tortoiseshell, Columnar Geometric, Bakelite Dabber	85.00
Vicky Tiel, Figural Dauber, Large	125.00
Vigny, Golliwog, Sticker, 2 In.	75.00

PETERS & REED Pottery Company of Zanesville, Ohio, was founded
y John D. Peters and Adam Reed in 1897. Chromal, Landsun,
Montene, Pereco, and Persian are some of the art lines that were made.
The company, which became Zane Pottery in 1920 and Gonder Pottery
n 1941, closed in 1957. Peters & Reed pottery was unmarked.

Bowl, Appliqued Flowers, Brown Glaze, Handles, 4 In.	30.00
Bowl, Landsun, 10 In.	35.00
Candlestick, Appliqued Wreath, Bell Shape, Large	40.00
Cuspidor, Moss Aztec, 5 x 6 In.	150.00
Flower Frog, Landsun, Leaf Shape, Blue, Green Matte Glaze, 5 1/2 x 2 In.	33.00
Jardiniere, Blue, 4 In.	50.00
Jardiniere, Chromal, 14 In.	450.00
Jardiniere, Floral & Drape, 10 In.	225.00
Jardiniere, Grape Vines, 6 In.	100.00
Jardiniere, Raised Geometric Band, Brown, Pale Green Matte Glaze, 3 In.	33.00
Jug, Wreath Design, Variegated Brown Glaze, Embossed, 5 In.	60.00
Pitcher, Dragon Handle, Light Green	350.00
Vase, Blue, Black & Yellow Brushed Over Red Clay, 9 In.	65.00
Vase, Blue, Red, Brown Highlights, 5 3/4 In.	44.00
Vase, Brown, Red, Blue Highlights, 3 1/2 In.	44.00
Vase, Chromal Landscape, Ivory, Blue, Umber Glaze, 1915, 6 x 4 1/2 In.	522.00
Vase, Chromal, Farm Scene, 7 1/2 In.	468.00
Vase, Landsun, 3 1/2 In.	60.00
Vase, Landsun, 4 In.	50.00
Vase, Matte Green, 8 In.	125.00 to 150.00
Vase, Molded Leaf, Branch Design, Deep Blue Glaze, 8 In.	66.00
Vase, Moss Aztec, 8 In.	95.00

Vase, Moss Aztec, Cyclamen, 10 In. 185.0
Vase, Moss Aztec, Leaves, With Long Stems, 8 In. 175.0
Vase, Moss Aztec, Stylized Roses, Green Over Brown Clay Body, Ferrel, 15 In. 358.0
Vase, Sewer Tile, Daisy Design, Brick Red, Green Glaze, 8 In. 83.0
Wall Pocket, Egyptian Head, Matte Green 275.0
Wall Pocket, Moss Aztec 150.0

PETRUS REGOUT, see Maastricht category.

PEWABIC POTTERY was founded by Mary Chase Perry Stratton in 1903 in Detroit, Michigan. The company made many types of art pottery, including pieces with matte green glaze and an iridescent crystalline glaze. The company continued working until the death of Mary Stratton in 1961. It was reactivated by Michigan State University in 1968.

PEWABIC

Bowl, Blue, 8 In. 500.0
Bowl, Flared Lip, Interior Cobalt Blue, Celadon With Gold, Signed, 4 x 5 In. 700.0
Bowl, Shimmering Burgundy Glaze Exterior, Gold Glaze Interior, Signed, 5 In. 495.0
Tile, Incised Geometric Design, Blue, Green Glaze, 5 1/2 In. 357.0
Vase, Black Dripping Glaze, Iridescent Ground, Signed, 3 x 2 1/2 In. 197.0
Vase, Blue Matte Glaze, 3 1/2 In. 330.0
Vase, Blue Matte Glaze, Broad Form, Marked, 4 In. 385.0
Vase, Blue Metallic Glaze, Gray Highlight Iridescent, 2 In. 286.0
Vase, Blue Metallic Glaze, Light To Navy Blue Iridescent, 11 In. 1760.0
Vase, Blue, Green Iridescent, 8 3/4 In. 1725.0
Vase, Blue, Green, Metallic Glaze, Purple Highlights, 11 1/2 In. 2310.0
Vase, Blue, Metallic, Gunmetal, Purple Glaze, 5 1/2 In. 825.0
Vase, Blue, Purple, Gunmetal Metallic Glaze, Impressed Mark, 10 In. 1760.0
Vase, Blue-Green Crystalline Glaze, Flaring Rim, Signed, 9 3/4 In. 2200.0
Vase, Brown, Blue, Tan Matte Over Green, Brown, Maple Leaves, 7 In. 715.0
Vase, Bud, Indigo Over Red Glaze, Paper Label, 5 x 2 1/2 In. 935.0
Vase, Bud, Purple Indigo Celadon Glaze, 4 1/2 x 4 In. 1210.0
Vase, Burgundy Luster, Celadon Glaze, Ribbed, 8 1/2 x 4 1/2 In. 1650.0
Vase, Cabinet, Turquoise, Silver, Red Glaze, 4 1/2 x 2 3/4 In. 880.0
Vase, Celadon, Blush Glaze, Bottle Shape, 5 x 3 3/4 In. 495.0
Vase, Celadon, Lavender Glaze, Flat Shoulder, Paper Label, 6 3/4 x 5 1/2 In. 1100.0
Vase, Cobalt Blue, Purple Celadon Glaze, 6 1/4 x 4 1/4 In. 2100.0
Vase, Cobalt Blue, Purple Glaze, Corseted Top, 4 3/4 x 3 1/2 In. 550.0
Vase, Copper Luster Glaze, 13 x 7 1/2 In. 2200.0
Vase, Deep Blue To Black Metallic Glaze, Gray, Blue Highlights, 7 1/2 In. 1045.0
Vase, Gold Luster, Green & Burgundy Glaze, Signed, 8 1/4 In. 1430.0
Vase, Gold Metallic, Blue, Gray Glaze, 5 1/2 In. 220.0
Vase, Gold To Cobalt Blue Matte Base, Cylindrical Center, 6 1/2 x 6 In. 1760.0
Vase, Indigo Luster, Purple Glaze, Ribbed, 5 x 4 In. 600.0
Vase, Lavender Celadon Glaze, Tapered, 5 1/4 x 4 In. 715.0
Vase, Lavender Glaze, Corseted Shoulder, 9 1/2 x 4 3/4 In. 660.0
Vase, Luster Drip Glaze, Gray, Rose, Tan & Yellow, Impressed Mark, 4 In. 665.0
Vase, Metallic Luster Glaze, Caramel, Pink & Yellow, Impressed Mark, 5 1/2 In. 990.0
Vase, Metallic Luster Glaze, Deep Blue, Impressed Mark, 6 1/2 In. 600.0
Vase, Metallic Luster Glaze, Green, Gray, Blues, Impressed Mark, 5 1/2 In. 465.0
Vase, Metallic Luster Glaze, Light Blue, Brown & Purple, Impressed Mark, 7 In. 770.0
Vase, Oatmeal Matte Glaze, Flared, Marked, 7 1/2 In. 286.0
Vase, Purple Glaze To Gold Base, Flat Shoulder, 10 1/2 x 6 1/2 In. 2530.0
Vase, Purple, Green Striated Glaze, 3 3/4 x 4 In. 825.0
Vase, Purple, Lavender, Green Glaze, 6 1/2 x 4 1/4 In. 885.0
Vase, Purple, Turquoise Glaze, Ribbed, Squatty, 3 1/2 x 5 1/2 In. 550.0
Vase, Red & Gold Glaze, Dripping Over Chinese Blue & Red, Signed, 7 1/2 In. 1760.0
Vase, Red Luster Metallic Glaze, Light Green Lowlights, 5 x 4 1/2 In. 550.0
Vase, Rose Pink Glaze, Gunmetal, 3 1/2 x 4 In. 715.0
Vase, Stovepipe Neck, Purple & Red Lustered Glaze, Paper Label, 4 x 3 In. 330.0
Vase, Tan Matte Drip Over Brown, 4 In. 360.0
Vase, Taupe Umber Glaze, Black Matte Ground, Paper Label, 7 1/2 x 4 1/2 In. 1980.0
Vase, Turquoise Luster, Vermilion Ground, Squatty, 2 1/2 x 3 3/4 In. 110.0

EWTER is a metal alloy of tin and lead. Some of the pewter made after 840 has a slightly different composition and is called *Britannia metal*. his later type of pewter was worked by machine; the earlier pieces ere made by hand. In the 1920s pewter came back into fashion and ieces were often marked *Genuine Pewter*. Eighteenth-, nineteenth-, nd twentieth-century examples are listed here.

Ashtray, Horse, 1940s	75.00
Basin, Barber's, England, c.1750	350.00
Basin, Burford & Green, c.1750, 12 In.	110.00
Basin, Samuel Danforth, Eagle Touch, 8 In.	192.00
Basket, Kayserzinn, Floral Relief Design, Signed, 9 x 11 1/2 In.	316.00
Bowl, Baptism, Boardman Family, 5 x 7 7/8 In.	880.00
Bowl, Compton, England, 13 1/4 In.	198.00
Bowl, Townsend & Compton, England, 13 In.	192.00
Box, Ashbil Griswold, V.W. Alford, Round, Hinged Lid, Divided Interior, 4 1/2 In.	220.00
Box, Rokesley, Enameled Panel, Green Leaves, Red Ground, c.1910, 1 1/2 x 5 3/4 In.	1200.00
Box, Soap, Hinged Lid, Late 18th Century, 4 1/4 In.	150.00
Box, Tobacco, Engraved, 2 Eagles, c.1800, 3 x 2 x 3/4 In.	145.00
Candlestick, Archibald Knox, 3 Leaves, Enamel Circles On Base, 9 1/2 In., Pair	1315.00
Candlestick, Baluster Form, 10 In., Pair	154.00
Candlestick, Lotus Leaf Pattern, Art Nouveau, 11 1/2 In.	180.00
Candlestick, Meriden, Removable Bobeche, 6 5/8 In.	3302.00
Candlestick, Neoclassical, Bands Of Bright-Cut Engraving, c.1810, 8 1/2 In., Pair	175.00
Candlestick, Pricket, Tripod Base, Ball Feet, Double Acorn Knops, c.1690, 9 In., Pair	1250.00
Candlestick, Pushup, Beaded, 9 In., Pair	300.00
Candlestick, Reed & Barton, c.1860, 11 In., Pair	575.00
Candlestick, Sellew & Co., With Bobeches, Cincinnati, 8 In., Pair	1100.00
Candlestick, Zeister, Tulip Bulb Shape, Holland, 3 1/4 x 2 1/4 In., Pair	15.00
Carrier, Food, Teapot Shape, Royal Portrait Medallions, Dragon Spout, Lid Handle	185.00
Chalice, Original Tinning, American, 19th Century, Pair	220.00
Charger, Engraved Scene, Man At Waterfall, Woman On Horse, 1793, 13 In.	220.00
Charger, Frederick Bassett, New York City, 1761-1780, 14 3/4 In.	1265.00
Charger, Hallmarked, Incised London, 16 1/2 In.	195.00
Charger, John Townsend, Fen Church Street, London, England, 16 1/2 In.	330.00
Charger, Robert Bush & Co., 14 7/8 In.	220.00
Charger, Robert Clothyer, 18 In.	220.00
Charger, Samuel Ellis, 16 1/2 In.	330.00
Charger, Temple & Reynolds, Engraved Monogram On Rim, 21 3/4 In.	852.00
Charger, Thomas Swanson, London, 1753-1783	138.00
Charger, William Hunter, England, 15 In.	209.00
Coaster, Wine, Vintage Design, England, 6 3/4 In., Pair	77.00
Coffeepot, Rufus Dunham, Lighthouse Shape, 10 In.	357.00
Coffeepot, Thomas D. Boardman & Co., 1825, 11 1/2 In.	675.00
Cuspidor, Scroll Handle, Continental, 1753, 3 1/2 In.	275.00
Dish, Alms, Wrigglework, Germany, 17th Century	1450.00
Dish, Deep Well, Wavy Edge, c.1750, 12 In.	275.00
Dish, Ebenezer Southmayd, 11 1/2 In.	302.00
Dish, G. Voltlander, Angel Touch, Continental, 8 1/2 In.	220.00
Dish, Single Reeded, Joseph Danforth, c.1779, 13 1/4 In.	525.00
Dish, Tudrig, Art Nouveau, Reticulated Floral, Enameled Interior, England, 10 In.	192.00
Flagon, Engraved St. Ninian's Relief Church, 1775, 9 3/4 In.	1350.00
Flagon, Kayserzinn, Art Nouveau, Embossed Floral, Horse, Hound, c.1890, 13 In.	495.00
Flagon, Richard Pitt, c.1770, 11 1/2 In.	1850.00
Humidor, Slave Head Tobacco, Interior Press Weight, 1790-1820, 5 1/2 x 3 1/2 In.	400.00
Inkwell, Underplate, Blown Out Bees, Kayserzinn	400.00
Jug, Cream, Footed, Edward Quick, London, 1759	2100.00
Jug, Scorn Finial, Bellied Form, 18th Century, 10 3/4 In.	195.00
Ladle, Twisted Baleen Handle, 12 3/4 In.	115.00
Lamp, Whale Oil, R. Gleason, 6 3/4 In.	300.00
Medallion, Liberty Bell, 4 Stars, c.1800, 3 In.	45.00
Mold, Aspic, Asparagus Top, 3-Part, English Registry Mark, 8 In.	115.00
Mold, Food, Fruit On Cover, Removable Base, English Registry Mark, 1 Qt., 6 5/8 In.	190.00
Mold, Ice Cream, E. & A. Co., Banana	65.00

Mold, Ice Cream, Grape Cluster 65.00
Mug, Tavern, WR Crowned Mark On Lip, 18th Century, London, 1 Qt. 250.00
Mug, Tulip, James Yates, Tinned Finish, 19th Century, 6 1/2 In. 175.00
Pitcher, Bird Shape, France, c.1910 .... 1275.00
Pitcher, Hinged Cover, Sellew & Co., Handle, Cincinnati, 8 3/4 In. 220.00
Pitcher, Owl, Liberty & Co., Incised Design, Blue Ceramic Eyes, England, 8 x 6 1/2 In. . 375.00
Pitcher, R. Dunham, Westbrook, Maine, 6 3/4 In. 358.00
Plate, Boardman & Co., New York, Eagle Touch, 10 3/4 In. 275.00
Plate, Boardman, 9 1/4 In. 350.00
Plate, Buford & Green, c.1748, 10 3/4 In. 95.00
Plate, Castle With Moat, Flock Of Birds, Wriggle Work, 1760s, 8 3/4 In. 125.00
Plate, Crowned Rose, Rampant Lion In Wreath With XX, London, 9 1/2 In. 150.00
Plate, Engraved, Saint Peter & Saint Paul, Continental, 18th Century, 15 In. 275.00
Plate, Johann Sprandel, Continental, 18th Century, 10 1/2 In. 110.00
Plate, John Dolbeare, Rim Stamped, Initialed & Dated 1751, 9 1/2 In. 450.00
Plate, John Townsend, Wavy Edge, London, 9 3/4 In. 295.00
Plate, Love Touch, 7 7/8 In. 165.00
Plate, Raised Central Boss, Continental, Late 16th Century, 12 7/8 In. 695.00
Plate, Rotgert Arends II, Master's Mark, 13 1/2 In. 260.00
Plate, S. Kilbourn, 7 3/4 In. 135.00
Plate, Samuel Ellis, c.1750, 8 1/2 In. 125.00
Plate, Sun & Stars Design, Hallmarked, Initialed, Early 1800s, 8 3/8 In. 250.00
Plate, Thomas Alderson, King George IV Royal Cipher On Rim, 1820 .... 495.00
Plate, Thomas Badgeer, Stamped PW, 8 1/2 In. 165.00
Plate, Thomas Danforth Boardman, 2 Eagles, Hartford, Connecticut, 7 3/4 In. 165.00
Plate, Thomas Danforth I, Rampant Lion Touch, Massachusetts & Connecticut, 8 In. ... 220.00
Plate, Thomas Danforth III, Eagle Touch, Philadelphia, 7 3/4 In. ....137.00 to 150.00
Plate, William Eddon, England, c.1730 .... 350.00
Porringer, Cast Crown Handle, S.G., 5 1/2 In. 192.00
Porringer, Cast Flower Handle, 5 In. 165.00
Porringer, Coronet Handle, c.1780, 4 1/2-In. Bowl 295.00
Porringer, Roswell Gleason, 3 Heart & Crescent Handle, 1822, 3 5/8 In., Pair 350.00
Pot, Leonard, Reed & Barton, England, 12 1/4 In. 192.00
Pot, Sellew & Co., Cincinnati, 11 1/4 In. 275.00
Salt Box, 2 Touchmarks, 18th Century, 8 x 6 In. 275.00
Soup, Dish, Nordingen Mark, Single Reeded Rims, Cast Leaf Design, 8 1/2 In., Pair . 175.00
Spoon, Cast Design, 1861, 8 In., 12 Piece 28.00
Spoon, Luther Boardman Touch, Cast Handle, Wire Rack, Set Of 22 .... 260.00
Spoon, Shaped Handle, Stamped Floral Design, England, 19th Century, 12 Piece 230.00
Sugar & Creamer, Sellew & Co., Cincinnati, 6 3/8 x 6 7/8 In. 495.00
Sugar Bowl, Sheldon & Feltman, Albany Touch, 7 5/8 In. 95.00
Tall Pot, Boardman & Hart, 11 1/2 In. 245.00
Tall Pot, G. Richardson, Boston, 10 1/2 In. 302.00
Tea Set, Child's, Teapot, Sugar, Creamer, 4 Cups & Saucers, 2 1/2 In., 11 Piece 70.00
Tea Set, Hand Hammered, Liberty, 4 Piece 650.00
Teapot, A. Griswold, Eagle Touch, 6 3/4 In. 195.00
Teapot, A. Griswold, Eagle Touch, Meriden, Ct., 8 1/8 In. 195.00
Teapot, Allover Wrigglework, Dutch, 1709, Small 1950.00
Teapot, Dixon & Son, Oblong Boat Shape, Ebonized Handle, Claw Feet 66.00
Teapot, F. Porter, Engraved Line Design, c.1835, 11 1/2 In. 170.00
Teapot, G. Richardson Touch, 9 1/4 In. 248.00
Teapot, J. Danforth, Wooden Wafer Finial, 7 1/4 In. 165.00
Teapot, James Dixson & Sons, Paneled, England, 11 In. 165.00
Teapot, L. Boardman, South Reading, Mass., 7 1/2 In. 138.00
Teapot, Leonard, Reed & Barton, Wooden Finial & Handle, 10 1/2 In. 126.00
Teapot, Savage, Midd Ct., 7 3/4 In. 258.00
Tray, Calling Card, Cherub Holds Up Tray, Germany, c.1880 .... 145.00
Tureen, Soup, Kayserzinn, Poppies, 12 In. 288.00
Vase, Art Nouveau, 3 Handles, 4 3/4 In. 60.00
Vase, Baluster Form, France, 18th Century, 7 In., Pair 33.00
Vase, Kayserzinn, Art Nouveau, 23 1/2 In., Pair 3750.00
Wine Can, Wrigglework Design, Initials, Continental, Date 1729 .... 295.00

HOENIX BIRD, or Flying Phoenix, is the name given to a blue-and-hite kitchenware popular between 1900 and World War II. A variant known as Flying Turkey. Most of this dinnerware was made in Japan or sale in the dime stores in America. It is still being made.

Bowl, Japan, 5 1/2 In.	22.00
Butter, Cover	90.00
Candy Dish	65.00
Chocolate Pot, Scalloped	125.00
Cup & Saucer	10.00 to 15.00
Dish, Pickle	50.00
Hair Receiver, Cover, Liner	44.00
Plate, 8 In.	35.00
Plate, 9 1/2 In.	45.00
Plate, 10 In.	50.00
Tea Strainer, Japan	25.00
Teapot, Japan, 4 1/2 In.	75.00

HOENIX GLASS Company was founded in 1880 in Pennsylvania. The rm made commercial products, such as lampshades, bottles, and assware. Collectors today are interested in the "Sculptured Artware" ade by the company from the 1930s until the mid-1950s. Some eces of Phoenix glass are very similar to those made by the onsolidated Lamp and Glass Company. Phoenix made Reuben Blue, vender, and yellow pieces. These colors were not used by Con-olidated. In 1970 Phoenix became a division of Anchor Hocking, then as sold to the Newell Group in 1987. The company is still working.

Vase, Daisy, Blue Ground, 9 1/2 In.	250.00
Vase, Dancing Girl, Brown, 11 1/2 In.	640.00
Vase, Fish, White, 9 In.	125.00
Vase, Foxglove, Gold Flowers, White Ground, 10 1/2 In.	195.00
Vase, Freesia, 8 1/2 In.	195.00
Vase, Leaping Deer, Ivory, 10 1/2 In.	1375.00
Vase, Philodendron, Blue, 11 1/2 In.	190.00
Vase, Umbrella, Thistle, White, 18 In.	400.00
Vase, Wild Rose, Blue, 10 1/2 In.	300.00

HONOGRAPHS, invented by Thomas Edison in the 1880s, have been ade by many firms. This category also includes other items associ-ed with the phonograph. Jukeboxes and records are listed in their vn categories.

Adapter, Stereo Cassette, 8-Track Player To Cassette Player, Sparkomatic, Box	20.00
Bohland & Fuchs, Gramophone Graslitz, Boheme, Brass Horn, 1905	4446.00
Columbia, Electric Turntable, Italian Renaissance	2500.00
Columbia, Modan, Brass Horn	875.00
Columbia, Regent, Desk Top	875.00
Davenola, Upright	350.00
Edison, Cylinder, 6-Ft. Brass Horn	4500.00
Edison, Fireside Model 1, Oak, Cylinder, Cygnet Horn No. 10, Pat. Oct. 1905	935.00
Edison, Home, 2-Minute Cylinder Records, Patent 1898	750.00
Edison, Home, Black Horn, Brass Flared End, Model C Reproducer, Pat. 1906	415.00
Edison, Home, Oak, Morning Glory Horn, 18 Cylinders, Not Running, 16 1/2 In.	605.00
Edison, Model C, Mahogany, Records, Floor	245.00
Edison, Model D, Cylinder, Plays 4 To 2 Minute Records, Morning Glory Horn	605.00
Edison, Opera, Mahogany Case & Horn, 23 Cylinders, 33 1/2 In.	2365.00
Edison, Standard Model E, Oak, Internal Horn, Molded Case, Open Spool Front	185.00
Edison, Standard, Brass Horn, Pat. Nov. 1903, 5 Cylinders, Banner Decal	440.00
Edison, Standard, E. Cylinder, Oak Case, 20 Cylinders	3000.00
Edison, Standard, Oak, Cygnet Horn, Banner Decal, Mode H Reproducer	440.00
Edison, Standard, Oak, Tin Morning Glory Horn, Black Paint, 40 Cylinders	520.00
Edison, Tin Morning Glory Horn, Oak Case, 18 Cylinders	605.00
Edison Gold Moulded Records, No. 9160, Cylinder, Original Tube	25.00
Emerson, Popeye Dance Party, Blue, Pressed Board Case, 12 x 10 x 5 In.	40.00
Emerson Wondergram, Presented To Marlene Dietrich By Harold Arlen, 1960	632.00

Gramophone, Thorens, 10 x 8 1/4 In. 285.0
Quartersawn Oak, Tin Morning Glory Horn, Label, 72 Cylinders, 13 In. 605.0
Thorens Excelda Cameraphone 350.0
Victor, Model II, Oak Horn, Oak Case 2850.0
Victor, Model V, Black Morning Glory Horn 2600.0
Victor, Model VV-IXA, Table Model, Mahogany Case, Lift Top, Speaker Doors 165.0
Victor, Monarch, Front Mount, Brass Horn 2600.0
Victor, Monarch, Morning Glory Horn, Flowers Inside 2550.0
Victor, No. 3, Morning Glory Horn 1250.0
Victor, Schoolhouse, Oak Horn 3200.0
Victor II, Brass Bell Horn . . . . .1250.00 to 1400.0
Victor II, Oak Horn 2600.0
Victor III, Oak Horn, Matching Base Cabinet 4500.0
Victor VI, Mahogany, Ornate Molded Case, Spear Tip Horn, No. 2 Reproducer 3410.0
Victor VII, Oak, Black & Gold Morning Glory Horn, Label 1760.0
Victor/Victrola XXV, Oak, Gold & Black Metal Morning Glory Horn, Floor 2090.0
Victrola, Model 500, Records, 1920s 700.0

PHOTOGRAPHY items are listed here. The first photograph was a view
from a window in France taken in 1826. The commercially successful
photograph started with the daguerreotype introduced in 1839. Today
all sorts of photographs and photographic equipment are collected.
Albums were popular in Victorian times. Cartes de visite, popular after
1854, were mounted on 2 1/2-by-4-inch cardboard. Cabinet cards were
introduced in 1866. These were mounted on 4 1/4-by-6 1/2-inch cards.
Stereo views are listed under Stereo Card. The cases for daguerreo-
types are listed in the Gutta-Percha category. Stereoscopes are listed in
their own section.

Album, Admiral Dewey, Portrait On Celluloid Front, Velvet Back Cover, 6 In. 165.0
Album, Carte De Visite, Officers & Troops In 19th Connecticut Infantry 3840.0
Album, Family, 24 Cartes De Visite, 7 Tintypes, Leather, 1870s, 5 1/4 x 6 In. 45.0
Album, Ormolu Liberty Bells, Velvet, Mirror Insert, Rack, 1989, 9 x 11 In. 145.0
Ambrotype, 2 Affectionate Young Dandies, 1/2 Plate 95.0
Ambrotype, 2 Gamblers, Sharing Whiskey, 1/4 Plate, Gutta-Percha Case 975.0
Ambrotype, Baby, In Buggy, With Fido, 1/6 Plate 297.0
Ambrotype, Barn, Corn & Flour Sign On Top, 1857 . . . . 770.0
Ambrotype, Confederate Officer, 1/9 Plate 770.0
Ambrotype, Confederate Soldier, S. Whitfield, Gilt Buttons On Coat, 1/6 Plate 797.0
Ambrotype, Confederate Soldier, Seated, 1/4 Plate, 3 1/4 x 4 1/4 In. 1100.0
Ambrotype, Confederate, Seated, Gilt Buttons, F.W. Davis, 1/6 Plate 660.0
Ambrotype, Portrait, Corn & Wheat On Union Case 110.0
Ambrotype, Soldier, Seated In Spindle Back Chair, Half Case, 1/6 Plate 440.0
Ambrotype, Virginia Confederate Private, Cavalry Jacket, 1/9 Plate 550.0
Cabinet Card, 2 Cowboys, Seated, H.M. Rice, On Card, 4 x 5 In. 85.0
Cabinet Card, Boomers On Canadian River Log Jam, 30 People 125.0
Cabinet Card, California Sheep Herders, 1880-1890, Oversized 110.0
Cabinet Card, Captain In Uniform, Wearing Indiana Camp GAR Ribbon 55.0
Cabinet Card, Deceased Baby, Flower Draped Wicker Buggy 90.0
Cabinet Card, Family On Porch, Black Woman Back Steps With Laundry, 1880s 75.0
Cabinet Card, General Tom Thumb & Wife, Autographed By Both, August, 1881 . . . . . 85.0
Cabinet Card, Man, Bib Shirt, Revolver & Sheath Knife, Gem Studio, 1880s 95.0
Cabinet Card, Man, No Arms, Eating With His Feet 195.0
Cabinet Card, Old Judge, Boston 800.0
Cabinet Card, Policeman, Full Dress Uniform 75.0
Cabinet Card, Ragged Old Black Man 63.0
Cabinet Card, RR Baseball Team, Parsons, Kans., Grandstand 50.0
Cabinet Card, Sitting Bull, Gilbert, 1891 . . . . 800.0
Cabinet Card, Sitting Bull, Palmquist & Jurgens, Autographed, 1884 . . . . 660.0
Cabinet Card, Yellow Dog, Indian, F. Jay Haynes, 1880 . . . . 550.0
Cabinet Card, Young Man, Tuxedo, Holding Violin 40.0
Camera, 7-Up Can 50.0
Camera, AGFA, Ansco, Black, Readyset Special Lens, 5 1/2 x 3 x 1 1/4 In. 57.0
Camera, AGFA, Clipper, Model PD-16, Extendable Front, 1930s, Box, 5 1/2 In. 34.0

Camera, AGFA, Folding, Black, Tan Carrying Case, Prewar 24.00
Camera, AGFA, Isolette, Bellows Style Lens, Leather, Case, Germany, 6 3/4 In. 57.00
Camera, AGFA, PD-16 Clipper, Black Metal, Extensible Front, 5 x 3 1/2 In. 26.00
Camera, AGFA, Solinette, Black Case, Silver Toned Top, 1950s, 5 x 3 x 1 1/2 In. 63.00
Camera, Al-Vista Panoramic, Leather Case, Multiscope & Film Co., c.1900 .... 1000.00
Camera, Argus, C2, Brick Style, Range Finder, Leather Case, 1930s, 5 x 3 x 2 In. 47.00
Camera, Argus, C3 Matchmatic, LC3 Meter, Brown Leather Case, 5 x 3 x 2 In. 29.00
Camera, Argus, C3, Brick Style, Black, Olive, Brown Leather Case, 5 x 2 1/2 In. 29.00
Camera, Bolex Paillard, Movie, 16mm, Grip Mount, 7 x 9 1/2 x 2 In. 20.00
Camera, Bolsey, Jubilee, Flash, Leather Carrying Case, 1950s, 5 x 3 In. 26.00
Camera, Box, R & O Co., Brass & Mahogany, Red Leather, Tripod 335.00
Camera, Budweiser Can 50.00
Camera, Canon, G-III QL, Case 50.00
Camera, Exakta VX500, To Marlene Dietrich From Yul Brenner 2587.00
Camera, Folding, Kodak, Vigilant Junior Six-20, 1940s, 6 1/2 x 3 1/2 In. 46.00
Camera, Graflex, Graphic 35, Gray Case, Silver Toned Top, 5 x 3 x 1 1/2 In. 30.00
Camera, Herold, Spartus Co-Flash, Bakelite Case, With Flash, c.1962, Box, 5 In. 29.00
Camera, Kit, Kodak, Brownie, 8 Movie, Box, 1960s 56.00
Camera, Kodak Brownie Hawkeye, Black Plastic, Attached Lens 10.00
Camera, Kodak Duaflex II, Plastic Strap, Fixed Focus Lens, Flash, 620 Film 15.00
Camera, Kodak, Anniversary, Box, 1929 .... 90.00
Camera, Kodak, Brownie, Flash Six-20, With Flash Attachment, 3 1/4 x 3 In. 26.00
Camera, Kodak, Brownie, Hawkeye, Flash, Black Plastic, Box, 4 1/2 x 3 x 3 In 34.00
Camera, Kodak, Brownie, Holiday Flash, Dakon Lens, Brown Bakelite Case, 4 In. 29.00
Camera, Kodak, Brownie, Star Flash, Instructions In Box 70.00
Camera, Kodak, Instamatic 124, Gray, Metal, Plastic, Box, 1969, 4 x 2 In. 30.00
Camera, Kodak, Instamatic, c.1950 .... 35.00
Camera, Kodak, Jiffy Six-20, Pop-Out Art Deco Front, 1930s, 6 x 3 x 1 1/2 In. 26.00
Camera, Kodak, Pony 135, Model B, Black, Gray Plastic, Box, 1950s, 5 x 3 In. 24.00
Camera, Kodak, Pony IV, Plastic & Aluminum Body, Brown Leather Case 47.00
Camera, Kodak, Retina IIIC, Black Case, Silver Toned Top, Late 1950s, 5 x 3 In. 144.00
Camera, Kodak, Retina-Compur-Rapid, Six-20 Case, Germany, 1930s, 4 3/4 In. 75.00
Camera, Kodak, Starmeter, Electric Light Meter, Box 37.00
Camera, Kraft Velveeta Shells & Cheese, Plastic, 4 1/2 x 2 1/2 In. 28.00
Camera, Land, Polaroid, Model 95A 50.00
Camera, Leica, 50 mm, Case, 1937 .... 350.00
Camera, Leica, Model M-3, Single Stroke Conversion ....*Illus* 1375.00
Camera, Magnacam, Wrist A Matic, Plastic, Leather Band, Unused In Box, 1981 ...... 132.00
Camera, Minox C, Flash, Chrome, Black Leatherette Cases, Storage Case, Manual 275.00
Camera, Movie, Cine-Kodak Eight-25, Case, 1940s, 6 x 4 x 1 1/2 In. 23.00
Camera, Movie, Keystone, KA-1 Electric Eye, 8mm, 3 Rotating Lenses, 5 In. 30.00
Camera, No. 110, Book Shape, Webster Dictionary 25.00
Camera, Photak, Foldex 20, 105mm Octivar Lens, Leather Case, 1950s, 6 x 4 In. 46.00
Camera, Polaroid, 420 Automatic Land, Gray Plastic, Black Strap, 8 x 6 x 3 In. 29.00
Camera, Polaroid, J33 Land, Leather Carrying Case, Instruction Booklet 41.00
Camera, Polaroid, Model 110A, Flash, Booklet, Accessories, Leather Case 39.00
Camera, Polaroid, SX70 .... 50.00
Camera, Seneca, Box 75.00

Photography, Camera, Leica, Model M-3,
Single Stroke Conversion

**Color pictures taken today should
last about 50 years; if protected in
albums, about 100 years.
Use albums with safe adhesive
and plastic—those labeled
"archival" or "no PVC."**

Camera, Twinflex, Matched Lenses, Black Plastic, Box, 4 1/2 x 3 x 2 In.	26.0
Camera, Viewmaster Personal Stereo	330.0
Camera, Vitalux, Black, Brown Case, Lixtus Light Meter, Germany, c.1940	51.0
Camera, Whittaker, Micro 16 Pixie, Black Plastic, Tan Leather Case, 1 1/2 In.	75.0
Camera, Zeiss Ikon, Contaflex Synchro-Compur, Tessar Lens, Case, Germany	190.0
Camera, Zeiss Ikon, Ikomatica, Leather Case, Germany	60.0
Camera, Zeiss Ikon, Nettar, Prontor-S Novar-Anastigmat 75mm Lens, 5 x 3 In.	138.0
Carte De Visite, Barnum Circus Freaks, Albino Family, Sepia, Brady, 4 x 2 1/2 In.	30.0
Carte De Visite, Bearded Black Men, Arm In Arm, C.R. Rees & Co., 1868	65.0
Carte De Visite, Black Siamese Twins, Joined At Back, Faux Crowns	50.0
Carte De Visite, Captain Gleason, Brady, Tax Stamp	110.0
Carte De Visite, Civil War Soldier	60.0
Carte De Visite, General Alexander Stewart Webb, Medal Of Honor Winner	424.0
Carte De Visite, General Braxton Brass, Confederate Uniform	145.0
Carte De Visite, General Grant, Children	38.0
Carte De Visite, General Greene	18.0
Carte De Visite, General Sherman & Staff, Morning Of Atlanta Battle	425.0
Carte De Visite, John Wilkes Booth . . . . .255.00 to 275.0
Carte De Visite, Samuel Colt	1610.0
Carte De Visite, Susan B. Anthony & Elizabeth Cady Stanton	600.0
Carte De Visite, Tom Thumb & The Little People, Age 12 Years	25.0
Carte De Visite, Tom Thumb's Family	12.0
Carte De Visite, Tom Thumb's Wedding	38.0
Daguerreotype, Baby Picture, 1/4 Plate	40.0
Daguerreotype, Black Soldier, White Woman & Child, Full Uniform, 1/6 Plate	1000.0
Daguerreotype, Boy & Girl, Standing Together, Whitmore, 1/6 Plate, 1851	130.0
Daguerreotype, Boy & His Dog, 1/6 Plate	950.0
Daguerreotype, Boy & His Rabbit, Tinted Face, 1/6 Plate	1695.0
Daguerreotype, House With Arbor, Man & Woman, Horse & Buggy, 1/6 Plate	1850.0
Daguerreotype, Middle-Aged Man, Holding Walking Stick, 1/6 Plate	235.0
Daguerreotype, Sergeant, Spur Trigger Smith & Wesson, Bowie Knife, 1/9 Plate	450.0
Daguerreotype, Traveling Butcher, 1850s	5500.0
Daguerreotype, Woman, Seated, With Bonnet, Marked, Scovills, 1/6 Plate	80.0
Lantern, Dark Room, Kerosene	125.0
Lantern, Dark Room, Kodak, Red & Amber Lenses	225.0
Lens, Argus, Telephoto & Wide View, Black Leather Case, 6 x 2 1/2 In., Pair	83.0
Light, Dark Room, Tin, Red Glass, Dietz Burner, Some Paint	40.0
Magic Lantern, 2 Original Celluloid Films	185.0
Magic Lantern, Bijou, Slides	215.0
Magic Lantern, Brevete SGDG, Tin, Brass, 5 Controls	185.0
Magic Lantern, Building Shape, George Carette & Co., 13 3/4 In.	7406.0
Magic Lantern, Glass Slide, Instructions, Tickets, Exhibition Poster, 1885, 7 1/2 In.	143.0
Magic Lantern, McAllister's Gem, Focusing Tube, 28 Slides, Case, 11 3/16 In.	57.0
Magic Lantern, Original Lenses, Lantern & 4 Slides, Tin & Brass, 19th Century	150.0
Magic Lantern, Queen & Co., Leather Case, 19 In.	440.0
Photograph, A Rock Garden Of Cape Cod, Signed Sawyer, Frame, 13 x 10 In.	275.0
Photograph, Alive & Well!, Bob & Emmett Dalton, Tackett, Kansas, 1892	800.0
Photograph, Armed Tombstone Cowboy	1840.0
Photograph, Blacksmith Shop, Working On Wagon Wheel, 6 1/2 x 4 1/4 In.	41.0
Photograph, Bob Weir, Woodstock Ticket, Signed By Ritchie Havens	500.0
Photograph, Card Players, 4 Men, Albertson, Kansas, Early 1900s, 6 x 4 In.	30.0
Photograph, Cowboy On Horse, Woolly Chaps, Sepia, 8 x 10 In.	35.0
Photograph, Cowgirl, 6 Gun Rig, Gauntlets, Boots, Coiled Rope, c.1910	145.0
Photograph, Dumbo, Elephant, Shot Near Railroad Engine, Canada, 8 x 10 In.	23.0
Photograph, Frank Buck, Circus, 8 x 10 In.	20.0
Photograph, Grant, Colfax, Cardboard, Jugate	350.0
Photograph, Hanging Emil Fricker, Edwardsville, Ill., 1926, 8 x 10 In., 4 Piece	350.0
Photograph, Hanging Of Lincoln Conspirators, A. Gardner, July 1865, 7 x 8 In.	7700.0
Photograph, High School Baseball Team, Uniforms, 1910, 14 x 12 In.	55.0
Photograph, Indian, Blanket Around, Platinum, 1900s, 7 x 11 In.	625.0
Photograph, Josephine Marcus Eart, Wife Of Wyatt Earp	2750.0
Photograph, La Habra Ca. Corn Festival, Parade View, 1959, 8 x 10 In.	37.0
Photograph, Man In Bonnet, Leather, Hinged, Red Velvet, 2 x 3 In. . . . .*Illus*	1200.0

Photography, Photograph, Man
n Bonnet, Leather, Hinged,
Red Velvet, 2 x 3 In.

Photography, Photograph,
Wedding, Beros Studio,
Cleveland, 1940s, 9 x 7 In.

Photograph, Mark Twain, Rocking Chair, On Porch, 7 x 5 In.	52.00
Photograph, Merke's Store Front, Butchers, Products, 1920s, 8 x 10 In.	30.00
Photograph, Minnesota Soldier, Campaign Against Sioux Uprising, 1862	1500.00
Photograph, Navajo Boy, Moon	3220.00
Photograph, Parade Float, Horse Drawn, Dallas, Stock Show, 1905	75.00
Photograph, Saloon Interior, 12 Men, Bartender, Orient Pecos 89, 7 x 5 In.	31.00
Photograph, Sunset After Appomattox, Lee, Carl Guthers, Frame, 1897, 9 x 13 In.	110.00
Photograph, Vanishing Race, Curtis	4313.00
Photograph, Wedding, Beros Studio, Cleveland, 1940s, 9 x 7 In. .... *Illus*	12.00
Projector, Keystone View Co.	45.00
Projector, Tru Vue, 10 Film Strips, Theater Box, 1960s	175.00
Stereoscope, Binocular Style, 25 Slides, France	275.00
Tintype, 2 Union Privates, Holding Revolver, 1/6 Plate	1320.00
Tintype, 2 Women In Old Car, Coney Island, 1909	50.00
Tintype, 4 Women On Bicycles	50.00
Tintype, 5 Confederate Officers	65.00
Tintype, 5 Officers, 1/2 Plate	650.00
Tintype, Abraham Lincoln, Beardless, 1/6 Plate	2750.00
Tintype, Boston Police Officer, On Cap Badge, 1/6 Plate	115.00
Tintype, Butcher Holding Utensils	25.00
Tintype, Cavalry Soldier, Coat, Beard, 1/6 Plate	137.00
Tintype, Civil War Train, 4 1/4 x 6 3/8 In.	190.00
Tintype, Dr. Lewis B. Kay, In Uniform, 1863	750.00
Tintype, Fireman, With Big Hat, Gold Tint Brocade, 1/9 Plate	117.00
Tintype, Frank & Jessie James & Friend, Fort Smith	6000.00
Tintype, Indian War, 2 Men Reclining, 1/6 Plate	40.00
Tintype, John Wilkes Booth, 3/4 Plate	1200.00
Tintype, Little Girl, Tinted, Full Plate	65.00
Tintype, Man Playing Cornet, Other Playing Violin, Leather Case	270.00
Tintype, Man, In Suit	30.00
Tintype, Older Man & Wife, GAR Badges & Coat, 1/6th Plate	100.00
Tintype, Scottish Highlander, Kilt, Tam	250.00
Tintype, Union Sailor, Double Brass 6 Button Jacket, 1/9 Plate	190.00
Tintype, Union Soldier, Seated, Holding Kepi, Alonzo Armington, 1/9 Plate	275.00

'IANO BABY is a collector's term. About 1880, the well-decorated
ome had a shawl on the piano. Bisque figures of babies were designed
o help hold the shawl in place. They range in size from 6 to 18 inches.
Most of the figures were made in Germany. Reproductions are being
nade. Other piano babies may be listed under manufacturers' names.

Crawling, White Gown, Blue Ribbon & Bow, Heubach, 7 1/2 In.	195.00
Holding Baby, Girl, Bisque, 12 In.	400.00
Playing With Toes, Bonnet, Short Gown, Heubach, 4 1/4 In.	250.00
Sitting Up, Bisque, Cherub Girl, Butterfly On Knee, Yellow Dress, 10 In.	95.00
Sitting Up, Boy, Blowing Bubbles, Heubach, 9 1/2 In.	595.00

PICKARD China Company was started in 1898 by Wilder Pickard. Hand-painted designs were used on china purchased from other sources. In the 1930s, the company began to make its own china wares in Chicago, Illinois. The company now makes many types of porcelains, including a successful line of limited edition collector plates.

Bottle, Hand Painted Floral, Gold Leaf & Trim, Stopper, 5 In.	75.0
Bowl, Berry Design, Gold, Signed, Nessy, Mark, 1905, 7 1/2 In.	115.0
Bowl, Gold Loop Handles, Creamy Interior, Gold Line Trim, 7 1/2 In.	65.0
Bowl, Nuts & Leaves, Signed, Vokral, 8 1/2 In.	135.0
Bowl, Raspberries & Leaves, Bow Handles, Gold Scalloped Trim, Signed, 7 In.	245.0
Bowl, Ruffled Edge, Poppies, Gold Trim, Signed, LOH, Mark, 1905-1910	255.0
Cake Plate, Classic Ruins By Moonlight, 10 1/2 In.	275.0
Cake Platter, Open Handles, Gold Edge, White, 11 In.	65.0
Candlestick, Allover Gold, Engraved, Flared Square Base, 9 In., Pair	275.0
Candy Dish, Gold Florals & Trim, Signed, Minnie Pickard, 1903, 7 In.	225.0
Candy Dish, Perforated Handle, 1919	35.0
Coffee Set, Honeysuckle, Service For 4, c.1910, 10 Piece	695.0
Coffee Set, Shamrock, 3 Piece	450.0
Coffeepot, Gold Handle, Spout, Green, Mark, 1903-1905, 8 3/4 In.	330.0
Dish, Lovers On A Swing, Painted, 5 In.	265.0
Dish, Mint, Red Poppies, Gold Trim, Signed, Fuchs, 1905, 6 In.	135.0
Jug, Lemonade, Wide Gold Band, Handle	245.0
Nappy, Quatrefoil Inside Cherries & Peaches, Signed, Nessy, 1912, 5 7/8 In.	285.0
Pitcher, Lemonade, Encrusted Honeysuckle, Wide-Mouth, Jaegere Co.	1650.0
Pitcher, Lemonade, Gold, Signed, Lind, 1905-1910	605.0
Pitcher, Poppies, With Gold, Signed, 7 In.	175.0
Plate, Classic Ruins, Signed, Chalinor, 1912, 8 1/2 In.	265.0
Plate, Dessert, Roses, Floral, Vines, Gold Trim, 1912, 6 1/2 In.	150.0
Plate, Garden Scene, Floral, Signed, Challinor, 9 In.	325.0
Plate, Large Lily, Signed, 9 In.	250.0
Plate, Poppy, Gold Trim, Signed, 9 In.	250.0
Plate, Setting Sun Over Green Breakers, Signed, Heidrich, 1918-1922, 9 1/2 In.	33.0
Powder Jar, 3 Gold Feet, Hand Painted Violets, Signed, Reury	150.0
Salt & Pepper, Allover Gold, 5 In.	50.0
Sugar & Creamer, Allover Gold, Etched Floral	70.0
Sugar & Creamer, Argenta Linear	100.0
Sugar Cube Holder, Gold & Green Clovers, Gold Feet, Handles & Rim, 7 3/4 In.	110.0
Syrup, Underplate, White & Gold, Floral Border	55.0
Tankard, Floral, 2 Gold Keys Crossed Over Coat Of Arms, Bagpipes, Signed, 7 In.	425.0
Toothpick, Gold Floral	35.0
Tray, Hunting Dogs In Meadow, Signed, Farrington, Round, 16 In.	3000.0
Vase, 2 Women Being Serenaded, Painted, 10 In.	395.0
Vase, 3 Dark Orange Poppies, Gold, Rust, Brown, Signed, Gasper, 9 In.	368.0
Vase, Hand Painted, Art Nouveau, c.1895, 7 1/2 In.	287.0
Vase, Pond Lily, Signed, Keates, 6 1/2 In.	350.0

PICTURE FRAMES are listed in this book in the Furniture category under Frame.

PICTURES, silhouettes, and other small decorative objects framed to hang on the wall are listed here. Sandpaper pictures are black and white charcoal drawings done on a special sanded paper. Some other types of pictures are listed in the Print and Painting categories.

Calligraphy On Paper, Eagle & Banner, Horace Spencer, Frame, 5 1/8 x 7 3/4 In.	425.0
Charcoal & Ink, Young Woman, Walnut Shadowbox, 15 x 13 In.	70.0
Cut Paper, Angels, Heart, Birds & Animals, White, Black Ground, Frame, 14 x 12 In.	395.0
Cut Paper, Memorial, Woman Died 1882, Frame, 14 x 20 In.	110.0
Diorama, 2 Horses & Riders Jumping, Wax, Under Glass, 19th Century, 5 1/2 x 8 In.	55.0
Diorama, Alpine Scene, Mixed Media, Shadowbox Frame, 23 1/2 x 31 1/4 In.	430.0
Diorama, Racing Yacht, 3 Masts, American Flag, Painted Seascape, Shadowbox Case	450.0
Diorama, Ship Scene, American Flag, Wood, 6 5/8 x 9 7/8 In.	99.0
Engraving, Farmland Scenes, Colored, Black & Gilt Glass Mats, 14 x 19 In., Pair	245.0
Engraving, Mr. Willm. Long On Bertha, Colored, 19th Century, Frame, 27 x 30 In.	120.0
Etching, Building Dover Pier, Joseph Pennell, 1910, 9 3/8 x 12 3/8 In.	250.0

Etching, Fiddler & The Hurdy-Gurdy Boy, 5th State, Adriaen Van Ostade, 5 3/4 x 5 In. . . . 250.00
Etching, Young Girl Sleeping, Dolls Watching, Stephen Ferris, 1884, 16 x 25 In. 1500.00
Ink, On The Crooked Trail, Dale Petit, 9 3/4 x 12 3/4 In. 130.00
Ink & Pencil On Paper, Portrait, Young Man, Eglomise Frame, 7 x 6 In. 385.00
Ink On Paper, Mythological, Men & Demons Battle, Bolognese School, 19 x 22 In. 800.00
Needlework, Beaded, English Manor Home, Gilt Frame, 6 x 9 In. 145.00
Needlework, Crewel, Ship With 9 Flags, Rose Border, Oval Frame, 15 x 21 In. 1380.00
Needlework, Cross Stitch, Woman, Garden, Sarah Justin, c.1836, 16 1/2 x 17 1/2 In. 66.00
Needlework, Embroidered Silk, Mrs. Beach's Academy, Mass., 1807, 17 x 22 1/2 In. 290.00
Needlework, Embroidery On Silk, Young Woman, Dog, Walnut Frame, 9 1/2 x 7 1/2 In. . . 395.00
Needlework, Hooked, Cornucopia, Blue-Gray Ground, Frame, 22 x 53 In. 495.00
Needlework, Landscape, Figures Beneath Tree, Giltwood Frame, 21 x 22 In. 865.00
Needlework, Millet's The Gleaners, 1940, 18 x 24 In. 55.00
Needlework, Mourning, 2 Ladies, 2 Girls Flanking Urn, 1825, Pa., 16 1/4 x 16 In. 11500.00
Needlework, Operatic Scene, Courting Couple, Mauve, White, Green, 31 x 23 In. 490.00
Needlework, Silk, Bird Scene, Satin Ground, Ebonized Frame, 1660, 15 x 18 1/2 In. . . . 6325.00
Needlework, Silk, Couple, Strolling Through Garden, Ebonized Frame, 7 x 8 In. 4600.00
Needlework, Silk, Female, Standing, Giltwood Frame, 1660, 12 x 11 3/4 In. 2990.00
Needlework, Silk, Landscape, Exotic Bird, Insect, Tree, Ebonized Frame, 11 3/4 In. 4600.00
Needlework, Silk, Landscape, Shepherdess, Seated, Sheep Dog, Flock, 14 x 12 In. 483.00
Needlework, Silk, Narrative Of Joseph, Ebonized Frame, 1660, 7 x 12 1/2 In. 1495.00
Needlework, Silk, Woman, Holding A Serpent & Book, Gilt, Ebonized Frame, 18 In. . . . 1035.00
Needlework, Silk, Woman, Standing With Fruit, Flowering Trees, Frame, 12 x 11 In. . . . 2185.00
Needlework, Vase Of Flowers, Multicolored, Needlepoint, 31 x 25 In. 300.00
Needlework, Winged Angel Carrying 2 Children, Oval Frame, Black Ground, 23 In. 345.00
Needlework, Woman & Tree By Lake, Frame, 31 x 19 1/4 In. 185.00
Needlework, Wool, Colorful Bird In Tree With Berries, Frame, 17 In. 300.00
Needlework, Wool, Spotted Leopard, Tree & Palm Tree, 12 1/2 x 16 1/2 In. 1150.00
Pastel On Paper, Portrait, Man & Woman, Oval, Black Matte, Frame, 13 x 10 In., Pair . 600.00
Pastel On Paper, Young Woman, Pearls In Her Hair, Oval, Gold Frame, 18 In. 250.00
Pencil & Graphite On Paper, Landscape, Mill, Stream, Rowboat, Frame, 18 x 26 In. . . 80.00
Pinprick, Valentine, Hand Colored, Cutout, Emily Miles, Frame, 1830, 10 In. 28.00
Sandpaper, Landscape, Pastel, Frame, 1830s, 10 1/2 x 14 In. 775.00
Silhouette, Child With Doll, Gilt Frame, 7 3/8 x 5 1/8 In. 412.00
Silhouette, G. Washington, Hollow Cut, Black Lacquer Frame, 7 5/8 x 6 1/2 In. 2200.00
Silhouette, Gentleman, Frock Coat, Maple Frame, Oval, 7 3/4 x 5 In. 315.00
Silhouette, Girl, Full-Length, Gilt Accents, Frame, 8 1/2 x 6 1/4 In. 425.00
Silhouette, Man & Woman, Double, 19th Century, 4 x 3 3/4 In. 235.00
Silhouette, Man & Woman, Pair, Hollow Cut, Ink, Watercolor, Gilt Frame, 6 x 8 In. . . . 355.00
Silhouette, Man & Woman, William Bache, Round Black Frame, 3 7/8 In., Pair 220.00
Silhouette, Man & Young Woman, Ogee Frame, 13 x 10 In. 220.00
Silhouette, Old Woman, Hollow Cut, Blue Painted Ground, Frame, Full Size, 21 x 17 In. 110.00
Silhouette, Slave, Toiling With Cotton Bales, Pale Blue Ground, 1850, 6 1/2 x 8 In. 450.00
Silhouette, Woman, Baby & Child, Ink Wash Ground, Ogee Frame, 13 x 10 In. 385.00
Silhouette, Woman, Cutout Litho Blue Dress, Black Cloth Back, Frame, 6 x 5 In. 600.00
Silhouette, Woman, Hollow Cut, Brushed Ink Detail, Cloth Back, Frame, 5 x 4 1/2 In. . . 575.00
Silhouette, Woman, Hollow Cut, Watercolor & Ink, Black Cloth Back, Frame, 5 x 4 In. . 2365.00
Silhouette, Woman, Portrait, Brushed Ink Bodice, Gilt, Black Frame, 5 x 4 1/4 In. 330.00
Silhouette, Woman, Portrait, Hollow Cut, 19th Century, Frame, 4 1/2 x 3 1/8 In. 250.00
Silhouette, Young Man & Woman, Ivory, Oval, S. Cowan, 3 x 4 In., Pair 230.00
Silhouette, Young Man, Label On Back, Hollow Cut, 6 x 4 In. 220.00
Silhouette, Young Mother & Child, Seated Under Tree, 1815, 10 1/2 x 13 1/2 In. 6325.00
Theorem, Basket Of Fruit, Frame, 11 x 13 1/2 In. 287.00
Theorem, On Paper, Peacock In Tree, Watercolor, Pine Frame, 12 x 8 1/2 In. 425.00
Theorem, Rooster, Tulips, Sponge Painted Frame, Bill Rank, 17 1/2 x 15 1/2 In. 245.00
Theorem, Rose, Birds, Watercolor, Graphite Wash, J. Whatman, Frame, 1830, 11 x 11 In. 495.00
Theorem, Watercolor, 2 Puppies Playing, Brown, Tan, Green, Black, Frame, 11 x 15 In. . 1100.00
Theorem, Watercolor, Birds, Flower, Fruit, Gilt Frame, 22 x 28 In. 220.00
Theorem, Watercolor, Vase Of Flowers, Blue, Green, Yellow, Red, Black, Frame, 14 In. . 1430.00
Tinsel, Basket Of Fruit, Gilded Frame, Victorian, 7 1/2 x 9 1/2 In. 225.00
Tinsel, Cornucopia, Flowers, Black Ground, Frame, 16 x 16 In. 275.00
Tinsel, Cranes Within Landscape, Empire Giltwood Frame, 27 x 33 In. 805.00
Tinsel, Urn Of Flowers, Black & Gilt Frame, c.1870, 12 1/2 x 10 1/2 In. 210.00

Watercolor, Classical Villa, Mary Philbrook, Frame, 7 x 10 In. 110.00
Watercolor, Cottage Scene, Frame, Signed, M.H. Humphrey, 1839, 7 1/4 & 6 In., Pair .. 495.00
Watercolor, Cove With Boats, Signed LR, 10 1/2 x 13 1/2 In. 50.00
Watercolor, Haying Scene, Horses, Men, F.F. English, Frame, 24 x 47 In. 715.00
Watercolor, Landscape, Harold Walker, Matted, Frame, 1890, 20 x 25 In. 100.00
Watercolor, Landscape, House, England, Gilt Gesso Frame, 7 1/2 x 7 In. 200.00
Watercolor, Landscape, Trees, Brush, Sky, MacKnight, 14 x 22 In. 935.00
Watercolor, Portrait, English Officer, Full Dress Uniform, 19th Century, 6 x 4 In. 195.00
Watercolor, Portrait, Gentleman, Mr. E. Wyndham, Jan. 13, 1827, Pastorini, 6 x 5 In. ... 300.00
Watercolor, Portrait, Girl, Full-Side, Marion Bewsley, May 7, 1837, 5 x 3 3/4 In. 230.00
Watercolor, Portrait, Man & Woman, F. Maybe, 1825, Frame, 8 x 11 In. 3525.00
Watercolor, Portrait, Man & Woman, Frame, 3 1/4 x 2 7/8 In., Pair 525.00
Watercolor, Portrait, Man, Black Frock Coat, Frame, 4 7/8 x 3 7/8 In. 550.00
Watercolor, Portrait, Monk, Antoine Thomas, France, 1821, 5 1/2 x 6 3/4 In. 135.00
Watercolor, Portrait, Perry & Mrs. Lucky Perry, Gilt Frame, 14 x 18 In. 3965.00
Watercolor, Portrait, Young Man, Profile, Frame, 3 3/8 x 2 7/8 In. 550.00
Watercolor, Red Flower, Yellow & Green, Emily Nye, Frame, 4 x 5 In. 275.00
Watercolor, River Scene, Farmhouse, Barns, Carl Weber, 13 x 26 In. 385.00
Watercolor, Seascape, W. Williams, 8 3/4 x 20 In. 250.00
Watercolor, Sheep Grazing, Signed R.L. Johnston, Gilt Frame, 17 x 23 In. 550.00
Watercolor, Study For Copper Kettle, Seymour Remenick, 7 1/2 x 10 1/2 In. 110.00
Watercolor, Vase Of Flowers, Red, Yellow, Blue, Green, Pink, Frame, 11 x 9 In. 600.00
Watercolor, Venetian Scene, Arthur Mountford, Matted, Frame, 21 3/4 x 30 In. 465.00
Watercolor, Vestals, White Paper On Board, Henry Ryland, 3 x 2 In., Set Of 4 .... 820.00
Watercolor, Woman, Child, Walking On Footbridge, Ricci, 21 x 17 In. 600.00
Watercolor, Woman, Elaborate Bonnet, Frame, Felt Liner, 5 1/2 x 4 3/4 In. 485.00
Watercolor & Gouache, Night Lights, Gloucester Harbor, N. Johnson, 8 1/2 x 6 In. ... 135.00
Watercolor & Graphite, Portrait, Young Lady, Gilt Frame, 3 7/8 x 3 In. 345.00
Watercolor & Ink, Bird On Branch, Cherries, Frame, 5 1/8 x 3 1/2 In. 935.00
Watercolor & Ink, Bird, Butterfly, Frame, 9 x 10 In. 495.00
Watercolor & Ink, Captain Stancliffee, Frame, 5 1/2 x 4 5/8 In. 495.00
Watercolor & Ink, Portrait, Man & Woman, Together In Frame, 7 x 9 In. 1760.00
Watercolor & Ink, Stylish Couple, Pinpricks, Black Ground, Frame, 8 x 6 In. 220.00
Watercolor & Pencil, Boat, Ironclad Essex, July 22, 1862, Frame, 12 x 18 In. 220.00
Watercolor & Pencil, Girl, Design On Floor, 1867, Frame, 9 1/2 x 7 3/8 In. 880.00
Watercolor On Board, Lake, Birch Trees Sheep, Howard, Frame, 10 1/4 x 19 1/4 In. .. 195.00
Watercolor On Ivory, Mourning, Marble Tomb, Urn, Gold Bars, 3 1/8 x 2 1/2 In. 635.00
Watercolor On Ivory, Portrait, Charles Dickens, Signed, Frame, 2 3/4 x 3 1/8 In. 485.00
Watercolor On Ivory, Portrait, Franklin Pierce, Leather Case Frame, 3 1/8 x 2 5/8 In. ... 750.00
Watercolor On Ivory, Portrait, Napoleon, 2 1/4 x 3 1/8 In. 490.00
Watercolor On Ivory, Young Woman, Frame, 2 3/4 x 2 1/4 In. 290.00
Watercolor On Velvet, Shepherdess & Shepherd, Frame, 20 x 25 In. 135.00

PIERCE, see Howard Pierce category.

PIGEON FORGE Pottery was started in Pigeon Forge, Tennessee, in 1946. Red clay found near the pottery was used to make the pieces. Molded or thrown pottery with matte glaze and slip decoration was made. The pottery is still working.

The Pigeon Forge Pottery Pigeon Forge Tenn

  Sugar & Creamer, White Flowers, Beige Ground, 4 x 4 1/2 In. ....*Illus* 45.00

Pigeon Forge, Sugar &
Creamer, White Flowers,
Beige Ground, 4 x 4 1/2 In.

Vase, Cylindrical, 4 In.	20.00
Vase, Signed, 3 1/2 In.	30.00

PILKINGTON Tile and Pottery Company was established in 1892 in England. The company made small pottery wares, like buttons and hatpins, but soon started decorating vases purchased from other potteries. By 1903, the company had discovered an opalescent glaze that became popular on the Lancastrian pottery line. The manufacture of pottery ended in 1937 but decorating continued until 1948.

Bottle, Band Of Fish, Gold, Purple Luster Glaze, Marked, 7 3/4 x 5 In.	1760.00
Tile, Tree, Broad Leaves, Silver, Red Ground, Metallic Glaze, Frame, 3 x 6 In.	319.00 to 415.00
Vase, Fulper Glaze, 1910, 7 1/2 In.	125.00
Vase, Stylized Lions Under Frothy Green Glaze, Richard Joyce, 8 x 5 3/4 In.	920.00

PINCUSHION DOLLS are not really dolls and often were not even pincushions. Some collectors use the term *half-doll*. The top half of each doll was made of porcelain. The edge of the half-doll was made with several small holes for thread, and the doll was stitched to a fabric body with a voluminous skirt. The finished figure was used to cover a hot pot of tea, powder box, pincushion, whisk broom, or lamp. They were made in sizes from less than an inch to over 9 inches high. Most date from the early 1900s to the 1950s. Collectors often find just the porcelain doll without the fabric skirt.

Attached To Cushion, Legs, Germany	50.00
Bisque, Blond Wig, Jointed Arms	95.00
Half, Arms Away, Attached Hands, 1920s Dress, 4 In.	45.00
Half, Arms Away, China, Gray Bun, Sausage Curls, Germany, 2 1/2 In.	20.00
Half, Extended Arms, Gray Wavy Hair, Brimmed Hat, 6 1/4 In.	28.00
Half, Powder Box, Ucagco, 5 1/2 In.	30.00
Nude, Composition	75.00

PINK SLAG pieces are listed in this book in the Slag category.

PIPES have been popular since tobacco was introduced to Europe by Sir Walter Raleigh. Carved wooden, porcelain, ivory, and glass pipes may be listed here. Meerschaum pipes are listed under Meerschaum.

Box, Shaped Backboard, Pierced Hanger, 1 Drawer, Pine & Maple, 1780s, 18 In.	1380.00
Briar, Figurehead With Putti, Garland Design, 8 1/2 x 3 1/2 In.	431.00
Briar, Green Bakelite, Wooden, Rhinestones	50.00
Burl, Carved Melons, Bowl Cover, 19th Century, 12 1/2 In.	250.00
Carved Wood, Glass Eyes, Brass, 3 1/2 x 2 In.	295.00
Case, Brass, Inlaid Heart, Holland, 18th Century, 10 In.	950.00
Case, For Clay Pipe, France, c.1750	185.00
Case, For Clay Pipe, Wood, c.1750, 10 1/4 In.	295.00
Copper Bowl, Carved Frog, Pewter & Brass Base, 22 In.	300.00
Opium, Iron Bowl & Mouth Piece, Cane Stem, Japan, 18th Century	85.00
Porcelain Bowl, Carved Wooden Stem, Germany, 29 In.	110.00
Red Clay, 18 Presentation Signatures, 6 5/8 In.	55.00

PISGAH FOREST pottery was made in North Carolina beginning in 1926. The pottery was started by Walter R. Stephen in 1914, and after his death in 1941, the pottery continued in operation. The most famous kinds of Pisgah Forest ware are the cameo type with designs made of raised glaze and the turquoise crackle glaze wares.

Bowl, Mottled Exterior, Turquoise Interior, W.B. Stephen, 1936, 11 In.	143.00
Jar, Cover, West Ashville, 1935	35.00
Pitcher, 3 1/2 In.	48.00
Pot, Tin Glaze, Light Blue	330.00
Sugar & Creamer, Turquoise Glaze	150.00
Tea Set, White Cameo Indian & Farm Scene, Robin's-Egg Blue, 4 Piece	800.00
Tea Set, White Cameo Wagon Scene, Deep Sage Green, 3 Piece	770.00
Vase, Aubergine Wine Glaze, White Interior Porcelain, 1953, 6 In.	99.00
Vase, Blue Snowflake, White Crystals, Walter Stephen, 1949, 5 1/2 In.	220.00
Vase, Blue, 1941, 8 In.	95.00

Vase, Blue, Purple Glaze, Walter Stephen, 5 1/2 x 7 In. 115.00
Vase, Blue-Green Crystalline Glaze, Signed, 6 x 4 1/4 In. 522.00
Vase, Blue-Green Glaze, 1920-1930, 5 1/2 In. 55.00
Vase, Camel Color Exterior, Celadon Cream Interior, Crystalline Glaze, 5 In. 440.00
Vase, Celadon Flambe Glaze, Blue & White Crystals, Signed, 5 x 7 In. 825.00
Vase, Celadon, Pink Glaze, 1949, 5 1/2 x 5 1/2 In. 990.00
Vase, Celadon, Pink, 1946, 5 x 3 1/2 In. 440.00
Vase, Cream, Celadon Flambe Glaze, Blue, White Crystals, 8 3/4 x 5 1/2 In. 715.00
Vase, Glossy Cream To Moss Flambe Glaze, Crystals, Baluster Shape, 7 1/2 In. 412.00
Vase, Gray Green, Handle, 6 1/2 x 6 In. 55.00
Vase, Gray, Beige Glaze, 6 1/4 x 4 1/2 In. 385.00
Vase, Green & Red Lustered Crystalline Glaze, Signed, 6 x 4 1/2 In. 935.00
Vase, Green Crystalline Glaze Over Caramel, Blue High Glaze, 8 In. 550.00
Vase, Ivory Glaze, 1934, 6 In. 115.00
Vase, Ivory, Amber Glaze, Blue-Gray Crystals, 1940, 5 x 4 1/2 In. 495.00
Vase, Light Blue, 1941, 6 x 4 In. 38.00
Vase, Purple, 1937, 8 In. ....45.00 to 50.00
Vase, Silver, White Crystalline Glaze, Blue Interior, Pink, 1953, 3 3/4 x 6 In. 374.00
Vase, Turquoise Glaze, Bright Rose Interior, 1940, 4 7/8 In. 77.00
Vase, White, Blue, Green Glaze, 5 1/4 x 4 In. 495.00
Vase, White, Celadon, Blue Glaze, 1949, 9 x 5 1/2 In. 1100.00
Vase, White, Cream Glaze, White, Blue, Green Crystals, 1949, 5 x 3 1/2 In. 350.00
Vase, White, Umber Glaze, White, Blue Crystals, Squatty, 1941, 4 1/2 x 6 In. 440.00

PLANTERS PEANUTS memorabilia is collected. Planters Nut and Chocolate Company was started in Wilkes-Barre, Pennsylvania, in 1906.
The Mr. Peanut figure was adopted as a trademark in 1916. National
advertising for Planters Peanuts started in 1918. The company was
acquired by Standard Brands, Inc., in 1961. Standard Brands merged
with Nabisco in 1981. Some of the Mr. Peanut jars and other memorabilia have been reproduced and, of course, new items are being made.

Ashtray, Bisque 150.00
Ashtray, Mr. Peanut, Standing Behind 1/2 Shell, Bisque, 4 1/2 x 3 In. 44.00
Bank, Mr. Peanut, Cast Iron, 1970s 95.00
Bank, Mr. Peanut, Full Color 35.00
Bank, Mr. Peanut, Plastic 9.00
Belt, Mr. Peanut, Metal Buckle, 1950s, 31 x 2 In. 25.00
Blotter, Mr. Peanut, Old Truck With Mr. Peanut On Side, 1930 .... 18.00
Blotter, Truck, With Mr. Peanut On Side, 1930 .... 10.00
Book, Paint Book, Dated 1950 ....25.00 to 35.00
Bookmark, Die Cut 12.00
Box, Mr. Peanut, 1930, 3 x 7 x 1 In. 16.00
Bracelet, Charm, Mr. Peanut & Peanuts, 1941 .... 125.00
Calendar, 1979-1980, Mr. Peanut, Display Dates Promotional, Plastic, 6 In. 5.00
Cap, Mr. Peanut, Inset Cap-C, Cardboard, 1948, 12 In. 28.00
Clock, Alarm, Mr. Peanut, Metal, Lux, 1960s 85.00
Container, Mr. Peanut, Papier-Mache, 13 In. 750.00
Cookie Cutter, Figural, Mr. Peanut, 2 Different Cutters, 1940-1950, 6 In. 20.00
Cookie Jar, Mr. Peanut ....65.00 to 75.00
Costume, Mr. Peanut, Commercial, 1950s, 43 In. 475.00
Figure, Peanut Man, Wooden 345.00
Jar, Apothecary, 75th Anniversary 35.00
Jar, Blown-Out Peanut Each Corner 245.00
Jar, Cover, Leap Year, 1940 .... 95.00
Jar, Embossed Planters & Mr. Peanuts, Counter Type, 12 1/4 In. 230.00
Jar, Mr. Peanut On All Sides, Pennant & Peanut On Lid, Octagonal ....150.00 to 195.00
Jar, Streamline, Embossed Front, Green Metal Top, Mr. Peanut & Lettering 75.00
Light Pull, Figural Mr. Peanut, 1940 .... 4.00
Marble Bag, Mr. Peanut, 1940 .... 20.00
Mitt, Oven, Figural 25.00
Mug, Mr. Peanut, Plastic, 1960s 20.00
Nodder, Mr. Peanut, Lego, 1960s, 7 In. 207.00

Nut Chopper, Mr. Peanut, Tin Dome Cap, 4 x 4 In.	28.00
Nut Dish Set, Tin, World's Fair, 1939, 5 Piece	11.00 to 28.00
Peanut Butter Maker, Emenee, 1960s, Box	65.00
Pen, Ball-Point	20.00
Pencil, Mechanical	20.00
Pocket Protector, Mr. Peanut On Front	45.00
Salt & Pepper, Figural, Plastic	175.00
Salt & Pepper, Glass Eye, Porcelain, 4 1/2 In.	95.00
Salt & Pepper, Range Size, 5 In.	35.00
Scale, Full Figure Of Mr. Peanut, 4 Ft.	16500.00
Sign, Mr. Peanut, Standing, With Sign, Planters, First In Flavor, 6 x 14 In.	235.00
Swizzle Stick, Mr. Peanut, Everybody Loves A Nut, Plastic	5.00
Tin, 1919	65.00
Tin, 75th Anniversary	1.00 to 5.00
Tin, Planters Peanut Oil, Mr. Peanut, Red, Blue, Recipes On Side, 1 Gal.	110.00
Tray, Mr. Peanut	20.00
Truck, Pressed Steel, Lincoln, 1950s, 14 In.	495.00
Wall Pocket, Mr. Peanut	255.00
Whistle, Mr. Peanut, Blue Plastic	2.00

PLASTIC objects of all types are being collected. Some pieces are listed in other categories; gutta-percha cases are listed in photography, celluloid in its own category.

Apron, Reddy Kilowatt, Tea Type, Plastic, 1950s	35.00
Ashtray, Horseshoe, Cream, Good Luck 1939, Redwood Empire, 2 3/4 In.	49.00
Bowl, Fruit, Pan Am Airline, Brown & White	4.00
Bowl, White, Weird Harold Picture In Bottom, General Foods, 1976	25.00
Box, Dresser, Gold Medallion, Art Deco, 1940s, 7 x 5 1/2 x 2 In.	28.00
Cigarette Holder, Black Shaft, England, 3 In.	10.00
Coaster Set, Piel's Beer, Bert & Harry, Unopened, 3 Piece	29.00
Comb, Art Deco Style, Tortoise Color, Green Rhinestones, 5 1/2 In.	85.00
Comb, Tortoise Color, White Rhinestones, Gold Scroll Trim, 4 1/2 In.	95.00
Dresser Set, Tiger Striped, 2 Round Containers, 9 Piece	110.00
Egg Timer, Isle Of Man, Figural, Plastic	32.00
Humidifier, Roly Poly Bakerman, Figural, Box, 1 1/2 In.	15.00
Lamp, Wall, Ivory Plastic, Paper Pleated Shade, 12 x 9 In.	35.00
Mug, Scooby Doo, Orange, 1983, 14 Oz.	15.00
Pitcher, 2 Cups, Kool-Aid, Smiling Face, White, 3 Piece	22.00
Powder Box, Pierrot The Clown, Orange, Painted, Art Deco, Round	60.00
Switch Plate, Electric, 3 Little Pigs, 1950s, Original Package	32.00
Swizzle Stick, Carved Little People, 1930s, 12 Piece	75.00
Swizzle Stick, Golf Clubs, Biloxi, 6 Piece	18.00

PLATED AMBERINA was patented June 15, 1886, by Joseph Locke and made by the New England Glass Company. It is similar in color to amberina, but is characterized by a cream colored or chartreuse lining (never white) and small ridges or ribs on the outside.

Bowl, Stripes, 8 In.	6500.00
Creamer, Applied Amber Handle, Squatty	4400.00
Pitcher, Ribbed, Applied Amber Handle, 7 In.	7500.00
Tumbler, 4 In.	2000.00

PLIQUE-A-JOUR is an enameling process. The enamel is laid between thin raised metal lines and heated. The finished piece has transparent enamel held between the thin metal wires. It is different from cloisonne because it is translucent.

Bowl, Pink, Blue, Gold, Red, Black, 5 In.	94.00
Bowl, Viking Boat Form, Stylized Foliage, Enamel, 1900, 7 3/4 In.	3450.00
Dish, Blue, Green, Rose, 5 In.	55.00
Pendant, Dancing Girl, Diamonds On Gown, Ruby, Pearl, France, 1900, 3 In.	4600.00
Sherbet Cup, Enameled, Peacocks, Grape Clusters, Moscow, 1910, 5 In.	5750.00
Spoon, Shovel Shape, 2 3/4 In.	225.00

POLITICAL memorabilia of all types, from buttons to banners, is collected. Items related to presidential candidates are the most popular, but collectors also search for material related to state and local offices. Many reproductions have been made. A jugate is a button with photographs of both the presidential and vice presidential candidates. In this list a button is round, usually with a straight pin or metal tab to secure it to a shirt. A pin is brass, often figural, sometimes attached to a ribbon.

Ashtray, Cowboy Hat Shape, Facsimile Signature On Side, 1960s	48.0
Autograph, Robert Morris, Signer Of Declaration Of Independence, 1795	750.0
Badge, Cleveland And Stevenson, 1892	50.0
Badge, Fremont, Lincoln & Harding	550.0
Badge, Kemp For President, Lee's Back Jack, '96	7.5
Badge, McKinley & Hobart, Brass Shell, Jugate Portrait, 2 1/2 In.	48.0
Badge, Satin Covered Button, Senator Kennedy, 1960, 1 3/4 In.	200.0
Badge, Watch Fob, Sons Of Revolution, Gold & Enamel, Eagle At Top, 1894	750.0
Badge, Westminster College, Harry Truman, Winston Churchill, Fulton, Mo., 1946	575.0
Bandana, Democratic Tariff Reform, Red & White Graphics, Eagle, Flags, 1890	125.0
Bandana, Harrison, Reed, Pictures Both, Our Choice, White Silk, Square	150.0
Bandana, Teddy Roosevelt, Progressive, Battle Flag, 1912, 24 x 21 In.	.60.00 to 175.00
Bandana, Teddy Roosevelt, Protection To American Industries, 1904, 22 x 24 In.	300.0
Banner, Women's Suffrage Era, Felt	600.0
Book, Coloring & Story, John F. Kennedy As Told By Caroline, Kanrom, 1962	9.0
Book, Nixon Yearbook, Campaign, 100 Pages, 1968	15.0
Book, Speaking My Mind, Ronald Reagan, Signed, 1989	495.0
Book, White House Gallery, Presidential Portraits, Up To McKinley, 16 x 20 In.	190.0
Bookends, Theodore Roosevelt, Copper Plate, 6 1/2 In.	75.00
Booklet, Elect Dewey, Platform, Bios Of Candidates, 1944, 2 1/2 x 4 In., Set Of 2	23.0
Booklet, Franklin Roosevelt Inaugural, Gilt Federal Eagle, Limited Edition, 1933	110.00
Bookmark, President, Wendell Wilkie, Vice President, Charles McNary, Jugate	110.00
Bottle, Promotional, Garfield, 20th President, Gold Borders	2860.00
Bottle, Quick Peace Cologne, Hand Giving Peace Sign, 9 In.	38.00
Bowl, 1840 Presidential Campaign, Columbian Star, John Ridgeway, 13 1/4 In.	1430.00
Brooch, Lincoln, Albumen Photo, Beveled Glass, Brady, 1 3/8 x 1 5/8 In.	550.00
Brooch, Miniature On Ivory, Andrew Jackson, Beveled Glass, 1 x 3/4 In.	4850.00
Brooch, William H. Harrison, Log Cabin Style, Cider Barrel, 1 In.	850.00
Bubble Gum Cigars, Nixon, Win With Dick, Box, 8 x 4 1/4 In.	90.00
Bumper Sticker, Eat Beans & Hobo Stew Or Beat Nixon In '72, 1972	13.00
Bust, George Washington, Sunburst, Stars, Success To The United States, Brass	350.00
Bust, Lincoln, Bronzed, 2 1/2 In. *Illus*	12.00
Bust, Lincoln, Reverse Winged Liberty & 2 Slaves At Monument, Bronze, 3 1/4 In.	375.00
Button, Anti-Mondale, Fritz & Tits, Head Of Each, 1 In.	4.00
Button, Ban The Bomb, Blue On Green, Early 1960s, 1 3/4 In.	8.00
Button, Ban The Bullet, New York Workshop In Non-Violence, Blue, White, 1 1/2 In.	12.00
Button, Boycott Non-Union Lettuce, Red, Yellow Ground, 1 1/2 In. *Illus*	33.00
Button, Clothing, Kneeling Slave, Am I Not A Man & A Brother, 1790s	650.00
Button, Colin Powell For President, 1996, 1 In.	4.00

Condition, size, and small details determine the value of political buttons. To be sure the description is accurate for buying, selling, or insurance, just put the buttons on the glass top of a photocopying machine. Make copies of both the front and the back.

Political, Bust, Lincoln, Bronzed, 2 1/2 In.

Political, Button, Boycott
Non-Union Lettuce, Red,
Yellow Ground, 1 1/2 In.

Political, Button, Kill
For Peace, 1 1/4 In.

Button, Congregation For Peace & Democracy, Silver On Blue, 1939 .... 18.00
Button, Coolidge Dawes Club, Albany Country, Celluloid, 1924, 7/8 In. .... 325.00 to 400.00
Button, De Berry For President, Pictures Head, Black & White, 3/4 In. 10.00
Button, Dewey & Bricker, 1 1/4 In. 9.00
Button, Dewey & Bricker, Red, White & Blue, 7/8 In. 7.50
Button, Dicky Poo For '72, Caricature, Full Color, 7/8 In. 20.00
Button, Dole & Kemp, Green, Yellow, Brown & Black, White Ground, Jugate, 9 In. 20.00
Button, Flasher, From Nixon To Agnew, Vari-Vue, 2 1/2 In. 10.00
Button, For Vice President, Calvin Coolidge, Center Picture, Red Border, 1 1/4 In. 600.00
Button, Franklin D. Roosevelt, Picture, 1 In. 18.00
Button, Goldwater In '64, Black & Gold, Star, 1 In. 6.00
Button, I'm An IKE Block Buster, 1 1/4 In. 30.00
Button, Ike, Rhinestone, 2 In. 100.00
Button, Jesse Jackson, The Rainbow Coalition, Logo, Enameled, 1 In. 2.00
Button, JFK, Inaugural, Celluloid, 1961, 6 In. 15.00
Button, Kennedy, He Will Win, Flasher, 2 1/2 In. 12.00
Button, Kill For Peace, 1 1/4 In. ....*Illus* 39.00
Button, King Lyndon The First, Caricature, Red Ground, 5/8 In. 15.00
Button, Lady Bird Special, Whistle-Stop Tour, 1964, Celluloid, 3 In. 30.00
Button, Landon, Knox, Celluloid, 7/8 In. 225.00
Button, LBJ For USA, Welcome Lady Bird On Reverse, Flasher, 3 In. 5.00
Button, Love It Or Leave It, Red, Blue On White, 1 3/4 In. 8.00
Button, Lyndon Johnson & Bobby Kennedy, 1/1/4 In. 4.00
Button, Mario Cuomo In '85, 3 In. 2.00
Button, McGovern, Eagleton, Come Home America, Celluloid, Jugate, 3 1/2 In. 10.00
Button, McKinley At Home, Celluloid, 1 1/2 In. 400.00
Button, McKinley, Hobart, Painted Brass, 1 1/4 In. 148.00
Button, McKinley, Roosevelt, Original Union Label, 1900, 7/8 In. 42.00
Button, Mobilize For Peace, White On Blue, 1930s, 1 3/4 In. 28.00
Button, Nixon & Agnew, Red, Blue, White Border, 1 In. 5.00
Button, Nixon Now, Blue Print, 7/8 In. 4.00
Button, No Third Term, Uncle Sam, Thumbs Down, 1940, 3/4 In. 25.00
Button, Our Next President, Barry Goldwater, Red, White & Blue, Center Picture, 4 In. .. 20.00
Button, Pat Paulsen For President, White & Blue, 1 In. 8.00
Button, Peace Brother, 1 1/2 In. ....*Illus* 9.00
Button, Peace Symbol, 1 1/4 In. ....*Illus* 17.00
Button, Robert Dole, Picture, 9 In. 12.00
Button, U.S. For IKE, Photograph, Stand Or Hang, Celluloid, 9 In. 75.00
Button, Uncle Sam Hanging Hitler From Tree, Let's Pull Together, 3 In. 375.00
Button, Vote For Peace, Clark, President, 3/4 In. 4.00
Button, Vote Libertarian Party, Oval, 3/4 In. 6.00
Button, Vote SLP, Socialist Labor Party, 3/4 In. 5.00
Button, Vote Socialist Workers, 1968, 7/8 In. 5.00
Button, Wallace, LeMay, White Print On Blue, 1 1/2 In. 6.00
Button, Warren G. Harding, Picture, 1 In. 20.00
Button, Wings For Willkie, Fighter Plane, 1939, 1 In. 15.00
Button, WPA, Clip-On 65.00
Button, Yanks, Are Not Coming, National Maritime Union, 1 In. .... 30.00 to 58.00
Button, Yanks, Let's Have Peace & Plenty, Red, White, Blue, 1 In. 27.00
Button, Yanks, National Maritime Union Of America, Red, White, Blue, 1 In. 28.00

Political, Button, Peace
Brother, 1 1/2 In.

Political, Button, Peace
Symbol, 1 1/4 In.

Can, Soda, Goldwater, Contents	8.00
Cane, Grover Cleveland, Pewter Bust	200.00
Cane, Walking, Jimmy Carter, 1976	40.00
Cane, Walking, Jimmy Carter, Jimmy For President Handle, 1976	12.00
Card, Playing, John F. Kennedy	25.00
Cloak, Garfield, Arthur, Painted Canvas, c.1881, 30 In.	1092.00
Cookie Cutter, Elephant, Vote Republican, Red, White & Blue Box, c.1952, 3 x 2 In.	12.00
Cuff Links, Cleveland & Hendricks, Photographs Mounted In Brass Cuffs, 7/8 In.	75.00
Cuff Links, Lyndon B. Johnson, Gold Washed, Box	20.00
Cup, Paper, Coffee With The Kennedys, 1960s	95.00
Decal, Landon & Knox For Congress, 1936, 4 x 10 In.	20.00
Decal, Window, Eisenhower, Young Republican, 1956	3.00
Decanter, Truman, Presidential	25.00
Document, Signed By John Quincy Adams, Henry Clay, March 21, 1826	835.00
Fan, Bush, Quayle, Jugate, Red, White & Blue	3.00
Fan, Clinton & Gore, Jugate, 1992	3.00
Fan, Hand Held, Goldwater, Elephant On Front, Flasher Eyes	18.00
Fan, Picture Of Clinton & Hillary, Red, White & Blue, 1992	4.00
Figure, Andrew Jackson, President, Plastic, Painted, Marx, 3 In.	1.00
Figure, Franklin Roosevelt, President, Plastic, Painted, Marx, 3 In.	1.00
Figure, U.S. Presidents, Washington To Nixon, Display, Marx, 37 Piece	225.00
Flag, Antenna, Lyndon B. Johnson, New Jersey, 1964	7.00
Flag Banner, Henry Clay, Election Of 1844	5000.00
Handkerchief, Barry Goldwater, 16 x 16 In.	10.00
Handkerchief, Presidential Victims Of Assassins, Silk, Frame, 19 1/2 x 18 1/2 In.	55.00
Hat, Paper, Win With Adlai & Estes, White, Red Stripe, Blue Lettering	8.00
ID Badge, 1968 Republican National Convention, Radio-TV, Bronze Colored, 1 3/8 In.	24.00
Kerchief, President Hoover Campaign, 1932, 17 x 17 In.	100.00
Key, McGovern, Skinny Cat, 2 1/4 In.	200.00
Key Chain, Jimmy Carter, Peanut Shape, With Carter Smile, Gold Metal	2.00
Land Grant, James Monroe, Signed & Dated, Frame, 1818	575.00
Land Grant, John Quincy Adams, Frame, Dated January 13, 1827	550.00
Lantern, Tin, 4 Years More Of Full Dinner Pail, McKinley & Roosevelt, 8 In.	745.00
Letter, Rutherford B. Hayes, To His Family Doctor, 1875	575.00
License Plate, Attachment, Hoover For President	25.00
License Plate Attachment, Goldwater Campaign, Eagle At Top Corners, 1964	14.00
License Plate Attachment, Perot, California, 1992, 2 1/3 x 5 In.	3.00
Lighter, Goldwater Campaign, Why Not Victory, Elephant With Glasses, 1964	48.00 to 80.00
Lunch Bucket, McKinley, 1 1/4 In.	75.00
Mask, Halloween, J.F. Kennedy, Plastic, 1960s, Child's	25.00
Mask, Jack & Jackie Kennedy, 1960s, 9 In., Pair	45.00
Mask, Nixon, CF Manufacturing, 1989	9.00
Match Book, Lyndon B. Johnson, LBJ For USA On Reverse, 1964	2.00
Medal, Republican Convention, 1952	30.00
Medallion, Inaugural, Johnson, Sterling Silver, 1965	80.00
Mirror, Harold Korn For Congress, Pocket	38.00
Mug, McGovern As Knight With Peace Shield, Glass, Shakey's Pizza, 1972, 6 In.	30.00
Mug, Teddy Kennedy, 1976, 4 In.	35.00
Paddle, Slogan, Goldwater In '64, Let's Spank LBJ, Yellow & Black, 3 x 8 In.	38.00

Patch, NRA Employee, Eagle, White, Blue, Red, 1930s, 3 In. 30.00
Pennant, 37th Presidential Inauguration, White, Blue & Red Lettering, 1973, 25 In. 9.00
Pennant, Civilian Conservation Corps, Green & Yellow, Felt, 1930s 60.00
Pennant, Keep Coolidge, 1924, 11 x 30 In. 150.00
Photograph, Ben Butler For President, Working Man's Friend, Frame, 1884 .... 900.00
Photograph, Buffalo Soldiers, Blacks, Served In Spanish-American War 1774.00
Photograph, Calvin Coolidge, Fishing, 1927 .... 85.00
Photograph, F.D. Roosevelt, Swing Frame 12.00
Photograph, Pres. Jimmy Carter, Rosalynn, Black & White, Autographed, 8 x 10 In. 25.00
Photograph, Truman, Autographed, White House Mailer, Jan. 19, 1953, 11 x 14 In. 231.00
Pillow, Don't Forget Pearl Harbor, We Will Win, Square, 15 In. 58.00
Pipe, Briar, Franklin D. Roosevelt, Hand Carved, 7 In. 125.00
Plate, Cleveland, Thurman, Sepia Transfer, 8 In. 115.00
Plate, Dewey, Cobalt Blue Border, Polychrome Transfer, 8 In. 70.00
Plate, John Hay, Yellow Border, Chestnuts, Commemorative, 1903, 8 In. 80.00
Plate, McKinley, Hobart, Sepia Transfer, 8 In. 90.00
Plate, Republican Centennial, Profiles Of Lincoln & Eisenhower, 1954, 10 In. 20.00
Plate, William Henry Harrison, Hero Of Thames, Name & Crossed Cannon, 9 In. 2000.00
Postcard, Anti-John F. Kennedy, SOB Club, We Miss Ike, We Even Miss Harry 18.00
Postcard, Barry Goldwater On Front, Tuesday Is Election Day, Sure To Vote, 1968 ..... 48.00
Postcard, Billies, Goats, Will Capture Teddy Bears Den, Omaha, 1908 .... 160.00
Postcard, Coolidge, Dawes, Full Color Jugate, 1924 .... 28.00
Postcard, D.C. Suffrage Parade, Head Of Suffragette Parade Passing Treasury, 1913 .... 16.00
Postcard, Dwight David Eisenhower, 34th President Of Washington, D.C., 1953 .... 2.00
Postcard, Elephant Expelling Gas On Donkey, Gone With The Wind, 1940s 22.00
Postcard, Flasher, Teddy Roosevelt, 1904 .... 40.00
Postcard, Grant, Lincoln & Wilson, Red, White & Blue, 1915 .... 65.00
Postcard, Ku Klux Klan, Who Is Better Citizen, Rail Splitter, Milan, Illinois 200.00
Postcard, Lyndon Johnson & Family, The First Family 2.00
Postcard, McKinley For President, Stands For Honest Money & Chance To Earn It 300.00
Postcard, Memorial, Martin Luther King, Photograph, Slogan At Bottom, 1929-1968 ... 2.00
Postcard, Nancy Reagan, Nancy Getting Kiss From Dog 3.00
Postcard, Pres. Nixon & Family At Piano, 1968 Campaign 10.00
Postcard, Pro-Socialism, Symbols Of Class Struggle, Appeal To Reason 250.00
Postcard, Temperance, Poem, Downfall Of Family Man To His Drink 75.00
Postcard, Vote For Your Future, Vote Republican, Eisenhower, Nixon, 1952 .... 18.00
Postcard, Votes For Women, 1914 Calendar, Artist Signed, B.M. Boye 484.00
Postcard, Votes For Women, Ain't Man Generous, Everything But That Vote!, Wall 39.00
Postcard, Votes For Women, I Should Worry!, I Have No Vote, Wall 96.00
Postcard, Votes For Women, I Speak For Myself, Signed, Wall 36.00
Postcard, Votes For Women, No Taxation, Little Girl With Sword, Signed, Wall 55.00
Postcard, Votes For Women, Something To Say, For Work Of A Day, For Taxes We Pay . 49.00
Postcard, Whose Going To Wear The Pants, Woman's Movement, Leather, 1907 ...... 30.00
Postcard, William J. Bryan, The Next President Of U.S., P. Sanders, 1908 .... 40.00
Postcard, Worker's Union, Workmen's Circle Of America, Text In Yiddish, 1917 ...... 85.00
Poster, Anti-Bryan, McKinley, Frame, 20 x 27 In. 100.00
Poster, Antiwar, 2 Hippies Hitchhiking To Toronto, 1968, 21 x 29 In. 28.00
Poster, Antiwar, LBJ's Face, Would You Die To Save This Face, 1968, 21 x 29 In. 28.00
Poster, Antiwar, Uncle Sam Wants You, 1920s Red Army Soldier, Factory, 1968, 29 In. . 32.00
Poster, Disaster Follows Sabotage, 4 Horsemen Of Apocalypse, 1953, 13 x 18 In. 25.00
Poster, Eisenhower, Fabric On Card Stock, Bachrach Photograph, 14 1/2 x 18 In. 12.00
Poster, Eldridge Cleaver, Black Panther Party Minister, Black, White, 23 x 29 In. 80.00
Poster, Humphrey, Muskie, Plastic, 20 x 30 In. 5.00
Poster, Jane Fonda Supports Black Panthers, Blue, Cardboard, 1970, 14 x 22 In. 163.00
Poster, Longshoremen, Pro-Vietnam War March, Blue, White, N.Y., 1967, 14 x 20 In. 77.00
Poster, Lyndon Johnson Senatorial, Cardboard, 1941, 11 x 14 In. 100.00
Poster, McGovern vs. Nixon Election, 1972, 19 1/4 x 29 In. 30.00
Poster, Mourning, Lincoln, Garfield, 25 x 33 In. 200.00
Poster, Nixon, Nation Needs Coolness More Than Clarion Calls, 1972, 17 x 22 In. 14.00
Poster, Nixon, This Time Vote Like Your Whole World Depended On It, 21 x 13 In. 18.00
Poster, Sabotage, Today's Menace, Red, Black, White, Paper, 1952, 13 x 18 In. 535.00
Poster, Security Is Everybody's Business, Pro-Worker, 1912, 16 x 20 In. 135.00

Poster, Sisters, Women's Liberation Center Of New York, Paper, 20 x 30 In. 27.00
Poster, Speak-Out On Abortion, All Women Welcome, Blue, Puce, 1971, 11 x 17 In. 50.00
Poster, Theodore Roosevelt, For Governor, 16 x 24 In. 50.00
Poster, Women's Day, Bay Area Women's Struggles, Red, Blue, 1973, 15 x 22 In. 36.00
Razor, Straight, Portraits Of James Cox & Franklin Roosevelt, 1920 . . . . 3000.00
Ribbon, Jugate, William Jennings Bryan & Arthur Sewall, 1896 . . . . 100.00
Ribbon, McKinley, Gubernatorial Campaign, Late 1800s 150.00
Ribbon, Official Host, Eisenhower, Nixon, 1956, 5 x 2 In. 25.00
Ribbon, Teddy Roosevelt Campaign, 1904 . . . . 150.00
Ribbon, Ulysses Grant, Eagle Above Portrait, Slogan, 4 1/2 In. 150.00
Ribbon, Vote Yes On The Constitutional Amendment, Blue, White Silk, 1 1/4 x 4 In. 175.00
Salt & Pepper, John F. Kennedy 50.00
Salt & Pepper, Nixon, Metal Milk Can, Picture On Box Cover, Lampkin 28.00
Scarf, John F. Kennedy, Portrait, 1960s 10.00
Sheet Music, All The Way With LBJ, Photograph On Front, 1964 . . . . 26.00
Sheet Music, End Of Perfect Day, Carrie Jacobs, Statue Of Liberty On Front 18.00
Sheet Music, Happy Landin' With Landon, 1936 . . . . 20.00
Sheet Music, John F. Kennedy, Inaugural, The New Frontier, Portrait On Front 48.00
Sheet Music, Thomas E. Dewey March, 1952 . . . . 10.00
Sheet Music, We Want Willkie, Portrait On Cover, Red, White & Blue 42.00
Sign, Order Of United Americans, New York State, c.1880, 12 1/2 x 26 In. 345.00
Sign, Yard, Elect Perot President, 1992, 22 x 14 In. 5.00
Snuffbox, Zachary Taylor, Old Rough & Ready 1275.00
Spoon, Franklin Delano Roosevelt, Silver Plate 10.00
Spoon, John F. Kennedy, Silver Plate 10.00
Spoon, Teddy Roosevelt, Sly Fox Back, Sterling Silver, June 6, 1906 . . . . 150.00
Stetson Hat, Goldwater, Plastic, 1964, Miniature 20.00
Stetson Hat, Lyndon B. Johnson, Plastic, 1964, Miniature 20.00
Stickpin, Owl, Debs, Brass 400.00
Tab Button, Kennedy, Black & White 1.50
Textile, Franklin Pierce Portraits & Eagle Pattern, Cotton, Frame, 10 1/2 x 9 In. 605.00
Thimble, LaFollette, Wheeler, Aluminum 125.00
Thimble, Nixon For Congress, Put The Needle In The PAC 75.00
Toy, John F. Kennedy, Rocker, Plays Happy Days Are Here, Windup, Lamer, Box, 1963 . . 325.00
Tray, Theodore Roosevelt, Rough Rider Image, Leading Charge Up San Juan Hill 592.00
Watch, Spiro Agnew, Caricature 60.00
Watch Fob, Cox, Best Ever, Mirror Back 4500.00
Watch Fob, Myron T. Herrick For Governor 50.00
Watch Fob, Warren Harding, Best Ever 2500.00
Wooden Nickel, Anti-JFK, 1962 . . . . 3.00

POMONA glass is a clear glass with a soft amber border decorated with pale blue or rose-colored flowers and leaves. The colors are very, very pale. The background of the glass is covered with a network of fine lines. It was made from 1885 to 1888 by the New England Glass Company. First grind was made from April 1885 to June 1886. It was made by cutting a wax surface on the glass, then dipping it in acid. Second grind was a less expensive method of acid etching that was developed later.

Bowl, Amber Stained, 1st Grind, 3 x 4 1/2 In. 275.00
Bowl, Cornflower Design, Ruffled Top, 2nd Grind, 2 1/2 x 5 1/2 In. 225.00
Champagne, Amber Stained, Stemmed, 2nd Grind, 5 In. 245.00
Finger Bowl, Light Amber Stain, 1st Grind 45.00
Punch Cup, Cornflower Design, 1st Grind, 2 3/4 In. . . . . .145.00 to 150.00
Punch Cup, Cornflower Design, Handle, 2nd Grind 145.00
Punch Cup, Inverted Thumbprint, Amber Stained, New England 45.00
Toothpick, Tricornered Top, Amber Stain, 2 In. 175.00
Tumbler, Cornflower Design, Amber Stain Top & Leaves, 2nd Grind, 3 3/4 In. . . . .125.00 to 135.00
Tumbler, Cornflower Design, Frosted, 2nd Grind 55.00
Tumbler, Diamond-Quilted, Blue Cornflower Design, 2nd Grind, 4 In. 95.00

PONTYPOOL, see Tole category.

POPEYE was introduced to the Thimble Theater comic strip in 1929. The character became a favorite of readers. In 1932, an animated cartoon featuring Popeye was made by Paramount Studios. The cartoon series continued and became even more popular when it was shown on television starting in the 1950s. The full-length movie with Robin Williams as Popeye was made in 1980.

Airplane, Marx	750.00
Bank, American Bisque Co.	335.00 to 450.00
Bank, Bust, Plastic, 1979, Large	35.00
Bank, Dime Registering, Tin Lithograph, 1929	175.00
Bank, Popeye Sitting On Rope, Play Pal Plastics, 7 1/2 In.	40.00
Bank, Swee'pea, Sitting, Yellow Sleepers, Painted, Ceramic, 7 1/2 In.	330.00
Bendiface, Foam Rubber, Squeeze To Form Different Shapes, 1968	16.50
Book, Big Little Book, Popeye, Olive & Wimpy On Cover, c.1935	72.00
Book, Coloring, 1938	22.00
Book, Flip, 8 Pages, 2 x 3 In.	44.00
Book, Pop-Up, Popeye & The Pirates	375.00
Book, Popeye Plays Nursemaid To Swee'pea	22.00
Box, Music, Pop-Up, Mattel, 1961	25.00
Box, Pencil, 1934	80.00
Candy Container, PEZ	77.00
Cap, Sailor, Picture On Top, Dark Blue, 1940s	125.00
Christmas Light Covers, Characters, Plastic, Red, White, Blue, Yellow, 1930s	85.00 to 125.00
Cookie Jar, Olive Oyl's Head, Green Hat & Collar, American Bisque, 10 1/2 In.	120.00
Cookie Jar, Olive Oyl, American Bisque	1550.00
Cookie Jar, Pipe, American Bisque	1500.00
Cookie Jar, Popeye & Wimpy, McCoy	60.00
Cookie Jar, Popeye's Head, Blue Hat Cover, 9 1/2 In.	205.00
Cookie Jar, Swee'pea, American Bisque, 9 In.	2975.00
Doll, King Features, 17 In.	23.00
Doll, Swee'pea, Cloth, Vinyl, 1985, 18 In.	30.00
Figure, Blowing Bubble Popeye, Battery Operated, Linemar, 12 In.	1145.00
Figure, Brutus, Lead, 1929	60.00
Figure, Cardboard, 1940s, 8 1/2 In.	30.00
Figure, Cast Iron, Hubley, 1929, 3 1/2 In.	350.00
Figure, Olive Oyl, Lead, 1929	60.00
Figure, Popeye & Olive Oyl, With Spinach Can	90.00
Figure, Popeye, Carrying Parrot Cages, Windup, Marx, 1932, 8 1/2 In.	450.00
Figure, Popeye, Standing With Stationary Parrot On Wheelbarrow, Marx	750.00 to 1100.00
Figure, Riding Spinach Cycle, Cast Iron, 1930s	950.00
Figure, Wimpy, Cast Iron, Hubley, 1929, 3 1/2 In.	350.00
Game, Card, Ed-U-Cards, Box	28.00
Game, Ring Toss, 1950s	55.00
Glass, Character, Coca-Cola, 8 Piece	30.00
Gumball Machine, Hasbro, 1968, 13 In.	25.00
Harmonica, Metal, Larami, On Card, 1983	18.00
Hot Water Bottle, Figural Popeye, Duarry, Spain, 12 In.	83.00
Lamp, Figural, Lamp Post, Cast Metal, Original Pipe, 1930s	475.00
Lamp, Figural, White Metal, Color Shade, Popeye, Olive & Wimpy, c.1935, 15 1/2 In.	330.00
Light Bulb, Figural Filament, Crystal Lamp, 1930s	895.00
Lighter, Slogan & Profile Embossed Both Sides, Brass, 1/2 In.	110.00
Lighter, Storm Master, Images Of Popeye, Donald Duck, Wimpy, Archie & Others	50.00
Lighter, Zippo, With Olive Oyl At The Tees	17.00
Lunch Box, No Thermos, 1980	55.00
Mold, Chocolate, Popeye, 2 Part, Closure Clamp, Single, 7 1/2 In.	145.00 to 495.00
Motorcycle Patrol, Rubber Tires, Cast Iron, Hubley, 1938, 8 3/4 In.	2300.00
Mug, Figural Head	25.00
Mug, Olive Oyl, Vandor, 1980	115.00
Napkin Ring, Bakelite	115.00
Night-Light, Vinyl, Alan Jay, 1959	65.00
Pail, Popeye At The Beach, Jeep & Sweet Pea, Tin Lithograph, T. Cohn, c.1936, 12 In.	687.00
Pail, Popeye The Sailor, Tin Lithograph, Handle, T. Cohn, c.1933, 4 3/4 In.	210.00

Paint Set, 1933, 6 x 4 1/2 In. 44.00
Paint Set, American Crayon Co., 1933 .... 30.00
Pencil Box, Popeye, Olive & Wimpy, Eagle Pencil Co., 1919-1929 ....70.00 to 100.00
Pencil Sharpener, Bakelite, K.F.S. Inc., 1930, 1 3/4 In. ....65.00 to 80.00
Pencil Sharpener, Tin Lithograph, 3 In. 330.00
Pipe, Kazoo, 1934 .... 100.00
Plate, Child's, Popeye, Olive, Swee'pea, Wimpy, Brutus, Plastic, 1972, DEKA, 9 1/2 In. . 25.00
Popeye Getar, Removable Pipe, No Music, Box, 1950s 125.00
Projector, Give-A-Show, Box, Kenner, 1960 .... 65.00
Punching Bag, J. Chein Co., 1930s 1150.00
Puppet, Push, Olive Oyl, Turns & Bends, Kohner 39.00
Puzzle, Frame, Popeye Fishing, 1960s, 10 In. 20.00
Record, Figural, 45 RPM, Holder, 1966 .... 19.00
Record, Fleas, Cardboard Holder, Small Record, L976 .... 6.00
Ring, Flasher, Popeye Switches To Nephew, Square Top, Silver Plastic, 1950-1960 ..30.00 to 45.00
Salt & Pepper, Popeye & Olive Oyl, Vandor, 1980 .... 110.00
Sheet Music, I'm Popeye The Sailor Man, Movie Popeye The Sailor, 1934 .... 73.00
Soaky, Popeye, 1960s, Colgate, 9 In. 40.00
Sparkler, 1959, Chein, Box 450.00
Spinach Wagon, With Repro Driver 800.00
Telephone, Figural, Comvu Corp., 1982 ....85.00 to 125.00
Toothbrush Holder, Bisque, 1930s 525.00
Toy, Barrel, Windup, Tin, Chein 800.00
Toy, Bellhop Carries Parrots In Cage, Windup 200.00
Toy, Bubble Blowing Popeye, Linemar, 1950s, 8 1/2 In. 1450.00
Toy, Eccentric Airplane, Marx, 1940, Box ....550.00 to 910.00
Toy, Express, With Blow Me Down Airport, Marx, Box 1870.00
Toy, Figure, Vinyl Head & Arms, Soft Filled Body, Uneeda, 1970s, 7 In. 69.00
Toy, Jack-In-The-Box, Lid Opens To Plastic Popeye Head, Mattel, 1957 .... 60.00
Toy, Jigger, Box, Marx, 1936, 9 1/2 In. 2860.00
Toy, Jumping Jack, Popeye In Can Of Spinach 125.00
Toy, Motorcycle, Popeye Rider, Cast Iron, Hubley, 5 x 8 In. 660.00
Toy, Olive Oyl On Tricycle, Windup, Linemar 895.00
Toy, Paddlewagon, Corgi, Box, 1967, 5 1/2 In. 450.00
Toy, Popeye Express, Overhead Airplane, Tin, Box 1295.00
Toy, Popeye In The Rowboat, Hoge Mfg. Co., 14 In. 6000.00
Toy, Popeye The Sailor, Bubble Blowing Pipe, Plastic, White, Boat Shape, 5 In. 35.00
Toy, Popeye, In Barrel, Windup, Chein, 1932 .... 295.00
Toy, Rollerskater, Linemar ....750.00 to 1095.00
Toy, Skating, Windup, Marx 695.00
Toy, Spinach Patrol 695.00
Toy, Strength Tester, Holgate, Wooden 55.00
Toy, The Champ, Clockwork, Tin & Celluloid Figures, Box 1485.00
Toy, Tricky Walker, Windup, Tin, Jaymar Inc., 6 In. 250.00
Toy, Walker, Popeye, Pushing Can Of Spinach, KFS, 3 In. 55.00
Watering Can, Spinach Farm, Popeye, Olive & Swee'pea, T. Cohn, New York, 6 1/2 In. ... 440.00

PORCELAIN factories that are well known are listed in this book under
the factory name. This category lists pieces made by the less well-
known factories.

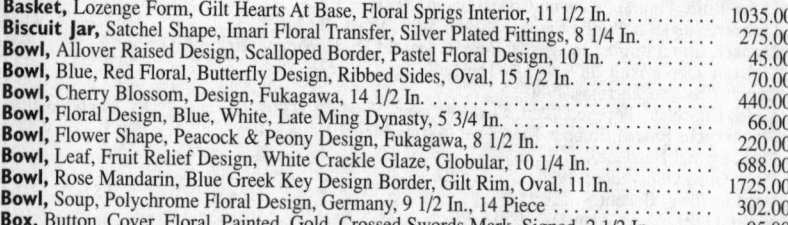

Basket, Lozenge Form, Gilt Hearts At Base, Floral Sprigs Interior, 11 1/2 In. 1035.00
Biscuit Jar, Satchel Shape, Imari Floral Transfer, Silver Plated Fittings, 8 1/4 In. 275.00
Bowl, Allover Raised Design, Scalloped Border, Pastel Floral Design, 10 In. 45.00
Bowl, Blue, Red Floral, Butterfly Design, Ribbed Sides, Oval, 15 1/2 In. 70.00
Bowl, Cherry Blossom, Design, Fukagawa, 14 1/2 In. 440.00
Bowl, Floral Design, Blue, White, Late Ming Dynasty, 5 3/4 In. 66.00
Bowl, Flower Shape, Peacock & Peony Design, Fukagawa, 8 1/2 In. 220.00
Bowl, Leaf, Fruit Relief Design, White Crackle Glaze, Globular, 10 1/4 In. 688.00
Bowl, Rose Mandarin, Blue Greek Key Design Border, Gilt Rim, Oval, 11 In. 1725.00
Bowl, Soup, Polychrome Floral Design, Germany, 9 1/2 In., 14 Piece 302.00
Box, Button, Cover, Floral, Painted, Gold, Crossed Swords Mark, Signed, 2 1/2 In. 95.00
Box, Dresser, Enameled Colonial Courting Couple, Rochelle, France, 8 1/2 In. 605.00
Box, Hen On Nest, 9 1/4 In. 275.00

Box, Lift Top, Blue, Gold, Transfer Design, Ormolu Mounts, Continental, 4 x 1 1/2 In. ...	132.00
Box, Man, Woman, Child & Trees On Cover, Floral, Gold Scroll, Sampson & Co.	127.00
Box, Polychrome Floral & Gilt Design, Germany, 8 x 6 x 5 1/4 In.	66.00
Box, Scenic Cover, Oriental Design, 2 1/2 In.	140.00
Candlestick, Cherub Design, 1 With Ewer, 1 Carrying Wheat, Germany, 9 In., Pair	259.00
Candlestick, Putti Seated On Tree Trunk, 10 1/2 In., Pair	165.00
Centerpiece, 3 Children, Polychrome, Mark, Wahliss, 7 5/8 In.	495.00
Centerpiece, Footed, Dots, Oriental Floral & Bird, Burslem, England, 11 1/2 In.	172.00
Chopstick Rest, Gourd, Rabbit, Cat & Mask, 4 Piece	198.00
Coffee Mug, Polychrome, Meissen Style, Continental, 19th Century, 3 In., 7 Piece	110.00
Compote, 4 Figures Of Children, Applied Leaves, Flowers On Bowl Base, 8 In.	173.00
Compote, Child's, Bisque, Footed, Wildflowers, France, c.1850, 2 1/2 In., Pair	300.00
Compote, Floral Bouquet, White Panels, White Biscuit Cherub, France, 11 In., Pair	173.00
Compote, Landscape Design, Red & Gilt Rim, France, 8 3/4 x 2 3/4 In., Pair	44.00
Compote, Pierced Bowl, Applied Leaves, Flowers, Germany, 12 1/4 In.	460.00
Cracker Jar, Roses, Pink, Gold Transfer, Royal Munich	350.00
Cup & Saucer, Pink, Animal Heads, Large ....*Illus*	25.00
Cup & Saucer, Polychrome, Friendship, Germany, Large	22.00
Dessert Set, Floral Design, Dresden Style, Germany, 8-In. Plates, 18 Piece	55.00
Dinner Set, Roses, Violets, Tureen, Plates, Bowls, Child's, France, 1880, 32 Piece	650.00
Dish, Entree, Cover, Rose Mandarin, Gilt Bamboo-Shaped Handle, 5 x 9 1/2 In.	1610.00
Dish, Entree, Cover, Rose Mandarin, Pinecone Finial, Oval, 11 In.	1092.00
Dish, Gilded, Multicolored Floral Center, Oval, Germany, 11 1/4 In.	50.00
Dish, Passion Floral Design, Blue, White, Late Ming, 5 1/2 In.	55.00
Dish, Yellow Kid, British Outfit, Settle Irish Question	725.00
Door Push, White Headed Sea Eagle & Golden Eagle, Painted, 1900, 11 In., Pair	225.00
Dresser Jar, Porcelain Hinged Cover, Multicolored Figural Panel, 4 In.	220.00
Egg, Easter, Floral Design, Russia, Late 19th Century, 4 1/2 In., 3 Piece	1035.00
Eggcup, Chicks, White, Gold, Japan, 4 Piece	55.00
Ewer, Relief Foliage, Light Blue Ground, France, 1880, 24 In., Pair	5460.00
Eye Bath, Shells & Fluting, Floral Spray, Vishe, 1767, 1 3/4 In.	1035.00
Figurine, Buddha, Standing On Lotus Throne Holding A Pearl, 1800, 17 1/4 In.	605.00
Figurine, Cat, Brown Glaze, 3 7/8 In.	60.00
Figurine, Colonial Woman & Man, Germany, 12 In., Pair	95.00
Figurine, Cupid & A Young Woman, White Glaze, France, 10 3/4 & 10 7/8 In., Pair	172.00
Figurine, Cupid, Painted, White, Black, Powolny, VWGK Mark, c.1907, 7 In.	1645.00
Figurine, Dachshund, Sleeping, Glazed, Gray Collar, Wiener Werkstatte, c.1910, 9 In.	290.00
Figurine, Flower Sellers, St. Cloud, c.1745, 8 7/8 x 9 In.	3450.00
Figurine, Oriental Woman, Blanc De Chine, 13 In., Pair	135.00
Figurine, Peasant Girl, Peeling Orange, Germany, 14 In.	28.00
Figurine, Rabbit, White English Bobby Suit, Artone, 4 1/2 In.	50.00
Figurine, Rearing Horse, White, Michael Powolny, c.1910, 10 1/8 In.	495.00
Figurine, Winter, Woman With Muff, Johanna Meier-Michel, 9 1/4 In.	1230.00
Figurine, Winter, Woman With Muff, Polychrome, Emil Meier, c.1920, 11 3/4 In.	1315.00
Figurine, Young Girl Holding Lamb, Signed Cuny Sagan, 26 In.	460.00
Fish Set, Fish Design, Water Grasses, Sauce Boat, Undertray, Austria, 14 Piece	330.00

Porcelain, Cup & Saucer, Pink,
Animal Heads, Large

Porcelain, Platter, Art Deco, Oval, Japan, 12 1/4 In.

Porcelain, Vase, Gilt Bat & Shou
Design, Blue, White, 15 3/4 In.

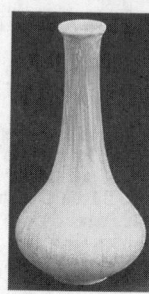

Porcelain, Vase, Bud,
Brown & Celadon
Flambe, Robineau,
6 x 3 In.

Porcelain, Vase,
Woman Portrait,
Hand Painted,
Gilt Trim,
Germany, 10 In.

Ginger Jar, Wooden Cover, Mythological Figural, Blue, White, Globular, 8 1/2 In.	3300.00
Group, 2 Birds, Painted, White, Green, Yellow, Powolny, c.1907, 2 In.	655.00
Group, Children, Goat, Sheep, Germany, 8 1/2 In.	374.00
Group, Chinese Man, Horse, Susi Singer, Weiner Werkstatte, c.1921, 7 3/4 In.	2465.00
Group, Married Couple, Polychrome, Mark, Hugo Freidrich Kirsch, 9 In.	535.00
Headrest, Modeled As Crouching Cat, Under Blanket, Cizhou, 10 1/2 In.	687.00
Incense Burner, Domed Red Cover, Gilt Crane, Pine, Bamboo & Prunus, 2 5/8 In.	55.00
Insert-Platter, Rose Mandarin, Rectangular, 11 1/4 In.	632.00
Jar, Cover, Enameled Floral, Diapered Borders, Bronze Mount, Oriental Mark, 9 In.	1320.00
Jar, Cover, White Hawthorn Blossom Design, Brass Base, Blue, White, 18 In., Pair	1400.00
Jar, Potpourri, Enameled Deer & Birds, Silver Sterling Foot, Squatty, Bulbous	55.00
Jardiniere, Bat & Floral Design, 9 x 12 In.	275.00
Jardiniere, Ram's-Head Handles, Underplate, Gilt, Germany, 7 1/4 In., Pair	86.00
Jug, Floral Design, Applied Handle, Blue, White, Stopper, 9 In.	45.00
Jug, Milk, Floral Design, White Body, Coral Handle, Russia, 6 1/2 In.	1150.00
Jug, Milk, Wave, Scroll Bases, Coral Handles, Russia, 19th Century, 7 3/4 In.	2300.00
Kettle, Hot Water, With Stand, France, 11 In.	55.00
Letter Rack, Blue & White, 6 1/2 In.	48.00
Mug, Coffee, Big Game Animals Portrayed, 11 Oz.	7.00
Mug, Handle, Black, Gold Scenic Band Around Body, Signed, 5 1/2 In.	15.00
Pitcher, 2 Men Bowling Scene, Silver Luster Trim, Thos. Maddock's Sons, 12 In.	55.00
Pitcher, Boy Scene, Peach Ground, Mask Spout, Amer. Porcelain Mfg., 1844, 6 In.	1150.00
Pitcher, Boy, Baseball Uniform, Wringing Goose's Neck, Transfer, 5 1/4 In.	75.00
Pitcher, Flowers & Butterflies, Gilt, J.P., France, 6 1/2 In.	150.00
Plaque, Antigone & Ismene, Signed, c.1900, 8 5/8 x 5 3/8 In.	862.00
Plaque, Duchess Of Richmond, Holding Walking Stick, Gilt Frame, 7 x 5 In.	92.00
Plaque, Hand Painted Young Peasant Boy, Venetian Frame, Grison, 7 1/2 In.	230.00
Plaque, Hunting Hound Chasing Grouse, Antique Frame, 1771, 8 x 15 1/2 In.	2000.00
Plaque, Oriental, Girl With Wise Man, Polychrome Enamel, Carved Frame, 22 In.	137.00
Plaque, Rugh, Germany, Early 20th Century, 5 3/4 x 4 In.	575.00
Plate, Gilt, Cobalt Blue Design, Floral Panels, 7 3/4 In., Pair	150.00
Plate, Military, Nicholas I, Inscribed, Imperial Eagles, Gilt Border, 1829, 9 In.	10350.00
Plate, Multicolored Floral, Reticulated Border, Schumann, 7 1/2 In., Pair	110.00
Plate, Oyster, Polychrome, Late 19th Century, 9 1/2 In.	143.00
Plate, Raphael Service, Alexander III, St. Petersburg, 1890, 9 1/2 In.	5750.00
Plate, Safari, Lion Center, Big Game Animals On Rim, 10 In.	25.00
Platter, Art Deco, Oval, Japan, 12 1/4 In. .... *Illus*	9.50
Platter, Blue Designed Edge, No. 2E & F, 13 1/2 x 10 1/4 In.	16.00
Platter, Blue Greek Key Border, Court Scene, Rose Mandarin, 11 1/4 In.	805.00
Platter, Blue Greek Key Border, Figural Scene With Boat, Rose Mandarin, 17 In.	3450.00
Platter, Court Scenes, Rose Mandarin, 15 3/4 In.	1035.00
Platter, Well & Tree, Figural Design, Rose Mandarin, 17 1/2 In.	3450.00
Service For 12, Cobalt & Gold Pattern, Aynsley, 1930, 80 Piece	3850.00
Serving Dish, Oval, Footed, Rose Mandarin, 3 3/4 x 15 3/4 In.	2300.00
Serving Dish, Polychrome, Lobster Form Handle, Continental, 14 In.	50.00

Spill Vase, Applied Cactus Florals, Double Root, Sitzendorf, 1870, 3 x 5 In. 85.00
Stand, Cachepot, Floral, On Stand, 5 1/2 In., Pair 172.00
Tankard, Clusters Of Blueberries, Gold Handle, Signed, Schmid, France, 13 1/2 In. 165.00
Tankard, Purple Grapes, Gold Signed, Germany, 13 In. 275.00
Tea Set, Blue, Gilt Border, England, c.1790, 22 Piece 1210.00
Tea Set, Child's, Floral Enamel, Purple, Yellow, Red, Box, 21 Piece 88.00
Tea Set, Child's, Polychrome Floral, Pink Band, Gold Trim, 17 Piece 198.00
Tea Set, Enameled Floral Magenta & Blue Border, England, 10 Piece 330.00
Tea Set, Iron Red & Blue, Gilt, 1810, 14 Piece 575.00
Teapot, Cover, Applied Flowers, Leaves, Floral Panels, Globular, C. Saxonian, 6 In. 403.00
Teapot, Dome Lid, Gilt Ball Finial, Rose Mandarin, 6 1/2 In. 977.00
Teapot, Mushroom Knop, Octagonal Spout, Silver Mounted, St. Cloud, 1745 .... 8625.00
Teapot, Purple Pansies, Gold Trim, White Ground, Wood 45.00
Teapot, Woman, With Flowers, Cobblestone, Large 55.00
Tureen, Sauce, Cover, Gilt Bud Finial, Twig Handles, Rose Mandarin, 6 x 8 In. 1092.00
Tureen, Sauce, Underplate, Enameled Scene Panels, Green Border, Branch Handle 185.00
Tureen, Soup, Cover, Red & Blue Flowers, Gilt Vines, England, 1820, 10 3/4 In. 690.00
Tureen, Soup, Cover, Ribboned Florals, Scattered Sprigs, Doccia, 1770, 11 In. 2587.00
Urinal, Hand Painted, Blue & White, Japan, 19th Century, 22 1/2 In. 998.00
Urn, Cover, Aqua, White & Gilt Trim, France, 11 3/4 In., Pair 1210.00
Urn, Cover, Fruiting Finial, All Over Flowers, White Ground, 16 In. 5462.00
Urn, Dome Cover, Children, China, 19th Century, 10 In., Pair 715.00
Urn, Dome Cover, Flower Cluster Finial, French Mount, China, 1840, 22 In., Pair 6050.00
Urn, Landscape Scene, Polychrome Enameled, Satyr Head Handles, 9 1/4 In., Pair 330.00
Urn, Mantel, Reticulated Lid, Pinecone Finial, Gilt Bronze Mount, 17 In., Pair 3850.00
Urn, Portrait, Woman, Bust, Painted, c.1840, 7 In., Pair 132.00
Urn, Troubadour & Woman With Child Scene, Fruit, Flowers, Gilt, 9 In., Pair 330.00
Vase, Bladder Form, Full Relief Dragon Entwined About Neck, Sky Blue, 9 1/2 In. 1375.00
Vase, Bud, Brown & Celadon Flambe, Robineau, 6 x 3 In. ....*Illus* 3300.00
Vase, Bud, Orchid Shape, Lavender Tipped Petals, 3 1/4 In, Pair 45.00
Vase, Cluster Of Shells, Coral, Seaweed, Cobalt Blue Ground, Pedestal, 11 In. 2875.00
Vase, Cornucopia, Polychrome & Gilt, Jacob Petite, 1880, 10 x 11 1/2 In., Pair 1400.00
Vase, Cover, Floral Design, Dolphin Handles, Blue Ground, Bloch & Achille, 9 In. 489.00
Vase, Cover, Scrolled Foliate Design, Cartouches, Cobalt Blue Ground, 20 In. 4600.00
Vase, Dragon, Lotus Design, Blue, White, Rectangular, 15 3/4 In. 715.00
Vase, Eggshell, Yellow Carnation, Teardrop, Rosenburg, 1908, 10 3/8 In. 3750.00
Vase, Fired-Gold Body, 2 Ram's Head Handles, Hand Painted Fruit, 12 In. 1725.00
Vase, Gilt Bat & Shou Design, Blue, White, 15 3/4 In. ....*Illus* 910.00
Vase, Hand Painted Scenes Of Women & Children, Gold Bands, France, 21 In., Pair 1300.00
Vase, Insects, Birds, Floral Scene, Dragon Handles, Cobalt Blue, 18 In., Pair 2185.00
Vase, Peacock Feathers, White Slip Trailing, Ed. Colonna, 1900, 12 3/8 In. 2625.00
Vase, Portrait, Woman, Scrolled Foliate, Burgundy Luster Ground, Oval, 34 In. 2875.00
Vase, Sprinkling-Can Shape, Polychrome Flowers, Transfer & Gilt, 6 1/4 In. 55.00
Vase, Tortoise Climbing Blue Mountain, Pear Shape, Makazu Kozan, 8 1/4 In. 935.00
Vase, Underwater Landscape Below A Sky Scene, Blue, Maurice Daurat, 13 In. 3680.00
Vase, Waisted, Simulated Rock Glaze, Signed, Japan, 20th Century, Square, 10 In. 110.00
Vase, White Japanese Blossoms Around Top, Taxile Doat, 1908, 5 7/8 In. 1150.00
Vase, Woman & Cherub, Seated, Flowers, Metal Rim, Sevres Type, Cartier, 23 In. 3162.00
Vase, Woman Portrait, Hand Painted, Gilt Trim, Germany, 10 In. ....*Illus* 330.00

POSTCARDS were first legally permitted in Austria on October 1, 1869.
The United States passed postal regulations allowing the card in 1872.
Most of the picture postcards collected today date after 1910. The amount
of postage can help to date a card. The rates are: 1872 (1 cent), 1917 (2
cents), 1919 (1 cent), 1925 (2 cents), 1928 (1 cent), 1952 (2 cents), 1959
(3 cents), 1963 (4 cents), 1968 (5 cents), 1973 (8 cents), 1975 (7 cents),
1976 (9 cents), 1978 (10 cents), 1981 (12 cents), 1985 (13 cents), 1985
(14 cents), 1988 (15 cents), 1991 (19 cents), 1995 (20 cents).

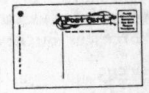

A. Dickinson, Witch Hazel, Dividing The Farm, Puzzle, 1930s, Large 15.00
A. Dickinson, Witch Hazel, Witch With Wand, 1930s 15.00
Advertise With Color, Harry H. Brumann, New York, 1948 .... 175.00
Blackbird, Habitat-Coonland, Ulman, 1905 .... 85.00
Border Girl, Holding Rifle, Next To Horse, Boots, Pants, Signed, R. Margin, 1906 ..... 68.00

Budweiser Beer, Reception Room, 1950s	15.00
Cape Smythe Whaling & Trading Co., Eskimo Children Playing In Snow	15.00
Catalina Island, 1900-1947, 3 x 5 In., 14 Piece	45.00
Ceramics, Modern Arts & Crafts, Severin Brothers, Zurich, Diveky Design	250.00
Country Club Beer, Building Scene, 1936, Unused	11.00
Czechoslovakia Exposition, Agriculture, Industry & Ethnology, 1902	200.00
Dayton Flood, Fire District, Photograph, 1913	20.00
Dr. Pepper, Good For Free Drink Of Dr. Pepper's Phos-Ferrates, Late 1890s	375.00
F & C Calendar Girl, Varnishes, Flood & Conklin, New Jersey, 1907	200.00
Football Player, Brains Have Gone To His Feet, Foxed, Hill, 1906	18.00
Fourth Of July, 6 Flags, Statue Of Liberty, 1900s, 3 x 5 In.	25.00
Googly Dolls, Glass Eyes, Unused, Glassine Envelope, c.1920, 3 x 4 In., 5 Piece	525.00
Griswold Hotel, New London, Connecticut, Hand Colored, 1910	5.00
Hanging, Blood Of Black Jack After Hanging, Head Snapped Off	250.00
Harvard, Queens College, Raphael Tuck	150.00
Hold-To-Light, Broadway	35.00
Hold-To-Light, Central Park	35.00
Hold-To-Light, Faneuil Hall, Boston	35.00
Hold-To-Light, La Porte Of St. Denis	7.00
Hotel Carlton, Rehoboth Beach, Delaware, Linen, Autos On Front, 1940s	3.00
I Can't Bear To Leave, Berthoud, Colorado, Leather, 1906	13.00
Illusion, Fade-Away Girl, Edward Gross, 1909	65.00
Indian, Chief Blackhawk, Wearing War Bonnet, Germany, 1907	19.00
Indian, Chief Little White Cloud, With Bow	19.00
Indian, Woman, Datsolalee Washoe Basket, Sepia, Smith & Co., 1910	50.00
Indians Of Montana, 5 Men, War Bonnets, Photograph, Roahen, 1924	23.00
Industry, Map & Commerce, Japan, 1929	100.00
Jack Dempsey, World's Fair	25.00
Jubilee Festival, Exhibition & Fair Of Czechoslovakian Singers, 1928	200.00
Lynching, August 11, 1913	1075.00
Lynching Of Leo Frank, Anti-Semitism, 1915	500.00
Maurice Baths, Gym & Massage, Hot Springs, c.1910	18.00
Mountain Lodge, N.M. On Route 66, Linen, 1950	4.00
Native Berry Sellers, Women With Berry Buckets, 1910	17.00
Old Cowgirl, Weathered Woman, Standing, In Cowgirl Outfit	113.00
Old Orchard Maine Pier, Strollers, Colored, 1910	7.50
Pawnee Bill, Rival To Buffalo Bill, Looking Sideways, Wearing Hat	30.00
Photograph Of 10th Cavalry Soldier	350.00
Reno Bank Club, Interior, Photograph, 1930s	18.00
Roadside Wedding Chapel, Yuman, Photograph, 1930s	10.00
Ronald McDonald, 1970	14.00
Sokol, Dodge, Nebraska, 1911	60.00
St. Patrick's Day, Let Erin Remember, Germany	15.00
Stained Glass Window, M. Mink, Paris, 1903	400.00
Stegmaier Brewing Company, Unused, 1950s	8.00
Stein Series, Boat Design, Gold Embossed, Fabric Art Co., 1908	25.00
Stein Series, Indian Hunting Scene, Gold Embossed, Fabric Art Co., 1908	25.00
Sugar Factory, Smokestack, Scottsbluff, Nebraska, 1909	11.00
Texas Rice Day, Golden Sheaf, September 30th	65.00
Titanic, White Star Liner, Struck Iceberg Off Newfoundland, England, 1912	300.00
Valentine, 12 Piece	20.00
Wiedmann's Brewery, Factory Scene, Unused, 1936	40.00
Woman & Russian Wolfhound, Hand Tinted, 1912	20.00
Worcester Buckeye, Mower, 1912	35.00

POSTERS have informed the public about news and entertainment events since ancient times. Nineteenth-century advertising or theatrical posters and twentieth-century movie and war posters are of special interest today. The price is determined by the artist, the condition, and the rarity. Other posters may be listed under Movie, Political, and World War I and II.

Ben Hogan, Follow The Sun, 1951, 28 x 22 In.	300.00
Buffalo Bill's Wild West Show, Full Color, 40 x 27 In.	3850.00

Century Magazine, Woman, Floral, Frame, Leyendecker, 1896, 20 x 14 In. 715.00
Cheyenne Cowboy & Indian Frontier Celebration, 1911, 42 x 28 In. 3850.00
Circus, Christy Bros. 5 Ring Wild Animal Show, Frame, 1920s, 27 1/4 x 41 In. 395.00
Circus, Group, Lithographs Of Scenes, Neal Walters, 1940s, 22 x 18 In. 200.00
Clyde Beatty-Cole Bros. Circus, c.1915, 28 x 21 In. 155.00
Daisy's Red Ryder BB Gun, Red Ryder & Little Beaver, Christmas, 1941, 17 x 22 In. . . 485.00
Eddie Stanky, Promoting Rollfast Bicycles, Orange, White, Black, 1950, 14 x 20 In. . . . 175.00
Edward Penfield, Brown, Black, Beige, Custom Frame, 16 x 23 In. 700.00
Freak Show, 3 Colors, Cardboard, 1930s, 14 x 22 In. 150.00
H. Rap Brown, FBI Wanted, Riot Scene, Black, White, Brown, 1967, 10 1/2 x 16 In. . . . 140.00
International Air Race, St. Louis, 1923, 14 x 22 In. 250.00
J.B. Ford Company, Wyandotte Indian With Bow & Arrow, Tin Frame, 38 x 28 In. 1550.00
Jacob Hoffmann Brewing Co., 1890s, 34 x 21 In. 200.00
Katie Emmett's Great Play, The Waifs Of New York, 19th Century, 21 x 28 In. 65.00
Killarney & The Rhine, Vot Did He Say, 19th Century, 28 1/2 x 21 In. 110.00
Mail Pouch, Union Maid, Man Diving, Shark, Board, 1930s, 10 x 14 In. 225.00
Milky Way Candy Bar, Art Linkletter Holding CBS Microphone, 15 x 20 In. 24.00
Minnesota State Fair & Expo, 1915, 28 x 42 In. 200.00
Molson Beer, Polar Bear, Walrus & Moose, In Saloon, 18 x 23 In. 12.00
Molson Beer, St. Bernard Pouring Beer For Skier, 18 x 23 In. 12.00
Monteith Comedy Co. In Dilemma, 19th Century, 19 x 28 In. 66.00
Moore & Vivian's Comedy Co., Hold On Gol Darn You, 19th Century, 21 x 27 In. 66.00
Morrison's Faust, The Prison, 19th Century, 29 1/2 x 20 In. 66.00
Pat Rooney Comedy Co., In Lord Rooney, 19th Century, 29 x 20 1/2 In. 165.00
Reno & Ford's Comedians In Joshua Simpkins, 19th Century, 26 1/2 x 21 In. 65.00
Royal Baking Powder, Gingerbread Man Book Picture, 1930s, 20 x 29 1/2 In. 75.00
Sells Circus, Pawnee Bill's Wild West, 1887, 10 x 28 In. 950.00
Shenandoah Cigar, Paper, 25 x 18 In. 160.00
Ski, Flexible Flyer, c.1935, 37 x 24 In. 195.00
Star Wars, Please Look Me Over, Advertising On Back, 1980, 18 x 23 In., 3 Piece 45.00
Star Wars-Empire Strikes Back, Han & Luke On Hoth, Coca-Cola, 1980, 19 x 25 In. . 46.00
Star Wars-Empire Strikes Back, Luke On Dagobah, Coca-Cola, 1980, 17 x 25 In. . . . 46.00
Sugar Cane Train, Amid Cane Fields, Lahaina, Hawaii, 22 x 34 In. 19.00
Toys & Cheerios, Star Wars, 27 x 18 In. 95.00
Virgil The Magician, Cardboard, 1940, 14 x 22 In. 85.00
Winchester, Cut-Away Of M-55, Single Shot .22 Automatic, Paper, 14 x 35 In. 85.00
Winchester Ammo, On Board, Shrink Wrap, Painted By Dwyer, 1954, 28 x 21 In. 100.00
Wrought Iron Bridge Co., Over Mississippi River, Frame, 20 x 24 In. 148.00

POTLIDS are just that, lids for pots. Transfer-printed potlids had their
heyday from the 1840s to the early 1900s. The English Staffordshire
potteries made ceramic containers with decorative lids for bear's
grease, shrimp or meat paste, cold cream, and toothpaste. Printed
advertising and pictures of historical events, portraits of famous people, or scenic views were designed in black and white or color.
Reproductions have been made.

Angel's Dandruff Eradicator, Pheasants, Black On White, 3 In. 350.00
Dr. Harvey's Pomade, Lizard, Black On White, 3 In. 600.00
F. & R. Pratt, Fishing Scene, Man & 3 Children At Water, 4 In. 30.00
Jules Hauel, River Scene, Black On White, 4 1/8 In. 800.00
Liston's Extract Of Beef, Chicago, Black On White, 2 In. 100.00
Shakespeare's Home, Polychrome Transfer, 4 In. 65.00
Street Scene, England 60.00

POTTERY and porcelain are different. Pottery is opaque; you can't see
through it. Porcelain is translucent. If you hold a porcelain dish in front
of a strong light, you will see the light through the dish. Porcelain is
colder to the touch. Pottery is softer and easier to break and will stain
more easily because it is porous. Porcelain is thinner, lighter, and more
durable. Majolica, faience, and stoneware are all pottery. Additional
pieces of pottery are listed in this book in the Art Pottery category and
under the factory name.

Bean Pot, Cover, Tan Glaze, Applied Handles, White Glaze Interior, 6 1/2 x 5 In. 80.00

Pottery, Bowl, Red,
Blue & Yellow
Stripes, Rosenthol
Netter, Italy, 1950s

Pottery, Creamer, Bird,
Yellow, Japan, 4 1/2 In.

Bottle, Narrow Neck, Overall Brown Markings, Sung, 7 1/4 In. 460.00
Bowl, Apple Green, Mahogany Brown Flambe Glaze, Natzler, 6 1/2 x 2 1/4 In. 2200.00
Bowl, Brown Metallic Glaze, Silver Crystalline Luster, Natzler, 6 1/2 x 2 In. 1760.00
Bowl, Calligraphic Markings, Blue Glaze, M. Fosdick, 14 3/4 In. 357.00
Bowl, Citron Yellow Matte Glaze, Orange, Red Clay Body, Natzler, 5 x 2 In. 1650.00
Bowl, Copper Crystalline Glaze, Low, Natzler, 1 1/2 x 10 1/2 In. 6600.00
Bowl, Copper Matte Glaze, Natzler, Signed, 5 1/2 x 1 3/4 In. 1540.00
Bowl, Coupe Shape, Brown, Yellow Flambe Glaze, Scheier, 3 x 6 In. 330.00
Bowl, Crackled Yellow Glaze, Bronze Band, Lucie Rie, 7 3/4 In. 3025.00
Bowl, Flambe, Leaf Shape, Blue, Footed, Valley Wieselthier, 14 In. 175.00
Bowl, Flared, Turquoise Volcanic Glaze, Natzler, 2 1/4 x 4 3/4 In. 2310.00
Bowl, Flower Frog, Flare, Red, Catalina Island 350.00
Bowl, Gold Flambe Glaze, Footed, 3 x 4 1/4 In. 1870.00
Bowl, Green & Blue Drip Glaze, Pacific Clay, 5 x 10 1/2 In. 247.00
Bowl, Green Lava Matte Glaze, Natzler, Signed, 10 3/4 x 3 In. 4125.00
Bowl, Green, Blue High Glaze, Natzler, 6 x 2 In. 1980.00
Bowl, Green, Blue, Yellow, Rose Glaze, Cole, 1962, 2 7/8 x 11 In. 165.00
Bowl, Green, Footed, Catalina Island, 11 In. 150.00
Bowl, Green, Yellow, Blue, Brown Volcanic Glaze, Natzler, 5 1/2 x 2 1/5 In. 2090.00
Bowl, Layered Rim, 5 Pad Feet, Plum Tree Pottery, John Glick, 20th Century, 7 In. 58.00
Bowl, Light Blue, Cream Glaze, Flared, Natzler, 3 1/2 In. 550.00
Bowl, Lime, Blue High Glaze, Natzler, 7 1/2 x 2 In. 1760.00
Bowl, Mardi Gras, Footed, Marc Bellaire, 6 1/2 In. 85.00
Bowl, Matte White Glaze, Bronze Colored Rim, Lucie Rie, 5 1/4 In. 1980.00
Bowl, Orange Dripping Matte Glaze, Natzler, 3 x 5 1/2 In. 3300.00
Bowl, Overlapping, Undulating Rim, Plum Tree Pottery, John Glick, 14 In. 115.00
Bowl, Pale Blue Glaze, Footed, Natzler, 2 1/2 x 6 1/4 In. 1540.00
Bowl, Peach Glaze, Gray, Natzler, 4 In. 330.00
Bowl, Red, Blue & Yellow Stripes, Rosenthol Netter, Italy, 1950s .... *Illus* 3.00
Bowl, San Ildefonso, Black On Black, Juanita, c.1930, 7 In. 450.00
Bowl, Sang-DeBoeuf Glaze, Natzler, 2 x 5 In. 1870.00
Bowl, Serving, Transfer Painted, Orange Ground, Flowers, Stand, England, 9 In., Pair ... 575.00
Bowl, Squat, Dripping Hare's Fur Amber Glaze, Pillin, 6 1/2 x 9 1/4 In. 220.00
Bowl, Tea, Conical, Hare's Fur Glaze, Sung, 7 1/8 In. 287.00
Bowl, Tea, Hare's Fur Glaze, Sung, 5 In. 287.00
Bowl, Turquoise Dripping Crystalline Glaze, Natzler, 2 3/4 x 5 1/2 In. 2970.00
Bowl, Turquoise, Footed, Catalina Island, 10 1/2 In. 325.00
Bowl, Verte De Wine Glaze, Red Clay Body, Natzler, 1946, 5 1/2 x 2 In. 520.00
Bowl, Wax-Resist Brown Interior, Pink Veins, P. Bogatay, 1934, 6 1/4 In. 825.00
Bowl, White Matte Glaze, Red Clay Body, Natzler, 6 x 2 1/2 In. 1100.00
Bowl, Woman, Holding 2 Cats, White Ground, Pillin, 2 3/4 x 8 In. 220.00
Bowl, Yellow High Glaze, Square, Natzler, 5 x 3 1/2 In. 1100.00
Bowl, Yellow Lava Glaze, Dark Brown Highlights, Natzler, 6 1/2 In. 2530.00
Bowl, Yellow, Brown Hare's Fur Matte Glaze, Natzler, 2 1/2 x 7 In. 2200.00
Bowl, Yellow, Cream Glaze, Thumb Grooved Handle, Jack Kiser, 1930s, 4 x 13 In. 44.00
Box, Incense, Monkey & Man Finial, Signed, 1 1/2 In. 66.00
Bust, Girl In Bonnet With Lace Trim, 19 In. 330.00
Candlestick, Blue, Catalina Island, 3 1/4 In., Pair 350.00
Candlestick, Turquoise, Catalina Island, 5 1/2 In., Pair 295.00

Charger, Oxblood & Charcoal Glaze On Interior, T. Takaesu, 1963, 13 In. 440.00
Coffee Server, Red, Catalina Island 200.00
Coffee Set, Hollywood Ware, Matte Green Glaze, Tudor Potteries, Signed, 8 In., 3 Piece 45.00
Creamer, Bird, Yellow, Japan, 4 1/2 In. . . . . *Illus* 10.00
Crock, Butter, W.A. Macquir & Co., Cobalt Blue Flowers, Applied Rim Handles, 13 In. . 385.00
Cup & Saucer, Tea, Caneware, Children Relief, Turner, 1790, 5 1/2 In. 630.00
Custard, Blue, Catalina Island 63.00
Decanter, Wine, Conical, Trees, Fruit, Glazed, Art Deco, Hand Painted, Japan, 11 In. . . . 174.00
Dish, 2 Harlequins, Dancing, Brown Ground, Pillin, Round, 6 In. 190.00
Dish, Gunmetal Crystalline Glaze, Pink Luster, Natzler, 3/4 x 4 3/4 In. 1100.00
Dish, Loaf, Combware, Tan, Brown & White, 18th Century, 16 In. 1650.00
Dish, Lotus Form, Speckled White Glaze, Shino, 8 1/2 In. 66.00
Figurine, American Indian Couple, Frank Lloyd Wright, 16 1/2 x 12 In., Pair 3250.00
Figurine, Boy, In Cloak & Hat, Glazed, England, 7 1/2 In. 86.00
Figurine, Cat, Hanging, Dark Yellow, Blue & White Hearts, Fife Pottery, 19 In. 245.00
Figurine, Cranes, Incised Feathers, Beak Pointing Upwards, Blue, 59 In., Pair 7475.00
Figurine, Dog, Ohio White Clay, Gold Paint, Rectangular Base, Clyde Little, 1920, 7 In. . 440.00
Figurine, Dog, Seated, White Clay, Brown Mottled Glaze, 9 In. 65.00
Figurine, Dog, Seated, With Basket, Tan Clay, Green Glaze, 4 3/4 In. 245.00
Figurine, Dog, Sitting, Buff, Blue & Brownish Yellow Sponged, Ohio, 8 1/2 In. 990.00
Figurine, Dog, White Clay, Brown Trim, Blue Eyes, Ohio, 6 3/4 In. 665.00
Figurine, Flamingo, Pink, California Pottery, 1950s, 5 3/4 In., Pair 40.00
Figurine, Flamingo, Pink, Maddux Pottery, California, 1950s, 9 1/2 In. 47.00
Figurine, Little Girl Between Large Flowers, S. Boru, 6 In. 247.00
Figurine, Little Nell, Circus Figure, V. Schreckengost, 1935, 4 In. 3850.00
Figurine, Man's Head, 2 Holes, 3 1/4 In. 165.00
Figurine, Mouse, Gray, Big Pink Ears, Thelma Winter, 1950s, 5 In. . . . . *Illus* 325.00
Figurine, Oh Joy, Hand Painted, De Lee Art, Signed, 8 In. 27.50
Figurine, Oriental, Boy & Girl, White, Yellow, SBM Calif., 8 In., Pair . . . . *Illus* 35.00
Figurine, Pig, Brown Splotches, Bennington Type Glaze, 1875-1890, 8 1/8 In. 185.00
Figurine, Pig, Gray Tan Glaze, 1880-1895, 6 5/8 In. 200.00
Figurine, Pluto, Howling, Tan, Black & Rose Glaze, Brayton Laguna, 6 In. 110.00
Figurine, Pony, Black & Cream, Morten Studio, 4 1/2 In. 55.00
Figurine, Ram, Glazed Kaolin, 19th Century, 5 3/4 In. 6325.00
Figurine, Rocker, Scroddleware, Red & Yellow, 1864, 7 1/2 In. 270.00
Figurine, Squirrel With Nut, Brown, Olive & Yellow Painted, 8 1/2 In. 355.00
Flowerpot, Attached Underplate, Brown Albany Slip, Buff Clay, New Geneva, 4 5/8 In. . 70.00
Flowerpot, Attached Underplate, Finger Crimped Rim, Tan, 2 Tone, Brown, 5 1/2 In. . . . 127.00
Goblet, 3 Roosters, Blue-Green Ground, Pillin, 4 In. 165.00
Honey Pot, Mottled Brown Glaze, With Runs, Peoria Pottery 225.00
Jar, Advertising Richardson Pottery, Inscribed Sizes, Salisbury Gathering, 1870 . . . . 6500.00
Jar, Apothecary, Blue Glaze, Incised Lines, 2 Handles, Red Ink Stamp, 1941, 7 x 27 In. . . 303.00
Jar, Glazed Yellowware, Pacific Clay, Signed, 4 1/2 x 8 In. 22.00
Jar, Glazed Yellowware, Pacific Clay, Signed, 8 1/2 x 10 In. 22.00
Jar, Stylized Mask, Banded Design, Mock Ring Handles, Globular, Han Dynasty, 8 In. . . 440.00

Pottery, Figurine, Mouse, Gray, Big Pink
Ears, Thelma Winter, 1950s, 5 In.

Pottery, Figurine, Oriental, Boy & Girl, White, Yellow, SBM
Calif., 8 In., Pair

Jug, Bellarmine, Tigerware, c.1600, 9 1/2 In. 1650.0

Jug, Grotesque, 2 Faces, Double Ear Handles, Green Ash Glaze, Teeth, L. Meaders, 10 In. 880.0

Jug, Grotesque, Devil's Head, Green Ash Glaze, Stone Teeth, Lanier Meaders, 8 1/4 In. .. 770.0

Jug, Grotesque, Green Ash Glaze, David Meaders, 6 In. 165.0

Jug, Grotesque, Red Clay, Amber Glaze, Brown Pottery, Arden, N.C., 6 7/8 In. 135.0

Jug, Memorial, Wellington, Died Sept. 14, 1852, Dark Brown, 7 1/2 In. 295.0

Jug, Puzzle, Initials On Front, England, 1920, 5 In. 450.0

Jug, Salt Glaze, Brown, Allover Blue Floral, Orange Peel Handle, 1983, 16 In. 220.0

Lamp, Monkey, Glass Eyes, Austria 1175.0

Mug, Monterey Brown, Catalina Island, After Dinner 55.0

Mug, Yellow, Catalina Island, After Dinner 55.0

Pie Dish, Fluted Edge, Red, Brown Glaze, Black Specks Highlights, Cole, 2 x 10 In. ... 55.0

Pipe, Monkey's Head, Green Glazed Buff Clay, Mid-19th Century, 1 3/4 In. 75.0

Pipe Holder, Catalina Island, White Glaze, Red Island Clay Body, 1 1/2 x 4 In. 60.0

Pitcher, Blue On White Sponge Glaze, Thumb-Grooved Handle, Cole, 8 1/4 In. 66.0

Pitcher, Cover, Green Variegated Glaze, Incised Lines Shoulder, Handle, Cole, 11 In. ... 110.0

Pitcher, Cover, Lazy Daisy, Iroquois, Ben Seibel 75.0

Pitcher, Dark Brown Floral Slip, Tan Ground, New Geneva, 6 5/8 In. 355.0

Pitcher, Gray, Black Floral Design, New Geneva, 6 5/8 In. 195.0

Pitcher, Gray, Black Floral Design, New Geneva, 7 1/2 In. 165.0

Pitcher, Gray, Dark Brown Floral Design, 5 1/2 In. 248.0

Pitcher, Grayish Tan, Black Floral Design, New Geneva, 6 7/8 In. 220.0

Pitcher, Green, Blue Splotches, Tan Glaze, Thumb-Grooved Handle, D. Auman, 11 In. .. 110.0

Pitcher, Painted & Incised Abstract Design, Cream Ground, Picasso, 1969, 12 In. 1870.0

Pitcher, Scroddleware, Brown, Pale Yellow, Lead Glaze, England, 1730, Small 325.0

Pitcher, Stylized Lilies, Leaves, Black & White Ground, Pablo Picasso, 11 1/2 In. 4125.0

Pitcher, Tan, Dark Brown Floral Design, New Geneva, 6 1/2 In. 330.0

Pitcher, Tan, Dark Brown Floral Design, New Geneva, 7 7/8 In. 303.0

Planter, Cat, Lina, Turquoise, Catalina Island 150.0

Planter, Flamingo, No. 819, Brad Keeler 100.0

Planter, Goldilocks, NAPCO 40.0

Planter, Head, Soldier, Hole In Hat, Morton Pottery, 6 1/2 In. 145.0

Planter, Prayer Lady, Pink 50.0

Plate, 2 Peasant Figures, Green Ground, M. Heaton, Square, 9 1/4 In. 220.0

Plate, 3 Women, Light Blue Ground, Acrobats, Chaim Gross, 9 1/2 x 13 1/2 In. 355.00

Plate, Dinner, Harvest Time, Iroquois, Ben Seibel, 10 In. 10.00

Plate, Happy Mortal Who Knows, Pleasures A Pipe Bestows, Fornasetti, 6 1/2 In. 27.00

Plate, Yellow, Catalina Island, 6 1/4 In. 47.00

Platter, Woman Hunter, Brown, Other Green, Gio Ponti, Ginori, 1920s, 14 In., Pair 6000.00

Pot, Moon, Glassy Gray & Beige Glaze, Signed, T. Takaesu, 9 3/4 x 9 In. 935.00

Relish, Lobster, No. 871, Brad Keeler 95.00

Shaker, Tulip, White, Catalina Island 60.00

Pottery, Vase, Eskimo Mother & Child, Matthew Adams, 1950s, 12 In.

Pottery, Vase, Turquoise, Carved Hearts, Circle & X Design, Raymor, 1950s, 7 1/2 In.

Pottery, Vase, Figural, Nancy, Girl With Basket, Walter Wilson, 9 In.

Pottery, Vase, Bowling Pin Shape, Green & Dark Blue, Raymor, 10 In.

Teapot, Alligator, Figural, Made In Japan, 5 1/2 In.	22.00
Teapot, Apache Red Glaze, Pacific Clay, Signed, 6 x 12 In.	93.00
Teapot, Design Transfer, C. Dresser, Old Hall, Oval, 1880s, 4 1/4 In.	2250.00
Tray, Reeded Handle, Rim, Plum Tree Pottery, John Glick, 20th Century, 22 1/2 In.	172.50
Tray, Teardrop Shape, Woman, Holding A Bouquet, Pink Ground, Pillin, 10 x 5 In.	165.00
Tray, Yellow, Fluted, Catalina Island, 9 1/2 In.	150.00
Tumbler, Turquoise, Catalina Island	38.00
Vase, 4 Female Nudes, Blossoms, Jens Jensen, 1927, 9 5/8 In.	10175.00
Vase, Abstract Floral Design, Bottle Shape, Peter Voulkos, 10 3/4 In.	1210.00
Vase, Abstract Floral, Drip Glaze At Rim, Elizabeth Lincoln, 1926, 8 3/8 In.	467.00
Vase, Bladder Shape, High Relief Dragon About The Neck, Seal Mark, 4 1/2 In.	165.00
Vase, Blue Glaze, Cream Highlights, Flared, Natzler, 7 In.	3080.00
Vase, Blue, Gray, Black, Handle Design, Baudisch, Weiner Werkstatte, c.1927, 10 In.	1315.00
Vase, Blue, Green High Glaze, Red Highlights, Pillin, 12 x 11 1/2 In.	1100.00
Vase, Bottle Shape, Burnt Orange, Umber Matte Glaze, Natzler, 16 1/2 x 4 1/2 In.	5775.00
Vase, Bowling Pin Shape, Green & Dark Blue, Raymor, 10 In. ....*Illus*	85.00
Vase, Brown, Ivory Swirled Stripes, Red Clay Ground, North Carolina, 7 In.	22.00
Vase, Chartreuse Glaze, Red Clay Body, Natzler, Signed, 1947, 3 1/2 In.	1320.00
Vase, Closed Rope Handles, Lime Green, Orange Glaze, Carolina Craft, 8 1/2 In.	660.00
Vase, Conical Chalice Form, Sky & Cloud Glaze, Light Blue, Red Body, Natzler, 10 In.	1760.00
Vase, Dawn Celadon Glaze, Gray, Blue Highlights, Natzler, 5 1/2 In.	2090.00
Vase, Eskimo Mother & Child, Matthew Adams, 1950s, 12 In. ....*Illus*	193.00
Vase, Fan Shape, Crimped, Green, Mottled, Williamsburg, 3 3/4 In.	25.00
Vase, Figural, Nancy, Girl With Basket, Walter Wilson, 9 In. ....*Illus*	25.00
Vase, Flaring Rim, Green Vertical Lines, Bronze Bands, Lucie Rie, 11 In.	7150.00
Vase, Floral & Geometric Design, Semicircular, Alhambrian, England, 7 1/2 In.	77.00
Vase, Flower, Green Over White Glaze, Loop Handles, J.B. Cole, 5 1/2 & 3 In.	66.00
Vase, Green & Brown Lava Glaze, Teardrop Shape, Natzler, Signed, 9 In.	3575.00
Vase, Green Over Yellow, Red Glaze, Footed, J.B. Cole, 1940-1950, 7 5/8 In.	99.00
Vase, Gunmetal To Rose, Crystal Formations, Purple Base, Natzler, Ink Mark, 8 x 3 In.	5225.00
Vase, Incised Geometric Design, Earl Menzel, 1951, 6 In.	220.00
Vase, Incised Primitive Men & Fish, Mahogany, Gray, Green Ground, Scheier, 6 In.	220.00
Vase, Light Blue & Pink Mottled Glaze, Gladding-McBean, Signed, 8 In.	45.00
Vase, Light Green Glaze, Light Rose Interior, Gladding-McBean, Signed, 12 In.	66.00
Vase, Lime Green Matte Glaze, Red Clay, Natzler, 10 x 5 1/2 In.	1760.00
Vase, Medium Blue Glaze Interior, Fluted Top, W. Gordy, 4 7/8 In.	165.00
Vase, Mottled Purple Glaze, Black Volcanic Drip On Side, E. Littlefield, 1931, 9 In.	715.00
Vase, Nude, Blue, Art Deco, 8 In.	80.00
Vase, Orange Matte Glaze, Sgraffito Design, Shows Red Clay, Natzler, Signed, 4 1/2 In.	2860.00
Vase, Orange, Charcoal Glaze, Yellow, Bulbous, Pillin, 9 x 9 In.	286.00
Vase, Painted, Yellow Ground, Brown Branches, Max Lauger, c.1921, 5 7/8 In.	370.00
Vase, Persian Deer Pattern, Poole, Impressed Mark, 1930, 10 In.	290.00
Vase, Serpent, Pink Glaze, Pacific Clay, Signed, 9 1/2 x 13 In.	110.00
Vase, Swirlware, Medium Green Glaze Interior, W. Gordy, 2 5/8 x 4 1/4 In.	100.00
Vase, Turquoise, Carved Hearts, Circle & X Design, Raymor, 1950s, 7 1/2 In. .....*Illus*	20.00
Vase, Turquoise, Rectangular, Glidden, 7 1/2 x 4 1/2 x 2 1/2 In.	50.00
Vase, Woman On Horse, Beige Ground, Bottle Shape, Pillin, 8 1/4 In.	440.00
Vase, Yellow Matte Glaze, Maroon On Pink Lines, Handles, Gambone, 15 In.	355.00
Vessel, Moose In Tall Trees, Black Ground, Russel Crook, 8 In.	1875.00
Vessel, Stovepipe Neck, Incised Undulations, Dark Gray, Bohrod & Ball, 14 1/2 In.	880.00
Water Cooler, Cream, Signed California Pottery	55.00

POWDER FLASKS AND POWDER HORNS were made to hold the gunpowder used in antique firearms. The early examples were made of horn or wood; later ones were of copper or brass.

POWDER FLASK, Brass, Animals, Works Until We 3 Meet Again, Civil War	95.00
Cattle Horn, Curved, Black, Wood Top, Bottom, Leather Strap, 12 In.	20.00
Copper, Brass Top, Musket & Shotgun Size, American Flask Co.	150.00
Disk Form, Large Suspension Rings, Moroccan, 4 1/2 In.	150.00
Hunting Scene, 19th Century	75.00
POWDER HORN, Carved, Dog Head Spout, c.1860, 10 In.	975.00
Cow, Carved, Allover Scene Dog Chasing Deer, 1800-1812, 12 In.	225.00
Engraved, British Royal Coat-Of-Arms, Stylized Blossoms, Putnum, 1757	3740.00

Engraved, Edward J. Abbet, Carved Pictures, Revolutionary War 1350.00
Engraved, Houses, Ship, Birds, Trees, Signed, John Brooks, 1779, 8 1/8 In. 4315.00
Engraved, Houses, Trees, Windmill, Fish, Signed, John Grant, 1762, 11 In. 3450.00
Engraved, Serpents, Bird, Fish, Trees, Swags, Signed, Gedison Dennison, 1775 .... 2415.00
Engraved, Serpents, Fish, Signed, Prince Freeman, N.Y., 1756, 9 In. 2590.00
Engraved, Ship, Animals, Dark Brown, Marked, Chandler, 18th Century, 11 In. 800.00
Engraved, Stylized Blossoms, Stag, Rooster, Signed, C. Schell, 1759, 12 1/2 In. 3450.00
Engraved Eagle On Shield, Death Before Dishonor, R.L. Miller, 1972 .... 125.00
Engraved Meeting House & American Ship, 9 1/4 In. 825.00
Foliate Border, Hearts, Patriotic Banner, E.K.B., 1831, 6 1/2 In. 1955.00
Laurel Heart Surround, Captain Jacob Morgan, Ft. Lebanon, 1756 .... 3450.00
Pennsylvania German Folk Art, Molded Cherry Butt, Brass Tip ....80.00 to 120.00
Pewter Screw Tip, Embossed Leather 2300.00
Scrimmed Eagle, Federal Shield, Cross & Anchors, Wood Plug, c.1860, 11 In. 450.00
Thick Wooden Pegged Base, Banded Spout & Iron Suspension Rings, 8 In. 85.00
Wooden Pegged Base, Forged Iron Ring, Suspension Cord, 14 In. 135.00
Wooden Plug With Metal Strap, 1800s, 8 1/2 In. 25.00

PRATT ware means two different things. It was an early Staffordshire pottery, cream-colored with colored decorations, made by Felix Pratt during the late eighteenth century. There was also Pratt ware made with transfer designs during the mid-nineteenth century in Fenton, England. Reproductions of the transfer-printed Pratt are being made.

PRATT
FENTON

Compote, Highland Music, 2 Handles, Oval, 1855, 12 1/4 In. 170.00
Figurine, Eagle, Blue, Brown Sponged Plumage, Wings Slightly Spread, 1810, 5 In. 1150.00
Figurine, Fortuna, Holding Cornucopia, Glazed, Base, Pearlware, c.1790, 6 1/4 In. 316.00
Figurine, Horse With Ocher Coat, Brown Hooves, White Saddle Blanket, 1800, 6 In. ... 1725.00
Figurine, Winter, Standing, Cut-Corner Base, 1800, 9 1/4 In. 460.00
Figurine, Woman, Mandolin, Standing, Rocky Base, 1795, 9 1/2 In. 1035.00
Jar, Pomade, Polychrome, The Village Wedding David Teniers, Mid-19th Century, 4 In. .. 88.00
Perfume Bottle, Orange Peel Ground, Oval, 1800, 3 1/8 In. 255.00
Pitcher, Children In Hearts, Both Sides, 5 In. 375.00
Pitcher, Fair Hebe, 6 In. 1450.00
Pitcher, Figural, Bear, Holding Monkey, Removable Head 3200.00
Pitcher, Pink Luster Deer, 1830s, 5 1/4 In. 450.00
Plate, State House In Philadelphia, 1776, Gilt Frame, 8 1/2 In. 138.00
Platter, 1840, 16 3/4 x 13 1/4 In. 201.00
Snuff Box, Cover, Dog, Lying On Pillow, Pearlware, Late 18th Century, 1 7/8 In. 1150.00
Toby Jug, Cover, Man Seated On Green Chair, Wearing Yellow Coat, 1800, 10 In. 1035.00
Toby Jug, Cover, Man, Yellow Faced, Wearing Blue Ocher Waistcoat, 1810, 9 7/8 In. ... 575.00
Toby Jug, Man Wearing Blue, Yellow, Ocher-Striped Coat, Holding Spotted Jug, 9 In. ... 402.00
Toby Jug, Man Wearing Blue-Dotted Waistcoat, Blue Edge, Brown Branch, 9 In. 1150.00
Toby Jug, Man Wearing Brown Ocher-Dotted Waistcoat, Holding Jug, 1810, 9 1/2 In. ... 575.00
Toby Jug, Martha Gun, Wearing White Hat, Ocher Cuffed Dress, Holding Bottle 1035.00
Toby Jug, Pearlware Glaze, Man Wearing Ocher Edge Tricornered Hat, 1790, 10 In. 402.00
Vase, Tulip, Heart Shape, Green Cartouche, Blue Acanthus Leaves, 8 In., Pair 1495.00

PRESSED GLASS was first made in the United States in the 1820s after the invention of glass pressing machines. Hundreds of patterns of pressed glass were made in complete table settings. Although the Boston and Sandwich Works was the most famous of the pressed glass factories, there were about sixteen other factories making pressed glass from 1830 to 1850, and still more from 1850 to 1900, when pressed glass reached its greatest popularity. It is now being widely reproduced. The pattern names used in this listing are based on the information in the book *Pressed Glass in America* by John and Elizabeth Welker. There may be pieces of pressed glass listed in this book in other categories, such as Lamp, Ruby, Sandwich, and Souvenir.

100-Eye pattern is listed here as Hundred Eye.
1000-Eye pattern is listed here as Thousand Eye.
101 pattern is listed here as One-Hundred-One.
8-0-8 pattern is listed here as Eight-0-Eight.
Acanthus pattern is listed here as Ribbed Palm.

Acorn Band, Butter, Cover 45.00
Acorn Medallion pattern with beading is listed here as Beaded Acorn Medallion.
Acorn Variant, Butter, Cover, Flint 65.00
Acorn Variant, Sauce, Flint, 4 In. 11.00
Actress, Celery Vase 140.00
Actress, Compote, Cover, 7 In. ....125.00 to 150.00
Actress, Creamer 75.00
Actress, Goblet ....85.00 to 95.00
Actress, Jam Jar, Cover 135.00
Actress, Sugar & Creamer 56.00
Admiral Dewey pattern is listed here as Spanish American.
Adonis, Compote, Cover, 8 In. ....115.00 to 125.00
Alabama, Butter, Cover, 7 3/4 In. 28.00
Alabama, Toothpick 65.00
Alabama, Tumbler 75.00
Alaska, Berry Bowl, Blue Opalescent 225.00
Alaska, Butter, Cover, Vaseline 350.00
Alaska, Cruet, Blue Opalescent 345.00
Alaska, Table Set, Blue Opalescent 695.00
Alaska, Water Set, Blue Opalescent 895.00
Albany, Celery Vase 18.00
Albany, Cruet, Stopper 45.00
Albany, Tray, 9 In. 18.00
Albany, Tumbler, Ruby Stained 69.00
Albany, Wine, Ruby Stained 65.00
Alligator Scales With Spearpoint, Tumbler, Etched 18.00
Amazon, Champagne 26.00
Amazon, Goblet 23.00
Amberette, Bowl, Square, Amber, Frosted, 6 In. 175.00
Amberette, Sauce, 4 1/4 In. 14.00
Amberette, Sauce, Satin 28.00
Apollo, Tumbler, Water, Frosted 18.00
Arched Grape, Goblet 25.00
Arched Leaf, Compote, Flint, 7 1/2 In. 28.00
Arched Leaf, Sugar, Cover, Flint 85.00
Argus, Eggcup, Flint 21.00
Argus, Goblet, Flint 45.00
Argus, Sugar, Cover, Flint 70.00
Argus, Wine, Flint 45.00
Arrowhead, Sugar, Cover 18.00
Art, Bowl, Footed, 8 In. 40.00
Ashburton, Champagne, Flint 60.00
Ashburton, Claret, Flint ....55.00 to 65.00
Ashburton, Eggcup, Flint ....22.00 to 45.00
Ashburton, Goblet, Flint, 6 In. 95.00
Ashburton, Mug, Flint, 4 1/4 In. 65.00
Ashburton, Sugar, Cover, Flint 95.00
Ashburton, Whiskey, Cut, Flint 75.00
Ashburton, Wine 25.00
Ashburton With Sawtooth, Pony Mug 75.00
Ashburton With Sawtooth, Whiskey 39.00
Atlanta, Wine 18.00
Atlas, Champagne 35.00
Atlas, Tumbler, Water 18.00
Austrian, Goblet ....35.00 to 45.00
Baby Face, Goblet 375.00
Baby Thumbprint pattern is listed here as Dakota.
Balder pattern is listed here as Pennsylvania.
Balky Mule pattern is listed here as Currier & Ives.
Ball & Swirl, Goblet 10.00
Ball & Swirl, Pitcher, Water 45.00
Baltimore Pear, Plate, 1950 .... 25.00
Bamboo, Compote, 8 3/4 x 7 In. 35.00

Banded Buckle, Honey, 3 1/2 In. 6.00

Banded Buckle, Whiskey 55.00

Banded Cube, Goblet 13.00

Banded Cube, Sauce, Etched, 4 In. 7.00

Banded Portland, Goblet, Amber Stained 85.00

Banded Portland, Goblet, Maiden's Blush 80.00

Banded Portland, Saltshaker, Maiden's Blush 55.00

Banded Raindrop, Cup & Saucer 18.00

Bar & Diamond pattern is listed here as Kokomo.

Barberry, Bowl, Cover, 8 x 5 In. 59.00

Barberry, Butter, Cover 55.00

Barberry, Compote, 8 In. 20.00

Barberry, Goblet 25.00

Barberry, Tumbler, Footed 35.00

Barley, Bowl, Oval, 10 In. . . . . .18.00 to 38.00

Barley, Butter, Cover . . . . .42.00 to 45.00

Barley, Cake Stand, 10 1/2 In. 42.00

Barley, Goblet 35.00

Barley, Pitcher, Water . . . . .45.00 to 50.00

Barley, Sauce, Footed, 4 1/4 In. 7.00

Barley & Oats pattern is listed here as Wheat & Barley.

Barley & Wheat pattern is listed here as Wheat & Barley.

Barred Forget-Me-Not, Compote, Cover, 7 7/8 x 10 1/2 In. 85.00

Barred Forget-Me-Not, Wine 40.00

Barred Oval, Goblet 40.00

Barred Star, Goblet 20.00

Barrel Excelsior, Goblet, Flint 50.00

Barrel Honeycomb, see also the related pattern Honeycomb.

Barreled Block pattern is listed here as Red Block.

Basket Weave, Cup . . . . .12.00 to 20.00

Basket Weave, Goblet . . . . .28.00 to 40.00

Basket Weave, Pitcher, Water, Amber 55.00

Basket Weave, Plate, Handles, Blue, 8 3/4 In. 20.00

Beaded Acorn, Pitcher, Buttermilk, Blue 24.00

Beaded Acorn Medallion, Goblet 33.00

Beaded Band, Goblet 30.00

Beaded Band, Sauce, 4 1/4 In. 5.00

Beaded Bull's-Eye & Drape pattern is listed here as Alabama.

Beaded Circle, Sauce, Flint, 4 In. 10.00

Beaded Circle, Sugar, Cover 120.00

Beaded Dewdrop pattern is listed here as Wisconsin.

Beaded Grape, Bowl, Square, 5 1/2 In. 25.00

Beaded Grape, Butter, Cover, Square 57.00

Beaded Grape, Pitcher, Water, Green 80.00

Beaded Grape, Tumbler, Green 42.00

Beaded Grape, Wine 35.00

Beaded Grape Medallion, Banded, Spooner 30.00

Pressed Glass,
Barred Oval

Pressed Glass,
Bird &
Strawberry

Pressed Glass,
Columbian Coin

Beaded Grape Medallion, Banded, Tumbler, Footed 45.00
Beaded Grape Medallion, Butter, Cover 50.00
Beaded Grape Medallion, Eggcup 40.00
Beaded Grape Medallion, Goblet 30.00
Beaded Grape Medallion, Pitcher, Amber 120.00
Beaded Loop, Berry Bowl, Oval, 6 3/4 In. 27.00
Beaded Loop, Cake Stand, 10 1/2 In. 47.00
Beaded Loop, Compote, Jelly ....25.00 to 32.00
Beaded Loop, Goblet ....35.00 to 40.00
Beaded Loop, Mug, Footed 40.00
Beaded Loop, Tumbler, Water 55.00
Beaded Mirror, Celery Vase, Flint ....55.00 to 65.00
Beaded Mirror, Goblet 26.00
Beaded Mirror, Sugar, Cover 45.00
Beaded Oval & Scroll, Goblet 35.00
Beaded Rosette, Goblet 40.00
Beaded Swirl, Wine 18.00
Beaded Tulip, Goblet 43.00
Beaded Tulip, Sauce 8.00
Bearded Head pattern is listed here as Viking.
Beatty Rib, Celery Vase, Opalescent 45.00
Beatty Rib, Spooner, Opalescent 35.00
Beautiful Lady, Banana Stand 35.00
Beautiful Lady, Cake Stand, 8 3/4 In. 35.00
Belcher Loop, Goblet 18.00
Bellflower, Bowl, Scalloped, 8 In. 80.00
Bellflower, Butter, Cover 102.00
Bellflower, Celery Vase, Single Vine 130.00
Bellflower, Champagne, Flint 175.00
Bellflower, Compote, Flint, Scalloped Edge, 8 x 4 3/4 In. 95.00
Bellflower, Cordial, Barrel Shape, Knob Stem, Rayed Base 95.00
Bellflower, Goblet, Banded, Flint 45.00
Bellflower, Goblet, Green 210.00
Bellflower, Wine, Barrel, Knob Stem, Flint 75.00
Bent Buckle pattern is listed here as New Hampshire.
Berkeley, Sugar, Cover 35.00
Beveled Diamond & Star pattern is listed here as Albany.
Beveled Star, Spooner, Green 20.00
Bible, Match Holder 35.00
Big Button, Cruet 45.00
Big Button, Sauce, Ruby Stained, 4 1/4 In. 15.00
Big Button, Tumbler, Water, Ruby Stained 35.00
Bigler, Compote, Flint, 6 x 5 3/4 In. 65.00
Bigler, Goblet, Flint 40.00
Birch Leaf, Sauce, Blue 12.00
Bird & Roses, Goblet 55.00
Bird & Strawberry, Butter, Cover 195.00
Bird & Strawberry, Cake Stand, 9 In. ....65.00 to 75.00
Bird & Strawberry, Creamer ....25.00 to 95.00
Bird & Strawberry, Pitcher 325.00
Bird & Strawberry, Tumbler 50.00
Blackberry, Goblet 25.00
Blaze, Eggcup, Flint 40.00
Blaze, Tumbler, Footed, Flint 40.00
Blaze & Mirror, Goblet, Flint 55.00
Bleeding Heart, Bowl, 7 3/4 In. 30.00
Bleeding Heart, Creamer 20.00
Bleeding Heart, Goblet ....25.00 to 40.00
Bleeding Heart, Tumbler ....75.00 to 95.00
Block & Fan pattern is listed here as Romeo.
Block & Fine Cut pattern is listed here as Fine Cut & Block.
Block & Honeycomb, Eggcup 15.00

Block & Honeycomb, Goblet . . . . .12.00 to 18.00

Block & Honeycomb, Salt, Master 22.00

Block & Lattice pattern is listed here as Big Button.

Block & Rosette, Cake Stand, 8 1/2 In. 95.00

Block & Spearpoint, Goblet, Ruby Stained 38.00

Block & Star pattern is listed here as Valencia Waffle.

Block & Thumbprint, Salt, Flint, Master 23.00

Block & Thumbprint, Tumbler, Footed 18.00

Bluebird pattern is listed here as Bird & Strawberry.

Bowtie, Bowl, 8 In. 30.00

Bowtie, Cake Stand 75.00

Box-In-Box, Toothpick 30.00

Box-In-Box, Tumbler, Water, Ruby Stained 45.00

Bradford Blackberry, Butter, Cover, Flint 195.00

Bradford Blackberry, Goblet, Flint 95.00

Bradford Grape pattern is listed here as Bradford Blackberry.

Brilliant, Goblet, Flint 65.00

Broken Column, Celery Dish 45.00

Broken Column, Compote, 7 3/4 x 7 1/2 In. 75.00

Broken Column, Creamer, Ruby Stained Notches 125.00

Broken Column, Cup & Saucer 45.00

Broken Column, Goblet 85.00

Broken Column, Salt & Pepper, Ruby Stained Notches 375.00

Bryce pattern is listed here as Ribbon Candy.

Bucket pattern is listed here as Oaken Bucket.

Buckle, Champagne, Flint 165.00

Buckle, Eggcup 24.00

Buckle, Sugar, Cover 75.00

Buckle, Tumbler, Footed, Flint 35.00

Buckle & Star, Compote, 10 x 6 In. 25.00

Buckle & Star, Goblet 35.00

Budded Ivy, Goblet 35.00

Bulging Loops, Water Set, Red, 6 Piece 500.00

Bull's Eye With Diamond Point, Water Set, Ruby Stained, Pitcher, 5 Piece 300.00

Bull's-Eye, Tumble-Up Set, Flint 250.00

Bull's-Eye & Bar, Eggcup 135.00

Bull's-Eye & Daisy, Goblet, Amethyst Stained Eyes 35.00

Bull's-Eye & Daisy, Goblet, Ruby Stained Eyes 35.00

Bull's-Eye & Daisy, Tumbler, Amethyst, Gold Trim, 4 In. 20.00

Bull's-Eye & Fan, Cake Stand, 9 In. 27.00

Bull's-Eye & Fan, Compote, 5 In. 25.00

Bull's-Eye & Fan, Creamer, 5 1/2 In. 27.00

Bull's-Eye & Fleur-De-Lis, Decanter, Flint, Pt. 295.00

Bull's-Eye & Fleur-De-Lis, Goblet, Flint 85.00

Bull's-Eye & Fleur-De-Lis, Sugar, Cover, Flint 80.00

Bull's-Eye & Prism, Goblet, Flint 95.00

Bull's-Eye & Rosette, Whiskey, Flint 45.00

Bull's-Eye & Spearhead, Goblet 55.00

Bull's-Eye Band, Wine 16.00

Bullet, Table Set, 4 Piece 950.00

Bumble Bee Honeycomb, Goblet, Flint 28.00

Button Arches, Creamer, Ruby Stained, Souvenir, Revere Beach, 1907, 2 3/4 In. 15.00

Button Arches, Mug, Ruby Stained, Souvenir, Revere Beach, 1906, 2 7/8 In. . . . . . .15.00 to 21.00

Button Arches, Syrup, Ruby Stained 185.00

Cabbage Rose, Compote, 10 1/4 x 8 1/2 In. 55.00

Cabbage Rose, Goblet 40.00

Cable, Eggcup, Etched, Flint 95.00

Cable, Goblet, Flint 95.00

Cable, Spooner . . . . .20.00 to 55.00

Cable With Fan, Sauce, Flint, 4 In. 8.00

California pattern is listed here as Beaded Grape.

Camel Caravan, Goblet 68.00

Canadian, Goblet 55.00

Candlewick as a pressed glass pattern is properly named *Banded Raindrop*. There is also a pattern called *Candlewick*, which has been made by Imperial Glass Corporation since 1936. It is listed in this book in the Imperial Glass category.

Candy Ribbon pattern is listed here as Ribbon Candy.

Cane, Bowl, Waste	30.00 to 40.00
Cane, Goblet	30.00 to 45.00
Cane, Plate, Amber, 4 1/2 In.	9.00 to 12.00
Cape Cod, Compote, Tall	72.00
Cape Cod, Plate, 10 In.	45.00
Capitol Building, Goblet	25.00

Cardinal pattern is listed here as Cardinal Bird.

Cardinal Bird, Butter, Cover	145.00
Cardinal Bird, Goblet	25.00 to 38.00
Carolina, Cake Stand, 11 In.	75.00
Celtic Cross, Celery Vase	45.00
Celtic Cross, Creamer	50.00
Celtic Cross, Goblet	45.00
Celtic Cross, Spooner	45.00

Centennial, see also the related patterns Liberty Bell, Viking, and Washington Centennial.

Centennial, Goblet	24.00 to 38.00
Centennial, Mug	65.00
Chain, Spooner	28.00
Chain, Wine	20.00
Chain & Shield, Goblet	35.00
Chain & Star Band, Goblet	28.00

Chain With Diamonds pattern is listed here as Washington Centennial.

Chain With Star, Cake Plate, Handle	25.00
Champion, Spooner, Amber	50.00
Chandelier, Pitcher	110.00
Chandelier, Sauce, 4 In.	12.00 to 18.00
Chandelier, Tumbler, Water	45.00
Checkerboard, Tumbler, 4 1/2 In.	21.00
Cherry Lattice, Butter, Cover, Gold Trim	55.00
Chrysanthemum Leaf, Toothpick, Gold Trim	75.00
Chrysanthemum Sprig, Sugar, Cover, Gold Trim, Marked	225.00
Chrysanthemum Sprig, Tumbler, Blue, Gold Trim	125.00
Civil War, Tumbler, 4 3/4 In.	175.00
Clear Block, Goblet, Blue Top	48.00
Clear Block, Sugar	12.00
Clear Circle, Sugar, Cover	44.00
Clear Diagonal Band, Goblet	18.00
Clear Ribbon, Goblet, Etched	27.00
Clio, Pitcher, Water	45.00
Coachman's Cape, Goblet	32.00

Coin Spot pattern is listed in this book in its own category.

Colonial, Toothpick, Blue, 2 Handles	35.00
Colorado, Butter, Cover, Green, Gold Trim	125.00
Colorado, Sauce, Green, Footed, 4 3/4 In.	15.00
Colorado, Spooner, Green, Gold Trim	70.00
Colorado, Toothpick, Green	23.00
Columbian Coin, Goblet, Wine, Gold Trim	135.00
Columbian Coin, Toothpick	55.00
Columned Thumbprints, Creamer	15.00
Comet, Goblet, Flint	135.00

Compact pattern is listed here as Snail.

Coral Gable, Goblet	20.00
Corcoran, Goblet	28.00
Cord Drapery, Punch Cup	15.00
Cord Rosette, Goblet	35.00
Cordova, Syrup	85.00
Cornell, Punch Bowl, 13 1/4 x 6 1/2 In.	85.00
Cornucopia, Tumbler	40.00

Cosmos pattern is listed in this book as its own category.

Cottage, Goblet	36.00
Cottage, Pitcher, Milk	49.00
Creased Ashburton, Goblet	55.00
Crescent & Fan, Whiskey	8.00
Croesus, Butter, Cover, Green, Gold Trim	200.00
Croesus, Celery Vase, Green, Gold Trim	395.00
Croesus, Creamer, Amethyst	145.00
Croesus, Cruet, Green, Gold Trim	295.00
Croesus, Pitcher, Green, Gold Trim	250.00
Croesus, Salt & Pepper, Green	250.00
Croesus, Sauce, Footed, Green, Gold Trim	33.00
Croesus, Tumbler, Amethyst, Gold Trim	30.00
Crossed Disks, Eggcup, Handles	13.00
Crossed Ovals, Wine	20.00
Crossed Pressed Leaf, Sugar	18.00
Crown Jewels is listed here as Chandelier.	
Crusader Cross, Goblet	30.00
Crystal, Celery Vase	15.00
Crystal, Eggcup	15.00
Crystal, Goblet	15.00
Crystal Wedding, Creamer, Frosted	70.00
Crystal Wedding, Spooner, Ruby Stained	40.00
Crystalina, Sauce, Amber Stained	15.00
Cube, Goblet, Square Stem, Etched	15.00
Cupid & Venus, Celery Vase	40.00
Cupid & Venus, Compote, Cover	125.00
Cupid & Venus, Spooner	45.00
Cupid & Venus, Wine	70.00 to 90.00
Currant, Pitcher	250.00
Currant, Spooner	20.00 to 45.00
Currier & Ives, Decanter, Wine	125.00
Currier & Ives, Goblet	25.00
Curtain, Saltshaker	15.00
Curtain Tieback, Cake Stand, 8 1/2 In.	49.00
Curtain Tieback, Goblet	28.00
Cut Log, Celery Vase, Monogram	15.00
Cut Log, Compote, 6 x 5 In.	35.00
Cut Log, Creamer, 5 1/4 In.	45.00
Cut Log, Goblet	35.00
Cut Log, Sauce, Footed, 4 3/8 In.	22.00
Czarina, Toothpick	28.00
Dahlia pattern is listed here as Square Fuchsia.	
Daisies In Oval Panels pattern is listed here as Bull's-Eye & Fan.	
Daisy & Button, Butter Chip, Apple Green, Square	15.00
Daisy & Button, Celery Vase	23.00
Daisy & Button, Match Safe, Amber	115.00
Daisy & Button, Plate, Amber, 10 In.	30.00
Daisy & Button, Plate, Square, Ruby Stained Daisies, 7 In.	18.00
Daisy & Button, Salt, Boat Shape	15.00
Daisy & Button, Sauce, Square, Amber Stained Buttons, 3 1/2 In.	12.00
Daisy & Button, Toothpick, Hat, 2 1/2 In.	15.00 to 25.00
Daisy & Button, Toothpick, Kettle, Blue, 2 1/2 In.	25.00
Daisy & Button, Tumbler, Water	18.00
Daisy & Button With Crossbar, Sauce, Octagonal, Amber Stained Daisies, 5 In.	15.00
Daisy & Button With Narcissus, Wine Set, Decanter, Tray, 6 Wines, 8 Piece	145.00
Daisy & Button With Thumbprint, Goblet, Blue Stained Panels	40.00
Daisy & Button With Thumbprint, Pitcher, Water, Blue Stained Panels	85.00
Daisy & Button With V Ornament, Mug	18.00
Daisy & Button With V Ornament, Sauce, Amber, 4 1/2 In.	13.00
Daisy & Button With V Ornament, Toothpick, Amber	25.00
Daisy & Button With V Ornament, Tumbler, Water, Amber	22.00
Daisy & Fern, Sugar Shaker, Vaseline	225.00
Daisy Whorl, Tumbler, Footed	15.00

Pressed Glass,
Dakota

Pressed Glass,
Dewdrop With Star

Pressed Glass,
Duquesne

Dakota, Butter, Cover, Etched .... 55.00 to 85.00
Dakota, Cake Stand, 9 In. .... 55.00 to 70.00
Dakota, Celery Vase, Etched ....　37.00
Dakota, Compote, Etched, 7 x 7 1/2 In. .... 35.00 to 40.00
Dakota, Creamer, Etched ....　65.00
Dakota, Goblet .... 22.00 to 30.00
Dakota, Pitcher, Water, Etched, 11 In. 125.00
Dakota, Shaker, Blossoms & Berry Etch, Cranberry Stained, Pair 220.00
Dakota, Tankard, 10 In. ....　95.00
Dakota, Tumbler, Water, Etched ....　45.00
Dart Bar, Goblet, Ruby Stained ....　25.00
Deer & Dog, Goblet ....　65.00
Deer & Dog, Pitcher, Etched 110.00
Deer & Pine Tree, Bread Tray, Blue .... 85.00 to 95.00
Deidre, Goblet ....　38.00
Delaware, Berry Bowl, Green, Gold Trim ....　25.00
Delaware, Butter, Cover, Rose Stained, Gold Trim 125.00
Delaware, Pin Tray, Rose Stained, Gold Trim, 4 3/4 In. ....　65.00
Delaware, Pitcher, Green, Gold Trim, 9 1/2 In. 295.00
Delaware, Salt & Pepper, Green, Gold Trim 495.00
Delaware, Sauceboat, Rose Stained, Gold Trim, 3 1/4 In. ....　35.00
Dewberry, Tumbler, Gold Trim ....　13.00
Dewdrop, Goblet ....　25.00
Dewdrop, Mug, 2 Handles, 3 5/8 In. ....　7.50
Dewdrop & Raindrop, Punch Cup ....　6.00
Dewdrop Band, Goblet ....　10.00
Dewdrop With Star, Sauce, 4 In. ....　5.50
Dewey, see also the related pattern Spanish American.
Dewey, Creamer, Green ....　65.00
Dewey, Inkwell 715.00
Diagonal Block Band, Goblet ....　3.00
Diagonal Sawtooth Band, Wine ....　28.00
Diamond, Punch Bowl Set, Child's, 7 Piece 125.00
Diamond & Bull's-Eye Band, Bowl, 8 3/4 In. ....　95.00
Diamond & Bull's-Eye Band, Goblet ....　65.00
Diamond & Bull's-Eye Band, Tumbler, Etched ....　50.00
Diamond & Long Sunburst, Plate, 9 In. ....　15.00
Diamond & Long Sunburst, Toothpick .... 30.00 to 55.00
Diamond Band, Goblet ....　18.00
Diamond Cut With Fan pattern is listed here as Holbrook.
Diamond Cut With Leaf, Goblet ....　20.00
Diamond Medallion pattern is listed here as Grand.
Diamond Point, Cake Stand, Columnar Base, c.1850, 6 1/2 x 13 In. 245.00
Diamond Point, Creamer, Flint, Handle ....　55.00
Diamond Point, Goblet, Flint .... 30.00 to 55.00
Diamond Point, Spooner, 6 In. ....　50.00
Diamond Point, Sugar Shaker, Rose Stained, 4 In. 115.00

Diamond Point, Syrup Pitcher, Rose Stained, 4 1/2 In. 225.00
Diamond Point, Wine, Flint . . . . .65.00 to 90.00
Diamond Point With Panels, Celery Vase, Flint 95.00
Diamond Point With Panels, Tumbler, Footed, Flint, 3 3/4 In. 37.00
Diamond Point With Panels, Wine, Flint 75.00
Diamond Prisms, see also the related pattern Albany.
Diamond Quilted, Bowl, 6 1/4 In. 13.00
Diamond Quilted, Compote, 5 1/2 In. . . . . .15.00 to 22.00
Diamond Quilted, Dish, Amber, Tricornered, Leaf Edge, 8 1/4 x 4 3/4 In. 15.00
Diamond Quilted, Goblet, Yellow 30.00
Diamond Rosettes, Sugar, Cover, Flint 50.00
Diamond Spearhead, Compote, Green Opalescent, 8 1/2 In. 395.00
Diamond Sunburst, Goblet 30.00
Diamond Thumbprint, Butter, Cover, Flint 125.0
Diamond Thumbprint, Compote, Flint, 9 1/2 x 11 In. . . . . .140.00 to 242.00
Diamond Thumbprint, Pitcher, Water, Flint 595.00
Diamonds In Diamonds, Goblet 18.00
Diamonds With Double Fans, Goblet 25.00
Dickinson, Goblet, Flint 69.00
Dirigo Pear, Sauce, Handles, 4 x 5 In. 10.00
Divided Diamonds, Butter, Cover, Flint 65.00
Divided Hearts, Eggcup, Flint 75.00
Divided Hearts, Goblet, Flint 95.00
Divided Squares, Creamer, Amber Stained 25.00
Divided Squares, Sauce, Tricornered, Amber, 4 1/4 In. 14.00
Doric pattern is listed here as Feather.
Dotted Loop, Wine 23.00
Double Block, Wine 15.00
Double Loop pattern is listed here as Ribbon Candy.
Double Spear, Spooner 35.00
Doyle's Shell, Wine 18.00
Draped Red Block, Goblet 55.00
Draped Red Block, Tumbler, Water 40.00
Drapery, Eggcup 24.00
Drapery, Goblet 28.00
Drum, Creamer, Individual 50.00
Drum, Mug, 2 In. 45.00
Duchess, Table Set, Green, Gold Trim, 4 Piece 475.00
Duchess Loop, Wine, Flint 25.00
Duncan Block, Carafe . . . . .35.00 to 55.00
Duncan Block, Goblet, Ruby Stained 50.00
Duncan Block, Punch Cup, Amber Stained, Etched 13.00
Duquesne, Goblet 13.00
E Pluribus Unum pattern is listed here as Emblem.
Earl pattern is listed here as Spirea Band.
Early Moon & Star, Sugar, Cover, Flint 95.00
Early Thistle, Goblet 65.00
Early Thumbprint, Goblet, Flint 85.00
Eastern Star, Goblet 17.00
Egg In Sand, Goblet 27.00
Egyptian, Bread Tray, Cleopatra, 13 x 8 1/2 In. 75.00
Egyptian, Celery Vase 125.00
Egyptian, Goblet . . . . .40.00 to 65.00
Eight-O-Eight, Sugar, Cover, Etched 33.00
Elegant, Goblet, Flint 45.00
Elk Medallion, Goblet 145.00
Elmino, Goblet, Etched 13.00
Elongated Honeycomb, Champagne, Flint 45.00
Emblem, Relish, 5 3/4 x 9 7/8 In. 25.00
Empress, Butter, Cover, Gold Trim 125.00
Empress, Cruet, Green, Gold Trim 375.00
English Hobnail Cross pattern is listed here as Amberette.
Esther, Cake Plate, Green, Gold Trim 65.00

Pressed Glass,
Excelsior

Pressed Glass,
Frosted Circle

Pressed Glass,
Fan With Diamond

Esther, Goblet, Amber Stained, Enameled Design	125.00
Etched Dakota pattern is listed here as Dakota.	
Euclid, Goblet	16.00
Euclid, Sherbet	11.00
Eureka, Butter, Cover, Flint	45.00
Eureka, Goblet, Flint	39.00
Everglades, Berry Set, Vaseline, Opalescent	695.00
Excelsior, Eggcup, Flint	21.00
Excelsior, Goblet, Flint	55.00
Eyewinker, Compote, 7 1/2 x 6 In.	45.00
Falcon Strawberry, Goblet	34.00
Falmouth Strawberry, Goblet	75.00
Fan With Diamond pattern is listed here as Shell.	
Fancy Diamonds, Tumbler, Water	12.00
Feather, Cake Stand, 9 1/4 In.	40.00
Feather, Creamer	20.00 to 45.00
Feather, Goblet	60.00
Feather, Pitcher, Milk	75.00
Feather, Plate, 10 In.	30.00
Feather, Salt & Pepper	185.00
Feather, Spooner	28.00 to 45.00
Feather, Toothpick	90.00
Feather, Wine	40.00
Feather Duster, Goblet	35.00
Feather Duster, Tumbler, Green	18.00
Feeding Swan, Goblet, Etched	53.00
Feeding Swan, Pitcher, Etched, 7 3/4 In.	65.00
Festoon, Cake Stand, 9 In.	35.00
Festoon, Tumbler, Water	22.00
Festoon & Grape pattern is listed here as Grape & Festoon.	
Fickle Block, Cake Stand, 9 3/4 In.	30.00
Fickle Block, Cup & Saucer	15.00
Findlay Bull's Eye, Pitcher, Water	75.00
Findlay Bull's Eye, Tray, 8 In.	18.00
Fine Cut, Spooner, Amber	30.00
Fine Cut, Toothpick, Hat, Amber, 2 1/4 In.	25.00
Fine Cut & Block, Bowl, Amber, Footed	55.00 to 65.00
Fine Cut & Block, Compote, Cover, Blue Stained Blocks, 8 x 15 In.	275.00
Fine Cut & Block, Creamer, Amber	55.00 to 60.00
Fine Cut & Block, Pitcher, Amber	85.00
Fine Cut & Block, Pitcher, Water, Stained Blocks	185.00 to 195.00
Fine Cut & Block, Waste Bowl, Amber	65.00
Fine Cut & Block, Wine, Stained Blocks	75.00
Fine Cut & Feather pattern is listed here as Feather.	
Fine Cut & Panel, Goblet	22.00 to 35.00
Fine Cut & Panel, Plate, 7 In.	10.00
Fine Diamond Point, Eggcup, Flint	27.00

Fine Prism, Wine, Flint	25.00
Fine Rib, Butter, Cover, Flint	125.00
Fine Rib, Eggcup, Flint	55.00
Fine Rib, Whiskey, Flint	18.00
Fine Rib With Cut Ovals, Wine, Flint	210.00
Fishbone, Goblet	13.00 to 38.00
Fishscale, Compote	15.00
Fishscale, Pitcher, Milk	45.00
Fishscale, Plate, 7 In.	35.00
Flamingo Habitat, Goblet	35.00
Flamingo Habitat, Tankard	150.00
Flat Diamond, Goblet	20.00
Flat Diamond, Spooner	20.00
Flattened Sawtooth, Spill, Flint	35.00
Fleur-De-Lis, Goblet	38.00
Fleur-De-Lis & Drape, Champagne	45.00
Fleur-De-Lis & Drape, Plate, Green, 8 In.	18.00
Flora, Spooner, Green, Gold Trim	65.00
Florette, Biscuit Jar, Pigeon Blood	275.00
Florida pattern pieces are listed here as Sunken Primrose if made of clear class.	
Flower Band, Frosted, Sauce, Footed, 4 1/2 In.	13.00
Flower Flange pattern is listed here as Dewey.	
Flower Medallion, Butter, Cover, Flint	115.00
Flute, Eggcup, Flint	15.00 to 18.00
Flute, Whiskey, Handle, Flint	30.00
Flute With Bull's-Eye, Wine, Flint	40.00
Fluted Scrolls, Cruet, Blue Opalescent	295.00
Flying Pheasant, Goblet, Etched	95.00
Flying Stork, Goblet	75.00
Forget-Me-Not, Celery Vase	38.00
Forget-Me-Not, Mug, Child's, Ribbed	22.00
Four-Row Honeycomb, Champagne, Flint	45.00
Frazier, Sugar, Cover, Enameled	33.00
Frazier, Tumbler, Water, Enameled	15.00
Frost Crystal, Sauce, Ruby Stained, 4 In.	13.00
Frost Crystal, Wine	20.00
Frosted patterns may also be listed under name of main pattern.	
Frosted Circle, Bowl, 6 In.	32.00
Frosted Crane pattern is listed here as Frosted Stork.	
Frosted Eagle, Butter, Etched	250.00
Frosted Eagle, Celery Vase	85.00
Frosted Flower Band pattern is listed here as Flower Band, Frosted.	
Frosted Foot, Sauce, Footed	19.00
Frosted Leaf, Marmalade, Cover	145.00
Frosted Ribbon With Double Bars, Celery Vase	39.00
Frosted Royal, Pitcher, Ivy	80.00
Frosted Stork, Bread Tray, Leaf Spray Handle	165.00
Frosted Stork, Creamer	35.00
Frosted Stork, Goblet	65.00
Frosted Waffle pattern is listed here as Hidalgo.	
Fuchsia, Honey, 3 1/2 In.	8.00
Fuchsia, Spooner	35.00
Galloway, Dish, Olive, 6 1/2 x 4 1/4 In.	18.00
Galloway, Goblet	75.00
Galloway, Punch Cup	13.00
Galloway, Toothpick	30.00
Galloway, Tumbler, Water	35.00
Galloway, Wine	45.00
Garden Fruits, Creamer, Applied Handle	23.00
Garden Fruits, Goblet	15.00
Garfield Drape, Butter, Cover	95.00
Garfield Drape, Creamer	35.00 to 38.00
Garfield Drape, Spooner	38.00

Giant Baby Thumbprint, Goblet, Flint	85.00
Giant Prism, Pitcher, Water, Flint, Applied Handle	350.00
Girl With Fan, Goblet	68.00
Good Luck pattern is listed here as Horseshoe.	
Goose Boy, Cake Stand 8 3/4 In.	275.00
Goose Boy, Compote, 8 x 9 In.	250.00
Gooseberry, Tumbler, Bar, Handle	35.00
Goosegirl, Compote, 8 1/4 x 8 1/4 In.	250.00
Gothic, Celery Vase	95.00
Gothic, Eggcup, Flint	45.00
Gothic, Goblet, Flint	85.00
Graduated Diamonds, Goblet	20.00
Grand, Celery Vase	25.00
Grand, Goblet	27.00
Grand, Spooner	18.00 to 45.00
Grant Memorial, Plate, Yellow, 10 In.	65.00
Grape, see also the related patterns Beaded Grape, Beaded Grape Medallion, and Magnet & Grape.	
Grape & Cable pattern is listed in this book in the Northwood category.	
Grape & Festoon, Butter, Cover	42.00
Grape & Festoon, Goblet	25.00
Grape & Festoon, Spooner	35.00
Grape & Festoon With Shield, Dish, Honey, 3 1/2 In.	6.00
Grape & Festoon With Shield, Goblet	65.00
Grape & Gothic Arches, Goblet, Custard, Nutmeg Stained	48.00
Grape Band, Goblet	30.00
Grape Band, Whiskey	35.00
Grapevine With Ovals, Mug, Child's, Handle	21.00
Grasshopper, Compote, Insect	55.00
Grasshopper, Creamer, No Insect	25.00
Grogan, Wine	16.00
Hairpin, Decanter, Flint, Qt.	95.00 to 110.00
Hairpin, Goblet	223.00
Hairpin, Whiskey, 2 1/2 In.	10.00 to 15.00
Halley's Comet, Wine	15.00
Hamilton, Eggcup, Flint	45.00
Hamilton, Spooner, Flint	40.00
Hamilton With Clear Leaf pattern is listed here as Hamilton With Leaf.	
Hamilton With Frosted Leaf, Goblet, Flint	85.00
Hamilton With Leaf, Goblet, Flint, Low Stem	85.00
Hamilton With Leaf, Sugar, Cover, Flint	65.00
Hamilton With Leaf, Whiskey, Flint	100.00 to 110.00
Hand, Celery Vase	35.00
Hand, Goblet	40.00
Hand, Pitcher, Water	110.00
Harp, Cake Stand, Blue	32.00
Harp, Spill, Flint	60.00
Hawaiian Lei, Bowl	15.00 to 18.00
Hawaiian Lei, Cake Stand, 9 In.	33.00
Hawaiian Lei, Plate, 10 In.	15.00
Hawaiian Pineapple, Goblet, Flint	125.00
Heart Band, Mug, Ruby Stained	10.00 to 15.00
Heart With Thumbprint, Creamer, Green, Individual	40.00
Heart With Thumbprint, Ice Bucket	135.00
Heart With Thumbprint, Mug	13.00
Heart With Thumbprint, Nappy, Tricornered	25.00
Heart With Thumbprint, Rose Bowl, 2 1/4 In.	35.00
Hercules Pillar, Tumbler, Footed	20.00 to 35.00
Herringbone, Goblet	23.00
Herringbone Buttress, Berry Set, Gold Trim	295.00
Hexagon Block, Bowl, Canoe Shape, 1880, 13 In.	75.00
Hexagon Block, Sauce, Amber Stained, Etched, 4 1/4 In.	10.00
Hexagon Block, Tumbler, Ruby Stained	195.00

Hickman, Creamer, Green, Individual 18.00
Hickman, Goblet 40.00
Hickman, Rose Bowl, 5 In. 25.00
Hickman, Syrup 110.00
Hidalgo, Celery Dish, Etched 22.00
Hidalgo, Goblet, Ruby Stained 40.00
Hinoto pattern is listed here as Diamond Point with Panels.
Hobnail pattern is in this book as its own category.
Hobnail With Thumbprint Base, Spooner, Amber 25.00
Hobnail With Thumbprint Base, Waste Bowl, Amber 25.00
Holbrook, Celery Dish, 11 1/4 x 4 3/4 In. 20.00
Holbrook, Rose Bowl, 4 In. 33.00
Holbrook, Sugar, Cover, Small 20.00
Homestead, Tumbler, Gold Trim 22.00
Honeycomb, Decanter, Flint, Qt. 75.00
Honeycomb, Eggcup, Flint 18.00
Honeycomb, Goblet ....10.00 to 20.00
Honeycomb, Tumbler, Footed 23.00
Honeycomb, Whiskey, Flint, Handle 55.00
Honeycomb With Diamonds, Eggcup, Flint 18.00
Honeycomb With Diamonds, Wine, Flint 23.00
Honeycomb With Ovals, Eggcup, Flint, Etched 33.00
Hops Band, Creamer, Applied Handle 33.00
Hops Band, Eggcup 20.00
Hops Band, Goblet 18.00
Hops Band, Spooner 23.00
Horn Of Plenty, Celery Vase, Flint 150.00
Horn Of Plenty, Compote, Flint, Waffle Base, 7 x 5 1/2 In. 115.00
Horn Of Plenty, Dish, Honey 15.00
Horn Of Plenty, Eggcup 45.00
Horn Of Plenty, Goblet, Flint 80.00
Horn Of Plenty, Plate, Flint, 6 In. 110.00
Horn Of Plenty, Spooner ....45.00 to 55.00
Horse Mint, Goblet, Gold Trim 14.00
Horsehead Medallion, Celery Vase 55.00
Horseshoe, Cake Stand, 9 1/2 In. 125.00
Horseshoe, Compote, Cover, 7 In. ....135.00 to 145.00
Horseshoe, Goblet 40.00
Horseshoe, Pitcher, Water 135.00
Horseshoe, Plate, 7 In. ....30.00 to 55.00
Horseshoe, Sugar, Cover 125.00
Hotel Argus, Goblet 15.00
Huber, Ale, Flint, 5 3/4 In. 30.00
Huber, Celery Vase, Flint 39.00
Huber, Compote, Flint, 7 x 7 1/2 In. 65.00
Huber, Creamer, Flint, Applied Handle 95.00
Huber, Eggcup, Flint, Vintage Etched 25.00
Huber, Goblet, Flint ....18.00 to 20.00

Pressed Glass,
Hairpin

Pressed Glass,
Hidalgo

Pressed Glass,
Iconoclast

Huber, Salt, Footed, Individual 10.00
Huber, Wine, Flint, Etched, 10 Panel 24.00
Huckle pattern is listed here as Feather Duster.
Hundred Eye, Goblet 15.00
Icicle With Loops, Goblet, Flint 38.00
Iconoclast, Goblet, Flint 75.00
Ida pattern is listed here as Sheraton.
Illinois, Creamer, 2 1/2 In. 18.00
Illinois, Plate, Square, 7 In. 20.00
Independence Hall, Champagne 33.00
Independence Hall, Mug 70.00
Indiana Swirl pattern is listed here as Feather.
Intaglio, Creamer, Opalescent 38.00
Interlocking Hearts, Goblet 32.50
Interlocking Hearts, Wine 17.50
Inverted Fan & Feather, Butter, Cover, Custard 65.00
Inverted Fan & Feather, Creamer, Green 34.50
Inverted Fan & Feather, Sugar, Cover, Custard 135.00
Inverted Fan & Feather, Tumbler, Water 20.00
Inverted Fern, Eggcup, Flint 30.00
Inverted Fern, Goblet, Flint 45.00
Inverted Fern, Sauce, Flint, 4 In. 10.00
Inverted Prism, Sugar & Creamer, Cover 75.00
Inverted Strawberry, Sugar, 2 Handles, Green 35.00
Inverted Thistle, Cake Stand, 8 In. 55.00
Inverted Thumbprint, Goblet, Amber, Souvenir, Bennington 28.00
Inverted Thumbprint, Punch Cup, Amber, Applied Handle 5.00
Inverted Thumbprint, Sugar, Cover ....28.00 to 30.00
Inverted Thumbprint, Wine, Amber 18.00
Inverted Thumbprint & Star, Goblet, Blue 30.00
Iris With Meander, Pitcher, Water, Blue, Gold Trim 110.00
Iris With Meander, Tumbler, Water, Blue, Gold Trim 40.00
Isis, Spooner 18.00
Ivy In Snow, Compote, Cover 200.00
Ivy In Snow, Tumbler, Water 23.00
Jacob's Ladder, Goblet 65.00
Jacob's Ladder, Salt, Master ....22.00 to 25.00
Jacob's Ladder, Sauce, 4 1/2 In. 8.00
Jasper pattern is listed here as Late Buckle.
Jersey Swirl, Jam Jar, Metal Cover 28.00
Jersey Swirl, Plate, 6 In. 9.00
Jersey Swirl, Plate, Amber, 10 In. ....18.00 to 20.00
Jewel & Fan, Bowl, Green Opalescent, Oval 18.00
Jewel Band, Wine 20.00
Jeweled Heart, Berry Set, Opalescent, 5 Piece 85.00
Jeweled Heart, Sauce, Ruffled Edge, Opalescent 15.00
Jeweled Heart, Tumbler, Blue 30.00
Jeweled Moon & Star pattern is listed here as Moon & Star Variant or Moon & Star.
Job's Tears pattern is listed here as Art.
Jubilee pattern is listed here as Hickman.
Jumbo, Compote, 8 In. 450.00
Jumbo & Barnum, Goblet 750.00
Kamoni pattern is listed here as Pennsylvania.
Kansas, Toothpick 55.00
Kayak, Tray, 10 In. 18.00
Kayak, Wine 18.00
Kentucky, Sauce, 3 3/4 In. ....7.00 to 13.00
Kentucky, Wine 35.00
King's 500, Tumbler, Cobalt, Gold Trim 55.00
King's 500, Water Set, 6 Piece 850.00
King's Crown, see also the related pattern Ruby Thumbprint.
King's Crown, Plate, Square, 7 In. 50.00
King's Crown, Tumbler, Blue, Gold Trim 28.00

Pressed Glass,
Inverted Thumbprint

Pressed Glass,
Liberty Bell

King's Crown, Wine ....14.00 to 18.00
Klondike pattern is listed here as Amberette.
Knobby Bull's-Eye, Goblet 18.00
Kokomo, Compote ....14.00 to 35.00
Kokomo, Cruet, Stopper, 8 In. 45.00
Kokomo, Goblet 25.00
Kokomo, Spooner, Ruby Stained 55.00
Kokomo, Wine 27.00
Lace Band, Creamer, Etched 27.00
Lacy Daisy, Sauce, 4 In. 5.50
Lacy Daisy, Spooner 18.00
Lacy Feather, Sauce, Flint, Blue, 4 5/8 In. 165.00
Lacy Medallion, see also the related pattern Princess Feather.
Ladder With Diamonds, Butter, Cover, Gold Trim 40.00
Ladder With Diamonds, Goblet 22.00
Late Block, Tumbler, Water, Ruby Stained 30.00
Late Buckle, Sauce, 4 1/4 In. 6.00
Late Buckle, Wine 27.00
Late Thistle pattern is listed here as Inverted Thistle.
Later Sawtooth, Goblet 18.00
Later Sawtooth, Wine 13.00
Lattice, Compote, 8 1/4 x 8 In. 25.00
Leaf & Dart, Sugar, Cover 35.00
Leaf & Dart, Wine ....30.00 to 45.00
Leaf & Flower, Celery Vase, Frosted 45.00
Leaf In Oval, Plate, 10 1/4 In. 20.00
Leaf Medallion, Tumbler, Green, Gold Trim 50.00
Leaf Umbrella, Salt & Pepper, Cased Cranberry 245.00
Leaf Umbrella, Sauce, Cased Cranberry 65.00
Leaf Umbrella, Sugar Shaker, Cased Blue 395.00
Lee, Champagne, Flint 165.00
Lee, Wine, Flint 125.00
Leverne pattern is listed here as Star in Honeycomb.
Liberty Bell, Butter, Cover 125.00
Liberty Bell, Compote, 7 7/8 x 4 1/4 In. 55.00
Liberty Bell, Creamer ....95.00 to 125.00
Liberty Bell, Goblet 38.00
Liberty Bell, Plate, 6 1/4 In. ....45.00 to 60.00
Liberty Bell, Relish, Shell Handles, 7 x 11 1/4 In. 65.00
Lily-Of-The-Valley, Celery Vase 65.00
Lily-Of-The-Valley, Compote, 8 1/4 x 7 1/8 In. 55.00
Lily-Of-The-Valley, Creamer, 3-Footed 95.00
Lily-Of-The-Valley, Goblet ....13.00 to 20.00
Lily-Of-The-Valley, Pitcher, Water 55.00
Lily-Of-The-Valley, Spooner ....20.00 to 55.00
Lincoln Drape, Compote, Flint, 7 x 5 1/4 In. 125.00
Lincoln Drape, Eggcup ....40.00 to 55.00

Lincoln Drape, Goblet, Flint 125.00
Lined Smocking, Tumbler, Flint, 3 3/8 In. 55.00
Lion, Creamer, Cable Rim 225.00
Lion, Frosted, Butter, Cover 150.00
Lion, Frosted, Cake Stand, Square 195.00
Lion, Frosted, Compote, Cover, 10 1/2 In. ....70.00 to 120.00
Lion, Frosted, Pitcher, 9 1/2 In. 340.00
Lion, Pitcher, Applied Handle, Scalloped Edge, 9 In. 85.00
Lion, Syrup, Pewter Hinged Cover, Rim, Handle, 9 In. 290.00
Lion & Baboon, Tray, Ice Cream, Amber 100.00
Lion's Leg pattern is listed here as Alaska.
Lippman pattern is listed here as Flat Diamond.
Little Ladders, Banana Stand 55.00
Locket On Chain, Cruet 250.00
Log & Star, Cruet, Amber 55.00
Log Cabin, Creamer 70.00
Log Cabin, Pitcher 349.00
Log Cabin, Table Set, 4 Piece 800.00
Loganberry & Grape, Sauce, Footed, 4 In. 6.00
Long Buttress, Saltshaker 18.00
Loop, see also the related patterns Seneca Loop and Yuma Loop.
Loop, Champagne 42.00
Loop, Spooner 22.00
Loop, Sugar 6.00
Loop, Tumbler, Flint, Footed 45.00
Loop & Argus, Cordial 28.00
Loop & Argus, Whiskey, 3 1/2 In. 16.00
Loop & Crystal, Whiskey, Flint, 3 1/8 In. 18.00
Loop & Dart, Eggcup 25.00
Loop & Dart, Sauce, 4 In. 5.00
Loop & Dart, Spooner 24.00
Loop & Dart, Sugar, Cover 40.00
Loop & Dart With Diamond Ornaments, Compote, 7 1/2 In. 15.00
Loop & Dart With Diamond Ornaments, Eggcup 23.00
Loop & Dart With Round Ornament, Creamer, Flint 65.00
Loop & Dart With Round Ornament, Eggcup, Flint 40.00
Loop & Dart With Round Ornament, Goblet, Flint 49.00
Loop & Fan, Goblet 28.00
Loop & Moose Eye, Creamer, Flint, Molded Handle 55.00
Loop & Moose Eye, Eggcup ....23.00 to 30.00
Loop & Moose Eye, Goblet, Flint 45.00
Loop & Moose Eye, Sugar, Cover, Flint 45.00
Loop & Moose Eye, Whiskey, Flint 45.00
Loop & Pyramid, Goblet 20.00
Loop With Fisheye, Goblet 20.00
Loops & Drops pattern is listed here as New Jersey.
Lotus, Dish, Oval 10.00
Lotus, Goblet 85.00
Louis XV, Sauce, Oval, Footed, Green, Gold Trim 22.00
Magnet & Grape, Goblet, Flint 195.00
Magnet & Grape With American Shield & Frosted Leaf, Goblet, Flint 350.00
Magnet & Grape With Stippled Leaf, Goblet 23.00
Magnolia, Goblet 45.00
Maiden Fern, Goblet 18.00
Maine, Cake Stand, 9 1/4 In. 65.00
Maine, Table Set, 4 Piece 195.00
Maine, Wine 35.00
Majestic, Sauce, 4 In. 5.00
Majestic, Spooner, Ruby Stained 45.00
Majestic, Syrup, Ruby Stained 350.00
Majestic, Tumbler, Water, Ruby Stained 40.00
Manhattan, Sauce, 4 1/2 In. 10.00
Manhattan, Toothpick 28.00

Manting, Goblet, Flint 69.00
Manting, Whiskey, Flint 55.00
Maple Leaf, Platter, 13 x 9 1/2 In. 25.00
Maple Leaf, Sauce, Yellow, Handles, 5 3/4 In. ....10.00 to 13.00
Mardi Gras, Whiskey 25.00
Marlboro, Pitcher, Water 55.00
Marlboro, Tumbler 17.00
Marquisette, Goblet 28.00
Marquisette, Spooner 22.50
Marsh Fern, Compote, 8 1/4 x 7 1/4 In. 28.00
Martha's Tears, Goblet 20.00
Maryland, Cake Stand, 8 1/2 In. 40.00
Maryland, Dish, Sweetmeat, Cover 35.00
Mascotte, Cake Stand, 10 In. 85.00
Mascotte, Compote 45.00
Mascotte, Creamer, Etched 45.00
Massachusetts, Cruet 40.00
Massachusetts, Goblet 55.00
Massachusetts, Vase, 9 3/4 In. ....25.00 to 65.00
Massachusetts, Whiskey 15.00
Massachusetts, Wine 40.00
Master Argus, Goblet, Flint 75.00
McKinley, Mug 25.00
McKinley, Platter, 10 x 8 1/2 In. 30.00
Medallion, Goblet 25.00
Medallion, Sauce, Amber, 4 1/4 In. 7.00
Medallion, Spooner, Amber 35.00
Medallion, Waste Bowl, Apple Green 58.00
Medallion Sunburst, Cake Stand, 8 3/4 In. 28.00
Melrose, Celery Vase 23.00
Melrose, Plate, 8 In. 10.00
Memphis, Punch Cup 15.00
Menagerie, Sugar, Bear, Child's 120.00
Michigan, Compote, 5 3/4 In. 24.00
Michigan, Pitcher, Water, 10 In. ....35.00 to 75.00
Michigan, Punch Cup ....10.00 to 15.00
Michigan, Relish, Gold Rim, 8 In. 15.00
Milton, Goblet 20.00
Minerva, Cake Stand, 10 In. 135.00
Minerva, Goblet 75.00
Minerva, Pitcher, Water 160.00
Minerva, Plate, 7 5/8 In. ....55.00 to 85.00
Minnesota, Carafe 45.00
Minnesota, Punch Cup 10.00
Minnesota, Tumbler, Footed, 4 In. 17.00
Mirror, Compote, 7 x 5 3/4 In. 45.00
Mirror, Goblet, Flint ....20.00 to 50.00
Mirror & Fan, Wine, Green 13.00

Pressed Glass,
Lily-Of-The-Valley

Pressed Glass,
Medallion

Pressed Glass,
Oval Miter

Mitered Diamond, Bowl, Amber, Square, 7 1/2 In.	23.00
Mitered Frieze, Goblet	18.00
Mitered Sawtooth, Spooner, Child's	26.00
Moon & Star, Cake Stand, 9 1/4 In.	65.00
Moon & Star, Goblet, Gold Trim	45.00
Moon & Star, Salt & Pepper, Blue	30.00
Moon & Star, Syrup, Hollow Handle, Tin Hinged Lid, Pewter Finial, 8 1/4 In.	165.00
Moon & Star Variant, Goblet	30.00
Moose-Eye In Sand, Goblet	28.00
Morning Glory, Eggcup, Flint	145.00
My Lady's Work Box, Goblet	20.00
Nail, Goblet	36.00
Nailhead, Cake Stand, 10 In.	40.00
Nailhead, Creamer	28.00
Nailhead, Goblet	28.00
Nestlings, Wine	45.00
New England Pineapple, Compote, Flint, 8 x 4 1/2 In.	95.00
New England Pineapple, Decanter, Flint, Pewter Stopper, Qt.	325.00 to 395.00
New England Pineapple, Eggcup	50.00 to 60.00
New England Pineapple, Goblet, Flint	80.00 to 150.00
New England Pineapple, Tumbler, 3 3/4 In.	66.00
New Hampshire, Cake Stand, 7 3/4 In.	45.00
New Hampshire, Toothpick	20.00
New Hampshire, Wine	18.00
New Jersey, Sauce, 4 1/4 In.	9.00
New Jersey, Table Set, Gold Trim, 4 Piece	185.00
New Jersey, Tumbler	25.00 to 35.00
New Jersey, Wine	34.00
New York Honeycomb, Celery Vase, Flint	35.00
New York Honeycomb, Champagne, Flint	20.00 to 35.00
New York Honeycomb, Goblet, Blue	55.00
New York Honeycomb, Goblet, Etched	15.00
New York Honeycomb, Sugar, Flint	15.00
New York Honeycomb, Wine	13.00 to 23.00
New York Honeycomb, Wine, Yellow	115.00
Nova Scotia Starflower, Compote	25.00
Nursery Tales, Punch Set, Child's, 7 Piece	250.00
O'Hara's Diamond, Plate, Green, 10 In.	15.00
Oak Leaf Band With Loops, Goblet, Flint	55.00
Oak Wreath, Goblet	45.00
Oaken Bucket, Matchholder, Pail, Amber, Bail Handle	25.00
Oaken Bucket, Pitcher, Blue	125.00
Oaken Bucket, Pitcher, Water	65.00
Old Abe pattern is listed here as Frosted Eagle.	
One-Hundred-One, Plate, 7 In.	16.00
One-O-One pattern is listed here as One-Hundred-One.	
One-Thousand Eye pattern is listed here as Thousand Eye.	
Open Plaid, Goblet	18.00
Open Rose, Eggcup	20.00
Open Rose, Goblet	28.00
Open Rose, Relish, Oval	17.00 to 21.00
Open Rose, Spooner	37.00
Open Rose, Sugar, Cover	55.00
Oregon, see also the related pattern Beaded Loop.	
Oval Miter, Goblet	20.00
Oval Panels, Goblet	22.00 to 35.00
Oval Star, Punch Set, Child's, 5 Piece	100.00
Oval Thumbprint, Goblet, Ruby Stained, Souvenir, Augusta, Me.	20.00
Overall Hob, Spooner, Opalescent	30.00
Overall Hob, Toothpick, Opalescent	28.00
Overall Lattice, Wine	15.00
Overshot, Dish, Ice Cream, Flint, 5 1/2 In.	10.00
Paddlewheel, Cruet	23.00

Palm & Scroll, Pitcher, Water, Green 85.00
Palm & Scroll, Sauce, Green, 4 1/2 In. 13.00
Palm Leaf Fan, Wine 35.00
Palm Wreath, Goblet 30.00
Palmette, Goblet 35.00
Palmette, Sauce, 4 In. 7.00
Palmette, Tumbler, Footed 45.00
Paneled 44, Butter, Cover, Rose Stained, Gold Trim 145.00
Paneled 44, Goblet, Pink Stained 25.00
Paneled 44, Pitcher, Gold Trim 100.00
Paneled Cane, Goblet 11.00
Paneled Cherry, Goblet 28.00
Paneled Daisy, Bowl, Oval 13.00
Paneled Daisy, Goblet 25.00
Paneled Daisy, Plate, 9 In. ....16.00 to 18.00
Paneled Dewdrop, Cordial 39.00
Paneled Dewdrop, Goblet 35.00
Paneled Diamonds, Goblet 15.00
Paneled Diamonds & Flowers, Goblet 26.00
Paneled Fern, Sugar, Cover, Flint 43.00
Paneled Finetooth, Whiskey, Flint 95.00
Paneled Forget-Me-Not, Goblet 35.00
Paneled Forget-Me-Not, Sauce, Handle, 4 In. 6.00
Paneled Forget-Me-Not, Spooner 30.00
Paneled Herringbone, Bowl, Green, Oval ....13.00 to 15.00
Paneled Herringbone, Sauce, Green, 4 1/2 In. 5.00
Paneled Herringbone, Tumbler, Water, Green 20.00
Paneled Holly, Tumbler, Blue Opalescent 100.00
Paneled Iris, Punch Cup 4.00
Paneled Jewels, Goblet, Blue 45.00
Paneled Nightshade, Goblet 30.00
Paneled Ovals, Eggcup, Flint 35.00
Paneled Ovals, Goblet, Flint 75.00
Paneled Sprig, Sugar, Cover, Milk Glass 110.00
Paneled Wheat, Sauce, 4 1/4 In. 5.00
Paneled Zipper, Sauce, 4 1/2 In. 7.00
Pathfinder, Goblet 18.00
Pavonia, Creamer 35.00
Pavonia, Pitcher, Water ....65.00 to 80.00
Pavonia, Tumbler ....19.00 to 30.00
Peerless, Celery Vase 35.00
Peerless, Champagne 75.00
Peerless, Eggcup, Saucer Base 18.00
Peerless, Goblet 25.00
Peerless, Plate, 6 In. 20.00
Peerless, Salt, Footed, Individual 15.00
Peerless, Whiskey 35.00
Pennsylvania, see also the related pattern Hand.
Pennsylvania, Celery Tray, 11 x 4 3/4 In. 24.00
Pennsylvania, Decanter, Stopper, Handles 95.00
Pennsylvania, Goblet 20.00
Pennsylvania, Plate, 8 In. 36.00
Pennsylvania, Whiskey 9.00
Pequot, Goblet 65.00
Pequot, Sugar, Cover 75.00
Pillar, Goblet, Flint 85.00
Pillared Crystal, Goblet ....20.00 to 45.00
Pinafore pattern is listed here as Actress.
Plain Smocking pattern is listed here as Smocking.
Pleat & Panel, Dish, Rectangular, 9 x 5 1/2 In. 30.00
Pleat & Panel, Goblet ....35.00 to 40.00
Pleat & Panel, Sauce, Handle 15.00
Pleat Band, Plate, 6 In. 25.00

Pressed Glass,
Princess Feather

Pressed Glass,
Prism

Pleating, Sauce, Ruby Stained, 4 In. 10.00
Pleating, Spooner, Ruby Stained 55.00
Plume, Bowl, Square, 8 1/4 In. 25.00
Plume, Goblet . . . . .20.00 to 36.00
Plume, Sauce, Square, 4 3/4 In. 8.00
Pogo Stick, Cake Stand 45.00
Polar Bear, Goblet, Frosted 145.00
Polar Bear, Pitcher, Frosted 450.00
Portland, Candlestick, Pair 75.00
Portland, Goblet 30.00
Portland, Sugar & Creamer, Gold Trim, Miniature 30.00
Portland, Toothpick 23.00
Portland With Diamond Point Band pattern is listed here as Banded Portland.
Powder & Shot, Goblet, Flint 65.00
Prayer Rug pattern is listed here as Horseshoe.
Pressed Diamond, Bowl . . . . .18.00 to 25.00
Pressed Diamond, Pitcher, Water, Amber 65.00
Pressed Diamond, Saltshaker, Amber 18.00
Pressed Leaf, Eggcup, Flint 20.00
Pressed Leaf, Goblet 20.00
Pressed Leaf With Chain, Goblet 30.00
Primrose, Plate, Handles, 9 In. 13.00
Primrose, Sauce, Blue, 4 In. 8.00
Prince Albert, Tumbler, Water 15.00
Princess Feather, Goblet . . . . .25.00 to 35.00
Princess Feather, Spooner 33.00
Priscilla, Cake Stand, 9 1/2 In. 65.00
Priscilla, Toothpick 35.00
Prism, Compote, Flint 20.00
Prism, Eggcup, Flint, Double 35.00
Prism & Block Band, Goblet 30.00
Prism & Daisy Bar, Goblet, Blue 35.00
Prism & Flattened Sawtooth, Goblet, Flint 65.00
Prism & Flattened Sawtooth, Spill, Flint 40.00
Prism & Flute, Tumbler, Footed 39.00
Prism Arc, Wine 13.00
Prism With Diamond Points, Eggcup 20.00
Prism With Loops, Goblet 19.00
Queen, Goblet . . . . .30.00 to 45.00
Queen, Sauce, Blue, 4 In. 8.00
Rail Fence Band, Goblet 15.00
Raindrop, Plate, Yellow, 10 1/8 In. 20.00
Red Block, Decanter, Stopper 115.00
Red Block, Goblet 35.00
Red Block, Goblet, Ruby Stained 25.00
Red Block, Pitcher, Water 115.00
Red Block, Wine, Ruby Stained 40.00
Reverse 44 pattern is listed here as Paneled 44.
Reverse Torpedo pattern is listed here as Diamond & Bull's-Eye Band.

Ribbed Acorn, Dish, Honey, Flint 8.00

Ribbed Grape, Goblet, Flint 75.00

Ribbed Grape, Spooner 45.00

Ribbed Ivy, Butter, Cover, Flint 95.00

Ribbed Ivy, Eggcup, Flint 30.00

Ribbed Ivy, Sauce, Flint, 4 In. 11.00

Ribbed Palm, Celery Vase, Flint 125.00

Ribbed Palm, Eggcup, Flint .... 33.00 to 45.00

Ribbed Palm, Goblet, Flint 30.00

Ribbed Palm, Sugar, Purple-Blue 2475.00

Ribbed Pineapple pattern is listed here as Prism & Flattened Sawtooth.

Ribbon Candy, Cake Stand, Green 100.00

Ribbon Candy, Plate, 8 3/8 In. 35.00

Ripple, Eggcup 20.00

Ripple, Goblet 25.00

Ripple, Plate, 6 In. 23.00

Ripple, Sugar 20.00

Ripple Band pattern is listed here as Ripple.

Rising Sun, Goblet, Pink Stained Suns 30.00

Rising Sun, Tumbler, Water, Gold Trim 14.00

Riverside's Victoria, Syrup 225.00

Riverside's Victoria, Toothpick 40.00

Roanoke, Bowl, Ruby Stained Edge 25.00

Roanoke, Sauce, 4 1/2 In. 6.00

Rochelle pattern is listed here as Princess Feather.

Roman Key, Butter, Cover 40.00

Roman Key, Champagne, Flint 65.00

Roman Key, Frosted, Eggcup, Flint 55.00

Roman Key, Frosted, Goblet, Flint 60.00

Roman Key, Sauce, Etched 6.00

Roman Rosette, Creamer 38.00

Roman Rosette, Pitcher, Milk 65.00

Roman Rosette, Sauce, 4 In. .... 9.00 to 15.00

Romeo, Celery Vase 35.00

Romeo, Cracker Jar, Cover 59.00

Romeo, Goblet 55.00

Romeo, Waste Bowl 39.00

Rose In Snow, Goblet 30.00

Rose In Snow, Mug 40.00

Rose In Snow, Pitcher, Water 125.00

Rose In Snow, Plate, Amber, 9 1/2 In. 55.00

Rose In Snow, Whiskey, Applied Handle 65.00

Rose Leaves, Goblet 20.00

Rose Sprig, Goblet 45.00

Rose Sprig, Tumbler, Handle, Yellow 110.00

Rosette, Bowl, Cover, Large 30.00

Rosette, Goblet 65.00

Rosette, Plate, Handles, 9 In. 20.00

Rosette & Palms, Celery Vase 28.00

Rosette & Palms, Goblet, Wine 20.00

Rosette & Palms, Pitcher, Water 58.00

Rosette Medallion pattern is listed here as Feather Duster.

Royal, Spooner, Amber Stained 39.00

Royal, Wine 13.00

Royal Crystal, Pitcher, Water, Bulbous 115.00

Royal Crystal, Tumbler, Water, Ruby Stained 45.00

Royal Ivy, Pitcher, Water, Frosted 75.00

Royal Ivy, Pitcher, Water, Ruby Stained, Frosted 275.00

Royal Ivy, Toothpick 150.00

Royal Oak, Sauce, Frosted 13.00

Ruby Thumbprint, see also the related pattern King's Crown.

Ruby Thumbprint, Bottle, Castor, Etched 75.00

Ruby Thumbprint, Tankard, Etched 200.00

S-Repeat, Berry Bowl, Green, Gold Trim 60.00
Sandwich Loop, see also the related pattern Hairpin.
Sandwich Star, Dish, Sweetmeat, Cover, Flint 95.00
Sandwich Star & Buckle, Spill 65.00
Santa Maria, Plate, 8 In. 20.00
Sawtooth, Creamer, Applied Handle, Flint 85.00
Sawtooth, Eggcup, Flint 45.00
Sawtooth, Goblet 20.00
Sawtooth, Sauce, Canary, 4 In. 23.00
Sawtooth & Star, Sauce, Footed, 4 In. 5.00
Sawtooth Band pattern is listed here as Amazon.
Sawtooth Circle, Salt, Flint, Master 35.00
Scalloped Daisy, Tumbler, Ruby Stained 45.00
Scalloped Daisy & Fans, Goblet, Green, Gold Trim 35.00
Scalloped Lines, Eggcup 13.00
Scalloped Lines, Goblet 23.00
Scalloped Swirl, Toothpick, Ruby Stained, Souvenir .40.00 to 70.00
Scalloped Swirl, Wine, Ruby Stained 55.00
Scarab, Goblet, Flint 195.00
Scroll Bands, Pitcher, Water, Green, Gold Trim 95.00
Scroll With Cane Band, Carafe, Ruby Stained 145.00
Scroll With Cane Band, Toothpick 35.00
Scroll With Flowers, Eggcup, Handle 15.00
Scroll With Flowers, Goblet, Wine 25.00
Sedan pattern is listed here as Paneled Star & Button.
Selby, Goblet 15.00
Semi-Loops, Goblet 18.00
Seneca Loop, Goblet 18.00
Sequoia, Creamer 15.00
Sequoia, Plate, Amber, 5 1/4 In. 10.00
Sequoia, Tumbler, Water 12.00
Shell, Compote, Cover, 7 3/4 x 9 1/2 In. 60.00
Shell & Jewel, Cake Stand 110.00
Shell & Tassel, Berry Bowl, With Spoon 145.00
Shell & Tassel, Butter Chip 7.00
Shell & Tassel, Goblet 35.00
Shell & Tassel, Pitcher, Round 135.00
Sheraton, Goblet 30.00
Sheraton, Pitcher, Milk 45.00
Shoshone pattern is listed here as Victor.
Shrine, Butter, Cover 85.00
Shrine, Compote, Jelly 25.00
Shrine, Goblet 65.00
Six Panel Finecut, Goblet 24.00
Six Panel Finecut, Goblet, Amber Stained 60.00
Skilton, Bowl, 7 3/4 x 2 1/2 In. 13.00
Skilton, Celery Vase 30.00
Skilton, Goblet, Ruby Stained 75.00

Pressed Glass,
Shell & Jewel

Pressed Glass, Shell & Tassel

Smocking, Goblet, Knob Stem, Flint 115.00
Smocking, Sugar, Cover, Flint 70.00
Snail, Butter, Cover ....90.00 to 125.00
Snail, Rose Bowl, Double 45.00
Snail, Sugar, Cover ....70.00 to 85.00
Snail, Tankard, 12 1/2 In. 140.00
Snake Drape, Goblet 25.00
Snow Band, Goblet 20.00
Snowdrop, Sauce, Handles, Small 7.00
Spanish American, Pitcher, Water 75.00
Spanish Coin pattern is listed here as Columbian Coin.
Spearpoint Band, Spooner, Ruby 40.00
Spirea Band, Goblet ....23.00 to 35.00
Spirea Band, Plate, Blue, 10 3/4 x 8 1/2 In. 18.00
Square Fuchsia, Bowl, Oval, 6 x 8 3/4 In. 17.00
Square Fuchsia, Cake Stand, 8 3/4 In. ....40.00 to 55.00
Square Fuchsia, Goblet 38.00
Square Fuchsia, Wine, 4 1/2 In. ....22.00 to 65.00
Square Panes, Compote, Cover, Base Etched, 6 1/2 x 7 1/2 In. 50.00
Square Panes, Goblet ....35.00 to 45.00
Squirrel, Pitcher, Water 175.00
Star & Feather, Plate, Blue, 7 In. 17.00
Star & Punty pattern is listed here as Moon & Star.
Star In Honeycomb, Compote, 8 x 7 1/4 In. 25.00
Star In Honeycomb, Sauce, 5 1/4 In. 8.00
Star In Honeycomb, Wine 28.00
Star Rosetted, Goblet 18.00
Star Rosetted, Sauce, 4 1/4 In. 5.00
Starred Cosmos, Water Set, 6 Piece 125.00
Stars & Bars, Cruet Set, Cruet, Salt & Pepper, Tray, Dark Blue, 4 Piece 185.00
Stars & Stripes, Goblet, Wine 10.00
States pattern is listed here as The States.
Stedman, Eggcup, Flint 20.00
Stedman, Goblet, Flint 35.00
Stedman, Sauce, Flint, 4 In. 14.00
Stippled Cherry, Plate, 6 In. 17.00
Stippled Dahlia pattern is listed here as Square Fuchsia.
Stippled Fans, Toothpick 25.00
Stippled Fleur-De-Lis, Goblet, Blue 65.00
Stippled Fleur-De-Lis, Tumbler, Water, Blue 39.00
Stippled Forget-Me-Not, Cake Stand, 8 In. ....57.00 to 65.00
Stippled Forget-Me-Not, Cup & Saucer ....20.00 to 30.00
Stippled Forget-Me-Not, Goblet 40.00
Stippled Fuschia, Goblet 35.00
Stippled Grape & Festoon, Goblet 20.00
Stippled Ivy, Goblet ....30.00 to 35.00
Stippled Ivy, Tumbler, Footed 35.00
Stippled Medallion, Eggcup, Flint 20.00
Stippled Paneled Flower pattern is listed here as Maine.
Stippled Scroll pattern is listed here as Scroll.
Stippled Star, Spooner 28.00
Strawberry, Whiskey 65.00
Strawberry & Currant, Goblet ....30.00 to 35.00
Sunbeam, Champagne ....15.00 to 20.00
Sunbeam, Sugar, Individual, Green 15.00
Sunburst, Goblet 20.00
Sunburst, Plate, 10 3/4 In. 16.00
Sunburst Medallion, Goblet 20.00
Sunflower, Cruet 40.00
Sunk Honeycomb, Butter, Cover, Ruby Stained 135.00
Sunk Honeycomb, Decanter, Wine, Floral Design, Ruby 325.00
Sunk Honeycomb, Mug, Ruby Stained, 2 3/4 In. 15.00
Sunk Honeycomb, Pitcher, Milk 45.00

If you have an alarm system, set it each time you leave the house, not just at night. Most home burglaries are during the day or early evening.

Pressed Glass, Thumbprint

Sunken Primrose, Plate, 7 1/2 In.	15.00
Sunken Teardrop, Creamer	12.00
Sunrise pattern is listed here as Rising Sun.	
Swag With Brackets, Jelly, Green Opalescent	28.00
Swag With Brackets, Toothpick, Amethyst, Gold Trim	95.00
Swan, Compote, 8 x 8 1/2 In.	55.00
Swan, Creamer, Amber	68.00
Swan, Sauce, 4 1/2 In.	10.00
Sylvan, Toothpick	18.00
Sylvan, Whiskey	7.00
Tarentum's Verona, Punch Cup, Ruby Stained	14.00
Tarentum's Virginia, Carafe	47.00
Tarentum's Virginia, Goblet	55.00
Teardrop pattern is listed here as Teardrop & Thumbprint.	
Teardrop & Tassel, Butter, Cover	120.00
Teardrop & Tassel, Creamer	40.00
Teardrop & Thumbprint, Goblet	50.00
Teardrop & Thumbprint, Tumbler, Water, Etched	22.00
Tennessee, Creamer	38.00
Tennessee, Pitcher, Milk	75.00 to 95.00
Texas, Butter, Cover	145.00
Texas, Cake Stand, 9 In.	95.00 to 145.00
Texas, Goblet	100.00
The States, Sauce, Gold Trim, 5 3/4 In.	8.00
The States, Wine	23.00
Thousand Eye, Butter, Cover, Amber	80.00
Thousand Eye, Cake Stand, Amber, 9 In.	95.00
Thousand Eye, Compote	28.00 to 45.00
Thousand Eye, Goblet	35.00 to 45.00
Thousand Eye, Mug, Amber	18.00 to 22.00
Thousand Eye, Plate, Amber, Square, 7 3/4 In.	17.00 to 40.00
Thousand Eye, Saltshaker	30.00 to 34.00
Thousand Eye, Tumbler, Blue	35.00
Thousand Eye Band, Wine, Etched	18.00
Three Bar Waffle, Syrup	50.00
Three Face, Goblet, Etched	150.00
Three Graces, see also the related pattern Three Face.	
Three Panel, Butter, Cover	45.00
Three Panel, Creamer, Blue	50.00
Three Panel, Spooner, Amber	28.00
Three Row Argus, Salt, Flint, Master	22.00
Three Sisters pattern is listed here as Three Face.	
Thumbelina, Tray	50.00
Thumbprint, Cheese, Cover	150.00
Thumbprint, Compote, Low, Footed, Flint	110.00
Thumbprint, Pitcher, Amber, Footed	45.00

Tiny Lion, Celery Vase, Etched 40.00
Torpedo, Celery Vase, 6 1/2 In. 28.00
Torpedo, Cup & Saucer ....49.00 to 65.00
Torpedo, Goblet 55.00
Transcontinental Railroad, Platter, 12 x 9 In. 75.00
Tree Bark, Pitcher, Water 50.00
Tree Of Life, Bowl, Amber, 5 3/8 In. 18.00
Tree Of Life, Cake Stand, With Hand, 8 1/2 In. 100.00
Tree Of Life, Celery Vase 55.00
Tree Of Life, Pitcher, Water 85.00
Tree Of Life, Sauce, Leaf, Amber, 7 1/2 x 4 3/4 In. 12.00
Triple Triangle, Goblet 40.00
Triple Triangle, Mug, Ruby Stained 33.00
Triple Triangle, Wine, Ruby Stained, Etched 45.00
Truncated Cube, Creamer, Ruby Stained 24.00
Truncated Cube, Wine 13.00
Tulip, Pitcher, Water, Flint 425.00
Tulip & Honeycomb, Butter, Cover, Child's 32.00
Tulip Petals, Whiskey, Flint 30.00
Tulip Variant, Compote, Flint, 6 1/4 x 6 1/4 In. ....75.00 to 105.00
Tulip With Sawtooth, Decanter, Scalloped Foot, Flint, Qt. 135.00
Tulip With Sawtooth, Goblet ....40.00 to 70.00
Tulip With Sawtooth, Salt, Master ....15.00 to 35.00
Two Panel, Creamer ....23.00 to 40.00
Two Panel, Goblet ....30.00 to 45.00
Two Panel, Pitcher, Water, Blue 95.00
Two Panel, Salt, Oval, Amber, Individual 18.00
Two Panel, Sauce, Oval, Amber 9.00
U.S. Coin, Compote, Cover ....450.00 to 595.00
U.S. Coin, Goblet, Frosted Dimes ....320.00 to 575.00
U.S. Coin, Sauce, 3 3/4 In. 40.00
U.S. Coin, Tumbler, Water, 1879, Coin In Bottom 225.00
Valencia Waffle, Creamer ....55.00 to 65.00
Valencia Waffle, Goblet 20.00
Valencia Waffle, Pitcher, Water, Amber 65.00
Vermont, Creamer, Green, 4 In. 40.00
Vermont, Goblet, Green, Gold Trim ....45.00 to 68.00
Vermont, Pitcher, Green 75.00
Vermont, Toothpick ....35.00 to 65.00
Vermont, Tumbler, Custard 110.00
Victor, Banana Stand, 9 x 7 In. 57.00
Victor, Cake Stand, Green 45.00
Victor, Carafe 65.00
Victor, Spooner, Green 45.00
Viking, Celery Dish 40.00
Viking, Creamer 38.00
Viking, Salt, Master 48.00
Waffle, Celery Vase, Scalloped Edge, 8 3/4 In. 17.00
Waffle, Eggcup, Flint 40.00
Waffle, Sweetmeat, Cover, Flint 125.00
Waffle, Whiskey, Flint 110.00
Waffle & Thumbprint, Compote, Flint, 6 1/4 x 4 3/4 In. 115.00
Waffle & Thumbprint, Decanter, Flint, Pt. 75.00
Waffle & Thumbprint, Goblet, Flint 90.00
Washington, Celery Vase, Flint 145.00
Washington & Lafayette, Mug 26.00
Washington Centennial, Celery Vase, Footed 43.00
Washington Centennial, Compote, 8 1/8 x 8 3/8 In. 38.00
Washington Centennial, Goblet 40.00
Washington Centennial, Platter, Independence Hall, Bear Claw Handles, Oval 120.00
Water Lily & Cattails, Sauce, Opalescent, 4 1/2 In. 6.00
Waterford Inverted Thumbprint, Goblet, Amber 18.00
Westward Ho, Bread Plate, Bison, Deer & Log Cabin, 14 In. 165.00

Pressed Glass,
Square Fuchsia

Pressed Glass,
U.S. Coin

Westward Ho, Celery Vase	160.00 to 170.00
Westward Ho, Compote, Cover, Deer, Buffalo Scene, Cabin Design, 14 1/2 In.	70.00
Westward Ho, Goblet	95.00
Wheat & Barley, Compote, Amber, 8 1/2 x 6 1/2 In.	40.00
Wheat & Barley, Creamer	30.00
Wheat & Barley, Sauce, Footed, Amber, 4 In.	10.00
Wheat & Barley, Tumbler	35.00
Wheel & Tassel, Creamer	45.00
Whitton, Wine	20.00
Wildflower, Compote, Cover, Blue, 8 In.	125.00
Wildflower, Creamer, Amber	30.00
Wildflower, Goblet	23.00 to 40.00
Wildflower, Pitcher, Water	55.00
Wildflower, Plate, Blue, 10 In.	45.00
Wildflower, Saltshaker, Amber	35.00
Wildflower, Sugar, Cover, Blue	55.00
Willow Oak, Compote	23.00
Willow Oak, Creamer	35.00
Willow Oak, Goblet	40.00 to 65.00
Willow Oak, Pitcher, Water	40.00 to 58.00
Willow Oak, Plate, Blue, 10 In.	40.00
Willow Oak, Tumbler, Water	40.00
Windflower, Compote, Cover, Low Stem	59.00
Windflower, Eggcup	35.00
Winona pattern is listed here as Barred Hobnail.	
Wisconsin, Cake Stand, 8 1/2 In.	45.00
Wisconsin, Celery Dish, 11 x 5 1/2 In.	45.00
Wisconsin, Pitcher, Milk, 9 In.	65.00
Wisconsin, Toothpick	35.00
Wooden Pail pattern is listed here as Oaken Bucket.	
Wreath & Shell, Berry Bowl, 8 1/2 In.	45.00
Wreath & Shell, Butter, Vaseline	250.00
Wreath & Shell, Celery, Vaseline	225.00
Wreath & Shell, Sauce, Footed, Green Opalescent, 4 3/8 In.	18.00
Wreath & Shell, Spooner, Vaseline	125.00
Wreath & Shell, Tumbler, Footed, Opalescent	375.00
X-Ray, Butter, Cover, Amethyst, Gold Trim	250.00
X-Ray, Creamer, Green, Gold Trim, Individual	55.00
X-Ray, Cruet, Green, Gold Trim	225.00
X-Ray, Salt & Pepper	225.00
X-Ray, Sugar, Cover, Individual	25.00
X-Ray, Syrup, Green, Gold Trim	175.00
X-Ray, Toothpick, Green, Gold Trim	25.00 to 80.00
Yoked Loop, Compote, Low Stem, Flint, 7 In.	20.00
Yoked Loop, Goblet, Flint	29.00
Yoked Loop, Sugar, Flint	20.00
Yuma Loop, Goblet	18.00
Zipper, Goblet	23.00
Zipper Slash, Celery Vase, Etched	30.00
Zipper Slash, Champagne	30.00

Zipper Slash, Goblet, Satin, Vintage Etch, Amber Stain 52.00
Zipper Slash, Wine 22.50
Zippered Block, Pitcher, Water 145.00

PRINT, in this listing, means any of many printed images produced on
paper by one of the more common methods, such as lithography. The
prints listed here are of interest primarily to the antiques collector, not
the fine arts collector. Many of these prints were originally part of
books. Other prints will be found in the Advertising, Currier & Ives,
Movie, and Poster categories.

Aldin, 4 Golfers, Walking Between Holes, England, 1925, 14 x 22 1/4 In. 1400.00
Alken & McLean, Symptoms, Comic, Matted, Frame, 13 7/8 x 15 3/8 In., 5 Piece 190.00

Audubon bird prints were originally issued as part of books printed
from 1826 to 1854. They were issued in two sizes, 26 1/2 inches by 39
1/2 inches and 11 inches by 7 inches. The quadrupeds were issued in
28-by-22-inch prints. Later editions of the Audubon books were done
in many sizes, and reprints of the books in the original size were also
made. The bird pictures have been so popular they have been copied in
myriad sizes by both old and new printing methods. This list includes
originals and later copies because Audubon prints of all ages are sold
in antiques shops.

J.W.Audubon

Audubon, American Goldfinch, 1828, 19 1/2 x 12 1/4 In. 5460.00
Audubon, Blue Winged Yellow Warbler, 1827, 19 3/8 x 12 1/4 In. 2585.00
Audubon, Blue Yellowback Warbler, 1827, 19 5/8 x 12 1/4 In. 1840.00
Audubon, Bonaparte's Flycatcher, 20 3/4 x 12 5/8 In. . . . . .1610.00 to 1840.00
Audubon, Children's Warbler, 1828, 19 1/2 x 12 1/4 In. 1150.00
Audubon, Prairie Chickens, 1860, Large Folio 1250.00
Audubon, Prairie Warbler, 1827, 19 1/2 x 12 1/4 In. 1265.00
Audubon, Prothonotary Warbler, 1826, 20 3/8 x 12 3/8 In. 975.00
Audubon, Red Headed Woodpecker, 1827, 25 3/8 x 21 5/8 In. 5175.00
Audubon, Song Sparrow, 1827, 19 1/2 x 12 1/4 In. 1265.00
Audubon, White Throated Sparrow, 1826, 20 1/2 x 12 7/8 In.   1495.00
Audubon, Yellow Billed Cuckoo, Frame, 1826, 21 x 26 1/4 In.   4885.00
Benton, Jessie James, 1936, 18 3/4 x 23 1/2 In. 8050.00
Bishop, Game Bird, Frame, 13 x 14 1/2 In., Set Of 6 . . . .   300.00
Comte, Ponte De Nice, Pencil Signed, 1933, 15 1/2 x 19 In. 130.00
Curtis, Botanical, Floral, Frame, 37 1/4 x 28 3/4 In., Pair 440.00
Dow, Ipswich Print, Trees Against Yellow, Brown, Blue Sky, Oak Frame, 6 x 3 In. 1100.00
Fox, Blue Lake, Frame, 14 x 20 In. 95.00
Fox, Venetian Gardens, Frame, 17 x 14 In. 38.00
Gallagher, Old Timer, Golf Scene, Frame, Boston, 1925, 7 1/2 x 9 1/2 In. 300.00
Gutmann, A Little Bit Of Heaven, Frame 80.00
Gutmann, Butterflies & Daisies, Tin Oval Frame, 7 1/2 x 9 1/2 In. 115.00
Gutmann, Little Boy Blue, 7 1/2 x 9 1/2 In. 125.00
Gutmann, Symphony, Frame, 7 1/2 x 9 1/2 In. 495.00
Howard Chandlers Christy, Young Lady Golfer, Jacket, Frame, 14 x 22 In. 525.00

Icart prints were made by Louis Icart, who worked in Paris from 1907
as an employee of a postcard company. He then started printing magazines and fashion brochures. About 1910 he created a series of etchings of fashionably dressed women and he continued to make similar
etchings until he died in 1950. He is well known as a printmaker,
painter, and illustrator. Original etchings are much more expensive
than the later photographic copies.

Icart, Autumn Leaves, Aquatint, 1926, 21 1/4 x 17 In. 1265.00
Icart, Baby Doll, Signed, 1924, 17 1/4 x 12 3/4 In. 1725.00
Icart, Black Bows, Signed, 17 x 12 In. 920.00
Icart, Carmen, Paris, France, Signed, 1927, 21 x 14 1/4 In. 865.00
Icart, Cigarette, Matted, Frame, Signed, 1931, 14 3/8 x 17 5/8 In. 2185.00
Icart, Curious, Etched, Color, No. 84, 8 1/4 x 10 3/8 In. 520.00
Icart, Don Juan, Eglomize Matte, Frame, Edition D'Art, Paris, France, 1928, 20 x 14 In. . .   800.00
Icart, Eve, Matted, Frame, Oval, 1928, 14 x 19 1/2 In. 550.00

Icart, Hat Box, Matted, Frame, Signed, 1914, 13 5/8 x 10 1/4 In. 920.00
Icart, Incident, Color Etching, No. 90, 1920, 8 1/4 x 10 3/8 In. 520.00
Icart, Les Quais, Matted, Frame, Signed, 1929, 14 x 7 1/4 In. 1380.00
Icart, Lilies, Matted, Frame, Signed, 1934, 27 3/4 x 18 7/8 In. 2590.00
Icart, Mockery, Aquatint, 1928, 15 1/4 x 19 In. 1380.00
Icart, Smoke, Frame, Signed, 1926, 18 x 24 1/4 In. 1380.00
Icart, Snack, Matted, Frame, Oval, Signed, 1927, 18 1/2 x 14 In. 1380.00
Icart, Spanish Night, France, Signed, 1926, 20 3/4 x 13 In. 920.00
Icart, Werther, Matted, Frame, Signed, 20 x 13 3/4 In. 930.00
Icart, Wishing Well, Signed, 17 3/4 x 12 In. 800.00
J.L. Marks, Young Willy & My Little Donkey, Gilt Frame, 8 1/2 x 5 1/2 In., Pair 145.00
Jacoulet, A Beauty Of Palao, Mandarin Duck Seal, 1935 .... 1320.00
Jacoulet, Beauty Of Yap With Orchids, 1934 .... 3300.00
Jacoulet, Chamorro Beauty In Green Costume, Rainbow Series, 1934 .... 885.00
Jacoulet, Chamorro Beauty In Red Costume, Rainbow Series, 1934 .... 935.00
Jacoulet, Chinese Puppets, Mandarin Duck Seal 935.00
Jacoulet, Fisherman Of Sawara, Mandarin Duck Seal, 1936 .... 495.00
Jacoulet, Fleurs Du Soir, Silver On Japan Paper, Signed, 1941, 15 1/2 x 11 7/8 In. 1265.00
Jacoulet, Green Caterpillar, Good Luck Hammer Seal, 1936 .... 550.00
Jacoulet, L'Etoile De Cobi, Signed, 1951, 15 1/2 x 12 In. 1725.00
Jacoulet, La Chenille Vert Coree, Brown Mica Ground, Frame, 21 3/4 x 17 1/4 In. 230.00
Jacoulet, Old Writings, Ivy Seal, Frame, 21 3/4 x 17 1/4 In. 230.00
Jacoulet, Oriental Woman, Leaning On Brown Bag, Frame, 12 x 15 In. 525.00
Jacoulet, Rich Korena Of Seoul, Fan Seal, 21 1/4 x 16 1/4 In. 9900.00
Jacoulet, Tattooed Woman Of Falalap, Mandarin Duck Seal, 1935 .... 5500.00
Jacoulet, The Crab, 1935 .... 2750.00
James King, Duchess Of Orleans As Hebe, Mezzotint, 19th Century, Frame, 12 x 8 In. .. 90.00

Japanese woodblock prints are listed as follows: Print, Japanese, name
of artist, title or description, type, and size. Dealers use the following
terms: Tate-e is a vertical composition. Yoko-e is a horizontal composition. The words Aiban (13 by 9 inches), Chuban (10 by 7 1/2 inches),
Hosoban (12 by 6 inches), Oban (15 by 10 inches), and Koban (7 by 4
inches) denote size. Modern versions of some of these prints have been
made.

Japanese, Azuma, Red Room, Frame, 21 1/2 x 21 3/4 In. 320.00
Japanese, Hei Kawanishi, The Pond, 1957, 19 1/2 x 13 1/2 In. 45.00
Japanese, Hiroshige, Kamewari Pass In Echigo Provence, 8 1/2 x 13 1/2 In. 255.00
Japanese, Hiroshige, Meandering River, Bridge, 1849, 9 x 13 3/4 In. 110.00
Japanese, Hiroshige, Woman Descending Mountain, 4 x 5 In. 290.00
Japanese, Hosoda Yeishi, Fukujin Takara-Awase Household Gods, 1795 .... 1800.00
Japanese, Kanamaro, Hawk In Pine Tree, Frame, Early 19th Century ....*Illus* 880.00
Japanese, Katsushika Hokusai, Catching Fish With Nets 330.00
Japanese, Kawano, Woodpecker, Green-Skinned Alien Girl, Frame, 15 & 10 In., Pair ... 50.00
Japanese, Kawase Hasui, Blue River Scene, Trees, Arts & Crafts, 4 1/2 x 7 In. 495.00

Print, Japanese,
Kanamaro, Hawk In
Pine Tree, Frame,
Early 19th Century

Print, Japanese,
Utagawa Kuniyoshi,
Warrior, 8 x 10 In.,
Pair, 1 Shown

Japanese, Kawase Hasui, Gatakudari In Shiobara, 9 1/4 x 14 1/4 In. 325.00
Japanese, Kawase Hasui, Misty Morning, 9 1/2 x 14 1/2 In. 345.00
Japanese, Kawase Hasui, Pondside In Night, 14 1/2 x 9 1/2 In. 345.00
Japanese, Kawase Hasui, Rain At Mackawa In Soshu District, 9 1/4 x 14 1/2 In. 400.00
Japanese, Kikugawa Eizan, 3 Geisha, 14 7/8 x 10 1/4 In. 325.00
Japanese, Kiyoshi Saito, Seated Woman, 15 1/2 x 10 1/2 In. 825.00
Japanese, Kunichika, Procession Of Shogun Crossing Bridge, Triptych, 14 x 9 In. 325.00
Japanese, Toyokuni III, Feudal Lord Calling On Sweetheart, 14 x 9 1/2 In. 322.00
Japanese, Utagawa Kuniyoshi, Warrior, 8 x 10 In., Pair ....*Illus* 1000.00
Japanese, Yoshida, Bamboo Wood, Frame, 14 3/4 x 9 3/4 In. 175.00
Japanese, Yoshida, Fujiyama From Miho, 1937, 15 x 9 1/2 In. 200.00
Japanese, Yoshida, In A Temple Yard, Frame, 14 3/4 x 9 1/2 In. 200.00
Japanese, Yoshida, Stratum, 1964, 20 x 12 1/2 In. 145.00
Japanese, Yoshitoshi Mori, Procession, 1971, 17 3/4 x 21 3/4 In. 120.00
Japanese, Yoshitoshi Mori, Samurai, Color, Signed, 17 x 28 In. 250.00
Jean-Paul Carriere, Japanese Doll Under Water With Fish, Aquatint, 1929, 15 x 19 In. . 1400.00
Kasimir, Carmel By The Sea, Cypress Tree, Aquatint, Signed, 13 5/8 x 10 3/8 In. 690.00
Kasimir, Fulton Fish Market, New York, Aquatint, 1936, 17 x 11 7/8 In. 800.00
Kent, Diver, Wood Engraving, Signed, 1931, 7 7/8 x 5 1/2 In. 1610.00
Kent, Wayside Madonna, Wood Engraving, 1927, 10 3/8 x 5 1/2 In. 315.00
Luigi Lucioni, Barn With Settling Silo, Etching & Drypoint, Frame, 9 x 12 In. 120.00

Nutting prints are now popular with collectors. Wallace Nutting is known for his pictures, furniture, and books. Nutting *prints* are actually hand-colored photographs issued from 1900 to 1941. There are over 10,000 different titles. Wallace Nutting furniture is listed in the Furniture category.

Wallace Nutting

Nutting, Blacksmith Shoeing A White Horse 800.00
Nutting, Blowing Bubbles, 5 x 9 In. 740.00
Nutting, Brandywine Battle Site 615.00
Nutting, Christmas At The Farm, 11 x 14 In. 1070.00
Nutting, Dog-On-It, Frame, 7 x 11 In. ....*Illus* 1165.00
Nutting, Eventful Journey, 13 x 16 In. 740.00
Nutting, Four O'Clock, 13 x 16 In. 855.00

Print, Nutting,
Dog-On-It, Frame,
7 x 11 In.

Print, Nutting, Meeting Place, 18 x 22 In.

Print, Nutting, Snow Road, Frame

Nutting, Fredericksburg Cottage 550.00
Nutting, Lane In Sorrento, 11 x 17 In. 505.00
Nutting, Let's Wade 1870.00
Nutting, Little River With Mt. Washington, Frame, 9 1/2 x 6 In. 110.00
Nutting, Little River With Mt. Washington, Frame, 17 x 11 In. 75.00
Nutting, Meeting Place, 18 x 22 In. ....*Illus* 2255.00
Nutting, On The Slope, 6 x 9 In. 245.00
Nutting, Parting Of The Ways 550.00
Nutting, Snow Road, Frame ....*Illus* 1633.00
Nutting, Swimming Pool, Frame, 12 1/2 x 10 1/2 In. 85.00
Nutting, The Quilting Party, Frame 230.00
Nutting, Tree Lined Stream, Frame, 18 1/2 x 22 1/2 In. 165.00

Parrish prints are wanted by collectors. Maxfield Frederick Parrish
was an illustrator who lived from 1870 to 1966. He is best known as a
designer of magazine covers, posters, calendars, and advertisements.

Parrish, Aucassin Seeks For Nicolette, 1903, 17 x 11 1/2 In. 410.00
Parrish, Canyon, Frame, 1924, 12 x 15 In. 195.00
Parrish, Cleopatra, 1917, 8 1/2 x 9 1/2 In. 195.00
Parrish, Daybreak, 1922, 17 1/2 x 10 In. ....240.00 to 300.00
Parrish, Daybreak, 1922, 9 1/2 x 6 In. ....85.00 to 100.00
Parrish, Dinkey Bird, 11 x 16 In. 200.00
Parrish, Dreaming, 1928, 18 x 30 In. ....1225.00 to 1450.00
Parrish, Dreaming, 1928, 6 x 10 In. 225.00
Parrish, Ecstasy, Edison-Mazda, 1930, 20 x 14 1/2 In. ....*Illus* 800.00
Parrish, Eventide, Matted, 1944, 16 1/2 x 12 1/2 In. 175.00
Parrish, Garden Of Allah, 1918, 15 x 30 In. ....135.00 to 250.00
Parrish, Garden Of Allah, 9 x 18 In. 185.00
Parrish, Gardens Of Isola Bella, 5 x 8 In. 95.00
Parrish, Hilltop, 12 x 20 In. ....*Illus* 400.00
Parrish, Hilltop, 18 x 30 In. 875.00
Parrish, House Of Art, 2 Girls By Pool, 18 x 12 In. 295.00
Parrish, Interlude, 1924, 15 x 12 In. ....165.00 to 192.00
Parrish, Jack Frost, 1936, 13 x 12 1/2 In. 385.00
Parrish, Lampseller Of Bagdad, Edison-Mazda, 1923, 23 x 14 1/2 In. ....*Illus* 625.00
Parrish, Land Of Make Believe, 1912, 11 x 9 In. 305.00
Parrish, Romance, 1925, 12 x 24 In. 1500.00
Parrish, Rubaiyat, Fancy Cut Frame, 1917, 8 x 30 In. ....750.00 to 895.00
Parrish, Sing A Song Of Six-Pence, 1910, 7 5/8 x 16 1/4 In. 3685.00
Parrish, Stars, 1927, 10 x 18 In. 214.00
Parrish, Sugar Plum Tree, 1905 ....750.00 to 925.00
Parrish, Wynken Blynken & Nod, 1905, 14 1/2 x 10 1/4 In. 440.00

Print, Parrish, Ecstasy, Edison-
Mazda, 1930, 20 x 14 1/2 In.

Print, Parrish, Hilltop,
12 x 20 In.

Print, Parrish, Lampseller Of Bagdad,
Edison-Mazda, 1923, 23 x 14 1/2 In.

Sadler, My Love To You & Same To You Dear, Mahogany Frame, 16 x 21 In., Pair 165.00
Woodblock, Arts & Crafts, Cabin Among Tall Trees, Oak Frame, 7 x 5 In. 230.00
Woodblock, Arts & Crafts, Cryptomeria Trees In Mayajima, Frame, 10 x 15 In. 770.00
Woodblock, Arts & Crafts, Landscape, Black, Blue, Brown Paper, Oak Frame, 14 x 5 In.   470.00
Woodblock, Ono Bakufu, Arts & Crafts, Salmonids, 3 Fish, 15 1/2 x 11 In. 525.00
Woodblock, William Rice, Harbor Scene, Blue Tug, Green, Ocher, 1920, 9 x 11 In. 1540.00
Woodblock, William Rice, Lone Rock, Crashing Waves, c.1925, 5 x 6 3/4 In. 605.00
Woodblock, William Rice, New England Sheep Barn, c.1920, 8 1/2 x 11 3/4 In. 1430.00
Woodblock, William Rice, River Willows, c.1912, 6 x 9 In. 2200.00
Woodcut, Bertha Lum, Chinese Funeral, Pencil, 5 1/8 x 3 3/8 In. 176.00
Woodcut, Bertha Lum, Land Of The Bluebird, Pencil, No. 97, 1916, 16 3/8 x 9 5/8 In. . .   1045.00
Woodcut, Bertha Lum, The Piper, Jizo, The Divinity, 1916, 9 1/2 x 13 5/8 In. 1320.00
Woodcut, Bertha Lum, Wedding Banners, Pencil, 1924, 8 1/2 x 11 1/4 In. 660.00
Woodcut, Forest Scene, Redwoods, Forest Floor With Trunks, Frame, 1910, 9 x 12 In. . .   2200.00

PURSES have been recognizable since the eighteenth century, when leather and needlework purses were preferred. Beaded purses became popular in the nineteenth century, went out of style, but are again in use. Mesh purses date from the 1880s and are still being made. How to carry a handkerchief and lipstick is a problem today for every woman, including the Queen of England.

2 Felt Dancing Figures, Dancing On Black & Pink Floor, Vinyl, 1950s 18.00
2 Tray Design, Pearl Gray Oval Base, Ascot, 4 x 7 1/8 In. 145.00
Alligator, Brown, With Change Purse, Coblentz 150.00
Alligator, Clutch, Suede Lining, 9 x 17 In. 125.00
Alligator, Vassar 75.00
Aluminum, Pressed Floral Pattern, 2 Swing Handles 95.00
Appliqued Flowers, Beaded Bottom Edge, Rialto 125.00
Beaded, Birds Facing Each Other, Cornucopia Other Side, 1835 . . . .   165.00
Beaded, Black, Czechoslovakia 35.00
Beaded, Blue, Yellow Bird Design 150.00
Beaded, Brown, Blue, Red, Yellow & Green Floral Design, Cast Metal Filigree, 6 In. . . .   110.00
Beaded, Cathedral Scene, Silvered Filigree Frame & Chain, Germany 220.00
Beaded, Clutch, Black Glass Beads, 9 x 5 3/4 In. 150.00
Beaded, Deep Red Glass, Beaded Handle, Art Deco, 5 1/4 In. 95.00
Beaded, Drawstring, Dusty Olive, Silk Ball Cord 135.00
Beaded, Drawstring, Floral Design, Fringed 28.00
Beaded, Floral Design, Fringe, 1920s, 10 x 13 In. 225.00
Beaded, Floral Garden Pattern, Fringe, 8 1/2 x 9 In. 180.00
Beaded, Foldover Style, Gold Seed Beads, Scarab Design, Metal Frame, 9 x 8 In. 125.00
Beaded, Lady's Blue, Copper Luster, Applied Floral Design, 9 In. 130.00
Beaded, Loops, Blue Iridescent, Gilt Fittings, Chain, 7 1/2 In.   72.00
Beaded, Loops, Multicolored Flowers, Orange Bakelite Frame, Art Deco, 8 3/4 x 7 In. . .   325.00
Beaded, Pagoda Trees, Filigree Frame, 7 x 8 In. 150.00
Beaded, Pink & White Flowers, Black, Belgium 65.00
Beaded, Polychrome Flowers, Metallic Brown Ground, Gilt Fittings, 7 1/2 In. 137.00
Briefcase Style, Single Moving Handle, Silver Fittings, 8 x 5 In. 125.00
Burled Chocolate Brown, Hidden Friction Catch, Hexagonal, Llewellyn 202.00
Caman, Tan, Brown Leather Lining, Compartments, 10 x 6 In.   23.00
Chatelaine, Double, Green Velvet, Finger Ring & Clip 200.00
Clutch, Lucite, Clear, Carved Diamond Pattern 70.00
Clutch, Rhinestone Closure 50.00
Coin, Beaded, House Scene 65.00
Crocheted, Popcorn Design, Plastic Closure & Handle, 8 In. 23.00
Crocodile, Black, Mallette, Hermes, 1960s 4025.00
Flexible Fabric, Clear Top & Bottom, Single Handle, Dorest-Rex, 5 1/8 x 5 1/8 In. 90.00
Gold, Mother-Of-Pearl Frame, Whiting Davis 60.00
Gold & Rhinestone Cat, Shoulder Strap, Judith Leiber Style 500.00
Gold Mesh, Rhinestone Clasp, Whiting & Davis 35.00
Gold Mesh, Sapphire & Sea Pearls, Inner Beveled Mirror 1950.00
Gold Straw Basket, Mesh Handles, Pink Velvet Top & Front, Midal Of Miami 30.00
Gold Woven Metal Sides, Black Plastic, Red Cotton Lining, Dorset-Rex 95.00
Ivory, Silver Mounts, Japan, 3 1/2 x 5 In. 250.00

Purse, Leather, Tooled, Flowers & Leaves, Brown, 1960s, 9 x 7 In.

Be careful when choosing a purse to use with a vintage gown. The fabric could be damaged by the rough surface of a beaded bag or a jeweled closure.

Leather, Butterscotch Bakelite Frame, Small	14.00
Leather, Tooled, Flowers & Leaves, Brown, 1960s, 9 x 7 In. ....*Illus*	175.00
Leather, Twist Lock, Gemco	90.00
Lizard, Scarlet, Kelly, 1972	3105.00
Lucite, Carved Clear, Rhinestones, Llewellyn, 9 x 4 1/2 In.	290.00
Lucite, Carved Top, Scalloped Edge, 4 Carved Leaves, Silver Bottom Band, Llewellyn	190.00
Lucite, Gray, Rhinestone Clasp, 4 x 7 In.	125.00
Lucite, Hinged Top, Cream Color, 1940s	85.00
Lucite, Mirror Under Lid, Black, 6 1/2 x 8 1/2 In.	145.00
Lucite, Pearly White, Double Handle, Triple Curve Top, Bailey	225.00
Mesh, 14K Gold, Lipstick, Engraved Diamond & Floral Design Frame, 1920s, 2 In.	175.00
Mesh, 18K Gold, 2 Topaz On Clasp, Mesh Divider, 1920s, 2 1/4 x 3 5/8 In.	700.00
Mesh, Arched Shape Frame, 18K Yellow Gold, c.1903	400.00
Mesh, Armor, Silk Lining, Metal Frame, Chain Handle, Whiting & Davis	65.00
Mesh, Art Deco, Cream, Salmon, Black, 5 1/2 x 3 1/2 In.	235.00
Mesh, Compact On Top	125.00
Mesh, Double Handle, Zipper Closure, Ring Pull, Whiting & Davis, 4 1/2 x 5 3/4 In.	55.00
Mesh, Floral, Fringed, Mandalian, Flat	125.00
Mesh, Gilt Metal, Chain, 4 1/2 In.	27.00
Mesh, Gold, Taffeta Lined, Knob Clasp, Snake Handle, Whiting & Davis, 8 x 6 1/4 In.	75.00
Mesh, Gold, Whiting & Davis	50.00
Mesh, Goldtone, Pierced Frame, Lining, Frame, Marked, Whiting & Davis, 6 3/4 In.	85.00
Mesh, Red, Green, Gold Snaps, Germany, 4 1/2 x 3 1/2 In.	110.00
Mesh, Rhinestone Clasp, Whiting & Davis	100.00
Mesh, Sapphire Clasp, Whiting & Davis	125.00
Mesh, Scalloped Bottom, Embossed Frame, 5 1/2 x 5 In.	75.00
Mesh, Silver Chain, 1 1/2 In.	275.00
Mesh, Sterling Silver, Chatelaine, Hallmark, England	180.00
Mesh, Sterling Silver, Signed A.S.E., 1920s, 5 x 4 3/4 In.	325.00
Necessaire, Bakelite, Rhinestones, Tassels, Concealed Lipstick, Black	300.00
Needlework, Flame Stitch Design, Monogrammed, 7 In.	575.00
Needlework, Strawberry & Diamond, 4 x 5 In.	495.00
Opaque Black, Carved Bow Design, Plastic Latch & Feet, Llewellyn, 7 x 5 1/2 In.	80.00
Petit Point, Etched Pearl Frame, Flowers, 5 x 5 1/4 In.	185.00
Plastic, Beaded, White, Large	10.00
Plastic, Coral, Shells, Faux Pearls, 8 In.	20.00
Plastic, Dark Gray, Interlocking Circle Pattern, Dooner, 8 1/8 x 4 1/2 x 6 1/2 In.	175.00
Plastic, Lucite, Pearly White, Button Catch, Rialto	85.00
Plastic, Pearlized Blue, Rigid Upright Handle, Gold Trim, 1950s	160.00
Plastic, Pearly White Base, 4 Spherical Feet, Rialto	180.00
Plastic, Rounded Corners, Colored Alternating Stripes, Wilardy, 7 1/2 In.	205.00
Plastic, Tortoiseshell Colored & Olive Squares, 1960-1970, 7 1/4 In.	45.00
Plastic, Wicker Style, Applied Plastic Flowers, Pearlescent Handles	29.00
Plastic & Cloth, Poodle, Rhinestones & Sequins, 10 1/2 In.	45.00
Sateen, Black, Mirror, Velvet Lining, Box, Zell	40.00
Satin, Black, Dancing Putti, Pierced Silver Frame, Floral Silver Chain, Vivaldi, Germany	70.00
Sequin, Brown & Bronze, Loops For Drawstrings, France	40.00
Silk, Floral Design, Flat Bow At Closure, Goldtone Link Straps, Emilio Pucci	143.00
Silk, Shoulder, Pucci	64.00

Silk Twill, Aztec Style Design, Cream Ground, Emilio Pucci, 1950s 345.00
Sterling Silver, Kerr 235.00
Sterling Silver, Serpent & Mesh Design, Victorian, 6 In. 120.00
Straw, Poodles Under Plastic, White Brocade Ground, Princess Charming Hollywood ... 65.00
Tortoiseshell, Plastic Cover, Olive Green, 7 1/4 In. 45.00
Velvet, Black, Envelope Style, 2 Rhinestone Ornaments, Eisenberg, 12 x 6 In. 350.00
Velvet, Black, Long Gold Chain, Box, Gucci 115.00
Wallet, Needlework, Flame Stitch, Embroidered Name At Top, Wait Fenner, c.1750 .... 1450.00
Wicker, Beige, Floral Design Under Clear Plastic, Pearlized Trim & Handles 26.00

QUEZAL glass was made from 1901 to 1924 by Martin Bach, Sr., in Queens, New York. Other glassware by other firms, such as Loetz, Steuben, and Tiffany, resembles this gold-colored iridescent glass. Martin Bach died in 1921. His son-in-law, Conrad Vahlsing, Jr., went to work at the Lustre Art Company about 1920 and his son, Martin Bach, Jr., worked at the Durand Art Glass division of the Vineland Flint Glass Works after 1924.

Quezal

Bowl, Overall Blue Iridescence, Silver Base, 6 3/4 In. 275.00
Bowl, Ruffed Edge, Gold Finish Inside, Gold & Green Lattice Outside, Signed, 6 1/2 In. .. 1210.00
Bowl, Stretched Edge, Gold Mirror Finish Interior, Gold, Green Lattice Exterior, 6 In. ... 1331.00
Compote, Crimped Rim, 3 Broad Green Leaves, White, Gold, 5 1/2 In. 2415.00
Lamp, Mantel, Opal Shade, Gold Outline Feather Design, Tripod Base, Signed, Pair 858.00
Salt, Pink Iridescent, 16-Panel Shape, Sterling Silver Overlay, 2 1/2 In., Pair 990.00
Salt Dip, Gold Aurene, Silver Overlay, 1 1/2 In. ....*Illus* 330.00
Shade, 5 Gold Feathers, Pulled From Rim, Golden Interior, 5 1/8 In., 5 Piece 747.00
Shade, 10-Panel, Gold Aurene, 2 1/4 x 4 5/16 x 4 1/8 In. 165.00
Shade, Allover Gold Iridescent, Oyster White Ground, Signed, 5 x 7 1/4 In. 525.00
Shade, Bell Form, Gold Iridescent, Signed, 5 1/2 x 2 1/4 In. 125.00
Shade, Diamond Pattern, 2 1/4 x 5 x 5 In. 330.00
Shade, Gold Aurene Over Calcite, 3 1/2 x 4 1/4 In. 110.00
Shade, Gold Threaded, Bell Form, Green & Gold Leaf Design, Signed, 5 3/4 In., 4 Piece 517.00
Shade, Hanging, Hooked Design, Gold, Lavender, Rose, Blue, 11 1/2 In. 1331.00
Shade, Mushroom Cap, 4 Pulled, Hooked Feathers, Lime, Green, 12 1/2 x 5 3/4 In. 1380.00
Shade, Pulled Feather, 2 1/4 x 5 1/8 x 4 3/4 In., Pair 440.00
Shade, Ruffled Edge, Gold Trellis, Opalescent, 6 7/8 In. 685.00
Shade, White Hooked Feather, Gold Iridescent, 5 1/4 x 2 1/8 In. 225.00
Shade, White Oyster Form, Gold White Hook Design, Purple Iridescent, Signed, 5 In. ... 350.00
Shade, Yellow & White, Ribbed, 5 In. 95.00
Vase, Amber, Green, Gold Feathers, Gold Iridescent Rim, Flared, 4 1/2 In. 920.00
Vase, Blue Iridescent, Signed, 10 1/2 In. 1375.00
Vase, Crimped Lip, Pulled Gold Features, Iridescent, Gold Interior, 9 1/4 In. 1100.00
Vase, Gold Iridescent Design, Pulled & Hooked Tracery, Amber, Signed, 8 1/2 In. 990.00
Vase, Gold, Green, Vertically Lined Leaf Design, 6 In. 1610.00
Vase, Iridescent Ribbon Design, 9 In. 880.00
Vase, Jack-In-The-Pulpit, Gold, Pansy Face, Lavender, Rose, Green, Blue, Signed, 7 In. . 1980.00
Vase, Jack-In-The-Pulpit, Green, Pulled Spearlike Leaf, Iridescent, Signed, 11 In. 2640.00

Quezal, Salt Dip, Gold Aurene, Silver Overlay, 1 1/2 In.

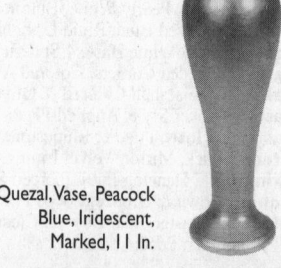

Quezal, Vase, Peacock Blue, Iridescent, Marked, 11 In.

Vase, Jack-In-The-Pulpit, Pansy Face, Gold, Lavender, Rose, Green, Blue, 12 In. 2178.00
Vase, Jack-In-The-Pulpit, Stretched Edge, Pulled Spear Leaf Design, Green, 11 In. 2904.00
Vase, Opal Iridescent, Gold Luster Spots, Iridescent Tear Drops, Signed, 5 In. 1045.00
Vase, Peacock Blue, Iridescent, Marked, 11 In. . . . .*Illus* 1100.00
Vase, Pulled Feather, Green, Gold Interior, Gold On Ivory Ground, 8 In. 1980.00
Vase, Tiny Prunts Design, Cerise, Aqua, Gold Luster Spots, Signed, 5 In. 1150.00
Vase, Trumpet, Green, Gold Pulled Feathers, Gold Interior, White Ground, 14 In. 1150.00
Vase, White Pulled, Hooked Feathers, Gold Iridescent, Amber Body, 8 1/2 In. 690.00
Vase, White Spatter On Clear, Black Base, Signed, 11 1/2 In. 325.00
Vase, White, Yellow Feathering, Green Trailing On Shoulder, Amber Iridescent, 5 In. . . . 1150.00

QUILTS have been made since the seventeenth century. Early textiles
were very precious and every scrap was saved to be reused. A quilt is
a combination of fabrics joined to a filler and a backing by small
stitched designs known as quilting. An appliqued quilt has pieces
stitched to the top of a large piece of background fabric. A patchwork,
or pieced, quilt is made of many small pieces stitched together.
Embroidery can be added to either type.

Amish, Diamond In The Square, Star Flower, Diamond Feather Quilting, 78 x 76 In. 6900.00
Amish, Patchwork, Friendship Pattern, Tan, Blue Baskets, Green Border, c.1930, 84 In. . . 625.00
Amish, Patchwork, Lone Star, 4 Rows Of Border, Hearts In Corners, 76 x 74 In. 550.00
Amish, Patchwork, Lone Star, Multicolored, Navy Ground, 1931, 84 x 83 In. 1455.00
Amish, Patchwork, Lord's Prayer, Red, Green Border, Green Binding, 1900, 69 x 61 In. . 4025.00
Amish, Patchwork, Sunshine & Shadow, Sawtooth Edge, 83 x 83 In. 715.00
Amish, Patchwork, Sunshine & Shadow, Yellow, Brown Binding, c.1910, 84 x 81 In. 450.00
Amish, Triple Irish Chain, Dark Colors, 93 x 105 In. 895.00
Appliqued, 4 Floral Medallions, Red, Khaki, Goldenrod Star Centers, 83 x 85 In. 385.00
Appliqued, 6 Clusters Of Cotton Seed, Bird Border, Floral, Pa., Late 19th Century, 90 In. 2070.00
Appliqued, 9 Clusters Of Flowers, Pale Yellow Patches, Early 19th Century, 84 x 92 In. . 575.00
Appliqued, 9 Floral Medallions, Red, Green, Bird & Vine Border, 86 x 86 In. 1320.00
Appliqued, 9 Medallions, Red, Green, Yellow, Blue, White, Green Binding, 86 x 86 In. . . 425.00
Appliqued, 9 Oak Leaf Pinwheels, Red, Green, Goldenrod, 70 x 71 In. 165.00
Appliqued, 9 Rose Medallions, Pink, Medium Green, White, Vine Border, 84 x 55 In. . . . 220.00
Appliqued, 9 Stylized Floral Medallions, Vine Border, J. Howard, 1860, 86 x 86 In. 385.00
Appliqued, 15 Floral Medallions, Tulips, Reds, Greens, 72 x 84 In. 665.00
Appliqued, 18 Pinwheels, Red, Blue, Teal Green, Red & Green Border, 90 x 94 In. 330.00
Appliqued, 20 Floral Medallions, Vine Border, Red Green, Blue Binding, 77 x 94 In. . . . 325.00
Appliqued, 30 Squares, Paisley Inner Border, 1780s, 88 x 101 1/2 In. 2550.00
Appliqued, 35 Blocks, Center Verse, Presented To Rev. M.E. Stokes, 79 1/2 x 92 In. 9000.00
Appliqued, American Flag, Red, White & Blue, White Border, 1940, 73 x 83 In. 3680.00
Appliqued, Baskets Of Lilies In 16 Squares, Diamond, Diagonal Lines, 1888, 74 x 74 In. . 1035.00
Appliqued, Dogwood Blossoms, White, Brown, Goldenrod, Green Ground, 74 x 82 In. . . . 275.00
Appliqued, Drunkard's Path, Calico Patches, White Ground, 78 x 72 In. 1035.00
Appliqued, Flag & Star, Embroidered, Stephen Douglas To Fitzpatrick, 1860, 25 x 36 In. 250.00
Appliqued, Floral Medallion, Red, Green, Goldenrod, Crib, 28 1/2 x 28 1/2 In. 28.00
Appliqued, Floral, Calico On White, Stylized Blossoms, 78 x 80 In. 690.00
Appliqued, Iris, Purple, Lavender, Green, Helen M. Johnson, 1928, 78 x 80 In. 550.00
Appliqued, Meandering Vine, Berry Border, White Ground, Crib, 60 x 63 In. 1725.00
Appliqued, Morning Glories, Embroider, Name, Sylvia Harris, 1936, 67 x 82 In. 198.00
Appliqued, Pineapple Block, Red Paisley Border, 80 x 84 In. 632.00
Appliqued, Pinwheel In Sun, 9 Blocks, Blue Green Background, 76 x 74 In. 402.00
Appliqued, Pinwheel, Corner Plumes, Deep Pink & White, 77 x 81 In. 385.00
Appliqued, Potted Flowers, Green Calico, Red Border, 78 x 80 In. 160.00
Appliqued, Red & White Leaf, Starred, Lobed Circle, 1861, 76 x 95 In. 315.00
Appliqued, Repeating Design Of Seated Cats, c.1930, 84 1/2 x 63 In. 1265.00
Appliqued, Stylized Floral Medallions, Green, Red, Orange, Vine Border, 78 x 81 In. . . . 715.00
Appliqued, Stylized Flowers, Red, Green, Goldenrod, 74 x 74 In. 495.00
Appliqued, Sunbonnet Babies, Pink, White, 68 x 91 In. 150.00
Appliqued, White Squares, Feather Wreaths, Flowers & Vine Border, 70 x 84 In. 605.00
Crazy, Embroidered Silk & Velvet, 1890s, 58 x 57 1/2 In. 690.00
Crazy, Pieced, People, Flowers, Animals, Nursery Characters, L.M., 70 x 76 In. 495.00
Cross Stitch Embroidery, Central Floral Medallion, Green & Blue Border, 76 x 86 In. . 105.00
Linsey Woolsey, Gold 1 Side, Other Brown, Cutout Post Ends, Repaired, 94 x 96 In. . . . 385.00

Linsey Woolsey, Green & Blue, 84 x 98 In. 121.00
Patchwork, 20 Floral Medallions, Multicolored, White Ground, 70 x 86 In. 165.00
Patchwork, 30 Squares, Different Names, Sarah Yound, 1852, 84 x 98 In. 690.00
Patchwork, 36 Basket Squares, Multicolored & White, Grayish Beige, 72 x 81 In. 165.00
Patchwork, 48 State Flowers, Embroidered Squares, 65 x 76 In. 220.00
Patchwork, Baskets Of Flowers, Meandering Feather Border, 82 x 85 In. 330.00
Patchwork, Bow Tie Squares, White, Deep Blue Calico Ground, 66 x 85 In. 248.00
Patchwork, Center Compass Star, Diamond & Rope Twist Quilting, 86 x 88 In. 2760.00
Patchwork, Checkerboard, Prints & Solids, 79 x 79 In. 60.00
Patchwork, Chintz & Other Prints, 37 1/2 x 39 1/2 In. 330.00
Patchwork, Concentric Squares, Postage Stamp Squares, Multicolored, 88 x 92 In. 275.00
Patchwork, Courthouse Square, Multicolored, 88 x 73 In. 330.00
Patchwork, Diamond & Lightning Bolt, Faded Salmon, White, Red Binding, 80 x 82 In. . 165.00
Patchwork, Diamond In Square, 9 Patch Design, Calico, 80 x 61 In. 1150.00
Patchwork, Double Wedding Ring, 86 x 95 In. 187.00
Patchwork, Embroidered, Rob Peter To Pay Paul, Red, White, Blue, 1909, 72 x 82 In. .. 260.00
Patchwork, Flower Basket, Red Flowers In Green Baskets, 91 x 73 In. 345.00
Patchwork, Flower Garden, Dark Colors, Knotted, 71 x 78 In. 90.00
Patchwork, Flying Geese, Corner Date, Jan. 13, 1899, 71 x 79 In. 660.00
Patchwork, Flying Geese, White Ground, Triple Border, 98 x 95 In. 660.00
Patchwork, Grandmother's Flower Garden, 76 x 84 In. 105.00
Patchwork, House Pattern, Pink, White, 72 x 79 In. 165.00
Patchwork, Irish Chain, Blue & White, Sawtooth Border, 82 x 82 In. 240.00
Patchwork, Irish Chain, Blue Print & White, 69 x 82 In. 385.00
Patchwork, Irish Chain, Navy Blue Star Print, White, 74 x 74 In. 385.00
Patchwork, Joseph's Coat, Stripes, Shell Quilting, 82 x 86 In. 1495.00
Patchwork, Laurel Wreath, Floral Garlands, Blue, Green, Yellow, 1850, 82 x 83 In. 3220.00
Patchwork, Leaf Pattern, Blue & White, 72 x 72 In. 385.00
Patchwork, Log Cabin, Concentric Diamond, White, Red Border, 83 x 88 In. 330.00
Patchwork, Log Cabin, Satins & Silks, c.1875, 66 x 75 In. 1904.00
Patchwork, Multicolored Prints, Navy Blue & White, 68 x 79 1/2 In. 247.00
Patchwork, Nine Patch, Calicos Set On Yellow Field, 41 x 41 In. 195.00
Patchwork, Nine Patch, Red Border, 91 x 88 1/2 In. 192.00
Patchwork, Nine Patch, Red, White & Blue, Crib 355.00
Patchwork, Ocean Waves, Calico, White Ground, 1885, 75 x 87 In. 1380.00
Patchwork, Ohio Star, Blue, Red & Yellow, 84 x 83 In. 165.00
Patchwork, Optical Star, Cradle 287.00
Patchwork, Pineapple, Blue & White, 63 x 74 In. 275.00
Patchwork, Pink Calico, Pink Border, Crib, 33 x 37 In. 115.00
Patchwork, Postage Stamp Squares, White, Red Binding, 66 x 78 In. 440.00
Patchwork, Postage Stamp, 83 x 74 In. 2490.00
Patchwork, Repeating Geometric Design, Blue On White Ground, 77 x 76 1/2 In. 345.00
Patchwork, Repeating Notched Cross, Pink Calico On White Ground, 74 x 73 1/2 In. 201.00
Patchwork, Signed Squares, Circle & Heart Border, Calico, 1850, 84 x 98 In. 1275.00
Patchwork, Small Squares, Multicolored, Deep Pink Calico Border, 80 x 86 In. 412.00
Patchwork, Snowflake, Turquoise & White, Doll's 40.00
Patchwork, Star Of Bethlehem, Blue, Pink, Yellow, Green, White Ground, 75 x 76 In. ... 805.00
Patchwork, Star Of Bethlehem, White Background, Pink & Green Border, 85 x 85 In. ... 715.00
Patchwork, Star, Calico, Natural Green, c.1870, 7 1/2 x 7 1/2 In. 560.00
Patchwork, Starburst Pattern, Multicolored, Light Blue Ground, 77 x 80 In. 374.00
Patchwork, Triangle Patches, Blue Print, 68 x 81 In. 385.00
Patchwork, Triple Irish Chain, 1930s, 72 x 85 In. 175.00
Patchwork, Tumbling Blocks, Bright Solid Colors, Orange Border, 63 x 88 In. 165.00
Patchwork & Appliqued, 25 Blocks, Forming Geometric Design, 84 x 84 In. 1610.00
Patchwork & Appliqued, 9 Squares Of Floral Pinwheels, Vines, 84 x 84 In. 4025.00
Patchwork & Appliqued, Star Of Bethlehem, Ocean Wave Quilting, 84 x 84 In. 3000.00
Patchwork & Quilted, Diamond In The Square, Silk Damask, 96 1/2 x 104 In. 7130.00
Trapunto, Grapevines, Flowers, Homespun Linen, B. Barton, Wife, 75 x 82 In. 1900.00

QUIMPER pottery has a long history. Tin-glazed, hand-painted pottery
has been made in Quimper, France, since the late seventeenth century.
The earliest firm, founded in 1685 by Jean Baptiste Bousquet, was
known as HB Quimper. Another firm, founded in 1772 by Francois

Eloury, was known as Porquier. The third firm, founded by Guillaume Dumaine in 1778, was known as HR or Henriot Quimper. All three firms made similar pottery decorated with designs of Breton peasants and sea and flower motifs. The Eloury (Porquier) and Dumaine (Henriot) firms merged in 1913. Bousquet (HB) merged with the others in 1968. The group was sold to a United States family in 1984. The American holding company is Quimper Faience Inc., located in Stonington, Connecticut. The French firm has been called Societe Nouvelle des Faienceries de Quimper HB Henriot since March 1984.

HR. Quimper

Ashtray, Peasant Design, 1930	50.00
Bank, Pig, 4 x 8 In.	95.00
Bank, Piggy, 1940s	498.00
Bottle, Figural, Man, Woman, 12 In., Pair	725.00
Bowl, Man & Woman In Wooden Shoes, Pecheurs, 4 1/2 x 9 1/2 In.	220.00
Box, Henriot, 4 1/2 In.	75.00
Box, Yellow, 4 x 5 In.	85.00
Charger, Facing Couple, Man & Woman, Yellow, Signed, 14 In., Pair	300.00
Charger, Peasant, 13 In.	650.00
Cup & Saucer, Man Smoking Pipe, Pecheurs, France	66.00
Cup & Saucer, Peasant Panel, Octagonal	125.00
Dish, Serving, Handle, Divided, 1920s	395.00
Figurine, Young Girl, Kerchief In Hand, Berthe Savigny, 1920s, 8 1/2 In.	460.00
Knife Rest, Pecheurs, France, 3 Piece	110.00
Lamp, Peasant Man & Woman, Handles, Signed, 15 In., Pair	995.00
Pitcher, Milk, H.B., France, 6 1/2 In.	132.00
Plate, Blue Danube, 10 In.	18.00
Plate, Mayflower Ship Scene In Center, Red, Blue Leaf Border, 4 1/4 In.	165.00
Plate, Mother's Day, 1982	75.00
Plate, Peasant Lady, 10 In.	65.00
Plate, Rooster & Flowers, Geometric Rim, 9 1/2 In.	135.00
Plate, Woman, Standing, Floral Border, 6 Sides, 7 1/2 In.	138.00
Platter, Fish, Peasant Couple, 23 x 11 1/2 In.	360.00
Puzzle Jug, Flowers, Pierced Neck, HB Mark, France, 19th Century, 7 3/4 In.	375.00
Relish, 2 Sections, Handle, Pecheurs, France, 2 1/2 x 7 1/4 In.	38.00
Salt & Pepper, Florals, Polychrome, Signed, 3 1/2 In.	110.00
Sauce, Double-Spouted, Pecheurs, France, 7 1/2 In.	88.00
Trivet, Man & Woman In Wooden Shoes, Pecheurs, France, 8 1/2 In.	137.00
Vase, Man & Woman In Wooden Shoes, 2 Handles, Pecheurs, 9 1/2 In.	143.00
Wall Pocket, Peasant Lady	80.00

RADFORD pottery was made by Alfred Radford in Broadway, Virginia, Tiffin and Zanesville, Ohio, and Clarksburg, West Virginia, from 1891 until 1912. Jasperware, Ruko, Thera, Radura, and Velvety Art Ware were made. The jasperware resembles the famous Wedgwood ware of the same name.

RADURA.

Plate, Indian Cameo, 7 1/4 In.	78.00
Vase, Brown Trees & Shrubbery, Golden Mushroom Ground, 1933, 13 5/8 In.	275.00
Vase, Thera, Nasturtium, Bulbous, 12 In.	770.00

RADIO broadcast receiving sets were first sold in New York City in 1910. They were used to pick up the experimental broadcasts of the day. The first commercial radios were made by Westinghouse Company for listeners of the experimental shows on KDKA Pittsburgh in 1920. Collectors today are interested in all early radios, especially those made of Bakelite plastic or decorated with blue mirrors. Figural advertising radios and transistor radios are also collected.

Addison, Model A2A, Ivory Trim	475.00
Advertising, Campbell's Soup, Can Form, AM, Hong Kong, Box	55.00
Advertising, Champion Spark Plug	135.00 to 185.00
Advertising, Cheeseburger, AM	55.00
Advertising, Chesterfield Cigarettes	120.00
Advertising, Coors Can, Box	35.00
Advertising, Gulden's Mustard, Figural, Box	95.00

Advertising, Gulf Auto Battery Shape, Plastic, Box, Hong Kong 60.00
Advertising, Hamm's Beer, Bear, Plastic Figure, 15 In. 150.00
Advertising, Heinz Ketchup Bottle 28.00
Advertising, L & M Cigarettes 120.00
Advertising, Lark Cigarettes 120.00
Advertising, Michelin Man, Figural, Italy, 1960s 395.00
Advertising, Mr. Peanut, Figural 98.00
Advertising, Nestle Crunch Bar 45.00
Advertising, Schlitz, Globe Shape, Plastic, Metal, Battery Operated, 8 x 5 1/2 In. ... 45.00
Advertising, Sunoco Gas Pump, Custom Blended, Transistor 65.00
Advertising, Tropicana Orange 30.00
Advertising, Yago Sangria Bottle, Box 65.00
Archer, Road Patrol, AM-FM, Plastic, Red, Black, For Bicycle, 5 x 3 1/4 x 3 In. .. 55.00
Bee Gees, Transistor, Pocket, AM, Orange Plastic, Paste-On Label 40.00
Bendix, No. 526C, Green Marbleized Catalin, Black Grill & Louvers, 12 x 6 1/2 In. 660.00
Bulova, Tube, Blue Plastic 45.00
Cabbage Patch Kids, Yellow Plastic, Vinyl Strap, 1983 .... 23.00
Capehart, Cream Plastic, Gold Colored Numbers, Not Working, 8 1/2 x 7 In. 25.00
Catalin, Emerson Tombstone 1400.00
Catalin, Motorola, Model 50XC, Tortoise Case 850.00
Catalin, Sentinel, Model 1U284NA 950.00
Cheeseburger, Side-Mounted Rotary Tuner & Volume Dial, Strap, 5 In. 26.00
Clock, Admiral, Model 5A32, Brown 30.00
Crosley, Grandfather Clock Form, Converted To Quartz, 66 1/2 In. 168.00
Crosley, Model 10-139, Green 125.00
Cruiser Form, AM, Japan 105.00
Emerson, Built Into Highboy, Phonograph, High-Legged Case, 42 x 23 1/2 In. 385.00
Fada, Bullet, Butterscotch 1100.00
Fada, Bullet, Butterscotch & Red 950.00
Fada, Model 845 .... 285.00
Farnsworth, Floor Model, Mahogany, 1930 .... 500.00
General Electric, Alarm, Clock, Model 506, Ivory, Plastic, Vacuum Tubes, 11 x 6 In. 65.00
General Electric, Clock Radio, White Plastic Case, Black & Silver Dial, Japan 39.00
Graphophone, Horn, White 550.00
Hallicrafters, Model S-38A, Short-Wave, Gray Steel Case, 4-Band Selector 75.00
Magnavox, Model 23, AM, Transistor, Box 35.00
Marconi, Kyowa, AM, Clear Plastic, Light Blue Dial, 3 In. 26.00
Microphone Shape, AM/FM, Taiwan 60.00
Mork & Mindy, Egg Shape, Box 45.00
Motorola, Catalin, Butterscotch, Green Figural S Grill & Handle, 10 x 6 In. 1320.00
Night-Light, Real Ghostbusters, Marshmallow Man, Green Base, Box 25.00
Peanut Form, Face Of Jimmy Carter, AM, Hong Kong, Box .... 60.00 to 90.00
Philco, Heterodyne Super 9 Model, 1930s 350.00
Philco, Model 46-420, AM, Brown, Bakelite, Controls On Top, 11 x 7 In. 70.00
Philco, Model 87, Cabinet, Double Doors, Tapestry Covered Speaker, c.1930s, 47 In. ... 154.00
Polaroid 600 Plus, AM/FM, Telescopic, Box, 6 In. 20.00
RCA Victor, Model 8-X-8N, AM, Twin Speakers, White Plastic, Phono Jack, 12 x 7 In. .. 33.00
Robot Form, Star Command, AM, Hong Kong, 1977 .... 60.00
Shaggy Dog, Disney Premium, Transistor, Box 50.00
Spartan, No. 517, Walter Dorwin Teague, Art Deco, Mirrored Glass, 1936, 16 1/2 x 8 In. 1980.00
Spirit Of '76, Transistor 30.00
Sunglasses, Transistor, Ross, Box, 1960s 75.00
Super Spy, Time Bomb Toy, HG Toys, Display Card, 1960s 28.00
True-Tone, Metal Fake Wood Case, Curved, Waterfall Style, Bakelite Knobs, 1930s-1940s 47.00
Western Electric, Crystal, With Earphones, 1918 .... 125.00
Westinghouse, Dual Speakers, AM, Tube Type, Turquoise Plastic, 1950s 29.00
Westinghouse, H769P7A, Transistor .... 20.00 to 40.00
Westinghouse, Model 38917, AM-FM, Brown Plastic Case, 180 Degree Tuner .... 20.00 to 40.00
Zenith, 7H820W, AM, 2 FM Bands, White Bakelite, Rotary Dial, FM Decal On Back ... 87.00
Zenith, Model 114C, AM, Brown & Cream Case, Plastic, 10 1/2 x 5 1/2 x 6 In. 24.00
Zenith, Model 6D815, Brown 20.00
Zenith, Model 7G01, AM-FM, Brown Plastic Case, 360 Degree Tuner, Handle 50.00
Zenith, Tombstone Style, Model 715 .... 125.00

RADIO MICROPHONE, Astatic, Model D-104, 12 In. 83.00
  Philmore, Hand Held, 1930s 25.00
  Turner, Dynamic Model 330, Aluminum, Wood Case, 5 In., 15-In. Case 60.00

RAILROAD enthusiasts collect any train memorabilia. Everything is
wanted, from oilcans to whole train cars. The Chessie system has a
store that sells many reproductions of their old dinnerware and uniforms.

Ashtray, C & O, Glass, Chessie Center 25.00
Ashtray, Southern Ry, Stamped Copper 60.00
Booklet, Colorado Mountain Playgrounds, Union Pacific Railroad, 1927, 48 Pages 30.00
Booklet, Denver & Rio Grande Western Railway, 1880s, 80 Pages, 5 x 7 1/2 In. 100.00
Booklet, New York Central Railway, Hudson River, 1926, 46 Pages 9.00
Booklet, Oregon Railroad & Navigation Co., 1904 .... 95.00
Booklet, Union Pacific Denver & Gulf Railroad, Rockies, 31 Pages, 5 x 7 1/2 In. 75.00
Bowl, Northern Pacific, 1930, Small 55.00
Bowl, Southern Pacific, Prairie Mountain Wildflower 110.00
Calendar, 1956, Chesapeake & Ohio, Chessie Cat, Young Boy & Trains, 15 x 23 In. 22.00
Cap, Pullman Porter 115.00
Card, Playing, C & O RR 35.00
Card, Playing, Soo Line RR 20.00
Card, Playing, Southern Pacific RR 15.00
Case, Pillow, Pullman 8.50
Cup, Southern Pacific, Prairie Mountain Wildflowers, Backstamped 60.00
Cuspidor, Nashville, Chattanooga & St. Louis, Raised Letters 225.00
Eggcup, B & O Railroad, Centenary 580.00
Headlight, Gas Powered, 3 Piece Glass Face, Tille Hendon Co., 1900s 350.00
Knife, Dinner, Santa Fe RR 12.00
Lamp, Caboose, Side Lamps, C & O, 1920s, Pair 300.00
Lamp, Station, Desk, Atlantic Boast Line, Cast Metal & Brass, 1800s 1000.00
Lantern, Conductors, A & W, Nickeled Brass 575.00
Lantern, Florida East Coast Railway, 1944 .... 150.00
Lantern, NYCRR, Dietz 100.00
Lantern, Santa Fe Railroad 80.00
Lantern, Tall Globe, Pennsylvania Railroad, Handlan 45.00
Lock, Alton & Southern, Brass, Brass, Adlake, 3 1/2 In. 20.00
Menu, Dining Car, Intercolonial RR, 1908 .... 38.00
Menu, Union Pacific, Streamliner, City Of Portland, 1950 .... 10.00
Number Plate, Boiler, Locomotive, 1880 .... 95.00
Padlock & Key, Wells Fargo Express, South Pacific Railroad 55.00
Paperweight, North Western Line 85.00
Pin, Lapel, Lehigh Valley Railroad, Safety Always, Clear Record, 3/4 In. 30.00
Pin, National Railroad Brotherhood, 15 Year, Screw Back, 1940s 8.00
Plate, Missouri Pacific, State Flower, Steam Engine Service 225.00
Plate, Pullman, Indian Tree, 9 In. 150.00
Plate, Union Pacific, Circus, Bareback Rider, 8 1/4 In. 95.00
Platter, Milwaukee Traveler, 10 x 8 In. 85.00
Postcard, Michigan Central Railroad, Colored, 1934 .... 85.00
Poster, Illinois Central Railroad, Loading Timber Products, 26 1/2 x 20 In. 100.00
Poster, Illinois Central, Procedures For Loading Timber Products, 26 1/2 x 20 In. 50.00
Poster, On Fabric, Streamliner, c.1935, 20 x 41 In. 660.00
Schedule, Northern Pacific, Passenger Train, September 30, 1956 .... 12.00
Seat, Parlor Car, 1890s, Pair 395.00
Sign, Great Northern Railway, Goat On Mountain Logo, Porcelain, Round, 22 In. 1050.00
Sign, Purple Atlantic Coast Line, Metal, 24 In. 350.00
Sign, Station 1 Mile, Raised Letters, Pole Mounted, Early 1800s 500.00
Spoon, Serving, Canadian National Railways, Silver 40.00
Stock Certificate, Fair Oaks Transit, 1912 .... 10.00
Switch Key, Nickel Plate Road, Tubular Brass, Adlake, 2 1/8 In. 25.00
Teapot, B & O Railroad, Centenary, With Cover 825.00
Timetable, Atlantic Coast Line, April 25, 1954 .... 15.00
Timetable, Big 4, July 1, 1923 .... 18.00
Timetable, Condensed, Seaboard Railroad, April 29, 1962 .... 5.00

Timetable, Fall River Line Tours, 1890 .... 85.00
Timetable, New York, New Haven, Hartford Railroad, November 17, 1940 .... 15.00
Timetable, Nickel Plate Railroad, 1900 .... 75.00
Timetable, Pennsylvania Railroad, September 29, 1940, To And From The South 15.00
Timetable, Southern Pacific, Sunset Route, April 28, 1957 .... 5.00
Timetable, Union Pacific, September 1957 To January 1958 .... 15.00
Transit, Bronze, Great Northern Railroad, Box, 8 1/2 x 20 In. 1200.00
Water Bucket, Northern Pacific Railway Co., Collapsible, Twill, Metal Frame, 11 In. .. 50.00
Wax Sealer, Union Pacific 350.00

RAZORS were used in ancient Egypt and subsequently wherever shaving was in fashion. The metal razor used in America until about 1870 was made in Sheffield, England. After 1870, machine-made hollow-ground razors were made in Germany or America. Plastic or bone handles were popular. The razor was often sold in a set of seven, one for each day of the week. The set was often kept by the barber who shaved the well-to-do man each day in the shop.

Blade, Bingham, Straight, Tortoise Handle, Gold Schooner On Blade, Box 95.00
Blade Bank, Barber Man 95.00
Blade Bank, Gay Blades Quartet 95.00
Duplex, Safety, Green Molded Handle, Leather Snap Case 23.00
Engraved Eagle On Blade, General Taylor Razor, Horn Handle 350.00
Iroquois Beer, Plastic Handle 25.00
Keen Kutter Jr., Box 35.00
King Oscillator, Box 85.00
Leslie Leeds, Safety, Lawn Mower Style Blade Strap, Box 185.00
Nude Woman Bathing On Handle 135.00
Pal-Injecto-Matic, Plastic Travel Case, Box 5.00
Remington, Lektronic IV, Electric, White Plastic, 6 Razors, 3 1/2 x 3 1/2 In. 25.00
Rools, Safety, Enclosed In Comb Container, Leather Strap, Stone, England 185.00
Schick, Eversharp, Bakelite Handle 65.00
Shapleigh Hardware, Signed 65.00
Sharpener, Syracuse, N.Y., Pat. 1888 .... 195.00
Star Safety Razor, Tin 42.00
Straight, 7 Day, Lined Oak Case 265.00
Straight, Bone Handle, Carved Young Woman, Civil War Era 95.00
Straight, Celluloid Handle, Windmill & Sailboat Carved In Handle, Box 150.00
Straight, Figural Indian Chief, Symbol, Black Handle, Swastika On Blade 275.00
Straight, Nude Woman, Celluloid Case, Morely 50.00
Strap, We'll Beat 'Em All Like Certified Checks, Clydesdale Shell 40.00
W.H. Morley & Son, Clover Brand, Hollow Ground, Square Point 35.00
Wald, Straight, Box 25.00
Winchester, Straight, Box 125.00
Yellow Kid, Straight 25.00

REAMERS, or juice squeezers, have been known since 1767, although most of those collected today date from the twentieth century. Figural reamers are among the most prized.

Apollo, Bernard Rice & Son, Silver Plate 125.00
Basket, Juice Squeezer, Brown Ceramic 100.00
Blue Onion, 2 Piece 20.00
Cambridge Glass, Green 200.00
Clear Glass, Small 10.00
Clown Head, Orange Collar, 2 3/4 In. 35.00
Crisscross, Cobalt Blue 250.00
Crisscross, Crystal 4.00
Crisscross, Lemon 325.00
Crisscross, Orange ....250.00 to 375.00
Custard Glass 20.00
Duck, Large 125.00
Duck, Small ....85.00 to 95.00
Face, Black, Goebel 875.00
Federal, Amber 8.00

Fleur-De-Lis, Red, Yellow 650.00
Fry, Emerald Green 750.00
Glass, High Sided, Grapefruit 40.00
Greyline, Red Wing 1650.00
Jeannette, Pink 175.00
Jennyware, Pink 70.00
Lemon, Applewood, 1870s 210.00
Lemon, Iron Hinge, Maple, 15 1/2 In. 115.00
Lemon, Japan 55.00
Lemon Shape, China, Japan, 3 Piece 12.00
Lime Green Glass, 1930s, Large 30.00
Lindsay, Green 475.00
Lindsay, Pink 425.00
Pear, Japan ....50.00 to 55.00
Puddinhead, Ceramic 78.00
Sunkist, Black ....700.00 to 800.00
Sunkist, Blue 200.00
Sunkist, Chalaine Blue ....200.00 to 295.00
Sunkist, Crown Tuscan ....350.00 to 375.00
Sunkist, Green 40.00
Sunkist, Jade 95.00
Sunkist, Jadite 65.00
Sunkist, Medium Jade 95.00
Sunkist, Milk Glass ....10.00 to 40.00
Sunkist, Pale Jade 295.00
Sunkist, Pink 65.00
Sunkist, Tan 300.00
Sunkist, White 15.00
Sunkist, White Opalescent 35.00
Sunkist, Yellow 75.00
Townsend, Lemon, Hinged, Ovala, Cast Iron, 1863 .... 150.00
Ultramarine, Jeannette Glass 165.00
Wagner, Aluminum 30.00
White Vitrock, Orange Juice 40.00

RECORDS have changed size and shape through the years. The cylinder-shaped phonograph record for use with the early Edison models was made about 1889. Disc records were first made by 1894, the double-sided disc by 1904. High-fidelity records were first issued in 1944, the first vinyl disc in 1946, the first stereo record in 1958. The 78 RPM became the standard in 1926 but was discontinued in 1957. In 1932, the first 33 1/3 RPM was made but was not sold commercially until 1948. In 1949, the 45 RPM was introduced. Compact discs became available in the U.S. in 1982 and many companies began phasing out the production of phonograph records.

Album, Audience Of One, David Soul, 33 RPM, 1977 .... 10.00
Album, Doris Day & Frank Sinatra, Young At Heart, Columbia, 45 RPM, 1954 .... 24.00
Album, Evel Knievel, Press Conference, Ballad, Sound City Studios, 33 1/3 RPM, 1974 . 34.00
Album, Gentlemen Prefer Blondes, Soundtrack, Marilyn Monroe, 33 1/3 RPM, 1978 .... 50.00
Album, I'm In The Mood For Love, Jayne Mansfield, LP 24.00
Album, Mamas & The Papas Deliver, Dunhill, In Shrink Wrap, 5 Records 505.00
Album, Partridge Family, 33 1/3 RPM, With Shopping Bag 30.00
Alice In Wonderland, Golden, 78 RPM, 1951 .... 16.00
All In The Family, Archie & Edith, Side By Side, RCA, 1973, Stereo 24.00
Alvin & The Chipmunks, Liberty, 45 RPM, 1960s 7.00
Andy Griffith, Destry, 33 RPM, 1959 .... 35.00
Andy Griffith, What It Was, Was Football, Capitol, 45 RPM, 1950s ... 45.00
Annette, Ma He's Making Eyes At Me, Disneyland, 45 RPM, 1950-1960 .... 8.00
Aristocats, Soundtrack, Phil Harris, Sterling Holloway, Stereo, Book, Disneyland, 1970 . 15.00
Bang The Drum Slowly, Soundtrack, Paramount, Stereo, 1973 .... 18.00
Bee Gees, Vanity Fair, Picture Inside Cover, 1979 .... 45.00
Bill Cosby, Fat Albert, When I Was A Kid, 1971 .... 16.00
Budweiser, Polkas, Tavern In Town, 6 Songs, 33 1/3 RPM 10.00

Casey At The Bat, Lionel Barrymore, Baseball Cover, LP 15.00

Danny Kaye, Gilbert & Sullivan, Decca, 33 RPM, 1949 .... 15.00

Dean Martin, Bells Are Ringing, Stereo, Capitol, 1960 .... 24.00

Dick Clark, All Time Hits, Vol. 3, 45 RPM, 1950s 15.00

Gone With The Wind, London Symphony, Stereo, Pickwick, 1967 .... 15.00

Jayne Mansfield, An Evening With Jayne, Hollywood Record, Album, 33 1/3 RPM 47.00

Monkees, Day Dream Believer, 45 RPM, 1960-1986 .... 12.00

Monkees, I'm A Believer/Steppin' Stone, Davy, Lifting Board, 45 RPM, 1960s 13.00

Monkees, Nice To Be With You, Group Photo On Front Sleeve, 45 RPM, 1960s 19.00

Monkees, Pleasant Valley Sunday, Group Photo On Sleeve, 45 RPM, 1960s 15.00

Monkees, Valleri, Taploca Tundra, 45 RPM, 1960s 9.00

Move Over Babe Here Comes Henry, Richard Wylie, 45 RPM 7.50

Picture, Frank Zappa, Goblin Girl, Pink Napkins, Barking Pumpkin Records, 1980 ..... 24.00

Picture, Frank Zappa, Untitled, Black & White Photo, 1979 .... 31.00

Picture, Fred Blassie, I Bite The Songs, Pencil Neck Geek, Rhino Records, 1983 ..... 23.00

Picture, Heartlight, Neil Diamond, Columbia, 1982 .... 25.00

Picture, Led Zeppelin, BBC Concert, Limited Edition, 1000 Copies, Image Disc, 1979 .. 28.00

Picture, On The Way To The Sky, Neil Diamond, CBS, 1981 .... 26.00

Picture, Wahi Aloha, Eddie Spencer & The Kings Of Hawaii, Lei Records, 1977 .... 23.00

Purple People Eater, Holder, 45 RPM 10.00

Ricky Nelson, Garden Party, Decca, 45 RPM, 1972 .... 5.00

Shirley Bassey, James Bond, Goldfinger, United Artists, 45 RPM, 1964 .... 8.00

Smothers Brothers, Curb Your Tongue, Knavel, 1960s 12.00

Smothers Brothers, It Must Have Been Something I Said, Mercury, 1960s 12.00

Snoopy, A Charlie Brown Christmas, 1977 .... 15.00

Utica Club, Natural Carbonation Beer Drinking Song, 45 RPM, 1960s 5.50

Victor Borge, Caught In The Act, Columbia, 1950s 15.00

Wagon Train, Picture Of Ward Bone On The Sleeve, Golden, 78 RPM, 1957 .... 12.00

What Made The Red Man Red, Peter Pan, Little Golden, 78 RPM, 1952 .... 19.00

Witch Doctor, Holder, 45 RPM 10.00

RED WING Pottery of Red Wing, Minnesota, was a firm started in 1878. The company first made utilitarian pottery. In the 1920s art pottery was made. Many dinner sets and vases were made before the company closed in 1967. Rumrill pottery was made for George Rumrill by the Red Wing Pottery and other firms. It was sold in the 1930s. For more information, see *Kovels' Depression Glass & Dinnerware Price List.*

Bob White, Basket, 12 In. 50.00

Bob White, Beverage Server, Stopper, Warmer 100.00

Bob White, Bowl, 9 In. 15.00

Bob White, Bowl, Salad, 12 In. 45.00

Bob White, Bowl, Vegetable, Divided 30.00

Bob White, Butter, 1/4 Lb. 75.00

Bob White, Casserole, 1 Qt. 30.00

Bob White, Casserole, 2 Qt. 30.00

Bob White, Cookie Jar ....75.00 to 100.00

Bob White, Creamer 25.00

Bob White, Cup & Saucer ....9.00 to 12.00

Bob White, Gravy Boat ....30.00 to 45.00

Bob White, Gravy Boat, Cover & Stand 85.00

Bob White, Hors D'Oeuvre Server 40.00

Bob White, Mug 85.00

Bob White, Pitcher, 8 In. 50.00

Bob White, Pitcher, 11 1/2 In. 45.00

Bob White, Pitcher, 12 In. ....35.00 to 45.00

Bob White, Pitcher, 60 Oz. ....40.00 to 45.00

Bob White, Plate, 6 1/2 In. ....3.50 to 8.00

Bob White, Plate, 8 In. 4.50

Bob White, Plate, 10 1/2 In. 12.00

Bob White, Platter, 13 In. 80.00

Bob White, Platter, Small 35.00

Bob White, Relish, 3 Sections ....30.00 to 45.00
Bob White, Salt & Pepper ....30.00 to 32.00
Bob White, Salt & Pepper, Bird Shape 35.00
Bob White, Shaker, Bird 25.00
Bob White, Tray, French Bread, 24 In. 80.00
Bob White, Trivet 250.00
Bob White, Tumbler 160.00
Capistrano, Bowl, 2 Sections 28.00
Capistrano, Bowl, Cereal 8.00
Capistrano, Plate, 10 In. 12.50
Cherry Band, Pitcher, 1 Qt. 350.00
Cherry Band, Pitcher, 2 Qt. 750.00
Driftwood, Creamer 10.00
Egyptian, Vase, Green & White, 15 In. 230.00
Fondoso, Cookie Jar ....65.00 to 95.00
Grayline, Casserole & 4 Custard Cups 1000.00
Incised Peasant, Cookie Jar 44.00
Jack Frost, Cookie Jar 695.00
Katrina, Clock 190.00
Katrina, Cookie Jar, Tan & Brown ....77.00 to 150.00
King Of Tarts, Cookie Jar, Blue Speckled 1200.00
Lotus, Casserole, Cover, 1 Qt. 75.00
Lute Song, Plate, 10 1/2 In. 10.00
Magnolia, Saucer 1.50
Magnolia, Wall Pocket 175.00
Nokomis, Planter, Elephant 225.00
Nokomis, Vase, 7 In. 365.00
Nokomis, Vase, 8 In. ....275.00 to 325.00
Nokomis, Vase, 9 In. 340.00
Nokomis, Vase, Blank, Gray & Black Painted Crystalline, Signed, 12 7/8 In. 440.00
Provincial Ware, Casserole, Individual 10.00
RoundUp, Bowl, Vegetable, Divided 165.00
RoundUp, Bread Plate 30.00
RoundUp, Cookie Jar ....350.00 to 475.00
RoundUp, Plate, 6 1/2 In. 40.00
RoundUp, Plate, 10 1/2 In. ....60.00 to 65.00
RoundUp, Platter, 13 In. 90.00
RoundUp, Salt & Pepper, Tall 152.00
RoundUp, Sugar 85.00
RoundUp, Teapot 450.00
Smart Set, Bowl, 6 1/2 In. 10.00
Smart Set, Bowl, 9 In. 15.00
Smart Set, Bowl, Salad, Large 25.00
Smart Set, Casserole, 2 Qt. 60.00
Smart Set, Cup & Saucer 8.00
Smart Set, Pitcher, 7 In. 15.00
Smart Set, Server, Cover, 2 Handles, 8 In. 45.00
Smart Set, Server, Divided, 14 In. 30.00
Sponge Band, Bowl, 8 In. 75.00
Stoneware, Birch Leaves, Jug, Beehive, 3 Gal. 300.00
Stoneware, Bottle, Pig 550.00
Stoneware, Bowl, Pedestal, Zephyr, Pink 25.00
Stoneware, Churn, 8 Gal. 1500.00
Stoneware, Cooler, Ice Water, Wing, 3 Gal. ....360.00 to 525.00
Stoneware, Crock, Big Wing, 50 Gal. ....875.00 to 1250.00
Stoneware, Crock, Button Lid, Wing, 1 Gal. 450.00
Stoneware, Crock, Salt Glaze, Cobalt Design, 4-Rib Cage Swirl, 4 Gal. 110.00
Stoneware, Crock, Wing, 40 Gal. 900.00
Stoneware, Figurine, Cowboy & Cowgirl, Hand Painted 400.00
Stoneware, Figurine, Elephant, 4 In. 175.00
Stoneware, Fruit Jar, Blue Letters, 1/2 Gal. 210.00
Stoneware, Jar, Beater, Blue Bands, 4 3/4 In. 80.00

Red Wing, Stoneware, Vase, Green & Brown,
8 1/2 x 3 3/4 In.

**Treat your antiques like your
grandparents: Have proper
respect for their age, but don't
exaggerate their fragility.**

Stoneware, Jar, Butter	160.00
Stoneware, Jar, Fruit, Stone Union Mason, Blue Lettering, 8 In.	385.00
Stoneware, Jar, Pantry, Blue Bandit, 5 Lb.	495.00
Stoneware, Jug, Beehive, 2 Gal.	115.00
Stoneware, Jug, Beehive, Wing With Oval, 5 Gal.	190.00
Stoneware, Jug, Elephant Ear, Beehive, Minnesota Oval, 3 Gal.	4000.00
Stoneware, Jug, Steuben County Wine Co., 2 Gal.	195.00
Stoneware, Lamp, Elephant, Yellow	165.00
Stoneware, Pitcher, Quail, 12 In.	35.00
Stoneware, Planter, Duck	95.00
Stoneware, Planter, Piano	150.00
Stoneware, Planter, Reclining Muses Sides, Bronze Finish	55.00
Stoneware, Planter, Seal	90.00
Stoneware, Sugar, Pineapple Shape	50.00
Stoneware, Teapot, Bronze Finish, Eva Zeisel	230.00
Stoneware, Teapot, Wreath, Yellow	66.00
Stoneware, Vase, Decorator Brass Line, Black, 8 In.	45.00
Stoneware, Vase, Fan, Blue, Pink Inside, 7 1/2 In.	48.00
Stoneware, Vase, Green & Brown, 8 1/2 x 3 3/4 In. ....*Illus*	28.00
Stoneware, Vase, Green & White, 15 In.	230.00
Stoneware, Vase, Lion, 7 In.	375.00
Stoneware, Vase, Nude Handle, Cobalt Blue, 11 In.	2640.00
Stoneware, Vase, Yellow, Leaf Design, Flared Rim, 6 3/4 In., Pair	38.00
Tampico, Bowl, Vegetable, 8 In.	25.00
Tampico, Cake Stand, Pedestal	50.00 to 65.00
Tampico, Cup & Saucer	15.00
Tampico, Gravy Boat	25.00
Tampico, Plate, 6 In.	9.00
Tampico, Plate, 10 In.	12.00
Tampico, Sugar	15.00
Terra Craft, Vase, 9 In.	120.00
Town & Country, Plate, 10 1/2 In.	16.00 to 25.00
Town & Country, Salt & Pepper	45.00 to 55.00
Vase, Deer & Woman's Face, 7 In.	75.00
Village Brown, Pitcher, 8 Cup	40.00
Village Green, Cooler, Lid, Spigot Stand, 2 Gal.	110.00

REDWARE is a hard, red stoneware that originated in the late 1600s and
continues to be made. The term is also used to describe any common
clay pottery that is reddish in color.

Baby Bear, Dark Stain, Incised Initials C.T. & Porky, 10 In.	165.00
Bank, Figural, Bust Of Abraham Lincoln, Channeled Base, 5 1/4 x 3 1/4 In.	4600.00
Bank, George Washington Bust	6900.00
Bank, House, Birds On Roof, Cat Climbing Side, Slot On Chimney, 4 1/2 In.	6900.00
Bank, Human Head Form, Slot Is Open Mouth, 5 5/8 In.	750.00
Bank, Leonard On Front, Monkey Over Coin Slot, Manganese Design	7400.00
Bank, Onion Shape	1900.00
Bank, Saint Bernard	3737.00

Bank, Yellow Slip, Clear Glaze, 19th Century, 8 3/4 In. 1380.00
Basket, Pierced Lid, Knob Finial, Rope Twist Handle Headed By Masks, 8 1/2 In. 6900.00
Bean Pot, Molded Strap Handle Over Vase Of Fruit, Simon Singer, 1880s, 5 3/4 In. 460.00
Bottle, Incised Eagle, 1814, 5 1/2 In. 1265.00
Bowl, Bands Of Rings & Squiggle Work In White Slip, Green Glaze, 11 1/4 In. 1955.00
Bowl, Bands Of White Slip Squiggle Work, Mottled Glaze, 12 In. 7130.00
Bowl, Coggled Rim, Yellow Slip Ware, 13 x 2 3/4 In. 770.00
Bowl, Yellow Slip Decorated, Coggled Rim, Word Cake Appears, 12 In. 275.00
Bowl, Yellow Slip Design, Luchia, Europe, 8 1/2 x 3 1/4 In. 71.50
Charger, Coggled Rim, Yellow Slip Design, Dark Overglaze, 12 In. 192.00
Cigar & Match Holder, Lion 650.00
Creamer, Gray Tin, Gallery Lip, 4 1/2 In. 80.00
Crock, Double Incised Band, Handle, Dark Glaze, 5 3/4 In. 110.00
Crock, Red, Black Design, Incised Band, 10 3/4 In. . . . . .148.00 to 163.00
Crock, Sawtooth Design Lip, Ear Handles, August 20, 1838, 1 Gal. 1980.00
Cup & Saucer, Daubs Of Brown Glaze, Handle Tapering To Foot, 3 1/8 In. 633.00
Cuspidor, Cream Slip, Brown & Green Glaze, Shenandoah, 6 1/4 In. 515.00
Cuspidor, John Bell, 4 1/2 In. 425.00
Dish, Coggled Rim, Brown, Yellow Slip Design, 7 1/4 In. 192.00
Dish, Coggled Rim, Orange, Yellow Slip Design, 7 1/4 In. 165.00
Dish, Loaf, Coggled Edge, 3 Yellow Horizontal Bands, 15 5/8 In. 2530.00
Dish, Loaf, Coggled Edge, Yellow Squiggle Design, 19th Century, 14 In. 2530.00
Dish, Loaf, White & Brown Slip & Green Glaze, John Bell, 13 1/2 In. 1955.00
Figurine, Dog, Basket In Mouth 2310.00
Figurine, Dog, Seated, Brown, Hand Tooled Chair & Pad Lock, 8 1/4 In. 357.00
Figurine, Dog, Seated, Unglazed, Tooled Coat, Newcomerstown, 9 1/2 In. 2310.00
Figurine, Dog, Spaniel, 7 1/4 In. 3500.00
Figurine, Eagle, 1814, 7 1/2 In. 9200.00
Figurine, Frog, Green, 6 In. 330.00
Figurine, Sheep, Next To Tree Trunk, Oval Plinth, 6 1/4 x 5 In. 3680.00
Figurine, Woman With Child, Painted, 5 3/4 In. 143.00
Flask, Indian Profile, Incised, T. Flows, Black Glaze, Early 19th Century, 5 3/4 In. 1100.00
Flowerpot, Attached Underplate, White Slip, Green Glazed, 8 1/2 In. 495.00
Flowerpot, Coggle Wheel Rim, Attached Conforming Saucer, White Slip, 6 1/4 In. 633.00
Flowerpot, Rosettes Above Tapering Body, Floral Over Acorn Drop, 12 1/4 In. 288.00
Flowerpot, Waynesboro Glaze, 5 1/4 In. 1095.00
Jar, Brown Glaze, W. Smith, Womelsdorf, Pa., 5 1/2 In. 93.00
Jar, Cover, Manganese Slip Design, Ridged Rim, Applied Molded Handle, 9 In. 1265.00
Jar, Cover, Red Glaze Bottom Border, Body Of Green Glaze, Red Splotches, 7 In. 2200.00
Jar, Green Glaze Rim, Egg Shape, 19th Century, 9 In. 150.00
Jar, Interior Glaze, John Bell, Waynesboro, Egg Shape, 7 1/2 In. 137.00
Jar, Mottled Green Brown Glaze, Applied Ribbed Handles, Egg Shape, 18 3/4 In. 440.00
Jar, Ribbed Strap Handle, Egg Shape, 9 In. 220.00
Jar, Sgraffito Design At Sides, Eagle Holding Banner, Liberty, 1809, 9 1/4 In. 5750.00
Jar, Storage, Orange Glaze, 19th Century, 10 In. 135.00
Jar, Tooled Lines, Amber Glaze, 2 Strap Handles, Egg Shape, 5 5/8 In. 190.00
Jar, Yellow Slip Sgraffito, Applied Rope Handles, 8 In. 785.00
Jar, Zigzag Design, Green Amber Glaze, 6 5/8 In. 175.00
Jug, Blue, Green, Tan, Ribbed Strap Handle, 5 1/2 In. 165.00
Jug, Brown Glaze, Moravian, 11 In. 67.00
Jug, Bulbous Shape, Dark Brown Slip, Wheel Thrown, Applied Handle, 7 In. 110.00
Jug, Center Band Of Incised Squiggle Design, Signed E + K 1854, 13 1/4 In. 1495.00
Jug, Clear Glaze, Overall Black Speckles, Ribbed Strap Handle, 6 5/8 In. 175.00
Jug, Dark Brown Manganese, Applied Molded Handle, 19th Century, 8 x 5 In. 575.00
Jug, Green, Rust, White, Double Handles, 8 In. 165.00
Jug, Green, White, Pumpkin, Ribbed Strap Handle, 6 In. 175.00
Jug, Slip Washed & Glazed, Egg Shape, Applied Handle, 4 3/4 In. 8625.00
Jug, Strap Handle, Clear Glaze, Black Splotches, Egg Shape, 9 In. 110.00
Jug, Strap Handle, Yellow Running Slip, Pumpkin Glaze, 9 In. 275.00
Jug, Wine, Applied Masks, Leaves, Berries, White Slip & Manganese Glaze, 6 In. 575.00
Lamp, Fat, Manganese Glaze, 5 7/8 x 4 1/2 In. 690.00
Match Case, Hanging, Owl On Front, Yellow Ground, Round, 3 1/2 In. Diam. 220.00

Mug, Handle, Brown & Cream Glaze, Signed, Shenandoah, 3 1/2 In. 1207.00
Mug, Hunt Relief, Silvered Trim Lines, Impressed Mark, Samuel Hollins, 5 3/8 In. 920.00
Mug, Strap Handle, Molded Bands, Hayes & Wheeler Mug, 6 In. 522.00
Mustard Pot, Green, Brass Top Closure, England, 4 1/4 x 4 3/4 In. 38.00
Pie Plate, Coggled Rim, Yellow Slip Design, 8 1/2 In. 385.00
Pitcher, Coggle-Wheel Design, 8 1/4 In. 695.00
Pitcher, Hunting Scene, Multiglaze, 8 In. 4900.00
Pitcher, Incised Rings, Butterscotch Glaze, 19th Century, 8 In. 175.00
Pitcher, New Geneva, Black Slip Freehand Floral Design, 7 In. 330.00
Pitcher, New Geneva, Brown Slip Freehand Floral Design, 5 In. . . . . .192.00 to 358.00
Pitcher, New Geneva, Brown Slip Freehand Floral Design, 7 In. 165.00
Pitcher, New Geneva, Brown Slip Stenciled Scroll Design, 7 In. 190.00
Pitcher, New Geneva, Red Brown Slip Freehand Floral Design, 8 In. . . . . .165.00 to 330.00
Pitcher, Pineapple, Multiglaze, 6 In. 1675.00
Pitcher, Slip Colored, Green To Rust, Wheel Thrown, Applied Handle, c.1920, 7 1/2 In. . 600.00
Plate, 3-Line, Slip, Serrated Edge, 8 In. 175.00
Plate, Center Pot With Tulips, Stems, Brown & Green Glaze, J. Medinger, 8 3/4 In. 1035.00
Plate, Coggle Wheel Rim, Flowerpot Center, Tulips, Daubs Of Green, 11 3/4 In. 9200.00
Plate, Coggled Wheel Rim, 2 Quill Squigglework In White Slip, 13 3/8 In. 1725.00
Plate, Eagle With Breast Plate, Crimped Rim, 1809, 8 3/4 In. 1840.00
Plate, Sgraffito Grapes & Tulips, White Slip, 1796, 11 In. 440.00
Plate, Stylized Flower & Flowerpot, White & Brown, 6 1/4 In. 805.00
Plate, Yellow Glaze, Green & Red Daubs, Incised Tobacco Leaf, 10 In. 8050.00
Plate, Yellow Slip Pinwheel, 7 1/2 In. 137.00
Plate, Yellow Slip Wavy Line Design, 7 1/2 In. 165.00
Plate, Yellow, Slip Decorated, Tooled Rim, 9 3/4 In. 395.00
Pot, Finial Cover, Applied Handle, Raised Finial, Dark Green Metallic Glaze, 4 In. 38.00
Shaving Dish, Design Of Comb, Razor, Scissors & Cloth, Yellow Slip, 8 1/4 In. 2990.00
Shaving Mug, 3 1/4 In. 450.00
Teapot, Cover, Silver Mounts, Flowering Branches, Wooden Handle, 1755, 4 In. 748.00
Teapot, England, c.1800, 4 3/4 In. 172.00
Tobacco Jar, Cover, Ribbed, Twisted Rope Handles, Finial, Signed, Shenandoah, 7 In. . . 1092.00
Wall Pocket, Brown, Yellow Bands, 1798, 6 1/2 In. 165.00
Washboard, Wooden Frame, Mottled Brown On Orange Glaze, 12 x 7 In. 1100.00
Whistle, Bird, Slip Design, Pair 275.00

REGOUT, see Maastricht category.

RICHARD was the mark used on acid-etched cameo glass vases, bowls, night-lights, and lamps made in Lorraine, France, during the 1920s. The pieces were very similar to the other French cameo glasswares made by Daum, Galle, and others.

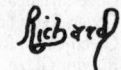

Vase, Amethyst Floral On Powder Blue Ground, Signed, 4 In. 550.00
Vase, Cobalt Florals, Orange Ground, Signed, 4 1/4 In. 275.00
Vase, Mountain & Lake, Cobalt Blue, Orange Ground, 13 1/2 In. . . . .*Illus* 2310.00

What to do when the power fails? If only a few rooms are affected, the problem may be an overloaded circuit. Turn off major appliances and the light switches and replace any burned-out fuses or rest the circuit breaker. When you turn appliances and lights back on, if the power fails again, call an electrician.

Richard, Vase, Mountain & Lake, Cobalt Blue, Orange Ground, 13 1/2 In

RIDGWAY pottery has been made in the Staffordshire district in England since 1808 by a series of companies with the name Ridgway. The transfer-design dinner sets are the most widely known product. They are still being made. Other pieces of Ridgway are listed under Flow Blue.

Bowl, Oriental Birds, 1814	185.00
Bowl, Vegetable, Cover, Handles, Scalloped, 1927, 10 x 8 1/2 In.	175.00
Butter, Flow Blue	25.00
Dish, Serving, Ironstone, Floral, Cobalt Blue, Gilt Edge, Openwork Handles, 11 In.	145.00
Eggcup, Osborne, Flow Blue	125.00
Mug, Coaching Days, Black Transfer, Brown Glaze, Silver Luster Rim & Handle, 4 In.	10.00
Pitcher, Raised Figural Motif, Applied Handle, Tan, 8 3/4 In.	35.00
Pitcher, Seaweed, Flow Blue, 6 1/2 In.	195.00
Plate, City Hall Of New York, Medallion Design, Rose, Leaf Border, 9 3/4 In.	220.00
Plate, Ruggles House, Black, 10 In.	175.00
Plate, Turkey, Flow Blue, 10 In.	110.00
Platter, Gainesborough, Flow Blue, 16 1/4 x 11 3/4 In.	55.00
Platter, Garland Design, Scalloped Edge, Cobalt Blue, 1912, 17 1/2 x 14 In.	165.00
Platter, Lonsdale, Gold Trim, Flow Blue, 16 In.	265.00
Platter, Oriental, Blue, White, 17 In.	265.00
Soup, Dish, Oriental Birds, Black	150.00
Soup, Dish, Pembroke Hall, Dark Blue, 10 In.	175.00
Sugar, Shoe Blossom, Flow Blue	300.00
Tea Set, Chintz, Blue & White, c.1882, 15 Piece	550.00
Teapot, Rosebud Finial, Peking, 1845, 8 3/4 In.	400.00 to 750.00
Tureen, Gravy, Cover, Undertray, Trinity Hall, Cambridge, Dark Blue	925.00
Vase, Chinese, Flow Blue, 8 1/4 In.	265.00

RIFLES that are firearms are not listed in this book. BB guns and air rifles are listed in the Toy category.

RIVIERA dinnerware was made by the Homer Laughlin Co. of Newell, West Virginia, from 1938 to 1950. The pattern was similar in coloring and in mood to Fiesta and Harlequin. The Riviera plates and cup handles were square. For more information, see *Kovels' Depression Glass & Dinnerware Price List.*

Blue, Cup	7.00
Blue, Tumbler, Handle	75.00
Cobalt Blue, Plate, 7 In.	50.00
Green, Bowl, Oatmeal, 6 In.	85.00
Green, Casserole, Cover	95.00
Green, Cup	7.00 to 12.00
Green, Plate, 6 In.	7.00 to 8.00
Green, Teapot	175.00
Green, Tumbler, Handle	75.00
Ivory, Bowl, Round, 9 In.	20.00
Ivory, Butter, 1/2 Lb.	155.00
Ivory, Plate, 9 In.	10.00
Ivory, Tumbler, Handle	150.00
Light Green, Plate, 9 In.	10.00
Light Green, Shaker	5.00
Light Green, Sugar	8.00
Mauve, Cup	12.00
Mauve, Pitcher, Juice	350.00
Mauve, Shaker	5.00
Red, Bowl, 5 In.	6.50
Red, Casserole, Cover	150.00
Red, Creamer	7.00
Red, Cup	7.00
Red, Soup, Flat	15.00 to 32.00
Yellow, Bowl, 5 In.	6.50
Yellow, Cup	7.00
Yellow, Platter, Lug Handle, 11 1/2 In.	20.00

Yellow, Sugar 6.5

Yellow, Tumbler, Handle 75.0

ROBLIN Art Pottery was founded in 1898 by Alexander W. Robertson and Linna Irelan in San Francisco, California. The pottery closed in 1906. The firm made faience with green, tan, dull blue, or gray glazes. Decorations were usually animal shapes. Some red clay pieces were made.

Cauldron, Dark Brown Matte Glaze, 2 1/2 x 2 Ft. 230.0

Vase, Brown Bisque, Urn Form, 2 In. ....120.00 to 145.0

Vase, Peacock Feathers, Gourd Shape, 10 1/4 In. 1540.0

ROCKINGHAM, in the United States, is a pottery with a brown glaze that resembles tortoiseshell. It was made from 1840 to 1900 by many American potteries. Mottled brown Rockingham wares were first made in England at the Rockingham factory. Other types of ceramics were also made by the English firm. Related pieces may be listed in the Bennington category.

Bank, Washington, On Horse, 6 1/2 In. 355.0

Bottle, Book Shape, Departed Spirits, 5 1/2 In. 300.0

Bottle, Flower Urn Both Sides, 10 In. 115.0

Bottle, Toby, Man Astride Barrel, 10 In. 66.0

Bowl, Tulips On Edge & Base, Brown, Cream Mottled, 10 1/2 x 3 In. 86.0

Butter Tub, Cover, Yellowware, Ribbed 130.0

Chamberstick, Grape & Vine Molded Base, 4 1/2 x 1 3/4 In., Pair 250.0

Coffeepot, Chinese Men 66.0

Cuspidor, 8 1/4 In. 45.0

Figurine, Bull, c.1860 .... 1150.0

Figurine, Dog, Brown Over Yellowware, 1840, 10 1/2 In. 950.0

Figurine, Dog, Seated, Free Standing Front Legs, 10 3/4 In. 300.0

Figurine, Dog, Sitting, Brown Glaze, 11 x 8 x 6 In. 285.0

Figurine, Poodle, Coleslaw On Head, Nose & Ears, Hindquarters 95.0

Jug, Cover, Wire Bale, Wooden Hale 440.0

Picture Frame, Brown Mottling, White Base, Oval, 8 x 7 In. 225.0

Pitcher, Cupid & Psyche, Molded, 9 In. 100.0

Pitcher, Foliage, 9 1/8 In. 100.0

Pitcher, Hunter & His Dog Design, Brown & White, 9 In. 165.0

Spoon Rest, Mammy Face 185.0

Tureen, Soup, Pale Yellow Leaves, Bands, Apple Green, Fired-Gold Trim, 12 In. 630.0

ROGERS, see John Rogers category.

ROOKWOOD pottery was made in Cincinnati, Ohio, from 1880 to 1960. All of this art pottery is marked, most with the famous flame mark. The R is reversed and placed back to back with the letter P. Flames surround the letters. After 1900, a Roman numeral was added to the mark to indicate the year. The name and some of the molds were purchased in 1984. A few new pieces were made, but these were glazed in colors not used by the original company.

Ashtray, Advertising, Boss Kerosene Ranges, Logo, 1947, 5 3/4 In. 38.00

Ashtray, Black High Glaze, 1957, 6 1/2 In. 350.00

Ashtray, Fox, Beige High Glaze, 1946, 6 3/4 In. 275.00

Ashtray, Frog, Open Mouth, Gunmetal Brown Glaze, 2 3/4 In. 302.00

Ashtray, Harp, Light Green High Glaze, 1927, 5 1/2 In. 195.00

Ashtray, Light Brown High Glaze, 1947, 6 1/2 In. 250.00

Ashtray, Tan High Glaze, 1949, 6 1/2 In. 275.00

Bookends, Artichoke, Brown High Glaze, 1956, 3 1/2 In. 250.00

Bookends, Eagle, Gray 600.00

Bookends, Elephant, Brown Matte Glaze, 1921, 5 1/2 In. 375.00

Bookends, Liberty Bell, Green Matte 400.00

Bookends, Light Brown Glaze, 1945, 5 1/2 In. 395.00

Bookends, Owl, Brown High Glaze, 1949, 4 1/2 In. 275.00

Bookends, Owl, Double, Mottled Brown Flambe Matte, Impressed, 1929, 7 In. 425.00

Bookends, Owl, Yellow, Green High Glaze, 1946, 6 In. 275.00

Bookends, Peacock, 1921 . . . . 375.00
Bookends, Rook, Standing In Open Book, Green Glaze, 1924, 7 In. 525.00
Bookends, Seated Woman, Reading Book, 6 x 6 1/2 In. 655.00
Bookends, Ships, Ivory Color, William McDonald, 1925, 5 5/8 In. 138.00
Bookends, Trees, Green, Brown Matte Glaze, William McDonald, 1929, 5 1/2 In. 880.00
Bookends, Trees, Matte, Light Green & Rust, 1929, 6 In. 550.00
Bookends, Union Terminal, Presentation, 1933, 4 5/8 In. 5500.00
Bowl, Birds On Interior, Matthew Andrew Daly, 1884, 10 In. 350.00
Bowl, Floral, Mottled Green Over Blue Glaze, 1921, 8 In. 165.00
Bowl, Flower Form, Blue Glaze, 1928, 13 5/16 In. 165.00
Bowl, Squat, Banded Dentil, Brown Matte Glaze, 1922, 6 In. 175.00
Bowl, Stylized Geometrics, Molded Leaves, Blue, Green Matte Glaze, 9 x 3 In. 286.00
Bowl, Stylized Paisley Border, Sara Sax, 1928, 3 x 6 1/2 In. 880.00
Bowl, White Matte, Blue Interior, 2 Handles, 1921, 10 1/2 In. 225.00
Bowl, With Frog, Octagonal, Gold, 1920s, 8 In. 125.00
Bowl, Yellow Matte Glaze, 6 In. 200.00
Box, Dogwood, Turquoise High Glaze, 1944, 4 1/2 x 3 1/4 In. 135.00
Bust, Young Woman, 1931, 8 1/4 In. 155.00
Cake Plate, Blue Ship, 1925, 14 In. 522.00
Candleholder, Flowers, Light Green Matte Glaze, Pair 225.00
Candlestick, Blue, 6 1/2 In., Pair 735.00
Candlestick, Egyptian Maidens, Blue, 1920, 12 In., Pair 695.00
Candlestick, Embossed Grape Leaves, Matte, 1922, Pair 275.00
Candlestick, Light Blue Glaze, 1920, 6 In., Pair 250.00
Candlestick, Pink, Flowers, No. 2311, 1921, 1 1/2 In., Pair 86.00
Chandelier, Architectural Faience, Embossed Fruit, 6 1/8 x 12 1/2 In. 605.00
Charger, Blue Viking Ships On Border, Ivory Ground, 13 3/4 In. 172.00
Chocolate Pot, Amelia B. Sprague, 1894 . . . . 995.00
Chocolate Pot, Brown Glaze, 1920, 10 1/2 In. 395.00
Chocolate Pot, Holly, With Berries, Gray To Rose, 1903, 10 In. 2250.00
Clock, Black Panther, 1950, 7 1/2 In. 600.00
Compote, Cherub Design On Pedestal, Cobalt Blue Glaze, 1920, 10 1/2 In. 595.00
Creamer, Orange Floral Motif, Brown Glaze, 1899, 2 1/2 In. 190.00
Cup, On Pedestal, Blue, 1931 . . . . 110.00
Doorstop, Cat, Cobalt High Glaze, 1924, 8 1/2 In. 3520.00
Ewer, Clover Blossoms, Yellow, Green, Brown Ground, Standard Glaze, 1894, 9 In. 825.00
Ewer, Dogwood, Yellow, Orange, Green Ground, Standard Glaze, Anna Valentien 522.50
Ewer, Dragons Around Body, Kataro Shirayamadani, 1894, 17 1/8 In. 3850.00
Ewer, Flowers, Trumpet Vine, Standard Glaze, Sallie Toohey, 1893, 9 x 4 In. 1650.00
Ewer, Goldstone & Tiger Eye, Albert R. Valentien, 22 In. 1980.00
Ewer, Oak Leaf & Acorn Design, Carrie Steinle, 1899, 8 1/8 In. 770.00
Ewer, Signed, Artus Van Briggle, 1888, 7 1/2 In. 3000.00
Ewer, Silver Overlay, Pansies Under Floral Overlay, Josephine Zettel, 1896, 7 In. 1320.00
Ewer, Virginia Creeper Leaves, Vines & Berries, Sallie Coyne, 6 1/2 In. 550.00
Figurine, Dog, Boxer, Butch, Seated, 4 1/2 In. 440.00
Figurine, Duck, Aqua, 4 In. 75.00
Figurine, Fawn, Ivory Matte Glaze, 1930, 6 1/2 In. 200.00
Flower Bowl, Stylized Flowers Rim, Mauve Ground, 3-Footed, 1921, WEH, 6 In. 190.00
Flower Frog, Turtle, 1930, 2 7/8 In. 495.00
Humidor, Blue Matte Glaze, 1929, 6 3/4 In. 250.00
Humidor, Green High Glaze, 1920, 4 1/2 In. 275.00
Inkwell, Large Bird Standing On Leaf Form, Logo, 6 1/2 x 11 In. 1190.00
Jar, Cover, Hanging Flowers, Brown Butterfat Ground, Charles Todd, 1918, 6 In. 770.00
Jar, Potpourri, Yellow Flowers, Black, Yellow Ground, Shirayamadani, 1923, 6 In. 3575.00
Jug, Clover Design, Standard Glaze, Josephine Zettel, 1895, 4 1/2 In. 550.00
Jug, Cream, Blue Glaze, 1919, 3 1/2 In. 85.00
Jug, Portrait, Portuguese Man, Stopper, Constance Baker, 1899, 10 x 6 In. 1870.00
Lamp, Shade, Green High Glaze, 1950, 13 1/2 In. 225.00
Lamp Base, Triple Seahorse, Rose Fechheimer, c.1905, 15 1/4 In. 3850.00
Loving Cup, Green High Glaze, 1937, 6 1/2 In. 250.00
Mug, Modeled Peacock Feather, 2 Tones Of Green & Blue, 4 3/4 In. 440.00
Mug, Wiedeman Brewing Co., Pewter Lid, 1948, 5 3/8 In. 605.00
Paperweight, Bull, Light Brown, Butcher's Supply Co., 1949 . . . . 65.00

Paperweight, Cat, Chartreuse High Glaze, Louise Abel, 6 7/8 In. 660.00
Paperweight, Elephant, 1928, 3 1/2 In. ....250.00 to 300.00
Paperweight, Elephant, Light Blue Matte Glaze, 1945, 3 1/2 In. 295.00
Paperweight, Elephant, Seated, Kataro Shirayamadani, 1947, 3 3/4 In. 605.00
Paperweight, Fruit Basket, Sallie Toohey, 1927, 3 1/8 In. 550.00
Paperweight, Goat, 1930, 6 1/4 In. 192.00
Paperweight, Rook, Advertising, Tan & Dark Blue 975.00
Paperweight, Ship, McDonald, White Matte, 1928 .... 395.00
Paperweight, Squirrel, 1928, 4 1/8 In. 440.00
Pin Tray, Nude Figure, 1924 .... 260.00
Pitcher, Clouds, Spiders & Spider Webs, N.J. Hirschfeld, c.1882, 6 1/2 In. 805.00
Pitcher, Tricornered, Incised Oak Leaves, Blue Ground, Albert Pons, 1900, 6 In. ... 467.00
Pitcher, Yellow Blossoms, Olive-Green Ground, Valentien, 1887, 12 x 6 In. 825.00
Planter, Stylized Leaves, Brown-Green Glaze, 8 3/4 In. 550.00
Plaque, Landscape Scene, Lake, Trees, Mountains, Blue, Ivory, Pink, 8 x 11 In. 2645.00
Plaque, Landscape Scene, Vellum, 1913, 4 x 8 In. 2185.00
Plaque, Sailing Ship, 12 In. 850.00
Plaque, Snow Clad Hillside, Pale Purple, Gray, Vellum, Epply, 6 x 8 In. 1375.00
Plaque, Snow Scene, Wind-Swept Tree, Pink Sky, Frame, McDermott, 1915, 11 In. 4675.00
Plaque, Snow-Capped Rockies, Meadow, Vellum, McDermott, 1916, 8 x 10 In. 4400.00
Plaque, Tree Along A Lake, Pale Brown, Pink, Vellum, Mahogany Frame, 5 x 7 In. 1760.00
Plaque, Vellum Glaze, Various Colors, Sara Sax, 1915, 12 1/8 x 9 In. 7475.00
Plaque, Winter Scene, Trees Along A Stream, Pale Blue, Gray, Frame, 8 x 5 In. 2090.00
Plaque, Woodland Scene, Vellum Glaze, E.T. Hurley, 1939, 11 1/2 x 6 3/4 In. 4400.00
Plate, Blue Ship, c.1930, 9 1/8 In., 6 Piece 412.00
Sign, Advertising, 2 Sides, 1925, 3 3/4 x 12 1/2 In. 1760.00
Sign, Dealer's, Rust Rook, Rookwood Pottery, Fine Tiles, 1926 .... 1200.00
Sugar & Creamer, Ship, Blue 145.00
Tankard, Beet Red High Glaze, 1949, 5 In. 159.00
Tea Set, Iris Glaze, Sallie Coyne, 3 Piece 2900.00
Tile, 4-Petal Leaf Design, Yellow, Green, Rose Ground, Oak Frame, 4 In. 154.00
Tile, Basket Of Fruit, 2 Humming Birds, Multicolored Glaze, Frame, 6 x 12 In. 1430.00
Tile, Blue Ship, 1925, 6 In. 357.00
Tile, Garden Scene, Trees, Wide Oak Frame, Square, 12 In. 2530.00
Tile, Gazebo Scene, Blue, Green Trees, Light Blue Sky, 1904, 12 In. 2640.00
Tile, Geometric Design On 4 Sides, Red Flower, Gray Border, Frame, 4 In. 468.00
Tile, Geometric Design, Blue, Cream, Yellow Matte, Wide Oak Frame, 4 In. 198.00
Tile, Geometric Design, Yellow, Blue Glaze, Frame, 4 In. 176.00
Tile, Green, Brown Leaves, Brown Vines, Black, Tan Ground, Oak Frame, 4 x 5 In. .. 440.00
Tile, Incised Tree Landscape, Blue To Green With Trees Reflected In Water, 8 In. 2970.00
Tile, Raised Classical Figures, Light Blue Matte Glaze, Ivory, 8 x 19 In. 920.00
Tile, Raised Design, Blue, Tobacco Glaze, Oak Frame, 4 In. 165.00
Tile, Raised Greek Key Design, Gray Matte Glaze, Rose Ground, Oak Frame, 4 In. ... 231.00
Tile, Sailing Ship, Matte, Dark Green, Tobacco Brown, Red Glaze, Oak Frame, 12 In. ... 862.00
Tile, Ship At Sea Scene, With Fish At Bottom, Multicolored, Frame, 6 In. 660.00
Tile, Stylized Blossoms & Leaves, Deep Rose Ground, Cushion, Square, 4 In. 385.00
Tile, Stylized Flowers Design, Blue, Green, Tobacco, Oak Frame, 4 In. 132.00
Tile, Stylized Flowers, Leaf Design, Yellow, Brown, Green, Blue Ground, Frame, 4 In. .. 176.00
Tile, Stylized Green Flower, Bone Ground, Arts & Crafts, Impressed Mark, 4 In. 495.00
Tile, Trees, Red Leaves, Brown & Tan Ground, Frame, Square, 18 In. 6050.00
Tile, Tulip, Pink, Cream Colored Leaves, Light Green Ground, Frame, 6 In. 1540.00
Tile, Windmill Design, White Matte, Dark To Light Blue Ground, 1919, 6 In. 286.00
Tile, Yellow Geometric Flowers Design, Green, Yellow Lion, Oak Frame, 4 In. 440.00
Tray, Brown Matte Glaze, Incised Peacock Feather Design, 1921, 7 x 3 In. 176.00
Tray, Incised Geometric Design, Brown, Blue, Green Matte Glaze, 1910, 10 In. 242.00
Tray, Long Leaf, Light Blue High Glaze, 1950, 15 In. 135.00
Tray, Owl, Green Matte Glaze, 1905, 4 In. 1870.00
Trivet, Matte Red Glaze, Logo, 6 In. 98.00
Vase, 2 Female Figures Draped Around Rim, Anna M. Valentien, 1910, 6 In. 3850.00
Vase, Abstract Flowers Design, Vera Tischler, 1924, 6 1/2 In. 250.00
Vase, Apples, Grapes, Vines, Peach Rose Matte Ground, Charles Todd, 1917, 16 In. 3080.00
Vase, Bamboo Tree Design, Yellow Matte Glaze, 1921, 6 1/2 In. 385.00
Vase, Band Of Stylized Flowers, Garnet Turquoise Matte Glaze, 1915, 14 x 10 In. 3190.00

Vase, Banded Daisy Design, Brown High Glaze, 1952, 6 In. 139.00
Vase, Berries & Leaves, Pink & Green Glaze, 1921, 4 1/2 In. 175.00
Vase, Berries, Leaves, Green, Yellow, Black, White, Mauve Rim, Sara Sax, 8 1/4 In. 3250.00
Vase, Birch Trees, Blue Matte Ground, Kataro Shirayamadani, 1911, 9 In. 2475.00
Vase, Birds & Trees Under Standard Glaze, Signed, 5 1/2 x 6 In. 197.00
Vase, Birds In Flight, Brown, Ocher, Pale Green, Yellow Ground, 14 In. 2185.00
Vase, Black Iris Glaze, Peacock Feather Design, Carl Schmidt, 1908, 9 1/2 In. 6500.00
Vase, Blossoms, Blue Vines, Blue, Pink & Green Ground, Charles Todd, 1922, 8 1/2 In. . 2860.00
Vase, Blue Dragonflies, Deep Red Ground, Matte Glaze, 1905, 7 In. 3190.00
Vase, Blue, Green Flowers, Vellum, Shirayamadani, 1935, 8 1/2 x 5 In., Pair 1610.00
Vase, Blue, Green Glaze, Fluted Neck, 1964, 10 In. 185.00
Vase, Blue, Green Matte Glaze, 1920, 8 1/2 In. 440.00
Vase, Branches Of Palm Fronds, Amber, Green, Brown, Mary Nourse, 1903, 12 1/2 In. .. 1610.00
Vase, Brown Flowers, Blue, Yellow Centers, Charles Todd, 1913, 8 In. 605.00
Vase, Brown Matte Glaze, Red, Blue Ground, Albert Pons, 1907, 6 1/2 In. 605.00
Vase, Bud, Sailboat Against Horizon, Harriette Strafer, 1895, 5 3/4 In. 4070.00
Vase, Butterfat Glaze, Kay Ley, 1945, 6 3/8 In. 825.00
Vase, Butterfly, Green High Glaze, 1945, 4 1/2 In. 165.00
Vase, Carved Flowers, Blue, Green, Purple Matte Glaze, William Hentschel, 1914, 7 In. . 990.00
Vase, Carved Oak Leaves, Vines Around Top, Green Matte Glaze, Cecil Duell, 9 In. 660.00
Vase, Carved Vines, Grape Clusters, Green Matte Glaze, Sallie Toohey, 1905, 7 In. 1100.00
Vase, Cattail, Brown High Glaze, 1959, 5 In. 195.00
Vase, Cherries, Laura E. Lindeman, 1904, 5 1/8 In. 275.00
Vase, Cherry Blossom Branches, Margaret McDonald, 1923, 8 1/2 In. 715.00
Vase, Cherry Blossoms, Green Base, Pale Red Ground, Vellum Glaze, 7 In. 690.00
Vase, Cherry Blossoms, Iris Glaze, Lenore Asbury, 10 1/2 In. 3500.00
Vase, Clover Design, Green Matte Glaze, Sallie Toohey, 1905, 4 In. 660.00
Vase, Coromandel Glaze, 1932, 3 3/4 In. 522.00
Vase, Dark Green High Glaze, 1946, 13 In. 250.00
Vase, Day Lilies, 2 Birds, High Glaze, Arthur Conant, 1922, 17 1/2 In. 3900.00
Vase, Decorative Band, Yellow Matte Glaze, 1940, 5 In. 140.00
Vase, Deep Purple Matte Crystalline Glaze, Black Highlights, 1919, 7 In. 660.00
Vase, Dogwood Blossoms, Lorinda Epply, 1907, 8 In. 660.00
Vase, Dogwood Branch, Brown, Green Ground, Standard Glaze, Edward Hurley, 8 x 4 In. 605.00
Vase, Dolphin Handles, Pale Green High Glaze, 1946, 10 In. 189.00
Vase, Dragonflies, Blue, Yellow, Blue, Green Matte Ground, Charles Todd, 1912, 7 In. .. 1650.00
Vase, Dusty Rose Flower, Matte Glaze, No. 1698, 3 3/4 x 6 In. 230.00
Vase, Dutchman Portrait, Grace Young, 1903, 8 In. 1750.00
Vase, Exotic Birds, Flowers, Gray, Vibrant Blue Body, Edward Hurley, 10 In. 3500.00
Vase, Fern Design, Rose, Green Matte Glaze, Shirayamadani, 1915, 8 In. 440.00
Vase, Fern, Crackled Yellow Matte Glaze, 1916, 7 7/8 In. 110.00
Vase, Figure Of Woman Draped Around Rim, Rose Moss Glaze, 1901, 3 x 4 In. 2530.00
Vase, Fish, Brown, Green Iris Glaze, Edward T. Hurley, 1904, 6 1/2 x 5 In. 1100.00
Vase, Fish, Green, Blue, 4 x 7 In. 975.00
Vase, Fish, Swimming, Pale Turquoise, Dark Blue, Vellum, Edward T. Hurley, 10 In. 1840.00
Vase, Fish-Scale Pattern, Turquoise Blue, Cylindrical, No. 2769, 1924, 7 1/4 In. 144.00
Vase, Fleshy Pink Red Roses, Green Flowers, Red Ground, Hattie Wilcox, 1901, 9 In. ... 9900.00
Vase, Flower On Branch, Double Handles, Constance A. Baker, c.1900, 7 In. 137.00
Vase, Flowers & Butterflies, Blue Shaded To Gray, Lenore Asbury, 11 In. 1705.00
Vase, Flowers Bouquet Design, Ivory Glaze, Pink, Yellow, Blue, Green, Sara Sax, 5 In. .. 625.00
Vase, Flowers Design, Dark Brown, Blue Body, Wilhelmine Rehm, 1945, 9 1/4 In. 295.00
Vase, Flowers Design, Yellow, Green, Pink Ground, Vellum, 8 3/4 x 3 1/2 In. 690.00
Vase, Flowers, 3 Panels, Green Matte Glaze, Brown Highlights, 1921, 7 1/2 In. 220.00
Vase, Flowers, Bulbous, Mauve Over Pink, 1934, 5 In. 165.00
Vase, Flowers, Indigo, Oriental Style, Light Apricot, William Hentschel, 7 x 3 In. 1100.00
Vase, Flowers, Jewels, Jens Jensen, 7 In. 800.00
Vase, Flowers, Leaves, Blue, Peach Matte Ground, Charles Todd, 1920, 15 x 7 In. 5500.00
Vase, Flowers, Orange Poppies, Brown, Green Ground, Standard Glaze, 9 x 6 In. 825.00
Vase, Flowers, Pale Pink Tulips, Ivory, Blue Ground, Shirayamadani, 1945, 6 In. 825.00
Vase, Flowers, Pink, Ivory Anemones, Green Ground, Vellum, Conant, 7 x 3 In. 990.00
Vase, Flowers, Poppies, Brown Ground, Standard Glaze, Mary Nourse, 1903, 10 x 4 In. . 935.00
Vase, Flowers, Poppy, Standard Glaze, Jeannette Swing, 1903, 7 1/2 x 3 1/4 In. 715.00
Vase, Flowers, Red, Yellow, Blue, Charles Todd, 1918, 6 1/4 In. 550.00

Vase, Flowers, Standard Glaze, Edward T. Hurley, 1898, 8 1/2 In. 895.00
Vase, Flowers, Stylized Taupe, Blue Roses, Brown, Black, Elizabeth Barrett, 6 x 5 In. 825.00
Vase, Flowers, Wax Matte, Blue & Cream, Jens Jensen, 1934, 4 In. 695.00
Vase, Flowers, Yellow Tulips, Celadon Stems, Black, Green Ground, Iris Glaze, 9 In. 1980.00
Vase, Fluted Top, Magnolia Flowers, Kataro Shirayamadani, 1946, 7 1/2 In. 880.00
Vase, Fruit Branches, Flared Lip, Light Green, Ocher, Brown Ground, 1900, 13 In. 1035.00
Vase, Fruit, Flowers & Birds, Yellow High Glaze, Arthur Conant, 1921, 12 1/2 In. 9075.00
Vase, Geese, Pale Blue, Yellow, Vellum, Edith Noonan, 1907, 7 In. 1540.00
Vase, Geometric Design At Top, Matte, Yellow, 1923, 9 1/2 In. 286.00
Vase, Geometric Design, Green Matte Glaze, 1905, 6 In. 308.00
Vase, Geometric Design, White Ground, Ruben Earl Menzel, 1952, 7 3/4 In. 4495.00
Vase, Geometric, Green Matte Glaze, 1901, 3 x 1/2 In. 275.00
Vase, Geometric, Row Of Arches, Dark & Light Brown, Green Ground, Jens Jensen, 6 In. 632.00
Vase, Glossy Turquoise Glaze, Buff Clay Body, 20 x 16 In. 1210.00
Vase, Green, Red Glaze, 1916, 8 1/2 x 7 In. 374.00
Vase, Green, Standard Glaze, 4 1/2 In. 295.00
Vase, Green, Yellow Drip Glaze, 1951, 3 1/2 In. 295.00
Vase, Hawthorne Berries & Leaves, Plum Ground, Matte, 1905, 6 In. 3750.00
Vase, Incised Design, Black High Glaze, 1925, 8 1/4 In. 495.00
Vase, Incised Design, Green Matte Glaze, Maroon Highlights, 1905, 10 1/2 In. 1100.00
Vase, Incised Geometric Design, Matte, Maroon, Light Green Ground, 1913, 8 In. 605.00
Vase, Incised Vertical Leaves, Blue, Green, Maroon, William Hentschel, 1910, 4 In. 880.00
Vase, Incised, Turquoise High Glaze, 2 Handles, 1939, 8 1/2 In. 245.00
Vase, Indian Portrait, Adeliza D. Sehon, 1900, 8 1/4 In. 2640.00
Vase, Indian Portrait, Grace Young, 1901, 9 1/2 In. 6050.00
Vase, Indian Portrait, Ho-Wear Comanche, Sturgis Laurence, 1898, 9 In. 2300.00
Vase, Iris Blossoms, Flowers, Edward Diers, 1902, 7 5/8 In. 4370.00
Vase, Iris Blossoms, Lenore Asbury, 1908, 8 In. 1650.00
Vase, Iris Glaze, Pond Scene, Trees, Birds, Gray, Yellow, Green, Rothenbusch, 12 In. 2495.00
Vase, Iris Glaze, Tulip Design, Sara Sax, 1905, 10 1/2 In. 2900.00
Vase, Iris Glaze, White Poppy Motif, K. Van Horne, 1908, 7 In. 2200.00
Vase, Japanese Plum Blossoms, High Glaze, Shirayamadani, 1924, 5 1/2 In. 3500.00
Vase, Japanese Scene, 2 Chickens, Arthur Conant, 1919, 9 In. 7700.00
Vase, Jewel Porcelain, Painted Flowers, Blue Berries, Fred Rothenbusch, 1924, 6 In. 1760.00
Vase, Landscape, Blue, Pink, Green, Impressed Logo, Vellum, 1919, 10 3/4 In. 975.00
Vase, Landscape, Bushy Green Palms, Birds, Salmon, Vellum, Edward Hurley, 7 x 5 In. . 1760.00
Vase, Landscape, Impressed Logo, Vellum, 1919, 10 3/4 In. 975.00
Vase, Landscape, Trees, Blue, Green, Light Pink, Lenore Asbury, 1916, 9 1/2 In. 1320.00
Vase, Large Phoenix, Orange, Brown, Matthew A. Daly, 1898, 15 1/2 In. 3450.00
Vase, Lilies-Of-The-Valley, Iris Glaze, Carl Schmidt, 1909, 9 1/8 In. 7975.00
Vase, Lilies-Of-The-Valley, Pink Ground, Carl Schmidt, 1909, 8 1/4 x 4 1/2 In. 3080.00
Vase, Matte Glaze, Deco Frieze, Anna M. Valentien, 1904, 6 In. 995.00
Vase, Matte Glaze, Geometric Design, Elizabeth Barrett, 1944, 9 In. 325.00
Vase, Matte Glaze, Stylized Vine Design, Dark Blue, Brown, Charles Todd, 1920, 5 In. . . 295.00
Vase, Matte, Green, Pink Glaze, 1907, 8 1/2 In. 605.00
Vase, Mexican Design, Yellow, Green High Glaze, 1941, 5 1/2 In. 145.00
Vase, Molded Floral, Leaf Design, Yellow Matte Glaze, 1922, 9 In. 990.00
Vase, Molded Geometric Design, Green Matte Glaze, 1920, 9 1/2 In. 605.00
Vase, Molded Leaf & Flower, Green, Blue, Yellow Matte, 1918, 6 In. 286.00
Vase, Molded Leaves, Blue Matte Glaze, 1922, 7 In. 412.50
Vase, Molded Poppies, Matte, Yellow Glaze, 1924, 11 In. 2420.00
Vase, Molded Vertical Leaves, Medium Brown Matte Glaze, 1919, 11 1/2 In. 825.00
Vase, Nasturtium, Brown, Green Ground, Standard Glaze, Albert Valentien, 9 In. 1100.00
Vase, Oriental Figure Design, W.E. Hentschel, 1921, 8 x 10 In. 3500.00
Vase, Oxblood, Variegated Glaze, 1926, 15 5/8 In. 1980.00
Vase, Painted Irises, Dark Blue, Gray, Yellow Highlights, Green Foliage, 20 In. 3800.00
Vase, Palm Trees Reflected In Water, Vellum, Green, Cream, Edward Hurley, 9 In. 5750.00
Vase, Pastel Flowers, Ivory Ground, Gray Rim & Interior, Egg Shape, 5 In. 305.00
Vase, Pastoral Landscape, Frederick Rothenbusch, 1923, 7 1/4 In. 990.00
Vase, Peacock Feather Design, Rose, Green Matte Glaze, 1919, 8 In. 220.00
Vase, Pentagonal Rim, Diamond Design, Brown Matte Glaze, 1914, 8 1/2 In. 440.00
Vase, Pillow, Standard Glaze, 4 1/2 In. 245.00
Vase, Pink Magnolia On Cobalt, Wax Gloss, Jens Jensen, 6 In. 665.00

Vase, Pink, Green Flowers, Blue, Green Ground, 1905, 6 1/2 x 4 In. 1035.00
Vase, Raised Blossom Design Rim, Matte Glaze, 1910, 10 In. 355.00
Vase, Raised Flowers Design, Pink & Green Matte, 1927, 6 1/2 In. 385.00
Vase, Raised Flowers Design, Wax Matte Glaze, Blue Body, 1925, 8 1/2 In. 770.00
Vase, Raised Flowers Motif, Blue Glaze, 1928, 4 3/4 In. 150.00
Vase, Raised Flowers, Green, Rose Glaze, W. Hentschel, 1910, 10 x 6 1/2 In. 862.50
Vase, Red Flowers, Green Ground, Charles S. Todd, 1915, 7 1/4 x 4 1/4 In. 2530.00
Vase, Red, Green Flowers, Leaves, Black Outline, Vellum, Rose, Elizabeth Lincoln, 9 In. 862.00
Vase, Roses, Pink, Green, Blue, Cream, Vellum Glaze, 12 In. 1725.00
Vase, Scenic, Brown Trees By Mountain Lake, Vellum, Asbury, 1915, 8 x 5 In. 2310.00
Vase, Scenic, Castle By Lake, Purple Hills, 8 5/8 In. 10450.00
Vase, Scenic, Fred Rothenbusch, 1929, 13 1/4 In. 6325.00
Vase, Scenic, Vellum, Pink & Blue, 6 1/2 In. 1600.00
Vase, Scenic, Vellum, S.E. Coyne, 1912, 9 In. 1675.00
Vase, Sea Horses, Green Against Ocean Blue Ground, Sallie Toohey, 6 1/2 In. 1265.00
Vase, Seagulls, Open Wings, Green, 8 1/2 In. 1750.00
Vase, Sparrows, Oriental Grasses, Green, Brown, Gold Glaze, M. McDonald, 6 In. 385.00
Vase, Sprays Of White Jonquils, Yellow Centers, Sara Sax, 1908, 10 1/4 In. 7700.00
Vase, Spring Landscape, Young Trees, Lorinda Epply, 1908, 8 3/4 In. 1035.00
Vase, Squeezebag Design, Cactus, Aventurine Glaze, W. Hentschel, 1931, 6 In. 4400.00
Vase, Stork Design, Embossed, Green Matte Glaze, 1937, 11 1/4 In. 275.00
Vase, Stylized Bushes, Flowers, Blue Exterior, Rose Interior, 1917, 8 3/4 In. 795.00
Vase, Stylized Leaf Design, Brown Matte Glaze, Purple Highlights, 1910, 6 In. 550.00
Vase, Stylized Leaf, Blossom Design, Green, Yellow Matte Glaze, 1931, 7 1/2 In. 660.00
Vase, Stylized Leaves, Moss Matte Ground, W.T. Hentschel, 1926, 8 1/2 In. 1540.00
Vase, Stylized Light Green Water Lilies, Sea Green, Matthew Daly, 1900, 11 x 4 In. 5500.00
Vase, Trunks Of Trees Silhouetted Against Yellow Sky, E.T. Hurley, 1908, 8 1/2 In. 1980.00
Vase, Turquoise High Glaze, 1926, 4 In. 135.00
Vase, Vellum Glaze, Grape Design, Sallie Coyne, 1930, 7 x 5 1/2 In. 760.00
Vase, Vellum, Lenore Asbury, 1917, 10 In. 2950.00
Vase, Vertical Leaf Design, Blue Matte Glaze, 1923, 6 In. 495.00
Vase, Virginia Creeper Design, Standard Glaze, Sallie Toohey, 1900, 19 1/2 In. 1650.00
Vase, Walking Geese, White Matte Glaze, 1941, 5 In. 165.00
Vase, White Floral Design, Ivory Glaze, Gray Body, Kay Ley, 1946, 13 1/4 In. 995.00
Vase, White Matte Glaze, 1939, 6 In. 195.00
Vase, White Matte Glaze, 1944, 5 In. 149.00
Vase, White Matte Glaze, 1944, 9 In. 325.00
Vase, Winter Landscape, Misty Vellum Glaze, Edward T. Hurley, 1912, 8 5/8 In. 825.00
Vase, Wisteria Vines, Spider Webs, Brown, Yellow, Green Body, Kay Ley, 7 In. 895.00
Vase, Yellow Wild Rose, Elizabeth Lincoln, 1897, 3 In. 302.00
Wall Pocket, Cicada, 1922, Pair 2400.00
Wall Pocket, Matte Glaze, Art Nouveau, 1921 . . . . 500.00

ROSALINE, see Steuben category.

ROSE BOWLS were popular during the 1880s. Rose petals were kept in
the open bowl to add fragrance to a room, a popular idea in a time of
limited personal hygiene. The glass bowls were made with crimped
tops, which kept the petals inside. Many types of Victorian art glass
were made into rose bowls.

Amethyst, Applied Flower & Leaf Pattern, 4 In. 307.00
Basket, Applied Artichokes, Leaf Design, Moore, England, 1880, 3 3/4 In. 66.00
Basket, Applied Floral, Leaf Design, Blue, Gold, Bronze, Moore, 1880, 5 In. 99.00
Blue, Lavender Enameled Leaf Design, White Lining, 8-Crimp Top, 4 3/8 In. 110.00
Canary Yellow, Herringbone, Satin Finish 70.00
Green, Enameled, Rossler, Large 120.00
Hanging Hearts, Custard Yellow, Purple Iridescent Hearts & Vines 175.00
Hanging Hearts, Turquoise, Purple Iridescent Hearts & Vines 150.00
Mother-Of-Pearl, Diamond-Quilted, Lavender, 3 In. 77.00
Opalescent, Fenton 65.00
Orange, White Opalescent Swirls, 6-Crimp Top, 2 3/4 x 2 3/4 In. 110.00
Pheasants, Signed, Stinton 145.00
Pink Cased, Yellow, Gold Design, 3 x 4 1/4 In. 44.00

Pink Satin, 4 1/2 In. 22.00
Pink Satin, Shell Pattern, 3 1/2 In. 60.00
Sapphire Blue, Crimped Top, Enameled Flowers, 4 3/4 x 5 3/8 In. 195.00
Satin Glass, Apricot To Pale Orange, 4 Dimpled Sides, Victorian 85.00
Satin Glass, Blue, 4 3/4 In. 22.00
Satin Glass, Blue, 5 1/2 In. 33.00
Satin Glass, Cherub Design, Blue To White, Victorian, 4 In. 175.00
Satin Glass, Pink, 4 1/2 In. 22.00
Vaseline Glass, Spanish Lace, 1929 .... 110.00

ROSE CANTON china is similar to Rose Medallion, except no people are
pictured in the decoration. It was made in China during the nineteenth
and twentieth centuries in greens, pinks, and other colors.

Bowl, Cartouche Panels, Landscape, Floral Spray, 19th Century, 10 1/4 In. 920.00
Bowl, Cover, Floral Reserves, Birds & Butterflies, Square, 9 1/4 In. 22.00
Cup & Saucer, Bat Design, After Dinner, 10 Sets 137.00
Cup & Saucer, Bouillon, Cover, 4 Sets 50.00
Dish, Shrimp, Foliage, Gilt Edging, Hand Painted, Soft Colors, 11 In. 795.00
Plate, Bat Design, 10 In., 12 Piece 100.00
Platter, Serving, 19th Century, 16 In. 230.00
Punch Bowl, Alternating Panels Of Roses & Landscapes, 15 3/4 In. 1850.00

ROSE MEDALLION china was made in China during the nineteenth and
twentieth centuries. It is a distinctive design picturing people, flowers,
birds, and butterflies. Pieces are colored in greens, pinks, and other
colors. It is similar to Rose Canton.

Berry Bowl, Figural & Floral Reserves, Flange, 6 In. 70.00
Bowl, Cover, Landscape Scenes Front & Back, Handle, 9 1/2 In. 385.00
Bowl, Figural & Floral Reserves, Serrated Rim, Pierced Handle, 10 1/4 In. 190.00
Bowl, On Pedestal, 10 x 4 1/4 In. 495.00
Bowl, Shrimp, Figural & Floral Reserves, 10 3/4 In. 160.00
Bowl, Vegetable, Panels Of Flowers, Birds, Butterflies, 9 x 7 1/4 In. 460.00
Bowl, Wooden Stand, 6 1/2 x 14 1/4 In. 55.00
Brush Box, Cover, Woman, Golden Hair, 7 1/2 x 3 1/2 In. 395.00
Candlestick, Pair, 10 1/4 In. 1200.00
Charger, Mandarin Pattern, 16 1/4 In. 440.00
Chop Plate, Mandarin Scenes, 13 1/4 In. 357.00
Cup & Saucer 125.00
Cuspidor, Mandarin Scenes, 9 x 6 1/4 In. 358.00
Dish, Figural & Floral Reserves, Double Pierced Handles, 7 1/4 In. 90.00
Dish, Lobed Ovoid, Gilt Trim, 10 3/4 x 8 3/4 In. 165.00
Dish, Serving, Hexagonal, 9 1/2 In. 330.00
Dish, Underplate, Mandarin, Reticulated Rims, Oval, 11 In. 715.00
Plate, Alternating Figural & Floral Reserves, Butterfly Center, 9 1/2 In., Pair 22.00
Plate, Birds & People, China, 6 In. 15.00
Plate, Birds & People, China, 7 1/2 In. 30.00
Plate, Birds & People, China, 9 1/2 In. 48.00
Plate, Figural & Floral Reserves, Flange, 8 1/2 In. 90.00
Plate, Figural & Floral Reserves, Flange, Scalloped, 8 1/2 In. 40.00
Plate, Figural & Floral Reserves, Hexagonal, 5 1/2 x 8 In. 170.00
Platter, Alternating Figural & Floral Reserves, Oval, 10 In. 100.00
Platter, Alternating Figural & Floral Reserves, Oval, 11 In. 120.00
Platter, Mandarin Scenes, Chinese Character Inscription On Back, 13 1/2 In. 330.00
Platter, Oval, 10 In. 100.00
Platter, Round, 18 3/4 In. 412.00
Platter, Sanded Bottom, 18 In. 1250.00
Platter, Tree & Well, Mandarin Scenes, 16 1/2 In. 330.00
Punch Bowl, 15 3/4 In. 870.00
Punch Bowl, Birds & Butterflies, 14 1/2 In. 605.00
Punch Bowl, Early 19th Century, 16 In. 950.00
Relish, Shell Form 165.00
Soup, Dish, Figural & Floral Reserves, 9 1/2 In. 100.00
Sugar, 4 1/4 In. 66.00

Sugar & Creamer, Figural & Floral Reserves, Bamboo Handles 225.00
Teapot, 6 1/2 In. 357.00
Teapot, Dome Top, Mandarin Pattern, 8 1/2 In. 660.00
Teapot, Dome Top, Orange Peel, 9 1/2 In. 995.00
Teapot, Drum Form, 5 In. 120.00
Teapot, Figural & Floral Reserves, Gooseneck Spout, Bamboo Handle, 7 In. 300.00
Teapot, Mandarin Scenes, Wicker Cozy, 5 1/4 In. 85.00
Tile, Courtyard Figures, Round, 9 1/2 In., Pair 575.00
Tray, Figures & Floral Reserves, Brocade Ground, Oval, 14 3/4 In. 187.00
Tureen, Mandarin, Gilt Handles, Finial, 11 1/4 In. 1100.00
Urn, Palace, Allover Roses & Vines, Butterflies, Chinese Life Scenes, 62 In. 805.00
Vase, 4 Dignitaries Amid Taoist Emblems, Butterfly Handles, 1840s, 9 In. 330.00
Vase, Alternating Figural & Floral Reserves, Gilt Foo Dogs, Scalloped, 24 In. 3080.00
Vase, Cover, Foo Dog Finial, 11 1/2 In. 247.00
Vase, Figural & Floral Reserves, Applied Foo Dogs & Lizards, 7 In. 80.00
Vase, Interior Scene, Gilt Foo Dogs & Lizards, 9 1/2 In. 210.00
Vase, Interior Scenes, Converted To Lamp, Baluster, Rim Repair, 9 In. 55.00
Vase, Urn Shape, 9 1/4 In., Pair 330.00

ROSE O'NEILL, see Kewpie category.

ROSE TAPESTRY porcelain was made by the Royal Bayreuth factory of
Tettau, Germany, during the late nineteenth century. The surface of the
porcelain was pressed against a coarse fabric while it was still damp,
and the impressions remained on the finished porcelain. It looks and
feels like a textured cloth. Very skillful reproductions are being made
that even include a variation of the Royal Bayreuth mark, so be careful when buying.

Candleholder, 3 Color Roses 860.00
Clock, 3 Color Roses 856.00
Creamer, 3 1/2 In. 192.00
Creamer, Corset, Pink Roses ....225.00 to 275.00
Dish, Leaf, 3 Colors, 5 In. 180.00
Figurine, Shoe 495.00
Hair Receiver, Pink Roses, 3 Gold Footed, Blue Mark, 3 x 4 In. 325.00
Match Holder, Pink Roses, Green Ground, Wall Mount 570.00
Pitcher, Pinched Spout, Gold Handle, 3 3/4 In. ....150.00 to 320.00
Plate, 6 In. 120.00
Sugar, Cover 265.00
Tray, Dresser, Pink Roses, White & Yellow Rose Interior, Blue Mark, 10 In. 375.00
Vase, Stag In Stream, 4 In. 385.00

ROSEMEADE Pottery of Wahpeton, North Dakota, worked from 1940 to
1961. The pottery was operated by Laura A. Taylor and her husband,
R.I. Hughes. The company was also known as the Wahpeton Pottery
Company. Art pottery and commercial wares were made.

Ashtray, Columbia Falls, Mt., Black, Small 160.00
Ashtray, Tennessee 50.00
Bank, Bear 400.00
Bank, Elephant 275.00
Bank, Hippo, Aqua, Marked 450.00
Creamer, Corn 25.00
Figurine, Bear, Seated, 3 In. 65.00
Figurine, Buffalo, Tan 160.00
Figurine, Cock Pheasant, 14 1/2 In. ....425.00 to 450.00
Figurine, Elephant, Pink, Large 200.00
Figurine, Mountain Goat, 3 1/4 x 3 1/4 In. 75.00
Figurine, Penguin, Female, Miniature 95.00
Flower Frog, Fish, Pink ....40.00 to 45.00
Flower Frog, Pheasant 95.00
Mug, Incised Prairie Rose, Pink, 4 In. 50.00
Mustache Cup, Advertising 175.00
Paperweight, Minnesota Centennial 150.00

Planter, Lamb, Pink	60.00
Plaque, Fish, 6 In.	195.00
Salt & Pepper, Black Bear	55.00
Salt & Pepper, Brown Bears	40.00
Salt & Pepper, Brussels Sprouts	40.00 to 50.00
Salt & Pepper, Cat, Sitting, Red	95.00
Salt & Pepper, Chicken, Small	30.00
Salt & Pepper, Cucumber	35.00 to 50.00
Salt & Pepper, Deer, Lying	130.00
Salt & Pepper, Dog Head	95.00
Salt & Pepper, Dog, Begging	55.00
Salt & Pepper, Donkey, Label	60.00
Salt & Pepper, Elephant, Blue	85.00
Salt & Pepper, Elephant, Pink, Brown	55.00
Salt & Pepper, Fish, Green	75.00
Salt & Pepper, Fish, Tail Up	45.00
Salt & Pepper, Golden Pheasant	195.00
Salt & Pepper, Greyhound	85.00
Salt & Pepper, Kangaroo	65.00 to 125.00
Salt & Pepper, Mallard Duck	90.00
Salt & Pepper, Oxen	95.00
Salt & Pepper, Pelican	60.00
Salt & Pepper, Pheasant, Male, Large	175.00
Salt & Pepper, Pheasant, Tail Down	75.00
Salt & Pepper, Pheasant, Tail Up	35.00 to 45.00
Salt & Pepper, Pig	100.00
Salt & Pepper, Poodle Head	165.00
Salt & Pepper, Potato	250.00
Salt & Pepper, Quail	50.00
Salt & Pepper, Red Ox	95.00
Salt & Pepper, Skunk, Large	45.00
Salt & Pepper, Skunk, Miniature	50.00 to 75.00
Salt & Pepper, Turkey, Miniature	225.00
Spoon Rest, Cactus	70.00

ROSENTHAL porcelain was made at the factory established in Selb, Bavaria, in 1880. The factory is still making fine-quality tablewares and figurines. A series of Christmas plates was made from 1910. Other limited edition plates have been made since 1971.

Bowl, Pleated Type, White	45.00
Box, Cover, Studio Line, Signed, Peynet	175.00
Cake Plate, Burgundy, Gold Trim	50.00
Coffee Set, Helena, Whiteware, 1930s, 15 Piece	165.00
Coffee Set, Pompadour, Gold Trim, 3 Piece	114.00
Cup & Saucer, Die Fledermaus, Footed, After Dinner	55.00
Figurine, 2 Geese, 5 1/2 In.	125.00
Figurine, Bird, On Branch, 6 In.	175.00
Figurine, Boy, Nude, Kicking Ball, 4 In.	175.00
Figurine, Boy, Nude, Playing With Animal, 8 In.	175.00
Figurine, Boy, With Lamb	145.00
Figurine, Cat & 2 Kittens, 5 In.	185.00
Figurine, Cat, Lying On Stomach, 6 1/2 In.	165.00
Figurine, Dachshund Puppy, Reclining, Heidenreich, 7 1/2 x 5 In.	285.00
Figurine, Dog, Long Eared Puppy, Seated, Black & White	195.00
Figurine, Fawn, Reclining, 5 In.	150.00
Figurine, Guinea Fowl, 6 In.	175.00
Figurine, Horse, Bisque, 11 x 18 In.	395.00
Figurine, Lady, No. 1512, 10 In.	200.00
Figurine, Lady, No. 1518, 9 3/4 In.	200.00
Figurine, Lippizaner Horse, Rearing, 11 In.	200.00 to 300.00
Figurine, Penguin, 3 In.	75.00
Figurine, Princess, With Frog	245.00
Figurine, Rabbit, Laughing, Small	75.00

Figurine, Victorian Woman, Fanning, Mid-20th Century, 8 1/2 In.	80.00
Figurine, Waiter, Black, Wearing Turban, Carrying Tray Of Food	225.00
Figurine, Woman, Dancing, Mid-20th Century, 14 1/4 In.	46.00
Ginger Jar, Lid, Stylized Floral Meanders, Gilt Grapes & S Scrolls, 1930s, 8 In.	176.00
Lamp, Owl, Brown, Gray, Yellow Glass Eyes, 7 In.	275.00
Plate, Orchid Design, Pastel Tones, Porcelain, 1891-1907, 7 1/2 In.	11.00
Plate Set, Queen's Rose, 8 Piece	100.00
Plate Set, Service, Ivory, Green, Gold, 10 1/2 In., 12 Piece	357.00
Soup, Dish, Fruit, Flanged, 11 In., Pair	90.00
Tray, Dresser, Crossed Swords, 11 1/2 In.	115.00
Tureen, Soup, Ivory Rose, 4 Qt.	145.00
Vase, Free Form, 3 Colors, 5 In.	68.00
Vase, Gray With Gold & Black Ferns, Hand Painted, Signed, 13 In.	185.00
Vase, Hand Painted, Selb Germany, Signed, 8 In.	125.00
Vase, Oriental Design, 1930s, 12 In.	65.00
Vase, Owls, On Branch, 7 In.	85.00
Vase, Signed, Madeira Yang, 4 1/2 In.	40.00
Vase, Stylized Bird Cage, Charcoal, 1950s, 8 In.	65.00
Vase, White Crackle Glaze, Fritz Heidenreich, 1950, 11 1/2 x 6 1/2 In.	165.00

ROSEVILLE Pottery Company was organized in Roseville, Ohio, in
1890. Another plant was opened in Zanesville, Ohio, in 1898. Many
types of pottery were made until 1954. Early wares include Sgraffito,
Olympic, and Rozane. Later lines were often made with molded decorations, especially molded flowers and fruit. Pieces are marked *Roseville*.

Roseville
U.S.A.

Apple Blossom, Basket, Blue, 12 In.	325.00
Apple Blossom, Basket, Green, 12 In.	250.00 to 275.00
Apple Blossom, Basket, Hanging, Green	185.00
Apple Blossom, Basket, Pink, 8 In.	300.00
Apple Blossom, Bookends, Pink	250.00
Apple Blossom, Ewer, Green, 8 In.	250.00
Apple Blossom, Ewer, Pink, 8 In.	200.00
Apple Blossom, Ewer, Pink, 15 In.	400.00
Apple Blossom, Jardiniere, Pedestal, Blue, 25 In.	925.00 to 2100.00
Apple Blossom, Jardiniere, Pedestal, Pink, 25 In.	1450.00
Apple Blossom, Jardiniere, Pedestal, Pink, 31 In.	935.00
Apple Blossom, Tea Set, 3 Piece	325.00
Apple Blossom, Vase, 8 In.	154.00
Apple Blossom, Vase, 18 In.	550.00
Apple Blossom, Vase, Flared Rim, Blue, Signed, 12 1/4 In.	395.00
Apple Blossom, Vase, Green, 10 In.	200.00
Apple Blossom, Vase, Pink, 10 In.	250.00
Apple Blossom, Wall Pocket, Green	230.00 to 275.00
Apple Blossom, Window Box, Blue	195.00
Apple Blossom, Window Box, Green	160.00
Aztec, Vase, Spherical Top, Signed, 11 In.	165.00
Aztec, Vase, Stylized Trees, Matte Blue Ground, Cylindrical, 10 In.	110.00
Baneda, Ice Bucket, Green	1250.00
Baneda, Jardiniere, Green, 5 In.	425.00
Baneda, Jardiniere, Green, 8 In.	220.00
Baneda, Jardiniere, Green, 10 In.	1700.00 to 1800.00
Baneda, Urn, Green, 6 In.	575.00
Baneda, Vase, Green, 2 Handles, 8 In.	770.00 to 1925.00
Baneda, Vase, Green, 9 In.	775.00
Baneda, Vase, Pink, 5 In.	350.00
Baneda, Vase, Pink, 6 In.	425.00
Baneda, Vase, Pink, 10 In.	1045.00
Baneda, Vase, Pink, Pear Shape, 6 In.	360.00 to 500.00
Bittersweet, Cornucopia, Green, 4 In.	125.00 to 130.00
Bittersweet, Planter, Hanging, Original Chains	200.00
Bittersweet, Window Box, Green, 10 x 3 1/4 In.	165.00
Blackberry, Basket, Hanging	900.00 to 1200.00
Blackberry, Jardiniere, Pedestal	5200.00

Blackberry, Vase, 2 Handles, 10 In. 715.00
Blackberry, Vase, 2 Handles, Spherical, 6 In. 300.00
Blackberry, Vase, 8 In. 710.00
Blackberry, Wall Pocket 1200.00
Bleeding Heart, Bookends, Blue 100.00
Bleeding Heart, Bowl, Pink, 4 In. 85.00
Bleeding Heart, Console, Blue 375.00
Bleeding Heart, Cornucopia, 6 In. . . . . .95.00 to 110.00
Bleeding Heart, Ewer, Pink, 10 In. 275.00
Bleeding Heart, Jardiniere, Pedestal, 9 In. 990.00
Bleeding Heart, Vase, Blue, 7 In. 190.00
Bleeding Heart, Vase, Pink, 20 In. 675.00
Bleeding Heart, Wall Pocket, Signed, 8 1/2 In. 825.00
Bridge, Pitcher, Landscape, 5 1/2 In. 88.00
Bushberry, Basket, 12 In. 525.00
Bushberry, Basket, Hanging, Green, 6 In. 350.00
Bushberry, Bowl, Green, 3 In. 149.00
Bushberry, Bowl, Orange, 3 In. 75.00
Bushberry, Ewer, Blue, 10 In. 330.00
Bushberry, Ewer, Brown, 6 1/4 In. 88.00
Bushberry, Ewer, Green, 10 In. 300.00
Bushberry, Jardiniere, Brown, Pedestal, 8 In. 800.00
Bushberry, Mug, Green, 3 1/2 In. 135.00
Bushberry, Pitcher, Cider, Brown 500.00
Bushberry, Tea Set, Green, 3 Piece 280.00
Bushberry, Vase, Blue, 6 In. . . . . .125.00 to 165.00
Bushberry, Vase, Brown, 4 In. 75.00
Bushberry, Vase, Green, 9 In. 175.00
Bushberry, Wall Pocket, Blue 350.00
Carnelian I, Candlestick, Blue 45.00
Carnelian I, Compote, Blue, 5 In. 110.00
Carnelian I, Flower Frog, Blue, 4 1/2 In. 145.00
Carnelian I, Vase, Brown, 10 In. 250.00
Carnelian I, Vase, Fan, Blue & White, 6 In. 90.00
Carnelian I, Vase, Green Gold, 7 In. 150.00
Carnelian I, Wall Pocket, Green, 8 In. . . . . .250.00 to 350.00
Carnelian I, Wall Pocket, Turquoise, 8 In. 275.00
Carnelian II, Bowl, Mottled Turquoise, 9 1/2 In. 250.00
Carnelian II, Flower Frog, Mottled Green, Ink Stamp 45.00
Carnelian II, Urn, Mottled Purple, 5 In. 225.00
Carnelian II, Vase, Double Handle, Green, 9 In. 150.00
Carnelian II, Vase, Pink, Purple, Bulbous, 9 In. 550.00
Cherry Blossom, Bowl, Pink, 4 In. 350.00
Cherry Blossom, Candlestick, 2 Handles, Flowers, Cream, Brown, Label, 4 In., Pair . . . 450.00
Cherry Blossom, Lamp, Green 800.00
Cherry Blossom, Vase, Blue, 8 In. 1100.00
Cherry Blossom, Vase, Blue, 10 In. 1100.00
Cherry Blossom, Vase, Brown, 5 In. 425.00
Cherry Blossom, Wall Pocket, Blue, 8 In. 1600.00
Chloron, Planter, 6 x 19 x 6 1/2 In. 715.00
Chloron, Planter, Gallon Shape, 6 x 21 x 5 1/4 In. 715.00
Clematis, Basket, Hanging, Green 165.00
Clematis, Candlestick, Green, 4 1/2 In. 36.00
Clematis, Cookie Jar, Green, Blue . . . . .375.00 to 475.00
Clematis, Creamer, Blue 80.00
Clematis, Teapot, Rust . . . . .125.00 to 145.00
Clematis, Vase, Blue, 2 Handles, 7 In. 275.00
Clematis, Vase, Yellow, 2 Handles, Spherical, 8 In. 415.00
Clematis, Wall Pocket, Brown 200.00
Clemena, Flower Frog, Brown, 4 In. 225.00
Columbine, Basket, Handle, Yellow Flowers, Green Leaves, Blue Ground, 12 In. 450.00
Columbine, Basket, Hanging, Pink, Green 385.00
Columbine, Console, Pink, 10 In. 190.00

Columbine, Flower Frog, Blue 195.00
Columbine, Urn, Pink, 8 In. 245.00
Columbine, Vase, Blue, 10 In. 135.00
Columbine, Vase, Blue, 2 Angular Handles, Signed, 8 In. 165.00
Columbine, Vase, Pink, 4 In. 235.00
Cosmos, Basket, Brown, 10 In. 225.00
Cosmos, Basket, Hanging, Gray, Pink, 12 In. 625.00
Cosmos, Basket, Hanging, Green, 5 In. 450.00
Cosmos, Bowl, Blue, 14 In. 240.00
Cosmos, Cornucopia, Tan, 6 In. 130.00
Cosmos, Jardiniere, Tan, 6 In. ....110.00 to 175.00
Cosmos, Vase, Apricot, 10 In. 350.00
Cosmos, Vase, Blue, 9 In. 300.00
Cosmos, Vase, Blue, Bud, 7 In. 125.00
Cosmos, Vase, Green, 8 In. 235.00
Cosmos, Vase, Tan, 3 In. 285.00
Creamware, Pitcher, 11 1/2 In. 800.00
Dahlrose, Bowl, Handles, 10 In. 165.00
Dahlrose, Candlestick 135.00
Dahlrose, Console Set, Candlestick, 3 1/2 In., 3 Piece 335.00
Dahlrose, Console, Oval, 10 In. 325.00
Dahlrose, Jardiniere, 4 In. ....125.00 to 135.00
Dahlrose, Jardiniere, 8 In. 175.00
Dahlrose, Vase, 6 In. 100.00
Dahlrose, Vase, Bud, Triple 150.00
Dahlrose, Window Box, Brown Ground, 6 x 6 In. 450.00
Dawn, Vase, Green, 12 In. 235.00
Dawn, Vase, Pink, 6 In. 99.00
Dog & Pheasant, Vase, Pillow, Signed, 9 In. 2800.00
Dogwood I, Umbrella Stand, 20 1/2 In. 880.00
Dogwood II, Basket, 8 1/2 In. 140.00
Dogwood II, Jardiniere, Pedestal, 20 In. 1050.00
Dogwood II, Lamp 850.00
Dogwood II, Planter, 6 x 13 In. 330.00
Dogwood II, Vase, 9 In. 155.00
Dogwood II, Wall Pocket, 10 In. ....625.00 to 650.00
Donatello, Bowl, Flower Frog, 6 In. 120.00
Donatello, Cuspidor 300.00
Donatello, Jardiniere, 6 In. 150.00
Donatello, Jardiniere, 8 In. 175.00
Donatello, Jardiniere, Cream, 9 In. 250.00
Donatello, Pitcher, 6 1/2 In. 65.00
Donatello, Vase, 8 In. 175.00
Donatello, Wall Pocket, 9 In. 200.00
Donatello, Wall Pocket, 11 1/2 In. 325.00
Earlam, Bowl, Blue, Green Glaze, 4 In. 250.00
Egypto, Jardiniere, 4 Handles, 5 1/2 In. 85.00
Egypto, Pitcher, Rozane, 7 1/2 In. 255.00
Egypto, Urn, Scrolled Handles, 12 1/2 In. 660.00
Egypto, Vase, Handle, 10 In. 525.00
Falline, Vase, Blue, 12 1/2 In. 1650.00
Falline, Vase, Brown, 6 In. 495.00
Falline, Vase, Brown, 8 In. 795.00
Ferrella, Bowl, Red, Flower Frog, 9 1/2 In. 220.00
Ferrella, Candlestick, Gray & Tan, 4 In. ....295.00 to 300.00
Ferrella, Urn, Red, 8 In. 1150.00
Ferrella, Vase, Brown, 2 Handles, 9 In. 525.00
Ferrella, Vase, Pink, 5 In. 550.00
Ferrella, Vase, Red, 6 In. 600.00
Ferrella, Vase, Red, Flared Lip, 2 Handles, 9 In. 250.00
Ferrella, Vase, Red, Ribbed, 2 Handles, 5 In. 660.00
Ferrella, Wall Pocket, Red, 7 In. ....600.00 to 770.00
Florane, Bowl, 7 In. 45.00

Florane, Vase, 10 In. 135.00
Florentine, Bowl, Brown, 5 In. 75.00
Florentine, Bowl, Brown, 7 In. 55.00
Florentine, Jardiniere, Brown, 7 In. 200.00
Florentine, Vase, Footed, Brown, 4 In. 80.00
Florentine, Vase, Footed, Brown, 10 In. 175.00
Foxglove, Basket, Green, 8 In. 185.00
Foxglove, Bookends, Pink 325.00
Foxglove, Console, Green, Pink, 12 In. ....225.00 to 235.00
Foxglove, Jardiniere, Blue, Pedestal, 20 In. 1550.00
Foxglove, Pedestal, Blue 385.00
Foxglove, Vase, Blue, 15 In. 475.00
Foxglove, Vase, Blue, 16 In. 650.00
Foxglove, Vase, Green, 4 In. 315.00
Foxglove, Vase, Green, 14 In. 600.00
Foxglove, Vase, Green, 15 In. 550.00
Foxglove, Vase, Pink, 5 In. 135.00
Foxglove, Vase, Pink, 16 In. 750.00
Foxglove, Vase, Pink, Green, Pillow 165.00
Foxglove, Wall Pocket, Blue 425.00
Foxglove, Wall Pocket, Green 425.00
Freesia, Basket, Brown, 8 In. 150.00
Freesia, Basket, Orange, Hanging 325.00
Freesia, Bowl, Orange, 4 In. 85.00
Freesia, Console, Brown, 16 In. 175.00
Freesia, Jardiniere, Brown, Pedestal, 8 In. ....825.00 to 875.00
Freesia, Jardiniere, Green, Pedestal, 24 In. 1295.00
Freesia, Jardiniere, Pink, Pedestal, 20 In. 1850.00
Freesia, Teapot, Matte Green, 8 In. 110.00
Freesia, Vase, Brown, 6 In. 85.00
Freesia, Vase, Green, 8 In. 165.00
Freesia, Vase, Orange, Bud, 7 In. 85.00
Fuchsia, Flower Frog, Green ....375.00 to 695.00
Fuchsia, Jardiniere, Brown, 4 In. 150.00
Fuchsia, Vase, Brown, 6 In. ....150.00 to 200.00
Fuchsia, Vase, Green, 7 In. 175.00
Fuchsia, Vase, Green, 10 In. 500.00
Fuchsia, Vase, Green, 18 In. 1500.00
Fuchsia, Wall Pocket, Blue 1100.00
Futura, Jardiniere, Brown, 8 In. 1000.00
Futura, Jardiniere, Gray, 6 In. 300.00
Futura, Jardiniere, Pedestal, Pink, Blue, 28 1/2 In. 1115.00
Futura, Jardiniere, Pink, Blue, 10 In. 1100.00
Futura, Urn, Stepped, Brown, 10 In. 1350.00
Futura, Vase, 2 Tapered Ribbed Handles, Flared Rim, Blue, 13 In. ... 1980.00
Futura, Vase, Black Flame, 7 In. 675.00
Futura, Vase, Blue Glaze, 3 Sides, Flared, Stepped Foot, 8 In. ... 275.00
Futura, Vase, Coral, Brown Glaze, 4 Sides, Stepped Foot, 12 In. ... 660.00
Futura, Vase, Green, Raised Pine Branch, 2 Handles, 10 In. ... 715.00
Futura, Vase, Pink, Gray, Footed, 7 In. 467.50
Futura, Vase, Pink, Turquoise Glaze, Ribbed, 2 Handles, 6 In. ... 165.00
Futura, Vase, Yellow, 7 In. ....195.00 to 200.00
Futura, Wall Pocket, Tan, 8 In. ....850.00 to 1195.00
Gardenia, Bookends, Green 260.00
Gardenia, Console, Blue, 10 In. 195.00
Gardenia, Vase, Gray, 8 In. 165.00
Gardenia, Vase, Tan, 6 In. 85.00
Gardenia, Vase, Tan, 12 In. 165.00
Gardenia, Wall Pocket, Green 275.00
Gardenia, Window Box, Gray 12.00
Good Night, Candlestick ....425.00 to 450.00
Holland, Pitcher, Tan, 9 1/2 In. 165.00
Hyde Park, Ashtray, Burnt Orange, 7 1/2 In. 20.00

Hyde Park, Ashtray, Green, 7 1/2 In.	35.00
Imperial II, Vase, Glossy Lavender, Matte Turquoise Glaze, 5 In.	165.00
Imperial II, Vase, Matte Celadon Glaze, Raised Geometric Band, Pink Ground, 9 In.	1045.00
Imperial II, Vase, Matte Cobalt Blue, Yellow Crystalline Glaze, Ribbed, 9 In.	550.00
Imperial II, Vase, Matte Yellow Crystalline Glaze, Cobalt Blue, 11 In.	1100.00
Imperial II, Vase, Mottled Red Glaze, Ribbed Top, Bulbous, 7 In.	525.00
Imperial II, Vase, Mottled Yellow, Green Glaze, Beehive, 5 In.	275.00
Imperial II, Vase, Pink, 7 In.	175.00 to 345.00
Iris, Basket, Blue, 8 In.	300.00
Iris, Basket, Hanging, Blue	395.00
Iris, Pitcher, Blue, 10 In.	325.00
Iris, Planter, Rose, Yellow, Stand, 8 In.	500.00
Iris, Vase, Blue, Brown, 15 In.	1200.00
Iris, Vase, Pink, 12 1/2 In.	1500.00 to 1900.00
Iris, Vase, Tan, 6 In.	75.00
Ixia, Candlestick, Yellow & Pink, Signed, 3 In., Pair	140.00
Ixia, Ginger Jar, Yellow, 12 In.	300.00
Ixia, Vase, Light Green, 8 In.	275.00
Ixia, Vase, Yellow, Purple, 6 In.	165.00
Jonquil, Basket, 8 1/2 In.	440.00
Jonquil, Vase, 2 Handles, Flared Rim, Bulbous, Paper Label, 9 In.	462.00
Jonquil, Vase, 2 Handles, Gourd Shape, 8 In.	330.00
Jonquil, Vase, 4 In.	235.00
Jonquil, Vase, 7 In.	360.00 to 415.00
Jonquil, Vase, 8 In.	310.00 to 325.00
Jonquil, Vase, 9 In.	450.00
Jonquil, Vase, Elongated Scalloped Rim, Squat, 4 In.	275.00
Juvenile, Creamer, Goose	400.00
Juvenile, Creamer, Rabbit, 3 In.	175.00
Juvenile, Eggcup, Chick	220.00
Juvenile, Eggcup, Double, Chicks	380.00
Juvenile, Mug, Chicks	95.00
Juvenile, Pitcher, Milk, Nursery Rhyme	400.00
Juvenile, Plate, Chicks	145.00
Juvenile, Plate, Nursery Rhyme, Rolled Edge, 8 In.	99.00 to 165.00
Juvenile, Sugar & Creamer, Chicks	275.00
Knights Of Pythias, Tankard Set, 7 Piece	1100.00
La Rose, Vase, Signed, 9 In.	285.00
Laurel, Bowl, Gold, 7 In.	185.00 to 200.00
Laurel, Candlestick, Green, 5 In.	175.00
Laurel, Vase, 2 Small Handles, Signed, 14 In.	416.00
Luffa, Cornucopia, Green, 6 In.	300.00
Luffa, Vase, Brown, 8 In.	275.00
Luffa, Vase, Green, 6 In.	165.00
Luffa, Vase, Green, 9 In.	110.00 to 190.00
Magnolia, Ashtray, Blue	110.00 to 120.00
Magnolia, Basket, Brown, 10 In.	300.00
Magnolia, Candlestick, Brown, Pair	125.00
Magnolia, Console, Blue	135.00
Magnolia, Cookie Jar, Tan	450.00
Magnolia, Flowerpot, Blue	140.00
Magnolia, Mug, Blue	165.00
Magnolia, Pitcher, Cider, Tan	195.00 to 200.00
Magnolia, Sugar & Creamer, Blue	150.00
Magnolia, Teapot, Tan, 8 In.	245.00
Magnolia, Vase, Blue, 6 In.	85.00
Magnolia, Vase, Blue, 7 In.	99.00 to 125.00
Magnolia, Vase, Blue, 14 In.	450.00
Magnolia, Vase, Blue, 15 In.	335.00
Magnolia, Vase, Brown, 6 In., Pair	130.00
Magnolia, Vase, Brown, 8 In.	130.00
Magnolia, Vase, Double, Green, 9 In.	33.00
Magnolia, Vase, Green, 15 In.	335.00 to 385.00

Ming Tree, Basket, Blue, 8 In. 88.00
Ming Tree, Basket, Green, 8 In. 125.00
Ming Tree, Basket, White, 14 In. 300.00
Ming Tree, Bookends, 5 1/2 In. 90.00
Ming Tree, Candlestick, Turquoise, Pair 125.00
Ming Tree, Pitcher, Green, 10 In. 235.00
Ming Tree, Vase, Blue, 8 In. 125.00
Ming Tree, Vase, Green, 14 In. 525.00
Ming Tree, Wall Pocket, Blue, 8 In. 330.00
Ming Tree, Window Box, Green, 10 In. ....150.00 to 165.00
Mock Orange, Basket, Footed, Green, 8 In. 175.00
Monticello, Bowl, White, Black, Green, 13 In. 600.00
Monticello, Console, Blue 400.00
Monticello, Urn, Brown, 7 In. 425.00
Monticello, Vase, Blue, 4 In. 225.00
Monticello, Vase, Blue, 5 In. ....350.00 to 460.00
Monticello, Vase, Blue, 9 In. 990.00
Monticello, Vase, Blue, 10 In. 990.00
Monticello, Vase, Brown, 5 In. 325.00
Monticello, Vase, Green, 8 In. ....425.00 to 595.00
Monticello, Vase, White, Black, Green, Brown, 9 In. 990.00
Monticello, Wall Pocket, Tan, 5 In. 350.00
Morning Glory, Basket, Green, Footed, 10 1/4 In. 990.00
Morning Glory, Urn, Green, 4 In. 495.00
Morning Glory, Urn, White, 9 In. 275.00
Morning Glory, Vase, Green, 9 In. 190.00
Morning Glory, Vase, Green, 10 In. 410.00
Morning Glory, Vase, Green, 14 In. 1870.00
Morning Glory, Vase, White, 8 In. 410.00
Moss, Bowl, Green, Pink, 6 In. 225.00
Moss, Console, Blue, 12 In. 400.00
Moss, Vase, Blue, 6 In. ....195.00 to 315.00
Moss, Vase, Blue, 12 In. 775.00
Mostique, Bowl, Green, Brown, Blue, Purple, 9 In. 110.00
Mostique, Jardiniere, Brown, Green, Pedestal, 28 1/2 In. 660.00
Mostique, Jardiniere, Mustard, Green, 8 In. 55.00
Mostique, Vase, Green, 10 In. 195.00
Mostique, Vase, Mustard, 6 In. 115.00
Mostique, Vase, Stylized High Glaze Blossoms, Gray Ground, 10 In. 255.00
Mostique, Vase, Tan, Green, Blue Stylized Design, 8 In. 165.00
Mostique, Vase, Textured Gray Ground, Ink Mark, 12 In. 265.00
Orian, Vase, White, 14 In. ....375.00 to 475.00
Peony, Bookends, Green 165.00
Peony, Bowl, Green, 10 In. 150.00
Peony, Jardiniere, Green, 4 In. 450.00
Peony, Jardiniere, Pink, 4 In. 50.00
Peony, Planter, Green 155.00
Peony, Teapot, Gold Trim, Tan 195.00
Peony, Vase, Gold, 8 In. 140.00
Peony, Vase, Gold, 15 In. 395.00
Peony, Vase, Green, 15 In. 125.00
Peony, Vase, Green, 18 In. 425.00
Peony, Vase, Yellow, 6 In. 100.00
Peony, Vase, Yellow, 18 In. 495.00
Persian, Jardiniere, 8 1/2 In. 300.00
Pine Cone, Ashtray, Blue 250.00
Pine Cone, Ashtray, Blue, Semicircular, 2 1/2 In. 412.00
Pine Cone, Ashtray, Green 90.00
Pine Cone, Basket, Blue, 10 In. ....365.00 to 605.00
Pine Cone, Basket, Green, 10 In. 165.00
Pine Cone, Basket, Hanging, Brown, 15 In. 595.00
Pine Cone, Bookends, Brown 250.00
Pine Cone, Bowl, Blue, 9 In. 385.00

Pine Cone, Bowl, Boat Shape, Green, 3 x 6 In.	375.00
Pine Cone, Console, Blue, 9 In.	450.00
Pine Cone, Cornucopia, White, 6 In.	55.00
Pine Cone, Ewer, Green	450.00
Pine Cone, Flowerpot, Saucer	325.00
Pine Cone, Jardiniere, Brown, 8 In.	130.00
Pine Cone, Jardiniere, Green, Pedestal, 20 In.	2500.00
Pine Cone, Pitcher, Blue, Handle, 15 1/2 In.	660.00
Pine Cone, Pitcher, Brown, 9 In.	540.00
Pine Cone, Planter, Green, 3 1/2 In.	100.00
Pine Cone, Sugar & Creamer, Green, Brown	65.00
Pine Cone, Teapot, Green Brown	65.00
Pine Cone, Umbrella Stand, Blue, 10 In.	3630.00
Pine Cone, Umbrella Stand, Blue, 20 In.	1850.00
Pine Cone, Umbrella Stand, Brown, 20 In.	825.00
Pine Cone, Urn, Blue, 8 In.	385.00
Pine Cone, Urn, Green, 5 In.	365.00
Pine Cone, Vase, Blue, Pillow, 8 In.	385.00
Pine Cone, Vase, Brown, 9 In.	250.00
Pine Cone, Vase, Brown, Bud, 7 1/2 x 5 In.	375.00
Pine Cone, Vase, Brown, Pillow, 6 In.	3745.00
Pine Cone, Vase, Bud, Green	325.00
Pine Cone, Vase, Green, 6 In.	135.00
Pine Cone, Vase, Green, 7 In.	190.00
Pine Cone, Vase, Green, 11 In.	385.00
Pine Cone, Vase, Green, Pillow, 7 In.	80.00
Pine Cone, Wall Pocket, Double, Green, Paper Label	375.00
Pine Cone, Window Box, Brown, 10 In.	235.00
Pine Cone, Window Box, Green, 16 In.	300.00
Poppy, Ewer, Green, 10 In.	275.00
Poppy, Ewer, Pink, 10 In.	225.00
Poppy, Ewer, Pink, 18 In.	750.00
Poppy, Flowerpot, Green, 5 In.	190.00
Poppy, Jardiniere, Pink, 6 In.	170.00
Poppy, Umbrella Stand, Whiplash Stems, Green, 21 x 10 In.	990.00
Poppy, Urn, Handles, Green, 6 In.	200.00
Poppy, Vase, Green, Pink, 6 In.	225.00
Primrose, Ewer, Blue	140.00
Primrose, Flowerpot, Saucer	225.00
Primrose, Vase, 2 Handles, 9 In.	220.00
Primrose, Vase, Blue, 8 In.	90.00
Primrose, Vase, Brown, 8 In.	475.00
Primrose, Vase, Pink, 8 In.	225.00
Raymor, Bean Pot, Autumn Brown, Mottled, 4 Qt.	85.00
Raymor, Bean Pot, Orange	75.00
Raymor, Butter, Cover, Dark Green	155.00
Raymor, Casserole, Large	130.00
Raymor, Creamer, Terra-Cotta	38.00
Raymor, Cruet, Vinegar, Avocado Green	65.00
Raymor, Plate, Black, 8 In.	16.00
Raymor, Plate, Brown, 10 In.	24.00
Raymor, Plate, White, 10 In.	24.00
Raymor, Ramekin, Cover, Avocado Green, Mottled, Individual	35.00
Raymor, Vase, Label, Green, 9 In.	320.00
Raymor, Vase, Yellow, 12 In.	125.00
Rosalie, Pitcher & Bowl, Creamware, Pitcher, 11 1/2 In.	800.00
Rosecraft, Bowl, Blue, 2 1/2 In.	32.00
Rosecraft, Vase, Panel, Brown, 8 In.	425.00
Rosecraft, Vase, White, Label, 6 In.	200.00
Rosecraft Hexagon, Vase, Blue, 6 In.	175.00
Rosecraft Hexagon, Vase, Green, 7 In.	425.00
Rozane, Basket, Green, Handle, 8 In.	110.00
Rozane, Ewer, Daffodil, 11 In.	88.00

Rozane, Jardiniere, Pedestal, Brown, 18 In. 140.00
Rozane, Vase, Artist Signed, 16 In. 500.00
Rozane, Vase, Berries, 4 Sides, 6 In. 220.00
Rozane, Vase, Daffodil, Scalloped Rim, Signed, 9 In. 360.00
Rozane, Vase, Dog & Pheasant, Signed, Pillow, 9 x 11 In. 2100.00
Rozane, Vase, Flowers, Leaves, 8 In. 140.00
Rozane, Vase, Pillow, 9 In. 1800.00
Rozane, Vase, Poppies, 11 In. ....220.00 to 550.00
Rozane, Vase, Portrait Of Lion, Dunlavy, Pillow, 10 x 10 In. 2200.00
Rozane, Wall Pocket, White, 8 In. 110.00
Russco, Vase, Blue, 9 In. 100.00
Russco, Vase, Butterscotch, Ocher, 8 In. 175.00
Russco, Vase, Gold, 8 In. ....140.00 to 160.00
Russco, Vase, Maroon, 8 In. 95.00
Russco, Vase, Orange, 8 In. 125.00
Russco, Vase, Turquoise Blue, Footed, Stacked Handles, 9 In. 135.00
Savona, Vase, White, 12 In. 195.00
Silhouette, Basket, Blue, 6 In. 115.00
Silhouette, Basket, Blue, 8 In. 195.00
Silhouette, Candlestick, Red, 3 In., Pair 120.00
Silhouette, Console Set, Turquoise, Leaves, White, 3 Piece 185.00
Silhouette, Cornucopia, White, Pale Green 95.00
Silhouette, Ewer, Red 125.00
Silhouette, Vase, 8 In., Pair 120.00
Silhouette, Vase, Rose, 8 In. 143.00
Snowberry, Ashtray, Blue 115.00
Snowberry, Basket, Blue, 12 In. 395.00
Snowberry, Basket, Hanging, Green, 10 In. 145.00
Snowberry, Basket, Pink, 7 In. 190.00
Snowberry, Basket, Pink, 10 In. 195.00
Snowberry, Candlestick, Rose, 2 Handles, 4 In. 22.00
Snowberry, Cornucopia, Blue, 6 In. 55.00
Snowberry, Ewer, Blue, 15 In. 115.00
Snowberry, Ewer, Green, 15 In. 350.00
Snowberry, Jardiniere, Green, 6 In. 100.00
Snowberry, Sugar & Creamer, Blue, White, 2 Piece 150.00
Snowberry, Urn, Green, 8 In. 195.00
Snowberry, Vase, Blue, 9 In. ....175.00 to 190.00
Snowberry, Vase, Green, 6 In. 125.00
Snowberry, Vase, Light Pink, 6 In. 125.00
Snowberry, Vase, Pink, 7 In. ....120.00 to 125.00
Snowberry, Vase, Pink, 18 In. 700.00
Snowberry, Wall Pocket, Blue, 5 1/4 In. 275.00
Snowberry, Wall Pocket, Pink 200.00
Snowberry, Window Box, Blue 155.00
Spanish Moss, Blue, Pedestal, Jardiniere, 8 In. 825.00
Sunflower, Bowl, 4 In. 795.00
Sunflower, Urn, Stepped, 10 In. 1350.00
Sunflower, Vase, 10 In. 2100.00
Sunflower, Vase, 5 In. 575.00
Sunflower, Vase, 8 In. 900.00
Sunflower, Vase, Angular Handles, 6 In. 600.00
Sunflower, Vase, Brown, Green, 2 Open Handles, 4 In. 550.00
Sunflower, Vase, Double Handle, 4 In. 495.00
Sunflower, Vase, Green, Blue, 2 Open Handles, 5 In. 660.00
Sunflower, Vase, Green, Blue, 2 Open Handles, 6 In. 715.00
Sunflower, Wall Pocket, Orange 225.00
Teasel, Vase, Blue, 2 Handles, 4 In. 66.00
Teasel, Vase, Cream, 14 In. 650.00
Teasel, Vase, Red, 2 Handles, 8 In. 80.00
Thorn Apple, Bookends, Pink & Green 240.00
Thorn Apple, Ewer, Blue 250.00
Thorn Apple, Vase, Blue, Bud, 6 In. 190.00

Thorn Apple, Vase, Pink, 2 Handles, Pillow, 6 In. 110.00
Thorn Apple, Wall Pocket, Blue 425.00
Topeo, Bowl, Dark Red, 11 1/2 In. 195.00
Tourmaline, Console, Turquoise, Pink, 8 In. 300.00
Tourmaline, Ginger Jar, Cover, 10 In. 375.00
Tourmaline, Urn, Blue, 8 In. 225.00
Tourmaline, Vase, Blue, Pillow, 6 In. 165.00
Tourmaline, Vase, Orange, 7 In. 150.00
Tourmaline, Vase, Turquoise, 6 In. 125.00
Tuscany, Candlestick, Pink 40.00
Tuscany, Flower Frog, Gray & Green, 6 In. 90.00
Tuscany, Lamp, Pink, 12 In. 300.00
Tuscany, Vase, 2 Handles, Pink, 6 In. 210.00
Tuscany, Vase, Gray, Green Handles, 8 In. 245.00
Tuscany, Vase, Gray, White Glaze, 2 Open Handles, 10 In. 231.00
Tuscany, Vase, Pink, 5 In. 95.00
Tuscany, Vase, Pink, 6 In. 111.00
Tuscany, Vase, Pink, 9 In. 185.00
Tuscany, Wall Pocket, Blue 195.00
Velmoss, Jardiniere, Pedestal, Blue, 29 1/2 In. 1045.00
Velmoss, Vase, Blue, 10 In. 165.00
Velmoss, Vase, Blue, 2 Handles, 7 In. 200.00
Velmoss, Vase, Cream, 6 In. 88.00
Velmoss, Vase, Paper Label, Cream, 10 In. 335.00
Venetian, Pitcher, 7 1/2 In. 100.00
Vista, Basket, Handle, 8 In. 350.00
Vista, Umbrella Stand, 20 In. 935.00
Vista, Vase, Buttressed Handles, 10 In. 385.00
Vista, Vase, Closed-In Top, Flared Foot, 10 In. 385.00
Vista, Vase, Green, 10 In. 800.00
Vista, Vase, Landscape Design, 14 In. 1045.00
Vista, Vase, Square Handles, Bulbous, 9 In. 530.00
Volpato, Dish, Cover, Fluted, Footed, Ivory, Silver Label, 4 3/4 x 5 1/4 In. 275.00
Water Lily, Basket, Handle, Blue, 12 In. 100.00
Water Lily, Bookends, Blue 245.00
Water Lily, Bookends, Pink 250.00
Water Lily, Console, Pink 150.00
Water Lily, Cookie Jar, Blue 400.00
Water Lily, Cookie Jar, Tan 550.00
Water Lily, Dish, Blue, 12 In. 100.00
Water Lily, Ewer, Blue, 6 In. 110.00
Water Lily, Ewer, Blue, 15 In. 375.00
Water Lily, Ewer, Pink, 15 In. 400.00
Water Lily, Vase, Blue, 8 In. .... 75.00 to 125.00
Water Lily, Vase, Pink, Green, Floor, 15 In. 450.00
Water Lily, Vase, Rose, 8 In. 175.00
White Rose, Basket, Blue, 10 In. 360.00
White Rose, Candlestick, Brown & Green, 2 In., Pair 135.00
White Rose, Console, Brown & Green, 10 In. 185.00
White Rose, Ewer, Blue, 6 In. .... 125.00 to 165.00
White Rose, Jardiniere, Blue, 6 In. 150.00
White Rose, Jardiniere, Pedestal, 20 In. 1100.00
White Rose, Pitcher, Pink, 10 In. 275.00
White Rose, Vase, Blue, 8 In. 220.00
White Rose, Vase, Blue, 15 In. 475.00
White Rose, Vase, Double, Blue, 4 In. 77.00
White Rose, Vase, Tan, 7 In. 340.00
Wincraft, Basket, Hanging, Tan 150.00
Wincraft, Bookends, Green .... 125.00 to 135.00
Wincraft, Bowl, Blue, 14 In. 120.00
Wincraft, Candlestick, Yellow 125.00
Wincraft, Console, Yellow 90.00
Wincraft, Creamer, Blue 85.00

Wincraft, Sugar & Creamer, Apricot 105.00
Wincraft, Tea Set, Green ....150.00 to 425.00
Wincraft, Vase, Chartreuse, 8 In. 150.00
Wincraft, Vase, Green, 6 In. 125.00
Wincraft, Vase, Yellow, Pillow 75.00
Wincraft, Window Box, Chartreuse 195.00
Wincraft, Window Box, Yellow, Green, 12 In. 105.00
Windsor, Basket, Blue, Geometric Band, 8 1/2 In. 247.00
Windsor, Vase, Blue, 7 In. 395.00
Windsor, Vase, Blue, Embossed Rectangles Around Collar, 6 In. 400.00
Windsor, Vase, Blue, Green Fern Leaves, Gourd Shape, 2 Handles, 7 In. 660.00
Windsor, Vase, Orange, Green Geometric Band, 2 Handles, 6 In. 80.00
Windsor, Vase, Orange, Spherical, 6 In. 110.00
Wisteria, Candlestick, Brown, Pair 750.00
Wisteria, Console, Brown, 12 In. 450.00
Wisteria, Jardiniere, Blue, Pedestal, 8 In. 4000.00
Wisteria, Jardiniere, Brown, 8 In. 1400.00
Wisteria, Urn, Blue, 7 In. ....710.00 to 850.00
Wisteria, Vase, Blue, 6 In. 325.00
Wisteria, Vase, Blue, Bulbous, 7 In. 770.00
Wisteria, Vase, Brown, 7 In. 475.00
Woodland, Vase, Flower, 7 In. 850.00
Zephyr Lily, Ashtray, Blue 50.00
Zephyr Lily, Basket, Hanging, Brown, 5 In. 210.00
Zephyr Lily, Bowl, Blue, 10 In. 225.00
Zephyr Lily, Bowl, Footed, Blue, 10 In. 110.00
Zephyr Lily, Candlestick, Blue, 2 In., Pair 150.00
Zephyr Lily, Candlestick, Green, 2 In. 25.00
Zephyr Lily, Console, Tan, 10 In. ....140.00 to 200.00
Zephyr Lily, Cookie Jar, Tan 475.00
Zephyr Lily, Cornucopia, Green 110.00
Zephyr Lily, Ewer, Brown, 15 In. 385.00
Zephyr Lily, Jardiniere, Brown, Pedestal, 20 In. 525.00
Zephyr Lily, Pitcher, Batter, Blue 495.00
Zephyr Lily, Planter, Green, 8 In. 295.00
Zephyr Lily, Plate, Blue, 14 In. 195.00
Zephyr Lily, Tea Set, Green 400.00
Zephyr Lily, Vase, Blue, 7 In. 145.00
Zephyr Lily, Vase, Blue, Bud, 7 1/2 In. 70.00
Zephyr Lily, Vase, Tan, Embossed, 7 In. 80.00
Zephyr Lily, Wall Pocket, Brown, Green 190.00
Zephyr Lily, Wall Pocket, Green 300.00
Zephyr Lily, Window Box, Brown, Green, 8 In. 100.00

ROWLAND & MARSELLUS Company is part of a mark that appears on
historical Staffordshire dating from the late nineteenth and early twentieth centuries. Rowland & Marsellus is the mark used by an American
importing company in New York City. The company worked from
1893 to about 1937. Some of the pieces may have been made by the
British Anchor Pottery Co. of Longton, England, for export to a New
York firm. Many American views were made. Of special interest to
collectors are the plates with rolled edges, usually blue and white.

Pitcher, American Pilgrims, Blue & White 225.00
Plate, Alaska, Yukon, Pacific Exposition, 1907, 10 In. ....*Illus* 77.00
Plate, Bermuda, Somers Island, Tower, 1609-1909, 10 In. ....*Illus* 39.00
Plate, Indianapolis, Indiana, 10 In. ....*Illus* 55.00
Plate, Kansas City, 10 In. ....*Illus* 33.00
Plate, Provincetown, Massachusetts, 10 In. ....*Illus* 121.00
Plate, Scenes Of Virginia On Border, Center Portrait Of Rebecka, 10 In. 77.00
Plate, Souvenir Of Alaska, Pacific Exposition, 1909, 10 In. 77.00
Plate, Souvenir Of Portland, Oregon, 10 In. 46.00
Plate, Souvenir Of St. Augustine, Florida, 10 In. 57.00
Plate, St. Louis, Missouri, 10 In. ....*Illus* 55.00

Front row: Rowland & Marsellus, Plate, Alaska, Yukon, Pacific Exposition, 1907, 10 In.
Rowland & Marsellus, Plate, Provincetown, Massachusetts, 10 In.
Rowland & Marsellus, Plate, Bermuda, Somers Island, Tower, 1609-1909, 10 In.
Back row: Rowland & Marsellus, Plate, Indianapolis, Indiana, 10 In.
Rowland & Marsellus, Plate, Kansas City, 10 In.
Rowland & Marsellus, Plate, Tacoma, Washington, 10 In.
Rowland & Marsellus, Plate, St. Louis, Missouri, 10 In.

Plate, Tacoma, Washington, 10 In.	*Illus*	55.00
Plate, Tampa Bay, Florida, 10 In.		85.00

ROY ROGERS was born in 1911 in Cincinnati, Ohio. In the 1930s, he made a living as a singer; in 1935, his group started work at a Los Angeles radio station. He appeared in his first movie in 1937. From 1952 to 1957, he made 101 television shows. The other stars in the show were his wife, Dale Evans, his horse, Trigger, and his dog, Bullet. Roy Rogers memorabilia is collected, including items from the Roy Rogers restaurants.

Bank, Boot Shape, Metal	95.00
Bedspread, Dale Evans	165.00
Bedspread, Poplin, Beige, Roy On Trigger, Pat Brady In Nelly Belle Jeep, Twin	310.00
Binoculars ....60.00 to	90.00
Book, Comic, Trigger, No. 12, 1954, 10 Cents	20.00
Book, Little Golden Book, Dale Evans & The Lost Gold Mine, 1954	20.00
Book, Paint, Unused, 1944	75.00
Book, Roy Rogers & The Brasada Bandits, Whitman	25.00
Book, Roy Rogers & The Raiders Of Sawtooth Ridge, Whitman, 1946, 6 x 8 In.	30.00
Box, Roy Rogers Yo-Yo	35.00
Button, Roy & Trigger, Celluloid, Black Ribbon, Gilt Boot, 1950s, 2 In.	30.00
Camera, Flash, Hopalong & Topper, Box	220.00
Cap Gun ....75.00 to	145.00
Cap Gun, Double Holsters	70.00
Cap Gun, Kilgore, No. 2066, Nickel Finish, White Plastic Grips, 9 In.	325.00
Cap Gun, Kilgore, Revolving Cylinder, Nickel Finish, White Plastic Grip, 1955	650.00
Cap Gun, Leslie-Henry, Nickel Finish, White Plastic Grips, 1950s, 9 In.	425.00
Clock, Alarm, Toy, Rogers & Trigger, Box	286.00
Cup, Figural, Plastic	35.00
Dale Evans, Coloring Book, Whitman, 1951	55.00
Dale Evans Paper Dolls, Whitman, 1954	80.00
Decal Set, Dale Evans	25.00
Drapes, Pair	175.00
Figure, Dale Evans, On Horse	150.00
Fix-It Stagecoach, Box	245.00
Flashlight	40.00
Guitar, Toy, Wood, Plastic, Yellow, Cartoon Cowboy Designs, 31 In.	155.00

Gun, Leather Holster, 2 1/2-In. Gun 45.00
Harmonica 95.00
Hat, 1950s 125.00
Holster Set, 1950s 405.00
Jacket, Leather, Fringed, 1950s 290.00
Knife, Pocket, Roy, Trigger, 2 Blades, Celluloid Grips, Colonial, Providence, R.I. 41.00
Lamp, Dale Evans, Signed, Pair 650.00
Lantern 130.00
Lobby Card, Trails Of Robin Hood 90.00
Lucky Horseshoe, Black Rubber 23.00
Lunch Box, Roy Rogers & Dale Evans, Metal, No Thermos, 7 1/4 x 8 3/4 In. 65.00
Lunch Box, Roy Rogers & Dale Evans, Metal, Red Band 145.00
Lunch Box, Vinyl 125.00
Magazine Cover, Life, July 12, 1943 .... 38.00
Moccasins, Roy On Trigger, Child's 175.00
Mug, Quaker Oats 30.00
Paint Set, Paint By Numbers, Box 95.00
Paint Set, Toycraft 135.00
Paper Doll, Roy Rogers & Dale Evans, Whitman, 1954 .... 80.00
Pencil Case, Vinyl, 1950s, 2 1/2 x 7 1/2 In. 35.00
Plate, 9 1/2 In. 80.00
Poster, Roy Rogers In Person, Picture, Restaurant, Double Sided, 1980s, 28 x 34 In. 175.00
Press Book, Heart Of The Golden West, 1955 .... 18.00
Record, Three On One, 45 RPM, Golden, 1960s 45.00
Ring, Microscope 95.00
Ring, Square, Sterling Silver 650.00
Saddle, Leather 1100.00
Sheet Music, Bible Tells Me So, Dale Evans & Roy Rogers, 1955 .... 19.00
Sheet Music, Dust, Under Western Stars, 1938 .... 50.00
Shirt, 1950s 135.00
Song Book, 56 Pages, 1943 .... 45.00
Telephone, Box 325.00
Tent, Canopy Entrance, Large 290.00
Thermos, 1955 .... 70.00
Tie Slide, Silver 55.00
TV Guide Cover, July 17, 1954 .... 175.00
View-Master, King Of The Cowboys, No. 945, 1950 .... 15.00
Yo-Yo, Roy & Trigger, Plastic, Paper Insert Front & Back, 1950, 3 In. .... 13.00 to 18.00

ROYAL BAYREUTH is the name of a factory that was founded in Tettau, Bavaria, in 1794. It has continued to modern times. The marks have changed through the years. A stylized crest, the name *Royal Bayreuth*, and the word *Bavaria* appear in slightly different forms from 1870 to about 1919. Later dishes may include the words *U.S. Zone*, the year of the issue, or the word *Germany* instead of *Bavaria*. Related pieces may be found listed in the Rose Tapestry, Sand Babies, Snow Babies, and Sunbonnet Babies categories.

Ashtray, Highland Sheep Scene 65.00
Bowl, Corinthian, 3 In. 70.00
Bowl, Goats, Oval 110.00
Bowl, Nautilus Shell, 10 In. 195.00
Bowl, Red Poppy, 8 In. 350.00
Bowl, Soldier On Arabian Horse, Handles .... 95.00 to 98.00
Bowl, Tomato, 4 1/2 In. .... 350.00 to 395.00
Box, Cover, Multicolored Art Nouveau Lady 2500.00
Box, Cover, Musicians Scene, 2 x 4 In. 110.00
Box, Playing Cards, Ship Scene 175.00
Box, Tomato, Large 50.00
Candleholder, Basset Hound, Brown, 4 1/2 In. 425.00
Candleholder, Brittany Women 275.00
Candleholder, Man With Chickens, Blue Mark, 5 In. 165.00
Candleholder, Rose 600.00
Candy Dish, Pearl Grape Wreath, Blue Mark 50.00

Chamberstick, Corinthian 55.00
Chocolate Pot, Little Bo Peep, 6 1/4 In. 350.00
Coffeepot, Cover, 2 Chinoiserie Figures Holding Parasols, Red, 1730, 7 In. 2587.00
Coffeepot, Exotic Bird In Flight, 3 Chinoiserie Figures, Brown, Red, 7 In. 3737.00
Cracker Jar, Babes In The Woods 650.00
Cracker Jar, Grape 550.00
Creamer, Alligator, 4 1/2 In. ....295.00 to 350.00
Creamer, Apple, 3 3/4 In. ....100.00 to 245.00
Creamer, Bull, 4 In. 195.00
Creamer, Butterfly, 4 1/4 In. 1150.00
Creamer, Butterfly, Open Wing 225.00
Creamer, Candle Girl, Pinch Spout, Brown 145.00
Creamer, Cat, 5 In. ....225.00 to 295.00
Creamer, Cavern Scene, Blue Mark 75.00
Creamer, Chick, 4 In. 250.00
Creamer, Chrysanthemum, Blue Mark, 3 1/2 In. 275.00
Creamer, Clown, 4 1/2 In. 600.00
Creamer, Coachman 265.00
Creamer, Coachman, 4 3/4 In. 375.00
Creamer, Corinthian, Pinched Spout, 4 3/4 In. 65.00
Creamer, Cover, Red Poppy 400.00
Creamer, Cows, 4 In. 225.00
Creamer, Crow, 4 3/4 In. 195.00
Creamer, Dachshund, 4 1/4 In. 225.00
Creamer, Devil & Cards, 4 In. 175.00
Creamer, Devil & Cards, Blue Mark 265.00
Creamer, Duck, Multicolored, 4 1/2 In. 395.00
Creamer, Elk, 4 1/2 In. 110.00
Creamer, Fox Hunt 65.00
Creamer, Girl With Basket, 4 1/4 In. 450.00
Creamer, Highland Goat Scene, Pinch Spout 225.00
Creamer, Highland Sheep Scene 195.00
Creamer, Hunt Scene, Man With Gun 175.00
Creamer, Hunt, 3 In. 85.00
Creamer, Hunting Scene, Fox Hounds ....125.00 to 175.00
Creamer, Lamplighter, 4 1/2 In. 250.00
Creamer, Lemon, 3 3/4 In. 150.00
Creamer, Little Boy Blue 115.00
Creamer, Lobster, 4 In. ....125.00 to 190.00
Creamer, Monk, 4 1/2 In. 860.00
Creamer, Monkey, 4 1/4 In. 400.00
Creamer, Mountain Goat, 3 3/4 In. 275.00
Creamer, Mountain Goat, 4 1/2 In. ....120.00 to 145.00
Creamer, Mountain Goat, Blue Mark, 4 1/2 In. 160.00
Creamer, Orange, 4 1/2 In. 205.00
Creamer, Pansy, 4 In. 260.00
Creamer, Parakeet, Green, 3 3/4 In. 250.00
Creamer, Parrot Handle, 5 1/4 In. 395.00
Creamer, Peasant Musicians 150.00
Creamer, Peasant Musicians, 3 1/2 In. 175.00
Creamer, Pelican, Pink, 4 3/4 In. 215.00
Creamer, Platypus, 4 In. 900.00
Creamer, Poodle, Black, 4 1/2 In. 245.00
Creamer, Poodle, Gray, 4 1/2 In. 225.00
Creamer, Poppy, 4 1/2 In. 275.00
Creamer, Poppy, White, 3 3/4 In. 95.00
Creamer, Red Devil, Full Bodied, 3 3/4 In. 285.00
Creamer, Robin, 4 In. ....135.00 to 375.00
Creamer, Rooster, 4 1/4 In. 375.00
Creamer, Sand Babies, Blue Mark, 4 1/2 In. 295.00
Creamer, Santa Claus, 4 1/4 In. 2200.00
Creamer, Scottish Highland Cattle Scene, 2 Handles 225.00
Creamer, Seal, 4 In. 250.00

Creamer, Shell Shape, Murex, 3 3/8 x 2 3/4 x 5 1/4 In. 85.00
Creamer, Spiky Shell, White Satin Finish, 4 1/2 In. 175.00
Creamer, St. Bernard, 3 1/2 In. . . . . .225.00 to 285.00
Creamer, Water Buffalo, 3 3/4 In. 195.00
Cup & Saucer, Floral Design, Gold Handle, Demitasse 22.00
Cup & Saucer, Poppy, Red 160.00
Dish, Brittany Girl, Maple Leaf Shape 120.00
Dish, Lemon, Flower, Green Ground, 6 3/4 In. . . . . .38.00 to 45.00
Ewer, Shawl Lady, 4 In. 175.00
Hair Receiver, Poppy, Footed 110.00
Hatpin Holder, Hunting Scene, Rider On Horse, Dogs, Blue Mark 265.00
Hatpin Holder, Owl, Figural 725.00
Hatpin Holder, Rose Tapestry, Flared Base, 1902, 4 1/2 In. 82.00
Humidor, Cavalier Lighting Pipe 390.00
Match Holder, Boy & Donkey 375.00
Match Holder, Goat, Wall Mount 530.00
Match Holder, Hanging, Red Clown 550.00
Match Holder, Hanging, Tapestry, Sheep 485.00
Match Holder, Santa In Red Suit, Holds Christmas Bag, 5 1/4 In. 5175.00
Mug, Beer, Elk 325.00
Nappy, Little Miss Muffet, Handle, Ruffled, Blue Mark 185.00
Pipe Holder, Basset Hound, Black 395.00
Pitcher, 3 Arabs On Horseback, Pinched Top 185.00
Pitcher, Apple 625.00
Pitcher, Art Nouveau Lady 2300.00
Pitcher, Babes In Woods . . . . .400.00 to 485.00
Pitcher, Brittany Girl, 10 In. 495.00
Pitcher, Cows, Green Bottom, Blue Mark, 4 In. 95.00
Pitcher, Dutch Woman & Child, Child Forms Handle, 5 In. 1155.00
Pitcher, Eagle 1650.00
Pitcher, Elk, 7 In. . . . . .550.00 to 600.00
Pitcher, Elk, Blue Mark, 5 In. 285.00
Pitcher, Figural, Fish, 7 1/2 In. 2090.00
Pitcher, Lady & Horse, 4 3/4 In. 425.00
Pitcher, Little Boy Blue, Floral, Green, Pink, Yellow, 3 1/2 In. 200.00
Pitcher, Lobster 495.00
Pitcher, Man With Pipe, Signed, 9 In. 285.00
Pitcher, Milk, Seahorse Handle 385.00
Pitcher, Milk, Skiff With Sail 195.00
Pitcher, Milk, Watermelon 550.00
Pitcher, Mountain Goat Tapestry, Pinch Spout 225.00
Pitcher, Mountain Goat, Pinch Spout 225.00
Pitcher, Peering Lady, Gold Rim, 5 In. 325.00
Pitcher, Rose Tapestry, Applied Handle, 1902, 3 1/2 In. 192.00
Pitcher, Sand Babies 98.00
Pitcher, Sunbonnet Babies, 4 In. 195.00
Pitcher, Woman & Horse, Signed 425.00
Planter, Cottage By Waterfall, Handles 150.00
Planter, Oak Leaf, White, Small 325.00
Plaque, Woman Descending Staircase With Candle 225.00
Plate, Christmas, 1967 . . . . 87.50
Plate, Christmas, 1968 . . . . 87.50
Plate, Christmas, 1969 . . . . 87.50
Plate, Floral, Hand Painted Centers, 11 In. 120.00
Plate, Green Leaf Under Plate 19.00
Plate, Man, Fishing, 8 In. 95.00
Plate, Man, Hunting, 8 In. 95.00
Plate, Multicolored, Anheuser-Busch, Brown Emblem, Green Wreaths, 8 In. 675.00
Plate, Peacock, Blue Mark, 9 1/2 In. 600.00
Plate, Sunbonnet, 6 In. 140.00
Porridge Set, Jack In Beanstalk, Little Boy Blue, Bopeep, 3 Piece 250.00
Relish, Shell 225.00
Relish, Spiky Shell 175.00

Rose Bowl, Leaf Underplate, Pink, White, 5 3/4 In. 295.00
Salt, Elk ....60.00 to 200.00
Salt, Red Pepper 285.00
Salt & Pepper, Elk 125.00
Salt & Pepper, Poppy, Lavender Satin 350.00
Salt & Pepper, Purple Grape, Blue Mark 75.00
Salt & Pepper, Spiky Shell 150.00
Salt & Pepper, Tomato 110.00
Strainer, Tea, Red Poppy 395.00
Sugar, Cover, Spiky Shell 175.00
Sugar, Cover, Turtle 1500.00
Sugar & Creamer, Figural, Red Poppy, Signed, 3 1/2 x 5 In. 70.00
Tea Caddy, 2 Chinamen Seated On Either Side Of Potted Palm, Red, 4 In. 2875.00
Teapot, Orange 350.00
Teapot, Rural Scene, Brown, Yellow, Green, 1902 .... 198.00
Teapot, Spiky Shell 350.00
Tile, Tea, Beach Babies 150.00
Toothpick, Arab, On Donkey, Footed 100.00
Toothpick, Boy With Turkeys 200.00
Toothpick, Cavalier Musician 140.00
Toothpick, Clown, Red 525.00
Toothpick, Coachman 600.00
Toothpick, Dutch Girl Pulling Wagon, Tub Shape 77.00
Toothpick, Grecian Design, 3 Handles 65.00
Toothpick, Heron, Tricorner 120.00
Toothpick, Horses & Riders 105.00
Toothpick, Lamplighter, Green 700.00
Toothpick, Man Lighting Pipe, Brown & Green Ground 71.00
Toothpick, Mountain & Sheep, 2 Handles 60.00
Toothpick, Peasant Musicians, 3 Handles 55.00
Toothpick, Penguins, Yellow Ground, Triangular Shape, Blue Mark, 2 3/4 In. 187.00
Toothpick, Red Pepper 285.00
Toothpick, Spiky Shell 95.00
Toothpick, Woman On Horse, Man On Ground, Gypsy Kettle Shape 55.00
Trivet, Sand Babies, Marked 95.00
Vase, Art Nouveau Lady, 3 Sections, Portrait, 7 3/4 In. 2500.00
Vase, Black Corinthian, Conical, 8 1/2 In. 225.00
Vase, Candle Girl, Pink Rim 4 1/2 In. 195.00
Vase, Cavalier, Cobalt Blue & Salmon Top, 5 1/4 In. 65.00
Vase, Cavaliers, Toasting Each Other, 3 Ornate Olive Green Handles, 9 In. 138.00
Vase, Fly Fisherman, 5 1/2 In. 110.00
Vase, Lady With Horse, Signed, 3 1/2 In. 145.00
Vase, Lady With Purple Hat, 7 1/2 In. 350.00
Vase, Lady With Purple Hat, Handle, 5 In. 225.00
Vase, Little Boy Sitting On Log, Between Donkeys, 4 1/2 In. 125.00
Vase, Peasant Musicians, Corset Shaped, Mandolin, 7 3/4 In. 295.00
Vase, Portrait, Man, Lighting Pipe, 5 1/2 In. 90.00
Vase, Roses, Blue Mark, 10 In. 225.00
Wall Pocket, Grape 395.00
Waste Bowl, 2 Birds In Flight Above Peasant, Yellow, 1730-1740, 6 In. 5462.00

ROYAL BONN is the nineteenth- and twentieth-century trade name for
the Bonn China Manufactory. It was established in 1755 in Bonn,
Germany. A general line of porcelain was made. Many marks were
used, most including the name *Bonn*, the initials *FM*, and a crown.

Clock, Floral Case, Light Green, Ansonia Clock Company, 15 x 13 In. 660.00
Clock, Floral Case, Red Brown, Ansonia Clock Company, 14 x 14 In. 522.00
Ewer, Red, Pink Flowers, Raised Gold Handle, 10 3/8 In. 75.00
Jardiniere, Floral, Gilt Design, Handle, Footed, 15 In. 242.00
Urn, Windmill, Sailing Ships Scene, Floral Motif, Blue, White, 9 3/4 In. 80.00
Vase, Female, Flowers, c.1900, 8 1/4 In. 575.00
Vase, Floral Design, 6 In. 50.00
Vase, Light Green Floral Design, Applied Side Handles, Flame Finial, 12 In. 140.00

Vase, Raised Gold Flowers, Floral Sprays, Link Handles, Footed, 20 x 5 In. 240.00
Vase, Sand Tapestry, 4 Multicolored Panels, Gold Band Top, F.A. Mehlem, 8 In. 330.00
Vase, Stylized Flowers, Viking Ship At Sea, 2 Handles, 13 1/2 In. 522.00
Vase, Woman's Portrait, Outdoor Scene, Bright Pink, Fancy Gold Trim, 14 In. 1160.00

ROYAL COPENHAGEN porcelain and pottery have been made in
Denmark since 1772. The Christmas plate series started in 1908. The
figurines with pale blue and gray glazes have remained popular in this
century and are still being made. Many other old and new style porcelains are made today.

Bowl, American Revolutionary War Scenes, Geo. Washington, 7 x 13 In. 1650.00
Bowl, Blue Lace, Footed, 7 In. 365.00
Bowl, Open Lace, Blue, Fluted 135.00
Bowl, Strawberry Plant Center, Serrated Rim, Square, 9 In. 865.00
Butter Pat, Blue Fluted 34.00
Candlestick, Leaf, Lion Design, Cobalt Blue, Regency, 9 In., Pair 46.00
Chamberstick, Blue Fluted Half Lace Pattern, Finger Handle, Brass, 4 In. 44.00
Chop Plate, Floral Spray, Reticulated Rim, 14 1/2 In. 920.00
Cup & Saucer, Flora Danica 495.00
Figurine, 3 Kittens, Sleeping 135.00
Figurine, Agnette & Merman, Signed, 22 In. 1100.00
Figurine, Baby Robin, No. 2238 .... 65.00
Figurine, Boy In Raincoat, No. 3556, 7 In. 150.00
Figurine, Boy On Gourd, No. 4539, 4 1/2 x 4 1/2 In. 100.00
Figurine, Boy On Rock, No. 1659, 12 In. 975.00
Figurine, Boy, Whittling, No. 905, 7 1/2 In. ....165.00 to 175.00
Figurine, Children, Playing, No. 1568, 4 1/2 In. 140.00
Figurine, Children, Reading, No. 1567, 3 3/4 In. 120.00
Figurine, Dog, Wire Terrier, No. 3165, 4 1/2 x 4 1/2 In. 150.00
Figurine, Foal, Lying Down, No. 5691 .... 150.00
Figurine, Fox, Curled Around 4 Pups, 6 1/2 x 4 1/2 In. 325.00
Figurine, Fox, Sitting 145.00
Figurine, Girl Bathing, No. 1229, 1935, 5 In. 195.00
Figurine, Girl Milking Cow 275.00
Figurine, Girl Standing, No. 1251, 7 1/2 x 4 In. 125.00
Figurine, Girl With Calf, No. 779, 6 1/2 x 6 1/2 In. 235.00
Figurine, Girl With Doll, No. 1938, 4 3/4 x 4 1/2 In. ....245.00 to 250.00
Figurine, Girl, Knitting, No. 1314, 5 3/4 x 3 1/2 In. 250.00
Figurine, Girl, With Teddy Bear, No. 1879, 5 1/8 In. 290.00
Figurine, Goose Girl, No. 528, 7 1/2 In. 175.00
Figurine, Madonna, Baby, White, 8 1/2 In. 75.00
Figurine, Man, With 2 Calves, 1858, 9 x 7 In. 400.00
Figurine, Nestling Sheep, No. 2709, 4 In. 75.00
Figurine, Satyr, On Columnar Plinth, Lizard, Porcelain, 8 1/2 In. 250.00
Figurine, Young Girl, Blue Polka Dot Dress, Holding Doll, No. 3539, 5 x 2 In. 86.00
Mustard, Flora Danica 195.00
Plaque, Christmas 1954 .... 110.00
Plate, Bead & Sprig Borders, Porcelain, 10 1/4 In. 110.00
Plate, Bicentennial, 1978, Electromagnetism 35.00
Plate, Christmas, 1914, Sparrows In Tree At Church Of Holy Ghost 180.00
Plate, Christmas, 1925, Street Scene From Christianshavn 80.00
Plate, Christmas, 1931, Mother And Child 100.00
Plate, Christmas, 1934, The Hermitage Castle 210.00
Plate, Christmas, 1935, Fishing Boat Off Kronborg Castle 310.00
Plate, Christmas, 1945, A Peaceful Motif 225.00
Plate, Christmas, 1952, Christmas In The Forest 140.00
Plate, Christmas, 1956, Rosenborg Castle 200.00
Plate, Christmas, 1957, The Good Shepherd 125.00
Plate, Christmas, 1958, Sunshine Over Greenland 125.00
Plate, Christmas, 1961, The Training Ship 135.00
Plate, Christmas, 1962, The Little Mermaid At Wintertime ....185.00 to 195.00
Plate, Christmas, 1982, Waiting For Christmas 25.00
Plate, Christmas, 1992, The Royal Coach 65.00

Plate, Flora Danica, Factory Mark, 20th Century, 11 1/2 In. 1265.00
Plate, Osterland, 1972 .... 25.00
Plate, Scalloped, Hand Painted, 6 1/4 In. 25.00
Plate, Statue Of Liberty, 8 In. 75.00
Salt Box, Pheasant, Blue, 1923 Mark 80.00
Sauceboat, Flora Danica 3600.00
Sugar & Creamer, Chocolate, Flora Danica 1200.00
Tray, Pen, Blotter, Butterfly, Set 48.00
Tureen, Sauce, Cover, 7 In., Pair 276.00
Tureen, Soup, Flora Danica, Botanical Specimens, Twig Handles, 14 In. 5750.00
Vase, 2 Flying Swans, Landscape, 1955, 12 1/2 In. 302.00
Vase, Faience, 1989-1928, 8 In. ....130.00 to 155.00
Vase, Flying Geese, 1955, 12 1/2 In. 214.00
Vase, Hand Painted Under Glaze, Blackberry Design, Signed, 5 1/2 In. 165.00
Vase, Schooner Design, Mounted As A Lamp, Tapered, 32 1/2 In. 431.00

ROYAL COPLEY china was made by the Spaulding China Company of Sebring, Ohio, from 1939 to 1960. The figural planters and the small figurines, especially those with Art Deco designs, are of great collector interest.

Ashtray, Horse Head 30.00
Bank, Pig, For My Cadillac, 7 1/2 In. 50.00
Bank, Pig, Pink Bow Tie, 6 1/4 In. ....55.00 to 65.00
Figurine, Barefoot Boy & Girl, Red Hat, Pair 75.00
Figurine, Bear, With Mandolin ....65.00 to 85.00
Figurine, Blue Jay, 8 In. 50.00
Figurine, Cockatoo 50.00
Figurine, Dog, In Picnic Basket 70.00
Figurine, Dog, Raised Paw 50.00
Figurine, Elephant, Stuffed ....60.00 to 65.00
Figurine, Parrot, Lime Green 40.00
Figurine, Swallow 50.00
Figurine, Teal Hen & Drake 200.00
Figurine, Titmouse, 8 In. 50.00
Head Vase, Blackamoor, 9 In. 90.00
Head Vase, Woman 45.00
Pitcher, Fruit, Tan Pome 75.00
Planter, Chartreuse Deer Leaping, Dark Green Border 20.00
Planter, Clown 140.00
Planter, Dog With Wagon 35.00
Planter, Mallard Duck, Split Neck, Red Breast, 8 In. 25.00
Planter, Oriental Boy, Green, Yellow 25.00
Planter, Pirate Head, Large 40.00
Planter, Rabbit 45.00
Vase, Chinese Girl, Label, 8 In. 20.00
Vase, Fish, 8 1/2 In. 35.00
Vase, Gold Trim, 7 In. 20.00
Wall Pocket, Cream, Light Brown, Salt 45.00
Wall Pocket, Old Woman 75.00
Wall Pocket, Oriental Girl, Pursing Lips 30.00
Wall Pocket, Oriental Girl, Smiling 30.00

ROYAL CROWN DERBY Company, Ltd., was established in England in 1890. There is a complex family tree that includes the Derby, Crown Derby, and Royal Crown Derby porcelains. The Royal Crown Derby mark includes the name and a crown. The words *Made in England* were used after 1921. The company is now a part of Royal Doulton Tableware Ltd.

Box, Mandarin, Cobalt Blue Design, Porcelain, 4 1/4 In. 220.00
Candlestick, Cobalt Blue, Mandarin Design, Porcelain, 10 In., Pair 1200.00
Dinner Service, Imari, 134 Pieces 4600.00
Dish, Cover, Oriental Pattern, 11 1/2 In. 285.00
Figurine, Lamb, Long Point Ears, Short Full Tail 95.00

Lighter, Table, Imari Pattern 100.00
Plate, Cobalt Blue, Mandarin Design, Porcelain, 10 1/2 In., 12 Piece 1250.00
Plate, Red Leaves, 8 1/2 In. 22.00
Tureen, Notched Cover, Cobalt Blue, Mandarin Design, 11 3/4 In. 1000.00
Vase, Floral Design, Raised Gilt Rim, Teal Blue Ground, 1896, 12 In. 290.00
Vase, Rocaille, Multicolored, Beige Ground, Gilt Highlights, 10 In. 175.00

ROYAL DOULTON is the name used on Doulton and Company pottery made from 1902 to the present. Doulton and Company of England was founded in 1853. Pieces made before 1902 are listed in this book under Doulton. Royal Doulton collectors search for the out-of-production figurines, character jugs, vases, and series wares. Some vases and animal figurines were made with a special red glaze called flambe. Sung and Chang glazed pieces are rare. The multicolored glaze is very thick and looks as if it were dropped on the clay.

Animal, Bird, Owl, Flambe, 12 1/4 In. 490.00
Animal, Bird, Peacock, HN 2577 .... 220.00
Animal, Cat, Lucky The Cat, K 12, 2 1/2 In. 125.00
Animal, Cat, Persian, HN 999 .... 155.00
Animal, Cat, Sitting, HN 2259, Flambe, 11 1/2 In. 495.00
Animal, Dog With Bone, HN 1159, 3 1/2 In. ....50.00 to 70.00
Animal, Dog, Airedale, HN 1024, 4 In. 275.00
Animal, Dog, American Foxhound, HN 2525, 5 In. 650.00
Animal, Dog, Boxer, HN 2643, 5 1/2 In. ....125.00 to 160.00
Animal, Dog, Bull Terrier, K 14, 1 1/2 In. 325.00
Animal, Dog, Bulldog, HN 1047, 3 In. 170.00
Animal, Dog, Bulldog, HN 1074, 3 In. 225.00
Animal, Dog, Bulldog, Union Jack, HN 6406, 6 In. 395.00
Animal, Dog, Cocker Spaniel, HN 1002, 6 1/2 In. 450.00
Animal, Dog, Cocker Spaniel, HN 1036, 5 In. 150.00
Animal, Dog, Cocker Spaniel, HN 1037, 3 1/2 In. 140.00
Animal, Dog, Cocker Spaniel, HN 1187 .... 160.00
Animal, Dog, Collie, HN 1057, 7 1/2 In. ....675.00 to 700.00
Animal, Dog, Dalmatian, HN 1113, 5 1/2 In. ....125.00 to 215.00
Animal, Dog, English Setter, HN 1050, 5 In. ....125.00 to 150.00
Animal, Dog, English Setter, HN 1051, 4 In. 195.00
Animal, Dog, French Poodle, HN 2631, 5 In. 225.00
Animal, Dog, Greyhound, HN 1065, 8 1/2 In. 1400.00
Animal, Dog, Greyhound, HN 1067, Small 425.00
Animal, Dog, Irish Setter, HN 1054, 7 1/2 In. 650.00
Animal, Dog, Pekinese, HN 1011, 6 1/2 In. 750.00
Animal, Dog, Pekinese, HN 1012, 3 In. 135.00
Animal, Dog, Rough Haired Terrier, HN 1007 .... 200.00
Animal, Dog, Scottish Terrier, HN 1016, 3 1/2 In. ....125.00 to 165.00
Animal, Dog, Sealyham, HN 1030, 5 In. 775.00
Animal, Duck, Drake, HN 2591, 2 1/2 In. 15.00
Animal, Elephant & Young, Flambe, HN 3548, 4 In. 220.00
Animal, Fox, Sitting, Flambe Sung, HN 2634 .... 160.00
Animal, Horse, Chestnut Mare And Foal, HN 2522, 6 1/2 In. 650.00
Animal, Horse, Gude Mare Gray, HN 2570, 9 In. 350.00
Animal, Kitten, Lying On Back, HN 2579, 1 1/2 In. 95.00
Animal, Leopard On Rock, HN 2638 .... 260.00
Animal, Penguin, K 23 .... 110.00
Animal, Tiger, On Rock, HN 2639, 11 1/2 In. 1500.00
Ash Pot, Falstaff 75.00
Ash Pot, Parson Brown 125.00
Ash Pot, Sairey Gamp 150.00
Ashtray, Dick Turpin 85.00
Biscuit Jar, Flambe Sung, Elephant Finial 2200.00
Bottle, Landscape Scene, Shepherd, Brown Glossy Glaze, 2 Handles, 7 x 5 In. 275.00
Bottle, Zorro 65.00
Bowl, All Fools Are Not Knaves, But All Knaves Are Fools, Crombie Figures 475.00
Bowl, Butterfly Luster, Yellow Ground, Octagonal, Artist, 1918, 9 1/2 In. 230.00

Bowl, Cereal, Bunnykins, Game Of Golf, Vernon, c.1930 .125.00 to 150.00
Bowl, Fox Hunting, 18 1/2 In. 110.00
Bowl, Fruit, Skating, 10 In. 302.50
Bowl, Fruit, Willow, 1902-1922, 7 x 3 1/2 In. 135.00
Bust, Mr. Pickwick 115.00
Bust, Sam Weller 100.00

Royal Doulton character jugs depict the head and shoulders of the subject. They are made in four sizes: large, 5 1/4 to 7 inches; small, 3 1/4 to 4 inches; miniature, 2 1/4 to 2 1/2 inches; and tiny, 1 1/4 inches. Toby jugs portray a seated, full figure.

Character Jug, 'Arriet, Large 165.00
Character Jug, 'Arriet, Small 150.00
Character Jug, 'Arry, Large . . . . .165.00 to 300.00
Character Jug, Anne Boleyn, Large . . . . .65.00 to 80.00
Character Jug, Antony & Cleopatra, Large 200.00
Character Jug, Athos, 7 1/2 In. 73.00
Character Jug, Auld Mac, Large 85.00
Character Jug, Auld Mac, Small 48.00
Character Jug, Bacchus, Large . . . . .70.00 to 120.00
Character Jug, Bacchus, Small 65.00
Character Jug, Beefeater, Large 90.00
Character Jug, Ben Franklin, Small 50.00
Character Jug, Busker, Large 175.00
Character Jug, Buzfuz, Odd Size 195.00
Character Jug, Buzfuz, Small 125.00
Character Jug, Captain Cuttle, Small 125.00
Character Jug, Captain Henry Morgan, Large . . . . .70.00 to 90.00
Character Jug, Captain Hook, Large . . . . .495.00 to 750.00
Character Jug, Cardinal, Small 55.00
Character Jug, Catherine Of Aragon, Large . . . . .80.00 to 95.00
Character Jug, Clown, White Hair, Large 950.00
Character Jug, Cook & The Cheshire Cat, Large 15.00
Character Jug, David Copperfield, Tiny 50.00
Character Jug, Dick Turpin, Large 135.00
Character Jug, Dick Turpin, Small 80.00
Character Jug, Don Quixote, Large 135.00
Character Jug, Falconer, Large . . . . .80.00 to 110.00
Character Jug, Fat Boy, Miniature 60.00
Character Jug, Fortune Teller, Large 250.00
Character Jug, Fortune Teller, Miniature 450.00
Character Jug, Fortune Teller, Small 400.00
Character Jug, Gaoler, Miniature 160.00
Character Jug, Gardener, Large . . . . .150.00 to 240.00
Character Jug, General Custer & Sitting Bull, Large 145.00
Character Jug, George Washington, Large 100.00
Character Jug, Gondolier, Large 600.00
Character Jug, Gone Away, Large 110.00
Character Jug, Granny, Small 55.00
Character Jug, Grant & Lee, Large 225.00
Character Jug, Groucho Marx, Large 170.00
Character Jug, Guardsman, Large 85.00
Character Jug, Gulliver, Small 500.00
Character Jug, Henry Morgan, Large 80.00
Character Jug, Henry VIII, Large 65.00
Character Jug, Jester, Small 60.00
Character Jug, Jockey, Large 350.00
Character Jug, John Barleycorn, Large 225.00
Character Jug, John Barleycorn, Small 60.00
Character Jug, John Peel, Miniature 65.00
Character Jug, John Peel, Small . . . . .60.00 to 95.00
Character Jug, John Peel, Tiny 165.00
Character Jug, Lobster Man, Large . . . . .105.00 to 110.00

Character Jug, Long John Silver, Large ....66.00 to 88.00
Character Jug, Louis Armstrong, Large 195.00
Character Jug, Lumberjack, Large 75.00
Character Jug, Mephistopheles, Large 2200.00
Character Jug, Mephistopheles, Small ....725.00 to 925.00
Character Jug, Merlin, Large 60.00
Character Jug, Monty, Large 100.00
Character Jug, Mr. Micawber, Miniature 45.00
Character Jug, Mr. Micawber, Small 70.00
Character Jug, Mr. Pickwick, Large 125.00
Character Jug, Mr. Pickwick, Miniature 85.00
Character Jug, Mr. Pickwick, Tiny 225.00
Character Jug, Mr. Quaker, Large 625.00
Character Jug, Neptune, Large 105.00
Character Jug, Night Watchman, Miniature 160.00
Character Jug, Old Charley, Large ....75.00 to 115.00
Character Jug, Old Charley, Miniature 55.00
Character Jug, Old Charley, Small 45.00
Character Jug, Old King Cole, Small 145.00
Character Jug, Old Salt, Large 82.00
Character Jug, Old Salt, Small 40.00
Character Jug, Paddy, Large 82.00
Character Jug, Parson Brown, Small 85.00
Character Jug, Pied Piper, Miniature 85.00
Character Jug, Pied Piper, Small ....100.00 to 150.00
Character Jug, Poacher, Large ....86.00 to 125.00
Character Jug, Punch & Judy Man, Large 600.00
Character Jug, Queen Victoria, Large 150.00
Character Jug, Queen Victoria, Small 100.00
Character Jug, Ringmaster, Large 200.00
Character Jug, Rip Van Winkle, Small 45.00
Character Jug, Robin Hood, Large 148.00
Character Jug, Robin Hood, Small 35.00
Character Jug, Robinson Crusoe, Large 75.00
Character Jug, Ronald Reagan, Large 475.00
Character Jug, Sairey Gamp, Large ....90.00 to 115.00
Character Jug, Sairey Gamp, Tiny 90.00
Character Jug, Sam Johnson, Large ....275.00 to 285.00
Character Jug, Sam Weller, Miniature 80.00
Character Jug, Santa Claus, Reindeer Handle, Large ....100.00 to 185.00
Character Jug, Santa Claus, Sack Of Toys Handle, Large 250.00
Character Jug, Scaramouche, Large 100.00
Character Jug, Simon The Cellarer, Large 120.00
Character Jug, Simon The Cellarer, Small 65.00
Character Jug, Sleuth, Large 80.00
Character Jug, Smuggler, Large 110.00
Character Jug, St. George, Large 275.00
Character Jug, Toby Philpots, Large 125.00
Character Jug, Tony Philpots, Small 75.00
Character Jug, Town Crier, Large 150.00
Character Jug, Vicar Of Bray, Large 215.00
Character Jug, Viking, Large 137.00
Coffeepot, Arcadia 175.00
Cup, Bunnykins, Golf Scene, Bunny In Knickers Swinging Club, Vernon 250.00
Cup & Saucer, Bouillon, White, Encrusted Gold, 12 Sets 470.00
Cup & Saucer, Coaching Days 85.00
Cup & Saucer, He That Always Complains, Is Never Pitied, Crombie Figures 275.00
Dish, Gleaners, Oval, 11 1/4 x 9 In. 45.00
Ewer, Dickens, Fighting Fish, 13 In. 850.00
Ewer, Floral Design, Green, Brown, Blue, 1902, 6 1/2 In. 77.00
Ewer, Lily Design, Brown, Gold Border, Cobalt Blue, 8 1/4 In. ....118.00 to 198.00
Figurine, Adrienne, HN 2152 .... 175.00
Figurine, Afternoon Tea, HN 1747 ....265.00 to 500.00

Figurine, Alice, HN 2158 .... 175.00
Figurine, All Aboard, HN 2940 .... 200.00
Figurine, Alsatian, HN 1117 .... 175.00
Figurine, Amy, HN 3316 .... 575.00
Figurine, Anna, HN 2802 .... 160.00
Figurine, Annabella, HN 1875 .... 750.00
Figurine, Apple Maid, HN 2160 .... 425.00
Figurine, Ascot, HN 2356 .... 250.00
Figurine, Auctioneer, HN 2988 .... 200.00
Figurine, Autumn Breezes, HN 1911 .... 125.00
Figurine, Autumn Breezes, HN 1913 .... 325.00
Figurine, Autumn Breezes, HN 1934 ....132.00 to 375.00
Figurine, Autumn Breezes, HN 2147 ....375.00 to 475.00
Figurine, Ballerina, HN 2116 .... 265.00
Figurine, Balloon Man, HN 1954 ....115.00 to 225.00
Figurine, Beat You To It, HN 2871 .... 215.00
Figurine, Beggar, HN 2175 .... 450.00
Figurine, Belle, HN 2340 .... 110.00
Figurine, Belle, HN 3703 .... 350.00
Figurine, Biddy Penny Farthing, HN 1843 .... 172.00
Figurine, Blacksmith, HN 2782 .... 200.00
Figurine, Blithe Morning, HN 2021 .... 110.00
Figurine, Blithe Morning, HN 2065 .... 121.00
Figurine, Bluebeard, HN 2105 ....450.00 to 650.00
Figurine, Boatman, HN 2417 .... 210.00
Figurine, Bon Appetit, HN 2444 .... 275.00
Figurine, Boy With Turban, HN 1214 .... 575.00
Figurine, Bride, HN 2873 .... 110.00
Figurine, Bride, HN 3284 .... 170.00
Figurine, Broken Lance, HN 2041 .... 400.00
Figurine, Bunnykins, Mr. Bunnybeat 125.00
Figurine, Bunnykins, Rise & Shine 69.00
Figurine, Bunnykins, Santa, 4 1/4 In. 80.00
Figurine, Bunnykins, Touchdown 65.00
Figurine, Buzfuz, HN 538 .... 70.00
Figurine, Carpenter, HN 2678 .... 225.00
Figurine, Carpet Seller, HN 1464 .... 325.00
Figurine, Cassim, HN 1231 .... 315.00
Figurine, Cellist, HN 2226 .... 425.00
Figurine, Charlie Chaplin, HN 2771 .... 325.00
Figurine, Charlotte, HN 2423 .... 275.00
Figurine, Cherie, HN 2341 ....100.00 to 200.00
Figurine, Chief, HN 2892 .... 140.00
Figurine, Christmas Morn, HN 1992 ....145.00 to 270.00
Figurine, Christmas Parcels, HN 2851 .... 350.00
Figurine, Christmas Time, HN 2110 ....400.00 to 450.00
Figurine, Cissie, HN 1809 .... 95.00
Figurine, Clockmaker, HN 2279 .... 300.00
Figurine, Cookie, HN 2218 .... 175.00
Figurine, Coralie, HN 2307 ....150.00 to 200.00
Figurine, Cradle Song, HN 2246 .... 465.00
Figurine, Craftsman, HN 2284 .... 300.00
Figurine, Daffy-Down-Dilly, HN 1712 .... 137.00
Figurine, Daisy, HN 3805 .... 270.00
Figurine, Darling, HN 1985 .... 60.00
Figurine, Deidre, HN 2020 .... 375.00
Figurine, Denise, HN 2273 .... 300.00
Figurine, Doctor, HN 2858 .... 225.00
Figurine, Dorcas, HN 1491 ....595.00 to 695.00
Figurine, Eleanor Of Provence, HN 2009 .... 625.00
Figurine, Embroidering, HN 2855 ....137.00 to 245.00
Figurine, Enchantment, HN 2178 ....100.00 to 275.00
Figurine, Fair Lady, HN 2193 .... 100.00

Figurine, Fair Lady, HN 2835 .... 225.00
Figurine, Fat Boy, HN 2096 .... 365.00
Figurine, Fleur, HN 2368 ....65.00 to 137.50
Figurine, Foaming Quart, HN 2162 .... 250.00
Figurine, Fragrance, HN 2334 ....121.00 to 150.00
Figurine, French Peasant, HN 2075 .... 500.00
Figurine, Friar Tuck, HN 2143 .... 400.00
Figurine, Frodo, HN 2912 .... 120.00
Figurine, Galadriel, HN 2615 .... 130.00
Figurine, Gardening Time, HN 3401 .... 175.00
Figurine, Genevieve, HN 1962 .... 295.00
Figurine, Genie, HN 2989 ....192.00 to 275.00
Figurine, Gimli, HN 2922 .... 175.00
Figurine, Gollywog, HN 2040 ....275.00 to 300.00
Figurine, Good Catch, HN 2258, 7 1/2 In. ....80.00 to 190.00
Figurine, Good King Wensceslas, HN 2118 .... 500.00
Figurine, Goody Two Shoes, HN 1905 .... 250.00
Figurine, Gossips, HN 2025 ....395.00 to 600.00
Figurine, Grace, HN 2318 ....93.00 to 225.00
Figurine, Gypsy Dance, HN 2230 .... 350.00
Figurine, Happy Anniversary, HN 3097 .... 160.00
Figurine, Homecoming, HN 3295 .... 275.00
Figurine, Honey, HN 1909 .... 295.00
Figurine, Hornpipe, HN 2161 .... 1050.00
Figurine, Hostess Of Williamsburg, HN 2209 .... 440.00
Figurine, Idle Hours, HN 3115 .... 65.00
Figurine, Irene, HN 1621 .... 345.00
Figurine, January, HN 2697 .... 150.00
Figurine, Jean, HN 2032 .... 374.00
Figurine, Jersey Milkmaid, HN 2057 ....190.00 to 345.00
Figurine, Jester, HN 1702 .... 950.00
Figurine, Jester, HN 2016 .... 465.00
Figurine, John F. Kennedy, White Suit, HN 2893 .... 8500.00
Figurine, Jovial Monk, HN 2144 .... 275.00
Figurine, Julia, HN 2705 .... 125.00
Figurine, June, HN 2991 .... 175.00
Figurine, Lady Charmian, HN 1949 .... 325.00
Figurine, Lady Diana Spencer, HN 2885 .... 750.00
Figurine, Lambing Time, HN 1890 .... 325.00
Figurine, Last Waltz, HN 2315 ....93.00 to 128.00
Figurine, Leaping Salmon, Flambe, HN 666, 12 1/2 In., Pair 3000.00
Figurine, Leda & The Swan, HN 2826 .... 690.00
Figurine, Legolas, HN 2917 .... 130.00
Figurine, Leisure Hour, HN 2055 ....345.00 to 650.00
Figurine, Lights Out, HN 2262 .... 225.00
Figurine, Little Boy Blue, HN 2062 ....125.00 to 225.00
Figurine, Little Bridesmaid, HN 1433 .... 275.00
Figurine, Little Bridesmaid, HN 2196 .... 95.00
Figurine, Lizzie, HN 2749 .... 225.00
Figurine, Lobsterman, HN 2317 .... 275.00
Figurine, Lorna, HN 2311 .... 175.00
Figurine, Lucy, HN 2863 .... 165.00
Figurine, Mandy, HN 2476 .... 125.00
Figurine, Margaret Of Anjou, HN 2012 .... 650.00
Figurine, Marguerite, HN 1928 .... 400.00
Figurine, Marie, HN 3357 .... 125.00
Figurine, Marjorie, HN 2788 .... 225.00
Figurine, Market Day, HN 1991 ....270.00 to 295.00
Figurine, Mary, HN 2374 .... 400.00
Figurine, Mary, HN 3375 .... 525.00
Figurine, Mary, Mary, HN 2044 .... 300.00
Figurine, Mask Seller, HN 1361 .... 1150.00
Figurine, Mask Seller, HN 2103 .... 125.00

Figurine, Master Sweep, HN 2205 .... 650.00
Figurine, Master, HN 2325 ....140.00 to 250.00
Figurine, Matilda, HN 2011 .... 625.00
Figurine, Maureen, HN 1770 .... 350.00
Figurine, Maxine, HN 3199 .... 175.00
Figurine, Maytime, HN 2113 .... 450.00
Figurine, Melanie, HN 2271 .... 275.00
Figurine, Mendicant, HN 1365 ....190.00 to 225.00
Figurine, Michele, HN 2234 .... 225.00
Figurine, Milady, HN 1970 .... 750.00
Figurine, Minuet, HN 2019 ....250.00 to 325.00
Figurine, Miss Demure, HN 1402 .... 325.00
Figurine, Modesty, HN 2744 .... 200.00
Figurine, Mother's Help, HN 2151 .... 220.00
Figurine, Mr. Micawber, HN 2097 .... 350.00
Figurine, Mr. Pickwick, HN 2099 ....350.00 to 500.00
Figurine, Mrs. Fitzh Bert, HN 2007 .... 795.00
Figurine, My Pretty Maid, HN 2064 .... 450.00
Figurine, New Bonnet, HN 1728 .... 895.00
Figurine, Nicola, HN 2839 ....230.00 to 350.00
Figurine, Ninette, HN 2379 .... 300.00
Figurine, Old Balloon Seller, HN 1315 ....80.00 to 350.00
Figurine, Old King Cole, HN 2217 .... 218.00
Figurine, Old King, HN 2134 .... 595.00
Figurine, Orange Lady, HN 1953 .... 193.00
Figurine, Pamela, HN 3223 .... 190.00
Figurine, Pantalettes, HN 1362 .... 375.00
Figurine, Parson's Daughter, HN 564 .... 575.00
Figurine, Partners, HN 3119 .... 225.00
Figurine, Pearly Boy, HN 2767 .... 250.00
Figurine, Pearly Girl, HN 2036 .... 135.00
Figurine, Pearly Girl, HN 2769 .... 250.00
Figurine, Penelope, HN 1901 ....350.00 to 375.00
Figurine, Philippa Of Hainault, HN 2008 .... 625.00
Figurine, Phyllis, HN 1698 .... 950.00
Figurine, Pied Piper, HN 2102 .... 280.00
Figurine, Pillow Fight, HN 2270 .... 225.00
Figurine, Pirouette, HN 2216 .... 300.00
Figurine, Poacher, HN 2043 .... 425.00
Figurine, Potter, HN 1493 .... 350.00
Figurine, Princess Of Wales, HN 2887 .... 1750.00
Figurine, Regal Lady, HN 2709 .... 275.00
Figurine, Rita, HN 1448 .... 1095.00
Figurine, Rosalind, HN 2393 .... 165.00
Figurine, Rose, HN 1368 ....58.00 to 100.00
Figurine, Rosemary, HN 3143 .... 275.00
Figurine, Royal Governor's Cook, HN 2233 .... 475.00
Figurine, Salome, HN 3267 .... 700.00
Figurine, Samantha, HN 2954 .... 225.00
Figurine, Sandra, HN 2162 .... 250.00
Figurine, Sandra, HN 2275 .... 200.00
Figurine, Schoolmarm, HN 2223 ....209.00 to 275.00
Figurine, Sharon, HN 3603 .... 250.00
Figurine, She Loves Me Not, HN 2045 .... 255.00
Figurine, Sheila, HN 2742 ....145.00 to 190.00
Figurine, Silks & Ribbons, HN 2017 .... 172.00
Figurine, Single Red Rose, HN 3376 .... 300.00
Figurine, Sir Walter Raleigh, HN 2015 .... 900.00
Figurine, Skater, HN 2117 ....295.00 to 475.00
Figurine, Snake Charmer, HN 1317 .... 180.00
Figurine, Sophie, HN 3257 .... 225.00
Figurine, Southern Belle, HN 2229 ....157.00 to 495.00
Figurine, Spring Flowers, HN 1807 ....325.00 to 445.00

Figurine, St. George, HN 2051 .... 450.00
Figurine, Suitor, HN 2132 .... 395.00
Figurine, Summer's Day, HN 2181 .... 250.00
Figurine, Summer, HN 2086 .... 475.00
Figurine, Suzette, HN 2026 .... 425.00
Figurine, Sweet April, HN 2215 .... 450.00
Figurine, Sweet Lavender, HN 1373 .... 650.00
Figurine, Sweet Seventeen, HN 2734 .... 250.00
Figurine, Symphony, HN 2287 .... 225.00
Figurine, Tess, HN 2865 .... 175.00
Figurine, This Little Pig, HN 1793 ....138.00 to 175.00
Figurine, Tinkle Bell, HN 1677 ....55.00 to 100.00
Figurine, Tootles, HN 1680 .... 75.00
Figurine, Top O' The Hill, HN 1834 .... 300.00
Figurine, Top O' The Hill, HN 1849 .... 275.00
Figurine, Town Crier, HN 2119 .... 157.00
Figurine, Toymaker, HN 2250 .... 325.00
Figurine, Wee Willie Winkle, HN 2050 .... 300.00
Figurine, West Indian Dancer, HN 2384 .... 1000.00
Figurine, Wigmaker Of Williamsburg, HN 2239 .... 250.00
Figurine, Willy Won't He, HN 2150 .... 550.00
Figurine, Wintertime, HN 3060 .... 275.00
Figurine, Wizard, HN 2877 .... 325.00
Figurine, Yeoman Of The Guard, HN 2122 .... 850.00
Figurine, Young Master, HN 2872 .... 375.00
Flask, Dewars, Oyez-Oyez, Signed Noke 275.00
Humidor, 6 Different Enameled Fish 395.00
Jardiniere, Oyama Pattern, Floating Dragons, Flames, 12 1/8 x 14 3/8 In. 440.00
Jug, Golf, Every Dog Has His Day, Every Man His Hour, Crombie 1500.00
Jug, Oliver Twist, 5 1/2 In. 175.00
Lighter, Falstaff 125.00
Lighter, Lawyer 225.00
Lighter, Old Charley 150.00
Liquor Container, Captain Cook 125.00
Liquor Container, Falstaff 150.00
Liquor Container, Rip Van Winkle 150.00
Loving Cup, Crombie Figures, 2 Handles, 1925, 11 1/2 x 9 1/2 In. 4000.00
Loving Cup, King Edward VIII, 1936, 10 1/2 In. 775.00
Mask, Fate, HN 1782, 1935, 10 1/2 In. 1840.00
Mask, Friar Of Orders Gray, HN 1733, 1935, 10 In. 460.00
Mask, Greta Garbo, Brown-Blond Hair, HN 1593, 1935, 7 5/8 In. 285.00
Mask, Jester, Grinning, HN 1609, 1935, 2 7/8 In. 460.00
Mask, Lady In Powdered Wig, Gray Hair, HN 1672, 1935, 4 In. 460.00
Mask, Lady In Stylish Hat, HN 1612, 1935, 2 3/4 In. 490.00
Mask, Madame Pompadour, HN 1817, Fred Moore, 1938, 7 3/4 In. 1090.00
Mask, Marlene Dietrich, Brown Hair & Eyes, HN 1591, 1935, 8 In. 285.00
Mask, St. Agnes, Richard Garbe, HN 1786, 1935, 11 In. 1035.00
Mask, Sweet Anne, Blond Hair, HN 1590, 1935, 8 In. 260.00
Mug, Bunnykins, Barbara Vernon 68.00
Mug, Cricket Scene, Dickens, Dauthery, 6 In. 600.00
Mug, Golfing Scene, Dickens, 6 In. 450.00
Mug, Monk, Dickens, 6 In. 200.00
Plaque, Babes In The Woods, Girl With Basket, England, Burslem, 10 x 8 In. 1525.00
Plate, Bunnykins, Barbara Vernon 25.00
Plate, Canterbury Pilgrims 85.00
Plate, Castle Scene, Men In Boats On River, Rust, Brown, Green, 10 1/2 In. 35.00
Plate, Cornell University, Blue & White, 10 In. 55.00
Plate, Crombie Figures, Crackle, 10 1/4 In. 150.00
Plate, Dessert, Black Design On White, Yellow Trim, 12 Piece 595.00
Plate, Doctor, 10 1/2 In. 30.00
Plate, Fisherman, 10 1/2 In. 94.00
Plate, Fisherwoman 125.00
Plate, Golf, Give Losers Leave To Speak, Winners To Laugh, Crombie 225.00

Plate, Golf, Proverb, An Oak Is Not Felled By 1 Blow, 10 In.	200.00
Plate, Golf, Proverb, Fine Feathers Make Fine Birds, 10 In.	125.00
Plate, Greek Key Gilt Band, 9 In., 10 Piece	93.00
Plate, Gypsies, 10 1/4 In.	38.00
Plate, He Hath Good Judgment, Who Relieth Not Wholly On His Own, 10 In.	225.00
Plate, Jackdaw Of Rheims, 13 In.	165.00
Plate, Landscape, Village Scene, Oak Branch, Acorn Border, 15 1/4 In.	35.00
Plate, Mayor	130.00
Plate, William Shakespeare	125.00
Sugar, Tony Weller	750.00
Sugar & Creamer, Arcadia	85.00
Tankard, Oliver Twist	185.00
Teacup, Saucer, Berry Design, Black & White, 12 Piece	66.00
Teapot, Arcadia	225.00
Teapot, Bunnykins, Large	75.00
Teapot, Canterbury Pilgrims, 1909-1933	215.00
Tobacco Jar, Golfer, Addressing His Ball	300.00
Toby Jug, Falstaff, Large	450.00
Toby Jug, Henry The V, 6671, 7 1/4 In.	295.00
Tray, Coaching Days, Street Scene, Noke, 8 1/2 x 10 In.	345.00
Tray, Portulaca Florals, Blue & Bronze Ground, 10 1/2 x 5 1/2 In.	85.00
Urn, Cover, Highland Cattle Scene, Purple Mountain, Green, Gold, 1878, 32 In.	3025.00
Vase, Babes In The Woods, Woman Sheltering Child With Cloak, 11 1/2 In.	1575.00
Vase, Babes In The Woods, Woman Sheltering Child With Cloak, 6 3/4 In.	665.00
Vase, Chang, Green, Blue, White Crackle Glaze, Red Flambe Ground, Noke, 4 In.	925.00
Vase, Flambe, Black Landscape, Printed Mark, 4 1/4 In.	170.00
Vase, Flambe, Veined Bright Red, Dark Blue Glossy Glaze, 10 x 6 1/2 In.	225.00
Vase, Kingsware, Verse, Dr. Johnson Tavern Scene, 10 3/4 In.	325.00
Vase, Scenes In Citadel & Cairo, Gilt Handle & Base, 10 In.	795.00
Vase, Ship At Sea, Dark Brown, Mottled Green, Yellow, 6 In.	100.00

ROYAL DUX is the more common name for the Duxer Porzellan-manufaktur, which was founded by E. Eichler in Dux, Bohemia, in 1860. By the turn of the century, the firm specialized in porcelain statuary and busts of Art Nouveau–style maidens, large porcelain figures, and ornate vases with three-dimensional figures climbing on the sides. The firm is still in business.

Bowl, Female, Tending A Fishing Net Atop Shell Form Bowl, 18 1/2 In.	489.00
Bust, Female, Raised Leaves & Berries, Early 20th Century, 14 In.	287.00
Bust, Woman With Hand Harp	110.00
Centerpiece, Naiads, 3 Women, Waves, Shell, White, Gold Highlights, 19 5/8 In.	1150.00
Compote, Female, Atop A Shell Form Bowl, Early 20th Century, 14 1/2 In.	747.00
Compote, Leaf, Floral Design, Central Tree-Form Support, 20th Century, 20 In.	632.00
Figurine, 2 Ladies, Holding A Basket, Ivory, Gold, 19 In., Pair	1800.00
Figurine, Bird Dog, With Pheasant, 20 In.	595.00
Figurine, Boy In Fisherman's Hat, Pink Triangle, 15 In.	295.00
Figurine, Deer, Prancing, Small	50.00
Figurine, Elephant, 6 In.	125.00
Figurine, Elephant, Raised Trunk, 10 x 13 In.	165.00
Figurine, Elk, With Jumping Fox	135.00
Figurine, Female, With A Harp, Scroll Banding To Raised Base, 14 1/4 In.	172.00
Figurine, Figural Flower Basket, Lady, Draped, Soft Buff, Green, Ivory, 20 1/2 In.	484.00
Figurine, Fisher Boy, Pink Triangle Mark, 21 In.	275.00
Figurine, Fisherman Holding Creel, Signed, 17 1/2 In.	385.00
Figurine, Fisherman, Holding Creel Over His Shoulder, Soft Green, Ivory, 17 In.	423.50
Figurine, German Shepherd, Pink Triangle, 10 1/2 x 6 In.	175.00
Figurine, Girl, Holding Gown & Mirror	195.00
Figurine, Man & A Woman At Water Fountain, Porcelain, 24 In., Pair	550.00
Figurine, Man On Elephant, Signed, Porcelain, 26 1/2 In.	275.00
Figurine, Owl, White, 10 In.	75.00
Figurine, Parakeets, Pair	125.00
Figurine, Spaniel	65.00
Figurine, Tazzas With Putti, Woman, Supporting Shell, Porcelain, 19 1/2 In.	800.00

Figurine, Woman, Ball Gown, 8 In. 195.00
Figurine, Woman, Black Glaze, Pink Triangle .... 125.00 to 130.00
Figurine, Woman, Draped Flower Basket, Green & Ivory, 20 1/2 In. 440.00
Figurine, Woman, Seated, With Sheaf Of Wheat, 21 In. 303.00
Figurine, Woman, Sitting On Edge Of Shell, 8 x 7 In. 330.00
Figurine, Woodpecker 100.00
Group, 2 Women Filling Water Jug, Red Marbleized Basin, 8 x 10 In. 220.00
Vase, Bisque, Female Figure To 1 Side Of Leaf, Floral Body, 19 1/4 In. 287.50
Vase, Boy On Nautilus Shell, Black & Gold Highlights, 9 In. 220.00
Vase, Floral, Pink Triangle, Mark, 12 In. 285.00
Vase, Girl With Flowing Hair, 11 1/2 In. 475.00
Vase, Lady's Face On Front, 2 Handles, 7 3/4 In. 215.00
Vase, Roses & Buds, Pastel Ground, 4 Loop Handles, 9 3/4 In. 160.00

ROYAL FLEMISH glass was made during the late 1880s in New Bedford, Massachusetts, by the Mt. Washington Glass Works. It is a colored satin glass decorated with dark colors and raised gold designs. The glass was patented in 1894. It was supposed to resemble stained glass windows.

Lamp, Coin Medallions, Winged Griffin Supporting Shade, 19 In. 495.00
Vase, Leaves & Flowers, Jeweled Berries, 9 In. 1100.00

ROYAL HAEGER, see Haeger category.

ROYAL IVY pieces are listed in the Pressed Glass category by that pattern name.

ROYAL NYMPHENBURG is the modern name for the Nymphenburg porcelain factory, which was established at Neudeck-ob-der-Au, Germany, in 1753 and moved to Nymphenburg in 1761. The company is still in existence. Marks include a checkered shield topped by a crown, a crowned *CT* with the year, and a contemporary shield mark on reproductions of eighteenth-century porcelain.

Cup & Saucer, Coffee, Black Bird Perched In Small Tree, 1765, 3 In. 862.00
Figurine, Short Hair Fox Terrier, Standing, 6 1/2 In. 275.00
Plate, Man Standing Beside Traveler, Red, Green, Brown, Kaltner, 9 In. 1265.00
Tea Set, Traveling, Gilt Metal, French, 1920s, 13 Piece 517.00

ROYAL OAK pieces are listed in the Pressed Glass category by that pattern name.

ROYAL RUDOLSTADT, see Rudolstadt category.

ROYAL VIENNA, see Beehive category.

ROYAL WORCESTER is a name used by collectors. Worcester porcelains were made in Worcester, England, from about 1751. The firm went through many different periods and name changes. It became the Worcester Royal Porcelain Company, Ltd., in 1862. Today collectors call the porcelains made after 1862 *Royal Worcester.* In 1976, the firm merged with W. T. Copeland to become Royal Worcester Spode. Some early products of the factory are listed under Worcester.

Biscuit Jar, Cover, Melon, Gold Top, Base 1210.00
Bowl, Molded Leaves, Multi Floral Design, Basket Weave, 1887 .... 357.00
Coaster, Birds, Box, 4 Piece 55.00
Compote, Foliage Spray, Clover Leaf Foot, 1875, 3 x 9 1/4 In., Pair 230.00
Compote, Pierced Basket Weave, Tree Trunk, 3 Shell Dishes, 1882, 13 7/8 In. 1725.00
Dish, Sardine, Cover, Twisted Knot Finial, Gold Highlights, Blue, White, 6 In. 80.00
Dish, Serving, Floral, Ivory Ground, 3 Sections, Marked, 10 5/8 In. 220.00
Dish, Shell, Tan, Cream, Serrated Edge, Gold Trim, 4 x 4 1/2 In. 50.00
Ewer, 1886, 8 1/2 In. 275.00
Ewer, Design, Ivory Ground, Gilt Bamboo Handle, Marked, 6 3/4 In. 165.00
Ewer, Floral Design, Enamel, England, Late 19th Century, 12 1/2 In. 201.00
Ewer, Floral, Gilt, Ivory Ground, Magenta Transfer Mark, 7 1/2 In. 275.00
Ewer, Floral, Ivory Ground, Gilt Lizard Handle, Marked, 12 1/2 In. 385.00
Ewer, Gold Floral Filigree, Apricot Ground, 6 3/4 In. 110.00
Figurine, Blue Tit, No. 3199, 1937, 2 1/4 In. 75.00
Figurine, Crabapple & Butterflies, Dorothy Doughty, 1942, 10 5/8 In. 300.00

Several types of glue are needed to repair broken pottery and porcelain. Commercial glues found in a local hardware store are often satisfactory. Read the labels. Some types work only with pieces that are porous, others only with pieces that are not porous. Instant glue is difficult to use if the break is complicated.

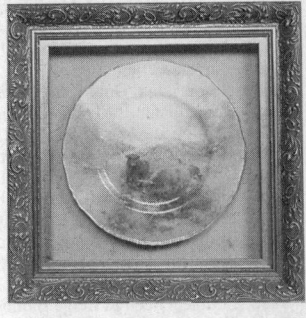

Royal Worcester, Plate, Mountain, Cattle, Stinton, c.1900, Frame, 10 1/2 In.

Figurine, Dairy Shorthorn, Doris Lindner	700.00
Figurine, Duchess Dress, Dorothy Doughty, Box, 1936	350.00
Figurine, Egyptian Female Musician, Leaning On Column, Purple, 13 In.	660.00
Figurine, Extinct Carolina Parakeet, 16 1/4 In.	440.00
Figurine, Golden Crowned Kinglet Cock, Wooden Case, Dorothy Doughty	1150.00
Figurine, Grandma's Dress, Doughty	100.00
Figurine, Grandmother's Dress, No. 3435, 1960	125.00 to 245.00
Figurine, Hog Hunting, Wooden Base, 1961, 10 In.	1195.00
Figurine, Indian, No. 3071, Signed, F.G. Doughty	200.00
Figurine, Invitation, Yellow Flowered Gown, Holding Fan, 1978, 6 1/2 In.	225.00
Figurine, Kingfisher, Dorothy Doughty, 12 1/4 In.	2100.00
Figurine, Magnolia Warbler Cock, Wooden Case, Dorothy Doughty, 15 In.	1800.00
Figurine, Magnolia Warbler Hen, Wooden Case, Dorothy Doughty, 15 In.	1800.00
Figurine, Mockingbird Cock, Wooden Case, Dorothy Doughty, 11 In.	1150.00
Figurine, Mockingbird Hen, Wooden Case, Dorothy Doughty, 10 1/4 In.	1150.00
Figurine, Mockingbirds, Hen & Cock, Doughty, 1940s, 10 3/4 In.	632.00
Figurine, Orange Blossom & Butterflies, No. 2620, D. Doughty, 8 In., Pair	500.00
Figurine, Parakeet, c.1936, 6 1/2 In.	22.00
Figurine, Parula Warbler, Dorothy Doughty, Pair	1017.00
Figurine, Peter Pan, No. 3011, 7 3/4 In.	180.00
Figurine, Red Cardinal Cock, Wooden Case, Dorothy Doughty, 11 1/2 In.	1200.00
Figurine, Red Cardinal Hen, Wooden Case, Dorothy Doughty, 9 3/4 In.	1200.00
Figurine, Red-Eyed Vireo, Wooden Case, Dorothy Doughty	510.00
Figurine, Saturday's Child, Works Hard For A Living, No. 3524	85.00
Figurine, Scarlet Tanager Cock, Wooden Case, Dorothy Doughty, 12 In.	750.00
Figurine, Scarlet Tanager Hen, Wooden Case, Dorothy Doughty, 11 In.	750.00
Figurine, Seated Artisan, Beside Grinding Wheel, 6 1/4 In.	198.00
Figurine, Sister, No. 3149, 6 3/4 In.	265.00
Figurine, Woodland Dance, No. 3076, 4 x 4 In.	300.00
Figurine, Yankee, Natural Colors, Ivory Ground, Impressed Mark, 1902, 7 In.	345.00
Jug, Lizard, Basket Weave, Deep Rust, Gold, Beige, 1912, 6 In.	385.00
Pie Bird, Blue & White, Box	150.00
Pitcher, Crane, 10 In.	265.00
Pitcher, Cranes In The Moonlight, Horn Handle, 10 In.	495.00
Pitcher, Cream, Purple Floral Design, England, 4 In.	22.00
Pitcher, Floral, Branch Handle, 8 In.	175.00
Pitcher, Floral, Gilt Dragon Handle, Cream Ground, Squat	253.00
Pitcher, Floral, Ivory Ground, Marked, 5 1/4 In.	155.00
Pitcher, Floral, Leaf Design, Applied Gold Handle, Beige Ground, 1890, 8 In.	192.00
Pitcher, Floral, Stag Horn Handle, Horn Shape, 9 In.	220.00
Pitcher, Florals On Gold, Gold Handle, c.1899, 8 3/4 In.	260.00
Pitcher, Flowers, Gold, 6 In.	75.00
Pitcher, Gilt Floral Glass, Narrow Spout, Bulbous, Circular, 1888, 7 3/4 In.	86.00
Pitcher, Ivory, Salt Glaze, Pewter Lid, Dated 1962, 8 In.	350.00

Pitcher, Mulberry Floral, Mask Spout, 7 In. 125.00
Plate, Floral, Gold Trim, 1887 .... 75.00
Plate, Mountain, Cattle, Stinton, c.1900, Frame, 10 1/2 In. ....*Illus* 1540.00
Plate, Petunia Center, Signed 45.00
Plate, Tewkesbury, Gold Rim, Signed Nickolls, 10 3/4 In. 175.00
Smoke Set, Game Bird Scenes, Sterling Band, Signed By Artist, 6 Ashtrays 950.00
Teapot, Applied Lotus Leaves, Gilt, Melon, Printed Mark, 1888, 6 In. 230.00
Toothpick Holder, Bamboo Pattern, Gold Leaves 55.00
Urn, Berry, Spider Motif, Applied Handles, 16 In. 525.00
Urn, Cover, Polychrome Enameled Holly, 9 1/4 In. 275.00
Vase, Art Nouveau, Floral Designs, Gilt Gothic Handles, 7 1/4 In., Pair 427.00
Vase, Bird Perched On Branch, Pierced Handles, Rim, 19th Century, 16 In. 920.00
Vase, Bottle Shape, Gold Handles, Maroon, Golf Fern, 1878, 14 1/2 In. 660.00
Vase, Bud, Floral, 7 In. 55.00
Vase, Double, Green & Beige Bamboo Handle, Gold Leaves, 5 x 8 In. 250.00
Vase, Floral, Ivory Ground, Gilt Reticulated Handles & Lip, Marked, 13 In. 385.00
Vase, Flowers, Gold, 8 In. 295.00
Vase, Lamp, Scene, Hand Painted, 31 In. 500.00
Vase, Nautilus Shell On Coral, Gold Shells, Ferns, Bronze Root Stem, 8 1/4 In. 880.00
Vase, Reticulated & Jeweled, G. Grainger, 1901, 11 In. 1695.00
Vase, Sabina Ware, Blue, Green Polychrome, 12 In. 220.00
Vase, Shell Shape, Hanging, Marked, 11 In. 275.00

ROYCROFT products were made by the Roycrofter community of East
Aurora, New York, in the late nineteenth and early twentieth centuries.
The community was founded by Elbert Hubbard, famous philosopher,
writer, and artist. The workshops owned by the community made furniture, metalware, leatherwork, embroidery, and jewelry. A printshop
produced many signs, books, and the magazines that promoted the say-
ings of Elbert Hubbard. Furniture by the Roycroft community is listed
in the Furniture category.

Ashtray, Copper, Hammered, Beaded Rim, 1910-1912, Square, 5 1/2 In. ....355.00 to 550.00
Bean Bag, Clownie, Yellow Polkadot Outfit, Paper Tag, 8 x 4 1/2 In. 110.00
Blotter, Copper, Hammered, Tooled Linear Design, Rivets, 4 x 4 In., 4 Piece 175.00
Blotter, Leather, Tooled Trefoil Floral Design, 7 1/2 x 7 1/2 In. 275.00
Bookends, Basket Of Flowers, Rounded Triangular Form, Pair 375.00
Bookends, Copper, Hammered, Convex Form, Tooled Edge, 4 x 3 In. 230.00
Bookends, Copper, Hammered, Curled-Up Edges, Marked, 5 1/2 x 3 3/4 In. 220.00
Bookends, Copper, Hammered, Curved Support, Stamped, 3 1/4 In. 103.00
Bookends, Copper, Hammered, Embossed Trillium, Orb & Cross Mark, 5 1/2 In. 220.00
Bookends, Copper, Hammered, Gnarled Tree Design, Impressed Mark, 4 x 6 1/2 In. 4125.00
Bookends, Copper, Hammered, Quatrefoil Design Corners, 3 1/2 x 5 1/2 In. 520.00
Bookends, Copper, Hammered, Strap Work, Original Patina, Circular, 4 x 5 In. 660.00
Bookends, Copper, Hammered, Tooled Flowers, Original Patina, 5 x 4 1/2 In. 495.00
Bookends, Leather, Quatrefoil Design Top, 3 1/2 x 4 1/2 In. 465.00
Bookends, Leather, Tooled Floral Design, 5 1/2 In. 715.00
Bookends, Ship, Brass, 5 x 6 In. 250.00
Bookends, Viking Ship, Circular Relief 245.00
Bookends, Wood, Original Finish, Burned Mark, 7 x 8 In. 385.00
Bookrack, 9 Volumes Of Elbert Hubbard's Selected Writings, 9 x 15 In. 560.00
Bowl, Copper, Hammered, Broad Leaves, Orb Mark, 9 1/2 x 4 In. 4125.00
Bowl, Copper, Hammered, Design Around Rim, 1912-1917, 6 1/2 x 3 In. 660.00
Bowl, Copper, Mottled Relief Design, 6 In. 198.00
Box, Incised Geometric Design, Pyramid Rivets, Marked, 3 3/4 x 10 1/2 In. 3965.00
Candleholder, Copper, Hammered, Original Brass Patina, Curled Feet, 8 x 3 In. 330.00
Candleholder, Copper, Hammered, Riveted Handle, Rolled Edge, 5 In. 330.00
Candlestick, Copper, Hammered, 4 Flat Bands, Original Dark Patina, 12 In. 2860.00
Candlestick, Copper, Hammered, Rolled Edge, Riveted Handle, ER, 5 1/2 In. 330.00
Candlestick, Twisted Stem, Flared Foot, Hammered Finish, Marked, 12 1/4 In. 660.00
Chair, 1 Vertical Slat, Tacked-On Leather Seat, 51 In. 1870.00
Chair, Bedroom, Dark Finish, 43 1/2 In. 1320.00
Cigarette Case, Brass, Hinged Copper Binding, Book Form, 1912-1920, 3 x 4 In. 550.00
Crumber Set, Copper, Hammered, Marked, 9 x 12 In., 2 Piece 165.00

Desk Box, Hinged Lid, Stamp Holder, Tooled Floral Design, Marked, 7 1/2 x 4 1/2 In. . .	990.00
Desk Set, Copper, Poppy, Hammered, Blotter & 2 Pen Trays, 1912-1915	2200.00
Fernery, Copper, Tooled Blossoms & Stems, Round Footed, 7 x 3 1/2 In.	1870.00
Frame, Double, Copper, Hammered, Blossom Corners, 8 3/4 x 11 1/2 In.	880.00
Holder, Napkin, Leather, Arts & Crafts, 1 1/2 x 1 1/2 In.	285.00
Holder, Pencil, 5-Tube, Marked	120.00
Holder, Poker Chip, Copper, Hammered, With 100 Chips, 5 x 6 1/2 In.	770.00
Holder, Scissors, Leather, Tooled Oak Leaf & Acorn Pattern, Triangular, 1912, 4 In.	220.00
Incense Burner, Copper, Hammered, Motto, Box	650.00
Inkwell, Copper, Hammered, Original Patina, 2 1/2 x 3 In.	330.00
Inkwell, Copper, Hammered, Original Patina, Circular, 5 x 3 In.	330.00
Inkwell, Copper, Hammered, Radial Hammered Edge, Original Patina, 2 x 3 In.	121.00
Jug, Pottery, Brown, 4 1/2 In.	20.00
Jug, Pottery, Brown, 5 1/2 In.	70.00
Lamp, Copper, Hammered, Brown Glass Shade, Base Handle, Impressed Mark, 10 In. . . .	2200.00
Lamp, Table, Trapezoid Shade, Panels Of Slag Glass, 26 In.	5290.00
Letter Opener, Copper, Hammered & Tooled Design, 9 In.	175.00
Letter Opener, Copper, Hammered, Curled & Impressed Design, Marked, 9 1/2 In.	120.00
Letter Opener, Copper, Hammered, Saber Form, 9 In.	120.00
Letter Rack, Copper, Arts & Crafts Design, Twisted Ropework, 7 x 4 1/2 In.	660.00
Mat, Leather, Arts & Crafts Design, Square, 6 In.	285.00
Pen Tray, 2 Stylized Floral Designs At Each End, Original Patina, 8 1/2 In.	121.00
Pen Tray, Copper, Hammered, Original Patina, 9 1/2 In.	300.00
Pin Tray, Copper, Hammered, Round, Marked, 6 In.	175.00
Pouch, Leather, Arts & Crafts, Grapes & Leaves, Folded, Snap, 6 x 6 1/2 In.	285.00
Punch Set, Brown Glaze, Hallmark, Bowl & 6 Cups, 10 3/8 In.	345.00
Purse, Clutch, Leather, Floral Design, Child's, 5 1/2 x 3 In.	255.00
Purse, Leather, Arts & Crafts Floral Design, Fitted Mirror, Laced, 1912, 7 1/2 x 9 In. . . .	440.00
Purse, Leather, Pine Needles, Cones, Coin Purse, Mirror, Gunmetal Frame, 8 x 6 In. . . .	770.00
Purse, Leather, Woman Cameo, Laced Frame & Strap, Scheidemantel, 1918, 5 x 9 In. . . .	605.00
Salt & Pepper, Geometric Design, 4 In.	770.00
Sconce, Copper, Hammered, 4-Sided Tulip Bobeche, Marked, 10 In.	935.00
Sconce, Copper, Hammered, Rolled Corners & Piecrust Edge, Hanging, 1912, 12 In. . . .	825.00
Tray, Copper, Hammered, 1912-1915, Round, 12 1/2 In.	990.00
Tray, Copper, Hammered, 2 Handles, Marked, 19 In.	605.00
Tray, Copper, Hammered, Curved Rim, Original Patina, 5 In.	187.00
Tray, Copper, Hammered, Mahogany Frame & Handles, 12 x 18 In.	1430.00
Tray, Copper, Hammered, Recessed Center, Original Patina, 6 In.	110.00
Tray, Copper, Hammered, Triangular Design At Corners, 3 1/2 x 7 1/2 In.	175.00
Tray, Copper, Hammered, Trillium Center, Rolled Edge, Oval, 3 x 8 In.	220.00
Tray, Fruit, Copper, Raised Beaded Rim, Round, 8 In.	550.00
Vase, Bullet, Copper, Hammered, Rose Band, Arts & Crafts, Orb Mark, 6 In.	2090.00
Vase, Copper, 4 Sides, Cutout Top, Silver Design, Karl Kipp, 7 In.	770.00
Vase, Copper, Glass Holder, Round Base With 3 Vertical Rods, Marked, 8 1/2 In.	880.00
Vase, Copper, Hammered Beauty, Brass, Original Patina, 12 x 6 In.	1430.00
Vase, Copper, Hammered Beauty, Stovepipe Neck, Squat, New Dark Patina, 18 In.	1870.00
Vase, Copper, Hammered, 4 Folded Leaflike Designs At Top, Cylindrical, 8 1/2 In.	1320.00
Vase, Copper, Hammered, 6 Vertical Panels, Enameled, Marked, 5 In.	1430.00
Vase, Copper, Hammered, 8 Cutouts At Top, Original Patina, Tapered, 7 In.	7150.00
Vase, Copper, Hammered, American Beauty, Dark Verdigris Patina, 21 In.	1725.00
Vase, Copper, Hammered, Band & Rivet Design, Flared, 15 In.	3190.00
Vase, Copper, Hammered, Flared Rim & Base, Rivet Design Lower Shoulder, 21 In.	4850.00
Vase, Copper, Hammered, Flared Rim, Ovoid, Orb & Cross Mark, 8 In.	1100.00
Vase, Copper, Hammered, Green Enameled, Walter Jennings, 6 In.	2090.00
Vase, Copper, Hammered, Medium Patina, Marked, 18 x 8 In.	1840.00
Vase, Copper, Hammered, Original Patina, Marked, 4 1/2 In.	495.00

ROZANE, see Roseville category.

ROZENBURG worked at The Hague, Holland, from 1890 to 1914. The most important pieces were earthenware made in the early twentieth century with pale-colored Art Nouveau designs.

Coffeepot, Domed Cover, Eggshell, Painted Flower, 1903, 6 1/2 In.	3888.00

RRP is the mark used by the firm of Robinson-Ransbottom. It is not a mark of the more famous Roseville Pottery. The Ransbottom brothers started a pottery in 1900 in Ironspot, Ohio. In 1920, they merged with the Robinson Clay Product Company of Akron, Ohio, to become Robinson-Ransbottom. The factory is still working.

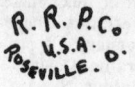

Bowl, Brown Band, Yellowware, 10 In.	30.00
Cookie Jar, Cow Over Moon, Gold	235.00
Cookie Jar, Hall 5 Band, Chinese Red	85.00
Cookie Jar, Owl, Cookie Stories	100.00
Cookie Jar, Sailor Jack, 1943	185.00
Planter, Snail, Yellow & Green	60.00

RS GERMANY is part of the wording in marks used by the Tillowitz, Germany, factory of Reinhold Schlegelmilch from 1914 until about 1945. The porcelain was sold decorated and undecorated. The Schlegelmilch families made porcelains marked in many ways. See also ES Germany, RS Poland, RS Prussia, RS Silesia, RS Suhl, and RS Tillowitz.

Basket, Candy, Oval, Twisted Handle, Orchid Design, Gold Trim, 4 x 8 In.	120.00
Berry Bowl, Square, 5 x 4 1/2 In.	20.00
Bowl, Floral, Pierced Rim, 9 1/4 In.	60.00
Bowl, White Flowers, Surreal Green, Gold Enamel, 9 In.	22.00
Box, Trinket, Cover, Shape Of Man's Collar, Gold Trim	40.00
Cake Plate, Cottage Scene, Maiden, 2 Yoked Oxen, 10 In.	235.00
Cheese Server, Floral Design, 2 Tiers, Marked, 8 1/2 In.	38.00
Cheese Server, Pink Roses, Green Leaves	125.00
Chocolate Pot, Apricot & White Flowers, Shaded Ground, 10 1/2 In.	115.00
Chocolate Set, Dogwood & Pine, Cream Satin Ground, 9 Piece	295.00
Chocolate Set, White Lilies, 11 Piece	450.00
Cologne Bottle, Pink, White, Rose Design	75.00
Cup & Saucer, Green On White, Gold Trim	44.00
Cup & Saucer, Steeple Mark, Demitasse	60.00
Dish, Cheese & Cracker, Pink Orchid Design, Signed, 8 1/2 In.	85.00
Dish, Triangular, Flower, Fruit Design, Gold Band, Signed, 1916	11.00
Dresser Set, White Roses, Green, Gold Design, Green Mark With Star, 8 1/4 In.	129.00
Hat Pin Holder, Red Iris, Red Wreath Mark, 4 1/2 In.	82.00
Mug, Puck	69.00
Plate, Floral Design, Gold Edge, Purple Flowers, Marked, 9 3/4 In.	5.50
Plate, Lilacs, White, Green, Pink, Green & Gold Trim, 11 1/4 In.	110.00
Powder Box, Cover, Pale Roses, Dappled Gold, Round, 4 1/2 In.	80.00
Sauceboat, Underplate, Blue Flowers, Gold Trim	45.00
Sugar & Creamer, Butterflies, Floral, Blue Mark With Star, Pair	65.00
Tray, Dresser, White Roses, 10 In.	154.00
Tray, Pastel Flowers, Cloverleaf-Shaped Handle, 8 1/2 In.	70.00
Vase, Cobalt Blue, 9 In.	250.00
Vase, Cottage Scene With Farmer, 3 1/2 In.	195.00

RS POLAND (German) is a mark used by the Reinhold Schlegelmilch factory at Tillowitz from about 1946 to 1956. After 1956, the factory made porcelain marked PT Poland. This is one of many of the RS marks used. See also ES Germany, RS Germany, RS Prussia, RS Silesia, RS Suhl, and RS Tillowitz.

Bowl, Crowned Cranes, Mold 90, 5 3/4 In.	465.00
Luncheon Set, Rose Design, 26 Piece	2500.00
Server, Center Handle, Lavender & Pink Roses, Gold Trim, 11 x 8 In.	515.00
Shaving Mug, Daffodil, Tulip Design	150.00
Vase, Crowned Cranes, Salesman Sample Size, 3 1/2 In.	410.00
Vase, White & Brown Pheasants, Gold Trim Handles, 9 7/8 In.	595.00
Vase, White Roses, Yellow Centers, Green Foliage, Signed, 7 1/4 In.	85.00

RS PRUSSIA appears in several marks used on porcelain before 1917. Reinhold Schlegelmilch started his porcelain works in Suhl, Germany, in 1869. See also ES Germany, RS Germany, RS Poland, RS Silesia, RS Suhl, and RS Tillowitz.

Bell, Wooden Clapper	195.00

Berry Set, Floral, Holly, Gold Scalloped Edge, Porcelain, 9 1/2 In., 7 Piece 121.00
Berry Set, Molded Flowers, Purple-Red Border, Floral Inside, Signed, 9 Piece 475.00
Biscuit Jar, Hidden Image, Signed, 7 x 6 In. ....480.00 to 950.00
Biscuit Jar, Roses & Snowballs, Green Trim 275.00
Bowl, Blown-Out Gold Roses At Border, 10 In. 595.00
Bowl, Blown-Out Sunflower, Gold Edged Leaves On Central Poppies, 10 1/2 In. 258.00
Bowl, Blue Iris, 8 1/2 In. 110.00
Bowl, Castle Scene, 10 1/4 In. 165.00
Bowl, Floral, Gilt, 10 1/4 x 3 In. 161.00
Bowl, Floral, Gold Trim, 11 In. 165.00
Bowl, Floral, Green, White, Red Mark, 10 1/2 In. 230.00
Bowl, Floral, Pastel Pink, Blue, Yellow, Scroll Mold, 11 x 11 1/2 In. 385.00
Bowl, Gold Iris Design, Rose Variation, Lady, Watering Flowers, 10 1/2 In. 23.00
Bowl, Gold Roses & Floral Design, Red, Gold, Daisy Shape, 10 In. 495.00
Bowl, Hidden Image, 10 1/4 In. 430.00
Bowl, Icicle Mold, Dark Pink Roses, Red Mark, 22 In. 275.00
Bowl, Iris, Pink Poppies, Daisies On Green, Red Mark, 10 1/2 In. 300.00
Bowl, Lily, Beige, Gold Scrolled Border, Green, Cream, 11 In. 165.00
Bowl, Mill Scene, Stipple-Tapestry Texture Effect, Mold No. 217, 10 3/4 In. ... 1185.00
Bowl, Molded Leaves, Grapes, Pink, White Roses On Base, Yellow, Gold, 11 In. 70.00
Bowl, Mums, Beaded Scalloped, Green, Gold Trim, 10 In. 19.00
Bowl, Orchid, Creme, Fleur-De-Lis, Floral Center, 10 1/2 In. 248.00
Bowl, Poppies, Scalloped, Red Mark, 10 1/2 In. 325.00
Bowl, Romantic Scene, Magenta, Gold, Green Glaze, 10 In. 165.00
Bowl, Scalloped Edge, Gold, Violet Flowers, 1900, 12 1/2 x 9 1/4 In. 55.00
Bowl, Sheepherder, Outer Pointed Border, Green, Gold, Pink, 11 In. 220.00
Bowl, Swans, Gold Beaded, Scalloped Rim, Beige, White, 10 In. 165.00
Bread Tray, Rose Design, Green, Peach, Pink, Gold Trim, 12 1/2 x 9 In. 154.00
Cake Plate, Floral Design, Blue, Pink, White, Gold, Crimped Rim, Scalloped, 11 In. ... 110.00
Cake Plate, Forget-Me-Not, Beige Flowers, Pink Luster Rim, 10 3/4 In. 195.00
Cake Plate, Hidden Image, 12 In. 375.00
Cake Plate, Mold No. 51, 12 In. 150.00
Cake Plate, Point & Clover, Open Handles, Dark Pink, White Roses, 10 In. 298.00
Cake Plate, Red Floral, Open Handles, Red Mark, 9 1/2 In. 110.00
Celery Dish, Dogwood Blossoms, Gold Enamel, Scalloped Rim, 12 1/4 x 6 In. 110.00
Celery Dish, Iris, 12 In. 175.00
Chocolate Pot, Poppies, Daisies 175.00
Chocolate Pot, Swans, Eggshell, Blue, Green, White, 10 In. 300.00
Chocolate Set, Laurel Chain Design, Green, Gold Trim, 6 Piece 1100.00
Chocolate Set, Peonies & Wild Flowers, 9 3/4-In. Pot, 7 Piece 522.00
Cracker Jar, Cover, Yellow, Gold Orchids, Handle, Beige, 9 1/2 x 5 1/2 In. 300.00
Cracker Jar, Surreal Dogwood, Red Mark 185.00
Cracker Jar, Yellow, Pink & White Roses, Handles, Footed, Tiffany Highlights 400.00
Creamer, Mill Scene, Mold 501, Red Mark 175.00
Cup & Saucer, Multicolored Luster, Satin Finish 175.00
Cup & Saucer, Purple, Stippled Floral Mold, Child's 75.00
Hatpin Holder, Red Mark 225.00
Mug, Floral, Yellow 250.00
Pitcher, Lemonade, White, Pink Surreal Blossoms & Fans, Scalloped Top, 6 In. 250.00
Plate, Bird Design On Branch, Hand Painted, 8 In. 66.00
Plate, Gibson Girl, 10 1/2 In. 550.00
Plate, Orchids, Floral Center, White, 8 1/2 In. 33.00
Plate, Peafowl, Red Mark, 9 7/8 In. 675.00
Plate, Poppies, 9 In. 215.00
Plate, Serving, Gold Scallops, Orchids, Rose Garlands, Cobalt Blue Edge, 8 1/2 In. 165.00
Plate, Serving, Pink & White Flowers, Yellow Ground, 11 In. 55.00
Plate, Yellow Roses, 9 In. 185.00
Powder Box, Cover 65.00
Sugar & Creamer, White Roses 82.00
Sugar & Creamer, White, Gold, Pink, On Square Pedestals 82.00
Syrup, Swan Scene, Mold 542, Red Mark, Satin Finish 275.00
Tankard, Stippled Floral 525.00
Tea Set, Floral, Pink Borders, 21 Piece, Child's 795.00

Teapot, Floral, Child's, 10 1/2 In. 225.00
Toothpick, Rose Design, 6 Panels, Footed, Green Wreath, Signed, 2 In. 104.50
Toothpick, Stippled Floral, Magnolia 175.00
Tray, Dresser, Gold Floral Border, Oval 225.00
Tray, Dresser, Mill Scene 650.00
Tray, Dresser, Mums, Green Ground 135.00
Vase, Floral, Purple, Pink, Yellow, Gold Handle, Turquoise, Green Ground, 9 In. 110.00
Vase, Pillow, Mill Scene, Gold Jewels, Blue-Green, Signed, 7 1/2 x 7 1/2 In. 850.00

RS SILESIA appears on porcelain made at the Reinhold Schlegelmilch factory in Tillowitz, Germany, from the 1920s to the 1940s. The Schlegelmilch families made porcelains marked in many ways. See also ES Germany, RS Germany, RS Poland, RS Prussia, RS Suhl, and RS Tillowitz.

Goblet, Cover, Engraved Foliate Scrolls, Butterflies & Squirrels, 1730s, 14 3/8 In. 1035.00
Gravy Boat 30.00

RS SUHL is a mark used by the Erdmann Schlegelmilch factory in Suhl, Germany, between 1900 and 1917. The Schlegelmilch families made porcelains in many places. See also ES Germany, RS Germany, RS Poland, RS Prussia, RS Silesia, and RS Tillowitz.

Coffee Set, Pot, Creamer, Sugar, 6 Cups & Saucers, Figural Scene 1675.00
Cup & Saucer, Man & Woman Scene, Gold Rim, Florals, Flower Handle, Beehive 100.00
Vase, Melon Eaters, 9 In. 660.00

RS TILLOWITZ was marked on porcelain by the Reinhold Schlegelmilch factory at Tillowitz from the 1920s to the 1940s. Table services and ornamental pieces were made. See also ES Germany, RS Germany, RS Poland, RS Prussia, RS Silesia, and RS Suhl.

Basket, Bird Of Paradise 150.00
Bowl, Cover, Floral Design, With Parrots 225.00
Cake Plate, Green, Yellow, Brown Lilies, Blue Glaze, 1930, 9 3/4 In. 15.00
Toothpick, 3 Handles, Silver Deposit, Signed 65.00
Toothpick, Silesia, Hexagonal, Silver Handles, Rim & Design 125.00

RUBENA is a glassware that shades from red to clear. It was first made by George Duncan and Sons of Pittsburgh, Pennsylvania, about 1885. This coloring was used on many types of glassware. The pressed glass patterns of Royal Ivy and Royal Oak are listed under Pressed Glass.

Celery Vase, Thumbprint, Enameled Bird, Silver Plate, James Tufts, 8 In. ....*Illus* 852.00
Cracker Jar, Fan & Strawberry, Sterling Silver Cover, 7 x 6 In. 1150.00
Creamer 170.00
Creamer, Paneled, Clear Handle, 5 In. 44.00
Pitcher, Coinspot, Cranberry Rim, Clear Ribbed Handle, 7 1/2 In. 165.00
Pitcher, White Opalescent Spiral Stripes, Clear Applied Handle, 8 x 6 1/2 In. 275.00
Sugar, Cover 185.00
Tumbler, Overshot, 3 1/2 In. 33.00
Vase, Craquelle, 10 3/4 In. 88.00

Be sure ladders, trash cans, sheds, and cars are not close to the house. A burglar can use them to climb up to a second-story window.

Rubena, Celery Vase, Thumbprint, Enameled Bird, Silver Plate, James Tufts, 8 In.

RUBENA VERDE is a Victorian glassware that was shaded from red to green. It was first made by Hobbs, Brockunier and Company of Wheeling, West Virginia, about 1890.

Epergne, 3-Lily, 20 In.	800.00
Pitcher, Water, Opalescent Hobnails	495.00
Sauce, Opalescent Hobnails	60.00
Tumbler, Hobnail, 3 7/8 In.	110.00

RUBY GLASS is the dark red color of the precious gemstone known as a *ruby*. It was a popular Victorian color that never went completely out of style. The glass was shaped by many different processes to make many different types of ruby glass. There was a revival of interest in the 1940s when modern-shaped ruby table glassware became fashionable. Sometimes the red color is added to clear glass by a process called flashing or staining. Flashed glass is clear glass dipped in a colored glass, then pressed or cut. Stained glass has color painted on a clear glass. Then it is refired so the stain fuses with the glass. Pieces of glass colored in this way are indicated by the word *stained* in the description. Related items may be found in other categories, such as Cranberry Glass, Pressed Glass, and Souvenir.

Basket, Big Cookies, 1935, 10 In.	150.00
Berry Set, Ruby Thumbprint, Boat-Shape Master, 5 Piece	150.00
Biscuit Jar, Florette	300.00
Bowl, Pineapple, Ruffled Edge, 3 Footed, 11 In.	135.00
Creamer, Flowers	150.00
Goblet, Swirl	80.00
Pitcher, Ruffled Neck	50.00
Powder Jar, Woman, 5 In.	35.00
Saltshaker, Flowers	60.00
Toothpick, Gold Trim	25.00
Vase, 12 In.	125.00

RUDOLSTADT was a faience factory in the Thuringia region of Germany from 1720 to about 1791. In 1854, Ernst Bohne began working in the area. From about 1887 to 1918, the New York and Rudolstadt Pottery made decorated porcelain marked with the RW and crown familiar to collectors. This porcelain was imported by Lewis Straus and Sons of New York, which later became Nathan Straus and Sons. The word *Royal* was included in their import mark. Collectors often call it *Royal Rudolstadt*. Most pieces found today were made in the late nineteenth or early twentieth century. Additional pieces may be listed in the Kewpie category.

Bust, Old Woman, Wearing Ruffled Bonnet, Holding Jar, 1800, 7 In.	137.50
Creamer, Hand Painted Open Roses, Gold Rim Band, Black Outlined, 3 In.	30.00
Dresser Set, Pink Rose, 4 Piece	200.00
Ewer, Ivory, Brown, Gold, Applied Bamboo Handle	220.00
Plate, Blossom, 8 In.	40.00
Vase, Cream, Pink, Heavenly Blue, 14 1/2 In.	325.00
Vase, Pale Blue Tapestry Finish, Flowers, 8 1/4 In.	55.00
Vase, Purple Flowers, Swirled Base, Flared, Gold Handles, Beige, 1887-1918, 12 In.	192.00

RUGS have been used in the American home since the seventeenth century. The oriental rug of that time was often used on a table, not on the floor. Rag rugs, hooked rugs, and braided rugs were made by housewives from scraps of material.

Afghan, Overall Dark Brown, Blue, Dark Burgundy Ground, 4 Ft. 5 In. x 6 Ft.	275.00
Afshar, Red Border, Salmon Spandrels, Blue Ground, 4 Ft. 11 In. x 6 Ft. 2 In.	1090.00
Aubusson, Central Oval Medallion, Pink, Green, 8 Ft. 11 In. x 11 Ft. 9 In.	2530.00
Aubusson, Floral Garland Medallion Field, Corner Vases, 16 Ft. 1 In. x 13 Ft. 2 In.	5635.00
Aubusson, Overall Polychrome Floral Vinery, France, 1880, 14 Ft. x 9 Ft. 11 In.	6325.00
Bakhtiari, Floral, Red, Ivory, Pale Gold, 6 Ft. 10 In. x 4 Ft. 6 In.	748.00
Bakhtiari, Palmette, Midnight Blue Field, 6 Ft. 10 In. x 4 Ft. 3 In.	489.00

Baluchi, Diagonal Stripes, Camel Triangle Border, 5 Ft. 4 In. x 2 Ft. 10 In. 230.00
Baluchi, Flower Heads, Red Border, 4 Ft. 6 In. x 2 Ft. 8 In. 288.00
Bergama, Brown Spandrels, Lavender Border, Red Ground, 3 Ft. 5 In. x 4 Ft. 10 In. 545.00
Bergama, Prayer Design, Teals & Corals, 3 Ft. 7 In. x 5 Ft. 6 In. 2900.00
Bidjar, 3 Central Medallions, 3 Borders, 7 Ft. 4 In. x 4 Ft. 4 In. 345.00
Bidjar, Midnight Blue Ground, Rust Border, 3 Ft. 9 In. x 9 Ft. 3 In. 220.00
Bidjar, Spandrels On Red Ground, 4 Ft. x 5 Ft. 9 In. 192.00
Bokhara, Overall Gul Design, Geometric Border, Red, 5 Ft. 4 In. x 8 Ft. 230.00
Bokhara, Runner, 9 Ft. 1 In. x 2 Ft. 8 In. 275.00
Bokhara, Teal Green Ground, Ivory & Salmon Multiple Borders, Wool, 8 x 10 Ft. 275.00
Caucasian, Central Medallion, Brick Red Field, 4 Ft. 11 In. x 6 Ft. 3 In. 605.00
Chinese, 2 Floral Groups, Leaf Design, 11 Ft. 9 In. x 8 Ft. 9 In. 1100.00
Chinese, Floral Medallion, Midnight Blue Field, 10 x 8 Ft. 865.00
Chinese, Floral, Red, Pink, Green, Gold Ground, 4 Ft. 10 In. x 3 Ft. 2 In. 187.00
Chinese, Geometric, Olive Field, Ivory Border, 5 Ft. x 3 Ft. 9 In. 1265.00
Chinese, Herringbone Design, Blue Border, Symbols, Wool, 14 Ft. x 8 Ft. 3 In. 3450.00
Chinese, Open Floral Design, Floral Borders, Red, Tan, 9 x 12 Ft. 460.00
Chinese, Overall Floral Design, Cream Field, Yellow, 8 x 10 Ft. 175.00
Chinese, Pastel Floral Sprays, Beige, Gray, 6 x 4 Ft. 165.00
Chinese, Rust Red, Midnight Blue Ground, Ivory Border, 4 Ft. 2 In. x 6 Ft. 7 In. 440.00
Derebend, Bag Face, White, Tan, Red Geometric Design, Blue Ground, 18 x 19 In. 94.00
Donegal, Floral, Blue Ground, G. Morton & G.K. Robertson, Runner, 1900, 9 Ft. 7125.00
Ersari, 2 Rows Of Red Roses, Ivory Field, 4 Ft. 6 In. x 1 Ft. 2 In. 345.00
Ersari, 28 Geometric Arasi Guls, Brown Field, 8 Ft. 5 In. x 11 Ft. 10 In. 550.00
Ersari, 3 Heart Medallions, Red Border, 4 Ft. 7 In. x 1 Ft. 4 In. 460.00
Ersari, Allover Geometric Pattern, Center Medallion, 8 Ft. 8 In. x 13 Ft. 7 In. 770.00
Ersari, Chuval Guls, Magenta, Rust Red Field, Silk, 4 Ft. 2 In. x 2 Ft. 4 In. 345.00
Ersari, Plant Design, Multicolored Border, 6 Ft. 4 In. x 4 Ft. 374.00
Grenfell, Burgundy, Rust, Gold & White, 2 Ft. 9 In. x 3 Ft. 9 In. 3500.00
Grenfell, Deer Eating Foliage, 1930s, 13 1/2 x 16 1/8 In. 402.00
Grenfell, Hooked, Sailboat, 10 1/2 x 9 In. 225.00
Hamadan, Blue Ground, Red Border, Runner, 3 Ft. 5 In. x 8 Ft. 9 In. 605.00
Hamadan, Botehs In Center, White Florals, Deep Rose Ground, 4 Ft. x 6 Ft. 10 In. 385.00
Hamadan, Burgundy Spandrels, Dark Blue Ground, Blue Border, 4 Ft. 6 In. x 7 Ft. 2 In. 440.00
Hamadan, Dark Brown Ground, Ivory & Camel Borders, 4 Ft. 1 In. x 8 Ft. 6 In. 605.00
Hamadan, Faded Red Ground, Midnight Blue Border, 5 Ft. 3 In. x 6 Ft. 2 In. 770.00
Hamadan, Overall Floral Design, Red Field, 2 Ft. 8 In. x 4 Ft. 4 In. 200.00
Hamadan, Salmon Spandrels, Gray Ground, Light Blue Border, 4 Ft. 4 In. x 6 Ft. 5 In. .. 275.00
Heriz, Brown, Sage Eggplant Medallion, Rose Field, 13 x 10 Ft. 1495.00
Heriz, Gabled Medallion, Floral, Terra-Cotta Red Field, 11 Ft. x 8 Ft. 6 In. 3450.00
Heriz, Ivory Spandrels, Rust Ground, Midnight Blue Border, 5 Ft. 5 In. x 8 Ft. 2 In. 385.00
Heriz, Medallion, Gabled, Palmette Pendants, 13 Ft. x 9 Ft. 6 In. 1100.00
Heriz, Overall Serrated Leaves, Terra-Cotta Red Field, 12 Ft. x 9 Ft. 2 In. 2990.00
Heriz, Rosettes, Palmettes, Royal Blue Field, 11 Ft. 6 In. x 8 Ft. 7 In. 6325.00
Heriz, Spandrels, Light Blue Ground, Camel & Rust Border, 3 Ft. x 4 Ft. 9 In. 495.00
Hooked, 15 Triangular Blocks, Alternating Upside Up & Down, Wool, 19 x 32 In. 2185.00
Hooked, 2 Birds, Flowering Tree, Floral Borders, Yarn, 35 x 54 In. 95.00
Hooked, 2 Deer, Striped Ground, Rag, Mounted On Stretcher, 24 3/4 x 35 1/2 In. 440.00
Hooked, 2 White Spaniels, Black Spots, Picket Fence, Rag, 25 x 45 In. 90.00
Hooked, 4 Flowers, Striated Black & Green Field, 1930s, 17 1/2 x 39 1/2 In. 175.00
Hooked, Abstract Geometric Design, 21 x 33 3/4 In. 175.00
Hooked, Baby Blocks, Wool & Cotton, 1920s, 21 1/4 x 57 1/2 In. 400.00
Hooked, Birds On Branch, 2 Flowers, 17 1/4 x 35 1/2 In. 250.00
Hooked, Black Horse, Red Bird, Brown Ground, Black Border, Rag, 22 x 31 In. 300.00
Hooked, Black, Cat, Seated By 4 Black Kittens, Turquoise, 27 x 43 In. 4370.00
Hooked, Blue Bird, Flowering Tree, Red, Pink Ground, Gray Stripe, Rag, 26 x 40 In. ... 110.00
Hooked, Cat, Black Edging & Spots On Green Ground, Wool, 21 x 32 In. 2990.00
Hooked, Center Domestic Animal & Vase Of Flowers, 1920s, 34 1/4 x 40 In. 400.00
Hooked, Checkerboard, Gray Ground, Floral Border, Rag & Yarn, 22 x 32 In. 330.00
Hooked, Checkerboard, Striped Border, Mounted On Stretcher, 20 x 35 In. 110.00
Hooked, Compass Star Design, Multicolored, Rag, 56 In. 250.00
Hooked, Compass Star, Red, Gray, Black, Blue, Yellow, Round, 55 In. 412.00
Hooked, Cottage & Trees, Rag & Yarn, 26 x 35 In. 110.00

Hooked, Crowing Rooster, Yarn, 19 x 33 1/2 In. 220.00
Hooked, Dog, Standing In Landscape, Brown, White, Black, Orange, 1900, 36 x 66 In. . . 805.00
Hooked, Farm Scene, Cow, Sheep, Buildings, Early 20th Century, 29 x 52 In. 300.00
Hooked, Field Of Flowering Vines, Exotic Birds, Gray Field, 29 1/2 x 57 1/2 In. 400.00
Hooked, Figural, 2 Horses, Linen Ground, Frame, 19th Century, 28 x 48 1/2 In. 520.00
Hooked, Figural, Trotting Horse, Striped, Scalloped, Foliate Border, 1922, 29 x 39 In. . . . 1050.00
Hooked, Floral & Geometric, 20th Century, 24 1/2 x 56 In. 300.00
Hooked, Floral & Geometric, Hearth, Field Of Stars, Diamond Border, 39 x 84 In. 2415.00
Hooked, Floral Spray Of Blossoms, Red, Pink, Maroon, Green, 108 x 131 In. 3162.00
Hooked, Floral, Beige, Ivory, Pink & Green Shades, 102 x 133 In. 385.00
Hooked, Flowers, Charcoal & Black Ground, Braided Edge, 36 x 49 In. 395.00
Hooked, Flowers, Geometric Designs, Yarn & Rag, Burlap Back, 114 x 144 In. 2750.00
Hooked, Forest Green Peacock, Tail In Full Plume, Wool & Cotton, 35 1/2 In. 4370.00
Hooked, Geometric, Pink, Yellow, Lavender, Gray, Blue, 182 x 108 In. 8050.00
Hooked, Gray Dog Center, Florals At Sides, c.1920, 21 x 53 In. 695.00
Hooked, Horse & Carriage, Cream Ground, Scalloped Border, 22 1/2 x 35 1/2 In. 325.00
Hooked, Horse Standing Within Black Border, Brown, White, Blue, 33 x 58 In. 805.00
Hooked, Light & Dark Square, 18 x 70 In. 210.00
Hooked, Maine Landscape Scene, Rag, Mounted On Stretcher, 27 1/2 x 34 3/4 In. 440.00
Hooked, Man With Horse, Colt, Barn, Rag, 18 x 34 In. 195.00
Hooked, Masted Schooner On Open Water, 17 x 20 1/2 In. 175.00
Hooked, Mat, Black Field, Striated Borders, Frame, 15 3/4 x 36 3/4 In. 260.00
Hooked, Mennonite, Floral & Heart, Green, Blue, Red, Pink, Orange, 47 x 39 In. 3162.00
Hooked, Mounted On Stretcher, 32 x 45 In. 950.00
Hooked, Pair Of Dogs In Landscape, Early 20th Century, 23 x 35 In. 175.00
Hooked, Pastel Flowers, Geometric Grid, Beige Ground, 63 x 101 In. 220.00
Hooked, Peacock, Yellow Standing Rose Sprigs, Dark Green Ground, 23 x 36 In. 1150.00
Hooked, Polychrome Floral, Black Scalloped Border, c.1930, 29 x 36 1/2 In. 150.00
Hooked, Prancing Horse, Black Field, Geometric Border, Frame, 1840s, 32 x 39 In. 920.00
Hooked, Racing Horses, Mary Smythe Perkins, 31 x 57 In. 8500.00
Hooked, Red Hearts & Blue Stars, 50 x 80 In. 2990.00
Hooked, Red Schoolhouse, Multicolored Flowers, 18 x 34 1/2 In. 550.00
Hooked, Reserve Of Bird Hunting Scene, Cream, Late 19th Century, 28 1/2 x 52 In. 865.00
Hooked, Reserve Of Horse, Stars & Hearts Border, Late 19th Century, 40 x 49 In. 1380.00
Hooked, Rising Sun, 27 1/2 x 37 1/2 In. 350.00
Hooked, Roses With Arabesques, Open Gold Ground, 85 x 73 In. 165.00
Hooked, Sailing Ship, Rocky Shoreline, 8 x 12 In. 265.00
Hooked, Scotty Dog, 20 x 32 1/2 In. 250.00
Hooked, Stag, Gray Ground, Geometric Floral Border, Rag, 26 x 47 In. 225.00
Hooked, Stylized Floral & Cross Design, Late 19th Century, 140 x 89 In. 1150.00
Hooked, Stylized Floral, Gray Striped Ground, Rag, 28 x 49 In. 100.00
Hooked, Tan Horse, Brown Harness, Navy Blue & Black Ground, Rag, 25 x 29 In. 165.00
Hooked, Trotting Horse, Green Field, Frame, Feb. 14, 1922, 29 x 39 1/2 In. 1100.00
Hooked, U.S. Map, States, Name & Flower, Multicolored, Beige, Wool, 84 x 108 In. . . . 495.00
Hooked, Variegated Fields Of Rural Scenes, Stair Runner, 20th Century, 188 In. 1495.00
Hooked, Vase Of Flowers, Black Field, 1921, 19 1/2 x 33 1/2 In. 460.00
Hooked, Village Scene, Four-Horse Carriage, 36 x 75 In. 935.00
Hooked, Welcome, 1920s, 16 x 47 In. 225.00
Hooked, Welcome, Mother Cat & Kitten, Floral Border, Half-Round, 1920s 450.00
Iranian, Floral, Blue, Red, Tan, Blue Ground, 13 Ft. x 8 Ft. 6 In. 825.00
Isfahan, Palmettes, Floral Border, 12 Ft. 3 In. x 13 Ft. 7 In. 2200.00
Ivory Spandrels, Dark Blue Ground, Runner, 2 Ft. 10 In. x 8 Ft. 990.00
Karabagh, 3 Medallions, Midnight Blue Field, 6 Ft. 5 In. x 4 Ft. 690.00
Karabagh, Concentric Hooked Medallions, Rust Field, Green Border, 6 Ft. x 4 Ft. 2 In. . 550.00
Karabagh, Dark Blue Ground, Dark Red Border, 4 Ft. 7 In. x 8 Ft. 3 In. 1430.00
Karabagh, Polychrome Herati Design, Raspberry Field, 12 Ft. 11 In. x 6 Ft. 4 In. 3450.00
Karabagh, Prayer, Dark Red-Brown Border, Camel Ground, 3 Ft. 3 In. x 4 Ft. 5 In. 385.00
Karaja, 3 Medallions, Navy Blue Field, Red Border, 4 Ft. 8 In. x 3 Ft. 8 In. 575.00
Karaja, 3 Medallions, Rust Field, Blue Border, 4 Ft. x 3 Ft. 6 In. 287.00
Kashan, Circular Star Medallion, Ivory Field, 7 Ft. x 4 Ft. 6 In. 920.00
Kashan, Medallion Centered On Floral Field, 8 Ft. 10 In. x 12 Ft. 7 In. 660.00
Kashan, Red Rust Spandrels, Blue Ground, Border, 8 Ft. 9 In. x 12 Ft. 3025.00
Kashan, Red, Blue, Signed, 6 Ft. 8 In. x 4 Ft. 6 In. 4025.00

Kazak, Blue Spandrels, Camel Ground & Border, Wool, 6 x 9 Ft. 550.00
Kazak, Brick Field, Teal, Ivory & Gold, 5 x 8 Ft. 4400.00
Kazak, Brown, Tan, Blue Ground, Ivory Border, 2 Ft. 6 In. x 4 Ft. 8 In. 424.00
Kazak, Geometric, Blue, Green, Gold, White, Black, Red, 6 Ft. 8 In. x 4 Ft. 7 In. 2530.00
Kazak, Geometric, Red, Green, Red Ground, 3 Borders, 5 Ft. 2 In. x 7 Ft. 2 In. 825.00
Kazak, Medallion, Geometric Border, Ivory, Green, Blue, 5 Ft. 8 In. x 8 Ft. 6 In. 1650.00
Kazak, Rust, Beige, Pale Blue, Browns, 5 Ft. 8 In. x 10 Ft. 4 In. 330.00
Kazak, Sea Green Partial Medallion, Madder Field, 7 Ft. x 5 Ft. 2 In. 1840.00
Kazak, Serrated Diamond Medallions, Red Field, 3 Ft. 8 In. x 3 Ft. 2 In. 690.00
Kerman, Beige, Blue Floral Field, Birds, 13 x 23 Ft. 5175.00
Kerman, Celadon Green Medallion, 20 Ft. 3 In. x 11 Ft. 7 In. 6440.00
Kerman, Center Floral Medallion, Green Field, 8 Ft. 8 In. x 11 Ft. 5 In. 440.00
Kerman, Circular Medallion, Flowering Vines, Ivory Field, 11 Ft. 2 In. x 8 Ft. 9 In. 6900.00
Kerman, Ivory Ground, Magenta Border, 7 Ft. 7 In. x 9 Ft. 8 In. 825.00
Kerman, Mauve, Ivory, Blue Field, 9 Ft. 1 In x 6 Ft. 10 In. 575.00
Kerman, Overall Palmette Design, Midnight Blue Field, 7 Ft. 2 In. x 4 Ft. 8 In. 1265.00
Kerman, Prayer Design, Ivory Field, Border, 11 Ft. 4 In. x 9 Ft. 2760.00
Kerman Laver, Prayer, Tree Of Life Design, 6 Ft. 10 In. x 4 Ft. 5 In. 1870.00
Kilim, 6 Serrated Squares, Ivory Field, 7 Ft. 9 In. x 4 Ft. 8 In. 575.00
Kilim, Hooked Hexagons, Ivory Border, 11 Ft. 4 In. x 5 Ft. 1610.00
Kilim, Paired Boteh, Brown Field, Gold Border, 6 Ft. x 3 Ft. 9 In. 1035.00
Kilim, Stylized Rose Filled Cartouches, Lilac Ground, 11 Ft. 8 In. x 5 Ft. 3 In. 1725.00
Kuba-Shirvan, Prayer, Midnight Blue Ground, Ivory Ground, 3 Ft. 4 In. x 7 Ft. 2540.00
Kurd, Herati Design, Navy Blue Field, Red Border, 9 Ft. 9 In. x 4 Ft. 6 In. 635.00
Kurd, Stepped Hexagonal Medallion, Rust Field, 7 Ft. 6 In. x 3 Ft. 4 In. 460.00
Lillihan, Floral, Navy Blue, Blue, Red, 7 Ft. 9 In. x 10 Ft. 2 In. 205.00
Lillihan, Medallion, Floral Sprays, Red Border, 5 Ft. 8 In. x 3 Ft. 9 In. 748.00
Machine Woven, Opticical Pattern, 1960s, 7 Ft. 6 In. x 4 Ft. 11 In. 415.00
Machine Woven, Sunburst Design, Brown & Beige, 1930s, 13 Ft. 8 In. x 10 Ft. 6 In. .. 3000.00
Machine Woven, Wool, Ship In Harbor, Beige, Wool, Art Deco, 2 Ft. 11 In. x 2 Ft. 7 In. .. 45.00
Mahajiran Sarouk, Mottled Purple, Red Ground, Dark Blue Border, 2 Ft. x 2 Ft. 6 In. .. 300.00
Mahal, Mustaufi Design Overall, Blue Field, 14 Ft. 9 In. x 12 Ft. 11 In. 8050.00
Malayer, Boteh Rows, Leafy Vines, Red Border, 6 Ft. 8 In. x 4 Ft. 6 In. 865.00
Malayer, Dark Brown Ground, Ivory Border, 3 Ft. x 4 Ft. 10 In. 715.00
Malayer, Diamond Medallion, Ivory Field, 6 Ft. 8 In. x 4 Ft. 4 In. 1840.00
Malayer, Flowerhead Medallion, Brown Palmette, 6 Ft. 8 In. x 5 Ft. 1380.00
Malayer, Red Ground, Camel Border, 4 Ft. 3 In. x 6 Ft. 8 In. 2200.00
Mosul, Red Spandrels, Blue Ground, 4 Ft. x 5 Ft. 9 In. 825.00
Needlepoint, Center Floral Medallion, Multiple Borders, 4 Ft. 6 In. x 6 Ft. 305.00
Needlepoint, Floral, Pink, Blue, Tans & Greens, Ivory Ground, 9 x 12 Ft. 880.00
Needlepoint, Tan & Pink Roses, Gray & White Grid, Black Border, 7 x 7 Ft. 220.00
Needlepoint, Victorian, Columns Of Red & Green Plants, 10 Ft. 7 In. x 7 Ft. 5 In. 4900.00
Oushak, Foliate, Ivory Field, Salmon, Pale Blue, 10 Ft. x 8 Ft. 3 In. 748.00
Oushak, Hooked Medallion, Sky Blue Field, 9 Ft. 10 In. x 6 Ft. 9 In. 400.00
Penny, Black, Colorful Applique, Wool Felt, 1 Ft. 10 In. x 3 Ft. 7 In. 28.00
Penny, Gray Wool, Olive Twill, Red Felt, White Flannel Ground, 27 x 51 In. 165.00
Perpedil, Multicolored Serrated Hexagons, 6 Ft. x 4 Ft. 3 In. 2070.00
Persian, 2 Rosettes, Leaf, Ivory Border, 1 Ft. 10 In. x 1 Ft. 8 In. 316.00
Persian, Blue Oval Medallion, Cranberry Field, 3 Ft. 5 In. x 4 Ft. 10 In. 460.00
Persian, Blue, Beige Foliate, Crimson Field, 6 Ft. 10 In. x 5 Ft. 375.00
Persian, Dark Blue Ground, Plum Border, 9 Ft. 4 In. x 13 Ft. 1375.00
Persian, Geometric Medallions, Ivory, Indigo, Red, 10 x 5 Ft. 345.00
Persian, Herati Design, Light Brown Field, 9 Ft. 6 In. x 5 Ft. 4 In. 400.00
Persian, Hexagonal Medallion, Terra-Cotta Red Field, 15 Ft. 6 In. x 11 Ft. 5750.00
Persian, Hooked Diamonds, Midnight Blue Field, 5 Ft. 6 In. x 3 Ft. 6 In. 345.00
Persian, Indented Diamond Medallion, Rust Field, 7 Ft. x 4 Ft. 5 In. 1610.00
Persian, Northwest, Dark Red Ground, Ivory Border, Runner, 3 Ft. 10 In. x 10 Ft. 4 In. .. 605.00
Persian, Orange Foliate, Blue Field, 6 Ft. 9 In. x 3 Ft. 8 In. 748.00
Qum, Stars, Spandrels, Ivory Ground, Light Blue Border, Wool, 4 x 7 Ft. 360.00
Sarouk, 3 Medallions, Burgundy Ground, Multiple Borders, 2 Ft. 6 In. x 10 Ft. 2 In. ... 220.00
Sarouk, Blue, Charcoal Ground, 3 Ft. 3 In. x 5 Ft. 2 In. 770.00
Sarouk, Blue, Charcoal Ground, Red Border, 2 Ft. 11 In. x 4 Ft. 11 In. 385.00
Sarouk, Burgundy Ground, Midnight Blue Border, Fringed, 4 Ft. 4 In. x 6 Ft. 6 In. 660.00

Sarouk, Dark Red Ground, Ivory Border, 11 Ft. 4 In. x 15 Ft. 9 In.	3300.00
Sarouk, Floral Sprays, Wine Red Field, 6 Ft. 10 In. x 4 Ft. 2 In.	1840.00
Sarouk, Foliate, Red Field, Blue Border, 13 Ft. 6 In. x 10 Ft. 4 In.	805.00
Sarouk, Geometric Medallion, Red Field, 12 Ft. x 9 Ft. 2 In.	3910.00
Sarouk, Light Burgundy, Midnight Blue Border, Fringed, 10 Ft. 4 In. x 17 Ft.	4400.00
Sarouk, Overall Floral Design, Red Field, 8 Ft. 7 In. x 11 Ft. 9 In.	5750.00
Sarouk, Red Field, Palmette, 11 Ft. 6 In. x 8 Ft. 6 In.	2185.00
Sarouk, Red, Blue, 5 Borders, c.1930, 11 Ft. 8 In. x 8 Ft. 4 In.	1100.00
Sarouk, Red, Purple Ground, Camel Border, Fringed, 2 Ft. 4 In. x 4 Ft. 8 In.	605.00
Sarouk, Stylized Floral Urns, Red, Blue, Beige, 6 Ft. 8 In. x 4 Ft. 2 In.	1375.00
Sarouk, Stylized Flowers, Center Medallion, Red Ground, 9 x 12 Ft.	2100.00
Sennah, Black Ground, Rust Border, 3 Ft. 8 In. x 6 Ft. 9 In.	1870.00
Shiraz, Dark Blue Ground, Brown Border, 2 Ft. 8 In. x 4 Ft. 2 In.	330.00
Shirvan, 2 Columns, Guls, Navy Blue Field, 5 Ft. 6 In. x 3 Ft. 4 In.	978.00
Shirvan, Abrash Blue Ground, White Border, 3 Ft. 8 In. x 5 Ft. 7 In.	550.00
Shirvan, Geometric Flowers, Blue, White, Orange, 3 Ft. 4 In. x 4 Ft. 8 In.	1925.00
Shirvan, Geometric, Light Red Ground, White, Tan Border, 7 Ft. 8 In. x 5 Ft. 5 In.	1155.00
Shirvan, Prayer, 6 Medallions, Navy Blue Field, 5 Ft. 8 In. x 3 Ft. 9 In.	865.00
Tabriz, Circular Medallion, Rosettes, Violet Blue Field, 10 x 9 Ft. 2 In.	1725.00
Tabriz, Diamond Medallion, Vine Border, 12 Ft. 5 In. x 8 Ft. 5 In.	3450.00
Tabriz, Light Blue Spandrels, Ivory Ground, Blue Border, 5 Ft. 11 In. x 9 Ft. 6 In.	880.00
Tabriz, Medallion, Rust Spandrels, Celadon Ground, 1920, 12 Ft. 9 In. x 9 Ft. 3 In.	4600.00
Tabriz, Multicolored Floral, Geometric Design, Red, 8 Ft. 1 In. x 10 Ft. 3 In.	805.00
Tabriz, Overall Herati Design, Medallion, Green, Blue Field, 13 Ft. 8 In. x 9 Ft. 8 In.	4025.00
Tabriz, Overall Palmette Design, Ivory Field, Tan Border, 11 Ft. 9 In. x 9 Ft.	980.00
Tabriz, Red Medallion, Blue Field, 6 Ft. 6 In. x 9 Ft. 10 In.	715.00
Tekke, Ivory, Black & Orange, Red Ground, 3 Ft. 7 In. x 4 Ft. 1 In.	305.00
Tekke, Prayer, Ivory, Dark Blue & Rust, Maroon Ground, 3 Ft. 9 In. x 4 Ft. 8 In.	120.00
Tufted, Modern Design, Gray, Brown & Gold Shades, Betty Joel, 1930, 4 Ft. x 2 Ft. 7 In.	4875.00
Turkish, Prayer, Turquoise, Maroon, Pink & Ivory Field, Silk, 2 Ft. 6 In. x 4 Ft. 6 In.	745.00
Turkish, Tribal, Geometric Medallion, Plain Tomato Field, 7 x 9 Ft.	770.00
Yomud, 9 Chuval Guls, Aubergine Field, 3 Ft. 8 In. x 2 Ft. 8 In.	431.00
Yuruk, Orange Border, Blue Spandrels, Burgundy Ground, 4 Ft. 6 In. x 6 Ft. 3 In.	468.00
Yuruk, Stepped Diamonds, Royal Blue, Apricot Border, 6 Ft. x 3 Ft. 4 In.	345.00

RUMRILL Pottery was designed by George Rumrill of Little Rock, Arkansas. From 1933 to 1938, it was produced by the Red Wing Pottery of Red Wing, Minnesota. In 1938, production was transferred to the Shawnee Pottery in Zanesville, Ohio. Production ceased in the 1940s.

RumRill

Bookends, Polar Bear, Jet Black Glaze	522.00
Figurine, Lady On Turtle, 10 1/2 In.	450.00
Jug, Stopper, Red Wing	95.00
Pitcher, Ball Shape, Mottled Green	75.00
Pitcher, Orange, Tray, 7 In.	25.00
Pitcher, Water, Matte Blue	50.00
Vase, Art Deco, Ball Shape, Mottled Blue, 6 In.	125.00
Vase, Beige, Brown Interior, 10 1/2 In.	90.00
Vase, Blue, 7 1/2 In.	65.00
Vase, High Glaze, Handles, 9 In.	125.00
Vase, Mermaid, Green, 9 In.	95.00
Vase, Olive, Gold, 5 3/4 In.	75.00
Vase, Water Lilies, Turtles, Light Purple, 6 1/2 In.	220.00

RUSKIN is a British art pottery of the twentieth century. The Ruskin Pottery was started by William Howson Taylor, and his name was used as the mark until about 1899. The factory, at West Smethwick, Birmingham, England, stopped making new pieces in 1933 but continued to glaze and sell the remaining wares until 1935. The art pottery is noted for its exceptional glazes.

Candlestick, Blue, Purple Luster Iridescent Glaze, Impressed Marks, 8 In., Pair	220.00
Lamp, Yellow, Pearl Luster Glaze, No Shade, 9 In.	185.00
Vase, Beaker Shape, Celadon, Purple, Oxblood Glaze, Marked, 1906, 9 x 5 1/2 In.	1100.00

Vase, Blue, Green Grape Design, Raspberry, Pink Glaze, Marked, 7 1/2 x 4 1/4 In. 330.00
Vase, Light Blue Luster Glaze, Green Iridescent, 8 In. 176.00
Vase, Orange Luster, 10 1/2 In. 110.00
Vase, Purple, Green, 11 In. 2200.00
Vase, Purple, Oxblood Crystalline Glaze, 1906, 9 3/4 x 4 1/4 In. 467.50
Vase, Speckled Purple, Green, Blue & White Glaze, 1906, 6 In. 2625.00
Vase, Yellow Luster Glaze, Green, Brown Iridescent, Impressed Marks, 14 In. 355.00

RUSSEL WRIGHT designed dinnerwares in modern shapes for many companies. Iroquois China Company, Harker China Company, Steubenville Pottery, and Justin Tharaud and Sons made dishes marked *Russel Wright.* The Steubenville wares, first made in 1938, are the most common today. Wright was a designer of domestic and industrial wares, including furniture, aluminum, radios, interiors, and glassware. Dinnerwares and other pieces by Wright are listed here. For more information, see *Kovels' Depression Glass & Dinnerware Price List.*

Russel Wright MFG. BY STEUBENVILLE

American Modern, Bowl, Vegetable, Divided, Cedar Green ....65.00 to 75.00
American Modern, Bowl, Vegetable, Granite Gray 26.00
American Modern, Butter, Cover, Cedar Green 475.00
American Modern, Butter, Cover, Granite Gray 250.00
American Modern, Carafe, Granite Gray 250.00
American Modern, Casserole, Bean Brown 45.00
American Modern, Casserole, Cover, Granite Gray 55.00
American Modern, Celery Dish, White 30.00
American Modern, Coffeepot, Black Chutney ....150.00 to 225.00
American Modern, Creamer, Granite Gray 9.00
American Modern, Creamer, Seafoam 15.00
American Modern, Cup & Saucer, Bean Brown 38.00
American Modern, Cup & Saucer, Chartreuse 9.00
American Modern, Cup & Saucer, Coral ....5.00 to 7.00
American Modern, Cup, Granite Gray ....6.00 to 12.00
American Modern, Cup, Seafoam Green, After Dinner 13.00
American Modern, Pitcher, Chartreuse 70.00
American Modern, Pitcher, Cover, Chartreuse 340.00
American Modern, Pitcher, Granite Gray 60.00
American Modern, Pitcher, Seafoam 145.00
American Modern, Pitcher, Water, Cedar Green 130.00
American Modern, Pitcher, Water, Coral 85.00
American Modern, Plate, Cantaloupe, 8 In. 38.00
American Modern, Plate, Chartreuse, 6 1/4 In. 5.00
American Modern, Plate, Chartreuse, 10 In. 6.00
American Modern, Plate, Coral, 6 1/4 In. 12.00
American Modern, Plate, Seafoam, 10 In. 45.00
American Modern, Platter, Chartreuse, Rectangular, 13 1/4 In. 20.00
American Modern, Relish, Chartreuse, Raffia Handle, Divided ....150.00 to 225.00
American Modern, Salt & Pepper, Bean Brown 20.00
American Modern, Salt & Pepper, Seafoam Green 10.00
American Modern, Saucer, Coral 4.00
American Modern, Soup, Dish, Lug, Coral 10.00
American Modern, Sugar & Creamer, Cantaloupe 85.00
American Modern, Sugar & Creamer, White, Box 135.00
American Modern, Sugar, Cover, Chartreuse 10.00
American Modern, Sugar, Cover, Coral 16.00
American Modern, Teapot, Bean Brown 150.00
American Modern, Teapot, Black Chutney 120.00
American Modern, Teapot, Granite Gray 70.00
Casual, Casserole, Cover, Pink Sherbet, 4 Qt. 90.00
Casual, Coffeepot, Avocado Yellow, After Dinner 80.00
Casual, Cup & Saucer, Sugar White 12.00
Casual, Plate, White, 6 1/2 In. 8.00
Iroquois, Bowl, Cereal, Aqua, 5 In. 45.00
Iroquois, Bowl, Vegetable, Lemon Yellow, Open, 10 In. 35.00
Iroquois, Carafe, Pink Sherbet ....200.00 to 225.00

Iroquois, Carafe, White	145.00
Iroquois, Casserole, Divided, Avocado Yellow, 10 In.	55.00
Iroquois, Casserole, Ice Blue, Handle, 2 Qt.	65.00
Iroquois, Mug, Ice Blue	45.00
Iroquois, Mug, Pink Sherbet	85.00
Iroquois, Plate, Cantaloupe, 6 1/2 In.	18.00 to 20.00
Iroquois, Plate, Ice Blue, 9 1/2 In.	6.00
Iroquois, Salt & Pepper, Pink Sherbet	10.00
Iroquois, Soup, Dish, Gumbo, Charcoal	55.00
Iroquois, Sugar & Creamer, Stacking, Sugar White	32.00 to 40.00
Iroquois, Sugar, Ice Blue	20.00
Iroquois, Teapot, Lemon Yellow	140.00
Suede, Ashtray, Sterling, Gray	85.00
Theme Formal, Cordial, 3 Oz.	200.00
White Clover, Clock, Kitchen, Harker	35.00

SABINO glass was made in the 1920s and 1930s in Paris, France. Founded by Marius-Ernest Sabino (1878–1961), the firm was noted for Art Deco lamps, vases, figurines, and animals in clear, colored, and opalescent glass. Production stopped during World War II but resumed in the 1960s with the manufacture of nude figurines and small opalescent glass animals. The new pieces are a slightly different color and can be recognized.

Sabino
France

Bowl, Roman Scenes, Black Ground, Signed, 1930, 4 1/2 x 9 1/2 In.	825.00
Figurine, Butterfly, Opalescent	115.00
Figurine, Frog, On Log, 3 5/8 In.	35.00
Lamp, Ceiling, Stylized Flower Heads Band, Circular Gray Shade, Bronze, 25 In.	1035.00
Plaque, 3 Nudes, Fountain, Wolfhound, Opalescent, 5 x 12 In.	495.00
Vase, 2 Figures Intertwined, Band Of Flower Heads, Leaf Border, Orange, 7 In.	546.00
Vase, Nude Women Each Side, Blossoming Flower Beds, Signed, 7 1/2 x 9 1/2 In.	1709.00

SALOPIAN ware was made by the Caughley factory of England during the eighteenth century. The early pieces were blue and white with some colored decorations. Another ware referred to as *Salopian* is a late nineteenth-century tableware decorated with color transfers.

Salopian

Bowl, Classical Figures, Floral Design, Scalloped Rim, c.1780, 7 In.	395.00
Bowl, Classical Figures, Florals, c.1780, 6 1/2 In.	325.00
Bowl, Figures, Waterfall, Boat & Pagoda Scene, Floral Spray Border, 3 x 6 In.	330.00
Cup & Saucer, Farm Scene, Girl, With Sheep, Acorn Leaf, Floral Border, No Handle	385.00
Mug, Cider, Classical Figures, Initialed, c.1780, 6 In.	650.00
Pitcher, Cream, Stag, Squatty, 4 x 5 3/4 In.	358.00
Plate, A Present For John, Central Medallion, c.1810, 6 1/2 In.	475.00
Plate, Acorn, Floral, Foliate, Blue Edge, Roman Key Type Border, 7 1/4 In.	330.00
Plate, Exotic Bird, Floral, Leaf & Floral Border, 7 1/2 In.	330.00
Plate, Harvest Scene, Man, With Wheat Flail, Floral Spray Border, 8 1/4 In.	300.00
Plate, Soup, Eagle Overlooking Sheep & Shepherds, Floral Border, 8 In.	170.00
Teapot, Floral, Foliate Design, Robin, Squat, Gray Ground, 5 1/2 x 10 In.	495.00

SALT AND PEPPER SHAKERS in matched sets were first used in the nineteenth century. Collectors are primarily interested in figural examples made after World War I. *Huggers* are pairs of shakers that appear to embrace each other. Many salt and pepper shakers are listed in other categories and can be located through the index at the back of this book.

A.O. Smith Harvestore System, White Top & Grid	85.00
Alcatraz Convicts	50.00
Alligator & Baby, Black	75.00
American Bisque, White, Gold	12.00
Aunt Jemima & Uncle Mose, F & F, 5 In.	35.00 to 60.00
Babies In Basket	75.00
Ball Mason Jar, Zinc Lid, Miniature	65.00
Bananas, Tray, 4 1/2 In. *Illus*	8.00
Barbie	20.00

Salt & Pepper, Bear, Huggers, Yellow & Black, Van Tellingen, 3 In.

Salt & Pepper, Dutch Boy & Girl, Huggers, Van Tellingen, 3 1/2 In.

Salt & Pepper, Prayer Lady, Blue & White, 4 1/2 In.

Barbie & Ken	30.00
Bart & Lisa, 3 1/2 In.	26.00
Baseball	10.00
Baumont's Acorn, Pink To White, Original Tops	115.00
Bear, Huggers, Yellow & Black, Van Tellingen, 3 In. *Illus*	45.00
Beehive & Bear, Huggers, Fingerhut	30.00
Beer Stein, Germany	16.00
Bell Boy, Carrying 2 Glass Shakers In Brass Holders, 1930s	125.00
Bellhop, Suitcase	25.00
Betsy Ross & Bill Of Rights, Enesco, Box	35.00
Big Boy & Hamburger, EBR Inc., 1995	15.00
Bill Of Rights, Enesco	22.00
Binoculars & Case, 3 In.	15.00
Black Cat, Rhinestone Eyes	26.00
Black Man & Woman, Seated, 2 1/2 In.	40.00
Borden, Elsie The Cow, Original Foil Label, Stamped, 1943	150.00
Boy & Dog, Huggers, Van Tellingen	70.00
Bunny, Huggers, Van Tellingen	125.00
Buster Brown & Tige	48.00
Candy Cane & Guy, Anthropomorphic Christmas Set, 4 3/4 In.	49.00
Cat & Ball Of Yarn, Huggers, Norcrest	28.00
Cat-In-The-Hat	225.00
Chef & Woodstock	28.00
Chicago Cubs, Ceramic, Sticker, 2 1/2 In.	30.00
Civil War Hat	25.00
Clown & Seal, Van Tellingen	80.00
Col. & Mrs. Sanders, Plastic, Margarot Corp, 1972, 4 In.	195.00
Collar & Polka Dot Bow Tie, 3 In.	24.00
Confederate Hat, Gray, Black Visor, Confederate Flag, 2 1/2 In.	20.00
Cooperstown Baseball Boys	125.00
Cutie Pie, Blue, NAPCO	45.00
Dean Martin & Jerry Lewis	150.00 to 225.00
Delphite, Basket Weave	20.00
Dog & Cat	40.00
Donald Duck, Leed's China	95.00
Dutch Boy & Girl, Huggers, Van Tellingen, 3 1/2 In. *Illus*	35.00
Elsie & Elmer, Borden	105.00 to 145.00
Elsie The Cow, Stack, Foil Label, Backstamped The Borden Co., 1943	150.00
Elves On Stump, Twin Winton	20.00
Eskimo	40.00
Filter Queen, Box	30.00
Fireplace & Stack Of Logs, 2 1/2 In.	18.00
Flamingo Snow Dome	32.00
Flintstones, Bedrock City	15.00
Fred Flintstone & Barney Rubble	125.00
G.E. Refrigerator, Milk Glass, Label	75.00
Gas Pump, Humble Esso, Decals, 2 3/4 In.	38.00

Gas Pump, Phillips 66, Plastic, Box, 2 3/4 In. ....55.00 to 60.00
Gas Pump, Richfield Oil, Plastic, 2 5/8 In. 132.00
Genie, Gold Lamp, Vallona Starr ....45.00 to 85.00
Gingham Dog & Calico Cat, Brayton Laguna 90.00
Girl & Sailor, Huggers, Van Tellingen 25.00
Girl & White Lamb, Van Tellingen 35.00
Goetz Country Club Beer, Box 28.00
Greyhound Bus, Box 85.00
Gumby & Pokey, Clay Art 25.00
Gun & Bullet, 4 In. 24.00
Head On Shoulders 75.00
Heinz Ketchup Bottle, Plastic, 4 In. 24.00
Humpty Dumpty, Regal ....75.00 to 135.00
Indians, Nodder 120.00
James Dean, 4 1/4 In. 26.00
Jonah & Whale ....50.00 to 70.00
Kangaroo, Twin Winton 75.00
Kangaroo & Baby In Pouch, 5 1/2 In. 24.00
Kellogg's Snap & Pop 35.00
Ken-L-Ration Cat & Dog, Plastic, Fitz & Floyd, 1950s ....20.00 to 28.00
Kermit & Miss Piggy, Cut In Half, Sigma 80.00
Kit & Kat, Vandor 40.00
Laurel & Hardy, Beswick 175.00
Leaf People, Convention, Regal 135.00
Little Lulu, Ceramic, 1950s, 9 In. 450.00
Love Bugs, Maroon, Bendel 100.00
Love Bugs, Van Tellingen 70.00
Ludwig & Donald Duck 90.00
Lunch Box, Thermos, Yellow, Red, 2 & 3 In. ....*Illus* 10.00
Maggie & Jiggs, Chalkware, Painted 85.00
Mammy, Black, F & F 45.00
Mammy & Pappy, Black, 8 In. 145.00
Mammy & Uncle Mose, Fitz & Floyd, 3 1/2 In. 55.00
Mary & Lamb, Van Tellingen 55.00
Max & Ray Camel, Figural, Plastic, 1993, 4 1/4 In. 60.00
Mickey Mouse & Wheelbarrow, 5 In. 55.00
Millie & Willie, Kool Cigarettes 25.00
Miss Cutie Pie, Pink 40.00
Monkey & Baby, CAS 85.00
Mouse & Cheese 40.00
Native With Watermelon ....45.00 to 60.00
Nipper, RCA Victor, His Master's Voice, Lenox, 1930s ....85.00 to 150.00
Old McDonald Boy & Girl, Regal 55.00
Peek-A-Boo, Van Tellingen 415.00
Peerless Beer, Figural, Plastic, Heartland, 5 In. 195.00
Pelican, Germany 15.00
Piano & Piano Stool, 2 1/2 In. 16.00
Pig & Sausage, 2 1/4 In. 24.00
Pillsbury Doughboy 65.00

Salt & Pepper,
Lunch Box,
Thermos, Yellow,
Red, 2 & 3 In.

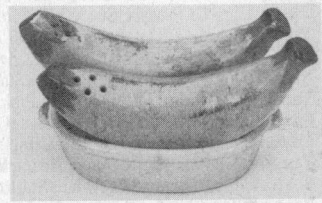

Salt & Pepper, Bananas, Tray, 4 1/2 In.

Pixieheads, In Race Car 65.00
Plaid Dog & Cat, Brayton 45.00
Popeye & Olive 'Oyl, Vandor 100.00
Poppin' Fresh, 1974 .... 35.00
Prayer Lady, Blue & White, 4 1/2 In. ....*Illus* 30.00
Puffer Belly, Locomotive & Tender, Cast Metal 50.00
Purple Grapes, Black Metal Vine 26.00
Quail 45.00
Red Riding Hood & Big Bad Wolf, 1943, 3 In. 50.00
Redcap 48.00
Sad-Eye Cat & Trash Can, Pottery, 1960s, 4 3/4 In. 35.00
Sailor & Mermaid, Van Tellingen ....125.00 to 160.00
Sailor Elephant, Twin Winton 20.00
Salty & Peppy, Pearl China, 7 In. ....110.00 to 175.00
Salty & Peppy, Racing Cars, 3 1/2 In. 35.00
Sealtest, Wooden Cow Holder 45.00
Smokey The Bear ....10.00 to 85.00
Snow Dome, Canadian Mountie, 1 Piece Set 38.00
Squirt, Bottle, Green Glass, Plastic Cap, Box, Mexico, 4 1/2 In. 25.00
Squirt, Glass, 1974 .... 19.00
Teapot Shape, Black Face, Pottery, Wire Handles 29.00
Three Stooges 22.00
Valentine Couple 90.00
Valentine Kids 195.00
Vegetable Head, Napco 35.00
Walking Elephant With Clown & Dog, Nodder 250.00
Westinghouse Washer & Dryer, Plastic, 1950s ....15.00 to 35.00
Winking Cat, Enesco, Box 15.00
Woody Woodpecker & Girl Friend 75.00

SALT GLAZE has a grayish white surface with a texture like an orange
peel. It is a method of decoration that has been used since the eighteenth century. Salt-glazed pieces are still being made.

Chicken Waterer, Cobalt Design, Projecting Tray, Domed Hood, 10 1/2 In. 1265.00
Coffeepot, Floral, Staffordshire, Mid-18th Century, 3 In. 1840.00
Crock, 2 Speckled Birds, Ear Handles, 6 Gal. 350.00
Crock, C. Hart & Son, 19th Century, 7 x 8 In. 95.00
Crock, Cake, Blue Design 450.00
Dish, Leaf Shape, Molded, Bird On Branch, Staffordshire, 1760, 9 5/8 In. 1150.00
Dish, Scalloped, Floral Scroll, Basket Weave Border, Staffordshire, 1760, 8 In. 1955.00
Figurine, Dog, Seated, Slipcast, Staffordshire, 1750, 4 1/2 In. 690.00
Flask, Ovoid, 8 1/2 In. 175.00
Jar, Cover, Cobalt Glazed Dog, White's, c.1895, 7 In. 155.00
Jar, Portrait Of General Frederick Von Steuben, 1 Side, Spirit Of '76 Other, 8 1/4 In. 950.00
Jug, Bear Shape, Allover Clay Shreds, Staffordshire, 1740, 10 In. 2185.00
Jug, Portrait Of Benjamin Franklin One Side, Spirit Of '76 On Other, 8 In. 275.00
Jug, Portrait Of General Friedrich Von Steuben 1 Side, Spirit Of '76 Other, 8 1/4 In. 350.00
Jug, Puzzle, Pear Shape, Flowers, Milled Border, Blue, Staffordshire, 7 In. 2300.00
Mug, Fraternal Crescent, Dolgeville, New York, 1894 .... 190.00
Pitcher, Polychrome Raspberry Design, 6 In. 110.00
Plate, Dot, Diaper & Basket Pattern, England, 1740, 9 1/2 In. 285.00
Plate, King Of Prussia, Success To King, Staffordshire, 1756, 9 1/4 In. 630.00
Platter, Circle & Dot, Scalloped, Staffordshire, 1760, 13 1/2 In. 1725.00
Sauceboat, Sheep, Cow Panels, Reedwork, Landscape, Staffordshire, 1760, 2 3/8 In. 805.00
Stand, Holds Round Dish, Pierced, Staffordshire, 1755, 1 1/8 x 2 1/4 In. 230.00
Teapot, Flowering Fruiting Plant, Pink, Yellow, Staffordshire, 1750, 5 In. 460.00
Teapot, Howdah, Vine Handle, Camel Shape, Staffordshire, 1750, 5 In. 5460.00
Teapot, King Of Prussia Portrait, Eagle, Globular, Staffordshire, 1760, 3 1/4 In. 5750.00
Teapot, Leaf Handle & Spout, Enameled, Globular, Staffordshire, 1765, 4 1/2 In. 690.00
Teapot, Leaf Shape, Hexagonal, Staffordshire, 1755, 4 1/2 In. 2070.00
Teapot, Tropical Birds & Oak Leaves, Quatrefoil, Staffordshire, 1750, 5 1/2 In. 1150.00
Tumbler, Floral, Staffordshire, Mid-18th Century, 3 In. 920.00

AMPLERS were made in America from the early 1700s. The best xamples were made from 1790 to 1840. Long, narrow samplers are sually older than square ones. Early samplers just had stitching or lphabets. The later examples had numerals, borders, and pictorial dec- rations. Those with mottoes are mid-Victorian. A revival of interest in he 1930s produced simpler samplers, usually with mottoes.

ABCDE

3 Story Federal House, Abigail Sawyer's, Aged 11, 1817, Frame, 17 x 17 5/8 In.	7475.00
Alphabet, 4 Dogs, Red, Blue, Green, Mary Johnson, 1858, 12 x 9 In.	165.00
Alphabet, Ann Armistead, August 24th, 1787, Silk On Linen, 16 x 14 In.	1760.00
Alphabet, Geometric Designs, Animals, People, Blue & White, 1748, 13 x 8 In.	220.00
Alphabet, House, Flanked By Trees, Signed, Amy Jenks, 1798, 15 1/4 x 12 1/8 In.	1725.00
Alphabet, House, Tree Scene, Augusta Jane Woodward, 1854, 13 x 18 In.	475.00
Alphabet, How Blest The Maid, Berry & Vine Border, Nancy Brown, 13, 13 x 12 In. . . .	385.00
Alphabet, Loudon County, A.E. Smallwood, 1843, 13 x 16 In. . . . .*Illus*	1760.00
Alphabet, Numbers, Floral, Rachel Lippincott, West Hill Seminary, 1820, 10 x 8 In.	880.00
Alphabet, Numbers, Verse, Mary Dunbar, Aged 7, 1795, Frame, 16 1/2 x 13 1/2 In.	632.00
Alphabet, Numbers, Tree & Flowers, 1826, Frame, 4 3/4 x 7 In.	325.00
Alphabet, Patience Margaret Heather, 1828, Silk On Homespun, Frame, 26 x 21 In.	3265.00
Alphabet, Trees, Flowers, Ivy, Sarah Share, October 1804	275.00
Alphabet, Verse, Harriott Lews, 8 Years, Chester Co., Pa., 1833, Frame	985.00
Alphabet, Verse, Urns, Willow, Floral, Silk On Linen, Deborah F. Howard, 1835, Frame .	275.00
Alphabet, Village Scene, Adult Figures, Blue, Brown, 1818, 16 x 15 In.	6900.00
Alphabets, 2 Birds Perched On Stylized Vase Of Flowers, K. Ridgway, N.J., 1800	4600.00
Alphabets, Blue, Green, Yellow, White Silk & Linen, 16 1/2 x 9 3/4 In.	3737.00
Alphabets, Floral, Fruit, Linen Homespun, M. Wing, Ohio, 1826, 18 5/8 In.	4400.00
Alphabets, Green House, Floral Vine Border, M. Littlefield, 1803	1495.00
Alphabets, Harriet Hales, 14 Years Of Age, August 17, 1818, Silk On Linen, 14 x 13 In. .	302.00
Alphabets, House, Blue, Green, Yellow, Linen & Homespun, M. Husted, Frame, 20 In. .	440.00
Alphabets, Numbers, Scene, Margaret MacArthur, Frame, 17 x 11 3/4 In.	546.00
Alphabets, Numerals, Flowers, Birds, Silk On Linen, 1826, Tray Frame, 23 x 19 In.	385.00
Alphabets, Verse, Floral Border, Green, Pink, Elizabeth Plume, 1794, Frame, 13 In. . . .	1430.00
Alphabets, Vine Border, Green, Blue, Anne M. Dowell, 15 x 20 In.	3162.00
Birds, Flowers, Verse, Jane Stillman, 12 Years, 1833, Butternut Frame	1250.00
Blossoming Vine, Baskets Of Fruit, Floral Clusters, 1803, 16 x 15 In.	7475.00
Church, Below A Grapevine, Green, Red, Blue, Signed, Ann Fordham, Age 11, 17 In. . . .	230.00
Courting Man & Woman Beside Tree, Green Ground, Silk, 7 x 10 In.	4830.00
Double Alphabet, Verse Over Brick House, Mary Foster Her Work, Frame	1395.00
Elizabeth Scott, 1827, Silk On Homespun, Frame, 20 1/2 x 18 1/2 In.	550.00
Ellen Ware, 9 Years Old, Border Of Flowers, Trees & Birds, 1846	412.00
Eunice N. Schrack, Flowers, Birds, Butterfly, Geometric Border, 1827, 17 x 17 In.	770.00
Family, Turkey, Butterfly, Catherine Anne Taylor, Silk On Wool, Frame, 1919, 9 1/2 In. . .	625.00
Family Record, McGilveray Family, Merrimack, N.H., 1827, 17 1/8 x 18 3/8 In.	4887.00
Family Register, 3 Ladies Wearing Empire Gowns, Linen Ground, 1826, 17 x 17 In. . . .	2300.00
Fanny Farmer, 12 Years Old, 1868, Silk On Cotton, Frame, 10 x 8 1/2 In.	385.00

Hanging textiles should be given a rest from time to time. The weight of the hanging causes strain on the threads. If the textile is taken down and stored for a few months, the threads will regain some strength.

Sampler, Alphabet, Loudon
County, A.E. Smallwood,
1843, 13 x 16 In.

Farm House, White Silk Stitches, Mary Dunn, 1797, 14 x 12 In. 1610.00
Floral Medallion, Stylized Medallion, Coral, Linen Ground, 22 x 22 1/2 In. 6900.00
Floral Spray, Red, Pink, Green, Blue, Brown Silk, Linen Ground, 1794, 14 x 17 In. 1150.00
Flowers, Baskets, Floral Vines, Ann Drinkwater, N.J., 1823, Silk, 21 x 18 In. 5750.00
Flowers, Birds, Fish In Center, Blue, Green, Red, Yellow, Brown, 7 x 8 1/2 In. 1495.00
Flowers, Verse, Margaret A. Reed, Silk On Linen, 1835, 25 x 17 In. 805.00
Friendship, Family Of Singing Monkeys, Frame, 28 1/2 x 16 1/2 In. 518.00
Georgian House, Anna McGeorge, 1769, Frame, 12 3/8 x 12 1/4 In. 316.00
Handkerchief, Birds, Flowerpots, Church Steeple, Dated 1843, 8 x 7 In. 225.00
Henrietta Kay, Wrought In 1816, Frame, 8 1/2 x 7 1/4 In. 575.00
Joan Price, 8 Years, Year Of Our Lord 1800, Cotton On Linen, 15 1/2 x 11 1/4 In. 500.00
Letters, Watch & Play, Red, Greens, Pinks, Eleanor Tyson, 1897, 12 x 14 In. 295.00
Mary Amanda Vaughan, Born 1812, Silk On Linen, Queen's Stitching, 16 3/4 x 17 In. . 2688.00
Mary Pollad, Born July 7th, 1809, Wrought 1824, Frame, 23 5/8 x 17 1/2 In. 2415.00
Mercy Lawrence Worken, 10 Years, July 12, 1833, Silk On Linen, Frame, 20 x 20 In. . 345.00
Numerals, Elisabeth Blyth, Age 12, Floral Border, 19th Century, 9 x 16 3/4 In. 305.00
Peacocks, Animals, Stylized Flowers, Blue, Red, Green, Yellow, 1826, 16 x 16 In. 3450.00
Pious Verse, Bird Scene, Mary Balm, 10 Years, 1772, Frame, 12 1/2 x 11 1/2 In. 1092.00
Pious Verse, Cornelia Donaldson, Aged 9 Years, July 6th, 1822, Frame, 18 x 14 In. 1495.00
Pious Verse, Eliza Ann Hayward, Aged 12, April 24th, 1827, Frame, 17 x 13 3/4 In. 2875.00
Pious Verse, Harriet Lewis, 8 Years, Finished July 14, 1830, Frame, 16 1/2 x 11 In. 460.00
Quaker, Stylized Vine & Leaf Border, Dark Brown Silk, 1818, 11 x 13 1/2 In. 8050.00
Religious Poem, Sarah Ann Kingsford, Honington School, 1848, 12 x 13 In. 635.00
Sarah Ann Leadbetter, Born 1823, Died 1844 Of Typhus Fever, 6 5/8 x 8 1/4 In. 517.00
Stylized Floral Vines, Green, Gold, Brown, White Silk, 1802, 17 x 13 3/16 In. 3450.00
Stylized Urn, Flanked By Birds, Red Silk, White Linen Ground, 1788, 4 3/4 x 10 In. . . . 805.00
Stylized Urn With Flowers, Blue, Green, Cream, Ann Cleverley, 1836, 16 x 13 In. 2530.00
Stylized Vine Border, Blue, Pink, Green, Brown, Mary Beal, 1802, 20 x 15 In. 2070.00
Trees, Flowers, Animals, Stylized Fine Border, S. Whittles, Linen Homespun, 21 In. . . . 715.00
Urn With Birds, Red Silk On White Linen Ground, German, 1788, 5 x 10 In. 605.00
Verse, Alphabet Border, Mary Gibbs, Aged 11, 1761, Frame 1900.00
Verse, Blue, Green, Brown, Black, Portland, Maine, Mary Portland, 16 x 11 In. 7475.00
Verse, Floral, Birds, Strawberry Border, Margaret Garrigues, 1830, 21 1/2 x 16 In. 935.00
Verse, House, Animals, Mary Cottom, Aged 10 Years, 1829, Frame, 18 x 13 1/4 In. 1045.00
Verse, House, Flowers, Hearts, Silk On Linen, Mary Cottom, Age 10, 1829 . . . . 1045.00
Verse, Potted Flowers, Ivy Border, Stitched On Paper, Hettie Garges, 1877 . . . . 577.00
Verse, Stylized Rosebud Border, Green, Blue, Gold, Mary Ann Scott, 1831, 20 x 17 In. . . 8050.00
Verse Titled Virtue, Martha Morphet, 11 Years, 1813, Bird's-Eye Frame, 23 x 18 In. . . . 1350.00
View Of Lake Lugano, Clarissa Fuller, 1821, Frame, 16 1/4 x 20 1/4 In. 2530.00
Vine & Floral Border, Green, Gold, Easton School, N.J., 16 x 12 In. 2990.00
Vine & Floral Border, Green, Yellow, Brown, White Silk, 21 x 17 In. 5750.00
Vine & Leaf Border, Pine Grove School, N.J., 1813, 17 5/8 x 15 5/8 In. 6900.00
Watch & Pray, Eleanor Tyson, Fancy Border, 1897, 12 x 14 In. 295.00
Waterford School, Elizabeth Homer Kay, Wrought In 1809, Frame, 17 x 16 1/4 In. 1725.00

SAMSON and Company, a French firm specializing in the reproduction of collectible wares of many countries and periods, was founded in Paris in the early nineteenth century. Chelsea, Meissen, Famille Verte, and Chinese Export porcelain are some of the wares that have been reproduced by the company. The firm uses a variety of marks on the reproductions. It is still in operation.

Figurine, Elephant, Standing On Ormolu Mounted Base, France, 1890 . . . . 431.00
Figurine, Lady, Floral Skirt, Green Bodice, 9 1/2 In. 58.00
Plate, Armorial, Oliphant Impaling Browne, Gilt, 19th Century, 9 13/16 In., Pair 630.00
Teapot, Armorial Shield, Floral, Gold, Strawberry Finial, Lowestoft Mark, 5 1/4 In. 165.00

SAND BABIES were used as decorations on a line of children's dishes made by the Royal Bayreuth China Company. The children are playing at the seaside. Collectors use the names *Sand Babies* and *Beach Babies* interchangeably.

Plate, 8 3/4 In. 175.00
Tray, 9 3/4 x 7 In. 370.00

ANDWICH GLASS is any of the myriad types of glass made by the Boston and Sandwich Glass Works in Sandwich, Massachusetts, between 1825 and 1888. It is often very difficult to be sure whether a piece was really made at the Sandwich factory because so many types were made there and similar pieces were made at other glass factories. Additional pieces may be listed under Pressed Glass and in related categories.

Candlestick, Canary Yellow, 7 In., Pair	260.00
Candlestick, Canary, 11 1/2 In., Pair	2100.00
Candlestick, Dolphin, Clambroth, 9 1/2 In., Pair	800.00
Celery Vase, Floral, Leaf, Cranberry Threading, 8 x 4 1/2 In.	225.00
Cologne, Grape Leaf, Blue, White, Stopper, 7 In.	1500.00
Cruet, Gold Design, Scrolled Vines, Flowers, Blue, Silver Deposit, 13 1/2 In.	550.00
Decanter, Diamond-Quilted, 11 1/2 In., Pair	175.00
Lamp, Banquet, Leaf & Vine, Blue, 19 1/2 x 6 1/2 In.	900.00
Lamp, Fluid, Loop, 10 In.	2200.00
Lamp, Stand, Milk Glass Base, Shade, 12 x 19 1/2 In.	1100.00
Lamp, Star & Punty, Milk Glass	1100.00
Perfume Bottle, Amber, 6 In.	200.00 to 400.00
Pitcher, Juice, Green	180.00
Rose Bowl, White, Pink Interior Rim, 4-Petals, Applied Amber Feet, 5 1/2 In.	88.00
Salt, Christmas, Dana K. Alden's, Table Salt Bottles, All Colors, Box, 6 Piece	660.00
Smoke Bell, Cranberry Cut To Clear, Floral, Ruffled Edge, 9 1/4 In.	605.00
Smoke Bell, Engraved Fern, Cobalt Blue Rim, 7 In.	230.00
Toothpick, Hat Shape, Cobalt Blue, 2 1/4 In.	605.00
Tumbler, Morning Glory, Footed, c.1850, 5 In.	200.00
Tureen, Doll's, Blue, 3 In.	412.00
Vase, Hobnail With Leaf, Green, 1850-1870, 11 1/2 In.	500.00
Vase, Icicles Applied Down From Top, Pedestal Foot, 10 1/4 In.	695.00
Witch's Ball, Aqua, White Opaque Swirl	357.00

SARREGUEMINES is the name of a French town that is used as part of a china mark. Utzschneider and Company, a porcelain factory, made ceramics in Sarreguemines, Lorraine, France, from about 1775. Transfer-printed wares and majolica were made in the nineteenth century. The nineteenth-century pieces, most often found today, usually have colorful transfer-printed decorations showing peasants in local costumes.

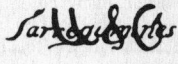

Chamberstick, Lily Pad & Bud Form, Signed, c.1890, 6 1/4 In.	50.00
Figurine, Madonna, 17 In.	45.00
Pitcher, 6 3/4 In.	100.00
Pitcher, Brown Drip	150.00
Pitcher, Brown, Tan Crystalline, 7 In.	110.00
Pitcher, Intertwined Fish Spout, Glass Base & Handles, Signed, 1875, 12 1/2 In.	840.00
Pitcher, Kate Greenaway Children	89.00
Pitcher, Seated Man, 12 In.	180.00
Platter, Leaf & Fruit, Majolica, 13 In.	125.00
Salt, Double, Figural, Ducks, Turtle Held By Both, Signed, 5 1/2 In.	110.00
Stein, Hand Painted, Family Crest, Pewter Lid, 1 Liter	225.00
Tureen, Boar's Head, Snout Lid, Ears & Head Top	3500.00
Urn, Cobalt Blue, Gilt Trim, Turquoise Interior, 11 3/4 x 16 In.	850.00

SASCHA BRASTOFF made decorative accessories, ceramics, enamels on copper, and plastics of his own design. He headed a factory, Sascha Brastoff of California, Inc., in West Los Angeles, from 1953 until about 1973. He died in 1993. Pieces made by Matt Adams after he left the factory are listed here with his name.

Ashtray, Abstract, Signed, 7 3/4 In.	15.00
Ashtray, Eskimo, Hood, 7 In.	95.00
Ashtray, Horse Design, Gray, Black Ground, 6 1/2 x 5 In.	30.00
Ashtray, Leaf Design, Forest Green, Square, 9 In.	75.00
Ashtray, Rooftops, 8 In.	65.00
Bowl, Green Leaf Design, Signed, 5 In.	45.00

Bowl, Horse, 10 In. 175.00
Bowl, Turbaned Dancer, Tricornered, 10 In. 35.00
Bowl, White Shell, Blue Mist 75.00
Box, Cigarette, Oriental Design 75.00
Box, Circus Pony Dancing, Silver 800.00
Box, Cover, Igloo, 7 x 5 In. 95.00
Box, Cover, Jeweled Bird 50.00
Charger, Brass, Enameled, 10 In. 60.00
Charger, Winter Scene, Matt Adams 225.00
Compote, Polar Bear 65.00
Dish, Horse, Green Ground, 6 1/4 In. 24.00
Dish, Houses, Square, 7 1/2 In. 65.00
Figurine, Bear, Blue Resin 325.00
Figurine, Bear, Marigold, Turned Head, 7 In. 325.00
Figurine, Bear, Peek-A-Boo, Blue, Pair 600.00
Figurine, Pelican, Green Resin, 11 In. 125.00
Figurine, Rooster, Gold & Black, 17 In. 450.00
Lamp, Mosaic, No Shade 225.00
Mug, Igloos 45.00
Plate, Enamel On Brass, 10 In. 65.00
Plate, Folk Dancer, 10 In., Pair 270.00
Plate, Rooftops, 10 In. 60.00
Relish, 2 Sections, Pink, Splashed With Silver, 10 In. 95.00
Salad Set, Surf Ballet, Large Bowl & 6 Small 175.00
Sign, Dealer, Jewelry 650.00
Smoking Set, Lighter & Ashtray 85.00
Tray, Allover Modern Design, Black Glaze, Signed, 9 In. 22.00
Tray, White Glaze, Hand Painting, Signed, Matt Adams, 6 In. 22.00
Vase, Alaska, 8 In. 55.00
Vase, Floral, 12 1/2 x 6 In. 50.00

SATIN GLASS is a late nineteenth-century art glass. It has a dull finish
that is caused by hydrofluoric acid vapor treatment. Satin glass was
made in many colors and sometimes has applied decorations. Satin
glass is also listed by factory name, such as Webb, or in the Mother-of-
Pearl category in this book.

Basket, Deep Purple Interior, White, Frosted Rope Handle, 8 x 8 In. 200.00
Biscuit Jar, Leaf, Scroll Design, Embossed, Gold Cover, Handle, 8 In. 176.00
Biscuit Jar, Silver Plate Cover, Bird Finial, Paneled Ribs, 19th Century, 8 1/2 In. 103.00
Bowl, Mother-Of-Pearl, Moire, Raspberry, 4 x 10 In. 295.00
Bowl, Mother-Of-Pearl, White Exterior, Pink, Yellow, Pale Blue, White, 5 x 8 In. 400.00
Bowl, Raspberry, Wavy Lines, Fluted, 10 x 4 In. 250.00
Cologne Bottle, Rose, Red, Opalescent Glass Interior, Screw Cap, 4 In. 345.00
Dish, Ruffled, Amethyst To White, Enameled Daisies, Silver Plated Base, 14 1/2 In. 330.00
Eggcup, Floral Spray Enamel, Cranberry 880.00
Lamp, Drapery, Pink, 8 1/2 In. 254.00
Mug, Pink & Gold Loops, White Ground, Frosted Reeded Handle, 3 1/2 In. 175.00
Perfume Bottle, Pale Blue, White Lining, Stoppers, 2 1/2 x 2 1/4 In., Pair 450.00
Pitcher, Mother-Of-Pearl, Water, Raspberry To Pink, 9 In. 245.00
Pitcher, Water, Mother-Of-Pearl, Blue, Heart Shaped Top, Bulbous, 8 1/2 x 6 In. 250.00
Pitcher, White Raised Accents, Blue, Pleated Ruffled Top, Blue Handle, 8 x 6 In. 105.00
Rose Bowl, Diamond-Quilted, Mother-Of-Pearl, Rose To Pink To White, 2 3/4 In. 375.00
Rose Bowl, Flowers, Leaf Overlay, 8-Crimp Top, White Lining, 3 3/8 In. 135.00
Rose Bowl, Mother-Of-Pearl, Avocado Green Ribbon, White Lining, 3 x 3 5/8 In. 235.00
Rose Bowl, Ribbon Pattern, 9-Crimp Top, White Lining, 2 3/8 x 3 3/4 In. 225.00
Tumbler, Rainbow, Florette, 3 7/8 In. 66.00
Vase, Beige, Enameled Wild Rose Design, Bulbous, 10 In. 11.00
Vase, Cream, White Interior, Sea Green, Pale Yellow, Barney English, 8 x 4 1/2 In. 275.00
Vase, Diamond-Quilted, Blue, Cut Velvet, 7 1/2 x 3 1/2 In. 110.00
Vase, Floral, Branches, Foliage, Peach Overlay, Ruffled, Applied Feet, 5 3/4 In. 135.00
Vase, Floral, Pink To White, Pillow Body, Crimped Top, Handles, 8 3/4 In., Pair 675.00
Vase, Mother-Of-Pearl, Herringbone, Pink, Yellow, Blue, 8 1/2 x 4 1/2 In. 300.00
Vase, Mother-Of-Pearl, Wafer Foot, White Lining, Chartreuse Green Ribbon, 3 In. 175.00

Vase, Pink & White Swirl, Applied Frosted Amber Base, 9 In., Pair 60.00
Vase, Ruffled Opening, Quilted, Blue, c.1800, 8 In. 550.00
Vase, Swirl, Crimped Rim, Green, Rose Body, 7 1/2 In. 805.00
Vase, White Daisies, Pink Overlay, White Lining, 6 1/2 In. 165.00
Vase, Yellow Spirals, Amber, Blue, England, 7 In. 575.00

ATSUMA is a Japanese pottery with a distinctive creamy beige cracked glaze. Most of the pieces were decorated with blue, red, green,
range, or gold. Almost all Satsuma found today was made after 1860.
During World War I, Americans could not buy undecorated European
orcelains. Women who liked to make hand painted porcelains at
ome began to decorate plain Satsuma. These pieces are known today
s *American Satsuma*.

Bottle, Figural Design, Blue Ground, Cylinder, Meiji Period, 2 1/4 In. 55.00
Bowl, Allover Chrysanthemum & Floral, 7 1/4 In. 97.00
Bowl, Beggar's, 8 Immortals, Globular Form, 9 In. 412.00
Bowl, Chrysanthemums, Signed, 4 3/4 In. 40.00
Bowl, Lohan & Dragon Interior, Dragon Exterior, Flower Form, Signed, 7 1/4 In. 522.00
Censor, Figural Design, Blue Field, Cylinder, Marked, Meiji Period, 5 1/2 In. 77.00
Charger, Lohan, Dragon, Raised Relief, Early 20th Century, 12 1/4 In. 690.00
Charger, One Thousand Flowers, Chrysanthemum Form, Signed, Box, 12 1/4 In. 825.00
Dish, Kannon & Dragon, Crashing Between Waves, 19th Century, 7 1/4 In. 863.00
Figurine, Nio, Dressed In Moriage Type Brocade, 22 In., Pair 1155.00
Inkstand, Attached Underplate, Gold, Allover Beaded Features, Porcelain, 4 In. 350.00
Jar, Cover, Coin Gold, Enamel, Figures, Flowers, Geometric Designs, Marked, 4 x 5 In. .. 165.00
Jar, Cover, Landscape, Naturalistic Flowers, Bamboo, Blue Ground, 6 In. 3450.00
Jar, Floral, Gilt, Rust & Ivory Ground, Repaired Handle, 13 1/2 In. 220.00
Jar, Flowers, Blue Ground, Gilt Trim, 12 In. 120.00
Jar, Fu Lion Finial, Floral & Figural Reserve, Allover Gilt, 28 In. 210.00
Jar, Ginger, Peacock & Flowers, 8 1/2 In. 35.00
Pitcher, Cover, Lohan Design, Dragon Handle, Globular, Meiji Period, 4 In. 66.00
Pitcher, Enameled Flowers & Birds, Silver Plated Collar, Lid & Handle, 10 3/4 In. 880.00
Tea Bowl, Room Interiors, Landscape, Interior Underwater Palace Of Dragon, 5 In. 1840.00
Tea Caddy, Ho Bird & Chrysanthemum Design, Silver Cover, 4 1/2 In. 165.00
Tea Set, Cobalt, Figural Scenes, Creamer, Sugar, Cover, Teapot, 6 1/2 In., 3 Piece 86.00
Teapot, Samurai & Women With Boys, Blue Ground, 3 In. 690.00
Urn, Cover, Lions On Handles & Cover, 49 x 29 In. 4500.00
Urn, Geishas In Landscape, Dragon Handles, 37 1/2 In. 303.00
Urn, Hand Painted Flowers & Pagoda, Green Field, c.1900, 19 3/4 In. 143.00
Vase, 2 Figures, Gilt, Dark Green Ground, 18 In. 135.00
Vase, Allover Chrysanthemum & Floral, Ovoid Form, 4 1/2 In. 97.00
Vase, Allover Gold Design, Woman & Playing Children, 10 In. 850.00
Vase, Bird, Floral Design, Dragon Between Border, Early 20th Century, 24 In. 1955.00
Vase, Blue, Gold, Floor, 18 1/2 In. 450.00
Vase, Bottle, Relief Dragon, Globular, Signed, Kinkozan, Meiji Period, 5 1/4 In. 165.00
Vase, Figural Landscape, Baluster Form, Signed, 5 In. 522.00
Vase, Figures, 18 In. ....*Illus* 5000.00
Vase, Floral Design, Hexagonal Form, Meiji Period, 4 7/8 In. 220.00

Satsuma, Vase,
Figures, 18 In.

Satsuma, Vase,
White,
Turquoise,
Black, Gold
Design, 6 1/2 In.

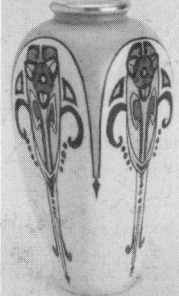

**Remove the remains of
gum, adhesive tape, and
other sticky tapes by
rubbing the glue with
lemon juice.**

Vase, Flowering Cherry Blossoms, Pink, White Petals, 6 1/2 In. 460.00
Vase, Gold Butterflies, Black, Gold Leaves, White Mum Enamel, 6 3/4 In. 17.00
Vase, Gold, Polychrome, Pottery, 12 In. 55.00
Vase, Hand Painted Florals, Ovoid, Double Handles At Neck, c.1900, 16 In. 85.00
Vase, Inverted Pear Shape, Raised Cherry Blossom Design, Meiji Period, 6 1/2 In. 770.00
Vase, Landscape, 2 Dragons On Floral Ground, Floral Panels, 15 In. 3335.00
Vase, Moriage Slip Design, Handles, Warriors, Priests On Each Side, Gold, 15 In. 30.00
Vase, Panels Of Figures In Landscape, 14 In., Pair 1265.00
Vase, Samurai, 1 With Women & Children In Garden Setting, Blue Ground, 7 In. 920.00
Vase, Scenes Of Bathing Men, Signed, 19th Century, 5 7/8 In., Pair 2200.00
Vase, White, Turquoise, Black, Gold Design, 6 1/2 In. . . . . *Illus* 135.00
Wine Pot, Floral Brocade Ground, Inverted Pear Shape, 3 5/8 In. 440.00

SATURDAY EVENING GIRLS, see Paul Revere Pottery category.

SCALES have been made to weigh everything from babies to gold.
Collectors search for all types. Most popular are small gold dust scales
and special grocery scales.

Analytical, Balance, Central Scientific Co., Mahogany Case, 17 1/2 In. 180.00
Analytical, Balance, Mahogany Case, Black Glass Top, 20 In. 126.00
Analytical, Voland Model No. 320, Glass, Metal Case, 21 x 18 1/2 x 9 1/2 In. 75.00
Analytical Balance, Chainomatic, Christian Beeker, Mahogany Case, 19 In. 214.00
Avery, Franklin Bros., Dickenson, 19th Century, 5 Lb. 250.00
Balance, 3 Weights, Carved Wooden Box, 18th Century, 3 1/2 x 3 1/2 In. 450.00
Balance, Aluminum Frame, Brass Hopper Arm, Edinburgh, Cast Iron Base, 33 In. 121.00
Balance, Brass Pans On Cast Iron Base 77.00
Balance, Coal, S.C.W.S. Lt., Edinburgh, Scoop, 36 x 38 In. 735.00
Balance, Howe Scale Co., Iron, Brass Scoop, Pat. Dec. 1882, Countertop, 23 x 10 In. . . . 165.00
Balance, Howe Scale Co., Iron, Brass, Iron, Brass, Brass Scoop, 15 x 10 In. 75.00
Balance, Mahogany Base, Drawer, Weights, 18 1/2 x 13 In. 345.00
Balance, Marshall Co., Wooden, Weights 35.00
Balance, Traveling Chain, Iron, Brass Pans, Aluminum Dial, 22 1/4 x 26 In. 165.00
Bathroom, Roto-Dial Health-O-Meter 48.00
Brass, Weights On Wooden Base, Mortar, Pestle 60.00
Brass Face, Landers, 80 Lbs. 55.00
Brass Pans, Marked W & T Avery, Gold Rush Era, Tin Case, 8 Weights, 6 1/8 In. 190.00
Candy, National, 8 x 10 In. 350.00
Coin Operated, Floor Model, 1 Cent, Porcelain, 300 Lbs., 13 x 35 x 20 In. 58.00
Double Pan, Brass, Marble, Mahogany, Mid-19th Century, 21 x 10 In. 357.00
Egg, Acme Egg Grading Scale, Specialty Mfg. Co., Pat. 1924 . . . . 55.00
Egg, Jiffy-Way, Silver Metal, Green Enamel Painted, 8 x 5 1/2 x 2 3/4 In. 48.00
Egg, Notched Wooden Base, Milk Glass Egg 37.00
Fairbanks, Platform, Iron, Brass, 4 Lb. 45.00
Folding, Traveling, Aluminum, Iron, 17 3/4 x 18 In. 22.00
Gold, Henry Troemner, Brass Beam & Pans, 3 Weights, Box With Drawer 365.00
Gold, Henry Troemner, Philadelphia, Marble, Mahogany 275.00
Gold, Label Of Joseph Richardson, Lid Marked T. Parry, c.1760 . . . . 695.00
Gold, Original Weights, Stamped WT In Shield, Line Design On Wood Box, 7 3/8 In. . . . 295.00
Grain, Hanging, O'Haus, Hanging, 2 Qt. Dry 110.00
Grain, Hanging, Winchester, Brass, Small 275.00
Hanging, Fairbanks, Brass 330.00
Hanging, Purine, Weighs Up To 6 Lbs. 18.00
Hide, Cast Iron & Brass 160.00
Kasco Feeds, Hanging, Weight The Milk, Weight The Feed, Metal, 16 x 4 1/2 In. 145.00
Laboratory, Beam, Fisher Scientific, Platform, 12 x 11 1/4 In. 95.00
Laboratory, W.M. Welch Scientific Co., Iron, Black Paint, Part Label, 16 1/2 x 17 In. . . . 85.00
Lollypot, Aristocrat, Peerless, Blue Porcelain, 1916 . . . . 1000.00
Merchant's, Grain, Fairbanks, Brass Bucket 175.00
Micromer Dodge Mfg. Co. 375.00
Milk, Hanson, Up To 40 Lb. 25.00
Pharmaceutical, Henry Troemner, Wooden Case, Glass Hinged Top, Pans, 13 x 6 x 7 In. . . 220.00
Pharmaceutical, Henry Troemner, Wooden, 1/2 Oz. Capacity 130.00
Philadelphia, Scoop & Scale Co., Hanging, 30 Lbs. Capacity 75.00
Postal, Inland Postal Rates, Wooden Base, Weights 50.00

Postal, J.E. Ratcliff, Brass, Wooden Base, Box, 11 5/8 x 7 x 6 In. 358.00
Postal, Salter, Porcelain Dial, Square, 15 Lb. 45.00
Prescription, Army Style, Oak Box, Wooden Weights, 6-In. Beam 175.00
Quintenez, Potato, Platform, Wooden, Iron, 100 Kilograms, 36 x 19 x 28 In. 275.00
Seed, Fairbanks Morse, Iron, Brass, Cup 195.00
Spring Balance, Chatillion's Improved, Hanging, Weight By Oz. 55.00
Store, Metal, Pat. Oct. 19th, 1912, 8 1/2 x 6 1/2 x 8 1/2 In. 20.00
Weighing, American Cutlery Co., Pat. 1906, Scoop, 4 Lbs. 38.00
Weighing, American Housekeepers, Pat. May 15, 1877, 9 1/2 In. 100.00
Weighing, Buffalo Scale Co., Brass, Nickel Plated, Counter, 26 x 7 1/2 In. 305.00
Weighing, Candy, Scale, STD Computing, Fan Dial, 20th Century, 3 Lb. 75.00
Weighing, Chicken, Penn Scale Mfg. Co., Chicken Scoop, Up To 20 Lbs. 45.00
Weighing, Counter, Henry Troemner, Red Paint, Weights, 11 In. 65.00
Weighing, Dayton-The Computing Scale Co., Gold Paint, Stenciled, Fan Dial, Counter . . 240.00
Weighing, Dodge Micrometer, Brass Scoop, Counter, 17 1/2 x 13 1/2 In. 330.00
Weighing, Dollydale, Scoop, Robson Corporation 45.00
Weighing, Fairbanks, Newspapers, Periodicals, Iron, Brass, 9 1/2 In. 75.00
Weighing, George Smith, Black, Yellow, Green Board, Boston, 1845, 8 7/16 x 11 In. 863.00
Weighing, George Smith, Gold, Brown, Black, Pastel Green, Boston, 1846, 8 1/2 In. 1035.00
Weighing, Howe, 1 Platform, Iron, Weights 65.00
Weighing, Micrometer, Dodge Mfg. Co., Yonkers, N.Y., Marble Base, Double, 9 x 12 In. 495.00
Weighing, Roman Meal Diet Scale, Plastic Scoop, Instructions 11.00
Weighing, Steelyard, Large Hook, Round Weight 65.00
Weighing, Winchester Chodrometer, Brass, Fitted Wooden Case 800.00

SCHAFER & VATER, makers of small ceramic items, are best known for their amusing figurals. The factory was located in Volkstedt-Rudolstadt, Germany, from 1890 to 1962. Some pieces are marked with the crown and R mark, but many are unmarked.

Creamer, Asian Boy, Making Grotesque Face, 3 1/2 In. 125.00
Creamer, Buster Brown 145.00
Creamer, Clown, 4 1/2 In. 100.00
Creamer, Figural, Woman With Cape, 4 In. 275.00
Decanter, Girl With Beer Stein, Barrel, German Slogan, Blue Glaze, 9 1/2 In. 1200.00
Figurine, Dog, Comical, Rectangular Base, Signed, 5 1/2 x 2 3/8 In. 125.00
Figurine, Man In Top Hat, Monocle, Wood Stick Legs 165.00
Hatpin Holder, Lighthouse Form, Flowers 195.00
Humidor, Man Smoking Pipe, Lavender 525.00
Jar, Cover, Grecian Figures, 4 In. 60.00
Pitcher, Witch 95.00
Pitcher, Woman With Fan, Witch Type Hat, Blue, 4 In. 135.00
Shaving Mug, Elephant, 4 In. 135.00
Shaving Mug, Elk Head, Brown & Rust 75.00
Vase, Woman's Face, Handles, 6 In. 75.00

SCHNEIDER Glassworks was founded in 1913 at Epinay-sur-Seine, France, by Charles and Ernest Schneider. Art glass was made between 1913 and 1930. The company still produces clear crystal glass.

Bowl, Glossy Orange, Wrought Iron Frame, Signed, 3 1/4 x 4 7/8 In. 330.00
Bowl, Stylized Etched Flower Heads, Branches, Orange, Green, White, Signed, 6 In. 657.00
Bowl, Swirls Raised On 3 Purple Bead Feet, Flattened, Flared, Signed, 9 In. 462.00
Compote, Mottled White, Black, Red Stem, Amber, Blue, Signed, 11 x 8 1/2 In. 1320.00
Compote, Striped Stem, 3 Glass Beads, Metal Tripod Base, 7 x 14 In. 977.00
Compote, Tango Red, Applied Purple, Black Stem, Folded Rim, 6 1/4 x 15 In. 518.00
Pitcher, Mottled Orange, Aubergine Base, Angular Handle, Signed, 6 1/2 In. 395.00
Vase, Applied Red Bands & Spots, Controlled Air Bubbles, Bulbous, Footed, 12 In. 5750.00
Vase, Aqua Mottling, Tapering Cylinder, 2 Teardrop Handles, Signed, 11 In. 822.00
Vase, Blood Orange & Custard, Flared Rim, Amethyst Stem, Amber Bands, 13 In. 1092.00
Vase, Etched Foliate Design, Mottled Yellow, Amber Body, Red, Olive Green, 3 In. 546.00
Vase, Half Cobalt, Half Yellow, Oval, Flared Rim, Signed, 10 In. 625.00
Vase, Ice Bucket Form, 2 Applied Knobs, Etched, France, 8 1/2 In. . . . . 220.00 to 385.00
Vase, Mottled Orange, 3 Applied Yellow Prunts, Signed, 22 x 7 In. 800.00
Vase, Mottled White, Purple, Green Ground, Flared, 19 1/2 x 5 1/4 In. 450.00

Vase, Mottled Yellow, Orange, Purple Ground, Applied Purple Foot, Signed, 18 In. 400.00
Vase, Mottled, 5 Repeat Pendent Berries, Signed, 19 In. 1980.00
Vase, Orange, Amber, 16 Ribs, Elongated Neck, 20 In. 230.00
Vase, Pink Satin Body, Etched Flowering Blossom, Signed, 15 In. 1495.00
Vase, Pink, Pearl White Highlights, Squared Edge, Bulbous, 14 1/8 In. 9200.00
Vase, Purple & Blue Streaks, Footed, Oval, Everted Rim, Signed, 17 1/2 In. 1068.00
Vase, Scarab, 3 Tall Beetles, Mottled Orange, Tortoiseshell Brown, Etched, 16 In. 1495.00
Vase, Spotted Vine, Mottled Aubergine, Blue, White, Etched, 22 In. 1380.00
Vase, Stylized Blossoms, Dots, Yellow Speckled Orange Layers, Footed, 12 In. 1380.00
Vase, Stylized Geometric Design, Orange, Tortoiseshell Brown, Etched, 7 In. 920.00
Vase, Stylized Poppy Blossoms, Mottled Tortoiseshell Brown, Orange, 22 In. 1495.00
Vase, Stylized Rose Blossoms, Mottled Pink, White, Orange Layers, 16 In. 1093.00
Vase, Swirled, Orange, Deep Purple, Applied Side Handles, 1930, 10 In. 4025.00
Vase, Yellow & Rose Swirls, Shaded To Purple, Marked, 18 In. 2875.00
Vase, Yellow, Burgundy Interior, Applied Double Amethyst Handles, 6 In. 863.00
Vase, Yellow, Orange, Mottled, 2 Violet Ribbons On Neck, Footed, Signed, 16 In. 3287.00

SCIENTIFIC INSTRUMENTS of all kinds are included in this category. Other categories such as Barometer, Binoculars, Dental, Nautical, Medical, and Thermometer may also price scientific apparatus.

Air Pump, Wooden Base, Brass Mechanism, 2 Blown-Glass Chambers 790.00
Anemometer, Wind Speed In Feet Per Second, Wind Velocity, Case 795.00
Bell Jar, Laboratory, With Vacuum Pump, 13 x 25 x 22 In. 248.00
Chronograph, 2-Tone Gold Plated Case, Russia 175.00
Chronometer, Parkinson & Frodsham, Mahogany Box, c.1820 .... 2070.00
Chronometer, Seconds & State Of Wind Dials, Mahogany Box, 5 In. 3450.00
Compass, Brass, Silver Dial, 1880, 2 5/8 In. 17.00
Compass, Brass, Silver Dial, Dark Brass, A. Chandler, 1840, 13 1/8 In. 2185.00
Compass, Equinoctial Dial, Hour Ring, Compass, Vogler, 1770s, 2 In. 3162.00
Compass, Equinoctial, L. Grassl, Leveling Bob, Hour Ring, 3 5/8 In. 3162.00
Compass, G.L. Whitehouse, Brass, Ivory, Ebony Case, 1840, 14 In. 5520.00
Compass, Marble Arms & Mfg. Co., Brass, Double Pin, 2 3/4 In. 51.00
Compass, Marble's Gladstone Mich., Brass, Pin Fastener, 1 1/2 In. 55.00
Compass, Paper Dial Hand Colored, Brass, Pocket, 18th Century 215.00
Compass, Pocket, Brass, Waterproof, Luminous Dial, Marble, Card, 1 In. 69.00
Compass, Pocket, Mahogany Case, 1825, 2 1/4 x 2 1/4 In. 230.00
Compass, Ritchie, Gimble, Box, 3 1/2 x 5 In. 25.00
Compass, Surveyor's, Brass Cover, 1835, 4 7/8 x 3 1/2 x 2 1/4 In. 1495.00
Compass, Surveyor's, Brass, Silver Dial, 1830, 5 3/4 In. 1090.00
Compass, Surveyor's, Mahogany Case, 30th Regiment Of Maine, 1864 .... 2200.00
Compass, Surveyor's, W. & L.E. Gurley, Silver Dial, 2 Level Dials, Case 1200.00
Compass, Surveyor's, W.L. Potts, Brass, Level, 14 3/4 In. 1725.00
Compass, Vernier, Dovetailed Mahogany Box, Brass Cover, 15 In. 1150.00
Compass-Sundial, Stockert, Paper Dial, Wooden Case, c.1760, 2 1/2 In. 450.00
Magnifying Glass, Folds Up, Germany, Turn Of The Century, Box 41.00
Magnifying Glass, Jeweler's, Brass, c.1900, 2 In. 35.00
Magnifying Glass, Jeweler's, Wood Handle, Mid-19th Century, 2 In. 30.00
Microscope, Achromatic, 1845 .... 1800.00
Microscope, Ball & Socket Joint At Base, Brass, France, c.1860, 10 In. 520.00
Microscope, Binocular, Double Mirror, Carl Zeiss, 1950, 14 5/8 In. 546.00
Microscope, Brass Compound, Monocular, England, 1865, 20 In. 1955.00
Microscope, Cary, Mahogany Case, Lens Holder, 1875, 7 In. 748.00
Microscope, Cary, Mahogany Case, Rack, Pinion Focusing, 12 In. 690.00
Microscope, Drum, Fitted Mahogany Case, England, 1820, 10 x 7 In. 745.00
Microscope, Drum, Mahogany Case, Glass Slide, 3 x 1 1/8 In. 430.00
Microscope, Ernst Leitz Wetzlar, Brass, Box, 14 In. 518.00
Microscope, Iron Base, Fitted Wooden Box, France, 20th Century, 17 In. 85.00
Microscope, Ivory Handle, Screw Barrel, 1825, 3 1/4 x 1 1/8 In. 575.00
Microscope, Library, Brass, Barrel, Rack, Gear Focus, 1900, 5 x 1 1/4 In. 316.00
Microscope, Monocular, Calibrated Draw Tube, Brass Case, 17 In. 5175.00
Microscope, Monocular, Case With Drawer, 7 1/2 x 1 1/4 In. 1610.00
Microscope, Monocular, Diaphragm With Tube, 1870, 14 1/4 In. 1380.00
Microscope, Monocular, Morocco Case, Japanned Black, 1920, 6 In. 345.00

Microscope, Monocular, Natchet Et Fils, Brass, Case, 1870, 10 3/4 In.	630.00
Microscope, Monocular, Rack Pinion Focus, Brass Case, 13 3/4 In.	1090.00
Microscope, Monocular, Silver Dial, 1894, 13 1/4 x 9 In.	1840.00
Microscope, Natchet A Paris, Mahogany Case, 1860, 11 In.	260.00
Microscope, Paul Roecsler, Mahogany Case, 1875, 7 3/4 x 4 1/2 In.	920.00
Microscope, Rosewood, 3-Sections, Barrel With Lenses, 1800, 17 In.	690.00
Octant, Ivory Graduated Scales, Brass Hardware, c.1830	895.00
Orrery, Brass Horizon Ring, Ebonized Standard, 13 In.	5175.00
Orrery, Middle Candle, Lunar & Solar Eclipses, Brass Disk, c.1880	6500.00
Protractor, Interpolation Grids, Hand Engraved, Mid-18th Century	225.00
Semi-Circumferentor, Brass, Mahogany, 3 1/2 In.	690.00
Semi-Circumferentor, Cased, Hardwood Base, 1770, 8 5/8 x 4 In.	860.00
Sextant, Ebony, Bone & Brass, 19th Century	220.00
Sextant, Pocket, Solid Brass, Silver Scale, 1852, 3 1/8 In.	400.00
Sextant, Stanley, Reflecting Mirrors, Adjustable, Brass, 3 3/4 In.	120.00
Sextant, Stanley, Screw-On Cover, Magnifying Lens, Brass, 3 In.	300.00
Slide Rule, 13-Inch Double Slide, 13 Logarithmic Scales, 1800, 13 In.	345.00
Slide Rule, 15-Inch Simplex Slide, Celluloid-Clad Mahogany, 1920	145.00
Spyglass, Wooden Barrel, Leather, Brass Tube, Revolutionary War	625.00
Surveyor's Sight, Wooden Case, Hand-Cut Screws, 18 5/8 In.	200.00
Tape, Surveying, On Spool, Cripple Creek	37.00
Telescope, A. Barbou, Brass, Mahogany Tripod, Fitted Box, 1900, 55 In.	6600.00
Telescope, Astronomical, Transit, Brass, Ivory Scale, 1860, 20 In.	7475.00
Telescope, Atelier De Brocanteur, 2 Sights, 1904	440.00
Telescope, Brass, Fitted Case, c.1900	2650.00
Telescope, Brass, Leather, Brass Knob, 39 1/4 In.	115.00
Telescope, E.C. Benedicte, Brass, Mahogany Stand, England, 48 In.	1955.00
Telescope, L. Black & Co. Opticians, Detroit, Mi., 30 In.	190.00
Telescope, Plastic, Metal, Focal, Japan, Tan Case, 13 In. Extended	20.00
Telescope, Reflecting, Edwin Stevens, Brass Tube, 5 Eye Pieces, Tripod	660.00
Telescope, Refracting, 19th Century	1800.00
Telescope, Refracting, Mahogany Case, Pedestal, 1910, 4 1/2 In.	4600.00
Telescope, Ross Mfg., London, England, 3 Piece	750.00
Telescope, Surveyor's, Alidade, Green Leather Finish, 1905, 11 1/4 In.	1090.00
Telescope, Surveyor's, Wye, Adjustable, Tripod Mount, Walnut Case	595.00
Telescope, Wottway Co., Brass, World War II, With Stand, 1942	575.00
Telescope Set, Ross Of London, 9, 10 & 12 Power, 3 Piece	750.00
Ticker Tape Machine, Edison, Wooden, Iron & Glass, 45 In. *Illus*	13750.00
Transit, Builder's, Mahogany Box, 1905, 9 x 7 3/4 In.	630.00
Transit, Compass, Brass Plumb Bob, 1874, 13 1/2 x 11 In.	1840.00
Transit, Engineer's, 4 Screw Leveling, 1891, 12 1/2 In.	1380.00
Transit, Engineer's, Black Dial, Silver Ring, 1872, 13 3/4 In.	1495.00
Transit, Flat Plate, Single Vernier, Brass Finish, 1850, 13 In.	1725.00
Transit, Mahogany Box, Green Leather Finish, 1890, 12 In.	920.00

Scientific Instrument, Ticker
Tape Machine, Edison, Wooden,
Iron & Glass, 45 In.

Collectors in a warm, humid climate like Hawaii
have special problems. If you collect metal,
leather, wool, or textiles, beware. Store pieces
in an airtight container or in a place with good
air circulation, like a half-filled closet. Keep
textiles clean and dry. Best method: After
washing, dry in the sun. Use mothballs or cedar
closets for textiles. Metal will rust if not kept
away from salt air and humidity. Storage in a
plastic bag is usually acceptable.

SCRIMSHAW is bone or ivory or whale's teeth carved by sailors and others for entertainment during the sailing-ship days. Some scrimshaw was carved as early as 1800. There are modern scrimshanders making pieces today on bone, ivory, or plastic. Other pieces may be found in the Ivory and Nautical categories.

Box, Whalebone, Mahogany Cover & Pine Base, Brass Tacks, Oval, 8 1/4 In.	3410.00
Busk, Engraved Filled With Black, Brown & Green Ink	1650.00
Busk, Whalebone, Carved, Columbia With Flag, American Eagle, 13 In.	1320.00
Busk, Whalebone, Floral Design, 1840	450.00
Busk, Whalebone, Mermaid At Mid-Section	1650.00
Clothespin, Whalebone, 5 3/4 In.	160.00
Corkscrew, Tooth, Whale, Carved, 4 In.	380.00
Figurine, Bone, Elder, Holding Fan & Staff, China, 17 In.	575.00
Knife, Both Sides Depicting 3-Masted Ship, Sailors, Exotic Wood, 10 1/2 In.	402.00
Powder Horn, Engraved, Revolutionary War, 12 In.	1895.00
Powder Horn, Horses, Dogs & People, c.1870	2950.00
Seaming Tool, Whale Bone, Shadow Box Frame, 5 x 1 1/4 In.	460.00
Swift, Whalebone	2310.00
Tooth, Whale, Angel Holding Banner, Remember Me - Love, 6 In.	1322.00
Tooth, Whale, Bone, Yellow, Red, Blue, 19th Century, 4 x 4 1/4 In.	1725.00
Tooth, Whale, Cutting In & Capture Of Whales	3740.00
Tooth, Whale, Masonic Symbols Covering Entire Surface, 5 3/4 In.	1600.00
Tooth, Whale, Portrait, President James Garfield, Patriotic Designs	2200.00
Walrus Ivory, Figurine, Polar Bear, Eskimo, 4 In.	395.00
Whistle, Tooth, Whale	175.00

SEBASTIAN MINIATURES were first made by Prescott W. Baston in 1938 in Marblehead, Massachusetts. More than 400 different designs have been made, and collectors search for the out-of-production models. The mark may say *Copr. P. W. Baston U.S.A.*, or *P. W. Baston, U.S.A.*, or *Prescott W. Baston*. Sometimes a paper label was used.

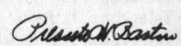

American Remembers	85.00
Fireman	28.00
George Washington	30.00
John Alden, 1939	20.00
Michigan Millers	250.00
Mr. Obocell	50.00
Sign, Dealer's, Male Bellringer, Standing Next To Logo, 4 3/4 In.	65.00
Twain's Home	550.00
William & Hannah Penn, Pair	200.00
Woman In Shoe	500.00

SEG, see Paul Revere Pottery category.

SEVRES porcelain has been made in Sevres, France, since 1769. Many copies of the famous ware have been made. The name originally referred to the works of the Royal Porcelain factory. The name now includes any of the wares made in the town of Sevres, France. The entwined lines with a center letter used as the mark is one of the most forged marks in antiques. Be very careful to identify Sevres by quality, not just by mark.

Bowl, Center, Frosted Figural Of Atlas On Base, With Arms Extended, 10 x 9 3/4 In.	518.00
Bowl, Figural Panel On Front, Floral Panel On Back, Gilded Ormolu Frame	6000.00
Bowl, Gilt Lacy Order On Rim, Decagonal, 1765-1775, 11 3/8 In.	1495.00
Bowl, Painted Birds, Blue Celeste Ground, Gilt Bronze Base, 1880s, 6 1/2 In.	862.00
Box, Hinged Cover, Floral Panel, Red, Pink, Porcelain, Signed, 3 In.	50.00
Box, Trinket, Gold-On-Gold Painted Lid, Green Ground, 5 1/2 In.	990.00
Box, Trinket, Hinged, Floral Motif, Gilt Metal Mounted, 7 In.	546.00
Butter, Attached Stand, Gilt Bands On Rim & Above Base, 1786, 7 3/4 In.	1035.00
Cachepot, Panels Of Birds, Rose Ground, 1870s, 10 1/2 In.	1092.00
Candy Dish, Boat Shape	80.00
Centerpiece, 4 Youths In Procession, Freeform Base, White Biscuit, 20 1/4 In.	316.00
Charger, Man & Woman, Seated, Playing Table Game, 13 1/4 In.	185.00

Sevres, Console, Figural Panel Front,
Floral Panel Back, Gilt Ornate Frame

Sevres, Plate, Portrait, Ladies Of French Court, 9 1/2 In., 8 Piece

Clock & Candelabra, 3-Light, Gilt Bronze, Louis XV, 16 In., 3 Piece 2700.00
Compote, Figural Landscape, Bronze, Polychrome Transfer, 5 1/4 In., Pair 173.00
Console, Figural Panel Front, Floral Panel Back, Gilt Ornate Frame ....*Illus* 6000.00
Cream Jug, Floral Sprays, Gilt Floral Terminals, 1770, 3 3/8 In. 402.00
Cup, Ice, Kidney-Shaped Front Panel, Painted Exotic Bird, c.1771, 2 5/8 In. 2070.00
Cup & Saucer, Laurel Garland Under Border, Dotted Trelliswork, 1773, 12 Sets 1265.00
Cup & Saucer, Roses Suspended From Bowknotted Ribbon, 1786, 3 x 2 In. 1150.00
Dish, Rose Sprig Center, Wreath Of Flowers, 1775, 11 7/16 In. 2587.00
Figurine, Turtle, 4 1/2 In. 55.00
Inkstand, Tray, Gilt Bands, Interior Floral Sprays, Fluid Lamp, 1756, 13 1/2 In. 2876.00
Jardiniere, Sprays Of Flowers, Trelliswork Design, 20th Century, 10 x 12 In. 288.00
Jug, Milk, Pear Shaped, Floral Spray Under Spout, Trelliswork, Branch Handle, 3 In. 2587.00
Lamp, Base, Mythological Frieze Of Male & Female Nudes, 1951, 23 3/4 In. 2990.00
Lamp, Figural, Classical, On Aladdin Form, Bronze Base, Electric, Pair 2750.00
Lamp Base, Vase Form, Figures & Foliage, Multicolored, 18 In. 288.00
Pitcher, Floral, White, Gold Trim, 1900-1908 .... 170.00
Plate, Man & Woman By Trees, Floral Medallions, Blue Border, 7 3/4 In. 27.00
Plate, Painted Floral Bouquet Center, Vines, Alternating Foliate, 1921, 9 1/4 In. 2415.00
Plate, Portrait, Ladies Of French Court, 9 1/2 In., 8 Piece ....*Illus* 770.00
Pot, Multicolored Floral Panels, Brass Base, Blue, White, 5 1/2 In. 320.00
Soup, Dish, Center Bouquet Of Roses, Morning Glories, Border Vine, 1792, Pair 805.00
Sugar, Cover, Double Walled, Reticulated Porcelain, Bamboo Handles, 1862 .... 950.00
Tazza, Allover Angel, Cherub, Pink, Gilt Ground, Wood Pedestal, 6 x 8 3/4 In. 863.00
Tazza, Cherubic Design, Royal Crest, Celeste Blue, Gold Border, 19th Century, 8 x 4 In. .. 212.00
Tazza, Figural Scene, Gilt Rococo Motifs, Bleu De Roi Ground, 1900, 5 x 8 In., Pair 7150.00
Urn, Allegorical Figures, Cupid, Landscape Scene On Reverse, 19th Century, 26 In. 4310.00
Urn, Allover Landscape, Allegorical Design, Gilt, Pink Floral Swags, 11 In. 115.00
Urn, Allover Multicolored Floral, Putti Design, Cobalt Blue, Gilt Highlights, 10 In. 430.00
Urn, Continual Figural & Landscape, Scrolled Handles, Female Busts, 1880s, 22 In. 1265.00
Urn, Continuous Napoleonic Scene, Berried Leaves & Eagles, 38 1/2 In. 6325.00
Urn, Lady & Cherubs, Hand Painted, Figural Handles, Cobalt Blue, White 4900.00
Urn, Porcelain, Continuous Hunting Scene, Cobalt Borders, 1890s, 29 1/2 In., Pair 6900.00
Urn, Turquoise & Blue, Foliage & Flowers, Bronze Bracket Base, 1930s, 18 1/2 In., Pr. .. 8625.00
Urn, Venus & Cupids, Classical Terms In Niches, Doves, Nests, Bronze, 34 In. 2530.00
Urn, Winged Putti, Garlands Of Flowers, White Ground, Signed, 22 In. 3795.00
Vase, Couple, Courting, Green, Painted Reserves, Champleve Top, Marble Base, 17 In. .. 345.00
Vase, Cover, Cartouches, Figural Landscape, Pink Ground, 11 In., Pair 1380.00
Vase, Cover, Figural Landscape, Light Blue Borders, 12 In. 230.00
Vase, Cover, Stylized Foliage, Pale Gray, Gray Foot, Marcel Prunier, 19 1/2 In. 4600.00
Vase, Cover, Winged Putto Finial, Opposing Figural Panels, Gilt Borders, 27 In. 3740.00
Vase, Stylized Leaf, Floral Design, Gilt Ground, Enamel, France, 6 In. 633.00

SEWER TILE figures were made by workers at the sewer tile and pipe
factories in the Ohio area during the late nineteenth and early twentieth centuries. Figurines, small vases, and cemetery vases were favored.
Often the finished vase was a piece of the original pipe with added decorations and markings. All types of sewer tile work are now considered
folk art by collectors.

Baby Bulldog, Rectangular Base, 3 3/4 In. 148.00
Bank, Pig, Initialed E.D., 8 3/4 In. 165.00

Bank, Pig, Seated, Incised To Pat My Godfather, 9 1/4 In. 220.00
Birdhouse, 8 1/2 In. 165.00
Dog, Dachshund, Seated, Black, 12 1/4 In. 220.00
Dog, Seated, Flat Head Type, Tooled, 11 1/2 In. 2310.00
Dog, Seated, Ohio, 11 In. 550.00
Dog, Seated, Raised Paw, Ohio, 9 3/8 In. 545.00
Duck, 14 1/2 In. 825.00
Eagle, 6 3/4 In. 55.00
Eagle, Signed, F.O.E., 1944, 8 In. 55.00
Fawn, 11 In. 248.00
Figurine, Dog, Seated, Dark Brown Glaze, 10 1/4 In. 220.00
Horse Head, Seated, 5 5/8 In. 55.00
Jar, Molded Art Deco Designs, Oval, 19 In. 55.00
Lion, Brown Repaint, Rectangular Base, 10 In. 220.00
Lion, Repaired, 4 5/8 In. 100.00
Owl, On Base, Initials E.J.E., Ohio, 14 In. 1575.00
Planter, Basket, Tooled Bark Finish, 10 In. 220.00
Planter, Stump, Incised Memorial Inscription, 22 1/2 In. 330.00
Planter, Stump, Small Bird In 1 Crook, 12 1/4 In. 165.00
Planter, Tree Trunk Form, Signed, B.H., 16 In. 200.00
Planter, With Vine, Marked, Alice Blanton, 12 1/2 x 12 1/2 In. 165.00
Raccoon, Chuck Milburn, 13 In. 230.00
Squirrel With Nut, Initialed E.D., 9 In. 55.00

SEWING equipment of all types is collected, from sewing birds that
held the cloth to tape measures, needle books, and old wooden spools.
Sewing machines are included here. Needlework pictures are listed in
the Picture category.

Ball, Bone, Mahogany Handle, c.1820-1860, 9 In. 185.00
Basket, Armadillo, Gold Satin Lining 80.00
Bird, Brass, Engraved, Dated 1853 .... 150.00
Bird, Clamp, Brass, 1853 .... 160.00
Bird, Clamp, Cast Iron 110.00
Bird, Dog, Metal, 3 1/2 In. 1700.00
Bird, Pincushion, Brass 150.00
Box, Brass, Brazed Seam, Pincushion Top, Fabric Lined, 19th Century, 2 1/4 In. 175.00
Box, Carved & Painted, 1860 .... 1400.00
Box, Cathedral Style, Mahogany, Pincushion, Drawers, Lid, 7 x 5 x 7 In. 330.00
Box, Cover Is Pincushion, Green Fabric Lining, 19th Century, 2 1/4 x 3 3/4 In. 145.00
Box, Decorated, Poplar, Black Paint, Gold Stencil, Drawer, Turned Feet, 7 x 8 x 6 In. 358.00
Box, Gilt Stenciling, Mother-Of-Pearl Lid, Wallpaper Interior, On Stand, 26 1/2 In. 2200.00
Box, Grape Leaf, Interior Ivory Fittings, Lower Drawer, Writing Surface, 1820s 1950.00
Box, Hanging, Brown Finish, Early 20th Century, 21 1/2 In. 138.00
Box, Inlaid Wood, Pincushion, Secret Compartments, England, 13 1/4 x 9 In. 295.00
Box, Lift Top, Compartmented, Ivory Implements, Drawer, 5 5/8 x 12 In. 1610.00
Box, Multicolored Design, White Ground, Scandinavian 2475.00
Box, Needlework Picture Of Stag On Lid, Velvet Sides, 6 1/4 x 7 3/4 In. 110.00
Box, Paper Covered, Hexagonal, Applied Beaded Velvet Flowers, Velvet Top, 6 In. 330.00
Box, Square Corner Posts, 1 Drawer, Penciled May 22, 1870, 9 x 8 1/4 In. 192.00
Cabinet, Spool, see Advertising category under Cabinet, Spool.
Caddy, Mahogany, Marquetry, Urn Finial, Scroll Handles, Inlaid Interior, 16 1/2 In. 2090.00
Caddy, Spool, Acorn Shape, Pedestal, Wooden 125.00
Caddy, Thread, Green Paint, Yellow Striping, 2 Metal Rods, Scrolled End, 13 1/2 In. 357.00
Case, Carp Shape, Silver Plate, Blue Velvet, Scale, Fin, Eye, 1820, 4 In. 977.00
Case, Thread, Sterling Silver, Unger 190.00
Clamp, Punch & File Design, Homespun Cushion, Forged Iron 425.00
Darner, Sterling Silver Handle & Collar, 6 1/2 In. 95.00
Darning Egg, Milk Glass 25.00
Gauge, Hem, Sterling Silver ....65.00 to 100.00
Kit, German Porcelain, Original Box, 19th Century 2250.00
Kit, Gulf Oil Co. ....12.00 to 45.00
Loom Light, Iron, Blacksmith Made, Mid-18th Century, 17 In. 350.00
Machine, Domestic, 1890, 14 x 20 In. 133.00

Machine, Featherweight Convertible, No. 222, Accessories, Case, Buttonholer	750.00
Machine, Portable, New Singer Queen, Electric, Given To Dorothy Lamour, 1950	373.00
Machine, Rosewood, Cast Iron	1035.00
Machine, Singer, Featherweight, Case & Accessories	295.00
Machine, Singer, Featherweight, Case, Manual, Attachments, 1964	255.00
Machine, Singer, Featherweight, Model, 221, Case	315.00
Machine, Wilcox & Gibbs, Electric	275.00
Machine, Wilcox & Gibbs, Manual, Box, c.1910	210.00
Needle Case, Art Nouveau, Sterling Silver	110.00
Needle Case, Buster Brown Needles, Buster & Tige, Silk	300.00
Needle Case, Fish Form, Wooden, c.1820	135.00
Needle Case, Ivory, Lady, Wearing A Bonnet, Dress, Flat Oval Base, 1790, 3 In.	1092.00
Needle Case, Lady Prim, 6 3/4 x 4 1/4 In. ....*Illus*	4.00
Needle Case, Steeple Chase, The Winner, 4 3/4 x 4 1/2 In. ....*Illus*	3.00
Needle Case, Tin, Boyee	75.00
Needle Case, Umbrella Shape, Bakelite	30.00
Needle Case, Victorian, Blown Glass	72.00
Needle Pack, Threader, C.C. Howard Furniture Co., 7 x 4 3/4 In. ....*Illus*	6.00
Needlebook, Peach Sweet Scotch Snuff	15.00
Niddy Noddy, Carved Shaft, Late 18th Century, 7 1/2 In.	245.00
Pattern, Devil's Costume, Butterick, Small, 1921	45.00
Pinball, Silk, Knitted, Oval, Red, Yellow, White, Sarah Hockey, Pennsylvania, 1796, 2 In.	610.00
Pincushion, Banjo Player	25.00
Pincushion, Basket Shape, Silver Head, Yellow Velvet, England, 1909, 3 Piece	747.00
Pincushion, Beaded, Red, Scalloped, Red Ground, 8 1/2 In.	60.00
Pincushion, Bird, Hanging, Beaded, Blue, Bird On Tail, American Indian, 8 In.	88.00
Pincushion, Buffalo Hoof	95.00
Pincushion, Clamp, 1840s	245.00
Pincushion, Duck, 4 In.	9.00
Pincushion, Figural, Shoe Roller Skate, Metal	195.00
Pincushion, Heart Shaped, Silver Plated, Box ....64.00 to 70.00
Pincushion, Needle & Thimble Drawer, Mahogany Floral Inlays, 6 3/8 In.	395.00
Pincushion, Red, Yellow, White Silk, Crown & Hearts, Sarah Hockey, 1796, 2 In.	610.00
Pincushion, Roll, Purple Velvet, Black Leather, 3 Graduated Wool Needle Holders	230.00
Pincushion, Silver Kangaroo On Cover, Red Velvet	475.00
Pincushion, Silver Plate, Engraved Your Friend	85.00
Pincushion, Tape Measure, Cat At Sewing Machine, Ceramic, 6 In.	55.00
Pincushion, Thread Caddy, Drawer, Walnut	95.00
Pincushion, Yellow Kid, Metal, 1890s, 3 1/2 In.	350.00
Pincushion Dolls are listed in their own category.	
Rack, Bobbin, Fitted With Spools Of Thread, Hardwood, Shoe Feet, 29 In.	247.00
Scissors, Embroidery, Carved Roses, Sterling Silver, Germany	85.00
Shuttle, Tatting, Celluloid, Chased Design, Metal	18.00
Shuttle, Tatting, Red Plastic	5.00
Spool Cabinets are in the Advertising category under Cabinet, Spool.	

Sewing, Needle Case, Lady Prim,
6 3/4 x 4 1/4 In.

Sewing, Needle Pack, Threader, C.C.
Howard Furniture Co., 7 x 4 3/4 In.

Sewing, Needle Case, Steeple
Chase, The Winner,
4 3/4 x 4 1/2 In.

Spool Holder, Pincushion, Metal, 3 1/2 In. 12.00
Stand, Whale Ivory & Whalebone, 4 Tiers, 9 1/2 In. 6160.00
String Winder, Mortised, Pegged & Chamfered, Red Paint, 1800s, 8 3/4 In. 85.00
Swift, Triple, Whalebone Staves, Ivory Finials, Clamp 2750.00
Swift, Whalebone, Ivory Clamp, Ivory Finial, Fabric Ties, 24 In. 1045.00
Swift, Whalebone, Nantucket 3800.00
Tape Loom, Chestnut, New England, 18th Century, 28 In. 595.00
Tape Loom, Oak, Mid-17th Century, 6 1/4 In. 1350.00
Tape Loom, Poplar, Old Dark Brown, 7 1/4 x 18 3/4 In. 485.00
Tape Measure, Bemberg Rayon, Red, White, Blue, Celluloid, 1 1/2 In. 40.00
Tape Measure, Black Fly On Red Egg 68.00
Tape Measure, Cat, Celluloid 90.00
Tape Measure, Court Lady, Celluloid, Germany, Prewar, 2 1/2 In. 152.00
Tape Measure, Covered Wagon, Plastic 125.00
Tape Measure, Decorated Cake, Celluloid, Germany, Prewar, 1 1/8 In. 224.00
Tape Measure, Dog, Celluloid, Tail Pull, Movable Head, Germany, Prewar, 2 1/2 In. ... 242.00
Tape Measure, Domed Top, Loop Finial, Scrolled Foliage, Glass Stopper, 2 1/4 In. ... 690.00
Tape Measure, Elephant, Howdah & Rider, Celluloid, Germany, 2 In. 140.00
Tape Measure, Equestrian With Whip, Celluloid, 2 In. 272.00
Tape Measure, Fish, Souvenir Of Catalina Island, Celluloid 90.00
Tape Measure, Fluted Case, Carved Wood, Leaf, Floral Design, Nailhead Trim, 1790 ... 1380.00
Tape Measure, General Electric, 1920 Refrigerator 55.00
Tape Measure, Golden Gate 25.00
Tape Measure, Hamilton Brown Shoe Co., American Lady Shoes, Office Building 35.00
Tape Measure, Home Federal, Des Moines, Cigarette Lighter Shape, 1962 .... 12.00
Tape Measure, Hoover, Canister Type ....28.00 to 30.00
Tape Measure, Indian Head, Celluloid 120.00
Tape Measure, Iron, Brown Slag Glass Handle, Wire Crank, 2 1/8 In. 165.00
Tape Measure, Iron, Green Slag Glass Handle, Ball Crank, Replaced Tape, 2 1/8 In. ... 175.00
Tape Measure, Iron, Orange & White Slag Glass Handle, Ball Crank, 2 1/8 In. 120.00
Tape Measure, John Deere, Plastic ....55.00 to 80.00
Tape Measure, Kangaroo, Baby In Pouch, Celluloid 88.00
Tape Measure, Kangaroo, Celluloid 45.00
Tape Measure, Lion, Crown Forms Pincushion, Scissors Holder, Ceramic, 6 1/4 In. ... 45.00
Tape Measure, Mammy Head, Celluloid 180.00
Tape Measure, Penguin, Occupied Japan, 3 In. 180.00
Tape Measure, Pig, Plastic ....35.00 to 40.00
Tape Measure, Pig, Wearing Top Hat, Celluloid 65.00
Tape Measure, Pincushion, Iron Shape 10.00
Tape Measure, Plum, Celluloid, Fly Pull, Germany, Prewar, 2 In. 247.00
Tape Measure, Queen Quality Shoes, Celluloid, 1 3/4 In. 55.00
Tape Measure, Rabbit With Egg, Celluloid, Germany, 2 1/2 In. 133.00
Tape Measure, Rabbit, Celluloid 90.00
Tape Measure, Renown Ranges 30.00
Tape Measure, Sadiron 55.00
Tape Measure, Ship, Celluloid 118.00
Tape Measure, Sitting White Cat, Pink Pillow Is Pin Box, Porcelain, Napco, 4 In. 85.00
Tape Measure, Squaw In Blanket 125.00
Tape Measure, Star Kist Tuna 40.00
Tape Measure, Swashbuckler, Celluloid, Germany, 2 In. 93.00
Tape Measure, Turtle Shell, Pull My Head, But Not My Leg, 2 x 1/2 In. 150.00
Tape Measure, Water Mill, Composition, England, 2 In. 170.00
Tape Measure, Yellowstone, Plastic 40.00
Thimble, Caswell Coffee, Metal 24.00
Thimble, Embossed Grapes, 1907, Child's 68.00
Thimble, Griswold 800.00
Thimble, Queen Victoria Pictured, Enamel, Sterling Silver, Date On Back, 1819-1901 ... 295.00
Thimble, Sterling Silver, Pat'd. 5-28-1889, Size 12 .... 35.00
Thimble, Velvet Case, 1910 .... 135.00
Thimble Holder, Sterling Silver, Marked F & B 175.00
Thread Holder, Bear, Carved, Pincushion Backpack, 2 Piece 155.00
Thread Holder, Ivory, Barrel Shape, Suspended From Arched Swivel Basket, 5 In. 2760.00
Thread Holder, Sunflower Design, Swing Handle, Early 19th Century, 7 1/4 In. 690.00

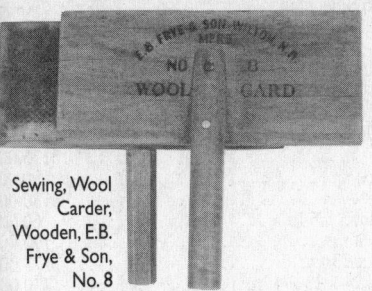

Sewing, Wool
Carder,
Wooden, E.B.
Frye & Son,
No. 8

If you scorch a textile while ironing, try this old trick: Rub a cut onion over the scorch, then soak the cloth in cold water for I hour. Rewash and then iron.

Vise, Miniature Drawer & Pincushion Top, Metal Framed 140.00
Vise, Pincushion Top, Mirror On Opposite Side 310.00
Wool Carder, Wooden, E.B. Frye & Son, No. 8 . . . . *Illus* 28.00
Yarn Winder, Click Mechanism, J. Roy, Wooden, 40 In. 137.00
Yarn Winder, Iron, Brown & Sharpe Mfg. Co., Bell Measure, 22 x 20 x 12 In. . . . . :. 440.00
Yarn Winder, Oak, Quartersawn, Sawtooth Edge 175.00
Yarn Winder, Tiger Maple 195.00

SHAKER items are characterized by simplicity, functionalism, and orderliness. There were many Shaker communities in America from the eighteenth century to the present day. The religious order made furniture, small wooden pieces, and packaged medicines, herbs, and jellies to sell to *outsiders*. Other useful objects were made for use by members of the community. Shaker furniture is listed in this book in the Furniture category.

Basket, Braided Handle, Wrapped Center, 2 x 3 1/2 In. 173.00
Basket, Carved Handle, Red Decorative Lines At Top, 6 x 10 1/2 x 9 1/2 In. 144.00
Basket, Cover, Square Handle, 5 1/2 x 13 In. 230.00
Basket, Splint, Bentwood Rim Handles, 5 x 12 In. 302.00
Basket, Splint, Carved Handle, Round, 6 x 12 In. 184.00
Basket, Splint, Handles, Wood Loop Handle, Patina, 4 x 12 1/2 x 9 In. 201.00
Bottle, Asthma Cure, Case 400.00
Box, 2-Finger, Bentwood, Grayish Brown Paint, 4 1/2 In. 275.00
Box, 2-Finger, Inscribed S.M., 2 1/4 x 6 In. 116.00
Box, 3-Finger, Pantry, Copper Nails, 3 x 6 In. 175.00
Box, 3-Finger, Pine Top, Green Scalloped Sides, White Dots, 1868, 1 1/2 x 3 1/2 In. 1725.00
Box, 4-Finger, Oval, Green Paint, Copper Tacks, 4 1/2 x 12 In. 1650.00
Box, Bentwood, Black Ink Graining, Copper Tacks, Harvard, 4 3/4 In., Pair 495.00
Box, Bentwood, Oval, Beech, Pine, Sponged Green Over Blue, 12 1/2 In. 990.00
Box, Bentwood, Oval, Blue, Green, Gray Paint, Iron Tacks, 6 3/8 In. 660.00
Box, Bentwood, Oval, Natural Finish, Copper Tacks, 9 In. 550.00
Box, Bentwood, Oval, Worn Red Paint, 11 1/2 In. 1430.00
Box, Copper Nails, Round, Handle, 3 3/8 x 7 5/8 In. 225.00
Box, Detached Pincushion Top, Grain Painted, Oval 517.00
Box, Gold Building With Spire, Rosewood Graining, Steel Tacks, Harvard, 5 In. 247.00
Box, Painted, Oval, 1850s, 13 x 15 In. 1350.00
Box, Seed, Harvard 6575.00
Box, Seed, Interior Label, Mount Lebanon 5275.00
Box, Sewing, Mahogany, Flame Veneer, Ivory Finial, Eyelets, 2 Drawers, 9 x 6 x 9 In. . . . 1100.00
Box, Stave Constructed, Copper Tacks On Lid Band, Interlocking Bands, 12 1/2 In. 220.00
Broadside, Shaker's Pure Lemon Syrup 3512.00
Brush, Red Felt Above Bristles, 10 1/2 In. 120.00
Brush & Mirror, Child's, Mother-Of-Pearl Inlay, 4 9/16 In. 200.00
Bucket, Bale Handle, Blue, 4 1/2 In. 258.00
Bucket, Pine, Stave Constructed Body, 2 Iron Rings, Bail Handle 1610.00
Butter Tub, Alligator Style, Beveled Top Edge, Grain Paint, Brown, 9 1/4 x 4 1/2 In. . . . 144.00
Churn, Butter, Buttonhole Laps, 22 In. 650.00
Gate, Wooden, Cherry, Turned Posts With Finials, 30 x 39 In. 330.00

Gavel, Call To Order, Walnut, Swing Clapper Side To Side	290.00
Mirror, Mahogany, Child's, 4 In.	125.00
Mittens, Hooked, Wool, White, Red Rose	220.00
Pail, Interlocking Staves, Metal Rod Bail, Wooden Handle, Titled Good Girl	990.00
Peeler, Apple, 3 Wooden Gears, Hand Cranked, Old Chatham	475.00
Press, Food & Herb, Tin Pan, Wood Blocks, Solid Walnut, 13 1/2 x 12 5/8 In.	255.00
Quilt Rack, Mortised & Pinned, Semi-Circular Top Rail, 47 1/2 x 38 In.	330.00
Rack, Wall, Peg, Red Wash	5175.00
Sander, Rosewood, 2 5/8 x 2 9/16 In.	90.00
Sewing, Caddy, Mahogany, Square, 7 1/2 In.	130.00
Sprinkler, Water, Dampen Things Before Ironing, Tin, 3 5/8 In.	60.00
Tray, Collection, Tin, Black, Oval, 5 1/4 x 6 1/8 In., Pair	190.00
Tray, Sorting, Cherry, 4 Sides, Cutout Handles, 4 1/2 x 33 x 20 In.	173.00
Wash Tub, Beveled Top Edge, 2 Handles, Red Paint, 24 x 15 3/4 In.	230.00
Wheelbarrow, 8-Spoke Wooden Wheel, Metal Rods, Curved Handles, Green, 81 In.	690.00

SHAVING MUGS were popular from 1860 to 1900. Many types were made, including occupational mugs featuring pictures of men's jobs. There were scuttle mugs, silver-plated mugs, glass-lined mugs, and others.

2 Birds & Flowers, Name, Sealey Southard, Germany	145.00
Bust, Black Man's Head, Austria, c.1920	350.00
Crossed Rifles, Joseph Consiglio, 106th Infantry, 1917	275.00
Double Fraternal Emblems, Odd Fellows & Knights Of Pythias, Gold Name	225.00
Drape & Red Poppy, White & Ivory Ground, W.E. Carpenter, 3 1/2 In.	94.00
Duck In Evergreen, Green Scene, Red Mark, Gaston 3	300.00
Floral, Dancing Couple On Front, Yellow Ground	45.00
Flowers & Bird, Luster China, Bavaria	29.00
Laughing Black Man, Porcelain, America, 1890-1935, 4 3/8 In.	465.00
Leonard Vienna Austria, J. Downing, 4 In.	690.00
Name Levi Darrah In Gold, Civil War Veteran, Late 19th Century	325.00
Occupational, Apothecary, Druggist, S.R. Romoff, Germany	715.00
Occupational, Beer Wagon, Barrels, T. Schoonmaker, Limoges, 3 5/8 In.	935.00
Occupational, Bull's Head & Butcher Cutlery, G.M. Hardendorf, 3 1/4 x 5 In.	58.00
Occupational, Butcher, Gold Trim, 3 3/4 x 3 1/4 In.	135.00
Occupational, Carpenter Planning A Board, S.F. Morrison, Germany, 3 3/4 In.	275.00
Occupational, Carpenter, Gold Lettering	300.00
Occupational, Cowboy	195.00
Occupational, Crossed Baseball Bats, Player, Mike J. Barry, Germany, 3 3/4 In.	2530.00
Occupational, Derrick Inside A Building, Chas. J. Kiers, 3 5/8 In.	6600.00
Occupational, Drapery Cutter, Drapes & Scissors, Name In Gold	195.00
Occupational, Horse Drawn Stake Wagon, C.W. Miller, Chicago, Ill., 3 5/8 In.	635.00
Occupational, Horse, Delivery Wagon, Vinegar & Cider, Edward H. May	3080.00
Occupational, Jr. Order Of United Auto Mechanics, 1885-1925, 3 3/4 In.	2475.00
Occupational, Locomotive & Coal Tender, Gold Band Base, Briggs, 4 x 5 In.	120.00
Occupational, Locomotive & Tender, Ed. Bryant, 1885-1925, 3 7/8 In.	210.00
Occupational, Lunch Wagon, Made From Railroad Car, D.D. Molanip, 3 1/2 In.	1015.00
Occupational, Man, Driving Express Wagon	1050.00
Occupational, Man, Operating Oil Derrick Type Machine	6600.00
Occupational, Music Store Scene, M.B. Franklin, 3 3/4 In.	715.00
Occupational, Railroad Passenger Car, D.F. Bower, Germany, 3 3/4 In.	415.00
Occupational, Railroad, Gold Rings On Rim, 4 x 3 3/4 In.	160.00
Occupational, Salesman, Hand Presenting Calling Card, Name In Gold 195.00 to 375.00
Occupational, St. Louis Electric Grinding Co., Barber Supplies, France, 3 7/8 In.	465.00
Occupational, Trolley, New York Railroad Co., J. Frank, 1912, 3 3/4 In.	2420.00
Toby Figure On Sides, Tree Branch Handle, Brown, Cream, 4 In.	200.00

SHAWNEE POTTERY was started in Zanesville, Ohio, in 1937. The company made vases, novelty ware, flowerpots, planters, lamps, and cookie jars. Three dinnerware lines were made: Corn, Lobster Ware, and Valencia (a solid color line). White Corn pattern utility pieces were made in 1945. Corn King was made from 1946 to 1954; Corn Queen, with darker green leaves and lighter colored corn, from 1954 to 1961.

Shawnee produced pottery for George Rumrill during the late 1930s.
The company closed in 1961.

Bank, Winnie Pig, Butterscotch	450.00
Bank, Winnie Pig, Chocolate	575.00
Bookends, Dog Head, 4 3/4 In.	45.00 to 55.00
Bookends, Flying Geese, 6 In.	70.00
Bowl, Corn King, 6 3/4 In.	55.00
Bowl, Vegetable, Corn Queen, 9 In.	24.00 to 42.00
Box, Cigarette, Arrowhead On Cover, Brown, 4 1/2 x 3 1/2 In.	275.00
Butter, Corn King	70.00
Butter, Cover, Corn Queen	29.00 to 42.00
Casserole, Corn King, Cover, 11 In.	50.00 to 85.00
Casserole, Corn King, Individual	125.00
Casserole, Lobster, 2 Qt.	55.00 to 60.00
Casserole, Lobster, Individual, 10 Oz.	30.00 to 42.00
Casserole, Sundial, With Stand, Pink, Black, 1 1/2 Qt.	60.00
Coffeepot, Sunflower, 6 1/4 In.	95.00
Cookie Jar, Cover, Corn Queen	143.00 to 190.00
Cookie Jar, Drum Major, Gold Trim	420.00 to 975.00
Cookie Jar, Dutch Boy, Blue Pants	95.00 to 175.00
Cookie Jar, Dutch Boy, Gold, Decals	325.00
Cookie Jar, Dutch Girl, Gold Trim, Decals	225.00 to 300.00
Cookie Jar, Dutch Girl, Tulip	349.00
Cookie Jar, Elephant, White	55.00
Cookie Jar, Happy, Gold Trim, Patches	250.00
Cookie Jar, Jack, Striped Pants	169.00
Cookie Jar, Jo Jo Clown	300.00 to 500.00
Cookie Jar, Little Chef, Multicolored	125.00
Cookie Jar, Lucky Elephant, 1993	350.00
Cookie Jar, Lucky Elephant, Gold, Green Collar	795.00
Cookie Jar, Muggsy	195.00 to 450.00
Cookie Jar, Muggsy, Gold Trim	850.00 to 900.00
Cookie Jar, Owl	135.00 to 175.00
Cookie Jar, Puss 'n Boots	150.00 to 225.00
Cookie Jar, Puss 'n Boots, Long Tail	175.00
Cookie Jar, Puss 'n Boots, White Bow, Gold Trim	495.00 to 595.00
Cookie Jar, Sailor Boy, Black Hair	550.00
Cookie Jar, Sailor Boy, Blond Hair	575.00
Cookie Jar, Smiley Pig, Chrysanthemum	3265.00
Cookie Jar, Smiley Pig, Clover Buds	400.00
Cookie Jar, Smiley Pig, Gold Trim	300.00
Cookie Jar, Smiley Pig, Gold, Blue Neckerchief, Decals	300.00 to 550.00
Cookie Jar, Smiley Pig, Shamrocks, No Gold	175.00
Cookie Jar, Smiley Pig, Tulip	250.00
Cookie Jar, Smiley Pig, Yellow Neckerchief, Gold Trim	795.00
Cookie Jar, Winking Owl	125.00
Cookie Jar, Winking Owl, Gold Trim	325.00
Cookie Jar, Winnie Pig, Blue Collar, Gold Trim	395.00 to 595.00
Cookie Jar, Winnie Pig, Shamrocks	320.00
Cookie Jar, Winnie Pig, Shamrocks, Gold Trim	485.00
Creamer, Corn King	18.00 to 30.00
Creamer, Corn Queen	30.00
Creamer, Elephant, Gold Trim	80.00
Creamer, Elephant, White	55.00
Creamer, Pennsylvania Dutch	95.00
Creamer, Pig, Yellow, Blue Neckerchief	115.00
Creamer, Puss 'n Boots	90.00
Creamer, Puss 'n Boots, White	35.00 to 40.00
Creamer, Puss 'n Boots, Yellow, Green	65.00 to 140.00
Creamer, Smiley Pig, Gold Trim	220.00
Creamer, Smiley Pig, Peach Flower	69.00
Creamer, Smiley Pig, Yellow, Blue Neckerchief	85.00 to 125.00
Creamer, Snowflake, Turquoise	18.00

Creamer, Sunflower . . . . .65.00 to 95.00
Dish, Fruit, Corn Queen, 6 In. . . . . .8.00 to 25.00
Figurine, Darn-Aide, Blue 95.00
Figurine, Deer 35.00
Figurine, Dutch Boy & Girl 55.00
Figurine, Elephant, Green 20.00
Figurine, Pekingese . . . . .68.00 to 75.00
Figurine, Squirrel . . . . .65.00 to 69.00
Figurine, Teddy Bear 65.00
Figurine, Tumbling Bear 75.00
Figurine, Turtle, Yellow 30.00
Lamp, Clown 55.00
Lamp, Elephant, Original Shade 95.00
Lamp, Mother Goose 85.00
Lamp, Wall, Embossed Flowers . . . . .40.00 to 125.00
Mixing Bowl, Corn King, 5 1/2 In. . . . . .40.00 to 48.00
Mixing Bowl, Corn Queen, 5 In. 29.00
Mixing Bowl, Corn Queen, 6 1/2 In. . . . . .19.00 to 34.00
Mixing Bowl, Corn Queen, 8 In. 39.00
Mug, Corn King, 8 Oz. . . . . .45.00 to 50.00
Mug, Corn Queen, 8 Oz. . . . . .19.00 to 34.00
Pie Bird, Blue 40.00
Pitcher, Bo Peep, Blue Bonnet . . . . .115.00 to 135.00
Pitcher, Bo Peep, Green Bonnet . . . . .100.00 to 135.00
Pitcher, Bo Peep, Lilac Bonnet 115.00
Pitcher, Chanticleer . . . . .65.00 to 140.00
Pitcher, Corn King . . . . .35.00 to 65.00
Pitcher, Little Boy Blue . . . . .130.00 to 150.00
Pitcher, Smiley Pig, Apple 275.00
Pitcher, Smiley Pig, Cloverbud, Red Bandanna . . . . .175.00 to 185.00
Pitcher, Smiley Pig, Gold Decals 375.00
Pitcher, Smiley Pig, Gold Trim, Red Feet 325.00
Pitcher, Smiley Pig, Peach, Blue Flowers . . . . .165.00 to 210.00
Planter, Bicycle Built For Two 90.00
Planter, Boot, Embossed, Blue, 7 In. 25.00
Planter, Chick & Egg Cart 35.00
Planter, Circus Train 30.00
Planter, Clown 45.00
Planter, Duck, With Cart 15.00
Planter, Elephant . . . . .75.00 to 85.00
Planter, Giraffe . . . . .40.00 to 55.00
Planter, Girl, At Gate 9.00
Planter, Locomotive, Black 50.00
Planter, Old Mill . . . . .25.00 to 26.00
Planter, Top Hat 15.00
Planter, Train, White Design, 4 Piece 325.00
Planter, Turtle, Yellow 30.00
Plate, Corn King, 7 1/2 In. 40.00
Plate, Corn King, 10 In. . . . . .35.00 to 45.00
Plate, Corn King, 12 In. 55.00
Plate, Corn Queen, 7 1/4 In. . . . . .3.00 to 7.00
Platter, Corn Queen, 12 In. . . . . .19.00 to 39.00
Pot, Grease, Fern 65.00
Relish, Corn King 40.00
Relish, Cover, Lobster 85.00
Salt & Pepper, Bo Peep & Sailor 45.00
Salt & Pepper, Chanticleer, Large 70.00
Salt & Pepper, Chanticleer, Small . . . . .35.00 to 40.00
Salt & Pepper, Chef . . . . .35.00 to 45.00
Salt & Pepper, Corn King, Large 25.00
Salt & Pepper, Corn Queen, Small 20.00
Salt & Pepper, Cottage . . . . .250.00 to 295.00

Salt & Pepper, Dutch Boy & Girl, Large .... .30.00 to 65.00
Salt & Pepper, Farmer Pig 15.00
Salt & Pepper, Fruit, Large 40.00
Salt & Pepper, Jack & Jill 45.00
Salt & Pepper, Lobster, Claw .... .35.00 to 56.00
Salt & Pepper, Muggsy 65.00
Salt & Pepper, Muggsy, Gold Trim, Large .... .150.00 to 325.00
Salt & Pepper, Muggsy, Small .... .55.00 to 65.00
Salt & Pepper, Owl, Blue Eyes .... .25.00 to 39.00
Salt & Pepper, Owl, Green Eyes .... .20.00 to 65.00
Salt & Pepper, Puss 'n Boots, Gold Trim .... .20.00 to 50.00
Salt & Pepper, Puss 'n Boots, White .... .35.00 to 48.00
Salt & Pepper, Rooster 65.00
Salt & Pepper, Smiley Pig & Winnie Pig 75.00
Salt & Pepper, Smiley Pig, Gold Decal, Large .... .120.00 to 200.00
Salt & Pepper, Smiley Pig, Gold Decal, Small .... .35.00 to 95.00
Salt & Pepper, Smiley Pig, Green Neckerchief, Large 165.00
Salt & Pepper, Smiley Pig, Yellow Neckerchief, Small 135.00
Salt & Pepper, Watering Can .... .15.00 to 45.00
Salt & Pepper, Winnie Pig & Smiley Pig 68.00
Salt & Pepper, Winnie Pig, Small 60.00
Saltshaker, Corn Queen, 3 1/4 In. 7.00
Saltshaker, Corn Queen, 5 1/4 In. 10.00
Sprinkler, Water 25.00
Teapot, Corn King .... .85.00 to 125.00
Teapot, Corn King, Individual 285.00
Teapot, Corn Queen, Individual .... .55.00 to 110.00
Teapot, Cover, Corn Queen 170.00
Teapot, Elephant, Blue 175.00
Teapot, Elephant, Yellow .... .225.00 to 295.00
Teapot, Granny Ann, Gold Trim 190.00
Teapot, Granny Ann, Gold Trim, Decals 130.00
Teapot, Granny Ann, Green, Lavender .... .130.00 to 150.00
Teapot, Granny Ann, Peach 105.00
Teapot, Granny Ann, Peach Apron 105.00
Teapot, Granny Ann, Purple Apron .... .130.00 to 195.00
Teapot, Pennsylvania Dutch 50.00
Teapot, Pennsylvania Dutch, Individual 125.00
Teapot, Snowflake 300.00
Teapot, Sunflower 100.00
Teapot, Tom, Red, Blue, Yellow .... .115.00 to 140.00
Teapot, Tom, White .... .95.00 to 110.00
Vase, Cornucopia, Burgundy, 6 In. 25.00
Vase, Giraffe & Baby, 10 1/2 In. 79.00
Vase, Texture, Woodtone, Square, 9 In. 30.00

SHEARWATER pottery is a family business started by Mr. and Mrs. G. W. Anderson, Sr., and their three sons. The local Ocean Springs, Mississippi, clays were used to make the wares in the 1930s. The company is still in business.

Figurine, Bird, Cream 200.00
Figurine, Lion, Slinking, Blue, Green 200.00
Pitcher, Blue Rain Glaze, Wide Handle, Blue Interior, 1950s, 5 7/8 In. 100.00
Pitcher, Dusty Green & Gunmetal, 5 In. 85.00
Pitcher, Green Matte Glaze, Signed, 1940s, 5 1/8 In. 154.00
Pitcher, Green, Signed, 5 1/2 In. 60.00
Pitcher, Turquoise & Copper Luster Glaze, Allover Drip Glaze, Signed, 5 In. 88.00
Vase, Aqua Glaze, 6 1/4 In. 140.00
Vase, Blue To Green-Gray, Signed, 7 In. 95.00
Vase, Cylinder, Green, 12 In. .... .100.00 to 125.00
Vessel, Light Matte Green, Gunmetal Glaze, Squat, 5 1/2 x 7 1/2 In. 275.00

SHEET MUSIC from the past centuries is now collected. The favorites are examples with covers featuring artistic or historic pictures. Early sheet music covers were lithographed, but by the 1900s photographic reproductions were used. The early music was larger than more recent sheets, and you must watch out for examples that were trimmed to fit in a twentieth-century piano bench.

A Love Like This, For Whom The Bell Tolls, Gary Cooper, Ingrid Bergman, 1943	25.00
A Man Chases A Girl, There's No Business Like Show Business, M. Monroe, 1948	18.00
A Song Is Born, Danny Kaye, 1932	27.00
A Warming Up In Dixie, E.T. Paull, 1899	30.00
Alone, Marx Brothers, Allan Jones & Kitty Carlisle, 1935	17.00
Amelia Earhart's Last Flight, Picture Of Amelia & Plane, 1939	20.00
Army Hit Kit, Graphic Black On Cover	15.00
As Time Goes By, Casablanca, Humphrey Bogart, Ingrid Bergman, 1931	36.00
At Mail Call Today, Gene Autry, Showing Sgt. Autry In Uniform On Cover, 1945	18.00
At The Baby Parade	50.00
Battleship Oregon, Black, White	45.00
Bewitched, Television Show, 1964	35.00
Blue Monday, Jayne Mansfield, Domino, Ewell	15.00
Blue Moon, With A Song In My Heart, Susan Hayward, Rory Calhoun, 1934	15.00
Born To Be Kissed, Jean Harlow & Howard Dietz, 1935	50.00
Bringing Up Father On Broadway, McManus, Cartoon Cover, 1920	50.00
Build A Little Home, Eddie Cantor, Roman Scandals On Cover, 1933	8.00
But Beautiful, Bob Hope, Bing Crosby, Dorothy Lamour On Mule On Cover, 1947	6.00
But Where Are You, Fred Astaire, Ginger Rogers, Irving Berlin Inc., 1936	14.00
Cantina Band, Star Wars, Logo, 1977	20.00
Cry, Baby Cry, Judy Garland, 1938	33.00
Deep Water, Kate Smith	10.00
Easter Parade, Judy Garland & Fred Astaire On Cover, 1940	22.00
El Dorado, Movie, John Wayne, Robert Mitchum, 1966	40.00
Four Little Blackberries	25.00
Gracie Allen, Vote For Gracie, Campaign Song For Her Bid, 1940	15.00
Happiest Day Of My Life, Royal Wedding, Astaire, Powell & Lawford, 1951	13.00
Have Yourself A Merry Little Christmas, Meet Me In St. Louis, Garland, 1944	22.00
Hear No Evil, See No Evil, Miss Sadie Thompson, Rita Hayworth, 1953	20.00
Hit Parade Of 1941, Frances Langford	20.00
I Can't Give You Anything But Love, Judy Holiday, Broderick Crawford, 1950	20.00
I Got Rhythm, Girl Crazy, Judy Garland, Mickey Rooney, 1930	25.00
I Know A Band That Needs No Leader, Black Band	14.00
I Never Felt This Way Before, Bundle Of Joy, Debbie Reynolds, Eddie Fisher, 1956	10.00
I Wanna Be A Dancin' Man, Belle Of New York, Fred Astaire	42.00
I Want My Mammy, Eddie Cantor, 1921	20.00
I'm Forever Thinking Of You, Rolf Armstrong, 1920	15.00
Is It True What They Say About Dixie, 1936	20.00
Just As The Ship Went Down, Titanic Sinking Picture, 1912	30.00
Last Train To Clarksville, Monkees, 1966	16.00
Little Women, Katharine Hepburn, 1933	24.00
Love Me Tender, Elvis Presley, 1956	35.00
Mammy Let Me Sing & I'm Happy, Al Jolson, 1929	23.00
Memories Are Made Of This, Dean Martin, 1955	9.00
Moonlight Becomes You, Bob Hope, Bing Crosby, Dorothy Lamour On Cover	9.00
My Golden Flower, Dolly Lewis, 1941	20.00
My Old Flame, Belle Of The Nineties, Mae West, 1934	20.00
Oh Why, Oh Why, Did I Ever Leave Wyoming, Jerry Colonna, 1946	8.00
Old Black Joe, Painted Cover	20.00
Olympia Waltz, Green, Black, White	50.00
One Look At You, Broadway Serenade, Jeannette MacDonald	28.00
Our Love Affair, Strike Up The Band, J. Garland, M. Rooney, 1940	11.00
Papa's Delicate Condition, Jackie Gleason, 1962	39.00
Pasadena Rose Bowl, 1939	12.00
Peace Ship, Henry Ford, Ford At Top, 1916	125.00
Peggy Sue, Buddy Holly, 1957	25.00
People Like You & Me, Orchestra Wives, Glen Miller, 1942	20.00

Perfect Song, Theme Of Pepsodent Amos 'n Andy Hour, 1930	25.00
Political, Harry David, Ohio Governor, 1924	25.00
Quaker State Oil, Radio Shoe Theme, 1930	35.00
Second Hand Rose, My Man, Fannie Brice, 1921	28.00
Seeing's Believing, Belle Of New York, Fred Astaire	23.00
Stout-Hearted Men, New Moon, Nelson Eddy, Jeannette MacDonald, 1927	30.00
Take Me Home, Old Black Man, Cotton Pickers, 1877	35.00
The Man That Got Away, A Star Is Born, Judy Garland, 1954	16.50
Tramp, Tramp, Tramp, The Boys Are Marching, Civil War Era, 1864	65.00
Treasure Island Memories, San Francisco, 1940	16.00
Tuxedo Junction, Glen Miller	15.00
Wedding Of The Chinee & The Coon, 1897	30.00
When Teddy Roosevelt Comes Marching Home, 1910	25.00
Why Dance, Kate Smith	10.00
Without Your Love, Pick A Star, Laurel & Hardy, 1937	25.00
Yellow Rose Of Texas, Dedicated To President Franklin Roosevelt, 1936	15.00
You Say You Care, Gentlemen Prefer Blonds, M. Monroe, J. Russell, 1949	25.00

SHEFFIELD items are listed in the Silver-English and Silver Plate categories.

SHELLEY first appeared on English ceramics about 1912. The Foley China Works started in England in 1860. Joseph Ball Shelley joined the company in 1862 and became a partner in 1872. Percy Shelley joined the firm in 1881. The company went through a series of name changes, and in 1910 the then Foley China Company became Shelley China. In 1929 it became Shelley Potteries. The company was acquired in 1966 by Allied English Potteries, then merged with the Doulton group in 1971. The name *Shelley* was put into use again in 1980. A trio is the name for a cup, saucer, and cake plate set.

Ashtray, Blue Rock	55.00
Ashtray, Melody, Chintz, 4 1/2 In.	150.00
Ashtray & Cigarette Holder Set, Rosebud, Dainty	68.00
Berry Bowl, Blue Rock, Dainty, 5 1/2 In.	50.00
Bouillon, Underplate, 2 Handles, Harebell, Oleander	95.00
Bouillon, Underplate, Georgian, Gainsborough	68.00
Bowl, Blue Rock, Blue Trim, 6 1/2 In.	55.00
Bowl, Cereal, Harebell, Oleander, 6 1/4 In.	45.00
Bowl, Harmony Ware, Orange & Yellow, c.1939, 8 1/2 In.	295.00
Bowl, Melody, Chintz, Green Trim, Square, 6 1/2 In.	115.00
Breakfast Set, Blue Rock, 10 Piece	345.00
Butter, Cover, Maytime, Green Trim, Chintz, 5 1/2 x 7 x 3 In.	295.00
Cake Plate, Blue Rock, Blue Trim, 8 In.	125.00
Cake Plate, Green Trim, Handles, 1933, 8 In.	150.00
Cake Plate, Harmony Ware, Blue, Gray & White Swirls, Pedestal, 1920s, 8 In.	120.00
Cake Plate, Orange, Dainty, Tab Handle	195.00
Cake Plate, Posie Spray, Green Trim, c.1936, 8 1/4 x 9 3/4 In.	125.00
Cake Plate, Syringe, Tab Handles, Regent, 1932, 8 x 9 1/2 In.	140.00
Coffeepot, Blue Rock, Individual	200.00
Coffeepot, Bridal Rose	350.00
Coffeepot, Flashes & Flowers, Queen Anne, 1929, 7 In.	375.00
Coffeepot, Harebell, 6 Cup	350.00
Coffeepot, Melody, Blue Trim	425.00
Coffeepot, Melody, Chintz, Henley, 7 In.	575.00
Coffeepot, Pink, Dainty, Demitasse	160.00
Coffeepot, Rose Pansy	245.00
Coffeepot, Sheraton, Gainsborough, Red Trim, 6 Cup	545.00
Condiment Set, Melody, Salt, Pepper & Mustard, Tray	350.00
Creamer, Blue, Daisy	45.00
Creamer & Sugar, Maytime	160.00
Creamer For One, Blue Rock	48.00
Creamer For Two, Stocks	65.00
Creamer For Two, Violets	65.00
Cup, Primrose	28.00

Cup, Violets 25.00
Cup, Woodland 25.00
Cup & Saucer, Begonia, Dainty ....68.00 to 95.00
Cup & Saucer, Blue Daisy, Oleander ....65.00 to 95.00
Cup & Saucer, Blue Poppy, Dainty 68.00
Cup & Saucer, Blue Rock, Dainty, Demitasse 68.00
Cup & Saucer, Blue Rock, Fluted 58.00
Cup & Saucer, Blue Spray, Demitasse 50.00
Cup & Saucer, Blue Spray, Henley, Blue Trim 75.00
Cup & Saucer, Blue Trim, Demitasse 58.00
Cup & Saucer, Briar Rose 125.00
Cup & Saucer, Celandine, Dainty 65.00
Cup & Saucer, Charm, Henley 70.00
Cup & Saucer, Chelsea 95.00
Cup & Saucer, Chintz ....85.00 to 150.00
Cup & Saucer, Crochet, 1940s ....50.00 to 52.00
Cup & Saucer, Daffodil Time 55.00
Cup & Saucer, Damsons, Queen Anne, 1938 .... 185.00
Cup & Saucer, Drifting Leaves 47.00
Cup & Saucer, Floral, Blue Trim 70.00
Cup & Saucer, Green, Daisy 125.00
Cup & Saucer, Green, Daisy, Chintz 95.00
Cup & Saucer, Harebell 62.00
Cup & Saucer, Heather 55.00
Cup & Saucer, Mauve, Dainty ....125.00 to 150.00
Cup & Saucer, Maytime, Demitasse 115.00
Cup & Saucer, Melody ....95.00 to 125.00
Cup & Saucer, Morning Glory, Dainty 70.00
Cup & Saucer, Old Mill ....40.00 to 58.00
Cup & Saucer, Pink, Dainty, Demitasse 125.00
Cup & Saucer, Plate, Melody, 8 In 125.00
Cup & Saucer, Polkadot 70.00
Cup & Saucer, Regency, Dainty 60.00
Cup & Saucer, Regency, Gold Handle, Demitasse 48.00
Cup & Saucer, Rock Garden, Chintz ....85.00 to 125.00
Cup & Saucer, Rock Garden, Oleander 150.00
Cup & Saucer, Rose & Pansy, Forget-Me-Nots, Blue Trim 68.00
Cup & Saucer, Rose Bud, Dainty, Demitasse ....50.00 to 70.00
Cup & Saucer, Rose Spray ....65.00 to 155.00
Cup & Saucer, Rose, Pansy, Forget-Me-Not, Dainty, Blue Trim 68.00
Cup & Saucer, Rosebud ....49.00 to 62.00
Cup & Saucer, Rosebud, Dainty, Rosebud Handle 225.00
Cup & Saucer, Sheraton, Gainsborough, Pink, Gold Trim 85.00
Cup & Saucer, Small Red Roses, Dainty, Green Trim 68.00
Cup & Saucer, Stocks 65.00
Cup & Saucer, Stocks, Demitasse 50.00
Cup & Saucer, Summer Glory, Yellow ....70.00 to 150.00
Cup & Saucer, Violet 165.00
Cup & Saucer, Vogue, Triangular Handle 250.00
Cup & Saucer, White, Dainty, Gold Trim, Gold Handle, Demitasse 48.00
Cup & Saucer, Wild Anemone 65.00
Cup & Saucer, Wild Flowers, Demitasse 50.00
Cup & Saucer, Woodland 62.00
Cup & Saucer, Woodland, Demitasse 70.00
Dish, Pancake, Cover, Blue Rock, 6 In. 200.00
Eggcup, Blue Rock 50.00
Eggcup, Bridal Rose 50.00
Eggcup, Rambler Rose, Double 54.00
Eggcup, Underplate, Duck 125.00
Eggcup, White, Dainty, Double 45.00
Figurine, Bride & Groom, Mabel Lucie Attwell, 6 1/2 In., Pair 1000.00
Gravy Boat, Regency, 32 Piece 1450.00
Honey Pot, Old Foley, 3 In. 75.00

Jam Jar, Chintz	50.00
Jam Pot, Rosebud	125.00
Loving Cup, Bermuda, 350th Celebration, Blue Clipper Ship, 1959, 7 In.	200.00
Luncheon Set, Phlox, Regent, 1933, 10-In. Tray, 7 Piece	425.00
Mug, Mabel Lucie Atwell	195.00
Nut Dish, Oval, Pink, Dainty, 5 1/2 x 4 In.	75.00
Nut Dish, Pink Center Flower, Yellow Flower Around Border, Blue Trim	59.00
Nut Dish, Pink Flower, Yellow Flowers Border, Scalloped	60.00
Nut Dish, Roses, Violets, Pansies, Double Handle, Pink Trim	58.00
Plate, Black Trees, Square, 1926, 6 1/4 In.	48.00
Plate, Blue Rock, Blue Trim, 8 In.	65.00
Plate, Blue Rock, Dainty, 8 In.	60.00
Plate, Chintz, 8 In.	125.00
Plate, Crochet, Gold Trim, 7 In.	48.00
Plate, Dessert, Blue, Dainty	60.00
Plate, Floral Center, Cobalt Rim, Gold, 10 1/2 In.	95.00
Plate, Hand Painted, Pink & Gold Design, Roses, Dainty, 6 In.	48.00
Plate, Harebell, Oleander, 6 In.	40.00
Plate, Harebell, Oleander, 11 In.	110.00
Plate, Maytime, Gold Trim, Chintz, 8 In.	88.00
Plate, Melody, 8 In.	125.00
Plate, Old Sevres, Chelsea Bird Center, 1914, 8 In.	95.00
Plate, Ovington, 8 In.	70.00
Plate, Pink Rose, Dainty, Gold Design, 6 In.	48.00
Plate, Primrose, Dessert	55.00
Plate, Rock Garden, 7 In.	75.00 to 85.00
Plate, Rock Garden, 8 In.	95.00 to 125.00
Plate, Rose Spray, 8 In.	80.00
Plate, Rosebud, 6 1/2 In.	32.00
Plate, Rosebud, Dainty, Green Trim, 7 1/4 In.	60.00
Plate, Rosebud, Dainty, Green Trim, 11 In.	115.00
Plate, Rosebud, Green Trim, 8 In.	60.00
Plate, Sheraton, Pink, 11 In.	110.00
Plate, Summer Glory, 8 In.	35.00
Platter, Blue Trim, 13 In.	250.00
Salt & Pepper, Maytime	160.00
Sandwich Plate, Fruit, Tab Handles, Queen Anne, 1927, 8 In.	85.00
Sandwich Plate, Melody, Chintz, Tab Handles, 8 1/4 In.	185.00
Saucer, Blue Rock	10.00
Saucer, Blue, Dainty	20.00 to 28.00
Saucer, Rosebud	18.00
Snack Set, Bridal Rose, Cup & Plate	125.00
Soup, Dish, Blue Rock, Blue Trim, 8 In.	65.00
Sugar, Creamer & Tray, Blue, Dainty	150.00
Sugar, Creamer, Tray, Regency	145.00
Sugar, Pink Polkadot	48.00
Sugar & Creamer, Blue	55.00
Sugar & Creamer, Blue Poppy, Dainty	95.00
Sugar & Creamer, Blue Rock	65.00
Sugar & Creamer, Blue, Dainty	115.00
Sugar & Creamer, Bridal Rose, Small	110.00
Sugar & Creamer, Crochet, Gold Trim, 3 1/2 In.	150.00
Sugar & Creamer, Daisy, Green	95.00
Sugar & Creamer, Forget-Me-Not	60.00
Sugar & Creamer, Mauve	125.00
Sugar & Creamer, Meissenette, Dainty	120.00
Sugar & Creamer, Pansy, Tray	175.00
Sugar & Creamer, Pink, Dainty, Demitasse	95.00
Sugar & Creamer, Poppy, Vincent, 1924, 2 1/2 In.	130.00
Sugar & Creamer, Primrose	85.00
Sugar & Creamer, Rosebud	85.00
Sugar & Creamer, Tiger Lily, Yellow, Royal Winton	125.00
Tea Set, Duchess, Green, Gainsborough, 1945, 21 Piece	1025.00

Tea Set, Pink, Queen Anne, Black, 10 Piece 1200.00
Teapot, Bridal Rose . . . . 195.00 to 375.00
Teapot, Gray, Dainty 450.00
Teapot, Melody 500.00
Teapot, Rose Pansy 240.00
Toothpick, Begonia 38.00
Toothpick, Bramble 45.00
Tray, Bramble, Dainty, Blue Trim, Oval, 5 1/2 x 9 In. 85.00
Tray, Regency, Dainty, Gold Trim, 5 1/2 x 9 In. 65.00
Tray, Sandwich, Begonia, 5 x 14 In. 150.00
Trio, Blue Daisy, Chintz, Henley, 8-In. Plate 185.00
Trio, Daisy, Queen Anne, 1926, 6 1/4-In. Plate 225.00
Trio, Harebell, Gold Trim, Ripon, 8-In. Plate 145.00
Trio, Hydrangea, Dainty, 6 1/4-In. Plate 150.00
Trio, Phlox, Regent, Bright Green Trim & Handle, 1933 . . . . 145.00
Trio, Regency, Dainty, White, Gold Trim 110.00
Trio, Sunrise & Trees, Queen Anne, 1929, 6 1/4-In. Plate 225.00
Vase, Bud, Marina, Lord Nelson 165.00
Vase, Storks, Red, 1912, 3 5/8 In. 95.00
Vase, Swirl Design, Yellow, Orange, Purple Green, Blue, Black Ground, 5 In. 105.00

SHIRLEY TEMPLE, the famous movie star, was born in 1928. She made
her first movie in 1932. Thousands of items picturing Shirley have
been and still are being made. Shirley Temple dolls were first made in
1934 by Ideal Toy Company. Millions of Shirley Temple cobalt blue
glass dishes were made by Hazel Atlas Glass Company and U.S. Glass
Company from 1934 to 1942. They were given away as premiums for
Wheaties and Bisquick. A bowl, mug, and pitcher were made as a
breakfast set. Some pieces were decorated with the picture of a very
young Shirley, others used a picture of Shirley in her 1936 *Captain
January* costume. Although collectors refer to a cobalt creamer, it is
actually the 4 1/2-inch-high milk pitcher from the breakfast set. Many
of these items are being reproduced today.

Ad, Full Page, Lane Cedar Chest, 1964 . . . . 10.00
Bank, Cast Iron 195.00
Book, About Me, Box, 5 Piece 185.00
Book, Poor Little Rich Girl 25.00
Book, Shirley Temple & The Spirit Of Dragonwood, Whitman 22.00
Book, Storytime Favorites, Shirley Photograph On Cover, 1960 . . . . 15.00
Book, The Little Colonel, 1938 . . . . 10.00
Bowl, Cereal, Cobalt Blue 15.00
Box, Trinket, Cover 15.00
Cards, Bridge, Unopened 135.00
Carriage, Doll, Porcelain Face On Sides, Wicker, Shirley Hubcaps 950.00
Chair, The Little Princess, 1939 . . . . 3737.00
Coin, Storybook NBC TV, 1938, 1 1/4 In. 78.00
Doll, Character, Composition, Ideal, 1930s, 17 In. 220.00
Doll, Composition Head, Tin Sleep Eyes, 6 Upper Teeth, Ideal, 11 In. 750.00
Doll, Composition, 1930s, 13 In. 515.00
Doll, Composition, Flirty Eyes, Open Mouth, 27 In. 1450.00
Doll, Flirty Eyes, Dress, Vinyl, 1950s, 17 In. 138.00
Doll, Flirty Eyes, Organdy Dress, 27 In. 950.00
Doll, Ideal, Composition, 1934, 22 In. 220.00
Doll, Ideal, Composition, Mohair Wig, 1936, 18 In. 145.00
Doll, Ideal, Composition, Mohair Wig, Box, 20 In. . . . . *Illus* 2000.00
Doll, Ideal, Composition, Sleep Eyes, 5 Teeth, Tag, Collector's Pen, 1934, 11 In. 550.00
Doll, Ideal, Flirty Sleep Eyes, Mohair Wig, 1930s, 24 In. 204.00
Doll, Ideal, Plastic, Original Box, 17 In. 352.00
Doll, Ideal, Red Polka Dot Dress, Red Shoes 185.00
Doll, Ideal, Vinyl, Plastic, Collector's Pen, c.1957, 17 In. 88.00
Doll, Ideal, Wee Willie Winkie, Sleep Eyes, 1957, Box, 12 In. . . . . *Illus* 600.00
Doll, Original Clothes, 1985, 34 In. 250.00
Doll, Vinyl, Box, Unused, 1973 . . . . 65.00

Shirley Temple,
Doll, Ideal,
Composition,
Mohair Wig,
Box, 20 In.

Shirley Temple, Doll, Ideal, Wee Willie
Winkie, Sleep Eyes, 1957, Box, 12 In.

Figurine, Capt. January, Shirley Dancing, Shirley Wearing Sailor Outfit	55.00
Figurine, Cat At Base, Salt Glaze, 5 In.	80.00
Fountain Pen, 1935	75.00
Hanger, Clothes, Blue Cardboard	65.00
Magazine, Look, Shirley Temple With Santa Claus, Dec. 21, 1937	40.00
Magazine, Photoplay, Shirley Temple Cover, June, 1937	35.00
Magazine, Screenland, Shirley On Cover, 1936	45.00
Paper Doll, 5 Outfits, 1930s	125.00
Paper Doll, Dolls & Dresses, Saalfield, 1937, Uncut	220.00
Paper Doll, Whitman, 1976, Uncut	15.00
Photograph, Black & White, 8 x 10 In.	40.00
Photograph, Shirley, Envelope, Theater Give Away, 1930s, 8 x 10 In.	15.00
Pitcher, Cobalt Blue	35.00 to 40.00
Playhouse	75.00
Postcard, Each Different, 5 Piece	4.00
Record, Shirley Temple 19 Songs, Fox, 1950s	36.00
Sheet Music, Animal Crackers In My Soup	18.00
Sheet Music, Come & Get Your Happiness, Rebecca, Sunny Brook Farm, 1938	27.00
Sheet Music, Dimples	20.00
Sheet Music, Good Ship Fair	15.00
Sheet Music, Goodnight My Love, 1936	25.00
Sheet Music, On The Good Ship Lollipop, Bright Eyes, 1934	18.00 to 22.00
Tablet, School, Ruled Paper, Color Photo On Cover, 5 1/2 x 9 In.	35.00
Watch, Pocket	200.00

SHRINER, see Fraternal category.

SILVER DEPOSIT glass was first made during the late nineteenth century. Solid sterling silver is applied to the glass by a chemical method so that a cutout design of silver metal appears against a clear or colored glass. It is sometimes called silver overlay.

Bottle, Gin, Arts & Crafts, 10 In.	95.00
Bowl, Floral Design, 12 1/2 In.	105.00
Bowl, Flowers, 3 Sections, 9 3/4 In.	50.00
Bowl, Roses, Ruffled, 13 In.	50.00
Cocktail Set, Diamond Lattice & Scrolls	80.00
Decanter, Floral Etched Panels & Stopper, German Silver, 9 3/4 In.	357.00
Decanter, Scrolled Openwork Foliate Design, c.1900, 12 In., Pair	2070.00
Decanter, Stopper, Scrolling Design, Monogrammed FGS, 7 1/2 In.	425.00
Decanter, Wreath & Thistle Design, Orange Lawn Tennis Club Horse Show, 1926	585.00
Flask, Scrolled Foliate, Cap Foot, Alvin, 1900, 5 1/2 In.	290.00
Perfume Bottle, Melon Ribs, Steeple Stopper, 7 1/2 In.	275.00
Plate, Wreaths, Bows, Garland Design, 6 3/4 In.	11.00
Plate Set, Black Glass, 4 Piece	68.00

Vase, Acid Cut To Form Poppies, Green, Square, 4 5/8 In. 44.00
Vase, Emerald Green, Scrolled Foliage, 1900, 16 In. 1093.00
Vase, Monogram On Neck, Ruffled, 10 1/2 In. 175.00
Vase, Oriental Scene, Rockwell, 14 1/2 In. 500.00
Wine Set, Blown Orvieto, Purple, 5 Piece 110.00

SILVER FLATWARE includes many of the current and out-of-production
silver and silver-plated flatware patterns made in the past eighty years.
Other silver is listed under Silver-American, Silver-English, etc. Most
silver flatware sets that are missing a few pieces can be completed
through the help of one of the silver matching services that advertise
in many of the national publications.

SILVER FLATWARE PLATED, Ambassador, Tureen Ladle, Rogers, c.1919 .... 65.00
  Arcadian, Crumber, Rogers 49.00
  Berkshire, Berry Spoon, 1847 Rogers 25.00
  Christopher Wren, Tea Set, Tray, Wallace, 6 Piece 4750.00
  Columbia, Tomato Server, Rogers 64.00
  Gardenia, Rogers, 78 Piece 120.00
  Grape, Dinner Knife, Solid Handle, French Blade, Rogers, 1910, 6 Piece 100.00
  Heritage, Pastry Spoon, International 18.00
  LaVigne, Bouillon Spoon, Rogers 13.00
  Lily Of The Valley, Berry Spoon, Case, Set Of 4 .... 110.00
  Little Miss Muffet, Fork, Child's 13.00
  Mayflower, Sugar Tongs, Claw, Rogers, 1912 .... 28.00
  Vintage, Salad Fork, Rogers 35.00
SILVER FLATWARE STERLING, Acorn, Salad Set, Georg Jensen 695.00
  Acorn, Salt Serving Set, Raised Fruit, Gold Wash, Jensen 695.00
  Adam, Carving Knife & Fork, Whiting 50.00
  Adam, Cheese Scoop, Whiting 125.00
  Adam, Cold Meat Fork, Whiting 75.00
  Altair, Butter Knife, Master, Watson Newell 45.00
  Altair, Ice Cream Spoon, Watson Newell 145.00
  American Beauty, Bonbon, Shiebler 70.00
  American Beauty, Sardine Fork, Shiebler 60.00
  American Beauty, Sugar Tongs, Shiebler, 5 1/4 In. 70.00
  American Classic, Ladle, Shreve, Crump & Low, 7 In. 240.00
  American Classic, Sugar Spoon, Easterling 12.00
  American Classic, Teaspoon, Easterling 9.00
  Ancestry, Cake Server, Weidlich 24.00
  Ancestry, Can Opener, Bar, Weidlich 16.00
  Andante, Sugar Shell, Gorham 26.00
  Angelique, Iced Tea Spoon, International 24.00
  Angelique, Pasta Scoop, International 30.00
  Angelique, Salad Fork, International 28.00
  Angelique, Sugar Tongs, International 28.00
  Antique, Dinner Fork, Gorham 34.00
  Arlington, Sardine Fork, Towle 50.00
  Aspen, Place Setting, Gorham, 4 Piece 52.00
  Autumn Leaves, Sugar Spoon, Reed & Barton 17.00
  Awakening, Gravy Ladle, Towle 48.00
  Awakening, Luncheon Knife, Towle 22.00
  Baltimore Rose, Bonbon Spoon, Schofield 40.00
  Baltimore Rose, Fork, Monogram, Schofield 85.00
  Baltimore Rose, Luncheon Fork, Schofield 24.00
  Baltimore Rose, Pastry Fork, Schofield, Monogram 50.00
  Basket Of Flowers, Sugar Shell, Dominick & Haff 55.00
  Bead, Teaspoon, Whiting 12.00
  Betsy Patterson, Salad Fork, Stieff, 8 Piece 200.00
  Bridal Bouquet, Cold Meat Fork, Alvin 30.00
  Bridal Rose, Preserve Spoon, Alvin 85.00
  Bridal Rose, Salad Set, Alvin, 9 1/8 In. 550.00
  Bridal Veil, Place Setting, International, 4 Piece 56.00
  Buttercup, Butter Pick, Gorham, 5 7/8 In. 45.00

Buttercup, Fish Fork, Gorham 48.00
Buttercup, Fish Slice, Gorham 250.00
Buttercup, Ice Cream Spoon, Gorham, 12 Piece 352.00
Buttercup, Jelly Server, Gorham 35.00
Buttercup, Knife, Gorham, 9 5/8 In. 26.00
Buttercup, Oyster Ladle, Gorham, 12 In. 275.00
Buttercup, Place Knife, Gorham 28.00
Buttercup, Punch Ladle, Gorham 395.00
Buttercup, Salad Fork, Gorham 28.00
Buttercup, Stuffing Spoon, Gorham 295.00
Cambridge, Dessert Spoon, Gorham 20.00
Cambridge, Punch Ladle, Gorham 425.00
Camellia, Butter Knife, Gorham, Individual 9.00
Candlelight, Poultry Shears, Towle 95.00
Canterbury, Cucumber Server, Towle 185.00
Canterbury, Olive Fork, Towle 55.00
Canterbury, Seafood Fork, Towle 20.00
Carnation, Sugar Tongs, Wallace 35.00
Chantilly, Lettuce Fork & Spoon, Gorham 125.00
Chantilly, Luncheon Knife, Gorham 22.00
Chantilly, Sauce Ladle, Gorham 35.00
Chapel Bells, Cocktail Fork, Alvin 12.00
Chateau Rose, Dinner Set, Alvin, 74 Piece 950.00
Chateau Rose, Luncheon Fork, Alvin 25.00
Chateau Rose, Teaspoon, Alvin 17.00
Chrysanthemum, Cold Meat Fork, Durgin, 9 1/8 In. 275.00
Chrysanthemum, Fish Knife, Tiffany 185.00
Chrysanthemum, Jelly Server, Durgin 175.00
Chrysanthemum, Preserve Spoon, Durgin, 9 1/8 In. 300.00
Chrysanthemum, Teaspoon, Monogram, Tiffany, 1880, 2 Troy Oz. 80.00
Chrysanthemum, Tomato Server, Tiffany 425.00
Classic Rose, Gravy Ladle, Reed & Barton 49.00
Clermont, Lettuce Fork, Gorham 75.00
Cluny, Butter Knife, Master, Gorham 225.00
Cluny, Soup Ladle, Gorham 795.00
Coligni, Teaspoon, Gorham, 7 Piece 110.00
Colonial, Cheese Knife, With Picks, Gorham 95.00
Commonwealth, Ice Cream Fork, Watson, 12 Piece 154.00
Corinthian, Cream Ladle, Gorham 155.00
Corsage, Bonbon Spoon, Stieff 45.00
Cottage, Dessert Spoon, Gorham 28.00
Courtship, Salad Fork, International 21.00
Craftsman, Potato Server, Towle 28.00
Crown Princess, Potato Server, International 27.00
Cynthia, Potato Server, Kirk 27.00
Damask Rose, Citrus Spoon, Oneida 18.00
Damask Rose, Potato Server, Oneida 28.00
Dancing Surf, Fish Knife, Kirk 15.00
Dauphine, Bouillon Spoon, Wallace 13.00
Dawn Mist, Carving Set, Wallace 22.00
Dawn Mist, Olive Fork, Wallace 13.00
Dawn Mist, Serving Spoon, Pierced, Wallace 31.00
Dawn Rose, Place Setting, International, 4 Piece 68.00
Dawn Star, Fork, Wallace, 7 1/8 In. 13.00
Dawn Star, Gravy Ladle, Wallace 24.00
Debutante, Carving Set, Richard Dimes 23.00
Debutante, Cold Meat Fork, Richard Dimes 41.00
Decor, Teaspoon, Gorham 20.00
Deerfield, Cocktail Fork, International 10.00
Deerfield, Cold Meat Fork, International 42.00
Deerfield, Potato Serving Fork, International 32.00
Della Robbia, Ice Cream Fork, Alvin 17.00
Della Robbia, Potato Serving Fork, Alvin 27.00

Della Robbia, Steak Carving Set, Alvin 41.00
Della Robbia, Sugar Spoon, Alvin 18.00
Dorothy Vernon, Fish Fork, Whiting 60.00
Dresden, Teaspoon, Dated In Bowl, Easter 1896, Whiting 25.00
Du Roi, Soup Spoon, Oval, Cartier 25.00
DuBarry, Soup Spoon, International, 12 Piece 292.00
Duke Of York, Place Fork, Whiting 21.00
Duke Of York, Teaspoon, Whiting 15.00
Egyptian, Cream Ladle, Gorham 350.00
Egyptian, Serving Spoon, Whiting 175.00
El Grandee, Sugar Spoon, Towle 29.00
English Gadroon, Luncheon Fork, Gorham 20.00
English Gadroon, Teaspoon, Gorham 13.00
English King, Cold Meat Fork, 8 5/8 In. 205.00
English King, Sugar Sifter, Tiffany, 7 In. 295.00
English Provincial, Cocktail Fork, Reed & Barton 11.00
English Provincial, Gravy Ladle, Reed & Barton 42.00
Etruscan, Bouillon Spoon, Gorham 28.00
Etruscan, Cocktail Fork, Gorham 11.00
Etruscan, Cream Soup Spoon, Gorham 34.00
Etruscan, Tablespoon, Gorham 42.00
Etruscan, Teaspoon, Gorham 11.00
Eugenie, Cheese Scoop, Watson Newell 45.00
Exeter, Dinner Fork, England, 1859, 6 Piece 350.00
Fiddle, Dessert Spoon, England, 1818-1824 .... 60.00
Fiddle Thread, Pie Server, Engraved Blade, Ball & Black 425.00
Fiorito, Seafood Fork, Shiebler 35.00
Flora, Olive Fork, Shiebler 85.00
Flora, Teaspoon, Shiebler 60.00
Fontainebleau, Gravy Ladle, Gorham 155.00
Fontainebleau, Salad Serving Fork, Gorham, 10 3/8 In. 350.00
Fontainebleau, Sugar Tongs, Gorham ....135.00 to 150.00
Francis I, Cream Soup Spoon, Reed & Barton 65.00
Francis I, Dinner Knife, Reed & Barton 50.00
Francis I, Grapefruit Spoon, Reed & Barton 60.00
French Antique, Baby Fork, Cartier 11.00
Gainsborough, Place Setting, Alvin, 4 Piece 60.00
Georgian, Asparagus Server, Hooded, Towle, 9 3/4 In. 900.00
Georgian, Tomato Server, Towle 155.00
Grand Baroque, Asparagus Server, Wallace 295.00
Grecian, Pudding Spoon, Gorham 350.00
Greenbrier, Fork, Gorham, 7 1/4 In. 14.00
Greenbrier, Soup Spoon, Gorham 16.00
Heiress, Cocktail Fork, Oneida 14.00
Hepplewhite, Asparagus Fork, Reed & Barton 245.00
Hepplewhite, Ice Cream Fork, Monogram, Reed & Barton 132.00
Honeysuckle, Mustard Ladle, Whiting 95.00
Honeysuckle, Sugar Tongs, Whiting, 5 1/2 In. 75.00
Horizon, Place Setting, Easterling, 4 Piece 52.00
Imperial Chrysanthemum, Fish Serving Fork, Gorham, 8 1/2 In. 250.00
Imperial Chrysanthemum, Pastry Fork, Gorham 65.00
Imperial Chrysanthemum, Teaspoon, Gorham, 6 Piece 120.00
Imperial Queen, Asparagus Server, Whiting 395.00
Intaglio, Claret Ladle, Reed & Barton 225.00
Irian, Berry Spoon, Wallace, 9 5/8 In. 275.00
Iris, Cream Ladle, Gorham 350.00
Iris, Serving Spoon, Gorham, 1871, 4 Oz. 546.00
Ivy, Youth Set, Case, 3 Piece 225.00
Kenilworth, Master Butter, International 45.00
Kensington, Ice Cream Spoon, Gorham 38.00
Keystone, Pickle Fork, Whiting 25.00
King, Berry Spoon, England, Pair 460.00
King Christian, Teaspoon, Wallace, 11 Piece 77.00

King Edward, Butter Knife, Gorham 15.00
King Edward, Salad Fork, Gorham 24.00
King George, Ice Cream Fork, Gorham 55.00
King George, Pea Spoon, Gorham 350.00
King George, Pie Server, Gorham 275.00
King George, Stuffing Spoon, Gorham 495.00
King's, Tablespoon, Geo. Adams, 1840 .... 125.00
La Parisienne, Cold Meat Fork, Reed & Barton 195.00
Lady Mary, Baked Potato Server, Watson 19.00
Lady Mary, Cocktail Fork, Watson 9.00
Lady Mary, Cold Meat Fork, Watson, 7 3/4 In. 27.00
Lady Mary, Cream Soup Spoon, Watson 12.00
Lancaster, Cucumber Server, Gorham 75.00
Lancaster, Fried Oyster Server, Gorham, 8 1/4 In. 250.00
Lancaster, Teaspoon, Gorham, 6 3/4 In. 6.00
Larkspur, Cream Soup Spoon, Wallace 8.00
Lasting Spring, Serving Spoon, Oneida 18.00
Lasting Spring, Teaspoon, Oneida, 5 7/8 In. 6.00
Lenox, Butter, Master, Gorham 12.00
Leonore, Bread Knife, Manchester 14.00
Leonore, Fruit Knife, Manchester 7.00
Leonore, Gumbo Spoon, Manchester 14.00
Les Cinq Fleurs, Salad Server, Reed & Barton, 12 Oz., Pair 345.00
Les Six Fleurs, Serving Fork & Spoon, Fluted, Reed & Barton 295.00
Lexington, Baked Potato Server, Dominick & Haff 16.00
Lexington, Bouillon Spoon, Dominick & Haff 6.00
Lily, Pickle Fork, Whiting 65.00
Lily, Pie Server, Watson 325.00
Lily, Salad Set, Watson Newell 400.00
Lily Of The Valley, Ladle, Double Lip, Georg Jensen 250.00
Litchfield, Dessert Spoon, International 9.00
Lorna Doone, Bouillon Spoon, Alvin 6.00
Lorna Doone, Citrus Spoon, Alvin 9.00
Lorna Doone, Sugar Spoon, Alvin 7.00
Lotus, Chipped Ice Tongs, Watson Newell 75.00
Lotus, Cream Soup Spoon, Watson Newell 35.00
Louis XIV, Teaspoon, Towle, 5 3/4 In. 8.00
Louis XV, Soup Ladle, Gorham 209.00
Louvre, Cold Meat Fork, Wallace 65.00
Louvre, Fruit Spoon, Wallace 17.00
Lucerne, Sugar Spoon, Wallace 35.00
Lyric, Sugar Spoon, Gorham 12.00
Madeira, Sugar Spoon, Towle 9.00
Mademoiselle, Baked Potato Server, International 18.00
Madison, Serving Spoon, Pierced, Wallace 18.00
Madison, Serving Spoon, Wallace 16.00
Majestic, Dessert Spoon, Alvin 15.00
Margaret Rose, Baked Potato Server, National 15.00
Margaret Rose, Cream Soup Spoon, National 7.00
Margaret Rose, Dinner Fork, National, 8 7/8 In. 8.00
Marguerite, Berry Spoon, Gorham 100.00
Marguerite, Cucumber Server, Gorham 65.00
Marguerite, Lettuce Fork, Gorham 78.00
Marguerite, Olive Spoon, Gorham 40.00
Marie Antoinette, Butter Knife, Alvin 9.00
Marie Louise, Iced Tea Spoon, Blackington 19.00
Mayflower, Egg Spoon, Kirk 65.00
Meadow Rose, Luncheon Fork, Watson Newell 35.00
Medallion, Gravy Ladle, Gorham, 8 In. 300.00
Medallion, Mustard Ladle, Gorham 135.00
Medallion, Sifter Ladle, Wood & Hughes 225.00
Medallion, Teaspoon, S.D. Brower 75.00
Melrose, Butter Knife, Gorham 14.00

Miss Alvin, Place Setting, Alvin, 4 Piece	52.00
Monterey, Pea Spoon, Alvin	275.00
Monticello, Baby Fork, Rogers, Lunt & Bowlen	45.00
Monticello, Bouillon Ladle, Rogers, Lunt & Bowlen	225.00
Morning Glory, Jelly Cake Server, Alvin	250.00
Morning Glory, Pea Spoon, Alvin, 8 5/8 In.	350.00
Mythologique, Stuffing Spoon, Gorham	495.00
Newport Scroll, Cheese Cleaver, Gorham	18.00
Newport Scroll, Lasagna Server, Gorham	21.00
Newport Shell, Cheese Scoop, Frank Smith	85.00
Newport Shell, Cold Meat Fork, Frank Smith	95.00
Newport Shell, Horseradish Spoon, Frank Smith	55.00
Old Baronial, Butter Knife, Gorham	13.00
Old Baronial, Citrus Spoon, Gorham	44.00
Old Baronial, Ice Cream Spoon, Gorham	50.00
Old Colonial, Lettuce Spoon, Towle	175.00
Old English, Cheese Scoop, Towle	95.00
Old English, Jelly Knife, Towle	100.00
Old French, Fork, Gorham, 7 In.	18.00
Old Master, Gravy Ladle, Towle	59.00
Old Medici, Gravy Ladle, Gorham	165.00
Old Medici, Tablespoon, Gorham	58.00
Old Newbury, Demitasse Spoon, Towle	20.00 to 22.00
Old Newbury, Dinner Fork, Towle	37.00
Old Newbury, Fish Fork, Individual, Towle	35.00 to 59.00
Old Newbury, Soup Spoon, Towle, 7 1/8 In.	33.00 to 39.00
Old Newbury, Sugar Spoon, Towle, 5 1/2 In.	27.00
Old Newbury, Teaspoon, Towle	22.00
Olympian, Ice Cream Spoon, Tiffany	85.00
Olympian, Punch Ladle, Monogram, Tiffany, 9 Oz.	863.00
Onslow, Salad Fork, Tuttle	43.00
Orange Blossom, Asparagus Server, Alvin	485.00
Orange Blossom, Carving Set, Alvin	275.00
Orange Blossom, Dessert Spoon, Alvin	55.00
Orange Blossom, Gumbo Spoon, Alvin	75.00
Orchids, Seafood Fork, Towle	30.00
Palm Beach, Cream Soup Spoon, Buccellati	24.00
Palm Beach, Fish Knife, Buccellati	30.00
Pansy, Master Butter, International	45.00
Passaic, Butter Knife, Master, Unger Brothers	150.00
Pembroke, Ladle, Gorham, 1895, Small	40.00
Phoebe, Confection Scoop, Watson Newell	110.00
Plymouth, Oyster Ladle, Gorham, 13 In.	250.00
Poppy, Fork, Gorham, 6 7/8 In.	13.00
Princess Ingrid, Carving Fork, Stainless Prongs, Whiting	54.00
Princess Ingrid, Fork, Whiting, 7 1/8 In.	45.00
Princess Ingrid, Salad Fork, Individual, Whiting, 6 1/4 In.	35.00
Princess Ingrid, Soup Spoon, Round Bowl, Whiting	36.00
Princess Ingrid, Tablespoon, Whiting, 8 5/8 In.	75.00
Princess Ingrid, Teaspoon, Whiting, 6 1/8 In.	24.00
Pynchon, Sardine Fork, Lunt	40.00
Pynchon, Sugar Shell, Lunt, 1910	45.00
Radiant, Berry Spoon, Whiting	90.00
Radiant, Cold Meat Fork, Whiting	70.00
Radiant, Sugar Shaker, Whiting	65.00
Radiant, Sugar Tongs, Whiting	30.00
Raphael, Breakfast Knife, All Silver, Gorham	50.00
Renaissance, Salad Set, Dominick & Haff, 9 In.	575.00
Repousse, Bowl, Floral Motif, Gorham, 9 1/2 In.	4313.00
Repousse, Cold Meat Fork, Kirk	195.00
Richelieu, Dinner Fork, Tiffany	55.00
Rococo, Asparagus Fork, Dominick & Haff	1325.00
Rococo, Dessert Spoon, Dominick & Haff	35.00

Rococo, Mustard Ladle, Dominick & Haff	65.00
Rococo, Oyster Fork, Dominick & Haff	18.00
Rose, Berry Spoon, Stieff	119.00
Rose, Salad Set, Stieff, 2 Piece	195.00
Rose Point, Gravy Ladle, Wallace	59.00
Rose Tiara, Salad Fork, Gorham	27.00
Royal Rose, Salad Fork, Wallace	34.00
Salem, Ice Cream Fork, Rogers	8.00
Sea Sculpture, Demitasse Spoon, Gorham	21.00
Shannon, Gumbo Spoon, Dominick & Haff	16.00
Shannon, Place Setting, Dominick & Haff, 4 Piece	64.00
Southern Charm, Gravy Ladle, Alvin	31.00
Southern Charm, Place Setting, Alvin, 4 Piece	48.00
Southern Grandeur, Cold Meat Fork, Easterling	40.00
Southern Grandeur, Cream Soup Spoon, Easterling	19.00
Southern Grandeur, Salad Fork, Easterling	23.00
Spanish Provincial, Place Setting, Towle, 5 Piece	89.00
Splendor, Butter Fork, International	10.00
Splendor, Citrus Spoon, International	11.00
Splendor, Dessert Spoon, International	17.00
Spring Bouquet, Baked Potato Server, International	26.00
Spring Bouquet, English Server, International	23.00
Spring Bud, Place Setting, Alvin, 4 Piece	60.00
Stanton Hall, Butter Fork, Oneida	14.00
Stanton Hall, Cake Breaker, Oneida	23.00
Stardust, Baked Potato Server, Century	26.00
Stardust, Butter Fork, Master, Century	11.00
Sterling Beauty, Butter Fork, Weidlich	11.00
Sterling Beauty, Dinner Fork, Weidlich, 7 3/4 In.	20.00
Sterling Beauty, Gumbo Spoon, Weidlich	15.00
Stradivari, Dinner Setting, Wallace, 8 Piece	89.00
Trajan, Berry Spoon, Gold Wash Bowl, Reed & Barton, 9 3/4 In.	165.00
Trianon, Serving Spoon, Pierced Filigree, Dominick & Haff	110.00
Tulipan, Gravy Ladle, Frank Smith	55.00
Tulipan, Pickle Fork, Frank Smith	35.00
Versailles, Crumber, Gorham	385.00
Versailles, Ladle, Gorham, c.1888, 9 In.	325.00
Versailles, Tomato Server, Gorham	85.00
Viola, Berry Spoon, Wood & Hughes	110.00
Viola, Meat Fork, Splayed Tines	125.00
Violet, Ice Tongs, Wallace, 6 1/4 In.	85.00
Violet, Salad Fork, Wallace	55.00
Violet, Soup Ladle, Whiting	285.00
Watteau, Cheese Knife, Durgin	90.00
Watteau, Ice Cream Spoon, Durgin, 6 Piece	160.00
Watteau, Sugar Shell, Durgin	40.00
Waverly, Cheese Scoop, Wallace	55.00
Waverly, Ice Cream Knife, Wallace	165.00
White Paisley, Teaspoon, Gorham	16.00
Winterset, Cake Fork, Buccellati	29.00
Winterset, Cocktail Fork, Buccellati	23.00
Winthrop, Olive Spoon, Monogram, Gorham	48.00
Woodlily, Cold Meat Fork, Frank Smith	85.00
Woodlily, Dinner Fork, Frank Smith	40.00
Woodlily, Sugar Tongs, Frank Smith	40.00

SILVER PLATE is not solid silver. It is a ware made of a metal, such as nickel or copper, that is covered with a thin coating of silver. The letters *EPNS* are often found on American and English silver-plated wares. Sheffield is a term with two meanings. Sometimes it refers to sterling silver made in the town of Sheffield, England. In this section, Sheffield refers to a type of silver plate, usually English.

Asparagus Tongs, Germany	75.00

Basket, Footed, Victorian, 2 1/2 x 9 1/2 In. 27.00
Basket, Green Glass Insert, Art Deco, WMF 175.00
Basket, Sweetmeat, Embossed Hats & Flowers, Cobalt Blue, 7 1/8 In. 175.00
Basket, Victorian, Frosted, Basket Weave Design, Meriden Frame, 8 x 7 In. 192.00
Biscuit Box, Fawn Finial, Victorian, 8 1/2 In. 500.00
Bottle, Hot Water, Gilette, Dated 1915 . . . . 85.00
Bowl, Centerpiece, Glass, Oval, Floral Garland, 4 Supports, England, 12 x 6 In. 330.00
Bowl, Relief Gourd & Vine Design, Footed, WMF, 8 1/4 In. 220.00
Bowl, Rim Design, E.G. Webster & Son 17.00
Box, Document, Inside Top Gold Plated, Barbour Bros., c.1890, 3 3/4 x 17 In. 695.00
Bride's Basket, Blue Bowl, Bee In Bottom, Enameled Flowers, Wilcox, 9 3/4 In. 575.00
Butter, Cover, Revolving Lid, Lion Head, Claw Foot 50.00
Candelabrum is listed in its own category.
Candlesticks are listed in their own category.
Case, Calling Card, Floral Body, Building On Reverse, England, 3 1/2 In. 85.00
Chafing Dish, Allover Foliate, Scroll Design, Turned Wood Handle, Wallace, 12 In. 65.00
Chafing Dish, Stand With Tray, Rogers Brothers 110.00
Coaster, Wine, Sheffield, England 176.00
Coaster, Wine, Turned Wooden Bottom, Sheffield, 7 1/2 In. 100.00
Coffee & Tea Set, Stag Legs, Dog Finials, Meriden, 6 Piece 275.00
Coffee Set, Stylized Leaf & Stem Handle, Dodge, 3 Piece 55.00
Coffee Urn, Band Of Stripes On Body, Harp Form Handles, Reed & Barton, 18 In. 805.00
Coffeepot, Ebony Swing Handle, Plinth Base, England, 10 1/2 In. 115.00
Compote, Figural, Girl & Puppy, Meriden, 5 1/2 In. 45.00
Compote, Shaped Vintage Design, Engraved Crest, Late 19th Century, 13 3/8 In. 315.00
Console Set, Fisher, 10-In. Bowl, 3 Piece 110.00
Cooler, Wine, Urn Shape, Double Handled, International, 10 3/4 In. 45.00
Cruet Set, 6 Cut Glass Bottles, Stand 45.00
Cup, Wine Taster, England 95.00
Dish, Boat Shape, Art Deco, 19 In. 70.00
Dish, Lobster, Figural, Oval, 10 In. 165.00
Dish, Potato, Ruby Lined, Lion's Heads, Pierced, Sheffield, 10 In. 1700.00
Dish, Serving, Acanthus Leaf, Shell, Gadroon Borders, 10 3/8 In. 1610.00
Dish, Serving, Lobster Salad, Lobster Form Finial, 4 1/2 x 9 1/2 x 5 1/2 In. 44.00
Dish, Vegetable, Floral & Scroll Border, Gorham, 11 In. 253.00
Dish, Warming, Double Compartment, Shell, Scroll Border, 28 x 19 x 10 In. 633.00
Epergne, 3-Light Candelabra, 3 Hanging Baskets, Mappin & Webb, 26 In. 4600.00
Epergne, 7 Trumpet Form, Scrolled Frame, Bun Feet, 19th Century, 15 1/4 In. 1725.00
Epergne, Center Trumpet With 3 Small Trumpets, Ruffled, 13 5/8 In. 325.00
Ewer, Hinged Lid, Classical, J.T. & Co., 8 5/8 In. 90.00
Fish Service, Mappin & Webb, 6 Knives, 6 Forks 143.00
Fish Service, Simulated Ivory Handles, Case, 6 Knives, 6 Forks 66.00
Fish Serving, Fork & Knife, Chased Floral Motif, England 460.00
Fish Set, Ivory Handles, Case, 13 Piece 99.00
Flagon, Short Spouts, Shellwork Framing, c.1769, 11 5/8 In. 2875.00
Flask, Tree & 3 Figures, Screw Cap, 5 In. 70.00
Garniture Set, Egyptian Revival Style, 3 Piece 4400.00
Kettle, Beehive, Electroplate, C. Dresser, Elkington & Co., England, 1885, 9 5/8 In. 3000.00
Kettle, Stand, Burner, Electroplate, C. Dresser, Hukin & Heath, England, 1878, 8 In. 1780.00
Knife & Fork, Fish, Ivory, Sheffield, 1896, Pair 350.00
Lantern, Coach, Beveled Glass, Draperies On Side Panels, Urn Finial, 29 In., Pr. 172.00
Lazy Susan, Tureen, 3 Casseroles, 2 Bowls, Shaker, Ladle, Wood Handles, 23 In. 920.00
Luncheon Set, Mother-Of-Pearl Handles, 12 Knives, 12 Forks 357.00
Measure, Tankard, Sheffield, 7 In. 100.00
Mirror, Plateau, Sheffield, c.1810, 25 1/2 x 16 In. 995.00
Napkin Rings are listed in their own category.
Pitcher, Chased Acorn Branch Design, Acorn Leaf Border, 1855, 11 1/2 In. 489.00
Pitcher & Bowl, Art Nouveau, Portrait Of Woman Embossed On Sides, c.1880 . . . . 3850.00
Platter, Hot Water Reservoir, Removable Top, Well & Tree, Sheffield, 25 In. 605.00
Punch Ladle, Carved Bone Handle, Sheffield, England 100.00
Salt, Figural, Woman Supporting Shell With Children, 5 1/4 In. 247.00
Salt, Shell On Wheels, Topped By Knight On Horseback, 4 In. 495.00
Salver, Gadroon Border, Ball, Claw Feet, Footed, England, 22 In. 575.00

Sconce, 2-Light, Baroque Cartouches, Flaming Urns, Electrified, 13 In., 6 Piece 8050.00
Server, Classical, Oblong Top, End Handles, Glass Insert, 14 x 25 x 32 In. 660.00
Server, Swivel Dome Lid, 2 Oval Inserts, Mappin & Webb, London, 12 In. 330.00
Spoon, Souvenir, see Souvenir category.
Spoon Warmer, Nautilus, Shell On Rocks & Seaweed, England, 6 1/2 In. 145.00
Spooner, Nautilus Shell Shape, Hinged Lid, 1870s ....181.00 to 250.00
Tea & Coffee Set, Rogers, Monogram, c.1870 .... 925.00
Tea Set, Art Deco, Floral Garlands, S-Scroll Handles, 1920s, 4 Piece 495.00
Tea Set, Barrel, Electroplate, C. Dresser, Hukin & Heath, England, 1878, 3 Piece 3562.00
Tea Set, James W. Tufts, 1919, 4 Piece 750.00
Tea Set, Old English Melon, Community Plate, 26-In. Tray, 5 Piece 138.00
Tea Set, Raised Iris Motif, Teapot, Coffeepot, Creamer, Sugar, WMF, 9 Piece 2630.00
Tea Set, Tray, Goldfeder, 4 Piece 595.00
Teapot, Beaded Border, Bone Finial, 6 In. 115.00
Teapot, Lions' Heads, Eastlake Style 95.00
Teapot, Rogers 800, Footed, 10 In. 35.00
Tip Tray, Porcelain Center, Springfield F & M Insurance Co., 3 3/4 In. 65.00
Toothpick, Goat 175.00
Tray, Calling Card, Female, Flowing Hair Forms Handles, W.M.W., c.1909, 9 In. 247.00
Tray, Tea, Chased Floral, Foliate Handle, Gadroon Border, 30 1/2 In. 316.00
Tray, Tea, Oval, Reed & Barton, 22 In. 55.00
Urn, Hot Water, Cover, Engraved Floral Garlands, Crest, Sheffield, 14 3/4 In. 577.00
Urn, Hot Water, Flowers & Foliage At Shoulder, Dragon-Head Crest, Sheffield 747.00
Urn, Hot Water, Scalloped, Square Base, Spurred Ball & Claw Feet, Squat 440.00
Urn, Hot Water, Sheffield, c.1800, 14 In. 495.00
Urn, Owl Finial, Arches, Cherubs, Flaming Urn, Hoof Feet, Wilcox, c.1870, 14 In. 325.00
Vase, Engraved B, Cartier, 11 3/4 In. 150.00
Vase, Trumpet, Oval Base, 19th Century, 24 1/4 In., Pair 978.00
Waiter, Handles, Simpson, Hall, Miller & Co, Oval 450.00
Warmer, Serving, 4 Dishes, Tureen, Covers, Base Holds Hot Water, 28 x 17 In. 1375.00
Whiskey, Jack Daniels, Towle, Pair 15.00
Wine Cooler, Applied Foliate Band To Foot, Rim, 2 Foliate Handles, 10 In., Pair 863.00
Wine Cooler, Ring Handle, Liner, England, 7 In., Pair 247.00
Wine Cooler, Silver On Copper, Victorian, England, 10 In. 143.00
Wine Jug, Wheel-Cut Dove Design, Teardrop Shape, Silver Top, Handle, 11 In. 259.00

SILVER, SHEFFIELD, see Silver Plate; Silver-English categories.

SILVER-AMERICAN. American silver is listed here. Coin and sterling silver are included. Most of the sterling silver listed in this book is subdivided by country. There are also other pieces of silver and silver plate listed under special categories, such as Candelabrum, Napkin Ring, Silver Flatware, Silver Plate, Silver-Sterling, and Tiffany Silver.

SILVER-AMERICAN, Basket, Fruit, Pierced Scroll Design, 4-Footed, Handle, Towle, 10 3/8 In. 403.00
Basket, Hammered, Rolled Rim, Randahl, 5 1/2 x 5 In. 465.00
Basket, Leaf, Applied Grapevine, Shiebler, 1890, 11 In. 3680.00
Basket, Pierced Flower Shape, Base & Handle Joined At Top, Towle, 13 In. 805.00
Basket, Repousse, Manor House Scene, Floral Borders, S. Kirk & Son Co. 275.00
Basket, Repousse, Scalloped Pedestal, Oval, S. Kirk & Son, 5 3/4 In. 415.00
Basket, Sweetmeat, Swing Handle, Presentation, Lincoln & Foss, 1854 .... 357.00
Berry Spoon, Chased Stem, Gilded Bowl, Flower Design Bowl, Knowles, 1880 .... 195.00
Bowl, Applied Copper, Bronze, Circular, Gorham, 12 In. 3220.00
Bowl, Basket Weave Sides, Floral Trophies Within Gadrooning, Gorham, 8 In. 143.00
Bowl, Bead, Leaf Pattern, Garland, Floral Rim, Gorham, 10 1/4 In. 863.00
Bowl, Berry In Calyx Design, Signed, Arching Lines, A. Stone, 8 In. 4295.00
Bowl, Chased Vintage, Footed, Engraved 1850, Ball, Black & Co., 5 5/8 In. 440.00
Bowl, Chased Wheat Sheaves Border, Handles, 1850, Ball, Black & Co. 1035.00
Bowl, Classical Foliage, Arches, Shreve & Co., 1910, 24 1/4 In. 4600.00
Bowl, Embossed Fisherman, Hunter & Horseback Rider, Kirk 3575.00
Bowl, Foliate Design, A. Stone, 7 1/4 In. 3440.00
Bowl, Governor Wentworth, Cut Corners, Shreve, Crump & Low, 4 x 8 In. 175.00
Bowl, Hammered, 5 Lobed Form, Randahl, 9 x 2 In. 200.00
Bowl, Hammered, Elaborate Monogram, 3 Curved Feet, Kalo, 4 x 3 In. 385.00

Bowl, Hammered, Pierced Floral Base, Scalloped, Randahl, 5 1/2 x 3 In. . . . . 770.0●

Bowl, Handles, Marshall Field, 6 In. . . . . 350.0●

Bowl, Ice, Glass Liner, Watson, Retailed By Caldwell, c.1920, 6 In. . . . . 315.0●

Bowl, Kirk & Son, 8 In. . . . .*Illus*   688.0●

Bowl, Marie Antoinette, Gorham, 11 In. . . . . 950.0●

Bowl, Montieth, Order Of Thistle, Applied Putto Masks, Gorham, 12 1/2 In. . . . . 4310.0●

Bowl, Pierced Rim Rolls Down & Out, Black, Starr & Frost, 13 In. . . . . 632.0●

Bowl, Scalloped Edge, Kalo, 6 x 9 3/4 In. . . . . 430.0●

Bowl, Scalloped Rim, Katherine Pratt, Arts & Crafts, 5 In. . . . . 197.0●

Bowl, Serving, 2 Handles, Handwrought, Kalo Shop, Chicago, 6 x 14 1/2 In. . . . . 2200.0●

Bowl, Underplate, International, 9 1/2 x 9 1/2 In. . . . . 165.0●

Bowl, Vegetable, Cover, Standing Lion With Shield Finial, Gorham, 1871 . . . . 3025.0●

Box, Heart Shape, Foliage Wags On Cover, Cornucopias, Howard, 4 3/4 In. 920.00

Box, Jewelry, Repousse Floral, Velvet Lining, Jacobi & Jenkins, 7 In. 1092.00

Box, Pill, Vegetable Design, Gorham 125.00

Bread Plate, Monogram, Shreve & Co., 6 13/16 In., 12 Piece . . . . 875.0●

Brush & Comb Set, Nylon Bristles, Saart, Box, 1940s, 5 & 7 1/4 In., 3 Piece . . . . 113.0●

Cake Basket, Elliptical, Beaded Rim, Center Greek Key, Jones, Ball & Co., 1853 . . . . . . 725.00

Cake Basket, Thomas Fletcher, 18 In. . . . . 700.0●

Cake Plate, Chased Poppy Border, 1900, Black, Starr & Frost, 11 1/16 In. 633.00

Cake Stand, Floral Rim, Monogram, Shreve & Co., 5 1/4 x 9 1/2 In. 330.00

Candelabrum is listed in its own category.

Candlesticks are listed in their own category.

Case, Coin, Globe Shaped, Engraved Scroll Design, 1 Troy Oz. . . . . 115.0●

Castor, Cover, Trellis, Octagonal, Peter Quintard, 1735, 5 3/8 In. 10350.00

Centerpiece, Fisherman, Hunter & Horseback Rider, Footed, S. Kirk . . . .*Illus* 3575.00

Chafing Dish, 3 Rabbits Near Burner, Oak Handle, Heinrich, 1907, 13 In. 4600.00

Chalice, Fleur-De-Lis, Urn Form, R & W Wilson, 1828, 7 1/4 In. 990.00

Chocolate Pot, Hinged Lid, Kirk & Sons, c.1890, 10 1/2 In. 990.00

Coaster, Monogram, Kirk, 12 Piece 165.00

Cocktail Shaker, Crown Finial Cap, Black, Starr & Gorham, 25 Oz., 3 Pt. 520.00

Coffee Set, Grapevine Handles & Finials, K Monogram, Schofield, 3 Piece 1200.00

Coffee Set, Jacobi & Jenkins, After Dinner, c.1906 . . . . 1175.00

Coffee Set, Melon Form, Scrollwork Handles, Spout, 1900, 79 Oz., 5 Piece 1006.00

Coffee Set, S. Reed, 1810-1834, 3 Piece 1955.00

Coffeepot, Chased With Dragonfly, Insects, Dominick & Haff, 1881, 11 In. 2185.00

Coffeepot, Urn Form, Circular Pedestal Base, Scroll Handle, 10 In., 28 Oz. 345.00

Compote, 3 Scenes Around Rim, Pedestal, Ball, Black & Co., 1865, 12 In. 1725.00

Compote, Hammered, 5 Lobed Form, Monogram, Kalo, 9 x 4 In. 440.00

Compote, Lobed, Scroll Handles, Oval, Kirk, c.1885, 11 1/2 In., Pair 2587.00

Compote, Pierced Trefoil, Applied Openwork Foliage, Gorham, 1870, 12 In. 1725.00

Creamer, Medallion, Acanthus Chasing At Spout, Spherical, Gorham 550.00

Cup, Chased Floral, Word Bettie, New Orleans, 4 3/8 In. 412.00

Cup, Coin, Beaded Handle, R & W Wilson, Phila., 1825, 2 3/4 In. 225.00

Silver-American, Centerpiece, Fisherman, Hunter
& Horseback Rider, Footed, S. Kirk

Silver-American, Bowl,
Kirk & Son, 8 In.

Cup, Cover, 2 Handles, Black, Starr & Frost, 90.3 Oz., 18 In. 5750.00
Cup, Eggnog, Kirk, 3 In., 8 Piece 385.00
Cup, Embossed Rabbit, Kalo, Inscribed Berry, Christmas, 1916, 2 x 3 3/8 In. 550.00
Cup, Julep, Presentation Engraving, Henry Mahler, 5 1/4 In. 795.00
Cup, Martini, International, 23 Oz., 12 Piece 172.00
Demitasse Set, Royal Danish, Gray, International, 4 Piece 1150.00
Dish, Condiment, Fluted, Embossed Design, Square, Gorham/Whiting, 5 In. 45.00
Dish, Cover, Chippendale, Oval, Gorham, 10 1/8 In. 220.00
Dish, Entree, Monogram, Scalloped Removable Rim, Reed & Barton 55.00
Dish, Floral Repousse, Flanged, Steiff, 7 1/4 In., Pair 385.00
Dish, Grape, Bead Borders, Fox On Tendrils, Ball, Black & Co., 1865, 16 In. 2010.00
Dish, Ice Cream, Violet Rim Relief, Hammered Ground, Gorham, 17 In. 8050.00
Dish, Presentation Inscription, Leaf Form, Gorham, 13 In. 220.00
Dish, Shell Shape, Monogram, Gorham, 9 x 9 x 17 In. 247.00
Dish, Vegetable, Cover, Floral Matte Ground, Dominick & Haff, 12 In. 4600.00
Dish, Windsor, Pierced Rose Design Rim, Reed & Barton 165.00
Epergne, Classical Woman Stem, 2 Baskets, Krider & Biddle, 1865, 21 In. 9775.00
Epergne, Classical Woman Stem, 2 Dishes, Wood & Hughes, 1870, 22 In. 5750.00
Feeder, Invalid, Coin, Monogram, Ball Black & Co., 6 1/4 In. 495.00
Flagon, Embossed Flowers, Arms, Satyr Head Spout, S. Kirk, 1830, 17 In. 6900.00
Flask, Man's, Screw-Off Lid, Ribbed Design, International Silver, 3/4 Pt. 88.00
Flask, Woman's, Cherub, Engraved Flowers, Hinged Cap, Reed & Barton, 6 In. 520.00
Fork, Serving, A. Stone, c.1912, 8 In. 362.00
Fork & Spoon, Salad, Pierced, Chased Foliate Design, A. Stone, 1915, 9 1/4 In. 1714.00
Gravy Boat, Dominick & Haff, 1894 .... 750.00
Grinder, Pepper, Chased Floral Design, Monogram, Gorham, 1898, 1/2 In. 115.00
Hook, Chatelaine, Inverted Heart, John Adam, Jr., Virginia, 1800, 2 1/8 In. 805.00
Ice Cream Fork, Shell & Seaweed Bowl, Gorham, c.1900, 6 1/8 In., 12 Piece 4600.00
Jug, Chased, Figural Spout, S. Kirk, 11 Oz., 4 1/2 In. 950.00
Julep Cup, Coin, Monogram, S. Kirk & Son, 3 3/8 In., 6 Piece 330.00
Kettle, Hot Water, Shreve & Co., 1860 .... 1955.00
Knife, Fruit, Gorham, Pocket 48.00
Loving Cup, 2 Handles, Jerry Travers, 1905, 5 1/2 In. 250.00
Loving Cup, 2 Handles, Jerry Travers, 1905, 7 In. 350.00
Loving Cup, Baluster Form, Applied Scrolling, 20th Century, 6 3/4 In. 345.00
Loving Cup, Chased With Dolphin Masks, Gorham, 1899, 9 3/4 In. 14950.00
Loving Cup, Chased With Thistles, Flute Handles, Gorham, 1905, 10 In. 7475.00
Mug, C-Scroll & Foliate, Lemuel Hurlbut, 1839-1850, 4 1/8 In. 200.00
Mug, Coin, Embossed, Engraved Medallion, Footed 55.00
Mug, Coin, Paneled, Inscription, Chased Rim, Davis, Palmer & Co. 120.00
Mug, Coin, Paneled, Scroll Handle, Inscription, Gale, Wood & Hughes, 1836 .... 65.00
Mug, Inscribed, J. Foster, 1814, 3 1/2 In. 517.00
Mug, Star In Circle Banding, Redman, 1817, 3 1/2 In. 316.00
Mug, T.C. Garrett & Co., 4 In. 220.00
Mustard Pot, Gale & Hayen, c.1849 .... 550.00
Napkin Rings are listed in their own category.
Nut Dish, Pierced, Gorham, Monogram, 8 Piece 165.00
Pitcher, Baluster, Bright Cut Geometric Band, Floral Band Base, 12 Oz. 253.00
Pitcher, Bar, J.E. Caldwell, c.1885, 6 In. 950.00
Pitcher, Chased Floral, Monogram, Lebkuecher & Co., 10 3/8 In. 825.00
Pitcher, Coin, Cattails, Inscription, Crosby, Hunnewell & Morse, 10 In. 1380.00
Pitcher, Coin, J.B. Jones, 10 In. 1045.00
Pitcher, Coin, Natural Floral Sprig, Handle, Ball, Black & Co., 11 In. 1093.00
Pitcher, Floral Rococo Design, Greek Key Foot, R & W Wilson, 7 5/8 In. 522.00
Pitcher, Francis I, Reed & Barton 7000.00
Pitcher, Hammered, Rolled Rim, Inscription, Monogram, Kalo, 6 1/2 In. 2750.00
Pitcher, Hinged Lid, Ebony Handle, Allan Adler, 11 In. 935.00
Pitcher, Water, Ewer Form, Wedgwood Pattern, International, 10 1/2 In. 769.00
Pitcher, Water, Flowers & Thistles, S. Kirk & Son, 1880, 17 In. 2300.00
Pitcher, Water, Gorham, Whiting, 5 1/2 Pt. 355.00
Pitcher, Water, Openwork Vine Footed, Oval Shape, Dominick & Haff 2320.00
Pitcher, Water, Pine Cone & Needle Design, Cowell & Hubbard, 10 1/2 In. 1870.00
Pitcher, Water, Stand, Chased Masks, Bands & Swags, Gorham, 1908, 12 In. 5460.00

Pitcher, Water, Tree Shape, Vine, Branch Handle, R & W Wilson, 1840, 14 In. 5750.00
Plate, Floral Border, Central Monogram, Kirk, 6 3/8 In., 8 Piece 632.00
Plate, Initialed S, International, 6 In., 8 Piece 115.00
Plate, Trophy, Santa Barbara Riding & Hunt Club, Dodge, 1931, 10 In. 660.00
Platter, Chased Circle & Wave, A. Stone, 10 1/2 In., Pair 2350.00
Platter, Openwork Foliate Handles, Oval, Richard Dimes, c.1908, 13 x 9 In. 795.00
Porringer, Angular Rim, Open Strapwork Handle, Van Voorhis, c.1769, 7 In. 860.00
Porringer, Coin, Cast Handle, Monogram, 5 1/4 In. 990.00
Porringer, Coin, Handle, William Jones, 5 1/4 In. 1045.00
Porringer, Key Hole Handle, Daniel DuPuy, 1785, 7 1/2 In. 2300.00
Porringer, Strapwork Handle, Daniel Van Voorhis, New York, 1769, 7 In. 860.00
Punch Bowl, Bombe, Inscriptions, Gorham, 1903, 19 In. 6325.00
Punch Bowl, Grapevine Feet, George W. Shiebler, 1905, 9 3/4 x 14 In. 5750.00
Punch Ladle, Martele, Gorham, 19 In. 4290.00
Punch Ladle, Shell Form Bowl, Twist Handle, Pear Shaped End 385.00
Punch Set, Embossed & Chased Chinoiserie Scenes, Schofield, 13 Piece 4600.00
Punch Set, Grapevine Mounts, Paw Feet, Gorham, 13 Piece 9350.00
Punch Set, Polished, Coat Of Arms, Graff, Washbourne & Dunn, 26 Piece 6610.00
Salad Set, Fork & Spoon, Pierced, Foliate Design, Arthur Stone, Mark, 1915 . . . . 1495.00
Salt, Open, Repousse, With Spoon, Stieff, Pair 440.00
Salver, Chased, Repousse Border, Footed, A.E. Warner, 10 In. 415.00
Salver, Chased, Repousse Border, Inscription, 1861, S. Kirk & Son, 7 1/2 In. 275.00
Salver, Diapered Center, S. Kirk, c.1885, 8 In. 595.00
Samovar, Presented To Postmaster Of Philadelphia, 1844 . . . . 7450.00
Sauce Ladle, Oval Handle, Monogram, J. Howell & Co., c.1802 . . . . 44.00
Sauceboat, Floral & Scroll Border, Scroll Feet, Black, Starr & Frost, Oval 165.00
Server, Fish, Engraved Floral Border On Blade, Albert Coles, 11 5/8 In. 172.00
Serving Spoon, Richard Humphreys, c.1772 . . . . 195.00
Serving Tongs, Hanover, Claw Form Fork, Gorham, 1895, 2 Troy Oz., Pair 144.00
Shaker, Sugar, London, Gorham, 1930, 8 In. 235.00
Shoehorn, Woman & Flowers, Unger Bros. 68.00
Soup Ladle, Fiddle Handle, Monogram, Samuel Williamson, c.1800 . . . . 275.00
Soup Ladle, Medallion Handle With Devil's Mask, Ford & Tupper, 1880s 310.00
Spoon, Bright Cut Handle, W.G. Forbes, 8 7/8 In., 5 Piece 385.00
Spoon, Coin Silver, J.T. Young, Petersburg 286.00
Spoon, Coin Silver, S. Kirk, Baltimore 88.00
Spoon, Coin Silver, W.G. Forbes, New York 385.00
Spoon, Fiddle & Shell Handle, Bailey & Kitchen, 1850s, Pair 45.00
Spoon, Rattail, L.S. Stowe, 6 In. 165.00
Sugar, Cover, Acorn, Oak Leaf Pattern, S-Scrolled Handles, 23 Oz. 322.00
Sugar, Elliptical Form, Foliate Banding, c.1790, 5 3/4 In. 1610.00
Sugar, Fleur-De-Lis, Coin, Lincoln & Foss, 5 1/4 x 4 3/8 In. 330.00
Sugar & Creamer, Band Of Birds, Branches, Gorham, 1873, 6 1/2 In. 460.00
Sugar & Creamer, Coin, Repousse Band, Paw Footed, Handle, N.Y., 6 1/4 In. 440.00
Sugar & Creamer, Coin, Scroll Handles, John W. Forbes 2200.00
Sugar & Creamer, Flower Bud Finial, Foliate Banding, c.1830, 8 1/2 In. 402.00
Sugar & Creamer, Peter L. Krider, c.1855 . . . . 550.00
Sugar Tongs, Fiddle Handle, Oval Nips, Monogram, Philadelphia 38.00
Tablespoon, Coin, Fiddle Handle, Simmons & Williamson, 9 In., Pair 45.00
Tablespoon, Coin, Turned Fiddle Handle, Simon Wedge, 1774-1823, 6 Piece 305.00
Tablespoon, Fiddle Handle, Monogram, J. Warner, c.1800 . . . . 38.00
Tablespoon, W.H. Calhoun, Nashville, c.1860 . . . . 40.00
Tankard, Stepped Domed Cover, Scroll Handle, Wm. Cowell, 1730, 7 In. 6900.00
Tazza, Oak Tree Shape, Rock Base, S. Kirk & Son, 9 1/4 In., Pair 4025.00
Tazza, Openwork Rim, Draped Putto Stem, Gorham, 1871, 12 1/4 In. 2300.00
Tazza, Repousse, Low, S. Kirk & Son, Inc. 135.00
Tea & Coffee Set, Bombe Form, Tray, Gorham, 1901, 6 Piece 9775.00
Tea & Coffee Set, Cinderella, Gorham, 1926, 6 Piece 4995.00
Tea & Coffee Set, Eastern Stylistic Influence, Whiting, 1888, 5 Piece 3600.00
Tea & Coffee Set, Floral Repousse, Square Handles, A.E. Warner, 5 Piece 4950.00
Tea & Coffee Set, Fruit Banding, William B. North, 1822, 4 Piece 3220.00
Tea & Coffee Set, Monogram M, Gorham, 7 Piece 3850.00
Tea & Coffee Set, Scrolled Handle & Spout, Gale & Willis, 1880s, 9 Piece 7475.00

Tea & Coffee Set, Tapering Lozenge Shape, Tray, Durgin, 7 Piece 5500.00
Tea Service, Empire Style, Garret Forbes, c.1835, 3 Piece 3150.00
Tea Set, Classic Floral Design, Monogram, Gorham, 1868, 5 Piece 2420.00
Tea Set, Coin, Floral, Acanthus, N.J. Bogert, 3 Piece 1430.00
Tea Set, Coin, Melon Rib, N. Taylor & Co., 1825, 3 Piece 1870.00
Tea Set, Coin, Paneled Bowls, Monogram, Flower Finial, N.J. Bogert, 4 Piece 2090.00
Tea Set, Devonshire, Reed & Barton, 3 Piece 9500.00
Tea Set, Empire Style, Garret Forbes, c.1835, 3 Piece 3185.00
Tea Set, Engraved Flowers, Gorham, c.1868, 5 Piece 2400.00
Tea Set, Fluted Sides, Engraved Tassels & Swags, Wood Handles, Lunt, 5 Piece 288.00
Tea Set, Fluted Urn Form, Finials, Charles Boehme, 1800, 3 Piece 4312.00
Tea Set, Monogrammed On Bottom, Bigelow, Kennard & Co., 1891, 3 Piece 550.00
Tea Set, Prelude, International, 5 Piece 2200.00
Tea Set, Prelude, International, 6 Piece 1650.00
Tea Set, Sugar & Creamer, Cover, Teapot, J. & I. Cox, New York, 3 Piece 1380.00
Tea Set, Urn Finials, Beaded Edge, Van Voorhis, 1751-1824, 3 Piece 5175.00
Tea Set, Vase Shape, Acanthus Leaves, Anthony Rasch & Co., 1820, 3 Piece 2875.00
Tea Set, Victorian, Gorham, 1869, 3 Piece 2400.00
Tea Tray, Scrolled Foliage, 2 Handles, Oval, William Forbes, 1839, 31 In. 10350.00
Tea Urn, Chased Birds, Floral, Angular Handles, S. Kirk & Son, 1880, 14 In. 6325.00
Teapot, Alexander S. Gordon, c.1795 .... 2250.00
Teapot, Lobed Corners, Rose & Anthemia Rims, J. Lownes, c.1805, 10 1/2 In. 1150.00
Toast Rack, Angular, Electroplate, C. Dresser, Tiffany, 1880s, 5 1/2 In. 2250.00
Tongs, Asparagus, Bright Cut Engraved Floral Handle, Bailey & Co. 373.00
Tongs, Basket Of Flowers, Mott & Co., c.1835, 6 1/2 In. 295.00
Tongs, Coin, Griffen & Hoyt 125.00
Tongs, Coin, Hyde & Nevins 125.00
Tongs, Feathered Edge, Design On Bowl Back, Caleb Beal, 1780s 250.00
Tongs, Raised Shell, William Gale, c.1825, 6 1/4 In. 100.00
Tongs, Sugar, William Stoddard Nichols, 1785 .... 55.00
Tray, Floral Repousse Border, Center Monogram, Meriden Co., 13 In. 120.00
Tray, Francis I, Reed & Barton, 11 1/2 In. 3835.00
Tray, Openwork Foliate Handles, A. Stone, 12 x 9 In. 2240.00
Tray, Presentation, Shell & Scroll Border, Durgin, 30 x 18 In. 1980.00
Tray, Sandwich, Monogram, Dominick & Haff, 11 In. 44.00
Tray, Smoker's, Graff, Washbourne & Dunn, 9 1/4 x 8 1/2 In. 330.00
Tray, Strawberry, Strawberry Leaf Form, 3 Ball Feet, Wallace, 10 3/4 In. 253.00
Tray, Tea, Foliate, Mosgrove Center, Handles, P.L. Krider, 1865, 33 In. 6900.00
Tray, Wreath Center, Floral Repousse Border, Stieff, 12 In. 605.00
Trivet, 3 Sections, Octagonal, 4 Paw Feet, F. Bucher & Sons, c.1877, 13 In. 1725.00
Trophy Cup, Crittenden, 2 C-Scroll Handles, S. Kirk & Son, 1905, 13 1/2 In. 1925.00
Tumbler, Hammered, Monogram, Inscription, Kalo, 1937, 5 In. 220.00
Tumbler, Rolled Edge, Footed, Black, Starr & Frost, 6 In., 12 Piece 5400.00
Tureen, Cover, Cows & Men & Dogs, Lion Mask, S. Kirk & Son, 1880, 13 In. 7475.00
Tureen, Cover, Stag Hunt, Ring Handles, Boat, S. Kirk & Sons, 1961, 13 In. 6900.00
Tureen, Soup, Birds & Flowers, Lion Head Ring Pulls, S. Kirk, c.1885 .... 2850.00
Urn, Cover, Baluster Shape, Scroll Handles, Durgin, 1900, 18 In. 1150.00
Vase, Oak Branches Girdle, Handles, Reed & Barton, 1910, 26 In. 6325.00
Vase, Oak Sprays, Pine Cones, Handles, Shreve & Co., 1910, 21 1/2 In. 5175.00
Vase, Swirling Foliage, Gorham, 1898, 15 1/8 In. 7475.00
Vase, Trumpet Shape, Applied, Pierce Rose Design, Redlich, 11 5/8 In. 690.00
Vase, Trumpet, Etched Floral, Filigree Frame, Bailey, Banks & Biddle 330.00
Waiter, Raised Beaded Rim, Monogram, John David, Round, 1790, 8 1/8 In. 6325.00
LVER-AUSTRIAN, Basket, Handle, Rose Twig, Wimmer, Wiener Werkstatte, 1908, 6 In. . 1645.00
Cup & Saucer, Stylized Leaves, Otto Prutscher, Eduard Friedmann, c.1911 .... 2055.00
Soup Ladle, Lion Mask On Back, Overlapping Scales, I.J. Wurth, 1780, 14 1/2 In. 5750.00
Sugar Tongs, Spring Loaded, Mid-19th Century, 7 In. 154.00
Tray, Lilies, Entwined, 2 Handles Of Cast Lilies, Foliage, 1905, 27 1/2 In. 6670.00
Tray, Square Form, Shaped Edge, 20th Century, 14 1/8 In. 316.00
Vase, Footed, Hammered, JH Monogram, Wiener Werkstatte, 1925, 13 In. 2465.00
LVER-BELGIAN, Dish, Strapwork, Husks, Baroque Cartouche, Buysens, 1718, 9 In. 5750.00
Snuffer Tray, Winged Cherub Heads, 3 Bud Feet, Van Sychen, c.1700, 10 1/2 In. 8050.00
LVER-BOLIVIAN, Pitcher, Ribbed, Entwined Branch With Serpent Handle, 13 1/4 In. 2300.00

Silver-Continental,
Chalice, Champleve
Plaques, Gemstones,
Gilt Metal, 10 In.

Silver-Continental,
Ewer, Art Nouveau,
Floral Design, Glass

SILVER-CHINESE, Case, Card, Dragon Design, 4 x 2 1/2 In. 198.00
   Cup, Carved Cherry Blossoms Rim, 2 Handles, 17 3/4 In. 1100.00
   Tea Set, Chased & Engraved, Figural Handles, Marked Coin, 3 Piece 330.00
   Teapot, Chased Stylized Dragons, Key Fret Border, Woven Bamboo Handle 316.00
   Vase, Floral Design, Metal Mounts, Teardrop Form, 7 3/4 In. 220.00
SILVER-CONTINENTAL, Basket, Fruit, Vine Swing Handle, Grape & Leaf Rim, 11 1/2 In. . 550.00
   Bowl, Floral Garlands, Birds, Putti Scene, 19th Century, 10 x 2 1/2 In. 132.00
   Box, Jewelry, Foliage, Cameos & Intaglios, Handle, 4 Scroll Feet, 7 1/4 In. 2875.00
   Box, Tea, Rose Repousse Corners To Lid, Key Lock, 19th Century 522.00
   Box, Tobacco, Cover, Chariot, Drawn By Eagles, 3 1/8 In. 6900.00
   Chalice, Champleve Plaques, Gemstones, Gilt Metal, 10 In. ....*Illus* 2200.00
   Coffee Service, Child's, Dolphin Feet, Sea Serpent Handles, 3 Piece 2090.00
   Compote, Female Figure, Partly Draped, 4 Handles, Silver Rim, 10 In. 2070.00
   Ewer, Art Nouveau, Floral Design, Glass ....*Illus* 1980.00
   Ewer, Wine, Glass Body, Cherub & Foliate, Late 19th Cent., 10 In., Pair 1925.00
   Figure, Pheasant, Strutting, Portuguese, 20th Century, 17 1/4 In., Pair 4025.00
   Figure, Swan, Centerpiece, Hinged Wings, Flexible Neck, Portuguese, 30 In. 9775.00
   Knife, Fruit, Split Bladed, Angular Handle, Pair 265.00
   Salt, Dolphin Stem, Shell With Mythical Boy With Spear & Horn, 4 1/2 In. 247.00
   Salt, Figural, Unicorn Pedestal, Shell Shape, Playing Horn, 4 1/2 In. 192.00
   Spice Tower, Filigree Panel & Door, Foliage, 1830s, 12 In. 8050.00
   Spice Tower, Flag Finial, Engraved Crowned Flowers, 18th Century, 7 In. 4312.00
SILVER-DANISH, Bowl, Centerpiece, Leaves, Berried Branches, Fluted Rim, 9 1/2 In. 7475.00
   Bowl, Fruit, Foliage, Berries On Openwork Stem, Georg Jensen, 1945, 7 3/4 In. 6440.00
   Bowl, Openwork Foliate Scroll, Flared Rim, J. Rohde, 1919, 5 3/4 In. 9775.00
   Bowl, Openwork Leaf, Berry Globular Stem, Beaded Rim, Georg Jensen, 9 Oz. 1380.00
   Bowl, Silver Cover, Blossom Pattern, 2 Handles, Georg Jensen, 1945, 12 In. 6325.00
   Cocktail Shaker, Lid, Foliage, Stepped Foot With Pearls, Georg Jensen, 12 In. 2645.00
   Compote, Fruiting Grapevine Base, Scrolled Lobed Stem, Georg Jensen, 5 In. 2070.00
   Compote, Gold Wash Interior, Scroll Handles, Footed, 20th Century, 10 In. 374.00
   Compote, Grapevine Pattern, Georg Jensen, 1945-1951, 12 1/8 In. 10550.00
   Cup, Acorn Pattern, Georg Jensen, 2 1/2 In. 595.00
   Dish, Hammered, Crown Mark, Oval, Georg Jensen, 1925-1932, 2 x 5 In. 863.00
   Dish, Lobed Stem With Stylized Leaves, Decagonal Foot, Georg Jensen, 5 In. 517.00
   Dish, Vegetable, Blossom Pattern, Georg Jensen, 1925-1932, 12 In. 5462.00
   Pitcher, Lobed Vase Shape, Anthemion Handle, Georg Jensen, 1933, 9 1/4 In. 3737.00
   Porringer, Hammered, Beaded Rim, Ebony Handle, Georg Jensen, 10 In. 1150.00
   Salt, Open & Pepper, With Spoon, Cactus, Georg Jensen 250.00
   Sauceboat, Ladle, Double Lipped, Georg Jensen 2300.00
   Sugar Tongs, Pyramid, Georg Jensen 175.00
   Tea Service, Blossom Pierced Cover, Circular Base, Georg Jensen, 8 Piece 2875.00
   Tray, Sugar Cube, Georg Jensen 70.00
   Tureen, Blossom Finial, Handles, Openwork, Georg Jensen, 1945 .... 6210.00
SILVER-DUTCH, Basket, Engraved Leaf Pattern, Pierced Border, Handle, 28 Troy Oz. 805.00
   Coffee Set, Bakelite Handle, Franz Hingelberg Aarhus, 1932, 3 Piece 2810.00

Figurine, Pheasant, Boot Button Eyes, Inner Stopper, 1924, 21 In.	1725.00
Flask, Courting Couples Design, Foliage, Ribbed Glass, 1900, 5 In.	230.00
Muffineer, Geometric Florals, Monogram & Crest, 8 1/4 In.	385.00
Mustard, Strapwork & Husks On Reserves, Foliage On Cover, 1728, 7 In.	6900.00
Sauceboat, Double Lipped, Gilt Interior, Hourdoucq, 1779, 8 Oz., 6 In.	2300.00
Spoon, Ship Finial, 7 1/2 In.	104.00
Teapot, Baluster Finial, Scroll & Tassel Design, Eagle Head Spout, Honing, 6 In.	1265.00
Vase, Contemporary, Bonebakker & Zoon, 6 5/8 In.	550.00

SILVER-ENGLISH. English sterling silver is marked with a series of four or five small hallmarks. The standing lion mark is the most commonly seen sterling quality mark. The other marks indicate the city of origin, the maker, and the year of manufacture. These dates can be verified in many good books on silver.

SILVER-ENGLISH, Asparagus Tongs, Teardrop Shaped Design, Mulford Wendell & Co.	374.00
Bell, George II, 1756, 4 3/8 In.	2300.00
Bowl, Enameled Copper Frieze, O. Baker, Liberty, 1899, 8 5/8 In.	11250.00
Bowl, Lion's Mask & Ring Handles, Claw Feet, Elkington & Co., 1919, 14 In.	1610.00
Bowl, Openwork, Swing Handle, Cobalt Blue Insert, Birmingham, 1921, 5 In.	316.00
Box, Feather, Crown & Fox On Lid, Fleur-De-Lis, Signed, Oval, 1677	2100.00
Box, Tobacco, Cover, Arms Under Foliate Mantle, J. Sutton, 1699, 3 1/2 In.	4600.00
Caddy Spoon, George Baskerville, 1798, 5 Troy Oz.	173.00
Caddy Spoon, Shell Form Well, Hester Bateman, London, George III, 1783	522.00
Cake Basket, Beaded Borders, Scrolls, Oval, H. Bateman, 1786, 13 1/2 In.	6325.00
Cake Basket, Pierced Sides, Ceres Masks, E. Aldridge, George II, 1745, 14 In.	6900.00
Cake Basket, Swing Handle, Thomas Robbins, George III, 1804	1430.00
Cake Basket, Wirework Sides & Handle, Matthew Boulton, 1801, 13 1/4 In.	2875.00
Candelabrum is listed in its own category.	
Candlesticks are listed in their own category.	
Cann, Repoussé Floral & Foliage, Cast Handle, W. & J. Priest, 3 3/4 In.	110.00
Carving Set, Bone Handles, 2 Knives, 1 Fork, 3 Piece	66.00
Castor, Cover, Pierced Foot, Cylindrical, Charles II, 1680, 8 In.	1725.00
Castor, Thomas Satchwell, 1773, 5 In.	395.00
Chamberstick, Snuff, Beaded Rim, Hester Bateman, 1781, 4 1/2 In., Pair	4950.00
Christening Bowl, Spoon, Noah's Ark, Wm Hutton & Sons, Sheffield, 1908	535.00
Cigarette Case, Applied Bowed Flanges, Omar Ramsden, 1938, 3 1/2 In.	322.00
Coaster, Wine, Beaded Rim, 5 In., Pair	275.00
Coffee Strainer, Sheffield, Early 19th Century, 6 In.	275.00
Coffee Urn, Reel Shaped Cover, Square Foot, J. Robins, 1780, 14 1/2 In.	1840.00
Coffeepot, Baluster Finial, Engraved Arms, S. Pantin, c.1715, 9 3/4 In.	2875.00
Coffeepot, Flower Spray Finial, Trailing Flowers, F. Crump, 1763, 12 1/2 In.	4025.00
Coffeepot, Gold-Washed Baluster, Wooden Handle, George III, 13 In.	1380.00
Coffeepot, Hinged Lid, Black Finial, Birmingham, 1897, 9 In.	550.00
Coffeepot, Lighthouse Form, Wood Handle, Monogram, Chester, 1908	154.00
Cooler, Wine, Engraved Contemporary Arms, Liner, W. Elliott, 1820, 83 Oz.	6325.00
Creamer, Cow, Garland Of Flowers On Cover, Fly Finial, Schuppe, 1761, 6 In.	8050.00
Creamer, Engraved Double-Headed Eagle, c.1783-1784, 6 1/4 In.	154.00
Creamer, Engraved Ship Crest, Raised On 4 Ball Feet, 1793, 4 Oz.	115.00
Cup, Caudle, Ribbed Midband, Twin Lyre Handles, Philip Rollos Jr., 1711	1650.00
Cup, Cover, Band Of Sloping Gadroons, R. Cooper, William III, 1700, 8 3/8 In.	9200.00
Cup, Engraved Arms, Gilt Interior, T. Wallace, 1804, 5 3/4 In., Pair	3162.00
Dessert Fork, Thomas Barker, 1805, 12 Piece	1200.00
Dish, Contemporary Arms & Crest, W.K. Reid, William IV, 1833, 13 In., Pair	4887.00
Dish, Entree, Cover, Reeded Stirrup Handles, Gadrooned Rim, R. Garrard, 1857	1250.00
Dish, Plated Cover, Pomegranate Finial, Mortimer & Hunt, 1839, 11 3/4 In., Pr.	4312.00
Dish, Vegetable, Cover, Foliate Ring Handle, George III, 1803, 9 1/8 In.	6670.00
Ewer, Cover, Baluster, Beaded, Chased Floral, Scroll, George III, 12 3/8 In.	1093.00
Ewer, Huguenot Style, Female Handle, Fraser & Haws, 1880, 14 In.	5175.00
Figurine, Classical Woman, Flowers, Marble Base, Paul Storr, 1832, 13 In.	2200.00
Fish Slice, Floral Scroll Design, Carved Ivory Handle, 1891, 13 7/8 In.	345.00
Fish Slice, Ivory Handle, Sheffield, 1906, 13 In.	173.00
Flask, Faceted Glass Body, Monogrammed Amber Stopper, 1929, 4 7/8 In.	345.00
Fork, Fiddle, J. & J. Williams, 1859, 6 Piece	350.00

Fork, Fiddle, Thread, R. Turner, 1809, 6 Piece 380.00
Fork, George I, Rat Tail Pattern, 3 Prongs, P. Hanet, 1723, 3 Piece 143.00
Fork, King's Honeysuckle, William Eley II, 1824, 11 Piece 950.00
Frame, Ribbon-Tied Floral Design, Rectangular, 7 In. 66.00
Frame, Sterling, Bracket Form, Oval View, Floral Design, 6 1/2 x 12 In. 264.00
Fruit Knife, Engraved Crest, London, 1818, 8 Piece 110.00
Funnel, Wine, Repousse, HC, 1792, 5 1/2 In. 1295.00
Inkstand, Egg & Dart Border, 2 Inkwells, Seal Compartment, Hunt, 1854 .... 1955.00
Inkstand, Leaf Form, Twig Supports, Apple Form Seal Box, Hennell, 1845, 8 In. 3737.00
Inkstand, Scrolled Shells & Leaves, 2 Bottles, IC, George III, 1807, 11 1/2 In. 2070.00
Jug, Cream, Baluster Form, Leaf Design, Hester Bateman, 1781, 4 1/2 In. 412.00
Jug, Cream, Helmet Form, Beaded Rim, Hester Bateman, George III, 1785, 6 In. 550.00
Jug, Cream, Helmet Form, Square Base, Hester Bateman, London, 1787, 5 In. 357.00
Kettle, On Stand, Hunt & Roskell, 1857, 12 In. 1500.00
Lamp, George V, Ball Shape, Flame Finial Holds Wick, Asprey & Co. 175.00
Lemonade Set, Cylindrical, Geometric Design, A.G. Styles, 7 Piece 5175.00
Lighter, Seated Irish Wolfhound Form, John S. Hunt, 1851, 8 1/2 In. 2875.00
Loving Cup, Foliate, Aviary, The Stratford On Avon, 1876, 8 1/2 In. 125.00
Marrow Scoop, Ivory Handle, Hester Bateman, George III 385.00
Marrow Scoop, Shield Handle, William Eley, Fearn & Chawner, 10 In. 190.00
Marrow Scoop, Thomas Chawner, George III, 1775, 8 3/8 In. 172.00
Mote Spoon, Pierced, Spearhead Handles, Hester Bateman, c.1780, 4 Piece 605.00
Mug, Double Scroll Handle, Monogram, Fuller White, 1760, 6 1/4 In. 1840.00
Napkin Rings are listed in their own category.
Pepper Castor, Engraved Crest, London, 1744 .... 247.00
Pepper Shaker, Chased & Engraved Design, Jabez Daniel, London, 1750, 5 In. 192.00
Pepper Shaker, Engraved, Thomas Smith, London, c.1772, George III, 5 In. 192.00
Platter, Meat, Oval, William Sumner, London, George III, 1804, 19 x 13 3/4 In. 2090.00
Porringer, Keyhole Design Handle, William Moulton III, 5 In. 1895.00
Porringer, Palm & Acanthus, Engraved Arms, Crossed Plumes, Fowles, 1678 .... 6900.00
Pot, Pomade, William & Mary, Slip-On Cover, Plumes, A. Nelme, 1690, Pair 2300.00
Punch Bowl, Chased Leaf & Acanthus Leaf Bands, Hunt & Roskell, 1889, 7 In. 978.00
Punch Ladle, Shell Form Well, Hester Bateman, London, 1779, 14 In. 825.00
Salt, Cobalt Blue Insert, Figural Footed, Chased Floral, 1853, 3 1/4 In. 300.00
Salt, Triton & Shell, Ball Feet, Paul Storr, George III, 1813, 4 3/4 In. 9775.00
Salt, With Spoon, Shell Form, In Case, Set Of 4 .... 143.00
Salt Spoon, Ivory Handle, FC Mark, Birmingham, 1826-1827, Pair 88.00
Salver, 3 Scroll Feet, Scroll Rim With Shells, George IV, 1829, 14 1/4 In. 2070.00
Salver, Chippendale Rim, Center Arms In Foliate Strapwork, Hindmarsh, 1738 .... 5750.00
Salver, Coat Of Arms, Engraved Design, 4-Footed, J. Carter, George III, 13 In. 2070.00
Salver, Engraved & Crested, Robert Garrard, 1848, 10 1/2 In. 1275.00
Salver, Engraved Arms Center, Floral Sprays, R. Rugg, George III, 1783, 16 In. 5750.00
Salver, Engraved Arms Center, Ribbon-Tied Frame, R. Rugg, 1773, 12 In. 3162.00
Salver, Engraved Arms In Baroque Cartouche Center, E. Bornock, 1729, 13 In. 3162.00
Salver, Pierced Rim, Trailing Flowers, Panel Feet, Hannam & Mills, 1764, 14 In. 3737.00
Salver, Shell Border, 3 Hoof Feet, Hannan & Crouch, George III, 1765, 13 In. 1650.00
Salver, Shells At Intervals Border, 3 Claw Feet, R. Rugg, 1767, 14 1/4 In. 3450.00
Sauce Ladle, Eagle Head End, Bowl Cast As Shell, c.1747, 6 3/4 In., Pair 5175.00
Sauce Ladle, Engraved Crest, Hester Bateman, George III, 1788, 4 Piece 1540.00
Sauceboat, C-Form Handle, Vermeil Interior, Samuel Hennel, George III, 1807 .... 410.00
Sauceboat, Crest On Sides, Scroll & Hoof Feet, W. Grundy, 1753, 7 3/4 In. 6612.00
Sauceboat, Leaf Design, 3 Legs, Scroll Handle, Hester Bateman, 1781, 5 1/2 In. 935.00
Sauceboat, Repousse Design, 3 Hoof Legs, Hester Bateman, 1787, 6 In. 825.00
Sauceboat, Shaped Rim With Shells, Scroll Handle, W. Fountain, 1814, 8 1/2 In. 2300.00
Sauceboat, Thomas Heming, 1770, 3 x 6 1/2 In., Pair 1250.00
Saucepan, Baluster, Turned Wood Handle, George III, 1810, 10 1/2 In. 1840.00
Scissors, Grape, Foliate Handles, 20th Century 400.00
Serving Spoon, Figural Handle, James Franklin, London, 1845, In Case, Pair 247.00
Serving Spoon, Zigzag Border, Monogram, Hester Bateman, George III, 1783 .... 550.00
Shaving Set, Mug, Cover, Brush, Birmingham, 1890s 325.00
Snuffbox, Engraved Anchor & Motto Center, Ledsam, Vale & Wheeler, 1829 .... 316.00
Spoon, Apostle, Saint Jude, 19th Century, 7 1/4 In. 110.00
Stirrup Cup, Collar Initialed JW To JW, John Edwards, 6 Oz., 4 3/8 In. 4600.00

Stirrups, William Barret, London, George III, 1800, Pair 1430.00
Strainer, Engraved Crest, R. & G. Garrard & Co., Mid-19th Century 110.00
Stretcher, Glove, Mosaic Design Handle, D. & S., 8 5/8 In. 172.00
Stuffing Spoon, Thomas Ollivant, London, 1795, 3 Troy Oz. 173.00
Sugar, Acanthus Border & Foot, 2 Handles, Benjamin Smith, 1829, 5 x 9 In. 302.00
Sugar, Birmingham, 1886, 7 1/2 In. 200.00
Sugar Basket, Swing Handle, Pierced Panels, Hester Bateman, 1788, 7 In. 1100.00
Sugar Tongs, Acorn Terminals, Hester Bateman, London, George III, 1780 .... 275.00
Sugar Tongs, Bright Cut Border, Robert Cox, George III, 1760s 132.00
Tankard, Domed Cover, Applied Strap, Hester Bateman, 1787, 8 1/2 In. 5390.00
Tankard, Engraved Vacant Cartouche, Scroll Handle, J. Leach, Queen Anne, 1702 ..... 4312.00
Tankard, Open Thumblift, Handle, Richard Gurney & Thomas Cooke, George II 2860.00
Tankard, Pear Shape, Scroll Handle, William Grundy, 1765 .... 2420.00
Tea & Coffee Set, Shellwork & Flowers, Monogram, Carrington, 1904, 6 Piece 4312.00
Tea Caddy, Beaded Rims, Ribbonwork Borders, H. Bateman, 1782, 5 1/4 In. 6325.00
Tea Caddy, Cover, Urn Finial, Bright Cut Borders, Crest In Oval, 4 In. 3737.00
Tea Caddy, Domed Cover, Borders Of Foliage, Baron's Coronet, Hennell, 1792 .... 4025.00
Tea Caddy, Domed Cover, Engraved Arms & Crest, R. Sharp, 1790, 6 In. 6900.00
Tea Caddy, Engraved Contemporary Initials Within Ribbon, Denziloe, 1782 .... 3162.00
Tea Caddy, Flower Finial, Floral Garlands, Charles Fox, 1833, 7 5/8 In. 1955.00
Tea Caddy, Hinged Cover, Double, Basket Form, J. Emes, 1799, 7 In. 4600.00
Tea Caddy, Rocaille Design, George III, 1770, 5 1/2 In. 2760.00
Tea Set, Regency, Gadrooned Rim, Foliate Finial On Teapot, 1816, 54 Oz. 2760.00
Tea Set, Ribbed Bodies, Wood Handles, Monogram, Crest, 1890-1910, 6 Piece 1870.00
Teapot, Engraved Rococo Band Around Cover, P. & E. Wakelin, 1765, 4 1/4 In. 2587.00
Teapot, Engraved Strapwork & Female Masks, A. Buteux, George II, 1729, 4 In. 8050.00
Teapot, Fluted Sides, Spout, Ivory Handle & Finial, R. Hennell, George III, 5 In. 747.00
Teapot, Hinged Lid, Black Handle & Finial, Birmingham, 1886, 6 In. 450.00
Teapot, Inverted Pear Shape, Shaw & Priest, 1759, 5 1/4 In. 2300.00
Toast Rack, Octagon Handle, Engraved Crest, Hester Bateman, 1790, 7 In. 1320.00
Tray, Flowers & Foliage Rim, Shell & Scroll Handles, E. Barnard, 1849, 32 In. 8912.00
Tray, Galleried, Oval, 4 Openwork Feet, Mappin & Webb, 17 In. 4370.00
Tray, Oval, Beaded Rim, John Scofield, London, George III, 1786, 10 1/4 In. 231.00
Tray, Scalloped, Beaded & Leaf Border, Arms, C. Boyton, 1899, 32 In. 4600.00
Tureen, Cover, Contemporary Crest, Samuel Hennell, 1819, 9 3/4 In. 7475.00
Tureen, Cover, Fluted Body, Lion Finial, Hallmark, c.1790, 12 x 19 In. 5462.00
Tureen, Sauce, Crests & Coronets Cover, Craddock & Reid, 1822, 8 In., Pair 4600.00
Tureen, Soup, Bombe, Feet Headed By Busts Of Hounds, T. Howell, 1809, 15 In. 8625.00
Tureen, Soup, Cover, Boat Form, Loop Handles, J. Schofield, 1793, 17 5/8 In. 6900.00
Tureen, Soup, Cover, Pomegranate Finial, Sheffield, c.1820, 16 1/2 In. 4025.00
Tureen, Soup, Heraldic Finial, Sarcophagus Form, Paw Feet, H. Nutting, 1807 .... 6900.00
Waiter, Engraved Arms Center, Hoof Feet, J. Tuite, 1732, 6 In., Pair 4025.00
Wine Funnel, Georgian 165.00
SILVER-FRENCH, Beaker, Tulip Form, 2 Alternating Designs, 3 In. 4600.00
Centerpiece, Round Stepped Base, 4 Pearl Scroll Feet, Pearl Rim, 8 3/4 In. 4140.00
Coffeepot, Hinged Cover, Chased With Trumpet Flowers, G. Keller, 1900, 8 In. 2070.00
Coffeepot, Wooden Handle, Second Standard, 8 In. 467.00
Cup & Saucer, Silver Holder Keeps Drinker From Spillage, Boullemer, 1715 .... 3450.00
Dish, Vegetable, Cover, Stepped Rim, Rectangular Flared Body, 1930, 11 In. 3450.00
Pitcher, Sprays Of Flowers, Forked Branch Handle, A. Debain, c.1890, 16 In. 4887.00
Salt, Clusters Of Shells Between Lion Mask, Paw Feet, Odiot, 1830s, 4 In., Pair 3737.00
Sauceboat, Floral Swags, Portrait Medallions, Hallmarks, 6 1/4 In. 220.00
Tea Caddy, Double, Flower Spray Finial, c.1840, 4 3/4 In. 2185.00
SILVER-GERMAN, Beaker, Pomegranate Finial, Flowers On Body, Rosenberg III, 1682 ... 3450.00
Biscuit Jar, Oval Panels, Fruit, Gold Wash, Augsburg, c.1800, 10 In. 3737.00
Bowl, Rosebud, Reticulated, Flower Basket, Garlands, 3 Putti, 8 In. 275.00
Bowl, Scalloped Floral Edge, Melon Ribbed, Flowers, 11 x 3 1/2 In. 220.00
Box, Infant Music Party On Hinged Cover, Storck & Sinsheimer, 12 1/4 In. 3162.00
Box, Repousse Children At Play, Oval, 3 In. 165.00
Bread Tray, Reticulated Design, Birds & Flowers, Footed, 12 x 8 x 2 In. 330.00
Casket, Napoleonic Scenes, Cover, Napoleon On Horseback Finial, 14 In. 6900.00
Cup, Cover, Ostrich Form, Detachable Head, Ruby Glass Eyes, 10 3/4 In. 5175.00
Cup, Engraved Ribbon-Tied Swags Of Fruit, Treffler I, c.1700, 4 5/8 In. 2300.00

Cup, Flaring Sides, Floral Repousse Reserves, 19th Century 880.00
Cup, Flaring Sides, Machined Finish, 19th Century 935.00
Cup, Floral Finial, Standing Pineapple, Woodsman Stem, Linden, 1620 .... 4312.00
Dish, Sweetmeat, Scroll Handles, Foliate Strapwork, Biller II, c.1700, 5 1/8 In. 1725.00
Dish, Venus In Shell Boat, Pulled By Cupid, Schurmann, c.1870, 8 In. 1150.00
Goblet, Presentation, Beer Meister, Gold Gilded Interior, 1899, 13 3/4 In. 1600.00
Jug, Claret, Duck Form, Schleissner, Early 20th Century, 11 In. 2587.00
Platter, Oval Form, Beaded Rim, Engraved Crest, 19th Century, 18 1/2 In. 489.00
Stein, Brewery, Cover, Gold Wash Interior, Francois Sy, Emil Wagner, 14 In. 1495.00
Sugar, Basket, Floral Fruit, Swing Handle, Removable Interior Bowl, 1880s 258.00
Sugar Box, Hinged Cover & Handle, Bands Of Strapwork, IC, 3 3/4 In. 4830.00
Tea Caddy, Scenes Of Sacrifice Of Isaac, T GS, 1760, 6 In. 4312.00
Tray, Art Nouveau, Allegorical Frolicking Youths, Handles, WMF, 14 In. 250.00
Tray, Mounted Brazilian Gold & Silver Coins, 1898 U.S. Gold Coin, 20 In. 5750.00
Tray, Reticulated, Rosebud, Putti Medallions, Putti In Relief, 9 x 9 In. 300.00
SILVER-GUATEMALAN, Beaker, Gilt Interior, c.1800, 9 Oz., 4 1/8 In. 3162.00
SILVER-HUNGARIAN, Beaker, Chased Fruit, Lobate Strapwork, Koszeghy, c.1680, 6 In. .. 8625.00
Beaker, Strapwork Grotesque Masks, Kreisch I, c.1660, 7 In. 9775.00
Breakfast Service, Fitted Satin Lined Box, Late 19th Century, 6 Piece 2530.00
Tea & Coffee Set, Tray, Lobed Fluted Pear Form, Rose Finials, 5 Piece 3737.00
SILVER-INDIAN, Tea Set, Rib, Cobra Handles, Elephant Finial, 5 3/4-In. Pot, 3 Piece 440.00
Tureen, Soup, Cover, Elephant Finial, Ladle, 9 1/2 x 11 1/2 In. 440.00
SILVER-IRISH, Bowl, Floral Scrolls, Dolphin & Chinese Man, S. Walker, c.1759, 5 1/4 In. .. 385.00
Butter, Underplate, Repousse Floral Motif Cover, Floral Finial, 1821, 6 1/2 In. 805.00
Cake Basket, Pierced Sides, Band Of Linked Quatrefoils, Graham, c.1750, 14 In. 5175.00
Coffee Set, Applied Banded Design, Wood Handle, Dublin, 1920-21, 3 Piece 715.00
Coffee Urn, Vase Form, Festoons, Contemporary Arms, Breading, 1789, 18 1/4 In. 4312.00
Creamer, Floral & Repousse Design, Lyre Handle, Webbed Feet, Andrew Goodwin 550.00
Cup, Twin Scroll Handles, Engraved Crest, Robert Calderwood, 7 1/2 In. 2310.00
Jug, Claret, Armada Pattern, Gilt Interior, JS, 1865, 15 In. 3335.00
Plate, Reeded Rims, Ribbons, Engraved Arms, Laughlin, 1760, 9 3/4 In., 6 Piece 8625.00
Salver, Shell & Scroll Rim, Engraved Arms, 4 Hoof Feet, J. Le Bass, 1813, 21 In. 5175.00
Sauceboat, Floral Design, Birds & Lion, Paw Feet, 6 5/8 In. 495.00
Sauceboat, Scene Of Cows & Flowers, Cherub Feet, A. Goodwin, c.1739, 6 In. 742.00
Sauceboat, Swan, Dolphin & Leaf Body, Lyre Handle, Shell Feet, 1760s 357.00
Serving Spoon, Dublin, 1828 .... 135.00
SILVER-ITALIAN, Box, Turtle Shape, Shell Hinged, Signed, Ni Notto, 10 3/4 In. 4255.00
Tureen, Soup, Cover, Lobed & Fluted Bombe Sides, Buccellati, c.1970, 13 1/2 In. 4600.00
SILVER-JAMAICAN, Sugar, Cover, Inverted Pear Form, C. Allan, 1750s, 7 3/4 In. 4312.00
SILVER-JAPANESE, Teapot, Ceremonial 375.00
SILVER-MEXICAN, Box, Janna Thomas, Taxco, Signed 250.00
Cake Stand, Center Floral Handle, 3 Graduated Trays, Torre Blanca 685.00
Casket, Trunk Form, Aztec Figures, Hammered Ground, 12 In. 1437.00
Coffee Set, After Dinner, Conquistador, 3 Piece 330.00
Coffeepot, Paneled Baluster Form, Acorn Finial, Scrolled Handle, 10 1/2 In. 405.00
Cup, Child's, Incised Design, Applied Handle, Spratling, 3 1/2 In. 465.00
Dish, Central Handle, Sectioned, Heart Form, 12 In. 88.00
Dish, Condiment, Sterling, 5 Compartments, Round, 13 1/2 In. 165.00
Dish, Serving, Chamfered Corners, Rectangular, 1 1/2 x 9 x 15 In. 165.00
Dish, Serving, Scalloped, Oval, 14 x 10 In. 295.00
Dish, Vegetable, Chamfered Corners, 1 1/2 x 10 x 10 In., Pair 192.00
Salt, Applied Medallion, Footed, Spoon, Spratling, 2 1/2 x 1 1/2 In., Pair 880.00
Salt & Pepper, Joined Concave Triangular Segments, Antonio Pineda 690.00
Salt & Pepper, Sterling, Marked, Janna 144.00
Tea & Coffee Set, Rosebud Handles & Finials, Scalloped Oval Tray, 6 Piece 8050.00
Tea Set, Melon Rib, Rope Twist Handles, Tray, 5 Piece 880.00
Tea Set, Paneled Baluster Form, Molded Floral Designs, 91 Oz. 805.00
Tray, Shallow Rim, Sterling, Circular, 8 x 8 In. 58.00
SILVER-NORWEGIAN, Bowl, Paneled, Hammered Surface, Wood Trunk Supports, 9 3/4 In. .. 2587.00
SILVER-PERUVIAN, Ashtray, 4 In., 3 Piece 44.00
Bowl, Paul Revere Style, Boardman, Engraved Names, 5 x 9 1/4 In. 132.00
Bowl, Vegetable, Applied Border, 12 1/2 In. 154.00
Bowl, Vegetable, Double, Cover, Applied Border, 12 1/2 In. 192.00

Butter, 4 In. 88.00
Coffee Set, Coffeepot, Sugar, Cover, Creamer, 3 Piece 275.00
Dish, Bread, Applied Border, 12 1/2 In. 110.00
Dish, Footed, Applied Border, 2 x 6 In., Pair 77.00
Dresser Set, Mirror, Hairbrushes, Clothes Brushes, 6 Piece 165.00
Finger Bowl, Applied Border, 4 3/4 x 2 1/4 In., 12 Piece 302.00
Gravy Boat, Tray, Applied Border, 9 1/2 In. 165.00
Ornament, Table, Fighting Cock, Pair 1045.00
Pitcher, Water, Swirl Form, Applied Border, 8 3/4 In. 330.00
Plate, Dinner, Applied Border, 11 In., 12 Piece 1760.00
Platter, Applied Border, Oval, 22 In. 357.00
Platter, Applied Border, Rectangular, 17 1/2 x 10 In. 302.00
Platter, Applied Border, Round, 14 In. 176.00
Platter, Applied Border, Round, 16 In. 247.00
Platter, Fish, Applied Border, Oval, 24 1/2 In. 275.00
Platter, Meat, Applied Border, Oval, 19 In. 330.00
Punch Set, 4 Ivory Balls Separate Base From Bowl, 11 Piece 1540.00
Shaker, Martini, 10 1/2 In. 165.00
Shaker, Pepper, 4 In., 6 Piece 110.00
Smoking Set, 12 1/2 In., 2 Piece 143.00
Table Tableau, Mirrored, Applied Border, 21 x 18 In. 330.00
Tea Set, Swirl Form, Applied Border, 8 Piece 2860.00
Vase, Flower, Globe Form, 2 Handles, 7 1/4 In. 154.00
SILVER-POLISH, Box, Sugar, Hinged, Cover, Lion Finial, T. Klimaszewki, c.1810, 6 3/8 In. .. 2300.00
SILVER-PORTUGUESE, Inkstand, Hinged Cover, Stepped Rectangular, 1930s, 12 In. 4125.00
Pitcher, Footed, Elongated Handle, 18th Century, 10 1/2 In. 797.00

SILVER-RUSSIAN. Russian silver is marked with the Cyrillic, or
Russian, alphabet. The numbers 84, 88, or 91 indicate the silver con-
tent. Russian silver may be higher or lower than sterling standard.
Other marks indicate maker, assayer, or city of manufacture. Many
pieces of silver made in Russia are decorated with enamel. Faberge
pieces are listed in their own category.

SILVER-RUSSIAN, Beaker, Multicolored Scroll & Foliate, Gilt Wash Interior, 3 1/2 In. 460.00
Bowl, Ladle, Chased With Flowers, Shellwork, Scrolls, 1833, 7 1/4 x 12 In. 690.00
Box, Carved With Strapwork, Gilded Interior, 4 Bracket Feet, Moscow, 5 In. 920.00
Cake Basket, Foliage Design, Swing Handle, Oval, Moscow, 1900, 8 3/4 In. 345.00
Cake Basket, Rococo Ornament, Swing Handle, Moscow, 1890, 9 1/2 In. 2587.00
Chalice, Engraved Evangelists, Repousse, 19th Century, 9 In. ....*Illus* 1650.00
Cigar Box, Gilded, Paper Tax Bands, Wood Grain, Moscow, 1900, 5 1/2 In. 2587.00
Cigar Box, Table, Carved Paper Tax Bands, Alexander Lokin, 1890, 4 1/8 In. 2300.00
Cigar Case, Chased With Wavy Design, Gilded Interior, 1847, 5 In. 1610.00
Cigar Case, Enameled, Flowers, Foliage, Stippled Ground, 4 3/4 In. 2587.00
Cigar Case, Scrolled Foliage, Hinged Half-Cover, Rectangular, 1856, 5 1/8 In. 1840.00
Cigarette Case, Applied Gold Charms, Signatures, 1900, 4 1/4 In. 1150.00
Cigarette Case, Cover, Foliage, Enameled, Moscow, 1910, 4 1/2 In. 4887.00
Cigarette Case, Dove Design On Cover, Rectangular, Moscow, 1910, 4 In. 1495.00
Cigarette Case, Enameled, Flowers, Foliage, Moscow, 1910, 4 1/4 In. 1610.00
Cigarette Case, Gold, Inscribed 1899, 3 3/4 x 2 1/2 x 5 1/8 In. 330.00
Cigarette Case, Plumed Exotic Birds Amidst Foliage, Stippled Ground, 4 In. 2070.00
Cordial, Stem, Floral Engraving, C.K. 65.00
Cross, Altar, Reliquary, Silver Gilt, 1886, 16 In. ....*Illus* 2200.00
Easter Egg, Stylized Foliage, Peach, Pale Blue, Dark Blue Ground, 1900, 3 In. 2300.00
Egg, Gilt Wasps, Vines, Cartouches, Garnet Cabochons, Ovchinnikov 4890.00
Flask, Applied Gold Monogram, Screw-On Top, 1887, 6 3/8 In. 2185.00
Inkwell, Domed, Fox's Head Shape, 4 Ball Feet, Old Russian Style Border, 4 In. 1725.00
Jug, Claret, Scroll Design, Silver Mounted Grapevine, Hinged Cover, 1900, 9 In. 690.00
Kovsh, Bearded Sage, Lion Handle, Gray, Green Ground, Moscow, 1910, 7 In. 5750.00
Kovsh, Foliage, Green, Blue, Cream Ground, Enamel Border, 1900, 3 3/4 In. 920.00
Kovsh, Foliage, Pale Green Ground, Scroll Handle, Ring Foot, 1900, 6 In. 3162.00
Kovsh, Lobed Figure Covered With Foliage, Hook Handle, Moscow, 1910, 6 In. 3450.00
Salt, Footed, Engraved Floral Glass Insert, Dated 1886, 1 1/2 In. 125.00
Samovar, Bulbous Body, Square Base, Wood Fittings, 1900, 25 1/2 In. 690.00

Silver-Russian,
Chalice, Engraved
Evangelists, Repousse,
19th Century, 9 In.

Silver-Russian,
Cross, Altar,
Reliquary, Silver Gilt,
1886, 16 In.

Snuffbox, Engraved Design, 1888	425.00
Snuffbox, Niello, Cover, Scrolled Foliage Border, Moscow, 1852, 3 3/4 In.	2185.00
Spoon, Demitasse, Parcel Gilt, 1895, 4 1/4 In., Pair	220.00
Stirrup Cup, Stag Form, Gild Interior, St. Petersburg, 1870, 4 In.	6612.00
Tankard, Barrel Form, Foliate Cartouche, Hinged Cover, Moscow, 1894, 6 In.	1610.00
Tea Set, Ivory Handles & Finial, Grigoriev, 1834, 6 Piece	5600.00
Teapot, Enameled, Blue Sky, Scroll Handle, Hinged Cover, 1886, 4 1/4 In.	1150.00
Vase, Foliage, Cylindrical, Inscribed, 1900, 7 3/8 In.	920.00
Vase, Square Section, 4 Sides With Silver Vases Of Flowers, Notched Rim, 5 In.	2300.00
Whiskey, Engraved, Dated 1896, 4 In., Pair	165.00
Wine, 1895, 2 1/2 In.	60.00
Wine, 2 1/2 x 2 1/2 In.	50.00
Wine, Cut Design, Pedestal, 3 3/4 In.	125.00
SILVER-SCOTTISH, Cup & Saucer, 6 1/4 In.-Saucer	465.00
Letter Opener, Form Of Dress Sword, Monogram	220.00
Sugar, Cover, Gadroons, Ball Finial, c.1720, 4 3/4 In.	3162.00
SILVER-SPANISH, Box, Putto Finial, Beaded Borders, Fleur-De-Lis, Gilt Silver, 4 3/4 In.	4025.00
Chamber Pot, Everted Rim, Stylized Leaf & Scroll Handle, 1830s, 8 1/4 In.	3737.00

SILVER-STERLING. Sterling silver is made with 925 parts silver out of
1,000 parts of metal. The word *sterling* is a quality guarantee used in
the United States after about 1860. The word was used much earlier in
England and Ireland. Pieces listed here are not identified by country.
Other pieces of sterling quality silver are listed under Silver-American,
Silver-English, etc.

SILVER-STERLING, Basket, Pierced, Oval, Ball Feet, 12 x 7 In.	247.00
Bowl, Centerpiece, Repousse Footed, Waterfall Design	4000.00
Bowl, Flowers In Relief, Monogram, 9 1/2 x 3 In.	300.00
Bowl, Pierced Cherry & Foliate Border, 2 x 10 In.	247.00
Box, Polychrome Floral, Blue & White Enamel, 1 9/16 In.	275.00
Candelabrum is listed in its own category.	
Candlesticks are listed in their own category.	
Case, Calling Card, Phoenix Bird, Blue Enamel Design, 4 In.	450.00
Cigar Case, Engraved, Presentation Inscription, 5 x 2 1/2 In.	220.00
Cigar Cutter, 2-End, Desk Top	295.00
Cigar Cutter, Embossed Nude	95.00
Cigarette Case, Lighter, Fitted, Engraved Leaf Design, Marked Silver 950, 4 In.	143.00
Condiment Set, Rickshaw	115.00
Creamer, Inscribed Richard & Mary Jan 2nd 1869, Leather Case, 7 1/2 In.	265.00
Dresser Set, Art Nouveau Style, c.1903, 7 Piece	525.00
Dresser Set, Parrots, Foliage, Art Deco	650.00
Dresser Set, Woman's, Turquoise, Hand Mirror, Comb, 2 Piece	110.00
Flask, Dragonflies, Hammered Finish, 5 3/8 In.	440.00
Gravy Boat, Greek Key Design, Coughlan, Early 20th Century, 5 1/2 x 9 In.	175.00
Holder, Dance Card	235.00

Horn, On Marble Base, 5 1/4 x 7 In. 143.00
Lipstick Holder, Engraved Swirls On Sides, Mirror Inside, 2 1/4 x 3/4 In. 40.00
Mirror, Hand, Engraved B On Back, 11 x 5 1/4 In. 30.00
Mug, Embossed, Engraved Andrew 65.00
Napkin Rings are listed in their own category.
Pepper Mill 55.00
Pill Box, Horse Applied To Horseshoe 65.00
Pin, Flower Holder 125.00
Pitcher, Cylindrical Body, Ebony Handle, 9 3/4 In. 2587.00
Pitcher, Marked J. Goldstein, 16 Troy Oz., 7 7/8 In. 286.00
Pitcher, Water, Beaded Border, Monogram, 8 In. 121.00
Platter, R.W. & S., 19 x 12 1/2 In. 495.00
Pot, Mustard, Hinged Cover, Spoon, Handle, Footed, Blue Glass Liner, 3 x 2 In. 150.00
Salt, Cup Form, Fitted Leather Case, HB Stamwood, c.1820, 3/4 x 1 3/8 In., 6 Piece 103.00
Salt, Georgian Design, Shell & Leaf Border, Lion Head & Claw Feet, Pair 135.00
Salt & Pepper, Pear Form Bodies, 3 Hoof Feet, 4 1/2 In. 55.00
Saltshaker, Floral Repousse, L.S. Lee, 5 1/2 In. 38.00
Samovar, Flame Finial, Scalloped Rim, Square Base, Sheffield, 18 In. 220.00
Shot Measure, Just A Thimble Full 45.00
Spoon, Tea Caddy, Ship Handle 65.00
Spoon, Souvenir, see Souvenir category.
Sugar Shaker, Engraved Crystal, 5 1/2 In. 132.00
Tag, Engraved Scotch & Whiskey 40.00
Tea Ball, Chain 65.00
Tea Ball, Teapot Shape, Signed 60.00
Tea Set, Floral Relief Rims & Handles, Toodnow & Jenks, c.1900, 3 Piece 632.00
Tea Set, Kenilworth, Plain, 5 Piece 5900.00
Toothpick, Top Hat Form 60.00
Tray, Everted Border, Scrolling Foliage, Presentation, c.1900, 29 34 In. 4600.00
Tray, TMW Monogram, Compass Mark, Round, 1908, 11 3/4 In. 115.00
Vase, Contemporary, Borgila, 5 7/8 In. 410.00
Vase, Paneled, Foliate Engraved, Weighted Pedestal, 14 In. 440.00
Whistle, Key Chain, Relief Floral Design, 1 1/2 In. 40.00

SINCLAIRE cut glass was made by H.P. Sinclaire and Company of
Corning, New York, between 1905 and 1929. He cut glass made at
other factories until 1920. Pieces were made of crystal as well as
amber, blue, green, or ruby glass. Only a small percentage of Sinclaire
glass is marked with the S in a wreath.

Basket, Aster-Type Flower, Signed, 16 1/2 x 11 1/2 In. 900.00
Bowl, Center, Atlanta Engraving, Elfin Green, Rolled Edge, 12 In. 250.00
Bowl, Pillar Optic Design, Amber, 14 In. 95.00
Candleholder, Intaglio Engraved On Mushroom Top, Signed, 3 1/2 In., Pair 15.00
Compote, Pillar Optic, Amber, 14 In. 125.00
Plate, Flutes & Panel, Signed, 8 1/4 In. 70.00
Tray, Bull's Eye, Hobstars, Fans, Stars With Hobstar Center, Signed, 8 1/2 x 10 In. 425.00
Tray, Snowflakes & Holly, Square, Signed, 10 x 8 1/4 In. 1300.00
Vase, Fan, Engraved Floral Spray 2 Sides, Amber, 8 In. 150.00
Vase, Green, 14 In. ....98.00 to 125.00

SKIING, see Sports category.

SLAG GLASS resembles a marble cake. It can be streaked with different
colors. There were many types made from about 1880. Caramel slag is
the incorrect name for Chocolate glass. Pink slag was an American
Victorian product made by Harry Barstow and Thomas E.A. Dugan at
Indiana, Pennsylvania. Purple and blue slag were made in American
and English factories. Red slag is a very late Victorian and twentieth-
century glass. Other colors are known but are of less importance to the
collector. New versions of chocolate glass and colored slag glass are
being made.

Caramel slag is listed in the Chocolate Glass category.
Green, Lamp, 8 Rectangular Panels, 20 x 13 In. 575.00

Green, Sugar, Cover 90.00
Pink, Punch Set, Inverted Fan & Feather, 12 Matte Cups, 13 Piece 14500.00
Pink, Toothpick 650.00
Purple, Basket, Grape Design 59.00
Purple, Bowl, Rose Pattern, 9 In. 135.00
Purple, Bowl, Ruffled, 8 In. 95.00
Purple, Cruet, Stopper 75.00
Purple, Figurine, Owl 68.00
Purple, Platter, Daisy 95.00
Purple, Soap Dish 45.00
Purple, Toothpick, Scroll & Acanthus 500.00
Red, Eggcup, Chicken, 4 1/8 x 4 3/4 In. 11.00

SLEEPY EYE collectors look for anything bearing the image of the nineteenth-century Indian chief with the drooping eyelid. The Sleepy Eye Milling Co., Sleepy Eye, Minnesota, used his portrait in advertising from 1883 to 1921. It offered many premiums, including stoneware and pottery steins, crocks, bowls, mugs, and pitchers, all decorated with the famous profile of the Indian. The popular pottery was made by Western Stoneware, Weir Pottery Company, and other companies long after the flour mill went out of business in 1921. Reproductions of the pitchers are being made today. The original pitchers came in only five sizes: 4 inches, 5 1/4 inches, 6 1/2 inches, 8 inches, and 9 inches. The Sleepy Eye image was also used by companies unrelated to the flour mill.

Crock, Butter, Stoneware 525.00
Crock, Salt 450.00
Label, Barrel, Lithographed, Frame, 16 In. 495.00
Mug, Blue & White, Bottom Ink Stamp, 4 1/4 In. 135.00
Mug, Commemorative, Blue, 1980, 4 1/4 In. 90.00
Pillow Cover, Chief Old Sleepy Eye, President Monroe, 1824 .... 700.00 to 1000.00
Pitcher, Commemorative, Green, 1987 .... 45.00
Pitcher, No. 1, Blue & Gray, Western Stoneware Circle Mark, 4 In. 525.00
Pitcher, No. 1, Blue & White, 4 In. .... 105.00 to 220.00
Pitcher, No. 1, Blue Rim, Maple Leaf Mark, 4 In. 900.00
Pitcher, No. 1, Brown, 4 In. 2100.00
Pitcher, No. 2, Blue & Gray, 5 1/4 In. .... 450.00 to 495.00
Pitcher, No. 2, Blue & White, 5 1/4 In. .... 210.00 to 500.00
Pitcher, No. 3, Blue & White, 6 1/2 In. 185.00
Pitcher, No. 4, Blue & White, 8 In. .... 400.00 to 450.00
Pitcher, No. 4, Lakins Christmas, Blue & White, 8 In. 2200.00
Pitcher, No. 5, Blue & White, 9 In. .... 130.00 to 190.00
Plate, Commemorative, 1976 .... 70.00
Plate, Commemorative, 1977 .... 45.00
Plate, Commemorative, 1978 .... 35.00
Plate, Commemorative, 1980 .... 40.00
Plate, Commemorative, 1989 .... 65.00
Plate, Commemorative, 1990 .... 33.00
Salt Bowl, Flemish Blue, Gray, Embossed Design, 6 1/2 In. 330.00
Stein, Blue & Gray, 7 3/4 In. 695.00
Stein, Brown & White, 7 3/4 In. 850.00
Stein, Brown & Yellow, 7 3/4 In. 575.00
Stein, Chestnut, Brown, 1952, 40 Oz. 225.00
Stein, Cobalt Blue, 7 3/4 In. 2200.00
Stein, Green & White, 7 3/4 In. 7100.00
Vase, Cattails, Indian Head, 8 1/2 In. 295.00

SLIPWARE is named for *slip,* a thin mixture of clay and water, about the consistency of sour cream, which is applied to pottery for decoration. It is a very old method of making pottery and is still in use.

Cup, Fuddling, Yellow Glaze, White Slip, Redware Body, 1786, 7 3/4 In. 1725.00
Tray, Bread, Coggled Edge, 3 Slip Trailed Squiggles, Lined, 8 x 12 In. 412.00

SLOT MACHINES are included in the Coin-Operated Machine category.

SMITH BROTHERS glass was made after 1878. Alfred and Harry Smith had worked for the Mt. Washington Glass Company in New Bedford, Massachusetts, for seven years before going into their own shop. They made many pieces with enamel decoration.

Smith Bros. Co.

Biscuit Jar, Pink Roses, Raised Gold Leaves, Gold, Melon Ribbed, 1886, 7 In.	1045.00
Bowl, Melon Shape, Blue Pansies, Blue Beaded Top, 1800s, 2 1/2 x 4 In.	125.00
Jar, Enamel Daisy Design, Signed, 2 1/4 x 3 1/4 In.	200.00
Rose Bowl, Bulbous, 2 Sprays Of Daisy Flowers, Beige, 4 1/2 In.	325.00
Salt, Melon Ribbed Body, Small Flowers & Buds, Beaded Top, 1 1/4 x 2 In.	92.00
Sugar & Creamer, Lion, Melon Ribbed, Red	550.00
Sugar & Creamer, Middletown Quadruple Plated Frame, Ornate Handle	300.00
Toothpick, Wild Rose, Blue Leaves, White Ground, Beaded Top, 5 3/4 In.	495.00
Toothpick, Wild Rose, Blue Leaves, White Ground, Beaded Top, Ribbed, 3 In.	495.00
Vase, Double Canteen, Floral Design, Pale Green Ground, 7 x 8 x 2 In.	90.00
Vase, Girl Feeding Chickens, Allover Pink, Signed, 5 3/4 In.	165.00
Vase, Petticoat Ring, Kate Greenaway Figures, Soft Beige, 6 1/2 In., Pair	675.00
Vase, Yellow, Orchid Pansies, Beige, White Opal Lining, 1880s, 4 In.	138.00

SNOW BABIES, made from bisque and spattered with glitter sand, were first manufactured in 1864 by Hertwig and Company of Thuringia. Other German and Japanese companies copied the Hertwig designs. Originally, Snow Babies were made of candy and used as Christmas decorations. There are also Snow Babies tablewares made by Royal Bayreuth. Copies of the small Snow Babies figurines are being made today and can easily confuse the collector.

Candy Container, Child Laying On Tummy, Flocked Sled, Holding Skis, 2 1/2 In.	225.00
Creamer, Bulbous, 3 1/2 In.	120.00
Figurine, 2 Babies On Sled	595.00
Figurine, 3 Babies On Sled, Germany, c.1910, 3 In.	225.00
Figurine, Baby On Bear, 2 In.	150.00
Figurine, Elf, Riding Horse, 1 1/2 In.	150.00
Figurine, On Sled Pulled By 2 Dogs, Germany, Prewar, 3 In.	126.00
Figurine, On Sled Pulled By Reindeer, Germany, Prewar, 3 In.	112.00
Figurine, Reclining, Germany, 3 1/2 In.	185.00
Figurine, Skater, Painted, Germany, Prewar, 2 1/4 In.	247.00
Figurine, Standing, 1 1/2 In.	65.00

SNUFF BOTTLES are listed in the Bottle category.

SNUFFBOXES held snuff. Taking snuff was popular long before cigarettes became available. The gentleman or lady would take a small pinch of the ground tobacco or snuff in the fingers, then sniff it and sneeze. Snuffboxes were made of many materials, including gold, silver, enameled metal, and wood. Most snuffboxes date from the late eighteenth or early nineteenth centuries.

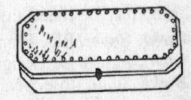

Agate & Sterling Silver, Birmingham, 1897, 1 1/2 x 2 In.	625.00
Bone, Rotating Model, Brass Hinges, Napoleonic Wars, P.O.W., 1 5/8 x 1 1/16 In.	375.00
Boy Lighting Pipe, Garden, 1785, Rectangular, China, 3 1/8 In.	3160.00
Brass, Engraved Flowers On Lid, W. Yates, 1846, 2 1/2 In.	220.00
Brass, Oval, Engraved T. Sherwood, 1882, 2 1/2 In.	110.00
Brass, Sir Ralph Abercrombie Cover, 2 1/2 In.	250.00
Burl Imitating Sunburst, Tortoiseshell Lined, c.1815, 2 1/8 x 1 1/4 In.	275.00
Burled Sycamore, 19th Century	85.00
Carved & Painted Horn, Adam & Eve With Apple, Interior Erotic Scene, 4 1/2 In.	750.00
Copper, Lead Lined, Book Shape, 3 x 2 1/2 In.	78.00
German Silver, Scene Of Sailor, Ship & Lighthouse, 1860, 3 1/4 In.	145.00
Gold, Enameled, Allegorical Scene On Cover, Blue Stripes, White Border, 3 In.	4025.00
Gold, Enameled, Alpine Scene On Cover, Leaf Tip Border, Blue, 1810, 3 In.	9775.00
Gold, Enameled, Hinged Lid, Black Geometric Design, Blue Ground, 1815, 3 In.	10350.00
Gold, Enameled, Hinged Lid, Cameo Female Head Figure, Leaf Tip Border, 2 In.	2300.00
Gold, Enameled, Hinged Lid, Garden Scene, Blue, Pearl Border, 1805, 3 In.	5750.00

Gold, Enameled, Hinged Lid, Maiden In Forest, White Flower Border, Base, Blue	5465.00
Gold, Foliage Design, Shell Thumbpiece, Rectangular, Continental, 1850, 2 In.	920.00
Gold, Green, Gold Leaf Tip Border, Red, Gold Ground, Paris, 1780, 3 1/2 In.	5750.00
Gold, Peasants With Their Flock Scene On Cover, Continental, 1820, 3 1/2 In.	1840.00
Lacquer, Brass & Pewter Inlay, 1870	110.00
Lacquer, Miniature Painting Called Scandal	250.00
Paktong, Band Design Cover, Oval	185.00
Papier-Mache, Hand Painted, Landscape On Cover, 19th Century, 3 In.	150.00
Porcelain, Figure Of Woman, Quimper, 1904	285.00
Porcelain, Heart Shaped, Boy Playing Flute, Quimper, Klate, 19th Century	454.00
Pressed Burl, Peasant Celebration, Tortoiseshell Interior, 1830, 3 1/8 In.	595.00
Silver, Chased & Engraved, Engraved, Wm. Summers, 1882, 2 7/8 In.	7500.00
Silver, Hardstone Mounted, Stylized Foliage, 1880s, 3 1/4 In.	3105.00
Walnut Burl, Barrel Form, Pin Hinge, Scalloped Grooves, Lined, Scotland, 3 1/4 In.	450.00
Wood, Brass Wire Inlay Design, Thistle, Bird On Branch, Shoe Form, 1878, 4 1/4 In.	275.00
Wood, Faux Grained Book, Lead Lining, c.1820, 3 3/8 x 2 In.	475.00

SOAPSTONE is a mineral that was used for foot warmers or griddles because of its heat-retaining properties. Soapstone was carved into figurines and bowls in many countries in the nineteenth and twentieth centuries. Most of the soapstone seen today is from China or Japan. It is still being carved in the old styles.

Bookends, Carved, With Vase Of Flowers, Early 20th Century, 5 x 7 In., Pair	115.00
Bookends, Pair	35.00
Figurine, Bird, In Fruit Tree, 9 1/2 x 6 1/4 In.	35.00
Figurine, Buddha, Seated, Cream, White, 19th Century, 1 3/8 In.	345.00
Figurine, Caballo, Of Seated Horse, Green, Black Formica Base, 12 In.	578.00
Figurine, Female Head, Scrolled Headdress, Signed, Schatzberg, 1983, 19 In.	275.00
Figurine, Foo Lion Finial, Rectangular, 19th Century, 4 In.	110.00
Figurine, Immortal, Standing, Head Bent Down, Carrying Woven Basket, 4 In.	230.00
Figurine, Man Smoking Pipe, 2 Children Playing, Signed, 5 1/4 In.	115.00
Figurine, Ram & Kids, Wooden Base, 6 In.	50.00
Goblet, Turned, America, Early 19th Century, 5 5/8 In.	395.00
Salt, c.1840, 1 1/2 x 2 3/4 In.	135.00
Vase, Bird Of Paradise & Floral, 9 /4 In.	187.00
Vase, Double Urn Form, Carved Flowers & Jardinieres, c.1900, 6 3/4x 9 1/2 In.	65.00
Vase, Floral, 11 3/4 In.	110.00
Vase, Floral, Aviary Design, Green, Beige, 11 In.	70.00

SOFT PASTE is a name for a type of pottery. Although it looks very much like porcelain, it is a chemically different material. Most of the soft-paste wares were made in the early nineteenth century. Other pieces may be listed under Gaudy Dutch or Leeds.

Bowl, Cover, Blue Floral, Leaf Design, 5 x 5 In.	35.00
Bowl, Impressed Design, 2 Carp, Floral Border, China, 18th Century, 11 In.	374.00
Bowl, Soup, Rose, Scalloped Border, 8 1/4 In.	44.00
Creamer, King's Rose, Vine Border	90.00 to 126.00
Cup & Saucer, Blue & Brown Tulip, 3-In. Saucer	66.00
Cup & Saucer, Kings Rose, Oyster Pattern, Solid Border, Handleless	40.00
Cup & Saucer, Swirled Fluting, Polychrome Design	66.00
Dish, Oval, Straight Sides, Bird's-Head Handles, Blue Transfer, 9 3/4 x 16 In.	130.00
Jug, Cream, Flowering Prunus Branches, S-Scroll Handle, St. Cloud, 1745, 3 1/4 In.	1610.00
Jug, Milk, Foliate Molded, 3 Prunus Sprigs, Silver Rim, St. Cloud, 1750, 4 5/8 In.	4312.00
Mug, Red, Blue & Green Stripes, Octagonal, 4 In.	132.00
Plate, King's Rose, 10 In.	110.00
Plate, Portrait General LaFayette, Welcome To Land Of Liberty, 7 In.	1150.00
Plate, Queen's Rose, 6 1/2 In.	50.00
Plate, Queen's Rose, Vine Border, 10 In.	110.00
Plate, Wood's Rose, Scalloped Edge, 9 In.	120.00
Sugar, Cover, Christmas Eve Pattern, Deep Blue Transfer, 6 1/2 In.	180.00
Teapot, Adam, Black Transfer, Canary Yellow, 3 1/2 In.	467.00
Teapot, Cover, Brown, Yellow, Orange Bands, Ribbon Twist, Green Leaves, 6 1/4 In.	58.00
Teapot, King's Rose, Solid Border, 5 1/2 In.	440.00

Teapot, Rose, Broken Solid Border, 5 3/4 In.	110.00
Teapot, Rose, Scalloped Borders, 5 1/2 In.	137.00
Vase, Moriage Floral Design, 13 In.	66.00
Vase, Polychrome Birds, Bamboo Designed, Allover Craquelure, 13 In., Pair	825.00

SOUVENIRS of a trip—what could be more fun? Our ancestors enjoyed the same thing and souvenirs were made for almost every location. Most of the souvenir pottery and porcelain pieces of the nineteenth century were made in England or Germany, even if the picture showed a North American scene. In the twentieth century, the souvenir china business seems to have gone to the manufacturers in Japan, Taiwan, Hong Kong, England, and America. Another popular souvenir item is the souvenir spoon, made of sterling or silver plate. These are usually made in the country pictured on the spoon. Related pieces may be found in the Coronation and World's Fair categories.

Ashtray, Astronauts On Moon, Peoria Journal Star	20.00
Ashtray, Citadel, Milk Glass	2.00
Ashtray, Fish, Cape Cod, Green, Treasure Craft	15.00
Ashtray, Pond, 2 Flamingos, Florida, 1950s, 5 x 3 1/2 In.	50.00
Baby Shoe, High Top, Silver, Gorham	135.00
Berlin Wall Fragment, Sold Through Ronald Reagan Presidential Library	20.00
Bowl, XIII Olympic Winter Games, Clear Glass, 1980, 6 1/4 x 1 5/8 In.	12.00
Box, Shell Covered, Detroit, 9 In.	55.00
Button, Flasher, Moon Landing	6.00
Creamer, Child's, Lacy Medallion, Green, Gold Trim	24.00
Cup, Stillwater, Okla.	25.00
Hula Dancer, Aloha Hawaii, Ceramic, Flexible Waist, Silk Thread Grass Skirt, 8 In.	190.00
Knife, Folding, Paris, Eiffel Tower, Swiss Army Crest, 6 Blades, 1940s	38.00
Lamp, New York City, Red, Plastic, Lighted Top, 1939, 8 In., Pair	60.00
Lighter-Cigarette Case, Mt. Fuji, Pagoda, Flowers, Japan & Korea Map, Lido, 4 1/2 In.	94.00
Matches, Stork Club, Jumbo, 1940s	35.00
Medal, Pony Express, Oregon Trail Memorial Ass'N., Nickel Silver, 1860-1935	3.00
Mirror, Chelan, Washington, Bungalow Grill, Girl & Collie, 1940s, 11 x 4 In.	52.00
Mug, Beer, Harvard Rowing, 1900s	100.00
Mug, Bob Hope's Head, Ceramic	100.00
Pen Holder, Dallas Texas, Texas Ranger Of 1860, One Riot-One Ranger, 3 In.	40.00
Pennant, Hawaii, 1960s	15.00
Pennant, Indian Pow-Wow, Spokane, June 1913, Felt	95.00
Pennant, University Of Hawaii, White, On Green, Felt, 1915	95.00
Pennant, Wapakoneta, Oh., Home Of Astronaut Neil Armstrong, Felt, 9 x 18 In.	15.00
Pillow Cover, Panama Canal, Gold, 14 x 14 In. *Illus*	5.00
Pin, California Diamond Jubilee, Celluloid, Paper Insert, Pinback, 1925	5.50
Pin Tray, Gays Mills, Wis.	25.00
Pin Tray, Horseshoe	25.00
Plate, Butter, American Airlines Logo On Front, 3 3/4 In.	15.00
Plate, Erie Pennsylvania Court House, German Porcelain Lusterware, 5 3/4 In.	28.00

To get wrinkles out of old felt pennants, put the pennant face down on an ironing board. Then dampen a terry-cloth towel, squeeze it out, lay it over the pennant, and iron the towel with a warm iron. The method won't work on newer fiber-paper pennants, but it works on felt pennants made through the mid-1960s.

Souvenir, Pillow Cover, Panama Canal, Gold, 14 x 14 In.

Plate, Lamoni, Iowa, 6 In. 25.00
Plate, Niagara Falls, Bavarian China Lusterware, 7 3/4 In. 38.00
Plate, Nova Scotia, Foley, 7 In. 28.00
Scarf, Charlie Pride 8.00
Spoon, Battleship Maine, 1890s 9.00
Spoon, Miner, Figural Handle, Pueblo, Colorado 42.00
Spoon, Silver Plate, Birth Of Israel, Baby Face, 1948 .... 75.00
Spoon, Silver Plate, Carlsbad Cavern 33.00
Spoon, Silver Plate, John Kennedy 12.00
Spoon, Silver Plate, Omaha 100th Anniversary 22.00
Spoon, St. Louis, Eads Bridge, Touring Car Handle 110.00
Spoon, Sterling Silver, Colorado School Of Mines, Miner & Donkey 50.00
Spoon, Sterling Silver, Evanston, Wyoming, Cowboy Roping Steer 22.00
Spoon, Sterling Silver, McPherson, Kansas, Holly Berries 15.00
Spoon, Sterling Silver, New York Times Building, Figural Handle, Demitasse 45.00
Spoon, Sterling Silver, Oakland California, Fish Handle 25.00
Spoon, Sterling Silver, Patrick Henry Bust Handle 25.00
Spoon, Sterling Silver, Pittsburg, Outline Of City On Handle 28.00
Spoon, Sterling Silver, Roosevelt Bears, 3 1/2 In. 130.00
Spoon, Sterling Silver, Washington, D.C., White House, Bayonet Handle, 1892 ... 40.00
Ticket, Funeral Of General Grant, Frame, 1885, 4 x 2 1/2 In. 35.00
Toy, Bricks, Philadelphia Bicentennial, Slide Top Box, 1882, 26 Piece 110.00

SPANGLE GLASS is multicolored glass made from odds and ends of colored glass rods. It includes metallic flakes of mica covered with gold, silver, nickel, or copper. Spangle glass is usually cased with a thin layer of clear glass over the multicolored layer. Similar glass is listed in the Vasa Murrhina category.

Basket, Overlay, White Lining, Clear Thorny Applied Handle, 6 1/4 In. 175.00
Basket, Rose To Pink To White, Twisted Crystal Handle, Melon Ribbed, 7 1/2 In. 57.00
Basket, Silver Mica Over Opaque White, Crystal Rope Handle, 11 x 9 1/2 In. 172.00
Basket, Thorn Handle 145.00
Cruet, Pink, Silver Mica In Tree Of Life Design, White Lining, Stopper, 7 1/4 In. 275.00
Pitcher, Rib Blowouts, Heart-Shaped Pouring Spout, Silver Mica, 1883, 8 In. 575.00
Vase, Blue, Amber Case, Hobbs, 7 In. 225.00

SPANISH LACE is a type of Victorian glass that has a white lace design. Blue, yellow, cranberry, or clear glass was made with this distinctive white pattern. It was made in England and the United States after 1885. Copies are being made.

Bottle, Barber 95.00
Bottle, Barber, Cranberry, 8 1/8 In. 220.00
Bottle, Water, Reverse Swirl, Large 215.00
Bowl, 8 1/2 In. 15.00
Bowl, Ruffled, Cranberry 175.00
Bowl, Ruffled, Cranberry, Griffin, 4 1/2 x 10 In. 250.00
Butter, Cover, Vaseline 450.00
Lamp Base, Night, Burner 175.00
Rose Bowl, White 55.00
Sugar Shaker, Cranberry ....480.00 to 550.00
Toothpick, Reverse Swirl 135.00
Tumbler, Sateen Swirl 85.00

SPATTER GLASS is a multicolored glass made from many small pieces of different colored glass. It is sometimes called *End-of-Day* glass. It is still being made.

Basket, Pink, White, Amber Exterior, White Interior, Clear Thorn Handle, 7 x 5 In. 99.00
Basket, Pink, White, Amber Exterior, White Interior, Thorn Handle, 8 In. 99.00
Basket, Star Shape, Pink, Yellow Exterior, White Interior, Thorn Handle, 1880, 6 In. 250.00
Basket, White, Pink, Frosted Green, 7 1/2 In. 95.00
Basket, Yellow Exterior, Pink, Yellow, White Interior, Twisted Thorn Handle, 8 In. ..88.00 to 99.00
Bear, Blown, Clear Cased, 1880-1885 .... 185.00
Box, Yellow & White Cased In Crystal & Yellow, 1 1/4 x 2 1/8 In. 150.00

Cologne Bottle, Dresser, Stopper, Leaf Mold, Vaseline, Shiny 495.00
Cologne Bottle, Red, White, Blue, Applied Clear Rigaree, Stopper, 7 3/8 In. 550.00
Cruet, Stopper, Leaf Mold, Cranberry, Cased 595.00
Cruet, Stopper, Leaf Mold, Vaseline, Shiny 450.00
Pitcher, Raised Rib Design, Allover Cranberry, White, Bulbous, 8 1/2 x 6 1/2 In. 200.00
Pitcher, Raised Rib Design, Allover White, Dark Pink Pleated Top, Handle, 8 In. 150.00
Pitcher, Water, Leaf Umbrella, Cranberry 595.00
Pitcher, Water, Leaf Umbrella, Yellow Cased, Shiny ....495.00 to 595.00
Vase, Applied Glass Acorns, Oak Leaves, Enameled, Ormolu Feet, Yellow, 7 In. 193.00
Vase, Flared, 8 In. 30.00
Vase, Orange, Blue, 5 3/4 In. 28.00

SPATTERWARE is the creamware or soft paste dinnerware decorated
with colored spatter designs. The earliest pieces were made in the late
eighteenth century, but most of the spatterware found today was made
from about 1800 to 1850, or it is a form of kitchen crockery with added
spatter designs, made in the late nineteenth and twentieth centuries.
The early spatterware was made in the Staffordshire district of England
for sale in America. The later kitchen type is an American product.

Basket, Square, Thorny Handle, White Interior, 5 1/2 In. 165.00
Bowl, School House, Green On Black Field, Staffordshire, c.1840, 6 1/2 In. 1150.00
Bowl, Sugar, Cover, Holly Berry, Red Berries, Black Vine, Open Handles, 4 x 5 In. 523.00
Bowl, Vegetable, Adam's Rose, Blue, Green & Black, 11 1/4 In. 465.00
Bowl, Wine & Green, Name Isabel, 3 In. 195.00
Chamber Pot, Peafowl, Blue 3000.00
Chamber Pot, Peafowl, Red 3000.00
Coffeepot, Fort, Blue 1900.00
Compote, Rainbow, Octagonal, Blue & Red Bands, Staffordshire, 1840, 11 1/2 In. 1725.00
Creamer, 4-Part Flower, Blue, 4 1/4 In. 220.00
Creamer, Adam's Rose, Paneled, Yellow, 5 3/4 In. 825.00
Creamer, Cluster Of Buds, Blue, Bulbous, 4 In. 770.00
Creamer, Peafowl, Blue, 5 1/8 In. 220.00
Creamer, Peafowl, Blue, Red, Yellow, Green & Black, Octagonal, 5 1/2 In. 330.00
Creamer, Peafowl, Red, Blue, Yellow & Black, 4 In. 1045.00
Creamer, Rose Design, Black, Brown, Green Foliage, 3 3/4 In. 522.00
Creamer, Rose Design, Bulbous, Red & Green, 4 In. 330.00
Creamer, Thistle, Blue, 4 1/2 In. 330.00
Creamer, Townhouse, Green Trees, Staffordshire, c.1840, 2 1/2 In. 2530.00
Cup, Cannonball Design, Handleless, 2 1/2 x 4 In. 132.00
Cup, School House, Red Ground 209.00
Cup & Saucer, Acorn, Red, Handleless 660.00
Cup & Saucer, Alternating Chevron Pattern, Red & Green, Staffordshire, 6 In. 3737.00
Cup & Saucer, Apple Green 245.00
Cup & Saucer, Blue On White, Red & Green Flower, Marked, c.1835 .... 250.00
Cup & Saucer, Child's, Green Design, Red Stripe, Handleless 105.00
Cup & Saucer, Deer, Blue 1500.00
Cup & Saucer, Deer, Brown Transfer, Staffordshire, 1850s, 5 1/2 In. 1495.00
Cup & Saucer, Dove 1500.00
Cup & Saucer, Fort, Red 1700.00
Cup & Saucer, Loop, Handleless, Child's 5720.00
Cup & Saucer, Parrot, Dark Blue 1100.00
Cup & Saucer, Peafowl, Brown, Set Of 6 .... 2300.00
Cup & Saucer, Peafowl, Green ....200.00 to 425.00
Cup & Saucer, Peafowl, Green, Handleless 742.00
Cup & Saucer, Peafowl, Perched On Branch, Staffordshire, c.1840, 5 3/4 In. 862.00
Cup & Saucer, Peafowl, Red 425.00
Cup & Saucer, Peafowl, Red, Blue, Yellow, Black, Handleless 467.00
Cup & Saucer, Rainbow, Black Peafowl, Red & Purple, Handleless, 5 In. 575.00
Cup & Saucer, Rainbow, Rose Design, Red, Purple, Handleless 1210.00
Cup & Saucer, Red, Blue, Green, 3 Piece, Handleless 495.00
Cup & Saucer, Rooster, Blue 1350.00
Cup & Saucer, School House Design, Red Border, Handleless 1700.00
Cup & Saucer, Shed, Yellow Door, Blue Roof, Staffordshire, c.1840 .... 632.00

Cup & Saucer, Thistle, Red & Yellow 2500.00
Cup & Saucer, Thistle, Red & Yellow, Staffordshire, c.1840, 6 In. 1840.00
Cup & Saucer, Tree 1100.00
Cup & Saucer, Tree, Blue Border, Green Leaves, Handleless, c.1840, Child's 258.00
Cuspidor, Woman's, Blue, 4 3/4 x 3 1/4 In. 190.00
Flask, Boot-Form, Multicolored, c.1840, 5 1/2 In. 1975.00
Mixing Bowl, Blue & White, Molded Arch, 12 1/4 x 6 In. 245.00
Mug, Peafowl, Blue, Red, Yellow, Green, Black, Leaf Handle, 3 1/8 In. 715.00
Mush & Milk Set, Gaudy Stick 290.00
Pepper Pot, Rainbow, Purple, Blue, 5 1/8 In. 5500.00
Pitcher, Adam's Rose, Blue, 9 7/8 In. 467.00
Pitcher, Band Of Leaves & Cherries, Lavender, 11 In. 517.00
Pitcher, Cluster Of Buds, Blue & Red, Green Leaves, 10 3/4 In. 5390.00
Pitcher, Milk, Peafowl, Red, 6 1/2 In. 2500.00
Pitcher, Milk, Profile Tulip 2500.00
Pitcher, Rainbow, Alternating Bands Of Blue & Red, Staffordshire, 1840, 7 3/4 In. 1380.00
Pitcher, Raised Diamond Pattern, Green, Brown Glaze, 9 In. 35.00
Pitcher, Red, White, Fluted Handle, 8 3/4 In. 125.00
Pitcher, Thorn Handle, 11 1/2 In. 115.00
Pitcher, Tulip, 7 3/4 In. 2200.00
Pitcher & Bowl, Birds, Black, Pitcher 12 In., Bowl 14 In. ....*Illus* 4400.00
Pitcher & Bowl, Rainbow, Alternating Red & Green, Staffordshire, 12 In. 1840.00
Plate, Adam's Rose, Blue Border, Red, Green, Blue, Black, 8 1/2 In. 275.00
Plate, Bull's-Eye, 9 1/2 In. 1137.00
Plate, Castle, Brown, Red Fort, Green Trees, 9 5/8 In. 330.00
Plate, Cockscomb, Paneled, Red Flower, Green Foliage, 9 3/4 In. 5775.00
Plate, Dahlia, Red, Blue Flower, Green Sprigs, 9 1/4 In. 385.00
Plate, Parrot, Blue, On Black Branch, Blue Border, 7 1/4 In. 345.00
Plate, Peafowl, Blue, 9 3/4 In. 1750.00
Plate, Peafowl, Blue, Orange, Red, Black, 8 1/4 In. 550.00
Plate, Peafowl, Blue, Yellow, Green, Black, 8 1/8 In. 440.00
Plate, Peafowl, Incised Leeds-Type Border, 7 In. 675.00
Plate, Peafowl, Red, 8 3/8 In. 687.00
Plate, Peafowl, Red, 10 In. 1550.00
Plate, Peafowl, Red, Green, Black, Yellow, 8 1/4 In. 495.00
Plate, Peafowl, Yellow, 7 1/2 In. 3800.00
Plate, Pineapple, Blue Ground, 8 In. 660.00
Plate, Pomegranate, Blue, 8 1/2 In. 385.00
Plate, Rainbow, 7 In. 165.00
Plate, Rainbow, Olive Brown, Red, Bull's-Eye Center, 8 3/8 In. 192.00
Plate, Red Design, Central Swag, 9 1/4 In. 165.00
Plate, Red, Green Center & Border, 9 1/2 In., 8 Piece 660.00
Plate, Schoolhouse, Blue, Red, 8 1/4 In. 2090.00
Plate, Schoolhouse, Brown, Green, Red Banded Border, c.1840, 7 1/2 In. 1955.00

Spatterware, Platter, Rainbow, Purple, Blue, 14 x 17 3/4 In.;
Spatterware, Pitcher & Bowl, Birds, Black, Pitcher 12 In., Bowl 14 In.

Plate, Schoolhouse, Red Band, c.1840, 8 In.	862.00
Plate, Schoolhouse, Red, Blue, 8 1/2 In.	220.00
Plate, Star, Red, Green, Blue, 9 1/2 In.	467.00
Plate, Thistle, Red & Green, 7 1/4 In.	2250.00
Plate, Thistle, Red, 8 1/4 In.	137.00
Plate, Tulip, Blue, 6 1/2 In.	192.00
Plate, Tulip, Green & Blue, 8 1/4 In.	1900.00
Plate, Tulip, Red, Blue, Green & Black, Purple Border, 8 3/8 In.	550.00
Plate, Tulip, Red, Green, Black, Yellow, 8 In.	1980.00
Plate, Wigwam, Flanked With Trees, Red, c.1840, 8 1/2 In., 5 Piece	1380.00
Platter, Eagle, Blue, 16 In.	660.00
Platter, Fort, Brown & Black, Staffordshire, c.1840, 10 1/2 x 13 1/2 In.	2300.00
Platter, Peafowl, Octagonal, 13 1/2 In.	907.00
Platter, Rainbow, Blue & Purple, Oval Bull's-Eye Center, 13 5/8 In.	605.00
Platter, Rainbow, Purple, Blue, 14 x 17 3/4 In. *Illus*	2310.00
Saucer, Cluster Of Buds, Blue Ground, 5 1/2 In.	100.00
Soup, Coupe, Peafowl, Red, Blue, Green, On Black Branch, 10 In.	660.00
Soup, Coupe, Rainbow, Blue, Black, 8 1/4 In.	935.00
Sugar, Adam's Rose, Brown, 5 In.	247.00
Sugar, Cluster Of Buds, Pink Ground, 3 1/2 In.	120.00
Sugar, Cover, Blue & Red	650.00
Sugar, Cover, Double Loop, Green, Purple, Yellow & Black, 4 In.	3520.00
Sugar, Cover, Peafowl, In Tree, Rainbow Spatter Rim, 4 7/8 In.	330.00
Sugar, Cover, Peafowl, Red, 7 3/4 In.	165.00
Sugar, Cover, Thistle, Gray & Yellow, Staffordshire, c.1840, 5 In.	1840.00
Sugar, Fort, Blue, 4 1/2 In.	375.00
Sugar, Parrot, Red & Blue, On Black Branch, Urn Form, Staffordshire, 4 1/2 In.	400.00
Sugar, Rainbow, Red & Green, 4 3/8 In.	247.00
Sugar, Red & Blue, 5 1/4 In.	137.00
Teapot, Hollyberry, Molded Panels, Blue, 9 1/4 In.	522.00
Teapot, King's Rose, 5 5/8 In.	165.00
Teapot, Peafowl, Red, 7 1/4 In.	1650.00
Teapot, Rainbow, Yellow, Blue, Green, Brown, 6 1/2 In.	6710.00
Teapot, Townhouse, Blue Doors, Trellis, Green Trees, Staffordshire, Child's	1265.00
Teapot, Tree, Green & Black, Molded Flower Finial & Handle, 6 In.	330.00
Teapot, Windmill, Embossed Leaf Handle	2750.00
Toddy, Tulip, Green, Purple, Black, Yellow, Ocher, Red, 6 1/2 In.	770.00
Tureen, Cover, Green Trees, Finial, Handles, Octagonal Form, 8 x 9 1/4 In.	4600.00

SPELTER is a synonym for a zinc alloy. Figurines, candlesticks, and other pieces were made of spelter and given a bronze or painted finish. The metal has been used since about the 1860s to make statues, tablewares, and lamps that resemble bronze. Spelter is soft and breaks easily. To test for spelter, scratch the base of the piece. Bronze is solid; spelter will show a silvery scratch.

Candlestick, Knight Form, Arm Upswept To Support Candle, 19th Century, 14 3/4 In.	115.00
Figurine, La Melodie, 21 1/2 In.	550.00
Figurine, Warrior, Bronze Patina, Blackened Base, 16 In.	180.00
Lamp, Man, With Hunting Dog, Gun, Green Dome Shade, 11 1/2 x 8 1/2 In.	170.00
Lamp, Moorish Figures, Pair	2450.00
Vase, Ladies' Heads & Poppies, Signed, Flora, Art Nouveau, 10 3/4 In.	290.00

SPINNING WHEELS in the corner have been symbols of earlier times for the past 100 years. Although spinning wheels date back to medieval days, the ones found today are rarely more than 200 years old. Because the style of the spinning wheel changed very little, it is often impossible to place an exact date on a wheel.

Flax, 1850	200.00 to 500.00
Flax, J. McKee	350.00
Floral & Geometric Carving, Scandinavian, 36 In.	255.00
Maple, Porcelain Studs, 19th Century, 31 x 35 In.	165.00
Oak, 36 In.	302.00
Oak, Stamped M.P.	132.00

Worn Paint, 18th Century 650.00
Yarn Winder, 12 Spokes, Bobbin Mechanism, Sheet Metal Hand, 49 1/2 In. 1495.00

SPODE pottery, porcelain, and bone china were made by the Stoke-on-Trent factory of England founded by Josiah Spode about 1770. The firm became Copeland and Garrett from 1833 to 1847, then W.T. Copeland or W.T. Copeland and Sons until 1976. It then became Royal Worcester Spode Ltd. The word *Spode* appears on many pieces made by the factories. Most collectors include all the wares under the more familiar name of Spode. Porcelains are listed in this book by the name that appears on the piece. Related pieces are listed under Copeland and Copeland Spode.

Bowl, Cereal, Indian Tree, Orange, Brown, Green 28.00
Coffee Set, Lancaster, Cobalt Blue, 27 Piece 7900.00
Cup & Saucer, Buttercup .... .40.00 to 63.00
Cup & Saucer, Fitzhugh, Blue & White, 20 Piece 145.00
Cup & Saucer, Golden Clipper 300.00
Plate, Baroda, 10 In. 35.00
Plate, Child's, 7 3/4 In. 25.00
Plate, Christmas, 1970 .... 45.00
Plate, Christmas, 1971 .... 45.00
Plate, Fleur-De-Lis, Red, Dinner 70.00
Plate, Floral Clusters, Sprig Of Pink Roses, Cobalt Blue Ground, Oval, 10 3/8 In., Pair .. 1725.00
Plate, Pastry, Shima, Handles 60.00
Plate, Scenes Of Boston, 10 In. 75.00
Plate, Shima, 10 In. 45.00
Plate, Stylized Floral, New Stone Mark, 19th Century, 8 In., Pair 280.00
Plate, Tower, Blue, 7 1/2 In. 30.00
Plate, Wicker Lane, Luncheon 28.00
Plate & Mug, Farm Animals, Kiddieware, 2 Piece 75.00
Platter, Basket Weave, 13 1/2 In. 15.00
Platter, Multicolored Floral Design, Feldspar, 15 1/2 In. 140.00
Platter, Peacock, Rose, Green, Turquoise, Yellow, Ocher, Blue, Spearhead Border, 20 In. . 865.00
Platter, Well & Tree, Oval, 1815-1820, 20 5/16 In. 635.00
Soup, Cream, Cowslip 25.00

SPONGEWARE is very similar to spatterware in appearance. The designs were applied to the ceramics by daubing the color on with a sponge or cloth. Many collectors do not differentiate between spongeware and spatterware and use the names interchangeably. Modern pottery is being made to resemble the old spongeware, but careful examination will show it is new.

Bank, Bottle Shape, Blue Polka Dots On Neck, Stenciled Blue Initials J.W.B. 745.00
Bank, Piggy, Blue & White 350.00
Bedroom Set, Bowl & Pitcher, Yellow, Green, Gold Trim, 5 Piece 300.00
Bowl, Basket Weave, Flower Design, Star Bottom, Star Pottery, Akron, 10 x 5 In. 195.00
Bowl, Blue & White, 10 In. 110.00
Bowl, Blue & White, Fluted, 11 In. 95.00
Bowl, Blue, 4 x 10 In. 44.00
Bowl, Brown & Butterscotch, 19th Century, 8 1/2 In. 150.00
Cuspidor, Blue, 7 x 5 In. 38.00
Cuspidor, Blue, Inscription Souvenir, Miniature 295.00
Dish, Blue, White, Serpentine Rim, 6 1/2 x 8 1/2 In. 192.50
Figurine, Rabbit, Blue, 7 3/4 In. 95.00
Frame, Picture, 8 x 10 In. 125.00
Mixing Bowl, Blue Bandings, Blue, Gray, 4 x 12 In. 176.00
Pitcher, Barrel, Blue & White, 8 In. 325.00
Pitcher, Flower Design On Both Sides, Blue & White, Mid-19 Century, 5 x 9 In. 275.00
Pitcher, Tankard, Blue & White, 9 In. 295.00
Teapot, Blue & White 1295.00
Teapot, Blue, 1850 .... 325.00
Teapot, Domed Lid, Blue & White, 6 In. 192.50

SPORTS equipment, sporting goods, brochures, and related items are listed here. Items are listed by sport. Other categories of interest are Bicycle, Card, Fishing, Sword, and Toy, and Trap.

Auto Racing, Badge, Pit Pass, NASCAR Daytona International Speedway, Brass, 1961 .	200.00
Auto Racing, Helmet, Soap Box Derby, 1957 All-American, Blue, Pressed Fiber	45.00
Auto Racing, Watch, Indy 500, Presented To Winning Pit Crew, 1959	2100.00
Auto Racing, Wine Bottle, Mario Andretti, Cabernet Sauvignon, 1990, Unopened	125.00
Baseball, Almanac, Baseball Players' Photographs, 1954	50.00
Baseball, Ashtray, Minnesota Twins, World Series, 1965 .88.00 to 150.00
Baseball, Ball, Autographed, Chicago Cubs, 1945	110.00
Baseball, Ball, Autographed, Nixon, Eisenhower, Feller	300.00
Baseball, Ball, Autographed, Stan Musial, With 1963 Topps Card, Wood Base	60.00
Baseball, Bank, American League, 10 Bats On Stand, Team Insignias, Plastic, 6 In.	55.00
Baseball, Bank, Cleveland Indian, 6 1/2 In. . . . . *Illus*	225.00
Baseball, Bat, Babe Ruth Day, April 27, 1947	2000.00
Baseball, Bat, Babe Ruth Model, Hillerich & Bradsby	85.00
Baseball, Bat, Chevrolet Advertising, 18 In.	10.00
Baseball, Bat, George Brett Model, Louisville Slugger, 1983	45.00
Baseball, Bat, Mickey Mantle, No. 3 Louisville Slugger, 32 In.	100.00
Baseball, Booklet, Souvenir, American League Golden Anniversary, 1950, 83 Pages	25.00
Baseball, Button, Card, Hank Aaron Night, 500th Home Run, August 23, 1968	23.00
Baseball, Button, Chicago White Sox, American League Champs, 1959, 2 1/4 In.	28.00
Baseball, Button, Yankee, Ball & Mitt, 1940s	75.00
Baseball, Candy Bar Wrapper, Ruth's Home Run Bar, 1920s, 5 x 7 In. . . . . *Illus*	880.00
Baseball, Costume, Milwaukee Braves, Headdress, Tom-Tom, Hatchet	325.00
Baseball, Cuff Links, Los Angeles Dodgers, Enamel, Red, White & Blue	45.00
Baseball, Figure, Ed Mathews, Hartland, Box	350.00
Baseball, Figure, Hank Aaron, Hartland, Box, With Tag	450.00
Baseball, Figure, Stan Musial, Hartland, Box	400.00
Baseball, Figure, Ted Williams, Gartlan	450.00
Baseball, Figure, Ted Williams, Pewter	650.00
Baseball, Figure, Warren Spahn, Hartland, Box	300.00
Baseball, Flip Book, Baltimore Orioles, Baseball Signals, Gillette, 1957	150.00
Baseball, Glass, Wrigley Field, 1969	25.00
Baseball, Glove, Big Mac, MacGregor, No. K2997, Taiwan, Medium	40.00
Baseball, Glove, Bill Doak Model, Rawlings, 1922 Patent . . . . *Illus*	175.00
Baseball, Glove, Bob Doerr Model, Globe, Laced Back	59.00
Baseball, Glove, Catfish Hunter Model, Wilson	49.00
Baseball, Glove, Curt Blefary Model, XPG12, Owner's Name On Wrist	39.00
Baseball, Glove, Eddie Mathews Hall Of Fame Model, T-648, Rawlings, 1960s	46.00
Baseball, Glove, Gil Hodges Model, Demkert	150.00
Baseball, Glove, Gil Hodges Model, Wilson, 1950s	50.00
Baseball, Glove, Hank Bauer Model, Rawlings Playmaker, 1950s . . . . *Illus*	50.00
Baseball, Glove, Mickey Mantle Model, Rawlings . . . . .80.00 to 90.00

Sports, Baseball, Bank, Cleveland Indian, 6 1/2 In.

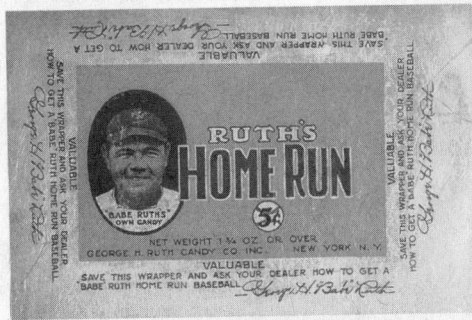

Sports, Baseball, Candy Bar Wrapper, Ruth's Home Run Bar, 1920s, 5 x 7 In.

Baseball, Glove, Mickey Mantle Model, Spalding 75.00
Baseball, Glove, Nolan Ryan Model, Autographed 60.00
Baseball, Glove, Ryne Sandberg Model, Black, Rawlings, Child's Size 30.00
Baseball, Glove, Yogi Berra Model, Spalding, Catcher's Mitt 60.00
Baseball, Highway Sign, New York Mets, World Champions, Metal, 1986, 7 x 21 Ft. ... 320.00
Baseball, Jacket Patch, Cleveland Indians, Chief Wahoo, 1948 .... 90.00
Baseball, Jacket, Chicago Cubs, Souvenir, Blue Satin, Cotton Lining, Snap Front, Small . 34.00
Baseball, Jersey, Cotton, Portman Sporting Goods, Peoria, Ill., 1950s-1960s, Size 42 .... 52.00
Baseball, Jersey, Wool, Short Sleeves, Fairdale, No. 16, MacGregor, Size 42 .... 69.00
Baseball, Key Ring, Babe Ruth, Medallion, Wheaties Cereal Premium 100.00
Baseball, Magazine, Capper's Farmer, Babe Ruth Cover, May 1935 .... 55.00
Baseball, Mitt, Catcher's, Sears & Roebuck, Box, c.1936 .... 300.00
Baseball, Model Kit, Willie Mays, Aurora, Unassembled, 1965 .... 229.00
Baseball, Pass, Lifetime, Ernie Banks, Baseball Hall Of Frame, Credit Card Size 1515.00
Baseball, Pen, Red Sox, 1930s 45.00
Baseball, Pennant, Boston Red Sox, Worlds Champions, 1918 .... 648.00
Baseball, Pennant, Dodgers vs. Phillies, National League Series, Tan, 1977, 29 1/2 In. .. 25.00
Baseball, Pennant, New York Yankees, Team Photo, 1962 .... 135.00
Baseball, Photograph, Babe Ruth, Autographed, 3 x 5 In. 1200.00
Baseball, Pocket Scorer, Celluloid, John H. Tietz, Grocer, 3 3/4 x 2 In. 38.00
Baseball, Postcard, Babe Ruth's Band, St. Mary's School, 1920s 32.00
Baseball, Press Pin, New York Yankees, Japan Tour, 1955 .... 145.00
Baseball, Program, Kansas City Royals, Awards Dinner, George Brett Autograph, 1975 .. 20.00
Baseball, Program, Negro League All-Star Game, Comiskey Park, 1947, 8 1/2 x 10 In. .. 195.00
Baseball, Program, World Series, 1923, Yankees vs. Giants 830.00
Baseball, Program, World Series, 1948, Cleveland Indians vs. Boston Braves ......*Illus* 75.00
Baseball, Program, World Series, 1964 .... 60.00
Baseball, Record, Great Moments In Cubs Baseball, 33 1/3 RPM, Cover, 1971 .... 30.00
Baseball, Record, Joe DiMaggio, 45 RPM, 1950s ....*Illus* 150.00
Baseball, Record, Talking Baseball Card, Reggie Jackson, World Series, Oct. 18, 1977 .. 25.00
Baseball, Scorecard, Yankees vs. White Sox, 1932 .... 90.00
Baseball, Sheet Music, Babe Ruth, We Know What He Can Do, 1st Edition 175.00
Baseball, Sign, Entrance, Fenway Park, Boston Red Sox, 1980s, 6 Ft. 1495.00
Baseball, Sweater, Cincinnati Reds, Black, V Neck, No. 27, Lin Les Label, China 75.00
Baseball, Ticket, Complimentary, Comisky Park, 1932 .... 35.00
Baseball, Ticket, Connie Mack Stadium, Final Game, Unused, 1970 .... 95.00
Baseball, Tobacco Felt, Eddie Ainsmith, Washington, 5 x 7 1/2 In. 65.00
Baseball, Tobacco Felt, Roy Hartzell, New York, 5 x 7 1/2 In. 65.00
Baseball, Tobacco Felt, Steve O'Neill, Cleveland, 5 x 7 1/2 In. 65.00
Basketball, Ball, Bob Pettit, Rawlings, Herculite, 1950s 670.00
Basketball, Glass, U. Of Kentucky, Logo, Schedule, 1987-1988, 5 1/4 In., Pair 25.00
Basketball, Jacket, USA Olympic Dream Team, Players, Facsimile Autographs, Medium . 60.00
Basketball, Jersey, Michael Jordon, Autographed, Not Game-Worn 395.00
Basketball, Poster Puzzle, USA Dream Team, Barcelona, Box, 1992, 300 Piece 26.00
Basketball, Wristwatch, Michael Jordan, He's Back, Commemorative, Signature, Case .. 195.00
Billiards, Table, Mahogany, Foldover, c.1860 .... 8500.00
Billiards, Table, Oak, Slate Top, Ivory Insets, Holt Co., No. 2059, c.1840, 97 In. 3300.00

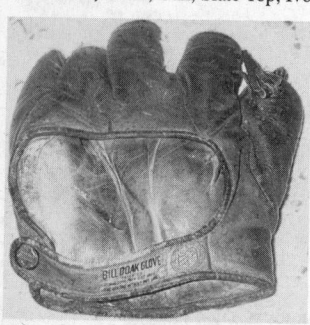

Sports, Baseball,
Glove, Bill Doak
Model, Rawlings,
1922 Patent

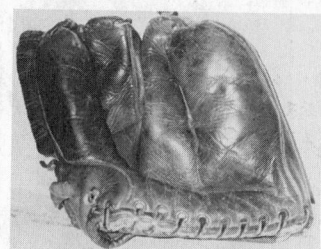

Sports, Baseball, Glove, Hank Bauer
Model, Rawlings Playmaker, 1950s

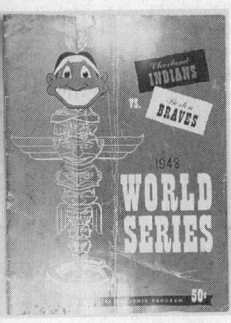

Sports, Baseball, Program, World Series, 1948, Cleveland Indians vs. Boston Braves

Sports, Baseball, Record, Joe DiMaggio, 45 RPM, 1950s

Sports, Boxing, Ring Magazine, Jake LaMotta Cover, Oct. 1949

Bowling, Trophy, Ladies, High Series, Metal, Bakelite Base, Dodge Trophies, 1939, 8 In.	23.00
Boxing, Belt Buckle, Muhammad Ali, 1970s	20.00
Boxing, Book, Art Of Boxing & Sparring, Johnson Smith Co., 1936, 32 Pages	25.00
Boxing, Book, The American Fistiana, Published 1843, 30 Pages	1380.00
Boxing, Button, I Want To Go The Louis-Nova Fight, Yellow, Black, 4 In.	190.00
Boxing, Button, Mohammed Ali (Cassius Clay), Full Length Photo, 3 1/2 In.	8.00
Boxing, Clock, Joe Louis World Champion, Metal, Electric	1500.00
Boxing, Matchbook, Schmeling vs. Louis, Jumbo, Complete	185.00
Boxing, Medal, Golden Gloves, Pinback, Ribbon, Clear Stones, 10 Karat, 2 In.	172.00
Boxing, Medal, Golden Gloves, Ribbon	95.00
Boxing, Medal, Jack Dempsey vs. Tommy Gibbons Fight, July 1923	106.00
Boxing, Poster, Joe Frazier vs. Muhammad Ali, Signed By Both, Frame, March 8, 1971 .	115.00
Boxing, Poster, Sonny Liston vs. Cassius Clay, Feb. 25, 1964, 27 x 41 In.	550.00
Boxing, Ring Magazine, Jake LaMotta Cover, Oct. 1949 . . . . *Illus*	40.00
Boxing, Robe, White Satin, Muhammad Ali, Everlast, Signed On Pocket Cuff, Size 44 . .	800.00
Boxing, Ticket, Jake Kilrain vs. Frank Slavin, 1896	2000.00
Boxing, Ticket, Joe Louis vs. Max Schmeling, Unused, June 22, 1938	977.00
Cricket, Card Set, British, Players Cigarettes, 1938, Set Of 50	55.00
Fencing, Mask, Kendo, Japan, 12 x 8 x 8 In.	285.00
Football, Ball, 29th Annual Oyster Bowl, Va. Tech vs. William & Mary, 1975	25.00
Football, Ball, Bart Starr, Facsimile Autograph, MacGregor Official, 1960s	585.00
Football, Ball, Kansas City Chiefs, Facsimile Team Autographs, 1968	35.00
Football, Ball, Missouri Tigers, Big 8 Champs, To John Ayers, 22 Autographs, 1969	40.00
Football, Ball, Y.A. Tittle, Facsimile Autograph, Pass Perfect Model, No. F 1134, Wilson	36.00
Football, Bank, Cardinals, Football Shape, Pottery	30.00
Football, Book, The Fighting Irish, Notre Dame Football Throughout The Years, 1976 . .	45.00
Football, Figure, Bo Jackson, Raiders, Starting Lineup, 2 Cards, Box, 1990, 4 In.	24.00
Football, Figure, Jim Kelly, Buffalo Bills, Starting Lineup, Box, 1990, 4 1/4 In.	30.00
Football, Frank Gifford's Football Guidebook, 1965, 5 x 9 In.	20.00
Football, Glass, Be A Packer Backer, Miller Life, 1950s, 4 In.	65.00
Football, Glass, Rose Bowl, Ohio State vs. California, 1950, 16 Oz. . . . . .25.00 to 50.00
Football, Jersey, L.A. Raiders, White, No. 32, Sand-Knit, Size 40	46.00
Football, Lighter, Engraved Steelers Helmet Logo, Brushed Finish, Zippo, 1973	37.00
Football, Lunch Box, Hall Of Fame Enshrinement Brunch, 1988	20.00
Football, Lunch Box, NFL Quarterback	105.00
Football, Pennant, Cleveland Browns, 1950s	75.00
Football, Photograph, Amos Alonzo Stagg, Signed	135.00
Football, Photograph, Cabinet Card, Football Player, 1900	45.00
Football, Program, 1st Super Bowl, Green Bay vs. Kansas City, 1967	116.00
Football, Program, Orange Bowl, Clemson vs. Miami, 1951	95.00
Football, Program, Penn State vs. Pittsburgh, Player Photos, Nov. 20, 1954	20.00
Football, Program, Princeton, Leather Cover, Football Shape, 216 Pages, 1904	90.00
Football, Program, Rose Bowl, Alabama vs. Stanford, 1925	325.00

Football, Program, Rose Bowl, Northwestern vs. California, Photos, 1949 . . . . 25.00

Football, Program, Rose Bowl, Pittsburgh vs. University Of Southern California, 1933 . . 225.00

Football, Ruler, Pottstown Firebirds, Affiliate Of Philadelphia Eagles, 1968 . . . . 7.00

Football, Wastebasket, Green Bay Packers, Pictures Of 22 Players, 1971 . . . . 125.00

Golf, Ashtray, Golf Ball, White Metal, Cast Brass 70.00

Golf, Ball, Arch Colonel, Mesh Pattern, 4 Green Squares Each Pole 65.00

Golf, Ball, Colonel, Bramble Pattern, Little Paint, 1910s 275.00

Golf, Ball, Dunlop Junior, Bramble Pattern, No Paint 175.00

Golf, Ball, Dunlop, Souvenir, St. Andrews, Scotland, Wood Base, In Wrapper, 1950s 20.00

Golf, Ball, Goodyear, Mesh Pattern, Blue & Red D Each Pole, 1920s 175.00

Golf, Ball, Wilson, Large Mesh Pattern, Original Paint 65.00

Golf, Ballot Box, Walnut, Vote With Ball, Y 1 Side, N Other, 9 1/2 x 10 1/2 In. 950.00

Golf, Club, Driver, St. Andrews, Gold Socket Head, Full Ivory Face, Brass Screws 300.00

Golf, Club, Driver, Transitional, Beechwood Head, Wooden Shaft, Edinburgh, 1895 . . . . . 350.00

Golf, Club, Lead-Filled Holes In Face, John Randall Patent 165.00

Golf, Club, Master, Adjustable, Gold, Blue, Breitenbaugh 2200.00

Golf, Club, Master, Adjustable, Left & Right Hand Golfers, Bremer & Co., 1915 . . . . 2000.00

Golf, Club, Niblick, T. Stewart Rut, Stamped G. Thom, 2 x 2 3/4-In. Head 500.00

Golf, Club, Putter, Arnold Palmer, Wilson, Regripped 600.00

Golf, Club, Putter, Chrome, Wilson, No. 8802 . . . . 350.00

Golf, Club, Putter, Crescent, Baseball Mark, Russet Grip, 1905 . . . . 250.00

Golf, Club, Putter, Crescent-Shape Head, Leather Grip, J.H. Dwight, 1911 . . . . 2500.00

Golf, Club, Putter, Mallet Head, Wooden Shaft, Harry Lee, 1903 . . . . 300.00

Golf, Club, Putter, Otto Hackbarth, Aluminum Mallet Head, Wooden Shaft, 1915 . . . . 400.00

Golf, Club, Putter, Presentation, Douglas H. Alexander, Sterling Silver, 1963 . . . . 75.00

Golf, Club, Putter, Spalding R, Wooden Mallet Head, Brass Face, Russet Grip, 1903 . . . . 375.00

Golf, Club, Putter, Spalding, Smooth Face, Brass Head, Stamped Shafts, 1898 . . . . 250.00

Golf, Club, Putter, Walter Travis, Wooden Mallet, Leather Wrap Grip, 1904 . . . . 300.00

Golf, Club, Putter, Wood Shaft, Schenectady 275.00

Golf, Club, Putter, Wooden Mallet Head, Flat Black Toe 325.00

Golf, Club, Putter, Wooden Mallet Head, Leather Grip, J. Cockburn, 1920 . . . . 500.00

Golf, Club, Wooden Shaft, 5 Piece 110.00

Golf, Club, Wooden Shaft, T. Morris 250.00

Golf, Coaster, Mickey Wright & Sam Snead, Wilson, Pair 18.00

Golf, Inkwell, Pine Grove Inn, Pewter, Wood, Silver Plate, Kirk Stieff 275.00

Golf, Magazine, Golfers Magazine, Leo Diegel On Cover, 1931 . . . . 40.00

Golf, Magi-Groove, Swing Improvement Device, Art Wall Jr., Box, 1960 . . . . 45.00

Golf, Marker, Ball, 1926 . . . . 440.00

Golf, Marker, Ball, Mark Fore, Brandell Co., Plastic, Box, 1966 . . . . 30.00

Golf, Marker, Ball, Omnes 550.00

Golf, Swing Practicing Machine, Revball, England, 1940s, 22 In. 385.00

Golf, Trophy, Bob Hope Desert Classic, Val St. Lambert, 1968, 15 In. 1500.00

Hockey, Glass, Chicago Blackhawks, Heavy Bottom, 1970s, 16 Oz. 20.00

Hockey, Jersey, New York Rangers, V-Neck, Red, White, Blue, Gerry Cosby, Canada . . . 26.00

Hockey, Program, Chicago Blackhawks, 1940 . . . . 25.00

Hockey, Puck, Autographed, Henri Richard 40.00

Hockey, Stick, Autographed, Paul Coffey 85.00

Hockey, Stick, Winchester, 1920s 600.00

Horse Racing, Decanter, Pimlico Preakness, 100th Anniversary 75.00

Horse Racing, Glass, Kentucky Derby, 1945 . . . . 950.00 to 1500.00

Horse Racing, Glass, Kentucky Derby, 1949 . . . . 110.00

Horse Racing, Glass, Kentucky Derby, 1950 . . . . 300.00

Horse Racing, Glass, Kentucky Derby, 1951 . . . . 375.00 to 525.00

Horse Racing, Glass, Kentucky Derby, 1952 . . . . 200.00

Horse Racing, Glass, Kentucky Derby, 1955 . . . . 90.00

Horse Racing, Glass, Kentucky Derby, 1958 . . . . 100.00 to 125.00

Horse Racing, Glass, Kentucky Derby, 1960 . . . . 45.00

Horse Racing, Glass, Kentucky Derby, 1961 . . . . 75.00

Horse Racing, Glass, Kentucky Derby, 1962 . . . . 55.00

Horse Racing, Glass, Kentucky Derby, 1964 . . . . 20.00 to 35.00

Horse Racing, Glass, Kentucky Derby, 1965 . . . . 25.00

Horse Racing, Glass, Kentucky Derby, 1967 . . . . 32.00

Horse Racing, Glass, Kentucky Derby, 1968 . . . . 35.00

Horse Racing, Glass, Kentucky Derby, 1981 .... 15.00
Horse Racing, Glass, Kentucky Derby, 1985 .... 20.00
Horse Racing, Glass, Kentucky Derby, 1986 .... 20.00
Horse Racing, Glass, Kentucky Derby, 1987 .... 20.00
Horse Racing, Glass, Kentucky Derby, 1992 .... 10.00
Horse Racing, Glass, Kentucky Derby, Aluminum, 1940 .... 400.00
Horse Racing, Glass, Kentucky Derby, Jigger, 1945 .... 950.00
Horse Racing, Glass, Preakness, 1975 .... 75.00
Horse Racing, Glass, Preakness, 1978 .... 55.00
Horse Racing, Glass, Preakness, 1983 .... 25.00
Horse Racing, Harness, Decatur, Illinois, Woman In 1903 Car, 1907 .... 850.00
Horse Racing, Program, Kentucky Derby, 1937 .... 395.00
Horse Racing, Program, Kentucky Derby, 1948 .... 20.00
Horse Racing, Program, Kentucky Derby, 1957 .... 25.00
Horse Racing, Program, Kentucky Derby, 1970 .... 75.00
Horse Racing, Program, Kentucky Derby, 1990 .... 25.00
Horse Racing, Ribbon, Blue, Devonwood Stables, Hunter Jumper Show 7.00
Hunting, Duck Stamp, Arkansas, 1st Of State 435.00
Hunting, Goose Call, Box Type, Bellows & Brass Horn, Canada, Early 1900s ... 450.00
Hunting, License, Alabama, 1927-1928 .... 50.00
Hunting, License, Deer, Michigan Resident, 1929 .... 110.00
Ice Skating, Figure Skates, Hand Forged, Russia 135.00
Ice Skating, Medal, Mayor Thompson's Relay, Brass, Pinback, Chicago, 1920, 1 1/2 In. .. 28.00
Ice Skating, Program, Sonja Henie, 1940 .... 15.00
Ice Skating, Program, Sonja Henie, 1950 .... 35.00
Ice Skating, Program, Sonja Henie, Black Velvet 30.00
Ice Skating, Program, Sonja Henie, Red Flocking, Gold Stamp, 1948 .... 50.00
Motorcycling, Trophy, Milton Field Meet, Second Place, 1959, 8 In. 75.00
Motorcycling, Trophy, Second Place, Engraved Brass Plate, 1956, 3 1/2 In. ... 57.00
Nodders are listed in the Nodder category.
Olympics, Kerchief, Flags Of All Countries, Blue Frame, 16 In. 275.00
Olympics, Pin, USA, 1988 .... 3.00
Olympics, Poster, Official Movie, Frame, 1948, 16 x 38 In. 300.00
Pool, Table, Brunswick, Saratoga Model, 1906 .... 3000.00
Pool, Table, Plywood, Rack With Scorekeeper, Balls, Cues, Rule Book, Portable, 77 In. ... 220.00
Riding, Spurs, Buermann Dropshank 275.00
Riding, Spurs, For Competitions, Leather Straps, England, 1930s 20.00
Roller Blades, Very First Roller Blades, Sidewalk Skates, Rubber Wheels, Box, 1950s .. 100.00
Roller Skating, Skates, Roller Drome Queen, White, Travel Case, Ware Bros., 1940s ... 30.00
Skateboard, Roller Derby No. 10, Wooden, Enamel Paint, Red & White, 19 x 4 1/2 In. . 40.00
Skiing, Skis & Poles, Wooden, Early 1900s 125.00
Snowshoes, Bear Paw, Pair 495.00
Snowshoes, Metal 195.00
Snowshoes, Snocraft, Pair 100.00
Snowshoes, Varnished, 48 x 14 In. 85.00
Snowshoes, Wood, Leather, Walter York Mfg., Caratunk, Maine, 37 1/2 In. 84.00
Soap Box Derby, Helmet, Blue, Fiber Composition, Canvas Ear Flaps, 1952 ... 38.00
Tennis, Book, Off The Court, Arthur Ashe, 1st Printing, Autographed, 1981 ... 150.00
Tennis, Racket, Dayton Steel, c.1920, All Metal Except Handle 20.00
Tennis, Racket, Winchester 595.00
Tennis, Trophy, Sagamore On Lake George, Copper & Silver, 1913 .... 775.00
Track & Field, Medal, Nude Mercury & Hercules, Sterling Silver, 1915, 2 In. ... 110.00

STAFFORDSHIRE, England, has been a district making pottery and porcelain since the 1700s. Hundreds of kilns are still working in the area.
Thousands of types of pottery and porcelain have been made in the many
factories that worked and still work in the area. Some of the most famous
factories have been listed separately, such as Adams, Davenport,
Ridgway, Rowland & Marsellus, Royal Doulton, Royal Worcester,
Spode, Wedgwood, and others. Some Staffordshire pieces are listed
under categories like Fairing, Flow Blue, Mulberry, Shaving Mug, etc.

Bank, Spaniel's Head, 4 1/2 In. 253.00
Basket, Fruit, Reticulated, Blue & White, 4 x 9 1/4 In., Pair 700.00

Basket, Moss & Flowers, 2 1/2 x 2 1/2 In. 30.00
Basket, Reticulated Valanced Rim, Black, Circular, 1760, 9 15/16 In. 1840.00
Basket, Stand, Handle, Salt Glaze, Pierced Basket Weave, 1760, 9 In. 975.00
Bottle, Chinese Figures, Floral, Salt Glaze, 1760, 7 3/4 In. 860.00
Bowl, Agate, Browns Stained With Blue To Cream, 1750, 4 In. 575.00
Bowl, Cereal, Brown, Green 13.00
Bowl, English Country House, Dark Blue Transfer, 11 1/2 x 5 1/2 In. 385.00
Bowl, Floral, Cobalt Blue, Rectangular Handle, c.1860, 14 x 8 In. 150.00
Bowl, Fruit, Beauties Of America, Octagon Church, Blue & White, 1814, 10 In. 1495.00
Bowl, Lafayette At Franklin's Tomb, Enoch Wood 1100.00
Bowl, Table Rock, Niagara, Beaded Rim, Hudson River Views, 12 In. 1200.00
Bowl, Urns Of Flowers, Dark Blue Transfer, 9 1/2 x 4 1/4 In. 357.00
Bowl, Vegetable, Brown, Green, 8 In. 35.00
Bowl, Vegetable, Columbus, Dark Blue Transfer, 12 3/4 In. 660.00
Bust, Boy & Girl, 18th Century, 7 3/4 In., Pair 690.00
Bust, George Washington, Blue Coat, Black Base, Enoch Wood, 1818, 8 1/2 In. 1875.00
Bust, Payta-Kootha, Shawnee Warrior, 7 1/2 In. 192.00
Butter, Cover, Brown, Green 49.00
Butter Chip, Landing Of The Founding Fathers, Enoch Wood, 3 1/4 In., 6 Piece 200.00
Cake Plate, Willow, Scalloped, Gold Trim, S. Radford, 1880-1891, 9 In. 45.00
Canister, Tea, Chinese Figural Panels, Green Glaze, 1765, 4 3/8 In. 2530.00
Canister, Tea, Creamware, Stars & Dots, Rectangular, 1765, 3 3/8 In. 805.00
Canister, Tea, Pineapple, Green & Yellow Glaze, 1765, 4 3/8 In. 4310.00
Coffeepot, Applied Relief, Floral Sprigs, Vines, Pale Blue, 1755, 7 In. 5175.00
Coffeepot, Domed Cover, Hunting Dog, Dark Blue Transfer, 12 1/4 In. 605.00
Coffeepot, Domed Cover, Stag Design, Blue, 1830, 12 1/2 In. 475.00
Coffeepot, Domed Cover, Wadsworth Tower, Dark Blue Transfer, 11 In. 2365.00
Coffeepot, Floral, Translucent, Fluted Spout, Scrolled Handle, Pear Shape, 9 In. ... 745.00
Coffeepot, Hinged Plain Edge Collar, Curved Spout, Strap Handle, 11 In. 460.00
Coffeepot, New Orleans, Black, Stevenson, 9 In. 750.00
Coffeepot, Pear Shape, Crabstock Spout, Strap Handle, 6 In. 460.00
Coffeepot, Pear Shape, Lady Holding Bird, Green, 8 1/2 In. 1495.00
Compote, European Ruin Scenes, Brown Transfer, 11 x 6 1/2 In. 520.00
Creamer, Calico Cow, Blue, Marked Calico, Burleigh, 3 1/4 In. 55.00
Creamer, Church & Woman With Child, Dark Blue Transfer, 3 3/4 In. 302.00
Creamer, Cover, Cow, Ribbed Rectangular Base, 1800, 5 1/8 In. 230.00
Creamer, Cow, Stopper, Mid-19th Century 595.00
Creamer, Crow's Nest From Bull's Hill, Blue 195.00
Creamer, Horse Drawn Sleigh, Dark Blue Transfer, Enoch Wood, 5 3/4 In. 550.00
Creamer, Milkmaid Milking Cow, Mottled Burgundy, 5 1/2 x 6 In. 287.00
Creamer, Oriental Scene, Dark Blue Transfer, 5 1/8 In. 275.00
Creamware, Basket, 6 Panels, Diamond-Shaped Sprays Of Daisies, 10 In. 2070.00
Creamware, Basket, Tortoiseshell, Green, Gray, Teal Blue, Brown Ground, 8 In. 805.00
Cup & Saucer, Brown, Green 13.00
Cup & Saucer, Centennial Boston Tea Party, Faneuil Hall, 1873 .... 200.00
Cup & Saucer, God Speed The Plough, c.1900 .... 125.00
Cup & Saucer, Lafayette At Franklin's Tomb 395.00
Cup & Saucer, Landing Of Lafayette 302.00
Cup & Saucer, Ship, American Flag, Wood & Sons 770.00
Cup & Saucer, Thatched Cottage With Mother & Child, Dark Blue 225.00
Dipper, Toddy, Salt Glaze, Pinched Spout, 1750, 1 5/8 In. 1090.00
Dish, 12 Sprigs Of Fruit On Rim, Scalloped Edge, Green Creamware, 11 In. 1955.00
Dish, Cover, Hen On Nest, White Bisque, Red Comb, Green Nest With Eggs, 6 In. ... 365.00
Dish, Cress, Salt Glaze, Molded Floral Scrolls, Scalloped Rim, 1750, 11 In. 690.00
Dish, Hen On Nest, Eggcup Insert, 7 1/2 In. 632.00
Dish, Leaf Shape, Salt Glaze, Bird On Leafy Branch Inside, 1760, 9 1/2 In. 1725.00
Feeder, Invalid, Scene Of Still Life, Flower In Vase, Dark Blue Transfer, 3 In. 220.00
Figurine, 2 British Drummers & Union Jack, 7 1/4 In. 201.00
Figurine, 3 Men Drinking, 6 1/2 In. 185.00
Figurine, Benjamin Franklin, 19th Century, 15 1/2 In. 920.00
Figurine, Benjamin Franklin, Tricorner, Document, 15 1/2 In. 440.00
Figurine, Boy & Girl Under Tree Canopy, Sheep & Dog, 5 1/2 x 3 1/4 In. 90.00
Figurine, Cat, Seated, c.1860, 7 1/2 In., Pair 1495.00

Figurine, Charity, Hooded Garment, Holding Infant, 9 1/2 In. 931.00
Figurine, Child, On Dog, Marked, 5 1/2 In., Pair 155.00
Figurine, Child, On Swimming Swan, 8 In. 270.00
Figurine, Cleopatra, Reclining, Rocky Floral Freeform Base, 19th Century, 12 In. 285.00
Figurine, Cow, Standing, Russet-Brown Hide, Gray Nose, Hooves, 17 In. 1035.00
Figurine, Dog, Dalmatian, Cobalt Blue Base, 1860, 5 In., Pair 750.00
Figurine, Dog, English Poodle, Brown & White, 4 In. 210.00
Figurine, Dog, Poodle, c.1870, 9 1/2 In., Pair 1200.00
Figurine, Dog, Poodle, Painted Faces, Gilt Collars, 5 1/2 In., Pair 140.00
Figurine, Dog, Poodle, Seated, White, Textured Fur, Gilt Collar, c.1840, 5 1/2 In. 2185.00
Figurine, Dog, Pug, Agate, Brown & Cream, Rectangular Base, 1755, 2 3/4 In. 1610.00
Figurine, Dog, Seated, Brown & White, Black, Gilt, 13 3/4 In., Pair 595.00
Figurine, Dog, Seated, Red & White, 3 3/4 In., Pair 176.00
Figurine, Dog, Seated, Red & White, 10 In. 60.00
Figurine, Dog, Seated, White, Sanded Coat, Black Trim, Yellow Collar, 3 1/2 In. 165.00
Figurine, Dog, Spaniel, Red & White, 1840, 9 1/2 In. 425.00
Figurine, Dog, Spaniel, Red & White, 6 1/4 In. 325.00
Figurine, Dog, Spaniel, White, 7 1/2 In., Pair 355.00
Figurine, Dog, Spaniel, White, Gold Trim, 14 In., Pair 385.00
Figurine, Dog, Spaniel, White, Silver Luster, 8 In., Pair 575.00
Figurine, Dog, White Glaze, England, 19th Century, 9 In., Pair 335.00
Figurine, Dog, White, Copper Luster, Pair 745.00
Figurine, Dog, White, Glass Eyes, 13 In., Pair 1000.00
Figurine, Faith, 8 1/2 In. 135.00
Figurine, Fish Seller, Neal, c.1800 . . . . 650.00
Figurine, Garibaldi, Polychrome With Gilt, 19 3/8 In. 415.00
Figurine, Girl, With Fawn, 6 7/8 In. 190.00
Figurine, Harvesters, 14 In. 350.00
Figurine, John Wesley, In Pulpit, Angels Adorn Top 185.00
Figurine, Lamb, Foliate, Green, Brown, Yellow Spots, Cream Ground, 1840 . . . . 460.00
Figurine, Lamb, Grassy Mound, Blossom In Mouth, 4 In. 60.00
Figurine, Leopard, 8 1/2 In. 3740.00
Figurine, Lion, Glass Eyes, 19th Century, 13 x 9 1/2 In., Pair 795.00
Figurine, Little Red Riding Hood, 19th Century, 10 1/8 In. 172.00
Figurine, Lovers, 10 1/2 In. 220.00
Figurine, Man & Woman, On Clock, Oval Base, 13 1/2 In. 115.00
Figurine, Man & Woman, On Goat, 6 In., Pair 75.00
Figurine, Man & Woman, Under Grape Arbor, Gold Highlights, 14 x 9 In. 115.00
Figurine, Man, Holding Apple, Victorian, 8 1/2 In. 85.00
Figurine, Paul & Virginia, 14 x 11 1/2 In. 1500.00
Figurine, Peasant Man & Woman, Pair 350.00
Figurine, Peasant Woman, Creamware, Brown & Green, 1755, 4 1/4 In. 345.00
Figurine, Prince Of Wales, Queen Victoria, 16 In., Pair . . . . *Illus* 880.00
Figurine, Rabbit, Freeform Rocky Base, Salt Glaze, 1755, 2 3/8 In. 920.00
Figurine, Ram, Against Tree Stump, Green Horns, Orange Spots, White, 1840 . . . . 195.00
Figurine, Robert Burns, 13 In. 495.00
Figurine, Rooster, Perched On Flowering Shrub, Polychrome, 9 In., Pair 520.00

Every collection as well as every collector should have a smoke detector nearby.

Staffordshire, Figurine, Prince
Of Wales, Queen Victoria,
16 In., Pair

Figurine, Sheep, Reclining, 1860, 2 1/2 In. 250.00
Figurine, Sir R. Peel, 19th Century, 10 In. 230.00
Figurine, St. George Slaying Dragon 170.00
Figurine, Stag, Recumbent, Majolica, Base, Removable Antlers, 1875, 11 In. 1840.00
Figurine, Uncle Tom's Cabin, Little Eva Sitting On Knee, 9 1/4 In. 575.00
Figurine, Victoria & Prince Albert, On Thrones, 6 3/4 In., Pair 65.00
Figurine, Whippets, Seated, Blue, Gilt Oval Bases, 8 3/4 In., Pair 92.00
Figurine, Zebra, 9 x 8 In. 675.00
Group, 2 Women, Standing, Flanking Column, 5 1/4 In. 200.00
Group, Children, Bocage, Applied Leaves To Base, Walton, England, 1825, 8 In. 905.00
Group, Children, With Lamb, 1860, 6 1/2 In. 250.00
Group, Scottish Courting Couple, 1860-1870, 10 In. 675.00
Group, Shepherds, Sheep, Standing, Two Lambs Recumbent, 1820, 6 In. 1840.00
Group, Youth, Playing Violin, Young Woman Dancing Under Arbor, 7 1/2 In. 143.00
Incense Burner, Cottage, 2 Chimneys, Applied Grass & Bird, 4 3/4 In. 38.00
Inkwell, Dog, Recumbent, Gold Collar, Black Snout, 4 x 6 In., Pair 518.00
Inkwell, Man & Woman On Horseback, Polychrome Enamel, 5 1/4 In., Pair 155.00
Inkwell, Washington On Horse, Polychrome & Gold Trim, 8 In. 550.00
Jar, Cover, Cruise Scenes, Blue, Blue Trim, Art Deco, 5 x 4 x 3 In. 355.00
Jug, Buff, Blue, Brown Clay, Lion-Paw Feet, 1760, 4 In. 748.00
Jug, Cream, Agate, 3 Mask & Claw Feet, Pear Shape, 1750, 3 1/4 In. 2185.00
Jug, Cream, Cow Shape, Milkmaid, Sponged Yellow Brown Spots, White, 5 In. 632.00
Jug, Cream, Cow Shape, Ocher Milkmaid, Blue Sponged Base, 1840, 5 1/2 In. 920.00
Jug, Cream, Cow Shape, Yellow, Olive Green, Olive Spots, Green Base, 5 1/2 In. 437.00
Jug, Cream, Cow, Milkmaid In Hat, c.1840, 6 In. 635.00
Jug, Cream, Drabware, Applied Floral, White Mask & Claw, 1740, 3 3/4 In. 1150.00
Jug, Cream, Floral Landscape, Salt Glaze, Pear Shape, Mid-18th Century, 3 In. 920.00
Jug, Cream, Sprig Of 2 Small Blossoms, S-Scroll Handle, Pointed Spout, 3 In. 1035.00
Jug, Cream, Translucent Brown & Green, Pear Shape, 18th Century, 3 1/2 In. 230.00
Jug, Hot Milk, Cover, Solid Agate, Pulled Loop Handle, Pear Shape, 7 In. 4312.00
Jug, Milk, Pulled Loop Handle, Pear Shape, 1750, 5 In. 3162.00
Jug, Milk, Scalloped Rim, Pale Blue Green, Ocher, Pear Shape, 3 5/8 In. 805.00
Jug, Pastoral Scene, Cows, Cottage, c.1820, 6 1/4 In. 395.00
Mug, 2 Ships, Seaweed & Shell Border, Shipping Series 1250.00
Mug, Cover, Creamware, Combed Surface Agate, 1800, 6 1/8 In. 4600.00
Mug, English Country House, Dark Blue Transfer, 3 7/8 In. 220.00
Mug, Floral, Luster & Polychrome Floral, 3 In. 44.00
Mug, Grandmamma's Tales, Young Man Shooting Cock Sparrow, 2 1/2 In. 71.00
Mug, Queen Victoria Commemorative, Magenta, R. & C., 3 1/4 In. 231.00
Mug, Red Brown Body, Blue Underglaze, Cream Spotted Interior, 4 In. 1265.00
Obelisk, Monument, Agate Clay, Burslem, Ra. Wood, '85, 12 In. 545.00
Pastille Burner, English Country House, c.1860, 6 In. 595.00
Pen Holder, Cover, Light Blue Transfer, Leaf Handle, Interior Ridges, 8 3/4 In. 220.00
Pepper Pot, Landing Of Lafayette 1155.00
Pitcher, Bust Of Harrison, Log Cabin, Magenta Transfer 10450.00
Pitcher, Combware, 1700-1720, 7 In. 1250.00
Pitcher, Figural, Lord Nelson, 11 3/4 In. 170.00
Pitcher, Milk, Abbey Ruins, Pink & White, Mayer, 8 1/2 In. 88.00
Pitcher, Residence Of Late Richard Jordan, N.J., Blue Transfer, 7 1/4 In. 265.00
Pitcher, T. Goodwin Wharf, Baltimore, Light Blue Transfer, 18 In. 355.00
Pitcher & Bowl, Lafayette At Tomb Of Franklin 4950.00
Pitcher & Bowl, Lucerne, Blue Transfer, Incised W.P. & Co., 11 x 12 In. 297.00
Plaque, William Ewart Gladstone, Green, Gold Border 95.00
Plate, Adam's Rose, 9 1/2 In., Pair 253.00
Plate, Albany State Capital, 9 In. 55.00
Plate, America & Independence, Dark Blue Transfer, 7 3/4 In. 355.00
Plate, America & Independence, States Rim, Dark Blue Transfer, 10 1/2 In. 357.00
Plate, Baltimore & Ohio Railroad, 10 1/4 In. 880.00
Plate, Baltimore & Ohio Railroad, Dark Blue, Enoch Wood, 9 1/4 In. 770.00
Plate, Bird In Tree, Blue & Green Spatter Border, 9 1/2 In., Pair 690.00
Plate, Boat, Old Man Sailing Toy Boat In Bucket For Child, Verse, 7 1/2 In. 132.00
Plate, Boston Hospital, Dark Blue, Stevenson, 9 In. 350.00
Plate, Capitol Washington, Shell Boarder, Wood & Sons, 7 5/8 In. 935.00

Plate, Catskill House, Hudson, Dark Blue, Wood & Sons, 6 In. 750.00
Plate, Chief Justice Marshall, Troy, Wood & Sons, 8 3/8 In. 605.00
Plate, Church In City Of New York, Dark Blue, Stubbs, 6 1/4 In. 775.00
Plate, Cologne, Red Transfer, Ralph Stevenson & Son, 10 1/2 In. 65.00
Plate, Cowle Harbour, Wood & Son, 6 3/8 In. 143.00
Plate, Cromwell Dismissing Parliament, Blue, Jones & Son, 16 1/2 In. 695.00
Plate, Dam & Waterworks, Philadelphia, Blue Transfer, 10 1/8 In. 160.00
Plate, English Cathedral With Fisherman, Dark Blue Transfer, 10 1/8 In. 165.00
Plate, Falls Of Montmorenci, Shell Border, Enoch Wood, 8 1/2 In. 350.00
Plate, Ft. Edward, Hudson River View, Black Transfer, 5 1/2 In. 10.00
Plate, Fulham Church, Middlesex, Dark Blue, 8 3/4 In. 75.00
Plate, Gentlemen's Cabin, Boston Malls, Black Transfer, 8 1/4 In. 135.00
Plate, Grand Canyon, Blue, 10 In. 90.00
Plate, Harvard College, Medium Blue, 10 1/8 In. 110.00
Plate, Harvard Hall, Jackson, Brown Transfer, 6 3/4 In. 110.00
Plate, Hollywell Cottage, Cavan, Dark Blue, Riley, 10 In. 225.00
Plate, Holme, Regents Park, Dark Blue, Enoch Wood, 10 In. 195.00
Plate, June, Daisy Border, Dixon 225.00
Plate, Knighthood Conferred On Don Quixote, Dark Blue, 10 In. 137.00
Plate, La Grange, 1840s, 10 1/4 In. 350.00
Plate, Leaf Molded Gadroon Rim, Manganese Brown, Teal Blue, Green, 7 In. 460.00
Plate, Lewis & Clark Centennial, Deep Blue, 1905, 10 In. 110.00
Plate, Louis Napoleon, My Uncle's Nephew, Astride Horse, Bird Rim, 7 1/2 In. 66.00
Plate, MacDonnough's Victory, Dark Blue, 9 In. 350.00
Plate, Marine Hospital, Louisville, Dark Blue Transfer, Wood & Sons, 9 3/8 In. .. 247.00
Plate, Medium Blue Transfer, Spotted Deer, 1810, 8 1/2 In. 155.00
Plate, Molded Leaves & Flowers Borders, Salt Glaze, 1860, 9 1/4 In. 490.00
Plate, Moulon Sur La Marne A Charenton, Dark Blue, Enoch Wood, 9 1/8 In. 145.00
Plate, Near Fishkill, Dark Blue Transfer, 7 3/4 In. 93.00
Plate, Pass In Catskill Mountains, Wood & Son, 7 1/2 In. 330.00
Plate, Philadelphia, Cities Series, Dark Blue, 6 3/4 In. 825.00
Plate, Phillip's Chapel, Regent's Street, Dark Blue, 10 In. 225.00
Plate, President's House, Washington, Brown Transfer, 10 1/2 In. 275.00
Plate, President's House, Washington, Purple Transfer, 10 3/8 In. 275.00
Plate, Quebec, Dark Blue, 9 In. 275.00
Plate, R. Hall's Select Views, Warleigh House, Dark Blue Transfer, 8 1/8 In. 187.00
Plate, Race Bridge, Philadelphia, Sepia Transfer, 9 In. 155.00
Plate, Sacred To Memory Of George III, Died 29th Of Jan. 1820, 10 In. 1250.00
Plate, Sancho, Priest & Barber, Dark Blue, 8 1/4 In. 110.00
Plate, Table Rock & Niagara Falls, Conch Shell Border, Enoch Wood, 10 In. 475.00
Plate, Texian Campaign, 7 In. 655.00
Plate, Texian Campaign, 9 3/4 In. 755.00
Plate, Texian Campaign, Battle Of Chapultepec, Brown Transfer, 9 3/8 In. 210.00
Plate, The Baltimore & Ohio Railroad, Shell Border, 9 1/4 In. 660.00
Plate, Trenton Falls, Enoch Wood, 6 3/4 In. 345.00
Plate, View Near Conway, New Hampshire, Red Transfer, 9 1/8 In. 60.00
Plate, View Of Trenton Falls Wood, Dark Cobalt Blue, 7 1/2 In. 300.00
Plate, Vue De Chateau Ermenonville, Dark Blue, Enoch Wood, 10 In. .... 175.00 to 225.00
Plate, Washington, Delaware, Blue 50.00
Plate, Water Landscape, Figures, Lilac, Salt Glaze, Octagonal, 1760, 8 1/4 In. 1090.00
Plate Set, Dessert, Flower Filled Vases & Baskets, 9 In., 7 Piece 172.00
Plate Set, Rococo, Green Floral Border, John Maddocks & Sons, 8 7/8 In., 6 Piece 60.00
Platter, Abbey Ruins, Pink & White, Mayer, 13 In. 143.00
Platter, Brown, Green, 12 In. 38.00
Platter, Cambrian, Brown Transfer, Phillips, 19 In. 412.00
Platter, Canova, Blue & White, 17 1/2 In. 121.00
Platter, Center Scene, Green Border, Podmore, Walker, 13 1/2 In. 175.00
Platter, Christianburg, Danish Settlement, Africa, Enoch Wood, 20 1/2 In. 1695.00
Platter, Cleopatra, Floral Landscape, Architectural Ruins, Fruit Border, 17 In. .. 170.00
Platter, Colonial Scene, c.1850, 16 x 12 In. 195.00
Platter, Detroit, Cities Series, Dark Blue, 18 1/2 In. 4800.00
Platter, England River Scene, Medium Blue Transfer, Ironstone, 20 In. 275.00
Platter, Ermine In Panels, Green, Blue, Yellow, Gray Glaze, Oval, 1770, 14 In. 1035.00

Platter, Ermine Rim, Green, Yellow, Gray Mottled Ground, 1760, 14 In. 633.00

Platter, Fonthill Abbey, Wiltshire, Dark Blue, 16 3/4 In. 950.00

Platter, Fruit & Flower, Tree & Well, Dark Blue Transfer, Stubbs & Kent, 18 In. 1210.00

Platter, Gray, Seashells, Stubbs, 12 1/2 x 9 3/4 In. 135.00

Platter, Green Leaf Design, Cream Ground, 21 1/2 x 17 In. 60.00

Platter, Iron Works At Saugerties, Purple, Jackson, 13 1/4 In. 595.00

Platter, Ironstone, Oval, Edward F. Bodley & Son, 1885, 15 7/8 x 19 5/8 In. 170.00

Platter, Landing Of General Lafayette, 17 In. 1320.00

Platter, London Views, St. George's Chapel, Dark Blue Transfer, 16 5/8 In. 660.00

Platter, Madras, Brown Transfer, 1880s, 18 x 14 In. 85.00

Platter, Oriental Design, Scalloped Edge, Pink & White, 20 In. 247.00

Platter, Oriental Figures, Floral Border, Black, Blue Transfer, 13 In. 170.00

Platter, Peace & Plenty, Dark Blue, Clews, 15 In. 1100.00

Platter, Piccolo Bent, Blue Transfer, 10 1/2 In. 137.00

Platter, Residence Of Late Richard Jordan, Red Transfer, 15 7/8 In. 715.00

Platter, Sandusky, Dark Blue Transfer, 16 5/8 In. 8525.00

Platter, Turkey, 21 1/2 In. 95.00

Platter, Upper Ferry Bridge Over River Schuylkill, Blue Transfer, 18 3/4 In. 1705.00

Punch Bowl, Armorial, 3 English Coats Of Arms, Foliate Border, Black, 1760 . . . . 2875.00

Punch Pot, Chinoiserie Lady Holding Parasol, Spherical, Red, 1760, 7 In. 517.00

Punch Pot, Cover, Chinoiserie Couple Standing, Swag Border Red, 8 In. 920.00

Punch Pot, Cover, Wavy Lines, Chevrons, Loop Handle, Cylindrical, Red, 7 In. 1150.00

Punch Pot, Cover, Wavy Lines, Diamonds, Leafage, Molded Handle, Red, 7 In. 460.00

Punch Pot, Foliate Rim, Crabstock Spout, Handle, Brown, Black, 1766, 7 In. 460.00

Sauceboat, 3 Cows, Calf Standing, Green, Brown, Yellow, 1765, 7 3/16 In. 9200.00

Sauceboat, 3 Roses On Each Side, Pulled Strap Handle, Gray, 1765, 6 9/16 In. 2300.00

Sauceboat, Double Spout, Strap Handle, Salt Glaze, Oval, 1760, 6 7/8 In. 1380.00

Sauceboat, Green Foliate, Manganese Brown, 1765, 6 7/8 In. 1150.00

Sauceboat, Scalloped Rim, Cream, Teal, Dark Brown, Oval, 1750, 7 In. 4025.00

Saucer, Charles Ford, Gold Trim, 1874-1904, 5 In. 20.00

Saucer, Lewis & Clark Centennial, 1905, 6 1/8 In. 55.00

Saucer, Scene Of Early Railroad With Engine, 1 Car, Dark Blue, 5 7/8 In. 275.00

Saucer, Washington At Tomb 200.00

Shell, Creamware, Brown & Blue Glazed, 1750, 6 1/2 In. 805.00

Soup, Dish, Guy's Cliff, Warwickshire, Blue, Enoch Wood, 8 3/4 In. 165.00

Soup, Dish, Octagon Church, Dark Blue, 9 7/8 In. 425.00

Soup, Plate, Acropolis, Violet Transfer, 10 1/4 In., Pair 121.00

Spill Holder, Double Swan, 19th Century 225.00

Sugar, Cover, Mount Vernon, Seat Of Late George Washington, 5 3/4 In. 359.00

Sugar, Cover, Shell & Seaweed, Peaked Knop Finial, Scrolled Handles 303.00

Sugar, Man In Sleigh, Enoch Wood 95.00

Sugar, Thatched Cottage, Dark Blue 315.00

Sugar & Creamer, Brown, Green 39.00

Tankard, Tavern Scene, Brown Top, Stoneware, Mid-18th Century, 8 3/8 In. 575.00

Tea Caddy, Applied Front & Reverse Foliate Scrolls, Orange, Brown Ground, 4 In. 1610.00

Tea Caddy, Dot Star Diaperwork, Manganese Brown, Teal Blue, 3 5/8 In. 460.00

Tea Caddy, European Lady Strolling Beside Companion, Biscuit, 5 In. 977.00

Tea Caddy, Figure Of Flora, Green Ground, 1765, 6 7/16 In. 1495.00

Tea Caddy, Green, Manganese Gray, Brown, Ocher, Diamond Shape, 5 In., Pair 3737.00

Tea Caddy, Star Diaperwork Under Arches, Milled Edges, 4 1/4 x 5 In. 2875.00

Tea Caddy, Trellis Cartouche, Foliate Scrolls, Green, Teal Blue, 1755, 6 1/4 In. 1725.00

Tea Set, Black Tracery, Green Band, Red Drop Design, 16 Piece, Child's 595.00

Teapot, Agate Pecten Shell, Dolphin Handle, Buff, Blue, Brown, 5 In. 7475.00

Teapot, Agate Pecten Shell, Pulled Loop Handle, Teal Blue, Cream, 6 In. 9775.00

Teapot, Boston Tea Party, Black Transfer On Gold, Arthur Wood 100.00

Teapot, Chinese Boy Kneeling Among Vines, Lamprey Handle, 3 7/8 In. 2300.00

Teapot, Chinese Molded Relief, Salt Glaze, Hexagonal, 1760, 5 In. 1955.00

Teapot, Cluster Of Grapes, Pineapples, Green, Yellow, Brown, 1765, 4 In. 5175.00

Teapot, Domed Cover, Solid Agate, Pulled Loop Handle, Teal Blue, Brown, 4 In. 4887.00

Teapot, Figural, Camel With Howdah, Chinese Designs, c.1750 . . . . 5462.00

Teapot, Floral, Bird Finial, 3 Mask & Claw Feet, Globular, 1740, 3 5/8 In. 860.00

Teapot, Floral, White Crabstock Handle, Drabware, Globular, 1740, 2 5/8 In. 2415.00

Teapot, Fluted Scallop Shell, Pulled S-Scroll Handle, Dark Brown, 6 In. 8625.00

Teapot, Fruiting Grapevines, Beadwork Border Base, Tapered Spout, 4 In.	805.00
Teapot, Jackfield Type, Black Glaze, Crabstock Handle, Globular, 1765, 7 3/4 In.	230.00
Teapot, Jackfield Type, c.1765	1250.00
Teapot, Lafayette At Franklin Tomb, Dark Blue Transfer	715.00
Teapot, Peg Leg, 10 In.	82.00
Teapot, Pineapple, Cabbage Spout, Dolphin Handle, 1765, 5 1/4 In.	3220.00
Teapot, Pompeii, Brown Transfer, c.1839-1846, 10 x 7 In.	275.00
Teapot, Prunus, Pale Buff, Crabstock Spout & Loop Handle, 5 In.	3162.00
Teapot, Red, Brown, Chocolate Brown, Pulled S-Scroll Handle, 5 In.	3737.00
Teapot, Residence Of Late Richard Jordan, Brown Transfer, 8 1/4 In.	715.00
Teapot, Scrolling Vine, S-Shaped Leaves, Teal Blue Underglaze, 4 In.	1035.00
Teapot, Sculpted Surfaces, Agate Ware, Bird Form, c.1750	5750.00
Teapot, Tudor Rose Blossoms, Crabstock Spout, Handle, Knop, Spherical	2875.00
Teapot, Tudor Rose Blossoms, Green, Ocher Gray Ground, 1755, 4 In.	2300.00
Teapot, Windsor Pattern, Dark Blue Transfer, Mellor, Venables & Co., 9 1/2 In.	192.00
Toby Jugs are listed in their own category.	
Tray, Bread, Combed Slipware, Raised Sides, 19th Century, 12 x 15 In.	400.00
Tray, Pin, Cobalt Blue Rim, 1930, 7 1/2 In.	22.00
Tray, R. Hall's Select Views, Castle Prison, Dark Blue Transfer, 10 5/8 In.	165.00
Tureen, Caister Castle, Norfolk, Dark Blue Transfer, 17 In.	780.00
Tureen, Cover, Undertray, LaGrange	6160.00
Tureen, Gravy, Tray, Vevay, Medium Dark Blue, Henshall	1400.00
Tureen, Letter From Wilkie's, Dark Blue Transfer, Ladle Notch, Clews, 16 In.	3740.00
Tureen, Sauce, Italian Scenery, Dark Blue Transfer, Terni, 6 1/4 In.	440.00
Tureen, Sauce, Oriental Scenes, Leaf Handles, Dark Blue Floral Transfer, 6 3/4 In.	302.00
Tureen, Soup, Capitol, Washington, Chickweed Border, Light Blue	1695.00
Vase, Boy & Girl, Colorful Clothes, 10 In.	325.00
Vase, Bud, Golfer, Tom Morris Jr., Standing Beside Tree, Pre-1920	300.00
Vase, Cover, Peonies, Lotus, Red, White Stippled Blue Dragons, Handles, 29 In.	4600.00
Vase, Peacock, Flowering Tree, Lion Handles, Ironstone, Meigh, c.1825, 15 In.	990.00
Vase, Spill, Black & White Spotted Hound, Chasing Stag, White Ground, 8 3/4 In.	258.00
Vase, Spill, Huntsman & Dog, Mid-19th Century, 13 In.	135.00
Vase, Young Tom Morris, Winner Of British Open 4 Times	330.00
Wash Bowl, Erie Canal Views, Dark Blue, Enoch Wood, 12 In.	1395.00

STANGL Pottery traces its history back to the Fulper Pottery of New Jersey. In 1910, Johann Martin Stangl started working at Fulper. He bought into the firm in 1913, became president in 1926, and in 1929 changed the company name to Stangl Pottery. The pottery made dinnerwares and a line of limited-edition bird figurines. The company went out of business in 1978. The numbers used by Stangl for the bird figures indicate two birds in one figure by adding the letter *D,* for double.

Amber Glo, Bowl, Vegetable, Round	20.00
Amber Glo, Dish, Vegetable, Divided	28.00
Amber Glo, Salt & Pepper	18.00
Amber Glo, Sugar & Creamer, Cover	26.00
Apple Tree, Cigarette Box	90.00
Ashtray, California Quail	65.00
Ashtray, Canada Goose, Oval, 10 1/2 In.	40.00 to 45.00
Ashtray, Canvasback, Square, 9 In.	45.00
Ashtray, Duck, Oval	35.00
Ashtray, Golfer	95.00
Ashtray, Leaping Deer	40.00
Ashtray, Mallard	90.00
Ashtray, Pheasant	50.00
Ashtray, Porpoise, Square	45.00
Ashtray, Rainbow Trout	55.00
Ashtray, Ruffed Grouse	80.00
Ashtray, Town & Country, Bathtub, Green	35.00
Bird, Allen Hummingbird, No. 3634	110.00
Bird, Bird Of Paradise, No. 3408	35.00
Bird, Blackpoll Warbler, No. 3810	105.00
Bird, Blue-Headed Vireo, No. 3448	77.00

Bird, Bluebird, No. 3276 ....70.00 to 125.00
Bird, Bluebirds, Double, No. 3276D ....135.00 to 150.00
Bird, Bobolink, No. 3595 .... 110.00
Bird, Brewer's Blackbird, No. 3591 .... 135.00
Bird, Broadtail Hummingbird, No. 3626 .... 110.00
Bird, Cardinal, No. 3444 .... 88.00
Bird, Cerulean Warbler, No. 3456 .... 66.00
Bird, Chestnut-Backed Chickadee, No. 3811 ....82.00 to 150.00
Bird, Chestnut-Sided Warbler, No. 3812 .... 55.00
Bird, Chickadees, No. 3581 .... 165.00
Bird, Cock, Pheasant, No. 3492 .... 185.00
Bird, Cockatoo, No. 3405 .... 55.00
Bird, Cockatoo, No. 3580 .... 132.00
Bird, Cockatoo, No. 3584 .... 450.00
Bird, Drinking Duck, No. 3250E 85.00
Bird, Evening Grosbeak, No. 3813 .... 100.00
Bird, Feeding Duck, No. 3250C 85.00
Bird, Flying Duck, No. 3443 ....300.00 to 425.00
Bird, Golden Crown Kinglet, No. 3848 .... 77.00
Bird, Goldfinch, No. 3849 .... 150.00
Bird, Goldfinches, No. 3635 .... 286.00
Bird, Gray Cardinal, No. 3596 ....66.00 to 75.00
Bird, Hen, No. 3446 .... 132.00
Bird, Hen, Pheasant, No. 3491 ....165.00 to 185.00
Bird, Hen, Yellow, No. 3286 .... 129.00
Bird, Hummingbirds, Double, No. 3599D 225.00
Bird, Indigo Bunting, No. 3589 .... 80.00
Bird, Kentucky Warbler, No. 3598 .... 55.00
Bird, Key West Quail Dove, No. 3454 ....260.00 to 300.00
Bird, Kingfishers, Double, No. 3406D ....121.00 to 135.00
Bird, Magnolia Warbler, No. 3925 .... 1100.00
Bird, Nuthatch, No. 3593 ....35.00 to 55.00
Bird, Oriole, No. 3402S ....44.00 to 100.00
Bird, Orioles, Double, No. 3402D ....55.00 to 100.00
Bird, Owl, No. 3407 .... 375.00
Bird, Parakeets, Double, No. 3582 .... 175.00
Bird, Parrot, No. 3449 .... 145.00
Bird, Parula Warbler, No. 3583D ....55.00 to 66.00
Bird, Pheasant, No. 3457 .... 150.00
Bird, Prothonotary Warbler, No. 3447 .... 75.00
Bird, Red-Faced, Warbler, No. 3594 .... 55.00
Bird, Rieffers Hummingbird, No. 3628 ....95.00 to 150.00
Bird, Rivoli Hummingbird, No. 3627 .... 99.00
Bird, Rooster, Yellow, No. 3285 .... 148.00
Bird, Rufous Hummingbird, No. 3585 .... 66.00
Bird, Standing Duck, No. 3250A 65.00
Bird, Titmouse, No. 3592 .... 88.00
Bird, Western Tanagers, Double, No. 3750D 375.00
Bird, Wilson Warbler, No. 3597 ....44.00 to 50.00
Bird, Wren, No. 3401 .... 55.00
Bird, Wrens, Double, No. 3401D 75.00
Box, Applied Flowers Pink Bisque, Oval 5 1/4 In. 195.00
Coaster, Duck 40.00
Coaster, Game Birds, 4 Piece 120.00
Coaster, Holly 20.00
Country Garden, Bowl, Salad, 10 In. 48.00
Country Garden, Bread Tray 50.00
Country Garden, Celery Dish 25.00
Country Garden, Chop Plate, 12 In. 40.00
Country Garden, Chop Plate, 14 In. 55.00
Country Garden, Mug 35.00
Country Garden, Plate, 6 In. 8.00
Country Garden, Plate, 10 In. 18.00

Country Garden, Relish	30.00
Country Garden, Sugar & Creamer	27.00
Country Life, Chop Plate	250.00
Della Ware, Plate, Morning Glories, 15 In.	27.00
Figurine, Draft Horse, Sticker, No. 3244	140.00 to 160.00
Figurine, Elephant, Black	125.00
Fruit, Bread Tray	45.00
Fruit, Cigarette Box	125.00
Fruit, Cookie Jar	150.00
Fruit, Plate, 8 In.	25.00
Fruit & Flowers, Bowl, Vegetable, Divided	55.00
Fruit & Flowers, Cake Stand	60.00
Fruit & Flowers, Chop Plate, 14 In.	70.00
Fruit & Flowers, Cup & Saucer	22.00
Fruit & Flowers, Plate, 6 In.	11.00
Fruit & Flowers, Plate, 10 In.	22.00
Fruit & Flowers, Platter, Oval, 14 3/4 In.	65.00
Golden Blossom, Sugar & Creamer	25.00
Golden Grape, Bowl, 12 In.	17.00
Golden Grape, Plate, 10 In.	8.00
Granada, Candy Dish, Gold, 2 Sections	22.00
Hen, Plate, Deviled Egg	125.00
Hen & Rooster, Salt & Pepper	125.00
Holly, Mug, 2 Cup	32.00
Jeweled Christmas Tree, Plate, 8 In., Pair	35.00
Jeweled Christmas Tree, Plate, 10 In.	50.00
Kiddieware, Cup & Saucer, Plate, Child's Set, Little Bo Peep	200.00
Kiddieware, Cup & Saucer, Plate, Indian Campfire	225.00
Kiddieware, Cup, Bo Peep	54.00
Kiddieware, Cup, Bowl, Plate, Circus Clown	275.00
Kiddieware, Cup, Carousel, Blue Border	35.00 to 45.00
Kiddieware, Cup, Little Quackers	35.00
Kiddieware, Cup, Mealtime Special	50.00
Kiddieware, Dish, ABC	85.00
Kiddieware, Dish, Ducky Dinner	60.00
Kiddieware, Dish, Five Little Pigs	150.00
Kiddieware, Dish, Kitten Capers	95.00 to 150.00
Kiddieware, Dish, Mealtime Special	110.00
Kiddieware, Mug, Jack & Jill, Musical	175.00 to 250.00
Kiddieware, Plate, Kitten Capers	85.00 to 95.00
Kiddieware, Plate, Little Bo Peep	85.00
Kiddieware, Plate, Little Boy Blue	70.00
Kiddieware, Plate, Little Quackers	150.00
Magnolia, Coffeepot, Individual	35.00
Orchard Song, Butter, Cover	40.00
Orchard Song, Plate, 8 In.	6.00
Orchard Song, Plate, 10 In.	15.00
Orchard Song, Teapot, 6 Cup	45.00
Pig At Fence, Plate, 8 In.	75.00
Rooster, Plate, 6 In.	15.00
Rose, Flowerpot, 4 1/2 In.	30.00
Terra Rose, Basket, 8 In.	35.00
Terra Rose, Vase, Horsehead Blue	350.00 to 400.00
Thistle, Cup	6.00
Thistle, Cup & Saucer	11.00
Thistle, Dish, Fruit, 5 1/2 In.	10.00
Thistle, Plate, 6 In.	5.00
Thistle, Plate, 8 In.	10.00
Thistle, Salt & Pepper	20.00
Thistle, Sugar & Creamer	22.00
Town & Country, Bean Pot, Brown	50.00
Town & Country, Bowl, Blue	30.00
Town & Country, Butter, Cover, Green	40.00 to 50.00

Town & Country, Candleholder, Finger Ring, Blue 40.00
Town & Country, Casserole, Cover, Green, 2 Qt. 55.00
Town & Country, Casserole, Green, 3 Qt. 50.00
Town & Country, Casserole, Pink, Caughley, 3 Qt. 125.00
Town & Country, Cup, Blue 55.00
Town & Country, Flowerpot, Brown, 3 3/4 In. 10.00
Town & Country, Gravy Boat, Blue, Stand 60.00
Town & Country, Napkin Ring, Blue, Set Of 4 ....65.00 to 75.00
Town & Country, Pitcher & Bowl, Blue, Large 285.00
Town & Country, Pitcher & Bowl, Yellow, Small 140.00
Town & Country, Pitcher, Blue, 2 1/2 Qt. ....60.00 to 65.00
Town & Country, Pitcher, Green, 2 1/2 Qt. ....38.00 to 50.00
Town & Country, Plate, Blue, 8 In. 20.00
Town & Country, Plate, Blue, 10 In. 35.00
Town & Country, Plate, Yellow, 10 In. 20.00
Town & Country, Platter, Blue, 15 In. 65.00
Town & Country, Sugar & Creamer, Cover, Blue 65.00
Tulip, Bean Pot, Cover, Yellow ....60.00 to 65.00
Tulip, Casserole, Cover, Yellow, 8 In. 40.00
Tulip, Cookie Jar, Blue 65.00
Tulip, Creamer, Yellow 8.00
Tulip, Cup & Saucer, Yellow 14.00
Tulip, Plate, 10 In. 12.00
Tulip, Platter, Yellow, 14 In. 45.00
Tulip, Soup, Dish, Lug, Yellow 12.00
Tulip, Sugar, Cover, Yellow 8.00
Vase, Black, Gold, Signed 125.00
Wig Stand, Blond, Ceramic Base 250.00
Wig Stand, Brunette, Wooden Base 250.00

STEINS have been used by beer and ale drinkers for over 500 years. They have been made of ivory, porcelain, stoneware, faience, silver, pewter, wood, or glass in sizes up to nine gallons. Although some were made by Mettlach, Meissen, Capo-di-Monte, and other famous factories, most were made by less important German potteries. The words *Geschutz* or *Musterschutz* on a stein are the German words for *patented* or *registered design*, not company names. Steins are still being made in the old styles. Lithophane steins may be found in the Lithophane category.

2 Deer, Transfer & Enameled, Brown, Porcelain Inlaid Lid, Glass, 1/2 Liter 185.00
2 Women In Musical Scene, Etched, Inlaid Lid, 1 Liter 165.00
3 Rows Of Cards, Etched, Cards On Inlaid Lid, 2 Liter 405.00
Amber Glass, Enameled Design, Pewter Top, 7 In. 120.00
Applied Glass Prunts With Enameled Dots, Amber Glass, 1896, 8 1/2 In. 120.00
Augustinerbrau Munchen, Etched, Pewter Cover, 1/4 Liter 75.00
Avon, Indians Of The American Frontier, Relief Design, Box, 1988 .... 31.00
Barrel Shape, Cobalt Blue, Closed Hinged Pewter Lid, Glass, 1/3 Liter 230.00
Bicycle Form, Man, Riding Bicycle, Pewter Lid, Amber Glass, 1/2 Liter 197.00
Boot, Anybody Who Can Drink This Is Truly A Man, Stoneware, Germany, 11 1/2 In. 385.00
Bowling Pin, Pottery Cover, 1/2 Liter 125.00
Bowling Pin, Tan, Green, Inlaid Cover, 1/2 Liter 250.00
Boy, Riding Stick Horse, In Soldier Uniform, Stoneware, Pewter Lid, 1/4 Liter 165.00
Brewery Burger Brau, Transfer & Enameled, Engraved Logo On Pewter Lid, 1/4 Liter . 275.00
Brewery Leist Brau, Brewery Logo Engraved On Pewter Lid, 1 Liter 1655.00
Budweiser, Bud Man, Metal Thumblift, Ceramarte, Brazil, 7 1/2 In. 205.00
Budweiser Printed On Wagon, St. Louis Engraved On Bottom, Lid, 1/2 Liter 117.00
Butcher, 1 Large Scene, Pewter Lid, Lithophane Bottom, 1/2 Liter 305.00
Cards, Etched, Inlaid Lid, 1/2 Liter 250.00
Children Scene, Stork, Pewter Cover, 1/2 Liter 260.00
Chimney Sweeps, Stoneware, Pewter Lid, 1 Liter 447.00
Choir With Birds & Music, Transfer & Enameled, Pewter Lid, 1 Liter 165.00
Christmas, Winter Festivities, Pewter Lid, Limited Edition, Munich, 1979 .... 43.00
City Of Rothenburg, Pewter Cover, 1/2 Liter 73.00

Crest With Lions, Engraved Floral On Pewter Cover, 1/2 Liter 115.00
Cucumber, Porcelain Lid, Schierholz, 1/2 Liter 237.00
Cut Star Design, Green Transfer, Porcelain Inlaid Lid, Glass, 1/2 Liter 95.00
Deer Head, Porcelain Inlaid Lid, Glass, 1/2 Liter 99.00
Diana & Hunters, Etched & Glazed, Hunter With Horn In Center, Inlaid Lid, 1/2 Liter . 350.00
Diana & Hunters, Etched, Inlaid Lid, Gerz, 1/2 Liter 260.00
Drunken Scene, Etched, Pewter Lid, Hauber & Reuther, 1/2 Liter 245.00
Dutch Mother With 2 Boys Smoking Behind Her, Stoneware, Pewter Lid, 1 Liter .. 195.00
Dutch Scene With Children, Etched & Glazed, Pewter Lid, 1 Liter 359.00
Embossed Hunters & Dogs, Chasing Deer, Pewter, Germany, 1960 .... 170.00
Firemen Equipment, Enameled Verse, Pewter Cover, 1/2 Liter 220.00
Flapper, Leading 6 Characters, Frothing Steins, Stoneware, Frische Mass, Signed, 1 Liter 235.00
Floral, Star Design, Prism Glass Inlaid Lid, Glass, 1/2 Liter 230.00
Fox Hunting Scene, Etched, Pewter Lid, Hauber & Reuther, 1/2 Liter 220.00
Fritz Heckert Style, Enameled Crest, Glass, 6 1/4 In. 165.00
Frog Party, Pewter Lid & Thumb Rest 950.00
Gargoyles Around Body, Amber, Pewter Lid, Amber Glass, 1/2 Liter 245.00
Gentleman Rabbit, 1/2 Liter 3000.00
Glass, Applied Imperial Crests, Flags, Equestrian Figure Finial, West Germany, 4 1/2 In. . 36.00
Gooseman, 1/2 Liter 1725.00
Hunter In Forest, Pewter Lid, 1/2 Liter 110.00
Hunter With Woman, Lithophane Of Hunter, Porcelain, Pewter Lid, 1/2 Liter 150.00
Hunting, Frieze Of Stags, Continental Silver Top, 5 1/2 In. 690.00
Jubilant Deer Hunter, Mountain Chalet, Cobalt Blue Ground, Thewalt, 1960s, 1/2 Liter 165.00
Kaiser Portrait, Oak Leaves, Equestrian Figure At Finial, Pottery, Pewter Lid, Small ... 40.00
Mack Truck, Whiskey, Gold Bulldog Top, Fire Trucks On Body 35.00
Man Playing Accordion, Bavarian Verse, Pottery, Pewter Lid, 1/2 Liter 285.00
Man With Pipe In Hand, Green Hat, Figural, West Germany, 9 In. 175.00
Men, Leaving Gasthaus, Etched, Inlaid Lid, Gerz, 1/2 Liter 110.00
Men At Table, Etched, Inlaid Lid, 1/2 Liter 140.00
Mettlach steins are listed in the Mettlach category.
Miller, Birth Of A Nation, 1st Edition 25.00
Monk, Figural, J. Reinemann Munchen, 9 1/2 In. 190.00
Monk, Inlaid Lid, Goebel, Full Bee, 1950, 1/2 Liter 330.00
Monk, Red Robe, Porcelain, Inlaid Lid 198.00
Munich Child, Inlaid Cover, 1/8 Liter 79.00
Munich Child, Transfer & Enameled, Pewter Lid, 1 Liter 435.00
Munich Scene, Child On Barrel, Pewter Lid, Glass, 1/2 Liter 195.00
Musical & Drinking Scene, Etched, Inlaid Lid, 1/2 Liter 162.00
Musicians, Gray Ground, Pewter Fittings, Germany, 12 1/2 In. 190.00
People Scene, Dancing, Ribbed, Green, Glass, Pewter Base, Cover, 1/2 Liter 160.00
Pewter Base & Lid, Glass, Dated 1819, 9 7/8 In. 300.00
Poodle, Porcelain Lid, Schierholz, 1/2 Liter 253.00
Potato Head, Porcelain Lid, Schierholz, 1/2 Liter 245.00
Rams' Heads At Sides, Encased In French Pewter, Hinged Lid, 15 1/4 In. 395.00
Regimental, 2-Sided Scene, Bird Thumblift, Porcelain, 1903-1905, 1/2 Liter 330.00
Regimental, 2-Sided Scene, Eagle Thumblift, Porcelain, 1/2 Liter 695.00
Regimental, 2-Sided Scene, Griffin Thumblift, Porcelain, 1/2 Liter 265.00
Regimental, 2-Sided Scene, Infantry, Porcelain, Eagle Thumblift, 1/2 Liter 440.00
Regimental, 2-Sided Scene, Sachsen Thumblift, 1901-1903, 1/2 Liter 440.00
Regimental, 4-Sided Scene, Bird Thumblift, 1904-1906, 1/2 Liter 358.00
Regimental, 4-Sided Scene, Griffin Thumblift, Porcelain, 1/2 Liter 396.00
Regimental, 4-Sided Scene, Griffin Thumblift, Porcelain, Pewter Lid, 1909, 1/2 Liter ... 330.00
Regimental, 4-Sided Scene, Lion Thumblift, 1907-1910, 1/2 Liter 660.00
Regimental, 4-Sided Scene, Lion Thumblift, Porcelain, 1/2 Liter 462.00
Regimental, 4-Sided Scene, Lion Thumblift, Porcelain, 1910-1912, 1/2 Liter 605.00
Regimental, 4-Sided Scene, Lion Thumblift, Porcelain, Prism Inlaid Lid, 1/2 Liter 350.00
Regimental, 6-Sided Scene, Porcelain, Plain Pewter Lid, 1899, 1/2 Liter 110.00
Regimental, Battle Scene, Pewter Lid, Dumler & Breiden, 1 Liter 454.00
Regimental, Bavarian Machine Gun Company, 1/2 Liter 2127.00
Regimental, Iron Cross With Colors Of German Flag, Pewter Lid, 1914, 1/2 Liter 554.00
Reineman Munchen, Munich Child, Twin Tower Thumblift, 1 Liter 375.00
Sad Radish, Porcelain, Musterschutz, Schierholz 300.00

Scene Of 2 People Playing Lawn Tennis, Inlaid Sailboat On Porcelain Lid, 1/2 Liter . 1525.00
Shield & Tree, Enameled Design, Pewter Top With Dragon, Germany, 13 3/4 In. 110.00
Skull, Porcelain, Inlaid Lid, E. Bohne & Son, 1/2 Liter 300.00
Skull, Porcelain, Pewter Lid, P.M. Bavaria, 1/4 Liter 111.00
Skyline Of Frankfurt, Stoneware, Brewery Logo Engraved On Pewter Lid, 1 Liter 395.00
Soldier, 1/2 Liter 1550.00
Star On Base Underside, Floral, Glass, Prism Inlaid Lid, 1/2 Liter 186.00
Stroh's Bohemian Beer, Tan, Ivory, Brazil, 1985, 7 1/2 In. 25.00
Sweetheart, Young Lovers On Park Bench, Porcelain Top, Pewter Thumblift, 4 In. 30.00
Transfer & Enameled, Beer Brewer, 3 Large Scenes, Pewter Lid, 1/2 Liter 355.00
Transfer & Enameled, Blacksmith, 1 Large Scene, Pottery, Pewter Lid, 1/2 Liter 368.00
Transfer & Enameled, Chamois In Mountains, Pewter Lid, Glass, 1/2 Liter 177.00
Transfer & Enameled, Man Who Works Furnace, 1 Front Scene, Pewter Lid, 1/2 Liter . 665.00
Transfer & Enameled, Pewter Lid, 1 Liter 465.00
Transfer & Enameled, Third Reich, Eagle With Swastika, Pewter Lid, 1/2 Liter 732.00
Turner Design, Stoneware, Inlaid Lid, 1/2 Liter 177.00
Woman, Playing Guitar, Stoneware, Pewter Lid, 3 Liter, 13 1/4 In. 180.00
Woman, Playing Trumpet For Sheepherder, Etched, Sheep On Inlaid Lid, 1/4 Liter 150.00

STEREO CARDS that were made for stereoscope viewers became popular after 1840. Two almost identical pictures were mounted on a stiff cardboard backing so that, when viewed through a stereoscope, a three-dimensional picture could be seen. Value is determined by maker and by subject. These cards were made in quantity through the 1930s.

Alone At Last, Keystone 25.00
Before & After Marriage, Keystone 10.00
Buffalo Bill, W.F. Cody In Full Regalia, Stacy, Brooklyn 600.00
Buffalo Bill's Wild West, Black, White, 7 1/2 x 9 1/2 In. 300.00
Cowboy, Cowboy Clothes, Postcard 65.00
French Cook, Keystone, 11 Cards 60.00
Lilly Langtry, Lafayette, Dublin, Ireland, 1884 .... 85.00
Lincoln Street, Sitka, Alaska & Kettle River, Minnesota Pineries, 1900s, Pair 14.00
Mormons Making Tunnel No. 3, Union Pacific Railroad Series 175.00
Portrait, Pawnee Chief, Peter La Chere, 1868 .... 400.00
President Taft 15.00
Sioux Indians & Wigwams, Near St. Paul, 1862 .... 175.00
Union Elevator, Omaha, Neb., 1880 .... 44.00
Wedding, Keystone, 6 Cards 25.00

STEREOSCOPES were used for viewing stereo cards. The hand viewer was invented by Oliver Wendell Holmes, although more complicated table models were used before his was produced in 1859. Do not confuse the stereoscope with the stereopticon, a magic lantern that used glass slides.

Alan Beckers, Rosewood Veneer, Holds 36 Cards, With Cards, Pat. 1857-1859 .... 880.00
Slant Top Oak Case, Cast Iron Viewing Port & Coin Slot, c.1920 .... 345.00

STERLING SILVER, see Silver-Sterling category.

STEUBEN glass was made at the Steuben Glass Works of Corning, New York. The factory, founded by Frederick Carder and T.G. Hawkes, Sr., was purchased by the Corning Glass Company. They continued to make glass called *Steuben*. Many types of art glass were made at Steuben. The firm is still making exceptional quality glass but it is clear, modern-style glass. Additional pieces may be found in the Aurene, Cluthra, and perfume bottle categories.

Basket, Blue, Purple Highlights, Applied Blue Handle, 12 x 9 In. 3000.00
Basket, White Exterior, Blue, Blue Aurene Handle, 2 Prunts, 9 1/4 x 7 3/4 x 5 In. 1800.00
Bowl, Applied Celeste Blue Threading, 3 x 12 In. 170.00
Bowl, Applied Ornaments On Base, Incised Label, 6 5/8 x 5 In. 275.00
Bowl, Applied Scroll Feet, Incised Label, 7 3/4 x 3 In. 275.00
Bowl, Celeste Blue, 12 In. 150.00
Bowl, Classic Shape, Gold Iridescent, Carder, 3 x 6 In. 460.00
Bowl, Flared Lip, Applied Prunts Stem, Marked, 7 1/2 x 4 3/4 In. 275.00

Bowl, Flared, Ruby, 13 1/8 x 3 In.	25.00
Bowl, Flat Rimmed, 8 In.	65.00
Bowl, Footed, 1938, 12 In.	400.00
Bowl, Gold, 10 Ribs, Scalloped Rim, Carder, 5 1/4 In.	374.00
Bowl, Gold, Blue Highlights, Silver Plate Holder, 11 1/2 x 10 In.	650.00
Bowl, Jade Green, Scalloped, Signed, 4 1/2 x 8 In.	175.00
Bowl, Rose Quartz, Scalloped Rim, Blossoms, Crackled, 3 Twig Feet, 7 x 8 In.	1715.00
Bowl, Verre De Soie, Melon Optic, 8 In.	165.00
Candleholder, 2-Light, Scroll Design, Signed, 4 3/4 x 6 3/4 In., Pair	560.00
Candleholder, Cobalt Blue, Marked, Fleur De Lis, 3 Piece	495.00
Candlestick, Amethyst, Spiral Banding, High Domed Foot, Pair	425.00
Candlestick, Jade, Green, Flared Ruffled Bobeche, Signed, 5 In., Pair	517.00
Candlestick, Pomona Green, Mushroom Shape, Signed, 3 3/4 x 4 1/8 In.	195.00
Candlestick, Twisted Neck, Flat Rimmed Bobeche, Signed, 6 1/2 In.	488.00
Centerpiece, Deep Purple, Gold, Cobalt Blue, Scalloped, 8-Spaced Crimps, 4 x 12 In.	2300.00
Champagne, Alabaster Rope Twist Stem, 5 1/2 In.	110.00
Compote, 12-Ribbed Bowl, Conforming Stem & Base, Signed, 5 In.	805.00
Compote, Air-Twist Ball Stem, Black, 5 1/4 x 10 In.	220.00 to 330.00
Compote, Amethyst, Rolled Edge, 7 In.	275.00
Compote, Applied 8 Banana Designs, Lemon Squeezed Base, 20th Century, 15 In.	575.00
Compote, Blue, Crimped, Rope Twist Stem, Carder, 10 x 7 1/2 In.	1265.00
Compote, Cover, Apple Finial, 10 In.	325.00
Compote, Floral Design, Rope Twist Stem	225.00
Compote, Green Machine Threading Engraved Cat	285.00
Compote, Ivrene Round Foot, Ruffled Edge, 10 In.	520.00
Compote, Pomona Green, Crystal	50.00
Console, Marina, 11 In.	225.00
Console Set, Pomona Green, Pedestal Base, Fleur-De-Lis, 14 1/2 x 4 In., 3 Piece	660.00
Cordial Set, Black, 1925-1932, 6 Piece	480.00
Dish, Cover, Ram's Head	295.00
Dish, Olive, John Greves, 1939, 5 5/8 In.	110.00
Ewer, Rosaline, Alabaster, 15 In.	900.00
Figurine, American Eagle, Perched On Ball, 4 3/4 x 5 1/2 In.	515.00
Figurine, Apple, Signed	110.00
Figurine, Banana, Signed	175.00
Figurine, Cat, Reclining, Signed, 5 3/4 In.	172.00
Figurine, Frog, Applied Eyes, Feet, Crystal, Signed, 4 3/4 In.	400.00
Figurine, Frog, Seated, 3 In.	115.00
Figurine, Frog, Seated, Signed Underfoot, Original Box, 2 1/4 In.	50.00
Figurine, Owl, Frosted Eyes, Signed, 5 1/2 In.	230.00
Figurine, Penguin, Signed, 3 1/2 In.	110.00
Figurine, Rabbit, Signed, 3 3/4 In.	350.00
Finger Bowl, Underplate, Gold Aurene On Calcite, 5 In., 24 Piece	4400.00
Finger Bowl, Underplate, Pomona Green, Ribbed, Signed	60.00
Flask, Wild Quail, Leather Fitted Box & Certificate, 8 1/4 In.	880.00
Goblet, Baluster Teardrop Stem, Signed, 6 3/4 In., 12 Piece	1725.00
Goblet, Cerise Ruby, 6 Piece	575.00
Goblet, Green Cut To Clear, Thistles, Leaves & Stem On Bowl, Signed	260.00
Goblet, Water, Trumpet Shape, Box & Felts, Signed, 7 1/4 In., 12 Piece	990.00
Ice Bucket, Signed, 7 x 5 In.	90.00
Necklace, Rosebud, 14K Yellow Gold Chain, Red Leather Case, 17 1/2 In.	660.00
Paperweight, Gilt Metal Eagle Finial, Incised Label, Fitted Box, 5 3/4 In.	385.00
Pitcher, Alabaster, Black Handle, Urn Form, 9 3/4 In.	750.00
Plate, Bristol Yellow, 10 In., 4 Piece	600.00
Plate, Oriental Jade, 9 In.	195.00
Plate, Pomona Green, Engraving, Signed	100.00
Plate, Red, Carder, 16 Ribs	690.00
Plate, Snowy Owl, 10 In.	795.00
Plate, Wild Turkey, Audubon, 10 In.	345.00
Platter, Amethyst, Signed, 14 In.	150.00
Salt, Aurene & Calcite, Footed, Paper Label	225.00
Sculpture, Ladder Of Dreams, Prismatic Tablet, 2 Boys & Girl, 11 3/4 In.	6900.00
Sculpture, Stars & Stripes, Signed, 4 x 4 In.	1495.00

Sculpture, Wilderness Serenade, Engraved Moon & Stars, Signed, 7 In.	3255.00
Shade, Calcite, Blue Border, Gold, 4 1/4 In.	175.00
Shade, Ceiling, Foliate Design, Ivrene, 4 Holes For Hanging, Signed, 17 1/2 In.	402.00
Shade, Intaglio, Ivy Leaves, Insect, Iridescent Border, 10 In.	2760.00
Shade, Pulled Feather, 2 1/4 x 5 1/2 x 6 In.	192.50
Sherbet, Amethyst Ribbed, Clear Stem, Signed, 3 3/4 In.	50.00
Sherbet, Gold Aurene On Calcite, 3 3/4 In.	172.00
Urn, Amber, Floral, Leaf, 9 x 7 1/2 In.	75.00
Urn, Celeste Blue, Fruit Design	600.00
Urn, Cover, Aqua, Applied Pear Knob, Ribbed Leaf, Carder, 14 1/2 In.	978.00
Urn, Cover, Cobalt Blue	495.00
Vase, Alabaster, Applied Green, Gold Aurene, 1910, 7 In.	5500.00
Vase, Amber, Gold, Rose, Blue Iridescent, Ribbed, Signed, 4 1/2 In.	495.00
Vase, Applied Blue Threading, 5 3/4 x 4 In.	95.00
Vase, Aurene Ribs, Rose, Blue Highlights, Signed, 5 In.	605.00
Vase, Blue Green, Leaves, Carder, 1916, 5 1/8 In.	5750.00
Vase, Blue, Double M Handles, Signed, F. Carder, 10 In.	1320.00
Vase, Blue, Purple, Green Iridescent, Blue Aurene, 1920, 8 1/4 In.	690.00
Vase, Celeste Blue, Footed, 8 In.	195.00
Vase, Cerise Ruby, 5 1/2 In.	475.00
Vase, Cobalt Blue, Iridescent, Flared Rim, Carder, 8 In.	860.00
Vase, Cut Garlands Of Flowers, 8 In.	325.00
Vase, Etched Mansard, Repeating Art Deco Blossoms, Marked, Fleur-De-Lis, 6 In.	1715.00
Vase, Fan Shape, Blue Threading, 7 3/4 In.	137.00
Vase, Fan, Amber Ribbed, 6 In.	175.00
Vase, Fan, Jade Green, Alabaster Stem, Foot, 16 Vertical Ribs, 11 x 9 In.	675.00
Vase, Fir Cone Etch, Spherical Body, Green, Carder, 7 x 7 1/2 In.	1035.00
Vase, Florentia, Pink Floral, Satin Ground, 6 In.	4345.00
Vase, Gazelle, Ivory, Carder, 10 3/4 In.	2300.00
Vase, Green, Rib Molded, Rectangular, Carder, 9 1/2 x 5 3/4 In.	290.00
Vase, Grotesque, Amethyst To Clear, c.1920, 11 In.	550.00
Vase, Grotesque, Green To Clear, 8 In.	350.00
Vase, Grotesque, Ivory, 12 In.	350.00
Vase, Ivory, Paneled, Black Base, 7 3/4 x 8 3/4 In.	440.00
Vase, Ivory, Raised Flared Rim, Oval, 8 1/4 In.	518.00
Vase, Jade Green On Alabaster, Sherwood Stylized Blossoms, 7 In.	977.00
Vase, Jade Green, Alabaster Handles, Carder, 10 1/4 In.	748.00
Vase, Lavender, Rose Iridescent, Green, Ivory Pulled Chain, Gourd Shape, 6 In.	1150.00
Vase, Millefiori, Green, Gold White Flowers, Iridescent, Signed, 1900, 4 1/2 In.	1840.00
Vase, Oriental Poppy, Integrated Opal Stripes, 6 In.	1587.00
Vase, Sculptured, Chrysanthemums, Signed, 13 In.	3335.00
Vase, Silverina, Green, Cylindrical, 8 In.	250.00
Vase, Silverina, Medium Green, 7 x 5 In.	450.00
Vase, Spanish Green, Ribbed Optic, Signed, 6 3/4 x 6 3/4 In.	50.00
Vase, Swirl, Amber Flip, Signed, 8 x 6 In.	125.00
Vase, Swirl, Green, Signed, 7 x 6 1/2 In.	70.00
Vase, Verre De Soie, Floriform, 19 In.	600.00
Vase, Verre De Soie, Iridescent, 6 In.	66.00
Vasse, Cornucopia Form, Copper Wheel Engraving, Signed, Pre-1932	175.00
Wine, Cerice Ruby, Engraved Grapes	95.00
Wine, Gold Iridescent, Rope Twisted Stem, Signed, 4 In.	225.00
Wine, Trumpet Shape, Box & Felts, Signed, 6 In., 12 Piece	880.00

STEVENGRAPHS are woven pictures made like fancy ribbons. They were manufactured by Thomas Stevens of Coventry, England, and became popular in 1862. Most are marked *Woven in silk by Thomas Stevens* or were mounted on a cardboard that tells the story of the Stevengraph. Other similar ribbon pictures have been made in England and Germany.

Bookmark, A Blessing, Floral, Black Silk	60.00
Bookmark, A Happy Christmas To You	145.00
Bookmark, Good Old Days, Coach & Four, Frame, 9 3/4 x 12 3/4 In.	137.00
Bookmark, Lincoln Portrait, Emancipation Proclamation, Flag, Shield, 11 In.	295.00

McKinley & Hobart, 2 3/4 x 8 In. 225.00
Ribbon, George Washington, Philadelphia Exposition, 1876, 12 In. 175.00
Shakespeare, Views Of Stratford On Avon 325.00
Signing Of Declaration Of Independence, Woven Silk, 7 x 2 1/2 In. 450.00

TEVENS & WILLIAMS of Stourbridge, England, made many types of
glass, including layered, etched, cameo, and art glass, between the
1830s and 1930s. Some pieces are signed *S & W*. Many pieces are dec-
rated with flowers, leaves, and other designs based on nature.

Basket, 2 Large Strawberries, Green Leaves, Stem, Amber Handle, 13 In. 650.00
Basket, 4 Pink & White Floral, Amber Thorn Handle, Rose Lining, 13 In. 850.00
Basket, Amber & Cranberry Leaf, Amber Handle, 7 1/2 In. 225.00
Basket, Applied Amber Design, Turquoise, Blue Exterior, White, 10 In. 225.00
Basket, Applied Glass Design, Pink, White, Amber, Green Flowers, 11 In. 700.00
Basket, Applied Leaves, Amber Apples & Feet, Square, 7 1/2 x 6 In. 632.00
Basket, Leaf Form Bowl, Frosted Thorn Handle, Orange Enamel, 14 In. 230.00
Basket, Overlay, Applied Leaves, Pink Lining, Amber Handle, 9 1/2 In. 650.00
Basket, Ruffled Leaves, Pink Lining, Stems Of Leaves Form Feet, 8 1/2 In. 550.00
Basket, White Lining, Floral Design, White, Blue Flowers, 8 1/4 x 6 In. 250.00
Bowl, Applied Floral Design, Gold, Scalloped Edge, 1886, 9 1/2 In. 248.00
Candleholder, Pink Jade, Alabaster Stem, 1880, 9 In. 193.00
Compote, Alabaster Stem, Signed, 4 3/4 In. 345.00
Cruet, Vinegar, Opaque White, Amber Applied Handle & Stopper, 8 In. 165.00
Decanter, Cactus Rose, Blossoms On Spiked Leaf-Forms, 15 1/2 In. 1455.00
Pitcher, 3 Pink, White Flowers, With Amber Centers, Handle, 7 x 4 In. 250.00
Pitcher, Yellow & Pink Opalescent Stripe, Clear Ground, 6 x 5 In. 225.00
Rose Bowl, Arboresque, White & Cranberry, Wishbone Feet, 4 x 3 3/4 In. 195.00
Rose Bowl, Cranberry, Polished Pontil, Fluted, 1880s, 4 1/2 x 5 1/4 In. 143.00
Rose Bowl, Crimped Edge, Zippered Sides, 1886, 2 In. 220.00
Rose Bowl, Pompeiian Swirl, Brown To Gold, Blue Lining, 5 x 5 1/4 In. 850.00
Vase, Amber Branch, Leaves & Ruffled Edge, Applied Feet, 10 In. 295.00
Vase, Amber Edging Around Ruffle, Cream Lining, 9 1/2 In. 550.00
Vase, Amber Ruffled Leaves At Sides, Rose Lining, Loop Feet, 6 1/2 In. 225.00
Vase, Amber, Green, Cranberry Ruffled Leaves, Rose Overlay, 6 1/2 In. 265.00
Vase, Applied Flowers & Leaves, Rose, Pink, White, Ruffled Top, 11 x 4 In. 220.00
Vase, Applied Glass Flower, Rim, Pink Cased, 5 In. 110.00
Vase, Applied Pale Pink Rigaree, White Opalescent Stripes, 10 x 4 In. 70.00
Vase, Applied Sapphire Blue Rigaree Around Neck, Deep Amber, 5 x 7 In. 155.00
Vase, Custard, Applied Amber Branch, Edge, Thorn Handles, 1886, 10 In. 193.00
Vase, Deep Amber, 4 Applied Green Teardrops, Rose, Leaf Base, 7 x 5 In. 50.00
Vase, Intaglio Ferns, Blue Feet & Stripes, 3 5/8 In. 225.00
Vase, Lacy Intaglio Designs, White Lining, Intaglio Overlay, 4 1/4 In. 195.00
Vase, Pompeiian Swirl, Amberina, White Lining, Satin, 11 x 6 In. 950.00
Vase, Pompeiian Swirl, Lime Green, White Lining, Bulbous, 10 3/4 In. 850.00
Vase, Protruding Poppy, Leaves, Stem, Green, Yellow, 10 In. 190.00
Vase, Rose Shaded To Pink, Yellow & White Flowers, Leaves, 8 In. 325.00
Vase, Ruffled Clear Leaves, Amber Loop Feet, 6 1/2 In. 245.00
Vase, Ruffled Top, Amber Edging, Amber Handle, Pink Overlay, 10 3/4 In. 495.00
Vase, Silver Top, Cranberry Bottom, Embedded Threading, 6 1/2 In. 550.00
Vase, Silverina, Applied Green Veining, Amethyst, Green Ground, 6 In. 3200.00
Vase, White, Pink Floral, Amber Handle, Edge, White Lining, 10 3/4 In. 495.00

STIEGEL TYPE glass is listed here. It is almost impossible to be sure a
piece was actually made by Stiegel, so the knowing collector refers to
this glass as *Stiegel type*. Henry William Stiegel, a colorful immigrant
to the colonies, started his first factory in Pennsylvania in 1763. He
remained in business until 1774. Glassware was made in a style popular in Europe at that time and was similar to the glass of many other
makers. It was made of clear or colored glass and was decorated with
enamel colors, mold blown designs, or etching.

Creamer, 15 Diamonds, Emerald Green, Egg Shape, 3 1/8 In. 2750.00
Creamer, Diamond Design, Sapphire Blue, 18th Century 435.00
Sugar, Cover, Expanded Diamond, Cobalt Blue, Pontil, 6 In. 1210.00

STONEWARE is a coarse, glazed, and fired potter's ceramic that is used to make crocks, jugs, bowls, etc. It is often decorated with cobalt blue decorations. In the nineteenth and early twentieth centuries, potters often decorated crocks with blue numbers indicating the size of the container. A "2" meant 2 gallons. Stoneware is still being made.

Bank, Acorn Finial, Globular Tapering Body, Wilhemina Silber, 1873, 6 In.	9775.00
Bank, Piggy, Blue Base Glaze, Green Variations, Incised Eye Pupils, Seagrove	110.00
Bank, Salt Glaze, Coin Slot At Base, Incised John Kelly, Dec. 25th, 1872, 6 1/2 In.	9200.00
Basin, Scene Of Perseus & Andromeda, Tin Glazed, Italy, 23 In.	1265.00
Batter Jug, Cobalt Swirl Around Spout, Handle Loops, Bail Handle, 4 Qt.	175.00
Beaker, Etched & Glazed, 4 1/2 In.	90.00
Bean Pot, Alkaline Glaze, Allover Black Glossy Glaze, Late 19th Century, 11 x 28 In.	22.00
Bell, Desert Sunset, 6 1/2 In.	30.00
Birdhouse, Thickly Applied Glaze, Crushed Glass Glaze, Mr. Craig, 8 1/4 In.	467.00
Bottle, Salt Glaze, Cream Colored, Charlotte, North Carolina, 1880, 9 5/8 In.	996.00
Bowl, Allover Embossed Design, Blue, 8 In.	65.00
Bowl, Blue Interior, Incised Abstract Designs, Brown Exterior, Pond Farm, 6 1/2 In.	880.00
Bowl, High Glass Exterior, Semigloss Crimson Interior, 9 1/2 In.	550.00
Bowl, Paneled, Spongeware, 4 In.	95.00
Bowl, White Glaze, Blue Stenciled Bands, Flower, 10 In.	80.00
Bust, Addison, White, Black Basalt Base, Turner, 1800, 9 1/2 In.	1150.00
Bust, Milton, White, Black Basalt Base, Turner, 1800, 10 1/8 In.	920.00
Butter, Stags On Cover, Hunting Scene	475.00
Canister, Tea, Stoneware Lid, Blue & White, 7 In.	150.00
Canteen, Embossed, Bardwell's Root Beer, 2 Elk On Reverse, c.1870, 10 In.	925.00
Chicken Waterer, Double Knob Finial, Arched Hood, Foliate, 7 1/4 In.	1610.00
Churn, Albany Slip Glaze, Green, Brown, Lug Loop Handles, Brown Bros., 16 In.	100.00
Churn, Albany Slip Glaze, Red, Brown Exterior, Black Interior, 2 Handles, 17 In.	110.00
Churn, Alkaline Glaze, Red Clay Body, 1-Loop 1-Lug Handles, 14 1/6 In.	44.00
Churn, Allover Light Green Glaze, Loop Handle, Sterrett Co., 15 1/2 In.	55.00
Churn, Applied Ear Handles, Cobalt Blue Quill Work, 6, Squiggle Design, 19 1/2 In.	110.00
Churn, Applied Handle, Wooden Lid, Handle, Dasher, Blue Lower, 4, 16 In.	350.00
Churn, Applied Handles, Cobalt Blue Floral Design, 6 1/8 In.	358.00
Churn, Blue Bird Design, Handles, Holed Lid Insert, Whites, Utica, 3 Gal.	1438.00
Churn, Cobalt Blue Applied Handles, No. 2, Egg Shape, 14 In.	190.00
Churn, Cobalt Blue Bird On Perch, Applied Shoulder Handles, 17 1/2 In.	495.00
Churn, Salt Glaze, 3 Handles, 2-Loop 1-Lug Handle, Pittman & Bros., 18 5/8 In.	88.00
Cider Set, Covered Tureen, 8 Mugs, 20th Century	125.00
Cooler, Barrel Shape, Bird On Branch Design, Cobalt Blue Bands, 14 In.	275.00
Cooler, Cobalt Blue Vine Design, Applied Shoulder Handles, Egg Shape, 16 In.	330.00
Cooler, Foliate Sprigs & 3, Bands Of Gadrooning, Samuel A. Smith, 9 1/2 In.	518.00
Cooler, Ice Tea, Lid, 2 Gal.	2500.00
Cooler, Radium Treatment, Salt Lake, Utah, Blue & White, 2 Gal.	850.00
Cooler, Woman, Wishing Well, Bundle Of Flowers, Robinson Clay Products, 12 In.	258.00
Creamer, Albany Slip Glaze, Allover Black Glossy Glaze, S.R. Rogers, 4 3/8 In.	22.00
Creamer, Arc & Leaf, Blue	65.00
Crock, 2 & Line Design, Cake, Tab Handles, Penna., 2 Gal., 7 1/2 x 11 1/2 In.	425.00
Crock, 3 Brown Bands, Impressed Boston, 1804, 13 In., 3 Gal.	330.00
Crock, A. Conrad, Shinnston, W.Va., c.1880, 21 In., 10 Gal.	995.00
Crock, Arhens, Clark & Fox Co., 9 1/2 x 14 In.	245.00
Crock, Blue Cobalt Stencil, Taylor Richmond, Va., 10 1/2 In.	145.00
Crock, Blue Cobalt Stencil, Wm. Kinnier, Virginia, 10 In.	72.00
Crock, Blue Design, Gray Ground, Salt Glaze, Incised Bands, Applied Handles, 13 In.	78.00
Crock, Blue Floral Design, Salt Glaze, Incised Band, Gray Ground, 7 1/2 In.	193.00
Crock, Blue Floral, Gray Ground, Applied Handles, Mullen & Connolly, N.J., 3 Gal.	110.00
Crock, Blue Floral, Gray Ground, Salt Glaze, S.L. Pewtress & Co., 3 Gal.	132.00
Crock, Blue Floral, O.L. & A.K. Ballard, Burlington, Vt., Salt Glaze, Handles, 10 In.	110.00
Crock, Blue Floral, Salt Glaze, Brown Ground, Richard C. Remmey, Penn., 9 In.	250.00
Crock, Blue Leaf, Gray Ground, Salt Glaze, Single Incised Band, 8 3/4 In.	100.00
Crock, Blue Speckled Bird, Foliage, Handles, F.A. Plaisted & Co., 3 Gal.	715.00
Crock, Blue Stencil Label, Shaw & Phister, 103 & 105 E. Pearl St., Cin., O., 9 1/2 In.	220.00
Crock, Blue Vine Design, Gray Ground, Salt Glaze, Incised Band, 9 In.	110.00

Crock, Butter, Blue, White, 8 1/4 In. 85.00
Crock, Butter, Blue, White, Robinson Clay Products Co., Akron, Ohio, 7 In. 138.00
Crock, Butter, Blue, White, Robinson Clay Products Co., Akron, Ohio, 8 1/4 In. 165.00
Crock, Butter, Cover, Cobalt Blue Design, 8 In. 220.00
Crock, Butter, Lambrecht, 1 Lb. 75.00
Crock, Cobalt Blue 2, Stripes, Flared Lip, 11 3/4 x 7 1/2 In. 80.00
Crock, Cobalt Blue Brushed Floral, Handles, Wm. E. Warner, 3, 9 3/4 In. 330.00
Crock, Cobalt Blue Cottage, R.O. Whittemore, 7 3/4 x 8 3/8 In. 1035.00
Crock, Cobalt Blue Stylized Floral, 2, Rim Handles, N.A. White & Son, 9 In. 220.00
Crock, Cobalt Floral, 2 Handles, Nichols & Boynton, 25 In. 165.00
Crock, Cobalt Flower, Flared Rim, Molded Handles, Egg Shape, 5 Gal. 440.00
Crock, Cover, Cobalt Blue Brushed Design, Shoulder Handles, 11 In. 605.00
Crock, Cover, Flower Finial, Cowden & Wilcox, Penna., 10 7/8 In. 575.00
Crock, Cover, Green Glaze, Incised Banding, Signed, I.S. Stahl, July 6, 1939, 6 In. 330.00
Crock, Cover, Molded Scene Of Hunters With Stag, Blue & White, 8 1/4 In. 357.00
Crock, Cover, Monmouth, 4 In. 25.00
Crock, Cover, Wire Bail & Wood Handle, Molded Pebble, Raised Leaves, 8 x 7 In. 192.00
Crock, Cowden & Wilcox, Floral Stenciled, Molded Handles, Egg Shape, 4 Gal. 38.00
Crock, Cowden & Wilcox, Triple Floral, 3 Gal. 1705.00
Crock, Daisy & Lattice, 10 In. 125.00
Crock, Elaborate Dog, Ground Cover, 5 Gal. 3025.00
Crock, Flower, John Burger, 9 In., 2 Gal. 400.00
Crock, Ft. Edward, N.Y., 3 Gal, 10 1/2 x 10 3/4 In. 245.00
Crock, Full Eagle, Stenciled Flowers, A. Conrad, 14 In., 2 Gal. 825.00
Crock, Gray Blue, Floral Design, Impressed Label, S. Risley Nor-Ich, 10 In. 137.00
Crock, Gray, Cobalt Blue Floral & Beaded, Applied Handle, 3 7/8 In. 105.00
Crock, Henry Clay, Cobalt Blue Floral, Dark Gray, Handles, 1844, 12 1/4 In. 6600.00
Crock, Jas. Benjamin, Stoneware Depot, Cincinnati, O., 2 x 9 In. 138.00
Crock, Jas. Hamilton & Cox, Gray & Blue, 10 In. 110.00
Crock, Ohio, Oval, Cobalt Blue Highlighted, 2, N. Tracy, 11 3/4 In. 220.00
Crock, Outdoor Scene, Mountains, Lake & Trees, N. Clark, c.1850, 3 Gal., 10 In. 1100.00
Crock, Oval, Stedman & Seymour, 1 Gal. 192.00
Crock, T. Crafts & Co., Whatley, Impressed Blue Label, Egg Shape, 11 1/2 In. 165.00
Crock, Tree & Grass, Strap Handles, Salt Glaze, 3 1/2 In. 4025.00
Cuspidor, Cobalt Blue Floral, 8 3/4 x 4 3/4 In. 205.00
Cuspidor, Cobalt Blue Floral, 8 x 4 In. 190.00
Cuspidor, R.C.R., Phila., Gray, Cobalt Slip Design, 1855-1875, 4 1/2 x 8 3/4 In. 330.00
Decanter, Around The World, Blue & Beige Ground, William Whiteley Co 38.00
Dispenser, Alkaline Glaze, Allover Dripping-Style Glaze, Hutchinson, 16 7/8 In. 440.00
Dispenser, Water, Fruit & Leaf Design, 19 1/2 x 9 1/2 In. 175.00
Figurine, Dog, Redware, Glazed, John Bell, Mid-19th Century, 8 1/2 In. 2200.00
Figurine, Dog, Sitting, Worn White Paint Over Brown Glaze, 10 3/4 In. 495.00
Figurine, Dog, White, Hand Painted, 12 1/4 In. 72.00
Figurine, Horse, Red, Brown, Dark Green Splotches, M. Rogers, 6 3/4 x 9 1/2 In. 80.00
Figurine, Nottingham Stoneware Bear, Removable Head 2250.00
Flagon, Pewter Mounted, Continental, 15 1/2 In. 374.00
Flask, Pig, Gray Salt Glaze, Shenandoah Valley, Va., c.1880, 6 In. 1650.00
Flowerpot, Attached Basin, Stylized Tulips, c.1880, 6 1/2 In. 748.00
Foot Warmer, Blue & White, Logan Pottery Co. 175.00
Gate Weight, Faceted, Blacksmith-Made Iron Ring, 18th Century 190.00
Jar, A. Conrad, New Geneva, Pa., 4, Cobalt Blue Applied Shoulder Handles, 15 In. 115.00
Jar, Abstract Face, MacQuoid, 1 1/2 Gal. 1650.00
Jar, Alkaline Glaze, Light Green, 2 Handles, Rolled Rim, 15 x 41 1/2 In. 935.00
Jar, Alkaline Glaze, Lime Glaze, Semi-Flattened Style Handles, 1960, 11 In. 132.00
Jar, Applied Handle, Stencil, T.F. Reppert, Successor To Jas. Hamilton & Co., 15 In. 220.00
Jar, Applied Shoulder Handle, Floral Design, 3, Hamilton Greensboro, Pa., 13 In. 578.00
Jar, Applied Shoulder Handles, Cobalt Blue Brushed Floral Design, 4, Oval, 15 In. 495.00
Jar, Applied Shoulder Handles, Cobalt Blue Flower, Oval, 15 In. 55.00
Jar, Applied Shoulder Handles, Cobalt Blue Quill Work, Feather, 3, Oval, 12 In. 192.00
Jar, Basket Of Flowers, New York Stoneware Co., 15 1/2 In., 5 Gal. 750.00
Jar, Bird, Branch, Cobalt Blue, Handles, Wooden Lid, New York Stoneware Co., 11 In. .. 440.00
Jar, Brown Glaze, Square, 1 Gal. 1980.00
Jar, Brushed & Stenciled Label, Hamilton & Jones 4, Oval, 14 1/2 In. 495.00

Jar, Burger & Lang, Rochester, N.Y., Cobalt Blue Flower & No. 2, Handles, 11 In. 330.0
Jar, Canning, Alkaline Glaze, Mid-19th Century, 7 3/8 In. 88.0
Jar, Canning, Blue Stencil Label, Benjamin Stoneware Depot, Zanesville, O., 9 In. 55.0
Jar, Canning, Blue, Stencil Label, Jacob Vossler, 112 W. Court St., Cin., O., 10 In. 190.0
Jar, Canning, Brushed Cobalt Blue Commas & Stripes, 8 In., Set Of 3 . . . . 440.0
Jar, Canning, Cobalt Blue Leaf Design, 9 In. 110.0
Jar, Canning, Cobalt Blue Stenciled Design, Red, 8 In. 214.0
Jar, Canning, Cobalt Blue Stenciled Flowers, Stripes, 8 In. 225.0
Jar, Canning, Cobalt Blue Stenciled Rose, 6 In. 302.0
Jar, Canning, Cobalt Blue Tulip Flowers, 9 1/2 In. 95.0
Jar, Canning, D. Albright, Cobalt Blue Design, Red Clay, Egg Shape, 10 1/2 In. 160.0
Jar, Canning, E.J. Miller, Alexa., 7 1/2 In. 60.0
Jar, Canning, Marked Lid, Pat. Mar. 1st–April 18, 1881 . . . . 22.0
Jar, Carved, Foo Dog Finials, Ring Handles, Gray Putty, Amber Figure, 3 5/8 In. 50.0
Jar, Cobalt Blue Floral, Impressed 3, Applied Shoulder Handles, Egg Shape, 14 In. 245.0
Jar, Cobalt Blue Floral, J. Swank & Co., 3 Gal. 200.0
Jar, Cobalt Blue Flower & 4, Applied Shoulder Handles, 13 1/2 In. 165.0
Jar, Cobalt Blue Repeated Design, Shenandoah Valley, 1/2 Gal. 35.0
Jar, Cobalt Blue, Straight & Wavy Lines, Hamilton & Jones 2, 10 In. 330.0
Jar, Cover, Albany Slip Glaze, Dark Brown Glaze, 20th Century, 8 1/2 In. 88.0
Jar, Cover, Barrel, Brown Albany Slip, Sgraffito Flowers & 1883, 4 3/4 In. 190.0
Jar, Cover, Haxstun & Co., Stylized Floral, Quill Work, Shoulder Handles, 11 1/2 In. 302.0
Jar, Cover, Male Profile In Center Of Star, T. Harrington, 3 Gal., 13 1/2 In. 3250.0
Jar, Cover, Molded Eagle & Stars, Tan Amber Glaze, Ear Handles, 4 3/4 In. 160.0
Jar, D.L. Ratcliff & Co. Dry Goods, Cobalt Blue, Egg Shape, 15 3/4 In. 440.0
Jar, Dark Green Glaze, Egg Shape, 3 7/8 In. 50.0
Jar, E.S. & B., Cobalt Blue, Shoulder Handles, 12 3/4 In. 71.0
Jar, Edward Heazelton, Pittsburgh, Pennsylvania, 3 Gal., 13 1/2 In. 1175.00
Jar, Floral Band, Cobalt Blue, Incised 4, Applied Shoulder Handles, 15 1/4 In. 220.00
Jar, Floral Design, Cobalt Blue, Handles, F.B. Norton, Worcester, Mass., 2, 11 In. 280.0
Jar, Flower & 2 Cobalt Blue Applied Shoulder Handles, Egg Shape, 11 1/2 In. 190.0
Jar, Freehand Floral Design, Incised A.W. Boughner, 4 Gal., 14 1/2 In. 1275.0
Jar, Geddess, N.Y., Cobalt Blue Bird & 3, Shoulder Handles, Egg Shape, 12 1/2 In. 715.0
Jar, Gray Salt Glaze, Buck & Russell, 3, Cobalt Blue Flower, Shoulder Handles, 13 In. . . 385.00
Jar, Gray Salt Glaze, Penna., 5 In. 100.00
Jar, Hamilton & Jones, Blue Design, 10 In. 110.00
Jar, I.M. Mead, Cobalt Blue Daubs At Handles, No. 2 On Lid, 11 3/4 In. 192.00
Jar, Impressed Boston On Banner, 19th Century, 2 Gal., 13 1/2 In. 431.00
Jar, Impressed Cowden & Wilcox, Blue Bird On Leafy Branch, No. 4, 13 In. 660.00
Jar, L. Lehman & Co., Cobalt Blue Flower & 1 1/2, Shoulder Handles, 11 1/4 In. 165.00
Jar, Leaf & 3, Cobalt Blue, Applied Shoulder, Egg Shape, 12 1/4 In. 165.00
Jar, Lime Alkaline, Collar Rim, Handle, Mid-19th Century, 7 3/4 In. 88.00
Jar, Man In The Moon, Cowden & Wilcox, 2 Gal. 2200.00
Jar, Pouring, Alkaline Glaze, Medium Green Glaze, Handle, 7 3/8 In. 110.00
Jar, Raised Slip Design, Cobalt Blue, Ear Handles, B.C. Millburn, 11 1/2 In. 1100.00
Jar, S. Purdy, Ohio, Cobalt Over Name, Oval, 3 Gal. 155.00
Jar, Salt Glaze, Ovoid, Bell & Sons, 1 Gal. 255.00
Jar, Shoulder Handles, N. Clark & Co., Cobalt Blue Leaf, 11 1/2 In. 275.00
Jar, Songbird, Cobalt Blue, White & Wood, Gray, c.1880, 2 Gal. 495.00
Jar, Stylized Flower With Face, Cowden & Wilcox, 4 Gal. 15125.00
Jar, Tobacco, Cover, Hunting Dog Design, Cobalt Blue 285.00
Jar, Urn & Flowers, N. Clark, Oval, 3 Gal. 1870.00
Jar, Wide Mouth, Edgefield Pottery, c.1850, 15 In., 4 Gal. 1645.00
Jug, 3 & Wavy Lines, Strap Handle, Cobalt Blue, Egg Shape, 15 1/2 In. 95.00
Jug, 3 Cobalt Blue Tulips, S.T. Brewer, Havana, N.Y., 2 Gal. 195.00
Jug, Albany Slip, Black Collar, Neck-Roll Style Handle, 5 3/8 In. 100.00
Jug, Alkaline Glaze, Orange, Black Glaze, 2 Handles, Late 19th Century, 16 In. 440.00
Jug, Allover Glaze, Alkaline Glaze, Double Dip Highlights, 14 1/2 In. 110.00
Jug, Applied Strap Handle, Oval, Incised Design, 11 1/2 In. 220.00
Jug, Barmann Kruge, Strap Handle, Germany, 11 In. 522.00
Jug, Batter, Lid, Wooden Grip, Stylized Floral, Cowden & Wilcox, 9 1/4 In. 3220.00
Jug, Ben. Jackson, Jr. & Co., Gray, Cobalt Blue Design, Applied Handle, 15 1/4 In. 330.00
Jug, Bird On Branch, Cobalt Blue Quill Work, Seymour & Bosworth, 3, 15 1/2 In. 330.00

Jug, Blue Cobalt Stencil, Donaho, Wheeling, W. Va., 11 In.	67.00
Jug, Blue Floral Design, Gray Ground, Cowden & Wilcox, Harrisburg, Pa, 14 In.	300.00
Jug, Blue Impressed Label, I. Seymour, Oval, 11 1/4 In.	302.00
Jug, Blue Tulip Design, Oval, Norton Bennington, 2 Gal.	575.00
Jug, Brown Glaze, D. Goodale, Hartford, Conn., Oval, c.1820, 11 In.	195.00
Jug, Charles Hood Liquors, Pittsburgh, Pennsylvania, 3 Gal., 14 1/2 In.	460.00
Jug, Chicken Waterer, Colorado Advertising, 1 Gal.	195.00
Jug, Claret, Hinged Cover, Silver Mounted, C. Dresser, Hukin & Heath, 1881, 9 In.	3000.00
Jug, Classical, White, Glazed Brown Slip Neck & Handle, Turner, 1800, 9 3/4 In.	345.00
Jug, Cloverdale Lithia Water Co., Harrisburg, Pa., 1 Gal.	28.00
Jug, Cobalt Flowers, Strap Handle, Cowden Wilcox, Harrisburg, Pa, 16 In.	275.00
Jug, D. Roberts & Co., Utica, Cobalt Blue Flower, Strap Handle, 14 In.	165.00
Jug, Dillon & Troy, 1 Gal.	320.00
Jug, Double Flower, Sipe & Sons, Cobalt Blue, 12 1/2 In.	209.00
Jug, Double, Incised With 4 Fish, Bird, Stylized Flowers, Leaves, 1835, 11 In.	2300.00
Jug, E.L. Stork Georgia, Alkaline Glaze, Yellow Top Handle, 12 1/4 In.	121.00
Jug, E.W. Farrington, Elmira, N.Y., Cobalt Blue, Applied Handle, 10 3/4 In.	305.00
Jug, Face, Alkaline Glaze, Applied Ears, White Clay Teeth, L. Meaders, 9 5/8 In.	1045.00
Jug, Face, Gray Salt Glaze, Cobalt Design, Jerry Brown Hamilton, 10 In.	165.00
Jug, Face, Green Ash Glaze, White Eyes & Teeth, Lanier Meanders, 10 In.	495.00
Jug, Face, Grimacing Visage Back Side, 1898	2745.00
Jug, Face, Red Clay, Green Glaze, Chester A. Arthur, Grace Nell Hewell, 10 In.	138.00
Jug, Face, Red Clay, Green Glaze, Grover Cleveland, Grace Nell Hewell, 11 In.	138.00
Jug, Face, Red Clay, James K. Polk & Grace Nell Hewell, 10 5/8 In.	110.00
Jug, Feldhoff & Co. Wines & Liquors, Shamokin, Penna., Brown, Gray, 1 Gal.	100.00
Jug, Floral Design On Gray Salt Glaze, Strap Handle, N. Clark Jr., 3, 14 1/2 In.	330.00
Jug, Floral Design, N. Clark Jr. Athens, N.Y., Cobalt Blue, Strap Handle, 17 In.	264.00
Jug, Floral, Strap Handle, T. & L.P. Norton, Cobalt Blue, 15 1/2 In.	275.00
Jug, Flower & 4, Strap Handle, Cobalt Blue, Egg Shape, 17 1/4 In.	415.00
Jug, Flower, Cowden & Wilcox, Pa. 4, Cobalt Blue, Egg Shape, 16 In.	275.00
Jug, Flower, Harrisburg, Pa., Strap Handle, Cobalt Blue, Egg Shape, 12 In.	165.00
Jug, Flower, M. Clark Jr., Strap Handle, Cobalt Blue, 13 1/2 In.	302.00
Jug, Flower, Strap Handle, Chollar Darby & Co., Cobalt Blue, 13 In.	220.00
Jug, Flowers, Cobalt Blue, Strap Handle, Cowden Wilcox, Harrisburg, Pa., 16 In.	275.00
Jug, Foliage Scroll, Cobalt Blue Slip, Strap Handle, 11 1/4 In.	110.00
Jug, Foliage, Richard C. Remmey, 9 3/8 In.	2070.00
Jug, Germa-Vici Co., Syracuse, N.Y., Bail Handle, 1/2 Gal.	65.00
Jug, Gilson & Co., Reading, Pa., Egg Shape, 1830s, 1 Gal.	285.00
Jug, Goodwin & Webster, Strap Handle, Label, Egg Shape, 11 3/4 In.	110.00
Jug, GR Medallion, Floral Design, Globular, Westerwald, 18th Century, 9 3/4 In.	690.00
Jug, Gray Band, Brown Glaze, Impressed Boston, Strap Handle, Egg Shape, 15 In.	235.00
Jug, Gray Blue Slip, Floral Design, Handle, New York Stoneware Co., 13 3/4 In.	192.00
Jug, Gray, Molded Floral Cartouches, Globular, Pewter Mounted, Westerwald, 8 In.	575.00
Jug, Hunting Party, White, Brown Slip Neck, Handle, Turner, 10 In.	690.00
Jug, Incised Van Dye & Andas, Camden, N.Y., Brown Glaze, 1 Gal.	145.00
Jug, J.A. Franz Groceries & Liquor, Albany Slip, 8 In.	247.00
Jug, Jesse Bollinger Druggist & Grocer, Hanover, Pa., 1 Gal.	465.00
Jug, John Hay, N. Y., Lincoln's Private Secretary, Blue Script	450.00
Jug, Johnson Apple Cider, Portland, Oregon Advertising	950.00
Jug, Label, Jas. Benjamin, Stenciled Label, Strap Handle, Wooden Cork, 11 1/4 In.	220.00
Jug, Lime Glaze Allover, Alkaline Glaze, Streaked Glaze, Timmerman, 11 3/8 In.	100.00
Jug, Lime Glaze, Akaline Glaze, Thumb-Pressed Handle, 16 1/2 In.	88.00
Jug, M.L. Hessberg & Son, 2 Gal.	230.00
Jug, Paducah, Kentucky, Miniature	65.00
Jug, Pouring Spout, Strap Handle, Bangor, Maine, Albany Slip Glaze, 10 In.	71.00
Jug, Pouring Spout, Strap Handle, Satterlee & Mary, Blue Quill Work, 14 1/2 In.	302.00
Jug, Pullman Company, Deodorizer, Brown Top, Blue Letters	45.00
Jug, Quill Work Foliage, Satterlee & Mory, Strap Handle, 13 3/4 In.	220.00
Jug, Rogers & Co. Boston 3, Floral Design, Quill Work, Strap Handle, 16 In.	412.00
Jug, Salt Glaze, Incised L. & B.G. Chace, Somerset, Egg Shape, c.1830, 11 In.	125.00
Jug, Shield Label, Hamilton & Jones, Green Glaze Blob 1 Side, 11 1/2 In.	135.00
Jug, Single Large Tobacco Leaf, 2 Gal.	2310.00
Jug, Squirrels & Branches, Stiff & Sons, Lambeth, 1875, 9 5/8 In.	575.00

Jug, Tulip, 3, Cobalt Blue, Oval, 15 1/2 In. 275.0
Jug, Tyler & Dillon, Albany, Strap Handle, Egg Shape, 10 5/8 In. 104.0
Jug, Washington, Fife & Drummers, Gray Blue Bark Ground, Centennial, 8 1/2 In. 190.0
Jug, Weaver Bros., Knoxville, 1 Gal. 350.0
Jug, West Troy Pottery 2, Cobalt Blue Bird On Branch, Quill Work, 13 3/4 In. 330.0
Jug, White House Vinegar, 1/2 Gal. 55.0
Jug, White, Brown Glaze, Molded Acanthus, Handle, Mary Campbell, 1858, 7 In. 65.0
Jug, Wire Bale, Wooden Handle, Tin Lids, Cobalt Blue At Ears & Spout, 9 1/2 In. 275.0
Keg, Keystone Pottery, Inscribed Star & Heart, Bung Hole, 1897, 15 1/2 x 9 In. 3700.0
Milk Bowl, Cobalt Blue Floral & 1, Pour Spout, 11 1/4 x 4 5/8 In. 495.0
Mixing Bowl, Swing Handle, Green Medallions Of Fruit, 19th Century, 10 In. 300.0
Mold, Food, Rabbit 325.0
Mortar & Pestle, Best Composition, Wooden Handle, Marked, 5 1/8 In. 285.0
Mug, Barrel, Albany Slip Glaze, Incised Rings At Top, W. Gordy, 1939, 4 1/2 In. 55.0
Mug, Gurd's Ginger Beer, The Perfect Drink, Barrel Shape 85.0
Mug, Hand Painted Cowboy, Blue, White, M.A. Hadley, 5 In. 35.0
Mug, Pink Luster Design, Yellow, 2 1/2 In. 330.0
Pail, Batter, Floral, Cowden & Wilcox 4400.0
Pitcher, Advertising, Schroeder Bros., Postville, Iowa, Blue & Gray 423.0
Pitcher, Alkaline Glaze, Brown, Orange Glaze, Henrys, Alabama, 6 1/8 In. 385.0
Pitcher, Allover Medium Green Glaze, Charles Lisk, 1980s, 15 3/4 In. 121.0
Pitcher, Avenue Of Trees, 2 Qt. 55.0
Pitcher, Blue, Grapes, White Interior 160.0
Pitcher, Brushed Design, Applied Handles, P.D. Gwaltney, 11 3/4 In. 1045.00
Pitcher, Calgary Brewery, Horseshoe Logo, J. Maddock & Sons 75.00
Pitcher, Cobalt Blue Floral, Applied Handle, 10 3/4 In. 385.00
Pitcher, Cobalt Blue Flower Basket, F.B. Norton & Co., Mass., 2 Gal. .... *Illus* 2860.00
Pitcher, Concentric Ring Sponging Above & Below Blue Band, 8 1/2 In. 150.00
Pitcher, Cowden & Wilcox, Cobalt Blue Flower, Applied Handle, 12 In. 485.00
Pitcher, Dutch Boy, Dutch Girl, Windmill, 7 In. 115.00
Pitcher, Emily Lulley's Dry Goods Store, 1880s 1092.00
Pitcher, Face, Red Clay, Green Ash Glaze, Cleater Meaders, 10 3/4 In. 110.00
Pitcher, Flemish Pattern, Whites Utica, 8 In. 295.00
Pitcher, Gray, Allover Embossed Blue Aster Design, 8 In. 150.00
Pitcher, Hunting Scene, 7 In. 450.00
Pitcher, Milk, Cow, Blue & White, 7 In. 225.00
Pitcher, Peacock, Rockingham Style Glaze, 8 In. 65.00
Pitcher, Rose, Fishscale, 8 In. 140.00
Pitcher, Thumb-Groove Handle, Orange Lead Glaze, 1930s, 8 7/8 In. 467.00
Pitcher, Toby Style, 3 Spout Top Arms, 1970s, 8 3/8 In. 302.00
Planter, Alkaline Glaze, Khaki Glaze, 3 Slit-Holes On Sides, 1930s, 5 1/4 In. 55.00
Planter, Stump Form, F.B. Norton, Mass., 1865-1880, 11 In. 316.00
Platter, Kings Rose, Pierced Edge, 11 In. 825.00
Pot, Cover, Cupids, Flying Floral Sprays, Rocaillerie Engine, Turned Ring Border 1955.00
Pot, Pansy, Allover Blue Glossy Glaze, Flower Holes, W. Gordy, 1936, 5 In. 66.00
Punch Bowl, 2 Cups, Sky Blue, Bybee Pottery, 6 3/8 x 13 1/4 In. 100.00
Punch Pot, Cover, 2 Cupids Flying, Applied Relief, Reeded Spout, 1761, 7 5/16 In. .. 805.00
Rum Pot, Cover, Cobalt Blue Feather Leaves & Tulips, Egg Shape, Penna., 11 In. 395.00
Salt Box, Black Berry Pattern, Blue & White, Cover 225.00

When cleaning ceramics be sure to remove your rings so you don't scratch the dishes. Wear tight sleeves to avoid snagging any figurine's arms or legs. Hold pieces with both hands. Don't pick up teapots by handles or spouts.

Stoneware, Pitcher, Cobalt Blue Flower Basket, F.B. Norton & Co., Mass., 2 Gal.

Salt Box, Butterfly Pattern, Blue & White, Maple Lid	175.00
Snuff Jar, Minnesota Stoneware, 1 Gal.	65.00
Soap Dish, New York State, Lion's Head Design, Blue	145.00
Sugar, Cover, Turquoise Glaze, Interior Frogskin Slip Glaze, 4 In.	1375.00
Tankard, Gray, Orange Peel Glaze, V. Owens, Thumb-Grooved Handle, 6 In., 4 Piece	100.00
Tankard, White Classical Relief, White, Metal Mounted Rim, Turner, 1800, 5 1/4 In.	375.00
Teapot, Cover, Phoenix In Flight, Red, Jacobus De Caluwe, 1710-1730, 5 In.	1495.00
Teapot, Herculancum, White, Basket Weave, Landscape Medallion, 1805, 6 In.	1265.00
Teapot, Red, Silver Gilt Mounts, Impressed Mark, Germany, 18th Century, 6 In.	1200.00
Teapot, White Classical Relief, Brown Ground, Square, Turner, 1800, 4 1/2 In.	805.00
Urn, Cobalt Flowers, 2 Birds On Branches, Inverted Rim, Salt Glaze, 16 3/4 In.	3220.00
Urn, EW Mort Alum Well, Va., Handle, 3 Gal.	175.00
Vase, Alkaline Glaze, Red Brown Glaze, Brown Bros., 1926-1927, 5 7/8 In.	66.00
Vase, Applied Silver Luster Ivy, Gray, 8 3/4 In., Pair	90.00
Vase, Gourd Form, Woman, Nude, Drinking From A Stream, Gray, Brown, 7 3/8 In.	2185.00
Water Filter, Cover, Blue Stripes, 21 1/2 In., 2 Piece	72.00

STORE fixtures, cases, cutters, and other items that have no advertising as part of the decoration are listed here. Most items found in an old store are listed in the Advertising category in this book.

Cabinet, Display, Oak Shelves, Glass Door & Sides, Cabriole Legs, 58 x 35 x 15 In.	275.00
Cabinet, Haberdashery, Stacked Shelves, Glass Front Doors, 3-Way Mirror, 10 Sections	6310.00
Cabinet, Oak, 9 Drawers, Glass Front, 48 x 36 In.	1650.00
Carrier, Farm Fresh Eggs, Locking Lid, Interior Dividers, Early 1900s	225.00
Case, Display, Cigar, Walnut, Tin-Lined Humidor	850.00
Case, Display, Mahogany, Brass-Edged Glass Top, c.1900, 36 x 53 In., Pair	4200.00
Case, Display, Pharmacy, Oak, Leaded Glass Insert, Glass Doors & Shelves, 84 In.	2000.00
Coffee Grinders are listed in their own category.	
Cutter, Cheese, Computing Scale Co., Dayton, Oh., Iron, Original Paint, Wooden, 1903	170.00
Desk, Post Office, Pine, 2 Hinged Tops, 7 Compartments, 65 1/2 In.	805.00
Desk, Post Office, Walnut, Drawers Over Shelf, Moore's Patent, 61 1/2 In.	5060.00
Mannequin, Head, Leather Cap	900.00
Popcorn Machine, With Peanut Roaster, Holkum & Hoke	2500.00
Sign, Straight Razor, Closed, Hand Carved Wood, 12 In.	55.00
Tobacco Cutter, The Champion, Enterprise Mfg. Co.	100.00

STOVES have been used in America for heating since the eighteenth century and for cooking since the nineteenth century. Most types of wood, coal, gas, kerosene, and even some electric stoves are collected.

Cook, Child's, Tinplate, 3 Oven Doors, 4 Burners, Black Paint, 1890, 16 In.	500.00
Cook, South Bend, No. 818, Woodburning, Malleable Range Co.	1500.00
Cook, Tappan, Trade Winds Frost Killer, Model 220	1000.00
Cook, Wood, 2 Warmer Plates, 2-Door Oven, Findley Stove Works, 1855	2000.00
Heating, 1 Burner, Cast Iron, Victorian, 1850s	150.00
Heating, Adams & Westlake, Oil, Cast Iron, Pressed Steel Sadiron Heater, 31 In.	245.00
Heating, Delft Tile Covered, Integral Fender, Murdoch Parker Stove Co., 1850	2200.00
Heating, Heater, Iron, 3 Legs, Godin-Lemaire Brevet, 27 In.	740.00
Heating, Iron, Repainted, Union Stove Works, Phil B, 27 In.	330.00
Heating, Perfection, Smokeless Oil, Blue Porcelain, Nickel Plated, 1900s	80.00
Kerosene, Tin, Steel & Brass, Bunsen-Davy Hartford, Conn., 10 1/2 In.	60.00
Laundry, Child's, 3 Legs, Cast Iron, France, 14 In.	800.00
Parlor, Neoclassical Design Ormolu Mounts, Enameled, France, 30 1/2 x 22 1/2 In.	55.00
Parlor, Nickel Plated Iron, 1890, 12 1/2 x 20 1/2 In.	40.00
Propane, White Porcelain, Curved Legs, Estate Stove Co.	1300.00
Radiator, Nickel Plated Cast Iron, Pressed Steel, Colin & Co., 30 In.	85.00

STRETCH GLASS is named for the strange stretch marks in the glass. It was made by many glass companies in the United States from about 1900 to the 1920s. It is iridescent. Most American stretch glass is molded; most European pieces are blown and may have a pontil mark.

Bowl, Blue, 2 1/4 x 8 1/2 In.	22.00
Bowl, Footed, Frosted White, Iron Cross, 11 In.	150.00
Bowl, Imperial, Red, 7 1/2 In.	55.00

Candlestick, Royal Blue Iridescent, 7 In. 30.00

Compote, Footed, Frosted White, Iron Cross, 8 In. 125.00

Compote, Green, Footed, 6 1/4 In. 60.00

Nut Bowl, Signed, Hoare, 5 In. 50.00

Pitcher, Red, Yellow Glass Base, 1960s, 18 x 6 In. 28.00

Plate, Gold Aurene, 9 In. 65.00

Vase, Imperial, Gold Iridescent, Signed, 6 1/4 In. ....44.00 to 82.00

Vase, Jack-In-The-Pulpit, Pulled-Feather Base, Butterscotch, 14 In. 270.00

SUMIDA, or Sumida Gawa, is a Japanese pottery. The pieces collected by that name today were made about 1895 to 1970. There has been much confusion about the name of this ware, and it is often called *Korean Pottery.* Most pieces have a very heavy orange-red, blue, or green glaze, with raised three-dimensional figures as decorations.

Bowl, 4 Figures Peering Over Rim, Marked, Meiji Period, 12 In. 440.00

Bowl, 4 Male Figures Peering Over Rim, c.1890, 7 In. 500.00

Bowl, Floral Design, Celadon Glaze, 12th Century, 2 x 4 1/2 In. 575.00

Chocolate Pot, Relief Figural Design, 8 1/2 In. 165.00

Jar, Tobacco, c.1900 .... 850.00

Pitcher, Okame Relief, Signed, 1900, 7 In. 220.00

Tankard Set, Tankard & 3 Cans, Orange Glaze, Japan, c.1900 .... 650.00

Teapot, Lions, Orange 750.00

Vase, Applied Man & Woman, Orange, Seal Signature, 8 1/2 In. 250.00

Vase, Embossed Oriental Figures, Orange, 12 1/4 In. 295.00

Vase, Pear Shape, Gray, Pale Celadon Glaze, 18th Century, 9 1/2 In. 1035.00

Vase, Warrior Figure, Holding Child, Mt. Fuji On Reverse, Square, c.1900, 9 1/2 In. 300.00

SUNBONNET BABIES were first introduced in 1900 in the book *The Sunbonnet Babies.* The stories were by Eulalie Osgood Grover, illustrated by Bertha Corbett. The children's faces were completely hidden by the sunbonnets. The children had been pictured in black and white before this time, but the color pictures in the book were immediately successful. The Royal Bayreuth China Company made a full line of children's dishes decorated with the Sunbonnet Babies. Some Sunbonnet Babies plates have been reproduced, but are clearly marked.

Cake Plate, Washing, Bavaria Backstamp, 10 1/4 In. 400.00

Candleholder, Shield Back 595.00

Candleholder, Shield Back, Scrubbing, Bavaria Backstamp, 4 3/4 In. 600.00

Cheese Server, Cover, Child's 625.00

Chocolate Pot, Cover, Blue Backstamp, 6 In. 950.00

Creamer, Mending, 2 3/4 x 4 In. 108.00

Creamer, Mending, Double Spout, 3 In. 550.00

Creamer, Royal Crownford 45.00

Creamer, Wash Day, 3 1/2 In. 300.00

Flowerpot, Fishing, 3 In. 450.00

Hair Receiver Set, Ruffled, 2 Piece 650.00

Hatpin Holder 695.00

Nappy, Ring Handle, 5 1/2 In. 475.00

Pin Box, Cover, Blue Backstamp, 5 In. 400.00

Plate, Mending, Flared Rim, 4 1/4 In. 115.00

Postcard, Days Of Week Series 65.00

Salt & Pepper 185.00

Sugar & Creamer, Open Boat Shape 375.00

Tumbler, Ironing, Marked, 3 1/2 In. 375.00

SUNDERLAND luster is a name given to a special type of pink luster made by Leeds, Newcastle, and other English firms during the nineteenth century. The luster glaze is metallic and glossy and appears to have bubbles in it. Other pieces of luster are listed in the Luster category.

Chamber Pot, Iron Bridge, Interior Comic Transfer 950.00

Pink, Creamer, 3 1/2 In. 115.00

Pink, Creamer, Black Ship Transfer, 3 1/4 In. 115.00
Pink, Pedestal Base, 5 In. 140.00
Pitcher, United States & Macedonian, Enterprise & Boxer, Green, 1812, 10 In. 2100.00
Plaque, Prepare To Meet Thy God, Pink Luster Frame, Black Print, 8 x 9 In. 172.00

UPERMAN was created by two seventeen-year-olds in 1938. The first issue of *Action* comics had the strip. Superman remains popular and became the hero of a radio show in 1940, cartoons in the 1940s, a television series, and several major movies.

Bank, Dime Register, Tin Lithograph, 1940s 250.00
Billfold, 1966 .... 45.00
Book, Coloring, Superman To The Rescue, Whitman, Uncolored, 1964 .... 24.00
Box, Pencil, Cardboard, 1940s, 8 3/4 x 5 1/4 In. 65.00
Cake Topper Set, Plastic, Package, 1978, 6 Piece 15.00
Cookie Jar, In Telephone Booth, Ceramic 475.00
Cup, Plastic, 1978, 20 Oz. 9.00
Doll, Composition, Wood, Cloth Cape, Jointed, Ideal Toy Corp., 1930s, 13 In. 825.00
Doll, Ideal, 14 In. 1320.00
Doll, Ideal, Composition & Wood, Cloth Cape, Jointed Toy Corp., 1930s, 13 In. 825.00
Doll, Wood & Composition, Jointed, Cloth Cape, 13 In. 1540.00
Figure, Plastic, Blue Cape, Movable, DC, 1984, 4 3/4 In. 29.00
Figure, Superman, Plastic, Jointed, Kenner, Plastic Pack, 1986, 5 In. 18.00
Figure, Superman, Rubber, Plastic, Blister Pack, 1974, 4 In. 20.00
Figure, Superman, With Cape, Mego, 1971, 8 In. 35.00
Game, 1966 .... 195.00
Game, Superman Match It, Ideal, 1979 .... 18.00
Horseshoe Set, Box 75.00
Kryptonite Rock, Glow-In-The-Dark, Original Box, 1978 .... 29.00
Lunch Box, Metal, Aladdin, 1978 .... 30.00
Lunch Box, Superman II, Plastic, Dome, With Thermos 30.00
Lunch Box, Superman, Flying, White Lettering, Metal 400.00
Necktie, Descending From Sky, Synthetic Fabric, Child's, 1940s 90.00
Nutcracker, Wooden, 1979, 10 1/2 In. 35.00
Paint By Number Set, 16 Watercolor Tablets, Tray, Transogram, 1954, 11 x 17 In. 110.00
Playset, Fortress Of Solitude, Vinyl, 1973 .... 50.00
Playset, Superman, Vinyl, Ideal, 1973 ....45.00 to 85.00
Puzzle, 1966, 8 x 11 In. 20.00
Quoit & Horseshoe Set, Box 150.00
Ray Gun, Krypton 250.00
Record Player, Fiberboard, Superman Cartoon Illustration, 1950s 80.00
Ring & Card, Nestle Chocolate Premium, 1976 ....30.00 to 40.00
Shade, Glass, Superman & Emblem Picture, Square, 1978, 13 In. 95.00
Shoes, Shower, Child's, 1970, 8 In. 20.00
Thermos, Red Cap, Canada, 1967 .... 40.00
Toy, Tank, Turn-Over, Battery Operated 595.00
Valentine, Unused, 1941 .... 55.00
Wallet, 1966 .... 45.00
Wristwatch, Dabbs, Box, 1977 .... 150.00
Wristwatch, Fossil, Limited Edition, 1993 .... 150.00
Wristwatch, Marx, Plastic, Original Card, 1977 .... 35.00
Wristwatch, New Haven, Half Figure, Pigskin Band, 1939 .... 175.00

SUSIE COOPER began as a designer in 1925 working for the English firm A.E. Gray & Company. In 1932 she formed Susie Cooper Pottery, Ltd. In 1950 it became Susie Cooper China, Ltd., and the company made china and earthenware. In 1966 it was acquired by Josiah Wedgwood & Sons, Ltd. The name Susie Cooper appears with the company names on many pieces of ceramics.

Breakfast Set, Azalea, Green, White Ground, Pink Interior, 13 Piece 150.00
Cup & Saucer, Cream Sgraffito Fruits & Leaves, Salmon Pink 30.00
Cup & Saucer, White, Fluted, Wedgwood 25.00
Platter, Tiger Lily, 18 In. 120.00

SWANKYSWIGS are small drinking glasses. In 1933, the Kraft Food Company began to market cheese spreads in these decorated, reusable glass tumblers. They were discontinued from 1941 to 1946, then made again from 1947 to 1958. Then plain glasses were used for most of the cheese, although a few special decorated Swankyswigs have been made since that time. A complete list of prices can be found in *Kovels' Depression Glass & Dinnerware Price List.*

Antique, Blue, 3 3/4 In.	4.00
Antique, Brown, 3 3/4 In.	4.00
Antique, Green, 3 3/4 In.	4.00
Antique, Orange, 3 3/4 In.	4.00
Band No. 3, Blue & White, 3 3/8 In.	4.00
Bustlin' Betsy, Brown, 3 3/4 In.	4.00
Bustlin' Betsy, Green, 3 3/4 In.	4.00
Bustlin' Betsy, Orange, 3 3/4 In.	4.00
Bustlin' Betsy, Red, 4 3/4 In.	20.00
Bustlin' Betsy, Yellow, 3 3/4 In.	4.00
Checkerboard, Red & White	10.00
Cornflower, No. 2, Blue, 3 1/4 In.	5.00
Daisy, Green, 3 1/4 In.	3.00
Daisy, Red, 4 1/2 In.	5.00
Daisy, Red, White & Green, 4 1/2 In.	5.00
Daisy, White, 4 1/2 In.	5.00
Duck & Horse, Kiddie Kup, Black, 3 3/4 In.	6.00
Forget-Me-Not, Dark Blue, 3 1/2 In.	3.00
Forget-Me-Not, Light Blue, 3 1/2 In.	3.50
Forget-Me-Not, Light Blue, 3 1/4 In.	5.00
Forget-Me-Not, Yellow, 3 1/2 In.	3.00
Kiddie Kup, Orange, 3 1/4 In.	5.00
Kiddie Kup, Red, Canada	5.00
Posy Cornflower, No. 1, Light Blue, 3 1/2 In.	5.00
Posy Cornflower, No. 2, Blue, 3 1/2 In.	4.00
Posy Cornflower, No. 2, Red, 3 1/2 In.	4.00
Posy Cornflower, No. 2, Yellow, 3 1/2 In.	3.50 to 4.00
Posy Jonquil, Yellow, 3 1/2 In.	4.00
Posy Tulip, No. 3, Blue, 3 1/4 In.	3.00
Posy Tulip, Red, 3 1/2 In.	4.00 to 5.00
Posy Tulip No. I, Red, 3 1/4 In.	5.00
Posy Tulip No. 3, Red, 3 3/4 In.	3.00
Posy Tulip No. 3, Red, 4 1/2 In.	5.00
Posy Violet, 3 1/2 In.	5.00
Stars, Black, 3 1/2 In.	5.00

SWORDS of all types that are of interest to collectors are listed here. The military dress sword with elaborate handle is probably the most wanted. Be sure to display swords in a safe way, out of reach of children.

American Field Officer's, Scabbard, 29 7/8 In.	245.00
Bayonet, Case, Ammo Pouch, Buckle, Belt	695.00
Bayonet, Gilt Panels, Scroll Work, Royal Arms Of Spain, Brass Hilt, Ivory Grip, 15 In.	1380.00
Cavalry, Iron Bar Guard, Leather Grips, Confederate, 34 1/2-In. Blade	950.00
Dagger, Left Hand, Stiletto Blade, Punched & Incised Pattern, Spain, 22 1/4 In.	2300.00
Dagger, Pierced Along Middle, Crowned Arms Of Savoy, Bone Hilt, 11 1/2 In.	1380.00
Double-Edged Blade, Gold Inlay, Horn Handles, Steel Mounts, Russia, 23 In.	275.00
Dragoon, U.S., Back Strap & Pommel, Wire-Wrapped Leather Grip, 1833, 34 In.	475.00
Foot Officer's, Model 1850, Scabbard	935.00
Foot Officer's, Schuyler, Hartley & Graham	1870.00
Fraternal, Swordfish Bill, 19th Century, 47 1/2 In., Pair	110.00
GAR, Officer's, Scroll Form Shell Guard, Leather Grip, Civil War, 28 3/4-In. Blade	275.00
Mounts, Japan, 38 In.	220.00
Officer's, Brass Hilt, Cyrillic Inscription, Bulgaria, 1900-1910, 32-In. Blade	950.00
Officer's, British Infantry, Scabbard, Dumbbell Blade, 1895, 32 1/2 In.	325.00
Officer's, Cavalry, Curved Blade, Sharkskin Cover, Hawks & Co., England, 1896, 35 In.	315.00
Officer's, Cavalry, Curved Broad Fullered Blade, Brass Hilt, 1872, 34 In.	375.00

Officer's, Imperial German, Sword Knot & Dress Strap, 1880, 29 3/4 In.	150.00
Officer's, U.S. Infantry, Carved Ivory Grip, Checkered Band, War Of 1812, 32 In.	850.00
Officer's, U.S. Militia, Gilt Brass Hilt, Reeded Bone Grip, Civil War, 27 1/2-In. Blade	275.00
Presentation, Lt. Colonel, 147 Pennsylvania Infantry	3650.00
Rapier, Swept Hilt, Globular Pommel, Turks' Heads Blade, Italy, 42 1/2 In.	2012.00
Rapier, Swept Hilt, Slender Blade, 2-Stage Faceted Pommel, Turks' Heads Grip, 41 In.	2587.00
Saber, American Artillery Officer's, Gilt Hilt, Floral Knuckle Bow, Bone Grip, c.1812	350.00
Saber, Cavalry, Scabbard, Brass 3-Branch Hilt, Leather Covered Handle, 1863	522.00
Saber, Cossack Cavalry, D-Form Knuckle Guard, Brass Hilt, 1880, 32 In.	185.00
Saber, German Cavalry, Brass, Sharkskin, Engraved, Scabbard, 38 In.	100.00
Saber, Silver Mounted, Leather Grip, Leather-Covered Scabbard, Poland, 31 1/4 In.	7820.00
Samurai, Scabbard, Wakizashi, Hand-Forged Blade, Silver Overlay Habaki, 25 In.	187.00
Samurai, Wooden Scabbard, Leather Covered, Cloth-Wrapped Handle, 32 1/2 In.	385.00
Scottish Officer's, Basket Hilt, Sharkskin Grip, Humphrey's & Crooks, 38 In.	1200.00
Silver Hilt, Colichemarde Blade, Spanish Rococo Patterns, 30 1/2 In.	1610.00
Silver Hilt, Oval Medallions Of Military Trophies, Silver Wire Grip, 32 1/4 In.	920.00
Silver Hilt, Short, Hanger, Leather Scabbard, Revolutionary War Period	2530.00
U.S. Foot Officer's, Scabbard, U.S. & Stand Of Flags On Blade, Brass Hilt, 1850	605.00
Wooden, Hand Guard On Hilt, Natural Patina, 40 In.	105.00

SYRACUSE is a trademark used by the Onondaga Pottery of Syracuse, New York. The company was established in 1871. It is still working. The name became the Syracuse China Company in 1966. It is known for fine dinnerware and restaurant china.

SYRACUSE
China

Bowl, Cereal, Wayne	32.00
Bowl, Fruit, Coralbel	20.00
Bowl, Fruit, Radcliffe	18.00
Bowl, Plate & Cup, Child's, Circus Design, 3 Piece	85.00
Place Setting, Mayview, Federal Shape, Gold Trim, 6 Piece	400.00
Plate, Coralbel, 8 In.	295.00
Plate, Grandma Moses, Sugaring Off, 12 In.	65.00
Plate, Grandma Moses, Taking In The Laundry, 12 In.	65.00
Platter, Coralbel, 14 In.	295.00
Platter, George Washington, C & O RR	150.00
Platter, Rosalie, 16 In.	50.00
Soup, Cream, Bracelet, Old Ivory	125.00
Tureen, Soup, Cover, Rosalie	75.00

TAPESTRY, PORCELAIN, see Rose Tapestry category.

TEA CADDY is the name for a small box made to hold tea leaves. In the eighteenth century, tea was very expensive and it was stored under lock and key. The first tea caddies were made with locks. By the nineteenth century, tea was more plentiful and the tea caddy was larger. Often there were two sections, one for green tea, one for black tea.

Bird's-Eye Maple, Octagonal, 4 3/4 x 4 1/4 x 6 1/4 In.	303.00
Black Lacquer, Gilded Chinoiserie Design, Paw Feet, 8 In.	302.00
Black Lacquer, Gilt, Brass Handles & Feet, Cut Glass Mixing Bowl, c.1790	1650.00
Black Lacquer, Gold, Pewter Liner, Chinoiserie, Early 19th Century, 6 In.	247.00
Brass, Double Eagle Design On Lid, Russia, 4 In.	27.00
Burl Walnut, Hinged Lid, Brass Monogram, Early 19th Century	302.00
Burl Walnut, Marquetry, Stenciled, George III, c.1800, 4 1/2 In.	172.00
Ceramic, Music Conductor, Baton, Musicians, Hand Painted, France, 5 1/2 In.	95.00
Cherry, Inlay, Swags, Diamond Compass Star, 12 1/2 In.	2310.00
Chrysanthemum Plants, Famille Verte, China, 1700, 5 1/2 In.	630.00
Cover, Armorial, Hexagonal, China, 1740, 5 In.	1380.00
Fruitwood, Apple Form, George III, c.1800, 4 1/2 In.	2645.00
Fruitwood, Hinged Lid, Paper Scroll Inlay, Octagonal, Glazed Panels, 5 1/4 In.	3450.00
Fruitwood, Pear Form, England, 5 In.	742.00
Fruitwood, Pear Form, George III, c.1800, 6 In.	3105.00
Fruitwood, Pear Form, George III, Early 19th Century, 7 In.	2012.00
Mahogany, 2 Fitted Compartments, Glass Bowl, Georgian, 6 3/4 x 13 1/2 In.	172.00
Mahogany, Brass Line & Circle Inlay, Lidded Compartments, Regency	305.00
Mahogany, Checker Banded Borders, Hexagonal, 6 1/2 In.	373.00

Mahogany, Hepplewhite, Inlaid Woods, Lead Foil Lining, 3 3/4 x 4 x 4 1/4 In. 330.00
Mahogany, Inlay, 3 Compartments With Covers, Bun Footed, 18th Century 475.00
Mahogany, Inlay, Late George III, 19th Century, 5 1/4 x 9 1/4 In. 345.00
Mahogany, Lines & Floral Inlay, Dovetailed Corners 235.00
Mahogany, Original Silver Mounted Jars, London, 1817, 13 In. 4500.00
Mahogany, Rococo Brass Handle & Feet, Walnut Secret Drawer, 1760, 9 1/2 In. 950.00
Mahogany, Sarcophagus Shape, 2 Interior Lidded Wells, String Inlay, 12 In. 172.00
Mahogany & Oak, Chippendale 325.00
Mahogany & Satin Wood, Acorn & Leaf Medallions, 3 Canisters, 8 1/4 In. 467.00
Mahogany Inlay, Cut Glass Mixing Bowl, England, c.1810, 6 1/2 x 11 1/2 In. 850.00
Mahogany Veneer, Fans & Flowers, 3 Sections, Secret Drawer, 10 1/2 In. 165.00
Mahogany Veneer, Figured, Line & Floral Inlay, 4 1/2 In. 137.50
Mahogany Veneer, Inlaid, Turned Feet, Finial, 3 Inside Compartments, 11 In. 385.00
Papier-Mache, Black & Gold Paneled Lid, Figures & Flowers, 8 x 12 In. 630.00
Papier-Mache, Mother-Of-Pearl, England, 1840s 165.00
Pewter, Peasants At Work In Field, German Verse, 7 In. 860.00
Pine, Faux Grained, American 195.00
Pottery, Flow Blue Spider Web Design, Sponged Gilding, Pauline Pottery, 5 x 3 In. 385.00
Rosewood, 2 Interior Caddies, Mixing Well 172.00
Rosewood, Domed Cover, Fitted Interior, Bun Footed, Regency, 5 1/2 In. 172.00
Rosewood, Foliage Inlaid, Rectangular, 19th Century, 9 In. 259.00
Rosewood, Interior Covered Compartments, Brass Mount, Crystal Bowl, Regency 440.00
Rosewood, Mother-Of-Pearl, Beveled Sloping Top, Rectangular, 6 1/2 x 9 x 5 In. 172.50
Satinwood, Inlaid Monogram Interior, 2 Caddies & Well, George III, 6 x 12 In. 230.00
Silver, Lion Final Cover, Desert Scene, 4 Footed, 5 1/2 x 3 1/4 In. 250.00
Silver Plate, 2 Compartments, Engraved Design 100.00
Sterling Silver, Reeded Design, Hester Bateman, London, England, 1789, 3 1/2 In. . . . 1155.00
Sterling Silver, Roger Williams Silver Co., 4 In. 88.00
Tole, Mahogany Canted Lid, D-Shape Base, Labeled Tea, 19th Century, Pair 2760.00
Tortoiseshell, 2 Lidded Compartments, 1860s, 5 x 7 1/2 In. 2587.00
Tortoiseshell, Serpentine Front, Victorian, 11 1/2 In. 575.00
Tortoiseshell, Stepped Cover, Bow Front, 2 Lidded Wells, 19th Century 862.00
Tortoiseshell Veneer, Bowfront, Inlaid Mother-Of Pearl, 6 x 8 3/4 In. 1610.00
Tortoiseshell Veneer, Ivory Edge Inlay, 2 Lidded Compartments, 8 In. 137.50

TEA LEAF IRONSTONE dishes are named for their decorations. There
was a superstition that it was lucky if a whole tea leaf unfolded at the
bottom of your cup. This idea was translated into the pattern of dishes
known as *tea leaf.* By 1850, at least twelve English factories were
making this pattern, and by the 1870s, it was a popular pattern in many
countries. The tea leaf was always a luster glaze on early wares,
although now some pieces are made with a brown tea leaf.

Bowl, Adams, 5 1/2 In. 29.00
Bowl, Cereal, Copper Trim, Adams, 6 5/8 In. 30.00
Bowl, Fruit, 8 In. 22.00
Bowl, Fruit, Copper Trim, Adams, 5 3/8 In. 27.00
Bowl, Teaberry, Clemenston, 10 In. 150.00
Bowl, Vegetable, Copper Trim, Oval, Adams, 9 3/4 In. . . . . .45.00 to 90.00
Bowl, Vegetable, Cover, Copper Trim, Oval, Adams 88.00
Bowl, Vegetable, Cover, Oval, Adams 239.00
Bread Plate, Copper Trim, Adams, 6 1/4 In. 17.00
Bread Plate, Gold Trim, Flintridge, 6 3/8 In. 20.00
Butter, Cable, Shaw 230.00
Butter, Cover, Little Cable, Furnival . . . . *Illus* 200.00
Cake Plate, Adams 175.00
Chamber Pot, Square, Mellor Taylor . . . . *Illus* 230.00
Creamer, Adams 40.00
Creamer, Bamboo, Meakin 110.00
Creamer, Fishhook, Meakin 170.00
Creamer, Gold Trim, Flintridge 70.00
Creamer, Red Cliff 65.00
Cup & Saucer, Adams 50.00
Cup & Saucer, Chinese, Shaw 80.00

Tea Leaf, Ironstone, Relish,
Lily Of The Valley, Shaw

Tea Leaf Ironstone, Chamber
Pot, Square, Mellor Taylor

Tea Leaf Ironstone, Butter,
Cover, Little Cable, Furnival

Cup & Saucer, Footed, Gold Trim, Flintridge, 2 1/2 In.	56.00
Cup & Saucer, Red Cliff	45.00
Cup & Saucer, Shaw, 1882-1889	35.00
Cuspidor, Shaw, Pre-1882	1150.00
Dish, Cover, Leopard Crouching On Cover, Continental, 1930, 6 x 8 1/2 In.	390.00
Gravy Boat, Attached Underplate	160.00
Gravy Boat, Attached Underplate, Gold Trim, Flintridge	142.00
Gravy Boat, Bamboo, Meakin	55.00
Gravy Boat, Copper Trim, Adams	120.00
Gravy Boat, Copper Trim, Underplate, Adams	150.00
Gravy Boat, Red Cliff	50.00
Gravy Boat, Underplate, Adams	147.00
Pitcher, Copper Trim, Adams, 6 3/4 In.	139.00
Pitcher, Empress, Adams	80.00
Plate, Adams, 6 1/4 In.	17.00
Plate, Adams, 8 1/2 In.	25.00
Plate, Adams, 10 3/8 In.	46.00
Plate, Copper Trim, Adams, 7 3/4 In.	25.00
Plate, Copper Trim, Adams, 8 In.	25.00
Plate, Copper Trim, Adams, 10 1/8 In.	50.00
Plate, Dinner, Red Cliff, 10 In.	42.00
Plate, Gold Trim, Meakin, 7 7/8 In.	40.00
Plate, Salad, Meakin, 7 7/8 In.	30.00
Plate, Salad, Red Cliff, 8 3/8 In.	29.00
Platter, Copper Trim, Adams, 11 1/2 In.	97.00
Platter, Copper Trim, Adams, 13 1/2 In.	119.00
Platter, Gold Trim, Meakin, 12 3/8 In.	149.00
Platter, Gold Trim, Rectangular, Meakin, 12 3/4 In.	75.00
Platter, John Edwards, 16 x 12 In.	44.00
Platter, Meakin, Rectangular, 12 3/8 In.	140.00
Punch Bowl, Cable, Shaw	375.00
Relish, Adams	44.00
Relish, DeSoto, Shaw	250.00
Relish, Lily Of The Valley, Shaw ....Illus	250.00
Salt & Pepper, Gold Trim, Flintridge	65.00
Saucer, Copper Trim, Adams	16.00
Shaving Mug, Scroll, Meakin	100.00
Soap Dish, Clemenston	525.00
Soup, Cream, Saucer, Adams ....69.00 to 72.00	
Soup, Cream, Underplate, Gold Trim, Flintridge	77.00
Soup, Dish, Copper Trim, Adams, 8 In.	49.00
Soup, Dish, Cream, Underplate	75.00
Soup, Dish, Meakin, 8 3/4 In.	45.00
Sugar, Chelsea	30.00
Sugar, Cover, Copper Trim, Adams	79.00
Sugar, Cover, Gold Trim, Flintridge	89.00
Sugar, Fishhook, Meakin	75.00
Sugar, Mellor Taylor	70.00
Teapot, Copper Trim, Adams	55.00
Teapot, Copper Trim, Meakin	175.00
Teapot, Teaberry, Clemenston	425.00

Toothbrush Holder, Ruffled Top, Meakin 168.00
Tureen, Soup, Cable, Shaw 420.00
Waste Bowl, Shaw 70.00

TECO is the mark used on the art pottery line made by the American
Terra Cotta and Ceramic Company of Terra Cotta and Chicago,
Illinois. The company was an offshoot of the firm founded by William
D. Gates in 1881. The Teco line was first made in 1885 but was not
sold commercially until 1902. It continued in production until 1922.
Over 500 designs were made in a variety of colors, shapes, and glazes.
The company closed in 1930.

$$\mathsf{T_{C}^{E}}$$

Bowl, Matte Glaze, Green, Impressed Mark, 9 1/2 x 2 1/2 In. 330.00
Bowl, Squat, Closed, Matte Glaze, Raspberry, 2 1/2 x 4 1/2 In. 220.00
Candlestick, Circular Form, Square Handles, Matte Glaze, Blue, Signed, 5 In., Pair 495.00
Jardiniere, Water Lily Design, Reticulated Leaves, Matte Glaze, Green, 9 3/4 x 10 In. . . 12100.00
Mug, Raised Cattails & Leaves, Matte Glaze, Green, Gunmetal, 6 In. 325.00
Tea Set, Art Nouveau Design, Matte Glaze, Gray-Beige, Signed, 5 Piece 715.00
Tile, Incised Frog, Matte Glaze, Green, Butterscotch, Blue, Signed, Square, 8 In. 3440.00
Vase, 2 Buttressed Handles, Matte Glaze, Deep Blue, 5 1/2 x 2 3/4 In. 825.00
Vase, 2 Buttressed Handles, Matte Glaze, Mustard, Impressed Mark, 5 1/2 In. 715.00
Vase, 2 Buttressed Handles, Matte Glaze, Yellow, 6 1/2 x 2 1/4 In. 1045.00
Vase, 2 Buttresses Top To Bottom, Matte Glaze, Green, Gates, 11 1/2 In. 2090.00
Vase, 2 Buttresses, Matte Glaze, Green, Charcoal Highlights, Mundie, 11 In. 1430.00
Vase, 2 Handles, Matte Glaze, Green, 9 In. 715.00
Vase, 2 Open Handles, Matte Glaze, Green, 4 In. 522.50
Vase, 3 Buttresses Top To Bottom, Matte Glaze, Green, 8 1/2 In. 2420.00
Vase, 4 Buttressed Handles, Matte Glaze, Brown, Cylindrical, 6 1/2 x 2 1/4 In. 1320.00
Vase, 4 Buttressed Handles, Matte Glaze, Green, Impressed Mark, 7 In. 1045.00
Vase, 4 Buttresses, Closed, Matte Glaze, Gray, Impressed Mark, 7 In. 605.00
Vase, 4 Buttresses, Double Gourd Form, Matte Glaze, Green, 6 1/2 In. 1045.00
Vase, 4 Buttresses, Swollen Form, Matte Glaze, Green, Charcoal Highlights, 7 In. 1100.00
Vase, 4 Leaves From Shoulder To Rim, Matte Glaze, Green, 10 1/2 x 5 1/2 In. 1650.00
Vase, 4 Open Handles, Bulbous Base, Flared Lip, Matte Glaze, Green, 6 1/2 In. 1430.00
Vase, 4 Open Handles, Impressed Mark, Matte Glaze, Green, 7 In. 1045.00
Vase, 4 Protruding Lobes, Matte Glaze, Green, Gunmetal, Signed, 9 In. 1430.00
Vase, 4 Sculpted Leaves, Organic Form, Matte Glaze, Green, 14 1/2 x 7 x 14 In. 4950.00
Vase, 4 Sides Flared, 4 Small Open Handles, Matte Glaze, Green Mark, 9 In. 3300.00
Vase, 4 Whiplash Handles, Matte Glaze, Green, 11 1/4 x 4 3/4 In. 1870.00
Vase, Bulbous Top, Flared Tapered Base, Matte Glaze, Green, Impressed Mark, 9 In. 495.00
Vase, Bulbous, Fluted Neck, Matte Glaze, Green, Charcoal Highlights, 7 1/2 x 16 In. 1650.00
Vase, Bulbous, Matte Glaze, Green, 5 In. 440.00
Vase, Buttressed Handles, Matte Glaze, Green, Mark, 6 In. 450.00
Vase, Closed Buttresses, Molded Leaf Design, Matte Glaze, Green, 12 In. 1760.00
Vase, Dimpled, Matte Glaze, Brown, 4 1/2 In. 385.00
Vase, Dimpled, Matte Glaze, Green, Impressed Mark, 4 In. 410.00
Vase, Flared Rim, Matte Glaze, Green, 8 x 3 1/2 In. 440.00
Vase, Flared, Matte Glaze, Brown, V-Shaped Feet, Impressed Mark, 9 In. 2200.00
Vase, Flared, Squat, Aventurine Glaze, 5 3/4 x 4 1/2 In. 467.50
Vase, Handles, Matte Glaze, Purple, Impressed Mark, 8 1/2 x 5 1/2 In. 410.00
Vase, Impressed Mark, Matte Glaze, Green, 4 In. 385.00
Vase, Impressed Mark, Matte Glaze, Green, 20 In. 1870.00
Vase, Lilies, Matte Glaze, Green, Impressed Mark, 13 In. 770.00
Vase, Matte Glaze, Blue, 4 In. 176.00
Vase, Matte Glaze, Brown, 7 In. 187.00
Vase, Pinched, Matte Glaze, Green, 6 In. 850.00
Vase, Reticulated Top, Matte Glaze, Mustard, Fritz Albert, 5 1/2 x 6 In. 2640.00
Vase, Round Bottom, Flaring Neck, Crystalline Glaze, 5 3/8 In.   302.00
Vase, Series Of Ridges, Matte Glaze, Green, Hugh Garden, 11 In. 2200.00
Vase, Shouldered Form, Matte Glaze, Green, 8 In. 319.00
Vase, Tapered, Matte, Die Stamp, 9 1/2 x 10 In. 1430.00
Vase, Triangular Form, Matte Glaze, Green, Signed, 7 3/4 In. 1320.00
Vase, Triangular Form, Matte Glaze, Yellow-Green, Fritz Albert, 7 5/8 In. 495.00
Vase, Tulip Shape, Matte Glaze, Green, Fernand Moreau, 11 3/4 x 5 1/2 In. 4125.00

Vase, Waisted Form, Matte Glaze, Green, Impressed Mark, 9 1/2 In. 715.00
Vase, Woman & Man Nude Figures, Matte Glaze, Green, Impressed Mark, 17 In. 2310.00
Wall Pocket, Matte Glaze, Green, Impressed Mark, 15 x 8 1/2 x 3 3/4 In. 2070.00
Wall Pocket, Vertical Leaves, Matte Glaze, Green, Impressed Mark, 8 1/2 x 16 In. 1760.00

TEDDY BEARS were named for a president of the United States. The first
teddy bear was a cuddly toy said to be inspired by a hunting trip made
by Teddy Roosevelt in 1902. Morris and Rose Michtom started selling
their stuffed bears as *teddy bears* and the name stayed. The Michtoms
founded the Ideal Novelty and Toy Company. The German version of
the teddy bear was made about the same time by the Steiff Company.
There are many types of teddy bears and all are collected. The old ones
are being reproduced. Other bears are listed in the Toy section.

Bing, Mohair, White, Felt Pads, Fully Jointed, Shoebutton Eyes, 1910, 15 In. 1265.00
Brown, Jointed, Germany, 20 In. 220.00
Caramel, Jointed, 3 In. 275.00
Chiltern, Mohair, Golden, Black Nose, Mouth, Amber Bead Eyes, 1935, 20 In. 450.00
Clemens, Mohair, Gold, Excelsior Stuffing, Fully Jointed, Glass Eyes, c.1940, 17 In. 287.00
Golden Brown, Jointed Arms & Legs, Germany, 6 In. 55.00
Golden Brown, Jointed, Germany, 13 In. 357.00
Hermann, Light Gold, Jointed, Tags, 1983, 10 In. 135.00
Hermann, Mohair, Gold, Fully Jointed, Shoebutton Eyes, 1920s, 19 In. 172.00
Hermann, Original Chest Tag, 1960s, 11 In. 165.00
Ideal, Mohair, Amber, Swivel Head, Black Shoebutton Eyes, 1906, 15 In. 1400.00
Ideal, Mohair, Swivel Head, Felt Paws, Jointed, Amber Bead Eyes, 1950, 19 In. 350.00
Jopi, Musical, Plays When Tummy Is Squeezed, 18 In. 2500.00
Kinser, Baby Sister, Leather Paws, Bonnet, Tags, 1983, 19 In. 175.00
Knickerbocker, Silent Voice Box, Mohair, Gold, Embroidered, Jointed, 10 In. 165.00
Lee, Plush, Brown, In Lee Brand Blue Denim Bib Overalls, 13 In. 75.00
Light Brown, Jointed, Germany, 14 In. 357.00
Light Brown, Jointed, Germany, 16 In. 220.00
Low-Nap Cloth, Gold, Felt Paws, Jointed, Glass Eyes, 13 1/2 In. 220.00
Merrythought, Mohair, Gold, Reticulated Limbs, Oilcloth Pads, England 255.00
Mohair, Amber, Shaved Nose, Black Claws, Amber Bead Eyes, 1925, 22 In. 600.00
Mohair, Blond, Brown Embroidery, Excelsior Stuffing, Jointed, Steel Eyes, 9 1/2 In. 546.00
Mohair, Blond, Embroidered, Fully Jointed, Black Steel Eyes, 1910, 17 In. 515.00
Mohair, Blond, Excelsior Stuffing, Fully Jointed, Shoebutton Eyes, 1910, 12 In. 260.00
Mohair, Blond, Excelsior Stuffing, Fully Jointed, Shoebutton Eyes, 1910, 18 In. 1035.00
Mohair, Brown, Curly, On All Fours, Glass Eyes, Early 20th Century, 9 x 14 In. 1380.00
Mohair, Brown, Woven, Embroidered, Fully Jointed, Shoebutton Eyes, 11 In. 115.00
Mohair, Cinnamon, Long, Hump, Felt Pads, Wheels, Glass Eyes, 1920, 21 In. 1000.00
Mohair, Cinnamon, Swivel Head, Excelsior Stuffing, Hump, 10 In. 2700.00
Mohair, Cream Color, Long & Curly, Fully Jointed, 1930s, 25 In. 950.00
Mohair, Curly, Yellow, Excelsior Stuffing, Fully Jointed, Glass Eyes, 1920, 26 In. 285.00
Mohair, Gold, Hump, Jointed, Shoebutton Eyes, 24 In. 875.00
Mohair, Gold, Reticulated Limbs, Velvet Paw Pads, Red Ribbon, Glass Eyes, 18 In. 220.00
Mohair, Gold, Swivel Head, Excelsior Stuffing, Hump, 18 In. . . . . *Illus* 2500.00
Mohair, Gold, Swivel Head, Excelsior Stuffing, Long Arms, Glass Eyes, 17 In. 325.00
Mohair, Gray, Felt Paws, Embroidered, Jointed, Glass Eyes, 17 1/4 In. 355.00
Mohair, Snout Nose, Jointed, Shoebutton Eyes, Germany, 1920, 11 In. 950.00
Mohair, Yellow, Extended Snout, Black Disc Eyes, 1940, 25 In. 375.00
Mohair, Yellowish Gold, Reticulated Limbs, Felt Paw Pads, Metal Nose, 13 In. 247.00
Pink, Straw Stuffing, Jointed, 14 In. 135.00
Plush, Amber, Elongated Torso, Jointed Arms, Amber Bead Eyes, 1935, 19 In. 500.00
Plush, Purple, Rose, Ivory, Pivot-Jointed Arms, Electric Eyes, 1907, 21 In. 600.00
Plush, Swivel Head, Snout Nose, Felt Paws, Amber Bead Eyes, 1935, 22 In. 500.00
Schuco, Bigo-Bello, Light Gold 150.00
Schuco, Brown, Jointed, 3 In. 275.00
Schuco, Mohair, Amber, Plush Body, Snout Nose, Felt Paws, 1945, 10 In. 750.00
Schuco, Mohair, Brown, Swivel Head, Black Nose, Shoebutton Eyes, 3 In. 1000.00
Schuco, Tricky, Mohair, Brown, Amber Eyes, Stitched-On Ear, Felt Paws, 8 In. 1450.00
Smokey Bear, Shovel, Smokey On Hat & Belt, 13 In. 40.00
Steiff, Baby, Mohair, Brown, Seated, Stitched Ears, Tan Feet, Bead Eyes, 17 In. 1000.00

Teddy Bear,
Mohair, Gold,
Swivel Head,
Excelsior Stuffing,
Hump, 18 In.

Teddy Bear, Steiff,
Mohair, Pale Gold,
Jointed, 17 In.

Steiff, Baby, White, 6 In. 99.00
Steiff, Bears In Circus Wagon, Box, 6 In. 425.00
Steiff, Buttons, Original Tag, Post-1950s, 12 In. 132.00
Steiff, Cinnamon, Embroidered, Fully Jointed, Steel Eyes, Button In Ear, 1906, 9 In. 2990.00
Steiff, Dark Brown, Button In Ear, Tag, 1970s, 9 In. 100.00
Steiff, Golden Brown, Jointed, 9 In. 330.00
Steiff, Jackie, Mohair, Gold, Felt Paws, Amber Bead Eyes, 1953, 14 In. 850.00
Steiff, Jointed, c.1970, 21 In. 275.00
Steiff, Light Yellow, Excelsior Stuffing, Fully Jointed, 1906, 12 In. 1725.00
Steiff, Mohair, Amber, Jointed, Black Shoebutton Eyes, 1910, 16 In. 2500.00
Steiff, Mohair, Amber, Swivel Head, Shoebutton Eyes, 13 In. 1300.00
Steiff, Mohair, Blond, Embroidered Nose, Jointed, Glass Eyes, 1950s, 13 In. 300.00
Steiff, Mohair, Blond, Excelsior Stuffing, Fully Jointed, Glass Eyes, 1950s, 13 In. 290.00
Steiff, Mohair, Blond, On Irish Mail Cart, Wood Wheels, Steel Eyes, 1920, 10 In. 2415.00
Steiff, Mohair, Brown, Suspended On Silver Chains, Felt Paws, 12 In. 2100.00
Steiff, Mohair, Caramel Color, Fully Jointed, Button In Ear, 12 In. 905.00
Steiff, Mohair, Champagne, Swivel Head, Plush, Felt Paws, 12 In. 1500.00
Steiff, Mohair, Embroidered, 1903 Anniversary, Certificate, Box, 1980s, 16 In. 260.00
Steiff, Mohair, Gold, Black Embroidery, Jointed, Steel Eyes, 5 1/2 In. 1035.00
Steiff, Mohair, Gold, Straw Stuffing, Painted, 1950s, 13 1/2 In. 425.00
Steiff, Mohair, Honey Color, Fully Jointed, Bead Eyes, Button In Ear, 3 1/2 In. 357.00
Steiff, Mohair, Light Brown, Swivel Head, Jointed, Amber Bead Eyes, 5 1/2 In. 325.00
Steiff, Mohair, Pale Gold, Jointed, 17 In. ....*Illus* 7200.00
Steiff, Mohair, Yellow, Black Embroidery, Fully Jointed, 3 3/4 In. 517.00
Steiff, Nimrod, Hunters, Set No. 1024, Boxed Set Of 3, 7 3/8 x 15 1/2 x 10 1/4 In. 145.00
Steiff, On Wheels, 1920, 23 In. 1250.00
Steiff, Petsy, Gold, 5 1/2 In. 99.00
Steiff, Plush, Cinnamon, Hump, Swivel Joints, Button In Ear, 1910, 17 In. 1495.00
Steiff, Plush, Tan, Green Clothes, West Germany, 7 In. 40.00
Steiff, Somersault, White, Box, 11 In. 295.00
Steiff, Squeaker, Silver Color, Brown Stitched Nose, Black Glass Eyes, 1920s, 17 In. 1950.00
Steiff, Tan Plush, Elongated Nose, Excelsior Stuffing, Button In Ear, 13 In. 1265.00
Steiff, Tan, Yellow Ribbon, Chest Tag, 5 1/2 In. 275.00
Steiff, White & Off White, 2-Prong Blank Button, 12 In. 1200.00
Steiff, Zotty, Raised Script Button, 8 In. 185.00
White, Jointed, England, 25 In. 88.00
White, Jointed, Germany, 22 In. 605.00

TELEPHONES are wanted by collectors if the phones are old enough or
unusual enough. The first telephone may have been made in Havana,
Cuba, in 1849, but it was not patented. The first publicly demonstrated
phone was used in Frankfurt, Germany, in 1860. The phone made by
Alexander Graham Bell was shown at the Centennial Exhibition in
Philadelphia in 1876, but it was not until 1877 that the first private
phones were installed. Collectors today want all types of old phones,
phone parts, and advertising. Even recent figural phones are popular.

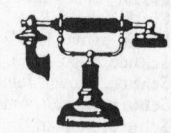

Alf, Television Series 95.00
Almanac, Bell System, 1931 .... 10.00

American Telephone & Telegraph, Candlestick, Oak Bell Box, Patent 1913, 12 In. 210.00
Automatic Electric, Model 40, Brass Bells, Dial, Art Deco, 1930 .... 199.95
Beetle Bailey 175.00
Booth, Original Telephone, Instructions, Manchester, England 3000.00
Booth, Tin Panels, Seat, Sliding Wooden Doors 1250.00
Booth, Windows, Seat, Ledge, Tin Paneling, Lamp 1250.00
Brass, Nickel Plated, Bakelite, Polychrome Transfer Design, France, 13 1/2 In. 110.00
Buzz Lightyear, Moveable Arms, Box, 16 In. 125.00
Candlestick, Rotary Dial, Ringer Box 145.00
Charlie Tuna, Box 75.00
Cuff Links, Bell System, Classic Silver, Blue-Trim Bell 45.00
Heinz Ketchup 45.00
Kellogg, Candlestick 110.00
Kellogg, Wall, Walnut Case, 32 In. 357.00
Kermit The Frog ....140.00 to 275.00
La Campania, Spain, 1910, 27 In. 350.00
Man, Tetley Tea, Canada 125.00
Mirror, Missouri & Kansas Telephone Company, Pocket 60.00
Paperweight, Telephone Pioneers Of America, Bell Shape, Cobalt Glass, 3 In. 40.00
Princess, Brown Plastic Shell, Push-Button, 1960s 46.00
Regal, Steel, Bakelite Handset, Brass Bells, Mute Button, Belgium, 1926 .... 150.00
Sign, Bell Logo, Bell System Public Telephone, Convex, Porcelain, Round, 7 In. 65.00
Sign, Bell System Telephone & Telegraph, Porcelain, Convex, 8 In. 120.00
Sign, Porcelain, 8 x 31 1/2 In. 110.00
Snoopy & Woodstock, American Telecommunications Co., 1976, 13 In. ....60.00 to 100.00
Spiderman 40.00
Star Trek 145.00
Stromberg-Carlson, Black & White Marbleized Plastic, Inside Dial, 1978 .... 22.00
Stromberg-Carlson, Candlestick, Nickel Plated Head 200.00
Tennis Shoe, Sports Illustrated 30.00
Volkswagen, 8 In. 35.00
Wall, Country Wood, Brass Bells, Dial, 1920s 300.00
Wall, Oak, Crank, 1913, 23 In. 230.00
Wall, Wood, Crank & Bands On Bakelite Handset, Coil Cord, c.1920 .... 300.00
Weird Alien, Box 75.00
Western Electric, Brass, Pat. Jan. 26, 1915 .... 295.00
Western Electric, Brown Bakelite, 1930s 27.50
Western Electric, Candlestick, Brass 175.00
Western Electric, Candlestick, Brass, Wood Subset, Brass Bells, 1919 .... 600.00
Western Electric, Model 202, Metal Base, Bakelite Handset, Brass Bells, 1920s .160.00 to 330.00
Western Electric, Model 302, Bakelite Hand Set, Internal Brass Bells, 1939 .... 160.00
Western Electric, Wall, Oak Case, Note Shelf 190.00

TELEVISION sets are twentieth-century collectibles. Although the first
television transmission took place in England in 1925, collectors find
few sets which pre-date 1946. The first sets had only five channels, but
by 1949 the additional UHF channels were included. The first color
television set became available in 1951.

Arvin, 2 Knobs, 21-In. Screen, 1953 .... 25.00
Emerson, Phonograph, Cabinet, 2 Doors, 10-In. Screen 75.00
Hallicrafters, Brown Bakelite Case, 12-In. Screen 85.00
Motorola, Wooden, Table Top, 10-In. Screen, 1948 .... 75.00
Philco, Pedestal, 10-In. Screen 1000.00
Philco, Predicta, Futuristic Design 850.00

TEPLITZ refers to art pottery manufactured by a number of companies
in the Teplitz-Turn area of Bohemia during the late nineteenth and
early twentieth centuries. The Amphora Porcelain Works and the
Alexandra Works were two of these companies.

Basket, Floral, Green, Gold Trim, 2 Handles, 6 x 8 In. 295.00
Basket, Peasant Woman, Carrying Basket On Back, Tan Clothes, Gold, Amphora, 16 In. . 550.00
Basket, Peasant Woman, Emptying Apron Of Greens, Tan, Gold, 18 1/2 In. 550.00
Bust, Young Gentleman, Pedestal, 7 1/2 In. 85.00

Candy Dish, Art Nouveau, 2 Tiers	65.00 to 85.00
Ewer, Green Jewels, 3 Gold Handles, Amphora, 7 1/2 x 5 In.	385.00
Ewer, Portrait, Raised Design In Gold & Blue, Gray Ground, 9 In.	285.00
Ewer, Water Lily & Lily Pad Design, Amphora, 11 3/4 In.	330.00
Figurine, Guinea Fowl, 7 x 9 In.	82.00
Figurine, Rebecca At The Well, 19th Century, 28 1/2 In.	2950.00
Jar, Cover, Figural, Elephant, Amphora, 8 x 9 In.	1695.00
Jug, Milk, Boy Giving Girl A Bouquet, 5 1/2 In.	250.00
Lamp, Pheasants With Geometrics, 2 Handles, Amphora, 6 x 12 In.	385.00
Pitcher, Girl & Dog, Enameled, 3 x 5 1/2 In.	38.50
Pitcher, Large Bird On Branch, Green, Gold & White, Signed, 11 In.	230.00
Pitcher, Spout On Each Side, Blue, Yellow, Handle, Amphora, 10 In.	350.00
Vase, 2 Flowers & Vines With Leaves, Amphora, 13 x 10 1/2 In.	475.00
Vase, 2 Girls Blowing Bubbles, Gray Speckles, Open Handles, Amphora, 5 1/4 In.	100.00
Vase, Applied 4 Gilt Branches Sprouting, Pink Roses, Amphora, 1900, 16 In.	3450.00
Vase, Applied Blackberry Cluster, Cream Basket Weave, Braided Handles, 10 x 9 In.	650.00
Vase, Basket Form, 3 Cherubs Mounted To 1 Side, Amphora, 18 In.	230.00
Vase, Bearded Man Portrait, Enameled, Amphora, 9 In.	125.00
Vase, Classical Form, Greek Key, C. Dresser, Linthrope, Amphora, 1880, 21 1/2 In.	1030.00
Vase, Covey Of Bats Above Glistening Waters, Tan, Yellow, Green, Amphora, 21 In.	6325.00
Vase, Dragon, Outspread Wings, Coiled Tail, Leafy Trees, Tan, Ivory, Amphora, 21 In.	5175.00
Vase, Floral Border, Multicolored, Amphora, 17 In.	550.00
Vase, Forest Scene, 2 White, Black Geese, Dark Green Body, Amphora, 14 In.	2420.00
Vase, Frieze Of Butterflies, Bees, Green, Enameled, Blue Ground, Amphora, 1900, 7 In.	690.00
Vase, Girl Climbing On Side, Attached At Hands & Feet, Gourd, Cream, Amphora, 5 In.	130.00
Vase, Jeweled, Amphora, Signed, 5 In.	290.00
Vase, Large Vulture, Thorny Vines, Berries, Enameled, Amphora, 15 1/2 x 12 1/2 In.	137.00
Vase, Medallions, Portrait Of Lady, Red & Brown, Signed, 6 x 8 1/4 In.	172.00
Vase, Overall Leafage, Gold Iridescent & Spotted Green Glaze, Signed, 11 In.	517.00
Vase, Portrait In Medallion, Iridized Finish, 4 1/2 In.	82.00
Vase, Rose Outline In Black, 4 Buttress Handles, Amphora, 10 3/8 In.	247.00
Vase, Roses, Amphora, 12 In.	350.00
Vase, Scarabs Near Top, 9 In.	66.00
Vase, Trees, Applied Pinecones, Green, Tan, Red, Amphora, 9 In.	715.00
Vase, Woman, Carrying A Jar, Bronze, Enameled, 2 Handles, 5 1/2 In.	125.00
Vase, Women Harvesting Wheat, Amphora, 10 1/8 In.	302.00
Vase, Young Women, Green, Brown Butterflies, Tan, Brown, Green Ground, 11 In.	308.00

TERRA-COTTA is a special type of pottery. It ranges from pale orange to dark reddish-brown in color. The color comes from the clay, which is fired but not always glazed in the finished piece.

Angel, Majolica Glaze, Early 20th Century, 18 In., Pair	5800.00
Bust, Girl, Louise Brogniart, 1777, 17 1/2 In.	7475.00
Bust, Young Augustus, Brown Painted Finish, 20 In.	862.00
Figurine, Bacchanalian Scene, Inlaid Maple Pedestal, 61 In., Pair	5750.00
Figurine, Bathing Venus	605.00
Figurine, Children & Goat, France, 18th Century	7800.00
Figurine, Female, Playing The Lute, Male, Playing The Guitar, France, 11 In., Pair	2070.00
Figurine, Gypsy Man & Woman, Hand Painted, 21 1/2 In., Pair	725.00
Figurine, Jockey On Horse, Painted, Wiener Werkstatte, 1920s, 7 1/4 In.	1500.00
Figurine, Lions, Resting On Hind Legs, Rectangular Plinth, 29 1/4 In., Pair	9200.00
Figurine, Nude Woman, Rockery Base, T. Bochs, Early 20th Century, 15 x 13 In.	220.00
Head, Black Minstrel Man & Woman, Hanging, American, 6 x 4 1/2 In., Pair	650.00
Humidor, Bust Of Devil, On Barrel, 7 1/2 In.	350.00
Jardiniere, Dragon Raised Relief Design, 10 x 15 In.	235.00
Lamp, Grecian Figures Embossed, Black, 20th Century, 27 In.	11.00
Matchbox, Brown Glaze, Embossed, Oval, 1890, 5 In.	75.00
Matchbox, Cover, Figural, African Head, Black, Red, White, 5 In.	110.00
Plaque, Benjamin Franklin, Wearing A Fur Cap, Oval, 1777, 4 1/8 In.	2185.00
Teapot, Dragon Spout, Handle, 2 Joined Forms, C. Dresser, Watcombe, 1875, 4 In.	1310.00
Tobacco Jar, Brown & Yellow Glaze, John W. Clough, 5 1/2 x 5 In.	175.00
Tobacco Jar, Greyhound, Reclining, On Cover, Gadroon Border, 6 x 7 In.	115.00

Umbrella Stand, Tree Stump Form, Applied Blossoming Plant, England, 20 In.	690.00
Vase, Blue, Gilt, Dragons, Oriental, 18 1/2 In.	80.00

EXTILES listed here include many types of printed fabrics and table
nd household linens. Some other textiles will be found under
Clothing, Coverlet, Quilt, Rug, etc.

Antimacassar, Crocheted, Cupid, Early 1900s	35.00
Antimacassar, Crocheted, God Bless America, Early 1900s	40.00
Apron, Robin Hood Flour Sack	35.00
Bandanna, Centennial Exposition, Memorial Hall, Red Star Border, 1876	110.00
Banquet Cloth, Mythological & Winged Figures, Linen, 1920s, 156 x 84 In.	1700.00
Bath Mat, Chenille, Golden Yellow, Navy & Black Line Center, 16 x 34 In.	10.00
Bath Set, Chenille, Black & White, 3 Piece	8.00
Bed Cover, Embroidered Irises & Crocuses, Neutral Ground, Arts & Crafts, 94 x 62 In.	275.00
Bedspread, Chenille, Lavender, White Wavy Line Pattern, Full Size	20.00
Bedspread, Chenille, Salmon, Melon, Wavy Line Pattern, Full Size	8.00
Bedspread, Chenille, White, Blue Trim, Full Size	65.00
Bedspread, Foliate & Geometric Designs, Lucy Coffin, 1836, 99 x 99 In.	316.00
Bedspread, Hand Crochet, Twin Size, Pair	115.00
Bell Pull, Needlepoint, Flowers On Celery Field, 42 In.	28.00
Bell Pull, Silk & Wool, Gros & Petit Point, Late Victorian, 54 In.	144.00
Blanket, Hudson Bay, Wool, Horner	95.00
Blanket, North Dakota State, Pendleton	30.00
Blanket, Red & Black Plaid, Wool, 3 Sections, 1850s, 96 x 98 In.	325.00
Blanket, Wool, Homespun, Crewel Embroidery, Floral Design, 70 x 76 In.	330.00
Cushion, 6 Pointed Star, Beadwork Center Design & On Star Points	105.00
Flag, 167th Infantry Regimental, Silk, Eagle, Spanish American War, 1902	3250.00
Flag, American, 13 Stars, Framed, Under Glass, 20 x 15 In.	460.00
Flag, American, 26 Stars, Great Star Pattern, c.1837, 26 1/2 x 28 3/4 In.	2310.00
Flag, American, 26 Stars, Henry Clay Portrait, Clay & Frelinghuysen, 26 x 27 In.	4950.00
Flag, American, 34 Stars, Hand Sewn, Woven Cotton, 48 x 84 In.	900.00
Flag, American, 42 Stars, Parade, 54th Massachusetts Infantry, July 18, 1890	9350.00
Flag, American, 45 Star, Silk, 17 1/2 x 26 1/2 In.	240.00
Flag, American, 46 Stars, Hand Sewn, Wool & Silk, c.1907, 75 x 40 In.	110.00
Flag, American, 48 Stars, U.S. Ensign, No. 6, Valley Forge Flag Co., 8 x 16 In.	175.00
Flag, American, Printed Silk, 40th State, 12 x 16 In.	225.00
Flag, American, Red, White, Blue, Blue Binding, 1939-1944, 68 x 84 In.	1150.00
Flag, Haitian Voodoo, Sequined, 30 x 28 In.	192.00
Flag, Union Jack, 48 Stars, Stars Both Sides, Brass Hook & Grommets, 77 x 56 In.	185.00
Flag, United States, 13 Stars, Pieced & Hand Stitched Stripes, Frame, 15 x 21 In.	660.00
Hammock, Transportation Design, Brown & Yellow, 1920s	2500.00
Handkerchief, 1876 Centennial Exhibition, Red Border, Brown Ink, 23 x 26 In.	285.00
Handkerchief, Western Design, 13 x 13 In. ....*Illus*	10.00
Handkerchief, Who Killed Cock Robin, 12 x 11 1/4 In.	125.00
Hanging, Crocheted Animals On Woven Backing, Granny Donaldson, Pre-1959, 40 In.	385.00
Historical, Linen, Blue Printed Scene Of G. Washington, Frame, 15 1/2 x 15 1/2 In.	330.00
Lap Robe, Sleigh, Stripes Of Velvet, Lined, 47 x 58 In.	50.00
Lap Robe, Sleigh, Twill Backing, 19th Century, 52 1/2 x 61 In.	165.00
Luncheon Set, Lilac Organdy, Embroidered Hydrangeas, Maghab, 1950s	100.00
Luncheon Set, Linen, Rose Applique On Cream, 4 Plate Mats, 4 Napkins, Box, 1950s	35.00
Mats, Needlework, Couple Dressed In Folk Costume, Dancing Jig, 1920s, Set Of 8	200.00
Mattress Cover, Homespun, Blue, White Check, Black Ribbon Ties, 67 x 68 In.	192.00
Mattress Cover, Homespun, Blue, White Check, White Tape Ties, 64 x 68 In.	275.00
Mattress Cover, Homespun, Blue, White, Tan Check, White Check, 61 x 72 In.	220.00
Mattress Cover, Homespun, Red, Blue & White Plaid, White Back, 55 x 61 In.	203.00
Napkin, Damask, B & O Railroad Dining Car	30.00
Napkin, Damask, Canadian Pacific Railroad	20.00
Needlework, Panel On Silk, Gilbert Family At Tomb, Painted Faces, Frame, 21 x 24 In.	2035.00
Panel, Aubusson Tapestry, Palm Leaves, Vines, Metallic Thread Border, 100 x 41 In.	8625.00
Panel, Embroidered, Blossoming Fruit Trees, Birds, 35 x 96 In.	4312.00
Panel, Embroidered, Eagle, American Flag, Brown, White, Black, Red, Blue, 25 x 25 In.	192.00
Panel, Embroidered, Eagle, Flag, Brown, Gold, Red, Blue, White, Frame, 21 1/2 In.	165.00
Panel, Flamestitch, Brilliant Colors, S.J. & 1777, Frame, 6 1/4 x 8 3/4 In.	1250.00

Soiled white quilts or fabrics in good condition can be helped. Soak the textile in the washing machine in a solution of warm water and I cup or more powdered dishwasher detergent for I hour. Then put on the gentle wash cycle for a few minutes. Rinse thoroughly.

Textile, Handkerchief,
Western Design, 13 x 13 In.

Panel, Needlework, Couple & Children, Floral, Sequins, Silk, Frame, 19 x 18 In. 110.00
Panel, Needlework, Figural Design, Mounted In Tray, China, 23 x 12 In. 44.00
Panel, Tobit, On Throne, Tobias Cures Blindness With Gall Of Fish, 42 5/8 x 60 In. 4025.00
Pillow, Esso Tiger 42.00
Pillow, Inflatable, Pop Art Design, Peter Max, Signed, c.1969, 15 x 16 In., Set Of 8 ..... 320.00
Pillow, Victorian Lady, Hand Painted, 21 x 21 In. 335.00
Pillow Case, Using 40 Cigarette Silks, Linen Backing 50.00
Purse, Pearlized, Plastic, Upright Rigid Handle, Gold Trim, Rectangular, 1950s 235.00
Runner, Drawn Work, Silk, 24 x 88 In. 185.00
Scarf, Abstract Design, Silk, Emilio Pucci 230.00
Scarf, Hooked, Field Of Flowering Plants, Gold Field, 14 x 38 In. 115.00
Scarf, Rialto, Stylized Venetian Scene, Silk Twill, Hermes 201.00
Shawl, Embroidered Oriental Silk, Black & White 210.00
Shawl, Paisley, Wool, 70 x 70 In. 330.00
Sleeping Bag, Dukes Of Hazzard 55.00
Tablecloth, Battenburg Lace, Round, 54 In. 65.00
Tablecloth, Chintz Appliqued, Wreath Of Blossoming Branches, 39 x 39 In. 805.00
Tablecloth, Crochet, White, 1940s, 46 x 64 In. 75.00
Tablecloth, Cutwork, Embroidery, Islet Lace, Figural Inserts, Italy, 120 x 70 In. 2200.00
Tablecloth, Floral, Lace, P. De Venice, 97 x 65 In. 518.00
Tablecloth, Graphics Of Black Folks, Yellow, Red, 50 x 50 In. 145.00
Tablecloth, Hand Crocheted Lace, Ecru, 48 x 60 In. 50.00
Tablecloth, Lace, Buildings, 12 Napkins, Venice, 19th-20th Century, 72 x 102 In. 121.00
Tablecloth, Lace, Cutwork Linen, Tree, Goddess, Fruit, Cherubs, 1920s, 138 x 80 In. ... 1500.00
Tablecloth, Linen, Overshot, Lace Border, 60 x 65 In. 82.00
Tablecloth, Square Panels, Inset With Lace, Lace Trim, Linen, 250 x 89 In. 1035.00
Tapestry, 2 Women & 2 Men, France, 18 x 18 In. 45.00
Tapestry, Aubusson, Demeter In Lush Landscape, Harvesters, 100 x 137 In. 9775.00
Tapestry, Aubusson, France, 18th-19th Century, 26 x 62 In. 880.00
Tapestry, Aubusson, Hunt Scene Within Golden Border, 57 x 91 In. 1610.00
Tapestry, Aubusson, Pastoral, Woman, 2 Musicians, Trompe L'Oeil Frame, 70 x 73 In. ... 4600.00
Tapestry, Cherub, Fruit & Parrot Design, Belgium, 18th-19th Century, 19 x 73 In. 1155.00
Tapestry, Floral Design, 19th Century, 77 x 78 In. 1150.00
Tapestry, Garden Scene, Figures In 18th Century Costume, Wooden Frame, 26 x 60 In. . 55.00
Tapestry, Hunting Scene, Dogs, Red Border, Flemish, 18th Century, 57 x 82 In. 5750.00
Tapestry, Joan Of Arc, Silk, Frame, 10 x 15 In. 90.00
Tapestry, Medieval Couple, In Forest, 31 x 52 In. 115.00
Tapestry, Medieval Scene, 34 x 52 In. 230.00
Tapestry, Needlepoint, 1880s, 9 x 7 Ft. 5800.00
Tapestry, Needlework, Floral, Frame, 13 x 7 In. 33.00
Tapestry, Needlework, Prayer Rug Style, Tree-Of-Life Mihrab, Persia, 59 x 35 In. 165.00
Tapestry, Stylized Birds, Fruits, Foliage, Black Ground, Bleynie, 1940, 43 x 78 In. 4600.00
Tapestry, Venetian Scene, Buildings, Canals, Gondolas, Belgium, 20 x 54 In. 165.00
Tea Cozy, Battenburg Lace, Flower Designs, 12 x 16 In. 115.00
Tea Cozy, Crazy Quilt, Victorian, 5 In. 165.00

Tea Cozy, Quilted Silk, Floral, Pink 55.00
Tea Cozy, Quilted, Turquoise Flowers, Green Leaves, England 88.00
Tea Cozy, Victorian, Silk & Velvet 67.00
Towel, Hand, Cross-Stitched, Peacocks, Fringed Edge, Wool On Linen, 1850, 57 In. 575.00
Towel, Show, Mennonite, Linen, Jonathen Stouffer, Lancaster County, 1847 .... 995.00
Towel, Show, Pennsylvania German, Linen, Flowers, Birds, Elizabeth Houder, 1839 .... 425.00
Towel, Tea, Embroidered Black Girl, 7 Piece 65.00
Valance, Conestoga Wagons, Plains Indians, Cotton, In Plastic Package, 1960s 25.00
Valance, Embroidered Phoenix & Butterflies, Chinese, Silk, Frame, 76 1/2 In. 440.00
Wall Hanging, Ancestor Man, No. 5775, Turquoise, Kay Finch, 26 In. 275.00
Wall Hanging, Needlework, Oriental Prayer Design, 19th Century, Austria, 49 x 27 In. .. 66.00
Window Shade, Hand Painted, Border, Scrolls, Fruit, Wood Rod, 31 x 70 In., Set Of 3 .. 715.00
Window Shade, Painted, Domestic Scene, For Office Of State Council Of Penn., 57 In. . 3630.00

THERMOMETER is a name that comes from the Greek word for heat.
The thermometer was invented in 1731 to measure the temperature of
either water or air. All kinds of thermometers are collected, but those
with advertising messages are the most popular.

7-Up, Bottle, Canada, 1940s, 6 x 15 In. 230.00
7-Up, Round, 9 In. 150.00
AC Spark Plugs, Round, 1940s 200.00
American Express, 1950s 165.00
B-1 Lemon-Lime, 16 1/2 x 4 1/2 In. 70.00
Bavarian's Beer, Plastic, Round, 1960s, 11 In. 33.00
Bireley's, Tin 165.00
Champion Spark Plugs, Wooden, 21 x 5 1/8 In. 120.00
Clark Bar, Wood, 1920, 5 1/4 x 19 In. 137.00
Country Kitchen Bread, Glass 70.00
Desk, Equestrian Weight, Bronze, Signed, Zimmerman, Germany, 8 1/2 In. 374.00
Diaper Dan, Black 65.00
Diet Dad's Root Beer, 12 Women 175.00
Diet Rite Cola, Wall, Aluminum, Glass, 1970s, Round, 12 In. 55.00
Dr Pepper, 1960 .... 60.00
Dr Pepper, 1970s 70.00
Dr. Pepper, Hot Or Cold, 1950s, 6 1/2 x 16 In. 200.00
Dr. Well's Soda, 1950s 120.00
Dunham's Coconut, Brass Frame, Round, 11 3/4 In. 192.00
Ex-Lax, Porcelain, 5 Colors, 39 x 8 In. 175.00
Farmers Elevator Grain & Supply, Pinup Type Lady, On Phone, Mirror 150.00
Frostie Root Beer, 1940s, 8 x 36 In. 345.00
Grand Prize, Brass, Glass Face, Round, 9 In. 175.00
Hires Root Beer, Blue & White, Drink Hires, With Bottle, Tin, 26 1/2 x 8 In. 135.00
Hydrometer, Mahogany Board, Andrew J. Lloyd, Boston, 2 1/2 x 14 In. 287.50
Indianapolis Indian Glove, Wooden, 10 5/8 x 4 In. 110.00
Interlux International Paint Company, Glass, Metal, Round, 12 In. 170.00
Jap Rose Soap, Cobalt Blue, Porcelain, 1915 .... 286.00
John Deere 50.00
John S. Mullenite, Pure Milk From Accredited Herd, Baby Picture, 4 x 6 In. 12.00
Ken-L Meal, For Best Results Feed Your Dog Ken-L Meal, 1950s, 7 x 27 In. 219.00
Listerine Antiseptic, Porcelain, 30 x 12 1/2 In. 600.00
Lowney's Chocolate Bars, Porcelain 400.00
Mail Pouch Tobacco, Porcelain .... 150.00 to 250.00
Manchester Bank Of St. Louis, Porcelain 35.00
Marvel Cigarettes, 1940s 110.00
McCord, Square 125.00
Mission Orange, Bottle, 1940s-1950s, 5 x 17 In. 109.00
Mission Orange, Bottle, 1950s, 5 x 17 In. 175.00
Mission Orange Soda, Bottle, Tin, 17 In. 60.00
Moxie, Image Of Moxie Man, 9 1/2 x 25 In. 489.00
Nature's Remedy, Cardboard, 1930s 100.00
Nature's Remedy, Porcelain 160.00
Neon Co., Metal, 13 In. 40.00
Nesbitt Orange, Bottle Shape, 16 In. 65.00

Nesbitt's Range Soft Drink 175.00
Neuweiler, Tin, Round, 12 In. 35.00
Nu-Grape, 1950s 90.00
O'Keefe Beer & Ale, Tin, 8 3/4 In. 70.00
Octagon Soap, A Good Soap, For All Uses, Octagon, Beige, Wood, 18 x 4 In. 110.00
Old Export, Tin Face, Round, 12 In. 44.00
Old Ranger Beer & Ale, Hornell Brewing Co., Metal, Glass Front, 10 In. 55.00
Orange Crush, Bottle Cap, 1950s, 6 x 16 In. 149.00
Orange Crush, Bottle, 1930s-1940s, 6 x 19 In. 210.00
Orange Crush, Die Cut Bottle, 1950s 150.00
Orange Crush, Thirsty? Crush That Thirst, Orange, Black Cap, Tin, 15 1/2 x 6 In. 95.00
Prestone Antifreeze, Porcelain, 36 x 9 1/4 In. 100.00
Quaker State Motor Oil, Round, 12 In. 55.00
Quench, Tin 150.00
Ramon's Brownie & Pink Pills, 9 x 21 In. 365.00
RC Cola, Bottle, 1960s, 5 x 17 In. 265.00
RC Cola, Round, 12 In. ....125.00 to 160.00
Red Seal Batteries, Porcelain, Red, White & Blue, 27 x 7 In. 90.00
Royal Crown Cola, Sign, Early 1940s, 20 x 25 In. 91.00
Royal Crown Soda 3.00
Sauer's Flavoring Extracts, 17 Awards, Wooden, 7 x 24 In. 345.00
Senator's Club Beer, Round, 10 In. 73.00
Shell, Porcelain, Pat. Mar. 16, 1915, 27 x 7 In. 3820.00
Singer Sewing Machine, Heavy Porcelain, 7 x 35 In. 3000.00
Sprague, Pam, 12 x 12 In. 95.00
Squirt, Bottle & Squirt Kid 145.00
Standard Oil, Box ....65.00 to 70.00
Standard Oil Co., Metal, 11 1/2 x 3 In. ....20.00 to 28.00
Sun Crest, Round 170.00
Sun Crest Orange, Switch To The Best Drink, 1940s-1950s, 6 x 16 In. 80.00
Sunbeam Bread, Sunbeam Girl, Square, 1970 .... 200.00
Table, Obelisk Form, Brass, Marble Base, 10 1/2 In. 488.00
Tums For The Tummy, Metal, Small 75.00
Wall, Black Walnut, Germany 605.00
Wall, Brass Scale, Walnut Back, Signed Fisher, Late 18th Century, 10 In. 850.00
Westinghouse, Betty Furness, Set 18.00
Winnipeg Free Press, First With The News, Porcelain, 39 x 8 In. 185.00
Winston Cigarette, Round, 9 In. ....45.00 to 60.00
Wool Soap For Toilet & Bath, Round, 6 In. 250.00

TIFFANY is a name that appears on items made by Louis Comfort
Tiffany, the American glass designer who worked from about 1879 to
1933. His work included iridescent glass, Art Nouveau styles of
design, and original contemporary styles. He was also noted for
stained glass windows, unusual lamps, bronze work, pottery, and silver. Other types of Tiffany are listed under Tiffany Glass, Tiffany
Gold, Tiffany Pottery, or Tiffany Silver. The famous Tiffany lamps are
listed in this section. Tiffany jewelry is listed in the jewelry and wristwatch categories. Reproductions of some types of Tiffany are being
made.

Louis C. Tiffany

Ash Receiver, Bronze, Bird Bearing Oviform Ashtray, Marked, 1899, 29 In. 5750.00
Ash Receiver, Bronze, Iridescent Amber, Impressed Mark, 1899-1918, 31 In. 8050.00
Ashtray, Floor, Wrought Iron, Standard Cast, Circular Base, Medium Brown, 28 In. 1380.00
Ashtray, Gold Dore Finish, Handle Each End, Bronze, Signed, 4 In. 135.00
Blotter Ends, Zodiac 175.00
Bookends, Griffowl, Owl Head, Bronze, Marked, 5 1/8 In. 550.00
Bookends, Raised Scenic, Trees, Mountains, Grass, Bronze, Signed, 4 1/2 x 5 In. 1500.00
Bowl, Gold, Copper Dragonfly, Seed Pods, Petal Rim, 1880, 4 1/4 In. 5462.00
Box, Cigar, Pine Needle, Bronze, Gold Beaded, Amber Glass Liner, 4 x 12 In. 1265.00
Box, Coffer Style, Bronze, Dore, Dome Top, Classical Column & Frieze, 8 x 3 In. 2200.00
Box, Cover, Incised Geometric, Raised Snake Heads, Gold Dore, Marked, 8 x 5 x 3 In. .. 660.00
Box, Indian, Hinged Cover, Geometric Pattern Around Body, Signed, 5 1/2 x 3 In. 450.00
Box, Stamp, Venetian, Chain Link Closure, 3 Section, Gold Dore Finish, Signed, 4 In. 450.00

Tiffany, Inkwell,
Turtleback
Pattern

Don't store foods or beverages in crystal bowls or bottles for long periods of time. Acidic juice, vinegar, and alcoholic beverages will leach out the lead in the glass. It is unhealthy to drink the liquid.

Bronze, Bulldog, Figural, Prone Position, Ears Up, Impressed Tiffany Studios 933, 2 In. .	345.00
Candelabrum, 3-Light, Adjustable Holder, Snuffer, Ribbed Base, Bronze, 22 In.	3837.00
Candlestick, Bronze, Blown-Out Favrile Glass Single Standard, Signed, 14 3/4 In.	2185.00
Candlestick, Bronze, Favrile, Serpent Head, 2 Serpentine Arms, Dark Green, 7 1/2 In. . .	575.00
Candlestick, Bronze, Intaglio Finish, Swirled Circular Foot, 1899, 8 In., Pair	920.00
Candlestick, Gilt Bronze, Green Glass Candle Cup, Enameled, 1918-1928, 9 In., Pair . . .	1035.00
Candlestick, Zodiac, Bronze, Octagon Base, Square Holders, Signed, Pair	2500.00
Chandelier, Bronze, 20 Tiles, Blue, Silver, Green Iridescent, Brown, 1900, 24 In.	2300.00
Clock, Bronze, Classical, Glass 4 Sides, 1900, 13 x 9 x 6 In.	990.00
Clock, Bronze, Geometric, Scroll Design, Rectangular, 6 1/2 In.	1100.00
Clock, Carriage, Favrile, Bronze, Amber Glass, Grapevine, Marked, 1899, 5 1/2 In.	3220.00
Clock, Desk, Bronze & Onyx, Double Dial, c.1920	1750.00
Clock, Enamel, Twisted Wire Filigree, Pink, Rose, 1918-1928, 7 1/2 In.	4312.00
Clock, Gilt Bronze, Arched Hood, Scrolled Acanthus, 1899-1918, 7 1/2 In.	3162.00
Clock, Gold & Silver Patina, Signed On Dial & Mechanism, 14 x 13 In.	5995.00
Clock, Mantel, Brass, Foliate Design, c.1900, 12 In.	546.00
Clock, Mantel, Gothic, Mercury Filled Pendulum, Arched Case, Brass, 10 In.	374.00
Clock, Zodiac, Symbols Allover, Bronze, Signed, 4 x 4 1/2 In.	1500.00
Compote, Renaissance Revival Band Around Bowl, Gold Interior, 1853, 10 In.	1782.50
Container, Gold-Washed Egg, Silver Prunus Blossoms, Stems, 4 3/8 x 5 1/2 In.	920.00
Desk Set, Grapevine, Bronze & Green Slag Glass, 12 Piece	3025.00
Fan, Ivory, Chantilly Lace, Box	150.00
Figurine, Art Deco Japanese Woman, Gold Leaf Over Bronze, 7 In., Pair	200.00
Frame, Bronze, Geometric Designs Applied At Corner, 1899, 6 1/2 In.	1150.00
Frame, Pine Needle, Glass Overlaid With Bronze, Signed, 8 3/8 x 6 7/8 In.	1725.00
Inkstand, Green Patina, Bronze	850.00
Inkwell, American Indian, Bronze	595.00
Inkwell, Double, 2 Hinged Covers, Bronze Ball Feet, Glass & Bronze, Signed, 5 1/2 In. .	2500.00
Inkwell, Favrile, Hinged Lid, Pierced Leafage, Green, Dark Brown Patina, 4 In.	2875.00
Inkwell, Turtleback Pattern . . . . *Illus*	1760.00
Inkwell, Venetian, Bronze, Hinged Cover, Ermine Border, Dore, 2 5/8 x 3 x 3 In.	585.00
Inkwell, Zodiac, Polychrome	350.00
Jar, Cover, Pulled Green Feathers, Silver Rim, Signed, 6 In.	990.00
Lamp, 3-Light, Lily, Glass & Bronze, Signed, 8 3/4 In.	4025.00
Lamp, 4 Dragonflies & Fly, Domed Shade, Blue, Gold, 15 1/4 In.	7475.00
Lamp, Abalone & Allover Gilt Panels, Amber Panel Shade, 1905, 16 1/2 In.	5625.00
Lamp, Acorn, Favrile, White Glass Striated, Green, Brown Patina, 16 1/2 In.	6325.00
Lamp, Acorn, Green To White Base, Bronze, 16 In.	9500.00
Lamp, Adjustable, Green Cased Glass Shade, Favrile, Bronze, 1899, 23 1/4 In.	5175.00
Lamp, Arrowroot, Favrile, Bronze, White Blossoms, Conical Leaded Glass Shade	18400.00
Lamp, Bamboo, Spreading Tree Trunk Shape, Swirl Shade, Bronze, 14 1/2 In.	3000.00
Lamp, Bridge, Favrile, Amber Glass Shade, White, Intaglio Finish, 55 In.	8625.00
Lamp, Bronze Stand, Art Nouveau Lines, Ball Knob Of Glass, Swirls	5225.00
Lamp, Bronze, Allover Green & White Striated Glass Shade, 1899-1928, 17 1/4 In.	5750.00
Lamp, Bronze, Iridescent Amber Flower Shade, 1892-1902, 19 3/4 In.	4310.00
Lamp, Candlestick, Bronze, Queen Anne's Lace, Bell Shade, Green Glass, 24 In.	975.00
Lamp, Candlestick, Twisted Stem, Leaf Design Fittings, Favrile, Signed, 14 In., Pair	3220.00
Lamp, Chandelier, Iridescent Glass Prisms, Alternating Chains, Favrile, 1899, 24 In.	3165.00

If you live in an earthquake area, a few precautions may help limit damage. Be sure there is a lip on the edge of a shelf that holds dishes and glassware. String a fishing line across the front of a shelf holding baskets or other very light objects to help keep them from falling. Use dental wax to stick the objects to the shelf.

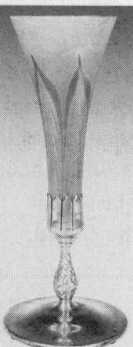

Tiffany Vase, Pulled Feather; Trumpet, Bronze Base, Signed LCT, c.1906, 11 3/4 In.

Lamp, Cypriote Shade, Bronze, 20 In.	1200.00
Lamp, Cypriote, Mottled Blue Glass, Gilt Bronze Pedestal, Signed, 18 In.	715.00
Lamp, Daffodil, Bronze, White Glass Segments, Yellow, Green, Domed Shade, 20 In.	21850.00
Lamp, Dogwood, Foliage, Mottled Spring Green, Yellow, Amber, 29 In.	12075.00
Lamp, Dogwood, Red, Pink, White, Yellow Centers, Bronze, 1920, 25 In.	24150.00
Lamp, Dragonfly, Bronze, 5 Intaglio Dragonflies, Gold Iridescent, 14 x 7 In.	5750.00
Lamp, Favrile, 32 Amber Iridescent Pendent Prisms Shade, Brown, 17 In.	5750.00
Lamp, Favrile, 6-Light, Adjustable, Lily, Brown Patina, 22 In.	8050.00
Lamp, Favrile, Azure Blue Honeycomb Form Tiles, Domed Shade, 19 In.	1840.00
Lamp, Favrile, Bronze, Harvard, Octagonal Leaded Glass Shade, Blue, Green, 26 In.	13800.00
Lamp, Favrile, Bronze, Pulled Feather, Green Top, 6 1/2 In.	8800.00
Lamp, Favrile, Bronze, Scroll Design, Domed Shade, Celadon, Gold, 20 In.	8050.00
Lamp, Favrile, Green Leafage, Tendrils, Amber Shade, Bronze, 15 In.	7475.00
Lamp, Favrile, Wave Design, Caramel Vertical Rows, Domed Shade, 13 In.	8050.00
Lamp, Gilt Bronze Shade, Favrile Prisms, Organic Form Base, Bronze, Signed, 17 In.	2005.00
Lamp, Gold Iridescent Art Glass Shade, Bronze Pedestal Footed, Signed, 12 In.	3025.00
Lamp, Greek Key, Mottled Golden Yellow, Conical Shade, 25 1/2 In.	4370.00
Lamp, Inverted Daffodils, Mottled Yellow, Amber, Conical Shade, 26 In.	5750.00
Lamp, Leaf & Vine, Band Of Striated Leaves, Telescopic Arm, Signed, 26 In.	7475.00
Lamp, Linenfold, Zodiac Base, Bronze, 1940, 18 1/4 In.	5175.00
Lamp, Oil, 3-Arm Shade Mount, Birds In Branches, Bronze, 1918, 12 1/2 In.	4025.00
Lamp, Pansy, Multicolored Blossoms, Purple, Blue, Domed Shade, 22 In.	23000.00
Lamp, Pansy, Spring Green, Emerald Green, Domed Shade, 21 x 18 In.	6900.00
Lamp, Peony Blossoms, Mottled, Salmon, Rose, Fuchsia, Magenta, 26 In.	2530.00
Lamp, Piano, 3-Lily, Gold Dore Bronze Base, Favrile	4900.00
Lamp, Pomegranate, Favrile, Geometric Tiles, Domed Shade, 1928, 22 In.	17250.00
Lamp, Scarab, Beetle Form Shade, Bronze, Favrile Glass, 8 1/8 In.	4379.00
Lamp, Student, Damascene Favrile Glass, Smocked Diamond Design, Signed, 21 In.	10580.00
Lamp, Swirling Leaves, Amber Ripple Glass, Emerald Green Ground, 18 x 23 In.	9900.00
Lamp, Water Lilies, White, Green Pads, Caramel Slag Glass Shade, Brown, Green, 17 In.	715.00
Lamp, Weight-Balance, Bronze Base, Gold Casing On Shade, Bronze, Signed, 14 In.	4000.00
Lamp, Weight-Balance, Pulled Feathers In Shade, Gilt Bronze, Favrile, 1928, 14 In.	3450.00
Lamp, Wire Mesh & Enamel, Silvered Bronze Base, Signed	4950.00
Lamp, Zodiac Shade, Bronze, Impressed Mark, 11 x 9 In.	2310.00
Lamp, Zodiac, Turtleback Tiles In Pivoting Shade, Bronze, Favrile, 1918, 14 1/2 In.	5750.00
Letter Clip, Zodiac, Brown Patina, Bronze	295.00
Letter Holder, American Indian, Bronze, Frog, Serpent, Geometric Forms, Gold, 6 In.	430.00
Letter Holder, Grapevine, Green Glass, Bronze	425.00
Letter Opener, Adam, Design In Curved Handle, Gold Dore, Signed, 10 In.	250.00
Letter Opener, Bronze, Blue Glass	195.00
Letter Opener, Heraldic, Green Enamel, Silvered Shield Handle Sides, Signed, 9 1/2 In.	250.00
Letter Opener, Louis XVI, Floral Wreath On Handle, Gold Dore, Signed, 10 In.	250.00
Letter Rack, Pine Needle, Green Slag Glass, Bronze, Signed, Square, 4 In.	650.00
Loving Cup, Favrile, 3 Green Leaf, Scrolled Vines, 3 Applied Reeded Handles, 8 In.	2530.00
Match Safe, Zodiac, Bronze	75.00
Match Stand, Disked Tray, Gilt Bronze, Signed, 4 In.	200.00

Matchbox, Art Deco, 14K Rose Gold, 1920, 1 3/4 x 2 1/2 In. 650.00
Mirror, Lily Pad, Coiling, Bronze, Brown, Green Patina, 1899-1918, 19 In. 11500.00
Paper Clip, Zodiac 150.00
Paperweight, Favrile, Planter Shape, Green Leaf, Vines, 2 1/8 x 6 1/2 In. 575.00
Pen Brush, Zodiac 125.00
Pen Tray, Pine Needle, Green Glass Under Bronze, Signed, 9 1/2 In. 350.00
Pen Tray, Spider Web, Brass & Chocolate Glass, 9 3/4 x 3 In. 187.00
Plate, Bronze Dore Finish, New York, 9 In. 66.00
Scale, Postal, Pine Needle .... .525.00 to 550.00
Screen, Tea, 3-Panel, Grapevine, Overlaid Grapevine Openwork, Signed 978.00
Screen, Tea, 3-Panel, Mottled, Overlaid With Pine Needle Openwork, Signed, 7 1/2 In. ... 1265.00
Toothpick, Gold Favrile, Marked, 1 15/16 In. 247.00
Tray, Floral Design, Bronze, Gold Dore Patina, Impressed Mark, 6 In. 220.00
Tray, Raised Scalloped Rim, Green Panels, Amethyst Rib Stripes, Signed, 6 1/2 In. 330.00
Vase, Pulled Feather, Trumpet, Bronze Base, Signed, LCT, c.1906, 11 3/4 In. ......*Illus* 2310.00
IFFANY GLASS, Bowl, 10-Scalloped Rim, Gold Iridescent, 2 1/4 x 4 In. 490.00
Bowl, Center, Favrile, 10 Lily Pads, Honey, Amber, Orange, Gold Body, 5 x 9 In. 1610.00
Bowl, Crimped Rim, Gold Iridescent, 3 x 1 In. 132.00
Bowl, Diamond Pattern, Raised On Transparent Disk Foot, Yellow, 6 1/4 In. 316.00
Bowl, Favrile, Flared Rim, 8 Pulled Green Feather Design, 4 x 7 1/4 In. 518.00
Bowl, Favrile, Flared Rim, Blue Base, 3 x 6 1/2 In. 546.00
Bowl, Favrile, Fluted, Crimped Rim, Gold, Rose Iridescent, 1924, 6 1/2 In. 360.00
Bowl, Favrile, Ribbed, Gold, Rose Iridescent, 7 x 2 1/4 In. 525.00
Bowl, Favrile, Ribbed, Pink, Gold, Blue Iridescent, 3 x 1 In. 121.00
Bowl, Flower, 5 Green Lily Pads, Gold Iridescent Luster, 10 1/2 In. 1840.00
Bowl, Lily Pad, Gold, Green Iridescent, 10 In. 1610.00
Bowl, Lobed, Circular, Etched Leaf Vine Design, L.C.T.-Favrile No. 6596, 10 In. 1095.00
Bowl, Pink Latticinio, Pedestal, Signed, 5 1/4 In. 1050.00
Bowl, Rib-Mold, Ruffled Rim, 4 Ruffled Feet, Gold, 3 1/2 x 6 In. 460.00
Bowl, Ruffled Edge, Signed, 1920, 4 1/2 In. 275.00
Bowl, Ruffled Rim, 14 Rib Oval, Purple Pulled Feather, Signed, 2 3/4 x 5 In. 657.00
Bowl, Scalloped Flaring Rim, Paneled Body, Amber, Favrile, 1893, 6 3/4 In. 920.00
Bowl, Side Handles, Amber, 2 In. 175.00
Bowl, Undertray, 8 Ruffled Rims, Gold Iridescent, 5 3/4 x 6 3/4 In. 635.00
Bowl, Yellow, Vines, Flared Rim, L.C. Tiffany-Favrile No. 17305, 1925, 8 In. ...805.00 to 1150.00
Cologne, Favrile, 8 Applied Prunts, Gold Iridescent Stopper, 7 1/4 In. 2415.00
Compote, 5-Ruffled Rim, Gold, Blue Iridescent, 4 3/4 x 5 In. 1035.00
Compote, Amber, Gold Iridescent, Flared Rim, 5 3/4 x 10 1/4 In. 690.00
Compote, Blossom Rim, Flared, Petals From Disk Foot, Blue Iridescent, 6 In. 2530.00
Compote, Favrile, Gold Iridescent, Scalloped 1850.00
Compote, Favrile, Morning Glory Blossoms, Gold Iridescent, 1900, 10 1/8 In. 1265.00
Compote, Favrile, Ribbed, Gold, Yellow Iridescent, 6 x 4 In. 550.00
Compote, Favrile, Scalloped Rim, Cobalt Blue Iridescent, Disk Foot, 4 x 10 In. 2760.00
Compote, Floriform, 5 Ruffled Blossoms, Gold, 5 In. 750.00
Compote, Internal Leaf Pattern, Flared Rim, Pink Opalescent, 3 x 5 1/4 In. 635.00
Compote, Leaf, Vine Interior Design, 10-Ribbed Disk Foot, Gold, 4 1/4 x 8 1/4 In. 290.00
Compote, Stylized Leaf Design, Opalescent To Periwinkle Blue, Signed, 4 1/4 In. 495.00
Decanter, Knobbed Stopper, Gold Iridescent, Walled Bottle Form, 11 1/2 In. 805.00
Decanter Set, Pinched Sides, Iridescent Gold, Signed, 10 1/4 In., 8 Piece 2950.00
Finger Bowl, Iridescent, Gold, Faceted Design, 2 1/8 x 4 1/4 In., 10 Piece 7475.00
Finger Bowl, Underplate, Favrile, Engraved, Grapes & Leaves, Green Gold 2250.00
Flowerpot, Favrile, Gold Iridescent, 4 Pulled Feet, Marked, 2 1/2 x 3 In. 575.00
Globe, Swirling Damascene Trailing, Favrile, Signed, 11 x 10 In. 3737.00
Goblet, Iridescent Gold, Signed, 9 1/2 In. 247.00
Goblet, Princess, Favrile, Iridescent Amber, Inscribed, 1892, 12 Piece, 7 In. 9775.00
Lantern, Hall, Favrile, Amber Body, Bronze, Brown Patina, 25 In. 6900.00
Loving Cup, 3 Handles, Gold Iridescent Body, Signed, 6 In. 635.00
Paperweight, Cut Glass, Diamond Cut & Shape, Ten Billion Dollars, 4 In. 395.00
Pen Tray, Pine Needle, 3 Sections, Green, 9 In. 325.00
Pitcher, Favrile, Gold, Bulging Sides, Scroll Handle, Cylindrical, 1910, 6 In. 750.00
Plate, Favrile, 14-Ribbed Card Tray Form, Ambergris, 7 3/4 In. 259.00
Rose Bowl, Favrile, 4 Pink Roses, Lime Green Leafage, 1892-1906, 3 x 5 In. 9775.00
Salt, Bean Pot Shape, Loop Handles, Signed 250.00

Salt, Favrile, Wide Top Opening, Gold Iridescent, Signed, 1 x 1 3/4 In. 300.0

Salt, Gold, Aurene, Ruffled Border, Marked, 2 3/4 In. 220.0

Salt, Ruffled Rim, Iridescent Gold, Favrile, Signed 215.0

Salt, Ruffled, Blue 450.0

Shade, Acorn Design, Dichroic Glass, 14 In. 4000.0

Shade, Acorn Pattern, Geometric Ground, Green, Red Mottled, 1899, 16 In. 6900.0

Shade, Acorn, Leaded Favrile, Transparent Glass Segments, Yellow, Green, 3 In. 3680.0

Shade, Damascene, Green Wavy Design Outside, Signed, 7 In. 3105.0

Shade, Diamond Pattern Teardrop Form, Gold Favrile, Signed, 8 In. 593.0

Shade, Lily, 8-Rib, Scalloped, Favrile Blossom, Signed, 4 1/2 In. 1315.0

Shade, Lily, Ruffled Rim, Iridescent Gold, 4 1/2 In., 3 Piece 3220.0

Shade, Ruffled Rim, Iridescent Gold, Favrille, 4 1/2 In., 3 Piece 1840.0

Tile, Geometric Raised Pattern, 4 x 4 In. 125.0

Vase, 10 Ribs, Oval Body, Gold Iridescent, 5 1/2 In. . . . . .978.00 to 1150.0

Vase, 18 Ribs, Swirl Design, Cobalt Blue, Conical Oval, 6 1/4 In. 1380.0

Vase, 5-Fold Flare Top, Signed, Favrile, 4 1/2 In. 2500.0

Vase, Amber Iridescent, Applied Ribbing, Favrile, 1928, 17 3/4 In. 2590.0

Vase, Amber Iridescent, Floriform, Bulbous, Favrile, 1899-1928, 14 3/4 In. 2070.0

Vase, Amber Iridescent, Pulled Green Leafage, Bronze, Favrile, 1918, 25 In. 4890.0

Vase, Applied 2 Scroll Handles, Amber Iridescent, Everted Rim, Favrile, 12 In. 1610.0

Vase, Aquatic, Sea Green Ribs, Favrile, Signed, 7 x 6 In. 700.0

Vase, Black, Dark Cobalt Blue, Pulled Swirled Design, 4 1/4 x 6 In. 2990.0

Vase, Blue Green, Signed, 9 In. 1650.0

Vase, Bronze, Amber, Pink-Blue Iridescent, Red, Green Mottled, Favrile, 12 In. 805.0

Vase, Bronze, Gold Dore, Favrile, 13 1/2 In. 990.0

Vase, Bronze, Ribbed Body, Blue Enamel Teardrop Design, Favrile, 1918, 17 In. 1380.0

Vase, Bud, Heart Leaves, Vines, Blue, Green, Purple Iridescent, Favrile, 1919, 6 In. 1725.0

Vase, Chain Pattern Trailing, Gold Latticed Trailings, Favrile, 1899, 4 3/8 In. 4025.0

Vase, Cobalt Blue Iridescent, Favrile, 1916-1917, 18 In. 2875.0

Vase, Cypriote, Favrile, Applied Trailing, Turquoise Iridescent, Gray, 14 1/2 In. 13800.0

Vase, Diamond-Quilted, Flared Rim, Cobalt Blue, 3 1/2 x 5 In. 1150.0

Vase, Favrile, 8 Pulled Brown Amber Leaf Forms, Gold Iridescent Accent, 10 In. 1840.0

Vase, Favrile, Deep Cobalt Blue Iridescent, 5 3/4 In. 977.5

Vase, Favrile, Emerald Green Leaf Design, Gold, Amber, 12 In. 1150.0

Vase, Favrile, Rib-Molded, White Opalescent Top, Gold Pulled Border, 5 3/4 In. 2990.0

Vase, Favrile, Scalloped Rim, 4 Peg Feet, Gold, 4 x 6 In. 690.0

Vase, Favrile, Split Swirl Design, 2-Tone Iridescent, Gold, Purple, Blue, 11 In. 1495.0

Vase, Feathering, Blue Dashes, Gold, Amber, Baluster, Favrile, 12 1/8 In. 1380.0

Vase, Fluted Top, Pedestal Foot, Gold, Rose Iridescent, Favrile, 4 1/2 In. 715.0

Vase, Gold Iridescent, Ruby Face Form, Leaves & Vines Imbedded, Signed, 5 In. 1540.0

Vase, Hourglass, Amber, Pink Iridescent, 1900, 8 1/2 In. 1035.0

Vase, Intaglio, Crimped Rim, Blooming Iris, Favrile, 1921, 14 5/8 In. 3740.0

Vase, Iridescent Gold & Purple, Pinched Shoulders, Favrile, Signed, 4 1/2 In. 440.0

Vase, Ivory Iridescent Rim, Olive, Green Scrolls, Favrile, 1900, 7 In. 1150.0

Vase, Jack-In-The-Pulpit, Favrile, Stretched Rim, Gold Iridescent, 18 3/8 In. 11500.0

Vase, Jack-In-The-Pulpit, Iridescent Gold, Signed, 13 1/2 In. 8050.0

Vase, Knopped Base, Amber Iridescent, Pink, Floriform, Favrile, 1909, 11 In. 1380.0

Vase, Lava, Applied Gold Lava Highlights, Aqua, Blue Ground, Favrile, 3 3/4 In. 8050.0

Vase, Leaf Swirls, Pods, Double-Hooked, Lavender, Emerald Green, Gold Top, 9 In. 825.0

Vase, Mahogany, Petals Outlined In Red, Cupped Foot, Signed, 9 In. 3737.0

Vase, Mushroom Shape, Green Iridescent, Gold, 2 1/4 x 2 1/4 In. 900.0

Vase, Narcissus, Favrile, 10 Narcissus Blossoms, Red, Yellow Centers, 16 In. 17250.0

Vase, Oyster White To Vaseline, Bean Pot Form, Signed, 2 x 2 1/2 In. 575.0

Vase, Paperweight, Crocus Blossoms, Green, Amber Leafage, Favrile, 1912, 5 In. 6037.0

Vase, Paperweight, Stylized Leaf Design, Brown Ground, Signed, 3 In. 460.0

Vase, Paperweight, Yellow Millefiore Blossoms, Favrile, 1909, 5 1/2 In. 7475.0

Vase, Pastel Blue Morning Glory, Sapphire Blue Throat, Signed, 9 1/2 In. 1455.0

Vase, Pulled Zigzag, Black, Blue, Gold, Favrile, 6 In. 2530.0

Vase, Rib-Molded Amber Body, Gold, Angular, Gold Iridescent, 9 In. 980.0

Vase, Ribbed, 2 Open Handles, Gold, Green, Rose, Blue Iridescent, Favrile, 3 In. 495.0

Vase, Ribbed, Gold, Rose Iridescent, Favrile, 5 In. 660.0

Vase, Ruffled Edge, Pulled Feather Design, Signed, 3 x 5 In. 1050.0

Vase, Ruffled Rim, Pedestal Base, Signed, 4 3/4 In. 650.0

Vase, Selenium Red, Favrile, 1919, 8 In. 3165.00
Vase, Swirled Blue, Green, Amber, Pale Green, Favrile, 1895, 11 1/2 In. 4600.00
Vase, Teardrop, Green Pointed Leaves, Gold Ground, Iridescent, Favrile, 10 In. 750.00
Vase, Tel El Amarna, Egyptian Chain Trailed Pattern, Ruby Red, 1910, 8 In. 10350.00
Vase, Tel El Amarna, Favrile, Spherical Form, Tomato Red Iridescent, 5 3/8 In. 8625.00
Vase, Trailing Wild Roses, Thorny Branches, Cobalt Blue, Favrile, 1918, 18 In. 11500.00
Vase, Trumpet, Gold Iridescent, 1916, 15 In. 2090.00
Vase, Trumpet, Pulled Feather Design, Cobalt Blue, Blue Iridescent, 8 In. 1840.00
Vase, Undulating Rim, Gold Iridescent, Favrile, 17 3/4 In. 5750.00
Vase, White Opalescent, Olive Green Leafage, Floriform, Favrile, 1925, 15 1/2 In. 8050.00
Wine, Favrile, Metallic Gold, Stemmed, 4 Piece 2400.00
Wine, Green Gold, Engraved Grapes & Leaves, 3 1/2 In. 1450.00
TIFFANY GOLD, Dresser Set, Bombe Form, Monogram, 18K Gold, 1930, 5 Piece 4025.00
Pot, 18K Gold, Initials & Dates, Demitasse, 1920, 9 In. 3735.00
TIFFANY POTTERY, Cup & Saucer, Oriental Design, Gilt 46.00
Vase, Brown, Black, Green Glaze, Marked, 5 1/2 In. 525.00
Vase, Forest Green & Cobalt Blue Glaze, Signed, 5 7/8 In. 2875.00
Vase, Silvered Bronze Overlay, Pansy Border, Favrile, Signed, 8 1/2 In. 9775.00
TIFFANY SILVER, Basket, Bread, Sprays Of Wheat, Handles, Pedestal Foot, 1855, 15 In. 1840.00
Basket, Pierced, Oval, c.1894, 1 1/2 x 9 In. 680.00
Bell, Dinner, Moresque Ornament Base, Bacchante Handle, 1869, 6 1/2 In. 2300.00
Bowl, Chrysanthemum, 10 In. 1250.00
Bowl, Clover Pattern, Pair 1035.00
Bowl, Fruit, Openwork Band, Reeded Rim Handle, 1907, 8 7/8 In. 230.00
Bowl, Golf Trophy, 1949, 6 In. 135.00
Bowl, Lotus Plants, Spot Hammered Ground, 1887, 8 1/2 In. 6325.00
Bowl, Perched Herons On Floral Handles, 1875-1891, 13 In. 5175.00
Bowl, Shrimp, Chased Floral & Palm Leaf, Cover On Drain, 7 x 5 In. 880.00
Bowl, Underplate, Band Of Children At Work & Play, Monogrammed, 7 1/4 In. 665.00
Box, Cigar, Bamboo Pattern, Cedar Lined, 20th Century, 8 1/8 x 9 1/2 In. 4312.00
Bread Tray, Reeded & Scalloped Rim, Handles, 1910s, 11 1/4 In. 247.00
Butter, Cover, Leaf Chased Border, Serpentine, Drain 330.00
Case, Dressing, Leather, Silver Fittings, 1925, 18 Piece, 15 3/4 In. 2875.00
Cigar Caddy, Silver Gilt Interior, 1870, 9 In. 2700.00
Cocktail Shaker, Silver Cover & Spout, Hawkes Crystal Container, 9 3/8 In. 230.00
Cocktail Shaker, Strainer Spout, 1930, 10 1/2 In. 1955.00
Cup, Arabesque Design, Applied Flower Heads, Horn Handles, 1885, 9 1/4 In. 5462.00
Decanter, Sterling Top, 1902 1907, 11 1/2 In. 1725.00
Desk Set, Grapevine, Apricot Glass, 8 Piece 4200.00
Dish, Condiment, Cover, Glass Lined, On Tray, Floral Garlands, 10 3/4 In. 515.00
Hair Brush, Floral, Fern Design, 1891-1902, 5 1/2 In., Pair 330.00
Kettle-On-Stand, Hot Water, 14 1/2 In. 5290.00
Magnifying Glass, Scroll & Rosette Chased Handle, Round Frame 308.00
Mug, Child's, Engraved Kittens, Ridged Handle, 1902-1907, 3 3/4 In. 1090.00
Nutmeg Grater, Hinged Drop Cover, Cylindrical, 1855, 2 3/4 In. 920.00
Pastry Tongs, Chased & Engraved, Pierced Holders, Marked, 1869 .... 385.00
Pepper Shaker, 5 In. 210.00
Pitcher, Repousse, Chased, Monogram, 4 Claw Feet, Baluster, 11 1/8 In. 3735.00
Pitcher, Repousse, Presentation, Gadrooned, Monogram On Handle, 1917, 7 In. 2070.00

Silver polish can be made at
home from a cup of cigar ashes,
2 tablespoons bicarbonate of
soda, and enough water to make
a paste. The only problem is
finding a cigar smoker.

Tiffany Silver,
Pitcher, Water,
Repousse, Engraved
Floral & Leaf Bands

Pitcher, Scroll Foliate Design, 4 Paw Feet, Monogram, 9 7/8 In. 3737.00
Pitcher, Water, Flowers & Ferns, Monogram, 1885, 12 1/4 In. 3450.00
Pitcher, Water, Foliage, Foliate Garlands, Sterling, 9 1/4 In. 1840.00
Pitcher, Water, Repousse, Engraved Floral & Leaf Bands ....*Illus* 3850.00
Plate, Dessert, Gadroon Rim, 9 In., 12 Piece 5750.00
Plate, Gadrooned & Foliate Border, Contemporary Arms, 1907, 10 In., 12 Piece 9775.00
Pot, Chased Foliage, Hammered Ground, Demitasse, 1885, 9 1/4 In. 2070.00
Salt, 3 Ducks Support As Legs, 3 In. 145.00
Salt & Pepper, Cabochon Turquoises, 1897, 2 1/4 In., Pair 4600.00
Sugar & Creamer, Beaded Border Around Body, Flowers, 1880s, 2 1/2 In. 400.00
Sugar & Creamer, Thread Mold Rim, Urn Shape, C-Form Handles 200.00
Sugar Sifter, Indian War Dance, Pierced, Chicago Columbian Expo, 1893, 8 In. 3160.00
Telephone Dialer 26.00
Thermometer, Monogram, Honeywell, Marked, 2 1/2 In. 145.00
Tray, Card, Scalloped Rim, 1907, 6 1/2 x 6 1/2 In. 175.00
Tray, Lemon, Wave Chased Border, 8 In. 165.00
Tray, Roll, Openwork Sides, Thread Mold Rim, Monogram, 11 1/4 In. 310.00
Tray, Serpentine, Molded Edge, 13 In. 880.00
Tureen, Cover, Embossed & Chased Flowers, Oval, 1880, 13 3/4 In. 5750.00
Vase, Square, Stylized Floral Spray, Bracket Feet, c.1875, 8 1/4 In. 3450.00
Vase, Stylized Blossoms, Elongated Baluster, 2 Scroll Handles, 1907, 12 In. 2585.00
Wine Cooler, Arms, Handles, Vase Form, 4 Lion Monopods Base, 1865, 13 In. 9200.00
Yo-Yo 525.00

TIFFIN Glass Company of Tiffin, Ohio, was a subsidiary of the United
States Glass Co. of Pittsburgh, Pennsylvania, in 1892. The U.S. Glass
Co. went bankrupt in 1963, and the Tiffin plant employees purchased
the building and the inventory. They continued running it from 1963 to
1966, when it was sold to Continental Can Company. In 1969, it was
sold to Interpace, and in 1980, it was closed. The black satin glass,
made from 1923 to 1926, and the stemware of the last twenty years are
the best-known products.

Ashtray, Empress, Twilight, Paneled Sides, Square, 10 1/2 In. 195.00
Ashtray, Ribbon, Clear, Killarney Green, Square 275.00
Candlestick, Cherokee Rose, 2-Light, Pair 135.00
Candlestick, June Night, 2-Light, Pair 125.00
Champagne, Cherokee Rose 22.00
Champagne, Empress, Pink 18.00
Champagne, Mt. Vernon 24.00
Champagne, Silhouette 8.00
Cocktail, June Night 12.00
Compote, Cherokee Rose, Ball Stem 115.00
Cordial, Queen Astrid 35.00
Flower Arranger, Black, Clear, 25 1/4 In. 125.00
Goblet, Byzantine, Yellow, 9 Oz. 20.00
Goblet, Cherokee Rose 25.00
Goblet, Cocktail, Byzantine, Yellow 15.00
Goblet, Cordial, Flanders 50.00
Goblet, Cordial, Flanders, Pink 85.00
Goblet, Cordial, June Night, 1 Oz. 40.00
Goblet, Draped Nude, Satin Stem 150.00
Goblet, Empress, Pink, 9 Oz. 37.00
Goblet, Flanders, Pink, 10 Oz. 41.00
Goblet, June Night, 9 Oz. 22.00
Iced Tea, Cherokee Rose 2.00
Jar, Heinz, 21 In. 90.00
Lamp, Owl, 8 In. 665.00
Lamp, Water, Optic, 13 In. 195.00
Pitcher, Killarney Green, Mica Flecks, Clear Handle, Oval 650.00
Plate, Byzantine, Yellow, 7 1/2 In. 15.00
Plate, Cadena, Yellow, 10 In. 45.00
Plate, June Night, 8 1/4 In. 10.00
Relish, Cherokee Rose, 3 Sections, 12 In. 80.00

Relish, June Night, 3 Sections, 12 1/2 In. 65.00
Sherbet, Byzantine, Yellow 13.00
Sugar, Pearl Edge, Green 12.00
Tumbler, Mt. Vernon, 10 Oz. 28.00
Tumbler, Rose Marie, 10 Oz. 15.00
Tumbler, Silhouette, 10 Oz. 10.00
Tumbler, Twilight, Footed, 10 Oz. 20.00
Vase, Blue Controlled Bubble Ball Stem, Clear Body, 9 In. 210.00
Vase, Bud, Cherokee Rose, 8 In. 40.00
Vase, Bud, June Night, 10 1/2 In. 35.00
Vase, Crackle, Teardrop Shape, 8 1/2 In. 475.00
Vase, Desert Red Controlled Bubble Ball Stem, Clear Body, 9 In. 210.00
Vase, Flanders, 15 In. 110.00
Vase, Twilight, 5 1/4 In. 65.00
Wine, Flanders 22.00

ILES have been used in most countries of the world as a sturdy build-
 g material for floors, roofs, fireplace surrounds, and surface top-
ngs. Many of the American tiles are listed in this book under the
ctory name.

3 Parrots On Tree Limb, Table Top, 1920s, 6 Piece 1100.00
Boch Freres La Louviere, Women In Kitchens, Signed, France, 5 1/2 In., Pair 247.00
Cunard Line Dock, Calendar, 1912, Lithographed, 3 1/4 x 4 5/8 In. 45.00
Cupid, Courtyard, 2 Doves, Lucien Boullemier, 12 1/4 x 15 1/4 In. 460.00
Floral, Majolica, J.& J.G., 1881, 4 Piece 350.00
Floreat, Story-Telling, Salopian, Maw, England, 1920, 6 x 6 In., 7 Piece 325.00
Flowers & Leaves, Blue & Gray, Semimatte, California Art, 6 In. 120.00
Fu Lions, Yellow & Green, Roof, Chinese, 9 In., Pair 65.00
Green Tree, Brown Matte, Ivory Ground, Arts & Crafts, 6 In. 176.00
Incised Blue Flowers, Green Leaves, Peach Ground, Square, Arts & Crafts, 5 1/2 In. 286.00
Ivy, Fruit, Tulip, Wheeling, 6 In. 18.00
Landscape, Figure, Seated, Blue, Copper Red Glaze, Porcelain, China, 15 In. 55.00
Landscape, Mill, Hand Painted, Terra-Cotta, Gilt Frame, Bouquet, 1872, 16 x 24 In. 1100.00
Landscape, Triptych, Tillinghast, Pre-1927 .... 675.00
Man With Bow On Horse, Polychrome, Persia, Square, 8 In. 33.00
Mythical Beast, Roof, Green & Yellow, 10 In. 690.00
Stylized Leaf Design, Red Cherries, Green Stems, Cream Ground, Arts & Crafts, 6 In. .. 330.00
Stylized Lime Green, Purple Flowers, Gray Ground, Oak Frame, Arts & Crafts, 6 In. ... 357.50
Stylized Peacock Feather, Yellow, Blue, Green, F.H. Rhead, 5 1/2 In. 286.00
Tree Scene, Lake & House In Background, Multicolored, Oak Frame, Claycraft, 4 x 8 In. 660.00
Warrior Riding A Buddhist Lion, Roof, Glazed, Green & Pink, 14 In., Pair 1150.00
Woman In Feathered Hat, Stove, Beaver Falls, 3 In. 75.00

NWARE containers for household use have been made in America
nce the seventeenth century. The first tin utensils were brought from
urope, but by 1798, tin plate was imported and local tinsmiths made
e wares. Painted tin is called tole and is listed separately. Some tin
tchen items may be found listed under Kitchen. The lithographed tin
ntainers used to hold food and tobacco are listed in the Advertising
tegory under Tin.

Box, Candle, Hanging, Cylindrical, 14 1/2 In. 220.00
Box, Tinder, Striker & Flint, Oval, Top & Bottom Sections, c.1800, 3 7/8 In. 320.00
Box, Tinder, Striker, Flints, Candleholder, Round, 4 1/4 In. 335.00
Box, Tinder, Striker, Flints, Candleholder, Square, 2 7/8 In. 365.00
Candlestand, Weighted Conical Base, Crimped Pan, 27 3/4 In. 440.00
Comb Case, Tooled Eagle On Crest, Embossed, 7 1/4 In. 70.00
Foot Warmer, Punched Tin, Walnut, 11 1/4 x 11 1/2 x 8 In. 250.00
Hip Bath, Painted, France, c.1870, 38 In. 950.00
Lantern, Candle, 19th Century, 10 3/4 In. 245.00
Mold, Candle, 12 Tube, 1 Handle, Raised Base, 10 3/4 x 7 In. 120.00
Mold, Candle, 12 Tube, Dish Top & Bottom Plates, 11 x 9 In. 175.00
Mold, Candle, 12 Tube, Ear Handle, 10 3/4 In. 148.00
Mold, Candle, 12 Tube, Handles, 11 1/2 In. 66.00

Mold, Candle, 20 Tube, 11 3/4 x 7 In.	82.0
Mold, Candle, 24 Tube, Ear Handle, 11 In.	247.0
Mold, Candle, 24 Tube, Wick Rod, Notched Top, Double Ear Handles, 11 3/4 In.	330.0
Mold, Candle, 36 Tube, Ear Handles, 11 3/4 x 21 In.	303.0
Mold, Candle, 48 Tube, Ear Handle, Curved Foot, 10 1/2 x 14 3/4 In.	467.0
Rattle, Embossed For A Good Child, c.1900	95.0
Roaster, Coffee, Handmade, c.1849, 3 1/4 x 9 1/8 In.	155.0
Sconce, Candle, Circular Crimped Crest, 11 1/4 In.	245.0
Sconce, Candle, Crimped Oval Reflectors, 4 1/2 In., Pair	550.0
Teapot, Punched, American, c.1870	2475.0
Wax Pouring Vessel, 3 Cylindrical Spouts, Handle, 15 In.	72.0

TOBACCO CUTTERS may be listed in either the Advertising or Store categories.

TOBACCO JAR collectors search for those made in odd shapes and colors. Because tobacco needs special conditions of humidity and air, it has been stored in special containers since the eighteenth century.

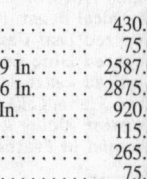

Acorn Finial, Chippendale Base, Brass, England, c.1790, 5 1/2 In.	295.0
Balding Fat Man, Full Figure, High Glaze, German	195.0
Blackamoor, Head Of Man With Turban, 7 1/2 In.	250.0
Cat, Majolica, 7 1/2 x 8 1/2 In.	495.0
Dwarf In Sack, Set On Lid, Terra-Cotta, 8 In.	278.0
Earth Tones, Gouda	275.0
Elk Finial, Horn Handles, Germany, 6 1/2 In.	93.0
Golfer, Googly-Eyed Boy, Yellow Jacket, Red Tie, Green Vest, Germany	265.0
Grays, Duck, Copper Trim, England	70.0
Head Of Black Man Smoking Pipe, 1920s, 4 1/2 In.	210.0
Monogrammed Lid, Silver Plate & Glass, Octagonal Body, 6 In.	92.0
Panther Head, Austrian, 7 1/2 x 8 1/2 In.	690.0
Porcelain, American Indian's Head, Germany, 5 1/4 In.	160.0
Wolf, 5 In.	195.0

TOBY JUG is the name of a very special form of pitcher. It is shaped like the full figure of a man or woman. A pitcher that shows just the top half of a person is not correctly called a toby. More examples of toby jugs can be found under Royal Doulton and other factory names.

Admiral Jelhoe, Hell Five Jack, Wilkinson, 1918, 10 In.	430.0
Benn Gunn, W.R. Midwinter Ltd., Staffordshire	75.0
Collier, Brown Slip, Tricornered Hat, Manganese, Loop Handle, Staffordshire, 9 In.	2587.0
Cover, Admiral Lord Howe, Brown Slip, Tricornered Hat, Staffordshire, 9 13/16 In.	2875.0
Cover, Pale Blue Face, Wearing Brown Slip Tricornered Hat, Staffordshire, 10 In.	920.0
Field Marshall Haig, Push & Go, Wilkinson, Printed Mark, 1917, 11 In.	115.0
Home Brewed Ale, Staffordshire, Cover, 19th Century, 11 In.	265.0
Lion Cub, Kevin Francis, 4 In.	75.0
Man, Creamware Brown Eyes, Manganese Tricornered Hat, Staffordshire, 10 In.	4887.0
Man, Gray Hair, Gray Tricornered Hat, Sitting On White Chair, Staffordshire, 10 In.	1265.0
Man, Gray Tricornered Hat, Pale Yellow Waistcoat, Staffordshire, 1780, 9 7/8 In.	1035.0
Man, Jolly Sailor, Old Salt, Mermaid Handle, Royal Doulton Seal Base, 7 1/4 In.	48.0
Man, Manganese Warty Face Hat, Wearing Prussian Blue Coat, Staffordshire, 6 In.	805.0
Man, Seated In Green Chair, Holding Brown Jug, Staffordshire, 1780, 10 In.	1265.0
Martha Gunn, Pale Green Washed Hat, Cobalt Blue Dress, Staffordshire, 11 In.	5175.0
Pitcher, Gentleman With Red Jacket, 19th Century, 10 3/4 In.	115.0
Pitcher, Man Holding Ale Pitcher, Removable Hat, Staffordshire, 8 3/4 In.	100.0
Winston Churchill, And May God Defend The Right, Wilkinson, 12 In.	1035.0

TOLE is painted tin. It is sometimes called *japanned ware* , *pontypool*, or *toleware*. Most nineteenth-century tole is painted with an orangered or black background and multicolored decorations. Many recent versions of toleware are made and sold. Related items may be listed in the Tin category.

Basket, Bread, Rolled Sides, Crystalline Interior, Fruit & Flower On Sides, 12 In.	4370.0
Bathtub, Wood Stand	1725.0
Bowl, Flower, Gold, Swan Neck Handles, France, 17 In.	400.0
Box, Deed, Dome Top, Blue Japanning, Yellow Stripes, 4 7/8 In.	50.0

Box, Deed, Dome Top, Floral, Dark Brown Japanning, 10 In. . . . . .605.00 to 935.00
Box, Deed, White Band, Floral, Original Dark Brown Japanning, Brass Handle 165.00
Box, Gold Design, Quatrefoil Reserve, Flowers, Victorian, 14 In. 150.00
Bread Tray, Floral, Black Ground, Brown Crystallized Paint Center, 12 1/2 In. 360.00
Bread Tray, Floral, Black Paint, 7 x 14 In. 770.00
Caddy, Wine, Pierced Rim, Gilt Design, France 275.00
Candlestick, Black Paint, Yellow, Red, Green Foliage, Side Push-Up, 5 1/4 In. 220.00
Canister, Tea, Band Of Stylized Fruit, Brown & Green Flowers, c.1825, 5 1/4 In. 3680.00
Canister, Tea, Red Flower, Fillips, Black Ground, 19th Century, 5 3/4 In. 1035.00
Cash Drawer, Blue, Red & Gold Lithograph, Hinged Lid, Germany, 2 x 1 3/8 In. 65.00
Coal Hod, Floral, Black Ground, Urn Shape, Cast Iron Fittings, 18 x 23 In. 797.00
Coal Hod, Hunt Scene, Gilding On Black Ground, 18 In. 302.00
Coffeepot, Hinged Lid, Red & Brown Fruit & Flowers, Red Body, 8 3/4 In. 5175.00
Coffeepot, Hinged Lid, Strap Handle, Stylized Flower, Buds, Black, 7 3/4 In. 3450.00
Inkstand, 2 Pots On Tray, Green, Flower Design, France 140.00
Jardiniere, Red Paint, Lion Mask Handles, 7 x 6 3/4 In., Pair 805.00
Jardiniere, Ribbon Twist Border, Ring Handle, Dark Green Ground, Cylindrical, 8 x 7 In.   920.00
Jardiniere, Strapwork, Foliate Arabesque, Lion Mask Ring Handles, Red, 8 x 5 In., Pair .   1610.00
Jardiniere, Waisted Body, Trailing Ring Handles, Paw Feet, Green, 8 1/2 In., Pair 2590.00
Lamp, Betty, Red Paint Traces, Hearts 175.00
Lamp, Candle, Adjustable Socket & Shade, Snuffer, Striping, Brown Japanning, 19 In. . .   935.00
Lamp, Candle, Shade, Black Paint, Brass Trim, 15 In., Pair 715.00
Lamp, Painted, Red, White, Gold, Rumford, 13 In., Pair 660.00
Matchbox, Trefoil Crest, Floral, Black Paint, Hanging, 6 In. 65.00
Mug, Flower, Dark Brown Japanning, 5 3/4 In. 960.00
Mug, Strap Handle, Stylized Red Fruit, Green Foliage, 19th Century, 5 In. 2760.00
Sconce, Candle, Polychrome Floral, Black Ground, Crimped Crest, 13 3/4 In. 110.00
Table, Iron Base, Scrolled Legs, Sheet Metal Foliage, Irish, 29 1/2 x 52 1/2 In. 2310.00
Tea Caddy, Mustard & Red, Black Ground, 3 1/2 x 6 In. 750.00
Tea Canister, Wood Cover, Gold Calligraphy, Black Ground, 19th Century, 27 In., Pair .   525.00
Teapot, Floral, Hinged Cover At Spout, Wood Handle, 8 In. 395.00
Teapot, Hinged Cover, Stylized Floral Over Copper, Wooden Handle 135.00
Tray, Birds, Flowers, Black Paint, Coffee Table Base, 29 x 31 1/4 x 18 1/2 In. 690.00
Tray, Capriccio Amidst Ruins, Continental, Early 19th Century, 30 In. 1955.00
Tray, Center Design, Rectangular Octagonal, 1840-1850, 8 x 15 In. 425.00
Tray, Crystalline Interior, Meandering Tulips & Leaves, Rolled Edges, 1830s, 12 In. 1380.00
Tray, Cutlery, 2 Lids, Black & Gold Paint 110.00
Tray, Depicting Annunciation, Flower-Filled Borders, Mid-19th Century, 24 In. 400.00
Tray, Georgian Style, Painted Flowers, Folding Stand, 27 In. 980.00
Tray, Gilt Flowers, Black Ground, 30 1/2 In. 550.00
Tray, Gilt Flowers, Geometric, Bamboo Style Legs, 19th Century, 25 1/4 x 30 In. 1955.00
Tray, Gold Designs Of Youth, Early Dress, Shooting Bird With Slingshot, 22 1/2 In. 195.00
Tray, In Wooden Table Stand, Stenciled Hunt Scene, 22 3/4 x 29 In. 247.00
Tray, Neoclassical Scene, Painted, 19 x 31 x 22 3/4 In. 1265.00
Tray, Neoclassical, Marco Polo Schooner Approaching Harbor, Black Ground, 24 In. 935.00
Tray, Peacock, 19th Century, 11 x 14 In. 165.00
Tray, Polychromed Leaf & Rose, Tan, Brown Band, Octagonal, 24 In. 45.00
Tray, Rooster, Gold, Red, Black & White, Georges Briard, 25 In. 75.00
Tray, Rural Scene, Steam Powered Train, 30 1/2 In. 1210.00
Tray, Serving, Green Flowers, Brown, Red Ground, England, 28 1/2 In. 1955.00
Tray, Ship Scene, Flying American Flag, Red, Green Rim, 1854, 16 1/2 In. 330.00
Tureen, Green 4-Leaf Clovers, Gilt Borders, White Porcelain, 1880, 4 In. 525.00
Urn, Gilded Flowers & Rain, Black, Brass Base, Tin & Pewter, 15 In. 467.00
Urn, Maritime Scenes, Lion's Head Handles, 14 In., Pair 5465.00
Vase, Oriental, Green, White, Blue Floral Design, Red, Enameled, 14 In. 700.00

OM MIX was born in 1880 and died in 1940. He was the hero of over
)0 silent movies from 1910 to 1929, and 25 sound films from 1929
▶ 1935. There was a Ralston Tom Mix radio show from 1933 to 1950,
ut the original Tom Mix was not in the show. Tom Mix comics were
ublished from 1942 to 1953.

Book, Big Little Book, The Fighting Cowboy, 1935 . . . .   40.00
Book, Big Little Book, Tom Mix & The Hoard Of Montezuma, No. 1462, 1937 . . . .   37.00

Book, Big Little Books, The Fighting Cowboy, 1935 .... 40.00
Decoder, Sunburst, Movable Disk, 1937, 1 3/4 x 2 In. 36.00
Knife, Ralston Straight Shooters, Pocket ....65.00 to 90.00
Ring, Look-Around, 1945 .... 150.00
Ring, Siren 125.00
Ring, Sliding Whistle, 9 1/2 In. 200.00
Ring, Tiger Eye 275.00
Rocket Parachute, Premium, Mailer 165.00
Signal Arrowhead, Lucite 60.00
Telescope, Bullet, Ralston 70.00
Watch, Sun, Aluminum, c.1935, 2 1/8 In. 75.00
Watch Fob, Gold Ore 60.00
Whistle, Bird, With Instructions & Mailer 195.00

TOOLS of all sorts are listed here, but most are related to industry. Other
tools may be found listed under Iron, Kitchen, Tinware, and Wooden.

Anvil, Clockmaker's, Dominy Family, New York, 18th Century, 6 1/2 In. 295.00
Anvil, Cooper's, Steel Mounted On Tapered Wooden Base, C.W. Smith, Canada, 18 In. ... 175.00
Auger, Iron Blade, Wooden Turning Handle, Norway, 1836 .... 80.00
Ax, Belt, Hickory Handle, Leather Case, Blacksmith Made, c.1830, 16 1/2 In. 185.00
Ax, Broad, Halberd, Curved Back, Colonial, 1750 .... 1475.00
Ax, Miner's Guild, Iron Head, Fruitwood Haft, Horn Panels Of Flowers, Saxon, 1687 ... 3450.00
Ax, Side, Cooper's, 2 Touchmarks, France, 27 In. 350.00
Ax, Throwing, Persian, Silver Inlaid Designs, Snakeskin Wrapped Shaft 250.00
Ax, Winchester, Boy's, Numbered Handle 130.00
Bar Clamp, Cabinetmakers, Wooden, c.1905 .... 39.00
Beader, Hand, Windsor 225.00
Bear Trap, 41AX Kodiak Bear Trap, Hudson Bay, Herters 600.00
Bee Smoker, Hand Held, Woodsman, Pat. 1876 .... 30.00
Bench, Cobbler's, Pine, 44 In. 165.00
Blackjack, Olice, Leather Encased 40.00
Blow Torch, Gasoline, Brass Tank, Steel Burner, Turner Brass Works, Sycamore, Ill. 26.00
Board, Smoothing, Horse Handle, Red & 2 Shades Of Green, 24 3/4 In. 330.00
Boot Pull, Ivory, Pair 95.00
Bootjack, Figured Bird's-Eye Maple 110.00
Bootjack, Lobster 95.00
Bootjack, Wooden, Place For Shoebutton Hooks, Folding 50.00
Boring Machine, Post & Beam Construction, 5 Bits, Tools, Portable 165.00
Box, Cabinet Maker's, 6 Raised Panels, 1900, 5 3/4 x 16 3/8 x 33 In. 125.00
Box, Machinist's, 5 Drawers, Open Upper Section, Carrying Handle, Gerstner 295.00
Brace, Brass Mounted, Pilkington, Pedigor & Storr 1300.00
Brace, Model 2528, Brass, G. Horton, 1850, 13 1/2 In. 1400.00
Brace, Ultimatum, Wm. Marples & Sons, Boxwood, 1854 .... 4000.00
Brace, Undertaker's, Folding, Screwdriver Bit, Rosewood Head, 10 In. 750.00
Branding Iron, Sheep, Letter W, Iron, 18th Century, 14 In. 40.00
Brush, Horse, US Cavalry, Marked 125.00
Cage, Cricket, Wire & Wood, 6 x 6 1/2 In. 95.00
Caliper, Brass Legs, 4 3/8 In. 235.00
Caliper, Cord Wood, Brass Corner Bracing, 10-Spoked Weighted Wheel, 42 1/2 In. 1600.00
Caliper, Iron Legs, 3 3/4 In. 160.00
Caliper, Iron Legs, A.Y. Boyd, 6 3/4 In. 165.00
Caliper, Iron Legs, J. Eastman, 7 In. 495.00
Caliper, Leg Shape, Women's Clothes Top, Brass, 10 In. 375.00
Caliper, Outside, Starrett, No. 38, 12 In. 15.00
Caliper Rule, Lufkin, No. 171, 6 In. 25.00
Caliper Rule, Stanley, No. 36, 6 In. 30.00
Candle Snuffer, Steel, England, c.1860, 8 In. 95.00
Carpenter's Chest, Cherry, Interior Tray & Saw Holder, 12 x 28 3/4 In. 220.00
Carrier, Log, Splint 75.00
Chest, Machinist, Oak 185.00
Chest, Stanley, Liberal Education, Pleasure & Profit In Set Of Tools, 4 x 25 In. 95.00
Chest, Walnut, Single Wide Boards, Paneled Lid, Dovetailed, Refinished, 49 1/2 In. 440.00
Chisel, Socket, Winchester, No. 4705, 3/4 In. 45.00

Cleaver, Butcher's	75.00
Clothes Brush, G-Man, Wooden, Black, Decal	85.00
Coin Detector, Counterfeit, Gold-Silver, Pat. 1877	185.00
Comb, Graining, Steel, Case, 19th Century, 5 1/2 In., Pair	225.00
Curling Iron, Heater, Alligator Base	175.00
Cutter, Groove, Stanley, 1901	65.00
Dibber, Garden, 1 Carved, 1 Turned, 18th Century, Pair	145.00
Dibber, Garden, Wooden, Early 19th Century, 16 1/2 In.	95.00
Drafting Set, Leroy, Dovetailed Wooden Box	50.00
Drill, Archemedian, A.H. Reid	50.00
Drill, Bow, George Buck Of London, Ebony & Brass, 10 1/2 In.	200.00
Drill, Bow, Octagonal Handle, Rosewood, Brass & Ivory, 13 In.	325.00
Drill, Chain, Goodell-Pratt, With Chain	20.00
Drilling Machine, N. Dramer, Silver, Wooden, Ivory	245.00
Dryer, Candle, Walnut	85.00
Farrier's, Wrought Iron Handle Shape Of Horse's Hoof	395.00
Flashlight, Bell System, 1896	40.00
Flashlight, Winchester, 1926	50.00
Flashlight, Winchester, 6 Cell, 14 1/2 In.	45.00
Floor Mat, Steel, Heart Shaped Segments, Rolls Up, 17 3/4 x 30 In.	302.50
Foot Rest, Shoeshine, Brass, Pair, 16 In.	110.00
Gauge, Butt, Stanley, No. 95	10.00
Gauge, Butt, Stearns, Nickel, No. 2 1/2 In.	10.00
Gauge, Measures Rhinestones	8.00
Gauge Bit, Stanley, No. 49, Original Box, 1940	55.00
Glove Form, Curtin-Herbet, With Heater, 34 1/2 In.	11.00
Gunpowder Tester, Iron, Blacksmith-Made, Late 17th Century, 9 1/2 In.	875.00
Hammer, Wrap-Around, Solomon S. Anderson, New Berlin, N.Y., Patented 1845, 11 In.	695.00
Handcuffs, American Munitions	100.00
Handcuffs, Crockett & Kelley	175.00
Handcuffs, Peerless	100.00
Handcuffs, Smith & Wesson, Box	145.00
Hat Blocking, Form, Stetson Style, c.1875	325.00
Hatchet, Claw, 4 In.	20.00
Hatchet, Stanley, No. 59-122, With Label, 14 In.	35.00
Hay Rake, Horse-Drawn, Red Paint, Salesman Sample, 19th Century, 18 In.	985.00
Hobble, Small Animal, Chain, Carved Wooden Cuffs, Leather Keepers, 18th Century	295.00
Hoe & Pitchfork, Iron, Blacksmith-Made, Wooden Handle, 18th Century, Pair	195.00
Holder, Yarn, Spherical Container, Turned Base	82.00
Iron, Curling, Mustache, Sterling Silver	65.00
Iron, Hat, McDonald, Rotary, Chrome Plated, Box, 10 In.	230.00
Jack, Conestoga Wagon, 1806, 21-In. Block	165.00
Jig, Dowel, Stanley, No. 59, Box	55.00
Lawn Mower, Cast Iron, Salmon Paint, Charter Oak Manufacturing Co., 1875, 58 In.	1395.00
Lawn Mower, Maytag	800.00
Lawn Mower, Savage, Push-Type	185.00
Lawn Mower, Sears Craftsman, 2 Cycles	150.00
Letter Sealing Wax Set, Dennison, Brass Lamp, Tools & Wax Assortment, Box	195.00
Level, 2 Sighting Posts, Japanned Finish, Brass Top Plate, A.E. Hyde, 18th Century	175.00
Level, Brass Plated, Disston, 26 In.	40.00
Level, Broad Tipped, Diss & Morse, 28 In.	50.00
Level, H.M. Pool, With Eagle, 24 In.	75.00
Level, Stanley, Brass, Wood, 1908, 27 In.	26.00
Level, Stanley, No. 01, Wooden, 1900, 28 In.	35.00
Level, Stanley, No. 3, 28 In.	35.00
Level, Stanley, No. 96, Rosewood, Brass Bound	150.00
Level, Stratton, B.B. Rose, With Eagle, 28 In.	195.00
Level, Stratton, Dandy, Wooden, 12 In.	40.00
Loom, Weaver's, Floor Stand, Mahogany, Adjustable Angle, 20th Century	247.00
Loop, Jeweler's, Leather Case, 10x	10.00
Malt Fork, England, 1820	495.00
Manicure Set, Painted Celluloid Flip-Top Container, 4 Tools, Germany, 1 x 2 1/2 In.	35.00
Miner's Cap, Canvas, Reflector, Brass Buy's Dropper Carbide Light	50.00

Miter Saw Box, Keen Kutter 300.0

Mold, Horse Collars, Harris Saddlery Co., Illinois, Oak 720.0

Mold, Plaster, Eagle, Bundled Arrows, Wooden Frame, 7 x 12 In. 465.0

Monkey Wrench, Ford, Script 10.0

Monkey Wrench, Wooden Grips, Coss Co., 12 In. 35.0

Nail Puller, Keen Kutter 15.0

Niddy Noddy, Hardwood, Relief Carved, Martin, 1806, 9 3/4 In. & 18 In., Pair 248.0

Padlock, Brass, Iron, Horseshoe Shape Shank, Signed Segal, Key, 5 In. 65.0

Pattern, Foundry, Eagle, Montalto On Base, Wooden, Black Paint, 13 1/4 In. 300.0

Pinchers, Blacksmith's, Keen Kutter, 16 In. 45.0

Pipe Tongs, Brass, Scalloped Design, 1750 .... 295.0

Pipe Tongs, Leg Shape, England, 18th Century, 6 3/4 In. 295.0

Pipe Tongs, Scissors, Blacksmith-Made, 10 1/2 In. 115.0

Pitchfork, Iron, Early 18th Century 195.0

Plane, Beader, Hand, Stanley, No. 66 .... 88.0

Plane, Bedrock, No. 606, Stanley 145.0

Plane, Belt Maker's, Stanley, No.11, 1907 .... 125.0

Plane, Blind Nail, Stranahan's Patent, July 20, 1886 .... 400.0

Plane, Block, Stanley, Low Angle 58.0

Plane, Block, Stanley, No. 15, 1890, 7 In. 100.0

Plane, Block, Stanley, No. 9 1/2, Lateral Adjustment Lever, 1930 .... 30.0

Plane, Block, Union, Knuckle-Joint 65.0

Plane, Bottom, Union, No. 22, Wooden 45.0

Plane, Carriage Maker's Rabbet, Stanley, No. 10, 1/2 In. 250.0

Plane, Chamfer, Bull-Nose Attachment, Stanley, No. 72 1/2, Box, 6 Cutters 850.0

Plane, Circular, Cooper's, Stanley, No. 113, Pistol Grip Handle 62.0

Plane, Circular, Stanley, No. 20 1/2, Japanned 160.0

Plane, Circular, Stanley, No. 20, c.1910 .... 175.0

Plane, Combination, Stanley, No. 45, Tin Box, Set Of Blades 225.0

Plane, Combination, Stanley, No. 50, 13 Cutters, Box 95.0

Plane, Combination, Stanley, No. 55 .... 475.0

Plane, Cutter, Set Of Blades, Tin Box 225.0

Plane, Dado, Stanley, No. 39 .... 96.0

Plane, Dado, Stanley, No. 39-1/2 .... 105.0

Plane, Double End Block, Stanley, No. 130, New In Box 125.0

Plane, Fibre Board Beveler, Stanley, No. 194 .... 75.00 to 110.0

Plane, Floor, Stanley, No. 74, c.1900 .... 295.0

Plane, Gage Jack, Stanley, No. G-5, 1920 .... 90.0

Plane, Gage Smooth, Stanley, No. G-4 .... 225.0

Plane, Jointer, Stanley, No. 7, 1st Model 65.0

Plane, Jointer, Stanley, No. 7, Box, 1950s 85.0

Plane, Jointer, Stanley, No. 7c, 22 In. 90.0

Plane, Jointer, Stanley, No.7, Type 6, 1888-1890 .... 35.0

Plane, Junior Jack, Stanley, No. 5-1/4 .... 80.0

Plane, Match, Stanley, No. 148 .... 135.0

Plane, Molding, 2 Blades, Cherry 65.0

Plane, Plow, Rosewood Screw Arms, Ivory Tips, J.P. Millener 3500.0

Plane, Plow, Slide Arm, H. Chapin 90.0

Plane, Rabbet, Stanley, No. 289 .... 185.0

Plane, Router, Stanley, No. 71 1/2, Cutters & Fence 50.0

Plane, Router, Stanley, No. 72 1/2, Type 4 .... 45.0

Plane, Scraper, Cabinet Maker's, Stanley, No. 87 .... 1400.0

Plane, Scraper, Cabinet, Stanley, No. 112 .... 145.00 to 185.0

Plane, Scrub, Stanley, No. 40, c.1898 .... 65.0

Plane, Scrub, Stanley, No. 40, c.1907 .... 95.0

Plane, Smooth, Stanley, No. 1, c.1907 .... 850.0

Plane, Smooth, Stanley, No. 21, Wooden Bottom, c.1900 .... 195.0

Plane, Smooth, Stanley, No. 4c, Type 9, 10 In. 40.0

Plane, Smoothing, Norris, A5 .... 695.0

Plane, Spiers, 8 In. 185.0

Propeller, From Taylor Cub, Wooden, 1940, 60 In. 675.0

Protractor, Stanley, Diamond Form Plate On Lid, Hinged Oak Box, c.1890, 5 1/2 In. 35.0

Punch Nail 27.0

Rake, Garden, Blacksmith-Made Iron, 10 Tines, 18th Century 295.00
Rake, Hay, Wooden 137.00
Reel, Hose, Marked O.K. No. 1 .... 50.00
Rod, Surveyor's Numbered, Brass Plate, Black Numbers, Points, Red Zero, 81 x 2 In. ... 29.00
Rope, Horsehair, Yuma Prison, 24 Ft. 295.00
Rule, Corrugated, Stanley, No. 2, c.1900 .... 520.00
Rule, Lufkin, No. 38LD, Brass Bound, Arch Joint, 24 In. 45.00
Rule, Stanley, No. 54, Arch Joint 60.00
Rule, Stephens, No. 46, Arch Joint 45.00
Rule, Zigzag, Stanley, No. 2 .... 425.00
Saw, Keyhole, Winchester 225.00
Saw, Panel, Henry Disston & Son, Clean Stamp 75.00
Saw, Treadle, Pinstriping, Barnes 950.00
Scissors, Cigar, Engraved 12K Gold 225.00
Scoop, Cranberry, Steel Tines, Root Handle, Dark Varnished Finish, 16 In. 275.00
Scorp, Treen Worker's, Iron, Blacksmith-Made, JHT, Mid-18th Century 350.00
Scraper, Beer, Whale Bone 75.00
Scraper, Pull, Holt Mfg. Co., Brass, Red Paint Traces 175.00
Scraper, Veneer, Stanley, No. 12, Marked Blade 60.00
Sharpening, Walnut Case, Mid-18th Century 185.00
Sharpening Stone, Coffin Shape, Wood Encased, Handle, America, 18th Century 150.00
Shoehorn, Brass, Closed & Seamed Handle, c.1750, Pair 145.00
Slitter, Leather, Pistol Handle, Osborne & Co. 60.00
Spokeshave, Stanley, No. 151 .... 30.00
Stand, Shoe, Cobbler's, Sears Roebuck, Cast Iron, c.1935 .... 25.00
Steam Iron, Tailor's, 2 Crows Eating Corn Handle, Pat. Sept. 9, '73, 10 1/4 In. 690.00
Steel Tape, Keuffel & Esser, 50 Ft. 35.00
Stick, Laundry 75.00
Stool, Shoeshine, Victorian, Fitted 55.00
Stretcher, Glove, Gold Monogram 50.00
Tape Loom, Heart Cutout On End, Dry Red Paint, Carved Initials M.A.G., 1835 .... 795.00
Tester, Cheese, Whitesmithed Iron, English, 18th Century 110.00
Trammel, 3 Prong Hook, Wrought Iron, 24 1/4 In. 210.00
Trimmer, Wick, Steel, W.B. Barnard, 1864, 6 In. 135.00
Trolley, Rope, Pegged Construction, Square Nails, 2 Ft. 250.00
Work Bench, Maple, Vise, Brass Rules, 3 Drawers, Paneled Door, 20 x 50 x 32 In. 660.00
Wrench, Pipe, Winchester, No. 1001 .... 65.00
Wrench, Screw Adjust Nut, Twist Handle, 21 In. 150.00
Yoke, Human, Wooden 110.00

TOOTHPICK HOLDERS are sometimes called *toothpicks* by collectors.
The variously shaped containers used to hold small wooden toothpicks
are made of glass, china, or metal. Most of the toothpick holders are
Victorian. Additional items may be found in other categories, such as
Bisque, Silver Plate, Slag Glass, etc.

Baby Owl, Milk Glass 48.00
Barrel, Souvenir, Shrine, Niagara Falls, 1905 .... 210.00
Bead Swag, Ruby Stained 60.00
Boot, Green, Glass 22.00
Daisy & Button, Amber 25.00
De Laval Cream Separator Co., Wall Hanging, Double 110.00
Dogs, With Cat Cornered In Doghouse, Porcelain 55.00
Fig Shape, Enameled Floral Sprays, Opaque Satin, Mt. Washington, 1 3/4 In. 742.00
Hand, Holding Ribbed Vase, Milk Glass 38.00
Hat, Uncle Sam's, Glass 50.00
Indian, Lemon Custard Glass, 2 In. 25.00
Inverted Strawberry, Aqua, Opalescent, Near Cut 45.00
Inverted Thumbprint, Blue, Tricornered 550.00
Iris With Meander, Amethyst 50.00
Iris With Meander, Blue Opalescent ....125.00 to 200.00
Jeweled, Heart, Amethyst 42.00
Just Out, Chick With Egg, Porcelain, 3 1/2 In. 22.00
Medallion Sunburst 35.00

Orinda	20.00
Plain Scalloped Panel, Green, Gold Trim	25.00
Pleat & Bow, Frosted With Flowers	55.00
Ribbed Spiral, White Opalescent	45.00
Scalloped Swirl, Ruby	60.00
Sprinkling Can, Glass	65.00
St. Clair Indian, Signed	45.00
Sunbeam	30.00
USA Bicentennial, Red Glass, Gold Letters	18.00
Vermont, Green Trim	95.00
Woodpecker, Sitting On Hollow Log, Gold Finish, Iron, 4 In.	44.00
Yellow & Pink Floral, Mt. Washington	695.00

TORQUAY is the name given to ceramics by several potteries working near Torquay, England, from 1870 until 1962. Until about 1900, the potteries used local red clay to make classical-style art pottery vases and figurines. Then they turned to making souvenir wares. Items were dipped in colored slip and decorated with painted slip and sgraffito designs. They often had mottoes or proverbs, and scenes of cottages, ships, birds, or flowers. The *Scandy* design was a symmetrical arrangement of brushstrokes and spots done in colored slips. Potteries included Watcombe Pottery (1870–1962); Torquay Terra-Cotta Company (1875–1905); Aller Vale (1881–1924); Torquay Pottery (1908–1940); and Longpark (1883–1957).

TORQUAY

Ashtray, Motto Ware, Better To Smoke Here Than Hereafter	30.00
Ashtray, Motto Ware, Who Burnt The Tablecloth?	30.00
Bowl, Diving Kingfisher, Pedestal, 4 In.	60.00
Bowl, Stylized Leaves Outside, Cream Inside, Blue Ground, 3 x 4 In.	75.00
Candleholder, Motto Ware, A Safe Conscience Makes A Sound Sleep	120.00
Chamberstick, Motto Ware, Last In Bed Put Out The Light	125.00
Cheese Dish, Cover, Cottage, Motto Ware, Dartmouth	60.00
Condiment Set, Cottage, 3 Piece	125.00
Console, Pink, 15 1/2 In.	125.00
Cup & Saucer, Carriageware, Shamrocks, Child's	35.00
Cup & Saucer, Cottage, 4-Line Verse On Back, 4 1/2 In.	145.00
Cup & Saucer, Dartmouth, Shamrocks, Child's, 2 In.	45.00
Cup & Saucer, Devon Cottage, Dartmouth, Child's, 2 In.	55.00
Dish, Yellow Flowers On Dark Green, 5 1/2 In.	65.00
Hatpin Holder, Keep Me On The Dressing Table, Marked, Longpark, 5 In.	60.00
Mustard, Cover, Cottage, 4 In.	95.00
Pitcher, Motto Ware, Guid Volks Be Scarce, 5 1/2 In.	95.00
Plate, Cottage, Motto Ware, Dartmouth, 10 In.	60.00 to 65.00
Plate, Sailing Ship, 10 In.	37.00
Teapot, Kingfisher, Large	140.00
Vase, Daffodil, 3 Handles, 8 In.	140.00
Vase, Kingfisher, Dark Blue, 10 In.	245.00
Vase, Sailboat, Watcombe, 3 1/4 In.	45.00
Vase, Tintern Abbey, Longpark, 6 In.	395.00

TORTOISESHELL is the shell of the tortoise. It has been used as inlay and to make small decorative objects since the seventeenth century. Some species of tortoise are now on the endangered species list, and old or new objects made from these shells cannot be sold legally.

Box, Circular, Figure By A Riverscape, Ivory, France, Late 19th Century, 3 In.	489.00
Box, Hinged Cover, Silver Inlaid, Ivory Bands, Light Blue Silk, 8 7/8 In.	2300.00
Box, People Salvaging A Wrecked Schooner, Continental, 18th Century, 4 In.	1380.00
Comb, Folding, Carved, Indian With Headdress, 18th Century	4025.00
Needle Case, 1 3/4 x 1 1/8 In.	365.00
Tea Caddy, Blond, 2 Covered Interior Compartments, 19th Century, 8 In.	862.00
Tea Caddy, Hinged Lid, Sarcophagus Form, Ivory, Bun Feet, Regency, 8 In.	2300.00
Tea Caddy, Rectangular Form, Silver Metal, Ivory, Bun Feet, Victorian, 5 3/4 In.	1725.00
Tea Caddy, Regency, Cushion Shape, 2 Interior Lidded Compartments, 8 In.	1265.00
Tea Caddy, Regency, Sarcophagus Shape, 2 Lidded Wells, 12 1/4 In.	1265.00

ORTOISESHELL GLASS was made during the 1800s and after by the andwich Glass Works of Massachusetts and some firms in Germany. ortoiseshell glass is, of course, named for its resemblance to real shell rom a tortoise. It has been reproduced.

Bowl, Oxblood Spatter, Amber Feet, 5 x 8 In. 135.00
Jar, Amber Stem On Cover, Apple Shape, Mottled, 7 1/4 In. 95.00
Vase, Pontil, Footed, France, 19th Century, 10 1/2 In. 181.00

OY collectors have special clubs, magazines, and shows. Toys are lesigned to entice children, and today they have attracted new interest mong adults who are still children at heart. All types of toys are col- ected. Tin toys, iron toys, battery operated toys, and many others are ollected by specialists. Dolls, Games, Teddy Bears, and Bicycles are isted in their own categories. Other toys may be found under company or celebrity names.

6 Million Dollar Man & Repair Station, Kenner 100.00
Accordion, Plastic, Emenee, Box .... .25.00 to 35.00
Acrobat, Whimsical, Hand Painted, Germany, 19th Century, 5 In. 60.00
Acrobat, Wood Acrobats Fit Together, Crandall, Box, Patented 1867, 9 x 5 In. 700.00
Airplane, Air Force Fighter, Sparking, 10 In. 165.00
Airplane, Air Mail, Rapid-Fire Motor, Pressed Steel, Keystone, c.1935, 24 x 24 In. 1320.00
Airplane, Airforce, Tin Lithograph, Japan, Box 45.00
Airplane, American Airlines, Flagship, Pressed Steel, 4 Propellers, 27-In. Wingspan 500.00
Airplane, American Eagle, Die Cast, Hubley, Box, 1971, 10 In. 82.00
Airplane, Autogyro, Die Cast, White, Blue Propeller, Tootsietoy, 1930s, 4 1/4 In. 150.00
Airplane, Biplane, Gas Engine, Lime Green, Cox, 8 1/2 In., 10-In. Wingspan 20.00
Airplane, Bomber, U.S. Navy, Blue & Silver, Tootsietoy 195.00
Airplane, Caledonian Airlines, Travel Agent's Model, 10-In. Wingspan 45.00
Airplane, Carousel, Windup, Battery Operated, Landing Lights, Tin Lithograph, 12 In. .. 1325.00
Airplane, Cessna, Sky Taxi, Friction, Tin, Japan, Box, 1960s, 10 1/2 In. 175.00
Airplane, Cessna, Skymaster, Box, 11 1/2 In. 650.00
Airplane, Challenger, Plastic, Bomb, Gas Engine, AMF Wen-Mac, Box, 12 1/2 In. 100.00
Airplane, Cream, Red, 13-In. Wingspan 475.00
Airplane, Dagwood's Solo Flight, Windup, Tin Lithograph, Celluloid Propeller, Marx ... 660.00
Airplane, Fighter, Red, Hubley, 12-In. Wingspan 120.00
Airplane, Flying Racer, Super Springmaster, Silver & Red, 43-In. Wingspan 29.00
Airplane, Hawker Hurricane, No. 11, Die Cast, Propeller, Londontoy, Canada, 4 1/2 In. ... 52.00
Airplane, Jet Fighter, Tin, Box, 1950s 95.00
Airplane, Jet, Fighter, Sparking, Friction, Tin, Cragstan, Japan, Box, 1950s, 8 In. 167.00
Airplane, Knight Fighter, Friction, Tin Lithograph, Japan 90.00
Airplane, Lindy, Cast Iron, Arcade, 4 In. 173.00
Airplane, Loop The Loop, Silver, Marx 425.00
Airplane, Loop The Loop, Windup, Tin, Occupied Japan, Box 315.00
Airplane, Mail, Die Cast, Tan, Rotating Propeller, Tootsietoy 55.00
Airplane, Monoplane, Open Cockpit, Spiral Around Pylon, Gunthermann 2200.00
Airplane, Navy Fighter, Die Cast Metal, Hubley, Box, 1950s, 6 1/2 In. 152.00
Airplane, P-38 Fighter, Sealed Box, Hubley 475.00
Airplane, P-51, Gas Powered, Testor's, Box, 13 1/2-In. Wingspan 25.00
Airplane, Pan American, DC-6, Stamped Metal, Wood Wheels, Marx, 27 1/2 In. 57.00
Airplane, Pan American, DC-7, Handle Activates Props, 1950s 350.00
Airplane, Patrol, Friction, Tin, Plastic Propeller, Japan, Box, 1950s, 12 1/2 In. 75.00
Airplane, PF-256, Sparking, Friction, Tin, Yone, Box, 1960s, 7 1/2 In. 95.00
Airplane, Red & White, Remote Control, 6-In. Wingspan 595.00
Airplane, Red Fuselage, Blue Wings, Wood Wheels, Wyandotte 185.00
Airplane, Rubber, Stahlwood, Box 325.00
Airplane, Seaboard World Airlines, 4 Propellers, Battery Operated, Tin 325.00
Airplane, Seaplane, 6-Engine, Marcus & Co., 1935 .... 890.00
Airplane, Seaplane, Battery Operated, Remco, Box, 12-In. Wingspan 360.00
Airplane, Silver, Red Wings, Metal, Rubber Wheels, Hubley, 7 1/2 In. 40.00
Airplane, Sky Skipper, Die Cast Metal, Gabriel, Box, 1977, 9 In. 85.00
Airplane, Spirit Of St. Louis, Marklin, 22 In. 750.00
Airplane, Trans-Canada Airlines, Friction, Tin, 15 1/2-In. Wingspan 275.00

Toy, Bear, Papa, Smoking, Battery Operated,
San, Japan, 1950s, 8 In.

Toy, Bed, Doll's, Pine, Yellow Paint, 19th
Century, 12 x 9 1/2 x 10 In.

Airplane, Tri-Motor, Turner, 24-In. Wingspan, 29 In. 995.00
Airplane, Twin Jet, Friction, Molded Plastic, Marx, Box, 6 In. 46.00
Airplane, U.S. Army, Monoplane, Die Cast, Blue, Rubber Tires, Barclay, 1930s, 3 x 4 In. 63.00
Airplane, U.S. Mail, Electric Lights, Steelcraft 575.00
Airplane, White, Doug Corrigan, 1940s, 13 In. 265.00
Airplane, Windup, Red, Yellow Wings, Tin, Marx, 5 x 6 In. 109.00
Airplane, Windup, Wilson, 10-In. Wingspan 25.00
Airplane, Windup, Yellow, Red, Blue, Tin, 9 In., Pair 225.00
Airplane, World War II, British R.A.F., Windup, Tin, England, 1940s, 10 x 8 1/2 In. 229.00
Airplane, World War II, Russian, Black Rubber 35.00
Airplane, Yanozawa Comet, Box 1200.00
Airport, Nonstop Action, Windup, Ohio Art 285.00
Alabama Coon Jigger, Windup, Tin, Lehmann, 10 In. 467.00
Alligator, Allie, Windup, Steiff, 14 In. 220.00
Alligator, Painted Eyes, Leather Feet, Schoenhut, 12 In. 230.00
Alligator With Black Man, Windup, Chein 185.00
Ambulance, Ford 3 Ton 4x4, No. 63, Lesney, Matchbox, 1959 .... 37.00
Ambulance, Red Cross, White Top, Black Wheels, Driver, Germany, 11 In. 750.00
Ambulance, Rescue, Tonka, 9 In. 125.00
Andy Brown, Sparks Through Glass Eyes, Germany, 1930s, 7 In. 760.00
Archery Set, Glassflex, Instructions 50.00
Armoire, Doll's, Wood, Curved Cornice, Ormolu, France, c.1880, 20 In. 1300.00
Astronaut, Red, Cragstan, 10 In. 275.00
Baby, Crawling, Windup, Celluloid, White Clothes, Polka Dots, Box, 1960s, 3 x 4 1/4 In. 40.00
Badge, Sheriff, Wyatt Earp 30.00
Badge, Wyatt Earp, Sheriff, 1957 .... 25.00
Ballerina, Lever Action, Marx, 1930s 175.00
Banjo, Tin Lithograph, Germany, 17 In. 99.00
Barnacle Bill, Windup, Chein 375.00
Bath Set, Doll's, Kilgore, 4 Piece 135.00
Bears are also listed in the Teddy Bears category.
Bear, Chews, Rotates, Raises & Lowers Drinking Cup, Windup 150.00
Bear, Circus, Gold Mohair, Amber Glass Eyes, Red Harness, 10 In. 110.00
Bear, Cleans Glasses, Windup, Tin, Plush, 6 1/2 In. 100.00
Bear, Drummer, Plush, Key Wind, Alps, Japan, Box, 8 In. 135.00
Bear, Head & Paws Move, Windup, Real Fur, Ives, 1890s 350.00
Bear, Jolly Guitarist, Windup, Plush Bear, Tin, TN, Japan, Box, 1950s, 8 3/4 In. 179.00
Bear, Jumping Rope, Windup, Tin Lithograph, Metal Rope, TN, Japan, 5 1/2 In. 101.00
Bear, Mama Bear Feeding Baby, Battery Operated, Japan, 9 1/2 In. 200.00
Bear, Mama, Vacuuming, Battery Operated, 7 1/2 In. 210.00
Bear, Mohair, Wheeled Base, Brown, Leather Collar, Shoebutton Eyes, 1920, 12 In. 290.00
Bear, Mohair, Wheeled Base, Light Brown, Squawk Box, c.1930, 12 x 28 x 21 In. 357.00
Bear, Papa, Smoking, Battery Operated, San, Japan, 1950s, 8 In. ....*Illus* 72.00
Bear, Riding, Brown Mohair, Steel Frame & Wheels, Steiff, 1920, 15 x 21 In. 345.00

Bear, Riding, Growler, Mounted On 4 Wheels, Steiff, 26 x 38 In. 660.00
Bear, Riding, Tricycle, Windup, Mohair Head, Glass Eyes, Flannel Clothes, 6 3/4 In. 460.00
Bear, Sneezes, Holds Tissue Box, Battery Operated, Linemar, 1950 .... 285.00
Bear, Telephone, Battery Operated, Linemar 255.00
Bear, Walking, Key Wind, Japan, Box 125.00
Bear, Walking, Windup, Chein, 4 1/2 In. 100.00
Bear, Walking, Windup, Modern Toys, Japan, Box, 4 x 3 1/2 x 2 In. 72.00
Beaver, Button & Tag, Steiff, 9 In. 125.00
Bed, Doll's, 4-Poster, Rope Mattress, Pillow, Walnut, 9 1/2 In. 135.00
Bed, Doll's, Brass, 4 Poster, Pillow & Mattress, Bedspread, 17 x 12 x 11 In. 125.00
Bed, Doll's, Bunk, Maple, 13 x 27 In. 75.00
Bed, Doll's, Cannonball, Birch, Turned Posts, 17 1/4 x 26 1/2 In. 660.00
Bed, Doll's, Cannonball, Rope, Birch, Ticking Mattress, 12 x 19 In. 247.00
Bed, Doll's, Cast Iron, Filigree Design, 15 x 8 3/4 In. 82.00
Bed, Doll's, Painted White Enamel, Cast Iron, 19 x 21 In. 650.00
Bed, Doll's, Pegged & Nailed, Mattress Ticking & Bed Linens, 19 1/2 In. 295.00
Bed, Doll's, Pine, Yellow Paint, 19th Century, 12 x 9 1/2 x 10 In. ....*Illus* 2530.00
Bed, Doll's, Tester, Walnut, Carved Cornice & Legs, 21 1/2 In. 687.00
Bed, Doll's, Tin, Amsco, Pair 45.00
Bed, Doll's, Turned Posts, Yellow Paint, 12 In. 2530.00
Bed, Doll's, Wood, Mattress, Sheet, Patchwork Quilt, 19th Century, 16 x 11 x 14 In. 115.00
Bed, Doll's, Wrought Iron, Green Paint, 31 x 16 x 23 In. 99.00
Bell Ringer, Frog, Riding Turtle, Horsedrawn, Cast Iron, 1880s 250.00
Bell Ringer, Harold Lloyd, Tin, Plunger Action, Germany, 1920s 435.00
Bell Ringer, Little Nemo & Mr. Flip, Iron, 1880s 650.00
Bell Ringer, Loco-Trix, Pull Toy, Metal & Wood 150.00
Bell Ringer, Monkey, Hits Log With Coconut, 1890s 575.00
Bell Ringer, Monkey, Moves Up & Down Playing Drums, Tin, Dressed, 1900 .... 225.00
Bell Ringer, Patty Cake, Baker's Man, Pull Toy, Mechanical, Chad Valley, 12 In. 145.00
Bicycles are listed in their own category.
Bicycle, Joe Palooka, 5 In. 42.00
Bicycle, Kiddy Cyclist, Windup, Unique Art, 8 5/8 In. 176.00
Bird, Bellows, Chirps, Wheeled Platform, Germany, 1900 .... 385.00
Bird, Pecking, Flapping Wings, Yellow Body, Occupied Japan 165.00
Black Dancers, Clockwork, Wood Platform, Ives 1540.00
Blender, Suzy Homemaker, Topper, Box 55.00
Blimp, Texaco, Limited Edition, Die Cast 60.00
Blocks, Building, Wood Lithograph, Animals, McLoughlin, 1880 .... 495.00
Blocks, Wood, Wooden Box, Label, Early 19th Century 135.00
Boat, Aircraft Carrier, Battery Operated, Linemar, Box 275.00
Boat, Arkansas Traveler, Aluminum, 17 In. 300.00
Boat, Battleship, Converts To Ocean Liner, Friction, Tin Lithograph, Japan, 12 In. 123.00
Boat, Cabin Cruiser, Red Bottom, 31 In. 2670.00
Boat, Cabin Cruiser, Tin Lithograph, Chein, Box, 15 In. 275.00
Boat, Convoy, Plastic, 3 Ships, 1 Submarine, Original Bag, Display Card, 6 1/2 x 10 In. .. 29.00
Boat, Cruiser, Miss Sakura, Battery Operated, 21 1/2 In. 675.00
Boat, Destroyer, Battery Operated, Wood, Japan, 33 In. 385.00
Boat, Dreadnought, Pull Toy, Wood, c.1930, 14 In. 85.00
Boat, Ferry, Sandy Andy, Tin, Red, Yellow, 5 x 4 x 13 In. 161.00
Boat, Gunboat, Friction, Pressed Steel, Schieble, c.1914, 10 In. 220.00
Boat, Gunboat, Steam, Bassett Lowke, 26 In. 2850.00
Boat, Marcella, Pressed Steel, Green, Gray, Orkin, Boston, 1920s, 18 1/2 In. 460.00
Boat, Navy M-205 Missile, Windup, Tin Lithograph, Plastic Propeller, Japan, 9 1/2 In. .. 90.00
Boat, Ocean Liner, 2 Lifeboats, Copper Hull, White Deck, Black Trim, Ives, 13 In. 288.00
Boat, Ocean Liner, Clockwork, Gray, White Copper Stacks, 18 In. 287.00
Boat, Ocean Liner, Windup, Caretta, 1915, 17 In. 6500.00
Boat, Pacific Sidewheeler, Tinplate, Hand Painted, 1880s 1980.00
Boat, PT-107, Remote Control, Tin Lithograph, Linemar, Japan, 11 In. 115.00
Boat, Racing, No. 43, Key Wind, Stand, Directions, Lionel, 1939, 18 In. 357.00
Boat, River, Windup, Wood & Brass, Tin Lithograph Figures, Liberty Toys, 1920s 1650.00
Boat, Sailboat, Red, White, Tin, Columbia, 21 In. 230.00
Boat, Scullers, 4 Crew Rowers & Coxwain, Pull Toy, Cast Iron, 10 In. 935.00
Boat, Side-Wheeler, Providence, Reed, Wood, Lithograph, Late 19th Century, 20 In. 690.00

Boat, Side-Wheeler, Wilkins Puritan, Cast Iron, Painted, 1900, 11 In. 430.0
Boat, Speedboat, Clockwork, Key Inside, Lionel-Craft, 1930s, 16 3/4 In. 287.0
Boat, Speedboat, Sea Queen, 1950s 95.0
Boat, Speedboat, Windup, Lindstrom Tool & Toy Co., 20 1/2 In. 275.0
Boat, Steamboat, Friction, Tin Lithograph, Heiss, c.1910, 6 3/4 In. 90.0
Boat, Texaco Tanker, Plastic 135.0
Boat, Tugboat, Radio Controlled 350.0
Boat, Tugboat, Shamrock, Brass, 11 In. 600.0
Boat, Tugboat, Wooden, Painted, 40 x 24 In. 3300.0
Boat, Windup, Wood, Adjustable Centerboard, Tin Outboard Motor, c.1930, 23 In. 200.0
Bonanza, Hoss Cartwright, Spurs, 10-Gallon Hat, American Character, Box, 1966, 8 In. . 80.0
Boxers, Knockout Champs, Windup, Marx, Box 750.0
Boxers, Windup, Black, Wheeled Platform, Celluloid, 1930s 265.0
Boxing Gloves, Sears & Roebuck, Box, c.1939 . . . . 300.0
Boy, Highchair, Penny Toy, Tin Lithograph, Bottom Platform Flips Up 145.0
Boy, Raising Hat, Pip-Squeak, Wood & Wire Body, Red Suit, Germany, 14 1/4 In. 1700.0
Brooklyn Bum, Pip-Squeak 175.0
Buffet, Doll's, Antique Ivory, Hand Painted Floral Sprays, Mirror, 1 Drawer, 2 Doors . . . 235.0
Bull, Bubbling, Bucks & Blows Bubbles, Battery Operated, Japan, Box, 1950s 300.0
Bull, Ferdinand, Tail Spins, Windup, Marx, c.1938, 4 x 4 In. 325.0
Bull Fighter, Sword, Windup, Wheeled Platform, Lithograph, Germany, 1920s 350.0
Bunny, Walking, Vibrates, Key Wind, Papier-Mache, Germany, 1925, 7 In. 225.0
Bunny, Wood Wheels, Brown, Stitched Ears & Tail, Black Bead Eyes, Steiff, 1919 . . . . . 600.0
Bureau, Doll's, Eastlake, Walnut, 5 Drawers, Mirror, 6 1/2 x 11 1/2 x 20 In. 220.0
Bus, Animals, Tin, Japan, 4 In. 30.0
Bus, Army Post Office, Military Mail, Friction, Tin Lithograph, Japan, 6 In. 52.00
Bus, Bowen Motor Coach, Arcade, 1936 . . . . 4000.0
Bus, Cast Iron, Painted, Blue, Nickel Plated Wheels, Arcade, 1920s, 4 5/8 In. 145.0
Bus, Century Of Progress, Cast Iron, 10 1/2 In. 195.0
Bus, Century Of Progress, Cast Iron, Arcade, 10 In. 425.0
Bus, Chicago Motor Coach, Art Deco Style, Arcade 1050.0
Bus, Continental Trailways, Friction, Tin Lithograph, Japan, 1960s, 6 1/2 In. 41.00
Bus, Double-Decker, Berlin, Tan, King Size, No. K-15, Matchbox, Box 57.00
Bus, Double-Decker, Cast Iron, Arcade, 8 In. 750.00
Bus, Double-Decker, Driver, 1933, Kenton, 10 In. 750.00
Bus, Double-Decker, Friction, Red, Minic Toys, England 375.00
Bus, Double-Decker, Horsedrawn, Colman's Mustard & Pear's Soap, Germany 2035.00
Bus, Double-Decker, Kenton, 6 1/2 In. 750.00
Bus, Double-Decker, London, Green, Cream, Rubber Tires 34.00
Bus, Double-Decker, Sticker, Arcade 375.00
Bus, Greyhound Lines, Windup, Tin Lithograph, J. Chein & Co., 6 In. 145.00
Bus, Greyhound, Die Cast, Rubber Tires, Painted, Tootsietoy, 1940s, 6 In. 29.00
Bus, Greyhound, Friction, Tin Lithograph, Japan, 1960s, Original Bag, 6 1/2 In. 41.00
Bus, Greyhound, Friction, Tin, Japan, 15 In. 165.00
Bus, Greyhound, White Bottom, Arcade, 1937 . . . . 500.00
Bus, Highway Express, Friction, Tin, TN, 1960s, 11 1/2 In. 45.00
Bus, Interstate, Strauss, Box, 10 1/2 In. 935.00
Bus, Orange, Cast Iron, Dent, 8 1/2 In. 700.00
Bus, Parlor Coach, Blue, Gold Stripe, Arcade, 13 In. 3400.00
Bus, Pickwick Nite Coach, Kenton, 11 In. 990.00
Bus, Routemaster, Corgi 20.00
Bus, Santa Fe Trailways, Nickeled Grill, Red & Beige Paint, Arcade 2300.00
Bus, School, Die Cast, Hubley, Box, 1960 . . . . 75.00
Bus, Shore Line Red Ball Express, Red, Yellow & Black, Upton, 12 In. 350.00
Bus, Touring, Tinplate, Lithograph, 6 Wheels, Jep, France, Early 1920s 1650.00
Bus, Trans-American, Red & Silver, Tootsietoy 195.00
Bus, Transport, Light Green, Buddy L, 28 In. 4000.00
Bus, Volkswagen, Friction, Tin, Red, Cream, Endoh, Japan, Box, 1950s, 6 In. 114.00
Bus, Windup, Tin, Wells Of London, 1940s, 6 In. 345.00
Buttercup, Windup, Crawler, Tin, Germany, Mid-1920s, 7 1/2 In. 260.00
Butterfly, Windup, Articulated Wings, Tin, Souvenir Of Chicago Theater, 2 1/8 In. 49.00
Cable Car, San Francisco, Friction, Tin Lithograph, Japan, 6 1/2 In. 100.00
Cable Car, San Francisco, Friction, Tin, Rubber & Plastic Tires, Japan, Box, 7 In. 155.00

Cable Car, Tin, Hand Painted, Steam Powered, Germany, 4 1/2 x 10 1/2 x 14 In. 300.00
Cable Car, Windup, Technoflex 330.00
Cage, 7 Sheep, Sheep Dog, Polychrome, Japan, 4 In., 8 Piece 250.00
Calliope, Barnum's, Pull Toy, Wheels, Chromolithograph, Wood, 31 In. 140.00
Calliope, Plays Piano Rolls, Coin Operated 4500.00
Camel, 1 Hump, Schoenhut 360.00
Camera, Yogi Bear, Hanna Barbera, Box 210.00
Camper & Boat, Sears, Structo, Box 275.00
Candy Store, Lollipop's Sweet Shop, Lithograph, Accessories, England, 14 In. 265.00
Cannon, Big Bang, Cast Iron & Sheet Steel, Army Green, Red Wheels, 24 In. 55.00
Cannon, Cast Iron, 1895, 5 In. 145.00
Cannon, Die Cast, Spring-Loaded Barrels, Britains, England, 4 x 1 3/4 x 1 3/4 In., Pair .. 44.00
Cap Gun, Agent Zero M, Camera Unfolds Into Gun, Plastic, Mattel, 1964, 7 In. 40.00
Cap Gun, Bango, Cast Iron 85.00
Cap Gun, Bronco 85.00
Cap Gun, Bulldog, Cast Iron, 4 3/4 In. 176.00
Cap Gun, Colt 45, Hubley 165.00
Cap Gun, Cowboy, Longhorn Grip 100.00
Cap Gun, Desert Patrol Luger, Silencer & Plastic Bullets 66.00
Cap Gun, Detective Special, Repeater, Metal, On Card, Roth American, 1950s-1960s ... 25.00
Cap Gun, Dragnet, Plastic, On Card, Webb Graphic, 1955 .... 50.00
Cap Gun, Dragnet, Snub Nose, Box 195.00
Cap Gun, G-Man, Plastic & Metal 195.00
Cap Gun, Gold Cylinder, 45 Cap, Hubley 195.00
Cap Gun, Lion, Cast Iron, Copper, c.1900 .... 75.00
Cap Gun, Lion, Hubley, 1880s 375.00
Cap Gun, Nigger Head, Cast Iron, Ives, 1887 .... 1200.00
Cap Gun, Rex Ranger, Repeating Rifle, Marx, Box 60.00
Cap Gun, Rick-O-Shay, Hubley ....125.00 to 135.00
Cap Gun, Secret Agent Hideaway, Hamilton, Box ....35.00 to 40.00
Cap Gun, Sniper, Plastic, 16-In. Barrel, Hubley, 1965, 22 In. 80.00
Cap Gun, Stallion, Nichols 45, Box ....145.00 to 350.00
Cap Gun, Strato Space, Chrome, Die Cast, 1950s, 8 In. 250.00
Cap Gun, Texan Jr., Hubley 40.00
Cap Gun, Texan Jr., Hubley, Box 150.00
Cap Gun, Texas, Star Grips, L. & H. 45.00
Cap Gun, Trooper, No. 240, Hubley, Box 100.00
Cap Gun, Trooper, Painted Grips, Hubley, 1960s 45.00
Car, 007 Secret Agent, Chevrolet, Battery Operated, Mystery Action, 14 In. 295.00
Car, Andy Gump, Tootsietoy 375.00
Car, Aston Martin, James Bond, Box, 11 In. 275.00
Car, Aston Martin, James Bond, Gold Plated, Corgi, 1960s 2556.00
Car, Berolina Convertible, Navy Blue, Red Trim, Cloth Top, Lehmann, 6 3/4 In. 1380.00
Car, Beverly Hillbillies, Ideal, Box 1195.00
Car, BMW MII, Corgi 44.00
Car, Buick, 1957 Model, Convertible, Windup, Bump & Go, Tin, Japan, 7 In. 210.00
Car, Buick, Convertible, Hubley 140.00
Car, Buick, Kojak Figure, Corgi 52.00
Car, Buick, Riviera, Corgi, Box 85.00
Car, Busy Lizzie, Windup, Tin, Lehmann, 6 3/4 In. 275.00
Car, Cadillac, Convertible, Tan, Dinky 85.00
Car, Cadillac, Convertible, Yellow, Dinky 85.00
Car, Cadillac, Die Cast Metal, Maroon Paint, Rubber Tires, Structo, 1950s, 6 1/2 In. 40.00
Car, Cadillac, Friction, Bandai, Box, 1959, 12 In. 595.00
Car, Camaro, 1967 Model, Friction, Tin, Japan, 1967, 13 1/2 In. 495.00
Car, Chevrolet, 1955 Model, Linemar, 11 In. 750.00
Car, Chevrolet, Convertible, Bandai, 10 In. 475.00
Car, Chevrolet, Convertible, Friction, Stamped Metal, Turquoise, 1963, 17 In. 402.00
Car, Chevrolet, Friction, Stamped Metal, Rubber Tires, 1963, 8 In. 98.00
Car, Chevrolet, Friction, Stamped Metal, Rubber Tires, Asahi Toy Co., 1955 .... 155.00
Car, Chevrolet, Impala SS, Friction, Stamped Metal, Red, Rubber Tires, 8 1/4 In. 99.00
Car, Chevrolet, Sedan, Friction, Stamped Metal, Linemar, Japan, 1953, 8 1/2 In. 168.00
Car, Chevrolet, Tin, Battery Operated, Linemar, 11 In. 2400.00

Car, Chitty Chitty Bang Bang, Corgi . . . . .170.00 to 185.0
Car, Chitty Chitty Bang Bang, Mattel, Box 95.0
Car, Chrysler, Windup, Dark Khaki-Brown, 4 Door, 4 x 5 x 16 In. 700.0
Car, Circus, Windup, Tin Lithograph, KO, Japan, 4 1/2 In. 300.0
Car, Clockwork, Lady Driver, Cast Iron & Pressed Steel, Wilkins 5400.0
Car, College Jalopy, Battery Operated, Tin, Linemar, Box 172.0
Car, Convertible, Rubber Tires, Cast Pot Metal, Faith Mfg. Co., 1930s, 10 1/2 In. 350.0
Car, Corvette, 1963 Model, White, Ichida, Box, 12 In. 1400.0
Car, Corvette, Battery Operated, Mystery Action, Tin, Red, Taiyo, Japan, 1968, 10 In. 100.0
Car, Cougar, Battery Operated, Mystery Action, Tin, Red, Taiyo, Japan, 1968, 10 In. 80.0
Car, Coupe, 1930s Model, Cast Iron, Williams 90.0
Car, Coupe, Airflow, Wyandotte 150.0
Car, Coupe, Art Deco Style, Marx, 1930s 130.0
Car, Coupe, Blue, Rumble Seat In Back, Nickel Wheels, Arcade, 5 x 2 In. 75.0
Car, Coupe, Dayton, Dark Blue Body, Silver Tires, 18 In. 225.00
Car, Coupe, Red Rumble Seat, Rubber Tires, Cast Iron, 6 1/2 In. 125.00
Car, Coupe, Red, Reversible, Marx 565.00
Car, Coupe, White Rubber Tires, Steel Wheels, Kingsbury, 1931, 13 In. 230.00
Car, Crash, Indian, 4 Cylinder, Driver, Decals, Hubley, 11 1/2 In. 5170.00
Car, Crash, Nickel Wheels, Molded Driver, Hubley, c.1930, 4 3/4 In. 445.00
Car, Crazy, College Jalopy, Marx, Box 695.00
Car, Crazy, Rodeo Joe, Windup, Tin Lithograph, Unique Art, 1930s, 7 In. 200.00
Car, DeSoto, Blue Cast-Iron Body, Chrome Grill, Rubber Tires, Arcade 50.00
Car, Dodge, Convertible, Female Driver, Friction, Tin, Plastic, Red, Japan, 7 1/2 In. 94.00
Car, Driver, Tut-Tut, Lehmann 850.00
Car, Electro-Mercedes, Convertible, White, Schuco, 1963 . . . . 900.00
Car, Ferrari, 1950s Model, Coupe, Blue, Japan, 5 1/2 In. 95.00
Car, Ferrari, Berlinetta Le Mans, Die Cast, Red, Corgi, 4 In. 20.00
Car, Ferrari, Hood Ornament, License Plate, Tin Lithograph, Bandai, 11 1/4 In. 315.00
Car, Fire Chief's, Hill Climber 895.00
Car, Fire Chief, Courtland 75.00
Car, Fire Chief, Electric Lights, Kingsbury 795.00
Car, Fire Chief, Pressed Steel, Metal Wheels, Red Enamel, 1930s, 15 In. 146.00
Car, Fire Chief, With Siren, Friction, Tin, Box, 1940-1950 . . . . 230.00
Car, Ford, 1934 Model, Cast Iron, Arcade 800.00
Car, Ford, 1934 Model, Sedan, 7 In. 400.00
Car, Ford, 1956 Model, Convertible, Red & White, Haji, 12 In. 3200.00
Car, Ford, Convertible, Green, Haji, 1950s, 7 In. 185.00
Car, Ford, Convertible, Japan, 1953, 9 In. 325.00
Car, Ford, Coupe, Arcade 325.00
Car, Ford, Firebird, Gold, 1968 . . . . 210.00
Car, Ford, Galaxie, 1960 Model, Blue & White, Taguchi Toy, 6 1/2 In. 185.00
Car, Ford, Model T, Cast Iron, Arcade, 5 In. 300.00
Car, Ford, Model T, Sedan, Cast Iron, Arcade, 5 In. 278.00
Car, Ford, Sedan, 4-Door, Canada, 1920s, 6 3/4 In. 250.00
Car, Ford, Station Wagon, Ambulance, 8 1/2 In. 360.00
Car, Ford, T-Bucket, Battery Operated, Box, 11 1/2 In. 450.00
Car, Futuristic, Friction, Plastic, Mattel, 1960s 75.00
Car, Golden Jubilee, Driver Shifts & Steers, Battery Operated, 9 1/2 In. 175.00
Car, Highway Patrol, Friction, Japan 85.00
Car, Highway Patrol, Marked Police Dept. No. 1, Friction, Tin Lithograph, 5 1/2 In. 24.00
Car, House Trailer, Friction, Tin Lithograph, Indianhead Logo, Japan, 1950s, 8 In. 54.00
Car, Jaguar, Red, Dinky Toy 165.00
Car, Jalopy, Windup, Tin, Marx, 8 In. 195.00
Car, La Salle, Wyandotte, 1930, 25 1/2 In. 695.00
Car, Lancia Fulvia Sport Zagato, Die Cast, Doors Open, Front Seats Fold, Corgi, 4 In. 50.00
Car, Limousine, Handbrake, Head Lamp, Key Wind, Tin Lithograph, c.1912, 10 In. 1150.00
Car, Limousine, Windup, Tin Lithograph, Red, Bing, Germany, 1910, 5 1/4 In. 690.00
Car, Lincoln, Blue, Green Body, 4-Door, Pressed Steel, 26 x 10 1/2 In. 2875.00
Car, Lotus Elan, Friction, Red & Black, Bandai, Box, 1960s, 8 In. 125.00
Car, Lotus, Die Cast, Green Paint, No. 19, Matchbox, Lesney, England, 2 3/4 In. 26.00
Car, Mercedes Benz, Friction, Blue, Tin, Japan, Box, 1960s, 7 1/2 In. 95.00
Car, Mercedes, With Hitler, Nazi Flag, Box, 1936 . . . . 75.00

Toy, Car, Racing, Key Wind, Tin, Marklin, Model
1107R, 15 In.

**Old metal toy trucks were made
of iron or tin, not brass or
aluminum, the metals favored
by some reproductions.**

Car, Mercedes-Benz 300, Windup, Chrome, Kolner, British Zone, Germany, 5 In.	75.00
Car, Mercedes-Benz 375, Tele-Magic, Plastic, Gama, W. Germany, Box, c.1960, 13 In.	91.00
Car, Mercedes-Benz, Red, Bandai, 8 In.	65.00
Car, Mercury, 4-Door, Friction, Stamped Tin, Red, White, Japan, 1960s, 6 In.	29.00
Car, Mercury, Station Wagon, Friction, Stamped Tin, Red, White, Japan, 1960s	46.00
Car, MGA Coupe, 1960s Model, 2-Tone Green, 10 In.	325.00
Car, Mighty Maverick, Die Cast, Metallic Green, Hot Wheels, 1969, 2 1/2 In.	24.00
Car, Military, Saladin Scout Car, Die Cast, Crescent, Box, 1950s, 4 1/2 In.	35.00
Car, Milton Berle, Marx, Box	385.00
Car, Minister Deluxe, Tin Lithograph, Pink, Japan, Box, Early 1950s, 10 In.	251.00
Car, Model T, Coupe, Cast Iron, Arcade, 5 In.	250.00 to 300.00
Car, Moko, Chauffeur, Windup, Tin, Green, Black, Yellow, Germany, c.1920, 9 1/2 In.	1045.00
Car, Monkee Mobile, Musical, Figures In Car, Japan, Box	750.00
Car, Monkey Driver, Windup, Tin Lithograph, Hess, 2 1/4 x 4 1/2 x 6 In.	700.00
Car, Mystery, Police Car, Tin, Plastic, Batteries, TN, Japan, Box, 1950s, 9 1/2 In.	137.00
Car, Mystery, Tin Lithograph, Mechanical, Red, Black Striping, Wolverine, 1930s, 13 In.	130.00
Car, Old Jalopy, Windup, Tin, Marx, 1940, 7 In.	225.00
Car, Oldsmobile, 1956 Model, Remote Control, Radicon, 14 In.	675.00
Car, Oldsmobile, 1968 Model, Toronado, Ichiko, 17 1/2 In.	395.00
Car, Oldsmobile, Super 88, Man From Uncle, 1/43 Scale, No. 497-A2, Corgi, 1966-1969	138.00
Car, Packard, 2-Door, Red, Gold Trim, Turner, 6 x 9 x 26 In.	1725.00
Car, Police, Cougar, Black, White, Box	175.00
Car, Police, With Siren, Friction, Tin, Box, 1940s-1950s	201.00
Car, Pontiac, GTO, Red Plastic, Dealer Promotional, MPC, 1970, 8 In.	120.00
Car, Porsche, Rally, Battery Operated, TPS, 1971	70.00
Car, Race, Bearcat, Windup, Tin, 7 In.	225.00
Car, Racing Set, Grand Prix, Shell Oil, Technofix	95.00
Car, Racing Set, Jackie Stewart California Speedway, Aurora Products, 1975	37.00
Car, Racing Set, Record Breakers-World Of Speed, 18-Ft. Track, Hasbro, Box, 1989	25.00
Car, Racing Set, Slot Car, AFX Aurora Winners Circle	25.00
Car, Racing, Adjustable Front Axle, Tin, Strauss, 9 In.	400.00
Car, Racing, Agajanian, With Driver, 1952	9800.00
Car, Racing, Cast Iron, Die Cast, Rubber Tires, Gray, Red Hood, Hubley, 8 In.	144.00
Car, Racing, Champion's, 18 In.	5500.00
Car, Racing, Corvette, Snake, Hot Rod, Battery Operated, Japan, 10 In.	100.00
Car, Racing, Die Cast, Car Union, Marklin	225.00
Car, Racing, Die Cast, Mercedes, Marklin	225.00
Car, Racing, Indy 500, Slush Cast, Metal Wheels, Green, 1930s, 5 1/2 In.	46.00
Car, Racing, Indy 500, Temco, Box, 1960	175.00
Car, Racing, Indy, Best Plastic Corp., Display Case, 1960s	45.00
Car, Racing, Jaguar, Battery Powered, Tin, Metallic Pink, Japan, 1950s, 8 1/2 In.	160.00
Car, Racing, Key Wind, Tin, Marklin, Model 1107R, 15 In. ... *Illus*	1650.00
Car, Racing, Molded Driver, Blue Body, Cast Iron, Arcade, 5 1/2 In.	144.00
Car, Racing, No. 5, Yellow, Hubley, 9 1/4 In.	1750.00
Car, Racing, Oh-Boy	3750.00
Car, Racing, Paggo Jet Racer, Clockwork, California	350.00
Car, Racing, Porsche, Acrobatic, Battery Operated, Box, 10 1/2 In.	295.00
Car, Racing, Porsche, Convertible, Windup, White, 3 3/4 In.	195.00
Car, Racing, Porsche, Yellow, Tin, Japan, 10 In.	295.00

Car, Racing, Pusher, Olson Rice 395.00

Car, Racing, Red Devil, No. 5, Aluminum, Iron Hood Opens, Hubley ....1950.00 to 2250.00

Car, Racing, Silver Jet, Driver, Tin, Plastic Tires, Japan, 1960s, 3 x 10 In. 100.00

Car, Racing, Speed King, Friction, Japan, Box, 6 In. 250.00

Car, Racing, Stock Car, Friction, Japan, Box 125.00

Car, Racing, Studio Racer, Windup, Schuco, 5 1/2 In. 265.00

Car, Racing, Windup, Green, Tin, 13 In. 225.00

Car, Racing, Windup, No. 5, Tin, White, Red, Black, Marx, 5 In. 40.00

Car, Racing, Windup, Red Flasher, Tin, Strauss, 9 In. 400.00

Car, Racing, Windup, Tin, Marx, 1930s 375.00

Car, Racing, Yellow, Rubber Balloon Tires, Cast Iron, Hubley, 9 1/2 In. 2875.00

Car, Radio, Windup, Swiss, Jibby, Box, 1948, 6 In. 575.00

Car, Ranch Wagon, Ford, Bandai, Box, 12 In. 325.00

Car, Red Planet, Psychedelic, Friction, Tin, Japan, 1950s, 10 In. 160.00

Car, Reo, Rumble Seat, Cast Iron, Arcade, 9 In. 4200.00

Car, Roadster, Driver, Windup, Tin, G & K Gundka, Germany, 5 1/4 In. 445.00

Car, Roadster, High Boy, Purple, Red Seat, Gold Wheels, Republic 100.00

Car, Roadster, Pressed Steel, Wood Tires, Wyandotte, c.1935, 6 In. 203.00

Car, Roadster, Tan, Red Fenders, Green Wheels, Kingsbury 345.00

Car, Roadster, Windup, Structo, 15 In. 440.00

Car, Rolls-Royce, Convertible, Cream, Bandai, 12 In. ....185.00 to 295.00

Car, Rolls-Royce, Friction, Box, 9 In. 250.00

Car, Rolls-Royce, Silver Cloud, Tin Lithograph, Japan, 3 1/2 x 11 1/2 In. 83.00

Car, Sedan, 1920s-Style, Lever Motor, Tin, Black, Red & Gold Striping, Japan, 7 In. 50.00

Car, Sedan, 2-Door, Cast Iron, Painted, Red, A.C. Williams, 1920s, 4 1/4 In. 115.00

Car, Sedan, Center Door, Arcade, Cast Iron, 1920s, 6 1/2 In. 575.00

Car, Sedan, Driver, Tin, Georg Fischer, 4 1/2 In. 137.00

Car, Sedan, Tin Lithograph, Penny Toy, Germany, 2 1/2 In. 50.00

Car, Sedan, Windup, Dark Maroon, Red, Electric Lights, 1930s, Kingsbury 405.00

Car, Sedan, Windup, Green, 4-Door, Keystone, 4 x 4 1/2 x 14 In. 345.00

Car, Sedan, Wyandotte, 14 In. 425.00

Car, Shore Patrol, Lever Action, Tin, Prewar, Japan, 7 In. 125.00

Car, Sky Show, Hot Wheels 300.00

Car, Skyliner, Convertible, Battery Operated, Tin, Red, Yellow, Japan, 9 x 3 1/2 x 3 In. ... 80.00

Car, Sport Roadster, Driver, Friction, Pressed Steel, Schieble, c.1920, 12 1/2 In. 302.00

Car, Sportsman, Convertible, Pressed Steel, Rubber Tires, Wyandotte, 12 In. 825.00

Car, Station Wagon, Wood & Fiberboard, Buddy L, 29 In. 55.00

Car, Station Wagon, Woodie, No. 530 47, Molded Rubber, Sun Rubber Co., 4 In. 99.00

Car, Studebaker, 1955 Model, Red & Black, Linemar, 4 1/2 In. 125.00

Car, Studebaker, Convertible, Pink, Hubley, 5 In. 280.00

Car, Studebaker, Friction, Red, 9 In. 275.00

Car, Studebaker, Take-Apart, Cast Iron, Hubley, 5 In. 450.00

Car, Subway, Comic Lines Express, Friction, Japan, Box, 7 1/4 In. 50.00

Car, Thunderbird, 1963 Model, Battery Operated, Japan, 11 In. 225.00

Car, Thunderbird, Convertible, Friction, AMT, 1957, 7 In. 85.00

Car, Thunderbird, Promotional, Friction, Plastic, Green, White, 1958, 8 In. 92.00

Car, Touring, 4 Door, Arcade, Cast Iron, 6 1/2 In. 75.00

Car, Touring, Blue & Gray Paint, Cast Iron, Arcade, 5 In. 105.00

Car, Touring, Blue, Nickel Wheels, Arcade, 4 1/2 In. 58.00

Car, Touring, Driver, Friction, Pressed Steel, Clark, c.1897, 7 1/2 In. 302.00

Car, Touring, Images Of Passengers In Windows, Distler, 4 In. 1320.00

Car, Traffic Cycle, Windup, Tin Lithograph, Rubber Wheels, Driver 3220.00

Car, Traffic, Indian, Swivel Head, Stake Body, Nickel Plated Wheels, Hubley, 9 In. 4400.00

Car, Van, Parcel Delivery, Tonka, 1954, 12 In. 375.00

Car, Volkswagen, Beetle, Tonka 48.00

Car, Volkswagen, Boat, Trailer, Motor & Sunroof, Battery Operated, Box 210.00

Car, Volkswagen, Deluxe, Die Cast, Blue, Dinky Toys, England, 3 3/4 In. 37.00

Car, Volkswagen, Forward & Back Motion, Battery Operated, Lighted Engine, Box 120.00

Car, Volvo, 1960s Model, 144 Sedan, Bandai, Box, 8 In. 185.00

Car, Whoopee Car, Windup, No. 150, Tin Lithograph, Marx, Box, 1930s, 7 In. 745.00

Car & Boat, Tin Lithograph, Indian Head Logo, Lucy Toy, Japan, 1950s, 7 In. 44.00

Car Transport, Mack, 4 Cars, Die Cast, Yellow, Tootsietoy, Box, 1930s, 11 In. 230.00

Carpenter's Tool, Wood Hinged Box, Boycraft, 1930s, 17 x 7 x 4 1/5 In. 88.00

Carriage, Doll's, Folding, Early 20th Century, 32 In. 82.00
Carriage, Doll's, Fringed Canopy, Pillow, Wood, 1880, 22 x 31 In. 316.00
Carriage, Doll's, Metal Frame, Wheels, Rubber Tires, Wicker, 1920s, 32 x 32 In. 450.00
Carriage, Doll's, Oilcloth Cover, Painted, Black Scroll Design, 19th Century, 20 x 21 In. 144.00
Carriage, Doll's, Red Paint, Late 19th Century, 36 In. 220.00
Carriage, Doll's, Red, Blue, Yellow Leather, Wood Wheels, 38 x 26 In. 500.00
Carriage, Doll's, Stroller, Fruitwood, Red Velvet, Louis Badeuille, France, c.1855, 16 In. 1200.00
Carriage, Doll's, Wicker, 3 Wheels, c.1920, 21 In. 55.00
Carriage, Doll's, Wicker, Articulated Bonnet, Whitney Carriage Co., 1920s 200.00
Carriage, Doll's, Wicker, Brown, c.1920, 29 In. 110.00
Carriage, Doll's, Whitney Carriage Co., Leominster, Mass., c.1925, 37 x 40 In. . . 200.00
Carriage, Kumfy-Kab Co., Wicker, Painted, Upholstered, Label 95.00
Carrier, Car, Ford Falcons, Tonka, Box 395.00
Carrying Case, Barbie, Vinyl, Supersize, Mattel, 1976, 18 In. 150.00
Carrying Case, Hot Wheels, Vinyl, Mattel, 1970s, 9 1/2 x 6 1/2 x 3 In. . . . . .20.00 to 29.00
Cart, 1 White & 1 Brown Oxen, Red Wagon, Gold, Brown, 2 x 3 In. 1300.00
Cart, Busy Delivery, Black Pinocchio, Marx, 1930s, 9 x 8 In. 975.00
Cart, Doctor's, Horsedrawn, Cast Iron, Wilkins 850.00
Cart, Doll's, Tin, Original Hood, Marklin, c.1910, 5 In. 121.00
Cart, Go Cart, Friction, Tin, Japan, 5 In. 95.00
Cart, Goat, 2 Wheels, Red Cart, Blue Base, Tin, 3 1/4 x 4 3/4 x 10 1/2 In. 1700.00
Cart, Goat, Yellow, Cast Iron, Kenton, Early 20th Century, 7 1/2 In. 345.00
Cart, Horse Drawn, 2 Wheels, Female Passenger, Nickel Plate, Cast Iron, Schimer 600.00
Cart, Mule Drawn, 2 Wheels, Cast Iron, Japanned, 4 1/2 In. 1350.00
Cart, Pony, Chester Gump, Arcade 975.00
Cart, Zebra, Driver, Daredevil, Windup, Tin, Lehmann, 7 1/2 In. 495.00
Cart & Horse, Chariot Style, Tin, Althof Bergman, c.1880, 8 In. 220.00
Case, Wardrobe, Barbie & Ken, Vinyl, 1963 . . . . 45.00
Cash Register, Ben Franklin, Tin 150.00
Cash Register, Tin, Yellow, Topple, 8 In. 450.00
Cash Register, Tom Thumb 20.00
Cat, Blond Mohair, Button Eyes, Jointed Arms, 12 In. 60.00
Cat, Collapsible, Fisher-Price 185.00
Cat, Felix, Composition, Movable Arms 995.00
Cat, Felix, Jointed, Label, Wood, Schoenhut, 1925, 4 In. 385.00
Cat, Felix, Leather Ears, Felix Decal On Chest, Schoenhut, 1924, 8 1/8 In. 375.00
Cat, Felix, Leather Ears, Paper Labels On Feet, 1923, 12 In. 2600.00
Cat, Felix, On Scooter, Windup 900.00
Cat, Felix, Sparking, Box 3190.00
Cat, Felix, Squeaker In Chest, Glass Eyes, Metal Nose, 1920s, 15 In. 485.00
Cat, Figaro, Windup, Tin, Box 385.00
Cat, Pull Toy, Mouth Opens, Cat Meows, Mohair Covered, 11 In. 143.00
Cat, Sitting, Pip-Squeak, Gray Mohair, Glass Eyes, 5 In., Pair 99.00
Cat, Stuffed, White, Germany, 11 In. 88.00
Cat, Stuffed, White, Jointed Head, Germany, 14 In. 110.00
Cat, With Ball, Tin Lithograph, Lever Action, Marx, 1930s, 8 1/2 In. 190.00
Cat, With Ball, Windup, Tin Lithograph, U.S. Zone, Germany, 1940s 55.00
Chair, Doll's, Bentwood 88.00
Chair, Doll's, Salon, Faux Bamboo, Tufted Blue Silk, France, c.1880, 11 In., Pair 1200.00
Chair, Doll's, Stenciling On Top Rail, c.1870 . . . . 185.00
Chair, Little Lounger, Captain Kangaroo, Cardboard, Mail-In Offer, 1958 . . . . 175.00
Chair, Mission, Paper Label 800.00
Chair, Rocking, Doll's, Ladder Back, Rush Seat, Acorn Finials, 13 In. 143.00
Chalkboard, Triangular Collapsible Stand, Lithograph, 46 In. 77.00
Charlie Brown, Cloth Shirt, Pants, Pocket Dolls, 1960s 55.00
Chest, Doll's, 2 Drawers, Wood, Marble Top, Bombe Front, Cabriole Legs, France, 11 In. 550.00
Chickens, In Coop, Pip-Squeak, Feathers, Softwood Coop, Germany 65.00
Chickens, Pecking, Finger Activated, Tin, 4 In. 357.00
Cinderella's Coach, Pull Toy, Wood, Lithograph, Top Lifts Off, American, c.1890, 16 In. 1000.00
Circus, Charben, Clowns & Animals, Britains 325.00
Circus, Humpty Dumpty, Tent, Clown, Donkey, Elephant, Schoenhut, Base 9 x 18 In. . . . 860.00
Circus, Wire Cage, Chair, Ball, Hoop, Barrel, Stools, Table, Ladder, Schoenhut, 8 7/8 In. . 430.00
Circus Cage, 3 Pip-Squeak Animals, On Wheels 390.00

Circus Cage, Animal, Corgi 65.00
Circus Cage, Royal Circus, Horsedrawn, Lion, Cast Iron, Yellow, Black, Blue, 15 1/2 In. 242.00
Circus Wagon, 2 Bears, Steiff, Box, 14 In. 595.00
Circus Wagon, Animal Cage, Chipperfield 96.00
Circus Wagon, Bear Cage, Hubley 2250.00
Circus Wagon, Cage, Pulled By Elephant, Windup, Tin Lithograph, 1930 .... 170.00
Circus Wagon, Horse Drawn, 4 Horses, Wood 595.00
Circus Wagon, Horse Drawn, Driver, Bear, 2 Riders, Cast Iron, Kenton, 13 1/2 In. 250.00
Circus Wagon, Overland Circus, Band, Musicians & Driver, Kenton, 16 x 7 1/2 In. 650.00
Circus Wagon, Overland Circus, Horses, Driver, Polar Bear, Kenton, 14 In. 105.00
Circus Wagon, Overland Circus, Horses, Driver, Polar Bear, Kenton, Box, 14 In. 330.00
Circus Wagon, Painted Yellow & Black, Cast Iron, Hubley 550.00
Circus Wagon, Pip-Squeak, Wood Cage, Iron Wheels, 4 Animals, 13 1/2 In. 412.00
Clancy The Great, Battery Operated, 1963 .... 90.00
Clown, Bobbing Head, Painted Papier-Mache, 8 1/2 In. 100.00
Clown, Cart With Donkey, Windup, Cloth & Flocking, Lehmann, 7 1/2 In. 110.00
Clown, Composition Head, Tin, Arms Make Balls Rotate On Dishes, Japan 135.00
Clown, Happy 'n Sad, Plays Accordion, Battery Operated, Side To Side Action 195.00
Clown, Happy The Violinist, Windup, Box 250.00
Clown, Juggler, Key Wind, Schuco, Box 650.00
Clown, Juggler, Windup, Schuco 110.00
Clown, Juggling Ball, Tin Lithograph, Japan, 8 In. 275.00
Clown, Marching, One-Man Band, Windup, Tin Lithograph, Painted, Japan, 11 1/2 In. ... 92.00
Clown, Monkey Whirligig, Parasol Spins, Windup, Celluloid, 7 In. 1990.00
Clown, Motodrill, Windup, Tin, Key & Box, Schuco, 5 In. 3780.00
Clown, Musicians, Fiddler & Drummer, Felt Costumes, Schuco, 4 3/8 In., 2 Piece 137.00
Clown, On Elephant, Celluloid, Japan, 1930s 495.00
Clown, On Horse, Wheels, Windup, 1890s 750.00
Clown, On Stilts, Playing Violin, Windup, Tin 395.00
Clown, On Trapeze, Windup, Celluloid, 1930s 195.00
Clown, Pip-Squeak, 2 Faces, Plastic, Composition & Cloth, 7 3/4 In. 440.00
Clown, Roller Skating, Windup, Box 270.00
Clown, Roly Poly, Papier-Mache, 5 In. 125.00
Clown, Standing, 2 Faces, Plaster Faces, Schoenhut 195.00
Clown, Weightlifter, Windup, Tin Lithograph, Print Suit, Germany, Early 1900s, 7 1/2 In. 1092.00
Clown, White Chair, Ladder, Schoenhut 150.00
Clown, Windup, Celluloid, C.K., Japan, Box, 1930s, 8 In. 230.00
Clown, Windup, Tin Lithograph, Felt, Schuco, 1940s, 3 3/4 In. 355.00
Clown & Devil, Papier-Mache Heads, Cloth Body, Pull String, Heads Change, 10 3/4 In. 148.00
Coach, Gunthermann, Driver 1250.00
Coach, Parlor, White Tires, Arcade, 13 In. 1850.00
Coffee Grinder, Windup, Musical, Wood Crank, Die-Cut Top, 3 1/4 In. 45.00
Colorforms, Play Set, Circus, World's Best Loved Clown, Emmett Kelly, 1960 .... 38.00
Colorforms, Play Set, Dukes Of Hazard, Box 30.00
Coon Jigger, EPL, No. 685, Windup, Tin, Lehmann, Early 1900s, 10 In. 400.00
Couch, Doll's, Fainting Couch, Turned Wood Legs, Silk Tapestry, 35 x 13 x 16 In. ... 375.00
Covered Wagon, 1849 Pioneer, 2 Oxen, Slush Mold, Red Spoked Wheels, 7 In. 20.00
Covered Wagon, 2 Horses, Driver, Kenton, Cast Iron, Box, 15 In. 385.00
Covered Wagon, Cloth Top, Cast Iron, Original Box, Kenton, 15 In. 468.00
Cow, Moo Cow, Raises Head & Moos, Fisher-Price, 10 In. 270.00
Cow, Pull Toy, Papier-Mache Covered, Move Head To Activate Mooing 632.00
Cow, Walking, Tongue Moves In & Out Of Mouth, Tin, 1940s, 5 In. 145.00
Cow, Wood, Papier-Mache, Amber Felt Covering, Glass Eyes, Paint, Red Base, 8 3/4 In. . 215.00
Cowboy, Die Cast, Crescent, Box, c.1950, 19 Piece 173.00
Cowboy, Horse & Saddle, Plastic, Painted, Hartland Plastics, 7 In. 60.00
Cowboy, Mexican, On Horse, Metal Stand, Britains, 1971 .... 25.00
Cowboy, On Horse, Lasso, Windup, Tin Lithograph, Marx, Box, 1930s, 7 In. 430.00
Cowboy, On Rocking Horse, Windup, Tin Lithograph, Y Mark, Japan, 7 x 2 x 6 1/2 In. .. 90.00
Cowboy, Ride 'Em Cowboy, Celluloid, Marx, 7 In. 82.00
Cowboy, Rodeo, Rocking Platform, France, Box, 1960s 175.00
Cowboy, Whoopee, Marx 450.00
Cowboy & Indian Set, Wood Stage, 4 Composition Horses, 10 Piece 65.00
Cradle, Doll's, Hood, Pine, Red Paint, A Present For Dorothy, c.1860, 18 In. 535.00

Cradle, Doll's, Pine, c.1800, 18 In. 150.00
Cradle, Doll's, Softwood, Dark Graining, Striping, Stenciled, Blue Interior, 15 1/2 In. . . . 300.00
Cradle, Hooded, Old Blue Paint, Child's 675.00
Cradle, Pine, Knobs For Roping, Grain Painted, Continental, c.1850, 30 x 15 In. 350.00
Crane, Lionel, Electro-Magnetic, 1940 . . . . 395.00
Crane, Mobile, Structo 95.00
Crapshooter, Table, Dice, Battery, Tin, Rubber, Cragstan, Y Mark, Japan, 9 In. 100.00
Crib Toy, Rings 'n Beads, Bakelite, Tykie Toy 55.00
Crow, Hopper, Windup, Tin Lithograph, Linemar 80.00
Cupboard, Doll's, Walnut, Arched Glass Door, Drawer, Late 19th Century, 29 In. 1350.00
Cyclist, Kiddy, Unique Art 175.00
Dairy Wagon, Horse, Driver, H. P. Hood & Sons, Schoenhut, Early 20th Century, 25 In. . 3105.00
Dancer, Black, Penny Toy, Tin Lithograph, Distler, Germany, Early 20th Century, 3 In. . . 200.00
Dancer, Hula, Windup, 1960s, 6 In. 60.00
Dancer, Man & Woman, Windup, Painted Tin, Bavaria, 8 In. 522.00
Dancing Man, Wood Springs, Fasteners, Red, Black, Green & White Paint, 16 In. 50.00
Dawn's Fashion Show, Box 110.00
Deep Sea Diver, Plastine, Box 230.00
Depot, Glendale, Electric, Baggage, Cart & Bench, Marx, Box, 13 3/4 In. 145.00
Depot Wagon, 2 Riders, Carpenter 3800.00
Desk, School, Metal, Attachable Seat, Red, White, Yellow, Marx, 1950s, 19 x 28 x 17 In. 80.00
Digger, On Mack Truck, Rubber Tires, Hubley, 13 In. 3300.00
Dinosaur, Dino, Flintstones, Riding, Plastic, Wheels, 1960s, 18 In. 90.00
Diver & Torpedo, Cast Iron, Wood Wheels, Painted, Manoil, 3 1/2 In. & 3 1/4 In. 26.00
Dog, Astro Dog, Barks, Wags Tail, Walks, Battery Operated, Box 225.00
Dog, Bimbo, Betty Boop's, 11 In. 995.00
Dog, Bulldog, Pull Toy, Head Nods, Pull Leash, Mouth Opens, Barks, Wheeled Platform . 1395.00
Dog, Button, Steiff, c.1908, 10 In. 522.00
Dog, Dachshund, Pull Toy, Papier-Mache, Iron, Leather Muzzle, France, c.1900, 9 In. . . . 1650.00
Dog, Dachshund, Straw-Stuffed Brown Mohair, Glass Eyes, Steiff, 1900, 13 1/2 In. 185.00
Dog, Dachshund, Waldi, Speaker, Tags, Steiff 295.00
Dog, Flipo, Windup, Tin Lithograph, Marx, Box, 1930s 185.00
Dog, Huckleberry Hound, Pip-Squeak, Hanna-Barbera 35.00
Dog, Itchy, Windup, Celluloid 65.00
Dog, Papier-Mache, Black Mask Face, Brown, Amber Eyes, France, 1900, 8 In. 600.00
Dog, Poodle, Jumps Through Hoop, Windup, Hand Painted 590.00
Dog, Pull Toy, Mohair Plush, Glass Eyes, Cast Iron Wheels, Steiff, c.1908, 8 In. 600.00
Dog, Pulling Wicker Cart, 2 Boys, Papier-Mache, Wood Base, Germany, c.1900, 11 In. . . 3500.00
Dog, Puppy, Skipping, Windup, TN, Box 155.00
Dog, Red & White Bow, Ear Button, Steiff, c.1908, 11 1/2 In. 745.00
Dog, Salon, White Plush, Wool, Fluffy Ears, Seated On Haunches, France, 3 1/2 In. 450.00
Dog, Schnauzer, Steiff, 11 In. 175.00
Dog, Scottie, Wags Tail, Head Nods, Windup, Plastic, Yellow, Red Jacket, Occupied Japan 85.00
Dog, Smokes Pipe, Remote Control, Plush, Felt, Tin, Metal Tires, SAN, Japan, 9 In. 160.00
Dog, Snoopy Sniffer, No. 180, Pull Toy, Wood, Vinyl Ears, Fisher-Price, 13 In. 35.00
Dog, Spitz, Pull Toy, Steiff, Button 1510.00
Dolls are listed in their own category.
Dollhouse, 5 Rooms, Wood, Painted, Electrified, Early 20th Century, 18 x 12 x 26 In. . . . 1595.00
Dollhouse, 6 Rooms, Wood, Electrified, Accessories, Late 19th Century, 75 x 52 In. 2300.00
Dollhouse, Bliss, 2 Rooms, Front Opens, c.1880, 9 x 5 x 12 In. 962.00
Dollhouse, Bungalow, 2 Story, 3 Rooms, Yellow, Red Roof, Furniture, 1920s, 19 In. 1150.00
Dollhouse, Cottage, Working Lights, 22 x 25 x 17 In. 250.00
Dollhouse, Dream House, 50 Pieces Of Furniture, Box 125.00
Dollhouse, Georgian Facade, 6 Rooms, Wallpaper, Rugs, Chandeliers, Electrified 495.00
Dollhouse, Gottschalk, 2 Story, Lithograph On Wood, Saxony, 1870s, 18 1/4 In. 9200.00
Dollhouse, Louis Badeuille, 2 Story, Fruitwood, Carved, France, 1855, 18 In. 3800.00
Dollhouse, Masonite Half-Timbered, Furniture & Accessories, Tootsietoy, 10 In. 460.00
Dollhouse, Schoenhut, Fiberboard, Wood, Simulated Block, Cardboard Furniture, 1930s . 575.00
Dollhouse, Tootsietoy, No. 12, 1927 . . . . 195.00
Dollhouse Furniture, Armoire, Bed, Maple, Steeple Crest, Bamboo Columns, 1900 . . . 800.00
Dollhouse Furniture, Bathtub, White, Kilgore 65.00
Dollhouse Furniture, Chairs, Empire, Red, Cotton Seats, Saxony, 1850, 3 In., 4 Piece . . 460.00
Dollhouse Furniture, Cradle, Wardrobe & Dresser, Box 115.00

Dollhouse Furniture, Crib, Chein 90.00

Dollhouse Furniture, Dining Room Chair, Renwall, 5 Piece 10.00

Dollhouse Furniture, Dining Room, Stromecker, Box, 8 Piece 110.00

Dollhouse Furniture, Fainting Couch, Brown Oilcloth, Button Tuck 595.00

Dollhouse Furniture, Fireplace, Pine, Marbleized Paint, 8 1/4 In. 137.00

Dollhouse Furniture, High Chair, Cast Iron, Kilgore 100.00

Dollhouse Furniture, Ice Cream Set, Bentwood, 2 Caned Chairs, Thonet, 3 Piece 895.00

Dollhouse Furniture, Living Room, Dining Room, Bliss, Box, 10 Piece 595.00

Dollhouse Furniture, Petite Princess, Box, 28 Piece 228.00

Dollhouse Furniture, Settee, Two Chairs, Adrian Cooke, Cast Metal, 1895, 1 In. 60.00

Dollhouse Furniture, Tootsietoy, 30 Piece 90.00

Dollhouse Furniture, Washing Machine, Drying Rack, Basket, Pins, Converse, Wood .. 195.00

Dollhouse Furniture, Wicker Settee, Wood, 10 Piece 55.00

Donkey, On Wheels, Button, Steiff, 1930s, 21 x 21 In. 395.00

Drawing Set, James Bond, Spy-O-Graph, Instructions, Lighted Drawing Desk 136.00

Dress Shop, Fifth Avenue, For Little Dolls, Patterns, Ruler, Transogram, Box, 1930s 23.00

Dresser, Doll's, Walnut, Dark Finish, 3 Drawers, Mirror, 15 x 7 x 28 1/2 In. 235.00

Drinking Captain, Tin, Vinyl, Cloth, Batteries, S & E, Japan, Box, 1950s, 12 In. 110.00

Drinking Happy Bird, Clear Glass, Painted Features, Plastic Stand, Taiwan, Box, 6 In. . 25.00

Dromedary, Brown & Tan, Dresden, 2 In. 85.00

Drum, Peanuts, Lithograph 75.00

Drum, Polychrome Lithograph Eagle & Shield, Tin, Wood, Cord, Leather, 2 Sticks, 8 In. . 302.00

Drum, Tin Lithograph, Graphics Of Airplanes & Zeppelins, 9 1/2 In. 195.00

Drum Major, Windup, Tin, Wolverine, 13 1/2 In. 192.00

Drummer, Arthur A-Go-Go, Battery Operated, Tin ....*Illus* 143.00

Drummer Boy, Windup, Tin, Celluloid Head, On Wheels, Fukuda Toy Co., 9 In. ... 395.00

Duck, Quacking, Windup, Tin Lithograph, Kohler, Box, 4 1/2 In. 65.00

Duck, Wobbling, Pull Toy, Papier-Mache, 1930s 245.00

Egg, Musical, Crank, 1950s 17.00

Elephant, Button, Steiff, c.1952, 6 In. 71.00

Elephant, Collapsible, Fisher-Price 185.00

Elephant, Jumbo, Tin, Pull Toy, 10 In. 27.00

Elephant, Leather Ears & Tusks, Hemp Tail, Schoenhut, Box, 1929, 10 3/8 In. 630.00

Elephant, Musical, Fisher-Price 70.00

Elephant, Painted Eyes, Leather Ears, Tusks, Hemp Tail, Schoenhut, Box, 1929, 9 x 6 In. 635.00

Elephant, Windup, Tin, West Germany 242.00

Emergency Medical Kit, CHIPS, Empire, Box 30.00

Engine, Clockwork, E. Planck, 11 1/2 x 9 3/4 In. 1250.00

Erector Set, Classic Ferris Wheel, Electric, Manual, 1939, 8 1/2 In. 295.00

Erector Set, Gilbert, Father & Son On Box, 1930s, 18 x 10 x 3/4 In. 67.00

Erector Set, Gilbert, No. 1, Papers & Box 50.00

Erector Set, Gilbert, No. 6 1/2, Metal, Red, 1954 ....82.00 to 107.00

Erector Set, Gilbert, No. 7 1/2, Ferris Wheel, 1935 .... 175.00

Erector Set, Mysto, No. 2A, Steel Girders, 1912 .... 107.00

Erector Set, Rocket Launcher, No. 10053, Metal Carrying Case, Plastic Rocket, 1959 .. 168.00

Eskimo, On Skis, Celluloid Propeller, Bing, 1910 .... 2635.00

Eskimo, On Skis, Wheel, Honoring Admiral Perry's Expedition, Celluloid, Plush, 1910 .. 4620.00

Keep lead soldiers away from fresh paint, oak and other fresh wood, paper, and cardboard. All of these emit acidic vapors that attack the lead and cause corrosion.

Toy, Drummer, Arthur
A-Go-Go, Battery
Operated, Tin

Express Wagon, Gold Stencil, Wood, Pat. Jan. 12, 1869, 15 In. 1185.00
Farm Wagon, McCormick Deering Weber, 2 Horses, Cast Iron, Arcade, 1900, 11 In. . . . 440.00
Farmer, On Tractor, Penny Toy, Tin Lithograph, Germany, 3 3/4 In. 170.00
Fawn, Straw Stuffed, Felt Covered, Pewter Button, Tag, Steiff, 4 1/4 In. 145.00
Ferris Wheel, 3 Chairs, Riders, Windup, Tin, Germany, 7 1/4 In. 300.00
Ferris Wheel, 6 Seats, Tin Lithograph, Chein, Box, 13 x 17 In. 425.00
Ferris Wheel, Electric, 19 x 22 x 13 In. 375.00
Ferris Wheel, Folk Art, Electric, 19 x 22 x 13 In. 375.00
Fiddler, Boy Scout, Schuco, 5 In. 560.00
Fiddler, Dutch Boy, Windup, Felt Over Tin, Wood Shoes, Schuco, 5 1/2 In. 240.00
Fire Cycle, Battery Operated, TN 750.00
Fire Hydrant, Twirling Tail, Windup, Plastic, Marx, Hong Kong, 6 1/2 In. 32.00
Fire Pumper, 2 Firemen, 2 Horses, Gong Bell, 1905, 18 In. 1295.00
Fire Pumper, 2 Horses, Red, Black, Gold, Cast Iron, Dent, 20 x 7 1/2 In. 300.00
Fire Pumper, 6 Firemen, Arcade, 1930, 13 In. 850.00
Fire Pumper, Cast Iron, Driver, Rubber Tires, Hubley, 11 1/4 In. 825.00
Fire Pumper, Cast Iron, Overpainted Wheels, 1920s, 6 1/4 In. 130.00
Fire Pumper, Driver, Horse On Wheels, Rear Kick Wheel, Cast Iron 3850.00
Fire Pumper, Friction, Tin Lithograph, Japan, c.1945, 5 1/2 In. 150.00
Fire Pumper, Gong Bell, Driver, Kingsbury, 1915, 11 1/2 In. 425.00
Fire Pumper, Horse Drawn, Cast Iron, Early 20th Century, 12 In. 105.00
Fire Pumper, Horse Drawn, Cast Iron, Ives & Blackslee Co., 1890, 20 In. 920.00
Fire Pumper, Horse Drawn, Driver, Cast Iron, Early 20th Century, 11 In. 115.00
Fire Pumper, Red, Gold Boiler, 2 Yellow Ladders, Pressed Steel, 7 x 12 x 26 In. 500.00
Fire Pumper, Red, Gold Boiler, Bell, Pressed Steel, 9 x 13 x 31 In. 900.00
Fire Pumper, Red, Gold, Black Rubber Tires, Cast Iron, Hubley, 12 x 7 1/2 In. 431.00
Fire Pumper, Red, Gold, White Rubber Tires, Cast Iron, Hubley, 8 x 5 In. 316.00
Fire Pumper, Red, Wood Steering Wheel, Bell, Siren, Keystone, 8 x 10 In. 500.00
Fire Set, Chief's Car, Hose-Reel Truck, Harley-Davidson Patrol Cycle, Red, 3 Piece 2640.00
Fire Truck, 3 Horses, Gold Trim, Water Tower, Cast Iron, 3 x 8 In. 2550.00
Fire Truck, 3 Ladders, Steel, Structo, 1940s 245.00
Fire Truck, Aerial Ladder, Fireman, Friction, Tin Lithograph, Japan, Box, 1950s, 11 In. . 90.00
Fire Truck, Aerial Ladder, Kingsbury 200.00
Fire Truck, Aerial Ladder, Pressed Steel, Doepke, American La France, 33 1/2 In. 225.00
Fire Truck, Aerial, Hydraulic, No. 205-B, Bell, Buddy L, Pre-1932, 34 In. 385.00
Fire Truck, Battery Operated, Mystery Action, Bump & Go, Tin, Japan, Box, 13 In. 330.00
Fire Truck, Electric, Tin, Rubber Tires, Distler, W. Germany, Box, 1950s, 10 In. 200.00
Fire Truck, Friction, Plastic, Marx, 12 In. 95.00
Fire Truck, Hook & Ladder, 3 Horses, 2 Fireman, 3 Iron Ladders, 1903, 19 In. 895.00
Fire Truck, Hose & Reel, Kenton, Cast Iron, 8 3/4 In. 600.00
Fire Truck, Hose Reel, Red, Yellow Grill, Rubber, Keystone, 30 x 8 1/2 In. 475.00
Fire Truck, Ladder, Aerial, Kingsbury 395.00
Fire Truck, Ladder, Aerial, Red, Nickel-Plated Ladder, Keystone, 9 x 10 x 31 In. 850.00
Fire Truck, Ladder, Driver, Arcade, 24 In. 950.00
Fire Truck, Ladder, Kenton, 15 1/2 In. 650.00
Fire Truck, Ladder, Wyandotte, Box, 27 In. 295.00
Fire Truck, Ladders, Wyandotte, 1939 . . . . 30.00
Fire Truck, Mighty Mo, Friction, Ideal 55.00
Fire Truck, Old Fashioned, Tin, Japan, Box, 9 1/2 x 4 1/2 x 7 In. 190.00
Fire Truck, Pioneer, Mack Bulldog, Cast Iron 2450.00
Fire Truck, Pontiac, Arcade, 10 In. 555.00
Fire Truck, Ride-On, Extendable Ladder, Red Plastic, Eldon, 1960s 75.00
Fire Truck, Snorkel, Corgi, Box 125.00
Fire Truck, Structo, 1950s 75.00
Fire Truck, Windup, Plastic, Sanders, 12 In. 95.00
Fire Truck, Windup, Tin, U.S. Zone Germany, 4 1/2 In. 125.00
Fire Wagon, 1 Running Horse, Red Wagon, 6 Firemen, Ives, 1890s, 19 3/8 In. 1840.00
Fire Wagon, 3 Horses, Driver, Cast Iron, 16 1/2 In. 27.00
Fire Wagon, 3 Horses, Driver, Cloth Hose, 22 In. 470.00
Fire Wagon, Hook & Ladder, Horsedrawn, Red, Green Drivers, 25 x 9 In. 900.00
Fire Wagon, Horse Drawn, Fireman, Hubley, 1907, 11 In. 585.00
Fire Wagon, Horse Drawn, Hose Reel, Black Horse, Cast Iron, 2 3/4 x 5 In. 450.00
Fire Wagon, Horse Drawn, Hose, Driver, Green, Red Wheel, Cast Iron, Hubley, 3 x 5 In. 700.00

Fireman, Climbing, Step Action, Marx, Box, 9 In. 268.00
Fireman, Climbing, Windup, Tin, Marx 295.00
Fish, Plastic Tail Moves Back & Forth, Windup, Chein, 1950s, 11 1/2 In. ... 160.00
Flashlight, Captain Ray-O-Vac, Rocket Ship, Box 325.00
Flashlight, Signal, Sergeant Preston, Mailer 95.00
Flying Saucer, 2 Pilots, Friction, Makes Whirring Sound, Haji 145.00
Flying Saucer, Battery Operated, Japan 195.00
Flying Saucer, Pilot, Sparking, Red & Blue Windows, Tin, Marubishi 150.00
Football Player, Windup, Molded Head, Wheels, S Mark, Japan, 4 1/2 In. .. 45.00
Fortress, Built-Rite, No. 100, Die Cut, Lithograph, Warren Paper Products, Box, 1940s . 89.00
Fox, Standing, Steiff, 7 In. 135.00
Fozzie Bear, Light Brown Fur, Jim Henson Muppet, Plastic Hat, Fisher-Price, 1976 .... 15.00
Frankenstein, Battery Operated, 1960s, 12 In. 1295.00
G.I. Joe, Action Team Vehicle 75.00
G.I. Joe, Adventure Team Commander, Simulated Hair, Beard, 12 In. 85.00
G.I. Joe, Adventure Team Vehicle, Amphibious, Box, 13 In. 45.00
G.I. Joe, Australian Jungle Fighter, Accessories 375.00
G.I. Joe, Australian Jungle Fighter, Window Box 2495.00
G.I. Joe, British Commando, Accessories 450.00
G.I. Joe, Canteen 35.00
G.I. Joe, Danger Of Depths 290.00
G.I. Joe, Dragonfly Copter, 1st Edition, 1983 .... 48.00
G.I. Joe, French Resistance Fighter, Accessories 375.00
G.I. Joe, German Storm Trooper, Accessories 450.00
G.I. Joe, Green Airbourne, Accessories 1495.00
G.I. Joe, Green Camouflage Uniform, Boots, Hasbro, Copyright 1964, 11 In. 310.00
G.I. Joe, Helmet, Combat, Hasbro 95.00
G.I. Joe, Jouncing Jeep, Unique Art 150.00
G.I. Joe, Jouncing Jeep, Unique Art, Box 295.00
G.I. Joe, K-9 Pups, Windup, Unique Art, Box .... 175.00 to 250.00
G.I. Joe, Mess Kit 45.00
G.I. Joe, Navy Seal, Box 95.00
G.I. Joe, Russian Soldier, Accessories .... 450.00 to 650.00
G.I. Joe, Secret Of Mummy's Tomb 250.00
G.I. Joe, Skystryker, Hasbro, 1983 .... 65.00
G.I. Joe, Space Capsule, Space Suit, Box, 1966, 14 In. ..... 170.00 to 325.00
G.I. Joe, Talking, Beard, Pull Chain, 1960s, 11 1/2 In. 55.00
G.I. Joe, Talking, World War II Soldier, 12 In. 185.00
G.I. Joe, Tan Bush Jacket, Green Trousers, Jointed, Hasbro, 12 In. 85.00
Games are listed in their own category.
Garage, 2 Cars, Racing Boat, Tin, Bing, 1912, 6 1/2 x 8 In. 750.00
Garage, Carmatic Door, Tin Lithograph, Marx 110.00
Garage, Esso, Tin, Kibri, 11 In. 235.00
Garage, Honeymoon, Marx 125.00
Garage, Tin, Bing, 3 1/4 x 6 In. 145.00
Garage, Town Garage, Runabout, Limousine, Parker Bros., Box, c.1910, 10 1/2 x 8 In. .. 1595.00
Gas Pump, Tin, 7 1/4 In. 175.00
Gas Pump Set, Tin, Marx 325.00
Gas Station, Prewar, Germany, 4 In. 175.00
Gas Station, Sunny Side Service Station, Tin, Store, Air Pump, Oil Cart, Lighted Ramp . 85.00
Giraffe, Painted Eyes, Leather Ears, Cotton Tail, Schoenhut, 11 5/8 In. 315.00
Giraffe, Windup, Germany, 1950s, 6 3/4 In. 75.00
Girl, Horses, Wheels, Windup, Bisque, Tin, Label, France, Box, c.1875, 12 1/2 In. 8250.00
Give-A-Show Set, Frankenstein Jr., Hanna-Barbera, Kenner, Box, 1967 ..... 148.00
Glider, Snoopy's Good Grief Glider, Spring Loaded Launcher, Questar, Box, 1970s 30.00
Globe, Accordion Fold, The Earth & Its Inhabitants, In 3 Languages, Box, 3 In. 190.00
Gnomes, Hammers & Anvil, Finger Activated, Johann Meier, 4 In. 275.00
Goat, Pulling Cart, Cast Iron, Late 19th Century, 6 In. 176.00
Goat, Rocky Mountain, Steiff, 5 1/2 In. 145.00
Goat, Snucky, Mohair, Glass Eyes, Button, Tags, Steiff, 6 In. .... 80.00 to 85.00
Goat, Yellow Kid, Goat-Drawn Cart, One Hand Extended, Cast Iron, 8 In. 735.00
Goose, Egg Laying, Hand Painted Tin, Germany, 5 1/2 In. 120.00
Goose, Egg Laying, Windup, White & Orange Plastic, 3 Wood Eggs, Marx, 9 In. 40.00

Goose, Windup, Golden Goose, Tin, 3 Wood Eggs, Box, Pat. July 8, 1924, 4 1/2 x 9 In. . . .   44.00
Goose, Wings Flap, Windup, Tin, Germany 95.00
Grasshopper, Pull Toy, Hubley, 4 x 9 1/2 In. . . . . .905.00 to 1100.00
Grinder, Food, Darling 38.00
Grinding Wheel, Man, Standing, Lithograph, Tin, Girard Co., 4 x 6 In. . . . . .125.00 to 175.00
Guitar, Beany & Cecil 95.00
Guitar, Buck Jones, Wood 395.00
Guitar, Cowboy, Wood, 37 In. 300.00
Guitar, Tin, Wood, 1930s, 12 In. 35.00
Gumby, Package, 1983, 16 In. 25.00
Gun, Air Pistol, Air Arms ProSport, Model 820-825, Premier Lights, 12 In. 575.00
Gun, Air Pistol, Benjamin, Model 250 . . . .   60.00
Gun, Air Pistol, Benjamin, Model 362, .22 Cal. 90.00
Gun, Air Pistol, Benjamin, Model G 75.00
Gun, Air Pistol, Burris Pistol Scope, With Rings 100.00
Gun, Air Pistol, Bushnell Scope, Model 10X 90.00
Gun, Air Pistol, Challenger Arms, Plainsman, .22 Cal., 1950s 150.00
Gun, Air Pistol, Crosman, Model 106, Pump, .22 Cal. 65.00
Gun, Air Pistol, Crosman, Model 116 . . . .   40.00
Gun, Air Pistol, Crosman, Model 400, Cross Bolt Safety 90.00
Gun, Air Pistol, Crosman, Model 451, 6 Shot Semi-Automatic 195.00
Gun, Air Pistol, Daisy, Model 25, 1936 . . . .   85.00
Gun, Air Pistol, Diana, Model 35, Magnum, 1960s 138.00
Gun, Air Pistol, El Gamo Falcon, Underlever 62.00
Gun, Air Pistol, Giffard, Rear Sight 40.00
Gun, Air Pistol, Haenel, Model 100, Bluing 90.00
Gun, Air Pistol, HyScore, Model 800, Sling Shot, .22 Cal., 8-In. Barrel 60.00
Gun, Air Pistol, Mega-Dart, Rubber Bands, Camo-Black Finish, .38 Cal. 150.00
Gun, Air Pistol, Mendoza Magnum, Monte Carlo Stock 200.00
Gun, Air Pistol, Sharp U-FP, Target Grips, Shoulder Stock 250.00
Gun, Air Pistol, Walther, Model LP53, Accessories, Box & Papers 225.00
Gun, Air Rifle, Beeman, Model R-10, .177 Cal., Box & Papers 300.00
Gun, Air Rifle, Quackenbush XL, .22 Cal., Box & Papers 350.00
Gun, Air Rifle, Sheridan Blue Streak, CO 2, Blued, Walnut, 1960s 100.00
Gun, Anti-Aircraft, 105mm, Tin Lithograph, Clicker, Marx, 10 In. 64.00
Gun, Astro Ray, Red & White Morse Code Sender, Brass Dart, Ohio Art 50.00
Gun, Atomic Disintegrator, Hubley, 1940s 373.00
Gun, BB Crosman, Scout, Pneumatic, Small 18.00
Gun, BB, Daisy, Model 101-36, Iron Lever, 1930s 40.00
Gun, BB, Daisy, Model 105-B, Lever Action, Plastic Stock 12.00
Gun, BB, Daisy, Targeteer, Nickel Plated, 1950s, 10 1/2 In. 80.00
Gun, Clicker, Me & My Buddy, Tin, Wyandotte, 1950s, 7 In. 130.00
Gun, Clicker, Tin Lithograph, Ohio Art, 8 In. 45.00
Gun, Cork, Double Barrel, Daisy, Box 15.00
Gun, Cosmic Ray Gun, Sparking, Plastic, Ranger Steel Products, Box, 1950s 83.00
Gun, Cosmic Ray, Ranger Steel Products, Box, 1950s, 8 In. . . . .*Illus*   83.00
Gun, Daisy Rifle, Ricochet, Box 145.00
Gun, Dart, Crack Shot, No. 25, Metal, Spring Firing, Wyandot, Box, 8 In. 25.00
Gun, Derringer, 2 Shot, Micklog, 1900s 35.00

Toy, Gun, Space, Tin, Japan, Box,
1950s, 9 In.

Toy, Gun, Cosmic Ray, Ranger
Steel Products, Box, 1950s, 8 In.

Toy, Gun, Numatic Space, Steel,
Shoots Paper, 1950s, 6 1/2 In.

Gun, Disintegrator, Die Cast, Hubley 485.0

Gun, Field, Replica Of WWI 75mm Howitzer, Cast Iron, 8 In. 69.0

Gun, Machine Gun, Squirt, Rambo, Box 20.0

Gun, Machine Gun, World War II Style, Tripod, Hand Crank, Pressed Steel, 23 1/2 In. ... 180.0

Gun, Machine, Space King, Battery Operated, Tin, Box 125.0

Gun, Machine, Tripod, Revolving Clip, Two Bullets, Tin Lithograph 225.0

Gun, Numatic Space, Steel, Shoots Paper, 1950s, 6 1/2 In. ....*Illus* 39.0

Gun, Ray Gun, Sparking, Piston Action, Sound, KO, Yoshiya 150.0

Gun, Rocket, Plastic, Gray, Spaceship Shape, Superior, 8 x 5 x 3 1/2 In. 38.0

Gun, Space, Plastic, 1950s, 10 In. 40.0

Gun, Space, Squirt Gun, Noisemaker, Sparking, 1960s, 8 1/2 In. 50.0

Gun, Space, Tin, Japan, Box, 1950s, 9 In. ....*Illus* 165.0

Gun, Sparking, G-Man, Marx, Box 95.0

Gun, Squirt, Batwing Shape 10.0

Gun, Squirt, Bubble Blaster, Pink, Bubble Fluid, Knickerbocker, Box, 1955 .... 35.0

Gun, Squirt, Daisy, No. 9 .... 65.0

Gun, Squirt, Derringer 5.0

Gun, Squirt, G.I. Joe Performing Space Walk On Handle, Hasbro 250.0

Gun, Squirt, Wizard, Cast Iron, 1896, 5 In. 140.0

Gun, Submachine, Caps, Plastic, Metal, Crank On Side, Mattel, 12 1/2 In. 40.0

Gun, Target, Corsman Skanaker 385.0

Gun & Holster Set, BB Gun, Daisy, No. 179, Instructions, Target Set 48.0

Gun & Holster Set, BB, Crosman V, Model 300, Spring Piston 100.0

Gun & Holster Set, Cap Gun, 2 Guns, Leatherette, Tin Conchos, Steer Head, 1950s ... 41.0

Gun & Holster Set, Cap Gun, Pony 15.0

Gun & Holster Set, Cap Gun, Stallion, Jeweled Holster 150.0

Gun & Holster Set, Hubley, Cap Gun, Texan, Twin Holsters 200.0

Gun & Holster Set, Lasso-Em Bill, Box 250.0

Gun & Holster Set, Mattel, Cap Gun, Fanner 50, Leather Holster & Belt, 5-In. Barrel .. 98.0

Gun & Holster Set, Mattel, Shootin' Shell, Snub Nose 38 .... 195.0

Gun & Holster Set, Paladin, Black Leather, Metal Buckle, 2 Chess Knights 126.0

Gun & Holster Set, Texan Jr., Cap Gun, Leather Holster & Belt, 8 In. 400.00

Gun & Holster Set, Texan Jr., Leather Holster, Belt, Steel Buckle, 1940s 64.00

Gun Carrier, Bren, Die Cast, Green, Lone Star Products, England, 3 1/2 x 2 x 1 1/2 In. ... 34.00

Gyro Copter, With Hanger, Palmer, 7 In. 125.00

Ham & Sam, Minstrel Team, Strauss, 1921, 7 In. 1200.00

Handcar, Clown, Holly & Polly, Box 75.00

Handcar, Hoky-Poky, Windup, Wyandotte, 1950s, 6 In. 295.00

Handcar, Moon Mullins & Kayo, Windup, Marx, 1930s 650.00

Handcar, Peter Rabbit, Track, Lionel, 1930s 1100.00

Handcar, Railroad, Windup, Tin Lithograph, Germany, 4 1/2 x 1 3/4 x 3 1/2 In. 126.00

Hanger, Rocket, Tin Lithograph, 1950s, 8 x 11 In. 125.00

Hansom Cab, Horse Drawn, Driver, Cast Iron, Pratt & Letchworth, c.1900, 12 1/2 In. ... 1540.00

Hansom Cab, Horse Drawn, Driver, Passenger, Kenton, Cast Iron, Box, 15 1/4 In. 330.00

Hansom Cab, Horse Drawn, Gray Horse, Black Cab, White Trim, Cast Iron, 2 x 6 In. ... 700.00

Hansom Cab, Original Driver, 1880, P & L, 12 In. 1750.00

Happy The Violinist, Cloth Costume, Box, 8 1/2 In. 300.00

Hat & Mask, Zorro, 1950s 60.00

Hay Wagon, Black Driver, Mule, Cast Iron, 1900 .... 450.00

Hedgehog, Steiff, c.1950, 7 In. 110.00

Helicopter, Battery Operated, Tin, Japan, 10 In. 375.00

Helicopter, Cable Crank Mechanism, Helibus 150.00

Helicopter, Hubley 65.00

Helicopter, Piasecki Hup-2, Double Rotors, Friction, Tin, TN, Japan, Box, 10 In. ... 180.00

Helicopter, Police-Fire Chief, Windup, Tin, Plastic, Japan, Box, 1950s, 6 1/4 In. ... 22.00

Helmet, Lost In Space, Remco 295.00

Herb Box, Doll's, Tin Lithograph, Cord Handle, Germany, Late 19th Century, 3 In. ... 250.00

Hobo, Monkey With Accordion & Cymbals, Battery Operated 350.00

Hoisting Tower, Buddy L 895.00

Honeymoon Express, Windup, Tin Lithograph, Marx, 1920s, 9 1/2 In. ....125.00 to 225.00

Hoop, Painted Wood, Metal Bells, American, Early 20th Century, 31 In. 170.00

Hoop, Wood, Handle Rolls, Decorated Wood Spindles, Tin Buttons, American, 20 In. ... 800.00

Horse, Cozner Galloper, Windup, Tin, Clockwork, Ives, 1870s, 11 In. 5995.00

Horse, Dapple Gray, Paper Tack, Papier-Mache, 1900-1920, 8 x 9 In., Pair 155.00
Horse, Gliding, Dapple Gray, Glass Eyes, Horsehair, 39 In. 460.00
Horse, Iron Wheels, Leather Saddle, Cast Iron, Stieff, 1908, 4 Ft. 2800.00
Horse, Laminated Wood, Gesso, Brown Repaint, Saddle, Pull Toy, 29 x 27 1/2 In. 495.00
Horse, On Wheels, Papier-Mache, Mohair Mane, Leatherette Bridle & Saddle, 8 1/2 In. . 125.00
Horse, Platform Wheels, Horsehide Covering, Black Wheels, Pull Toy 1150.00
Horse, Platform Wheels, Mohair Burlap Cover, Leather Bridle, Reins, 19 In. 450.00
Horse, Rocking, 4 Wheels, Cast Iron, Bell Toy, c.1895 . . . . 350.00
Horse, Rocking, Attached Windsor Chair, Polychrome Paint 625.00
Horse, Rocking, Hand Carved, Painted, 1890 . . . . 995.00
Horse, Rocking, Hide Cover, Glass Eyes, Horsehair Mane, Tail, Plywood Platform, 46 In. 920.00
Horse, Rocking, Hide Covered 250.00
Horse, Rocking, Horsehair Tail, Carved & Painted Wood, 20th Century 285.00
Horse, Rocking, Indian Rider, Windup, Composition, Wood, Germany, c.1915, 7 In. 460.00
Horse, Rocking, Leather Saddle, Reins, Carved, Painted Wood, 19th Century, 48 1/2 In. . 920.00
Horse, Rocking, Stationary Base, 35 In. 330.00
Horse, Rocking, Stick Legs, Original Paint & Tail, 1850s 1400.00
Horse, Swings Back & Forth On Base, Wood, Dapple Gray Paint, Glass Eyes, 40 x 34 In. 578.00
Horse, Trotter, Windup, Tin Horse, Celluloid Driver, Bestmade, Japan, 1950s, 7 In. 210.00
Horse, Wood, Black Mohair, Orange Harness, Red Trim, Steel Wheels, Pull Toy, 11 In. . . 205.00
Horse, Wood, Papier-Mache, Dapple Gray Paint, Red Base, Pull Toy, Germany, 8 In. . . 165.00
Horse, Wood, Smoked Dapple Gray Paint, Paper Blanket, Cloth Harness, Pull Toy, 6 In. . 77.00
Horse & Buggy, Upholstered Seat, Glass Eyes, c.1910, 20 x 60 In. 4950.00
Horse & Wagon, Arcade 375.00
Horse & Wagon, Bakery, Cast Iron, 1907 . . . . 395.00
Horse & Wagon, Barrel, Black Driver, Cast Iron, Wilkins, 1895, 21 In. 1250.00
Horse & Wagon, Brown, Gray Horse, Driver, Green Wagon, Cast Iron, Ives 1500.00
Horse & Wagon, Carpenter's, Cast Iron, Harrison, New York, 1881, 19 In. 2530.00
Horse & Wagon, City Sprinkler, Driver, Hubley 1250.00
Horse & Wagon, Coal, 2 Wheels, Black Horse, Blue Wagon, Cast Iron, 2 x 7 In. 430.00
Horse & Wagon, Dairy, Sheffield Farms Co., Wood, Rich Toy, 1930, 20 1/2 In. 630.00
Horse & Wagon, Driver, Wilkins, Cast Iron, 13 x 7 In. 1950.00
Horse & Wagon, Dump, Contractor's, Cast Iron, Painted, Arcade, 1920s, 14 In. 170.00
Horse & Wagon, Express, Painted Wood, American, Late 19th Century, 31 In. 920.00
Horse & Wagon, Gravel, Sand, 2 Horses, Driver, Green Wagon, Cast Iron, 3 In. 250.00
Horse & Wagon, Gray Beauty Pacers, Wood, Tin, Iron Wheels, Gibbs No. 50, 19 In. . . . 95.00
Horse & Wagon, Grocery, Sheffield Farms, Rich Toy, c.1930, 9 1/2 x 22 In. 345.00
Horse & Wagon, Ice, 2 Horses, Enclosed Wagon, Cast Iron, Hubley, c.1906, Oversized . 860.00
Horse & Wagon, Ladder, 3 Horses, Cast Iron, Wood Ladders, Early 1900s, 24 1/2 In. . . . 975.00
Horse & Wagon, Ladder, Cast Iron, c.1910, 21 In. 110.00
Horse & Wagon, Log, Black Horse, Driver, Yellow Wagon, Cast Iron, 4 In. 650.00
Horse & Wagon, Milk, Marx, Box, 1930s 696.00
Horse & Wagon, Milk, Tin Lithograph, Converse, 17 In. 230.00
Horse & Wagon, Red, Green, Cast Iron, 15 x 5 In. 175.00
Horse & Wagon, Rider, Cast Iron, Green, Red, Gray, Late 19th Century, 8 In. 210.00
Horse & Wagon, Sand & Gravel, Shellacked Horses, Arcade, 1920, 15 In. 115.00
Horse & Wagon, Wood, Glass Eyes, Harness & Whip, Pull Toy, 51 In. 415.00
Horse Race, Windup, Celluloid, Occupied Japan 220.00
House, Humphrey Mobile, Wheels, Smokestack, Windup, Tin, Wyandotte, 1940s 600.00
House Trailer, 1955 Ford Station Wagon, White Lettering, Box, 7 1/2 In. 425.00
House Trailer, 2-Tone 1956 Cadillac, White Trailer, Black Lettering, Box 740.00
Hubbell's Grand Jubilee Dancers, Walnut Box, Windup, With Box, c.1875, 5 In. 4400.00
Huckleberry Hound, Ride Em' Cowboy, 1960s 95.00
Hurricane Spotter 225.00
Ice Skates, Leather, Union Hardware Co., 1894 . . . . 135.00
Ice Skates, Union Hardware, c.1908 . . . . 9.00
Ice Wagon, Horsedrawn, Black Horse, Green Wagon, Cast Iron, 2 x 3 In. 172.00
Icebox, Zinc Lined, Colorado Refrigerator, Geo. Scipel, Easton, Pa., 1880, 23 x 13 In. . . 1155.00
Indian, Brave Eagle, Warrior, Beats Drum, Battery, Plastic, Tin, Box, 12 In. 160.00
Indian Boy In Canoe, Friction, Tin, Rubber Tires, Yanoman, Japan, 5 1/4 In. 105.00
Iron, Aluminum, Wood Handle, Electric, Dolly Dell Quality Toys, Omaha, Box, 5 In. . . . 34.00
Iron, Deco, Electric, 5 1/2 x 9 In. 45.00
Iron, Sunny Suzy, Electric 20.00

Ironing Board, Wood 35.0

Jack-In-The-Box, Alvin The Chipmunk, 1984 .... 35.0

Jack-In-The-Box, Cat In The Hat 175.0

Jack-In-The-Box, Clown, Bell Rings When Cranked, Ohio Art 150.0

Jack-In-The-Box, Off To See The Wizard, Ohio Art 175.0

Jack-In-The-Box, Papier-Mache Head, Germany, 4 1/4 In. 170.0

Jack-In-The-Box, Porky Pig, Metal, Mattel, 1960s 450.0

Jack-In-The-Box, Snoopy, Metal, 1966 .... 55.0

Jack-In-The-Box, Super Chef 285.0

Jack-In-The-Box, Timmy The Tiger, Mattel, 1960s 25.0

James Bond, 007 Secret Agent, Scuba Gear, No. 3, On Card, Gilbert, 1965, 3 1/2 In. ... 46.0

James Bond, Moonraker, Original Box, 1979, 12 1/2 In. 170.0

James Bond, Secret Agent, Goldfinger, On Card, Gilbert, 1965, 3 1/4 In. 50.0

Jazzbo Jim, Alabama Coon Jigger Base, Windup, Strauss, 1910, 10 In. .... 300.00 to 695.0

Jazzbo Jim, Dances On The Roof, Unique Art, 1921, 9 1/2 In. 650.0

Jeep, Army, Plastic, Green, Marx Toys, 5 In. 30.0

Jeep, Battery Operated, Japan, Box 95.0

Jeep, Fire, Tonka, 1963 .... 210.0

Jeep, G.I. Joe, Windup, Tin, Unique Art, 1950s, 8 In. 245.0

Jester, Lester, Twirls Cane, Shakes Head, Body Moves, Windup, Tin, Alps, 9 1/2 In. .. 495.0

Jigger, Somstepa Coon, Marx, 8 In. 595.0

Jingle Dingle, Ring-O-Bell, HG Toys, 1950s, 11 In. 46.0

Jouncing, Unique Art 225.0

Jr. Ironer, Windup, Tin, Japan, 1940s 55.0

Jumping Jack, Wood, Painted, Natural Patina, Composition Head, 15 In. 33.0

Kaleidoscope, Hand Crank, 2 Color Round Glass Panes, 19th Century 195.0

Kangaroo, Pip-Squeak, Glass Eyes 1450.0

Kentucky Derby, Lead Horses, Strings To Inside Bar, Turn Handle To Race 325.0

Kib-Itz, Wood, Painted, String Strung, Box, 1940s 32.0

Kiddie-Kar-Kid, H.C. White Co., Boy On Car, Composition, Cloth, Wood, 1924, 10 In. .. 285.0

Kitchen, Sink, Recirculating Running Water, Stove Top, Oven, Alps 125.0

Kitchen Set, Modern, Accessories, Instructions, Marx, Box 350.0

Kite, Fireball Twig, Kit ....20.00 to 30.0

Kite, G.I. Joe, Plastic, Keel-Style, Original Package, 1982, 42 In. 20.0

Kite, Space Scenes, Planets, Spacemen, Rockets, 1950s 20.0

Kite, Uncle Sam Image, Hi Flyer Mfg. Co., 1930s 125.0

Kite, Yellow, Give-Away, 1950s 12.0

Ladybug, Stuffed, Knickerbocker, 1950s, 16 1/2 In. 50.0

Lamb, Bead Eyes, Pile Wool, Felt Face, Ears & Legs, Ear Button, Steiff, c.1913, 4 5/8 In. 575.0

Lamb, Wood & Steel, Woolly Coat, Felt & Glass Eyes, Pull Toy, Steiff, 14 x 14 In. 1210.0

Lamb, Woolly Coat, Wood Wheels, Bead Eyes, Bells, Pull Toy, Steiff, 11 x 11 3/4 In. ... 385.0

Lantern, Doll's, Tole, White Ground, Court Scenes, France, Early 19th Century, 2 In. .. 1000.0

Laurel & Hardy, Pip-Squeak, Pair 50.0

Leopard, Lying Down, Mohair, Button With Tag, Plastic Eyes, Unjointed, Steiff, 12 In. .. 88.0

Leopard, Saber Tooth, Windup, Label, Marx 150.0

Li'l Abner Dogpatch Band, Windup, Unique Art, Box ....750.00 to 800.0

Linus, Peanuts, Vinyl, Painted, 1950s, 9 In. 75.0

Lion, Cub, Reclining, Steiff, 9 In. 110.0

Lion, Leo, Reclining, Steiff, 17 In. 250.0

Lion, Steiff, c.1956, 21 In. 66.0

Log Cabin, Curtains, Chimney & Porch, 13 In. 195.00

Log Wagon, Black Driver, Pulled By 2 Oxen, Cast Iron, Hubley 975.00

Louis Armstrong, Plays Trumpet, Kicks, Hat Bounces, Windup, Tin, Japan, 10 In. 285.00

Lucy, Peanuts, Plastic Body, Rubber Head, Skediddle Kiddle, Mattel, 1968, 5 In. 52.00

Lucy, Peanuts, Vinyl, Plastic, Yellow Dress, United Feature Syndicate, 1950s, 9 In. 99.00

Maggie & Jiggs, Battling, Tin Lithograph, Couple On Wheels, c.1930, 7 In. 805.00

Magic Set, Dr. Doolittle 45.00

Magic Set, Rootie Kazootie, Zenith 75.00

Magic Slate, Captain Kangaroo & Mr. Moose 48.00

Magic Trick Set, Chandu, Orange, Brown, Black Box, Crystal Ball, Wood Wand, 1933 .. 200.00

Mammy, Windup, Tin, Lindstrom, 10 In. 220.00

Man, Neanderthal, Schuco, 11 In. 150.00

Marble & Bag, Leather, Indian Chief, Clay Marbles 150.00

Merry-Go-Round, Airplanes, Horses, Wolverine, 1930s ....325.00 to 425.00
Merry-Go-Round, Mounted On Truck, Buddy L 145.00
Merry-Go-Round, Tin, Chein, 11 x 10 In. 300.00
Merrymakers, Windup, Tin Lithograph, Marx, 1930s 750.00
Merrymakers, Windup, Tin Lithograph, Marx, Box, c.1935, 9 In. ....1375.00 to 1495.00
Mickey Rooney's One Man Band, Musical Instruments, 18 x 9 In. 85.00
Microscope, S-25, Carrying Case, Tools, Gilbert 36.00
Microscope, Space Patrol ....57.00 to 75.00
Mighty Mouse, Plush, Red, Yellow, Black, White, 21 In. 37.00
Milk Wagon, Cast Iron, Kenton, 12 1/2 In. 550.00
Milk Wagon, Horse Drawn, Black Horse, Red Wheels, Cast Iron, 3 x 5 In. 200.00
Milk Wagon, Rich's, Tin Lithograph, Wood, Rich Toy, 1930s, 20 In. 285.00
Minstrel, Playing Accordion, Hand Painted, Tin Lithograph 2200.00
Minstrel Team, Ham & Sam, Strauss 990.00
Mobile, Peter Rabbit, Chick, Windup, Tin Lithograph, Lionel Corp., New York 400.00
Model Kit, Airplane, Boeing 747, Pan Am, Minicraft, 11 x 13 In. 57.00
Model Kit, Airplane, Curtiss Jenny, Plastic, Unassembled, Lindberg, Box, 1/48 Scale ... 25.00
Model Kit, Airplane, Engine, Model 19, Olson & Rice 45.00
Model Kit, Airplane, F4U-5 Corsair, Plastic, Lindberg, 1960 .... 29.00
Model Kit, Airplane, F4U-5 Corsair, Plastic, Revell, 1963 .... 30.00
Model Kit, Airplane, Famous Fighters, Fokker D-VIII, Aurora, Box 35.00
Model Kit, Airplane, Flying White House, E-4 Boeing, Airfix, Unassembled, 1/144 Scale .. 20.00
Model Kit, Airplane, P-47D Thunderbolt, Lindberg, Late 1950s 31.00
Model Kit, Boat, Outboard Motor, No. 43, Battery, Plastic, Metal, Johnson, Japan, Box .. 70.00
Model Kit, Boat, Royal Louis Ship, Box 10.00
Model Kit, Boat, Russian Submarine, Aurora, Sealed Box 40.00
Model Kit, Bride Of Frankenstein, Aurora, Box 75.00
Model Kit, British Scout, Plastic, Aurora 125.00
Model Kit, Car, 1928 Model A Ford, Plastic, AMT, 1960s, 1/25 Scale 46.00
Model Kit, Car, Chevrolet Impala Convertible, AMT, 1964, 1/25 Scale 46.00
Model Kit, Car, Mercedes-Benz 190 SL, No. 1239, Plastic, Revell, Box, 1960s 40.00
Model Kit, Diver, James Bond 007, Japan, Box, 1965 .... 260.00
Model Kit, Dr. Jekyll, Aurora 75.00
Model Kit, Dracula, Aurora 45.00
Model Kit, Frankenstein, Aurora, Box, Gigantic 2995.00
Model Kit, Guillotine, Aurora 225.00
Model Kit, Helicopter, Sikorsky HO4S-1 .... 15.00
Model Kit, House, Addams Family, Aurora 295.00
Model Kit, Invisible Engine, 4-Cylinder, Plastic, Battery, Gescha, Germany, 8 x 4 In. ... 30.00
Model Kit, Jeep, U.S. Army, M-10, Balsa & Cardboard, Megow, Red Box, 1943 .... 46.00
Model Kit, Mummy's Chariot, Aurora 250.00
Model Kit, Mummy, Aurora, Box 600.00
Model Kit, Neanderthal Man, Aurora, Sealed Box 70.00
Model Kit, Nike Hercules, Revell, Unopened, 1/40 Scale 18.00
Model Kit, Road Runner 40.00
Model Kit, Snoopy, Surfing, Monogram, 1973, 10 x 6 In. 46.00
Model Kit, Spacecraft, Apollo Lunar Module, Airfix, Sealed, 1/72 Scale 18.00
Model Kit, Starship Enterprise, Next Generation, No. 6102, Playmates, Box, 15 In. 25.00
Model Kit, Steve Canyon, Aurora, Sealed Box 190.00
Model Kit, Tarzan, Aurora, Box 225.00
Model Kit, Three Musketeers, Aurora 125.00
Model Kit, Wolfman, Aurora, Box 275.00
Model Kit, Wonder Woman, Aurora, Box 125.00
Model Kit, Zorro, Aurora 125.00
Monkey, Circus, Acrobatic Marvel, On Rocking Base, Windup, Tin Lithograph, Marx ... 165.00
Monkey, Circus, Windup, Tin, Plush, TN, Japan, Box, 7 1/2 In. 95.00
Monkey, Combing Hair, Battery Operated, Celluloid 125.00
Monkey, Crapshooting, Battery Operated, Cragstan 120.00
Monkey, Drinking, Battery Operated 120.00
Monkey, Drinking, Windup, Marx 95.00
Monkey, Frankie The Roller Skating Monkey, Tin, Plush, Alps, Japan, Box, 1950s, 12 In. . 120.00
Monkey, Hula Hoop, Windup, Mechanical, Tin, Plush, Plaything, Japan, Box, 10 In. 110.00
Monkey, Jocko, Climbing, Tin Lithograph, Linemar, 1950s, 6 1/2 In. 70.00

Take batteries with you to toy sales if you plan to buy a battery-operated toy. Check to see if the toy really works.

Reproduction cast-iron toys and banks are heavier and thicker than the originals.

Toy, Monkey, Playing
Guitar, Battery
Operated

Monkey, On Tricycle, Pull Toy, Legs Move With Front Wheel, Cast Iron, 8 In.	3410.00
Monkey, Orangutan, Yes-No, U.S. Zone Tag	395.00
Monkey, Playing Guitar, Battery Operated ....*Illus*	121.00
Monkey, Playing Guitar, Windup, Celluloid, Occupied Japan	200.00
Monkey, Playing Trumpet, Battery Operated	225.00
Monkey, Pull Toy, Mohair Plush, Cast Iron Base, Rubber Wheels, Steiff, Late 1940s, 9 In.	650.00
Monkey, Rock 'n Roll, Battery Operated	185.00
Monkey, Sambo Minstrel Man, Plucks Guitar, Windup, Prewar Japan	400.00
Monkey, Schoenhut	300.00
Monkey, Shoeshine, Battery Operated, Japan, Box	85.00
Monkey, Skipping, Battery Operated, Box	35.00
Monkey, Tumbling, Battery Operated, Box	65.00
Monkey, Velveteen, Dakin, 1961	20.00
Monkey, With Coconut, Cracks Coconut On Log To Ring Bell, Cast Iron, Pull Toy	245.00
Monkey, With Cymbals, Original Clothing, Tin, 10 In.	100.00
Monkey, Wood With Mohair, Felt Clothing, Glass Eyes, Label, Germany, 10 1/2 In.	350.00
Monkey, Yes-No, Mohair, Felt, Cotton, Glass Eyes, Schuco, 1916, 11 1/2 In.	200.00
Monkey, Yes-No, Mohair, Glass Eyes, U.S. Zone, Germany, Schuco, Late 1940s, 10 In.	375.00
Monkey, Zippo The Climbing Monkey, Tin, Pull String Make Legs Move, 9 x 4 1/2 In.	28.00
Monster, Ultra Seven, Plastic, Bullmark Toys, Japan, Unopened Bag, 9 1/2 In.	120.00
Mortimer Snerd's Hometown Band, Windup, Tin Lithograph, Marx, 1930s, 8 3/4 In.	975.00
Mother Goose, Whirl Around The Head, 1940s	30.00
Motorcycle, 1914 Sunbeam, Models Of Yesteryear, No. Y-8, Lesney, Matchbox, Box	57.00
Motorcycle, Army, Rider, Gray, Plastic, Tin Wheels, Box, 1950s	290.00
Motorcycle, Clown Rider, Lehmann	750.00
Motorcycle, Clown Rider, Windup, Tin Lithograph, 5 1/2 In.	210.00
Motorcycle, Clown, Lithograph, Mettoy, Prewar, 7 In.	1200.00
Motorcycle, Delivery, Bump & Go, Windup, Tin Lithograph, Japan, 6 In.	225.00
Motorcycle, Delivery, Speed Boy, Marx	325.00
Motorcycle, Driver, 1950s Model, Battery Operated, Modern Toys, Japan, 8 x 11 In.	385.00
Motorcycle, Flip-Over, Friction, Tin, Alps, 1950s, 5 In.	215.00
Motorcycle, Harley-Davidson, Friction, Plastic, Maroon, Matchbox, 1981, 6 In.	23.00
Motorcycle, Indian Police, Red, Silver Trim, Rubber Wheels, 8 In.	465.00
Motorcycle, Indian, Cast Iron, Red, Black Rubber Tires, Hubley, c.1930, 8 In.	330.00
Motorcycle, Indian, Driver, Crash Car, Hubley, c.1930, 11 1/2 In. ....*Illus*	5170.00
Motorcycle, Indian, Traffic Car, Swivel Head, 9 In. ....*Illus*	4400.00
Motorcycle, Moto Police Gorgo, Tin Lithograph, Box, 8 1/2 In.	275.00
Motorcycle, Patrol, Molded Driver, Rubber Tires, Hubley, 1930s, 6 1/4 In.	415.00
Motorcycle, Police, Mars	250.00
Motorcycle, Policeman, 3 Wheeler	65.00
Motorcycle, Policeman, Cast Iron, Painted, Bowed Legs, 1930s, 2 1/2 In.	32.00
Motorcycle, Policeman, Cast Iron, Red Paint, White Rubber Tires, 4 In.	60.00
Motorcycle, Policeman, Cast Iron, Rubber Tires, Enamel Painted	80.00
Motorcycle, Policeman, Cast Metal, Blue, White Rubber, Tires, 1920s, 7 In.	585.00
Motorcycle, Policeman, Champion, White Rubber Tires, Red Wood Hubs, 1930, 5 In.	935.00
Motorcycle, Policeman, Windup, Marx, 1920s, 9 In.	350.00

Motorcycle, Racing, Driver, Technofix, U.S. Zone, Germany, c.1948, 7 In. . . . .*Illus* 330.00
Motorcycle, Racing, Sidecar, Box, 1960s, 4 1/4 In. 204.00
Motorcycle, Revs Up, Rider Gets On & Off, Battery Operated, Tin, 1950s, 12 In. 745.00
Motorcycle, Rider, Champion, Japan, 10 In. . . . . .175.00 to 225.00
Motorcycle, Rider, George Fischer, 1914, 6 In. 675.00
Motorcycle, Rider, Sidecar, Horn, Windup, Tin Lithograph, 12 In. 225.00
Motorcycle, Rider, Sidecar, Nosco 150.00
Motorcycle, Rider, Sidecar, Orange, Cast Iron, 1930, 4 In. 190.00
Motorcycle, Rider, Sidecar, Passenger, Harley-Davidson, Cast Iron, 9 In. 605.00
Motorcycle, Rider, Solo, Electric, Orange, Rubber Tires, Hubley 595.00
Motorcycle, Sidecar, Nosco 350.00
Motorcycle, Sidecar, Windup, Tin, U.S. Zone 190.00
Motorcycle, Speed Box, Windup, Tin, Marx, Box, 1938, 9 In. . . . .*Illus* 1045.00
Motorcycle, Speed Racer, Cast Iron, Hubley 250.00
Motorcycle, Sunbeam, Sidecar, Marusan, Box 2850.00
Motorcycle, Windup, Clockwork, Tin 330.00
Motorcycle, Windup, Tin, Technofix, No. 4 . . . . 260.00
Mouse, Merry Mousewife, No. 662, Fisher-Price, 1962 . . . . 45.00
Mouse, Pippy, Velvet, Button, Tag In Ear, Stieff, 4 3/4 In. 120.00
Mouse, Standing, Black Velveteen, Corduroy, Yellow, White Skirt, Felt Ears, 16 1/2 In. . . 316.00
Mouse, Tumbling, Windup, Schuco, 4 1/4 In. 80.00
Mr. Potato Head, Styrofoam Head, Plastic Accessories, Hasbro, 1950s 50.00
Mule, Balky Mule, EPL, No. 425, Windup, Tin Lithograph, Lehmann, c.1915, 7 In. 230.00
Mule, Balky Mule, Pulling Carriage, Windup, Tin, Lehmann, 7 x 5 x 2 In. 300.00
Music Box, Humpty Dumpty, Windup, 6 1/2 In. 85.00
Music Box, Punch & Judy, Lithograph Rocking Chime, Cardboard Back, 8 3/4 In. 182.00
Music Box, Three Little Pigs, 3-Dimensional, Jaymar, 1940s 295.00
Musical Chime, Tin Cylinder, Wood Handle, Push Toy, Fisher-Price, 1950s, 8 x 23 In. . . . 30.00
Musicians, Rabbit & Frog, Gunthermann 2750.00
Mystery Ball, Gravity Toy, Fernand Martin, France 725.00
Native On Alligator, Windup, Chein, 15 In. . . . . .225.00 to 265.00
Negro Dude, Pip-Squeak 695.00
Newsboy, Windup, Tin Lithograph, Rubber-Like Face, Felt Clothes, TN, Japan, 6 In. 182.00
Night-Light, Fred Flintstone, Hanna-Barbera, 1984 . . . . 45.00
Noah's Ark, 11 Animals, Wood, Polychrome, 6 1/4 In. 515.00
Noah's Ark, 84 Pairs Of Animals, Dove On Roof 7700.00
Noah's Ark, Cut-Paper Detail, 14 Carved Animals, Brown Finish, Germany, 21 In. 525.00
Organ, No. 130, Crank Handle, Box 70.00
Ostrich, Schoenhut . . . . .650.00 to 850.00
Oven, Cast Iron, Utensils, Marvel 440.00
Owl, Steiff, 9 1/2 In. 30.00
Owl, Woodsy Owl, Cloth, Knickerbocker, 1973, 16 In. 40.00
Ox Cart, Plantation, Black Driver, Cast Iron, Kenton, 1910, 12 In. 330.00
Pail, Boats, Tin Lithograph, Chein 75.00
Pail, Felix, Riding A Horse Chased By Boy, Cover, 8 In. 75.00
Pail, Hanna-Barbera Characters, Tin Lithograph, 8 In. 350.00
Pail, Raggedy Ann & Raggedy Andy, Chein, 1972 . . . . 55.00
Pail, Sea Creatures, Ohio Art 25.00
Pail, Three Little Pigs, Fern Bissell Peat . . . . .100.00 to 125.00
Pail, Treasure Island, Tin 65.00

Toy, Motorcycle, Indian, Driver, Crash Car, Hubley, c.1930, 11 1/2 In.

Toy, Motorcycle, Indian, Traffic Car, Swivel Head, 9 In.

Toy, Motorcycle, Racing, Driver, Technofix,
U.S. Zone, Germany, c.1948, 7 In.

Toy, Motorcycle, Speed Box, Windup, Tin,
Marx, Box, 1938, 9 In.

Paint Box, Alice In Wonderland, Hasbro, 1969, 14 x 18 In. 45.0
Paint Box, Faux Leather Paper Cover, Bourgeois Aine, France, 1890, 16 x 11 In. 1000.0
Paint Box, Little Artist, 3 Porcelain Basins, Paintbrush, Paints, Child's 22.0
Paint Box, Nursery Rhymes, Tin Lithograph, 1930s 45.0
Parachute, Spring Loaded, Pops From Pack, Releases Chutist, Clockwork, Bing 2880.0
Parachutist, Cloth Gear, Helmet & Harness, Silk Parachute, Bing, 1920s 1640.0
Parrot, Lora The Parrot, Original Button & Tag, Steiff, c.1967, 9 In. 70.0
Party Pop Up, Boy, Bisque Head, Papier-Mache Flower, On Stick, France, 1860, 6 In. ... 800.0
Patrol Wagon, White, Black Tires, Electric Lights, Kingsbury 795.0
Peacock, Windup, Tin Lithograph, Japan 195.0
Pedal Car, Airplane, U.S. Mail, Steelcraft, c.1930 .... 3500.0
Pedal Car, Airplane, U.S. Navy Patrol, Silver, Propeller, Steelcraft, 1940s 2990.0
Pedal Car, Atomic Missile, Murray Jet, Chain Drive, 2 Tone Stratosphere Blue 2200.0
Pedal Car, Auburn Super Charger, 1937 .... 5500.0
Pedal Car, Austin J40, Pressed Steel, Blue, Electric Headlights, England, 1950s, 61 In. ... 1610.0
Pedal Car, Bugatti, Eureka, 45 In. 2000.0
Pedal Car, Buick, American National, 1933 .... 4500.0
Pedal Car, Buick, Skylark, BMC, 1950s 250.0
Pedal Car, Buick, Steelcraft, 1929, 38 In. 4500.0
Pedal Car, Champion, Murray, 1958 .... 600.0
Pedal Car, Chrysler Airflow, Skippy, c.1936, 52 In. 7500.0
Pedal Car, Chrysler, Battery Operated, Blue, White Top, Japan, 8 In. 195.0
Pedal Car, Dump Truck, Jetline, 1953 .... 695.0
Pedal Car, Dump Truck, Mack, Steelcraft, 65 In. 6000.0
Pedal Car, Earth Mover, Murray 695.0
Pedal Car, Fantasy, Fiberglass, Plush Interior, Metal Wheels & Bumpers, 57 In. 1320.0
Pedal Car, Fire Chief, AMF 295.0
Pedal Car, Fire Chief, Rickenbacker, Steel, Wood, American National, 1920s, 42 In. 1840.0
Pedal Car, Fire Truck, Ladder, 1923 .... 6800.0
Pedal Car, Fire Truck, Ladder, Murray, 1960 .... 250.0
Pedal Car, Fire Truck, Pontiac, 1948 .... 575.0
Pedal Car, Ford Capri, Battery Operated, Red, Black Wheels, Japan, 11 In. 150.0
Pedal Car, Garton, 1950s 250.0
Pedal Car, Green Upholstery, Rubber Spoked Wheels, Mors, 1907 .... 4620.0
Pedal Car, Highway Patrol, Black, White Body, Black Lettering, 1948 .... 38.0
Pedal Car, Kodak, Yellow, Black, Red, 1941 .... 36.0
Pedal Car, Mercury Cougar, Battery Operated, Bandai, Box, 10 In. 250.0
Pedal Car, No. 7, Red & Black, Gold Trim, American National, c.1910 .... 4800.0
Pedal Car, Packard, Steelcraft, 1927, 48 In. 6500.0
Pedal Car, Pierce Arrow, Steelcraft, c.1935, 46 In. 4500.0
Pedal Car, Racing, Chain Drive, Murray, 1962 .... 495.0
Pedal Car, Racing, Futuristic, 1950s 385.0
Pedal Car, Racing, Indy 500, Metal 295.0
Pedal Car, Racing, Miller, Hammered-Aluminum Body, Engine, Wire Wheels, 1970 .... 7700.0
Pedal Car, Rickenbacker, 1927 .... 6500.0
Pedal Car, Skippy, 1937 .... 2500.0
Pedal Car, Spirit Of America, Orange & Black, Steelcraft 9900.0
Pedal Car, Station Wagon, Murray, 1953 .... 350.0
Pedal Car, Thistle, Station Wagon, 1950s 227.0

Pedal Car, Tot Rod, Murray 119.00
Pedal Car, Tractor, Cast Metal, White & Silver Paint Overall, Farmall, 21 In. 1320.00
Pedal Car, Train, Locomotive & Tender, Casey Jones, Garton, 1961 .... 2500.00
Pencil Case, Gunsmoke, Snap-Open, Photo Of Matt Dillon, Cardboard, Hasbro, 1961 ... 30.00
Perfume Sample Box, Doll's, Heavy Paper, 6 Glass Bottles, France, c.1880, 2 In. 650.00
Phonograph, General Phonograph Mfg., 20 In. 275.00
Phonograph, Windup, Tin Lithograph, Outside Horn, Bing 425.00
Piano, Doll's, Gold Stenciled Front, 12 x 24 In. 495.00
Piano, Mahogany Finish, Stool, Schoenhut, 20 In. 250.00
Piano, Uncle Sam's Baby, Black, Gold Accents, Pressed Steel, 11 x 12 In. 225.00
Piano, Upright, Cherubs Playing Music, 8 Keys, Wood, Lithograph, Bliss, c.1900, 10 In. . 525.00
Piano, Upright, Lithographs On Panels, 15 Keys, Bliss, c.1911, 11 1/2 x 16 3/7 In. 115.00
Pig, Drummer, Windup, Schuco 325.00
Pig, Flutist, Key Wind, Schuco, Box 650.00
Play Pen, Doll's, Cabbage Patch 50.00
Play Set, Betsy McCall Fashion Designer, Desk, Patterns, Pencils, Directions, Box, 1961 45.00
Play Set, Corner Grocer Backdrop, Tin Lithograph, Wolverine, 30 x 11 1/2 x 2 In. 52.00
Play Set, Creeple Peeple Thingmaker, Mattel, Box, 1965, 13 x 15 x 4 In. 90.00
Play Set, Doll Baby Feeding, American Metal Specialties Corp., Box, 18 x 14 x 4 In. 87.00
Play Set, Fast Draw, Mattel, Box 225.00
Play Set, Flintstones, Box 435.00
Play Set, Modern Ranch House, Marx, Box 125.00
Play Set, Motorcycle, Marklin, Box 125.00
Play Set, Soldiers Of Fortune, Tin Lithograph, Soldiers, Howitzer, Marx, 1930s, 28 Piece 555.00
Play Set, Tinker Junior, Wood, Tinkertoy, Cylinder, 9 In. 25.00
Play Set, Troll Village, Marx, Box, 1965 .... 115.00
Pokey, Gumby, Signed By Gloria & Art Clokey, Jesco, Hong Kong, 4 3/4 x 4 1/2 In. 78.00
Police Wagon, Windup, Tin Lithograph, Dumlog Tires, 6 In. 110.00
Policeman, Keystone Cop, Composition, Painted, 13 In. 135.00
Policeman, On Tricycle, Bell In Back, Windup, Tin, Plastic, Suzuki, Japan, 1950s, 4 In. .. 150.00
Policeman, Traffic Cop, Arms Operate With Magnets, Instructions, Box, 1925, 8 In. 550.00
Pool Table, Spring-Loaded Sticks, Tin, U.W.A., 13 In. 145.00
Pool Table, Sticks & Balls, 1931 .... 150.00
Pool Table, Wood Balls, Gotham Steel Corp. 75.00
Pretzel Jetzel Factory, Transogram, Box, 1965 .... 45.00
Projector, Kodatoy, 5 Early Disney Films, Kodak 35.00
Purse, Blondie & Dogwood, Red, 1950s 125.00
Purse, Doll's, Leather, Gold Tooling, Silver Clasp, France, c.1865, 1 1/4 In. 375.00
Purse, Doll's, Reticule, Brown Fabric, Turquoise Beads, France, c.1870, 1 1/2 In. 325.00
Rabbit, Button In Ear, Steiff, 1950, 13 In. 158.00
Rabbit, Easter Bunny, On Tricycle, Windup, Plastic, Tin, Suzun Of Japan, 4 In. 160.00
Rabbit, Peter Rabbit, Composition, Straw Cloth Body, Harrison Caddy, 17 In. 245.00
Rabbit, Pip-Squeak, Blue Ribbon Around Ankles, 9 In. 195.00
Rabbit, Pip-Squeak, Floppy Ears 875.00
Rabbit, Pulling Cart, Plastic Rabbit, Marx, Box, 4 1/2 x 7 In. 65.00
Rabbit, Rubber Ears, Tin Lithograph, Kohler, Box, 4 x 4 1/4 In. 65.00
Rabbit, Sleeping, Plush, Yellow, Pink Ribbon, Gund, Box, 12 In. 50.00
Raccoon, Cosy Raccy, Steiff, 10 In. 155.00
Racing Set, Ford Pickup Pulling Mustang, Wix, Box 80.00
Radiotron Man, Plexiglas, Wood Case, Maxfield Parrish 2250.00
Ramp Walker, 2 Penguins, Plastic Wrap, Hong Kong 40.00
Ramp Walker, Girl, Red Shawl, USA Pat. No. 2140275 .... 75.00
Ramp Walker, Penguin, Sled 30.00
Ramp Walker, Wood, 4 1/2 In. ....*Illus* 25.00
Range, Eagle, Gas, Cast Iron, Hubley, 1920s, 3 1/2 In. 150.00
Rattle, Brownie Head, Sterling Silver & Mother-Of-Pearl, Bells, 1880s, 3 3/4 In. 143.00
Rattle, Rabbit With Carrot, Pink, Celluloid, 1950s, 5 In. 45.00
Rattle, Tin, Bone Handle & Knob, c.1875, 7 In. 95.00
Rattle, Tin, Whistle In Handle, Stamped Hearts & Diamonds, 4 1/2 In. 25.00
Rattle & Whistle, Buttercup, Tin, 1930s 150.00
Rattle & Whistle, Happy Hooligan & Jiggs, Tin 150.00
Refrigerator, California Refrigerator, George Sciple Mfg. Co. 2500.00
Refrigerator & Stove, Metal, 1940s 200.00

Rhinoceros, Schoenhut 500.00
Rickshaw, Masuyama, Man Pulling, Woman With Parasol, Lehmann, c.1930, 7 1/2 In. . . 1150.00
Rickshaw, Mikado Family, Pulled By Man, Lehmann 3200.00
Ring, G-Man 10.00
Robot, Acrobat, Japan, Box 75.00
Robot, Astronaut, Propeller Helmet, Paddle Feet, Windup, NASA Logo, SY 250.00
Robot, Attack Robot, Battery Operated, Tin, Plastic, Black, Red, Japan, 29 In. 390.00
Robot, Battery Operated, Tin Lithograph, Plastic Dome, Japan, 1950s 1288.00
Robot, Bump & Go, Lights Flash, China 10.00
Robot, Chief Robotman 1050.00
Robot, Commando, Ideal, Box 375.00
Robot, Dux-Astroman 695.00
Robot, Junior, Talking, Remote Control, Radio Shack 65.00
Robot, Key Wind, Sparking, Tin Lithograph, Green, N Mark, Japan, Box, 5 1/4 In. 266.00
Robot, Lavender, Rolls Forward, Face Lights Up, Battery Operated, Masudaya, 15 In. . . 4890.00
Robot, Lionbot, Die Cast 185.00
Robot, Lost In Space, Plastic, Blue, Red, Clear, Remco, 1966, 12 1/2 In. 150.00
Robot, Lost In Space, Plastic, Walks Forward, Flashing Lights, Hong Kong, 1977 . . . . . . 295.00
Robot, Monster, Helmet Opens, Lighted Dinosaur, Walks, Arms Move, Battery Operated 95.00
Robot, Moon Explorer . . . . .535.00 to 650.00
Robot, Mr. Sandman, Shovel In Hands Becomes Handle, Sprinkler Head, Wolverine 895.00
Robot, Radar, Battery Operated, Lithographed Legs & Face, Nomura, 1950s, 8 In. 2590.00
Robot, Robbie, Box, 14 In. 3500.00
Robot, Rock 'Em Sock 'Em, Box 200.00
Robot, Rotomatic, Japan, 1960s, 11 In. 295.00
Robot, Smoking, Eyes Light, Arms Move, Battery Operated, Red, Silver, Linemar, Box . 6100.00
Robot, Space Astronaut, Battery Operated 1450.00
Robot, Star Strider AIJI-01, Battery Operated, Tin, Blue, SH Mark, Japan, Box, 12 In. . . 275.00
Robot, Walks, Fires Gun, Battery Operated, Tin Lithograph, Painted, 12 1/2 In. 316.00
Robot, Walks, Rotates, Fires & Flashes, Battery Operated, Tin, Box 55.00
Robot, Warning, Speaks English & Japanese, Blinking Light 200.00
Robot, Windup, Plastic, Blue, Red, Japan, 2 3/4 In. 30.00
Robot, Windup, Sparking, Tin, Green, N Mark, Japan, 5 In. 150.00
Robot, Windup, Walking Legs, Sparking Chest, SY 350.00
Robot, With Gears, Tin & Plastic, 12 In. 195.00
Robot, Zoomer, Blue & Silver 325.00
Rocket Racer, Windup, Marx 425.00
Rocket Ship, Astro 40.00
Roller Coaster, 2 Cars, Chein, 1930 . . . . 325.00
Roller Coaster, 2 Cars, Chein, 1950s 350.00
Roller Skates, Tu-Weeler, 1931 . . . . 75.00
Rollo-Chair, Black Man Pushes Carriage, Windup, Tin, Strauss, 1921 . . . . 575.00
Roly Poly, Clown, Felt Suit, Composition, 8 In. 450.00
Roly Poly, Inspector, Tobacco 450.00
Roly Poly, Jester, Holding Punch Figure, Schoenhut 1200.00
Roly Poly Chime Ball, Fisher-Price, 1966 . . . . 10.00
Ronald McDonald, Standing By Glow-In-The-Dark Star, 1988, 3 In. 25.00

**Wooden boxes, toys, or decoys
should not be kept on the fireplace
mantel or nearby floor area when
the fire is burning. The heat dries
the wood and the paint.**

Toy, Ramp Walker,
Wood, 4 1/2 In.

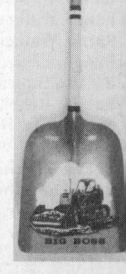

Toy, Shovel,
Bulldozer, Blue
Pan, Big Boss,
13 1/2 x 4 1/2 In.

Rooster, Pip-Squeak, Hen House, Germany 225.00
Rooster, Pip-Squeak, In Case, 1900s 195.00
Rooster, Pip-Squeak, Papier-Mache, Wood Bellows, 4 1/4 In. 82.00
Rooster, Rock-A-Tot, Riding Toy, Wood, White, Red Comb, Green Rockers 250.00
Rooster, Tag, Steiff, c.1950, 7 1/4 In. 71.00
Rooster & Chick, Wolverine, Box 880.00
Sail Way Carnival, 3 Children In Boats, Spin Around, Unique Art 465.00
Sailor, Dancing, Columbia On Hat, Lehmann, 1903, 7 1/2 In. 690.00
Satellite, Astronaut Floats In Air, Battery Operated, Japan 395.00
Scooter, Arrow Deluxe, Steel Frame & Wheels, Stripes, 43 In. 137.00
Scooter, Bonzo, Pull Toy, Chein 650.00
Scooter, Ice Cream, Courtland, Box 350.00
Scooter, Krazy Kat, Nifty, 1932, 7 x 6 In. 450.00
Scooter, Zundapp Bella, Friction, Tin, Technofix, 1950s, 6 1/2 In. 350.00
Seal, Steel Frame, Rubber Wheels, Ivory Mohair, Straw Stuffing, Pull Toy, Steiff, 28 In. . 195.00
Seal, Swimming, Windup, Hand Painted Tin & Wood, 6 In. 55.00
Seesaw, Windup, Celluloid, Tin, 6 1/2 In. 195.00
Service Station, Cars, Renwal 235.00
Service Station, Municipal Airport, 2 Pumps, Tin Lithograph, Marx, c.1930, 5 x 6 In. .. 650.00
Service Station, Roof Sign, Working Car Wash, Keystone, Box, c.1949 .... 480.00
Service Station, Texaco, Complete, Unused, Box 200.00
Sewing Machine, Barbie, Box 25.00
Sewing Machine, Battery Operated, Original Wrench & Instructions, Box, 7 x 4 x 6 In. . 75.00
Sewing Machine, Bell 175.00
Sewing Machine, Betsy Ross, Metal, Green 85.00
Sewing Machine, British Zone, Germany 145.00
Sewing Machine, Cast Iron, Oak Base, Electric Motor, Wilcox & Gibbs, Pat. 1894 ..... 65.00
Sewing Machine, Elect Kramer, Child's 35.00
Sewing Machine, Holly Hobbie 25.00
Sewing Machine, Junior Miss, Singer, France 70.00
Sewing Machine, Little Comfort, Automatic, Wood Box, c.1897, 3 x 8 x 7 In. 518.00
Sewing Machine, Little Modiste, Red Metal, Japan 25.00
Sewing Machine, Little Mother 125.00
Sewing Machine, Metal, Wood Base, Kananee, U.S. Zone Germany, Box, 10 x 5 In. ... 85.00
Sewing Machine, Montgomery Ward 35.00
Sewing Machine, Mueller, Germany 495.00
Sewing Machine, No.1 Princess, Treadle, Decker Mfg. Co. Ltd., Detroit, Mich. 2530.00
Sewing Machine, Pretty Maid, Tin, Blue & Silver, Marx 75.00
Sewing Machine, Renwal 10.00
Sewing Machine, Singer, Box ....52.00 to 98.00
Sewing Machine, So Big, Marx, Box 135.00
Sewing Machine, Spencer, 1910 .... 450.00
Sewing Machine, Stitchwell, Early 1900s 500.00
Sewing Machine, Treadle, Cast Iron & Oak, Ideal Label, 30 1/2 In. 19.00
Sewing Set, Nancy & Sluggo, Box, 1949, 16 In. 100.00
Sheriff, 2 Guns, Battery Operated, Cragstan 150.00
Shmoo, Vinyl, Bells Inside, Copyright UFS, 1950s, 6 In. 145.00
Shovel, Bulldozer, Blue Pan, Big Boss, 13 1/2 x 4 1/2 In. ....*Illus* 15.00
Shovel, Steam, Pressed Steel 104.00
Shrink Machine, Futuristic Look, Wham-O, 1968 .... 45.00
Sign Set, Airport, Scale Models, Cragstan Industries, Box, 2 3/4 In., 8 Piece 23.00
Siren, Bicycle, CHIPS, Package, 1970s 20.00
Siren, G-Man, Windup, Tin, Courtland, 4 In. 65.00
Skateboard, Chicago, Chicago Roller Skate Co., Oak, Box, c.1950 .... 100.00
Skaters, Man & Woman, Windup, Celluloid, Occupied Japan 225.00
Sled, Floral Design, Red, c.1880 .... 495.00
Sled, Joseph, Dark Red & Black Paint, Gold Striping, Wood, 38 In. 745.00
Sled, Painted Red, River Scene, Pine, Iron Blades, 1870s, 30 3/4 In. 785.00
Sled, Painted, Shaped Platform, Persimmon Design, c.1860, 32 x 12 1/2 In. 795.00
Sled, Pine & Wrought Iron, Carved, Painted, William Hust Stencil, c.1870, 34 x 13 In. .. 1285.00
Sled, Portland Racer, Painted Snow Scene 990.00
Sled, Push, Child's, Wood, Black & Red Paint, Upholstery, Late 19th Century, 50 In. 285.00
Sled, Scenic Design, Mustard, c.1870 .... 695.00

Sled, Speedaway, Paris Mfg. Co., 30 1/2 In. 55.0
Sleigh, Wood, Winter Landscapes Painted On Sides, 38 1/4 x 44 In. 770.0
Smoking MacGregor, Steamer Trunk, Battery Operated, Tin, TN, Japan, 11 In. 160.0
Snail, Velvet, Multicolored, Vinyl Shell, Rubber Antennae, Tag, Steiff, 1960s, 6 1/2 In. .. 315.0
Snoopy, Astronaut, Spacesuit, Accessories, Determined Prod., Box, 1969, 9 In. ...224.00 to 415.0
Snoopy, Beach Outfit, Plastic, Movable, Knickerbocker Toy Co., 1970s, 8 In. 60.0
Snoopy, Blue Jeans, Sweater, Movable, Knickerbocker Toy Co., 1970s, 8 In. 65.0
Snoopy, Canteen, Children's, Plastic, Vinyl Carrier, Snoopy Selling Lemonade, 6 x 5 In. . 25.0
Snoopy, Flying Ace, Jointed, Goggles, Leather Flight Helmet, Pocket Dolls, 1960s, 7 In. . 50.0
Snoopy, Pilot, Plastic, Cloth Flight Helmet, Pocket Dolls Production, 1960s, 7 In. 60.0
Snoopy, Pilot, Plastic, Vinyl, Brushed-Felt Flight Helmet, United Features, 1966, 7 In. .. 78.0
Snoopy, Plastic, Hong Kong, 1960s, 7 In. 35.0
Snoopy, Plastic, Movable Arms, Legs, Knickerbocker Toy Co., 1970s, 9 In. 50.0
Snoopy, Rubber, Vinyl, Safari Style Jacket, Determined Products, Korea, 1970s, 9 In. ... 52.0
Snoopy, Sno-Cone Machine, Shaped Like Snoopy's Doghouse, Playskool, Box 30.0
Snowmobile, Goes Uphill, Sound, Japan, Box, 1960s, 8 In. 300.0
Sofa, Doll's, Mahogany, Carved, Red Upholstery, Victorian, 35 In. 110.0
Soldier, 11th Hussars, Prince Albert's Own, Britains, Box, 2 1/2 In., 8 Piece 650.0
Soldier, 16th Century Knights In Armor, Britains, No.1307, Box, 9 Piece 75.0
Soldier, Arabs Of The Desert, Britains, 11 Piece 55.0
Soldier, Arabs Of The Desert, No. 164, Britains, Box, 6 Piece 144.0
Soldier, Artillery, Trucks, Airplanes, Metal, Midgetoy, Box, 20 Piece 82.0
Soldier, Australian Jungle Fighter Set, Window Box 2495.0
Soldier, Bandsman Playing Flute, Lead, 1930s, 3 In. 25.0
Soldier, Beating Drum, Windup, Tin Lithograph, Wolverine, 13 In. 225.0
Soldier, Black Watch, No. 11, Britains ....125.00 to 150.0
Soldier, British Commando, Accessories 450.0
Soldier, Camel Corps Of Egyptian Army, No. 48, Britains, Box, 6 Piece 175.0
Soldier, Civil War Union Infantry, No. 2059, Britains, Box 185.0
Soldier, Coronation Series, Procession, Die Cast, Johillco, Box, c.1953, 53 Piece 175.0
Soldier, Drummer Boy, Chein 175.0
Soldier, Drums & Bugles Of The Line, Britains, c.1945, 6 Piece 235.0
Soldier, French Resistance Fighter, Accessories 375.0
Soldier, German Storm Trooper, Accessories 450.0
Soldier, Gordon Highlanders, Britains ....145.00 to 165.0
Soldier, Japanese, Accessories 650.0
Soldier, Lancer Group, Die Cast, Britains, England, Original Card, 3 In., 4 Piece 40.0
Soldier, Medical Personnel, Nurses, Doctor, Stretcher Team, Britains 44.0
Soldier, Queen's Own Hussars, No. 8, Britains, Box, 5 Piece 120.0
Soldier, Roman Chariots & Figures, Johillco, 6 Piece 22.0
Soldier, Royal Scots Greys, Britains 30.0
Soldier, Russian Infantryman, Accessories 450.0
Soldier, Sharpshooter, Crawls On Stomach, Windup, Occupied Japan, 8 In. 100.0
Soldier, U.S. Cavalry, Britains, No. 229, Box, 5 Piece 120.0
Soldier, U.S. Federal Troops, Paint, Pfeiffer, 1898, 6 Piece 185.0
Soldier, U.S. Marine Corps Color Bearer, USMC Flag, Hand Painted, England, 4 In. 25.0
Soldier, Union Artillery, Britains, Box 265.0
Soldier, Windup, Tin, Prewar Germany, 7 In. 275.0
Soldier Boy, Drummer, Felt Outfit, Tin Helmet, 5 In. 510.0
Space Commando, Battery Operated, Japan, Box 2450.0
Space Satellite, Launching Station, Tin Lithograph, Marx, 9 1/2 x 12 x 6 In. 116.0
Space Station, Planet-Y, Pilot, Rotating Upper Half, Battery Operated, Sound, TN 425.0
Spaceship, Apollo, Lights, Sound, Tin, Battery Operated, Alps, Japan, 9 In. 130.0
Spiderman, On Motor Bike, Plastic, Red, Black, Blue, Buddy L, 4 In. 29.0
Squirrel, Possy The Squirrel, Tag, Steiff, c.1950, 7 In. 71.0
Squirrel, Steiff, 1930s 70.0
Stage Coach, 2 Horses, Driver, Plastic, 1/25 Scale, 1960s, 11 x 5 In. 30.0
Stake Wagon, Donkey Drawn, Black Driver, Tin, Cast Iron, 3 3/4 x 4 3/4 In. 250.0
Stan Laurel, Vibrates & Moves, Windup, Vinyl, Harmon Pictures Corp., 1968, 6 In. 35.0
Steam Engine, Brass & Metal, Minor No. 1, Mamod, England, 5 1/2 x 5 1/2 x 3 In. 57.0
Steam Engine, Horizontal, Ernst Planck, 10 1/2 In. 1350.0
Steam Engine, Pulleys, Gauges, Rumely, 18 x 8 1/2 x 8 1/2 In. 650.0
Steam Engine, Road Roller, Buddy L, 1920s 15000.0

Steam Engine, Vertical Boiler, Runs On Sterno Or Alcohol, Red Injun Brand, 1930s ... 175.00
Steam Shovel, Battery Operated, Stamped Metal, Orange, Japan, 7 x 6 In. 115.00
Steam Shovel, Mack, Hercules, Tin Lithograph, Chein, Late 1920s, 27 1/2 In. 2530.00
Steam Shovel, Mechanical, Courtland, Box 135.00
Steam Shovel, No. 106, Steel, Orange, Structo, Box 350.00
Steam Shovel, Panama, Hubley 2090.00
Steam Shovel, Riding, Keystone 175.00
Steamroller, Keystone, No. 60, Pressed Steel, Black, Green, Red Wheels, 1931, 20 In. ... 750.00
Steamroller, Rangeley Rod Co., c.1920 .... 300.00
Steamroller, Tin, Metal Rolled Roof, 1920s, 11 1/2 In. 195.00
Steamroller, Tin, Plastic, White, Blows Bubbles, Modern Toys, Japan, 1960s, 4 x 10 In. . 165.00
Steamroller, Windup, Tin, 1930, 11 1/2 In. 230.00
Store, Kiddie Grocery Store, Utensils, Products, Braun's Animal Cracker Tin, 1930s 150.00
Stove, 5 Pots & Covers, Electric, Germany, 1910 .... 2410.00
Stove, Accessories & Cooking Pots, Cast Iron, Kenton, 1910s, 6 1/2 x 8 7/8 In. 115.00
Stove, Bucks Junior, Cast Iron, Nickel Plated, 22 In. 1485.00
Stove, Crescent 55.00
Stove, Crescent, Cast Iron, Accessories, Sample, 12 In. 300.00
Stove, Eagle, Pots, Lid Lifter, Cast Metal 45.00
Stove, Electric Range, Marklin, 1940 .... 85.00
Stove, Electric, 1930s 125.00
Stove, Electric, Pressed Steel, Marklin, 15 x 15 x 8 1/2 In. 581.00
Stove, Estate Fresh Air Oven, Enameled Steel, Nickel Fittings, 15 In. 2420.00
Stove, Favorite Stoves & Ranges, Cast Iron, 23 In. 93.00
Stove, Myers, Osborn & Co., Iron, 1884, Golden Star, 13 In. 130.00
Stove, Potbellied, Cast Iron, Spark, 13 1/2 In. 250.00
Stove, Restaurant Type, With 5 Pots, 14 In. 825.00
Stove, Spark, Lid Lifter, Black Finish, Cast Iron, 13 7/8 In. 325.00
Stove, Venus, Cooking Pot, Fry Pan, Lifter, Cast Iron & Tin 225.00
Street Cleaner, Tidy Tim, Windup, Tin, Marx, 1933, 9 x 7 In. ....450.00 to 785.00
Stroller, Doll's, Cast Iron, Kilgore, Orange 625.00
Stroller, Doll's, Rolled Wicker, Curlicue Design, Unpainted, Victorian 350.00
Stroller, Doll's, Tin Lithograph, 16 In. 325.00
Sulky, Removable Driver, Cast Iron, Kenton 325.00
Surrey, 2 Horses, Kenton, c.1940, 11 In. 77.00
Sweeper, Baby Sweeper, Bissell 195.00
Sweeper, Broom & Dustpan, 1950s 98.00
Table, Doll's, Drop Leaf, Wood, Drawer, Turned Legs, France, c.1875, 9 In. 325.00
Table, Doll's, Maitrise, Cabriole Legs, Top Flips Up, Garden Scene, France, 7 In. 750.00
Tank, Assault, Gama, Box, 5 1/2 In. 480.00
Tank, Clockwork, White Lettering, Box, 3 3/4 In. 225.00
Tank, Gama, 6035 T-60, Box 1100.00
Tank, M-18, Bump & Go, Tin Lithograph, Battery Powered, Japan, 8 In. 75.00
Tank, M-35, Battery Operated, Tin, Green, Brown, Cragstan, Japan, Box, 8 x 4 x 4 In. 150.00
Tank, Mack, Orange, Rubber Balloon Tires, Cast Iron, 5 3/4 x 2 x 2/34 In. 350.00
Tank, MX, Battery Powered, Bump & Go, Tin Lithograph, Movable Turret, Japan, 9 In. . 77.00
Tank, Soldier, Windup, Orange, Blue, Tin Lithograph, Marx, 1930s, 9 In. 145.00
Tank, Space, Windup, Rex Mars, All Tin, Marx 375.00
Tank, Strange Explorer, Gorilla Comes Out Of Bottom, Battery Operated 545.00
Tank, Windup, Tin Lithograph, Prewar, Japan 100.00
Tank, Windup, Tin, Camouflage Paint, Germany, 2 3/4 x 1 1/2 x 1 1/4 In. 86.00
Target, Air Rifle, Daisy, Ward's, Box, 1950s 200.00
Target, Daisy, Cork, Ward's, Box, 1950s 200.00
Target, Shooting Gallery, Cast Iron, Eagle, 13 In. 300.00
Target, Shooting Gallery, Clown, Barrel Body, Painted, 13 1/2 In. 385.00
Target, Shooting Gallery, Metal, Ohio Art, Box 95.00
Target, Shooting Gallery, Tin Lithograph, Gun & 2 Darts, Ohio Art 175.00
Taxi, Ford Galaxie, Ambulance, Family Sedan, Japan, Box, 1964, 7 In., 6 Piece 169.00
Taxi, Mohawk, Yellow, 8 1/2 In. 375.00
Taxi, Stamped Tin, Rubber Tires, Antenna, Friction, Green, White, Japan, 6 In. 23.00
Taxi, Thomas Taxi, Rubber Wheels, Checkered Design Sticker, Plastic, 4 1/2 In. 35.00
Taxi, Tricky Taxi, Windup, Tin, Orange, Black, Cream, Marx, 4 1/2 In. 110.00
Taxi, Tricky Taxi, Windup, Tin, Red & White, Marx, 4 1/2 In. 290.00

Toy, Train, Marvel, Superhero Express,
Windup, Box

Toy, Train Set, Lionel,
Locomotive, Green,
Brass Trim, 5 Piece

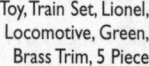

Taxi, Windup, Yellow, Chein	295.0
Taxi, Yellow Cab, Arcade, 8 In.	975.0
Taxi, Yellow Cab, Driver, Arcade, 7 3/4 In.	800.0
Taxi, Yellow Cab, Mohawk	325.0
Taxi, Yellow Cab, Molded Driver, Arcade, 8 1/4 In.	316.0
Taxi, Yellow Cab, Orange, Nickel Wheels, Cast Iron, Arcade, 8 In.	400.0
Tea Set, Doll's, China, Blue, White, With Shelf, Japan, Box, 20th Century, 22 Piece	49.0
Tea Set, Doll's, Porcelain, Floral Design, France, Box, Service For 6	265.0
Tea Set, Floral Decals, Gold Rim, Madame Alexander, Box, 8 Piece	175.0
Tea Set, Occupied Japan, 9 Piece	125.0
Teddy Bears are also listed in the Teddy Bear category.	
Teething Ring, Teddy Bear Holding Bells, Mother-Of-Pearl Mouthpiece, 3 7/8 In.	375.0
Telegraph Set, Standard Telegraph Signal, Strauss Toy, Box	35.0
Telephone, Chatters, Pull Toy, Fisher-Price	30.0
Telephone, Romper Room Snoopy	15.0
Telephone Lineman, Climbs Pole, Battery Operated	350.0
Theatre, Guignol, La Poupee Modele, Cardboard, France, c.1900, 12 x 18 In.	2500.0
Theatre, Marionette, Windup, Celluloid Figures Dance On Metal Platform, 1920s	650.0
Thresher, McCormick-Deering, Gray, Red Plates, Cast Iron, Arcade, 10 In.	254.0
Tiger, Beige Velvet, Black Stripe, Glass Eyes, Straw Stuffing, 11 1/2 In.	60.0
Tiger, Bengal, Battery Operated, Box, 1961	195.0
Tiger, Riding Scooter, Windup, Marx	57.0
Tiger, Tag, Steiff, c.1950, 15 In.	88.0
Tin Man, Galvanized Sheet Metal, Gold Paint, 14 1/2 In.	303.0
Tinker Toy, Zoo, Plastic, Wood, No. 727, Tinkertoy, Cylinder, 11 In.	30.0
Tool Chest, No. 16, 2 Boys Building A Chest, Wood, Gilbert, 21 x 12 1/2 In.	105.0
Top, Gulliver's Travels, Animated Movie Characters, Tin Lithograph, Chein, c.1939	85.0
Top, Irving's Wizard Top, Metal, 1902	20.0
Top, Snoopy & The Gang, Tin, Red Push Handle, 1966	25.0
Tractor, 6 Wheels, Foden, King Size, No. K-12, Green, Matchbox, England, Box	46.0
Tractor, BJ & The Bear, Road Champs, Die Cast, Kenworth, Display Card, 2 1/2 In.	25.0
Tractor, Cast Iron, Arcade, 1920s	95.0
Tractor, Cultivision Farmall, Nickel Driver, Rubber Tires, Arcade, 5 x 7 In.	990.0
Tractor, Fordson, Cast Iron, Red, Gold Wheels, 4 In.	65.0
Tractor, Fordson, Power Major, Box	150.0
Tractor, Hubley, 12 x 7 1/2 In.	95.0
Tractor, John Deere Harvester, Silver, Green Trim, Vindex, 13 1/2 In.	7150.0
Tractor, John Deere, 1960	175.0
Tractor, Pressed Metal, 2 Farming Attachments, 5 In.	16.0
Tractor, Rubber, Metal Axles, Red, Black, Auburn, 3 1/2 x 3 In.	23.0
Tractor, Structo, Pat. Sept. 28, 1920, 8 1/2 In.	295.0
Tractor, Tonka, Red	120.0
Tractor, Trailer, Case Comfort King	180.0

Tractor, Windup, Tin Lithograph, Red, Blue, Gama, Western Germany, 4 In.	46.00
Tractor & Wagon, Row Crop, Oliver, Cast Metal, 18 In.	350.00
Tractor Trailer, GMC, 13-Wheel Machinery Hauler, Smitty Toys, 1945-55, 26 In.	200.00
Traffic Signal, Stop-And-Go, Tin & Steel, Chein, c.1930, 10 1/2 In.	330.00
Train, American Flyer, Windup, O Gauge, Streamlined, 3-Piece Train	345.00
Train, Baggage Cart, Railway Express, Pressed Steel, 23 1/2 In.	275.00
Train, Black Fire, Engine & Tender, 3 1/2 In.	5130.00
Train, Black Fire, Live Steam, Tender, London-Midland Scotland Lines	9000.00
Train, Bliss, Buffalo, Wood, Paper Lithograph, Removable Roof, c.1900, 45 In.	7190.00
Train, Fallows, Locomotive, Steam, Venus, Tin, Painted, 1880s, 6 In.	315.00
Train, Fisher-Price, No. 999, Huffy Puffy Train, Engine, Caboose, 2 Cars, 1963	35.00
Train, Folk Art, Clowns, Wood, Cloth, Paper, Yellow Paint, 12 3/4 & 6 1/2 In, 7 Piece	635.00
Train, Ives, Locomotive, No. 3, Windup, Clockwork, Tin Lithograph	1815.00
Train, Keystone, Pullman Car, No. 6800, Black & Red, 10 1/2 x 26 In.	395.00
Train, Lionel, Box Car, Baby Ruth, X1004, 1949	22.00
Train, Lionel, Flat Car, Airplane, No. 6800, 1957	80.00
Train, Lionel, Gondola, N.Y.C., No. 6062, 1959	24.00
Train, Lionel, Hopper Car, Stamped Metal, Green, Black, New York Central, 1930s	59.00
Train, Lionel, Locomotive & Tender, No. 224, Steam, O Gauge, 18 In.	165.00
Train, Lionel, Locomotive, No. 252, Electric, Stamped Metal, Painted, O Gauge	255.00
Train, Lionel, Locomotive, Switch, Santa Fe, No. 634, Diesel, Plastic, Blue, 10 In.	60.00
Train, Lionel, Locomotive, Union Pacific, No. 202, Diesel, Plastic, Orange, 10 In.	55.00
Train, Lionel, Turbo Missile Launching Car, No. 3349, 1962	28.00
Train, Lionel, ZW Transformer, 275 Watts	325.00
Train, Locomotive, Lionel, No. 2348, Minneapolis & St. Louis	350.00
Train, Locomotive, Overland Express, Windup, Tin Lithograph, Yone, Japan, Box, 7 In.	55.00
Train, Locomotive, Pacific Railway Electric, Friction, Tin Lithograph, Japan, Box, 6 In.	78.00
Train, Locomotive, Red, Stamped Steel, 8 In.	155.00
Train, Locomotive, Ride-On, Leather Seat, Iron Wheels, Rubber Tires, 1900, 49 1/2 In.	2595.00
Train, Locomotive, Tender, 2 Passenger Cars, Windup, Tin, Germany, Box, c.1910	635.00
Train, Marklin, Steam Locomotive & Tender, HR66/12920, O Gauge	1300.00
Train, Marvel, Superhero Express, Windup, Box *Illus*	9075.00
Train, Marx, Army Supply, 2 Buildings, 1950s	350.00
Train, Marx, Streamline, Commodore Vanderbilt Locomotive, Tender, Tanker, Gondola	115.00
Train, Rapid Transit Car, Friction, Sheet Steel, Blue, Red, Yellow, Doors Open, 20 1/2 In.	190.00
Train, Revell, Chu Chu, Plastic, Trigger Mechanism, Box, 1950s	55.00
Train, Steam Engine, Horizontal, Wood, Early 20th Century, 6 In.	115.00
Train, Steam Engine, Stationary, Germany, 7 In.	35.00
Train, Tin, Locomotive & 2 Cars, France, c.1870, 2 3/4 x 8 1/4 In.	375.00
Train Accessories, Central Station, Original Glass, Marklin, 1900	3500.00
Train Accessories, Freight Station, Platform, Maroon Roof, Green Station, Lionel, 18 In.	375.00
Train Accessories, Grand Central Station, Tin, Electrified, Marx, 16 3/4 In.	357.00
Train Accessories, Ives, Twist Bridge	5720.00
Train Accessories, Railroad Crossing Signal, Lighted, 9 In.	40.00
Train Accessories, Railroad Station, 2 Buildings, Corrugated Tin Arch, 18 x 13 In.	1995.00
Train Accessories, Railroad Station, City, Green Roof, Lionel, 8 1/2 x 19 1/2 In.	1150.00
Train Accessories, Street Lamps, Metal, Fluorescent, Aristo-Craft, Japan, Box, 2 Piece	38.00
Train Set, American Flyer, Model 901, Cast Iron, Tin, Box	198.00
Train Set, Aurora, Railmaster, Display Base, Red Ball Express	70.00
Train Set, Issmayer, Windup, Tin Lithograph, Track, Box, c.1900, 5-In. Engine	990.00
Train Set, Lionel, Locomotive & 3 Cars, Standard Gauge, Boxes, 1926	775.00
Train Set, Lionel, Locomotive, Coal Tender, Transformer, Track, 5 Piece	175.00
Train Set, Lionel, Locomotive, Green, Brass Trim, 5 Piece *Illus*	2700.00
Train Set, Lionel, Locomotive, No. 1601, Original Blister-Pack Carton	4070.00
Train Set, Lionel, Log Loader & Log Dump Car, 1950	395.00
Train Set, Lionel, No. 324E, Baby State, Standard Gauge	2420.00
Train Set, Lionel, Texas Special, Alcoa, Diesel Freight, Box	395.00
Train Set, Marx, O Gauge, Double Engine, Tinplate, No Tracks, 1941, 7 Piece	650.00
Train Set, Marx, Union Pacific Streamline, No. 1093, Green & Cream, Box	275.00
Train Set, Weeded Dart, Alcohol Burning, Track, 8-In. Engine, 4 Piece	825.00
Train Set, Wood, No. 1486, Frankfurt, Germany, Box, 1961, 8 Piece	69.00
Training Center, Army & Air Force, Tents, Office Equipment, Marx, Box, 12 In.	1000.00
Transporter, Race Car, Ecurie Ecosse, 2 Mercedes, Corgi	135.00

Traveling Salesman, Windup, Celluloid & Metal, Box, 4 In. 225.C
Tricycle, Horse, Gold Art 500.C
Troll House, Mattel 25.C
Trolley, Bell, 10 Separate Tin People, Friction, Japan, 7 In. 165.C
Trolley, Bell, Windup, Kingsbury, 9 In. 365.C
Trolley, Dent, Cast Iron 650.C
Trolley, Toonerville, Cast Iron, Dent, Box 1250.C
Trolley, Toonerville, Pot Metal 350.C
Trolley, Toonerville, Windup, Tin, Fontaine Fox 345.C
Trolley Car, Windup, Tin Lithograph, Tramway Co., Red, Gray, Germany, 1920, 6 3/4 In. 200.C
Truck, Aerial Ladder, Tonka, 1961 .... 225.C
Truck, Army, Canvas Top, Pressed Steel, Keystone 650.C
Truck, Army, Olive, Kingsbury 288.0
Truck, Army, Searchlight, Friction, Tin, Rubber Tires, Japan, 4 In. 50.0
Truck, Automatic Tilter, Driver, Windup, Germany, 1920s, 9 1/2 In. 1195.0
Truck, Bedford Evening News Van, No. 42A, Matchbox 50.0
Truck, Bell Telephone, Green, Gold Trim, Nickel Plated Wheels, 3 x 5 In. 1035.0
Truck, Beverly Hillbillies, 4 Figures, Bench, Chair, Table, Ladder, Tire, Tied On Truck .. 400.0
Truck, Brinks Armored, Accessories, Buddy L, Box 1000.0
Truck, Cannon, Brown, Kingsbury, 15 In. 225.0
Truck, Cannon, Pressed Steel, Sonny, 1920s 695.0
Truck, Car Carrier, 4 Cars, Structo, 1950s 85.0
Truck, Car Carrier, Racing Cars, Buddy L 95.0
Truck, Car Carrier, Ramp, Wyandotte 110.0
Truck, Cargo, Texaco, With Skychief Gas Pump, Red Body, Chrome Fender, 1940 ..... 46.0
Truck, Cement Mixer, Buddy L 850.0
Truck, Cement Mixer, Foden, Swivel Mixer, No. 26, Lesney, Matchbox, 1956 .... 41.0
Truck, Cement Mixer, Green & Red, Buddy L 195.0
Truck, Cement Mixer, Hubley, Cast Iron, 3 5/8 In. 295.0
Truck, Cement Mixer, Jaeger, Cast Iron, Nickel Plated, Kenton, 1930, 6 5/8 In. 375.0
Truck, Cement Mixer, Mack, Hubley 1760.0
Truck, Cement Mixer, Structo, 22 In. ....150.00 to 200.0
Truck, Circus Animal, Trailer, Dinky Toy 595.0
Truck, Coal, Black Driver, Cast Iron, Hubley, 1920s 5390.0
Truck, Crane, Renwal 50.0
Truck, Delivery, Bond Bread, Friction, Tin Lithograph, Linemar, Japan, 3 In. 40.0
Truck, Delivery, Chivers & Sons, Metal, Plastic Wheels, Painted, Corgi, 5 In. 40.0
Truck, Delivery, Coca-Cola, Delicious & Refreshing, Red, White, Ertl, 1954 .... 85.0
Truck, Delivery, Coca-Cola, White Body, Black Tires, Buddy L 325.0
Truck, Delivery, Coca-Cola, Work Refreshed, Yellow, Red Lettering, Ertl, 1954 .... 88.0
Truck, Delivery, Fanny Farmer Candy, Red & White, 8 1/4 In. 120.0
Truck, Delivery, Heinz Pickles, Metalcraft, Box 850.0
Truck, Delivery, Howard Johnson's, Push Toy, Marx 150.0
Truck, Delivery, Ice Cream, Blue Cab, Orange Box, Cast Iron, Kilgore, 6 x 2 In. 350.0
Truck, Delivery, John Wanamaker, No. 54, Wood, 1920, 11 In. 875.0
Truck, Delivery, Milk, Plastic, 1950s 50.0
Truck, Delivery, See's Candies 18.0
Truck, Delivery, Wrigley's Spearmint, Green, Rear Doors Open, Buddy L, 14 In. 325.0
Truck, Driver, Side Dumper, Bonnet, Windup, 8 In. 490.0
Truck, Dump, Blue, Cast Iron, Arcade, 4 In. 50.0
Truck, Dump, Contractor's, Cast Iron, Kenton, 1920s, 8 In. 650.0
Truck, Dump, Crank-Up, Cast Iron, Arcade, 1924 .... 875.0
Truck, Dump, Dodge, Turner, 1939 .... 295.0
Truck, Dump, Green Body, Rubber Tires, Cast Iron, Arcade, 3 1/2 In. 86.0
Truck, Dump, Green, White Balloon Wheels, Pressed Steel, Wyandotte, 1930s, 15 In. ... 275.0
Truck, Dump, Hi-Side, Marx, Box 500.0
Truck, Dump, Highway Department, Tonka 225.0
Truck, Dump, Hydraulic, Green & White, Buddy L, 1954 .... 225.0
Truck, Dump, Hydraulic, No. 201A, Steel, Rubber Tires, Buddy L, c.1930, 24 1/2 In. 1090.0
Truck, Dump, Lift, Perforated Grill, Black, Nickel, Red, Wheels, 1925 .... 500.0
Truck, Dump, Mack, Blue, Arcade, 8 1/2 In. 431.0
Truck, Dump, Mack, Blue, Red, Nickel Wheels, Kilgore, 9 In. ....230.00 to 259.0
Truck, Dump, Mack, Gray, Arcade 2750.0

Truck, Dump, Mack, No. 28, Orange, Die Cast, Matchbox, Lesney, England, 2 1/2 In. . . . 26.00
Truck, Dump, No. 38, Pressed Steel, Black, Red Chassis, Keystone, c.1927, 26 1/2 In. . . . 345.00
Truck, Dump, No. 434, Yellow, Red, Electric Headlights, Buddy L, 1935, 19 1/2 In. 285.00
Truck, Dump, Pressed Steel, Buddy L, 26 In. 6325.00
Truck, Dump, Ratcheting, Buddy L 1100.00
Truck, Dump, Red Body, Green Dump, Nickel Wheels, Arcade, 6 In. 85.00
Truck, Dump, Sand & Gravel, Metalcraft, St. Louis, Mo. 450.00
Truck, Dump, Sturditoy, c.1920, 24 In. 735.00
Truck, Dump, Turner, 1930 . . . . 475.00
Truck, Dump, Windup, Kingsbury 345.00
Truck, Dump, Wolverine, 1950s, 13 In. 165.00
Truck, Express, Buddy L 875.00
Truck, Extension Ladder, Tin Lithograph, Cragstan, Japan, Box, 1960s, 14 1/4 In. 80.00
Truck, Flat Bed & Steam Shovel, Structo, 1950 . . . . 3550.00
Truck, Freighter, Double, Cooper-Jarrett, Die Cast, Blue, Matchbox, England, Box, 11 In. 120.00
Truck, Gasoline, Battery Operated, Hong Kong, 1977, 13 1/4 In. 60.00
Truck, Gasoline, Lubrite, Red, Mack Labels On Cab, Nickel Plated Driver, Arcade, 13 In. 2300.00
Truck, Gasoline, Mobil, Friction, Tin, Japan, Box, 1950s . . . . .250.00 to 475.00
Truck, Gasoline, Pure Oil Company, Nickel Bumper, Headlights & Spotlight, Blue Tank . 1600.00
Truck, Gasoline, Shell Oil, Friction, Japan, 1950s, 13 1/2 In. 245.00
Truck, Gasoline, Shell Oil, Tootsietoy 50.00
Truck, Gasoline, Sinclair, Pressed Steel, Marx 350.00
Truck, Gasoline, Texaco, Pressed Steel, Painted, Plastic Tires, Buddy L, 1950s, 23 1/2 In. 189.00
Truck, Gasoline, Texaco, Tilt Cab, Red, White Lettering, Ertl 24.00
Truck, Grain Hauler, Dark Green Cab, Light Green Trailer, Dunwell 175.00
Truck, Grain Hauler, Tonka, 1955 . . . . 325.00
Truck, Hydraulic, Orange Cab, Black Bed, Pump, Keystone, 28 x 9 x 10 In. 450.00
Truck, Ice Cream, White Body, Bandai, Box, 6 1/2 In. 450.00
Truck, Ice, Ice & Tongs, Pressed Steel, Marx, 11 In. 100.00
Truck, Ice, Ice & Tongs, White Flatbed, Black Wheels, Buddy L 625.00
Truck, Ice, Tin, Marx, 1950s, 11 In. 145.00
Truck, Land Rover Safari, Die Cast, No. 12, Matchbox, Lesney, England, 2 3/4 In. 26.00
Truck, Log, Structo 150.00
Truck, Lorry, Anti-Aircraft, Die Cast, Lone Star Products, England, 5 1/2 In. 44.00
Truck, Lumber, Buddy L 1250.00
Truck, Mack, Gasoline, Driver, Cast Iron, Arcade, 12 1/2 In. 1950.00
Truck, Mail, Black Cab, Green Body, Keystone, 27 x 8 x 11 1/2 In. 1300.00
Truck, Military, Siren, Slush Cast Metal, Khaki Paint, 1930s 36.00
Truck, Military, Tin, No. J-1555, Sample Tag, Linemar, Box, 7 x 2 3/4 x 2 3/4 In. 90.00
Truck, Milk & Cream, Toyland, White, Box 445.00
Truck, Milk, Borden's, White, Kingsbury 170.00
Truck, Milk, Friction, Tin, Linemar, 5 1/2 In. 225.00
Truck, Moving Van, Allied Van Lines, Black, Orange, Buddy L, 29 In. 775.00
Truck, Moving Van, Allied Van Lines, Tonka, Box, 1961, 9 In. . . . . .195.00 to 225.00
Truck, Moving Van, Lumar Van Lines, Metal, Marx, 18 1/2 In. 275.00
Truck, Moving Van, Mayflower, Limited Edition, Ralstoy, Box, 1/42 Scale 95.00
Truck, Moving Van, United Van Lines, Dobson The Mover, Tonka, 1957 . . . . 1950.00
Truck, Oil Tanker, Texaco, Box 175.00
Truck, Oil, Wood Wheels, Running Boards, Wyandotte 125.00
Truck, Overland, Turner 1250.00
Truck, Panel, Green, Black Pinstripes, Keystone, 22 1/2 x 6 1/2 In. 400.00
Truck, Pastry, Renault, Patisserie Marcel Gardet, Paris, Die Cast, Corgi, England, 5 In. . . 30.00
Truck, Pickup, Cast Iron, Freidga, 7 1/2 In. 550.00
Truck, Pickup, Chevrolet, Black, 1958, 8 In. 225.00
Truck, Pickup, Chevrolet, El Camino, Friction, Green, White Roof, Japan, Box, 8 In. 67.00
Truck, Pickup, Chevrolet, El Camino, Friction, Stamped Metal, Japan, 1958, 8 1/4 In. . . . 202.00
Truck, Pickup, Flivver, No. 210, Pressed Steel, Decal, Buddy L, c.1920s, 12 In. . .700.00 to 805.00
Truck, Pickup, Ford, Fairlane, 1957 Model, Friction, Tin, Green, Orange, Japan, 11 In. . . 99.00
Truck, Pickup, Red, Pressed Steel, Nylint, 1960s, 11 In. 150.00
Truck, Pickup, State Highway, Tonka, 1956 . . . . 325.00
Truck, Pickup, Willys, Accessories, Marx, 1950 . . . . 625.00
Truck, Produce, Friction, Tin Lithograph, Green, Japan, 4 In. 36.00
Truck, Red Baby Express, International Harvester, Pressed Steel, 1924 . . . . 2000.00

Truck, Rescue Squad, Tonka, 1956 .... 275.0
Truck, Rescue Squad, Tonka, 1958 .... 250.0
Truck, Rescue, Auburn, Blue Rubber, Black Rubber Tires, Steel Axles, 5 1/2 In. 23.0
Truck, Road Grader, Tonka, Orange 195.0
Truck, Road Roller, Driver, Cast Iron, Painted, Green, Hubley, 1930, 7 1/2 In. 345.6
Truck, Road Scraper, Orange & Yellow, Tonka 95.0
Truck, Rocket Launcher, Ideal, Box 110.0
Truck, Sand Loader, Battery Operated, Japan, Box 195.0
Truck, Searchlight, Hausser 1150.0
Truck, Stake, Diamond T, Hubley, 6 3/4 In. 175.0
Truck, Stake, Girard Stearbird, Red, Electric Lights 75.0
Truck, Stake, Green, Orange, Chein, 19 In. 985.0
Truck, Stake, Livestock, Tonka, 1957 .... 345.0
Truck, Stake, Model A Ford, Cast Iron, Nickel-Plated Wheels, Arcade, 1930s, 5 In. 115.0
Truck, Stake, Model T, Blue, Arcade 285.0
Truck, Stake, Motor Driven, Pressed Steel, Green, Red Wheels, Kingsbury, 1925, 11 In. . 345.0
Truck, Telephone, Bell Telephone, Hubley, 1950s, 9 In. ....60.00 to 90.0
Truck, Telephone, Bell Telephone, Pole Wagon, Winch, Hubley, 10 In. 750.0
Truck, Telephone, Bell Telephone, Rubber Balloon Tires, Cast Iron, 9 1/2 x 5 In. 405.0
Truck, Tow, American Motor Club, Nylint 95.0
Truck, Tow, B.F. Goodrich, Metalcraft ....395.00 to 425.0
Truck, Tow, B61, Open Hood, Doors, 1960 .... 214.0
Truck, Tow, Red, Green, Nickel Plated Wheels, Arcade, 8 1/2 In. 431.0
Truck, Tow, Smith-Miller 1895.0
Truck, Tow, Structo, 1960s 145.0
Truck, Tow, Texaco, Red Body, Black Fenders, 1960 .... 200.0
Truck, Trailer, Livestock, Marx 100.0
Truck, Troop Carrier, No. 380, Tonka, Box, 1960s 105.0
Truck, U.S. Army, Friction, Tin Lithograph, Rubber Tires, Cloth Bed Cover, 10 In. 78.0
Truck, U.S. Artillery, Sonny, Steel, Dayton Toy & Specialty Co., Late 1920s, 23 1/2 In. .. 400.0
Truck, U.S. Mail, Packed, No. 45, Pressed Steel, Rubber Tires, Keystone, 1926, 26 In. .. 860.0
Truck, U.S. Mail, Pressed Steel, Sturdity, 1920s, 25 In. ....2300.00 to 2750.0
Truck, With Car Carrier, Buddy-L, Box, 28 x 6 In. 250.0
Truck & Horse Trailer, Blue, Tonka, 1959 .... 250.0
Truck & Horse Trailer, Friction, Tin Lithograph, Japan, 9 In. 52.0
Trumpet Player, Windup, Tin, Vinyl, Cloth, TN, Japan, Box, 1950s, 10 In. 179.0
Trunk, Doll's, 12 x 8 x 8 In. 95.0
Trunk, Doll's, Metal, Blue, 20 1/2 In. 60.0
Trunk, Steamer, Doll's, Wood, Canvas, Leather, Brass, Vuitton, Late 19th Century, 11 In. 2000.0
Turtle, Windup, Tin Lithograph, Gunthermann, 1920s, 4 1/2 In. 180.0
Typewriter, Junior, Dial, Marx, Box 65.0
Typewriter, Marxwriter, Marx 50.0
Typewriter, Simplex, No. 1, Box 125.0
Typist, Miss Friday The Typist, 6 Actions, Nomura Toys Ltd., Box, 8 In. 135.0
U-Haul Set, Truck, Open Trailer, Covered Trailer, Nylint, 1970s, 3 Piece 120.0
Uncle Sam, Flag, Wood Silhouette, Cloth Flag, Red, Blue, Black & White Paint, 13 In. .. 205.0
Valise, Doll's, Wood Frame, Red Leather, Triple-Domed Top, France, c.1865, 2 In. 275.0
Van, Charlie's Angels, Die Cast, On Card, Corgi, 1978 .... 25.0
Van, Express, Friction, Stamped Tin, Rubber Tires, Red, Silver, Japan, 5 1/2 In. 34.0
Van, GMC, Steelcraft 895.0
Van, Refrigerator, Corner, Box 148.0
Ventriloquist's Dummy, Papier-Mache Head, Wood & Cloth Body, Homemade, 39 In. .. 72.0
View-Master, Bugs Bunny & Elmer Fudd, The Hunter, No. 800, 1951 .... 10.0
View-Master, Captain Kangaroo 25.0
View-Master, Charlie Brown, GAF, Canister Box, 1974 .... 35.0
View-Master, Cisco Kid & Pancho, No. 960, 1950 .... 15.0
View-Master, Flintstones, Group Of Bedrock Characters, 1962 .... 24.0
View-Master, Flintstones, Pebbles & Bamm-Bamm, 2 Children In Adventures, 1966 .... 19.0
View-Master, Hula Dancers Of Hawaii, 1951 .... 8.0
View-Master, Land Of The Giants 95.0
View-Master, Little Black Sambo, Booklet, No. 8, 1948 .... 15.0
View-Master, Lost In Space 125.0

View-Master, Magic Carpet, Booklet, No. 51, 1951 .... 5.00
View-Master, Moonraker 35.00
View-Master, Pee Wee's Playhouse, Gift Set, Unopened, Box, 1988 .... 40.00
View-Master, Sam & The Flying Saucer Pirates, Booklet, No. 6, 1951 .... 8.00
View-Master, Sam In Darkest Africa, Booklet, No. 4, 1951 .... 8.00
View-Master, Sam In The Land Of Ice, Booklet, No. 5, 1951 .... 8.00
View-Master, Scooby Doo 18.00
View-Master, Six Million Dollar Man 20.00
View-Master, Time Tunnel 95.00
View-Master, Twin Cities & Southern Minnesota, 1952 .... 4.00
View-Master, Voyage To Bottom Of Sea 65.00
View-Master, Winnie The Pooh 18.00
View-Master, Woody Woodpecker, Pony Express Ride, No. 820, 1951 .... 10.00
Village, Nuremburg, Houses, Church, City Arches, Trees, People, Late 19th Century 345.00
Violinist, Happy, Sways Back & Forth, Plays Violin, Tin, 9 In. 475.00
Waffle Iron, Cast Iron 35.00
Wagon, Boy Scout, Wood Spoke Wheels, Red Paint, Lewis Gear Mfg., 32 In. 445.00
Wagon, Driver, No. 131, Wood, Pull Toy, Fisher-Price, 17 In. 29.00
Wagon, Pumpkin Paint, Paris, Maine 325.00
Wagon, Red & Mustard Paint, Black Stenciling, Late 19th Century 435.00
Wagon, St. Claus, Dealer In Good Things, Wood, 15 x 27 1/2 In. 825.00
Wagon, Studebaker Junior, Metal Fittings, Dog-Cart Harness, 42 In. 330.00
Wagon, Wood, Iron Frame & Wheels, 4 Coin Springs, Hand Brake, 32 x 12 x 14 In. 500.00
Walker, Black, Paper Lithograph, On Wood, 1920s, 13 1/2 In. 225.00
Walker, Funny Face, No. 535, Windup, Tin Lithograph, Marx, Box, 1930s, 11 In. . 1150.00
Walker, Old Black Joe, Clockwork, Lead Head, Wood Frame, Moves Legs, c.1880, 9 In. .. 1955.00
Wash Tub, Copper, Co. K.C. Kans. Pat. August 11, 1925 .... 385.00
Washboard, Glass Insert, Small 10.00
Washing Machine, Columbia, Wood, Cast-Iron Agitator, 18 In. 633.00
Washing Machine, Drumm's Little Champion, Wood, Metal Base, Stenciled, 11 In. 605.00
Washing Machine, Hand Crank, Wood, Cast Iron, 15 1/4 In. 415.00
Washing Machine, Jiffy-Jeff, Electric, Jefferson Electric Mfg. Co., 10 In. ... 305.00
Washing Machine, Kiddie, Pressed Steel, Tin, 12 In. 525.00
Washing Machine, Sunny Suzy, Wringer 45.00
Washing Machine, Wood, Tin, Labels, Victor Toy Co., 8 In. 230.00
Washing Machine, Wringer Washer, Glass Tub, Wolverine 165.00
Washing Machine, Wringer, Horseshoe Brand Relief, Bucket, Legs, Hand Crank, 12 In. . 275.00
Washstand, Doll's, 1 Long Drawer, 2 Doors, White Paint, Floral 325.00
Weasel, Wiggy, Synthetic White Fur, Plastic Eyes, Embroidered, Steiff, 1970, 7 5/8 In. .. 260.00
Wheelbarrow, Red Rabbit, Wood, 25 In. 110.00
Whip-It Playland, 4 Cars Go Around Track, Tin Lithograph, Chein, 19 x 10 In. 500.00
Whirligig, Comic Figure In Canoe, Wood, Tacks, Yellow, Red & Blue Lacquer, 15 In. 110.00
Whirligig, Dragonfly, Wood, Black, Green & Orange Paint, 13 In. 170.00
Whistle, Penny Toy, Seamed Construction, Marked B, Brass, 14 In. 215.00
Whistle, Spaceship, Blue Hard Plastic, 1950s 95.00
Whistle, Squirrel & Cage, Tin, 4 3/4 In. 192.00
Wimpy, Tricycle, Celluloid Arms, Linemar 1250.00
Wishnik Troll House, Vinyl, Ideal, 1965 .... 25.00
Wringer, Little Dot, Simmons Hardware Co., Inc., 7 1/4 In. 440.00
Wringer, No.1 Gem, American Wringer Co., N.Y., 7 1/4 In. 150.00
Xylophone, Pull Toy, Fred Flintstones, Fisher-Price 395.00
Xylophone, Tiny Teddy, No. 635, Fisher-Price 70.00
Yo-Yo, Bozo, Metal, 1 1/2 In. 45.00
Yo-Yo, Duncan, 1950 .... 10.00
Yosemite Sam, Hat, Gun, 1968 .... 36.00
Zebra, Schoenhut 400.00
Zeppelin, 3 Children Watching Airships Spin, Plink-Plunk Music, Hopewell, Crank, 8 In. 577.00
Zeppelin, Cast Iron, Silver, 1930s, 4 3/4 In. 85.00
Zeppelin, Die Cast, Silver, 1920s, 4 1/2 In. 150.00
Zeppelin, Newton Aero Circus, 2 Airplanes, Paper Wings Rotate, Cast Iron, Box 1155.00
Zeppelin, Propeller Spins, Windup, Tin, Chein, c.1930, 9 In. 685.00
Zeppelin, Twin Flyer, Tin Lithograph, Pull Toy, Hopewell 1485.00
Zeppelin, Windup, Tin, Strauss, 1930s, 9 1/2 In. 200.00

TRAMP ART is a form of folk art made since the Civil War. It is usually made from chip-carved cigar boxes. Examples range from small boxes and picture frames to full-sized pieces of furniture.

Box, Applied Diamonds, Mottled Brown, Mustard Ground, c.1920 .... 175.C
Box, Blue Ground, Cast Iron Bale, 8 1/4 In. 165.C
Box, Hinged Lid, Chip Carved, Triangular & Rectangular Pyramids, 9 x 16 In. 330.C
Cabin, Crown Of Thorns Style, Early 20th Century, 20 x 22 x 19 In. 395.C
Cabinet, Wall, Swivel Mirror, Fitted Interior, 1 Drawer, 29 1/2 In. 287.C
Chess Set, Hand Carved Wooden Arab Armies, 1920s, 4 In. 135.0
Doll Furniture, Bed & 2 Chairs, Cigar Box Construction 650.0
Frame, Double, 2 Mirrors, 1930s, 19 x 26 In. 475.0
Frame, Layered Rosettes, Crossed Arms, 20 x 28 In. 425.0
Frame, Layered Rosettes, Crossed Arms, Maple Wood, 20 x 24 In. 225.0
Frame, Square, 6 x 7 In. 75.0
Frame, Triangular, 6 7/8 x 9 3/8 In. 65.0
Mirror, Crest, Heart Shape Carving, 2 Short Drawers Over 2 Long Drawers, 24 In. 1150.0
Table, Center, 10-Sided Top, Allover Chip-Carved Raised Panel, 1870, 30 In. 1265.0
Walking Stick, Carved Insects, 35 In. 125.0
Watch Holder, Pyramid, 2 Sections, Upper Central Viewing Hole, 22 x 12 In. 460.0

TRAPS for animals may be handmade. One of the most unusual is the mousetrap made so that when the mouse entered the trap, it was hit on the head with a mallet. Other traps were commercially manufactured and often are marked with the name of the manufacturer. Many traps were designed to be as humane as possible, and they would trap the live animal so it could be released in the woods.

Bear, Grizzly, No. 15, MacKensie District Fur Co., c.1886 .... 575.0
Bear, Kodiak, Hudson Bay, 46 x 20 In. Diam. 800.0
Bear, Swivel Chain, Ring, American Fur Co., 46 In. 400.0
Fly, Glass, Bell Shape 50.0
Fly, Glass, Blown, Applied Seal, Piece A Mouche, Vic Truchot, France, 1860, 7 In. 176.0
Fly, Glass, Blown, Turquoise, Allover Thumbprint, 1880-1920, 6 In. 1320.0
Fly, Glass, Pat. Oct. 18, 1890, ABM Base, American, 1890-1910, 2 Piece, 6 3/4 In. 176.0
Insect, Purple Glass 85.0
Mouse, Choker, 4 Holes, Wooden 22.0
Mouse, Elgin 25.0
Mouse, Iron, Blacksmith-Made, Oak Top & Bottom, Late 18th Century 875.0
Mouse, McGill 12.0
Mouse, Runaway 18.0
Mouse, Wire Frame, Round Internal Mechanism, 1850s, 8 x 4 1/2 In. 125.0
Rat, Automatic 17.0
Rat, Step-It 25.0
Squirrel 295.00

TREEN, see Wooden category.

TRENCH ART is a form of folk art made by soldiers. Metal casings from bullets and mortar shells were cut and decorated to form useful objects, such as vases.

Ashtray, 303 Enfield Artillery Shell Base, World War II 55.00
Ashtray, Aluminum Base, Brass Shell With Projectile In Center, World War II 29.00
Candlestick, Triangular Bayonet, Twisted Into Scroll, 1860-1870 .... 55.00
Shovel, Coal, French Bayonet, 1870 .... 85.00
Vase, 1918, 14 In. 200.00
Vase, Copper, Large 68.00
Vase, Verdun, 8 In. 60.00

TRIVETS are now used to hold hot dishes. Most trivets of the late nineteenth and early twentieth centuries were made to hold hot irons. Iron or brass reproductions are being made of many of the old styles.

Brass, 2 Cutout Hearts, England, 1860s, 10 In. 75.00
Brass, Give Your Heart To God Now, 9 1/4 In. 120.00
Brass, Griffin-Style Figures, Claw Footed, 10 1/2 In. 50.00

Brass, Horseshoe, Handle, Center 1888	95.00
Brass, Iron, Kettle Shelf, Turned Wooden Handle, Pullout Rods, 6 x 16 In.	93.50
Brass, Luxfer Prism Co., 5 3/4 In.	50.00
Brass, Man O' War, 4 1/2 In.	35.00
Brass, Rosewood Handle, 13 1/2 In.	71.00
Brass, Urn With Wreath, 12 In.	75.00
Brass Over Iron, Lyre Form, 13 In.	35.00
Brass Over Iron, Tall Flower Design, 12 1/4 In.	16.00
Coffeepot, Griswold No. 7	90.00
Ember Receptacle, Brass & Forged Iron	325.00
Griswold, No. 1725, 5 In.	22.50
Hearth, Queen Anne, Brass & Iron, Wooden Handle, Penny Feet, 11 1/4 x 13 In.	230.00
Iron, 2 Interlaced Hearts, Heart-Shaped Handle, 4 Footed, 7 In.	1150.00
Iron, 4 Hearts Cut In Top, Penny Feet, Warming, c.1840	365.00
Iron, Colt, Flat Iron, 6 1/2 In.	85.00
Iron, George Washington Bust, 19th Century, 9 1/4 In.	175.00
Iron, George Washington Portrait, 9 1/4 In.	300.00
Iron, Griswold	95.00
Iron, Heart Center, Handle, 12 In.	355.00
Iron, Heart Shape, Loop Handle, 3 Feet	467.00
Iron, Heart Shape, Tapering Loop Handle, Flattened Disc Feet, 6 1/2 In.	633.00
Iron, Insect Design, 9 In.	245.00
Iron, Poppy Plant Design, Key Border, 12 In.	38.00
Iron, Revolving, 26 x 12 In.	110.00
Iron, Scroll Design, Spade Footed, 9 3/4 In.	245.00
Iron, Tapered Legs, Round, Stand, American, 1750, 12 1/2 In.	175.00
Iron, Tooled Leaf Design, Turned-Up Feet, 10 1/2 In.	330.00
Iron, Triangular, 3 Feet, Maple Handle, c.1800, 11 x 4 1/8 In.	145.00
Warmer With Rest & Fork, Iron, 25 1/4 In.	180.00

TRUNKS of many types were made. The nineteenth-century sea chest was often handmade of unpainted wood. Brass-fitted camphorwood chests were brought back from the Orient. Leather-covered trunks were popular from the late eighteenth to mid-nineteenth centuries. By 1895, trunks were covered with canvas or decorated sheet metal. Embossed metal coverings were used from 1870 to 1910. By 1925, trunks were covered with vulcanized fiber or undecorated metal.

Dome Top, Dovetailed, Chrome Yellow Paint, 14 x 27 1/2 In.	287.00
Dome Top, Floral Within Painted Oval, Tan Ground, Early 19th Century, 11 x 24 In.	1035.00
Dome Top, Painted Design, Iron Strap Hinges, Cotter Pinned Handles, K.N.D., 1780	1100.00
Immigrant's, Original Painted Design, 1853, 25 1/2 x 45 In.	925.00
Leather, Painted Village Scene, Brass Studded, England, 18 x 36 In.	1090.00
Leather Covered, Metal Straps & Handles, Custom Stand, 19th Century	447.00
Leather Covered, Yellow Paint, 27 In.	95.00
Louis Vuitton, Early 20th Century, 13 x 43 1/2 x 21 1/2 In.	575.00
Louis Vuitton, Leather	2900.00
Louis Vuitton, Suitcase, Leather, 17 1/2 x 27 1/2 In.	775.00
Mahogany, Dome Top, Dovetailed, Original Pine Graining, 24 1/4 In.	192.50
Pine, Cast-Iron Handles, Gold Name Plate, Henry Belleman, 17 x 25 In.	190.00
Pine, Dome Top, Swirled Green Pattern, 19th Century, 11 x 29 x 14 In.	632.00
Pine, Dome Top, Yellow Design Against Black Ground, 19th Century, 29 In.	632.00
Poplar, Leather Trim, Tin Corner Braces, Brass Tacks, Black Paint, Initials, 23 3/4 In.	195.00
Red Lacquer, Gilt Floral & Figures, China, 26 x 16 x 10 1/2 In.	22.00
Suitcase, Leather, Embossed Dragon, Boxer Rebellion	498.00
Vanity Case, Leather, Red, Fitted With Bottles, Brushes, Gustave Keller	460.00

TUTHILL Cut Glass Company of Middletown, New York, worked from 1902 to 1923. Of special interest are the finely cut pieces of stemware and tableware.

Basket, Vintage, Glass Handle, 14 1/2 x 10 In.	3750.00
Basket, Wild Rose, Applied Twisted Rope Handle, 6 x 6 1/4 In.	1850.00
Basket, Wild Rose, Crystal Handle, 5 1/2 x 6 In.	1293.00
Tray, Vintage, Oval, Signed, 7 1/4 x 5 1/2 In.	550.00

TYPEWRITER collectors divide typewriters into two main classifications: the index machine, which has a pointer and a dial for letter selection, and the keyboard machine, most commonly seen today. The first successful typewriter was made by Sholes and Glidden in 1874.

Blickensderfer 7, Wood Base	85.0
Hall, Cased, 80 Alpha, Numeric Symbols, National Typewriter Co., 1890, 15 In.	333.0
Olivetti Lettera 22, Case, To Marlene Dietrich From Noel Coward, 1960s	4600.0
Remington, Lady's, St. Paul's Merchant's Carnival, People's Church, 1890	121.0
World, 43 Alpha, Numeric Symbols, Directions For Using, 1886	374.0

TYPEWRITER RIBBON TINS are now being collected. The lithographed tin containers have been used since the 1870s. Most popular with collectors are tins with pictorial graphics.

Tin, American Ace	15.0
Tin, American Flier, Ribbon	50.0
Tin, Amneco	36.0
Tin, Battleship, Blue, White, Black, Square, 2 1/8 In.	10.00 to 16.0
Tin, Black Hawk, Indian Shooting Arrow, Black & White, Round	15.0
Tin, Broadway	60.0
Tin, Burroughs	3.0
Tin, Chief Typewriter Ribbon, Copper	45.0
Tin, Codo Typocraft, Blue & White, Square	20.00 to 44.0
Tin, Curtis-Young	10.00 to 18.0
Tin, Dandy-Line Brand, Square, Round Corners	75.0
Tin, Diamond	15.00
Tin, Dri Kleen	12.00
Tin, Economique	10.00 to 29.0
Tin, Emerald Brand	42.0
Tin, Foyers Best	36.0
Tin, High Point	25.00
Tin, Hub Brand	15.00
Tin, Just-Rite	60.00
Tin, Kee Lox Ivory Brand, Blue & White, Round	6.00 to 8.00
Tin, Lith-O-Rite	15.00
Tin, Manhattan	15.00 to 25.00
Tin, Marvello	15.00 to 21.00
Tin, Miller Line, Yellow & Black, Round	3.00 to 10.00
Tin, Monogram	15.00
Tin, Montague	14.00 to 29.00
Tin, Perm-O-Rite	56.00
Tin, Popular Quality, Blue & White, Red Letters, Round, 2 1/2 In.	78.00
Tin, Red Feather Brand, Red, Round, 2 1/2 In.	50.00
Tin, Super Shell, Orange & Red, Square, Round Corners	183.00

UHL pottery was made in Evansville, Indiana, in 1854. The pottery moved to Huntingburg, Indiana, in 1908. Stoneware and glazed pottery were made until the mid-1940s.

Jug, Acorn	65.00
Jug, Baseball	45.00 to 55.00
Jug, Football	55.00
Jug, J.T. Doores & Co., Bowling Green, Ky., Handle, 4 Gal.	550.00
Pitcher, Spongeware, Bulbous Base, Labeled, 6 1/2 In.	770.00
Teapot, Blue, Stoneware	185.00 to 225.00
Vase, Yellow, 8 In.	60.00 to 125.00

UMBRELLA collectors like rain or shine. The first known umbrella was owned by King Louis XIII of France in 1637. The earliest umbrellas were sunshades, not designed to be used in the rain. The umbrella was embellished and redesigned many times. In 1852, the fluted steel rib style was developed, and it has remained the most useful style.

Handle, Gold Scrollwork & Floral, Oriental, 6 In.	57.00
Parasol, Child's, Bunnies, Monkeys, Birds, Scalloped, Oriental Boy Handle	22.00
Parasol, Gold Fittings, Sheaf Of Wheat Ivory Handle, 25 In.	230.00

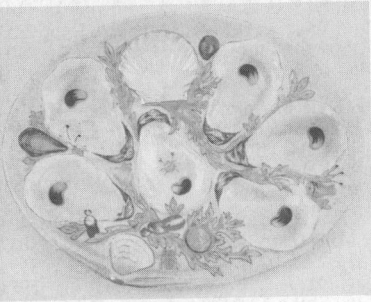

Union Porcelain Works,
Oyster Plate,
7 Wells, 10 1/4 In.

Union Porcelain
Works, Vase,
Turtle, 9 In.

Parasol, Handle, 3 Mice On Tree Branch, Gathering Berries, 6 3/8 In. 115.00
Parasol, Handle, Magnifying Glass, Mother-Of-Pearl Panels, 15 1/2 In. 165.00
Parasol, Handle, Smoky Quartz, With Tortoise, Enameled Silver & Rubies 7500.00
Parasol, White Linen, Embroidered, Burl Handle, c.1900 .... 165.00
Peter Max, Vinyl, Allover Design, People, Heads, Stars, Planets, Signed, 26 1/2 In. 125.00

UNION PORCELAIN WORKS was established at Greenpoint, New York, in 1848 by Charles Cartlidge. The company went through a series of ownership changes and finally closed in the early 1900s. The company made a fine quality white porcelain that was often decorated in clear, bright colors.

UNION
PORCELAIN
WORKS
GREENPOINT
N.Y.

Oyster Plate, 7 Wells, 10 1/4 In. ....*Illus* 525.00
Vase, Turtle, 9 In. ....*Illus* 1200.00

UNIVERSITY OF NORTH DAKOTA, see North Dakota School of Mines category.

VAL ST. LAMBERT Cristalleries of Belgium was founded by Messieurs Kemlin and Lelievre in 1825. The company is still in operation. All types of table glassware and decorative glassware have been made. Pieces are often decorated with cut designs.

Val St Lambert

Bowl, Frosted Lion On Bottom, 6 In. 47.00
Bowl, Hand Cut & Engraved, Signed, 8 3/4 In. 110.00
Candleholder, 6-Paneled Stem, Hexagon Base, Polished Pontil, Signed, 9 In. 66.00
Candlestick, Gardenia, 10 In., Pair 275.00
Candlestick, Signed, Pair 250.00
Paperweight, Iceberg 65.00
Paperweight, Lion, Etched, 2 x 3 In. 22.00
Pitcher, Iris, Leaf Relief, Purple Etched Ground, Curved Handles, 1900, 11 In. 1035.00
Plate, Pilgrim Fathers 225.00
Plate, Zodiac 225.00
Vase, 4 Pansies, Stems, Buds, Chartreuse, Yellow, Green Ground, 7 1/2 x 2 In. 200.00
Vase, Acid Cutback, Green Neck, Green Ground, Belgium, 1920, 8 In. 825.00
Vase, Deep Cranberry, Amber, Gold Stone, 9 x 6 In. 225.00
Vase, Deep Cranberry, Amber, White Swirls With Gold Accents, 10 1/2 x 5 In. 125.00
Vase, Deep Cranberry, Amber, White, Gold Accents, 12 x 6 In. 150.00
Vase, Emerald Bows & Swags, Clear Frosted Ground, 8 1/2 In. 385.00
Vase, Emerald Cutting Of Florals, Frosted Ground, Signed, 7 1/2 In. 660.00
Vase, Floral Design, Signed, 9 1/4 In. 90.00
Vase, Floral Motif, Green, Signed, 16 1/2 In. 50.00
Vase, Floral Motif, Lavender, 16 1/2 In. 380.00
Vase, Lime, Green, Transparent Glass Elliptical, Acid-Stamped, 5 1/4 x 7 In. 345.00

VALLERYSTHAL Glassworks was founded in 1836 in Lorraine, France. In 1854, the firm became Klenglin et Cie. It made table and decorative glass, opaline, cameo, and art glass. A line of covered, pressed glass animal dishes was made in the nineteenth century. The firm is still working.

Vallerysthal

Dish, Cover, Squirrel With Acorn 48.00
Dish, Cow Cover, Oblong, 4 1/4 x 7 In. 125.00
Dish, Dog On Carpet Cover, Blue 225.00

Dish, Duck Cover, Swimming, Blue, 6 1/4 In. .... 140.
Dish, Fish Cover .... 225.
Dish, Hen On Nest Cover, Basket Weave Base, Amethyst, 6 3/4 In. .... 70.
Dish, Rabbit On Egg Cover, Textured Finish, 4 3/4 In. .... 190.

VAN BRIGGLE pottery was made by Artus Van Briggle in Colorado Springs, Colorado, after 1901. Van Briggle had been a decorator at Rookwood Pottery of Cincinnati, Ohio. He died in 1904. His wares usually had modeled relief decorations and a soft, dull glaze. The pottery is still working and still making some of the original designs.

Ashtray, Turquoise .... 30.00 to 40.0
Bowl, Embossed Poppy Blossoms, Blue Over White Matte Glaze 1906 5 In. .... 303.
Bowl, Floral Design, Matte Red, Blue Glaze, 1920s, 7 1/2 x 5 1/2 In. 319.0
Bowl, Flower Frog, Blue Mermaid, Large .... 595.
Bowl, Incised Leaves & Berries, Matte Blue Glaze, 1907-1912, 3 1/2 x 2 In. 176.0
Bowl, Molded Floral Design, Matte 2-Tone Blue Glaze, 1920s, 5 1/2 x 3 1/2 In. 99.0
Bowl, Molded Floral Design, Matte Dark Blue, Red, 1930, 5 1/2 x 3 1/2 In. 99.0
Bowl, Molded Floral Design, Matte Red, Dark Blue Glaze, 3 1/2 In. 154.0
Bowl, Molded Floral Design, Matte, Deep Red Glaze, Dark Blue, 1920, 6 x 3 In. 154.0
Bowl, Swirling Molded Flowers, Matte Navy Blue, Light Blue, 7 1/2 x 4 In. 297.0
Bowl, Yucca, Yellow, Green, 1920s 225.0
Ewer, White, 6 1/2 In. 50.0
Figurine, Elephant, Mauve, 4 1/2 x 8 In. 200.0
Figurine, Owl, 9 1/2 In. 100.0
Flower Frog, Triple, Blue, 1914 .... 300.0
Lamp, Damsel Of Damascus, Original Shade, Turquoise .... 395.00 to 475.0
Lamp, Dogwood, Turquoise Blue Overspray Butterfly, Floral Shade, 1970, 33 In. 165.0
Lamp, Girl, On Fence, White Shade, Red, Pair 400.0
Lamp, Girl, Urn On Shoulder, Blue, Green 350.0
Lamp, Persian Rose, Ming Blue, Celluloid Shade, Butterflies & Grasses, 11 In., Pair 400.0
Lamp, Table, With Shade, Mountain Craig Brown 450.0
Lamp, Woman On Rock, Shade 325.0
Mug, Toasting, Green, Eagle, 1905 .... 290.0
Paperweight, Elephant 25.0
Pitcher, White, 4 In. 30.0
Planter, Embossed Tulips, Dark Blue Matte Glaze, 1908-1911, 5 x 6 In. 825.0
Plaque, Big Buffalo, Turquoise, 6 In. 85.0
Plate, Embossed Large Poppy, Red On Blue Ground, Signed, 1907, 8 1/2 In. 990.0
Tile, 3 White Geese, Yellow Bills, Green, Dark Blue, Aqua Ground, 6 In. 1760.0
Tile, Blue Bird, Perched On Tree Limb, Light Blue Ground, Frame, 6 In. 880.0
Tile, Sailing Ships, White Sails Against Blue Water, Oak Frame, 6 In. 1045.0
Tile, Stylized Landscape, Polychrome Glazes, Frame, Signed, 6 In. 2530.0
Tile, Tree Scene, Hills, Blue Sky, Matte Glaze, 6 In. 2640.0
Tile, Tree Scene, Purple Hills, Arts & Crafts, 6 In. 2530.0
Vase, 2 Women, Flowing Dresses, Matte Purple Glaze, Maroon, 7 In. 3300.0
Vase, 3 Embossed Butterflies, Blue, 3 1/4 x 3 1/2 In. 195.0
Vase, 3 Indian Heads, 12 1/2 In. 168.0
Vase, 3 Indian Heads, Blue & Green, Label, 11 3/8 In. 355.0
Vase, 3 Indian Heads, Brown & Green Glaze, Logo, 11 1/4 x 5 1/4 In. 197.0
Vase, 4 Buttresses At Base, Blue-Green Matte Glaze, 1920, 8 In. 286.0
Vase, 4 Raised Leaves, Matte Dark Green Glaze, Brown, Marked, 6 1/4 x 4 In. 546.0
Vase, Black Glaze Finish, Laura Lie, 10 1/2 In. 115.0
Vase, Blue, Green Matte Glaze, Spherical, 1907, 5 x 6 In. 330.0
Vase, Blue, Green Matte, Signed, 1920s, 6 1/4 In. 125.0
Vase, Bud, 3 Sections, Black, White Drip, Colorado Springs, Co., 7 In. 28.0
Vase, Bulbous, Molded Leaves, Rose Pink Glaze, 2 Handles, 1904, 10 x 6 In. 1980.0
Vase, Crocus With Roots, Aqua, 7 In. 70.0
Vase, Dark Green Matte Glaze, Spherical, 1903, 5 1/2 x 6 In. 660.0
Vase, Deep Amethyst Glaze, 2 Handles, 6 In. 135.0
Vase, Dragonflies, 2-Tone Blue Matte Glaze, 1907-1912, 3 In. 880.0
Vase, Dragonflies, Matte Green, 1907-1912, 8 In. 715.0
Vase, Embossed Iris, Blue Matte Glaze, 1908, 10 x 4 In. 750.0
Vase, Flared, Dark Green Matte Glaze, 1905, 6 1/2 x 3 1/2 In. 1320.0

Van Briggle, Vase,
Stylized Spiderwort,
Green Matte,
Pinched Handles,
1903, 6 In.

Keep burglars away from your house. Cut hedges back to 3 feet high if near first-story windows. Keep tree branches trimmed so a burglar can't climb up to a second-floor window. If you plant shrubs that hide doors and windows, pick those with prickers and sharp thorns. Cacti are good in a warm climate.

Vase, Floral, Green Matte Glaze, Artist, 3 1/2 In.	990.00
Vase, Green Matte Glaze, 1906, 7 x 6 1/2 In.	522.50
Vase, Green, Brown Matte Glaze, Molded Leaves, 1920, 11 1/2 In.	275.00
Vase, Irises, Red, Blue Matte Glaze, 1907-1912, 16 In.	1980.00
Vase, Large Leaf Design, Pink Matte Glaze, Incised Mark, Pre-1920s, 7 1/2 In.	385.00
Vase, Leaf & Berry, Thick Green Matte, Incised Mark, 1905, 7 x 4 In.	660.00
Vase, Leaves Alternating Stylized Blossoms, Light & Dark Green Matte, 7 1/2 In.	1000.00
Vase, Lorelei, Woman Draped Around Rim, Maroon Matte Glaze, 1920, 9 In.	1000.00
Vase, Lorelei, Woman Draped Around Rim, Turquoise Blue, 10 x 4 In.	1000.00
Vase, Lorelei, Woman Draped Around Rim, Yellow Glaze, Signed, 9 1/4 In.	3300.00
Vase, Lorlei, Matte Light Blue, Green Glaze, 1940, 11 In.	360.00
Vase, Maroon Matte Glaze, 1904, 7 In.	176.00
Vase, Maroon Matte Glaze, Green, Blue, 1904, 13 In.	1320.00
Vase, Matte 2-Tone Blue Glaze, 2 Handles, 1920s, 8 In.	253.00
Vase, Matte Green Glaze, Marked, 1904, 8 x 5 1/2 In.	747.00
Vase, Matte Maroon, Green Highlights, 1907-1912, 5 In.	605.00
Vase, Ming, Turquoise, Dated 1920	175.00
Vase, Molded Blue Trefoils, Light Green Matte Ground, 1903, 6 x 2 3/4 In.	1870.00
Vase, Molded Butterflies, Maroon, Blue Matte, 4 In.	300.00
Vase, Molded Daffodils, Frothy Blue Glaze, Signed, 14 In.	5225.00
Vase, Molded Daisies, Green, Rose, Pink Glaze, 1904, 5 x 10 1/2 In.	1100.00
Vase, Molded Floral Design, 2-Tone Blue Matte Glaze, 1920, 14 In.	385.00 to 412.00
Vase, Molded Floral Design, Rose Pink Matte Glaze, 1916, 7 1/2 In.	220.00
Vase, Molded Flowers, Stems, Green Against Brown Matte Ground, 10 1/2 In.	121.00
Vase, Molded Iris Blossoms, Raspberry Pink Matte Glaze, 5 x 3 In.	660.00
Vase, Molded Leaves, Green Matte Glaze, 1907-1911, 11 x 3 1/4 In.	1320.00
Vase, Molded Leaves, Mustard Matte Glaze, 1908-1911, 3 x 6 In.	770.00
Vase, Molded Leaves, Stems, Berries, Rose, Light Green Matte Glaze, 1904, 8 In.	1925.00
Vase, Molded Peacock Feathers, Blue Green Matte Glaze, 1911, 14 x 7 In.	2090.00
Vase, Molded Poppies, Frothy Medium Green Matte Glaze, 1908, 9 x 4 In.	605.00
Vase, Molded Stylized Thistle, Medium Green Glaze, Signed, 1906, 8 x 6 In.	935.00
Vase, Molded Stylized Trefoils, Stems, Persian Rose Matte Glaze, 1908, 5 In.	467.50
Vase, Molded Thistles, Green Matte Glaze, Protruding Shoulder, 1906, 8 In.	990.00
Vase, Molded, Incised Poppy Design, 2-Tone Blue Matte Glaze, 1920s, 8 In.	253.00
Vase, Mulberry & Dark Turquoise, Drip Glaze At Handle, 1920s, 7 1/4 In.	450.00
Vase, Pink Matte Glaze, 1906, 9 1/2 x 7 1/2 In.	770.00
Vase, Poppies, Whiplash Stems, Green, Blue Matte Glaze, 1916, 7 In.	605.00
Vase, Poppy Design, Dark Maroon, Blue Glaze, 6 1/2 In.	176.00
Vase, Purple Matte Glaze, 1905, 8 x 4 In.	880.00
Vase, Red Purple Matte, 1906, 7 In.	176.00
Vase, Seashell, Blue Matte Glaze, 12 In.	65.00
Vase, Stylized Blossoms, 4 Long Stems, 1916, 7 3/4 x 4 1/4 In.	990.00
Vase, Stylized Blossoms, Blue Matte Glaze, Metallic Flecks, 1907, 5 1/2 In.	1100.00
Vase, Stylized Daisies, Swirling Leaves, Purple To Red Glaze, Signed, 11 x 12 In.	1650.00
Vase, Stylized Dandelion Around Rim, Green Glaze, Signed, 1907, 7 5/8 In.	880.00
Vase, Stylized Floral, Blue-Green Glaze, Signed, 1916, 7 1/2 In.	550.00
Vase, Stylized Floral, Moonglo Matte Glaze, Colorado Springs, Co., 1970, 8 In.	33.00

Vase, Stylized Floral, Turquoise, 3 1/4 In. ....

Vase, Stylized Peacock Feathers, Blue, Maroon, 4 Handles, 14 In. 88.0

Vase, Stylized Spiderwort, Green Matte, Pinched Handles, 1903, 6 In. .... *Illus* 605.0

Vase, Swirled Blue Leaves, Stems, Maroon Ground, 1920-1930, 13 In. 1375.0

Vase, Trumpet, Floral Design, Turquoise Ground, 5 x 3 3/4 In. 308.0

Vase, Tulip Design, Thick Maroon Matte Glaze, Light Green, 1905, 7 In. ...... 45.00 to 48.0

Wall Pocket, 1920, 10 1/2 In. 1045.0

295.0

VASA MURRHINA is the name of a glassware made by the Vasa
Murrhina Art Glass Company of Sandwich, Massachusetts, about
1884. The glassware was transparent and was embedded with small
pieces of colored glass and metallic flakes. The mica flakes were
coated with silver, gold, copper, or nickel. Some of the pieces were
cased. The same type of glass was made in England. Collectors often
confuse Vasa Murrhina glass with aventurine, spatter, or spangle glass.
There is uncertainty about what actually was made by the Vasa
Murrhina factory. Related pieces may be listed under Spangle Glass.

Basket, Amber Cased, Ruffled Edge, Twisted Amber Thorny Handle, 10 3/8 In. 245.0

Basket, Aqua Interior, Yellow & Tan Spatter Center, Mica Flakes, 10 1/2 In. 295.0

Basket, Blue Cased, Clear Thorn Handle, Ruffled Edge, Mica Flakes, 8 x 5 In. 175.0

Basket, Blue Spatter, 11 In. 95.0

Basket, Coral Design, Briar Handle, Mica Flakes, 9 1/4 x 5 3/4 In. 275.0

Basket, Cranberry Cased, White Lining, Clear Thorn Handle, Mica Flakes, 9 In. 192.0

Basket, Cranberry, Melon Shaped, 9 In. 145.0

Basket, Jack-In-The-Pulpit, Ruffled Edge, Mica Flakes, 11 1/2 In. 265.0

Basket, Spatter Center, Clear Handle, Clear Handle, Mica Flakes, 10 1/2 In. 345.0

Basket, Tan, Aqua, Yellow Spatter Center, White To Deep Rose Interior, 10 In. 345.0

Basket, White Lining, Clear Briar Handle, Mica Flakes, 9 1/4 x 5 3/4 In. 325.0

Finger Bowl, Pink, Swirled 45.0

Pitcher, Pink, Ruby, Applied Fluted Handle, Mica Flakes, 9 In. 138.0

Rose Bowl, Blue Cased, Hexagonal Crimped Top, 3 3/4 x 3 3/8 In. 100.0

Rose Bowl, Pink, White, Mica Flakes, 4 1/2 In. 83.0

Rose Bowl, Rose Cased, White Lining, Octagonal Crimped Edge, Mica Flakes, 3 In. ... 110.0

Vase, Blue Green, 11 1/2 x 5 In. 80.0

Vase, Coral Design, White Lining, Mica Flakes, 7 3/8 In., Pair 295.0

Vase, Yellow, Pink, Red, White, 7 1/2 In. 65.0

VASART is the signature used on a late type of art glass made by the
Streathearn Glass Company of Scotland. Pieces are marked with an
engraved signature on the bottom. Most of the glass is mottled or
shaded.

Vasart

Basket, Purple, Signed, Cluthra, 3 3/4 x 6 In. 25.00

Vase, Oyster White & Blue, Cluthra Type, Corset Shape, 8 In. 172.00

VASELINE GLASS is a greenish-yellow glassware resembling petroleum
jelly. Some vaseline glass is still being made in old and new styles.
Pressed glass of the 1870s was often made of vaseline-colored glass.
Additional pieces of vaseline glass may also be listed under Pressed
Glass in this book.

Bowl, Amberette, Scalloped Edge, Large 125.00

Bowl, Fluted Scrolls, Opalescent, Footed, 6 1/2 In. 29.50

Candlestick, Dolphin, Petal Holder, Square Pedestal, Flint, 10 1/2 In. 55.00

Compote, Clark's Teaberry Gum, Pedestal .... 150.00 to 350.00

Compote, Cover, Thumbprint 185.00

Compote, Thumbprint, Lattice 95.00

Cordial, Crescent 26.00

Creamer, Fluted Scrolls, Scroll Feet, Reeded Handle, 5 1/4 In. 70.00

Eggcup Set, Opalescent, Silver Plated Stand, Salt Center, 8 x 4 x 6 1/2 In. 195.00

Goblet 55.00

Jar, Preserve, Cover, Early American, 6 In. 250.00

Perfume Bottle, Multicolored, Stopper, 6 3/4 In. 200.00

Sugar & Creamer, Hobnail 60.00

Toothpick, Swan 20.00

VENETIAN GLASS, see Glass-Venetian category.

ENINI glass was first designed by Paolo Venini, who established his
actory in Murano, Italy, in 1925. He is best known for pieces of mod-
rn design, including the famous *handkerchief* vase. The company is
ill working. Other pieces of Italian glass may be found in the Glass-
Contemporary, Glass-Midcentury, and Glass-Venetian categories of
his book.

venini
mmrano
ITALIA

Bottle, Applied Opaque Green Glass, Stopper, Hexagonal, Paolo Venini, 1950, 8 In.	1500.00
Bottle, Black, Ball Form Stopper, Fulvio Bianconi, c.1950, 18 In.	2420.00
Bottle, Black, White, White Conical Stopper, Fulvio Bianconi, 1950, 19 In.	825.00
Bottle, Giada, Dark Opaque, Internal Copper Design, Stopper, Zuccheri, 1960	210.00
Bottle, Inciso Blue Sommerso, Amethyst Stopper, 1950s, 8 In.	465.00
Bottle, Inciso Green, Stopper, Paolo Venini, 1950s, 8 In.	240.00
Bottle, Light Amber, Squat Body, Incised Lined Stopper, Venini, 1960, 7 In.	470.00
Bottle, Light Green, Red, Light Green Conical Stopper, Fulvio Bianconi, 19 In.	880.00
Bottle, Royal Blue, Yellow, Green Bands, Acid Stamp, Paolo Venini, 13 In.	220.00
Bottle, Sommerso, Amber, Horizontal Lines, Paolo Venini, 1950s, 7 1/2 In.	305.00
Bowl, A Bollicine, Green, With Pestle, Carlo Scarpa, 1930s, 3 In.	220.00
Bowl, Leaf, Tyra Lundgren, 1938	1250.00
Bowl, Royal Blue, Shallow Egg Shape, Paolo Venini, c.1950, 11 x 2 In.	825.00
Cane, Orange Glass	1275.00
Decanter, Incisco, Paolo Venini, 1956	2000.00
Decanter Set, Mezza Filigrana, Signed, c.1946, 7 Piece	2645.00
Egg, A Canne, Alternating Spiral, Red & Blue, Engraved, 5 In.	130.00
Figurine, Acrobat Standing On Head, Black Hat, Gloves, 13 1/2 In.	500.00
Figurine, Chicken, Opaque White, Black Design, Murano, Fulvio Bianconi, 1950s, 7 In. .	3575.00
Figurine, Dove, Tyra Lundgren, 1936	950.00
Flask, Pilgrim, Clear Blue, c.1925, 10 1/2 In.	275.00
Lamp, Hurricane, Red, Blue Vertical Bands, Fulvio Bianconi, 1950, 12 In.	880.00
Obelisk, Internal Coral, Fulvio Bianconi, c.1950, 16 In.	825.00
Obelisk, Translucent Green Body, Hexagonal, Paolo Venini, 1950s, 12 In.	1045.00
Paperweight, Orange, White, Black Swirling Canes, 1960, 6 In.	176.00
Pitcher, Blue, Green Vertical Canes, Paolo Venini, 1950s, 9 In.	468.00
Pitcher, Orange Vertical Bands, Applied Handle, Bianconi, 1950, 9 In.	495.00
Pitcher, Tessuto Red, Blue, Green, Amethyst, Vertical Canes, Paolo Venini, 1950s, 9 In. .	550.00
Shade, Lamp, Tessuto Yellow & White Stripes, 12 In.	475.00
Sorbet Cup, Green & Purple Sofiati, c.1920, 6 Piece	220.00
Timer, Clessidre, Incalmo, Green & Red Basin, Murano, 9 1/2 In.	880.00
Tumbler, A Canne, 1950s, 10 Piece	1500.00
Tumbler, Red Vertical Canes, Blue, Green, Purple, Amber, Paolo Venini, 6 In.	360.00
Vase, A Canne, Alternating Pink & White Latticinio, Bianconi, Murano, 1950s, 6 In.	355.00
Vase, Bright Blue, Heavy Vertical Ribs, Rolled Lip, N. Martinuzzi, 1920s, 9 x 9 In.	440.00
Vase, Clear, Blue Inner Layer, Zigzag, Square, F. Bianconi, 1958, 5 In.	1760.00
Vase, Deep Red Case With Amber, Paolo Venini, 1960s, 5 In.	165.00
Vase, Emerald Green, Applied Ring Foot, Controlled Bubbles, Martinuzzi, 1920s, 9 In. . .	355.00
Vase, Gray, Light Amber Vertical Bands, Bianconi, 10 In.	1045.00
Vase, Handkerchief, Pink Zanfirico, 6 x 9 1/2 In.	110.00
Vase, Handkerchief, Red & White, Signed, 10 In.	895.00
Vase, Handkerchief, White & Eggplant, Signed, 1983, 12 x 13 In.	605.00
Vase, Handkerchief, White Zanfiricio, Signed, 5 1/2 x 9 In.	330.00
Vase, Mezza Filigrana, Clear Spirals, Pinched Cylinder, Signed, 10 1/2 In.	690.00
Vase, Mezza Filigrana, Elliptical, 9 In.	1200.00
Vase, Pezzato, Triangular Form, Patchwork, Red, Blue, Green & Clear, 8 3/4 In.	7187.00
Vase, Purple Fine Lines, Paolo Venini, c.1950s, 6 x 4 In.	1210.00
Vase, Quadrilobato, Tessuto Mosaico, Amethyst Canes, Bianconi, 1957, 9 In.	6050.00
Vase, Red, Blue, Green Diagonal Canes, Fulvio Bianconi, c.1950, 9 In.	3300.00
Vase, Red, Blue, Green, Cigar Form, Fulvio Bianconi, c.1950, 11 In.	5500.00
Vase, Rows Of Amber & Clear Glass, c.1960, 8 7/8 In.	3450.00
Vase, Sommerso, Blue & Pink, Teardrop, Murano, 1950s, 14 In.	935.00
Vase, Spichi, Flared Form, Vertical Bands In Black, Teal, Yellow & Clear, 9 1/2 In.	8050.00
Vase, Translucent Gray, White Cane Segments, Paolo Venini, 3 x 5 In.	2420.00
Vase, Trumpet, Bright Blue, Vertical Ribs, Napoleone Martinuzzi, 1920s, 13 In.	660.00
Vase, Vetro Pezzato, Patchwork, Flared, Fulvio Bianconi, 1950s, 9 3/8 In.	11245.00

VERLYS glass was made in France after 1931. It was made in the United States from 1935 to 1951. The glass is either blown or molded. The American glass is signed with a diamond-point-scratched name, but the French pieces are marked with a molded signature. The designs resemble those used by Lalique.

Bowl, Chrysanthemum, Satin, 9 In.		555.0
Bowl, Leaves, Oval, 14 In.		400.0
Bowl, Orchid, Dusty Rose, 14 In.		66.0
Bowl, Thistle, 10 In.		295.0
Bowl, Thistle, Directoire Blue, 8 1/2 In.		100.0
Bowl, Water Lily, 11 In.		25.0
Bowl, Wild Duck, 13 1/2 In.		60.0
Vase, Love Bird, Marked, 6 1/2 x 2 3/4 In.		170.0
Vase, Mandarin, 9 In.		150.0

VERNON KILNS was the name used after 1958 by Vernon Potteries, Ltd. The company, which started in 1931 in Vernon, California, made dinnerware and figurines until it closed in 1958. Collectors search for the brightly colored dinnerware and the pieces designed by Rockwell Kent, Walt Disney, and Don Blanding. For more information, see *Kovels' Depression Glass & Dinnerware Price List.*

1776, Bowl, Salad, Large		95.00
Alaska, Sugar & Creamer, 4 Scenes		85.00
Aztec, Bowl, Vegetable		45.00
Bits Of Old South, Chop Plate, Down On The Levee, 14 In.		175.00
Black Hills, South Dakota, Plate, Marked, 8 1/2 In.		8.00
Brown-Eyed Susan, Sauce Boat		25.00
California, Teapot, Orange, Angular Handle		60.00
Casual California, Bowl, Salad, Turquoise, 10 In.		50.00
Chatelaine, Coffeepot, Topaz		265.00
Chatelaine, Plate, Bronze, 4 Corner Decoration, 10 1/2 In.		30.00
Chatelaine, Plate, Platinum, 1 Leaf, 10 1/2 In.		25.00
Chatelaine, Salt & Pepper, Platinum		90.00
Chatelaine, Sugar Cover, Platinum		45.00
Chicago Fair, Plate		28.00
Connecticut, Plate, Multicolored		38.00
Coral Reef, Salt & Pepper, Blue		65.00
Early California, Muffin Tray, Cover, Light Blue		55.00
El Camino Real Mission, Plate, 14 In.		65.00
Frontier Days, Chop Plate, 14 In.		175.00
Frontier Days, Platter, Oval, 12 In.		75.00
Fruitdale, Soup, Dish, 8 1/2 In.		14.00
Hawaiian Flowers, Chop Plate, Blue, 14 In.		155.00
Hawaiian Flowers, Chop Plate, Maroon, 12 In.		150.00
Hawaiian Flowers, Coffeepot, Maroon		95.00 to 125.00
Hawaiian Flowers, Creamer		40.00
Hawaiian Flowers, Cup & Saucer		60.00
Hawaiian Flowers, Cup & Saucer, Blue		59.00
Hawaiian Flowers, Plate, Bread & Butter		20.00
Hawaiian Flowers, Salt & Pepper, Blue		49.00 to 55.00
Historic Boston, Plate		28.00
Homespun, Chop Plate, 12 In.		20.00
Homespun, Pitcher, 2 Qt.		35.00
Homespun, Plate, 6 In.		3.00
Homespun, Sugar & Creamer		18.00
Kentucky, Ashtray		30.00
Lei Lani, Chop Plate, 14 In.		195.00
Lei Lani, Chop Plate, 17 In.		250.00
May Flower, Salt & Pepper		35.00
Moby Dick, Chop Plate, 12 In.		175.00
Moby Dick, Chop Plate, 14 In.		125.00
Moby Dick, Chop Plate, Brown, 14 In.		325.00

Moby Dick, Plate, Blue, 9 1/2 In.	65.00 to 75.00
Moby Dick, Plate, Brown, 7 1/2 In.	40.00
Moby Dick, Plate, Brown, 9 1/2 In.	69.00
Moby Dick, Tumbler, Blue	125.00
Music Master, Plate, Greig, 8 1/2 In.	25.00
Music Master, Plate, Liszt, 8 1/2 In.	25.00
Music Master, Plate, Mendelssohn, 8 1/2 In.	25.00
Music Master, Plate, Schubert, 8 1/2 In.	25.00
Napa Valley, Plate, 8 1/2 In.	28.00
Native California, Plate, Bread & Butter, 6 In.	6.00
Native California, Platter, 14 In.	25.00
Opera, Plate, Faust, 8 1/2 In.	20.00
Organdie, Bowl, 10 1/2 In.	75.00
Organdie, Butter Chip, 2 1/2 In.	25.00
Organdie, Butter Chip, 2 1/2 In., 4 Piece	85.00
Organdie, Candlestick	50.00
Organdie, Casserole, Cover, Round	45.00
Organdie, Flowerpot, Saucer, 5 In.	60.00
Organdie, Pitcher, Syrup	70.00
Organdie, Tidbit, 2 Tiers	35.00
Organdie, Tumbler, Straight Side, 5 In.	25.00
Our America, Plate, Brown, 8 1/2 In.	45.00
Raffia, Pitcher, 2 Qt.	45.00
Romeo & Juliet, Platter, 11 In.	65.00
Salamina, Chop Plate, 12 In.	225.00
Salamina, Plate, 9 1/2 In.	125.00 to 230.00
Santa Barbara, Bowl, Vegetable, 9 In.	18.00
Santa Barbara, Plate, 9 1/2 In.	10.00
Sherwood, Pitcher, 2 Qt.	45.00
Starburst, Butter, Cover	55.00
Texas, Lone Star State, Plate	22.00
Trade Winds, Pitcher, 2 Qt.	45.00
Trade Winds, Teapot	45.00
University Of Notre Dame, Plate, 10 1/2 In.	25.00
University Of Washington, Plate, 10 1/2 In.	35.00
Will Rogers, Plate	30.00
Winchester, Teapot, '73	125.00

VERRE DE SOIE glass was first made by Frederick Carder at the Steuben Glass Works from about 1905 to 1930. It is an iridescent glass of soft white or very, very pale green. The name means *glass of silk*, and it does resemble silk. Other factories have made verre de soie, and some of the English examples were made of different colors. Verre de soie is an art glass and is not related to the iridescent, pressed, white carnival glass mistakenly called by its name. Related pieces may be found in the Steuben category.

Basket, Ruffled Edge, Iridescent, 10 3/4 x 8 1/2 In.	700.00
Jar, Dresser, Gilt Ribbons, Laurel Leaves, Enameled Flowers, 5 1/2 In.	175.00
Vase, Applied Vines, Leaves, Global, 4 1/2 In.	220.00

VIENNA, see Beehive category.

VIENNA ART plates are round metal serving trays produced at the turn of the century. The designs, copied from Royal Vienna porcelain plates, usually featured a portrait of a woman encircled by a wide, ornate border. Many were used as advertising or promotional items and were produced in Coshocton, Ohio, by J.F. Meeks Tuscarora Advertising Co. and H.D. Beach's Standard Advertising Co.

Plate, Jamestown, 1607-1907, Pat. Feb. 21, 1905, 10 1/2 In.	33.00
Plate, Lad In Garden, Cherubs, Green Band, Birds, 1905, 10 1/2 In.	45.00
Plate, T.C. Gleason & Co., Knights Of Columbus, 10 1/8 In.	33.00
Plate, Woman Portrait, Pat. Feb. 21st, 1905, 10 1/8 In.	50.00
Plate, Woman, Low-Cut Transparent Gown, 1905, 10 In.	75.00

Plate, Woman, Red Tam, Sheer Blouse, 1908-1912, 10 1/2 In. . . . . .115.00 to 200.0

VILLEROY & BOCH Pottery of Mettlach was founded in 1841. The firm made many types of wares, including the famous Mettlach steins. Collectors can be confused because although Villeroy & Boch made most of its pieces in the city of Mettlach, Germany, they also had factories in other locations. The dating code impressed on the bottom of most pieces makes it possible to determine the age of the piece. Additional items, including steins, may be found in the Mettlach category.

Bowl, 9 1/2 x 4 1/4 In.	65.0(
Bowl, Vegetable, Blue Onion, Round, 1900, 9 1/2 In.	100.0(
Bowl, Vegetable, Cover, Onion, 1900, 9 1/2 In.	140.0(
Charger, Windmill Scene, Blue, White, Signed, A. Heide, 17 In.	165.0(
Chop Plate, Gaudy Stick, Spatter, 16 1/4 In.	413.0(
Pitcher, Floral, Yellow, Green, Brown, Orange, Green, 7 In.	88.0(
Plaque, Lilies Of The Valley, 12 In.	180.0(
Plate, Child's, Blue Cameo Design Of Children, White Ground, 7 1/2 In.	44.0(
Soap, Dish, Salmon Liner, Mulberry, Gold, 1874, 7 In.	27.5(
Syrup, Onion Pattern, Pewter Top, 1870s	75.0(
Tea Set, Flower & Bird Pattern, 12 Piece	450.0(
Tureen, Vegetable, Cover, Bouillabaisse, 70 Oz.	275.0(
Vase, Applied Duck Relief, Bamboo, 11 x 5 1/4 x 4 In.	285.00

VOLKMAR pottery was made by Charles Volkmar of New York from 1879 to about 1911. He was associated with several firms, including the Volkmar Ceramic Company, Volkmar and Cory, and Charles Volkmar and Son. Volkmar had been a painter, and his designs often look like oil paintings drawn on pottery.

VOLKMAR
Corona, N.Y

Plate, Mountain Scene, White, Blue, Signed, 8 1/2 In.	154.00
Vase, High Glaze, 5 1/4 In.	300.00
Vase, Pansies, Crown Point, 4 In.	450.00
Vessel, Matte Brown & Green Glaze, Squat, Signed, 1910, 4 1/4 x 6 1/2 In.	220.00

VOLKSTEDT was a soft-paste porcelain factory started in 1760 by Georg Heinrich Macheleid at Volkstedt, Thuringia. Volkstedt-Rudolstadt was a porcelain factory started at Volkstedt-Rudolstadt by Beyer and Bock in 1890. Most pieces seen in shops today are from the later factory.

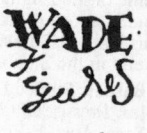

Figurine, Cupid & Psyche, Mounted To A Rock, Circular Base, White Biscuit, 13 In.	230.00
Figurine, Female, Flanked By Cherubs, White, Germany, c.1900, 7 3/4 In.	115.00
Group, 8 Figures Clad In 18th-Century Dress, White, 13 3/4 x 27 In.	1495.00

WADE pottery is made by the Wade Group of Potteries started in 1810 near Burslem, England. Several potteries merged to become George Wade & Son, Ltd. early in the twentieth century, and other potteries have been added through the years. The best-known Wade pieces are the small figurines given away with Red Rose Tea and other promotional items. The Disney figures are listed in this book in the Disneyana category.

WADE
figures

c. 1936+

Bank, Pig	55.00
Dish, Cat, Small	20.00
Dish, Cover, Copper Luster, Marked, 1957, 6 x 4 3/4 In.	50.00
Figurine, Bartender Bear	50.00
Figurine, Fireside Friend	75.00
Figurine, Fish Porter	175.00
Figurine, Gingerbread Boy, Large	50.00
Figurine, Gingerbread Boy, Small	30.00
Figurine, Humpty Dumpty, 2 3/4 In.	35.00
Figurine, Jack & Jill	35.00
Figurine, Lester Leprechaun	70.00
Figurine, Little Jack Horner, 3 In.	35.00
Figurine, Mr. & Mrs. Duck	250.00

Pitcher, Bushnell's Pub	38.00
Pitcher, Copper Luster, Festival, 6 1/2 In.	55.00
Pitcher, Grant's 8 Scotch, 3 Sides, Cobalt Blue, Gold, 6 1/2 In.	45.00
Pitcher, Ships, Clouds	160.00
Teapot, Paisley Chintz	385.00

WAHPETON POTTERY, see Rosemeade category.

WALLACE NUTTING photographs are listed under Print, Nutting. His reproduction furniture is listed under Furniture.

WALRATH was a potter who worked in New York City; Rochester, New York; and at the Newcomb Pottery in New Orleans, Louisiana. Frederick Walrath died in 1920. Pieces listed here are from his Rochester period.

Walrath Pottery

Bowl, 3 Sculpted Frogs, Sitting Atop Carved Leaves, Green, Yellow Glaze, 9 x 3 In.	2750.00
Chamberstick, Gray, 5 In.	250.00
Figurine, Woman, Green & Brown Matte Glaze, Incised Mark, 4 1/2 x 3 x 1 In.	330.00
Vase, Floral, Brown, Yellow, Green, Green Ground, 8 In.	4125.00
Vase, Pink, Mauve Roses, Deep Green Foliate Design, Heather Green Ground, 14 In.	8050.00

WALT DISNEY, see Disneyana category.

WALTER, see A. Walter category.

WARWICK china was made in Wheeling, West Virginia, in a pottery working from 1887 to 1951. Many pieces were made with hand painted or decal decorations. The most familiar Warwick has a shaded brown background. The name *Warwick* is part of the mark and sometimes the mysterious word *IOGA* is also included.

Creamer, Pansy, Embossed Design	225.00
Cuspidor, Crab Apples, Brown, 6 1/2 In.	195.00
Pitcher, Lemonade, Beechnuts, Brown To Orange	115.00
Tankard, Bulldog, Champion Rodney Stone	32.00
Tankard Set, Dog Series, Hand Painted, 9 Piece	725.00
Tray, Dresser, Pansy	225.00
Vase, Green Base Fading To Light Green, 2 Red Roses, 2 Pink Roses, 10 3/8 In.	170.00
Vase, Hibiscus, Twig Handle, Brown, 10 1/2 In.	120.00
Vase, Madam Le Brun, IOGA, 11 1/2 In.	195.00
Vase, Pillow, Woman Portrait, Brown, Blue, 8 1/4 In.	195.00
Vase, Thelma, Matte Finish, IOGA, 9 In.	115.00
Vase, War & Victory Symbol Design, Bronze, Black Marble Base, 10 In., Pair	4400.00
Vase, Woman, Holding Long-Stemmed Yellow Roses, Twig Handles, 12 In.	225.00

WATCH pockets held the pocket watch that was important in Victorian times because it was not until World War I that the wristwatch was used. All types of watches are collected: silver, gold, or plated. Watches are arranged by company name or by style. Pocket watches are listed here; wristwatches are a separate category.

Bijou Watch Co., Woman's, Lapel, Ornate Hands On Dial, 14K Yellow Gold	375.00
Bulova, Accutron, Railroad Approved	165.00
Bunn Special, Gold Filled Hunting Case, 24 Jewel	1200.00
Canadian Pacific Railway, 17 Jewel, Gold Filled Case, American	175.00
Charles LeRoy, Gilt Case, Shepherdess With Sheep, Fusee Enamel, c.1820	2400.00
Chronometer, Pocket, Gilt Pivot Detent Movement, White Metal Dial, 18K Gold	2300.00
D. Delacaux, 23 Jewel, Time & Observation Register, Key Wind, 18K Gold Case	2750.00
E. Gubelin, Blue Enamel Stripes, Sterling Silver, Purse, 1 1/2 In.	100.00
Elgin, 15 Jewel, 14K Solid Gold	395.00
Elgin, Hunting Case, Gold Plated	275.00
Elgin, Hunting Case, Separate Seconds Face, 14K Gold, 1899, 1 1/2 In.	315.00
Elgin, Open Face, 15 Jewel, Box	145.00
Elgin, Silver Metal Case, White Face, Separate Seconds Dial, 1 3/4 In.	99.00
Enamel & Gilt-Metal, Roman Numerals, France, 2 1/2-In. Face	57.00
Enamel Form, Gold, White Enamel Dial, Flower Heads, Seed Pearls	2530.00

Gallet, Stop, 7 Jewel 150.0

Gruen, Open Face, 19 Jewel, 14K Gold 180.0

Hamilton, 14K Gold, Open Face, 1 3/4 In. 143.0

Hamilton, 23 Jewel, Masonic Dial, 14K Gold, Box & Papers, c.1922 .... 1400.0

Hamilton, Navigator, 24-Hour Dial, 22 Jewel 245.0

Hamilton, No. 940, 21 Jewel, Lever Set, Porcelain Railroad Dial 265.0

Hamilton, Roland, 22 Jewel, Black Dial, 14K Gold 285.0

Hampden, Open Face, Swivel Stem, 17 Jewel 88.0

Howard, 17 Jewel, Seconds Register At 3 O'Clock, Gold Filled Case 150.0

Howard, Boston, 19 Jewel, 14K Gold Open Face Case 950.0

Howard, Open Face, 17 Jewel, 14K White Gold 198.0

Hunting Case, 3 Colors, Sidewinder, Swiss 83.0

Hunting Case, Chronograph, Calendar & Moon Phases, Foliate Monogram, 18K Gold .. 1840.0

Hunting Case, Dairyman & Maid Within Interior, White Enamel Dial, 18K Gold 4600.0

Hunting Case, Key Wind, Gold Dial, Gold Case 495.0

Hunting Case, White Porcelain Dial, 18K Gold 3001.5

Illinois, 19 Jewel, 3 Adjustments, Double Roller 70.0

Illinois, Bunn Special, 60 Hour, 14K Gold Filled 795.0

Illinois, Bunn Special, Silveroid, 21 Jewel, Silver Metal, Seconds Dial, 2 1/4 In. .. 225.0

Illinois, Great Northern Railroad Locomotive On Back, 17 Jewel 150.0

Ingraham, Sentinel, Travel Case 20.0

J.J. Drielsma, 18K Gold, Hunting Case, Jeweled Movement, Liverpool, England, 2 In. .. 302.0

Longines, 15 Jewel, Sterling Silver, Chain, Bigelow Kennard & Co., Inc., Boston .. 175.0

Longines, 19 Jewel, Silver Matte Dial, Arabic Numerals, 8-Day Deck, 1925, 3 x 5 In. .. 4025.0

Missouri Pacific, 21 Jewel, Train Case, 18 Size 500.0

Morris, Hunting Case, Silver, Enamel & Gold, Aviation Subject 1750.0

Movado, Sterling Silver, Purse, c.1950 .... 500.0

New York Watch Co., Floral Hunting Case, 15 Jewels, J.C. Perry, 18K Gold 1017.0

Omega, 15 Jewel, 3 Dials, 4 Hands 250.0

Open Face, Nickel Lever Movement, White Enamel Dial, Arabic Numerals, 18K Gold .. 1840.0

Open Face, White Dial, Blue Numerals, Diamond-Set Fleur-De-Lis, 18K Yellow Gold .. 287.0

R. Roskell, Open Face, Gilt Crank Lever Movement, Gold Dial, Blue Enamel, 18K Gold 1725.0

Rockford, Key Wind, Coin Silver, Open Face 200.0

Rockford, Solid Gold Transition, Key Wind, 11 Jewel, 1878 .... 750.0

Roux Bordier & Co., Fusee Enamel, Quarter Hour Repeating, c.1800 .... 2700.0

South Bend, 19 Jewel, 14K Gold, Open Face 300.0

Springfield, Back Opens To Inner Mechanism, Etched Flower On Outer Case .. 200.0

T.F. Cooper, Jeweled, Key Wind, Coin Silver, England 150.0

Tissot, World Time, Automatic, 17 Jewel, 14K Gold 2500.0

Waltham, 18K Gold, Open Face, Minute & Second Hand, Engraved 1919, 1 3/4 In. 115.0

Waltham, Bicycle Rider On Dial, 1891 .... 385.0

Waltham, Demi-Hunter, Black Enamel Roman Numerals 900.0

Waltham, Double Dial, Chronograph, Jeweled Movement, Brass Gears, 18K Gold 4000.0

Waltham, Pendant, 4 Colors Of 14K Gold, 19th Century 800.0

Waltham, Riverside Maximus, 23 Jewel, Presentation, 18K Gold, c.1908 ..... 575.0

Waltham, Seconds Dial, Engraved Flora & Scroll Case, 14K Yellow Gold 230.00

Woman's, Pendant, 14K Yellow Gold, 3 Stones, Closed Face, 14K Gold Slide Chain 862.00

Woman's, Pendant, Pagoda Form, 14K Gold, Gold Chain, 24 In. 522.00

Zeppelin, Around The World 300.00

WATCH FOBS were worn on watch chains. They were popular during
Victorian times and after. Many styles, especially advertising designs,
are still made today.

Anheuser-Busch, Brass, Paint Gone, Pre-Prohibition 18.00

Art Nouveau, Swirl Design, Coral, Carnelian, Topaz, 18K Gold, 1915, 19-In. Chain 400.00

Auto Hill Climb, June 11, 1910, Represents 1 Dollar, Metal, 1 3/4 x 1 1/2 In. 88.00

Buffalo Head 110.00

Caterpillar 12.00

Cincinnati Horseshoe, Manufacturers Of Horse & Mule Shoes, Leather Strap 40.00

Columbia Exposition, 1894 .... 35.00

Esco Construction Equipment, Relief Image Of Scoop, Rectangle, 1 1/2 x 1 In. 57.00

Green River Whiskey 25.00

Ham, Swifts Premium 12.00

Haynes-Kokomo, Indiana, 1910-Era Auto, Tin Coated Brass, Leather Strap, 1 1/2 In. 20.00
Hires Root Beer, Little Boy Pointing, Logo 85.00
Human Hair, 6 Coiled Strands, Gold Metal Ends, Chain, Victorian, 2 1/4 In. 35.00
Kansas War Maneuvers, 1912 .... 37.00
Lindbergh, New York To Paris, With Compass 200.00
Lion Co. & R., Set On Initial Seal, Chain With Swivel Loop 110.00
Lone Wolf Club 50.00
Oklahoma International Petroleum Exposition, Oil Wells & Airplane, Brass 45.00
Polarine, Metal, Leather Band, 5 1/2 In. 120.00
Pope Pius XI, Chicago, 1926 .... 20.00
Saucer's Extracts, Richmond, 10 Medals Won At World's Fair, Gilt 100.00
Spanish American War Reunion, New Orleans, 1931 .... 20.00
Statue Of Liberty 55.00
Texaco Petroleum Products, Embossed Lettering Both Sides, 1 1/4 In. 187.00
Union Railroad Co., For Service ....100.00 to 125.00

WATERFORD type glass resembles the famous glass made from 1783 to
1851 in the Waterford Glass Works in Ireland. It is a clear glass that
was often decorated by cutting. Modern glass is being made again in
Waterford, Ireland, and is marketed under the name *Waterford*.

Biscuit Jar 70.00
Decanter, Center Star, Raised Diamonds, Stopper, 10 In. 230.00
Decanter, Crystal, 9 In. 90.00
Finger Bowl, Diamond Cut Band & Lower Body, Footed, Signed, 4 3/4 In. 30.00
Jar, Cover, Regency, Stippled Diamond, Urn Shape, 19th Century, 14 In. 1650.00
Lamp, Cut, Cylindrical Shape, Brass Plate Base, 13 In., Pair 300.00
Liqueur Set, Colleen, 4 Piece 120.00
Pitcher, Tapered & Paneled Sides, Signed, 7 1/4 In. 258.00
Sherry, Sheila, c.1970, 5 1/2 In., 9 Piece 315.00
Tumbler, Diamond Cut, 5 In. 165.00
Vase, Allover Geometric Design, Pinched Circular Shape, 8 In. 125.00
Vase, Baluster Form, Signed, 7 In. 70.00
Wine, Lismore 40.00

WATT family members bought the Globe pottery of Crooksville, Ohio,
in 1922. They made pottery mixing bowls and tableware of the type
made by Globe. In 1935 they changed the production and made the
pieces with the freehand decorations that are popular with collectors
today. Apple, Starflower, Rooster, Tulip, and Autumn Foliage are the
best-known patterns. Pansy, also called Rio Rose, was the earliest pattern. Apple, the most popular pattern, can be dated from the leaves.
Originally, the apples had three leaves; after 1958 two leaves were
used. The plant closed in 1965. For more information, see *Kovels'
Depression Glass & Dinnerware Price List.*

Apple, Baker, Stand, No. 96 .... 250.00
Apple, Bean Pot, 3 Leaves, No. 76 .... 250.00
Apple, Bean Pot, Cover 135.00
Apple, Bowl, Salad, No. 74 .... 45.00
Apple, Casserole, French Handle, Individual, No. 18 .... 90.00
Apple, Chop Plate, No. 49 .... 275.00
Apple, Cookie Jar, Tapered, Cone-Top, No. 91 .... 800.00
Apple, Creamer, No. 62 ....90.00 to 150.00
Apple, Ice Bucket, Cover, No. 59 .... 200.00
Apple, Jar, Grease, No. 01 .... 375.00
Apple, Mixing Bowl Set, No. 6, No. 7, No. 8 .... 450.00
Apple, Mixing Bowl, 2 Leaves, No. 6 .... 95.00
Apple, Mixing Bowl, No. 64 .... 50.00
Apple, Pie Plate, No. 33 .... 75.00
Apple, Pitcher, 2 Leaves, No. 69 .... 300.00
Apple, Pitcher, 3 Leaves, Ice Lip, No. 17 .... 150.00
Apple, Pitcher, Land-O-Lakes Creameries, No. 15 .... 80.00
Apple, Pitcher, No. 15 ....75.00 to 95.00
Apple, Pitcher, No. 16 .... 110.00

Apple, Salad Bowl, 3 Leaves, No. 106 . . . . 500.0
Autumn Foliage, Bowl, Spaghetti, No. 39 . . . . 148.0
Cherry, Bowl, Spaghetti, No. 39 . . . . 95.0
Cherry, Pitcher, Plain Lip, No.16 . . . . 210.0
Cherry, Popcorn Bowl, No. 55 . . . . 275.0
Cherry, Saltshaker, Barrel 65.0
Coffeepot, Dogwood, Gray, Orchard Ware 65.0
Cookie Jar, Policeman . . . . .1500.00 to 1800.0
Dogwood, Gravy Boat, Gray, Orchard Ware 45.0
Dogwood, Teapot, Gray, Orchard Ware 55.0
Dogwood, Tumbler, Gray, Orchard Ware 28.0
Dutch Tulip, Baker, No. 68 . . . . 65.0
Dutch Tulip, Creamer, No. 62 . . . . .210.00 to 275.0
Dutch Tulip, Pitcher, No. 15 . . . . .130.00 to 300.0
Esmond, Cookie Jar, Happy-Sad Face, No. 34 . . . . 225.0
Nassau, Cruet Set, No. 126 . . . . 60.0
Orchard Ware, Pitcher, Black Beauty, Plain Lip 100.0
Orchard Ware, Pitcher, Cinnamon Drip, No. 15 . . . . 65.0
Orchard Ware, Pitcher, Cinnamon Drip, No. 16 . . . . 65.0
Pansy, Bowl, Spaghetti, No. 39 . . . . 120.0
Pansy, Casserole, Cover, Individual, No. 18 . . . . .89.00 to 195.0
Pansy, Pitcher, No. 17 . . . . 250.0
Peedeeco, Casserole, Stick Handle, Individual, No. 18 . . . . 20.0
Rio Rose, Mixing Bowl, No. 9 . . . . 75.0
Rooster, Bowl, Spaghetti, No. 39 . . . . 325.0
Rooster, Casserole, French Handle, Individual, No. 18 . . . . 200.0
Rooster, Creamer, No. 62 . . . . 260.0
Rooster, Mixing Bowl, No. 64 . . . . .100.00 to 110.0
Rooster, Pitcher, No. 15 . . . . .180.00 to 195.0
Rooster, Pitcher, No. 16 . . . . 125.00
Rooster, Pitcher, Refrigerator, No. 69 . . . . 225.00
Starflower, Bowl, 5 Petals, No. 55 . . . . 120.00
Starflower, Cookie Jar, No. 21 . . . . 230.00
Starflower, Ice Bucket, No. 59 . . . . 200.00
Starflower, Jar, Grease, 5 Petals, No. 47 . . . . 300.00
Starflower, Mug, 4 Petals, No. 501, 4 Piece 95.00
Starflower, Pitcher, 5 Petals, No. 17 . . . . 120.00
Starflower, Platter, No. 31 . . . . 60.00
Teardrop, Bean Pot, Tab Handles, No. 76 . . . . .80.00 to 95.00
Teardrop, Pitcher, No. 15 . . . . .45.00 to 95.00
Teardrop, Pitcher, No. 62 . . . . 75.00
Tulip, Baker, Cover, No. 600 . . . . 340.00
Tulip, Creamer, No. 62 . . . . .150.00 to 275.00

WAVE CREST glass is an opaque white glassware manufactured by the
Pairpoint Manufacturing Company of New Bedford, Massachusetts,
and some French factories. It was decorated by the C.F. Monroe
Company of Meriden, Connecticut. The glass was painted in pastel
colors and decorated with flowers. The name *Wave Crest* was used
after 1898.

**WAVE CREST
WARE**

Atomizer, Transfer 225.00
Biscuit Jar, Barrel Form, Floral Design, 8 1/2 In. 188.00
Biscuit Jar, Bell Form, Acanthus, Floral Design, 8 In. 170.00
Biscuit Jar, Cafe Au Lait Coloring, Flowers, Silver Fittings, Signed 325.00
Biscuit Jar, Cover, Butterscotch, White, Lavender Flowers, 7 In. 135.00
Biscuit Jar, Embossed Crest, Barrel Shape, Silver Plated, C.F. Monroe, 10 1/2 In. . . 675.00
Biscuit Jar, Embossed, Egg Crate Shape, Blue, Hand Painted Flowers, 10 1/4 In. 885.00
Biscuit Jar, Pink Floral Design, 7 1/2 In. 75.00
Biscuit Jar, Pink Transfer Design, Handle, C.F. Monroe Co., 11 x 5 In. 125.00
Biscuit Jar, Scroll Design, Pink Flowers, Silver Plate Cover, 7 In. 200.00
Bonbon, Venetian Scene, C.F. Monroe, 7 x 6 In. 1200.00
Bowl, Enamel Floral Sprays, Electroplate Rim, Signed, 3 3/4 x 6 In. 288.00
Box, 2 Cherubs Frolicking, Hinged Cover, 3 1/2 x 4 1/4 In. 250.00

Box, Blown-Out Baroque Shell, Pink & Blue, 5 1/2 In. . . . . .475.00 to 500.00
Box, Cigarette, Blue, Purple Flowers, Yellow Ground, Signed, 4 1/4 x 3 In. 500.00
Box, Collars & Cuffs, Signed, 6 x 7 1/4 In. 1150.00
Box, Cover, Pink Flowers On Cover, Sides, 6 In. 489.00
Box, Dresser, Baroque Shell, Hand Painted Florals, 7 1/2 In. 403.00
Box, Dresser, Blue, White Flowers, Lavender Ground, 5 1/2 In. 150.00
Box, Dresser, Brass Rim, Enameled Flowers, 5 7/8 In. 110.00
Box, Dresser, Gilded Brass Rim, Scroll Designs, Polychrome Flowers, Signed, 4 In. 82.00
Box, Dresser, Pale Yellow, Hand Painted Flowers, 4 In. 300.00
Box, Dresser, Pansies, Ivory Ground, Gilt Metal Rim, Rococo Handles, Red Mark, 7 In. . 190.00
Box, Dresser, Relief Design, Flowers, Enamel, 3 1/2 In. 165.00
Box, Egg Crate Shape, Collars & Cuffs, Daisies, Pink Ground, C.F. Monroe, 6 In. 1450.00
Box, Egg Crate Shape, Light Blue, Yellow Lilies, Lavender & Gold Enamel, 7 x 7 In. . . . 1570.00
Box, Glove, Floral Design, Blue, 9 x 5 In. 100.00
Box, Hand Painted Flowers On Lid & Base, Shell Design, Circular 395.00
Box, Hand Painted Maiden Hair Fern, Forget-Me-Nots, Hinged Cover, 4 x 7 In. 550.00
Box, Helmschmied Swirl, Polychrome Violets, Lined, 4 1/2 In. 385.00
Box, Helmschmied Swirl, Raised Roses, Hinged Cover 350.00
Box, Niagara Falls Scene, Cream Background, Blue Forget-Me-Nots, 5 1/4 In. 790.00
Box, Pale Yellow Flowers, Circular Swirl, Hinged Cover 350.00
Box, Pink Clover, Green Leaves On White, Hinged Cover, 4 1/2 x 6 In. 510.00
Box, Portrait, Landscape Scene, 2 Cherubs, Yellow Daisies, 4 x 7 In. 850.00
Box, Portrait, Woman, Wearing Hat, Glossy Green, Gold Ground, 4 x 7 In. 900.00
Box, Shell, Blue, Footed, 4 In. 325.00
Box, Shell, Petit Point Design, Purple, Blue, Pink, White, Hinged Cover, 4 x 7 In. 450.00
Box, Swirl, Purple, Blue Flowers, Enameled, Hinged Cover, 5 x 6 1/2 In. 275.00
Box, Swirl, Yellow, White, Flowers, Enameled, Hinged Cover, 3 1/4 x 3 In. 150.00
Box, Yellow Floral Design, Pale Blue, White Ground, Hinged Cover, 3 1/2 x 4 In. 150.00
Creamer, Helmschmied Swirl, Pink Roses 110.00
Creamer, Helmschmied Swirl, Roses 95.00
Fernery, Daisies, Blue 325.00
Fernery, Egg Crate Shape, Square 275.00
Fernery, Ferns & Flowers, Blown Out, Brass Ormolu Rim, Brass Insert 425.00
Humidor, Cigarettes, Floral & Scenic, Word In Lavender Enamel, 3 3/4 In. 1035.00
Plate, Lily Pond, Blue Ground, Reticulated, C.F. Monroe, 7 In. 750.00
Salt & Pepper, Sunburst Design, Ring Neck, Sterling Top, 3 1/2 In. 38.00
Saltshaker, Tulip, House Scene, Original Top, Pair 55.00
Spooner, Helmschmied Swirl, Pink Roses 195.00
Sugar Shaker, Brass Cover, Melon Ribs, Polychrome Florals, Signed, 4 3/4 In. 220.00
Sugar Shaker, Paneled, Sprigs Of Johnny-Jump-Ups, Silver Plated Cover, 3 In. 585.00
Syrup, Blue & White Blossoms, Silver Plated Cover & Collar 485.00
Vase, Bud, Cream, Blue Flowers, Metal Rim & Base, 5 In. 320.00

WEAPONS listed here include instruments of combat other than guns,
knives, rifles, or swords. Firearms are not listed in this book. Knives
and swords are listed in their own categories.

Billy Club, Police, Hardwood, Leather Strap, 1930s-1940s, 13 In. 95.00
Cannonball, Broad Arrow Mark, England, c.1750, 4 In. 450.00
Crossbow, With Windlass, Early 15th Century 750.00
Priming Wire, Cleaning Touchholes Of Cannons, Iron, Revolutionary War, 23 In. 185.00

WEATHER VANES were used in seventeenth-century Boston. The direc-
tion of the wind was an indication of coming weather, important to the
seafaring and farming communities. By the mid-nineteenth century,
commercial weather vanes were made of metal. Today's collectors
often consider weather vanes to be examples of folk art, even though
they may not have been handmade.

Arrow, Gilt Copper, Late 19th Century, 43 3/4 In. 805.00
Arrow, Gilt Iron & Copper, Late 19th Century, 39 1/2 In. 805.00
Arrow & Star Banneret, Painted Wood, 19th Century 1380.00
Automobile, Copper, Yellow, 4 Wheels, Black Wood Base, 11 In. 4025.00
Banner & Arrow, Bullet Hole, Gilt Zinc, 19th Century, 42 In. 2530.00
Banneret, Hand Form, Gilt Copper, Bullet Hole, 26 1/4 In. 1265.00

Baseball & Bat, Copper 5750.0
Blackhawk, Copper, Late 19th Century, 26 In. 1380.C
Blackhawk Horse 2300.C
Bull, Standing, Copper, Sheet-Copper Ears, Allover Verdigris, 22 In. 6900.C
Cock, Copper, Worn Gilt, Replaced Foot, 23 In. 2420.C
Codfish, Articulated Gills, Tail, Metal Rod Support, Wood Base, White, 30 In. 1035.C
Codfish, Large Sheet Metal Fins, Wooden Body, Glass Eyes, 30 In. 770.0
Cow, Bullet Holes, Copper, 19th Century, 16 1/2 x 30 1/2 In. 4312.0
Cow, Molded Zinc, Late 19th Century, 29 In. 230.0
Doughboy, Painted Flag, Verdigris Surface, Copper, 36 1/2 In. 4600.0
Doughboy, WW I, Copper, With Rifle & American Flag, Gray, Green, 36 1/2 In. 6750.0
Eagle, 72-In. Arrow 9500.0
Eagle, Copper, On Sphere, Gilt Traces, Arrow, 30 In. 1815.0
Eagle, Copper, Perched On An Orb, Allover Verdigris, Late 19th Century, 32 In. 9200.0
Eagle, Copper, Perched On Orb, Arrow Directionals, 29 1/4 In. 6900.0
Eagle, Copper, Pine, Perched On Orb, Green Over Gold, 23 1/2 In. 1150.0
Eagle, Full-Bodied, On Rod & Arrow, Cast Iron, 43 In. 138.0
Eagle, Full-Bodied, Perched On Ball Above Arrow, 49 1/2-In. Wingspan 4025.0
Fierce Dragon's Head, Baring Teeth, Iron, Germany, 10 3/4x 15 1/2 In. 2587.0
Fish, Bullet Holes, Gilt Copper, Late 19th Century, 35 1/2 In. 3220.0
Fish, Copper, Allover Verdigris, Black Metal Base, 19th Century, 8 3/4 In. 3162.0
Fish, On Spire Standard, Weathered Gray Patina, 67 In. 440.0
Fox, Running, Copper, Head Up, Ears Pricked, Black Metal Stand, 12 In. 14950.0
Grasshopper, Copper, Verdigris Patina, 20th Century, 31 In. 288.0
Greyhounds, Male Figure, Iron, 1915, 16 1/8 In. 1725.0
Half Moon, Copper, With Face, Spirals, Arrow, 67 In. 5500.0
Horse, Galloping, Tin, Wood Base, Mid-19th Century, 25 x 20 In. 1017.0
Horse, Running, Blackhawk, Full-Bodied, Fiske, c.1870 . . . . 2400.0
Horse, Running, Cast Head, Copper Body, Light Green Paint, 30 In. 805.0
Horse, Running, Copper, Allover Verdigris, Black Base, 18 3/4 In. 6900.0
Horse, Running, Copper, Allover Verdigris, Mounted On Black Base, 15 In. 5750.0
Horse, Running, Copper, Black Metal Base, 20 1/4 In. 8050.0
Horse, Running, Copper, Bullet Holes, 30 In. 747.0C
Horse, Running, Copper, Full-Bodied, Black Metal Base, Zinc, 27 3/4 In. 5750.0
Horse, Running, Copper, Full-Bodied, Driver, Wearing Cap, 20 In. 2875.0
Horse, Running, Copper, Harris & Co., 48 In. 3025.0C
Horse, Running, Copper, Zinc Ears, Black Hawk, 26 3/4 In. 3690.0C
Horse, Running, Full-Bodied, Gold Gilt, Zinc, 54 In. 2012.5C
Horse, Running, Gilt Copper, Late 19th Century, 29 In. 4025.0C
Horse, Running, Gilt, Wooden Base, Ethan Allen, 29 x 20 In. 192.5C
Horse, Running, Sheet Metal, Late 19th Century, 27 In. 431.0C
Horse, Running, Tin, Cast-Iron Arrow, 15 1/2 x 10 1/2 In. 192.50
Horse & Jockey, Painted, Copper, 19th Century, 15 1/2 x 29 In. 2300.00
Humpback Whale Mother & Calf, Wooden, 33 In. 302.00
Indian, Sheet Metal, Astride Standing Horse, Black, 22 In. 1150.00
Jockey, Painted, Wire Wheel Sulky, Running Horse, Cast Iron, 33 In. 3162.00
Merino Ram, Articulated Horns, Ears, Eyes, Black Metal Base, 28 x 26 In. 4600.00
Pig, Copper, 5-Pointed Star, Allover Verdigris, Early 20th Century, 52 1/2 In. 2070.00
Pig, Copper, Allover Verdigris, Curly Tail, Molded Eye, 18 In. 13800.000
Rooster, Bullet Hole, Gilt, Zinc, 1860s, 26 x 21 In. 2645.00
Rooster, Bullet Holes, Gilt Copper, Late 19th Century, 28 1/4 x 28 1/2 In. 4600.00
Rooster, Gilt Over Copper, Iron Stand, Bullet Holes, 28 1/2 x 24 In. 770.00
Rooster, Hollow Body, Copper, 24 In. 1045.00
Rooster, Sheet Metal, Gold Paint, Black Metal Base, 32 1/4 x 29 1/2 In. 1724.00
Rooster, Sheet Steel, 20th Century, 24 3/4 x 21 1/4 In. 357.00
Rooster, Sheet Steel, Old Paint, Replaced Rod, 32 1/2 In. 365.00
Rooster, Silhouette, Copper, Green, 19 In. 190.00
Rooster, Silhouette, Sheet Steel, Worn Red, Silver & White, Wooden Base, 36 In. 190.00
Rooster, Standing Upright, Bullet Holes, 34 In. 7975.00
Sailboat, Copper, Single Mast, Under Full Sail, Allover Verdigris, 29 1/2 In. 1380.00
Sailboat, Iron, Blacksmith Construction, Rivets, Primitive, 20 1/2 In. 247.00
Sailing Ship, Copper, 1940s, 23 x 20 In. 225.00
Schooner, Painted Wood & Zinc, 20th Century, 20 x 35 1/2 In. 316.00

Schooner, Painted Wood & Zinc, Early 20th Century, 29 x 41 In.	1150.00
Scroll Banner, Bullet Holes, Gilt Copper, 37 3/4 x 49 5/8 In.	1955.00
Squirrel, Copper, 2 Squirrels, 1 Lunging For Acorn, 35 In.	6900.00
Steamship, Copper, Boston, 26 In.	950.00
Swordfish, Silhouette, Sheet Steel, 15 In.	440.00
Wingover Airplane, Hand Carved, 19 In.	125.00

WEBB glass is made by Thomas Webb & Sons of Ambelcot, England. Many types of art and cameo glass were made by them during the Victorian era. Production ceased by 1991, and the factory was demolished in 1995. Webb Burmese and Webb Peachblow are special colored glasswares of the Victorian era. They are listed at the end of this section. Glassware that is not Burmese or Peachblow is included here.

Webb

Bowl, Coralene Blue Flowers, Green Leaves, Red Satin Interior, 8 1/4 In.	385.00
Bowl, Mother-Of-Pearl, Rainbow, Raspberry Prunt Thorn Footed, Signed, 5 x 5 1/2 In.	1500.00
Bride's Bowl, Enameled, E.G. Webster Holder, 11 In.	935.00
Cologne, Blossoming Leaf Vines, Stylized Border, Red, White, Screw Cap, 5 1/2 In.	1495.00
Cologne, Etched Blossoms, 4 Panels, Amber, Yellow, 5 In.	818.00
Cup & Saucer, Cranberry Cut To Clear, Blossoms, Cameo, 2 3/4 & 5 In.	550.00
Jug, Bird, Floral Design, Citron Yellow Body, Handle, Cameo, 4 3/4 In.	88.00
Lamp, Floral, Butterflies, Blue Ground, Cameo, 18 In. *Illus*	17250.00
Perfume Bottle, Citron, Roses, White Cameo, Silver Hinged Cover, Square, 5 In.	2750.00
Perfume Bottle, Large Butterfly, Palm Leaves, Blue, White Cameo, 8 In.	1250.00
Pin, Rolling, Cobalt Blue, Finial Ends, Signed, 14 In.	450.00
Pitcher, Brown, Cream Lining, Satin Applied Handle, 3 3/4 x 2 1/2 In.	195.00
Rose Bowl, Diamond-Quilted, Amberina To Orange, White Lining, 3 1/2 In.	550.00
Scent Bottle, Amber Ground, Butterfly, Rose Branch, White Cameo, 1900, 6 In.	690.00
Scent Bottle, Red Ground, Butterfly, Rose Branch, White Cameo, 1900, 5 In.	1150.00
Tumbler, Amber, Coralene Floral Leaf Design, Applied Rigaree, 19th Century, 5 In.	66.00
Vase, Amber, Rose, 1 Blue Band, Mushroom Shape, 2 1/2 x 4 1/2 In.	1600.00
Vase, Applied Floral Design, Maroon, Gold, Pale Blue Lining, Ball Shape, 10 1/2 In.	220.00
Vase, Basket Weave, Brown To Tan To Gold To Cream, White Lining, Satin, 5 1/2 In.	850.00
Vase, Blue To Sky Blue To White, Clear Edge, Enameled Floral, 5 x 6 In.	425.00
Vase, Blue, Peach, White, Ruffled Edge, 1890, 4 In.	195.00
Vase, Blue, Wild Rose, Butterfly, Pillow Shape, White Cameo, Marked, 7 1/2 x 6 1/2 In.	2750.00
Vase, Brown To Gold, Satin, Floral Design, White Interior, 10 1/2 x 4 In.	450.00
Vase, Bud, Gold Enameled Design, 8 1/4 In.	303.00
Vase, Cut Fruit & Leaf Laden Branches, Gourd Shape, Solid Top, Stem Handle, 7 1/4 In.	3705.00
Vase, Deep Purple, Blue, Gold Iridescent, 8 1/4 x 4 1/2 In.	175.00
Vase, Enameled Lace, Pink Ground, Signed, 10 In.	325.00
Vase, Floral, Blue Ground, White Cameo, Bulbous, Ruffled & Crimped Edge, 4 x 3 In.	475.00
Vase, Flower & Acorn, Mother-Of-Pearl, Bridal White, Pocket Shape, 3 1/2 x 6 1/2 In.	650.00
Vase, Flowers, Leaves, Stems, Rose Ground, White Cameo, 10 In.	2310.00
Vase, Flowers, Scrolling Leaves, Star Cut Base, Early 20th Century, 8 1/4 In.	460.00
Vase, Fuchsia Design, Enameled, 3 1/4 In.	220.00

Be sure copies of lists of valuables, photographs, and other information can be found in case of an insurance loss. Give copies to a trusted friend. Do not keep them in the house. If you keep them in your safe deposit box, be sure you have a key off site. The key could be lost in a house fire.

Webb, Vase, Grape Picker, Brown Ground, Cameo, Woodall, 8 1/2 In.

Webb, Lamp, Floral, Butterflies, Blue Ground, Cameo, 18 In.

Vase, Gold Design, Floral, White Interior, Pyramid Shape, 3 Gold Ball Feet, 8 1/2 In. . . . 247.50
Vase, Gold Florals, Gold Dragonfly On Back, Off-White Interior, 4 1/4 In. 195.00
Vase, Gold Flowers & Fern Leaves, Gold Butterfly On Back, Orange Cameo, 7 1/2 In. . . 245.00
Vase, Gold Flowers & Vines, Gold Butterfly On Back, 4 In. 145.00
Vase, Grape Picker, Brown Ground, Cameo, Woodall, 8 1/2 In. . . . .*Illus* 37375.00
Vase, Grape, Vine Motif, Faceted Body, Hexagonal Stem, 11 1/2 x 8 In. 201.00
Vase, Jack-In-The-Pulpit, Pink & White Stripes, Bulbous, 6 x 5 In. 375.00
Vase, Moroccan Ware, Flowers, Foliage, Dots, Opaque White, 1879, 5 1/2 In. 225.00
Vase, Mother-Of-Pearl, Basket Weave, Blue To Pale Blue, Cream Interior, 7 x 5 In. 750.00
Vase, Mother-Of-Pearl, Butterscotch, 7 1/4 In. 82.50
Vase, Pink & White Stripes, Satin, Bulbous, 1885, 4 x 8 In. 425.00
Vase, Pink Satin, Bird, Butterfly, 7 1/2 In., Pair 500.00
Vase, Pink, Floral Branches, Ribbed, White Cameo, 8 In. 1430.00
Vase, Red, Cased In Yellow, Butterfly, Gilt Vines, White Cameo, 1900, 6 In., Pair 690.00
Vase, Rose Blossoms, Buds, White Cameo, Oval, England, 7 In. 1840.00
Vase, Rose To Green, Cream Lining, Bottle Shape, 9 In. 335.00
Vase, Seashell, 5 Shells On Seaweed Clusters, Red, White Cameo, Etched, 5 1/2 In. 2645.00
Vase, Small Brown Bird, Salmon Pink To Yellow, Rust Flowers, 8 1/4 In. 1200.00
Vase, Spring Flowers, Gold Leaf, White Cameo, Enameled, Rolled Edge, 8 1/2 In., Pair . 150.00
Vase, Yellow To Pale Yellow, Satin, White Lining, Gourd Shape, 10 1/2 In. 285.00

WEBB BURMESE is a colored Victorian glass made by Thomas Webb
& Sons of Stourbridge, England, from 1886.

Lamp, Fairy, Satin, 4 x 2 3/4 In., Pair 350.00
Perfume Bottle, Blue Butterfly, Oval Teardrop Shape, Signed, 5 In. 990.00
Pitcher, Cream, Grapes, Leaves, Vine, Hexagonal, 3 x 3 1/2 In. 350.00
Toothpick 395.00
Toothpick, Hexagonal, 2 3/4 In. 195.00
Vase, Bud, Enameled, Flowers, Silver Plated Frame, 8 1/4 In. 515.00
Vase, Bud, Gold Berries, Leaves, Dimpled Etch, Bulbous, 1880s, 6 In. 330.00
Vase, Green Leaves & Berries, Petal Top, Satin, 3 1/2 In. 475.00
Vase, Green, Brown Flowers, Canary Yellow, Salmon, Satin, 9 In. 719.00
Vase, Hexagonal, 3 5/8 In. 195.00
Vase, Ribs, Ruffled Edge, 4 1/4 In. 225.00
Vase, Swirl, 4 Gold Flowers, Rigaree Edge, Bulbous, 4 x 3 In. 200.00
Vase, Vine & Ivy Leaves, Bottle Shape, Signed, 10 1/4 In. 895.00

WEBB PEACHBLOW is a colored Victorian glass made by Thomas
Webb & Sons of Stourbridge, England, from 1885.

Bowl, Blue Interior, Pink Base, Red Top, 1880s, 5 x 3 In. 110.00
Celery Vase, Basket Weave, 6 5/8 In. 853.00
Cologne Bottle, Rose, Amber, Gold Prunus Blossoms, Butterfly, 5 In. 747.50
Flask, Figural, Eagle Head, Opal White Interior, 6 1/2 In. 1495.00
Jug, Bird & Floral, Citron Yellow Body, Satin Handle, Cameo, 4 3/4 In. 66.00
Lamp, Fairy, Clarke Base, 2 5/8 In. 330.00
Pot, Crimped Rim, 2 x 3 In. 143.00
Vase, Enameled Florals, Butterflies, Red To Light Pink, White Interior, 6 In. 220.00
Vase, Gold Flowers, Leaves & Branches, Dragonfly, 3 1/2 In. 295.00
Vase, Pine Needles, Trailing Prunus Blossoms, Gold Trim, 11 1/4 In. 750.00
Vase, Silver Florals, Gold Stems & Leaves, Off-White Interior, 5 1/8 In. 210.00

WEDGWOOD, one of the world's most successful potteries, was
founded by Josiah Wedgwood, who was considered a cripple by his
brother and was forbidden to work at the family business. The pottery
was established in England in 1759. A large variety of wares has been
made, including the well-known jasperware, basalt, creamware, and
even a limited amount of porcelain. There are two kinds of jasperware.
One is made from two colors of clay, the other is made from one color
of clay with a color dip to create the contrast in design. The firm is still
in business. Other Wedgwood pieces may be listed under Flow Blue,
Majolica, or in other porcelain categories.

WEDGWOOD

Bank, Peter Rabbit 45.00
Basket, Queensware, Chestnut, Ivory Color, Openwork Lattice Cover, 1770s 2300.00

Bidet, Queensware, Wooden Stand, Impressed Mark, 1800, 20 1/4 In. 400.00
Biscuit Jar, Jasperware, Silver Plated Hinged Lid & Underplate, Blue, 8 In. 575.00
Bookends, Jasperware, Light Blue, Medallions, Rosewood, Adjustable, 16 In. 490.00
Bottle, Sherry, Sandeman 45.00
Bough Pot, Jasperware, Green, Handles, c.1800, 7 1/2 x 10 1/2 In. 1250.00
Bowl, Black Basalt, Bellflowers, Acanthus, Oak Leaf Acorn Border, 12 In. 1495.00
Bowl, Butterfly Luster, Octagonal, 4 3/8 In. 325.00
Bowl, Cover, Wildlife, Floral Design, Rabbit Handle, 19th Century, 9 1/4 In. 230.00
Bowl, Creamware, Masonic Symbols, Etruscan Lodge 327, Marked, 1807, 12 In. 2070.00
Bowl, Dragon Luster, 1920, 8 In. 285.00
Bowl, Dragon Luster, Blue, Mother-Of-Pearl Interior, Octagonal, 1920, 7 3/4 In. 515.00
Bowl, Fairyland Luster, 8 Interior Inscriptions, 1923 . . . . 4485.00
Bowl, Fairyland Luster, Elves, Black, Mother-Of-Pearl, 1920, 5 In. 690.00
Bowl, Fairyland Luster, Gold, Cobbled Medallion, Purple, Crimson, 1920, 9 In. 1265.00
Bowl, Fairyland Luster, Landscape Scene, Trees, 9 In. 1540.00
Bowl, Fairyland Luster, Leap-Frogging Elves, Octagonal, 1920, 9 In. 3737.00
Bowl, Hummingbird Luster, Blue Mottled Exterior, Gold, Orange Interior, 11 In. 1955.00
Bowl, Hummingbird Luster, Blue, Orange Mottled Interior, 1920, 8 7/8 In. 690.00
Bowl, Jasper Dip, Blue, Cupids At Play, Reading Lesson, Marked, 1785, 6 1/4 In. 1610.00
Bowl, Jasperware, Black, White Classical Dancing Hours, 1956, 10 1/8 In. 690.00
Bowl, Jasperware, Black, White Classical Dancing Hours, 1959, 10 1/4 In. 545.00
Bowl, Jasperware, Blue, Alternating Acanthus Leaves & Palmettes, 6 In. 690.00
Bowl, Jasperware, Children, Blue, Lady Templetown, 1785, 5 5/8 In. 805.00
Bowl, Primrose, 8 In. 95.00
Bowl, Queensware, Centenary Of Montreal, Black Transfer, 1945, 12 1/4 In. 260.00
Bowl, Sacrifice, White On Lilac, 8 In. 285.00
Bowl, Vegetable, Cover, Chapoo, 1850, 12 x 9 1/2 In. 862.50
Box, Jasperware, Bust Of Churchill, Blue, 3 In. 95.00
Box, Onyx, Jasperware Medallion On Hinged Cover, 4 x 7 1/4 In. 630.00
Bust, Eisenhower, Basalt 75.00
Bust, George II, Black Basalt, Parade Armor, Marked, 1780, 9 3/4 In. 1090.00
Bust, Homer, Black Basalt, Waisted Round Socle, 1790, 13 1/2 In. 1150.00
Bust, Lincoln, Basalt 75.00
Bust, Mercury, Black Basalt, Signed, 20 In. 1380.00
Bust, Paris, Carrara, Waisted Round Socle, Impressed Mark, 1860, 18 1/4 In. 1035.00
Bust, Princess Elizabeth, Moonstone, Artist, 1937, 15 3/4 In. 1150.00
Bust, Queen Elizabeth II & Duke Of Edinburgh, Black Basalt, 9 In., Pair 345.00
Bust, Rousseau, Black Basalt, Stepped Square Base, 18th Century, 6 1/2 In. 515.00
Bust, Shakespeare, Black Basalt, Waisted Round Socle, 1775, 14 In. 3450.00
Bust, Sir Isaac Newton, Black Basalt, Turned Socle, Bentley, 1775, 6 In. 975.00
Bust, Swift, Black Basalt, Waisted Round Socle, Bentley, 1775, 18 In. 8050.00
Bust, Watt, Carrara, Raised Round Base, E.W. Wyon, 1859, 14 3/4 In. 515.00
Butter, Cover, Atlanta, Flow Blue 330.00
Butter, Cover, Jasperware, Blue, White Floral & Leaf, Cylindrical, c.1790, 5 In. 375.00
Butter, Cover, Stand, Jasperware, Blue, Boys At Play, Domestic Scene, 1785, 7 In. 1265.00
Candleholder, Black Basalt, Children Playing, Rosso Antico, 1800, 3 1/4 In. 475.00
Candlestick, Black Basalt, Dolphin Shape, Shell Base, 1971, 9 In., Pair 1380.00
Candlestick, Dolphin, Green Glaze, Shell Base, Impressed Mark, 9 7/8 In. 260.00
Candlestick, Jasperware, Yellow, Black & White Classical, Marked, 6 3/4 In. 165.00
Candlestick, Jasperware, Yellow, Black Classical, 1930, 5 In., Pair 575.00
Canister, Young America Clipper Ship, 5 In. 120.00
Charger, Earthenware, Silver Luster 3-Masted Ship, A. Powell, 1923, 18 3/8 In. 1035.00
Charger, Majolica, Sea Nymph Thetis, Riding Serpent, 1872, 15 1/4 In. 1150.00
Cheese Dome, Jasperware, Cover, Tray, Green, White, Mid-19th Century, 11 In. 165.00
Chess Piece, Drabware, King, With Child, Impressed Mark, 1800, 4 1/4 In. 805.00
Chess Piece, Jasperware, King & Queen, Royal Blue, Pair 285.00
Clock Case, Jasperware, White Classical, Lilac, Green, Impressed Mark, 6 3/4 In. 630.00
Coffee Can, Jasper Dip, Saucer, White Classical, 3 Colors, 1870, 5 1/2 In. 1265.00
Compote, Majolica, Argenta Ware, Grapevine Border, Pierced, 1871, 11 In. 260.00
Compote, Pomona, Black Basalt, Impressed Mark, 9 x 11 3/4 In. 1840.00
Creamer, Belle Fleur 20.00
Creamer, Jasperware, Tankard Shape, Classical Women & Cupid, 1915, 4 1/8 In. 88.00
Creamer, Jasperware, Yellow, Black Classical Figures, 3 3/4 In. 100.00

Cup, Black Basalt, Musicians & Instruments, With Bentley, c.1775, 2 1/2 In. 1955.00
Cup, Cover, Stand, White Biscuit, Trembleuse, Scrolled Panels, 1830, 4 1/2 In. 515.00
Cup, Jasperware, Diceware, Green, Yellow Quatrefoils, White Ground, 1795, 2 In. 1380.00
Cup & Saucer, Belle Fleur 16.00
Cup & Saucer, Chinese, Flow Blue, After Dinner 65.00
Cup & Saucer, Jasperware, Blue, White Lady Templetown, Children, 5 1/8 In. 690.00
Cup & Saucer, Jasperware, Classical Scenes, Dark Blue, White, 1890 . . . . 55.00
Cup & Saucer, Queensware, Floral, Double Entwined Handle, 1780, 5 1/8 In. 474.00
Cuspidor, Majolica, Mottled Blue, Brown & Yellow, Impressed Mark, 1885, 7 In. 345.00
Custard Cup, Jasperware, Lilac, Applied White Latticework, 1 5/8 In. 920.00
Dish, Black Basalt, Running Anthemion Border, Crest, 18th Century, 5 1/2 In. 745.00
Dish, Cheese, Jasperware, White Classical Figures, Garlands, Lavender 275.00
Dish, Cover, Creamware, Grapevine Design 35.00
Dish, Heart, Jasperware, Dark Blue, White Slip Floral, Harry Barnard, 4 5/8 In. 460.00
Dish, Queensware, Armorial, Maria Palette, Maria Lyons Brighton, 1883, 12 In. 170.00
Egg Stand, Drabware, Salt Cellar Center, 6 Holes, 19th Century, 7 1/8 In. 315.00
Eggcup, Jasperware, Black, White 55.00
Figurine, 2 Toucan, Black Basalt, Glass Eyes, 1913, 5 1/4 In. 920.00
Figurine, Black Basalt, Reclining Baby, Head On Fruit Basket, 18th Century, 5 In. 745.00
Figurine, Black Basalt, Recumbent Lion, 6 1/4 In. 690.00
Figurine, Black Basalt, Sleeping Boy, Rectangular Base, 18th Century, 4 5/8 In. 230.00
Figurine, Boy, Sleeping, Jasparware, White, Blue Base, Green, 1785, 5 1/8 In. 3335.00
Figurine, Fallow Deer, Moonstone, John Skeaping, 1927, 7 1/4 In. 230.00
Figurine, Hedgehog, Black Basalt, Pierced For Bulbs, England, 6 1/2 In. 630.00
Figurine, Lion, Recumbent, Black Basalt, England, 10th Century, 6 1/4 In. 690.00
Figurine, Polar Bear, Gray & Rust Glaze, John Skeaping, 1930-1940, 9 In. 1840.00
Flower Frog, Psyche, Sitting On Rock, Holding Staff 375.00
Garden Seat, Greek Musician, Blue Transfer, Thomas Allen, 1882, 17 3/8 In. 4885.00
Garden Seat, Majolica, Rubena, Pillow Form Seat, Scrolled Legs, 17 3/4 In. 5750.00
Garden Seat, Mosaic & Floral Paneled, Transfer, Hexagonal, 1861, 17 1/2 In. 400.00
Goblet, Cover, Jasperware, Light Blue, Lilac, White Classical, 7 1/2 In. 630.00
Group, Charity, Pearlware, Enameled, Impressed Title, Factory Mark, 8 1/2 In. 375.00
Humidor, Jasper Dip, Green, 8 In. 330.00
Inkstand, Black Basalt, 2 Pots, Urn Form Quill Holder, 1785, 2 7/8 In. 1150.00
Inkstand, Drabware, 3 Round Pots, Set In Pen Tray, 1830, 8 3/8 In. 170.00
Jar, Biscuit, Jasperware, Blue, Silver Plated Fittings, 6 1/2 In. 165.00
Jar, Cigarette, Jasperware, White On Lilac, 4 3/4 In. 120.00
Jardiniere, Stand, Pearlware, Slip Designed, Drapery Swags, 5 3/4 In., Pair 1495.00
Jug, Bellarmine, Drabware, VA Medallion, Sgraffito Design, 1876, 7 1/4 In. 285.00
Jug, Black Basalt, Helmet Shape, Bentley, 1775, Marked, 4 5/8 In. 1265.00
Jug, Black Basalt, Helmet, Bacchanalian Boys, Bentley, 1780, 11 1/4 In. 3335.00
Jug, Caneware, Sportive Love & Charlotte At Tomb Werther, 1800, 4 1/4 In. 630.00
Jug, Etruscan, White On Lilac, 1/2 Pt. 155.00
Jug, Jasperware, Blue, Helmet, Boys At Play, Lady Templetown, 1785, 5 In. 1265.00
Jug, Longfellow, Black Transfer, Gilt, Impressed Mark, 1880, 6 3/4 In. 115.00
Jug, Majolica, Frog, Seated On Eggplant, Impressed Mark, 1872, 4 In. 1725.00
Jug, Majolica, Reed Pattern, Dark Blue Ground, Impressed Mark, 1868, 7 In. 860.00
Jug, Queensware, Commemorative, Irish Volunteers, c.1780, 8 1/2 In. 4312.00
Jug, Queensware, Death Of Wolfe Transfer, Sea Battle, 1778, 8 3/4 In. 3735.00
Jug, Queensware, Figures & Music Landscape Transfer, Marked, 1790, 9 1/2 In. 975.00
Jug, Queensware, Perseveranti Dabitur Motto, 1780, 9 3/4 In. 920.00
Jug, Upper Polished Surface, Bacchanalian Boys, With Bentley, c.1780, 11 In. 3335.00
Lamp, Cover, Black Basalt, Acanthus, Bellflowers, Oak Leaf Acorn Border, 9 In. 1610.00
Match Holder, Classical Scene, Blue & White, 2 1/2 In., 2 Piece 125.00
Medallion, Black Basalt, Ben Franklin, Self Frame, Bentley, 1777, 3 1/8 x 4 In. 2875.00
Medallion, Black Basalt, Christ Portrait, Profile, 18th Century, 4 1/4 x 5 5/8 In. 860.00
Medallion, Black Basalt, Storming Bastille, King's Paris Arrival, 3 1/4 In., Pair 1265.00
Medallion, Jasper Dip, Dark Blue, Fame Inscribing A Tablet, 1790, 3 1/2 x 5 In. 690.00
Medallion, Jasperware, White, Night Shedding Poppies, Bentley, 4 x 6 In. 1265.00
Mold, Gelatin, Queensware, Inner Tube Hand Painted, 18th Century, 10 1/2 In. 4025.00
Mold, Gelatin, Queensware, Iron Bridge At Wearmouth Scene, 18th Century, 5 In. 4310.00
Mortar & Pestle, Stoneware, Wooden Handle, Mid-19th Century, 5 1/8 In. 290.00
Mug, Jasperware, Commemorative, Washington, Franklin, Blue, c.1875, 7 1/2 In. 375.00

Mug, Queensware, Blind Man's Bluff Transfer, 1775, 6 In. 1610.00
Mug, Queensware, Investiture Of Charles, 1968 . . . . 75.00
Mug, Shakespeare, Anniversary, 1964 . . . . 50.00
Perfume Bottle, Jasperware, Blue, Classical Relief, 18th Century, 4 5/8 In. 805.00
Pipe, Jasperware, Dark Blue, Staite's Pat. & Factory Mark, 3 1/2 In. 290.00
Pitcher, Basin Pomegranate Stylized Pods Leaves Ivory Ground, 10 x 8 In. 660.00
Pitcher, Black Basalt, Classical Figures, Grape & Leaf Rim, 6 In. 187.00
Pitcher, Chapoo, Bulbous, 1850, 6 In. 690.00
Pitcher, Classical Figures, Rosette Above & Below, 5 1/2 In. 100.00
Pitcher, Cover, Queensware, Etruscan Borders, Marked, 1780, 10 In. 630.00
Pitcher, Garfield, Red Brown Transfer, Gilt, 7 3/8 In. 440.00
Pitcher, Hunting Scenes, Hound Handle, Silver Gilt, 6 In. 175.00
Pitcher, Jasperware, Classical Figures, Blue, Marked, England, 5 7/8 In. 105.00
Pitcher, Jasperware, Green, White Classical Figures, Band, Rope Handle, 8 1/2 In. 165.00
Pitcher, Jasperware, Purple, White Classical Figures, Marked, 6 3/4 In. 770.00
Pitcher, Jasperware, Stylized Floral Bands, Blue Ground, 9 In. 230.00
Plaque, Black Basalt, Frightened Horse, George Stubbs, 1973, 9 1/4 x 15 1/4 In. 545.00
Plaque, Black Basalt, Herculaneum Dancer, Self Frame, 1775, 14 5/8 In. 6325.00
Plaque, Fairyland Luster, Enchanted Palace, Rectangular, 1976, 8 x 11 1/2 In. 1610.00
Plaque, Jasper Dip, Discovery Of Achilles, 14 In. 9200.00
Plaque, Jasperware, Apotheosis Of Virgil, Blue & White, Frame, 14 3/4 In. 4140.00
Plaque, Jasperware, Blue, An Offering To Peace, Marked, 5 1/8 x 9 3/8 In. 690.00
Plaque, Jasperware, Blue, Domestic Employment, Frame, 3 3/4 x 5 In., Pair 860.00
Plaque, Jasperware, Choice Of Hercules, Black, Wooden Frame, 6 x 18 In. 1495.00
Plaque, Jasperware, Green, White Classical Templetown Figures, 3 x 9 1/2 In. 575.00
Plaque, Jasperware, Light Blue, Muses Classical Relief, Frame, 1895, 4 x 10 7/8 In. 745.00
Plaque, Jasperware, Lilac Classical, White, 19th Century, 2 x 8 5/8 In., Pair 860.00
Plaque, Jasperware, Minerva & Blind Justice, Blue, 1780, 6 1/2 In., Pair 2530.00
Plaque, Jasperware, Yellow, White Nude Children, 5 In. 520.00
Plaque, Othello, Gilt Foliate Ground, Thomas Allen, 1881, Round, 15 1/8 In. 4310.00
Plaque, Romeo, Thomas Allen, 1881, Round, Impressed Mark, 15 In. 4310.00
Plaque, Sir John Falstaff, Gilt Foliate Ground, Thomas Allen, Round, 1881, 15 In. 5310.00
Plaque, White House, 5 1/2 In. 125.00
Plate, Blue Transfer, Kings Chapel, Boston, 9 1/4 In. 22.00
Plate, Blue Transfer, Mayflower Arriving In Provincetown Harbor, 1620, 9 1/4 In. 22.00
Plate, Blue Transfer, Niagara Falls, 9 1/4 In. 22.00
Plate, Christmas, 1970, Christmas In Trafalgar Square 68.00
Plate, Christmas, 1971 . . . . 68.00
Plate, Christmas, 1972 . . . . 68.00
Plate, Christmas, 1982, 8 1/2 In. 60.00
Plate, Etruscan, Winter, March, 1920, 10 1/4 In. . . . . .44.00 to 88.00
Plate, Home Of Emerson, Cabbage Rose Border, Cobalt Blue & White, 9 In. 40.00
Plate, Ivanhoe, Flow Blue, 10 In. 75.00
Plate, Jasperware, Cupid, Pink, 9 1/2 In. 135.00
Plate, Jasperware, Zodiac 20.00
Plate, Kate Greenaway Months, Rust Border, 1880, 10 1/2 In. 165.00
Plate, Majolica, Ocean, Argenta Ware, Oval, 1875, 25 3/4 In. 2070.00
Plate, Queensware, Blue, White Band, Gilt Rim, 1790, 8 In. 34.00
Plate, Rebecca Repelling Templar, 10 In. 95.00
Plate, Trophy, Jasperware, Lilac, White Classical Center, Black Ground, 7 1/4 In. 1380.00
Plate, Willow, 1900, 10 1/2 In. 55.00
Plate Set, Queensware, Each Different Cherubs, E. Lessore, 1863, 9 In., 12 Piece 2530.00
Platter, Chapoo, 1850, 15 3/4 x 12 1/4 In. . . . . .287.00 to 400.00
Platter, Geneva Pattern, Blue Transfer, Ironstone, 1847, 15 3/4 In. . . . . .110.00 to 121.00
Platter, Landscape, Flow Blue, 1911, 11 x 15 In. 235.00
Platter, Meat, Willow, 1840-1860, 18 x 14 In. 295.00
Platter, Pearlware, Nankin, 1867, 17 x 21 In. 650.00
Platter, Queensware, Black Transfer Landscape Scene, Oval, 15 x 18 3/8 In. 805.00
Pot, Dome Cover, Widow Warburton Finial, Black Basalt, 10 5/8 In. 385.00
Potpourri, Cover, Ivory Vellum, Insect Lid, Gilt, Leaves & Vines, 1885, 7 3/4 In. 490.00
Punch Bowl, Fairyland Luster, Night Poplar Trees, Day Trees Interior, 1920, 9 In. 4025.00
Punch Bowl, Harvard, Blue & White 230.00
Rum Pot, Cover, Dancing Maidens, Trefoil Overhead Handle, 1779, 6 3/4 In. 2530.00

Sauceboat, Queensware, Salt Glaze Style, Rococo Shape, 1770, 8 In. 745.00
Soup, Dish, Beatrice, Brown & White Transfer, 1881 .... 65.00
Stirrup Cup, Hare Head, Black Basalt, 19th Century, 5 7/8 In. 1495.00
Sugar, Chapoo, 1850 .... 546.00
Sugar, Cover, Black Basalt, Hieroglyphs, Crocodile Finial, Rosso Antico, 5 In. 1265.00
Sugar, Cover, Caneware, Bacchanalian Boys, Marked, 1780, 4 1/4 In. 745.00
Sugar & Creamer, Whitehall 75.00
Syrup, Fallow Deer, Tankard Style 325.00
Tankard, Jasperware, Green, 8 1/4 In. 295.00
Tankard, Jasperware, Psyche & Cupid, Light Blue 150.00
Tankard, Queensware, Hunting Scene Transfer, 1770, 4 3/4 In. 515.00
Tea Bowl, Saucer, Jasperware, Blue, Children, Lady Templetown, 1785, 5 In. 575.00
Tea Set, Bone China, Gilt Handles & Finial, Silver Form, Marked, 12 Piece 170.00
Tea Set, Chinese Bird & Flower, Bone China, 1815, 23 Piece 920.00
Tea Set, Floral, Gilt, Wooden Tripod Stand, Printed Mark, 1880, 17 Piece 1090.00
Tea Set, Jasperware, Terra-Cotta, White Classical, 1957, 4 Piece 400.00
Teakettle, Cover, Black Basalt, Encaustic, Trefoil Overhead Handle, 1780, 5 In. 2760.00
Teapot, Black Basalt, Allover Scrolled Flowers, Marked, 1775, 5 In. 6325.00
Teapot, Black Basalt, Bulbous, 1780, 3 1/2 In. 1265.00
Teapot, Black Basalt, Egyptian Hieroglyphs, Crocodile Finial, 7 1/4 In. 1715.00
Teapot, Black Basalt, Howling Spaniel Finial, Overall Dimpled Surface, c.1775 ...... 6325.00
Teapot, Black Basalt, Sybil Finial, Impressed Mark, 9 1/4 In. 315.00
Teapot, Blue Transfer, Oaklands Pattern, SYP, 1909, 7 3/4 In. 110.00
Teapot, Caneware, Bamboo Shape, 5 Sides, Bentley, 1780, 4 1/2 In. 2990.00
Teapot, Caneware, Molded Foliate Pattern, Mythological Characters, 5 In. 23.00
Teapot, Cauliflower, c.1770 .... 7475.00
Teapot, Classical Figures, Blue Jasper Dip, Impressed Mark, England, 6 In. 132.00
Teapot, Commemorative, George III, Charlotte Sophia Wedding, c.1763 .... 9775.00
Teapot, Cover, Black Basalt, Barrel Form, Bamboo Handle, 5 1/4 & 3 5/8 In. Pair 460.00
Teapot, Cover, Black Basalt, Beehive Shape, Reeded Loop Handle, 4 In. 400.00
Teapot, Cover, Black Basalt, Commemorative, 5 3/4 & 4 1/2 In., Pair 1495.00
Teapot, Cover, Black Basalt, Infants Playing, Sibyl Knop, 1880, 4 1/4 In. 575.00
Teapot, Cover, Black Basalt, Swan Form, Flowerhead Knop, Oval Stand, 7 In. 400.00
Teapot, Cover, Chapoo, 1850, 9 In. 460.00
Teapot, Cover, Commemorative, Black Basalt, Lion's Head Spout, Serpent Handle 977.00
Teapot, Jasperware, Blue, Acanthus Leaves & Palmettes, 1785, 5 In. 975.00
Teapot, Pearlware, Blue Transfer, Peony Printed Design, SYP, 5 1/2 In. 345.00
Teapot, Praised Admiral Rodney, Naval Hero, c.1770 .... 3737.00
Teapot, Queensware, Black Transfer, Inscription, Globular, 1776, 5 In. 1380.00
Teapot, Queensware, Calico Pattern, Globular, 1770, 5 1/4 In. 3735.00
Teapot, Queensware, Chintz Pattern, Globular, 1775, 5 1/4 In. 3795.00
Teapot, Queensware, Exotic Birds Transfer, Globular, 1775, 5 In. 490.00
Teapot, Queensware, Flowers, Leaf Spout, Double Entwined Handle, c.1770, 6 In. 1610.00
Teapot, Queensware, Queen Charlotte, Black Transfer, 1763, 4 1/4 In. 6325.00
Teapot, Queensware, Strawberry Design, Globular, 1770, 5 1/2 In. 6725.00
Teapot, Redware, Enameled, Polychrome Floral, Early 19th Century, 10 In. 165.00
Teapot, Tortoiseshell, c.1760 .... 2300.00
Tile, Scenes Of Boston, Calendar On Reverse, 1907 .... 85.00
Tile, Scenes Of Boston, Calendar On Reverse, 1919 .... 85.00
Tobacco Jar, Cover, Jasperware, Lilac, Green, White Ground, 6 1/2 In. 690.00
Tray, Caneware, Leaf Border, Gilt, 18th Century, 9 1/8 In. 2875.00
Tray, Fairyland Luster, Lily, Blue, Purple, Green, Mother-Of-Pearl Ground, 9 In. 2300.00
Tray, Jasperware, Heart, Lilac ....35.00 to 40.00
Tray, Jasperware, Pink, Square 45.00
Tray, Lilac, 4 1/2 In. ....35.00 to 40.00
Tray, Portland, Blue, Square, 4 In. 40.00
Tray, Tea, Jasperware, Blue, Floral, Guilloche, 1780, Impressed Mark, 10 x 13 In. 805.00
Tureen, Sauce, Cover, Queensware, Greek Bands, 18th Century, Marked, 5 In. 805.00
Tureen, Sauce, Ivanhoe, Flow Blue 185.00
Tureen, Soup, Cover, Oregon, Scrolled Handles, Flow Blue 720.00
Tureen, Soup, Cover, Stand, Queensware, Leaf Handles, 18th Century, 18 x 12 In. 690.00
Tureen, Soup, Irene, Flow Blue ....795.00 to 895.00
Urn, Black Glaze, Signed, 9 1/2 In., Pair.................................... 770.00

Urn, Caneware, Crater, Grapevine, Pierced Disc Cover, Impressed Mark, 13 In. 690.00
Urn, Dairy, Cover, Queensware, Handles, Endsleigh Dairy, Marked, 1820, 15 In. 2300.00
Vase, 2 Floral, Leaf Garlands, Applied Scrolled Handles, Terra-Cotta, 16 1/2 In. 3450.00
Vase, Arcadian, Black, 7 1/2 In. 170.00
Vase, Black Basalt, Auro, Gilded Slip Floral, Impressed Mark, 15 7/8 In. 690.00
Vase, Black Basalt, Blossoms, Palmette Motifs, Loop Handles, 11 3/8 In. 1150.00
Vase, Black Basalt, Dancing Figures, Scroll Handles, Bentley, 1778, 15 In. 6900.00
Vase, Black Basalt, Grecian Design, Flowers & Grapes In Top Band, 7 x 6 In. 550.00
Vase, Bone China, Blue Luster, Vine & Floral Border, Square, 1920, 7 1/2 In. 345.00
Vase, Cover, Black Basalt, Scrolled Handles, Bentley, 1775, 12 3/4 In. 4310.00
Vase, Cover, Black Basalt, Sphinx Handles, Bentley, Wafer Mark, 1775, 6 In. 3450.00
Vase, Cover, Jasperware, Black, White Muses, Impressed Mark, 11 1/4 In., Pair 2530.00
Vase, Cover, Queensware, Drapery Swags, Botanical Border, Marked, 11 In. 690.00
Vase, Cover, Victoria Ware, White Dancing Hours, Blue Ground, Marked, 7 3/4 In. 860.00
Vase, Creamware, Grape Vines, Foliage, Strawberry Band, Mid-19th Century, 6 In. 86.00
Vase, Encaustic, Classical Scenes, Handles, 1780, 10 1/2 In. 3450.00
Vase, Fairyland Luster, Black, Gold, Blue, Green, Crimson, Gilt Edge Border, 8 In. 2990.00
Vase, Fairyland Luster, Persian Celtic Border, Mother-Of-Pearl Ground, 9 In. 4025.00
Vase, Floral, Iron Red Ground, Gilt, Flow Blue, 4 In., Pair 400.00
Vase, Flowers & Grapes In Band At Top & Bottom, 7 x 6 In. 550.00
Vase, Hummingbird, Luster, Mottled Blue, Orange Mottled Interior, 5 1/8 In., Pair 575.00
Vase, Incised Floral, Yellow Ground, Alfred H. Powell, 1930, 4 3/4 In. 630.00
Vase, Ivory Glazed, Bottle Form, Floral Design, Gilt, 1885, 14 1/4 In. 745.00
Vase, Jasperware, Black, 7 1/2 In. 190.00
Vase, Jasperware, Black, White Classical Figure, Impressed Mark, 9 1/2 In. 630.00
Vase, Jasperware, Blue, Broken Column, c.1800 . . . . 5000.00
Vase, Jasperware, Blue, White Classical, Portland, 1840, 10 1/8 In. 2415.00
Vase, Jasperware, Classical Ladies, Lion Head Masques On Sides, 1892-1915, 7 In. 225.00
Vase, Jasperware, Teal, Bud 80.00
Vase, Majolica, Sunflower, Deep Blue Ground, Impressed Mark, 1875, 12 In. 1725.00
Vase, Marsden Art Ware, Bottle Form, Leaves & Floral, Buff Ground, 1885, 7 In. 460.00
Vase, Marsden Art Ware, Flowers & Leaves, Blue Ground, Marked, 1885, 6 In. 1380.00
Vase, Moonstone, Floral, Millicent Taplin, 1935, 9 1/4 In. 690.00
Vase, Potpourri, Cover, Pearlware, Floral Sprays, Green Ground, 16 In. 1725.00
Vase, Sun-Lit, Glazed Caneware Body, Trellis Borders, Millicent Taplin, 8 3/4 In. 315.00
Vase, Taperstick, Cover, Black Basalt, Bentley, Wafer Mark, 1775, 8 1/2 In. 2185.00
Wall Pocket, Majolica, Bird's Nest, Oak Branches, Impressed Mark, 1874, 9 In. 1725.00

WELLER pottery was first made in 1873 in Fultonham, Ohio. The firm
moved to Zanesville, Ohio, in 1882. Art wares were introduced in
1893. Hundreds of lines of pottery were produced, including
Louwelsa, Eocean, Dickens Ware, and Sicardo, before the pottery
closed in 1948.

LOUWELSA
WELLER

Angry Duck, Ornament, 10 x 15 In. 7500.00
Ardsley, Bowl, Kingfisher, 16 1/2 x 3 1/2 In. 330.00
Ardsley, Vase, Green, Brown, 9 In. 77.00
Art Nouveau, Vase, 8 In. 120.00
Atlantic, Vase, 9 In. 200.00
Atlas, Bowl, Star Shape, Blue, Ivory Lining, 9 1/4 In. 65.00
Aurelian, Vase, Berry Design, Signed Kapps, 8 1/2 In. 110.00
Baldin, Umbrella Stand 750.00
Baldin, Vase, Blue, 6 In. 250.00
Baldin, Vase, Bud, 7 In. . . . . .90.00 to 125.00
Baldin, Wall Pocket 600.00
Barcelona, Vase, 8 In. 500.00
Barcelona, Vase, 14 In. 550.00
Bedford Matte, Umbrella Stand, Umbrella, Foliate Design, Green Glaze, 10 1/4 In. 330.00
Bedford Matte, Vase, 4 Vertical Columns Each Side, Geometric, Green Glaze, 5 In. 385.00
Blossom, Vase, Handled, Footed, 8 In. 45.00
Blue Ware, Jardiniere, Figure Playing Flute Among Trees, 6 1/2 In. 247.00
Bonito, Jardiniere, 7 1/2 In. 250.00
Bonito, Vase, 6 x 5 In. 130.00
Bouquet, Vase, Matte Green, 12 In. 145.00

Brighton, Figurine, Blue Bird, 6 In. 250.00
Brighton, Figurine, Blue Bird, 8 In. 250.00
Brighton, Figurine, Cardinal, 5 1/2 In. 357.00
Brighton, Figurine, Cardinal, 8 x 6 1/2 In. 1210.00
Brighton, Figurine, Kingfisher, 6 1/2 In. 295.00
Brighton, Figurine, Kingfisher, 9 In. 325.00
Brighton, Figurine, Kingfisher, On Stump With Openings For Flowers, 5 1/2 In. 230.00
Brighton, Figurine, Parrot, 8 In. 470.00
Brighton, Figurine, Parrot, 12 1/2 In. 1320.00
Brighton, Figurine, Parrot, On Hanging Stand, 13 In. 550.00
Brighton, Figurine, Pheasant, Green, Yellow, 11 1/2 x 7 In. 415.00
Brighton, Flower Frog, 2 Bluebirds, 4 In. 264.00
Brighton, Flower Frog, 2 Robins, 5 1/2 In. 132.00
Brighton, Flower Frog, Woodpecker 175.00
Brighton, Wall Pocket, Kingfisher, 12 In. 253.00
Bronze Ware, Vase, Hammered, Blue Mottled Mouth, Signed, 11 x 5 In. 770.00
Burntwood, Jardiniere, 12 In. 275.00
Burntwood, Vase, Birds, 12 In. ....225.00 to 250.00
Burntwood, Vase, Vegetation, Signed, 10 1/2 In. 275.00
Cactus, Figurine, Camel, Yellow, 4 In. 88.00
Cactus, Figurine, Pan With Lily, 5 In. 110.00
Cactus, Planter, Rabbit, Duck, Yellow, 6 1/2 In. 66.00
Camelot, Vase, Geometric, Cream, Brown Ground, 4 1/2 In. 265.00
Chase, Vase, 5 1/2 In. 275.00
Chase, Vase, Cobalt, 11 In. 550.00
Chengtu, Vase, 8 In. 125.00
Chengtu, Vase, 16 In. ....275.00 to 285.00
Claywood, Pedestal, 17 1/2 In. 325.00
Claywood, Umbrella Stand, Grapes, 19 1/2 In. 395.00
Cloudburst, Vase, Glazed In Luster Colors, 10 3/4 In. 522.00
Coppertone, Candleholder, Turtle, Pair 600.00
Coppertone, Cigarette Holder, Frog, 4 1/2 x 4 In. ....350.00 to 395.00
Coppertone, Figurine, Frog, Logo, Signed, 5 1/2 In. 990.00
Coppertone, Figurine, Frog, On All Fours 275.00
Coppertone, Figurine, Frog, Water Lily, 4 1/2 In. 305.00
Coppertone, Flower Frog, Duck, 11 1/2 In. 2860.00
Coppertone, Flower Frog, Lily 250.00
Coppertone, Flower Frog, With Waterlily, 4 x 4 In. 275.00
Coppertone, Garden Figure, Frog With Banjo, 12 1/4 In. 8800.00
Coppertone, Vase, 2 Handles, 12 In. 385.00
Coppertone, Vase, 8 1/2 In. 340.00
Coppertone, Vase, Closed Handles, Spherical, 7 x 9 In. 425.00
Coppertone, Vase, Cylinder, 13 In. 650.00
Coppertone, Vase, Green Matte Over Gray, Incised Mark, 8 1/2 x 6 1/2 In. 440.00
Coppertone, Vase, Marked, 6 1/2 In. 60.00
Coppertone, Vase, Trumpet Shape, 6 1/2 In. ....145.00 to 175.00
Cornish, Vase, Matte Brown, Black, 3 In. 165.00
Cretone, Vase, Deer & Flower Design, Hester Pillsbury, Signed, 6 7/8 In. 660.00
Delsa, Vase, Green, Yellow, 12 In. 99.00
Dickens Ware I, Orange Poppies, Stylized Leaves, Blue Ground, 11 1/2 In. 275.00
Dickens Ware I, Vase, Floral, 7 x 9 1/2 In. 400.00
Dickens Ware II, Mug, American Indian, Polychrome, 6 In. 220.00
Dickens Ware II, Mug, Hunter, Sea Birds, Crashing Waves, Charles B. Upjohn, 5 5/8 In. .. 385.00
Dickens Ware II, Pitcher, Monk, Blue Glaze Ground, Gibson, 13 x 6 In. 935.00
Dickens Ware II, Tobacco Jar, Chinaman, 6 In. 935.00
Dickens Ware II, Tobacco Jar, Irishman, 6 1/2 In. 495.00
Dickens Ware II, Tobacco Jar, Turk, 7 In. 605.00
Dickens Ware II, Vase, Dragon, Wrap Around, Shaded Persian Blue Ground, 16 In. 385.00
Dickens Ware II, Vase, Flower Lady, 12 In. 1050.00
Dickens Ware II, Vase, Golfing Scene, Golfer & Caddy, Signed, 9 1/4 In. 2200.00
Dickens Ware II, Vase, Pillow, Drinking Monk, Charles Upjohn, Pillow, 5 In. .. 525.00
Dickens Ware II, Vase, Portrait, Blue Glaze, Floral Design On Sides, 11 3/4 In. 770.00
Dickens Ware II, Vase, Victorian Figural Scene, 9 1/4 In. 880.00

Dickens Ware III, Mug, Monk Shaving, 5 1/2 In. 525.00
Dupont, Vase, 8 In. 235.00
Eocean, Cup, Green Fish, Light Green Ground, 3 1/2 In. 143.00
Eocean, Jonquils, Vase, 2 Handles, 11 1/2 In. 880.00
Eocean, Tankard, Dark Red Cherry Design, 10 In. 465.00
Eocean, Vase, Dark, Light Pink Leaves, Berries, Green To Pink Ground, 16 1/4 In. 825.00
Eocean, Vase, Flowers, Berries, Green Leaves, Shaded Green To Ivory, 10 In. .... .660.00 to 715.00
Etna, Bowl, Stylized Red Roses, Black, Yellow, Black Ground, 10 In. 165.00
Etna, Jardiniere, Incised Red Flowers, Green Leaves, Brown Ground, Marked, 7 In. 253.00
Etna, Vase, Chrysanthemums, Shaded Ivory To Green Ground, 14 1/2 In. 825.00
Etna, Vase, Stylized Cherry Design, Black Ground, 3 1/8 x 4 3/4 In. 110.00
Flemish, Basket, 4 1/2 In. 66.00
Flemish, Basket, Handles, 6 1/2 x 8 1/2 In. 115.00
Flemish, Basket, Hanging, Chains 175.00
Flemish, Jardiniere, 7 1/2 In. 200.00
Flemish, Tub ....150.00 to 175.00
Florenzo, Basket, Flowers, Green, Cream, 7 In. 27.50
Florenzo, Vase, Foral, Water Lily, 6 1/2 In. 187.00
Floretta, Mug, Brown, 5 In. 110.00
Floretta, Tankard, Pink Flowers, Green Leaves, Green, Gray, Pink Ground, 12 1/2 In. 355.00
Forest, Basket, 8 In. 300.00
Forest, Bowl, 4 Feet, 6 1/2 x 3 In. 88.00
Forest, Jardiniere, 7 In. ....300.00 to 350.00
Forest, Lamp, 11 1/2 In. 1150.00
Forest, Planter, 4 In. 135.00
Forest, Teapot, High Glaze, 5 7/8 In. 220.00
Forest, Vase, 8 In. 150.00
Forest, Vase, Matte Brown, Cream, Green, 16 x 4 1/2 In. 60.00
Forest, Wall Pocket, Squirrel, 9 In. 275.00
Geode, Vase, Blue Stars & Comets, Signed, 3 3/4 In. 440.00
Glendale, Vase, 8 In. 625.00
Glendale, Vase, 13 In. 1600.00
Glendale, Vase, Bird Beside Nest, Mottled Pink Glaze, 6 3/4 In. 220.00
Gloria, Vase, 2 Handles, 6 1/2 In. 95.00
Gloria, Vase, Green, 6 In. 22.00
Green Matte, Jar, 12 x 10 In. 145.00
Green Matte, Vase, Leaf Design, Glaze, 8 x 7 In. 265.00
Greenaway, Jardiniere, House, Windmill Scene, Marked, 8 1/2 x 12 In. 176.00
Greenbriar, Vase, Handle, 15 1/2 In. 525.00
Greora, Vase, 9 In. 225.00
Greora, Vase, Matte Green, Brown, 12 1/2 In. 60.00
Hudson, Decanter, Blue 450.00
Hudson, Vase, Berries & Flowers On Branch, 2 Handles, 6 1/2 In. 522.00
Hudson, Vase, Blue, Clusters Around Shoulder, Royal Blue Ground, 9 3/4 x 5 In. 355.00
Hudson, Vase, Bud, Pansy, Blue, 9 3/4 In. 275.00
Hudson, Vase, Clover, 2 Handles, Shaded Blue Ground, 6 1/2 In. 880.00
Hudson, Vase, Daffodils, Yellow, Green, Gray, Green Ground, Square, 9 1/2 In. 385.00
Hudson, Vase, Daisies, Shaded Pink To Green Ground, M. Ansel, 8 3/4 In. 495.00
Hudson, Vase, Floral, Royal Blue Ground, 8 3/4 x 4 1/4 In. 385.00
Hudson, Vase, Floral, Stylized Branches, Ivory Ground, 8 1/4 x 5 In. 330.00
Hudson, Vase, Flowers, Sage Green To Pink Ground, Artist, 7 3/4 In. 190.00
Hudson, Vase, Grapes, Wrought Iron Stand, Sara Reid McLaughlin, 27 1/8 In. 3410.00
Hudson, Vase, Irises, Signed Pillsbury, 6 In. 450.00
Hudson, Vase, Jonquils, Angular Handles, Shaded Blue Ground, 9 3/4 In. 715.00
Hudson, Vase, Landscape, 3 Houses & Picket Fence Along Road, McLaughlin, 9 In. 2970.00
Hudson, Vase, Lotus Flower, White, 10 In. 165.00
Hudson, Vase, Multicolored Flowers, Dark Band, Cream Ground, 10 In. 385.00
Hudson, Vase, Nasturtium, Shaded Blue, Green, Pink Ground, 11 3/4 In. 1045.00
Hudson, Vase, Pale Blue Roses, White, 9 1/4 In. 400.00
Hudson, Vase, Roses, Pink, Blue, Cylinder, 13 1/2 In. 522.00
Hudson, Vase, Spanish Ship Under Full Sail, Painted By Hester Pillsbury, 8 5/8 In. 4510.00
Hudson, Vase, Stylized Floral, Royal Blue Ground, 8 1/3 x 3 1/8 In. 245.00
Jap Birdimal, Vase, 3 Blue Fish, Black Outline, Pale Green Ground, 6 In. 715.00

Kenova, Vase, Woman, Medallions, 6 In. 275.00
Kingfisher, Flower Frog 425.00
Knifewood, Bowl, Swans, 3 1/2 In. 220.00
Knifewood, Vase, Florals, Cream & Green, Signed, 7 In., Pair 197.00
LaSa, Vase, Bulbous, 4 In. 250.00
LaSa, Vase, Landscape, Iridescent, 7 In. 495.00
LaSa, Vase, Landscape, Tree, Nacreous Glaze, 8 1/2 In. ....355.00 to 440.00
LaSa, Vase, Palm Tree Design, Gold, Red, Purple Iridescent, 12 In. 465.00
LaSa, Vase, Palm Trees, Flared, 9 1/2 In. 595.00
Lavonia, Wall Pocket, Stylized Victorian Designs, Mauve To Aqua, 10 3/4 In. 192.00
Lido, Vase, White Matte Glaze, Yellow Base, 1872, 11 In. 30.00
Lorber, Jardiniere, Satyr, 14 In. 1475.00
Louella, Bowl, 5 x 2 In. 33.00
Louwelsa, Candleholder, Floral Design, 7 In. 175.00
Louwelsa, Jardiniere, 12 1/2 In. 200.00
Louwelsa, Lamp Base, Floral, 3 Handle Style, Signed, 11 1/4 x 11 1/4 In. 500.00
Louwelsa, Lamp Base, Grape Leaves, Vines, Standard Glaze, Signed, 25 In. 330.00
Louwelsa, Pitcher, Indian Portrait, Signed, 10 3/4 In. 795.00
Louwelsa, Pitcher, Lybarger, 10 7/8 In. 220.00
Louwelsa, Roses, Hexagonal, 5 1/2 x 2 3/4 In. 75.00
Louwelsa, Vase, Flowers, Dark Glaze, Signed, Hester Pillsbury, 13 1/2 In. 1595.00
Louwelsa, Vase, Nasturtium & Stylized Stems, Browns, Sage Green Ground, 12 x 6 In. .. 385.00
Louwelsa, Vase, Persian Cat, Brown Glaze, Hester Pillsbury, Pillow, 7 1/2 x 8 In. 3190.00
Louwelsa, Vase, Renaissance Gentleman With Ruffled Collar, Pillow, 11 In. 355.00
Louwelsa, Vase, Signed, Knott, 8 x 11 In. 285.00
Louwelsa, Vase, Spade Form, Poppy On Brown, Green Field, 6 1/2 In. 85.00
Luster, Bowl, 9 1/2 x 6 In. 77.00
Malverne, Pot, Strawberry 275.00
Malverne, Vase, Green, Red Buds, Unmarked, Pillow, 6 1/4 In. 82.50
Mammy, Cookie Jar 650.00
Mammy, Cookie Jar, Watermelon, 11 In. 1000.00
Mammy, Sugar & Creamer ....1250.00 to 1650.00
Mammy, Teapot, 8 In. ....550.00 to 650.00
Marbelized, Vase, 6 In. 80.00
Marbelized, Vase, Orange & White, Marbelized, Goblet Shape, 10 In. 200.00
Marbleized, Flower Frog, White & Orange, 4 In. 40.00
Marvo, Flower Frog, Blue 55.00
Marvo, Vase, 9 1/2 In. 95.00
Marvo, Vase, Green, 8 In. ....100.00 to 145.00
Marvo, Wall Pocket, 7 In. 150.00
Mermaids, Vase, Ivory, 13 In. 165.00
Muskota, Bowl, Squirrel, 7 x 5 In. 264.00
Muskota, Bowl, Swan, 10 x 4 1/2 In. ....550.00 to 600.00
Muskota, Figurine, Dog, 6 In. 660.00
Muskota, Figurine, Kingfisher, 8 1/2 In. 198.00
Muskota, Figurine, Nude, With A Swan, 7 1/2 x 7 In. 770.00
Muskota, Flower Frog, Nude, White 350.00
Muskota, Flower Frog, Raised Flowers 115.00
Muskota, Flower Frog, Swan, 6 In. 165.00
Muskota, Flower Frog, Turtle, 5 In. 185.00
Nile, Vase, 9 In. 200.00
Oak Leaf, Console, Dusty Blue, 8 x 12 In. 95.00
Orris, Wall Pocket, Brown, Green 150.00
Panella, Vase, Blue, 4 1/2 In. 33.00
Panella, Wall Pocket, Blue, 8 In. 165.00
Patricia, Bowl, Swan Head Handles, Green, Brown, 10 x 6 1/2 In. 176.00
Patricia, Bowl, Swan Head Handles, White, 8 x 5 In. 77.00
Patricia, Vase, Duck Heads, Crystalline Glaze, Signed, 11 5/8 In. 770.00
Patricia, Vase, Swan Head Handles, White, 4 In. 33.00
Pearl, Wall Pocket, 8 1/2 In. 140.00
Pussy Willow, Vase, Green, 7 In. 125.00
Roba, Ewer, 6 In. 90.00
Rochelle, Bowl, Blackberry Design, 2 Handles, 9 1/4 x 3 1/4 In. 99.00

Rochelle, Vase, Multicolored Floral Design, Black Berries, Blue, Gray Ground, 11 In. . . .	880.00
Rochelle, Vase, Pink Cherries, Green Leaves, Gray To Pink, Black Ground, 8 1/2 In.	242.00
Roma, Bowl, 2 Twig Handles, 7 x 3 In.	33.00
Roma, Bowl, 4 x 2 In.	33.00
Roma, Bowl, 8 In.	50.00
Roma, Compote, Buttressed Pedestal, 5 3/4 In.	72.00
Roma, Jardiniere, Pedestal, 29 1/2 In.	1800.00
Roma, Planter, Embossed, Fruit, Polychrome, Ivory Ground, 4 1/2 In.	44.00
Roma, Planter, Roses, Pierce Lattice Fence, Square, 8 In.	105.00
Roma, Planter, White Floral Cameo, Soft Gold Ground, 3-Footed, 7 1/2 In.	22.00
Roma, Vase, Double Bud	70.00
Roma, Vase, Embossed, Fruit, 2 Handles, Ivory Ground, 7 In.	55.00
Roma, Vase, Green, Cream, 6 In.	88.00
Roma, Wall Pocket, Flowers On Trellis, Bumble Bee, Signed, 5 5/8 In.	302.00
Sabrinian, Bowl, 3 x 6 1/2 In.	240.00
Sabrinian, Wall Pocket, Label	725.00
Seneca, Vase, Blue, 8 In.	99.00
Sicardo, Candleholder, Reverse Painted Shade, Signed	385.00
Sicardo, Vase, Blown-Out 4 Part Top, Florals, Signed, 5 3/4 In.	990.00
Sicardo, Vase, Chrysanthemum, Sea Foam Green Ground, 6 x 4 In.	880.00
Sicardo, Vase, Corn Cobs, Leaves, Embossed, 3 Sides, 5 In.	550.00
Sicardo, Vase, Daisies, Purple, Green, Scalloped Rim, 2 Handles, 5 1/2 In.	1650.00
Sicardo, Vase, Floral, Green, Gold, Pink, 6 In.	595.00
Sicardo, Vase, Green, Gold Swirls, 6 Sides, Blue Accents, Deep Red Ground, 8 x 4 In. . .	605.00
Sicardo, Vase, Maple Leaves, Scalloped Rim, 3 Sides, 7 1/4 In.	660.00
Silvertone, Basket, 8 In.	350.00
Silvertone, Vase, Flowers, Berries, Handles, 7 In.	395.00
Silvertone, Vase, Handles, 6 In.	230.00
Silvertone, Vase, Lavender, Green, 12 In.	550.00
Silvertone, Vase, Trumpet With Lily, 11 In.	450.00
Softone, Basket, Drape Design, Blue, 4 In.	40.00
Softone, Vase, Blue, 5 In.	45.00
Softone, Vase, Floral Design, Blue, White Cameo, 9 In.	40.00
Souevo, Vase, Dark Blue Over Dark Brown, 10 In.	209.00
Souevo, Vase, Tan, Light, Dark Brown, 2 Handles, 10 In.	231.00
Tile, Classical Female Figure, Signed, 16 7/8 In.	465.00
Turada, Pitcher, Dark Blue, 17 In.	1150.00
Tutone, Vase, 6 In. . . . . .140.00 to 285.00	
Warwick, Vase, 4 In.	110.00
Warwick, Vase, Bud, 7 In.	50.00
Wild Rose, Vase, Green, 14 In.	150.00
Wild Rose, Vase, Green, White, Brown, 11 In.	77.00
Wild Rose, Vase, Orange, 6 1/2 In.	33.00
Woodcraft, Bowl, Squirrel On Branch, 3 In.	95.00
Woodcraft, Bowl, Squirrel, 5 1/2 In.	143.00
Woodcraft, Flower Frog, Bee On Top, 3 1/2 x 2 1/2 In.	176.00
Woodcraft, Garden Figure, Squirrel, 12 In.	950.00
Woodcraft, Jardiniere, Woodpecker On The Side, 6 In.	415.00
Woodcraft, Mug, 3 Foxes On Front, 6 In.	264.00
Woodcraft, Planter, Fox	350.00
Woodcraft, Planter, Foxes & Tree, Brown, Green, 7 1/2 x 4 In.	165.00
Woodcraft, Vase, 3 Foxes, 5 1/2 In.	275.00
Woodcraft, Vase, 3 Foxes, 8 In.	275.00
Woodcraft, Vase, 9 In. . . . . .110.00 to 175.00	
Woodcraft, Vase, Bud, Green, Brown, Pink, 10 In.	175.00
Woodcraft, Vase, Double, Bud	115.00
Woodcraft, Vase, Owl, 14 In.	2000.00
Woodcraft, Wall Pocket, Squirrel . . . . .375.00 to 400.00	
Woodcraft, Window Box, Green	78.00
Woodrose, Jardiniere, 7 In.	45.00
Woodrose, Jardiniere, 8 In.	180.00
Woodrose, Plate, Blue Berries, Wood Tone Ground, 6 In.	33.00
Woodrose, Wall Pocket, Brown	65.00

Xenia, Floral Design, Vase, Red, Green Outline, Stems, Slate Green Ground, 6 In.	715.00
Zona, Dish, Feeding, Bunny & Bluebird On Sides	75.00
Zona, Pitcher, Kingfisher & Tree, Half Kiln Stamp, 8 1/4 In.	300.00 to 450.00
Zona, Pitcher, Kingfisher, Green, 8 In.	165.00
Zona, Plate, 7 In.	40.00

WEMYSS ware was made by Robert Heron in Kirkaldy, Scotland, from
1850 to 1929. It is a colorful peasant-type pottery that is occasionally
found in the United States.

Figurine, Pig, Red, Brown, 7 x 4 In.	200.00
Jam Jar, Roses On Blue, Yellow & Green, Robert Heron	495.00
Mug, Roses, Large	445.00

WESTMORELAND GLASS was made by the Westmoreland Glass
Company of Grapeville, Pennsylvania, from 1890 to 1984. They made
clear and colored glass of many varieties, such as milk glass, pressed
glass, and slag glass.

Beaded Edge, Berry Bowl	8.00
Beaded Edge, Cup & Saucer, Cherry Decoration	15.00
Beaded Edge, Cup, Apple Decoration, Milk Glass	13.00
Beaded Edge, Plate, Peach Decoration, 10 1/2 In.	24.00
Beaded Grape, Ashtray, Square, 6 1/2 In.	12.00
Beaded Grape, Bowl, Cover, Milk Glass, Footed, 7 In.	35.00
Beaded Grape, Bowl, Cover, Square, 4 In.	30.00
Beaded Grape, Bowl, Flared, Footed, 9 In.	45.00
Beaded Grape, Bowl, Square, Footed, 9 In.	55.00
Beaded Grape, Box, Cigarette, 4 x 6 In.	35.00 to 40.00
Beaded Grape, Dish, Cover, Square, 4 In.	30.00
Beaded Grape, Honey, Cover, Roses & Garland, 5 In.	35.00 to 45.00
Beaded Grape, Puff Box, 4 In.	25.00
Cat, Dish, Cover, Reclining, Milk Glass, 5 1/2 In.	135.00
Checkerboard, Water Set, Blue, 7 Piece	160.00
Colonial, Cruet, Blue, Stopper, 2 Oz.	85.00
Della Robbia, Bowl, Pastel Stain, 4 1/2 In.	28.00
Della Robbia, Cake Stand, Stained	85.00
Della Robbia, Candy Dish, Dome Cover	21.00
Della Robbia, Plate, 10 In.	85.00
Doric, Bowl, Milk Glass, Oval, 12 In.	30.00
Doric, Dish, Sweetmeat, Ruffled Edge, Footed, Almond	17.00
Doric, Soap Dish, Leaf Shape, Footed	18.00
Eagle, Dish, Cover, Purple Slag, Carnival Glass	240.00
English Hobnail, Ashtray, Square	15.00
English Hobnail, Bon Bon, Handle, Hexagonal	10.00
English Hobnail, Butter, Cover, 6 1/2 x 5 In.	25.00
English Hobnail, Goblet, Green, 8 Oz.	23.00
English Hobnail, Sherbet, Amethyst Base	13.00
English Hobnail, Sugar & Creamer, 4 1/2 In.	15.00
English Hobnail, Water Set, Luvay Red, Ball Pitcher, 7 Piece	495.00
Fan & File, Punch Cup, Child's	2.50
Figurine, Butterfly, Light Blue, 2 1/2 In.	23.00
Figurine, Butterfly, Pink, 2 1/2 In.	20.00
Figurine, Cardinal, Pink, 5 1/8 In.	24.00
Figurine, Robin, Blue Mist, 5 1/8 In.	24.00
Figurine, Robin, Red, 5 1/8 In.	28.00
Figurine, Santa On Sleigh, Milk Glass	110.00
Figurine, Wren, Light Blue, 2 1/2 In.	23.00
God & Home, Water Set, Blue, 7 Piece	165.00
Hen On Nest Cover, Dish, Chocolate, 7 1/2 In.	300.00
Lamp, Fairy, Ruby Stained Top	445.00
Lattice Edge, Bowl, Milk Glass, Large	25.00
Lattice Edge, Candlestick, 4 In.	21.00
Maple Leaf, Bowl, Ruffled & Crimped Edge, 7 1/2 In.	30.0

Maple Leaf, Compote, Crimped Edge	21.00
Maple Leaf, Sugar & Creamer	15.00
Old Quilt, Candy Dish, Cover	20.00
Old Quilt, Cheese Dish, Cover	35.00
Old Quilt, Cruet	25.00
Old Quilt, Salt & Pepper	25.00
Old Quilt, Sugar & Creamer	25.00
Paneled Grape, Basket, Milk Glass, Oval, 6 1/2 In.	30.00
Paneled Grape, Bowl, 10 1/2 In.	100.00
Paneled Grape, Bowl, Flared, 12 1/2 In.	295.00
Paneled Grape, Bowl, Flared, Oval, 11 In.	100.00
Paneled Grape, Bowl, Footed, Oval, 10 1/2 In.	85.00
Paneled Grape, Bowl, Scalloped Edge, Milk Glass, 9 1/2 In.	125.00
Paneled Grape, Bowl, Skirted Foot, Crimped Edge, 9 In.	60.00
Paneled Grape, Butter, Cover, 2 1/4 In. . . . . .23.00 to 30.00
Paneled Grape, Cake Stand	85.00
Paneled Grape, Candlestick, 3-Light, Pair	375.00
Paneled Grape, Candlestick, 4 In., Pair	27.00
Paneled Grape, Candy Dish, Crimped & Ruffled Edge, 3-Footed, 8 In.	35.00
Paneled Grape, Cheese Dish, Cover, White	60.00
Paneled Grape, Compote, 4 1/2 In.	30.00
Paneled Grape, Compote, Crimped Edge, 6 In.	40.00
Paneled Grape, Compote, Golden Sunset, 7 In.	40.00
Paneled Grape, Creamer, Milk Glass . . . . .18.00 to 23.00
Paneled Grape, Cruet	22.00
Paneled Grape, Cup & Saucer, Milk Glass . . . . .21.00 to 25.00
Paneled Grape, Decanter, Milk Glass, 9 1/2 In.	120.00
Paneled Grape, Epergne, Milk Glass, 9 1/2 In.	125.00
Paneled Grape, Flower Pot	48.00
Paneled Grape, Goblet, 9 Oz. . . . . .18.00 to 20.00
Paneled Grape, Goblet, Blue Opalescent, 9 Oz.	30.00
Paneled Grape, Gravy Boat, Underplate	70.00
Paneled Grape, Iced Tea, Milk Glass	25.00
Paneled Grape, Jardiniere, 5 In.	27.00
Paneled Grape, Jardiniere, Cupped, 4 In.	19.00
Paneled Grape, Jug, 2 Pt.	37.00
Paneled Grape, Pitcher, 16 Oz.	48.00
Paneled Grape, Planter, 6 x 9 In.	40.00
Paneled Grape, Plate, 8 1/2 In.	22.00
Paneled Grape, Plate, 10 1/2 In.	40.00
Paneled Grape, Plate, Blue Opalescent, 6 In.	12.00
Paneled Grape, Plate, Blue Opalescent, 10 In.	29.00
Paneled Grape, Punch Cup	12.00
Paneled Grape, Punch Ladle	95.00
Paneled Grape, Punch Set, Scalloped Edge, 15 Piece	550.00
Paneled Grape, Salt & Pepper	40.00
Paneled Grape, Salt & Pepper, Footed	25.00
Paneled Grape, Sauce, Handle, Round, 5 In.	22.00
Paneled Grape, Sherbet	15.00
Paneled Grape, Sugar & Creamer, Footed, Individual	25.00
Paneled Grape, Sugar & Creamer, Large	45.00
Paneled Grape, Torte Plate, 14 1/2 In.	120.00
Paneled Grape, Tumbler, 8 Oz.	20.00
Paneled Grape, Vase, Bell Shape, 6 In.	20.00
Paneled Grape, Vase, Bell Shape, Footed, 9 1/2 In.	30.00
Paneled Grape, Vase, Bell, Footed, Blue Opalescent, 9 In.	29.00
Paneled Grape, Vase, Bud, 10 In.	17.00
Paneled Grape, Vase, Rose, Footed, 18 In.	55.00
Princess Feather, Plate, 8 In.	10.00
Queen Victoria's Hands, Dish, Milk Glass	45.00
Uncle Sam, Toothpick, Hat Shape, Milk Glass	30.00
Wedding, Bowl, Milk Glass, 10 In.	60.00

WHEATLEY Pottery was established in 1880. Thomas J. Wheatley had worked in Cincinnati, Ohio, with the founders of the art pottery movement, including M. Louise McLaughlin of the Rookwood Pottery. Wheatley Pottery was purchased by the Cambridge Tile Manufacturing Company in 1927.

Mug, Front Shield, Pretzel Handle, Compliments Of Fleischman Co., 7 1/4 In.	275.00
Vase, Alternating Leaves & Buds, Ocher Matte Glaze, 5 3/4 x 6 3/4 In.	2750.00
Vase, Buttressed Batwing Handles, 20 5/6 In.	5775.00
Vase, Conical Floor, Green Matte Glaze, 4 Buttressed Handles, 18 1/2 x 9 1/2 In.	3575.00
Vase, Embossed Scarabs, Papyrus Plants, Green Matte Glaze, 7 3/4 x 4 In.	1210.00
Vase, Leathery Green Matte Glaze, Bulbous, 6 x 6 1/2 In.	550.00
Vase, Molded Leaves & Buds, Over 3 Open Buttresses, Green Matte Glaze, 11 In.	4950.00
Vase, Overlapping Leaves, Bat Wing Handles, Cafe-Au-Lait Glaze, 20 5/8 In.	5775.00
Vase, Peacock Leaves, Matte Green Glaze, 10 x 8 In.	990.00
Vase, Pillow, Daisies, Celadon, Black Ground, Oval, 9 1/4 x 6 3/4 In.	110.00
Vase, Thick Glaze, 3 Angular Handles, 4 1/2 In.	220.00
Vessel, Green Glaze, Overlaid Silver Leaves & Branches, Signed, 11 In.	2750.00
Wall Pocket, Molded Leaves, Buds, Green Matte Glaze, 8 x 5 1/4 x 5 1/2 In.	715.00

WHEELING Pottery Company of Wheeling, West Virginia, worked from 1879 to about 1923. The firm went through a number of mergers and name changes during that time. Pottery, semiporcelain, artware, and sanitary wares were made.

Punch Cup, Drape, Pink To White, Applied Clear Handle	175.00

WHIELDON was an English potter who worked alone and with Josiah Wedgwood in eighteenth-century England. Whieldon made many pieces in natural shapes, like cauliflowers or cabbages.

Figurine, Pug Dog, Patchwork Glaze, 7 In.	440.00
Plate, Pheasant, F. Winkle & Co., 12 Piece	100.00
Stand, Sprigs Of Fruit, Green Glaze, Earthenware, 1760, 12 In.	1265.00
Teapot, Pineapple Pattern, Globular, 1760, 5 In.	1955.00

WILLETS Manufacturing Company of Trenton, New Jersey, began work in 1879. The company made Belleek in the late 1880s and 1890s in shapes similar to those used by the Irish Belleek factory. They stopped working about 1912. A variety of marks were used, all including the name Willets.

Mug, Bead & Scroll Handle, White Interior, Black Exterior, Band Of Grapes, 5 1/2 In.	45.00
Mug, Berries & Vines, Dragon Handle, 6 In.	275.00
Salt, Roses	50.00
Vase, Flowers On Top, Gold Band, 12 1/2 In.	240.00
Vase, Rose Design, Hand Painted, Pear Shape, Belleek, 10 In.	522.00

WILLOW pattern has been made in England since 1780. The pattern has been copied by factories in many countries, including Germany, Japan, and the United States. It is still being made. Willow was named for a pattern that pictures a bridge, birds, willow trees, and a Chinese landscape. Most pieces are blue and white.

Bowl, Blue, Crown Pottery, 8 In.	98.00
Bowl, Cereal, Homer Laughlin, 6 In.	15.00
Bowl, Cereal, Japan, 6 In.	12.00 to 14.00
Bowl, Cover, Allerton	65.00
Bowl, Cover, Brown & Steventon, 9 In.	145.00
Bowl, Cranberry, Homer Laughlin, 5 In.	39.00
Bowl, Dessert, Japan, 5 3/8 In.	12.00
Bowl, Fruit, Japan, 5 3/8 In.	12.00
Bowl, Salad, Japan, 9 3/4 In.	48.00
Bowl, Vegetable, Allerton, 9 1/4 x 7 1/8 In.	85.00
Bowl, Vegetable, Allerton, Oval	55.00
Bowl, Vegetable, Cover, Homer Laughlin	120.00
Bowl, Vegetable, Homer Laughlin, 9 In.	42.00
Bowl, Vegetable, Japan, 10 1/4 In.	45.00

Bowl, Vegetable, Oval, Homer Laughlin, 8 3/4 In. 33.00
Bowl, Vegetable, Oval, Japan, 10 3/8 In. 59.00
Bowl, Vegetable, Scalloped, Bowknot Border, Blue, Booths, 1912, 8 1/2 In. 75.00
Bowl & Pitcher, Wedgwood 1450.00
Box, Cover, Square, Japan, 4 In. 45.00
Bread Plate, Homer Laughlin, 6 1/4 In. 8.00
Bread Plate, Japan, 6 In. ....7.00 to 11.00
Bread Plate, Occupied Japan, 6 1/4 In. 8.00
Butter, Square, Japan 55.00
Cake Plate, Handles, Adderlyware, 1919-1947, 9 1/2 In. 65.00
Cake Plate, Scalloped, Gold Trim, Handles, England, 1880, 9 In. 65.00
Canister Set, Regal China, England, 4 Piece 190.00
Canister Set, Square, 4 Piece 450.00
Casserole, Cover, Ridgway 90.00
Cheese Truckle, Red, J. Dimmock, 1862-1876, 12 1/2 x 2 In. 250.00
Chop Plate, Japan 40.00
Coffeepot, Burleigh 80.00
Coffeepot, Cover, Japan, Miniature 69.00
Compact, Powder 170.00
Creamer, Homer Laughlin, 3 1/2 In. ....26.00 to 27.00
Creamer, Japan 15.00
Cruet, Mustard, Lid, Japan 17.00
Cup & Saucer, Allerton 18.00
Cup & Saucer, Allerton, 6 Piece 45.00
Cup & Saucer, England, 20th Century 35.00
Cup & Saucer, Geisha In Cup Bottom 25.00
Cup & Saucer, Gold Trim, Cauldon, 1905-1920, 3 In. 45.00
Cup & Saucer, Homer Laughlin, 2 3/8 In. ....20.00 to 21.00
Cup & Saucer, Japan, 2 1/4 In. ....16.00 to 33.00
Cup & Saucer, Round Handle, Homer Laughlin ....20.00 to 21.00
Dish, Pickle, Leaf Shape, England, 1880, 5 1/2 x 4 1/2 In. 175.00
Eggcup, Double, Allerton 28.00
Eggcup, Double, Handles, Bowknot Border, Gold Trim, 1910 .... 65.00
Eggcup, Japan, 3 3/4 In. 15.00
Gravy Boat, J. Steventon & Sons 55.00
Gravy Boat, Ridgway 23.00
Grill Plate, Arthur J. Wilkinson, 1907, 10 1/2 In. 85.00
Grill Plate, Child's 55.00
Grill Plate, Japan, 10 In. 12.00
Grill Plate, Ridgway 25.00
Ice Cream Scoop 69.00
Jug, Cream, Sparrow Beak, Booths, 1912-1930, 4 1/2 In. 195.00
Ladle, Gravy, Curved Handle, 7 In. 110.00
Lamp, Kerosene 50.00
Mold, Pudding, 3 5/8 x 5 3/4 In. 48.00
Mug, Doulton, 4 x 4 In. 75.00
Pitcher, Bridge & Trees ....*Illus* 220.00

Willow, Pitcher, Bridge & Trees

**Rubber cement solvent, available at art
supply and office supply stores, has many
uses. Put a few drops on a paper towel and
rub off ink smudges, adhesive tape glue, or
label glue from glass or porcelain.**

Pitcher, Milk, Allerton, 6 In. 150.00
Pitcher & Bowl, Wedgwood 1450.00
Planter, Cat, Japan 120.00
Plate, 2 Temples, Butterfly Border, England, 1851-1885, 9 In. 95.00
Plate, Adams, 10 1/2 In. 22.00
Plate, Cartwright & Edwards, 1857, 6 In. 38.00
Plate, Dessert, 6 1/4 In. 8.00
Plate, Homer Laughlin, 10 In. ....18.00 to 19.00
Plate, Homer Laughlin, 7 3/8 In. 8.00
Plate, Homer Laughlin, 9 1/8 In. ....11.00 to 12.00
Plate, Japan, 6 In. 5.00
Plate, Japan, 9 In. ....10.00 to 13.00
Plate, Japan, 9 3/4 In. ....19.00 to 21.00
Plate, Japan, 10 In. 10.00
Plate, Moriyama, 9 3/4 In. 12.00
Plate, Occupied Japan, 9 1/4 In. 14.00
Plate, Salad, Pink, Ridgway 18.00
Plate, Scalloped, Baker, Bevins & Irwin, 1813-1838, 10 In. 75.00
Platter, Allerton, 15 3/8 x 12 1/4 In. 150.00
Platter, Marked Stoneware T.W., 15 3/4 In. 115.00
Platter, Meat, 1870, 15 1/2 x 12 1/2 In. 225.00
Platter, Meat, 1880, 21 1/2 x 16 1/2 In. 525.00
Platter, Meat, Blue C Mark, 1870, 14 x 11 In. 175.00
Platter, Meat, Bowknot Border, Gold Trim, Booths, Oval, 1912, 16 x 12 1/2 In. 145.00
Platter, Meat, England, 1880, 17 1/2 x 14 In. 295.00
Platter, Meat, Wood, Challinor & Co., 1860-1864, 16 x 12 1/2 In. 235.00
Platter, New Wharf Pottery, 11 3/4 In. 40.00
Platter, Serving, Homer Laughlin, Oval, 11 3/4 In. 39.00
Platter, Serving, Oval, Japan, 12 1/2 In. 36.00
Platter, Staffordshire, Adams, 13 1/2 In. 176.00
Platter, Warranted Staffordshire Mark, c.1830-1840, 12 1/2 x 16 In. 225.00
Platter, Well & Tree, Royal Arms Mark, Pre-1837, 20 1/2 x 16 1/2 In. 625.00
Salt & Pepper, Japan ....35.00 to 36.00
Saucer, Homer Laughlin 7.00
Saucer, Homer Laughlin, 6 1/4 In. 7.00
Saucer, Occupied Japan 9.00
Saucer, Shellware, England, 20th Century 16.00
Shaker, Raised Pattern, Japan 85.00
Soup, Coupe, Homer Laughlin, 8 In. 19.00
Soup, Dish, Bennett, 7 1/2 In. 8.00
Soup, Dish, Homer Laughlin, 7 1/4 In. 19.00
Soup, Dish, Ridgway 18.00
Sugar, Cover, Handle, Homer Laughlin 39.00
Sugar, Cover, Japan ....47.00 to 49.00
Sugar, Handle, Homer Laughlin, 8 1/4 In. 27.00
Sugar & Creamer, J. Steventon & Sons 65.00
Sugar & Creamer, John Steventon 75.00
Teapot, Bow Knot Gold Border, Booth, 1900s 145.00
Teapot, Japan ....98.00 to 100.00
Tray, Card, Flow Blue, Johnson Bros., 6 x 5 In. 60.00
Tureen, Sauce, Cover, Dillwyn & Co., Swansea, Wales, 1824-1880, 7 x 4 In. 185.00
Tureen, Sauce, Tray 190.00
Vegetable, Homer Laughlin, Oval, 9 In. 42.00
Vegetable, Homer Laughlin, Round, 8 3/4 In. 39.00
Waste Bowl, Ching Pattern, Dagger Border, Alcock, 1870 .... 45.00

WINDOW glass that was stained and beveled was popular for houses during the late nineteenth and early twentieth centuries. The old windows became popular with collectors in the 1970s; today, old and new examples are seen.

Arts & Crafts, Geometric Prairie Design, Caramel Square, 19 1/2 x 15 In. 385.00
Chinese, Elmwood, Fitted Without Nails, 3 Panels 950.00

Kitchen, Dark Finish, Traces Of Design, 31 1/2 In., 9 Piece 346.00
Leaded, 4 Medallions, Leaf Design Center, Frank Lloyd Wright Style, 32 x 20 In. 230.00
Leaded, Apple Tree, Colorful Landscape, 29 x 65 In. 975.00
Leaded, Arched Wood Frame, Last Supper, Lower Dedicatory Plaque, 66 x 29 3/4 In. ... 880.00
Leaded, Casement, Center Floral, Opalescent Colored & Clear, G.W. Maher, 22 1/2 In. ... 1495.00
Leaded, Casement, Center Floral, Opalescent Green & Yellow, G.W. Maher, 19 1/2 In. ... 2185.00
Leaded, Centered Floral Design, Opalescent Green & Yellow, G.W. Maher, 19 1/2 In. ... 1955.00
Leaded, Central Tulip Design, Prairie School, 64 x 12 In., Pair 253.00
Leaded, Colonial Caning, White Glass, Encased Gold Foil, 1900, 63 1/2 x 14 In. 2300.00
Leaded, Foliate, Red, White Glass, 1900, 29 3/4 x 13 3/4 In. 1725.00
Leaded, Fruit Grapevine, High Relief Grapes, Green, Blue, White, Tiffany, 43 In., Pair .. 11500.00
Leaded, Geometric, Cream & Gold Iridized, 2 Replaced Segments, 27 x 36 In. 4675.00
Leaded, Horizontal Bands At Top & Bottom, Frank Lloyd Wright, 42 x 25 In. 2415.00
Leaded, Panel, Mounted, Frank Lloyd Wright, 28 3/8 x 37 In. 8215.00
Leaded, Skylight Alcove, Lappet, Amber Glass Segments, Crown In Shield, 16 x 38 In. . 2875.00
Leaded, Snowball Bush In Blossom, Against Mottled Purple Ground, 1900, 31 In. 4025.00
Leaded, Stained Glass, American, Exterior Reinforcing Rods, 1880, 72 x 22 In., Pair ... 1750.00
Leaded, Stained Glass, Dodge Brothers Logo Center, Cobalt Blue, 48 x 48 In. 2420.00
Leaded, Stained Glass, Flower, Multicolored Geometric, Late 19th Century, 45 x 28 In. . 880.00
Pane, Pressed Glass, Fiery Opalescent, 6 1/2 x 8 In. 150.00
Transom, 3 Bohemian Glass Panels, Floral, Wooden Frame, 15 x 53 In. 270.00

WOOD CARVINGS and wooden pieces are listed separately in this book.
Many of the wood carvings are figurines or statues. There are also
wooden pieces found in other categories, such as Kitchen.

American Eagle, Bellamy-Type, Walnut, c.1880, 8 1/2 x 14 1/2 In. 295.00
American Eagle, White Trim, 10 In. 475.00
Angel, Kneeling, Right Hand Raised, Alceo Dossena, 1930s, 67 3/4 In. 5175.00
Bald Eagle, Driftwood Base, A.J. King ....*Illus* 1540.00
Bear, Sign, Parks & Recreation, California, Round, 10 In. 45.00
Bird, Blue Jay, Original Paint, Whittled Tree Trunk Base, 10 3/4 In. 192.00
Bird, Carved, Gold Paint, Ruby Glass Eyes, 5 1/4 In. 38.00
Bird, Least Tern, Painted, A.E. Crowell, Life-Size ....*Illus* 5280.00
Bird, Nesting, White Bird With Long Tail, Red Rectangular Base, 4 1/2 In. 2645.00
Bust, Cleric, England, 17th Century, 12 1/2 In. 990.00
Bust, Haitian General Jean Dessalines, 14 In. 132.00
Bust, Wooden Indian, Attached To Ashtray, C.M. Russell, 1900, 4 x 5 In. 60.00
Cherubim, Curly Hair, Gilt Wings, Germany, 7 1/2 In., Pair 1840.00
Christ On Road To Calvary, 1540s, 15 5/8 x 13 1/8 In. 3450.00
Columbia River, Human Face From Columbia River, 6 x 4 In. 88.00
Columbia River, Human Head Stone, 9 x 5 In. 165.00
Corpus Christi, 16 1/2 In. 575.00
Cowboy On A Horse, Painted, On Stand, Roy Lennberg, Signed, Dated '78, 16 In. 100.00
Demilunes, Sunburst Pattern, Blue, Green, 19th Century, 15 1/2 In., Pair 1495.00
Eagle, Mahogany, Old Finish, 3-Dimensional, 26 3/4 In. 3410.00

Wood Carving,
Bald Eagle,
Driftwood Base,
A.J. King

Wood Carving, Bird, Least Tern, Painted,
A.E. Crowell, Life-Size

Wood Carving, St. Joseph,
Altar Niche, Mexico,
19th Century, 37 In.

**Never use olive oil to treat a wooden bowl.
It will turn rancid. If you used an olive
oil–based salad dressing in the bowl at a
meal, be sure to rinse the bowl.**

Eagle, On Branch, Old White & Black Repaint, 27 1/2 In.	1320.00
Eagle, On Rocky Base, Painted, Glass Eyes, 49 1/2 In.	1375.00
Eagle, Resting On Ball, Turned Base, Detachable Wings, 15 In.	575.00
Eagle, Shield, Arrows, Bellamy Style, 20th Century, 44 In.	935.00
Eagle's Head, 3 Dimensional, Yellow Paint, Walnut Back, 10 1/2 In.	1430.00
Ear Of Corn, Crab Apples & Grasshopper, Japan, 1890, 8 In.	245.00
Elephant, Asian, Recumbent, 49 In.	2875.00
Fish, Cardboard Fins, Painted, On Raised Panel Board From Door, 11 x 15 In.	3000.00
Kylin, Polychromed, 37 In.	880.00
Magdalene, Crowned, Draped, Holding Chalice, 1530s, 37 3/4 In.	4830.00
Man, Tobacco Store, Tobacco Leaf Skirt, 1860-1900, 56 In.	1600.00
Mask, African, Carved, Ceremonial, 1920, 19 x 10 In.	88.00
Mask, African, Painted Wall, Kenya, 1988, 9 x 5 In., Pair	40.00
Mask, Guro Tribe, Ram Horns, Ivory Coast, 15 1/2 x 8 In.	175.00
Mask, Tibetan, 14 x 10 In.	295.00
Mermaid, Lounging, On Pedestal, Cherry & Oak, Bill Jackman, 72 In.	412.00
Monkey, Seated, Plate In Left Hand, Castanets In Other, Walnut & Pine, 64 In.	6900.00
Nun, Walnut, Brass Plaque, J. Rotermundt Nurnberg, 19 1/2 In.	135.00
Panel, Oak, Musical Instruments, In High Relief, 51 1/2 x 28 In.	1265.00
Panel, Portrait Of Saint, Painted, South America, 19th Century, 21 x 13 In.	165.00
Parrot, On Post, Staring Down At Mouse At Base, Glass Eyes, 1940, 28 In.	815.00
Peasant, Germany, 1920s, 8 1/4 In., 8 Piece	175.00
Plaque, Eagle, Shield & Banner, Don't Give Up The Ship, c.1900, 28 In.	3400.00
Saint Francis, Polychrome, Square Base, 18th Century, 24 1/4 In.	1155.00
Saint Peter, Standing With Book In Left Hand, Key In Right, 15 1/4 In.	1150.00
Salt, Walnut, Penna., 1750-1780, 2 In.	235.00
Saxophone, High Relief, Black Walnut, 18 1/2 x 9 3/4 x 3 In.	475.00
Scepter, Red Paint, Gold Trim, 26 In.	93.50
Shrine, Temple, Red Lacquer & Gilt, Oriental, 26 1/2 In.	135.00
St. Joseph, Altar Niche, Mexico, 19th Century, 37 In. ....*Illus*	2530.00
St. Joseph & Christ Child, Polychrome, Austria, 17th Century, 32 In.	4400.00
St. Michael, 27 In.	2500.00
Toucan, Joseph A. Moyer, 1949, 6 1/2 In.	2145.00
Trumpeting Angel, Painted, 19th Century, 28 In.	2185.00
Virgin & Child, Child On Left Hip, 15th Century, 13 3/8 In.	5750.00
Virgin Immaculata, Hands Joined In Prayer, 1680s, 15 1/2 In.	4887.00
Woman With Cane, Black Paint, Brown Varnish, 9 3/4 In.	435.00

WOODEN wares were used in all parts of the home. Wood was used for
many containers and tools. Small wooden pieces are called *treenware*
in England, but the term woodenware is more common in the United
States. Additional pieces may be found in the Advertising, Kitchen,
and Tool categories.

Altar, Gothic Style, Fenestrated Doors, Painted Cherubs On Porcelain, 6 x 15 In.	121.00
Ashtray, Silent Butler, Girl Silhouette, Polychrome Paint, 25 1/2 In.	82.00

Barrel, Oak, Split Staves, Iron Rings, c.1880, 33 1/4 In. 475.00
Bellman, 3-D, Googly Eyes, Holds Ashtray, Painted Red & Black, 36 1/2 In. 850.00
Bellows, Painted, Pink & Green Floral Motif, Miniature, 11 In. 86.00
Bootjack, Folding, Curly Maple 85.00
Bowl, Abalone, Carved Facial Features, Inlaid Abalone Eyes, Oval, 18 1/2 In. 1955.00
Bowl, Brass Nailheads At Rim, 5 1/4 x 14 In. 300.00
Bowl, Burl Ash, Brown Finish, 12 3/4 x 4 3/4 In. 1150.00
Bowl, Burl Ash, Scrubbed, 11 x 3 3/4 In. 970.00
Bowl, Burl Ash, Turned Exterior, Notch In Rim, 6 3/4 x 2 1/4 In. 385.00
Bowl, Burl, Ash, Cutout Rim Handles, Oval, 7 7/8 x 8 7/8 x 2 3/4 In. 2640.00
Bowl, Burl, Dark Finish, 5 3/4 In. 310.00
Bowl, Burl, Dark Finish, 6 1/4 In. 190.00
Bowl, Burl, Mounted On Board, Black Interior, 19 x 26 x 15 In. 192.00
Bowl, Burl, Scrubbed, 17 1/4 x 5 1/2 In. 1430.00
Bowl, Burl, Warm Brown Finish, 10 In. 770.00
Bowl, Curly Maple, Treen, Brown Finish, 6 1/2 In. 100.00
Bowl, Dough, Hand Turned, 19th Century, 12 x 17 In. 350.00
Bowl, Grooved Design On Outside, 7 x 12 In. 300.00
Bowl, Grungy Finish, Red Paint, 5 x 16 In. 144.00
Bowl, Maple Burl, Lathe Turned, 19th Century, 3 1/2 x 10 3/4 In. 895.00
Bowl, Pine, Dark Finish, Korea, 13 x 19 1/2 x 21 In. 50.00
Bowl, Pine, Worn Brown Finish, Dovetailed Joints, Octagonal, 22 x 23 x 6 In. 245.00
Bowl, Poplar, Worn Gray Patina, 14 1/2 x 5 1/4 x 4 1/2 In. 150.00
Bowl, Primitive, Protruding End Handles, 19 1/2 x 28 1/2 In. 300.00
Bowl, Sugar, Cover, Apple Form, Mid-19th Century, 5 3/4 In. 350.00
Bowl, Sugar, Cover, Maple, Brown Paint, Late 18th Century, America, 3 1/2 In. 295.00
Bowl & Ladle, Ash Burl, 19th Century, 18 3/4-In. Ladle, Bowl 16 3/4 x 5 1/4 In. 3800.00
Box, Cover, Bentwood, Worn Green Paint, Over Blue, 10 In. 275.00
Box, Hinged Lid, Lion Paw Feet, Silver Plated, Faux Tortoiseshell, 9 1/2 In. 3737.00
Bucket, Brick's Mince Meat, Paper Label 135.00
Bucket, Butter, Hickory & Pine, Lapped Construction, Splint Lock, 4 1/2 x 6 In. 450.00
Bucket, Lid, Pine, Stave Constructed, Steel Bands, Painted, 12 1/2 In. 247.00
Bucket, Mahogany, Slatted Sides, Brass Insert, Lion's-Head Mounts, 12 1/2 x 12 In. 4312.00
Bucket, Old Green Paint 200.00
Bucket, Peat, George III, Brass Handle, Mahogany, Copper Lined, 10 3/4 In. 2185.00
Bucket, Stave Constructed, Yellow Graining, Stenciled, Wire Bail, 6 5/8 In. 825.00
Bucket, Stave Construction, Wire Bands, Bail, Wooden Handle, Pat. Jan. 14, '90, 12 In. . 55.00
Bucket, Stave, Wire Metal Bands, Wire Bail, Diamond Fasteners, Red Stain 105.00
Bucket, Sugar, Stave Construction, Copper Tacks, Wire Bail, Wooden Handle, 6 1/2 In. . 355.00
Bucket, Sugar, Tin Cover, Stave Construction, Yellow Varnish, 13 1/2 In. 110.00
Bucket, Tree Trunk Form, Handles 44.00
Busk, Geometric Chip Carving, Pinwheel, Heart, Inscribed A.D. 1776, A.A., 13 In. 770.00
Canteen, Carved Oak, Forged Iron Handle, Revolutionary War, 5 3/8 x 11 5/8 In. 385.00
Canteen, Pewter Top, Boer War 55.00
Carrier, Bentwood, Finger Construction, Yellow Over Red, Swivel Handle, 9 3/4 In. 385.00
Carrier, Bucket, Pine, Iron Hangers, 40 In. 145.00
Castor, Pepper, American, 18th Century, 5 1/8 In. 295.00
Chalice, Communion, Ephrata Cloister Congregation, Cherry, 1780s, 8 1/4 In. 8500.00
Comb, 18th Century, 4 1/2 In. 210.00
Dipper, Curly Maple, Natural Shaped Bowl, Refinished, 12 In. 110.00
Dipper, Horse Head Handle, 5 1/2 In. 230.00
Dipper, Natural Growth Wood, Burl Bowl, Curly Handle, 12 3/4 In. 220.00
Firkin, Painted Design, Mustard Ground, Strapped & Pegged, Signed LHW, 7 In. 135.00
Gavel, Auctioneer's, 11 In. 17.00
Humidor, Dunhill, Burl Walnut, Ebonized Wood, c.1920 . . . . 1595.00
Humidor, Owl, Glass Eyes, Hinged Lid, Side Pockets For Cigars, 15 In. 1200.00
Humidor, Painted, Walnut, Lion On Top 4675.00
Jar, Cover, Poplar, Green & Yellow Vinegar Paint, 4 1/2 In. 300.00
Jar, Cover, Wire Bail, Barrel Shape, Treenware, 4 1/2 In. 66.00
Jar, Curly, Treenware, Acorn Finial, Pease, 6 1/2 In. 825.00
Jar Set, Cover, Wire Bail, Treenware, Largest-6 In., 4 Piece 1980.00
Keg, Rum, Staved, Forged Iron Bands, Wrought Iron Rivets, Marked JBB, 7 7/8 In. 195.00
Liqueur Set, Burled Walnut Case, 4 Blown Glass Decanters, 16 Glasses, 14 x 11 In. 2310.00

Mask, Movable Lower Jaw, Demonic Expression, Lacquer, Japan, 12 In. 385.00
Milk Bottle, Carnival, Apple Green Paint, 7 3/8 In., Pair 75.00
Mold, Candle, 24 Tube, J. Walker, Livonia, N.Y. 1595.00
Mold, Cigar, 1897 .... 100.00
Paddle, Butter, Ash, Curved Burl Bowl, 12 In. 1155.00
Paddle, Butter, Curly Maple, Carved Man Handle, 10 In. 770.00
Paddle, Butter, Maple, Carved Hook Handle, 10 1/2 In. 220.00
Paddle, Butter, Maple, Stylized Sleeping Bird, Handle, 6 5/8 In. 1155.00
Paddle, Curly Maple, Heart Handle, 8 In. 495.00
Piggin, Staved White Pine, Wrapped Willow, Figural Cutout Handles, 15 1/2 In. 78.00
Rack, Drying, Pine, Red Brown, Shoe Feet, Mortised Construction, 29 x 30 In. 355.00
Rack, Towel, Stenciled Oilcloth, On Frame, 2 Bars Each End, Hanging, 20 x 32 In. 180.00
Rolling Pin, Curly Maple, 19th Century, 16 In. 195.00
Seed Planter, Stenciled Label, Norcross & Boynton, Monmouth, Me., 39 1/2 In. 154.00
Spoon, Chestnut, Design On Handle, 6 3/4 In. 220.00
Stamp Box, Shaped Like Swiss Lion, 3 x 4 1/2 x 2 1/2 In. 50.00
Stand, Wig, 18th Century, 11 1/2 In. 250.00
Stand, Wig, Turned Standard, Late 18th Century, 13 In. 195.00
Stein, Barrel Shape, Horizontal Bands On Body, Wood Handle, 1/2 Liter 77.00
Sugar, Cover, Treenware, 5 In. 300.00
Swift, Table Clamp, 21 In. 28.00
Swift, Table Clamp, 22 In. 40.00
Tankard, Burl, Allover Design, Handle, Norway, 1750 .... 1800.00
Tankard, Carved Form Solid Log Including Handle, 18th Century, 1 Pt., 8 7/8 In. 190.00
Teapoy, Amboyna, William IV, Hinged Top, 4 Compartments, 2 Wells, 30 In. 1380.00
Tray, Cutlery, Curly Maple, Dovetailed, Scalloped Sides, c.1840, 14 x 8 In. 425.00
Tub, Stave, Wire Bands, Blue Paint, Cutout Handles, 23 In. 412.50
Urn, Cutlery, Regency, Mahogany, Painted Classical Chariot Scene, 24 In., Pair 7425.00
Wall Pocket, Walnut, Square Framed Print, Leather Hinges, Match Holder, Victorian 245.00
Wall Shelves, Gilded Eagle, Foliate Design, 13 In., Pair 325.00
Washtub, Painted Blue, Amish 375.00

WORCESTER porcelains were made in Worcester, England, from 1751.
The firm went through many name changes and eventually, in 1862,
became The Royal Worcester Porcelain Company Ltd. Collectors
often refer to *Dr. Wall*, Barr, *Flight*, and other names that indicate time
periods or artists at the factory. It became part of the Royal
Worcester Spode Ltd. in 1976. Related pieces may be found in the Royal
Worcester category.

Basket, Rural Scene, 8 1/2 x 5 1/2 x 2 1/4 In. 172.00
Biscuit Jar, Pheasant, Hand Painted, Garland Trim, Lock & Co., Stinton, 9 1/4 In. 450.00
Coffee Cup, Bell Shaped, 2 Plum Quails Beneath Stylized Prunus Tree, 2 In. 1092.00
Cup & Saucer, Blue Bands, Gilt, Barr Period 110.00
Cup & Saucer, Caudle, Chrysanthemums, Prunus Branches, 1770, 2 1/4 In. 745.00
Cup & Saucer, Dr. Wall, Pearlware, Crest Mark, Handleless 165.00
Cup & Saucer, Dragon In Compartments, Blue Fret Marks, 1770, 4 1/2 In. 515.00
Cup & Saucer, Japan Pattern, Imari Palette, Fret Mark, 1770 .... 490.00
Dish, Berry, Cobalt Blue, Orange, Brown, Shells, Flight Barr & Barr, 7 In., Pair 11500.00
Dish, Leaf Shaped, 2 Overlapping Leaves, Pink, Red, Blue, Green, Yellow, 1758, 3 In. .. 1380.00
Dish, Leaf Shaped, 2 Overlapping Lettuce Leaves, Red Scallop & Dot Border, 10 In. 1840.00
Dish, Lobed, Rose Plums, Green Leaves, Gilt Scalloped Rim, 1775, 9 In. 1380.00
Dish, Saucer, River Scene, Clusters Of Rose, Purple Fruit, 1780, 7 1/8 In. 575.00
Dish, Scalloped, Flowering Prunus Branch, Gilt Red Border, Oval, 2 In. 1035.00
Dish, Serving, Leaf Form, Yellow-Brown, Gold Highlights, 12 In. 132.00
Dish, Sweetmeat, 2 Stems, Purple Edged, Veined Black, Dotted Stem Handle, Pair 1955.00
Dish, Sweetmeat, 2 Twigs Of Rose Leaves, 2 Rose Buds, Red Branch Handle, 6 In. 1610.00
Dish, Sweetmeat, Reclining Boy & Girl, 8 In., Pair 725.00
Inkwell, Mug, Cossack Horses, 4 1/4 In. 374.00
Jug, Leaf, Dragon & Crab, Dragon Shrouded In Clouds, C-Scrolled Handle, 8 In. 2990.00
Mug, Armorial Landscape, Trees, Bushes, Ridged Loop Handle, Green, Yellow, 4 In. 690.00
Mug, Beckoning Chinaman, Purple, Red, Yellow, Green, Blue, Rose, 1756, 5 1/2 In. 805.00
Mug, Blue-Scaled Exotic Bird Amid Shrubbery, Rose Red, Yellow, 1770, 6 In. 2070.00
Plate, Armorial, Gadroon Edge, Floral Cartouches, 1820, 10 1/4 In. 545.00

Worcester, Plate, Oriental Bridge Scene,
Gold Trim, 7 1/4 x 6 1/8 In.

**If garage windows are painted,
burglars won't be able to tell if
cars are home or not. Use
translucent paint to get light in
the closed garage, if it has an
entrance to your house.**

Plate, Basket Molded Brown Jackal, Green Foliate Garlands, 1780, 8 1/8 In. 1150.00
Plate, Blue-Scaled Spray Of Yellow, Purple, Rose Red Flowers, Trellis Border, 9 In. 1037.00
Plate, Botanical Pictures, Green Ground Banding, Chamberlain, 10 In., 8 Piece 460.00
Plate, Cobalt Blue, Puce Shells, Red Berries, Brown, Flight Barr & Barr, 9 In., Pair 11500.00
Plate, Commemorative, Spanish Armada, Tomato Red Ground, Chamberlain, 9 In. 460.00
Plate, Commemorative, Spanish Armada, Tomato Red Ground, Chamberlain, Pair 977.00
Plate, Embossed Leaves & Rosebud, 1910, 9 In. 135.00
Plate, Floral, Wide Blue Ground Border, Gilt, Late 18th Century, 8 In., Pair 860.00
Plate, Oriental Bridge Scene, Gold Trim, 7 1/4 x 6 1/8 In. . . . . *Illus* 65.00
Plate, Stag Crest, Motto, Gilt Floral Border, Barr, Flight & Barr, 1810, 9 1/4 In. 400.00
Sauceboat, Crane Standing Beneath Branch, Scalloped Rim, 1752, 7 1/2 In. 920.00
Sauceboat, Leaf Molded, Butterfly Hovering Near Floral Spray, 1756, 7 In. 1380.00
Soup, Dish, Flight, Barr & Barr, 11 Piece 3400.00
Sugar, Cover, Dr. Wall, Blue & White, 1785, 4 1/2 In. 115.00
Tea Caddy, Bird Perched On Leafy Branch, Rose, Purple Red, 1772, 5 1/8 In. 575.00
Teapot, Blue Oriental Landscape, Globular, 1765, 3 In. 460.00
Teapot, Flower Baskets, Gilt, Dark Puce Enamel, 18th Century, Globular, 5 1/2 In. 285.00
Tray, Serving, Light Blue Florals, Dark Blue Border, 1883, 16 x 10 In. 100.00
Tureen, Cover, Bird Nesting, Black, Red Beak, 1756, 7 1/4 In. 1380.00
Tureen, Sauce, Cover, Exotic Bird Amid Shrubbery Insects, Oval, 1770, 7 In. 1150.00
Vase, Cover, Regent, Cylindrical Body, Brown, Tan, Red, Blue, Gray, Gilt, 9 In. 1035.00
Vase, Flower, Double Beige Handle, Gold Leaves, 8 In. 220.00
Waste Bowl, Molded Spiral Flutes, Blue Rim, Gilt, 6 1/4 In. 110.00

WORLD WAR I and World War II souvenirs are collected today. Be
careful not to store anything that includes live ammunition. Your local
police will tell you how to dispose of the explosives. See also Sword
and Trench Art.

WORLD WAR I, Booklet, Camp Grant, 1917 . . . . 25.00
Bugle, Brass, U.S. Regulation 75.00
Canteen, Water, U.S., Dated 1918 . . . . 40.00
Compass, Linsatic, Case 95.00
Fan, Wood Brise, Sticks Shaped Like 6 Heads Of State Who Signed Peace Accord 412.00
Game, Checker, Given To Dough Boys By Y.M.C.A., Case 20.00
Helmet, Crossed Rifle Badge 25.00
Helmet, Spike, Germany 375.00
Helmet, Spike, No Chin Strap, Large 295.00
Matchbook, Red Cross, Uncle Sam, Arms Around Sailor & Soldier 6.00
Medal, Ace, Saving Service, Satin Ribbon, Arm Holding Torch, Pinback, Oval 270.00
Patch, Polar Bear, Russia Painted On Helmet 1650.00
Postcard, Our World War Allies, Statue Of Liberty On World 10.00
Poster, Enlistment, With Lions, England, 31 x 22 In. 150.00
Poster, U.S. Army Recruiting, Soldiers, Pennsylvania, Canvas Mounted, 1914 . . . . 375.00
Siren, Hand Crank, Chemical Klaxon 225.00
Uniform, Army Doctor's, Worn Gas Mask, Equipment 850.00
Uniform, Marine Cops, Enlisted Dress, Blue 150.00

Uniform, Polar Bear, North Russia Patch, Helmet .... 875.
Walking Stick, Eagle's Head Form, Below Green Lizard, Wood, 39 In. .... 1150.
WORLD WAR II, Ammo Pouch, 3 Pockets, Black Leather .... 25.
Armband, Swastika, Germany .... 50.
Backpack, Germany, Canvas Body, Fur Back, Leather Straps, Internal Pockets .... 50.
Badge, Patrolman, Franklin County Council Of Defense, Nickel Finish, Pinback .... 29.
Bag, Bread, Italian Campaign Period, Germany .... 45.
Banner, Swastika, Germany, 10 x 5 Ft. .... 275.
Buckle, Belt, Hitler Youth, Celluloid Insert .... 75.
Cartridge Belt, USMC, Webb, Metal Buckle, Holds Carbine Mag Pouches .... 16.
Drawing, Prison Camp, By Prisoner Of War, Colored Pencil .... 80.
Flag, Flying Tigers, Squadron, Silk, 3 x 5 Ft. .... 650.
Flare Gun, Lifeboat .... 75.
Gas Mask, For Civilian Use, Filter & Instruction Papers 25.0
Goggles, Third Reich, Sand & Dust, Clear Lens, Envelope 10.0
Grenade, Dummy, German, Wooden Grip, Screw Base 30.0
Hat, General's, Visor, Germany 795.0
Helmet, Black, No Liner, Germany 50.0
Helmet, Paratroop, Green Painted Steel Shell, Leather Liner, Ear Flaps, Germany 75.0
Jacket, 5th Air Force, Leather Chit, Size 42 .... 2200.0
Jacket, A-2 Pilots, Leather Chit, Sterling, Colonial Eagles, Size 42 .... 1850.0
Jacket, Army Air Corp, B-15, Several Tears On Sleeves 390.0
Jacket, Flight, Army Air Corp., Leather, China Burma India Theatre, Patches 1600.0
Jeans, U.S.N., Blue Denim, Button Fly, Unissued 190.0
Machine Gun, MG-34, On Tripod 575.0
Map, Japanese Facilities Along Coasts 22.0
Matchbook, Match 'Em Bond For Bomb-Buy War Bonds, Hitler, Empty, 1940s 15.0
Microphone & Headpiece, Aircraft Carrier 125.0
Military Sword, Floral Design On Grip, Black House, Japan, 38 In. 132.0
Panties, Souvenir, Remember Pearl Harbor, Silk-Type Fabric, 6 x 7 3/4 In. 45.0
Pants, Leather, U.S. Air Force 50.0
Pin, 31 Regt. Genie, Bulldozer, Enameled 65.0
Pin, Nazi, Party Membership 14.0
Plate Set, MacArthur, Arnold, Marshal, Adm. King, Salem Pottery, 10 In., 4 Piece 125.0
Postcard, I Am A Visitor At Fisherman's Wharf, San Francisco, For Service Men 9.0
Poster, Anti-Hitler, We've Made A Monkey Out Of You, 1943, 15 x 20 In. 15.0
Poster, Are You Playing Square?, Car At Gas Pump, Cromwell, 1944, 14 x 20 In. 45.0
Poster, Christmas Overseas Ma, Santa With Helmet, 1945, 21 x 27 In. 60.0
Poster, Eisenhower, Back 'Em Up, Buy Extra Bonds, 20 x 28 In. 95.0
Poster, Find Your War Job, Yellow Field, 1943, 16 x 22 In. 37.0
Poster, Giant Spider Hirohito, Attacking Republic Of China, 1930s, 18 x 26 In. 63.0
Poster, I'm Counting On You, Uncle Sam, Finger To Lips, 1943, 20 x 28 In. 65.0
Poster, I'm In This War Too, Women's Army Corps, Graves, 1944, 13 x 19 In. 40.0
Poster, Keep Your Red Cross At His Side, Whitman, 1944, 14 x 20 In. 35.0
Poster, Save Fuel For Bombers, Hitler & Tojo Caricatures, 20 x 24 In. 75.0
Poster, Someone Talked, Sailor Drowning, Siebel, 1942, 22 x 28 In. 100.0
Poster, Till We Meet Again, Buy War Bonds, 1942, 22 x 28 In. 60.0
Poster, V-Mail Letter Forms, Multicolored, Schlaikler, 1942, 22 x 28 In. 75.0
Sake Cup, Leaping Horse Design, Gold Inscription, Japan 35.0
Shirt, U.S.N., Cotton, Long Sleeves, 2 Pockets, Unissued, Size 14 1/2 .... 57.0
Sign, Air Raid Warden, Porcelain, White Ground, Red Lettering, 3 x 9 In. 55.0
Siren, Air Raid, Battle Of Malta, Hand Cranked 475.00
Telescope, Brass, With Stand For Desk, Wottway Co., Ltd., 10 Power, 1942 ...... 575.00
Trousers, Khaki, Cotton, Aviation Cadet Trousers, Unissued, Tags, 1941 .... 69.00
Trousers, Khaki, Cotton, Button Fly, Size 28 x 31 In. 48.00
Trousers, U.S.N., Cotton Twill, Button Fly, Unissued, Tags, Size 30 x 31 In. 86.00
Visor Cap, Officer's, Third Reich, Chin Cord, Braided Aluminum Wire 35.00
Wallet, War Bond, 1940 .... 10.00
War Bond, Frame, 1940 .... 400.00

WORLD'S FAIR souvenirs from all of the fairs are collected. The first
fair was the Great Exhibition of 1851 in London. Other important exhi-
bitions and fairs include Philadelphia, 1876 (Centennial); Chicago,

893 (World's Columbian); Buffalo, 1901 (Pan-American); St. Louis, 904 (Louisiana Purchase); San Francisco, 1915 (Panama-Pacific); hiladelphia, 1926 (Sesquicentennial); Chicago, 1933 (Century of rogress); Cleveland, 1936 (Great Lakes); San Francisco, 1939 Golden Gate International); New York, 1939 (World of Tomorrow); eattle, 1962; New York, 1964; Montreal, 1967; New Orleans, 1984; sukuba, Japan, 1985; Vancouver, B.C., 1986; Brisbane, Australia, 988; Seville, Spain, 1992; and Genoa, Italy, 1992. Memorabilia of airs include directories, pictures, fabrics, ceramics, etc.

Ashtray, 1939, New York, Trylon & Perisphere, Ceramic, 5 x 8 In.	15.00
Ashtray, 1939, New York, Trylon & Perisphere, Plastic, 5 1/2 In.	60.00
Ashtray, 1939, San Francisco, Golden Gate Bridge	65.00
Ashtray, 1939, San Francisco, Golden Gate International, Horseshoe Shape	20.00
Ashtray, 1962, Seattle, Silver Plate	12.00
Badge, 1893, Manhattan Day, Columbian Exposition, White Ribbon	27.00
Badge, 1893, New York, Columbian Exposition, 1492-1892, Ribbon	32.00
Badge, 1901, Buffalo, Pan-American Exposition, Pinback, Gilt Brass, 2 Piece	28.00
Bank, 1939, New York, Trylon & Perisphere, Globe, Blue, Box, Instructions	95.00
Bank, 1939, New York, Trylon & Perisphere, Globe, Brown Ceramic, Gold Trim	75.00
Banner, 1904, St. Louis, Portraits, Jefferson, Napoleon, Teddy Roosevelt, 1803-1904	235.00
Book, 1933, Chicago, Century Of Progress, Poles In America, 263 Pages, 9 x 11 In.	45.00
Book, 1939, New York, World's Fair Views, Black & White Prints, 48 Pages	30.00
Bookends, 1939, Trylon & Perisphere, Ceramic	100.00
Booklet, 1915, San Francisco, Red Book Of Views, Envelope, 75 Pages	25.00
Booklet, 1933, Chicago, Pabst Blue Ribbon, Century Of Progress, 14 Pages	12.00 to 25.00
Booklet, 1933, Chicago, Pennsylvania Railroad	15.00
Booklet, 1939, New York, World's Fair Yale Lock	8.00
Booklet, 1964, New York, Picture Of Pavilions On Back, 3 x 4 In.	12.00
Bookmark, 1939, New York, Metal	25.00
Bottle, 1893, Chicago, Peachblow, Pear, Etched	175.00
Box, Hair Pin, 1901, Buffalo, Pan American, Aluminum	22.00
Bracelet, 1893, Chicago, Sterling Silver	200.00
Bracelet, 1939, New York, Sterling Silver	325.00
Button, 1909, Seattle, Alaska-Yukon, Hudson-Fulton Celebration, Celluloid, Pinback	18.00
Card, Playing, 1933, Chicago, Belgian Village, Plastic Case	75.00
Card, Playing, 1933, Chicago, Century Of Progress	23.00
Coaster, 1933, Chicago, Century Of Progress, Golden Pavilion Of Jehol, 3 In., Pair	9.00
Compact, 1934, Chicago, Century Of Progress, Silver Plate	15.00 to 45.00
Compact, 1939, New York, Trylon & Perisphere, Gold Tone	50.00
Cookbook, 1893, Columbian Exposition, Choice Receipts Walter Baker, Mass.	35.00
Crumb Tray, 1933, Chicago, Metal, Fair Scenes	20.00
Cup, 1894, San Francisco, Cut Glass, Ruby Flash, Ella On Side, 2 3/4 In.	50.00
Cup, 1904, St. Louis, Cascade Garden	28.00
Cup, 1904, St. Louis, Diamond Cut Glass, Ruby Flash, Vera On Side, 2 3/4 In.	40.00
Cup & Saucer, 1962, Seattle, Century 21 Exposition, Pottery, White, Gold Trim	17.00
Fan, 1939, New York, Electric Fan Of Tomorrow	950.00
Fan, 1939, New York, Metal Plate Front, 9 1/4 x 9 In.	560.00
Flag, 1939, New York, Cloth, 14 3/4 x 68 1/2 In.	240.00
Folder, 1933, Chicago, Blatz Beer, Die Cut Cardboard, Inside Ads, 6 x 14 In.	20.00
Glass, 1939, New York, Clear, Fireworks In Sky, Blue Wraparound Design, 5 In.	22.00
Glass, 1962, Seattle, Century 21 Exposition, Space Needle, Monorail, Clear, 4 3/4 In.	7.00
Glass, 1964, New York, World's Fair	12.00
Glass Set, 1962, Seattle, Wire Carrier, 8 Piece	75.00
Glass Set, 1964, New York, Scenes Of The Fair, 8 Piece	12.00
Globe, 1933, Chicago, Building View, Miniature	45.00
Hat, 1933, Chicago, Smile With Al, Metal, Cloth String, 2 x 3 3/4 x 4 3/4 In.	94.00
Hot Plate, 1933, Chicago, Century Of Progress, Aluminum Cover, 8 x 6 In.	14.00
Lantern, 1933, Chicago, Chase, 5 1/2 In.	125.00
License Plate Attachment, 1933, Chicago, Metal, 5 x 5 In.	110.00
Lighter, 1962, Seattle, Space Needle, 10 1/2 In.	135.00
Lucky Penny, 1937, Cleveland, Great Lakes Exposition, Gold Plated Over Metal	17.00
Mailer, 1915, San Francisco, Exposition City, Accordion, Photograph, 6 x 4 In.	4.00

Map, 1939, New York, Shell Oil Company 20.0
Map, 1939, World's Fair, Globe Indemnity 14.0
Mirror, 1901, Buffalo, Pan-American Exposition, Wabash Railroad, Pocket 110.0
Mug, 1933, Chicago Century Of Progress, Nude Woman Handle, 6 1/2 In. 110.0
Napkin Ring, 1904, St. Louis, Enameled, Aluminum, Engraved Border, 1 5/8 In. 25.0
Necklace, 1939, New York, Original Box 75.0
Pamphlet, 1933, Chicago, 27 New Recipes, Wilson's Certified Sliced Bacon, 20 Pg. ... 6.0
Pamphlet, 1933, Chicago, Royal Scot Train, Great Britain, 5 1/2 x 8 1/2 In. 9.0
Paperweight, 1893, Chicago, Virginia State Building, Milk Glass, Libbey 65.0
Paperweight, 1894, San Francisco, Mechanical Arts Building, Glass, 4 In. 65.0
Paperweight, 1904, St. Louis, Mound Coffin Co. 225.0
Paperweight, 1939, San Francisco, Lucky Horseshoe, Medal, 2 1/8 x 2 3/8 In. 23.0
Pass, Admission, 1938, New York, Trylon & Perisphere, 3 1/2 In. 25.0
Pencil, 1939, San Francisco, Mechanical, Golden Gate, 10 1/2 In. 39.0
Pencil, 1962, Seattle, Space Needle, Wooden, Yellow Tassel On Eraser 12.0
Pennant, 1933, Chicago, Century Of Progress, Felt, Hall Of Science, 12 x 29 In. 38.0
Pennant, 1939, New York, Trylon & Perisphere, Felt, 23 1/2 x 9 In. 30.0
Picture Puzzle, 1933, Cellophane Wrapper & Box, 12 x 18 In. 85.0
Pin, 1939, New York, World Of Tomorrow 35.0
Pin, Sharpshooter's, 1933, Chicago, Silver Plated, Owen's-Illinois 16.0
Pin Tray, 1909, Seattle, Alaska-Yukon Pacific Exposition, Metal, 5 1/2 x 4 In. 22.0
Plaque, 1939, New York, The World Of Tomorrow, Aluminum, Hammered, 19 In. 450.0
Plaque, 1967, Montreal, 8 Pavilions, Bronze, Creation Universelle, Inc., 7 In. 18.0
Plate, 1900, Universal Exposition Paris 75.0
Plate, 1904, St. Louis, Captain John Smith, Blue 175.0
Plate, 1904, St. Louis, Louisiana Purchase, Blue 185.0
Plate, 1909, Seattle, Territory Of Hawaii, O.P. Co., Syracuse China, 8 3/4 In. 135.0
Plate, 1915, San Diego, Panama-California Exposition, San Diego Scenes 110.0
Plate, 1962, Seattle, Space Needle, Pottery, White, Gold Trim, 4 In. 2.0
Plate, 1964, New York, Tower Of Light, Pool Of Industry, Sky Ride, Green, 9 In. 15.0
Plate, 1974, Spokane, United States Pavilion, Plastic, 9 1/2 In. 18.0
Postcard, 1904, St. Louis, Hold To Light, Palace Of Agriculture 50.0
Postcard, 1904, St. Louis, Palace Of Mines & Metallurgy 20.0
Postcard, 1904, St. Louis, Palace Of Transportation Views 18.0
Postcard, 1915, San Francisco, Panama Pacific Exposition, Unused 90.0
Postcard, 1930, Stockholm, Elsie, Borden 30.0
Postcard, 1933, Chicago, Century Of Progress Exposition 3.0
Postcard, 1939, Elsie 30.0
Postcard, 1939, New York 2.0
Postcard, 1939, San Francisco, Golden Gate International Exposition 2.0
Program, 1935, San Diego Exposition, California-Pacific 30.0
Purse, Coin, 1893, Chicago, Government Building, Metal, Leather, 2 5/8 x 1 3/4 In. ... 37.0
Purse, Doll's, 1878, Paris, France, Brass, Fabric, Engraving Of Building, 3 x 1 1/2 In. 475.0
Razor, Straight, 1893, Chicago, Silver Steel, Case, 8 7/8 In. 16.5
Record, 1964, New York, Triumph Of Man, Travelers Insurance, 33 1/3 RPM, 7 In. 14.0
Ribbon, 1893, Chicago, Columbian Exposition, Star Spangled Banner, Silk, 13 In. 150.0
Ring, 1904, St. Louis, Sterling Silver, Thomas Jefferson Bust, Size 4 1/2 .... 85.0
Ring, 1939, San Francisco, Golden Gate, Tower Of Sun Logo, Silver Plated Metal 29.0
Salt & Pepper, 1939, New York, Trylon & Perisphere Shaped, On Base, 3 1/2 In. 52.0
Salt & Pepper, 1939, New York, Trylon & Perisphere, Orange Plastic, 3 1/2 In. 58.0
Saltshaker, 1893, Chicago, World's Columbian, Lay Down, Egg Shape, Blue, 3 In. 225.0
Scarf, 1962, Seattle, Monorail, Hydro-Electric Exhibit, Rayon, Silk, Square, 30 In. 18.0
Schedule, 1958, Brussels Universal, TWA Airline, 9 x 4 In. 24.0
Spinner, 1939, New York, Metropolitan Life Insurance, Trylon & Perisphere, Brass 5.0
Spinner Medal, 1915, San Francisco, Risque Bear Scene, Silver Plate Bronze 10.0
Spoon, 1901, Buffalo, Pan-American Exposition, Sterling Silver, 3 3/4 In. 15.0
Spoon, 1904, St. Louis, Cascade Gardens, Jefferson Handle, Silver Plate, 4 3/8 In. ... 15.0
Spoon, 1904, St. Louis, Cascade Gardens, Steamboat, Silver Plate, 5 1/2 In. 22.0
Spoon, 1933, Chicago, Fort Dearborn Administration Building 12.0
Spoon, 1939, New York, Demitasse, 4 Piece 125.0
Spoon, 1964, New York, Unisphere Cutout View Handle, Silver Plate, 4 In. 5.0
Ticket, 1893, Chicago, Eagle In Center, Oct. 9, 2 x 4 In. 25.0
Ticket, 1939, San Francisco, Incubator Babies, Blue, White, 3 3/4 In. 3.0

Ticket, 1939, San Francisco, Tower Of Sun & Bridges, 3 3/4 In.	3.00
Ticket Stub, 1933, Chicago, Century Of Progress, Logo, 3 1/2 x 2 1/4 In.	3.00
Tie Clasp, 1933, Chicago, Skyline, Brass Plated Elongated Penny, Frame, 2 3/4 In. . . .4.00 to 15.00	
Tin, 1893, Chicago, Wax Museum Advertising, England, 2 x 6 x 1 In.	75.00
Tip Tray, 1933, Chicago, Century Of Progress	16.00
Tip Tray, 1964, New York, Unisphere, Flags & People, U.S. Steel, 7 1/8 x 5 In.	7.00
Towel, 1893, Chicago, Columbian Exposition, Christopher Columbus, Indians	90.00
Towel, 1939, New York, Fairfax, Unopened Wrapper	35.00
Toy, Bus, 1933, Chicago, Century Of Progress, Arcade, Painted, 10 In., 2 Piece	395.00
Tray, 1964, New York, Peace Through Understanding, Tin, 12 In. . . . . .6.00 to 25.00	
Tray, 1967, Montreal, Major Pavillions, Anchor Industries, Plastics, 15 x 11 In.	12.00
Trivet, 1893, Chicago, Cracked Word, 7 3/4 In.	22.00
Tumbler, 1939, New York, Theme Building	45.00
Umbrella, 1933, Chicago, Century Of Progress, Japan	100.00
Urn, 1904, St. Louis, Brass, Small	20.00
View-Master, 1964, New York, With Reels	50.00
View-Master Reel, 1939, New York, Treasure Island	30.00
View-Master Reel, 1939, San Francisco, Golden Gate, 7 Color Views, Pair	22.00
Wagon, Radio Flyer, 1933, Chicago, Century Of Progress, 5 In.	85.00
Walking Cane, 1934, Chicago, 6 Scenes, Metal	65.00
Watch Fob, 1893, Chicago, Watch Opener, Compliments Of Keystone	38.00
Watch Fob, 1905, Portland, Lewis & Clark Centennial, Brass, Shield Shape	37.00
Watch Fob, 1915, San Francisco, Panama-Pacific International Expo, Metal	28.00
Zither, 1904, St. Louis, Menzenhauer Guitar-Zither, Oscar Schmidt, 13 x 19 In.	195.00

WRISTWATCHES came into use during World War I. Wristwatches are
listed here by manufacturer or as advertising or character watches.
Pocket watches are listed in the Watch category.

Advertising, BMW, Woman's, Logo, Gold Metal, Battery Operated, Alligator Band	18.00
Advertising, Brach's Peppermint Candy, Plastic, Red Bezel & Band	14.00
Advertising, Camel Cigarette Pack	45.00
Advertising, Charlie Tuna, Starkist, Pink Plastic Case	112.00
Advertising, Chevrolet, Blue Logo, Battery Operated, Leather Band	10.00
Advertising, Colgate, Brush, It's Still Working, Digital, Blue Plastic Band	10.00
Advertising, Crayola Crayon, Sweephand	40.00
Advertising, Famous Grouse Whiskey	35.00
Advertising, Guinness Time, Animated, Toucan, Chrome Bezel Case, 1930s, 2 In.	290.00
Advertising, Joe Camel	65.00
Advertising, Kool Aid, Digital	10.00
Advertising, LA Gear	35.00
Advertising, Mr. Peanut, Original Band	75.00
Art Nouveau, Platinum, Diamond, Sapphire, Rectangular, Fine Mesh Band, 1915	550.00
Art Nouveau, Star, Leaf & Floral Designs, White Gold, Platinum, Diamonds, 1915	450.00
Baume & Mercier, Rope Strand Bracelet, Quartz Movement, 14K Yellow Gold	148.00
Benrus, Gold Toned Case, Speidel Flex Band, Seconds Dial, c.1940s, 1 In.	40.00
Benrus, Man's, Automatic, Gold Filled Case, Steel Back, Expansion Band	60.00
Bercona, Sport, Steel Case, Speidel Flex Band, White Face, 1 In.	25.00
Bracelet, Movado, 14K Yellow Gold	287.00
Breguet, Skeletonized Lever Movement, Sapphire Crystal, c.1988, 18K Gold	8625.00
Bucherer, Woman's, 14K Gold Band, Black Dial, 1940s	275.00
Bulgari, Date Below 6 O'Clock, Quartz, 18K Gold Buckle, c.1978	1840.00
Bulova, 30 Jewel, Hour Hand, Center Rotating Disc, Speidel Band, 14K Gold Case	350.00
Bulova, 5th Ave., N.Y. Gents, Gold Filled, 1943	65.00
Bulova, Alarm, Manual Wind, 1967	95.00
Bulova, Art Deco Designs, Silver Metal Case, Flex Band, 1 x 3/4 In.	60.00
Bulova, Curvex Style, 17 Jewel, Oblong Gold Filled Case	60.00
Bulova, Gold Toned Case, Speidel Flex Band, Seconds Dial, Blue Plastic Box, 1 In.	50.00
Bulova, Rectangle, 14K Gold, 17 Jewel, Seconds Dial, Leather Strap, Black Case	130.00
Cartier, Circular Nickel Lever Movement, White Matte Dial, 1990, 18K Gold	3220.00
Cartier, White Matte Dial, Roman Numerals, 1990, 18K White Gold	2185.00
Chalet, Diver's, Steel Case, Black Face, 60 Meter Depth, Date Window, 1 In.	25.00
Character, Alien, Figural, Wrap Around Wrist, Package	15.00
Character, Barbie, 3 Bands, Red Plastic Display Box, 1971	150.00

Character, Barbie, Original Band, 1950s 95.0

Character, Bozo The Clown 60.0

Character, Donkey, Democrat, Timex 38.C

Character, Dukes Of Hazzard, Alarm, Musical, Unisonic, 1981, Plastic Box ...... 15.00 to 30.0

Character, Felix The Cat, Digital, 3-D Flicker Face, Vinyl Band, On Card 18.0

Character, Frankenstein, Fossil 65.0

Character, Globetrotters 65.0

Character, Jack & Jill 65.0

Character, Lucy, Peanuts, White Rubber & Vinyl Band, Timex, 1970s 44.0

Character, Marvin The Martian, Hologram Face, Novelty Watch, Plastic Holder 45.0

Character, Pebbles, Flintstones, Yellow Vinyl Wrist Band, Swiss, 1972 .... 23.0

Character, Smokey The Bear, Box 170.0

Character, Snoopy In Center, Red Watch Face, Red Vinyl Band, Timex, 1970s 50.0

Character, Snoopy, Blue Rubber & Vinyl Band, Timex, 1970s 52.0

Character, Snoopy, Red Baron, Timex, Case ....65.00 to 75.0

Character, Strawberry Shortcake 12.0

Character, Tom Corbett, Original Band, Planets & Rocket Ship 195.0

Character, Tony The Tiger 17.5

Character, Woody Woodpecker 100.0

Character, Zorro, Box 165.0

Demco, Woman's, Hidden Face, Hinged Cover, 10 Diamonds, 17 Jewel, 6 1/4 In. ... 450.0

Elgin, Lord, 10K Gold Bezel, Steel Back, Speidel Flex Band, Rectangular Face, 1 In. ... 40.0

Elgin, White Gold Filled, Art Deco, 21 Jewel 55.00

Elgin De Luxe, 10K Gold Filled, Seconds Dial, Leather Strap 110.0

Favre Leuba, Steel Case, Harpoon Style, Flex Band, Geneva, 1 In. 50.00

Girard Perregaux, 14K Yellow Gold 230.0

Girard Perregaux, Cut & Single Diamonds, White Gold Links, Platinum 1980.0

Girard Perregaux, Gyromatic, 17 Jewel 150.00

Glycine, Airman Special, White Metal, Spiedel Band, Date Window 325.00

Gruen, Woman's, 17 Jewel, 14K Gold Case, Speidel Flex Band, 1/2 In. 30.00

Hamilton, Driving, Woman's, 14K Gold, c.1940 .... 1000.00

Hamilton, Gold Filled Front, Back, Tonneau Case 85.00

Hamilton, Presentation, 14K Gold, Leather, Seconds Dial, Celluloid Case, 1948 .... 139.00

Helbros, Woman's, Square Case, Gilt Finish, Expansion Band, 1950s 45.00

Ingraham, White Metal Case, Rounded Rectangle Face, Leather Band 47.00

Jaeger Le Coultre, Gold Toned Case, Flex Steel Band, 1 In. 110.00

Juvenia, Linear Sapphire Motif, Diamond Corners, 18K Gold, Round, 1925 .... 600.00

Krieger, Woman's, Mother-Of-Pearl Dial, Stainless Steel, Quartz, Box 430.00

Le Coultre, 17 Jewel, Gold Filled, 1940s 100.00

Le Coultre, Automatic Up/Down Indicator, Sweep Seconds, Brickwork Band 632.00

Le Coultre, Ball & Leaf Design, Silver Silk Cord, 14K Gold, 1940s, 6 1/4 In. ... 650.00

Le Coultre, Teardrop Lugs, 18K Gold, c.1950 .... 1800.00

Longines, Bracelet, 14K Black, Gold Filled 70.00

Longines, Woman's, 14K Yellow Gold, Closed Case, Chain Marked 15c 287.00

Movado, Astronic, Silverized Dial, Moon Phase, Day & Date 345.00

Movado, Bracelet, Hinged Cover, Quartz, 14K Yellow Gold 431.00

Movado, Moon Phases, 15 Jewel, 18K Pink Gold, c.1955 .... 2530.00

Movado, Woman's, 14K Gold, Square Dial, Integral Link Bracelet 258.00

Nardin, 2-Color Gold, Snake Link Bracelet, Rubies & Diamonds 2185.00

Nardin, Single Button Chronograph, 18K Gold, c.1925 .... 5750.00

Omega, 18K Yellow Gold, Goldtone Arabic Numerals, Cream Dial 460.00

Omega, Seamaster, Automatic Chronometer, Date, Second Hand 862.00

Omega, Seamaster, Automatic Movement 115.00

Omega, Woman's, 14K Gold Case & Band, 1960s 225.00

Parsifal, White Enamel Dial, Date Box, Leather Strap, Stainless Steel 345.00

Patek Philippe, 28 Jewel, Nickel Lever Movement, Blue Matte Dial, 18K Gold 3450.00

Patek Philippe, Bracelet, Nickel Lever Movement, Silver Dial, 18K White Gold 6900.00

Patek Philippe, Bracelet, Silver Matte Dial, Baton Numerals, 1980, 18K Gold 7475.00

Patek Philippe, Bracelet, Textured Black Matte Dial, Baton Numerals, 21 Jewel 13800.00

Patek Philippe, Bracelet, Textured Black Matte Dial, Baton Numerals, 29 Jewel 6900.00

Patek Philippe, Bracelet, White Matte Dial, Roman Numerals, 1985, 18K Gold 9487.00

Patek Philippe, Circular Nickel Movement, Silver Matte Dial, 1953, 18K Gold 3740.00

Patek Philippe, Gilt Lever Movement, Champagne Matte Dial, 1914, 18K Gold 2530.00
Patek Philippe, Gilt Lever Movement, Champagne Matte Dial, 1920, 18K Gold 5750.00
Patek Philippe, Gilt Lever Movement, Champagne Matte Dial, Arabic Numerals 4600.00
Patek Philippe, Gilt Lever Movement, Roman Numerals, 1917, 18K Gold 2645.00
Patek Philippe, Nickel Lever Movement, Arabic, Baton Numerals, 18K Gold 2760.00
Patek Philippe, Nickel Lever Movement, Pink Matte Dial, 1950, 18K Pink Gold 6325.00
Patek Philippe, Nickel Lever Movement, Roman Numerals, 18K Pink Gold 4312.00
Patek Philippe, Nickel Lever Movement, Silver Matte Dial, Baton Numerals 18400.00
Patek Philippe, Nickel Lever Movement, White Matte Dial, 18K Pink Gold 6037.00
Patek Philippe, Silver Matte Dial, Baton Numerals, 1926, 25 Jewel 5462.00
Patek Philippe, Silver Matte Dial, Baton Numerals, 1952, 18K Gold 3450.00
Patek Philippe, White Enamel Dial, Arabic Numerals, 1910, 18K Gold 4312.00
Patek Philippe, Woman's, 18K Gold, Curved Teardrop Lugs, Square Face, 1940s 1800.00
Piaget, 2-Tone Gold Bracelet, Leather Box, Slipcase, Guarantee, c.1990 .... 3450.00
Piaget, Bracelet, Black Matte Dial, 18K White Gold, Gilt Baton Numerals 1610.00
Piaget, Swiss Movement, Goldtone Dial, Brilliant Cut Diamond Frame 2530.00
Piguet, Bracelet, Textured Blue Dial, 18K White Gold, Baton Numerals, 1960 .... 2645.00
Pucci, Turquoise, White & Purple, Exchangeable Bands, Box 287.00
Rhone, 18 Jewel, Framed In Diamonds, Diamond Set Box Link Bracelet 230.00
Rolex, 14K Yellow Gold, Goldtone Dial, Ostrich Strap 805.00
Rolex, Double-Sunk White Enamel Dial, Roman Numerals, 9K Pink Gold 2415.00
Rolex, Oyster, Gold Screw-Down Crown, Black Matte Dial, 1939 .... 8337.00
Rolex, Oyster, Nickel Lever Movement, Textured Black Dial, 1955 .... 2645.00
Rolex, Oyster, Screw-Down Crown, Champagne Matte Dial, 1980, 18K Gold 4370.00
Rolex, Oyster, Screw-Down Crown, Nickel Lever Movement, 14K Gold 3450.00
Rolex, Oyster, Screw-Down Crown, Pink Matte Dial, 1970, 18K Pink Gold 5462.00
Rolex, Oyster, Screw-Down Crown, Pink Matte Dial, Baton Numerals, 1945 .... 3737.00
Rolex, Oyster, Screw-Down Crown, Pink Matte Dial, Pink, Gold Bezel, 1939 .... 10062.00
Rolex, Oyster, Screw-Down Crown, Purple Enamel Dial, 18K Pink Gold 6900.00
Rolex, Oyster, Screw-Down Crown, Silver Matte Dial, 27 Jewel, 18K Pink Gold 4312.00
Rolex, Oyster, Screw-Down Crown, Silver Matte Dial, Arabic Numerals, 1940 .... 8050.00
Rolex, Oyster, Screw-Down Crown, Silver Matte Dial, Gold Bezel, 1937 .... 2645.00
Rolex, Oyster, Screw-Down Crown, Silver Matte Dial, Pink Gold Bezel, 1946 .... 6900.00
Rolex, Oyster, Screw-Down Crown, Silver Matte Dial, Roman Numerals, 9K Gold 4312.00
Rolex, Oyster, Self-Winding, Tudor Prince, 1942 .... 195.00
Rolex, Oyster, Tudor, Leather Strap, 14K Gold Over Stainless Steel 795.00
Rolex, Woman's, 2-Tone Silver Dial, Leaf Tip Bezel, 1934, 9K Gold 1725.00
Rolex, Woman's, Gold, 2 Diamonds, Round Head, Mesh Band, 1950s 750.00
Rolex, Woman's, Silvertone Dial, Jubilee Bracelet 1035.00
Ruhla, Chronograph, Anti-Magnetic, Steel Waterproof Case, East Germany, Box 347.00
Snoopy, With Tennis Racket, Blue Denim Watch Face, Tennis Ball Second Hand 65.00
Swiss, Woman's, Cover, Milli-Nugget Style, Diamonds, Oval Opals, Gold Bracelet 695.00
Swiss, Woman's, Platinum, 8 Diamonds, 18K Gold, Black Ribbon Band, 1920s 350.00
Tavannes, Luminescent Hands, Separate Seconds Dial 179.00
Tavannes, Reverso, Stainless Steel, c.1940 .... 2000.00
Tissot, Seastar Seven, Steel Case, Flex Band, Date Window, 1 In. 40.00
Universal, 2-Dial Chronograph, Sweep Seconds Hand, Lizard Strap, 18K Gold 977.00
Vacheron & Constantin, 17 Jewel, Black Face, Leather Strap, Gold Case 1045.00
Vacheron & Constantin, 18 Jewel, Second Hand, 18K Pink Gold, c.1960 .... 2587.00
Vacheron & Constantin, Circular Nickel Lever Movement, 1970, 18K Gold 1610.00
Vacheron & Constantin, Gilt Lever Movement, Roman Numerals, 18K Gold 5750.00
Vacheron & Constantin, Silver Matte Dial, Baton Numerals, 1955, 18K Gold 2070.00
Waltham, Buckle Ribbon Band, 14K White Gold Case, Leather Box, 1933 .... 55.00
Waltham, Gold Toned Case, Leather Band, Separate Seconds, Face, 1 In. 50.00
Waltham, Sweep Seconds Dial, Kreisler Cordovan Band 172.00
Waltham, Woman's, 14K Gold, Diamonds Around Face, Black Band 60.00
Westclox, World Time 90.00
Woman's, 14K Yellow Gold, Diamonds On Covered Face, Flexible Band, 1950s 535.00
Woman's, 18K Gold, Diamonds, Dark Blue & White Enamel Design, 1920s 700.00
Woman's, Goldtone Dial, Black Roman Numerals, 18K Yellow Gold 920.00
Woman's, Staggered 1 Link-2 Link Bracelet, 17 Jewel, Case, 1950s 395.00

YELLOWWARE is a heavy earthenware made of a yellowish clay. It
varies in color from light yellow to orange-yellow. Many nineteenth-
and twentieth-century kitchen bowls and jugs were made of yellowware. It was made in England and in the United States. Another
form of pottery that is sometimes classed as yellowware is listed in this
book in the Mocha category.

Bank, Dog, Seated, Green & Brown Running Glaze, 7 1/2 In.	1150.0
Bank, Parrot	450.0
Bank, Piggy, Green Spongework	145.0
Bowl, 3 Brown Bands, 10 3/4 In.	30.0
Bowl, 5 Bands, 19th Century, 7 x 14 In.	145.0
Bowl, 6 Panels, 9 In.	115.0
Bowl, Blue Bands, Large	65.0
Bowl, Blue Seaweed Design, White Band, East Liverpool, Ohio, 11 x 5 1/4 In.	220.0
Bowl, Lattice, Applied Floral Design, 6 1/2 In.	70.0
Bowl, Mixing, Brown Stripes	30.0
Bowl, Mixing, Molded Ribs, Brown Bands, 11 1/2 In.	65.0
Bowl, Spinach & Eggs Glaze, 2 3/4 In.	80.0
Bowl, Wide Brown Band, 5 1/2 x 3 In.	35.0
Bowl, Yellow On Yellow Squares, Molded Leaf Edge, 11 In.	60.00
Bowl Set, Miniature, 6 Piece	300.0
Butter Mold, Grape Design, 3 1/2 x 7 x 8 In.	45.00
Candy Dish, Woven Clay Strips, England	125.00
Chamber Pot, Embossed, 7 In.	110.00
Crock, Butter, Lid, Cream & Brown Bands	165.00
Dish, Fluted Edge, 15 1/4 In.	30.00
Figurine, Cat, Seated, Circlets Border, Brown Band, Strap Handle, 4 7/16 In., Pair	632.00
Figurine, Dog, Seated, Mottled Blue & Black Glaze, Ohio, 10 In.	4400.00
Figurine, Dog, Seated, Open Front Legs, Blue Mottled Glaze, 9 1/2 In.	2200.00
Figurine, Eagle, Outstretched Wings, 7 3/4 x 17 1/2 In.	6200.00
Fruit Jar, Robert Arthues, 1 Pt.	250.00
Humidor, Gilt Design, 10 In.	265.00
Humidor, Hinged Brass Cover	240.00
Inkwell, Dog, Green, Brown, 6 1/8 In.	440.00
Jar, Cover, Blue Seaweed, White Bands, Blue Stripes On Cover, Ohio, 5 1/4 In.	138.00
Jug, Molded Anchor On Sides, Rockingham Type Glaze, Signed, 1880s, 9 1/4 In.	375.00
Match Holder, Figural, Boy In Straw Hat, Tree Stump	225.00
Mixing Bowl, Blue, White Bands, No. 5	34.00
Mixing Bowl, Blue, White Bands, No. 8	30.00
Mold, Cake, Rabbit	75.00
Mold, Fruit, Rockingham Glaze	375.00
Mug, Trifle For Ralph, Leaf Decorated Handle, 2 1/4 In.	325.00
Pan, Bundt Cake, Swirl, Sponge Glaze	60.00
Pan, Milk, Rolled Rim, 13 In.	165.00
Pie Bird, Stamped Nut Brown	95.00
Pie Pan	95.00
Pitcher, Brown, Green Drip Glaze, 5 In.	65.00
Pitcher, Grape In Shield, Large	195.00
Pitcher, Milk, Black Glaze Outside, Dark Red Sponge Circles	275.00
Teapot, Embossed Flowers	335.00
Teapot, Sponge Spatter, Blue Sponging, Green, Clear Glaze, 9 In.	220.00
Urinal, Bird Design, 1840-1850, 6 1/2 In.	33.00

ZANE Pottery was founded in 1921 by Adam Reed and Harry
McClelland in South Zanesville, Ohio, at the old Peters and Reed
Building. Zane pottery is very similar to Peters and Reed pottery, but
it is usually marked. The factory was sold in 1941 to Lawton Gonder.

Bowl, Brick Red, Red & Green Glossy Interior	95.00
Plate, Landsun Drip, Flame Pattern, 10 In.	275.00
Vase, Green, Brown, Blue Drip Over Yellow, 11 1/2 In.	297.00
Vase, Moss Aztec, Green, Brown Matte, 4 Handles, 5 x 2 In.	60.00
Vase, Raised Floral Design, Green Matte Glaze, 8 x 18 In.	275.00
Wall Pocket, Moss Aztec, Leaf, Berry Design, Green, Brown Matte, 9 1/2 In.	60.50

ANESVILLE Art Pottery was founded in 1900 by David Schmidt in anesville, Ohio. The firm made faience umbrella stands, jardinieres, nd pedestals. The company closed in 1962. Many pieces are marked ith just the words *La Moro*.

LA MORO

Vase, Brown, Floral Design, La Moro, 9 In. 300.00
Vase, Drippy Glaze, 8 In. 35.00

SOLNAY pottery was made in Hungary after 1862 and was character-
zed by Persian, Art Nouveau, or Hungarian motifs. A series of new
solnay figurines with green-gold luster finish is available in many
hops today. Early Zsolnay was not marked, but by 1878 the tower
ademark was used.

ZSOLNAY
PÉCS

Ashtray, Heart Shaped, Flower Center, 4 3/4 In. 22.00
Basket, Lace, Egg Shaped, 1887-1889, 8 1/2 x 6 1/2 In. 795.00
Ewer, Iridescent Green, 14 In. 225.00
Figurine, Remorse, Nude, Green, Blue-Gold, Stamped, 1930s, 8 3/4 x 5 1/4 In. 495.00
Jar, Cover, Horses & Chariots, Gold & Green Glaze, 5 1/8 In. 55.00
Jug, Aqua Green, Bubble Textured Surface, Applied Medallions, Gold Trim, 9 1/4 In. ... 260.00
Jug, Locomotive Going Up Around Body, Billowing Smoke, Handle, Signed, 17 In. 2000.00
Plate, Iridescent, Persian Design, Embossed Mark, Signed, 10 1/2 In. 360.00
Vase, Bird, Foliage, Double Gourd Form, 7 1/2 In. 145.00
Vase, Blue Spots On Green, Iridescent, Scalloped Edge, 3-Footed, Signed, 9 In. 575.00
Vase, Blue, Green Iridescent, Signed, 11 1/2 In. 515.00
Vase, Enameled, Oxblood & Green, Applied Arboreal Handles, 11 1/4 In. 740.00
Vase, Iridescent Swirl, Blue-Green Design, Signed Funfkirchen, 11 1/2 In. 468.00
Vase, Molded Flower & Leaf Design, Blue, Green, Gold Iridescent, 10 In. 110.00

INDEX

This index is computer-generated, making it as complete as possible. References in uppercase type a
category listings. Those in lowercase letters refer to additional pages where the piece can be found. The
is also an internal cross-referencing system used in the main part of the book, so if you look for a Kewp
doll in the Doll category, you will be told it is in its own category. There is additional information at th
end of many paragraphs about where to find prices of pieces similar to yours.

K O V E L S

ORDERS & INQUIRIES TO: **CROWN PUBLISHERS, INC.**
RANDOM HOUSE, 400 HAHN ROAD, WESTMINSTER, MD 21157
ATTN: ORDER DEPARTMENT
SITE: www.randomhouse.com

Sales & Title Information:
1-800-733-3000
For order entry:
FAX# **1-800-659-2436**

_____

ADDRESS _____

_____ STATE _____ ZIP _____

send me the following books:

NO.	QTY.	TITLE		PRICE	TOTAL
80344-1	___	Kovels' Antiques & Collectibles Price List — *current edition*	PAPER	$14.95	_____
58012-8	___	Kovels' American Art Pottery: The Collector's Guide to Makers, Marks, and Factory Histories	HARDCOVER	$60.00	_____
54668-X	___	American Country Furniture 1780 –1875	PAPER	$16.95	_____
70137-5	___	Dictionary of Marks—Pottery and Porcelain	HARDCOVER	$17.00	_____
55914-5	___	Kovels' New Dictionary of Marks	HARDCOVER	$19.00	_____
56882-9	___	Kovels' American Silver Marks	HARDCOVER	$40.00	_____
88435-6	___	Kovels' Bottles Price List— *current edition*	PAPER	$16.00	_____
80310-7	___	Kovels' Depression Glass & Dinnerware Price List — *current edition*	PAPER	$16.00	_____
57806-9	___	Kovels' Know Your Antiques Revised and Updated	PAPER	$16.00	_____
58840-4	___	Kovels' Know Your Collectibles Updated	PAPER	$16.00	_____
88381-3	___	Kovels' Quick Tips: 799 Helpful Hints on How to Care for Your Collectibles	PAPER	$12.00	_____
50168-7	___	The Label Made Me Buy It: From Aunt Jemima to Zonkers—The Best Dressed Boxes, Bottles & Cans from the Past (Available October 1998)	HARDCOVER	$40.00	_____
	___	TOTAL ITEMS		TOTAL RETAIL VALUE	_____

CHECK OR MONEY ORDER ENCLOSED
MADE PAYABLE TO CROWN PUBLISHERS, INC.
or telephone 1-800-733-3000
(No cash or stamps, please)

Shipping & Handling Charge
$2.00 for one book;
50¢ for each additional book.
Please add applicable sales tax._____

CHARGE: ☐ Master Card ☐ Visa ☐ American Express
Account Number (include all digits) Expires: MO.___ YR.___

TOTAL AMOUNT DUE _____

_____

_____

PRICES SUBJECT TO CHANGE WITHOUT
NOTICE. If a more recent edition of a price
list has been published at the same price, it
will be sent instead of the old edition.

Thank you for your order

Signature
- -